A COMPENDIOUS AND COMPREHENSIVE Law Dictionary;

ELUCIDATING

THE TERMS,

AND

General Principles

OF

LAW AND EQUITY.

By THOMAS WALTER WILLIAMS, Esq.

Of the Inner Temple, London, Barrister at Law,

AUTHOR OF THE LAW RELATIVE TO THE DUTY AND OFFICE OF A JUSTICE OF THE PEACE, &c. &c.

With a New Introduction by Bryan A. Garner

THE LAWBOOK EXCHANGE, LTD.
Clark, New Jersey

ISBN 978-1-58477-680-2

Lawbook Exchange edition 2006, 2025

The quality of this reprint is equivalent to the quality of the original work.

THE LAWBOOK EXCHANGE, LTD.
33 Terminal Avenue
Clark, New Jersey 07066-1321

Please see our website for a selection of our other publications and fine facsimile reprints of classic works of legal history:
www.lawbookexchange.com

Library of Congress Cataloging-in-Publication Data

Williams, Thomas Walter, 1763-1833.
A compendious and comprehensive law dictionary : elucidating the terms and general principles of law and equity / Thomas Walter Williams ; introduction by Bryan A. Garner.
p. cm.
Originally published: London : Gale and Fenner, 1816.
Includes bibliographical references and index.
ISBN-13: 978-1-58477-680-2 (alk. paper)
ISBN-10: 1-58477-680-3 (alk. paper)
1. Law--Dictionaries. I. Title.
K50.W545 2006
340.03--dc22 2006000377

Printed in the United States of America on acid-free paper

INTRODUCTION

Bryan A. Garner

In some ways, the career of the barrister and legal lexicographer Thomas Walter Williams (1763–1833) finds parallels in the career of Henry Campbell Black (1860–1927). Like Black, Williams "was not much known as a pleader, his repute chiefly resting on his writings."[1] And both men published copiously. Williams abstracted many acts of Parliament and wrote several books, among them *A Compendious Digest of the Statute Law* (2 vols., 1787, and later editions); *Original Precedents and Conveyances* (4 vols., 1788–1792); *The Whole Law Relative to the Duty and Office of a Justice of the Peace* (3 vols., 1793–1795); *An Abridgment of Cases Argued and Determined During the Reign of George III* (5 vols. 1798–1803);[2] *The Practice of the Commissioners, Assessors, and Other Officers Under the Acts Relating to the Assessed Taxes* (1804); and *The Farmer's Lawyer* (1819).[3]

The main difference between the two authors is that Black came to be celebrated for his *Dictionary of Law*, whereas Williams has remained relatively obscure despite his lexicographic endeavors. The *Dictionary of National Biography* (1917) reports that he published *A General Dictionary of the Law* in 1812, followed by the present work in 1816. Today both volumes are rare, and copies are extraordinarily difficult to obtain in the antiquarian-book trade.

---

1 21 *Dictionary of National Biography* 457 (1917).

2 In 1932, Cowley referred to Williams's abridgment of cases argued as one of "[t]wo minor common law abridgments [that] appeared before the close of the [18th] century." John D. Cowley, *A Bibliography of Abridgments, Digests, Dictionaries and Indexes of English Law to the Year 1800* lxv–lxvi (1932).

3 21 *DNB* 457.

INTRODUCTION

In his dictionary, Williams's stated purpose was to "combine . . . within a moderate compass, an exposition of all the known Terms, and general Principles of Law and Equity." In his note "To the Public," he mentions having minutely examined all the "Interpreters of the Law" as well as the "larger Law Dictionaries." He concludes with the claim that his dictionary "contains an accurate exposition of a very great variety of words, terms, and rules, not to be found in any other Dictionary on the same subject now extant."

Certainly his coverage has a greater scope than any contemporaneous one-volume law dictionary of similar size. In Williams, the letter *A* contains 492 headwords, an impressive number. In Jacob's abridged dictionary of 1743, there are 317 headwords under *A*. And in Potts's *Compendious Law Dictionary* (1803) — surely the closest competitor to Williams — there are 246.

A comparison with Potts's dictionary shows that Williams does include many more terms, and they're treated more informatively. There are many notes on terms' derivation, history, statutes, related principles, and more. Also, the language is more modern, and even today Williams is markedly easier to understand than Potts. Potts tends to be terse, even cryptic at times; Williams is explanatory, tending toward verbosity.

Of course, many definitions in these earlier dictionaries are precisely the same — word for word. In addition to the work of Potts and any of various editions of Jacob, Williams may have drawn on John Cowell's *Interpreter* (1607, 1684, 1708, 1727, or maybe another edition), John Rastell's *Termes de la Ley* (1624, 1636, 1685, 1721, or maybe another edition), Timothy Cunningham's *New and Complete Law-Dictionary* (editions of 1764, 1771, and 1783), Richard Burn's *New Law Dictionary* (2 vols., 1792), and perhaps even *The Student's Law-Dictionary* (1740). The wordings of many entries are remarkably alike. What Williams did was blend encyclopedic comprehensiveness with a greater degree of readability.

INTRODUCTION

This dictionary marks an important stage toward the evolution of the modern law dictionary: it is half dictionary, half encyclopedia. Much if not most of the text is copied from earlier sources — the usual practice in those days — but Williams has often modernized the language to make it more accessible.

Williams may have been ahead of his time in producing a handy quarto edition of a law dictionary. Apart from various editions of *Termes de la Ley*, huge folios, such as those by Jacob and Cunningham, seem to have been the order of the day. It wasn't until precisely a century after Williams — with the publication of James A. Ballentine's *Law Dictionary*[4] — that short, small law dictionaries gained popularity. In some sense, Williams's work might be considered a predecessor of today's pocket law dictionaries. It wasn't until there was a large body of law students that people really needed a portable reference of this kind.

LawProse, Inc.
Dallas, Texas
March 2006

---

4 San Francisco: Bancroft-Whitney Co., 1916.

A

COMPENDIOUS

AND

COMPREHENSIVE

Law Dictionary;

ELUCIDATING

THE TERMS,

AND

General Principles

OF

LAW AND EQUITY.

By THOMAS WALTER WILLIAMS, Esq.

Of the Inner Temple, London, Barrister at Law,

AUTHOR OF THE LAW RELATIVE TO THE DUTY AND OFFICE OF A JUSTICE OF THE PEACE, &c. &c.

LONDON:

PRINTED FOR GALE AND FENNER, PATERNOSTER ROW.

1816.

W. Flint, Printer, Old Bailey, London.

TO THE PUBLIC.

In preparing the present Work, the object has been to combine, upon a correspondent scale, and within a moderate compass, an exposition of all the known Terms, and general Principles of Law and Equity, without entering into a diffuse detail of the various abstract points which have arisen from the discussion of those principles, in different cases.

In the performance of this undertaking, the most ancient and learned Interpreters of the Law, upon whose labours the larger Law Dictionaries are obviously founded, have been minutely examined; the Statutes have also been strictly attended to, and the best Authorities relied on.

Under these circumstances, it is presumed, that the volume now offered to public notice, will be found, upon examination, to be eminently useful, as a portable and convenient book of reference; and the more so, as it contains an accurate exposition of a very great variety of words, terms, and rules, not to be found in any other Dictionary on the same subject, now extant.

Inner Temple,
1st of July, 1816.

A

GENERAL DICTIONARY

OF

LAW AND EQUITY.

AB, When the name of a place begins with *Ab*, it denotes that either the place belonged to some abbey, or that an abbey was founded there: thus *Abingdon* in *Berkshire* took that name soon after *Cissa* king of the West Saxons had founded the abbey there; for before it was called *Cloveshoe*. *Cowel. Blount.*

ABACOT, the cap of state used in old time by our English kings, wrought up in the figure of two crowns. *Chron. Ang.* 1463. *Spelman. Cowel.*

ABACTORS, (*Abactores*, ab *abigendo*,) were stealers of cattle or beasts by herds or great numbers. *Blount. Cowel.*

ABACUS, (*Arithmetic*) or the art of numbering, from the *abacus* or table on which dust was strewed, and whereon the ancients set down their figures: hence also *abacista* an arithmetician. *Cowel. Blount.*

ABANDONMENT, (*on marine insurances*) is the exercise of a right, which the assured has, to call upon the underwriters or insurers to accept of what is saved, and to pay the full amount of the insurance, as if a total loss had happened, where the matter insured is, by some of the usual perils of the sea, become of little value.

Abandonment is as ancient, as the contract of insurance itself, and must be total and not partial of any particular part of the property insured. 1 *Ter. Rep.* 608. 2 *Bur.* 697. 1211.

And in all cases the insured has a right to elect whether he will abandon or not. *Park.* 144. 2 *Bur.* 697. 1211.

For this purpose as soon as the insured receives accounts of such a loss as entitles him to abandon, and not before, 2 *Bur.* 1211. he must in the very first instance make his election whether he will abandon or not; and if he abandon, he must give the underwriters notice in a reasonable time, otherwise he will be taken to waive his right to abandon, and can never after recover for a total loss. 1 *Ter. Rep.* 608.

But if the insured hearing that his ship is much disabled, and has put into port to repair, express his desire to the underwriters to abandon, and be dissuaded from it by them, and they order the repairs to be made, they are liable to the owner for all the subsequent damage occasioned by that refusal, though it amount to the whole sum insured, for they have by their own act superseded the necessity of notice. 2 *Ter. Rep.* 407.

The insured may abandon to the underwriters, and call upon them for a total loss, if the damage exceed half the value, if the voyage be absolutely lost or not worth pursuing, if further expence be necessary, and the insurer will not engage at all events to bear that expence, though it should exceed the value or fail of success; but he cannot abandon, unless at some period or other of the voyage there has been a total loss. 1 *Ter. Rep.* 187. *Park.* c. 9.

Also if neither the thing insured, nor the voyage be lost, and the damage does not amount to a moiety of the value, he shall not be allowed to abandon. 2 *Bur.* 1211. 3 *Atk.* 195. 2 *Bur.* 683.

And the right to abandon, must depend on the nature of the case, at the time of the action brought, or at the time of the offer to abandon: therefore where there was a capture and re-capture, and it was stated that at the time of the offer to abandon, the peril was over, as the ship was safe in port, and had suffered no damage, the court held that the insured had no right to abandon. 2 *Bur.* 1198. 1 *Black. Rep.* 276.

When the underwriter has discharged his insurance, and the abandonment is made, he stands in the place of the insured, and is entitled to all the advantages resulting from that situation, in case the ship or property is not totally lost, or is afterwards restored by recapture. *Park. c.* 9. 1 *Vez.* 98.

ABANDUN, (*Abandonum*) any thing sequestered, proscribed: *abandon, i. e. in bannum res missa:* a thing *bann'd* or *denounced* as forfeited and lost: to *abandon* or *desert* or *forsake* as lost and gone. *Cowel.*

ABARNARE, to detect and discover to a magistrate any secret crime: from the Saxon *abarian*, to uncover, disclose or make bare. *Cowel* B.

ABARSTICK, insatiable, from *a* privative, and the Saxon *Berstan, disrumpi.*

ABATE, seems to be derived from the French word *abattre destruere, prosternere*, to fell, break down or destroy, and is used in various senses in the law; as for instance, to abate a castle or fort is to beat it down, *old Nat. Brev.* 45 *St. Westm.* 1. *c.* 17. *abattre maison*, to ruin or cast down a house and level it with the ground. *Cowel. Blount.*

ABATEMENT of *Freehold.* An abatement in this sense is where a person dies seised of an inheritance, and before the heir or devisee enters, a stranger who has no right makes entry and gets possession of the freehold: this entry of him is called an *abatement*, and he himself is denominated an abator: this expression of *abating* which is derived from the French, is a figurative expression, and signifies to quash, bear down, or destroy: and in the present sense denotes that the rightful possession or freehold of the heir or devisee is overthrown by the intrusion of a stranger. 3 *Black. Com.* 168. 1 *Inst.* 277. *Comyns' Dig. Abatement.*

This abatement of a freehold is somewhat similar to an immediate occupancy in a state of nature, which is effected by taking possession of the land the same instant that the prior occupant by his death relinquishes it. But this, however agreeable to natural justice, considering man merely as an individual, is diametrically opposite to the law of society, and particularly the law of England; which, for the preservation of public peace, hath prohibited as far as possible all acquisitions by mere occupancy; and hath directed that lands on the death of the present possessor, shall immediately vest either in some person expressly named and appointed by the deceased as his devisee, or, on default of such appointment, in such of his next relations as the law hath selected and pointed out as his natural representative or heir: every entry therefore of a mere stranger, by way of intervention between the ancestor and heir or person next entitled, which keeps the heir or devisee out of possession, is one of the highest injuries to the rights of real property. 3 *Black. Com.* 168, 9.

ABATEMENT *of Nuisances*, is a species of remedy allowed by the law to the party injured by a *Nuisance*, to abate, destroy, remove, or put an end to the same by his own act: thus whatsoever unlawfully annoys or doth damage to another is, in contemplation of law, a nuisance, and such nuisance may be abated, that is, taken away or removed by the party aggrieved thereby, so as he commits no riot in the doing of it: as for instance, if a house or wall is erected so near to mine that it stops my ancient lights, which is a *private* nuisance, I may enter my neighbour's land and peaceably pull it down: or if a new gate be erected across the public highway, which is a *common* nuisance, any of the king's subjects passing that way may cut it down and destroy it. And the reason why the law allows this private and summary method of doing one's self justice, is because injuries of this kind, which obstruct or annoy such things as are of daily convenience and use, require an immediate remedy, and cannot wait for the slow progress of the ordinary forms of justice. 5 *Rep.* 101. 9 *Rep.* 55. *Salk.* 459. *Cro. Car.* 184. 3 *Black. Com.* 5. 6.

ABATEMENT *amongst Legatees.* If a man bequeaths specific legacies and pecuniary legacies, and the estate falls short to answer the pecuniary legacies, they shall abate in proportion, but nothing shall be abated from the specific legacies. 2 *Fonbl.* 369.

And as all legatees are on a deficiency of assets to be paid in proportion, so if the executor pay one of the legatees, yet the rest shall make him refund in proportion: and even if one of the legatees get a decree for his legacy and is paid, and afterwards the assets appear to have been originally deficient, yet the legatee who received shall refund: but if the executor had at first enough to pay all the legacies, and afterwards by his wasting the assets they became deficient, in such case the legatee who has received his legacy shall not be compelled to refund, but shall retain the advantage of his legal diligence, which the other legatees neglected by not bringing their suit in time, before the wasting by the executor: whereas if the other legatees had commenced their suit before such waste committed, they might have met with the like success, *et vigilantibus non dormientibus jura, Ibid.* 371. 1 *Pere. Wms.* 595. 2 *Pere. Wms.* 146. 2 *Bro. Ch. Rep.* 305.

But though a legatee who has received his legacy may if the assets were originally deficient, be called upon by other legatees to refund, yet he is not bound to refund at the suit of the executor unless the payment by the executor was compulsory. 2 *Vern.* 205. or the deficiency created by debts which did not appear till after payment of the legacy, 1 *Ch. Ca.* 136. but the executor will in such case be personally liable. 1 *Ch. Rep.* 71. but if there be a deficiency to pay debts, a legatee who has received his legacy, is in all cases liable to refund to creditors. 1 *Vern.* 94. 2 *Vent.* 360. *Anst.* 113. 2 *Fonbl.* 371, 2.

Although specific legatees are not to abate in proportion with other legatees, where there is a deficiency to pay debts, yet they must abate proportionably amongst themselves, if there be a deficiency of general assets. 2 *Fonbl.* 372. 2 *P. W.* 381. So where the testator doth bequeath any thing in satisfaction or recompence of some injury by him done; this legacy is not to abate any more than a specific legacy. 2 *Fonbl.* 373.

But if a man devise specific and pecuniary legacies, and afterwards says that such pecuniary legacies shall come out of all his personal estate, or words tantamount, or if there is no other personal estate than the specific legacies, they must be intended to be subject to the pecuniary legacies, otherwise he must mock the legatees. *Ibid.*

ABATEMENT, *Plea of.* This is a plea put in by the defendant, in which he alleges some matter to shew that he ought not to be impleaded; or if impleaded, not in the manner and form in which he is, therefore praying that the writ or plaint do abate, that is, cease against him for that time. 1 *Bac. Ab. Comyns' Dig. Co. Lit.* 303.

The order of pleading in abatement is, 1*st. To the jurisdiction of the court*; 2*ndly, To the ability of the plaintiff or person impleading;* and 3*dly, To the ability of the defendant or person impleaded. Co. Lit.* 303. *Comyn's Dig. tit. Ab.*

And as these pleas enter not into the merits of the cause, but merely tend to delay it, it is provided by *statute* 4 & 5 *Ann. c.* 16. *s.* 11. that *no dilatory plea shall be received in any court of record, unless the party by affidavit prove the truth of it, or shew some probable matter to induce the court to believe the fact true.*

Pleas in abatement must be pleaded within four days (the first and last both inclusive) after the declaration is delivered, if it be in term time; but if in vacation, or within less than four days from the end of the term, it may be pleaded (there being a special imparlance) within the first four days inclusive of the next term, *as of the preceding term;* and within that time it must be filed, (for it is not sufficient that it be *delivered only*) whether a rule to plead be given or not: Sunday is reckoned as one of the four days, though it happens to be the last, in which case the plea must be filed on the Saturday. *Cro. Jac.* 82. 3 *Ter. Rep.* 185. *Imp. K. B.* 239. *C. P.* 319. 1 *Ter. Rep.* 277. 689. 5 *Ter. Rep.* 210. 3 *Ter. Rep.* 642.

It is not an issuable plea within an order for time to plead upon the usual terms, and it is inadmissible after the rule for pleading is expired, or after forfeiture of a bail bond. 1 *Bur.* 59. *Barnes* 331. 2 *Salk.* 519.

I. *Plea to the jurisdiction of the court.* The pleas to the jurisdiction are, 1st, that the land is ancient demense; 2dly, within a county palatine; 3dly, within the cinque ports; 4thly, that the defendant has privilege, 1. as a peer; 2. as baron of the cinque ports; 3d. as officer to a court; 4. as a tinner; 5. as a minter only impleadable before the warden of the mint.

A plea to the jurisdiction of the court must be put in before any imparlance, for by craving leave to imparl, the defendant submits to the jurisdiction. 1 *Bac. Abr. Gilb. Hist. C. P.* 187. 22 *H.* 6. 7. *Barnes* 331.

But after a general special imparlance, that is, an imparlance with a general saving of all manner of exceptions, it seems that it may be pleaded; but the granting of such an imparlance is discretionary in the court, and it cannot be had but by special motion. 2 *Black. Rep.* 1094. 1 *Lut.* 46. 12 *Mod.* 529. *Hard.* 365. *Raym.* 34.

The plea must run that the defendant comes *in propriâ personâ*, and not by his attorney, for he cannot plead *by attorney* without leave of the court first had, which leave acknowledges the jurisdiction; for an attorney is an officer of the court; and if defendant puts in a plea by an officer of the court, that plea must be supposed to be put in by leave of the court. *Bac. Abr.* 2.

Every plea to the jurisdiction must state another jurisdiction. *Doct. pl.* 234. *Cowper* 172. 1 *Vez.* 203. 2 *Vez.* 357.

And the defendant must make but half defence, for if he makes full defence *quando et ubi curia consideraverit*, he submits to the jurisdiction of the court. *Co. Lit.* 127. *Gilb. Hist. C. P. Vent.* 334.

II. *Plea to the ability of the plaintiff or person impleading.*

(1. *Outlawry in the plaintiff.*) Outlawry in the plaintiff is a good plea in abatement, for he thereby loses his *liberam legem*, and is out of the protection of the law; for not having been answerable to the law, he ought not to have any privilege or benefit from it. 1 *Bac. Abr.* 3.

It cannot be pleaded without concluding *prout patet per recordum*, 3 *Lev.* 29. *Com.* 307.

And an express averment that the plaintiff and person outlawed are the same person is not necessary: it is sufficient if the identity be apparent on the face of the plea. *Lut.* 40. 2 *Mod.* 267.

This disability is only pleadable when the plaintiff sues in his own right, for if he sues *in right of another*, as executor, administrator, or as mayor with his community, outlawry shall not disable him, because the person whom he represents has the privilege of the law. *Co. Lit.* 128. *Gilb. Hist. C. P.* 197. 1 *Vern.* 184.

When outlawry is pleaded in abatement the plaintiff shall not reply that the outlawry is erroneous, for it is good until reversed. *Lut.* 36. *Ord. in Ch.* 97.

Outlawry in a court of inferior jurisdiction

cannot be pleaded in any of the courts of Westminster, for the party is only ousted of his law within the inferior jurisdiction. *Gilb. Hist. C. P.* 200. 1 *Bac. Abr.* 4.

Outlawry in a personal action, *it is said* goes only to *personal* actions in respect of the person; but outlawry in felony goes to actions generally. *Doct. pl.* 397. and see 33 *Hen.* 6. 19.

But outlawry does not entirely abate the writ, but is only a temporary impediment that disables the plaintiff from proceeding; for upon obtaining a charter of pardon, or reversing the outlawry, he is restored to his law, and can oblige the defendant to plead to the same writ. *Co. Lit.* 128. *Doct. pl.* 397. *Ord in Ch.* 97.

Outlawry may be pleaded always in *abatement*, but not in bar, unless the cause of action be forfeited. *Co. Lit.* 128 b. *Doct. pl.* 395.

And in pesonal actions where the damages are uncertain, outlawry cannot be pleaded in bar; but in actions on the case, where the debt to avoid the wager of law is turned into damages, outlawry may be pleaded in bar; for it was vested in the king by the forfeiture as a debt certain and due to the outlaw, and the turning it into damages, whereby it becomes uncertain, shall not divest the king of what he once lawfully possessed. 2 *Lutw.* 1604. 3 *Lev.* 29. 2 *Vent.* 281. 3 *Leon.* 197. *Cro. Eliz.* 204. *Owen* 22.

And outlawry may be pleaded in bar after it has been pleaded in abatement, because the thing is forfeited, and the plaintiff has no right to recover. 10 *Hen.* 7. 11. 42 *Lutw.* 1604.

(2. *Excommunication of plaintiff.*) It may be pleaded in abatement, that the demandant or plaintiff is excommunicated. *Co. Lit.* 134. *a.* 1. *Lut.* 17.

And it is a good plea, though he sue in the *right of another*, as an executor, or administrator: for an excommunicate person is excluded from the body of the church, and is incapable to lay out the goods of the deceased to pious uses. *Gilb. Hist. C. P.* 203. *Co. Lit.* 134.

But excommunication is no plea to the next friend of an infant. *Pr. Reg. Ch.* 278.

And excommunication is no plea on a *qui tam* action, because it is for example, and the statute having given the informer an ability to sue, and not excepted excommunicated or other disabled persons from the liberty of informing, he is enabled to sue by the statute, notwithstanding the censures of the church. 12 *Co.* 61. *Gilb. Hist. C. P.* 203.

And the plea of excommunication must state the precise time when the party was excommunicated. *Cro. Jac.* 82.

A replication that the plaintiff has *appealed* from the sentence, is bad, for the sentence is in force until it is repealed; and while it is in force the plaintiff cannot appear in any of the courts of justice, but he may reply that he is absolved, for then his disability is taken away: the absolution must, however, appear to have been by the same bishop who excommunicated, or by the archbishop upon appeal. *Bro. Excom.* 3. 3 *Bulst.* 72. 20 *Hen.* 6. 25. *Gilb. Hist. C. P.* 204. *Moor* 775.

(3. *Attainder of plaintiff.*) It may also be pleaded in abatement that the plaintiff is attainted of *treason* or *felony*, or attainted in a *præmunire*, for all such persons are incapable of bringing any action, being wholly out of the protection of the law. *Co. Lit.* 128, 129, 130, a. *Noy* 1. *Show*, 55. *Gilb. Hist. C. P.* 205. *Doct. pl.* 10.

(4. *Popish Recusancy by plaintiff.*) This disability of popish recusancy convict is by virtue of the statute 3 *Jac.* 1. *c.* 5. which disables the party to all intents and purposes whatsoever, except when he sues for lands, tenements, leases, annuities, rents, and hereditaments, or the issues or profits thereof, which are not to be seized into the hands of the king, his heirs, or successors: but this cannot be pleadable now against those papists who (see PAPISTS) may conform to *statute* 18 *Geo.* 3. *c.* 60. and *statute* 31 *Geo.* 3. *c.* 32. and take the oaths therein prescribed.

(5. *Alien enemy.*) An alien enemy cannot have any action real, personal, or mixt, nor can an alien friend have any, except a personal action. *Dyer* 2. b. 19 *Ed.* 4. 6. 6 *Ter. Rep.* 23.

And it may be pleaded in abatement that he is an alien, if he be an alien enemy. *Co. Lit.* 129. *Ast. Entries*, 11.

And as he cannot sue directly in his own name, so neither can he sue indirectly in the name of a trustee. 6 *Ter. Rep.* 23.

But this is to be understood as to cases where he sues *proprio jure*, for it is said that he may sue *en autre droit*, as executor or the like: nor is it any exception that the testator was an alien enemy, unless it be shown that he was so at the time of his death: and if he were resident here when he died, the court will intend that he was so with the king's licence. *Skin.* 370. *Lutw.* 35.

So if an alien comes here under letters of safe conduct, or resides here by the king's licence, he is to be deemed an alien friend, and the plea of alienage will be unavailable. *Ld. Raym.* 282. *Salk.* 46. *Lutw.* 34.

Therefore in pleading *alienage*, it is necessary to aver that the plaintiff is *an alien enemy*, and when so pleaded, the plaintiff, if he has a protection, must state it in his replication whether it be general or special, and should conclude with an averment. 2 *Str.* 1082. 2 *Atk.* 397. *Fortes.* 221. 1 *Mod.* 150. *Lutw.* 34. *Ld. Raym.* 282.

Alienage may be pleaded either in bar or in abatement; but with this difference, that alienage can be only pleaded in *abatement* to an *alien in league*, but may be pleaded in *bar* to an *alien enemy*, because the cause of action is forfeited to the king, as a reprisal for the damages committed by the dominion in enmity. *Bro. Den.* 10. *Co. Lit.* 129 b. 1 *Bac. Abr. tit. Ab.*

(6. *Coverture of plaintiff.*) It may also be pleaded to the person of the plaintiff, that she is a feme covert, and, as it seems, that she is the wife of the defendant: and to a plea of coverture the plaintiff may reply that she is sole, which shall be tried by the country. *Co. Lit.* 132. *b. Ast. Ent.* 9, 10. 17 *Ed. III.* 20 b. 1 *Bro. Ent.* 63.

So in an action by husband and wife, it may be pleaded that she was not covert at the day of the writ purchased; or that they never were married; or that there was a divorce between them, and so she is not his wife; but it is no plea if there be a divorce, though the divorce only be *a mensa et thoro*. *Th. Dig. L.* 11. *c.* 2. *s.* 8. *Sho.* 50. 39 *Ed.* 3. 32. 1 *Comyns* 12.

So it is no plea if the queen consort sues alone. *Co. Lit.* 133. a.

Also if a feme sole plaintiff, after the verdict, and before the day in bank, takes husband, she shall have judgment, and the defendant cannot plead this coverture, for he has no day to plead it at. *Cro. Car.* 132. 1 *Buls.* 5.

(7. *Want of proper parties.*) It may be pleaded in abatement to the ability of the demandant or plaintiff, if he sues alone when others ought to join with him in the action, that *another who ought to join is not named*, such as 1. a coparcener; 2. a joint-tenant; 3. a tenant in common; 4. a joint-contractor, co-obligor, or copartner; 5. an executor suing without naming the others; and 6. the like of administrators.

But if a man plead that the plaintiff hath nothing but jointly with another, who is alive and not named, he ought to shew by his plea where he is living: for the issue shall be joined upon the life, and not upon the death, which comes on the part of the tenant or defendant. 22 *Ed.* 3. 8. 1 *Comyns* 13.

It may also be pleaded in abatement to the person of the plaintiff, that there *never* was any such person *in rerum natura*, or *that* there *never* was one of the plaintiffs *in rerum naturâ*, or that there *never* was such an one *in rerum naturâ* as A, who is named another defendant; and no such person *in rerum naturâ* as to one abates the whole writ: but that there was no such person *at the day of the original purchased*, is ill, for it ought to be alleged that he was dead *before* the original purchased, or that there *never* was such a person *in rerum naturâ*. *Bro.* 25. 70 *Th. Dig. l.* 11. *Ast. Ent.* 10. *Bendl. pl.* 196. *Com.* 18, 19.

(8. *Misnomer of the plaintiff.*) The defendant may also plead misnomer of the plaintiff if his *christian* name be mistaken, or if his *christian* name be omitted, though he be known by the name by which he sues: for he can have but one name of baptism, and ought to sue by his true name, and not by the name by which he is known. *Th. Dig. L.* 3. *c.* 1. *s.* 7. but if a bond or other specialty security be given to Elizabeth, and an action is brought in the name of Elizabeth, the defendant shall not plead that the plaintiff's name is Isabel. *Bunb.* 101.

So if a peer of the realm sue, he ought to sue by his name of baptism as an earl, or the like. *Th. Dig. L.* 3. *c.* 1. *s.* 6.

But a plaintiff may sue by his name of confirmation. *Th. Dig. L.* 3. *c.* 1. *s.* 7. *R.* 2. *Rol.* 135. (A.)

And a corporation aggregate shall sue by its name of incorporation, without the name of its chief magistrate. 2 *Inst.* 666.

And where it appeared that the plaintiffs were incorporated by the name of *the mayor and burgesses of Stafford*, "*in the county of Stafford*," and they sued merely in the name of *the mayor and burgesses of the borough of Stafford*, omitting the words *in the county of* Stafford: it was held that this misnomer was pleadable in abatement, and that it could not be taken advantage of in any other way. 1 *Bos. & Pul. Rep.* 40.

So if the surname of the plaintiff be omitted, it may be pleaded in abatement; or if it be mistaken, or if his name of baptism be joined by his name of office, it is not sufficient without his surname, as A. parson of D. *Comyns' Dig. tit. Ab.*

But if the surname *by which he is known* is added, it is sufficient. *Th. Dig. L.* 2. *c.* 2. *s.* 1.

And the plaintiff may reply to the plea of misnomer, that he is as well known *by one name* as the other. *Comyns' Dig. tit. Ab.*

So if it be said A, the daughter or son or duke, archbishop, or bishop of B, it is good, and not pleadable in abatement. *Ibid.*

But if the plaintiff has a name of dignity, as an earl, bishop, knight, or the like, and it be omitted or mistaken, it may be pleaded in abatement. *Ibid.*

But a dignitary of another realm, as of *France*, or the like, need not be so named. *Ibid.*

So if the plaintiff sues for any thing relating to his office, such as a sheriff, prebendary, precentor, or the like, he ought to name himself by the name of his office, otherwise it may be pleaded in abatement. *Ibid.*

So if a plaintiff sues, and to his name of baptism adds a wrong addition, it may be pleaded in abatement. *Ibid.*

III. *Plea to the ability of the defendant or person impleaded.*

(1. *Plea by defendant of privilege.*) The officers of each court enjoy the privilege of being sued only in those courts to which they respectively belong; the reason whereof

is because of the duty they are under of attending those courts, and lest their client's cause should suffer if they were drawn to answer to actions in other courts. 2 *Mod.* 297. *Vaughan,* 155. 2 *Hen.* 7. 2. 2 *Rol. Abr.* 272. 1 *Lutw.* 44. 639.

Whenever therefore an attorney is sued out of his own court, he may say that he is *attorney* of another court, but the plaintiff may reply that he is a husbandman, or the like in the country, and traverse his being an attorney. *Lutw.* 44. 639. *Bro. Traver.* 27.

But this privilege is not the privilege of the officers, but of the suitors and attendance is the ground and foundation of it: it must therefore be alleged that the officers are actually attendant in their respective courts, otherwise the plea will be disallowed. 2 *Wils.* 42. 228. 1 *Str.* 546. 4 *Bur.* 2109. *Andr.* 45.

And the plaintiff must have the same remedy against the officer in his own court, as in that where he sues him, for if money be attached by foreign attachment in the sheriff's court of London, he shall not have his privilege; because in that case the plaintiff would be remediless. *Saund.* 67, 68. *Gilb. Hist. C. P.* 209, 210. *Sid.* 362. 2 *Keb.* 346. *pl.* 24. 2 *Lem.* 156. *pl.* 190.

So if a writ of entry, or other real action, be brought against an attorney of the king's bench, he cannot plead his privilege; because if this should be allowed, the plaintiff would have a right without a remedy, for the king's bench hath not cognizance of real actions. *Sand.* 67. *Gilb. Hist. C. B.* 210.

So if an attorney of the common pleas be sued in an *appeal,* he shall not have his privilege; for his own court hath no coguizance of this action; nor if sued as *bail.* *Rep.* and *Cas. Prac. C. P.* 64. *Gilb. Hist. C. P.* 110.

The privilege which the courts indulge their officers with is restrained to those suits only which they bring, or which are brought against them in their own right; for if they sue or are sued as executors or administrators, they then represent common persons, and are to have no privilege. *Hob.* 177. *Gilb. Hist. C. P.* 211. 17 *Viner* 517. 1 *Bac. Abr.* 8.

So if an officer of one court sue an officer of another, the defendant shall not have his privilege; for the attendance of the plaintiff is as necessary in his court, as that of the defendant in his, and therefore the cause is legally attached in the court where the plaintiff is an officer. *Gilb. Hist. C. P.* 211. *Godb.* 81. *pl.* 95. *Brownl.* 37. 2 *Black. Rep.* 1325.

So if a privileged person bring a joint action, or if an action be brought against him and others, he shall not have his privilege. *Gilb. Hist.* 212. *Dyer* 377. *Godbol.* 10. 2 *Lev.* 129.

An officer shall not have his privilege against the king, for as the xecutive power is lodged in the king, it would be unreasonable that his court, which gives relief to private persons, should protect any subject from being brought to justice for offending against the laws which concern the whole commonwealth. *Fortes.* 342. *Gilb. Hist. C. P.* 208.

But in an action *qui tam,* at the suit of an *informer,* he shall have his privilege. *Lil. Reg.* 7. 3 *Lev.* 398. *Lutw.* 193.

If an attorney of the common pleas be *in custodia maresch.* for want of bail, at the suit of A, he may plead his privilege, but if he be in such custody at the suit of A and B, who declare against him as so; if he has waved his privilege as to A, he cannot take advantage of it against B. 2 *Rol. Abr.* 275. *pl.* 7. *Salk.* 1. *pl.* 3. 5 *Mod.* 310. 3 *Lev.* 343. *Ld. Raym.* 135.

After a general imparlance, an officer cannot plead his privilege, because by imparling he affirms the jurisdiction of the court. *Bro. Priv.* 25. 22 *Hen.* 6. 7. *Sid.* 29, *Hard.* 365. *Lutw.* 46. *Salk.* 1. *Show* 522.

He may plead as well to an action on a bill of exchange, as to any other personal action. *Doug.* 312.

But an attorney has not any privilege to be sued in Middlesex; it is enough that he be sued in his own court. *Fortes.* 343, 344. 4 *Bur.* 2027.

(2. *Plea by defendant of misnomer and want of addition.*) Misnomer is a good plea in *abatement;* for since names are the only marks and *indicia* of things which human kind can understand each other by, if the name be omitted or mistaken, there is a complaint against no one. 1 *Bac. Abr.* 9.

But though a defendant may, by pleading in *abatement,* take advantage of a misnomer when there is a mistake in the writ or declaration, as to the name of baptism or surname, yet in such a plea he must set forth his right name, so as to give the plaintiff a better writ. *Finch.* 363. 9 *Han.* 51. *pl.* 3.

And it is pleadable only in abatement. 2 *Bl. Rep.* 1120.

One defendant cannot plead *misnomer* of his companion, for the other defendant may admit himself to be the person. *Lutw.* 36.

The defendant, though his name be mistaken, is not obliged to take advantage of it; and therefore if he be impleaded by a wrong name, and afterwards impleaded by his right name, he may plead in bar the former judgment and aver that he is *one and the same person.* 2 *Str.* 1218.

In case of felony at common law, if a person were indicted by a wrong name, he could not plead misnomer, but was obliged to plead to the felony; for the fact being sworn against the party present, it was thought that there could be no injury by the *misnomer,* as there might be, where the party appeared by attorney; and felons generally go by no certain name, nor have they any fixed habitation. *Cro. Car.* 104. 21 *E.* 4, 72. 2 *Inst.* 670. *Sid.* 40. *Lit. Rep.* 8.

But now the party accused, may take advantage of *misnomer*, or the want of *addition:* however, if he do, he must plead over to the felony; but though such plea be found for him, he is not to be discharged, but must be indicted over again, neither shall such plea, if found against him, be peremptory, but he shall be tried on his plea in chief. 2 *Hawk. P. C.* 186,7.

And it is now necessary to set forth the state, place of abode, and dignity of the person impleaded, lest an innocent person suffer, by having the same name with the real defendant; for 1 Hen. 5. c.5, enacts, *that in all personal actions, appeals, and indictments, there shall be added to the names of the defendants, their estates, degrees, mystery, and place of abode.*

Additions which are inducements to the action must be made use of; as if one is liable as heir, he must be named heir, so, if as an executor he must be named as such. 1 *Bac. Ab.* 10.

And mistakes in such additions are good objections in abatement, both at law and in equity. *Rast.* 324. 11 *Hen.* 7. 11. *Mitf. Eq.* 192. *Pr. Reg.* 278.

And if the defendant plead a mistake in the addition, he must set forth his right addition. 2 *Str.* 816. 10 *Mod.* 208. 2 *Ld. Raym.* 1178, 1541.

(3. *Plea by defendant of coverture.*) Coverture is a good plea in abatement on a writ brought against a feme covert as sole, but it cannot be pleaded after an imparlance. *Reg. pl.* 290. *Lutw.* 23, 24. 3 *Ter. Rep.* 627.

And if a feme covert sued as sole, do not plead her coverture, but neglect to do it, and there be a recovery against her as a feme sole, the husband may avoid it by writ of error, and may come in at any time and plead it. *Lutw.* 24. *Style* 254. 2 *Rol. Rep.* 53.

A feme covert defendant may plead, that she is the wife of the plaintiff. *Th. Dig. l.* 11. *c.* 2. *s.* 7. 12 *Ed.* 3. 481. *Ray.* 395.

And she may plead the same, although her husband lives out of the realm, *per Lit.* 18 *Ed.* 4. 4. Although she has given a bail bond, for if she be covert, it is not her deed. 1 *Sal.* 7. *Mod. Cas.* 311.

So if an action be brought in an inferior court against a feme sole, and pending the suit, she intermarry, and afterwards remove the cause by *habeas*, and the plaintiff declare against her as a feme sole, she cannot plead coverture at the time of suing the *habeas*. *Barnes* 355.

To a plea of coverture, the plaintiff may reply that the defendant was not covert. *Cl. Ass.* 15. but a replication that the defendant was separated from her husband, and having alimony under a decree of the ecclesiastical court, made the promises on her own account as feme sole, 5 *Ter. Rep.* 679. or that she was living in adultery, 4 *Ter. Rep.* 766, or living apart from the husband, carrying on a separate trade is bad. 6 *Ter. Rep.* 604.

(4. *Plea in abatement by defendant for want of proper parties.*) A defendant may also plead in abatement, that he is not a person able to answer without another not named, who has equal right with himself. *Brac. l.* 5. *de exceptionibus, c.* 26.

As if a *parcener* be sued, she may plead that there is another co-heir not named. *Th. Dig. l.* 5. *c.* 1. *s.* 2, 3, 5.

So if a *joint-tenant* be sued, he may plead in abatement that he holds jointly with such a one, who is alive, and not named. *Comyns, Dig. tit. Ab.*

Also, if a man sue a personal action against a *tenant in common*, touching the lands held in common, without naming his companion, he shall plead that he held in common the day of the writ purchased. *Comyn's Dig. tit. Ab.*

So if an action be sued against a *husband* alone, where *the wife* ought to be joined, it may be pleaded in abatement, that he holds jointly with his *wife* not named. *Ast. Ent.* 10.

So, if there be *co-obligors, joint-contractors*, or *copartners*, and one only is sued without the other of them, it may be pleaded in abatement, that the other is alive not named. *Ast. Ent.* 7. *Cro.Eliz.* 355. *Lutw.* 696.

And copartnership must be pleaded in abatement, and cannot be given in evidence to *nonsuit* the plaintiff on the trial. 5 *Burr.* 2611.

So, if debt be brought against an *heir* in gavelkind, it may be pleaded that there is another coheir not named. 11 *Hen.* 7. *c.* 12.

But against an heir on the part of the father, and an heir on the part of the mother, the writs ought to be several, 11 *Hen.* 7. 12; and it is the same against an heir and the executors. 18 *Ed.* 3. 4.

So if one executor or administrator be sued, it may be pleaded that there is another executor or administrator not named. *Rast. Ent.* 324, 325.

So if one executor or administrator be misnamed, the other may plead that there is another executor (naming him by his true name) not named. *Th. D. l.* 11. *c.* 5. *s.* 15.

(5. *Plea in abatement by defendant in real actions.*) So if a *real action* be sued against *several*, it may be pleaded in abatement that they hold *severally*, *Lutw.* 11; or that one of them holds parcel of the land as *tenant in severalty*. *Th. Dig.* 11 *c.* 31. *s.* 7.

So in an action against several, the one may take the *entire tenancy* on himself and demand judgment of the writ, or may take the entire tenancy upon himself as to part, and plead as to the other. *Th. Dig.* 11. *c.* 33. *s.* 5. *Sav.* 116.

So if the tenant plead *non tenure*, the writ shall abate. *Cro. Eliz.* 559. *Ast. Ent.* 10. *Lutw.* 37. 581,b.

So if he plead a special *non tenure*, as that he has common, and puts the cattle into the land as in his common, without that, that he has any other possession, and that such a one is tenant of the freehold. *Th. Dig. l.* 11. *c.* 22. *s.* 48.

Or that he holds only for years, by statute, elegit, or other occupation, and that another is tenant of the freehold. *Ibid. s.* 48.

But non tenure of parcel shall only abate for that parcel. St. 25 *Ed.* 3. *c.* 16.

Upon a plea of non tenure, if it be found for the defendant, judgment shall be, that the defendant go quit: but the demandant may enter. *Comyn's Dig. tit. Ab.*

So if the tenant *disclaims*, the writ shall abate; but an action accrues to the demandant by a writ of right upon the *disclaimer*. *Th. Dig. l.* 11. *c.* 34. *s.* 2.

If the tenant disclaims, the judgment shall be, that the tenant go without day, and after such judgment the defendant may enter. *Lit. s.* 691.

So the tenant may plead that *the demandant himself* was seised on the day of the writ purchased; or that he was seised of parcel. *Th. Dig. l.* 11. *c.* 35. *s.* 1—18—4—6; but it is no plea in an action upon the *stat.* 8 *Hen.* 6. for a *forcible entry*. *Th. Dig. l.* 11. *c.* 35. *s.* 16; nor in trespass, that the plaintiff was possessed of the goods taken. *Ibid. c.* 36. *s.* 2. nor in replevin. *Ibid. c.* 36. *s.* 3.

ABATEMENT, *plea of to the count or declaration.*) The first act, *after the appearance of the parties, and the admittance of the jurisdiction, and the abilities of both parties (plaintiff and defendant)* is, that the party suing, counts or declares; and afterwards the party impleaded, that is the deforceant in real, or defendant in personal actions, may demand oyer of the writ: and then if there be any fault or insufficiency in the count or declaration for a cause apparent in itself; or if there be a variance between the count or declaration and the writ, or between the writ and the record, specialty or the like-mentioned in the count or declaration, and the writ, or between the writ and the record, specialty, or like-mentioned in the count or declaration; the party impleaded ought to shew it and plead. *Th. Dig. l.* 10. *c.* 1. *s.* 5. *Fitz. Count,* 27.

As in real actions, it may be pleaded in abatement, that the lands, tenements, or other things are not demanded by their proper names, or in the proper order in which they ought. *Comyn's Dig. tit. Ab.* or that the same thing is *twice demanded*, as if the demand be of a manor and rent, when the rent is parcel of the manor. *Th. Dig. l.* 8. *c.* 25. *s.* 1. So also it may be pleaded in abatement to the demand, that the *demand* is mistaken, or that the demand is of a manor, whereas the tenements put in view, are two houses, or the like, and not a manor. 6 *Ed.* 3. 242. *Th. Dig. l.* 8. *c.* 27. *s.* 9. *Comyn's Dig. tit. Ab.*

So also it may be pleaded in abatement, that the plaint is of two several and *distinct causes* of action; as where the plaint is of two trespasses depending upon two separate and distinct titles. *Reg. Pl.* 282, 283.

Also it may be pleaded that the plaint is not in a proper action; as that the plaintiff hath declared in an action on the case, when he ought to have an account, *Reg. Pl.* 283; or that he hath brought an action upon the case, when he ought to have brought trespass. *Th. Dig. l.* 10. *c.* 27. *s.* 3.

But in an action upon the case for money received to his use, it is no plea in abatement, that he received as bailiff. 1 *Show.* 71.

So also it may be pleaded in abatement, that the count *or* declaration shews a demand before a cause of action, as in a *scire facias* by an administrator, tested 12th Feb. the defendant upon *oyer* of the administration, dated 26th March afterwards, may plead in abatement, that the action was sued before a cause of action. 2 *Lev.* 197. So in an assumpsit upon a promise to pay within 7 years, if brought before the 7 years expired. *Bend. pl.* 93, or in debt before the day of payment arrived. *Hob.* 245. *Ast. Ent.* 7.

So in an action against an administrator, it may be pleaded in abatement, that the writ was *tested* before administration granted; or against an executor, that the testator was alive at the time of the writ purchased; or in debt against an heir, that his ancestor was alive the day of the original purchased. *Lutw.* 8, 14, 15, 16.

So also *default of legal form* may be pleaded in abatement, as that the count does not pursue the legal form: as in a *writ of right, formedon*, and the like, that no *espleas* are alleged. *Bro. Count.* 7. In prohibition that it is not alleged, that the writ of prohibition was delivered to the defendant, though this is not traversable. *Bro. Count.* 11.

Upon a plea to the count or declaration, there is no other judgment but *quod quer, nil capiat, per breve*, and therefore a fault herein abates the writ. *Bro. Count.* 8, 12, 24. 60. 64, 74.

If the count or declaration varies in form, the defendant may plead *the variance* in abatement, for the plaintiff has abated his own writ, by prosecuting it in a different manner; but if it varies in substance, the defendant may move it in arrest of judgment, because the court has no authority to proceed, a different matter being prosecuted from that which the writ has given authority to the court to take cognizance of. *Cro. Eliz.* 722. *Cro. Ja.* 651. *Jones* 304.

But the defendant cannot plead a variance between the writ and count or declaration, without praying oyer of the writ, and shewing it to the court. 2 *Wils.* 85, 395.

The declaration varying from the writ, as by laying the cause of action in the reign of a present king, when the writ supposed it to have been in the reign of a former king, or by giving the defendant a name different from that in the writ, as where the writ calls him A B, of London, *Alderman,* and the plaintiff declares against him as A B of London, *Esquire,* or where the declaration is otherwise defective, in not pursuing the writ, or not setting forth the cause of action with that certainty the law requires, or in laying the offence in a different county from that in which the writ is brought; in all such cases, the defendant may plead in abatement. *Fitz. Nat. Brev.* 219, 230. *Yelv.* 120. *Finch.* 357. *Latch.* 173. *Allen* 17, 18.

But the writ may in some cases be general, and the declaration special; as where a statute gives an action, but does not prescribe any form of the writ, the writ framed by the common law will serve, and the special matter may be set forth in the declaration. *Doct. pl.* 84.

It may also be pleaded in abatement, that there is *another action brought for the same thing,* for the law abhors multiplicity of actions; and therefore whenever it appears on record, that the plaintiff has sued out two writs against the same defendant for the same thing, the second writ shall abate, for if it were allowed that a man should be twice arrested, or twice attached by his goods, for the same thing, by the same reason he might suffer *in infinitum*; and it is not necessary that both should be pending at the time of the defendant's pleading in *abatement,* for if there was a writ in being at the time of suing out the second, it is plain the second was vexatious and ill, *ab initio.* 1 *Bac. Abr. tit. Ab.*

So also may it be pleaded to an information *qui tam,* 2 *Hawk. P. C.* 275. but to defeat an informer by a plea of this kind of his right of suing, a defendant must shew a prior right attached in somebody else, and therefore if the pendency of another action, by another person for the same offence brought in the same term, be pleaded in abatement, it must be shewn on what particular day, such other action was commenced, that its priority may be ascertained: so if both actions were commenced on the same day, the defendant, it seems, may shew that the action which he states, was prior in point of time on that day, notwithstanding it was formerly holden, that in that case, the right was attached in neither, and the court could give no judgment. 3 *Bur.* 1423. 1 *Bl. Rep.* 437. 2 *Lev.* 141. 2 *Str.* 1169.

But it is no good plea in *abatement* of an indictment, as it is of an appeal or information, that there is another indictment against the defendant for the same offence, but in such a case, the court in discretion, will quash the first indictment. 2 *Hawk. P. C.* 367.

And on a plea in abatement, of another action pending, it must appear plainly to be for the same thing; for an assise of lands in one county, shall not abate an assise in another county, for these cannot be the same lands. 4 *H.* 6. 24. *Doct. pl.* 10.

In *general* writs as *trespass,* and the like, where the special matter is not alleged, the defendant cannot plead in abatement another action depending for the same matter, without alleging that the plaintiff, hath declared in it, for without such allegation it cannot be traversed, whether it be for the same matter or not: but it is otherwise when the first is a *special* writ, and sets forth the particular demand, for there the court can readily see, that it is for the same thing, and therefore the first shall abate the second writ, it being apparently brought for the same thing. *Lit. Pr. Reg.* 8. 2 *Barnard,* 143. 5 *Co.* 61. *Doct. pl.* 11, 12. *Th. Dig. l.* 11. *c.* 39. *s.* 19.

An action depending in an inferior court, cannot be pleaded to an action brought in one of the courts at Westminster, for the same thing, and upon a demurrer to such a plea, the court will give judgment against the defendant *quod respondeat ouster.* 5 *Co.* 62. *Dyer* 92, 93. *Fitzgib.* 313.

If a second writ be brought, tested the same day the former is abated, it shall be deemed to be sued out after the abatement of the first. *Gilb. Hist. C. P.* 260.

And if an action pending in the same court, be pleaded to a second action brought for the same thing, the plaintiff may pray that the record may be inspected by the court, or demand oyer of it, which if not given him in convenient time, he may sign his judgment. *Dyer* 227. *Carth.* 453, 517. *Ld. Raym.* 347, 550. 6 *Mod.* 122.

The pendency of a prior action may be pleaded either in bar or abatement, although it is said in the case of *Baines* v. *Blackbourne,* to be pleadable only in bar. 3 *Bur.* 1423. *Sayer's Rep.* 216.

To an action of debt on a judgment recovered, the defendant cannot plead a writ of error brought, and pending either in bar or in abatement: but the court on a summary motion, will direct the proceedings to be stayed pending the writ of error. *Carth.* 136. 1 *Bac. Abr. tit. Ab. N.*

Abatement by a defect in the writ.] The preceding objections being matters *dehors,* must be shewn to the court: and must be pleaded in proper time and manner as already observed, but for defects in the writ itself, the court may *ex officio* abate it. 1 *Bacon's Abr.* 17.

Herein the law hath been very strict in obliging men to keep to the legal forms it prescribes, and therefore in the writ which is the foundation of the whole proceedings, it requires full certainty and exactness, as that no person be arrested or attached by his goods, unless there appear sufficient grounds to warrant such proceedings, so that if the writ vary materially from that in the register, or be defective in substance, the party may take advantage of it. 9 *Hen.* 7. 16. 10 *Ed.* 3. 1. *pl.* 2. *Hob.* 1, 51, 57, 84. *Carth.* 172. *Cro. Jac.* 376,7.

But though the writ vary from the register, yet if it be warranted by the modern precedents, this shall not abate it. *Hob.* 84.

And there is a difference between original and judicial writs, for in the former, matter of form abates them as well as substance, but in the latter it is otherwise, for if the substance be good, the want of form will be aided. 41 *Ed. III.* 13, 14.

ABATEMENT *by demise of the king.*] At common law, all patents of justices, commissions civil and military, were determined by the death of the king; and all suits depending in the king's courts were discontinued, so that the plaintiffs were obliged to commence new actions, or to have re-summons or attachment on the former processes, to bring the defendants in, but to prevent the inconvenience, expense, and delay, which this occasioned, were the *statutes* of 1 *Ed.* 6. *c.* 7. and 1 *Ann. st.* 1. *c.* 8. *s.* 1. passed. 1 *Bacon's Abr. tit. Ab.* which acts are in substance as follows:

By stat. 1 *Ed.* 6. *c.* 7. *By the death of the king, no action, suit, bill, or plaint depending between party and party in any court of record, shall be discontinued, and put without day, but the process, pleas, demurrers, and continuances, shall stand good in the same condition as if the king had lived.*

But this stat. does not extend to actions in a county court or other court not of record. 7 *Co.* 30. b. nor to actions in which the original is not returned, for before the return it is not depending. 7 *Co.*30. *a.* 1 *And.* 44-5. *Bend* 79.

And now, by stat. 1 *Ann. c.* 8. it is enacted, that *no writ, plea, or process, or other proceeding on any indictment or information, or for any debt or account to her majesty or successors shall be discontinued, and put without day by her or their death, but shall continue in force and may be proceeded upon.*

And no original writ, writ of nisi prius, commission, process or proceeding out of any court of equity or upon any office or inquisition, nor any writ of certiorari, or habeas corpus in any cause, criminal or civil, nor any writ of attachment or process for contempt, shall be abated or discontinued by the death of the queen or her successors.

ABATEMENT *by the death of parties.*] The death of the plaintiff or defendant before interlocutory judgment is an abatement of the suit; but where there are more than two or more plaintiffs, or defendants, the general rule was, before the stat. of 8 & 9 *Wil.* 3. 9. hereafter noticed, that although the death of one of the parties may happen, pending the writ, and yet the plea is in the same condition, as if such party were living, there such death makes no alteration; for where the death of the parties makes no change of proceedings it would be unreasonable that the surviving parties should make any alteration in the writ; for if such writ and process were changed, it would set rights but in the same condition they were in at the death of the parties, and it would be absurd that what made no alteration should change the writ and the process. 1 *Bacon's Abr. tit. Ab.*

This rule, however, respecting the non-abatement of a suit, by the death of one of the parties, where there were two or more plaintiffs or defendants, where such death made no alteration in the proceedings laid down as above by the Lord Chief Baron *Gilbert*, though founded in reason was not uniformly supported by authorities, and the aid of the legislature became requisite for the purpose of enforcing it.

Accordingly it was enacted by *stat.* 8. *and* 9. *Wil. III. c.* 11. that *if there be two or more plaintiffs or defendants, and one or more of them shall die, if the cause of action survive to the surviving plaintiff or plaintiffs, or against the surviving defendant or defendants, the writ or action shall not be thereby abated, but such death being suggested on the record, the action shall proceed at the suit of such surviving plaintiff or plaintiffs against such surviving defendant or defendants.* s. 7.

Although this statute makes mention only of actions at law, yet it hath been construed to prevent the abatement of a suit in equity, provided that the subject matter of the suit be not affected by it. 1 *Atk.* 291.

And the formal suggestion of the death need be only on the plea roll; nothing more, is necessary on the *nisi prius* roll, than merely to point out to the judge what he is try, and between whom. 1 *Burr.* 362.

By the same *stat.* 8 & 9 *Will.* 3. *c.* 11. it is also enacted, *that if any plaintiff happen to die after an interlocutory judgment, and before a final judgment obtained therein*, the said action shall not abate *by reason thereof, if such action might originally be prosecuted or maintained by the executors or administrators of such plaintiff: and if the defendant die after such interlocutory judgment, and before final judgment therein obtained*, the said action shall not abate, *if such action might originally be prosecuted or maintained against the executors or administrators of such defendant; and the plaintiff*, or *if he be dead, after such interlocutory judgment, his executors or administrators shall and may have a* scire facias *against the defendant if living, after such interlocutory judgment; or if dead after, then against his executors or administrators to shew cause why damages in such action should not be assessed and recovered by him or them ; and if such defendant, his executors or administrators shall appear at the return of such writ and not shew or allege any matter sufficient to arrest the final judgment or being returned warned, or upon two writs of* scire facias *it be returned that the defendant his executors or administrators, had nothing whereby to be summoned,* or could not be found in the *county, shall make default,* that thereupon a writ of inquiry of *damages shall be awarded, which being executed and returned, judgment final shall be given for the said plaintiff his executors or administrators prosecuting such writ or writs of* scire facias, *or against such defendant his executors or administrators respectively.*

And agreeable to the equity of this statute, where the plaintiff died after a rule by consent to refer the matter to the prothonotary, and before the report made, The court allowed his executors to be made a party to the rule, and directed the prothonotary to proceed without the defendant's consent.

Manner of pleading in abatement.] The defendant cannot plead two outlawries or two excommunications in abatement, for this would be duplicity in pleading, and duplicity is a fault in abatement as well as in bar. *Carth.* 8, 9.

In pleas of abatement which relate to the person there is no necessity of laying a venue, for all such pleas are to be tried where the action is laid. *Salk.* 4. *Carth.* 363. 12 *Mod.* 125, 195.

If a defendant plead matter in abatement, and conclude in bar, this shall be esteemed a plea in bar, and the court will give final judgment thereupon, because by pleading to the action the writ is admitted to be good, and he puts the whole matter upon his plea. 2 *Rol. Rep.* 64. *Lev.* 312. *Mod.* 214. 2 *Sand.* 128.

So if a man plead in bar and conclude in abatement, this shall be esteemed a plea in bar, because he could have no writ, if he could have no action; and where there could be no action the dispute about the writ would be insignificant. 6 *Mod.* 103. *Lut.* 34, 36. 10 *Hen.* 7. 11.

A plea in abatement may be good though it contains matter in bar; but this is to be understood of such pleas as may be pleaded either in disability or in bar, as *outlawry* and the like. 6 *Mod.* 215. 10 *Hen.* 7. 11.

If a matter which may be pleaded either in abatement or bar, be pleaded in abatement only, if the plaintiff reply or demur in bar, this will be a discontinuance, because the plaintiff does not maintain his writ, and the defendant may have other matter in bar of which he would hereby be excluded. 1 *Bac. Abr. tit. Ab.* P.

But if the defendant begin such plea in bar, and conclude in abatement, or plead in abatement and conclude in bar, then the plaintiff may reply or demur to it, either as a plea in abatement or in bar; and if he demur or plead to it as a plea in bar, then the judgment is final, for he has closed with the defendant to put the plea to the judgment of the court as a bar to the action. *Vent.* 136. *Lutw.* 36. 3 *Mod.* 281.

All pleas to the jurisdiction conclude to the cognizance of the court, praying *judgment whether the court will have further cognizance of the suit;* pleas to the disability conclude to the person by praying *judgment, if the said A. the plaintiff ought to be answered;* and pleas in abatement (when the suit is by original), concludes to the writ or declaration by praying *judgment of the writ or declaration,* and that it may be quashed *cassetur,* made void or abated: but if the action be by bill, the bill must pray *judgment of the bill,* and not of the declaration, the bill being here the original, and the declaration only a copy of the bill. 5 *Mod.* 132. 3 *Black. Com.* 303.

And it is said to be the conclusion of a plea, and not the matter of it, that makes a plea in abatement, so that should a man plead a plea, that for the matter of it might have been pleaded in bar, and concludes *petit quod breve cassetur,* it would be but a plea in abatement, and the judgment would be no other than a *respondeat ouster:* so *vice versa,* a plea in abatement, pleaded in form of a plea in bar, would be a plea in bar though an ill one. 10 *Mod.* 112. *Show.* 4.

If a dilatory plea be pleaded, and the plaintiff take issue upon it, he may conclude with a *petit judicium et damna,* because there final judgment shall be; but if a dilatory plea be pleaded, which the plaintiff does not deny, but confess and avoid, he must conclude in maintenance of his writ; as if the defendant plead an attainder in disability of the plaintiff, and he plead a pardon, he must not conclude with a *petit judicium et damna,* but in maintenance of his writ. 6 *Mod.* 236. 3 *Mod.* 281.

If the defendant demur in *abatement,* the court will give final judgment, because there can be no demurrer in abatement; for if the matter of abatement be *de hors,* it must be pleaded, if intrinsic, the court will take notice of it themselves. *Salk.* 210. *pl.* 9. 6 *Mod.* 195, 198.

If on a plea in abatement a *respondeat ouster* is awarded, and afterwards the defendant pleads in chief, and there is a verdict for the plaintiff, yet if the plea in abatement does not appear to have been entered on the *nisi prius* record, judgment will be arrested; for it being entered on the plea roll (which was in court) it must be entered on the *nisi prius* roll, otherwise it does not appear that it was a verdict in the same cause. *Carth.* 447, 499. *Ld. Raym.* 329. 5 *Mod.* 399.

The judgment for the defendant on a plea in abatement is *quod breve vel narratio cassetur,* and for the plaintiff a *respondeat ouster;* but if issue be joined on a plea in abatement, and it be found for the plaintiff, it shall be peremptory against the defendant, and the judgment shall be *quod recuperet*, because the defendant choosing to put the whole weight of his cause on this issue, when he might have had a plea in chief, it is an admission that he had no other defence. *Yelv.* 112. 2 *Show* 42. *Str.* 532. *Cath.* 138. 1 *Wils.* 302.

But on a demurrer to a plea in abatement, the judgment against the defendant shall be only to *answer over*, because the issues in fact are within the conusance of the party: issues in law are not. *Th. Dig. l.* 16. *c.* 11. *s.* 12. 1 *Lev.* 163.

And the same judgment shall be given, though the defendant join in demurrer to it as to a plea in bar, because the fault originates with the plaintiff. 1 *Vent.* 135.

And upon a *respondeat ouster*, no notice need be given of it, for the defendant is supposed to be attending his cause in the paper to maintain his plea. *Salk.* 7. *pl.* 18.

And on the filing of a plea in abatement the plaintiff may if he think fit enter a *nil capiat per breve*. *Barnes* 257. *Salk.* 4. *pl.* 11.

ABATOR, is a person that abateth, that is, intrudeth into a house or land void by the death of the former possessor, and not yet entered or taken up by his heir. *Cowel.*

ABATUDE, that is diminished, *moneta abatuda*, is money clipped or diminished in value. *Cowel. Blount. Du Cange in verbo.*

ABAWED, that is, terrified; from the French *echabir*; *attonitum reddere*. *Cowel. Blount.*

ABBACY, in Latin *abbatia* or *abbathia*, is the same as to the government of a religious house and the revenues thereof, subject to an abbot, as a bishoprick is to a bishop.

ABBAT or ABBOT, (in Latin *abbas*, French *abbe*, and Saxon *abbud*,) was before the dissolution of the monasteries in the reign of Henry the eighth, the spiritual lord or governor who had the rule and government of such religious house. *Cowel. Blount.*

At the time of the dissolution of these religious houses, these spiritual persons consisted of ninety-six mitred abbots and two priors. 1 *Black.* 155.

Such as were mitred had episcopal authority within their limits, being exempted from the jurisdiction of the diocesan, but the other sort of *abbots* were subject to the diocesan in all spiritual government. *Cowel. Blount.*

The mitred abbots were lords of parliament, and called abbots sovereign, and abbots general, to distinguish them from the other abbots. The lords priors also had exempt jurisdiction, and were likewise lords of parliament. *Cowel. Blount.*

However by statute 27 *Hen.* 8. *cap.* 28. all abbeys, monasteries, priories, and other religious houses, not above the value of 200*l.* *per ann.* were given to the king, who sold the lands at low rates to the gentry. And in 29 *Hen.* 8. the rest of the abbots made voluntary surrenders of their houses to obtain favour of the king: and *anno* 31 *Hen.* 8. a bill was brought into the house to confirm those surrenders; which passing, completed the dissolution, except the hospitals and colleges, which were not dissolved, the first till the 33d, and the last till the 37th of *Hen.* 8. when commissioners were appointed to enter and seize the said lands and hereditaments.

ABBATIS, an avener or steward of the stables; the word was sometimes used for a common hostler. *Cowel. Blount.*

ABROCHMENT, (*abbrocamentum*) The buying up of wares before they are exposed to sale in a fair or market, and selling the same by retail; which is a forestalling of a market or fair. *Cowel. Blount.*

ABBUTTALS, (from the French *abbuter* or *aboutir*, to limit or bound) are the buttings and boundings of lands, either to the east, west, north, or south, shewing on what other lands, highways, or other places they abut, or are limited and bounded.

ABDICATE, (*abdicare*) to renounce or refuse any thing. *Terms de Ley* 5. *Cowel. Blount.*

ABDICATION, (*abdicatio*) in general, is where a magistrate or person in office, renounces and gives up the same, before the term of service is expired. And this differs from resignation, in that, *abdication* is done purely and simply; whereas *resignation* is in favour of some other person. *Chamb. Dict.*

It is said to be a renunciation, quitting, and relinquishing, so as to have nothing further to do with a thing; or the doing of such actions as are inconsistent with the holding of it. *Ibid.*

Thus on king *James's* leaving the kingdom, the lords and commons met in a convention, and both houses resolved, that he had *abdicated the government, and that the throne was thereby vacant*. By this vote the government was allowed to subsist, though the executive magistrate was gone, and the kingly office to remain, though king James was no longer king: and thus the constitution was kept entire, which upon every sound principle of government must otherwise have fallen to pieces, had the royal authority been abolished, or even suspended, for that would have levelled all distinctions of honour, rank, offices, and property, would have annihilated the *sovereign* power, and in consequence have repealed all positive laws, and would have left the people at liberty to have erected a new system. *Black. Com.* 212, 213.

ABDITORIUM, an abditory or hiding-place, to hide and preserve goods, plate, or money; or a chest in which reliques were kept, as mentioned in the inventory of the church of *York*. *Mod. Aug. p.* 173. *Cowel. Blount.*

ABDUCTION

ABDUCTION (*of children*) is an injury offered to a person, considered in the relation of a parent, and is of two kinds: but Blackstone states it to be a matter of doubt whether it be a civil injury or not; as before the abolition of the tenures in chivalry it was equally a doubt, whether an action would lie for taking and carrying away any other child besides the heir: some holding that it would not, upon the supposition that the only ground or cause of action was losing the value of the heir's marriage: and others holding that an action would lie, for taking away *any* of the children, for that the parent hath an interest in them all, to provide for their education (*Cro. Eliz.* 770); if therefore before the abolition of these tenures it was an injury to the father to take away the rest of his children as well as his heir, (as *Blackstone* inclines to think it was,) it still remains an injury, and is remediable by a writ of *ravishment*, or action of trespass *vi et armis, de filio, vel filia rapto vel abducto, Fitz. N. B.* 90. in the same manner as the husband may have it for the abduction of his wife. 3 *Black. Com.* 140.

Of a Ward.] Of a similar nature to the last is the *abduction* of a ward from the guardian: and the like actions, *mutatis mutandis*, as are given to fathers, the guardian also has for recovery of damages, when his ward is stolen or ravished away from him. *Fitz. Na. Br.* 139.

And though guardianship in chivalry is now totally abolished, which was the only beneficial kind of guardianship to the guardian, yet the guardian in socage was always (*Fitz. Nat. Br.* 139) and is still entitled to an action of ravishment, if his ward or pupil be taken from him: but then he must account to his ward or pupil for the damages which he so recovers. *Hale on Fitz. N. B.* 139.

And as guardian in socage was also entitled at common law to a writ of *right of ward, de custodia terræ et hæredis*, in order to recover the possession and custody of the infant: so according to the opinion of Blackstone is he at this day still entitled to sue out this antiquated writ. 3 *Black. Com.* 141.

But a more speedy and summary method of redressing all complaints relative to wards and guardians, hath of late obtained, by an application to the court of chancery, which is the supreme guardian, and has the superintendant jurisdiction of all the infants in the kingdom. *Ibid.*

And it is expressly provided by statute 12 *Car.* 2. *c.* 24. that testamentary guardians may maintain an action of ravishment or trespass for recovery of any of their wards, and also for damages, to be applied to the use and benefit of the infants.

Of an Heiress.] The *forcible abduction* and *marriage* of a female, which is vulgarly called *stealing an heiress*, is an offence punishable by the statute law: for by 3 *Hen.* 7. *c.* 2, it is enacted, that *if any person shall for lucre take any woman, being maid, widow, or wife, and having substance either in goods or lands, or being heir apparent to her ancestors, contrary to her will; and afterwards she be married to such misdoer; or by his consent to another; or defiled: such person, his procurers and abettors, and such as knowingly receive such, shall be deemed principal felons;* and by 39 *Eliz. c.* 9. the *benefit of clergy is taken away* from all such felons, who shall be principals, procurers, or accessaries *before* the fact.

In the construction of this statute it hath been determined, 1st. that the indictment must allege, that the taking was for lucre, for such are the words of the statute. 1 *Hawk. P. C.* 110. 2dly, in order to shew this, it must appear that the woman has substance either real or personal, or is an heir apparent, 1 *Hale P. C.* 660. 1 *Hawk. P. C.* 109: 3dly, it must appear that she was taken away against her will; 4thly, it must also appear, that she was afterwards married or defiled, and though possibly the marriage or defilement might be by her subsequent consent, being won thereunto by flatteries after the taking, yet this is felony, if the first taking were against her will, 1 *Hal. P. C.* 661. and so *vice versa*, if the woman be originally taken away by her own consent, yet if she afterwards refuse to continue with the offender, and be forced against her will, she may from that time as properly be said to be taken against her will, as if she never had given any consent at all; for till the force was put upon her, she was in her own power, 1 *Hawk. P. C.* 110. It is held that a woman thus taken away and married, may be sworn and give evidence against the offender, though he is her husband *de facto*, contrary to the general rule of law, because he is no husband *de jure*, in case the actual marriage was also against her will, 1 *Hal. P. C.* 661; but in cases where the actual marriage is good by the consent of the inveigled woman, obtained after her forcible abduction, Sir Matthew Hale seems to question how far her evidence should be allowed; but other authorities seem to agree, that it should even then be admitted; esteeming it absurd that the offender should thus take advantage of his own wrong, and that the very act of marriage, which is a principal ingredient of his crime, should (by a forced construction of law) be made use of to stop the mouth of the most material witness against him. 4 *Black. Com.* 208.

An inferior degree of the same kind of offence, but not attended with force, is punished by the statute 4 & 5 *Phil.* & *Mar. c.* 8. which enacts, that "*if any person above the age of fourteen, unlawfully shall convey or take away any woman-child unmarried*, (which is held (2 *Str.* 1162) to extend to bastards as well as to legitimate children) *within the age of sixteen years, from the possession and against the will of the father, mother, guardians, or governors, he shall be imprisoned two years, or fined at the discretion of the justices: and if he deflowers such maid or woman-child, or without the consent of parents contracts matrimony with her, he shall be imprisoned five years, or fined at the discretion of the justices, and she shall forfeit all her lands to her next of kin during the life of her said husband:* so that as these stolen marriages under the age of sixteen, were usually upon mercenary views, this act, besides punishing the seducer, wisely removed the temptation. 4 *Black. Com.* 209.

It has been decided in the court of exchequer, that she forfeits her lands only during the life of her husband, *Amb.* 73. though the more natural construction of the statute seems to be, that the next heir shall retain them during the life of the wife, even after the death of the husband. 1 *Brown* 25.

But the latter part of the above act is now rendered almost useless by provisions of a very different kind, which make the marriage under certain circumstances totally void. See 26 *Geo.* 2. *c.* 33. under title MARRIAGE, and 4 *Black. Com.* 210.

Of a Wife.] Abduction or *taking away* a man's wife, is an offence, and may be either by fraud and persuasion or open violence, though the law in both cases supposes force and constraint, the wife having no power to consent: and therefore a remedy is given to the husband for this injury, by writ of *ravishment*, or action of *trespass vi et armis de uxore rapta et abducta, Fitz. Nat. Br.* 89. 3 *Black.* 139.

This action lay at the common law; and thereby the husband shall recover, not the possession of his wife, but damages for taking her away. 2 *Inst.* 434. 3 *Black.* 139.

And by stat, *West.* 1. 3 *Ed.* 1. *c.* 13. the offender shall also be imprisoned two years, and be fined at the pleasure of the king: both the king and husband may therefore prosecute: and the husband is also entitled to recover damages in an action on the case against such as persuade and entice the wife to live separate from him, without a sufficient cause. *Bull. N. P.* 74. 3 *Black.* 139.

The old law was so strict in this point, that if a man's wife missed her way upon the road, it was not lawful for another man to take her into his house, unless she was benighted and in danger of being lost or drowned, *Bro. Abr. Tres.* 223. but a stranger might carry her behind him on horseback to market, to a justice of the peace for a warrant against her husband, or to the spiritual court to sue for a divorce. *Bro. Abr. Tres.* 307. 440. 3 *Black.* 139.

ABEARANCE. For recognizances to be of good *abearance*. See title SURETY.

ABECHED, (from the French *abecher*, to feed) is an old word, which signifies to be satisfied. *Cowel. Blount.*

ABEREMURDER, (*aberemurdrum*) plain or downright murder; as distinguished from the less heinous crimes of manslaughter and chancemedley. It is derived from the Saxon *æbere*, apparent, notorious, and *mord*, murder; and was declared a capital offence, without fine or commutation, by the laws of *Canute, cap.* 93. and of *Hen.* 1. *cap.* 13. *Spelm. Cowel. Blount.*

ABESSED, that is, humbled, (from the French *abaisser*) to depress, and hence the English words *base* and *abase*.

ABET, (*abettare*) from the Saxon *a*, and *bedan* or *beteren*, to stir up or excite; or from the French *bouter, impellere* or *excitare*. In our common law it signifies as much as to encourage or set on; the substantive *abetment* implies the same, *Staundf. Pl. Cr.* 105. And both are always taken in the worst sense, as *abettor* (*abettator*) is an instigator or setter on; one that promotes or procures a crime. *Old. Nat. Br.* 21. *Abbettors* of murder are such as command, procure, or counsel others to perpetrate the murder; and in some cases these *abettors* shall be taken as principals, in others but as accessaries; their presence or absence, at the time of committing the fact, making the difference. *Co. Lit.* 475. *Hawk. P. C. part* 2.

There are also *abettors* in treason, but they are as principals, for there are no accessaries in treason. *Fleta. lib.* 1. *c.* 34. *Cowel. Blount.*

ABEYANCE, or *abbayance*, (from the French *bayer*) to expect. It is what is in expectation, remembrance, and contemplation of law. *Cowel. Blount.*

According to a received principle of law, the fee-simple or inheritance of lands and tenements is gererally vested and resides in some person or other; though divers inferior estates may be carved out of it: as if one grants a lease for 21 years, or for one or two lives, the fee-simple remains vested in him and his heirs; and after the determination of those lives or years, the land reverts to the grantor or his heirs, who shall hold it again in fee-simple. 2 *Black.* 106.

Yet sometimes it has been said, that the fee may be in *abeyance*, that is, as the word signifies, in expectation, remembrance, and contemplation in law; there being no person in *esse* in whom it can vest and abide, though the law considers it as always potentially existing, and ready to vest, whenever a proper owner appears. 2 *Black.* 106.

Thus in a grant to *John* for life, and afterwards to the heirs of *Richard*, the inheritance is plainly neither granted to *John* nor *Richard*, nor can it vest in the heirs of *Richard* till his death, for *nemo est hæres viventis*; it hath therefore been said to remain in waiting in *abeyance*, or *in nubibus*, or *in gremio legis*, during the life of *Richard*, after whose death, the heir has a good remainder, as a purchaser, and it ceases to be in abeyance. *Cowel. Blount. Co. Lit.* 342. 2 *Black.* 106.

But the late Mr. Fearne has produced anthorities which prove beyond all doubt, that "where a remainder of inheritance is limited in contingency by way of use, or by devise, *the inheritance in the mean time,* if not otherwise disposed of, *remains in the grantor and his heirs*, or in the heirs of the testator, until the contingency happens to take it out of them. *Fearne's Cont. Rem.* 513.

And although different opinions appear to have prevailed, in respect to the admission of this doctrine, *in conveyances at common law,* yet Mr. *Fearne* adduces (*Cont. Rem.* 526.) arguments and authorities, which render the doctrine as unquestionable in this case, as in the two former of uses and devises. 2 *Black. Com.* 107.

And therefore professor *Christian,* in a note on the above case, as put by *Judge Blackstone,* observes, that if John should determine his estate either by his death, or by a feoffment in fee, which amounts to a forfeiture in the lifetime of Richard, under which circumstances the remainder never could vest in the heirs of Richard, in that case the grantor or his heir may enter and resume the estate. 2 *Black.* 107. *n.* by *Chr.*

So also it hath been said, that if a man be a patron of a church, and presents one to the same, there the fee of the lands and tenements pertaining to the rectory is in the parson; but if the parson die, and the church become void, then is the fee in *abeyance,* until there be a new parson presented, admitted, and inducted; for the patron hath not the fee, but only the right to present, the fee being in the incumbent that is presented. *Terms de Ley,* 6.

The frank-tenement of the glebe of a parsonage, during the time the parsonage is void, is in no man; but *in abeyance* or expectation, belonging to him who is next to enjoy it. *Lit.* 647. 2 *Black.* 107.

But professor *Christian* observes upon these two last cases, that from the doctrine now established by *Fearne,* there does not seem to be any necessity to resort to *abeyance* to explain the residence of the inheritance, or of the freehold: *in the first case* the whole fee simple is conveyed to a sole corporation, the parson and his successors; but if any interest is not conveyed, it still remains in the grantor and his heirs, to whom upon the dissolution of the corporation, the estate will revert: and in the *second* case, the freehold seems in fact, from the moment of the death of the person to vest and abide in the successor, who is brought into view, and notice by the institution and induction: for after induction, he can recover all the rights of the church which accrued from the death of the predecessor. 2 *Black.* 107. n. (3.) by *Chr.*

And it is clear that a fee-simple in *abeyance* cannot be charged until it comes *in esse,* so as to be certainly charged or aliened; though by possibility it may fall every hour. *Co. Lit.* 378.

ABGATORIA, *abgetorium,* the alphabet, *A, B, C, &c.* This seems to be an Irish word, as the Irish still call the alphabet *abghittin. Cowel.*

ABIGEVUS, for *abigens,* signifies a thief who hath stolen many cattle. *Bract. Tract.* 1. *l.* 1. 3. *cap.* 6. 105. *a. Cowel. Blount.*

And the Roman law punished more severely than other thieves, the *abigei* or stealers of cattle. 4 *Bl.* 239. 240.

ABISHERSING, is to be quit of amercements. It originally signified a forfeiture or amercement; and is most probably *mishersing* or *miskering,* according to the learned *Spelman.* By some, it hath been termed a liberty or freedom, because, wherever this word is used in a grant or charter, the persons to whom made, have the forfeitures and amercements of all others, and are themselves free from the controul of any within their fee. *Rastal's Abr. Terms de Ley. Cowel. Blount.*

ABJURATION, (*abjuratio*) a forswearing or renouncing by oath, signifies a sworn banishment, or an oath taken to forsake the realm for ever. *Staundf. Pl. C. l.* 2. *c.* 40. Formerly in king Edward the Confessor's time, and other reigns down to the 22 *Hen.* 8. (in imitation of the clemency of the Roman emperors towards such as fled to the church) if a person accused of any crime (except treason or sacrilege) could fly to a church or church-yard before his apprehension, he might not be taken from thence to be tried for his crime; but on confession thereof before the justice, or before the coroner, he was admitted to his oath to abjure or forsake the realm; which privilege he was to have forty days, during which time any person might give him meat and drink for his sustenance, but not after, on pain of being guilty of felony. *Cowel. Blount.* and *Horn's Mirror. lib.* 1. And if during this 40 days privilege, he was apprehended and arraigned in any court for the felony he might plead the privilege of sanctuary, and had a right to be remanded: but by this abjuration his blood was attainted, and he forfeited all his goods and chattels. *Mir. c.* 2. *s.* 13. 2 *Hawk. P. C. c.* 335. 2 *Hawk. P. C. c.* 52.

But at last, this punishment being but a perpetual confinement of the offender to some sanctuary, wherein (upon abjuration of his liberty and free habitation) he would chuse to spend his life, as appears by the stat. *anno* 22 *Hen.* 8. *c.* 14. it is enacted, by 21 *Jac.* 1. *cap.* 28. "That thence after; no sanctuary or privilege of sanctuary shall be allowed:" whereupon this abjuration ceased. 2 *Inst.* 629. *Oath of. See* OATHS.

ABOLITION, a destroying or effacing, or putting out of memory: it also signifies the leave given by the king, or judges, to a criminal accuser to desist from further prosecution. *Stat.* 25 *Hen.* 8. *c.* 21. *Cowel. Blount.*

ABRIDGE, (*abbreviare*) is derived from the French word *abbreger,* to make shorter in words and still retain the sense and substance. But in law it signifies the making a declaration or count shorter, by subtracting or severing some of the substance from it: for instance, a man is said to abridge his plaint in assise; and a woman her demand in action of dower, where any land is put into the plaint or demand, which is not in the tenure of the defendant; for if the defendant pleads non-tenure, joint-tenancy, or the like, in abatement of the writ as to part of the lands, the plaintiff may leave out those lands, and pray that the tenant may answer to the rest. The reason of this abridgment of the plaint is, because the certainty is not set down in such writs, but they run in general; and though the demandant hath abridged his plaint in part, yet the writ will be good for the remainder. *Brook. tit. Abridgment*, *vide* 21 *Hen.* 8. *c.* 3. and *Cowel* and *Blount.*

ABROCAMENTUM, the buying goods by the wholesale before they are brought to the market, and selling them again in parcels.

ABROGATE, (*abbrogare*) to disannul or take away any thing: as to abrogate a law, that is, to lay aside or repeal it. *Cowel. Blount.*

ABSENTEES, or *des absentees*, was a parliament so called, held at Dublin 10th May, 8 *Hen.* 8. And mentioned in letters patent, dat. 29 *Hen.* 8. 4 *Co. Inst.* 354. *Cowel. Blount.*

ABSOLVE, (*absolvere*) to absolve one excommunicated, or to pardon, or set free from excommunication. *Vide* Assoile.

ABSOLUTIONS, from Rome, high treason, &c. *Stat.* 23 *Eliz. c.* 1.

ABSONIARE, was a word used by the English Saxons in the oath of fealty, and signified to shun or void. *Cowel. Blount.*

ABSQUE HOC, (without this, that, &c.) are words of exception made use of in a traverse; as the defendant pleads that such a thing was done at B, &c. *absque hoc*, that it was done at, &c. *Mod. Ca.* 103.

ACCAPITUM, and *accapitare*, the same with relief due to lords of manors.—*Capituli domino, accapitare, i. e.* to pay a relief to the chief lord. *Fleta, l.* 2. *c.* 50. *Cowel. Blount.*

ACCEDAS AD CURIAM, is a writ that lies where a man hath received false judgment in a hundred court or court-baron. It is directed to the sheriff; and issued out of the Chancery, but returnable into B. R. or C. B. And is in the nature of the writ *de falso judicio*, which lies for him that had received false judgment in the county-court. In the Register of Writs, it is said to be a writ that lies as well for justice delayed, as for false judgment; and that it is a species of the writ *recordari*, the sheriff being to make record of the suit in the inferior court, and certify it into the king's court. *Reg. Orig.* 9. 56. *F. N. B.* 18. *Dyer*, 169. *Cowel. Blount.*

ACCEDAS AD VICECOMITEM. This is a writ directed to the coroner, commanding him to deliver a writ to the sheriff; who, having a writ called a *pone* delivered to him, suppresseth it. *Reg. Orig.* 83. *Cowel. Blount.*

ACCEPTANCE, (*acceptatio*) is the taking and accepting of any thing in good part, and as it were a tacit agreement to a preceding act, which might have been defeated and avoided, if such acceptance had not been. *Cowel. Blount.*

Thus, where the condition of a bond is to pay money, *acceptance* of another thing is good. But if the condition is not for money, but a collateral thing it is otherwise. *Dyer*, 56. 9 *Rep.* 79. And the *acceptance* of uncertain things, as customs or the like, made over, may not be pleaded in satisfaction of a certain sum due on bond. *Cro. Car.* 193. If a woman hath title to an estate of inheritance, as dower, or the like, she shall not be barred by any collateral satifaction or recompence: and no collateral *acceptance* can bar any right of inheritance or freehold, without some release or the like. 4 *Rep.* 1. When a man is entitled to a thing in gross, he is not bound to *accept* it by parcels; and if a lessor distrains for rent, he is not obliged to *accept* part of it; nor in action of detinue, part of the goods. 3 *Salk.* 2.

If a man be bound in 200 quarters of corn, with condition to pay 20*l.* the obligor may, by agreement, give the obligee any other thing in satisfaction of the money; but if the condition had been to pay 100 quarters of corn, there the acceptance of money; or any other thing, had not been good, because the contract was not made for money, but for a collateral thing. *Peyto's* case, 9 *Rep.* 79. And yet it seems reasonable, if the obligee *agrees to accept, and does accept the same in satisfaction* and discharge, that the obligor should plead the same, if the agreement is by deed. *Morgan.*

Debt upon bond, conditioned for the obligor to make an assurance of such lands to such uses as in the condition mentioned: the defendant pleaded, that he had made a feoffment of the same lands to other uses than in the condition expressed, which the obligee had accepted; and upon demurrer it was adjudged an ill plea; for the obligor ought not to vary from the uses set forth in the condition. 1 *Brownl.* 60.

Acceptance of a *less* sum may be in satisfaction of a *greater* sum, if it be before the day on which the money becomes due: for where a lesser sum is paid before it is due, and the payment is accepted, it shall be good in satisfaction of a greater sum. Thus in debt upon bond, conditioned to pay 8*l.* &c.; defendant pleaded payment of 5*l.* before the day mentioned in the condition, which the obligor accepted in satisfaction of the bond; and upon demurrer this was adjudged a good plea. *Moor* 677. *Vide* 3 *Bul.* 301.

But if the defendant plead payment *generally*, without alleging, that it was *in satisfaction* of the debt, it is as bad on demurrer. 5 *Rep.* 117.

But payment after the day of a *less* sum is not good, as the bond is forfeited, at *common law;* and there is not any statute to relieve. Thus, debt upon bond, conditioned, that in consideration the plaintiff had paid 12*l.* to the defendant, he became bound to pay the plaintiff 12*l.* if he lived one month after the date of that bond; and if not paid at that time, then to pay to him 14*l.* if he lived six months after the date of the bond; the defendant pleaded, that, *after* the six months, he paid the plaintiff 8*l.* and then gave him another bond in the penalty of 20*l.* conditioned to pay him 10*l.* on a certain day, in full satisfaction of the other bond, and that the plaintiff did accordingly accept the said bond; upon a demurrer to this plea it was held ill; for admitting that one bond might be given in satisfaction of another, yet it cannot be after the other is forfeited, as it was in this case; because after the forfeiture the penalty is vested in the obligee, and a less sum cannot be a satisfaction for a greater. 1 *Lut.* 464.

But by the stat. 12 *Ann. c.* 16. payment *after the day* specified in the condition, may be pleaded.

It hath been adjudged, that the acceptance of one bond cannot be pleaded in satisfaction of another bond. *Cro. Car.* 85. *Moore* 872. *Cro. Eliz.* 716, 727. 2 *Cro.* 579. because the acceptance of a new bond to pay money at another day, could not be a present satisfaction for the money due on the day when it was to be paid on the old bond. *Hob.* 68. But it is otherwise where the second bond is not given by the original *obligor*, as if a defendant be sued as heir, and he plead that his ancestor, the obligor, died intestate, and that *W. R.* administered, who gave the plaintiff another bond in satisfaction of the former: there a verdict must be taken for the defendant: and this is the distinction, *viz.* that if the obligor, who gave the first bond, likewise give the second, it will not discharge the first; but in case the second bond be not given by him who gave the first, but by his administrator, which mends the security, (because he may be chargeable *de bonis propriis:*) for that reason the second bond will be a discharge of the first. 1 *Mod.* 225.

ACCESSARY, *(particeps criminis)* from the Latin word *accedo: qui alium accedit in vitio impetrando,)* signifies a man that is guilty of a felonious offence, not principally, but by participation, as by command, advice, or concealment, and is of two sorts, 1st, before the offence or fact; 2dly, after the offence.

—— *Before the fact.*] An accessary *before* the fact is he, that being absent at the time of the felony committed doth yet procure, counsel, command, or abet another to commit a felony, and it is an offence greater than the accessary after; and therefore in many cases clergy is taken away from accessaries *before*, which yet is not taken away from accessaries *after*, as in petit treason, murder, robbery, and wilful burning, but by 4 & 5 *P.* & *M. c.* 4. 1 *Hale's History of the Pleas of the Crown* 615 —If the commander or counsellor be present, he is a principal. *H. H. P. C.* 616. Words which sound in bare permission, make not an accessary, as if A. says he will kill I. S. and B. says, you may do your pleasure for me, this makes not B. accessary, 1 *H. H. P. C.* 616. 21 *Hen.* 7, 36, 37. *Cromp.* 41. *b.* If A. hires B. to mingle or lay poison for C. and B. doth it accordingly, and C. is poisoned; B. though absent, is principal, and A. is accessary; but if A. were present at the mingling or laying of the poison, though both were absent at the taking of it, yet both are principal, for they are both equally acting in the poisoning. But if A. buys the materials of the poison, knowing and consenting to the design, and deliver them to B. to mingle and apply it, or lay it in the absence of A. here it seems A. is only accessary before. *H. H. P. C.* 616. See 3 *Inst. p.* 50. *State Tr. vol.* 1. *p.* 329.

There cannot be an *accessary* before the fact in manslaughter, because it is committed of a sudden, and unpremeditated. *H. P. C.* 317. He who counsels or commands any evil shall be adjudged *accessary* to all that follows upon it, but not to any thing else. If a person commandeth another to beat such a person, and he beats him so that he dies of his wounds, the person commanding will be *accessary* to the murder. *Ibid.*

But if the command had been to beat another person, or to burn such a house, and he burns another, he that commandeth will not be *accessary.* 3 *Inst.* 51. If I command a person to do an unlawful act, as to rob A. B. at one place, and he doth it at another; or to rob him on such a day, and he doth it not himself, but procures another to do it; or to kill by poison, and he does it by violence; in all these cases I shall be *accessary:* but where the command is to kill A. B. and he killeth A. D. this difference in substance will not make the commander *accessary.* *Plowd.* 475. If a man counsels a woman to murder the child in her womb, and the woman murder her child after it is born, he is *accessary* to the murder. *Dyer* 185.

—— *After the fact.*] An *accessary* after the fact is he that receives, assists or comforts any man that hath committed murder or felony, which hath come to his knowledge; but this doth not extend to a woman who receives or assists her husband, though a husband receiving his wife will be *accessary:* and a servant may be *accessary* in relieving his master, or assisting him in his escape. 3 *Inst.* 108.

If the wife alone, the husband being ignorant of it, do knowingly receive a felon, the wife is accessary and not the husband. 1 *H. H. P. C.* 621.

But if felons come to the house of D. and M. his wife, and M. know them to be felons, though D. doth not, and both D. and M. receive and entertain them, but M. consents not to the felony: adjudged that this makes not M. accessary. 3 *Inst.* 108. *cap.* 47. cites *Mi.* 37 *E.* 3. *Dey's* case.

But if the husband and wife both receive a felon knowingly, it shall be judged only the act of the husband, and the wife shall be acquitted. 1 *H. H. P. C.* 621.

If a felon comes to the house of another, and he permits him to escape without arrest, knowing him to have committed felony, this doth not make a man accessary; but if he takes money of the felon to suffer such escape, it makes him an accessary: and so it is if he shut the fore door of his house, whereby the pursuers are deceived, for here is not a bare omission, but an act done. 1 *Hale's Hist. P. C.* 619.

Accessaries *after* the fact can only be in felonies, and in those felonies where, by the law, judgment of death regularly ought to ensue; and therefore there is no accessary in petit larceny, homicide *per infortunium* or homicide *se defendendo.* 1 *H. H. P. C.* 618.

By statute 3 *W.* & *M.* *c.* 9. *s.* 4. "Receivers of stolen goods, knowing them to be stolen, are to be deemed accessaries after the fact, and suffer as such." But because these receivers often concealed the principal felons, and thereby escaped being punished as accessaries; therefore by 1 *Ann. c.* 9. *s.* 2. it is enacted, that "whosoever shall buy or receive stolen goods, knowing them to be stolen, may be prosecuted for a misdemeanor, and punished by fine and imprisonment, though the principal felon be not convicted;" and this shall exempt them from being punished as accessaries, if the principal shall afterwards be convicted. But by 5 *Ann. c.* 31. *s.* 5, it is enacted, that "if any person shall receive or buy knowingly any stolen goods, or knowingly harbour or conceal any felon, he shall be taken as accessary to the felony, and shall suffer as a felon." This statute does not take away the benefit of clergy; but by statute 4 *Geo.* 1. *c.* 11. *s.* 1. such person may be transported for fourteen years. And by this last mentioned statute it is also enacted, that "whosoever shall take a reward under the pretence of helping any one to stolen goods, shall suffer as a felon, as if he himself had stolen them, unless he cause such felon to be apprehended and brought to trial, and give evidence against him."

If any person, knowing another to have committed piracy, shall on the land or sea receive, entertain, or conceal him, or receive or take into their custody any ship, vessel, or goods, which have been piratically taken, he shall be adjudged accessary to the piracy. 11 & 12 *W.* 3. *cap.* 7. *s.* 9, 10.

—— *In what Offences.*] As to felonies at common law it is said, that accessaries both before and after are included: and as to felonies by act of parliament; regularly if an act of parliament enact an offence to be felony, though it mention nothing of accessaries before or after, yet virtually and consequentially those, who counsel or command the offence, are accessaries before, and those that knowingly receive the offender, are accessaries after; as in the case of rape made felony by the statute of *Westminster* 2. *c.* 34. 1 *H. H. P. C.* 613. 2 *Inst.* 434. *Staundf. P. C. lib.* 1. *c.* 47.

But if the act of parliament, that makes the felony, in express terms comprehend *accessaries before*, and makes no mention of *accessaries after*, namely, receivers or comforters, there it seems there can be no accessaries after; for the expression of procurers, counsellors, abettors, (all which import accessaries *before*,) makes it evident, that the law-makers did not intend to include accessaries after, which is an offence of a lower degree than accessaries before; as the statute of 8 *Hen.* 6. *c.* 12. for stealing of records, the statute 33 *Hen.* 8. *c.* 8. for witchcraft, &c. 1 *H. H. P. C.* 614.

In the highest capital offence, namely, high treason, there are no accessaries, neither before nor after; for all consenters, aiders, abettors, and knowing receivers and comforters of traitors are principals. 1 *H. H. P. C.* 613.

In cases that are criminal but not capital, as in trespass, mayhem, or premunire, there are no accessaries, for all the accessaries before are in the same degree as principals; and accessaries after by receiving the offenders, cannot be in law under any penalties as accessaries, unless the acts of parliament that induce those penalties, do expressly extend to receivers or comforters, as some do. 1 *H. H. C. P.* 613. And though generally an act of parliament, creating a felony, renders (consequentially) accessaries before and after within the same penalty, yet the special penning of the act of parliament in such cases sometimes varies the case. Thus the statute of 3 *Hen.* 7. *c.* 2. for taking away maidens, &c. makes the offender, and the procuring and abetting, yea, and wittingly receiving also, to be all equally principal felonies, and excluded of clergy. 1 *H. H. P. C.* 614.

—— *Proceedings against.*] By the statute 2 & 3 *Ed.* 6. *c.* 24. the accessary is indictable in that county where he was accessary, and shall be tried there, as if the felony had been committed in the same county; and the justices, before whom the accessary is, shall write to the justices before whom the principal is attainted, for the record of the attainder. 1 *Hale's Hist. P. C.* 623. This writing is to be by writ in the king's name, under the teste of the justice so sending it. *Dyer* 253. *b.* The accessary may be indicted in the same indictment with the principal, and that is the best and most usual way; though he may be indicted in another indictment, but then such indictment must contain the certainty and kind of the principal felony. 1 *H. H. P. C.* 623.

Formerly it was held, that the accessary might be tried and punished as if the principal had been attainted; and this, although the principal was admitted to his clergy, pardoned, or otherwise delivered before attainder. And if the principal be erroneously attainted, yet the accessary shall be put to answer, and shall not take advantage of the error in that attainder; but the principal reversing the attainder, reverseth the attainder of the accessary. 1 *H. H. P. C.* 625.

Where the principal is not attainted, but discharged by being burnt in the hand only, the accessary after the fact, ought to be discharged without burning in the hand, on being put to his book. *Cro. Car.* 566. *pl.* 3. *Hill.* 15 *Car. B. R. Steven's Case.*

But now the accessary shall not be constrained to answer to his indictment, till the principal be tried; yet if he will waive that benefit, and put himself upon his trial before the principal be tried, he may; and his acquittal or conviction upon such trial is good. But it seems necessary in such case to respite judgment till the principal be convicted and attainted; for if the principal be after acquitted, that conviction of the accessary is annulled, and no judgment ought to be given against him; but if he be acquitted of the accessary, that acquittal is good, and he shall be discharged. 1 *H. H. P. C.* 623, 624.

And it seems to be settled at this day, that if the principal and accessary appear together, and the principal plead the general issue, the accessary shall be put to plead also; and that if he likewise plead the general issue, both may be tried by one inquest; but that the principal must be first convicted; and that the jury shall be charged, that if they find the principal not guilty, they shall find the accessary not guilty. But it seems agreed, that if the principal plead a plea in bar, or abatement, or a former acquittal, the accessary shall not be forced to answer, till that plea be determined; for if it be found for the principal, the accessary is discharged; if against the principal, yet he shall after plead over to the felony, and may be acquitted. 1 *H. H. P. C.* 624. 2 *Hawk.* 323. Where there are two principals, the attainder of one of them gives sufficient foundation to arraign the accessary. *Jenk. Cent.* 76. *Hawk. P. C.* tit. *Accessary.*

ACCOLA, an husbandman who came from some other parts or country to till the lands, *eo quod adveniens terram colat.*—And is thus distinguished from *Incola, viz.* Accola *non propriam, propriam colit* Incola *terram.* Du Fresne. *Cowel. Blount.*

ACCOLADE, (from the French *accoller, collum amplecti,*) a ceremony used in knighthood, by the king's putting his hand upon the knight's neck. *Cowel. Blount.*

ACCOMPLICES. Since the course of admitting approvements (see *Approver,*) hath been disused, all the good that could be expected from the method of approvement, or the confession and appeal of an *accomplice,* is fully provided for by divers statutes. 4 *Black.* 330.

Thus by 4 & 5 *Will.* & *Mar. c.* 8. in highway robberies—by 6 & 7 *Will.* 3. *c.* 17. and 15 *Geo.* 2. *c.* 28. in clipping and coining—by 10 & 11 *Will.* 3. *c.* 23. and 5 *Ann. c.* 31. in burglary, house-breaking, horse stealing, and shop lifting, it is enacted, that if any such offender therein, *being out of prison,* shall discover two or more persons who have committed the like offences so as they may be convicted thereof, he shall in case of burglary or house-breaking, receive a reward of 40*l.* for each, and in general be entitled to a *pardon* of all capital offences, excepting only murder and treason, and of the latter also in the case of coining.

The foregoing acts relate only to persons who are at large; and to entitle themselves to a pardon they must actually convict two offenders at the least, for if their confession be such on their trial, as the jury gives no credit to, they are liable to prosecution. *Cowper's Rep.* 335.

Also by 5 *Geo.* 3. *c.* 14. persons stealing *fish* out of private waters, surrendering to a justice and convicting one or more of their accomplices—by 12 *Geo.* 3. *c.* 48, offenders using *stamps,* a second time, being out of prison, and convicting one or more of their accomplices—or by 8 *Geo.* 2. *c.* 20. destroying locks on navigable rivers, and being out of prison, convicting one or more accomplices, are respectively entitled to a pardon.

Likewise by 6 *Geo.* 1. *c.* 28. offenders opposing the execution of process in the *mint,* not being in prison, discovering and convicting two accomplices are entitled to a reward of 40*l.* for each—by 6 *Geo.* 1. *c.* 21. persons to the number of eight and armed, resisting officers of customs, discovering within two months two accomplices, are entitled to a reward of 40*l.* for each, on their conviction—by 8 *Geo.* 1. *c.* 18. receivers of foreign goods, who within two months discover two accomplices (the goods recovered to the king's use exceeding 50*l.*) are entitled to a reward of 40*l.* for each on conviction: and by 9 *Geo.* 2. *c.* 35. offenders who have assembled armed to be aiding in the removing of goods, being three or more in company, who shall within three months discover two accomplices, are entitled to a reward of 50*l.* for each upon conviction, besides which, all such offenders so discovering such accomplices, are by the said several acts, by such conviction to have a pardon of their own offences therein.

Also by 19 *Geo.* 2. *c.* 31. *s.* 10, 11. persons discovering any person guilty of any of the following offences, viz. in assembling armed, to the number of three, to assist in the illegal exporting or removing of goods, or appearing in disguise with such goods, or who shall resist officers in the execution of their duty, from whom the benefit of clergy is taken, (see *Smuggling*,) and against whom a proclamation shall have issued for his surrender, shall have a reward of 500*l*. and any *accomplice* not proclaimed, who shall discover and apprehend any other offender, *shall be pardoned*, and have a share of the reward; and if any of the said offenders, before proclaimed, discover two or more accomplices, they shall have a reward of 50*l*. for each on conviction, and be moreover entitled to a pardon of his own offence, and all other like offences before committed.

Also by 29 *Geo*. 2. *c*. 30. persons stealing lead, iron, copper, brass, bell-metal, or solder, discovering *two* or more buyers or receivers thereof, or *any person* to whom it was offered to be sold, pawned, or delivered, without his apprehending of the offender, are on conviction of such persons to be entitled to a pardon.

Also by 2 *Geo*. 3. *c*. 28. persons stealing part of the cargo of any vessel in the Thames, convicting *two* or more buyers or receivers thereof, are entitled to a pardon.

Also by 22 *Geo*. 3. *c*. 28. felons without benefit of clergy, *under fifteen years of age*, who shall convict two buyers or receivers of the stolen goods, are likewise entitled to a pardon.

And it is usual to insert in the acts which establish and regulate state lotteries, a clause, whereby accomplices discovering an offender in counterfeiting lottery orders, are entitled to a pardon.

All such *accomplices* as are described in the above statutes, and also those persons to whom the king, by special proclamation in the Gazette, or otherwise, has promised his pardon, and who come in under the royal faith and promise, and discover their accomplices according to the terms prescribed, have a right to a pardon. *Cowper's Rep*. 334.

A practice has also been introduced and adopted in analogy to the old law of approvement, by which an *accomplice* may be entitled to *a recommendation to the king's mercy*, but not to a *pardon* as of legal right; which he may plead in bar, or avail himself on his trial. It is where an accomplice having made a full and fair confession of the whole truth, is in consequence thereof admitted evidence for the crown; and that evidence is afterwards made use of to convict the other offenders: if he act fairly and openly and discover the whole truth, though he is not entitled of right to a pardon, yet the usage, the practice, and the lenity of the court, is to stop the prosecution against him: and he has an equitable title to a recommendation for the king's mercy:—it holds out a kind of hope, that accomplices who behave fairly and disclose the whole truth, and bring others to justice, should escape punishment and be pardoned. *Cowper's Rep*. 336.

But a justice of the peace cannot pardon the offender, and tell him he shall be a witness against others: he cannot select whom he pleases, to pardon or prosecute, and the prosecutor has even a less pretence to select, than the justice of the peace: however, if the justices deceive the accomplice under a promise or assurance, or hope of pardon from them, which in strictness they have no right to make, yet if he make a full and fair disclosure, at the time of his examination of all he knows, he will be entitled to *a recommendation to mercy*; and the king's bench will in this case bail him, in order that he may apply for the king's pardon; or the justices of gaol delivery, on all the circumstances relative to the prisoner's claims of indemnity being laid before them, will exercise their discretion in deferring the trial accordingly. *Cowper's Rep*. 336.

ACCOMPT, (*computus*) is taken for a writ or action which lies against a bailiff or receiver, who ought to render an account to his lord or master, but refuseth. *F. N. B*. 116. *Cowel*. *Blount*.

If I make J. S. my bailiff or receiver, and he make a *deputy*, I must have accompt against the bailiff or receiver himself, and not against the deputy, for the receipt of the deputy was to the use of *his* master. *Fitz. N. B*. 119. b. 4 *Leo*. 32.

A *bailiff* who is understood to be a servant, who hath administration and charge of lands, goods, and chattels to make the best benefit for the owner, may be charged in *accompt*, for the profits which he hath raised or made, his reasonable charges and expences deducted. *Co. Lit*. 172. *a*.

But he cannot be charged as a *receiver*, (who is one who receiveth money, and is to render an account of it, but is not allowed any charges or expences, except what are agreed on by the parties,) for if such *bailiff* were to be charged as a receiver, he would lose the allowance of his charges and expences. *Co. Lit*. 172. *a*. *Rol. Abr*. 119.

In *assumpsit* for money received *ad computandum*, and verdict for the plaintiff, it was moved in arrest of judgment, that this action did not lie, but *accompt*; for if a man receives money to a special purpose, as to account, or to merchandize, it is not to be demanded of the party as a duty, till he has neglected or refused to apply it according to the trust, under which he received it; and the declaration must shew a misapplication or a breach of trust: but this objection being taken after verdict, it was holden that such verdict had aided the declaration, and that in such a case it must be intended that there was proof to the jury, that the defendant refused to account, or had done something else that rendered him an absolute debtor. *Salk*. 9. *pl*. 2. 2 *Show. Rep*. 301.

The writ of *account de compulo*, (*Fitz. N. B*. 116.) commands the defendant to render a just account to the plaintiff, or shew the court good cause to the contrary. 3 *Black.* 162.

And the process in *account* is summons, *pone*, and distress, and upon a *nihil* returned, the plaintiff may proceed to outlawry. And it is to be observed, that the statute of limitations, 21 *Jac.* 1. *c.* 16. doth not bar a man who is *a merchant* from bringing his action of *accompt*, for merchandize at any time, though all other actions of *accompt* are within the statute. *Morgan, tit. Ac.*

And the defendant cannot in an action of *accompt*, pay money into court as he may in an assumpsit. *Bul. N. P.* 128.

——*Judgment in.*] In an action of *accompt* there are two judgments, the first is *quod computet*, after which the court assigns *auditors*, usually *two of the officers of the court*, who are armed with authority to convene the parties before them, *de die in diem* at any day or place, that they shall appoint, till the *account* is determined; the time by which the account is to be settled is prefixed by the court; but if the account be of a long and confused nature, the court, on application, will enlarge the time: if either of the parties think they do them injustice, they may apply to the court, and if the defendant denies any article, or demurs to any demand, it is to be tried and determined in court. *Mod.* 42 *Brown.* 24. *Co. Ent.* 46. *Lutw.* 49. *Rast* 14. *Lutw.* 50.

Whatever might have been pleaded in bar to this action in the first instance, shall never be allowed of, as a good discharge upon the judgment *quod computet* before the auditors; as, if the defendant plead that *he never was his receiver*, or the like: but it is a good discharge before the auditors for a factor to say, that in a tempest the goods were cast overboard, or that he was robbed of the goods, without default or negligence. 1 *Bac. Abr. tit. Ac. F.*

So it is a good discharge, before the auditors, if the receiver renders back the money delivered to him to make profit of it, and swears that after the time he received it, he found that he durst not buy for fear of loss, for he is not obliged to run any hazard himself. *Ibid.*

And nothing can be pleaded before auditors contrary to what has been pleaded in the action, and found by the verdict: thus, if the plea of *plene computavit* be found against the defendant, he shall account before the auditors, for the whole money he is charged with, for this plea admits the receipt of the whole. 1 *Lutw.* 63.

And where a defendant, charged as surviving bailiff, of goods delivered to him and his co-bailiff, to be merchandized, and to render an account, had gone to issue upon this fact, viz. whether upon his delivering over the goods to the deceased bailiff all his (the defendant's) concerns in the trust, care, and management thereof ceased, and was at an end; which issue was found against him, it was holden that he could not afterwards plead before the auditors, that he delivered the goods over to the co-bailiff, with the consent of the plaintiff: for this matter might have been given in evidence upon the former issue: and the consequence of admitting it, to be put in issue before the auditors, would have been either two verdicts the same way, which would have been nugatory, or two contradictory verdicts, which would have entangled the court so much, that they would not have known what judgment to have given, *Godfrey* v. *Saunders*, 3 *Wils.* 114.

The *second* or next judgment after the *first quod computet*, is when the account is finished, that the defendant pay the plaintiff so much as he is found in arrear. 1 *Brown* 24. *Cro. Eliz.* 86. 3 *Bl. Com.* 163.

Upon the first judgment a *capias ad computandum* lies, and if a *non est inventus* be returned upon it, an *exigent* issues. 1 *Bac. Abr. tit. Ac. G.*

It is usual to bail the defendant, if he be taken on the *capias*, though by the rigour of the law, he is to account (*in vinculis*) that is, in prison. *Ibid.*

If the defendant make default, after the interlocutory judgment, at the day assigned by the auditors, final judgment shall be entered for the sum demanded by the plaintiff. *Cro. Eliz.* 806. 3 *Wils.* 117. *Co. Lit.* 139 b. 11 *Co.* 39. 27 *E.* 387. 2 *Rol. Abr.* 131. *pl.* 4.

So if there be judgment on demurrer, to an insufficient plea, before the auditors. *Ibid.*

But if final judgment be entered in the first instance, the court will set it aside, on motion, as irregular. *Cas. B. R. H.* 394. *And.* 29.

It seems to be questionable, whether *in all cases*, damages are recoverable in account: but it is clear, that if the defendant resist the plaintiff's claim, by pleading, or where an increase is received by a receiver *ad merchantizandum*, there shall be judgment for damages. *Jenk.* 288. 1 *Rol. Abr.* 575. 1 *Leo.* 302. 2 *Leo.* 118. 3 *Wils.* 117.

It hath been holden that the *first* judgment is not such, as can be revived by *scire facias*, upon the death of the plaintiff, before the accounts taken; or as, a writ of error can be brought upon; and yet the plaintiff cannot be nonsuited after it. 1 *Bac. Abr. tit. Ac. G.*

After final judgment, the plaintiff ought to pray that the defendant's body may be taken in execution; or he may pray an elegit if he refuses the body: and in the *Reg.* 137. there is a writ to the gaoler to receive the body of the defendant after final judgment. *Lutw.* 51. 1 *Bac. Abr. tit. Ac. G.*

The proceedings in this action being difficult, dilatory, and expensive, it is now seldom used, especially if the party have other remedy, as debt, covenant, case; or if the demand be of consequence and the matter of an intricate nature; for in such case it is more advisable to resort to a court of equity, where matters of accompt are more commodiously adjusted, and determined more advantageously for both parties; the plaintiff being entitled to a discovery of books, papers, and the defendant's own oath; and on the other hand the defendant being allowed to discount the sums paid or expended by him; to discharge himself of sums under 40*s.* by his own oath; and if by answer or other writing he charges himself, by the same to discharge himself, which will be good, if there be no other evidence: further, all reasonable allowances are made to him; and if after the accompt is stated, any thing be due to him upon the balance, he is entitled to a decree in his favour. 1 *Bac. Abr. Tit. Ac.*

However from the experiment made of this action in the case of *Godfrey* v. *Saunders*, 3 *Wils.* 94. a matter (which had been fruitlessly depending in chancery upwards of twelve years, but was thoroughly examined and finally determined in this form of action in the course of two years,) it may still, notwithstanding its general disuse, be proper to give *in this place*, the leading principles on which it may be proceeded in.

—— *Where it lies.*] By the common law account lay only against a guardian in socage, bailiff, or receiver, or by one in favour of trade and commerce, naming himself merchant, against another naming himself merchant, and the executors of a merchant; for between these there was such a privity, that the law presumed them conusant of each others disbursements, receipts, and acquittances. 1 *Bac. Abr. tit. Ac.*

But the stat. 13 *Ed.* 3. *c.* 23. gives an action of *account* to the executors of a merchant; the stat. 25 *Ed.* 3. *c.* 5. to executors, of executors; the stat. 31 *Ed.* 3. *c.* 11. to administrators: and by the stat. 3 & 4 *Ann. c.* 16. actions of *account* may be brought against the executors and administrators of every guardian, bailiff and receiver, and by one joint-tenant, tenant in common, his executors and administrators against the other as bailiff, for receiving more than his share, and against their executors and administrators.

ACCOMPTANT GENERAL, a new officer in the court of Chancery, appointed by act of parliament, to receive and account for all money belonging to the suitors of the court, in the place of the masters, which monies are to be paid into the Bank, with the privity of such accomptant general, and laid out in the 3 per cent. consols, in trust for the parties, and to be taken out by order of the court; and he shall only keep the account with the Bank, for the Bank is to be answerable for all money received by them, and not the accomptant general. 12 *Geo.* 1. *c.* 32. No fees shall be taken by this officer or his clerks, on pain of being punished for extortion; but they are to be paid salaries.

Counterfeiting the hand of the accomptant general is felony without clergy. 12 *Geo.* 1. *c.* 32. *s.* 9.

ACCORD and SATISFACTION. Accord is an agreement between two or more persons, where one is injured by a trespass, or offence done, or on a contract, to give on the one part and receive on the other, some recompence as a satisfaction: this agreement when executed and performed, shall be a good bar in law, if the other party after the *accord* performed, bring any action for the same. *Termis de Ley.*

For in all personal injuries, the law gives damages as an equivalent, and when the party accepts of an equivalent, there is no injury or cause of complaint, and therefore accord and present satisfaction is a good plea: but if the wrong doer only promise a future satisfaction, the injury continues till satisfaction is actually made; and consequently there is a cause of complaint in being; and if the trespass were barred by this plea, the plaintiff would have no remedy for the future satisfaction, for that supposes the injury to have continuance. 5 *E.* 4. 7. *Plow.* 5 b. *Roll. Abr.* 129. *Raym.* 450. 2 *Keb.* 332. 2 *Jones*, 158, 168. But if the defendant has promised to pay the plaintiff so much as a satisfaction, in case the plaintiff will not sue for the trespass, *assumpsit* will lie on that promise. 1 *Bac. Abr. tit. Ac.*

Accord with satisfaction is a good plea in all personal actions, where damages only are to be recovered; and in all actions which suppose a wrong *vi et armis*, where a *capias* and *exigent* lie at the common law; in trespass and ejectment, detinue, and the like, *accord* is a good plea: so in an appeal of maihem. But in real actions it is not a good plea. 4 *Rep.* 1, 9, 70. 9 *Rep.* 77.

So when a duty in certain accrues by the deed, *tempore confictionis scripti*, as by covenant, bill, or obligation, to pay a certain sum of money; this certain duty takes its essence originally and only by writing, and therefore ought to be avoided by matter of as high a nature, though the duty be merely in the personalty. 6 *Co.* 43. *Lutw.* 358. *Cro. Jac.* 254.

Thus if the debt is *certain*, on a deed or obligation, the accord and satisfaction must also be by deed and so pleaded, 2 *Wils.* 86. and for how far the *acceptance* of one bond in lieu of another, or for a less sum than the sum secured will be good. See title *Acceptance.*

But if in covenant against a lessee, a breach is assigned, in not repairing the house, the defendant may plead an *accord* between himself and the plaintiff and execution thereof, *in satisfactione, et exoneratione reparationum præd.* for no certain duty accrued by the deed, and the action is founded upon a *tort* or *default* subsequent to the deed, and damages are only to be recovered, which are in the personalty. *Palm.* 110. *All.* 39. *Cro. Jac.* 304. *Co. Ent.* 117. *Yelv.* 125. 1 *Bac. Abr. tit. Ac. B.*

It is to be observed, that accord *executed* only is pleadable in bar, and *executory* not. 1 *Mod.* 69. Also in pleading it, it is the safest to plead it by way of satisfaction, and not of accord alone. For if it be pleaded by way of accord, a precise execution thereof in every part must be pleaded: but, by way of satisfaction, the defendant need only allege, that he paid the plaintiff such a sum, in full satisfaction of the accord, which the plaintiff received, 9 *Rep.* 80. The defendant must plead, that the plaintiff accepted the thing agreed upon in full satisfaction. And if it be on a bond, it must be in satisfaction of the money, mentioned in the condition, and not of the bond; which cannot be discharged but by writing under hand and seal. *Cro. Jac.* 254, 650.

ACCOUNT *in* EQUITY.] A court of equity will entertain jurisdiction of a suit, though remedy might perhaps be had in the courts of common law: the ground upon which the courts of equity first interfered in these cases, seems to have been the difficulty of proceeding to the full extent of justice in the courts of common law; or perhaps to prevent multiplicity of suits. *Mitford* 109-10.

Thus though accounts may be taken before auditors in an action of *accompt* in a court of common law (see title *Accompt*) yet a court of equity by its mode of proceeding is enabled to investigate more effectually long and intricate accounts in an adverse way, and to compel payment of the balance which ever way it turns. *Ibid.* 110.

And the interference of courts of equity is peculiarly effective in correcting errors, or detecting fraud in accounts, relied upon as stated and settled, by allowing the plaintiff, in case of specific error alleged and proved, to surcharge and falsify, and in the case of fraud opening the whole account: and a party who is at liberty to surcharge and falsify, is not merely confined to errors in fact, but may take advantage of errors in law. 2 *Atk.* 112. 119. 1 *Fonbl.* 15.

The jurisdiction exercised by courts of equity in matters of account, is however, in many cases bounded by the discovery; as where a suit is instituted for an account of waste of timber, without praying injunction, the plaintiff will have a decree for an account of the timber felled, though he cannot have a decree for relief: so where the bill seeks an account of ore dug, because the working of a mine is a kind of trade. 1 *Fonbl.* 13, 14.

Neither will equity in all cases decree an account of mesne profits, for "where a man has title to the possession of lands and makes an entry, whereby he becomes entitled to damages at law, for the time that possession was detained from him, he shall not after his entry, turn that action at law into a suit in equity, and bring a bill for an account of the profits, except in the case of an infant, or some other very particular circumstances," which particular circumstances extend to all those cases which involve an equity, which the plaintiff cannot make available at law. *Fonbl.* 14.

To a bill for an account, a plea of a stated account is a good bar. 1 *Vern.* 180. 2 *Atk.* 1. But it must shew that the account was in writing, or at least it must set forth the balance, 2 *Atk.* 399. And if the bill charges that, the plaintiff has no counterpart of the account, the account should be annexed by way of schedule to the answer, that if there are any errors upon the face of it, the plaintiff may have an opportunity of pointing them out. 3 *Atk.* 303. Also if error or fraud are charged, they must be denied by the plea as well as by way of answer. *Gilb. Ch.* 56. And if neither error nor fraud is charged, the defendant must by the plea, aver that the stated account, is just and true to the best of his knowledge and belief. 3 *Atk.* 70. And the delivering up of vouchers at the time the account was stated seems to be a proper averment in a plea of this nature, *Gilb. Ch.* if the fact was such. *Mitf.* 208—9.

ACCOUPED, his conscience accouped him thereof: from the Latin *adculpare.* *Cowel. Blount.*

ACCROCHE, (from the French *accrocher*). To hook or grapple unto. It signifies as much as to encroach: thus the *accroaching* or attempting to exercise royal power (a very uncertain charge,) was in 4 *Ed.* 3. held to be treason, in a knight of Hertfordshire who forcibly assaulted and detained one of the king's subjects till he paid him 90*l.* The French use it for delay; as, *accrocher un process,* to stay the proceedings in a suit. *Cowel. Blount.* 4 *Black.* 75—6. 1 *Hal. P. C.* 80.

ACCUSATION, (*accusatio*) To charge any person with a crime. By Magna Charta, no man shall be imprisoned or condemned on any *accusation,* without trial by his peers, or the law. None shall be vexed upon any accusation, but according to the law of the land: and no man may be molested by petition to the king, &c. unless it be by indictment, or presentment of lawful men, or by process at common law. 25 *Ed.* 3. 28 *Ed.* 3. *c.* 3. None shall be compelled to answer an accusation to the king, without presentment, or some matter of record. *Stat.* 42 *Ed.* 3. Promoters of suggestions are to find surety to pursue them, and not making them good, shall satisfy damages to the party accused, and pay a fine to the king. 38 *Ed.* 3. *c.* 9. In treason there must be two lawful accusers. *Stat.* 5 & 6 *Ed.* 6. *c.* 11. *s.* 12. 1 *P* & *M.* *c.* 10. *s.* 11.

ACEPHALI, the levellers in the reign of king *Hen.* 1. who acknowledged no head or superior. *Leges H.* 1. They were reckoned so poor that they had not a tenement by which they might acknowledge a superior lord. *Du Cange.* *Cowel.* *Blount.*

AC ETIAM BILLÆ, the words or a clause added to a writ, where the action requires bail. The statute 13 *Car.* 2. *c.* 2. enjoins the cause of action to be particularly expressed in the writ or process, to hold a person to bail, by inserting therein, after the words *to answer in a plea of trespass*, and also *according to the custom of the court in a certain plea of trespass on the case upon promises to the value of* 20*l.* &c. but it ought not to be made out against a peer of the realm, or upon a penal statute, or against an executor or administrator, or for any debt under 10*l.* in the superior courts. Nor in any action of account, action of covenant, or the like, unless the damages are 10*l.* or more: nor in trover, action of trespass, or for battery, wounding or imprisonment; except there be an order of court for it, or a warrant under the hand of one of the judges of the court out of which the writ issues. The sum sworn to by the plaintiff, is to be marked on the back of the process: and then the sheriff or like officer, must arrest the body of the defendant, and return the writ with a *cepi corpus* indorsed thereon. 3 *Black.* 288.

ACHAT, (French *achet*) signifies a contract or bargain. Purveyors by statute 36 *Ed.* 3. were called *achators*, from their frequent making of bargains. *Cowel.*

ACHERSET, a measure of corn, conjectured to be the same with our quarter or eight bushels. *Cowel.*

ACHOLITE, (*acholitus*) an inferior church servant, who, next under the subdeacon, followed or waited on the priests or deacon, and performed the meaner offices of lighting the candles, carrying the bread and wine, and paying other servile attendance.

This officer, an *acholite*, was in our old English called a colet, from which appellation came the family of dean *Colet* founder of St. Paul's School. *Cowel.*

ACKNOWLEDGMENT MONEY, is a sum paid in some parts of England by tenants on the death of their landlords, as an acknowledgment of their new lords. *Cowel. Blount.*

ACQUITANDIS PLEGIIS, a writ of *justices*, lying for the surety against a creditor, who refuses to acquit him after the debt is satisfied. *Reg. of Writs*, 158. *Cowel. Blount.*

ACQUIETANTIA DE SHIRIS ET HUNDREDIS, to be free from suits and services in shires and hundreds. *Cowel.*

ACQUIETARE, is a law word, signifying *quietum reddere. Dr. Wilk. Gloss.* And it also sometimes signifies to pay. *Mon. Angl. tom.* 1. *fol.* 199. *Cowel. Blount.*

ACQUITTAL, (from the French word *acquitter*, and the Latin compound *acquietare*) to free, acquit, or discharge; it most commonly signifies a deliverance and setting free of a person from the suspicion or guilt of an offence; as, for instance, he that on a trial is discharged of a felony, is said to be *acquietatus de felonia*; and if he be drawn in question again for the same crime, he may plead *auter foits acquit*; as his life shall not be twice put in danger for the same offence. 2 *Inst.* 385. And when two are indicted, the one as principal, and the other as accessary, the principal being discharged, the accessary of consequence will be acquitted by law. *Staunf. P. C.* 168.

And when a person is found Not guilty of the offence by a jury, on verdict, he is acquitted in fact. But in murder, if a man is *acquitted*, appeal may be brought against him. 3 *Inst.* 273.

And by statute 3 *Hen. c.* 1. if either principal or accessary be *acquitted* on an indictment for murder, the court may remit him to prison or bail him till the year and day (for appeal) be passed.

If one be acquitted on an indictment charging the offence at one time, and be afterwards indicted again in the same county, for such offence as committed at another time; here, notwithstanding that variance, the party may plead *auter foits acquit*, by averring it to be the same felony: so where a person is indicted a second time, for the felony, but at another vill, &c. 2 *Hawk.* 370. Where a man is discharged on special matter, found by the grand jury, yet he may be indicted *de novo* seven years afterwards, and cannot plead this acquittal; as he may upon the special matter found by the petit jury, and judgment given thereon. *Ibid.* 246.

And if a person is lawfully acquitted on a malicious prosecution, he may bring his action for damages, after he hath obtained a copy of the indictment; but it is usual for the judges of gaol delivery to deny a copy of an acquittal to him who intends to bring an action thereon, when there was probable cause for a criminal prosecution. *Carth. Rep.* 421.

ACQUITTAL also signifies in another sense, to be free from entries and molestations by a superior lord, for services issuing out of lands: for where there is a *lord mesne* and *tenant*, the tenant must do his service to the *mesne* only, and not to divers lords for one parcel of land. *Co. Lit.* 100. *Cowel. Blount.*

ACQUITTANCE, (*acquietantia*,) signifieth a release or discharge in writing, of a sum of money, or debt due, as, where a man is bound to pay rent, reserved upon a lease, &c. and the party to whom due, on receipt thereof, gives a writing under his hand witnessing that he is paid: this will be such a discharge in law, that he cannot demand and recover the sum or duty again, if the acquittance be produced. *Terms de Ley* 15. *Dyer* 6, 25, 51.

An acquittance is a discharge and bar in the law to actions. And if one acknowledges himself to be satisfied by deed, it may be a good plea in bar, without any thing received;

but an acquittance, without seal, is only evidence of satisfaction, and not pleadable. *L. D.* by *Morg.*

It is observed, that a general receipt or acquittance in full of all demands, will discharge all debts, except such as are on specialty, *viz.* bonds, bills, and other instruments sealed and delivered; on which account those can be destroyed only by some other specialty of equal force, such as a general release, or the like. There being this difference between that and the general acquittance. *Cro. Jac.* 650.

But the producing an acquittance will not bar the action, if the plaintiff can by any means shew a mistake, and that he has not been paid, or paid so much as the acquittance is for. *L. D.* by *Morg.*

In some cases payment may be refused, unless an acquittance is given. Thus the obligor is not bound to pay money upon a single bond, except an acquittance be given him by the obligee; nor is he obliged to pay the money before he hath the acquittance. But in case of an obligation with a condition, it is otherwise; for there one may aver payment. And by 3 & 4 *Ann. c.* 16. If an action of debt is brought upon a single bill, and the defendant hath paid the money, such payment may be pleaded in bar of the action.

A servant may give an acquittance for the use of his master, where such servant usually receives his master's money, and a master shall be bound by it. *Co. Lit.* 112.

ACRE, (from the German *acker*, i. e. *ager*) a parcel of land, containing in length forty perches, and in breadth four perches; or in proportion to it, be the length or breadth more or less. By the customs of various countries, the perch differs in quantity, and consequently the acre of land. It is commonly but 16 feet and a half, but in *Staffordshire* it is 24 feet. According to the statute 34 *Hen.* 8. concerning the sowing of flax, it is declared that 160 perches make an *acre*, which is forty multiplied by four; and the ordinance of measuring land, 35 *Ed.* 1. agrees with this account. *Cowel. Blount.*——But the word *acre* formerly meant any open ground or field, as *castle-acre, long-acre, west-acre,* &c. and not a determined quantity of land. *Cowel.*—Also *acre*, or *acre-fight,* is an old sort of duel fought by single combatants, English and Scotch, between the frontiers of their kingdoms, with sword and lance; and this duelling was called camp-fight, and the combatants champions, from the open field that was the place of trial. *Cowel.*

ACROISIA, blindness: but the right word is *acrusia. Dufresne. Cowel. Blount.*

ACTILIA, military utensils. *Du Cange. Cowel. Blount.*

ACTION, (*actio.*) Men in civil society are obliged to have recourse to the law and courts of justice for redress, when injured, and thereby measure their damages; this application is what is generally termed bringing an action, and *an action* (*actio*) as defined by *Bracton, nihil aliud est quam jus prosequendi in judicio quod sibi debetur*; or otherwise, a legal demand of one's right. *Co. Lit.* 285. 2 *Inst.* 40.

And actions are divided into criminal or civil: as for instance, *criminal actions,* are to have judgment of death, as appeals of death, robbery, &c. or only to have judgment for damage to the party, fine to the king, and imprisonment, as appeals of maihem, &c. *Co. Lit.* 284. 2 *Inst.* 40.

And civil actions are divided into real, personal, or mixed.

ACTIONS *real*] or relating unto lands are either *droitural* or in the right, or *possessory*: and the distinction between *droitural* and *possessory* depends on, whether it seek to recover the property or the possession: if the former, the action is *droitural,* if the latter, it is *possessory,* and *Finch* states this correctly; "real actions," says he, "where a freehold is to be recovered, are *possessory* or *droitural,* possessory, which are to recover a *possession,* as all assises, writs of *ayel, besayel,* and *cosinage*—*droitural* or *in the right,* which are to recover a possession mixed with the right: and both these may either be of a possession or right in himself, or descended from his ancestors, which we call *auncestral. Finche's Law,* 257, 8. and 1 *Bac. Abr.* 47. note by *Gwillim, E.* 6.

But the proceedings in these real actions being dilatory and expensive, and in many cases concluding the party upon one trial, a more commodious method was contrived to dispute the title of lands, which began in the reign of *Hen.* 7. in this manner; by forming a term for years; and then the lessees, bringing an *ejectment* to recover the term, and thereby to assert the title of the lessor of the plaintiff, in which, if they recovered, the courts of law likewise gave an *habere facias possessionem* to recover the term itself (for this see *Ejectment.*) *Fitz. N. B.* 220. 3 *Black.* 206.

ACTIONS *personal*] are such whereby a man claims a debt, a personal duty, or damages in lieu thereof; and, likewise whereby a man claims satisfaction in damages for some injury done to his person or property: the former are said to be founded *ex contractu,* that is, on contract: the latter *ex delicto,* that is upon *torts* and wrongs: of the former nature are all actions upon *debt* or *promises*: of the latter all actions for trespasses, nuisances, assaults, defamatory words, and the like. 3 *Black.* 117.

ACTIONS *mixed*] are suits partaking of the nature of the other two wherein some real property is demanded, and also personal damages for a wrong sustained; as, for instance: an action of waste: which is brought by him who hath the inheritance, in remainder or reversion, against the tenant for life, who hath committed waste therein, to recover not only the land wasted, which would make it merely a *real* action; but also treble damages; in pursuance of the statute of *Gloucester*, 6 *Ed.* 1. *c.* 5. which is a *personal* recompence; and so both being joined together, denominate it a mixed action. 3 *Black.* 118.

Parties to action dying.] Many personal actions die with the person. Thus if a lessee for years commit waste, and dies, action of waste may not be had against his executor or administrator, for waste done by the deceased. And where a keeper of a prison permits one in execution to escape, and afterwards dieth, no action will lie against his executors. But this must be understood, of that kind of keeper, to whom the prison actually belongs, as the *marshal*, the *warden* of the Fleet, not of a gaolor who acts as servant to a sheriff, for in such case, the death of the gaoler, is not any bar to an action against the sheriff, to whom in fact, the prison actually belongs.

So in *assault*, *battery*, *slander*, or other personal injuries; if either he that is the aggressor, or the party injured, die, the action is gone. But in other actions it is otherwise, for they survive.

Actions *local.*] Actions real and mixed, ejectment, waste, trespasses, *quare clausum fregit*, &c. are to be laid in the same county where the land lieth.

——— *transitory.*] Personal and transitory actions, as debt, detinue, assault and battery, &c. may be brought in any county, (except it be against officers of places, &c. by statute 21 *Jac.* 1.) *Co. Lit.* 282. Or against officers acting under particular acts of parliament, which frequently direct actions against them, to be laid in the respective counties, where the facts happen.

If the defendant is desirous to change the venue in transitory actions he must move the court on affidavit, that if the plaintiff hath any cause of action, such cause accrued in the county of, &c. and not where the plaintiff hath laid it, &c. and such motion must be made before issue joined; for by joining issue, he agrees with the plaintiff, as to the manner of bringing the action, and though the court seldom refuses on such an affidavit to change the venue, yet if, before or after the motion made, the plaintiff will enter into a rule, to offer material evidence, in the county where he laid his action, the cause will be tried there. 1 *Sid.* 44. 2 *Salk.* 669, 670.

But though the court, on application, seldom refuses to change the venue, yet there are cases in which the judges have refused; as where a peer of the realm brings an action of *scandalum magnatum*, the court will not change the venue; because a scandal raised on a peer reflects on him through the whole kingdom. 2 *Mod.* 215. 1 *Lev.* 56. *S. P.* A serjeant at law, barrister, attorney, or any other privileged person, whose attendance is necessary at Westminster-hall, may lay his action in *Middlesex*, though the cause of action accrued in another county; and the court, on the usual affidavit, will not change the venue. 2 *Salk.* 668, 670. 2 *Show. Rep.* 176, 177, 242. *S. P.*

Limitation of actions.] Actions are likewise *limited*, and cannot be determined except within a certain time.

Thus by statute 32 *Hen.* 8. *c.* 2. A writ of right for recovery of lands is to be brought within *sixty* years.

By 21 *Jac.* 1. *c.* 16. Writs of *formedon* for any title to lands in *esse*, are to be sued within *twenty* years.

Actions of debt, on the case, of account, detinue, trover, and trespass, are to be brought within *six* years.

Of assault and battery within *four* years.

And slander within *two* years.

But the right of action in these cases is saved to infants, feme coverts, and persons beyond sea. And on a fresh promise the time limited may be enlarged; also the taking out and filing of a writ, is a good commencement of an action to avoid the statute of limitations, if continuances be entered, to the time of declaring. 1 *Lill.* 19.

Joint actions] are where several persons are equally concerned, and the one cannot bring the action, or cannot be sued, without the other.

Several actions] are where persons are to be severally charged, as on trespass committed by many it is several. 2 *Leon* 77.

Parties to actions.] In all actions there must be a person able to sue; the party sued must be one sueable for the thing laid; and the plaintiff is to bring his right and proper action which the law gives him for relief. 1 *Shep. Abr.* 20.

A man attainted of treason or felony, convict of recusancy, an outlaw, excommunicated person, convict of *præmunire*, an alien enemy, &c. cannot bring an action, till pardon, reversal, absolution, &c. But executors or administrators, being outlawed, may sue in the right of the testator or intestate, though not in their own right. A feme covert must sue with her husband; and infants are to sue by guardian, &c. *Co. Lit.* 128. Actions may be brought *against* all persons, whether attainted of treason or felony, a convict recusant, outlawed, and excommunicate, &c. and a feme covert must be sued with her husband. 6 *Rep.* 3. *Salk.* 5.

Action on the case] is a general action given for redress of wrongs and injuries, *done without force*, and not particularly provided against by law, in order to have satisfaction for damage: and in actions upon the case, the like process is to be had as in actions of trespass or debt. 19 *H.* 7, *c.* 9. *Terms de Ley* 17.

In all cases where a man has a temporal loss, or damage by the wrong of another, he may have an action upon the case to be repaired in damages. But the particular damage must be specially alleged.

This action lies in a great variety of instances, of which the chief are,

1. Action on the case for *words:* which is brought for words spoken or written which affect a person's life, reputation, office, or trade, or tend to his loss of preferment, in marriage or service, or to his disinheritance, or which occasion him any particular damage. *Comyn's Dig.*

2. Action on the case likewise lies upon an *assumpsit* or undertaking; and such actions are founded on a contract either express or implied by law, and gives the party damages in proportion to the loss he has sustained by the violation of the contract. 4 *Co.* 92. *Moore* 667.

3. An action on the case likewise lies against carriers and others upon the custom of England: thus, if a person deliver goods to a common carrier, to carry them to a certain place, and he loseth them, action upon the case lies against him; for by the common custom of the realm he ought to carry them safely: it is the same of a common hoyman or lighterman, who is a water-carrier of goods; but goods in this case may be thrown overboard in a tempest, to preserve the passenger's lives in the lighter, &c. and no action lies. 2 *Bulst.* 280. And if a common carrier is robbed of goods, he is chargeable for them, because he had his hire, and took upon himself the safe delivery of the goods. 1 *Danv.* 13.

So also a common inn-keeper is chargeable for goods stolen in his house, and though the inn-keeper be not of sound memory, it is said action lies against him: but if the inn-keeper be an infant, no action will lie against such infant; but the owner must be a guest. *Moor* 177. *Latch* 127. 8 *Rep.* 33. And if an inn-keeper refuse to entertain his guest, action on the case may be brought against him. *Dyer* 158.

This action also lies for deceit in contracts, bargains, and sales: as if a man sell by false weights or measures, or sells wine or other things, knowing the same to be corrupt, as good and not corrupt, though without warranty, action lies. *Dyer* 75. 4 *Rep.* 18. *Cro. Jac.* 270. *Danv.* 173.

So if a man sells a horse, and warrants him to be sound, if he be not, action on the case lies. But if he hath at the time visible infirmities, which the buyer may see, action on the case will not lie. *Yelv.* 114. *Cro. Jac.* 675.

If a surgeon neglects his patient, or applies unwholesome medicines, whereby the patient is injured, this action lieth. 3 *Black.* 122.

And if a counsel retained to appear on such a day in court, doth not come, by which the cause miscarries, action lies against him: so if after retainer, he become of counsel to the adversary against the plaintiff. 1 *H.* 6. 18.

For stopping up a water-course or way, breaking down a party wall, stopping up ancient lights, and for any private nusance to a man's water, light, or air, whereby a person is damnified, this action lieth. *Cro. Eliz.* 527. *Yelv.* 159. Where a smith promises to shoe my horse well, if he pricks him, action on the case lies; and so when he refuses to shoe him; on which I travel without, and my horse is damaged, action lies: so where goods pawned are not delivered, on offering the money. *Ibid.*

Where any one personates another, cheats at gaming; or where a surety is not saved harmless, this action lieth. 2 *Inst.* 193. So for the excessive use of an *horse.* *Cro. Eliz.* 14. 8 *Rep.* 146. For keeping a dog accustomed to bite sheep, if the owner know the vice of the dog. But not if it be without his consent, and he did not know the dog was accustomed to bite. 1 *Danv. Abr.* 19. *Hetl.* 171.

Action on the case will lie against a gaoler for putting irons on his prisoner; or putting him in the stocks, or not giving sufficient sustenance to him, being committed for debt. *F. N. B.* 83. Also masters may have action against servants, stewards or bailiffs, for any special abuse or negligence. Also for taking or enticing them away. *Lane* 68. *Cro. Eliz.* 777. 1 *Shep. Abr.* 52, 59.

If I trust one to buy a lease or other thing for me, and he buyeth it for himself, this action lies against him. *Bro.* 117.

Where a man is disturbed in the use of a seat in the church; the keeping of his courts; in taking the profits of his office; action on the case will lie. *Bendl.* 89. *Lib. Intr.* 5. *Moor* 987. And for setting up a new mill on a river, to the prejudice of another who hath an ancient mill, an action will lie. *Lib. Intr.* 9. Action on the case likewise lies for and against commoners, for injuries done in commons; as for surcharging. *Style* 164. Digging pits or the like. *Sid.* 106. *Cro. Jac.* 165. 2 *Inst.* 474.

Action on the case may likewise be brought for malicious prosecutions: where a suit is without ground, and one is arrested, action on the case lies for unjust vexation: and for falsely and maliciously arresting a person, for more than is due to the plaintiff, whereby the defendant is imprisoned, for want of bail; or if it be on purpose to hold him to bail, action on the case will lie, after the original action is determined. 1 *Lev.* 275. 1 *Salk.* 15.

Actions on the case likewise lie for conspiracy, escape, and rescous, nusances, and the like, which see under their proper titles.

Action *upon a statute.*] Upon every statute made for the remedy of any injury, mischief, or grievance, an action lies by the party grieved, either by the express words of the statute, or by implication; and such action shall be either by an action for a recompence to the party in damages, or by way of prohibition by writ, for that purpose. 2 *Inst.* 55. 118. 10 *Co.* 75 b. *Comyn's Dig.*

And if a statute gives a remedy in the affirmative (without a negative expressed or implied) for a matter which was actionable by the common law, the party may sue at the common law as well as upon the statute, for this does not take away the common law. 2 *Inst.* 200.

But if a man brings his action at the common law, he waives his remedy by the statute. 4 *Rol.*

Action *upon a statute, qui tam.*] Actions *qui tam*, which are sometimes called *popular actions*, are such as are given by acts of parliament, which impose a penalty and create a forfeiture for the neglect of some duty, or commission of some crime, to be recovered by action or information, at the suit of him who prosecutes, as well in the king's name as his own. 1 *Bac. Abr. tit. Ac.* 9 b. But without such penalty be given no person can sue, for the whole penalty goes to the king. 2 *Hawk. P. C.* 377.

In those actions or informations, the party who prosecutes has, by commencing his suit such an interest in the penalty, that the king cannot suspend or discharge the suit, as to the part, he the plaintiff, is entitled to, 2 *Hawk. P. C.* 392.

And wherever a statute prohibits a thing, as being an immediate offence against the public good in general, under a certain penalty, and the penalty or part of it, is given to him who will sue for it, any person may bring such action or information and lay his demand *qui tam.* *Co. Ent.* 375. *Lutw.* 133. 138. *Dyer* 95. 346. and 139.

But an act which gives a remedy only to the party *grieved*, is not to be considered as a *penal* act; for the king cannot discharge it, or proceed in it after the death of the party. *Cas. temp. Hard.* 412. *Andr.* 115. 2 *Ter. Rep.* 148. *Wood's Inst.* 535. *Show.* 354.

By *stat.* 21 *Jac.* 1. *c.* 4. All offences against penal statutes prosecuted by any common informer (except in recusancy, maintenance, customs, transporting gold or silver, or munition wool or leather) shall be determined by action, plaint, bill, information, or indictment before the justices of assise, of *nisi prius*, of *oyer* and *terminer*, gaol delivery, or before justices of the peace having power to hear and determine the same, and shall be laid in the proper county.

Although by the above *stat.* of 21 *Jac.* 1. no action of debt or information or other suit whatever can be brought on any penal statute in any of the courts at *Westminster Hall* for an offence not excepted by the statute, yet when a subsequent statute gives an action of debt or any other remedy for the recovery of a penalty in any court of record, generally, it so far impliedly repeals the restraint of 21 *Jac.* 1. and consequently leaves the informer at his liberty to sue in the courts of Westminster Hall. 1 *Bac. Abr. tit. Ac.* 9 t.

Penal actions, though the judgment may in some cases be followed by legal disabilities, are considered as civil proceedings; they are founded upon the implied contract, which every one is under by the fundamental constitution of government, to obey the directions of the legislature, and to pay the forfeiture incurred by his disobedience to such persons as the law requires; therefore the affirmation of a *quaker* is admissible in them; the proceedings may be *amended* and a *new trial* may be had after a verdict for the defendant. 3 *Black.* 159. 1 *Str.* 136. 2 *Str.* 1227. 1 *Wils.* 124. 4 *Ter. Rep.* 753.

An informer on a popular statute shall in no case whatsoever have his costs, unless they be expressly given him by such statute, for the common law gives costs in no cases, and the stat. of Gloucester only gives costs where *damages* are recovered, which a penalty cannot be said to be. 1 *Bac. Abr. Ac. g. h.*

But wherever a statute gives a certain penalty to *the party grieved*, he is entitled to his costs by the *stat.* of *Gloucester*, otherwise it would be in vain for him to sue, since in many cases the costs would exceed the penalty. *Ibid.*

But by 18 Eliz. c. 5. and 27 Eliz. c. 10. *If any informer shall delay his suit, or discontinue, or become nonsuit, or have the trial passed against him, he shall pay the defendant his costs.*

ACTION PREJUDICIAL, (otherwise called preparatory, or principal) is an action which arises from some doubt in the principal; as in case a man sues his younger brother for lands descended from his father, and it is objected against him that he is a bastard; now this point of bastardy is to be tried before the cause can any further proceed: and therefore it is termed *prejudicialis, quia prius judicanda.* *Bract. lib.* 3. *c.* 4. *num.* 6. *Cowel. Blount.*

ACTION OF A WRIT, is a phrase of speech used; when one pleads some matter, by which he shews the plaintiff had no cause to have the writ he brought, yet it may be that he may have another writ or action for the same matter. Such a plea is called a plea to the action of the writ; whereas, if by the plea it should appear that the plaintiff hath no cause to have an action for the thing demanded, then it is called a plea to the action. *Cowel. Blount. Termes de la Ley.*

ACTIONARE, i. e. *In jus vocare*, or to prosecute one in a suit at law. *Thorn's Chron. Cowel. Blount.*

ACTON BURNEL. A statute so called, made 13 *Ed.* 1. *ann.* 1285. ordaining the statute merchant for recovery of debts: it was so termed from a place named Acton Burnel, a castle in Shropshire, where it was made. *Cowel. Blount.*

ACTOR, the proctor or advocate in civil courts or causes. *Actor dominicus*, was often used for the lord's bailiff or attorney. *Actor ecclesiæ* was sometime the forensic term for the advocate or pleading patron of a church. *Actor villæ* was the steward or head bailiff of a town or village. *Cowel.*

ACTS OF PARLIAMENT, are the *leges scriptæ*, the written and positive laws of the kingdom, which are statutes, acts or edicts made by the king's majesty, by and with the advice and consent of the lords spiritual and temporal, and commons in parliament assembled. *Cowel. Blount.* 8 *Rep.* 20.

The oldest of these now extant, and printed in our statute books, is the famous *magna charta*, as confirmed in parliament, 9 *Hen.* 3: though doubtless there were many acts before that time, the records of which are now lost, and the determinations of them perhaps at present currently received for the maxims of the old common law. 1 *Black.* 85.

The words of acts of parliament shall be taken in a lawful sense: and some acts extend by equity to other things than are mentioned therein. *Co. Lit.* 24, 381. For which see title *Statutes.*

By 33 *Geo.* 3. *c.* 13. the clerk of the parliament is to indorse on every act, the time it receives the royal assent, which shall be its commencement, where no other is fixed.

By 41 *Geo.* 2. *sess.* 2. *c.* 90. the statutes of England and Great Britain, printed by the king's printer, shall be conclusive evidence in Ireland, and Irish statutes, prior to the union, so printed there, shall be evidence in Great Britain. *s.* 9.

By 48 *Geo.* 3. *c.* 106. when bills for continuing expiring acts, shall not pass before such acts expire, such continuing acts shall have effect from the date of the expiration of the act intended to be continued.

ACTUARY, (*actuarius*) a clerk that registers the acts and constitutions of the convocation: also the register in the court christian.

ADCREDULITARE, to purge one's self of an offence by oath. *Qui in collegio fuerit ubi aliquis occisus est, adcredulitet se quod eum non percussit. Legis Inæ. c.* 36. *Blount.*

ADDITION, (*additio*) signifies a title given to a man besides his christian and surname, setting forth his estate, degree, trade, and the like. As, for example; additions of estate, are yeoman, gentleman, esquire. *Additions* of degree, are knight, earl, marquis, and duke: additions of trade, are merchant, clothier, carpenter, or the like. There are likewise additions of place of residence, as London, York, Bristol, &c. And these additions were ordained that one man might not be grieved or molested for another: and that every person might be certainly known, and bear his own burden. And if one be of the degree of a duke, an earl, &c. he shall have the addition of the most worthy dignity. 2 *Inst.* 669. But the titles of duke, marquis, and earl, are not properly additions, but names of dignity. *Terms de Ley* 20. And the title of knight or baronet, is a part of the party's name, and ought to be rightly used; but the titles of esquire, gentleman, yeoman, &c. being no part of the name, but additions as people please to call them, may be used or not used, or if varied is not material. 1 *Lill.* 34. An earl of Ireland is not an addition of honour here in England, but such a person must be written by his christian and surname, with the addition of esquire only: and sons of English noblemen, although they have given them titles of nobility in respect of their families; if you sue them, they must be named by their christian and surnames, with the addition of esquire, as such a one esquire, commonly called lord A. &c. 2 *Inst.* 596, 666.

And by stat. 1 *Hen.* 5. *cap.* 5. it is enacted, that *in suits or actions where process of outlawry lies*, additions *are to be made to the name of the defendant, to shew his estate, mystery, and place of dwelling; and that writs not having such* additions *shall abate, if the defendant takes exception thereto, but not by the court ex officio.*

By pleading to issue, the party passes by the advantage of exception for want of addition; for by the common law it is good without addition, and the statute gives remedy only by exception. *Cro. Jac.* 610. 1 *Roll.* 780. And no addition is necessary, where process of outlawry doth not lie. 1 *Salk.* 5.

ADELING, or ETHLING, (from the Saxon *ædelan*, i. e. *nobilis*) was a title of honor amongst the Angles; properly belonging to the successor of the crown: for king Edward the Confessor having no issue, and intending to make Edgar, his nephew, the heir of the kingdom, gave him the stile and title of Adeling *Spelm. Gloss. Cowel. Blount.*

ADEMPTION *of a legacy;* that is, *the taking away of a legacy;* and arises from a supposed alteration of a testator's intent, as where a testator applies a sum of money, or gives a security for the same purposes, for which he had before given a legacy, or sells stock or calls in a security specifically bequeathed, if *no cause* appears for his so doing. *Amb.* 57. 3 *Atk.* 68, 183. 1 *Atk.* 426. *Amb.* 401.

AD INQUIRENDUM, is a judicial writ commanding inquiry to be made of any thing relating to a cause depending in the king's courts. *Reg. Judic. Cowel. Blount.*

ADJOURNMENT, (*adjournamentum*) The same with the French word adjournment, and signifies a putting off until another day, or to another place. *Cowel. Blount.*

And the substance of the adjournment of courts is to give licence to all parties that have any thing to do in court to forbear their attendance till such a time. Every last day of the term, and every eve of a day in term, which is not *dies juridicus*, or a law day, the court is adjourned. 2 *Inst.* 26.

The terms may be adjourned to some other place, and there the King's Bench and other courts at Westminster be held: and if the king puts out a proclamation for the adjournment of the term, this is a sufficient warrant to the keeper of the great seal to make out writs accordingly; and proclamation is to be made, appointing all persons to keep their day, at the time and place to which, &c. 1 *And.* 279. 1 *Lev.* 176.

Though by magna charta the court of common pleas is to be held at Westminster, yet necessity hath sometimes superseded the law, as in the case of a plague, a civil war, &c. Thus in 1 *Car.* 1. a writ of adjournment was delivered to all the justices, to adjourn two returns of Trinity term: and in the same year Michaelmas-term was adjourned until *crastino animarum* to Reading; and the king by proclamation signified his pleasure, that his court should be there held. *Cro. Jac.* 13, 27. *Anno* 17 *Car.* 2. The court of B. R. was adjourned to Oxford, because of the plague; and from thence to Windsor; and afterwards to Westminster again. 1 *Lev.* 176, 178.

If the judges of the court are divided in opinion, two against two, upon a demurrer or special verdict (not on a motion) the cause must be adjourned into the Exchequer Chamber, to be determined by all the judges of England. 3 *Mod.* 156. 5 *Mod.* 335.

If justices or others authorized by commission, sit by force of such commission, and do not adjourn the commission, it is determined. 4 *Inst.* 265.

ADIRATUS, a price or value set upon things stolen or lost, as a recompence to the owner. *Bract. l.* 3. *tract.* 2. *cap.* 32. *Cowel. Blount.*

ADJUDICATION, (*adjudicatio*) a giving or pronouncing by judgment, a sentence or decree. *Cowel. Blount.*

ADJURA REGIS, a writ brought by the king's clerk presented to a living, against those that endeavour to eject him, to the prejudice of the king's title. *Reg. of Writs*, 61. *Cowel. Blount.*

AD LARGUM, at large: and there is title at large, assise at large, verdict at large, to vouch at large. *Cowel.*

ADLEGIARE, or *aleier*, in French, is to purge himself of a crime by oath. *Brompt. Chron. cap.* 4. and *cap.* 13. *Du Cange. Cowel. Blount.*

ADMEASUREMENT, (*admensuratio*) is a writ which lies against such persons as usurp more than their share, to bring them to reason. It lies in two cases; one is termed admeasurement of dower (*admensuratio dotis*) where a man's widow after his decease holdeth from the heir more land, as dower, than of right belongs to her: and the other is admeasurement of pasture (*admensuratio pasturæ*) which lies between those that have common of pasture appendant to their freehold estates, or common by vicinage, where any one or more of them surcharge the common. *Reg. Orig.* 156, 171.

ADMINICLE, (*adminiculum*) signifies aid, help, or support; being used to this purpose, in stat. 1 *Ed.* 4. *cap.* 1.

ADMINISTRATOR, (*Latin*) is one that hath the goods of a man dying intestate committed to his charge by the ordinary, for which he is accountable when thereunto required. *Cowel. Blount.*

Appointment of.] The bishop of the diocese where the party dies, is regularly to grant administration: but when the person dying hath goods in several dioceses, which are *bona notabilia*, administration must be granted by the archbishop of the province, in his prerogative court, or it will be void. 1 *Plowd.* 281.

And by statute 31 *Ed.* 3. *cap.* 11. (*Ad. D.* 1357.) *Where a man dieth intestate, the ordinaries shall depute the next and most lawful friends to administer his goods, which deputies shall have action to demand and recover as executors, the debts due to the intestate, and shall answer also to others to whom the said dead person was holden and bound, in the same manner as executors, and shall be accountable to the ordinaries as executors.*

And it is enacted by the statute 21 *Hen.* 8. *cap.* 5. *sec.* 13. *In case any person die intestate, or the executors refuse to prove the testament, then the ordinary shall grant administration to the widow, or next of kin, or to both, by discretion of the ordinary, taking surety for true administration.*

Where divers persons be in equality of kindred, the ordinary is to be at liberty to accept one or more, taking nothing for the same, as in probate of testaments, unless the goods of the deceased amount to above the value of an hundred shillings. s. 4.

As the law is now settled administration must be granted, 1st, To the husband, of the wife's goods and chattels. 2. To the wife, of the husband's goods and chattels. 3. If there be no husband or wife, to the children, sons or daughters. 4. If there be no children alive, to the father or mother. 5. Then to a brother or sister of the whole blood, or of the half blood. (And the brother of the half blood shall exclude the uncle of the whole blood; and the ordinary may grant administration to the sister of the half, or the brother of the whole blood, at his own discretion.) 1 *Vent.* 425. *Aleyn.* 36. *Style*, 74. 6. And if there be none such, to the next of kin, as uncle, aunt, or cousin. 7. Then to a creditor of the deceased. 8. And for want of all these, to any other person, at the discretion of the ordinary: or the ordinary may grant to a stranger letters *ad colligendum bona defuncti*, to gather up the goods of the deceased; or may take them into his own hands, to pay the deceased's debts, in such order as an executor or administrator ought to pay them; but it is said, he or the stranger who hath letters *ad colligendum*, cannot sell them, without making themselves executors of their own wrong, and action lies only against the ordinary, &c. *Wood's Inst.* 333.

Administration likewise may be granted *durante minori ætate* of an infant executor or administrator. As if one makes an infant his executor, or dies intestate, and the right of administration devolves upon an infant, in these cases the ordinary is to grant administration during the minority of the infant, *i. e.* in the first case till he arrives at the age of seventeen, and in the latter till he arrives at the age of twenty-one, because an infant cannot, before his full age, give bond to administer faithfully. *Godolph.* 102. 5 *Co.* 29. *Hob.* 250. *Yelv.* 128.

And it is discretionary in the ordinary to whom to grant it, and therefore he is not obliged within the statute 21 *H.* 8. *c.* 5. to grant it to the next of kin either of the deceased, or the infant. *Hob.* 250. 1 *Vent.* 219. 1 *Keb.* 549. 3 *Mod.* 24. 1 *New Abr.* 381.

Administration also may be granted *de bonis non*, where the first administrator dies, without having administered all the intestate's goods. 2 *Bac. Abr. tit. Ex.* and *Ad.*

So if an executor dies intestate, administration *de bonis non cum testamento annexo* of the testator must be granted by the ordinary, for they are not devolved on his administrator, he having had them in *auter droit*, but if the executor dies and makes an executor, then the trust is devolved on him, and after payment of the debts and legacies of the first testator, he has an absolute property in the goods. *Ibid.*

If the executor dies before probate, his executor cannot be executor to the first testator, but instead of an administration *de bonis non*, an immediate administration is granted. *Ibid.*

So if an executor refuses, administration with the will annexed, is to be granted to another. *Ibid.*

Besides all these administrations, there is administration *durante absentia extra regnum*, where a person is absent abroad; and administration *pendente lite*, which may be granted by the ordinary as well as *durante minori ætate.* *Ibid.*

In these cases administration is to be granted to the next of kin to the first testator or intestate; but if the testator appoints a residuary legatee, such legatee is intitled to administration. *Ibid.*

Interest of.] An administrator, by virtue of his administration, hath interest in all the chattels, real and personal, of the intestate, and in all the goods and chattels, either in possession or action, in like manner as an executor in the goods of the testator deceased. And all these goods and chattels which belonged to the intestate at the time of his death, and which come to the hand of the administrator, shall be assets, or sufficient goods and chattels, to make him chargeable to the creditors, as executors are to creditors and legatees. Before they come to his hands he is not chargeable. *Wood's Inst.* 339.

An administrator cannot take advantage by his administration, (unless by paying his own debt first, if it is equal in degree with others, or by taking the goods and chattels as they are appraised) because the surplusage must be distributed amongst the next of kin, if there are any kin, according to the statute of the 22 & 23 *Car.* 2. *c.* 10. If a debtor takes administration of the goods and chattels of his creditor, this shall not discharge the debtor; but his debt shall be *assets*; because the intestate did no act to free him from the debt. Whereas, by making a debtor executor, the testator doth thereby release the debt. When an administrator (as well as an executor) hath paid funeral charges, debts, &c. with his own money, he may retain so much of the goods of the intestate, in kind, according to the value, and shall have property in them. For by such payment the property is altered from the intestate to the administrator. *Wood's Inst.* 339.

As to the *power* of an administrator, no one, not an executor, can legally do any act, relative to the estate or concerns of the deceased, till an administration is granted to him; but after the administration is granted, his *power* is almost equal with that of an executor. Yet if there are many administrators, one of them cannot sell goods, release debts, &c. without the other, but they must all join, because they have but one authority. See 30 *Car.* 2. *c.* 7. 4 & 5 *W.* & *M.* *c.* 24.

With regard to the *office* and *duty* of an administrator, it is the same with that of an executor, as to the burial of the deceased and payment of funeral charges, the making of an inventory of his goods and chattels, the payment of debts, and the passing of an account.

But with respect to his distributing the effects of the intestate, that is regulated by the statute of *distribution*, that is, the 22 & 23 *Car.* 2. *c.* 10. by which it is enacted, that *all ordinaries and ecclesiastical judges (upon granting administration) must take bond of the administrator with two or more sureties, with condition that the administrator shall make a true and perfect inventory of all the goods and chattels of the deceased, and exhibit it into the registry of the ordinary's court by such a day: and to administer according to law, and to make a true and just account thereof, and to make distribution of the surplusage as followeth:* viz. *one third to the wife of the intestate, the residue among his children, and such as legally represent them if any of them be dead, other than such children (not heirs at law) who shall have any estate by settlement of the intestate in his life-time, equal to the other shares. Children, other than heirs at law, advanced by settlements or portions not equal to other shares, shall have so much of the surplusage as shall make the estate of all to be equal. But the heir at law shall have an equal part in the distribution with the other children, without any consideration of the value of the land which he hath by descent or otherwise from the intestate.*

If there be no children, nor legal representatives of them, one moiety shall be allotted to the wife; the residue equally to the next of kindred to the intestate, in equal degree, and those who represent them. s. 5.

No representation shall be admitted among collaterals after brothers and sisters children. And if there be no wife, all shall be distributed amongst the children; and if no child, to the next of kin to the intestate in equal degree, and their representatives. s. 6.

No such distribution shall be made till one year after the intestate's death; and every one, to whom any shares shall be allotted, shall give bond with sureties in the said courts, that, if debts afterwards appear, he shall refund his ratable part thereof, and of the administrator's. s. 7.

In all cases where the ordinary hath used to grant administration cum testamento annexo, *he shall continue so to do.* s. 8.

But by statute 1 *Jac.* 2. *cap.* 17. *No administrator shall be cited into court to render an account of the personal estate of his intestate, otherwise than by an inventory thereof, unless at the instance of some person in behalf of a minor, or having a demand out of such estate as a creditor, or next of kin; nor shall be compellable to account before an ordinary or judge empowered by the act of* 22 & 23 *Car.* 2. *cap.* 10. *otherwise than as aforesaid.* s. 6.

If after the death of a father, any of his children shall die intestate, without wife or children, in the life-time of the mother, every brother and sister, and their representatives, shall have equal share with her. s. 7.

If after the death of the father the son die intestate, without issue, but leaving a wife, a mother, brother, sisters, and nieces, the intestate's wife shall have but one moiety, and as to the other, the intestate's brothers, sisters, and nieces, shall come in for an equal share thereof with the mother. 2 *P. Williams* 344.

But if a child dies intestate and unmarried, the father surviving has the child's whole estate at this day, 1 *P. Williams* 48. And this without taking administration to him. *Pr. Ch.* 260.

The clause in the act of 22 & 23 *Car.* 2. *c.* 10. *by which it is provided, that that act shall not prejudice the customs of the city of London and province of York, shall not extend to such part of any intestate's estate, which an administrator, by virtue of his being so, by pretence of any custom may claim, to exempt the same from distribution.* s. 8.

It has been resolved likewise, that the half blood shall have a share upon a distribution equally with the whole blood. *Wood's Inst.* 341.

By stat. 29 Car. 2. cap 3. *The act of* 22 & 23 Car. 2. cap. 10. *shall not extend to the estates of feme coverts that die intestate, but their husbands may have administration of their personal estates, and recover and enjoy the same as they might have done before the making of the said act.*

And since the stat. 22 & 23 *Car.* 2. *c.* 10. the ordinary may grant administration to the wife or next a-kin, at his election, also the ordinary may grant administration *quoad* part to the wife, and as to the other part, to the next of-kin. 1 *Sid.* 179. *Raym.* 93. 1 *Show.* 351. 1 *Salk.* 36.

If there be grandfather, father, and son, and the father dies intestate, the son shall have the administration, and not the grandfather. 2 *Vern.* 125.

If a father die intestate, leaving only one son, which son also dies intestate, administration should be granted, to the next of kin, of the son, and not the father. 3 *Mod.* 58. *Shower* 26. and 2 *Vern.* 274.

If a person die intestate, leaving two, who are next a-kin, in equal degree to him, and one of them die intestate within the year, and before distribution; such an interest is vested in him, that his next of kin shall have administration. *Show.* 25.

Administration may be granted to the grandmother, in preference to the aunt; for she is as near of kin as the aunt, or rather nearer, because she is in the right line ascending. 1 *Salk.* 38, 39.

——— *Suits by and against,*] Actions will lie both against and for an administrator in like manner as for and against an executor, and he shall be charged to the value of the goods, and no further; unless it be by his own false plea, or by wasting the goods of the intestate. An executor or administrator shall never be charged *de bonis propriis,* bnt where he doth some wrong; as by selling the testator's goods, and converting the money to his own use, concealing or wasting them, or by pleading what is false. *Dyer* 210. 2 *Roll. Rep.* 295. But this plea must be of a fact, within his own knowledge. If an administrator plead *plene administravit,* and it is found against him, the judgment shall be *de bonis propriis,* because it is a false plea, and that upon his own knowledge. 2 *Cro.* 191. *Contra* where he pleads such a plea, and that he hath no more than to satisfy such a judgment, &c. the recovery shall be *de bonis testatoris,* &c. 2 *Rol. Rep.* 400. This must mean, where such plea is true in fact. Upon *plene administravit* pleaded by an administrator, the plaintiff must prove his debt, or he shall recover but a penny damages, though there be assets; because the plea only admits the debt, but not the *quantum*. 1 *Salk*. 296.

Special bail is not required of administrators in any action brought against them for the debt of the intestate; except where they have wasted the goods of the deceased: nor shall costs be had against administrators. 2 *Bac. Abr.* and 1 *Comyn's Dig. Ex.* and *Ad.* If a stranger that is not administrator, take the goods and administer in his own wrong, he shall be charged and sued as an executor. *Terms de Ley* 24. And generally an administrator shall be charged by others, for any debt or duty due from the deceased, as he himself might have been charged in his lifetime; so far as he hath any of the intestate's estate, to discharge the same. *Co. Lit.* 219. *Dyer* 14.

An administrator's power is given by the administration, therefore he can do nothing until that be granted; and yet as to goods taken away before, the administration shall relate, so as to give the administrator an action for them. *Fitzherb.* 2. 6. If a man have judgment for land in a real or mixed action, and for damages, and then dies; his executor or administrator, not the heir, shall have execution for the damages; but not for the land. *Fitz. Admin.* 53. *March.* 9.

——— *Grant of administration, how revoked.*] The ordinary ought not to repeal letters of administration which he hath duly granted; but if they are granted to such persons who ought not by law to have them, he may revoke them. 1 *Lill.* 38. As where a person is a lunatic, or the like. And if granted where not grantable, they may be repealed by the delegates. 1 *Lev.* 157, 186. If administration is granted, and afterwards a will is produced and proved, the administration shall be revoked; and all acts done by the administrator are void. 2 *Rol. Abr.* 907. If a citation is granted against a stranger administrator, and his administration is revoked by sentence, yet all acts done by him *bona fide* as administrator are good till the revocation; the administration being only voidable. 6 *Rep.* 18. 8 *Rep.* 135. But if there is any fraud, a creditor may have relief upon the stat. 13 *Eliz. cap.* 5. for letters of administration obtained by fraud are void. 3 *Rep.* 78. 6 *Rep.* 18, 19. 8 *Rep.* 143. If an administrator give goods away, and then administration is revoked or repealed, it is said the gift is good; except it be by *covin*, when it shall be good only against a creditor by statute: and where the administrator, after many goods administered, had his administration revoked, and it was committed to *B.* who sued the first administrator for goods unduly administered; it was held, that there was no remedy but in chancery. 6 *Rep.* 19. *Clayt.* 44. 4 *Shep. Abr.* 89. See *Hob.* 266.

But *Morgan*, the valued and much lamented friend of the editor of this present Dictionary, in the 10th edit. of *Jac. L. D.* suggests that in such a case as this, the second administrator might maintain an action at law against the first, for money had and received, or trover for any goods remaining in his possession or by him converted, and not duly administered.

ADMINISTRATRIX, (*Lat.*) A woman, who hath goods and chattels of an intestate, committed to her charge, in like manner as an administrator. *Blount.*

ADMIRAL, (*admiralius, admirallus, admiralis, capitaneus,* or *custos maris*) is derived of the French *amerel*, and signifies an high officer or magistrate, that hath the government of the king's navy. *Cowel. Blount.* This word is also said to have its derivation from the Saxon *aen mereal*, over all the sea: and in ancient time the office of the admiralty was called *custodia maritimæ Angliæ*. *Co. Lit.* 260. It appears that anciently the admirals of England had jurisdiction of all causes of merchants and mariners, happening not only upon the main sea, but in all foreign parts within the king's dominions, and without them, and were to judge them in a summary way, according to the laws of Oleron, and other sea laws. 4 *Inst.* 75. In the time of king *Ed.* 1. and king *John*, all causes of merchants and mariners, and things arising upon the main sea, were tried before the lord admiral; but the first title of admiral of England, expressly conferred upon a subject, was given by patent of king *Rich.* 2. to the earl of Arundel and Surry. Of late times this high office has been generally executed by commissioners; who by stat. 2 *W.* & *M. cap.* 2. are empowered to use and execute the like authorities as lord admiral.

ADMIRALTY, *Court of.* The high court of Admiralty, 4 *Inst.* 134, 147. held before the lord high admiral of England, or his deputy stiled the judge of the admiralty; is not only a court of civil, but also a court of criminal jurisdiction. 4 *Black.* 268.

The court of admiralty hath been time out of mind, and so it was said in the time of *Ric.* 1. which also appears by several records in the time of *Hen.* 3. *Ed.* 1. and other reigns. *Co. Lit.* 260 b. 4 *Inst.* 145. 1 *Rol. Abr.* 528. *Seld. Mare Cl. l.* 2. *c.* 14.

This court hath cognizance of all crimes and offences committed either upon the sea or on the coasts out of the body or extent of any English county, and is regulated by the following acts:

By 13 *Rich.* 2. *st.* 1, *c.* 5. "upon complaint of incroachments made by the admirals and their deputies, the admirals "and their deputies shall meddle with nothing done within the realm, but only "with things done upon the sea"

By 15 *Ric.* 2. *c.* 3. *all contracts, pleas and quarrels, and other things done within the bodies of counties by land or water, and of wreck, the admiral shall have no conusance, but they shall be tried, by the law of the land; but of the death of the man, and of mayhem done in great ships, being in the main stream of great rivers, beneath the points near the sea, and in no other place of the same river, the admiral shall have conusance; and also to arrest ships in the great flotes, for the great voyages of the king and the realm, saving to the king his forfeitures; and shall have jurisdiction in such flotes during such voyages, only saving to lords, their liberties.*

By 2 *Hen.* 4. c. 11. reciting the 13 *R.* 2. c. 5. it is enacted, *that he that finds himself aggrieved against the form of the statute, shall have his action, by writ grounded upon the case, against him that so pursues in the admiralty, and recover double damages against him, and he shall incur the pain of* 10l. *if he be attainted.*

By 28 *Hen.* 8. *cap.* 15. "all felonies and robberies upon the sea, or in any haven, creek or place, where the admiral has jurisdiction, shall be tried in such places in the realm, as shall be limited by the king's commission, in like form, as if committed upon the land; and such commissions shall be had under the king's great seal, directed to the admiral or to his lieutenant, or deputies, and to three or four such other substantial persons, as shall be named, or by the lord chancellor for the time being, to hear and determine such offences after the common course of the laws of the land used for felonies and robberies, &c. done and committed upon the land within this realm."

"And if any person happen to be indicted for any such offence done upon the seas, or in any other place above limited, then such order, process, judgment and execution, shall be had, as against felons, for felony upon the land, and such as shall be convict, shall suffer such pains of death, losses of lands, goods and chattels, as if they had been attainted, and convicted of such offence, done upon the land; and also, shall be excluded from the benefit of the clergy."

And by 11 & 12 *W.* 3. *cap.* 7. "their aiders and comforters, and the receivers of their goods are made accessaries, and to be tried as pirates by 28 *Hen.* 8. *cap.* 15."

This is now the only method of trying maritime felonies in the court of admiralty; the judge of the admiralty still presiding therein, as the lord mayor is the president of the session of *oyer* and *terminer* in London.

But *the jurisdiction of the commissioners appointed under* 28 Hen. 8. c. 15. *being confined to the offences therein mentioned,* The *Stat.* 39 *Geo.* 3. c. 15. enacts, "that every offence committed upon the high seas shall be subject to the same punishment, as if it had been committed upon the shore, and shall be tried in the same manner as the crimes enumerated in the 28 *Hen.* c. 15. are directed to be tried."

And *as persons, tried for murder under that statute, could not be found guilty of manslaughter, and where the circumstances made the same manslaughter, were acquitted entirely,* the said stat. 39 *Geo.* 3. *cap.* 15. enacts, "that where persons tried for murder or manslaughter committed on the high seas, are found guilty of manslaughter only, they shall be subject to the same punishment as if they had committed such manslaughter upon the land.

The jurisdiction of the lord-admiral, therefore, is confined to the main sea, or coasts of the sea, not being within any county. Thus, the admiralty hath cognisance of the death or maim of a man, committed in any ship riding in great rivers, beneath the bridges thereof, next the sea: but by the common law, if a man be killed upon any arm of the sea, where the land is seen on both sides, the coroner is to inquire of it, and not the admiral; for the county may take cognisance of it; and where a county may inquire, the lord admiral has no jurisdiction. 3 *Rep.* 107.

All ports and havens are *infra corpus comitatus,* and the admiral hath no jurisdiction of any thing done in them: between high and low water-mark, the common law and admiral have jurisdiction by turns; one upon the water and the other upon the land. 3 *Inst.* 113.

The admiralty is said not to be a court of record, by reason it proceeds by the civil law. 4 *Inst.* 135. But the admiralty has jurisdiction, where the common law can give no remedy; and therefore of all maritime causes, or causes arising wholly upon the sea, it hath cognizance. 1 *Com. Dig.* The admiralty hath jurisdiction in cases of freight, mariners' wages, breach of charter-parties, though made within the realm; if a penalty be not demanded: and likewise in case of building, mending, saving, and victualling ships, so as the suit be against the ship, and not against the parties only. 2 *Cro.* 216. Mariners' wages are contracted on the credit of the ship, and they may all join in suits in the admiralty; whereas at common law they must all sever: the master of a ship contracts on the credit of the owners, and not of the ship; and therefore he cannot prosecute in the admiralty for his wages. 1 *Salk.* 33. It is allowed by the common lawyers and civilians, that the lord admiral hath cognisance of seamens' wages, and contracts and debts for making ships; also of things done in navigable rivers, concerning damage done to persons, ships, goods, annoyances of free passage, &c. And of contracts, and other things done beyond sea, relating to navigation and trade by sea. *Wood's Inst.* 218. But if a contract be made beyond sea, for doing of an act or payment of money within this kingdom; or the contract is upon the sea, and not for a marine cause, it shall be tried by a jury; for where part belongs to the common law, and part to the admiral, the common law shall be preferred. And contracts made beyond sea may be tried in *B. R.* and a fact be laid to be done in any place in England, and so tried here. 2 *Bulstr.* 322.

Where a contract is made in England, and there is a conversion beyond sea, the party may sue in the admiralty, or at common law. 4 *Leon.* 257. An obligation made at sea, cannot be sued in the admiral's court; because it takes its course, and binds according to the common law. *Hob.* 12.

But if a ship is taken by pirates upon the sea, and the master, to redeem the ship, contracts with the pirates to pay them 50*l.* which he does by money borrowed, and on bond, he may sue in the admiralty for the 50*l.* because the original cause rose upon the sea, and what followeth was but consequential. *Hard.* 183.

If goods delivered on shipboard are imbezzled, all the mariners ought to contribute to the satisfaction of the party, that lost his goods, by the maritime law, and the cause is to be tried in the admiralty. 1 *Lill.* 368. By the custom of the admiralty, goods may be attached in the hands of a third person, *in causa maritima & civili*, and they shall be delivered to the plaintiff after defaults, on caution to restore them, if the debt, &c. be disproved in a year and a day; and if the party refuse to deliver them, he may be imprisoned *quousque, &c. March Rep.* 204.

The court of admiralty may cause a party to enter into bond in nature of caution or stipulation, like bail at common law; and if he render his body, the sureties are discharged; and execution shall be of the goods, or of the body, &c. not of the lands. *Godb.* 260. 1 *Shep. Abr.* 129. 1 *Salk.* 33. *T. Ray.* 78. 2 *Lord Ray.* 1286. *Fitzg.* 197.

The admiralty court may award execution upon land; though not hold plea of any thing arising on land. 4 *Inst.* 141. And upon letters missive or request, the admiralty here may award execution on a judgment given beyond sea, where an Englishman flies or comes over hither, by imprisonment of the party, who shall not be delivered by the common law. 1 *Roll. Abr.* 530. When sentence is given in a foreign admiralty, the party may libel for execution of that sentence here; because all courts of admiralty in Europe are governed by the civil law. *Sid.* 418. Sentences of any admiralty in another kingdom are to be credited, that ours may be credited there, and shall not be examined at law here; but the king may be petitioned, who may cause the complaint to be examined; and, if he finds just cause, may send to his embassador where the sentence was given, to demand redress; and, upon failure thereof, will grant letters of marque and reprisal. *Raym.* 473.

If one is sued in the admiralty, contrary to the statutes 13 *R.* 2. *st.* 1. *c.* 5. & 15 *R.* 2. *c.* 3. he may have a *supersedeas*, to cause the judge to stay the proceedings, and also have action against the party suing. 10 *Rep.* 75. A ship being privately arrested by admiralty process only, and no suit, it was adjudged a prosecution within the meaning of the statutes; and double damages, recovered. 1 *Salk.* 31, 32. And if an erroneous judgment is given in the admiralty, appeal may be had, to delegates appointed by commission, out of chancery, whose sentence shall be final, *Stat.* 8 *Eliz. cap.* 5.

Appeals may be brought from the inferior admiralty courts to the lord high admiral: but the lord warden of the cinque ports hath jurisdiction of admiralty exempt from the admiralty of England. A writ of error doth not lie upon a sentence in the admiralty, but an appeal. 4 *Inst.* 135. 339.

ADMISSION *of a clerk*, (*admissio*) is when a patron of a church having presented to it, the bishop upon examination admits the clerk, by saying *admitto te habilem*. *Co. L.* 344. *a.* It is properly the ordinary's declaration that he approves of the presentee, to serve the cure of the church to which he is presented. *Co. L.* 344. *a.* All persons are to have episcopal ordination before they are admitted to any parsonage or benefice; and if any shall presume to be admitted, not having such ordination, &c. he shall forfeit 100*l.* *Stat.* 13 & 14 *Car.* 2. *c.* 4. No person is to be admitted into a benefice with cure of 30*l. per ann.* in the king's books, unless he is a batchelor of divinity at least, or a preacher lawfully allowed by some bishop, &c. Action of the case will not lie against the bishop, if he refuse to admit a clerk to be qualified according to the canons (as for any crime or impediment, illiterature, &c.) but the remedy is by writ *quare non admisit*, or *admittendum clericum* brought in that county where the refusal was. 7 *Rep.* 3.

ADMITTENDO CLERICO, is a writ granted to him who has recovered his right of presentation against the bishop in the common pleas, to admit his clerk. *Reg.* 33. *a. Cowel. Blount.*

ADMITTENDO IN SOCIUM, a writ for associating certain persons to justices of assize. *Reg. Orig.* 206. And knights and other gentlemen of the county are at this day usually associated with judges in holding their assizes on the circuits.

ADNICHILED, signifies annulled, cancelled, or made void. *Stat.* 28 *Hen.* 8. *Cowel. Btount.*

ADQUIETO, the same as *acquietare*, that is, to pay. *Blount.*

AD QUOD DAMNUM, is a writ which ought to be issued before the king grants certain liberties, as a fair, market, &c. which may be prejudicial to others: it is directed to the sheriff to inquire what damage it may do, for the king to grant a market, fair, &c. *Terms de Ley* 25. *Blount.*

The writ *ad quod damnum* is also had for the turning and changing of ancient highways; which may not be done without the king's licence obtained by this writ, on inquisition found, that such a change will not be detrimental to the public. *Vaugh.* 341. Ways turned without this authority are not esteemed highways, so as to oblige the inhabitants of the hundred to make amends for robberies; nor have the subjects an interest therein to justify going there. 3 *Cro.* 267.

The river Thames is an highway, and cannot be diverted without an *ad quod damnum*, and to do such a thing ought to be by patent of the king. *Noy* 105.

If there be an ancient trench or ditch coming from the sea, by which boats and vessels used to pass to the town, if the same be stopped in any part, by outrageousness of the sea, and a man will sue to the king to make a new trench, and to stop the ancient trench, &c. they ought first to sue a writ of *ad quod damnum*, to enquire what damage it will be to the king or others. *F. N. B.* 265. *E.*

And if the king will grant to any city the assise of bread and beer, and the keeping of weights and measures, an *ad quod damnum* shall be first awarded, and when the same is certified, &c. then to make the grant. *F. N. B.* 225. *E.*

ADRECTARE, *addressare*, i. e. *ad rectum ire, recto stare*, to do right, satisfy or make amends. *Gerv. Dorobern. anno* 1170. *Cowel. Blount.*

AD TERMINUM QUI PRETERIIT, a writ of entry, that lies for the lessor and his heirs, where a lease has been made of lands or tenements, for term of life, or years; and after the term is expired, the lands are withheld from the lessor by the tenant, or other person that possesseth the same: and it likewise lies for the heir of the lessor. *F. N. B.* 201.

But the modern and most easy way of recovering possession, is by ejectment: after judgment in which, the annual value of the premises, during the wrongful holding, may be recovered, in an action of trespass, for the mesne profits, in which may also be recovered, the costs of ejectment.

And now by statute 4 *Geo.* 2. *c.* 28, a tenant wilfully holding over, after demand and notice in writing for delivering possession, shall pay double the yearly value.

ADVENT, (*adventus*) a time containing about a month preceding the feast of the nativity of Christ. It begins from the Sunday that falls either upon St. Andrew's day, being the 30th of November, or next to it, and continues to the feast of Christ's nativity, commonly called Christmas. *Blount.*

AD VENTREM INSPICIENDUM. This is a writ at common law, which lies for the heir presumptive, to examine, whether the widow, who is suspected to feign herself with child in order to produce a supposititious heir to the estate, be with child or not; and if she be, to keep her under proper restraint till delivered.

ADVENTURE, a thing sent to sea, the adventure whereof the person, sending it, stands to out and home. *Lex Mercat.* Vide *Adventure.*

ADVERTISEMENTS, see *Stamps, Stolen Goods, Theft, Bote,* and other titles.

AD VITAM AUT CULPAM, (according to the statute 28 *Geo.* 2. *c.* 7. on *Scotch Jurisdictions.* is the same as *quamdiu se bene gesserit* in England) and imports that the office granted to be so held, can only be determined by the death or delinquency of the possessor.

ADULTERY, (*adulterium, quasi ad alterius thorum, anno* 1 *Hen.* 7. *cap.* 7.) and in divers old authors termed *advowtry*, is the sin of incontinence between two married persons; and if but one of the persons be married, it is nevertheless adultery: but in this last case it is called single adultery: to distinguish it from the other, which is double. The Julian law, among the old Romans, made it death. And by a law of *William the Conqueror*, whoever forced a woman was to lose his genitals, the offending parts. But in most countries at this time the punishment is by fine, and sometimes banishment: in England it is punished in the ecclesiastical courts by fine, penance, divorce *a mensa et thoro*, &c. and in the *common law* courts, by a compensation in damages to be assessed by a jury, on the trial of an action for *crim. con.* See *Cowel. Bracton. Blount.*

If a wife elope from her husband, and live with the adulterer, (without being reconciled to the husband) she shall forfeit her dower. *Co. Lit.* 36. 2 *Inst.* 435. And even though with her husband's consent, she live in adultery, yet she shall lose her dower. 2 *Inst.* 435.

So also in the case of elopement, and living with an adulterer, the ecclesiastical court does not allow *alimony*. 1 *Black.* 441, 442.

ADVOCATE, is the same by the civil and ecclesiastical laws as a counsellor by the common law; and who assists his client with advice and pleads for him. *Cowel. Blount.*

ADVOCATI, were those which we now call patrons of churches, and reserved to them, and their heirs, a liberty to present a person on any avoidance. *Blount.*

ADVOCATIONE DECIMARUM, a writ that lies for tithes, demanding the fourth part, or upwards, that belong to any church. *Cowel. Blount. Reg. Orig.* 29.

ADVOW, (*advocare, to avow*) that is, to justify or maintain an act formerly done. For example: one takes a distress for rent, and he that is distrained sues the replevin: now the distrainer, justifying or maintaining the act is said to *advow* or *avow*: and hence comes *avowment* and *avowry*. *Old Nat. Br.* 43.

ADVOWEE, or *avowee*, (*advocatus*) is used for him that hath right to present to a benefice: and by 25 *Ed.* 3. *stat.* 5. we find *advowee paramount* is taken for the king, the highest patron.—*Advocatus est ad quem pertinet jus advocationis alicujus ecclesiæ, ut ad ecclesiam, nomine proprio non alieno, possit præsentare. Fleta, lib.* 5. *c.* 14.

ADVOWSON, (*advocatio*) signifies the right of presentation to a church or benefice: and he who hath this right to present, is stiled *patron*: because they that originally obtained the right of presentation to any church, were maintainers of, or benefactors to, the same church. When the christian religion was first established in England, kings began to build cathedral churches, and to make bishops; and afterwards in imitation of them, several lords of manors founded particular churches on some part of their own lands, and endowed them with glebe, reserving to themselves and their heirs a right to present a fit person to the bishop, when the same should become void: and this is called an *advowson*, and he that hath this right of presentation is termed the patron, it being presumed that he who founded the church, will avow and take it into his protection, and be a patron to defend it in its just rights. *Cowel. Blount.* 1 *Nels. Abr.* 184. 2 *Black. Com.* 21—3.

And advowsons are of two kinds, namely, *appendant* and in *gross*.

Advowson appendant] Is a right of presentation dependant upon a manor, lands, or the like, and passes in a grant of the manor as incident to the same; and when manors were first created, and lands set apart to build a church on some part thereof, the advowson or right to present to that church became appendant to the manor. 1 *Comyn's Dig. tit. Ad.*

Advowson in gross] Is a right subsisting by itself, belonging to a person, and not to a manor, lands, or the like. So that when an advowson appendant is severed by deed or grant from the corporeal inheritance to which it was appendant, then it becomes an advowson in gross. *Co. Lit.* 121, 122. 2 *Black.* 22, 23.

And the law in this case, of a common person, is thus set down by Rolle, out of the antient books: if a man seised of a manor to which an advowson is appendant, aliens that manor, without saying with the appurtenances (and much more without naming the advowson) yet the advowson shall pass; for it is parcel of the manor. 2 *Rol. Abr.* 60.

But with respect to the king, by the statute *de prærogativa regis*, 17 *Ed.* 2. *c.* 15. When the king giveth or granteth land or a manor with appurtenances; without he make express mention in his deed or writing, of advowson of churches when they fall, belonging to such manor or land, at this day the king reserveth to himself such advowsons, albeit that among other persons it hath been observed otherwise.

Advowsons are also either presentative, collative, or donative.

Advowson presentative] Is, where the patron hath a right to present or offer his clerk to the bishop or ordinary of the diocese, and moreover to demand of him to institute his clerk, if he finds him canonically qualified, and this is the most usual advowson. *Co. Lit.* 120. 2 *Black.* 22.

Advowson collative] Is that advowson which is lodged in the bishop; for collation is the giving of a benefice by a bishop, when he is the original patron thereof, or he gains a right by lapse: in which case the bishop cannot present to himself, but he does by an act of *collation*, or conferring the benefice the whole that is done in common cases by both presentation and institution. 2 *Black.* 22. For institution is given by the bishop upon a presentation of a patron; but collation is an immediate institution, because the bishop is both patron and ordinary. Institution and collation are in effect (for the most part) the same, and are terms made use of to distinguish the persons, who have the power to bestow the benefice. *Cowel.* 157.

Advowson donative] Is, when the king or other patron (in whom the advowson of the church is lodged) does, by a single donation in writing, put the clerk into possession, without presentation, institution, or induction. Donatives are either of churches parochial, chapels, prebends, &c. and may be exempt from all ordinary jurisdictions, so that the ordinary cannot visit them, and consequently cannot demand procurations. If the true patron of a church or chapel donative doth once present to the ordinary, and his clerk is admitted and instituted, it becomes a church presentative, and shall never have the privilege of a donative afterwards. Yet if a stranger presents to such a donative, and institution is given, all is void. *Id.* 158.

The right of donation descends to the heir (the ancestor dying seised, where the church became void in his life-time) and not to the executor, which it would had it been a presentative benefice. 2 *Wilson Rep.* 150, 1.

There is not any case in the books to exclude the heir of a donative from his turn in this case. And a patron of a donative can never be put out of possession by an usurpation. *Ibid.*

ADVOWSON OF THE MOIETY OF THE CHURCH, (*advocatio medietatis ecclesiæ*) Is where there are two several patrons and two several incumbents in one and the same church, the one of the one moiety, and the other of the other moiety thereof. *Co. Lit.* 17 b. *Medietas advocationis*, a moiety of the advowson, is where two must join in the presentation, and there is but one incumbent; as where there are two parceners: and though they agree to present by turns, yet each of them hath but the moiety of the church. *Co. Lit.* 17 b. But by 7 *Ann. c.* 18. where coparceners, joint-tenants, or the like, are seised of an advowson, and a partition is made to present by turns, each of them shall be seised of his separate estate.

ADVOWSON OF RELIGIOUS HOUSES, where any persons founded any house of religion, they had thereby the advowson or patronage thereof, like unto those who built and endowed parish churches. *Kennet's Paroch. Antiq.* 147, 163.

AERIE, (*aerie accipitrum*) airy of goshawks, is the proper term for hawks, for that which of other birds we call a nest. *Stat.* 9 *H.* 3. c. 12. and is said by *Spelman* to come from the French word *aere,* a hawk's nest. *Cowel. Blount.*

ÆSTIMATIO CAPITIS, (*pretium hominis*) king Athelstane ordained that fines should be paid for offences committed against several persons according to their degrees and quality, by estimation of their heads. *Cress. Ch. Hist.* 834. *Leg. Hen.* 1. *Cowel. Blount.*

ÆTATE PROBANDA, a writ that lay to inquire, whether the king's tenant holding in chief by chivalry, was of full age to receive his lands into his own hands. It was directed to the escheator of the county; but is now disused, since wards and liveries are taken away by the statute. *Reg. Orig.* 294. *Cowel. Blount.*

AFFEERERS, (*afferatores*) from the Fr. *affier,* to affirm. They are those that in courts-leet, upon oath, settle and moderate the fines and amercements, imposed on such persons as have committed faults, arbitrarily punishable, *viz.* that have no express penalty appointed by statute: and they are also appointed for moderating amercements, in courts baron. The persons nominated to this office affirm upon their oaths what penalty they think in conscience ought to be inflicted on the offenders. This word is used *stat.* 25 *Ed.* 3. *c.* 7. Where mention is made, that the justices before their rising in every sessions shall cause the amerciaments to be affeered. And this seems to be agreeable to magna charta, by which it is ordained, that persons are to be amerced after the manner of the fault; and the amerciaments shall be assessed by the oath of honest and lawful men of the vicinage. 9 *Hen.* 3. *cap.* 14. *Com. Dig.* 4 *V. tit. Leet,* (O. 2.) *Cowel. Blount.* 4 *Black.* 380.

AFFIANCE, the plighting of troth between a man and a woman, upon agreement of marriage: it is derived from the Latin word *affidare,* and signifies as much as *fidem ad alium dare.* *Lit. sect.* 39.

AFFIDARE, to plight one's faith, or give or swear fealty. *Blount.*

AFFIDATIO DOMINORUM, an oath taken by the lords in parliament, *anno* 3 *Hen.* 6. *Rot. Parl. Blount.*

AFFIDATUS, signifies a tenant by fealty, also a retainer. *Blount.*

AFFIDARI, *seu affidari ad arma,* to be mustered and inrolled for soldiers upon an oath of fidelity. *Dom de Farendon MS.* 55.

AFFIDAVIT, (the perfect tense of the verb *affido*) signifies in law an oath in writing; and to make affidavit of a thing, is to testify it upon oath An affidavit generally speaking, is an oath in writing, sworn before some judge, or officer of a court, or other person who hath authority to administer such oath, to evince the truth of certain facts therein contained; and the true place of habitation, and true addition of every person who shall make an affidavit, is to be inserted in his affidavit. 1 *Lill. Abr.* 44. 46. 3 *Black.* 304.

And an affidavit must set forth the matter positively, and all material circumstances attending it, that the court may judge whether the deponent's conclusion be just or not. As, for instance, on motion to put off a trial for want of a material witness, it must appear that endeavours were made use of to have him at the time appointed, and that he cannot possibly be present, though he may on further time given. *Farres.* 121. *Comb.* 421, 422. 1 *Bac. Abr. tit. Aff.*

Affidavits are usually for holding persons to bail, certifying the service of process, or other matters touching the proceedings in a cause; or in support of, or against motions, in cases, where the court has to determine matters in a summary way.

Affidavit annexed to a Bill of Interpleader.] In bills of interpleader, the party who prefers it must make affidavit that he does not collude with either of the other parties. *Mitford* 49.

——— *To a bill to perpetuate the testimony of witnesses.*] To avoid objection to a bill framed on the ground, that before the facts can be investigated in a court of law, the evidence of a material witness is likely to be lost by his death or departure from the realm, it seems proper to annex to it an affidavit of the circumstances by which the evidence intended to be perpetuated is in danger of being lost. 1 *Peere Wms.* 117. 3 *Peere Wms.* 77. 1 *Atk.* 450. *Mitford* 51.

And unless such an affidavit be annexed to the bill a demurrer will hold. *Mitford* 131.

The principle on which it is required in these cases to annex to the bill an affidavit of the circumstances, which render the examination of witnesses proper in a court of equity, though the matter is capable of being made immediately the subject of a suit at law, seems to be this; namely, that the bill tends to alter the ordinary course of the administration of justice which ought not to be permitted, upon the bare allegation of a plaintiff in his bill. *Mitford* 132.

——— *to a Bill for a discovery of a Deed and Relief.*] If a person exhibits a bill in equity for the discovery of a deed, and prays relief thereupon, he must annex an affidavit to his bill, that he has not such deed in his possession or power, and that he knows not where they are unless in the hands of the defendant; for otherwise he takes away the jurisdiction of the common law courts, without shewing any probable cause why he should sue in equity. 1 *Chan. Ca.* 11, 231. 1 *Vern.* 59, 180, 247. *Mitford* 52.

But if he seeks discovery of the deed only, or that it may be produced at a trial at law, he need not annex such affidavit to his bill; for it is not to be presumed that in either of these cases, he would do so absurd a thing, as exhibit a bill, if he had the deed in his possession. 1 *Vern.* 180, 147. *Mitford* 53.

It is also unnecessary in the case of a bill for the discovery of a cancelled instrument, and to have another deed executed, for if the plaintiff had the cancelled instrument in his hands, he could make no use of it at law, and indeed the relief prayed is such as a court of equity only can give. *Mitford* 113.

——— *To obtain leave to file a bill of review.*] If the object of a bill of review be to reverse a decree signed and inrolled *upon discovery of some new matter,* the leave of the court must be first obtained, and this will be not granted, but upon allegation upon oath, that *the new* matter could not be produced or used by the party claiming the benefit of it, at the time when the decree was made. *Mitford* 78, 79.

And as the office of a *supplemental bill, in nature of a bill of review,* is to supply the defect which occasioned the decree on the former bill; it is also necessary to obtain the leave of the court to bring a supplemental bill of this nature, and the same affidavit is required for this purpose, as is necessary to obtain leave to bring a bill of review on discovery of new matter. *Mitford* 82.

AFFINAGE, (Fr. *affinage*) refining of metal, *purgatio metalli; inde,* fine and refine. *Blount.*

AFFIRM, (*affirmare*) signifies to ratify or confirm a former law or judgment. *Cowel. Blount.*

AFFIRMATION, The people called quakers, are in cases, where an oath is required from others, allowed to make a solemn AFFIRMATION that what they say is true; and if they make a false affirmation, they are subject to the penalties of perjury: but this relates only to oaths to the government, and in *civil* matters; for quakers may not give testimony on affirmation, in any criminal cause. 7 & 8 *W.* 3. *c.* 34. and 22 *G.* 2. *c.* 46.

AFFORARE, to set a value or price on a thing. *Charta anno* 1316. *apud. Thorn. Du Cange. Blount.*

AFFORATUS, appraised or valued, as things vendible in a fair or market. *Cartular Glaston. MS. f.* 58. *Cowel. Blount.*

AFFORCIAMENT, (*afforciamentum*) a fortress, strong hold, or other fortification. *Pryn Animad. on Coke, fol.* 58. *Cowel. Blount.*

AFFORCIARE, to add, increase, or make stronger. *Bract. lib.* 4. *c.* 19. *viz.* Let the witnesses be increased. *Blount.*

AFFOREST, (*afforestare*) to turn ground into a forest. *Chart. de Forest. c.* 1.

AFFRAY, is derived from the French word *effrayer,* to affright, and it formerly meant no more; as where persons appeared with armour or weapons not usually worn, to the terror of others. *Stat.* 2 *Ed.* 3. *c.* 3. But now it signifies a fighting between two or more in some *public place,* to the terror of his majesty's subjects: for if the fighting be *in private* it is no *affray* but an *assault.* 4 *Black.* 145. and there must be a stroke given, or offered, or a weapon drawn, otherwise it is not an affray. 3 *Inst.* 158. And sir Edward Coke emphatically says, that an affray is a public offence to the terror of the king's subjects, and so called, because it affrighteth and maketh men afraid. 3 *Inst.* 158.

From this it is said, that no quarrelsome or threatening words whatsoever shall amount to an affray. But yet it seems certain, that in some cases, there may be an affray, where there is no actual violence; as where a man arms himself with dangerous and unusual weapons, in such a manner, as will naturally cause a terror to the people; which is said to have been always an offence at the common law, and is strictly prohibited by statute 2 *Ed.* 3. *c.* 3. 1 *Hawk. P. C.* 135.

A *constable* may require affrayers to depart, and if they resist, he may call others to his assistance; who, if they refuse to assist him, may be fined and imprisoned: and a *private person, or stander-by,* may put a stop to an affray, and seize the offenders, where persons are assembled in a tumultuous manner to break the peace. 3 *Inst.* 158. *H. P. C.* 135. And in case a person be dangerously wounded, any man may apprehend the offender, and carry him before a justice, in the same manner as a constable. *Dalt.* 35. In a very dangerous affray, a constable can justify commitment, till the offenders find sureties for the peace. *Lamb.* 139. He may likewise put the affrayers in the stocks till he can procure proper assistance to convey them to gaol. *Dalt.* 38.

If an affray be in an house, the constable may break open the doors to preserve the peace; and if affrayers fly to an house, and he follow with fresh suit, he may break open the door to take them. 1 *Hawk.* 137.

But in cases of affray, the constable must apprehend the persons offending before the affray is over, or else he may not do it without a warrant from a justice, except it be in an extraordinary case; as where a person is wounded dangerously. *Dalt.* 36. In the case of a sudden affray, through passion or excess of drinking, the constable may put the persons in prison, if there be one in the vill, until the heat of their passion and intemperance is over, though he deliver them afterwards; or till he can bring them before a justice of peace, and that to avoid the present danger. 2 *Hale's Hist. P. C.* 90, 95. If a constable is hurt in an affray, he may have his remedy by action of trespass, and have damages; but the affrayers, if they are hurt, shall have no remedy. *Lamb.* 141. And where any other persons receive harm from the affrayers, they may have remedy by action against them. *Dalt.* 35.

A justice of peace may commit affrayers, until they find sureties for the peace. But he cannot without a warrant authorize the arrest of any person for an affray out of his own view; yet he may make his warrant to bring the offender before him, to compel him to find sureties for the peace. 1 *Hawk.* 137.

It is inquirable in the court-leet; and punishable by justices of peace in their sessions, by *fine and imprisonment*. And it differs from assault, in that, it is a wrong to the public; whereas assault is of a private nature. *Lamb. lib.* 2. yet indictment lies, as being a breach of the public peace.

And the measure of punishment for affrays must be regulated by the circumstances of each case: for where there is any material aggravation, the punishment proportionally encreases: as where two persons coolly and deliberately engage in a *duel*, this being attended with an apparent intention and danger of murder, and being a high contempt of the justice of the nation, is a strong aggravation of the affray, though no mischief has ensued,—So also another aggravation is, when thereby the officers of justice are disturbed in the due execution of their office: or where a respect to the particular place ought to restrain and regulate men's behaviour, as in the king's courts, palaces, and the like, or a church or church-yard 4 *Black.* 145.

AFFREIGHTMENT, (*affretamentum*) the freight of a ship, from the French *fret*, which signifies the same. *Cowel. Blount.* See *Charter-Party.*

AFFRI, vel *affra*, bullocks, or horses or beasts of the plough. *Spel. Gloss. Cowel. Blount.*

AFRICAN TRADE. See *Slave Trade.*

AGALMA, the impression or image of any thing on a seal. *Cowel. Blount.*

AGE, (*ætas*, French *age*,) generally signifies from his birth to any certain time, or the day of his death: it also hath relation to that *æra* or period of time wherein men live.

But in the law it is particularly used for those special times which enable persons of both sexes to do certain acts, which before through want of years and judgment they are prohibited to do. *Co. Lit.* 78.

And the ages of male and female are different for different purposes, 1 *Black.* 463. As for example; *a man* at twelve years of age ought to take the oath of allegiance to the king: *at fourteen* which is his age of discretion, he may consent to marriage, and choose his guardian —And if his discretion be actually proved, may make his testament of his *personal* estate; at *seventeen* he may be an executor; and at twenty-one he may alien his lands, goods, and chattels. *Co. Lit.* 78. 4 *Black.* 463.

A woman at *seven* years of age may be betrothed or given in marriage: at *nine* is dowable: at *twelve* she may consent or disagree to marriage; and if proved to have sufficient discretion may bequeath her personal estate: at *fourteen* she is at years of discretion, and may chuse a guardian: at *seventeen* may be an executrix: and at *twenty-one* she may alienate her lands, &c. *Co. Lit.* 78.

The age of twenty-one is the full age of man or woman; which enables them to contract and manage for themselves, in respect to their estates, until which time they cannot act, with security to those who deal with them; for their acts in most cases are either void or voidable. *Perk.* But a person under twenty-one may contract for necessaries suitable to his quality; and it shall bind him. *Co. Lit.* 171.

The *full age* in males and females being twenty-one years, that age is considered to be *completed* on the day preceding the anniversary of a person's birth, who till that time is an infant, and so stiled in law. 1 *Black.* 403.

Thus if the party be born on the first of January, he is of age to do any legal act on the morning of the last day of December, though he may not have lived twenty-one years by nearly forty-eight hours: the reason assigned is, that in law there is no fraction of a day: and if the birth were on the *first second of one day*, and the act on the *last second* of the other, then twenty-one years would be complete: and in the law it is the same, whether a thing is done upon one moment of the day or another. 1 *Black. Com.* 463. 4 *Mod. Cas.* 260.

The law of England does in some cases privilege an infant, under the age of twenty-one, as to common misdemeanors; so as to escape fine, imprisonment, and the like: and particularly in cases of omission; as not repairing a bridge, or a highway, and other similar offences: for not having the command of his fortune till twenty-one, he wants the capacity to do those things which the law requires. *Hale's P. C.* 20, 21, 22.

But where there is any notorious breach of the peace, as a riot, battery, or the like, (which infants when full grown are at least as liable as others to commit) for these an infant above the age of fourteen is equally liable to suffer, as a person of the full age of twenty-one. 4 *Black.* 22.

Persons under the age of fourteen are not generally punishable for *capital* crimes. *Co. Lit.* 247. 2 *Roll. Abr.* 547.

But this general rule, however, as to *capital* crimes, hath its exceptions founded on the nature of the case, and the judgment of the infant. For, although under the age of fourteen, if he display a discretion to discern between good and evil, the maxim of the law as it now stands, and has stood ever since the reign of *Ed.* 3. is that *malitia supplet ætatem:* and it would be absurd to measure the capacity of doing ill, or contracting guilt, rather by years and days, than the strength of the delinquent's judgment. 4 *Black.* 22, 23.

Thus a girl of thirteen has been burnt for killing her mistress; and one boy of ten and another of nine years old, who had killed their companions, have been sentenced to death; and he of ten years actually hanged, because it appeared upon their trials, that the one hid himself, and the other hid the body he had killed; which hiding manifested a consciousness of guilt, and a discretion to discern between good and evil. 1 *Hale P. C.* c. 26, 27.

Thus also in very modern times, a boy of *ten* years old was convicted on his own confession, of murdering his bedfellow: there appearing in his whole behaviour a variety of acts done with that deliberation, which shewed his judgment sufficiently ripe to render him accountable for his actions: and as the sparing of this boy merely on account of tender years might be of dangerous consequence to the public, by encouraging a notion that children might commit such atrocious crimes with impunity, it was unanimously agreed by all the judges, that he was a proper subject of capital punishment. *Forster* 70-2.

However, under seven years of age, an infant cannot be guilty of felony; for then a felonious discretion is almost an impossibility in nature: but at eight years old he may be guilty of felony. *Mir.* c. 4. s. 16. 1 *Hale P. C.* 27. *Dall. Just.* 147. 4 *Black* 23.

And there was an instance in the last century, where a boy of *eight* years old was tried at Abingdon, for firing two barns; and it appearing that he had malice, revenge, and cunning, he was found guilty, condemned, and hanged accordingly. *Emlyn.* 1 *Hale P. C.* 25.

As to how far infants may be admitted to give evidence, it is to be observed, that, all persons may be witnesses who appear to have a competent knowledge of the nature and consequences of an oath: and that therefore infants of very tender years, may be witnesses. *Co. Lit.* 6. 1 *Bac. Abr. tit. Evidence.*

Thus an infant of nine years has been allowed to give evidence. 1 *Hale P. C.* 263.

And an infant under the age of seven years may be a witness in a criminal prosecution, provided such infant appears, upon examination, to possess a sufficient knowledge of the nature and consequences of an oath, for there is no precise or fixed rule, as to the time, within which infants are excluded from giving evidence: their admissibility depends, upon the sense they entertain of the danger and impiety of falsehood, which is to be collected from their answers to questions propounded to them by the court: but if they are found incompetent to take an oath, their testimony cannot be received. *Leach's C. L.* 104, 180.

And to prevent a want of due justice, Mr. *Justice Rooke*, in a criminal prosecution that was coming on to be tried before him at *Gloucester*, finding that the principal witness was an infant, who was wholly incompetent to take an oath, postponed the trial till the following assizes, and ordered the child to be instructed in the mean time by a clergyman, in the principles of her duty, and the nature and obligation of an oath: at the next assizes the prisoner was put upon his trial, and the child was produced as witness; and being found by the court upon examination, to have a proper sense of the nature of an oath, was sworn: and upon her testimony, the prisoner was convicted and afterwards executed: this was afterwards mentioned by *Rooke, J.* at the Old Bailey, 1795, in the case of *Patrick Murphy* for a rape on a child of seven years: and he said that upon a conference with the other judges, upon his return from the circuit, they had unanimously approved of what he had done. *Gwillim* on *Bac. Abr. tit. Ev.* 577.

AGE-PRIER, (*ætatem precari*, or *ætatis precatio*) is, when an action being brought, against a person under age, for lands which he hath by descent, he by petition or motion shews the matter to the court, and prays that the action may stay till his full age, which the court generally agrees to. *Terms de Ley* 30. *Cowel. Blount.* This is called *parol demurrer*, *i. e.* a staying or delaying of the plea or suit. *Parol* signifies the plea or suit, *demurrer* to stay or abate. See *Parol Demurrer.*

AGENFRIDA, the true lord or owner of any thing. *Cowel. Blount.*

AGENHINE, a guest at an inn after three nights, who was then accounted one of the family. *Cowel. Blount.*

AGENT. An agent is a person employed to enter into contracts, manage property, or transact business for another; and whatever acts he may do in such capacity, are to be taken to have been done for the use and benefit of his principal.

Therefore where an agent has been employed, his principal has, in equity, in many cases, a right to a discovery of his transactions, and to demand the property with which he has been entrusted, or the value of it, *against those with whom the agent has had dealings:* and therefore where a merchant, who had employed a factor to sell his goods, filed a bill against the persons to whom the goods had been sold, for an account, and to be paid the money for which the goods had been sold, and which had not been paid to the factor, a demurrer was over-ruled. *Mitf.* 142.

But if an agent or factor sell goods at a less price than he is commissioned, the sale will bind the principal for the convenience of trade. *Ambler*, 498.

But a trustee or particular *agent*, shall not be allowed to become the purchaser, of that which he holds in trust, and thereby raise an interest in himself opposite to that of his principal. 2 *Fonbl. Eq.* 187.

And notice to the *agent* or purchaser for another, is a good notice to the principal, because it is a presumptive notice to the party. 2 *Fonbl.* 153.

Where a man acts in execution of the authority given him by another, either expressly or impliedly; that it is, by relation, the act of that other, and he acquires no right, nor brings any obligation on himself: yet if a verdict is obtained against an *agent* or trustee, equity will not relieve against such verdict, but will decree that he shall be reimbursed by his principal, and stand in the place of the creditor. 1 *Fonbl.* 296-7.

And the difference is, where the *agent* undertaking for, or on the behalf of another, has an authority so to do, and where he has not. If he has not, then it is a fraud; and he ought himself to be liable: but where there is such an authority given, it is *only* acting for another, like the case of a *factor* or *broker*, acting for their principals, who were never held to be personally liable: but to protect themselves from being so personally bound, they must strictly preserve their authority. 4 *Bur.* 2108. 6 *Ter. Rep.* 411.

AGENT AND PATIENT, The agent is doer of a thing, and the patient the party suffering the thing to be done: as where a woman endows herself of the best part of her husband's possessions, this being the sole act of herself to herself, makes her *agent and patient*. Also if a man be indebted unto another, and afterwards he makes the creditor his executor, and dies, the executor may retain so much of the goods of the deceased as will satisfy his debt; and by this retainer he is agent and patient, that is, the party to whom the debt is due, and the person that pays the same. But a man shall not be judge in his own cause, *quia iniquum est aliquem suæ rei esse judicem*. 8 *Rep.* 138. *Cowel. Blount.*

AGILD, from the Saxon *a* priv. and *zeldan selvert, quasi sine mulcta*, signifies to be free from penalties, not subject to the customary fine or imposition. *Cowel. Blount.* *Agilde* was also taken to be a person so vile, that whoever killed him was to pay no mulct for his death. *Ibid.*

AGILER, from the Saxon *a gile*, observer or informer. *Ibid.*

AGILLARIUS, an hey-ward, herd-ward, or keeper of cattle in a common field. Towns and villages had their hey-wards, to supervise and guard the greater cattle, or common herd of kine or oxen, and keep them within due bounds; and if these were servile tenants, they were privileged from all customary services to the lord, because they were presumed to be always attending their duty, as a shepherd on his flock. And lords of manors had likewise their hey-wards, to take care of the tillage, harvest work, &c. and see that there were no encroachments made on their lordships. *Cowel, Blount*, and others. This is now in most places the business of bailiffs: yet in many manors the custom continues.

AGIST, (from the French *giste*, a bed or resting-place,) signifies to take in and feed the cattle of strangers in the king's forest, and to gather up the money due for the same. *Chart. de Foresta*, 9 *Hen.* 3. *c.* 9. The officers appointed for this purpose are called *agisters*, or *gist-takers*, and are made by the king's letters patent: there are four of them in every forest wherein the king hath any pawnage. *Manw. For. Laws* 80. They are also called, according to *Cowel*, *agistators*, to take an account of the cattle agisted.

AGISTMENT, (*agistamentum*,) is where other men's cattle are taken into any ground, at a certain rate per week: it is so called, because the cattle are suffered *agiser*, that is, to be levant and couchant there: and many great farms are employed to this purpose. 2 *Inst.* 643.

Our graziers call cattle which they thus take into keep, guisements; and to guise or juice the ground, is when the occupier thereof feeds it not with his own stock, but takes in the cattle of others to agist or pasture it. *Cowel. Blount.*

Agistment is likewise the profit of such feeding in a ground or field: and extends to he depasturing of barren cattle of the owner, for which tithes shall be paid to the parson. *Ibid.*

There is agistment of sea-banks, where lands are charged with a tribute to keep out the sea. *Terræ agistatæ* are lands whose owners are bound to keep up the sea-banks. *Ibid. Spelm. on Romney-Marsh.*

AGITATIO ANIMALIUM IN FORESTA, the drift of beasts in the forest. *Leg. Forest. Cowel. Blount.*

AGIUS, (Gr. *i. e. holy.*)—*Ego triumphalem trophæum agiæ crucis impressi.* *Mon. Angl. p.* 15, 17.

AGNUS DEI, a piece of white wax in a flat oval form, like a small cake, stamped with the figure of a lamb, and consecrated by the pope. *Cowel.*

And by 13 *Eliz. c.* 2. "to *import any ag-*" *nus dei*, crosses, beads, or other supersti-" tious things, pretended to be hallowed by " the bishop of Rome, and tender the same " to be used, or to receive the same with " such intent, and not discover the offender, " or if a justice of the peace knowing there- " of, shall not within fourteen days disclose " it to a privy counsellor, they all incur a " præmunire." See *Papists.*

AGNATI, the relations by the *father*, who

were preferred by the Roman laws to the *cognati*, or relations by the *mother*: till the edict of the emperor Justinian, *Nov.* 118, abolished all distictions between them. 2 *Black.* 235.

AGRARIA LEX, a law made by the Romans for the distribution of lands among the common people. *Cowel.*

AGREEMENT, is the consent of two or more persons, concerning, the one in parting with, and the other receiving some property, right, or benefit. 1 *Bac. Abr. tit. Agr.*

And it is defined to be *aggregatio mentium in re aliqua facta vel facienda*, and it ought to be so certain and complete, that each party may have an action upon it. *Plow. Com.* 5, *a.* 6. *a.*

To an agreement or contract, there is not any prescribed form of words, but such words as shew the assent of the parties are sufficient, so as the agreement be certain and complete, and therefore it is not material by which of the parties the words of the agreement or contract are used, if the assent of the other appears.

And there are three sorts of agreements: 1st. *An agreement executed* already at the beginning, as where money is paid for the thing agreed, or other satisfaction made at the time of the execution: 2dly, where an *assent* subsequent is given to an act precedent; as where one doth such a thing, and another person *agrees* or *assents* to it afterwards, and by such *assent* the agreement is also *executed*: 3dly, an *agreement executory*, is an agreement to execute a deed, pay a sum of money, or perform some act at a future day. *Plowd. Com.* 8 9. *Terms de Ley.* 31.

How enforced.] In many cases the party injured by breach of an agreement may either have a remedy by action at common law, or by recourse to a court of equity; but here a general rule must be observed, that wherever the matter put in question by the bill is merely in damages, there the remedy is at law; because the damages cannot be ascertained by the conscience of the chancellor; and therefore must be settled by a jury. 1 *Bac. Abr. tit. Agr. b.*

For it is the rule of courts of equity not to entertain the suit unless the plaintiff wants the thing in specie, and cannot have it in any other way. Therefore in general they will not allow a bill for a specific performance of contracts of stock, corn, hops, or other articles of merchandize, but will leave the party to his remedy at law. 2 *Bro. Ch. Rep.* 343. 1 *Pere Wms.* 570. 5 *Vin. Abr.* 538—540. *Bunb.* 135. 2 *Eq. Cas. Abr.* 161.

But if there be matter of fraud mixed with the damages, and a bill is filed for an injunction upon this equitable suggestion, that the covenant was obtained by fraud; and then the defendant files his cross bill for relief upon the covenant, the court will retain it, because the validity of the covenant is disputed in that court, and on an head properly cognizable there; and therefore if the validity of the deed be established, the court will direct an issue for the quantum of the damages. *Ch. Rep.* 158. *Abr. Eq.* 17.

So where the agreement is to do something in *specie*, as to convey lands, execute a deed, or the like, there it will be proper to apply to a court of equity for a specific execution, to which the party is entitled, if the agreement be good and sufficiently proved, when otherwise, he could only recover damages at law. *Ch. Cas.* 42.

And it is now by a series of decisions established, that courts of equity may decree a contract to be performed in *specie* at least, wherever a court of law would give damages, for the non-performance of it; but which damages would not be an adequate compensation for the non-performance, the party wanting the thing in specie. 1 *Fonbl.* 30.

However, though equity will in general enforce the specific performance of contracts, if the party wants the thing in *specie*, and cannot have it in any other way, yet if the breach of contract can be or was intended to be compensated in damages, courts of equity will not interpose. 2 *Bro. Rep.* 341. 1 *Pere Wms.* 570. *Bunb.* 135.

And in the exercise of this equitable jurisdiction, the court may either direct the master to enquire, what damage the plaintiff hath sustained by the defendant's non-performance of his agreement, and upon the report, decree satisfaction; *or*, otherwise, send it to be tried at law upon a *quantum damnificatus*; when the bill prays a specific performance of such agreement, which cannot be decreed, as where the defendant has *by sale of the estate, or the like,* put it out of his power. *Abr. Eq. Cas.* 18. *pl.* 7. 1 *Fonbl.* 389.

But here it must be observed, that agreements, out of which an equity can be raised, for a decree in specie, ought to be obtained with all imaginable fairness, and without any mixture tending to surprize or circumvention, and that they be not unreasonable in themselves. *Abr. Eq.* 17. 1 *Bac. Abr.* 109.

But inadequacy of price simply andof itself, independently of any other circumstances, is not a ground with the court to annul an agreement, though executory, still less is it a ground to rescind one already executed: and in *Heathcote* v. *Paignon*, 2 *Bro. Ch. Rep.* 167. *Lord Thurlow* admitted, that mere inadequacy of price was scarcely sufficient, but said, that *there was a difference between that and evidence arising from in-*

adequacy: if there is such inadequacy as to shew that the person did not understand the bargain he made, or was so oppressed that he was glad to make it, knowing its inadequacy, it will shew a command over him, which may amount to fraud. 1 *Fonbl.* 128.

And where agreements are endeavoured to be set aside for supposed weakness of understanding, for breach of confidence, or other substantive reason, the inequality of the terms may be a material ingredient in the case as evidence of imposition. 3 *Woodes* 455.

It is also to be observed, that where an agreement appears to be very unequal, the courts will lay hold of very slight circumstances, to avoid enforcing the execution of it; as where the plaintiff had not made out his title by the time stipulated; a circumstance which in general has not any weight with them. 2 *Bro. Ch. Rep.* 396. 1 *Atk.* 12.

But as these cases, and all others on this head, depend so much upon circumstances, and are to stand or fall, according to the degrees of fraud or circumvention attending them, and proved in the cause, or by what appears unreasonable on the face of them; it is only to be observed, that a court of equity will much more easily be prevailed on, to dismiss a bill which prays a specific execution of an unreasonable agreement, than set aside an agreement, though not strictly fair on a bill for that purpose, for this deprives the party of what he had a right to by law; and that when such agreements are set aside, it must be on refunding what was *bona fide* paid, making allowances for improvements. 1 *Bac. Abr.* 111.

Thus the court will not compel a purchaser to take a title which is at all doubtful. 1 *Br. Ch. Rep.* 75. 4 *Br. Ch. Rep.* 80. Nor will they interpose where a party has forborne to insist upon an agreement for several years, unless the delay can be accounted for, by special circumstances: nor in case of a written agreement afterwards discharged by parol: nor in the case of a sale by auction, where an accident has happened to cast a damp upon the sale; as where the vendor's agent, *known to be such to the company present*, bid for the purchase: nor if the agreement be to do a thing which would tend to extortion or promote inebriety: nor if damages be stipulated, though in general they will in the case of a penalty, designed merely as a medium for securing the performance of the contract: nor will they interpose if the agreement be founded on an illegal consideration, as that of stifling a prosecution for felony or for fraud. *Ibid.*

And as solemn conveyances, releases, and agreements by parties are not slightly to be blown off and set aside, equity will not void *a reasonable and fair agreement*, though founded on mistake; or though the party were intoxicated, or in prison, at the time he entered into it, or some paternal authority were exerted, and some benefit accrue to the father under it: nor will the court decree a forfeiture after an agreement, in which, if it were a mistake, it was a mistake of all the parties to it. *Ibid.*

As to voluntary agreements.] It is laid down that as men have a right to their acquisitions, so may they dispose of them at their pleasure, and without valuable consideration; but if a man promises to convey lands, or to give goods, *without valuable consideration, or without delivering possession* of them, this alters no property, nor has the party any remedy at law or equity, it being *nudum pactum unde non oritur actio.* 3 *Co.* 81. *b.* 2 *Black. Com.* 443. *Dy.* 336. *b.* 2 *Buls.* 225.

But if it be done, by deed duly executed under seal, this is good in law, though there be *no* consideration, or no delivery of possession, because a man is estopped to deny his own deed, or affirm any thing contrary to the manifest solemnity of contracting. *Plow.* 308, 309. *Yelv.* 196. *Cro. Jac.* 270. *Brown* 111. 3 *Bur.* 1637. 2 *Bl.* 446. 1 *Fonbl.* 335.

And equity will not carry a merely voluntary contract beyond the letter of it. 2 *Vern.* 692. And in decreeing the execution of agreements, it regards the intent of the parties, and does not confine itself, to the strictly legal operation of the words; where therefore marriage articles, *literally*, taken would give the husband or wife an estate tail, it decrees a strict settlement; for otherwise the provisions for the issue, the object of the settlement, might be defeated. 1 *Bac. Abr.* 113.

Also in contracts, proper for a specific performance, equity considers them often as actually performed, from the time they are entered into: thus money agreed to be laid out in land, it considers as land, and it will go to the *heir* and not to the executor. 1 *Pere Wms.* 483. *Pr. Ch.* 540. 2 *Pere Wms.* 171. 3 *Pere Wms.* 221. And land agreed to be sold, it treats as money, which thus circumstanced, will be deemed as part of the personal estate. 2 *Vern.* 295. 1 *Br. Ch. Rep.* 236, 368. thus investing each with the qualities of the other. 1 *Bac. Abr.* 113.

Parol agreements.] By statute 29 *Car.* 2. *c.* 3. "no action shall be brought whereby "to charge any executor or administrator, "upon any special promise to answer damages out of his own estate, or whereby "to charge the defendant, upon any special "promise to answer for the debt, default, or "miscarriages of another person or to "charge any person upon any agreement, "made upon consideration of marriage, or "upon any contract or sale of lands, tenements or hereditaments, or any interest in "or concerning them, or upon any agree-

" ment that is not to be performed, within " the space of one year, from the making " thereof, unless the agreement upon which " such action shall be brought, or some " *memorandum* or note thereof shall be in " writing, signed by the party to be " charged therewith, or some other per- " son by him thereunto lawfully authorised." *s.* 4.

In the construction of this statute, the following points have been resolved.

1st. That if there be a *parol agreement* for the purchase of lands, and a bill brought for a specific execution thereof, and the substance of the agreement set forth in the bill be confessed by the defendant's answer, without insisting on any fraud, that in such case the court will decree a specific execution, because there is no danger of perjury, which was the principal thing the statute intended to prevent, and he has thereby taken away the necessity of proof. *Abr. Eq.* 19. and 1 *Treatise on Eq.* 178.

Upon this point Mr. *Fonblanque* admits, that if a defendant confess the agreement charged in the bill, there is no danger of fraud or perjury in decreeing the performance of such agreement; but he very judiciously observes, that it is of considerable importance to determine, whether the defendant be bound to confess or deny a merely parol agreement, not alleged to be in any part executed, or if he do confess it, whether he may not insist on the statute in bar of the performance. 1 *Fonbl.* 178. *n. d.*

2d. That if a parol agreement be carried into execution by one of the parties as by delivering possession, and such execution be accepted by the other, he that accepts it must perform his part; for where there is a performance, the evidence of the bargain does not lie merely upon the words, but upon the fact performed, and it is unconscionable, that the party, that has received the advantage, should be admitted to say that such contract was never made. 1 *Fonbl. B.* 1. *c.* 3. *s.* 8.

And the general rule is, that the acts must be such as could be done with no other view, or design than to perform the agreement, and not such as are merely *introductory* or ancillary: the giving of possession, is therefore, to be considered, as an act of part performance, but giving directions for conveyances, and going to view the estate are not. Payment of money is also said to be an act of part performance: but it seems that payment of a sum by way of earnest is not. 1 *Fonbl.* 186. *Amb.* 586. 1 *Bro. Rep.* 412. 3 *Vez. Jun.* 34, 379. 1 *Atk.* 12.

3d. That if a parol agreement is agreed to be reduced into writing, and signing and reducing the same into writing, be prevented by fraud, it may be decreed in equity; as if upon a marriage treaty, instructions are given by the husband to draw a settlement, and by him *privately* countermanded, and afterwards he draws in the woman by professions, and assurances of such settlement to marry him. *Abr. Eq.* 19. *Fonbl.* 184. *Pr. Ch.* 526. 5 *Vin. Abr.* 521. 1 *Vern.* 296.

And although parol agreements are bound by the statute, and agreements are not to be part parol and part in writing; yet a deposit or collateral security for the performance of the written agreement, is not within the purview of the statute. *Treatise of Eq.* 186.

4th. That where in consideration of a parol agreement the plaintiff had expended great sums of money about the premises, and charged, that part of the agreement was, that *the agreement should be put into writing*, there the lord keeper over-ruled a plea of the statute of frauds. 2 *Ch. Cas.* 135.

And the want of such circumstance in another case was held fatal to the agreement, though the plaintiff alleged that he had expended considerable sums, on the premises, on the faith of it. 1 *Vern.* 151.

But in the case of *Seagood* v. *Meale, Pr. Ch.* 561. it is said, that " where a man on " promise of a lease to be made to him, " lays out money on improvements, he " shall oblige the lessor afterwards to exe- " cute the lease, because it was executed on " the part of the lessee," and upon this *dictum*, Mr. *Fonblanque* justly observes, that it is sanctioned by the spirit of equity, and seems to do away the decisions, which require, even under the circumstance of the premises being improved, an averment of its being part of the parol agreement, that it should be reduced into writing. 1 *Fonb.* 187.

So where the plaintiff pursuant to a parol agreement for a building lease, proceeded to pull down part, and build part, and before any lease executed, the owner of the soil died, equity decreed a building lease to be made, according to the agreement. 2 *Vern.* 456.

And when this court, does assist the common law, and enforce the performance of the agreement in *specie*, in these cases, it does it, upon important reasons, *viz.* because otherwise there would be a great burthen and penalty upon the party, if, having performed part, by which he himself has a *loss*, and the other a *benefit*, he should not have a reciprocal performance. *Treatise of Eq. c.* 1. *s.* 5. *c.* 3. *s.* 1—9.

But there is a difference to be taken where the money is laid out in *lasting improvements*, and where for fancy and humour: for it is clear that a bill would hold, *so far as to be restored to the consideration money*, expended in valuable improvements; for a lease, though void for want of legal ceremonies, is yet a sufficient colour to possess: and the difficulty seems to be, that the act *makes void the estate, but does not say that the agreement itself shall be void*, so that possibly, a man may recover damages for the non-performance of it, and then there is no doubt to decree it in equity. *Treatise of Eq.* 187—8.

See also Age—Baron and Feme—Marriage—Infant—Lunatics.

AGRI, in our law, denotes arable land in the common fields. *Fortescue.*

AID, (*auxilium*) is all one with the French *aide*, and in general acceptation is understood to be a subsidy granted to the crown. By the ancient or rather *feudal* law of the land, the king and any lord of the realm might lay an aid upon their tenants, for knighting an eldest son, or marriage of a daughter; but these tenures were abolished by 12 *Car.* 2. *c.* 24.

And by stat. 34 *Ed.* 1. c. 1. It is ordained that the king shall levy no aid or tax without his parliament.

AID OF THE KING, (*auxilium regis*) If a man be impleaded, and cannot make a defence, he may petition or pray in aid of the king; and aid of the king shall be granted in all actions, where the king may have prejudice; as in all *real actions* where the title of the king appears to be, and also in all *personal actions* where the interest of the king may be concerned, as in ejectment against the king's lessee, trespass, replevin, case, debt or other personal action against the king's farmer or officer. *Rol. Abr. Comyn's Dig.*

In these cases, the proceedings are stopped till the king's council are heard to say what they think fit, for avoiding the king's prejudice: and this aid shall not in any case be granted after issue; because the king ought not to rely upon the defence made by another. *Jenk. Cent.* 64. *Terms de Ley* 35. *Stat.* 4 *Ed.* 1. and 14 *Ed.* 3.

AID-PRAYER *of a common person* (*auxilium petere*) a word anciently made use of in pleading, for a petition in court to pray in aid from the reversioner or remainder-man, or other having interest, when the title of the inheritance is in question. *Comyn's Dig. tit. Aid.*

But this ancient mode of praying aid has long since been disused, and a more convenient course introduced, by the practice of letting parties into the liberty of filing bills of interpleader in a court of equity.

AIEL, (of the French *aieul*, i. e. *avus, the grandfather*) was a writ, now in disuse, which anciently lay where a man's grandfather being seised of lands, a stranger abated and dispossessed the heir. *Fitz. N. B.* 221.

ALIAMENTA, includes any liberty of passage, open way, water-course, &c. for the ease and accommodation of tenants. *Kitch.*

AL, (*ald*) words which begin with *al* or *ald* in the names of places, signify antiquity; as Alborough, Aldworth, &c. *Cowel. Blount.*

ALANERARIUS, a manager and keeper of dogs, for the sport of hawking, from *alanus*, a dog, known to the ancients. *Du Fresne.* But Blount renders it a faulconer.

ALBA, (the *alb*) a surplice or white sacerdotal vest, anciently used by officiating priests. *Blount.*

ALBA FIRMA. This word is used by my lord Coke, and seems to signify a tenure. 2 *Inst.* 10. When quit-rents, payable by freeholders of manors, were reserved in silver, or white money, they were anciently called white rents, or blanch farms, *reditus albi*; in contradistinction to rents reserved in work, grain, &c. which were called *reditus nigri*, or *blacke maile.* 2 *Inst.* 19.

In Scotland this kind of small payment is called blanch-holding, or *reditus albæ firmæ.* 2 *Black.* 42. n.

ALBERGELLUM, signifies a defence for the neck. *Hovedon* 611.

ALBINATUS JUS, (derived from *alibi natus*) the *droit d' aubaine* or right, which existed in France before the late revolution, whereby the king at the death of an *alien* became entitled to all that he was worth, unless he had a peculiar exemption. 1 *Black.* 372. *Spelm. Glos.* 24.

ALBUM, is a word made use of for white rent, paid in silver. *Rot. Parl.* 6 *H.* 3.

ALDER, signifies the first; as alder best, is the best of all; alder liefest, the most dear. *Blount.*

ALDERMAN, (Saxon *ealdorman*, Latin *aldermannus.*) This was one of the three degrees amongst the Saxons. *Ætheling* was the first, and *Thane* the lowest, but *alderman* was the same as our earl; the word was disused in the latter ages of the Saxons, and in its place the word earl was introduced. It is certain that it was used in the reign of *Æthelstan.* *Cowel. Blount.*

It literally imports no more than *elder*, but among the Saxons it signified a duke, an *earl*, a *nobleman*; but then he was called *Heretoga*, viz. *Mercna Heretoga*, that was, alderman of *Mercland*; which title he had in relation to his military power: but the title alderman shewed his civil jurisdiction, which title afterwards was applied to a judge, as in the reign of *Edgar*, *Alwin*, the son of *Æthelstane* is called *aldermanus totius Angliæ*, that is according to *Spelman*, *Justiciarius Angliæ.* *Ibid.*

There was likewise *aldermanus hundredi*, which dignity was first introduced in the reign of *Hen.* 1. among whose laws we find, *præsit autem singulis hominum novinis decimus et toti simul hundredo unus de melioribus et vocetur* aldermannus, *qui dei leges et hominum jura, vigilante studiat observantia promovere.* Du Cange. Cowel. Blount.

But at this day, and long since, those are called aldermen who are associates to the chief civil magistrate of a city or town corporate. *Stat.* 24 *H.* 8. *cap.* 13. *Spelman.*

And an alderman ought to be an inhabitant of the place, and resident where he is chosen; and if he removes, he is incapable of doing his duty in the government of the city or place, for which he may be disfranchized. *Mod. Rep.* 36.

ALÆ ECCLESIÆ, the wings or side-isles of the church, from the French *Les ailes de l'Esglise. Cowel. Blount.*

ALECENARIUM, a sort of hawk called a lanner. *Ibid.*

ALEHOUSES, By 5 *Ed.* 6. *c.* 25, no person shall keep an alehouse, unless licensed in sessions; or by two justices (one of the *quorum*) on pain of three days imprisonment, and a fine to be imposed by the quarter sessions. The justices have power to put them down, and to take recognizances for keeping good order; but this act shall not restrain the selling of malt liquors in fairs.

By 1 *Jac.* 1. *c.* 9. alehouse-keepers permitting townsmen to sit tippling, are liable to ten shillings penalty, and on non-payment to be imprisoned till paid; and persons tippling therein, are to forfeit three shillings and fourpence, or sit in the stocks four hours.

By 4 *Jac.* 1. *c.* 4. selling ale to an unlicensed alehouse-keeper, except for his own private use, incurs a penalty of six shillings and eight-pence for every barrel, to be recovered at the quarter-sessions.

By 4 *Jac.* 1. *c.* 5. persons convicted of drunkenness are to forfeit five shillings, or be put in the stocks six hours.

If convicted a second time, to be bound over to their good behaviour; but the prosecution must be within six months. *Ibid.*

By 7 *Jac.* 1. *c.* 10. an alehouse-keeper, convicted under either of the two last acts, is disabled to keep an alehouse for three years.

By 21 *Jac.* 1. *c.* 7. one witness, or the party's own confession, shall be sufficient; and the oath of the party confessing shall convict others.

By 1 *Car.* 1. *c.* 14. alehouse-keepers permitting any person whatsoever to sit tippling, shall incur the penalty of 1 *Jac.* 1. *c.* 9. Vintners, keeping inns or victualling houses, to be also liable.

By 3 *Car.* 1. *c.* 4. persons, keeping alehouses without licence, are to forfeit twenty shillings to the poor, or be whipped; and for the second offence, to be committed to the house of correction for a month; but any person may, during a fair, sell malt liquors in booths.

By 7 & 8 *Will.* 3. *c.* 19. alehouse-keepers were restrained from using plate; but by 9 *Geo.* 3. *c.* 11. that part of the act was repealed.

By 2 *Geo.* 2. *c.* 28. and 26 *Geo.* 2. *c.* 31. no licence shall be granted, but at a general meeting of justices, on September the first, or within twenty days after, and the same shall be made but for one year; notice is likewise to be given of the time and place for granting them; and persons selling brandy are to be licensed, and subject to the same rules as common alehouse-keepers.

By 17 *Geo.* 2. *c.* 17. victuallers having a licence to retail spirits shall not, during the time of that licence, exercise the trade of a distiller, grocer, or chandler, or keep a brandy-shop for sale of any spirits, upon pain of forfeiting the licence, and also 10*l.* for every offence. Persons selling a less quantity than two gallons shall be deemed retailers. And the licence shall not extend to any other than the house mentioned in it.

By 26 *Geo.* 2. *c.* 13. justices being brewers, inn-keepers, distillers, victuallers, or maltsters are prohibited from granting of licences for selling of ale, beer, or spirits. *s.* 12.

But by 39 *Geo.* 3. *c.* 86. if in cities and towns any justice shall be incapable by reason of his dealing in spirits, a justice of the county at large may act. *s.* 3.

By 26 *Geo.* 2. *c.* 31. justices licensing alehouses are to take a recognizance in the sum of 10*l.* for the maintenance of good order; which recognizance must be sent to the clerk of the peace, on penalty of 3*l.* 6*s.* 8*d.* *s.* 1.

Licences are to be granted to none, unless they were licensed the year preceding, or can produce certificates (except in cities and towns corporate, *s.* 16) of their good fame. *s.* 2.

Where a justice shall adjudge the recognizance to be forfeited, he is to summon the party to the quarter sessions, and the jury finding him guilty, the recognizance is to be estreated, and he is to be disabled from selling beer or spirits for three years. *Ibid.*

Where a justice shall suspect that any victualler sells ale or the like, without a license, he may summon him and the officer who surveys him, and examine such officer upon oath. *Ibid.*

A justice, upon information that any person is reasonably suspected of selling ale, without a license, is to summon the party and evidence before him; and persons summoned not appearing are to forfeit 10*l.* *Ibid.*

The rights of the universities to grant licenses are reserved. The times of granting licences for common inns and alehouses in any city or town corporate are not altered. Parishioners are likewise declared to be competent witnesses. *Ibid.*

By 30 *Geo.* 2. *c.* 24. publicans permitting journeymen, servants, or apprentices to game in their houses, are to forfeit 40*s.* and for the second and every subsequent offence 10*l.* which penalties are to be levied by distress and sale.

By 9 *Geo.* 3. *c.* 6. the powers, directions, and penalties, provided and established by any act made since 8 *Geo.* 2. as to selling spirituous liquors, without licence, may be exercised, but transporting and whipping are to cease.

By 43 *Geo.* 3. *c.* 69. retailers of wine and

spirits are to take out an annual excise-licence, and pay

For every licence to retail foreign wines in England, if the party has not a spirit or beer licence, 5*l.* 4*s.*

——— if the party has a beer licence, but not one for spirits, 4*l.* 4*s.*

——— if he has also a spirit licence, 2*l.* 4*s.*

For every licence to retail foreign wines in Scotland, if the party as not a spiri. or beer licence, 3*l.* 6*s.* 8*d.*

——— if he has a beer licence, but not one for spirits, 2*l.* 13*s.* 4*d.*

——— if he has also a spirit licence, 1*l.* 6*s.* 8*d.*

For every licence to retail spirits in Great Britain, if the party's house be rated under 15*l.*—4*l.* 4*s.*

	£.		£.	£.	*s.*	*d.*
—— if rated	at 15	and under	20 —	5	2	0
—— if ——	at 20	and under	25 —	5	10	0
—— if ——	at 25	and under	30 —	5	18	0
—— if ——	at 30	and under	40 —	6	6	0
—— if ——	at 40	and under	50 —	6	14	0
—— if ——	at 50	or upwards	—	7	2	0

By 30 *Geo.* 3. *c.* 38. the licences are to continue in force till Oct. 10, ensuing the granting thereof, and if granted between the 5th of April and Oct. 10, a rateable proportion only to be charged. *s.* 8.

The licences are to be renewed annually, and persons retailing without a licence, or not renewing it, forfeit 50*l.* *s.* 9.

On death or removal of licenced persons, the commissioners of excise may authorise the executors or assignees to carry on the trade, for the remainder of the term: one licence is sufficient for a partnership in a house; and the licence is not to authorise the party to retail in any other house, than that for which it was granted. *s.* 10.

This is not to prejudice the privileges of the two universities, nor the company of vintners, or any town corporate; but freemen of the vintners' company by redemption are to take out licences: and the letters patent for licencing taverns at St. Albans are confirmed. *s.* 11, 12, 13.

Persons selling foreign wine in less quantities, than equal to the measure first imported, or British made wines, in the quantity of twenty-five gallons or under, or spirits in less than two gallons, shall be deemed retailers. *s.* 15.

By 48 *Geo.* 3. *c.* 143. the stamp duties on licences to retail ale shall after Oct. 10 cease, and in lieu thereof the alehouse-keeper, or victualler, shall take out an excise licence for the purpose, and pay for the same a licence duty of 2*l.* 2*s.*

Which licences shall be taken out from the excise within ten days next after the date of the justices' licence, and shall continue in force until the 10th of October ensuing, and no longer; and such licence is to be renewed annually within ten days after the expiration of the former, and no one shall retail ale, beer, or the like, without such annual excise licence on pain of 50*l* *s.* 3, 4, 5.

On death or removal, the executors or assignees may sell under the licence. *s.* 6.

Excise licences are not to be granted, except to such persons only, as have been previously licenced by the justices, and this act does not affect any former regulations, as to licences to be granted by the magistrates; and clerks to justices are entitled to the same fees as heretofore. *s.* 10.

If persons be disabled by conviction to keep an alehouse, they are to forfeit this licence, and cannot afterwards sell any liquors thereunder. *s.* 11.

By 32 *Geo.* 3. *c.* 59. if alehouse-keepers die, or remove, before the expiration of their licences, new ones may be granted to the executors, or new tenants, till the next licencing day, obtaining within thirty days after such death or removal, the usual certificate, and entering into the recognizances; which certificates and recognizances are to be sent to the clerk of the peace to be renewed. *s.* 1.

In Middlesex and Surry, the justices at the general licencing meetings, are to appoint special ones, not less than six nor more than eight, in each year: at which they may grant, on the removal of licenced persons, a continuance of the licence, or a new one to the succeeding occupier, producing the certificate and entering into the recognizance. *s.* 3.

But no new licences are to be granted, at the petty sessions, to houses not licenced at the general licencing day. *s.* 4.

Nothing herein is to extend to alter the times of granting licences; or oblige persons, licenced the year preceding to produce certificates. *s.* 5.

Persons entering into licenced houses, without the authority of the justices, are liable to the penalty, for retailing without licence. *s.* 6.

But persons, obtaining the necessary certificates, are indemnified till the petty sessions. *s.* 7.

Clerk of the peace is to record the continuance of licences. *s.* 8.

No person shall sell wine by retail, to be drank in his own house without having a beer licence, and justices are to have the same jurisdiction over such retailers of wine, as they have over sellers of beer, who are to be subject for retailing wine without a licence to the same penalties as for retailing ale without licence. *s.* 9.

This act is not to extend to the vintners' company, the universities, or St. Albans; but freemen of the vintners' company by purchase since October 11, 1792, are not exempted. *s.* 11.

By 35 *Geo.* 3. *c.* 113. persons selling, or

permitting to be sold, in their houses, excisable liquors by retail without a licence shall forfeit 20*l.* and the costs of conviction. *s.* 1.

Any justice may determine complaints; and if the penalties are not paid on conviction, if the party is present, or if absent, within three days after notice thereof, the same may be levied by distress. *s.* 2.

The officers are to execute their warrants agreeably to 27 *Geo.* 2. *c.* 20: the provisions of which, and of 33 *Geo.* 3. *c.* 55. (see *Distress*), as to execution of warrants, are to extend to this act. *Ibid.*

Distress may be sold within four days, and the officer to be allowed not exceeding 5*s.* per day, and his assistants 2*s.* *s.* 3, 4.

Half of the penalty to be to the informer, and the other half to the poor of the parish; and if sufficient distress cannot be found, the justice may commit the offender for not exceeding six, nor less than three calendar months. *s.* 5.

The leaving a summons at the place where the offence is committed, and affixing a copy thereof at the door, is sufficient to compel persons to answer informations for selling liquors by retail without licence. *s.* 6.

Retailers, are to make previous entry at the excise, office of all places used for laying beer, ale, cyder, perry, and other exciseable liquors, on pain of 50*l.* and places not entered to be deemed concealed places. *s.* 7.

Such liquors, and goods, and chattels, found where any offence is committed, to be liable to distress. *s.* 8.

Persons making entry to be deemed retailers: justices may summon excise officers, to produce entries, and stock books, and may examine them on oath; and may summon retailers to produce licences; and for not producing them may adjudge the defaulters guilty. *s.* 9.

Penalty of 10*l.* on witnesses not attending summonses, to be levied by distress, and if sufficient cannot be found, the party may be committed for not exceeding six months: the penalty to be applied to the use of the poor of the parish. *s.* 10.

Goods liable to seizure may be distrained wherever found, and justices may indorse warrants for seizing goods removed into their jurisdictions. *s.* 11.

Appeals are allowed to the next quarter sessions, unless held within six days after conviction, and then to the next subsequent sessions, which may finally determine such appeals, and adjudge costs. *s.* 12.

Justices may mitigate penalties, in the case of a first offence, but not to less than 10*l.* Inhabitants may be witnesses, and penalties are to be determined in six months. *s.* 13, 14, 15.

The act is not to prohibit the selling ale, or beer, at fairs. *s.* 17.

By 38 *Geo.* 3. c. 54. he penalty in the last act is not to extend to beer, or ale, sold in casks containing not less than five gallons, or in bottles not less than two dozen quarts. *s.* 13.

ALER SAN JOUR, (French) to go without day, *viz.* to be finally dismissed the court, because there is no further day assigned for appearance. *Kitch.* 146. *Cowel. Blount.*

ALE-SILVER, a rent or tribute annually paid to the lord-mayor of London, by those that sell ale within the liberty of the city. *Antiq. Purvey.* 183. *Cowel. Blount.*

ALESTAKE, a may-pole called alestake, because the country people drew much ale there: but it is not the common may-pole, but rather a long stake drove into the ground, with a sign on it, that ale was to be sold. *Cowel.*

ALE-TASTER, is an officer appointed in every court leet, sworn to look to the assize and goodness of ale and beer, &c. within the precincts of the lordship. *Kitch.* 46. In London there are ale-conners, who are officers appointed to taste ale and beer, &c. in the limits of the city. *Cowel. Blount.*

ALFET, (Saxon *alfæth*) a cauldron or furnace, wherein boiling water was put for a criminal to dip his arm in up to his elbow, and there hold it for some time. *Du Cange. Cowel. Blount.*

ALIAS, a second or further writ, issued from the courts at Westminster, after a *capias*, &c. sued out without effect. *Cowel. Blount.*

ALIAS DICTUS, (or *otherwise called*) is the manner of description of a defendant in pleadings, better omitted as a variance may be fatal.

ALIEN, (*alienus, alienigena*) an alien is, one *born in a strange country, out of the allegiance of the king*: but a man born out of the land, if it be within the limits of the king's obedience beyond sea; or born of English parents out of the obedience of the king, if the parents at the time of the birth were of such obedience, is no alien. 1 *Bac. Abr. tit. Al.* a.

If an English merchant goes beyond sea, and takes an alien wife, the issue shall inherit him; but it is not so, if an English woman goes beyond sea, and takes an alien husband, the children there born shall not inherit her. *Cro. Car.* 601, 602. *Lit. Rep.* 22, 24. 1 *Sid.* 198. 4 *Ter. Rep.* 300. 1 *Bac. Abr. tit. Al.* a.

An alien cannot hold land by descent or purchase, or be tenant by the curtesy, or in dower. 5 *Rep.* 502. In case an alien purchase land, the king upon office found shall have it. *Co. Lit.* 2. So if an alien purchase any estate of freehold in houses, lands, tenements or hereditaments, the king upon office found shall have them. If an alien be made denizen and purchase and, and die without issue, the lord of the fee shall have the escheat, and not the king. But as to a lease for years, there is a difference between a lease for years of a house for the habitation of a merchant stranger being an alien, whose king is in league with ours: and a lease for years of lands, meadows, pastures, woods, and the like. For if he take a lease for years of lands, upon office found the king shall have it. But of a house for habitation, he may take a lease for years as incident to commerce, for without an habitation he cannot merchandize or trade. But if he depart or relinquish the realm, the king shall have the lease. So if he die possessed thereof, neither his executors or administrators shall have it, but the king: for he had it only for habitation, as necessary to his trade or traffic, and not for the benefit of his executor or administrator. But if the alien be no merchant, then the king shall have the lease for years, though it were for his habitation, and so it is if he be an alien enemy. *Co. Lit.* 2 *b.*

Aliens may obtain goods and personal estate, by trade, &c. And may maintain actions for the same, they may also have actions of assault and battery, and for support of their credit. 2 *Bulst.* 134. But they cannot bring any real action, unless it be for an house for necessary habitation, being for the benefit of trade. 7 *Rep. Calvin's Case.* And an alien enemy cannot maintain any action whatsoever, nor get any thing lawfully within this realm. *Terms de Ley* 6.

An alien friend may be an administrator, and shall have administration of leases, as well as personal things, because he hath them in another's right, and not to his own use. *Cro. Car.* 8. 1 *Vent.* 417. *S. C.* cited.

But it has been long doubted, whether an alien enemy should maintain an action as executor; for on the one hand it is said, that by the policy of the law, alien enemies shall not be admitted to actions to recover effects, which may be carried out of the kingdom, to weaken onrselves and enrich the enemy; and therefore public utility must be preferred to private convenience; but on the other hand it is said, that these effects of the testator are not forfeited to the king by way of reprisal, because they belong not to the alien enemy, for he is to recover them for others; and if the law allows such alien enemies, to possess the effects, as well as an alien friend, it must allow them power to recover, since in that there is no difference, and by consequence he must not be disabled to sue for them; if it were otherwise it would be a prejudice to the king's subjects, who could not recover their debts, from the alien executor, by his not being able to get in the assets of the testator. *Cro. Eliz.* 683. *Molloy* 870. *Carter* 49, 191. *Skin.* 370.

An alien enemy coming into this kingdom, and *taken in war*, shall suffer death by the martial law; and not be indicted at the common law. *Molloy de jur. Marit.* 417.

But an alien whilst he resides here is generally subject to our laws, and owes a local and temporary allegiance to the sovereign, by whose authority those laws are administered, and by whom his person and property are protected: consequently if during such residence he commit an offence, which in the case of a natural born subject would amount to treason, he may be dealt with as such; and this whether his sovereign be in amity, or at enmity with us. 1 *Woodes* 379. *Fost.* 185. 1 *Hawk. P. C. c.* 17. *s.* 5. 32 *Hen.* 8. *c.* 16. *s.* 9.

Aliens are subject to and shall have the benefit of the statutes against bankrupts. 21 *Jac.* 1. *c.* 19. *s.* 15.

The property of an alien resident abroad, consisting of stock in the public funds, or other personal effects in this country, is subject to the control of the court of chancery. 1 *Atk.* 19.

But if an alien, resident abroad, dies intestate, his whole property here is distributable according to the laws of the country where he so resided; but the residence must be stationary, not occasional, else the municipal institutions will not attach upon the property. *Ambl.* 25, 415.

No alien shall be returned on any jury, nor be sworn for trial of issues between subject and subject, &c. but where an alien is party in a cause depending, the inquest of jurors are to be half denizens, and half aliens: but in cases of high treason, this is not allowed. 2 *Inst.* 17. An alien shall not have any vote in choice of knights of the shire, or burgesses to parliament. *Hob.* 270. And persons that are aliens, or born out of the realm, are incapable to be members of parliament, enjoy offices, &c. *Stat.* 12 *W.* 3, *cap.* 2.

ALIENATION, (from *alienare*, to alien) is the act whereby one man transfers the property and possession of lands or tenements, or other things to another.

ALIMONY, (*alimonia*,) signifies nourishment or maintenance: and in a legal sense, is taken for that allowance which a married woman sues for either in the chancery or spiritual court, and is entitled, except in the cases of elopement or adultery, to recover from her husband, during any separation. *Terms de Ley* 38. *Co. Lit.* 335. *a.*

The spiritual court is, however, the proper court to sue in for alimony. 12 *Rep.* 30. *Moor* 874.

But if there is a *trust fund*, equity will interpose: for in *Williams* v. *Callow*, the court appear to have decreed the wife a separate maintenance *out of a trust fund*, on account of the cruelty and ill behaviour of the husband, though there was no evidence of a divorce or agreement that the fund in dispute should be so applied. 2 *Vern.* So where the husband had quitted the kingdom, lord *Hardwicke* decreed the wife the interest of *a trust fund*, till he should return and maintain her as he ought. 2 *Atk.* 96.

ALLAUNDS, *ab alanis, Scythæ gente*, harehounds. *Cowel.*

ALLAY, (French, in Latin *allaya,*) signifies what used for the tempering and mixing other metals with silver or gold. This allay is to augment the weight of the silver or gold, so as it may defray the charge of coinage, and to make it the more fusile. *Lownd's Essay upon Coins, page* 19, & 9 *H.* 5. *St.* 1. *c.* 11.

ALLEGIANCE, *allegiantia,* (formerly called *ligeance,* from the Latin *alligare* and *ligare,* i. e. *ligamen fidei*) is the allegiance, or faith and obedience, which every subject owes to his prince. It is either perpetual, where one is a subject born; or where one hath the right of a subject by naturalization, &c. or is temporary, by reason ef residence in the king's dominions. *Co. Lit.* 2. 329. 2 *Inst.* 741.

The duty of allegiance arising from birth is perpetual and unalienable, and it is not in the power of any private subject to shake off his allegiance, and transfer it to a foreign prince: who cannot by naturalizing, or employing a subject of Great Britain, dissolve the bond of allegiance between that subject and the crown; but when by treaty, especially if ratified by act of parliament, the king cedes any island or region to another state, the inhabitants of such ceded territory, though born under the allegiance of our king, or being under his protection whilst it appertained to his crown and authority; become effectually, aliens, or liable to the disabilities of alienage in respect to their future concerns with this country. *Fost.* 59. *Dy.* 298. *b.* 300. *b.* 1 *Woodes* 382.

All persons above the age of twelve years are to be required to take the oath of allegiance in courts-leet. And there are several statutes requiring the oath of allegiance and supremacy, &c. to be taken under penalties.

ALLEGIARE, to defend or justify by due course of law. *Cowel. Blount.*

ALLER GOOD, the word *aller* is used to make what is added to signify superlatively; as *aller good* is the greatest good. *Cowel. Blount.*

ALLEVIARE, signifies to levy or pay an accustomed fine. *Brady's Pref. Cowel. Blount.*

ALLOCATION, (*allocatio*) in a legal sense, is an allowance made upon account in the *exchequer*; or more properly a placing or adding to a thing. *Ibid.*

ALLOCATIONE FACIENDA, a writ directed to the lord treasurer, and barons of the exchequer, upon complaint of some accountant, for allowing to such accountant such sums of money as he hath lawfully expended in his office. *Reg. Orig.* 206.

ALLOCATO COMITATU, is a new writ of exigent allowed, before any other county court holden, on the former not being fully served, or complied with, &c. *Fitz. Exig.* 14.

ALLODIAL. This is where an inheritance is held without any acknowledgment to any lord or superior; and therefore is of another nature from that which is feodal. *Allodial* lands are free lands, which a man enjoys without paying any fine, rent, or service to any other. *Cowel. Blount.* 2 *Black.* 47, 60, 105.

ALLUMINOR, (from the French *allumer,* to lighten, or kindle,) is used for one who coloureth or painteth upon paper or parchment, and the reason is, because he gives light and ornament by his colours to the letters or other figures. The word is used, in stat. 1 *R.* 3. *c.* 9. at this day he is called a *limner. Cowel. Blount.*

ALLUVION, is where land is gained from the sea side by the washing up of sand and earth, so as in time to make *terra firma.* 2 *Black.* 261.

ALMANACKS. The courts must take notice of the almanacks as part of the law of England, in respect to the returns of writs, and otherwise; but the almanack to go by is that annexed to the book of Common Prayer. *Mod. Cas.* 41, 81.

Whether such a day of the month was on a Sunday or not, and so not a *dies juridicus,* is triable by the country or the almanack. *Dyer* 182. *pt.* 55.

And the court may judicially take notice of almanacks, and be informed by them. 1 *Leo.* 242. *pl.* 328. *Cro. Eliz.* 227.

ALMARIA, for *armaria:* the archives of a church, a library. *Cowel. Blount.*

ALMNER, or ALMONER, (*eleeomsinarius,*) an officer of the king's house, whose business it is, to distribute the king's alms, every day. *Fleta, lib.* 2. *cap.* 22. *Cowel. Blount.*

ALMSFEOH, or *almesfeoh,* Saxon for *alms money:* it has been taken for what we call *Peter pence,* first given by *Ina* king of the West Saxons, and anciently paid in England on the first of August. It was likewise called *romefeoh, romescot,* and *heorthpenning. Selden's Hist. Tithes.* 217.

ALMUTIUM, a garment which covered the head and shoulders of priests. *Cowel. Blount.*

ALNAGE, (French *aulnage*) signifies a measure, particularly the ell. *Ibid.*

ALNAGER, or *aulnager,* (French *alner,* Latin *ulniger*) is properly a measure by the ell; and the word *aulne* in French signifieth an ell. *Cowel. Blount.*

ALNETUM, a place where alders grow; or a grove of alder trees. *Cowel. Blount.*

ALODIUM, or *allodium,* in domesday signifies a free manor: and *alodarii* lords of free manors, or lords paramount. *Co. Lit.* 1, 5. *Cowel. Blount.*

ALOVERIUM, a purse. This word is mentioned in *Fleta, lib.* 2. *c.* 82. *par.* 2.

ALTARAGE, (*altaragium,*) the offerings made upon the altar, and also the profit that arises to the priest by reason of the altar, *obventio altaris. Terms de ley* 39. 2 *Cro.* 516.

And where *altaragium* is mentioned in old

endowments, and *supported by usage*, it will extend to small tithes, but not otherwise. *Bunb.* 79.

ALTERATION, (*alteratio*,) is the changing of a thing: and when witnesses are examined upon exhibits, &c. they ought to remain in the office, and not to be taken back into private hands, by whom they may be altered. *Hob.* 254.

ALTERATION *of a deed*: a deed may be avoided, if there be any rasure, interlining, or other alteration in any material part; unless a memorandum be made thereof at the time of the execution and attestation. 11 *Rep.* 27. 2 *Black.* 308.

ALTO ET BASSO. By this is meant the absolute submission of all differences. *Cowel. Blount.*

AMABYR, *vel* AMVABYR, a custom in the honour of *Clun*, belonging to the earls of Arundel: *Precium virginitatis domino solvendum* LL. *eccl. Gul.* Howeli Dha, *regis* Walliæ. *Puella dicitur esse desertum regis, & ob hoc regis est de ea* amvabyr *habere*. This custom *Henry* earl of Arundel released to his tenants. *Anno* 3 & 4 *P.* & *M. Cowel.*

AMBACTUS, a servant or client. *Cowel.*

AMBASSADOR, (*legatus*.) An ambassador is a person sent by one sovereign prince to another, to transact in the place of his sovereign such matters as relate to both states. The manner of appointing and receiving public ministers, and their duty, power, and privileges, are chiefly regulated by the civil law or law of nations, and our law pays the greatest regard to the rules thereof. 1 *Bac. Abr.* 141.

Ambassadors are either *ordinary*, or *extraordinary*; the *ordinary* ambassadors are those who reside in the place whither sent; and the time of their return being indefinite, so is their business uncertain, arising from emergent occasions; and commonly the protection and affairs of the merchants is their greatest care: the *extraordinary ambassadors* are made *pro tempore*, and employed upon some particular great affairs, as condolements, congratulations, or for overtures of marriage, or the like. Their equipage is generally very magnificent; and they may return without requesting of leave, unless there be a restraining clause in their commission. *Molloy* 144.

By the laws of nations, none under the quality of a sovereign prince can send any ambassador: a king that is deprived of his kingdom and royalty, hath lost his right of legation. 4 *Inst.* 53.

Ambassadors may, by a precaution, be warned not to come to the place where sent; and if they then do it, they shall be taken for enemies; but being once admitted, even with enemies in arms, they shall have the protection of the laws of nations, and be preserved as princes. *Moll.* 146.

An ambassador, guilty of treason against the king's life, may be condemned and executed; but for other treasons, he shall be sent home, with demand to punish him, or to send him back to be punished. 4 *Inst.* 152. 1 *Roll. Rep.* 185.

If a foreign ambassador commits any crime here, which is *contra jus gentium*, as treason, felony, &c. or any other crime against the law of nations, he loseth the privilege of an ambassador, and is subject to punishment as a private alien; and he need not be remanded to his sovereign, but of curtesy. *Danv. Abr.* 327. But if a thing be only *malum prohibitum* by an act of parliament, private law, or custom of the realm, and it is *contra jus gentium*, an ambassador shall not be bound by them. 4 *Inst.* 153. And it is said ambassadors may be excused of practices against the state where they reside, (except it be in point of conspiracy, which is against the law of nations) because it doth not appear whether they have it *in mandatis*; and then they are excused by necessity of obedience. *Bac. Max.* 26.

By the civil law, the person of an ambassador may not be arrested; and the moveable goods of ambassadors, which are accounted an accession to their persons, cannot be seized on, as a pledge, nor for payment of debts, though by leave of the king or state, where they are resident; but on refusal of payment, letters of request are to go to his master, &c. *Molloy* 157. *Danv.* 328.

Also by *Ann.* 7. *c.* 12. "an ambassador, or "public minister, or his domestic servants, "registered in the secretary's office, and "thence transmitted to the sheriff's office of "*London* and *Middlesex*, are not to be arrested: if they are, the process shall be "void, and the persons suing out and executing it, shall suffer such penalties and corporal punishments, as the lord chancellor or "either of the chief justices shall think fit." Also the goods of an ambassador, or of his servants, shall not be distrained.

The privilege of a public minister is annexed to his situation: it is the privilege of the state that sends him out, and not that of the individual: he cannot therefore waive it or forfeit it by becoming a trader; but a consul or any person acting in an office of that kind it seems is not entitled to privilege. *Cas. temp. Talb.* 281.

AMBIDEXTER, (Latin,) one that can use his left hand as well as his right; or that plays on both sides. But in a legal sense, it is taken for a juror or embraceor, who takes money of both parties for giving his verdict; and such a one shall be imprisoned, never more be of a jury, and further punished at the king's pleasure. 5 *Ed.* 3. *c.* 10. *Crompt. Just.* 156.

AMBRA, (Saxon *amber*, Latin *amphora*,) a vessel among the Saxons: it contained a measure of salt, butter, meal, beer, &c. *Leg. Inæ West Saxon. Cowel. Blount.*

AMBRY, the place where the arms, plate, vessels, and every thing which belonged to housekeeping were kept; and probably the ambry at Westminster is so called, because formerly set apart for that use: or rather the *aumonery*, from the Latin *eleemosynaria*, an house adjoining to an abbey, in which the charities were laid up for the poor. *Cowel. Blount.*

AMENABLE, (French *amener*,) in our ancient law books is commonly applied to a woman, that is governable by her husband. But in the modern sense, it signifies to be responsible, or subject to answer within the jurisdiction of a court of justice. *Cowel. Blount.*

AMENDMENT, (*emendatio*) AT LAW: the correction of an error committed in any process, which may be amended after judgment; and if there be any error in giving the judgment, the party is driven to his writ of error; though where the fault appears to be in the clerk who writ the record, it may be amended. *Terms de Ley* 39.

At common law there was little room for amendments, which appears by the several statutes of *amendments and jeofails. Brit.* 2. 8 *Co.* 156. 4 *Inst.* 235.

Original writs are not amendable at common law, for if the writ be not good, the party may have another: judicial writs may and have been often amended. 8 *Rep.* 157.

Whatever at common law might be amended in civil cases, was at common law amendable in criminal cases, and so it is at this day; resolved by *Holt* Ch. J. *Powell* and *Powis* J. 1 *Salk.* 51. *pl.* 14.

The statutes of amendment are the following: By Statute 14 *Ed.* 3. *c.* 6. It is asserted, that "by the misprision of a clerk "in any place wheresoever it be, no "process shall be annulled or discontinued, by mistaking in writing one syllable or one letter too much or too "little; but as soon as the thing is perceived, by challenge of the party, or in other "manner, it shall be hastily amended in due "form, without giving advantage to the "party that challengeth the same, because "of such misprision."

This statute is confirmed by statute 4 *Hen.* 6. *c.* 3. with an exception, that *it shall not extend to process on outlawry, or to records or processes in Wales.* But according to 2 *Sand.* 40. this last exception, and the like exception in 8 *Hen.* 6. *c.* 15. seem to be annulled by the statute 27 *Hen.* 8. *c.* 26. by which it is enacted, that *the laws of England shall be used, practised and executed in Wales.*

The statute 8 *Hen.* 6. *c.* 12. *gives power to judges to amend what they shall think in their discretion to be the misprision of their clerks in any record, process, and plea, warrant of attorney, writ, panel, or return.*

By statute 8 *Hen.* 6. *c.* 15. "The king's "justices, before whom any misprision shall "be found, be it in any records or processes "depending before them, as well by way of "error as otherwise, or in the returns of the "same, by sheriffs, coroners, bailiffs of "franchises, or any other, by misprision of "the clerks of any of the said courts, or of "the sheriffs, coroners, their clerks, or other "officers clerks, or other ministers whatsoever, in writing one letter or one syllable "too much or too little, shall have power to "amend the same."

A declaration grounded on an original writ may not be amended, if the writ be erroneous: though if it be on a bill of *Middlesex* or a *latitat*, it is amendable. 1 *Lill. Abr.* 67. Declarations upon any penal statutes, *qui tam, &c.* may not be amended after issue joined. 2 *Mod.* 144. And indictments of treason, and felony, writs of appeal, &c. are excepted out of the statutes of amendments; though some things are amendable at common law. *Mod. Cas.* 269.

A plaintiff may amend his declaration in matter of form after a general issue pleaded, before entry thereof, without payment of costs: if he amend in substance, he is to pay costs, or give imparlance; and if he amend after a special plea, though he would give imparlance, he must pay costs. 1 *Lill.* 58. A declaration in ejectment laid the demise before the time; this was not amendable, for it would alter the issue, and make a new title in the plaintiff. 1 *Salk.* 48. The plaintiff declared on the statute of *Winton* for a robbery done to himself, when it should have been of his servants; he had leave to amend. 3 *Lev.* 347. If a defendant pleads a plea to the right, or in abatement, the plaintiff may amend his declaration; but not where he demurs, for this fault may be the cause of the demurrer. 1 *Salk.* 50. A demurrer may be amended, after the parties have joined in demurrer, if it be only in paper. *Style* 48.

As to the amendments of records, &c. an issue entered upon record, with leave of the court may be amended; but not in a material thing, or in that which will deface the record. 1 *Lill. Abr.* 61. A record may be amended by the court in a small matter, after issue joined, so as the plea be not altered. *Danv. Abr.* 338.

If on a writ of error a record is amended in another court, in affirmance of the judgment, it must be amended in the court where judgment was given. *Hardr.* 505.

Where the record of *nisi prius* does not agree with the original record, it may be amended after verdict, provided it do not change the issue: but a record shall not be amended to attaint the jury, or prejudice the authority of the judge. A general or special verdict may be amended by the notes of the clerk of assise in civil causes; but not in criminal actions. 1 *Salk.* 47.

The issue roll shall be amended by the imparlance roll, which is precedent: but a roll may not be amended after verdict, when there is nothing to amend it by; though surplusage may be rejected, and so make it good. *Cro. Car.* 92. 1 *Sid.* 135.

AMENDMENT IN EQUITY.] If any necessary parties are omitted, or unnecessary parties are inserted in a bill, the court, upon application, will in general permit the proper alterations to be made. *Mitford*, 39.

And a bill may be amended before or after appearance and answer, and new parties added even after publication passed, where there are not proper parties. *Ibid.*

But after the parties are at issue, and witnesses have been examined, no part of the pleadings can be amended, but under very special circumstances; but if no witness has been examined, an amendment may be permitted, though publication may have passed. *Milford* 258.

Also after a demurrer to a whole bill, it seems not to be strictly regular to permit an amendment of the bill in part. *Mitford* 13. nor where it is dismissed upon the merits. 2 *Pere. Wms.* 401.

The plaintiff may amend at any time after the defendant has appeared and taken an office-copy of the bill *without costs*, undertaking to amend the defendant's office-copy of the bill: but if he would amend, and require an answer to the amendment after answer filed, it is on payment of 20*s.* costs, which he must pay before he proceeds, otherwise he is irregular. *Ibid.*

Where an improper submission was made in the bill of an infant, the court allowed it to be amended on the hearing of the cause. 2 *Pere. Wms.* 386.

There are no certain rules, respecting the amendment of answers, but they are in the discretion of the courts: the admission of a fact is never suffered to be struck out, but on an affidavit of surprize, or the defendant being ill-advised: but where an amendment is admitted in the bill; where, through inadvertency a mistake is made as to a fact or date; where there is no danger of perjury; where the case depends upon old documents, lies pretty much in the dark, and new matter discovered, which affords the defendant a good defence; the courts have allowed amendments to be made either by striking out passages, or making new facts, and this after issue joined, or upon the hearing of the cause. 1 *Eq. Cas. Abr. tit. Am.*

If new matter has arisen, the practice is to add it by way of supplemental answer: for the defendant will not be permitted to take the old answer off the file. *Ibid.*

An answer shall not be amended after an indictment for perjury preferred, or threatened: yet if there were circumstances extremely strong, to shew that it was only a mere mistake, it might be otherwise. 1 *Br. Ch. Rep.* 419.

An infant may amend his answer, when he comes of age, and therefore no exceptions can be taken to it. *Bunb.* 338.

Where it appears, that either the examiner is mistaken in taking a deposition, or the witness in making it, it may be amended after publication. 2 *Pere. Wms.* 646.

A mistake in the title of an order, was allowed to be amended, though it was for the purpose of charging a surety, who had entered into a recognizance to abide the order of hearing. 2 *Vern.* 376. 1 *Eq. Cas. Abr. tit. Am.*

But where there was a mistake in the title of the interrogatories, neither the depositions were permitted to be read, nor the title to be amended, though most of the witnesses were gone abroad. 1 *Eq. Cas. Abr tit. Am.*

AMERCIAMENT, *amerciamentum*, (from the French *merci*) signifies the pecuniary punishment of an offender against the king, or other lord in his court, that is found to be in *misericordia*, i. e. to have offended, and to stand at the mercy of the king or lord. *Cowel. Blount.* Amerciament is properly a penalty assessed by the peers or equals of the party amerced, for the offence done; for which he putteth himself at the mercy of the lord. *Terms de Ley* 40. And by the statute of Magna Charta, a freeman is not to be amerced for a small fault, but proportionable to the offence, and that by his peers. 9 *H.* 3. *c.* 4. The difference between amerciaments and fines, is this; fines are said to be punishments certain, and grow expressly from some statute; but amerciaments are such as are arbitrarily imposed. *Kitch.* 78. Also fines are imposed and assessed by the court: amerciaments by the country: and no court can impose a fine, but a court of record: other courts can only amerce. 8 *Rep.* 39, 41.

A court-leet can amerce for public nuisances only. 1 *Saund.* 135. For a fine and all amerciaments in a court-leet, a distress is incident of common right: but for amerciament in a court baron, distress may not be taken but by prescription. 11 *Rep.* 45. When an amerciament is agreed on, the lord may have an action of debt, or distrain for it, and impound the distress, or sell it at his pleasure: but he cannot imprison for it. 8 *Rep.* 41, 45. 1 *Wils. Rep.* 248. In courts baron the amerciaments ought to be affeered; but it is otherwise of fines imposed by a court of record. 2 *Inst.* 27. An amerciament of a freeholder must be affeered by freeholds of the manor, or debt will not lie for it. 1 *Wils. Rep.* 2—20. In the court baron, tenants not doing suit of court, persons making any incroachments, not performing what is ordered, or for other misdemeanors there punishable, are to be amerced: these amerciaments are made upon presentment of the jury; and if they are grounded upon a void presentment, the amerciaments are also void. 1 *Lill. Abr.* 72.

There is also amercement in pleas in the courts of record, when a defendant delays to tender the thing demanded by the king's writs, on the first day. *Co. Lit.* 116. And in all personal actions without force, as in debt, detinue, &c. if the plaintiff be nonsuited, barred, or his writ abate for matter of form, he shall be amerced: but if on judicial process, founded on a judgment and record, the plaintiff be nonsuited, barred, &c. he shall not be amerced. 1 *Nels. Abr.* 206. And an infant, if nonsuited, is not to be amerced: it is otherwise when at age. *Jenk. Cent.* 258. But now the *capias pro fine* is taken away, by 2 *W.* & *M. c.* 12.

Sheriffs are to be amerced for the faults of their officers; and clerks of the peace are amerceable in B. R. for gross faults in indictments removed thither. *Hill.* 21 *Car.* The amerciament of the sheriff, or other officer of the king, is called amerciament royal. *Terms de Ley.* A town shall be amerced for the escape of a murderer, in the day-time: and if the town be walled, it is said, it shall be subject to amercement, whether by day or night. 3 *Inst.* 53.

AMESSE, (from the Latin *amictus*) is taken for a priestly garment. *Cowel. Blount.*

AMICIA, (the same with *almutium*) a cap made with goats or lambs skins: that part whereof which covered the head was square, and one part of it hung behind, and covered the neck. *Monasticon,* 3 *tom. p.* 36.

AMICTUS, was the uppermost of the six garments worn by priests, tied round the neck, and it covered the breast and heart. Amictus, *alba, cingulem, stola, manipulus,* & *planeta,* were the six garments of the priests. *Cowel.*

AMICUS CURIAE, if a judge is doubtful or mistaken in matter of law, a stander-by may inform the court, as *amicus curiæ.* 2 *Co. Inst.* 178.

AMITTERE LEGEM TERRÆ, to lose and be deprived of the liberty of swearing in any court: or according to *Coke* to become infamous, and incapable of being an evidence. *Glanvil, lib.* 2.

AMMOBRAGIUM, a service.—*in com.* Flint. conjectured to be the same as CHEVAGE by *Spelm.*

AMNESTY, (*amnestia, oblivio*) an act of pardon or oblivion.

AMNITUM INSULÆ, isles upon the west coast of Britain. *Blount.*

AMORTIZATION, (*amotizatio,* French *amortissement*) is an alienation of lands or tenements in mortmain, *viz.* to any corporation or fraternity, and their successors, &c. see *Mortmain.*

AMORTIZE, (French *amortir*) is to alien lands in mortmain. See *Mortmain.*

AMPLIATION, (*ampliatio*) an enlargement, but in sense of law it is a referring of judgment, till the cause is further examined. *Cowel.*

AMY, (*amicus*) A *prochein amy* is the next friend suing for an orphan or infant. And infants are to sue by *prochein amy* (*i. e.* next friend) or guardian: and defend by guardian. *Alien amy* is a foreigner here subject to some prince in friendship with us.

AN, JOUR ET WASTE, (French) years day and waste; a forfeiture of lands to the king incurred by tenants committing felony, afterwards the lands escheat, to the lord.

ANCESTOR, (*antecessor*) one that has gone before in a family: and the law makes a difference between an *ancestor* and a *predecessor;* the one being applied to a natural person and his ancestors, and the other to a corporation and their predecessors. *Co. Lit.* 78 b.

ANCESTREL, as homage ancestrel, what relates to or hath been done by one's ancestors. *Cowel. Blount.*

ANCHOR, is a measure of brandy, &c. containing ten gallons. *Lex. Mercat.*

ANCHORAGE, (*ancoragium*) a duty taken of ships for the use of the haven where they cast anchor. *MS. Arth. Trevor, Ar.* The ground in ports and havens belonging to the king, no person can let any anchor fall there on, without paying therefore to the king's officers appointed by patent. *Cowel. Blount.*

ANCIENTS, gentlemen of the inns of court. In Gray's inn the society consists of benchers, ancients, barristers, and students under the bar; and here the ancients are of the oldest barristers. In the Middle Temple, such as have gone through, or are past their readings, are termed ancients; the inns of Chancery consist of ancients and students or clerks; and from the ancients one is yearly chosen the principal or treasurer. *Cowel. Blount.*

ANCIENT DEMESNE, (*vetus patrimonium domini*) all those lands which were in possession of *Edward* the confessor, and afterwards came to William the conqueror, and were by him set down in a book called *domesday,* about the 28th year of his reign, under the title *de terra regis,* are *ancient demesne* lands. *Kitch.* 98.

But the lands which were in the possession of Edward the confessor, and were given away by him, are not at this day ancient demesne, nor any others, except those writ down in the book of *domesday;* and therefore, whether such lands are ancient demesne or not, is to be tried only by that book. 1 *Salk.* 57. 4 *Inst.* 269. *Hob.* 188. 1 *Brownl.* 43.

But if the question is, whether lands be parcel of a manor which is ancient demesne, this shall be tried by a jury. *Salk.* 56, 774. 1 *Com. Dig. tit. Abatement.*

Tenants in ancient demesne had many immunities and privileges granted to them; as to try the right of their property in a peculiar court of their own, called a court of ancient demesne, by a peculiar process, called *a writ of right close;* not to pay toll or taxes, not to contribute to the expenses of the knights of the shire; not to be put on juries and the like. 2 *Black.* 99.

Lands holden by this tenure are a species of copyhold, and as such preserved and exempted from the operations of the stat. of *Car.* 2. and they cannot be conveyed from man to man by the general common law conveyances; but must pass by surrender to the lord, or his steward, in the manner of common copyholds, yet with this distinction, that in the surrender of these lands in *ancient demesne*, it is not used to say *to hold at the will of the lord* in their copies, but only *to hold* according to the custom of the manor. *Kitchen* 194. 2 *Black.* 100.

ANCIENTY, (French *ancienete*, Latin *antiquitas*) eldership or seniority. *Cowel. Blount.*

ANCILIARY: courts of equity in many cases will act as *anciliary* to the administration of justice in other courts by removing impediments to the fair decision of a question. Thus if an ejectment be brought to try a right to land, in a court of common law, a court of equity will restrain the party in possession, from setting up any title which may prevent the fair trial of the right; as a term for years, or other interest in a trustee, lessee, or mortgagee. *Mitf.* 121.

But this will not be done in every case; for as the court proceeds, upon the principle, that the party in possession ought not in conscience, to use an accidental advantage to protect his possession against a real right in his adversary, if there is any circumstance which meets the reasoning upon this principle, the court will not interfere. *Ibid.* 122.

Therefore if the possessor is a purchaser for a valuable consideration, without notice of the title of the claimant, this is a title in conscience equal to that of the claimant, and the court will not restrain the possessor, from using any advantage he may be able to gain to defend his possession. It can hardly appear upon the face of a bill, that the defendant is in such a situation, and therefore the benefit of this defence, must generally be taken by plea: but if the case should be so stated, the defendant might demur; because the case stated would appear to be such in which a court of equity ought not to assume jurisdiction. *Ibid.* 122.

So if the matter suggested in a bill as an impediment to the determination of a question in a court of ordinary jurisdiction, in fact is not so, the defendant may also demur, for then there is no pretence for the interference of a court of equity: therefore, where a bill was filed for a discovery of the value of the respective real estates of the inhabitants of a parish, in which a church rate had been assessed, and of the application of the money collected, a demurrer was allowed, because the ecclesiastical court, to which the ordinary jurisdiction belonged, was capable of compelling the discovery. 1 *Atk.* 288. 1 *Vez.* 205. 2 *Vez.* 451. *Mitf.* 122, 151.

So also if a bill is brought to aid by a discovery, the prosecution or defence of any proceeding, not merely civil, in any other court, as an indictment or information (or an action by a common informer for the recovery of money, won at play, under the statute against gaming. *Holloways' case, Anstr. Rep.*) A court of equity will not exercise its jurisdiction to compel a discovery, and the defendant may demur. 2 *Vez.* 398. *Mitf.* 150.

ANDENA, a swath in mowing: it likewise signifies as much ground as a man can stride over at once. *Ibid.*

ANELACIUS, a short knife or dagger.

ANFELDTYHDE, or *anfealtihle*, according to the Saxon law, a simple accusation. *Cowel. Blount.*

ANGARIA, (from the French *angarie*) personal service which tenants were obliged to pay to their lords. *Cowel. Blount.*

ANGELICA VESTIS, a monkish garment which laymen put on a little before their deaths, that they might have the benefit of the prayers of the monks. *Monasticon*, 1 *tom.* *p.* 632.

ANGEL, signifies in the computation of money, ten shillings of English coin.

ANGILD, (*angildum*) the bare single valuation or compensation of a criminal; from the Saxon *an* one, and *gild*, payment, mulct, or fine; *twigild* was the double fine, and *trigild* the treble, according to the rated ability of the person. Law of *Ina*, *c.* 20. *Spelm. Cowel. Blount.*

ANHLOTE, a single tribute or tax, such as pay his part and share, as scot and lot. *Leg. W.* 1. *c.* 64. *Cowel. Blount.*

ANIENS, (French) void, being of no force. *F. N. B.* 214.

ANNALES, yearlings, or young cattle of the first year. *Cowel. Blount.*

ANNATS, (*annates*) this word has the same meaning with first-fruits. *Cowel. Blount.*

ANNEALING OF TILE, (*anno* 17 *Ed.* 4.) from the Saxon *onælan accendere*, signifies the burning or hardening of tile.

ANNIENTED, (from the French *anneanter*) abrogated, frustrated, or brought to nothing. *Lit. c.* 3. *sect.* 741.

ANNIVERSARY DAYS, (*dies anniversarii*) solemn days appointed to be celebrated yearly, in commemoration of the death or martyrdom of saints; or the days whereon, at the return of every year, men were wont to pray for the souls of their deceased friends, according to the custom of the Roman Catholics, mentioned in the statute of 1 *Ed.* 6. *cap.* 14. and 12 *Car.* 2. *cap.* 13. This was in use among our ancient Saxons. See *Lib. Rames. sec.* 134.

ANNI NUBILES, (Latin) when a woman is under 12 years of age, her age to marry, she is said to be *infra annos nubiles*, and unmarriageable; so that it signifies the marriageable age of a woman. 2 *Co. Inst.* 434.

ANNO DOMINI, the computation of time from the incarnation of Jesus Christ, which is generally inserted in the dates of all public writings, with an addition of the year of the king's reign. The Romans began their æra of time from the building of Rome; the Grecians computed by olympiads; and the Christians reckon from the birth of Jesus Christ. *Cowel. Blount.*

ANNOISANCE, ANNOYANCE, or *noisance*, is a word used for any hurt done to a place, as a highway, bridge, river, or the like, or to any private place, by laying any thing therein that may breed infection, by incroachments, or such like means; and it is also taken for the writ brought upon such a transgression. This word is mentioned *anno* 22 *H.* c. 5. *Cowel. Blount.*

ANNUA PENSIONE, an ancient writ now disused, for providing the king's chaplain unpreferred, with a pension. It was brought where the king had due to him an annual pension from an abbot or prior, for any of his chaplains whom he should nominate, (being unprovided of livings) to demand the same of such abbot or prior. *Reg. Orig.* 165, 307.

ANNUALE, the yearly rent or income of a prebendary. *Cowel. Blount.*

ANNUALIA, a yearly stipend assigned to a priest for celebrating an anniversary, or for saying continued masses one year, for the soul of a deceased person. *Cowel. Blount.*

ANNUITY. An annuity strictly taken, is a yearly payment (*annus redditus*) of a certain sum of money granted to another in *fee-simple, fee-tail*, for *life* or *years*, charging the person of the grantor only. 1 *Bac. Abr. tit. An.*

If payable out of lands, it is properly called *a rent charge*, but if both the person and estate be made liable, as they most commonly are, then it is generally called an annuity. *Ibid.*

A rent charge is, where the owner of the rent hath no future interest or reversion expectant in the land: as where a man by deed maketh over to others his whole estate in fee-simple, with a certain rent payable thereout; and adds to the deed a covenant or clause of distress, that if the rent be in arrear or behind, it shall be lawful to distrain for the same: in this case the land is liable to distress, not of common right, but by virtue of the clause in the deed, and therefore it is called *a rent charge*, because in this manner, the land is charged with a distress for the payment of it, and if the grant be without clause of distress, then it is *a rent seck, redditus siccus*, or barren rent. 2 *Black.* 41. 1 *Bac. Abr. tit. Am.*

And if the annuitant die before the quarterly day of payment arrives, nothing is due for the intermediate time that may have elapsed since the last quarterly day of payment and the day of his death, unless it is otherwise provided by the deed creating the annuity. 3 *Atk.* 260.

There are now very few, if any, grants of annuities, without a covenant for payment, and therefore, where a distress cannot be made, or is not approved of, the grantee may bring an action of covenant, and recover the arrears in damages, with costs of suit. And that action is now usually brought, real actions and writs of annuity being much out of use. *Morgan.*

ANNUITIES FOR LIVES. The practice of purchasing *annuities for lives* at a certain price or premium, instead of advancing the same sum on an ordinary loan, arises usually from the inability of the borrower to give the lender a permanent security, for the return of the money borrowed at any one period of time; he therefore stipulates (in effect) to repay annually during his life, some part of the money borrowed; together with legal interest, for so much of the principal, as annually remains unpaid, and an additional compensation for the extraordinary hazard run, of losing that principal entirely, by the contingency of the borrower's death: all which considerations being calculated and blended together, will constitute the just proportion or quantum of the annuity, which ought to be granted. 2 *Black.* 461.

The real value of that contingency must depend on the age, constitution, situation and conduct of the borrower, and therefore the price of such annuities, cannot, without the utmost difficulty, be reduced to any general rules: so that if, by the terms of the contract, the lender's principal is *bona fide* (and not colourably, *Carth.* 67.) put in jeopardy, no inequality of price will make it an *usurious bargain*; though under some circumstances of imposition, it may be relieved against in equity. *Ibid.*

To throw, however, some check upon improvident transactions of this kind, which are usually carried on with privacy, *it is enacted* by 17 *Geo.* 3. *c.* 26. that "a memorial of all "deeds, bonds, or other instruments for "granting life annuities, shall within twenty "days after the execution thereof, be inrolled "in the court of chancery; which shall contain the date, names of the parties, and witnesses; otherwise every such deed, bond, "or the like, shall be void." *s.* 1.

"Before judgment shall be entered of "record, upon any warrant of attorney, for "recovering any annuity already granted, "and before execution shall be sued out, on "any judgment already entered, a memorandum shall be enrolled as aforesaid." *s.* 2.

"All future deeds, bonds and instruments "for granting of annuities, shall contain the "consideration, and the names of the parties "at length, and if any part of the consideration shall be returned, or any notes shall "not be paid when due, the court where the "action is brought, may stay the proceedings, and order the deeds, bonds, and other "instruments to be cancelled." *s.* 3, 4.

"The clerk of the enrolments in chancery "shall keep a particular roll for annuities, "wherein he shall specify the time of enrolment. His fees are, one shilling for the first 200 words, sixpence for each 100 words after, and one shilling for a search." *s*. 5.

"All contracts for the purchase of annuities, with any person under the age of twenty-one years of age shall be void; and any person procuring or soliciting any minor, to grant an annuity, or any solicitor, scrivener, or broker taking more than 10*s*. *per cent.* for procuring money for annuities, shall be punished by fine and imprisonment." *s*. 6, 7.

"Act not to extend to annuities, or rent charges by will, marriage settlement, or for advancement of a child; nor, if secured on lands of equal or greater value, if the grantor is seised in fee or tail, or if secured by stocks actually transferred, if the dividend is of greater value; nor to voluntary annuities without a pecuniary consideration, nor if granted by corporations, or by authority of act of parliament, or if under 10*l*. *per ann.* unless there be more than one from the same grantor to, or in trust for the same grantee." *s*. 8.

A deed not registered according to the directions of the above act is absolutely void, and not merely voidable. 2 *Ter. Rep.* 603. 4 *Ter. Rep.* 463, 494, 500, 694, 790, 824. And if the security be set aside for want of complying with the formalities of the act, the consideration if fair and legal may be recovered back by the grantee in an action of assumpsit against the person actually receiving such consideration money, but not against a surety. 1 *Ter. Rep.* 732. 2 *Ter. Rep*. 366.

ANNULUM ET BACULUM, the ancient mode of granting the investitures of bishopricks, was *per annulum et baculum*, by the prince delivering to the prelate a ring and pastoral staff, and crosier. 1 *Black.* 378—9.

ANNUM LUCTUS. The civil law ordained, that no widow should marry *infra annum luctus*, to prevent, amongst other inconveniences, that which arises from a man's dying, and his widow soon after marrying again, and having a child born within such a time, as that by the course of nature it may be the child of either husband: in which case it is said to be more than ordinarily legitimate, inasmuch as he may when he arrives at years of discretion, choose which of the fathers he pleases. *Co. Lit.* 8. 1 *Black.* 456.

ANTEJURAMENTUM, and *præjuramentum*. By our ancestors called *juramentum calumniæ*; in which both the accuser and the accused were to make this oath before any trial or purgation, *viz.* the accuser was to swear, that he would prosecute the criminal; and the accused was to make oath on the very day, that he was to undergo the ordeal, that he was innocent of the crime of which he was charged. *Leg. Athelstan. apud Lambard* 23. If the accuser failed to take this oath, the criminal was discharged; and if the accused did not take his, he was intended to be guilty, and not admitted to purge himself. *Leg. Hen.* 1. *c*. 66.

ANTISTITIUM, a word used for monastery in our old histories. *Blount.*

ANTITHETARIUS, signifies where a man endeavours to discharge himself of the fact of which he is accused, by recriminating and charging the accuser with the same fact. *Cowel. Blount.*

APATISATIO, an agreement or compact made with another. *Ibid.*

APORIARE, to be brought to poverty. It hath been used sometimes to signify shun or avoid. *Ibid.*

APOSTACY, a total renunciation of Christianity, by embracing either a false religion, or no religion at all: this offence could only take place in such as had once professed the true religion, and the perversion of a Christian to Judaism, Paganism, or other false religion, was punished by the emperors *Constantius* and *Julian* with confiscation of goods, to which the emperors *Theodosius* and *Valentinian* added capital punishment, in case the apostate endeavoured to pervert others to the same iniquity: the zeal of our ancestors also induced them to adopt the same severity in this country: for we find by *Bracton* *l*. 3, *c*. 9. that in his time apostates were burnt to death. 4 *Black.* 43,

This punishment, however, has long since become obsolete; and the offence of *apostacy*, was for a long time cognizable only in the ecclesiastical courts, where the offender might be corrected, *pro salute animæ*. *Ibid.*

But about the close of the seventeenth century, the civil liberties to which we were then restored, being used as a cloak of maliciousness, and the most horrid doctrines, subversive of all religion, being publicly avowed, both in discourse and writing, it was thought necessary again for the civil power to interpose, by not admitting the professors of such doctrines to the privileges of society, who maintained principles, so destructive of all moral obligation. *Ibid.*

To this end it was enacted by stat. 9 & 10 *Wil. c*. 32. that *if any person educated in, or having made profession of the Christian religion, shall by writing, printing, teaching, or advised speaking, deny the Christian religion to be true, or the holy Scriptures to be of divine authority, he shall upon the first offence be rendered incapable to hold any office or place of trust; and for the second be rendered incapable of bringing any action, being guardian, executor, legatee, or purchaser of lands, and shall suffer three years imprisonment without bail: but* (to give room for repentance as Judge Blackstone observes, 4 *Com.* 44.) *if within four months after the first conviction, the delinquent will in open court, publicly renounce his error, he is discharged for that once from all disabilities.*

APOSTARE, to violate: wilfully to break or transgress the laws. *Cowel. Blount.*

APOSTATA CAPIENDO, a writ, now out of use, that formerly lay against one who, having entered and professed some order of religion, broke out again, and wandered up and down the country, contrary to the rules of his order: it was directed to the sheriff for the apprehension of the offender, and delivery of him again to his abbot or prior. *Reg. Orig.* 71, 267.

APOTHECARIES, are exempted from serving offices, by 6 *Will.* 3. *c.* 4.

APPARATOR, or APPARITOR, a messenger that serves the process of the spiritual court. His duty is to cite the offenders to appear; to arrest them; and to execute the sentence or decree of the judges, &c. *Cowel. Blount.*

APPARATOR COMITATUS, an officer formerly called by this name; for which the sheriffs of Buckinghamshire had a considerable yearly allowance; and in the reign of queen Elizabeth, there was an order of court for making that allowance: but the custom and reason of it are now altered. *Hale's Sher. Acco.* 104.

APPARLEMENT, (from the French *pareillement*, i. e. in like manner) signifies a resemblance or likelihood, as apparlement of war. 2 *R.* 2. *Stat.* 1. *c.* 6.

APPARURA, furniture and implements. *Carrucaram apparura* is plough-tackle, or all the implements belonging to a plough. *Cowel. Blount.*

APPEAL, *appellum*. [From the French *appeller:* the verb active, which signifies to call upon, summon or challenge one, and not the verb neuter which signifies the same, as the ordinary sense of *appeal* in English. 4 *Black.* 312. n. i.] An appeal in the general use of the word, signifies any complaint to a superior court of an injustice done by an inferior one; but it here means an original suit at the time of its first commencement. 3 *Black.* 362. 4 *Black.* 312.

But an appeal, when spoken of as a criminal prosecution (as it is here) is the party's private action, seeking revenge for the injury done him, and at the same time prosecuting for the crown, in respect of the offence against the public. 1 *Bac. Abr. tit. Ap.*

Though this be a legal suit, and therefore to be carried on in a reasonable way, yet as none of the statutes of amendment or jeofail extend to it, the utmost exactness is required in the proceedings: and in modern times, from the great difficulty, attendant upon a prosecution of this kind, and the little encouragement given to it by the judges, from its vindictive nature, it is a course of proceeding now rarely resorted to.

This private process, for the punishment of public crimes, had probably its original in those times when a private pecuniary satisfaction, called a *weregild*, was constantly paid to the party injured, or his relations, to expiate enormous offences: as, therefore, during the continuance of this custom, a process was certainly given, for recovering the *weregild*, by the party to whom it was due, it seems that when these offences by degrees grew no longer redeemable, the private process was still continued, in order to insure the infliction of punishment upon the offender, though the party injured was allowed no pecuniary compensation for the offence. 4 *Black.* 313.

Of these appeals, there were anciently several kinds, which seem obsolete at this day; as appeals of treason, within the realm which might be sued by courts of law, or before parliament. 2 *Inst.* 132. *Bract.* 118. 2 *Hawk. P. C.* 161.

But that in the first was *virtually* abolished by 5 *Ed.* 3. *c.* 9. *s.* 2. 5 *Ed* 3. *c.* 22. and in the second, expressly by 1 *Hen.* 4. *c.* 14. 4 *Black.* 314.

However, the jurisdiction of the constable and marshal, in relation to appeals of treasons *committed out of the realm*, seems to continue still in force; for so late as 7 *Car.* 1. an appeal of treason, supposed to be committed beyond sea, was actually commenced before the constable and marshal; who, for want of sufficient proof to clear the truth, awarded that a duel should be fought between the parties, for the final determination of the matter. *Rushworth's Collect. part* 2. *vol.* 1. *p.* 112.

Appeals *de pace, de plagis,* and *de imprisonamento,* are out of use, and have been turned to actions of trespass for many hundred years past; also the whole learning of appeals of arson seems obsolete at this day. *Co. Lit.* 288. *a.*

The only appeals, therefore, that may be brought at this day, seem to be those of *death, larceny,* and *rape,* which are capital appeals, and that of *mayhem,* which is considered as a trespass. 1 *Bac. Abr.* 190.

APPEAL OF DEATH, which is now chiefly in use, is a vindictive action which the law gives a wife against her husband's murderer, and to the *male* heir at law, against one who kills his ancestor, which, being the suit of the subject, the king cannot pardon. *Ibid.*

At the common law, before magna charta, 9 *Hen.* 3. *c.* 34. a woman as well as a man might have had an appeal of death of any of her ancestors. But by magna charta, *c.* 34. a woman cannot sue an appeal for the murder of any one, but her husband. 2 *Inst.* 68.

The wife is to be a wife *de facto* to be intitled to appeal; and if she marries again, before the appeal is brought, or whilst the same is depending, her appeal will be gone. 2 *Inst.* 68, 317.

The husband shall not have an appeal for the death of his wife, but the heir only.

Danv. Abr. 488. An heir shall not have appeal for the death of a man married, except the wife kill the husband; in which case the heir may prosecute the appeal. 1 *Leon.* 326. *Co. Lit.* 33.

And if the wife dies within the year, the heir shall have no appeal. *Keilw.* 120.

And by the stat. *Glocester*, 6 Ed. 1. c. 9. *all appeals of death must be sued within a year and a day, after the completion of the felony, by the death of the party*, which according to 4 *Black.* 314. seems to be only declaratory of the common law.

These appeals may be brought, *previous to any* indictment; and if the appellor be acquitted thereon, he cannot afterwards be indicted for the same offence. 4 *Black.* 314.

But if a murderer be acquitted upon indictment, or found guilty, and pardoned by the king, the wife or heir may bring appeal. *Wood* 629. 4 *Black.* 314.

And therefore when a person is indicted for murder, and acquitted thereupon, he is to be bailed till the year and day is past, allowed for bringing the appeal, if an appeal be intended. 3 *Hen.* 7. *cap.* 1.

But if he hath been found guilty of manslaughter on an indictment, and hath had the benefit of clergy, and suffered the judgment of the law, he cannot be afterwards appealed; for it is a maxim of the law that *nemo bis punitur pro eodem delicto.* 4 *Black.* 315.

If the appellee be found guilty, he shall suffer the same judgment, as if he had been convicted by indictment: but with this remarkable difference, that in an indictment, which is at the suit of the king, the king may pardon and remit the execution: but on an appeal, which is at the suit of a private subject, to make an atonement for the private wrong, the king can no more pardon it, than he can remit the damages on an action of battery: an appeal being for retribution or satisfaction as far as the law can give it, that is, *life* for *life.* 4 *Black.* 316. 3 *Inst.* 131. *Staund.* 147—8.

However, the punishment of the offender may be remitted and discharged, by the concurrence of all parties interested; and as the king by his pardon may frustrate an indictment, so the appellant by his release may discharge an appeal *nam quilibet rotest renunciare juri pro se introductu.* 4 *Black.* 316.

APPEAL OF MAIHEM, is the accusing one that hath maimed another: but this being generally no felony, it is in a manner but an action of trespass; and nothing is recovered by it but damages. 3 *Inst.* 63.

APPEAL OF RAPE, lies where a rape is committed on the body of a woman. 3 *Inst.* 30. A feme covert, without her husband, may bring appeal of rape: and the *stat.* 11 *Hen.* 4. *cap.* 13. gives power where a woman is ravished, and afterwards consents to it, for a husband, or a father, or next of kin, there being no husband, to bring appeal of rape: also the criminal, in such case, may be attainted at the suit of the king. 3 *Inst.* 131. 6 *R.* 2. *cap.* 6.

Appeal of Rape may be brought in any reasonable time. *H. P. C.* 186. And though formerly the defendant might have his clergy, it is taken away by the stat. 18 *Eliz. cap.* 17. *Dyer* 201.

APPEAL OF ROBBERY, a remedy given by the common law, where a person is robbed of his goods, &c. to have restitution of the goods stolen: as they could not be restored on indictment at the king's suit, this appeal was judged necessary. 3 *Inst.* 242. If a man robbed make fresh pursuit after, and apprehend and prosecute the felon, he may bring appeal of robbery at any time afterwards. *Staundf.* 62.

For the party robbed, shall not be bound to bring it within a year and a day, as he must do in appeal of murder. 4 *Leon.* 16.

APPEAL TO ROME. By the stat. 24 *Hen.* 8. *c.* 12. and 25 *Hen.* 8. *c.* 19, 21. to appeal to Rome from any of the king's courts, to sue to Rome for any licence of dispensation, or to obey any process from thence, are made liable to the pains of *præmunire.*

APPEARANCE to actions, signifieth the defendant's filing common or special bail, when he is served with a copy of, or arrested on any process out of the courts at Westminster. *Show* 165.

For the time and manner of entering, which appearances, see the practice of the respective courts, as detailed under the proper titles relative thereto, in this Dictionary.

APPENDANT, (*appendens*) is a thing of incorporeal inheritance, belonging to another inheritance that is more worthy. As an advowson, common, court, or the like, which may be appendant to a manor: common of fishing, appendant to a freehold: land appendant to an office: a seat in a church to a house. But land is not appendant to land, both being corporeal, and one thing corporeal may not be appendant to another that is corporeal; but an incorporeal thing may be appendant to it. *Co. Lit.* 121. 4 *Rep.* 86. *Danv. Abr.* 500.

A way thus may be *quasi* appendant to the house or land, and as such pass by grant thereof. *Co. Lit.* 172. b. *Cro. Jac.* 190.

APPENDITIA, the appendages or pertinences of an estate. Hence our pentices or pent-houses, are called *appenditia domus*, &c. *Cowel. Blount.*

APPENNAGE, or *apennage*, (French) is derived from *appendendo*; or the German word *apanage*, signifying a portion. It is used for a child's part or portion; and is properly the portion of the king's younger children in France, where by a fundamental law, called the law of apennages, the king's younger sons have duchies, counties, or baronies granted to them and their heirs, &c. the reversion being reserved to the crown, and all matters of regality as to coinage, and levying taxes in such territories. *Spelm. Gloss. Cowel. Blount.*

APPENSURA, the payment of money at the scale or by weight. *Ibid.*

APPODIARE, is a word used in old historians, and signifies to lean on, or prop up any thing. *Ibid.*

APPOINTMENT. An appointment generally considered in this place, as one of the common law conveyances, is a deed or instrument of a derivative nature, relative to or dependant on some precedent deed or assurance, in which a power to appoint to certain uses, has been created or reserved to the party thereby granting or appointing: the person taking under an appointment must therefore be considered as taking, under the power, by which the appointment is authorised, precisely in the same manner as if his name had been inserted in the original instrument by which the power was granted; with this difference, that if the appointment be made by DEED, the estate appointed will, by force of the statute of uses, immediately vest in the appointee, in like manner as if he had been named in the instrument creating the power; but if the appointment be made by *will* the appointee will be considered in all respects as a *devisee*, and subject to the same chance of lapse, in case of his death in the life time of the devisor, as is incident to the ambulatory nature of a will. *Co. Lit.* 80. 2 *Ter. Rep.* 241, 251, 787. See titles *Powers, Uses.*

APPONERE, to pledge or pawn. *Acceptâ à fratre Gulielmo summâ non modicâ Normanniam illi apposuit. Neubrigensis, lib.* 1. c. 2.

APPORTIONMENT, (*apportionamentum*) is a dividing of rent into parts, according as the land out of which it issues, is divided among two or more. As if a stranger recovers part of the land, a lessee shall pay, having regard to that recovered, and what remains in his hands. Where the lessor recovers part of the land, or enters for a forfeiture into part thereof, the rent shall be apportioned. *Co. Lit.* 148. So if a man leases three acres, rendering rent, and afterwards grants away one acre, the rent shall be apportioned. *Co. Lit.* 144. So lessee for years, leases for years, rendering rent, and after devises this rent to three persons, this rent may be apportioned. *Danv. Abr.* 505.

But as rent is not due till the last minute of the natural day, if the lessor dies after sun-set and before midnight, the rent shall go to the heir and not to the executor, and so there can be no apportionment. *Co. Lit.* 202. 2 *Saund.* 287. 1 *Salk.* 578. *Prc. Ch.* 555.

Before the stat. 11 *Geo.* 2. *c.* 19. by the death of a tenant for life in an intermediate quarter; such quarter was lost, for the law would not suffer his representatives to bring an action for the use and occupation, much less if there was a lease, and the remainder-man had no right because the rent was not due in his time; nor could equity relieve against his hardship by apportioning the rent. 1 *Pere. Wms.* 392.

But now by stat. 11 Geo. 2. c. 19. *if any tenant for life shall die before or on the day on which any rent shall become due, his executors or administrators may recover from the under-tenant if he died on the day when the rent became due, the whole, or if before such day then a proportion of such rent.* s. 15.

And by an equitable construction of the above statute, its provisions have been extended to tenants in tail, where leases are determined by their deaths. *Amb.* 198. 2 *Bro. Ch. Rep.* 659.

But though the executor of tenant for life is now entitled to an apportionment of the rent, yet *the dividends* of money directed to be laid out in lands, and in the mean time to be invested in *government securities*, and the interest, and dividends to be applied as the rents and profits would, in case it were laid out in land, were held not to be apportionable, though tenant for life died in the middle of the half year. 3 *Atk.* 502. *Ambl.* 279. 2 *Vez.* 672. 3 *Atk.* 260.

However, where the money was laid out in *mortgage*, till a purchase could be made, the interest was held to be apportionable under this distinction, that interest on a mortgage was in fact due from *day to day*, and so not properly an apportionment; whereas the dividends accruing from the public funds are made payable on certain days, and therefore not apportionable. 2 *Pere. Wms.* 176, 501.

Regularly at law a rent-charge, issuing out of land, may not be apportioned: nor shall things entire, as if one holds lands by service to pay yearly to the lord, at such a feast, a horse, &c. *Co. Lit.* 149. But if part of the land, out of which a rent-charge issues, descends to the grantee of the rent, this shall be apportioned. *Danv.* 507.

So if a grantee of rent releases part of the rent to the grantor, this doth not extinguish the residue, but it shall be apportioned: for here the grantee dealeth not with the land, only the rent. *Co. Lit.* 148. On partition of lands, out of which a rent is issuing, the rent shall be apportioned. *Danv. Abr.* 507.

A man purchases part of the land where he hath common appendant, the common shall be apportioned: of common appurtenant it is otherwise, and if by the act of the party, the common is extinct. 8 *Rep.* 79. If where a person has common of pasture *sans number*, part of the lands descends to him, this being intire and uncertain cannot be apportioned: but if it had been common certain, it should have been apportioned. *Co. Lit.* 149.

APPORTUM, (from the French *apport*) the revenue or profit which a thing brings in to the owner: and it was commonly used for a corody or pension. *Cowel. Blount.*

APPOSAL OF SHERIFFS, the charging

them with money received upon their accounts in the exchequer. *Stat.* 22 & 23 *Car.* 2.

APPRAISEMENT, *commission of,*] anciently in the case of the seizure of treasure trove, wrecks, waifs, and estrays, by the king's officer for his use, an information was usually filed in the king's exchequer, and thereupon a proclamation was made for the owner (if any) to come in and claim the effects; and at the same time there issued *a commission of appraisement* to value the goods in the officer's hands; after the return of which, and a second proclamation had, if no claimant appeared, the goods were supposed derelict and condemned to the use of the crown. *Gilb. Ex. cap.* 13. 3 *Black.* 262.

And since, in later times, forfeitures of goods, as well as personal penalties have been inflicted by act of parliament for transgressions against the laws of the customs, the same process has been adopted in order to secure the forfeited goods for the public use, though the offender himself escape the reach of justice. 3 *Black.* 362.

APPRAISERS of goods are to be sworn to make true appraisement; and, valuing the goods too high, shall be obliged to take them at the price appraised. *Stat.* 11 *Ed.* 1. *Stat. Acton Burnel.*

APPRENDRE, (French) a fee or profit *apprendre,* is fee or profit to be taken or received. *Anno* 2 & 3 *Ed.* 6. *cap.* 8. *Cowel. Blount.*

APPRENTICE, (from *apprendre,* to learn) signifies a young person bound for a term of years, by deed indented, or indentures, to serve some masters, and be maintained and instructed by him. 1 *Black.* 245.

This is usually done to some tradesman or artificer, who upon certain covenants is to teach him his mystery or trade: and these apprentices are servants by covenant, and for a term, usually seven years. *Smith's Rep. Angl. lib.* 3. *cap.* 8.

And an apprentice must, by 5 *Eliz. c.* 4. *s.* 25. be by deed, and cannot be discharged without deed, and he must be retained therein by the name of an *apprentice* expressly, otherwise he is no apprentice, though bound. 4 *Bac. Abr. tit. Mas. & Ser.*

And as an apprentice can only be bound by deed, so it is necessary, according to the custom of some places, that such deed or indenture be inrolled; as in London, (except with the Waterman's company, which is only a voluntary society,) if the indentures be not inrolled before the chamberlain within a year, upon a petition to the mayor and aldermen, &c. a *scire facias* shall issue to the master, to shew cause why not inrolled; and if it was through the master's default, the apprentice may sue out his indentures, and be discharged: otherwise, if through the fault of the apprentice; as if he would not come to present himself before the chamberlain, &c. for it cannot be inrolled, unless the apprentice be in court and acknowledge it. 2 *Rol. Rep.* 305. *Palm.* 361. 1 *Mod.* 271. 6 *Mod.* 69. *Salk.* 68.

And as an apprenticeship by 5 *Eliz. c.* 4. *s.* 25. can only be created by *indenture,* where the writing, by which one person agreed to serve another for seven years, began, *this indenture witnesseth,* but was in fact a deed poll, and not indented or cut out at the head scallopwise, it was holden that the master could not maintain any action upon it, against a person for enticing away and detaining his apprentice. 1 *Sess. Cas.* 222.

Who may bind themselves apprentices.] By the common law infants, or persons under the age of twenty-one years, cannot bind themselves apprentices, in such a manner as to intitle their masters to an action of covenant, or other action against them for departing from their service, or other breaches of their indentures; which makes it necessary, according to the usual practice, to get some of their friends, to be bound for the faithful discharge of their offices, according to the terms agreed on. 11 *Co.* 89. b. 2 *Inst.* 379, 580. 3 *Leon.* 63. *Foresl.* 15. And notwithstanding the 5 *Eliz. c.* 4. *s.* 43. enacts, that *although persons bound apprentices shall be within age at the time of making their indentures, they shall be bound to serve for the years in their indentures contained, as if they were at full age at the time of making them;* it hath been held, that although an infant may voluntarily bind himself an apprentice, and, if he continue an apprentice for seven years, he may have the benefit to use his trade; yet neither at the common law, nor by any words of the abovementioned statute, can a covenant or obligation of an infant, for his apprenticeship, bind him; but if he misbehave himself, the master may correct him in his service, or complain to a justice of peace, to have him punished according to the statute: but no remedy lieth against an infant upon such covenant. *Cro. Car* 179. *Cro. Jac.* 194. *S. P.* 4 *Bac. Abr. tit. M.*

But although an infant cannot bind himself apprentice, so as to entitle his master to an action of covenant, for breach of any of the clauses of the indenture, yet it should seem, though the point has never been directly determined, that if in fact he does bind himself, he is not afterwards at liberty to avoid a contract which is so notoriously for his benefit. 2 *Str.* 1066. *Burr. Setl. Cas.* 91. *Cas. Temp. Hard.* 323. *Cald.* 26. 6 *Ter. Rep.* 557. 652.

And it has been determined that an indenture of apprenticeship to an infant is not void, but only voidable. 4 *Ter. Rep.* 196.

By the custom of London an infant unmarried, and above the age of fourteen, may bind himself apprentice to a freeman of London, by indenture with proper covenants; which covenants, by the custom of London, shall be as binding as if he were of full age *Moor.* 134. 2 *Bulst.* 192. 2 *Rol. Rep.* 305. *Palm.* 361. 1 *Mod.* 271. 2 *Keb.* 687.

Jurisdiction of justices of the peace.] By 5 *Eliz.* c. 4. "if any person under the age "of 21 years, shall be required by any "householder having and using half a "plough land in tillage, to be an appren- "tice, and to serve in husbandry, or in any "other kind of art, mystery, or science in "the act mentioned, and shall refuse, then "upon complaint to one justice, of the coun- "ty, mayor, bailiff, or head officer of the "city or place, they shall have authority "to send for the person refusing, and if "they think him fit to serve, they shall, if "he refuse to be bound as an apprentice, "commit him into ward until he will be "bounden to serve." *s.* 35.

"And if any such master shall misuse or "evil entreat his apprentice, or the said "apprentice shall have any just cause to "complain, or the apprentice do not his "duty to his master: then the said master "or apprentice, being grieved, shall repair "unto one justice or the chief magistrate, "who shall take such order and direction "between them, as the equity of the cause "shall require, and if for want of good con- "formity in the master, the justice or ma- "gistrate cannot compound and agree the "matter between them, then they shall take "bond of the master to appear at the next "sessions, and upon his appearance at the "sessions, and hearing of the matter before "the five justices there, or four of them at "the least, (1 *qu.*) in counties; and in cities "or towns corporate before the chief magis- "trate and three others; they shall have au- "thority by writing under their hands and "seals to pronounce and declare that they "have discharged the said apprentice, and "the cause thereof, and the said writing "being so made and inrolled with the clerk "of the peace or town clerk, shall be a suf- "ficient discharge for the said apprentice; "and if the default shall be found to be in "the apprentice, then the said justices and "magistrates shall cause such due correction "and punishment to be ministered unto "him, as by their discretion shall be thought "meet." *Ibid.*

"The justices are authorized to grant war- "rants to apprehend apprentices who shall "abscond from service, and to imprison "them until they demean themselves pro- "perly." *s.* 47.

An apprentice apprehended under this act, cannot object in his defence, that he had been bound contrary to the directions of the act, and had therefore run away to avoid the indenture. *Cald.* 26.

For if the indentures be executed, contrary to the provisions of the act, they are not absolutely void, but only voidable, and the apprentice cannot, while they remain unvacated, set up a criminal act (which his absconding is) as a rightful act of avoidance; if, therefore, it should become under any circumstances necessary to avoid the *indentures* for any informality, or on the ground that the apprentice is above the age of 21, the proper course to be taken, is to sue out an *habeas corpus*, directed to the master to bring up the body of the apprentice, in order to his being discharged: in which case the court above, will take all the circumstances into consideration, and if they see fit, order the apprentice to be discharged and the indentures delivered up to be cancelled; but till then he is subject to all the covenants, into which he has entered, and all the statutes made in relation to apprentices. *Editor.*

By 20 *Geo.* 2. *c.* 19. "any two justices "may upon complaint of any parish ap- "prentice, or of any other apprentice, up- "on whose binding no larger sum than 5*l.* "was paid, summon the master and upon "satisfactory proof of ill-usage, they may "discharge the apprentice: and the justices "upon the complaint of masters against "such apprentices, and proof upon oath "may commit the offender to the house of "correction for not exceeding one calendar- "month, or may discharge such person, "but parties aggrieved, may appeal to the "next quarter general sessions."

By 6 *Geo.* 3. *c.* 25. "if any apprentice, ex- "cept such with whom 10*l.* were paid, shall "absent himself during the term, he shall "serve for so long as he shall absent him- "self, over and beyond the term of his ap- "prenticeship, unless he make satisfaction "to his master, and if he refuse, one justice "on complaint of the master (at any time "within seven years after the expiration of "the apprenticeship, *s.* 5.) may determine "the satisfaction that shall be made. If "the apprentice do not conform, the justice "may commit him to the house of correc- "tion for not exceeding three months; but "the parties grieved may appeal to the next "general or quarter sessions, giving six days "notice, but the privileges of the stanna- "ries, the chamberlain of London and the "courts in the city are saved."

The order of discharge need not be mutual; therefore if the justices order that the apprentice shall be discharged from his master, they need not discharge the master from his covenants, for where the apprentice is discharged, the other is no longer master. 5 *Mod.* 139. 2 *Salk.* 471. But the particular cause of the discharge must be stated, and appear on the face of the order. 2 *Str.* 704. *Cas. Tem. Hard.* 101. 2 *Str.* 1014.

A person after three years service, plainly appearing to be a natural ideot was discharged, and the order affirmed. *Str.* 114. but a master cannot send an apprentice away on account of his being sick, or so lame as to be unable to work, or having the king's evil to such a degree as to be incurable. 1 *Str.* 99. neither can the sessions discharge an apprentice *on general allegations* of unkind usage by the master, and the declaration of the master, that he will not take his apprentice again. 2 *Str.* 704. *Cas. Temp. Hard.* 101. But a *neglect* on the part of the master to instruct his apprentice in the mysteries of that trade he was bound to learn, is a sufficient cause of discharge. 1 *Const.* 515.

Formerly it was held that an order on the master to return money had with an apprentice was good. 2 *Barn. K. B.* 244, 296. *Sess. Cas.* 190. 1 *Const.* 515. but in the *K.* v. *Vandeleer*, it was decided that the justices cannot order monies to be returned on discharge of an apprentice. 1 *Str.* 69. Which last case is only affected in some degree by the subsequent statute of 32 *Geo.* 3. *c.* 57. *infra.*

By 43 *Eliz. c.* 2. "the churchwardens and "overseers, by the assent of two justices, "may bind poor children apprentices when "they shall see convenient, till such man-"child shall come to the age of (twenty-one "years 18 *Geo.* 3. *c.* 4) and such woman-"child also to the age of twenty-one years, "or the time of her marriage: the same to "be as effectual as if the child was of full "age, and by indenture or covenant bound "him or herself." *s.* 5.

By 21 *Jac.* 1. *c.* 28. all persons to whom the churchwardens and overseers of the poor (according to 43 *Eliz. c.* 2.) bind any poor children apprentices, may take and keep them as apprentices.

And by 8 & 9 *Will.* 3. *c.* 30. if the person to whom such poor children shall be appointed to be bound, shall refuse to receive and provide for them, and execute the other part of the indentures, on oath thereof by one of the churchwardens or overseers before two justices, he shall forfeit 10*l.* to be levied by distress, and applied, to the use of the poor of the parish, saving to the party to whom the child shall be appointed to be bound, if he think himself aggrieved thereby, his appeal to the next general or quarter sessions.

By 32 *Geo.* 3. *c.* 57. "covenants for the "maintenance of *parish apprentices*, with "whom no more than 5*l.* shall be given, "shall continue in force no longer than "three months after the death of the mas-"ter, and a proviso to this effect is to be in-"troduced in the indenture, and if omitted, "the covenants shall nevertheless continue "no longer in force." *s.* 1.

"Within three months after the death of "a master, two justices may order such ap-"prentices, to serve the residue of their "time, with the widow, husband, son, or "daughter, brother or sister, or executor or "administrator, on application by them for "that purpose." *s.* 2.

"And the said provisions, which are to take "place on the death of the original master, "are to extend to subsequent ones." *s.* 3.

"If no such application be made, or the "justices should not think fit, that the ap-"prenticeship should be continued, it shall "be at an end." *s.* 4.

"This act is to extend, to such parish ap-"prentices only, as shall be living with the "master." *s.* 5.

"And instead of bringing actions on the "covenant, two justices may order the ne-"cessary sums for maintenance and cloth-"ing of such apprentices, to be levied by "distress." *s.* 6.

"Masters may assign over parish appren-"tices, with the consent of two justices: "and the justices may discharge such ap-"prentices, whose masters cannot employ "or maintain them: but nothing herein is "to extend to any parish apprentice, with "whom more than 5*l.* shall be given." *s.* 9.

Justices discharging any apprentice, "under 20 *Geo.* 2. *c.* 19. may order his clothes "to be delivered up, and a sum not exceed-"ing 10*l.* to be paid the parish officers, for "placing him out again, and may compel "the parish officers to enter into a recogni-"zance to prosecute masters, for ill treat-"ment of apprentices." *s.* 11.

"Justices may order any master, con-"victed under the last act, when liable to "take a parish apprentice, to pay to the "parish officers a sum not exceeding 10*l.* "nor less than 5*l.* for the purpose of binding "out the child." *s.* 12.

"Masters may appeal to quarter sessions, "and on notice of such appeal, no distress is "to be made till after the quarter sessions, "and the penalty for not appearing to sup-"port the appeal is 40*s.*" *s.* 12.

"Apprentices discharged for ill behaviour, "may be sent to the house of correction, for "not exceeding three calendar months. *s.* 13.

"And all persons aggrieved may appeal "to the quarter sessions." *s.* 14.

And by 33 *Geo.* 3. *c.* 55. justices may impose fines not exceeding 40s. on masters for ill-usage of an apprentice, whether bound by the parish or otherwise, where not more than 10*l.* was paid on the binding, to be applied for the benefit of the apprentice, and levied by distress, and for want of distress to be committed for not exceeding ten days, but the party may appeal to the quarter sessions.

As by the above statute of *Eliz.* the justices of the peace have a power of imposing an apprentice on a master, of whatever trade, occupation, or profession he may be: in consequence thereof an indictment lies for disobedience to their orders, either in not receiving, or receiving and after turning off, or not providing for such apprentice; for though an act of parliament may prescribe an easier way of proceeding by complaint, yet that does not exclude the remedy by indictment. 6 *Mod.* 163. 1 *Salk.* 381.

And a person *occupying* lands in a parish, *although he reside out of it*, is compellable to receive a parish apprentice: for it is one of the modes by which the poor are to be relieved. And the words *occupier* and *inhabitant* are for this purpose synonimous. 5 *Ter. Rep.* 107. 1 *Const.* 549. 13 *Ter. Rep.* 523.

With regard to the *assigning* of apprentices, it is clear, that except in the case of a parish apprentices by the above statute 32 *Geo.* 3. *c.* 57. an apprentice is not assignable. He cannot be bound nor discharged without deed. 1 *Salk.* 68. *pl.* 7. *Mich.* 13. *W.* 3. *B. R.*

But though an apprentice is not assignable, yet if he be made a party to the assignment, a contract between him and the two masters, that he shall serve the latter may be valid. *Ed.*

And neither a parish indenture nor a common indenture, though voidable, can be avoided, except by the consent of all the parties to it. *Bur. Set. Cas.* 249.

Therefore an infant apprentice and his master, with the consent of the parish officers and two justices, may vacate the indentures. *Cald.* 126.

Parish indentures must be assented to by two justices in the presence of each other, for if it be done by them separately, or the one in the absence of the other, the indenture is void. 3 *Ter. Rep.* 380. And the justices cannot order, nor can the indentures covenant, that the master at the end of the term, shall give his apprentice two suits of cloaths, one for holidays and the other for working days or the like, for this sounds like wages, and they can only order maintenance, and not even that after the term ended. *Foley* 225. And after the master has signed the counter part of the indenture, he cannot appeal to the sessions. 1 *Const.* 555.

Whatever an apprentice gains, is for the use of his master; and whether he was legally bound or no, is not material, if he was an apprentice *de facto*. *Salk.* 68. If an apprentice marries, without the master's privity, that will not justify his turning him away, but he must sue on his covenant. 2 *Vern.* 492. By the custom of the city of *London* a freeman may turn away his apprentice for gaming. *Ibid.* 241. But if a master turns an apprentice away on account of negligence, &c. who himself has been guilty of laches, such as not inrolling the indentures, equity may decree him to refund part of the money given with him. 1 *Vern. Rep.* 460. And in the case of bankruptcy of the master, before the expiration of the term, the apprentice may have a proportion of the premium paid, deducting for the time which he has served. 1 *Atk.* 149. and an apprentice is not obliged to serve his master's executors for the remainder of his term. 2 *Vez.* 35.

Apprenticeship necessary to the exercising of a trade.] At common law every person might follow what lawful trade he pleased, which being inconvenient in many instances, and a detriment to the public, in permitting persons to exercise trades in which they had little or no skill or experience; to prevent this mischief, and the better to train up and inure persons to labour and industry from their youth, and thereby make them more skilful and expert. 11 *Co.* 53. 2 *Buls.* 191. *Skin.* 133. *Sand.* 312. It is enacted by the 5 *Eliz. c.* 4. *s.* 31. "That it shall not be lawful for any person "to set up, occupy, use, or exercise any "craft, mystery or occupation, now used or "occupied within the realm of *England* or "*Wales*, except he shall have been brought "up therein seven years, at the least, as an "apprentice; nor to set any person on "work in such mystery, art or occupation, "except he shall have been apprentice, as is "aforesaid; or else having served as an ap-"prentice, as is aforesaid, shall or will be-"come a journeyman, or hired by the year; "upon pain that every person willingly offend-"ing, or doing the contrary, shall forfeit and "lose for every default forty shillings for every "month, one half to the king and the other "half to the prosecutor.

But the resolutions of the courts have in general rather confined than extended the provision contained in this restrictive clause, for under the words *now used*, it hath been held that no trades are within the statute but such as were exercised at the time of making it. 2 *Salk.* 611. *Palm.* 528. 1 *Sid.* 175. and for trading in a country village apprenticeships are not requisite. *Carth.* 163. 1 *Vent.* 51. 2 *Keble.* 583. also the following a trade for seven years without any effectual prosecution (either as a master or a servant) is sufficient without an actual apprenticeship; for the words are, having served *as an apprentice*, and there can be no doubt but the legislature intended that the tradesman should have served an actual apprenticeship, but from the words *as an apprentice*, this being a penal statute, the judges have determined, that he serves as an apprentice, who for seven years has been working *as a master*, or as the *master's wife*. 2 *Wils.* 168. 1 *Barnard* 367. For more on the subject of apprentices, see *Williams's Justice*.

APPROPRIATION, (*appropriatio*,) from the French *approprier*, i. e. *aptare accomodare*. A parson has, during his life, the freehold in himself of the parsonage house, the glebe, the tithes, and other dues: but these are sometimes *appropriated*; *appropriation* therefore signifies the severance of a benefice ecclesiastical, (which originally and in nature is *juris divini et in patrimonio nullius*,) to the proper and perpetual use of some bishoprick, prebend, college, or other spiritual corporation, either sole or aggregate: and it is so called, because parsons, not being ordinarily accounted *domini*, but *usu fructuarii*, having no right of fee simple, are by reason of their perpetuity accounted owners of the fee simple, and therefore called *proprietarii*, 1 *Black.* 383. *Cowel. Blount.*

These appropriations could be originally made to none but to such spiritual corporation as was patron of the church, the whole being nothing else but an allowance for the patrons to retain the tithes and glebe in their own hands, without presenting any clerk, they themselves undertaking to provide for the church. *Plow.* 496, 500. 1 *Black.* 384.

Before the time of *Ric.* 2. it was lawful (as it seems) to *appropriate* the whole fruits of a benefice. But that king ordained that in every licence of *appropriation* made in chancery, it should be expressly contained, that "the diocesan of the place should provide a convenient sum of money to be yearly paid out of the fruits towards the sustenance of the poor in that parish, and that the vicar should be well and sufficiently endowed." See 15 *Ric.* 2. *c.* 6.

To make an appropriation (after licence obtained of the king in chancery) the consent of the diocesan patron and incumbent was necessary when the church was full: and it is even said the diocesan and the patron might conclude it. *Plow.* 496. And the priest of every parish in which these appropriations have been made is called *vicar quasi vice fungens rectores*. *Cowel. Blount.*

When the appropriations were thus made, the appropriators and their successors became perpetual parsons of the church, and they must sue and be sued in all matters concerning the rights of the church by the name of parsons. 1 *Black.* 385. *Hob.* 307.

Before the dissolution of the monasteries and other religious houses in the reign of *Hen.* 8. the appropriations belonging to such houses amounted to more than one third of all the parishes in England. *Seld. c.* 9. *Spelm.* 35. and these at their disssolution by the statutes 27 *Hen.* 8. *c.* 28. and 31 *Hen.* 8. *c.* 13. would by the rules of the common law have been *disappropriated*; had not a clause in those statutes intervened *to give them to the king in as ample a manner* as those houses held the same at the time of their dissolution. 1 *Black.* 386. for by the common law if the corporation which has the appropriation is dissolved, the parsonage becomes *disappropriate*: because the perpetuity of parson is gone, which is necessary to support the appropriation.

From these two roots have sprung all the lay appropriations or secular parsonages which we now see in the kingdom, they having been afterwards granted out from time to time by the crown. 1 *Black.* 386. and according to *Spelm.* on *Tithes, c.* 29. the latter are now called *impropriations*, as being improperly in the hands of laymen.

This appropriation (besides being subject to severance by the dissolution of the corporation to which it is annexed, as above mentioned) may be also severed and the church become disappropriate, if the patron or proprietor presents a clerk to the diocesan, and he institutes and inducts him to the parsonage: for that once done, the benefice returns to its former nature, the incumbent so instituted and inducted is to all intents and purposes complete parson; and the appropriation being thus severed, can never be reunited again, unless by a repetition of the original solemnities. *Fitz. N. B.* 35. *Co. Lit.* 7. 1 *Black.* 385.

APPROPRIARE COMMUNIAM, to discommon, and inclose any parcel of land, that was before open common. *Paroch. Antiq.* 336. *Cowel. Blount.*

APPROVE, (*approbare*,) to augment a thing to the utmost: to approve land is to make the best benefit of it, by increasing the rent, &c. 2 *Inst.* 474.

APPROVEMENT, (an ancient expresssion signifying the same as *improvement*,) is where the lord makes an inclosure of part of the waste for himself, leaving sufficient common with egress and regress for the commoners. *Reg. Jud.* 8, 9. And any person who is seised in fee of part of a waste, may approve besides the lord of the manor, provided he leaves a sufficiency of common for the tenants of the manor. 4 *Ter. Rep.* 445.

APPROVER or PROVER, (*approbator*) If a person indicted of treason or felony, not disabled to accuse, upon his arraignment, before any plea pleaded, and before competent judges, *confesseth the indictment*, and takes an oath to reveal all treasons and felonies that he knoweth of; and therefore prays a coroner to enter his appeal, or accusation against those that are partners in the crime contained in the indictment; such a one is an approver. 3 *Inst.* 129. *H. P. C.* 192.

This ancient course of admitting the approver thus to *appeal*, hath been long since discontinued, and the doctrine on the subject is now become a matter of more curiosity than use: it is therefore only necessary to observe, 1st, that it was entirely in the discretion of the court to suffer one to be an approver or not; 2dly, that if he failed to convict the appellee, he was to receive judgment, to be hanged upon his own confession of the indictment; and *lastly*, that all the good which could be expected to be derived from approvements, is now obtained from the admitting of accomplices to give evidence under the statutes and circumstances mentioned under the title Accomplices.

APPROVERS, *anno* 9 *H.* 6. Bailiffs of lords in their franchises are called their approvers. And in the stat. 1 *Ed.* 3. *c.* 8. Sheriffs are called the king's approvers.

APPRUARE, to take to his own use or profit. *Cowel. Blount.*

APPURTENANCES, (*pertinentia*) derived from the French *appartenir*, to belong to, signify things both corporeal and incorporeal appertaining to another thing as principal: as hamlets to a chief manor; and common of pasture, piscary, &c. Also liberties and services of tenants. *Brit. cap.* 39. Out-houses, yards, orchards, and gardens are appurtenant to a messuage. 1 *Lill. Abr.* 91. Lands cannot, in the true sense of the words *cum pertinentiis*, be appurtenant to the house. *Plowd.* 170. *Cro. El.* 704.

Therefore lands will not pass by the word appurtenances, but only such things which do properly belong to the house. *Godb.* 352. *S. C. Cro. Car.* 57. *Hutt.* 85. *Lill. Rep.* 8. *S. C.*

Grant of a manor, without the words *cum pertinentiis*, it is said, will pass all things belonging to the manor. *Owen's Rep.* 31. A turbary may be appurtenant to a house; so a seat in a church, but not to land: for the things must agree in nature and quality. 3 *Salk.* 40. *Plo. Com.* 103 *b.* 104 *b.* 170.

AQUAGE, (*aquagium, quasi aquæ agium*, i. e. *aquæductus & aquægangium,*) a watercourse. *Cowel. Blount.*

ARABANT, (*ad curiam domini*) was intended of those who held by the tenure of ploughing and tilling the lord's lands within the manor. *Cowel. Blount.*

ARACE, (*angl.*) to rase, from the French *arracher, evellere. Ibid.*

ARAHO, *in araho conjurare, i. e.* to make oath in the church, or some other holy place; for, according to the Ripuarian laws, all oaths were made in the church upon the relics of saints. *Cowel. Blount.*

ARATRUM TERRÆ, as much as can be tilled with one plough. *Aratura terræ* is the service which the tenant is to do for his lord in ploughing his land. *Cowel. Blount.*

ARBITRAMENT, (*arbitrium* or *award*, which see) is the sentence or determination pronounced by arbitrators, and published when they have heard all parties. 8 *Rep.* 98.

ARBITRATOR, is a person indifferently chosen by third persons, between whom there are any matters in dispute, to determine all such matters in controversy, according to his own judgment, whether they relate to matters of law or fact. *See title* AWARD.

ARCA CYROGRAPHICA, *sive cyrographorum judæorum*, this was a common chest with three locks and keys, kept by certain Christians and Jews, wherein all the contracts, mortgages, and obligations belonging to the Jews were kept, to prevent fraud; and this by order of K. *Rich. I. Hoveden's Annals, p.* 745. *Cowel. Blount.*

ARCHBISHOP, (*archiepiscopus*) is the chief of the clergy in his province, and is that spiritual secular person, who hath supreme power under the king in all ecclesiastical causes. An archbishop is said to be inthroned, when a bishop is said to be installed. 3 *Salk.* 72. 1 *Roll. Rep.* 328. 2 *Roll.* 440.

And archbishops have also the titles and style of *Grace* and *Most Reverend Father in God*. The bishops have *Lord and Right Reverend Father in God by divine permission.*

And at this day, the ecclesiastical state of England and Wales is divided only into two provinces or archbishopricks; to wit, Canterbury and York. Each archbishop hath within his province bishops of several dioceses. The archbishop of CANTERBURY hath under him within his province, of ancient foundations, Rochester, London, Winchester, Norfolk, Lincoln, Ely, Chichester, Salisbury, Exeter, Bath and Wells, Worcester, Coventry and Litchfield, Hereford, Landaff, St. David's, Bangor and St. Asaph; and four founded by king *Henry* 8, erected out of the ruins of dissolved monasteries, *viz.* Gloucester, Bristol, Peterborough and Oxford.—The archbishop of YORK hath under him four, *viz.* the bishop of the county palatine of Chester, newly erected by king *Henry* 8, and annexed by him to the archbishoprick of York; the county palatine of Durham, Carlisle and the isle of Man, annexed to the province of York by king *Henry* 8. but a greater number this archbishop anciently had, which time hath taken from him. *Co. Lit.* 94.

The archbishop of Canterbury is now stiled *metropolitanus & primus totius Angliæ;* and the archbishop of York styled *primus & metropolitanus Angliæ*. They are called archbishops in respect of the bishops under them; and metropolitans, because they were consecrated at first in the metropolis of the province. 4 *Inst.* 94. Both the archbishops have distinct provinces, wherein they have suffragan bishops of several dioceses, with jurisdiction under them. And each hath two concurrent jurisdictions, one as ordinary, or the bishop himself within his diocese; the other has superintendance throughout his whole province of all ecclesiastical matters, to correct and supply the defects of other bishops. The archbishop of Canterbury hath the privilege to crown all the kings of England, and to have prelates to be his officers; as for instance, the bishop of London is his provincial dean; the bishop of Winchester, his chancellor; the bishop of Lincoln, his vice-chancellor; the bishop of Salisbury, his precentor; the bishop of Worcester, his chaplain; &c. It is the right of the archbishop to call the bishops and clergy of his province to convocation, upon the king's writ: he hath a jurisdiction in cases of appeal, where there is a supposed default of justice in the ordinary; and hath a standing jurisdiction over his suffragans: he confirms the election of bishops, and afterwards consecrates them, &c. And he may appoint coadjutors to a bishop that is grown infirm. He may confer degrees of all kinds; and censure and excommunicate, suspend or depose, for any just cause, &c. 2 *Roll. Abr.* 223. And he hath power to grant dispensations in any case, formerly granted by the see of Rome, not contrary to the law of God: but if the case is new and extraordinary, the

F 2

king and his counsel are to be consulted. *Stat.* 25 *H.* 8. *c.* 21, 28. *H.* 8. *c.* 16. § 6. He may retain eight chaplains: and, during the vacancy of any see, he is guardian of the spiritualties. *Stat. ibid.* and 21 *H.* 8. *c.* 13

The archbishop of Canterbury hath the precedency of all the clergy; next to him the archbishop of York; next to him the bishop of London; next to him the bishop of Durham; next to him the bishop of Winchester; and then all the other bishops of both provinces after the seniority of their consecration; but if any of them be a privy counsellor, he shall take place next after the bishop of Durham. *Co. Lit.* 94. 1 *Ought. Ord. Jud.* 486.

The archbishop of York hath the privilege to crown the queen consort, and to be her perpetual chaplain. *Chamberlain's Present State,* 65.

The archbishop of Canterbury is the first peer of the realm, and hath precedence, not only before all the other clergy, but also (next and immediately after the blood royal) before all the nobility of the realm: and as he hath the precedence of all the nobility, so also of all the great officers of state. *God.* 13.

The archbishop of York hath the precedence over all dukes, not being of the blood royal; as also before all the great officers of state, except the lord chancellor. *God.* 14.

ARCHDEACON, (*archidiaconus*) is one that hath ecclesiastical dignity, and jurisdiction over the clergy and laity next after the bishop throughout the diocese, or in some part of it only. An archdeacon is now allowed to be an ordinary, as he hath a part of the episcopal power lodged with him. He visits his jurisdiction once every year: and he hath a court, (which he may hold in person or before a judge appointed by himself to set in his absence, who is called his official. 3 *Black.* 64.) where he may inflict penance, suspend, or excommunicate persons, prove wills, grant administrations, and hear causes ecclesiastical, &c. subject to appeal to the court of the bishop of the diocese. It is one part of the office of an archdeacon to examine candidates for holy orders, and to induct clerks within his jurisdiction, upon receipt of the bishop's mandate. 2 *Cro.* 556. 1 *Lev.* 195. *Wood's Inst.* 30. 24 *Hen.* 8. *c.* 12.

Archdeaconries are commonly given by bishops, who therefore prefer to the same by collation: but if an archdeaconry be in the gift of a layman, the patron presents, to the bishop, who institutes; and then the dean and chapter induct him, that is, after some ceremonies, place him in a stall in the cathedral church. *Wats. c.* 15.

Archdeacons, by 13 & 14 *Car.* 2. *c.* 4. are to read the Common Prayer and declare their assent thereunto, and also subscribe the same before the ordinary; but they are not obliged by 13 *Eliz. c.* 12. to subscribe and read the thirty-nine articles. *Wats. c.* 15. And they are to take the oaths as o her persons qualifying for offices.

It hath been held, that where the archdeacon hath a peculiar jurisdiction, he is totally exempt from the power of the bishop, and the bishop cannot enter there, and hold court; and in such case, if the party who lives within the peculiar be sued in the bishop's court, a prohibition shall be granted; for the statute intends that no suit shall be *per saltum*: but if the archdeacon hath not a peculiar, then the bishop and he have a concurrent jurisdiction, and the party may commence his suit either in the archdeacon's court or the bishop's, and he hath election to choose which he pleaseth: and if he commence in the bishop's court, no prohibition shall be granted; for if it should, it would confine the bishop's court to determine nothing but appeals, and render it incapable of having any causes originally commenced there. *L. Raym.* 123.

ARCHERY, a service of keeping a bow, for the use of the lord to defend his castle. *Co. Litt. sect.* 157.

ARCHES COURT, (*curia de arcubus*) The chief and most ancient consistory court belonging to the archbishop of *Canterbury* for debating of spiritual causes. It is so called from the church in *London*, commonly called *St. Mary le Bow*, (where it was formerly held) which church is named *Bow Church* from the steeple, which is raised by pillars, built *arch wise*, like so many bent bows. *Cowel.*

The judge of this court is styled the Dean of the *Arches* court: he hath extraordinary jurisdiction in all ecclesiastical causes, except what belong to the prerogative court; also all manner of appeals from bishops, or their chancellors or commissaries, deans and chapters, archdeacons, *&c.* first or last are directed hither: he hath ordinary jurisdiction throughout the whole province of *Canterbury*, in cases of appeals; so that upon any appeal made, he, without any further examination of the cause, sends out his citation to the appellee, and his inhibition to the judge from whom the appeal was made. 4 *Inst.* 337. But he cannot cite any person out of the diocese of another, unless it be on appeal, *&c.* 23 *Hen.* 8. *c.* 9.

In another sense the dean of the *arches* has a peculiar jurisdiction of thirteen parishes in *London*, called a deanery, (being exempt from the authority of the bishop of *London*) of which the parish of *Bow* is the principal. The persons concerned in this court are the judge, advocates, registers, proctors, *&c.* And the foundation of a suit in these courts is a citation for the defendant to appear; then the libel is exhibited, which contains the action, to which the defendant must answer; whereupon the suit is contested, proofs are produced, and the cause determined by the judge, upon hearing the advocates on the law and fact; when follows the sentence or decree thereupon.

This court (as also the court of peculiars, the admiralty court, the prerogative court, and the court of delegates for the most part) is now held in the hall belonging to the college of Civilians, commonly called Doctors Commons. *Floy.* 21.

From this court the appeal is to the king in Chancery; by the 25 *Hen.* 8. *c.* 19.

ARCHIVES (*archiva,* from *arca,* a chest) The *Rolls,* or any place where ancient records, charters, and evidences, belonging to the crown and kingdom, are kept; also the *Chancery, Exchequer Office, &c.* And it hath been sometimes used for repositories in libraries. *Cowel. Blount.*

ARENTARE, To rent out, or let at a certain rent. *Ibid.*

ARERIESMENT, Surprise, affrightment. *Ibid.*

ARGENTUM ALBUM, Silver coin, or pieces of bullion that anciently passed for money. *Spelm. Gloss. Cowel. Blount.*

ARGENTUM DEI, God's penny. Money given in earnest upon the making of any bargain; hence comes *arles,* earnest. *Cowel. Blount.*

Until this day, upon bargains in the north, the purchasers of cattle and the like in fairs, or elsewhere, claim from the vendors what they call God's penny. *Editor.*

ARGIL, or ARGOIL, Clay, lime, and sometimes gravel; also the lees of wine, gathered to a certain hardness. *Law Fr. Dict. Cowel. Blount.*

ARGUMENTOSUS, a word which signifies *ingenious,* mentioned by *Neubrigensis, lib.* 1. *c.* 14. *Cowel. Blount.*

ARIERBAN. The edict of the king, commanding all his tenants to come into the army: if they refuse, then to be deprived of their estates. *Ibid.*

ARIETUM LEVATIO, an old sportive exercise, supposed to be the same with running at the *quintal. Cowel.*

ARISTOCRACY, is that form of government which is lodged in *a council,* composed of select members. 1 *Black.* 49.

ARMA DARE, to dub or make a knight. The word *arma,* in these places, signifies only a sword; but sometimes a knight was made by giving him the whole armour. *Cowel. Blount.*

ARMA DEPONERE, was enjoined when a man had committed an offence. *Cowel. Blount.*

ARMA LIBERA, a sword and a lance, which were usually given to a servant when he was made free. *Leg. Will. cap.* 65.

ARMA MOLUTA, sharp weapons that cut, opposed to such as are blunt, which only break or bruise. *Bract. lib.* 3. *Cowel. Blount.*

ARMA REVERSATA, this was a punishment when a man was convicted of treason or felony. *Cowel. Blount.*

ARMIGER (*Esquire*), a title of dignity, belonging to such gentlemen that bear arms: and these are either by *courtesy,* as sons of noblemen, eldest sons of knights, *&c.* or by *creation,* such as the king's servants, *&c.* The word *armigeri* has been also applied to the higher servants in convents. *Paroch. Antiq.* 576. *Cowel.*

ARMISCARA, was an ancient mode of punishment decreed or imposed on an offender, by the judge, to carry a saddle at his back as a token of subjection. *Cowel.*

ARMS, in the understanding of law, are such things as a man wears for his defence, or takes into his hands, or useth in anger to strike or cast at another. *Crompt. Inst.* 65.

By the common law, it is an offence for persons to go or ride *armed* with dangerous and unusual weapons: but gentlemen may wear common *armour* according to their quality, *&c.* 3 *Inst.* 160, *&c.* But by Stat. 2 *Ed.* 3. *c.* 3, none shall come with *force* and *arms* before the king's justices, nor ride *armed* in an affray of the peace, on pain to forfeit their *armour,* and suffer imprisonment, *&c.*

ARMS, (*insignia,*) are also in heraldry ensigns of honour; the origin of which was to distinguish commanders in war; who being in a coat of mail, which covered their persons, could not be distinguished but by a certain badge painted on their shields, which was called their *arms.*

ARNALDIA, *arnoldia;* a sort of disease that makes the hair fall off, like the *alopecia,* or like unto a distemper in foxes. *Rog. Hoveden,* p. 693. *Cowel.*

ARNALIA, *arable grounds,* in *Domesday,* tit. *Essex.*

AROMATARIUS, (*Lat.*) a word often used for a *grocer.* 1 *Vent.* 142.

ARPEN, or *arpent,* signifies an acre or furlong of ground: and according to Domesday-book 100 perches make an *arpent. Cowel. Blount.*

ARPENTATOR, a measurer or surveyor of land. *Ibid.*

ARQUEBUSS, (Fr. *arquebuse,*) a short hand-gun, a caliver or pistol; mentioned in some of our ancient statutes. *Law Fr. Dict.*

ARRAIATIO PEDITUM, is used in *Pat.* 1. *Ed.* 2, for the *arraying* of foot-soldiers, *Cowel. Blount.*

ARRAIERS, (*arraiatores,*) officers who had the care of the soldiers *armour,* and whose business it was to see them duly accoutred. *Cowel. Blount.*

ARRAIGN, (from the *Fr. arraisonner,* i. e. *ad rationem ponere,* to call a man to answer in form of law). To *arraign* a prisoner is nothing else but to call the prisoner to the bar of the court to answer the matter charged upon him in the indictment; the mode of doing which is as follows: The prisoner is to be called to the bar by his name, and during his arraignment may stand at the bar of the court in irons, for the court has no authority to order them to be taken off till the prisoner has pleaded, and the jury are charged to try him. 4 *Black.* 322. *Leach.* 34.

When he is brought to the bar he is called upon by name to hold up his hand, which, though it may seem a trifling circumstance, yet it is of this importance, that by the holding up of the hand *constat de persona*; and he owns himself to be of that name by which he is called: however it is not an indispensable ceremony, for being calculated merely for the purpose of identifying the person, any other acknowledgment will do as well; therefore, if the prisoner obstinately and contemptuously refuses to hold up his hand, but confesses he is the person named, it is fully sufficient. 2 *Hal. P. C.* 219. *Raym.* 408.

After his *arraignment*, as above, his fetters are to be taken off, and he is to be treated with all the humanity imaginable: But the prisoner is to hold up his hand only in treason and felony. 2 *Inst.* 315.

Upon his arraignment the indictment is to be read to him distinctly, and he is then to be asked whether he be guilty of the crime whereof he stands indicted, or not; and in this stage of the proceedings against him he either *stands mute*, or *confesses the fact*, or else he pleads to the indictment. 4 *Black.* 323, 324.

ARRAY, (*arraya* sive *arraiamentum*,) an old *French* word, signifying the ranking or setting forth of a jury of men empanelled upon a cause. 18 *H.* 6. *c.* 14. And when we say to *array* a panel, that is, to set forth the men empanelled one by another. *F. N. B.* 157. To *challenge the array* of the panel is at once to except against all persons *arrayed* or empanelled, in respect of partiality, or some default in the sheriff. *Co. Lit.* 156. If the sheriff be of affinity to either of the parties, or if any one or more of the jurors are returned at the nomination of either party, or for any other partiality, the *array* shall be *quashed*.

ARRAY (*commission of*). Previous to the reigns of *H.* 8, and *Eliz.* to protect the realms from domestic insurrection and from invasion, it was usual for our princes to issue, under the authority of certain acts of parliament, (the whole of which were repealed by stat. 1 *Jac.* 1. *c.* 25. 21 *Jac.* 1. *c.* 28.) *Commissions of array*, and send into every county officers in whom they could confide, to muster and *array* (or set in military order) the inhabitants of every district; and the form of the *commission of array* was settled in parliament in the reign of 5 *Hen.* 4. so as to prevent the insertion therein of any new penal clauses. 1 *Black.* 410.

But it was provided that no man should be compelled to go out of the kingdom at any rate, nor out of his shire, but in cases of urgent necessity; nor to provide soldiers, unless by consent of parliament. *Stat.* 1 *Ed.* 3. *stat.* 2. *c.* 5, 7. 1 *Black.* 411. Afterwards about the reign of king *Hen.* 8. or some of his immediate successors, the lieutenants of counties began to be introduced, as standing representatives of the crown, to keep the counties in military order. 1 *Black.* 411.

The introduction of these *commissions of lieutenancy*, which contained in substance the same powers as the old *commissions of array*, caused the latter to fall into disuse. *Ibid.*

ARREARAGES, (*arreragia*, from the French *arriere, retro*, behind,) is money unpaid at the due time, as rent behind; the remainder due on an account, or a sum of money remaining in the hands of an accountant. *Cowel. Blount.*

ARRECTATUS, one suspected of any crime. *Spelm. Gloss.* Hence *arrected*, reckoned, or considered. 1 *Inst.* 153. b.

ARRENATUS, *arraigned*, accused. *Rot. Parl.* 21. *Ed.* 1.

ARRENTATION, (from the Spanish *arrendar*,) signifies the licensing the owner of lands in the forest to inclose them with a low hedge and small ditch, according to the assise of the forest, under a yearly rent: *saving the arrentations* is a saving power to give such licences. *Ordin. Forestæ*, 34 *Ed.* 1.

ARREST OF JUDGMENT. To move in *arrest of judgment* is to show cause why judgment should not be staid, notwithstanding the verdict given; for in many cases, though there be a verdict, no judgment can be had. And the causes of arrest of judgment are, 1st, where the declaration varies totally from the original writ; 2dly, where the verdict materially differs from the pleadings, and issue thereon, or 3dly, if the case laid in the declaration is not sufficient in point of law to found an action: and this is an invariable rule with regard to arrests of judgment upon matter of law, that *whatever is alleged in arrest of judgment must be such matter as would upon demurrer have been sufficient to overturn the action or plea*; but if a declaration or plea omits to state some particular circumstance, without proving of which at the trial, it is impossible to support the action or defence, this omission after a verdict shall be aided; for the court must conclude that after a verdict under the inspection of a judge, those circumstances were proved. 3 *Black.* 393, 394.

Four days are allowed to move in *arrest of judgment*; and the defendant hath all the term wherein the verdict was given to speak any thing to arrest it, if the plaintiff hath not given his four day rule, and signed his judgment: after which defendant is put to his writ of error. 2 *Lill.* 93.

On motion in *arrest of judgment*, if the court be divided, two judges against two, the plaintiff must have his judgment; unless a rule be made at first to stay all proceedings until the court otherwise order, &c. which rule is now always made. 2 *Lill. Abr.* 118.

Judgment may be also arrested in *criminal* cases as well as civil, if the indictment be insufficient. 3 *Inst.* 210. Therefore whenever a party appears in person, either upon a capital or inferior conviction, he may at this period offer any exceptions to the indictment in arrest or stay of judgment; as for want of sufficient certainty in setting forth either the person, the time, the place or the offence; and if the objections be valid, the whole proceedings shall be set aside; but the party may be indicted again. 4 *Black.* 374.

ARREST OF INQUEST, is to plead in arrest of taking the inquest upon the former issue, and to show cause why an inquest should not be taken. *Bro.* tit. *Repleud.*

ARREST *in civil actions.* An *arrest* is the beginning of imprisonment, where a man is first taken, and restrained of his liberty, by power of a lawful warrant, in execution of the command of some court, or officer of justice. 2 *Shep. Abr.* 299. *Wood's Inst.* 575.

And *arrests* are either in *civil* or *criminal* cases; and there is this difference between arrests in *civil* and *criminal* cases, that none shall be arrested for debt, trespass, or the like, or other cause of action, but by virtue of a precept or commandment, out of some court: but for treason, felony, or breach of the peace, any man may arrest without warrant or precept. *Terms de Ley* 54.

The arrest must be a corporal seizing or touching the defendant's body; after which the bailiff may justify breaking open the house in which he is, to take him if he escape. 3 *Bl.* 288.

When a person has committed treason or felony, doors may be broke open to arrest the offender. *Plowd.* 5 *Rep.* 91. But if a bailiff find an outer door open he may open the inner door to make an arrest. *Comber.* 327. And so also he may break open the inner door to arrest an inmate or lodger, if he gain peaceable entrance at the outer door, for the lodger's door is not to be considered as an outer door, and so protected. *Gunsel's Case, Cowp. Rep.* 1.

The bailiff's fee for an arrest in civil actions is by an ancient statute, but fourpence, and the sheriff's twenty pence: and bailiffs cannot legally take any thing but what is allowed by this statute and other subsequent acts. For taking fees not warranted by law they shall render treble damages to the party grieved, and incur a forfeiture of 40*l.* *Stat.* 23 *H.* 6. *cap.* 10. But now the master allows for arrests on mesne process, within the bills of mortality, 10*s.* 6*d.* and without, 1*l.* 1*s.* and 1*s.* per mile. *Imp. Sheriff* 122.

Every warrant to issue upon any writ to arrest any person shall have the same day and year set down thereon as on the writ, under the penalty of 10*l.* 6 *Geo.* 1. *c.* 21.

And an arrest in the *night* as well as the day is lawful. 9 *Rep.* 66.

But by *Stat.* 29 *Car.* 2. *c.* 7, no writ, process, warrant, *&c.* (except in cases of *treason, felony*, or for *breach of the peace*) shall be served on a *Sunday*, on pain that the person serving them shall be liable to the suit of the party grieved, and answer damages, as if the same had been done without writ. But a person may be retaken on a *Sunday*, where arrested the day before, *&c.* *Mod. Cas.* 231. And a man may be taken on a *Sunday* on an escape warrant: when he goes at large out of the rules of the *King's Bench* or *Fleet* prison, *&c.* *Stat.* 5 *Ann. c.* 9. Also bail may take the principal on a *Sunday*, and confine him till *Monday*, and then render him. 1 *Nels.* 258. But a party cannot be arrested on a *Sunday* on an attachment for non-performance of an award, it being only in the nature of a civil execution. 1 *Ter. Rep.* 266.

Also to restrain the abuses of gaolers and sheriffs officers in arrests it is provided by *Stat.* 32 *Geo.* 2. *c.* 28, "that the officer shall not "carry his prisoner to any tavern, alehouse, "or the like, without his consent; nor charge "him for any liquor but such as he shall "freely call for, nor demand for caption or "attendance any other than his legal fee, "nor exact any gratuity-money, nor carry "his prisoner (not being in execution) to gaol "within twenty-four hours after his arrest, "unless the prisoner refuse to go to some "safe house (not his own) of *his own choosing*: "nor shall any officer take for the diet, lodg-"ing, or expences of his prisoner, more than "shall be allowed by order of sessions. Bai-"liffs are also to show a copy of the writ to "prisoners, and permit perusal thereof; "and prisoners may send for their own vic-"tuals, bedding, and the like."

Persons privileged from arrests.] Peers of the realm — Members of parliament — Peeresses by birth — Peers of Scotland or Ireland sitting in parliament, or peeresses by marriage; but not if they afterwards intermarry with commoners; — Members of convocation actually attending thereon — Bishops, Ambassadors, or the domestic servants of an Ambassador, really and *bonâ fide* in that capacity — The king's servants — Marshal of B. R. — Warden of the Fleet — Clerks, attornies, and all other persons attending the courts of justice — Clergymen during the performance of divine service, and not merely staying in the church with a fraudulent design—Suitor's witnesses subpœna'd, and other persons necessarily attending any court of record upon business — Bankrupts coming to surrender, or within 42 days after their surrender — Witnesses properly summoned before commissioners of bankrupt, or other commissioners under the great seal, but not creditors going to prove their debts — Heirs, executors, and administrators, unless it be on their own personal contracts — Sailors and soldiers, unless the debt is 20*l.* — Members of corporations aggregate, and hundredors, cannot be arrested in their corporate capacity; nor femes covert.

By 11 & 12 *Will.* 3. *c.* 9, no person is to be held to bail in *Wales* on process out of the courts at *Westminster* for less than 20l.

By 12 *Geo.* 1. *c.* 29, and 5 *Geo.* 2. *c.* 27, made perpetual by 21 *Geo.* 2. *c.* 3, on writs out of a superior court, *where the cause of action is under* 10*l.* the defendant shall not be arrested, but only personally served with a copy of the process; and if he doth not appear at the return, the plaintiff may enter appearance for him, and proceed.

And no person shall be arrested or held to bail *where the cause of action is for* 10*l.* or upwards, unless an affidavit of the amount of debt be made and filed, and specified on the back of the writ. *Ibid.*

By 19 *Geo.* 3. *c.* 70, no person shall be arrested upon any process issuing out of inferior courts, where the cause of action doth not amount to 10*l.* but the like copy of process may be served, for 2*s.* 6*d.* and the like procedings had thereupon as directed by 12 *Geo.* 1. *c.* 29, *s.* 1.

Proceedings in inferior courts (having jurisdiction) in causes of 10*l.* or upwards, shall be the same as by the 12 *Geo.* 1. *c.* 29, are ordered in cases of 40*s.* or upwards. *s.* 2.

So much of all acts for recovery of small debts, as authorizes imprisonment of defendants for less than 10*l.* are repealed. *s.* 3.

By 43 *Geo.* 3. *c.* 46, no person shall be arrested on process of any court in *England* or *Ireland* for a cause of action not originally sufficient to require bail. *s.* 1.

Persons arrested on mesne process, instead of giving bail may deposit with the sheriff the sum indorsed on the writ, with 10*l.* to answer costs: which deposit shall be paid into court, and on the defendant's perfecting bail be repaid him: or on bail not being put in, be paid over to the plaintiff by order of the court. *s.* 2.

Wherever the plaintiff shall not recover the amount of the sum for which the defendant was held to bail (without probable cause,) defendant shall be entitled to costs under a rule of court. *s.* 3.

In actions on judgments plaintiffs are not entitled to costs unless by rule of court.

On mesne process, after return thereof, defendants in custody may in vacation justify bail before one of the judges. *s.* 6.

ARREST in *criminal cases.*] To this arrest, in all treasons, felonies, &c. all persons whatsoever are, without distinction, liable: but no man is to be arrested unless charged with such a crime as will at least justify holding him to bail when taken; and in general an arrest may be made in all criminal cases four ways: 1. by *warrant*: 2. by an officer without warrant; 3. by a private person, also without a warrant; 4. by an hue and cry (for which see title *Hue and Cry*). 4 *Black.* 289.

1. *Arrest by warrant.*] A warrant may be granted in extraordinary cases by the privy council, or secretaries of state, but ordinarily by justices of the peace; this they may do in any cases where they have a jurisdiction over the offence, in order to compel the person accused to appear before them. 2 *Hawk. P. C.* 84. And this extends to all *treasons, felonies,* and *breaches of the peace*; and also to *all such offences* as they have power to punish: for Sir *Matthew Hale*, with invincible authority, maintains, 1. That a justice of peace hath power to issue a warrant to apprehend a person accused of felony *though* not yet indicted: and, 2. That he may also issue a warrant to apprehend a person *suspected* of felony, though the original suspicion be not in himself but in the party that prays his warrant, because he is a competent judge of the probability offered to him of such suspicion. 2 *Hale P. C.* 108.

But in both cases it is fitting to examine upon oath the party requiring the warrant, as well to ascertain that there *is* a felony or other offence actually committed, without which no warrant should be granted; as also *to prove* the crime and probability of suspecting the party against whom the warrant is prayed. 2 *Hal. P. C.* 108.

This warrant ought to be under the hand and seal of the justice; should set forth the time and place of making, and the cause for which it is made; and should be directed to the constable or other peace officer (or, it may be, to any private person by name, *Salk.* 176) requiring him to bring the party either generally before any justice of the peace for the county, or only before the justice who granted it; the warrant in the latter case being called a special warrant. 2 *Hawk. P. C.* 82.

But a general warrant to apprehend all persons suspected, without naming or particularly describing any person in special, is illegal, and void for its uncertainty, for it is the duty of the magistrate, and ought not to be left to the officer, to judge of the ground of suspicion. 1 *H. P. C.* 580. 2 *Hawk. P. C.* 82.

And a warrant to apprehend all persons guilty of a crime therein specified is no legal warrant: for the point upon which its authority rests is a fact to be decided upon by a subsequent trial; namely, whether the person apprehended thereupon be really guilty or not: it is therefore in fact *no* warrant at all, for it will not justify the officer who acts under it: whereas a warrant *properly framed,* (even though the magistrate who issues it should exceed his jurisdiction) will by *stat.* 24 *Geo.* 2. *c.* 44, at all events indemnify the officer who executes the same ministerially. 4 *Black.* 290, 291.

And when a warrant is received by the officer he is bound to execute it so far as the jurisdiction of the magistrate and himself extends. *Ibid.*

A warrant from the chief or other justice of the court of king's bench *extends all over the kingdom*, and is tested or dated *England*, not any particular county. *Ibid.*

But the warrant of a justice of the peace in one county cannot be executed in *any other county* until it be backed, that is, signed by a justice of the peace in such other county, authorizing its execution there. 4 *Black.* 292, and 23 *Geo.* 2. *c.* 26. 24 *Geo.* 2. *c.* 55. and 13 *Geo.* 3. *c.* 31.

2. *Arrests by officers without warrant.*] These may be executed, 1, By a justice of the peace, who may himself apprehend, or cause to be apprehended by word of mouth only, any person committing a felony or breach of the peace in his presence. 2. The sheriff, and 3, the coroner may apprehend any felon within the county without warrant. 4. The constable also hath great original and inherent authority with regard to arrests: he may *without warrant* arrest any one for a breach of the peace *committed in his view*, and carry him before a justice of the peace. 4 *Black.* 292.

And in case of felony *actually* committed, or a dangerous wounding, whereby felony is likely to ensue, he may upon probable suspicion arrest the felon; and for that purpose is authorized (as upon a justice's warrant) to break open doors, and even to kill the felon if he cannot be otherwise taken; and if he or his assistants be killed in attempting such arrests, it is murder in all concerned. 2 *Hale P. C.* 88. 96. 5, Watchmen, *viz.* either those appointed by the *Stat.* of *Winchester*, 13 *Ed.* 1. *c.* 4, to keep watch and ward in all towns from sun-setting to sun-rising, or such as are mere assistants to the constables, may, *virtute officii*, arrest all offenders, and particularly night-walkers, and commit them to custody till the morning. *Ibid.* 98.

3. *Arrests by private persons without warrant.*] Any private person (and *a fortiori*, a peace officer,) that is present when any felony is committed, is bound by the law to arrest the felon, on pain of fine and imprisonment, if he escapes through the negligence of the by-standers. 2 *Hawk. P. C.* 74. And they may justify breaking open doors upon following such felon; and *if they kill him*, provided he cannot be otherwise taken, it is justifiable: though if *they are killed* in endeavouring to make such arrest it is murder. 2 *Hale's. P. C.* 77.

Also, where a felony has been actually committed, a private person acting with a good intention, and upon such information as amounts to a reasonable and probable ground of suspicion, is justified in apprehending the suspected person *without a warrant*, in order to carry him before a magistrate. *Cald.* 291.

But if a private person deliver another into the custody of a constable upon a suspicion, which appears afterwards to be unfounded, as to their party; the person so arrested may maintain an action of trespass for an assault and false imprisonment against such private person, although a felony may have been actually committed. 6 *Ter. Rep.* 315. And yet a peace officer upon a reasonable charge of felony may, as already mentioned, justify an arrest without a warrant, even where no felony has been committed. *Doug.* 343.

But a private person cannot justify breaking open doors to arrest upon a *reasonable suspicion*; and if either party kill the other in the attempt it will be manslaughter. 2 *Hale P. C.* 82, 83. and it is no more than manslaughter, because there is no malicious design to kill: but it amounts to so much, because it would be of most pernicious consequence, if under pretence of suspecting felony any private person might break open a house, or kill another: and also because such arrest upon suspicion is barely *permitted* by the law, and not *enjoined*, as in the case of those who are present when a felony is committed. 4 *Black.* 293.

ARRESTANDIS BONIS NE DISSIPENTUR. A writ which anciently lay for a man whose cattle or goods were taken by another, who during the contest did or was like to make them away, not being of ability to render satisfaction. *Reg. Orig.* 126.

ARRESTANDO IPSUM QUI PECUNIAM RECEPIT, &c. An ancient writ that lay for apprehending a person who had taken the king's prest-money to serve in the wars, and hid himself when he should go. *Reg. Orig.* 24.

ARRESTO FACTO SUPER BONIS MERCATORUM ALIENIGENORUM, an ancient writ that lay for a denizen against the goods of *aliens* found within this kingdom, in recompense of goods taken from him in a foreign country, after denial of restitution. *Reg. Orig.* 129. *Cowel. Blount.*

ARRETTED, *arrectatus, quasi, ad rectum vocatus*, is where a man is convened before a judge, and charged with a crime. *Staundf. Pl. Co.* 45. *Littleton*, cap. *Remitter. Bract. lib.* 3. *tract.* 2. *cap.* 10. *Cowel. Blount.*

ARROWS. By an ancient statute all heads for *arrows* shall be well brazed, and hardened at the points with steel, on pain of forfeiture and imprisonment: and to be marked with the mark of the maker. *Stat.* 7 *H.* 4. *c.* 7.

ARRURA, in the black book of *Hereford*, *De Operationibus* Arruræ, signifies days work of ploughing; for anciently customary tenants were bound to plough certain days for their lord. *Una arrura*, one day's work at the plough: and in *Wiltshire*, earing is a day's ploughing. *Paroch. Antiq.* p. 41. *Cowel. Blount.*

ARSER IN LE MAIN, burning in the hand, is the punishment of criminals that have the benefit of clergy. *Terms de Ley.*

ARSON, (from *ardeo*, to burn) is the maliciously, voluntarily, and actually burning of the house, or out-house of another man, not putting fire only into a house, or any part of it, without burning; though if part of the house is burnt; or if the fire doth burn, and then goeth out of itself, it is felony. 2 *Inst.* 188. *H. P. C.* 85. 4 *Black.* 220. and not only the bare dwelling-house, but all out-houses that are parcel thereof, though not contiguous thereto, nor under the same roof, as barns and stables, may be the subject of arson. 1 *Hale P. C.* 567.

But if a house is fired by negligence or mischance, it cannot amount to *arson.* 3 *Inst.* 67. *H. P. C.* 85.

However by 6 *Annæ*, c. 31, servants, through negligence or carelessness setting on fire any dwelling-house, or out-house, shall forfeit 100*l.* to be levied by warrant of two justices, and paid to the churchwardens of the parish, to be distributed to the sufferers by the fire, or on default shall be sent to the house of correction, and there kept to hard labour eighteen months.

Formerly great niceties and distinctions prevailed concerning what should or should not be considered as amounting to *arson*, and previous to 43 *Geo.* 3. *c.* 58. it seems to have been settled, 1st. That one seised in fee of a house standing by itself at a distance from all others, does not commit felony in burning the same. 1 *Hawk. c.* 39. *s.* 3.

2dly, That a man possessed of a house for a term of years, or being a bare tenant from year to year, was not, in wilfully burning the house of his landlord, guilty of arson. 1 *Hawk. c.* 39. *s.* 3. *Cro. Car.* 376. *Leach's Cro. Law* 217, 219, 238. *Cald.* 397.

But by 43 *Geo.* 3. *c.* 58. (*Lord Ellenborough's act*) it is now enacted that " if any " person shall wilfully, maliciously, and un- " lawfully set fire to any house, barn, gra- " nary, hop-oast, malt-house, stable, coach- " house, out-house, mill, warehouse, or " shop, whether the same shall then be *in* " *the possession of the person so setting fire* " *to the same*, or *in the possession of any other* " *person*, or *of any body corporate*, with intent " thereby to injure or defraud his majesty, or " any of his subjects, *or* any body corporate, " then the person so offending, his counsel- " lors, aiders, and abettors, knowing of and " privy to such offence, shall be *felons*, " and suffer death without benefit of cler- " gy."

For the punishment of other offences by *wilfully burning stacks of corn, ships*, &c. which do not come under the denomination of *arson*, see title Felony.

ARSURA, the trial of money by fire, after it was coined. *Cowel. Blount.*

ART AND PART, is a term used in *Scotland* and the north of *England;* when one charged with a crime, in committing the same was both a contriver of and acted his part in it. *Cowel. Blount.*

ARTHEL, a *British* word, and more truly written *arddel*, signifying to avouch; as if a man were taken with stolen goods in his hands, he was to be allowed a lawful *arthel* (or vouchee) to clear him of the felony. The privilege of *arthel* occasioning a delay and exemption of criminals from justice, provision was made against it by *Stat.* 26. *H.* 8. *c.* 6. *Cowel. Blount.*

ARTICLES of the NAVY. The method of ordering seamen in the royal fleet, and keeping up a regular discipline there, is directed by certain express rules and articles enacted by the authority of parliament: in these *articles of the navy* almost every possible offence is set down, and the punishment thereof annexed; in which respect the seamen have much the advantage over their brethren in the land-service, whose *articles of war* are not enacted by parliament, but framed from time to time at the pleasure of the crown. 1 *Black.* 420.

The acts of parliament here referred to, and by which these articles are established, are *Stat.* 22 *Geo.* 2. *c.* 33. and *stat.* 19 *Geo.* 3. *c.* 17.

The Stat. 22 *Geo.* 2. *c.* 33. contains the articles and orders following:

1. Officers are to cause public worship, according to the liturgy of the church of England, to be solemnly performed in their ships, and take care that prayers and preaching by the chaplains be performed diligently, and that the Lord's day be observed.

2. Persons guilty of profane oaths, cursing, drunkenness, uncleanness, &c. to be punished as a court martial shall think fit.

3. If any person shall give or hold intelligence to or with an enemy without leave, he shall suffer death.

4. If any letter or message from an enemy be conveyed to any in the fleet, and he shall not in twelve hours acquaint his superior officer with it, or if the superior officer, being acquainted therewith, shall not reveal it to the commander in chief, the offender shall suffer death, or such punishment as a court martial shall impose.

5. Spies and persons endeavouring to corrupt any one in the fleet, shall suffer death, or such punishment as a court martial shall impose.

6. No person shall relieve any enemy with money, victuals or ammunition, on like penalty.

7. All papers taken on board a prize shall be sent to the Court of Admiralty, &c. on penalty of forfeiting the share of the prize, and such punishment as a court martial shall impose.

8. No person shall take out of any prize any money or goods, unless for better securing the same, or for the necessary use of any of his Majesty's ships, before the prize shall be condemned; upon penalty of forfeiting his share, and such punishment as shall be imposed by a court martial.

9. No person on board a prize shall be

stripped of his cloaths, pillaged, beaten, or ill-treated, upon pain of such punishment as a court martial shall impose.

10. Every commander, who, upon signal or order of fight, or sight of any ship which it may be his duty to engage, or who, upon likelihood of engagement, shall not make necessary preparations for fight, and encourage the inferior officers and men to fight, shall suffer death, or such punishment as a court martial shall deem him to deserve. And if any person shall treacherously or cowardly yield or cry for quarter, he shall suffer death.

11. Every person who shall not obey the orders of his superior officer, in time of action, to the best of his power, shall suffer death, or such punishment as a court martial shall deem him to deserve.

12. Every person, who, in time of action, shall withdraw or keep back, or not come into the fight, or do his utmost to take or destroy any ship which it shall be his duty to engage, and to assist every ship of his Majesty or his allies, which it shall be his duty to assist, shall suffer death,—*or such punishment as a court martial shall deem him to deserve.* 19 *Geo.* 3. *c.* 17.

13. Every person, who through cowardice, &c. shall forbear to pursue the chase of any enemy, &c. or shall not assist to relieve a known friend in view, to the utmost of his power, shall suffer death,—*or such punishment as a court martial shall deem him to deserve.* 19 *Geo.* 3. *c.* 17.

14. If any person shall delay or discourage any action or service commanded, upon pretence of arrears of wages, or otherwise, he shall suffer death, or such punishment as a court martial shall deem him to deserve.

15. Every person who shall desert to the enemy, or run away with any ship, ordnance, &c. to the weakening of the service, or yield up the same cowardly or treacherously to the enemy, shall suffer death.

16. Every person who shall desert, or entice others so to do, shall suffer death, or such punishment as a court martial shall think fit. If any commanding officer shall receive a deserter, after discovering him to be such, and shall not with speed give notice to the captain of the ship to which he belongs, or if the ship is at a considerable distance, to the secretary of the Admiralty, or commander in chief, he shall be cashiered.

17. Officers and seamen of ships appointed for convoy of merchant ships, or of any other, shall diligently attend upon that charge according to their instructions; and whosoever shall not faithfully perform their duty, and defend their ships in their convoy, or refuse to fight in their defence, or run away cowardly and submit the ships in their convoy to hazard, or exact any reward for convoying any ship, or misuse the master or mariners, shall make reparation of damages, as the court of Admiralty shall adjudge; and be punished criminally by death, or other punishment, as shall be adjudged by a court martial.

18. If any officer shall receive or permit to be received on board any goods or merchandize, other than for the sole use of the ship, except gold, silver, or jewels, and except goods belonging to any ship which may be shipwrecked, or in danger thereof, in order to the preserving them for the owners, and except goods ordered to be received by the lord high Admiral, &c. he shall be cashiered, and rendered incapable of further service.

19. Any person making or endeavouring to make any mutinous assembly, shall suffer death. Any person uttering words of sedition or mutiny shall suffer death, or such punishment as a court martial shall deem him to deserve. If any officer, mariner, or soldier, in or belonging to the fleet, shall behave himself with contempt to his superior officer, being in the execution of his office, he shall be punished according to the nature of his offence by the judgment of a court martial.

20. Any person concealing any traiterous or mutinous practice or design, shall suffer death, or such punishment as a court martial shall think fit. Any person concealing any traiterous or mutinous words, or any words, practice, or design, tending to the hindrance of the service, and not forthwith revealing the same to the commanding officer, or being present at any mutiny or sedition, shall not use his utmost endeavours to suppress the same, shall be punished as a court martial shall think he deserves.

21. Any person finding cause of complaint of the unwholesomeness of victuals, or upon other just ground, shall quietly make the same known to his superior, who, as far as he is able, shall cause the same to be presently remedied; and no person upon any such or other pretence shall attempt to stir up any disturbance, upon pain of such punishment as a court martial shall think fit to inflict.

22. Any person striking any his superior officer, or drawing or offering to draw or lift up any weapon against him, being in the execution of his office, shall suffer death. And any person presuming to quarrel with any his superior officer, being in the execution of his office, or disobeying any lawful command of any his superior officer, shall suffer death or such other punishment as shall be inflicted upon him by a court martial.

23. Any person quarreling or fighting with any other person in the fleet, or using reproachful or provoking speeches or gestures shall suffer such punishment as a court martial shall impose.

24. There shall be no wasteful expence or embezzlement of any powder, shot, &c. upon penalty of such punishment as by a court martial shall be found just.

25. Every person burning or setting fire to any magazine, or store of powder, ship,

&c. or furniture thereunto belonging, not then appertaining to an enemy, shall suffer death.

26. Care is to be taken that through wilfulness or negligence no ship be stranded, run upon rocks or sands, or split or hazarded, upon pain of death, or such punishment as a court martial shall deem the offence to deserve.

27. No person shall sleep upon his watch, or negligently perform his duty, or forsake his station, upon pain of death, or such punishment as, &c.

28. Murder,

29. And buggery or sodomy, shall be punished with death.

30. Robbery shall be punished with death, or otherwise as a court martial shall find meet.

31. Every person knowingly making or signing, or commanding, counselling, or procuring the making or signing, any false muster, shall be cashiered and rendered incapable of further employment.

32. Provost marshal refusing to apprehend or receive any criminal, or suffering him to escape, shall suffer such punishment as a court martial shall deem him to deserve. And all others shall do their endeavours to detect and apprehend all offenders, upon pain of being punished by a court martial.

33. If any flag officer, captain, commander or lieutenant, shall behave in a scandalous, infamous, cruel, oppressive or fraudulent manner, unbecoming his character, he shall be dismissed.

34. Every person in actual service and full pay, guilty of mutiny, desertion, or disobedience, in any part of his Majesty's dominions on shore, when in actual service relative to the fleet, shall be liable to be tried by a court martial, and suffer the like punishment as if the offence had been committed at sea.

35. Every person in actual service and full pay, committing upon shore, in any place out of his Majesty's dominions, any crime punishable by these articles shall be liable to be tried and punished as if the crime had been committed at sea.

36. All *other crimes* not capital, not mentioned in this act, shall be punished according to the laws and customs at sea.

No person to be imprisoned for longer than two years.—Court martial not to try any offence (except the 5th, 34th, and 35th articles) not committed upon the main sea, or in great rivers beneath the bridges, or in any haven, &c. within the jurisdiction of the Admiralty, or by persons in actual service and full pay, except such persons and offences, as in 5th article;—nor to try a land officer or soldier on board a transport ship.

The lord high Admiral, &c. may grant commissions to any officer commanding in chief any fleet, &c. to call courts martial, consisting of commanders and captains. And if the commander in chief shall die or be removed, the officer next in command may call courts martial. No commander of chief in a fleet, &c. of more than five ships, shall preside at any court martial in foreign parts, but the officer next in command shall preside.

If a commander in chief shall detach any part of his fleet, &c. he may empower the chief commander of the detachment to hold courts martial during the separate service.

If five or more ships shall meet in foreign parts, the senior officer may hold courts martial and preside thereat.

Where it is improper for the officer next to the commander in chief to hold or preside at a court martial, the third officer in command may be empowered to preside at or hold a court martial.

No court martial shall consist of more than thirteen, nor less than five persons.

Where there shall not be less than three, and yet not so many as five of the degree of post captain or superior rank, the officer who is to preside may call to his assistance as many commanders under the degree of a post captain, as, together with the post captains, shall make up the number five, to hold the court martial.

After trial begun, no member of a court martial shall go on shore, until sentence, except in case of sickness, upon pain of being cashiered.

Proceedings shall not be delayed, if a sufficient number remain to compose the court, which shall sit from day to day (except Sunday) till sentence be given.

Nor shall the proceedings of courts martial be delayed by the absence of any members, if enough remain to make a court, but no members shall be absent except on some extraordinary occasion. 19 *Geo.* 3. *c.* 17. *s.* 1, 2.

The judge advocate, and all officers constituting a court martial, shall be upon oath. —Persons refusing to give evidence may be imprisoned.—Sentence of death within the narrow seas (except in case of mutiny) shall not be put in execution till a report be made to the lord high admiral, &c.—Sentence of death beyond the narrow seas, shall not be put in execution but by order of the commander in chief of the fleet, &c.—Sentence of death in any squadron, detached from the fleet, shall not be put in execution (except in case of mutiny) but by order of the commander of the fleet, or lord high admiral, &c.—And sentence of death passed in a court martial, held by the senior officer of five or more ships met in foreign parts (except in case of mutiny) shall not be put in execution but by order of the lord high admiral, &c.

The powers given by the said articles shall remain in force with respect to crews of shpis wrecked, lost, or destroyed, until they be discharged or removed into another ship, or a court martial shall be held to inquire of the causes of the loss of the ship. And if upon inquiry it shall appear, that all or any of the officers and seamen did their utmost to save the ship, and behaved obediently to their superior officers, their pay shall go on: as also shall the pay of officers and seamen taken by the enemy, having done their best to defend the ship, and behaved obediently. If any officer shall receive any goods on board, contrary to the 18th article, he shall further forfeit the value of such goods, or 500*l.* at the election of the informer; one moiety to the informer, the other to Greenwich chest.

ARTICLES of WAR. The crown, with regard to military offences, has almost an absolute legislative power; for his majesty, by the *annual mutiny act*, "may form *articles* "*of war*, and constitute courts martial, with "power to try *any crime by such articles*; "and inflict penalties by sentence or judg-"ment of the same, not extending to life or "limb, except for crimes expressly declared "to be so punishable by the act."

ARTICULI CLERI, (*articles of the clergy*) are statutes containing certain *articles* relating to the church and clergy, and causes ecclesiastical. 9 *E.* 2. *Stat.* 1. *c.* 14. 9 *E.* 3. *Stat.* 1.

ARTICULUS, an *article*, or complaint, exhibited by way of libel, in a court christian. *Cowel. Blount.*

ARTIFICERS, or workmen, are taken for such as are masters of their art, or whose calling and employment doth consist chiefly of manual labour. For the acts relating to *artificers* or workmen, see title *Manufactures.*

ARUNDINETUM, a ground or place where reeds grow. 1 *Inst.* 4.

ARVIL-SUPPER, a feast or entertainment made at funerals, in the north part of *England*: *arvil bread* is the bread delivered to the poor at funeral solemnities. *Cowel.*

ASCESTERIUM, (*archisterium, arcisterium, acisterium, alcisterium, architrium*) is a *Greek* word, and signifies a monastery. It often occurs in old histories. *Du Cange.*

ASPORTATION, the *carrying away* of goods; thus in all felonies there must not only be *a taking*, but a *carrying away*: *cepit et asportavit* was the old law Latin: and a *bare removal* from the place in which he found the goods, though the thief does not quite make off with them, is a sufficient *asportation*, or carrying away. 4 *Black.* 231.

ASSACH, or *assath*, was a custom of purgation used of old in *Wales*, by which the party accused did clear himself by the oaths of 300 men. It is mentioned in ancient *MSS.* and prevailed till the time of Henry 5. when it was abrogated. 1 *H.* 5. *c.* 6.

ASSART, (*assartum*) Fr. *assartir*, to make plain. *Manwood*, in his *Forest Laws*, says it is an offence committed in the forest, by pulling up the woods by the roots that are thickets and coverts for the deer, and making the ground plain as arable land; this is esteemed the greatest trespass that can be done in the forest, to vert or venison, as it contains in it waste and more; for whereas waste of the forest is but the felling down the coverts, which may grow up again, *assart* is a plucking them up by the roots, and utterly destroying them, so that they can never afterwards spring up again. *Manwood*, *part* 1, *p.* 171. *Cowel. Blount.*

ASSAULT (*assultus*). At this day no words whatsoever, be they ever so provoking, can amount to an assault. 1 *Hawk. P. C.* 134.

To strike a man, though he be not hurt with the blow, is an assault: and to strike at a person, notwithstanding he be neither hurt nor hit, hath been so adjudged. 22 *Lib. Ass. pl.* 60. For assault doth not always necessarily imply a hitting, or blow; because in trespass for assault and battery a man may be found guilty of the assault, and excused of the battery. 25 *Ed.* 3. *c.* 4. If a person in anger lift up or stretch forth his arm, and offer to strike another or menace any one with any staff or weapon, it is trespass and assault in law; and if a man threaten to beat another person, or lie in wait to do it, if the other is hindered in his business, and receives loss thereby, a special action on the case, laying the damages with a *per quod*, may be brought for the injury. *Lamb. lib.* 1. 22 *Ass. pl.* 60.

In many cases a man may justify an assault; thus, to lay hands gently upon another, not in anger, is no foundation of an action of trespass and assault: the defendant may justify *molliter manus imposuit* in defence of his person or goods, or of his wife, father, mother, or master; or for the maintenance of justice. *Bract.* 9 *E.* 4. 35 *H.* 6. *c.* 51.

But a master cannot justify an assault in defence of a servant. *L. Raym.* 62.

If an officer, having a warrant against one who will not suffer himself to be arrested, beat or wound him in the attempt to take him, he may justify it; so if a parent in a reasonable manner chastise his child, or master his servant, being actually in his service at that time, or a schoolmaster his scholar, or a gaoler his prisoner, or even a husband his wife (for reasonable and proper cause); or if one confine a friend who is mad, and bind and beat him in such manner as is proper in his circumstances; or if a man force a sword from one who offers to kill another; or if a man gently lays his hand on another, and thereby stay him from inciting a dog against a third person; if I beat one (without wounding him, or throwing at him a dangerous weapon) who wrongfully endeavours with violence to dispossess me of my lands or goods, or the goods of another delivered to me to be kept for him, and who *will not desist upon my laying my hands gently on him*, and disturbing him; or if a man beat, wound, or maim one who makes an assault upon his person, or that of his wife, parent, child, or master; or if a man fight with, or beat one who attempts to kill any stranger, if the beating was actually necessary to obtain the good end proposed, or rendered necessary in defence of the person so laying his hands on, by an assault from the other; in these cases it seems the party may justify the assault and battery. 1 *Hawk. P. C.* 130.

And on an indictment the party may plead Not Guilty, and give special matter in evidence; but in an action he must plead it specially. 6 *Mod.* 172.

For an assault the wrong-doer is subject both to an action at the suit of the party, wherein he shall render damages, and also to an indictment at the suit of the king, wherein he shall be fined according to the heinousness of the offence. 1 *Hawk.* 134.

But if both are depending at one time, unless in very particular cases, the attorney general will, on application, grant a *nolle prosequi*, if the party will not discontinue his action.

By 8 & 9 *W.* 3. *c.* 11, it is enacted that "where there are several defendants to any action of assault, *&c.* and one or more acquitted, the person so acquitted shall recover costs of suit, unless the judge certify that there was a reasonable cause for making such person a defendant or defendants to such action."

And where the jury who try the action shall give less damages than 40*s.* the plaintiff shall be allowed no more costs than damages, unless the judge before whom the cause is tried shall certify under his hand on the back of the record that an *actual battery* (and not an assault only) was proved. 21 *Jac.* 1. *c.* 16.

ASSAY *of weights and measures*, (from the Fr. *essay*, *i. e.* a proof or trial) is the examination of weights and measures by clerks of markets, *&c. Cowel. Blount.*

ASSAYER OF THE KING, *(assayator regis)* an officer of the king's mint, for the trial of silver; he is indifferently appointed between the master of the mint and the merchants that bring silver thither for exchange. *Cowel. Blount.*

ASSAYERS of plate made by *goldsmiths.* The *assaying* and marking gold and silver plate is regulated by statute.

ASSAYSIARE, a word used in old charters for to take fellow judges. *Cowel. Blount.*

ASSECURARE, (*adsecurare*) to make secure by pledges, or any solemn interposition of faith. *Hoveden, anno* 1174. *Cowel. Blount.*

ASSEMBLY UNLAWFUL, (from the Fr. *assembler, i e. aggregare*) to flock together. It is the meeting of three or more persons to do an unlawful act, although they do it or not: as to assault or beat any person; enter into houses, or lands, *&c. West. Symb. part.* 2. *sect.* 65. 3 *Inst* 9. See *Riots.*

ASSENT, or consent, when necessary in Law. See *Agreements, Executors, Legacies,* and other proper titles.

ASSESSORS, those that *assess* public taxes, for which see title *Taxes.*

ASSETS, (Fr. *assez*, i. e. *satis*) signifies goods and chattels in the hands of the executor or administrator sufficient or enough to discharge that burden which is cast upon the executor or administrator in satisfying the debts and legacies, so far as such goods and chattels extend. 2 *Black.* 510.

Assets by descent, or *real*, is where a man hath lands in fee simple, and dies seised thereof, the lands which come to his heir are assets *real:* and where the ancestor is bound in an obligation, such lands shall be assets, and the heir shall be charged as far as the land to him descended will extend. *Terms de Ley. Cowel. Blount.*

But by stat. 3 *Will.* and *Mar. c.* 14. "the heir is made liable to the value of the land by him sold, in action of debt brought against him by the obligee, who shall recover to the value of the said land, as if the debt was the proper debt of the heir; but the land which is sold or aliened *bona fide* before the action brought shall not be liable to execution upon a judgment recovered against the heir in any such action."

By *Stat.* 29 *Car.* 2. *c.* 3. Lands of *cestui que trust* shall be assets by descent; s. 1. and estates *pur autre vie* shall be assets in the hands of the heir, if it come to him by reason of a special occupancy, and if it be not devised, and there is no special occupant, it shall go to the executors or administrators of the party that had the estate thereof by virtue of the grant, and shall be assets in their hands. Sec. 12. And in such last case, viz. if there is no special occupant thereof, or it be not devised by 14 *Geo.* 2. *c.* 20. such estates *pur autre vie*, after payment of debts, shall be distributed in the same manner as the personal estate of the testator or intestate.

Lands by descent in ancient demesne will be assets in debt. But a copyhold estate descending to an heir is not assets: nor is any *right* to an estate assets, without possession, &c. till recovered and reduced into possession. *Danv.* 577.

An *annuity* is no assets, for it is only a *chose en action. Br. Assets per Descent, pl.* 26.

Equity of redemption of an estate mortgaged, and a term for years to attend the inheritance are assets. 3 *Leon.* 32.

ASSEWIARE, to draw or drain water from marsh grounds. *Cowel. Blount.*

ASSIDERE, or *assedare*, to tax equally. *Ibid.*

ASSIGN, (*assignare*) hath two significations, one *general*, as *to set over a right* to another, or *appoint a deputy*, *&c.* And the other *special*, to set forth or point at, as we say, to *assign error*, assign *false judgment*, *waste*, *&c.* *F. N. B* 19. 112. *Reg. Orig.* 72. *Cowel. Blount.* Also justices are said to be assigned to take assises. *Stat.* 11 *H.* 6. *c.* 2.

ASSIGNEE, (*assignatus*) one that is assigned or appointed by another to do any act, or perform any business. It also signifies one that taketh any right, title, or interest in things by assignment from an assignor. These assignees may be by deed, or in law: assignee *by deed* is when a lessee of a term sells and assigns the same to another, that other is his assignee by deed: assignee *in law* is he upon whom by law the property devolves, without any appointment of the person; thus an executor is assignee in law to the testator. *Dyer* 6.

ASSIGNMENT, (*assignatio*) is the transferring and setting over to another of some right, title, or interest.

But a possibility, right of entry, title for condition broken, a trust, or thing in action, or cause of suit, cannot be granted or assigned over. *Co. Lit.* 214.

Yet though a bond, being a chose in action, cannot be assigned over so as to enable the assignee to sue in his own name, yet he has by the assignment such a title to the paper and wax that he may keep or cancel it. *Co. Lit.* 232.

Also in equity a bond is assignable for a valuable consideration paid, and the assignee alone becomes entitled to the money; so that if the obligor, after notice of the assignment, pays the money to the obligee, he will be compelled to pay it over again. 2 *Vern.* 595.

But the assignee must take it subject to the same equity that was in the hands of the obligee. 2 *Vern.* 428.

An *office of trust* is not grantable or assignable to another; *Dyer* 7, neither can a personal trust which one man reposes in another, such as a trusteeship, executorship, or the like, be assigned over, however able such assignee may be to execute it. 1 *Bac. Abr.* tit. *As.* Nor can the full pay or the half pay of an officer in the army be assigned. 1 *Hen. Black.* 627. 4 *Ter. Rep.* 248. 3 *Ter. Rep.* 681. And by *Stat.* 1 *Geo.* 2. *st.* 2. *c.* 14. *s.* 7, all assignments of seamens wages are declared void.

Arrears of rent, and the like, as *choses in action*, are not assignable. *Skin.* 6.

ASSIMULARE, to put highways together: it is mentioned in *Leg. Hen.* 1. *c.* 8. *Cowel. Blount.*

ASSISA CADERE. This word signifies to be nonsuited; as when there is such a plain and legal insufficiency in a suit that the complainant can proceed no further on it. *Fleta, lib.* 4, *cap.* 15. *Bracton, lib.* 2, *cap.* 7. *Cowel. Blount.*

ASSISA CADIT IN JURATAM, is where a thing in controversy is so doubtful that it must necessarily be tried by a jury. *Fleta, lib.* 4. *c.* 15.

——— *in modum assisæ*, is when the defendant pleads to the assise without taking any exception to the count, declaration, or writ. *Cowel. Blount.*

ASSISA CONTINUANDA, an ancient writ directed to the justices of *assise* for continuation of a cause, when certain records alleged could not be produced in time by the party that had occasion to use them. *Reg. Orig.* 217. *Cowel. Blount.*

ASSISA PANIS ET CEREVISÆ, the power or privilege of assising or adjusting the weights and measures of bread and beer; *Cowel.*

ASSISA PROROGANDA, is a writ directed to the justices assigned to take assises for the stay of proceedings, by reason of the party's being employed in the king's business. *Reg. Orig.* 208. *Cowel. Blount.*

ASSISE (Fr. *assis*). This word is properly derived from the *Latin* verb *assideo*, to sit together; and is also taken for the court, place, or time when and where the writs or processes of assise are handled or taken. And in this signification assise is general, as when the justices go their several circuits with commission to take all assises; or special, where a special commission is granted to certain persons (formerly oftentimes done) for taking an assise upon one or two disseisins only. *Bract. lib.* 3. 1 *Inst.* 153. 3 *Black.* 185.

At this day all the counties in *England* are divided into six circuits; and the court of *Assise* and *Nisi prius* at this day in each county are composed of two judges, who are assigned by the king's special commission for every circuit, and hold their assises twice a year in every county, except *London* or *Middlesex*, where the king's courts of Nisi prius do sit in and after every term, before the chief or some other judge of the respective courts at *Westminster*. 3 *Black.* 57.

These judges upon their circuits sit by virtue of *five* several commissions. 3 *Blac.* 58.

1. The *commission of the peace*, in every county of the circuits; and all justices of the peace of the county are bound to be present at the assises; and sheriffs are also to give their attendance on the judges, or they shall be fined. *Bacon's Elem.* 15, 16, &c. 3 *Black. Com.* 58.

2. Of *oyer and terminer*, directed to them and many other gentlemen of the county, by which they are empowered to try treasons, felonies, &c. and this is the largest commission they have. *Ibid.*

3. Of *gaol delivery*, directed to the judges and the clerk of assise associate, which gives them power to try every prisoner in the gaol,

committed for any offence whatsoever, but none but prisoners in the gaol; so that one way or other they rid the gaol of all the prisoners in it. *Ibid.*

4. Of *assise*, directed to themselves only and the clerk of assise, to take assises, and do right upon writs of assise brought before them by such as are wrongfully thrust out of their lands and possessions: which writs were heretofore frequent, but now mens possessions are sooner recovered by ejectments, &c. *Ibid.*

5. Of *nisi prius*, directed to the judges and clerk of assise, by which civil causes grown to issue in the courts above, are tried in the vacation by a jury of twelve men of the county where the cause of action arises; and on return of the verdict of the jury to the court above, the judges there give judgment. *Ibid.*

In *Wales* there are but two circuits, *North* and *South Wales*; for each of which the king appoints two persons learned in the laws to be judges. *Stat.* 18 *Eliz. c.* 8.

ASSISE, *Writ of*, is a remedy which the law hath appointed for the restitution of a freehold, of which the party has been disseised, and appears to have been in the nature of a commission to put the disseisee in possession by trial at the assises. *Bac. Abr. Ass.*

The word *assise* is derived by sir *Ed. Coke*, 1 *Inst.* 153, from the Latin *assideo*, to sit together; and it signifies originally the jury who try the cause, and sit together for that purpose; and the reason, saith *Littleton*, (*Co. Lit.* 159,) why such writs at the begining were called assises was, for that in these writs the sheriff is ordered to summon a jury or assise, which is not expressed in any other original writ. *F. N. B.* 195.

This mode of proceeding is now seldom made use of except for the recovery of offices, being supplied by other actions less perplexed, and which yield a more expeditious remedy. *Bac. Abr. tit. Ass.*

It is therefore here only necessary to observe, that this remedy by writ of *assise* is only applicable to two species of injury by *ouster*, viz. *abatement*, and a recent or *novel disseisin* as follows. 3 *Black.* 185.

ASSISE of *Mort d'ancestor*. If the abatement happened upon the death of the demandant's *father* or *mother*, *brother* or *sister*, *uncle* or *aunt*, *nephew* or *niece*, the remedy is by an *assise* of *mort d'ancestor*, or the death of one's ancestor; and the general purport of this writ is, to direct the sheriff to summon a jury or assise, to view the land in question, and to recognize whether such ancestor were seised thereof on the day of his death, and whether the demandant be the next heir. *F. N. B.* 195. *Finch L.* 290. And in a short time after the judges usually come down by the king's commission to take the recognition of assise; when, if these points are found in the affirmative, the law immediately transfers the possession from the tenant to the demandant. If the abatement happened on the death of one's grandfather or grandmother, then an assise of *mort d'ancestor* no longer lies, but a writ of *ayle*, or *de avo*: if on the death of the great grandfather or great grandmother, then a writ of *besayle*, or *de proavo*; but if it mounts one degree higher, to the *tresayle* or grandfather's grandfather; or if the abatement happened upon the death of any collateral relation, other than those before mentioned, the writ is called a writ of *cosinage*, or *de consanguineo*. *Finch L.* 266, 267. And the same points shall be inquired of in all these actions *ancestrel*, as in an assise of *mort d'ancestor*, they being of the very same nature. *Stat. West.* 2. 13 *Ed.* 1. c. 20, Though they differ in this point of form, that these *ancestrel* writs, (like all other writs of *præcipe*) expressly assert the demandant's title, (*viz.* the seisin of the ancestor at his death, and his own right of inheritance) the assise asserts nothing directly, but only prays an inquiry whether those points be so. 2 *Inst.* 399. There is also another ancestrel writ, denominated a *nuper obiit*, to establish an equal division of the land in question, where on the death of an ancestor who has several heirs, one enters and holds the others out of possession. *F. N. B.* 197. *Finch L.* 293. But a man is not allowed to have any of these possessory actions for an abatement consequent on the death of any collateral relation, beyond the fourth degree. *Hale* on *F. N. B.* 221. though in the lineal ascent he may proceed *ad infinitum*. *Fitzh. Abr.* tit. *Cosinage*, 15. For the law will not pay any regard to the possession of a collateral relation, so very distant as hardly to be any at all. 3 *Black.* 185, 186.

It was always held to be law, *Bract. l.* 4. *de assis. mort antecessoris, c.* 13. *s.* 3. *F. N. B.* 196. that where lands were devisable in a man's last will by the custom of the place, there an assise of *mort d'ancestor* did not lie. For, where lands were so devisable, the right of possession could never be determined by a process which inquired only of these two points, the seisin of the ancestor, and the heirship of the demandant. And hence it might be reasonable to conclude, that when the statute of wills, 32 *Hen.* 8. *c.* 1, made all socage lands devisable, an assise of *mort d'ancestor* no longer could be brought of lands held in socage; (see 1 *Leon.* 267.) and that now, since the statute 12 *Car.* 2. *c.* 24, which converts all tenures, a few only excepted, into free and common socage, it should follow, that no assise of *mort d'ancestor* can be brought of any lands in the kingdom; but in case of abatements recourse must be properly had to the more ancient writs of entry.

ASSISE *of novel disseisin*, is so called because the justices *in eyre* went their circuits from seven years to seven years; and no assise was allowed before them, which commenced before the last circuit, which was called an *ancient* assise: and that which was upon a *disseisin* since the last circuit, an assise of *novel disseisin*. *Co. Lit.* 153. *b*.

This ASSISE of *novel disseisin* is an action of the same nature with the assise of *mort d'ancestor* before mentioned, in that herein the demandant's possession must be shown. But it differs considerably in other points, particularly in that it recites a complaint by the demandant of the disseisin committed, in terms of direct averment; whereupon the sheriff is commanded to reseise the land and all the chattels thereon, and keep the same in his custody till the arrival of the justices of assise (which, since the introduction of giving damages, as well as the possession, is now omitted). *Booth.* 262. And in the mean time to summon a jury to view the premises, and make recognition of the assise before the justices. *F. N. B.* 177. And if, upon the trial the demandant can prove, first, a title, next, his actual seisin in consequence thereof; and, lastly, his disseisin by the present tenant; he shall have judgment to recover his seisin, and damages for the injury sustained. 3 *Black.* 187.

The first process in this action is an original writ issued out of chancery, directed to the sheriff, commanding him to return a jury, who are called the recognitors of the assise. An assise is to be arraigned on the day the writ is returnable, on which day the defendant is to count, and the tenant is to appear and plead instantly, unless the court thinks proper to allow him an imparlance, which it is said cannot be without showing good cause. *Style's Reg.* 88.

But by 32 *Hen.* 8. *c.* 2, no manner of person shall sue, have, or maintain any assise of *mort d'ancestor*, *cosinage*, *ayle*, writ of entry upon disseisin done to any of his ancestors, or any other *action possessory* upon the possession of any of his ancestors, but only of the seisin of the ancestor within *fifty years* next before the teste of the writ. *s.* 2. Nor shall any person sue any action of or upon his own seisin or possession above *thirty* years next before the teste of the original writ. *s.* 3.

The process of assises in general is called by statute *West.* 2. 13 *Ed.* 1. *c.* 24, *festinum remedium*, in comparison of that by a writ of entry, in not admitting of many dilatory pleas and proceedings, to which other real actions are subject. *Booth.* 262. Costs and damages were annexed to these possessory actions by the statute of *Gloucester*, 6 *Ed.* 1. *c.* 1, before which the tenant in possession was allowed to retain the intermediate profits of the land to enable him to perform the feudal burdens incident thereunto. And, to prevent frequent and vexatious disseisins, it is enacted by the statute of *Merton*, 20 *H.* 3. *c.* 3, that if a person disseised recover seisin of the land again by assise of *novel disseisin*, and be again disseised of the same tenements by the same disseisor, he shall have a writ of *re-disseisin*; and, if he recover therein, the re-disseisor shall be imprisoned; and, by the statute of *Marlbridge*, 52 *Hen.* 3. *c.* 8, shall also pay a fine to the king. And by stat. *Westminster* 2. 13 *Ed.* 1. *c.* 25. In this suit, if the defendant fail to make good the exception which he pleads, he shall be adjudged a disseisor, without taking the assise; and shall pay the plaintiff double damages, and be imprisoned a year.

In like manner, by the same statute of *Merton*, when any lands or tenements are recovered by assise of *mort d'ancestor*, or other jury, or any judgment of the court, if the party be afterwards disseised by the same person against whom judgment was obtained, he shall have a writ of *post-disseisin* against him, which subjects the post-disseisor to the same penalties as a re-disseisor. The reason of all which, as given by sir Edward Coke, 2 *Inst.* 83, 84. *lib.* 4. *c.* 49, is because such proceeding is a contempt of the king's courts, and in despite of the law. See also *Bracton*, *lib.* 4. *c.* 49. 3 *Black.* 187, 188.

ASSISE OF THE FOREST, (*assisa de foresta*) is a statute touching orders to be observed in the king's forest. *Manwood* 35.

ASSISE also signifies an ordinance or statute of *assise*, setting down and appointing a certain measure, rate, or order for the things they concern, as the *stat. de assisa panis et cerevisa*, and other ancient statutes.

ASSISORS, (*assisores*) *Sunt qui assisas condunt aut taxationes imponunt.*—In Scotland (according to *Skene*) they are the same with our jurors. *Cowel. Blount.*

ASSISUS, rented or farmed out for such an assise, or certain assessed rent in money or provisions. *Cowel. Blount.*

ASSITHMENT, a weregeld, or compensation, by a pecuniary mulct: from the preposition *ad*, and the Sax. *sithe*, *vice*: *quod vice supplicii ad expiandum delictum solvitur. Cowel. Blount.*

ASSOCIATION, (*associatio*) is a writ or patent sent by the king, either at his own motion, or at the suit of a party plaintiff, to the justices appointed to take assises, or of *oyer* and *terminer*, &c. to have others *associated* unto them. And this is usual where a justice of assise dies: and a writ is issued to the justices alive to admit the person associated: also where a justice is disabled this is practised. *F. N. B.* 185. *Reg. Orig.* 201. 206. 223. The clerk of the assise is usually associate of course; in other cases some learned serjeants at law are appointed. *Br. Assis.* 386. *Mich.* 32 *H.* 6.

ASSOILE, (*absolvere*) to deliver from excommunication. *Staundf. Pl. Cr.* 72.

ASSUMPSIT, (from the Lat. *assumo*) is taken for a promise, by which a man assumes or takes upon him to perform or pay any thing to another: and it comprehends any verbal promise, made upon consideration. *Terms de Ley*.

And the law gives an action of *assumpsit* to a party injured by the breach or non-performance of a contract legally entered into: it is founded on a contract either express or implied by law, and gives the party damages in proportion to the loss he has sustained by the violation of the contract. 1 *Bac. Abr. tit. Ass.*

And in every action upon assumpsit there ought to be a valuable and meritorious, and not an idle or insignificant consideration, promise, and breach of promise. 1 *Leon.* 405. *Dyer* 336. 2 *Bulst.* 269.

But the law distinguishes between a general *indebitatus assumpsit*, and a *special assumpsit*: for though they come under the denomination of actions on the case, and the party is to be recompensed in damages alike in both, yet the first seems to be of a superior nature, and where debt will lie; for an action of assumpsit will lie in many cases where debt lies, and in many where it does not lie; but for a particular undertaking, or collateral promise to discharge the debt or duty of another, a special *assumpsit* must be brought. *Salk.* 23. 6 *Mod.* 128. 4 *Co.* 92. 2 *Bur.* 1008.

And a promise, according to sir William Blackstone, is in the nature of a verbal covenant, and wants nothing but the solemnity of writing and sealing to make it absolutely the same. If therefore it be to do any explicit act, it is an express contract, as much as any covenant; and the breach of it is an equal injury. The remedy indeed is not exactly the same: since, instead of an action of covenant, there only lies an action upon the case, for what is called the *assumpsit*, or undertaking of the defendant; the failure of performing which is the wrong or injury done to the plaintiff, the damages whereof a jury are to estimate and settle. Thus if a builder promises, undertakes, or assumes to C. that he will build and cover his house within a time limited, and fails to do it, C. has an action on the case against the builder, for this breach of his express promise, undertaking, or *assumpsit*; and shall recover a pecuniary satisfaction for the injury sustained by such delay. So also in the case before mentioned, of a debt by simple contract, if the debtor promises to pay it and does not, this breach of promise entitles the creditor to his action on the case, instead of being driven to an action of debt. Thus, likewise, a promissory note, or note of hand not under seal, to pay money at a day certain, is an express *assumpsit*; and the payee at common law, or by custom and act of parliament the indorsee, may recover the value of the note in damages, if it remains unpaid. Some agreements indeed, though ever so expressly made, are deemed of so important a nature, that they ought not to rest on verbal promise only, which cannot be proved but by the memory (which sometimes will induce the perjury) of witnesses.

To prevent which, the statute of frauds and perjuries, 29 Car. 2. c. 3, enacts, that in the five following cases no verbal promise shall be sufficient to ground an action upon, but at the least some note or memorandum of it shall be made in writing, and signed by the party to be charged therewith: 1. Where an executor or administrator promises to answer damages out of his own estate. 2. Where a man undertakes to answer for the debt, default, or miscarriage of another. 3. Where any agreement is made upon consideration of marriage. 4. Where any contract or sale is made of lands, tenements, or hereditaments, or any interest therein. 5. And, lastly, Where there is any agreement that is not to be performed within a year from the making thereof. In all these cases a mere verbal assumpsit is void. 3 *Black.* 157, 158.

Besides these express contracts there are others that are only implied by law.

This class of *implied contracts* are such as do not arise from the express determination of any court, or the positive direction of any statute, but from natural reason, and the just construction of law: which class extends to all presumptive undertakings or assumpsits, which, though never perhaps actually made, yet constantly arise from this general implication and intendment of the courts of judicature, that every man hath engaged to perform what his duty or justice requires. 3 *Black.* 161.

1. Thus if I employ a person to transact any business for me, or perform any work, the law implies that I undertook, or assumed to pay him so much as his labour deserved. And if I neglect to make him amends he has a remedy for this injury, by bringing his action on the case upon this implied assumpsit, wherein he is at liberty to suggest that I promised to pay him so much as he reasonably deserved, and then to aver that his trouble was really worth such a particular sum, which the defendant has omitted to pay. But this valuation of his trouble is submitted to the determination of a jury, who will assess such a sum in damages as they think he really merited. This is called an *assumpsit* on a *quantum meruit*. *Ibid.*

2. There is also an implied assumpsit on a *quantum valebant*, which is very similar to the former, being only where one takes up goods or wares of a tradesman without expressly agreeing for the price. There the law concludes that both parties did intentionally agree that the real value of the goods should be paid; and an action on the case may be brought accordingly, if the vendee refuses to pay that value. *Ibid.*

3. A third species of implied assumpsits is when one has had and received money

belonging to another, without any valuable consideration given on the receiver's part; for the law construes this to be money had and received for the use of the owner only; and implies, that the person so receiving promised and undertook to account for it to the true proprietor. And if he unjustly detains it, an action on the case lies against him for the breach of such implied promise and undertaking: and he will be made to repay the owner in damages equivalent to what he has detained in such violation of his promise. This is a very extensive and beneficial remedy, applicable to almost every case where the defendant has received money, which *ex æquo et bono* he ought to refund. It lies for money paid by mistake, or on a consideration which happens to fail, or through imposition, extortion, or oppression, or where undue advantage is taken of the plaintiff's situation. 4 *Burr.* 1012. 3 *Black.* 162.

4. Where a person has laid out and expended his own money for the use of another, at his request, the law implies a promise of repayment, and an action will lie on this assumpsit. *Cart.* 446. 2 *Keb.* 99. 3 *Black.* 162.

5. Likewise, fifthly, upon a stated account between two merchants, or other persons, the law implies that he against whom the balance appears has engaged to pay it to the other, though there be not any actual promise. And from this implication it is frequent for actions on the case to be brought, declaring that the plaintiff and defendant had settled their accounts together, *insimul computassent*, (which gives name to this species of assumpsit) and that the defendant engaged to pay the plaintiff the balance, but has since neglected to do it. But if no account has been made up, then the legal remedy is by bringing a writ of *account de computo*, *F. N. B.* 116. (for which see title ACCOMPT) commanding the defendant to render a just account to the plaintiff, or show the court good cause to the contrary. 3 *Black.* 162.

ASSUMPTION, the day of the death of a saint, so called, *Quia ejus anima in cœlum assumitur.* *Du Cange.* *Cowel.*

ASSURANCE, the legal evidences of the translation of property are called *the common assurances* of the kingdom; whereby every man's estate is assured to him, and all controversies, doubts, and difficulties, are either prevented or removed. 2 *Black.* 294.

There is also an *assurance* of ships, goods, and merchandise, for which see *Insurance.*

ASTER, and *Homo Aster,* a man that is resident. *Britton.* 151.

ASTRARIUS HÆRES, (from *Astre,* the hearth of a chimney) is where the ancestor by conveyance hath set his heir apparent and his family in a house in his life-time. *Co. Lit.* 8. *Cowel.* *Blount.*

ASTRUM, a house, or place of habitation, also from *astre.* *Ibid.*

ATHEGAR, a weapon among the Saxons, which seems to have been a hand-dart, from the Sax. *aeton,* to fling, or throw, and *gar,* a weapon. *Spelm.* *Cowel.*

ATH, ATHA, ATHE, an oath. *Cowel. Blount.*

ATHES, ADAA, a power or privilege of exacting and administering an oath in some cases of right and property; from the Sax. *ath, othe, juramentum.* *Cowel.* *Blount.*

ATIA, see *odio & atia,* an ancient writ of inquiry whether a person be committed to prison on just cause of suspicion. *Cowel. Blount.*

ATILIA, utensils or country implements. *Cowel.* *Blount.*

ATRIUM, signifies a court before the house, and sometimes a church-yard. *Ibid.*

ATTACH, (*attachiare,* from the French *attacher*) signifies to take or apprehend by commandment of a writ or precept. *Lamb. Eiren. lib.* 1. *cap.* 16. It differs from arrest, in that he who arresteth a man carrieth him to a person of higher power to be forthwith disposed of, but he that attacheth keepeth the party attached, and presents him in court at the day assigned. Another difference there is, that arrest is only upon the body of a man, whereas an attachment is oftentimes upon his goods. *Kitch.* 279.

ATTACHIAMENTA *bonorum,* a distress formerly taken upon goods or chattels, which was sued for personal estate, or debt, by the legal attachiators, or bailiffs, as security to answer an action. *Cowel.* *Blount.*

——— *de spinis et boscis* a privilege granted to the officers of a forest to take to their own use thorns, brush, and windfalls, within their precincts. *Ibid.*

ATTACHMENT, (from *attach*) is a process that issues at the discretion of the judges of a court of record against a person for some contempt, for which he is to be committed, and may be awarded by them upon a bare suggestion, or on their own knowledge, without any appeal, indictment or information; for though by the statute of *Magna Charta* none are to be imprisoned *sine judicio parium vel per legem terræ,* yet this summary method of proceeding being absolutely necessary to the furtherance and execution of justice, seems to have been long practised, and is certainly now established as part of the law of the land. *Lamb. Eiren. lib.* 1. *c.* 16. 1 *Bac. Abr.*

If any contempt arise in the face of the court, as by rude and contumelious behaviour, by obstinacy, perverseness, or prevarication, by breach of the peace, or any wilful disturbance whatsoever, the commitment is by rule of court, not on process, unless the party escape out of court before he is secured. *Jacob, tit. Attachment.* 4 *Black.* 285.

All courts of record have a discretionary power over their own officers, and are to see that no abuses be committed by them which may bring disgrace on the courts themselves;

therefore if a sheriff or other officer shall be guilty of a corrupt practice in not serving a writ, as if he refuse to do it unless paid an unreasonable gratuity from the plaintiff, or receive a bribe from the defendant, or give him notice to remove his person or effects, in order to prevent the service of any writ, the court which awarded it may punish such offences in such manner as shall seem proper by attachment. *Dyer* 218 2 *Hawk. P. C.* 142. 1 *Bac. Abr. tit. Attachment.*

But if there be no palpable corruption, nor extraordinary circumstance of wilful negligence or obstinacy, the judgment whereof is to be left to the discretion of the court, it seems not usual to proceed in this manner, but to leave the party to his ordinary remedy against the sheriff, either by action, or by rule to return the writ, or by an *alias* and *pluries*, which if he have no excuse for not executing, an attachment goes of course. *Hob.* 62. 264. *Noy* 101. *F. N. B.* 38. *Finch* 237. 5 *Mod.* 314, 315.

Abuses committed by attornies and solicitors, who are also officers of the respective courts, by gross instances of fraud and corruption, injustice to their clients, or other dishonest practice, may be punished by attachment. 4 *Black.* 283.

Those committed by jurymen in collateral matters relating to the discharge of their office, such as making default when summoned, eating or drinking without the leave of the court, and especially at the cost of either party, and other misbehaviour, or irregularities of a similar kind; but not in the mere exercise of their judicial capacities, as by giving a false or erroneous verdict, may be punished by attachment. 4 *Black.* 284.

Those committed by witnesses; by making default when summoned, refusing to be sworn or examined, or prevaricating in their evidence when sworn, may likewise be punished by attachment. 4 *Black.* 284.

For contempts against the king's writs, using them in a vexatious manner, altering the teste, or filling them up after sealed, &c. attachment lies. And for contempts of an enormous kind, in not obeying writs, &c. attachment may be issued against peers. 2 *Hawk.* 152, 153. For persuading jurors not to appear on a trial, attachment lies against the party for obstructing the proceedings of the court. 1 *Lill.* 121. The court of B. R. may award attachments against any inferior courts usurping a jurisdiction, or acting contrary to justice; as for proceeding after a *habeas corpus* issued, and a *supersedeas* to stay proceedings. And attachments may be granted against justices of peace for proceeding on an indictment after a *certiorari* delivered to them to remove the indictment. 1 *Lill.* 121. *Salk.* 207. So attachment lies against a lord that refuses to hold his court, after a writ issued to him for that purpose, so that his tenant cannot have right done him. *New Nat. Br.* 6. 27.

An attachment is also the proper remedy for disobedience to the rules of court; as of those made in ejectment and arbitrament. So where a defendant in account, being adjudged to account before the auditors, refuses to do it unless they will allow matter disallowed by the court before, or where one refuses to pay costs taxed by the master, whose taxation the law looks upon as a taxation by the court. 1 *Mod.* 21. 1 *Salk.* 71.

But an attachment is not granted for disobedience of a rule of *Nisi prius*, unless it be first made a rule of court; nor for disobedience of a rule made by a judge at his chamber, unless it be entered; nor for disobedience of any rule without personal service. 1 *Salk.* 84.

Also an attachment is proper for abuses of the process of the court; as for suing out execution where there is no judgment, bringing an appeal for the death of one known to be alive, making use of the process of a superior court, as a stale to bring a defendant within the jurisdiction of an inferior court, and then dropping it, using such process in a vexatious, oppressive, or unjust manner, without colour of serving any other end by it. 2 *Hawk. P. C.* 154.

Attachments for contempts (not committed in the face of the court) are usually granted on a rule to show cause, unless the offence complained of be of a flagrant nature, and positively sworn to; in which last case the party is ordered to attend, which he must do in person, as must every one against whom an attachment is granted; and if he shall appear to be apparently guilty, the court in discretion, on consideration of the nature of the crime, and other circumstances, will either commit him immediately, in order to answer interrogatories to be exhibited against him concerning the contempt complained of, or will suffer him to enter into recognizance to answer such interrogatories; which if they be not exhibited within four days, the party may move to have the rocognizance discharged; otherwise he must answer them, though exhibited after the four days; but in all cases, if he fully answer them, he shall be discharged as to the attachment, and the prosecutor shall be left to proceed against him for the perjury, if he thinks fit; but if he deny part of the contempts only, and confess other part, he shall not be discharged as to those denied, but the truth of them shall be examined, and such punishment inflicted as from the whole shall appear reasonable; and if his answer be evasive as to any material part, he shall be punished in the same manner as if he had confessed it. 2 *Hawk. P. C.* 141. 1 *Salk.* 84. 6 *Mod.* 73. 2 *Jones* 178.

Attachment in *courts of equity*, see *Chancery*, and other proper titles.

ATTACHMENT, *foreign*, is an attachment of the goods of foreigners found in some liberty, to satisfy their creditors within such liberty. *Carth. Rep.* 66. And by the custom of London, and some other places, a man may attach money or goods in the hands of a stranger, if there be no suit depending in any of the courts at Westminster concerning the same. *Cro. Eliz.* 691.

Foreign attachments in London upon plaint of debt are made after this manner, either in the court of the mayor or sheriff: *A.* oweth *B.* 100*l.* and *C.* is indebted to *A.* 100*l.* *B.* enters an action against *A.* of 200*l.* and by virtue of that action a serjeant *attacheth* 100*l.* in the hands of *C.* as the money of *A.* to the use of *B.* which is returned upon that action. The attachment being made, and returned by the serjeant, the plaintiff is immediately to fee an attorney, before the next court holden, or the defendant may then put in bail to the attachment, and nonsuit the plaintiff: four court days must pass before the plaintiff can cause *C.* the garnishee, in whose hands the money was attached, to show cause why *B.* should not condemn the 100*l.* attached in the hands of *C.* as the money of *A.* the defendant in the action (though not in the attachment) to the use of *B.* the plaintiff: and the garnishee *C.* may appear in court by his attorney, wage his law, and plead that he hath no money in his hands of the defendant's, or other special matter; but the plaintiff may hinder his waging of law, by producing two sufficient citizens to swear that the garnishee had either money or goods in his hands of *A.* at the time of the attachment, of which affidavit is to be made before the lord mayor, and being filed may be pleaded by way of estoppel: then the plaintiff must put in bail, that if the defendant come within a year and a day into court, and he can discharge himself of the money condemned in court, and that he owed nothing to the plaintiff at the time in the plaint mentioned, the said money shall be forthcoming, &c. if the garnishee fail to appear by his attorney, being warned by the officer to come into court to show cause as aforesaid, he is taken by default for want of appearing, and judgment given against him for the goods and money attached in his hands, and he is without remedy, either at common law, or in equity; for if taken in execution he must pay the money condemned, though he hath not one penny, or go to prison; but the garnishee appearing to show cause why the money or goods attached in his hands ought not to be condemned to the use of the plaintiff, having feed an attorney, may plead as aforesaid, that he hath no money or goods in his hands of the parties against whom the attachment is made, and it will then be tried by a jury, and judgment awarded, &c. but after trial, bail may be put in, whereby the attachment shall be dissolved, but the garnishee, &c. and his security will then be liable to what debt the plaintiff shall make out to be due upon the action: and an attachment is never thoroughly perfected till there is a bail, and satisfaction upon record. *Privileg. Lond.* *Comyns' Dig.* tit. *Attachment.*

ATTACHMENT, *Court of.* This is one of the courts held in the king's forests. *Manwood* 90, 99. For which see *Forests.*

Attachment, *privilege of.* See *Attornies.*

ATTAINDER. (*attincta* and *attinctura.*) When sentence is passed on a man who hath committed treason or felony, the immediate inseparable consequence from the common law is *attainder.* 4 *Black.* 380.

For when it is now clear beyond all dispute that the criminal is no longer fit to live upon earth, but is to be exterminated as a monster and a bane to human society, the law sets a note of infamy upon him, puts him out of its protection, and takes no further care of him than barely to see him executed. He is then called *attaint*, *attinctus*, stained or blackened. 4 *Black.* 380.

This is *after judgment and sentence pronounced*, for there is a great difference between a man *convicted* and attainted, though they are frequently through inaccuracy confounded together. *Ibid.*

After *conviction* only, a man is liable to none of these disabilities: for there is still in contemplation of law a possibility of his innocence: something may be offered in arrest of judgment: the indictment may be erroneous, which will render his guilt uncertain, and thereupon the present conviction may be quashed: he may obtain a pardon, or be allowed the benefit of clergy. both which, suppose some latent sparks of merit, which plead in extenuation of his fault. *Ibid.*

But *when judgment is once pronounced*, both law and fact conspire to prove him completely guilty, and there is not the remotest possibility left of any thing to be said in his favour. *Ibid.*

Upon judgment therefore of death, and not before, the attainder of a criminal commences: or upon such circumstances as are equivalent to judgment of death, as judgment of outlawry on a capital crime pronounced for absconding or flying from justice, which tacitly confesses the guilt: and therefore *either upon judgment of outlawry, or of death for treason or felony*, a man shall be said to be *attainted.* 4 *Black.* 380.

The consequences of *attainder* are *forfeiture* and corruption of blood. 4 *Black.* 381. For which see titles *Forfeitures* and *Corruption* of Blood.

Attainder, *Acts of.*] Also persons may be attainted by act of parliament. Acts of attainder of criminals have been passed in several reigns, on the discovery of plots and rebellions, from the reign of king Charles II. when an act was made for the attainder of several persons guilty of the murder of king Charles I. to this time; among which, that for attainting Sir John Fenwick, for conspiring against king William, is the most remarkable; it being made to attaint and convict him of high treason on the oath of one witness, just after a law had been enacted, that no person should be tried or attainted of high treason where corruption of blood is incurred, but by the oath of two lawful witnesses, unless the party confess, stand mute, &c. *Stat.* 7 & 8 *W.* 3. *cap.* 3. But in the case of Sir John Fenwick there was something extraordinary; for he was indicted of treason, on the oaths of two witnesses; though but one only could be produced against him on his trial. It was pretended Sir John had tampered with and prevailed on one of the witnesses to withdraw.

The 8 *W.* 3. *c.* 5. also required Sir George Barclay, major general Holmes, and other persons to surrender themselves to the lord chief justice, or secretaries of state; or to be attainted. By the 13 *W.* 3. *c.* 3. the pretended Prince of Wales was under attainder of treason, &c. And by 1 *Geo.* 1. *c.* 16. the late Duke of Ormond and others are attainted. And besides these acts of attainder, we have had bills for inflicting pains and penalties, as those against the late bishop of Rochester, &c. *Stat.* 9. *Geo.* 1. *c.* 17. See *Evidence.*

ATTAINT, (*attincta*) is a writ that lieth after judgment in any court of record, in an action real or personal, (where the debt or damages amount to above 40*s.* *Stat.* 5 & 34 *Ed.* 3. *c.* 7.) to inquire whether the jury gave a false verdict: that so, the judgment following thereupon may be reversed: and this must be brought in the life-time of him for whom the verdict was given, and of two at least of the juries who gave it. *Finch. L.* 484. 3 *Black.* 402.

This lay, at the common law, only upon verdicts in actions for such personal injuries as did not amount to *trespass:* for in *real wrongs,* the party injured had redress by writ of right; but after verdict against him in *personal suits,* he had no other remedy; and it did not lie in actions of *trespass* for a very extraordinary reason; because if the verdict was set aside, the king would lose his fine. *Bro. Abr. tit. Att.* But by stat. *Westm.* 1. 3 *Ed.* 1. *c.* 38. it was given in all pleas of land, franchise, or freehold, and by several subsequently in the reign of *Ed.* 3. viz. 1 *Ed.* 3. *c.* 6. 5 *Ed.* 3. *c.* 7. 28 *Ed.* 3. *c.* 8. 34 *Ed.* 3. *c.* 7. and 9 *Ric.* 2. *c.* 3, it was allowed in almost every action, except in a writ of right, for there no attaint lay, either by common law or statute, because it was determined by the grand assise, consisting of *sixteen* jurors. *Bro. Abr. Att.* 42. 3 *Black. Com.* 403.

The jury who are to try this false verdict must be twenty-four, and are called the grand jury; for the law wills not that the oath of one jury of twelve men should be *attainted,* or set aside by an equal number, nor by less indeed than double the former. 3 *Black.* 403.

He that brings the attaint can give no other evidence to the grand jury than what was originally given to the petit; for as their verdict is now trying, and the question is whether or no they did right upon the evidence that appeared to them, the law judged it the highest absurdity to produce any subsequent proof upon such trial, and to condemn the prior jurisdiction for not believing evidence which they never heard: but those against whom it is brought are allowed in affirmance of the first verdict to produce new matter; *Finch L.* 486, because the petit jury may have formed their verdict upon evidence of their own knowledge, which never appeared in court; and because very terrible was the judgment which the common law inflicted upon them if the jury found the verdict a false one. 3 *Black.* 403.

The judgment was, 1. That *they should lose their liberam legem, and become for ever infamous.* 2. That *they should forfeit all their goods and chattels.* 3. That *their lands and tenements should be seized into the king's hands.* 4. That *their wives and children should be thrown out of doors.* 5. That *their houses should be rased and thrown down.* 6. That *their trees should be rooted up.* 7. That *their meadows should be ploughed.* 8. That *their bodies should be cast into gaol.* 9. That *the party should be restored to all that he lost by reason of the unjust verdict.* *Glanv. lib.* 2. 3 *Black.* 403.

But as the severity of this *common law* punishment had the effect of preventing the law from being executed, therefore by *Stat.* 11 *Hen.* 7. *c.* 24, revived by 23 *Hen.* 8. *c.* 3, a more moderate punishment was inflicted upon attainted jurors, viz. *perpetual infamy;* and if the cause of action were above 40*l.* value *a forfeiture of* 20*l. a-piece by the jurors,* or if under 40*l. then* 5*l. a-piece, to be divided between the king and the party injured.* So that a man may now bring an attaint either upon the statute, or at common law, at his election; and in both of them may reverse the judgment. 3 *Inst.* 264. 3 *Black.* 404.

But the practice of setting aside verdicts upon motion, and granting New Trials, *has so far superseded the use of both sorts of attaints, that there is no instance of an attaint in our books since the reign of* Eliz. (see *Cro. Eliz.* 309. 3 *Black.* 404.) *And therefore it is unnecessary in this place to enlarge any further upon the subject.*

ATTAL SARISIN, the inhabitants and miners of Cornwall called an old deserted mine, that is given over, by this name of *attal Sarisin, i. e.* the leavings of the *Sarasins, Sassins,* or *Saxons.* *Cowel.*

ATTEGIA, (from the Lat. *ad* and *tego*) a little house. It is mentioned in Ethelward, *lib.* 4. Hist. Angl. *cap.* 3.

ATTENDANT, (*attendens*) signifies one that owes a duty or service to another, or in some sort depends on him. Where a wife is endowed of lands by a guardian, &c. she shall be attendant on the guardian, and on the heir at his full age. *Terms de Ley.*

ATTERMINING, (from the Fr. *attermine*) is used for a time or term granted for payment of a debt. *Ordinatio de libertatibus perquirendis, ann.* 27 *Ed.* 1. And in the stat. Westm. 2, it seems to signify the purchasing or gaining a longer time for payment of debts.—Atterminent *querentes usque in proximum parliamentum.* West. 2. c. 4. *Cowel. Blount.*

ATTILE, (*attilium, attilamentum*) the rigging or furniture of a ship. This word is mentioned in *Fleta, lib.* 1. *c.* 25. *Batellus,* (*i. e.* the boat) *cum omni onere & Attillamento. Cowel. Blount.*

ATTORNARE REM, to *attorn* or turn over money and goods, *viz.* to assign or appropriate them to some particular use and service. *Kennet's Paroch. Antiq. p.* 283.

ATTORNATO FACIENDO VEL RECIPIENDO, an ancient writ to command a sheriff or steward of a county-court, or hundred-court, to receive and admit an attorney to appear for the person that owes suit of court. *F. N. B.* 156. Every person that owes suit to the county-court, court-baron, &c. may make an attorney to do his suit. Stat. 20 *H.* 3. *c.* 10.

ATTORNEY, (*attornatus*) is one set in the place of another man, and who has authority given him to act in the place and stead of him by whom he is delegated, in private contracts and agreements, which authority must be by deed, that it may appear that the attorney has pursued his commission, and this is in general done by a power or letter of attorney executed under seal, though such a power may be and very frequently is contained in other deeds. 1 *Bac. Abr. tit. Attorney.*

Of this power all persons are capable, and therefore the same may be executed by infants, femes covert, persons attainted, outlawed, excommunicated, aliens, and others; for this being only a *naked authority,* the execution of it can be attended with no manner of prejudice to the persons under such incapacities or disabilities, or to any other person who by law may claim any interest of such disabled persons after their death. *Ibid.*

Attornies at Law. An attorney at law is a person duly admitted in the king's courts, and who is appointed by another person, usually denominated his *client,* to prosecute, or defend some suit on his behalf: and he is considered as a public officer belonging to the courts of justice in which he may be admitted.

And the following is the substance of the several acts relating to attornies.

By stat. Merton, 20 *Hen.* 3. *c.* 10, freemen owing suit to the county, tithing, hundred, wapentake, or to a court-baron, may do the same by an attorney.

By stat. of York, 12 *Ed.* 2. *c.* 1, tenants in assise may make attornies, and may plead by their bailiffs as heretofore.

By stat. of Carlisle, 15 *Ed.* 2. *stat.* 1, parties to fines shall appear personally. The lord chancellor, judges, and barons, may admit attornies in their respective courts, but such power is denied to their clerks and servants.

By 7 *Ric.* 2. *c.* 14, persons out of the realm, by the king's license, may make general attornies in writs of præmunire, and those attornies may make attornies under them.

By 4 *Hen.* 4. *c.* 18, all attornies shall be examined by the justices, and by their discretions be inrolled; and being of good fame, shall be sworn truly to serve in their office, and especially to make no suit in a foreign county; and if any attorney be found notoriously in fault, he shall forswear the court, and never after be received in any court of the king.

No officer of a lord of a franchise shall be attorney in any plea within the same. *Ibid.*

By 7 *Hen.* 4. *c.* 13, impotent persons may make attornies to traverse an erroneous outlawry.

By 29 *Eliz.* *c.* 5, defendants in suits on penal statutes, being bailable, may appear by attorney.

But by 31 *Eliz.* *c.* 10, this extends only to subjects, and free denizens, and not to aliens.

By 3 *Jac.* 1. *c.* 7, attornies or solicitors shall not be allowed fees to counsel without they produce tickets thereof signed by counsel; and they are to give in true bills to their clients. If they delay the client's suit, or demand more than fees and disbursements, they are to pay costs and treble damages, and be disabled. None shall be admitted attornies or solicitors in any court but persons brought up in that court, or well skilled. And no attorney shall permit another to follow a suit in his name under the penalty of 20*l.*

By 12 *Geo.* 1. *c.* 29, attornies or solicitors, convicted of forgery, perjury, or common barratry, acting in any court of record, are to be transported as felons in a summary way. *s.* 4.

By 2 *Geo.* 2. *c.* 23, attornies shall be sworn and admitted by the judges, who are to examine into their capacity before admission.

None shall act as a solicitor unless he take the oath, and be inrolled in the court of equity, where he must be previously examined. *Ibid.*

None shall act as an attorney or solicitor unless he has served a clerkship of five years, and been admitted, but he may with the consent of an attorney of another court sue out writs in such court. *Ibid.*

Clerks on the deaths of their masters may be turned over; and attornies and solicitors before admission are to take an oath to demean themselves honestly in their profession. *Ibid.*

No attorney shall have more than two articled clerks at one time: but the prothonotaries and secondary may have three. *Ibid.*

Sworn attornies, permitting others who are not, to issue out writs in their names, are disabled to practise. Attornies and solicitors are to be inrolled in the proper courts, and a sworn attorney may be admitted a solicitor, and a sworn solicitor in one court of equity may be admitted into any other court. *Ibid.*

The name of the attorney retained shall be written on every writ; attornies and solicitors shall not bring any action for fees till a month after delivery of bills; and parties may get them taxed in the mean time, and if reduced a sixth part the attorney is to pay the costs of taxation. *Ibid.*

Any person suing any process as an attorney or solicitor, without being admitted and inrolled, forfeits 50*l.* and is disabled to bring any action to recover his disbursements. *Ibid.*

This act shall not extend to the six clerks office in chancery, cursitors, the filazers, attornies and clerks in the exchequer, duchy court, or solicitors of the treasury. *Ibid.*

By 6 *Geo.* 2. *c.* 27, attornies of the superior courts, being qualified, may be admitted in inferior courts.

By 12 *Geo.* 2. *c.* 13, the not indorsing the attorney's name on warrants upon writs, shall not vitiate the same, for officers may indorse the attornies names upon writs

Attornies and solicitors may use abbreviations in their bills, and the act of 2 *Geo.* 2. is not to extend to any bill of fees between one solicitor and another. *Ibid.*

Persons unqualified acting in county courts forfeit 20*l.* and Quakers may be inrolled as attornies on their affirmation. *Ibid.*

No attorney, while he is in prison, or within the rules of one, shall commence any suit in his own name or another's, on pain of being struck off the roll, and incapacitated to act in future, and any person permitting him to sue in his name shall likewise be struck off the roll, and in like manner incapacitated. But he may carry on suits commenced before his confinement. *Ibid.*

By 22 *Geo.* 2. *c.* 46, persons bound to serve as clerks to attornies or solicitors, are to cause affidavit to be made within three months of the execution of such contracts, which affidavit is to be filed with the proper officer in the respective courts, whose fee thereon is half a crown. None are to be admitted before such affidavit be produced, and openly read in the court where such person shall be admitted an attorney or solicitor.

No attorney or solicitor shall take a clerk after discontinuing business; and clerks shall be employed in their proper business during the time of their contract. *Ibid.*

But if a clerk is turned over he may serve the remainder of his time, if an affidavit is made of the execution of the second contract, and filed according to the above directions as to the first. *Ibid.*

Clerks before they are admitted are to make affidavit of having served five years.

Sworn attornies or solicitors acting for persons not qualified are to be struck off the roll, and to be committed. *Ibid.*

Unqualified persons are not to act as attornies, or in the name of one, at sessions, under the penalty of 50*l.* The attornies of the duchy of Lancaster, the great sessions of Wales, or of Chester, Lancaster, or Durham, are excepted. *Ibid.*

No clerk of the peace, or under-sheriff, shall act as attorney at the quarter sessions for the county, under the penalty of 50*l.* *Ibid.*

Persons admitted sworn clerks in the six clerks office, or having served five years to one, may be admitted solicitors. Clerks may likewise be turned over, but no sworn clerk may have more than two clerks. *Ibid.*

By 23 *Geo.* 2. *c.* 26, solicitors in the courts of equity may be admitted attornies without fees or stamp.

By 24 *Geo.* 2. *c.* 42, attornies and solicitors are to be subject to the processes of the court of conscience for Westminster.

By 34 *Geo.* 3. *c.* 14, (which first imposed the duties on articles of clerkship) no clerk shall be admitted unless the indenture be inrolled with an affidavit within six months after the date, and every such clerk, previous to his being permitted to practise, shall make an affidavit of the payment of the duty. *s.* 2, 3.

If any person not admitted in one of the courts of great sessions in Wales, or counties palatine, shall in his own or any other name, sue out any writ in the courts at Westminster, without being admitted in one of them, he shall forfeit 100*l.* *s.* 4.

Persons admitted in any court at Westminster, who shall have paid the duty on the articles of clerkship, may be admitted in any of the other courts without payment of any further duty. *s.* 5.

And persons admitted in any one of the courts of great sessions in Wales, or counties palatine, who shall have paid the duty on articles of clerkship there, may be admitted in any other of the said courts without payment of further duty. *s.* 6, 7.

Articled clerks having paid the duty shall not be liable again on any new contracts with other masters. *s.* 8.

Parchment and paper for contracts to be stamped prior to being ingrossed; but only one part need be then stamped, and the duplicate shall be stamped after execution on proof of payment of duty. *s.* 11.

The usual allowance is to be made for prompt payment of the duty.

See also Stamps.

An attorney, solicitor, &c. having fees due to him, may detain writings until his just fees are paid: but if there be no fees due to him, the court, on motion, will compel the delivery of them. 1 *Lill.* 148. Any papers may be detained by an attorney till the money is paid for drawing them; but he cannot detain writings which are delivered to him on a special trust, for the money due to him in that very business, &c. if he doth, a rule may be obtained that he shall deliver them by such a day, or an attachment shall issue against him. *Mod. Cas. in Law and Equity* 306. The court will make a rule for delivery of writings, when they come to the attorney's hands by way of his business; and when they come to him in any other manner the party must bring his action. 1 *Salk.* 87.

Attornies have the privilege to sue and be sued only in the courts at Westminster, where they practise: they are not obliged to put in special bail, when defendants; but when they are plaintiffs they may insist upon special bail in all bailable cases. 1 *Vent.* 299. *Wood's Inst.* 450. But an attorney of one court may in that court hold an attorney of another court to bail; and attornies shall not be chosen into offices against their will. See *Privilege. Stamps.*

ATTORNEY OF THE DUCHY COURT OF LANCASTER, is the second officer in that court; and seems for his skill in law to be there placed as assessor to the chancellor, and chosen for some special trust reposed in him, to deal between the king and his tenants. *Cowel. Blount.*

ATTORNEY-GENERAL. This officer is made by letters patent, and his duty is to exhibit informations, and prosecute for the crown in matters criminal; and to file bills in the Exchequer for any thing concerning the king in inheritance or profits; and others may bring bills against the king's attorney. His proper place in court, upon any special matters of a criminal nature, wherein his attendance is required, is under the judges, on the left hand of the clerk of the crown; but this is only upon solemn and extraordinary occasions; for usually he does not sit there, but within the bar, in the face of the court. *Mich.* 22 *Car. B. R.*

ATTORNMENT, (*attornamentum*, from the Fr. *tourner*) the acknowledgment of a new lord on the alienation of lands, and the assent or agreement of the tenant to attorn; as, *I become tenant to the purchaser.* It may be made by payment of a penny rent to the grantee, or assent in writing. *Co. Lit.* 309.

But by 4 *Ann.* c. 16, it is enacted, that all grants and conveyances of manors, lands, rents, reversions, &c. by fine, or otherwise, shall be good without the attornment of the tenants of such lands, or of the particular tenant upon whose estate any such reversion, &c. shall be expectant or depending; but notice must be given of the grant to the tenant; before which he shall not be prejudiced by payment of any rent to the grantor, or for breach of the condition for non-payment. *s.* 9. And by 11 *Geo.* 2. *c.* 19, attornments of lands, &c. made by tenants to strangers shall be void, and their landlord's possession not affected thereby: though this shall not extend to vacate any attornment made pursuant to a judgment at law, or with consent of the landlord, or on a forfeited mortgage, &c.

ATTRAPER, (*Fr.*) taken, or seized. *Law Fr. Dict.*

AVAGE, or *avisage*, a rent or payment by tenants of the manor of Writtle in Essex, upon St. Leonard's day, 6th November, for the privilege of pawnage in the lord's woods, *viz.* for every pig under a year old, an halfpenny; for every yearling pig, one penny; and for every hog above a year old, twopence. *Blount.*

ADVANTAGIUM, profit and advantage. *Regist. Eccles. Christi Cantuar. MS. anno* 11 *Ed.* 2.

AUBAINE, DROIT DE. See *Albinatus jus.*

AUCTIONARII, *auxionarii*, sellers, regrators, or retailers. *Placit. Parl.* 18 *Ed.* 1. See *Excise.*

AUDIENCE COURT, (*curia audientiæ Cantuariensis*) is a court belonging to the archbishop of Canterbury, having the same authority with the court of arches, though inferior to it in dignity and antiquity. It is held in the archbishop's palace; and in former times the archbishops were wont to try and determine a great many ecclesiastical causes in their own palaces; but before they pronounced their definitive sentence they committed the matter to be argued by men learned in the law, whom they named their auditors: and so in time it grew to one special man, who at this day is called *causarum negotiorumque* audientiæ *Cantuariensis auditor officialis.* And to the office of auditor was formerly joined the chancery of the archbishop, which meddleth not with any point of contentious jurisdiction; that is, deciding of causes between party and party, but only such as are of office, and especially as are *voluntaria jurisdictionis*, as the granting the custody of spiritualties, during the vacancy of bishoprics, institutions to benefices, dispensations, &c. but this is now distinguished from the audience. The auditor of this court anciently by special commission was vicar-general to the archbishop, in which capacity he exercised ecclesiastical jurisdiction of every diocese becoming vacant within the province of Canterbury. 4 *Inst.* 337. But now the three great offices of official principal of the archbishop, dean or judge of the peculiars, and official of the audience are and have been for a long time past united in one person, under the general name of *Dean of the Arches*, who keepeth his court in Doctors Commons hall. *Johns.* 254.

The archbishop of York hath in like manner his court of audience. *Johns.* 255.

AUDIENDO ET TERMINANDO, a writ, or rather a commission to certain persons, when any insurrection or great riot is committed in any place, for appeasing and punishment thereof. *F. N. B.* 110. See *Oyer* and *Terminer.*

AUDITA QUERELA, is a writ that lies where a defendant against whom judgment is reversed, and who is therefore in danger of execution, or perhaps actually in execution, may be relieved upon good matter of discharge, which has happened since the judgment. 3 *Black.* 404.

This writ is granted by the lord chancellor to the justices of either bench, willing them to grant summons to the county where the creditor lives, for his appearance before them at a certain day. *F. N. B.* 102; upon which the justices shall hear the complaint, and do right. 1 *Mod.* 111.

Thus if the plaintiff hath given the defendant a general release, or if the defendant hath paid the debt to the plaintiff, without entering satisfaction on the record, in these and the like cases, wherein the defendant hath good matter to plead, but hath had no opportunity of pleading it, (either at the beginning of the suit, or *since the last continuance*) an *audita querela* lies in the nature of a bill in equity to be relieved against the oppression of the party. *Ibid.*

It also lies for bail when judgment is obtained against them by *scire facias* to answer the debt of their principal, and it happens afterwards that the original judgment against their principal is reversed; for here the bail, after judgment had against them, have no opportunity to plead this special matter, and therefore they shall have redress by *audita querela.* 1 *Rol. Abr.* 308, which is a writ of a most remedial nature, seems to have been invented, lest in any case there should be an oppressive defect of justice, where a party has a good defence, but by the ordinary forms of law had no opportunity to make it. 3 *Black.* 405.

But the indulgence now shown by the courts in granting a summary relief upon motion in cases of such evident oppression, has almost rendered useless the writ of *audita querela*, and driven it quite out of practice. *Ibid.*

If a statute be acknowledged to two, of which one is an infant, and they make a defeasance, and after sue execution contrary to it, an *audita querela* shall be brought against both; for it does not appear within the deed that he was an infant; also the deed of an infant is only voidable, and peradventure he will affirm it. 1 *Rol. Abr.* 312.

AUDITOR, (*Lat.*) is an officer of the king, or some other great person, who examines yearly the accounts of all under-officers, and makes up a general book, which shows the difference between their receipts and charge, and their several allowances, commonly called allocations; as the auditors of the exchequer take the accounts of those receivers who collect the revenues. 4 *Inst.* 106. Receivers-general of fee-farm rents, &c. are also termed auditors, and hold their audits for adjusting the accounts of the said rents at certain times and places appointed. And there are auditors assigned by the court to audit and settle accounts in actions of account, and other cases, who are proper judges of the cause, and pleas are made before them, &c. 1 *Brownl.* 24.

AUDITOR OF THE RECEIPTS, an officer of the exchequer, that files the teller's bills, and having made an entry of them gives the lord treasurer, &c. weekly, a certificate of the money received; he makes debentures to the tellers, before they pay any money, and takes their accounts: he also keeps the black book of receipts, and the treasurer's key of the treasury, and seeth every teller's money locked up in the treasury. 4 *Inst.* 107.

AUDITORES, is the same with *audientes*, i. e. the catechumens, or those who were newly instructed in the mysteries of the christian religion before they were admitted to baptism; and *auditorium* is that place in the church where they stood to hear, and be instructed. It is what we now call *navis ecclesia*: and in the primitive times the church was so strict in keeping the people together in that place, that the person who went from thence in sermon time was excommunicated. *Blount.*

AUDITORS OF THE IMPREST, are officers in the exchequer, who have the charge of auditing the great accounts of the king's customs, naval and military expenses, of the mint, &c. and any money imprested to men for his majesty's service. *Pract. Excheq.* 83.

Auditors in Accompt: see *Accompt.*

AVENAGE, (from the Lat. *avena*) a certain quantity of oats paid by a tenant to his landlord as a rent, or in lieu of some other duties. *Cowel. Blount.*

AVENOR, (*avenarius*, from the Fr. *avoine*, i. e. oats) is an officer belonging to the king's stables, that provides oats for his horses: he is mentioned 13 *Car.* 2. cap. 8.

AVENTURÆ, Adventures, or trials of skill at arms, and signifies military exercises on horseback. *Cowel. Blount.*

AVENTURE, (properly adventure) a mischance causing the death of a man: as where a person is suddenly drowned, or killed by any accident, without felony. *Co. Lit.* 391.

AVERA, (*quasi overa*, from the Fr. *ouvre* and *ouvrage*, *velut operagium*) signifies a day's work of a ploughman, formerly valued at 8*d.* It is found in *Domesday.* 4 *Inst.* 269.

AVERAGE, (*averagium*) is commonly used for a contribution that merchants and others make towards their losses, who have their goods cast into the sea for the safety of the ship, or of the other goods and lives of those persons that are in the ship, during the tempest. It is in this sense called average, because it is proportioned and allotted after the rate of every man's goods carried. By the laws of the sea, in a storm, when there is an extreme necessity, the goods, wares, guns, or whatsoever else is on board the ship, may (by consulting the mariners) be thrown overboard by the master, for the preservation of the ship; and it shall be made good by average and contribution. *Mod.* 297. But if the master takes in more goods than he ought, without leave of the owners and freighters, and a storm ariseth at sea, and part of the freighters goods are thrown overboard, the remaining goods are not subject to average, but the master is to make good the loss out of his own estate: and if the ship's gear or apparel be lost by storm, the same is not within the average. *Leg. Rhod.*

If goods are cast overboard before half the voyage is performed they are to be estimated at the price they cost; but if they are ejected afterwards, then at the price as the rest are sold at the port of arrival. *Leg. Oleron.* Where goods are given to pirates by way of composition to save the rest, there shall be average, by the civil law. *Moor* 297.

There is another species of average called *small*, or *petty* average; *petty average* consists in such charges and disbursements as according to occurrences, and the custom of every place the master necessarily furnishes for the benefit of the ship and cargo, either at the place of loading or unloading, or on the voyage: these charges are *lodemanaye*, or the hire of a pilot for conducting the vessel from one place to another; *towage, pilotage, light-money, beaconage, anchorage, bridge-toll, quarantine, river-charges, signals, instructions, passage-money* by castles, *expenses* for digging a ship out of ice when frozen up, that it may be brought into a proper harbour; and at London a custom, the fee paid at Dover pier. 4 *Bac. Abr.* 621.

A third species of average is that we are accustomed to meet with in bills of lading, *paying so much freight for the said goods, with primage or average accustomed:* in this sense it signifies a small duty which merchants who send goods in the ships of other men pay to the master, over and above the freight, for his care and attention to the goods so intrusted to him. *Ibid.*

AVERAGE OF CORN FIELDS, the stubble or remainder of straw and grass left in corn-fields after the harvest is carried away. In Kent it is called the gratten, and in other parts the roughings, &c. *Cowel. Blount.*

AVER CORN, is a reserved rent in corn, paid by farmers and tenants to religious houses, and signifies, by *Somner*, corn drawn to the lord's granary by the working cattle of the tenant. It is supposed that this custom was owing to the Saxon *cyriac sceat*, church-seed, a measure of corn brought to the priest annually on St. Martin's day, as an oblation for the first-fruits of the earth, under which title the religious had corn-rent paid yearly, as appears by an inquisition of the estate of the abbey of Glastonbury, *A.D.* 1201. *Cowel. Blount.*

AVER LAND seems to have been such lands as the tenants did plough and manure, *cum averiis suis*, for the proper use of a monastery, or the lords of the soil. *Mon. Angl. Cowel. Blount.*

AVER PENNY, (or average penny) money paid towards the king's averages or carriages, or to be freed thereof. *Rastal.*

AVER SILVER, a custom or rent formerly so called. *Cowel.*

AVERIA, cattle. *Spelman* deduces the word from the Fr. *ouvrer*, to work, as if chiefly working cattle; though it seems to be more probably from *avoir*, to have or possess; the word sometimes including all personal estate, as *catalla* did all goods and chattels. This word is used for oxen or horses of the plough; and in a general sense any cattle.

AVERIIS CAPTIS IN WITHERNAM, a writ for the taking of cattle to his use who hath cattle unlawfully distrained by another, and driven out of the county where they were taken, so that they cannot be replevied by the sheriff. *Reg. Orig.* 82. If the cattle are put into any strong place in the same county, the sheriff may take the *posse comitatus* and break into it, to make the replevin: but when they are driven out of the county he hath no authority to pursue them. Vide 1 & 2 *Ph. & Mar.* c. 12.

AVERIUM, the best live beast, due to the lord as an *heriot* on the death of his tenant.

AVERMENT, (*verificatio*, from the Fr. *averer*, i. e. *verificare, testari*,) is an offer of the defendant to make good or justify an exception pleaded in abatement or bar of the plaintiff's action: and it signifies the act, as well as the offer of justifying the exception; and not only the form, but the matter thereof. *Co. Lit.* 362. Averment is either general, or particular; general, which concludes every plea, &c. or is in bar, or in a replication, or other pleadings, containing matter affirmative, and ought to be with these words, 'and this he is ready to verify,' &c. Particular averment is when the life of tenant for life, or of tenant in tail, &c. is averred. *Ibid.*

AVERRARE, to carry goods in a waggon, or upon loaded horses, a duty required of some customary tenants. *Cowel. Blount.*

AUGEA, a cistern for water. *Cowel. Blount.*

AUGMENTATION, (*augmentatio*) the name of a court erected 27 *H.* 8. for determining suits and controversies relating to monasteries and abbey lands. The intent of this court was, that the king might be justly dealt with touching the profits of such religious houses as were given to him by act of parliament. It took its name from the augmentation of the revenues of the crown by the suppression of religious houses; and the office of augmentation, which hath many curious records, remains to this day, though the court hath been long since dissolved. *Terms de Ley* 68.

AVISAMENTUM, advice, or counsel. *Cowel. Blount.*

AULA, *i. e.* a court-baron. *Aula ecclesiæ* is that which is now termed *navis ecclesiæ*. *Ibid.*

AULNAGE. See ALNAGE.

AUMONE, (Fr. *aumosne*, alms) Tenure in aumone is where lands are given in alms to some church, or religious house, upon condition that a service or prayers shall be offered at certain times for the repose of the donor's soul. *Brit.* 164. *Cowel. Blount.*

AUNCEL-WEIGHT, (*quasi* hand sale weight, or from *ansa*, the handle of the balance) an ancient manner of weighing, by the hanging of scales or hooks at each end of a beam or staff, which by lifting up in the middle with one's finger or hand, discovered the equality or difference between the weight at one end, and the thing weighed at the other. This weighing, being subject to great deceit, was prohibited by several statutes, and the even balance commanded in its stead. 25 *Ed.* 3. *st.* 5. *c.* 9. 27 *Ed.* 3. *st.* 2. *c.* 10. 34 *Ed.* 3. *c.* 5. And see 8 *H.* 6. *c.* 5, and 22 & 23 *Car.* 2. *c.* 12, though in some parts of England the steelyards are still used.

AUNCIATUS, a word signifying antiquated. *Cowel. Blount.*

AVOIDANCE, in the general signification, is when a benefice is void of an incumbent, in which sense it is opposed to plenarty. Avoidances are either in fact, as by death of the incumbent, or in law, and may be by cession, deprivation, resignation, &c. In the first case,

Where the avoidance is by the death of the incumbent, or by his being made a bishop, in such cases the patron is to take notice of it at his peril; and the six months in which he is to present another shall be accounted from the death of the one, and the creation of the other; but if the avoidance be by resignation, which is the act of the party himself, or by deprivation, which is the act of the law, in both these cases the patron must have notice, and the six months shall be accounted from the time of the notice, and not from the resignation or deprivation. *Dyer* 327.

Where the patron himself took notice of a deprivation, which was obtained at his own prosecution, for not reading the thirty-nine articles; yet in such case lapse shall not incur without an actual notice of the deprivation given to him by the bishop: for it is he, and no other person, who is required by the law to give notice, and it must not be a general notice, but it must be particular, and the cause be expressed for which he was deprived. 6 *Rep.* 29.

Where the bishop refuseth to institute a clerk he must give notice of such refusal to the patron himself, if he is within that county where the church is become void; but if he is not in that county, then notice must be given at the door of that church; but where it is doubtful who is patron, and upon *jus patronatus* awarded it is found that such a one is patron, though it may happen he is not the true patron, yet if he gives him notice, and no presentation is made within six months after such notice, the bishop may collate to the church; and though that collation shall not bind the true patron, yet the bishop shall be excused from being a disturber. 1 *Leon.* 32.

There are avoidances by act of parliament, wherein there must be a judicial sentence pronounced to make the living void. If a man hath one benefice, with cure, &c. and take another with cure, without any dispensation to hold two benefices, in such case the first is void by the act 21 *Hen.* 8. *c.* 13, if it was above the value of 8*l.* During an avoidance it is said that the house and glebe of the benefice are in abeyance: but by stat. 28 *Hen.* 8. *cap.* 11, the profits arising during an avoidance, are given to the next incumbent towards payment of the first fruits; though the ordinary may receive the profits to provide for the service of the church, and shall be allowed the charges of supplying the cure, &c. for which purpose the churchwardens of the parish are usually appointed. The next avoidance of a church may be granted by deed, where the church is full: if a grant be made of the next avoidance when it shall happen, and the church is void at that time, this will make the grant void as to that very avoidance, but it may be good for the next turn after that.

And the distinction which hath obtained is this: if it come in question whether the church be full of an incumbent or not, the same shall be tried by the certificate of the bishop, who best knows of the institution; but if the issue to be tried be, whether the church be void or not, the same shall be tried by a jury at the common law, unless the issue to be tried be upon some special act of avoidance, for then the same shall be tried by the certificate of the bishop, so as the special cause of the avoidance be spiritual. *Gib.* 793. *Hughes, c.* 13. 1 *Burn E. L.* 78. And see 25 *Ed.* 3. *st.* 3. *c.* 8.

If a clerk is instituted to a benefice of the yearly value of 8l. and before induction accepts another benefice with cure, and is instituted, the first benefice is void by the statute 21 *H.* 8. *c.* 13. for he who is instituted, only, is properly said to have accepted a benefice within the words of the act. 4 *Rep.* 78.

The patron granted the next avoidance to two jointly and severally; adjudged, that this grant is not good, because an interest cannot be divided; so where there was a grant of the next avoidance to three; *habendum* to them and to each of them jointly and severally, the first presented the third, and adjudged good; but if the bishop had refused to admit the presentee, he might have failed in a *quare impedit*, because the severance in the *habendum* is void in law; but it is otherwise in case of an authority, for that may be divided. *Golds.* 142.

But if he is inducted into a second benefice, the first is void *in facto et jure*, and not voidable only, *quoad* the patron, and until he presents another; and in such case the patron ought to take notice of the avoidance at his peril, and present within the six months. *Cro. Car.* 258.

A grant of the next avoidance is no more than a chattel, and goes to executors. *Right Clerg.* 64.

AVOIRDUPOIS, or *averdupois*, (Fr. *avoir du poids*, i. e. *habere pondus, aut justi esse ponderis*) signifies a weight different from that which is called troy weight, which contains but twelve ounces in the pound, whereas this hath sixteen ounces: and in this respect it is probably so called, because it is of greater weight than the other. It also signifieth such merchandizes as are weighed by this weight; and is mentioned in divers statutes, as 9 *Ed.* 3. 27 *Ed.* 3. *c.* 10. 2 *R.* 2. *c.* 1. *Averium ponderis*, full weight, or avoirdupois. *Cart.* 3 *Ed.* 2.

AVOWEE, of a church benefice. See *Advowee.*

AVOWRY, (Fr. *advouerie*) is where a man takes a distress for rent or other thing, and the party on whom taken sues forth a replevin, then the taker shall justify his plea for what cause he took it; and if in his own right, he must shew the same, and avow the taking; but if he took it in right of another, he must make cognizance of the taking, as bailiff or servant to the person in whose right he took the same. *Terms de Ley* 70. 2 *Lill.* 454.

The avowant shall recover his damages and costs, for by 21 *Hen.* 8. *c.* 19. it is enacted, that "if in any replegiare for rents, &c. the "avowry, cognizance, or justification be found "for the defendant, or the plaintiff be non-"suit, &c. the defendant shall recover such "damages and costs as the plaintiff should "have had, if he had recovered. And by "17 *Car.* 2. *c.* 7. When a plaintiff shall "be nonsuit before issue in any suit of re-"plevin, &c. removed or depending in any "of the courts at Westminster, the defend-"ant making suggestion in the nature of an "avowry for rent, the court on prayer shall "award a writ to inquire of the sum in ar-"rear, and the value of the distress, &c. "Upon return whereof the defendant shall re-"cover the arrears, if the distress amounts "to that value, or else the value of the dis-"tress with costs; and where the distress is "not found to the value of the arrears, the "party may distrain for the residue. And "if the plaintiff be nonsuit, discontinue, or "have judgment against him, the defendant "shall recover double costs." 11 *Geo.* 2. *c.* 19. *s.* 22.

AURES, a punishment by the Saxon laws of cutting off the ears, inflicted on those who robbed churches, or were guilty of any other theft. *Fleta, lib.* 1. *c.* 38. *par.* 10. And this punishment also extended to many other crimes as well as theft. *Upton de Militari Officio, page* 140.

AURICULARIUS, a secretary, *Mon. Angl. p.* 120.

AURUM REGINÆ, the queen's gold, a duty anciently imposed to augment the queen's income. 1 *Black.* 221.

AUSCULTARE. Formerly, persons were appointed in monasteries to hear the monks read, and direct them how, and in what manner they should do it with a graceful tone or accent, to make an impression on their hearers, which was required before they were admitted to read publicly in the church; and this was called *auscultare*, viz. to read or recite a lesson.—*Quicunque lecturus vel cantaturus est aliquid in monasterio, si necesse habeat, ab eo, (viz. Cantore) priusquam incipiat, debet auscultare. Lanfrancus in Decretis pro ordine Benedict. c.* 5.

AUSTURCUS, and *Osturcus*, a goshawk; from whence we usually call a faulkoner, who keeps that kind of hawks, an ostringer. In ancient deeds there has been reserved, as a rent to the lord, *unum austurcum. Cowel. Blount.*

AUTER DROIT, is where persons sue or are sued in another's right; as executors, administrators, &c. 2 *Black.* 177.

AUTERFOITS ACQUIT, is a plea by a criminal that he was heretofore acquitted of the same treason or felony. 3 *Inst.* 213. There is also plea of *auterfoits attaint*, and *auterfoits convict*; that he was heretofore attainted or convicted of the same felony. But in appeal of death, *auterfoits acquit*, or *auterfoits attaint*, upon indictment of the same death, is no plea. *H. P. C.* 244. But in other cases where a person is attainted, it is to no purpose that he should be attainted a second time. And conviction of manslaughter, where clergy is admitted thereon, will bar any subsequent prosecution for the same death. 2 *Hawk. P. C.* 377.

AUTER VIE, *tenant pur*, where a man holds an estate by the life of another, he is usually called tenant *pur auter vie*. 2 *Black.* 120.

AUTHORITY, that power of acting which one man has, being transferred to another, is called an authority; and this the law allows of, for as a contract is no more than the consent of a man's mind to a thing, if such consent or concurrence appears; it would be very unreasonable to oblige him to be present at the execution of every contract, since it may be as well performed by any other person delegated for that purpose. 1 *Bac. Ab. tit. Auth.*

But such delegation or authority must be by deed, that it may appear that the attorney or substitute, had a commission or power to represent the party; also that it may appear that the authority was well preserved. *Co. Lit.* 48. b. 2 *Rolls. Abr.* 8. *Salk.* 96.

An authority may be delegated by deed indented, though the attorney be not party to the deed; because the attorney takes nothing by the deed, but has only a naked authority delegated to him; and therefore, since a man may take an estate in remainder, though he is no party to the deed, *a fortiori* one not party to the deed may receive a naked authority or power by it. 2 *Rol. Abr.* 8, 9.

One, who has an authority to do any act for another, must execute it himself, and cannot transfer it to another; for this being a trust and confidence reposed in the party cannot be assigned to a stranger whose ability and integrity were not so well thought of by him for whom the act was to be done. 9 *Co.* 77. *b.* 1 *Rol. Abr.* 330.

The authority given by letter of attorney must be executed during the life of the person that gives it; because the letter of attorney is to constitute the attorney by representative for such a purpose, and therefore can continue in force only during the life of me that am to be represented. 2 *Rol. Abr.* 9. *Co. Lit.* 52.

But if any corporation aggregate, as a mayor and commonalty, or dean and chapter, make a feoffment and letter of attorney to deliver seisin, this authority does not determine by the death of the mayor or dean, but the attorney may well execute the power after their death: because the letter of attorney is an authority from the body aggregate, which subsists after the death of the mayor or dean, and therefore may be represented by their attorney; but if the dean or mayor be named by their own private name, and die before livery, or be removed, livery after seems not good. *Co. Lit.* 52. 2 *Rol. Abr.* 12.

And where an interest is coupled with an authority, there it cannot be countermanded or determined. *And.* 1 *Dyer* 190.

If a man devise that his executors shall sell his land, this gives but a naked authority; and the lands, till the sale is made, descend to the heir at law; and in this case all must join in the sale; and if one die, it being a bare authority, cannot survive to the rest. *Co. Lit.* 112. *b.* 113. *a.* 181. *b.*

But if a man by will give land to executors to be sold, and one of them die, the survivors may sell; for the trust being coupled with an interest, shall survive together with it. *Co. Lit.* 113. *b.* 181. *b.*

AUTUMN, is the decline of the summer. And Lindewood tells us, in the following lines, when the several seasons of the year begin. *Cowel. Blount.*

Dat Clemens Hiemem, dat Petrus ver Cathedratus,
Æstuat Urbanus, Autumnat Bartholomæus.

AUTUMNALIA, those fruits of the earth which are ripe in autumn or harvest.

AUXILIUM AD FILIUM MILITEM FACIENDUM ET FILIAM MARITANDAM, an ancient writ formerly directed to the sheriff of every county where the king or other lord had any tenants, to levy of them an aid towards the knighting of a son, and the marrying of a daughter. *F. N. B.* 82. See *Aid.*

AUXILIUM CURIÆ, a precept or order of court for the citing or convening of one party, at the suit and request of another, to warrant some thing. *Kennet's Paroch. Antiq.* 477.

AUXILIUM FACERE ALICUI IN CURIA REGIS. To be another's friend and solicitor in the king's court; an office undertaken by some courtiers for their dependants in the country. *Paroch Antiq.* 126.

AUXILIUM REGIS, the king's aid, or money levied for the king's use, and the public service; as where taxes are granted by parliament. *Cowel. Blount.*

AUXILIUM VICECOMITI, a customary aid or duty anciently payable to sheriffs, out of certain manors, for the better support of their offices. *Cowel. Blount.*

AWAIT, seems to signify what we now call way-laying, or lying in wait to execute some mischief. *Stat.* 13 *R.* 2. *Stat.* 2. *c.* 1. It is ordained that no charter of pardon shall be allowed before any justice for the death of a man slain by await, or malice prepensed, &c.

AWARD, (from the *Fr. agard*) An award is the judgment and arbitration of one or more persons, at the request of two parties who are at variance, for ending the matter in dispute without public authority: and may be called an award, because it is imposed on both parties to be observed by them. *Dictum quod ad custodiendum seu observandum partibus imponitur. Spelm.*

The submission to an award may be by bond, covenant, or by an assumpsit or promise; or without all this, by a bare agreement to refer the matter to such a person or persons. 10 *Rep.* 131. *Dyer* 270.

If the submission be without deed, it may be revoked without deed, and the party shall lose nothing, for *ex nuda submissione non oritur actio.* 1 *Bac. Ab. tit. Arb.*

If the submission be by deed, it is of its own nature countermandable, though made irrevocable by the express words of the deed, for the arbitrators being constituted and put in the place of the parties by their consent to act for them, they can no longer act, than while they have such consent. *Ibid.*

But where a man obliges himself to stand to an award, if the party revokes it, according to his power, he hath forfeited his obligation, for the making the award becomes impossible by his own default, and therefore the obligation is simple; but if it be without obligation, he forfeits nothing. *Ibid.*

There is, however, an instance in 2 *Keb.* 10, 20, 24. and 231. of an action on the case, being maintained for the countermand of a parol submission; and there can be no doubt but that a parol submission amounts to a promise to perform.

If several plaintiffs or defendants submit themselves to an award, one cannot revoke the submission without the other, for joint acts are considered as the acts of one person, and there can be no revocation without the act of that person that made the submission. 28 *Hen.* 6. *c.* 6. *Brownl.* 62.

If a feme sole submits to arbitration, and afterwards marries, this is a revocation of the submission, and if it be by bond, the bond is forfeited. 2 *Keb.* 865. *Jones* 388.

And a submission may be made a rule of court, pursuant to the statute 9 & 10 *Will.* 3. c. 15. and it is said, that although the submission be by bond, yet the party may have it made a rule of court; in which case it is said he may proceed on the bond, and likewise have an attachment for not performing the award. *Salk.* 73. *pl.* 12. *Sid.* 54. *Raym.* 85.

By this *stat.* 9 & 10 *W.* 3. *c.* 15. it is enacted, that "submissions to awards, by "agreement of the parties, may be made a "rule of any of his majesty's courts of record; "and on a rule of court thereupon, the parties shall be finally concluded by such arbitrament: and, in case of disobedience "thereto, the party refusing to perform the "same, shall be subject to the penalties of "contemning a rule of court, &c. unless it "appears on oath that such award was procured by corruption or other undue means, "when it shall be set aside: so as complaint "thereof be made to the court before the last "day of the next term, after made and published."

The limitation under this stat. to the second term is confined merely to such objections as affect the conduct of the arbitrators: but objections which arise on the face of the award itself, may be made at any time. 2 *Burr.* 701. *Barnes* 56, 57.

Where the submission limits no time for the making of the award it shall be understood to be within convenient time, and if in such a case the party request the arbitrators to make an award, and they do not, a revocation afterwards will be no breach of the submission. 3 *Keble* 745.

An award can only be binding and effectual amongst those who are parties, therefore if a man submit *for himself and partner* all matters in difference between the partnership and another, the partner submitting shall be bound to perform the award, but *the other* shall not, because he is a stranger to the award. 2 *Mod.* 228.

So if the parson on the one hand, and some of the parishioners on the other, *in behalf of themselves, and the rest* of the inhabitants of the parish, but *without the* authority of the rest, submit to arbitration by bond, the parishioners submitting, shall alone be answerable for a breach of the award by any of the other parishioners. *Lit.* 30. *Hetl.* 4.

But if several persons on the one part, and several on the other, submit generally to any award, the arbitrators have not only power to determine matters between them jointly, but severally and distinctly also; and an award between one only, of the one side, and another on the other side, is good, for this is not doing less than the commission warrants, since there is an authority in it to determine matters distinctly between them for the submission is of all matters, so that it contains as well all things severally between each of them, as jointly between them all, and perhaps there may be no cause of award between the others. 1 *Bac. Abr. tit. Arb.* (C.)

—— *Of the award itself.*] If an award be made of any other thing than what is contained in the submission, it is void; for no acts are my own, or binding to me, unless done by me or by commission from me. *Plow.* 396. *Dyer* 242.

If arbitrators award to do an act to a stranger, this is good; for the stranger is put by the arbitrators in the place of the party, and they have power to award this act, since it is not impossible or unequal, and it is relating to the submission. *Mo.* 3, 359. 10 *Co.* 131. 3 *Leon.* 62. 1 *Rol. Abr.* 248. *Hard.* 46. 1 *Leon.* 316.

But an award that an act should be done by a stranger, is void; because he is not within the submission. *Hard.* 46.

An award may be good, though made of less than is contained in the submission; as if the submission be of all actions, trespasses, demands and controversies, and the award be made of some only, this is good; for no more shall be supposed to be made known to the arbitrator: and if there be other causes of action in being, and they be made known to the arbitrator, they must be shewn on the other side; and this as well where the submission is conditional by *ita quod*, as where it is absolute; for the award being made *de præmissis* shall be supposed to settle all things. *Hob.* 49. 8 *Co.* 98. *Cro. Jac.* 278. 1 *Sand.* 32. 1 *Brownl.* 63. 2 *Brownl.* 310. 1 *Sid.* 12. *Dyer* 216, 242. *Hard.* 45.

An award of one particular thing for the ending of an hundred matters in difference, is sufficient; as of a specific sum of money for arrears of rent, and for repairs. 1 *Lev.* 132. 1 *Keb.* 738.

The awarding of costs is incidental to the power of an arbitrator: the provision therefore on the reference, that the costs shall abide the event of the award, is a restriction of the power which he necessarily hath of giving costs at his election. 2 *Term Rep.* 644.

And the award of costs *to be taxed* by the proper officer, doth not include the costs of the reference, but is merely confined to the costs of the action. 1 *Hen. Black.* 213.

As an award is in nature of a judgment, *it ought to be wholly decisive*, for if it doth not determine the matter, it becomes a new controversy; therefore if the arbitrators award a bond for quiet enjoyment of lands, without appointing a certain sum, or direct one party to give to the other a good security for a certain sum of money, without saying what security, or to pay for so many quarters of malt sold according to the market price or without ascertaining what that price was, this is a void award, and the party is not obliged to give bond to the value of the land; for then the sense of the award must be supplied by averment; now if it hath the credit of a judgment, there can be no interpretation made of the award, but by the words of the award itself; for if it receives its meaning from any matters out of the award, the mind of the arbitrators is only guessed at, and not expressed; but the parties intended to be obliged only by what the arbitrators themselves declare to be their award, and the bond to be according to the value, they cannot assign their power to any person to assess the value. 5 *Co.* 77. *Cro. Eliz.* 432. 1 *Rol. Abr.* 263. *Moor* 359. 1 *Rol. Rep.* 271. *Dyer* 242. *Yelv.* 78.

But an award in the alternative, that the party shall do one thing or another, is not liable to the objection of uncertainty for which he has domain of the things he has performed the award; as if the award be, that he shall deliver up to the other party a certain deed, or pay him 50*l.*; and such an award in the alternative seems to be the best mode of compelling a party to exert himself to procure the performance of what is not immediately in his power. *Kyd*, 137.

An award made only on one side, without any thing on the other, is void in law: as that one shall pay or give bond for money to the other party, and he do nothing for it: but if it be to give bond to pay, or to pay a debt, and that the other shall be discharged of the debt, &c. this is good: so where it is that one party shall pay money to the other, and then the other shall release all actions to him. 8 *Rep.* 72, 98.

Thus in case of a trespass submitted, the arbitrators award that one shall pay the other 3*l.* this is void, because only on one side; for it is not said for what, and so the trespass is not discharged, and then the other party hath no advantage by the award; but if it were awarded *de et super præmissis*, it would be well enough; likewise if the award had been that he shall pay 3l. for a trespass, it had been good, and yet one only was to do an act, but then the trespass by that award had been discharged. 1 *Rol. Abr.* 253, 254. *Hob.* 49.

If the arbitrators award a thing impossible *ex natura rei*, it is void: as if they award a sum of money to be paid at a day past, it is void, 8 *Ed.* 4. 1. *b*. But if they award a thing which cannot be done, but is not in the nature of the act itself contradictory or repugnant; this may be a good award; for there is no construction to be made of the award, but by the words thereof. 1 *Rol. Abr.* 248.

An award to levy a fine is good; for though it is an act of the court, yet, by the law and public justice of the kingdom, it is not to be refused to any man; but if the award be to command the justices to do it, this is no good award; for the parties in effect pray leave to agree from the king himself, which is quite different from the nature of a command. 1 *Rol. Abr.* 249.

An award to pay so much *apud domum* J. S. good; for he is not bound to pay it in the house, but as near as he can to it, or it shall be intended a common inn; and if the party will not let him pay there, it has been said that the endeavour is sufficient; for they cannot award any thing that will make the party a trespasser. 1 *Rol. Abr.* 249. 1 *Rol. Rep.* 6. *Cro. Car.* 226. 2 *Bulst.* 39. 3 *Lev.* 153. An award that one of the parties shall do a thing out of his power, as to deliver up a deed which is in the custody of J. S. is void. 12 *Mod.* 585. If an arbitrator awards a thing against law, this is void. 1 *Rol. Abr.* 249. And a party is not to be made a judge in his own cause by award. 1 *Salk.* 71. And the award must be *final.* 1 *Bac. Ab. tit. Ar.*

——— *how enforced.*] The submission to arbitrators being made a rule of court, an attachment is granted against the party refusing to perform the award, as for a contempt of that court of which the submission is a rule. 1 *Bac. Ab. tit. Arb.* (H.)

The attachment in this case is in the nature of a civil execution, and therefore cannot be executed on a Sunday, but it is so far criminal, that the motion for it cannot be grounded on the affirmation of a quaker. *Ibid.*

But if the party dies, there is no remedy by attachment against his representatives, for the contempt dies with him. 2 *Vern.* 444.

The course of proceeding in order to obtain an attachment, is this: the award must be tendered to the party against whom it is intended to move, and if he refuse to accept it, affidavit of the due execution of the award, and of such tender and refusal must be made, and on that, an application to the court to make the order of *nisi prius* a rule of court; a copy of this rule must then be served on the party refusing to accept the award: if he still refuse to accept it, an affidavit must be made of personal service of the rule and of the disobedience to it, and then upon application grounded upon that affidavit, an attachment will be entered. *Kyd.* 216.

But it seems that where a reference is submitted to, under an order of the court of Chancery, the proper motion is not for an attachment, but that the party refusing to perform the award should stand committed: and notice of such motion must be served personally, and not on the clerk in court. 3 *Bro. Ch. Rep.* 361.

Where the award is to pay a sum of money, it is said that a bill in equity to compel performance, is improper, but where it is to do any thing in specie, as for the conveyance of an estate, or the like, a court of equity will sometimes lend the aid of its decrees to enforce the execution of it. And a bill in general, will lie for performance, either where the award hath been made, under a submission entered into by order of the court, or where, though the submission be voluntary, or the award defective in circumstances, the parties have long acquiesced in it, or it has been in part executed. 3 *Peere Wms.* 189, 190. 1 *Ch. Rep.* 86. 1 *Atk.* 62.

But a bill in equity, will not lie to carry into execution, an award in a voluntary submission, unless there has been an acquiescence in it by the parties to the submission on an agreement by them afterwards to have it executed. 1 *Atk.* 62.

When an award is put in suit at law, no extrinsic circumstances, nor any matter of fact *dehors* can be given in evidence to impeach it; if it be open therefore to any objection of this kind, the defendant must apply for relief, either to a court of equity by bill, or if the submission has been made a rule of any court of law, to the summary and equitable jurisdiction of that court, of which such submission has been made a rule. 2 *Wils.* 148.

These objections being in general founded on the mistakes or misconduct of the arbitrators who are judges chosen by the party himself, are received by the courts at first with a degree of caution and reserve, though if made out to their satisfaction, relief is certainly afforded. 2 *Vez.* 315. 1 *Atk.* 64. 1 *Salk.* 731.

Therefore if it appears, on a bill in equity to set aside an award, that the arbitrators went upon a plain mistake, either as to the law or the fact, the same is an error appearing on the face of the award, and is sufficient to set it aside. 2 *Vern.* 705.

So if the arbitrators have been guilty of gross fraud, partiality, or corruption, a bill may be filed in equity to set aside the award. 2 *Atk.* 64; 155. 2 *Vern.* 251, 315, 485, 514. *Amb.* 245.

If a bill to set aside an award for partiality or corruption, be filed against the arbitrators, those charges must not only be denied by way of averment in pleading the award, but such plea must be also supported by an answer, shewing the arbitrators to have been incorrupt and impartial. 2 *Atk.* 396, 50. *Mitf.* 209.

If a bill is filed to have the benefit of, or to impeach an award, and the arbitrators are made parties, not charged with partiality, they may demur to the whole bill, as well to discovery as relief, for the plaintiff can have no decree against them, nor can he read their answer against the other defendants. 2 *Vern.* 380. *Mitf.* 142.

But where an award has been impeached, on the ground of gross misconduct in the arbitrators, and they have been made parties to the suit, the court has gone so far as to order them to pay the costs, and therefore in such a case, it seems probable that a demurrer to the bill would not have been allowed. *Mitf.* 209.

A bill in equity will not lie against an arbitrator for a discovery of the grounds upon which he made his award, or of any fact which may have come to his knowledge from the confidence reposed in him as such arbitrator. 3 *Atk.* 644.

On a bill in equity to set aside an award, the court will not let the party go into any legal objections, except for partiality and corruption: but if the bill is for *an account*, and prays to set aside an award, there in order to let in such account, the plaintiff may make legal objections. *Amb.* 245.

AWM or AUME, (Teut. *ohm. i. e. cadus vel mensura*) a measure of Rhenish wine, containing forty gallons; mentioned in 1 *Jac.* 1. *c.* 33. and 12 *Car.* 2. *c.* 4. *Cowel. Blount.*

AXE and AXEN, comes from the Saxon verb *axian*, to demand, and from hence we have our English word *ask*. *Cowel.*

AYEL and BESAIEL. See titles *Aile* and *Besayle*.

AZALDUS, signifies a poor horse or jade. *Cowel. Blount.*

B

BACA, a hook or link of iron, or staple. *Cowel. Blount.*

BACCINIUM, or BACINA, a bason or vessel to hold water to wash the hands. *Ibid.*

BACHELERIA, the commonality as distinguished from baronage. *Ibid.*

BACHELOR, the most probable derivation of the feudal word *bachelor*, is from *bas* and *chevalier*, an inferior knight, and thence latinized into the barbarous word *baccalaureus*. *Ducange. Bac.*

And it is somewhat remarkable, that whilst this feudal word has long been appropriated to single men, another feudal term of higher degree, viz. *baron*, should in legal language, be applied to those who are married. *Christian's* note on 1 *Black.* 404.

The word bachelor is used in 13 *R.* 1. and signifies the same with knight-bachelor, which is the most ancient, though the lowest order of knighthood amongst us. *Cowel. Blount.* 1 *Black.* 404.

By 3 *E.* 4. *c.* 5. it is a simple knight, and not knight banneret, or knight of the Bath.

Also in the universities, the lowest graduates, are styled bachelors of arts, which is the first degree taken by students, before they come to greater dignity.

BACKBERINDE, (*Sax.*) signifieth bearing upon the back, or about a man. Bracton useth it for a sign or circumstance of theft apparent, which the civilians call *furtum manifestum*; for, dividing *furtum* into *manifestum* & *non manifestum*, he defineth the former thus; *furtum vero manifestum est, ubi latro deprehensus est seisitus de aliquo latrocinio, scil. handhabend,* & *backerind,* & *insecutus fuerit per aliquem cujus res illa fuerit.* *Bract. lib.* 3. *tract.* 2. *cap.* 32. *Cowel. Blount.*

BACKING OF WARRANTS, is the signing of an authority on the back thereof, by a magistrate of a different county from that mentioned in the body thereof, empowering the officer to execute the same in such other county. see 23 *Geo.* 2. *c.* 26. 24 *Geo.* 2. *c.* 55. and 13 *Geo.* 3. *c.* 31. under title ESCAPE.

BACO, is a bacon hog, as often used in old charters. *Blount.*

BACTILE, a candlestick properly so called, when formerly made *ex baculo* of wood, or a stick. *Cowel. Blount.*

BADGER, (from the Fr. *bagage*, a bundle, and thence is derived *bagagier*, a carrier of goods) signifies with us one that buys corn or victuals in one place, and carries them to another to sell and make profit by them. *Cowel. Blount.*

BAG, an uncertain quantity of goods and merchandize, from three to four hundred. *Lex Mercat'.*

BAGA, a bag or purse. *Cowel. Blount.*

BAGAVEL, the citizens of Exeter had granted to them by charter from K. *Edw.* 1. a collection of a certain tribute or toll upon all manner of wares brought to that city to be sold, towards the paving of the streets, repairing of the walls, and maintenance of the city, which was commonly called in old English *begavel, bethugavel,* and *chippinggavel.* *Ibid.*

BAHADUM, a chest or coffer; it is mentioned in *Fleta, lib.* 2. *c.* 21.

BAJARDOUR, (Lat. *bajulator*) a bearer of any weight or burden. *Cowel. Blount.*

BAIL, *ballium*, (from the Fr. *bailler*, which comes of the Greek Βάλλειν, and signifies to *bail* or to deliver into hands) is used in our common law for the freeing or setting at liberty of one arrested or imprisoned upon action, either civil or criminal, on surety taken for his appearance at a day and place certain. *Bract. lib.* 3. *tract* 2. *cap.* 8.

The person bailed, is supposed to continue in their friendly custody, instead of going to gaol, and therefore the bail may keep the person committed to them in their custody, for their indemnity. 4 *Inst.* 178, 179.

Or if he be at large, they may re-seize him, and bring him before a justice, to find new bail, or to be committed to prison, and this they may do upon a *Sunday*, so they may detain him in safe custody, remaining with him there, until by render, or *habeas corpus*, he can be turned over to the proper prison. *Hale P. C.* 96. *Mod. Cas.* 231, 247.

1. *Bail in civil cases.*] With respect to bail in civil cases it is to be observed, that there is both common and special bail: common bail is in actions of small concern (under the amount of 10l.) and it is called *common*, because any sureties in that case are taken; whereas in causes of greater weight, as actions upon bonds, or specialty, or other matters where the debt amounts to 10l. special bail or surety may be taken. 4 *Inst.* 179.

By *stat.* 23 *Hen.* 6. *c.* 9. sheriffs are to let to bail persons by them arrested by force of any writ, in any personal action, upon reasonable sureties, having sufficient within the county to keep their days in such place, &c. as the writs require.

And where the defendant has been arrested and discharged out of custody, upon giving a bail bond to the sheriff, he must at the return of the writ to discharge such bond, appear thereto, by *putting in special bail*, or as it is termed, *bail above*, so called in contradistinction to the sheriffs bail, or bail *below*, nor can he render himself in discharge of such bond after the return of the writ, without first putting in bail above. 5 *Burr.* 2683. But he may voluntarily surrender himself to the sheriff before the return of the writ.

If at the return of the writ the plaintiff dislike the security taken by the sheriff, and does not take an assignment of the bail bond, he may have the defendant brought up, by *ruling* the sheriff in the first instance to return the writ, and upon a return of *cepi corpus*, by ruling him in the next place to bring in the body: the intent of which is, to compel the sheriff to put in good bail above, which if not done in due time, the court on motion will grant an attachment against the sheriff, the consequence of which is, generally payment by the sheriff of the debt and costs, who seeks his remedy over against the officer, by whom the defendant was arrested, or his sureties, who have their remedy over against the principal and his bail.

But if the plaintiff take an assignment of the bail bond, though the bail is insufficient, yet the sheriff is not to be amerced. 1 *Salk.* 99. And by stat. 4 *Ann. c.* 16. *s.* 20. the plaintiff may now, under such assignment, sue in his own name.

By 43 *Geo.* 3. *c.* 46, persons arrested on mesne process, instead of giving bail, may deposit with the sheriff, the sum indorsed on the writ, with 10l. to answer costs, which deposit shall be paid into court, and on the defendant's perfecting bail be re-paid to him; or on bail not being put in, be paid over to the plaintiffs by order of the court. *s.* 3.

By stat. 4 & 5 *W.* & *M. c* 4, The judges of the courts at Westminster have power to appoint commissioners in every county to take recognisances of bail, in causes depending in their courts; and to make such rules for justifying the bail as they shall think fit, and the cognizees, unless they live in London or Westminster, or within 10 miles, may justify before commissioners; in the country, also, any judge of assise in his circuit, may take bails.

And by 43 *Geo.* 3. *c.* 46. defendants in custody on mesne process, after the return thereof, may on notice, justify bail before one of the judges in *vacation*. *s.* 6.

By 21 *Jac.* 1. *cap.* 26. enacts, that it is felony without benefit of clergy, to acknowledge, or procure to be acknowledged, any bail in the name of another person, not privy or consenting thereto, provided that it shall not corrupt the blood, or take away dower.

Stat. 4 & 5 *W.* & *M. cap.* 4. *s.* 4. enacts, that any person representing or personating another before commissioners appointed to take bail, shall be adjudged guilty of felony.

By 12 *Geo.* 1. *c.* 29. 5 *Geo.* 2. *c.* 27. and 19 *Geo.* 3. *c.* 70. none shall be held to special bail on process out of any court, where the cause of action doth not amount to 10l. or upwards; and an affidavit is to be made of the cause of action. And by 43 *Geo* 3. *c.* 46. no person shall be arrested on process of any court for a cause of action not originally sufficient to require bail. *s.* 1.

In actions of battery, trespass, slander, trover, or the like, though the plaintiff is like to recover large damages, *special bail is not to be had*, unless by order of the court, or one of the judges thereof, and the process is marked for special bail: nor is it required in actions of account, or of covenant, except it be to pay money; nor against heirs or executors, or administrators, for the debt of the testator, unless they have wasted the testator's goods. 1 *Danv. Abr.* 681. Nor against an attorney or officer of the court. *Mod. Rep.* 10.

Neither is an executor, administrator, or heir, upon the removal of a cause out of an inferior court, obliged to put in bail. 2 *Lev.* 204. 1 *Sid.* 418. 1 *Lev.* 945, 268. 2 *Jones* 82. 1 *Salk.* 98. *S. P. cont. Lit. Rep.* 81.

But if there be a *devastavit* suggested, which can only be on an action of debt on a judgment, they must find special bail. 1 *Lev.* 145. 1 *Sid.* 63. 1 *Salk.* 98.

If baron and feme are sued, the husband must put in bail for both, but if the husband does not appear upon the arrest, the wife must file common bail, before she can be discharged; for otherwise the plaintiff could not proceed to obtain judgment. *Golds.* 127. *Cro. Eliz.* 370. *Cro. Jac.* 445. *Style* 475. 1 *Mod.* 8. 6 *Mod.* 17, 105.

In all actions brought in *B. R.* upon any penal law, the defendant is only to put in common bail, except otherwise directed by the statute. *Yelv.* 53.

In *audita querela*, if the plaintiff is in execution, a recognizance of bail may be acknowledged, upon a writ commanding the justices to let him to mainprize. *Jenk. Cent.* 129.

For one taken on a writ of execution is not bailable by law; except an *audita querela* be brought. 1 *Nels. Abr.* 331.

Also if a writ of error is brought *after verdict*, bail must be put in, 3 *Jac.* 1. *c.* 8. 16 & 17 *Car.* 2. *c.* 8. *s.* 3. also in actions of debt on bond for payment of money only, debt for rent; and in ejectment, in which case the plaintiff in error may either become bound himself or find sureties. *Coke's Rep.* 142. But it is not necessary in actions on a bail bond. *Ib.* 7. Nor in error brought by executors or administrators.

On a *ca. sa.* against the defendant being returned *non est inventus*, a *scire facias* is to issue against the bail, or an action may be brought. Where a defendant renders his body in discharge of the bail, the plaintiff is by the rules of the court to make his choice of proceeding in execution, whether he will charge body, goods, or lands. 1 *Lill.* 183. And if the principal after judgment renders not himself in discharge of his bail, it is at the election of the plaintiff to take out execution either against him, or proceed against his bail: but if he takes the bail in execution, though he hath not full satisfaction, he shall never after take the principal; and if the principal be taken, he may not after meddle with the bail. *Ibid.*

There must be an *exoneretur* entered, to discharge the bail. If the defendant dies before a *ca. sa.* against him returned and filed, the bail will be discharged. 1 *Lill.* 177.

Before a *scire facias* taken out against bail, the principal may render his body in discharge of the bail: and if the bail bring in the principal before the return of the second *sci. fac.* against them, they shall be discharged. 1 *Roll. Abr.* 250. 1 *Lill.* 471.

If bail surrender the principal at or before the return of the second *scire facias*, it is good, although there be not immediate notice of it to the plaintiff, and if through want of notice he is at further charge against the bail, that shall not vitiate the surrender, but the bail shall not be delivered till they pay such charges: if at any time, after the return of the *capias*, the bail surrender the principal at a judge's chamber, and he thereupon is committed to the tipstaff, from whom he escapes, &c. this will not be a good surrender; but if it be before or on a *capias* returned, it is otherwise, the one being an indulgence, and the other matter of right. *Mod. Cas.* 238.

But the bail upon a writ of error cannot render the party in their discharge; because they are bound in a recognisance that the party shall prosecute the writ of error with effect, and pay the money if judgment be affirmed. 1 *Lill. Abr.* 173.

Neither an attorney nor his clerk shall be bail for any defendant in any civil action, nor any sheriff's officer or other person concerned in the execution of process, nor persons outlawed after judgment. *Reg. M.* 1654. *Cowp.* 228. *Doug.* 466. *Reg.* 14 *Geo.* 2.

A bail cannot be witness for the defendant at the trial; but the court, on motion, will discharge the bail, upon giving other sufficient bail. *Wood's Inst.* 582. *For the practice of the courts in respect to bail in civil actions.* See PRACTICE.

2. *Bail in criminal cases.*] Regularly for all offences, either against the common law, or act of parliament, that are below felony, the offender ought to be admitted to bail, unless it be prohibited by some special act of parliament. 4 *Black.* 297. 2 *Hal. P.C.* 127.

But by the *stat. Westm.* 1. 3 *Ed.* 1. *c.* 15. 23 *Hen.* 6. *c.* 9, and 1 & 2 *Ph. & Mar. c.* 13, at this day no justice of the peace can bail, 1, upon an accusation of treason; nor 2, of *murder*, nor, 3. in case of *manslaughter*, if the prisoner be clearly the slayer, and not barely suspected to be so; nor, 4, such as, being guilty of felony, have *broken prison*, because it not only carries a presumption of guilt, but is superadding one felony to another; 5, *persons outlawed.* 6, such as have *abjured the realm*; 7, *approvers*, and persons by them accused; 8. persons taken under the *mainour*, or in the fact of felony; 9, persons charged with *arson*; 10, *excommunicated persons*, taken by writ *de excommunicato capiendo*, *all of which are clearly not bailable*: BUT 1, As to *thieves openly defamed and known*; 2, *persons charged with other felonies, or manifold and enormous offences, not being of good fame*; and, 3, *accessaries to felonies*, that labour under the same want of reputation; *which are of a more dubious nature than the first ten, it is in the discretion of the justices whether they bail or not.*

And in the following cases the justices must admit offenders to bail upon offering sufficient surety, *viz.* 1, *persons of good fame*, charged with a bare suspicion of manslaughter, or other inferior homicide; 2, such persons being charged with *petty larceny*, or any felony not before specified; or, 3, with being *accessary* to any felony.

But where persons are arrested for manslaughter or felony, being bailable by law, they are not to be let to bail by justices of peace but in open sessions, or where two justices (*quorum unus*) are present; and the same is to be certified with the examination of the offender, and the accusers bound over to prosecute, &c. 3 *Hen.* 7. *c.* 3. 1 & 2 *P. & M. c.* 13. § 3.

Although a person under an actual arrest for any crime declared to be irrepleviable, cannot be bailed by any justice; yet if *a person at large be only accused* of any such crime, *on a slight suspicion*, before a justice of the peace, it seems that the justice of the peace ought not to commit him, but ought to take surety from him to appear before a proper court. 2 *Hawk. P. C.* 163.

And if there is no felony done he ought to be discharged. *Hal. P. C.* 98, 106.

Justices of gaol-delivery, *not being within the restraint of the stat. of Westm.* 1, which extends only to inferior magistrates, may bail persons convicted before them of homicide by misadventure, or self-defence, the better to enable them to purchase their pardon. *Cromp.* 154. *a.* *H. P. C.* 101. *F. N. B.* 246. *S. P. C.* 15.

Also it seems that in discretion they may bail a person convicted before them of manslaughter, upon special circumstances, as if the evidence against him were slight, or if he had purchased his pardon. *H. P. C.* 101. *Cromp.* 153.

The court of *B. R.* also bails in all cases, and may bail even in murder by the coroner's inquest, after examination into the depositions taken by the coroner. 1 *Salk.* 104. But if a criminal be indicted of murder, the court will not bail him; nor when a person is found guilty of any crime by the grand jury, because they cannot have notice of what evidence was before the jury. 1 *Salk.* 104.

But although this court is not tied down by the rules prescribed by the stat. West. 1. yet it will in discretion pay a due regard to those rules, and not admit a person to bail, who is expressly declared to be irreplevisable, without some particular circumstances in his favour. 2 *Inst.* 185, 186, 189. *H. C. P.* 104. 1 *Salk.* 61. 3 *Bulst.* 113. 2 *Hawk. P. C.* 113, 114. 5 *Mod.* 454.

The courts of King's Bench, Common Pleas and Exchequer, in term time, and the Chancery in the term or vacation, may bail persons by the *habeas corpus* act; but not such as are committed for treason, or felony specially expressed in the warrant of commitment, unless it be where a sessions is past from the time of commitment of the prisoner, without any prosecution, when he may be bailed. 2 *Hawk. P. C.* 107, 109, and *stat.* 16 *Car.* 1. *cap.* 10.

The *House of Lords* may also bail a peer committed upon an indictment for murder, if the indictment be removed before them by *certiorari*. *Skin.* 683.

Upon an impeachment for high crimes and misdemeanors the recognizance of bail is taken by order of the house of peers, at their lordships bar, the bail being previously approved by a committee, to whom it is referred to consider of their sufficiency; and the condition of the recognizance in such case is, that the criminal shall appear personally before the lords in parliament, and from day to day until the further order of the house. Dr. *Sacheverel's* case, 13th June 1709. *Warren Hastings'* ditto, 21st May 1787.

No person shall be bailed for felony by less than two; and it is said not to be usual for the King's Bench to bail a man on a *habeas corpus*, on a commitment for treason or felony, without four sureties; the sum in which the sureties are to be bound ought to be never less than 40*l.* for a capital crime; but it may be higher in discretion, on consideration of the ability and quality of the prisoner, and the nature of the offence; and the sureties may be examined on oath concerning their sufficiency, by him that takes the bail; and if a person be bailed by insufficient sureties, he may be required either by him who took the bail, or by any other who hath power to bail him, to find better sureties, and on his refusal may be committed; for insufficient securities are as none. *H. P. C.* 97. 2 *Hawk. P. C.* 88.

BAILIFF. (*ballivus*) Baily or *bailiff* (a word, according to Dr. *Johnson*, of doubtful etymology in itself, and borrowed from the French *baili*). But my Lord *Coke*, (*Co. Lit.* 61. *b.*) saith that it is an old Saxon word, which signifies a keeper or protector; and though there be several officers called bailiffs, whose offices and employments seem quite different from each other, yet doth something of keeping or protection belong to them all. 1 *Bac. Abr.* 361.

Hence the *sheriff* is considered as *bailiff* to the crown; and his county, of which he hath the care, and in which he is to execute the king's writs, is called his *bailiwick*; and the officers who by his precept execute writs and other process are called his *bailiffs*. *Ibid.*

There are likewise bailiffs of liberties, who are officers under lords, who have franchises exempt from the jurisdiction of the sheriff. *Ibid.*

There are likewise bailiffs of lords of manors, who collect their rents, and levy their fines and amerciaments. *Ibid.*

Also he is called a bailiff, who hath the administration, or charge of lands, goods, or chattels, to make the best benefit for the owner, against whom an action of *account* doth lie for the profits which he hath raised or made, or might by his industry and care reasonably have made, his reasonable charges and expences deducted. *Ibid.*

There are likewise those termed *bailiffs*, to whom the king's castles are committed, as the bailiff of Dover castle. *Ibid.*

The chief magistrates in divers ancient corporations are also called bailiffs, as in *Ipswich*, *Yarmouth*, *Colchester*, and other places. *Ibid.*

Besides these there are also bailiffs of the forest, of which you may read in *Manwood*, part 1, p. 113.

BAILIWICK, (*balliva*) is not only taken for the county, but signifies generally that liberty which is exempted from the sheriff of the county over which the lord of the liberty appointeth a bailiff, with such powers within his precinct as an under-sheriff exerciseth under the sheriff of the county; such as the bailiff of Westminster, &c. *Stat.* 27 *Eliz. cap.* 12. *Wood's Inst.* 206.

BAILMENT, properly so called, from the French *bailer*, to deliver, is a delivery of goods in trust, upon a contract expressed or implied, that the trust shall be faithfully executed on the part of the bailee, and the goods re-delivered as soon as the time or use for which they were bailed shall have elapsed, or be performed. 2 *Black.* 451. *Law of B.* 117.

In all cases of bailment the bailee is responsible to the bailor, if the goods are lost or damaged by his wilful default or gross negligence, or if he do not deliver up the chattels on lawful demand. 2 *Black.* 453.

And he hath therefore, such a special qualified property transferred from the bailor to himself in the goods, that he may, as well as the bailor, maintain an action against any stranger or third person who may injure or take away such goods; and this is reasonable, in order that he may thereby be always ready to answer the call of the bailor. *Ibid.*

And the degree of neglect which every bailee is answerable for is limited by Sir *Wm. Jones*, in his "Essay on the Law of Bailments," to three kinds; viz.

1. *Ordinary neglect*; which is the omission of that care which every man of common prudence, and capable of governing a family, takes of his own concerns.

2. *Gross neglect*; which is the want of that care, which every man of common sense, how inattentive soever, takes of his own property.

3. *Slight neglect*; which is the omission of that diligence which any circumspect and thoughtful persons use in securing their own goods and chattels.

The doctrine upon this subject is most learnedly, and elegantly treated of, by Sir William Jones in his essay, and is also exceedingly well exemplified in the case of Coggs and Bernard, *Ld. Raym.* 909, which was as follows: *the defendant did undertake to remove a quantity of brandy from Brook's Market to Water-Lane, and by reason of his neglect, one of the casks broke; and on Not guilty, a verdict was for the plaintiff: and in arrest of judgment two exceptions were taken: 1. Because in the declaration he was not alleged to be a common porter. 2. Because it was not averred that he had a reward.*

Ld. Ch. Ju. Holt, in his argument on this case, enumerated six species of bailment:

1st. A bare and naked bailment to another, to keep for the use of the bailor, which is called *depositum.*

2dly. A delivery of goods to another which are in themselves useful to keep, and these are to be restored again in specie, which is called accommodation.

3dly. A delivery of goods for hire, which is called *locatio*, or *conductio.*

4thly. A delivery by way of pledge, which is called *vadium.*

5thly. A delivery of goods to be carried for a reward.

6thly. Such a delivery as here in the case at bar, where the goods are delivered to do some act about them, as the carrying, and without a reward, which is called *mandatum* by *Bracton, lib.* 3. 100. In English an acting by commission

As to the first, if a person out of kindness keeps the goods of another, he shall not be answerable if they be stolen, without there be a particular default in him: and secondly, such a bailee is not chargeable for a common neglect, for it must be a gross neglect for which he shall be liable.

As to the *second bailment*, a lending gratis to use for his advantage; there the borrower is strictly bound to keep it, for if he be guilty of the least neglect he shall be answerable; as if I lend a horse to go to the North of England, and he goes to the West, and the horse is stole, he shall in that case be chargeable; for if he had gone as I directed, the horse, perhaps, would not have been stolen; this sort of bailment is mentioned in *Bracton* 90. but in this case, if the horse had been in the stable of the bailee, and stolen thence without his default, as perhaps the thieves might first have bound the bailee, and then have taken the horse, he shall not be answerable; but if he left the stable door open, he shall for that neglect be answerable: Bracton says he ought to take the utmost care, but in no place says he shall be charged where no default was in him.

As to the *third bailment*, where goods are hired out for a reward, *Bracton* 62, says, the hirer is to take all imaginable care, and to restore them at the time, and he is bound to such a care as a diligent master of a family useth to his family, which care, if he so useth, he shall not be bound; now the most diligent man is liable to be robbed, and therefore I collect, that if he be so careful, as according to Bracton's definition, and be robbed, he shall not be liable.

As to the *fourth bailment*, if goods be pawned, the pawnee has a special property, which is in nature of a security to compel the pawner to pay; and if the goods be the worse for using, the pawnee must not use them; as clothes, &c. but if they be not the worse for using, he may use them at his peril; as jewels pawned to a lady, and she keeps them in a box, and they are stolen, she shall not be charged; but if she goes abroad with them to a play, and there they are stolen, she shall be answerable. 2dly, If the pawnbroker be at charge in keeping of them, as if it were a horse, and he gives it meat, he may use it for the reasonable charge he has been at. *Bracton* 99. If a creditor takes a pawn, he is bound to restore it upon payment; but if he, notwithstanding all his diligence, lose it, he shall howsoever recover his debt, 29 *Ass. pl.* 28. for the law does not lay upon him an obligation to keep against all accidents; but if the money be tendered, and he afterwards detains, and then it is lost, he shall then be liable, for he is then a wrong-doer, and his keeping it after, is the occasion of its being stolen, and he is then answerable at all events.

As to the *fifth bailment*, goods to be carried for a reward. 1. If you deliver them to a public or common carrier, and they are stolen, he must be liable, for the law charges him at all events; yet the act of God, or the enemies of the queen, may excuse, and this is a political institution by the laws of England, that people may be safe in their dealing; for otherwise carriers, that are frequently trusted with things of greatest value, would be often tempted to confederate with thieves. 2dly, But he who has a particular private employment, though he has a reward, yet he is not bound against all events, as a factor or a bailiff; if they do to the best of their power; and that is Southcott's case, and he is bound no otherwise than as his master himself should do; for it were unjust to charge him with what he cannot prevent.

As to the *sixth bailment*, to this point; here is a man not intrusted to keep, but to carry, and not to have any thing for his pains, and through his negligence miscarries, though he be to have nothing, yet it appears there was a neglect, and for that reason he is chargeable; but if the goods had been misused by a third person in the way, as he carried them, and without any neglect of his, I hold that he would not then be liable, because he had nothing for a reward. In this case the court resolved that the plaintiff should have judgment. 1 *Bac. Abr.* 243. *Comyn.* 153. S. C. 2 *Ld. Raym.* 909. S. C. Vide also 2 *Inst.* 89. 4 *Rep.* 83. 1 *Rol. Abr.* 338. *Co. Lit.* 89. *a.* 4 *Co.* 83. *b.* *Doct. & Stud.* 129.

BALLOT for jurors. See *Jurors.*

BAIRMAN, a poor insolvent debtor left bare and naked. *Stat. Will. Reg. Scot. cap.* 17.

BAKERS, making bread under weight, deficient in goodness, &c. the same may be seized by justices of peace, &c. and penalties are inflicted by stat. So for selling their large bread at higher price than set. *Vide* 51 *H.* 3. *St.* 6. *Ord. pro pistor.* c. 2. 8 *Ann.* c. 18. 1 *Geo.* 1. *c.* 26. *s.* 5. &c. 3 *Geo.* 2. *c.* 29. *s.* 2. By the *stat.* 22 *G.* 2. *c.* 46. *s.* 21. Bakers are to mark on every loaf exposed to sale, a large W. to denote its being wheaten bread, and to denote its being household bread a large H. under the penalty of 20*s.* And within London and 12 miles of the Royal Exchange, they are restricted from baking, except within certain hours on Sunday. See *Bread. London.*

BALCANIFER, or *baldakinifer*, *i. e.* a standard bearer. *Cowel. Blount.*

BALE, (*Fr.*) a pack, or certain quantity of goods or merchandize; as a bale of silk, cloth, &c. This word is used in the statute 16 *R.* 2. and is still in use. *Ibid.*

BALENGER, by the *stat.* 28 *H.* 6. *c.* 5. seems to have been a kind of barge, or water vessel. But elsewhere it rather signifies a man of war. *Cowel. Blount.*

BALEUGA, a territory or precinct. *Ibid.*

BALISTARIUS, a balister or cross-bow man. *Ibid.*

BALIVA, is expounded to signify jurisdiction. *Co. Lit.* 105.

BALIVO AMOVENDO, a writ which anciently lay to remove a bailiff from his office, for want of sufficient land in the bailiwick. *Reg. Orig.* 78.

BALKERS, are derived from the word *balk*, because they stand higher, as it were on a balk or ridge of ground, to give notice of something to others. *Shep. Epitom.* vide *Conders.*

BALLARE, signifies *scopis expurgare.* It is mentioned in *Fleta*, *lib.* 2. *cap.* 87. *Cowel. Blount.*

BALLAST, signifies gravel, stones, or whatever else is used to poise ships, and make them go steady. *Cowel. Blount.*

BALLIUM, a sort of fortress or bulwark. *Cowel. Blount.*

BAN, or *bans*, (from the Brit. *ban.* i. e. *clamor*) is a proclamation, or public notice; any public summons or edict, whereby a thing is commanded or forbidden. It is a word ordinary among the feudists; and there is both *bannus* and *bannum* which signify two several things. This word *bans* we use here in England, especially in publishing matrimonial contracts, which is done in the church before marriage, to the end that if any man can speak against the intention of the parties, either in respect of kindred, precontract, or for other just cause, they may take their exception in time, before the marriage is consummated: and in the canon law, *bannæ sunt proclamationes sponsi & sponsæ in ecclesiis fieri solitæ.* But there may be a faculty or licence for the marriage, and then this ceremony is omitted; and ministers are not to celebrate matrimony between any persons without a licence, except the bans have been first published three several times; upon pain of suspension, &c. *Can.* 62. See MARRIAGE.

BANCALE, a covering of ease and ornament for a bench, or other seat. *Cowel. Blount.*

BANE, (from the Sax. *bana*, a murderer) signifies destruction or overthrow: as, I will be the bane of such a man, is a common saying; so when a person receives a mortal injury by any thing, we say it was his bane: and he who is the cause of another man's death, is said to be *le bane*, *i. e.* a malefactor. *Bract. lib.* 2. *tract.* 8. *cap.* 1.

BANERET, (*banerettus*, *miles vexilarius*) is a knight made in the field, with the ceremony of cutting off the point of his standard, and making it as it were a banner, and accounted so honourable that they are allowed to display their arms in the king's army as barons do, and may bear arms with supporters. They are next to the barons in dignity, and take place of all baronets; as we may learn by the letters patent for creation of baronets. *Cowel. Blount.*

But in order to entitle himself to this rank, he must have been created by the king in person in the field, under the royal banners, in time of open war, else he ranks after baronets. 4 *Inst.* 6. 1 *Black.* 403.

BANISHMENT, (Fr. *bannissement*) *Exilium, abjuratio,* is a forsaking or quitting of the realm; and a kind of civil death, inflicted on an offender: there were two kinds of it, one voluntary and upon oath, called abjuration; and the other upon compulsion for some offence. *Staundf. Pl. Cr. f.* 117. By magna charta, none shall be outlawed or banished his country, but by lawful judgment of his peers, or according to the law of the land. 9 *H.* 3. *c.* 29. And by the common law no person shall be banished, but by the authority of parliament; or in case of abjuration for felony, &c. but this is taken away by statute, 3 *Inst.* 115. *Stat.* 21 *Jac.* 1. *c.* 28. See Abjuration.

BANK, (Lat. *bancus,* Fr. *banque*) in our common law, is usually taken for a seat or bench of judgment; as *Bank le Roy,* the King's Bench, *Bank le Common Pleas,* Bench of Common Pleas, or the common Bench; called also in Latin *Bancus Regis,* and *Bancus Communium Placitorum. Cromp. Just.* 67, 91.

There are, in each of the terms, stated days, called days in bank, *dies in banco,* that is, days of appearance in the court of Common Pleas. They are generally at the distance of about a week from each other, and regulated by some festival of the church. On some one of these days in bank, all original writs must be made returnable; and therefore they are generally called the returns of that term. 3 *Black. Com.* 277.

BANK also signifies a place where a great sum of money is to let out to use, returned by exchange, or otherwise disposed of to profit: and *the Bank of England,* managed by a governor and directors, was established by parliament, by stat. 5 & 6 *Will.* & *Mar. c.* 20.

BANKERS, are those persons in whose hands money is deposited and lodged for safety, to be drawn out again as the owners have occasion for it. And the monied goldsmiths were the first who got the name of bankers in the reign of K. *Charles* the Second.

BANKRUPT, (*bancus ruptus*) is so called, because when the bank or stock is broken or exhausted, the owner is said to be a bankrupt. *Cowel.*

Summary of all the statutes relating to Bankrupts.] By 13 *Eliz. c.* 7. if any merchant, or other person using trade, bartery, or otherwise, in gross or by retail, or seeking his living by buying and selling, subject or denizen, shall depart the realm, keep his house, absent himself, suffer himself to be arrested for a debt not due, or to be outlawed, or yield himself to prison, or depart from his dwelling-house, with intent to defraud or hinder a just creditor, he shall be deemed a bankrupt.

The lord chancellor, on complaint in writing, may appoint commissioners, under the great seal, who are authorized to order the body, goods, and lands, freehold or copyhold, to be sold for satisfaction of creditors in equal portion. *Ibid.*

But the person to whom any copyhold shall be sold, shall compound with the lord of the manor for his fine, before he enters or takes any profit. *Ibid.*

The commissioners, on request, shall declare to the bankrupt, how they have bestowed his estate, and pay him the overplus. *Ibid.*

The commissioners may summon and examine all persons suspected of knowing or concealing a bankrupt's goods, debts, or effects. *Ibid.*

If such person refuse to swear, or to discover the truth, or if any persons fraudulently claim, or detain any goods, debts or tenements, they shall forfeit double the value concealed, to be levied and distributed by the commissioners amongst the creditors: and if there be an overplus, one moiety of such forfeitures shall be paid to the crown, the other to the poor. *Ibid.*

If the bankrupt doth not surrender himself, after five proclamations made near the place of his abode, he shall be out of the queen's protection, and if any persons conceal him, they shall be fined by the lord chancellor. *Ibid.*

A creditor, not satisfied his whole debt, shall have his remedy for the residue, as before this act. *Ibid.*

The commissioners may sell lands that come to the bankrupt before satisfaction is made to the creditors. *Ibid.*

This act does not extend to lands sold *bona fide,* before bankruptcy, and not to the use of the bankrupt himself.

By 1 *Jac.* 1. *c.* 15. any person using trade or the like, that shall fraudulently procure himself to be arrested, or his goods to be attached, or make any fraudulent grant of his estate, whereby his creditors may be defeated or delayed, or being arrested, shall thereon lie in prison six months shall be adjudged bankrupt.

Any creditors may share with the rest, within four months after the commission sued, and until distribution, contributing to the charges. *Ibid.*

Estates of a bankrupt conveyed to any of his children, or other persons, or debts transferred into other names, unless upon marriage, or for some valuable consideration, may be sold by the commissioners. *Ibid.*

The bankrupt not appearing on three notices left at his house, may be proclaimed a bankrupt, and not appearing on five proclamations, he may be apprehended. *Ibid.*

The commissioners may examine the offender, as to his estates, upon interrogatories. On refusal to answer fully, they may commit him, until he shall conform, and for perjury to the value of 10l. he is to stand on the pillory. *Ibid.*

Such persons as refuse, on summons, to appear and answer to interrogatories, may be committed until they submit; and witnesses sent for are to be allowed their charges, and shall be liable to the penalties of 5 *Eliz.* for perjury. *Ibid.*

Forfeitures by force of this act are to be recovered by creditors only. *Ibid.*

Debts due to the bankrupt may be assigned, but no debtor of the bankrupt is to be prejudiced on account of paying any debt to him, before he knew that he was become bankrupt. *Ibid.*

The commissioners in any action brought against them, may plead the general issue, and give the statute in evidence. *Ibid.*

If the bankrupt dies, after the commission is sued and dealt in, the commissioners may notwithstanding proceed in execution. *Ibid.*

By 21 *Jac.* 1. *c.* 19. all former statutes against bankrupts shall be largely and beneficially construed for the aid of the creditors.

Every person using trade, by bargaining, exchange, bartering, chevisance, or otherwise, in gross or by retail, or seeking his living by buying and selling, or using the trade or profession of a scrivener, who shall obtain any protection, other than lawful privilege of parliament, or exhibit any bill, to compel his creditors to accept less than their just debts, or procure longer days of payment, or upon any arrest for debt shall lie in prison two months or more, or being arrested for a debt of 100l. shall escape out of prison, or procure his enlargement by common or hired bail, shall be a bankrupt from the time of the first arrest. *Ibid.*

The commissioners may examine the bankrupt's wife for discovery of his estates, and on refusal, she is liable to the same penalties, as others are in like cases. *Ibid.*

If a bankrupt conceals goods to the value of 20l. fraudulently, or does not shew casual loss, whereby he became disabled, on indictment and conviction, he shall be set on the pillory. *Ibid.*

The commissioners may authorize persons to break open the bankrupt's house, doors, or chests, and to seize and order the body, goods and money as before appointed. *Ibid.*

The bankrupt's goods shall be divided rateably, notwithstanding any judgment bond, or attachment in London, so that execution was not executed before he became bankrupt. *Ibid.*

His goods shall be liable notwithstanding an extent, where the bankrupt was not originally debtor to the king. *Ibid.*

Goods in a bankrupt's possession, by consent of the owner, and whereof he is the reputed owner, may be sold. *Ibid.*

The commissioners, by deed inrolled, within six months, may sell the bankrupt's estates in tail, in possession, reversion or remainder, unless the remainder is in the king by his grant. *Ibid.*

Conditional estates granted by a bankrupt, may be redeemed by the commissioners and sold. *Ibid.*

No purchaser for valuable consideration, shall be impeached, unless the commission be sued within five years after the bankruptcy. *Ibid.*

All statutes against bankrupts shall extend equally to aliens as denizens, or natural born subjects. *Ibid.*

By 10 *Ann.* *c.* 15. the discharge of a bankrupt shall not extend to his partner, or one jointly bound with him.

By 7 *Geo.* 1. *c.* 31. creditors of a bankrupt, whose debts are payable at a future day, shall be admitted to a proportionable dividend, discounting at the rate of 5 per cent. and the bankrupt shall be discharged in the same manner, as if such debts had been due before he became bankrupt.

By 5 *Geo.* 2. *c.* 30. made perpetual by 37 *Geo.* 3. *c.* 124. if a bankrupt does not, within forty-two days after notice left at his house, or personal notice in case he is in prison, and notice in the London Gazette, surrender himself, and conform to the statutes by discovering his estate and effects, or if he embezzles goods to the value of 20l. or conceals books of account fraudulently, he shall suffer as a felon, without benefit of clergy, and his estate shall be divided amongst the creditors. *s.* 1.

The commissioners within the forty-two days, shall appoint not less than three meetings, the last to be on the forty-second day, whereof three weeks notice is to be given in the London Gazette. *s.* 2.

The lord chancellor may enlarge the time for a bankrupt's surrendering, not exceeding fifty days from the end of the forty-two days, by order made six days at least before the time he was to have surrendered. *s.* 3.

The bankrupt shall deliver up his accounts which are not seized, upon oath or affirmation, and upon notice he shall attend and assist the assignees. *s.* 4.

The bankrupt may inspect the accounts, and shall be free from arrests during the said forty-two days, or such further time as is allowed him to surrender, unless he was in custody at the time of his submission. If arrested within that time, on producing the notice or summons, he shall be discharged, and the officer detaining him shall forfeit 5*l.* a day to such bankrupt. *s.* 5.

Bankrupt in custody at the time of his surrender, shall be brought before the commissioners at the expence of the estate, and if in execution, they shall take his examination in prison. *s.* 6. *But see* 49 *Geo.* 3. *c.* 121. *s.* 13. *infra.*

Bankrupts discovering their estate and effects, shall, if the creditors are paid 10s. in the pound, be allowed 5l. per cent. out of the neat proceeds, so that it does not exceed 200l. and if they are paid 12s. 6d. in the pound, the bankrupt shall be allowed 7l. 10s. per cent. not exceeding 250l. in the whole, and if the creditors are paid 15s. in the pound, he shall be allowed 10l. per cent. not exceeding 300l. and such bankrupt shall be discharged from all debts due at the time he became bankrupt. *s.* 7.

If the neat produce of the estate discovered by the bankrupt does not amount to 10s. in the pound, he shall be allowed what the assignees and the commissioners think fit, not exceeding 3l. per cent. *s.* 8.

The future effects of bankrupts who shall have been discharged by any insolvent act, compounding with creditors, or by becoming bankrupt, shall be liable, unless the effects are sufficient to pay 15s. in the pound. *s.* 9.

No discovery shall entitle the bankrupt to the benefit of this act, unless the commissioners certify his conformity, and such certificate must be signed by [*three parts in five,* 49 *Geo.* 3. *c.* 121. *s.* 18.] in number and value of the creditors, whose respective debts are not less than 20*l.* The bankrupt must make oath or affirmation, that he did not obtain the signing thereof by fraud; and if he gives any securities, to induce creditors to sign the certificate, such securities shall be void. *s.* 10—11.

No bankrupt shall have any benefit under this act, who has given above 100l. on the marriage of any of his children, unless he can prove that he had sufficient effects to pay all his debts at that time; or that he has not lost at gaming 5l. in one day, or 100l. in one year, before he became bankrupt. *s.* 12.

The bankrupt after his certificate is allowed, shall be discharged from any execution, or detention in prison, for debt due at the time he became bankrupt. *s.* 13.

Judges, or justices of the peace, may grant warrants to apprehend bankrupts, who do not conform; when apprehended the gaolers are to give notice to the commissioners; and bankrupt's goods, books, and effects may be seized in any prison; but the bankrupt, so apprehended, on his conforming, may have the benefit of this act. *s.* 14, 15.

Bankrupt and others not answering the interrogatories of commissioners, may be imprisoned until they submit, but the warrant of commitment shall specify the question. *s.* 16, 17.

If an *habeas corpus* is brought on such commitment, the judge may recommit the prisoner, until he shall conform, though the form of the warrant is insufficient, unless it appear that he had answered all lawful questions; and the gaoler suffering the bankrupt to escape, or to go out of prison, shall forfeit 500l. for the benefit of the creditors, and if he refuses to shew his prisoner to a creditor, who has proved his debt, he shall in like manner forfeit 100l. *s.* 18, 19.

Persons discovering effects concealed by bankrupts, are to be allowed 5 per cent. thereout; and persons concealing the same are to forfeit 100l. and double the value to the creditors. *s.* 20, 21.

Creditors on bonds, notes, or bills, payable at a future day, may petition for commissions, and no commission shall be granted, unless the debt of a single petitioner amounts to 100l. of two creditors petitioning to 150l. or of three creditors to 200l. which must be sworn to or affirmed, and bonds must be given to prove the bankruptcy. *s.* 22, 23.

Where creditors have made a collusive composition with the bankrupt, to have more than the rest, they shall forfeit their whole debts, and pay back what they have received to the creditors; and the commission in such case, shall be superseded, and another granted to the other creditors. *s.* 24.

The charge of suing the commission shall be paid by the petitioners, and reimbursed out of the bankrupt's effects, and creditors shall be admitted without contributing. *s.* 25.

After the party is declared a bankrupt, the commissioners shall give notice in the Gazette, of the meetings; and creditors living remote may prove their debts by affidavit, or affirmation made before a master extraordinary; and, by letter of attorney, may vote in the choice of assignees, who shall keep accounts for the inspection of creditors. But no creditors shall vote for assignees, whose debt does not amount to 10*l.* *s.* 26, 27.

Mutual credits with the bankrupt, shall be settled according to the balance of account. *s.* 28.

Persons swearing to debts falsely, are to forfeit double the sum to the other creditors, and be liable to the statutes made against perjury. *s.* 29.

The commissioners may appoint assignees for securing the bankrupt's effects, who may be removed by the creditors at their meeting, and others chosen, and for not delivering up the effects to the new ones, after ten days notice, the first assignees shall respectively forfeit 200l. to the creditors. And notice of the removal of assignees, and appointment of others, in whom the effects are vested, shall be given in the Gazette. *s.* 30, 31.

Creditors, before the choice of assignees, may appoint the manner of paying the monies got in. *s.* 32. See also 49 *Geo.* 3. *c.* 121. *s.* 3. *infra.*

After four, and within twelve months, from the commission, assignees shall give twenty-one days notice in the Gazette, and creditors may come and prove their debts, and a dividend shall be directed. *s.* 33.

Assignees with the consent of creditors, may submit disputes to arbitration, and compound debts. *s.* 34, 35.

A bankrupt, after certificate allowed, shall attend and assist the assignees in settling his accounts, for 2s. 6d. a day; and if he refuses, may be committed till he shall conform. *s.* 36.

A final dividend shall be made within eighteen months, unless there is a suit depending, or some effects outstanding. *s.* 37.

No suit in equity shall be commenced without consent of a majority of the creditors. *s.* 38.

Bankers, brokers, and factors, shall be liable to the bankrupt laws; but no farmer, grazier, or drover of cattle, or receiver general of taxes, shall be liable thereto. *s.* 39, 40.

Proceedings may be entered on record, by direction of the lord chancellor, and may be searched, and copy of such record and of certificate allowed, shall be evidence to discharge bankrupts from actions, unless the creditor proves it was fraudulently obtained. *s.* 41.

No schedule shall be annexed to any assignment of the bankrupt's personal estate from the commissioners to the assignees: and if a commissioner takes above 20s. for each meeting, or orders any expence, he shall be disabled. *s.* 42.

Commissioners are to take an oath to act impartially, and enter a memorial thereof amongst the proceedings. *s.* 43, 44.

Commissions shall not abate by demise of the king, but if necessary to renew the same, through the death of the commissioners, the same shall be done for half fees. *s.* 45.

Fees of solicitors employed under commissions, are to be settled by a master in chancery, who is to have 20s. for so doing. *s.* 46.

By 19 *Geo.* 2. *c.* 32. creditors of bankrupts shall not be liable to refund to the assignees, monies, *bona fide* received in the course of trade, before notice of insolvency. *s.* 1.

Creditors on bottomree bonds, policies of insurance, and the like, shall be admitted to prove, as if the contingency had happened, and the bankrupt shall be discharged from the debt accordingly. *s.* 2.

By 24 *Geo.* 2. *c.* 57. certificates signed by fictitious creditors, unless the bankrupt discloses the fraud, shall be void. *s.* 9.

Letter of attorney from a creditor in foreign parts, attested by a notary public, shall be sufficient evidence to authorise his signing the certificate. *s.* 10.

By 4 *Geo.* 3. *c.* 33. the creditors of any merchant within the description of the laws relating to bankrupts, having privilege of parliament, may, upon affidavit made of the debt, and filed in any of the courts at Westminster, sue out a summons, or original bill, against such debtor: and if he shall not, within two months, pay, secure, or compound for the debt, he shall be adjudged a bankrupt; and a commission may be accordingly sued out against him. *s.* 1, 2.

But persons entitled to privilege are not to be arrested, except in cases made felony in the bankrupt laws. *s.* 3.

By 36 *Geo.* 3. *c.* 90. upon bankrupts refusing to transfer stock standing in their own right, the lord chancellor may order it to be transferred to the assignees.

By 45 *Geo.* 3. *c.* 124. traders having privilege of parliament, shall, within two months after summonses, under 4 *Geo.* 3. *c.* 33. enter an appearance, or be adjudged bankrupt. *s.* 1.

And traders having the privilege of parliament, disobeying the orders of the court of chancery or exchequer, and refusing to pay money according to the tenor thereof, shall be deemed bankrupts. *s.* 7.

But the personal liberty of members during privilege is saved.

By 46 *Geo.* 3. *c.* 135. all conveyances by, all payments to, and all contracts with, a bankrupt, made *bona fide* two months before the date of the commission of bankrupt shall be good. *s.* 1.

Bona fide creditors shall be admitted to prove debts, notwithstanding any secret act of bankruptcy. *s.* 2.

Mutual debts and credits may be set off, notwithstanding a secret act of bankruptcy. *s.* 3.

Certificates shall discharge bankrupts of debts provable under this act. *s.* 4.

And commissions of bankruptcy shall not be avoided by any secret act of bankruptcy, committed before the contracting of the petitioning creditor's debt. *s.* 5.

By 49 *Geo.* 3. *c.* 121. in all cases executions and attachments against the lands or goods of bankrupts levied more than two months before the commission, shall be valid, notwithstanding any prior act of bankruptcy, provided the party had no notice of such prior act of bankruptcy, and the issuing of a commission grounded upon an act of bankruptcy, though afterwards superseded, shall be deemed notice. *s.* 2.

If the creditors do not, before they proceed to the choice of assignees, direct how and with whom and where the monies arising from the bankrupt's estate, shall be paid, until the dividend takes place, the commissioners immediately after the choice of assignees, and at the same meeting, shall give directions thereon, and the assignees are to conform to such directions as often as 100*l.* shall be got in: but the monies are not to be directed to be paid to the commissioners or the solicitor, or into any banking house or other house of trade or business in which the commissioners or solicitor are interested or concerned: the assignees disobeying such directions are to be charged 20*l.* per cent. on the money retained or employed contrary thereto. *s.* 3—4.

The commissioners are not to declare a dividend till a true statement in writing be made upon oath by the assignees of their receipts and payments, to ascertain what dividend ought to be made, and what sum retained in hand. *s.* 5.

After Jan. 1. 1810, if assignees become bankrupt, having 100*l.* of the bankrupt's estate, their certificates shall not discharge their future effects in respect of so much thereof, with lawful interest, as shall not be paid by the dividends. *s.* 6.

The commissioners may direct the money paid in on bankrupt's estate, to be invested in exchequer bills, and also with whom and where they shall be deposited, until the dividend. *s.* 7.

Sureties and persons liable for the debts of the bankrupt, not paying until after the commission, may prove under the commission, after having paid such debts, not disturbing former dividends; and the persons hereby enabled to prove will be barred by the certificate in like manner as other creditors. *s.* 8.

Debts not payable at the time of the bankruptcy may be proved, deducting a rebate of interest. *s.* 9.

In actions brought by assignees, and also in suits in equity, by assignees, the commission and proceedings under it shall be sufficient evidence of the petitioning creditor's debt, and the trading and act of bankruptcy, unless notice in writing be given that those matters are to be disputed. *s.* 10—11.

No action shall be brought against assignees for dividends, but the remedy shall be by petition to the lord chancellor. *s.* 12.

Bankrupts in custody *in execution* may be brought before the commissioners by their warrant to be examined. *s.* 13.

Proving a debt under a commission, shall be deemed an election not to proceed against the bankrupt by action in respect of such debt. *s.* 14.

Persons effecting policies of insurance with under-writers, who become bankrupts, may prove the loss, though not interested in the policy, if the insured is not in that part of the kingdom. *s.* 16.

Annuity creditors may be admitted to prove the value under any commission, such value being ascertained by the commissioners. *s.* 17.

The signature and consent of *three parts in five* in number and value of the creditors of the bankrupt, to the allowance of his certificate and discharge, shall be sufficient to authorize all acts to be done by the lord chancellor and commissioners for his benefit. *s.* 18.

Bankrupts entitled to leases, or agreements for leases, delivering up the same to assignees are not liable afterwards for the rent nor in respect of the covenants. *s.* 19.

Practical summary of the subsisting bankrupt laws.] *Who may be made bankrupts.*—Under the above statutes, any merchant or other person using the trade of merchandize by way of bargaining, exchange, re-change, bartery, chevisance, or otherwise, in gross or retail, or seeking his trade or living by buying or selling, may be bankrupt. Also bankers, brokers, factors, dealers in coals, scriveners, vintners, brickmakers, butchers, bakers, brewers, clothiers, goldsmiths, iron manufacturers buying the same and working it up into goods, locksmiths, milliners, nailors, plumbers, salesmen, shoemakers, smiths, tanners, and indeed any person seeking his living by buying or selling any thing, though his dealing may not come under the denomination of any particular trade, may be a bankrupt as a dealer and chapman. 1 *Cooke B. L.* 37.

Persons exercising mere handicraft trades, where nothing is bought or sold, cannot by such trading become bankrupts; but where they purchase commodities, upon which bodily labour is afterwards bestowed in order to render them fit for sale, thereby enhancing their value, they may become bankrupts. *Ib.* 37.

Clergymen, barristers, and attornies, as such, are not liable to the bankrupt laws; but if they enter into a trade they are liable in that character. Infants and married women cannot be bankrupts, but a feme covert sole trader in the city of London may, according to the custom, be bankrupt. 1 *Cooke B. L.* 26.

Acts of bankruptcy]. Must be committed with an intent to defraud or delay creditors from recovering their just debts, and among these, are to be reckoned:

1. *Departing the realm*, by which a man withdraws himself from the reach of the law, which is an act of bankruptcy if done with a view to defraud his creditors, or if in fact they are delayed by such absence. *Bull. N. P.* 39.

2. *Beginning to keep house or otherwise to absent himself*, is an act of bankruptcy; keeping house without a denial to a creditor is not. 5 *T. R.* 575. And a mere denial may be explained by circumstances, such as sickness, company, business, or a late hour. 1 *Coke* 79. A mere order to deny, without an actual denial, is not sufficient. *Ib.* The denial must be to a creditor who has a debt due at the time. *Ib.* 82.

3. *Departing from his dwelling house*, if with a view of defrauding or delaying his creditors, is an act of bankruptcy. *Ib.* 85.

4. *Suffering himself to be outlawed*, is an act of bankruptcy, if suffered with an intent to defraud his creditors. *Ib.* 85.

5. *Yielding himself to prison for debt*, is an act of bankruptcy, where done voluntarily, if it can be ascertained that the person imprisoned is capable of paying. 1 *Cooke B. L.* 85.

6. *Willingly or fraudulently procuring his goods or effects to be attached or sequestered*, is an act of bankruptcy, being of course an attempt to prejudice the rest of his creditors. 2 *Com.* 478.

7. *Making fraudulent grant or conveyance of his lands, tenements, goods, or chattels*, is an act of bankruptcy; but it must be by deed; and must be of all his effects; a mere colourable reserve of part of the effects will not prevent the deed being deemed fraudulent; and it is fraudulent though made to a *bona fide* creditor, or even to trustees for the benefit of all the creditors except one. 1 *Burr.* 477. An assignment for the benefit of all the creditors has been held an act of bankruptcy unless they all concur in the deed. 1 *Cooke* 89.

8. *Procuring protection from arrests*, other than is afforded by privilege of parliament, is an act of bankruptcy, and also

9. *Lying in prison for two months or more upon arrest or other detention for debt*: the months are lunar months. *Ib.* 97.

10. *Escaping from prison* after an arrest for a just debt of 100l. or upwards, is an act of bankruptcy; and also

11. Neglecting to make satisfaction for any just debt of 100l. or upwards within two months, after process served upon him, having privilege of parliament. 4 *Geo.* 3. *c.* 33.

Petitioning creditor's debt.] No commission shall be granted unless the debt upon the petition of one creditor amounts to 100l.; of two, to 150*l.*; of three or more, to 200l. 5 *Geo.* 2. *c.* 30. *s.* 23.

The debt must be a legal and not an equitable one; therefore, the assignee of a bond cannot take out a commission. A debt at law, notwithstanding the statute of limitations has incurred will support a commission. 1 *Coke* 13. And also a solicitor's bill for fees notwithstanding an order has been obtained for taxing. *Ib.* 17. So also attornies or solicitors' bills, though not delivered a month, signed, the act requiring same, applying only to actions at law. A debt due from a partnership will support a separate commission against one of the partners. *Ex parte Crisp*, 1 *Atk.* 134. Creditor by bond, bill, or security for money payable at a future day, may sue out commission. 5 *Geo.* 2. *c.* 30. *s.* 22. Also indorsee of a bill or note after an act of bankruptcy. 2 *Wils.* 135. Creditor having debtor in execution cannot petition. 1 *Cooke* 25. Petitioning creditor has not the election of proceeding at law. *Ib.* 25.

Striking a docket] is done by applying to the clerk in the secretary of bankrupts office, for a bond to the lord chancellor, in the penalty of 200l. to prove the party a bankrupt, (which the clerk will fill up) this bond the petitioning creditor must execute, and likewise make an affidavit of his debt before a master in chancery if in town; or a master extraordinary in the country: in the latter case, such affidavit must not be sworn before the solicitor to the commission, or any of the intended commissioners; and, in a country commission, the bond is prepared and executed in the country and transmitted with the affidavit, and the bond should be executed in the presence of two witnesses, one the master extraordinary who takes the affidavit.

This bond being executed, and affidavit sworn, the clerk will prepare a petition to the lord chancellor, on behalf of the petitioning creditor, and get the commission sealed.

When the commission is sealed, the messenger being informed of the commissioners' names, will summon three of them to meet at some tavern, coffee-house, or other convenient place.

But if the commission is to be executed in the country, which can only be when the bankrupt resides above forty miles from London, the petitioning creditor names the commissioners; and by the lord chancellor's order of 12th August, 1800, there should be two barristers and three attornies in such commission.

If a creditor strikes a docket and does not proceed to seal a commission within four days after, exclusive, any other creditor may strike a new docket and obtain commission. Lord chancellor's order, 12 Feb. 1774. And any commission of bankrupt to be executed in the city of London, and not prosecuted within fourteen days from the date thereof, shall be supersedable; if in the country, twenty-eight days; but one day must elapse before supersedeas shall issue, and any solicitor first applying that day, for a new commission, shall be preferred to the former solicitor. Lord chancellor's order, 26 June, 1793.

Renewed commissions are granted where the original commissioners are dead, so that the original commission cannot be proceeded in, and is directed to new commissioners: it is obtained upon petition to the chancellor, stating the deaths of the commissioners and verified by affidavit.

Private meeting.] This meeting is had for the commissioners to find by proof an act of bankruptcy committed, to see the petitioning creditor's debt proved, and to declare the party a bankrupt accordingly; for this purpose the solicitor attends with the commission and witnesses.

The commissioners being met, and the commission produced, the three commissioners present administer an oath to each other for the faithful execution of their trust; and then proceed to take the proof of the petitioning creditor's debt, the trading, and acts of the bankruptcy, which are to be reduced into the form of depositions.

If the party is found to be a bankrupt, the commissioners sign proper warrants for seizing the bankrupt's effects, advertising the bankruptcy in the Gazette, and for the bankrupt to appear and surrender himself, &c. This first meeting, and till the seizure, is usually carried on with great secresy, to prevent any suspicion, and concealing or carrying away of the bankrupt's effects, by himself or others. And sometimes at this sitting, where an extent is expected on the bankrupt's effects, a provisional assignment is required to be made, which is only a temporary assignment, and usually made to the messenger until assignees are chosen in order to take place of an extent; but should only be executed when necessary.

First meeting.] At the first public meeting there is seldom any thing more to be done than the taking depositions of creditor's debts; if the bankrupt appears, a memorandum is made of it, and thereby further time is given him to make his examination; so there is if he does not.

At this meeting it is prudent for the bankrupt to surrender for the sake of protection, but it is doubtful whether a surrender at the private meeting will protect him. 2 *Cooke, p.* 21.

Debts are proved by the deposition of the creditors themselves, if in town, their clerks or servants not being allowed to prove for them; but if absent, any person may attend and make a claim of such debts, which the creditors must afterwards attend and substantiate. Claims should in strictness be struck out before the first dividend, though it is usual to let them remain until the final dividend, when they are struck out of course if not established. 2 *Cooke* 24. If any creditor resides in the country, his affidavit must be prepared, sworn before a master extraordinary, and then sent up to be exhibited to the commissioners at one of their public meetings; and care should be taken that such affidavit state the consideration upon which the debt arose, and also the security or securities (if any) which the creditor may have in his hands for the same, which must be sent up, with the affidavit to be exhibited.

Second meeting.] At the second public meeting, after taking depositions of such creditors debts as appear, the creditors who have proved their debts to be 10l. or above (for no other has a vote for choice of assignees) consult among themselves and chuse one or more, usually of the greatest creditors, to be assignee or assignees of the bankrupt's effects, which choice is determined by the major part in value of those who vote; and such creditors set their names to a memorandum of their making such choice, and thereby request the commissioners to assign the same to him or them accordingly; and the assignee or assignees signs his or their names thereunder, of their acceptance of such trust; if the bankrupt then appears to surrender, he must sign his surrender, and request further time to the last sitting to make his final examination and discovery.

Country creditors, who mean to vote in the choice of assignees, must execute a letter of attorney for that purpose to some person in town, which must be sent up, together with an affidavit of the execution thereof.

At this second meeting, the solicitor has an assignment of the bankrupt's effects ready ingrossed, to be executed by the commissioners. And it is also necessary for the solicitor who sued out the commission, to make out his bill of costs (inclusive of this sitting) that the same may be settled and allowed by the commissioners, and paid on behalf of his client, before he parts with the commission out of his hands; for the assignees may afterwards employ some other attorney to act for them under the commission; and, as the petitioning creditor is obliged to prosecute the commission until assignees are chosen, therefore the commissioners are empowered to settle and allow his bill, and to order the assignees to pay the same out of the first effects that shall come to their hands. Subsequent bills are settled by a master in chancery.

Before the creditors proceed to the choice of assignees, they are to direct how, with whom, and where the monies arising from the bankrupt's estate shall be paid or deposited, and if they do not, the commissioners, after the choice of the assignees, shall give proper directions in that behalf. 49 *Geo.* 3. *c.* 121. *s.* 3.

Third meeting.] The last or third public sitting is for the bankrupt to finish his examination and discovery of his effects; and the creditors to assent to or dissent from the allowance of his certificate; but depositions are still to be prepared for such creditors who come to prove their debts. *Green's B. L.*

The bankrupt, upon finishing his examination, must surrender up what money he has in his pocket, watch, silver-buckles, &c. to the assignees; they are seldom so strict as to keep all his money, but will return in proportion to the quantity; at this sitting it may be prudent for him to have a proper person to attend with his certificate, to request such of his creditors to sign it, as have proved debts to the value of 20l. or upwards respectively; and to witness their signing; which may save the trouble of going round to all of them separately afterwards, and forward the same so that he may get it allowed. *Green's Bank. L.*

One or more further meetings of the commissioners are often requisite to be had, either for making a dividend, or other purpose; notice is to be published in the Gazette, and 21 days notice given of the meeting (if it be for a dividend); if the bankrupt has occasion for the commissioners to certify the great seal of his conformity, he must have a meeting on purpose at his own expense. *Ibid.*

Dividends.] Persons chosen assignees shall, after the expiration of four months and within twelve months from the time of issuing such commission, cause 21 days notice to be given in the Gazette of the time and place the commissioners and assignees intend to meet and make a dividend; at which time the creditors who have not before proved their debts, shall be at liberty to prove the same; which meeting for the city of London, and all places within the bills of mortality, shall be at Guildhall; and upon every such meeting the assignees shall produce an account of their receipts and payments, and of what shall remain outstanding; and shall (if the creditors present require the same) be examined upon oath or solemn affirmation, touching the truth of such account, and the assignees shall be allowed all just allowances; and the commissioners shall order such part of the neat produce of the said bankrupt's estate, in the hands of the assignees, as they shall think fit, to be divided amongst the creditors, and shall make such order for a dividend in writing, and shall cause one part of such order to be filed amongst the proceedings under the commission, and shall deliver unto each of the assignees a duplicate of such order, which order shall contain an account of the time and place of making such order, and the sum total of the debts proved, and the sum total of the money remaining in the hands of the assignees; and how much in the pound is then ordered to be paid, and the assignees in pursuance of such order, and without any deed of distribution, shall forthwith make such dividend, and take receipts from each creditor. 5 *Geo.* 2. *c.* 30. *s.* 33. *Atk. Rep.* 88, 91. *ca.* 39. *id.* 107, 209.

Within eighteen months after the issuing forth of any such commission, the assignees shall make a second dividend, in case the estate was not wholly divided upon the first, and shall cause notice to be inserted in the Gazette, of the time and place the said commissioners intend to meet to make a second dividend, and for the creditors who shall not have before proved their debts, to come and prove the same; and at such meeting every assignee shall produce upon oath or affirmation his accounts; and what upon the balance shall appear to be in his hands shall by like order of the commissioners be forthwith divided, which second dividend shall be final, unless any suit shall be depending, or any part of the estate standing out, or unless some future estate of the bankrupt shall afterwards come to the assignee, in which case the assignees shall, as soon as may be, convert such future estate into money, and shall within two days after, by the like order of the commissioners, divide the same. Same stat.

Creditors not having proved their debts in time to receive the first dividend, may, upon obtaining an order for that purpose, be permitted to prove at a second or further dividend, and be paid equally with the creditors under the former dividend, and it is now the practice to permit such proof without any order, and the commissioners will direct that such creditors be paid, in the first place, equal to those who have proved before, and then direct an equal distribution of the residue. 1 *Cooke* 521.

Formerly a creditor might recover his dividend from the assignees by action of assumpsit, and the proceedings before the commissioners was conclusive evidence of the debt. *Doug.* 392. But now by 49 *Geo.* 3. *c.* 121. *s.* 12. No action can be brought against the assignees for any dividend, but the party must apply for payment by petition to the lord chancellor.

Assignees should make a dividend as early as possible after the time given by the statute, as they will otherwise become liable to interest in case they unnecessarily retain the money. 1 *Cooke* 273.

In case they do not make a dividend in due time, the commissioners ought to summon them to do it. *Atk. Rep.* 91. *ca.* 39.

The Commissioners.] The lord chancellor, &c. upon complaint in writing against a bankrupt, by petition, as before prescribed, must, by commission, appoint such persons as to him shall seem good; who, or the major part of them, may at their discretion take such order with the body of such person by imprisonment, also with his lands as well copyhold as freehold, which he had in his own right before he became a bankrupt; and also with such lands as such person hath purchased for money, or other recompence, jointly with his wife or child, or to the only use of such offender; or for such use or title us such offender then shall have in the same, which he may depart withal; or with any person of trust to any secret use of such offender; and also with his money, goods, merchandize, and debts; and cause the said lands, &c. to be appraised to the best value, and by deed indented to be inrolled sell the said lands; and of all deeds touching the same, belonging to such offender; and also of all fees, offices, goods and chattels; or otherwise to order the same for satisfaction of the creditors, to every of the creditors a portion rate like according to their debts; and every direction, and other thing done, by the person so authorised, shall be good against the said offender, his wife, heirs, children, and such persons as by such joint purchase with the offenders shall have any estate or interest in the premises, and against all other persons claiming by, from, or under such offender; or by acts done after such person shall become bankrupt; and also against the lords of manors, whereof the said copyhold lands are holden, provided that every person, to whom such sale of copyhold lands shall be made, shall, before they take any profit of the same, agree with the lords of manors for such fines, as have been accustomed to be paid; and upon such agreement the lords at the next court are to admit, &c. 13 *Eliz. c.* 30. *s.* 3.

The commissioners may examine the bankrupt upon interrogatories, touching the lands, goods, debts, books of account, and such other things as may tend to disclose his estate, or secret grants, and eloigning of his lands, goods, money, and debts, as they think meet. 1 *Jac. c.* 15. *sect.* 9. 5 *Geo.* 3. *c.* 30.

They may examine, as well by word of mouth as on interrogatories in writing, every bankrupt, touching all matters relating to his trade, dealings, and effects, and reduce into writing his answers had or taken before them as aforesaid, which examination, so reduced into writing, he shall sign and subscribe. 5 *Geo.* 2. *c.* 30. *sect.* 16.

They have power to examine his wife upon oath, for the discovery of his estate, goods, and chattels; and such wife refusing to appear, or to answer interrogatories, shall incur the same penalties, as are provided against such persons in like cases. 21 *Jac. c.* 19. *sect.* 6.

But she cannot be examined against her husband touching his bankruptcy, or whether he had committed any act of bankruptcy, or as to how and when he became bankrupt. *P. W. Rep.* 610. 12 *Vin. Abr.* 11. *pl.* 28.

The commissioners may examine, as well by word of mouth as on interrogatories in writing, all and every person, duly summoned before or present at any of their meetings, touching any act or acts of bankruptcy committed by him; and also take down, or reduce into writing, the answers of verbal examinations of every such person had or taken before them as aforesaid, which examination so taken down, or reduced into writing, the party examined shall sign or subscribe. 5 *Geo.* 2. *c.* 30. *sect.* 16.

In case any such person shall refuse to answer, or shall not fully answer to their satisfaction all lawful questions put to him by them, or the major part of them, as well by word of mouth as by interrogatories in writing, or shall refuse to sign and subscribe his examination, so taken or reduced into writing as aforesaid (not having a reasonable objection either to the wording thereof, or otherwise, to be allowed by the commissioners) they may, by warrant under their hands and seals, commit him to such prison as they shall think fit, there to remain without bail or mainprize, until such time such person shall submit himself to the commissioners, and full answer make to their satisfaction to all such questions as shall be put to him as aforesaid, and sign and subscribe such examination as aforesaid, according to the true intent and meaning of this act. See *Ld. Raym.* 100. 2 *Bur. Rep.* 1125.

In case any person shall be committed by the commissioners for refusing to answer, or not fully answering any question put to him by them, by word of mouth, or on interrogatories, they shall in their warrant of commitment specify such questions. *Same act, sect.* 17. *Atk. Rep.* 200.

The commissioners may commit a bankrupt refusing to be examined, &c. till he does submit himself to be examined. *Salk.* 151. See *Perrot's* Case in 2 *Bur. Rep.* 1123, 1216.

The commissioners have power to examine others as to what they know of any person's carrying away any part of the bankrupt's estate. 5 *Mod.* 309. *Comb.* 391. *Ld. Raym.* 467. *Com. Rep.* 80. *Ses. Cas.* 335. 2 *Stra.* 880. See Miller's Case in *Green,* 235.

The commissioners have power to sell, grant, and assign the bankrupt's estate, and effects; but they cannot bring an action; for their assigns must generally bring all actions. *Mod.* 30.

Formerly all the goods and chattels of a bankrupt, which he was possessed of at the time of his becoming a bankrupt might be sold by the commissioners, notwithstanding the bankrupt sold them in market overt; for the sale of the commissioners only had a relation to the first act of bankruptcy: but now by 46 *Geo.* 3. *c.* 135. *s.* 1. all contract with a bankrupt in *bona fide* made two months before the date of the commission are declared to be good, and no debtor of a bankrupt shall be in danger for paying a debt due to a bankrupt before he had notice that he was a bankrupt. 1 *Jac.* 1. *c.* 15. 2 *Show. Rep.* 522. 7 *Vin. Abr.* 108. 2 *Eq. Cas. Abr.* 396. *pl.* 3. *Atk. Rep.* 127, 157.

The creditors have a right to the bankrupts goods by the act of bankruptcy, and thereby they are bound: though until assignment by the commissioners the property is not transferred out of the bankrupt. *Salk.* 108. Therefore a creditor being in possession of the bankrupt goods by virtue of a *Fi. fa.* upon a judgment entered up after an act of bankruptcy proved, must waive the same, and come in under the commission.

The commissioners are to sell all the bankrupt lands in fee, for life, or years, and it will be binding against the bankrupt and his issue.

If a bankrupt hath lands in right of his wife, they may be sold during the coverture; but the dower of a bankrupt's wife cannot be sold, nor an estate settled to the separate use of wife and children.

They may sell all entailed lands in possession, reversion, or remainder; except entailed in the crown, of the gift of the king; and this shall bind the issue in tail, and all others which a common recovery might cut off. *Stat.* 21 *Jac. c.* 19. *s.* 12.

If a bankrupt grants his lands or goods in the names of other persons, the commissioners notwithstanding may make sale of them, but not lands, &c. conveyed *bona fide* two months before the date of the commission *c.* 7. *s.* 12. *Mo.* 594. *pl.* 805. *Mar.* 34. *pl. Stat.* 13 *El.* 67. 46 *Geo.* 3. *c.* 135. *s.* 1.

Lands held by a bankrupt in jointenancy, may be sold as to the moiety. *Atk. Rep.* 93. *ca.* 41. See *Bur. Rep.* 472. also lands devised to a bankrupt may be sold.

The commissioners have power to sell lands mortgaged, on tender and payment of the mortgage money. 2 *Rep.* 25. *Com. Dig.* 530. *Cro. Car.* 550.

Offices of inheritance may be sold, but not offices of trust annexed to the person for life. *Atk. Rep.* 210. *ca.* 217. *id.* 213.

If a bankrupt commits felony, his lands shall not escheat, but the commissioners may sell; and his creditors shall have his goods, not the king. 5 *Geo.* 2. *c.* 30.

The sale of bankrupt lands by the commissioners must, according to the statute, be by deed of bargain and sale inrolled.

And no purchase of lands *bona fide* sold, nor conveyances by bankrupts, made two calendar months previous to the date of commission, shall be impeached notwithstanding any previous act of bankruptcy, provided the person so contracting or dealing with bankrupt had no notice of any prior act of bankruptcy. 46 *Geo.* 3. *c.* 135. *s.* 1.

A man makes a bill of sale of some lands, and personal estate, to another, in trust to pay his debts; the trustee takes the whole into his possession, and becomes a bankrupt; his estate is not liable to the bankruptcy, either in law or equity. *P. Will. Rep.* 314. *pl.* 81.

Assignees.] The commissioners, after they have declared the person a bankrupt, are to cause notice thereof to be given in the Gazette, and appoint a time and place for the creditors to meet and chuse assignees; at which meeting the commissioners are to admit the proof of any creditor's debt, that lives remote from the place of meeting, by affidavit or affirmation; and also permit any person duly authorized by letter of attorney (oath or affirmation being made of the execution of it before a master in chancery ordinary or extraordinary, or *viva voce* before the commissioners, and in case of creditors residing in foreign parts, on affidavit or affirmation made before a magistrate, and which shall, together with his letter of attorney, be attested by a notary public) to vote in the choice of assignees, in the place of such creditor, and the commissioners are to assign the estate to such persons, as the major part in value of such creditors, according to the debts then proved, shall chuse; and the assignees are to keep books of account of all money and effects which they shall receive; to which book the creditors are to have free resort; no creditor or person in his behalf to vote in the choice of assignees whose debt does not amount to 10*l.* 5 *Geo.* 2. *c.* 30. *sec.* 26, 27.

Assignees are to pay and reimburse the petitioning creditor. 5 *Geo.* 2. *c.* 30.

Where there hath been mutual credit given, or mutual debts between the bankrupt and any other person, before the bankruptcy, the commissioners or assignees shall state the account, and one debt may be set off against another, and the balance only of such account claimed or paid. 5 *Geo.* 2. *c.* 30. *sect.* 28.

In case of mutual credit given by the bankrupt and any other person, or mutual debts between the bankrupt and any other person, one debt or demand may be set off against another, notwithstanding any prior act of bankruptcy committed before such credit was given to bankrupt, provided it was given two calendar months before issuing commission and creditor had no notice of such act. 46 *Geo.* 3. *c.* 135. *s.* 3.

They may, with the consent of the major part in value of the creditors, at any meeting, pursuant to notice in the Gazette, submit any difference to arbitration. 5 *Geo.* 2. c. 30. *sect.* 34.

They may, with the consent of the creditors, compound debts. *s.* 35.

They may, with the consent of the major part in value of the creditors, at any meeting, pursuant to notice in the Gazette, commence a suit in equity, but not without such consent. 2 *Black. Com.* 487. 1 *Atk. Rep.* 91. *ca.* 39. *id.* 107, 253.

As often as 100*l.* shall be received, they are to pay in the same in such manner and place, as the major part in value of the creditors present at the choice of assignees shall direct; and they are indemnified for what they shall do in pursuance of such direction of the creditors. 5 *Geo.* 2. *c.* 30. *sect.* 32.

And if the creditors do not before the choice of assignees, appoint how the monies shall be paid, the commissioners shall give directions in respect thereof, see 49 *Geo.* 3. *c.* 121. *s.* 3. *supra.*

They may discharge the solicitor to the commission, and employ whom they please, and therefore the former one is to deliver up all papers, &c. on being paid his bill. 7 *Vin. Abr.* 117. *pl.* 2.

They are to reward discoverers of bankrupt's effects 5*l.* per cent. and such further reward as the major part of creditors in value, at any meeting, shall think fit. 5 *Geo.* 2. *c.* 20. *sect.* 20.

The assignees after assignment, may bring actions for debts due to the bankrupt in their own names. The statute of limitations will run against the assignees from the time of the original promise made to bankrupt. 1 *Cooke* 273.

Assignees have the benefit of covenants of re-entry into lands.

Under the assignment of the bankrupt's estate, the assignees have power to do every act, the commissioners themselves might do, for the better enabling them to recover and get in the same, for the benefit of themselves and the rest of the creditors.

They may give notice in writing to the bankrupt, after he has obtained his certificate, and the same be confirmed, to attend them to settle accounts of his estate, or to attend any court of record to be examined touching the same, or for any other business the assignees judge necessary, for getting in his estate; for which attendance the assignees must allow the bankrupt 2*s.* 6*d.* a day; and if he neglects to attend, or refuses to assist in such discovery, without good cause shewn to, and allowed by the commissioners (the assignees proving such notice, and neglect, or refusal, on oath before the commissioners) the commissioners may issue their warrant for apprehending him, and commit him to the county gaol till he does conform, and he by the commissioners or order of lord chancellor or due course of law be discharged. 5 *Geo.* 2. *c.* 30. *s.* 36. 1 *Atk. Rep.* 148. *pl.* 8.

By virtue of the commissioners warrant they may break open chests, chambers, houses, shops, doors, &c. where he or his goods or estate shall be reputed to be, and seize upon and order the body, goods, money, &c. as to the commissioners shall be thought meet. 21 *Jac.* 1. *c.* 19. *s.* 8.

It is most justifiable for the assignees to act publicly in their office; as where a lease of the bankrupt's house is to be sold, to advertise the same, and sell by public sale; so of his goods and fixtures, &c. rather than by a private sale.

Assignees or solicitor to commission ought on no account to purchase, or be concerned in the purchase of any part of the bankrupt's property.

Creditors.] Every creditor of a bankrupt must prove his debt before the commissioners by himself, or by an affidavit sworn before a master, ordinary or extraordinary, in chancery, to be exhibited to and allowed by them. *Stat.* 21 *Jac. c.* 19. *s.* 9. 5 *Geo.* 2. *c.* 30. *s.* 29. 1 *Atk. Rep.* 77.

A plaintiff that hath a defendant's body in execution who becomes bankrupt, shall not come in to be relieved by the statutes. *Stone* 130, 131. *pl.* 50. 2 *Black. Com.* 487. 1 *Atk. Rep.* 262. *ca.* 142. *Bunb. Rep.* 33. *pl.* 50, 202. *pl.* 279. 7 *Vin. Abr.* 104. *pl.* 1.

But if the plaintiff recover damages against the defendant, and hath judgment, and then the defendant becomes bankrupt, the plaintiff is a creditor; for it is a debt due to him, and action of debt lies on the judgment. *Cro. Car.* 166. *pl.* 12. If defendant becomes bankrupt before judgment, the plaintiff shall not add his costs at law to his debt. *Atk. Rep.* 140. *ca.* 81.

Costs have relation to the verdict or interlocutory judgment, therefore if there be a verdict or interlocutory judgment before bankruptcy, costs may be proved though not taxed or ascertained until after. 1 *Cooke* 184.

Sureties, or bail, when they have paid the debt, may come in as creditors. *Com. Dig.* 527. *Atk. Rep.* 135, 238. *ca.* 130, 262. *ca.* 141. *Cro. Jac.* 127. *pl.* 17. But mortgagees, or persons that have a pledge of the bankrupt's goods, having security for their debts in their hands, are not creditors within the statute. 2 *Black. Com.* 487. *Com. Dig.* 527.

Those that attach goods of the bankrupt are to come in as creditors.

If an executor becomes bankrupt, a legatee is to be a creditor. *Com. Dig.* 527. See *Atk. Rep.* 102. *ca.* 51.

Aliens, as well as denizens, may come in as creditors; for all statutes concerning bankrupts extend to aliens, who shall be subject to the laws against bankrupts. 2 *Black. Com.* 474, 475.

A creditor having proved his debt under a commission, has nothing further to do than to wait for an order of a dividend to be made, and to receive the same.

In the distribution of the bankrupt's estate, no respect is to be had to debts upon judgments, recognizances, or specialties, beyond other debts. 1 *Atk. Rep.* 183, 229, 233. 1 *Bur. Rep.* 476, 477. After four months and distribution made, no creditor can come in to disturb it; but he may come in for the residue of which no distribution is made. *Hob. Rep.* 287. *pl.* 375.

But the court of chancery, hath sometimes allowed creditors, to come in after distribution, upon particular circumstances which have happened. And now generally, where one dividend has been made, and at the meeting for making a further, or final dividend, other creditors come in and prove their debts, (as they may) the commissioners will order such creditors to be first paid a proportion, equal to the first dividend, and then the remainder of the bankrupt estate, if any, to be divided amongst all the creditors, as is just and equitable, for otherwise where such creditors debts are small, or the dividend so, such creditors had better go without, than apply to the court for payment of a proportion to be made them.

If a debtor to a bankrupt pay him his debt voluntarily, he must pay it over again; but it is otherwise in case of payment by compulsion of law. 2 *Vern.* 258. 3 *Keb. Rep.* 232. *Vern.* 94.

And by statute 19 *Geo.* 2. *c.* 32. no person who is *bona fide* a creditor of any bankrupt for or in respect of any goods *bona fide* sold to such bankrupt; or of any bill of exchange *bona fide* drawn, negociated, or accepted by such bankrupt, in the usual and ordinary course of trade, shall be liable to re-pay to the assignee any money which before the suing forth of the commission was *bona fide*, and in the usual course of trade, received by such person of such bankrupt, before the person receiving the same shall have notice that he is become bankrupt, or is in insolvent circumstances. *Bur. Rep.* 32. 7 *Vin. Abr.* 69. *pl.* 6.

If creditor receives money or bills of exchange after act of bankruptcy committed, if no notice, and bills received before commission, payment is good. 2 *Vez.* 550.

Creditor lending money to bankrupt after commission, was excluded from coming in, being bound to take notice of issuing of commission. See *Green* 132. in notes. But lending money to tradesmen, knowing them to be in distressed or dubious circumstances, on mortgages or for lives, is not fraudulent, nor the contract, in case of bankruptcy, void. *Green* 102. in notes.

Rent due to a landlord is a debt of the highest nature, and affects the goods, chattels, and stock of the tenant upon the premises; and (if there is no seizure made by the landlord) in the case of an execution, a year's rent is to be reserved for him, by *stat.* 8 *Ann. c.* 14. *s.* 1.

But in commissions of bankruptcy, it is otherwise, and no commission can remove or carry away any goods belonging to the bankrupt, if the landlord seizes for the rent before the goods are removed, and he is to be first discharged, even if there are several years rent in arrear; and even after assignment and sale by the assignees under the commission. 1 *Atk. Rep.* 103. *ca.* 54. but if the landlord does not seize before the commission of bankruptcy carries away the goods from off the premises, he must then come in as a creditor for his rent, with the rest of the bankrupt's creditors. *Dav.* 314 *Atk. Rep.* 104. *ca.* 55. *id.* 105. 2 *Black. Com.* 487. See *Atk. Rep.* 102. *ca.* 52, 103. *ca.* 53, 54. *id.* 104. *ca.* 55.

Also if there are not sufficient goods upon the premises to pay the landlord's rent, he can then only take what goods there are upon the premises, and after they are appraised and sold, as the law, in cases of distress for rent, directs; then the landlord may come in as a creditor for the rent remaining due, to him, with the rest of the creditors under the commission. *Ibid.*

Apprentices, where the master becomes bankrupt, have no right of preference to other creditors, but the commissioners generally recommend it to the creditors, to allow a gross sum, out of the estate, for the purpose of binding them to another master. 1 *Cooke* 144.

Debts bearing interest.] For debts on specialty, the creditors shall have interest as well between the act of bankruptcy as before. 7 *Vin. Abr.* 110.

Where a bankrupt's estate is sufficient to pay every debt, with a large surplus left, creditors, whose debts carried interest, shall be allowed interest for their respective debts, from the time the computation of it was stopt by the commissioners, and the bankrupt or his representatives will be chargeable therewith: but such as are creditors by bond, not beyond their penalties. 1 *Atk. Rep.* 75. *ca.* 29.

There is no such rule, "that all interest on debts carrying interest shall cease from the time of issuing the commission." 1 *Atk. Rep.* 79, 244. *ca.* 132.

Where there is mutual credit between bankrupt and creditor, the commissioners ought to stop interest on both sides at the time of the bankruptcy, or compute interest on both till settling the account. 1 *Atk. Rep.* 80.

Interest on debts that carry interest shall be carried down to the date of the commission; but on a special deposit of goods or stock, interest stops from the time of the deposit, and a calculation shall be made of the value of the whole entire thing deposited, both principal and interest, be it stock or goods, according to the market price at the time of the deposit. *Atk. Rep.* 259. *ca.* 139.

If a trader, being indebted on simple contract, pledges goods for the payment, and promises interest, such creditor shall have interest, even between the act of bankruptcy and the commission. 7 *Vin. Abr.* 110.

A mortgagee shall have his interest run on, upon a bankrupt estate, because he hath a right *in rem*, but as to other interest it ceaseth on the bankruptcy. *Id. ib.* If mortgage is not adequate to payment of principal and interest, the mortgagee must apply by petition to have the security sold, and to be admitted a creditor for deficiency, but the interest is only to be calculated up to the date of commission. 1 *Cooke* 181.

The Bankrupt.] If a bankrupt shall not within forty-two days after notice in writing, left at his usual place of abode, or personal notice if he be in prison, and notice in the London Gazette, surrender himself to the commissioners, and subscribe the surrender, and submit himself to be examined upon oath, or affirmation, and discover all his effects, how he has disposed thereof (and all books, papers, and writings relating to the same) of which he was possessed, or interested, or whereby he has, or may expect, any possibility of advantage, (except such part as shall have been *bonâ fide* disposed of in the way of his trade, and except such money as shall have been laid out in the ordinary expense of himself and family) and also deliver up to the commissioners such part of his effects, and all books and writings relating thereto, as shall be in his power, (except the necessary wearing apparel of himself, his wife and children) and if he conceals or embezzles his estate to the value of 20*l.* or any books of account relating thereto, with intent to defraud his creditors, being convicted thereof by judgment or information, he is guilty of felony without clergy, and his goods and estate shall go among his creditors; and the commissioners are to appoint, within the 42 days, not less than three meetings, the last to be on the 42d day limited for his appearance, and three weeks notice is to be given in the Gazette of the time and place of such meeting. The lord chancellor, &c. may enlarge the time for such surrender and discovery, not exceeding 50 days from the end of the said 42 days (so as the order for enlarging the time be made in six days before the time on which the bankrupt is to surrender himself). 5 *Geo.* 2. *c.* 30. *s.* 1, 2, 3.

The act says 50 days, but the lord chancellor's order is for 49 days, because the 50th day may happen to fall on a Sunday; and is made on the bankrupt's petition.

Where a bankrupt did not surrender himself in due time, and there did not appear to be any intention of defrauding his creditors, lord chancellor Macclesfield, in several instances, superseded the commission, in order to prevent such a prosecution. *Atk. Rep.* 222.

And lord chancellor Hardwicke would not order the clerk of the commission to attend at the Old Bailey, with the proceedings upon a prosecution against the bankrupt for felony, in not surrendering himself according to the directions of the act of parliament. 1 *Atk. Rep.* 221. *ca.* 123.

Also if by an innocent default of the bankrupt he has neglected to surrender himself upon the day appointed, the lord chancellor may, upon petition, make order for the commissioners to be at liberty to appoint a new day for taking the examination. 1 *Cooke*, 434.

If a bankrupt is fearful of being arrested, on coming to surrender himself, he may apply to the commissioners for a warrant of protection for his person, which they will grant him, and which will secure his person from arrest and imprisonment till the time of his last examination, whether within the forty-two days or forty-nine days.

If the commissioners adjourn the last examination, the bankrupt's protection continues. 1 *Cooke*, 115. Bankrupt is protected against an attachment for non-payment of money, but not against being rendered by his bail. *Ib.* 119.

Bankrupt has no right to be maintained out of his effects during examination. 1 *T. R.* 157.

Upon the certificate of the commissioners that the commission is issued, and the person proved a bankrupt, the justices of *K. B. C. P.* and the barons of the exchequer and justices of the peace in England, Wales, or Berwick upon Tweed, on application, are to grant warrants for apprehending such person, and commit him to the gaol of the county where apprehended, there to remain until he be removed by order of the commissioners. And the gaoler must give notice to one of the commissioners of his being in custody, and the commissioners may seize the effects of such bankrupt (except the necessary apparel of himself, wife and children), and his books and writings which shall be then in his custody, or of any person in prison; and if any person so apprehended shall, within the time allowed, submit to be examined and conform as if he had surrendered, he shall have the same benefit as if he had voluntarily come in. 5 *Geo.* 2. *c.* 30. *s.* 14, 15.

If the bankrupt be in custody at the time of issuing the commission, and is willing to submit to be examined, and can be brought before the commissioners and creditors, the expence thereof shall be paid out of the bankrupt estate: and whether he is in custody on mesne process only, or in execution, he may now be brought before the commissioners by their warrant, in order to make his discovery. 5 *Geo.* 2. *c.* 30. *s.* 6. 49 *Geo.* 3. *c.* *s.* 13.

And the assignees are to appoint persons to attend such bankrupt in prison, and to prepare his books and writings in order to prepare his discovery; a copy whereof the assignees shall apply for, and the bankrupt shall deliver the same to their order ten days before the last examination. 5 *Geo.* 2. *c.* 30. *s.* 6.

Bankrupt having surrendered, may at seasonable times, before the expiration of the forty-two days, or such further time as shall be allowed him to finish his examination, inspect his books and writings in the presence of some person to be appointed by the assignees, and bring with him for his assistance such persons as he shall think fit, not exceeding two at a time, and make extracts and copies, to enable him to make discovery of his effects. 5 *Geo.* 2. *c.* 30. *s.* 5.

A bankrupt is free from arrests in going and coming to surrender himself to the commissioners, and from actual surrender for forty-two days, or such further time as shall be allowed him to finish his examination, provided he was not in custody at the time of surrender; and if he be arrested for debt, or on any escape warrant, coming to surrender, or after his surrender within that time, then on producing the summons or notice under the hands of the commissioners or assignees, and giving the officer a copy thereof, he shall be discharged; and if any officer detain such bankrupt he shall forfeit to the bankrupt, for his own use, 5*l.* for every day he detains him; and if any commission of bankruptcy, shall issue against any person, who shall have been discharged by virtue of this act, or shall have compounded with his creditors, or delivered to them his effects, and been released by them, or been discharged by any act of insolvency, then the body only of such person shall be free from arrest and imprisonment. 5 *Geo.* 2. *c.* 30. *s.* 9.

If a bankrupt, upon examination, be found to have fraudulently conveyed his goods, lands, or other estate to the value of 20*l.* to hinder the execution of the statutes, or to defraud creditors, and shall not upon examination discover, and if in his power deliver, to the commissioners, all the estate so conveyed or detained, or that he cannot make appear, that he has had some casual loss, whereby he is disabled to pay what he owed, he may be indicted for such fraud or abuse at the assizes or sessions of peace, and if convicted set in the pillory for two hours, and have one of his ears nailed to the pillory, and cut off. 21 *Jac.* 1. *c.* 19. *sec.* 7.

For an encouragement to bankrupts duly to submit and conform, an allowance is appointed them out of their estate, *viz.* 5*l. per cent.* if the net produce that shall be received after such allowance is sufficient to pay 10*s.* in the pound, so as such allowance does not amount to above 200*l.* and if the net produce be sufficient to pay 12*s.* 6*d.* in the pound, to be allowed 7*l.* 10*s.* *per cent.* so as such allowance does not amount to above 250*l.* and if the net produce be sufficient to pay 15*s.* in the pound, to be allowed 10*l. per cent.* so as such allowance does not amount to above 300*l.* and every such bankrupt, to be discharged from all debts, owing at the time he became a bankrupt; and if he be impleaded for any debt due before he became a bankrupt, he shall be discharged upon common bail, and may plead in general that the cause of action accrued before he became bankrupt, and the certificate of his conforming, and the allowance thereof, shall be sufficient evidence of the trading, bankruptcy, commission, and other proceedings precedent to the obtaining such certificate, unless the plaintiff can prove the said certificate was obtained unfairly, or make appear any concealment by such bankrupt to the value of 10*l.* But if the net produce does not amount to 10*s.* in the pound, he is to be allowed, so much only, as the assignees and commissioners think fit, not exceeding 3*l. per cent.* 5 *Geo.* 2. *c.* 30. *s.* 7, 8.

But no discovery entitles the bankrupt to the benefits of this act unless the major part of the commissioners certify to the lord chancellor that he has made a full discovery, and in all things conformed himself, and that there is no doubt of the truth of such discovery, and unless (*three parts* in five, both in number and value, of the creditors, 49 *Geo.* 3. *c.* . *s.* 18.) who must be creditors for not less than 20*l.* respectively, or some other person by them duly authorized, sign such certificate: but the commissioners are not to certify till they have proof, by affidavit or affirmation in writing, of such creditors signing the said certificate, and of the power by which any person is authorized to sign for any creditor, (which affidavit or affirmation, together with such authority to sign, shall be laid before the lord chancellor, &c. with the said certificate) and unless such bankrupt make oath or affirmation in writing that such certificate was obtained without fraud; and unless such certificate be allowed by the lord chancellor, &c. or by such two of the justices of *K. B.* and *C. P.* or barons of the exchequer, to whom the consideration of such certificate is referred by the lord chancellor, and any of the creditors are to be heard, if they think fit, against the making the certificate, and against the confirmation thereof. 5 *Geo.* 2. *c.* 30. *s.* 10.

Formerly the judges had the cognizance of certificates, but being found inconvenient, the great seal hath taken it to itself, 1 *Atk. Rep.* 87.

If a bankrupt who has obtained commissioners certificate of his conformity be taken in execution, or imprisoned on account of any debt, owing before he became a bankrupt, by reason, that judgment was obtained before certificate allowed, a judge of the court, wherein judgment was obtained, on the bankrupt's producing the certificate allowed. may order any sheriff or gaoler to discharge him without fee. 5 *Geo.* 2. *c.* 30. *sec.* 13.

But the discharge of a bankrupt, from debts owing by him when he became a bankrupt, shall not discharge him, who was his partner in trade, or stood jointly bound, or had made any joint contract with such bankrupt. 10 *An.* *c.* 15. *s.* 3.

Certificate.] In order, for a bankrupt to obtain his certificate, he should apply to the solicitor under the commission, or some other solicitor, to prepare his examination, and likewise draw up, and ingross his certificate, which *three parts* in five of his creditors (who are creditors for not less than 20*l.*) both in number and value must sign; for which purpose it is advisable for him to have some person to attend with the certificate at the third sitting, who with himself may request such creditors, as then appear to sign the same; this person must see them sign it, because he must make an affidavit thereof, before the commissioners will sign it; when he has got all the hands he can at this sitting, the same or any other person, may go round with him to the rest, and the persons who saw the same signed must make an affidavit thereof before a master in chancery, which being produced to the commissioners, they will compute the number of creditors, and the amount of their debts, and those who have signed; and if it appears that *three parts* in five, both in number and value, have signed the certificate, they will also then sign it; the bankrupt ought to have a meeting of the commissioners, at his own expense, on purpose to have it signed by them; though upon application to the commissioners, and on payment of their fees, when sitting at Guildhall, they will sign it; the affidavit or affidavits of seeing the creditors sign, as also any letter of attorney to authorize any one to sign for them, must be exhibited to the commissioners.

The bankrupt having his certificate signed by his creditors, and certified by the commissioners, by their signing thereof, is then to make an affidavit before a master in chancery of his having obtained the same fairly and without fraud; and the certificate, with the several affidavits and letters of attorney (if any), must be left at the secretary of bankrupts, who gives an authority for inserting the allowance of the certificate in the Gazette; and at the expiration of 21 days after, the lord chancellor will (if no cause shown) allow the certificate.

If it is intended to oppose the allowance of a certificate, a petition for that purpose must be lodged at the secretary of bankrupts before the time appointed for the allowance, and the bankrupt must also be served with the same, that he may have an opportunity of answering it, and the certificate is thereupon stayed until the hearing of the petition; and if an order is made to stay certificate, such order must be drawn up within three months, or the certificate will be allowed. *Lord Chancellor's Order*, 22 March, 1796.

A creditor only can petition; and any one may, though his debt is under 20*l.* 1 *Cooke*, 463.

All affidavits in support of petition to stay certificate shall be brought into the office, together with the petition, except such as shall be necessary in reply to affidavits in answer to it. *Lord Chancellor's Order*, 16 Nov. 1805.

Future effects.] If any person, declared a bankrupt by virtue of this act, shall at any time after purchase lands or chattels, or any lands or chattels shall descend or come to such bankrupts before their debts shall be fully satisfied or agreed for, the said lands and chattels shall by the commissioners be bargained, sold, extended, delivered and used for the payment of the said creditors, in like manner as other the lands and chattels of the said bankrupts. 13 *Eliz.* *c.* 7. *sec.* 11.

In case any commission of bankruptcy shall issue against any person, who after the 24th of June, 1732, shall have been discharged by virtue of this act, or shall have compounded with his creditors, or delivered to them his estate or effects, and been released by them, or discharged by any act for the relief of insolvent debtors, after the time aforesaid, then his future estate and effects only shall remain liable to his creditors, (his tools of trade, necessary household goods and furniture, and his necessary wearing apparel, and of his wife and children, only excepted) unless his estate shall produce clear, after all charges, sufficient to pay every one of his creditors 15*s.* in the pound for their respective debts. 5 *Geo.* 2. *c.* 30. *sec.* 9.

Upon motion for a new trial, the court held, that though, under the said statute, the future effects of a bankrupt, against whom two commissions had issued, were liable to be seized for the benefit of creditors, yet the bankrupt, had in the mean time such a property in them, as enabled him, to transact and sell to a *boná fide* purchaser. *Ashley* v. *Kell*, 2 *Stra.* 1207.

Supersedeas.] In order to supersede a commission of bankruptcy with the assent of the creditors, a petition must be ingrossed, and signed by all the bankrupt's creditors (be the debt ever so small) then lodged at the secretary of bankrupt's office: this petition requires no attendance, it is only to be served (with the lord chancellor's, &c. order thereon) upon all parties concerned.

The bankrupt must sign the prayer of the petition, and there must likewise be an affidavit of seeing the bankrupt sign, as also of the creditors signing their consent to the prayer of the bankrupt's petition.

But a commission of bankrupt cannot be superseded before the bankrupt has surrendered. 11 *Vesey, jun.* 409.

Solicitor.] All bills of fees or disbursements demanded by any solicitor employed under any commission of bankrupts, (that is, after the choice of assignees) shall be settled by one of the masters in chancery, and the master who shall settle such bill shall have for his care in settling the same, as also for his certificate thereof, 20*s* 5 *Geo.* 2. *c.* 30. *s.* 46.

The clerk to a commission may be discharged by the assignees, for they are trustees for the creditors, and may employ whom they please; and therefore the former clerk was ordered to deliver up all papers on being paid his bill. 7 *Vin. Abr.* 117. *pl.* 2.

BANKS, no town or freeman shall be distrained to make banks or bridges, but such as of old time have been used to make them. *Stat.* 9 *H.* 3. *c.* 15. See also *Bridges* and *Felony*.

BANNIMUS, the form of an expulsion of any member from the University of Oxford, by affixing the sentence in some public places, as a denunciation or promulgation of it. And the word *banning* is taken for an exclamation against, or cursing of another. *Cowel. Blount.*

BANNITUS, an outlaw, or banished man. *Ibid.*

BANNIATUS FORTIS, is used in the same sense as *bannitus*, signifying one outlawed or judicially banished.

BANNUM VEL BANLEUGA, the utmost bounds of a manor, or town, so used 47 *Hen.* 3. *Rot.* 44, &c. *Banleuga de Arundel* is taken for all that is comprehended within the limits or lands adjoining, and so belonging to the castle or town. *Seld. Hist. of Tythes, p.* 75. *Cowel. Blount.*

BARATRY. See *Barratry*.

BARBERS, were incorporated with the surgeons of London; but not to practise surgery, except drawing of teeth, &c. 32 *H.* 8. *c.* 42. but separated by 18 *Geo.* 2. *c.* 15.

BARBICAN, (*barbicanum*) a watch-tower, or bulwark. *Cowel. Blount.*

BARBICANAGE, (*barbicanagium*) money given for the maintenance of a barbican, or watch-tower; or a tribute towards the repairing or building a bulwark. *Cowel. Blount.*

BARCA, a barque: *navis mercatorum & quæ merces exportat.* Gloss. Sax. *Ælfrici*, a flotship. *Ibid.*

BARCARIUM, (*barcaria*) a sheep-cote, and sometimes used for a sheep-walk. *Ibid.*

BARGAIN AND SALE *of lands.* A *bargain and sale* in this respect is a contract in consideration of money, passing an estate in lands, tenements, and hereditaments, by *deed indented and inrolled.* 2 *Inst.* 672.

This mode of conveying lands is created and established by the 27 *Hen.* 8. *c.* 10. which executes all uses raised: but as this introduced a more secret mode of conveyancing, than that known to the policy of the common law, namely, the conveyance by *feoffment* with livery and seisin, the *enrolment* of the deed of bargain and sale, was made necessary by the 16th chapter of the same statute.

The stat. 27 *Hen.* 8. *c.* 10. enacts, that "where "any person is seised of, or in any lands to the "use, confidence or trust of any other person "or body politic, by reason of any *bargain*, "*sale*, feoffment or the like, such persons that "have any such use, shall be deemed in lawful seisin, estate, and possession thereof, to "all intents and purposes, of or in such like "estates, as they have in the use, and the "estate, right and possession of him so "seised to any use, shall be deemed and adjudged in him or them, which have the "use after such quality, manner, &c. as "they had before in or to the use."

But by 27 *Hen.* 8. *c.* 16. "no manors, "lands, tenements, or other hereditaments, "shall pass from one to another, whereby "any estate of inheritance of freehold shall "be made or take effect, or any use thereof "to be made *by reason only of any bargain and "sale*, except by writing indented, sealed, "and enrolled in one of the courts at Westminster, or else within the county where "the lands lie, before the *custos rotulorum*, and "two justices of the peace, and clerk of "the peace or two of them, whereof the "clerk of the peace to be one; the same inrolment to be made within six months [of "28 days, *Dyer* 907.] after the date of the "same writing indented. Provided this act "extends not to any lands lying within any "city, borough, &c. wherein the mayors, "&c. or other officers have used to enrol "deeds within their limits."

And by 5 *Eliz.* *c.* 26. "bargains and "sales of lands being within six months enrolled in the courts of the counties palatine of *Lancaster*, *Chester*, or *Durham*, shall "be as effectual as if enrolled in any of the "courts at Westminster."

The six months limited by these statutes for the enrolment of bargains and sales, are to be reckoned as lunar months, *viz.* after 28 days to the month, the day of the date taken exclusively. *Dyer* 90. 7 *Rep.* 40. 2 *Buls.* 8.

But the general method now used to convey estates, (except where it is otherwise directed by act of parliament, as in the case of the sale of lands to redeem land-tax, and the like) is by lease and release, whereby the possession and fee immediately pass without inrolment.

BARGAIN AND SALE *of goods*. There is a bargain and sale also, where a man makes a contract with another for the sale of goods or chattels, and at the same time makes the sale of them. *Com. Dig. tit. Bar.* and *Sale*, for which see *Bills* of sale.

BARGAINS, *catching*. See *Catching Bargains.*

BARKARY, (*barkaria, corticulus*) a tan-house, or place to keep bark in for the use of tanners. *Cowel. Blount.*

BARON, hath divers significations here in England. First, it is taken for a degree of nobility next to a viscount. *Bracton, lib.* 1. *cap.* 8.

There are also barons by office; as the barons of the Exchequer, barons of the Cinque Ports, &c. for which see the proper heads.

BARONY, (*baronia*) is that honour and territory which gives title to a baron; comprehending not only the fees and lands of temporal barons, but of bishops also, who have two estates; one as they are spiritual persons, by reason of their spiritual revenues and promotions: the other grew from the bounty of our English kings, whereby they have baronies and lands added to their spiritual livings and preferments. The baronies belonging to bishops are by some called *regalia*, because *ex sola liberalitate regum eis olim concessa, & a regibus in feudum tenenter. Blount.* Barony, *Bracton*, says (*lib* 2. *cap.* 34.) is a right indivisible, and therefore, if an inheritance be to be divivided, among coparceners, though some capital messuages may be divided, yet, *si capitale messuagium, si caput comitatus, vel caput baroniæ*, they may not be parcelled. In antient times thirteen knight fees and a quarter made a tenure *per baroniam*, which amounted to 400 marks per annum.

BARONET, (*baronettus*) is a dignity or degree of honour, of inheritance, created by letters patent, and usually descendible to the issue male: it hath precedency before all knights, except bannerets, made *sub vexillis regiis in exercitu regali in aperto bello, & ipso rege personaliter præsente.* (See *Banneret.*) This order of baronets was instituted by king James I. in the year 1611, with such precedency as aforesaid, and other privileges, in order to raise a competent sum for the reduction of the province of *Ulster*, and 100 gentlemen advanced each 1000*l.* for the grant of this title to them: for this reason, all baronets have the arms of *Ulster*, viz. a hand *gule*. or a bloody hand in a field *argent*, superadded to their family coat. Their number at first was to be but two hundred; but now they are without limitation. *Cowel. Blount.* 1 *Black.* 404.

BARON AND FEME, are husband and wife by our law; and they are adjudged but one person: that is, the very being or legal existence of the woman, is suspended during the marriage, or at least is incorporated and consolidated into that of the husband: under whose wing, protection, and *cover*, she performs every thing, and is therefore called in our law French, a *feme covert; fœmina viro cooperta:* she is said to be *covert-baron* or under the protection and influence of her husband, her *baron* or lord, and her condition during her marriage, is called her *coverture.* 1 *Black.* 442.

And professor *Christian* in a note hereon, observes, that whatever may be the origin of *feme covert*, it is not perhaps wholly unworthy of notice, that it nearly corresponds in its signification to the Latin word *nupta;* derived *a nubendo*, i. e. *tegendo*, because the modesty of the bride, it is said, was so much consulted by the Romans, upon that delicate occasion, that she was led to her husband's home *covered* with a veil. 1 *Black.* 442. *n.* 15.

Upon this principle of an union of person in husband and wife, a man cannot grant any thing to his wife, or enter into covenant with her, for the grant would be to suppose her separate existence, and to covenant with her, would be only to covenant with himself. *Co. Lit.* 112.

But the husband may grant to the wife by the intervention of trustees, and he may surrender a copyhold to her use. *Co. Lit.* 30. 4 *Co.* 29.

Upon this principle, it is also generally true, that all contracts and agreements made between husband and wife, *while single*, are avoided by the intermarriage. *Cro. Car.* 551.

A woman may, however, be attorney for her husband, for that implies no separation, but is rather a representation of her *baron* or lord. *Fitz. N. B.* 27. and a husband may also bequeath any thing to his wife by will, for that cannot take effect till the coverture is determined by his death. *Co. Lit.* 112.

Power of the husband.] The husband hath, by law, power and dominion over his wife, and may keep her by force within the bounds of duty: and he may correct or beat her, but not in a violent or cruel manner, for in such case, or if he but threaten to beat her outrageously, or use her barbarously, she may make him find surety of the peace, by suing a writ of *supplicavit* out of Chancery, or by preferring articles of the peace against him in the court of King's Bench, or before the justices of the peace, or she may apply to the spiritual court for a divorce *propter sævitiam. Crom.* 28. 136. *F. N. B.* 80. *Hett.* 149. *cont.* 1 *Sid.* 113, 116. *Dalt. c.* 68. *Lamb.* 78. *Crom.* 133. 1 *Hawk. P. C.* 253.

But a wife cannot, either by herself or her *prochein amy*, bring a *homine replegiando* against her husband, for he has by law a right to the custody of her, and may, if he think fit, confine her, but he must not imprison her; if he does, it will be a good cause for her to apply to the spiritual court for a divorce *propter sævitiam*; and the nature and proceedings in the writ *de homine replegiando* shew that it cannot be maintained by the wife against her husband. *Prec. in Ch.* 492.

However in cases of unreasonable and improper confinement, the court will relieve the wife on *habeas corpus*, *Ld. Ferrers's* case, 1 *Bur.* 634. and if upon the return of an *habeas corpus* sued out by the husband, to bring up the wife, it appears that he hath used her ill, and she exhibit articles of the peace against him, the court will not order her to be delivered to him. 4 *Burr.* 1991. And a wife separated by articles, in consideration of money received by the husband, with covenants from him, cannot be seized by him or forced to live with him. *Bur.* 542. 1 *Str.* 478.

From the time of the intermarriage, the law looks upon the husband and wife, but as one person, and therefore allows but of one will between them which is placed in the husband, as the fittest and ablest to provide for and govern the family, and for this reason, *the law gives the husband an absolute power of disposing of her personal property*, no act of hers being of any force, to affect, or transfer that, which by the intermarriage she hath resigned to him. 2 *Rol. Abr.* 347. 10 *Co.* 42. 2 *Inst.* 510. *Sid.*

Thus, all the personal estate, as money, goods, cattle, household furniture, and the like that were the property, and in the possession of the wife at the time of the marriage, are actually vested in the husband; so that of these he may make any disposition in his life time without her consent, or may by will, bequeath them, and they shall without any such disposition go to the executors or administrators of the husband, and not the wife, though she survive him. *Dr. & Stud. Di.* 1. *c.* 7. *Co. Lit.* 351.

And so it is of all chattels real, as a term for years, mortgages, estates by statute merchant, statute, staple, elegit and the like, of which he may in like manner dispose. 7 *H.* 62. *Roll. Abr.* 341. *Co. Lit.* 351. 2 *Atk.* 208. 1 *Peere Wms.* 407, 8.

But *the freehold and inheritance of the wife is subject to other rules and regulations*: for the husband, by the marriage, does not become absolute proprietor of the inheritance; but as the governor of the family, is so far the master of it, as to *receive the profits of it during her life*: therefore if a man marries a woman seized in fee, *he gains a freehold in right of his wife during her life*, but hath no power to make an absolute sale of it, without her consent. *Co. Lit.* 351. *Doug.* 329.

The law gives him the same right also over any *real estate* accruing to the wife during coverture, as if she were seised of it before marriage; so of *chattels real* accruing to the wife: it also gives him an absolute power over any *personal estate* or interest accruing to the wife by gift, devise, or her labour. *Co. Lit.* 351. *Salk.* 115. *Carth.* 251.

And where an executor paid a legacy to a feme covert, who lived separate from her husband, on a bill filed against the executor, he was decreed to pay it over again with interest. *Salk.* 115. *Vern.* 261.

Debts contracted by the wife before marriage.] In general, the husband is liable to the wife's debts, contracted before marriage, whether he had any portion with her or not; and this the law presumes reasonable, because, by the marriage, the husband acquires an absolute interest, in the personal estate of the wife. and has the receipt of the rents and profits of her real estate, during coverture; and that no person's act should prejudice another, the law makes the husband liable to those debts with which he took her attached. *F. N. B.* 265. 20 *Hen.* 6. 22. *b. Moor* 468. 1 *Rol. Abr.* 352. 3 *Mod.* 186.

But the debts must be recovered against the husband during the life of the wife, and therefore if a feme sole indebted, marries, and dies, the husband shall not be charged with her debts afterwards. 10 *H.* 6. 10, 12. 20 *H.* 6. 22. *Roll Abr.* 351.

So, though there be a judgment in debt, against a feme sole, and she afterwards marry and die; the baron shall not be charged therewith, for he is not liable to her debts before coverture, unless recovered in her life time. 3 *Mod.* 186.

If baron and feme are sued on the wife's bond, entered into by the feme before marriage, and judgment is had thereupon, and his wife dies before execution, yet the husband is liable; for the judgment has altered the debt. 1 *Sid.* 337.

And if there is any of the wife's personal property, which he did not reduce into possession before her death, which he must afterwards recover as her *administrator*, he will to the extent of the value of that property, be liable to pay his wife's debts *dum sola*, which remain undischarged during the coverture. 1 *Peere Wms.* 468.

Maintenance.] The husband is obliged to maintain his wife in necessaries: yet they must be according to his degree and his estate; to charge him; and necessaries may be suitable to a husband's degree of quality, but not to his estate; also they may be necessaries, but not *ex necessitate* to charge the husband. 1 *Mod.* 129. 1 *Nels. Abr.* 354. If a woman buys things for her necessary apparel, though without the consent of her husband, yet the husband shall be bound to pay it. *Brownl.* 47. And if the wife buys any thing for herself, children, or family, and the baron does any act precedent or subsequent whereby he shews his consent, he may be charged thereupon. 1 *Sid.* 120. Though the wife is very lewd, if she cohabits with her husband, he is chargeable for all necessaries for her, because he took her for better for worse: and so he is if he runs away from her, or turns her away: but if she goes away from her husband, *or lives in adultery with another man*, then as soon as such separation or *adultery* is notorious, whoever gives her credit doth it at his peril, and the husband is not liable *even for necessaries*, unless he take her again. 1 *Salk.* 119. 1 *Lev.* 5.

And *Ld. Kenyon* has held at *nisi prius*, that if a husband gives notice to a particular tradesman, not to deal with his wife, *unless she brings ready money*, that tradesman cannot maintain an action against the husband, *even* for necessaries. 1 *Black.* 442. *n.* 17. And what are necessaries must be ascertained by a jury from the rank and circumstances of the husband. *Ibid.*

But a prohibition in general, by putting her in the newspapers, is no legal nôtice not to trust her. 1 *Vent.* 42.

Although a husband be bound to pay his wife's debts for her reasonable provision, yet if she parts from him, especially by reason of any misbehaviour, and he allows her a maintenance, he shall never be charged with her debts, till a new cohabitation. *Mod. Cas.* 147, 171.

Where this is a separation by consent, and the wife hath a separate allowance, those who trust her, knowing of such separation and maintenance, do it upon her own credit. 1 *Salk.* 116. If a husband makes his wife an allowance for clothes, &c. which is constantly paid her, it is said he shall not be charged. 1 *Sid.* 109.

Crimes committed by the wife.] The will of the wife is subject to that of the husband; so that if they commit a felony together, she shall be neither principal nor accessary, for it shall be presumed, that this was by the coercion of the husband. *F. N. B.* 188.

But if husband and wife commit treason or murder, they shall be both found guilty, and the wife shall not be discharged, on presumption that it was by coercion of the husband. 1 *Hale's Hist. P. C.* 47. So if she commit a theft of her own voluntary act, or by the bare command of her husband, she is punishable as much as if she was sole, for a wife for her *own personal crimes* may be indicted without her husband. 9 *Rep.* 72. *H. P. C.* 65. *Dalt.* 27, 104. *Ass. pl.* 40. *Fitz. Coron.* 199.

And a feme covert, generally shall answer, as much as if she were sole, for any offence not capital against the common law or statute; and if it be of such nature, that it may be committed by her alone, without the concurrence of her husband, as by keeping a bawdy-house or the like, she may be punished for it without the husband by way of indictment, which being a proceeding grounded merely on the breach of the law, the husband shall not be included in it, for any offence to which he is no way privy. 9 *Co.* 71. *Hawk. P. C.* 3. See *Moor* 813. *Hob.* 93. *Noy* 103. *Savil.* 25. *Cro. Jac.* 482. 11 *Co.* 61.

Where a wife shall be considered as a feme sole.] A husband who has abjured the realm, or who is banished, is thereby *civiliter mortuus*; and being disabled to sue or be sued in right of his wife, she must be considered as a feme sole; for it would be unreasonable that she should be remediless on her part, and equally hard on those who had any demands on her, that not being able to have any redress from the husband, they should not have any against her. *Bro. Baron and Feme*, 66. *Co. Lit.* 133. 1 *Rol. Rep.* 400. *Moor* 851. 3 *Bulst.* 188. 1 *Bulst.* 140. 2 *Vern.* 104.

Where a married man is transported for any felony, the wife may be sued alone, for any debt contracted by her, after the transportation. So determined in a case before Mr. Justice Yates, at Carlisle, and afterwards in another case, before Lord Mansfield, in Kent, and both determinations acquiesced in. *Morgan's Ed. of Jac.*

And by the custom of London, if a feme covert trades by herself, in a trade with which her husband does not intermeddle, she may sue and be sued as a feme sole 10 *Mod.* 6.

In the case of a divorce, *a mensa et thoro* of which alimony is a consequence, the wife, it seems, becomes solely responsible to creditors. *Co. Bank. L.* 32.

And it hath been holden, that a wife who had a copyhold estate to her separate use, *and lived separate from her husband*, could surrender the same without her husband, *he having*, upon the separation, *covenanted* to join in the necessary conveyance of such estates, and to such uses as she should appoint. 1 *Hen. Black.* 334.

But it is in a court of equity where a feme covert is usually, and where, perhaps only, she can be properly considered as a feme sole; it being competent to this court to act upon her property in the hands of her trustees, and therefore to treat her as having interests and obligations distinct from those of her husband: if therefore, she claims any rights in opposition to those claimed by her husband, or if she lives separate from him, or disapproves the defence he wishes her to make, she may, in equity, obtain an order to defend a suit separately. If a husband is plaintiff in a suit and makes his wife a defendant, he is considered as thereby renouncing his *marital* right over her, and she is allowed to answer separately, without an order of the court for that purpose, and as she may defend a suit against her husband, so she may institute a suit against him. But the bill must be exhibited in her name, by her *prochein amy* or next friend, though she may defend without such protection, and the court will not permit a bill to be filed by any one without her consent. 1 *Bac. Abr. Ed.* 1807. *p.* 506, 7.

The general grounds upon which equity allows a wife to institute a suit against her husband, are where any thing is given to her separate use; or the husband refuseth to perform marriage articles, or articles for a separate maintenance; or where the wife having been deserted by her husband, hath during his absence acquired by her labour a separate property, of which he hath plundered her: and it will decree a specific performance of articles at the suit of the wife, though the husband offer to take her back again, if it appear that a *perpetual* separation was intended by the parties: but not so, where the separation is merely temporary, or there hath been a subsequent cohabitation: nor is it any answer to such a suit that his wife hath been guilty even of adultery: however in most cases where a wife comes into equity to support her possession independent of her husband, it must be a *meritorious* ground to entitle her to relief; and therefore the court will not decree maintenance where there is full proof of elopemeut and adultery. *Ibid.* 506.

When the property of a wife is in the power of a court of equity, it will not part with it, unless the husband make a proper settlement, or the wife upon examination in court, consent to his receiving it; and it will even prevent him from receiving the interest, that it may accumulate for her benefit, and it hath gone so far, as to restrain him, from proceeding in the spiritual court, for the wife's portion arising out of personal estate, because that court cannot oblige him to make an adequate provision on her. *Finch.* 143. 2 *Pere Wms.* 639. 3 *Pere Wms.* 12, 205. 1 *Sh.* 238. 1 *Vern.* 538. 3 *Atk.* 22.

And courts of equity will not allow a feme covert to part with her separate personal estate, without a previous examination and consent in court, in analogy to the caption of a fine at law, and such is the course of the court, where the trustees put the parties to file a bill. 1 *Pere Wms.* 768. 2 *Atk.* 67, 448, 452. 1 *Anst.* 277. 2 *Vez. Jun.* 448.

And in all instances, where the wife's examination and consent are taken, it must be personally in court, or if she is abroad by *dedimus*, as in the case of a fine. 2 *Vez.* 60. 3 *Bro. Ch. Ca.* 237.

However, if trustees pay the wife's separate fortune to the husband, it is irrecoverable. *Pr. Ch.* 414. 4 *Br. Ch. Rep.* 326.

BAR, or BARR, (Lat. *barra;* and in Fr. *barre*) in a legal sense, is a plea or peremptory exception of a defendant, sufficient to destroy the plaintiff's action. And it is divided into bar to common intendment, and bar special; bar temporary, and perpetual: bar to a common intendment is an ordinary or general bar, which usually is a bar to the declaration of the plaintiff: bar special is that which is more than ordinary, and falls out upon some special circumstance of the fact, as to the case in hand. *Terms de Ley.*

Bar temporary is such a bar that is good for the present, but may afterwards fail: and bar perpetual is that which overthrows the action of the plaintiff for ever. *Plowd.* 26. But a plea in bar, not giving a full answer to all the matter contained in the plaintiff's declaration is not good. 1 *Lill. Abr.* 211. If one be barred by plea to the writ, or to the action of the writ, he may have the same writ again, or his right action: but if the plea in bar, be to the action itself, and the plaintiff is barred by judgment, &c. it is a bar for ever in personal actions. 6 *Rep.* 7. And a recovery in debt is a good bar to action on the case for the same thing: also a recovery on *assumpsit* in case, is a good bar in debt, &c. *Cro. Jac.* 110. 4 *Rep.* 94.

In all actions personal, as debt, account, &c. a bar is perpetual, and in such case the party hath no remedy, but by writ of error or attaint; but if a man is barred in a real action, or judgment, yet he may have an action of as high a nature, because it concerns his inheritance; as for instance, if he is barred in a *formedon in descender*, yet he may have a *formedon* in the remainder, &c. 6 *Rep.* 7. It has been resolved, that a bar in any action real or personal by judgment upon demurrer, verdict, or confession, is a bar to that action, or any action of the like nature for ever: but, according to Pemberton chief justice, this is to be understood, when it doth appear that the evidence in one action would maintain the other; for otherwise the court shall intend that the party hath mistaken his action. *Skin.* 57, 58.

Bar to a common intent is good: and if an executor be sued for his testator's debt, and he pleadeth, that he had no goods left in his hands, at the day the writ was taken out against him, this is a good bar to a common intendment, till it is shewn, that there are goods; but if the plaintiff can shew by way of replication, that more goods have fallen into his hands since that time, then, except the defendant allege a better bar, he shall be condemned in the action. *Plowd.* 26. *Kitch.* 215. *Bro. tit. Barre.*

There is a bar material, and a bar at large: bar material may be also called special bar; as when one, in stay of the plaintiff's action, pleadeth some particular matter, *viz.* a descent from him that was owner of the land, &c. a feffoment made by the ancestor of the plaintiff, or the like: a bar at large is, when the defendant, by way of exception, doth not traverse the plaintiff's title, by pleading, nor confess, nor avoid it, but only makes to himself a title in his bar. *Kitch.* 68. 5 *H.* 7. 29.

This word bar is likewise used for the place where serjeants and counsellors at law stand to plead the causes in court; and where prisoners are brought to answer their indictments, &c. whence our lawyers, that are called to the bar, are termed barristers. 24 *H.* 8. *c.* 24.

See *Abatement, Action, Judgment, Pleading,* &c.

BARRASTER, BARRISTER, (*barrasterius*) is a counsellor learned in the law, admitted to plead at the bar, and there to take upon him the protection and defence of clients. *Fortesc.* The time before they ought to be called to the bar, by the ancient orders, was eight years, now reduced to five; and the exercises done by them (if they were not called *ex gratia*), were twelve grand moots performed in the inns of Chancery in the time of the grand readings, and twenty-four petty moots in the term times, before the readers of the respective inns: and a barrister newly called was to attend the six (or four) next long vacations the exercise of the house, *viz.* in Lent and Summer, and was thereupon for those three (or two) years stiled a vacation barrister. Also they are called *utter barristers, i. e.* pleaders *ouster* the bar, to distinguish them from benchers, or those that have been readers, who are sometimes admitted to plead within the bar, as the king, queen, or prince's counsel are. Barristers, who constantly attend the King's Bench, &c. are to have the privilege of being sued in transitory actions in the county of Middlesex. But a counsel cannot maintain any action for his fees, for a counsellor's fee is *honorarium quiddam,* non *mercenariam,* as that of an attorney or solicitor. 2 *Inst.* 213, 214, &c. *Wood's Inst.* 448.

BARRATOR, or BARRETOR, (Lat. *barractator*, Fr. *barrateur*) a common mover exciter or maintainer of suits and quarrels, either in courts or elsewhere in the country, and this offence consisting in all kinds of disturbances of the peace, and the spreading of false rumours and calumnies, whereby discord and disquiet may grow among neighbours, it is not material whether the suits commenced, be in a court of record, or not, or whether their quarrels relate to a disputed title of possession or not. *Co. Lit.* 368. *a. b.* 8 *Co.* 36. 6 *Hawk. P. C. B.* 1. *c.* 21.

But no one can be a barretor in respect of one act only; nor shall a man be adjudged a barretor for bringing any number of suits in his own right, though they are vexatious, especially, if there be any colour for them; for if they prove false, he shall pay the defendant costs. 1 *Rol. Abr.* 355. 3 *Mod.* 98.

Also an attorney, is in no danger of being convicted of barretry, in respect of his maintaining another, in a groundless action; to the commencing whereof he was no way privy. 3 *Mod.* 97.

A common solicitor, who solicits suits, is a common barretor, and may be indicted thereof, because it is no profession in law. 1 *Danv. Abr.* 725.

And a barrister at law entertaining a person in his house, and bringing several actions in his name, where nothing was due, was found guilty of barretry. 3 *Mod.* 97.

Barretors are punished by fine and imprisonment, and binding to the good behaviour, &c. And if they belong to the profession of the law, they ought to be further punished by disability to practice. 34 *Ed.* 3. *c.* 1. *Hawk. P. C.* 244.

And by 12 *Geo.* 1. *c.* 29. if an attorney or solicitor is convicted of barretry, he shall be transported as a felon in a summary way.

BARRATRY. In marine insurances, one of the risks insured against, is the barratry of the master or mariners.

And any act of the master or mariners which is of a criminal nature, such as a deviation for the purpose of smuggling or making capture, or which is grossly negligent, tending to their own benefit, to the prejudice of the owners of the ship, without their consent or privity, is barratry. 1 *Str.* 581. 2 *Str.* 1173. *Cowp.* 143. 1 *Ter. Rep.* 323.

And whatever is done by the captain to defeat or delay the performance of the voyage is barratry in him, it being to the prejudice of the owners. 6 *Ter. Rep.* 379.

But if the act of the captain be done, with a view to the benefit of his owners, as by deviation for the purpose of saving the ship or the like, and not to advance his own private interest, it is no barratry. *Cowp.* 154.

And an act of the captain, with the knowledge of *the owners of the ship,* though without the privity of the owner of the goods insured, is not barratry. 1 *Ter. Rep.* 323.

Neither can the master of the ship, if he be also owner be guilty of barratry, for no man shall be allowed to derive a benefit from his own crime, and which he would do, if he were permitted to recover against the insurers for a loss occasioned by his own act. 4 *Ter. Rep.* 33.

BARREL, (*barillum*) is a measure of wine, ale, oil, &c. Of wine it contains the eighth part of a tun, the fourth part of a pipe, and the moiety of a hogshead; that is, thirty-one gallons and a half. 1 *R.* 3. *c.* 13. Of beer, it contains thirty-six gallons; and of ale, thirty-two gallons. *Anno* 23 *H.* 8. *c.* 4. and 12 *Car.* 2. *c.* 23. It is declared, that the assise of herring barrels is thirty-two gallons wine measure, containing in every barrel usually a thousand full herrings. *Anno* 13 *El. c.* 11. The eel barrel contains thirty gallons. 2 *H.* 6. *c.* 13.

BARRIERS, (Fr. *barrieres*) *palæstra,* a martial exercise of men armed and fighting together with short swords, within certain bars or rails which separated them from the spectators, now disused in England. There are likewise barrier towns, or places of defence on the frontiers of kingdoms. *Cowel. Blount.*

BARROW, (from the Sax. *boerg*, a heap of earth) a large hillock or mount, raised or cast up in many parts of England, which seem to have been a mark of the Roman *tumuli*, or sepulchres of the dead. The Sax. *beora* was commonly taken for a grove of trees on the top of a hill. *Kennet's Gloss. Cowel. Blount.*

BARTER, (from the Fr. *baretre, circumvenire*) signifies to exchange one commodity for another, or truck wares for wares. *Anno* 1 *R.* 3. *c.* 9. And the reason may be, because they that exchange in this manner do endeavour, for the most part, one to overreach and circumvent the other. *Cowel. Blount.*

BARTON, is a word used in Devonshire, for the demesne lands of a manor; sometimes the manor-house itself; and in some places for out-houses and fold-yards. In the *stat.* 2 & 3 *Ed.* 6. *c.* 12. barton lands, and demesne lands, are used as synonyma. See *Berton.*

BAS CHEVALIERS, low or inferior knights by tenure of a bare military fee, as distinguished from bannerets, the chief or superior knights: hence we call our simple knights, *viz.* knights bachelors, bas chevaliers. *Kennet's Gloss. to Paroch. Antiq. Cowel. Blount.*

BASE COURT, (Fr. *cour basse*) is any inferior court, that is not of record, as the court baron, &c. *Kitch. fol.* 95, 96.

BASE ESTATE, (Fr. *bas estat*) is that estate, which base tenants have in their lands. And base tenants according to Lambert, are those who perform villainous services to their lords; *Kitchen, fol.* 41., makes base tenure and frank tenure to be contraries, and puts copyholders in the number of base tenants; where it may be gathered that every base tenant holds at the will of the lord: but there is a difference between a base estate and villenage; for to hold in pure villenage is to do all that the lord will command him; and if a copyholder have but a base estate, he not holding by the performance of every commandment of his lord, cannot be said to hold in villenage: copyholders are by the customs of manors, and continuance of time, grown out of that extreme servitude wherein they were first created. *Cowel. Blount.*

BASE FEE, is a tenure in fee at the will of the lord, distinguished from socage free tenure: but according to lord Coke, a base fee is what may be defeated by limitation, or on entry, &c. *Co. Lit.* 1, 18. *Bassa tenura,* or base tenure, was a holding by villenage, or other customary service, opposed to *alta tenura*, the higher tenure in *capite* or by military service, &c. *Consuetud. Domus de Farendon, MS.* 44.

BAS VILLE, the suburbs or inferior town, as used in France. *Cowel. Blount.*

BASELS, (*basseli*) a kind of coin abolished by king *Hen.* 2. *anno* 1158. *Hollingshed's Chron. p.* 67.

BASELARD, or BASILLARD, in the *stat.* 13 *R.* 2. *c.* 6. signifies a weapon, which Mr. Speight, in his exposition upon Chaucer, calls *pugionem vel sicam*, a poniard, *arrepto basillardo transfixit, &c. Cum alio basillardo penetravit latera ejus, &c. Knighton, lib.* 5. *pag.* 2731.

BASILEUS, from the Greek Βασιλευς, *Rex.* (Vide Gr. *Lexicon*) a word mentioned in several of our historians signifying the king, and seems peculiar to the kings of England. *Monasticon, tom.* 1. *p.* 65. *Ego Edgar totius Angliæ* basileus *confirmavi. Cowel. Blount.*

BASKET TENURE of lands. See *Canestellus.*

BASNETUM, a basnet, or helmet. *Cowel. Blount.*

BASSINET, a skin with which the soldiers covered themselves. *Ibid.*

BASTARD, (*bastardus*) from the Brit. *bastaerd, i. e. nothus* or *spurius*, is one that is born of any woman not married, so that his father is not known by the order of law; and therefore is called *filius populi*, the child of the people.—But if a woman be with child by a man, who afterwards marries her, and then the child is born, this child is no bastard: but if a man hath issue by a woman before marriage, and after they marry, the issue is a bastard by our law; but legitimate by the civil law. 2 *Inst.* 96, 97.

So if a man marries a woman grossly big with child by another, who shortly after is delivered, in our law the issue is no bastard. 1 *Danv. Abr.* 729. And where a child is born within a day after marriage between parties of full age, if there be no apparent impossibility, that the husband should be the father of it, the child is no bastard, but supposed to be the child of the husband. 1 *Rol. Abr.* 358. But if the husband be but eight or nine years of age, or if he be within the age of fourteen, the issue is a bastard: so where a husband is gelt, or hath lost his genitals, &c. which shews an impossibility to get a child, the issue of his wife, though born within marriage is a bastard. *Co. Lit.* 244. 1 *Danv.* 728.

Hence we perceive, that by the law of the land a person cannot, in general, be a bastard who is born after espousals, unless it be by a special matter. And it was formerly held, that if a woman eloped from her husband, and the husband was *within the four seas,* so that by intendment he might converse with his wife, and the wife had issue, the child was not to be a bastard: though it would be a bastard if born of a woman whose husband, at and from the time of the begetting to the birth, was *extra quatuor maria. Co. Lit.* 244. 2 *Salk.* 483.

But this strange doctrine has for some time

been overruled, and now not only proof of being out of the kingdom; but also every other kind of evidence tending to prove the impossibility or even improbability of the husband's being the father is admitted. 2 *Str.* 925. 3 *Peere Wms.* 365. 1 *Black. Com.* 457. 2 *Str.* 940, 1076. *Cas. Temp. Hard.* 379. *And.* 8. 4 *Ter. Rep.* 251, 356.

A divorce *causâ precontractus, causâ affinitatis, causâ frigiditatis,* &c. bastardises the issue, not for cause subsequent to the marriage; but if the man and woman continue husband and wife for all their lives, the issue cannot be a bastard, by divorce after their death. 1 *Danv.* 730. Where a woman, on divorce *a mensa & thoro,* lives in adultery with another, her children by such other are bastards, for children born in adultery are born out of the limits of matrimony. Though if husband and wife consent to live separate, the children born after such separation shall be taken to be legitimate, because the access of the husband may be presumed; but if it be found there was no access, then they are bastards. 1 *Salk.* 122.

Where a man hath issue a son by a woman before marriage, and afterwards marries the same woman, and hath issue a second son born after the marriage, the first of these is termed in law a bastard *eigne,* and the second a *mulier;* by the common law, such bastard *eigne* is as incapable of inheriting as if the father and mother had never married; but yet there is one case in which his issue was let into the succession, and that was by the consent of the lord and person legitimate; as if upon the death of the father the bastard *eigne* enters, and the *mulier* during his whole life never disturbs him, he cannot upon the death of the bastard *eigne,* enter upon his issue. *Lit. sec.* 399. *Co. Lit.* 245.

But to exclude the *mulier* from the inheritance there must not only be an uninterrupted possession of the bastard *eigne* during his life, but a descent to his issue. *Co. Lit.* 244. 1 *Rol. Abr.* 624.

If a woman hath a child forty weeks and eight days after the death of her husband, it shall be legitimate; the law having appointed no exact certain time for birth of legitimate issues. 1 *Danv.* 726. 2 *Lill. Abr.* 236.

If a man or woman marry a second wife or husband, the first being living, and have issue by such second wife or husband, the issue is a bastard. 39 *Ed.* 3. *cap.* 14. &c.

Bastard is *terminus a quo,* he is the first of his family, for he hath no relation, of which our law takes any notice; yet this must be understood as to civil purposes, there being a relation as to moral purposes; for he cannot marry his own mother, or bastard sister. 3 *Salk.* 66, 67.

A bastard cannot inherit land as heir to his father; nor can any person inherit lands as heir to him but one that is heir of his body. *Lit. sec.* 401.

But though he cannot inherit to any ancestor, yet when he hath gotten a name of reputation he may purchase by it; for all surnames were originally acquired by reputation. *Co. Lit.* 36. 6 *Co.* 65. But if a remainder be limited to the eldest issue of *T. S.* whether legitimate or illegitimate, and *T. S.* hath issue a bastard, he shall not take this remainder, for it is not vested in *T. S.* but is in *contingency,* and the certain time is not defined when this contingency shall happen; for the bastard at his birth does not acquire the reputation of being the issue of *T. S.* and since the bastard, when first in being, cannot take by virtue of this limitation, he can never take it; for he cannot be understood to be the person designed and marked out by these words, if after his birth it depends on the uncertainty of popular reputation, whether he should take the remainder or not; and such a designation of the person as contains no certainty in itself, or no relation to any other certain matter, that may reduce it to certainty, is a void limitation. *Co. Lit.* 3 *b.* 6 *Co.* 65.

But where a remainder is limited to the eldest son of *Jane S.* whether legitimate or illegitimate, and she hath issue, a bastard shall take this remainder, because he acquires the denomination of her issue by being born of her body; and so it was never uncertain who was designed by this remainder. *Noy* 35.

If a man, in consideration of natural affection and love, covenants to stand seised to the use of a bastard, this is not good, for he is not *de sanguine patris;* but it is said that a woman may give lands in frank-marriage with her bastard, because he is of the blood of the mother; but he hath no father but from reputation only. *Dyer* 374. *And.* 79. 6 *Co.* 77. *Noy* 35.

A court of equity, will not supply the want of a surrender, of a copyhold estate, in favour of a bastard, as it will for a legitimate child. *Preced. Chan.* 475.

A bastard by the common law is made incapable of any ecclesiastical benefice: for the sacraments ought not to be committed to infamous persons. *Fortescue* 88, 89.

How provided for by statute.] By stat. 18 *Eliz. c.* 3, and 3 *Car.* 1. *c.* 4, "a woman "with child of a bastard must be first examined by a justice of peace, and the fact "of her being with child proved by her oath, "and then the justice is to send his warrant "for the reputed father; when the party is "brought before the justice he must enter "into a recognizance with sufficient sureties for his appearance at the next sessions, &c. and he may be continued on "the recognizance till the woman is delivered of the child: after the child is born, "two justices (*quorum unus*) residing near-

"est the place, are to examine the matter "by witnesses, &c. and make their order "for relief of the parish from the bastard; "and if the two justices cannot agree they "may refer it to the sessions; also the "putative father may appeal from the order "of the two justices, or may give security "to the parish," &c.

"The two next justices of peace (one be- "ing of the *quorum*) may make orders for "punishing the mother and father of a bas- "tard child; and by order of the justices, "the churchwardens and overseers of the "poor may seize goods, and receive the "annual rents of lands, &c. of the father "and mother to discharge the parish; and "justices of the peace have power to com- "mit lewd women having bastards to the "house of correction for one year, &c. or "for a second offence, till she give security "for her good behaviour." 18 *Eliz. c.* 3. 13 and 14 *Car.* 2. *c.* 12. 7 *Jac.* 1. *c.* 4.

"If a single woman declares herself to be "with child of a bastard, and on oath before "a justice charge any person with getting it, "he may grant his warrant to apprehend "the person charged, and for bringing him "before any justice, &c. who may commit "him to gaol, or the house of correction, "unless he give security to indemnify the "parish, or enter into recognizance with "sureties, to appear at the next quarter- "sessions, and perform such order as shall be "made, pursuant to the statute 18 *Eliz. c.* 3.

"Unless two justices shall have certified in "writing to the next, or where such woman "shall not have been delivered, then to the "immediately next sessions, that an order "of filiation hath been already made on the "person charged; or that such order was "not then requisite to be made, on account "of the death of the child, or for other suf- "ficient reason, in each of which *first cases*, "the sessions may respite the recognizance "to the next sessions; and in either of the "*two last cases* wholly discharge the recog- "nizance." 49 *Geo.* 3. *c.* 68. *s.* 2.

"But no justice may send for or com- "pel any woman before she is delivered, "and one month after, to answer ques- "tions, &c." *Stat.* 6 *Geo.* 2. *c.* 31.

Upon these statutes it has been decided, 1. That the putative father shall be discharged if the justices at the sessions, upon hearing all the circumstances of the case, shall be of opinion that he is not the father of the child. 1 *Black.* 458.

2. That although by the 6 *Geo.* 2. *c.* 31, one magistrate may compel the person on whom the child is filiated, to indemnify the parish by a bond, with two sufficient sureties, yet the parish cannot take a gross sum of money, as 40*l.* or the like, to discharge the putative father totally: they can only take a security to indemnify themselves by weekly or other payments during the time the child remains chargeable; and all securities contrary hereto are void. 6 *East's Rep.* 192.

3. That under the statute of *Eliz.* the sessions have no power to compel the putative father to give security for the performance of the order of filiation, and maintenance; but that if the party do disobey such order, or the order by two justices out of sessions, he may be punished by indictment for such disobedience. 6 *Term Rep.* 147.

And so it is if the party under 6 *Geo.* 2. *c.* 31, instead of giving bond to indemnify the parish in the first instance, enter into a recognizance to appear at, and abide by the order of, the next sessions, he cannot even then be compelled to give security for the performance of the order of sessions; and the parish can only take their common law remedy by indictment, in case the order of filiation is disobeyed. *Ibid.*

But now by 49 *Geo.* 3. *c.* 68. "if the re- "puted father or mother on whom any order "of filiation or maintenance shall have been "made, shall neglect or refuse to pay, any "justice on complaint thereof by the over- "seers, and proof thereof, may issue his "warrant to apprehend the party, and un- "less some reasonable cause for the neglect "be shewn, he may commit them to the "house of correction, or common gaol, to "be kept to hard labour for three [lunar] "months, unless the money shall be sooner "paid. *s.* 3."

4. It has been held at *Nisi prius* that the heir of the principal, or the heir of the surety, inheriting lands from his ancestor, may at any distance of time be sued upon the bond, for the damages which the parish sustains, by maintaining the bastard in his old age, or his children, who have not obtained settlements in another parish or township. 1 *Black. Com.* 458.

By the 49 *Geo.* 3. *c.* 68. "the reputed "fathers of bastard children shall be charge- "able with the expences incident to the "birth, with the costs of apprehending and "of the order of filiation not exceeding 10*l.* "to be ascertained by the justices or court "of quarter sessions who shall make the "order of filiation." *s.* 1, 4.

"But persons aggrieved may appeal to "the quarter sessions, on giving 10 days "notice to the justices or one of them, and "also to the churchwardens and overseers, "and entering into a recognizance within "three days after such notice with sufficient "surety, to try the appeal, abide by the "order of sessions, and pay the costs award- "ed." *s.* 5.

"And no appeal shall in future be allow- "ed in any bastardy case without like no- "tice, and entering into a like recogni- "zance." *s.* 7.

Settlement of bastards.] Bastard children

gain a settlement in the parish where they are born. But if a woman big with child, pending an order of removal appealed against, be delivered, the child's settlement must follow that of the mother. 1 *Bac. Abr. tit. Bas.*

So it will be settled in the mother's parish, if she is apprehended for vagrancy, 17 *Geo.* 2. *c.* 5. So if born in gaol, 1 *Sess. Cas.* 94, or in a licensed lying-in hospital, or in any house of industry, 10 *Geo.* 3. *c.* 36; or under a certificate. *Bur. Set. Cas* 187. 264. 650. or during the suspension of an order of removal by reason of illness. 35 *Geo.* 3. *c.* 101. *s.* 6.

And where a bastard having a different settlement from its mother, lives with her for nurture, the parish where the bastard's settlement is must maintain it. *Doug.* 7, 9. *n.* 2. And if the parents neglect to provide for the sustenance of a bastard child, the parish where it is born must do it, though the justices make no order for that purpose. 1 *Hen. Black. Rep.* 253. *Doug.* 9.

If a woman be with child, and any one gives her a potion to destroy the child within her, and she takes it, and it works so strongly that it kills her, this is murder; for it was not given to cure her of a disease, but unlawfully to destroy the child within her, and therefore he that gives her a potion to this end must take the hazard, and if it kills the mother it is murder. 1 *Hal. P. C.* 429, 430.

And by 43 *Geo.* 3. *c.* 58. "Persons administering medicines to women, though "not quick with child, to procure miscarriage, are guilty of felony, and to be "punished by fine and imprisonment, the "pillory, or public or private whipping, or "to be transported for not exceeding 14 "years." *s.* 2.

If a man counsel a woman with child to destroy her infant when born, and the child being born, the woman in pursuance of that counsel kill the infant, this is murder in the mother, and the procurer is accessary. 1 *Hale's H. P. C.* 433.

And by 43 *Geo.* 3. *c.* 58, the trials of women for the murder of bastards shall proceed as in other cases of murder, *sec.* 3. And women acquitted of such murder, on the jury finding them to have been guilty of concealment of the birth, shall be imprisoned in the common gaol or house of correction for not exceeding two years. *sec.* 4.

BASTARDY, (*bastardia*) signifies a defect of birth, objected to one born out of wedlock. *Bract. lib.* 5. *c.* 19.

BASTARD-EIGNE, (Fr.) is where a man hath issue a son by a woman before marriage, and afterwards hath another son by the same woman in wedlock, the first of which is in the law termed a *bastard-eigne*.

BASTON, (Fr.) a staff, or club; and by our statutes, it signifies one of the warden of the Fleet's servants or officers who attend the king's courts with a red staff, for taking such into custody, who are committed by the court. 1 *R.* 2. *c.* 12. 5 *Eliz. c.* 23. See *Tipstaff.*

BASUS, *per basum tolnetum capere*, to take toll by strike, and not by heap. *Cowel.* *Blount.*

BATABLE GROUND, is taken for the land that lay between England and Scotland, heretofore in question, when they were distinct kingdoms, to which it belonged. It seems to mean, as if we should say, litigious or debatable ground, *i. e.* land about which there is debate; and by that name *Skene* calls ground that is in controversy. *Cam. Britan.* Tit. *Cumberland.* *Cowel.* *Blount.*

BATH, (Lat. *bathon*, called by the Britons *badizu*) has been termed the city of sick men: it is a place of resort in Somersetshire, famous for its medicinal waters. *Cowel.* *Blount.*

BATITORIA, a fulling-mill. *Ibid.*

BATTLE, (Fr. *battaile*) signifies a trial by combat, which was anciently allowed of in our laws, where the defendant in appeal of murder or felony might fight with the appellant, and make proof thereby whether he were culpable or innocent of the crime. *Glanv. lib.* 14. *c.* 1.

This trial by battle was before the constable and marshal, but, with all its ceremonies, is now disused. See *Glanv. lib.* 14. *Bracton, lib.* 3. *Britton, c.* 22. *Smith de Rep. Angl. lib.* 2. *Co. Lit.* 294, &c. 3 *Black.* 339.

BATTERY, (from the Fr. *battre*, to strike, or Sax. *batte*, a club) is an injury done to another in a violent manner, as by striking or beating of a man, pushing, jolting, filiping upon the nose, &c. And it is also defined by our law to be a trespass committed by one man upon another, *vi et armis et contra pacem*, &c. This offence is punishable by action and indictment; and on action for the injury at the suit of the party, the defendant shall render damages, &c. On indictment at the suit of the king, for a breach of the peace, he shall be fined according to the heinousness of the offence. *Dall.* 282. 1 *Hawk. P. C.* 134.

But a man may beat another, who first assaults him, in his own defence, and justify in an action by special pleading, as that the battery was occasioned by his own assault; or the defendant may give that in evidence upon *not guilty*, to an indictment: and the record of the conviction of the offender by indictment may serve afterwards for evidence in action of trespass for the same assault and battery. *Terms de Ley.* 2 *Rol. Abr.* 546.

BATUS, (Lat. from the Sax. *bat*) a boat, and *battellus*, a little boat. *Cowel.* *Blount.*

BAUBELLA, (*baubles*) a word mentioned

in *Hoveden* in *R.* 1, and signifies jewels or precious stones. *Ibid.*

BAUDEKIN, (*baldicum*, and *baldekinum*) cloth of *baudekin*, or gold: it is said to be the richest cloth, now called brocade, made with gold and silk, or tissue, upon which figures in silk, &c. were embroidered *Ibid.*

BAWDY-HOUSE, (*lupanar*, *fornix*) a house of ill fame, kept for the resort and commerce of lewd people of both sexes. The keeping of a bawdy-house comes under the cognizance of the temporal law, as a common nuisance, not only in respect of its endangering the public peace by drawing together dissolute and debauched persons, and promoting quarrels, but also in respect of its tendency to corrupt the manners of the people, by an open profession of lewdness. 3 *Inst.* 205. 1 *Hawk. P. C.* 196. Those who keep bawdy-houses are punished with fine and imprisonment; and also such infamous punishment, as pillory, &c. as the court in discretion shall inflict: and a lodger who keeps only a single room for the use of bawdry is indictable for keeping a bawdy-house. 1 *Salk.* 382. Persons resorting to a bawdy-house are punishable, and they may be bound to the good behaviour, &c. But if one be indicted for keeping or frequenting a bawdy-house, it must be expressly alleged to be such a house, and that the party knew it, and not by suspicion only. *Poph.* 208. And it is said that a constable, upon information that a man and woman are gone to a lewd house, or about to commit fornication or adultery, may, if he finds them together, carry them before a justice of peace *without any warrant*, and the justice may bind them over to the sessions. *Dalt.* 214.

It seems always to have been the better opinion, that a man may be bound to his good behaviour for haunting bawdy-houses with women of bad fame, as also for keeping bad women in his own house. 1 *Hawk.* 132.

Constables in these cases may call others to their assistance, enter bawdy-houses, and arrest offenders for breach of the peace: in London they may carry them to prison; and by custom of the city whores and bawds may be carted. 3 *Inst.* 206.

A wife may be indicted together with her husband, and condemned to the pillory with him for keeping a bawdy-house, for this is an offence as to the government of the house, in which the wife has a principal share; and also such an offence as may generally be presumed to be managed by the intrigues of her sex. 1 *Hawk.* 2.

But it is said a woman cannot be indicted for being a bawd generally, for that the bare solicitation of chastity is not indictable. 1 *Hawk.* 196. 1 *Salk.* 382.

It was always held infamous to keep a bawdy-house, yet some of our historians mention bawdy-houses publicly allowed here in former times, till the reign of *Hen.* 8. and assign the number to be eighteen, thus allowed, on the Bank-side in Southwark.

"If two inhabitants, paying scot and lot, "shall give notice to a constable of any "person keeping a bawdy-house, the constable shall go with them before a justice "of peace, and shall, (upon such inhabitants "making oath that they believe the contents of such notice to be true, and entering into a recognizance of 20*l.* each "to give material evidence of the offence) "enter into a recognizance of 30*l.* to prosecute with effect such person for such "offence at the next sessions; the constable shall be paid his reasonable expenses "by the overseers of the poor, to be ascertained by two justices; and if the offender "be convicted, the overseers shall pay to "the two inhabitants 10*l.* each. On the "constable's entering into such recognizance as aforesaid, the justice shall bind "over the person accused to the next sessions, and, if he shall think proper, demand security for such person's good behaviour in the mean time. A constable "neglecting his duty forfeits 20*l.* Any person appearing as master or mistress, or "as having the care or management of any "bawdy-house, shall be deemed the keeper "thereof, and liable to be punished as "such." *Stat.* 25 *Geo.* 2. *c.* 36.

BAY, or *pen*, is a pond-head, made up of a great height, to keep in water for the supply of a mill, &c. so that the wheel of the mill may be driven by the water coming thence, through a passage or flood-gate. A harbour where ships ride at sea, near some port, is also called a bay: and this word is mentioned *anno* 27 *Eliz.* *c.* 19. *Cowel. Blount.*

BEACON, (from the Sax. *beacen*, i. e. *signum*) a signal well known, being a fire maintained on some eminence near the coasts of the sea, to prevent invasions, &c. 4 *Inst.* 148. 8 *Eliz.* *c.* 13. Hence beaconage (*beaconagium*) money paid towards the maintenance of beacons; and we still use the word *beckon* to give notice unto. See *Stat.* 5 *Hen.* 4. &c. The king hath an exclusive power by commission under the great seal to appoint them. *Black. Com.* 1 *V.* 265. They are usually vested by letters patent in the office of lord high admiral. *Ibid.*

BEAD, or *bede*, (Sax. *bead*, *oratio*) a prayer, so that to say over beads is to say over one's prayers. They were most in use before printing, when poor persons could not go to the charge of a manuscript book; though they are still used in many parts of the world, where the Roman catholic religion prevails. They are not allowed to be brought into England, or any superstitious things to be used here under the penalty of a *præmunire*, by stat. 13 *Eliz.* *c* 2. *Cowel. Blount.*

BEAM, is that part of the head of a stag where the horns grow, from the Sax. *beam*, i. e. *arbor*, because they grow out of the head as branches out of a tree. Beam is likewise used for a common balance of weights in cities and towns. *Ibid.*

BEARERS, signify such as bear down or oppress others, and is said to be all one with maintainers.—Justices of assise shall inquire of, hear, and determine maintainers, bearers, and conspirators, &c. *Stat.* 4 *Ed.* 3. *c.* 11.

BEASTS OF CHASE, (*feræ campestres*) are five, *viz.* the buck, doe, fox, marten, and roe. *Manw.* part 1, pa. 342. Beasts of the forest (*feræ silvestres*) otherwise called beasts of venary, are the hart, hind, boar, and wolf. *Ibid. par.* 2. *c.* 4. Beasts and fowls of the warren are the hare, coney, pheasant, and partridge. *Ibid. Reg. Orig.* 95, 96, &c. *Co. Lit.* 233.

BEAU-PLEADER, (*pulchre placitando*, Fr. *beauplaider*, i. e. to plead fairly) is a writ upon the statute of Marlbridge, 52 *H.* 3. c. 11, whereby it is enacted, that neither in the circuits of justice, nor in counties, hundreds, or courts-baron, any fines shall be taken for fair-pleading, *viz.* for not pleading fairly or aptly to the purpose; upon which statute this writ was ordained, directed to the sheriff, bailiff, or him who shall demand such fine, and it is a prohibition not to do it: whereupon an *alias* and *pluries* and attachment may be had, &c. *New Nat. Brev.* 596, 597. And beau-pleader is as well in respect of vicious pleadings, as of the fair pleading, by way of amendment. 2 *Inst.* 122. *Cowel. Blount.*

BEDEL, (*bedellus*, Sax. *bydel*) a crier or messenger of a court, that cites men to appear and answer: and is an inferior officer of a parish, or liberty, very well known in London, and the suburbs. There are likewise university-bedels, and church-bedels, now called summoners and apparitors; and Manwood in his Forest Laws saith there are forest-bedels, that make all manner of garnishments for the courts of the forest, and all proclamations, and also execute the process of the forest, like unto bailiffs-errant of a sheriff in his county. *Cowel. Blount.*

BEDELARY, (*bedelaria*) is the same to a bedel as bailiwick to a bailiff. *Lit. lib.* 3. *cap.* 5.

BEDEREPE, alias *bidrepe*, (Sax.) is a service which certain tenants were anciently bound to perform, *viz.* to reap their landlord's corn at harvest, as some yet are tied to give them one, two, or three days work, when commanded. This customary service of inferior tenants was called in the Latin *precaria bedrepium*, &c. See *Magna Præcaria. Cowel. Blount.*

BEDEWERI, those which we now call banditti, profligate and excommunicated persons. The word is mentioned in *Mat. Par. ann.* 1258. *Cowel. Blount.*

BEER. See ALEHOUSES and EXCISE.

BEGGARS. See *Vagrants*.

BEHAVIOUR of persons. Vide SURETY.

BELGÆ, the inhabitants of Somersetshire, Wiltshire, and Hampshire. *Blount.*

BENEFICE, (*beneficium*) is generally taken for any ecclesiastical living or promotion, and all church preferments and dignities are benefices, but they must be given for life, not for years, or at will. 3 *Inst.* 155.

BENEFICIO PRIMO ECCLESIASTICO HABENDO, a writ directed from the king to the chancellor, to bestow the benefice that shall first fall in the king's gift, above or under such a value, upon such a particular person. *Reg. Orig.* 307.

BENEFIT OF CLERGY. See CLERGY.

BENEFIT CLUBS. By 33 *Geo.* 3. *c.* 54, any number of persons may form themselves into a society, and raise among themselves a fund for their mutual benefit, and may make rules, and impose fines; but the rules of such societies are to be exhibited to the justices in quarter sessions, who may annul or confirm them: the rules are to be signed by the clerk of the peace, and deposited with him; and no society is to be within the meaning of this act, till their rules have been confirmed. *s.* 1, 2.

No confirmed rule to be altered but at a general meeting of the society; and the alterations of the rules, are to be subject to the review of the quarter sessions. *s.* 3.

The societies may appoint officers, and securities are to be given for offices of trust, if required: and every such bond from treasurers or trustees, is to be given to the clerk of the peace; and from other persons to the treasurers or trustees; which bonds are not chargeable with stamp-duty. *s.* 4.

Powers of standing committees to be declared in the rules of the society; and if particular ones, entered in a book; and all committees are to be controllable by the society. *s.* 5.

Treasurers or trustees are to lay out the surplus of the contributions either in private securities to be approved of, or in the public funds, and to bring the proceeds to account for the use of the society. *s.* 6, 7.

Treasurers and trustees are to render accounts, and pay over balances; and in case of neglect, application may be made in a summary way, by petition to the court of chancery or exchequer, or great sessions. *s.* 8.

And no fee is to be taken for any proceedings in such courts. *s.* 9.

Executors and administrators, are to pay money due to societies, before any other debt. *s.* 10.

The effects of societies to be vested in the treasurers or trustees for the time being, who may bring and defend actions. *s.* 11.

Societies are to declare the purpose of their establishment, before the confirmation of their rules by the quarter sessions, and may inflict penalties for misapplication of money. The consent of five sixths at a general meeting is necessary for the dissolution of societies; and the stock is not to be divisible, but for the general purposes of the society. *s.* 12.

Their rules are to be entered in a book, and received in evidence. *s.* 13.

Societies may also receive donations in support of their stock. *s.* 14.

When members think themselves aggrieved, two justices on complaint may summon the officers, and on hearing of the parties they may make such order as shall seem just, which is not removable by certiorari. *s.* 15.

No member of any such society producing a certificate thereof, shall be removable from where he resides, till actually chargeable to the parish; but the signing of such certificate must be authenticated, by the oath of a witness, before a justice of peace. *s.* 17, 18.

And, on complaint of parish officers, any justice may summon persons bringing such certificates, to be examined, and make oath of their settlement; and copies of the examination, are to be given to the parties, which shall exempt them from future examination. *s.* 19.

Justices may declare, by an order in writing, the place of settlement of persons so examined, without issuing a warrant for removal; and copies of such orders, and of examinations, are to be returned to the parish officers; and persons aggrieved herein may appeal to the quarter sessions. *s.* 20, 21.

No person who shall reside in any parish, under this act, shall thereby acquire a settlement; nor for paying rates; nor any apprentice or servant to such persons. *s.* 22, 23, 24.

Bastards are to have their mother's settlement. *s.* 25.

Charges of maintaining or removing residents under this act to be reimbursed by the parish to which the parties belong. *s.* 26.

By 35 *Geo.* 3. *c.* 111. governors of institutions for the relief of the widows, orphans, and families of the clergy, and others in distressed circumstances, may frame rules, and present them for confirmation. *s.* 2.

Institutions where rules shall be confirmed may appoint treasurers, and be entitled to the benefit of this act. *s.* 3.

By 49 *Geo.* 3. *c.* 125. all societies established before Michaelmas 1796, whose rules have been since exhibited, or shall at any time hereafter be exhibited, to the justices at sessions, and approved of, shall be deemed to be within the benefit of 33 *Geo.* 3. *c.* 54. *s.* 2.

Two justices on complaint may enforce the observance of the rules of benefit societies, and in the case of the adjudication of monies in arrear, levy the same by distress, and sale of the goods, of the person on whom the order is made. *s.* 1.

On complaint of members, of relief refused, such justices may summon the proper officer, and on proof upon oath, order the money to be paid with costs, not exceeding 10*s.* which, if not forthwith paid in the presence of the justice, shall be levied on the monies and effects of the society, with the further costs of the distress and sale: and in default of distress on society monies or effects, the same shall be levied on those of the treasurer or other proper officer, and repaid out of the society's funds. *s.* 3.

The orders of the justices, upon the officers, shall be made out in the proper names of such officers, and served either personally, or by leaving the same at their dwelling houses. *s.* 4.

And all orders of the justices under this act shall be final, and not removed into any court of law, or restrained by injunction in equity. *s.* 5.

BENERETH, an ancient service which the tenant rendered to his lord with his plough and cart. *Lamb. Itin. p.* 222. *Co. Lit.* 86.

BENEVOLENCE, (*benevolentia*) is used in the chronicles and statutes, of this realm, for a voluntary gratuity given by the subjects to the king. *Stow's Annals, p.* 701, now given by way of taxes.

BENEVOLENTIA REGIS HABENDA, the form of purchasing the king's pardon and favour, in ancient fines and submissions, to be restored to estate, title, or place. *Paroch. Antiq.* 172. *Cowel. Blount.*

BENT, See SEA BANKS.

BERBIAGE, (*berbiagium*) *Nativi tenentes manerii de Calistoke reddunt per ann. de certo redditu vocat. berbiag. ad le Hokeday* xix. *s.* MS. Survey of the Duchy of Cornwall. *Cowel. Blount.*

BERBICARIA, a sheep-down, or ground to feed sheep. *Ibid.*

BERCARIA, (*berchery*, from the Fr. *bergerie*) a sheep-fold, or other inclosure for the keeping of sheep. *Ibid.*

BEREFELLARII: There were seven churchmen so called, anciently belonging to the church of St. John of Beverly. *Cowel. Blount.*

BEREFREIT, BEREFREID, a large wooden tower. *Ibid.*

BERGHMASTER, (from the Sax. *berg*, a hill, *mons quasi*, master of the mountains) is a chief officer among the Derbyshire miners, who also executes the office of a coroner. *Cowel. Blount.*

BERGMOTH, or BERGHMOTE, comes from the Sax. *berg*, a hill, and *gemote*, an assembly, and is as much as to say, an assembly or court upon a hill, which is held in Derbyshire for deciding pleas and controversies among the miners. *Ibid.*

BERIA, BERIE, BERRY, a large open field; and those cities and towns in England which end with that word, are built in plain and open places, and do not derive their names from boroughs, as Sir Henry Spelman imagines. Most of our glossographers in the names of places have confounded the word *berie* with that of *bury* and *borough*, as if the appellative of ancient towns; whereas the true sense of the word berie is a flat wide champaign, as is proved from sufficient authorities by the learned *Du Fresne*, who observes that *Beria Sancta Edmundi*, mentioned by *Mat. Par. sub. ann.* 1174, is not to be taken for the town, but for the adjoining plain. To this may be added, that many flat and wide meads, and other open grounds, are called by the name of beries, and berryfields: the spacious meadow between Oxford and Isley was in the reign of king Athelstan called Bery. *B.* Twine, MS. As is now the largest pasture ground in Quarendon in the county of Buckingham, known by the name of Beryfield. And though these meads have been interpreted demesne or manor meadows, yet they were truly any flat or open meadows that lay adjoining to any vill or farm; as Laleham Burway. *Cowel. Blount.*

BERRA, a plain open heath. *Berras assartare*, to grub up such barren heaths. *Ibid.*

BERNET, *incendium*, comes from the Sax. *byran*, to burn. It is one of those crimes which by the laws of *Hen.* 1. *cap.* 15, *emendari non possunt*. Sometimes it is used to signify any capital offence. *Leges Canuti apud Brompt. c.* 90. *Leg. Hen.* 1. *c.* 12. 47.

BERSA, (Fr. *bers*) a limit or bound. A park pale. *Cowel. Blount.*

BERSARE, (Germ. *bersen*, to shoot) *bersare in foresta mea ad tres arcus. Chart. Ranulph. Comit. Cestr. ann.* 1218. *viz.* to hunt or shoot with three arrows in my forest. *Bersarii* were properly those that hunted the wolf. *Ibid.*

BERSELET, (*berseletta*) a hound. *Ibid.*

BERTON, or BARTON, (*bertona*) is that part of a country farm, where the barns and other inferior offices stand, and wherein the cattle are foddered, and other business is managed. See *Claus.* 32 *Ed.* 1. *m.* 17. It also signifies a farm distinct from a manor: in some parts of the west of England they call a great farm a berton, and a small farm a living. *Bertonarii* were such as we now call farmers or tenants of *bertons*, husbandmen who held lands at the will of the lord. *Cowel. Blount.*

BEREWICHA, or BERWICA, villages or hamlets belonging to some town or manor. *Cowel. Blount.*

BERWICK. By *Stat.* 20 *Geo.* 2. *c.* 42, *sec.* 3, Wales and Berwick upon Tweed shall be included in all acts of parliament wherein the kingdom of England, or that part of Great Britain called England, shall be mentioned.

BERY, or BURY, the vill or seat of habitation of a nobleman, a dwelling, or mansion-house, being the chief of a manor, from the Sax. *beorg*, which signifies a hill or castle, for heretofore noblemens seats were castles, situate on hills, of which we have still some remains; as in Herefordshire there are the beries of Stockton, Hope, &c. It was anciently taken for a sanctuary. *Cowel. Blount.*

BESAILE, (from the Fr. *bisayeul, proavus*) i. e. *the father of the grandfather*) was a writ, now in disuse, which anciently lay at the common law, where the great grandfather was seised the day that he died, of any lands or tenements in fee-simple; and after his death a stranger entered the same day upon them and kept out the heir. *F. N. B.* 222.

BESCHA, (from the Fr. *bercher, fodere*, to dig) a spade or shovel. Hence perhaps, *una bescata terra inclusa—Mon. Ang. tom.* 2. *fol.* 642. may signify a piece of land usually turned up with a spade, as gardeners fit and prepare their grounds; or may be taken for as much land as one man can dig with a spade in a day. *Cowel. Blount.*

BESTIALS, (*bestials*) beasts or cattle of any sort. *Cowel. Blount.*

BETACHES. Laymen using glebe lands. *Parl.* 14 *Ed.* 2. *Ibid.*

BEVERCHES, bed-works, or customary services done at the bidding of the lord by his inferior tenants. *Ibid.*

BEWARED, an old Saxon word signifying expended; for before the Britons and Saxons had plenty of money, they traded wholly in exchange of wares. *Ibid.*

BIDALE, or BIDALL, (*precaria potaria*, from the Sax. *biddan*, to pray or supplicate) is the invitation of friends, to drink ale at the house of some poor man, who thereby hopes a charitable contribution for his relief: it is still in use in the West of England: and is mentioned 26 *Hen.* 8. *c.* 6. And something like this seems to be what we commonly call house warming, when persons are invited and visited in this manner on their first beginning house-keeping. *Ibid.*

BIDDING OF THE BEADS, (*bidding* from the Sax. *biddan*) was anciently a charge or warning given by the parish priest to his parishioners at some special times to come to prayers, either for the soul of some friend departed, or upon some other particular occasion. And at this day our ministers, on the Sunday preceding any festival or holiday in the following week, give notice of them, and desire and exhort their parishioners to observe them as they ought; which is required by our canons. See *Stat.* 27 *Hen.* 8. *c.* 26. *Cowel. Blount.*

BIDENTES, two yearlings or sheep of the second year. *Cowel. Blount.*

BIDUANA, a fasting for the space of two days. *Ibid.*

BIGA, *bigala*, a cart or chariot drawn with two horses, coupled side to side; but it is said to be properly a cart with two wheels, sometimes drawn by one horse; and in our ancient records it is used for any cart, wain or waggon. *Ibid.*

BIGAMUS, is a person that hath married two or more wives, successively after each other, or a widow; for the canonists account a man that hath married a widow, to have been twice married. It is mentioned in the statutes 18 *Ed.* 3. *c.* 2. 1 *Ed.* 6. *c.* 12. and 2 *Inst.* 273.

BIGAMY, (*bigamia*) signifies a double marriage, or marriage of two wives; one after another, and not the having of two together; more properly called polygamy.

And by 1 *Jac.* 1. *c.* 11. *if any person on being married, do afterwards marry again, the former husband or wife being living, it is felony.* Except 1, where either party has been continually *abroad* for seven years, whether the party in England hath notice of the other's being living or no; 2, where either of the parties hath been absent from the other seven years *within* this kingdom, and the remaining party hath had no knowledge of the other's being alive within that time; 3, where there is a divorce, (or separation *a mensâ et thoro*, 1 *Hawk.* 174.) by sentence in the ecclesiastical court;* 4, where the first marriage is declared absolutely void by any such sentence, and the parties loosed *â vinculo matrimonii*; or 5, where either of the parties was under the age of consent at the time of the first marriage.

And by 35 *Geo.* 3. *c.* 67. *persons convicted under* 1 *Jac.* 1. *c.* 11. *in England of bigamy, are made subject to the penalties inflicted for larceny*, i. e. *transportation, and returning before the expiration of the term for which they are transported, to be guilty of felony without benefit of clergy, and may be tried in the county where convicted or found at large.*

If one of the parties only be under the age of consent, the exception in 1 *Jac.* 1. extends as well to the party above the age, as to the other; because the power of disagreeing was equal on both sides. 4 *Black. Com.* 163.

In these cases, the first and true wife is not an admissible witness against her husband, but the second woman is competent to prove the marriage, *for* she is not his wife so much as *de facto*. 1 *Hale* 692, 3.

BIGOT, is a compound of several old English words, and signifies an obstinate person; or one that is wedded to an opinion, in matters of religion, &c. *Cowel. Blount.*

* In these three first cases, however, though the parties are excepted from *felony*, the second marriage is void.

BILAGINES, (Lat.) by-laws of corporations, &c. See *By-laws.*

BILANCIIS DEFERENDIS, a writ anciently directed to a corporation, for the carrying of weights to such a haven, there to weigh the wool that persons by our ancient laws were licensed to transport. *Reg. Orig.* 270.

BILINGUIS, signifies generally a double tongued man; or one that can speak two languages; but it is used in our law for a jury that passeth between an Englishman and a foreigner, whereof part ought to be English, and part strangers. Though this is properly a jury *de medietate linguæ*. 28 *Ed.* 3. *c.* 13. *Cowel. Blount.*

BILL, (*billa*) is diversly used: thus, in law proceedings, it signifies the *declaration* in writing, expressing either the wrong the complainant hath suffered by the party complained of, or else some fault committed against some law or statute of the realm. *Terms de Ley* 86. *Cowel. Blount.*

Also in criminal cases, when a grand jury upon a presentment or indictment find the same to be true, they indorse on it *billa vera*; and thereupon the offender is said to stand indicted of the crime, and is bound to make answer unto it: and if the crime touch the life of the person indicted; it is then referred to the jury of life and death, *viz.* the petty jury, by whom if he be found guilty, then he shall stand convicted of the crime, and is by the judge condemned to death. *Terms de Ley* 86. 3 *Inst.* 30.

BILL SINGLE, or PŒNAL: is a writing *under seal*, wherein one man is bound to another, to pay a sum of money on a day that is future: or presently on demand, according to the agreement of the parties at the time it is entered into, and the dealings between them; and is divided into several sorts, viz. a bill *single*, without a penalty, and a bill *penal*, under a penalty. *Cro. Eliz.* 548. 3 *Keb.* 176. *Rol. Abr.* 148. 2 *Rol.* 146. 22 *E.* 4. *c.* 22.

The first of *these bills hath long since fallen into disuse, from the introduction of bills of exchange, and the latter are seldom taken, the security by bond being preferable, and more generally resorted to.*

BILL IN EQUITY. Different kinds of bills are used in the courts of equity to answer the several purposes of instituting an original suit, of adding to, continuing or obtaining the benefit of a suit, of instituting a cross suit, of impugning the judgment of the court on a suit brought to a decision, and of carrying a judgment into execution. *Milf.* 31.

The several kinds of bills have been usually considered as capable of being arranged under three general heads: 1st, original bills; 2d, bills not original; 3d, bills in the nature of original bills. *Ibid.*

1. *Original bills*] are such as relate to some

matter, not before litigated in the court, by the same persons, standing in the same interests, and these may pray relief against an injury suffered, or only seek the assistance of the court, to enable the plaintiff to defend himself, against a possible future injury, or to support or defend a suit in a court of ordinary jurisdiction. *Ibid* 32.

Original bills are therefore again divided into 1st, *bills praying relief, 2dly, bills not praying relief.*

I. *Original bills praying relief,*] may be 1st, a bill praying the decree or order of the court, touching some right claimed by the person exhibiting the bill, in opposition to some right, claimed by some person against whom the bill is exhibited. *Ibid.*

This bill must shew the rights of the plaintiff, or person exhibiting the bill; by whom and in what manner he is injured; or in what he wants the assistance of the court; and that he is without remedy, except in a court of equity, or at least is properly relievable, or can be more effectually relieved there: having thus shewn the plaintiff's title to the assistance of the court, the bill may pray, that the defendant or person against whom the bill is exhibited, may answer upon oath the matters charged against him, and it may also pray the relief or assistance of the court, which the plaintiff's case entitles him to: for these purposes the bill must pray that a writ called a writ of *subpœna*, may issue under the great seal, which is the seal of the court, to require the defendant's appearance and answer to the bill; unless the defendant has privilege of peerage as a lord of parliament, or is made a defendant as an officer of the crown. *Mitf.* 37.

In the case of a peer or peeress, or lord of parliament, the bill must first pray the letter of the person holding the great seal, called a letter *missive*, requesting the defendant to appear to and answer the bill, and the writ of *subpœna* only in default of compliance with that request: and if the attorney-general is made a defendant, as an officer of the crown, the bill must pray instead of the writ of *subpœna*, that he being attended with a copy, may appear, and put in an answer. *Ibid* 38.

It is usual to add to the prayer of the bill, a general prayer for that relief which the circumstances of the case may require; that if the plaintiff mistakes the relief to which he is entitled, the court may yet afford him that relief to which he has a right. 2 *Atk.* 3. *Mitf.* 38.

Indeed it has been said, that a prayer of general relief, without a special prayer of the particular relief, to which the plaintiff thinks himself entitled, is sufficient; and that the particular relief which the case requires, may at the hearing, be prayed at the bar. But this relief must be agreeable to the case made by the bill, and not different from it; and the court will not in all cases be so indulgent, as to permit a bill framed for one purpose to answer another, especially if the defendant may be surprized or prejudiced; if therefore the plaintiff doubts his title to the relief he wishes to pray, the bill may be framed with a double aspect; that if the court determines against him in one view of the case, it may yet afford him assistance in another. 2 *Atk.* 325. *Mitf.* 39.

All persons concerned in the demand, or who may be affected by the relief prayed, ought to be parties, if within the jurisdiction of the court: but if any necessary parties are omitted, or unnecessary parties are inserted, the court upon application, will in general permit the bill to be amended, and the proper alteration made. *Mitf.* 39.

It is the practice to insert in a bill, a general charge, that the parties named in it combine together, and with several other persons unknown to the plaintiff, whose names, when discovered, the plaintiff prays he may be at liberty to insert in the bill. This practice is said to have arisen from an idea that without such a charge, parties could not be added to the bill by amendment; and in some cases, perhaps, the charge has been inserted with a view to give the court jurisdiction: but from whatever cause the practice has arisen, it is still adhered to, except in the case of *a peer*, who was never charged with combining with others to deprive the plaintiff of his right, either from respect to the peerage, or perhaps from apprehension, that such a charge might be construed a breach of privilege. *Mitf.* 40.

The rights of the several parties, the injury complained of, and every other necessary circumstance, as time, place, manner, or other incidents ought to be plainly, yet succinctly alleged. And whatever is essential to the rights of the plaintiff, and is necessarily within his knowledge, ought to be alleged positively, and with precision, and not by way of stating that *he has been so informed*, which is cause of demurrer. 1 *Vez.* 56; but the claims of the defendant may be stated in general terms; and if a matter essential to the determination of the plaintiff's claims, is charged to rest in the knowledge of the defendant, or must of necessity be within his knowledge, and is consequently the subject of a part of the discovery sought by the bill, a precise allegation is not required. *Mitf.* 41.

As the bill must be sufficient in substance, so it must have convenient form, and consist of those several parts which long practice has prescribed for such form.

After a bill is filed, for the purpose of preserving the property in dispute, or to prevent the evasion of justice, the court will, where necessary, make a special order on the subject, or issue a provisional writ; such as the *writ of injunction*, to restrain the defendant from proceeding at common *law* against the plaintiff, or from committing *waste*, or *doing any injurious act*:* the writ of *ne exeat regno*, if the suit is in *Chancery*, or an order in the nature of such writ, if it is in the Exchequer, to restrain the defendant from avoiding the plaintiff's demands by *quitting the kingdom;* and other writs of a similar nature: and where a bill seeks to obtain the special order of the court, or a provisional writ for any of these purposes, it is usual to insert in it, immediately before the prayer of process, a prayer for the order or particular writ, which the case requires: and the bill is then commonly called, from the writ so prayed, an *injunction bill*, or a bill for a writ *ne exeat regno*. *Mitf.* 46.

The form of every kind of bill bears a resemblance to that of an original bill; but there are necessarily some variations either arising from the purposes for which the bill is framed, or the circumstances under which it is exhibited, as will be shewn hereafter. *Mitf.* 47.

Every bill must be signed by counsel; and if it contains matter criminal, impertinent, or scandalous, such matter shall be expunged, and the counsel shall pay costs to the party aggrieved, but nothing relevant is considered as scandalous. *Rules and orders of Ch.* 93. 1 *Ch. Rep.* 194. 2 *Vez.* 24. *Mitf.*

2. *A bill of interpleader*, is where the person exhibiting the bill, claims no right, in opposition to the rights claimed by the persons, against whom the bill is exhibited, but prays the decree of the court, touching the rights of those persons, for the safety of the person exhibiting the bill. *Ibid.*

Where two or more persons, claim the same thing, by different or separate interests, and another person, not knowing to which of the claimants he ought of right to render a debt or duty, or to deliver property in his custody, fears he may be hurt by some of them, he may exhibit a *bill of interpleader* against them: in this bill, he must state his own rights, and their several claims, and pray that they may interplead, so that the court may adjudge to whom the thing belongs, and he may be indemnified: if any suits at law are brought against him, he may also pray that the claimant may be restrained from proceeding, till the right is determined. *Mitf.* 47, 8.

As the sole ground on which the jurisdiction of the court in this case is supported, is the danger of injury to the plaintiff, from the doubtful titles of the defendants, the court will not permit the proceeding to be used collusively to give an advantage to either party, nor will it permit the plaintiff to delay the payment of money, due from him by suggesting a doubt to whom it is due; therefore to a bill of interpleader *the plaintiff must annex an affidavit* that there is no collusion, between him and any of the parties; and if any money is due from him he must bring it into court, or at least offer so to do by his bill. *Mitf.* 49.

3. Bill praying the writ of certiorari to remove a cause from an inferior court of equity. *Ibid* 33.

When an equitable right is sued for, in an inferior court of equity, and by means of the limited jurisdiction of the court, the defendant cannot have complete justice, or the cause is without the jurisdiction of the inferior court; the defendant may file a bill in Chancery, praying a special writ, called a writ of *certiorari*, to remove the cause into the court of chancery. This species of bill, having no other object than to remove a cause from one inferior court of equity, merely states the proceedings in the inferior court, shews the incompetency of them, and prays the writ of *certiorari*; it does not pray that the defendant may answer, or even appear to the bill, and consequently it prays no writ of subpœna. *Mitf.* 49.

The proceedings upon the bill are peculiar, and are particularly mentioned in the books which treat of the practice of the court. In case the court of Chancery removes the cause from the inferior court, the bill exhibited in that court is considered as an original bill in the court of Chancery, and is proceeded upon as such. *Mitf.* 50.

II. *Original bills not praying relief*, may be, 1, a bill to perpetuate the testimony of witnesses; 2nd, a bill for the discovery of facts resting within the knowledge of the person against whom the bill is exhibited, or of deeds, writings, or other things in his custody or power. *Ibid.*

1. A bill to *perpetuate the testimony of witnesses* must state the matter touching which the plaintiff is desirous of giving evidence, and must shew that he has some interest in the subject, and pray leave to examine witnesses touching the matter so stated, to the end that their testimony may be preserved and perpetuated. *Mitf.* 50, 51.

The bill ought also to shew, that the facts to which the testimony of witnesses proposed to be examined, is conceived to relate, cannot be immediately investigated in a court of

---

* Under this rule the *bill quia timet* falls, which is founded upon the maxim, that equity prevents mischief, and such bills are proper in cases, where a person is entitled to any thing after a certain period, which in the interim is to be enjoyed by another, by whom it may be wasted or destroyed, or where a person is entitled to a thing after another's death, who is to have the use of that thing for life. 1 *Ch. Cas.* 223. or, where one may be injured by another's neglecting or refusing to do what in conscience he was bound to do. 1 *Vern.* 190.

law, as in the case of a person in possession without disturbance; or that before the facts can be investigated in a court of law, the evidence of a material witness is likely to be lost, by his death or departure from the realm. *Ibid* 51.

To avoid objection to a bill framed on the latter ground, it seems proper to annex to it an affidavit of the circumstances, by which the evidence intended to be perpetuated is in danger of being lost; a practice adopted in other cases, of bills which have a tendency to change the jurisdiction of a subject, from a court of law to a court of equity: it seems another requisite to a bill of this kind, that it should shew an interest in the defendant to contest the title of the plaintiff in the subject of the proposed testimony. *Mitf.* 51.

2. *Bill of discovery.* Every bill is in reality, *a bill of discovery*, but the species of bill usually distinguished by that title, is a bill for discovery of facts, resting in the knowledge of the defendant, or of deeds or writings, or other things in his custody or power, and seeking no relief in consequence of the discovery: this bill is commonly used in aid of the jurisdiction of some other court, as to enable the plaintiff to prosecute or defend an action at law, or proceeding before the king in council, or any other legal proceeding of a nature merely civil, before a jurisdiction, which cannot compel a discovery on oath; except that the court has in some instances refused to give this aid to the jurisdiction of inferior courts. A bill of this nature must state the matter, touching which a discovery is sought, the interest of the plaintiff and defendant in the subject, and the right of the first to require the discovery from the other. *Mitf.* 52.

If a bill seeking a discovery of deeds or writings, *also prays* such relief, as might be obtained at law, if the deeds or writings were in the custody of the plaintiff, he must annex to his affidavit, that they are not in his custody or power, and that he knows not where they are, unless they are in the hands of the defendant: but a bill for a discovery merely, or which only prays the delivery of deeds or writings, or equitable relief grounded upon them, does not require such an affidavit. *Mitf.* 52, 53.

III. *Bills not original.*] A suit imperfect in its frame, or become so, by accident, before its end has been obtained, may in many cases be rendered perfect by a new bill, which is not considered as an *original bill*, but merely as an addition to, or continuance of the former bill, or both. And a bill of this kind may be, 1, a supplemental bill; 2, a bill of revivor; 3, a bill of revivor and supplement.

1. *Supplemental bills*] are used where the imperfection of a suit arises from a defect in the original bill, or in the proceedings upon it, and not from any subsequent event. Thus a supplemental bill will lie for a further discovery, to put new matter in issue, or to add new parties, where it is too late to amend the original bill, and this may be done either before or after the decree, for it may be used either to aid or impeach the decree; but where an original bill may be amended, a supplemental bill will not lie. *Mitf.* 59.

So upon an event subsequent to the original bill, which gives a new interest to any one, not a party to the suit, as the birth of a tenant in tail; or a new interest to the party, as the happening of some other contingency; or upon an event which occasions an alteration in the interest of any of the parties to the suit, and does not deprive the plaintiff, suing in his own right, of his whole interest in the subject; or if one, not the sole plaintiff, is entirely deprived of his interest, the defect may be supplied by a supplemental bill. *Ib.* 60.

It is not accurately ascertained, how a suit becomes defective without abatement, and in what cases it abates, as well as becomes defective; but it may be collected, that if the interest of a party to the suit becomes vested in another, the proceedings are rendered defective in proportion, and though the parties to the suit may remain, the object in question cannot be obtained; and if such a change is the consequence of a party's death, whose interest is not determined by that event, or by the marriage of a female plaintiff, the proceedings become likewise abated or discontinued, either in part or in all. So, upon the death of one defendant, all proceedings abate as to him, but they do not abate upon the marriage of a defendant, though her husband must be named in the subsequent proceedings. *Ib.* 55.

Where the proceedings in the supplemental and original bills are in equal forwardness, one replication may be filed, and the causes consolidated; or where a replication may be filed in each cause, then, upon giving a rule to pass publication, the causes become consolidated, and are proceeded in as one. 1 *Fowl. Prac. in Exch.* 68.

2. *Bills of revivor*] must state the original bill, the proceedings, and the abatement; it must shew a title to revive, and charge that the cause ought to be revived, and stand as the original bill did at the time of abatement, praying that the suit may be revived accordingly; and in some cases, as a requisite admission of assets, it may be necessary to pray that defendant may answer the bill of revivor; and if defendant admits assets, the cause may proceed upon an order of revivor only; but if he does not admit them, the cause must be heard, in order to obtain the accounts of the deceased's estate to answer the demands against it; and therefore, if the bill should extend to the taking of the accounts, in case defendant does not admit assets, so far this is in nature of an original bill. *Mitf.* 70.

If the defendant to the original bill dies before he has put in a complete answer, though the bill of revivor may not require an answer, yet it should pray that the defendant in revivor should answer so much as remains unanswered, as well in the case of amendments as exceptions. *Ib.* 71.

3. *Bills of revivor and supplement*] are merely a compound of the two former sorts of bills, upon which, in their separate parts, they must be framed. If a suit is abated by any event, except the immediate cause of abatement, the rights of the parties are affected, as by a settlement or a devise, though a bill of revivor may continue the suit, yet to bring the whole matter before the court, the parties must add a supplemental bill to their bill of revivor, to shew how their rights are affected. So if any other cause of abatement is accompanied by any matter which ought to be stated to the court, to shew the rights of the parties, or to obtain the full benefit of the suit, that matter must be set forth by way of supplemental bill added to the bill of revivor. *Mitf.* 65.

IV. *Bills in the nature of original bills.*] Bills for the purposes of cross litigation of matters already depending before the court, of controverting, suspending, avoiding or carrying into execution a judgment of the court, or of obtaining the benefit of a suit, which the plaintiff is not entitled to add to or continue; or for the purpose of supplying any defect in it, have been generally considered under the head of bills in the nature of original bills, though occasioned by or seeking the benefit of former bills, and are, 1st, a cross bill; 2, a bill of review; 3, a bill in nature of a bill of review; 4, a bill to impeach a decree on the ground of fraud; 5, a bill to suspend or avoid the execution of a decree; 6, a bill to carry a decree into execution; 7, a bill in the nature of a bill of revivor; 8, a bill in nature of a supplemental bill.

1. *Cross bills*] are usually brought by a defendant, against a plaintiff in a former suit depending, either to obtain a necessary discovery or full relief to all parties: if a question arises between two defendants to an original bill, on which the court cannot make a complete decree without a cross bill; to bring every matter before the court, it is necessary for some or one of the defendants to the original bill to file a bill against the plaintiff and the other defendants in the original bill, and bring the point litigated properly before the court. A cross bill should state the original bill and proceedings, and the rights of the complainant, or the ground on which he resists the original plaintiff's claim, if such be the object of the cross bill; but if the cross bill be only intended as a defence, or to procure a determination of the matter already litigated, the complainant need not shew his equity to support the jurisdiction of the court. *Mitf.* 75.

Also bills may be filed by direction of the court, and they are brought where the suit already instituted is insufficient to bring all matters so before the court, as to enable it to decide on the rights of all the parties; and this frequently happens where persons in opposite interests, are original co-defendants, and the determination of their interests, is necessary to a complete decree: in such case, if a difficulty appears upon the hearing, which a cross bill has not been exhibited to remove, the court will direct a bill to be filed, to bring all the rights of the parties before the court, and will reserve the directions until the hearing of the new bill. *Jones* v. *Jones, T.* 1744; 3 *Atk.* 110. *Mitf.* 77.

2. *Bills of review*] are preferred to procure an examination and reversal of a decree, signed, and inrolled. It may be brought for error in the decree, or for new matter discovered. If for error of law, as where the person decreed against, is an infant, it can only be reversed upon that apparent ground, and such a bill may be brought without the previous leave of the court; but if to reverse a decree, signed and inrolled, upon discovery of new matter, leave of the court must be first obtained, and that cannot be had, but upon allegation upon oath, that the new matter could not be produced by the claimant, when the decree was made. If the court is satisfied that the new matter is material, and such as might have occasioned a different determination, a bill of review will be allowed. *Mitf.* 78.

It is a rule that a bill of review shall not prevent the execution of the decree impeached; and if money is directed to be paid, it ought to be paid before the bill of review is filed, though afterwards refunded. *Ib.* 80.

This bill should state the former bill and proceedings, the decree and matter of grievance thereby, and the ground of law or new matter, upon which the decree is sought to be impeached. On the ground of new matter, it seems, leave to file the bill should be obtained, though it is doubtful whether the fact of discovery is traversable, after leave given; the bill may pray simply that the decree may be reviewed, and reversed in the point complained of, if not carried into execution. *Ib.* 80.

A bill to review the reversal of a former decree, may pray that the original decree may stand; and it may also be made a bill of revivor, if the original suit has become abated; and if any event has happened since, a supplemental bill may be added; and particularly if any one, not a party to the original suit becomes interested, he must be made a party to the bill of review by way of supplement. *Ib.* 81.

To render a bill of review necessary, the original decree must be signed and inrolled; and where that has not been done, a decree may be examined and reversed upon a supplemental bill in nature of a bill of review, upon any new matter discovered. *Ib.* 82.

As a decree not signed and inrolled may be altered upon a re-hearing, so the office of the supplemental bill, in nature of a bill of review, is to supply the defect which occasioned the former decree. *Ib.*

It is necessary, in bringing this sort of supplemental bill, to make the same affidavit as in bringing a bill of review on discovery of new matter, and to obtain the leave of the court. The bill, in its frame, nearly resembles a bill of review, excepting, that instead of praying a review and reversal of the former decree, it prays that the cause may be heard; and with respect to the new matter, made the subject of a supplemental matter, to be reheard upon the original bill, and that plaintiff may be relieved as the supplemental bill requires. *Ib.*

3. *Bills in nature of bills of review*] may be brought for relief against error in a decree made against a person who had no interest, or not such, as to render the decree binding upon a claimant; as where a decree is made against a tenant for life only, a remainder man cannot defeat the proceedings against him, but by a bill, shewing the error in the decree, the incompetency of the tenant for life to sustain the suit, and the accruer of his own interest; whereupon he prays that the original proceedings may be reviewed, that the other party may appear and answer, and that the rights of the parties may be ascertained. *Mitf.* 83.

This bill may be brought without leave of the court. *Ib.*

4. *Bills to impeach a decree on the ground of fraud*] may be brought without leave of the court; the fraud used in obtaining the decree being the principal point in issue, and necessary to be proved before the decree can be investigated; and where a decree has been so obtained, the court will restore the parties to their original situation whatever their rights may be.—Besides cases of direct fraud, it seems, that where a decree is made against a trustee, the *cestuy que* trust not being before the court, and the trust not discovered, or against a person who has made some conveyance or incumbrance not discovered, or in favour or against an heir, where the ancestor, by his will, has disposed of the subject matter of the suit; the concealment of the trust, conveyance, or will, in such cases, is a fraud. So where a decree has been made against an infant, without actual fraud, it may be impeached by original bill. *Mitf.* 84.

This bill must state the decree and proceedings, and the circumstances of the fraud, and according to the nature of the fraud, and its operation, in obtaining an improper decree, so must the prayer of this bill be varied. *Ib.* 85.

5. *Bills to suspend or avoid the execution of a decree.*] For these matters a new bill may be brought; as where a mortgagor was obliged to quit the kingdom after the death of Charles I. to avoid the effects of his engagements with the royal party, upon a decree of foreclosure in case of non-payment of principal, interest, and costs; and having requested the mortgagee to sell the estate to the best advantage and pay himself, which the mortgagee acquiesced in: the court, on a new bill, enlarged the time for performing the decree, upon the ground of inevitable necessity, and made a new decree grounded on subsequent matter. *Mitf. on Plead.* 85. *Cocker* v. *Bevis*, *H.* 1666; 1 *Ch. Ca.* 61. *Venables* v. *Foyle*, *T.* 1663; 1 *Ch. Ca.* 3. *Whorewood* v. *Whorewood*, *H.* 1675; 1 *Ch. Ca.* 250. *Wakelin* v. *Walthell*, *M.* 1679; 2 *Ch. Ca.* 8.

6. *Bills to carry decrees into execution*] are generally necessary, where the parties have neglected to execute the decree, and their rights become afterwards so embarrassed, as to require the aid of the court in settling and ascertaining them. Such a bill is sometimes preferred by a person, not a party to the original suit, but claiming in a similar interest, or unable to obtain a determination of his own rights till the decree is executed; or it may be brought by or against an assignee.—The court, in these cases, only enforces the decree, and seldom varies it, unless on mistake; it has even refused to enforce the decree, though in other cases, the court, and the house of lords, have considered that the law of the decree ought not to be examined on these sorts of bills.—These bills may be brought to execute the judgment of an inferior court of equity, as a decree in Wales; and the court will, in such case, examine the justice of the decision, though affirmed in the lords. *Mitf.* 86.

This bill, though not strictly original, partakes of it; sometimes also of revivor or supplement, and sometimes of both, and it must be framed accordingly. *Ib.* 87.

7. *Bills, in the nature of bills of revivor,*] are proper where the interest of a party dying is transmitted to another, to be litigated in equity; as in case of a devise, where the suit cannot be revived by, or against the person, to whom the interest is so transmitted, but who, if he succeeds to that interest, is entitled to the benefit of the former suit. This bill must state the original bill and proceedings, the abatement and the transmission of interest; the validity of which must be charged, stating the rights that have accrued by it.—The bill is called original, for the want of that privity of title, between the parties to the former and the latter bill, though claiming the same interest, as would have permitted a revivor; therefore, when the validity of the transmission is established, the party to the new bill shall be equally bound or benefited by the original bill, as if

there had been such a privity; and the suit is considered as pending from the filing of the original bill, so as to have every advantage attending the institution of the original suit, or the continuance of it by revivor. *Mitf.* 88.

8. *Bills, in nature of supplemental bills,*] are preferred to obtain the benefit of the former proceedings, where the interest of a plaintiff or defendant, in his own right, wholly determines, and the same property becomes vested in another not claiming under him, and where the suit cannot be continued by bill of revivor, and its defects must be supplied by a supplemental bill. *Mitf.* 89.

This bill must state the original bill and proceedings, and the event which has determined the interest of the original plaintiff or defendant, and the manner in which the property has become vested in the person entitled. It must then shew the ground for granting the benefit of the former suit, and pray a decree adapted to the case of the plaintiff in the new bill. This bill, though in nature of a supplemental bill, is not an addition to the original bill, for an original bill draws to itself the advantages of the former proceedings. *Ib.*

BILLS, *by way of information,* in every respect follow the nature of other bills except in their style. When they concern the rights of the crown only, or those who take under its protection, they are exhibited in the name of the attorney or solicitor general as informant. *Mitf.* 22.

If the right of the queen is in question, the bill must be exhibited in the name of her attorney general. *Ib.*

But if the suit does not immediately concern the crown, its prosecution depends on some person as a relator, in whose name and under whose direction the suit is carried on, and he is considered answerable for the propriety and conduct of it. *Ib.*

Where there are several relators the death of one of them does abate the suit; but if all die, the court will stay proceedings till a new one be appointed; for there must be one person to sustain the suit, and if it be improperly brought, to pay the costs. 1 *Vez.* 72. 2 *Vez.* 327. *Mitf.* 91.

The proceedings upon an information can only abate by the defendant's death, or the determination of his interest, and an information by the attorney general alone, is not dismissible for want of prosecution, though it is *otherwise* if by a relator. 1 *Fowl.* 118.

And where a man prays a debt decreed by an English information to be due to the crown, he shall stand in its place, and have the aid of the crown in recovering it. *Ib.* 119.

Defence to bills in equity.] To a bill in equity, unless the sole object of it, is to remove a cause from an inferior court of equity, it is necessary for the person complained of, either to make defence, or to disclaim all right to the matters in question by the bill: for as the bill calls upon the defendant to answer the several charges it contains, he must do so; unless he can dispute the right of the plaintiff, to compel such an answer, either from some impropriety in requiring the discovery sought by the bill, or for some objection to the proceeding, to which the discovery is proposed to be assistant; or unless by disclaiming all right to the matters in question by the bill, he shews a further answer from him to be unnecessary. *Mitf.* 10, 11.

The grounds on which a defence may be made to a bill, either by answer, or by disputing the right of the plaintiff to compel the answer, which the bill requires, are various. The subject of the suit may not be within the jurisdiction of a court of equity; or some other court of equity may have the proper jurisdiction: the plaintiff may not be entitled to sue, by some personal disability: if he has no such disability, he may not be the person he pretends to be: he may have no interest in the subject, or if he has an interest, he may have no right to call upon the defendant concerning it: the defendant may not be the person he is alleged to be by the bill: or he may not have that interest in the subject, which can make him liable to the claims of the plaintiff: and finally if the matter is such as a court of equity ought to interfere in, and no other court of equity has the proper jurisdiction, if the plaintiff is under no personal disability, if he is the person he pretends to be, and has a claim of interest in the subject, and a right to call upon the defendant concerning it, if the defendant is the person he is alleged to be, and also claims an interest in the subject which may make him liable to the demands of the plaintiff: still the plaintiff may not be entitled, in the whole or in part, to the relief or assistance he prays; or if he is so entitled, the defendant may also have rights in the subject, which may require the attention of the court, and call for its interference to adjust the rights of all parties; the effecting complete justice, and finally determining as far as possible all questions concerning the subject, being the constant aim of courts of equity: some of these grounds may extend, only to entitle the defendant, to dispute the plaintiff's claim to the relief prayed by the bill, and may not be sufficient to protect him from making the discovery sought by it; and where there is no ground for disputing the right of the plaintiff to the relief prayed, or if no relief is prayed, yet if there is any impropriety in requiring the discovery sought by the bill, or if the discovery can answer no purpose, the impropriety or immateriality of the discovery, may protect the defendant from making it. *Mitf.* 12, 13.

The defence which may be made on these several grounds may be founded on matter apparent on the bill, or on a defect either in its frame, or in the case made by it, and may on the foundation of the bill itself demand the judgment of the court whether the defendant shall be compelled to make any answer to the bill, and consequently whether the suit shall proceed; or it may be founded in matter not apparent on the bill, but stated in the defence, and may on the matter so offered, demand the judgment of the court, whether the defendant shall be compelled to make any other answer to the bill, and consequently whether the suit shall proceed, except to try the truth of the matter so offered; or it may be founded on matter in the bill, or on further matter offered, or on both, and submit to the judgment of the court on the whole case made on both sides, and it may be more complex, and apply several defences, differently founded, to distinct parts of the bill. *Mitf.* 13.

The form of making defence varies, according to the foundation, on which it is made, and the extent in which it submits to the judgment of the court; if it rests on the bill, and on the foundation of matter there apparent demands the judgment of the court whether the suit shall proceed at all, it is termed *a demurrer:* if on the foundation of new matter offered, it demands the judgment of the court, whether the defendant shall be compelled to answer further, it assumes a different form, and is termed *a plea;* if it submits to answer generally the charges in the bill, demanding the judgment of the court on the whole case made on both sides, it is offered in a shape different, and is simply called *an answer:* if the defendant disclaims all interest in the matters in question by the bill, his answer to the complaint made is again varied in form, and is termed *a disclaimer.* *Mitf.* 13, 14.

And all these several forms of defence, and disclaimer, or any of them, may be used together, if applying to separate and distinct parts of the bill. *Ibid.*

See also *Chancery, Demurrer, Exchequer,* and *Pleadings.*

BILL OF EXCEPTIONS. At common law a writ of error lay for an error in law, apparent on the record, or for error in fact, where either party died before judgment; yet it lay not for an error in law, not appearing on the record; and therefore, where the plaintiff or demandant, tenant, or defendant, alleged any thing *ore tenus,* which was over-ruled by the judge, this could not be assigned for error, not appearing within the record, nor being an error in fact, but in law; and so the party grieved was without remedy. 2 *Inst.* 426. And therefore, by the stat. *Westm.* 2. 13 *Ed.* 1. *c.* 31. if the judge either in his directions or decisions misstates the law by ignorance, inadvertence or design, the counsel on either side may require him publicly to seal *a bill of exceptions,* stating the point wherein he is supposed to err, and this he is obliged to seal, for if he refuses so to do, the party may have a compulsory writ against him, (2 *Inst.* 487) commanding him to seal it, if the fact alleged, be truly stated: and if he returns that the fact is untruly stated, when the case is otherwise, an action will lie against him for making a false return. 3 *Black.* 372.

The exceptions ought to be put in writing *sedente curia,* in the presence of the judge who tried the cause, and signed by the counsel on each side; and then the bill must be drawn up and tendered to the judge that tried the cause, to be sealed by him; and when signed, there goes out a *scire facias* to the same judge *ad cognoscendum scriptum,* and that is made part of the record, and the return of the judge with the bill itself, must be entered on the issue-roll; and if a writ of error be brought, it is to be returned as part of the record. 1 *Nels. Abr.* 373.

These bills of exceptions, are to be brought before a verdict given, and extend only to civil actions, not to criminal. *Sid.* 85. 1 *Salk.* 288.

This bill of exceptions is in the nature of an appeal, examinable, not in the court out of which the record issues for the trial, at *nisi prius,* but in the next immediate superior court upon a writ of error after judgment given in the court below.

BILL OF EXCHANGE. A bill of exchange is a security, originally invented among merchants in different countries, for the more easy remittance of money from the one to the other, which has since spread itself into almost all pecuniary transactions. 2 *Black.* 466.

It is *an open letter of request,* from one man to another, desiring him to pay a sum mentioned therein, either to his own order, or to a third person, on his account; by which means a man at the most distant part of the world may have money remitted to him from any trading country. *Ibid.*

In common speech, such a bill is frequently called a *draft,* but a *bill of exchange* is the more legal as well as mercantile expression. *Ibid* 467.

The person, however, who writes this letter, is called in law the *drawer,* and he to whom it is written, the *drawee;* and the third person, or negotiator to whom it is payable (whether specially named, or the *bearer* generally) is called the payee. *Ibid.*

These bills are either foreign or inland, foreign when drawn by a merchant residing abroad upon his correspondent, or *vice versa,* and inland where both the drawer and drawee reside within the kingdom. *Ibid.* 467.

Promissory notes, or *notes of hand* are a plain and direct engagement in writing, to pay a sum specified at the time therein limited to a person therein named, or sometimes to his order, or often to the bearer at large. *Ibid.*

BILLS OF EXCHANGE.

1. *Bills and notes in general.*] The person who makes a bill is called the *drawer*, the person to whom it is addressed, the *drawee*; and the person in whose favour it is made, the *payee*; if the drawee accepts the bill, he is called the *acceptor*.

The person who signs a promissory note, is called the *maker*; and the person to whom it is payable the *payee*.

When a bill or note is indorsed, the person indorsing it, is called the *indorser*; and the person to whom it is indorsed, the *indorsee*.

A promissory note while in the hands of the payee resembles a bill of exchange, inasmuch as it is for the payment of a sum of money absolutely, and at all events; and when transferred, it is exactly similar to a bill of exchange. *Bayl.* 3. *Burr.* 669. 1224. 4 *Ter. Rep.* 148. 5 *Ter. Rep.* 482.

No particular words are necessary to make a bill of exchange or promissory note; any order or promise, which from the time of making it cannot be complied with, or performed without the payment of money is a bill or note. *Ld. Raym.* 1397. *Str.* 629. 8 *Mod.* 364.

Thus an order or promise to deliver, or that J. S. shall receive money, or to be accountable or responsible for it to him or order is a good bill, *Ibid.*

A note was in these words, "borrowed of J. S. 50*l.* which I promise not to pay;" and per *lord Macclesfield* the word *not* shall be rejected, for a man shall never say I am a cheat, and have defrauded. 2 *Atk.* 32.

But bills and notes must be for the payment of money *only*: and therefore an order, or promise to pay money, *and do some other act*, is not a bill or note. *Bull. N. P.* 272.

And they must be for the payment of money in specie: therefore an order or promise to pay money in *good East Indian bonds*, is not a bill or note.

Also by 48 *Geo.* 3. *c.* 88. "all promissory "and other notes, bills of exchange, or drafts "or undertakings in writing, for money or "goods, for less than 20*s.* in the whole, shall "be absolutely void, and persons uttering any "such shall forfeit, not exceeding 20*l.* nor "less than 5*l.* half to the informer, and half "to the poor; to be recovered, by a summary "conviction, before one justice: on which "parishioners may be evidence."

And by 17 *Geo.* 3. *c.* 30. made perpetual by 27 *Geo.* 3. *c.* 16. "all negotiable notes, "bills or drafts for more than 20*s.* and less "than 5*l.* issued in England, and the in-"dorsements thereon shall specify the names "and places of abode of the persons to whom "payable, and shall bear date when given "and be made payable within 21 days, and "the signing of every such bill or note and "indorsement thereof, shall be attested by "one witness, or else void.—Persons pub-"lishing or negotiating any such bills or "notes contrary to the method prescribed by "this act shall be subject to a penalty, of "not more than 20*l.* nor less than 5*l.* reco-"verable as under the first mentioned act."

But by 37 *Geo.* 3. *c.* 32. so much of the stat. 17 *Geo.* 3. *c.* 30. as relates to the making void notes under 5*l.* *payable on demand to bearer** is suspended *until two years after the expiration* of the restriction upon payment in cash by *the Bank of England* (56 *Geo.* 3. *c.* 21.) And if such notes are not paid within seven days after demand, the justices of peace may enforce payment thereof with costs.

A bill or note must be payable absolutely and at all events: and if it depend on any uncertainty, the instrument is not a bill or note. *Bayl.* 8.

Therefore an order or promise to pay money, provided the terms mentioned in certain letters shall be complied with, provided J. S. shall not be surrendered to prison within a limited time; provided J. S. shall not pay the money by a particular day; provided J. S. shall leave me sufficient, or I shall otherwise be able to pay it; or when J. S. shall marry, is no bill or note, on account of the contingency to which the payment is subjected. *Bay.* 8. 3 *Ld. Raym.* 67. 8 *Mod.* 363. 4 *Vin.* 240. *Burr.* 323. *Str.* 1151.

So an order or promise to pay out of my growing subsistence or fifth payment when due, or out of money when received, is no bill or note, on account of the uncertainty, whether the subsistence or payment will become due, or the money be received. *Fort* 281. 10 *Mod.* 294, 316. *Ld. Raym.* 1563. *Black.* 782. 3 *Wils.* 207.

So an order, to pay a sum of money, out of rents, or other money in the hands of the person, to whom it is addressed, is no bill, because it may be, that he has not rent or other money in his hands sufficient to discharge it. *Ld.Ray.* 1362. *Str.* 592. *Fort.* 282.

So an order from the owner of a ship to the freighter, to pay money on account of freight is no bill, because the quantum due for freight may be open to litigation; but such an order from the freighter is, because it is an admission that so much at least is due. *Str.* 1211. *Cowp.* 571.

And an order to pay money, as the *drawer's quarter's half pay by advance*, before the pay will be due, is a good bill; because it will be payable, though the half pay shall never become due. *Ld. Raym.* 1481. *Str.* 762. *Barnard.* 12.

So an order or promise to pay money when J. S. shall come of age, specifying the day when that event is to happen, is a good bill or note, because it is payable, though J. S. die in the interim. *Burr.* 220.

And an order or promise to pay within a limited time after a man's death, is a good

---

* But if payable *to order* or otherwise than on demand, the rules must be observed.—ED.

bill or note, because it must become payable at some time or other, though the exact period is uncertain. *Str.* 1217.

So an order or promise, to pay within a limited time, after the payment of money due from government, is a good bill or note, because it is morally certain that such payment will be made. *Str.* 24. 1 *Wils.* 262.

A bill or note payable to J. S. or order, is payable to order; a bill or note payable to J. S. or bearer, is payable to bearer, and in the latter case J. S. is a mere cypher. *Bayl.* 11. *Burr.* 1516.

It was for some time unsettled whether it was not essential, that a bill or note should be payable either to order, or to bearer, but it is now decided that it is not. 6 *Ter. Rep.* 123.

It was also for some time a matter of controversy whether it was not necessary that a bill or note should not express on the face of it to have been made for *value received*; but it is now settled, that it is not necessary. *Bayl.* 13. *Ld. Raym.* 1418.

The name of the person making it must be inscribed in the body, or subscribed at the bottom of every bill or note; and every bill must be written or signed by the person making it, or some one authorized by him for that purpose. *Bayl.* 13. *Ld. Raym.* 1484, 1542.

If any person signs his name, upon a blank paper, stamped with a bill stamp, and delivers it to another person to draw such bill as he may choose thereon, he is the drawer of any bill to which the stamp is applicable, which such person shall draw thereon. 1 *Hen. Black.* 313.

Bills are either *inland* or *foreign*: *inland*, when made and payable within this kingdom; and *foreign* when made or payable abroad—*inland* bills and notes seldom consist of more than one part: *foreign* bills in general consist of several, and the several parts of a bill are called a set: and each part contains a condition, that it shall be payable only so long, as all the others remain unpaid: in other respects, all are of the same tenor. *Bayl.* 14, 15.

This condition should be inserted in each part, and should in each, mention every other part of the set, for if a man with an intention to make a set of three parts, should omit the condition in the first, and make the second with a condition mentioning the first only, and in the third alone take notice of the other two (which by the way, is the mode pointed out by *Molloy, b.* 2. *c.* 10. *s.* 24. *Malyne's b.* 3, *c.* 5. *s.* 261, 2, and *Marius, p.* 7.) the might, perhaps, in some cases be obliged to pay each; for it would be no defence to an action on the second, that he had paid the third, nor to an action on the first that he had paid either of the others: but an omission is not perhaps material, which upon the face of the condition must necessarily have arisen from mistake, as if in the enumeration of the several parts one of the intermediate ones were to be omitted, as for instance, "pay this my first of exchange, second and *fourth* not paid." *Bayl.* 15.

Where a bill consists of several parts, each ought to be delivered to the person in whose favour it is made (unless one is forwarded to the drawee for acceptance, and in that case, the rest must be so delivered) otherwise there may be difficulties in negotiating the bill, or obtaining payment. *Ibid.*

Bills and notes are also unavailable both at law and in equity, unless written on paper, duly stamped according to the stat. 55 *Geo.* 3. *c.* 184. by which the following stamp duties have been imposed, *viz.*

Bill of exchange, viz. *inland* bill of exchange, draft, or order, for payment to the bearer, or to order, either on demand, or otherwise, *not exceeding two months after date, or sixty days after* sight, of any sum of money,

Amounting to 40*s.* and not exceeding 5*l.* 5*s.*	0	1	0
Exceeding 5*l.* 5*s.* and not 20*l.*	0	1	6
Exceeding 20*l.* and not 30*l.*	0	2	0
Exceeding 30*l.* and not 50*l.*	0	2	6
Exceeding 50*l.* and not 100*l.*	0	3	6
Exceeding 100*l.* and not 200*l.*	0	4	6
Exceeding 200*l.* and not 300*l.*	0	5	0
Exceeding 300*l.* and not 500*l.*	0	6	0
Exceeding 500*l.* and not 1000*l.*	0	8	6
Exceeding 1000*l.* and not 2000*l.*	0	12	6
Exceeding 2000*l.* and not 3000*l.*	0	15	9
Exceeding 3000*l.* -	1	5	0

Inland bill of exchange, draft or order, for the payment to the bearer, or to order at any time *exceeding two months after date, or sixty days after sight*, of any sum of money,

Amounting to 40*s.* and not 5*l.* 5*s.*	0	1	6
Exceeding 5*l.* 5*s.* and not 20*s.*	0	2	0
Exceeding 20*l.* and not 30*l.*	0	2	6
Exceeding 30*l.* and not 50*l.*	0	3	6
Exceeding 50*l.* and not 100*l.*	0	4	6
Exceeding 100*l.* and not 200*l.*	0	5	0
Exceeding 200*l.* and not 300*l.*	0	6	6
Exceeding 300*l.* and not 500*l.*	0	8	6
Exceeding 500*l.* and not 1000*l.*	0	12	0
Exceeding 1000*l.* and not 2000*l.*	0	15	0
Exceeding 2000*l.* and not 3000*l.*	1	5	0
Exceeding 3000*l.*	1	10	0

Inland bill, draft, or order, for the payment of any sum of money, though not made payable to the bearer, or to order, if the same shall be delivered to the payee, or some person on his or her behalf, the same duty as if payable to bearer or order.

Foreign bill of exchange, (or bill of exchange drawn in but payable out of Great Britain) if drawn singly, and not in a set, the same duty as on an inland bill of the same amount.

Foreign bills of exchange, drawn in sets; for every bill of each set, where the sum shall not exceed 100*l.*

shall not exceed 100*l.*	0	1	6
Exceeding 100*l.* and not 200*l.*	0	3	0

Exceeding 200*l.* and not 500*l.*	0	4	0
Exceeding 500*l.* and not 1000*l.*	0	5	0
Exceeding 1000*l.* and not 2000*l.*	0	7	6
Exceeding 2000*l.* and not 3000*l.*	0	10	0
Exceeding 3000*l.* -	0	15	0

Exemption.—All drafts or orders for the payment of money to the bearer on demand, and drawn upon any banker, or person acting as a banker, within ten miles of the place where such draft shall be drawn; provided such place shall be specified in such drafts; and provided the same shall bear date on the day on which the same shall be issued; and provided the same do not direct the payment to be made by bill, or promissory notes.

Promissory note for the payment, *to the bearer on demand*, of any sum of money,

Not exceeding 1*l.* 1*s.* -	0	0	5
Exceeding 1*l.* 1*s.* and not 2*l.* 2*s.*	0	0	10
Exceeding 2*l.* 2*s.* and not 5*l.* 5*s.*	0	1	3
Exceeding 5*l.* 5*s.* and not 10*l.*	0	1	9
Exceeding 10*l.* and not 20*l.*	0	2	0
Exceeding 20*l.* and not 30*l.*	0	3	0
Exceeding 30*l.* and not 50*l.*	0	5	0
Exceeding 50*l.* and not 100*l.*	0	8	6

Which said notes may be re-issued, after payment thereof, as often as shall be thought fit.

Promissory note, for the payment, *in any other manner than to bearer on demand*, but not exceeding two months after date, or sixty days after sight, of any sum of money,

Amounting to 40*s.* and not 5*l.* 5*s.*	0	1	0
Exceeding 5*l.* 5*s.* and not 20*l.*	0	1	6
Exceeding 20*l.* and not 30*l.*	0	2	0
Exceeding 30*l.* and not 50*l.*	0	2	6
Exceeding 50*l.* and not 100*l.*	0	3	6

These notes are not to be re-issued after being once paid.

Promissory note, for the payment, *either to the bearer on demand, or in any other manner than to bearer on demand*, but not exceeding two months after date, or sixty days after sight, of any sum of money,

Exceeding 100*l.* and not 200*l.*	0	4	6
Exceeding 200*l.* and not 300*l.*	0	5	0
Exceeding 300*l.* and not 500*l.*	0	6	0
Exceeding 500*l.* and not 1000*l.*	0	8	6
Exceeding 1000*l.* and not 2000*l.*	0	12	6
Exceeding 2000*l.* and not 3000*l.*	0	15	0
Exceeding 3000*l.*	1	5	0

These notes are not to be re-issued after being once paid.

Promissory note for the payment to the bearer, or otherwise, at any time *exceeding two months* after date, or *sixty days after sight*, of any sum of money,

Amounting to 40*s.* and not 5*l.* 5*s.*	0	1	6
Exceeding 5*l.* 5*s.* and not 20*l.*	0	2	0
Exceeding 20*l.* and not 30*l.*	0	2	6
Exceeding 30*l.* and not 50*l.*	0	3	6
Exceeding 50*l.* and not 100*l.*	0	4	6
Exceeding 100*l.* and not 200*l.*	0	5	0
Exceeding 200*l.* and not 300*l.*	0	6	0
Exceeding 300*l.* and not 500*l.*	0	8	6
Exceeding 500*l.* and not 1000*l.*	0	12	6
Exceeding 1000*l.* and not 2000*l.*	0	15	0
Exceeding 2000*l.* and not 3000*l.*	1	5	0
Exceeding 3000*l.* -	1	10	0

These notes are not to be re-issued after having been once paid.

By 31 Geo. 3. c. 25. All unstamped, or improperly stamped, bills or notes shall be void and unavailable: and it shall not be lawful for the commissioners to stamp the same at any time after they shall have been drawn. *s.* 19.

And by 55 *Geo.* 3. *c.* 184. If any person shall sign or issue, or accept or pay any unstamped bill or note, he shall forfeit 50*l.** *s.* 11.

Also if any person shall issue any bill or note for payment of money after date or sight, which shall bear date subsequent to the day when issued, so that it shall not in fact become payable in two months after date, or sixty days after sight, unless stamped as a bill or note, exceeding such two months or sixty days, he shall forfeit 100*l.* *s.* 12.

If any person shall issue any bill, draft, or order, payable to *bearer on demand*, upon any banker or firm, acting as such, which shall be dated on a subsequent day, or which shall not specify the place where issued, or which shall not fall within the exemption, as above mentioned, unless stamped as a bill, such person shall forfeit 100*l.* and any person knowingly receiving the same, 20*l.* and if any banker pay the same, he shall forfeit 100*l.* and moreover, not be allowed the money so paid in his account against the party. *s.* 13.

Any banker who shall have issued promissory notes for payment to bearer on demand, of any sum not exceeding 100*l.* may reissue the same as often as he thinks fit. *s.* 14. And that notwithstanding any alteration in the firm, or any alteration therein, as to any house or place, where the same were first made payable. *s.* 15.

Reissuable notes in circulation before or upon 31st August, 1815, are allowed to be reissued for three years only from their date; and if any banker or other person shall after 31st of August, 1815, issue any note, bearing date before or upon that day he shall forfeit 50*l.* *s.* 16. Notes issued with printed dates upon or before the same 31st of August, may be also reissued for three years from their date: but if any such notes *with printed dates*, be first issued after that day, the penalty is 50*l.* *s.* 17.

And after the said 31st of August, 1815, no banker shall issue any promissory note for payment of money to bearer on demand *with the date printed thereon*, on pain of 50*l.* *s.* 18.

If any person shall reissue any note, bill, draft or order, not allowed to be reissued:

* But by 37 Geo. 3. c. c. 136. The holder thereof, may in certain cases get them stamped upon paying certain Penalties.—See title STAMPS.

or after payment thereof, shall refuse or neglect to cancel the same, such person shall forfeit 50*l.* and in case of the same being reissued, he is also chargeable with a further duty, as if the same had been then first issued, and persons knowingly receiving the same, shall forfeit 20*l.* *s.* 19.

Reissuable notes are not to be issued by bankers or others without annual licence of 3*l.* 1. for each town or place where they are issued. *s.* 30.

Promissory notes payable to bearer on demand, made out of Great Britain shall not be circulated or paid in Great Britain, *unless stamped*, on pain of 20*l.* for each: but this does not extend to notes made and payable only in Ireland. *s.* 29.

A bill payable at sight, is not payable on demand, but the usual days of grace are to be allowed from the sight or demand. *Bayl.* 24.

If a bill or note is altered, although with the consent of all parties, *after* it has once issued, or *after* the time when it was originally payable, it requires a new stamp. *Ibid.* 5 *Ter. Rep.* 537.

No bill or note can properly be made or indorsed by, nor can a bill be properly addressed to any person incapable of making himself responsible for the payment. *Bayl.* 24.

Therefore an infant cannot make himself responsible for the payment, unless it be given for necessaries. *Carth.* 160. 3 *Salk.* 197. 1 *Ter. Rep.* 40. nor a feme covert, except in those instances in which she is considered as having an existence independent of her husband. *Bayl.* 25.

And a feme covert resident in this kingdom is considered as having an existence independent of her husband, where the husband is under a civil incapacity of being here as in cases of attainder and the like: and there are cases, in which it has been decided that she is to be considered as having an independent existence where she lives apart from her husband, and has a separate maintenance; but in the latter case in all actions brought against her, the husband must be joined for the sake of conformity. *Ld. Raym.* 147. *Bayl.* 25, 26.

But a feme covert is not to be so considered, though she may be, by particular custom, permitted to trade on her separate account. *Black.* 1081. 4 *Ter. Rep.* 361.

It has also been held, that no person, except an actual merchant, could draw a bill, but the contrary is now settled. *Lutw.* 891. 1585.

A bill may be drawn by the drawer at one place and addressed to himself at another place, but this in legal operation is rather a note than a bill. *Carth.* 509. *Burr.* 1077.

A bill or note, cannot be made payable to any person who is incapable of suing for its payment—such as a feme covert, who cannot sue for payment: but an infant can. *Bay.* 26.

But a bill may be made payable to the drawer. *Salk.* 130. And if a bill or note is made payable to a *fictitious person* not *in esse*, or his order, and is issued with an indorsement in blank, purporting to be made by him thereon, it is as against the drawer or maker to be considered as a bill or note *payable to bearer*, and so is the bill as against the acceptor, if he knew at the time of the acceptance, that the payee was a *fictitious* person. 1 *Hen. Black.* 313. 3 *Ter. Rep.* 174.

If a note be signed by *several* persons, but begins, I *promise*, it is several as well as joint. *Peake* 130.

The act of drawing bills implies an undertaking for the drawer to the payee, and every other person to whom the bill may afterwards be transferred, that the drawer is a person capable of making himself responsible for its payment, that he shall, if applied to for the purpose, express in writing upon the bill an undertaking to pay it, when it shall become payable, and that he shall then pay it, and subjects him, on a failure in any of these particulars, to an action at the suit of the payee or holder. *Bayl.* 29.

And the making of a note is an express engagement to the payee or person to whom it shall be transferred, to pay the money therein mentioned according to its tenor. *Ibid.*

II. *Indorsement of bills and notes.*] Bills or notes payable to *order* or to *bearer*, or containing any words to make them transferrable, may be indorsed or assigned over, so as to give the assignee a right against all the antecedent parties, whose names appear upon the bill or note: and bills or notes containing no words to make them negociable, may be indorsed or assigned over, so as to give such indorsee or assignee, a right upon them, against the immediate indorser, but not so as to give him a right against any of the antecedent parties. *Bay.* 30. *Salk.* 132.

Bills and notes are passed, either by delivery only, or by indorsement and delivery: thus bills and notes payable to order, are transferrable by the latter mode only; but bills and notes payable to bearer, may be by either. *Bayl.* 31, 32.

On a transfer by *delivery*, the person making it, ceases to be a party to the bill or note: but on a transfer by *indorsement*, he is to all intents and purposes chargeable as a new drawer. *ib.* and *Ld. Raym.* 442, 724, 929.

Upon bills and notes for the payment of less than 5*l.* the indorsement must be attested by one subscribing witness, and such indorsement must mention the place of abode of the indorsee, and bear date at or before the making of it. 17 *Geo.* 3. *c.* 30. *s.* 1.

But no particular words are essential on the indorsement of either bills or notes: the mere signature of the indorsee is in general sufficient. *Holt.* 117. *Ld. Raym.* 176, 810. 12 *Mod.* 192. 244. *Salk.* 126, 128, 130. *Ld. Raym.* 444.

An indorsement, which mentions the name of the person, in whose favour it is made, is called a full indorsement; an indorsement which does not, a blank one—a blank indorsement, so long as it continues blank, makes a bill or note payable to the bearer; and as long as the first indorsement continues blank, the bill or note, as against the payee, the drawer and acceptor is assignable by mere delivery, notwithstanding it may have upon it subsequent full indorsements. *Bay.* 31. *Doug.* 611, 633 *Peake* 225.

A full indorsement may specially restrain the negotiability of a bill or note: and an indorsement is restrictive, which either has *express words* making it so, or is made in favour of a person who cannot make a transfer: thus an indorsement in these words, *pay the contents* to J. S. only, to *J. S. for my use*, or (at least when addressed to the drawee) *the within must be credited to J. S.* is restrictive. *Bay.* 33. *Burr.* 1227. *Black.* 229. *Doug.* 615, 637.

But the mere omission of the words, *or to his order*, to give a power of transfer will not make an indorsement restrictive. *Com.* 311. *Str.* 557. *Bull. N. P.* 275. *Black.* 295. *Burr.* 1216.

A restrictive indorsement precludes the person in whose favour it is made from making a transfer, so as to give a right of action against the person making it, or any of the antecedent parties, and (where the restriction is expressed upon the bill or note) from retaining a payment to their prejudice. *Doug.* 615, 637.

An indorsement cannot be made for a part of, or less than the full sum, appearing to be due upon the bill or note, otherwise it would subject the party to a variety of actions. *Ld. Raym.* 360. *Carth,* 466. 12 *Mod.* 213. *Salk.* 65. 2 *Wils.* 262.

A transfer by *indorsement* will convey no title, except against the person making it, unless it is made by him who has a right to make the indorsement: therefore in case of a loss by theft or accident, if the bill or note be only transferrable by indorsement, the thief or finder cannot confer a title against the antecedent parties, for, unless the indorsement be made by the person, to whom the bill is payable, it is a forgery and can confer no title: but if such bill or note be payable to bearer, and therefore assignable by mere delivery, the thief or finder may confer a title against the antecedent parties, by transferring it. And consequently, an innocent holder thereof, for a fair and valuable consideration, may recover the amount thereof, though the party from whom he took it, having no title, cannot. 4 *Ter. Rep.* 28. *Ld. Raym.* 738. *Salk.* 126. 3 *Salk.* 71. *Burr.* 452, 1516.

And by 9 & 10 *Will.* 3. *c.* 17, "if any inland bill be lost, or miscarry within the "time limited for its payment, the drawer "shall on security given, upon request, to "indemnify him, if such bill shall be found "again, give another bill of the same tenor "with the first." *s.* 3.

The right to transfer a bill or note, is in the payee, or in the person to whom it has been transferred from him: therefore an indorsement by a person of the same name, with the person entitled to transfer it, is void (except against the person indorsing it, and the subsequent indorsers) though the person entitled to indorse it, was not particularly described upon the bill or note. 4 *Ter. Rep.* 28.

On a bill or note payable to A. for the use of B the right to indorse is in A. *Carth.* 5. 2 *Vent.* 307. *Skin.* 264.

On a bill or note payable to *several* persons, not in partnership, the right to indorse is in all collectively, and not in any individually, *Doug.* 653. *n.* 134. If a right to indorse a bill or note be in a feme sole, and she marry, it devolves upon her husband. *Str.* 516. 3 *Wils.* 5. If the person who has a right to indorse a bill or note, die, it devolves upon his personal representative, and, if he becomes bankrupt, on his assignees. 3 *Wils.* 1. *Str.* 1260 2 *Barnes* 137.

But if an executor or administrator indorse, he binds himself personally, and not the assets in his hands. 1 *Ter. Rep.* 487.

The indorsement of a bill or note may be made, either *before* the expiration of the time limited for its payment, or (unless the sum payable thereby be under 5*l.* 17 *Geo.* 3. *c.* 30. *s.* 1.) at any time afterwards. 1 *Show.* 163. *Ld. Raym.* 575.

But where a bill or note is indorsed over after the time appointed for its payment, if there is any fraud in the transaction, it ought to be left to the jury, upon the slightest circumstance to presume that the indorsee knew of such fraud. 3 *Ter. Rep.* 83. *n.* And though he was ignorant of the fraud, any objection which might have been taken against the indorsee may be taken against him, if the bill or note appeared upon the face of it, when he took it, to have been dishonoured. 3 *Ter. Rep* 80.

A bill or note dishonoured, cannot be indorsed or negotiated after it has been paid by the drawer, or first payee, for when it comes back to the drawer or first payee, and is taken up by him, its negotiability ceases. 1 *Hen Black.* 89. *n.*

If a man indorse his name on a copper plate, bill or note; made in blank, without any sum, date, or time of payment expressed therein he will be precluded from saying, that his indorsement was prior to the completion or issuing of the bill or note, even against a person who knew when he took it, in what state the bill was, at the time of the indorsement. *Doug.* 496, 514.

Upon the transfer of a bill drawn in sets, each part must be delivered to the person, in whose favour the transfer is made; otherwise the same inconveniencies may follow, which would ensue upon a neglect to deliver each of them to the payee. *Bay.* 41.

The indorsement of a bill or note, implies an undertaking from the indorsor, to the person in whose favour it is made, and every other person to whom the bill or note may afterwards be transferred, exactly similar to that which is implied by drawing a bill, except that in the case of a note, the stipulation with respect to the drawer's responsibility and undertaking, does not apply; and a transfer by delivery only, if made on account of an antecedent debt, implies a similar undertaking from the person making it, to the person in whose favour it is made. *Ibid.*

III. *Acceptance of bills of exchange.*] An acceptance is an engagement to pay a bill according to the tenor of the acceptance, and a general acceptance is an engagement to pay according to the tenor of the bill. *Bay.* 42.

This engagement is usually made by the person, on whom the bill is drawn, but on his refusal, it may be by some other person, expressing it to be for the honor of the drawer, and in either case, the acceptor will be bound. *Ld. Raym.* 575. 12 *Mod.* 410. *Com.* 76. *Burr.* 1672, 1674. *Cowp.* 571. *Doug.* 284, 297. 1 *Atk.* 611.

This acceptance, or engagement to pay, may be made before the bill is drawn, or afterwards, and it may be either verbally or in writing, and is either absolute or conditional; and when made after the drawing of the bill, is according to, or varying from its tenor. *Bay.* 44.

Thus a verbal promise, that *if the bill came back he would pay it*, was held a good acceptance. *Ann.* 75. And in a variety of other cases, parol acceptances have been held good. *Ann.* 74. 2 *Wils.* 9. 1 *Atk.* 612. *Burr.* 1662. 1 *Ter. Rep.* 182.

Also a conditional acceptance to pay *when goods consigned were sold*, *Str.* 1152. *When in cash for the cargo of a ship.* 2 *Wils.* 9. And that the bill would not be accepted till a navy bill was paid, *Cowp.* 572. have been deemed good acceptances.

So also a bill may be accepted, as already observed, varying from its tenor, as for instance, to pay 100*l.* instead of 127*l.* *Str.* 214. to pay at a date different from the time required by the bill, 11 *Mod.* 190. or to pay half in money and half in bills, *Comb.* 452. and the acceptor will be bound, if the holder, who may totally reject the same, acquiesce in such acceptances. *Comb.* 452.

An acceptance is seldom made, before the bill is drawn, by any other person than the drawee: afterwards for the purpose either of promoting the negotiation of a bill, when the drawee's credit is suspected, or to save the reputation, and prevent the prosecution of some of the parties, where the drawee cannot be found, is not capable of making himself responsible, or refuses acceptance, it is not uncommon; and it is called an acceptance for the honor of the person, on whose account it is made, and enures to the benefit of all the parties subsequent to such person. *Bayl.* 45.

Such of these acceptances, as are made with the former view, are considered as made, on account of the previous possession of the bill, at the time they are made; and such as are made with the latter, unless they declare the contrary, on account of the drawer. *Ibid.*

If a bill is drawn on several persons, not connected in co-partnership, an acceptance by one will bind him, but him only. *Bull. N. P.* 279. But in the case of two joint-traders, the acceptance of one, will bind both. *Mar.* 16. *Beawes* 228. *Molloy*, c. 10. *s.* 18.

A general acceptance of a bill drawn upon a man, by the description of servant, will bind him personally. *Ann.* 1. *Str.* 955.

An acceptance after the bill is drawn, may be made even after the time appointed for its payment. *Ld. Raym.* 364, 574. *Salk.* 127, 9. *Com.* 75. 12 *Mod.* 212, 410. And in such case, an acceptance to pay according to the tenor, will be considered as a general acceptance to pay on demand. *Ld. Raym.* 364, 574.

A written acceptance is either made upon the bill or elsewhere: and on a written acceptance by the drawee, his name need not appear; it is sufficient if he write upon the bill, not putting a direct negative upon its request, as, '*accepted*' '*presented*' 'sum' 'the day of the month' or 'a direction to a third person to pay it:' all these are *primâ facie* complete acceptances. *Comb.* 401. 1 *Atk.* 611. *Bull. N. P.* 270.

An express refusal to accept, written on a bill, is not an acceptance, though if the drawee intend it as a surprize upon the party, and to make him consider it as an acceptance, it seems that it may be otherwise. *Bayl.* 48.

A promise to accept, if made upon an executed consideration, or if it influences any person, to take or retain the bill, is a complete acceptance, as to the person to whom the promise is made, in the one case, and the person influenced in the other, and all the subsequent parties in each. *Ibid.*

Thus, a promise to accept such bills as B. should, after the expiration of a month, draw on account of a debt from C. to B. was held a complete acceptance. *Burr.* 1663.

But a promise to accept, made upon an executory consideration, such as when a credit is given to the party, by another house, is not binding so long as such consideration remains executory, unless it influences some person to take or retain the bill. *Burr.* 1666. *Bayl.* 49.

So a verbal promise to accept, though the party expressly defer a written acceptance, as where he says *leave the bill and I will accept it*, is a complete acceptance. *Molloy, b.* 2. *c.* 10. *s.* 20. So a verbal promise to accept a returned bill, when it shall come back, is binding if it do come back, *Ann.* 75.

An answer by the drawee when a bill is called for, "there is your bill," it is all right," is no acceptance. *Espin.* 27.

But an acceptance to pay when remitted for, is a conditional acceptance. *Str.* 1211. So an answer by a drawee who lived in London, that a ship was consigned to him and a person in Bristol, and that till he should know to which port the ship would come, he could not accept, connected with a subsequent answer that the bill was a good one, and would be paid, though the ship should be lost, was held a conditional acceptance only; it being clear that the drawee looked for an opportunity of reimbursing himself, and had three events in contemplation, the ship's arrival at Bristol, her arrival at London, and her loss: in the two latter, he should have the opportunity, and therefore accepted; on the former he should not, and did not accept it. 1 *Ter. Rep.* 182.

But an answer by the drawee, that he would pay, if J. S. would not, but that he must first apply to him, not that he thought he would pay, but because he judged it right to put him to the trial, with an assurance to the holder, that he might rest satisfied of the payment, was held an absolute acceptance. *Str.* 648.

If a man intends to make a conditional acceptance only, and gives that acceptance in writing, he should be careful to express the conditions therein, for, of any verbal condition he may annex to the acceptance, he will not be at liberty to avail himself, against any subsequent party, if either such party, or any intermediate one, between him and the person, to whom the acceptance was given, took the bill without notice of such condition, and gave a valuable consideration for it, and at all events the *onus* of proving such condition, will be upon the acceptor. *Bay.* 51.

But if an agreement to accept is conditional, and a third person takes the bill, knowing of the conditions, he takes it subject to them. *Doug.* 286, 299.

A conditional acceptance becomes absolute, as soon as its conditions are performed: thus an answer by the drawee, that he could not accept until a navy bill should be paid, was thought to operate as an absolute acceptance upon the payment of the navy bill. *Burr.* 1663. But if the drawee says he cannot accept without further directions from J. S., and J. S. afterwards desires him to accept, and draw upon A. B. for the amount, the mere drawing upon A. B. will not make this an acceptance, although the actual payment of the bill on him may. 1 *Ter. Rep.* 269.

An acceptance varying from the tenor, differs from it either in the *sum*, the *time*, the *place*, or *mode* of payment. *Bayl.* 52. But though any of these varied acceptances, bind the person making them, yet the holder of the bill is entitled, from the undertaking of the drawer and indorsors, to expect an absolute acceptance by the drawee. *Marius* 22. or if there be several not connected in partnership by each. *Molloy, b.* 2. *c.* 10. *s.* 18, 19. for the payment of the full sum of money, *Ibid s.* 20. mentioned therein, *Ibid, s.* 28. according to its tenor, specifying, *Ld. Raym.* 575. if none be mentioned for the purpose, a place for its payment, and expressing, *Beawes* 452. if the bill be payable within a limited time after sight, the time of its presentment for acceptance, and may reject any other. *Bayl.* 53.

And if upon the offer of any other acceptance, the holder does any act expressing a non-acquiescence therein, as if he gives notice to any of the antecedent parties generally, that acceptance is refused, or notes the bill for non-acceptance, the offer is not binding. 1 *Ter. Rep.* 182.

There is a case however, in *Beawes, s.* 222. in which it has been supposed to have been decided, that if the holder strikes out an acceptance which varies from the tenor of the bill, and substitutes an acceptance according to the tenor, he may afterwards restore the acceptance he struck out, and that such acceptance will continue binding; but it has been doubted, 4 *Ter. Rep.* 350. whether the determination went further, than to decide, that the alteration in the acceptance (though it annulled the acceptance, and discharged the acceptor), did not destroy the bill as to other parties. *Bayl.* 54.

The obligation of a complete acceptance may be waived, and this waiver may be either express or implied. *Ibid.*

An agreement to consider an acceptance as at an end, *Doug.* 236, 237, 248, 249. or a message, *ibid.* to the acceptor upon an accommodation bill, that the business was settled with the drawer, and he need not give himself any further trouble, is an express waiver: the receipt of the known consideration of the acceptance an implied one. *Doug.* 284, 297.

If the holder of the bill receives a part of the money, from the drawer, and takes a promise from him upon the back of the bill, for the payment of the residue, at an enlarged time, it is for a jury to say whether this is not a waiver of the acceptance; but it ought to be left to them with strong observations to shew that it is. *Doug.* 250.

But a neglect to call upon an acceptor, or the receiving a part from the drawer, or other indulgence shewn to any of the other parties, though for ever so long a time, shall not be considered as a waiver of the remedy against the acceptor. *Doug.* 235, 247.

IV. *Presentment of bills and notes.*] The party taking a bill or note, impliedly undertakes to the antecedent parties, who would be entitled to bring an action on paying it, to present in proper time the one, where necessary, for acceptance, and each for payment: to allow no extra time for payment, and to give notice without delay to such persons, of a failure in the attempt to procure a proper acceptance or payment; and a default in any of these respects will discharge such persons from all responsibility, on account of a non-acceptance or non-payment, and make the bill or note operate as a satisfaction of any debt or demand for which it was given. *Bayl.* 57. *Str.* 649, 792.

And by 3 & 4 *Ann. c.* 9. *s.* 7. (which also places promissory notes on the same footing as bills of exchange, *s.* 1.) it is enacted, that "if any person doth accept any such "bill of exchange, for and in satisfaction of "any former debt, the same shall be es-"teemed compleat payment of such debt, if "such persons, accepting of any such bill "for his debt, doth not take his due course "to obtain payment thereof, by endeavour-"ing to get the same accepted and paid, and "make his protest either for non-acceptance "or non-payment."

The presentment is to be made where the bill or note is payable. *Bayl.* 58. And if the drawee or maker cannot be found at the place, where the bill or note is payable, and it appears that he never lived there or has absconded, the bill or note is to be considered as dishonoured. *Ld. Raym.* 743. If he has only removed, the holder must endeavour, to find out, to what place he has removed, and make his presentment there. *Str.* 1087.

If on a presentment, it appears that the drawee or maker is dead, the holder should inquire after his personal representative, and, if he lives within a reasonable distance, present the bill or note to him. *Molloy, b.* 2. *c.* 10. *s.* 34.

If a bill or note is made payable at a banker's, it is sufficient to present it for payment at the banker's, and if the banker is himself the holder, it is sufficient for him to see whether he has effects in hand. 2 *Hen. Black.* 509.

A presentment should be made at a seasonable time, *Bayl.* 59, and if by the known custom of any place, bills and notes are only payable within limited hours, a presentment *there* out of those hours, is unreasonable. *Ibid.* And so is a presentment out of the hours of business to a person of a particular description, in a place, where, by the known custom of that place, all persons of his description, begin and leave off business at stated hours. *Ibid.*

A presentment for acceptance is not absolutely necessary, except upon bills payable within a limited time after sight. *Molloy, b.* 2. *c.* 10. *s.* 16. *Beawes, s.* 266.

No certain time is fixed, within which this presentment must be made, but it should be made within a reasonable time. 2 *Hen. Black.* 569, 570. And what shall be deemed a reasonable time, must depend upon the particular circumstances of each case, and it must always be left to the jury to say whether there has been an improper delay. 1 *Hen. Black.* 569.

No delay, warranted by the common course of business, is improper, nor is any delay, which is occasioned by keeping the bill in circulation, at a great distance from the place, where it is payable: but a delay by locking it up for any length of time is. *Hen. Black.* 565.

If a bill payable abroad at a certain time after sight, is taken in a course of negotiation, it is not necessary, to send it by the first opportunity, to the place where it is payable: and if a bill is payable in India 60 days after sight, it is not necessarily a neglect, to omit presenting it for acceptance for 26 days after its arrival. 2 *Hen. Black.* 565.

Upon a presentment for acceptance, the bill should be left with the drawee 24 hours, unless in the interim, he either accepts or declares a resolution not to accept. *Ld. Raym.* 281. But a bill or note must not be left, (unless it is paid) on a presentment for payment; if it be, the presentment is not considered as made until the money is called for. *Strange* 550.

A bill or note payable on demand, is payable immediately on presentment, and a bill payable at sight, is either payable immediately upon presentment, or within the days of grace afterwards, and each must be presented within a reasonable time after the receipt, or put into a course of negotiation. *Bayl.* 24, 62.

Upon bills or notes given by way of payment, or paid into a banker's, any time beyond that which the common course of business warrants, is unreasonable. *Str.* 416.

Upon a bill or note of this kind, given by way of payment, the course of business seemed formerly to allow the party to keep it, if it was payable in the place where it was given, until the morning of the next day of business after its receipt, and till the next post, if payable elsewhere, but not longer. *Ld. Raym.* 928. *Str.* 415, 416, 910, 1248. *Str.* 508, 1175.

Thus where a note of this kind, payable in London, was given there in the morning, a presentment the next morning was held sufficiently early: a presentment at two the next afternoon, too late. *Ld. Raym.* 928. *Str.* 415, 1248, 1175.

But in a very modern case, *Appleton v. Sweetapple, B. R. Mic. Ter.* 23 *Geo.* 3. where a similar note was given at one, and not presented till the next morning, two juries held the delay unreasonable; this, however, was against the opinion of the court, but being a second verdict upon a new trial they refused to interfere. *Bayl.* 65.

A bill or note of this kind given by way of payment to a banker, must be presented by him, as soon as if it had been paid into his hands, by a customer. *Black.* 1. And a bill or note of this kind paid into a banker's, if payable at the place where the banker lives, must be presented the next time the banker's clerk goes his rounds. *Ibid.*

A bill or note importing to be payable within a limited time, or at sight, is not in fact payable, until the third day after the expiration of that time, unless it happens that the last of the three days is a Sunday or great holiday, such as Christmas day, upon which no money is used to be paid; in which case the party ought to demand the money upon the second day, otherwise it will be at his own peril. 1 *Barnard.* 303. 4 *Ter. Rep.* 148. *Bayl.* 66. *Ld. Raym.* 743.

And by 39 & 40 *Geo.* 3 c. 42. "where "bills of exchange and promissory notes, "become due on *Good Friday*, the same shall "be payable on the day before, and the "holders thereof may protest the same, for "non-payment on such preceding day."

And a presentment on the *second* day, where the third is not a day of rest, is a nullity. *Espin.* 261.

These extra days are called *days of grace*; but different countries, vary in the number of days, allowed by way of grace. *Beawes, s.* 260.

Upon the last day of grace, and within a reasonable time, before the expiration of that day, a bill or note must be presented for payment. *Bayl* 67.

But if the holder makes a second presentment on that day, the drawer or maker is entitled to insist on paying it, when such presentment is made, without paying the fees of noting or protesting, notwithstanding such presentment is made, after the banking hours, and for the purpose of noting and protesting. 4 *Ter. Rep.* 170.

Upon a bill payable within a limited time after sight, the time must be computed from its presentment for acceptance. *Beawes, s.* 252. And upon a bill or note payable within a limited time after the date, where it has no date, from the day it issued. *Ld. Raym.* 1076.

Where the time, after the expiration of which, a bill or note imports to be payable, is limited by months, it is to be computed by *calendar* not lunar months. *Marius* 19. Thus on a bill or note payable one month after date, and dated the 1st of Jan. the month will not expire till the 1st of Feb. *Beawes, s.* 253.

Where the time is computed by days, the day on which the event happens, is to be excluded: thus on a bill or note payable 10 days after date, dated the 1st of Jan. the time does not expire till the 11th. *Ld. Raym.* 280. *Lutw.* 1591. 1 *Barnard* 303.

The bankruptcy or known insolvency of the drawee, or maker, is no excuse for a neglect to make a presentment, or to give notice. *Doug.* 497, 515.

Notice must be given of a failure, in the attempt to procure an acceptance, though the application for such acceptance, might have been unnecessary. *Burr.* 2670. 1 *Ter. Rep.* 712.

So if the drawee offer a partial or conditional acceptance, or an acceptance at an extended period, or if any other person offer an absolute one, though the holder may be willing to acquiesce in such acceptance, he must give notice. *Bayl.* 71. In that case, however, if he wishes to have the power of availing himself of it, he should mention in his notice, the acceptance offered: for a notice generally of non acceptance, shews he did not acquiesce in such offer. 1 *Ter. Rep.* 182.

A neglect to give notice, upon the refusal of any thing more, than a conditional acceptance, is done away by the completion of those conditions before the bill becomes payable; and a neglect upon the refusal of any thing more, than a partial acceptance, discharges the persons intitled to it only from their responsibility, on account of the non-payment of the residue. *Bayl.* 71.

The notice must come from the holder, and though there is no prescribed form for it, ought to import, that the holder looks on the person, to whom it is given, as liable, and expects payment from him. 1 *Ter. Rep.* 167.

To give this notice, *in the case of a foreign bill*, effect, it is necessary that a minute of the non-acceptance or non-payment, and a solemn declaration on the part of the holder, against any loss to be sustained thereby, (which minute and declaration is called a *protest*, and must on an action against the drawer, be proved. 2 *Ter. Rep.* 713. 5 *Ter. Rep.* 239.) should be made out by a notary public, or if there be no such notary, in or near the place, when the bill is payable, an inhabitant, in the presence of two witnesses, and that a copy, or some other memorial of it should accompany the notice. *Bayl.* 72,3.

And by 43 *Geo.* 3. c. 149. the following stamp duties are payable on the protest of bills or notes, *viz.*

Bills or notes not amounting to 20*l.*	0	2	0
Amounting to 20*l.* and not 100*l.*	0	3	0
———— to 100*l.* and not 500*l.*	0	5	0
———— to 500*l.* and upwards	0	10	0

Such protest may also be made on the *non-acceptance* of an *inland* bill, if such bill is for the payment of 5*l.* or upwards, within a limited time after date, and the value is expressed therein to have been received, 3 & 4 *Ann. c.* 9. *s.* 46. or after an acceptance written on such a bill for its non-payment, 9 & 10 *Will.* 3. *c.* 17. *s.* 1. but a protest cannot properly be made on any other inland bills. 4 *Ter. Rep.* 170. And a protest upon an inland bill is never necessary, where the bill is for the payment of less than 20*l.* 3 & 4 *Ann.* *c.* 9. *s.* 6. And on such as are for the payment of more, a neglect to procure it, only precludes the holder, from recovering against the drawer or indorsors, entitled to notice, any special damages, costs, or interest, occasioned by the non-acceptance, or non-payment. *Str.* 649, 910.

To such of the parties as reside in the place where the presentment was made, the notice must be given at the furthest, by the expiration of the day following the failure; to those who reside elsewhere by the next post. 1 *Ter. Rep.* 167. 2 *Hen. Black.* 565. *Malynes, b.* 3. *c.* 6. *s.* 1.

Sending notice by the post is sufficient; though there is no proof that it was received, and where there is no post, it is sufficient to send by the ordinary mode of conveyance. 2 *Hen. Black.* 509. Therefore in the case of a foreign bill, it is sufficient to send it by the first regular ship, bound for the place to which it is to be sent; and it is no objection, that if sent by a ship bound elsewhere, it would by accident have arrived sooner, though the owner wrote other letters by that ship to the place to which the notice was to be sent. 2 *Hen. Black.* 565.

The drawer of a bill, and (where the acceptance appoints the payment to be made elsewhere than at the acceptor's house) the acceptor, and every person who transfers a bill or note is, *primâ facie,* to be presumed entitled to bring an action on paying it, and therefore entitled to insist on a want of notice, or on a neglect to make a proper presentment, but the contrary may be proved. 1 *Ter. Rep.* 405. 2 *Ter. Rep.* 713. 1 *Ter. Rep.* 712. and payment of part, *Str.* 1246. or a promise to pay, 2 *Ter. Rep.* 713. *Buller* 276. after full notice of the default, sufficiently evinces the contrary; but a payment or promise without such notice, does not. *Burr.* 2670.

Proof that the drawer had no effects in the hands of the drawee from the time the bill was drawn until it became payable is sufficient, at least *primâ facie,* to shew, that the drawer would be entitled to bring no action on paying the bill, and has therefore no right to insist on notice, for in such case he cannot be injured by the want of notice. 2 *Ter. Rep.* 713. 1 *Ter. Rep.* 712.

If the payee of a note lends his name, merely to give it credit, and to enable the maker to raise money upon it, and knows at the time that the maker is insolvent, he is not entitled to notice, nor is it any defence to him, that the note was not properly presented for payment; for under such circumstances, the payee guarantees the payment, and no loss could happen to him, from the want of notice. 2 *Hen. Black.* 336. So if the payee lends his name to secure a composition from the drawer to a creditor, and takes effects of the drawer to answer it, he is not entitled to notice. *Espin.* 302.

But it is no excuse for *not having presented a note* in time for payment, that the defendant *indorsed* it to guarantee a debt from the maker, or that the defendant knew before it was due, that the maker could not pay it, and had desired a banker, at whose house it was made payable, to send it to him, and he would pay it: for, though the justice of such a case may be with the plaintiff, yet an indorsement by way of guarantee only, is liable to all the legal consequences of an indorsement, and the undertaking to pay, can only be taken to extend to such notes as are duly presented. 2 *Hen. Black.* 609.

Nor is it any excuse for not giving notice to the drawer of a bill, if he had effects in the hands of the drawee, that the drawee represented to the drawer when the bill was drawn, that he should not be able to provide for it, and that the drawer thereby understood that he should have to provide for it. *Espin.* 332.

Each party, immediately upon the receipt of notice, ought to give a fresh one to such of those persons, who are liable over to him, against whom he must prove notice. *Bayl.* 83.

V. *Remedies for non-acceptance or non-payment.*] Upon non-acceptance or non-payment, the holder of a bill or note may sue all the persons liable to him, on account of such non-acceptance or non-payment, either at the same time, or successively one after the other. *Bayl.* 84.

An indorsor, an acceptor for the honor of an indorsor or drawer, or the drawer, is, after payment by him, holder; but he holds in his original capacity, not as upon a transfer from the person he has paid. 10 *Mod.* 36. 1 *Wils.* 185. 4 *Bro. P. C.* 604.

So the bail of any of the parties who are sued, or any persons who pay the bill or note, on account of any of the parties, become, on payment, holders; and they hold as upon a transfer from the person for whom they made the payment, not as upon a transfer from the person they have paid. 4 *Ter. Rep.* 470. *Espin.* 112.

Thus if the maker of a note, or the acceptor of a bill, be sued by the indorsee, and the *bail* pay the debt and costs, this absolutely discharges the indorser, as much as if the principal had paid the note or bill, and the bail cannot afterwards recover against the indorsor in the name of the indorsee. 1 *Wils.* 46.

An action may be brought upon a non-acceptance against the drawer before the expiration of the time limited by the bill for its payment. *Bull. N. P.* 269. *Doug.* 55.

And all the antecedent parties are liable to the holder, on account of a non-acceptance or non-payment, and if the bill or note was transferred to him for a precedent consideration by delivery, the person who delivered it is also liable. *Bayl.* 86.

If the holder sues all the persons liable at the same time, it has been supposed that the court or a judge would not stay proceedings in one action, but upon payment of the money recoverable in that, and the costs in such of the rest in which judgment has not been obtained. *Black.* 749. But it has been recently determined in the case of a bill, that the acceptor is the only person against whom the plaintiff is entitled to the costs of *all* the actions, and that each of the other parties is entitled to a stay of proceedings upon paying the debt and costs in the action against him. 4 *Ter. Rep.* 691.

But though he may recover judgment in all the actions, he can only once recover the sum payable by the bill or note, and the costs; and if he rejects a tender of such sum and costs, the court will make an order to restrain him from taking out execution. 2 *Vez.* 115. *Str.* 515.

If the holder at first sue only some of the persons liable, he may at any time before satisfaction, sue all or any of the rest. *Bayl.* 87.

Obtaining a judgment is no satisfaction even as to the parties subsequent to him, against whom the judgment is obtained, for where to an action against the indorser of a bill, the defendant pleaded that the plaintiff had recovered a judgment against the drawer, still in force, the court of *King's Bench* on demurrer, held the plea good; but the court of Exchequer chamber, on a writ of error, held otherwise, and the judgment was reversed. 2 *Show.* 441, 494. *Lutw.* 882.

And the actual taking of a man in execution, and discharging him upon a letter of licence, is no satisfaction as to any of the antecedent parties. *Black.* 1235.

Nor is it a satisfaction, that one of the parties has been charged in execution, on the bill or note, and discharged as an insolvent, except as to the party at whose suit he was so charged. 4 *Ter. Rep.* 825.

Receiving dividends under a commission of bankrupt, is a satisfaction *pro tanto* only. *Bayl.* 88.

If more than one of the persons liable on account of the non-acceptance or non-payment of a bill or note become bankrupt, the holder may prove, under the separate commissions of each, the full amount of the money due to him upon the bill or note, at the time he makes his proof, and receive dividends under each upon the sums proved, until he shall in the whole have received such amount. 1 *Atk.* 109. 2 *Vez.* 113. *Cooke's B. L.* 170. But after the receipt of a dividend under one commission, he cannot prove under any of the rest, more than the sum remaining due, after deducting such dividend. *Ibid.* 1 *Atk.* 106. 2 *Peere Wms.* 89, 409.

So after a partial satisfaction, the holder must not in an action take a verdict for more than the sum remaining due; if he do, the court will either make him correct the verdict, and pay any expence the mistake may have occasioned, or grant a new trial. 1 *Hen. Black.* 88. *Cowp.* 571.

In an action upon a bill or note, the plaintiff is entitled to recover the money payable thereby, with interest in some cases, from the date of the note, as where it appears on the face of it to be for money lent, or is expressed to be payable with interest: but in general, the holder is entitled to interest, from the time it became due, or ought to have been regularly paid, down to the time of final judgment, together with all incidental expences occasioned by the non-acceptance or non-payment. *Black.* 761. *Pr. Reg.* 357. *Burr.* 1077. 1 *Wils.* 105. 2 *Ter. Rep.* 52.

Thus upon a bill or note payable on presentment or demand, interest must be computed from the presentment or demand. *Black.* 761. *Pra. Reg.* 357. 9 *Mod.* 138.

But a neglect to procure a protest upon any inland bill, for the payment of 20*l.* upon which a protest might have been made, will, as it seems, preclude the holder from recovering such interest or expences from any person entitled to notice of the non-acceptance or non-payment, from any other person not. 3 & 4 *Ann. c.* 9. *s.* 5. *Ld. Raym.* 992. 6 *Mod.* 80. *Salk.* 131. *Str.* 910. 9 & 10 *W.* 3. *c.* 17.

The only incidental expence, in the case of the person who made the presentment, is the charge of the notice: in the case of any antecedent party, that of the return of the bill or note must be added. *Bayl.* 92.

Upon a foreign bill, the re-exchange forms a part of the expence of the return, and let the bill be returned through ever so many hands, the drawer is liable for the re-exchange upon each return. 2 *Hen. Black.* 378.

And the drawer is liable for the re-exchange, and every other expence arising from the non-acceptance or non-payment, notwithstanding the dishonour of the bill is expressly ordered by the country on which it is drawn. *Ibid.*

On the return of a bill drawn here, for the payment of pagodas in the East Indies, the practice is to allow for the sum payable by the bill, interest, and all incidental charges, after the rate of 10*s.* for each pagoda, and 5*l.* per cent. thereon, from the expiration of 30 days after the bill's dishonour; and it has been determined that this practice was lawful, even where the price allowed for each pagoda, on the discount of the bill, was only 6*s.* 6*d.* 1 *Ter. Rep.* 52.

Under a commission of bankrupt, the holder of a bill or note is not entitled to any interest or charges accrued or incurred after the commission issued, nor where the act of bankruptcy, to which the commission relates, is ascertained, to any accrued or incurred after that act of bankruptcy. 1 *Atk.* 140. 2 *Bro. Ch. Ca.* 597.

The action usually brought on account of a bill or note, is a special action of assumpsit thereon: but perhaps a special action of debt; debt on an indebitatus, or an indebitatus assumpsit might be maintained thereon. *Bayl.* 95.

But instead of suing upon the bill or note, the holder may use it merely as evidence in another action. *Ibid.*

For a bill is *primâ facie* evidence of money lent by the payee to the drawer; and a *note* of money lent by the payee to the maker, and each consequently of money had, and received by the drawer or maker to the use of the holder, and of money paid by the holder to the use of the drawer or maker. *Ibid.* and *Ld. Raym.* 758. 12 *Mod.* 380. *Burr.* 1516, 1525.

An acceptance is also evidence of money had and received by the acceptor to the use of the holder, and of money paid by the holder to the use of the acceptor; and an indorsement, of money lent by the indorsee to the indorser. 3 *Ter. Rep.* 174, 182. *Bayl.* 96.

VI. *Evidence on bills or notes.*] To recover in respect of a bill or note upon a count for money lent, money paid, or money had and received, the plaintiff must prove such of those facts which are not admitted, which he ought to state upon the usual declaration in special assumpsit; and upon a special assumpsit, he must prove such of the facts which are not admitted, as appear upon the face of that declaration to be necessary. *Bayl.* 114.

An acceptance admits the ability of the drawer to make the bill, and, if made after sight of the bill, his signature: and though it may be a forgery of the drawer's hand, the acceptor is precluded from disputing it afterwards; for it is incumbent on him, previously to satisfy himself, that it is the drawer's hand. So also an indorsement admits the ability and signature of every antecedent party. *Str.* 648, 946. *Burr.* 1354. *Black.* 390. 1 *Ter. Rep.* 655. *Salk.* 127. *Ld. Raym.* 443. 12 *Mod.* 254. *Holt.* 117. 2 *Barnard.* 82.

But an *acceptance*, though made after sight of an indorsement, does not admit the ability or signature of the indorser. 1 *Ter. Rep.* 664. *Doug.* 630, 653.

In an action therefore, against the acceptor of a bill, or maker of a note, the plaintiff must prove the defendant's signature, and the necessary indorsement; and in the former case, if the acceptance was made without sight of the bill, the signature of the drawer in an action against the drawer of a bill, or the indorser of a bill or note, he must prove the defendant's signature, the necessary indorsements between him and the plaintiff, the presentment, the non-acceptance, or non-payment, and the notice for not giving it. *Bayl.* 116.

In the case of a *foreign* bill, if the plaintiff is bound to prove notice, he must also prove a protest. *Ibid.*

After a transfer by delivery, by a person not entitled to make such transfer, any subsequent holder must prove that either he or some intermediate person between him, and the person who so transferred it, took the bill or note *bona fide*, and gave a valuable consideration for it. *Ibid.*

A confession of the signature, is sufficient evidence against the party making it, but not against any other party; and it is sufficient, though made pending a treaty for a compromise. *Str.* 1051. 1 *Barnes* 317. *Espin.* 143.

In an action against the drawer of a lost bill, *Holt, C. J.* 12 *Mod.* 309. held proof that the defendant owned he had made the bill sufficient. So in an action against an indorser, proof that the defendant admitted to have received a bill, corresponding with that, upon which the action was brought, that after issue joined, he declared that he came to town to hasten the trial of a cause brought against him, on an indorsement he had made upon a bill, and that he carried the, case down by proviso, was held sufficient. 1 *Barnard.* 199.

But in an action by the indorsee of a *bill* against the drawer, proof that one of the indorsers had confessed his signature, is insufficient; and in an action against several drawers, indorsers, or acceptors, an admission upon the pleadings by one, of his signature, will not exempt the plaintiff from the necessity of proving it against the others, if they contest it. 1 *Barnes* 317. *Espin.* 125.

The signature of a *partner* or *servant*, importing to have been made on the partnership or master's account, is to be considered as the signature of the partnership or master. *Ld. Raym.* 175, 1484. *Doug.* 630.

But on a signature by a servant, the servant's authority must be proved. *Bayl.* 119. However, an authority by parol, is sufficient. 12 *Mod.* 564. and subsequent assent is evidence of precedent authority. *Comb.* 450. usual employ is also evidence of a general authority; and a general authority is supposed to continue until its determination is notorious, 12 *Mod.* 346. 10 *Mod.* 110. Therefore after the discharge of a servant usually employed, a man will be bound by his signature until his discharge is generally known. *Beawes, s.* 231. *Molloy, b.* 2. *c.* 10, *s.* 27.

Where a notice is sent by the post, proof of putting it into the post is sufficient. 2 *Hen. Black.* 509. And production of the instrument is sufficient evidence of a protest. 12 *Mod.* 345.

On a judgment by default in an action upon a bill or note, it need not be proved by evidence. *Str.* 1149. *Bayl.* 120.

The court will therefore, upon such judgment, if the bill or note is for the payment of British money, refer it to the proper officer, to ascertain the sum due for principal, interest and charges, and give the plaintiff final judgment without a writ of enquiry: and this is now the constant practice in the King's Bench and Common Pleas, but not in the Exchequer. 4 *Ter. Rep.* 279. 1 *Hen. Black.* 252, 529, 541. 1 *Anstr.* 249.

However, the court will not refer it, if the bill or note is for the payment of foreign money, but leave it to be ascertained on a writ of enquiry. 5 *Ter. Rep.* 87.

VII. *Defence against bills and notes.*] The only species of defence to an action in respect of a bill or note necessary to be mentioned, is that which is founded upon the want of a consideration for giving or transferring it, or an illegality in the consideration upon which it is given or transferred. *Str.* 647. *Bayl.* 121.

The debt of a third person, or a debt barred by the statute of limitations, by a discharge under an insolvent or fugitive act, by a bankruptcy and certificate, or by a composition is a good consideration. *Str.* 264. *Ld. Raym.* 389. 6 *Mod.* 309. *Burr.* 2630. *Black.* 703. *Cowp.* 290.

But if given as the consideration of signing a bankrupt's certificate, or withdrawing a petition against it, or joining in the acceptance of a composition, it is illegal. 1 *Hen. Black.* 647. 5 *Geo.* 2. *c.* 30. *s.* 11. 1 *Atk.* 105. 2 *Ter. Rep.* 763. 4 *Ter. Rep.* 166. 6 *Ter. Rep.* 263.

A bill or note given for past seduction will be valid: but for future prostitution, bad. *Burr.* 1568.

Dropping a criminal prosecution, or suppressing evidence thereon, a recommendation to an office in the king's household, though of a private nature, and not within the stat. 5 & 6 *Ed.* 3. A smuggling, an usurious or a stock-jobbing contract, is an illegal consideration. 3 *Peere Wms.* 279. 2 *Wils.* 349. 1 *Bro. Ch. Ca.* 114. *Black.* 445.

So money lost by gaming (except 9 *Ann. c.* 14. *s.* 9. in some part of a royal palace in which the king is then actually resident, the freehold and inheritance of which part is in the crown, and which is not in lease) or betting on the sides of persons so gaming, money knowingly lent for such gaming or betting, or money lent at the time and place of such play to any person, either then gaming or betting, or who shall, during the play, play or bet, is an illegal consideration. 9 *Ann. c.* 14. *s.* 1.

Under this act cricket, a horse-race, or a foot-race against time, hath been held a game. 1 *Wils.* 220. 2 *Wils.* but insuring in the lottery, not being known at the time of passing the act, is not. 1 *Hen. Black.* 29.

No person can insist upon a want of consideration, who has himself received one, nor can it ever be insisted on, if the plaintiff or any intermediate party between him and the defendant, took the bill or note *bona fide,* and upon a good consideration. *Com.* 43. 1 *Ter. Rep.* 40. 2 *Ter. Rep.* 71. 2 *Atk.* 182. *Bull. N. P.* 274. *Bayl.* 123.

In those cases in which a defendant *might* insist upon a *total* want of consideration, if there really was none, he may shew that the consideration does not extend to all the money payable by the bill or note, and the plaintiff shall only recover for the residue. *Peake* 61.

Wherever the defendant might insist that there was no consent, he may insist that the consideration was illegal: and in those cases in which the legislature has declared that the illegality of the consideration shall make the bill or note *utterly void, frustrate, and of none effect* to all intents and purposes whatsoever; he may insist upon such illegality to defeat the plaintiff's action, though the plaintiff or any of the parties between him and the defendant, may have become innocent indorsees, and taken the bill or note *bona fide,* and given a valuable consideration for it. *Str.* 1155. *Doug.* 708, 736.

These cases are, where the consideration is either wholly or in part, for signing a *bankrupt's certificate,* 5 *Geo.* 2. *c.* 30. *s.* 11. Money lost by *gaming* as aforesaid, or betting on the sides of persons so gaming, money knowingly lent for such gaming or betting, money lent at the time and place of such play, to any person either thus gaming or betting, or who shall, during the play, play or bet; 9 *Ann. c.* 14. *s.* 1. or money lent on an *usurious* contract. 12 *Ann. St.* 2. *c.* 16.

But if at the time of the making the bill or note, the consideration upon which it was accepted or given, was not illegal, any illegality in the consideration upon which it was afterwards transferred or indorsed over, will be no defence, if the plaintiff is an innocent holder *bona fide,* and upon a good consideration—therefore where the drawer of a bill for a good consideration, had discounted it with another, who took for the same at the rate of 18*l.* per cent. discount, and it afterwards came to the hands of the plaintiff, a *bona fide* holder: it was held that, although the bill would have been void in the hands of even an innocent holder, yet if it had been originally given on an usurious transaction, the usury in the intermediate transaction on the discount of it, did not make it void in the hands of the plaintiff who was an innocent indorsee. *Espin.* 274.

And by suffering a judgment by default, the defendant loses the opportunity, if he has any grounds of objecting to the sufficiency of the consideration. 4 *Ter. Rep.* 279.

BILL OF LADING, is a memorandum signed by masters of ships, acknowledging the receipt of the merchants goods, &c. Vide *Lex Mercatoria.*

BILL OF SALE, is a solemn contract under seal, whereby a man passes the right or interest that he hath in goods and chattels; for if a man promises or gives any chattels without valuable consideration, or without delivering possession, this doth not alter the property, because it is *nudum pactum unde non oritur actio;* but if a man sells goods by deed under seal duly executed, this alters the property between the parties, though there be no consideration, or no delivery of possession, because a man is estopped to deny his own deed, or affirm any thing contrary to the manifest solemnity of contracting. *Yelv.* 196. *Cro. Jac.* 270. 1 *Brown.* 111. 6 *Co.* 18. 1 *Bac. Abr. tit. Bill of Sale.*

But by stat. 13 *Eliz. cap.* 5. it is enacted "that all fraudulent conveyances of lands, "&c. goods and chattels, to avoid the debt "or duty of another, shall (as against the "party only, whose debt or duty is so endea-"voured to be avoided) be utterly void, ex-"cept grants made *bona fide,* and on a "good (which is construed a valuable) consi-"deration." And by the latter clause of that statute it is provided, "that all parties to "such fraudulent conveyance, who, being "privy thereunto, shall wittingly justify the "same to be done *bona fide* and on good con-"sideration, or shall alien or assign any "lands, lease or goods so to them conveyed "as aforesaid, shall forfeit one year's value "of the lands, lease, rent, common or other "profit out of the same, and the whole value "of the goods; and being thereof convicted "shall suffer half a year's imprisonment "without bail; the forfeiture to be divided "between the queen and the party grieved."

BILL OF STORE, a kind of licence granted at the custom-house to merchants, to carry such stores and provisions as are necessary for their voyage, custom free. A BILL OF SUFFERANCE is a licence granted to a merchant, to suffer him to trade from one English port to another, without paying custom. *An.* 14 *Car.* 2. *c.* 11.

BILLETS OF GOLD, (Fr. *billot*) are wedges or ingots of gold, mentioned in the statute 27 *E.* 3. *c.* 27. *Cowel. Blount.*

BILLET WOOD, is small wood for fuel, the assise of which was regulated by 43 *Eliz. c.* 14. 9 *An. c.* 15. 10 *An. c.* 6.

BILLINGSGATE market. See *London, Fish.*

BILLUS, a stick or staff, which in former times was the only weapon for servants. *Cowel. Blount.*

BINNARIUM, *binna, benna,* stews or water penned up for feeding and preserving of fish. *Ibid.*

BIOTHANETUS, one who deserves to come to an untimely end. *Ibid.*

BIRETTUM, a thin cap fitted close to the shape of the head: and is also used for the cap or coif of a judge, or serjeant at law. *Spelm.*

BISACUTUS, an iron weapon double edged, so as to cut on both sides. *Fleta, lib.* 1. *c.* 33. *Cowel. Blount.*

BISANTIUM, *besantine,* or *besant,* an antient coin first coined by the Western emperors at Bizantium or Constantinople. It was of two sorts gold and silver; both which were current in England. *Cowel. Blount.*

BI-SCOT, at a session of sewers, held at Wigenhale in Norfolk, 9 *Ed.* 3. it was decreed, that if any should not repair his proportion of the banks, ditches and causeys by a day assigned, 12*d.* for every perch unrepaired should be levied upon him, which is called a bilaw: and if he should not, by a second day given him, accomplish the same, then he should pay for every perch 2*s*; which is called bi-scot. *Hist. of Imbanking and Draining, f.* 254.

BISHOP, (*episcopus*) is the chief of the clergy in his diocese, and the archbishop's suffragan or assistant. He is elected by the king's *conge d' elire,* or licence to elect the person named by the king, directed to the dean and chapter; and if they fail to make election in twenty days, they incur the penalty of a *præmunire,* and the king may nominate, &c. by letters patent. *Stat.* 25 *H.* 8. *c.* 20. This was to avoid the power of the see of Rome. The dean and chapter having made their election, certify it to the king, and the archbishop, &c. And then the king gives the royal assent under the great seal, directed to the archbishop, commanding him to confirm and consecrate the bishop elect: and, on confirmation, a bishop hath jurisdiction in his diocese; but he hath not a right to his temporalities till consecration. The consecration of bishops, &c. is confirmed by act of parliament. *Palm. Rep.* 473.

It is held that a bishop hath three powers; 1st, his power of ordination, which is gained on his consecration, and not before; and thereby he may confer orders, &c. in any place throughout the world. 2. His power of jurisdiction, which is limited and confined to his see. 3. His power of administration and government of the revenues; both which last powers he gains by his confirmation: and some are of opinion, that the bishop's jurisdiction, as to ministerial acts, commences on his election. *Palm. Rep.* 473, 474, 475.

A bishop hath his consistory court, to hear ecclesiastical causes; and is to visit the clergy, &c. He consecrates churches, ordains, admits, and institutes priests; confirms, suspends, excommunicates, grants licences for marriage, makes probates of wills, &c. *Co. Lit.* 96. 2 *Rol. Abr.* 230. He hath his archdeacon, dean and chapter, chancellor, and vicar-general; to assist him: may grant leases for three lives, or twenty-one years, of land usually letten, reserving the accustomed yearly rents. *Stat.* 32 *H.* 8. *c.* 28. And by 1 *El. c.* 19. *s.* 5. Leases otherwise made are void.

BISHOPRICK, the diocese of a bishop, or that circuit, wherein he hath jurisdiction. 1 *Black.* 378. 4 *Black.* 107, 408, 423.

BISSA, (Fr. *biche*) *cerva major*, a hind. *Cowel. Blount.*

BISSEXTILE, (*bissextilis*) leap year, so called because the sixth day before the calends of March is twice reckoned, *viz.* on the 24th and 25th of February; so that the bissextile year hath one day more than the others, and happens every fourth year. This intercalation of a day was first invented by Julius Cæsar, to make the year agree with the course of the sun. And, to prevent all doubt and ambiguity that might arise thereupon, it is enacted by the statute *de anno bissextili*, 21 *H.* 3. That the day increasing in the leap year, and the day next before, shall be accounted but one day. *Brit.* 209. *Dyer* 17. The new stile to be used by *Stat.* 24 *Geo.* 2. *c.* 23.

BISUS, *bisius, mica bisa, panis bisius*, (Fr. *pain bis*) brown bread, a brown loaf. *Cowel.*

BLACK ACT, by 9 *Geo.* 1. *cap.* 22, persons hunting armed and disguised, and killing or stealing deer, or robbing warrens, or stealing fish out of any river, &c. or any persons unlawfully hunting in his majesty's forests, &c. or breaking down the head of any fish-pond, or killing, &c. of cattle, or cutting down trees, or setting fire to house, barn, or wood, or shooting at any person, or sending anonymous letters, or signed with fictitious name, demanding money, &c. or rescuing such offenders, are guilty of felony without benefit of clergy: made perpetual by 31 *Geo.* 2. *c.* 42. See also *Felony*.

BLACK-BOOK, is a book lying in the Exchequer. *Stat. Annals* 154.

BLACK-LEAD. By 25 *Geo.* 2. *c.* 10. entering mines of black-lead, with intent to steal, is made felony; and by the same act offenders committed or transported for entering mines of black-lead with intent to steal, escaping, or breaking prison, or returning from transportation, are excluded from clergy.

BLACK-MAIL, (Fr. *maillé*, a link of mail, or small piece of metal or money) signifies in the north of England, in the counties of Cumberland, Northumberland, and that quarter, a certain rent of money, (of baser quality than silver, *reditus albi*, 2 *Black.* 42.) corn, or other thing, anciently paid to persons inhabiting upon or near the borders, being men of name and power, allied with certain robbers within the said counties; to be freed and protected from the devastations of those robbers. *Anno* 43 *Eliz. cap.* 13. These robbers were called moss troopers, and several statutes have been made against them. The 9 *Ed.* 3. *c.* 4. mentions black money: and black rents are the same with black mail; being rents formerly paid in provisions and flesh. And by 18 *Car.* 2. *c.* 3. Notorious thieves, or spoil-takers in Northumberland or Cumberland are excluded clergy, or may be transported at the discretion of the judge.

BLACK-ROD, the gentleman usher of the black rod, is chief gentleman usher to the king; he belongs to the garter, and hath his name from the black rod, on the top whereof sits a lion in gold, which he carrieth in his hand. He is called in the Black-book, fol. 255. *Lator virgæ nigræ, & hostiarius*; and in other places *virgæ bajulus*. His duty is *ad portandum virgam coram domino rege ad festum sancti Georgii infra castrum de Windsore*: and he hath the keeping of the chapter-house door, when a chapter of the order of the garter is sitting; and in the time of parliament, he attends on the house of peers. His habit is like to that of the register of the order, and garter king at arms; but this he wears only at the solemn times of the festival of St. George, and on the holding of chapters. The black rod he bears, is instead of a mace, and hath the same authority; and this officer hath anciently been made by letters patent under the great seal, he having great power; for to his custody all peers, called in question for any crime, are first committed. *Cowel. Blount. Morgan.*

BLACKS OF WALTHAM, a set of desperate deer-stealers. See *Black Act.*

BLACKWELL-HALL. See *London.*

BLADARIUS, a corn-monger, meal-man, or corn-chandler. *Cowel. Blount.*

BLADE, (*bladum*) in the Saxon signifies generally fruit, corn, hemp, flax, herbs, &c. *Ibid.*

BLANCH FIRMES, in ancient times the crown-rents were many times reserved *in libris albis*, or *blanch firmes*: *reditus albi* in contradistinction to rents reserved in work, grain, or base money, which were called *reditus nigri*, or black mail. *Lowndes's Essay upon Coins, p.* 5. 2 *Black.* 42.

2. Blanch farm, according to Cowel and Blount, was also a white farm; that is, where the rent was paid in silver, and not in cattle. Blanks, being a kind of white money coined by *Hen.* 5. in those parts of France which were then subject to England, the value whereof was 8*d.* *Stow's Annals, p.* 586. These were forbidden to be current in this realm. 2 *Hen.* 6. *c.* 9.

BLANHORNUM, a little bell, or rather *ticinium*. *Cowel. Blount.*

BLANK-BAR, is used for the same with what we call a common bar, and is the name of a plea in bar, which, in an action of trespass, is put in, to oblige the plaintiff to assign the certain place where the trespass was committed. 2 *Cro. Rep.* 594.

BLANKS, in judicial proceedings, certain

void spaces sometimes left by mistake. A blank (supposing some thing material wanting) in a declaration, abates the same, 4 *Ed.* 4, 14. 20 *H.* 6, 18. And such a blank is a good cause of demurrer. Blanks in the imparlance roll aided after verdict for the plaintiff. *Hob.* 76. *Parker* v. *Parker*.

BIASARIUS, is a word used to signify an incendiary. *Cowel. Blount.*

BLASPHEMY, (*blasphemia*) is an injury offered to God, by denying that which is due and belonging to him, or attributing to him what is not agreeable to his nature. *Lindw. cap.* 1. And blasphemies of God, as denying his being, or providence, and all contumelious reproaches of Jesus Christ, &c. are offences by the common law, punished by fine, imprisonment, pillory, &c. 1 *Hawk. P. C.* 87. And by statute, if any one shall by writing, speaking, &c. deny any of the persons in the Trinity, to be God; assert there are more Gods than one, &c. he shall be incapable of any office; and for the second offence, be disabled to sue any action, to be executor, &c. and suffer three years imprisonment. 9 & 10 *W.* 3. *cap.* 32.

Likewise by 3 *Jac.* 1. *c.* 21. persons jestingly or prophanely using the name of God, or of Jesus Christ, or of the Holy Ghost, or of the Trinity, in any stage play, &c. incurs a penalty of 10*l*.

BLE, signifies sight, colour, &c. And blee is taken for corn: as to Boughton under the Blee, &c. *Cowel. Blount.*

BLENCH, a sort of tenure of land; as to hold land in blench, is by payment of a sugar-loaf, a couple of capons, a beaver-hat, &c. if the same be demanded in the name of blench, i. e. *Nomine albæ firmæ*. *Ibid.*

BLENCH-HOLDING, the white-rents, or blanch-farms, *reditus albi;* this small kind of payment is called in Scotland blench-holding, or *reditus albæ firmæ*. 2 *Black.* 42. *n.*

BLETA, (Fr. *bleche*) peat or combustible earth dug up and dried for burning. *Cowel. Blount.*

BLINKS, boughs broken down from trees, and thrown in a way where deer are likely to pass. *Ibid.*

BLISSOM, corruptly called blossom, is when a ram goes to the ewe, from the Teuton. Blets, the bowels. *Ibid.*

BLODEUS, (Sax. *blod*) deep red colour; from whence comes bloat and bloated, *viz.* sanguine and high coloured, which in Kent is called a blousing colour: and a blouse is there a red-faced wench. *Cowel. Blount.*

BLOOD, (*sanguis*) is regarded in descents of lands; for a person is to be the next and most worthy of blood, to inherit his ancestor's estate. *Co. Lit.* 13. See *Jenk. Cent.* 203.

Blood, *Corruption of.* See *Attainder, Forfeitures,* and *Pardon.*

BLOODWIT, or Bloudwit, compounded of the Sax. *blod,* i. e. *sanguis* and *wyte,* an old English word signifying *misericordia,* is often used in ancient charters of liberties for an amerciament for bloodshed. Skene writes it *bloudveit;* and says *veit* in English is *injuria;* and that *bloudveit* is an amerciament or unlaw (as the Scotch call it) for wrong or injury, as bloodshed is: for he that hath *bloudveit* granted him, hath free liberty to take all amerciaments of courts for effusion of blood. Fleta saith, *quod significat quietantium misericordiæ pro effusione sanguinis. Lib.* 1. *cap.* 47. And, according to some writers, *blodwite* was a customary fine paid as a composition and atonement for shedding or drawing of blood; for which the place was answerable, if the party was not discovered: and therefore a privilege or exemption from this fine or penalty, was granted by the king, or supreme lord, as a special favour. So king Henry II. granted to all tenants within the honour of Willingford, *ut quieti sint de hidagio & blodewite,* &c. *Paroch. Antiq.* 114. *Cowel. Blount.*

BLOODY-HAND, is one of the four kinds of circumstances by which an offender is supposed to have killed deer in the king's forest: and it is where a trespasser is apprehended in the forest, with his hands or other parts bloody, though he be not found chasing or hunting of the deer. *Manwood.* In Scotland, in such like crimes, they say taken in the fact, or with the red hand. See *Backberind. Cowel. Blount.*

BLUBBER, is whale-oil before it is thoroughly boiled and brought to perfection. *Ibid.*

BOCK-HORD, or book-hoard (*librorum horreum*) a place where books, evidences, or writings are kept. *Ibid.*

BOCKLAND, (Sax. *quasi* bookland) a possession or inheritance held by evidence in writing. Bockland signifies deed-land; and it commonly carried with it the absolute property of the land, wherefore it was preserved in writing, and possessed by the thanes or nobler sort, and was the same as *allodium,* descendable unto all the sons, according to the common course of nations and of nature, and therefore called gavelkind; devisable also by will, and thereupon termed *terræ testamentales. Spelm.* of *Feuds.* This was one of the titles which the English-Saxons had to their lands, and was always in writing. There was but one more, and that was folkland, *i. e. terra popularis,* which passed from one to another without any writing. See *Charter-land. Cowel. Blount.*

BOIA, chains or fetters, properly what we call bernicles. *Ibid.*

BOILING TO DEATH. The killing by poisoning was by stat. 22 *Hen.* 8. *c.* 9, made treason, and the delinquent subject to a more grievous and lingering death, than the common law allowed, namely, *boiling to death.*

This extraordinary punishment, seems to have been adopted by the Legislature, from the peculiar circumstances of the crime, which gave rise to it; for the preamble of the statute informs us, that John Roose, a cook, had been lately convicted, of throwing poison into a large pot of broth, prepared for the bishop of Rochester's family, and for the poor of the parish; and the said John Roose was by a retrospective clause of the same statute *ordered to be boiled to death*. And Ld. *Coke* mentions several instances of persons suffering this horrid punishment. 3 *Inst.* 48. *Christian* in *n.* 3. 4 *Black.* 196.

BOIS, (Fr.) wood, and *sub-bois*, underwood. *Boscus.* *Cowel.* *Blount.*

BOLHAGIUM, or *boldagium*, a little house, or cottage. *Ibid.*

BOLT. A *bolt* of silk or stuff seems to have been a long narrow piece; in the accounts of the priory of Burcester, it is mentioned. *Paroch. Antiq. p.* 574.

BOLTING, a term of art used in our inns of court, whereby is intended a private arguing of cases. The manner of it at Gray's-Inn is thus: An ancient and two barristers sit as judges, three students bring each a case; out of which the judges choose one to be argued, which done, the students first argue it, and after them the barristers. It is inferior to *mooting*, and may be derived from the Sax. *bolt*, a house, because done privately in the house for instruction. In Lincoln's-Inn, Mondays and Wednesdays are the *bolting-days*, in vacation time, and Tuesdays and Thursdays the *moot-days*. *Dugdale.* *Cowel.* *Blount.*

BONA FIDE. We say that is done *bonâ fide* which is done really, with a good faith, without any fraud or deceit. *Stat.* 13 *Eliz.* c. 5. 12 *Car.* 2. *c.* 18, &c.

BONA GESTURA, good abearing, or good behaviour. See *Surety*.

BONAGHT, or *bonaghty*, was an exaction in Ireland, imposed on the people at the will of the lord, for relief of the knights called *bonaghti*, who served in the wars. *Antiq. Hibern. p.* 60.

BONA NOTABILIA. Where a person dies having at the time of his death goods in any other diocese, besides his goods in the diocese where he dieth, amounting to the value of 5*l.* at least, he is said to have *bona notabilia*, and then probate of his will, or granting administration, belongs to the archbishop of the province: but this doth not prejudice those dioceses where, by composition or custom, *bona notabilia* are rated at a greater sum. *Can.* 92, 93. *Perkins, sec.* 489. And in the city of London *bona notabilia* are 10*l.* by composition. 4 *Inst.* 335. One that hath a debt upon bond or specialty, &c. in another diocese, hath *bona notabilia*. 1 *Rol. Abr.* 908. Though if a person happens to die in another diocese than that wherein he lives, on a journey, what he hath about him above the value of 5*l.* &c. shall not be *bona notabilia*. *Can.* 93.

There must be several administrations where a person dies leaving *bona notabilia* in each province of Canterbury and York; for administration granted in one province doth not extend to goods in the other, because the archbishops have distinct supreme jurisdictions; but then there is to be *bona notabilia* in several dioceses in each province. *Dyer* 305. 2 *Lev.* 86. If a man dies in one diocese without any goods, and leaves to the value of 5*l.* in another diocese, the archbishop of that province may grant administration, as he hath a general jurisdiction there; though such administration is voidable by sentence. *Cro. Eliz.* 457. But where a bishop grants administration, and there are *bona notabilia*, such administration is merely void for he hath no jurisdiction out of his diocese. 5 *Rep.* 30. 1 *Nels. Abr.* 381. Vide *Black. Com.* 2 *V.* 509, 510.

BONA PATRIA, an assise of countrymen or good neighbours. It is sometimes called *assisa bonæ patriæ*, when twelve or more men are chosen out of any part of the country to pass upon an assise, otherwise called *juratores*, because they are to swear judicially in the presence of the party, &c. according to the practice of Scotland. *Skene.* See *Assisors.*

BONA PERITURA, goods that are perishable. See *Wreck.*

BONCHA, a bunch, is derived from the old Lat. *bonna*, or *bunna*, a rising bank for the bounds of fields; and hence bown is used in Norfolk for swelling or rising up in a bunch or tumour, &c. *Cowel.* *Blount.*

BOND, is a deed or obligatory instrument in writing, whereby one doth bind himself and his heirs, executors, and administrators, to another, to pay a sum of money, or do some other act; as to make a release, surrender an estate, for quiet enjoyment to stand to an award, save harmless, perform a will, or the like. It contains an obligation, with a penalty: and a condition, which expressly mentions what money is to be paid, or other thing to be performed, and the limited time for the performance thereof; for which the obligation is peremptorily binding. It may be made upon parchment or paper, though it is usually on paper, and be either in the first or third person; and the condition may be either in the same deed, or in another, and sometimes it is included within, and sometimes indorsed upon the obligation; but it is commonly at the foot of the obligation. *Bro. Obl.* 67. And a memorandum on the back of a bond may restrain the same by way of exception. *Moor* 67.

This security is also called a specialty; the debt being therein particularly specified in writing, and the party's seal, acknowledging the debt or duty, and confirming the contract; rendering it a security of a higher nature than those entered into, without the solemnity of a seal; and therefore bonds or specialties shall be preferred to simple contracts in a course of administration; and from its being a higher security it is held that for a breach or non-performance an action of debt only will lie. 1 *Bac. Abr.* tit. *Oblig.* But if in a bond the obligor *binds himself*, without adding his *heirs, executors and administrators*, the executors and administrators shall nevertheless be bound, but not the heir. *Shep. Touch.* 369.

A bond is a chose in action which cannot be assigned over, so as to enable the assignee to sue in his own name; yet he has by the assignment such a title to the paper and wax that he may keep or cancel it. *Co. Lit.* 232.

Also in equity, a bond is assignable, for a valuable consideration paid, and the assignee alone becomes entitled to the money; so that if the obligor, after notice of the assignment, pays the money to the obligee, he will be compelled to pay it over again. 2 *Vern.* 595. *Abr. Eq.* 44.

But the assignee must take it subject to the same equity that it was subject to in the hands of the obligee. *Ibid.*

If a man enters into a bond of such a sum, on condition to be void on payment of a lesser sum, or if a man bind himself in the penalty of 100*l.* that he will pay 50*l.* by such a day; after the day of payment is past, the penalty or sum of 100*l.* is the legal debt; and for so much it hath been resolved, an executor of an obligor of such forfeited bond may cover the assets of his testator. *Cro. Car.* 490. 1 *Vent.* 354. 3 *Lev.* 368. *Hill.* 9 *Geo.* 2, in *B. R.* The *Bank of England* v. *Morris. Annaly's Rep. temp. Hardwicke*, 219, &c.

And as the penalty, by the bond's being forfeited, becomes the legal debt, so there was no remedy against such penalty, but by application to a court of equity, which relieves in those cases, on payment of principal, interest, and costs; also, though at law there can be no remedy beyond the penalty, because in that the obligee seems to have taken up his security, yet as it is on the foundation, of doing equal justice to both parties, that equity proceeds, it will, on any application for a favour from the obligor, compel him to pay the principal, interest, and costs, though exceeding the penalty. *Show. Par. Ca.* 15. *Abr. Eq.* 91, 92. 1 *Salk.* 154. 1 *Vern.* 342. 350. 2 *Vern.* 509.

And this rule of compelling the party to do equity, who seeks equity, seems to be the reason why an obligee shall have interest, after he has entered up judgment; for though in strictness it may be accounted his own fault, why he did not take out execution, and therefore not entitled to interest, yet, as by the judgment he is entitled to the penalty, it does not seem reasonable, that he should be deprived of it, but upon paying him principal and the interest, incurred as well before as after the entering up of the judgment. *Abr. Eq.* 92. 288.

It is said that there are only three things essentially necessary to the making a good obligation, *viz.* writing on paper or parchment, sealing and delivery. 2 *Co.* 5. *a. Noy* 21. 85. *Moor* 28. *Stil.* 97. 2 *Salk.* 462. 5 *Mod.* 281.

And the name of the obligor subscribed, it is said, is sufficient, though there is a blank for his christian name in the bond. *Cro. Jac.* 261. Vide *Cro. Jac.* 558. 1 *Mod.* 107.

An obligation is good though it wants a date, or hath a false or impossible date; for the date is not of the substance of the deed; and the day of the delivery of a deed or obligation is the day of the date, though there is no day set forth. 2 *Co.* 5. *Noy* 21. 85, 86. *Hob.* 249. *Stil.* 97. *Cro. Jac.* 136. 264. *Yelv.* 193. 1 *Salk.* 76.

A bond dated on the same day on which a release is made of all things *usque diem datus*, &c. is not thereby discharged. 2 *Rol. Rep.* 255.

If A and B enter into a bond, and set but one seal to it, and A execute it for himself and B, with the authority and in the presence of B, it is obligatory on both. Sir *W. Jones*, 268. 4 *Term Rep.* 313.

It is to be observed, that the condition of a bond must be to do a thing lawful; and therefore bonds restraining trade in general in any part of the kingdom, are unlawful and void, for they are against the good of the public, and the liberty of a freeman, and tend to a monopoly; but a condition, erstraining a man from exercising a particular trade in a certain *place*, or within certain limits, if done fairly, and upon a good and lawful consideration, is good. 1 *Bac. Abr.* tit. *Ob.* (K.)

Conditions of bonds are to be not only lawful but possible; and when the matter or thing to be done, or not to be done by a condition, is unlawful, or impossible, or the condition itself repugnant, insensible or uncertain, the condition is void, and in some cases the obligation also. 10 *Rep.* 120. But sometimes an obligation may be single, to pay the money, where the condition is impossible, repugnant, &c. 2 *Mod.* 285. If a thing be possible at the time of entering into the bond, and afterwards becomes impossible by the act of God, the act of the law, or of the obligee, it is become void; as if a man be bound to appear next term, and dies before, the obligation is saved. *Co. Lit.* 206.

Thus a condition of a bond was, that A. L. should pay such a sum upon the 25th of December, or appear in Hilary term after in the court of *B. R.* he died after the 25th of December, and before Hilary term, and had not paid any thing: in this case the condition was not broken for non-payment, and the other part is become impossible by the act of God. 1 *Mod. Rep.* 265. And when a condition is doubtful it is always taken most favourably for the obligor, and against the obligee; but so as a reasonable construction be made as near as can be according to the intention of the parties. *Dyer* 51.

If no time is limited in a bond for payment of the money, it is due presently, and payable on demand. 1 *Brownl.* 53.

The obligor or his servant, &c. may tender the money to save the forfeiture of the bond, and it shall be a good performance of the condition, if made to the obligee, though refused by him; yet if the obligor be afterward sued, he must plead that he is still ready to pay it, and tender the money in court. *Co. Lit.* 208.

And in case the condition of a bond is not performed, the bond becomes forfeited, or absolute at law, and charges the obligor while living, and after his death the obligation descends upon his heir, who on defect of personal assets is bound to discharge it, provided he has real assets by descent as a recompense; so that it may be called though not a *direct*, yet a collateral charge upon the lands. 2 *Black.* 340. And yet a bond does not seem properly to be called an encumbrance upon land, for it does not follow the land like a recognizance and a judgment; and even if the heir at law aliens the land, the obligor in the bond, by which the heir is bound, can have his remedy only against the person of the heir, to the amount of the value of the land; but he cannot follow it when it is in the possession of a *bona fide* purchaser. *Bul. N. P.* 175.

And by 4 *Ann.* c. 16, "if at any time "pending an action upon any bond with a "penalty, the defendant shall bring into "court where the action is depending, all "principal money and interest due on such "bond, and also all such costs as have been "expended in any suit or suits in law or "equity upon such bond, the said money "so brought in, shall be deemed and taken "to be in full satisfaction and discharge of "the said bond; and the court shall and "may give judgment to discharge every "such defendant of and from the same accordingly." *sec.* 14.

BONDAGE, is slavery, and bondmen, in Domesday, are called *servi*, but rendered different from *villani*. *Cowel. Blount.*

BOND-TENANTS, copyholders, and customary tenants, sometimes called bond-tenants. For, according to *Calthorpe* on copyholds, 51, 54, all those kinds of tenants agree in substance and kind of tenure; all their lands being holden in one general kind, that is by custom and continuance of time; and the diversity of their names doth not alter the nature of their tenure. 2 *Black.* 147, 148.

BONO ET MALO, writ *de*. It was anciently the course to issue special writs of *gaol-delivery*, for each particular prisoner, which were called the writs *de bono et malo*, but these being inconvenient and oppressive, a *general commission* for all the prisoners has long been established in their stead. 2 *Inst.* 43. 4 *Black.* 270.

BONIS NON AMOVENDIS, a writ directed to the sheriffs of London, &c. where a writ of error is brought, to charge them, that the person against whom judgment is obtained, be not suffered to remove his goods till the error is tried and determined. *Reg. Orig.* 131.

BOOKS. By 25 *Hen.* 8, *c.* 15, none shall buy, to sell again, printed books, ready bound, imported from beyond sea, under penalty of 6*s.* 8*d.* a book, and none shall buy any books by retail, imported by any stranger, under the like penalty.

By 3 and 4 *Ed.* 6, *c.* 10, popish books, missals, legends, and antiphoners, shall be abolished.

By 17 *Car.* 2. *c.* 4, a printed copy of every book shall be sent to the king's library, and to each of the two universities.

University printers shall deliver one copy of books printed there to the king's library, and to the vice-chancellor of each university, and two others for the public libraries there, on pain of 5*l.* each book. *Ibid.*

By *Stat.* 7 *Ann.* *c.* 14, *sec.* 10, if any book shall be taken, or otherwise lost out of any parochial library, any justice may grant his warrant to search for it; and if it shall be found, it shall by order of such justice be restored to the library.

By 8 *Ann.* *c.* 19, authors of books and their assigns shall have the sole right of printing them for fourteen years from the day of publishing; and others printing the same without their consent, shall forfeit the books, and one penny for every sheet.

The titles of copies shall be entered before publication, in the register-book of the company of Stationers, for inspection; the clerk of the company shall give a certificate thereof for sixpence. *Ibid.*

Nine copies of each book shall be delivered to the warehouse-keeper of the company of Stationers, for the use of the royal library, the libraries of Oxford and Cambridge, the libraries of the four universities in Scotland, of Sion college, and the library of the advocates at Edinburgh, within ten days after demand, on pain to forfeit the value of the books, and 5*l.* *Ibid.*

This act shall not restrain the importing of books in Greek, Latin, or any foreign language, printed beyond sea; nor extend to the right of the universities. *Ibid.*

The general issue may be pleaded by defendants, having acted under this act. *Ibid.*

After the first fourteen years the right of printing shall return to the author, if living for other fourteen years. *Ibid.*

The author of any pamphlet shall lose all property therein if the stamp-duties are not paid; and they shall have the printer or publisher's name thereon, on pain of 20*l.* *Ibid.*

By 12 *Geo.* 2. *c.* 36, the penalty of 5*l.* and double the value is inflicted on persons importing for sale books first written and printed in this kingdom, and re-printed abroad; but books not printed or re-printed in this kingdom within twenty years are excepted.

This shall not extend to books printed in England, and inserted in other larger tracts printed abroad. *Ibid.*

This act, by the last continuance of 22 *Geo.* 3. *c.* 13, was to continue in force till the year 1788, and is now expired, other provisions having been made by subsequent statutes.

By 15 *Geo.* 3. *c.* 53, the two universities in England, and four in Scotland, and the colleges of Eton, Westminster, and Winchester, shall have the sole right, for ever, of printing books which have or (not having been published or assigned) shall be bequeathed, or otherwise given by authors to any of the said universities, unless given for a term of years, or other limited time; and others printing such books forfeit the same, with one penny per sheet, half to the king, and the other to the prosecutor: but this act shall not give an exclusive right, longer than such book is printed at the universities or college press; and they are not to grant away their right, but may sell the copy, as authors can by 8 *Ann. c.* 19.

None are subject to penalty for printing books already given to the universities, unless entered at Stationers hall before 24th June 1775, and if hereafter given they are to be entered in two months after bequest known, and sixpence paid for each entry, which is to be inspected *gratis*, and sixpence for the certificate. The whole title to be entered. *Ibid.*

By 41 *Geo.* 3. (u. k.) *c.* 107, authors of books and their assigns shall have the sole right of printing them for 14 years, and booksellers in any part of the united kingdom, or British European dominions, who shall print, re-print, or import any such books, without the consent of the proprietor, shall be liable to an action for damages, and shall also forfeit the books to the proprietor, and 3*d.* *per* sheet, half to the king, and half to the informer; and authors shall have a second 14 years term if living at the end of the first. *sec.* 1.

Trinity-college, Dublin, shall for ever have the sole right of printing books given or bequeathed to them, unless they are given for a limited time only; and persons printing such books are liable to the same penalty as in the last clause; but this is to extend only to books printed at the college press; and the college may sell their copy-rights. *sec.* 3.

Booksellers shall not be liable to the penalty of 3*d.* per sheet unless the title to the copy-right be entered by the proprietor at Stationers' hall, London, nor if the consent of the proprietor be so entered, of which entries the clerk of the company is to give certificates, and make a half-yearly list of the books so entered for the use of Trinity-college. *s.* 4.

If the clerk refuses to make entries, parties may give notice in the London Gazette, and the clerk shall forfeit 20*l.* *s.* 5.

Two additional copies of books entered at Stationers' hall shall be delivered there for the use of the libraries of Trinity-college, and the king's Inns, Dublin. *s.* 6.

No person shall import into any part of the united kingdom, for sale, any book first composed and printed within the united kingdom, and re-printed elsewhere; and persons importing, selling, or keeping for sale, any such books, are to forfeit the same, and also 10*l.* and double the value, which books may be seized by officers of customs or excise, and made waste paper of, and the commissioners may reward them with not exceeding their value; but this clause is not to extend to books not printed in the united kingdom for 20 years, or books re-printed abroad, and inserted in larger works. *s.* 7.

BOOK OF RATES, the book declaring the duties of customs.

BOOTING, or BOTING CORN, rent-corn anciently so called. *Cowel. Blount.*

BORDAGIUM, the tenure called bord-lands. *Ibid.*

BORDARIA, a cottage, from the Sax. *bord, domus. Ibid.*

BORDARII, or BORDVANNI, these words often occur in Domesday, and some think they mean boors, husbandmen, or cottagers. In the Domesday inquisition, they were distinct from the *villani*, and seemed to be those of a less servile condition, who had a bord or cottage, with a small parcel of land allowed to them, on condition they should supply the lord with poultry and eggs, and other small provisions for his board or entertainment. Some derive the word *bordarii* from the old Gall. *bords*, the limits or extreme parts of any extent, as the borders of a country, and the borderers inhabitants in those parts, *quasi* borderers. *Spelman. Cowel. Blount.*

BORD-HALFPENNY, signifies a small toll, by custom paid to the lord of the town for setting up boards, tables, booths, &c. in fairs and markets. It is derived from three Saxon words, *bræd*, i. e. *board, helve*, in behalf of, and *penning*, a toll; which in the whole makes a toll for or in behalf of boards. *Cowel. Blount.*

BORDLANDS, the demesnes which lords keep in their hands for the maintenance of their board or table. *Bract. lib.* 4. *tract* 3. *c.* 9. *Cowel. Blount.*

BORDLODE, was a service required of tenants to carry timber out of the woods of the lord to his house; or it is said to be the quantity of food or provision which the *bordary* or *bordman* paid for the *bord-lands*. The old Scots had the term of *burd*, and *meet-burd* for victuals and provisions; and *burden-sack* for a sack full of provender, from whence, it is probable, came our burden. *Cowel. Blount.*

BORD-SERVICE, a tenure of bord-lands, by which some lands in the manor of Fulham in *com. Mid.* and elsewhere, are held of the bishop of London; and the tenants do now pay six-pence per acre in lieu of finding provision anciently for their lord's board or table. *Blount.*

BORD-BRIGCH, *borg-bryce*, or *burg-brych*, (Sax.) a breach or violation of suretyship, pledge-breach, or of mutual fidelity. *Ibid.*

BOROUGH, (Fr. *burg*. Lat. *burgus*. Sax. *borhoe*) signifies a corporate town, which is not a city, and also such a town or place as sends burgesses to parliament. *Verstegan* saith that burg, or burgh, whereof we make our borough, metaphorically signifies a town having a wall, or some kind of inclosure about it: and all places that in old time had among our ancestors the name of borough, were one way or other fenced or fortified. *Lit. sect.* 164. And why these were called free burghs, and the tradesmen in them free burgesses, was from a freedom to buy and sell without disturbance, exempt from toll, &c. granted by charter. Parliament boroughs are said to be either by charter, or towns holden of the king in ancient demesne. *Brady*. It is conjectured that borhoe, or borough, was also formerly taken for those companies consisting of ten families, which were to be pledges for one another. *Bract. lib.* 3. *tract.* 2. *cap.* 10. *Lamb. Duty of Const. p.* 8. Vide *Squire's Anglo-Saxon Government*, 236, 247, 251, 254, 258, 262, 264. Trading boroughs were first formed in the time of Alfred. *Squire* 247, 251. 1 *Black. Com.* 114. and 2 *Bl. Com.* 82.

BOROUGH COURTS, arose originally from the favour of the crown to those particular districts wherein we find them erected, upon the same principle that hundred courts, and the like, were established, for the convenience of the inhabitants, that they might prosecute their suits, and receive justice at home; and for the most part the courts at Westminster-hall have a concurrent jurisdiction with these, as also a superintendency over them; and the proceedings in these special courts ought to be according to the course of the common law, unless otherwise ordered by parliament; for though the king may erect new courts he cannot alter the established course of law. 3 *Black.* 80.

BOROUGH-HOLDERS, or BURSE-HOLDERS, *quasi* bourhoe-ealders, are the same officers with borough-heads, or head-boroughs, who, (according to *Lambert*) were the head men, or chief pledges of boroughs, chosen by the rest to speak and act in their names in those things that concerned them. See *Headborough*. 1 *Black. Com.* 114,356,406.

BOROUGH-ENGLISH, (Sax. *borhoe Englise*) so called, because, as some hold, it first prevailed in England, *Co. Lit.* 110, *b.*) is a customary descent of lands, in some ancient boroughs, and copyhold manors, that estates shall descend to the youngest son, or, if the owner hath no issue, to his younger brother, as in Edmuntun, &c. *Kitch.* 102. It has been observed, that the original of this old custom, proceeded from the lords of certain lands, having the privilege to lie with their tenants wives, the first night after marriage; wherefore in time the tenants obtained this custom, on purpose that their eldest sons (who might be their lord's bastards,) should be incapable to inherit their estates. *Præf.* 3 *Mod. Rep.*

But the reason of the custom of borough-English (*Littleton* says) is because the youngest is presumed in law to be least able to provide for himself. *Lit.* 165. This custom goes with the land, and guides the descent to the youngest son, although there be a devise to the contrary. 2 *Lev.* 138. If a man seised in fee of lands in borough-english, makes a feoffment to the use of himself, and the heirs male of his body, according to the course of the common law, and afterwards die seised, having issue two sons, the youngest son shall have the lands by virtue of the custom, notwithstanding the feoffment. *Dyer* 179.

If a copyhold in borough-english be surrendered to the use of a person and his heirs, the right will descend to the youngest son according to the custom. 1 *Mod.* 102. And a youngest son shall inherit an estate in tail in borough-english. *Noy* 106. But an heir at common law shall take advantage of a condition annexed to borough-english land, though the youngest son shall be entitled to all actions in right of the land, &c. 1 *Nels. Abr.* 396. And the eldest son shall have tithes arising out of land borough-english; for tithes, of common right, are not inheritances, descendable to an heir, but come in succession from one clergyman to another. *Ibid.* 347.

Borough-English land being descendable to the youngest son, if a younger son dies without issue male, leaving a daughter, such daughter shall inherit *jure repræsentationis.* 1 *Salk.* 243. It hath been adjudged where a man hath several brothers, the youngest may inherit lands in borough-english; yet it is said where a custom is, that land shall go to the youngest son, it doth not give it to the youngest uncle for customs shall be taken strictly; and those which fix and order the descents of inheritance can be altered only by parliament. *Dyer* 179. 4 *Leon.* 384. *Jenk. Cent.* 220.

By the custom of borough-english the widow shall have the whole of her husband's lands in dower, which is called her free-bench; and this is given to her the better to provide for the younger children, with the care of whom she is intrusted. *Co. Lit.* 39, 111. *F. N. B.* 150. *Mo. pl.* 566.

BOROUGH GOODS are devisable, as before the statutes of 33 *Hen.* 8. *c.* 1. and 34 *Hen.* 8. *c.* 5.

BOREL-FOLK, *i. e.* country people, from the Fr. *boure, floccus,* because they covered their heads with such stuffs. *Blount.*

BORROWING. If a man borrows money, corn, or such things of another; he may not expect the same again, but the like, or so much; but if one lend me a horse, &c. he must have the same restored. If a thing lent for use be used to any other end or purpose than that for which it was borrowed, the party may have his action on the case for it, though the thing be never the worse; and if what is borrowed be lost, although it be not by any negligence of mine, as if I be robbed of it; or where the thing is impaired or destroyed by my neglect, admitting that I put it to no more service than that for which borrowed, I must make it good: so where I borrow a horse, and put him in an old rotten house ready to fall, which falls on and kills him, I must answer for the horse. But if such goods borrowed perish by the act of God in the right use of them, as where I put the horse, &c. in a strong house, and it fall and kill him, or it dies by disease, or by default of the owner, I shall not be charged. *Co. Lit.* 89. 29 *Ass.* 28. 2 *H.* 7. 11. 2 *Black. Com.* 453. *See also* BAILMENT.

BORSHOLDERS. See *Borough-holders.*

BOSCAGE, (*boscagium*) is that food which wood and trees yield to cattle; as mast, &c. from the Ital. *bosco, silva;* but *Manwood* observes, to be quit *de boscagio,* is to be discharged of paying any duty of wind-fall wood in the forest. *Cowel. Blount.*

BOSCARIA, wood houses, from *boscus;* or ox houses from *bos. Mon. Angl. tom.* 2. *fol.* 302. *Cowel. Blount.*

BOSCUS, an ancient word used in our law, signifying all manner of wood: the Italians make use of *bosco* in the same sense; as the French do *bois.* Boscus is divided into high-wood or timber, *haut-bois,* and coppice or under-woods, *sub-bois*: but the high-wood is properly called *saltus,* and in Fleta we read it *maeremium. Cowel. Blount.*

BOSINNUS, a certain rustical pipe, mentioned in ancient tenures. *Ibid.*

BOSTAR, an ox-stall. *Ibid.*

BOTE, (Sax.) signifies a recompense, satisfaction, or amends; hence comes *manbote,* compensation, or amends for a man slain, &c. *Lamb cap.* 99. From hence likewise we have our common phrase *to-boot,* i. e. *compensationis gratia.* There are house-bote, plough-bote, &c. privileges to tenants in cutting of wood, &c. 2 *Black. Com.* 35.

BOTELESS, *sine remedio,* in the charter of *H.* 1. to *Tho.* archbishop of York, it is said, that no judgment or sum of money shall acquit him that commits sacrilege; but he is in English called boteless, *viz.* without emendation. *Lib. Albus penes Cap. de Suthnet. Int. Plat. Trin.* 12 *Ed.* 2. *Ebor* 48. We retain the word still in common speech; as it is booteless to attempt such a thing; that is, it is in vain to attempt it. *Cowel. Blount.*

BOTELLARIA, a buttery or cellar, in which the buts and bottles of wine, and other liquors are reposited. *Ibid.*

BOTHA, a booth, stall, or standing in a fair or market. *Ibid.*

BOTHAGIUM, *boothage,* or customary dues paid to the lord of the manor or soil, for the pitching and standing of booths in fairs or markets. *Ibid.*

BOTHNA, or BUTHNA, seems to be a park where cattle are inclosed and fed. Bothena, also signifies a barony, lordship, &c. *Ibid.*

BOTILER OF THE KING, (*pincernes regis*) is an officer that provides the king's wines, who (according to *Fleta*) may by virtue of his office take out of every ship laden with sale wines, *unum dolium eligere in prora navis ad opus regis, & aliud in puppe, et pro qualibet pecia reddere tantum* 20 *solid. mercatori. Si autem plura inde habere voluerit, bene licebit, dum tamen pretium fide dignorum judicio pro rege apponatur. Fleta, lib.* 2. *cap.* 21. This officer shall not take more wine than he is commanded, of which notice shall be given by the steward of the king's house, &c. on pain of forfeiting double damages to the party grieved; and also to be imprisoned and ransomed at the pleasure of the king. *Stat.* 25 *Ed.* 3. *cap.* 21. 45 *Ed.* 3. *c.* 3.

BOTTOMRY, or BOTTOMREE, (*fœnus nauticum*) is in the nature of a contract or mortgage, where the master of a ship borrows money upon the keel or bottom of his ship, and binds the ship itself, that if the money be not paid by the day assigned, the creditor shall have the ship. But it is generally where a person lends money to a merchant, who wants it to traffick, and is to be paid a greater sum at the return of the ship, standing to the hazard of the voyage; in regard to which, though the interest be greater than five per cent. or what is allowed by law, it is not usury. For money lent on a sea risque, is allowed a larger interest than money advanced on land, by reason it is furnished at the hazard of the lender, and if the ship perishes, the lender shares in the loss, and loses his whole money; so that there is no real security, as in case of lands, &c. And the greater the danger is, the greater may be the profit reasonably required for the money advanced. *Lex Mercat.* 122.

Money lent on bottomree is either on the bare ship (the usual way) or upon the person of the borrower, and sometimes upon both: the first is where a man takes up money, and obliges himself, that if such a ship shall arrive at such a port, then to repay perhaps in long voyages near double the sum lent; but if the ship happens to miscarry, then nothing. But when money is lent at interest, it is delivered at the peril of the borrower, and the profit of this, is merely the price of the loan; whereas the profit of the other, is a reward for the danger and adventure of the sea, which the lender takes upon himself and makes the interest lawful. *Sea Laws* 206, 207.

When the ship and tackle are brought home, they are liable as well as the person of the borrower for the money lent: but when the loan is not made upon the vessel, but upon the goods and merchandizes laden therein, which from their nature, must be sold or exchanged in the course of the voyage; then the borrower only is personally bound to answer the contract; who therefore, in this case is said to take up money at *respondentia.* 2 *Black.* 458.

In this, consists the difference between *bottomree* and *respondentia,* that the one is a loan upon the ship, the other upon the goods: in the former, the ship and tackle are liable, as well as the person of the borrower; in the latter for the most part, recourse must be had to the person only of the borrower. *Ibid.*

Another observation is, that in a loan upon *bottomree,* the lender runs no risk though the goods should be lost; and upon *respondentia* the lender must be paid his principal and interest, though the ship perish, provided the goods are safe; but in all other respects the contract of *bottomry* and that of *respondentia* are upon the same footing. 2 *Black.* 458.

By the *Stat.* 19 *Geo.* 2. *c.* 37. every sum lent on *bottomree* or at *respondentia,* upon any subject's ships to or from the East Indies, shall be lent only on the ship, or the merchandise laden on board her, and so expressed in the condition of the bond, and the benefit of salvage shall be allowed to the lender, who alone shall have right to make assurance on the money lent. And no borrower of money, on *bottomree* or at *respondentia,* as aforesaid, shall recover more on any assurance than the value of his interest exclusive of the money borrowed. And if the value of his interest doth not amount to the money borrowed, he shall be responsible to the lender for the surplus, notwithstanding the ship and merchandise be totally lost.

By 19 *Geo.* 2. *c.* 32. obligees in bottomree bonds are admitted to claim, and after the loss or contingency shall have happened, to prove their debts, in cases of bankruptcy, in like manner, as if the loss or contingency had happened, before the time of the issuing of the commission of bankruptcy against the obligor.

BOVATA TERRÆ, as much land as one ox can plough. *Cowel. Blount.*

BOVERIUM, or BOVERIA, an ox-house. *Ibid.*

BOVETTUS, a young steer or castrated bullock. *Ibid.*

BOVICULA, an heifer or young cow; which in the east riding of Yorkshire is called a *whee,* or *whey.* *Ibid.*

BOUCHE OF COURT, commonly called *budge of court,* was a certain allowance of provision from the king, to his knights and servants, that attended him in any military expedition. The French *avoir bouche a court,* is to have an allowance at court, of meat and drink: from *bouche* a mouth. But sometimes it extended only to bread, beer, and wine. *Ibid.*

BOUGH OF A TREE, seisin of land given by it, to hold of the donor. 1 *Mad. Exch.* 62.

BOUND, or BOUNDARY, (*bunda*) the utmost limits of land, whereby the same is known and ascertained. 4 *Inst.* 318. *Cowel. Blount.*

BOUND-BAILIFFS, are sheriffs officers, for executing of process. The sheriffs being answerable for their misdemeanors, the bailiffs are usually bound in a bond, for the due execution of their office, and thence are called bound-bailiffs, which the common people have corrupted into a much more homely appellation. 1 *Black. Com.* 345, 6.

BOUNTY OF Q. ANNE, for maintaining of poor clergymen, regulated by *Stat.* 2 & 3 *Ann. c.* 11. 1 *Geo.* 1. *c.* 10. 5 *Ann. c.* 24. 6 *Ann. c.* 27.

BOW-BEARER, an under officer of the forest, whose office is to oversee, and true inquisition make, as well of sworn men as unsworn in every bailiwick of the forest; and of all manner of trespasses done, either to vert or venison, and cause them to be presented, without any concealment in the next court of attachment, &c. *Crompt. Juris. fol.* 201.

BOWYERS, one of the ancient companies of the city of London.

BRACELETS, hounds, or rather beagles of the smaller and slower kind. *Cowel. Blount.*

BRACENARIUS, (Fr. *braconnier*) a huntsman, or master of the hounds. *Ibid. Rot.* 10. in *Dorso.*

BRACETUS, a hound: *brachetus* is in Fr. *brachet, braco canis sagax, indagator leporum*: so a braco was properly the large fleet hound; and brachetus, the smaller hound; and brachete the bitch of that kind. *Ibid.*

BRACINUM, a brewing: the whole quantity of ale brewed at one time, for which *tolsestor* was paid in some manors. Brecina, a brew-house. *Ibid.*

BRANDING *in the hand,* or *face,* was a punishment inflicted by law, for various offences, by burning, with a hot iron, after the offender had been allowed clergy. 4 *Black. Com.* 360, 370. now repealed by 5 *Ann. c.* 6. 19 *Geo.* 3. *c.* 74. and 39 *Geo.* 3. *c.* 45. by which two last acts whipping or imprisonment is substituted.

BRASSUM, signifies malt: in the ancient statutes brasiator is taken for a brewer, from the Fr. *brasseur;* and at this day is used for a maltster or malt-maker. *Cowel. Blount.*

BREACH OF CLOSE, every unwarrantable entry on another's soil, the law calls a trespass, by breaking his close, the words of the writ of trespass. 3 *Black. Com.* 209.

BREACH OF COVENANT, the not performing of any covenant, expressed or implied in a deed, or the doing an act, which the party covenanted not to do. 2. *Black. Com.* 155, 6.

BREACH OF DUTY, the not executing any office, employment or trust, &c. in a due and legal manner. 3 *Black. Com.* 163, 4.

BREACH OF PEACE, offences against the public peace, are either such as are an actual breach of the peace, or constructively so, by aiding to make others break it. 4 *Black. Com.* 142. &c.

BREACH OF POUND, the breaking any pound or place where cattle or goods distrained are deposited, to rescue such distress. 3 *Black. Com.* 146.

BREACH OF PRISON. Breach of prison, by the offender himself, when committed for any cause, was felony at the common law. 1 *Hal. P. C.* 607. So was conspiring to break it. *Bract. l.* 3. *c.* 9. But this severity is mitigated by the statute *de frangentibus prisonam.* 1 *Ed.* 2. But to break prison when lawfully committed for treason or felony, remains still felony at the common law: if on any inferior charge, it is still punishable, as an high misdemeanor, by fine and imprisonment. 2 *Hawk. P. C.* 128

BREACH OF PROMISE, (*violatio fidei*) is a breaking or violating a man's word. Breach also signifies where a person commits any breach of the condition of a bond, or covenant entered into. See *Action, Assumpsit, Bond, Condition,* and *Covenant.*

BREAD AND BEER, the assize of bread, beer, and ale, &c. is granted to the lord mayor of London and other corporations: bakers, &c. not observing the assise to be set in the pillory. *Stat.* 51 *H.* 3. *St.* 1. *ord. Pistor.* & 51 *H.* 3. *St.* 6. Vide 2 & 3 *Ed.* 6. *c.* 15.

BREAD OF TREET, or TRITE, (*panis tritici*) this is also mentioned in the statute 51 *Hen.* 3. of assise of bread and ale; wherein are particularised wastel bread, cocket bread, and bread of treet, which answer to the three sorts of bread now in use, called white, wheaten, and household bread. In religious houses they heretofore distinguished bread by these several names, *panis armigerorum, panis conventualis, panis puerorum, & panis famulorum. Antiq. Not. Cowel. Blount.*

The modern acts relating to the assise of bread are in substance and effect as follows:

By 31 *Geo.* 2. *c.* 29. the assise of bread shall be regulated by the price the grain, meal, or flour bears in the market, allowing sufficient profit to the baker.

Where an assise shall be set, no sort of bread (wheaten and household excepted) other than what is thereby allowed, is to be made for sale: under penalty of not more than 40*s.* nor less than 20*s.* and the assise shall be set according to the table annexed to the act. *Ibid.*

Returns shall be made weekly to the court of mayor and aldermen of London, by the meal weighers, of the prices which the several kinds of grain, meal and flour, fit for bread, publicly sell for in the markets of the city; the prices to be entered by them on a certain day in a book to be kept in the town clerk's office; and the assize and price of bread to be set the next day; and to take place according to order, and continue till a new assize be set; and to be published forthwith. Before any advance or reduction be made in the price of bread, the meal weighers are to leave at Baker's hall a copy of the returns made that day, that the company may have time to object thereto, before the assize be set. *Ibid.*

The court of mayor and aldermen, and magistrates in other cities, towns, and boroughs, may, in like manner, cause returns to be made them of the prices, which the several sorts of grain, meal and flour, fit for bread, shall be publicly sold at in the markets, within their jurisdictions. The prices to be entered and certified in a proper book; and the assize and price of bread, to be set within two days after; and to take place, and continue (not more than seven days) and to be published, as the court or magistrates shall direct. *Ibid.*

Two or more justices within their jurisdictions may set an assize of bread, and cause returns to be made by the clerks of the neighbouring markets of the price at which grain, meal and flour, shall be there sold; the returns to be made on a certain day, and to be entered and signed in a book to be kept for that purpose; the assize and price of bread to be set within two days after, and to continue (not more than fourteen days) and to commence and be published as shall be ordered. *Ibid.*

Bakers may see the returns, the day after the same shall be made, that they may have time to object to the advance or reduction to be made in the price of bread, before the assize be set, and bakers are not liable to pay fees on account of the assize of bread. *Ibid.*

Half peck and quartern loaves are to weigh, and be sold, in due proportion to the peck loaf. Magistrates shall direct how the assize of rye, barley, or mixed bread, when ordered to be made, shall be published. *Ibid.*

Where bread of a certain denomination and value shall be ordered, or allowed to be made, no bread of a different denomination is to be sold at the same time, upon pain of not more than 40*s.* nor less than 20*s.* *Ibid.*

The justices at a general or quarter sessions may fix the jurisdiction of any hundred or place within a certain district, so as the assize of bread set for the same may extend thereto. *Ibid.*

Entry shall be made by every clerk of the market in proper books, of the returns made by him; and of the rate at which the assize and price of bread shall be set from time to time, the said books to be open to the inspection of any inhabitant. *Ibid.*

No alteration is to be made in assize of bread, unless the price of wheat, or other grain, shall vary three-pence in the bushel from the last return. *Ibid.*

Any meal weigher, or clerk of the market, who shall neglect his duty, or make a false return, and any peace officer who shall disobey the warrant of any magistrate, or justice, or otherwise neglect his duty, is to forfeit not more than 5*l.* nor less than 20*s.* *Ibid.*

Any buyer, seller, or dealer, who shall refuse to disclose to the meal weighers in London, or clerks of the markets, in other places, the true prices, the several sorts of grain, meal, and flour, shall be bought or sold at in the public market, or shall give in a false price, is to forfeit not more than 10*l.* nor less than 40*s.* *Ibid.*

Where any false return shall be suspected to be made, the court, magistrate, or justice, may within three days summon any buyer, seller, or other person, likely to give information; and examine them upon oath, touching the prices of grain, meal, and flour, within seven days before, and any person not appearing thereto, or refusing to give evidence, forfeits not more than 10*l.* nor less than 40*s.* and forswearing himself, incurs the penalties of perjury; but the party summoned is not obliged to go above five miles, from home. *Ibid.*

When an order shall be made for making bread for sale, of any other grain than wheat, or of mixed meal or flour, bakers shall conform to such order, and make the bread of such weight and goodness and at such price, as shall be therein directed, on pain of forfeiting not more than 5*l.* nor less than 40*s.* *Ibid.*

The several sorts of bread made for sale are to be always well made, and in their degrees, according to the goodness of the meal the same ought to be made of, without any adulteration or mixture, except the genuine meal, salt, water, eggs, milk, and yeast, or such leaven as shall be occasionally allowed; upon penalty of the offender (not being the servant) forfeiting not more than 10*l.* nor less than 40*s.* or being imprisoned not more than one month, nor less than ten days. If the offender be a servant he is to forfeit, not more than 5*l.* nor less than 20*s.* or be imprisoned for the like time; and the magistrate may, out of the money of the forfeiture, publish in some newspaper the offender's name, place of abode, and offence. *Ibid.*

The penalty for adulterating corn, meal, or flour, whether at the time of the grinding, dressing, or bolting, or for selling the meal of one sort of corn for another sort; or any thing mixed which shall not be of the genuine meal of the grain the same is sold for; is not to exceed 5*l* or be less than 40*s.* *Ibid.*

Where bread shall be of a different mixture of corn, than what it is imported to be of, or is allowed, or where the mixture allowed of shall not be duly observed, or where any thing shall be sold as flour, which is not genuine, the penalty is the same as last mentioned. *Ibid.*

Where bread shall be made under weight, the offender forfeits not more than 5*s.* nor less than 1*s.* for every ounce deficient, and if under one ounce, not more than 2*s.* 6*d.* nor less than 6*d.* provided such bread complained of, if in any city, town corporate, or borough, be weighed before the justice, within twenty-four hours after the same shall be baked or sold: and if in any other place within three days after the baking, or sale thereof; unless such deficiency arose by accident, or through some contrivance. *Ibid.*

Wheaten bread made for sale is to be marked W. and household H. in order to ascertain under what denomination it was made and ought to be weighed; upon penalty of not more than 20*s.* nor less than 5*s.* *Ibid.* and also 3 *Geo.* 3. *c.* 11.

Bakers demanding or taking more than the assize price, or refusing to sell any of the sorts allowed or ordered, when he has more than enough for the use of himself or customers, forfeit not more than 40*s.* nor less than 10*s.* *Ibid.*

Bread of an inferior quality to wheaten, is not to be sold for more than household, on penalty of 20*s.* *Ibid.* and also 3 *Geo.* 3. *c.* 11.

Magistrates and justices, or peace officers by them authorised, may in the day-time, enter the houses and shops of bakers, and search for and weigh the bread therein, and may seize such as shall be defective in goodness, due baking, or weight, or not properly marked, or of any different sort than is allowed of, and dispose thereof at their discretion. *Ibid.* and also 3 *Geo.* 3. *c.* 11.

Where any miller, mealman, or baker, shall be suspected of adulterating meal, the magistrate may, upon information on oath, enter the premises of such suspected person himself, and make search, or may grant a search warrant to some peace officer, and such meal as shall be deemed to have been adulterated, may be seized, together with the mixtures: if seized by a peace officer it is to be carried before a magistrate; if seized by the magistrate, or adjudged by him adulterated, he may dispose thereof as he thinks fit. *Ibid.*

The miller, mealman, or baker in whose premises such mixtures shall be found, shall forfeit not more than 10*l.* nor less than 40*s.* unless it be made appear that the same were not intended for adulteration, but for some other lawful purpose; and part of the forfeiture may be applied in publishing the offender's name, abode, and offence. *Ibid.*

Opposing any search or seizure incurs a penalty of not more than 5*l.* nor less than 20*s.* and no miller, mealman, or baker shall act as a justice under this act, on pain of 50*l.* to the informer. *Ibid.* and also 3 *Geo.* 3. *c.* 11.

Where any baker shall, on complaint, make it appear, that the offence wherewith he was charged, and paid the penalty of, arose from the wilful default of his servant, the magistrate shall cause the party to be apprehended, and on conviction, shall decree a recompence to the master, and on non-payment thereof shall commit the offender, for any time not exceeding one month, unless payment is sooner made. *Ibid.* and also 3 *Geo.* 3. *c.* 11.

Offences against this act, are to be determined in a summary way, before a magistrate, with appeal to sessions, and all prosecutions must be commenced within three days after the offence. *Ibid.*

This act is not to extend to any custom in London, the privilege of any lords of leet, or the rights of the dean and high steward of Westminster, or of the universities of Oxford, or Cambridge. *Ibid.*

By 32 *Geo.* 2. *c.* 18. the unappropriated penalties and forfeitures under the above act, shall be distributed, one moiety to the prosecutor, where the offender shall be convicted by oath, or self confession; and the other moiety with the penalties on weighing, trying, or seizure of bread, by a magistrate, to such purposes as the magistrate shall think fit.

By 3 *Geo.* 3. *c.* 11. no assized bread, and priced bread shall be made at the same time in the same place, *viz.* no assize loaves of the price of three-pence and priced loaves called half quartern loaves, no twelve-penny loaves, and half peck loaves, nor assize loaves of eighteen-pence and priced loaves called peck; upon pain of forfeiting not more than 40*s.* nor less than 10*s.*

Justices at sessions, may appoint which of the sorts of assize or priced loaves, and what other sorts of bread, and of what grain shall be made for sale; they causing an entry to be made of such orders (which may be inspected) and a copy thereof shall be set up in some market or other public place, or published in the country newspapers. *Ibid.*

A like proportion, as to weight, is to be kept between the white and wheaten bread, and the wheaten and household assize bread, *viz.* wheaten assize loaves shall weigh three parts in four of the weight of household assize loaves, on pain of forfeiting not more than 40*s.* *Ibid.*

A proportion in the price is to be kept in the peck loaf, and half peck, and its other subdivisions, both in the wheaten, and the household bread, and the household bread is to be one fourth cheaper than the wheaten; on penalty of not more than 40*s.* nor less than 10*s.* *Ibid.*

Bread not made of wheat, shall be marked with such letters as the justices shall order, and where they neglect to make such order, the maker is to mark every such loaf with two distinct letters, on penalty of not more than 40*s.* nor less than 5*s.* for every unmarked loaf. *Ibid.*

By 13 *Geo* 3. *c.* 62. standard wheaten bread shall weigh three fourths of the wheat whereof made, and be marked S. W. The peck loaf to weigh 17 pound 6 ounces avoirdupoise, and lesser loaves in proportion; seven standard loaves equal to eight wheaten, and six household.

Standard wheaten bread shall not be sold as priced loaves at the same time. Magistrates may, whenever they think proper, set the price and assize of standard wheaten bread, according to the table to the act, and bakers are liable to the same penalties as for offences concerning wheaten or household bread by the laws in being. *Ibid.*

If a baker informed against for making, marking, baking, or selling standard wheaten bread, not the whole produce of the wheat, except bran, and weighing three fourths of the wheat, shall prove that he bought the flour of miller or mealman, and discover his place of abode, the baker is to be acquitted, and the miller or mealman become subject to the penalties in 31 *Geo.* 2. *c.* 29. *Ibid.*

Where the magistrates have set the price of standard wheaten bread, they may omit other sorts, and justices at the sessions may prohibit, for three months, the making or selling other than standard wheaten bread on one month's public notice, but the Baker's company of London may object to such prohibition; and penny and two-penny loaves may be sold as by 31 *Geo.* 2. and coarser bread subject to the same act, but if sold as priced bread, subject to the same penalties, and magistrates shall have all powers by any law in being, and the same privileges, but this act is not to extend to the custom of London or Westminster, or right of the universities of Oxford and Cambridge, and all laws concerning bread shall remain; in corporations where there are two bailiffs, one is to set the assize of bread.

By 33 *Geo.* 3. *c.* 37. the proviso limiting the time of conviction in *s.* 41. of 31 *Geo.* 2. *c.* 29. is repealed, and the prosecution may be commenced within seven days.

By 36 *Geo.* 3. *c.* 22. loaves may be made of wheat, deducting only 5lb. of bran per bushel, or mixed with other grain or potatoes, and sold at such prices as shall be deemed reasonable. *s.* 1.

If such bread be deficient in weight according to the assize prescribed by 31 *Geo.*

2. c. 29. or be not marked, the offender shall be liable to the penalties of that act. s. 3.

By 41 *Geo.* 3. (u. k.) c. 12. any person may make and sell loaves made of flour of the whole produce of the wheat, or with the bran taken therefrom at any price less than the assize price of the place. s. 1.

Household bread to be marked H. and mixed, with an X. and persons who shall not mark such bread, or not well make it, or adulterate it, or make it deficient in weight, shall be liable to the present penalties with respect to bread. s. 3, 4.

Acts in force to extend to this act. s. 5.

Half quartern loaves may be made, on which an assize and price shall be set, and the provisions of former acts are extended to such loaves. s. 6.

The rights of the city of London and Baker's company are reserved. s. 7.

By 37 *Geo.* 3. c. 98. within London, and ten miles of the Royal Exchange, corn meters are to make entries at the corn meter's office every Monday of the wheat worked in the preceding week: and the meal weighers are also to make their returns according to 38 *Geo.* 3. c. 55. (see title *Corn*), and corn factors are to deliver on demand true accounts in writing, of the quantities and prices of the wheat sold and delivered by them; and corn factors are to take an oath, that they will make such returns comformable to this act, and carrying on business without such oath, is a penalty of 50*l.* s. 1—6.

Bills of parcels are to be made of meal and flour sold and delivered, on pain of 40*s.* on both buyer and seller, and the prices are to be fixed at the time of sale, and before the delivery, on pain of 20*l.* on both buyer and seller. s. 7, 8.

Buyers and sellers upon request by the meal-weighers, are to disclose the true prices, and the court of mayor and aldermen, or lord mayor or justices, may order bills of parcels of meal or flour to be produced, and the same shall be so produced, on pain of 5*l.* s. 11, 12.

The weekly returns hereby directed to be made, shall be in lieu of so much only of those as are required by 31 *Geo.* 2. as relate to wheat, and meal and flour of wheat, and the returns of other grain shall be discontinued, and the quantities shall be computed by the Winchester bushel, and sack of 280lbs. weight. s. 13, 14.

The assize of bread shall be set every Tuesday, either from the price of wheat or from that of flour, and to take place from the following Thursday, within ten miles from the Royal Exchange (Westminster and Southwark, and the bills of mortality in Surry excepted): but before any advance or reduction can be made, the meal-weighers are to leave at Baker's hall a copy of the last returns. s. 15.

Six-penny, twelve-penny, and eighteen-penny loaves, are not to be sold at the same time as pecks, half-pecks, and quarterns. s. 17.

Any corn-meter, corn-factor, baker, or meal-weigher, who shall neglect his duty, shall forfeit not exceeding 10*l.* s. 18.

Any buyer or dealer, who shall refuse to disclose the true prices, shall forfeit not exceeding 10*l.* s. 19.

When any false return is suspected, the party likely to give information may be summoned, and refusing to attend or answer on oath, is a penalty of 10*l.* and persons forswearing themselves are subject to be prosecuted for perjury. s. 20.

Bakers are not to use alum in making bread for sale, on pain of forfeiting not exceeding 10*l.* nor less than 5*l.* or in default to be imprisoned, for not exceeding six nor less than two months. s. 21.

Wardmote inquests may enter bakers shops to weigh and try bread, and seize such as shall be found deficient, which shall be disposed of by the magistrates. Persons obstructing the search or seizure of bread, shall forfeit not exceeding 5*l.* nor less than 20*s.* s. 22, 23.

The returns are not to be inspected or made known, except to such magistrates and officers, as such returns are intended to be inspected and examined by, on pain of not exceeding 20*l.* nor less than 10*l.* s. 24.

The general clauses of 31 *Geo.* 2. c. 29. as to recovery of penalties, and the indemnity of justices, are extended to this act. s. 25, 26.

By 38 *Geo.* 3. c. 62. in setting the assise of bread 5*d.* per quarter is to be added to the average price of wheat, on account of the additional duty on salt.

By 38 *Geo.* 3. c. 55. bakers within London, and ten miles of the Royal Exchange, are to make their returns of meal and flour bought by them at the cocquet office at the Mansion house, every Saturday, before eleven, if they reside within the bills of mortality, and before five in the afternoon, out of those limits. s. 1—3.

Instead of the oath required of bakers by 37 *Geo.* 3. c. 37. that they will make true returns, they shall take the oath prescribed by this act, on pain of 5*l.* for making bread without taking the oath. s. 4.

The meal-weighers returns shall be prepared from the weekly accounts of meal and flour, and contain the quantities, sorts, and prices, and average prices. s. 5.

Penalty on bakers and meal-weighers for not making returns, and on peace officers for neglect of duty, not exceeding 10*l.* s. 6.

Penalty on bakers for receiving, and on

persons selling meal or flour for giving any allowance, so as that the corn shall be made less than stated in the weekly returns, not exceeding 10*l*. *s.* 7.

In setting the assize of bread, 5*d.* per quarter to be added to the average price of wheat, and 4*d.* per sack to the average price of flour, as an allowance for the additional duty on salt. *s.* 8.

Such parts of any acts as impose a penalty on bakers not marking loaves within the limits, are repealed, and such loaves as are wheaten are to be marked W. and such as are household H. on pain of not exceeding 5*s.* nor less than 1*s.* *s.* 10.

No baker within the limits shall be liable to penalty for deficiency in weight, unless ascertained within twenty-four hours after baking. *s.* 11.

No baker or other person shall ask more for his bread than the set price, nor refuse to sell to any person, who shall tender payment for loaves in his possession, more than necessary for the immediate use of his family or customers; on pain of not exceeding 40*s.* nor less than 10*s.* *s.* 12.

Penalty for selling bread inferior to wheaten, at a higher price than household, not exceeding 10*l.* nor less than 40*s.* *s.* 13.

Magistrates, or peace officers by their warrants, may at seasonable times search bakers premises, and if any adulterated flour, bread, alum, or other ingredient be found, it may be seized and disposed of. *s.* 14.

Penalty on bakers in whose premises shall be found any alum or ingredients for adulterating flour, not exceeding 20*l.* nor less than 10*l.*; and the penalty for obstructing any search or seizure, is not exceeding 10*l.* nor less than 5*l.* *s.* 15—16.

If any baker shall make it appear that any offence for which he shall have paid the penalty shall have been occasioned by the wilful default of a servant, the justice may order his servant to make recompence, and if unable, commit him to hard labour, for not exceeding one month. *s.* 17.

Persons forswearing themselves, are guilty of perjury, and the provisions of 31 *Geo.* 2. *c.* 29. for recovery of the penalties, are to extend to this act. *s.* 18—19.

By 39 & 40 *Geo.* 3. *c.* 74, the assize and weight of bread, may be set whatever the price of wheat may be, the proportions of the tables in the former acts, being observed, according to the schedule annexed to this. *s.* 1.

The lord mayor and aldermen of London, may set the assize and weight of bread whatever the price of wheat or flour may be. *s.* 2.

The penalties for selling bread deficient in weight, or higher than the assize price, to extend to persons acting contrary to this act. *s.* 3.

Magistrates may weigh bread made for sale at any time within forty-eight hours after it has been baked, for ascertaining whether it be deficient in weight. *s.* 4.

By 45 *Geo.* 3. *c.* 23. the allowance to the bakers of London, instead of that under 31 *Geo.* 2. *c.* 29. as amended by 37 *Geo.* 3. *c.* 98. shall be when the assize is set from wheat 16*s.* per quarter, or 2*s.* per bushel, and when from flour 13*s.* 4*d.* per sack, with an addition of 6*d.* per quarter, and 5*d.* per sack, for, and on account of the new duty on salt. See also *London—Bakers.*

BRECCA, (from the Fr. *breche*) a breach or decay. In some ancient deeds there have been covenants for repairing *muros & breccas, portas & fossata*, &c. *Cowel. Blount.*

BREDE, a word used by Bracton for broad; as too large and too brede, is proverbially too long and too broad. *Cowel. Blount.*

BREDWITE, (Sax. *bread* and *white*) a fine or penalty imposed for defaults in the assise of bread: to be exempt from which, was a special privilege granted to the tenants of the honour of Wallingford by *Hen.* 2. *Paroch. Antiq.* 114. *Cowel. Blount.*

BREHON, in Ireland the judges and lawyers were anciently styled brehons; and thereupon the Irish law called the brehon law. 4 *Inst.* 358. Vide *Edm. Spencer's* State of Ireland, *p.* 1513. *edit. Hughes.* In a parliament held at Kilkenny, 40 *Ed.* 3. under Lionel duke of Clarence, the then lieutenant of Ireland, the brehon law was formally abolished. 1 *Black. Com.* 100. It is described to have been *a rule of right unwritten but delivered by tradition from one to another, in which oftentimes there appeared great show of equity* in determining the right between party and party, but in many things repugnant both to God's laws and man's. 1 *Black.* 101. 4 *Black.* 313.

BREISNA, weather-sheep. *Cowel. Blount.*

BRENAGIUM, a payment in bran, which tenants anciently made to feed their lords hounds. *Blount.*

BRETOYSE, or BRETOISE, the law of the marches of Wales, in practice among the ancient Britons. *Cowel. Blount.*

BREVE, is any writ by which a man is summoned or attached to answer in action, or whereby any thing is commanded to be done in the king's courts, in order to justice, &c. It is called *breve* from the brevity of it. *Bract. lib.* 5. *Tract.* 5. *cap.* 17. *Cowel. Blount.*

BREVE PERQUIRERE, to purchase a writ or license of trial in the king's courts, by the plaintiff, *qui breve perquisivit*: and hence comes the usage of paying 6*s.* 8*d.* fine to the king, where the debt is 40*l.* and of 10*s.* where the debt is 100*l.* &c. in suits and trials for money due upon bond, &c. *Cowel. Blount.*

BREVE DE RECTO, a writ of right, or license for a person ejected out of an estate, to sue for the possession of it when detained from him. *Ibid.*

BREVIA TESTATA, mentioned by the feodal writers, *Feud. l.* 1. 64. were written memorandums introduced to perpetuate the tenure of the conveyance and investiture, when grants by parol only became the foundation of frequent dispute and uncertainty. To this end they registered in the deed the persons who attended as witnesses; and our modern deeds are in reality nothing more than an improvement or amplification of the *brevia testata*. 2 *Black. Com.* 307.

BREVIBUS ET ROTULIS LIBERANDIS, a writ or mandate to a sheriff to deliver unto his successor the county, and the appurtenances, with the rolls, briefs, remembrances, and all other things belonging to that office. *Reg. Orig. fol.* 295

BREWERS. See Excise.

BRIBERY, (from the Fr. *briber*, to devour or eat greedily) is a high offence, where a person in a judicial place takes any fee, gift, reward or brocage, for doing his office, but of the king only. 3 *Inst.* 145. But taken largely, it signifies the receiving or offering any undue reward to, or by any person concerned in the administration of public justice, whether judge, officer, or the like, to act contrary to his duty; and sometimes it signifies the taking or giving a reward for a public office. 3 *Inst.* 9. To take a bribe of money, though small, is a great fault; and judges' servants may be punished for receiving bribes. And though a bribe be refused the offerer is punishable. *Fortescue, cap.* 51.

Bribery in judicial or ministerial officers is punishable by fine and imprisonment. Before the statute 25 *Ed.* 3. bribery in a judge was looked upon as so heinous an offence that it was sometimes punished as high treason; and it is at this day punishable, with forfeiture of office, fine and imprisonment. In the reign of king James I. the earl of M. lord treasurer of England, being impeached by the commons for refusing to hear petitions referred to him by the king, till he had received great bribes, &c. was, by sentence of the lords, deprived of all his offices, and disabled to hold any for the future, or to sit in parliament; also he was fined fifty thousaud pounds, and imprisoned during the king's pleasure. 1 *Hawk. P. C.* 170. In the eleventh year of king George I. the lord chancellor M——— had a milder punishment: he was impeached by the commons with great zeal, for bribery, in selling the places of masters in chancery for exorbitant sums, and other corrupt practices, tending to the great loss and ruin of the suitors of that court; and the charge being made good against him, being before disseised of his office, he was sentenced by the lords to pay a fine of thirty thousand pounds, and be imprisoned till it was paid. *See the State Trials.*

By statute, the chancellor, treasurer, justices of both benches, barons of the exchequer, &c. shall be sworn not to ordain or nominate any person in any office for any gift, brocage, &c. 12 *R.* 2. *c.* 2. And the sale of offices concerning the administration of public justice, &c. is prohibited on pain of forfeiture and disability, &c. by 5 & 6 *Ed.* 6. *c.* 16. In the construction of the last mentioned statute, it has been resolved that the offices of the ecclesiastical courts are within the meaning of that act, as well as the offices in the courts of common law; and it hath been adjudged, that one who contracts for an office, contrary to the purport of the said statute 5 & 6 *Ed.* 6. *c.* 16. is so disabled to hold the same, that he cannot be restored to a capacity of holding it by any grant or dispensation whatsoever. *Cro. Jac.* 269, 386. *Hawk. P. C.* 171.

Officers of the revenue taking bribes are also punishable by particular statutes, as is also the offence of bribery at parliamentary elections; for which see Parliament.

BRIBOUR, (Fr. *bribeur*) seems to signify in some of our old statutes, one that pilfers other men's goods. 28 *Ed.* 2. *cap.* 1.

BRICOLLS, an engine mentioned in *Cowel* and *Blount*, by which walls were beat down.

BRICKS. By 17 *Ed.* 4. *c.* 4. plain tiles, roof tiles, corner tiles, and gutter tiles, shall be made good, and the earth whereof they shall be made, shall be digged and cast up before November 1, next before making, and turned before February 1, and not wrought till March 1, after.

The earth is not to be mixed with the marl, or chalk whereof they are made. Plain tiles to be $10\frac{1}{2}$ inches long, $6\frac{1}{4}$ inches broad, $\frac{1}{2}$ an inch and $\frac{1}{2}$ quarter thick, roof tile 13 inches long, $\frac{1}{2}$ an inch and $\frac{1}{2}$ quarter thick, with convenient depth, gutter and cover tile $10\frac{1}{2}$ inches long, with convenient thickness, breadth, and depth. *Ibid.*

Selling tiles contrary to the act, to forfeit to the buyer double value, and justices may determine offences, and assess on the offender for every 1000 plain tiles 5*s.* for every 1000 roof tiles 6*s.* 8*d.* and for every 100 corner or gutter tiles 2*s.* *Ibid.*

The justices may appoint searchers, who are to have of the tile-maker for searching 1000 plain tiles 1*d.* 100 roof tiles $\frac{1}{2}$, and for 100 corner and gutter tiles $\frac{1}{4}$; they are to present defaults, on pain of 10*s.* *Ibid.*

By 17 *Geo.* 3. *c.* 42. all bricks made in England for sale shall be $8\frac{1}{2}$ inches long, $2\frac{1}{2}$ inches thick, and 4 wide; and all pantiles $13\frac{1}{2}$ inches long, $9\frac{1}{2}$ inches wide, and $\frac{1}{2}$ inch thick; on pain of forfeiting for bricks or tiles made of less dimensions when burnt, as follows, *viz.* 20*s.* for every 1000 of bricks, and 10*s.* for every 1000 of pantiles. *Ibid.*

Mashes of sieves, for screening sea-coal ashes, not to be more than a quarter of an inch asunder. *Ibid.*

All contracts for engrossing of bricks and

tiles, or for hindering a free sale thereof, shall be void, and the maker shall forfeit 20*l.* his clerk or agent 10*l.* half to the poor, and the other to the informer. *Ibid.*

See also Excise, (*Bricks*).

BRIDGE, (*pons*) public bridges, which are of general convenience, are of common right, to be repaired by the whole inhabitants of that county in which they lie. *Hale's P. C.* 146. 13 *Co.* 33. *Cro. Car.* 365.

But a corporation aggregate, either in respect of a special tenure of certain lands, or in respect of a special prescription; and also any private person, by reason of such special tenure, may be compelled to repair them. *Hale's P. C.* 143. *Dalt. c.* 14. 6 *Mod.* 307.

And those who are bound to repair public bridges, must make them of such heighth and strength, as shall be answerable to the course of the water; and they are not trespassers if they enter on any land adjoining to repair them, or lay the materials necessary for the repairs thereon. *Dalt. cap.* 16.

If a man makes a bridge for the common good of the king's subjects, which becomes a public conveniency, the inhabitants of the county are bound to repair it. 2 *Inst.* 70. *Rol. Abr.* 368. *Salk.* 359. 6 *Mod.* 307.

But by 43 *Geo.* 3. *c.* 59. *no bridge erected in any county by private persons shall be deemed a county bridge, to be repaired by the inhabitants, unless built in a substantial manner, under the directions of the county surveyor and the quarter sessions. s.* 5.

Indictments for not repairing of bridges, will not lie, but in case of common bridges on highways; though it hath been adjudged they will lie for a bridge on a common footway. *Mod. Cas.* 256. Not keeping up a ferry, being a common passage for all the king's people, is also indictable, as well as not keeping up bridges. 1 *Salk.* 12.

The following is the substance and effect of the acts relating to bridges.

By magna charta, 9 *Hen.* 3. *c.* 15. no town or freeman shall be distrained to make bridges but such as have been accustomed.

By 22 *Hen.* 8. *c.* 5. four justices of the peace may hear and determine annoyances of bridges, and charge such as ought to repair them; and when it cannot be known who ought to repair, the county, cities or town corporate where it lies shall be charged.

The justices may tax the inhabitants with the assent of the constables, and appoint two collectors, and two surveyors, who shall repair the bridge, and the collectors and surveyors are to account to the justices. *Ibid.*

The justices may make process into every shire against offenders, where the bridge is in one county, and the persons who ought to repair in another; the sheriff is to execute the process, and the justices are to make allowances to the collectors and surveyors. *Ibid.*

This act is not to extend to the cinque ports. *Ibid.*

Three hundred feet in the highway from the ends of bridges, shall be repaired as often as necessary; for which purpose the justices are to act as above. *Ibid.*

By 1 *Ann. stat.* 1. *c.* 18. the quarter-sessions upon presentment that a bridge is out of repair, may assess every town and parish; the money to be levied by the constables, and paid to the high constables, who are to remit it to the treasurers appointed by the justices. Persons refusing to collect or pay the money, forfeit 40*s.* treasurers paying money without order of sessions to forfeit 5*l.* collectors of the rate to be allowed three-pence in the pound, inhabitants deemed good witnesses and no certiorari to be allowed.

By 12 *Geo.* 2. *c.* 29. no money shall be expended in the repair of bridges without the presentment of the grand jury.

By 14 *Geo.* 2. *c.* 33. justices at their quarter-sessions may purchase an acre of land for the building or enlarging of county bridges.

By 43 *Geo.* 3. *c.* 59. the surveyors of county bridges are empowered to get materials for the repair of bridges, in the same manner as surveyors of highways, under 13 *Geo.* 3. *c.* 78. and the quarter sessions may widen and improve or alter the situation of county bridges, on presentment of their insufficiency. *s.* 1, 2.

Tools and materials provided by the quarter sessions are vested in the surveyor: and inhabitants of counties may sue for damages done to bridges, in the name of the surveyor. *s.* 3, 4.

This act not to extend to bridges repaired by tenure. *s.* 7.

BRIDGEMASTERS, there are bridgemasters of London bridge, chosen by the citizens, who have certain fees and profits belonging to their office, and the care of the said bridge, and bridge-house estates. *Lex. Londin.* 283.

BRIEF, (*brevis*) an abridgement of the client's case, made out for the instruction of counsel, wherein the case of the party is to be briefly but fully stated.

BRIEF AL EVESQUE, a writ to the bishop, which in *quare impedit* shall go to remove an incumbent, unless he recover or be presented *pendente lite.* 1 *Keb.* 386.

BRIEFS, or licences to make collection for loss by fire. See *stat.* 4 & 5 *Ann. cap.* 14.

BRIGA, (Fr. *brigue*) debate or contention. *Cowel. Blount.*

BRIGANDINE, (Fr. in Lat. *lorica*) is a coat of mail or ancient armour, consisting of many jointed and scale-like plates, very pliant and easy for the body. *Cowel and Blount.*

BRIGANTES, a word used in Yorkshire, Lancashire, bishoprick of Durham, Westmorland and Cumberland. *Blount.*

BRIGBOTE or BRUG-BOTE, signifies to be freed from the reparation of bridges. It is compounded of the Sax. *brig*, a bridge, and *bote*, which is a yielding of amends, or supplying a defect: but this is more properly bruckbote, from the Germ. *bruck*, i. e. a bridge, and bote, a compensation; and it is used for the liberty or exemption of being free from tribute or contribution towards the mending or re-edifying of bridges. *Fleta, lib.* 1. *c.* 47. *Selden's Titles of Honour, fol.* 622. *Cowel. Blount.*

BROCAGE, (*brocagium*) the wages or hire of a broker; which is also termed brokerage. 12 *R.* 2. *c.* 2. and 11 *H.* 4. *Rot. Stat.* 31 *Ed.* 3. *Cowel. Blount.*

BROCELLA, signifieth a wood; and it is said to be a thicket or covert of bushes and brush wood. *Cowel. Blount.*

BROCHA, (from the Fr. *broche*) an awl, or large packing needle, the use whereof is very well known. A spit in some parts of England is called a *broche*; and from this word comes to pierce or broach a barrel. *Ibid.*

BROCHIA, a great can or pitcher. *Bract. lib.* 2. *tract.* 1. *cap.* 6. Where it seems that he intends *saccus* to carry dry, and *brochia* liquid things. *Ibid.*

BRODEHALFPENY, or BROADHALFPENY. See *Bordhalfpeny.*

BROKERS, (*broccatores, broccarii & auxionarii*) are those that contrive, make and conclude bargains and contracts between merchants and tradesmen, in matters of money and merchandize, for which they have a fee or reward. The original of the word is from a trader broken, and that from the Sax. *broc*, which signifies misfortune, which is often the true reason of a man's breaking; so that the broker came from one who was a broken trader by misfortune, and none but such were formerly admitted to that employment. *Cowel. Blount.*

By the *stat.* 8 & 9 *W.* 3. *cap.* 20. they are to be licensed in London by the lord mayor, who administers an oath, and takes bond for the faithful execution of their offices: if any persons shall act as brokers, without being thus licensed and admitted, they shall forfeit the sum of 500*l.* And persons employing them 50*l.* And brokers are to register contracts, &c. under the like penalty: also brokers shall not deal for themselves, on pain of forfeiting 200*l.* They are to carry about them a silver medal, having the king's arms, and the arms of the city, &c. and pay 40*s.* a year to the chamber of the city.

By 10 *Ann. c.* 19. brokers taking above 2*s.* 6*d.* per cent. for brokage of stocks, shall forfeit 20*l.* with costs.

By 6 *Geo.* 1. *c.* 18. all undertakings tending to the prejudice of trade, and all subscriptions thereto, or presuming to act as corporate bodies without legal authority, and all acting under obsolete charters, shall be deemed illegal and void. All such undertakings are deemed public nuisances, and shall incur a *præmunire.*

Merchants or traders may have an action to recover treble damages with costs against the undertakers, and brokers buying or selling any shares in such undertakings, shall forfeit 500*l.* and be disabled.

This act not to extend to undertakings established before 1718, the two assurance companies thereby erected, or the South Sea company; nor to restrain the carrying on of any home or foreign trade in partnership. *Ibid.*

South Sea and East India companies may advance money on bottomree to their captains or other servants. *Ibid.*

Not to extend to corporations formerly created, or to any subscriptions to be made to the capital of the South Sea, nor to the powers of the East India company. *Ibid.*

By 7 *Geo.* 2. *c.* 8. all premiums to deliver, accept, or refuse any stock or share therein, shall be void, and the money returned; in default, it may be recovered by action, with double costs; and persons entering into any such contract, shall forfeit 500*l.* the like penalty is inflicted on brokers, negotiating such contracts, and also on persons who agree to sell, and are not actually possessed of, or entitled to stock; and in this case brokers transacting agreements knowingly, shall forfeit 100*l.*

Brokers are to keep a book, called the brokers book, in which they shall enter all contracts and agreements, with the names of buyers and sellers, and day of making, to be produced when required, under 50*l.* penalty. *Ibid.*

No money shall be given to compound any difference, for not delivering stock, but the whole money agreed shall be paid, and the stock transferred, on pain of 100*l.* *Ibid.*

Persons liable to be sued on this act, shall be obliged to answer a bill in equity, brought for discovering such contract or wager, and the sum or premium given, the plaintiff giving security for answering costs. *Ibid.*

Stocks sold to be delivered at a certain day, and not paid for at the time agreed, may be sold to any others, and the buyer shall make good the damage. *Ibid.*

Such stock not being transferred at the time agreed, the buyer may purchase other stock, and recover his damage. *Ibid.*

This act is not to extend to contracts for stock pursuant to order of the court of chancery, nor to hinder persons from lending money on stock, or prevent the redelivering thereof, on payment of the money lent. *Ibid.*

There are likewise pawn-brokers, who commonly keep shops, and let out money to poor necessitous people upon pawns, for the most part on extortion. See *Pawn-Brokers.*

BROK, an old sword or dagger. *Cowel. Blount.*

BROSSUS, bruised or injured with blows, wounds, or other casualty. *Ibid.*

BROTHEL-HOUSES, lewd places, being the common habitation of prostitutes. King *Hen.* 8. by proclamation, in the 37th year of his reign, suppressed all the stews or brothel-houses, which had long continued on the bank side in Southwark, contrary to the law of God and of the land. 3 *Inst.* 205. A brothelman was a loose idle fellow; and a feme bordelier or brothelier, a common whore. And borelman is a contraction of brothelman. *Chaucer. Cowel. Blount.*

BRUERE. This the Latins call *erica*, and signifies heath ground; and *brueria*, briars, thorns, or heath, from the Sax. *brær*, briar. *Ibid.*

BRUILLUS, a wood or grove; a thicket or clump of trees in a park or forest. *Ibid.*

BRUILLETUS, a small coppice or wood. *Ibid.*

BRUSCIA, sometimes signifies a wood. *Ibid.*

BRUSUA and BRUSULA, brouse or brush-wood. *Ibid.*

BUBBLES, the South-sea project, and other schemes, to raise joint-stock companies, having a tendency to defraud the subject, are called by the name of bubbles. And the *stat.* 6 *Geo.* 1. *c.* 18. makes all such unwarrantable undertakings by unlawful subscriptions subject to the penalties of a *præmunire.* 4 *Black.* 117.

BUCKLARIUM, a buckler. *Cowel. Blount.*

BUCKSTALL, a toil to take deer, which by the *stat.* 19 *Hen.* 7. *c.* 11. is not to be kept by any person that hath not a park of his own, under penalties. See also 3 *Jac.* 1. *c.* 13. There is a privilege of being quit of amerciaments for buckstalls, 4 *Inst.* 306.

BUCKWHEAT, is the same with French wheat, used in many counties of this kingdom: in Essex it is called brank; and in Worcestershire, crap. It is mentioned in the *stat.* 15 *Car.* 2. *c.* 5.

BUCINUS, a military weapon for a footman. *Tenures, pag.* 74. *Cowel. Blount.*

BUGGERY, or *sodomy*, (from the Italian *buggerare*) is a carnal copulation against nature, and this is either by the confusion of species; that is to say, a man or a woman with a brute beast; or of sexes, as a man with a man, or man unnaturally with a woman. 12 *Co. Rep.* 36. This sin was brought into England by the Lombards. *Rot. Parl.* 50 *Ed.* 3. *numb.* 58. *Stat.* 25 *H.* 8. *cap.* 6. And in ancient times, it was punishable with burning, though others say with burying alive: but, at this day it is felony excluded clergy, and punished as other felonies. 25 *H.* 8. *cap.* 6. and 5 *Eliz. cap.* 17.

By the articles of the navy, (22 *Geo.* 2. *c.* 33.) if any person in the fleet shall commit the unnatural and detestable sin of buggery or sodomy, with man or beast; he shall be punished with death by the sentence of a court martial.

It is felony both in the agent and patient consenting, except the person on whom committed be a boy under the age of discretion; when it is felony only in the agent: all persons present, aiding and abetting to this crime, are all principals, and the statutes make it felony generally: there may be accessaries before and after the fact; but though none of the principal offenders shall be admitted to clergy, the accessaries are not excluded it. 1 *Hale's Hist. P. C.* 670.

In every indictment for this offence, there must be the words, *rem habuit veneriam & carnaliter cognovit, &c.* and of consequence some kind of penetration and emission must be proved; but any the least degree is sufficient. 1 *Hawk.* 6.

BULL, (*bulla*) a brief or mandate of the pope or bishop of Rome, from the lead or sometimes gold seal affixed thereto: but by the statute 28 *Hen.* 8. *c.* 16. it was enacted, that all bulls, briefs and dispensations had or obtained from the bishop of Rome, should be void. And by 13 *Eliz. c.* 2. (vide 23 *Eliz. c.* 1.) if any person shall obtain from Rome any bull or writing to absolve or reconcile such as forsake their due allegiance, or shall give or receive absolution by colour of such bull, or use or publish such bull, &c. it is high treason.

BULL AND BOAR, by the custom of some places, a parson may be obliged to keep a bull and a boar, for the use of the parishioners, in consideration of his having tithes of calves and pigs, &c. 1 *Roll. Abr.* 559. 4 *Mod.* 241.

BULLIO SALIS, as much salt as is made at one wealing or boiling: a measure of salt, supposed to be twelve gallons. *Mon. Angl. tom.* 2.

BULLION, (Fr. *billon*) the ore or metal whereof gold is made; and signifies with us gold or silver in billet, in the mass before it is coined. *Anno* 9 *Ed.* 3. *c.* 2. *Cowel. Blount.*

BULTEL, is the bran or refuse of meal after dressed; also the bag wherein it is dressed is called a bulter, or rather boulter. *Cowel. Blount.*

BUNDLES, a sort of records of the Chancery lying in the office of the Rolls; in which are contained, the files of bills and answers, of *hab. cor. cum causa, certiorari's*, attachments, &c. *scire facias's*, certificates of statute-staple, extents and liberates, *supersedeas's*, bails on special pardons, bills from the Exchequer of the names of sheriffs, letters patent surrendered and deeds cancelled, inquisitions, privy seals for grants, bills signed by the king, warrants of escheators, customers, &c. *Ibid.*

BURCHETA, (from the Fr. *berche*) a kind of gun used in forests. *Cowel. Blount.*

BURCIFER REGIS, purse-bearer, or keeper of the king's privy purse. *Pat.* 17 *Hen.* 8. *Cowel. Blount.*

BURDARE, to jest or trifle. *Mat. Paris, Addit. p.* 149. *Cowel. Blount.*

BURGAGE, (*burgagium*) an ancient tenure proper to boroughs, whereby the inhabitants by custom hold their lands or tenements of the king, or other lord of the borough, at a certain yearly rent. *Old Tenures.* It is a kind of socage tenure, and signifieth the service whereby the borough is holden; and the king hath nothing to do with the heirs of this land, whether they be under fourteen or above that age and under twenty-one. *Co. Lit.* 109. *Jenk. Cent.* 127. 2 *Black. Com.* 82. 4 *V.* 412.

BURG, a small walled town, or place of privilege, &c. See *Borough.*

BURG-BOTE, (from *burg, castellum,* and *bote, compensatio*) is a tribute or contribution towards the building or repairing of castles, or walls of a borough or city: from which divers had exemption by the ancient charters of the Saxon kings. *Fleta, lib.* 1. *c.* 47. *Cowel. Blount.*

BURGESSES, (*burgarii* & *burgenses*) are properly men of trade, or the inhabitants of a borough or walled town; but we usually apply this name to the magistrates of such a town, as the bailiff and burgesses of Leominster, &c. *Cowel. Blount.*

We now also call those burgesses, who serve in parliament, for any borough or corporation: and no man is qualified to be such a burgess, that hath not an estate of 300*l.* a year, clear of all incumbrances. 9 *Ann. cap.* 7. 33 *Geo.* 2. *c.* 20.

BURGH-BRECHE, a fine imposed on the community of a town, for a breach of the peace, &c. *Leg. Canuti, cap.* 55. *Cowel. Blount.*

BURGHERISTHE, or *burgheriche*, is a word used in Domesday, signifying *violatio pacis in villa. Blount.*

BURGMOTE, a court of a borough. *Cowel. Blount.*

BURGHWARE, (*quasi burgiver*) a citizen or burgess. *Ibid.*

BURGLARY, (*burglaria*, from the Sax. *burg, domus,* or *arx,* & *laron, furtum*) is a felony at common law, in breaking and entering the mansion house of another, or a church, or the walls or gates of a walled town in the night-time, to the intent to commit some felony, whether the intention be executed or not. 4 *Co.* 49. *H. P. C.* 80. 1 *Hawk. P. C.* 38.

When several come with a design to commit burglary, and one does it, while the rest watch near the house, here his act is, by interpretation, the act of all of them. *Wood.* 377. If thieves pretend business to get into a house by night, and thereupon the owner of the house opens his door, and they enter and rob the house, this is burglary. *Kel.* 42. Though in such a case, juries generally find guilty of the stealing, but not of the burglary. Also if a person be within the house, and steal goods, and then open the house on the inside, and go out with the goods, this is burglary, though the thief did not break the house. 3 *Inst.* 64. If a thief unlocks a door, or draws the latch of a room to rob, &c. or if one comes down a chimney, opens a window, breaks a hole in the wall, &c. all these are a breaking: and if the thief set his foot over the threshold of the door of the house, or put his hand, pistol, &c. within the door or window, it is an entry sufficient to make it burglary. *H. P. C.* 80, 81.

Every entrance into the house by a trespasser is not a breaking in this case, but there must be an actual breaking. As if the door of a mansion house stand open, and the thief enters, this is no breaking. So it is if the window of the house be open, and a thief with a hook or other engine draweth out some of the goods of the owner, this is no burglary, because there is no actual breaking of the house. But *any the least entry, either with the whole, or with but part of the body* or without any *instrument or weapon*, will be sufficient; therefore, if the thief breaketh the glass of the window, and with a hook or other engine draweth out some of the goods of the owner, this is burglary, for there was an actual breaking of the house. 3 *Inst.* 64. And these acts amount to an actual breaking, *viz.* opening the casement, or breaking the glass window, picking open the lock of a door, or putting back the lock, or the leaf of a window, or unlatching the door that is only latched. 1 *Hale H. P. C.* 552.

One of the servants of the house opened his lady's chamber door, which was fastened with a brass bolt, with design to commit a rape, (a felony at common law); and it was ruled to be burglary, and the defendant was convicted and transported. *Stran.* 481. *Kel.* 67.

Though the house is to be a mansion-house, and the out-houses adjoining to the mansion-house are part thereof, wherein this crime may be committed; yet a barn, stable, &c. at any distance from the house, is not. 4 *Rep.* 40. But part of a house divided from the rest, having a door of its own to the street, this is a mansion-house of him who hires it. *Kel.* 84.

To break and enter a shop, not parcel of the mansion-house, in which the shop-keeper never lodges, but only works or trades there in the day-time, is not burglary, but only larceny; but if he, or his servant, usually or often lodge in the shop at night, it is then a mansion-house, in which a burglary may be committed. 1 *H. H. P. C.* 557, 558.

It is not necessary to make it burglary, that any person be actually in the house at the very time of the offence committed. 1 *Hawk.* 103.

And if on a bare assault upon a house,

without entry, the owner fling out his money, it is no burglary. *Hawk. P. C. c.* 38.

The intention to commit felony to make burglary must be of such a fact, as was felony at common law; and not of a felony newly made by act of parliament: but the offences of burglary and felony may be joined in the same indictment; and where a man commits burglary, and at the same time steals goods out of the house, if he be acquitted of the burglary, he may notwithstanding be indicted of the larceny. 2 *Hale's Hist. P. C.* 245. Taking away goods from a dwelling-house in the night or day, where any person is therein; and breaking a shop, warehouse, &c. and taking away goods privately to the value of 5*s.* though no person be therein, is burglary, by *stat.* 3 *W.* & *M. c.* 9. 10 & 11 *W.* 3. *c.* 23. And a reward of 40*l.* is given by the statute for apprehending a burglar, and prosecuting him to conviction. 5 *Ann. cap.* 31.

And by *stat.* 12 *Ann. cap.* 7. if any person shall enter into the mansion-house of another, by day or by night, without breaking the same, with an intent to commit felony, or being in such house shall commit any felony, and shall in the night-time break the said house to get out, he shall be guilty of burglary, and ousted of the benefit of clergy, in the same manner as if he had broken and entered the house in the night-time, with intent to commit felony.

But it is not burglary if it appear upon the evidence, that there was so much *day-light* at the time, that the man's countenance might be discerned thereby. *Hawk. P. C. c.* 38. This capability of discernment does not, however, extend to *moon-light*, for then many mid-night burglaries would go unpunished. And besides, the malignity of the offence doth not so properly arise from its being done in the dark, as at the dead of night, when all the creation, except beasts of prey, are at rest, when sleep has disarmed the owner, and rendered his castle defenceless. 4 *Black.* 244.

BURI, a word signifying husbandmen. *Mon. Angl. tom.* 3. *p.* 183.

BURIALS. Persons dying are to be buried in woollen, on pain of forfeiting 5*l.* And affidavit is to be made of such burying before a justice, &c. under the like penalty. *Stat.* 30 *Car.* 2. *c.* 3.

BURNETA, cloth made of dyed wool. *Cowel. Blount.*

BURNING IN THE HAND. Vide *Branding.*

BURNING *of houses, out-houses*, &c. Vide *Arson.*

BURROCHIUM, a burrock, or small ware over a river, where wheels are laid for the taking of fish. *Cowel. Blount.*

BURSA, a purse. *Ibid.*

BURSARIA, the bursery, or exchequer of collegiate and conventual bodies; or the place of receiving and paying, and accounting by the *bursarii*, or *bursers*. *Paroch. Antiq. p.* 288. But the word *bursarii* did not only signify the bursars of a convent or college; but formerly stipendiary scholars were called by the name of *bursarii*, as they lived on the burse or fund, or public stock of the university. *Cowel. Blount.*

BURSE, (*bursa, cambium, basilica*) an exchange or place of meeting of merchants. *Ibid.*

BURSHOLDERS. See *Borough-holders.*

BUSONES COMITATUS: they are mentioned in Bracton, *lib.* 3. *tract.* 2. *cap.* 1. Cowel and Blount say *busones* is used for *barones.*

BUSSA, a old word signifying a great ship. *Cowel. Blount.*

BUSSELUS, a bushel; from *buza, butta, buttis*, a standing measure: and hence *butticella, butticellus, bussellus*, a less measure. Some derived it from the old Fr. *bouts*, leather continents of wine; whence come our leather budget and bottles. *Kennet's Gloss.*

BUSTA and BUSTUS, *busca*, and *buscus, etc.* The same with *brucia* and *brusula*. *Cowel. Blount.*

BUSTARD, a large bird of game, usually found on downs and plains, mentioned in *stat.* 25 *Hen.* 8. *cap.* 11.

BUTT, (*butticum*) a measure of wine, &c. well known among merchants, and containing 126 gallons of Malmsey wine. *Stat.* 1 *R. c.* 13.

BUTTER AND CHEESE. The following is the substance of the acts relating to butter and cheese:

By 9 *Hen.* 6. *c.* 8. a wey of cheese shall contain thirty-two cloves.

By 4 & 5 *W.* & *M. c.* 7. warehouse keepers, shippers, or others refusing to receive and ship butter, to forfeit 10*s.* for every firkin of butter, and 5*s.* for every wey of cheese. Masters of ships not taking on board, half such penalties. *s.* 4.

By 36 *Geo.* 3. *c.* 76. coopers shall make vessels, intended for packing of butter, of well-seasoned timber, and tight, and not leaky, in tubs weighing not less than eleven nor more than fifteen pounds, avoirdupois; firkins not less than seven, nor more than eleven pounds; and every half firkin not less than four, nor more than six pounds; and the same shall be capable of holding, tubs eighty-four pounds, avoirdupois, firkins fifty-six pounds, and half firkins twenty-eight pounds, of butter, on penalty of 10*s.* for each vessel made contrary to the above directions. *s.* 1.

Vessels are to be branded with the name of the maker, and the weight thereof, on penalty of 10*s.* *s.* 2.

Dairymen are to pack their butter in no other vessels, and before packing they shall soak and season them, and brand in the inside, on the bottom, and on the outside, at the top, and also on the bouge on the staves, their Christian and surnames, on pain of *5l.* *s.* 3.

The quantities packed shall be good and merchantable, and exclusive of the tare of the cask, eighty-four pounds net weight of butter in each tub, fifty-six pounds in firkins, and twenty-eight pounds in half firkins, and such butter shall not be mixed nor salted with great salt, on pain of *5l.* for each offence. *s.* 4.

Any farmer, dairyman, factor, or other person whomsoever, guilty of any fraud whatsoever, in respect of the said matters, shall forfeit *30l.* *s.* 5.

The full quantity of butter shall be delivered in the vessels, and if not, satisfaction may be recovered, with costs by action at law. *s.* 6.

Persons repacking butter in any vessel, for sale again, are to forfeit *5l.* but foreign butter may be repacked in vessels used for British butter, defacing the original marks, and branding instead thereof their own names, and the words foreign butter. *s.* 8.

Persons counterfeiting the names or marks of farmers, are to forfeit *30l.* *s.* 9.

Penalties not exceeding *5l.* are recoverable before one justice; if exceeding *5l* in courts of record, with costs; the whole to the informer. *s.* 10—14.

The act does not extend to vessels containing not more than fourteen pounds. *s.* 15.

By 38 *Geo.* 3. *c.* 73. persons making vessels for packing butter shall brand them with their name and place of abode, on pain of *10s.* and factors buying or selling butter in vessels not legally marked are to forfeit *20s.* Also dealers having in their possession butter in vessels not legally marked, are to forfeit *10s.* to be recovered as under last act; but this act does not extend to Scotland.

BUTTONS. See *Manufactures.*

BUTTS, the place where archers met with their bows and arrows to shoot at a mark, was called shooting at the butts. Also butts are the ends or short pieces of land in arable ridges and furrows; *buttum terræ*, a butt of land. *Cowel. Blount.*

BUTLERAGE OF WINES, signifies that imposition upon wine brought into the kingdom, which the king's butler may take of every ship, *viz.* *2s.* for every ton of wine imported by strangers. 1 *Black.* 314, 315.

BUTHSCARLE, *butsecarl, buscarles,* (*buscarli & buthsecarli*) mariners or seamen. *Selden's Mare Clausum, fol.* 184.

BUZONIS, seems to be the shaft of an arrow, before it is fledged or feathered. *Cowel. Blount.*

BYE, words ending in by or bee, signify a dwelling place or habitation, from the Sax. *bye. Ibid.*

BY-LAWS, (*bilagines*, from the Goth, *by*, *pagus*, and *lagen*, *lex*) A by-law is a private law or statute, made by those who are duly authorised thereunto by charter, prescription, or custom, for the conservation of order and good government within some particular place or jurisdiction. *Moor* 583. 5 *Co.* 62.

Such as orders and constitutions of corporations, for the governing of their members; of courts-leet and courts-baron; commoners or inhabitants in vills, made by common assent, for the good of those that made them, in particular cases, whereunto the public law doth not extend; so that they lay restrictions on the parties, not imposed by the common or statute law: guilds and fraternities of trades, by letters patent of incorporation, may likewise make by-laws, for the better regulation of trade among themselves, or with others. *Kitch.* 45, 72. 6 *Rep.* 63.

For a power of making by-laws is included in the very act of incorporating, and incident to every corporation aggregate, without express words in the charter; and all by-laws must ever be subject and squared to the rule of the general law of the realm, as subordinate to it, otherwise they will be void. *Hob.* 211. 1 *Black.* 475.

A by-law by a corporation may inflict a penalty, recoverable by distress, or action of debt, and be good. 1 *Danv. Abr.* 738. But it cannot be made with a penalty of imprisonment or forfeiture of goods and chattels. 5 *Co.* 64. 8 *Co.* 127. 2 *Inst.* 54. For a by-law may not be made *on pain of forfeiture of goods:* nor may it inflict imprisonment, being contrary to magna charta. 2 *Inst.* 54.

All by-laws are to be reasonable; and ought to be for the common benefit, and not private advantage of any particular persons; and must be consonant to the public laws and statutes, as subordinate to them. *Godsb.* 79. And by 19 *H.* 7. *c.* 7. by-laws made by corporations are to be approved by the lord-chancellor, or chief justices, on pain of *40l.*

C

CABALLA, (from the Lat. *caballus*) belonging to a horse. *Domesday.*

CABLISH, (*cablicium*) signifies brushwood, according to the writers of the forest laws: but according to *Spelman*, it is more properly windfall-wood, because it was written of old *cadibulum*, from *cadere*: or if derived from the Fr. *chabilis*, it also must be windfall-wood. *Cowel. Blount.*

CABLES. By 25 *Geo.* 3. *c.* 56. no person shall make or sell any cordage for shipping in which any hemp is used, called short chucking, half clean, whale line, or other toppings, codilla, or any damaged hemp, on pain of forfeiting the same, and also treble the value thereof.

Cables, hawsers, or ropes, made of materials not prohibited by this act, and whose quality shall be inferior to clean Petersburgh hemp, shall be deemed inferior cordage, and the same shall be distinguished by marking on the tally, staple or inferior. Manufacturers making default herein forfeit for every hundred weight of cordage 10*s*. *Ibid.*

Manufacturers are to affix their names and manufactory, to new cordage, before sold, under the like forfeiture: and putting a false name is a forfeiture of 20*l*. *Ibid.*

Persons making cables of old and overworn stuff, containing above seven inches in compass, shall forfeit four times the value. *Ibid.*

Vessels belonging to British subjects, having on board foreign made cordage, are to make entry thereof, on entering into any British port, on penalty of 20*s*. for every hundred weight. But this is not to extend to cordage, brought from the East Indies; nor to materials at present used by any vessels built abroad before this act. *Ibid.*

CACHEPOLUS or CACHERELLUS, an inferior bailiff, a catchpole. *Cowel. Blount.*

CADE, of herrings is 500, of sprats 1000. *Ibid.*

CADET, the younger son of a gentleman; now applied to a volunteer in the army, waiting for some post. *Ibid.*

CAEP GILDUM, the restoring goods or cattle. *Blount.*

CAGIA, a cage or coop for birds. *Cowel. Blount.*

CALAMUS, a cane, reed, or quill. *Ibid.*

CALANGIUM and CALANGIA, a challenge, claim, or dispute. *Ibid.*

CALCETUM, CALCEA, a causey or common hard way, maintained, and repaired with stones and rubbish, from the Lat. *calx*, chalk, Fr. *chaux*, whence their *chaussee* and our *causway*, or path raised with earth, and paved with chalk-stones, or gravel. *Calcearium operationes* were the work and labour done by the adjoining tenants: and *calcagium* was the tax or contribution paid by the neighbouring inhabitants towards the making and repairing such common roads; from which some persons were especially exempted by royal charter. *Kennet's Gloss. Cowel. Blount.*

CALEFAGIUM, a word signifying a right to take fuel yearly. *Blount.*

CALENDAR. By 24 *Geo.* 2. *c.* 23. the commencement of the year was regulated, and the calendar corrected, and settled according to the form specified in the book of common prayer.

And 25 *Geo.* 2. *c.* 30. enacts, that the opening of commons, and doing other things depending on the movable feasts shall be according to the new calendar.

CALENDAR OF PRISONERS. A list of all the prisoners names, in the custody of each sheriff. Where prisoners are capitally convicted at the assizes, the judge may command execution to be done, without any writ. And the usage now is, for the judge to sign the calendar, which contains all the prisoners names, with their several judgments in the margin, and this calendar is left with the sheriff. As, for a capital felony, it is written opposite to the prisoner's name, "hanged by the neck." Formerly in the days of Latin and abbreviation, "*sus. per coll.*" for "*suspendatur per collum.*" *Staundeford, P. C.* 182. And this is the only warrant that the sheriff has, for so material an act, as the taking away the life of another. 4 *Black. Com.* 396,7. But Professor *Christian*, in a note upon this observation of the learned commentator states, that "though it be true, that a marginal note of a calendar, signed by the judge, is the only warrant that the sheriff has for the execution of a convict, yet it is made with more caution and solemnity than above represented. At the end of the assizes, the clerk of assize makes out in writing, four lists of all the prisoners, with separate columns, containing their crimes, verdicts and sentences, leaving a blank column, in which, if the judge has reason to vary the course of the law, he writes opposite the names of the capital convicts, *to be reprieved, respited, transported,* &c. these four calendars, being first carefully compared together by the judge and the clerk of assize, are signed by them, and one is given to the sheriff, one to the gaoler, and the judge and the clerk of assize each keep another. If the sheriff receives afterwards no special order from the judge, he executes the judgment of the law in the usual manner, agreeably to the directions of his calendar. In every county, this important subject is settled with great deliberation by the judge and the clerk of assize, before the judge leaves the assize town; but probably in different counties, with some slight variation, as in *Lancashire*, no calendar is left with the gaoler, but one is sent to the Secretary of State. 4 *Black. Ed.* 1809. *p.* 404.

If the judge thinks it proper to reprieve a capital convict, he sends a memorial or certificate *to the king's most excellent majesty*, directed to the Secretary of State's office, stating that, from favourable circumstances appearing at the trial, he recommends him to his majesty's mercy, and to a pardon upon condition of transportation, or some slight punishment. This recommendation is always attended to. *Ibid.*

CALENDS, (*calendæ*) among the Romans was the first day of every month, being spoken of it by itself, or the very day of the new moon, which usually happen together: and if *pridie*, the day before, be added to it, then it is the last day of the foregoing month; as *pridie calend.* Septemb. is the last day of August. If any number be placed with it, it signifies that day in the former month, which comes so much before the month named; as the tenth calends of October is the 20th day of September; for if one reckons backwards, beginning at October, the 20th day of September makes the 10th day before October. In March, May, July, and October, the calends begin at the sixteenth day, but in other months at the fourteenth; which calends must ever bear the name of the month following, and be numbered backwards from the first day of the said following months. *Hopton's Concord, p.* 69. In the dates of deeds, the day of the month, by *nones, ides*, or *calends*, is sufficient. 2 *Inst.* 675. See *Ides.*

CALIBURNE, the famous sword of the great king Arthur. *Hovedon and Brompton in vita R.*

CALLING THE PLAINTIFF. It is usual for a plaintiff, when he or his counsel perceives that he has not given evidence sufficient to maintain his issue, to be voluntarily nonsuited, or withdraw himself: whereupon the crier is ordered to call the plaintiff; and if neither he, nor any one for him, appears, he is nonsuited, the jurors are discharged, the action is at an end, and the defendant shall recover his costs. In fact, neither the plaintiff nor any one for him appears, unless council, or party, insist on the evidence, such as it is, being sent to the jury, which is seldom done, unless council have very good reasons for it. A nonsuit is not (like a verdict) a bar to the plaintiff's bringing another action, when he can get better proof, &c. 3 *Black.* 376.

CALLIS, the king's highway, mentioned in some of our ancient authors. *Cowel. Blount.*

CAMERA, from the old Germ. *cam. cammer*, crooked; whence comes our English *kembo*, arms in kembo. But camera at first signified any winding or crooked plat of ground; as *unam cameram terræ*, i. e. a nook of land. *Du Fresne.* Afterwards the word was applied to any vaulted or arched building; and by degrees more particularly restrained to an upper room or chamber: and it is now often used in the law, in the business of a judge, where persons are to be brought before him *apud cameram suam situat.* in Serjeant's-Inn, &c. The present Irish use *cama* for a bed. See *Kennet's Gloss.*

CAMERA STELLATA. The Star Chamber.

CAMISIA, a garment belonging to priests, called the *alb.* *Cowel. Blount.*

CAMOCA, a garment made of silk, or something better. *Mon. Angl. Tom.* 3. 81.

CAMPANA BAJULA, a small hand-bell, much in use in the ceremonies of the Roman church; and retained among us by sextons, parish clerks and criers. *Cowel.*

CAMPARTUM, any part of a larger field or ground, which would otherwise be in gross or common. *Ibid.*

CAMPERTUM, is used for a corn-field. *Cowel. Blount.*

CAMPFIGHT, the fighting of two champions or combatants in the field. 3 *Inst.* 221.

CAMPUS MAII, or MARTII, was an assembly of the people every year upon May-day, where they confederated together to defend the country against foreigners and all enemies. *Cowel. Blount.*

CANCELLI. Lattice work. 2 *Black.* 308.

CANCELLING DEEDS. A deed may be cancelled and avoided; 1st, by razure, interlining, or other alteration in any material part; unless a memorandum be made thereof at the time of the execution and attestation. 11 *Rep.* 27. 2dly, by breaking off, or defacing the seal. 5 *Rep.* 23. 3dly, by delivering it up to be cancelled; that is, to have lines drawn over it in the form of lattice work or *cancelli*; though the phrase is now used figuratively for any manner of obliteration or defacing of it: 4thly, by the disagreement of such, whose concurrence is necessary in order for the deed to stand; as the husband, where a feme covert is concerned; an infant or person under duress, when those disabilities are removed, and the like; 5thly, by the judgment or decree of a court of judicature. This was anciently the province of the court of Starchamber, and now of the Chancery: as when it appears that the deed was obtained by fraud, force, or other foul practice, or is proved to be an absolute forgery. *Tothil Rep.* 24, in any of which cases, the deed may be avoided either in part or totally, according as the cause of avoidance is more or less extensive. 2 *Black.* 308, 309.

CANCELLING OF WILLS. Although a man make a last will and testament irrevocable in the strongest words; yet he is at liberty to revoke it; because his own act or words cannot alter the disposition of law so as to make that irrevocable which is in its own nature revocable: for this, said *Lord Bacon*, would be for a man to deprive himself of that which of all other things is most incident to human conditions; and that is, alteration or repentance. 8 *Rep.* 82. *Bac. Elem. c.* 19. 2 *Black.* 502.

CANDLEMAS-DAY, the feast of the purification of the blessed Virgin Mary, being the second day of February, instituted in memory and honour of the purification of the said virgin, in the temple of Jerusalem, the fortieth day after her happy child-birth, according to the law of Moses, and the presentation of our blessed Lord. It is called Candlemas, or a mass of candles, because before mass was said that day, the church consecrated and set apart, for sacred use, candles for the whole year, and made a procession with hallowed candles, in remembrance of the divine light, wherewith Christ illuminated the whole church at his presentation in the temple, when by old Simeon stiled, a light to lighten the Gentiles, and to be the glory of his people Israel. *St. Luke, cap.* 2 *ver.* 32.

This festival is *a dies non*, or no day in court, for the judges sit not.

CANES OPERTIÆ, dogs with whole feet, not lawed. *Cowel. Blount.*

CANESTELLUS, a basket. In the inquisition of serjeancies, and knight's fees, *anno* 12 & 13 of king John, for Essex and Hertford, it appears that one John of Liston held a manor by the service of making the king's baskets. *Ex Libro Rub. Scac. fol.* 137.

CANFARA. (See *Ordeal.*) A trial by hot iron, formerly used in this kingdom. *Cowel. Blount.*

CANIPULUS. This word hath been taken for a short sword. *Cowel. Blount.*

CANNA, a rod or distance in the measure of ground. *Ibid.*

CANON LAW. The canon law is a body of Roman ecclesiastical law, relative to such matters as that church either has, or pretends to have, the proper jurisdiction over. 1 *Black.* 82.

This is compiled from the opinions of the ancient Latin fathers; the decrees of general councils, and the decretal epistles and bulls of the holy see: all which lay in the same disorder as the Roman civil law; (See title *Civil Law.*) Till about the year 1151, one Gratian, an Italian monk, animated by the discovery of *Justinian's* Pandects, reduced the ecclesiastical constitutions into some method in three books; which he entitled *Concordia Discordantium Canonum*, but which are generally known by the name of *Decretum Gratiani*, these reached as low as the time of pope *Alexander* III. The subsequent papal decrees, to the pontificate of *Gregory* IX. were published in much the same method, under the auspices of that pope, about the year 1230, in five books, entitled *Decretalia Gregorii Noni.* A sixth book was added by *Boniface* VIII. about the year 1298, which is called *Sextus Decretalium:* the Clementine constitutions or decrees of *Clement* V. were in like manner authenticated in 1317 by his successor *John* XXII. who also published twenty constitutions of his own, called the *Extravagantes Joannis:* all which in some measure, answer to the novels of the civil law: to these have been since added some decrees of later popes, in five books, called *Extravagantes Communes.* And all these together, *Gratian's* decree, *Gregory's* decretals, the sixth decretal, the *Clementine* constitutions, and the *extravagants* of John and his successors, form the *corpus canonici*, or body of the Roman canon law. 1 *Black.* 82.

Besides these pontifical collections, which during the times of popery, were received as authentic in this island, as well as in other parts of Christendom, there is also a kind of national canon law, composed of *legatine* and provincial constitutions, and adapted only to the exigencies of this church and kingdom. The *legatine* constitutions were ecclesiastical laws, enacted in *national synods*, held under the cardinals *Otho* and *Othobon*, legates from pope *Gregory* IX. and pope *Clement* IV. in the reign of king Henry III. about the years 1220 and 1268. The *provincial* constitutions are principally the decrees of *provincial synods* held under divers archbishops of Canterbury from *Stephen Langton* in the reign of Hen. III. to *Henry Chichele*, in the reign of Hen. V., and also adopted by the province of York, in the reign of Hen. VI. At the dawn of the reformation, in the reign of king Hen. VIII. it was enacted in parliament, (25 *Hen.* 8. *c.* 19. *revived* and *confirmed* by 1 *Eliz. c.* 1.) that a review should be had of the canon law; and, till such review should be made, all canons, constitutions, ordinances, and synodals provincial, being then already made, and not repugnant to the law of the land, or the king's prerogative, should still be used and executed: *and as no such review has yet been perfected, upon this statute depends the authority of the canon law of England.* 1 *Black.* 83.

For as to the canons, enacted by the clergy under *James* I. in the year 1603, and never confirmed in parliament, it has been solemnly adjudged upon the principles of law and the constitution, that where they are not merely declaratory of the ancient canon law; but are introductory of new regulations, they do not bind *the laity*, not being confirmed by parliament: although the clergy are clearly bound by the canons confirmed by the king only. 1 *Black.* 83. 2 *Str.* 1057. 2 *Atk.* 605. 2 *Bl. Rep.* 968.

CANON RELIGIOSORUM, a book wherein the religious of convents had a fair transcript of the rules of their order, which were frequently read among them as their local statutes; and this book was therefore called *Regula* and *Canon*. *Kennet's Gloss.*

CANTEL, (*cantellum*) a lump, or a piece of any thing, as a cantel of bread, and the like.

CANTRED, (*cantredus*) a British word from *cant*, or *cantre*, which in the British tongue signifies *centum*, and *tret*, a town or village, is in Wales an hundred villages: for the Welsh divide their counties into *cantreds*, as the English do into hundreds. *Cowel.*

CAPACITY, (*capacitas*) the capacity or ability in contemplation of law, to give or take lands, or other things, sue or defend actions, or commit treason, felony, or other crimes, is treated of under *Infants, Ideots*, and other proper heads.

CAPE, (*Lat.*) is a writ judicial, touching plea of lands or tenements; so termed, as most writs are, of that word in it, which carries the chief intention or end thereof: and this writ is divided into *cape magnum*, or *grand cape*, and *cape parvum*, or *petit cape*, both of which take hold of things immovable. *Blount.*

The *grand cape*, is a writ that lies before appearance to summon the tenant to answer the default, and also over to the demandant: and in the *Old. Nat. Brev.* it is defined to be, where a man hath brought a *præcipe quod reddat* of a thing touching plea of land, and the tenant makes default at the day to him given in the original writ, then this writ shall go for the king to take the land into his hands; and if the tenant come not at the day given him thereby, he loseth his land, &c. See *Reg. Jud. fol.* 1. *Bract. lib.* 3. *tract.* 3. *c.* 1. *Blount.*

The *petit cape*, is where the tenant is summoned in a plea of land, and comes on the summons, and his appearance is recorded; if at the day given him he prays the view, and having it granted, makes default; then this writ shall issue for the king, &c. *Old Nat. Brev.* 162. The difference between the *grand cape* and *petit cape* is, that the *grand cape* is awarded upon the tenant's not appearing or demanding the view in such real actions, where the original writ does not mention the particulars demanded; and the *petit cape* is after appearance or view granted; and whereas the *grand cape* summons the tenant to answer for the default, and likewise over to the demandant: *petit cape* summons the tenant to answer the default only: and therefore it is called *petit cape*; though some say it hath its name, not because it is of small force, but by reason it consists of few words. *Reg. Jud. fol.* 2. *Fleta, lib.* 2. *c.* 44. *Blount.*

CAPE AD VALENTIAM. This is a species of *cape magnum*, and is where I am impleaded of lands, and vouch to warrant another, against whom the summons *ad warrantizandum* hath been awarded, and he comes not at the day given; then if the demandant recover against me, I shall have this writ against the vouchee, and recover so much in value of the lands of the vouchee, if he hath so much; if not, I shall have execution of such lands and tenements as shall after descend to him in fee; or if he purchases afterwards, I shall have against him a re-summons, &c. And this writ lies before appearance. *Old. Nat. Br.* 161. *Blount.*

CAPELLA. Before the word chapel was restrained to an oratory or depending place of divine worship: it was used also for any sort of chest, cabinet, or other repository of precious things, especially of religious reliques. *Kennet's Paroch. Antiq. p.* 580.

CAPELLUS, a cap, bonnet, or other covering for the head. *Blount.*

CAPIAS AD RESPONDENDUM, is a writ or process before judgment, to take the defendant and make him answer the plaintiff.

CAPIAS AD SATISFACIENDUM, is a judicial writ which issues after a judgment recovered; or the like. And by this writ the sheriff is commanded to take the body of the defendant in execution, and him safely to keep, so that he have his body in court at the return of the writ, to satisfy the plaintiff his debt and damages. When the body is taken upon a *ca. sa.* and the writ is returned and filed, it is an absolute and perfect execution against the defendant, and no other execution can be against his lands or goods. But where a person dies in execution, his lands and goods are liable to satisfy the judgment, by statute 21 *Jac.* 1. *c.* 24. *Rol. Abr.* 904. 1 *Lit. Abr.* 249.

CAPIAS UTLAGATUM, is a writ that lies against a person who is outlawed in any action, by which the sheriff apprehends the party outlawed, for not appearing upon the *exigent*, and keeps him in safe custody till the day of return, and then presents him to the court, there to be ordered for his contempt.

When a person is taken upon a *capias utlagatum*, the sheriff is to take an attorney's engagement to appear for him, where special bail is not required; and his bond with sureties to appear, where it is required. Stat. 4 & 5 *W. & M. c.* 18. This writ is either general against the body; or, special, against the body, lands and goods. And the plaintiff, (after an inquisition taken thereupon, and returned into the Exchequer) may have the lands extended, and a grant of the goods, &c. whereby to compel the defendant to appear; which when he doth, if he reverse the outlawry, the same shall be restored to him. *Old Nat. Br.* 154.

CAPIAS PRO FINE, is where one, who is fined to the king for some offence committed against a statute, does not discharge the fine according to the judgment; whereupon his body is to be taken by this writ, and committed to prison until he pay the fine. 3 *Rep.* 16.

CAPIAS IN WITHERNAM, a writ lying for cattle in withernam, which is, where a distress taken is driven out of the county, so that the sheriff cannot make deliverance in replevin, when this writ issues to the sheriff to take as many beasts of the distrainer, &c. *Reg. Orig.* 82, 83. Vide *Withernam.*

CAPIATUR, (judgment *quod*) formerly if final judgment was for the plaintiff, it was also considered that the defendant should be either amerced, for his wilful delay of justice in not immediately obeying the king's writ, by rendering the plaintiff his due, (5 *Rep.* 49.) or be taken up, (*capiatur*) to pay a fine to the king, in case of any forcible injury. But now by stat. 5 *W. & M. c.* 12. *capias* shall not issue for this fine, but plaintiff shall pay 6*s.* 8*d.* and be allowed it against defendant in costs. Therefore in judgments in Common Pleas, they enter that the fine is remitted: in King's Bench they take no notice of any fine or capias. *Salk.* 54. *Carth.* 390.

CAPITA, (*distribution by*) *i. e.* to every man an equal share of personal estate, when all the claimants claim in their own right, as in equal degree of kindred, and not *jure representationis.* 2 *Black. Com.* 517.

Capita, (*succession by*) where the claimants are next in degree to the ancestor, in their own right, and not by right of representation. 2 *Black. Com.* 217, 218.

CAPITALE, signifies a thing which is stolen or the value of it. *Leg. H.* 1. *cap.* 59. *Blount.*

CAPITALE VIVENS, hath been used for live cattle. *Ibid.*

CAPITE, *tenants in*, (from *caput*, i. e. *Rex, unde tenere in capite, est tenere de rege, omnium terrarum capite*) an ancient tenure, whereby a man held lands of the king immediately as of the crown, whether by knight's service, or in socage. *Kitch.* 129. *Dyer* 44. *F. N. B.* 5. 2 *Black.*

But tenure in *capite* is now abolished; and by stat. 12 *Car.* 2. *c.* 24. all tenures are turned into free and common socage: so that tenures hereafter to be created by the king are to be in common socage only; and not by *capite*, knight's service, or the like. *Blount.*

CAPITILITIUM, a word used to signify what we now call poll-money. *Blount.*

CAPITITIUM, a covering for the head. *Ibid.*

CAPITULI AGRI, the head-lands, lands that lie at the head or upper end of the land or furrows. *Kennet's Paroch. Antiq. p.* 137. *Cowel. Blount.*

CAPITULA RURALIA, assemblies or chapters held by rural deans and parochial clergy within the precinct of every distinct deanery; which at first were every three weeks, afterwards once a month, and more solemnly once a quarter. *Cowel.*

CAPTION, (*captio*) when any commission at law or in equity is executed, the commissioners subscribe their names to a certificate, testifying when and where the commission was executed; and this is called a *caption.*

Also where a man is arrested, the act of taking him is termed a *caption.* There is also the *caption* of an indictment, which is the setting forth of the style of the court before which the jurors made their presentment.

CAPTAIN, (*capitaneus*) one that leadeth or hath the command of a company of soldiers, or a ship of war. *Cowel. Blount.*

CAPTIVES, as in the goods of our enemy, so also in his *person* a man may acquire a sort of qualified property, by taking him a prisoner in war, at least till his ransom is paid. 2 *Black.* 402.

CAPTURE, (*captura*) signifies the taking of prizes, in time of war, which are to be divided between the captors, according to a particular act which passes at the commencement of every new war.

CAPUTAGIUM, head or poll-money. See *Chevage.*

CAPUT ANNI, new year's day, upon which of old was observed the *festum stultorum.* *Cowel. Blount.*

CAPUT BARONIÆ, is the castle or chief seat of a nobleman; which descends to the eldest daughter, if there be no son, and must not be divided among the daughters like unto lands, &c. *Ibid.*

CAPUT JEJUNII, in our records is used for Ash-Wednesday, being the head, or first day of the beginning of the Lent-fast. *Paroch. Antiq. p.* 132. *Cowel. Blount.*

CAPUT LOCI, the head or upper end of any place; *ad caput villæ*, at the end of the town. *Ibid.*

CAPUT LUPINUM, anciently an outlawed felon was said to have *caput lupinum*, and might be knocked on the head like a wolf. But now the wilful killing of such a one would be murder. 1 *Hal. P. C.* 497. 4 *Black.* 320.

CAR and CHAR, the names of places beginning with *car* and *char*, signify a city, from the British *caer*, viz. *Civitas*, as *Carlisle, Caerleon.* *Cowel. Blount.*

CARAVANNA, a caravan, or joint company of travellers in the eastern countries, for mutual conduct and defence. *Ibid.*

CARCAN, is sometimes expounded for a pillory. *Ibid.*

CARCATUS, signifies loaden: a ship with her freight. *Ibid.*

CARDS AND DICE. See STAMPS.

CARECTA and CARECTATA, a cart and cartload. *Cowel. Blount.*

CARETARIUS, or CARECTARIUS, a carter. *Ibid.*

CARISTIA, dearth, scarcity, dearness. *Ibid.*

CARITAS, *ad caritatem, poculum caritatis*, a grace cup; or an extraordinary allowance of wine, or other liquor, wherein the religious at festivals drank in commemoration of their founders and benefactors. *Cartular. Abbat. Glaston. A. S. f.* 29. *Ibid.*

CARK, a quantity of wool, whereof thirty make a sarpler. *Stat.* 27 *H.* 6. *c.* 2. *Ibid.*

CARNARIUM, a charnel house, or repository for the bones of the dead. *Ibid.*

CARNO. This word seems to signify an immunity or privilege, as appears in *Cromp. Jurisd. fol.* 191. *Ibid.*

CARPEMEALS, cloth made in the northern parts of England, of a coarse kind, mentioned in 7 *Jac.* 1. *cap.* 16.

CARR, in some places is a kind of cart with wheels, in others a slide drawn, and sliding on the ground. *Ibid.*

CARRAT, a weight of four grains in diamonds, &c. And this word it is said was formerly used for any weight or burden. *Cowel. Blount.*

CARRELS, closets, or apartments for privacy and retirement. Three pews or carrels, where every one of the old monks, after they had dined, did resort, and there study. *Davies Mon. of Durham, p.* 31.

CARRETA, hath been taken for a carriage, cart, or wain load; as *carreta fœni* is used in an old charter for a load of hay. *Cowel. Blount.*

CARRICK, or CARRACK, (*carrucha*) a ship of great burden, so called of the Italian word *carico* or *carco*, which signifies a burden or charge. *Cowel. Blount.*

CARRIERS. All persons carrying goods for hire, as masters, and owners of ships, lightermen, stage-coachmen, and the like, come under the denomination of common carriers, and are chargeable on the custom of the realm for their faults and miscarriages, and it is said that they are liable in respect of their reward, but the true ground of their liability is *the public employment* they undertake. *Co. Lit.* 89. *Rol. Abr.* 2, 338. *Salk.* 17. *pl.* 8. 143. *Ld. Raym.* 646, 917. 12 *Mod.* 487.

Also if a person who is no common carrier, takes upon himself to carry another man's goods, though the other promise him no reward, yet if the goods are lost or damaged, by such person's *own* default, the owner shall have an action against him, for by taking the trust on himself, he is obliged to execute it; but if the goods are misused by another, he is not liable. *Salk.* 26. *pl.* 12. 2 *Ld. Raym.* 907.

But the master of a stage-coach, *who only carries passengers for hire*, shall not be liable for the goods of his passengers that are lost, and therefore where A. delivered a trunk to the driver or servant, who lost it out of his possession, it was holden that the master was not liable in an action upon the case, on the custom of the realm: for though the servant received money for it, yet it was but a gratuity; and the master shall not be chargeable with the acts of his servant, otherwise than as he acts in execution of the authority given him. *Comyns*, 25. *pl.* 16.

But *if he carries goods as well as passengers for hire*, then he is a common carrier, and shall be liable. 2 *Show. Rep.* 128. *Salk.* 282.

And the post-master general doth not come under the denomination of a carrier; for he hath no hire; nor enters into any contract: the post-office is a branch of the public revenue, and a part of the police of the country created by act of parliament: and the salary annexed to the office of post-master, is for no other consideration, than the trouble of executing it: he is therefore not liable for any constructive negligence. 1 *Ld. Raym.* 646. *Carth.* 487. 12 *Mod.* 482. *Cowp.* 754.

Where goods are delivered to a carrier, and he is robbed of them, he shall be charged, and answer for them, because of the hire. 1 *Rol. Abr.* 338.

For a carrier who undertakes to carry goods, must deliver them safe at all events, except damaged by the act of God, or the king's enemies. 1 *Wils.* 281. 1 *Salk*, 18. 1 *Vent.* 190, 238.

If a common carrier, who is offered his hire, and who has convenience, refuses to carry goods, he is liable to an action in the same manner as an inn-keeper who refuses to entertain a guest, or a smith who refuses to shoe a horse. 2 *Show. Rep.* 327.

But if the porter of the inn puts up a package into the carriage, and the master as soon as he knows of it, says that he is already full, and refuses to take charge of it, the master shall not be liable. 2 *Show. Rep.* 128.

And if a common carrier between C. and D. receives goods, to be carried from C. to D. *and then forwarded to* E., and the carrier takes them safely to D. and there puts them in his warehouse to secure them until he can forward them by another conveyance, in such case, if they are destroyed by an accidental fire before he hath an opportunity of forwarding them, the carrier shall not be liable. 4 *Ter. Rep.* 581.

And if goods be delivered to a carrier to be carried from C. to D. and after their arrival at D. they are consumed by an accidental fire in the warehouse at D. where they are usually unloaded, but which does not belong to the carrier, in this case the carrier shall be liable, though all the profits of the cartage of the goods from D. to the consignee's house in that town, (charged and received by the carrier) belong to the warehouse-keeper, and not to the carrier; and the circumstance of its being known to the consignee does not vary the case. 5 *Ter. Rep.* 389.

For a carrier must see all things forthcoming which are delivered to him, let what will happen; *the act of God*, or *an enemy, perils* and *dangers of the seas excepted;* but for *fire, thieves*, and *other casualties*, he must answer. *Molloy, b.* 2. *c.* 2. *s.* 2. And the *act of God*, in this case, means such act, as could not happen by the intervention of man, as lightning and tempests. Inevitable accident happening by any human means, irresistible force, if not occasioned by the king's enemies, will not excuse, for *the carrier is in the nature of an insurer:* therefore, where a fire, *not occasioned by lightning*, began at another booth in a fair, than that wherein the goods were placed, and afterwards spread thither, and consumed the goods, the carrier was holden liable, though there was not the least negligence on his part. 1 *Ter. Rep.* 27.

If a carrier accept *generally*, he is liable to the value, whatever it may be. 1 *Vent.* 238. 3 *Keb.* 133. But he may accept conditionally, as, provided there be no money, or, it doth not exceed a certain amount: or in case of such excess, he may refuse to accept, without an additional premium; and if there be proof that the owner was apprized of his intention, such as by general advertisements or the like, though there be no personal communication, the carrier shall be considered as a *special* acceptor. 1 *Str.* 145. 4 *Burr.* 2298. And if the owner of the goods, thus knowing the conditions, conceals the real value, he is guilty of a fraud and imposition, and therefore he shall not only where there hath been an express declaration on the part of the carrier, that he will not be answerable beyond a certain amount without notice, not recover to that amount, but he shall not even recover back the money he may have paid for the carriage. 1 *Hen. Black.* 298.

So where a person delivered to a carrier's book-keeper two bags of money sealed up, to be carried from London to Exeter, and told him that it was 200*l.* and took his receipt for the same, with promise of delivery for 10*s. per cent.* carriage and risque: though it be proved that there was 400*l.* in the bags, if the carrier be robbed, he shall only answer for 200*l.* because there was a particular undertaking for the carriage of that sum and no more, and his reward, which makes him answerable, extends no farther. *Carthew's Rep.* 486.

A carrier who hath goods delivered to him, undertakes for his hire to deliver them safely, and though he hath the possession of them for no further purpose, yet he hath such a *qualified*, or *special limited property* therein, that he may bring trover and conversion against a stranger that takes them away, or he may sue the hundred when robbed of them, because he is answerable even in damages to the absolute owner. *Co. Lit.* 89. 4 *Co.* 83. 2 *Buls.* 311. *Sid.* 438. *Mod.* 30. 2 *Saund.* 47. *Yelv.* 44. *Dyer* 98.

So where goods are stolen from a carrier, he may bring an indictment against the felon as for his own goods, and the owner may likewise prefer an indictment against the felon. *Kel.* 39.

And, where a carrier entrusted with goods, opens the pack, and takes away and disposes of part of the goods, this, shewing an intent of stealing them, will make him guilty of felony. *H. P. C.* 61. And it is the same if the carrier receives goods to carry to a certain place, and carrieth them to some other place, and not to the place agreed, with intent to defraud the owner of them. 3 *Inst.* 367. So if a carrier, after he hath brought goods to the place appointed, take them away privately, he is guilty of felony; for the possession which he received from the owner being determined, his second taking is in all respects the same as if he were a mere stranger. 1 *Hawk. P. C.* 90.

By the 3 *Car.* 1. *c.* 1. *Carriers are not to travel on the Lord's day.*

By the stat. 3 *W.* & *M. c.* 12. "The justices are to assess the price of land carriage of goods to be brought into any place within their jurisdiction, by any common carrier, who is not to take more, under the penalty of 5*l.*"

And by 21 *Geo.* 2. *c.* 28. "A carrier is not to take more, for carrying goods from any place to London, than is settled by the justices for the carrying goods from London to such a place, under the same penalty."

By 24 *Geo.* 2. *c.* 8. "commissioners for regulating the navigation of the river Thames are to rate the price of water carriage."

By 30 *Geo.* 2. *c.* 22. "justices of the city of London to assess the rates of carrying goods between London and Westminster." And by 7 *Geo.* 2. *c.* 15. and 26 *Geo.* 3. *c.* 86. "ship-owners are not answerable for any embezzlement or robbery by the master or mariners beyond the value of the ship and freight nor for loss by fire."

CART-BOTE, the Saxon word *bote*, is of the same signification with the French word *estovers*, and cart-bote is wood, to be employed in making and repairing instruments of husbandry. 2 *Black. Com.* 35.

CARUCA, (Fr. *charrue*) a plough, from the old Gallic *carr*, which is the present Irish word for any sort of wheeled carriage: hence *charl* and *car*, a ploughman or rustic. *Cowel. Blount.* Vide *Karle.*

CARUCAGIUM, was a tribute imposed on every plough, for the public service; and as hidage was a taxation by hides, so carucage was by carucates of land. *Mon. Angl. tom.* 1. *f.* 294. *Blount.*

CARUCATE, or CARVE OF LAND, (*carucata terræ*) a plough land, anciently taken to be one hundred acres.

CARUCATARIUS, he that held lands in carvage, or plough-tenure. *Paroch. Antiq. p.* 354.

CASE. See *Action.*

CASSATUM and CASSATA, by the Saxons, called *hide*; by Bede, *familia*, is a house with land sufficient to maintain one family. *Cowel. Blount.*

CASHLITE, a Saxon word signifying a mulct. *Blount.*

CASSIDILE, a little sack, purse, or pocket. *Ibid.*

CASSOCK, or CASSULA, a certain garment belonging to the priest, *quasi minor cassa. Ibid.*

CASTEL, or CASTLE, (*castellum.*) In the time of *Hen.* 2. there were in England 1115 castles; and every castle contained a manor: but during the civil wars in this kingdom these castles were demolished, so that generally there is only the ruins or remains of them at this day. 2 *Inst.* 31.

CASTELLAIN, (*castellanus*) the lord, owner, or captain of a castle, and sometimes the constable of a fortified house. *Bract. lib.* 5. *tract.* 2. *cap.* 16.

CASTELLARIUM, CASTELLARII, the precinct or jurisdiction of a castle. *Mon. Angl. tom.* 2. *f.* 402.

CASTELLORUM OPERATIO, castle-work, or service and labour done by inferior tenants, for the building and upholding of castles of defence; towards which some gave their personal assistance, and others paid their contribution. *Cowel. Blount.*

CASTIGATORY for *scolds.* A woman indicted for being a common scold, if convicted, shall be sentenced to be placed on a certain engine of correction, called the trebucket, castigatory, or cucking stool, which in the Saxon language signifies the scolding stool; though now it is frequently corrupted into ducking stool, because the residue of the judgment is, that, when she is so placed therein, she shall be plunged in the water for her punishment. 3 *Inst.* 219. 4 *Black. Com.* 169.

CASTLE-WARD, (*castlegardum, vel wardum castri*) an imposition laid upon such persons as dwell within a certain compass of any castle, towards the maintenance of such as watch and ward the castle. *Magna charta, cap.* 19, 20. 32 *Hen.* 8. *cap.* 48. It is sometimes used for the circuit itself, which is inhabited by those that are subject to this service. Castle guard rents were paid by persons dwelling within the liberty of any castle, for the maintaining of watch and ward within the same. *Stat.* 22 & 23 *Car.* 2. *s.* 24. *sect.* 2.

CASTER, and CHESTER: the names of places ending in these words are derived from the Lat. *castrum*; for this termination at the end was given by the Romans to those places where they built castles. *Cowel. Blount.*

CASTRATION, the offence of mayhem by castration, is, according to all our old writers, felony; and this, although the mayhem was committed upon the highest provocation. *Bract. fol.* 144. 3 *Inst.* 62. 4 *Black. Com.* 206.

CASUAL EJECTOR, in ejectment a nominal defendant, and who continues such until appearance by or for the tenant in possession. 3 *Black. Com.* 202.

CASU CONSIMILI, *writ in.* Is a writ of entry granted where tenant by the curtesy, or tenant for life, aliens in fee or in tail, or for another's life; and is brought by him in reversion against the party to whom such tenant so aliens to his prejudice, and in the tenant's life time. It takes its name from this; that the clerks of the chancery did, by their common assent, frame it to the likeness of the writ called *in casu proviso*, according to the authority given them by the stat. *Westm.* 2. *cap.* 24. which statute, as often as there happens a new case in Chancery, something like a former, yet not specially fitted by any writ, authorises them to frame a new form answerable to the new case, and as like the former as they may. 7 *Rep.* 4. See *Fitz. Nat. Br. fo.* 206. *Blount.*

CASU PROVISO, *writ of entry in.* A writ of entry given by the statute of *Gloucester, cap.* 7. where a tenant in dower aliens in fee, or for life, &c. and lies for him in reversion against the alienee. *Fitz. N. B.* 205. This writ, and the writ of *casu consimili*, supposes the tenant to have aliened in fee, though it be for life only; and a *casu proviso* may be without making any title in it, where a lease is made by the demandant himself to the tenant that doth alien; but if an ancestor lease for life, and the tenant alien in fee, &c. the heir in reversion must have this writ with the title included therein. *F. N. B.* 206, 207.

CASUS OMISSUS: an expression signifying that some particular thing is omitted, or otherwise not provided against by statute.

CATALS, *catalla*, the same as goods and chattels.

CATALLIS CAPTIS NOMINE DISTRICTIONIS, was a writ, now obsolete, that anciently lay where a house is within a borough, for rent going out of the same; and warrants the taking of doors, windows, &c. by way of distress for the rent. *Old. Nat. Br.* 66.

CATALLIS REDDENDIS, an ancient writ, now disused, which lay where goods being delivered to any man to keep till a certain day, were not upon demand delivered at the day. It may be also called a writ of *detinue*: and is answerable to *actio depositi* in the civil law. See *Reg. Orig.* 139. and *Old. Nat. Br.* 63. *Blount.*

CATAPULTA, a warlike engine to shoot

darts: but it is rather taken for a cross-bow. *Cowel. Blount.*

CATASCOPUS. This word signifies an archdeacon. *Du Cange. Blount.*

CATCHING BARGAIN, is an hazardous bargain, made with a young heir, to have double and treble the sum lent, or some other unreasonable advantage after the death of the father or tenant for life, or some other contingency. In these catching bargains, courts of equity will sometimes interfere, and set them aside, if there are strong circumstances of fraud; and where they do interfere they will oblige the plaintiff to do equity to the defendant, by paying what was really lent. 1 *Fonbl.* 140. 1 *Atk.* 301. 352. 2 *Vez.* 125. 1 *Bro. Cha. Ca.* 149.

CATCHLAND. In Norfolk there were formerly some grounds not known to what parish they certainly belonged, so that the minister who first seized the tithes did, by that right of pre-occupation enjoy them for that year: and the land of this dubious nature was there called catchland, from this custom of seizing the tithes. *Cowel.*

CATCHPOLE, (*quasi*, one that catches by the poll,) now taken as a term of contempt. Sheriffs officers are now commonly so called, though in ancient times it was used without reproach. *Cowel. Blount.*

CATHEDRAL (*ecclesia cathedralis*), is the church of the bishop, and head of the diocese, wherein the service of the church is performed with great ceremony.

CATHEDRATIC (*cathedraticum*), is a sum of two shillings paid to the bishop by the inferior clergy, *in argumentum subjectionis et ob honorem* cathedræ. *Hist. procurat. et Synodals*, p. 82. *Cowel. Blount.*

CATZURUS, a hunting-horse. *Ibid.*

CAUDA TERRÆ, a land's end or the bottom of a ridge in arable land. *Cartul. Abbot. Glast. fol.* 117.

CAVEAT, is a kind of process in the spiritual court to stop the institution of a clerk to a benefice, or probate of a will, or the like. When a caveat is entered against an institution, if the bishop afterward institutes a clerk it is void; the *caveat* being a *supersedeas*: but a caveat has been adjudged void when entered in the lifetime of the incumbent. A caveat entered against a will stands in force for three months; and this is for the caution of the ordinary, that he do no wrong; though it is said the temporal courts do not regard these sort of caveats. 1 *Rol. Rep.* 191. 1 *Nels. Abr.* 416, 417. 3 *Black. Com.* 98. 246.

CAVERS, offenders, relating to the mines in Derbyshire, who are punishable in the berghmote, or miners court. *Cowel. Blount.*

CAULCEIS, *anno* 6 *Hen.* 6. *cap.* 5. Ways pitched with flint, or other stone. See *Calcetum Cowel. Blount.*

CAURCINES, (*Caurcini*) were Italians that came into England about the year 1235, terming themselves the 'pope's merchants,' driving no other trade than letting out money; and having great banks in England, they differed little from Jews, save that they were rather more merciless to their debtors. Some will have them called *Caursines*, *quasi, causa ursini*, bearish and cruel in their causes; others *coursini*, or *causini*, as coming from the isle of Corsica: but *Cowel* says they have their name from *Caorsium*, *Caorsi*, a town in Lombardy, where they first practised their arts of usury and extortion; from whence spreading themselves, they carried their accursed trade through most parts of Europe, and were a common plague to every nation where they came. The then bishop of London excommunicated them; and king *Hen.* 3. banished them from this kingdom in the year 1240. But being the pope's solicitors and money-changers, they were permitted to return in the year 1250; though in a very short time after they were driven out of the kingdom again for their intolerable exactions. *Mat Par.* 403. *Cowel. Blount.*

CAUSA MATRIMONII PRÆLOCUTI, a writ now in disuse, which anciently lay where a woman gave land to a man in fee-simple, &c. to the intent he should marry her, and he refused to do it in any reasonable time, being thereunto required. *Reg. Orig.* 66.

CAUSAM NOBIS SIGNIFICES, a writ directed to a mayor of a town, &c. who was by the king's writ commanded to give seisin of lands to the king's grantee, on his delaying to do it, requiring him to show cause why he so delays the performance of his duty. *Blount.*

CAUSEA, the same with *calcea*, *calceta*, which we call a causeway. *Ibid.*

CAUSES AND EFFECTS, (*cessante causâ cessat effectus*, i. e. when the cause ceaseth, the effect also ceaseth. *Noy's Max.* 4.) In most cases the law hath respect to the cause, or beginning of a thing, as the principal part on which all other things are founded: and herein the next, and not the remote, cause, is most looked upon, except it be in covinous and criminal things; and therefore that which is not good at first will not be so afterwards; for such as is the cause, such is the effect. *Plowd.* 208. 268. Thus if an infant or feme covert make a will, and publish it, and after die of full age, or sole, the will is of no force, by reason of the original cause of infancy and coverture. *Finch.* 12.

So if husband and wife be legally separated, or if the wife carry on a sole trade, as by the custom of London, and many places, she may, the husband is no longer liable to her debts, according to this maxim. 2 *Black. Rep.* 1179. 1 *Ter. Rep.* 5. *Cooke's Bankr. Laws* 36.

Also, if lessee commit waste, no action will lie, if the thing wasted be repaired before the commencement of the action, because the cause of the action has ceased. *Co. Lit.* 204.

CAUTION. In the spiritual court *caution* (a species of bail, 1 *Com. tit. Ba.* (D) shall be given, and it is *juratory*, when a man makes oath in small offences; *stare mandatis ecclesiæ: fide jussary*, when he gives an obligation with sureties to do so; and *pignoratitia*, when he gives pledges for the same intent; but an obligation can only be taken upon a writ *de cautione admittenda*. 1 *Lev.* 36.

CAUTIONE ADMITTENDA, is a writ that lies against a bishop, who holds an excommunicated person in prison for contempt, notwithstanding he offers sufficient caution or security to obey the orders and commandment of holy church for the future. *Reg. Orig.* 66. *See* BAIL.

CEAPGILDE, a word derived from the Sax. *ceap*, signifying *pecus*, cattle, and *gild*, i.e. *solutio*; and hence it is *solutio pecudis*: from this Saxon word gild it is very probable we have our English word yield; as yield, or pay. *Cowel. Blount.*

CELER LECTI, is the top, head, or tester of a bed. *Ibid.*

CELLERARIUS, the butler in a monastery: in the universities they are sometimes called *manciple*, and sometimes caterer, and steward. *Ibid.*

CENDULÆ, small pieces of wood laid in form of tiles, to cover the roof of a house. *Ibid.*

CENEGILD. This was an expiatory mulct, paid by one who had killed another, to the kindred of the deceased. *Spelm. Cowel. Blount.*

CENELLÆ, acorns, from the oak, in our old writings, *pessona cenellarum*, is put for the pannage of hogs, or running of swine, to feed on acorns. *Cowel.*

CENNINGA, was notice given by the buyer to the seller, that the thing sold was claimed by another, that he might appear and justify the sale. *Cowel. Blount.*

CENSARIA, a farm, or house and land, let *ad censum* at a standing rent: it comes from the Fr. *cense*, which signifies a farm, and hence *censarii*, farmers. *Ibid.*

CENSUALES, a species or class of the *oblati*, or voluntary slaves of churches or monasteries, *i. e.* those who to procure the protection of the church bound themselves to pay an annual tax or quit-rent out of their estates to a church or monastery. Besides this, they sometimes engaged to perform certain services. *Roberts. Hist. Emp. Cha.* Vth. 1 *V.* 271, 2. *Potgiesserus de Statu Servorum, lib.* 1. *cap.* 1, *sect.* 6, 7. *Cowel. Blount.*

CENSUMOTHIDUS, a dead rent, like that which we call *mortmain*. *Blount.*

CENSURE, a custom called by this name (from the Lat. *census*, which has been expounded to be a kind of personal money, paid for every poll) observed in divers manors in Cornwall and Devon, where all persons residing therein above the age of sixteen are cited to swear fealty to the lord, and to pay 11 pence *per* poll, and one penny *per annum* ever after; and these thus sworn are called *censers*. Survey of the Duchy of Cornwall. *Cowel. Blount.*

CENTENARII, were petty judges, under sheriffs of counties, that had rule of an hundred, and judged smaller matters among them. 1 *Vent.* 211. 1 *Black.* 116.

These inferior judges, called *centenarii*, were required to take an oath that they would neither commit any robbery themselves, nor protect such as were guilty of that crime. 1 *Black. Com.* 115.

CEOLA, a large ship. *Cowel. Blount.*

CEPI CORPUS, is a return made by the sheriff, upon a *capias*, or other process to the like purpose, that he hath taken the body of the party. *F. N. B.* 26.

CEPPAGIUM, the stumps or roots of trees which remain in the ground after the trees are felled, &c. *Fleta, lib.* 2. *cap.* 41. *Cowel. Blount.*

CERAGIUM, cerage, a payment to find candles in the church. *Cowel. Blount.*

CERTAINTY, is a plain, clear, and distinct setting down of things in writs, declarations, pleadings, and the like, so that they may be understood. 5 *Rep.* 121.

CERTIFICANDO DE RECOGNITIONE STAPULÆ, an ancient writ whereby the mayor of the staple was commanded to certify to the lord chancellor a statute staple taken before him, where the party himself detained it, and refused to bring in the same. *Reg. Orig.* 152.

CERTIFICATE, is a writing made in any court to give notice to another court of any thing done therein, which is usually by way of transcript, &c. And sometimes it is made by an officer of the same court, where matters are referred to him, or a rule of court is obtained for it, containing the tenor and effect of what is done. *Cowel. Blount. Morgan.*

CERTIFICATION OF ASSISE OF NOVEL DISSEISIN, (*certificatio assisæ novæ disseisinæ*, &c.) was an ancient writ (now obsolete) granted for the re-examining of a matter passed by assise before justices, directed to the sheriff to call both the party for whom the assise passed, and the jury that was impanelled on the same, before the said justices at a certain day and place, at which the same was to be examined: and it was called a certificate, because therein mention was made to the sheriff, that upon the party's complaint of the defective examination, as to the assise passed, the king had directed his letters patent to the justices *for the better certifying of themselves*, whether all points of the said assise were duly examined. *Reg. Orig.* 200. *F. N. B.* 181. *Bract. lib.* 4. *c.* 13. *Horne's Mirr. lib.* 3.

CERTIORARI. A *certiorari* is an original writ issuing out of the Chancery, or court of King's Bench, directed in the king's name to the judges or officers of inferior courts, commanding them to return the records of a cause or matter depending before them, to the end the party may have the more sure and speedy justice before him, or such other justices as he shall assign to determine the cause. *Fitz. N. B.* 245. A.

The other courts at Westminster may also issue a *certiorari* to remove proceedings of a civil nature, 2 *Ld. Raym.* 836. 1 *Salk.* 148. 1 *Hen. Black. Rep.* 552.

The court of King's Bench hath a superintendency over all courts of an inferior criminal jurisdiction, and may by the plenitude of its power award a *certiorari* to have any indictment removed and brought before itself; and when such *certiorari* is allowable, it ought of right to award it at the instance of the king, because every indictment is at the suit of the king, and he hath a prerogative of suing in what court he pleases. 2 *Hawk. P. C.* 27. § 27.

But there is a distinction between those cases, in which the crown is specially concerned, and prosecutes by the attorney-general; and those which are nominally at the suit of the crown; but in reality are prosecuted by a private person; in the former the crown hath a right to *demand* a *certiorari*, and the court are *bound* to grant it: in the latter it issues indeed of course; but upon good cause a *procedendo* may be awarded. 4 *Bur.* 2458.

But though the court is to grant it at the suit of the king, yet it hath a discretionary power in granting or refusing it at the suit of the defendant. 2 *Hawk. P. C. c.* 27. *sec.* 27.

This writ of *certiorari* is also not only used for the purpose of removing *legal*, but likewise *equitable* proceedings; for when an equitable right is sued for in an inferior court of equity, and by reason of the limited jurisdiction of the court the defendant cannot have complete justice, or the cause is without the jurisdiction of the inferior court, the defendant may file a bill in Chancery, praying this writ to remove the cause into the court of Chancery; and when the bill is filed he must enter into a bond with one surety, in the penalty of £.100 to the master of the Rolls, and the senior master in Chancery, to prove the suggestion of the bill within fourteen days; and in default of proof a *procedendo* may be applied for of course: but the plaintiff below, it seems, is not at liberty to make this application. 2 *Cha. Rep.* 109. *Pr. Reg.* 41. *Car. Rep.* 48. 1 *Vern.* 178. *Eq. Abr.* 80. *Harrison's Cha. Pr.* 119.

This writ of *certiorari* may be issued by the courts of Chancery and King's Bench, to remove the proceedings from any inferior courts, whether they be of ancient or newly created jurisdiction, unless the statute or charter, which creates them exempts them from such jurisdiction. 2 *Hawk. P. C. c.* 27. *sec.* 22.

Therefore the King's Bench may award such *certiorari* to justices in eyre, or gaol delivery, or of a county palatine, and to the college of physicians having a special power by statute to impose fines, and to justices of the peace, commissioners of sewers, the courts of the Cinque Ports, the courts of the grand sessions, and other courts in Wales, and also to a sheriff to return inquisitions taken under a private act. 1 *Bac. Abr. tit. Cer.* B.

In vacation time a *certiorari* to remove an indictment from the quarter sessions may be granted by any of the judges of *B. R.* but security is to be found before it is allowed, otherwise it is no *supersedeas*. *Mod. Ca.* 33. For by stat. 5 and 6 *W. & Mar. cap.* 11, no *certiorari* "is to be granted out of *B. R.* to "remove any indictment before justices of "peace at the sessions before trial, unless "motion be made in open court, and the "party indicted find security by two persons in 20*l.* each, to plead to the indictment in *B. R.* &c. And if the defendant "prosecuting the *certiorari* be convicted, "the court of *B. R.* shall order costs to the "prosecutor of the indictment."

CERT-MONEY, (*quasi* certain money) is head-money, paid yearly by the resiants of several manors to the lords thereof, for the certain keeping of the leet; and sometimes to the hundred: as the manor of Hook in Dorsetshire, pays *cert*-money to the hundred of Egerdon. In ancient records this is called *certum letæ*. *Cowel. Blount.*

CERVISARII. The Saxons had a duty called drinclean, that is, *retributio potus*, payable by their tenants; and such tenants were in Domesday called *cervisarii*, from *cervisia*, ale, their chief drink: though *cervisarius* vulgarly signifies a beer or ale brewer. *Ibid.*

CERURA, a mound, fence or inclosure. *Ibid.*

CESSAT EXECUTIO. In trespass against two persons, if it be tried and found against one, and the plaintiff takes his execution against him, the writ will abate as to the other; for there ought to be a *cessat executio* till it is tried against the other defendant. 10 *Ed.* 4. 11.

CESSAVIT. The writ of *cessavit* was a writ now in disuse which anciently lay, by the statutes of *Gloucester*, 6 *Ed.* 1. *c.* 4. and of *Westminster* 2, 13 *Ed.* 1. *c.* 21 and 41, when a man holding lands of a lord by a rent or other services, neglected or *ceased* to perform his services for two years together; or where a religious house held lands given it on condition of performing some certain spiritual service, as reading prayers, or giving alms, and neglected it, in neither of which cases if the *cesser* or neglect had continued for two years, the lord or donor and his heirs should have a writ of *cessavit* to recover the land itself; *eo quod tenens in faciendis servitiis per biennium jam cessavit*. *Fitz. N. B.* 208.

But by the statute of *Gloucester* the *cessavit* does not lie for lands let upon fee-farm rents, unless they have laid fresh and uncultivated for two years, and there be not sufficient distress upon the premises, or unless the tenant hath so inclosed the land, that the lord cannot come upon it to distrain. *Fitz. N. B.* 209. 2 *Inst.* 298.

But the same statute of *Gloucester* has provided further that upon tender of arrears and damages before judgment, and giving security for the future performance of the services, the process shall be at an end, and the tenant shall relieve him; and to this the stat. *West.* 2 conforms. *Finch* 270, 271.

CESSAVIT DE CANTARIA, was an ancient writ which laid where a man gave land to any house of religion, or parson, to say divine service, provide alms for the poor, &c. If the said services were not done in two years the donor or his heirs had this writ against him that held the land thus given, after such cessure. *Stat. West.* 2. *cap.* 41. *Cowel. Blount.*

CESSE, signifies an assessment or tax. *Ib.*

CESSION, (*cessio*) a ceasing, yielding up, or giving over: and is when an ecclesiastical person is created bishop, or a parson of a parsonage takes another benefice, without dispensation, or otherwise not qualified, &c. In both cases their first benefices are become void and are in the law said to be void by cession, without any resignation or deprivation; and to those benefices that the person had who was created bishop, the king shall present for that time, whoever is patron of them; and in the other case the patron may present. *Cowel. Blount.* 1 *Black.* 392.

CESSOR, (Lat.) a loiterer, but more particularly used for him who ceaseth, or neglects so long to perform a duty, that he thereby incurs the danger of the law. *Old Nat. Brev.* 136.

CESSURE, or *cesser*, is used for ceasing, giving over, or departing from. *Stat. W.* 2. *c.* 1.

CESTUI QUE TRUST, is he to whose use or benefit another man is enfeoffed or seised of lands or tenements. 1 *Rep.* 133.

CESTUI QUE USE, (Fr. *cestui à l' use de qui*) which signifies him to whose use any other man is enfeoffed of lands or tenements. 1 *Rep.* 133.

CESTUI QUE VIE, is he for whose life any lands or tenements are granted. *Perk.* 97.

CHACEA, is a station of game more extended than a park, and less than a forest, and is sometimes taken for the liberty of chasing or hunting within such a district. And according to *Blount* it hath another signification, *i. e.* the way through which cattle are drove to pasture, commonly called in some places a droveway. *Bracton, lib.* 4. *c.* 44. *Cowel. Blount.*

CHACEARE *ad lepores, vel vulpes*, to hunt hare or fox. *Ibid.*

CHACURUS, (from the Fr. *chasseur*) a horse for the chase, or rather a hound or dog, a courser. *Ibid.*

CHAFE, from the Fr. *chauffer*, to heat, whence our chafing-dish. *Ibid.*

CHAFEWAX, an officer in chancery, who fits the wax for sealing of the writs, and such other instruments as are there made to be issued out. *Ibid.*

CHAFFERS, seem to signify wares or merchandise; and we yet use chaffering for buying and selling, though we take it to be generally a kind of bartering of one thing for another. It is mentioned in stat. 3 *Ed.* 4. *c.* 4. *Ibid.*

CHAINS, (hanging in). By 25 *Geo.* 2. *c.* 37, the judge before whom a murderer is convicted shall, in passing sentence, direct him to be executed on the next day but one, (unless the same shall be Sunday, and then on the Monday following,) and that his body be delivered to the surgeons, to be dissected and anatomized; and that the judge may direct his body to be afterwards hung in chains, but in no wise to be buried without dissection. But a power is allowed to the judge, upon good and sufficient cause, to respite the execution, and relax the other restraints of this act. 4 *Black. Com.* 202.

CHALDRON, or CHALDER of coals, contains thirty-six bushels heaped up, according to the bushel sealed for that purpose at Guildhall, London. 16 *et* 17 *Car.* 2. *c.* 2.

CHALLENGE, *Calumnia* (from the Fr. *chalenger*) is used in the law for an exception to jurors, who are returned to pass on a trial; and this challenge to jurors is either made 1st. to the array, or 2d. to the poll. *Cowel. Blount.* 3 *Black.* 359.

CHALLENGES TO THE ARRAY, are at once an exception to the whole panel, in which the jury are arrayed, or set in order, by the sheriff in his return; and they may be made upon account of partiality, or some default in the sheriff, or his under-officer who arrayed the panel. And, generally speaking, the same reasons that before the awarding the *venire* were sufficient to have directed it to the coroners or elisors, will be also sufficient to quash the array, when made by a person or officer of whose partiality there is any tolerable ground of suspicion. Also, though there be no personal objection against the sheriff, yet if he arrays the pannel at the nomination, or under the direction of either party, this is good cause of challenge to the array. Formerly, if a lord of parliament had a cause to be tried, and no knight was returned upon the jury, it was a cause of challenge to the array: but an unexpected use having been made of this dormant privilege by a spiritual lord, (K. *v.* bishop of Worcester, M. 23 *Geo.* 2.

B. R. though his title to such privilege was very doubtful) 2 *Whitelocke* of Parl. 211, it was abolished by statute 24 *Geo.* 2, *c.* 18. Also, by the policy of the ancient law, the jury was to come *de vicineto*, from the neighbourhood of the vill or place where the cause of action was laid in the declaration; and therefore some of the jury were obliged to be returned from the hundred in which such vill lay; and if none were returned, the array might be challenged for defect of hundredors. Thus the Gothic jury, or *nembda*, was also collected out of every quarter of the country; " *binos, trinos, vel etiam senos,* " *ex singulis territorii quadrantibus.*" *Stiernhook* de jure *Goth. lib.* 1. *c.* 4. For, living in the neighbourhood they were properly the very country, or *pais*, to which both parties had appealed; and were supposed to know beforehand the characters of the parties and witnesses, and therefore the better knew what credit to give to the facts alleged in evidence. But this convenience was overbalanced by another very natural and almost unavoidable inconvenience; that jurors coming out of the immediate neighbourhood would be apt to intermix their prejudices and partialities in the trial of right. And this our law was so sensible of, that it for a long time has been gradually relinquishing this practice; the number of necessary hundredors in the whole pannel, which in the reign of *Ed.* 3d. were constantly six, *Gilb. Hist. C. c.* 8, being in the time of *Fortescue, De Laud.L.L.* 125, reduced to four. Afterwards, indeed, the stat. 35 *Hen.* 8. *c.* 6, restored the ancient number of six, but that clause was soon virtually repealed by stat. 27 *Eliz. c.* 6, which required only two. And sir *Ed. Coke* also, 1 *Inst.* 157, gives us such a variety of circumstances whereby the courts permitted this necessary number to be evaded, that it appears they were heartily tired of it. At length by stat. 4 & 5 *Ann. c.* 16, it was entirely abolished upon all civil actions, except upon penal statutes, and upon those also by the 24 *Geo.* 2. *c.* 18, the jury being now only to come *de corpore comitatus*, from the body of the county at large, and not *de vicineto*, or from the particular neighbourhood. The *array* by the ancient law may also be challenged, if an alien be party to the suit, and, upon a rule obtained by his motion to the court for the jury *de medietate linguæ*, such a one be not returned by the sheriff, pursuant to the stat. 28 *Ed.* 3, *c.* 13, which enacts, that where either party i an alien born, the jury shall be one half aliens, and the other denizens, if required, for the more impartial trial: a privilege indulged to strangers in no other country in the world, but which is as ancient with us as the time of king *Ethelred*, in whose stat. *de monticolis Walliæ* (then aliens to the crown of England), *cap.* 3, it is ordained that " *duodeni legales homines, quorum sex Walli* " *et sex Angli erunt, Anglis et Wallis jus* " *dicunto.*" But where both parties are aliens, no partiality is to be presumed to one more than another; and therefore by the statute 21 *Hen.* 6, *c.* 4, the whole jury are then directed to be denizens. And it may be questioned whether the statute 3 *Geo.* 2. *c.* 25, (before referred to) hath not in civil causes undesignedly abridged this privilege of foreigners, by the positive directions therein given concerning the manner of impanelling jurors, and the persons to be returned in such panel. So that the court might probably hesitate, especially in the case of special juries, how far it has now a power to direct a panel to be returned *de medietate linguæ*, and to alter the method prescribed for striking a special jury, or ballotting for common jurymen. 3 *Black.* 359. 361.

CHALLENGES TO THE POLLS, *in capita*, are exceptions to particular jurors, and seem to answer the *recusatio judicis* in the civil and canon laws, by the constitutions of which a judge might be refused upon any suspicion of partiality, *Cod.* 3, 1. 16. *Decretal. l.* 2. *t.* 28. *c.* 36. By the laws of England also, in the time of *Bracton, l.* 5. *c.* 15. and *Fleta, l.* 6. *c.* 37. a judge might be refused for good cause; but now the law is otherwise, and it is held that judges or justices cannot be challenged, *Co. Lit.* 294. For the law will not suppose a possibility of bias or favour in a judge, who is already sworn to administer impartial justice, and whose authority greatly depends upon that presumption and idea. And should the fact at any time prove flagrantly such, as the delicacy of the law will not presume beforehand, there is no doubt but that such misbehaviour would draw down a heavy censure from those to whom the judge is accountable for his conduct. 3 *Black.* 361.

But challenges to the polls of the jury (who are judges of fact) are reduced to four heads by sir *Ed. Coke* 1 *Inst.* 156. *propter honoris respectum; propter defectum; propter affectum;* and *propter delictum. Ibid.*

1. *Propter honoris respectum*: as if a lord of parliament be impanelled on a jury, he may be challenged by either party, or he may challenge himself. *Ibid.*

2. *Propter defectum*: as, if a juryman be an alien born, this is defect of birth; if he be a slave or bondman, this is defect of liberty, and he cannot be *liber et legalis homo.* Under the word *homo* also, though a name common to both sexes, the female is however excluded, *propter defectum sexus*; except when a widow feigns herself with child in order to exclude the next heir, and a supposititious birth is suspected to be intended; then upon the writ *de ventre inspiciendo*, a jury of women is to be impanelled to try the question, whether with child, or not *Cro. Eliz.* 566. But the principal de-

ficiency is defect of estate, sufficient to qualify him to be a juror. This depends upon a variety of statutes. And first, by the stat. *Westm.* 2, 13 *Ed.* 1, *c.* 38, none shall pass on juries in assises within the county but such as may dispend 20*s.* by the year at the least, which is increased to 40*s.* by the stat. 21 *Ed.* 1, *st.* 1, and 2 *Hen.* 5, *st.* 2, *c.* 3. This was doubled by the stat. 27 *Eliz.* *c.* 6, which requires in every such case the jurors to have estate of freehold to the yearly value of 4*l.* at least. But the value of money at that time decreasing very considerably, this qualification was raised by the statute 16 & 17 *Car.* 2, *c.* 3, to 20*l. per ann.* which being only a temporary act, for three years, was suffered to expire without renewal, to the great debasement of juries. However, by the stat. 4 & 5 *W. & M.* *c.* 24, it was again raised to 10*l. per ann.* in England, and 6*l.* in Wales, of freehold lands or copyhold; which is the first time that copyholders, as such, were admitted to serve upon juries in any of the king's courts, though they had before been admitted to serve in some of the sheriff's courts, by statutes 1 *Ric.* 3, *c.* 4, and 9 *Hen.* 8, *c.* 13. And, lastly, by stat. 3 *Geo.* 2, *c.* 25, any leaseholder for the term of five hundred years absolute, or for any term determinable upon a life or lives, of the clear yearly value of 20*l. per ann.* over and above the rent reserved, is qualified to serve upon juries. When the jury is *de medietate linguæ*, that is, one moiety of the English tongue or nation, and the other of any foreign one, no want of lands shall be cause of challenge to the alien; for as he is incapable to hold any, this would totally defeat the privilege. 3 *Black.* 362, 363.

3. Jurors may be challenged *propter affectum*, for suspicion of bias or partiality. This may be either a principal challenge, or to the favour. A principal challenge is such where the cause assigned carries with it *prima facie* evident marks of suspicion, either of malice or of favour; as, that a juror is of kin to either party within the ninth degree, *Finch L.* 401, that he has been arbitrator on either side; that he has an interest in the cause; that there is an action depending between him and the party; that he has taken money for his verdict; that he has formerly been a juror in the same cause; that he is the party's master, servant, counsellor, steward, or attorney, or of the same society or corporation with him: all these are principal cause of challenge; which, if true, cannot be over-ruled, for jurors must be *omni exceptione majores.* Challenges to the favour are where the party hath no principal challenge, but objects only some probable circumstances of suspicion, as acquaintance, and the like, the validity of which must be left to the determination of triors, whose office it is to decide whether the juror be favourable or unfavourable. The triors, in case the first man called be challenged, are two indifferent persons named by the court; and if they try one man and find him indifferent, he shall be sworn; and then he and the two triers shall try the next, and when another is found indifferent, and sworn, the two triers shall be superseded, and the two first sworn on the jury shall try the rest. *Co. Litt.* 158. 3 *Black.* 363.

4. Challenges *propter delictum* are for some crime or misdemeanor that affects the juror's credit, and renders him infamous. As for a conviction of treason, felony, perjury, or conspiracy; or if he hath received judgment of the pillory, tumbrel, or the like; or to be branded, whipped, or stigmatized; or if he be outlawed, or excommunicated, or hath been attainted of false verdict, *præmunire*, or forgery; or lastly, if he hath proved recreant when champion in the trial by battle, and thereby hath lost his *liberem legem.* A juror may himself be examined on oath of *voir dire, veritatem dicere*, with regard to the three former of these causes of challenge, which are not to his dishonour; but not with regard to this head of challenge, *propter delictum*, which would be to make him either forswear or accuse himself if guilty. 3 *Bl.* 364.

Besides these challenges, which are exceptions against the fitness of jurors, and whereby they may be excluded from serving, there are also other causes to be made use of by the jurors themselves, which are matter of exemption; whereby their service is excused, and not excluded. As by statute *Westm.* 2, 13 *Ed.* 1. *c.* 38, sick and decrepid persons, persons not commorant in the county, and men above seventy years old; and, by the stat. 7 & 8 *W.* 3. *c.* 32, infants under twenty-one. This exemption is also extended by divers statutes, customs, and charters, to physicians, and other medical persons, counsel, attorneys, officers of the courts, and the like; all of whom, if impanelled, must show their special exemption. Clergymen are also usually excused, out of favour and respect to their function: but if they are seised of lands and tenements they are in strictness liable to be impanelled in respect of their lay-fees, unless they be in the service of the king, or of some bishop: "*in obsequio domini regis, vel alicujus episcopi.*" *F. N. B.* 166. *Reg. Brev.* 179. 3 *Black.* 364.

CHAMBERDEKINS, or CHAMBERDEACONS, were certain poor Irish scholars, clothed in mean habit, and living under no rule: banished England by stat. 1 *Hen.* 5. *cap.* 7, 8. *Cowel. Blount.*

CHAMBERLAIN, (*camerarius*) is variously used in our laws, statutes and chronicles: as first, there is lord great chamberlain of England, to whose office belongs the government of the palace at Westminster, and upon all solemn occasions the keys of Westminster-Hall, and the court of Requests are delivered to him; he disposes of the sword of state to be carried before the king when he comes to the parliament, and goes on the right hand of the sword next to the king's person: he has the care of providing all things in the House of Lords in the time of parliament; to him belongs livery and lodgings in the king's court, &c. And the gentleman usher of the black rod, yeoman usher, &c. are under his authority. *Cowel. Blount.*

The lord chamberlain of the household has the oversight and government of all officers belonging to the king's chamber, (except the bed-chamber, which is under the groom of the stole), and also of the wardrobe; of artificers retained in the king's service, messengers, comedians, revels, musick, &c. The serjeants at arms are likewise under his inspection; and the king's chaplains, physicians, apothecaries, surgeons, barbers, &c. And he hath under him a vice-chamberlain, both being always privy counsellors. *Ibid.*

There were formerly chamberlains of the king's courts. 7 *Ed.* 6. *cap.* 1. And there are chamberlains of the exchequer, who keep a controlment of the pells of receipts and *exitus*, and have in their custody the leagues and treaties with foreign princes, many ancient records, the two famous books of antiquity called Domesday, and the Black Book of the Exchequer; and the standards of money, and weights and measures are kept by them. There are also under-chamberlains of the exchequer, who make searches for all records in the treasury; and are concerned in making out the tallies, &c. The office of chamberlain of the exchequer is mentioned in the stat. 34 & 35 *H.* 8. *cap.* 16. Besides these, we read of a chamberlain of North Wales. *Stow. p.* 641.

A chamberlain of Chester, to whom it belongs to receive the rents and revenues of that city; and when there is no prince of Wales, and earl of Chester, he hath the receiving and returning of all writs coming thither out of any of the king's courts. *Cowel. Blount.*

The chamberlain of London, who is commonly the receiver of the city rents payable into the chamber; and hath great authority in making and determining rights of freemen, concerning apprentices, orphans, &c. *Cromp. Jur.*

CHAMBERS OF THE KING, (*regiæ cameræ*) the havens or ports of the kingdom are so called in our ancient records. *Mare Claus. fol.* 242. *Cowel. Blount.*

CHAMBRE DEPINCT, anciently St. Edward's chamber, now called the painted chamber. *Ibid.*

CHAMPARTY, or CHAMPERTY, *campi partitio*, (from the Fr. *champ*, a field, and *parti* divided, or the Lat. *campus*, and *partitio*, because the parties in *champerty*, agree to divide the thing in question) this is a species of maintenance, and signifies a bargain with the plaintiff or defendant in any suit, to have part of the land, debt, or other thing sued for, if the party that undertakes it prevails therein. *Co. Lit.* 368.

This offence is punishable by common law and statute; and the *stat.* 33 *Ed.* 1. *stat.* 2. "makes the offenders liable to three years imprisonment, and a fine at the king's pleasure." And by the *stat.* 28 *Ed.* 1. *c.* 11. it is ordained, that "no officer, nor any other, shall take upon him any business in suit, to have part of the thing in plea; nor none upon any covenant, shall give up his right to another; and if any do, and be convicted thereof, the taker shall forfeit to the king so much of his lands and goods as amounts to the value of the part purchased, &c. for such maintenance."

In the construction of these statutes, it hath been adjudged, that under the word covenant, all kinds of promises and contracts are included, whether by writing or parol. *F. N. B.* 172. 2 *Inst.* 209. 2 *Rol. Abr.* 113.

Champerty in any action at law, seems to be agreed to be within the statute, and a purchase of land, pending a suit in equity concerning it, it hath also been holden to be within it, also a lease for life or years, or a voluntary gift of land pending a plea, is as much within the statute as a purchase for money. 1 *Hawk. P. C. c.* 84. *s.* 16.

But neither a conveyance executed, pending a plea, in consideration of a precedent honest debt, which is agreed to be satisfied with the thing in demand when recovered, or in pursuance of a precedent bargain, nor any surrender by a lessee to his lessor, nor any conveyance or promise thereof made by a father to his son, or by any ancestor to his heir apparent, nor a gift of land in suit, *after the end of it*, to a counsellor for his fee or wages, without any kind of precedent bargain relating to such gift, are within the meaning of the stat. 1 *Haw. P.C. c.* 84. *s.* 15, 18, 19, 20.

CHAMPERTORS, by statute, are those who move pleas or suits, or cause them to be moved, either by their own procurement, or by others, and sue them at their proper costs, to have part of the land in variance, or part of the gain. 33 *Ed.* 1. *stat.* 2.

CHAMPION, (*campio*) is taken in the law not only for him that fights a combat in his own cause, but also for him that doth it in the place or quarrel of another: these judicial combats, on the wager of battel by a defendant, have long since fallen into disuse. *Bract. lib.* 3. *tract.* 2. *cap.* 21. 3 *Black.* 341.

These champions were usually hired, and any one might hire them, except parricides, and those who were accused of the highest offences: before they came into the field, they shaved their heads, and made oath that they believed the persons who hired them, were in the right, and that they would defend their cause to the utmost of their power;

which was always done on foot, and with no other weapon than a stick or club, and a shield: and before they engaged, they always made an offering to the church, that God might assist them in the battle. On a drawn battle, the defendant maintained his possession, but if victory declared itself for either party, for him judgment was finally given. 3 *Black.* 340. *Bract. lib.* 2. *c.* 35.

CHAMPION OF THE KING, (*campio regis*) is an ancient officer, whose office it is at the coronation of our kings, when the king is at dinner to ride armed *cap-a-pee* into Westminster Hall, and by the proclamation of a herald make a challenge, that if any man shall deny the king's title to the crown, he is there ready to defend it in single combat, &c. Which being done, the king drinks to him, and sends him a gilt cup with a cover full of wine, which the champion drinks, and hath the cup for his fee. This office, ever since the coronation of king Richard II. when Baldwin Freville exhibited his petition for it, was adjudged from him to sir John Dymocke his competitor, (both claiming from Marmion), and hath continued ever since in the family of the Dymockes; who hold the manor of Scrivelsby in Lincolnshire, hereditary from the Marmions, by grand serjeantry, *viz.* that the lord thereof shall be the king's champion, as abovesaid. Accordingly sir Edward Dymocke performed this office at the coronation of king Charles II. *Cowel. Blount.*

And a person of the name of Dymocke performed it, at the coronation of his present majesty George the Third.

CHAMPS DES MARS, and *les champs de mai*, assemblies of the ancient Gauls, to deliberate on whatever related to the general welfare of the nation. These assemblies were called champs, because, according to the custom of all the barbarous nations, they were held in the open air, in some plain, capable of containing the vast number of persons who had a right to be present. They were denominated *champs de mars* and *de mai*, from the months in which they were held. Every freeman seems to have had a right to be present in these assemblies. 1 *Robert. Hist. Emp. C. v.* 357.

CHANCE, where a man commits an unlawful act, by misfortune, or chance, and not by design, this is a deficiency of the will; for here the will observes a total neutrality, and doth not co-operate with the deed; which therefore wants one main ingredient of a crime. 4 *Black. Com.* 26, 7.

And if any accident or mischief happens to follow from the performance of a *lawful* act, the party stands excused from all guilt: but if a man be doing any thing *unlawful*, and a consequence ensues which he did not foresee or intend, as the death of a man or the like, his want of foresight shall be no excuse; for being guilty of one offence, in doing antecedently, which in itself is unlawful, he is criminally guilty of whatever consequence may follow the first misbehaviour. 4 *Black. Com.* 26, 7.

But a very important distinction is made in such cases, *viz.* whether the unlawful act *is also in its original nature* wrong and mischievous, for a person is not answerable criminally for the incidental consequences of an unlawful act, which is merely a *malum prohibitum*; as from an unqualified person being in pursuit of game, he is answerable only to the same extent as a man duly qualified. *Fost.* 659. 1 *Hale P. C.* 475. See also *Chancemedley*.

CHANCELLOR, (*cancellarius*) for the office of lord high chancellor, see *Chancery*.

—— *Chancellor of the Duchy of Lancaster*, is the chief judge of the duchy court, held in Westminster-Hall. Under the chancellor of the duchy, are an attorney of the court, one chief clerk or register, and several auditors.

—— *Chancellor of the Exchequer*, a great officer, originally appointed for the qualifying extremities in the exchequer: he sometimes sits in court, and in the exchequer-chamber; and with the judges of the court, orders things to the king's best benefit. He hath by the stat. 33 *H.* 8. *c.* 39. power with others, to compound for the forfeitures upon penal statutes, bonds and recognizances entered into to the king: he hath also great authority in the management of the royal revenue, &c. which seems of late to be his chief business, being commonly the first commissioner of the treasury. And though the court of equity in the Exchequer-chamber was intended to be holden before the treasurer, chancellor, and barons; it is usually before the barons only. Where there is a lord-treasurer, the chancellor of the Exchequer is under treasurer. *Cowel. Blount.*

There is a chancellor of the Order of the Garter, *Stow's Annals*, 706. Chancellor of the Universities. See 9 *Hen.* 5. *c.* 8. Chancellor of the diocese, 32 *Hen.* 8. *c.* 15. Chancellor in cathedral churches. *Mon. Angl. tom.* 3. *p.* 24, 339. *Cowel. Blount.*

CHANCEMEDLEY. If a person casts (not intending harm) a stone, which happens to hit one, whereof he dies: or shoots an arrow in a highway, and another that passeth by is killed therewith: or if a workman, in throwing down rubbish from a house, after warning to take care, kills a person: or a school-master in correcting his scholar, a master his servant, or an officer in whipping a criminal, in a reasonable manner, happens to occasion his death: it is chancemedly and misadventure. 3 *Inst.* 56. *Dalt.* 351.

But if a man throws stones in a highway where persons usually pass: or shoots an arrow, &c. in a market place, among a great many people: or if a workman cast down rubbish from a house, in cities and towns, where people are continually passing: or a school-master, &c. correct his servant or scholar, &c. exceeding the bounds of moderation, it is manslaughter; and if with an improper instrument of correction, as with a sword or iron bar, or by kicking, stamping, &c. in a cruel manner, it is murder. *Terms de Ley, H. P. C.* 31, 58, &c. *Kel.* 40, 65, 113. If a man whips his horse in the street to make him gallop, and the horse runs over a child and kills it, it is manslaughter: but if another whips the horse, it is manslaughter in him, and chancemedley in the rider. *H. P. C.* 48, 59. And if two are fighting, and a third person coming to part them is killed by one of them, without any evil intent, yet this is murder in him; and not manslaughter by chancemedley or misadventure: and if they were met with prepensed malice, the one intended to kill the other, then it is murder in both. *Terms de Ley.* In chancemedley the offender forfeits his goods; but hath a pardon of course. *Stat.* 6 *Ed.* 1. *c.* 9.

CHANCERY, (*cancellaria.*) The high court of Chancery, is by much the most important of any of the king's superior and original courts of justice: and is next to the parliament, it has its name of Chancery *cancellaria,* from the judge who presides here: the *lord chancellor* who, sir Edward Coke tells us, is so called *a cancellendo,* from cancelling the king's letters patent, when granted contrary to law, which is the highest point of his jurisdiction. 4 *Inst.* 88.

But the office and name of chancellor, (however derived) was certainly known to the courts of the Roman emperors; where originally, it seems to have signified a chief scribe or secretary, who was afterwards invested with several judicial powers, and a general superintendency over the rest of the offices of the province. 3 *Black.* 46.

From the Roman empire, it passed to the Roman church, ever emulous of imperial state; and hence every bishop has to this day, his chancellor, the principal judge of his consistory. And when the modern kingdoms of Europe were established upon the ruins of the empire, almost every state preserved its chancellor, with different jurisdictions and dignities according to their different constitutions: but in all of them, it seems to have had the supervision of all charters, letters, and such other public instruments of the crown, as were authenticated in the most solemn manner; and therefore when seals came in use, he had always the custody of the king's great seal. 3 *Black.* 46, 47.

So that the office of chancellor, or lord keeper, (whose authority by stat. 5 *Eliz. c.* 18. is declared to be exactly the same) is with us at this day created by the mere delivery of the king's great seal into his custody. *Lamb. Archeion,* 65. 1 *Roll. Abr.* 385. Whereby he becomes, without writ or patent, an officer of the greatest weight and power of any now subsisting in the kingdom; and superior in point of precedency to every temporal lord. *Stat.* 31 *Hen.* 8. *c.* 10. He is a privy counsellor by his office, and, according to lord chancellor Ellesmere, prolocutor of the house of lords by prescription. To him belongs the appointment of all justices of the peace throughout the kingdom. *Ibid.*

Being formerly usually an ecclesiastic, (for none else were then capable of an office so conversant in writings), and presiding over the royal chapel, *Madox. Hist. of Exch.* 42. he became keeper of the king's conscience; visitor, in right of the king, of all hospitals and colleges of the king's foundation; and patron of all the king's livings under the value of 20*l.* per annum in the king's books. *Ibid.*

He is the general guardian of all infants, idiots, and lunatics; and has the general superintendance of all charitable uses in the kingdom. And all this over and above the vast and extensive jurisdiction which he exercises in his judicial capacity in the court of chancery: wherein, as in the exchequer, there are two distinct tribunals; the one ordinary, being a court of common law; the other extraordinary, being a court of equity. *Ibid.*

As to the Master of the Rolls, he hath judicial power; and is an assistant to the lord chancellor when present, and his deputy when absent, but he has certain causes assigned him to hear and decree, which he usually doth on certain days appointed at the chapel of the rolls, being assisted by one or more masters in chancery: he is, by virtue of his office, chief of the masters of chancery, and chief clerk of the petty-bag office. *Chan. Prac.*

The twelve Masters in Chancery sit some of them in court, and take notice of such references as are made to them, to be reported to the court, relating to matters of practice, the state of the proceedings, accounts, &c. and they also take affidavits, acknowledge deeds and recognizances, &c. *Ibid.*

The six Clerks in chancery transact and file all proceedings by bill and answer; and also issue out some patents that pass the great seal; which business is done by their under clerks, each of whom has a seat there, and whereof every six clerk has a certain number in his office, usually about ten. *Ibid.*

The Cursitors of the court, four and twenty in number, make out all original writs in Chancery, which are returnable in *C. B.* &c. and among these the business of the several counties is severally distributed. *Ibid.*

The Register is a place of great importance in this court, and he hath several deputies under him, to take cognizance of all orders and decrees, and enter and draw them up, &c. *Ibid.*

The *master of the subpœna office* issues out all writs of subpœna. *Ibid.*

The EXAMINERS are officers in this court, who take the depositions of witnesses, and are to examine them, and make out copies of the depositions. *Ibid.*

The *clerk of the affidavits* files all affidavits used in court, without which they will not be admitted. *Ibid.*

The *clerk of the rolls* sits constantly in the rolls to make searches for deeds, offices, &c. and to make out copies. *Ibid.*

The *clerks of the petty-bag office*, in number three, have great variety of business that goes through their hands, in making out writs of summons to parliament, *conges d' elire* for bishops, patents for customers; *liberates* upon extent of statute-staple, and recovery of recognisances forfeited, &c. And also relating to suits for and against privileged persons, &c. And the clerks of this office have several clerks under them. *Ibid.*

The *usher of the chancery* had formerly the receiving and custody of all money ordered to be deposited in court, and paid it back again by order.

But anno 12 *Geo.* 1. *c.* 32. a new officer was appointed by statute, called ACCOUNTANT-GENERAL, to receive the money lodged in court, and convey the same to the Bank, to be there kept for the suitors of the court.

Then there is a SERJEANT AT ARMS, by whom persons standing in contempt are brought up by his substitute as prisoners. *Chan. Pr.* 2.

A *warden of the Fleet*, who receives such prisoners as stand committed by the court, &c. *Chan. Pr.* 2.

And besides these officers, there is a clerk of the crown in chancery; clerk and controller of the hanaper; clerk for inrolling letters patent, &c. not employed in proceedings of equity, but concerned in making out commissions, patents, pardons, &c. under the great seal, and collecting the fees thereof. A clerk of the faculties for dispensations, licences, &c. Clerk of the presentations, for benefices of the crown in the chancellor's gift; clerk of appeals, on appeals from the courts of the archbishop to the court of chancery: and divers other officers, who are constituted by the chancellor's commission. *Chan. Pr.* 3.

The ordinary legal court of the chancellor is much more ancient than the court of equity. Its jurisdiction is to hold plea upon a *scire facias* to repeal and cancel the king's letters patent, when made against law or upon untrue suggestions; and to hold plea of petitions, *monstrans de droit*, traverses of offices, and the like; when the king hath been advised to do any act, or is put in possession of any lands or goods, in prejudice of a subject's right, (4 *Rep.* 54.) On proof of which, as the king can never be supposed intentionally to do any wrong, the law questions not but he will immediately redress the injury; and refers that conscientious task to the chancellor, the keeper of his conscience. It also appertains to this court to hold plea of all personal actions, where any officer or minister of the court is a party. (4 *Inst.* 80.) It might likewise hold plea (by *scire facias*) of partitions of lands in co-parcenery, (*Co. Litt.* 171. *F. N. B.* 62.) and of dower, (*Bro. Abr. tit. dower.* 66. *Moor.* 565.) where any ward of the crown was concerned in interest, so long as the military tenures subsisted; as it now may also do of the tithes of forest land, where granted by the king and claimed by a stranger against the grantee of the crown, (*Bro. Abr. tit. dismes.* 10.) and of executions on statutes, or recognizances in nature thereof by the stat. 23 *Hen.* 8. *c.* 6. (2 *Roll. Abr.* 469.) "but if any cause comes to "issue in this court, that is, if any fact be "disputed between the parties, the chancel-"lor cannot try it, having no power to sum-"mon a jury; but must deliver the record "*proprio manu* into the court of king's bench, "where it shall be tried by the country, and "judgment shall be there given thereon." (*Cro. Jac.* 12.) And, when judgment is given in chancery, upon demurrer or the like, a writ of error, in nature of an appeal, lies out of this ordinary court into the court of king's bench. (*Year Book*, 18 *Ed.* 3. 25. 17. *Ass.* 24. 29. *Ass.* 47. *Dyer*, 315. 1 *Roll. Rep.* 287. 4 *Inst.* 80.) But so little is usually done on the common law side of the court, that according to *Blackstone* there are no traces of any writ of error being actually brought, since the fourteenth year of queen Elizabeth, *A. D.* 1572. 3 *Black.* 48.

In this ordinary, or legal, court is also kept the *officina justitiæ*: out of which all original writs that pass under the great seal, all commissions of charitable uses, sewers, bankruptcy, idiocy, lunacy, and the like, do issue; and for which it is always open to the subject, who may there at any time demand and have, *ex debitio justitiæ*, any writ that his occasions may call for. These writs (relating to the business of the subject) and the returns to them were, according to the simplicity of antient times, originally kept in a hamper, *in hanaperio*; and the others (relating to such matters wherein the crown is immediately or mediately concerned) were preserved in a little sack or bag, *in parva baga*; and thence hath arisen the distinction of the *hanaper* office, and *petty bag* office, which both belong to the common law court in chancery. 3 *Black.* 48, 49.

But the extraordinary court, or court of equity, is now become the court of the greatest judicial consequence. This distinction between law and equity, as administered in different courts, is not at present known, nor seems to have ever been known in any other country at any time: and yet the difference of one from the other, when administered by the same tribunal, was perfectly familiar to the Romans; the *jus prætorium*, or discretion of the prætor, being distinct from the *leges* or standing laws: but the power of both centered in one and the same magistrate, who was equally intrusted to pronounce the rule of law, and to apply it to particular cases by the principles of equity. With us too, the *aula regia*, which was the supreme court of judicature, undoubtedly administered equal justice according to the rules of both or either, as the case might chance to require; and, when that was broken to pieces, the idea of a court of equity, as distinguished from a court of law, did not subsist in the original plan of partition. For though equity is mentioned by Bracton, (*l.* 2. *c.* 7. *fol.* 23.) as a thing contrasted to strict law, yet neither in that writer, nor in Glanvil or Fleta, nor yet in Briton (composed under the auspices and in the name of Edward I. and treating particularly of courts and their several jurisdictions) is there a syllable to be found relating to the equitable jurisdiction of the court of chancery. It seems therefore probable, that when the courts of law, proceeding merely upon the ground of the king's original writs, and confining themselves strictly to that bottom, gave a harsh or imperfect judgment, the application for redress used to be to the king in person assisted by his privy council, (from whence also arose the jurisdiction of the court of requests (*Smith's Commonwealth, b.* 3. *c.* 7.) which was virtually abolished by the statute 16 *Car.* 1. *c.* 10.) and they were wont to refer the matter either to the chancellor and a select committee, or by degrees to the chancellor only, who mitigated the severity or supplied the defects of the judgments pronounced in the courts of law, upon weighing the circumstances of the case. This was the custom not only among our Saxon ancestors, before the institution of the *aula regia* (*LL. Edg. c.* 2.) but also after its dissolution, in the reign of king Edward I. (*Lambard. Archeion.* 59.) if not that of Henry II. 3 *Black.* 50.

In these early times the chief juridical employment of the chancellor must have been in devising new writs, directed to the courts of common law, to give remedy in cases where none was before administered. And to quicken the diligence of the clerks in the chancery, who were too much attached to antient precedents, it is provided by statute *Westm.* 2. 13 *Edw.* 1. *c.* 24. that "whensoever from thenceforth in one case a "writ shall be found in the chancery, and "in a like case falling under the same right, "and requiring like remedy no precedent of "a writ can be produced, the clerks in chan-"cery shall agree in forming a new one: and, "if they cannot agree, it shall be adjourned "to the next parliament, where a writ "shall be framed by consent of the learned "in the law, lest it happen for the future that "the court of our lord the king be deficient "in doing justice to the suitors." And this accounts for the very great variety of writs of trespass on the case, to be met with in the register, whereby the suitor had ready relief according to the exigency of his business, and adapted to the specialty, reason, and equity of his very case. (*Lamb. Archeion.* 61.) Which provision (with a lttle accuracy in the clerks of the chancery, and a little liberality in the judges, by extending rather than narrowing the remedial effects of the writ) might have effectually answered all the purposes of a court of equity, except that of obtaining a discovery by the oath of the defendant. 3 *Black.* 51.

But when, about the end of the reign of king Edward III. uses of land were introduced, and, though totally discountenanced by the courts of common law, were considered as fiduciary deposits and binding in conscience by the clergy, the separate jurisdiction of the chancery as a court of equity began to be established (*Spelm. Gloss.* 106. 1 *Lev.* 242.); and John Waltham, who was bishop of Salisbury and chancellor to king Richard II. by a strained interpretation of the above-mentioned statute of *Westm.* 2. devised the writ of *subpœna*, returnable in the court of chancery only, to make the feoffee to uses accountable to his *cestuy que use:* which process was afterwards extended to other matters wholly determinable at the common law, upon false and fictitious suggestions; for which therefore the chancellor himself is by statute 17 *Ric.* 2. *c.* 6. directed to give damages to the parties unjustly aggrieved. But as the clergy, so early as the reign of king Stephen, had attempted to turn their ecclesiastical courts into courts of equity, by entertaining suits *pro læsione fidei*, as a spiritual offence against conscience, in case of non-payment of debts or any breach of civil contracts (*Ld. Lyt. Hen.* 2. *b.* 3. *p.* 361. *n.*); till checked by the constitutions of Clarendon (10 *Hen.* 2. *c.* 15.), which declared that *placita de debitis, quæ fide interposita debentur, vel absque interpositione fidei, sint in justicia regis:* therefore probably the ecclesiastical chancellors, who then held the seal, were remiss in abridging their own new-acquired jurisdiction; especially as the spiritual courts continued to grasp at the same authority as before, in suits *pro læsione fidei*, so late as the fifteenth century (*Yearb.* 2 *Hen. IV.* 10. 38. & *VI.* 29.), till finally prohibited by the unanimous concurrence of all the judges. However, it appears from the parliament rolls (*Rot. Parl.* 4 *Hen. IV. n.* 78. & 110. 3 *Hen. V. n.* 46.) that in the reigns of Henry IV. and V. the commons were repeatedly urgent to have the writ of *subpœna* intirely suppressed, as being a novelty devised by the subtilty of chancellor

Waltham, against the form of the common law; whereby no plea could be determined, unless by examination and oath of the parties, according to the form of the law civil, and the law of holy church, in subversion of the common law. But though Henry IV. being then hardly warm in his throne, gave a palliating answer to their petitions, and actually passed the statute 4 *Hen.* 4. *c.* 23. whereby judgments at law are declared irrevocable, unless by attaint or writ of error, yet his son put a negative at once upon their whole application: and in Edward VI. time, the process by bill and *subpœna* was become the daily practice of the court (*Rot. Parl.* 14 *Edw.* 4. *n.* 33. 3 *Black.* 52.)

But this did not extend very far; for in the antient treatise, intitled *Diversité des courtes* (*Tit. Chanc. fol.* 296. *Rastell's edit. A. D.* 1534.) supposed to be written very early in the sixteenth century, we have a catalogue of the matters of conscience then cognizable by *subpœna* in chancery, which fall within a very narrow compass. No regular judicial system at that time prevailed in the court; but the suitor, when he thought himself aggrieved, found a desultory and uncertain remedy, according to the private opinion of the chancellor, who was generally an ecclesiastic, or sometimes (though rarely) a statesman: no lawyer having sat in the court of chancery from the times of the chief justices Thorpe and Knyvet, successively chancellor to king Edward III. in 1372 and 1373, (*Spelm. Gloss.* 111. *Dougl. Chron. Ser.* 50.) to the promotion of sir Thomas More by king Henry VIII. in 1530. After which the great seal was indiscriminately committed to the custody of lawyers, or courtiers, or churchmen, according as the convenience of the times and the disposition of the prince required, till serjeant Puckering was made lord keeper in 1592: from which time to the present, the court of chancery has always been filled by a lawyer, excepting the interval from 1621 to 1625, when the seal was intrusted to Dr. Williams, then dean of Westminster, but afterwards bishop of Lincoln: who had been chaplain to lord Ellesmere, when chancellor. 3 *Black.* 53.

In the time of lord Ellesmere (*A. D.* 1616.) arose that notable dispute between the courts of law and equity, set on foot by sir Edward Coke, then chief justice of the court of king's bench; whether a court of equity could give relief after or against a judgment at the common law. This contest was so warmly carried on, that indictments were preferred against the suitors, the solicitors, the counsel, and even a master in chancery, for having incurred a *præmunire*, by questioning in a court of equity a judgment in the court of king's bench, obtained by gross fraud and imposition (*Bacon's Works, IV.* 611, 612, 632.) This matter, being brought before the king, was by him referred to his learned counsel for their advice and opinion; who reported so strongly in favour of the courts of equity, (*Whitelocke of Parl. ii.* 390. 1 *Chan. Rep. append.* 11.) that his majesty gave judgment on their behalf: but, not contented with the irrefragable reasons and precedents produced by his counsel, (for the chief justice was clearly in the wrong) he chose rather to decide the question by referring it to the plenitude of his royal prerogative. (1 *Chan. Rep. append.* 26.) Sir Edward Coke submitted to the decision, and thereby made atonement for his error: but this struggle, together with the business of *commendams* (in which he acted a very noble part) and his controlling the commissioners of sewers, were the open and avowed causes, first of his suspension, and soon after of his removal from his office. 3 *Black.* 54.

Lord Bacon, who succeeded lord Ellesmere, reduced the practice of the court into a more regular system; but did not sit long enough to effect any considerable revolution in the science itself: and few of his decrees which have reached us are of any great consequence to posterity. His successors, in the reign of Charles I. did little to improve upon his plan; and even after the restoration, the seal was committed to the earl of Clarendon, who had withdrawn from practice as a lawyer near twenty years; and afterwards to the earl of Shaftsbury, who had never practised at all. 3 *Black.* 54, 55.

Sir *Heneage Finch*, who succeeded in 1673, and became afterwards earl of Nottingham, was a person of the greatest abilities and most uncorrupted integrity: a thorough master and zealous defender of the laws and constitution of his country; and indued with a pervading genius that enabled him to discover and to pursue the true spirit of justice, notwithstanding the embarrassments raised by the narrow and technical notions which then prevailed in the courts of law, and the imperfect ideas of redress, which had possessed the courts of equity. 3 *Black.* 55.

The reason and necessities of mankind, arising from the great change in property by the extension of trade, and the abolition of military tenures, co-operated in establishing his plan, and enabled him in the course of nine years to build a system of jurisprudence and jurisdiction upon wide and rational foundations; which have also been extended and improved by many great men, who have since presided in chancery, and from that time to this, the power and business of the court have increased to an amazing degree. 3 *Black.* 55.

From this court of equity in chancery, as from the other superior courts, an appeal lies to the house of peers: but there are these differences between appeals from a court of equity, and writs of error from a court of law; 1st, that the former may be brought upon an interlocutory matter; the latter upon nothing, but only a definitive judgment; 2dly, that in writs of error, the house of lords pronounces the judgment: in appeals, it gives direction to the court below, to rectify its own decree. *Ibid.*

But this court of chancery, will not retain a suit by English bill under 10*l.* value, except in cases of charity, nor under the value of 40*s.* per ann. in lands, except for rent-service. *Eq. Cas. Abr.* 75.

For the practice of this court, see BILL IN EQUITY *and* PRACTICE.

CHANGER, an officer belonging to the king's mint, whose office consists chiefly in exchanging coin for bullion, brought in by merchants or others: it is written after the old way, *chaunger. Stat.* 2 *Hen.* 6. *cap.* 12. *Cowel. Blount.*

CHANTER, (*cantator*) a singer in the choir of a cathedral church. *Ibid.*

CHANTRY, or CHAUNTRY, (*cantaria*) a little church, chapel, or particular altar, in some cathedral church, &c. endowed with lands, or other revenues, for the maintenance of one or more priests, daily to sing mass, and officiate divine service for the souls of the donors, and such others as they appointed. *Ibid.*

CHAPEL, (*capella*, Fr. *chapelle*) is either adjoining to a church, for performing divine service; or separate from the mother-church, where the parish is wide, which is commonly called a chapel of ease. And chapels of ease are built for the ease of those parishioners who dwell far from the parochial church, in prayer and preaching only; for the sacraments and burials ought to be performed in the parochial church. 2 *Rol. Abr.* 340.

These chapels are served by inferior curates, provided at the charge of the rector, or vicar, or him that has the benefice, as the custom may be. And the curates are therefore removable at the pleasure of the rector or vicar. *Cowel. Blount.*

Public chapels, annexed to parish churches, shall be repaired by the parishioners, as the church is; if any other persons be not bound to do it. 2 *Inst.* 489.

CHAPELRY, (*capellania*) is the precinct and limits of a chapel.

CHAPERON, (Fr.) a hood or bonnet, anciently worn by the knights of the garter, as part of the habit of that noble order: but in heraldry, it is a little escutcheon fixed in the forehead of the horses that draw a hearse at a funeral. *Cowel. Blount.*

CHAPITERS, (Lat. *capitula*, Fr. *chapitres*, *i. e.* chapters of a book) signified in our ancient common law, a summary of such matters as were to be enquired of, or presented before justices in eyre, justices of assise, or of peace, in their sessions. *Britton, cap.* 3.

These chapiters are now those articles which are delivered by the justice in his charge to the inquest; whereas, in ancient times, they were first read in open court, and then delivered in writing to the grand inquest, for their better observance; and the grand jury were to answer upon their oaths to all the articles thus delivered them, and not put the judges to long and learned charges to little or no purpose, for want of remembering the same, as they do now, when they think their duty well enough performed, if they only present those few of many misdemeanors which are brought before them by way of indictment. *Horn's Mir. lib.* 3. *Des articles in Eyre. Cowel. Blount.*

CHAPLAIN, (*capellanus*) a priest or like spiritual person retained by the king, or some noble person, to instruct him and his family, and say divine service in his house. *Cowel. Blount.*

The king, queen, prince, princess, and royal family, may retain as many chaplains as they please; and the king's chaplains may hold any number of benefices of the king's gift, as the king shall think fit to bestow upon them. And this, even in addition to what they hold upon the presentation of a subject without dispensation: but a king's chaplain beneficed by the king, cannot afterwards take a living from *a subject*, but by a dispensation according to the stat. 1 *Salk.* 161.

An archbishop may retain eight chaplains; a duke, or a bishop, six; marquis, or earl, five; viscount, four; baron, knight of the garter, or lord chancellor, three; a duchess, marchioness, countess, baroness, the treasurer, and controller of the king's house, the king's secretary, dean of the chapel, almoner, and master of the rolls, each of them two; the chief justice of the king's bench, &c. one; all which may purchase a licence or dispensation, and take two benefices with cure of souls. *Stat.* 22 *H.* 8. *cap.* 13.

Also every judge of the king's bench and common pleas, and chancellor and chief baron of the exchequer, and the king's attorney and solicitor general, may each of them have one chaplain, attendant on his person, having one benefice with cure, who may be non-resident on the same, by stat. 25 *Hen.* 8. *cap.* 16.

And the groom of the stole, treasurer of the king's chamber, and chancellor of the duchy of Lancaster, may retain each one chaplain. *Stat.* 33 *Hen.* 8. *cap.* 28.

There is also a distinction between the king's chaplains and those of noblemen, for the king can give a leave to his chaplains for non-residence, even whilst they do not attend his household. But the chaplains of noblemen are only excused during their actual attendance upon lords or their ladies. 3 *Burn. Ec. L.* 290.

A chaplain must be retained by letters testimonial under hand and seal, or he is not a chaplain within the statute, so that it is not enough for a spiritual person to be retained by word only to be a chaplain. 4 *Rep.* 90.

CHAPTER, (*capitulum*) is a congregation

of clergymen consisting of *prebends* or *canons* under the dean in a cathedral church. This collegiate company is metaphorically termed *capitulum*, signifying a little head; it being a kind of head, not only to govern the diocese in the vacation of the bishoprick, but also in many things to advise and assist the bishop when the see is full, for which, with the dean, they form a council. *Co. Lit.* 103.

CHARGE to the GRAND JURY. The grand jury, previous to their sitting to receive indictments proposed before them are instructed in *the articles* of their enquiry by *a charge* from the judge, who presides on the bench, these articles were formerly reduced to writing, and delivered to the grand jury for their information. See *Chapiters.*

CHARGE AND DISCHARGE. A charge is a thing done, that bindeth him that doth it: and discharge is the removal, or taking away of that charge. *Terms de Ley.* Land may be charged divers ways; as by demise, mortgage, or grant of rent out of it, or by statutes, judgments, conditions, warranties, or the like. *Lit. sect.* 648. *Moor Ca.* 129. *Dyer* 10.

If rent be issuing out of a house, &c. and it falls down, the charge shall remain upon the soil. 9 *E.* 4. 20. But when the estate is gone, upon which the charge was grounded, there generally the charge is determined. *Co. Lit.* 349. And in all cases where any executory thing is created by deed, there by consent of all the parties it may be by deed defeated and discharged. 10 *Rep.* 49.

Charge and discharge in Equity. Where a decree or order of the court directs an account, or the like, to be taken and examined before one of the masters thereof, in such case, the plaintiff delivers in an account before the master, in the form of *a charge* against the defendant, which being examined and gone through, the defendant or adverse party must bring in his *discharge* against such *charge*, which being likewise examined and gone through, the master will exercise his judgment upon the evidence, and allow or disallow *the charge* or any part of it as he thinks proper, and so *è contra* as to the discharge, after which the report is made.

CHARITABLE CORPORATION. A society of persons, who in the early part of the reign of *Geo.* 2. obtained a statute to lend money to industrious poor, at 5*l.* per cent. interest on pawns and pledges, to prevent their falling into the hands of the pawnbrokers, and they were therefore called the charitable corporation: but they likewise took 5*l.* per cent. for the charge of officers, warehouses, &c. And in the 5th of *Geo.* 2. broke, and defrauded the proprietors of great sums. See 5 *Geo.* 2. *cap.* 31, 32. 7 *Geo.* 2. *cap.* 11.

CHARITABLE USES. The king as *parens patriæ*, has the general superintendance of all *charities*, which he exercises by the keeper of his conscience, the chancellor: and therefore whenever it is necessary, the attorney general at the relation of some informant (who is usually called *the relator*,) files *ex officio*, an information in the court of chancery, to have the charity properly established. 3 *Black.* 427.

Also by stat. 43 *Eliz.* *c.* 4. authority is given to the lord chancellor or lord keeper, and to the chancellor of the duchy of Lancaster respectively, to grant commissions under their several seals, to inquire into abuses of charitable donations, and rectify the same by decree; which may be reviewed in the respective courts of the several chancellors upon exceptions taken thereto. But though this is done in the petty bag-office, in the court of chancery, because the commission is there returned, it is not a proceeding at common law, but treated as an original cause in the court of equity. 3 *Black.* 428.

The evidence below is not taken down in writing, and the respondent, in his answer to the exceptions, may allege what new matter he pleases; upon which they go to proof, and examine witnesses in writing upon all the matters in issue: and the court may decree the respondent to pay all the costs, though no such authority is given by the statute. *Ibid.*

And as it is thus considered as an original cause throughout, an appeal lies of course from the chancellor's decree to the House of Peers. *Ibid.*

As to what shall be deemed a charitable use, the *stat.* 43 *Eliz.* *c.* 4. enacts, that "the commissioners shall inquire of the following uses as good and charitable: *viz.* for relief of aged and impotent and poor people; for maintenance of sick and maimed soldiers; schools of learning, free schools, scholars in universities; houses of correction; for repair of bridges, of seas and havens, of causeways, of churches, of seabanks, of highways; for education and preferment of orphans, for marriage of poor maids, for support and help of young tradesmen, of handicraftsmen, of persons decayed; for redemption, or relief of prisoners or captives, for ease and aid of poor inhabitants; concerning payment of fifteenths, setting out of soldiers, and other taxes."

Other gifts, provisions, and limitations, which, though not within the letter, have been held to be within the provisions of the statute, as money to maintain a preaching minister, or a schoolmaster: so for the building of an hospital for the relief of poor people. 2 *Ves.* 187. So for the king to fund a free-school, and make it a corporation of guardians, masters, and ushers, to give charity to them and theirs for necessaries to maintain them, and certain poor people under them: so for the building a sessions-house for a city or county; the making of a new or repair of an old pulpit in a church, or the buying a pulpit cloth or pulpit cushion, or the setting up of new bells, where none are, or amending them, where they are out of order. *Duke's Ch. Us.* 109. So a devise of money to a minister to preach an annual sermon, and keep a tomb-stone and inscription in repair, and to a corporation for keeping accounts thereof, is a charitable use. 1 *Vez.* 320 4 *Bro. Ch. Rep.* 67. *Fonbl.* 208. See also *Mortmain.*

CHARKS, are pit-coal when charred or charked, so called in Worcestershire; as sea-coal thus prepared at Newcastle is called coke. *Blount.*

CHARRE OF LEAD, is a quantity of lead consisting of thirty pigs, each pig containing six stone wanting two pounds, and every stone being twelve pounds. *Cowel. Blount.*

CHARTA, a word made use of not only for a charter, for the holding an estate, but also a statute. See *Magna Charta.*

CHARTE, a card, chart, or plan which mariners use at sea, mentioned 14 *Car.* 2. *cap.* 33. *Cowel. Blount.*

CHARTEL, (Fr. *cartel*) a letter of defiance, or challenge to single combat; in use heretofore to decide difficult controversies at law, which could not otherwise be determined. *Blount.*

CHARTER, (Lat. *charta*, Fr. *chartres*, i. e. *instrumenta*) is the written evidence of things done between man and man: and *charters* are divided into those of *the king*, and those of *private persons.* Charters of the king are those whereby the king passeth any grant to any person or body politic; as a charter of exemption, of privilege, pardon, or the like. *Bract. Lib.* 2. *c.* 26. *Brit. c.* 39. *Fleta, lib.* 3. *c.* 14. *Cowel. Blount.*

Charters of private persons are deeds and instruments for the conveyance of lands, &c. And the purchaser of lands shall have all the charters, deeds and evidences as incident to the same, and for the maintenance of his title. *Co. Lit.* 6. *Moor Ca.* 687.

CHARTERER, in Cheshire, a freeholder is called by this name. *Sir P. Ley's Antiq. fol.* 356.

CHARTER-GOVERNMENTS IN AMERICA. Our colonies in America, previous to the acknowledgment of the independance of the united states by 22 *Geo.* 3. *c.* 46. with respect to their interior polity, were properly of three sorts.

1. *Provincial establishments*, the constitutions of which depend on the respective commissions issued by the crown to the governors, and the instructions which usually accompany those commissions; under the authority of which, provincial assemblies are constituted with the power of making local ordinances, not repugnant to the laws of England. 1 *Black.* 108.

2. *Proprietary* governments, granted out by the crown to individuals, in the nature of *feudatory principalities*, with all the inferior regalities, and subordinate powers of legislation, which formerly belonged to the owners of counties palatine: yet still with these express conditions, that the ends for which the grant was made, be substantially pursued, and that nothing be attempted which may derogate from the authority of the mother country. *Ibid.*

3. *Charter* governments, in the nature of civil corporations, with the power of making by-laws, for their own interior regulation, not contrary to the laws of England; and with such rights and authorities as are specially given them in their several charters of incorporation. *Ibid.*

The form of government in most of them is borrowed from that of England. They have a governor named by the king (or in some proprietary colonies by the proprietor) who is his representative or deputy; they also have courts of justice of their own, from whose decisions an appeal lies to the king and council here in England. *Ibid.*

Their general assemblies, which are their house of commons, together with their council of state, being their upper house, with the concurrence of the king, or his representative, the governor, make laws suited to their emergency. *Ibid.*

CHARTER-LAND, (*terra per chartam*) is such as a man holds by charter, that is by evidence in writing otherwise called freehold. *Anno* 19 *H.* 7. *cap.* 13. This in the time of the Saxons was called *bockland*, which was held (according to Lambard) with more commodious and easy conditions than *folkland* was, *i. e.* lands held without writing. 2 *Black. Com.* 90.

CHARTER-PARTY, (Lat. *charta partita*, Fr. *chartre parti*, *i. e.* a deed or writing divided) is what among merchants and sea-faring men we commonly call a pair of indentures, containing the covenants and agreements made between them, touching their merchandize and maritime affairs. 2 *Inst.* 673. And charter-parties of affreightment settle agreements, as to the cargo of ships, and bind the master to deliver the goods in good condition at the place of discharge, according to agreement; and the master sometimes obliges himself, ship, tackle and furniture, for performance.

The common law construes charter parties, as near as may be, according to the intention of them, and not according to the literal sense of traders, or those that merchandize by sea, but they must be regularly pleaded. In covenant by charter-party, that the ship should return to the river of Thames, by a certain time, dangers of the sea excepted, and after in the voyage, and within the time of the return, the ship was taken upon the sea by pirates, so that the master could not return at the time mentioned in the agreement; it was adjudged that this impediment was within the exception of the charter-party, which extends as well to any danger upon the sea by pirates and men of war, as dangers of the sea by ship-wreck, tempest, &c. *Stile* 132. 2 *Rol. Abr.* 248.

A ship is freighted at so much per month that she shall be out, covenanted to be paid after her arrival at the port of London; the ship is cast away coming up from the Downs, but the lading is all preserved, the freight shall in this case be paid; for the money becomes due monthly by the contract, and the place mentioned is only to ascertain where the money is to be paid, and the ship is intitled to wages, like a mariner that serves by the month, who if he dies in the voyage, his executors are to be answered, *pro rata*. *Molloy de Jur. Maritim.* 260. If a part-owner of a ship refuse to join with the other owners in setting out of the ship, he shall not be intitled to his share of the freight; but by the course of the admiralty, the other owners ought to give security if the ship perish in the voyage, to make good to the owner standing out his share of the ship. Sir Lionel Jenkins, in a case of this nature, certified that by the law marine and course of the admiralty, the plaintiff was to have no share of the freight; and that it was so in all places, for otherwise there would be no navigation. *Lex Mercat.* 100. See *Freight.*

CHARTIS REDDENDIS, is a writ now in disuse which anciently lay against him that had charters or feoffment entrusted to his keeping, and refused to deliver them. *Reg. Orig.* 159.

CHASE, (Fr. *chasse*) is a great quantity of woody ground lying open, and privileged for wild beasts of the chase, which properly extend to the buck, doe, fox, martin, and roe, and in common and legal sense to all the beasts of the forest; which, besides the other, are reckoned to be hart, hind, hare, boar, and wolf, and in a word all wild beasts of venary, or hunting. *Co. Lit.* 233.

A chase is of a middle nature between a forest and a park, being commonly less than a forest, and not endowed with so many liberties, as the courts of attachment, swainmote, and justice-seat; though of a larger compass, and stored with greater diversity both of keepers, and wild beasts or game, than a park. *Manwood.*

A chase also differs from a forest in this, because it may be in the hands of a subject, which a forest in its proper and true nature cannot. *Crompt. Jurisd.* 148, 197.

For though the king may give or alienate a forest to a subject, yet it thereby loseth the true property of a forest, because the courts called the justice-seat, swainmote, &c. do forthwith vanish, none being able to make a lord chief justice in eyre of the forest, but the king, and yet it may be granted in so large a manner, as there may be attachment, swainmote, and a court equivalent to a justice-seat, and if such jurisdiction is not added in the grant, it becomes a chase, and trespassers in it are only punishable by the common law. *Manwood, part* 2. *c.* 3, 4. 4 *Inst.* 314.

A chase likewise differs from a park in that it is not inclosed; and also in that, a man may have a chase in another man's ground as well as his own, being indeed the liberty of keeping beasts of chace or royal game therein, protected even from the owner of the land, with a power of hunting them therein. 2 *Black. Com.* 38.

And if a person hath a chase in other men's grounds, and after purchaseth the grounds, the chase remaineth. 2 *Inst.* 318.

Also if a common person hath a chase in another's soil, the owner of the soil cannot destroy all the covert, but ought to leave sufficient thereof, and also browsewood, as hath been accustomed. 11 *Rep.* 22.

CHASOR, an hunting horse. *Dederunt mihi unum chasorem*, &c. *Leg. Will.* 1. *cap.* 22. *Blount.*

CHASTELLAINE, a noble woman: *quasi castelli domina.*

CHASTITY. The Roman law (*Ff.* 48, 8. 1.) justifies homicide in defence of the chastity either of one's self or relations; and so also, according to Selden, (*de Legib. Hebræor. l.* 4. *c.* 3.) stood the law in the Jewish republic. The English law likewise justifies a woman, killing one who attempts to ravish her. (*Bac. Elem.* 34. 1 *Hawk. P. C.* 71.) So the husband or father may justify killing a man, who attempts a rape upon his wife or daughter; but not if he takes them in adultery by consent, for the one is forcible and felonious, but not the other. 1 *Hal. P. C.* 485, 6. 4 *Black.* 181.

And without doubt the forcibly attempting a crime, of a still more detestable nature, may be equally resisted by the death of the unnatural aggressor. For the one uniform principle that runs through our own and all other laws seems to be this, that where a crime, in itself capital, is endeavoured to be committed by force, it is lawful to repel that force by the death of the party attempting. 4 *Black. Com.* 181.

CHATTELS, or CATALS, (from the Lat. *catalla*) which primarily signified only beasts of husbandry, or as we still call them cattle; but in its secondary sense it was applied to all *movables* in general. 2 *Black.* 385. And chattels are distributed by our law into two kinds, chattels real, and chattels personal. 2 *Black.* 386.

Chattels real are such as concern or savour of the realty or freehold, as terms for years of land, the next presentation to a church, estates by statute merchant, statute staple, elegit, or the like: and these are called real chattels, as being interests issuing out of or annexed to real estates, of which they have one quality, *viz. immobility*, which denominates them *real*: but want the other, *viz.* a sufficient legal indeterminate duration: and this want it is that constitutes them *chattels*: the utmost period for which they can last is fixed and determinate, either for such a space of time certain, or till such a particular sum of money be raised out of such a particular income. Thus a lease for years must necessarily fail at the end and completion of the term: the next presentation to a church is satisfied and gone the instant it comes into possession, that is, by the first avoidance, and presentation to the living; the conditional estates by statutes and elegits are determined as soon as the debt is paid; and if there be any other chattel real it will be found to correspond with the rest in this essential quality, that its duration is limited to a certain time, beyond which it cannot subsist. 1 *Inst.* 118. 2 *Black.* 386.

Chattels personal are properly and strictly speaking things *movable*, which may be annexed to or attendant on the person of the owner, and carried about with him from one part of the world to another. 2 *Black.* 387.

Thus gold, silver, plate, jewels, household-goods and wares in a shop, corn sown on the ground, carts, ploughs, coaches, saddles, cattle, as horses, oxen, kine, bullocks, sheep, pigs, and all tame fowls and birds, swans, turkeys, geese, poultry, are called personal in two respects, one because they belong immediately to the person of a man; and the other, for that being any way injuriously withheld from us we have no means to recover them but by personal action. *Co. Lit.* 118. *Noy* 49.

But deeds relating to a freehold, obligations, and the like, which are things in action, are not reckoned under goods and chattels; nor is money, or animals *feræ naturæ*. 8 *Rep.* 33. *Terms de Ley* 103. *Kitch.* 32.

CHAUD-MEDLEY, is of pretty much the same import with chance-medley. The former, in its etymology, signifies an affray in the heat of blood, or passion; the latter, a casual affray. The latter is in common speech too often erroneously applied to any manner of homicide by misadventure; whereas it appears by the stat. 24 *Hen.* 8, *c.* 5. and our ancient books, *Staundf. P. C.* 16, that it is properly applied to such killing as happens in self-defence, upon sudden rencounter. 3 *Inst.* 55, 57. *Foster* 275, 6. 4 *Black. Com.* 184.

CHAUMPERT, a kind of tenure mentioned in *Stat.* 35 *Ed.* 3, to the hospital of Bowes in the isle of Guernsey. *Cowel. Blount.*

CHAUNTER, a singer in a cathedral. *Ibid.*

CHAUNTRY-RENTS, are rents paid to the crown by the servants or purchasers of chauntry-lands. 22 *Car.* 2. *c.* 6.

CHEATS, are deceitful practices in defrauding or endeavouring to defraud another of his known right by means of some artful device, contrary to the plain rules of common honesty; as by playing with false dice, or by causing an illiterate person to execute a deed to his prejudice, by reading it over to him in words different from those in which it was written; or by persuading a woman to execute writings to another as her trustee, upon an intended marriage, which in truth contained no such thing, but only a warrant of attorney to confess a judgment; or by suppressing a will, and such like. 1 *Hawk.* 188.

And by 33 *Hen.* 8. *cap.* 1, "If any person "falsely and deceitfully get into his hands "or possession any money or other things "of any other persons by colour of any "false token, &c. being convicted, he shall "have such punishment by imprisonment, "setting upon the pillory, or by any corporal pain, except pains of death, as shall "be adjudged by the persons before whom "he shall be convicted." *Sec.* 2.

For this offence the offender cannot be fined, but corporal pain only inflicted if he be indicted on the statute. 3 *Inst.* 133.

But if he be indicted (as he may be) at common law, he may be fined and imprisoned. 4 *Black.* 158. 1 *Hawk.* 158.

And there are frauds which in a special case may not be helped civilly, and yet shall be punished criminally: as, if a minor goes about the town, and pretending to be of age defrauds many persons, by taking credit for a considerable quantity of goods, and then insisting on his nonage, the persons injured cannot recover the value of their goods, though they may indict and punish him for a common cheat. *Barl.* 100.

Also, by 30 *Geo.* 2. *c.* 24, persons convicted of obtaining money or goods by false pretences, or of sending threatening letters in order to extort money or goods, may be punished by fine and imprisonment, or by pillory, whipping, or transportation. But it has been determined on this statute that a false assertion or affirmation, without an artful device or contrivance, will not amount to a false pretence, and therefore it was held in the *K. v. Lara*, that it was not a false pretence within this statute to purchase goods and to give a bill for them drawn upon a banker with whom the drawer had no effects. 6 *Ter. Rep.* 565.

CHECK-ROLL, is a roll or book containing the names of such as are attendant on and in pay to the king or other great personages, as their household servants. *Stat.* 19 *Car.* 2. *cap.* 1. It is otherwise called the chequer-roll, and seems to take its etymology from the Exchequer. 14 *Hen.* 8. *c.* 3.

CHELINDRA, was a sort of ship. *Cowel. Blount.*

CHEST, an uncertain quantity of merchandise, wine, &c. *Cowel. Blount.*

CHESTER. See *Counties Palatine.*

CHEVAGE, (*chevagium*, from the Fr. *chef*, i. e. *caput*) was a tribute or sum of money formerly paid by such as held lands in villenage to their lords in acknowledgment, and was a kind of head or poll-money. *Cowel. Blount.*

CHEVANTIA, a loan or advance of money upon credit. *Ibid.*

CHEVERIL, (*cheverillus*) a young cock, or cockling. *Ibid.*

CHEVISANCE, (from the Fr. *chevissance*,) signifies an agreement or contract made in respect to the buying and selling of goods amongst traders, and is so used in stat. 13 *Eliz. c.* 7, relating to bankrupts.

CHEVITIÆ, and CHEVISCÆ, are heads of ploughed lands. *Cowel. Blount.*

CHIEF RENTS, the rents of freeholders of manors often so called, i. e. *reditus capitales.* They are also denominated quit rents, *quieti reditus,* because thereby the tenant goes quit and free of all other services. 2 *Black. Com.* 42.

CHIEF PLEDGE, (*plegius vel vas capitalis*) mentioned 20 *Hen.* 6. *c.* 8. See *Borough-head* and *Borough-holder.*

CHIEF (TENANTS IN). Tenants in *capite,* holding immediately under the king, in right of his crown and dignity. 2 *Black. Com.* 60.

CHILDREN, (in law) are a man's issue, begotten on his wife. The duties of children to their parents arise from a principle of natural justice and retribution: for to those who gave us existence we naturally owe subjection and obedience during our minority, and honour and reverence ever after: they who protected the weakness of our infancy are entitled to our protection in the infirmities of their age: they who by sustenance have enabled their offspring to prosper, ought in return to be supported by that offspring, in case they stand in need of assistance: upon this principle proceed all the duties of children to their parents which are enjoined by positive laws: thus a child is equally justifiable in defending the person or maintaining the cause or suit of a bad parent as a good one; and is equally compellable by the stat. 43 *Eliz. c.* 2, made for the relief of the poor, if of sufficient ability, to maintain and provide for a wicked and unnatural progenitor, as for one who has shown the greatest tenderness and parental piety. 1 *Black.* 453, 454.

See also *Age—Capacity—Infant,* and *Posthumous.*

CHILDWIT, (Sax.) was a fine or penalty of a bond-woman unlawfully gotten with child. And according to *Cowel* it signified a power to take a fine of a bond-woman gotten with child without the lord's consent: and within the manor of Writtle, in the county of Essex, every reputed father of a base child pays to the lord, for a fine, 3*s.* 4*d.* where it seems to extend as well to free as bond-women; and the custom is there called childwit to this day. *Blount.*

CHIMIN, (from the Fr. *chemin,* i. e. *via*) is a way; which is of two sorts: the king's highway, and a private way. *Comyns' Dig. tit. Chim.*

CHIMINAGE, (*Chiminagium*) is a toll due by custom for having a way through a forest. *Cromp. Jurisd.* 189. *Co. Lit.* 56. *Cowel. Blount.*

CHIMNEY-MONEY, otherwise called hearth-money, a duty imposed by 14 *Car.* 2, *c.* 2, on every fire-hearth and stove of every dwelling or other house within England and Wales, which being much complained of, as burthensome to the people, was taken off by 7 & 8 *W.* 3. *c.* 18, which substituted an equally grievous duty on windows.

CHIMNEY SWEEPERS. By 28 *Geo.* 3. *c.* 48. the churchwardens and overseers of parishes, with the consent of two justices, may bind any boy of the age of eight years or more, chargeable to the parish, or who begs, or with the consent of the parent, to be apprentice to a chimney sweeper, until 16 years of age.

His age to be mentioned in the indenture, as taken from the register, or where none according to information. *Ibid.*

The form of the indenture is given, but they are not chargeable with the duty now chargeable on parish indentures. *Ibid.*

Covenants for keeping boys under eight years are void; and taking them otherwise is 10*l.* penalty, and not less than 5*l.* *Ibid.*

Overseers of the poor of any township or village may act. *Ibid.*

Any justice may determine complaints between masters and apprentices. *Ibid.*

No one shall keep more than six apprentices at one time, on like pain, and every master is to affix a brass plate with his name and place of abode, on the front of a leathern cap for the boy to wear when upon duty, on like pain. *Ibid.*

Masters ill treating apprentices, or being guilty of a breach of covenant, subjected to like pain. *Ibid.*

Masters are not to let apprentices to hire, nor cause them to call the streets before seven, nor after twelve between Michaelmas and Lady Day; nor before five and twelve, between Lady Day and Michaelmas, on like pain. *Ibid.*

A magistrate may convict; and the penalties are recoverable by distress; but not to issue till six days after conviction, and order for payment served; appeal lies to the informer. *Ibid.*

CHIPP, CHEAP, CHIPPING, signifies the place to be a market-town, as Chippenham, &c. *Blount.*

CHIPPINGAVEL, or cheapingavel, toll for buying and selling. *Ibid.*

CHIRCHGEMOT, or CHIRGEMOT, (*ciregimot,* Sax.) a synod, or a meeting in a church or vestry. 4 *Inst.* 321. *Cowel. Blount.*

CHIROGRAPH, (*chirographium,* or *scriptum chirographatum*). Formerly when deeds were more concise than at present, it was usual to write both parts on the same piece of parchment, with some words or letters of the alphabet written between them, through which the parchment was cut, either in a straight or indented line, in such manner as to leave half the word CHIROGRAPH on in one part, and half in the other. Deeds thus made were denominated *syngrapha* by the canonists, and with us *chirographa*, or hand-writing; the word *cirographum* or *cyrographum* being usually that which is divided in making the indenture: and this custom is still preserved in making out the indentures of a fine. 2 *Black.* 296.

CHIROGRAPHER OF FINES, (*chirographus finitum et concordiarum* of the Greek Χειρογραφον, a compound of χειρ, *manus*, a hand, and γραφω, *scribo*, I write, a writing of a man's hand) signifies that officer in the Common Pleas who ingrosseth fines acknowledged in that court into a perpetual record, after they are examined and passed in the other offices, and that writes and delivers the indentures of them to the party: and this officer makes out two indentures, one for the buyer, another for the seller; and also makes one other indented piece, containing the effect of the fine, which he delivers to the *custos brevium*, which is called the foot of the fine. The chirographer likewise, or his deputy, proclaims all the fines in the court every term, according to the statute, and indorses the proclamations upon the backside of the foot thereof, and always keeps the writ of covenant, and note of the fine. 2 *Inst.* 468.

CHIVALRY, (*servitium militare*) comes from the Fr. *chevalier*, and in our law was used for a tenure of lands by knights service; whereby the tenant was bound to perform service in war unto the king, or the mesne lord of whom he held by that tenure.

It was only in the feoffment that the tenant held *per servitium militare*, without any specification of serjeanty, escuage, &c. Special, when it was declared particularly by what kind of knight-service the land was held.

By the stat. 12 *Car.* 2. *c.* 24, tenures by knights service of the king, or any other person *in capite*, &c. and the fruits and consequences thereof are taken away and discharged; and all tenures are to be construed and adjudged to be free and common socage, &c.

CHOP-CHURCH, (*ecclesiarum permutatio*) a vulgar expression, used to denote the exchange of benefices; thus to chop and change is a common expression. *Cowel. Blount.*

CHORAL, (*choralis*) any person admitted to sit and serve God in the choir, or chorus. *Ibid.*

CHOREPISCOPI, Suffragan or rural bishops, now abolished. *Kennet's Paroch. Antiq.* 639.

CHOSE, (Fr.) a thing; used in the common law with divers epithets; as, chose local, chose transitory, and chose in action. Chose local is such a thing as is annexed to a place, as a mill, and the like: and chose transitory is that thing which is movable, and may be taken away, or carried from place to place: chose in action is a thing incorporeal, and only a right, which may be recoverd by suit, as an annuity, a bond or obligation for debt, covenant, or the like. And, generally, all causes of suit for any debt, duty, or wrong, are to be accounted choses in action: and it seems a chose in action may also be called chose in suspence, because it hath no real existence or being, nor can properly be said to be in our possession until after a verdict. *Bro. tit. Chose in Action.* 1 *Lil. Abr.* 264. 2. *Black.* 390.

When bonds or other specialties or debts are assigned, it is done with power of attorney to receive and sue in the assignor's name; so that though in this case a chose in action may be said to be assignable over to a certain extent, yet it amounts to little more than a letter of attorney to sue for the debt. *Wood's Inst.* 282. 1 *Shep. Abr.* 337.

CHRISM, a confection of oil and balsam consecrated by the bishop, and used in the popish ceremonies of baptism, confirmation, and sometimes ordination. *Cowel. Blount.*

CHRISMALE, *Chrismal*, *Chrisom*, the face-cloth, or piece of linen laid over the child's head at baptism, which in ancient times was a perquisite due to the parish priest. *Ibid.*

CHRISMATIS DENARII, chrisom-pence, money paid to the diocesan, or to his suffragan, by the parochial clergy, for the chrisom consecrated by them about Easter, for the holy uses of the year ensuing. *Cartular.* Mons. *De Bernedy*, *Cotton.* MS.

CHRISTIANITATIS CURIA, the court christian, or ecclesiastical judicature. See *Court Christian.*

CHURCH, (*ecclesia*) is a temple or building consecrated to the honour of God and religion, and anciently dedicated to some saint, whose name it assumed; or it is an "assembly of persons united by the profes-"sion of the same christian faith, met to-"gether for religious worship;" and if it hath administration of the sacraments and sepulture, it is in law adjudged a church.

A church in general consists of three principal parts, that is, the belfrey or steeple, the body of the church with the aisles, and the chancel: and not only the freehold of the whole church, but of the church-yard, are in the parson or rector; and the parson may have an action of trespass against any one that shall commit any trespass in the church or church-yard; as in the breaking of seats annexed to the church, or the windows, taking away the leads, or any of the materials of the church, cutting the trees in the church-yard, &c. *Co. Lit.* 644, 645.

Also a man may be indicted for digging up the graves of persons buried, and taking away their burial-dresses, &c. the property whereof remains in the party who was the owner when used: and it is said an offender was found guilty of felony in this case, but had his clergy. *Co. Lit.* 113.

The property of the bells, books, and other ornaments, and the goods of the church, is in the parishioners; but the custody of them is in the church-wardens, who may maintain action of trespass against such as shall wrongfully take them away. 1 *Rol. Rep.* 255.

The use of the body of the church, and the seats fixed to the freehold, is common to all the parishioners that pay to the repairs thereof. The chancel of the church is to be repaired by the parson, unless there be a custom to the contrary; and for these repairs the parson may cut down trees in the church-yard, but not otherwise. 35 *E.* 1. *Stat.* 2. viz. *Stat. Ne Rector prosternat*, &c. By the common law parishioners of every parish are bound to repair the church: 1 *Salk.* 164. and the Spiritual court may compel the parishioners to repair the church, and excommunicate every one of them till it be repaired; but those that are willing to contribute shall be absolved till the greater part agree to a tax, when the excommunication is to be taken off; but the spiritual court cannot assess them towards it. 1 *Mod.* 194. 1 *Vent.* 367. For though this court hath power to oblige the parishioners to repair by ecclesiastical censures, yet they cannot appoint in what sum, or set a rate, for that must be settled by the church-wardens, &c. 2 *Mod.* 8.

Where a church is so much out of repair that it is necessary to pull it down, in such case, upon a general warning to the parishioners, the major part, meeting, may make a rate for pulling it down, and rebuilding it on the old foundation, and it shall be good. And if any parishioner refuse to pay his proportion, they may libel against him in the ecclesiastical court. 2 *Mod.* 222. And if a church be down, and the parish is increased, the greater part of the parish may raise a tax for he necessary enlarging it, as well as the repairing thereof, &c. 1 *Mod.* 237.

Church rates for repairs are to be made by the *church-wardens and the major part of the parishioners*, which shall bind the others, after a general notice given; and if the parishioners refuse or neglect to meet upon such notice, or if on meeting they refuse to make a rate, then the church-wardens and overseers of the poor may make a rate, and levy it on the inhabitants, being first confirmed by the ordinary or archdeacon. And rates for repairing of churches, &c. are of ecclesiastical cognizance, and to be recovered in the ecclesiastical court. Also if a parish is unequally rated, those who are aggrieved must plead it in the spiritual court, being sued there. 1 *Vent.* 367. 2 *Rol. Abr.* 291.

These rates must be made upon the whole parish, and not on particular persons; and the charge is in respect of the land, upon every occupier, &c. If the owner lives in another parish he shall be rated for repairs in the parish where the lands lie, and not where he lives; for though the charge is upon the person, yet it is in regard of his lands: if he let the same by lease, then he shall be charged in respect of the rent reserved, and the farmer shall make up the rest. 2 *Rol. Rep.* 270.

The communion tables are to be kept in repair in churches, and covered in time of divine service with a carpet, &c. And the Ten Commandments to be set up at the east end of every church or chapel, and other chosen sentences of scripture upon the walls. *Can.* 82, 83.

By 1 *Eliz. c.* 2.; 23 *Eliz. c.* 1.; and 3 *Jac.* 1, *c.* 4, every person is to repair to his parish church every Sunday, on pain of forfeiting 1*s.* for every offence; and being present at any form of prayer used contrary to the Book of Common Prayer, is punished with six months imprisonment, &c. Persons above sixteen years of age, who absent themselves from church above a month, are to forfeit 20*l. per* month to the king, and if they keep any inmate thus irreligiously disposed, in their houses, they forfeit 10*l. per* month. But protestant dissenters, not denying the Trinity, are exempted from the penalties by 1 *W. & M. c.* 18. And Roman catholics by 31 *Geo.* 3, *c.* 52.

No ill language is to be used, or noise made in churches or church-yards; and persons striking others there are to be excommunicated, and lose one of their ears: and a man may not lawfully return blows in his own defence in these cases. 5 & 6 *Ed.* 6. *cap.* 4. Disturbing dissenting or Roman catholic ministers officiating divine service, incurs three months imprisonment, and a forfeiture of 20*l.* by stat. 1 *M. cap.* 3, and 1 *W. & M. c.* 18. 31 *G.* 3. *c.* 52, any person may be indicted for indecent or irreverent behaviour in the church; and those that offend against the acts of uniformity are punishable either by indictment upon the statute, or by the ordinary, &c. See likewise *Mag. Chart.* 9 *Hen.* 3. *c.* 1.—5 *Ed.* 3.—13 *Ed.* 1, stat. 2. *c.* 6.—3 *Ed.* 1, stat. 2.—21 *Ed.* 1, *c.* 3.—9 *Ed.* 2, stat. 1, *c.* 10.—50 *Ed.* 3, *c.* 5.—1 *Ric.* 2, *c.* 5, and 15 *Ric.* 2, *c.* 15.

CHURCHWARDENS, (*ecclesiæ guardiani*) are ancient officers, chosen yearly in Easter week, by the minister and parishioners of every parish, to look to and take care of the church and church-yard, and the things belonging to the same.

They are to be chosen by the joint consent of the parishioners and minister; and by custom the minister may choose one, and the parishioners another; or by custom the parishioners alone may elect both, though it be against the canon. 1 *Vent.* 267.

They are sworn into their offices by the archdeacon; and if the archdeacon refuses to swear a churchwarden, a *mandamus* shall issue to compel him, *Cro. Car.* 551 for the parishioners are the proper judges of their ability to serve, and not the archdeacon who swears them. 5 *Mod.* 325.

All peers of the realm, by reason of their dignity, are exempt from the office of church-warden; *Gibs.* 215. So are all clergymen, by reason of their order, *Id.* In like manner all parliament men, by reason of their privilege. *Ibid.*

If an attorney be made a churchwarden of a parish, he shall have a writ of privilege, showing his privilege to be discharged thereof, by reason of his attendance in court. *Ibid.*

And no person living out of the parish, although he occupies lands within the parish, may be chosen churchwarden, because he cannot take notice of absences from church, nor disorders in it, for the due presenting of them. *Gibs.* 215.

Churchwardens are in the nature of a corporation to sue and be sued for the goods of the church. 2 *Cro.* 325. *Co.Lit.* 3. 1 *Rol. Abr.* 330. 1 *Rol. Abr.* 393. *Cro. Eliz.* 179.

But the churchwardens have no right to, or interest in, the freehold and inheritance of the church, which alone belongs to the parson or incumbent. *Comp. Incumb.* 381.

Also, churchwardens cannot release to the prejudice of the church; nor can they dispose of the church goods without the consent of the vestry. If they waste the goods of the church the new churchwardens may have actions against them, or call them to account before the ordinary; though the parishioners cannot have an action against them for wasting the church goods, for they must make new churchwardens, who must prosecute the former, &c. 1 *Danv. Abr.* 788. 2 *Cro.* 145. *Bro. Account,* 1.

But they have such a special property in the organ, bells, parish books, bible, chalice, surplice, &c. belonging to the church, that for the taking away, or for any damage done any of these, they may bring an action at law, and therefore the parson cannot sue for them in the spiritual court. 1 *Bac. Abr.* tit. *Churchwarden.*

General power of Churchwardens.] Besides their ordinary power, the churchwardens have the care of the benefice during its vacancy: and as soon as there is any avoidance they are to apply to the chancellor of the diocese for a sequestration; which being granted, they are to manage all the profits and expenses of the benefice for him that succeeds, plough and sow his glebes, gather in tithes, thrash out and sell corn, repair houses, &c. and they must see that the church be duly served by a curate approved by the bishop, whom they are to pay out of the profits of the benefice. 2 *Inst.* 489. They are to join with the overseers of the poor in making rates for the relief of the poor, setting up trades for employing them, placing out poor apprentices, settling poor persons, &c. and in the execution of their whole office, by statutes 43 *Eliz. c.* 2. 13 & 14 *Car.* 2. *c.* 12. 3 *W. & M. c.* 11, &c.

The churchwardens have no power to make any rate themselves, exclusive of the parishioners, their duty being only to summon the parishioners, who are to meet for that purpose, and when they are assembled a rate made by the majority present shall bind the whole parish, although the churchwardens voted against it. See *Comp. Incumb.* 389.

But if the churchwardens give the parishioners due notice that they intend to meet for that purpose, and the parishioners refuse to come, or being assembled, refuse to make any rate, they may make one without their concurrence; for as they are liable to be punished in the ecclesiatical courts for not repairing the church, it would be unreasonable that they should suffer by the wilfulness and obstinacy of others. 1 *Vent.* 367. 1 *Mod.* 79, 194.

The churchwardens, in summoning the parishioners need not do it from house to house, but a general public summons at the church is sufficient, and the major part of them that appear upon such summons will bind the whole parish. 1 *Vent.* 367. *Comp. Incumb.* 389.

Duty of Churchwardens.] The churchwardens are to take care of the repairs of the church; and if they erect, or add any thing new to the same, they must have the consent of the parishioners or vestry; and if in the church the license of the ordinary. 2 *Inst.* 489. 1 *Vent.* 367.

The churchwardens shall suffer no man to preach within their churches without producing his license: and they are to keep the keys of the belfrey, and take care that the bells be not rung without good cause, to be allowed of by the minister and themselves. *Can.* 50, 80.

Churchwardens are to see that all the parishioners duly resort to their parish-church, and there continue during the time of divine service. They are not to permit any to stand idle, walk, or make any noise in the church, or to contend for places, &c. they may apprehend those that disturb the minister, &c. and justify the appeasing any disorder in the church or church yard; they are to chastise disorderly boys, and take off the hats of those who would irreverently keep them on. 1 *Saund.* 13.

Further, they must search alehouses on Sundays, that there be no persons therein during divine service; and execute warrants against those who profane the Lord's Day, &c. Also levy penalties on persons not coming to church, against prophaners of the Sabbath in pastimes, tippling, &c. and for drunkenness, cursing and swearing, &c. by divers statutes. And they are to present to the ordinary all things presentable by the ecclesiastical laws, which relate to the church, the parson, and parishioners: these presentments are made upon oath, and usually twice a year, especially at the visitation: and what relates to the church, is chiefly of repairs, and whether there be a box for alms, in the church, a Bible, Common Prayer Book, and Book of Canons, a desk for the reader, cushion for the pulpit, a communion-table, table-cloth, cups and covers for bread, flagons, and font, a register-book, king's arms set up, Lord's Prayer, creed and commandments, in fair letters, &c.

What concerns the parson is, whether he reads the Thirty-nine Articles twice a year, and the Canons once in the year; preaches every Sunday good doctrine; reads the Common Prayer; celebrates the sacraments; preaches in his gown; visits the sick; catechises children; marries according to law, &c.

And what relates to the parishioners is, whether they come to church, and duly attend the worship of God, if baptism be neglected, women not churched, persons marrying in prohibited degrees, or without banns or licence, alms-houses or schools abused, legacies given to pious uses, &c. They must likewise present crimes and offences, such as drunkenness, fornication, adultery, incest, blasphemy, &c. and by statute popish recusants: and if they refuse to make presentments, the parsons or vicars, &c. may present to the bishop all crimes committed in their parishes. *Can.* 117. *Cro. Car.* 291. 1 *Vent.* 114.

It is their duty to collect the charity-money upon briefs, which are to be read in churches, and the sums collected, &c. to be indorsed on the briefs in words at length, and signed by the minister and churchwardens; after which they shall be delivered, with the money collected to the persons undertaking them, in a certain time, under the penalty of 20*l.* A register is to be kept of all money collected, &c. Also the undertakers in two months after the receipts of the money, and notice to sufferers, are to account before a master in chancery, appointed by the lord chancellor. *Stat.* 4 & 5 *Ann. c.* 14.

They are to sign certificates of receiving the sacrament by persons, to qualify them to bear offices, &c.

Churchwardens' accounts.] At the end of the year the churchwardens are to yield just accounts to the minister and parishioners, and deliver what remains in their hands to the parishioners, or to the new churchwardens: in case they refuse, they may be presented at the next visitation, or the new officers may by process call them to account before the ordinary, or sue them by writ of account at common law. And if all the parish have allowed their accounts of the church goods, the ordinary may nevertheless call them to account before him too, and punish them if he find cause; but in laying out their money, they are punishable for fraud only, not indiscretion. If their receipts fall short of their disbursements, the succeeding churchwardens may pay them the balance, and place it to their account. 1 *Rol. Abr.* 121. *Can.* 89, 109, &c. Disputes arising about churchwardens' accounts are to be decided before the ordinary: and for disbursements of any sum not exceeding 40*s.* the churchwardens' oath alone is a sufficient proof; but for all sums above, receipts are to be produced, &c. If churchwardens through improvidence, indiscretion, or negligence, either waste the church goods in their custody, or much damnify the parish; on proof thereof they may be removed at any time, by the authority of the ordinary. 8 *El.* 4, 6. 13 *Co.* 70.

The spiritual court can only order the churchwardens' accounts to be audited, but cannot make a rate to reimburse them, because they are not obliged to lay out money before they receive it. *Rep. temp. Hard. p.* 381. *Cro. Car.* 285, 286.

CHURCH-REEVE, is the same with churchwarden, (*reve* in the Sax. being as much as guardian in the French.) *Cowel. Blount.*

CHURCHESSET, or *churchset, ciricseat,* a Saxon word used in Domesday, which is interpreted *quasi semen ecclesiæ,* corn paid to the church. *Ibid.*

CHURCH-SCOT, customary oblations paid to the parish-priest; from which duties the religious sometimes purchased an exemption for themselves and their tenants. *Ibid.*

CHURLE, *ceorle, carl,* was in the Saxon time a tenant at will, of free condition, who held some land of the Thanes, on conditions of rents and services; which *ceorles* were of two sorts; one that hired the lord's tenementary estate, like our farmers; the other that tilled and manured the demesnes, (yielding work and not rent) and were thereupon called his sockmen or ploughmen. *Spelm.*

CINQUE-PORTS, (*quinque portus*). The cinque ports, as we now account them, are, Dover, Sandwich, Rumney, Winchelsea, and Rye; and to these we may add Hythe and Hastings, which are reckoned as part or members of the cinque ports: though by the first institution it is said that Winchelsea and Rye were added as members, and that the others were the cinque ports; there are also several other towns adjoining that have the privileges of the ports. These cinque ports have an especial governor, called lord warden of the cinque ports, and divers privileges granted them, as a peculiar jurisdiction; their warden having not only the authority of an admiral amongst them, but of sending out writs in his own name, &c. *Stat.* 32 *Hen.* 8. *c.* 48. 4 *Inst.* 222. To hold pleas, &c. and the king's writs do not run there; but on a judgment in any of the king's courts, if the defendant hath no goods, &c. but in the ports; the plaintiff may get the record certified into chancery, and from thence sent by mittimus to the lord warden to make execution. 4 *Inst.* 223. 3 *Leon.* 3.

The constable of Dover castle is lord warden of the cinque ports. And there are several courts within the cinque ports; one before the constable, others within the ports themselves, before the mayors and jurats; another, which is called *curia quinque portuum apud Shepway:* there is likewise a court of chancery, in the cinque ports, to decide matters of equity; but no original writs issue thence. 1 *Danv. Abr.* 793. The jurisdiction of the cinque ports is general, extending to personal, real, and mixed actions: and if any erroneous judgment is given in the cinque ports before any of the mayors and jurats, writ of error lies not in B. R. but it shall be redressed, according to the custom, by bill in nature of a writ of error *coram domino custode seu guardiano quinque portuum apud curiam suam, &c.* And in these cases the mayor and jurats may be fined, and the mayor removed, &c. 4 *Inst.* 334. *Crompt. Jurisd.* 138.

The cinque ports cannot award process of outlawry. *Cro. Eliz.* 910. And a *quo minus* from the Exchequer, lies to the cinque ports. *Ibid* 911. Also if a man is imprisoned at Dover by the lord warden, an *habeas corpus* may be issued; for the privilege that the king's writ lies not there is intended between party and party, and there can be no such privilege against the king; and an *habeas corpus* is a prerogative writ, by which the king demands an account of the liberty of the subject. *Cro. Jac.* 543. 1 *Nels. Abr.* 447.

Also a *certiorari* lies to the cinque ports, to remove indictments; for the jurisdiction that *brev. dom. regis non currit* is only in civil causes between party and party: but this has been held to extend only to indictments before the mayors, barons, &c. as justices of peace, on late statutes, &c. *Cro. Car.* 252, 253. 2 *Hawk. P. C.* 286, 287.

CIRCA, a watch; from which *circuitor; Cowel. Blount.*

CIRCADA, a tribute anciently paid to the bishop or archdeacon for visiting the churches. *Du Fresne.*

CIRCUITS, certain divisions of the kingdom appointed for the judges to go, twice a year, for administering of justice, in the several counties. These circuits are made in the respective vacations, after Hilary and Trinity terms. 3 *Black. Com.* 58. 4 *Black.* 415, 417.

CIRCUITY OF ACTION, (*circuitus actionis*) is a longer course of proceeding to recover a thing sued for than is needful: as if a person grant a rent-charge of 10*l.* per annum out of his manor of B. and after the grantee disseiseth the grantor of the same manor, who brings an assise and recovers the land, and 20*l.* damages, which being paid, the grantee brings his action for 10*l.* of his rent due during the time of the disseisin, which he must have had if no disseisin had been: this is called circuity of action, because as the grantor was to receive 20*l.* damages, and pay 10*l.* rent, he might have received but 10*l.* only for damages, and the grantee might have kept the other 10*l.* in his hands by way of retainer for his rent, and so saved his action, which appears to be needless. *Terms de Ley.*

CIRCUMSPECTE AGATIS, is the title of a statute made anno 13 *Ed.* 1. relating to prohibitions, prescribing certain cases to the judges, wherein the king's prohibition lies not. 2 *Inst.* 187.

CIRCUMSTANTIAL EVIDENCE, or the doctrine of presumption, takes place, next to positive proof: for when the fact itself cannot be demonstratively evinced, that which comes nearest to the proof of the fact is the proof of such circumstances which either necessarily or usually attend such facts; and these are called presumptions, which are only to be relied upon till the contrary be actually proved. *Co. Lit.* 373. 3 *Black. Com.* 371.

CIRCUMSTANTIBUS, *tales de:* signifies in our law the supplying or making up from the by-standers the number of jurors, if any impanelled appear not, or appearing are challenged by either party, by adding to them so many of those that are present or standing by that are qualified as will serve the turn. *Stat.* 35 *H.* 8. *cap.* 6. 3 *Black.* 365.

CITATION, (*citatio*) a summons to appear, applied particularly to process in the spiritual court, where they proceed according to the course of the civil and canon laws, by citation. But a person is not generally to be cited to appear out of the diocese, or peculiar jurisdiction where he lives; unless it be by the archbishop, in default of the ordinary; where the ordinary is party to the suit, in cases of appeal, or the like. And by law, a defendant may be sued where he lives, though the offence be in another diocese. 1 *Nels.* 449.

CITATIO AD INSTANTIAM PARTIS, is mentioned in 22 & 23 *Car.* 2. *c.* 9. for laying impositions on proceedings at law. *Blount.*

CITY (*civitas*). A city is a town corporate, which is or hath been the see of a bishop and hath a cathedral; and though the bishoprick be dissolved, as at Westminster, yet still it remaineth a city. *Co. Lit.* 109. 1 *Black.* 114.

CITIZENS, (*cives*) are either freemen, or such as reside and keep a family in the city, &c. and some are citizens and freemen; and some are not, who have not so great privileges as the others. 1 *Rol. Rep.* 105.

CIVIL LAW, is that civil or municipal law which the old Romans used, compiled from the laws of nature and of nations, and comprised in the *institutes*, the *code*, and the *digest* of the emperor *Justinian*, and the *novel constitutions* of himself and some of his successors. 1 *Black.* 80.

The whole civil law is contained in four books or tomes, 1. The code. 2. The pandects or digests. 3. The institutes. 4. The novels or authentics. *Ibid.*

1. The *code* is divided into twelve books,

and was the first book of the civil law, which the emperor Justinian ordered to be collected: it was published in the year 534, and contains the constitutions of fifty-six emperors, and their wise councils. *Ferriers Hist.*

2. The *digests or pandects*, were collected from the works and commentaries of the ancient lawyers, some whereof lived before the coming of our Saviour: this tome is divided into fifty books; and upon a more particular division, the whole digest is divided into seven parts. *Ibid.*

3. The *institutes* contain a system of the whole body of law, and are an epitome of the digest divided into four books; but sometimes they correct the digest: they are called institutes, because they are of instruction, and shew an easy way to the obtaining a knowledge of the civil law: but they are not so distinct and comprehensive as they might be, nor so useful at this time as they were at first. *Ibid.*

4. The *novels or authentics* were published at several times without any method: they are termed novels as they are new laws, and authentics, being authentically translated from the Greek into the Latin tongue; and the whole volume is divided into nine collations, constitutions or sections, and they again into 168 novels, which also are distributed into certain chapters. *Ibid.*

There are four species of courts in which the civil law is permitted under different restrictions to be used; 1st, the courts of the archbishop and bishop, and their derivative officers, usually called in our law, courts *Christian, curiæ Christianitatis*, or the ecclesiastical courts; 2d. the military courts; 3d. the courts of admiralty; 4th. the courts of the two universities. 1 *Black.* 83.

CIVIL LIST, is properly the whole of the king's revenue in his own distinct capacity. 1 *Black.* 332.

CLACK WOOL, is to cut off the sheep's mark, which makes it weigh lighter, as to force wool, signifies to clip off the upper and hairy part thereof; and to bard it, is to cut the head and neck from the rest of the fleece. *Stat.* 8 *H.* 6. *cap.* 22. *Cowel. Blount.*

CLADES, *clida, cleta, cleia*, from the Brit. *clie*, and the Irish *clia*, a wattle or hurdle. *Paroch. Antiq. p.* 575.

CLAIM, (*clameum*) is a challenge of interest in any thing that is in the possession of another, or at least out of a man's own, as claim by charter, by descent, &c. And claim is either verbal, where one doth by words claim and challenge the thing that is so out of his possession; or it is by an action brought, &c. and sometimes it relates to lands, and sometimes to goods and chattels. *Lit. Sect.* 420.

CLAIM OF LIBERTY, is a suit or petition to the king in the court of Exchequer, to have liberties and franchises confirmed there by the king's attorney-general. *Co. Ent.* 93.

CLAMEA ADMITTENDA IN ITINERE PER ATTORNATUM, an ancient writ now disused, by which the king commanded the justices in eyre to admit a person's claim by attorney who was employed in the king's service, and could not come in his own person. *Reg. Orig.* 19.

CLAP-BOARD, is a board cut in order to make casks or vessels. *Stat.* 35 *El. c.* 11. *Cowel. Blount.*

CLARENDON, (*constitutions* of) certain constitutions, made in the reign of *Hen.* 2. *A. D.* 1164, in a great council held at Clarendon, whereby the king checked the power of the pope, and his clergy, and greatly narrowed the total exemption they claimed from the secular jurisdiction. 4 *Black. Com.* 415.

CLARETUM, a liquor made of wine and honey, clarified or made clear by decoction: and it was from this, the red wines of France were called claret. *Cowel. Blount.*

CLARIGARIUS ARMORUM, an herald at arms. *Cowel. Blount.*

CLARIO, a trumpet. *Cowel. Blount.*

CLASSIARIUS, a seaman or soldier serving at sea. *Ibid.*

CLAUD, (Brit.) a ditch: from *claudere*, to enclose, or turn open fields into inclosures. *Ibid.*

CLAVES INSULÆ, is a term used in the Isle of Man, where all ambiguous and weighty cases are referred to twelve persons, whom they call *claves insulæ*, i. e. the keys of the island. *Ibid.*

CLAVIA, an ancient tenure, *viz.* by the serjeantry of the club or mace. *Brady* 22.

CLAVIGERATUS, a treasurer of a church. *Cowel. Blount.*

CLAUSE ROLLS, (*rotuli clausi*) contain all such matters of record as were committed to close writs: these rolls are preserved in the Tower. *Ibid.*

CLAUSTURA, brushwood for hedges and fences. *Ibid.*

CLAUSUM FREGIT, is a writ so called, because the defendant is summoned thereby to answer *quare clausum fregit* of the plaintiff, that is why he did such a trespass. It is the course of the common pleas, to declare in actions (especially upon an *assumpsit* or the like) upon a *quare clausum fregit* as they do on a *latitat* in the king's bench. 2 *Vent.* 192, 259.

But personal service of this writ of *quare clausum fregit* is not necessary; the defendant being to be summoned by the sheriff, which is done by the officers leaving a copy of the warrant, whereby he is directed to summon the party at his house; if the defendant does not appear at the return, a distringas issues to levy 40*s.* on the goods, and then a second to levy 4*l.* after which, if the defendant still continues in contempt, on affidavit and motion to the court, the issues to be distrained will be directed by the court to be increased to the full amount of the debt, and for default of appearance then the court will order the same to be sold.

CLAUSUM PASCHÆ, Stat. *Westm.* 1. *in crastino clausi paschæ*, or *in crastino octabis paschæ*, which is all one, that is the morrow of the *utas* of Easter. 2 *Inst.* 157.

CLAUSURA HEYÆ, the enclosure of a hedge. *Cowel. Blount.*

CLAWA, a close or small measure of land. *Ibid.*

CLEPTOR, this word is taken for a rogue or thief. *Ibid.*

CLERGY. (*clerus*) The clergy comprehends all persons in holy orders and in ecclesiastical offices, such as bishops, deans, parsons, vicars and like persons.

This venerable body of men, being separate and set apart from the rest of the people in order to attend the more closely to the services of Almighty God, have thereupon larger privileges allowed them by our municipal laws. 1 *Black.* 376.

Clergymen are liable to all public charges imposed by act of parliament, where they are not particularly excepted. But they are not to be chosen to any temporal offices, as the office of sheriff, bailiff, reeve, constable, or the like, (though they are sometimes in the commission of the peace, in which commissions they may either act as justices, or not act at their pleasure) nor are they to serve on juries, or obliged to appear at turns and leets; or to be pressed to serve in the wars in person, although by statutes they are compellable to contribute to the charge of a war, and to musters of the militia: their bodies are not to be taken upon statutes merchant or staple, &c. for the writ to take the body of the conusor is *si laicus sit*; and if the sheriff or any other officer arrest a clergyman upon any such process, it is said an action of false imprisonment lies against him that does it, or the clergyman arrested may have a *supersedeas* out of chancery. 2 *Inst.* 4. *Finch.* 88. 1 *Black.* 376.

Clergymen may not be arrested in the church, or church-yard, while attending on divine service, &c. (that is, for a reasonable time *eundo redeundo et morando* to perform divine service, 12 *Co.* 100.) on pain of imprisonment, and ransom at the king's pleasure, and likewise to make agreement with the party. 50 *Ed.* 3. *c.* 5. 1 *Ric.* 2. *c.* 16.

In cases also of felony, a clerk in orders shall have the benefit of his clergy, without being branded in the hand; and may likewise have it more than once. 2 *Inst.* 637. 4 *Hen.* 7. *c.* 13. 1 *Ed.* 6. *c.* 12. 1 *Black.* 377.

This is a privilege, peculiar to the clergy, that sentence of death can never be passed upon them for any number of manslaughters, bigamies, simple larcenies, or other clergyable offences: for a layman, even a peer may be ousted of clergy and will be subject to the judgment of death, upon a second conviction of a clergyable offence, thus if a layman has once been convicted of manslaughter, upon production of the conviction, he may afterwards suffer death for bigamy or any other felony within clergy, or which would not be a capital crime to another person not so circumstanced: but for the honor of the clergy, there are few or no instances in which they have had occasion to claim the benefit of this privilege. 1 *Black.* 377. 4 *Black.* 373. *Leon.* 312.

But clergymen have no privilege in petty larcenies, but they are liable to be whipped or transported, like other persons for a petty larceny, though they are subject to no corporal punishment whatsoever, upon being convicted of a grand larceny or any clergyable felony. *Christian*, (*n.* 3.) 4 *Black.* 373.

But as they have their privileges, so also they have their disabilities, on account of their spiritual avocations; thus "no person having been ordained to the office of priest or deacon, is capable of being elected to serve in parliament, and if he shall sit in the house, he forfeits 500*l.* per day, and becomes incapable of holding any office or profession under the king." 41 *Geo.* 3. *c.* 17.

And by stat. 21 *Hen.* 8. *c.* 13. they are not in general, allowed to take any lands or tenements to farm, upon pain of 10*l.* per month, and total avoidance of the lease.

But if they have not sufficient glebe, they may take a farm for the necessary expences and consumption of their household. 43 *Geo.* 3. *c.* 84.

Nor shall they upon like pain keep any farmhouse or brewhouse, or engage in any manner of trade, nor sell any merchandize, under the forfeiture of treble the value. *s.* 9.

This prohibition is consonant to the canon law. 1 *Black.* 377. But though a clergyman is subject to this penalty for trading, yet his contracts with others as a trader are valid, and he is liable to be made a bankrupt. 1 *Cooke's B. L.* 33.

CLERGY, Benefit of. I. Clergy, the *privilegium clericale*, or in common speech the benefit of clergy, had its original from the pious regard paid by christian princes to the church in its infant state; and the ill use which the popish ecclesiastics soon made of that pious regard. The exemptions which they granted to the church, were principally of two kinds: 1. Exemption of places consecrated to religious duties, from criminal arrests, which was the foundation of sanctuaries: 2. Exemption of the persons of clergymen from criminal process before the secular judge in a few particular cases, which was the true original and meaning of the *privilegium clericale*. 4 *Black.* 365.

But the clergy, increasing in wealth, power, honour, number, and interest, began soon to set up for themselves: and that which they obtained by the favour of the civil government, they now claimed as their inherent right: and as a right of the highest nature, indefesible, and *jure divino*. From the following text of scripture; "touch not mine anointed, and do my prophets no harm."

Keilw. 181. By their canon laws therefore and constitutions they endeavoured at, and where they met with easy princes obtained, a vast extension of these exemptions: as well in regard to the crimes themselves, of which the list became quite universal; as in regard to the persons exempted, among whom were at length comprehended not only every little subordinate officer belonging to the church or clergy, but even many that were totally laymen. 4 *Black.* 366.

In England however, although the usurpations of the pope were very many and grievous, till Henry the eighth entirely exterminated his supremacy, yet a total exemption of the clergy from secular jurisdiction could never be thoroughly effected, though often endeavoured by the clergy, *Keilw.* 180. and therefore, though the antient *privilegium clericale* was in some capital cases, yet it was not universally allowed. And in those particular cases, the use was for the bishop or ordinary to demand his clerks to be remitted out of the king's courts, as soon as they were indicted: concerning the allowance of which demand there was for many years a great uncertainty, 2 *Hal. P. C.* 377. till at length it was finally settled in the reign of Henry the sixth, that the prisoner should first be arraigned; and might either then claim his benefit of clergy, by way of declinatory plea; or, after conviction, by way of arresting judgment. This latter way is most usually practised, as it is more to the satisfaction of the court to have the crime previously ascertained by confession or the verdict of a jury; and also it is more advantageous to the prisoner himself, who may possibly be acquitted, and so need not the benefit of his clergy at all. 4 *Black.* 366.

Originally the law was held, that no man should be admitted to the privilege of clergy, but such as had the *habitum et tonsuram clericalem.* 2 *Hal. P. C.* 372. *M. Paris, A. D.* 1259. But in process of time a much *wider and more comprehensive criterion was established: every one that could read* (a mark of great learning in those days of ignorance and her sister superstition) *being accounted a clerk or* clericus, *and allowed the benefit of clerkship, though neither initiated in holy orders, nor trimmed with the clerical tonsure.* But when learning, by means of the invention of printing, and other concurrent causes, began to be more generally disseminated than formerly; and reading was no longer a competent proof of clerkship, or being in holy orders; it was found that as many laymen as divines were admitted to the *privilegium clericale:* and therefore by statute 4 *Hen.* 7. *c.* 13. a distinction was once more drawn between mere lay scholars, and clerks that were really in orders. And, though it was thought reasonable still to mitigate the severity of the law with regard to the former, yet they were not upon the same footing with actual clergy; being subjected to a slight degree of punishment, and not allowed to claim the clerical privilege more than once. Accordingly the statute directs, that *no person once admitted to the benefit of clergy, shall be admitted thereto a second time, unless he produces his orders:* and in order to distinguish their persons, all laymen who are allowed this privilege shall be burnt with a hot iron in the brawn of the left thumb. This distinction between learned laymen, and real clerks in orders, was abolished for a time by the statutes 28 *Hen.* 8. *c.* 1. and 32 *Hen.* 8. *c.* 3. but it is held (*Hob.* 294. 2 *Hal. P. C.* 375.) to have been virtually restored by statute 1 *Ed.* 6. *c.* 12. which statute also enacts that lords of parliament and peers of the realm, having place and voice in parliament, may have the benefit of their peerage, equivalent to that of clergy, for the first offence, (although they cannot read, and without being burnt in the hand,) for all offences then clergyable to commoners, and also for the crimes of house-breaking, highway-robbery, horse-stealing, and robbing of churches. 4 *Black.* 367.

After this burning the laity, and before it, the real clergy, were discharged from the sentence of the law in the king's courts, and delivered over to the ordinary, to be dealt with according to the ecclesiastical canons. Whereupon the ordinary, not satisfied with the proofs adduced in the profane secular court, set himself formally to work to make a purgation of the offender by a new canonical trial; although he had been previously convicted by his country, or perhaps by his own confession. *Staund. P. C.* 138. *b.* This trial was held before the bishop in person, or his deputy; and by a jury of twelve clerks: and there, first, the party himself was required to make oath of his own innocence; next, there was to be the oath of twelve compurgators, who swore they believed he spoke the truth; then, witnesses were to be examined upon oath, but on behalf of the prisoner only: and, lastly, the jury were to bring in their verdict upon oath, which usually acquitted the prisoner; otherwise, if a clerk, he was degraded, or put to penance, 3 *P. Wms.* 447. *Hob.* 289. A learned judge in the beginning of the last century, *Hob.* 291. remarks with much indignation the vast complication of perjury and subornation of perjury, in this solemn farce of a mock trial; the witnesses, the compurgators, and the jury, being all of them partakers in the guilt: the delinquent party also, though convicted before on the clearest evidence, and conscious of his own offence, yet was permitted and almost compelled to swear himself not guilty: nor was the good bishop himself, under whose countenance this scene of wickedness was daily transacted, by any means exempt from a share of it. And yet by this purgation the party was restored to his credit, his liberty, his lands, and his capacity of purchasing afresh, and was entirely made a new and an innocent man. 4 *Black.* 367, 8.

This scandalous prostitution of oaths, and the forms of justice, in the almost constant acquittal of felonious clerks by purgation, was the occasion, that, upon very heinous and notorious circumstances of guilt, the temporal courts would not trust the ordinary with the trial of the offender, but delivered over to him the convicted clerk, *absque purgatione facienda:* in which situation the clerk convict could not make purgation; but was to continue in prison during life, and was incapable of acquiring any personal property, or receiving the profits of his lands, unless the king should please to pardon him. Both these courses were in some degree exceptionable; the latter being perhaps too rigid, as the former was productive of the most abandoned perjury. As therefore these mock trials took their rise from factious and popish tenets, tending to exempt one part of the nation from the general municipal law; it became high time, when the reformation was thoroughly established, to abolish so vain and impious a ceremony. 4 *Black.* 368.

Accordingly the stat. 18 *Eliz. c.* 7 enacts, that, "for the avoiding of such perjuries "and abuses, after the offender has been al- "lowed his clergy, he shall not be delivered "to the ordinary, as formerly; but, upon "such allowance and burning in the hand, "he shall forthwith be enlarged and deli- "vered out of prison; with proviso, that the "judge may, if he thinks fit, continue the "offender in gaol for any time not exceeding "a year." And thus the law continued, for above a century unaltered; except only that the statute 21 *Jac.* 1. *c.* 6. allowed, that "women convicted of simple larcenies under "the value of ten shillings should" (not properly have the benefit of clergy, for they were not called upon to read; but) "be "burned in the hand, and whipped, stocked, "or imprisoned for any time not exceeding "a year." And a similar indulgence by the statutes 3 & 4 *W.* & *M.* *c.* 9. and 4 & 5 *W.* & *M.* *c.* 24. was extended to women, guilty of any clergyable felony whatsoever; "who "were allowed once to claim the benefit of "the statute, in like manner as men might "claim the benefit of clergy, and to be dis- "charged upon being burned in the hand, "and imprisoned for any time not exceeding "a year." The punishment of burning in the hand being found ineffectual was also changed by statute 10 & 11 *W.* 3. *c.* 23. into "burning in the most visible part of the "left cheek, nearest the nose:" but, such an indelible stigma being found by experience to render offenders desperate, this provision was repealed about seven years afterwards, by statute 5 *Ann.* *c.* 6. and, till that period, all women, all peers of parliament and peeresses, and all male commoners who could read, were discharged in all clergyable felonies; the males absolutely, if clerks in orders; and other commoners, both male and female, upon branding, and peers and peeresses without branding, for the first offence: yet all liable (excepting peers and peeresses) if the judge saw occasion, to imprisonment not exceeding a year. And those men, who could not read, if under the degree of peerage, were hanged. 4 *Black.* 368, 9.

Afterwards indeed it was considered, that education and learning were no extenuations of guilt, but quite the reverse: and that, if the punishment of death for simple felony was too severe for those who had been liberally instructed, it was, *a fortiori*, too severe for the ignorant also. And thereupon by the same statute 5 *Ann.* *c.* 6. it was enacted, that "if a person convicted of a clergyable "offence shall pray the benefit of this act, "he shall not be required to read, but shall "be taken to be, and punished as, a clerk "convict." And experience having shewn, that so very universal a lenity was frequently inconvenient, and an encouragement to commit the lower degrees of felony; and that, though capital punishments were too rigorous for these inferior offences, yet no punishment at all (or next to none) was as much too gentle; *it was farther enacted* by the same statute, that "when any person is convicted of "any theft or larceny, and burnt in the "hand for the same according to the ancient "law, he shall also, at the discretion of the "judge, be committed to the house of cor- "rection or public workhouse, to be there "kept to hard labour, for any time not less "than six months, and not exceeding two "years; with a power of inflicting a double "confinement in case of the party's escape "from the first." And it was also enacted by the statutes 4 *Geo.* 1. *c.* 11. and 6 *Geo.* 1. *c.* 23. that "when any persons shall be con- "victed of any larceny, either grand or pe- "tit, or any felonious stealing or taking of mo- "ney or goods and chattels either from the "person or the house of any other, or in any "other manner, and who by the law shall be "entitled to the benefit of clergy, and liable "only to the penalties of burning in the "hand or whipping, the court in their dis- "cretion, instead of such burning in the "hand or whipping, may direct such of- "fenders to be transported to America, (or, "by statute 19 *Geo.* 3. *c.* 74. to any other "parts beyond the seas) for seven years: "and if they return or are seen at large in "this kingdom within that time, it shall be "felony without benefit of clergy."

It is also enacted by the same statute, 19 *Geo.* 3. *c.* 74. that "instead of burning in "the hand (*which was sometimes too slight and "sometimes too disgraceful a punishment*) the "court in all clergyable felonies may im- "pose a pecuniary fine; or (except in the "case of manslaughter) may order the of- "fender to be once or oftener, but not more "than thrice, either publicly or privately "whipped; such private whipping (*to pre- "vent collusion or abuse*) to be inflicted in "the presence of two witnesses, and in case "of female offenders in the presence of fe- "males only. Which fine or whipping shall "have the same consequences as burning in "the hand; and the offender, so fined or "whipped, shall be equally liable to a sub- "sequent detainer or imprisonment."

And in consequence of these statutes, persons convicted of manslaughters, bigamies, and simple grand larcenies, are still asked what they have to say why judgment of death should not be pronounced upon them? And they are then told to kneel down, and pray the benefit of the statute. *Christian* in (*n.* 2.) 4 *Black.* 370.

In this state does the benefit of clergy at present stand; very considerably different from its original institution: the wisdom of the English legislature having converted, by gradual mutations, what was at first an unreasonable exemption of particular popish ecclesiastics, into a merciful mitigation of the general law, with respect to capital punishment. 4 *Black.* 372.

What persons are allowed the benefit of clergy.] At this day all clerks in orders are, without any branding, and of course without any transportation, fine, or whipping, (for those are only substituted in lieu of the other,) to be admitted to this privilege, and immediately discharged; and this as often as they offend. 2 *Hal. P. C.* 375. Again, all lords of parliament and peers of the realm having place and voice in parliament, by the statute 1 *Ed.* 6. *c.* 12, (which is likewise held to extend to peeresses*,) shall be discharged in all clergyable and other felonies, provided for by the act, without any burning in the hand or imprisonment, or other punishment substituted in its stead, in the same manner as real clerks convict: but this is only for the first offence. Lastly, all the commons of the realm, not in orders, whether male or female, shall *for the first offence* be discharged of the capital punishment of felonies within the benefit of clergy, upon being burnt in the hand, whipped, or fined, or suffering a discretionary imprisonment in the common gaol, the house of correction, one of the penitentiary houses, or in the places of labour for the benefit of some navigation; or in case of larceny, upon being transported for seven years, if the court shall think proper. 4 *Black.* 373.

A layman, who has once had the benefit of clergy, may be precluded from obtaining it a second time, by a counter-plea on the part of the prosecution, averring the identity of the prisoner's person, and that he had before been allowed the benefit of his clergy, though the second crime be quite different from the first. As a person convicted of bigamy is liable to suffer death for a manslaughter, or any other clergyable felony. *Leach.* 312.

For what crimes the benefit of clergy is to be allowed.] The benefit of clergy was not allowed at common law, neither in high treason, nor in *petit larceny*, nor in any mere misdemeanors, and therefore it may be laid down for a rule, that it was allowable only in *petit treason and capital felonies:* which for the most part became legally intitled to this indulgence by the statute *de clero*, 25 *Ed.* 3. *st.* 3. *c.* 4. which provides that clerks convict for treasons or felonies, touching other persons than the king himself or his royal majesty, shall have the privilege of holy church. But yet it was not allowable in all felonies whatsoever: for in some it was denied even by the common law, viz. *insidiatio viarum*, or lying in wait for one on the highway; *depopulatio agrorum*, or destroying and ravaging a country, 2 *Hal. P. C.* 33; and *combustio domorum*, or arson, that is, the burning of houses 1 *Hal. P. C.* 346. all which are a kind of hostile acts, and in some degree border upon treason. And farther, all these identical crimes, together with petit treason, and very many other acts of felony, are ousted of clergy by particular acts of parliament. 4 *Black.* 373.

Upon all which statutes we may observe the following rules: 1st, that in all felonies, whether new created or by common law, clergy is now allowable, unless taken away by express words of an act of parliament, 2 *Hal. P. C.* 330. 2nd, That where clergy is taken away from the principal, it is not of course taken away from the accessory, unless he be also particularly included in

---

* Upon the conviction of the duchess of Kingston for bigamy, it was argued by the attorney-general Thurlow, that peeresses were not entitled by this stat. of 1 *Ed.* 6. *c.* 12. like peers, to the privilege of peerage; but it was the unanimous opinion of the judges, that a peeress convicted of a clergyable felony, ought to be immediately discharged without being burnt in the hand, or without being liable to any imprisonment. 11 *H. St. Tr.* 264. If the duchess had been admitted, like a commoner, only to the benefit of clergy, burning in the hand at that time could not have been dispensed with.

The argument was, that the privilege of peerage was only an extension of the benefit of clergy, and therefore granted only to those who were or might be entitled to that benefit; but as no female, peeress or commoner, at that time was entitled to the benefit of clergy, so it was not the intention of the legislature to grant to any female the privilege of peerage.

the words of the statute. 2 *Hawk. P. C.* 341. 3. That, when the benefit of clergy is taken away from the offence, (as in case of murder, buggery, robbery, rape, and burglary,) a principal in the second degree, being present, aiding, and abetting the crime, is as well excluded from his clergy as he that is principal in the first degree: but 4. That, where it is only taken away from the person committing the offence, his aiders and abettors are not excluded, through the tenderness of the law, which hath determined that such statutes shall be taken literally, 1 *Hal. P. C.* 529. *Foster* 356, 357. 4 *Black.* 374.

The allowance of the benefit of clergy, operates as a statute pardon; but the consequences are, 1st. that by the conviction the offender forfeits all his goods to the king; which being once vested in the crown, shall not afterwards be restored. 2. That, after conviction, and till he receives the judgment of the law, by branding or some of its substitutes, or else is pardoned by the king, he is to all intents and purposes a felon, and subject to all the disabilities and other incidents of a felon. 3. That, after burning or its substitute, or pardon, he is discharged for ever of that, and all other felonies before committed, within the benefit of clergy, but not of felonies from which such benefit is excluded: and this by stat. 8 *Eliz. c.* 4. and 18 *Eliz. c.* 7. 4. That by the burning, or its substitute, or the pardon of it, he is restored to all capacities and credits, and the possession of his lands, as if he had never been convicted. 5. That what is said with regard to the advantages of commoners and laymen subsequent to the burning in the hand, is equally applicable to all peers and clergymen, although never branded at all, or subjected to other punishment in its stead: for they have the same privileges, without any burning, or any substitute for it, which others are entitled to after it. 2 *Hal. P. C.* 388, 9. 3 *Peere Wms.* 487. 5 *Rep.* 110. 4 *Black.* 373.

CLERICO ADMITTENDO. Upon a presentation to a benefice recovered in a *quare impedit*, or assise of *darrein presentment*, the execution is by this writ, directed not to the sheriff, but to the bishop or his metropolitan, requiring them to admit and institute the clerk of the plaintiff. 3 *Black. Com.* 413.

CLERICO INFRA SACROS ORDINES CONSTITUTO, NON ELIGENDO IN OFFICIUM, is a writ directed to those who have thrust a bailiwick, or other office upon one in holy orders, charging them to release him. *Reg. Orig.* 143.

CLERICO CAPTO PER STATUTUM MERCATORUM, &c. A writ for the delivery of a clerk out of prison, who is taken and imprisoned upon the breach of a statute merchant. *Reg. Orig.* 147.

CLERICO CONVICTO COMMISSO GAOLÆ IN DEFECTU ORDINARII DELIVERANDO, is an ancient writ that lay for the delivery of a clerk to his ordinary, that was formerly convicted of felony, by reason his ordinary did not challenge him according to the privileges of clerks. *Reg. Orig.* 69.

CLERK, (*clericus*) in the most general signification, is one that belongs to the holy ministry of the church; and is said to be properly a minister or priest in holy orders. *Cowel. Blount.* 1 *Black.* 388.

CLERK, in another sense, signifies a person who practises his pen in any court, or otherwise; of which clerks there are various kinds, in several offices, for the officers of the courts of law were formerly often clergymen; hence to this day their successors are denominated clerks. 1 *Black.* 16, 17.

CLERK OF THE ACTS, is an officer in the navy office, whose business is to record all orders, contracts, bills, warrants, &c. transacted by the lord high admiral, or lords commissioners of the admiralty, and commissioners of the navy. See 16 *Car.* 2. *c.* 5. and 22 & 23 *Car.* 2. *c.* 11.

CLERK OF AFFIDAVITS, in the court of chancery, is an officer that files all affidavits made use of in court.

CLERK OF THE ASSISE, is he that records all things judicially done by the justices of assise in their circuits. *Cromp. Jurisd.* 227. And this officer is associated to the judge in the commission of assise, to take assises, &c.

CLERK OF THE BAILS, an officer belonging to the court of king's bench. He files the bail pieces taken in that court, and attends for that purpose.

CLERK OF THE CHECK, is an officer in the king's court, so called, because he hath the check and controlment of the yeomen of the guard, and all other ordinary yeomen belonging either to the king, queen, or prince; giving leave, or allowing their absence in attendance, or diminishing their wages for the same: he also by himself or deputy takes the view of those that are to watch in the court, and hath the setting of the watch. 33 *H.* 8. *c.* 12. Also there is an officer of the same name in the king's navy at Plymouth, Deptford, Woolwich, Chatham, &c. 19 *Car.* 2. *c.* 1.

CLERK CONTROLLER OF THE KING'S HOUSE, is an officer in the king's court, that hath authority to allow or disallow charges and demands of pursuivants, messengers of the green cloth, &c. He hath likewise the oversight of all defects and miscarriages of any of the inferior officers; and hath a right to sit in the counting-house, with the superior officers, *viz.* the lord steward, treasurer, controller, and cofferer of the household, for correcting any disorders. 33 *H.* 8. *c.* 12.

CLERK OF THE CROWN, (*clericus co-*

ronæ) an officer in the king's bench, whose function is to frame, read and record all indictments against offenders there arraigned or indicted of any public crime. He is also termed clerk of the crown-office, and exhibits *informations*, by order of the court, for divers offences.

CLERK OF THE CROWN IN CHANCERY, is an officer in that court who continually attends the lord chancellor in person or by deputy: he writes and prepares for the great seal, special matters of state by commission, or the like, either immediately from his majesty's orders, or by order of his council, as well ordinary as extraordinary, *viz.* commissions of lieutenancy, of justices of assise, oyer and terminer, gaol delivery, and of the peace, with their writs of association, &c. All general pardons, at the king's coronation, or in parliament, where he sits in the lord's house in parliament time; and into whose office the writs of parliament, with the names of knights and burgesses elected thereupon, are to be returned and filed. He hath likewise the making out of all special pardons; and writs of execution upon bonds of statute staple forfeited; which was annexed to his office in the reign of queen Mary, in consideration of his chargeable attendance.

CLERK OF THE DECLARATIONS, an officer of the court of king's bench, that files all declarations in causes there depending.

CLERK OF THE DELIVERIES, is an officer in the Tower of London, who exercises his office in taking of indentures for all stores, ammunition, &c. issued from thence.

CLERK OF THE ERRORS, (*clericus errorum*) in the court of common pleas, transcribes and certifies into the king's bench the tenor of the records of the cause or action, upon which the writ of error, made by the cursitor, is brought there to be heard and determined. The clerk of the errors in the king's bench, likewise transcribes and certifies the records of causes in that court into the exchequer, if the cause or action were by bill: if by original, the lord chief justice certifies the record into the house of peers in parliament, by taking the transcript from the clerk of the errors, and delivering it to the lord chancellor, there to be determined, according to the statutes 27 *Eliz. c.* 8. and 31 *Eliz. c.* 1. The clerk of the errors in the exchequer also transcribes the records, certified thither out of the king's bench, and prepares them for judgment in the court of exchequer chamber, to be given by the justices of C. B. and barons there. *Stat.* 16 *Car.* 2. *c.* 2. 20 *Car* 2. *c.* 4.

CLERK OF THE ESSOINS, is an officer belonging to the court of common pleas, who keeps the essoin rolls; and the essoin roll is a record of that court: he has the providing of parchment, and cutting it out into rolls, marking the numbers thereon; and the delivery out of all the rolls to every officer of the court; the receiving of them again when they are written, and the binding and making up the whole bundles of every term; which he doth as servant of the chief justice. The chief justice of C. B. is at the charge of the parchment of all the rolls, for which he is allowed, as is also the chief justice of B. R. besides the penny for the seal of every writ of privilege and outlawry, the seventh penny taken for the seal of every writ in court under the green wax, or petit seal; the said lord chief justices having annexed to their offices or places, the custody of the said seals belonging to each court.

CLERK OF THE ESTREATS, (*clericus extractorum*) a clerk or officer belonging to the exchequer, who every term receives the estreats out of the lord treasurer's remembrancer's office, and writes them out to be levied for the king: and he makes schedules of such sums estreated as are to be discharged.

CLERK OF THE HANAPER, or HAMPER, is an officer in the chancery, whose office is to receive all the money due to the king, for the seals of charters, patents, commissions and writs; as also fees due to the officers for inrolling and examining the same. He is obliged to attendance on the lord chancellor daily in the term time, and at all times of sealing, having with him leather bags, wherein are put all charters, &c. After they are sealed, those bags, being sealed up with the lord chancellor's private seal, are delivered to the controller of the hanaper, who, upon receipt of them, enters the effect of them in a book, &c. This hanaper represents what the Romans termed *fiscum*, which contained the emperor's treasure; and the exchequer was anciently so called, because in *eo reconderentur hanapi & scutræ cæteraquæ vasa quæ in censum & tributum persolvi solebant;* or it may be for that the yearly tribute which princes received was in hampers or large vessels full of money.

CLERK OF THE INROLLMENTS, is an officer of the common pleas, that inrolls and exemplifies all fines and recoveries, and returns writs of entry, summons and seisin, &c.

CLERK OF THE JURIES, (*clericus juratorum*) an officer belonging to the court of common pleas, who makes out the writs of *habeas corpora* and *distringas*, for the appearance of juries; either in that court, or at the assises, after the jury or panel is returned upon the *venire facias:* he also enters into the rolls the awarding of these writs; and makes all the continuances from the going out of the *habeas corpora* until the verdict is given.

CLERK OF THE MARKET, (*clericus mercati hospitii regis*) is an officer of the king's house, to whom it belongs to take charge of the king's measures, and keep the standards of them, which are examples of all measures throughout the land; as of ells, yards, quarts, gallons, &c. And of weights, bushels, &c. And to see that all weights and measures in every place be answerable to the said standard. For the court of the clerk of the market, see *Courts*.

CLERK MARSHAL OF THE KING'S HOUSE, an officer that attends the marshal in his court, and records all his proceedings. 33 *H.* 8. *c.* 22.

CLERK OF THE NISCHILS, or NIHILS, (*clericus nihilorum*) an officer of the court of exchequer, who makes a roll of all such sums as are nihiled by the sheriffs upon their estreats of green wax, and delivers the same into the remembrancer's office, to have execution done upon it for the king.

CLERK OF THE ORDNANCE, is an officer in the Tower, who registers all orders touching the king's ordnance.

CLERK OF THE OUTLAWRIES, (*clericus utlagariarum*) an officer belonging to the court of common pleas, being the servant or deputy to the king's attorney-general, for making out writs of *capias utlagatum*, after outlawry; the king's attorney's name being to every one of those writs.

CLERK OF THE PAPER-OFFICE, is an officer in the court of king's bench, that makes up the paper-books of special pleadings and demurrers in that court.

CLERK OF THE PAPERS, an officer in the common pleas; who hath the custody of the papers of the warden of the Fleet, enters commitments and discharges of prisoners, delivers out day-rules, &c.

CLERK OF A PARISH. The parish clerk is regarded by the common law, as a person who has a freehold in his office, and therefore, though he may be punished, yet he cannot be deprived by ecclesiastical censures. 2 *Rol. Abr.* 234.

For it has been resolved, that if the parish clerk misdemean himself in his office, or in the church, he may be sentenced for it in the ecclesiastical court to excommunication, but not to deprivation. 2 *Brownl.* 38. And when a parish clerk is nominated, he is by common law an officer, and in for life without deed. 2 *Salk.* 536.

And a parish clerk may sue in court Christian for his fees. *Reg.* 52. 2 *Rol. Rep.* 71.

The parish clerk was formerly very frequently in holy orders, and some are so to this day: he is generally appointed by the incumbent, but by custom, may be chosen by the inhabitants, and if such custom appears, the court of king's bench will grant a *mandamus* to the archdeacon to swear him in; for the establishment of the custom turns it into a temporal right. *Cro. Car.* 589. 1 *Black.* 395.

CLERK OF THE PARLIAMENT ROLLS, (*clericus rotulorum parliamenti*) is he who records all things done in the high court of parliament, and ingrosseth them in parchment rolls, for their better preservation to posterity: of these officers there are two, one in the lords' house, and another in the house of commons.

CLERK OF THE PATENTS, or of the letters patent under the great seal of England, an office erected 18 *Jac.* 1.

CLERK OF THE PEACE, (*clericus pacis*) is an officer belonging to the sessions of the peace: his duty is to issue sessions, process, record the proceedings therein, and do particular acts directed by divers statutes.

The *custos rotulorum* of the county hath the appointment of the clerk of the peace, who may execute his office by deputy. 37 *H.* 8. *c.* 1. And if the clerk of the peace misdemeans himself, the justices of peace in quarter-sessions have power to discharge him; and the *custos rotulorum* is to choose another resident in the county, or on his default the sessions may appoint one: the place is not to be sold, on pain of forfeiting double the value of the sum given, and disability to enjoy it, &c. *Stat.* 1 *W.* & *M. sess.* 1. *c.* 21.

CLERK OF THE PELL, (*clericus pellis*) is a clerk belonging to the exchequer, whose office is to enter every teller's bill into a parchment roll called *pellis receptorum*, and also to make another roll of payments, which is termed *pellis exituum*; wherein he sets down by what warrant the money was paid. See *stat.* 22 & 23 *Car.* 2. *c.* 22.

CLERK OF THE PETTY-BAG, (*clericus parvæ bagæ*) an officer of the court of chancery. There are three of these officers, of whom the master of the rolls is the chief. Their office is to record the return of all inquisitions out of every shire; to make out patents of customers, guagers, controllers, &c. all *conges d' elire* for bishops, the summons of the nobility, and burgesses to parliament; commissions directed to knights and others of every shire, for assessing subsidies and taxes: all offices found *post mortem* are brought to the clerks of the petty-bag to be filed; and by them are entered all pleadings of the chancery concerning the validity of patents or other things which pass the great seal; they also make forth liberates upon extents of statutes staple, and recovery of recognizances forfeited, and all eligits upon them: and all suits for or against any privileged person are prosecuted in their office, &c.

CLERK OF THE PIPE, (*clericus pipæ*) is an officer in the exchequer who having the accounts of debts due to the king, delivered and drawn out of the remembrancer's offices, charges them down in the great roll, and is called clerk of the pipe from the shape of that roll, which is put together like a pipe: he also writes out warrants to the sheriffs to levy the said debts upon the goods and chattels of the debtors; and if they have no goods, then he draws them down to the lord treasurer's remembrancer, to write estreats against their lands. The ancient revenue of the crown stands in charge to him, and he sees the same answered by the farmers and sheriffs: he makes a charge to all sheriffs of their summons of the pipe, and green wax, and takes care to be answered on their accounts. And he hath the drawing and ingrossing of all leases of the king's lands; having a secondary and several clerks under him. In the reign of king Henry VI. this officer was called *ingrossator magni rotuli*. See *Stat.* 33 *H.* 8 *c.* 22.

CLERK OF THE PLEAS, (*clericus placitorum*) an officer in the court of exchequer, in whose office all the officers of the court, upon special privilege belonging unto them, ought to sue or be sued in any action, &c. In this office are also prosecuted actions at law, by other persons as well as officers of the court; but the plaintiff ought to be tenant, or debtor to the king, or some way accountant to him: now it is only matter of form. The clerk of the pleas has under him a great many clerks, who are attornies in all suits commenced or depending in the exchequer.

CLERK OF THE PRIVY SEAL, (*clericus privati sigilli.*) There are four of the officers which attend the lord privy seal: or if there be no lord privy seal, the principal secretary of state; writing and making out all things that are sent by warrant from the signet to the privy seal, and which are to be passed to the great seal: also they make out privy seals, upon a special occasion of his majesty's affairs, as for loan of money, and the like. He that is now called lord privy seal, seems to have been in ancient times called clerk of the privy seal; but notwithstanding to have been reckoned in the number of the great officers of the realm. *Stat.* 12 *R.* 2. *c.* 11. and 27 *H.* 8. *c.* 11.

CLERK OF THE ROLLS, an officer of the chancery, that makes search for, and copies deeds, offices, &c.

CLERK OF THE RULES, in the court of king's bench, is he who draws up and enters all the rules and orders made in court: and gives rules of course on divers writs: this officer is mentioned in the 22 & 23 *Car.* 2. *c.* 22.

CLERK OF THE SEWERS, an officer belonging to the commissioners of sewers, who writes and records their proceedings, which they transact by virtue of their commissions, and the authority given them by statute 13 *Eliz.* *c.* 9.

CLERK OF THE SIGNET, (*clericus signeti*) is an officer continually attendant on his majesty's principal secretary, who hath the custody of the privy signet, as well for sealing his majesty's private letters, as such grants as pass the king's hand by bill signed: and of these clerks or officers there are four, that attend in their course, and have their diet at the secretary's table.

CLERK OF THE KING'S SILVER, (*clericus argenti regis*) is an officer belonging to the court of common pleas, to whom every fine is brought after it hath passed the office of the *custos brevium*, and by whom the effect of the writ of covenant is entered into a paper-book; according to which all the fines of that term are recorded in the rolls of the court. After the king's silver is entered, it is accounted a fine in law, and not before.

CLERK OF THE SUPERSEDEAS, an officer belonging to the court of common pleas, who makes out writs of *supersedeas*, upon a defendant's appearing to the *exigent* on an outlawry, whereby the sheriff is forbidden to return the *exigent*.

CLERK OF THE TREASURY, (*clericus thesaurarii*) is an officer of the common pleas, who hath the charge of keeping the records of the court, and makes out all the records of *nisi prius;* also he makes all exemplifications of records being in the Treasury; and he hath the fees due for all searches. He is taken to be the servant of the chief justice, and removable at pleasure; whereas all other officers of the court are for life: there is a secondary, or under clerk of the Treasury for assistance, who hath some fees and allowances: and likewise an under-keeper, that always keeps one key of the treasury door, and the chief clerk of the secondary another; so that the one cannot come in without the other.

CLERK OF THE KING'S GREAT WARDROBE, an officer of the king's houshold, that keeps an account or inventory of all things belonging to the royal wardrobe. *Stat.* 1 *E.* 4. *c.* 1.

CLERK OF THE WARRANTS, (*clericus warrantorum*) an officer belonging to the common pleas court, who enters all warrants of attorney for plaintiffs and defendants in suits; and inrolls deeds of indentures of bargain and sale, which are acknowledged in the court or before any judges out of the court. And it is his office to estreat into the exchequer all issues, fines and amerciaments, which grow due to the king in that court, for which he hath a standing fee or allowance.

CLERONIMUS, an old word signifying heir.

CLIPPING *the coin.* By 5 *Eliz.* *c.* 11. "*clipping*, washing, rounding, or filing for "wicked gain's sake any of the money of "this realm or other money suffered to be "current here, shall be adjudged high trea-"son." And by stat. 18 *Eliz.* *c.* 1. (because the same law, being penal, ought to be taken and expounded strictly according to the words thereof, and the like offence not by any equity to receive the like punishment and pains) the same species of offence is described in other more general words, viz.

"impairing, diminishing, falsifying, scal-"ing, and lightening, and made liable to "the same penalties."

CLITONES, the eldest, and all the sons of kings. *Cowel. Blount.*

CLIVE, CLIFF. The names of places beginning or ending with these words signify a rock from the old Saxon. *Ibid.*

CLOTHES (spoiling). By 6 *Geo.* 1. *c.* 23, the wilful and malicious tearing, cutting, spoiling, burning, or defacing of the garments or clothes of any person passing in the streets or highways, with intent so to do, is felony.

This act was occasioned by the insolence and malicious practices of certain weavers, and others, who, upon the introduction of a new fabric, prejudicial to their own manufactures, made it their practice to deface them, either by open outrage, or by privily cutting, or casting *aqua fortis* in the streets upon such as wore them. 4 *Black.* 245.

CLOERE, a prison or dungeon; conjectured to be of British original: as the dungeon, or inner prison of Wallingford castle, *temp. Hen.* 2. was called *cloere brien*, i. e. *carcer brieni*, &c. *Cowel. Blount.*

CLOSE ROLLS and CLOSE WRITS, Grants of lands, &c. from the crown, are contained in charters or letters patent, that is, open letters, *literis patentes*, so called because they are not sealed up, but exposed to open view, with the Great Seal pendent at the bottom, and are usually addressed by the king to all his subjects at large. And therein they differ from other letters of the king, sealed also with the Great Seal, but directed to particular persons, and for particular purposes; which, therefore, not being fit for public inspection, are closed up and sealed on the outside, and are thereupon called writs close, *literæ clausæ*, and are recorded in the close rolls, in the same manner as the others are in the patent-rolls. 2 *Black. Com.* 346.

CLOSH, was an unlawful game forbidden by 17 *Ed.* 4, *c.* 3, and 33 *H.* 8. *c.* 9, and said to have been the same with our nine-pins. *Blount.*

CLOVE, is the two-and-thirtieth part of a weigh of cheese, *i. e.* eight pounds. 9 *H.* 6. *c.* 8.

CLOUGH, a word made use of for valley, in *Domesday* book. But among merchants it is an allowance for the turn of the scale on buying goods wholesale by weight. *Lex Mercat.*

CLUTA, (*Fr. clous*) shoes, clouted shoes, and most commonly horse-shoes: it also signifies the streaks of iron with which cart-wheels are bound. *Cowel. Blount.*

CLYPEUS, one of a noble family. *Blount.*

COADJUTOR, (Lat.) a fellow-helper or assistant, particularly applied to one appointed to assist a bishop, being grown old and infirm, so as not to be able to perform his duty. *Cowel. Blount.*

COALS. By 12 *Ann.* stat. 2, *c.* 17, the coal bushel shall contain one Winchester bushel and one quart, and the chalder shall contain 36 such bushels heaped.

By 15 *Geo.* 3, *c.* 27, the coal bushel shall be round, with an even bottom, nineteen inches and an half from outside to outside; to contain one Winchester bushel and one quart of water, allowing 36 bushels heaped to a chaldron, and 20 hundred, at 112 pounds avoirdupoise *per* hundred, to the ton. *Ibid.*

And by 28 *Geo.* 3. *c.* 53, persons united in covenant or otherwise, consisting of more than five, for the purchasing of coals, or regulating the trade, shall be deemed a combination to advance the price of coals, and may be punished in the King's Bench at Westminster. See also LONDON.

COLLIERIES. See MINES.

COATS OF ARMS. It is said that these were introduced about the reign of Richard the First, who brought them from the Croisade in the Holy Land, where they were first invented, and painted on the shields of the knights to distinguish the variety of persons of every Christian nation who resorted thither, and who could not when clad in complete steel be otherwise known or ascertained. 2 *Black. Com.* 306.

It is the business of the court military or the court of chivalry, according to sir Matthew Hale, to adjust the right of armorial bearings. 3 *Black. Com.* 105.

COCHERINGS, chief rents in Ireland. *Cowel. Blount.*

COCKET, (*cockettum*) is a seal belonging to the king's custom-house, or rather a scroll of parchment sealed, and delivered by the officers of the custom-house to merchants, as a warrant that their merchandises are customed. *Cowel. Blount.*

COCKSETUS, a boatman, cockswain or coxon. *Cowel.*

COCULA, a cogue, or little drinking-cup. *Cowel. Blount.*

CODICIL, (*codicillus*, from *codex*, a book, a writing) is a supplement to a will, where any thing is omitted which the testator would add, or which he would explain, alter, or retract; and it is the same with a testament, and taken as part thereof, and the testator may make as many codicils as he pleases. *West, Symb. p.* 636. *Swinb.* 1. *sec.* 1.

COFRA, a coffer, chest, or trunk. *Cowel. Blount.*

COFFERER OF THE KING'S HOUSEHOLD, is a principal officer of the king's house, next under the comptroller, who in the counting-house, and elsewhere, hath a special charge and oversight of other officers of the household, to all which he pays their wages: this officer passes his accounts in the Exchequer, and is mentioned in 39 *Eliz.* c. 7. *Ibid.*

COGGLE, a small fishing-boat, upon the coasts of Yorkshire. *Ibid.*

COGNATI, relations by the mother, as the *agnati* are relations by the father. 2 *Black.* 234.

COGNATIONE, a writ of cousenage. See *Cosenage.*

COGNISANCE, or cognizance, (Fr. *connusance*, Lat. *cognitio*) is used diversely in our law: sometimes it is an acknowledgment of a fine, or confession of a thing done; and there is a cognisance of taking a distress: as a bailiff to another; and it is the same as an avowry. Sometimes it is the hearing of a matter judicially; as to take cognisance of a cause; and sometimes it signifies a jurisdiction, as cognisance of pleas is a power to call a cause or plea out of another court, which none can do but the king, or by charter. This cognisance of pleas is a privilege granted by the king to a city or town, to hold plea of all contracts, &c. within the liberty of the franchise; and when any man is impleaded for such matters in the courts of Westminster, the mayor, &c. of such franchise, may ask cognisance of the plea, and demand that it shall be determined before them: but if the courts at Westminster are possessed of the plea before cognisance be demanded, it is then too late; and cognisance must be demanded before an imparlance. *Terms de Ley. Gilb. Hist. P. C.*

Cognisance also signifies the badge of a waterman or servant, which is usually the giver's crest, whereby he is known to belong to this or that nobleman or gentleman. 3 *Black. Com.* 3 *V.* 300. 4 *V.* 275.

COGNISOR, and COGNISEE. In a fine the cognisor is he who passeth or acknowledges a fine of lands or tenements to another; and the cognisee is he to whom the fine of the said lands, &c. is acknowledged.

COGNITIONES, ensigns and arms, or a military coat painted with arms. *Mat. Par.* 1250. *Cowel. Blount.*

COGNITIONIBUS MITTENDIS, was an ancient writ to one of the king's justices of the Common Pleas, or other that hath power to take a fine, who having taken the fine defers to certify it, commanding him to certify it. *Reg. Orig.* 68.

COGNOVIT ACTIONEM, is where a defendant acknowledges or confesses the plaintiff's cause against him to be just and true, and before or after issue suffers judgment to be entered against him without trial, upon which judgment may be entered up, and execution levied according to such terms as are therein agreed on by the parties. 1 *Rol.* 929. *Hob.* 178.

COGWARE, is said to be a sort of coarse cloths, made in divers parts of England. See 13 *R.* 2. *cap.* 10.

COHUAGIUM, a tribute anciently paid by those who met promiscuously in the market or fair. *Cowel. Blount.*

COIF, (*coifa*) the lawn coif which serjeants at law wear on their heads when they are created, hence they are called *serjeants* of the coif; and the use of it was anciently to cover *tonsuram clericalem*, otherwise called *corona clericalis*, because the crown of the head was close shaved, and a border of hair left round the lower part, which made it look like a crown. *Blount.*

COIN (*cuna pecunia*). Coin is a word collective, and so called from the most ancient having been square, with corners, and not round, as it now is. *Cromp. Jur.* 71. 220. It contains in it all manner of the several stamps and species of money in any kingdom: and this is one of the royal prerogatives belonging to every sovereign prince, that he alone in his own dominions may order and dispose the quantity, value, and fashion of his coin. But the coin of one king is not current in the kingdom of another; though our king by his prerogative may make any foreign coin lawful money of England at his pleasure, by proclamation. *Terms de Ley.*

By statute any person may break or deface pieces of silver money suspected to be counterfeit, or diminished otherwise than by wearing: but if such pieces on breaking, &c. are found to be good coin, it will be at the breaker's peril, who shall stand to the loss of it. 9 & 10 *W.* 3, *cap.* 21.

But it said that when a person has accepted of money in payment from another, and put the same into his purse, it is at his peril after his allowance; and he shall not then take exception to it as bad, notwithstanding he presently reviews it. *Ter. de Ley.*

COLIBERTS, (*coliberti*) were tenants in socage, and particularly such villeins as were manumitted or made freemen. *Domesday. Du Cange.*

COLLATERAL, (*collateralis*) from the Lat. *laterale*, sidewise, or that which hangeth by the side, not direct; as collateral assurance is that which is made over and above the principal deed itself: collateral security is where a deed is made of other lands beside those granted by the deed of mortgage: and if a man covenants with another, and enters into bond for performance of his covenant, the bond is a collateral assurance, because it is external, and without the nature and essence of the covenant. *Cromp. Juris.* 185. *Cowel. Blount.*

COLLATERAL CONSANGUINITY, or kindred. Collateral relations agree with the lineal in this, that they descend from the same stock or ancestor, but differ in this, that they do not descend from each other. Collateral kinsmen, therefore, are such as lineally spring from one and the same ancestor, who is the *stirps* or root, the *stipes*, trunk, or common stock from whence these relations are branched out. 2 *Black. Com.* 204.

COLLATERAL ISSUE, is where a criminal convict pleads any matter, allowed by law, in bar of execution, as pregnancy, the king's pardon, an act of grace, or diversity of person, *viz.* that he or she is not the same that was attainted, &c. whereon issue is taken, which issue is to be tried by a jury, *instanter*. 4 *Black. Com.* 389.

COLLATIO BONORUM, is in law where a portion or money advanced by the father to a son or daughter, is brought into hotchpot, in order to have an equal distributory share of his personal estate at his death, according to the intent of the stat. 22 & 23 *Car.* 2. *c.* 10. *Abr. Cas. Eq.* p. 254. 2 *Black. Com.* 517.

COLLATION OF A BENEFICE, (*collatio beneficii*) signifies the bestowing of a benefice by the bishop, when he hath right of patronage. And it differs from institution in this, that institution is performed by the bishop upon the presentation of another, and collation is his own act of presentation; and it differs from a common presentation, as it is the giving of the church to the parson, and presentation is the giving or offering of the parson to the church. But collation supplies the place of presentation and institution, and amounts to the same as institution, where the bishop is both patron and ordinary. 1 *Lil. Abr.* 273. Anciently the right of presentation to all churches was in the bishop, and now if the patron neglects to present to a church then this right returns to the bishop by collation: and if the bishop neglects to collate within six months after the lapse of the patron, then the archbishop hath a right to do it; and if the archbishop neglects, then it devolves to the king, the one as superior, to supply the defects of bishops, the other as supreme, to reform all defects of government. 1 *Inst.* 344. *Wood's Inst.* 159. 2 *Black. Com.* 22, 23.

COLLATIONE FACTA UNI POST MORTEM ALTERIUS, is a writ directed to the justices of the Common Pleas, commanding them to issue their writ to the bishop for the admission of a clerk in the place of another presented by the king, who died during the suit between the king and the bishop's clerk; for judgment once passed for the king's clerk, and he dying before admittance, the king may bestow his presentation on another. *Reg. Orig.* 31.

COLLATIONE HEREMITAGII, an ancient writ whereby the king conferred the keeping of an hermitage upon a clerk. *Reg. Orig.* 303. 308.

COLLATION OF SEALS. This was when upon the same label one seal was set on the back or reverse of the other. *Cowel. Blount.*

COLLATIVE ADVOWSONS. An advowson collative is where the bishop and patron are one and same person; in which case the bishop cannot present to himself; but he does, by the one act of collation, or conferring the benefice, the whole that is done in common cases, by presentation and institution. 2 *Black. Com.* 22, 23.

COLLEGE, (*collegium*) a particular corporation, company, or society of men, having certain privileges founded by the king's license, such as the colleges or universities at Oxford, Cambridge, and elsewhere. 4 *Rep.* 106, 108. *Roberts. Hist. Emp. Charles* V. 323.

COLLEGIATE CHURCH, consists of a dean or other president, and secular priests, as canons or prebendaries in the said church, as Westminster, Windsor, Winchester, &c.

COLLIGENDUM BONA DEFUNCTI, (letters *ad*). In defect of representatives and creditors to administer to an intestate, the ordinary may commit administration to such discreet person as he approves of, or grant him letters *ad colligendum bona defuncti*, which neither make him executor or administrator, his only business being to keep the goods in his safe custody, and to do other acts for the benefit of such as are entitled to the property of the deceased. 2 *Black. Com.* 505.

COLLOQUIUM, (*a colloquendo*) a talking together, or affirming of a thing, and the *colloquium* in pleading is the *discourse*, laid in declarations for words in actions of slander. *Mod. Cas.* 203. *Carthew* 90.

COLLUSION. (*collusio*), is a deceitful agreement or contract between two or more persons, for some evil purpose, as to defraud a third person, or the like. This collusion is either apparent, when it shows itself in the face of the act; or, which is more common, it is secret, where done *occulte*, or in the dark, covered over with a show of honesty. And it is a thing the law abhors; wherefore when found it makes void all things dependent upon the same, though otherwise in themselves good. *Co. Lit.* 109. 360. *Plowd.* 54.

COLONIES. See *Charter-governments*

COLONUS, a husbandman or villager, anciently bound to pay a yearly tribute, or at certain times in the year to plough some part of the lord's land. *Cowel. Blount.*

COLOUR, (*color*) signifies a probable plea, but what is in fact false, and hath this end, to draw the trial of the cause from the jury to the judges; and therefore colour ought to be matter in law, or doubtful to the jury. 1 *Rep.* 79. 108. *Terms de Ley*, 140. See *Doct. Plac.* 72, 73. 3 *Black. Com.* 309.

COLOUR OF OFFICE, (*color officii*) is

when an act is evilly done by the countenance of an office: and always taken in the worst sense, being grounded upon corruption, to which the office is as a shadow and colour. *Plowd. Comment.* 64.

COLPICES, (*colpicium, colpiciis,*) young poles, which being cut down make levers, or lifters. *Blount.*

COLPO, a small wax candle, *à copo de cere. Ibid.*

COMBARONES, the fellow barons, or commonalty of the Cinque Ports. But the title of barons of the Cinque Ports is now given to their representatives in parliament, and the word *combaron* is used for a fellow member, the baron and his combaron. *Cowel. Blount.*

COMBA TERRÆ, from the Sax. *cumbe,* Brit. *kum,* Eng. *comb,* a valley or low piece of ground or place between two hills. *Ibid.*

COMBAT, (Fr.) an ancient mode of trial between two champions, of a doubtful cause or quarrel, by the sword or bastons. See *Battle. Champion.*

COMBINATIONS to do unlawful acts are punishable by the common law before the unlawful act is executed; and this is to prevent the consequence of combinations and conspiracies, &c. 9 *Rep.* 57.

By 39 and 40 *Geo.* 2, c. 106, every workman who shall enter into any contract for obtaining an advance of wages, altering the usual time of working, decreasing the quantity of work, or the like (except contracts between masters and men) shall be committed to the common gaol for not more than three months, or the house of correction for not more than two, on conviction before two justices: as also any workmen entering into any combination for advancing wages, or the like, as above, or who shall wilfully and maliciously endeavour to prevent any workmen from hiring himself, or prevail on him to quit his employ, or who shall hinder any master from employing any person, or, without reasonable cause, shall refuse to work with any other workman, and also all persons who shall attend any meeting for the purpose of making any such illegal contract, or who shall summon, or by intimidation, or otherwise, endeavour to induce any journeyman to attend any such meeting for such purpose. *s.* 1, 2, 3, 4.

No person shall contribute for any expenses incurred for acting contrary to this act, or towards the support of any person to induce him not to work, on penalty not exceeding 10*l.* and any person collecting money for such purposes shall forfeit not exceeding 5*l.* one moiety to his Majesty, and the other to the informer and the poor of the parish. *s.* 5.

The offences shall be determined in a summary way before two justices, who shall fix the penalty, and if not paid shall cause it to be levied by distress, or in default thereof shall commit the offender to the common gaol or house of correction. *s.* 5.

Contributions made for any prohibited purposes shall be forfeited, one moiety to the king, and the other to the person who shall sue for the same. *s.* 6.

Persons liable to be sued for contribution money shall be obliged to answer, on oath, to any information in equity preferred against them by the attorney-general, or at the relation of any informer. *s.* 7.

Upon payment into court of the money remaining in the hands of any person, at the time of filing information, and making discovery of the securities, upon which other monies shall have been placed, the party shall be discharged from penalty, and no person is to be liable to penalty for money discovered by any answer to an information. *s.* 8.

Offenders may be compelled to give evidence, and shall be indemnified from prosecution for any offence whatever to which they give testimony. *s.* 9.

Justices may summon offenders: and on their not appearing, or in the first instance, may issue warrants for their apprehension, and also on their appearing, or on proof of their absconding, may convict or acquit the parties. *s.* 10.

Justices may summon witnesses, and for non-appearance, or refusal to give evidence, may commit them until they submit. *s.* 11.

Convictions are to be transmitted to the next general or quarter sessions, to be filed, and if appeal be made the justices shall then proceed to hear it. *s.* 13.

This act is not to abridge powers now given by law to justices touching combinations; nor empower manufacturers to employ workmen contrary to the provisions now in force for regulating the conduct of any particular manufacture, without a licence from a justice, who is empowered to grant the same in the case of misconduct on the part of a qualified workman. *s.* 15.

No master in the trade in which any offence is charged to have been committed, shall act as a justice under this act. *s.* 16.

All contracts between masters or other persons for reducing the wages of journeymen, or for altering the usual hours of working, or increasing the quantity of work, shall be void, and masters convicted thereof shall forfeit 20*l.* one moiety to his Majesty, and the other to the informer and the poor of the parish, which may be levied by distress, and if not paid the offender may be committed for not exceeding three, nor less than two, calendar months. *s.* 17.

Disputes between masters and workmen may be settled by arbitration. If arbitrators shall not decide the matter within three days after submission to their award, either party may require them to go before and state to a justice the points in difference, who shall finally determine the same. *s.* 18.

Persons summoned neglecting to attend the arbitrators, or refusing to be examined, may be committed by a justice till they submit. *Ibid.*

But the parties may extend the time limited for making the award, and the submission to arbitration and the award may be on unstamped paper, and each party to have a copy of the submission. *s.* 19, 20, 21.

If an arbitration be demanded, and the submission signed, and an arbitrator named by either party, and the other shall refuse to sign the submission and appoint his arbitrator, he shall on conviction forfeit 10*l.* half to the king, and the other to the poor of the parish, which may be levied by distress, or in default the offender may be committed for three months, or not less than two. *s.* 22.

If either party shall not perform what is directed by the award he may be committed till performance; but no person is to be deemed guilty in not attending at more than one arbitration at a time, or more than two in one day, and non-resident masters may appoint persons to act for them. *Ibid.*

Appeal may be made to the general sessions, or general quarter sessions, whose decision shall be final.

For combinations amongst particular manufacturers, see tit. *Manufacturers.*

COMBUSTIO PECUNIÆ, the ancient way of trying mixed and corrupt money, by melting it down upon payment into the Exchequer. *Lowndes's Essay on Coin*, p. 5.

COMITATUS, a county divided into hundreds and into tithings. *Mat. Paris. anno* 1234.

According to Lord Littleton, in his history of *Hen.* 2. *lib.* 2, *fol.* 217, each county was anciently an earldom, so that, previous to the reign of king Stephen, there were not any titular earls, nor more earls than counties, though there might be fewer, see also *Bract. l.* 3. *c.* 10.

COMITATU COMMISSO, is a writ or commission whereby a sheriff was authorized to take upon him the charge of the county. *Reg. Orig.* 295.

COMITATU ET CASTRO COMMISSO, a writ by which the charge of a county, together with the keeping of a castle, was committed to the sheriff. *Reg. Orig. Ibid.*

COMITIVA, a companion or fellow traveller. *Cowell. Blount.*

COMMANDERY, (*præceptoria*) was any manor or chief messuage, with lands or tenements thereto appertaining, which belonged to the priory of St. John of Jerusalem in England; and he who had the government of such a manor or house was styled the commander, who could not dispose of it but to the use of the priory, and only taking thence his own sustenance, according to his degree. Since the dissolution of this priory in the reign of *Hen.* 8. the name only of commanderies remains, the power being now extinct.

COMMANDMENT, (*præceptum*) is diversely taken, as the commandment of the king, when upon his own motion he hath cast any man into prison. Commandment of the justices, absolute or ordinary; absolute, where upon their own authority they commit a person for contempt, &c. to prison, as a punishment; ordinary is when they commit one rather for safe custody than for any punishment; and a man committed upon such an ordinary commandment is replevisable. *Staundf. P. C.* 72, 73.

In another sense of this word, magistrates may command others to assist them in the execution of their offices, for the doing of justice, and so may a justice of peace to suppress riots, apprehend felons; an officer to keep the king's peace, &c. *Bro.* 3. A master may command his servant to drive another man's cattle out of his ground, to enter into lands, seize goods, distrain for rent, or do other things, if the thing be not a trespass to others. *Fitz. Abr.* The commandment of a thing is good where he that commands hath power to do it: and a verbal command in most cases is sufficient, unless it be where it is given by a corporation, or when a sheriff's warrant is to a bailiff to arrest, &c. *Bro.* 288. *Dyer* 202.

But he that commandeth any one to do an unlawful act is accessary to it and all the consequences, if it be executed in the same manner as commanded: but if the commander revoke the command, or if the execution varies from it, or in the nature of the offence, in such case he will not be accessary. 2 *Inst.* 282. 3 *Inst.* 51. 57.

In trespasses an infant or feme covert may be guilty in respect of actual violence done by them in person, though not in regard to what shall be done by others at their command, because all such commands of theirs are void. *Co. Lit.* 357. 1 *Hawk.* 147. In trespass, &c. the master shall be charged criminally for the act of the servant, done by his command; but servants shall not be excused for committing any crime when they act by command of their masters, who have no authority over them to give such command. *Doct. et Stud. c.* 42. *H. P. C.* 66. *Kel.* 13. And if a master commands his servant to distrain, and abuses the distress, the servant shall answer it, to the party injured, &c. *Kitch.* 372.

COMMARCHIO, the confines of the land, whence, probably, comes the word marches. *Cowel. Blount.*

COMMENDAM, (*ecclesia commendata, vel custodia ecclesiæ alicui commissa*) is the holding of a benefice or church living, which being void, is commended to the charge and care of some sufficient clerk, to be supplied until it may be conveniently provided of a pastor, and he to whom the church is commended, hath the profits thereof only for a certain time, and the nature of the church is not changed thereby, but is as a thing deposited in his hands in trust, who hath nothing but the custody of it, which may be revoked. When a parson is made bishop, there is a cession or voidance of his benefice, by the promotion; but if the king by special dispensation gives him power to retain his benefice, notwithstanding his promotion; he shall continue parson, and is said to hold it *in commendam*. *Hob.* 144. *Latch.* 236.

But this is usually where the bishopricks are small, for the better support of the dignity of the bishop promoted, (as in the case of the late bishop of Rochester, and the benefice of St. Mary, Newington,) and it must be always before consecration: for afterwards it comes too late, because the benefice is then absolutely void. *Dyer.* 228. 3 *Lev.* 381. *Hob.* 143. *Danv.* 79.

And a commendam may be temporary for six or twelve months; two or three years, &c. or it may be perpetual, i. e. for life, and thus it is equal to a presentation, without institution or induction. *Vaugh.* 18.

COMMENDATORY, (*commendatarius*) is he that hath a church living or preferment *in commendam*. *Cowel. Blount.*

COMMENDATORY LETTERS, are such as are written by one bishop to another in behalf of any of the clergy, or others of his diocese, travelling thither, that they may be received among the faithful: or that the clerk may be promoted, or necessaries administered to others, &c. *Ibid.* and *Bede, lib.* 2. *c.* 18.

COMMENDATUS, one that lives under the protection of a great man. *Spelm. of funds, cap.* 20.

COMMERCE, (*commercium*), there is a difference between commerce and trade; the former relates to our dealings with foreign nations, or our colonies, &c. abroad, the other to our mutual trafficks and dealings among ourselves at home. *Lex. Mer.*

COMMISSARY, (*commissarius*) is a title in the ecclesiastical law, belonging to one that exerciseth spiritual jurisdiction, in places of a diocese which are so far from the episcopal city, that the chancellor cannot call the people to the bishop's principal consistory court, without their too great inconvenience. This commissary was ordained to supply the bishop's jurisdiction and office in the out places of the diocese: or in such places as are peculiar to the bishop, and exempted from the jurisdiction of the archdeacon: for where, either by prescription or composition, archdeacons have jurisdiction within their archdeaconries, as in most places they have, this commissary is superfluous and oftentimes vexatious, and ought not to be, yet in such cases a commissary is sometimes appointed by the bishop, he taking prestation money of the archdeacon yearly, *pro exteriori jurisdictione*, as it is ordinarily called. But this is held to be a wrong to archdeacons and the poorer sort of people. *Cowel's Interp.* 4 *Inst.* 338.

COMMISSION, (*commissio*) the warrant or letters patent, which all men exercising jurisdiction either ordinary or extraordinary, have to authorize them to enquire into, hear or determine any cause, action, or matter: as the commission of the judges, justices of the peace. *Bro. Abr.* 12. *Rep.* 39. 2 *Dyer.* 289.

COMMISSION OF ARRAY, before the establishment of the militia, it was usual for our princes to issue commissions of array, and send into every county officers in whom they could confide, to muster and array, (or set in military order), the inhabitants of every district. 1 *Black. Com.* 410, 11.

COMMISSION OF ASSOCIATION, is a commission to associate two or more learned persons with the justices, in the several circuits and counties of Wales. 18 *Eliz. c.* 9.

COMMISSION OF BANKRUPT, issues from the lord chancellor to certain commissioners appointed to take order with the bankrupt's lands and goods, for the satisfaction of the creditors. See *Bankrupt.*

COMMISSION OF CHARITABLE USES, goes out of the Chancery to the bishop and others, where lands given to charitable uses are misemployed, or there is any fraud or disputes concerning them, to enquire of and redress the abuse, &c. 43 *Eliz. c.* 4. See *Charitable Uses.*

COMMISSION OF DELEGATES, is a commission under the great seal to certain persons, usually two or three temporal lords, as many bishops, and two judges of the law, to sit upon an appeal to the king in the court of chancery, where any sentence is given in any ecclesiastical cause by the archbishop. *Stat.* 25 *H.* 8. *c.* 19. Now generally three of the common law judges, and two civilians, sit as delegates. *Cowel. Blount.*

COMMISSION TO ENQUIRE OF FAULTS AGAINST THE LAW, was an ancient commission sent forth on extraordinary occasions and corruptions. *Ibid.*

COMMISSION OF LUNACY, a commission out of Chancery to enquire whether a person represented to be a lunatic be so or not, that if a lunatic, the king may have the care of his estate, &c. 17 *Ed.* 2. *c.* 10.

COMMISSION OF THE PEACE, justices of the peace are appointed by the king's special commission under the great seal, the form of which was settled A.D. 1590, this appoints them all jointly and severally to keep the peace, and any two or more of them to enquire of and determine felonies and other misdemeanors: in which number some particular justices or one of them, are directed to be always included, and no business to be done without their presence; the words of the commission running thus: *quorum aliquem vestrum*, A. B. C. D. &c. *unum esse volumus*, whence the persons so named are usually called justices of the *quorum*. 1 *Black*. 351.

COMMISSION OF REBELLION, is a writ, which issues when a man after proclamation made by the sheriff, upon process out of the Chancery, on pain of his allegiance, to present himself to the court by a day assigned, makes default in his appearance: and this commission is directed to certain persons, to the end they, three, two, or one of them apprehend the party, or cause him to be apprehended as a rebel and contemner of the king's laws, wheresoever found within the kingdom, and bring or cause him to be brought to the court on a day therein assigned: this writ or commission goes forth after an attachment returned, *non est inventus, &c. Terms de Ley*.

COMMISSION OF SEWERS, is directed to certain persons to see drains and ditches well kept and maintained in the marshy and fenny parts of England, for the better conveyance of the water into the sea, and preserving the grass upon the land. See 23 *H*. 8. *c*. 5. 13 *Eliz*. *c*. 9.

COMMISSIONER, (*commissionarius*) is he that hath a commission, letters patent, or other lawful warrant to examine any matters or to execute any public office, or the like. And commissioners by the common law must strictly pursue the authority of the commission, and perform the effect thereof; and they are to observe the ancient rules of the courts whence they come; and if they do any thing for which they have not authority, it will be void. 2 *Co. Rep*. 25. *Co. Lit*. 157. The office of commissioners is to do what they are commanded; and it is necessarily implied, that they may do that also, without which, what is commanded cannot be done: and their authority when appointed on any statute law, must be used as the statutes prescribe. 12 *Rep*. 32.

COMMITTEE, are those to whom the consideration or ordering of any matter is referred by some court, or by consent of parties to whom it belongs: as in parliament where a matter is referred to the consideration of certain persons appointed by the house farther to examine it, they are thereupon called a committee. And when a parliament is called, and the speaker and members have taken the oaths, and the standing orders of the house are read, committees are appointed to sit on certain days, viz. the committee of privileges and elections, of religion, of grievances, of courts of justice, and of trade; which are the standing committees. But though they are appointed by every new parliament, they do not all of them act, only the committee of privileges; and this being not of the whole house, is first called in the speaker's chamber, from whence it is adjourned into the house, every one of the house having a vote therein, though not named, which makes the same usually very numerous: and any member may be present at any select committee; but is not to vote unless he be named. The chairman of the grand committee, who is always some leading member, sits in the clerk's place at the table, and writes the votes for and against the matter referred to them; and if the number be equal he has a casting voice, otherwise he hath no vote in the committee; and after the chairman hath put the question for reporting to the house, if that be carried, he leaves the chair, and the speaker being called to his chair, (who quits it in the beginning, and the mace is laid under the table) he is to go down to the bar, and so bring up his report to the table. After a bill is read a second time in the house of commons, the question is put, whether it shall be committed to a committee of the whole house, or a private committee; and the committees meet in the speaker's chamber, and report their opinion of the bill with the amendments, &c. And if there be any exceptions against the amendments reported, the bill may be recommitted: eight persons make a committee, which may be adjourned by five, &c. *Lex Constitutionis*, 147, 150.

COMMITTEE. The care and commitment of the custody of the persons and estates of ideots and lunatics are the prerogative of the crown, and are always entrusted to the person holding the great seal by the royal sign manual. By virtue of this authority, upon an inquisition finding any person an ideot or lunatic, grants of the custody of the person and estate of the ideot or lunatic are made to such persons as the lord chancellor, or lord keeper, or lords commissioners for the custody of the great seal for the time being think proper, and the person to whom these grants are made, are termed *their committees*; ideots and lunatics therefore can only sue by the committees of their estates. *Mitford*, 28.

COMMITMENT, is the sending of a person to prison by warrant or order, who hath been guilty of any crime: and all persons apprehended for offences which are not bailable, and all persons who neglect to offer bail for offences which are bailable, must be committed. 2 *Hawk. P. C.* 116, 117.

The privy council, or any one or two of them, or secretary of state, may lawfully commit persons for treason, and other offences against the state, as in all ages they have done. 2 *Hawk. P. C.* 117.

And by 2 & 3 *P. & M. c.* 10. Justices of peace shall examine persons brought before them for felony, or the like, or suspicion thereof, before they commit them to prison, and shall bind their accusers to give evidence against them.

Under this statute a justice of the peace may detain a prisoner a reasonable time, in order to his being brought up to be examined; and it is said, that three days is a reasonable time for this purpose. 2 *Hawk. P. C.* 119. *Dalt. c.* 125. 2 *Inst.* 52, 591.

Every commitment must be in writing, under hand and seal, and directed to the keeper of the prison. *Hawk. P. C.* 119.

And it may command the gaoler to keep the party in safe and close custody. 2 *Hawk. P. C.* 119.

But it ought to set forth the crime with certainty, whether the commitment be by the privy council, or any other authority, otherwise the officer is not punishable for suffering the party to escape; and the court before whom he is removed by *habeas corpus* ought to discharge or bail him; and this doth not only hold where no cause at all is expressed in the commitment, but also where it is so loosely set forth, that the court cannot judge whether it were a reasonable ground for imprisonment or not. 2 *Hawk. P. C.* 119.

And a commitment for high treason or felony in general, without expressing the particular species is not good, for under the *habeas corpus* act, the party may be admitted to bail, if it do not appear of what species of treason or felony he was guilty. 2 *Hawk. P. C.* 119. *Skin.* 596. 1 *Salk.* 347. S. C.

It is also safe to set forth that the party is charged upon oath; though not absolutely necessary. 2 *Hawk. P. C.* 120.

Every such *mittimus* ought to have a lawful conclusion, *viz.* that the party be safely kept till he be delivered by law, or by order of law, or by due course of law, or that he be kept (if committed only for want of bail), till he find bail; but a commitment till the person who makes it shall take further order, is not good. 2 *Hawk. P. C.* 120.

Also a commitment grounded on an act of parliament must be strictly conformable to the method prescribed by such statute. *Carth.* 152, 153.

All commitments must be to some prison within the realm of England. For by *stat.* 31 *Car.* 2. *cap.* 2. no subject of this realm, being an inhabitant of England, Wales, or Berwick, shall be sent prisoner into Scotland, Ireland, Jersey, Guernsey, Tangier, or into any parts, garrisons, islands, or places beyond the seas, within or without the dominions of his majesty.

By 14 *Ed.* 3. *c.* 10. " Sheriffs shall " have the custody of the gaols as before " this time they were wont to have, and " they shall put in such underkeepers for " whom they will answer." And by 5 *Hen.* 4. *cap.* 10. it is enacted, " that none be imprisoned by any justice of the peace, but " only in the common gaol, saving to lords, " and others who have gaols, their franchise " in this case."

But by 6 *Geo.* 1. *c.* 19. Vagrants and other criminals, offenders, and persons charged with small offences, may for such offences, or for want of sureties, be committed either to the common gaol or house of correction, as the justices in their judgment shall think proper.

And by the 3 *Hen.* 7. *c.* 3. The sheriff shall certify the names of all prisoners in his custody to the justices of gaol delivery.

As prisoners ought to be committed at first to the proper prison, so they ought not to be removed thence, except in some special cases; for by 31 *Car.* 2. *cap.* 2. " If " any subject of this realm shall be committed to any prison, or in custody of any " officer or officers whatsoever, for any criminal, or supposed criminal matter, that " the said prison shall not be removed from " the said person and custody, into the custody of any other officer or officers, unless it be by *habeas corpus*, or some other " legal writ; or where the prisoner is delivered to the constable or other inferior " officer, to carry such prisoner to some " gaol; or where any person is sent by " order of any judge of assize, or justice of " the peace, to any common workhouse, or " house of correction; or where the prisoner " is removed from one prison or place to " another within the same county, in order " to a trial or discharge by due course of " law; or in case of sudden fire or infection, " or other necessity; upon pain that he " who makes out, signs, or countersigns, " or obeys or executes such warrant, shall " forfeit to the party grieved 100*l.* for the " first offence, 200*l.* for the second, &c. 2 " *Hawk. P. C.* 118.

A person legally committed for a crime certainly appearing to have been done by some one or other, cannot be lawfully discharged by any other but by the king, till he be acquitted on his trial, or have an *ignoramus* found by the grand jury, or none to prosecute him on a proclamation for that purpose; by the justices of gaol delivery. 2 *Hawk. P. C.* 121.

COMMOIGNE, (*Fr.*) A word signifying a fellow monk, that lives in the same convent. 3 *Inst.* 15.

COMMONALTY, (*populus, plebs communitas*) *In art. super chartas,* 28 *Ed.* 1. *c.* 1. *Tout le Commune d' Engleterre* signifies all the people of England. 2 *Inst.* 539. But it is now generally used to design all such persons as are members of particular corporations, thus many companies incorporated are said to consist of masters, wardens, and commonalty, the first two being the chief, and the others such as are usually called of the livery.

COMMON, *communia*. Common is a right or privilege which one or more persons claim to take or use, in some part or portion of that which another man's lands, waters, woods, or the like, do naturally produce, without having an absolute property therein. It is called an incorporeal right, which lies in grant, as if originally commencing on some agreement between lords and tenants, for some valuable purposes, which by age being formed into a prescription continues, although there be no deed or instrument in writing which proves the original contract or agreement. 4 *Co.* 37. 2 *Inst.* 65. 1 *Vent.* 387.

There is not only common of pasture, but also common of piscary or fishing, common of estovers, common of turbary. But the word common in its most usual acceptation signifies common of pasture, which is divided into common in gross, common appendant, common appurtenant, and common per cause *de vicinage*. *Bur. Abr. Tit. Com.*

Common in gross is a liberty to have common alone, without any lands or tenements, in another person's land, granted by deed to a man and his heirs, or for life, &c. *F. N. B.* 31, 37. 4 *Rep.* 30.

Common appendant is a right belonging to a man's arable land, of putting beasts commonable into another's ground.

And common appurtenant is belonging to an estate for all manner of beasts commonable or not commonable. 4 *Rep.* 37. *Plowd.* 161.

Beasts commonable are horses, oxen, kine, and sheep; and *not commonable* goats, hogs, and geese. *Ibid.*

Common pur cause de vicinage, common by reason of neighbourhood, is a liberty that the tenants of one lord in one town have to common with the tenant, of another lord in another town; and is where the tenants of two lords have used, time out of mind, to have common promiscuously in both lordships lying together and open to one another. 8 *Rep.* 78.

Interest of the lord.] The property of the soil in the common is entirely in the lord; and the use of it, jointly in him and the commoners. 1 *Inst.* 122.

But the lord may agist the cattle of a stranger in the common by prescription: and he may licence a stranger to put in his cattle, if he leaves sufficient room for the commoners. 1 *Danv.* 795. 2 *Mod.* 6. Also the lord may surcharge an overplus of the common: and if where there is not an overplus the lord surcharges the common, the commoners are not to distrain his beasts: but must commence an action against the lord. *F. N. B.* 125. 1 *Danv.* 807. So if the lord makes a warren on the common, the commoners may not kill the conies; but are to bring their action, for they may not be their own judges. 1 *Rol.* 90, 405.

The lord however may distrain where the common is surcharged, and bring action of trespass for any trespass done in the common. 9 *Rep.* 113.

Also a lord may make a pond on the common: though he cannot dig pits for gravel or coal; the statutes of approvement being only by inclosure. 3 *Inst.* 204. 1 *Sid.* 106.

By stat. 20 *H.* 3. *c.* 4, lords may approve against their tenants, viz. inclose part of the waste, &c. and thereby discharge it from being common, leaving common sufficient; and neighbours as well as tenants claiming common of pasture, shall be bound by it. But if the lord encloses on the common, and leaves not common sufficient, the commoners may not only break the enclosures, but may put in their cattle, although the lord ploughs and sows the land. 2 *Inst.* 88. 1 *Rol. Abr.* 406.

Interest of the commoners.] A commoner hath only a special and limited interest in the soil, but yet he shall have such remedies as are commensurate to his right, and therefore may distrain beasts damage-feasant, bring an action on the case, &c. but not being absolute owner of the soil, he cannot bring a general action of trespass for a trespass done upon the common. See *Bridg.* 10, 11. *Godb.* 123, 124. 2 *Leon.* 201, 202.

But a commoner cannot regularly without there is a custom to do it, do any thing on the soil, which tends to the melioration or improvement of the common, as cutting down of bushes, fern, or the like, &c. 1 *Sid.* 251. 12 *Hen.* 8. 2. 13 *Hen.* 8. 15. 1 *Nils.* 642. For he has nothing to do with the soil, but only to take the grass with the mouth of the cattle. 1 *Rol. Abr.* 405. 2 *Bulst.* 116.

If the tenant of the freehold ploughs it, and sows it with corn, the commoner may put in his cattle, and therewith eat the corn growing upon the land; so if he lets his corn lie in the field beyond the usual time the other commoners may, notwithstanding put in their beasts. 2 *Leon.* 202, 203.

The commoner cannot use common but with his own proper cattle; but if he hath not any cattle to manure the land, he may borrow other cattle to manure it, and use the common with them; for by the loan, they are in a manner made his own cattle. 1 *Danv.* 798.

A commoner may distrain beasts put into the common by a stranger, or every commoner may bring action of the case, where damage is received. 9 *Rep.* 11. But one commoner cannot distrain the cattle of another commoner, though he may those of a stranger, who hath no right to the common. 2 *Lutw.* 1238.

Where a commoner surcharges the common, the other commoners may have a writ of admeasurement; and admeasurement is to be according to the quality and quantity of the freehold, and for all the cattle which are upon the land. It lies only by one commoner against another, but not against a commoner *sans number*, nor against the lord, in which case there must be an assize. 1 *Danv.* 809. If a man be disseised of his common, he shall have an assise. *New Nat. Br.* 399.

If any commoner incloses, or builds on the common, every commoner may have an action for the damage. Where turf is taken away from the common, the lord only is to bring the action: but it is said the commoners may have an action for the injury, by entering on the common, &c. 1 *Rol. Abr.* 89, 398. 2 *Leon.* 201.

If a commoner who hath a freehold in his common be ousted of, or hindered therein, that he cannot have it so beneficially as he used to do; whether the interruption be by the lord or any stranger, he may have an assize against him, but if the commoner hath only an estate for years, then his remedy is by action on the case. And if it be only a small trespass, that is little or no loss to the commoner, but he hath common enough besides, the commoner may not bring any action. 4 *Rep.* 37. 8 *Rep.* 79. *Dyer,* 316.

A commoner cannot dig clay on the common, which destroys the grass, and carrying it away doth damage to the ground: so that the other commoners cannot enjoy the common *in tam amplo modo* as they ought. *Godb.* 344.

A release of common in one acre, is an extinguishment of the whole right of common. 3 *Co.* 47.

COMMON OF ESTOVERS, is a right of taking wood out of another man's wood, for house-bote, plough-bote, and hay-bote. What botes are necessary, tenants may take, notwithstanding mention be not made thereof in their leases, but if a tenant take more house-bote than is needful, he may be punished for waste, *Terms de Ley.*

COMMON OF PISCARY, is a liberty of fishing in another man's water. Common of piscary to exclude the owner of the soil, is contrary to law: though a person by prescription may have a separate right of fishing in such water, and the owner of the soil be excluded; for a man may grant the water, without passing the soil: and if one grant *separaliam piscariam*, neither the soil nor the water pass, but only a right of fishing. 1 *Inst.* 4. 122, 164. 5 *Rep.* 34.

COMMON OF TURBARY, is a licence to dig turf upon the grounds of another or in the lord's waste. This common is appendant or appurtenant to an house, and not to lands; for turfs are to be burnt in the house: and it may be in gross; but it does not give any right to the land, trees, or mines. It cannot exclude the owner of the soil. 1 *Inst.* 4. 4 *Rep.* 37.

COMMON BENCH, (*bancus communis*, from the Sax. *banc*, bank, and thence metaphorically a bench, high seat or tribunal) the court of common pleas was anciently, and still at times, called in common bench, because the pleas or controversies between *common persons* are there tried and determined. *Camb. Britan.* 113.

This court of *common pleas* is referred to by the letters C. B. from *communi banco*, (or C. P.) And the justices of that court are stiled *justiciarii de banco*. See *Common Pleas.*

COMMON DAY OF PLEA IN LAND, an ordinary day in court, as *octabis hilarii, quindena paschæ*, &c. *Cowel. Blount.*

COMMON FINE, (*finis communis*) a small sum of money, which the resiants within the liberty of some leets pay to the lords, called in divers places head silver or head pence, in others cert money; and was first granted to the lord, towards the charge of his purchase of the court-leet, whereby the resiants have the ease to do their suit within their own manors, and are not compellable to go to the sheriff's turn: in the manor of Sheapshead in the county of Leicester, every resiant pays 1*d.* per poll to the lord at the court held after Michaelmas, which is there called common fine. For this common fine the lord may distrain; but he cannot do it without a prescription. 11 *Rep.* 44. It is also called the *leet penny.*

COMMONS HOUSE OF PARLIAMENT, is the lower house of parliament, so called, because the commons of the realm, that is the knights, citizens, and burgesses returned to parliament, representing the whole body of the commons, do sit there. *Crom. Jurisd.*

COMMON INTENDMENT, is the common meaning, sense, or understanding, according to the subject matter, not strained to any extraordinary or foreign sense. *Co. Lit.* 78. See *Co. Lit.* 303, *a*, *b*, &c.

COMMON LAW, (*lex communis*). The common law is grounded upon the general customs of the realm; and includes in it the law of nature, the law of God, and the principles and maxims of the law: it is founded upon reason; and is said to be the perfection of reason, acquired by long study, observation and experience, and refined by learned men in all ages. And it is the common birth-right, that the subject hath for the safe-guard and defence, not only of his goods, lands, and revenues; but of his wife and children, body, fame, and life also. *Co. Lit.* 97, 142,

According to Hale, the common law of England, is the common rule for administering justice, within this kingdom, and asserts the king's royal prerogatives, and likewise the rights and liberties of the subject: it is generally that law, by which the determinations in the king's ordinary courts are guided; and this directs the course of descents of lands; the nature, extent and qualification of estates; and therein the manner and ceremonies of conveying them from one to another; with the forms, solemnities, and obligations of contracts; the rules and directions for the exposition of deeds, and acts of parliament: the process, proceedings, judgments and executions of our courts of justice; also the limits and bounds of courts and jurisdictions; the several kinds of temporal offences and punishments, and their application, &c. *Hale's Hist. C. L.* 24, 44, 45.

COMMON PLEAS, (*communia placita*) is one of the king's courts now constantly held in Westminster-hall.

By the antient Saxon constitution, there was only one superior court of justice in the kingdom: and that had cognizance both of civil and spiritual causes; viz. the *wittenagemote*, or general council, which assembled annually or oftener, wherever the king kept his Easter, Christmas, or Whitsuntide, as well to do private justice as to consult upon public business. At the conquest the ecclesiastical jurisdiction was diverted into another channel; and the conqueror, fearing danger from these annual parliaments, contrived also to separate their ministerial power, as judges, from their deliberative, as counsellors to the crown. He therefore established a constant court in his own hall, thence called by Bracton, *l.* 3. *tr.* 1. *c.* 7. and other antient authors *aula regia* or *aula regis*. This court was composed of the king's great officers of state resident in his palace, and usually attendant on his person: such as the lord high constable and lord mareschal, who chiefly presided in matters of honour and of arms, determining according to the law military and the law of nations. Besides these, there were the lord high steward, and lord great chamberlain; the steward of the household; the lord chancellor, whose peculiar business it was to keep the king's seal, and examine all such writs, grants, and letters, as were to pass under that authority; and the lord high treasurer, who was the principal adviser in all matters relating to the revenue. These high officers were assisted by certain persons learned in the laws, who were called *the king's justiciars or justices*; and by the greater barons of parliament, all of whom had a seat in the *aula regia*, and formed a kind of court of appeal, or rather of advice, in matters of great moment and difficulty. All these in their several departments transacted all secular business both criminal and civil, and likewise the matters of the revenue: and over all presided one special magistrate, called the *chief justiciar* or *capitalis justiciarius totius Angliæ*; who was also the principal minister of state, the second man in the kingdom, and by virtue of his office guardian of the realm in the king's absence. And this officer it was who principally determined all the vast variety of causes that arose in this extensive jurisdiction; and from the plenitude of his power grew at length both obnoxious to the people and dangerous to the government which employed him, *Spelm. Gloss.* 331, 2, 3. *Gilb. Hist. C. P. introd.* 17. 3 *Black.* 37, 8.

This great universal court being bound to follow the king's household in all his progresses and expeditions, the trial of common causes therein was found very burthensome to the subject. Wherefore king John, who dreaded also the power of the justiciar, very readily consented to that article, which now forms the eleventh chapter of magna charta, and enacts, that "*communia placita non sequantur curiam regis, sed teneantur in aliquo loco certo.*" This certain place was established in Westminster-hall, the place where the *aula regis* originally sat, when the king resided in that city; and there it hath ever since continued. And the court being thus rendered fixed and stationary, the judges became so too, and a chief with other justices of the common pleas was thereupon appointed; with jurisdiction to hear and determine all pleas of land, and injuries merely civil between subject and subject. Which critical establishment of this principal court of common law, at that particular juncture, and that particular place, gave rise to the inns of court in its neighbourhood; and thereby collecting together the whole body of the common lawyers, enabled the law itself to withstand the attacks of the canonists and civilians, who laboured to extirpate and destroy it. 3 *Black.* 38, 39.

The *aula regia* being thus stripped of so considerable a branch of its jurisdiction, and the power of the chief justiciar being also considerably curbed by many articles in the great charter, the authority of both began to decline apace under the long and troublesome reign of king Henry III. And in further pursuance of this example, the other several offices of the chief justiciar were, under Edward I. (who new modelled the whole frame of our judicial polity,) subdivided and broken into distinct courts of judicature. A court of chivalry was erected, over which the constable and mareschal presided; as did the steward of the household over another, constituted to regulate the king's domestic servants. The high steward, with the barons of parliament, formed an august tribunal for the trial of delinquent peers; and the barons reserved to themselves in parliament the right of reviewing the sentences of other courts in the last resort. The distribution of common justice between man and man was thrown into so provident an order, that the great judicial officers were made to form a cheque upon each other: the court of chancery issuing all original writs under the great seal to the other courts; the common pleas being allowed to determine all causes between private subjects; the exchequer managing the king's revenue; and the court of king's bench retaining all the jurisdiction which was not cantoned out to other courts, and particularly the superintendance of all the rest by way of appeal; and the sole cognizance of pleas of the crown or criminal causes. For pleas or suits are regularly divided into two sorts; pleas of the crown, which comprehend all crimes and misdemesnors, wherein the king (on behalf of the public) is the plaintiff; and common pleas, which include all civil actions depending between subject and subject. The former of these were the proper object of the jurisdiction of the court of king's bench; the latter of the court of common pleas. Which is a court of record, and is stiled by Sir Edward Coke, 4 *Inst.* 99. the lock and key of the common law; for herein only can real actions, that is, actions which concern the right of freehold or the realty, be originally brought; and all other, or personal, pleas between subject and subject, are likewise here determined; though in some of them the king's bench has also a concurrent authority. 3 *Black.* 38, 39.

Thus in personal and mixed actions it hath a concurrent jurisdiction with the king's bench: but it hath no cognizance of pleas of the crown; and common pleas are all pleas that are not such. Also this court cannot regularly hold plea in any action, real or personal, &c. but by writ out of chancery returnable here, except it be by bill for or against an officer, or other privileged person of the court: and except as after mentioned. All actions belonging to this court, come hither either by original, as arrests and outlawries; or by privilege or attachment, for or against privileged persons; or out of inferior courts, not of record, by *pone, recordare, accedas ad curiam*, writ of false judgment, &c. Actions popular, and actions penal, of debt, &c. upon any statute, are cognizable by this court; and besides having jurisdiction for punishment of its officers and ministers; the court of common pleas may grant prohibitions to keep temporal and ecclesiastical courts within due bounds. 4 *Inst.* 99, 100, 118.

The judges of this court are at present four in number, one chief and three *puisne* justices, created by the king's letters patent, who sit every day in the four terms to hear and determine all matters of law arising in civil causes, whether real, personal, or mixed and compounded of both. These it takes cognizance of, as well originally, as upon removal from the inferior courts. But a writ of error, in the nature of an appeal, lies from this court into the court of king's bench. 3 *Black.* 40.

The other officers of the common pleas are the *custos brevium*, three prothonotaries and their secondaries, the clerk of the warrants, clerk of the essoins, fourteen filazers, four exigenters, a clerk of the juries, the chirographer, clerk of the king's silver, the clerk of the Treasury, clerk of the seal, of outlawries, and the clerk of the inrolment of fines and recoveries, clerk of the errors, &c. The *custos brevium* is the chief clerk in this court, who receives and keeps all writs returnable therein; and all records of *nisi prius*, which are delivered to him by the clerks of the assise of every circuit, &c. and he files the rolls together, and carries them into the treasury of records: he also makes out exemplifications, and copies of all writs and records, &c. The prothonotaries enter and inrol all declarations, pleadings, judgments, &c. and they make out all judicial writs, writs of execution, writs of privilege, procedendo's, &c. The secondaries are assistants to the prothonotaries in the execution of their offices; and they take minutes, and draw up all orders and rules of court. The filazers, who have the several counties of England divided among them, make out all mesne process, as *capias, alias, pluries*, &c. between the original writ and the declaration; and they make all writs of view, &c. The exigenters, appointed for several counties, make out all exigents and proclamations in order to outlawry. The clerk of the warrants, enters all warrants of attorney; inrols deeds of bargain and sale, and estreats all issues. The clerk of the essoins, keeps the roll of the essoins, wherein he enters them, and nonsuits, &c. The clerk of the juries, makes out all writs of *habeas corpora jurator'*, for juries to appear; and he enters the continuances till the verdict given. The clerk of the Treasury keeps the records of the court, and makes exemplifications of records, copies of issues, judgments, &c. The clerk of the seals, seals all writs and mesne process; also writs of outlawry and supersedeas, and all patents. The clerk of the outlawries, makes out the writs of *capias utlagatum*. The clerk of the errors, is for the allowance of writs of error, &c. The clerk of the inrolments of fines and recoveries, returns all writs of covenant, writs of entry and seisin, and inrols and exemplifies fines, &c. The clerk of the king's silver, enters the substance of the writ of covenant: and the chirographer ingrosseth all fines, and delivers the indentures to the parties, &c.

To these officers may be added, a proclamator; a keeper of the court; cryer; and tipstaffs; besides the warden of the Fleet. There are also attornies of this court, whose number is unlimited; and none may plead at the bar of the court, or sign any special pleadings, but serjeants at law. See PRACTICE.

COMMON PRAYER, *(preces publicæ)* is the liturgy, or prayers used in our church, prescribed by the book of common prayer: and established by stat. 1 *Eliz. c.* 2.

COMMON WEAL, is understood in our law to be *bonum publicum,* and is a thing much favoured; and therefore the law doth tolerate many things to be done for common good, which otherwise might not be done: and hence it is, that monopolies are void in law; and that bonds and covenants to restrain free trade, tillage, or the like, are adjudged void. 11 *Co. Rep.* 50. *Plowd.* 25. *Shep. Epit.* 270.

COMMORANCY, (*commorantia*, from *commoro*) an abiding, dwelling or continuing in any place; as a house, a vill, or the like, and sleeping there. *Dalt. tit. Poor,* &c. 4 *Black.* 273.

COMMORTH, or COMORTH, (*comortha*) from the Brit. *cymmorth,* i. e. *subsidium*; a contribution, formerly gathered at marriages, and when young priests said or sung the first masses, &c. *Cowel. Blount.*

COMMOTE, in Wales is half a cantred, or hundred, containing fifty villages. *Stat. Walliæ,* 12 *Ed.* 1.

COMMUNANCE. The commoners or tenants and inhabitants, who had the right of common, or commoning in open fields, &c. were formerly called the communance. *Cowel. Blount.*

COMMUNE CONCILIUM REGNI ANGLIÆ, the common council of the king and people assembled in parliament. *Ibid.*

COMMUNIA PLACITA NON TENENDA IN SCACCARIO, was an ancient writ directed to the treasurer and barons of the exchequer, forbidding them to hold plea between common persons in that court, where neither of the parties belong to the same. *Reg. Orig.* 187.

COMMUNI CUSTODIA, a writ which anciently lay for the lord, whose tenant holding by knight's service died, and left his eldest son under age, against a stranger that entered the land, and obtained the ward of the body. *F. N. B.* 89. *Reg. Orig.* 161. Since the stat. 12 *Car.* 2. *c.* 24. (which took away wardships,) of no use.

COMMUNITY, the people of the kingdom.

COMPANAGE, (Fr.) is all kind of food, except bread and drink. *Cowel. Blount.*

COMPANION OF THE GARTER, is one of the knights of that most noble order; at the head of which is the king, as sovereign. 24 *H.* 8. *c.* 13.

COMPASS, an instrument used in navigation, by the direction and assistance whereof vessels are steered to the most distant parts of the world. It was invented soon after the close of the holy war, and thereby navigation was rendered more secure as well as more adventurous, the communication between remote nations was facilitated, and they were brought nearer to each other. 1 *Roberts. Hist. Emp. C. V.* 78.

COMPELLATIVUM, an adversary or accuser. *Cowel. Blount.*

COMPERTORIUM, a judicial inquest in the civil law, made by delegates, or commissioners to find out and relate the truth of a cause. *Paroch. Antiq.* 575.

COMPOSITION, (*compositio*) an agreement or contract between a parson, patron and ordinary, &c. for money or other thing in lieu of tithes. Real compositions for tithes are to be made by the concurrent consent of the parson, patron and ordinary. Real composisions are distinguished from personal contracts; for a composition called a personal contract is only an agreement between the parson and the parishioners, to pay so much instead of tithes; and though such agreement is confirmed by the ordinary, yet (if the parson is not a party) that doth not make it a real composition, because he ought to be a party to the deed of composition. *March's Rep.* 87. The compositions for tithes made by the consent of the parson, patron and ordinary, by virtue of 13 *Eliz. c.* 10. shall not bind the successor unless made for twenty-one years or three lives, as in case of leases or ecclesiastical corporations, &c. Compositions were at first for a valuable consideration, so that though in process of time, upon the increase of the value of the lands such compositions do not amount to the value of the tithes, yet custom prevails, and from hence arises what we call a *modus decimandi. Hob.* 29.

COMPOSITIO MENSURARUM, is the title of an antient ordinance for measures, not printed. *Cowel. Blount.*

COMPOSTUM, dung, soil or compost laid on lands. *Ibid.*

COMPOUNDING FELONY, or *theftbote,* is where the party robbed not only knows the felon, but also takes his goods again, or other amends upon agreement not to prosecute. It was formerly held to make a man an accessary; but is now punished only with fine and imprisonment. 1 *Hawk. P. C.* 125.

And by stat. 25 *Geo.* 2. *c.* 36. even to advertise a reward for the return of things stolen, with no questions asked, or words to the same purport, subjects the advertiser and the printer to a forfeiture of 50*l.* each.

COMPRINT, intends a surreptitious printing of another bookseller's copy, to make gain thereby. See BOOKS.

COMPROMISE, (*compromissum*) is a mutual agreement between two or more parties at difference, to put an end to such difference upon certain terms agreed upon, such as by releasing, or the like, or referring the ending of the controversy to arbitrators: and West says it is the faculty or power of pronouncing sentence between persons at variance, given to arbitrators by the parties private consent. *West's Symb. sect.* 1.

COMPURGATOR, one that by oath justifies another's innocence, 3 *Black. Com.* 342, 3. 4 *Black.* 361, 407.

COMPUTATION, (*computatio*) is the true account and construction of time; and to the end neither party to an agreement, &c. may do wrong to the other, nor the determination of time be left at large, it is to be taken according to the just judgment of the law. 1 *Inst.* 46. 5 *Rep.* 1.

COMPUTATION of miles after the English manner, is allowing 5280 feet, or 1760 yards to each mile; and the same shall be reckoned not by strait lines, as a bird or arrow may fly, but according to the nearest and most usual way. *Cro. Eliz.* 212.

COMPUTO, (Lat.) is a writ to compel a bailiff, receiver or accountant, to yield up his accounts: it is founded on the statutes of *Westm.* 2. *cap.* 12. And also lies against guardians, &c, *Reg. Orig.* 135.

CONCEALERS, (*concelatores*, so called *à concelando*, as *mons a movendo*, by an antiphrasis) are such as find out concealed lands, *i. e.* such lands as are privately kept from the king by common persons, having nothing to shew for their title or estate therein. *Cowel. Blount.*

CONCESSI, a word of frequent use in conveyances, creating a covenant in law; as *dedi* makes a warrantry. *Co. Lit.* 384. This word is of a general extent, and said to amount to a grant, feoffment, lease and release, &c. 2 *Saund.* 96.

CONCIONATORS, common-council men, freemen, called to the hall or assembly, as most worthy. *Cowel. Blount.*

CONCLUSION, (*conclusio*) is when a man by his own act upon record hath charged himself with a duty or other thing, or confessed any matter whereby he shall be concluded: as if a sheriff returns that he hath taken the body upon a *capias*, and hath not the body in court at the day of the return of the writ; by the return, the sheriff is concluded from plea of escape, &c. *Terms de Ley.* In another sense, this word conclusion signifies the end of any plea, replication, &c. and a plea to the writ is to conclude to the writ; a plea in bar, to conclude to the action, &c. Conclusion of plea in bar shall be, *et hoc paratus est verificare*: of pleas tendering issue, *et de hoc ponit se super patriam. Kitch.* 219, 220. 3 *Black. Com.* 303. and *Co. Lit.* 303. *a. b*, &c.

CONCORD, (*concordia*) is an agreement made between two or more, upon a trespass committed; and is divided into concord executory and concord executed. *Plowd.* 5, 6, 8.

Concord is also an agreement between parties, who intend the levying of a fine of lands one to the other, how and in what manner the lands shall pass: and is the foundation and substance of the fine, and acknowledged by the party before one of the judges of C. B. or by commissioners in the country. *Cruise on Fines.*

CONCUBARIA, a fold, pen, or place where cattle lie. *Cowel. Blount.*

CONCUBEANT, signifies a lying together. *Stat.* 1 *H.* 7. *cap.* 6.

CONCUBINAGE, (*concubinatus*) in common acceptation is the state of living with a concubine; but in a legal sense, it is used as an exception against her that sueth for dower, alleging thereby that she was not a wife lawfully married to the party, in whose lands she seeks to be endowed, but his concubine. *Brit. c.* 107. *Bract. lib.* 4. *tract.* 6. *cap.* 8. *Cowel. Blount.*

CONDERS, (from the Fr. *conduire*, to conduct) are such as stand upon high places near the sea-coast, at the time of herring-fishing, to make signs with boughs, &c. to the fishermen at sea, which way the shoals of herrings pass; for this may be better discovered by such as stand upon some high cliff on the shore, by reason of a kind of blue colour which the herrings cause in the water, than by those that are in the ships or boats for fishing. These are otherwise called huers and balkers, directors and guiders, as appears by stat. 1 *Jac.* 1. *c.* 23. *Blount.*

CONDITION, (*conditio*) is a restraint annexed to a thing, so that by the non-performance, the party to it shall receive prejudice and loss; and by the performance, commodity and advantage: or it is a restriction of men's acts, qualifying or suspending the same, and making them uncertain whether they shall take effect or not; also it is defined to be what is referred to an uncertain chance, which may happen or not happen. *West's Symb. part* 1. *lib.* 2. *sect.* 156. And of conditions there are divers kinds, *viz.* conditions in deed and in law; conditions precedent, and subsequent; conditions inherent, and collateral, &c. *Bac. Abr. tit. Con.*

A condition in deed is that which is joined by express words to a feoffment, lease, or other grant; as if a man makes a lease of lands to another, reserving a rent to be paid at such a feast, upon condition if the lessee fail in payment, at the day, then it shall be lawful for the lessor to enter. *Ibid.*

Condition in law, or *implied*, is when a person grants another an office, as that of keeper of a park, steward, bailiff, &c. for term of life; here, though there be no condition expressed in the grant, yet the law makes one, which is, if the grantee do not justly execute all things belonging to the office, it shall be lawful for the grantor to enter and discharge him of his office. *Lit. lib.* 3. *c.* 5.

Condition precedent is when a lease or estate is granted to one for life, upon condition that if the lessee pay to the lessor a certain sum at such a day, then he shall have fee simple; in this case the condition precedes the estate in fee, and on performance thereof gains the fee-simple. *Bac. Abr. tit. Con.*

Condition subsequent, is when a man grants to another his manor of Dale, &c. in fee, upon condition that the grantee shall pay to him at such a day such a certain sum, or that his estate shall cease; here the condition is subsequent, and following the estate, and upon the performance thereof continues and preserves the same: so that a condition precedent doth get and gain the thing or estate made upon condition by the performance of it; as a condition subsequent keeps and continues the estate by the performance or the condition. 1 *Inst.* 201, 327. *Terms de Ley.* If one agree with another to do such an act, and for the doing thereof the other shall pay so much money; here the doing the act is a condition precedent to the payment of the money, and the party shall not be compelled to pay till the act is done: but where a day is appointed for the payment of money, which day happens before the thing contracted for can be performed, there the money may be recovered before the thing is done; for here it appears that the party did not intend to make the performance of the thing a condition precedent. 3 *Salk.* 95.

Inherent conditions are such as descend to the heir with the land granted, &c.

A collateral condition is that which is annexed to any collateral act.

Conditions are likewise affirmative, which consist of doing; negative, and consist of not doing: some are further said to be restrictive, for not doing a thing; and some compulsory, as that the lessee shall pay the rent, &c.

Also some conditions are single, to do one thing only; some copulative, to do divers things; and others disjunctive, where one thing of several is required to be done. *Co. Lit.* 201.

Among these several kinds of conditions, the cases which most frequently occur fall under the distinctions of conditions precedent and subsequent. We shall therefore speak of them more at large under the following divisions, wherein it is to be considered,

To what estates conditions may be annexed.] Conditions may be to any estate, whether in fee-simple, fee-tail, for life or years: they run with the estate, and bind in the hands of whomsoever they come. *Lit. Rep.* 128. But a condition may not be made but on the part of the lessor, donor, &c. For no man may annex a condition to an estate, but he that doth create the estate itself. 8 *Rep.* 75. *Bac. Abr. tit. Con.*

A condition that would take away the whole effect of a grant is void; and so it is if it be contrary to the express words of it. Conditions against law are void; but what may be prohibited by law, may be prohibited by deed. 1 *Inst.* 206, 220.

The word "if" will not always make a condition; but sometimes it makes a limitation, as where a lease is made for years, if A. B. lives so long. And this is contrary to a condition, for a stranger may take advantage of an estate determined thereby, &c. *Co. Lit.* 236. *Dyer* 300. *Upon condition,* is the most proper word to make a condition: *provided* is also as good a word, when not dependant upon another sentence; but in some cases, the word "provided" may make no condition, but be only a qualification or exemplication of a covenant. 2 *Danv.* 1, 2. And neither the word "provided" nor any other, makes a condition, unless it is restrictive. *Plowd.* 34, 1 *Nels.* 466.

Performance of conditions.] A condition may be well performed, when it is done as near to the intent as may be: for if the condition of a feoffment be, that the feoffee shall make an estate back to the feoffor and his wife, and the heirs of their two bodies, remainder to the right heirs of the feoffor; in this case, if the feoffor die before, the estate shall be made to the wife without impeachment of waste, the remainder to the heirs of the body of the husband begotten on the wife, &c. *Co. Lit.* 219. 8 *Rep.* 69. So if a condition be performed in substance and effect, it is good although it differs in words; as where it is to deliver letters patent, and the party bound having lost them, delivers an exemplification, &c. 2 *Danv.* 40.

So where there is a condition in a feoffment or lease, that if no distress can be found, the feoffor, &c. shall re-enter; if the place is not open to the distress, as if there be only a cupboard in the house, which is locked, &c. it is all one as if there was no distress there, and the feoffor, &c. may enter. 2 *Danv.* 46. When a rent is to be paid upon condition at a certain day, the lessor cannot enter for the condition broken, before demand of the rent. *Ibid.* 98. And the lessor ought to demand the rent at the day, or the condition shall not be broken by the non-payment of the rent. 1 *Rol. Abr.* 408.

No one can reserve the power or benefit of re-entry, on breach of a condition to any other but himself, his heirs, executors, &c. parties and privies in right and representation: But by the *stat.* 32 *H.* 8. *c.* 28, grantees of reversions may take advantage against lessees, &c. by action. 1 *Inst.* 214, 215. *Plowd.* 175.

Tenants by the curtesy, tenant in tail after possibility of issue extinct, tenant in dower, for life, or years, &c. hold their estates subject to a condition in law, not to grant a greater estate than they have, nor to commit waste, &c. 1 *Inst.* 233.

A condition in a will is a thing odious in law, which shall not be created without sufficient words. 2 *Leon.* 40. A devise to the heir at law, provided he pay to A.B. 20*l.* is a void condition, because there is no devise over to any other person to take advantage of the non-performance. 1 *Lutw.* 797. Yet conditional devises, as well of lands as of goods, are allowed by our law, and not being performed, the heir or executors shall take advantage of them. 1 *Nels.* 467.

Conditions precedent and subsequent.] Conditions precedent are such as must be punctually performed before the estate can vest; but on a condition subsequent, the estate is immediately executed: yet the continuance of such estate dependeth on the breach or performance of the condition. *Co. Lit.* 218. *Eq. Abr.* 108. As if I grant, that if A. will go to such a place, about my business, that he shall have such an estate, or that he shall have 10*l.* &c. this is a condition precedent. 1 *Rol. Abr.* 414.

But if A. makes a lease for five years to B. upon condition that if B. pays him 10*l.* within two years, that then he shall have a fee-simple in the lands, and make livery and seisin to B. this passes the freehold immediately, and B. has a fee conditional; because if the freehold was not to vest in B. till the condition performed, it would be difficult to determine in whom the freehold lay, for conditions may be inserted in such deeds as are perfected privately, which might prove greatly prejudicial to strangers. *Lit. sect.* 350. *Co. Lit.* 216, 217.

CONDUITS, for water in London, were formerly directed by the *Stat.* 35 *H.* 8. *c.*10. to be made and repaired, and the lord mayor and aldermen were to inquire into defaults therein, &c.

CONE AND KEY. A woman at the age of fourteen or fifteen years might take the charge of her house, and receive cone and key: that is, she was then deemed able to keep the accounts and keys of the house. *Bract. lib.* 2. *cap.* 37. *Glanv. lib.* 7. *c.* 9. *Cowel. Blount.*

CONEY-BURROWS, places where conies or rabbits breed and haunt, &c. And commoners cannot lawfully dig up coney-burrows in the common. 2 *Wils. Rep.* 51.

CONFEDERACY, (*confœderatio*) is when two or more combine together to do any damage or injury to another, or to do any unlawful act. And false confederacy between divers persons shall be punished, though nothing be put in execution: but this confederacy, punishable by law before it is executed, ought to have these incidents; first, it must be declared by some matter of prosecution, as by making of bonds or promises the one to the other; secondly, it should be malicious, as for unjust revenge; thirdly, it ought to be false against an innocent person; and lastly it is to be out of court voluntarily. *Terms de Ley.*

It is the practice to insert in a bill in equity, a general charge of *confederacy*, viz. that the parties named in it combine together, and with several other persons unknown to the plaintiff, whose names when discovered the plaintiff prays he may be at liberty to insert in the bill: this practice is said to have arisen from an idea, that without such a charge, parties could not be added to the bill by amendment, and in some cases perhaps the charge has been inserted with a view to give the court jurisdiction, and from whatever cause the practice has arisen, it is still adhered to, except in the case of a peer. *Mitford,* 40.

CONFESSION, (*confessio*) is where a prisoner being indicted of treason and felony, and brought to the bar to be arraigned; upon the indictment being read to him, and the court demanding what he can say thereto, he confesses the offence, and the indictment to be true. And where a prisoner confesses the fact, the court has nothing more to do than to proceed to judgment against him, *confessus in judicio pro judicato habetur.* 11 *Rep.* 30. 4 *Inst.* 66.

A demurrer also amounts to a confession of the indictment as laid, so far, that if the indictment be good, judgment and execution shall go against the prisoner. *Bro.* 86. *S. P. C.* 150. *H. P. C.* 246. And in criminal cases, not capital, if the defendant demur to an indictment, &c. whether in abatement, or otherwise, the court will not give judgment against him to answer over, but final judgment. 2 *Hawk.* 334.

Also it has been held, that wherever a man's confession is made use of against him, it must all be taken together, and not by parcels. 4 *Hawk. P. C.* 429. And no confession shall, before final judgment, deprive the defendant of the privilege of taking exceptions in arrest of judgment, to faults apparent in the record. *Ibid.* 333.

Confession is likewise in civil cases, where the defendant confesses the plaintiff's right of action to be good: (*see cognovit*) or in prosecutions under penal statutes, by which confession, there may be a mitigation of a fine, against the penalty of a statute, though not after verdict. *Finch.* 387. 2 *Keb.* 408. *Lamb. lib.* 4. *c.* 9.

CONFESSO. In courts of equity after an order for a sequestration issued, the plaintiff's bill is to be taken *pro confesso,* and a decree made accordingly. 3 *Black.* 444.

CONFESSOR, (Lat. *confessor, confessionarius*) hath relation to private confession of sins, in order to absolution: and the priest who received the auricular confession had the title of confessor, though improperly; for he is rather the confessee, being the person to whom the confession is made. This receiving the confession of a penitent, was in old English to shreve or shrive; whence comes the word beshrieved, or looking like a confessed or shrieved person, on whom was imposed some uneasy penance. The most solemn time of confession was the day before lent, which from thence is still called Shrove Tuesday. *Cowel. Blount.*

CONFIRMATION, (*confirmatio*, from the verb *confirmare, quod est firmum facere*) is an affirmative deed of conveyance at the common law, whereby an estate or right which is voidable is made sure and unavoidable; or a particular state is increased, or a possession made perfect. And it is a strengthening of an estate formerly made, which is voidable, though not presently void, as for example: a bishop granteth his chancellorship by patent, for term of the patentee's life; this is no void grant, but voidable by the bishop's death, except it be strengthened by the confirmation of the dean and chapter. *Wood Moor.* 180. 1 *Inst.* 296. *Plow.* 10.

CONFISCATE, From the Lat. *confiscare*, and that from *fiscus*, which signifies metonymically the Emperor's treasure; and as the Romans say, such goods as are forfeited to the emperor's treasury for any offence are *bona confiscata*, so we say of those that are forfeited to our king's exchequer. *Staund. P. C. lib.* 3. *cap.* 24.

Goods confiscated are generally such as are arrested and seized for the king's use: but *confiscare* and *forisfacere* are said to be *synonyma*: and *bona confiscata* are *bona forisfacta*. 3 *Inst.* 227. 1 *Black. Com.* 299. 4 *Ibid.* 370.

CONFORMITY to the church of England, the *Stat.* 1 *Eliz.* c. 2. see *Recusant*, prescribes a strict conformity to the church of England, and is still to be acted on, except when by subsequent acts certain non-conformists are tolerated in the exercise of their own religious rites.

CONFRAIRIE (*confraternitas*) a fraternity, brotherhood, or society. *Cowel. Blount.*

CONFRERES, (*confratres*) brethren in a religious house, fellows of one and the same society. *Ibid.*

CONFUSION, *property by*, where goods of two persons are so intermixed, that the several portions can no longer be distinguished, if the intermixture be by consent, it is supposed the proprietors have an interest in common, in proportion to their respective shares; but, if one wilfully intermixes his money, corn, or hay, with that of another man, without his approbation or knowledge, or cast gold in like manner into another's melting pot or crucible, our law does not allow any remedy in such case; but gives the entire property without any account to him, whose original dominion (or property) is invaded, and endeavoured to be rendered uncertain, without his own consent. 2 *Black. Com.* 405.

CONGEABLE, (from the Fr. *conge*, i. e. leave or permission) signifies in our law, as much as lawful, or lawfully done, or done with permission; as entry congeable, &c. *Lit. sect.* 420.

CONGE D' ACCORDER, (Fr.) leave to accord or agree, mentioned in the statute of fines. 18 *Ed.* 1.

CONGE D' ELIRE, (Fr. i. e. leave to choose) is the king's licence or permission sent to a dean and chapter to proceed to the election of a bishop, when any bishopric becomes vacant. 1 *Black. Com.* 379, 382. 4 *Ibid.* 414.

CONGIUS, an ancient measure, containing about a gallon and a pint. *Cowel. Blount.*

CONINGERIA, a coney-burrow or warren of conies. *Ibid.*

CONJUGAL RIGHTS, a suit for restitution of conjugal rights is one of the species of matrimonial causes: and is brought when either the husband or wife is guilty of the injury of subtraction, or lives separate from the other without any sufficient reason; in which case the ecclesiastical jurisdiction will compel them to come together again, if either party be weak enough to desire it, contrary to the inclination of the other. 3 *Black. Com.* 94.

CONJURATIO, is an oath, and *conjuratus*, the same with *conjurator*, viz. one who is bound by the same oath. *Conjurare* is where several affirm a thing by oath. *Mon. Angl. Tom.* 1. *p.* 207. *Cowel. Blount.*

CONJURATION, (*conjuratio*) signifies a plot or compact made by persons combining by oath, to do any public harm: but was more especially used for the having (as was supposed) personal conference with the devil, or some evil spirit, to know any secret or effect any purpose. The difference between conjuration and witchcraft was said to be, that a person using the one, endeavoured by prayers and invocations to compel the devil to say or do what he commanded him, the other dealt rather by friendly and voluntary conference, or agreement with the devil or familiar, to have his desires served, in lieu of blood or other gift offered. Both differed from enchantment or sorcery; because they were supposed to be personal conferences with the devil, and these were but medicines and ceremonial forms of words usually called charms, without apparition. *Lambarde. Cowel. Blount. Hale. Dalton.*

Hawkins, in his Pleas of the Crown, *lib.* 1. *p.* 5, says, that conjurors are those who by force of certain magic words, endeavour to raise the devil, and oblige him to execute their commands. Witches are such who by way of conference bargain with an evil spirit, to do what they desire of him: and sorcerers are those, who by the use of certain superstitious words, or by the means of images, &c. are said to produce strange effects, above the ordinary course of nature. All which were anciently punished in the same manner as heretics, by the writ *de hæretico comburendo*, after a sentence in the ecclesiastical court: and they might be condemned to the pillory, &c. upon an indictment at common law. 3 *Inst.* 44. *H. P. C.* 38.

By 9 *Geo.* 2. *c.* 6, where persons pretend to exercise any kind of witchcraft or conjuration, or undertake to tell fortunes, or from their skill in any crafty science to discover where goods stolen or lost, may be found, upon conviction, shall be imprisoned a year, and stand in the pillory once in every quarter, in some market-town, and may be ordered to give security for their good behaviour. See also *Vagrants.*

CONQUEST, countries got by, to be governed by the English laws, except otherwise settled by the capitulation of the people. 2 *Black. Com.* 48, 242.

CONSANGUINEO, is a writ mentioned in *Reg. Orig. de avo, proavo et consanguineo, &c. f.* 226.

CONSANGUINEUS FRATER, a brother by the father's side. 2 *Black. Com.* 232.

CONSANGUINITY, (*consanguinitas*) is a kindred by blood or birth, as affinity is a kindred by marriage: and it is considerable in the descent of lands, who shall take it as next of blood, &c. And also in administrations, which shall be granted to the next of kin. 1 *Black. Com.* 434. 2 *Black. Com.* 202.

CONSCIENCE, *courts of.* These were courts originally instituted by act of parliament, in London and Westminster, and other trading and populous districts, for the recovering of small debts not exceeding 40*s.* but many of them have now an extended jurisdiction for the recovery of small debts to the amount of 5*l.* as by 39 and 40 *Geo.* 3. *c.* civ. as to London, and 46 *Geo.* 3. *c.* lxxvii. and *c.* lxxxviii, as to Southwark and the west hundred of Brixton.

And by 26 *Geo.* 3. *c.* 38, debtors committed by courts of conscience for debts not exceeding 20*s.* shall not be imprisoned more than 20 days, and where the debt does not exceed 40*s*, not more than forty days, which prisoners are to be discharged without gaol fees, and gaolers demanding or taking the same are to forfeit 5*l.* on conviction, before two justices within two months; and the process of courts of conscience, shall not issue against both body and goods at the same time.

CONSECRATION. See *Bishops, Church.*

CONSENT, in all cases when any thing executory is created by deed, it may by consent of all persons that were parties to the creation of it by their deed, be defeated and annulled, and therefore it is said, that warranties, recognizances, rents, charges, annuities, covenants, leases for years, uses at common law, &c. may by a defeasance made with the mutual consent of all that were parties to the creation of them by deed, be annulled, discharged, and defeated. 1 *Rep.* 113. See *Age.*

CONSEQUENTIAL, damages. It is a fundamental principle in law and reason, that he who does the first wrong shall answer for all consequential damages. 12 *Mod.* 639. And though a man does a lawful thing, yet if any damage do thereby befal another, he shall answer if he could have avoided it; and this holds in all civil cases. As if a man lops a tree, and the boughs fall upon another, *ipso invito*, yet an action lies. So if a man shoots at butts, and hurts another unawares. So if I have land through which a river runs to your mill, and I lop the sallows growing on the riverside which accidentally stop the water so as your mill is hindered. So if I am building my own house, and a piece of timber falls on my neighbour's house, and breaks part of it. So if a man assaults me, and I lift up my staff to defend myself, and strike another in lifting it up. *Raym.* 422, 423.

So he that makes a fire in his field must see that it does no harm, and answer the damage if it does. 1 *Salk.* 13. Also if a man keeps a beast of a savage nature, as a lion, or the like, it is at his peril to keep him up, and he is answerable for all the consequences of his getting loose. *Gilb.* 187. 3 *Black. Com.* 153. But it is otherwise in criminal cases, for there *actus non facit reum nisi mens sit rea. Raym.* 422, 3.

So where one is party to a fraud, all which follows by reason of that fraud, shall be said as done by him, as if one trader *knowingly* give a false character of another, to a third person to obtain a credit, whereby the latter sustains a loss, he shall have his action on the case. *Cro. Jac.* 469. Action lies for threatening workmen to maim and prosecute them, whereby the master loses the selling of his goods, the men not daring to go on with their work. *Cro. Jac.* 567.

CONSERVATOR, (Lat.) a protector, preserver, or maintainer; or a standing arbitrator, chosen and appointed as a guarantee to compose and adjust differences that may arise between two parties, &c. *Paroch. Antiq. p.* 513. *Cowel. Blount.*

CONSERVATOR OF THE PEACE, (*conservator vel custos pacis*) is he that hath an especial charge to see the king's peace kept: and of these conservators Lambard saith, that before the reign of *Ed.* 3. who first created justices of the peace, there were divers persons that by the common law, had interest in keeping the peace; some whereof had that charge by tenure, as holding lands of the king by this service, &c. And others as incident to the offices which they bore, and so included in the same, that they were nevertheless called by the name of their office only: also some had it simply, as of itself, and were therefore named *custodes pacis*, wardens or conservators of the peace. Thus the chamberlain of Chester is a conservator of the peace in that county, by virtue of his office. 4 *Inst.* 212. So also sheriffs of counties are at common law conservators of the peace; but constables, though deemed conservators, were only subordinate to the conservators of the peace, as they are now to the justice. 1 *Black.* 350.

The king's majesty is, by his office and dignity royal, the principal conservator of the peace within all his dominions, and may give authority to any other to see the peace kept, and to punish such as break it: hence it is usually called the king's peace. The lord chancellor or keeper, the lord treasurer, the lord high steward of England, the lord mareschal, and lord high constable of England, (when any such officers are in being) and all the justices of the court of King's Bench, by virtue of their offices, and the master of the Rolls, by prescription, are general conservators of the peace throughout the whole kingdom, and may commit all breakers of it, or bind them in recognizances to keep it; the other judges are only so in their own courts. The coroner is also a conservator of the peace within his own county, as, also, is the sheriff, and both of them may take a recognizance or security for the peace. Constables, tithing-men, and the like, are also conservators of the peace within their own jurisdictions, and may apprehend all breakers of the peace, and commit them till they find sureties for their keeping it. 1 *Black. Com.* 350.

CONSERVATOR OF THE TRUCE AND SAFE CONDUCTS, (*conservator induciarum et salvorum regis conductuum*) was an officer appointed by the king's letters patent, whose charge was to inquire of all offences done against the king's truce and safe conducts upon the main sea, out of the liberties of the Cinque Ports, as the admirals customarily were used to do, and such other things as are declared 3 *Hen.* 5. *c.* 6. Two men learned in the law were joined to conservators of the truce, as associates; and masters of ships sworn not to attempt any thing against the truce, &c. And letters of request and of marque were to be granted when truce was broken at sea, to make restitution. *Stat.* 4 *Hen.* 5. *c.* 7. 4 *Black. Com.* 69.

There was anciently a conservator of the privileges of the Hospitallers and Templars. *West.* 2, *c.* 43. And the corporation of the great Level of the Fens consists of a governor, six bailiffs, twenty conservators, and commonalty. Stat 15 *Car.* 2. *c.* 17.

CONSIDERATIO CURIÆ, is the judgment of the court, and often mentioned in the books and law pleadings, *ideo consideratum est per curiam*, i. e. therefore it is considered and adjudged by the court.

CONSIDERATION, (*consideratio*) is the material cause, or *quid pro quo*, of any contract, without which it will not be effectual or binding. This consideration is either expressed, as when a man bargains to give so much for a thing bought, or to sell his land for 100*l.* or grants it in exchange for other lands; or where I promise that if one will marry my daughter, or build me a house, &c. I will give him a certain sum of money; or one agrees for 20*s.* to do a thing. Or it is implied, when the law itself enforces consideration; as where a person comes to an inn, and there staying, eats and drinks, and takes lodgings for himself and horse, the law presumes he intends to pay for both, though there be no express contract for it; and therefore if he discharge not the house the host may stay his horse; and so if a taylor makes a garment for another, and there is no express agreement what he shall have for it, he may keep the clothes till he is paid, or sue the party for the same. 5 *Rep.* 19. *Plowd.* 308. *Dyer.* 30. 337. Also there is a consideration of nature and blood; and valuable consideration in deeds and conveyances: but if a man be indebted to divers others, and in consideration of natural affection *gives all his goods* to his son, or other relation, this shall be consrued a fraudulent gift as against the creditors within the statute 13 *Eliz. c.* 5, because that act intends a valuable consideration. *Terms de Ley.*

But considerations of natural love, affection, marriage, and the like, are good to raise the uses of lands to a man's family: and yet if the uses are limited to a stranger, then it must be for a valuable consideration, not for love, affection, or the like. 1 *Inst.* 271. 1 *Rep.* 176.

And in case a deed of feoffment be made of lands, or a fine and recovery be passed, and no consideration is expressed in the deed, &c. for the doing thereof, it shall be intended by the law that it was made in trust for the use of the feoffor or conusor; for it shall be presumed he would not part with his land without a consideration; and yet the deed shall be construed to operate something, and that which is most reasonable. 1 *Lill. Abr.* 299.

A consideration also must be lawful to ground an *assumpsit.* 2 *Lev.* 161.

CONSIGNEE is the person to whom goods are assigned, or directed to be delivered over. *Lex Mercat.* See *Factor.*

CONSILIUM, (*dies consilii*) was a time allowed for one accused to make his defence, and answer the charge of the accuser; but it is now used for a speedy day appointed to argue a demurrer, which the court grants after the demurrer joined on reading the record of the cause, &c. 4 *Black. Com.* 349.

CONSIMILI CASU. See CASU CONSIMILI.

CONSISTOR, a magistrate so called. *Blount.*

CONSISTORY, (*consistorium*) signifies as much as *prætorium*, or tribunal: it is commonly used for a council-house of ecclesiastical persons, or place of justice in the Spiritual Court; a session or assembly of prelates. And every archbishop and bishop of every diocese hath a consistory court, held before his chancellor, or commissary in his cathedral church, or other convenient place of his diocese, for ecclesiastical causes. 4 *Inst.* 338.

CONSOLIDATION (*consolidatio*) is used for the uniting of two benefices into one in stat. 37 *Hen.* 8. *c.* 21. See *Union of Churches.*

There are also divers statutes for the *consolidation* of different taxes, such as of customs, excise, stamps, &c.

CONSORT, Queen. See QUEEN.

CONSPIRACY, (*conspiratio*) is an agreement of two or more persons falsely to indict one, or to procure him to be indicted of felony, riot, or other misdemeanor, who, after acquittal shall have a writ of conspiracy. See 33 *Ed.* 1. stat. 2. 4 *Ed.* 3. *c.* 11. 3 *Hen.* 7. *c.* 13. 1 *Hen.* 5. *c.* 3, and 18 *Hen.* 6. *c.* 12. And not only the old writ of conspiracy, which is a civil action at the suit of the party, but also an *action on the case, in the nature of a writ of conspiracy*, doth lie for a false and malicious accusation of any crime, whether capital or not capital, even of high treason; and though the bill of indictment is found *ignoramus*, or it does not go so far as an indictment. And the same damages may be recovered in such action as in a writ of conspiracy, where the party is lawfully acquitted by verdict. 1 *Rol. Abr.* 111, 112. 9 *Rep.* 56. See *Gilb. Ca.* 185. 10 *Mod.* 148. 214. *Salk.* 15.

And in action on the case *he need not aver* that he was lawfully acquitted, as he ought to do in a writ of conspiracy: but he must aver that the accusation was *falsa et malitiosa*, which words are necessary in the declaration; and it must appear that there was no ground for it. And as an action on the case may be prosecuted against one person, where the writ of conspiracy or indictment doth not lie but against two, this action is most commonly brought. 1 *Danv. Abr.* 208. 213. 2 *Inst.* 562, 638.

Conspirators may also be indicted at the suit of the king: and at the common law one may prefer an indictment against conspirators, who only conspire together, and nothing is executed: but a bare conspiracy will not maintain a writ of conspiracy at the suit of the party, because he is not damaged by it; though it is a ground for an indictment. 9 *Rep.* 56. 2 *Rol. Abr.* 77.

On an indictment for a conspiracy, if all the defendants but one are acquitted, that one must be acquitted also; because one person alone cannot be indicted for this crime: and husband and wife being but one person may not be indicted for a conspiracy, unless it be laid or proved that they conspired with others unknown. 2 *Rol. Abr.* 708. 3 *Mod.* 220. 1 *Vent.* 234. *Cro. Eliz.* 701.

If the parties are found guilty of the conspiracy, upon an indictment of felony at the king's suit, the consequence is that they shall lose their frank law (which disables them to be put upon any jury, to be sworn as witnesses, or to appear in person in any of the king's courts), and their lands, goods, and chattels are to be seized as forfeited, and their bodies committed to prison, which is called a villainous judgment. 2 *Inst.* 143. 222. *Crompt. Just.* 156, 810. But the usual punishment at this day on an indictment for a conspiracy is by fine and imprisonment, and sometimes pillory; and on writ of conspiracy, &c. the party shall be fined, and render damages. 1 *Hawk. P. C.* 193. *Moor.* And there are instances of parties being fined and having judgment of the pillory and to be burnt in the cheek with the letters F.C. i. e. *false conspirators.*

CONSPIRATORS (*conspiratores*), by 33 *E.* 1. stat. 2, are defined to be those that do bind themselves by oath, covenant, or other alliance, that every of them shall aid the other falsely and maliciously to indict persons; or falsely to move or maintain pleas, &c. And such as retain men in the country with liveries, or fees, to maintain their malicious enterprises, which extends as well to the takers as the givers; and stewards or bailiffs of great lords, who by their office or power undertake to bear and maintain quarrels, pleas, or debates, that concern other parties than such as relate to the estate of their lords or themselves. 2 *Inst.* 384. 562. And against conspirators, false informers, and embracers of inquest, the king hath provided a writ in the Chancery: and the justices of either bench, and justices of assise, shall on every plaint award inquest thereupon. Stat. 28 *E.* 1. *c.* 10.

CONSPIRATIONE, was the writ that anciently lay against conspirators. *Reg. Orig.* 134. *F. N. B.* 114.

CONSTABLE, (*constabularius*) is said by *Lambard* to be derived from the Sax. and compounded of the Saxon words *coning*, i. e. king, and *staple*, which signifies the stay or hold of the king: but however derived, it is at this day immaterial to consider, being now used in general acceptation for a well-known peace-officer. It is, however, diversely used in our law; first, for the *lord constable of England*, whose power was anciently so extensive, that some time since that office hath been thought too great for any subject, unless at the king's coronation, to complete the grandeur of that ceremony. This office was formerly of inheritance, and first created by Will. the conqueror: but Edward duke of Buckingham, the last inheritor, being attainted of high treason, *anno* 13 *Hen.* 8. the office became forfeited to the crown, and since that time it was never granted but *pro hac vice*, to be exercised at a coronation, &c.

Out of this high magistracy of the constable of England (says *Lambard*) were drawn those inferior constables which we call constables of hundreds and franchises; and the statute of Winchester, 13 *Ed.* 1, appoints for conservation of the peace, and view of armour, two constables in every hundred and franchise, who in Latin are called *constabularii capitales*, high constables, because continuance of time, and increase of people and offences, have under these made others necessary in every town, called petty constales, in Latin *sub-constabularii*, which are of like nature but of inferior authority to the other. *Cowel. Blount*

And there are other officers, whose duty is much the same with constables, as headboroughs, tithing-men, &c. of which the petty constable seems to be the principal officer, but in his absence, or where there is no petty constable, their duty is the same.

My Lord Coke says that both high constables and petty constables were created by 13 *Ed.* 1, *stat.* 2, *c.* 6, and that their duty was thereby limited, though subsequent statutes have enlarged their power. 4 *Inst.* 267. 2 *Danv. Abr.* 148.

Choice of Constables.] Anciently high and petty constables were appointed by the sheriff in his tourn, and sworn there as well as in the leet: and by the common law they ought to be chosen in the tourn or leet. *Dalt. cap.* 21. Of common right a constable is to be chosen by the jury in the leet, and if he be present, and refuse to be sworn, the steward may fine him; if he be absent he shall be sworn before justices of peace; and if such constable refuses to be sworn, the jury must present his refusal the next court, and then he shall be amerced, for the steward of the leet may not fine him if he is absent. 1 *Salk.* 175. 5 *Mod.* 130.

A high constable may be chosen at a court-leet by the steward, on presentment of the jury, when custom warrants it; but where such courts are not kept, or there is a neglect in choosing him, the justices at their quarter-sessions may choose and swear a high constable. 1 *Mod. Jus.* 133. And he may be sworn out of sessions by warrant from thence, and be elected out of the sessions by the greater number of justices in the division. *Ibid.* If one that is elected to the office of constable, being eligible, refuse to take the oath to serve in that office, a writ of *mandamus* may be had to compel him to do it. 1 *Lil. Abr.* 303. Or he may be indicted. And the justices of peace may appoint a constable in such place where there was never any before. 1 *Mod.* 13.

If constables, headboroughs, &c. die or go out of the parish, two justices of peace are to swear new ones till the lord of the manor hold a court-leet, or till the next quarter-sessions, who shall approve of them or appoint others: and if any of them continue above a year the justices of peace may discharge them, and put in others till the lord of the manor holds a court. By stat. 13 & 14 *Car.* 2, *cap.* 12, a constable's oath runs thus: "You shall well and truly serve "our sovereign lord the king, and the lord of "this leet (if sworn in a court-leet) in the of- "fice of constable, in and for the hundred of, "&c. or parish of, &c. for the year ensuing, or "until you shall be thereof discharged ac- "cording to due course of law: You shall "well and truly do and execute all things be- "longing to the said office, according to the "best of your knowledge. *So help you God.*"

At this day, however, high constables are generally chosen and sworn by the justices of peace in their sessions; and as to the *petty* constables, who are their assistants, in each town, parish, or vill, the choice of them properly belongs to the court-leet; but they are in some places elected by the parishioners, and sworn by a justice of peace, who on just cause may remove them. 4 *Inst.* 267.

These constables are appointed yearly, and are to be men of honesty, knowledge and ability, not infants, lunatics, &c. And if they refuse to serve they may be bound over to the sessions, and indicted, and fined and imprisoned. 8 *Rep.* 41. 5 *Mod.* 96.

And none are to be chosen constable who are not inhabitants. *Field's Par. Off.* 331. nor unless they be of an *abler* sort of inhabitants, 8 *Co.* 42; and within Westminster none of the age of 63 or upwards are to be chosen. 31 *Geo.* 2, *c.* 17. *sec.* 13. And the crown may exempt particular persons from serving, provided a sufficient number be left to serve. 1 *Ter. Rep.* 686. Also no man who keeps a public house ought to be a constable. 6 *Mod.* 41. But revenue officers, as such, are not exempt. *Espin. Ca.* 359. Nor are women, if chosen according to custom, in turn, in respect to the houses in a town, for the office is ministerial, and may be executed by deputy. 2 *Hawk. c.* 10. *s.* 37. Nor is a younger brother of the Trinity House exempted. 1 *Ter. Rep.* 679; or a captain in the guards, who is appointed in respect of lands in a town. 2 *Hawk. c.* 10. *s.* 41; or a practising physician, unless he be a member of the College of Physicians and practise in London, or within seven miles thereof. 32 *Hen.* 8. *c.* 40. But surgeons by the ancient custom of the realm, and the statutes 5 *Hen.* 8, *c.* 6, and 18 *Geo.* 2,

c. 15, s. 10, are exempt; and so also are apothecaries by 6 and 7 *Wil.* 3, *c.* 4. Likewise by 12 *W.* 3, *c.* 2, and 1 *Geo.* 1, *c.* 4, aliens naturalized are not eligible, for this is a civil office of trust, 5 *Burr. Rep.* 2799. Also by 1 *Wil. & Mar. c.* 18, *s.* 11, dissenting preachers, and by 31 *Geo.* 3, *c.* 32, Roman catholic priests, taking certain oaths, are exempted. Likewise by 10 and 11 *Wil.* 3, the prosecutors of *burglars, housebreakers*, persons privately stealing to the value of 5*s.* in any shop, warehouse, coach-house, or stable, and horse-stealers, are entitled to certificates to exempt them from parish and ward offices; but this does not exempt them if they are chosen constables for a manor, and not for a parish or ward. 2 *Burr.* 1182. By ancient custom also barristers, servants to members of parliament, and attornies, 2 *Hawk. c.* 10. *s.* 39, aldermen of London, 1 *Jones* 462. *Cro. Car.* 585, and the college barbers of Oxford and Cambridge are exempt. *Doug. Rep.* 531.

But physicians, apothecaries, and surgeons, are excused by statute from bearing the office of constable, or other parish office in London, or within seven miles thereof. See 5 *H.* 6. *c.* 6. 3 *H.* 8. *c.* 43. 5 *H.* 8. *c.* 6. and 6 *W.* & *M. c.* 4.

And by the last act, 6 *Wil.* & *Mar. c.* 4. apothecaries wherever they may reside, are in like manner exempt.

General duty of constables.] The HIGH CONSTABLE has the direction of the *petty* constables, *headboroughs, and tithingmen*, within his hundred: his duty is to keep the peace, and apprehend felons, rioters, &c. to make hue and cry after felons; and take care that the watch be duly kept in his hundred; and and that the statutes for punishing rogues and vagrants be put in execution. He ought to present unlawful games, tippling, and drunkenness; bloodshed, affrays, &c. He is to execute precepts and warrants, directed to him by justices of the peace, and make returns to the sessions of the peace to all the articles contained in his oath, or that concern his office: and shall also cause the petty constables, to make their returns. He is to return all victuallers and alehouse-keepers that are unlicensed; and all such persons as entertain inmates, who are likely to be a charge to the parish. He must likewise present the faults of petty constables, headboroughs, &c. who neglect to apprehend rogues, vagrants, and idle persons, whores, night-walkers, mothers of bastard children like to be chargeable to the parish, &c. And also all defects of highways and bridges, and the names of those who ought to repair them: scavengers who neglect their duty; and all common nusances in streets and highways: bakers who sell bread under weight; brewers selling beer to unlicensed alehouses; forestallers, regraters, ingrossers, &c. And at every quarter-sessions they are to pay to the treasurer of the county all such money as hath been received by them, of the churchwardens, &c. for the county rates. *Dalt. Ca.* 28. *Lamb.* 125. and 12 *Geo.* 2. *cap.* 29.

The authority of PETTY CONSTABLES, in their several towns, tithings, and boroughs, is generally the same as the high constable hath in his hundred: they are to keep the peace in the absence of the high constable; and assist him in making presentments at the assises and quarter sessions, of every thing that is amiss: they may command affrayers to keep the peace, and depart, &c. and may break into a house to see the peace kept; make fresh pursuit into another county, &c. Also they may command all persons to assist them, to prevent a breach of the peace; justify beating another if assaulted; and if they happen to be killed, doing their duty, it will be taken to be murder, or malice prepense; they may, without warrant from a justice of peace, take into custody any persons whom they see committing a felony or breach of the peace; but if a breach of the peace has been committed out of their sight, as an assault, an affray, or the like, they may not do it without a warrant from a justice. Neither can a constable detain a man at his pleasure; for he can only stay him for a reasonable time, to bring him before a justice to be examined, &c. And this detaining of an offender by the constable, it is said, may be for a day, (if he has reasonable cause for so doing,) without warrant, and be justified. *Dalt. c.* 1. 8 *Lamb.* 125. *H. P. C.* 135. 1 *Leon.* 307. *Moor* 408.

Petty constables are to execute all warrants of justices, and not dispute it, where the justice hath jurisdiction, and the warrant is lawful: and being sworn officers, they need not shew their warrants when they come to arrest any one. 10 *Rep.* 76.

But if any justice sends his warrant to a constable, &c. to bring a person before him to answer all such matters as shall be objected against him by another, and doth not set forth the special matter in the warrant, the warrant is unlawful; or if a justice of peace sends a warrant to a constable to take up one for slander, &c. the justices having no jurisdiction, in such cases, the constable ought not to execute it, because the constable, if he executes it, is liable to an action of false imprisonment. 2 *Inst.* 521.

And as the constable is the proper officer to a justice of peace, and bound to execute his lawful warrants; therefore where a statute authorises a justice to convict a person of any crime, and to levy the penalty, &c. without saying to whom such warrant shall be directed, the constable is the officer to execute the warrant, and must obey it. 5 *Mod.* 130. 1 *Salk.* 381. And if a warrant be directed to a *constable* by *name*, commanding him to execute, though he is not compellable to go out of his own parish, yet he may if he will, and execute it in any place in the county, and shall be justified by the warrant for so doing; but if the warrant be directed to all constables, &c. generally, no constable can execute the same out of his precinct. 1 *Salk.* 175. 3 *Salk.* 99.

It is at the election of a constable to carry an offender before any other justice than him who issued the warrant; if the warrant be not special, to bring the offender before the justice that granted it. 5 *Rep.* 59.

And by stat. 24 *Geo.* 2. *c.* 55. " a constable may execute a warrant in any other county, &c. if indorsed by a justice of such other county, &c. and carry the offender before a justice of such other county, &c. and if the offender shall give bail, the constable is to deliver the recognizance, examination or confession of the offender, and all other proceedings relating thereto to the clerk of assise, or clerk of the peace of the county, &c. where the offence was committed, under the penalty of 10*l*. But if the offence shall not be bailable, or the offender shall not give bail, the constable shall carry the offender before a justice of the county where the offence was committed."

A constable is not obliged to return a justice's warrant to the justice, but he may keep the same for his own justification, in case he should be questioned for his acting; but he must make a return to the justice of what he hath done upon it. 2 *Ld. Raym.* 1196.

As to the particular duty of constables, this depends on the provisions contained in numerous acts of parliament, which being in general to be carried into execution by the justices of peace, and under their special warrants, it is unnecessary in this place to enumerate all the objects of their duty, and more particularly as the constable is protected in the exercise of his office, and the execution of all warrants issued by the justices of the peace by the following statutes.

By 7 *Jac.* 1. *cap.* 5. if any action is brought against a constable, for any thing done by virtue of his office, he, and also all others who in his aid, or by his command, shall do any thing concerning his office, may plead the general issue, and give the special matter in evidence, and if he recovers he shall have double costs.

By the stat. 24 *Geo.* 2. *c.* 44. no action shall be brought against any constable, or other officer, or any person acting by his order, and in his aid, for any thing done in obedience to any warrant of a justice of peace, until demand of the perusal and copy of such warrant, and the same hath been refused or neglected by the space of six days; and in case after such demand, and compliance therewith, any action shall be brought against such constable, &c. without making the justice a defendant; then on producing and proving such warrant, the jury shall give a verdict for the defendant, notwithstanding any defect of jurisdiction in such justice; and if such action be brought jointly against such justice, and also against such constable, &c. then on proof of such warrant, the jury shall find for such constable, &c. and if the verdict shall be given against the justice, the plaintiff shall recover his costs against him, to be taxed, so as to include the costs plaintiff shall be liable to pay to such defendant, &c. No action shall be brought against any constable, &c. unless commenced within six calendar months after the act committed.

Stat. 27 *Geo.* 2. *cap.* 20. *sect.* 2. the constable executing a justice's warrant for levying a penalty, or other sum of money directed by any act of parliament, by distress, may deduct his own reasonable charges of taking, keeping, and selling the goods distrained; returning the overplus on demand, after such penalty or sum of money, and charges deducted.

By 18 *Geo.* 3. *c.* 19. constables every three months shall deliver to the overseers of the poor, an account of their expences for the parish, to be settled in 14 days, and paid, if approved, by the parish, if not, to be settled by a justice, with an appeal to the next general or quarter sessions, who may give costs, and in corporations or liberties not having four justices, appeal may be to the next general or quarter sessions of the county.

And by 41 *Geo.* 3. (u. k.) *c.* 78. when special constables shall be appointed in *England* to execute warrants in cases of felony, two justices may order proper allowances to be made for their expences and loss of time, which order shall be submitted to the quarter sessions. *s.* 1.

And two justices may in like manner, order allowances to be made to high constables in England for extraordinary expences incurred in the execution of their duties in cases of riot or felony. *s.* 3.

CONSTAT, (Lat.) is a certificate from the clerk of the pipe, and auditors of the exchequer, made at the request of any person who intends to plead or move in that court, for the discharge of any thing: and the effect of it, is the certifying what does constat upon record, touching the matter in question. 3 & 4 *Ed.* 6. *c.* 4. and 13 *Eliz.* *c.* 6.

CONSTITUTION, the form of government used in any place.

The pure principles of the British Constitution, many of which are pointed out in this Dictionary, under their different titles, cannot be better illustrated, than by referring to the elegant summary of *the rise, progress, and gradual improvements of the laws of England*, given by Sir William Blackstone in the *fourth volume* of his learned Commentaries, and wherein he has taken a chronological view of the state of our laws, and their successive mutations at different periods of time.

The several periods under which the learned Commentator considers the state of our legal polity, are the following six; I. From the earliest times to the Norman conquest; II. From the Norman conquest to the reign of king *Ed.* 1.; III. From thence to the reformation; IV. From the reformation to the restoration of king *Car.* 2.; V. From thence to the revolution in 1688.; VI. From the revolution to the present time.

I. With regard to the antient Britons, the aborigines of our islands, so little is handed down to us concerning them with any tolerable certainty, that inquiries here must be very fruitless and defective. However, from Cæsar's account of the tenets and discipline of the antient Druids in Gaul, in whom centered all the learning of these western parts, and who were, as he tells us, sent over to Britain, (that is, to the island of Mona or Anglesey,) to be instructed; we may collect a few points, which bear a great affinity and resemblance to some of the modern doctrines of our English law. Particularly, the very notion itself of an oral unwritten law, delivered from age to age, by custom and tradition merely, seems derived from the practice of the Druids, who never committed any of their instructions to writing: possibly for want of letters; since it is remarkable that in all the antiquities, unquestionably British, which the industry of the moderns has discovered, there is not in any of them the least trace of any character or letter to be found. The partible quality also of lands, by the custom of gavelkind, which still obtains in many parts of England, and did universally over Wales till the reign of Henry VIII. is undoubtedly of British original. So likewise is the antient division of the goods of an intestate between his widow and children, or next of kin: which has since been revived by the statute of distributions. And the same custom had continued from Cæsar's time, until altered by stat. 30 *Geo.* 3. *c.* 48.; that of burning a woman guilty of the crime of petit treason by killing her husband. 4 *Black.* 408.

The great variety of nations, that successively broke in upon and destroyed both the British inhabitants and constitution, the Romans, the Picts, and, after them, the various clans of Saxons and Danes, must necessarily have caused great confusion and uncertainty in the laws and antiquities of the kingdom; as they were very soon incorporated and blended together, and therefore, we may suppose, mutually communicated to each other their respective usages, (*Hal. Hist. C. L.* 62.) in regard to the rights of property, and the punishment of crimes. So that it is morally impossible to trace out, with any degree of accuracy, when the several mutations of the common law were made, or what was the respective original of those several customs we at present use, by any analization or resolution of them to their first and component principles. We can seldom pronounce, that *this* custom was derived from the Britons; *that* was left behind by the Romans; *this* was a necessary precaution against the Picts, *that* was introduced by the Saxons, discontinued by the Danes, but afterwards restored by the Normans. *Ibid.*

Wherever this can be done, it is matter of great curiosity, and some use: but this can very rarely be the case; not only from the reason above-mentioned, but also from many others. First, from the nature of traditional laws in general; which, being accommodated to the exigencies of the times, suffer by degrees insensible variations in practice (*Ibid.* 57.): so that, though upon comparison we plainly discern the alteration of the law from what it was five hundred years ago, yet it is impossible to define the precise period in which that alteration accrued, any more than we can discern the changes of the bed of a river, which varies its shores by continual decreases and alluvions. Secondly, this becomes impracticable from the antiquity of the kingdom and its government: which alone, though it had been disturbed by no foreign invasions would make it impossible to search out the original of its laws; unless we had as authentic monuments thereof, as the Jews had by the hand of Moses (*Ibid.* 59.) Thirdly, this uncertainty of the true origin of particular customs must also in part have arisen from the means, whereby christianity was propagated among our Saxon ancestors in this island, by learned foreigners brought over from Rome and other countries; who undoubtedly carried with them many of their own national customs; and probably prevailed upon the state to abrogate such usages as were inconsistent with our holy religion, and to introduce many others that were more conformable thereto. And this perhaps may have partly been the cause, that we find not only some rules of the mosaical, but also of the imperial and pontifical laws, blended and adopted into our own system. *Ibid.*

A farther reason may also be given for the great variety, and of course the uncertain original, of our antient established customs; even after the Saxon government was firmly established in this island: *viz.* the subdivision of the kingdom into an heptarchy, consisting of seven independent kingdoms, peopled and governed by different clans and colonies. This must necessarily create an infinite diversity of laws: even though all those colonies, of Jutes, Angles, Anglo-Saxons, and the like, originally sprung from the same mother-country, the great northern hive; which poured forth its warlike progeny, and swarmed all over Europe, in the sixth and seventh centuries. This multiplicity of laws will necessarily be the case in some degree, where any kingdom is cantoned out into provincial establishments; and not under one common dispensation of laws, though under the same sovereign power. Much more will it happen where seven unconnected states are to form their own constitution and superstructure of government, though they all begin to build upon the same or similar foundations. *Ibid.*

When, therefore, the West Saxons had swallowed up all the rest, and king Alfred succeeded to the monarchy of England, whereof his grandfather Egbert was the founder, his mighty genius prompted him to undertake a most great and necessary work, which he is said to have executed in as masterly a manner: no less than to new model the constitution; to rebuild it on a plan that should endure for ages; and, out of its old discordant materials, which were heaped upon each other in a vast and rude irregularity, to form one uniform and well-connected whole. This he effected, by reducing the whole kingdom under one regular and gradual subordination of government, wherein each man was answerable to his immediate superior for his own conduct and that of his nearest neighbours: for to him we owe that masterpiece of judicial polity, the subdivision of England into tithings and hundreds, if not into counties; all under the influence and administration of one supreme magistrate, the king; in whom as in a general reservoir, all the executive authority of the law was lodged, and from whom justice was dispersed to every part of the nation by distinct, yet communicating, ducts and channels; which wise institution has been preserved for near a thousand years unchanged, from Alfred's to the present time. He also, like another Theodosius, collected the various customs that he found dispersed in the kingdom, and reduced and digested them into one uniform system or code of laws, in his *dom-bec*, or *liber judicialis*. This he compiled for the use of the court-baron, hundred, and county-court, the court-leet, and sheriff's tourn; tribunals, which he established, for the trial of all causes civil and criminal, in the very districts wherein the complaint arose: all of them subject however to be inspected, controlled, and kept within the bounds of the universal or common law, by the king's own courts; which were then *itinerant*, being kept in the king's palace, and removing with his household in those royal progresses, which he continually made from one end of the kingdom to the other. *Ibid.* 411.

The Danish invasion and conquest, which introduced new foreign customs, was a severe blow to this noble fabric: but a plan, so excellently concerted, could never be long thrown aside. So that, upon the expulsion of these intruders, the English returned to their antient law; retaining however some few of the customs of their late visitants; which went under the name of Dane-Lage; as the code compiled by Alfred was called the West Saxon-Lage; and the local constitutions of the antient kingdom of Mercia, which obtained in the counties nearest to Wales, and probably abounded with many British customs, were called the Mercen-Lage. And these three laws were, about the beginning of the eleventh century, in use in different counties of the realm: the provincial polity of counties, and their subdivisions, having never been altered or discontinued through all the shocks and mutations of government, from the time of its first institution; though the laws and customs therein used, have often suffered considerable changes. *Ibid.* 412.

For king Edgar, (who besides his military merit, as founder of the English navy, was also a most excellent civil governor,) observing the ill effects of three distinct bodies of laws, prevailing at once in separate parts of his dominions, projected and began what his grandson king Edward the confessor afterwards completed, *viz.* one uniform digest or body of laws to be observed throughout the whole kingdom: being probably no more than a revival of king Alfred's code, with some improvements suggested by necessity and experience; particularly the incorporating some of the British or rather Mercian customs, and also such of the Danish as were reasonable and approved, into the West Saxon-Lage, which was still the groundwork of the whole. And this appears to be the best supported and most plausible conjecture (for certainty is not to be expected) of the rise and original of that admirable system of maxims and unwritten customs, which is now known by the name of the common law, as extending its authority universally over all the realm; and which is doubtless of Saxon parentage. *Ibid.*

Among the most remarkable of the Saxon laws we may reckon, 1. The constitution of parliaments, or rather, general assemblies of the principal and wisest men in the nation: the *wittena-gemote*, or *commune consilium* of the antient Germans; which was not yet reduced to the forms and distinctions of our modern parliament: without whose concurrence, however, no new law could be made, or old one altered. 2. The election of their magistrates by the people; originally even that of their kings, till dear-bought experience evinced the convenience and necessity of establishing an hereditary succession to the crown. But that of all subordinate magistrates, their military officers or heretochs, their sheriffs, their conservators of the peace, their coroners, their port-reeves, (since changed into mayors and bailiffs,) and even their tithing-men and borsholders at the leet, continued, some till the Norman conquest, others for two centuries after, and some remain to this day. 3. The descent of the crown, when once a royal family was established, upon nearly the same hereditary principles upon which it has ever since continued: only that, perhaps, in case of minority, the next of kin of full age would ascend the throne, as king, and not as protector; though, after his death, the crown immediately reverted back to the heir. 4. The great paucity of capital punishments for the first offence: even the most notorious offenders being allowed to commute it for a fine or *weregild*, or, in default of payment, perpetual bondage; to which our benefit of clergy has now in some measure succeeded. 5. The prevalence of certain customs, as heriots and military services in proportion to every man's land, which much resembled the feodal constitution; but yet were exempt from all its rigorous hardships: and which may be well enough accounted for, by supposing them to be brought from the continent by the first Saxon invaders, in the primitive moderation and simplicity of the feodal law; before it got into the hands of the Norman jurists, who extracted the most slavish doctrines and oppressive consequences out of what was originally intended as a law of liberty. 6. That their estates were liable to forfeiture for treason, but that the doctrine of escheats and corruption of blood for felony, or any other cause, was utterly unknown amongst them. 7. The descent of their lands to all the males equally, without any right of primogeniture; a custom, which obtained among the Britons, was agreeable to the Roman law, and continued among the Saxons till the Norman conquest: though really inconvenient, and more especially destructive to antient families; which are in monarchies necessary to be supported, in order to form and keep up a nobility, or intermediate state between the prince and the common people. 8. The courts of justice consisted principally of the county courts, and in cases of weight or nicety the king's court held before himself in person, at the time of his parliaments; which were usually holden in different places, according as he kept the three great festivals of Christmas, Easter, and Whitsuntide. An institution which was adopted by king Alonso VII. of Castile, about a century after the conquest: who at the same three great feasts was accustomed to assemble his nobility and prelates in his court; who there heard and decided all controversies, and then, having received his instructions, departed home. (*Mod. Un. Hist.* xx. 114.) These county courts, however, differed from the modern ones, in that the ecclesiastical and civil jurisdiction were blended together, the bishop and the ealdorman or sheriff sitting in the same county court; and also that the decisions and proceedings therein were much more simple and unembarrassed: an advantage which will always attend the infancy of any laws, but wear off as they gradually advance to antiquity. 9. Trials, among a people who had a very strong tincture of superstition were permitted to be by ordeal, by the corsned or morsel of execration, or by wager of law with compurgators, if the party chose it; but frequently they were also by jury, for whether or no their juries consisted precisely of twelve men, or were bound to a strict unanimity; yet the general constitution of this admirable criterion of truth, and most important guardian both of public and private liberty, we owe to our Saxon ancestors. Thus stood the general frame of our polity at the time of the Norman invasion, when the second period of our legal history commences. *Ibid.* 414.

II. This remarkable event wrought as great an alteration in our laws, as it did in our antient line of kings: and though the alteration of the former was effected rather by the consent of the people, than any right of conquest, yet that consent seems to have been partly extorted by fear, and partly given without any apprehension of the consequences which afterwards ensued. *Ibid.* 415.

1. Among the first of these alterations we may reckon the separation of the ecclesiastical courts from the civil; effected in order to ingratiate the new king with the popish clergy, who for some time before had been endeavouring all over Europe to exempt themselves from the secular power: and whose demands the conqueror, like a politic prince, thought it prudent to comply with, by reason that their reputed sanctity had a great influence over the minds of the people; and because all the little learning of the times was engrossed into their hands, which made them necessary men, and by all means to be gained over to his interests. And this was the more easily effected, because the disposal of all the episcopal sees being then in the breast of the king, he had taken care to fill them with Italian and Norman prelates. *Ibid.*

2. Another violent alteration of the English constitution consisted in the depopulation of whole countries, for the purposes of the king's royal diversion: and subjecting both them, and all the antient forests of the kingdom, to the unreasonable severities of forest laws imported from the continent, whereby the slaughter of a beast was made almost as penal as the death of a man. In the Saxon times, though no man was allowed to kill or chase the king's deer, yet he might start any game, pursue, and kill it, upon his own estate. But the rigour of these new constitutions vested the sole property of all the game in England in the king alone; and no man was entitled to disturb any fowl of the air, or any beast of the field, of such kinds as were specially re-

served for the royal amusement of the sovereign, without express licence from the king, by a grant of a chase or free warren: and those franchises were granted as much with a view to preserve the breed of animals as to indulge the subject. From a similar principle to which, though the forest laws are now mitigated, and by degrees grown entirely obsolete, yet from this root has sprung a bastard slip, known by the name of the game law, now arrived to and wantoning in its highest vigour: both founded upon the same unreasonable notions of permanent property in wild creatures; and both productive of the same tyranny to the commons; but with this difference, that the forest laws established only one mighty hunter throughout the land, the game laws have raised a little Nimrod in every manor. And in one respect the antient law was much less unreasonable than the modern: for the king's grantee of a chase or free warren might kill game in every part of his franchise; but now, though a freeholder of less than 100*l.* a year is forbidden to kill a patridge upon his own estate, yet nobody else, (not even the lord of the manor, unless he hath a grant of free-warren) can do it without committing a trespass, and subjecting himself to an action. *Ibid.* 415, 16.

3. A third alteration in the English laws was by narrowing the remedial influence of the county courts the great seats of Saxon justice, and extending the original jurisdiction of the king's justices to all kinds of causes, arising in all parts of the kingdom. To this end the *aula regis*, with all its multifarious authority, was erected; and a capital justiciary appointed, with powers so large and boundless, that he became at length a tyrant to the people, and formidable to the crown itself. The constitution of this court, and the judges themselves who presided there, were fetched from the duchy of Normandy: and the consequence naturally was, the ordaining that all proceedings in the king's courts should be carried on in the Norman, instead of the English language. A provision the more necessary, because none of his Norman justiciers understood English; but as evident a badge of slavery as ever was imposed upon a conquered people. This lasted till king Edward the third obtained a double victory, over the armies of France in their own country, and their language in our courts here at home. But there was one mischief too deeply rooted thereby, and which this caution of king Edward came too late to eradicate. Instead of the plain and easy method of determining suits in the county courts, the chicanes and subtilties of Norman jurisprudence had taken possession of the king's courts, to which every cause of consequence was drawn. Indeed that age, and those immediately succeeding it, were the era of refinement and subtilty. There is an active principle in the human soul, that will ever be exerting its faculties to the utmost stretch, in whatever employment, by the accidents of time and place, the general plan of education, or the customs and manners of the age and country, it may happen to find itself engaged. The northern conquerors of Europe were then emerging from the grossest ignorance in point of literature: and those who had leisure to cultivate its progress, were such only as were cloistered in monasteries, the rest being all soldiers or peasants. And, unfortunately, the first rudiments of science, which they imbibed were those of Aristotle's philosophy, conveyed through the medium of his Arabian commentators; which were brought from the east by the Saracens into Palestine and Spain, and translated into barbarous Latin. So that, though the materials upon which they were naturally employed, in the infancy of a rising state, were those of the noblest kind; the establishment of religion, and the regulations of civil polity, yet having only such tools to work with, their execution was trifling and flimsy. Both the divinity and the law of those times were therefore frittered into logical distinctions, and drawn out into metaphysical subtilties, with a skill most amazingly artificial; but which serves no other purpose, than to shew the vast powers of the human intellect, however vainly or preposterously employed. Hence law in particular, which (being intended for universal reception) ought to be a plain rule of action, became a science of the greatest intricacy; especially when blended with the new refinements engrafted upon feodal property; which refinements were from time to time gradually introduced by the Norman practitioners, with a view to supersede (as they did in great measure) the more homely but more intelligible, maxims of distributive justice among the Saxons. And to say the truth, these scholastic reformers have transmitted their dialect and finesses to posterity so interwoven in the body of our legal polity, that they cannot now be taken out without a manifest injury to the substance. Statute after statute has in later times been made, to pare off these troublesome excrescences, and restore the common law to its pristine simplicity and vigour; and the endeavour has greatly succeeded, but still the scars are deep and visible; and the liberality of our modern courts of justice is frequently obliged to have recourse to unaccountable fictions and circuities, in order to recover that equitable and substantial justice, which for a long time was totally buried under the narrow rules and fanciful niceties of metaphysical and Norman jurisprudence. *Ibid.* 417.

4. A fourth innovation was the introduction of the trial by combat, for the decision of all civil and criminal questions of fact in the last resort. This was the immemorial practice of all the northern nations; but first reduced to regular and stated forms among the Burgundi, about the close of the fifth century; and from them it passed to other nations, particularly the Franks and the Normans; which last had the honour to establish it here, though clearly an unchristian, as well as most uncertain, method of trial. But it was a sufficient recommendation of it to the conqueror, and his warlike countrymen, that it was the usage of their native duchy of Normandy. *Ibid.* 417.

5. But the last and most important alteration, both in our civil and military polity, was the engrafting on all landed estates, a few only excepted, the fiction of feodal tenure; which drew after it a numerous and oppressive train of servile fruits and appendages; aids, reliefs, primer seisins, wardships, marriages, escheats, and fines for alienation; the genuine consequences of the maxim then adopted, that all the lands in England were derived from and holden, mediately or immediately, of the crown. *Ibid.* 417.

The nation at this period seems to have groaned under as absolute a slavery, as was in the power of a warlike, an ambitious, and a politic prince to create. The consciences of men were enslaved by four ecclesiastics, devoted to a foreign power, and unconnected with the civil state under which they lived; who now imported from Rome for the first time the whole *farrago* of superstitious novelties, which had been engendered by the blindness and corruption of the times, between the first mission of Augustin the monk, and the Norman conquest; such as transubstantiation, purgatory, communion in one kind, and the worship of saints and images; not forgetting the universal supremacy and dogmatical infallibility of the holy see. The laws too, as well as the prayers, were administered in an unknown tongue. The ancient trial by jury gave way to the impious decision by battle. The forest laws totally restrained all rural pleasures and manly recreations. And in cities and towns the case was no better; all company being obliged to disperse, and fire and candle to be extinguished, by eight at night, at the sound of the melancholy *curfeu*. The ultimate property of all lands, and a considerable share of the present profits, were vested in the king, or by him granted out to his Norman favourites; who, by a gradual progression of slavery, were absolute vassals to the crown, and as absolute tyrants to the commons. Unheard of forfeitures, talliages, aids, and fines, were arbitrarily extracted from the pillaged landholders, in pursuance of the new system of tenure. And to crown all, as a consequence of the tenure by knight service, the king had always ready at his command, an army of sixty thousand knights or milites; who were bound upon pain of confiscating their estates, to attend him in time of invasion, or to quell any domestic insurrection. Trade or foreign merchandize, such as it then was, was carried on by the Jews and Lombards; and the very name of an English fleet, which king Edgar had rendered so formidable, was utterly unknown to Europe: the nation consisting wholly of the clergy, who were also the lawyers, the barons, or great lords of the land; the knights or soldiery, who were the subordinate landholders, and the burghers, or inferior tradesmen, who from their insignificancy happily retained, in their socage and burgage tenure, some points of their antient freedom. All the rest were villains or bondman. *Ibid.* 419.

From so complete and well concerted a scheme of servility, it has been the work of generations for our ancestors to redeem themselves and their posterity into that state of liberty which we now enjoy: and which therefore is not to be looked upon as consisting of mere encroachments on the crown, and infringements on the prerogative, as some slavish and narrow minded writers in the last century endeavoured to maintain; but as in general, a gradual restoration of that ancient constitution, whereof our Saxon forefathers had been unjustly deprived, partly by the policy, and partly by the force of the Norman. How that restoration, has in a long series of years, been step by step effected, I now proceed to inquire. *Ibid.*

William Rufus proceeded on his father's plan, and in some points extended it; particularly with regard to the forest laws. But his brother and successor Henry the first, found it expedient, when he first came to the crown, to ingratiate himself with the people; by restoring, (as our monkish historian tells us) the laws of king Edward the confessor. The ground whereof is this, that by charter he gave up the great grievances of marriage, ward, and relief, the beneficial pecuniary fruits of his feodal tenures; but reserved the tenures themselves, for the same military purposes that his father introduced them. He also abolished the *curfeu*; (*Spelm. Cod. L. L. W. I.* 228. *Hen. I.* 299). For, though it is mentioned in our laws a full century afterwards (*Stat. Civ. Lond.* 13 *Edw.* 1); Yet it is rather spoken of as a known time of night (so denominated from that abrogated usage) than as a still subsisting custom. There is extant a code of laws in his name, consisting partly of those of the confessor, but with great additions and alterations of his own;

and chiefly calculated for the regulation of the country courts. It contains some directions as to crimes and their punishments, (that of theft being made capital in his reign,) and a few things relating to estates, particularly as to the descent of lands, which being by the Saxon laws equally to all the sons, by the feodal or Norman to the eldest only, king Henry here moderated the difference; directing the eldest son to have only the principal estate, "*primum patris feudum*," the rest of his estates, if he had any others, being equally divided among them all. On the other hand, he gave up to the clergy the free election of bishops and mitred abbots; reserving however these ensigns of patronage, *conge d'r eslire*, custody of the temporalities when vacant, and homage upon their restitution. He lastly united again for a time the civil and ecclesiastical courts, which union was soon dissolved by his Norman clergy: and, upon that final dissolution, the cognizance of testamentary causes seems to have been first given to the ecclesiastical court. The rest remained in his father's time, from whence we may easily perceive how far short this was of a thorough restitution of king Edward's, or the Saxon laws. *Ibid.* 420.

The usurper Stephen, as the manner of usurpers is, promised much at his accession, especially with regard to redressing the grievances of the forest laws, but performed no great matter in that or in any other point. It is from his reign, however, that we are to date the introduction of the Roman civil and canon laws into this realm, and at the same time was imported the doctrine of appeals to the court of Rome, as a branch of the canon law. *Ibid.*

By the time of king Henry the second, if not earlier, the charter of Henry the first seems to have been forgotten: for we find the claim of marriage, ward, and relief, then flourishing in full vigour. The right of primogeniture seems also to have tacitly revived, being found more convenient for the public than the parcelling of estates into a multitude of minute subdivisions. However in this prince's reign much was done to methodize the laws, and reduce them into a regular order; as appears from that excellent treatise of Glanvil; which, though some of it be now antiquated and altered, yet when compared with the code of Henry the first, it carries a manifest superiority. (*Hal. Hist. C. L.* 138.) Throughout his reign also was continued the important struggle, which we have had occasion so often to mention, between the laws of England and Rome; the former supported by the strength of the temporal nobility, when endeavoured to be supplanted in favour of the latter by the popish clergy. Which dispute was kept on foot till the reign of Edward the first, when the laws of England, under the new discipline introduced by that skilful commander, obtained a complete and permanent victory. In the present reign of Henry the second, there are four things which peculiarly merit the attention of a legal antiquarian. 1. The constitutions of the parliament at Clarendon, *A. D.* 1164, whereby the king checked the power of the pope and his clergy, and greatly narrowed the total exemption they claimed from the secular jurisdiction: though his farther progress was unhappily stopped, by the fatal event of the disputes between him and archbishop Becket. 2. The institution of the justices in eyre, *in itinere*; the king having divided the kingdom into six circuits, (a little different from the present), and commissioned these new created judges to administer justice, and try writs of assize, in the several counties. These remedies are said to have been then first invented, before which all causes were usually terminated in the county courts, according to the Saxon custom; or before the king's justiciaries in the *aula regis*, in pursuance of the Norman regulations. The latter of which tribunals, travelling about with the king's person, occasioned intolerable expense and delay to the suitors; and the former, however proper for little debts and minute actions, where even injustice is better than procrastination, were now become liable to too much ignorance of the law, and too much partiality as to facts, to determine matters of considerable moment. 3. The introduction and establishment of the grand assize, or trial by special kind of jury in a writ of right at the option of the tenant or defendant, instead of the barbarous and Norman trial by battle. 4. To this time must also be referred the introduction of escuage, or pecuniary commutation for personal military service; which in process of time was the parent of the ancient subsidies granted to the crown by parliament, and the land tax of later times. *Ibid.* 422.

Richard the first, a brave and magnanimous prince, was a sportsman as well as a soldier: and therefore enforced the forest laws with some rigour, which occasioned many discontents among his people, though (according to Matthew Paris) he repealed the penalties of castration, loss of eyes, cutting off the hands and feet, before inflicted on such as transgressed in hunting; probably finding that their severity prevented prosecutions. He also, when abroad, composed a body of naval laws at the isle of Oleron; which are still extant, and of high authority; for in his time we began again to discover, that (as an island) we were naturally a maritime power. But with regard to civil proceedings we find nothing very remarkable in this reign, except a few regulations regarding the Jews, and the justices in eyre: the king's thoughts being chiefly taken up by the knight errantry of a croisade against the Saracens in the holy land. *Ibid.*

In king John's time, and that of his son Henry the third, the rigours of the feodal tenures and the forest laws were so warmly kept up, that they occasioned many insurrections of the barons or principal feudatories: which at last had this effect, that first king John, and afterwards his son, consented to the two famous charters of English liberties *magna carta*, and *carta de foresta*. Of these the latter was well calculated to redress many grievances, and encroachments of the crown, in the exertion of forest law; and the former confirmed many liberties of the church, and redressed many grievances incident to feodal tenures, of no small moment at the time; though now, unless considered attentively and with this retrospect, they seem but of trifling concern. But, besides these feodal provisions, care was also taken therein to protect the subject against other oppressions, then frequently arising from unreasonable amercements, from illegal distresses or other process for debts or services due to the crown, and from the tyrannical abuse of the prerogative of purveyance and preemption. It fixed the forfeiture of lands for felony in the same manner as it still remains; prohibited for the future the grants of exclusive fisheries; and the erection of new bridges so as to oppress the neighbourhood. With respect to private rights, it established the testamentary power of the subject over part of his personal estate, the rest being distributed among his wife and children; it laid down the law of dower, as it hath continued ever since, and prohibited the appeals of women, unless for the death of their husbands. In matters of public police and national concern, it enjoined an uniformity of weights and measures, gave new encouragements to commerce, by the protection of merchant strangers, and forbad the alienation of lands in mortmain. With regard to the administration of justice, besides prohibiting all denials or delays of it, it fixed the court of common pleas at Westminster, that the suitors might no longer be harassed with following the king's person in all his progresses: and at the same time brought the trial of issues home to the very doors of the freeholders, by directing assizes to be taken in the proper counties, and establishing annual circuits; it also corrected some abuses then incident to the trials by wager of law and of battle; directed the regular awarding of inquest for life or member, prohibited the king's inferior ministers from holding pleas of the crown, or trying any criminal charge, whereby many forfeitures might otherwise have unjustly accrued to the exchequer; and regulated the time and place of holding the inferior tribunals of justice, the county court, sheriff's tourn, and court-leet. It confirmed and established the liberties of the city of London, and all other cities, boroughs, towns, and ports of the kingdom. And lastly, (which alone would have merited the title that it bears, of the great charter), it protected every individual of the nation in the free enjoyment of his life, his liberty, and his property, unless declared to be forfeited by the judgment of his peers or the law of the land.* *Ibid.* 424.

However by means of these struggles, the pope in the reign of king John gained a still greater ascendant here, than he ever had before enjoyed; which continued through the long reign of his son Henry the third, in the beginning of whose time the old Saxon trial by ordeal was also totally abolished. And we may by this time perceive in Bracton's treatise, a still farther improvement in the method and regularity of the common law, especially in the point of pleadings. (*Hale Hist. C. L.* 156). Nor must it be forgotten, that the first traces which remain, of the separation of the greater barons from the less, in the constitution of parliament, are found in the great charter of king John, though omitted in that of Henry III. and that, towards the end of the latter of these reigns, we find the first record of any writ for summoning knights, citizens, and burgesses to parliament. And here we conclude the second period of our English legal history. *Ibid.*

III. The third commences with the reign of Edward the first; who hath justly been stiled our English Justinian. For in his time the law did receive so sudden a perfection, that Sir Matthew Hale does not scruple to affirm, (*Ibid.* 158), that more was done in the first thirteen years of his reign to settle and establish the distributive justice of the kingdom, than in all the ages since that time put together.

It would be endless to enumerate all the particulars of these regulations; but the principal may be reduced under the following general heads. 1. He established, con-

---

* The following is the celebrated 29th chapter of magna charta, the foundation of the liberty of Englishmen:

Nullus liber homo capiatur, vel imprisonetur aut disseisiatur de libero tenemento suo, vel libertatibus, vel liberis consuetudinibus suis, aut utlagetur, aut exulet, aut aliquo modo destruatur, nec super eum ibimus, nec super eum mittemus, nisi per legale judicium parium suorum vel per legem terræ. Nulli vendemus, nulli negabimus, aut differemus rectum vel justitiam.

firmed, and settled the great charter and charter of forests. 2. He gave a mortal wound to the encroachments of the pope and his clergy, by limiting and establishing the bounds of ecclesiastical jurisdiction: and by obliging the ordinary, to whom all the goods of intestates at that time belonged, to discharge the debts of the deceased. 3. He defined the limits of the several temporal courts of the highest jurisdiction, those of the king's bench, common pleas, and exchequer; so as they might not interfere with each other's proper business: to do which they must now have recourse to a fiction, very necessary and beneficial in the present enlarged state of property. 4. He settled the boundaries of the inferior courts in counties, hundreds, and manors confining them to causes of no great amount, according to their primitive institution; though of considerably greater, than by the alteration of the value of money they are now permitted to determine. 5. He secured the property of the subjects by abolishing all arbitrary taxes and talliages, levied without consent of the national council. 6. He guarded the common justice of the kingdom from abuses, by giving up the royal prerogative of sending mandates to interfere in private causes. 7. He settled the form, solemnities, and effect, of fines levied in the court of common pleas; though the thing itself was of Saxon original. 8. He first established a repository for the public records of the kingdom, few of which are ancienter than the reign of his father, and those were by him collected. 9. He improved upon the laws of king Alfred, by that great and orderly method of watch and ward, for preserving the public peace and preventing robberies, established by the statute of Winchester. 10. He settled and reformed many abuses incident to tenures, and removed some restraints on the alienation of landed property, by the statute of *quia emptores*. 11. He instituted a speedier way for the recovery of debts, by granting execution not only upon goods and chattels, but also upon lands by writ of *elegit;* which was of signal benefit to a trading people: and upon the same commercial ideas, he also allowed the charging of lands in a statute merchant, to pay debts contracted in trade, contrary to all feodal principles. 12. He effectually provided for the recovery of advowsons, as temporal rights in which, before the law was extremely deficient. 13. He also effectually closed the great gulph, in which all the landed property of the kingdom was in danger of being swallowed, by his reiterated statutes of mortmain; most admirably adapted to meet the frauds that had been then devised, though afterwards contrived to be evaded by the invention of uses. 14. He established a new limitation of property by the creation of estates tail; concerning the good policy of which, modern times have however entertained a very different opinion. 15. He reduced all Wales to the subjection, not only of the crown, but in great measure of the laws, of England, (which was thoroughly completed in the reign of Henry the eighth); and seems to have entertained a design of doing the like by Scotland, so as to have formed an entire and complete union of the island of Great Britain. *Ibid.* 426,7.

This catalogue might be continued much farther; but upon the whole, we may observe, that every scheme and model of the administration of common justice between party and party, was entirely settled by this king. (*Hal. Hist. C. L.* 162). And hast continued nearly the same in all succeeding ages, to this day; abating some few alterations, which the humour or necessity of subsequent times hath occasioned. The forms of writs by which actions are commenced, were perfected in his reign, and established as models for posterity. The pleadings, consequent upon the writs, were then short, nervous, and perspicuous; not intricate, verbose, and formal. The legal treatises written in his time, as Britton, Fleta, Hengam, and the rest, are for the most part law at this day, or at least were so, till the alteration of tenures took place. And to conclude, it is from this period, from the exact observation of *magna charta*, rather than from its making or renewal, in the days of his grandfather and father, that the liberty of Englishmen began again to rear its head; though the weight of the military tenures hung heavy upon it for many ages after. *Ibid.* 426,7.

A better proof of the excellence of his constitutions, cannot be given than that from his time to that of Henry the eighth, there happened very few, and those not very considerable, alterations in the legal forms of proceedings. As to matter of substance the old Gothic powers of electing the principal subordinate magistrates, the sheriffs, and conservators of the peace, were taken from the people in the reigns of Edward II. and Edward III. and justices of the peace were established instead of the latter. In the reign also of Edward the third the parliament is supposed most probably to have assumed its present form; by a separation of the commons from the lords. The statute for defining and ascertaining treasons was one of the first productions of this new modelled assembly; and the translation of the law proceedings from French into Latin another. Much also was done, under the auspices of this magnanimous prince, for establishing our domestic manufactures; by prohibiting the exportation of English wool, and the importation or wear of foreign cloth or furs; and by encouraging clothworkers from other countries to settle here. Nor was the legislature inattentive to many other branches of commerce, or indeed to commerce in general; for, in particular, it enlarged the credit of the merchant by introducing the statute-staple, whereby he might the more readily pledge his lands for the security of his mercantile debts. And, as personal property now grew by the extension of trade to be much more considerable than formerly, care was taken, in case of intestacies, to appoint administrators, particularly nominated by the law, to distribute that personal property among the creditors and kindred of the deceased, which before had been usually applied by the officers of the ordinary to uses then denominated pious. The statutes also of *præmunire*, for effectually depressing the civil power of the pope, were the work of this and the subsequent reign. And the establishment of a laborious parochial clergy, by the endowment of vicarages out of the overgrown possessions of the monasteries, added lustre to the close of the 14th century; though the seeds of the general reformation, which were thereby first sown in the kingdom, were almost overwhelmed by the spirit of persecution introduced into the laws of the land by the influence of the regular clergy. *Ibid.* 427, 428.

From this time to that of Henry VII. the civil wars and disputed titles to the crown gave no leisure for further juridical improvement: "*nam silent leges inter arma.*" And yet it is to these very disputes that we owe the happy loss of all the dominions of the crown on the continent of France, which turned the minds of our subsequent princes entirely to domestic concerns. To these likewise we owe the method of barring entails by the fiction of common recoveries, invented originally by the clergy, to evade the statutes of mortmain, but introduced under Edward the Fourth for the purpose of unfettering estates, and making them more liable to forfeiture: while on the other hand the owners endeavoured to protect them by the universal establishment of uses, another of the clerical inventions. *Ibid.* 428.

In the reign of king Henry VII. his ministers (not to say the king himself) were more industrious in hunting out prosecutions upon old and forgotten penal laws, in order to extort money from the subject, than in framing any new beneficial regulations. For the distinguishing character of this reign was that of amassing treasure in the king's coffers by every mean that could be devised; and almost every alteration in the laws, however salutary or otherwise in their future consequences, had this and this only for their great and immediate object. To this end the court of star-chamber was new modelled, and armed with powers the most dangerous and unconstitutional, over the persons and properties of the subject. Informations were allowed to be received in lieu of indictments at the assises and sessions of the peace, in order to multiply fines and pecuniary penalties. The statute of fines for landed property was craftily and covertly contrived to facilitate the destruction of entails, and make the owners of real estates more capable to forfeit as well as to aliene. The benefit of clergy, which so often intervened to stop attainders and save the inheritance, was now allowed only once to lay-offenders, who only could have inheritances to lose. A writ of *capias* was permitted in all actions on the case, and the defendant might in consequence be outlawed; because upon such outlawry his goods became the property of the crown. In short, there is hardly a statute in this reign, introductive of a new law, or modifying the old, but what either directly or obliquely tended to the emolument of the Exchequer. *Ibid.* 429.

IV. This brings us to the fourth period of our legal history, *viz.* the reformation of religion under Henry VIII. and his children, which opens an entirely new scene in ecclesiastical matters, the usurped power of the pope being now for ever routed and destroyed, all his connexions with this island cut off, the crown restored to its supremacy over spiritual men and causes, and the patronage of bishoprics being once more indisputably vested in the king. And had the spiritual courts been at this time re-united to the civil, we should have seen the old Saxon constitution with regard to ecclesiastical polity completely restored. *Ibid.* 429, 430.

With regard also to our civil polity, the statute of wills, and the statute of uses, (both passed in the reign of this prince) made a great alteration as to property: the former by allowing the devise of real estates by will, which before was in general forbidden, the latter by endeavouring to destroy the intricate nicety of uses, though the narrowness and pedantry of the courts of common law prevented this statute from having its full beneficial effect. And thence the courts of equity assumed a jurisdiction, dictated by common justice and common sense, which, however arbitrarily exercised, or productive of jealousies in its infancy, has at length been matured into a most elegant system of rational jurisprudence; the principles of which (notwithstanding they may differ in forms) are now equally adopted by the courts of both law and equity. From the statute of uses, and another statute of the same antiquity, (which protected estates for years from being destroyed by the reversioner,) a remarkable alteration took place in the mode of conveyancing: the ancient assurance by feoffment and livery upon the land being now very seldom practised since the more easy and more private invention of transferring property by secret conveyances to uses, and long terms of years being now continually created in mortgages and family settlements, which may be moulded to a thousand useful purposes by the ingenuity of an able artist. *Ibid.* 430, 431.

The further attacks in this reign upon the immunity of estates tail, which reduced them to little more than the conditional fees at the common law before the passing of the statute *de donis*, the establishment of recognizances in the nature of a statute-staple for facilitating the raising of money upon landed security, and the introduction of the bankrupt laws, as well for the punishment of the fraudulent, as the relief of the unfortunate, trader; all these were capital alterations of our legal polity, and highly convenient to that character which the English began now to re-assume, of a great commercial people. The incorporation of Wales with England, and the more uniform administration of justice, by destroying some counties palatine, and abridging the unreasonable privileges of such as remained, added dignity and strength to the monarchy, and, together with the numerous improvements before observed upon, and the redress of many grievances and oppressions which had been introduced by his father, will ever make the administration of Henry the Eighth a very distinguished era in the annals of juridical history. *Ibid.* 431.

It must, however, be remarked, that (particularly in his later years) the royal prerogative was then strained to a very tyrannical and oppressive height; and, what was the worst circumstance, its encroachments were established by law, under the sanction of those pusillanimous parliaments, one of which, to its eternal disgrace, passed a statute whereby it was enacted that the king's proclamations should have the force of acts of parliament; and others concurred in the creation of that amazing heap of wild and new-fangled treasons which were slightly touched upon in a former chapter. Happily for the nation this arbitrary reign was succeeded by the minority of an amiable prince, during the short sun-shine of which great part of these extravagant laws were repealed. And, to do justice to the shorter reign of queen Mary, many salutary and popular laws, in civil matters, were made under her administration; perhaps the better to reconcile the people to the bloody measures which she was induced to pursue for the re-establishment of religious slavery, the well-concerted schemes for effecting which, were (through the providence of God) defeated by the seasonable accession of queen Elizabeth. *Ibid.* 431, 432.

The religious liberties of the nation being by that happy event established (we trust) on an eternal basis, (though obliged in their infancy to be guarded against papists and other non-conformists by laws of too sanguinary a nature,) the forest-laws having fallen into disuse, and the administration of civil rights in the courts of justice being carried on in a regular course, according to the wise institutions of king Edward the First, without any material innovations, all the principal grievances introduced by the Norman conquest seem to have been gradually shaken off, and our Saxon constitution restored, with considerable improvements, except only in the continuation of the military tenures, and a few other points, which still armed the crown with a very oppressive and dangerous prerogative. It is also to be remarked, that the spirit of enriching the clergy, and endowing religious houses, had through the former abuse of it gone over to such a contrary extreme, and the princes of the house of Tudor and their favourites had fallen with such avidity upon the spoils of the church, that a decent and honourable maintenance was wanting to many of the bishops and clergy. This produced the restraining statutes, to prevent the alienations of lands and tithes belonging to the church and universities. The number of indigent persons being also greatly increased by withdrawing the alms of the monasteries, a plan was formed in the reign of queen Elizabeth, more humane and beneficial than even feeding and clothing millions, by affording them the means (with proper industry) to feed and to clothe themselves. And, the farther any subsequent plans for maintaining the poor have departed from this institution, the more impracticable, and even pernicious, their visionary attempts have proved. *Ibid.* 432.

However, considering the reign of queen Elizabeth in a great and political view, we have no reason to regret many subsequent alterations in the English constitution: For, though in general she was a wise and excellent princess, and loved her people; though in her time trade flourished, riches increased, the laws were duly administered, the nation was respected abroad, and the people happy at home; yet the increase of the power of the star-chamber, and the erection of the high commission court in matters ecclesiastical, were the work of her reign. She also kept her parliaments at a very awful distance; and in many particulars she at times would carry the prerogative as high as her most arbitrary predecessors. It is true, she very seldom exerted this prerogative so as to oppress individuals; but still she had it to exert; and therefore the felicity of her reign depended more on her want of opportunity and inclination, than want of power to play the tyrant. This is a high encomium on her merit; but at the same time it is sufficient to show, that these were not those golden days of genuine liberty that we formerly were taught to believe; for surely the true liberty of the subject consists not so much in the gracious behaviour, as in the limited power, of the sovereign. *Ibid.* 433.

The great revolutions that had happened in manners and in property had paved the way, by imperceptible yet sure degrees, for as great a revolution in government: yet, while that revolution was effecting, the crown became more arbitrary than ever by the progress of those very means which afterward reduced its power. It is obvious to every observer that, till the close of the Lancastrian civil wars, the property and the power of the nation were chiefly divided between the king, the nobility, and the clergy. The commons were generally in a state of great ignorance; their personal wealth, before the extension of trade, was comparatively small; and the nature of their landed property was such as kept them in continual dependence upon their feudal lord, being usually some powerful baron, some opulent abbey, or sometimes the king himself. Though a notion of general liberty had strongly pervaded and animated the whole constitution, yet the particular liberty, the natural equality, and personal independence of individuals, were little regarded or thought of; nay even to assert them was treated as the height of sedition and rebellion. Our ancestors heard with detestation and horror those sentiments rudely delivered, and pushed to most absurd extremes by the violence of a Cade and a Tyler, which have since been applauded, with a zeal almost rising to idolatry, when softened and recommended by the eloquence, the moderation, and the arguments of a Sidney, a Locke, and a Milton. *Ibid.* 434.

But when learning, by the invention of printing, and the progress of religious reformation, began to be universally disseminated; when trade and navigation were suddenly carried to an amazing extent, by the use of the compass, and the consequent discovery of the Indies, the minds of men thus enlightened by science, and enlarged by observation and travel, began to entertain a more just opinion of the dignity and rights of mankind. An inundation of wealth flowed in upon the merchants, and middling rank, while the two great estates of the kingdom, which formerly had balanced the prerogative, the nobility and clergy, were greatly impoverished and weakened. The popish clergy, detected in their frauds and abuses, exposed to the resentment of the populace, and stripped of their lands and revenues, stood trembling for their very existence. The nobles, enervated by the refinements of luxury, (which knowledge, foreign travel, and the progress of the politer arts, are too apt to introduce with themselves,) and fired with disdain at being rivalled in magnificence by the opulent citizens, fell into enormous expenses, to gratify which they were permitted, by the policy of the times, to dissipate their overgrown estates, and alienate their ancient patrimonies. This gradually reduced their power and their influence within a very moderate bound, while the king, by the spoil of the monasteries, and the great increase of the customs, grew rich, independent, and haughty; and the commons were not yet sensible of the strength they had acquired, nor urged to examine its extent by new burthens or oppressive taxations, during the sudden opulence of the Exchequer. Intent upon acquiring new riches, and happy in being freed from the insolence and tyranny of the orders more immediately above them, they never dreamed of opposing the prerogative to which they had been so little accustomed, much less of taking the lead in opposition, to which by their weight and their property they were now entitled. The latter years of Henry VIII. were therefore the times of the greatest despotism that have been known in this island since the death of William the Norman: the prerogative, as it then stood by common law, (and much more when extended by act of parliament,) being too large to be endured in a land of liberty. *Ibid.* 434, 435.

Queen Elizabeth, and the intermediate princes of the Tudor line, had almost the same legal powers, and sometimes exerted them as roughly, as their father Henry VIII. But the critical situation of that princess with regard to her legitimacy, her religion, her enmity with Spain, and her jealousy of the queen of Scots, occasioned greater caution in her conduct. She, probably, or her able advisers, had penetration enough to discern how the power of the kingdom had gradually shifted its channel, and wisdom enough not to provoke the commons to discover and feel their strength. She therefore drew a veil over the odious part of prerogative, which was never wantonly thrown aside, but only to answer some important purpose: and, though the royal treasury no longer overflowed with the wealth of the clergy, which had been all granted out, and had contributed to enrich the people, she asked for supplies with such moderation, and managed them with so much economy, that the commons were happy in obliging her. Such, in short, were her circumstances, her necessities, her wisdom, and her good disposition, that never did a prince so long and so entirely, for the space of half a century together, reign in the affections of the people. *Ibid.* 435.

On the accession of king James I. no new degree of royal power was added to, or exercised by, him; but such a sceptre was too weighty to be wielded by such a hand. The unreasonable and imprudent exertion of what was then deemed to be prerogative, upon trivial and unworthy occasions, and the claim of a more absolute power inherent in the kingly office than had ever been carried into practice, soon awakened the sleeping lion. The people heard with astonishment doctrines preached from the throne and the pulpit, subversive of liberty and property, and all the natural rights of humanity. They examined into the divinity of this claim, and found it weakly and fallaciously supported: and common reason assured them, that, if it were of human origin, no constitution could establish it without power of revocation, no precedent could sanctify, no length of time could confirm it. The leaders felt the pulse of the nation, and found they had ability as well as inclination to resist it; and accordingly resisted and opposed it, whenever the pusillanimous temper of the reigning monarch had courage to put it to the trial; and they gained some little victories in the cases of concealments, monopolies, and the dispensing power. In the mean time, very little was done for the improvement of private justice, except the abolition of sanctuaries, and the extension of the bankrupt laws, the limitation of suits and actions, and the regulating of informations upon penal statutes. For I cannot class the laws against witchcraft and conjuration under the head of improvements; nor did the dispute between lord Ellesmere and sir Edward Coke, concerning the powers of the court of chancery, tend much to the advancement of justice. *Ibid.* 436.

Indeed when Charles the first succeeded to the crown of his father, and attempted to revive some enormities, which had been dormant in the reign of king James, the loans and benevolences extorted from the subject, the arbitrary imprisonments for refusal, the exertion of martial law in time of peace, and other domestic grievances, clouded the morning of that misguided prince's reign; which, though the noon of it began a little to brighten, at last went down in blood, and left the whole kingdom in darkness. It must be acknowledged that, by the petition of right, enacted to abolish these encroachments, the English constitution received great alteration and improvement. But there still remained the latent power of the forest laws, which the crown most unseasonably revived. The legal jurisdiction of the star-chamber and high commission courts was also extremely great; though their usurped authority was still greater. And, if we add to these the disuse of parliaments, the ill-timed zeal and despotic proceedings of the ecclesiastical governors in matters of mere indifference, together with the arbitrary levies of tonnage and poundage, ship-money, and other projects, we may see grounds most amply sufficient for seeking redress in a legal constitutional way. This redress, when sought, was also constitutionally given: for all these oppressions were actually abolished by the king in parliament, before the rebellion broke out, by the several statutes for triennial parliaments, for abolishing the star-chamber and high commission courts, for ascertaining the extent of forest and forest laws, for renouncing ship-money and other exactions, and for giving up the prerogative of knighting the king's tenants *in capite*, in consequence of their feodal tenures: though it must be acknowledged that these concessions were not made with so good a grace, as to conciliate the confidence of the people. Unfortunately, either by his own mismanagement, or by the arts of his enemies, the king had lost the reputation of sincerity; which is the greatest unhappiness that can befal a prince. Though he had formerly strained his prerogative, not only beyond what the genius of the present times would bear, but also beyond the examples of former ages, he had now consented to reduce it to a lower ebb than was consistent with monarchial government. A conduct so opposite to his temper and principles, joined with some rash actions and unguarded expressions, made the people suspect that this condescension was merely temporary. Flushed therefore with the success they had gained, fired with resentment for past oppressions, and dreading the consequences if the king should regain his power, the popular leaders (who in all ages have called themselves the people) began to grow insolent and ungovernable; their insolence soon rendered them desperate: and despair at length forced them to join with a set of military hypocrites and enthusiasts, who overturned the church and monarchy, and proceeded with deliberate solemnity to the trial and murder of their sovereign. *Ibid.* 437.

The crude and abortive schemes for amending the laws in the times of confusion which followed, must be passed by: the most promising and sensible whereof (such as the establishment of new trials, the abolition of feodal tenures, the act of navigation, and some others) were adopted in the

V. Fifth period, which is after the restoration of king Charles II. Immediately upon which, the principal remaining grievance, the doctrine and consequences of military tenures, were taken away and abolished, except in the instance of corruption of inheritable blood, upon attainder of treason and felony. And though the monarch, in whose person the royal government was restored, and with it our antient constitution, deserves no commendation from posterity, yet in his reign, (wicked, sanguinary, and turbulent as it was,) the concurrence of happy circumstances was such, that from thence we may date not only the re-establishment of our church and monarchy, but also the complete restitution of English liberty, for the first time, since its total abolition at the conquest. For therein not only these slavish tenures, the badge of foreign dominion, with all their oppressive appendages, were removed from incumbering the estates of the subject; but also an additional security of his person from imprisonment was obtained, by that great bulwark of our constitution, the habeas corpus act. These two statutes, with regard to our property and persons, form a second magna charta, as beneficial and effectual as that of Running-Mead. That only pruned the luxuriances of the feodal system; but the statute of Charles the second extirpated all its slaveries; except perhaps in copyhold tenure; and there also they are now in great measure enervated by gradual custom, and the interposition of our courts of justice. Magna Carta only, in general terms, declared, that no man shall be imprisoned contrary to law: the habeas corpus act points him out effectual means, as well to release himself, though committed even by the king in council, as to punish all those who shall thus unconstitutionally misuse him. *Ibid*.

To these may be added the abolition of the prerogatives of purveyance and pre-emption; the statute for holding triennial parliaments; the test and corporation acts, which secure both our civil and religious liberties; the abolition of the writ *de hæretico comburendo*; the statute of frauds and perjuries, a great and necessary security to private property; the statute for distribution of intestates' estates, and that of amendments and jeofails, which cut off those superfluous niceties which so long had disgraced our courts; together with many other wholesome acts that were passed in this reign, for the benefit of navigation and the improvement of foreign commerce: and the whole, when we likewise consider the freedom from taxes and armies which the subject then enjoyed, will be sufficient to demonstrate this truth, "that the constitution of England had arrived to its full vigour, and the true balance between liberty and prerogative was happily established by law, in the reign of king Charles the second." *Ibid*. 438, 9.

It is far from my intention to palliate or defend many very iniquitous proceedings, contrary to all law, in that reign, through the artifice of wicked politicians, both in and out of employment. What seems incontestible is this, that by the law*, as it then stood, (notwithstanding some invidious, nay dangerous branches of the prerogative have since been lopped off, and the rest more clearly defined,) the people had as large a portion of real liberty, as is consistent with a state of society; and sufficient power, residing in their own hands, to assert and preserve that liberty, if invaded by the royal prerogative. For which I need but appeal to the memorable catastrophe of the next reign. For when king Charles's deluded brother attempted to enslave the nation, he found it was beyond his power: the people both could, and did, resist him; and, in consequence of such resistance, obliged him to quit his enterprize and his throne together. Which introduces us to the last period of our legal history; *viz*.

VI. From the revolution in 1688 to the present time. In this period many laws have passed; as the bill of rights, the toleration act, the act of settlement with its conditions, the act for uniting England with Scotland, under the title of Great Britain, and recently Great Britain with Ireland, and some others: which have asserted our liberties in more clear and emphatical terms; have regulated the succession of the crown by parliament, as the exigencies of religious and civil freedom required; have confirmed, and exemplified, the doctrine of resistance, when the executive magistrate endeavours to subvert the constitution; have maintained the superiority of the laws above the king, by pronouncing his dispensing power to be illegal; have indulged tender consciences with every religious liberty, consistent with the safety of the state; have established triennial, since turned into septennial, elections of members to serve in parliament; have excluded certain officers from the house of commons; have restrained the king's pardon from obstructing parliamentary impeachments; have imparted to all the lords an equal right of trying their fellow peers; have regulated trials for high treason; have afforded our posterity a hope that corruption of blood may one day be abolished and forgotten; have (by the desire of his present majesty) set bounds to the civil list, and placed the administration of that revenue in hands that are accountable to parliament; and have (by the like desire) made the judges completely independent of the king, his ministers, and his successors. Yet, though these provisions have, in appearance and nominally, reduced the strength of the executive power to a much lower ebb than in the preceding period; if on the other hand we throw into the opposite scale (what perhaps the immoderate reduction of the antient prerogative may have rendered in some degree necessary) the vast acquistion of force, arising from the riot act, and the annual expedience of a standing army; and the vast acquisition of personal attachment, arising from the magnitude of the national debt, and the manner of levying those yearly millions that are appropriated to pay the interest; we shall find that the crown has gra-

* The point of time at which Sir William Blackstone fixed this theoretical perfection of our public law, is the year 1679; after the habeas corpus act was passed, and that for licensing the press had expired; though the years which immediately followed it were times of great practical oppression. 1 *Black*. 439.

dually and imperceptibly, gained almost as much in influence, as it has apparently lost in prerogative. 4 *Black.* 440.

The chief alterations of moment (for the time would fail me to descend to *minutiæ*) in the administration of private justice during this period, are the solemn recognition of the law of nations with respect to the rights of embassadors: the cutting off by the statute for the amendment of the law, a vast number of excrescences, that in process of time had sprung out of the practical part of it: the protection of corporate rights by the improvements in writs of *mandamus*, and informations in nature of *quo warranto*: the regulations of trials by jury, and the admitting witnesses for prisoners upon oath: the farther restraints upon alienation of lands in mortmain: the annihilation of the terrible judgment of *peine fort et dure*: the extension of the benefit of clergy, by abolishing the pedantic criterion of reading: the counterbalance to this mercy, by the vast increase of capital punishment: the new and effectual methods for the speedy recovery of rents: the improvements which have been made in ejectments for the trying of titles: the introduction and establishment of paper credit, by indorsements upon bills and notes, which have shewn the legal possiblity and convenience (which our ancestors so long doubted) of assigning a chose in action: the translation of all legal proceedings into the English language: the erection of courts of conscience for recovering small debts, and (which is much the better plan) the reformation of county courts; the great system of marine jurisprudence, of which the foundations have been laid, by clearly developing the principles on which policies of insurance are founded, and by happily applying those principles to particular cases: and, lastly, the liberality of sentiment, which (though late) has now taken possession of our courts of common law, and induced them to adopt (where facts can be clearly ascertained) the same principles of redress as have prevailed in our courts of equity, from the time that lord Nottingham presided there; and this, not only where specially impowered by particular statutes, (as in case of bonds, mortgages, and set offs,) but by extending the remedial influence of the equitable writ of trespass on the case, according to its primitive institution by king Edward the first, to almost every instance of injustice not remedied by any other process. These, are all the material alterations that have happened with respect to private justice, in the course of the present century. 4 *Black.* 441, 2.

Thus, therefore, hath the learned commentator endeavoured to delineate some rude outlines of a plan for the history of our laws and liberties; from their first rise, and gradual progress among our British and Saxon ancestors, till their total eclipse at the Norman conquest; from which they have gradually emerged, and risen to the perfection they now enjoy, at different periods of time. For the fundamental maxims and rules of the law, which regard the rights of persons, and the rights of things, the private injuries that may be offered to both, and the crimes which affect the public, have been and are every day improving, and are now fraught with the accumulated wisdom of ages: that the forms of administering justice came to perfection under Edward the first; and have not been much varied, nor always for the better, since: that our religious liberties were fully established at the reformation: but that the recovery of our civil and political liberties was a work of longer time; they not being thoroughly and completely regained, till after the restoration of king Charles, nor fully and explicitly acknowledged and defined, till the era of the revolution. Of a constitution so wisely contrived, so strongly raised, and so highly finished, it is hard to speak with that praise, which is justly and severely its due: but it has defects, chiefly arising from the decays of time, or the rage of unskilful improvements in later ages. To sustain, to repair, to beautify this noble pile, is a charge intrusted principally to the nobility, and such gentlemen of the kingdom as are delegated by their country to parliament. The protection of the liberty of Britain is a duty which they owe to themselves, who enjoy it; to their ancestors, who transmitted it down; and to their posterity, who will claim at their hands this, the best birthright, and noblest inheritance of mankind. 4 *Black.* 443.

CONSTRUCTIVE TREASON. By the stat. 25 *Ed.* 3. *c.* 2. and stat. 39 & 40 *Geo.* 3. *c.* 93, treason is defined, to prevent the subject from becoming condemned for constructive treason. See title TREASON.

CONSUETUDINARIUS, a ritual or book, containing the rites and forms of divine offices, or the customs of abbies and monasteries. *Cowel. Blount.*

CONSUETUDINIBUS A SERVICIIS, is a writ of right close, which lies against the tenant that deforceth his lord of the rent or service due to him. *Reg. Orig.* 159. *F.N.B.* 151.

CONSUL, (Lat.) in our law books signifies an earl. *Bract. lib*, 1. *c.* 8. *Blount.*

At this day we have consuls abroad, whose duty it is to take care of the affairs and interests of merchants, in foreign kingdoms. They are appointed by the king.

CONSULTA ECCLESIA, a church full, or provided for, according to Cowel.

CONSULTATION, (*consultatio*) is a writ whereby a cause being removed by prohibition from the ecclesiastical court, to the king's court, is returned thither again; for if the judges of the king's court, upon comparing the libel with the suggestion of the party, find the suggestion false, or not proved, and therefore the cause to be wrongfully called from the ecclesiastical court, then upon this consultation or deliberation they decree it to be returned: whereupon the writ in this case obtained is called a consultation, and is in nature of a *procedendo*. *Reg. Orig.* 44

CONTEMPT, (*contemptus*) is a disobedience to the rules and orders of a court, which hath power to punish such offence; and one may be imprisoned *instanter* for a contempt done in court; but not for a contempt out of court, or a private abuse. *Cro. Eliz.* 689. But for a contempt out of court, an attachment may be granted, to bring in the offender to answer on interrogatories, and if he cannot acquit himself, he shall according to the nature of the case be fined or imprisoned. 1 *Lill.* 305. *Dyer*, 128, 177. 1 *Bulst.* 85. 12 *Rep.* 86. 4 *Black. Com.* 280.

CONTENEMENT, (*contenementum*) is said to signify a man's countenance or credit, which he hath together with, and by reason of, his freehold. But it is more properly that, which is necessary for the support and maintenance of men, agreeable to their several qualities, or states of life: and seems to be freehold land, which lieth to a man's tenement, or dwelling-house, that is in his own occupation. *Cowel. Blount.*

CONTINGENT LEGACY. If a legacy be left to any one, when he attains, or if he attains the age of twenty-one, it is contingent, and if he dies before that time, it is lapsed. *Dyer*, 59. 1 *Eq. Cas. Abr.* 295. But a legacy to one, to be paid when he attains the age of twenty-one years, is a vested legacy, an interest which commences in *præsenti*, although it be *solvendum in futuro:* and if the legatee dies before that age, his representatives shall receive it out of the testator's personal estate, at the same time it would have become payable, in case the legatee had lived. 2 *Black. Com.* 513.

CONTINGENT REMAINDER, contingent or executory remainders (whereby no present interest passes) are where the estate in remainder is limited to take effect, either to a dubious and uncertain person, or upon a dubious and uncertain event; so that the particular or intermediate estate may chance to be determined, and the remainder never take effect. 2 *Black. Com.* 169.

CONTINGENT USE, is a use limited in a conveyance of land, which may, or may not happen to vest, according to the contingency expressed in the limitation of such use: a use in contingency is such which by possibility may happen in possession, reversion or remainder. 1 *Rep.* 121. A remainder contingent is said to be an estate vested; but on such remainder in executory devises, the estate descends till the contingency happens, and nothing is vested till then. 1 *Vent.* 189.

CONTINUAL CLAIM, is a claim made from time to time, within every year and day, to land, or other thing, which in some respect we cannot attain without danger as if a person be disseised of land, into which, though he hath a right of entry, he dare not enter for fear of beating, &c. it behoves him to hold on his right of entry at his best opportunity, by approaching as near it as he can, once a year, as long as he lives, and to save the right of entry to his heir. *Lit. lib.* 3. *c.* 7.

Continual claim is where it is made, and repeated yearly, so as to be within a year and a day before the death of him that hath the lands; and if after he dies seised, so that his heir is in by descent, yet he that makes the claim may enter, &c. but if no claim be made, then the entry of the person disseised, &c. is taken away. 32 *H.* 8. *cap.* 33.

Though by the statute the disseisor is to have peaceable possession for five years, without entry or continual claim, for a descent on his death, to take away the entry of the disseisee, or his heir; after the five years, the disseisee is to make continual claim, as before the statute: the feoffee of a disseisor, abators, &c. are out of the statute. As to this claim, though the tenant die within the year and day, and it be but once made, it shall preserve the entry of him that maketh it: and if the ancestor claim, and the disseisor die, and then the ancestor dieth, now his heir may enter: but if an ancestor or predecessor, make a continual claim, and dieth, and the son or successor make no continual claim, and within the year and day after the claim made by the ancestor, the disseisor dies; this shall take away the entry of the son or successor, for the descent was cast in his time. *Co. Lit.* 250, 251.

If there be tenant for life, remainder for life, the remainder in fee, and the tenant for life alien in fee: if he in remainder for life maketh continual claim, before the dying seised of the alienee, and after the alienee die seised, and after that the remainder man for life dieth before any entry made by him: in this case he in remainder in fee shall have benefit by the claim of tenant for life, and he may enter upon the heir of the alienee, &c. *Lit. Sect.* 416.

This claim shall not avoid a descent, unless it be made by him that hath title to enter, and in whose life the dying seised was: and so it is for the continual claim of a tenant for life, to give him in remainder advantage, except the disseisor, &c. die in the life-time of tenant for life. *Co. Lit.* 250. 2 *Black. Com.* 316. 3 *Black.* 175.

CONTINUANCE, is the continuing of a cause in court, by an entry upon the records there for that purpose. *Kitch.* 262. 3 *Lev.* 431. 2 *Danv. Abr.* 150. *Cro. Jac.* 316, 317.

CONTINUANDO, is a word used in a special declaration of trespass, when the plaintiff would recover damages for several trespasses in the same action: and to avoid multiplicity of suits, a man may in one action of trespass recover damages for many trespasses, laying the first to be done with a *continuando* to the whole time, in which the rest of the trespasses were done; which is in this form, *continuando transgressionem prædictam*, &c. *a prædicto die*, &c. *usque talem diem*, including the last trespass. *Terms de Ley*.

CONTRABAND GOODS, (from *contra*, and the Ital. *bando*, an edict or proclamation) are those which are prohibited by act of parliament, or the king's proclamation to be imported into, or exported out of this into any other nation.

CONTRACAUSATOR, a criminal, or one prosecuted for a crime. *Cowel. Blount.*

CONTRACT, (*contractus*) is an agreement between two or more persons, with a lawful consideration or cause. *West. Symb. part* 1.

And every contract doth imply in itself an assumpsit in law, to perform the same; for a contract would be to no purpose, if there were no means to enforce the performance thereof. 1 *Lill. Abr.* 308.

But all contracts are to be certain, perfect, and compleat: for an agreement to give so much for a thing as it shall be reasonably worth, is void for uncertainty: so a promise to pay money in a short time, &c. or to give so much, if he likes the thing when he sees it. *Dyer*, 91. 1 *Bulst.* 92.

And by the statute of frauds, 29 *Car.* 2. c. 3. "all contracts, not to be performed in "a year, are to be in writing, signed by the "party, or no action may be brought on "them." However, if no day is set, or the time is uncertain, they may be good without it. And by the same statute, "no contract "for the sale of goods for 10*l.* or upwards, "shall be good, unless the buyer receive "part of the goods sold; or gives something "in earnest to bind the contract; or some "note thereof be made in writing, signed by "the person charged with the contract, &c.

CONTRAFACTION, (*contrafactio*) a counterfeiting; as *contrafactio sigilli regis*, counterfeiting the king's seal. *Cowel. Blount.*

CONTRA FORMAM COLLATIONIS, is a writ that lay where a man had given lands in perpetual alms, to any of the old houses of religion, as to an abbot and convent, or to the warden or master of any hospital and his convent, to find certain poor men with necessaries, and do divine service, &c. If they aliened the land, to the disherison of the house and church, then the donor or his heirs, should bring this writ to recover the lands. It was had against the abbot or his successor; not against the alienee, though he were tenant of the land: and was founded upon the statute of *Westm.* 2. c. 1. *Reg. Orig.* 238. *F. N. B.* 210.

CONTRA FORMAM FEOFFAMENTI, a writ that lies for the heir of a tenant enfeoffed of certain lands or tenements, by charter of feoffment from a lord to make certain services and suits to his court, who is afterwards distrained for more services than are mentioned in the charter. *Reg. Orig.* 176. *Old Nat. Br.* 162.

CONTRA FORMAM STATUTI, is the usual conclusion of every indictment, &c. laid on an offence created by statute.

CONTRAMANDATIO PLACITI, signifies a respiting or giving a defendant further time to answer; or a countermand of what was formerly ordered. *Leg. H.* 1. *c.* 59. *Cowel. Blount.*

CONTRAMANDATUM, is said to be a lawful excuse which the defendant in a suit by attorney alegeth for himself, to shew that the plaintiff hath no cause of complaint. *Cowel. Blount.*

CONTRAPOSITIO, a plea or answer. *Ibid.*

CONTRARIENTS. In the reign of *Ed.* 2. the earl of Lancaster taking part with the barons against the king, it was not thought fit, in respect of their great power, to call them rebels or traitors, but contrarients. *Ibid.*

CONTRA TENERE, to withhold. *Ibid.*

CONTRIBULES, *contribunales*, kindred or cousins. *Lamb.* 75. *Cowel. Blount.*

CONTRIBUTION, (*contributio*) is where every one pays his share, or contributes his part to any thing. One parcener shall have contribution against another; one heir have contribution against another heir, in equal degree: and one purchaser have contribution against another. Also conusors in a statute shall be equally charged, and not one of them solely extended. 3 *Rep.* 12, 13, &c.

Where goods are cast into the sea, for the safe-guard of a ship, or other goods, &c. aboard in a tempest; there is a contribution among merchants, towards the loss of the owners. 32 *H.* 8. *c.* 14.

CONTRIBUTIONE FACIENDA, is a writ which anciently lay where there were tenants in common, bound to do one thing, and one was put to the whole burden; or who jointly held a mill *pro indiviso*, and took the profits equally, and the mill falling into decay, one of them would not repair the mill; then the other was to have a writ to compel him to contribute to the reparations. And if there were three coparceners of land, that owed suit to the lord's court, and the eldest performed the whole; then she might have this writ to compel the others to make their contribution. So where one suit was required for land, and that land being sold to divers persons, suit was demanded of them all, or some of them by distress, as entirely as if all the land were still in one. *Reg. Orig.* 175. *F. N. B.* 162.

CONTROLLER, (Fr. *contrerolleur*, Lat. *contrarotulator*) is an officer having the supervision or controul of public accounts, &c.

And we have divers officers of this name; as controller of the king's household; of the navy; of the customs; of the excise; of the mint, &c.

CONTROVER, (*controuveur*) signifies in our law, one that of his own head devises or invents false news. 2 *Inst.* 227.

CONVENABLE, (Fr.) agreeable. 27 *Ed.* 3. *c.* 21. See *Covenable*.

CONVENIENT, (*conveniens*) *non solum quod licet sed quod est conveniens est considerandum, nihil quod est inconveniens est licitum.* 1 *Inst.* 66.

CONVENT, (*conventus*) signifies the fraternity of an abbey or priory: as *societas* doth the number of fellows in a college. *Bract. lib.* 2. *c.* 35.

CONVENTICLE, (*conventiculum*) a private assembly or meeting for the exercise of religion. And by 22 *Car.* 2. *cap.* 1. if any persons of the age of sixteen years, subjects of this kingdom, shall be present at any conventicle, where there are five or more assembled, they shall be fined 5*s.* for the first offence, and 10*s.* for the second; and persons preaching incur a penalty of 20*l.* Also suffering a meeting to be held in a house, &c. is liable to 20*l.* penalty. Justices of peace have power to enter such houses, and seize persons assembled, &c. And if they neglect their duty, they shall forfeit 100*l.* And if any constable, &c. know of such meetings, and do not inform a justice of peace or chief magistrate, he shall forfeit 5*l.* But the 1 *W.* & *M.* *c.* 18. ordains that protestant dissenters not denying the Trinity shall be exempted from the penalties: though if they meet in a house, with the doors locked, barred, or bolted, such dissenters shall have no benefit from that statute. Officers of the government, &c. present at any conventicle, at which there shall be ten persons, if the royal family be not prayed for in express words, shall forfeit 40*l.* and be disabled. *Stat.* 10 *Ann. c.* 2. See *Papists.*

CONVENTIO, is a word used in ancient law-pleadings, for an agreement or covenant, &c. *Cowel. Blount.*

CONVENTIONE, is a writ that lies for the breach of any covenant in writing, whether real or personal: and it is called a writ of covenant. *Reg. Orig.* 115. *F. N. B.* 145.

CONVENTION, is properly where a parliament is assembled, but no act is passed, or bill signed. See *Abdication.*

CONVENTION PARLIAMENT, the lords and commons convened, on the abdication of king James II. Anno 1689, and who settled king William and queen Mary on the throne, formed what was called the Convention.

CONVENTUALS, religious men united together in a convent or religious house. *Cowel.*

CONVENTUAL CHURCH, is a church that consists of regular clerks, professing some order of religion; or of dean and chapter, or other societies of spiritual men. *Cowel. Blount.*

CONVERSION, is where a person finding or having the goods of another in his possession, converts them to his own use, without the consent of the owner, and for which the proprietor may maintain an action of trover and conversion against him. And refusal to restore goods is, *prima facie*, sufficient evidence of a conversion, though it does not amount to a conversion. 10 *Rep.* 56. 3 *Black. Com.* 152.

CONVERSOS. The reformed Jews here in England were formally called conversos, because they were converted to the Christian religion. And king *Hen.* 3. built an house for them, called *Domus Conversorum*, in London, and allowed them a competent provision or subsistence for their lives; the Jews however, being afterwards banished, king *Ed.* 3. in the 51st year of his reign, gave this house for the keeping of the rolls; and it is said to be the same which is at this time enjoyed by the master of the rolls. *Blount.*

CONVEYANCE *of lands.* The conveyance of lands by feoffment, and livery and seisin, was formerly the general conveyance at common law; but after the statute of uses, it became the practice to make a lease for years upon a valuable consideration, and afterwards execute a release, which release operates upon the lease without an actual entry by the lessee so as to pass the reversion: because the statute executed the lease, and raises an use presently to the lessee: and it is said that Serjeant Moor was the first who practised this way. 2 *Mod.* 251, 252.

The most common conveyances now in use are deeds of gift, bargain and sale, feoffment with livery and seisin, lease and release, fines and recoveries, settlements to uses, &c. 2 *Lev.* 225. A feoffment without livery and seisin, will not enure as a grant; but where made in consideration of a marriage, &c. it has been adjudged, that it did enure as a covenant to stand seised to uses. 2 *Lev.* 213.

CONVICT, (*convictus*) is he that is found guilty of an offence by verdict of a jury. *Staund. P. C.* 186. And for the consequences of a conviction, see *Attainder.*

CONVICTION, (*summary*). A conviction, in the sense in which it is here used, is a record of the summary proceedings upon any penal statute, before one or more justices of the peace, or other persons duly authorized, in a case where the offender has been convicted and sentenced. *Boscaw.* 7. *Wms. Jus. tit. Conv.*

This mode was first introduced for the greater ease of the subject, by doing him speedy justice, and by not harrassing the freeholders with frequent and troublesome attendances to try every minute offence. 4 *Black. Com.* 280.

But such summary convictions are unknown at the common law, there being no intervention of a jury, and therefore this authority being special, and in restraint of the common law, it must appear on the face of the proceedings, to have been strictly pursued according to the letter of the act by which it was created; that the justice has jurisdiction in the case, and that rules similar to those adopted by the common law, in criminal prosecutions, and founded in natural justice have been observed; unless the statute does (as it doth in some instances, in giving particular forms of conviction) expressly dispense with the necessity of stating them. *Wms. Jus. tit. Con.*

And it is reasonable that these convictions should be construed with strictness, because they must be taken to be true against the defendant. 1 *Bur.* 613.

In these convictions, it is necessary that there should be, 1st, an information or charge against the defendant; 2dly, a summons or notice of such information in order that he may make his defence; 3dly, his appearance or non-appearance; 4thly, his defence or confession; 5thly, the evidence against him; and 6thly, the judgment on adjudication against him, and in general all those matters must be particularly set forth in the record of the conviction. *Wms. Jus. tit. Con.*

But for the ease of the magistrate this precise statement is in many instances dispensed with, by the statute which imposes the penalty, by allowing some concise form of conviction to be drawn up, and where an act directs that all convictions shall be made out *in the form* OR *to the effect following*, giving a particular form; a conviction containing all the substantial parts of the form prescribed will be good, although it be not in the express words thereof, or may contain something more than is directed, 4 *Ter. Rep.* 767. But where a form of conviction is prescribed by statute, it is in general *most safe* to adopt the *very words* used, and if the justices do vary therefrom, the conviction must be drawn up agreeable to the express provisions of the act. 6 *Ter. Rep.* 538.

Also in all instances convictions ought to be drawn up in form, and returned to the sessions to be there recorded, whether the defendant appeals or not, or whether an appeal is or is not given, that the crown may not be deprived of its share of the forfeitures. 2 *Ter. Rep.* 285.

CONVICT RECUSANT, according to the statutes. See *Recusants.*

CONVIVIUM, signifies the same thing among the laiety, as *procuratio* doth with the clergy, viz. When the tenant by reason of his tenure is bound to provide meat and drink for his lord once or oftener in the year. *Blount.*

CONVOCATION, (*convocatio*) is the assembly of all the clergy, to consult of ecclesiastical matters in time of parliament; and as there are two houses of parliament, so there are two houses of convocation; the one called the higher or upper house, where the archbishop and all the bishops sit severally by themselves: and the other the lower house of convocation: where all the rest of the clergy sit, i. e. all deans and archdeacons, one proctor for every chapter, and two proctors for all the clergy of each diocese, making in the whole number one hundred and sixty-six persons. Each convocation house hath a prolocutor, chosen from among themselves, and that of the lower house is presented to the bishops, &c.

The Archbishop of Canterbury is the president of the convocation, and prorogues and dissolves it by mandate from the king. The convocation exercises jurisdiction in making of canons, with the king's assent; for by the *stat.* 25 *H.* 8. *c.* 18, the convocation is not only to be assembled by the king's writ, but the canons are to have the royal assent; they have the examining and censuring of heretical and schismatical books, and persons, &c. But appeal lies to the king in Chancery, or to his delegates. 4 *Inst.* 322. 2 *Rol. Abr.* 225. The clergy called to the convocation, and their servants, &c. have the same privileges as members of parliament. *Stat.* 8 *H.* 6. *c.* 1.

CONUSANCE OF PLEAS, a privilege that a city or town hath to hold pleas. *Cowel. Blount.*

CONUSANT, (Fr. *connoisant*) knowing or understanding. *Co. Lit.* 159.

COOPERTIO, the head or branches of a tree cut down, though *coopertio arborum* is rather the bark of timber trees felled, and the chumps and broken wood. *Cowel.*

COOPERTURA, a thicket or covert of wood. *Chart de Foresta, cap.* 12. *Cowel. Blount.*

COPARCENERS, (*participes*) otherwise called *parceners*, are by law the issue female which in default of heirs male, come in equality, and have equal portions in the lands and inheritance of their ancestors. *Bract. lib.* 2. *cap.* 30.

COPARTNERSHIP, a copartnership is where two or more persons agree to stand share and share alike, or in some other proportion as to profit and loss, in any trade or bargain. See *Partners.*

COPE, is a custom or tribute due to the king, or lord of the soil, out of the lead mines in some part of Derbyshire. *Cowel. Blount.*

COPIA LIBELLI DELIBERANDA, is a writ that lies where a man cannot get the copy of a libel at the hand of a judge ecclesiastical, to have the same delivered to him. *Reg. Orig.* 51.

COPPA, a cop or cock of grass, hay or corn divided into tithable portions, as the tenth cock, &c. *Cowel. Blount.*

COPY, (*copia*) is in a legal sense the transcript of an original writing; as the copy of a patent, of a charter, deed, will, or the like; for how far copies are admitted as evidence, see *Evidence.*

COPYHOLD, (*tenura per copiam rotuli curiæ*) is a tenure for which the tenant hath nothing to shew but the copy of the rolls, made by the steward of the lord's court, on such tenant's being admitted to any parcel of land or tenement belonging to the manor. 4 *Rep.* 25. It is called base tenure, because held at the will of the lord: but though they are held by copy, yet are they a kind of freehold; *Kitch.* 81. However copyhold land cannot be made at this day: for the pillars of a copyhold estate are, that it hath been demised time out of mind by copy of court-roll; and that the tenements are parcel of or within the manor. 1 *Inst.* 58. 4 *Rep.* 24. A copyhold tenant had originally in judgment of law, but an estate at will; yet custom so established his estate, that by the custom of the manor it was descendible, and his heirs inherited it: and therefore the estate of the copyholder is not merely *ad voluntatem domini*, but *ad voluntatem domini secundum consuetudinem manerii*; so that the custom of the manor is the life of copyhold estates, for without a custom, or if copyholders break their custom, they are subject to the will of the lord: and as a copyhold is created by custom, so it is guided by custom. 4 *Rep.* 21.

Copyholds descend according to the rules and maxims of the common law, (unless in particular manors, where there are contrary customs of great antiquity); but such customary inheritances shall not be assets; to charge the heir in action of debt, &c. 3 *Rep.* 21. 1 *Vent.* 165. Copyholders hold their estates free from charges of dower, being created by custom, which is paramount to the title of dower. 4 *Rep.* 24. But by particular custom, there may be dower and tenancy by the curtesy. *Cro. Eliz.* 361. So by custom a copyhold may be entailed, and by custom the entail may be cut off by surrender. 1 *Inst.* 60.

So also by custom a recovery may be suffered of a copyhold: but a fine and recovery at common law will not destroy a copyhold estate: because common law assurances do not work upon the assurance of the copyhold.

And by 47 *Geo.* 3, *sess.* 2. *c.* 8, persons may appoint attornies for surrendering copyholds or customary estates, of which common recoveries are intended to be suffered.

Also copyholders may according to the custom of some manors, entail copyhold lands, and bar the entails and remainders, by committing a forfeiture, as making lease without licence, &c. and then the lord is to make three proclamations, and seize the copyhold, after which the lands are granted to the copyholder, and his heirs, &c. 2 *Danv. Abr.* 191. *Sid.* 314.

Copyholders shall neither implead nor be impleaded for their tenements by writ, but by plaint in the nature of a *real* action in the lord's court held within the manor: and if on such plaint, erroneous judgment be given, no writ of false judgment lies, but petition to the lord in nature of a writ of false judgment, wherein errors are to be assigned, and remedy given according to law. *Co. Lit.* 60. 1 *Brown.* 121.

But it is now the practice, (except where the statute of limitations has run against this possessory action,) to bring an ejectment to recover the possession of copyholds: for the defendant by the rule obliges himself to confess lease, entry, and ouster, and the title only can come in question on the trial. But the lessor of the plaintiff, before he brings his ejectment, should be admitted; unless he be the heir at law, in which case, if the ancestor, through whom he claims was admitted, and in possession, actual admission previous to the bringing the ejectment is not absolutely necessary.

A manor is lost when there are no customary tenants or copyholders: and if a copyhold comes into the hands of the lord in fee, and the lord leases it for one year, or half a year, or for any certain time, it can never be granted by copy after; but if the lord keeps the copyhold for a long time in his hand, it is no impediment but that he may after grant it again by copy. 2 *Danv. Abr.* 176, 177. And if a copyholder in fee accepts of a lease, grant, or confirmation of the same land from the lord, this determines his copyhold estate, for it is a surrender in law of his copyhold. 2 *Cro.* 16. *Cro. Jac.* 253. 3 *Leon.* 329.

A copyholder cannot convey or transfer his copyhold estate to another, otherwise than by surrender; which is the yielding up of the land by the tenant to the lord, according to the custom of the manor, to the use of him that is to have the estate. And if a lord of the manor for the time being, take a surrender, and before admittance dieth, the next lord shall be compelled to make admittance according to the surrender. *Co. Lit.* 59.

All grants of copyhold estates are to be according to the custom of the manor, and rents and services customary must be reserved; for what acts of the lord in granting copyholds are not confirmed by custom, but only strengthened by the power and interest of the lord, have no longer duration than the lord's estate continueth. *Comp. Court. Keeper.* 421.

And in voluntary admittances, if the lord admits any one contrary to custom, it shall not bind his heir or successor. 1 *Nels. Abr.* 493.

The lord of a manor may himself grant a copyhold estate at any place out of the manor; but the steward cannot grant a copyhold at a court held out of the manor. 4 *Rep.* 26. Though the steward may take surrenders out of the manor, as well as the lord. 2 *Danv. Abr.* 181.

In admittances, in court, upon voluntary grants, the lord is proprietor; in admittances upon surrender, the lord is not proprietor of the lands, but only a necessary instrument of conveyance; and in admittances by descent the lord is a mere instrument, not being necessary to strengthen the heir's title, but only to give the lord his fine. 4 *Rep.* 21, 22.

On surrender of a copyhold, the surrenderor or person making the same, continues tenant till the admittance of the surrenderee, and the surrenderee may not enter upon the lands, or surrender before admittance, for he hath no estate till then: though it is otherwise of the heir by descent, who is in by course of law, and the custom casts the possession upon him. *Comp. Court Keep.* 436. A surrender is not of any effect until admittance, and yet the surrenderee cannot be defrauded of the benefit of the surrender; for the surrenderor cannot pass away the land to another, or make it subject to any other incumbrances; and if the lord refuse the surrenderee admittance, he is compellable in Chancery, or by *mandamus. Comp. Cop. sect.* 39. And a grantee hath no interest vested in him till he is admitted; but admittance of a copyholder for life is an admittance of him in remainder; for they are but one estate; and the remainder-man may, after the death of tenant for life, surrender without admittance. 3 *Lev.* 308. *Cro. El.* 504.

Where a widow's estate is created by custom, that shall be an admittance in law: and her estate arising out of that of her husband's, his admittance is the admittance of her. *Hut.* 18. And she who hath a widow's estate by the custom of the manor, upon the death of her husband, need not pay a fine to the lord for the estate; for this is only a branch of the husband's. *Hob.* 181. For after the death of the baron the law casts the estate upon the wife, so that she shall have it before admittance, &c. 2 *Danv.* 184. But if a copyholder in fee surrenders to the use of another, and then dies; the surrenderee should have the land, free from the *free bench* or estate of the wife; because the wife's title thereto, doth not commence till after the death of her husband; but the plaintiff's title begins with the surrender; and the admittance relates to that, and it is the husband's dying seized only, which gives the widow a title. 1 *Inst.* 59. 1 *Salk.* 185. 4 *Mod. Rep.* 452, 453.

The widow's title commenceth not by the marriage; if it did, then the husband could do nothing in his life-time to prejudice it: but it is plain he may alien or extinguish his right, so as to bind the estate of the widow: the free bench grows out of the estate of the husband.

Admittances are never by attorney, for the tenant ought to do fealty: though surrenders are oftentimes by attorney. 2 *Danv.* 189.

The intent of surrenders is, that the lord may not be a stranger to his tenant, and the alteration of the estate. And if any person would devise a copyhold estate, he cannot do it by his will; but he must surrender to the use of his last will and testament; and in his will declare his intent. *Comp. Cop. sect.* 36, 39. And where a copyholder surrenders to the use of his will, the lands do not pass by the will, but by the surrender; the will being only declaratory to the uses of the surrender. 1 *Bulst.* 200. But in case of a will, the Chancery will supply the defect of a surrender, in the behalf of children, if not to disinherit the eldest son; and for the benefit of creditors, where a copyhold estate is charged by will with the payment of debts, for though there is no surrender to those uses, it will be good in equity. 4 *Rep.* 25. 1 *Salk.* 187. 3 *Salk.* 84. Yet it is held, that equity shall not supply the want of such surrender in favour of a grandchild; or bastard, who is not considered as a child, or a wife against the heir, nor in behalf of legatees; but where the surrender is refused by the lord, a will of copyhold may be sufficient without it. *Abr. Cas. Eq.* 122, 124.

A *cestui que trust* may devise an interest in land, &c. without surrender, and if copyhold lands are in mortgage, the mortgagor can dispose of the equity of redemption by will, without any surrender made; because he hath at that time no estate in the land, whereof to make a surrender. *Preced. Canc.* 320, 322.

By the general custom of copyhold estates, copyholders may surrender in court, and need not allege any particular custom to warrant it; but where they surrender out of court, into the hands of the lord by customary tenants, &c. custom must be pleaded. 9 *Rep.* 75. 1 *Rol. Abr.* 500. And surrenders out of court are to be presented at the next court; for it is not an effectual surrender till presented in court. Where a copyholder in fee surrenders out of court, and dies before it is presented; yet the surrender being presented at the next court, will stand good, and *cestui que use* shall be admitted; so if *cestui que use* dies before it is presented, his heir shall be admitted.

But if the surrender be not presented at the next court it is void. *Co. Lit.* 62. 2 *Danv.* 188.

Tenants refusing to make presentments, are compellable in the lord's court. And by surrender of copyhold lands to the use of a mortgagee, the lands are bound in equity, though the surrender be not presented at the next court. 2 *Salk.* 449. When a copyholder surrenders upon condition, and this is presented absolutely, the presentment is void; but where a conditional surrender is presented; and the steward omits entering the condition, on proof thereof the condition shall not be avoided; but the rolls shall be amended. 4 *Rep.* 25. A copyholder may surrender to the use of another, reserving rent, with a condition of re-entry for non-payment, and in default of payment may re-enter. *Ibid.* 21.

Fines are paid to the lord on admittances, and may be either certain by custom, or uncertain; a fine certain is to be paid presently on the admission; but if it be uncertain, the copyholder is to have notice and time to pay it. 4 *Rep.* 27. 13 *Rep.* 2.

Uncertain fines must be reasonable, such as a year, or at the utmost a year and a half's value which has been deemed a reasonable fine, but two years unreasonable. These fines are not due until after admission, and if not paid the lord may have his action of debt for the same, in which their reasonableness may be tried; or he may by custom in some places distrain.

An heriot is a duty to the lord, at the death of the tenant, and is the best beast or goods, found in the possession of the tenant deceased. *Plowd.* 96.

Relief is a sum of money which every copyholder in fee, or freeholder of a manor pays to the lord, on the death of his ancestor; and is generally a year's profit of his land. *Ibid.*

Services signify any duty whatsoever accruing unto the lord from tenants: and are not only annual and accidental; but corporal, as homage, fealty, &c. *Comp. Court Keep.* 7, 8, 9, &c.

And for heriots, reliefs, &c. the lord may distrain or bring action of debt. *Plowd.* 96.

Copyholds escheat, and are forfeited to the lord; either where the lands fall into the hands of the lord for want of an heir to inherit them; or where the copyholder commits felony, &c. But before the lord can enter on an estate escheated, the homage jury ought to present it. *Ibid.*

Upon the descent of any copyhold of inheritance, the heir by the general custom is bound upon three solemn proclamations, made at three several courts, to come in and be admitted to his copyhold; or if he faileth therein, this failure worketh a forfeiture.

And by *stat.* 9 *Geo.* 1. *c.* 29. "On default "of infant and feme coverts appearing "to be admitted tenants to copyhold "lands, the lord or his steward, may "name a person to be guardian or "attorney for them, and by such guardian "&c. admit them, and if the usual fine "be not paid in three months, being de- "manded in writing, the lord may enter "on the copyhold, and receive the rents, "&c. till the fine is paid with all charges. "And by this statute no infant or feme "covert shall forfeit any copyhold lands "for their neglect to come to court to be "admitted, or refusal to pay any fine."

The general custom of copyholds allows a copyholder to make a lease for one year of his copyhold estate and no more, without incurring a forfeiture. *Moor.* 184. *Salk.* 186. But if there is a custom to warrant it, a copyholder may make a lease for years, without forfeiture; so also with the licence of the lord, a copyholder may make a lease for years. *Cro. Jac.* 300. *Cro. Car.* 7. 4 *Rep.* 21 *to* 25.

If copyholder *for life* cuts down timber trees, the lord may take them, and it is a forfeiture of his copyhold: though such copyholder may take house-boot, hedge-boot, and plough-boot upon his copyhold, of common right, as a thing incident to the grant; if he be not restrained by custom, to take them by the assignment of the lord or his bailiff. But if under-lessee for years of a copyholder cut down timber, this shall not be a forfeiture of the copyhold estate, but the lord is put to his action on the case against the lessee. 1 *Bulst.* 150. *Style.* 233.

But the copyholder for life, committing waste, shall not forfeit the estate of him in remainder. *Cro. Eliz.* 880. A copyholder committing waste voluntary or permissive, that is a forfeiture: voluntary, as if he pull down any house, though built by himself, lop trees and fell them, plough up meadow, whereby the ground is made worse, &c. Permissive, if he suffer the roof of the house to let in rain, or the house to fall, or if he permit his meadow ground to be surrounded with water, so that it becomes marshy, or his arable land to be thus surrounded and become unprofitable, &c. these and the like are forfeitures. See 2 *Danv. Abr.* 192, 193, 196, &c. 1 *Nels. Abr.* 509, 510, &c. But it must be by his wilful default.

The court of Chancery will not relieve a copyhold tenant against a forfeiture, on committing voluntary waste by wilfully cutting down timber trees, or the like. But it doth for permissive waste, arising by neglect and laches, and when the estate is forfeited for non-payment of rent, a fine, or such things, where a value may be set on them, and compensation made the lord, the tenant may be relieved; for there the land is but in nature of a security for those sums. *Preced. Chanc.* 569, 572.

If a lease for years be made without licence, and not warranted by custom, and it be found to be a forfeiture at law, equity has nothing to do with it, to give any remedy.

COPYRIGHT, was by the common law of England, a perpetual and inviolable right vested in the author of any literary composition. But the enjoyment of this right has been abridged by the statute of Queen *Ann*, and all remedy for the violation of it, is now taken away by that statute, after the expiration of the two several terms specified in the act. 4 *Burr.* 2303.

By this stat. 8 *Ann. c.* 19. (amended by 15 *Geo.* 3. *c.* 53.) it is now declared that the author and his assigns shall have the sole liberty of printing and reprinting his works for the term of 14 years *and no longer*, and hath also protected that property by additional penalties and forfeitures, (see *Books*) directing further, that if, at the end of that time, the author himself be living, the right shall then return to him for another term of the same duration.

And by 41 *Geo.* 3. (u. k.) *c.* 107. in consequence of the Irish union, provisions similar to those in the stat. of queen *Ann*, are re-enacted and extended to the whole of the united kingdom (before that time no statute was existing in Ireland to protect copyright) these provisions ase also enforced by additional remedies and increased penalties, and an action on the ease for damages is specifically given to the party injured. See *Books*.

Where an author transfers *all his right or interest* in his publication, upon his surviving the first fourteen years, the second term will result to his assignee, and not to himself. 2 *Bro.* 80; and musical compositions are within the meaning and protection of the stat. *Cowp.* 623, but the representation on the stage of a dramatic performance not printed, is not such a publication, for which the author can maintain an action as for the invasion of his rights. 5 *Ter. Rep.* 245. But no one has a right to take down a play in short hand, and to print it before it is published by the author. *Amb.* 694.

A *fair* and *bona fide* abridgment of any book is considered a new work; and however it may injure the sale of the original, yet it is not deemed in law to be a piracy or a violation of the author's copyright. 1 *Bro.* 451. 2 *Atk.* 141.

But in such productions, and also history, chronology, dictionaries, and the like, it must be left to a jury to determine whether the publication complained of is a servile copy, and imitation, or an original work upon the same subject. 1 *East.* 358.

No one but the author or his assignee hath a right to print or publish original notes, or additions to an old work, although the chief copyright may be open, and any person have the liberty of printing and publishing the original work without the notes or improvements. *Christ. n.* 6. 2 *Black.* 407.

Also no one can be prosecuted for the penalties introduced by the statutes, viz. a forfeiture of one penny, (and in some cases three pence) for every sheet, and the sheets being defaced (*see Books*) unless the work is duly entered at Stationer's hall in London, according to the directions of the several statutes now in force; but an action may be brought, or an injunction obtained in a court of equity, though the publication be not entered in the register of the Stationer's company, or the author does not prefix his name to it. 1 *Black. Rep.* 330. 7 *Ter. Rep.* 620.

CORAAGE, (*coraagium*) was a kind of extraordinary imposition, growing upon some unusual occasion, and seems to have been of certain measures of corn; for *corus tritici* is a measure of wheat. *Bract. lib.* 2. *c.* 116. *Blount.*

CORACLE, a small boat used by fishermen on the river Uske, and some parts of the river Severn, made of split sally twigs interwoven, and on that part next the water covered with leather, capable of holding only one man, on a seat in the middle.

CORAM NON JUDICE, when a cause is brought, and determined in a court, whereof the judges have not any jurisdiction; it is said to be *coram non judice*, and void. 2 *Cro.* 351.

CORBEL, a nich in the wall of a church or other structure, in which an image is placed for an ornament or superstition; the niches remain on the outside of very many churches, though the little statues and reliques were most of them broken down in the puritannical rebellion. *Paroch. Antiq.* 575.

CORD OF WOOD, is a quantity of wood eight feet long, four feet broad, and four feet high. *Cowel. Blount.*

CORDAGE, (Fr.) is a general appellation for all stuff to make ropes, and for all kind of ropes belonging to the rigging of a ship. *Cowel. Blount.*

CORDINER, from the Fr. *cordouannier*, a shoemaker; we call him vulgarly a cordwainer; and so this word is used in divers statutes.

CORDUBANARIUS, also signifies a shoemaker. *Cowel. Blount.*

CORETES, from the Brit. *cored*, pools, ponds, &c. *Du Fresne. Cowel. Blount.*

CORUM FORISFACERE, was where a person was condemned to be whipped; which was anciently the punishment of a servant. *Ibid.*

CORN, *Offences concerning corn.* By 11

Geo. 2. *c.* 22, persons using violence to hinder the buying or carrying corn, on conviction, shall be imprisoned three months, and not less than one month, within which time they are to be publicly whipped.

By 36 *Geo.* 3. *c.* 9. persons hindering the buying of corn, or seizing it on its passage to any place, are to be committed to hard labour for not exceeding three months, nor less than one. *s.* 1.

Persons convicted of such offences a second time, or destroying store houses, or carrying corn therefrom, are to be transported for seven years. *s.* 2.

The hundred where any such offence is committed may be sued for damages not exceeding 100*l.*; but no person is to recover such damages unless notice be given of the offence, and recognizance entered into to prosecute known offenders, and if any offender be convicted within a year after the offence, the hundred is not liable to make satisfaction for such damages, and no such action is to be commenced until after the year, nor unless commenced within two years after the offence. *s.* 3, 5.

This is not to abridge any law for the punishment or suppression of such offences as aforesaid. *s.* 6.

Bounties and duties.] By 44 *Geo.* 3, *c.* 109, the bounties on British corn exported shall be as follows: *s.* 3.

Wheat at or under 48*s.* per quarter, bounty, 5*s.* and for wheat, flour, biscuit, &c. 1*s.* 6*d.* per cwt. and wheat meal 1*s.* 3*d.* per cwt.

——— if above 54*s.* per quarter no export allowed.

Rye at or under 32*s.* per quarter, bounty 3*s.* and rye meal or flour 9*d.* per cwt.

——— if above 54*s.* per quarter no export allowed.

Peas and beans at or about 35*s.* per quarter, exportable without bounty.

——— if above 35*s.* per quarter, no export allowed.

Barley or malt if at or under 28*s.* per quarter, bounty 2*s.* 6*d.* or for barley, beer, or big meal, 10*d.* per cwt.

——— if above 31*s.* per quarter no export allowed.

Oats, if at or under 16*s.* per quarter, bounty 2*s.* and for oatmeal per cwt. 1*s.*

——— if above 19*s.* per quarter no export allowed.

The duties on corn imported shall be as follows:

Wheat imported from Quebec, or the British plantations in America, if under 53*s.* per quarter, high duty, 24*s.* 3*d.* per quarter, or 6*s.* 6*d.* per cwt. for meal.

——— if at or above 53*s.* but under 56*s.* per quarter, first low duty, 2*s.* 6*d.* per quarter, or 1*s.* 6*d.* per cwt. for meal.

——— if at or above 56*s.* per quarter, second low duty, 6*d.* per quarter, or 2*d.* per cwt. for meal.

Wheat, when imported from any foreign country, if under 63*s.* per quarter, high duty, 24*s.* per quarter, or 6*s.* 6*d.* per cwt. for meal.

——— if at or above 63*s.* but under 66*s.* per quarter, first low duty, 2*s.* 6*d.* per quarter, or 1*s.* 2*d.* per cwt. for meal.

——— if at or above 66*s.* per quarter, second low duty, 6*d.* per quarter, or 1s. per cwt. for meal.

And malt made of wheat prohibited.

Rye, peas and beans, imported from Quebec, or the British plantations, if under 35*s.* high duty, 22*s.* per quarter.

——— if at or above 35*s.* and under 37*s.* per quarter, first low duty, 1*s.* 6*d.*

——— if at or above 37*s.* per quarter, second low duty, 3*d.* per quarter.

——— when imported from any other foreign country, if under 42*s.* per quarter, 22*s.* per quarter.

——— if at or above 42*s.* and under 44*s.* per quarter, first low duty, 1*s.* 6*d.* per quarter.

——— if at or above 44*s.* per quarter, second low duty, 6*d.*

And rye, ground, or malt made of rye, peas ground, and beans ground, prohibited.

Barley, beer, or big, and Indian corn and maize, imported from Quebec, or the British plantations, if under 26*s.* per quarter, high duty, 22*s.* per quarter.

——— if at or above 26*s.* and under 28*s.* per quarter, first low duty, 1*s.* 3*d.* per quarter.

——— if at or above 28*s.* per quarter, second low duty, 3*d.* per quarter.

——— if imported from any other foreign country, if under 31*s.* 6*d.* per quarter, high duty, 22*s.* per quarter.

Barley, if at or above 31*s.* 6*d.* and under 33*s.* per quarter, first low duty, 1*s.* 3*d.* per quarter.

——— if at or above 33*s.* per quarter, second low duty, 3*d.* per quarter.

And barley, Indian corn, or maize, beer, or big, ground, and malt made of barley, Indian corn, maize, beer, or big, prohibited.

Oats imported from Quebec, or the British plantations, if under 17*s.* per quarter, high duty, 6*s.* 7*d.* per quarter.

——— if at or above 17*s.* and under 18s. per quarter, first low duty, 1*s.* per quarter.

——— if at or above 18s. per quarter, second low duty, 2*d.* per quarter.

——— when imported from any other foreign country, if under 21*s.* per quarter, high duty, 6*s.* 7*d.*

——— if at or above 21*s.* and under 22*s.* per quarter, first low duty 1*s.* per quarter.

——— if at or above 22*s.* per quarter, second low duty, 2*d.* per quarter.

And malt made of oats prohibited.

Oatmeal, if imported from Quebec, or the British plantations, if under 16*s*. 6*d*. per boll, 128*lbs*. Scotch Troy, high duty 8*s*. per boll.

——— if at or above 16*s*. 6*d*. and under 17*s*. 4*d*. per boll, first low duty, 1*s*. per boll.

——— if at or above 17*s*. 4*d*. per boll, second low duty, 2*d*. per boll.

——— when imported from any other foreign country, if under 20*s*. per boll, high duty, 8*s*. per boll.

——— if at or above 20*s*. and under 21*s*. per boll, first low duty, 1*s*. per boll.

——— if at or above 21*s*. per boll, second low duty, 6*d*. per boll.

By 45 *Geo*. 3. *c*. 86, the importation and exportation of corn into and from Great Britain, shall be regulated by the average prices of the twelve maritime districts in England and Wales, as ascertained by the returns required by 31 *Geo*. 3, *c*. 30. *s*. 31, *infra*. And no corn shall be exported when the price in the preceding week is at the import rates. *s*. 1, 2.

And the orders in council, when issued for the importation of corn and grain from the British colonies in America, shall continue in force for six months. *s*. 3.

Corn Regulations.] By 31 *Geo*. 3, *c*. 30, so much of 15 *Car*. 2. *c*. 7, as prohibits the buying of corn to sell again, and the laying it up in granaries, is repealed; and it shall be lawful to buy corn to sell again, and lay it up in granaries, whatever the price may be. *s*. 2.

Bond is to be given for the due exportation of corn exported upon bounty, and the bounty is to be paid on oath that it is of British growth or produce, and a certificate from the proper officer of its having been duly exported. *s*. 5, 6.

Corn exported contrary to the act is forfeited, with the vessel; but if satisfactory proof be made that from the smallness of the quantity the same was on board without the privity of the owner or master, the vessel is not to be forfeited. *s*. 9.

Corn begun to be shipped outwards, or such part as shall be shipped within twenty days from the entry, may be exported, though the price in the mean time rise to the rates at which the exportation is prohibited. *s*. 10.

But the act is not to extend to corn for the sustenance of the crew of any vessel, or for victualling his Majesty's ships of war, forces, forts, or garrisons, or to beans exported to the British forts in Africa, or corn carried coastwise on sufferance. *Ibid*.

Or to certain quantities permitted to be exported to certain places mentioned in the table set forth in the act, for the due exportation whereof to which settlements and places bond is to be given. *Ibid*. and *s*. 7.

The inhabitants of Guernsey, Jersey, or Alderney, may transport directly from thence to Newfoundland, or the British colonies in America, for the use of the fishery, the corn allowed to be imported into those islands. *s*. 12.

In cases of war or distress his Majesty in council, when the parliament is not sitting, may allow certain further quantities of corn specified in the act, to be exported to the above places. *s*. 14.

Corn, grain, and flour imported may be landed without payment of duty, and warehoused under certain regulations. *s*. 19.

Foreign corn imported, and not warehoused, or delivered from the warehouse for home consumption, not to be exported from any port when British corn is not permitted to be exported therefrom. *s*. 20.

No debenture is to be made out for bounty on any corn shipped when it may be imported at the low duties. *s*. 22.

Foreign corn not warehoused, or meal made therefrom, if exported contrary to this act, to be forfeited, with the vessel. *s*. 23.

For ascertaining the prices of corn, the maritime counties of England are to be divided into the twelve districts herein specified, (including the cities which are counties of themselves,) *viz*. London, Essex, Kent, and Sussex, being the 1st district—Suffolk and Cambridge the 2d,—Norfolk the 3d,—Lincoln, and the east and north ridings of Yorkshire, including Kingston upon-Hull, the 4th,—Durham, Northumberland, and Berwick, the 5th,—Cumberland and Westmorland, the 6th,—Lancaster and Chester, the 7th,—Flint, Denbigh, Anglesea, Caernarvon, and Merioneth, the 8th,—Cardigan, Carmarthen, and Glamorgan, the 9th,—Gloucester, Somerset, Monmouth, and Bristol, the 10th,—Devon and Cornwall, the 11th,—and Dorset and Hants, the 12th district. *s*. 31.

And the several counties of Scotland form the 13th, 14th, 15th, and 16th dsstricts. *s*. 32, 33.

The exportation of corn to be regulated in London and Kent, Essex and Sussex, by the prices at the Corn Exchange: the proprietors whereof are to appoint an inspector of corn returns, who is to be sworn; and they are also to appoint an office for his use. *s*. 34, 35

The inspector is not removable, except by the London sessions. *s*. 36.

In case of sickness a deputy-inspector may be appointed. *s*. 37.

Corn-factors are to make a declaration in writing that they will make true returns to be delivered to the lord mayor, who is to grant a certificate thereof, to be registered with the inspector: and corn-factors acting without the delivery of such certificate, forfeit 50*l*. *s*. 38.

Factors are to make weekly returns to the inspector of corn returns, of the quantity of each sort sold, on penalty of 10*l.* which returns are to be entered in a book by the inspector, but not shown without proper authority on like penalty. *s.* 39, 40.

The inspector is to make up weekly accounts of the average quantity and price of each sort sold in London, and transmit the average prices every Friday to the receiver of corn-returns, who is to transmit a certificate thereof to the collectors of the customs within the district, as the price for exportation. *s.* 41.

The inspector is also to make up within seven days after 15th February, 15th May, 15th August, and 15th November, in every year, like accounts, and to transmit the average prices to the receiver of corn-returns, who is to transmit a copy thereof to the collectors of customs, as the rule for importation. *s.* 42. Inspector to deliver a copy of the average prices at the sessions, to be inserted in the Gazette. *s.* 43.

Factors are to pay to the inspector for corn brought into the Thames eastward of London bridge, 1*d.* per last, and for foreign corn 2*d.* and to deliver to him an account of the quantity. *s.* 45.

Inspector to deliver twice in the year to the London sessions an account of the money so received by him, which is to be disposed of in paying to the inspector not more than 200*l.* nor less than 100*l.* *per ann.* 2dly, so much to the proprietors of the Corn Exchange as will discharge the expense of providing the office; and 3dly, the residue, if any, to the receiver-general of the Customs. *s.* 45.

And the lord mayor and aldermen in sessions may order the beforementioned imposition of 1*d.* and 2*d.* per last to be levied by distress. *s.* 46.

In each of the eleven other districts (except counties of themselves) the justices in sessions are to appoint an inspector of corn-returns; and for such of them as are counties of themselves, the mayor and justices in their sessions are to appoint such inspector. *s.* 48, 49.

Such inspector may be removed, and in case of death or resignation other persons may be appointed by two justices till the quarter-sessions. *s.* 50.

Inspectors are to take an oath to make true returns, and dealers in corn for sale are to return to the inspectors accounts of the quantities bought by them in each week, and to make a declaration in writing that they will act conformable to the act, which declaration is to be delivered to a justice, to be filed by the clerk of the peace; and acting without, or making a false declaration, is a penalty of not exceeding 10*l.* nor less than 40*s.* *s.* 51, 52, 53.

Inspector is to enter the accounts of the quantities and prices of corn returned to him by the dealers, and return to the receivers of corn-returns, weekly, an account of the quantities and prices. *s.* 54.

By 33 *Geo.* 3. *c.* 65, the receiver of corn-returns is to make up the weekly average prices of corn and oatmeal sold in each of the towns in England, appointed by the last act, and to transmit the average prices in each district to the officer of customs, at the several ports as the rule for exportation. *s.* 2.

The receiver of corn within 7 days after 15th February, 15th May, 15th August, and 15th November, in each year is to state the average prices of corn and oatmeal in each district for the last six weeks, and transmit the same to the several officers of the customs, as the rule for import and export. *s.* 3.

Receivers of corn returns are to insert in the gazette, the weekly average prices of corn and oatmeal in each county, and the general aggregate prices in England, and the like average prices in Scotland monthly. *s.* 4.

In case a sufficient number of returns shall not be made from any districts, the receiver of corn returns is to transmit a certificate of the general average prices to the officers of customs therein, for the rule of import and export. *s.* 4.

Seed corn may at all times be carried coastwise, but when prohibited to be exported, bond must be given to secure its being only carried coastwise; oath must also be made that it is seed corn, and bond given that it shall not be used for any other purpose, and if used for any other purpose, the party is to forfeit treble the value. *s.* 13, 14.

By 31 *Geo.* 3. *c.* 30, the importation and exportation of corn is to be regulated in Scotland by certain rules. *s.* 57 to 61.

Accounts of the prices of corn are also to be taken in the several inland and other counties and places, in the act specified, for each of which an inspector of corn returns is to be appointed by the sessions, in like manner as for the maritime counties. *s.* 62, 64.

Such inspectors are to transmit to the receiver of corn returns a weekly account of the average prices sold in their districts, on penalty of 10*l.* *s.* 65.

Receiver of corn returns to cause an abstract of the average prices, from the last mentioned places to be inserted in the Gazette weekly, and to transmit certificates of the returns received four times in the year to the county treasurer. *s.* 66.

Places for taking the prices of corn may be changed. *s.* 67.

Returns from two-thirds of the places in corn districts to be sufficient for forming the average prices, and the average prices of the districts which have sent returns are to be transmitted as guides for importation or exportation in the districts from which sufficient returns have not been received. *s.* 68, 69.

Inspectors in England are to be paid quarterly out of the county rates, 5*s.* for each return from any city or town in the maritime counties, and 2*s.* for each return from cities and towns in the inland counties. *s.* 74.

The receiver of corn returns is to transmit, at the end of every year, a certificate of the number of returns received to the receiver general of the customs, who is to repay the county treasurers out of duties received, and if the duties on foreign corn imported be insufficient to make repayment, the receiver-general is to make up the deficiency. *s.* 75, 76.

The lords of the treasury are to appoint a receiver of corn returns, who is to take an oath to execute the office truly, who may send and receive papers free of postage. *s.* 77, 78, 79.

The collectors of the customs are to send weekly accounts of corn shipped to be carried coastwise at, or brought coastwise into their respective ports, to the receiver of corn returns, who is every three months to transmit an account thereof to the commissioners of customs. *s.* 80.

The treasury are to order an annual account to be transmitted from the customs, to the receiver of corn returns, of the corn exported. *s.* 81.

All corn shall be measured by the Winchester bushel, but when sold by weight, the following quantities are to be deemed equal to a bushel, wheat 57lb. rye 55lb. barley 49lb. beer or bigg 42lb. oats 38lb. wheat meal 56lb. wheat flour 45lb. rye meal 53lb. barley meal 48lb. beer or bigg meal 41lb. oatmeal 22lb. and the quantity of ground corn in sacks is to be determined by weighing two sacks out of twenty; and on doubts whether it be wheat meal or wheat flour, the officer may require a reasonable portion of every sack to be passed through a 14*s.* cloth. *s.* 82.

The inspector of corn returns is to make a comparison between the Winchester measure, and that used where he is inspector. *s.* 83.

The present practice of measuring corn within London is to continue, and the city tolls to be paid. *s.* 84.

No fee is to be taken for oaths. *s.* 86.

And the penalties may be recovered in the courts of record, or before two justices of the peace, who may levy the same by distress. *s.* 87, 88.

By 39 *Geo.* 3. *c.* 38, the average prices of middling British rapeseed at the place of importation shall be ascertained in like manner as the prices of corn. *s.* 2.

By 46 *Geo.* 3. *c.* 11, the act 45 *Geo.* 3. *c.* 86, *s.* 2, shall not prevent the carrying coastwise, or exporting corn for the use of his majesty's forces, or for the purposes mentioned in 31 *Geo.* 3. *c.* 30, and 33 *Geo.* 3. *c.* 65, although prohibited from being otherwise exported by reason of the price.

By 46 *Geo.* 3. *c.* 97, all bounties and duties payable on the interchange of corn and grain between Great Britain and Ireland shall cease, and corn and grain may be imported and exported between them whatever the price may be. *s.* 1.

But the exporter is to declare before the officer of customs, that such corn and grain is intended to be exported between the countries, and shall receive a coast cocquet; and no fee shall be taken by any officer of customs on account thereof, on pain of being dismissed, and rendered incapable of serving in the customs, excise, or any revenue office. *s.* 3.

Nothing in any acts in force shall prohibit the exportation from Ireland of a supply of corn, and the like for ship stores, or for provisioning forces or garrisons, or beans for the British forts in Africa, usually supplied from Great Britain, nor prohibit the like quantities mentioned in table C. of the British acts 31 *Geo.* 3. *c.* 30. *s.* 10, and 33 *Geo.* 3. *c.* 65, but if the price be above the price at which the export is allowed, the exporter to any place mentioned in the said table shall declare the place for which the same are exported. *s.* 5, 6.

And by 47 *Geo.* 3. *sess.* 1. *c.* 7, the act 46 *Geo.* 3. *c.* 97, is declared to extend only to corn and grain of the growth of Great Britain or Ireland.

CORNAGE, (*cornagium*, from the Lat. *cornu*) a horn, was a kind of tenure in grand serjeantry; the service of which was to blow a horn when any invasion of the Scots was perceived; and by this tenure many persons held their lands northward, about the wall commonly called the Picts wall. *Cambd. Britan.* 609. *Cowel. Blount.*

CORNARE, to blow in the horn. *Ibid.*

CORN RENTS. By 18 *El.* *c.* 6, on college leases, one-third of the old rent is to be reserved in wheat or malt, &c. The invention of lord treasurer Burleigh, and sir Thomas Smith, who observed the value of money to sink much, and the price of provisions to rise greatly, on our communication with the Indies; and therefore devised this method for upholding the revenues of the colleges. 2 *Black. Com.* 322.

CORNWALL, a royal duchy belonging to the Prince of Wales, abounding with mines, and having stannary courts, &c. See STANNARIES.

CORODY, (*corodium*) was a sum of money or allowance of meat, drink, and clothing due to the king from an abbey, or other house of religion, whereof he was founder, towards the sustentation of such a one of his servants as he thought fit, to bestow it upon. And the difference between a corody and pension was, that a corody was allowed towards the maintenance of any of the king's servants in an abbey; a pension was given to one of the king's chaplains, for his better maintenance, till he was provided of a benefice. *Fitz. Nat. Br.* 250. *Staundf. Prærog.* 44.

CORODIO HABENDO, a writ to exact a corody of an abbey or religious house. *Reg. Orig.* 264.

CORONA MALA or MALA CORONA, the clergy who abused their character were formerly so called. *Blount.*

CORONARE FILIUM, to make one's son a priest; *homo coronatus* was one who had received the first tonsure, as preparatory to superior orders; and the tonsure was in the form of a corona, or crown of thorns. *Cowel. Blount.*

CORONATION OATH, the original contract between the king and people is now comprized in the coronation oath, the articles which seem to be as ancient as the Mirrour of Justices, *cap.* 1. *s.* 2. and even as the time of *Bracton, lib.* 3. *c.* 9. 1 *Black.* 234, 235.

This oath, by *stat.* 1 *W.* & *M. st.* 1. *c.* 6, is to be administered to every king and queen, who shall succeed to the imperial crown of these realms, by one of the archbishops or bishops of the realm, in the presence of all the people; who on their parts do reciprocally take the oath of allegiance to the crown. This coronation oath is conceived in the following terms.

The archbishop or bishop shall say, "Will you solemnly promise and swear to govern the people of this kingdom of England, and the dominions thereto belonging, according to the statutes in parliament agreed on, and the laws and customs of the same." The king or queen shall say, "I solemnly promise so to do." Archbishop or bishop. "Will you to your power, cause law and justice, in mercy to be executed in all your judgments." King or queen, "I will." Archbishop or bishop. "Will you to the utmost of your power maintain the laws of God, the true profession of the gospel, and the protestant reformed religion established by the law. And will you preserve unto the bishops and clergy of this realm, and to the churches committed to their charge, all such rights and privileges as by law do or shall appertain unto them, or any of them." King or queen, "all this I promise to do." After this the king or queen, laying his or her hand upon the holy gospels, shall say, "the things which I have here before promised I will perform and keep: so help me God," and then shall kiss the book.

And it is required both by the bill of rights, 1 *W.* & *M. st.* 2. *c.* 2, and the act of settlement 12 & 13 *W.* 3. *c.* 2, that every king and queen of the age of twelve years, either at their coronation, or on the first day of the first parliament, upon the throne in the house of peers, (which shall first happen), shall repeat and subscribe the declaration against popery according to the 30 *Car.* 2. *st.* 2. *c.* 1.

This is most indisputably a fundamental and original express contract; and on the king's part expresses all the duties that a monarch can owe to his people, viz. to govern according to law; to execute judgment in mercy, and to maintain the established religion: though doubtless the duty of protection is impliedly as much incumbent on the sovereign before coronation as after: in the same manner as allegiance to the king becomes the duty of the subject immediately on the descent of the crown, before he has taken the oath of allegiance, or whether he ever takes it at all. 1 *Black.* 235, 6.

CORONATORE ELIGENDO, is a writ which lies on the death or discharge of any coroner, directed to the sheriff out of the Chancery, to call together the freeholders of the county, for the choice of a new coroner; and to certify into the Chancery: both the election and the name of the party elected, and also to give him his oath, &c. *Reg. Orig.* 177. *F. N. B.* 163.

CORONATORE EXONERANDO, is a writ for the discharge of a coroner for negligence, or insufficiency in the discharge of his duty; and where coroners are so far engaged in any other public business, that they cannot attend the office; or if they are disabled by old age or disease, to execute it; or have not sufficient lands, &c. they may be discharged by this writ. 2 *Inst.* 32. 2 *Hawk. P. C.* 44. But if any such writ be grounded on an untrue suggestion, the coroner may procure a commission from the Chancery, to inquire thereof; and if the suggestion be disproved, the king may make a *supersedeas* to the sheriff, that he do not remove the coroner; or if he hath removed him, that he suffer him to execute the office. *Reg. Orig.* 177, 8. *F. N. B.* 164.

CORONER, (*coronator, a corona*), is an ancient officer of this realm, so called because he deals wholly for the king and crown. *Bac. Abr. tit. Cor.*

Coroners are to be men of good ability, and have lands in fee in the county, where chosen, to answer all people; and if insufficient, the county shall answer for them. 2 *Inst.* 174.

And by 28 *Ed.* 3. *c.* 6, the coroner shall be chosen by the commons in full county, saving the franchises of the king and other lords. But the lord chief justice of the king's bench is the sovereign coroner of the whole kingdom in person wheresoever he is, 4 *Rep.* 57. And there are also special coroners within divers liberties, either in right of their offices according to custom, or by appointment agreeable to the king's charter, as granted to some corporations. *Cromp. Juris.* 102. 4 *Inst.* 271. 2 *Hale's Hist. P. C.* 53.

And thus there are coroners of the king's household, and of the verge of the king's palaces, of the admiralty, of London, Southwark, and other particular franchises.

Power of Coroners.] Coroners are conservators of the peace in the county where elected; and their authority is both judicial and ministerial. Judicial, where one comes to a violent death, and to take and enter appeals of murder, pronounce judgment upon outlawries, &c. And to inquire of lands and goods, and escapes of murderers, treasure trove, of persons riotously living, of deodands, wreck of the sea, &c. The ministerial power is where the coroners execute the king's writs, on exception to the sheriff, as being party, plaintiff, or defendant to a suit, kin to either of the parties, or on default of the sheriff in not making returns, &c. 4 *Inst.* 271. 1 *Plowd.* 73. And the authority of coroners does not determine by the demise of the king. 2 *Inst.* 174.

By the stat. *de officio coronatoris*, 4 *Ed.* 1. "The coroner is to go to the place where "any person is slain or suddenly dead, "and shall by his warrant to the bailiffs, "constables, &c. summon a jury out of the "four or five neighbouring towns, to make "inquiry upon view of the body; and the "coroner and jury are to inquire into the "manner of killing, and all circumstances "that occasioned the party's death, who "were present, whether the dead person was "known, where he lay the night before, "&c. Examine the body if there be any "signs of strangling about the neck, or of "cords about the members, &c. Also all "wounds ought to be viewed, and inquiry "made with what weapons, &c. And the "coroner may send his warrant for witnesses, and take their examination in "writing: and if any appear guilty of the "murder, he shall inquire what goods and "lands he hath, and then the dead body "is to be buried. A coroner may likewise "commit the person to prison who is by "his inquisition found guilty of the murder; and the witnesses are to be bound "by recognizance to appear at the next "assizes, &c."

When the jury have brought in their verdict, the coroner is to inroll and return the inquisition, whether it be brought in murder, manslaughter, &c. to the justices of the next gaol delivery of the county, or certify it into B. R. where the murderers shall be proceeded against. 2 *Rol. Abr.* 32. And upon an inquisition taken before the coroner, he must put into writing the effect of the evidence given to the jury before him; and bind them to appear, &c. which is to be certified to the court with the inquisition, and neglecting it he shall be fined. 1 & 2 *P. & M. cap.* 13. 1 *Lil. Abr.* 327.

The coroner may in convenient time take up a dead body that hath been buried, in order to view it; but if it be buried so long that he can discover nothing, from the viewing it; or if there be danger of infection, the inquest ought not to be taken by the coroner, but by justices of peace, by the testimony of witnesses; for none can take it on view, but the coroner. *Bro. Coron.* 167, 173.

And a coroner may find any nuisance by which the death of a man happens; and the township shall be amerced on such finding. 1 *Nels. Abr.* 536.

Coroners ought to sit and inquire on the body of every prisoner that dies in prison. 3 *Inst.* 134.

If a body is drowned and cannot be found to be viewed, the inquisition must be taken by justices of peace, on the examination of witnesses, &c. 5 *Rep.* 110.

A coroner's inquisition being final, the coroner ought to hear counsel and evidence on both sides. 2 *Sid.* 90, 101. Where a coroner would not admit of evidence against the king, to prove a *felo de se* to be *non compos mentis*, his inquisition was set aside; and a new inquisition taken, whereby it was found that the party was *non compos.* 2 *Hale's Hist. P. C.* 60. But though the coroner must admit evidence as well against the king's interest, as for it; yet if a person be killed by another, and it is certainly known that he did it, the coroner's jury are to hear the evidence only for the king; and inquire whether the killing were by malice, or without malice. 2 *Hale's P. C.* 60.

If there be an inquisition of manslaughter or murder, and also an indictment by the grand jury, against one, and he is arraigned, and found not guilty on the indictment; here it is necessary to quash the coroner's inquisition, or to arraign the party upon it, and acquit him on that also; for otherwise it stands as a record against him, whereon he may possibly be outlawed. 2 *Hale.* 65.

Fees of coroners.] By 3 *Hen.* 7. *cap.* 1. upon an inquisition taken on the view of the body, the coroner shall have 13*s.* 4*d.* fee of the goods of the murderer; and if he be gone, then out of the amercement of the town for the escape, but by 1 *H.* 8. *c.* 7, where a person is slain, drowned, or dead by misadventure, the coroner is to take no fee, on pain of 40*s.*

By *stat.* 25 *Geo.* 2. *c.* 29, however, every inquisition, (not taken upon the view of a body dying in gaol), which shall be taken by the coroner in any township or place contributory to the rates directed by *stat.* 12 *Geo.* 2. *c.* 29, the sum of 20*s.* and for every mile which he shall travel from the place of his abode, the further sum of 9*d.* shall be paid him out of the money arising by the said rates. And for every inquisition taken upon the view of a body dying in gaol, so much money, not exceeding 20*s.* shall be paid him as the justices at sessions shall think fit to allow, out of the money arising from the said rates. Provided that over and above the recompence hereby appointed for inquisitions taken as aforesaid, the coroner who shall take an inquisition upon the view of a body slain or murdered, shall have the fee of 13*s.* 4*d.* payable, by stat. 3 *H.* 7. *c.* 1. out of the goods of the slayer or murderer, or out of the amerciaments upon the township, if the slayer or murderer escape. And coroners taking further fees shall be guilty of extortion.

But no coroner of the king's household, and of the verge of the king's palaces, nor any coroner of the Admiralty, nor of the county palatine of Durham, nor of the city of London and borough of Southwark, or of any of the franchises belonging to the said city, nor any coroner of any city, borough, town, liberty or franchise not contributory to the rates directed by stat. 12 *G.* 2. *c.* 29. or within which such rates have not been usually assessed, shall be entitled to any fee, recompence, or benefit given by this act.

Punishment for misbehaviour.] If a coroner be remiss in coming to do his office, when he is sent for, he shall be amerced by virtue of the stat. *de coronatoribus*. *S. P. C.* 51. *Salk.* 377. *H. P. C.* 170.

And if a coroner hath been guilty of any corrupt practice, such as bribery, or the like, in taking the inquisition, a *melius inquirendum* may be awarded for taking a new one by special commissioners. And coroners concealing felonies, are to be fined, and suffer one year's imprisonment by 3 *Ed.* 1. *cap.* 9. Also for mismanagement in the coroner, filing the inquisition may be stopped, 1 *Mod.* 82.

If it be found before the coroner *super visum corporis*, that one was *felo de se*, the executors or administrators of the deceased, it is said, cannot traverse it. 3 *Inst.* 55. But it has been held that the inquest being moved into B. R. by *certiorari*, may be there traversed by the executor or administrator of the deceased. 2 *Hawk.* 54. And it hath been adjudged, that the inquisition of *felo de se* is traversable; though *fugam fecit* is not. 2 *Leon.* 152.

CORONER OF THE KING'S HOUSEHOLD, hath an exempt jurisdiction within the verge, and the coroner of the county cannot intermeddle within it; as the coroner of the king's house may not intermeddle within the county out of the verge. 2 *Hawk.* 45.

By the stat. 33 *H.* 8. 12. *Par.* 1 & 3. it is ordained, "that all inquisitions made upon "the view of persons slain, within any of "the king's palaces or houses, or any other "house or houses wherein his majesty shall "happen to be abiding in his royal person, "shall be taken by the coroner for the time "being of the king's household, without "any assisting of another coroner of any "shire within this realm, by the oaths of "twelve or more of the yeomen officers of "the king's household, returned by the two "clerks controllers, the clerks of the checks, "and the clerks marshal, or one of them, of "the said household, to whom the said coroner of the household shall direct his precept; and the said coroner shall certify "under his seal, and the seals of such persons as shall be sworn before him, all such "inquisitions before the master or lord steward of the household; who hath the appointment of such coroner," &c.

CORONER OF LONDON. By the charter of king *Ed.* 4. the mayor and commonalty of London may grant the office of coroner to whom they please; and no other coroner but he that belongs to the city, shall have any power there: also the lord mayor, &c. may chuse two coroners in Southwark. *Cit. Lib.* 46, 47. 1 *Lil. Abr.* 327.

CORONE, (*Fr.*) all matters of the crown, were heretofore reduced to this law head or title; they are the things that concern treason, felony, and divers other offences by the common law, and by statute. *Shep. Epit.* 367.

CORPORAL OATH. See *Oaths*.

CORPORATION, (*corporatio*) is a body politic or incorporate, so called, as the persons are made into a body, and of capacity to take and grant, &c. Or it is an assembly and joining together of many into one fellowship and brotherhood, whereof one is head and chief, and the rest are the body; and this head and body knit together, make the corporation: also it is constituted of several members like unto the natural body, and framed by fiction of law to endure in perpetual succession. *Bac. Abr.* tit. *Corp.*

Of corporations some are sole, some aggregate; sole, when in one single person, as the king, a bishop, dean, or the like. Aggregate, which is the most usual, consisting of many persons, as mayor and commonalty, dean and chapter, &c. Likewise corporations are spiritual or temporal; spiritual, of bishops, deans, archdeacons, parsons, vicars, and other ecclesiastical persons. Temporal, of mayors, commonalty, bailiffs and burgesses, &c. and some corporations are of a mixt nature, composed of spiritual and temporal persons, such as heads of colleges and hospitals, &c. And all corporations are said to be ecclesiastical, or lay.

Bodies politic or incorporate may be, 1st, by prescription; 2dly, by letters patent, or 3dly, by act of parliament; but they are most commonly by patent or charter. 1 *Inst.* 250. 3 *Inst.* 202. 3 *Rep.* 73.

In making aggregate corporations, there must be, 1. Lawful authority. 2. Proper persons to be incorporated. 3. A name of incorporation. 4. A place, without which no corporation can be made. 5. Words sufficient in law to make a corporation. 10 *Rep.* 29, 123. 3 *Rep.* 73.

London and many other places are corporations by prescription; but though a corporation may be by prescription, it shall be intended that it did originally derive its authority by grant from the king; for the king is the head of the commonwealth, and all the commonwealth, in respect of him, is but one corporation; and all other corporations are but limbs of the greater body. 1 *Lil. Abr.* 330. A mayor and commonalty or corporation, cannot make another corporation, or commonalty. 1 *Sid.* 290. But they may make a company or fraternity. 1 *Salk.* 193.

By 13 *Car.* 2. *c.* 1. no person shall bear the office of mayor, alderman, recorder, bailiff, town clerk, common council man, or other office in any corporation, unless he hath taken the sacrament, one year prior to his election; and he shall take the oaths of allegiance and supremacy when the oaths of office are administered, otherwise the election is void.

The 5 *Geo.* 1. *c.* 6. discharged members of corporations from all incapacities of the last act, incurred by not receiving the sacrament within a year before their election: and enacts that persons elected hereafter shall not be removed, unless prosecution is commenced within six months after election.

Jurisdiction of Corporations.] When a corporation is duly created, all incidents, as to purchase and grant, sue and be sued, &c. are impliedly annexed to it; and although no power to make by-laws is given by a special clause to a corporation, it is included by law in the very act of incorporating. *Co. Lit.* 264. And a new charter doth not merge or extinguish any of the ancient privileges of the old charter. And if an ancient corporation is incorporated by a new name, yet their new body shall enjoy all the privileges that the old corporation had. *Raym.* 439. 4 *Rep.* 37.

And there are usually granted in charters to corporations, divers franchises; as felons' goods, waifs, estrays, treasure trove, deodands, courts, and cognisance of pleas, fairs, markets, assise of bread and beer, &c. 4 *Rep.* 65. Also actions arising in corporations may be tried in the corporation courts, where such courts are erected by the charter; but if they try actions which arise not within their jurisdictions, and encroach upon the common law, they shall be punished for it. *Lutw.* 1571, 1572.

By 2 & 3 *Phil. & Mar. c.* 18. commissioners of peace and gaol delivery for a town corporate, are not superseded by a new commission or the county.

By 38 *Geo.* 3. *c.* 52. in actions in any court of record at Westminster, or indictments removed by certiorari, if the venue be laid in the county of any city or town corporate, the court may direct the issue to be tried by a jury of the county next adjoining. *s.* 1.

Bills of indictment for offences committed within the county of any city or town corporate, may be preferred to the jury of the county next adjoining. *s.* 2.

Indictments found by a grand jury of the county of any city or town corporate, or inquisitions taken before the coroner, may be ordered by the court of oyer there, to be filed with the proper officer of the next adjoining county, and defendants removed to the gaol thereof. *s.* 3.

The judges of the court of king's bench, or oyer and terminer, may on application of the prosecutor, cause persons in custody for offences committed within the county of any city or town corporate, to be removed into the custody of the sheriff of the next adjoining county for trial, and direct coroners to return to the court of oyer and terminer inquisitions. *s.* 4.

Recognizances for prosecutions are to be forfeited, if the parties on notice left at their abode of intention to prefer indictments in the next adjoining counties, do not appear. *s.* 5, 6.

But such recognizances are not to be estreated until the next following sessions for the adjoining county.

Persons taking such recognizances, are to return them to the next court of oyer and terminer, for the next adjoining county, upon notice of the intention to prosecute, in the next adjoining county: and after such notice, bills are not to be preferred at any sessions for the county of the city or town corporate. *s.* 7.

Justices of oyer and terminer of the next county may order the expences of prosecution to be paid, as if the indictment had been tried in the county of the city. *s.* 8.

York is to be considered as the next county to Kingston upon Hull, and Northumberland as next to Newcastle upon Tyne. *s.* 9.

The act does not extend to London, Westminster, Southwark, Bristol, Chester, or Exeter, except where the court of king's bench has concurrent jurisdiction: nor to take away any other ancient privileges of corporations, who shall not be liable to attend as jurymen upon the trial of any cause or indictment in the county at large. *s.* 10, 11.

Also, the act is not to authorise the preferring any bill of indictment, for an offence committed within the county of any city or town, to the jury of the next county, unless recognizances be entered in to pay the extra costs. *s.* 12.

In a case of sole corporation, as bishop, dean, parson, &c. no chattel, either in action or possession, shall go in succession; but the executors or administrators of the bishop, parson, &c. shall have them: but it is otherwise of a corporation aggregate, as a dean and chapter, mayor and commonalty, and the like: for they in the judgment of law never die. *Terms de Ley*.

But though a sole corporation cannot generally take in succession goods and chattels, &c. yet it may take a fee-simple in succession, by the word successors. *Co. Lit.* 8, 9. 46. And aggregate corporations may take not only goods and chattels, but lands in fee-simple, without the word successors, for the reason before mentioned. 4 *Inst.* 249. And succession in a body politic, is an inheritance in a body private. If a lease for years be made to a bishop and his successors, it is said his executors shall have it *in auter droit;* for regularly no chattel can go in succession in case of a sole corporation, no more than if a lease be made to a man and his heirs, which cannot go to his heirs. *Co. Lit.* 46.

Grants of corporations are to be by deed, under their common seal, and are good without delivery; for the common seal gives perfection to corporation deeds. *Danv.* 44. And the release of a mayor of a corporation, made in his own name, is not good in law; the corporation must join and do it by their common seal. *Terms de Ley*.

But though a corporation cannot do an act *in pais* without their common seal, they may do an act upon record; and the reason is, because they are estopped by the record to say it is not their act. 1 *Salk.* 192.

A promise to a corporation is good without deed. 2 *Lev.* 252.

And a corporation may do an act in that capacity, to one of themselves in his natural capacity; and any member in his natural capacity may perform an act to the corporation in its politic capacity; and so they may sue one another, in their distinct capacities. 1 *Shep. Abr.* 436.

A corporation cannot sue, or appear in person, but by attorney: they cannot commit treason or felony, or be excommunicate, &c. They may not be executors, or administrators, be joint-tenants, trustees, &c. Nor shall the members of a corporation be regularly witnesses for the corporation. 10 *Rep.* 32. 11 *Rep.* 98. *Co. Lit.* 134. But they may be disfranchised, and then be witnesses; though not surrender by consent. Yet in some cases the judges now admit their testimony without disfranchisement, where the interest is remote. Attachment doth not lie against a corporation. *Raym.* 152.

Corporations may have power not only to infranchise freemen, but to disfranchise a member, and deprive him of his freedom; if he doth any act to the prejudice of the body, or contrary to his oath, &c. Though for conspiring to do any thing contrary to his duty, or for words of contempt against the chief officers, he may not be disfranchised; but he may be committed till he find sureties for his good behaviour. 11 *Rep.* 98. 5 *Mod.* 257. A corporation cannot disfranchise for breach of a by-law. 1 *Lil.* 331. And one wrongfully disfranchised may be restored, and have his remedy by *mandamus*, &c. in B. R. And a freeman of a corporation cannot be removed from his freedom or place without good cause, and a custom to remove them *ad libitum* is void, because the party hath a freehold therein. *Cro. Jac.* 540.

By 7 *Geo.* 3. *c.* 48. in companies or corporations instituted for carrying on particular trades or dealing with joint stocks, no member shall vote in general courts, unless possessed of his stock six months (except acquired by bequest, marriage, succession to intestate's estate, custom of London, or settlement); the oaths are required to be conformable to this act.

No declaration of a dividend shall be made, but at one of the half yearly or quarterly general courts, at five months distance from the last preceding declaration; and for no more than the half year. And no question for a proposed increase of dividend shall be decided, but by ballot taken three days after breaking up of the court. *Ibid.*

Acts of corporations.] A corporation is properly an investing the people of the place with the local government thereof, and therefore their laws shall be binding to strangers; but a fraternity is some people of a place united together in respect of a mystery and business into a company, and their laws and ordinances cannot bind strangers, for they have not a local power. *Salk.* 193.

And by 19 *Hen.* 7. *c.* 7. no masters and wardens, or fellowships of any mystery, or other corporation, shall make any by-laws or ordinances in diminution of the king's prerogative, or against the common profit of the people; except the same be approved by the lord chancellor, treasurer, or chief justices, &c. on pain of 40*l*.

And such bodies corporate shall not make any acts or ordinances for restraining persons to sue in the king's courts for remedy, &c. under the like penalty. *Ibid.*

And ordinances made by corporations, to be observed, on pain of imprisonment, or of forfeiture of goods, &c. are contrary to magna charta. 2 *Inst.* 47, 54.

But penalties may be inflicted by by-laws, which may be recovered by distress or action of debt: and a custom for the lord mayor and aldermen of London, to commit a citizen for not accepting of the livery, &c. was held a good custom, being for the good government of the city. 5 *Mod.* 320.

Corporations may not, by bond, or otherwise, restrain any apprentice, &c. from keeping shop in the corporation under the penalty of 40*l*. *Stat.* 28 *H.* 8. *c.* 5.

And by 33 *Hen.* 8. *c.* 27. grants, leases, and the like, by the majority of a corporation shall be valid, against any negative voice or dissent of the minority, and any by-law or oath to the contrary shall be void.

Corporations dissolved.] A corporation may be dissolved, for it is created upon a trust; and if that be broken it is forfeited. 4 *Mod.* 58.

Corporations are dissolved by forfeiture of their charter, misuser, &c. upon the writ *quo warranto* brought; by surrender, or by act of parliament; and if they neglect to choose officers, or make false elections, &c. it is a forfeiture of the corporation. 4 *Rep.* 77.

But by stat. 11 *Geo.* 1. *c.* 4. where the election of mayors, or other chief officers shall not be made on the days appointed by charter or usage, the corporation shall not be thereby dissolved, but they may meet and proceed to election on the day after, and the mayor or chief officer absenting, the nearest in place may hold the court.

If no election be made, or one that becomes void, the king's bench may award a *mandamus*, for electing, and mayors so elected shall take the oaths before the presiding officer. *Ibid.*

No such election shall be valid, unless as great a number be present, as required by charter. *Ibid.*

Mayors voluntarily absenting themselves, shall suffer six months imprisonment, and be incapacitated. *Ibid.*

A return shall be made to the first writ of *mandamus*. *Ibid.*

By 2 *Ann.* *c.* 20. where persons intrude into the office of mayor, &c. of a corporation, a *quo warranto* shall be brought against the usurpers, who shall be ousted, and fined: and none are to execute an office in a corporation for more than a year.

And by 12 *Geo.* 3. *c.* 21. any person intitled to be admitted a citizen, burgess, or freeman, of any city, or corporation, applying to the mayor or chief officer for that purpose, and giving him notice, specifying the nature of his claims; shall if such mayor or head officer shall refuse to admit such person, and a *mandamus* shall issue for compelling his admission, have all costs from the mayor.

Freemen shall be admitted to inspect the entries of admission, and to take copies thereof. *Ibid.*

Mayor, bailiff, or other head officer, denying inspection of such entries, or to give copies thereof, shall for every refusal forfeit 100*l.* if sued for within one year. *Ibid.*

By 32 *Geo.* 3. *c.* 58. defendants to informations, in the nature of *quo warranto*, for the exercise of any office or franchise in corporations, may plead the holding of it six years, or more. *s.* 1.

And forfeiture of the office, within six years before information, may be replied to such plea. *s.* 2.

The title derived under an election, is not to be affected, on account of defect of title in the person electing, if he was in the exercise of his office six years previous to the information. *s.* 3.

Officers having the custody of corporation records, are to permit any member thereof to inspect the book of admission of freemen, on pain of 100*l.* *s.* 4.

CORPSE, *stealing of.* If any one in taking up a dead body steals the shroud, or other apparel, it will be felony. 3 *Inst.* 110. 12 *Rep.* 113. 1 *Hal. P. C.* 515. But stealing the corpse itself, is a misdemeanor only, and not felony. 4 *Black. Com.* 236.

CORPUS CHRISTI DAY, is a feast instituted in the year 1264, in honour of the sacrament: to which also a college in Oxford is dedicated. *Cowel. Blount.*

CORPUS CUM CAUSA, is a writ issuing out of the chancery, to remove both the body and record, touching the cause of any man lying in execution upon a judgment for debt, into the king's bench, &c. there to lie till he have satisfied the judgment. *F. N. B.* 251.

But by 2 *Hen.* 5. *st.* 1. *c.* 2. no *certiorari* or *corpus cum causâ* shall *discharge* one that is in prison upon an execution.

CORRECTOR OF THE STAPLE, was a clerk belonging to the staple, that wrote and recorded the bargains of merchants there made. 27 *Ed.* 3. *stat.* 2 *cap.* 22 & 23.

CORREDIUM and CONREDIUM. See Corody.

CORRUPTION OF BLOOD, (*corruptio sanguinis*) is an infection growing to the state of a man, and to his issue; and is where a person is attainted of treason or felony, by means whereof his blood is said to be corrupted, and neither his children, nor any of his blood, can be heirs to him or any other ancestor: also if he is of the nobility, or a gentleman, he and all his posterity by the attainder are rendered base and ignoble: but by pardon of the king, the children born afterwards may inherit the land of their ancestor, purchased at the time of the pardon or after; but so cannot they, who were born before the pardon. *Terms de Ley.*

Corruption of blood from an attainder is so high that it cannot be absolutely saved but by act of parliament; for the king's pardon doth not restore the blood so as to make the person attainted capable either of inheriting others, or being inherited himself by any one born before the pardon. 1 *Inst.* 391, 392. 2 *Hawk.* 458. A statute which saves the corruption of blood, impliedly saves the descent of the land to the heir; and it prevents the corruption of blood so far: also it saves the wife's dower, &c. But nevertheless the land shall be forfeited for the life of the offender. 3 *Inst.* 47. 1 *Hawk.* 107.

CORSELET, (Fr. in Lat. *corpusculum*) signifies a little body: and it was used with us for an armour to cover the body or trunk of a man, wherewith pikemen commonly set in the front and flanks of the battle were formerly armed, for the better resistance of the assaults of the enemy, and the surer guard of the soldiers placed behind, who were more slightly armed for their speedier advancing to and retreating from fire. *Cowel. Blount.*

CORSEPRESENT, (from the Fr. *corpse present*) is a word signifying a mortuary: and the reason why it was thus termed seems to be, that where a mortuary became due on the death of any man, the best or second beast was, according to custom, offered or presented to the priest, and carried with the corpse. *Ibid.* 4 *Black. Com.* 425.

CORSNED BREAD, (*panis conjuratus*) ordeal bread: it was a kind of superstitious trial used among the Saxons, to purge themselves of any accusation, by taking a piece of barley bread, and eating it with solemn oaths and execrations, that it might prove poison, or their last morsel, if what they asserted or denied were not punctually true. These pieces of bread were first execrated by the priest, and then offered to the suspected person to be swallowed by way of purgation: for they believed a person, if guilty, could not swallow a morsel so accursed; or if he did, it would choak him. *Cowel. Blount.*

CORTIS, (*curtis*) a court or yard before a house. *Blount.*

CORTULARIUM, (*curtilagium*) is also a yard adjoining to a country farm. *Ibid.*

CORUS, a certain corn-measure heaped up, (from the Hebr. *cora*, a hill:) eight bushels of wheat in a heap, making a quarter, are of the shape of a little hill; and probably a corus of wheat was eight bushels; for we read in Bracton, *decem. coros tritici sive decem quarteria. Bract. lib.* 2. *c.* 6. *Cowel. Blount.*

COSDUNA, an ancient word for custom or tribute. *Mon. Angl. tom.* 1. *p.* 562. *Ibid.*

COSENAGE, (from the Fr. *cousinage*, i. e. kindred, cousinship) a writ, now in disuse, which anciently lay for the heir where the *tresail*, that is, the father of the *besail*, or great grandfather, being seised of lands, a stranger entered and abated. *F. N. B.* 221.

COSENING, is an offence where any thing is done deceitfully, whether belonging to contracts or not, which cannot be properly termed by any special name. *West. Symb. p.* 2. *sect.* 68.

COSHERING. As there were many privileges inherent by right and custom, allowed in the feudal laws; so were there several grievous exactions imposed by the lords on their tenants, by a sort of prerogative or senioral authority, as to lie and feast themselves and their followers at their tenants houses, &c. which were called coshering. *Spelm. of Parliaments. MS.*

COSMAS, a word mentioned by Cowel and Blount for clean.

COSTARD, apple, whence costard-monger, i. e. seller of apples. *Cowel. Blount.*

COSTERA, coast, sea-coast. *Ibid.*

COSTS in general acceptation, are the expences incurred by proceedings at law or in equity, and these were not originally recoverable by the plaintiff or defendant at common law. 2 *Inst.* 288. *Hardr.* 152.

But as to the *Plaintiff's costs.*] By the statute of Gloucester, (6 *Edw.* 1.) *c.* 1. *s.* 2. it is provided, "that the demandant may recover "against the tenant the costs of his writ purchased (*which has been construed to extend* "*to the whole costs* of his suit, 2 *Inst.* 228.) "together with the damages given by that "statute; and that this act shall hold place, "in all cases where a man recovers damages." This was the origin of costs *de incremento. Gilb. Eq. Rep.* 195. And hence the plaintiff has, generally speaking, a right to costs, in all cases where he was entitled to damages, antecedent to, or by the provisions of, the statute of Gloucester 10 *Co.* 116. a.; as in *assumpsit*, covenant, debt on contract, case, trespass, replevin, ejectment, &c.; or where, by a subsequent statute, double or treble damages are given, in a case where single damages were before recoverable, 2 *Inst.* 289. *Cowp.* 368.; as upon the 2 *Hen.* 4. *c.* 11. for suing in the admiralty court, 10 *Co.* 116. a.b. *Dyer*, 159. b. *Carth.* 287. upon the 8 *Hen.* 6. *c.* 9. for a forcible entry, 10 *Co.* 115. b. *Co. Lit.* 257. b. 2 *Inst.* 289. *Cro. Eliz.* 582. or upon the 2 & 3 *W.* & *M. sess.* 1. *c.* 5. for rescuing a distress for rent, *Carth.* 321. 1 *Salk.* 205. 1 *Ld. Raym.* 19. *Skin.* 555. *Holt*, 172. *S. C.* And he has also a right to costs, in all cases where a certain penalty is given by statute to the party grieved, for otherwise the remedy might prove inadequate. *Cro. Car.* 560. 1 *Roll. Abr.* 574. *Skin.* 363. *Carth.* 230. 1 *Salk.* 206. 1 *Ld. Raym.* 172. *Say. Costs*, 11. *H. Black.* 10.

But the statute of Gloucester did not extend to cases where no damages were recoverable at common law, as in *scire facias*, prohibition, &c. *Comb.* 20.; nor where double or treble damages were given by a subsequent statute, in a new case where single damages were not before recoverable, as in waste against tenant for life or years, 2 *Hen.* 4. 17. 9 *Hen.* 6. 66. b. 10 *Co.* 116. b. 3 *Inst.* 289. upon the statute of Gloucester, (6 *Edw.* 1.) *c.* 5.; for not setting out tithes, *Moor*, 915. *Noy*, 136. *Hardr.* 152. upon the 2 & 3 *Edw.* 6. *c.* 13.; or for driving a distress out of the hundred. 2 *Inst.* 289. *Dyer*, 177. But see *Cro. Car.* 560. 1 *Roll. Abr.* 574. upon the 1 & 2 *Ph.* & *M. c.* 12. Nor does this statute extend to popular actions, where the whole or part of a penalty is given by statute to a common informer, as, upon the 5 *Eliz. c.* 4. *s.* 31. for exercising a trade, without having served an apprenticeship; or upon the statute of usury, 12 *Ann. stat.* 2. *c.* 16. In these and such like cases, therefore, the plaintiff is not entitled to costs, unless they are expressly given him by the statute; but wherever they are so given, he is of course entitled to them. 1 *Roll. Abr.* 574. 1 *Vent.* 135. *Carth.* 231. 1 *Salk.* 206. 1 *Ld. Raym.* 172. *Cas. Pr. C. B.* 87. *Barnes*, 124. *S. C. Cowp.* 366. *H. Black.* 10. *B. N. P.* 333.

Where single damages are given by a statute, subsequent to the statute of Gloucester, in a new case wherein no damages were previously recoverable, it has been doubted whether the plaintiff shall recover costs, if they are not mentioned in the statute. The rule in Pilford's case is, that he shall not, 10 *Co.* 116. a.; and accordingly it is holden, that he is not entitled to costs, in *quare impedit*, wherein damages are given by the statute of Westm. 2. (13 *Edw.* 1.) *c.* 5. *s.* 3. 2 *Hen.* 4. 17. 27 *Hen.* 6. 10. 10 *Co.* 116. a. 2 *Inst.* 289. 362. *Barnes*, 140. And see *Cro. Car.* 360. *Carth.* 231. *Cowp.* 367, 8. But the rule in *Pilfold*'s case is contradicted by lord Coke himself, 2 *Inst.* 289, who says that "this clause (respecting the statute of Gloucester's holding place, in all cases where a man recovers damages) doth extend to give costs, where damages are given to any demandant or plaintiff, in any action, by any statute made after this parliament." And the rule has been since narrowed by several modern decisions, from whence it may be collected that the plaintiff is entitled to costs in all cases where single damages are given by statute to the party grieved, although costs are not particularly mentioned in the statute. 2 *Wils.* 91. *Barnes*, 151. *S. C.* 3 *Bur.* 1723. 1 *T. R.* 71. But see the opinion of *Aston*, J. *contra.* *Cowp.* 367, 8.

In several of the foregoing cases, wherein costs were not recoverable by the plaintiff at common law, they are expressly given him by statute 8 & 9 *Will.* 3. *c.* 11, by which it is enacted, that "in all actions of waste, "and actions of debt upon the statute for "not setting forth tithes, wherein the single "value or damage found by the jury shall "not exceed the sum of twenty nobles; "and in all suits upon any writ or writs of "*scire facias*, and suits upon prohibitions, "the plaintiff obtaining judgment, or any "award of execution, after plea pleaded, "or demurrer joined therein, shall likewise "recover his costs of suit; and if the "plaintiff shall become nonsuit, or suffer "a discontinuance, or a verdict shall pass "against him, the defendant shall recover "his costs, and have execution for the same "by *capias ad satisfaciendum*, *fieri facias*, "or *elegit*."

Upon this statute there have been the following determinations:

In an action of debt for the penalty of the statute 2 & 3 *Ed.* 6. *c.* 13, for not setting out tithes, with a count for the single value, after a demurrer to the declaration the parties submitted to arbitration, and the arbitrator awarded the single value to less than 20 nobles (6*l.* 13*s.* 4*d.*), the court held that the plaintiff was not entitled to costs on the counts for the penalty, under the statute 8 & 9 *Wil.* 3. *c.* 11, the value not having been found by the jury; but they allowed him to have the costs taxed on the count for the single value. *H. Black.* 107. *Barnes* 150.

In *scire facias* the plaintiff is not entitled to costs unless the defendant has appeared and pleaded: and no costs are payable by the plaintiff on moving to quash his own writ before plea. *Cas. Pr. C. B.* 74. nor after a plea in abatement. 1 *Stra.* 638.

In prohibition the rule is that the plaintiff succeeding after a plea pleaded, or demurrer joined, ought to have his costs from the time of the suggestion, or first motion for a prohibition, and all costs incident and subsequent thereto. *Pr. Cas. C. B.* 11. 1 *Str.* 82. 2 *Str.* 1062. And where the defendant pleaded nothing to the merits, but only that he did not proceed in the spiritual court after the prohibition, the court held this not to be a plea within the statute, but a mere sham plea; and ordered the defendant to pay the plaintiff's costs of the proceedings in prohibition. *Barnes* 148. Where the defendant in prohibition lets judgment go by default, the plaintiff is entitled by the common law to a writ, to inquire of his damages for the contempt in proceeding after the prohibition delivered; and of consequence, by the statute of Gloucester, to his costs. *Cas. Pr. B. C.* 20. In this case, however, the plaintiff is only entitled to costs from the time that the rule for a prohibition was made absolute, as the defendant could not possibly be in contempt before. *Say. Costs*, 137. And where the plaintiff was nonsuited, it was holden that the defendant ought only to have the costs of the nonsuit, and not what were incurred by opposing the rule, to show cause why the writ of prohibition should not be granted. *Say*, *Costs* 21. If judgment be given for the plaintiff, as to part of what is in issue, he is entitled to costs, although a consultation be granted as to the residue. 2 *Str.* 1062, 3. And in like manner, if the defendant prevail as to part, he is entitled to costs. *Barnes* 138, 139. But it seems that if the defendant succeed upon demurrer he is not entitled to costs. *Brymer* and *Atkyns*, H. 29 *Geo.* 3. *C. B.* This being a *casus omissus* out of the statute, there is a proviso in the statute, *sec.* 5, that it shall not extend to executors or administrators; and hence it has been determined that in *scire facias*, 1 *Str.* 188, or prohibition, *Cas. Pr. C B.* 158, *Pr. Reg.* 118. *Barnes* 127, 129. *S. C.* they are not liable when plaintiffs, to the payment of costs.

The plaintiff's general right to costs being thus settled and established upon the footing of the statute of Gloucester, has been since altered, restrained, and modified by subsequent statutes. The first statute that restrained the plaintiff's right to costs, was the 43 *Eliz. c.* 6, (extended to Wales, and the counties palatine, by the 11 & 12 *W.* 3. c. 9.) by which it is enacted, "that if in "any personal action, to be brought in any "of her majesty's courts of Westminster, "not being for any title or interest of lands, "nor concerning the freehold or inheritance "of any lands, nor for any battery, it shall "appear to the judges of the same court, "and be so signified by the justices before "whom the same shall be tried, that the "debt or damages to be recovered therein "shall not amount to the sum of 40*s.* that "in every such case the judges or justices "before whom such action shall be pursued "shall not award to the plaintiff any more "costs than the sum of the debt or damages "so recovered shall amount to, but less at "their discretion." The intention of this statute was to confine trifling actions to inferior courts. *Gilb. Eq. Rep.* 196. And a certificate may be granted upon it at any time after the trial of the cause. *Say. Costs,* 18. 3 *T. R.* 38. (*d*) The first instance of a certificate being granted upon this statute was in the case of White *v.* Smith, E. 17 *G.* 2. wherein *Willes,* ch. jus. certified in an action for taking sand, 2 *Str.* 1232. 1 *Wils.* 93. S. C. 3 *Wils.* 325. And since that time certificates have been not unfrequent. *Say. Rep.* 250. 2 *Wils.* 258. 3 *T. R.* 37.

By 21 *Jac.* 1, *c.* 16, it is enacted, that "in all actions upon the case for slanderous "words, to be sued or prosecuted in any "of the courts of record at Westminster, "or in any court whatsoever that hath power "to hold plea of the same, if the jury upon "the trial of the issue in such action, or "the jury that shall inquire of the damages, "do find or assess the damages under 40s. "then the plaintiff or plaintiffs in such ac- "tion shall have and recover only so much "costs as the damages so given or as- "sessed amount unto, without any further "increase of the same, any law, statute, or "usage to the contrary notwithstanding." The operation of this statute is confined to actions for slanderous words spoken of the person, and does not extend to actions for slander of title, &c. *Cro. Car.* 141. 163. 1 *Str.* 645. wherein the special damage is the gist of the action: neither, for the same reason, does it extend to an action for special damage in consequence of words not in themselves actionable, 2 *Ld. Raym.* 831. 1 *Salk.* 206. 7 *Mod.* 129, S. C. *Barnes* 135. Though where the words are actionable in themselves a special damage will not take the case out of the statute. 2 *Ld. Raym.* 15 8. 2 *Str.* 936. S. C. *Barnes* 132. 142. 5 *Bur.* 1688. 2 *Black. Rep.* 1062. *Cas. Pr. C. B.* 137. *contra.* This statute applies to a writ of inquiry as well as a trial, where the damages are under 40*s.* 2 *Str.* 934; and a justification found for the plaintiff will not in that event entitle him to full costs. *Barnes* 128.

But the principal statute made for restraining the plaintiff's right to costs is the 22 & 23 *Car.* 2, *c.* 9, (extended to Wales and the counties palatine, by the 11 & 12 *Will.* 3, *c.* 9.) by which it is enacted, that "in all actions of trespass, assault and bat- "tery, and other personal actions, wherein "the judge at the trial of the cause shall "not find and certify under his hand, upon "the back of the record, that an assault and "battery was sufficiently proved by the "plaintiff against the defendant, or that the "freehold or title of the land mentioned in "the plaintiff's declaration was chiefly in "question, the plaintiff, in case the jury "shall find the damages to be under the "value of 40*s.* shall not recover or obtain "more costs of suit than the damages so "found shall amount unto." It seems to have been the intention of this statute that the plaintiff shall have no more costs than damages in any personal action whatsoever, if the damages be under 40*s.* except in cases of battery or freehold, and not even in these without a certificate. And this construction was adopted in some of the first cases that arose upon the statute; 3 *Keb.* 121. 247. But a different construction soon prevailed; and it is now settled that the statute is confined to actions of assault and battery, and actions for local trespasses, wherein it is possible for the judge to certify that the freehold or title of the land was chiefly in question. *T. Raym.* 487. *T. Jon.* 232. 2 *Show.* 258. S.C. 3 *Mod.* 39. 1 *Salk.* 208. 1 *Str.* 577. *Gilb. Eq. Rep.* 195. *Barnes* 134. 3 *Wils.* 322. S. C. *H. Black.* 294. Therefore it does not extend to actions of debt, covenant, *assumpsit,* trover, or the like; or to actions for a mere assault; or for criminal conversation, or battery of the plaintiff's servant, *per quod consortium vel servitium amisit.* 3 *Keb.* 31. 1 *Salk.* 208. 3 *T. R.* 391. 3 *Wils.* 319. 3 *Keb.* 184. 1 *Salk.* 208. 1 *Stra.* 192.

In actions for local trespasses the statute applies wherever an injury is done to the freehold. 2 *Vent.* 48. *Com. Rep.* 19. 1 *Salk.* 208. 1 *Stra.* 577. 633. 645. *Gilb. Eq. Rep.* 195. 2 *Stra.* 726. 2 *Ld. Raym.* 1444. or to any thing growing upon, *B. N. P.* 330. *Barnes,* 144, or affixed, *B. N. P.* 330. 1 *Stra.* 633. *Cas. Pr. C. B.* 86. *Barnes,* 121. to, the freehold: and in a modern case it was carried still farther: it was an action of trespass *quare clausum fregit*: the first count stated that the defendants broke and entered the close of the plaintiffs, and the grass of the plaintiffs there then growing, with their feet in walking trod down, spoiled, and consumed; and dug up and got divers large quantities of turf, peat, sods, heath, stones, soil and earth of the plaintiffs in and upon the place in which, &c. and took and carried away the same, and converted and disposed of the same to their own use. On the trial a verdict was found for the plaintiffs on the general issue, with 1*s.* damages. The question was, whether the plaintiffs were entitled to any more costs than damages under the statute 22 and 23 *Car.* 2, *c.* 9. And Lord *Mansfield* said that on a consultation with all the judges they were all of opinion that this case was within the statute, and that the *plaintiffs ought to have no more costs than damages.* That what had been called an *asportavit* in this declaration was a mode or qualification of the injury done to the land. The trespass was laid to have been committed on the land by digging, &c. and the *asportavit* as part of the same act; and on the trial of the issue the freehold certainly might have come in question. This is clearly distinguishable from an *asportavit* of personal property, where the freehold cannot come in question, and which therefore is not within the act. Thus after trees are cut down, and thereby severed from the freehold, if a trespasser comes and carries them away, that case is not within the statute, because the freehold cannot come in question; here it might. *Doug.* 779.

Where an injury is done to a personal chattel it is not within the statute. 3 *Keb.* 389. 469. *T. Jon.* 232. 1 *Salk.* 208. 1 *Stra.* 534. *Gilb. Eq. Rep.* 197. S. C. nor where an injury to a personal chattel is laid in the same declaration with an assault and battery, or local trespass. 3 *Mod.* 39. 1 *Salk.* 208. 1*Stra.* 192. 551. *Gilb. Eq. Rep.* 197. S. C. *Barnes*, 119, 120. 134. 3 *Wils.* 322 S. C. 2 *Stra.* 1130. *Say. Costs*, 39. And consequently in these cases, though the damages be under 40*s.* the plaintiff is entitled to full costs, without a certificate. But then it must be a substantive and independent injury; for where it is laid, or proved, merely in aggravation of damages, as a mode or qualification of the assault and battery, or local trespass, 1 *Stra.* 624. *Ante*, 22. or there is a verdict for the defendant, upon that part of the declaration which charges him with an injury to a personal chattel, 2 *Vent.* 180. 125. *Cas. Pr. C. B.* 118. it is within the statute. So where a *laceravit*, or tearing of the plaintiff's clothes, is laid in the declaration, *Say. Rep.* 91. 1 *T. R.* 655. *H. Black.* 291, or found by the jury to be merely in consequence of an assault and battery, the plaintiff, recovering less than 40*s.* damages, is not entitled to full costs without a certificate. *Ibid.* 24.

The certificate required by this statute need not, it seems, be granted at the trial of the cause, 11 *Mod.* 198. And where the defendant lets judgment go by default, *B. N. P.* 329, or justifies the assault and battery, or pleads in such a manner as to bring the freehold or title of the land in question, on the face of the record, 1 *Ld. Raym.* 76. 2 *Salk.* 665. S. C. a certificate is holden to be unnecessary; but where to a plea of a right of way there is a replication of *extra viam*, if the judge do not certify, the plaintiff is not entitled to more costs than damages. *Tidd*, 82. So where in an action for an assault and battery the defendant justifies the assault only, 3 *T. R.* 391, or an assault only is certified by the judge, 2 *Lev.* 102, the plaintiff recovering less than 40*s.* is not entitled to more costs than damages; though in the latter case to entitle him to full costs the judge may certify on the 8 and 9 *Wil.* 3. *c.* 11, that the assault was wilful and malicious. 3 *Wils.* 326. The award of an arbitrator is not tantamount to a judge's certificate under the 22 & 23 *Car.* 2, *c.* 9. 3 *T. R.* 138.

Where the plea or issue, though special, is collateral to the question of freehold or title to the land, as where the defendant justifies an entry as bailiff under process, and issue is joined upon the door's being shut, 2 *Barnard. K. B.* 277, or where upon a plea of a distress for rent there is an issue on the defendant's being bailiff, *Say. Rep.* 250, a certificate is necessary to entitle the plaintiff to full costs; and it is also necessary, where the plaintiff recovers less than 40*s.* damages, on a plea of not guilty to a new assignment. *Barnes*, 124. 129. S. C. *Id.* 149. *B. N. P.* 330. But where the plaintiff is entitled to costs upon the new assignment he is entitled to the costs of all the previous pleadings. 1 *T. R.* 636.

None of the statutes made for restraining the plaintiff's right to costs extend to actions brought in an inferior court, and removed by the defendant into a superior one, 2 *Lev.* 124. 4 *Mod.* 378, 379. 1 *Ld. Raym.* 395. *Cas. Pr. C. B.* 45. (*a*): and it has been holden that the 21 *Jac.* 1. *c.* 16, 1 *Salk.* 207, and the 22 & 23 *Car.* 2. *c.* 9, *Cas. Pr. C. B.* 45, only restrain the court from awarding more costs than damages: but the jury not being restrained thereby may give what costs they please.

The restraint put upon the plaintiff's general right to costs, by the 22 & 23 *Car.* 2. *c.* 9, has been since partly taken off, by 4 & 5 *W.* & *M. c.* 23. *s.* 10, which enacted that "if any inferior tradesman, apprentice, or other dissolute person shall presume to hunt, hawk, fish, or fowl, (unless in company with the master of such apprentice, duly qualified by law), such person shall be subject to the penalties of this act, and shall or may be sued or prosecuted for his wilful trespass, in such his coming on any person's land; and if found guilty thereof, the plaintiff shall not only recover his damages thereby sustained, but his full costs of suit; any former law notwithstanding. It has been holden that a clothier is an inferior tradesman, within the meaning of this statute; and it is said that the words "inferior tradesmen," extend to every tradesman who is not qualified to kill game. *Barnes*. 125, but this was doubted in a subsequent case. 2 *Wils*. 70. *Say. Costs*. 54. *S. C.* wherein the judges where divided in opinion, upon the question, whether a surgeon and apothecary should be considered as an inferior tradesman.

So, by the 8 & 9 *W*. 3. *c*. 11, *s*. 4, for the preventing of wilful and malicious trespasses, it is enacted, "that in all actions of trespass, to be commenced or prosecuted in any of his majesty's courts of record at Westminster, wherein at the trial of the cause it shall appear, and be certified by the judge under his hand, upon the back of the record, that the trespass, upon which any defendant shall be found guilty, was wilful and malicious, the plaintiff shall recover not only his damages, but his full costs of suit; the certificate required by this statute, need not be granted at the trial of the cause; 1 *T. R.* 636. 2 *Wils.* 21. *Doug. Oct.* 108, and it is said that the statute extends to every trespass, that is not accidental as well as trifling. 6 *Mod.* 153.

In the common pleas, where the declaration consists of several counts, and the plaintiff succeeds upon any one of them, he is entitled to the costs of the whole declaration; *B. N. P.* 335. 2 *Black. Rep.* 1199, though the defendant succeed upon the other counts. But it is otherwise in the king's bench; for there, neither party is allowed costs, as to those counts, the issues upon which are found for the defendant. *Say. Costs.* 212. *Dougl. Oct.* 677. 1 *Wils.* 331. In the latter court, where the plaintiff's declaration consisted of two counts, to one of which the defendant pleaded the general issue, which was found for the plaintiff, and to the other a justification, to which the plaintiff demurred, and judgment was thereupon given for the defendant; the court agreed, that the defendant could have no costs upon the demurrer. *Say. Costs.* 211. 2 *Bur.* 1232. But if there be two distinct causes of action, in two separate counts, and as to one the defendant suffers judgment to go by default, and as to the other takes issue, and obtains a verdict, he is entitled to judgment for his costs on the latter counts, notwithstanding the plaintiff is entitled to judgment and costs on the first count. 3 *T. R.* 654.

By the statute for the amendment of the law, (4 *Ann. c.* 16. *s.* 4, 5), it is enacted that "it shall be lawful for any defendant or tenant in any action or suit, or for any plaintiff in replevin, in any court of record, with the leave of the same court, to plead as many several matters thereto, as he shall think necessary for his defence."

"But if any such matter shall, upon a demurrer joined be judged insufficient, costs shall be given at the discretion of the court, or if a verdict shall be found, upon any issue in the said cause, for the plaintiff or demandant, costs shall be also given in like manner, unless the judge who tried the said issue, shall certify that the said defendant or tenant, or plaintiff in replevin, had a probable cause to plead such matter, which upon the said issue shall be found against him."

The certificate upon this statute is not required to be made in court, at the trial of the cause, *Barnes*. 141; and where the judge refuses to grant it, the court have not a discretionary power, whether they will allow the defendant any costs at all; but are bound by the statute to allow him some costs, though the quantum is left to their discretion. *Barnes*. 140. 2 *T. R.* 394, 5. The intention of the legislature was, that if there be several matters pleaded, some of which are found for the plaintiff, he shall be entitled to the costs of those, *Sayer*. 223; notwithstanding other matters are found for the defendant, which entitle him to judgment upon the whole record; unless the judge before whom the cause was tried, shall certify that the defendant had a probable cause to plead the matters which are found against him.

Thus in trespass, the defendant pleaded not guilty and several justifications; upon the trial, the plaintiff not proving his possession of the *locus in quo*, the defendant had a verdict; and by direction of Denison, J. the verdict was entered upon the general issue only; upon which there was a motion for a *venire de novo*; but the court refused the motion; saying the verdict was complete, and determined the cause; that the plaintiff was not entitled to damages; though they said, he might have insisted to have a verdict entered on the other issues, for the sake of costs, which he would be entitled to, unless the judge certified, that the defendant had probable cause to plead such plea. *B. N. P.* 335. But where the defendant in trespass in C. B. pleaded three different justifications, to three different counts, and on issue joined, had a verdict for him on two, and a verdict against him on the third; on motion this was holden not to be a case within the act, and that the plaintiff was entitled to costs at common law, on the whole declaration. *B. N. P.* 335.

Where the defendant pleads not guilty, and a justification, to which the plaintiff demurs, and the plaintiff has judgment on the demurrer, but is nonsuited on the plea of not guilty, he shall nevertheless be allowed the costs of the demurrer, which shall be deducted out of the costs allowed to the defendant. *Barnes*. 136. And if one of several pleas, pleaded by defendant, be adjudged bad on a demurrer to plaintiff's replication, the plaintiff is entitled to have the costs of those pleadings deducted, from the costs taxed for the defendant upon the *postea*, if afterwards upon the trial of the issues joined on the other pleas, the defendant should have a verdict; even though it should appear on the whole of the record, that the plaintiff had no cause of action. 2 *T. R.* 391. But if the plaintiff take issue on several pleas, one of which is insufficient in law, and has a verdict on all the issues, except that joined on the insufficient plea, which is found for the defendant, and afterwards judgment is entered for the plaintiff, still he shall not be allowed any costs, upon issue found for the defendant. 1 *T. R.* 266. *Barnes*. 133. And it has been resolved, at a meeting of all the judges, that if there be a certificate upon the 43 *Eliz.* the plaintiff shall not have the costs of any plea, pleaded with leave of the court; although the issue thereupon joined be found for him, and the judge have not certified, that the defendant had a probable cause for pleading the matter therein pleaded. *Say. Rep.* 260.

In *crim. con.* the defendant pleaded two pleas, viz. not guilty, and not guilty within six years; on the former, the plaintiff joined issue, and obtained a verdict, but to the latter there was a demurrer, and judgment against him; and it was holden, that the defendant should have the costs of the demurrer, but upon the trial, there should be no costs on either side. 2 *Bur.* 753. 2 *Wils.* 85. *S. C.*

The authority of this case, however, seems to be questionable, as to the costs of the trial, from a similar one that was differently determined in the court of common pleas, *Barnes*. 141. as well as from the reasoning that prevailed in several of the foregoing cases. *Tidd.* 35.

The avowant or defendant in replevin, though not within the words is plainly within the meaning of the statute, 4 *Ann.c.* 16. And accordingly, where some issues in replevin are found for the plaintiff, which entitle him to judgment, and some for the defendant, the latter must be allowed the costs of the issues found for him, out of the general costs of the verdict; unless the judge certify, that the plaintiff had a probable cause for pleading the matters, on which those issues are joined. 2 *T. R.* 235, And the general rule is said to be this, where several matters are pleaded by the plaintiff, some of which are found for him, and others for the defendant, so that the plaintiff is entitled to judgment; if the judge who tried the cause certify, that there was a probable cause for pleading those pleas, the master is not to deduct the costs of the issues so found for the defendant, but if there be no certificate, the defendant is entitled to have those costs deducted for him. 2 *T. R.* 237, 141, 144, 146. *Doug. Oct.* 708, 9.

Defendant's Costs.] No costs were recoverable by a defendant at common law. *Tidd.* 2, and the reason seems to be that if the plaintiff failed in his suit, he was amerced to the king *pro falso clamore*, which was thought to be a sufficient punishment, without subjecting him to the payment of costs. The first instance of costs being given to a defendant, was in a writ of right of ward, by the statute of Marlberge. 52 *Hen.* 3. *c.* 6. Afterwards costs were given to the defendant in error, by the 3 *Hen.* 7. *c.* 10; and in replevin, by the 7 *Hen.* 8. *c.* 4, and 21 *Hen.* 8. *c.* 19, &c. But in one of these cases, the defendant is to be considered as an actor; and in the other of them, the provision is virtually for the benefit of the plaintiff in the original action. *Say. Costs.* 70.

In error, brought by the defendant before execution, *Cro. Jac.* 636; or by the plaintiff upon a judgment for the defendant, if the judgment be affirmed, the writ of error discontinued, or the plaintiff in error nonsuited, the defendant in error is entitled to costs, by 3 *Hen.* 7. *c.* 10, and 8 & 9 *W.* 3. *c.* 11. *s.* 2; upon the former of which statutes it has been holden, that costs are recoverable in error, for the delay of execution, although none were recoverable in the original action. *Dyer.* 77. *Cro. Eliz.* 617. 659. 5 *Co.* 101. *S. C. Cro. Car.* 145. 1 *Str.* 262. 2 *Str.* 1084. By the 13 *Car.* 2. *stat.* 2. *c.* 2. *s.* 10, if the judgment be affirmed after verdict, the plaintiff shall pay to the defendant in error his double costs. And by the 4 *Ann. c.* 16. *s.* 25, for preventing vexation, from suing out defective writs of error, it is enacted, that "upon the quashing of any writ of error, for variance from the original record, or other defect, the defendant shall recover against the plaintiff in error his costs, as he should have had, if the judgment had been affirmed, and to be recovered in the same manner." 2 *Str.* 834. *Cas. Temp. Hardw.* 157. Which costs include those of the motion, for quashing the writ of error, 2 *Ld. Raym.* 1403. 1 *Str.* 606. 8 *Mod.* 316. And though no costs were recoverable in the original action, they are payable, on quashing a writ of error. 1 *Str.* 262. But where the defendant in error enters continuances, to defeat the writ of error, the plaintiff in error is not liable to costs on quashing it. 1 *Str.* 139. 2 *Str.* 834. *Barnes*, 250. And none of the statutes before mentioned give costs, upon the reversal of a judgment. 1 *Str.* 617.

In replevin, or second deliverance, the

defendant making avowry, cognizance, or justification, for rents, customs, or services, or for damage feasant, is entitled to costs by the 7 *Hen.* 8. *c.* 4, and 21 *Hen.* 8. *c.* 19. *s.* 3, if the avowry, cognizance, or justification be found for him, or the plaintiff be nonsuit, or otherwise barred; which statutes extend to avowries, &c. made by an executor, 2 *Rol. Rep.* 437; or for an estray, *Cro. Eliz.* 330; and as it should seem, for an amercement by court leet. *Cro. Jac.* 520. *Cro. Eliz.* 300; but not to pleas of *prisel en auter lieu*, upon which the writ is abated. *Com. Rep.* 122; or to pleas of property in the thing distrained. *Hardr.* 153. By the 17 *Car.* 2. *c.* 7. *s.* 2, the defendant obtaining judgment thereon, for the arrearages of rent, or value of the goods distrained is also entitled to his full costs of suit. And by the 11 *Geo.* 2. *c.* 19. *s.* 22, if the defendant avow, or make cognizance, according to that statute, upon a distress for rent, relief, heriot, or other service, and the plaintiff be nonsuit, discontinue his action, or have judgment against him, the defendant shall recover double costs of suit. But this latter statute does not extend to a seizure for a heriot custom. *Barnes.* 148.

At length by the statute 23 *Hen.* 8. *c.* 15, *s.* 1, it was enacted, that "in trespass upon the statute 5 *Rich.* 2, debt, covenant, detinue, account, trespass on the case, or upon any statute for an offence or wrong personal, immediately supposed to be done to the plaintiff, if the plaintiff, after the appearance of the defendant be nonsuited, or a verdict pass against him, the defendant shall have judgment to recover his costs against the plaintiff, to be assessed and taxed by the discretion of the judge or judges of the court, where such action shall be commenced or sued; and shall have such process and execution, for the recovery of the same against the plaintiff, as the plaintiff should or might have had against the defendant, in case judgment had been given for the plaintiff."

But by *s.* 2. of the same statute, it is provided that "every poor person, being plaintiff in any such action, who at the commencement of his suit shall be admitted, by the discretion of the judge or judges where the action is pursued, to have his process counsel of charity, without paying money or fee for the same, shall not be compelled to pay any costs, by virtue of this statute; but shall suffer other punishments, as by the discretion of the justices, before whom the suit shall depend, shall be thought reasonable."

Executors and administrators are not particularly excepted out of the statute 23 *Hen.* 8. *c.* 16, yet as that statute only relates to contracts made with, or wrongs done to the plaintiff, 2 *Str.* 1107; it has been uniformly holden, 2 *Cro. Eliz.* 503. *Cro. Jac.* 229. 2 *Bulst.* 261. 1 *Salk.* 207, 314. 3 *Bur.* 1586. *Say. Costs.* 97; that they are not liable to costs, upon a nonsuit or verdict, where they necessarily sue in their representative character, and cannot bring the action in their own right; as upon a contract entered into with the testator or intestate, *T. Jon.* 47. 2 *Ld. Raym.* 1414. 1 *Str.* 682. *S. C. Cas. Pr. C. B.* 157. *Pr. Reg.* 118. *S. C. Barnes.* 141; or for a wrong done in his lifetime, *Barnes.* 129. But where the cause of action arises after the death of the testator or intestate, and the plaintiff may sue thereon, in his own right, he shall not be excused from the payment of costs, though he bring the action as executor or administrator; as upon a contract express or implied, 6 *Mod.* 91, 181. 1 *Salk.* 207. *S. C.* 1 *Ld. Raym.* 436. 1 *Str.* 682. *Barnes.* 119. 2 *Str.* 1106. 4 *T. R.* 277; or in trover for a conversion, after the death of the testator or intestate. *Com. Rep.* 162. *Cas. Pr. C. B.* 61. *Barnes.* 132. *Cas. Temp. Hardw.* 204. But an executor or administrator is liable to costs, upon a judgment of *non pros, Cas. Pr. C. B.* 14. 157, 8. 3 *Bur.* 1585; and where he has knowingly brought a wrong action, or otherwise been guilty of a wilful default, he shall pay costs upon a discontinuance, *Cas. Pr. C. B.* 79. 3 *Bur.* 1451. 1 *Black. Rep.* 451. *S. C.*: or for not proceeding to trial according to notice, *Cas. Pr. C. B.* 158. 3 *Bur.* 1585; but otherwise he is not liable to costs, in either of these cases, 2 *Str.* 871. *Barnes.* 133. 4 *Bur.* 1927. Nor where he merely sues *en auter droit*, is he liable to costs, upon a judgment as in case of a nonsuit. 4 *Bur.* 1928.

The stat. 23 *Hen.* 8. *c.* 15, only relates to cases where the plaintiff is nonsuited, or has a verdict against him. But by stat. 8 *Eliz. c.* 2, "upon process issuing out of the court of king's bench, if the plaintiff do not declare in three days after bail put in, or if after declaration he do not prosecute his suit with effect, but willingly suffer the same to be delayed or discontinued, or he be nonsuited therein, the judges by their discretions, shall award to the defendant his costs, damages, and charges in that behalf sustained." This statute does not extend, any more than the former to actions brought by executors and administrators, in their representative character. *Cro. Eliz.* 69. *Cro. Jac.* 361. But if the plaintiff enter a *nolle prosequi*, the defendant is entitled to costs upon this statute. 3 *T. R.* 511.

The plaintiff is not entitled to costs in a popular action, for the whole or part of a penalty, given by statute to a common informer, unless they are expressly given him by the statute. *Tidd.* 47. Nor was the defendant entitled to costs, in such an action, until the statute 18 *Eliz. c.* 5. *s.* 3, (made perpetual by the 27 *Eliz. c.* 10), by which it is enacted, that "if any common informer shall willingly delay his suit, or shall discontinue or be nonsuit, or shall have the matter pass against him therein by verdict or judgment in law, the said informer shall pay to the defendant his costs, charges, and damages, to be assigned by the court, in which the suit shall be attempted;" with a proviso, that "this act shall not extend to any officer who in respect of his office, has heretofore usually sued upon penal laws; nor to any officer suing only for matters concerning his office." 2 *Ld. Raym.* 1333. *B. N. P.* 334. This law extends to actions brought upon a subsequent statute, or one that is repealed, 1 *Wils.* 177. *Hutt.* 35,6. 2 *Keb.* 106; and also to actions *qui tam*, for part of a penalty, as well as where the whole is given to a common informer, *Cowp.* 366; but it does not extend to actions, brought by the party grieved, upon a remedial statute. 1 *And.* 116. 2 *Leon.* 116. 4 *Leon.* 55. *Cro. El.* 177. *Hutt.* 22. 1 *Salk.* 30.

There being still many cases in which the defendant was not aided by the provisions of the before mentioned statutes, 2 *Leon.* 9. 3 *Leon.* 92. *B. N. P.* 334; it was enacted by the statute 4 *Jac.* 1. *c.* 3, that "if any person shall commence in any court, any action of trespass, *ejectione firmæ*, or any other action whatsoever, wherein the plaintiff or demandant might have costs, in case judgment should be given for him, and the plaintiff shall be nonsuited therein, after the appearance of the defendant, or a verdict shall pass against him by lawful trial, that then the defendant in every such action, shall have judgment to recover his costs against the plaintiff or demandant, to be assessed and levied in like manner as upon the 23 *Hen.* 8. *c.* 15." By this statute the defendant is entitled to costs, on a nonsuit or verdict, in all cases where the plaintiff would have been entitled to them, if he had obtained judgment. And though the declaration be insufficient, so that the plaintiff could not have had costs thereon, the defendant is nevertheless entitled to costs, for the unjust vexation. *Moor.* 625. 1 *Bulst.* 189. 3 *Bulst.* 248. *Hob.* 219. *Hutt.* 16 *S. C. Cro. Car.* 175. But see *Cro. Jac.* 158,9. *semb. contra.*

By the 13 *Car.* 2. *stat.* 2. *c.* 2. *s.* 3, it is enacted, that "upon an appearance entered for the defendant by attorney, of the term wherein the process is returnable, unless the plaintiff shall put into the court, from whence the process issued, his bill or declaration against the defendant, in some personal action or ejectment of farm, before the end of the term next following after appearance, a nonsuit for want of a declaration may be entered against him; and the defendant shall have judgment to recover costs against the plaintiff to be taxed and levied in like manner as upon the 23 *Hen.* 8. *c.* 15."

And still further to discourage the bringing of frivolous and vexatious actions, it is enacted by the statute 8 & 9 *W.* 3. *c.* 11, *s.* 2, that "if any person shall commence or prosecute any action, in any court of record wherein upon demurrer, either by plaintiff or defendant, demandant or tenant, judgment shall be given by the court against the plaintiff or defendant, the demandant or tenant shall have judgment to recover his costs, and have execution for the same by *capias ad satisfaciendum*, *fieri facias*, or *elegit*." This statute does not extend to demurrers to pleas in abatement, 1 *Ld. Raym.* 337. 1 *Salk.* 194. 12 *Mod.* 195. *Comb.* 482. *S. C.* 2 *Ld. Raym.* 992. 1 *Salk.* 194. 6 *Mod.* 88. *S. C.*; nor in any action, wherein the defendant would not have been entitled to costs upon a nonsuit or verdict. *Cas. Pr. C. B.* 25.

Where there are several defendants, who succeed in the action, the plaintiff may pay costs to which of them he pleases, 1 *Str.* 516. 2 *Str.* 1203; and if they fail, each of them is answerable for the whole costs. Thus, where an ejectment was brought against several defendants, who defended severally, and at the assizes one of them confessed lease, entry, and ouster, and had a verdict against him, but the others did not confess; the court upon application said, the officer must tax the same costs against all the defendants; and that if the plaintiff, after he had satisfaction against one should take out execution against another, the latter might apply to the court. *B. N. P.* 335, 6.

Where one of several defendants lets judgment go by default, and the other pleads a plea which goes to the whole, and shews that the plaintiff had no cause of action, if this plea be found for the defendant who pleaded it, he shall have costs; and being an absolute bar, the other defendant shall have the benefit of it, and shall not pay costs to the plaintiff. *Co. Lit.* 125. *Cro. Jac.* 134. 1 *Lev.* 63. 1 *Sid.* 76. 1 *Keb.* 284. *S. C.* 2 *Ld. Raym.* 1372. 1 *Str.* 610. 8 *Mod.* 217. *C. C. Cas. Pr. C. B.* 107. *Pr. Reg.* 102. *S. C.*

But where the plea does not go to the whole, but is merely in discharge of the party pleading it, there the other party shall not have the benefit of it; but shall pay costs, though it be found against the plaintiff. *Ibid.* 1 *Wils.* 89. 3 *T. R.* 656.

Before the statute 8 & 9 *W.* 3. *c.* 11, if one of several defendants was acquitted, he was not entitled to his costs; the courts construing the former acts to relate only to the case of a total acquittal of all the defendants. 2 *Str.* 1005. And see 1 *Salk.* 194. This being found inconvenient, it was enacted by the same statute, *s.* 1, that "where several persons shall be made defendants, to any action of trespass, assault, false imprisonment, or *ejectione firmæ*, and any one or more of them shall be, upon the trial thereof acquitted by verdict, every person so acquitted shall recover his costs of suit, in like manner as if the verdict had been given against the plaintiff, and acquitted all the defendants; unless the judge, before whom the cause is tried, shall immediately after the trial thereof, in open court certify upon the record under his hand that there was a reasonable cause for making such person a defendant." This statute is confined to the particular actions therein mentioned; and does not extend to an action of trespass upon the case, 2 *Str.* 1005; nor consequently to an action of trover, *Barnes.* 139; neither does it extend to an action of replevin. 3 *Bur.* 1284. 1 *Black. Rep.* 355. *S. C.*

When a feigned issue is ordered by a court of law, whether it be in a civil or criminal proceeding, the costs always follow the verdict, and must be paid to the party obtaining it. 1 *Lil. P. R.* 344. *Barnes.* 130. 1 *Wils.* 261. 331. *Say. Rep.* 24. 1 *Wils.* 324.

But when a feigned issue is ordered by a court of equity, the costs do not follow the verdict as a matter of course; but the finding of the jury is returned back to the court which ordered it, and the costs there are in the discretion of the court. *Ibid.* Where the issue is ordered by a court of law, on a rule for an information, *Say. Rep.* 229. 1 *Bur.* 605, or motion for an attachment, *Say. Rep.* 253, the costs of the original rule, or motion, do not in general follow the verdict, but only the costs of the feigned issue; which costs are to be reckoned from the time when the feigned issue was first ordered and agreed to, 1 *Bur.* 604. Yet where it was ordered by the consent-rule that the costs should abide the event of the issue, the court directed the whole costs to be paid under it. 2 *Bur.* 1021.

Double and treble Costs.] Where the plaintiff recovers single damages he is only entitled to single costs, unless more be expressly given him by the statute. But if double or treble damages be given by statute, in a case wherein single damages were before recoverable, the plaintiff is entitled to double or treble costs, although the statute be silent respecting them, *Say. Costs*, 228; as in an action upon the 2 *Hen.* 4, *c.* 11, for suing in the Admiralty court, &c. (*ante.*)

In some cases double and treble costs are expressly given to the plaintiff, as upon the game-laws by the statute 2 *Geo.* 3, *c.* 19, *s.* 5; and wherever a plaintiff is entitled to double or treble costs, the costs given by the court *de incremento* are to be doubled or trebled, as well as those given by the jury. 2 *Leon.* 52. *Cro. Eliz.* 582. 3 *Lev.* 351. *Carth.* 297. 321. 2 *Stra.* 1048. 1 *T. R.* 252.

But double or treble costs are not to be understood to mean, according to their literal import, twice or thrice the amount of single costs; for where a statute gives DOUBLE costs they are calculated thus: 1, the common costs, and then half the common costs. If TREBLE costs, 1st, the common costs; 2d, half of these, and then half of the latter. *Table of Costs in principio.*

Double or treble costs are also in some cases expressly given to the defendant, as in actions against parish officers, by 43 *Eliz.* *c.* 2, *s.* 19; against justices of the peace, constables, &c. by the 7 *Jac.* 1, *c.* 5, for distresses for rents and services; by the 11 *Geo.* 2, *c.* 19. *s.* 21, 22; and against officers of the excise or customs by 23 *Geo.* 3. *c.* 70, *s.* 34, and 24 *Geo.* 3, sess. 2, *c.* 47. *s.* 35. In these and such like cases, where it does not appear on the face of the record that the defendant is entitled to the benefit of the act, (as where he pleads the general issue) and there is no particular mode appointed for recovery of the costs, the proper mode, after a nonsuit or verdict for the defendant is to apply to the court, upon an affidavit of the facts, for leave to enter a suggestion on the roll. 1 *Stra.* 49, 50. *Cas. Pr. C. B.* 16. *Cas. Temp. Hardw.* 125. *Id.* 138. 2 *Stra.* 1021. S. C. *Say. Rep.* 214. 3 *Wils.* 442. And it cannot be done by rule of court, 1 *Stra.* 50, unless where the plaintiff moves for leave to discontinue on payment of costs; in which case the court may make it part of the rule that he shall pay double or treble costs. 2 *Stra.* 974. *Cas. Temp. Hardw.* 125. But where a particular mode is appointed by statute for the recovery of double or treble costs, as by the certificate of the judge who tried the cause on the 7 *Jac.* 1. *c.* 5, there that particular mode must be observed, 2 *Vent.* 45. *Doug. oct.* 307, 308: so that if the judge certify there is no need of a suggestion; and if he do not it is useless, except where judgment goes by default. *Cas. Temp. Hardw.* 138, 139.

Taxing of costs.] Costs are taxed as between party and party, by the master in the king's bench, or by one of the prothonotaries in the common pleas, upon a bill made out by the attorney for the party entitled, or more frequently without a bill, upon a view of the proceedings; and if there have been any extra expenses which do not appear on the face of the proceedings, there should be an affidavit made of such expenses, to warrant the allowance of them, which is called an affidavit of increased costs. *Imp. K. B.* 348.

It is usual among fair practisers to give notice to the opposite attorney of the time when the costs are intended to be taxed, but in order to enforce it there must be a rule to be present at taxing costs, which rule is obtained from the clerk of the rules in the king's bench, or one of the secondaries in the common pleas, and should be duly served; after which, if the costs are taxed without notice, the taxation is irregular, and the attorney liable to an attachment. *Impey*, 348.

The means of recovering costs as between party and party, are by action or execution, upon a judgment obtained for them, or by attachment, upon a rule of court. Thus in ejectment, where there is a verdict and judgment against the tenant, an action may be brought, or execution taken out thereon for the costs, *Run. Eject.* 140, 141; but where the plaintiff is nonsuited for not confessing lease, entry, and ouster, the lessor of the plaintiff must proceed by attachment, upon the consent rule. *Ibid.* 1 *Salk.* 259. *Barnes*, 182. And so where the nominal plaintiff is nonsuited upon the merits, or has a verdict and judgment against him, the only remedy is by attachment, against the lessor of the plaintiff. *Run. Eject.* 142, 143.

In proceeding by attachment a copy of the rule, with the officer's *allocatur* thereon, should be personally served on the party liable to the payment of costs; and at the same time the original rule should be shown to him, and a demand made of the payment of them, which demand may be made by the acting attorney in the cause, although he act in the name of another attorney. And if the costs be not paid, the court, upon an affidavit of the circumstances, will grant an attachment. In the king's bench the rule for an attachment is absolute in the first instance, and may be moved for on the last day of term. 3 *T. R.* 351. *Barnes*, 120. *Say. Rep.* 95. 5 *Burr.* 2686.

Besides the ordinary method of proceeding there are certain auxiliary means for the recovery of costs as between party and party: These means are by moving to stay the proceedings until security be given for the payment of costs, or until the costs are paid of a former action for the same cause, or by deducting the costs of one action from those of another. *Tidd*, 60, 61.

Thus in ejectment, 1 *Str.* 681, and actions *qui tam*, 1 *Stra.* 697. 705. *Barnes*, 126, where the plaintiff or his lessor is unknown to the defendant, the latter may call for an account of his residence, or place of abode, from the opposite attorney, and if he refuse to give it, or give in a fictitious account of a person who cannot be found, the court will stay the proceedings until security be given for the payment of costs. And in ejectment, where the lessor of the plaintiff is an infant, dead, or resident abroad, 1 *Str.* 694. 2 *Str.* 932. 1206. 1 *Wils.* 130. *Cowp.* 24. *Barnes*, 183. *B. N. P.* 111. *Cowp.* 128. *Barnes*, 147. 2 *Bur.* 1177. *Say. Costs*, 153, the court will stay the proceedings until a real and substantial plaintiff be named, or some responsible person undertake for the payment of costs. A similar undertaking is also required in an action for the mesne profits, brought in the name of the nominal plaintiff in ejectment. *Say. Rep.* 78.

But except in ejectment, 2 *Bur.* 1177. *Say. Costs*, 153, or actions *qui tam*, 1 *Stra.* 697. 2 *Stra.* 1206. 1 *Wils.* 266, it was not formerly usual to require security for costs where the plaintiff resided abroad, 2 *Str.* 1206. 1 *Wils.* 266. *Say. Costs*, 155. 2 *Bur.* 1026. 4 *Bur.* 1205. *Cowp.* 24. 158: for it was considered that such a proceeding might affect trade, by excluding foreigners from our courts, and would be a mean of clogging the course of justice. But now, although a plaintiff is not compellable to give security for costs, merely as a foreigner, if he reside in this country, yet, whether foreigner or native, if he reside abroad, out of the reach of the process of the court, the proceedings may be stayed till his return, or security be given for the payment of costs. 1 *T. R.* 267. 362. 491. These are the only grounds upon which the proceedings can be stayed for want of security for costs; it being holden that they shall not be stayed even in a *qui tam* action merely on account of the plaintiff's poverty, *Cowp.* 24. *Barnes*, 126, or in ejectment, where the lessor of the plaintiff is known of full age, and resident in this country. 1 *T. R.* 491.

In a second ejectment the court will stay the proceedings until the costs are paid of a prior one for the same case; and that whether it be brought in the same or a different court. 1 *Salk.* 255. 1 *Stra.* 548. 554. 2 *Stra.* 1152. 1206. 1 *T. R.* 492. K. B. *Pr. Reg.* 174. *Barnes*, 133. 2 *Black. Rep.* 304. 1158. 1180. C. B. And where the defendant in ejectment brings a writ of error before he has quitted possession, the court will stay the proceedings pending the writ of error. 1 *Salk.* 258, 9, and see 1 *Str.* 554.

But the vexation of the party is said to be the ground of these rules: 4 *Mod.* 379. 2 *Str.* 1152. And therefore if the second ejectment be brought by the defendant, or there appears to be no vexation, the court will not make a rule for staying the proceedings until the costs are paid of the former ejectment. 4 *Mod.* 379. 1 *Str.* 681. 2 *Str.* 1152. 1121. *Barnes*, 180.

In other cases it was not formerly usual to stay the proceedings in a second action until the costs were paid of a prior one, for the same cause, and particularly if the merits did not come in question on the former trial. But of late years it has been done, in several instances, on the ground of vexation: 2 *T. R.* 511. K. B. *Say. Costs*, 245. 247

2 *Black. Rep.* 741. 3 *Wils.* 149. S. C. C. B. and in one case, *Lampley* and wife v. *Sands*, H. 25 *Geo.* 3. K. B. where an action was brought by husband and wife, the court stayed the proceedings until the payment of costs in a former action, at the suit of the husband only, it being for the same demand. *Tidd*, 64, 65.

The practice of deducting or setting off the costs in one action against those in another, however agreeable to natural justice, does not seem to have obtained till lately, in the court of king's bench. 2 *Str.* 891. 1203. *B. N. P.* 336. 4 *T. R.* 124. But in the court of common pleas it has been frequently allowed; and that not only where the parties have been the same, *Barnes*, 145. 2 *Black. Rep.* 826. *B. N. P.* 336, but also where they have been in some measure different. Thus a party has been permitted to set off a separate demand for costs payable to himself alone, against a joint demand for costs payable by himself and others, *Barnes*, 146. But see *Barnes*, 130: and he has also been permitted to set off a joint demand for costs payable to himself and another, against a separate demand for damages and costs payable by himself only. *Say. Costs*, 254. 2 *Black. Rep.* 827. But where in an action of trespass against four defendants, the plaintiff obtained a verdict against one, and the other three were acquitted, the court would not suffer the costs of the three defendants who were acquitted to be deducted out of the plaintiff's costs, against that defendant who was found guilty, declaring the motion to be unprecedented. *Barnes*, 145. *B. N. P.* 336.

Where the application is made by the party to whom the larger sum is due, the rule is for a stay of proceedings, on acknowledging satisfaction for the lesser sum. *B. N. P.* 336. But where the lesser sum is due to the party applying, the rule is to have it deducted, and for a stay of proceedings on payment of the balance. *Say. Costs*, 254. 4 *T. R.* 124.

As between attorney and client, the former may maintain an action against the latter for the recovery of his costs. *Cro. Car.* 159, 160. But by the stat. 3 *Jac.* 1. *c.* 7, *s.* 1, "all attornies and solicitors shall give a true bill unto their masters or clients, or their assigns, of all charges concerning the suits which they have for them, subscribed with their hands and names, before such time as they or any of them shall charge their clients with any the same fees or charges." Upon this statute it was a good plea to an action brought by an attorney for his fees, that no bill had been delivered to the defendant, 3 *Keb.* 118. 514. *T. Raym.* 245. 3 *Salk.* 19. S. C. But see *Carth.* 57. 1 *Show.* 48. *Comb.* 126. S. C. or the statute might have been given in evidence on *non assumpsit*. 1 *Show.* 338. But if an attorney had delivered his bill to the defendant, after the arrest, and before the bill filed, it was well enough, 1 *Lil. P. R.* 145, but see 1 *Str.* 633. *Cas. Pr.* C. B. 27. S. C. And this statute did not extend to attornies in inferior courts, but only to those in the courts at Westminster. *Carth.* 147. 1 *Show.* 96. 1 *Salk.* 86. S. C. It should also seem that an attorney's bill could not have been taxed unless an action was depending thereon, nor without bringing the amount of it into court. To remedy these manifold inconveniences it was enacted by the stat. 2 *Geo.* 2, *c.* 23, *s.* 23, (made perpetual by 30 *Geo.* 2. *c.* 19, *s.* 75) that "no attorney of the court of king's bench, common pleas, or exchequer, &c. nor any solicitor in chancery, &c. shall commence or maintain any action or suit for the recovery of any fees, charges, or disbursements, at law or in equity, until the expiration *of one month* or more after such attorney or solicitor respectively shall have delivered unto the party to be charged therewith, or left for him at his dwelling-house, or last place of abode, a bill of such fees, charges, and disbursements, (*Barnes*, 243,) written in a common legible hand, and in the English tongue, except law-terms and names of writs, and in words at length, except times and sums, which bill shall be subscribed with the proper hand of such attorney or solicitor respectively.

"And upon application of the party chargeable, or of any other person in that behalf, unto the chancellor, or master of the rolls, or unto any of the courts aforesaid, or unto a judge or baron of any of the courts, in which the business, or the greatest part thereof, in amount, shall have been transacted; and upon the submission of the party or person aforesaid to pay the whole sum that upon taxation shall appear to be due, it shall be lawful for the said master of the rolls, or any of the courts aforesaid, or any judge or baron, to refer the said bill, although no action be then depending, to be taxed by the proper officer, without any money being brought into court; and if the attorney or solicitor, or the party chargeable, having notice, shall refuse or neglect to attend such taxation, the said officer may proceed to tax the bill *ex parte*, pending which reference and taxation no action shall be commenced.

"And upon the taxation the said party shall forthwith pay to the said attorney or solicitor, or to any person by him authorized to receive the same, that shall be present at the taxation, or otherwise unto such other person, or in such manner, as the court shall direct, the whole sum that shall be found to be due thereon, which payment shall be a full discharge of the said bill; and in default thereof the said party shall be liable to an attachment, or such other proceedings, at the election of the attorney or solicitor, as such party was before liable unto.

"And if, upon the taxation it shall be found, that such attorney or solicitor shall have been overpaid, then he shall forthwith refund, and pay unto the party all such money as the officer shall certify to have overpaid; and in default thereof, the said attorney or solicitor shall in like manner, be liable to an attachment, or to such other proceedings, at the election of the said party, as he would have been subject unto, if this act had not been made.

"And the said courts are to award the costs of such taxations to be paid by the parties, according to the event of the taxation: that is to say, if the bill taxed be less, by a sixth part, than the bill delivered then the attorney or solicitor is to pay the costs, but if it shall not be less, the court in their discretion shall charge the attorney or client, in regard to the reasonableness or unreasonableness of such bill."

But by the 12 *Geo.* 2. *c.* 13. *s.* 6, the said act 2 *Geo.* 2. shall not extend to any bill of fees, charges, and disbursements, due from any attorney or solicitor, to any other attorney or solicitor, or clerk in court; but every such attorney, solicitor, or clerk in court, may use such remedies for the recovery thereof, as he might have done before the making of the said act."

Upon the latter clause, there is a case in 1 *Wils.* 266. where a judge of the court of king's bench having made an order, to refer an agent's bill to be taxed, and the master not having obeyed it, the court was applied to, and held that the order was irregular; the master declaring, that he had never taxed a bill for agency. But it is now the uniform practice of both courts, *Doug. oct.* 199, 200. to refer an agent's bill to be taxed, upon the defendant's bringing into court the sum claimed by the plaintiff. It is not necessary, however, that such a bill should be signed, or delivered, before the commencement of an action. *Doug. oct.* 199. *in notis.*

If the whole bill be for conveyancing, or for business done at the quarter sessions, &c. it cannot be taxed. *Barnes,* 141,2. 4 *T. R.* 124. *Barnes,* 122. *C. B.* But where an attorney had delivered two separate bills, one of which was for fees and disbursements in causes, and the other for making conveyances, a rule was made for taxing both. *Say. Rep.* 233. *Say. Costs,* 320. *S. C.* And so, where it was moved, that the master might be directed to tax those articles in an attorney's bill, which related to conveyancing and parliamentary business, the rest being for management of causes in the court of king's bench, lord Mansfield said, there was no doubt but the master might tax the whole: that he recollected a case, where the fees paid to a proctor, for business done in the ecclesiastical court, made part of the bill; and it was determined, that, as the whole bill had been referred to the master, he might tax that part of it. *Doug. oct.* 199. *in notis.*

It is not necessary for the executor or administrator of an attorney, to deliver a bill of costs, for business done by his testator or intestate, before the commencement of an action, *Cas. Pr. C. B.* 58.; the statute 2 *Geo.* 2. *c.* 23. *s.* 23. being confined to actions brought by the attorney himself, and not extending to his personal representatives. And, in the court of common pleas, they will not suffer such a bill to be taxed, *Barnes,* 119, 122.: but in the court of king's bench it is otherwise, 2 *Str.* 1056. *Say. Costs,* 324,5. *Imp. K. B.* 482.; for there, the bill may be referred to be taxed, on the defendant's undertaking to pay what is due. *Tidd.* 75. An attorney delivered his bill, and, after his death, application was made to tax it, and above a sixth part was taken off; it was moved that the executrix might pay the costs, but the court held she should not, for the words of the act 2 *Geo.* 2. *c.* 23. *s.* 23. impose them upon the attorney or solicitor only, and the executrix is not to blame, if she stand upon his bill, or make out one from his books. 2 *Str.* 1056. *Say Costs,* 327

After an attorney's bill has been settled and paid, and the payment has been long acquiesced under, the court will not refer it to be taxed as a matter of course, *Say Costs,* 323. *Doug. oct.* 199. So where a bond had been given for the debt, five years before, and the vouchers had been delivered up, the court would not refer the bill to be taxed, saying, an attorney at this rate could never be safe, *Cas. Pr. C. B* 109. *Pr. Reg.* 37. *S. C.* And it is a general rule that an attorney's bill cannot be taxed, at the trial of an action brought upon it, nor after verdict, *Doug. oct.* 199 *K. B. Barnes,* 124 *C. B.*; for if the business was really done, (which must be proved at the trial,) the delay of the defendant, for more than a month, in objecting to the quantum, is an admission that he thinks it to be reasonable. *Tidd.* 76, 7.

But though an attorney's bill has been settled and paid, yet the court, under special circumstances, will refer it to be taxed; for the client may, by affidavit, shew, that the business charged was never performed, or that the charges are fraudulent: and where that is the case, neither payment, nor a release, nor a judgment for the money due, will preclude the court from referring the bill to be taxed. *Say. Costs,* 323. *Doug. oct.* 199. *S. P.*

It may also be taxed, though there was a special agreement, between the attorney and his client, that the former should be paid for his time, ot a certain rate by the day, besides his expences; or though he has obtained a warrant of attorney from his client, for confessing judgment for the money due upon his bill, and has entered judgment thereupon. *Say. Costs*, 321, 2,

The statute 2 *Geo.* 2. *c.* 23. *s.* 23. only requires the delivery of a bill, for the bringing of an action; and therefore, though an attorney cannot bring an action on his bill, till it has been delivered a month, that circumstance is not necessary to enable him to set it off. But he must not produce it at the trial by surprize. It is sufficient, in such case, to deliver it time enough, for the plaintiff to have it taxed before the trial. *Doug. oct.* 199. *in notis.*

If any attorney refuse to deliver a bill to his client, the latter may compel him, by taking out a summons before a judge; and if the attorney, on being served therewith, do not attend, an order will be made for delivering it, within a reasonable time. If he still neglect to deliver it, the order should be made a rule of court; and on serving the same, and making affidavit thereof, the court on motion will grant an attachment. The bill being delivered, the client may apply for a judge's summons, to shew cause why it should not be referred to the proper officer to be taxed; upon which an order will be made, the client undertaking to pay what shall appear to be due upon such taxation. If the attorney do not attend, an order will be made of course. *But the client cannot have a summons for delivery of the bill, and taxing it together. Imp. K. B.* 479, 480. *Barnes*, 126. *C. B.*

It was formerly necessary, in the king's bench, to have three appointments, in case the attorney did not attend, before the master could proceed *ex parte*. But, by a late rule, *H.* 32 *Geo.* 3. 4 *T. R.* 580. it is ordered, that "on every appointment to be made by the master, the party on whom the same shall be served, and required to attend, shall attend such appointment, without waiting for a second; or in default thereof, the master shall proceed *ex parte* on the first appointment."

Under the statute.] If a sixth part of the bill be taken off, the attorney is to pay the costs of taxation; but if less, the costs are in the discretion of the court. In the exercise of this discretion, however, the courts are governed by the statute: and accordingly, the costs of taxation have been always reciprocally given to the client or attorney, as a sixth part has, or has not been taken off. *Barnes*, 118. 147, 8.

To assist the attorney, in recovering his costs, he has a lien for the amount of his bill, upon the deeds, papers, and writings in his hands, belonging to his client, 4 *T. R.* 124. *Doug. oct.* 104,5.: and until that be paid, the court will not order them to be delivered up, 1 *Lil. P. R.* 142. 3 *T. R.* 275. Nor can an attorney be changed by his client, without leave of the court, or order of a judge, on payment of his bill, to be taxed by the proper officer. 1 *Lil. P. R.* 141. *Doug. oct.* 217. An attorney has also a lien, on the money recovered by his client, for his bill of costs. 4 *T. R.* 124. If the money come to his hands, he may retain it, to the amount of his bill: he may stop it *in transitu*, if he can lay hold of it: if he apply to the court, they will prevent its being paid over, till his demand is satisfied. And lord Mansfield declared he was inclined to go still farther, and to hold, that if the attorney give notice to the defendant, not to pay the money recovered by his client, till his bill be satisfied, a payment by the defendant, after such notice, would be in his own wrong, and like paying a debt which has been assigned, after notice. *Doug.* 100, 101. So in a late case, where the defendant applied to set off the debt and costs in one action, against those in another, the court would not suffer it to be done, until the attorney's bill was first discharged. 4 *T. R.* 123, 4. But the court will not go beyond those limits. And therefore where the defendant, not having had any notice to the contrary, compromised the debt and costs with the plaintiff, before his attorney had been paid, the court would not oblige the defendant to pay him. *Doug.* 226.

COSTS IN EQUITY. Costs in equity are in the discretion of the court upon all the circumstances of the case, though he who fails is *primâ facie* to be taken to be the person liable to the costs; and those parties who depend upon circumstances to govern the discretion of the court in withholding costs, must show the existence of those circumstances, in a sufficient degree to cut down the *primâ facie* claim of costs. 11 *Vez.* 458.

If the plaintiff obtains a decree, he has generally his costs of suit, but if it be against a trustee not in fault, but who desires only to be indemnified by the decree of the court in the performance of the trust, he shall pay no costs. *Pre. Chan.* 254. 3 *Peere Wms.* 347. 3 *Bro. Ch. Ca.* 90. 1 *Ves. jun.* 245.

And where trustees and executors are brought into court, they are entitled to costs, though they make a claim and fail, if merely by submission. 1 *Ves. J.* 205.

But the court will not give costs to a trustee, whose neglect has occasioned the suit. 5 *Vez.* 128. And where trustees are charged with a loss occasioned by their negligence, though without any corrupt motive, the costs follow of course. 6 *Vez.* 488. And notwithstanding a testator may direct that his executors for any expences they may be put to, shall be allowed their costs out of his estate, yet if they act fraudulently, the court will decree costs against them. 3 *Atk.* 126.

Where a cause is set down upon bill and answer only, or comes on after withdrawing the replication, it is discretionary in the court to dismiss with 40*s.* costs, or costs to be taxed, or no costs. *Wy. Pr. R.* 146.

Upon affidavit to satisfaction of the court, that the complainant lives beyond sea, he may be ordered to enter into 40*l.* security to pay costs, and so it will be if he is about to go to live, or stay long there. *Wy. Pr.* 146. 2 *Vez.* 557.

But the court will not order a plaintiff residing abroad to give security for costs where there are co-plaintiffs residing in England, for the defendant has a security for his costs against each of the plaintiffs. 6 *Vez.* 612.

And this security should be applied for before an order for time to answer is obtained, if it appears upon the bill, or is in the defendant's knowledge, that the plaintiff is beyond sea; otherwise it may be applied for in any stage of the cause. 6 *Vez.* 612. 10 *Vez.* 287.

Sometimes upon a full hearing, the court will, upon pronouncing a decree for the plaintiff, order the defendant to pay him his costs to that time, and if the court refers matters to a master, as accounts to be taken or the like, between plaintiff and defendant, the court commonly reserves costs in these cases till after the master hath made his report; and after he has made his report, the court gives either party liberty to apply for further directions as they shall think fit; whereon such order shall be made as shall be just, in which case, after the master has made his report, and the same is absolutely confirmed by the court, either party may apply by petition to the lord *chancellor* to have the cause heard on the master's report as to costs, which is always granted of course; and that order being drawn up, and served on the adverse clerk in court, and the cause being set down by the register to be heard upon the master's report, the court will order costs to be taxed by the said master, and paid by such party as the court shall think proper. *Har. Ch. Pr. cap.* 56. *Costs.*

On bills for a discovery and nothing more, the defendant is always entitled to and may move as a matter of course for his costs, after he has put in a full and sufficient answer. *Wy. Pr. R. Costs. Mitf.* 136.

After an order to have costs taxed, the clerk or solicitor for the party that is to have them, delivers in a bill thereof to the master, to whom they are referred, who gives the other side a copy of the charge, if desired, and on a request, he gives out a summons for the party to attend him at a certain time, and so from time to time till the whole costs are taxed, and then he reports the quantum to the court. *Wy. Pr. R.* 148.

The report being confirmed, and the order duly entered, there may be a subpœna to the party to pay them; and if upon due service thereof, the costs be not paid, then upon affidavit as to the default, an attachment, and further process of contempt to a sequestration go forth, if there be occasion. *Wy. Pr. R.* 328.

COT, in the old Saxon signifies cottage, and so is still used in many parts of England. *Cowel. Blount.*

COTARIUS, a cottager: the *cotarii*, or cottagers, are mentioned in Domesday. *Ibid.*

COTE and COT. The names of places which begin or end with these words or syllables, have the signification of a little house or cottage: there are likewise dove-cotes, which are small houses or places for the keeping of doves or pigeons. *Ibid.*

COTELLUS, COTERIA, both signify a small cottage, house or homestall. *Ibid.*

COTERELLUS. *Cotarius* and *coterellus*, according to Spelman and Du Fresne, are servile tenants: but in Domesday and other ancient MSS. there appears a distinction as well in their tenure and quality, as in their name. For the *cotarius* had a free socage tenure, and paid a stated firm or rent in provisions or money, with some occasional customary services; whereas the *coterellus* seems to have held in mere villenage, and his person, issue and goods, were disposable at the pleasure of the lord. *Paroch. Antiq.* 310. *Cowel. Blount.*

COTESWOLD, is used for sheep cotes and sheep feeding on hills: from the Sax. *cote* and *wold*, a place where there is no wood. *Cowel. Blount.*

COTGARE, a kind of refuse wool, so clung or clotted together, that it cannot be pulled asunder. See *stat.* 12 *Ric.* 2. *c.* 9. *Cowel. Blount.*

COTLAND and COTSETHLAND, land held by a cottager, whether in socage or villenage. *Cowel. Blount.*

COTSETHLA, COTSETLE, the little seat or mansion belonging to a small farm. *Ibid.*

COTSETHUS, a cottage-holder, who, by servile tenure, was bound to work for the lord. *Cowel.*

COTTAGE, (*cotagium*) is properly a little house for habitation, without any land belonging to it. See stat. 4 *Ed.* 1. *stat.* 1. But by 31 *El. cap.* 7. no man could build a cottage, unless he laid four acres of land thereto, except it were in a market-town or city, or within a mile of the sea, or for the habitation of labourers in mines, sailors, foresters, shepherds, &c. or a cottage erected by order of justices of peace, &c. for poor impotent people. But by 15 *Geo.* 3. *c.* 23. this stat. of 31 *Eliz.* was repealed.

COTUCA, coat armour. *Walsing.* 114. *Cowel. Blount.*

COTUCHANS, boors or husbandmen, of which mention is made in Domesday. *Ibid.*

COUCHER, or COURCHER, signifies a factor that continues abroad in some place or country for traffic; as formerly in Gascoign, for buying of wines. Stat. 37 *Ed.* 3.

c. 16. This word is also used for the general book wherein any corporation, &c. register their particular acts. 3 & 4 *Ed.* 6. c. 10. *Cowel. Blount.*

COVENABLE, (Fr. *covenable,* Lat. *rationabilis*) is what is covenient or suitable.—Every of the same three sorts of goods, &c. shall be good and covenable, as in old time hath been used. Stat. 31 *Ed.* 3. *cap.* 2. Covenably indowed, that is, indowed as is fitting. 4 *H.* 8. *c.* 12. See *Plowd.* 472. *Cowel. Blount.*

COVENANT, (*conventio*) is the consent and agreement of two or more persons to do or not to do some act or thing contracted between them. Also it is the declaration the parties make, that they will stand to such agreement, relating to lands or other things; and is created by deed in writing, sealed and executed by the parties: a covenant may likewise be implied in the contract, as incident thereto. 2 *Mod. Entr.* 91. And if the persons do not perform their covenants, an action of covenant is the remedy to recover a compensation in damages for the breach thereof. *Ibid.*

A covenant is generally either in fact or in law: in fact is that which is expressly agreed between the parties, and inserted in the deed; and in law, is that covenant which the law intends and implies, though it be not expressed in words; as if a lessor demise and grant to his lessee a house or lands, &c. for a certain term, the law will intend a covenant on the lessor's part, that the lessee shall, during the term, quietly enjoy the same against all incumbrances. 1 *Inst.* 384.

There is also a covenant real, and covenant personal: a covenant real is that, whereby a man ties himself to pass a thing real, as lands or tenements; or to levy a fine of lands, &c. And covenant personal, is where the same is annexed to the person and merely personal; as if a person covenants with another by deed to build him a house, or to serve him, &c. *F. N. B.* 145. 5 *Rep.* 10.

Covenants are likewise inherent, that tend to the support of the land or thing granted; or are collateral to it; and are affirmative, where somewhat is to be performed; or negative; executed, of what is already done, or executory: but a covenant being to bind a man, to do something *in futuro,* is for the most part executory, and can only be enforced and carried into execution by a court of equity. 1 *Vent.* 176. *Dyer* 112, 271.

There is this difference, however, between a covenant, and a condition; a condition broken, gives a right of entry, but covenant broken, gives an action only. *Owen* 54. Note also that a person cannot have action of covenant upon a verbal agreement, for it cannot be grounded without writing. *F. N. B.* 45.

All covenants between persons must be to do what is lawful, or they will not be binding; and if the thing to be done be impossible, the covenant is void. *Dyer.* 112.

An infant within age may bind himself apprentice; but neither at common law nor by statute, can he be bound by covenant for his apprenticeship, so as to make himself liable to an action of covenant, if he depart, &c. 1 *Cro.* 129. *Winch.* 68.

No cause of action arises on a covenant, till it is broken: and as to breaches of covenant, if a person by his own act disables himself to perform a covenant, or does any act to defeat the intent and use of it, it is a breach thereof. 5 *Rep.* 21.

In covenant that a person shall hold land free from all incumbrances, and be kept indemnified from arrears of rent; there, till an action is brought, or distress made, he is not indemnified; and a suit in chancery is no breach in such case; but where a jointure, or dower is recovered, it is. *Skin.* 397. *Moor* 159. *Palm.* 339.

When a covenant is to two persons jointly, one of them may not bring action of covenant, or plead alone, but both must join. 1 *Nals.* 558.

Covenants are generally taken most strongly against the covenantor, and for the covenantee. *Plowd.* 287. But it is a rule in law, that where one thing may have several intendments, it shall be construed in the most favourable manner for the covenantor. 1 *Lut.* 490. The common use of covenants is for assuring of land; quiet enjoyment free from incumbrances; for payment of rent reserved; and concerning repairs, &c. And in deeds of covenant, sometimes a clause for performance, with a penalty, is inserted in the body of the deed. Other times, and more frequently, bonds for performance, with a sufficient penalty, are given separate; which last being sued, the jury must find the penalty; but on covenant, only the damages. *Wood's Inst.* 250.

COVENANT TO STAND SEISED TO USES, is where a man that hath a wife, children, brother, sister, or kindred, doth by covenant in writing under hand and seal agree that for their or any of their provision or preferment, he and his heirs will stand seised of land to their use; either in fee-simple, fee-tail, or for life. The use being created by the stat. 27 *H.* 8. *c.* 10. which conveyeth the estate as the uses are directed; this covenant to stand seised is become a conveyance of the land since the said statute. The considerations of these deeds, are natural affection, marriage, &c. and the law allows in such cases consideration of blood and marriage, to raise uses, as well as money and other valuable consideration when a use is to a stranger. *Plowd.* 302. There are no considerations now, to raise uses upon covenants to stand seised, but natural love and affection, which is for advancement of blood; and consideration of marriage, which is the joining of the blood and marriage together: other considerations, as money, &c. for land, though the words in the deed are *stand seized*, yet they are bargains and sales, and without inrolment they raise no use. *Carter* 138. *Lil. Abr.* 353.

The usual covenant to stand seised to uses need not be by deed indented and inrolled. And where a man limits his estate to the use of his wife for life, this imports a sufficient consideration in itself: also, if a person covenants to stand seised to the use of his wife, son, or cousin, it will raise an use without any express words of consideration, for sufficient consideration appears. 7 *Rep.* 40.

In case of a covenant to stand seised, so much of the use as the owner doth not dispose of, remains still in him. 1 *Ventr.* 374. And where an use is raised by way of covenant, the covenantor continues in possession; and there the uses limited, if they are according to law, shall rise and draw the possession out of him: but if they are not, the possession shall remain in him until a lawful use ariseth. 1 *Leon.* 197. 1 *Mod.* 159, 160.

If on a covenant to stand seised to uses, no use doth arise, yet it may be good by way of covenant and give remedy to the covenantee in an action; as if the covenant be future, that, in consideration of a marriage, lands shall descend or remain to a son and the heirs of his body on the body of his wife, in this case the covenantee may have writ of covenant upon the covenant against the covenantor. But if a covenant be that a man and his heirs, shall from henceforth stand and be seised to such and such uses, and the uses will not arise by law; here no action of covenant lies on the covenant: for this action will never lie upon any covenant but such as is either to do a thing hereafter, or where the thing is already done, and not when it is for a thing present. *Plowd.* 307, 398. *Finch's Law.* 49.

COVERT BARON, a married woman. 1 *Black. Com.* 442.

COVERTURE, (Fr.) any thing that covers; as apparel, a coverlet, &c. but it is by our law particularly applied to the state and condition of a married woman, who is *sub potestate viri*; and therefore disabled to contract with any to the damage of herself or husband, without his consent and privity, or his allowance and confirmation thereof. *Bract. lib.* 1. *c.* 10. *lib.* 2. *c.* 15, *&c. Bro. Abr.* When a woman is married, she is called a feme covert; and whatever is done concerning her, during the marriage, is said to be during the coverture: all things that are the wife's, are the husband's; nor hath the wife power over herself, but the husband. And if the husband alien the wife's land, during the coverture, she cannot avoid it during his life; but after his death, she may recover by *cui in vita*. *Terms de Ley.* See *Baron* and *Feme.*

COVIN, (*covina*) is a deceitful compact between two or more to deceive or prejudice others, as if tenant for life or in tail, conspire with another, that he shall recover the land which he the tenant holds, in prejudice of him in reversion. *Plowd.* 546. Covin is commonly used as to conveyances of land by fine, feoffment, recovery, &c. where it tends to defeat purchasers of the land they purchase, and creditors of their just debts, and so it is used as to deeds of gift of goods; it may be likewise sometimes in suits of law, and judgments had in them. But wherever covin is, it shall never be intended, unless it appears and be particularly found: for covin and fraud though proved, must yet be found by the jury, or it will not be good to avoid the act. *Brownl.* 188. *Bridgm.* 112.

COUNSELLOR, (*consiliarius*) is a person retained by a client to plead his cause, in a court of judicature. A counsellor at law hath a privilege to enforce any thing which is informed him by his client, if pertinent to the matter, and is not to examine whether it be true or false; for it is at the peril of him who informs him. *Cro. Jac.* 90. But after the court hath delivered their opinions of the matter in law depending before them, the counsel at the bar are not to urge any thing further in that cause, 1 *Lil. Abr.* 355. A counsellor must not set his hand to a frivolous plea, to delay a trial; which argues ignorance or foul practice. *Ibid.* And as counsellors have a special privilege to practice the law, they are punishable by attachment, &c. for misbehaviour. 1 *Hawk. P. C.* 157.

And if a bill in equity signed, contain matters criminal, impertinent, or scandalous, the counsel who signed them, on its being referred to the master, and reported to be so, is in strictness to pay costs to the party aggrieved; but nothing relevant is considered as scandalous. 1 *Ch. Rep.* 194. 2 *Vez.* 24. Also if upon reference to the master, any part of an answer is reported to be impertinent, it will be struck out as such with costs, which likewise in strictness ought to be paid by the counsel, who signed the answer. *Mitf.* 253. And by 3 *Ed.* 1. *c.* 29, "any serjeant pleader or the like attainted of using deceit in the king's court, shall be imprisoned a year and a day, and thenceforth he shall not be heard to plead in the court." But by 5 *Eliz. c.* 14, no counsellor shall be punished for pleading or shewing forth a forged deed, or the like, not being privy to the forgery thereof.

By 3 *Jac.* 1. *c.* 5, no recusant convict shall

practice the common law as a counsellor, but by 31 *Geo.* 3. c. 32, Roman catholics taking the oaths prescribed by that act may act as barristers.

COUNT, signifies the declaration of the complainant in a real action. A declaration is applied to personal, so count is applicable to real causes; but count and declaration are oftentimes confounded, and made to signify the same thing. *F. N. B.* 16, 60.

COUNTEE, (Fr. *comte*) was the most eminent dignity of a subject, before the conquest; and those who in ancient times were created countees, were men of great estate: for which reason, and because the law intends that they assist the king with their counsel for the public good, and preserve the realm by their valour, they had great privileges; as they might not be arrested for debt or trespass, or be put on juries, &c. Of old the countee was *præfectus* or *præpositus comitatus*, and had the charge and custody of the county, but this authority the sheriff now hath. 9 *Rep.* 46. A countee or count, is an earl, in the law French. *Law Fr. Dict.*

COUNTENANCE. This word seems to be used for credit or estimation. *Old. Nat. Br.* 111.

COUNTER, (*computatorium* from the Lat. *computare*) is the name of two prisons in London, the Poultry counter, and Wood-street counter, for the use of the city to confine debtors, peace-breakers, &c. *Cowel. Blount.*

COUNTERFEITS, See *Cheats, Frauds.*

COUNTERMAND, is where a thing formerly directed to be executed, is afterwards by some act or ceremony countermanded and made void by the party that first did it. But an authority by deed, such as a letter of attorney or the like, can only be countermanded and avoided by an instrument executed with the same solemnity, that is, by a deed under seal.

COUNTERPART. When the several parts of an indenture are interchangeably executed by the several parties, that part or copy which is executed by the grantor is usually called the original, and the rest are counterparts; though of late it is most frequent (and better) for all the parties to execute every part; which renders them all originals. 2 *Black. Com.* 296.

COUNTERPLEA, is where the tenant in any real action, tenant by the curtesy, or in dower, in his answer and plea, vouches any one to warrant his title, or prays in aid of another, who hath a larger estate; as of him in reversion, &c. Or where one that is a stranger to the action, comes and prays to be received to save his estate; then that which the demandant allegeth against it, why it should not be admitted is called a counterplea; in which sense it is used *stat.* 25 *Ed.* 3. *cap.* 7. So that counterplea is in law a replication to aid prier; and is called counterplea to the voucher; but when the voucher is allowed and the vouchee comes and demands what cause the tenant hath to vouch him, and the tenant shews his cause, whereupon the vouchee pleads any thing to avoid the warranty; that is termed a counterplea of the warranty. *Terms de Ley.* 3 *Ed.* 1. *cap.* 39. If on demurrer to a counterplea of the voucher upon a warranty, it be found against the vouchee, judgment shall not be peremptory, but only *stet vocare*; it is otherwise upon a plea to the writ tried by the country. 4 *Rep.* 80. 10 *Rep.* 34.

COUNTER-ROLLS, are the rolls which sheriffs of counties have with the coroners of their proceedings, as well of appeals, as of inquest, &c. *Stat.* 3. *Ed.* 1. *c.* 10.

COUNTORS, (Fr. *contours*) have been taken for such serjeants at law, which a man retains to defend his cause, and speak for him in any court for their fees. *Horn's Mirror, lib.* 2. And as in the court of C. B. none but serjeants at law may plead; they were anciently called serjeant countors. 1 *Inst.* 17.

COUNTY, (*comitatus*) signifies the same with shire, the one coming from the French the other the Saxons; and contains a circuit or proportion of the realm, into which the whole land is divided for the better government of it, and the more easy administration of justice: so that there is no part of this kingdom that lies not within some county: and every county is governed by a yearly officer whom we call a sheriff. *Fortescue, cap.* 24. Of these counties there are in England forty, besides twelve in Wales, making in all fifty-two.

COUNTY PALATINE, there are four counties of special note, which are therefore termed counties palatine; as Lancaster, Chester, Durham, and Ely. 4 *Inst.* 204, 221.

These counties palatine are reckoned among the superior courts; and are privileged as to pleas, so as no inhabitant of such counties shall be compelled by any writ to appear or answer out of the same; except for error, and in cases of treason, &c. *Cromp. Juris.* 137. 1 *Danv. Abr.* 750.

But by 33 *Geo.* 3. *c.* 68, when final judgment shall be obtained in the courts of the great sessions in Wales or Chester, or the common pleas in Lancaster and Durham, and the persons or effects cannot be found within the jurisdiction of the court, any court of record at Westminster, upon affidavit filed, may issue execution. *s.* 1.

Counties palatine, with *jura regalia*, were probably erected at first, because they were adjacent to the enemies countries heretofore; as Lancaster and Durham to Scotland, and Chester to Wales; that the inhabitants might have administration of justice at home, and remain there to secure the country from incursions. 1 *Vent.* 155.

County palatine of Lancaster.] By 33 *Hen.* 6. c. 2, jurors who indict in the county of Lancaster, a foreigner dwelling in another county, must have lands, 5*l.* each, value.

By 37 *Hen.* 8. *c.* 19, fines levied in Lancaster shall be of like force, as fines acknowleged before the justices of the common pleas, and like proclamations shall be made in the sessions there.

By 5 & 6 *Ed.* 6. *c.* 26, on exigent, in any action in the king's bench or common pleas, awarded against any person dwelling in the county of Lancaster, a writ of proclamation shall be awarded to the sheriff, and all other process of outlawry shall be directed to the chancellor of the duchy who shall issue like writs, under the seal of the county palatine, to the sheriff.

By 2 & 5 *Ph.* & *M.* *c.* 20, duchy lands severed from the crown, and since re-united shall be again parcel of the duchy, as well those lying out of the county palatine of Lancaster, as those within the same, and shall pass under the duchy seal.

But lands in the principality of Wales, the duchy of Cornwall, and the counties of Chester and Flint, shall not be annexed to the duchy. *Ibid.*

By 17 *Geo.* 2. *c.* 7, the chancellor of the duchy may grant commissions to take affidavits.

By 22 *Geo.* 2. *c.* 46, the statute for further regulations of attornies, shall not deprive those of the duchy or county palatine of Lancaster, from acting within those jurisdictions.

Writs in the court of common pleas of Lancaster, shall be made returnable on the first Wednesday of any month, in vacation, or before justices of the sessions of assizes for the county of Lancaster, at the plaintiff's election, and the defendant at the day of return shall appear. *Ibid.*

By 34 *Geo.* 3. *c.* 58, no execution shall be stayed by writ of false judgment in any inferior court in the county of Lancaster, but on recognizance given, with two sureties for payment of the debt and costs, nor any action for less than 10*l.* be removed from any inferior court into the common pleas of the said county.

By 38 *Geo.* 3. *c.* 63, adjournments of the general court of quarter sessions of the peace for Lancaster are declared to be legal.

The justices are also authorized to hold an annual general sessions at Preston, for the county at large, and also a special general sessions at any time, upon a previous advertisement, and notice therein of the business to be brought forward. *Ibid.*

By 39 & 40 *Geo.* 3. *c.* 105, in the court of common pleas of Lancaster, the plaintiffs and defendants may plead and give evidence of any cause of action, or any thing in bar of any suit, provided the same shall happen prior to the issuing of the writ of *capias ad respondendum*, or prior to the day of actual service of any declaration in ejectment, notwithstanding the cause of action shall not have accrued prior to the teste and return of the writ, and no advantages shall be by reason taken of any action having accrued subsequent to such teste and return. *s.* 1.

Process issuing out of the said court may be returnable, according to the present practice, on any of the return days in Easter and Michaelmas terms, according to the court of common pleas at Westminster. *s.* 2.

But no final judgment shall be entered, or execution issued, within ten clear days, after the days of the return of the writ of inquiry, or *scire facias.* *s.* 3.

Parties are not to be debarred from moving in arrest of judgment. *s.* 4.

Counties Palatine of Chester.] By 1 *Hen.* 4. c. 18, process of outlawry in other counties, against persons in the county of Chester, may be certified into the county of Chester, and proceeded upon there.

By 32 *Hen.* 8. *c.* 43. sessions shall be kept in Chester twice in the year, viz. at Michaelmas and Easter.

By 38 *Hen.* 8. *c.* 13, the sheriff of Chester is to keep his court monthly, and with the two coroners sit to give judgment upon outlawries.

By 2 & 3 *Ed.* 6. *c.* 28, fines may be levied before the chief justice of Chester, or his deputy, of lands in the county palatine of Chester.

Recognizances of statute merchant, on the statute of Acton Burnel, acknowledged before the mayor of Chester, shall be good. *Ibid.* *c.* 31.

By 43 *Eliz.* *c.* 15, fines may be levied before the mayor of Chester, of lands within the county of the city of Chester, and writ of error lies thereon before the high justice of the said county.

By 22 *Geo.* 2. *c.* 46, writs of capias, and other mesne process in the court of session of Chester, may be made returnable at the first day of the next session, or on the first Wednesday of any month, in the vacations at the election of the plaintiff, and the defendant shall appear on the day of such return, or within eight days after.

By 26 *Geo.* 2. *c.* 34, the annual meeting for election of mayor and other officers of the city of Chester, shall be on the Friday next after October 20th yearly.

By 27 *Geo.* 3. *c.* 43, justices of the court of session for the county palatine of Chester, may empower persons to take affidavits in causes depending therein; and the prothonotary may take like affidavits.

Persons forswearing themselves are liable to the same penalties as for false affidavits in open court. *Ibid.*

The prothonotary is to make out the commission upon a fiat from the justices, or one of them, of which he is to make entry, and the fees for each commission are 2*s.* for the fiat, 4*s.* for the commission, besides duty and parchment, and 4*s.* for sealing the same: and the commissioners may take for swearing each affidavit 1*s.* but no affidavit shall be taken within a mile of Chester castle, during the county sessions. *Ibid.*

Justices of the said court may empower persons to take recognizances of bail, and the commission shall be made out by the prothonotary, upon the justice's fiat; and the said bail with an affidavit of the taking thereof, shall be sent to the prothonotary's office, within ten days, to be filed upon payment of 5*s.* 4*d.* and the following fees shall be paid for commissions and for taking recognizances, viz. 2*s.* for the fiat; and 7*s.* 6*d.* for the commission, besides duty and parchment; 4*s.* for the seal, 5*s.* for taking bail, and 1*s.* for swearing. *Ibid.*

The justices of the said court may make rules for justifying bail, by affidavits before the commissioners, and the power of the prothonotary, or his deputy, to take recognizances, shall not be affected by this act. *Ibid.*

If any person represent another in entering into special bail, he shall be adjudged a felon. *Ibid.*

County palatine of Durham.] By 27 *Hen.* 8. 24, bishops of Durham and their chancellors, shall be justices of the peace within that county palatine.

By 5 *Eliz. c.* 27, fines levied before the justices of assize at Durham, shall be as effectual for lands there, as fines in the common pleas.

By 31 *El. c.* 9, on exigent awarded against any person dwelling in the bishopric of Durham, a writ of proclamation shall be awarded, and the bishop, or chancellor, shall issue a mandate to the sheriff to make proclamation.

The bishop of Durham shall have a deputy in the king's bench and common pleas, to receive such writs of proclamation; and the bishop, or chancellor, not making true return of every such writ, shall forfeit 5*l.* *Ibid.*

All process against persons outlawed there, shall be directed to the bishop of Durham, or during vacancy, to the chancellor; and one fee only shall be taken for the proclamation, mandate, and execution. *Ibid.*

By 4 *Geo.* 3. *c.* 21, the chancellor and justices of the court of pleas, are empowered to issue commissions to proper persons to take and swear affidavits in causes depending in their respective courts, which affidavits are to be filed, and may be read in evidence.

The cursitor is to make out the commissions upon a fiat from the chancellor; or upon a fiat from two justices of the pleas, of which he is to make an entry. *Ibid.*

His fees for each commission are as follows, viz. 2*s.* for the fiat, 4*s.* for the commission, besides duty and paper, and 4*s.* for sealing, and the commissioners may take for swearing each affidavit, if in chancery 2*s.* and if in the court of common pleas 1*s.* *Ibid.*

Officers of the respective courts may take affidavits as heretofore.

By 14 *Geo.* 3. *c.* 46, persons apprehending offenders guilty of highway robbery, clipping, coining, or housebreaking, within the county palatine of Durham, shall receive the rewards made payable by the acts 4 *W.* & *M. c.* 6. and 7 *Will.* 3. 5 *Ann.* and 6 *Geo.* 1.

Disputes arising between parties apprehending offenders, shall be determined by the judges. *Ibid.*

The sheriff is to pay the reward, and be reimbursed by the commissioners of the treasury. *Ibid.*

In case any sheriff shall die, before a month after conviction, his successor shall pay the reward; and in case of default, shall forfeit double the sum, with treble costs of suit. *Ibid.*

COUNTIES CORPORATE. Besides the counties above mentioned, there are counties corporate. *Stat.* 3 *Ed.* 4. *c.* 5. And they are certain cities, with lands and territories, having liberties and jurisdiction by grant from the king. As the county of Middlesex annexed to the city of London by king *Hen.* 1. The county of the city of York, *anno* 32 *H.* 8. The county of the city of Chester, 42 *Eliz.* The county of the city of Bristol, Gloucester, Norwich, Worcester, &c. and the county of the town of Kingston upon Hull, Newcastle, &c. *Lamb. Eiren. lib.* 1. *Cromp. Just.* 69.

COUNTY COURT, (*curia comitatus*) the county court is a court incident to the jurisdiction of the sheriff, held every month, by the sheriff or his deputy; and by the stat. 2 *Ed.* 6. *c.* 25, no county court shall be adjourned longer than for one month, consisting of 28 days. 3 *Black.* 40, 41.

It had formerly, and now hath the determination of certain debts, &c. under 40*s.* And this court holdeth not plea (*de jurie*) of any debt or damage to the value of 40*s.* or above; nor of trepsass; *vi & armis*, &c. And the proceedings are removable from hence into the king's superior courts, by *pone* or *recordari.*

But of debt and other actions personal above that sum, the sheriff may nevertheless hold plea by force of a writ of justicies, which is in nature of a commission to him to do so. 4 *Inst.* 266. In this court the plaintiff takes out a summons, and if the defendant do not appear, an attachment or distringas is to be made out against him; but if the defendant appears, the plaintiff is to file his declaration, and after the defendant is to put in his answer or plea; and the plaintiff having joined issue, the trial proceeds, &c. whereupon, if verdict is given for the plaintiff, judgment is entered, and a *fieri facias* may be awarded against the defendant's goods, which may be taken by virtue thereof, and be appraised and sold to satisfy the plaintiff: but if the defendant hath no goods, the plaintiff is without remedy in this court; for no capias lies therein, but an action may be brought at common law, upon the judgment entered. *Greenwood of Courts, p.* 22.

COUNTY-RATES, the justices of peace at their quarter sessions may make one general rate, to answer all former distinct county rates, which shall be assessed on every parish, &c. and collected and paid by the high constables of hundreds to treasurers appointed by the justices: which money shall be deemed the public stock and be laid out in repairing of bridges, gaols, or houses of correction, on presentment made by the grand jury at the assizes or quarter sessions, of their wanting reparation; and the other purposes to which by law the county rates are applicable. But appeal lies by the churchwardens and overseers of the poor of the parishes to the justices at the next sessions against the rate on any particular parish. 12 *Geo.* 2. *c.* 9.

COUNTING HOUSE OF THE KING'S HOUSEHOLD, (*domus computus hospitii regis*) is usually called the green cloth, where sit the lord steward, treasurer of the king's house, the comptroller, master of the household, cofferer, and two clerks of the green cloth, &c. for daily taking the accounts of all expenses of the household, making provisions, and ordering payment for the same, and for the good government of the king's household servants, and paying the wages of those below stairs. *Stat.* 39 *Eliz. cap.* 7.

COURIER, (from the Fr. *courir* to run) an express messenger of haste. *Cowel. Blount.*

COURRACIER, a French word signifying a horse courser. 2 *Inst.* 719. *Ibid.*

COURT, (*curia*) signifies the king's palace or mansion; but is more especially the place where justice is judicially administered.

Of courts, some are of record, and some not, which are accounted base courts in respect of the rest; a court of record is that court which hath power to hold plea, according to the course of the common law, of real, personal, and mixed actions, where the debt or damage is 40*s.* or above: as the king's bench, common pleas, &c. 1 *Inst.* 117, 260, 4 *Rep.* 52. 2 *Rol. Abr.* 574.

A court not of record is where it cannot hold plea of debt or damages amounting to 40*s.* but of pleas under that sum, or where the proceedings are not according to the course of the common law, nor inrolled; as the county court, and the court baron, &c. 1 *Inst.* 117, 260. 4 *Rep.* 52. 2 *Rol. Abr.* 574.

The rolls of the superior courts of record are of such authority, as no proof will be admitted against them; and they are only triable by themselves. 3 *Inst.* 71. But as the county court, court baron, &c. are not courts of record, the proceedings therein may be denied, and tried by a jury: and upon their judgments a writ of error lies not; but writ of false judgment. 1 *Inst.* 117.

COURT OF ADMIRALTY, (*curia admiralitatis*) was erected by *Ed.* 3. for deciding maritime causes: but is not allowed to be a court of record, because it proceeds by the civil law. 4 *Inst.* 134, 135. This court hath jurisdiction only to determine causes arising wholly upon the sea, out of the jurisdiction of a county, and consequently judgment of a thing done upon land is void. 1 *Inst.* 260.

COURT BARON, (*curia baronis*) is a court which every lord of a manor hath within his own precinct; and it is inseparably incident to the manor; and must be held by prescription, for it cannot be created at this day. 1 *Inst.* 58. 4 *Inst.* 268. It must be kept on some part of the manor; and is,

1st, By common law, which is the barons or freeholders court, of which the freeholders being suitors are the judges, and this cannot be a court baron without two suitors at least.

2dly, By custom, which is called the customary court; and concerns the customary tenants and copyholders, whereof the lord or his steward, is judge. The court baron may be of this double nature, or one may be without the other, but as there can be no court baron at common law without freeholders, so there cannot be a customary court without copyholders or customary tenants. 4 *Rep.* 26. 6 *Rep.* 11, 12. 2 *Inst.* 119.

The freeholders' court which hath jurisdiction for trying actions of debt, trespasses, &c. under 40*s.* may be had every three weeks; and is something like a county court, and the proceedings much the same; though on recovery of debt, they have not power to make execution, but are to distrain the defendant's goods, and retain them till satisfaction is made.

The other court baron for taking and passing of estates, surrenders, admittances, &c. is held but once or twice in a year, (usually with the court leet), unless it be on purpose to grant an estate; and then it is holden as often as requisite. In this court the homage jury are to inquire that their lords do not lose their services, duties, or custom; but that the tenants make their suits of court: pay their rents, heriots, &c. and keep their lands and tenements in repair; they are to present all common and private nuisances, which may prejudice the lord's manor: and every public trespass must be punished in this court, by amercement on presenting the same. By statute, it shall be inquired of customary tenants, what they hold, by what works, rents, heriots, services, &c. And of the lord's woods and other profits, fishing, &c. *Stat. Extent. Manerii.* 4 *Ed.* 1. See *Compleat Court-keeper.*

COURT OF CHIVALRY, (*curia militaris*) otherwise called the court martial; the judges of it were the lord constable of England, and the earl marshal; this court is said to be the fountain of the martial law; and the office is now given to the earl marshal who hath both a judicial and ministerial power; for he is not only one of the judges, but to see execution done. 4 *Inst.* 123. *Wood's Inst. lib.* 4. *c.* 1.

COURT-CHRISTIAN, (*curia christianitatis*) is an ecclesiastical judicature, opposed to the civil court, or lay tribunal; and as in secular courts human laws are maintained; so in the court christian, the laws of Christ should be the rule. And therefore the judges are divines, as archbishops, bishops, archdeacons, &c. 2 *Inst.* 488.

COURT OF CONSCIENCE, (*curia conscientiæ*). See *Conscience, court of.*

COURT OF DELEGATES, (*curia delegatorum*) is so called, because the judges are delegated, and sit by force of the king's commission, under the great seal, upon appeals to the king in three cases. 1st, When a decree or sentence is given in an ecclesiastical cause by the archbishop, or any of his officials. 2dly, When any decree or sentence is given in an ecclesiastical cause, in places exempt, or peculiars, belonging to the king, or an archbishop. 3dly, When a sentence is given in the court of admiralty in a civil and marine cause, according to the civil law. 4 *Inst.* 339. *Stat.* 25 *Hen.* 8. *c.* 19.

COURTS ECCLESIASTICAL, (*curiæ ecclesiasticæ*) are those courts which are held by the king's authority as supreme governor of the church, for matters which chiefly concern religion. 4 *Inst.* 321. And the laws and constitutions whereby the church of England is governed, are; 1st, Divers immemorial customs. 2dly, Our own provincial constitutions, and the canons made in convocations, especially those in the year 1603. 3dly, Statutes or acts of parliament concerning the affairs of religion, or causes of ecclesiastical cognizance; particularly the rubricks in our common prayer book, founded upon the statutes of uniformity. 4th, The articles of religion, drawn up in the year 1562, and established by 13 *Eliz. cap.* 12. And it is said by the general canon law, where all others fail. *Wood's Inst. lib.* 4. *c.* 1. *s.* 26.

COURT OF HUSTINGS, (*curia hustingi*) is the highest court of record, holden at Guildhall for the city of London, before the lord mayor and alderman, the sheriffs, and recorder. 4 *Inst.* 247. For which see London.

COURT-LEET, (*leta visus francii plegii*) is a court of record ordained for punishing offences against the crown; and is said to be the most ancient court of the land. 2 *Danv. Abr.* 289.

A leet is incident to a hundred, as a court baron to a manor; for by grant of a hundred, a leet passeth, and a hundred cannot be without a leet. *Kitch.* 70. Leets may be held by charter or prescription; but are commonly claimed by prescription, and are to be kept twice a year, one time within a month after Easter, and the other within a month after Michaelmas, at a certain place within the precinct; these are the usual times of holding the leet; but if it hath been a custom to keep this court at any other time of the year, it is good if due warning be given. 1 *Inst.* 115. 2 *Inst.* 72. The steward is the judge of this court, as the sheriff is in the torn; and he hath power to elect officers, as constables, tithingmen, &c. as well as punish offenders. 6 *Rep.* 12. 2 *Inst.* 199. See Leet.

COURT OF MARSHALSEA, (*curia palatii*) a court of record to hear and determine causes, kept once a week in Southwark. See Marshalsea.

COURT MARTIAL, (*curia martialis*) is a court held both in the military and naval service for punishing offences.

COURT OF PIE POWDRE, (*curia pedis pulverisati*) is a court held in fairs to do justice to buyers and sellers, and for redress of disorders committed in them, so called because they are most usual in summer, when the suitors to the court have dusty feet, and from the expedition in hearing causes proper thereunto, before the dust goes off the feet of the plaintiffs and defendants. 4 *Inst.* 272. It is a court of record incident to every fair, and to be held only during the time that the fair is kept. *Doct. et Stud. c.* 5. As to the jurisdiction, the cause of action for contract, slander, &c. must arise in the fair, or market, and not before at any former fair, or after the fair: it is to be for some matter concerning the same fair or market, and be done, complained of, heard and determined, the same day. Also the plaintiff must make oath that the contract, &c. was within the jurisdiction and time of the fair. Stat. 17 *Ed.* 4. *c.* 2. 2 *Inst.* 220.

The court of *pie poudre* may hold a plea of a sum above 40*s.* and it is said judgment may be given at another fair, at a court held there; and a writ of error lies upon a judgment given. *Dyer* 133. *F. N. B.* 18. This court may not meddle with any thing done in a market without a special custom for it; but what is done in a fair only; and not there for slanderous words, unless they concern matters of contract in the fair, as, where it is for slandering the wares of another, and not of his person in the same fair. *Moor, ca.* 854. The steward before whom the court is held is the judge; and the trial is by merchants and traders in the fair; and the judgment against the defendant shall be *quod amercietur.* If the steward proceeds contrary to the statute 17*Ed.* 4. *c.* 2, he shall forfeit 5*l.*

COURT OF REQUESTS, (*curia requisitionum*) was a court of equity, of the same nature with the court of chancery, but inferior to it, and abolished by stat. 16 & 17 *Car.* 2. *c.* 10. 4 *Inst.* 97.

COURT OF THE LORD STEWARD OF THE KING'S HOUSE. The lord steward, or, in his absence, the treasurer and comptroller of the king's house, and steward of the Marshalsea, may inquire of, hear, and determine, in this court, all treasons, murders, manslaughters, bloodsheds, and other malicious strikings, whereby blood shall be shed, in any of the palaces and houses of the king, or in any other house where his royal person shall abide. And this jurisdiction was given by the statute 33 *Hen.* 8, *c.* 12. 3 *Inst.* 140. But this court was at first intended only to inquire of and punish felonies, &c. by the king's servants against any lord or other person of the king's council. 3 *Hen.* 7. *c.* 14.

COURT OF STAR-CHAMBER, (*curia cameræ stellatæ*) a court erected by 3 *Hen.* 7. *c.* 8, but dissolved by stat. 17 *Car.* 12. *c.* 10.

COURTS OF THE UNIVERSITIES. The courts of the two universities of Oxford and Cambridge are the chancellor's courts. These two learned bodies enjoy the sole jurisdiction, in exclusion of the king's courts, over all civil actions and suits whatsoever, where a scholar or privileged person is one of the parties, excepting in such cases where the right of freehold is concerned. And these, by the university charter, they are at liberty to try and determine, either according to the common law of the land, or according to their own local customs, at their discretion; which has generally led them to carry on their process in a course much conformed to the civil law. 3 *Black.* 83.

These privileges were granted that the students might not be distracted from their studies by legal process from distant courts, and other forensic avocations. And privileges of this kind are of very high antiquity, being generally enjoyed by all foreign universities, as well as our own, in consequence of a constitution of the emperor Frederick, *A. D.* 1158. *Cod.* 4. *tit.* 13. But as to England in particular, the oldest charter containing this grant to the university of Oxford was 28 *Hen.* 3. *A. D.* 1244. And the same privileges were confirmed and enlarged by almost every succeeding prince down to king Henry 8, in the 14th year of whose reign the largest and most extensive charter of all was granted. One similar to which was afterward granted to Cambridge in the third year of queen Elizabeth. But yet, notwithstanding these charters, the privileges granted therein, of proceeding in a course different from the law of the land, were of so high a nature that they were held to be invalid; for though the king might erect new courts, yet he could not alter the course of law by his letters patent. Therefore in the reign of queen Elizabeth an act of parliament was obtained, 13 *Eliz.* *c.* 29, confirming all the charters of the two universities, and those of 14 *Hen.* 8, and 3 *Eliz.* by name: which blessed act, as sir Ed. Coke intitles it, 4 *Inst.* 227, established this high privilege without any doubt or opposition, *Jenk. Cent.* 2. *pl.* 88. *Cent.* 3. *pl.* 33. *Hardr.* 504. *Godbolt*, 201. or, as sir Matthew Hale, *Hist. C. L.* 33, very fully expresses the sense of the common law, and the operation of the act of parliament, "although king Henry 8, 14 *A. R. sui*, "granted to the university a liberal charter "to proceed according to the use of the "university, *viz.* by a course much con- "formed to the civil law, yet that charter "had not been sufficient to have warranted "such proceedings without the help of "an act of parliament. And therefore in "13 Eliz. an act was passed, whereby that "charter was in effect enacted; and it is "thereby that at this day they have a kind "of civil law procedure, even in matters "that are of themselves of common law "cognizance, where either of the parties is "privileged." 3 *Black.* 84.

This privilege, so far as it relates to civil causes, is exercised at Oxford in the chancellor's court; the judge of which is the vice-chancellor, his deputy, or assessor. From his sentence an appeal lies to delegates appointed by the congregation, from thence to other delegates of the house of convocation; and if they all three concur in the same sentence it is final, at least by the statutes of the university, *tit.* 21, *sec.* 19, according to the rule of the civil law, *Cod.* 7.

70. 1. But if there be any discordance or variation in any of the three sentences, an appeal lies in the last resort to judges delegates, appointed by the crown under the great seal in chancery. 3 *Black.* 83.

But these particular jurisdictions, derogating from the general jurisdiction of the courts of common law, are ever taken strictly, and cannot be extended farther than the most explicitly express letter of their privileges will warrant. 3 *Black.* 83.

COURTS OF WALES (*curia principalitatis Walliæ*). The courts of the principality of Wales, and their jurisdiction, are settled by acts of parliament; and beside county-courts, hundred-courts, courts-leet, &c. by 34 and 35 *Hen.* 8, *c.* 26, *sec.* 5, it is enacted, that there shall be a court of grand sessions kept twice in every year in every of the 12 counties of Wales; and the justices of those courts may hold pleas of the crown in as large a manner as the king's bench, &c. and also pleas of assises, and all other pleas and actions real and personal, in as large a manner as the common pleas, &c. And errors in judgment before any of the justices in the great sessions shall be redressed by writ of error out of the chancery of England, returnable in *B R.* The proceedings in these courts are according to the laws of England. 3 *Black.* 77.

COURT-LANDS, Domains, or lands kept in the lord's hands to serve his family. *Cowel. Blount.*

COUSENAGE, an ancient writ. See *Cosenage.*

COUTHUTLAUGH, (from the Sax. *couth*, i. e. *sciens*, and *utlagh*, *ex lex*) a person that willingly and knowingly received a man outlawed, and cherished or concealed him, for which offence he was in ancient time to undergo the same punishment as the outlaw himself. *Bract. lib.* 3. *tract.* 2. *c* 13.

CRAIERA, (*crayer*) a small vessel of lading, a hoy, or smack. *Cowel. Blount.*

CRAIL, an engine made use of to catch fish. *Ibid.*

CRANAGE, (*cranagium*) is a liberty to use a crane for drawing up goods and wares of burthen from ships and vessels, at any creek of the sea, or wharf, unto the land and to make a profit of it; it also signifies the monies paid and taken for the same. *Cowel. Blount.*

CRANNOCK, an ancient measure of corn. *Ibid.*

CRASPICIS, is a word signifying a whale, viz. *piscis crassus. Ibid.*

CRASTINO SANCTI VINCENTII, the morrow after the feast of St. Vincent the martyr, *i. e.* the 22d of January, which is the date of the statutes made at Merton, *anno* 20 Hen. 3. There are likewise certain return days of writs in terms, in the courts at Westminster, beginning with *crastino, &c.* as *crastino animarum* in Michaelmas term; *crastino Purificationis beatæ Mariæ Virginis*, in Hilary term; *crastino Ascensionis Domini*, in Easter term; and *crastino Sanctæ Trinitatis*, in Trinity term.

CRATES (Lat.), is an iron grate before a prison, used in the time of the Romans. 1 *Vent.* 304.

CRAVARE, to impeach. *Cowel. Blount.*

CRAVEN, or CRAVENT, was a word of obloquy, where in the ancient trial by battle the victory should be proclaimed, and the vanquished acknowledge his fault, or pronounce the word *craven*, in the name of *recreantisse*, &c. and thereupon judgment was given forthwith; after which the recreant should become infamous, &c. 2 *Inst.* 248. 3 *Inst.* 221. 3 *Black. Com.* 340. *Ibid.* 4, 342.

CREAMER, a foreign merchant, but generally taken for one who has a stall in a fair or market. *Blount.*

CREANSOR, creditor, (of the Fr. *croyance*) signifies him that trusts another with any debt, money, or wares, in which sense it is used in *Old Nat. Br.* 66.

CREAST, or CREST, (*crista*) any imagery, or carved work, to adorn the head of wainscot, &c. like our modern cornice; but this word is now applied by the heralds to their devices set over a coat of arms. *Kennet's Paroch. Antiq.* 573.

CRECHE, a drinking-cup. *Cowel. Blount.*

CREDITORS. See *Bankrupt, Conscience, courts of*, and other titles.

CREEK, (*creca, crecca*) is a part of a haven where any thing is landed from the sea. *Cromp. Jurisd. fol.* 110.

CREMENTUM COMITATUS. The sheriffs of counties anciently answered in their accounts for the improvement of the king's rents above the ancient *vicontiel* rents, under the title of *crementum comitatus*, or *firma de cremento comitatus. Hale's Sher. Acc. p.* 36.

CREPARE OCULUM, to put out an eye, which had a pecuniary punishment annexed to it. *Cowel. Blount.*

CRETINUS, (*cretena*) a sudden stream or torrent. *Ibid.*

CROCARDS, a sort of old base money. *Ibid.*

CROCIA, the crosier or pastoral staff, so called *a similitudine crucis*, which bishops, &c. had the privilege to carry as the common ensign of their religious office, on being invested in their prelacies, by the delivery of such a crosier. *Cowel. Blount.*

CROCIARIUS, the crociary or cross-bearer, who, like our verger, went before the prelate and bore his cross. *Ibid.*

CROFT, (Sax. *croftum* and *crofta*) a little close adjoining to a dwelling-house, and enclosed for pasture or arable, or any particular use. *Ibid.*

CROISES, and *croisado*, are mentioned in our ancient law-books. *Ibid.*

CROK, (*crocus*) turning up the hair into curls or croks. *Ibid.*

CROP, (*croppa*) the seeds or products of the harvest in corn, &c. *Fleta, lib. cap.* 82.

CROSS BILL, in equity, when a defendant has any relief to pray against a plaintiff, he must do it by an original bill of his own, which is called a cross bill. 3 *Black.* 448.

CROSS-BOWS. None shall shoot in, or keep any cross-bow, hand-gun, hagbut, &c. but those who have lands of the value of 100*l.* *per ann.* and no person shall travel with a cross-bow bent, or gun charged, except in time of war; or shoot within a quarter of a mile of any city, or market-town, unless for defence of himself or his house, or at a dead mark, under the penalty of 10*l.* Stat. 33 *Hen.* 8. *cap.* 6.

CROSS REMAINDERS, are where *an estate tail* is limited to one person, and for *default of such issue* then over to another *in tail*, with or without other remainders over. 2 *Black.* 381.

CROSSES. By stat. 13 *Eliz. c.* 2, crosses, beads, &c. used by the Roman catholics, are prohibited to be brought into this kingdom on pain of a *præmunire*, &c.

CROWN, (*corona*) signifies the possessions and dignity of a king of any kingdom. The crown of England is, by common law and constitutional custom hereditary; and this in a manner peculiar to itself; as the right of inheritance may, *under peculiar circumstances*, from time to time be changed or limited by act of parliament, under which limitations the crown still continues hereditary. 1 *Black. Com.* 191. For after the abdication of *James* 2. the lords spiritual and temporal, and commons, lawfully representing all the estates of the people of the realm, invited over William prince of Orange, and the princess Mary, eldest daughter of *James* 2. to take care of their rights and liberties, whom they declared to be king and queen of England. And by stat. 1 *W. & M. c.* 2, reciting the declaration of the lords and commons for securing the liberties of the kingdom, upon which the prince and princess of Orange accepted the crown, the said prince and princess were recognised king and queen of England, &c. for their lives, and the life of the survivor of them; and after their deaths the crown was settled on the heirs of the body of the said princess, and for want of such issue to the princess Anne of Denmark, sister to the queen, and the heirs of her body.

Also by 12 *W.* 3, *c.* 2, (after the decease of queen Mary without issue) the princess Sophia of Hanover, daughter of Elizabeth, eldest daughter of *James* 1. was declared next in succession after king *William*, and the princess Anne, and their issue; and the crown to remain to the princess Sophia, and the heirs of her body, being protestants.

By virtue of which last statute his Majesty king *George* the first, eldest son of the princess Sophia, on the death of her majesty queen Anne without issue, the said princess Sophia being likewise dead, came to the possession of the crown of these realms. But by these last acts papists are rendered incapable to inherit the crown of England, and subjects are absolved from their allegiance to such persons coming to the crown. 1 *Black. Com.* 191.

CROWN-OFFICE. This is an office belonging to the court of king's bench, of which the king's coroner, or attorney there is commonly master; in which the attorney-general and clerk of the crown exhibit informations for crimes and misdemeanors, the one *ex officio*, and the other by order of court.

CROY, signifies marsh land. *Cowel. Blount.*

CROYSES, (*cruce signati*) is used by *Britton* for pilgrims, because they wear the sign of the cross upon their garments. *Bracton, lib.* 5, *par.* 2, *cap.* 2, and *par.* 5, *cap.* 9.

CRUSTUM, was a garment of purple, mixed with many colours. *Cowel. Blount.*

CRY DE PAIS. On a robbery, or other felony done, hue and cry may be raised by the country in the absence of the constable, which is called *cry de pais.* 2 *Hale's Hist. P. C.* 100.

CRYPTA, a chapel, or oratory under ground. *Cowel. Blount.*

CUCKING-STOOL, (*tumbrellum*) is an engine invented for the punishment of scolds and unquiet women, by ducking them in water, called in ancient times a tumbrel, and sometimes a trebuchet. *Lamb. Eiren. lib.* 1. *c.* 12. It was anciently also a punishment inflicted upon brewers and bakers transgressing the laws, who were thereupon in such a stool immersed over head and ears *in stercore*, some stinking water. *Blount.*

CUDE. A cude cloth is a chrysom or face-cloth for a child baptized. *Ibid.*

CUI ANTE DIVORTIUM, was a writ that a woman divorced from her husband had to recover lands and tenements which she had in fee simple, or in tail, or for life, from him to whom her husband did alienate them during the marriage, when she could not gainsay it. *Reg. Orig.* 233. *F. N. B.* 240. And the heir shall have a *sur cui ante divortium* where the wife dieth before the action brought, as well as she shall have a *sur cui in vita:* But of an estate-tail the heir shall not have *sur cui in vita ante divortium*, but shall be put to his *formedon* in the descender. *New Nat. Br.* 454. 3 *Black. Com.* 183.

CUI IN VITA, is a writ of entry which a widow has against him to whom her husband alienated her lands or tenements in his life-time, which must contain in it, that during his life she could not withstand it. *Reg. Orig.* 233. *F. N. B.* 193.

CULAGIUM, is when a ship is laid up in the dock to be repaired. *Cowel. Blount.*

CULPRIT, is a reply of a proper officer in

behalf of the king, affirming a criminal to be guilty after he had pleaded Not guilty, without which the issue to be tried is not joined. It is compounded of two words, *viz. cul* and *prit*, the one an abbreviation of *culpabilis*, and the other derived from the French word *prest*, i. e. ready, and is as much as to say that he is ready to prove the offender guilty. 4 *Black. Com.* 333.

CULTURA. This word is often found in old writings, and signifies a parcel of arable land. *Blount.*

CULVERTAGE, (*culvertagium*) is said by some persons to be derived from *culum & vertere*, to turn tail; and in this sense *sub nomine culvertagii* was taken to be on pain of cowardice, or being accounted cowards. But in the opinion of others it rather signifies some base slavery, or the confiscation of an estate, being a feudal term for the lands of the vassal, forfeited and escheating to the lord; and *sub nomine culvertagii*, in this signification, was under pain of confiscation. *Mat. Par.* 1212.

CULWARD, and CULVERD, words used for a coward, or cowardice. *Chart. Temp. Ed.* 1.

CUNA CERVISIÆ, a tub of ale. *Domesday. Cowel. Blount.*

CUNEUS, a mint or place to coin money: *cuneum monetum* signifies the king's stamp for coinage, and from the word *cune* is derived coin. *Ibid.*

CUNTEY-CUNTEY, was a kind of trial, as appears by *Bracton*, by the ordinary jury. *Bract. lib.* 4. *tract.* 3, *c.* 18.

CURAGULUS, one who takes care of a thing. *Mon. Ang. tom.* 2. *Cowel. Blount.*

CURA MONASTERII, an officer so called, who had the charge of a monastery.

CURATE, (*curatus*) is he who represents the incumbent of a church, parson or vicar, and officiates divine service in his stead. He is to be licensed and admitted by the bishop or ordinary; and when a curate has the approbation of the bishop he usually appoints the salary too; and in such case, if he be not paid, the curate has a proper remedy in the ecclesiastical court, by a sequestration of the profits of the benefice; but if he hath no license from the bishop he is put to his remedy at common law, where he must prove the agreement, &c. *Right. Clerg.* 127.

By 12 *An.* stat. 2, *c.* 12, when a rector or vicar presents a curate to the ordinary to be licensed, the ordinary may appoint a stipend to such curate, according to the cure, not exceeding 50*l.* nor less than 20*l.* *per ann.* And by 36 *Geo.* 3. *c.* 83, the bishop or ordinary may appoint a stipend to curates of 75*l.* *per ann.* where the incumbent does not reside four months, with the use of the parsonage house for 12 calendar months, or a further allowance of 15*l.* *per ann.* in lieu thereof, *sec.* 1. But the grant of the house may be revoked; and the curate neglecting to deliver it up is to forfeit his salary unpaid, and 50*l.* *sec.* 2. Churches augmented according to 1 *Geo.* 1. stat. 2, *c.* 10, by *queen Anne's* bounty, are to be deemed benefices presentative; and the officiating curate may have a like stipend, *sec.* 3. And bounties held with augmented cures may be held by the present incumbents, *s.* 4.

The bishop or ordinary may appoint the stipend to officiating curates of perpetual curacies not augmented, *sec.* 5. The ordinary may license curates employed, though no nomination shall have been made to him by the incumbent; and may revoke any license, subject to appeal to the archbishop.

By 43 *Geo.* 3. *c.* 84, and *c.* 109, curates may take leases of the impropriate parsonages of their parishes, but where not occupied by a spiritual person before July 1803, the license of the bishop shall be necessary, *sec.* 7, 8.

A curate having no fixed estate in his curacy, not being instituted and inducted, may be removed at pleasure by the bishop or incumbent. *Nog.* But there are perpetual curates, as well as temporary, who are appointed where tithes are impropriate, and no vicarage endowed: these are not removable; and the impropriators are obliged to find them, some whereof have certain portions of the tithes settled on them. Stat. 29 *Car.* 2. *c.* 8.

CURATOR, is the guardian of an infant. 1 *Black.* 460.

CURFEU, (of the Fr. *couvrir*, i. e. *tegere*, and *feu*, *ignis*,) signifies the ringing of a bell, or evening peal, by which William I. called the conqueror, commanded every person to rake up or cover over his fire, and put out his light. And in many places of England at this day, where a bell is customarily rung towards bed-time, it is said to ring *curfew*. *Stow's Annals.*

CURIA. This word was sometimes taken for the persons, as feudatory and other customary tenants, who did their suit and service at the court of the lord. *Kennet's Paroch. Antiq.* 139. See *Court.*

CURIA ADVISARE VULT, when judgment is staid on matters of difficulty requiring the deliberation of the judges, the entry is *curia advisare vult*. *Shep. Epit.* 682.

CURIA CURSUS AQUÆ, a court held by the lord of the manor of Gravesend for the better management of barges and boats using the passage on the river Thames from thence to London, and plying at Gravesend-bridge. See stat. 2 *Geo.* 2. *c.* 26.

CURIA CLAUDENDA, is a writ to compel another to make a fence or wall, which he ought to make between his land and the plaintiff's, on his refusing or deferring to do the same. *Reg. Orig.* 155.

CURIA DOMINI, the lord's house, hall,

or court, where all the tenants attend at the time of keeping courts. *Cowel. Blount.*

CURIA PENTICIARUM, is a court held by the sheriff of Chester, in a place there called the Pendice or Pentice: and it is probable its being originally kept under a Penthouse, or open shed covered with boards, gave it its denomination. *Ibid.*

CURNOCK, a measure containing four bushels, or half a quarter. *Fleta, lib.* 2. *c.* 12.

CURRICULUS, the year, or course of a year. *Cowel. Blount.*

CURSING. See SWEARING.

CURSITORS, (*clerici de cursu*) clerks belonging to the Chancery, who make out original writs; and are called clerks of course, in their oath appointed 18 *Ed.* 3. *stat.* 5. There are of these clerks twenty-four in number, which make a corporation of themselves; and to each clerk is allotted a division of certain counties, in which they exercise their functions. 2 *Inst.* 670.

CURSONES TERRÆ, is used for ridges of land. 14 *Ed.* 2. *Cowel. Blount.*

CURSORIÆ, a sort of light ships or swift sailers. *Ibid.*

CURTESY OF ENGLAND, (*jus curialitatis Angliæ*) is where a man taketh a wife seised in fee-simple, or fee-tail general, or as heiress in special tail, and hath issue by her, male or female, *born alive*, which by any possibility may inherit, and the wife dies; the husband holds the lands during his life; and is called *tenens per legem Angliæ*, or tenant by the curtesy of England; because this privilege is not allowed in any other country, except Scotland.

Four things are requisite to give an estate by the curtesy, *viz.* marriage, seisin of the wife, issue, and death of the wife. *Co. Lit.* 30. Therefore if land descend to the wife after the husband hath issue by her; or if the issue be dead at the time of her death, *being born alive;* the husband shall be tenant by the curtesy. And it is not material whether it was baptised, or ever heard to cry, for *if it is born alive*, it is enough. 1 *Nels. Abr.* 578. But the child must be such as by possibility may inherit; and therefore if land be given to a woman, and *the heirs* male of her body, and she takes husband and *hath issue a daughter*, and dies; as this issue cannot possibly inherit, the husband shall not be tenant by the curtesy. *Terms de Ley.*

If the child is ripped forth of the mother's belly, after her death, though it be alive, it will not entitle tenancy by the curtesy; for this ought to begin by the issue, and be consummate by the death of the wife, and the estate of tenant by the curtesy should avoid the immediate descent. *Ibid.*

But there is no tenancy by the curtesy of copyhold lands, except there be a special custom for it. *Plowd.* 263.

CURTEYN, (*curtana*) was the name of king Edward the confessor's sword: which is the first sword carried before the kings of England at their coronation: and it is said the point of it is broken as an emblem of mercy. *Mat. Paris. in Hen.* 3. *Cowel. Blount.*

CURTILAGE, (*curtilagium*) from the Fr. *cour*, court, and *Sax. leagh locus*) is a court-yard, back-side, or piece of ground lying near and belonging to a dwelling-house. 4 *Ed.* 1. *cap.* 1. 35 *H.* 8. *c.* 4. 39 *Eliz. c.* 10. 9 *Rep.* 64.

CURTILES TERRÆ, court lands. It is recorded, that among our Saxon ancestors, the Thanes or nobles who possessed Bock-land, or hereditary lands, divided them into inland and outland: the inland was that which lay most convenient for the lord's mansion house; and therefore the lords kept that part in their own hands, for the support of their families, and for hospitality: afterwards the Normans called these lands *terras dominicales*, the domains, or lord's lands: the Germans termed them *terras indominicatas*, lands in the lord's own use: and the Feudists, *terras curtiles*, lands appropriate to the court or house of the lord. *Spelm. of Feuds, c.* 5.

CUSTANTIA, the same with *custagium*, which signifies costs. *Cowel. Blount.*

CUSTODE ADMITTENDO, and CUSTODE AMOVENDO, writs for the admitting or removing of guardians. *Reg. Orig.*

CUSTODES LIBERTATIS ANGLIÆ AUTHORITATE PARLIAMENTI, was the style in which writs and all judicial process did run during the grand rebellion, from the murder of king Charles I. till the usurper Oliver was declared protector, &c. mentioned and declared to be traiterous, by statute 12 *Car.* 2. *c.* 3.

CUSTODIAM DARE, was taken for a gift or grant for life. *Du Cange.*

CUSTOM, (*consuetudo*) is a law not written, established by long usage, and the consent of our ancestors. And if it is universal, then it is common law: if particular to this or that place, then it is custom. 3 *Salk.* 112.

And general customs which are used throughout England, and are the common law, are to be determined by the judges: but particular customs, such as are used in some certain town, borough, city, &c. shall be determined by jury. *Doct. & Stud. c.* 7, 10. 1 *Inst.* 110. See also *London.*

CUSTOM OF MERCHANTS. These are particular customs prevailing among merchants which being in furtherance of trade, are supported by the common law, and upon those customs have originated the laws relating to bills of exchange, marine insurances, and many other matters.

CUSTOMS (*custuma*) are duties payable to the crown for goods exported and imported, and are due to the king of common right; first, because the subject hath leave to depart the kingdom, and to export the commodities thereof; secondly, for the interest which the king hath in the sea, and as he is guardian of, and maintains all the ports, wherein the commodities are exported or imported; and lastly, for that the king protects merchants from enemies and pirates. *Dyer* 43.

These duties have been from time to time settled by act of parliament, and as they now stand are ascertained and fully fixed by the tables and per centages contained in a very voluminous act, *viz.* 49 *Geo.* 3. *c.* 98.

These duties of customs began in the reign of *Ed.* 1. when the parliament granted him 3*d.* in the pound for all merchandizes exported and imported. *Dyer* 165.

And the following is a compendious summary of all such acts as relate generally to the customs, and what is termed smuggling, from the earliest period to the present time, so far as the same appear to remain in force.

By 27 *Ed.* 3. *stat.* 2. *c.* 16. credit shall be given to letters brought by merchants aliens, or to their oaths, of the value of their goods; and sheriffs, mayors, or other officers, wrongfully meddling with the goods of such merchants shall pay quadruple damages.

By 38 *Ed.* 3. *c.* 8. the owner of a ship shall not forfeit for a small thing therein, not customed, without his knowledge.

By 14 *Ric.* 2. *c.* 10. no customer or comptroller shall have any ship of his own, nor meddle with the freight of ships; and he shall not enjoy such office for life, but only during the king's pleasure. Also 17 *Ric.* 2. *c.* 5.

By 1 *Hen.* 4. *c.* 13. customers and comptrollers shall be resident upon their offices, without making any deputy.

By 4 *Hen.* 4. *c.* 20. merchandizes entering in, or going out, shall be charged and discharged in the great ports, and not in creeks, upon pain of forfeiture.

By 4 *Hen.* 4. *c.* 21. searchers shall not let their offices to farm, nor occupy them by deputy, nor take more than shall be ordained to them, nor be host to any merchant or mariner.

By 11 *Hen.* 4. *c.* 2. no common innkeeper in any city or borough, shall be a customer, comptroller, or searcher there.

By 13 *Hen.* 4. *c.* 5. all customers, comptrollers, and collectors, shall be constantly resident upon their offices, nor be absent three weeks, unless commanded of record.

By 3 *Hen.* 6. *c.* 3. customer, collector, or comptroller of the king's customs, concealing the same when entered and paid, shall forfeit the treble value of the merchandizes.

By 11 *Hen.* 6. *c.* 15. customers and comptrollers shall deliver warrants to discharge merchants that have paid their custom.

By 20 *Hen.* 6. *c.* 5. no customer, comptroller, or his servant, shall have any ship of his own, nor use merchandize, keep an inn, or a wharf, or be a factor to another.

By 28 *Hen.* 6. *c.* 5. officer of the customs making an arrest or distress upon any ships for an unlawful cause, shall pay 40*l.* on conviction.

By 31 *Hen.* 6. *c.* 5. no letters patent of the offices of searcher, gauger of wine, aulneger, finder, weigher, collector or comptroller, shall be made but by warrant from the treasury.

By 1 *Hen.* 7. *c.* 2. and 11 *Hen.* 7. *c.* 14. an alien made denizen shall pay the same customs as before.

By 1 *Hen.* 8. *c.* 5. one Englishman may custom goods in another Englishman's name, and a merchant stranger may custom goods in another's name.

Customing goods, whereby the king loseth his custom, forfeits the goods, and also the value of the goods, to the party grieved. *Ibid.* and by 2 & 3 *Ed.* 6. *c.* 22. he shall forfeit all his goods and chattels.

By 1 *Hen.* 8. *c.* 5. no citizen of London, inhabitant of Cinque Ports, or other person being free of butlerage, shall custom the wines of others.

By 14 & 15 *Hen.* 8. *c.* 4 an Englishman, sworn subject to a foreign prince, shall pay such customs as aliens do; and if they return and dwell again in the realm, they shall pay such customs as other Englishmen.

By 22 *Hen.* 8. *c.* 8. tables of the custom duties shall be set up in every city or town where demanded; on pain of 5*l.* in every city, and 40*s.* in every town, for every month's neglect herein.

The scavage tables in London shall be approved and signed by the chancellor, treasurer, president of the council, lord privy seal, lord steward, and the two chief justices or four of them. *Ibid.*

By 1 *Eliz.* *c.* 11. no customable goods shall be laden or discharged but in the daylight, and in open place where there is a customer, upon pain of forfeiture. Masters of vessels receiving or discharging the loading otherwise, forfeit 100*l.* and they are to give notice to the customer of their departure under the like penalty.

No master of a ship shall discharge the same, before he hath certified the custom, upon pain of 100*l.* and no man shall enter goods in the customer's book, but in the owner's name. *Ibid.*

The penalty of an officer of the custom-house, concealing an offence, is 100*l.* *Ibid.*

This act not to prejudice the inhabitants of Anglesey, Flint, and Caernarvon. *Ibid.*

By 12 *Car.* 2. *c.* 4. the penalty for not paying the old subsidy, was forfeiture of goods; but merchant strangers shall be well intreated, and such whose goods be taken by pirates, or perish in the sea, may newly ship other goods to the amount of those lost, without paying any duty; and goods shipped in caracs or galleys shall pay alien duties.

By 12 *Car.* 2. *c.* 19. if any persons convey away any goods without entry and agreement for the custom, the chief magistrate of the port may grant a warrant of assistance, to search for and seize the same within a month after.

By 13 & 14 *Car.* 2. *c.* 11. for preventing frauds and abuses in the customs, no ship arriving from beyond sea, shall be above three days coming from Gravesend to the place of her discharge in the Thames, unless hindered by winds or otherwise, and shall make true entry of the loading, on forfeiture of 100*l.*

Captains or other officers, shall take no goods on board ships outward bound, before entry thereof made at the custom-house, on the like pain. *Ibid.*

Officers of the customs may enter ships, and stay aboard to search; the penalty on embezzling or concealing goods is 100*l.* and persons beating or abusing the officers shall by the next justice of peace be committed to prison, and be fined not above 100*l.* *Ibid.*

Foreign built ships shall not have the privilege of English ships. *Ibid.*

No goods shall be water borne or landed, but in the presence of an officer of the customs, nor carried from one port to another, without a coquet. Officers of any port making false certificate, shall lose their employment, be incapacitated, and forfeit 50*l.* and any person counterfeiting a certificate, shall forfeit 100*l.* *Ibid.*

Owners of goods secretly conveyed beyond sea, uncustomed, shall forfeit the double value of the goods. *Ibid.*

For preventing frauds in colouring strangers goods, the merchant shall subscribe a bill of every entry. *Ibid.*

There shall be no party jury in actions concerning the customs. Allowances to merchants for damages in goods, shall be made upon oath. Goods brought from or carried into Scotland, shall pass through Berwick or Carlisle. The king may appoint further ports, except Hull, where merchandize shall be landed, and custom paid. *Ibid.*

None shall seize any ship or goods, for non-payment of customs, but officers of the customs. *Ibid.*

Informer not prosecuting to effect, officers of the custom may bring action by way of *devenerunt;* and no informer shall compound under a third part of the appraised value. *Ibid.*

Customers taking any bribe, or conniving at false entries, forfeit 100*l.* and are disabled. Persons revealing their offences to the lord treasurer within two months shall be acquitted. *Ibid.*

Foreign goods shall be landed at the most convenient keys, and there weighed, numbered, and marked. No packet boats shall carry goods, on pain of 100*l.* *Ibid.*

On seizure by the navigation act, the defendant may have a commission, and time to examine witnesses beyond sea. *Ibid.*

No writ of delivery shall be granted out of the court of exchequer for goods seized, but on good security, and for goods perishable only. *Ibid.*

One moiety of the forfeitures are to the king, and the other to the informer. All persons shall be aiding to officers of the customs, and be saved harmless; and officers of the customs shall be sworn for their faithfulness therein. *Ibid.*

Persons employed about the customs shall not demand more than the fees due by law, nor put any person out of his turn, on pain of double costs and damages. *Ibid.*

By 25 *Car.* 2. *c.* 6. the merchants, whether denizens or aliens, shall pay no more on exporting the native commodities of this realm, than the king's natural-born subjects (except for coals or manufactures wrought in this kingdom, or Berwick), and they shall pay no ships duties for fish caught by English ships, and exported in such ships with three-fourths English seamen.

By 2 *Will. & Mar. stat.* 2. *c.* 10. an officer of receipt for customs given upon East India goods, tobacco and the like, shall be within the city of London.

By 4 & 5 *Will. & Mar. c.* 15. the penalty for insuring goods prohibited, or goods without custom, is 500*l.*

By 6 *Will. & Mar. c.* 1. the commissioners and officers of the customs shall take an oath for the faithful execution of their office, upon pain of forfeiting the same.

By 6 & 7 *Will.* 3. *c.* 7. officers for extraordinary attendance may take such recompence from the merchant as the commissioners shall determine.

By 8 & 9 *Will.* 3. *c.* 36. any person may prosecute for the penalty for insuring goods without paying customs.

By 2 & 3 *Ann. c.* 9. the oath of the agent, or husband of any company, or servant of any merchant, on the importing or exporting of any goods, shall be sufficient.

By 8 *Ann. c.* 7. persons claiming goods seized, shall give security to answer costs.

By 8 *Ann. c.* 13. certificate goods relanded, shall be forfeited, and double the value of the drawback, with the vessel, and all things used in moving the goods. Officers conniving are to be incapacitated, and imprisoned for six months: and masters (besides the penalties) are to be imprisoned for the same time.

Officers embezzling any goods, are to forfeit double the value, with costs. *Ibid.*

By 12 *Ann. stat.* 2. *c.* 8. goods that have remained (by 12 *Geo.* 1. *c.* 28. six months) in her majesty's storehouses, uncustomed, shall be sold by auction.

Deputations of officers of the customs, shall continue in force, notwithstanding the death or removal of the commissioners who deputed them. *Ibid.*

By 5 *Geo.* 1. *c.* 11. foreign goods taken at sea (unless in case of necessity) to be run, are forfeited, and the master shall forfeit treble the value of such goods. *Ibid.*

Goods not reported, and found after clearing the ship, are forfeited. *Ibid.*

Goods prohibited to be worn here, and foreign goods relanded, are forfeited; and the master of the ship shall forfeit the value of such goods. *Ibid.*

The master permitting the package of certificate goods to be opened on board, without leave, forfeits 100*l.* *Ibid.*

Ships of fifty tons, or under, hovering on the coast, officers may enter and take an account of the lading, and demand security in treble the value of the goods; the master refusing to enter into bond, the foreign goods may be taken out of the ship, and secured, and custom paid; and wool and prohibited goods are forfeited. *Ibid.*

Goods saved out of any stranded ship, after salvage and charges paid, are liable to the customs. *Ibid.*

Officers making collusive seizures, are to forfeit 500*l.* and be incapacitated, and the importer is to forfeit treble the value of the goods. *Ibid.*

Officers or importer discovering his accomplices, in two months, shall be acquitted, and any other person discovering in three months, shall have half the king's share of the penalties, which are half to the king and half to the informer. *Ibid.*

By 6 *Geo.* 1. *c.* 21. in trials relating to excise or customs, if questions arise concerning the keeping of any office, or any one's being an officer, proof of the exercising such office may be given, without proving the handwriting of the commissioners.

Commanders of vessels in the king's service, may compel the master of any ship under fifty tons, hovering within two leagues of the shore, to come into port. *Ibid.*

Master suffering uncustomed goods, wool, woolfells, mortlings, yarn of wool, woolflocks, fullers-earth, or tobacco-pipe clay, to be taken out of, or put on board, besides former penalties, shall be imprisoned six months. *Ibid.*

Any offender in hindering officers in their duty, discovering before conviction, two of his accomplices, within two months, shall have 40*l.* for each, and be acquitted. Other persons discovering in three months, shall have 40*l.* over and above any other reward, to be paid by the cashier of the customs. *Ibid.*

An officer of the customs may stop and warehouse, till claimed, prohibited or customable goods, found in any boat or house. *Ibid.*

Proof must be in ten days after stopping; it shall lie on the claimer, and if he gets a verdict, he shall have reasonable costs. *Ibid.*

If the claimer make proof of his goods, or that they have received any damage, the goods shall be delivered, and he may sue the officers. *Ibid.*

Officers may prosecute notwithstanding the direction of the commissioners; so may the owners; and offences relating to the customs may be tried in any of the courts at Westminster, or in the exchequer in Scotland. *Ibid.*

By 8 *Geo.* 1. *c.* 18. made perpetual by 49 *Geo.* 3. *c.* 20. boats, barges, or the like, rowing or found with more than four oars above or below London bridge, shall be forfeited, and the owner, or person using the same, shall forfeit 40*l.* *Ibid.*

Such boats are to be burnt, or used as aforesaid: but this act is not to extend to the king's boats or galleys, to boats belonging to merchant ships, or to boats licenced by the admiralty, so as security be given that they shall not run uncustomed goods. *Ibid.*

Persons receiving or buying goods clandestinely run, shall forfeit 20*l.* Persons running goods, or receiving the same, may be arrested on a *capias* in the first instance. *Ibid.*

Seizures of vessels of fifteen tons or under, and of carriages, cattle, and the like, may be determined by two justices of the peace. *Ibid.*

Goods brought from one port in Great Britain to another, unshipped before cocquet delivered to the customer, are forfeited: and foreign goods landed without the presence of an officer of the customs, shall be forfeited. *Ibid.*

By 9 *Geo.* 1. *c.* 21. the customs of Great Britain may be put under one commission, or under several commissions for England, and Scotland respectively, as his majesty shall judge best.

Persons discovering frauds, shall have one half of the officer's share. Tobacco or foreign goods, carried coastways from any other port than the place from whence certified, are forfeited, and double the value; and the master of the ship shall forfeit the value of the goods. *Ibid.*

By 11 *Geo.* 1. *c.* 30. concealing goods liable to duties of customs or excise, forfeits the goods and treble value, and the value thereof shall be taken at the best rate.

Goods prohibited, or run, may be seized by any person, and warehoused, and offering such goods to sale, forfeits them and treble the value. *Ibid.*

The buyer shall also forfeit treble value, but both buyer and seller shall not be prosecuted for the same goods. *Ibid.*

If the prosecution be not commenced within a month, the warehouse-keeper may prosecute. *Ibid.*

No custom or excise officer shall deal in tea, coffee, brandy, or the like, on loss of office and 50*l.* *Ibid.*

On seizure of foreign goods for non-payment of duties, the proof shall lie on the owner. *Ibid.*

One or more justices of peace, where the seizure is made, may examine persons on oath to the value of the goods. *Ibid.*

After entry of goods for exportation, whereon there is a drawback, the searcher may open and examine any bale, chest, or the like, and on discovery of fraud, the owner shall forfeit the same, and lose the drawback. *Ibid.*

Customable goods shipped for exportation, without warrant or presence of an officer, are forfeited. *Ibid.*

Goods brought into the king's warehouses, remaining there six months, the duties not paid, may be publicly sold. *Ibid.*

Entering foreign goods for exportation, to get the drawback, and landing them in the isle of Man, shall forfeit treble the value of the goods, and the master, besides, shall be imprisoned six months. *Ibid.*

Persons in prison relative to the custom or excise, not pleading within one term, judgment may be entered by default, and execution awarded against body and estate. *Ibid.*

No information shall be filed for recovery of any penalty by the laws of the customs or excise, unless entered in the attorney-general's name, or of some officer. *Ibid.*

By 9 *Geo.* 2. *c.* 35. persons apprehending, or maimed in apprehending of offenders against this act by running goods, shall be allowed 50*l.* reward, and if killed, their executors shall have the same.

Such offenders discovering two or more accomplices, three months after the offence, to the commissioners of the customs or excise, shall be discharged, and have the fifty pounds reward. *Ibid.*

The proof of entry and payment of duties, shall lie on such offenders, and all goods, weapons, furniture, and packages shall be forfeited. *Ibid.*

The rewards shall be paid by the respective receivers general, by order of the commissioners, on the judge's certificate of the offender's conviction; and the commissioners are to adjust the shares in case of difference. *Ibid.*

Persons lurking within five miles of the sea, or a navigable river, with intent to assist in running goods, not giving a good account of themselves to a justice, shall be sent to the house of correction, and be whipt, and kept to hard labour, and 20*s.* per head to the informer of such offenders shall be paid by the commissioners. *Ibid.*

Such persons desiring time to clear themselves of the accusation, shall be only imprisoned till satisfaction, or security given not to offend again. *Ibid.*

Watermen, porters, or others, found with prohibited or run goods, shall forfeit treble the value, or be imprisoned for not more than three months. *Ibid.*

Vessels arriving from foreign parts, with six pounds of tea on board, or brandy or spirits in casks, under six gallons (except for the use of the seamen) hovering within two leagues of the shore, all such goods, with the packages, shall be forfeited. *Ibid.*

Foreign goods taken in, or put out of any vessel, within four leagues of the British coasts, without payment of customs (unless in apparent necessity) shall be forfeited, and the master shall forfeit treble the value, and the vessel, if not above 100 tons. *Ibid.*

Fifty pounds penalty on offering to bribe an officer to connivance; and actions of assault upon officers, may be tried in any county of England. *Ibid.*

All goods found concealed, after the master's report at the custom-house, are forfeited, and the master shall forfeit treble the value. *Ibid.*

Officers may go on board coasting vessels, and search for prohibited goods, and continue on board during the vessel's stay in port; and every person obstructing shall forfeit 100*l.* *Ibid.*

Alehouse-keepers or the like persons, knowingly harbouring any person against whom process hath issued, for obstructing officers, and after six days notice in the gazette, of such persons absconding, and writing fixed to the door of the church, shall forfeit 100*l.* *Ibid.*

Sheriffs, mayors, and like officers, on request in writing of a known solicitor for the customs or excise, shall grant special warrants for apprehending offenders, and they shall be indemnified from escapes. *Ibid.*

In trials of seizures, judges shall proceed to the merits of the cause, without inquiring into the fact or form of making the seizure. *Ibid.*

Officers and their assistants may oppose force to force, and if carried before a justice for wounding or killing, shall be admitted to bail. *Ibid.*

The court of king's bench, or court of justiciary in Scotland, may bail persons committed on this act. *Ibid.*

By 15 *Geo.* 2. *c.* 31. claimants of vessels seized for unlawful importation shall give security to pay costs.

By 19 *Geo.* 2. *c.* 34. made perpetual by 43 *Geo.* 3. *c.* 157. armed persons in the number of three, assembled to assist in the illegal exporting of wool, or other prohibited goods, or in the running of goods, or appearing in disguise with such goods, or who shall resist officers in the execution of their duty, are guilty of felony without clergy.

Orders for offenders to surrender in forty days, shall be published in two successive gazettes, and on their not surrendering, to be deemed convicted of felony without clergy. *Ibid.*

Persons harbouring such offenders shall be transported for seven years. *Ibid.*

Where officers are wounded in securing offenders, the hundred shall make full satisfaction and amends, and pay 100*l.* to the executors of each officer killed. *Ibid.*

Offenders discovering two or more accomplices shall receive 50*l.* and be acquitted. *Ibid.*

On information for seizures, if there was a probable cause for seizure, the person who seized shall not pay costs: and in actions for the seizure, if there was a probable cause, the defendant shall not be liable to costs. *Ibid.*

By 21 *Geo.* 2. *c.* 2. drawbacks shall be allowed on exportation within three years, except where any act of parliament has declared that no drawback shall be allowed.

By 28 *Geo.* 2. *c.* 21. no spirituous liquors imported in vessels under sixty gallons shall be entered or reported for exportation; and all tea above six pounds, found in British vessels (excepting those of the East India company) arriving from foreign parts, shall be forfeited.

By 3 *Geo.* 3. *c.* 22. vessels or goods seized by officers of the customs, shall be publicly sold after condemnation, at such places as the commissioners of the customs shall think proper.

By 5 *Geo.* 3. *c.* 43. unentered goods found concealed in packages sent to the king's warehouse, or brought on shore by special sufferance, and not specified, are forfeited.

Officers seizing and not prosecuting, instead of a moiety, shall have only one third of the value.

By 14 *Geo.* 3. *c.* 89. a *capias* requiring bail, may issue in the first process for smuggling.

The 12 *Geo.* 1. *c.* 28. as to informations is extended to suing of penalties for importing, wearing, or using prohibited goods, where the king is entitled to any part. *Ibid.*

By 16 *Geo.* 3. *c.* 48. bonds taken relating to the customs, and not prosecuted in five years (except for duties or money due to the crown, or for the good behaviour of officers) shall be void, and the commissioners shall order them to be cancelled. *s.* 2.

But by 48 *Geo.* 3. *c.* 84, all such bonds shall remain in force and may be prosecuted within two years from the time limited in the condition.

By 17 *Geo.* 3. *c.* 41, unshipping goods at sea from homeward bound East India ships at any distance from the coast, (unless through apparent necessity) is a forfeiture thereof, and of the vessel into which they are taken, and treble value for assisting; and putting on board East India ships, wine, brandy, or the like at sea, after clearance (except stores for the voyage) is the like forfeiture.

Bonds for the exportation of prohibited goods, or goods intitled to a drawback, shall not be discharged without a certificate of the landing; and commanders of ships to the Baltic shall give a particular of their landing to the British consul in ten days. *Ibid.*

By 18 *Geo.* 3. *c.* 40, the 17 *Geo.* 3. *c.* 41, as to certificates and proof for their discharge of bonds for exportation of goods prohibited is repealed; and the part relating to the Baltic is extended to Denmark, Norway, and Archangel.

By 19 *Geo.* 3. *c.* 48, masters of ships removing their vessels out of the stream, except to the lawful quays in the port of London, before the goods are discharged, forfeit 100*l.*

By 19 *Geo.* 3. *c.* 69, foreign brandy or other spirits imported from any part of Europe, in casks less than sixty gallons, (except two gallons for each seaman) shall be forfeited with the ship.

If tea, coffee, foreign brandy, or other spirits or goods liable to forfeiture, be found on board any ship in port, or within two leagues, not more than 200 tons, such ship and tackle shall be forfeited. *Ibid.*

The 8 *Geo.* 1. *c.* 18, is extended to boats with six oars, but not to commanders of the king's ships, nor to tow boats at Bristol. *Ibid.*

Ships and other things forfeited may be seized by officers of the customs or excise, and if not fit for the king's service shall be broken up and sold; and no writ of delivery shall issue out of the exchequer for any ship ordered to be burnt, or used for the king's service or broken up, unless the officer seizing shall delay proceeding three terms, and then not without good security for double value. *Ibid.*

Penalty 300*l.* on master of a ship coming from abroad (not an East India ship) having more than 100lb. of tea, or 100 gallons of spirits (above two gallons for each seaman) in casks under sixty gallons. *Ibid.*

Officers of the customs or excise may arrest the master and persons assisting in running goods, and justices of peace may commit them. *Ibid.*

And such master shall enter into a recognizance with one sufficient security for 300*l.* to enter appearance to informations, and refusing so to do shall be imprisoned. 26 *Geo.* 3. *c.* 77.

Two or more travelling together, armed or disguised, with horses or carriages, laden with more than 6lb. of tea, or five gallons of spirits, without a permit, may be arrested and committed, as also any one obstructing the officer, attempting a rescue, or damaging the casks, the officer to enter into a recognizance to prosecute, and the charges to be paid by the receiver-general of the customs. 19 *Geo.* 3. *c.* 69.

Persons so committed may be tried at the quarter sessions, and if convicted, to be committed for not more than three years nor less than one, or to serve the king by sea or land, and then not to be discharged in less than five years. *Ibid.*

By 24 *Geo.* 3. *c.* 47, if any vessel shall be found at anchor, or hovering on the coasts (unless by distress of weather) having on board any foreign spirits in a less cask than sixty gallons, or any wine in casks, six pounds of tea, or twenty pounds of coffee, such vessel with its cargo shall be forfeited; but on proof that such small quantities were on board without the privity of the owner or master, such vessel shall not be forfeited, if of more than 100 tons burthen, but the goods found on board shall be forfeited.

Cutters, luggers, shallops, or wherries shall be forfeited, and all armed vessels; but vessels may have two carriage guns, four pounders, and two muskets for every ten men. *Ibid.*

This is not to extend to vessels belonging to the revenue or government offices, or such as are licensed by the admiralty, or have arms on board for exportation, by way of merchandize. *Ibid.*

No fee is to be taken for licenses. Owners of licensed vesels shall bring their licenses to the proper officer at the port of exportation, and shall give security not to employ the vessel in the importation or landing of tea, or foreign spirits, or any prohibited goods.

If any person shall maliciously shoot at any ship belonging to the crown, or shoot at, or dangerously wound, any officer of the navy, customs, or excise, when acting in the execution of his duty, he shall suffer death as a felon. *Ibid.*

If any person be charged with any offence made felony by this act, before a judge of the court of king's bench, if in England, or before one of the lords of justiciary, if in Scotland, such judge shall return the information to one of the secretaries of state to be laid before the king in council; who may order the offender to surrender himself to such judge, who shall commit him: which order is to be published in the gazette, and transmitted to the sheriffs, who shall proclaim the same in two market towns; offenders not surrendering shall suffer death as felons, and the court may award execution against them, as if they had been convicted. *Ibid.*

Any person harbouring such offenders after the time appointed for their surrender, and being prosecuted within a year after, shall on conviction, be guilty of felony and be transported for seven years. *Ibid.*

This is not to prevent the apprehending such offenders by the ordinary course of law. Persons obstructing officers of the navy, customs, or excise, in execution of their duty, may be carried before a justice, who may commit them, and on conviction they are to be sent to hard labour on the Thames for three years; and persons charged with such offences may be committed until the next quarter sessions. *Ibid.*

Offences may be tried in any county, and persons charged with a misdemeanor shall not be admitted to bail, without entering into a recognizance to appear, and stand trial. *Ibid.*

Officers and seamen wounded in the revenue service shall be provided for by the treasury, and commissioners of customs shall reward officers, who shall take offenders against this act. *Ibid.*

If suspected vessels shall not bring to, when chased by any cutter in the service of the navy, having the proper pendant hoisted, the commander may shoot into them. Vessels not in the service of the navy, or customs or excise, shall not hoist such pendant on penalty of 500*l.* *Ibid.*

The penalties and restrictions in an act 8 *Geo.* 1. and in 19 *Geo.* 3. *c.* 69. relating to certain boats, are extended to boats exceeding twenty-eight feet in length, or more in proportion than three feet and an half in length to one in breadth. *Ibid.*

Masters of vessels arriving at any port in this kingdom, or going outwards in ballast, shall make a true report of their vessels. and answer questions relative to the voyage, put to them by the proper officer; on penalty of 100*l.* *Ibid.*

Wine imported in any vessel not exceeding sixty tons burthen, shall be forfeited, as also the vessel. Goods reported, contents unknown, may be opened, and if any prohibited goods are found, they shall be forfeited. *Ibid.*

Officers of customs shall have like power to seize tea and spirits removing without permit, as officers of excise; and seizures of horses, boats, and carriages, for remov ng of customable goods, shall be determined by two justices. *Ibid.*

Officers making any collusive seizure, or agreeing not to seize any ship or goods, or taking any bribe, shall forfeit 500*l.* and be incapacitated; and every person giving or offering such bribe, shall forfeit 500*l.* *Ibid.*

Vessels and goods forfeited by this act, or by 19 *Geo.* 3. *c.* 69. may be seized by any officer of customs or excise; but condemned vessels, if fit for his majesty's service, may be sold to the officers appointed by the admiralty. *Ibid.*

All the regulations in 23 *Geo.* 3. *c.* 70, (*see* EXCISE) touching actions to be brought against excise officers, and their aiders, are extended to officers of the customs. *Ibid.*

No claim shall be entered to any vessel

or goods seized, and returned into the exchequer, unless in the real names of the owners or proprietors thereof, which are to be sworn to before a baron, and taking a false oath incurs the pains of perjury. *Ibid.*

Every claimant of any vessel or goods seized (if resident in Great Britain) shall be bound with two sureties, in a penalty of 100*l.* to pay costs; but if not resident, his attorney shall be bound in like manner. *Ibid.*

By 26 *Geo.* 3. *c.* 40. no goods shall be imported into Great Britain, in any vessel belonging to British subjects, unless the master have on board a manifest, containing the particulars of the contents, where laden, the name and built of such ship, the tonnage, the commander's name, the port to which it belongs, and a true account of the whole cargo.

No wine shall be imported from any place not subject to the crown of Great Britain, unless the master has a proper manifest on board. *Ibid.*

And certificates are requisite on the importation of goods, as heretofore. *Ibid.*

Masters of vessels, before clearing out for Great Britain, from any of the British dominions in foreign parts, shall deliver a manifest to the chief officer of the customs. *Ibid.*

Truth of the manifest shall be verified on oath before the consul relative to wine shipped in foreign parts for Great Britain. *Ibid.*

Masters of vessels importing goods without a proper manifest, forfeit double the value of the goods, with the full duties. *Ibid.*

Masters of vessels, on arrival within four leagues of the British coast, are to produce their manifest to the first officer of the customs who shall come on board, and give him a copy thereof. Officer shall certify such production on the back of the original manifest, and transmit a copy to the proper officers at the port of consignment. The master is not required to give more than two copies of his manifest. *Ibid.*

The master neglecting to produce his manifest, or to give a copy thereof to the proper officer, forfeits double the value of the goods, and all the duties, and the officer neglecting to certify the production thereof forfeits 100*l.* *Ibid.*

Master and mate of any such vessel, who shall suffer bulk to be broken within the said limits, unauthorised by the proper officer, shall forfeit 200*l.* each (except through bad weather). *Ibid.*

Goods not stored in the main hold shall be taken an account of by the proper officer, who shall first come on board, who is to mark or seal the packages; and if any marks on such goods shall be defaced, with the privity of the master and mate, they shall forfeit 200*l.* each. *Ibid.*

Masters of every vessel importing such goods shall make entry upon oath, of her burthen and lading, before the chief officer at the port of importation; and deliver his manifest to him; on penalty of 200*l.* *Ibid.*

The master, if the goods reported do not agree with the manifest, shall forfeit 200*l.*; But if it is proved that the cargo was taken aboard in foreign parts, and that no part has been unshipped, or that the manifest is lost, or defaced without fraud, or incorrect only by mistake, the penalties are not to be incurred. *Ibid.*

Masters permitting goods to be thrown overboard or destroyed after arrival within the limits aforesaid, unless through necessity, shall forfeit 200*l.* *Ibid.*

Importers, within twenty days after the master's report, shall make entry, with the proper officer, of all goods imported by them, and pay the duties; unless such goods may be warehoused upon bond, *Ibid.*

No vessel shall be cleared out for foreign parts, until the master and mate have given bond not to land illegally any goods on board; and no bounty or drawback shall be allowed on any goods exported in bales press packed, unless the packer make oath of the quantity and quality of the goods packed. *Ibid.*

Masters who shall not deliver cocquets to the proper officer shall forfeit 100*l.* and if the cargo shall not be agreeable thereto, he shall likewise forfeit 20*l.* for every package missing. *Ibid.*

Debentures on exportation of goods entitled to a drawback or bounty, shall be made out in the names of the real owners; but companies trading by a joint stock may employ an agent. *Ibid.*

No bounty or drawback shall be paid for goods exported to Ireland, Guernsey or Jersey, without a proper certificate. *Ibid.*

Goods entitled thereto shall not be put on board by any persons (except revenue officers) other than such as shall be licensed by the commissioners of the customs, who are to grant such licences to the persons now entitled by law to carry goods on board, they finding proper security. *Ibid.*

Masters of vessels who shall neglect to bring to at the usual places appointed for stationing revenue officers, shall forfeit 100*l.* *Ibid.*

Revenue officers on board shall have free access to the cabin, and may open locks. *Ibid.*

No goods, the growth or manufacture of any country beyond the Cape of Good Hope, shall be brought into London or Westminster, Southwark or the bills of mortality without a proper certificate that the duties have been duly paid; on forfeiture thereof with the carriages. The proof of the place to which such goods were removing shall lie on the claimant; but goods that were bought openly, or are private property, and used as domestic furniture may be removed without forfeiture thereof. *Ibid.*

Commanders of the king's ships of war may seize any vessels or goods subject to forfeiture. *Ibid.*

Witnesses shall be examined on oath before the surveyors general of the customs; and persons making a false oath shall be deemed guilty of perjury. *Ibid.*

If in a trial for seizure of goods, wherein a verdict is given for the claimant, there shall appear to have been a probable cause for such seizure, the defendant shall not be liable to costs or damages. *Ibid.*

All vessels and goods seized and condemned in the British colonies in America, shall be sold there, by public auction. *Ibid.*

By 27 *Geo.* 3. *c.* 13. all goods imported shall be entered at the custom-house, and landed in the presence of an officer, except fish, British taken, and turbots and lobsters.

The value of non-enumerated goods, shall be ascertained by the importer or proprietor making a declaration according to the form in the act, which shall bind as fully, as if it had been made on oath: and if such goods be undervalued, they are to be taken for the use of the crown, paying to the proprietor for the same the entered value, with 10 per cent. thereon, and the duties paid; which goods so taken for the use of the crown may be sold; and if they produce more than all costs and charges, a moiety of the overplus may be given to the officers who examine them. *Ibid.*

There is a similar clause in respect to goods which may be exported chargeable with duties according to their value.

Collectors of the customs shall account for money received for sale of goods undervalued, as for duties. *Ibid.*

The portage to masters of ships shall cease. *Ibid.*

Cambrics or French lawns may be imported, worn, or sold; but cambrics imported in ships of less than sixty tons burthen, and in bales not containing the quantity of 100 pieces, and French wines in packages, containing less than three dozen quarts, shall be forfeited. *Ibid.*

The commissioners of customs may settle the accounts of the collectors or receivers, who have applied money belonging to one branch of the revenue to another. *Ibid.*

The East India company shall pay, at the times they become due by law, their duties to the receiver general of the customs, whose receipt shall be received as cash by the collector. *Ibid.*

Duties collected in the port of London, shall be paid to the receiver general, on the days they are received. *Ibid.*

Monies due on debentures for drawbacks or premiums, if due in London, shall be paid by the receiver general. *Ibid.*

Such debentures not due in London, may be paid by the respective collectors at the out-ports. *Ibid.*

If goods on which duties are payable according to weight, tale, gauge, or measure, be damaged on the voyage, a proportionable allowance shall be made out of the duties. *Ibid.*

Goods shall continue to be laden and unladen, and the officers of the customs shall attend at the same hours, and the same fees shall be received as now established by law. *Ibid.*

The duties and drawbacks on specific quantities of goods shall apply proportionably to any less quantities. *Ibid.*

By 27 *Geo.* 3. *c.* 31. the regulations of 26 *Geo.* 3. *c.* 40. shall not tend to beer exported.

By 27 *Geo.* 3. *c.* 32. any cutter, lugger, shallop, wherry, sloop, smack, or yawl belonging to his majesty's subjects, found within four leagues of the coast, whose bowsprit exceeds two thirds of the vessel in length, shall be forfeited. *Ibid.*

Names of boats belonging to such vessels shall be painted on their sterns, on penalty of being forfeited. *Ibid.*

Boats not belonging to vessels shall have their names and the owners painted on their sterns, on penalty of being forfeited, if found within the limits of any port or within four leagues of the coast; but this is not to extend to any vessel in his majesty's service. *Ibid.*

If vessels having a licence from the admiralty shall be found out of the limits thereof, they may be seized, unless it be made appear that they were driven thereout by distress of weather. *Ibid.*

The licences shall be produced to officers of the revenue, who shall board such vessels within four leagues of the coast, otherwise the vessel may be seized. *Ibid.*

Vessels seized may be disposed of agreeable to 24 *Geo.* 3. *c.* 47. *Ibid.*

The officers of the customs may open all bales, casks and packages, on board any vessel wherein any packages for exportation have been reported; but this is not to extend to vessels coming from Asia, Africa, or America. *Ibid.*

The manifest required by 26 *Geo.* 3. *c.* 40. shall for all ships within the limits of the East India company's charters be delivered to and authenticated by the person who shall deliver the last dispatches: and for ships from China, by the company's chief supercargo there. *Ibid.*

Commissioners of the customs may direct the hull of any vessel seized in America or the West Indies, to be broken up, and the materials sold. *Ibid.*

All seized goods shall be stamped before they are delivered from his majesty's warehouses; and if any officer neglects to stamp such goods, or accepts any fee for stamping them, he forfeits 200*l.* and is disabled from serving his majesty. *Ibid.*

Persons counterfeiting such stamps shall be guilty of felony without clergy. Goods with counterfeit stamps shall be forfeited, and the person in whose custody they are found, shall forfeit 500*l.* and unauthorised persons having stamps in their custody shall also forfeit 500*l.* *Ibid.*

Commissioners of the customs may restore goods, and other things seized, on being satisfied that the forfeiture arose, without any design of fraud in the proprietor, on such conditions as they may think reasonable; and if such conditions are not complied with, they may be condemned; but proprietors accepting such conditions are not entitled to any recompence on account of the seizure. *Ibid.*

By 28 *Geo.* 3. *c.* 34. the commissioners of the customs and excise shall out of the king's share of seizures, reward the officer seizing any vessel liable to be broken up after condemnation, by paying them 10*s.* per ton for all vessels exceeding 4 tons, and 40*s.* for every boat not exceeding 4 tons, and also one half of the produce of the materials after deducting the charges.

If it shall appear to the commissioners that any condemned vessel is not proper for smuggling, but may be employed in fair mercantile trade, such vessel may be sold and applied in like manner.

Goods seized in pursuance of any act relative to the trade and revenue of the British colonies in America, may by order of the judge be delivered, on security by bond to answer double the value in case of condemnation. *Ibid.*

The collector and comptroller are to inquire into the sufficiency of the security, and certify the same to the judge before delivery. *Ibid.*

And this act does not permit the delivery of any goods except such as are perishable, or where the prosecutor wilfully delays the suit. *Ibid.*

Any open boat belonging to his majesty's subjects, and being of the length of 23 feet and upwards, the length of which shall be greater than in the proportion of three feet and an half to one foot in breadth, to be measured by a straight line from the forepart of the stem to the aft-side of the transum or stern post aloft, found within any port or within four leagues of the coast shall be forfeited: and if any such open boat shall be eighteen feet long, and under twenty-four feet, from the fore-part of the stem to the aft-side of the transum or stern post aloft, and whose depth shall be more than in proportion of one inch and a quarter to every foot in length, the depth to be taken from the upper part of the plank next the keel to the top of the upper strake, it shall be forfeited with the vessel to which it belongs. *Ibid.*

All open boats belonging as aforesaid, of twenty-four feet and upwards, the depth of which shall be greater than in the proportion of one inch to one foot in length to be taken as aforesaid, shall be seized. *Ibid.*

But this act shall not authorise the seizing of any boat, on account of her built, employed in the navy, or revenue, or which is used on any canal, nor any boat licensed by the admiralty, if the licence is on board; nor any of the following open boats, *viz.*

	Plank in thickness In. qrs.	and timber sq. In. qrs.
An open boat from 23 to 25 feet in length having	¾	1 ¼
from 25 to 30 in length	1 ½	2
from 30 to 35 in length	1 ¾	3.
from 35 to 40 in length	2	4
from 40 to 50 in length	2	5
from 50 feet and upwards in leegth	3	6

By 28 *Geo.* 3. *c.* 37. "actions for any "thing done in pursuance of *any* act relating to the customs or excise, must be "brought in the proper county within three "months. The defendant may plead the "general issue, and if he succeeds, he has "treble costs." *Ibid.*

"If in an action for a seizure the claimer "recovers, he shall not have any costs; if "the court certifies that there was a probable cause of seizure, not greater damages "than 2*d.*; nor shall the defendant be imprisoned, or be fined above 1*s.*" *Ibid.*

"No writ shall issue against any person "acting under any act relating to the customs or excise, until one month's notice "shall be given of the cause of action, for "which the attorney is entitled to 20*s.* and "within that month the person may tender "amends. No evidence shall be received of "any act, except what is mentioned in the "notice; and if the defendant neglects to "tender amends within the month, he may "at any time before issue joined pay money "into court." *Ibid.*

By 30 *Geo.* 3. *c.* 43. the commissioners of the customs may order the expences of seizures of vessels to be paid out of his majesty's share of any seizure, and the officer to receive his full share of the net produce.

By 33 *Geo.* 3. *c.* 70. commissioners of the customs may direct their officers to examine goods damaged on the voyage, and to make a proportionable allowance out of the duties; but if the importer is not satisfied with the allowance, or the officers are incompetent to determine it, the directions of 27 *Geo.* 3. are to be followed. *s.* 5.

Vessels condemned, under 24 *Geo.* 3. *sess.* 2. *c.* 47. and which may be broken up or sold to private persons, may be sold to be used as privateers, and one moiety of the produce paid into the exchequer, and the other to the officer. *s.* 6.

By 34 *Geo.* 3. *c.* 50. persons obstructing officers of the navy, customs, or excise, in execution of their duty, may be prosecuted as for a misdemeanor, and shall not have time to traverse, but plead immediately, and if convicted they are to be sentenced to hard labour on the Thames, or some navigable river, or in the house of correction, for not exceeding three years. *s.* 5.

The 24 *Geo.* 3. *c.* 47. so far as relates to the vessels hereinafter mentioned to have arms on board is repealed. *s.* 6.

Every cutter, lugger, shalloon, wherry, smack, or yawl, of which the bottom is clench work, unless square-rigged, or fitted with a standing bowsprit, found within the limits of any of the ports, or within four leagues of the coast, or any distance as after mentioned, shall be forfeited with her furniture. *s.* 7.

Vessels having on board any spirits in any cask which shall not contain sixty gallons (except at the rate of two gallons for each seaman), or any wine in casks, (if the vessel shall not exceed sixty tons), or 6lb. of tea, or 20lb. of coffee, or any tobacco or snuff, exceeding together or separately 100lb.; or having on board any prohibited goods on a straight line between Walney and Great Ormshead, Burdsey Island and Shamble Head; the Lizard and the Prall; and the Prall and Bill of Portland; Cromer and the Spun Head; Flamborough Head to the Staples or the Mull of Galloway and Ayre in the Isle of Man; shall be forfeited with their furniture, as also open boats of the length of fourteen and under eighteen feet, and cutters, luggers, shallops, wherries, smacks, or yawls, to which they belong: but this is not to extend to whale-boats. *s.* 8, 9, 10.

Such last-mentioned vessels found within the said distances, having on board arms or ammunition without license, to be forfeited, except vessels from America, or the East or West Indies, or Africa, or the Mediterranean, or vessels in the service of the navy, victualling, ordnance, customs, excise, or post-office. *s.* 11.

By 35 *Geo.* 3, *c.* 31. the act 34 *Geo.* 3, *c.* 50, is extended to cutters, luggers, shallops, wherries, smacks, or yawls of any built whatever. *s.* 1.

By 36 *Geo.* 3, *c.* 82, no goods imported, (except diamonds, precious stones, and fresh fish,) shall be unshipped, though on Sundays or holidays, without the presence of the proper officer, on pain of forfeiture. *s.* 1.

Also, by 36 *Geo.* 3, *c.* 82, owners of vessels licensed pursuant to 24 *Geo.* 3. *sess.* 2, *c.* 47, are to give bond that if they are lost the license shall be delivered up, and the commissioners of the customs may at any time direct licenses to be cancelled. *s.* 3, 4.

By 39 & 40 *Geo.* 3, *c.* 51, the owner of every vessel licensed under 24 *Geo.* 3, *sess.* 2, *c.* 47, shall, before it sails, give bond that the same shall not be found within the limits prescribed by 34 *Geo.* 3, *c.* 50, or trade contrary to 27 *Geo.* 3. *c.* 32, and also that the vessels shall not be engaged in any other trade or employment than what is set forth in the license. *s.* 17.

By 42 *Geo.* 3. *c.* 82, vessels described in 24 *Geo.* 3. *c.* 41, or any other act, found hovering within eight leagues of the coast, shall be forfeited, with the cargo; and all pains and penalties, and all clauses in such acts relating to vessels described therein, found hovering within four leagues of the coast, shall extend to such vessels hovering within eight leagues, and their cargoes. *s.* 1, 2, 3.

And though in any trial it shall appear doubtful whether the vessel was within such limits, the jury shall find for the crown, if they are satisfied the vessel had prohibited goods on board. *s.* 4.

Officers of excise or customs may extinguish lights made for signals to smugglers (see 47 *Geo.* 3, sess. 2, *c.* 36, *s.* 37, infra) and convey offenders before a justice, who shall proceed against them as vagabonds, or take bail for their appearance. *s.* 10.

Persons so found making such lights shall be deemed rogues and vagabonds, within the meaning of 17 *Geo.* 2, *c.* 5, the powers of which act are extended to this for the purpose of punishing such offenders. *s.* 14. 12.

Persons shall be liable to be prosecuted only for one offence. *s.* 13.

By 43 *Geo.* 3, *c.* 68, pearls, emeralds, rubies, and other jewels, except diamonds, are to be entered and landed as other goods. *s.* 3.

Fish of British taking and curing caught by the crews of vessels built in Great Britain, Ireland, &c. and navigated and registered according to law, may be imported into Great Britain, duty free. *s.* 6.

Where goods on importation are chargeable according to the value, it shall be considered the same as at the port of their importation, which shall be ascertained according to 27 *Geo.* 3, *c.* 13, and if not truly valued, may be detained; and where on exportation according to the value, it shall be considered the same as at the port of exportation, &c. *s.* 12, 13.

If on making entry of such goods for exportation the real value cannot be ascertained, the officer of the customs may permit them to be exported upon oath that it cannot be ascertained, and bond being given for payment of the duties, and producing such documents as may be required by the commissioners of the customs. Bonds not chargeable with stamp-duties.

Penalty for making false declaration of the value of such goods, forfeiture of the real value. *s.* 14, 15.

If goods are detained for not being truly valued the commissioners of the customs, upon proof that no fraud was intended, may direct the entry to be amended upon such terms as to them shall appear reasonable. *s.* 16.

Where the duties on goods imported by the East-India company are charged according to the value, it shall be ascertained by the gross price at their public sales. *s.* 18.

Persons bringing goods from the limits of the East-India company's charters as presents, or for private use, may enter them with the officer of the customs, and the value shall be ascertained as prescribed with respect to goods not imported by the company. *s.* 21.

But no goods shall be entered unless on proof that they are imported for private use. *s.* 23.

Tonnage-duties on vessels entering inwards or outwards from foreign parts shall be paid each voyage, and shall be computed according to their register. *s.* 28.

The duties charged according to weight are to be paid for in proportion to the actual weight, &c. of the articles, *s.* 42, and the allowance in weighing of goods, called draft, shall be discontinued. *s.* 43.

The commissioners of customs may close the accounts of collectors or receivers, and correct any erroneous application of the duties, which corrections shall be allowed by the commissioners for auditing the public accounts. *s.* 47.

By 43 *Geo.* 3, *c.* 128, during hostilities commissioners of the customs or excise may sell condemned vessels (see 24 *Geo.* 3, *c.* 47. *s.* 34,) to be commissioned as privateers. *s.* 5.

By 45 *Geo.* 3, *c.* 121, if vessels of subjects coming from foreign parts shall be found in any part of the British or Irish channels, or high seas, within 100 leagues of the coasts of Great Britain or Ireland, having spirits in casks less than 60 gallons, except two gallons for each of the crew; tea exceeding 6 lbs. or tobacco or snuff in packages of less than 450 lbs. weight (except loose tobacco not exceeding 5 lb. for each of the crew) the whole goods and ships shall be forfeited, *s.* 1; and vessels taking such articles on board on the high seas are subject to the like forfeiture. *s.* 2.

No foreign spirits shall be imported, exported, or carried coastwise, at Guernsey, Jersey, Alderney, or Sark, in ships of less than 100 tons, and casks of 60 gallons; tobacco in like ships, and in packages of 450 lbs.; wine in ships of not less than 60 tons, and in hogsheads. *s.* 3.

But licensed boats, not exceeding 10 tons, having 10 gallons of spirits or under, in casks of less than 60 gallons, or tobacco, snuff, or tea, not exceeding 50 lbs. each, on board for the supply of the isle of Sark, are not seizable. *s.* 5.

And the act is not to prevent the importation or exportation at Guernsey, Jersey, Alderney, or Sark, of wine in bottles, packed in cases, containing six dozen quart bottles; but, before exportation to this kingdom, bond shall be entered into for duly landing thereof. *s.* 5.

Vessels having on board spirits, wine, or tobacco, in illegal packages, and found hovering within two leagues of the coast of Guernsey, Alderney, or Sark, shall be forfeited, as also the articles. *s.* 6.

Penalty on subjects (not being passengers only) found on board vessels liable to forfeiture, or assisting in unshipping, or concealing any spirits subject to forfeiture, treble the value of the goods, or 100*l.* and such persons may be taken before a justice, near the port to which the ship is brought, to be bailed or committed; or if desirous of entering into the navy or marines, they may be taken before officers, and entered for five years: officers discharging such persons shall be cashiered; and persons entering are acquitted of the penalty. *s.* 7.

And the commissioners of the customs and excise may reward officers and others, where men taken enter to serve his majesty. *s.* 8.

Persons taking horses for conveying articles liable to seizure, without owner's consent, to forfeit not exceeding 50*l.* nor less than 20*l.* *s.* 9.

Powers of officers of customs and excise under former acts, extended to vessels and goods liable to forfeiture under this act; and persons assaulting or resisting officers of army or navy, customs or excise, in execution of this act, shall be guilty of felony, and transported for seven years; and shooting at any ship, or officer, or persons aiding therein, felony without benefit of clergy. *s.* 10, 11.

Spirits seized shall be deposited in the king's warehouse in London, or at places appointed by the treasury, in Scotland or Ireland, and an account kept of quantity and strength. *s.* 13.

Tobacco and snuff shall also be conveyed to London, or to places appointed by the treasury, in Scotland or Ireland. *s.* 14.

The treasury may, if they see fit, order spirits to be re-distilled, to bring the same to a proper strength; and may order spirits either before or after such distillation, and also tobacco or snuff, seized and condemned, to be delivered to the victualling-office, for the use of the navy, or otherwise to be destroyed, giving at the same time such rewards as they think fit to settle to the officers of the customs, excise, navy, or army. *s.* 15.

The powers and privileges of officers of customs and excise extended to the commissioned officers of the navy or army; but ships seized by any officers of the army, navy, or marines, shall be delivered to the revenue officers. *s.* 16, 17.

By 46 *Geo.* 3. *c.* 82, no fee or gratuity shall be taken by the officers of the customs in the ports of London specified in the act, but such officers shall receive yearly salaries to be settled by the treasury, and if they do take fees, they shall be for the first offence peremptorily dismissed, and rendered incapable of again holding an office of customs or excise. *s.* 1.

But this does not extend to shares of seizures, penalties, and compositions, or allowances, or reward from the crown, to such officers. *s.* 2.

Landing waiters shall make out, and deliver to merchants, accounts of West India goods imported without fee. *s.* 4.

The said officers shall take an oath "for the faithful execution of their offices, and not to take any fees," instead of the oath under 6 and 7 *Will.* 3. *c.* 1, *s.* 5. *s.* 5.

No holidays shall be observed except Sundays, Christmas-day, Good Friday, public fasts, or thanksgivings, the Restoration of Charles II. and the birth-day of the king, queen, and prince of Wales. *s.* 6.

This act is not to alter the attendance of officers at the West-India, London, or East-India docks. *s.* 7.

Officers of the customs in the port of London shall attend from 10 Nov. to 9 May inclusive, from 9 to 4, and from 10 May to 9 Nov. from 8 to 4. *s.* 8.

And the commissioners of customs may enforce the attendance of any officers whenever the public service shall require. *s.* 9.

And offices usually exercised by deputies may continue to be so. *s.* 10.

By 46 *Geo.* 3. *c.* 150, all monies received by the receiver-general of the customs in England shall be paid into the Bank of England, who shall open an account thereof, *s.* 1.; but money not exceeding 1000*l.* at the close of each day may be retained for current payments. *s.* 2.

The Bank shall enter payments in a book, to be returned for inspection of the supervisor of the receiver-general's accounts. *s.* 3.

And the money placed at the Bank shall be paid into the Exchequer by weekly orders from the Treasury on the Bank; and the bank is restrained from making any other payments. *s.* 4.

But deductions on account of the civil list tax, and 1*s.* tax on salaries, or on account of the superannuation fund, money for repair of Dover harbour, or fees arising from vacant patent offices, need not be paid into the Bank. *s.* 6.

Drawbacks, bounties, and the like, shall be paid under the direction of the commissioners of customs, by draft, countersigned by the supervisor. *s.* 7.

Officers of the exchequer shall be furnished with appropriation paper. *s.* 7.

On the death or removal of the receiver general, the balance shall vest in his successor. *s.* 8.

The receiver general shall keep an account with the bank. *s.* 9.

Penalty on forging drafts, &c. felony without clergy. *s.* 10.

By 47 *Geo.* 3. sess. 1, *c.* 51, the treasury may extend the provisions of the act of 46 *Geo.* 3, *c.* 82, to such of the out-ports as they think fit, *s.* 1.; and no fee or gratuity, though freely offered, shall be taken by the officers or persons employed in the service of the customs, in any such port in Great Britain, on pain of being dismissed and rendered incapable of acting in any office of customs or excise, *s.* 2, except only that such officers may receive shares of seizures, or allowances from the crown, *s.* 3, and officers are to be sworn to act faithfully, and not take fees. *s.* 6.

After 5th July, 1807, no holidays shall be kept at the custom-house, in any port in Great Britain, except Christmas-day, Good Friday, days of general fast, or thanksgiving, the restoration of Charles II. the coronation, and the births of the king, queen, and prince of Wales. *s.* 8.

And the treasury may alter the hours of attendance in any port, except the port of London. *s.* 9.

By 47 *Geo.* 3, sess. 2, *c.* 66, every vessel rigged or fitted as a lugger, above 50 tons, shall be forfeited. *s.* 1.

But the owners of such vessels so rigged and fitted on 13th August 1807, not exceeding 50 tons, are to take out a licence from the customs within two months. *s.* 2.

Boats constructed to row with more than six oars found within the limits of any port, or in any part of the British or Irish channels, or elsewhere, within 100 leagues of any part of the coast, shall be forfeited. *s.* 3.

But this is not to extend to whale-boats, nor boats belonging to any merchant vessel exceeding 250 tons, nor to any life-boat, nor boats on rivers or inland navigations. *s.* 4.

No ships, vessels, or boats, shall be navigated with a greater number of men than in the proportions herein mentioned, *viz.* of 30 to under and above 5 tons, 4 men—of 60, or under and above 30 tons, 5 men—of 80, or under and above 60 tons, 6 men—of 100, or under and above 80 tons, 7 men—and above that tonnage one man for every 15 tons additional; or if a lugger the following proportions: if of 30 tons or under, 8 men—if of 50 tons or under, and above 30 tons, 9 men, on pain of forfeiture. *s.* 5.

Vessels are not to be forfeited for passengers only, or persons taken on board from distress, to be proved to the commissioners; nor are revenue vessels, or letters of marque, of any fishing vessels for excess of number of men to be forfeited. s. 6, 7.

Vessels owned in whole or in part by subjects, and manned as before, found within the limits, having on board any small cordage for slinging small casks, or any more ankers, half-ankers, or other small casks under 60 gallons, or any tin, or other cases, or bladders, of less content than 60 gallons, than shall be really necessary for the use of the vessel, or any materials for making the same, or any siphon, tube, hose, or implement for drawing any fluid more than is necessary, or having on board any articles adapted for the repacking of tobacco, shall be forfeited. *s.* 8.

And if any ship, vessel, or boat, shall be found hovering within four or eight leagues of such parts of the coasts of Great Britain or Ireland, as are in former acts specified, having on board, or having had on board, such articles as aforesaid, the same shall be forfeited. *s.* 9.

No tobacco or snuff shall be on board any vessel whatever within the said limits, separated or divided in any manner within the package, or having any other article introduced therein, on forfeiture of the vessel and goods. *s.* 10.

Vessels clearing out from Jersey, Guernsey, Alderney, and Sark, shall not break bulk or alter their cargo during the voyage, unless through distress, or some unavoidable cause. *s.* 11.

No vessel to sail from the said islands without a clearance, whether in ballast or with cargo, and if found light afterwards before delivery at the port of clearance, may be seized. *s.* 12.

Vessels are not to clear out from those islands with any greater proportion of men than allowed by this act, nor with any of the before-mentioned prohibited articles, on pain of forfeiture. *s.* 13.

Vessels belonging in whole, or part, to subjects, which shall take on board any spirits, tobacco, or snuff, or tea, in any foreign port at war with his majesty, more than necessary for the use of the men, without license from the privy council or admiralty, shall be forfeited if seized within six months. *s.* 14.

All protections of men found on board of vessels liable to seizure shall be forfeited, and the men impressed therefrom compelled to serve in the navy for five years, and afterwards, until the conclusion of any war in which his majesty may be engaged; and the commissioners of customs may reward persons taking such men. *s.* 15.

Powers of seizure given by any acts to officers of the army are extended to officers of the militia, volunteers, or other forces, while on service. *s.* 16.

All provisions in any act or acts respecting vessels found within four or eight leagues, shall extend to vessels found in any part of the British or Irish channels, or elsewhere on the high seas within 100 leagues of any part of the coasts of Great Britain or Ireland under any of the circumstances specified in such acts. *s.* 17.

Commissioners of the customs and excise may reward officers seizing vessels, or boats liable to be broken up, and not used in his majesty's service, or as privateers, with certain sums, according to their tonnage, *viz.* for vessels or boats seized and condemned exceeding 4 tons, 30*s.* per ton—not exceeding 4 tons, 40*s.* per ton—and for all ships, vessels, and boats, liable to be broken up, and at the time of seizure, light or in ballast, 20*s.* per ton. *s.* 18.

The rewards to the officers on penal prosecutions in the name of the attorney-general shall be, where they are carried on wholly at the charge of the crown, one fourth of the money recovered; when they are carried on wholly at the charge of the crown, except the charge of arresting the defendant, one moiety; and where they are carried on wholly at the charge of the officer, two thirds. *s.* 19.

On seizure of spirits, tobacco, or snuff, at sea, or in any port or harbour, or on shore, if the officer shall also arrest the persons on board, and convey them before some justice of the peace, he shall be paid one moiety of the value; and if he shall also seize the ship, vessel, or boat, or the cattle or cariages used in conveying the same, but shall not arrest the parties, or carry them before a justice, then the officer shall be only entitled to one third of the value of the spirits, tobacco, and snuff; and if he shall seize the same, and not seize the ship, boat, cattle, or carriage, nor arrest the parties, then he shall be entitled to only one fourth. *s.* 20.

Officers seizing carts, horses, cattle, or carriages, are upon their condemnation entitled to three fourths of the net proceeds, after costs deducted. *s.* 21.

And if prevented in seizing, the commissioners may reward their officers in not exceeding one moiety of the value. *s.* 22.

In cases of seizures by officers or privates in the army, or their aiding officers of customs or excise, the king in council may direct how and in what proportion the rewards by this or any other acts shall be distributed amongst them. *s.* 23.

The licenses for certain ships, vessels, and boats, under 24 *Geo.* 3, and other acts, are to be granted in future by the commissioners of the customs, and not the lords of the admiralty. s. 24.

And such licenses are to be without any stamp, or fee, or reward, or any payment whatever. *s.* 25.

Persons counterfeiting or altering such license to forfeit 500*l.* and on the licensed ship, vessel, or boat being lost, broken up, or otherwise disposed of, the license is to be delivered up to the collector of the customs within twelve months. *s.* 26, 27.

On penalties recovered under the license-bond, one half shall be paid to the officer seizing the ship, vessel, or boat, for which the bond was given. *s.* 28.

The treasury may direct seized spirits, tobacco, or snuff to be sold, either for home consumption or exportation, as shall appear most conducive to the protection of the revenue. *s.* 29.

Any warrant or non-commissioned officer, not under the rank of a serjeant, approved by the commanding officer, may patrole with soldiers, and make seizures without warrant from the commissioners of customs or excise, so that the seizures be deposited in the revenue warehouses. *s.* 30.

Salt exported from Guernsey, Jersey, Alderney, or Sark, shall only be exported in bulk or casks of 4 cwt. net, except it exceed not 2lb. for each man on board—and pepper in casks of 4 cwt. on pain of forfeiture with the vessel. *s.* 31.

All the powers in 24 *Geo.* 3. *c.* 47. for bringing vessels too, are extended to subsequent acts, and this act. *s.* 32.

The 62d section of 42 *Geo.* 3. *c.* 82. is repealed, and instead thereof it is provided, that persons making signals to smugglers, by lighting fires on the coast, shall be guilty of a misdemeanor, and may be arrested and carried before a justice of the peace, who may commit them to the assizes, where they shall be obliged to plead *instanter*, and if convicted, either forfeit 100*l.*, or be committed to gaol, to be kept to hard labour, for not exceeding one year. *s.* 33, 34.

And the proof of making the fires for some other purpose, and not with the intent charged, is to be with the defendant. *s.* 35.

Persons arrested and taken before a justice for any offence, under this act, or the acts of 42 & 45 *Geo.* 3. shall not be bailed, unless they enter into a recognizance themselves in 200*l.* and two sureties in 100*l.* each. *s.* 36.

Any person whatsoever may enter lands and extinguish fires. *s.* 37.

And as commissioners of customs or excise have power to elect as to the taking treble value or a penalty of 100*l.* from persons on board smuggling vessels, not proving themselves passengers, it is declared that an averment in the information that the commissioners of customs or excise had made their option in the recovery of penalties under 45 *Geo.* 3. *c.* 21. shall be sufficient proof of their determination. *s.* 38.

Every penalty of 100*l.* under the act of 45 *Geo.* 3. may be recovered either in the exchequer or before two justices of the peace. *s.* 39.

But persons prosecuted in the court of king's bench, may be proceeded against as offenders, under 45 *Geo.* 3. *c.* 10. § 41. *s.* 40.

Officers detaining persons are to be allowed by the commissioners 20*l.* for each. *s.* 41.

Officers and seamen in the service of the customs or excise, if wounded, or their families, if killed, to be provided for, out of the revenue, by warrant from the treasury. *s.* 42.

On mitigation of penalties, under the revenue laws, by the court of quarter sessions, or the justices of the peace out of sessions, they may require the offenders to enter into a recognizance for payment of double the sum for which convicted, in case they be again convicted within three years of a like offence. *s.* 43.

Justices of the peace nearest to the port (and also the court of king's bench, and justices of oyer and terminer and gaol delivery, 48 *Geo.* 3. *c.* 84. *s.* 8.), are also empowered to take cognizance of offences committed on the high seas. *s.* 44.

Penalties and seizures in the customs, under this act, are to be prosecuted and applied according to the law of customs. *s.* 45.

And penalties and seizures in the excise are to be prosecuted and applied according to law of excise. *s.* 46.

Persons giving or offering bribes, or making collusive agreements with officers, or non-commissioned officers of the army, navy, or marines, are to forfeit 100*l.* *s.* 47.

By 48 *Geo.* 3. *c.* 9. the office of surveyor of subsidies and petty customs in the port of London is abolished.

By 48 *Geo.* 3. *c.* 84. the licences to vessels exceeding fifty tons, granted under the last act, which extended only to vessels not exceeding fifty tons, are declared valid, *s.* 1, and such licences may be renewed within ten years of the first licence, *s.* 2; but no such vessel shall be navigated by more men than as follows, if of eighty tons or under, and above sixty tons, eleven men; a hundred or under, and above eighty tons, twelve men; and if of a hundred tons, one man for every ten tons additional tonnage, *s.* 3, and vessels having letters of marque are to be deemed vessels licensed. *s.* 4.

Non-commissioned officers of the army may stop persons liable to be detained, under any act relating to smuggling. *s.* 5.

Persons making seizures of spirits, tobacco, or snuff, and carrying any seamen found on board the vessel to any ship of war shall be rewarded. *s.* 6.

Unlicensed persons offering for sale any tea, spirits, tobacco, or snuff, and not having a permit, and hawkers so offering the same, though they have a permit, may be stopped, and proceeded against, and the party seizing shall have a reward of 5*l.* *s.* 7.

Persons sailing in any vessel on the enemy's coast with intent to take on board spirits, tea, tobacco, or snuff, to be transported for seven years, *s*. 9, and the offenders may be tried in any county. *s*. 10.

Persons committed for offences may be admitted to bail. *s*. 11.

So much of the acts 45 *Geo*. 3. and 47 *Geo*. 3. as are applicable to Guernsey, shall extend to the Isle of Man. *s*. 12.

Bonds entered into relating to the customs are to remain in force two years from the time limited in the condition. *s*. 13.

And bonds granted on licences are not to be cancelled until the licences shall have been delivered up twelve months. *s*. 14.

By 49 *Geo*. 3. *c*. 59. the importation of goods is allowed from the united states of America, in vessels of that country.

By 49 *Geo*. 3. *c*. 62. whenever any ship, vessel, or boat, for which the owners are required to have a licence, shall be found within four or eight leagues of the coasts of Great Britain or Ireland, or found in any part of the British or Irish channel, or elsewhere on the high seas within one hundred leagues of any part of the said coasts; and any person on board shall, during the chase, or previous to its being taken possession of, unship or throw overboard any part of the cargo, every person on board, not being a passenger, shall forfeit 100*l*. and the vessel and goods on board, shall be forfeited; and may be seized as under the Hovering acts; or every such person being a seaman, may be dealt with according to 47 *Geo*. 3. *sect*. 2. *c*. 66. *s*. 1.

The reward to the officers seizing spirits, sunk and concealed under water, within the said one hundred leagues, shall be one moiety of their value: any thing in 47 *Geo*. 3. *sect*. 2. *c*. 66. to the contrary notwithstanding. *s*. 2.

Persons liable to be detained under 45 *Geo*. 3. *c*. 121. and the said act of 47 *Geo*. 3. who shall be found unfit to serve in the navy, shall forfeit 100*l*. and give bail before two justices, to appear and answer to any information, that may be filed against him; or in default of finding bail, he shall be committed to gaol, until the penalty is paid. *s*. 3.

By 49 *Geo*. 3. *c*. 65. fines incurred against the laws relating to the customs, not exceeding 50*l*. may be recovered in a summary way, before two justices of the peace, who on non-payment, may levy the same by distress and sale, or, in default thereof, commit the offender to gaol for the space of six [*lunar*] months; a summons left in the parties' house is sufficient: the justices may mitigate the penalties one half; after the expiration of the imprisonment, the party is absolved from the payment of the penalties; and the information must be laid before the justices, before the expiration of six [*lunar*] months.

Uncustomable and prohibited goods, seized under the public acts, are to be carried to the Custom-house warehouse; and goods seized, as feloniously stolen, are to be deposited at the Thames or other public office, to be produced at the trial of the offender: but notice of such stopping is to be given to the Custom-house; and after trial, the goods are to be carried to the Custom-house.

Goods not carried to the Custom-house, as directed by this act, may be seized, or reseized, by officers of the customs; and the party neglecting, shall forfeit 20*l*.

CUSTOMS AND SERVICES, belonging to the tenure of lands, are such as tenants owe unto their lords; which, being withheld from the lord he may have a writ of customs and services. *Cowel. Blount.*

CUSTOS BREVIUM, is a principal clerk belonging to the court of common pleas, whose office is to receive and keep all the writs returnable in that court, and put them upon files, every return by itself; and to receive of the *prothonotaries* all the records of *nisi prius*, called the *postea's*. He makes entry likewise of all writs of covenant, and the concord upon every fine; and maketh forth exemplifications, and copies of all writs and records in his office, and of all fines levied. This officer is made by the king's letters patent.

In the court of king's bench, there is also a *custos brevium* and *rotulorum*, who fileth such writs as are in that court filed, and all warrants of attorney, &c. and whose business it is to make out the records of *nisi prius*, &c.

CUSTOS PLACITORUM CORONÆ, an officer which seems to be the same with him we now call *custos rotulorum*. *Bract. lib*. 2. *c*. 5.

CUSTOS ROTULORUM, is he who hath the custody of the rolls or records of the sessions of the peace, and also of the commission of the peace itself. He is always a justice of the peace of the *quorum* in the county where appointed, and usually some person of quality: but he is rather termed an officer or minister, than a judge. *Lamb. Eiren. lib*. 4. *cap*. 3. *p*. 373.

By 37 *H*. 8. *cap*. 1. the *custos rotulorum* in every county shall be appointed by a writing signed by the king's hand, which shall be a warrant to the lord chancellor to put him in commission: and he may execute his office by deputy; and hath power to appoint the clerk of the peace, &c.

And by stat. 1 *W*. & *M*. *c*. 21. the *custos rotulorum* is to nominate and appoint the clerk of the peace; but not to sell the place, on pain of forfeiting the office of *custos rotulorum*, and other penalties, &c.

CUSTOS OF THE SPIRITUALTIES, (*custos spiritualitatis*) is he that exerciseth the spiritual or ecclesiastical jurisdiction of a diocese, during the vacancy of any see; who with us in England is the archbishop by prescription: but (according to Gwyn) some deans and chapters challenge this right by ancient charters from the kings of this land. *Cowel. Blount.*

CUSTOS OF THE TEMPORALITIES, (*custos temporalium*) the person to whose custody a vacant see or abbey was committed by the king, as supreme lord; who, as a steward of the goods and profits, was to give an account to the escheator, and he unto the exchequer: his trust continued till the vacancy was supplied, and the successor obtained the king's writ *de restitutione temporalium*, which was usually after consecration. *Ibid.*

CUT-PURSE, a pick-pocket. 4 *Black. Com.* 341. 3 *Inst.* 68.

CUTTS, flat bottomed boats, built low and commodiously, used in the channel for transporting of horses. *Stow Annal. p.* 412.

CUTTER OF THE TALLIES, is an officer in the exchequer, to whom it belongs to provide wood for the tallies, and to cut the sum paid upon them, &c. *Cowel. Blount.*

CUVE, is a French word, in English *keeve*, from whence comes *keever*, a tub or vat for brewing. *Cowel.*

CYCLAS, a long garment close upwards, and open or large below. *Cowel. Blount.*

CYNEBOTE. This word signifies the same with *cenegild*. *Blount.*

CYRICHRYCE, (Sax.) *irruptio in ecclesiam. Leg. Eccl. Canuti Regis. Cowel. Blount.*

D

DA, (Fr.) a word affirmative for yes. *Law Fr. Dict.*

DAG, a gun; *un dagg*, a small gun, or hand-gun. *Cowel. Blount.*

DAGUS or DAIS, the chief or upper table in a monastery; from a cloth called *dais*, with which the tables of kings were covered. *Ibid.*

DAKIR. The stat. 41 *H.* 3. *st.* 1. *de compositione ponderum & mensurarum* ascertains a last of hides to consist of twenty dickers, and every dicker of ten hides. *Ibid.*

DALMATICA, a garment with large open sleeves, at first worn only by bishops, though since made a distinction of degrees; so called, because it came originally from *Dalmatia. Ibid.*

DALUS, DAILUS, DAILIA, a certain measure of land. In some places it is taken for a ditch, or vale, whence comes *dale*. The *dali prati* have been esteemed such narrow slips of pasture, as are left between the ploughed furrows in arable land; which in some parts of England are called *doles:* the present Welch use this word for low meadow by the river side. And this seems to be the original name and nature of Deal in Kent. *Cowel. Blount.*

DAMAGE, (*damnum*) signifies generally any hurt or hindrance that a man receives in his estate: but in its particular sense in this place signifies what the jurors are to enquire of and bring in, when an action passeth for the plaintiff: for after verdict given of the principal cause, the jury are asked touching costs and damages, which comprehend a recompence for what the plaintiff hath suffered, by means of the wrong done him by the defendant. *Co. Lit.* 257.

In *personal* and *mixed* actions, damages were recoverable at common law. And by the stat. of *Glouc.* 6 *Ed.* 1. *cap.* 1. damages are given in real actions, assises of *novel disseisin, mort d' ancestor*, &c. and shall be recovered against the alienee of a disseisor, as well as against the disseisor himself.

In a personal action, the plaintiff shall recover damages only for the tort done before the action brought; and therein he counts for his damages: but in a real action, he recovers his damages pending the writ; and therefore never counts for his damages. 10 *Rep.* 117. 2 *Inst.* 288.

In real actions, damages are assessed by writ of enquiry: but in other actions, when the jury find the issue for the plaintiff, they are to assess the damages. In debt, which appears certain to the court what it is, the damages assessed by the jury are small, in fact only nominal, as one shilling; and the master in B. R. taxeth the costs; which is added thereto, and called damages: but in actions where the damages are uncertain, as in actions upon the case, or the like, it is left to the jury to inquire of them. 1 *Lill.* 390.

Where excessive damages have been given, or there hath been any misdemeanor in executing a writ of enquiry, the court hath sometimes relieved the defendant by granting a new trial or awarding a new writ of enquiry. 2 *Danv.* 464. *Style* 465. 1 *Nels. Abr.* 587. But this is entirely in the discretion of the court, under all the circumstances of each particular case, and if upon a new trial or second writ of enquiry, the second jury should find damages to the same or a greater amount for a personal wrong, the court will not interpose on an opinion so expressed, though the damages may appear to them to be excessive, *Blanchard* v. *Cobb. Tr. Ter. B. R.* 48 *Geo.* 3. *Editor's MSS.*

In an action upon the case the jury may find less damages than the plaintiff lays in his declaration; but ought not to find more. And if they do, the plaintiff may release part of the damages, upon entering up his judgment. 10 *Rep.* 115. If he does not, but takes judgment for damages (exclusive of costs) to a larger amount, than laid in the declaration, it is error, and not within any of the statutes of amendment or jeofails. *Morg. L. D.*

In some cases double, treble, and other damages are allowed: but these are incurred by some particular statute. And if it be not found by the jury, that the plaintiff hath sustained some damage in cases where double or treble damages are inflicted, no damages can be awarded. 2 *Danv. Abr.* 449. See also Costs.

DAMAGE-CLEER, (*damna clericorum*) was a fee assessed of the tenth part in the common pleas, and the twentieth part in the king's bench and exchequer, out of all damages exceeding five marks, recovered in those courts, in actions upon the case, covenant, trespass, battery, &c. wherein the damages were uncertain; which the plaintiff was obliged to pay to the prothonotary, or the chief officer of the court wherein recovered, before he could have execution for the damages: this was originally a gratuity given to the prothonotaries and their clerks, for drawing special writs and pleadings; but it is now taken away by statute, and if any officer in the king's courts, take any money in the name of damage-cleer, or any thing in lieu thereof, he shall forfeit treble the value. Stat. 17 *Car.* 2. *c.* 6.

DAMAGE-FEASANT, or *faisant*, is where a stranger's beasts are found in another person's ground without his leave or licence, (and without the fault of the possessor of the close, which may happen from his not repairing his fences,) and there doing damage, by feeding, or otherwise, to the grass, corn, woods, or the like. In which case, the tenant whom they damage, may distrain and impound them, as well by night as in the day, and keep them till satisfaction be made of the damages. 2 *Danv. Abr.* 364. 3 *Black.* 7.

But if one comes to distrain damage-feasant, and to seize the cattle, and the owner drives them out before they are taken, he cannot distrain them damage-feasant, but is put to his action of trespass; for the cattle ought to be actually upon the land damage-feasant, at the time of the distress. 1 *Inst.* 161. 9 *Rep.* 22.

DAM, a boundary, or confinement; as to dam up, or dam out: *infra damnum suum*, within the bounds or limits of his own property or jurisdiction. *Bract. lib.* 2. *c.* 37.

DAMISELLA, a light damosell or miss. *Cowel. Blount.*

DAMNUM ABSQUE INJURIA. If one man sets up a trade in any particular place, another may do so likewise in the same place, though he draw away the business from the other; and this is *damnum absque injuria*: but he must not do any thing to disturb the other in the exercise of his business. 3 *Salk.* 10.

DAN. Anciently the better sort of men in this kingdom had the title of *dan*; as the Spaniards *don*, from the Lat. *dominus*. *Cowel. Blount.*

DANEGELT, or DANE-GOLD, (*danegildum*) compounded of the words *dane* and *gelt*, the latter in Dutch signifying money; was a tribute of 1*s.* and after of 2*s.* upon every hide of land through the realm, laid upon our ancestors by the Danes. *Camb. Brit.* 83, 142.

DANELAGE, was the law of the Danes when they governed a third part of this kingdom. 1 *Black. Com.* 65. 4 *Black.* 405.

DANGERIA, a payment in money made by forest tenants, that they might have liberty to plough and sow in time of pannage or mast-feeding. *Manw. For. Laws.*

DAPIFER, (*a dapes ferendo*) was at first a domestic officer, like unto our steward of the household: or rather clerk of the kitchen: but by degrees it was used for any fiduciary servant, especially the chief steward or head bailiff of an honour or manor. *Cowel.*

DARDUS, *i. e.* a dart: in Wales an oak is called a dar. *Cowel. Blount.*

DARE AD REMANENTIAM, to give away in fee, or for ever. *Glanv. lib.* 7. *cap.* 1.

DARREIN, is a corruption from the Fr. *dernier*, viz. *ultimus*, the last; in which sense we use it: as *darrein continuance*, &c. *Cowel. Blount.*

DARREIN PRESENTMENT, (*ultima præsentatio.*) See *Assise of Darrein Presentment.*

DATE *of a deed*, is the description of the time, *viz.* the day, month, year of our Lord, year of the reign, &c. in which the date was made. 1 *Inst.* 6. If in the date of a deed, the year of our Lord is right, though the year of the king's reign be mistaken, it shall not hurt it. *Cro. Jac.* 261. 2 *Salk.* 658. A deed is good, though it hath no date, or the date be mistaken, or though it hath an impossible date, as the 30th of February, &c. But he that doth plead such a deed, without any date, or with an impossible date, must set forth the time when it was delivered. 2 *Rep.* 5. 1 *Inst.* 46. For it is no deed till the delivery, and that is in the intendment of the law the date of it. *Mod. Ca.* 244. 1 *Nels. Abr.* 525.

A deed may be dated at one time, and sealed and delivered at another: but every deed shall be intended to be delivered on the same day it bears date, unless the contrary is proved. 2 *Inst.* 674. Though there can be no delivery of a deed before the day of the date; yet after there may. *Yelv.* 138. So that a deed may be dated back on a time past, but not at a day to come. 2 *Black. Com.* 304.

DATIVE, or DATIF, (*dativus*) signifies that which may be given or disposed of at will and pleasure. *Stat.* 9 *R.* 2. *c.* 4.

DAVACA TERRÆ DAWACH, a portion of land so called in Scotland. *Skene. Cowel. Blount.*

DAY, (*dies*) is a certain space of time, containing twenty-four hours; the natural day consists of twenty-four hours, and contains the solar day and the night; and the artificial day begins from the rising of the sun, and ends when it sets. *Co. Lit.* 135.

There are several return days in the terms, and if either of them happen upon a Sunday it is a *dies non juridicus*; and so is Ascension day in Easter term, St. John Baptist in Trinity term, All Saints and all Souls in Michaelmas term, and the Purification of the Virgin Mary in Hilary term. 2 *Inst.* 264.

Days in bank are the days when writs shall be returned, or when the party shall appear upon the writ served. *Stat.* 51 *H.* 3. *stat.* 2. *and stat.* 3. 32 *Hen.* 8. *cap.* 21. 3 *Black.* 377.

To be dismissed or go without day, is to be finally dismissed the court: and when the justices before whom causes were depending, do not come on the day to which they were continued, whether such absence be occasioned by death or otherwise, they are said to be put without day; but may be revived or recontinued by re-summons, re-attachments, &c. 2 *Hawk. P. C.* 300.

In action of trespass, if the day laid in the declaration be either before or after the actual day on which the trespass is committed, it is not material, if a trespass be proved. *Co. Lit.* 283, *a.*

When an act is to be done on a certain day, the party hath the whole of that day to perform the same, for the law rejects all fractions and divisions of a day, for the uncertainty. 4 *Rep.* 1. 1 *Inst.* 135.

DAY-WRIT, or RULE; the king may grant writ of *warrantia die* to any person, which shall save his default for one day, be it in plea of land or other action, and be the cause true, or not; and this by his prerogative. *Br. Prerogative, pl.* 142. cites *F. N. B.* 7.

It is against law to grant liberty to prisoners in execution, by other writs than day-writs, or rules. *Chan. Rep.* 67.

No prisoner committed for a contempt ought to have the benefit of the day-rule of going abroad in term time, for their imprisonment is their punishment for their contempt, or misbehaviour. 2 *Show.* 88. *pl.* 80.

DAYS-MAN, in the north of England, an arbitrator, or elected judge, is usually termed a dies-man or a days-man. *Cowel. Blount.*

DAYERIA, dairy, from *day, deie,* Sax. *dæg,* was at first the daily yield of milch cows, or profit made of them. *Ibid.*

DAYWERE OF LAND. As much arable land as could be ploughed up in one day's work; or one journey, as the farmers still call it. *Ibid.*

DEADLY FEUD, is a profession of an irreconcileable hatred, till a person is revenged even by the death of his enemy. It is mentioned in stat. 43 *El. c.* 13. And such enmity and revenge were allowed by the old Saxon laws; for where any man was killed, if a pecuniary satisfaction was not made to the kindred of the slain, it was lawful for them to take up arms against the murderer, and revenge themselves on him: and this is called deadly feud; which it is conjectured was the original of an appeal. *Blount.* 4 *Black.* 243.

DEAD MAN'S PART. See *Distribution.*

DEAD PLEDGE, (*mortuum vadium*) a pledge of lands or goods. See *Mortgage.*

DEAF, DUMB, and BLIND. A man who is born deaf, dumb, and blind, is looked upon by the law as in the same state with an ideot, or being supposed incapable of any understanding, as wanting senses that furnish the human mind with ideas. *Fitz. N. B.* 223. 1 *Black.* 304.

DE-AFFORESTED, this word signifies discharged from being forest; or that is freed and exempted from the forest laws. 17 *Car.* 1. *c.* 16.

DEAN, (*decanus,* from the Greek Δέκα, *decem*) is an ecclesiastical governor or dignitary, so called, as he presides over ten canons or prebendaries at the least. And we call him a dean, that is next under the bishop, and chief of the chapter, originally in a cathedral church, the rest of the society being called *capitulum,* the chapter. *Latch.* 237, 250. *Palm. Rep.* 460.

A dean and chapter are the bishop's council, to assist him in the affairs of religion, &c. to consult in deciding difficult controversies, and to consent to every grant which the bishop shall make to bind his successors, &c.

DEATH OF PERSONS, there is a natural death of a man, and a civil death: natural, where nature itself expires, and extinguishes; and civil, is where a man is not actually dead, but is adjudged so by law.

If any person for whose life any estate hath been granted, remain beyond sea, or is otherwise absent seven years, and no proof made of his being living, such person shall be accounted naturally dead; though if the party be after proved living at the time of eviction of any person, then the tenant, &c. may re-enter and recover the profits. Stat. 19 *Car.* 2. *c.* 6. And persons in reversion or remainder, after the death of another, upon affidavit that they have cause to believe such other dead, may move the lord chancellor to order the person to be produced; and if he be not produced, he shall be taken as dead; and those claiming may enter, &c. 6 *Ann. c.* 18.

DE BENE ESSE, is in law to take any act *as well done for the present;* subject when it comes to be more fully examined or tried, to stand or fall according to the merit of the thing in its own nature. Thus in equity, upon motion, the court will often order a defendant to be examined *de bene esse, viz.* that his depositions be taken, subject to be allowed or suppressed at the hearing of the cause, upon the full debate of the matter, as the court shall think fit; but in the interim they have a well being, or conditional allowance. 3 *Cro.* 68.

So also at common law, bail is taken *de bene esse,* that is, to be allowed or disallowed upon the exception, or approbation of the plaintiff's attorney, however, in the interim, they are good, or have conditional allowance: and so it is of declarations filed *de bene esse. Cowel. Blount.* 3 *Black. Com.* 383.

DEBENTURE. A debenture is a written instrument in the nature of a bond or bill issued from some public office to charge the government with the payment of money due and payable to individuals out of the public revenue, and these usually are in the exchequer customs and excise. Debentures are also given to the king's servants, for the payment of their wages, &c.

DEBET ET DETINET, an action shall be always brought in the *debet et detinet,* when he who makes a bargain or contract, or lends money to another, or he to whom a bond is made, bringeth the action against him who is bounden, or party to the contract and bargain, or unto the lending of the money, &c. See *New Nat. Br.* 119.

But if an action be brought against an executor or administrator, for the act of his testator or intestate, it must be laid in the *detinet* only; and if it is laid in the *debet et detinet,* the declaration may be demurred to. 5 *Rep.* 31.

DEBET ET SOLET, are formal words made use of in writs: thus if a person sues to recover any right, whereof his ancestor was disseised by the tenant of his ancestor, then he useth the word *debet* alone in his writ, because his ancestor only was disseised, and the estate discontinued; but if he sue for any thing that is now first of all denied him, then he useth *debet et solet,* by reason his ancestor *before* him, and he himself *usually* enjoyed the thing sued for, until the present refusal of the tenant. *Reg. Orig.* 140.

DEBT, (*debitum*) Debt in the usual acceptance of the word is a sum of money due from one person to another. But in the legal sense, it is taken to be an action which lieth where a man oweth another a certain sum of money, by obligation, or bargain for a thing sold, or by contract, &c. and the debtor will not pay the debt at the day agreed. *New Nat. Br.* 268.

Thus an action of debt lies upon a parol contract, as well as *assumpsit,* or action on the case. 1 *Lil.* 403. 9 *Rep.* 87.

As if I agree with a taylor for a certain price to make me a suit of clothes, the taylor may have *a general action* of debt against me for the money; though if the price is not agreed on, there lies action on the case only, or special action of debt upon the special contract, which the law may imply on a *quantum meruit. Wood's Inst.* 554. But as in all these actions of debt or parol contracts, the defendant may wage his law, an action *on the* case brought upon the promise of payment, wherein the defendant cannot wage his law, is now the most usual course of proceeding. 4 *Rep.* 93.

But if the debt due, be secured by bond, obligation, or other speciality, an action of debt only lies for recovery thereof and no other. *New Nat. Brev.* 268.

So if a man accepts a bribe or obligation for a debt due by simple contract, this extinguishes the contract, and he shall have his action of debt upon the obligation only, and not upon the contract. 13 *H.* 4. *c.* 1. 1 *Roll. Abr.* 604. *New Nat. Brev.* 268.

In debt upon an obligation, the defendant cannot plead *nil debet,* but must deny the deed by pleading *non est factum. Hard.* 332.

But if in a debt by simple contract, then he may plead *nil debet. Hob.* 218.

DEBT TO THE KING. This comprehends all things due to the king; as all rents, fines, issues, and amerciaments, and other duties received or levied by the sheriff; for debt in the larger sense signifies whatever any man owes. 2 *Inst.* 198. The king's debt is to be satisfied before that of a subject. *Mag. Char.* 618. 1 *Inst.* 130. See Extent.

DEBTEE EXECUTOR. See Executor.

DEBTORS. By 22 & 23 *Car.* 2. *c.* 20. no bailiff or officer shall carry persons in his custody to any tavern or alehouse, without their voluntary consent, nor charge such prisoners for any wine, ale, or victuals, but what they call for of their own accord; nor demand or receive any greater sum than by law ought to be taken.

All gaolers shall permit their prisoners to send for necessaries where they please; and they shall not take any greater fee for their commitment or discharge, than what is allowed. *Ibid.*

The lord chief justice shall enquire into all charities given for the benefit of poor prisoners: and the rates of fees of prisons, signed by the lords chief justices, shall be hung up in every prison, fairly written, and no other fees shall be demanded or received. *Ibid.*

Felons and prisoners for debt shall not be lodged together, but kept separate and in distinct rooms; and any one offending against any part of this act, shall forfeit his office, and treble damages to the party grieved. *Ibid.*

By 4 & 5 *Will. & Mar. c.* 21. plaintiff may deliver a copy of a declaration to a prisoner, or to the keeper of a prison, and if such prisoner do not plead, the plaintiff shall have judgment.

By 8 & 9 *Will.* 3. *c.* 27. keepers of the King's Bench, or Fleet, suffering prisoners to go at large, or out of the rules, without *habeas corpus*, or rule of court, shall be guilty of an escape.

Upon judgment in an action of escape, the marshal or warden's fees shall be sequestered for satisfaction, and if they bring error, they must put in special bail. *Ibid.*

The marshal or warden taking any reward to connive at prisoner's escape, shall forfeit 500*l.* and be disabled. But this does not extend to the taking security from prisoners who live within the rules only. *Ibid.*

No retaking on fresh pursuit shall be given in evidence on action of escape, unless specially pleaded; nor any special plea, unless upon oath that the escape was without consent. *Ibid.*

Prisoner in execution escaping, may be retaken by any new *capias*. *Ibid.*

Keeper's refusal to shew the prisoner to his creditor or attorney shall be adjudged an escape. *Ibid.*

Keepers are to give a note to any person wanting to charge a prisoner in execution, specifying his being in custody, on pain of 50*l.* *Ibid.*

The marshal and warden shall be answerable for escapes by their deputies, whom they have liberty to appoint. *Ibid.*

All conveyances of the inheritance of the King's Bench and Fleet prisons shall be inrolled in six months after execution, or else be void. *Ibid.*

Persons having cause of action against the warden of the Fleet, may file a bill against him in the common pleas or exchequer, and for want of a plea sign judgment. *Ibid.*

Plaintiffs may deliver a copy of declaration to a prisoner in the Fleet, or to the turnkey; and in default of a plea may sign judgment, on an affidavit of the delivering a declaration. *Ibid.*

No prisoner shall pay chamber rent longer than while in actual possession, and not more than 2*s.* 6*d.* per week; keeper taking or demanding more, shall forfeit 20*l.* *Ibid.*

By 1 *Ann. stat.* 2. *c.* 6. prisoner escaping out of the King's Bench or Fleet, a judge may grant warrants for retaking him, and thereupon he may be committed to the prison which the sheriff uses for debtors: the sheriff shall answer for such prisoner's escape after retaken; and bail for a prisoner retaken, may have a writ of detainer directed to the sheriff, who is to return the same, and whether the prisoner is in custody, on pain of 50*l.*

By 5 *Ann. c.* 9. confirming the above act, it is enacted, that an escape-warrant may be granted on affidavit made in the country; and persons may be apprehended by such a warrant on a Sunday.

Persons in custody for not performing a decree in chancery or the exchequer to pay money, afterwards escaping, the sheriff shall be liable to pay the same with costs. *Ibid.*

By 12 *Geo.* 2. *c.* 13. no attorney who shall be a prisoner, or within the rules, during such confinement, shall commence any action or suit. All proceedings therein shall be void, and he shall be incapacitated: but this is not to prevent his carrying on suits commenced before.

By 27 *Geo.* 2. *c.* 17. the prison of the court of King's Bench, with power of appointing the marshal, was revested in the crown, under certain provisions and regulations for execution of the office, and government of the prison.

The marshal, his officers, and prisoners, are subject to the rules in 2 *Geo.* 2. *c.* 22. (a temporary act, the clauses whereof are incorporated in 32 *Geo.* 2. *c.* 28.) and shall take no other fees than allowed thereby. *Ibid.*

The marshal shall have the appointment of inferior officers: both marshal and officers are liable to be amoved for non-residence, neglect of duty, or misbehaviour, as the court of king's bench shall judge, on motion in a summary way.

Selling the office of marshal, or inferior offices thereto belonging, incurs forfeiture and disability; and the marshal shall keep the prison in repair. *Ibid.*

By 32 *Geo.* 2. *c.* 28. no officer shall carry his prisoner to any tavern or other public-house, without his consent; nor charge him for liquor or other things, except such as he shall freely call for; nor demand for caption or attendance any other than his legal fee; nor exact any gratuity money; nor carry his prisoner to gaol within twenty-four hours after his arrest, unless he shall refuse to be carried to some safe house of his own appointment where arrested, or within three miles thereof.

Nor may the officer take for the lodging, diet, and other expences of such prisoner, more than shall be allowed in such cases by the sessions, a copy whereof shall be hung up in the sessions-house. *Ibid.*

Sheriffs and the secondaries of the counters, shall deliver printed copies of these clauses to bailiffs, and make it part of the condition of the bond to be given by them, that they shall show and deliver a copy of the said clauses to the prisoner, if carried to a public-house, to be by him read, or heard read, before any liquors or victuals be brought in, on pain on the officer, besides breach of covenant, of being punished for a misdemeanor. *Ib.*

Gaolers shall permit prisoners to send for what victuals, bedding, or linen, they please, without any restraint. *Ibid.*

The lords chief justices of the king's bench, common pleas, and exchequer, with the mayor and two aldermen of London, for the prisons within the city; and the chief justices and baron, with three justices of peace for Middlesex and Surrey, for the prisons in the said counties, shall settle the fees to be taken by gaolers, and make rules and orders: and the sessions elsewhere. *Ibid.*

Rules and orders for the better government of the gaols and prisoners therein, shall be made by the respective courts in Westminster hall for the gaols belonging to such courts, duplicates of which fees and orders shall be inrolled, and copies thereof hung up in courts of assize, sessions, and in prisons. *Ibid.*

The courts in Westminster are, every Michaelmas term, to inquire whether such tables of fees and orders are duly hung up and complied with, and shall give notice to the prisoners of the time of inquiry. *Ibid.*

Judges and justices of assizes shall make a like inquiry, and redress complaints, and charge grand juries to inquire. *Ibid.*

Courts of Westminster, judges of assize, justices of peace, and commissioners for charitable uses, may inquire of bequests to poor prisoners, and send for papers and persons, and settle the payment, recovery, and receipt of such bequests. *Ibid.*

Table of benefactions to be transmitted to, and registered by, the clerks of the peace, and also to the gaolers of the prisons to which the same relate, and to be hung up in such prisons. *Ibid.*

Where gaolers shall be guilty of extortion, or other abuses, the court, upon petition of the prisoner, is to examine into the same in a summary way, and redress the abuse and punish the offender. *Ibid.*

Gaolers shall take no other fees than what shall be allowed in the authenticated table of fees; and sheriffs or other officers offending against this act shall forfeit 50*l.* (besides other penalties) to the party aggrieved. *Ibid.*

" Any debtor charged in execution for " not more than 100*l.* (extended to 300*l.* " by 33 *Geo.* 3. *c.* 5,) may petition the court, " certifying therein the cause of imprisonment, with a schedule of his real and " personal estates at the time, and charges " affecting the same; and also the state of " his effects at the time of his first imprisonment, and the securities, bonds, notes, " and books relating thereto, with the particular witnesses. Fourteen days previous notice of such intended petition to " be given to the creditor, or his attorney, " at whose suit he is charged in execution; " and a copy of the schedule he intends to " deliver into court. Affidavit of the due " service of such notice to be delivered " at the same time with the petition into " court, and read openly; and a rule to be " made upon receiving the petition for " bringing the prisoner into court; and summoning the creditor, and the creditor appearing, or not appearing thereto, oath " being made of the due service of the " rule, the court to examine into the matter of the petition in a summary way, " and administer an oath to the prisoner.

" The court may thereupon order an assignment to be made, on the back of the " petition, of the prisoner's effects, subject to " former encumbrances to the creditor, who " may thereupon take possession, and sue " as an assignee of a bankrupt; and the " court shall order the prisoner to be discharged. *Ibid.*

" Assignee to make sale of and divide the " effects; but if the creditor shows cause of " disbelieving the prisoner's oath, and desires time for further information, the " court to remand the prisoner back to a " further day; objections to the form of the " schedule shall be made the first time the " prisoner is brought up. *Ibid.*

" The creditor not appearing the second " day or not making a further discovery, " the court to make a rule for discharge of " the prisoner, unless the creditor insist upon " his detention, and covenant to allow him " (3*s.* 6*d.* a week, 37 *Geo.* 3. *c.* 85.); but " upon failure, at any time, in the payment " thereof, the prisoner, upon application to " the court, shall be discharged upon executing such assignment and conveyance " as aforesaid. Prisoner refusing to take " the oaths, or being detected of falsity " therein, or refusing to execute an assignment of his estate, to be continued in execution. *Ibid.*

" Where more creditors than one insist on " the prisoner's detention, they are to pay " him each not exceeding (2*s.* 37 *Geo.* 3. " *c.* 85.) per week. *Ibid.*

" Prisoner charged in execution in county " and other gaols, distant from Westminster, " to proceed in like manner by petition and " affidavit; and the court to make a rule " thereupon, for his being brought up to the " next assizes; 1*s.* per mile to be paid to the " gaoler for his expences out of the prisoner's " estate or by the treasurer of the county. " *Ibid.*

" Creditors to be summoned, and a copy " of the rule served on them; and upon " affidavit made of such service the court " to appoint a time for hearing the matter " of the petition; and the creditors appear- " ing thereto, or not, proof being made of " their being duly served with the notice, " and copy of the schedule of the prisoner's " estate, the court to proceed therein in a " summary way, and administer the oath " to the prisoner, and make such order in " the premises as shall seem meet, and pro- " ceed as before concerning the prisoner's " discharge. *Ibid.*

" Prisoner refusing to deliver up his es- " tate and effects to satisfy his creditors, " they may compel him to be brought up, " and deliver into court a schedule of his " estate and effects, giving him twenty " days notice, in order that his estate and " effects may be divested out of him, and " assigned and conveyed as after directed. " Like notice to be given of such intention " to the other creditors, and also to the " sheriff and gaoler, requiring them to bring " up such prisoner, who is to be brought " up accordingly at the cost of the creditors, " with a copy of the detainer. Sheriffs and " gaolers making default on tender of " amends forfeit 20*l.* to the party aggrieved, " with treble costs. *Ibid.*

" Prisoner, upon proof of due notice as " aforesaid having been given him, is to " deliver in upon oath, to the court, a sche- " dule of his estate and effects, and signed " by him; and is to assign and convey " the same in trust for the benefit of his " creditors, they agreeing to his discharge, " and to take a dividend; but if any refuse, " then the same to be in trust, for the cre- " ditors, only requiring the prisoner to be " brought up. Overplus remaining, after " all charges to be paid to the prisoner. " Prisoner complying to the satisfaction of " the court to be set at liberty, paying " for his discharge fees. 2*s.* 6*d.* Future " effects of the prisoner liable to debts un- " satisfied; and no advantage to be taken " of the statute of limitation, unless he " was entitled thereto before he stood " charged in custody on the original suit.

" Prisoner neglecting or refusing to deli- " ver in a schedule of his estate and effects, " or to make an assignment and conveyance " thereof, to be transported for seven years; " and delivering a false account, to suffer the " pains and penalties of wilful perjury, and " be taken again in execution, and never " have the benefit of this act. *Ibid.*

" If the prisoner's effects shall not satisfy " his debt and gaol fees, the gaoler shall re- " ceive only a proportionable dividend with " the other creditors. *Ibid.*

" Prisoners discharged not liable to ar- " rests for the same debt, unless perjured; " but the judgment shall remain against " their effects. *Ibid.*

" Assignees of a prisoner's estate may " compound debts, and refer disputes to " arbitration, and may be removed by the " court on complaint of mismanagement. *Ibid.*

" None entitled to the benefit of this act " who has had the benefit of any act of " insolvency, unless compelled by a creditor " to deliver up his estate and effects." *Ibid.*

By 33 *Geo.* 3, *c.* 5, persons charged in execution for sums not exceeding 300*l.* to be entitled to the relief of the lords act (32 *Geo.* 2, *c.* 28), and debtors in execution for sums not exceeding 300*l.* may be compelled to deliver up their effects. *s.* 1, 3.

Persons committed on attachment for not paying money awarded by arbitrators, or on excommunications for ecclesiastical costs, are entitled to the benefit of the act. *s.* 4.

Debtors making it appear to the court that from ignorance or mistake they have not taken the benefit of the acts in time, shall be entitled thereto; and creditors may file interrogatories for the examination of prisoners before they take the benefit of the act. *s.* 5.

The act does not extend to debts due to the crown. *Ibid.*

By 37 *Geo.* 3. *c.* 85, debtors entitled to their discharge under 32 *Geo.* 2, *c.* 28, may be discharged, unless their creditors agree to pay them not exceeding 3*s.* 6*d.* weekly. *s.* 3.

When more creditors than one insist on a debtor's detention, they are each to pay him not exceeding 2*s.* weekly. *s.* 4.

By 48 *Geo.* 3. *c.* 123, persons in execution on judgment, in whatever court, whether of record or not, for any debt and damages not exceeding 20*l.* exclusive of costs recovered by such judgment, and who shall have laid in prison twelve calendar months, shall, on application to one of the superior courts at Westminster, be discharged; but persons fraudulently obtaining their discharge are liable to be taken in execution; and the estate and effects of debtors shall remain liable, notwithstanding their discharge; but debtors discharged are not liable afterwards to be arrested in any action to be brought on such judgment. *s.* 1.

DEBTS, priority of. See Executor.

DECEIT (*deceptio*) is a writ which lies to give damages in some particular cases of fraud, and principally where one man does any thing in the name of another, by which he is deceived or injured: as if one brings an action in another's name, and then suffers a nonsuit, whereby the plaintiff becomes liable to costs; or when one suffers a fraudulent recovery of land or chattels to the prejudice of him that hath right. It also lies in the cases of false warranties, and other subtle tricks, injuries, and devices contrary to good faith and honesty; but the *special action on the case* in nature of *deceit*, is now the ordinary remedy taken on these occasions. 3 *Black.* 165, 6.

DECENNARY, a town or tithing consisting (originally) of ten families of freeholders. Ten tithings composed an hundred. The institution of decennaries (or frankpledges) is imputed to Alfred. In these decennaries the whole neighbourhood or tithing of freemen were mutually pledges for each other's good behaviour. 1 *Black. Com.* 114. *Ibid.* 4. 249.

DECEM TALES, is when a full jury does not appear at a trial at bar; then a writ goes to the sheriff *apponere decem tales*, &c. whereby a supply is made of jurymen to proceed in the trial. *Cowel. Blount.*

DECIES TANTUM, is a writ that lies against a juror, who hath taken money of either party for giving his verdict; so called because it is to recover ten times as much as he took: and every person that will may bring this writ and recover the same, one half whereof shall be to the prosecutor, and the other to the king. This writ also lies against embraceors that procure such an inquest; who shall be further punished by imprisonment for a year. *Reg. Orig.* 188. *F. N. B.* 171. Stat. 38 *Ed.* 3. *c.* 13. But *decies tantum* does not lie against the embraceor, if he embrace and take no money, for he ought to take money, and also embrace. Yet it lies against the jurors, although they do not give a verdict, if they take money; and so it is said if they give a true verdict, *decies tantum* lies if they take money. *Dyer* 95. *New Nat. Br.* 380.

DECIMATION, (*decimatio*) the punishing every tenth soldier by lot: also tithing. *Cowel. Blount.*

DECINERS, DECENNIERS, or DOZINERS, (*decennarii*) such as were wont to have the oversight of the Friburghs, or views of frank-pledge, for the maintenance of the king's peace; and the limits or compass of their jurisdiction was called *decenna*, because it commonly consisted of ten households, as every person bound for himself and his neighbours to keep the peace was styled *decennier*. *Bract. lib.* 3. *tract.* 2. *cap.* 15.

DECLARATION, (*declaratio, narratio*) is an exposition of the writ, and shows in writing the cause of complaint of the plaintiff in an action against the defendant, wherein the party is supposed to have received some wrong. This ought to be plain and certain, because it impeaches the defendant, and compels him to answer thereunto; it must set forth the plaintiff's and defendant's names, the nature and cause of the action, the manner thereof, &c. and the damage received. 1 *Inst.* 17. *Wood's Inst.* 582. See PLEADING and PRACTICE.

DECREE. A decree is the judgment of a court of equity pronounced on the hearing of a cause; and it is of the like nature with a judgment at common law. *Chan. Rep.* 234.

A decree not signed and inrolled may be altered upon a re-hearing, without the assistance of a bill of review, if there is sufficient matter to revise it appearing upon the former proceedings, and the investigation of the decree must be brought on by a petition of re-hearing only. 2 *Vez.* 598. *Mitf.* 82.

But if the decree be signed and inrolled it can only be altered upon a bill of review, 1 *Chan. Cas.* 44. 2 *Fr.* 179, except it has been obtained by fraud, in which case it may be impeached by original bill, *Mitf.* 84, and where a decree has been so obtained the court will restore the parties to their former situation, whatever their rights may be, 2 *Bro. P. C.* 44.

A bill to set aside a decree for fraud must state the decree, and the proceedings which led to it, with the circumstances of fraud on which it is impeached: the prayer must be necessarily varied, according to the nature of the fraud used, and the extent of its operation, in obtaining an improper decision of the court. *Mitf.* 85.

The operation of a decree signed and inrolled has also been suspended on special circumstances, or avoided by matter subsequent to the decree, upon a new bill for that purpose: Thus, during the troubles, after the death of *Car.* 1. upon a decree for a foreclosure in case of non-payment of principal, interest, and costs, due on a mortgage, the mortgagor at the time of payment being forced to leave the kingdom, to avoid the consequences of his engagements with the royal party, and having regranted the mortgage, to sell the estate to the best advantage, and pay himself, which the mortgagee appeared to have acquiesced in, the court, upon a new bill enlarged the time for performance of the decree, upon the ground of the inevitable necessity which prevented the mortgagor from complying with the strict terms of it; and also made a new decree on the ground of new matter subsequent to the former decree. 1 *Cha. Ca.* 361. 2 *Cha. Ca.* 8. *Mitf.* 86.

Sometimes from the neglect of parties, or some other cause, it becomes impossible to carry a decree into execution without the further decree of the court: this happens generally in cases where parties having neglected to proceed upon the decree, their rights under it become so embarrassed by a variety of subsequent events, that it is necessary to have the decree of the court to settle and ascertain them. Sometimes such a bill is exhibited by a person who was not a party, nor claims under any party to the original decree; but claims in a similar interest, or is unable to obtain the determination of his own rights till the decree is carried into execution; or it may be brought by or against a person claiming as assignee of a party to the decree. *Mitf.* 86, 87.

The court in these cases in general only enforces, and does not vary, the decree; but, on particular circumstances, it has sometimes considered the directions, and varied them in case of mistake; and it has even refused to enforce the decree; though in other cases the court, and the house of lords on appeal, seem to have considered that the law of the decree ought not to be examined on a bill to carry it into execution. *Mitf.* 87.

Such a bill may also be brought to carry into execution the judgment of an inferior court of equity, if the jurisdiction of that court is not equal to the purpose; as in the case of a decree in Wales, which the defendant avoided by flying into England: but in this case the court thought itself entitled to examine the justice of the decision, though affirmed in the house of lords. *Mitf.* 87.

A bill for this purpose is, generally, partly an original bill, and partly in the nature of an original bill, though not strictly original; and sometimes it is likewise a bill of revivor, or a supplemental bill, or both; the frame of the bill is varied accordingly. *Mitf.* 88.

But if upon the face of a bill to carry a decree into execution the plaintiff appears to have no right to the benefit of the decree, the defendant may demur. *Mitf.* 167.

And if a plaintiff filing a bill to carry a decree into execution, has no right to the benefit of the decree, the defendant may plead the fact, if it is not so apparent on the bill as to admit of a demurrer. *Mitf.* 232.

A decree determining the rights of the parties, and signed and inrolled, may be pleaded to a new bill for the same matter, and this even if the party bringing the new bill was an infant at the time of the former decree; for a decree inrolled, as before observed, can only be altered upon a bill of review, but the decree must be in its nature final, or afterwards made so by order, or it will not be a bar. Therefore a decree for an account of principal and interest due on a mortgage, and for a foreclosure in case of non-payment, cannot be pleaded to a bill to redeem, unless there is a final order of foreclosure: nor can a decree which has been made upon default of the defendant, in not appearing at the hearing, be pleaded without an order making the decree absolute; the terms of such decree being always that it shall be binding on the defendant, unless on being served with a writ of subpœna for the purpose, he shall show cause to the contrary. *Mitf.* 195.

Upon a plea of this nature, so much of the former bill and answer must be set forth as is necessary to show that the same point was then in issue. 2 *Atk.* 603. 2 *Ves.* 577.

A decree or order dismissing a former bill for the same matter may be pleaded in bar to a new bill, if the dismission was upon hearing, and was not in terms directed to be without prejudice; but an order of dismission is a bar only where the court determined that the plaintiff had no title to the relief sought by his bill; and therefore an order dismissing a bill for want of prosecution is not a bar to another bill. 1 *Vern.* 310. 1 *Br. P. C.* 281. 1 *Ch. Ca.* 155. 1 *Atk.* 571.

DECRETALS, (*decretales*) are a volume or books of the canon law, so called, containing the decrees of sundry popes, or a digest of the canons of all the councils that pertained to one matter under one head. See *Canon Law.*

DECURIARE, signifies to bring into order. *Mon. Angl. tom.* I. *p.* 243. *Cowel. Blount.*

DEDBANA, (*ded bane*, Sax.) an actual homicide, or manslaughter. *Leg. H.* 1. *c.* 85.

DEDI, is a warranty in law, as if it be said in a deed or conveyance, that *A. B.* hath given, &c. to *C. D.* it is a warranty to him and his heirs. *Co. Lit.* 304.

DEDICATION-DAY, (*festum dedicationis*) the anniversary feast of dedication of churches, anciently celebrated not only by the inhabitants of the place, but those of neighbouring villages, by feasting and drinking, and in many parts of England they still meet every year in villages for this purpose, which are days called feasts or wakes. *Cowel. Blount.*

DEDIMUS POTESTATEM, is a writ issued out of the court of chancery to commissioners, authorizing them to take an answer,—to examine witnesses in a cause—to levy a fine in the common pleas, &c.

Also when any justice intends to act under any commission of the peace, he sues out a writ of *dedimus potestatem* from the clerk of the crown in chancery, empowering certain persons therein named to administer the usual oaths to him; which done he is at liberty to act. 1 *Black. Com.* 351.

DEDIMUS POTESTATEM DE ATTORNATO FACIENDO, a writ; anciently the parties could not make attornies in any action or suit without the king's writ of *dedimus potestatem*, to receive their attornies; but now the plaintiff or defendant may make attornies in suits without such writs. *New Nat. Br.* 55, 56.

DEED, (*factum*) is an instrument in writing, on parchment, or paper, *and under seal*, containing some conveyance, contract, bargain, or agreement between the parties thereto; and it consists of three principal points, writing, sealing, and delivery; writing, to express the contents — sealing, to testify the consent of the parties—and delivery, to make it binding and perfect. *Terms de Ley.*

And it seems that ten things are necessarily incident to a deed: 1. That it should be in writing. 2. That it be on parchment, vellum, or paper. 3. A person able to contract. 4. By a sufficient name. 5. A person able to be contracted with. 6. By a sufficient name. 7. A thing to be contracted for. 8. Apt words required by law. 9. Sealing: And, 10, delivery. *Co. Lit.* 35. *b.*

Every instrument in writing is not a deed; for a contract may be in writing and not by deed, (it being under seal,) and if so it is but as a parol agreement. 1 *Ld. Raym.* 28.

It is essential that all the matter thereof be written before *the sealing and delivery of it*: for if a man seals and delivers a blank piece of parchment or paper, although he therewith gives commandment that an obligation or other matter shall be written on it, which is done accordingly, yet this will not make it a good deed. *Co. Lit.* 171. *Perk. S.* 118, 119. See *Moor* 28. *Hetley* 136, 137.

A deed may be written in any hand, as in text, court, or Roman hand; or in any language, as in Latin or French, and is as good as a deed written in English and in common hand. 2 *Co.* 3.

If there be any alteration, erasure, or interlining made in any part of the deed before the delivery of it, this will not hurt the deed, but in all such cases it is proper to make a memorandum thereof, upon the back of the deed, and to give the witnesses notice of it (this is now usually done in the attestation of the deed thus: Sealed and delivered, the word —— being first interlined, &c.); for otherwise, if it be in any place material, as in the name of the grantor, grantee, in the limiting of the estate, or the like, and it cannot be proved to be done before the sealing and delivery of it, especially if it be a deed poll, it is very suspicious. *Co. Lit.* 37, 225. *Perk. S.* 125, 126, 127, 128. 155.

A deed sealed and delivered, it is said, may be good without signing; for the seal is the essential part of the deed: but it is usual to have deeds signed; and there must be witnesses to the sealing and delivery, who are to indorse or under-write their names thereon. 1 *Inst.* 7. 10 *Rep.* 93. The signing is of great use, for the subscribing witnesses to the deed may be dead, when proving their death, and the hand-writing of the party executing the deed, will be sufficient to establish the same. If a writing is not sealed, it cannot be a deed. 3 *Inst.* 169. 5 *Rep.* 23.

A deed may be good without all the orderly and formal parts; but if it be without delivery by the party himself, or his attorney lawfully authorized, to the party to whom made, or some other to his use, it is no deed. 1 *Inst.* 35. 2 *Rep.* 5.

Of deeds there are two sorts, deeds indented, and deeds poll; which names principally arise from the form of them, the one being cut in and out at top, dentwise, and the other plain; that is, shaved close, from whence it takes the name of deed poll. 2 *Black. Com.* 296.

A deed-poll is said to be a deed testifying that only one of the parties to the agreement hath put his seal to the same, where such party is the principal, or only person whose consent or act is necessary to the deed: and it is therefore a plain deed without indenting, and is used when the vendor, for example, only seals, and there is no need of the vendee's sealing a counterpart, because the nature of the contract is such as it requires no covenant from the vendee, &c. *Co. Lit.* 55.

Deeds by *indenture*, are, where there are several parts belonging to the feoffor, grantor, or lessor, who has one, and the feoffee, grantee, or lessee, who has another; and some other persons, as trustees, a third, &c. and the deed-poll which is single, and of but one part, is delivered to the feoffee, or grantee, &c. *Ibid.*

All the parts of a deed indented, in judgment of law, make but one entire deed; but every part is of as great force as all the parts together, and they are esteemed the mutual acts of either party, who may be bound by either part of the same, and the words of the indenture are the words of either party, &c. But a deed-poll is the sole deed of him that makes it, and the words thereof shall be said to be his words, and bind him only. *Plowd.* 134, 421. *Lit. sect.* 370.

Deeds have several formal parts, *viz.* the premises, *habendum*, *reddendum*, condition, covenants, warranty, date, sealing, &c.

The premises set forth the proper names of the parties, with their additions of place and quality: the lands and tenements intended to be conveyed, with the consideration of the deed, as money, natural love, &c. also the exceptions, if there be any, out of the land granted; as of timber, mines, &c. and in many deeds there may be an occasion for a recital of former deeds in the premises. 1 *Inst.* 6, 47, 201, 365. *Plowd.* 152. *Wood's Inst.* 224, 228.

The *habendum* fixes the certainty of the estate granted, for what time the grantee is to have it, and to what use: and it sometimes qualifies the estate, so that the general implication of it, which by construction of law passes in the premises, by the habendum may be controlled, but not if the estate is expressed in the premises. Likewise an habendum may explain the premises, to prevent wrong; and sometimes the premises are thereby enlarged. A freehold cannot be granted by deed with habendum at a day to come; and a deed or lease, habendum from henceforth, includes the day on which it was dated; but *habendum a die datûs* excludes it. *Ibid.*

The *reddendum* is that clause in the deed which reserves some new thing to the grantor, as rent, suit, service, &c. and is usually made by the words yielding, paying, doing, &c. A lessor cannot reserve to any but himself, his heirs and executors, &c. nor can he reserve to himself parcel of the annual profits, such as the herbage of the land, for that would be repugnant to the grant, it being a part thereof. *Ibid.*

Conditions and covenants in deeds are for the holding or not holding of the estate granted, on performance of some act: and a condition relating to a real estate is a quality annexed by him that hath the estate, interest, or right in the same, whereby the estate granted may be defeated, enlarged, or created, upon an uncertain event. Conditions are expressed by these words, *viz.* Upon condition, Provided, So that, &c. and Provided always, and it is covenanted, is a condition by force of the proviso, and a covenant by virtue of the other words; though sometimes a proviso shall amount to a covenant, and sometimes be taken for a limitation, exception, reservation, explanation, &c. *Ibid.*

The warranty in deeds is to secure the estate to the grantee and his heirs, &c. and is a covenant real, annexed to the land granted, by which the grantor and his heirs are bound to warrant the same to the grantee and his heirs, and that they shall quietly hold and enjoy it; or upon voucher, &c. the grantor shall yield other lands, to the value of what shall be evicted. Where a feoffor grants away all his estate in the land, and is not bound to warrant the title, but the feoffee is to defend it at his peril; the feoffor shall have all the deeds, as incidents to the land, although not granted in express words; but where the feoffor warrants the land it is otherwise: the feoffor shall have them to defend the title, and the feoffee must trust to his warranty, and have only such deeds as concern the possession, &c. *Ibid.*

In witness whereof, &c. ascertains the date of the deed; and is as well part of it as what is written before. 1 *Inst.* 6, 47, 201, 365. *Plowd.* 152. *Wood's Inst.* 224, 225.

In deeds, the consideration is a principal thing to give them effect: and the foundation of deeds ought always to be honest.

False English will not make a deed void: but rasure or interlineation in a material part, will render the same void, unless some memorandum be made thereof on the back of the deed, testifying its being done before sealing. 1 *Rol. Rep.* 40. And if words are blotted out in a deed, by a grantee or lessee himself, after execution, although it be not in a place material, it will make the deed void. *Dyer* 261.

When a chose in action is created by deed the destruction of such deed is the destruction of the duty itself; as in the case of a bond, bill, or the like, though it is not so where an estate or interest is created by a deed, which cannot be defeated by another deed. 3 *Salk.* 120.

An indorsement on a deed at or before the time of the sealing and delivery, is a part of the same; but if an indorsement be after the delivery it is a new deed. *Mod. Cas.* 237.

In deeds indented all parties are estopped, or concluded, to say any thing against what is contained in the deed, 1 *Inst.* 45. And where a deed is by indenture between parties, none can have an action upon that deed but he who is a party to it; but where it is a deed-poll one may covenant with another who is not a party to it, to do certain acts, for the non-performance whereof he may bring an action. 2 *Lev.* 74.

But deeds, if fraudulently made, when got by corrupt agreement, as on usurious contract, and when made by force or duress, &c. are void: so they are for uncertainty, and by reason of infancy, coverture, or other disability in the makers, &c. 2 *Rol. Abr.* 28. 1 *Inst.* 253. 11 *Rep.* 27.

And if a deed is obtained fraudulently, without consideration, or for an inadequate consideration; or if by fraud, accident, or mistake, a deed is framed contrary to the intention of the parties in their contract on the subject, the parties claiming under it may take the advantage of proceeding in a court of common law, against the conscience of the case; a court of equity will on this ground interfere to restrain proceedings at law until the matter has been properly investigated; and if it finally appears that the deed has been improperly obtained, or that it is contrary to the intention of the parties in their contract, will in the first case compel the delivery and cancellation of the deed; and in the second case will either rectify the deed according to the intention of the parties, or will restrain the use of it in the points in which it has been framed contrary to, or gone beyond, their intention in the original contract. And the instances of the exercise of the jurisdiction of courts of equity in these cases, and especially in the case of deed fraudulently obtained, are numerous. 3 *Lev.* 36. 1 *Vern.* 443, 446. 2 *Vern.* 123, 206. *Mitf.* 116.

On the ground of mistake the courts of equity have frequently interfered in a variety of instances, and particularly in the cases of defective securities for money, and of marriage settlements founded on previous articles, where the settlement has been contrary to the evident intention of the parties in the articles. *Mitf.* 116, 117.

DEEDS, stealing of. At common law,

bonds, bills, and notes, which concern mere choses in action, were held not to be such goods whereof larceny might be committed: but by *Stat.* 2 *Geo.* 2. *c.* 25, the stealing thereof shall be felony of like degree as in stealing of other goods of like value.

DEEMSTERS, (from the Sax. *dema*, a judge or umpire) are a kind of judges in the Isle of Man, who without process, or any charge to the parties, decide all controversies in the island; and they are chosen from among themselves. *Cam. Brit.*

DEER-FELD, a park, or deer-fold. *Cowel. Blount.*

DEER-HAYES, are engines, or great nets made of cords to catch deer; and no person not having a park, &c. shall keep any of these nets under the penalty of 40*s.* a month. Stat. 19 *Hen.* 7. *cap.* 11.

DEER-STEALERS. By 16 *Geo.* 3. *c.* 30, justices may order suspected houses to be searched for skins. *s.* 4.

Setting toils for deer to forfeit 10*l.* and not less than 5*l.* and for the second offence 20*l.* and not less than 10*l.* *s.* 7.

Pulling down pales, or inclosures of a park or like place, where deer are kept, incurs the same penalty, as the first for killing deer. *s.* 8.

Fire arms or the like, carried in parks, with intent to destroy deer, may be seized; and beating the keeper, or rescuing the prisoner, transportation for seven years. *s.* 9.

The penalties shall be applied one moiety to the king, and the other to the informer, to be levied by distress; and the offender, on non-payment, may be committed for one year, or till payment. *Ibid.*

It is necessary to observe that this act repealed 13 *Ric.* 2, *c.* 13. 19 *Hen.* 7, *c.* 11. 7 *Jac.* 1, *c.* 13. 3 *Jac.* 1, *c.* 13. 13 *Car.* 2, *c.* 10. 3 and 4 *Wil.* & *Mar.* *c.* 10. 5 *Geo.* 1, *c.* 15, and 10 *Geo.* 2, *c.* 32, so far as they respectively relate to deer. But it does not extend to Scotland.

By 42 *Geo.* 3, *c.* 107, persons who shall illegally hunt, snare, or shoot deer in any inclosure, and their abettors, shall be guilty of felony, and may be transported for seven years. *s.* 1.

Persons committing such offences in uninclosed grounds forfeit 50*l.* and keepers of deer offending shall forfeit double. *s.* 2.

The provisions of 16 *Geo.* 3, *c.* 30, are extended to this act, and in default of payment of the penalties, offenders may be committed for six months. *s.* 3.

Persons convicted of a second offence punishable by a pecuniary penalty, may be transported for seven years, and convictions for first offences shall be transmitted to quarter sessions, and filed for proof. *s.* 4, 5.

So much of 16 *Geo.* 3, *c.* 30, *s.* 1, as inflicts penalties for hunting or shooting deer is repealed. *s.* 6.

The act does not extend to Scotland. *s.* 7.

DE ESSENDO QUIETUM DE TELONIO, is a writ that lies for those who are by privilege free from the payment of toll, on their being molested therein. *F. N. B.* 226.

DE EXPENSIS MILITUM, a writ commanding the sheriff to levy the expenses of a knight of the shire for attendance in parliament, being 4*s.* *per diem* by statute: and there is a like writ *de expensis civium et burgensium*, to levy 2*s.* *per diem* for the expenses of every citizen and burgess of parliament. Stat. 23 *Hen.* 6. *cap.* 11. 4 *Inst.* 46.

DE FACTO, signifies a thing actually done, that is done indeed. A king *de facto* is one that is in actual possession of a crown, and hath no lawful right to the same; in which sense it is opposed to a king *de jure*, who has right to a crown, but is out of possession. 3 *Inst.* 7.

DEFAMATION, (*defamatio*) is when a person speaks scandalous words of another, whereby he is injured in reputation, for which the party offending shall be punished according to the nature and quality of his offence; sometimes by action on the case at common law, sometimes by statute, and sometimes by the ecclesiastical laws.

Defamation is also punishable by the ritual courts; in which it ought to have three incidents, *viz.* First, it is to concern matters spiritual, and determinable in the ecclesiastical courts; as for calling a man heretic, schismatic, adulterer, fornicator, &c. Secondly, that it be a matter spiritual only, for if the defamation concern any thing determinable at the common law, the ecclesiastical judges shall not have conusance thereof. And thirdly, although such defamation be merely spiritual, yet he that is defamed cannot sue for damages in the ecclesiastical courts; but the suit ought to be only for punishment of the fault by way of penance. *Terms de Ley.*

And by 27 *Geo.* 3, *c.* 44, suits in ecclesiastical courts for defamatory words shall be commenced within six months.

DEFAULT, (Fr. *defaut*) is commonly taken for non-appearance in court at a day assigned, though it extends to any omission of that which we ought to do. *Bract. lib.* 5. *tract.* 3. *Co. Lit.* 259. If a plaintiff makes default in appearance in a trial at law he will be non-suited; and where a defendant makes default without plea, judgment shall be had against him by default; but in that case a writ of inquiry is to be taken, because damages are uncertain. 1 *Salk.* 216.

For suffering judgment to go by default is an admission of the contract declared on. *Stra.* 612. And after the inquest is taken by default the defendant can make no suggestion on the roll. *Str.* 46.

DEFAULT IN CRIMINAL CASES. An offender indicted appears at the *capias*, and pleads to issue, and is let to bail to attend his trial, and then makes default; here the inquest in case of felony shall never be taken by default, but a *capias ad audiendam juratam* shall issue, and if the party is not taken, an *exigent*; and if he appear on that writ, and then make default, an *exigi facias de novo* may be granted; but where upon the *capias* or *exigent* the sheriff returns *cepi corpus*, and at the day hath not his body, the sheriff shall be punished, but no new exigent awarded, because in custody of record. 2 *Hale's Hist. P. C.* 202.

DEFAULT OF JURORS. If jurors make default, in their appearance for trying of causes, they shall lose and forfeit issues, unless they have any reasonable excuse proved by witnesses, in which case the justices may discharge the issue for default. Stat. 35 *H.* 8. *c.* 6.

DEFEASANCE, (from the Fr. *defaire*, to defeat) is a declaration relating to a deed that on some act being performed, the deed shall be defeated, and rendered void, as if it never had been made; and the difference between a common condition and a defeasance is, that the condition is annexed to, or inserted in the deed; and a defeasance is either a deed by itself, concluded and agreed on between the parties having relation to another deed, or it may (as in the case of a bond, warrant of attorney, or the like,) be indorsed on the back of the deed. 1 *Inst.* 236 *b.* 237. (*a*) 1 *Rep.* 113.

And to make a good defeasance it must be, 1st, by deed, (unless indorsed) for there cannot be a defeasance of a deed without deed; and a writing under hand doth not imply it to be a deed. 2dly. It must recite the deed it relates to, or at least the most material part thereof, (unless it be on the back, as mentioned before.) 3dly. It is to be made between the same persons that were parties to the first deed. 4thly. It must be made at the time, or after the first deed, and not before. 5thly. It ought to be made of a thing defeasible. 1 *Inst.* 236. 3 *Lev.* 234. *Wood's Inst. lib.* 2. *c.* 3.

DEFENCE, in a legal signification, is applicable to a plea, and is that which the defendant ought to make immediately after the count or declaration, *viz.* that he defends all the wrong, force, and damages, where and when he ought, &c. *Terms de Ley.*

When the plaintiff hath stated his case in the declaration, it is incumbent on the defendant within a reasonable time to make his defence and to put in a plea, or else the plaintiff will at once recover judgment by default, or *nihil dicit* of the defendant. 3 *Black.* 296.

Defence, in its true legal sense, signifies not a justification, protection, or guard, which is now its popular signification; but merely an opposing or denial (from the French verb *defender*) of the truth or validity of the complaint. It is the *contestatio litis* of the Civilians: a general assertion that the plaintiff hath no ground of action, which assertion is afterwards extended and maintained in his plea. For it would be ridiculous to suppose that the defendant comes and defends (or in the vulgar acceptation, justifies) the force and injury, in one line, and pleads that he is not guilty of the trespass complained of, in the next. And therefore in actions of dower, where the demandant does not count of any injury done, but merely demands her endowment. (*Rastal. Entr.* 234.) and in assises of land, where also there is no injury alleged, but merely a question of right stated for the determination of the recognitors or jury, the tenant makes no such defence. (*Booth of real Actions*, 118.) In writs of entry, (2 *Black. Com. Append. No.* 5. *sect.* 2.) where no injury is stated in the count, but merely the right of the demandant and the defective title of the tenant, the tenant comes and defends or denies his right, *jus suum*, that is, (as Blackstone understands it, though with a small grammatical inaccuracy) the right of the demandant, the only one expressly mentioned in the pleadings, or else denies his own right to be such, as is suggested by the count of the demandant. And in writs of right (3 *Black. Com. No.* 1. *sect.* 5.) the tenant always comes and defends the right of the demandant and his seisin, *jus prædicti S. et seisinam ipsius.* (*Co. Entr.* 182.) or else the seisin of his ancestor, upon which he counts, (as the case may be) and the demandant may reply, that the tenant unjustly defends his, the demandant's right, and the seisin on which he counts. (*Nov. Narr.* 230. *edit.* 1534.) All which is extremely clear, if we understand by defence on opposition or denial, but it is otherwise inexplicably difficult. [The true reason of this, says Booth (on real Actions, 94, 112.) I could never yet find.] 3 *Black. Com.* 297.

The courts were formerly very nice and curious with respect to the nature of the defence, so that if no defence was made though a sufficient plea was pleaded, the plaintiff should recover judgment: (*Co. Lit.* 127.) and therefore the book entitled *Novæ Narrationes* or the *Newtalys*, (*edit.* 1534.) at the end of almost every count, *narratio*, or tale, subjoins such defence as is proper for the defendant to make. For a general defence or denial was not prudent in every situation, since thereby the propriety of the writ, the competency of the plaintiff, and the cognizance of the court, were allowed. By defending the force and injury the defendant waved all pleas of misnomer; (*Thelo. Dig. l.* 14. *c.* 1. *pag.* 357.) by defending the damages, all exceptions to the person of the plaintiff; and by defending either one or the other when and where it should behove him, he acknowledged the jurisdiction of the court. [*En la defence sont iij choses on tendantz: per tant quil defende tort et force, home doyt entendre quil se excuse detort a luy surmys per conte, et fait se partie al ple; et per tant quil defende les damages, il affirme le partie able destre respondu; et per tant quil defende ou et quant il devera, il accepte la poiar decourte de conustre on trier courple.* (*Mod. Tenend. cur.* 408. *Edit.* 1534.) See also *Co. Lit.* 127.] But of late years these niceties have been very deservedly discountenanced; (*Salk.* 217. *Ld. Raym.* 282.) though they still seem to be law, if insisted on. *Carth.* 230. *Lord Raym.* 117. 3 *Black. Com.* 298.

DEFEND, (*defendere*) in our ancient laws and statutes, signifies to forbid: as in some parts of England we say, God defend, instead of God forbid. *Blount.*

DEFENDANT, (*defendens*) is the party that is sued in a personal action; as tenant is he that is sued in action real. *Cowel. Blount.*

DEFENDEMUS, is an ordinary word used in grants and donations; and hath this force, that it binds the donor and his heirs to defend the donee, if any one go about to lay any incumbrance on the thing given, other than what is contained in the deed of donation. *Bract. lib.* 2. *c.* 16. See *Warranty.*

DEFENDER OF THE FAITH, (*fidei defensor*) is a peculiar title belonging to the king of England, as *catholicus*, to the king of Spain; and *Christianissimus*, to the king of France, &c. These titles were given by the Popes of Rome; and that of *defensor fidei* was first conferred by Pope Leo the tenth, on king Henry the eighth, for writing against Martin Luther, and the bull for it bears date *quinto idus Octob.* 1521. *Lord Herbert's Hist. Hen.* 8. 105. But the Pope, on king Henry's suppressing the houses of religion, at the time of the reformation, foolishly sentenced him to be deprived of his title, and deposed from his crown; though in the 35th year of his reign his title, &c. was confirmed by parliament; which hath continued to be used by all succeeding kings to this day. *Lex Constitutionis*, 47, 48.

DEFENDERE SE PER CORPUS SUUM, to offer duel or combat as a legal trial and appeal. *Bract. lib.* 3. *cap.* 26.

DEFENDERE UNICA MANU. Words signifying to wage law, and a denial of the accusation upon oath. See *Manus. Cowel. Blount.*

DEFENSA, a park or place fenced in for deer. *Ibid.*

DEFENSIVA, the lords or earls of the marches, who were the wardens or defenders of their country, had the title of *defensiva. Ibid.*

DEFENSO, that part of any open field or place that was allotted for corn and hay, and upon which there was no common or feeding, was anciently said to be *in defenso:* so of any meadow ground, that was laid in for hay only. It was likewise the same of a wood, where part was inclosed and fenced up, to secure the growth of the underwood from the injury of cattle. *Mon. Angl. Tom.* 3. *p.* 306.

DEFENSUM, an inclosure of land, or any fenced ground. *Mon. Angl. tom.* 2. *p.* 114.

DEFORCEMENT, (*deforciamentum*) is where any one is cast out of his lands or possessions by force: or it is a with-holding lands or tenements by force from the right owner. *Co. Lit.* 331.

DEFORCEOR, *deforciator*, (from the French *forceur, expugnator*) signifies one that overcometh, and casteth out by force. *Britton, cap.* 53. *Old Nat. Brev. fol.* 118. *Lit. Discon. fol.* 117. *Bract. lib.* 4. *cap.* 1.

DEFORCIANT, mentioned in the stat. 23 *El. c.* 3. is the same with a *deforceor*. 2 *Black. Com.* 350. 3 *Black. Com.* 174.

DEFORCIATIO, is used for a distress, or holding of goods for satisfaction of a debt. *Paroch. Antiq.* 293.

DEGRADATION, (*degradatio*) otherwise called *deposition:* is an ecclesiastical censure, whereby a clergyman is divested of his holy orders, and there are two sorts of degrading, by the canon law; one summary, by word only; the other solemn by stripping the party degraded of those ornaments and rights which are the ensigns of his order or degree. *Selden's Titles of Hon.* 787.

There is likewise a degradation of a lord, or a knight, &c. at common law; when they are attainted of treason. And there may be also a degrading by act of parliament; as by stat. 13 *Car.* 2. *cap.* 16. where lord Monson, sir Henry Mildmay, and others, were degraded from all titles of honour, dignities, and pre-eminences, and none of them to bear or use the title of lord, knight, esquire, or gentleman, or any coat of arms for ever after. 1 *Black. Com.* 403.

DEHORS, (Fr.) a word used in ancient pleading, when a thing is without the land, &c. or out of the point in question. Vide *Hors de son fee. Cowel. Blount.*

DE INJURIA SUA PROPRIA, *absque tali causa*, are words used in a replication where the defendant has pleaded a justification in an action of trespass. 1 *Lil. Abr.* 427. *Cro. Eliz.* 539. 2 *Salk.* 628.

DEI JUDICIUM. The old Saxon trial by *ordeal* was so called; because they thought it an appeal to God, for the justice of a cause, and verily believed that the decision was according to the will and pleasure of Divine Providence. *Domesd. Cowel. Blount.*

DEIS, the high table of a monastery. *Ibid.*

DELATURA, a Saxon word, signifying an

accusation: and sometimes it hath been taken for the reward of an informer. *Leges H.* 1. *c.* 46. *Leges Inæ* 20. *apud Brompton.*

DELEGATES, are commissioners of appeal appointed by the king under the great seal; in cases of appeals from the ecclesiastical court, &c. by stat. 25 *Hen.* 8. *c.* 19. See *Court of Delegates.*

DELF, (from the Sax. *delfan*, to dig, or delve) is a quarry or mine, where stone or coal, &c. are dug. Stat. 31 *Eliz. cap.* 7.

DELIVERANCE. When a criminal is brought to trial, and the clerk in court asks him whether he is guilty, or not guilty, to which he replies not guilty, and puts himself on God and his country, the clerk wishes him a good deliverance. *Crown Cir. Com.*

DELIVERY OF DEEDS. See *Deed.*

DEMAND, (Fr. *demande*, Lat. *postulatum*) signifies a calling upon a man for any thing due. 8 *Rep.* 153.

And there are three sorts of demands; 1st, one in writing, without speaking, and that is in every *præcipe;* 2dly, one without writing, being a verbal demand of the person, who is to do or perform the thing; and 3dly, another made without either word or writing, which is a demand in law. 1 *Nels.* 630.

And an entry on land, and taking a distress, are a demand in law of the land and rent; so the bringing an action of debt for money due on an obligation is a demand in law of the debt. 1 *Lill.* 432.

And where there is a duty, which the law makes payable on demand, no actual demand need be made previous to suit; but if there is no duty till demand, in such case there must be a demand, to make the duty. *Trin.* 3 *Ann.* 1 *Lil.* 432. *Cro. Eliz.* 548. But upon a penalty the party need not make a demand; for if a man be bound to pay 20*l.* on such a day, and in default thereof to pay 40*l.* the 40*l.* must be paid without demand. 1 *Mod.* 89. So if a man leases land by indenture for years, reserving a rent payable at certain days, and the lessee covenants to pay the said rent at the days limited; the lessor is entitled to his rent, without demand, for the lessee is obliged to pay it at the days, by force of his covenant. 2 *Danv. Abr.* 101.

But if a lessor makes a lease rendering rent, and the lessee covenant to pay the rent, *being lawfully* demanded, the lessee is not bound to pay the rent, without a demand. *Ibid.* 102.

DEMANDANT, *(petens)* all civil actions are prosecuted either by demands or plaints, and the pursuer is called demandant, in actions real, and the plaintiff, in personal actions: in a real action, lands, &c. are demanded. *Co. Lit.* 127.

DEMESNE. Lands which are next or more convenient to the lord's mansion house, and which he keeps in his own hands for the support of his family, and hospitality, are called his *demesne*, but have not the same properties as ancient demesne. *Spelm.* 12.

DEMISE, (*dimissio*) is applied to an estate either in fee, for term of life or years, but commonly the latter: it is used in writs for any estate. 2 *Inst.* 483. The word demise in a lease for years, implies a warranty to the lessee and his assignee; and upon this word action of covenant lies against the heir of the lessor, if he oust the lessee: it binds the executors of the lessor, who has fee-simple, or fee-tail; where any lessee is evicted, and the executor hath assets; but not the lessor for life's executors, without express words, that the lessee shall hold his whole term. *Dyer* 257. *Jenk. Cent.* 35.

DEMISE and REDEMISE, the conveyance by demise and redemise is where there is a lease made from one to another at a pepper-corn or some other nominal rent. And the latter redemises to the first lessor the same land for a shorter term, subject to an actual rent; and this is most usually done upon the grant of a rent-charge, or annuity.

DEMURRER AT LAW, (in Latin *demorari in lege,* from the Fr. *demurer*) is an issue upon matter of law: thus when any action is brought, and the defendant saith that *the plaintiff's declaration is not sufficient for him to answer unto:* or when the defendant pleads, and the plaintiff says, *that it is not a sufficient plea in law*, and the defendant says, that it is a good plea; and thereupon both parties submit to the judgment of the court, this is a *moratur in lege.* 1 *Lil. Abr.* 435.

So that a demurrer is an issue joined upon matter of law, to be determined by the judges; and is an abiding in point of law, and a referring to the judgment of the court, whether the declaration or plea of the adverse party is sufficient in law to be maintained. *Finch, lib.* 4. *cap.* 40. 1 *Inst.* 71.

A demurrer admits the matter of fact, since it refers the law arising on the fact, to the judgment of the court; and therefore the fact is taken to be true on such demurrer, or otherwise the court has no foundation on which to make any judgment. *Gilb. Hist. of C. P.* 55.

When the court gives judgment on demurrer in debt for the plaintiff in the action, the judgment is for the plaintiff to recover his debt, costs, and damages; but if it be in action of the case, a writ of enquiry of damages must be awarded, before the plaintiff can have final judgment. If judgment on the demurrer is for the defendant in the action, the judgment is, that the plaintiff *nihil capiat per breve*, or *per billam*, and that the defendant *eat sine die.* *Wood's Inst.* 603.

DEMURRER IN EQUITY. A demurrer in equity, is a defence which rests on the bill, and on the foundation of matter there apparent, demanding the judgment of the court, whether the suit shall proceed at all. *Mitf.* 14.

DEMURRER

A demurrer being founded on the bill itself, necessarily admits the truth of the facts contained in the bill, or in that part of the bill to which it extends; and therefore, as no fact can be in question between the parties, the court may immediately proceed to pronounce its definitive judgment on the demurrer, which if favourable to the defendant, puts an end to so much of the suit as the demurrer extends to. A demurrer if allowed, consequently prevents any further proceeding. *Ibid.*

This demurrer is an allegation of a defendant, which admitting the matters of fact alleged in the bill to be true, shews that as they are therein set forth, they are insufficient for the plaintiff to proceed upon, or to oblige the defendant to answer, or that for some reason apparent on the face of the bill, or because of the omission of some matter which ought to be contained therein, or for want of some circumstance which ought to be attendant thereon, the defendant ought not to be compelled to answer, it therefore demands the judgment of the court, whether the defendant shall be compelled to make answer to the plaintiff's bill, or to some certain part thereof. *Mitf.* 99.

The causes of demurrer are merely upon matter in the bill, or upon the omission of matter which ought to be therein, or attendant thereon; and not upon any foreign matter alleged by the defendant. *Mitf.* 100.

The principal ends of a demurrer are, to avoid a discovery, which may be prejudicial to the defendant; to cover a defective title; or to prevent unnecessary expense: if no one of these ends is obtained, there is little use in a demurrer; for in general, if a demurrer would hold to a bill, the court, though the defendant answers, will not grant relief upon hearing the cause. *Ibid.*

The principal grounds of *objection to the relief* sought by an original bill, which can appear on the bill itself, and may therefore be taken advantage of by demurrer, are these, 1st, that the subject of the suit is not within the jurisdiction of a court of equity; 2dly, that some other court of equity has the proper jurisdiction; 3dly, that the plaintiff is not entitled to sue by reason of some personal disability. 4thly, that he has no interest in the subject, or no title to institute a suit concerning it. 5thly, that he has no right to call upon the defendant concerning the subject of the suit. 6thly, that the defendant has not that interest in the subject which can make him liable to the claims of the plaintiff. 7thly, that for some reason founded on the substance of the case, the plaintiff is not entitled to the relief he prays; *to these may be added,* 8thly, the deficiency of the bill to answer the purpose of complete justice; and, 9thly, the impropriety of confounding distinct subjects in the same bill, or of unnecessarily multiplying suits. *Mitf.* 102, 103.

And it has been said that a defendant may demur to a bill, if it appears upon the face of it to be *brought for a very small sum*; but it is most usual to apply to the court, that the bill may be dismissed. *Mosely* 47, 356. *Bunb.* 17. *Comyn* 715.

When the discovery sought by a bill can only be assistant to the relief prayed, a ground of demurrer to the relief will also extend to the discovery, but if the discovery may have a further purpose the plaintiff may be entitled to it, though he has no title to relief. *Mitf.* 103.

The objections to a bill, which are *causes of demurrer to discovery only*, are, 1st, that the case made by the bill is not such in which a court of equity assumes a jurisdiction to compel a discovery. 2dly, that the plaintiff has no interest in the subject, or no interest which entitles him to call on the defendant for a discovery. 3dly, that the defendant has no interest in the subject to entitle the plaintiff to institute a suit against him, even for the purposes of discovery. 4thly, although both plaintiff and defendant may have an interest in the subject, yet that there is not that privity of title between them which gives the plaintiff a right to the discovery required by his bill. 5thly, that the discovery, if obtained, cannot be material; and, 6thly, that the situation of the defendant renders it improper for a court of equity to compel a discovery. *Ibid.* 149.

Where *the sole object of a bill is to obtain a discovery*, some grounds of demurrer, which if the bill prayed *relief* would extend to a *discovery*, as well as to the relief, will not hold: thus a demurrer to a bill for a *discovery merely*, will not hold for want of parties; for the plaintiff seeks no decree: nor, in general, for want of equity in the plaintiff's case, for the same reason, nor because the bill is brought for the discovery of part of a matter, for that is merely a demurrer, because the discovery would be insufficient; but it should seem a demurrer would hold to a bill for discovery of several distinc matters against several distinct defendants for though a defendant is always eventually paid his costs upon a bill of discovery, if both parties live, yet the court ought not to permit him to be put to any unnecessary expense, as either the plaintiff or defendant may die pending the suit. *Ibid.* 163.

A demurrer must be signed by counsel; but is put in without oath, as it asserts no fact, and relies merely upon matter apparent on the face of the bill; it is therefore considered that the defendant may, upon the sight of the bill only, be enabled to demur thereto; and for this reason it is always made the special condition of an order, giving the defendant time to demur, plead, or answer to the plaintiff's bill, that he shall not demur alone. *Ibid.* 170.

Whenever, therefore, the defendant has

obtained an order for time, and is afterwards advised to demur, he must also plead to or answer some part of the bill: and it has been held, that answering to some fact immaterial to the cause, and denying combination, do not amount to a compliance with the terms of such an order; and therefore upon motion a demurrer accompanied by such an answer has been discharged. 2 *P. Will.* 286. And as the modern practice is according to the strictness of this rule, Ld. *Redesdale* is of opinion that where the defendant cannot answer further without over-ruling his demurrer, it may be better to relax the rule upon special application to the court, than to permit it to be evaded. *Mitf.* 170, 2.

A demurrer must express the several causes of demurrer; and in case the demurrer does not go to the whole bill it must clearly express the particular parts of the bill demurred to; if a demurrer is general to the whole bill, and there is any part, either as to the relief or the discovery, to which the defendant ought to put in an answer, it is generally considered that the demurrer being entire must be over-ruled. *Ibid.* 173.

But there are instances of allowing a demurrer in part; and a defendant may put in separate demurrers to separate and distinct parts of a bill for separate and distinct causes: for the same ground of demurrer frequently will not apply to different parts of a bill, though the whole is liable to demurrer; and in this case one demurrer may be over-ruled upon argument, and another allowed. *Ibid.*

If the plaintiff conceives that there is not sufficient cause apparent in his bill to support a demurrer put into it, or that the demurrer is too extensive, or otherwise improper, he may take the judgment of the court upon it; and if he conceives that by amending his bill he can remove the ground of demurrer, he may do so before the demurrer is argued, on payment of costs, which vary according to the state of the proceedings. *Ibid.* 174.

But after a demurrer to the whole of a bill has been argued and allowed, the bill is out of court, and therefore cannot be regularly amended: to avoid this consequence the court has sometimes, instead of deciding upon the demurrer, given the plaintiff liberty to amend his bill, paying the costs incurred by the defendant; and this has been frequently done in the case of a demurrer for want of parties. *Ibid.*

Where a demurrer leaves any part of a bill untouched, the whole may be amended, notwithstanding the allowance of the demurrer; for the suit in that case continues in court, the want of which circumstance seems to be the reason of the contrary practice, where a demurrer to the whole bill has been allowed. *Ibid.*

A demurrer being frequently a matter of form is not in general a bar to a new bill; but if the court upon a demurrer has clearly decided upon the merits of the question between the parties, the decision may be pleaded in bar of another suit. *Ibid.* 175.

A demurrer being always upon matter apparent upon the face of the bill, and not upon any matter alleged by the defendant, it sometimes happens that a bill, which if all the parts of the case were disclosed, would be open to a demurrer, is so artfully drawn as to avoid showing upon the face of it any cause of demurrer; in this case the defendant is compelled to revert to a plea by which he may allege matter which, if it appeared on the face of the bill, would be good cause of demurrer; for in many cases what is a good defence by way of plea is also good as a demurrer, if the facts appear sufficiently by the bill. *Ibid.*

DEMURRER TO EVIDENCE, is where a question of law doth arise thereupon: as if the plaintiff produces in evidence, any records, deeds, writings, &c. upon which a question of law arises, and the defendant offers to demur upon it; and then the plaintiff must join in demurrer, or wave his evidence. So if the plaintiff brings witnesses to prove a fact, and a matter of law ariseth upon it; if the defendant admits their testimony to be true, there also the defendant may demur in law: and so may the plaintiff demur upon the defendant's evidence. And in these cases, the counsel for the plaintiff and defendant agree the matter of fact in dispute, and the jury are discharged; and the matter of law is referred to the judges to determine. But where evidence is given for the king, in an information or other suit, and the defendant offers to demur upon it, the king's counsel are not obliged to join therein; but the court ought to direct the jury to find the special matter. And, indeed, because juries of late usually find a doubtful matter specially, demurrers upon evidence are now seldom used. 5 *Rep.* 104. 1 *Inst.* 72. 2 *Inst.* 426. If the court doth not agree to a demurrer, to the insufficiency of evidence in a civil cause, they ought to seal a bill of exceptions, &c. 9 *Rep.* 13. See *Bill of Exceptions.*

DEMURRER TO INDICTMENTS. If a criminal joins issue upon a point of law in an indictment or appeal, allowing the fact to be true, as laid therein, this is a demurrer in law: and if the indictment or appeal proves good in law, in the opinion of the judges, they proceed to judgment and execution, as if the party had been convicted by confession or verdict. 2 *Inst.* 178. *H. P. C.* 243. *S. P. C.* 160. 1 *Hawk. P. C.* 14.

DEMY SANGUE, is the half blood: where a man marries a woman, and hath issue by her a son, and the wife dying he marries another woman, by whom he hath also a son ; now these two sons, though they are called brothers, are but brothers of the half blood, because they had not both the father and mother: and therefore by law they cannot be heirs to one another; for he that claims as heir to another by descent must be of the whole blood to him from whom he claims. *Terms de Ley.*

But the half blood are entitled under the statutes of distribution to any equal share of the personal estate with the whole blood. Stat. 22 & 23 *Car.* 2, *c.* 10.

DEN. The names of places ending in den, as Biddenden, &c. signify the situation to be in a valley, or near woods, from the Sax. den, i. e. *vallis, locus sylvestris. Cowel. Blount.*

DEN AND STROND, is a liberty for ships or vessels to run or come ashore: and *Ed.* 1. by charter granted this privilege to the barons of the Cinque Ports. *Ibid.*

DENA TERRÆ, a hollow place between two hills; it is also used for a little portion of woody ground, commonly called a coppice. *Ibid.*

DENARII, a general term for any sort of *pecunia numerata*, or ready money. *Paroch. Antiq.* 320.

DENARII DE CARITATE, customary oblations made to cathedral churches about the time of Pentecost, when the parish priests and many of their people went in procession to visit their mother church. *Cowel. Blount.*

DENARIUS, an English penny. *Ibid.*

DENARIUS DEI, God's penny, or earnest money given and received by the parties to contracts, &c. *Ibid.*

DENARIUS S. PETRI, (called *Peter's pence*) an annual payment of one penny from every family to the pope, during the time that the Roman catholic religion prevailed in this kingdom, paid on the feast of St. Peter, finally abolished by 1 *Eliz. c.* 1.

DENARIUS TERTIUS COMITATUS. Of the fines and other profits of the county-courts, originally when those courts had superior jurisdiction before other courts were erected, two parts were reserved to the king, and a third part or penny to the earl of the county; who either received it in specie at the assises and trials, or had an equivalent composition for it out of the exchequer. *Parock. Antiq.* 418.

DENBERA, (from the Sax. *den*, a vale, and berg, a barrow or hog) a place for the running and feeding of hogs, wherein they are penned, by some called a swinecomb. *Cowel. Blount.*

DENIZEN, (Fr. *donaison*) is an alien enfranchised, and made a subject by the king's letters patent; and is called *donaison*, because his legitimation proceeds *ex donatione regis*, from the king's gift. 2 *Inst.* 741. This may be either *general*, as to be accounted in all things as a subject, or *particular*, enabling one to sue only. And in the charter, whereby a person is made a denizen, there is commonly contained some clause that expressly abridges him of that full benefit which natural subjects enjoy. *Bract. lib.* 5. *tract.* 5. *cap.* 25. 2 *Inst.* 741.

When the king makes a denizen by letters patent he may purchase lands, and his issue born afterwards may inherit them, but those he had before shall not. And though a denizen is enabled to purchase he cannot inherit the lands of his ancestors, but as a purchaser he may enjoy them; and he may take lands by devise. 1 *Inst.* 8. 5 *Rep.* 52. 11 *Rep.* 67. And aliens made denizens are incapable of offices in the government, or to be members of parliament, &c. by stat. 12 *W.* 3. *c.* 2. 1 *Geo.* 1. *c.* 4.

DENSHIRING OF LAND (so called from the original practice in *Devonshire*) is the casting parings of earth, turf, and stubble, into heaps, which when dried are burnt into ashes for a compost on poor barren land. *Cowel. Blount.*

DE NON DECIMANDO, a writ to be discharged of tithes. *Ibid.*

DE NON RESIDENTIA CLERICI REGIS, was an ancient writ where a parson was employed in the king's service, &c. to excuse and discharge him of non-residence. 2 *Inst.* 624.

DENTRIX, a fish with many teeth. *Cowel. Blount.*

DEODAND (*Deo dandum*) is a thing given to God, to appease his anger, where a person comes to a violent death by mischance, not by any reasonable creature, and is forfeited to the king, or the lord of the manor, as grantee of the crown; and if to the king, his almoner disposes of it by sale, and the money arising thereby, he distributes to the poor: also if forfeited to the lord of a liberty, it ought to be thus distributed. 3 *Inst.* 57. 5 *Rep.* 110. 1 *Nels.* 636. And it is described to be any movable thing inanimate, or beast animate, that doth cause or occasion the untimely death of any man by mischance (without fault of himself, or other person) in any county of England, (but not upon the sea or salt water) and *that thing*, and every thing *moving with it to the death*, is forfeited to the king, or grantee of the crown, if he dies within a year and a day after. 3 *Inst.* 57. 5 *Rep.* 110. *Keil.* 686.

Thus if a man in driving a cart falls so as the cart-wheel runs over him, and presses him to death, the cart-wheel is forfeited; and that only, as the immediate cause of his death, may be then seized by the lord of the manor, and converted to his own use. 1 *Nels.* 639. So if a horse strikes and kills a person, it is *deodand.* 3 *Inst.* 57.

And if a horse strikes a man, and afterward the owner sells the horse, and then the party that was stricken dies of the stroke, the horse, notwithstanding the sale, shall be forfeited as deodand. *Plowd.* 260. 5 *Rep.* 110.

But if a man riding over a river is thrown off his horse by the violence of the water, and drowned, his horse is not *deodand*, for his death was caused *per cursum aquæ*. 2 *Co.* 483.

Things fixed to the freehold, as a bell hanging in a steeple, a wheel of a mill, &c. unless severed from the freehold, cannot be deodands. 2 *Inst.* 281. And there is no forfeiture of a deodand till the matter is found of record by the jury that finds the death, who ought also to find and appraise the value of the deodand. 5 *Rep.* 110. 1 *Inst.* 144. After the coroner's inquisition the sheriff is answerable for the value, where the deodand belongs to the king, and he may levy the same on the town, &c. wherefore the inquest ought to find the value of it. 1 *Hawk.* 67.

DE ONERANDO PRO RATA PORTIONIS, was a writ, (now in disuse) which anciently laid where a person was distrained for rent, that ought to be paid by others proportionably with him. *F. N. B.* 234.

DEPARTURE, (in pleading) is where a defendant, who first pleading one thing in bar of an action, and being replied unto, in his rejoinder quits that and shows another matter, contrary to, or not pursuing his first plea, which is called a departure from his plea: also where a plaintiff in his declaration sets forth one thing, and after the defendant has pleaded, the plaintiff in his replication shows new matter different from his declaration, this is a departure; and for a departure in pleading a demurrer will lie. *Plow.* 7, 8. 2 *Inst.* 147.

DEPARTURE IN DESPITE OF THE COURT, and entry of it. See *Default.*

DEPARTURE OF GOLD AND SILVER. The parters or dividers of those metals, from others that are coarser. *Cowel. Blount.*

DEPOPULATIO AGRORUM, destroying and ravaging a country, an offence where the benefit of clergy was denied at common law. 2 *Hal. pl.* 333. 4 *Black. Com.* 366.

DEPOPULATION, (*depopulatio*) is a wasting or destruction; a desolation or unpeopling of any place, by fire, sword, pestilence, &c. 12 *Rep.* 30.

DEPOPULATORES AGRORUM, these were great offenders, by the ancient common law, so called because by prostrating and ruining of houses of habitation of the king's people, they, as it were, depopulated towns and villages, leaving them without inhabitants. Stat. 4 *Hen.* 4. *cap.* 2. 3 *Inst.* 204.

DEPOSITION, (*depositio*) is the testimony of a witness, otherwise called a deponent, put down in writing by way of answer to interrogatories exhibited for that purpose, in courts of equity, and the copies of such depositions regularly taken and published, are read as evidence at the hearing of the cause. *Practis. Attorn.* Edit. 1, *p.* 234. *Harrison's Prac.*

Depositions in the chancery after a cause is determined may be given in evidence in a trial at law, in a suit for the same matter, between the same parties, *if the party that deposed* be dead, but not otherwise; for if he be living he must appear in person in court, to be examined, &c. 1 *Lil. Abr.* 445.

Also in the courts of law, where witnesses in a cause are going to sea, or on long journies, the court will give leave to examine them *de bene esse* on interrogatories, at a judge's chamber, in the presence of the attornies on both sides. Also in the case of witnesses residing abroad, commissions frequently issue to take their depositions there, and such depositions in all such cases shall be admitted to be good evidence. *Ibid.*

Depositions of witnesses taken upon oath before a coroner, upon an inquisition of death, or before justices of peace on a commitment or bailment of felony, may be given in evidence at a trial for the same felony, if it be proved on oath that they are dead, or unable to travel, or kept away by the procurement of the prisoner; and oath must be made that the depositions are the same that were sworn before the coroner or justice, without any alteration. 2 *Hawk. P. C.* 429.

Deposition is also used in the law in another sense, *viz.* to signify the depriving of a person of some dignity; and deposition is also taken for death; and *dies depositionis* the day of one's death. *Litt. Dict.*

DEPRIVATION, (*deprivatio*) is depriving or taking away, as where a bishop, parson, vicar, or other ecclesiastical person, is deposed from his preferment. *Cowel. Blount.*

And the causes of deprivation are many: if a clerk obtain a preferment in the church by simoniacal contract; if he be an excommunicate, a drunkard, fornicator, adulterer, infidel, schismatic or heretic, or guilty of murder, manslaughter, perjury, forgery, &c. If a clerk be illiterate and not able to perform the duty of his church; if he is a scandalous person in his life and conversation; or bastardy is objected against him: if one be a mere layman, and not in holy orders; or under age, *viz.* the age of twenty-three years, be disobedient and incorrigible to his ordinary; or a nonconformist to the canons; if a parson refuse to use the common prayer, or preach in derogation of it; do not administer the sacraments, or read the articles of religion, &c. Or if any parson, vicar, &c. have one benefice with cure of souls, and take plurality, without a faculty or dispensation; or if he hath omitted to read and subscribe the thirty-nine articles, or if he commit waste in the houses and lands of the church, called dilapidations; all these have been held good causes for deprivation of priests. *Degg's Parson's Counsellor*, 98, 99, &c. 3 *Inst.* 204.

But where the living is made *ipso facto* void, as in avoidances by act of parliament, no previous declaratory sentence is necessary. *Can.* 122.

But where a benefice is only voidable, but not void before sentence of deprivation, the party must be cited to appear; there is to be a libel against him, and a time assigned to answer it, and also liberty for advocates to plead, and after all a solemn sentence pronounced.

If a deprivation be for a thing merely of ecclesiastical cognizance, no appeal lies; but the party has his remedy by a commission of review, which is granted by the king of mere grace. 26 *H.* 8. *Moor* 781.

DEPUTY, (*deputatus*) is he that exercises an office, &c. in another man's right, whose forfeiture or misdemeanor shall cause him whose deputy he is to lose his office. 1 *Lill. Abr.* 446.

And there is great difference between a deputy and assignee of an office; for an assignee has an interest in the office itself, and does all things in his own name; for whom his grantor shall not answer, unless in special cases. But a deputy has not any interest in the office, but is only the shadow of the officer, in whose name he does all things. And where an officer has power to make assigns, he may implicitly make deputies, for *cui licet quod majus est, non debet quod minus est non licere.* And a sheriff may make a deputy, or under-sheriff, although he have not such express words in the patent. *Cowel. Blount.*

So a bailiff of a liberty may make a deputy. *Cro. Jac.* 240. And a constable may make a deputy, who may execute the warrant directed to the constable. 2 *Danv.* 482.

So when an office of inheritance descends to an infant, idiot, or other incapacitated person, such may make a deputy of course. 9 *Rep.* 47. And where an office is granted to a man and his heirs he may make an assignee of that office, and by consequence a deputy. A deputy of an office has no interest therein, but doth all things in his master's name, and his master shall be answerable; but an assignee hath an interest in the office, and does all things in his own name, for whom his grantor shall not answer unless in special cases. *Terms de Ley.*

And the superior officer must answer for his deputy in civil actions, if he is not sufficient; but in criminal cases it is otherwise, where deputies are to answer for themselves. 2 *Inst.* 191, 446. *Doct. et Stud. c.* 42.

But a deputy cannot make a deputy, because it implies an assignment of his whole power, which he cannot assign over, but he may empower another to do a particular act. 1 *Salk.* 96. *Lit.* 379.

Judges, however, cannot act by deputy, but are to hold their courts in person; for they may not transfer their power over to others. 2 *Hawk. P. C.* 3.

Also a coroner ought not to execute his office by deputy, it being a judicial office of trust, and judicial offices are annexed to the person. 1 *Lill.* 446.

DE QUIBUS SUR DISSEISIN, is a writ of entry mentioned in our books treating of writs. *F. N. B.* 191.

DER (from the Sax. *deor, fera*). The names of places beginning with this word signify that formerly wild beasts herded together there. *Cowel. Blount.*

DERAIGN, or DEREYN, (*distrationare*) seems to be derived literally from the Fr. *destrayer*, i. e. to confound and disorder, or to turn out of course, or displace, as deraignment or departure out of religion. Stat. 31 *H.* 8. *cap.* 6. *Cowel. Blount.*

DERELICT (*derelictus*), is any thing forsaken or left, or wilfully cast away. 2 *Nels. Abr.* 903.

If the sea shrink back so slowly that the gain be by little and little, *i. e.* by small and imperceptible degrees, it is said it shall go to the owner of the lands adjoining. 2 *Black. Com.* 262.

But where an island in the sea is formed, or a large quantity of new land appears, it belongs to the king. 2 *Nels. Abr.* 903. 2 *Black. Com.*

DESCENDER, writ of *formedon* in. A writ which lies where a gift in tail is made, and the tenant in tail aliens the lands entailed, or is disseised of them and dies, the heir in tail shall have this writ against him who is then the actual tenant of the freehold. *F. N. B.* 211, 212. 3 *Black. Com.* 192.

DESCENT of lands, tenements, &c. See *Discent.*

DESCRIPTION (*descriptio*). In deeds and grants there must be a certain description of the lands granted, the places where the lands lie, and of the persons to whom granted, &c. to make them good. But wills are more favoured than grants, as to those descriptions; and a wrong description will not make a devise void if there be otherwise a sufficient certainty of what was intended by the testator. 1 *Nels. Abr.* 647.

DESERTION. If any one deserts from the king's armies in time of war, whether by land or sea, in England, or in parts beyond the seas, he is by the standing laws of the land (exclusive of the annual acts of parliament to punish mutiny and desertion), and particularly by stat. 18 *Hen.* 6, *c.* 19. and 5 *Eliz. c.* 5, guilty of felony, but not without benefit of clergy. But by stat. 2 & 3 *Ed.* 6. *c.* 2, clergy is taken away from such deserters, and the offence is made triable by the justices of every shire. 4 *Black. Com.* 101.

DE SON TORT DEMESNE, are certain words of form used in actions of trespass, &c. by way of replication to the defendant's plea, *i. e*, that he did it *of his own wrong*, without any such cause, &c. in manner and form, &c. 8 *Rep.* 67. 1 *Lil. Abr.* 428. 3 *Lev.* 65. 2 *Leon.* 108.

DESPITUS, signifies in our ancient lawbooks a contemptible person. *Fleta, lib.* 4, *cap.* 5, *par.* 4.

DESUBITO, to weary a person with continual barkings, and then to bite. *Cowel. Blount.*

DETACHIARE, to seize or to take into custody another person's goods, &c. by attachment or other course of law. *Cowel. Blount.*

DETERMINATION OF WILL, the exertion of any act of ownership by the lessor puts an end to or determines an estate at will. 2 *Black. Com.* 146.

DETINET, a word used in writs, which is necessary in the writ of *detinue*, &c. See *Lebet* and *Detinet*.

DETINUE, (*detinendo*) is a writ which lies, against him, who having goods or chattels delivered to keep, refuses to re-deliver them. In this action the thing detained is generally to be recovered, and not damages; but if one cannot recover the thing itself, he shall recover damages for the thing, and also for the detainer. *Wood's Inst.* 542. *Detinue* lies for any thing certain and valuable, wherein one may have a property or right; as for horse, cow, sheep, hens, dogs, jewels, plate, cloth, bags of money, sacks of corn, &c. It must be laid so certain, that the thing detained may be known and recovered; and therefore for money out of a bag, or corn out of a sack, &c. it lies not; for the money or corn cannot in this case be known from other money or corn; so that the party must have an action on the case, &c. 1 *Inst.* 226. *F. N. B.* 138.

In order, therefore, to ground an action of *detinue*, which is only for the detaining, these points are necessary; 1st, that the defendant came lawfully by the goods, as either by delivery to him, or finding them; 2dly, that the plaintiff have a property; 3dly, that the goods themselves be of some value; and, 4thly, that they be ascertained in point of identity. 3 *Black.* 151.

But there is one disadvantage which attends this action, *viz.* that the defendant is herein permitted to wage his law, that is, to exculpate himself by oath, denying the possession, &c. and thereby defeat the plaintiff of his remedy: which privilege is grounded on the confidence originally reposed in the bailee by the bailor, in the borrower by the lender, and the like; from whence arose a strong presumptive evidence that in the plaintiff's own opinion the defendant was worthy of credit. 3 *Black.* 151. *And for this reason the action itself is of late much disused, and has given place to the action of* Trover, *in which the defendant cannot wage his law. Ibid.*

DETINUE OF CHARTERS. A man may have a writ of detinue for deeds and charters concerning land; but if they concern the freehold, it must be in C. B. and no other court. *New Nat. Br.* 308. *Co. Lit.* 286. 1 *Rep.* 2. *F. N. B.* 138.

For detaining of deeds and charters concerning the inheritance of lands, or an indenture of lease, the defendant shall not wage law; but in a common action of detinue he may do it. 1 *Inst.* 295.

DETINUE OF GOODS IN FRANK-MARRIAGE, is on a divorce between a man and his wife; after which the wife shall have this writ of detinue for the goods given with her in marriage. *New Na'. Br.* 308.

DETRACTARE, signifies a punishment to be torn in pieces with horses. *Cowel. Blount.*

DETUNICARE, to discover or lay open to the world. *Ibid.*

DEVADIATUS, is where an offender is without sureties or pledges. *Ibid.*

DEVASTAVIT, or DEVASTAVERUNT BONA TESTATORIS, is a writ that lies against executors or administrators for paying debts upon simple contract, before debts on bonds and specialties, &c. after notice. 1 *Mod.* 175. 1 *Lev.* 215. For in this case they are liable to action as if they had squandered away the goods of the deceased, or converted them to their own use; and are compellable to pay such debts by specialty out of their own goods, to the value of what they so paid illegally. *Dyer* 232.

Where an executor, &c. pays legacies before debts, and has not sufficient to pay both, it is a *devastavit*. Also where an executor sells the testator's goods at an undervalue, it is a *devastavit*; but this is understood where the sale is fraudulent; for if more money could not be had, it is otherwise. *Kielw.* 59. 1 *Nels. Abr.* 649. Executors keeping the goods of the deceased in their hands, and not paying the testator's debts, or selling them, and not paying off debts, &c. or not observing the law which directs them in the management thereof; or doing any thing by negligence or fraud, whereby the estate of the deceased is misemployed, are a *devastavit*, or waste; and they shall be charged for so much *de bonis propriis*, as if for their own debt. 8 *Rep.* 133. But the fraud or negligence of one executor is not chargeable on the rest, where there are several executors. 1 *Rol. Abr.* 929.

If an executor or administrator confesses judgment, or suffers it to go by default, he thereby admits assets, and is estopped to say the contrary in an action on such judgment, suggesting a *devastavit*. 1 *Wils.* 258.

DEVENERUNT, a writ, now disused, which was heretofore directed to the escheator on the death of the heir of the king's tenant under age, and in custody, commanding the escheator that by the oaths of good and lawful men he inquire what lands and tenements by the death of the tenant came to the king, *Dyer* 360.

DEVEST, (*devestire*) is opposite to invest. As invest signifies to deliver the possession of any thing to another, so devest signifies the taking it away. *Feud. lib.* 1, *cap*, 7. *Cowel. Blount.*

DEVISE, (from the Fr. *deviser*, to divide or sort into parcels) signifies a gift, or disposition of any lands or tenements by will in writing; and he who gives away, or in any wise disposes of or limits his lands in this manner, is called the devisor; and he to whom the lands are given or limited, the devisee. See WILLS.

DEVOIRES OF CALEIS, were the customs due to the king, for merchandise brought into or carried out of Calais, when our staple remained there. *Cowel. Blount.*

DEXTRARIUS, is understood to take the right hand of another. And the word *dextarios* has been used for light horses, or horses for the great saddle. *Ibid.*

DEXTRAS DARE, shaking of hands in token of friendship; or a man's giving up himself to the power of another person. *Ibid.*

DIARIUM, is taken for daily food, or as much as will suffice for the day. *Ibid.*

DIASPERATUS, stained with many colours. *Ibid.*

DICA, a tally for accounts, by number of taillees, cuts, or notches. *Ibid.*

DICKAR, or DICKER OF LEATHER, is a certain quantity, consisting of ten hides, by which leather is bought and sold: there are also dickers of iron, containing ten bars to the dicker. This word is thought to come from the Greek δεκας, which signifies ten. *Ibid.*

DICTORES and DICTUM, the one signifies arbitrators, and the other the arbitrament. *Ibid.*

Dictum also signifies any casual or extrajudicial opinion delivered by a judge in the argument of a case before the court.

DICTUM DE KENELWORTH, an edict or award, between king *Hen.* the Third and his barons and others, who had been in arms against him: so called because it was made at Kenelworth castle in Warwickshire, *anno* 51 *Hen.* 3. *Cowel. Blount.*

DIEM CLAUSIT EXTREMUM, was a writ issued out of the court of chancery to the escheator of the county upon the death of any of the king's tenants *in capite*, to inquire by a jury of what lands he died seised, and of what value, and who was the next heir to him; and the same ought to be granted at the suit of the next heir, &c. for upon that, when the heir came of age, he was to sue livery of his lands out of the king's hands. *F. N. B.* 251. *Ibid.*

DIES NON. There are several days in the different terms called *dies non juridica*, on which the courts at Westminster do not transact any business; they are the following, *viz.* the *Lord's day*, throughout the whole year; in *Easter term*, *Ascension day*; in *Trinity term*, *St. John Baptist*, when it falls in that term; and in *Hilary term* the *day of the purification* of the Virgin Mary.

DIES DATUS, is a day or time of respite given to the defendant in a suit by the court. *Broke.*

DIES MARCHIÆ, was the day of congress or meeting of the English and Scotch, appointed annually to be held on the marches or borders, to adjust all differences between them, and preserve the articles of peace. *Cowel. Blount.*

DIETA, a day's journey. *Omnes rationibilis dieta constat ex viginti miliaribus. Fleta, lib.* 4, *c.* 22, and in this sense it is used by *Bracton, lib.* 3, *tract.* 2, *c.* 16.

DIET, (*conventus*) an assembly, as the diet of the empire, of Ratisbon, &c.

DIEU ET MON DROIT, God and my Right, the motto of the royal arms, intimating, that the king of England holds his empire of none but God; first given by king *Rich.* 1. *Cowel. Blount.*

DIEU SON ACT. It is a maxim of law that the act of God shall prejudice no man. Therefore, if an accident happens by tempest, thunder, or lightning, without the intervention of man, this shall excuse one who would otherwise be liable, as a common carrier, for the goods which he is intrusted to carry; or a lessee for life or years, in respect of waste or damage. 4 *Rep.* 63. 11 *Rep.* 82. 1 *Ter. Rep.* 27. 5 *Ter. Rep.* 389. 4 *Ter. Rep.* 581.

DIFFACERE, to destroy; and *diffactio* is a maiming any one. *Leg. H.* 1. *c.* 64. 92. *Cowel. Bloutt.*

DIFFORCIARE, RECTUM, to take away, or deny justice. *Mat. Paris. anno* 1164. *Cowel. Blount.*

DIGEST, the book of Pandects of the civil law, which has its name from its containing *Legalia præcepta excellenter digesta. Du Cange.*

DIGNITY. (*dignitas*) Dignity may be divided into superior and inferior: as the titles of duke, earl, baron, &c. are the highest names of dignity; and those of baronet, knight, serjeant at law, &c. the lowest. The omission of a name of dignity may be pleaded in abatement; and so it may be where a peer who has more than one name of dignity is not named by the most noble. 1 *Hawk. P. C.* 185, 239. But no temporal dignity of any foreign nation can give a man a higher title here than that of esquire. 2 *Inst.* 667.

DIGNITARIES, (*dignitarii*) are those who are advanced to any dignity ecclesiastical; as a bishop, dean, archdeacon, prebendary, &c. But there are simple prebendaries, without cure or jurisdiction, which are not dignitaries. 3 *Inst.* 155.

DILAPIDATION, (*dilapidatio*) is where an incumbent on a church living suffers the parsonage house or outhouses to fall down, or be in decay for want of necessary reparation: or it is the pulling down or destroying any of the houses or buildings, belonging to a spiritual living, or destroying of the woods, trees, &c. appertaining to the same; for it is said to extend to the committing or suffering any wilful waste in or upon the inheritance of the church. *Degg's Paris. Couns.* 89.

By the old canons, and our own provincial constitutions, the clergy are bound sufficiently to repair the houses belonging to their benefices; which, if they neglect or refuse to do, the bishop may sequester the profits of the benefice for that purpose, &c. *Rights Clerg.* 143.

The prosecution in these cases may be brought either against the incumbent himself, or against his executors or administrators; and the executor or administrator of him in whose time it was done or suffered must make amends to the successor: and if you proceed against the incumbent, then it is proper in the spiritual court: likewise you may proceed in that court against an executor, or the successor may have an action of the case or debt at the common law, in which action he shall recover damages in proportion to the dilapidations. 1 *Nels. Abr.* 656. *Pars. Couns.* 97, 98.

By statute, if any parson, &c. shall make a gift of his goods and personal estate to defraud his successor, as to dilapidations, such successor may have the same remedy in the spiritual court against the person to whom such gift is made, as he might have against the executors of the deceased parson. 13 *Eliz. cap.* 10. And money recovered for dilapidations, is to be employed in the reparations of the same houses suffered to be in decay, or the party recovering shall forfeit double the value of what he receives, to the king, by *Stat.* 14 *Eliz. cap.* 11.

If a parson suffers dilapidations, and afterwards takes another benefice, whereby his former benefice becomes void, his successor may have an action against him, and declare that by the custom of the kingdom he ought to pay him *tantas denariorum summas quantæ sufficient ad reparandum, &c.* 3 *Lev.* 268. In case a parson comes to a living, the buildings wherof are in decay by dilapidations, and his predecessor did not leave a sufficient personal estate to repair them, so that he is without remedy; he is to have the defects surveyed by workmen, and attested under their hands in the presence of witnesses, which may be a means to secure him from the encumbrance brought upon him by the fault of his predecessor. *Country Parson's Companion,* 60.

By 17 *Geo.* 3. *c.* 53, the incumbent of any ecclesiastical living, whereon there is no house of habitation, or one that is so ruinous or mean that one year's net income will not build or repair it, after an estimate, on oath, laid before the ordinary and patron, may borrow not more than two years income, and mortgage the living for twenty-five years, or till repaired, with interest and costs, which mortgage shall bind the succeeding incumbents.

The mortgagee is to execute a counterpart, which is to be registered by the register of the diocese for 5*s.* to pay 1*s.* for a search, and a copy to be evidence. *Ibid.*

On failure of payment of principal and interest, forty days after due, the mortgagee may distrain. *Ibid.*

The money borrowed, to be paid to a person nominated by the ordinary, who is to give security, and contract and pay for the work, and the surplus is to be laid out in lasting improvements by order of the ordinary, patron, and incumbent. *Ibid.*

The ordinary to inquire into the condition of the buildings, when the incumbent entered; every incumbent to pay the interest yearly, and 5 *per cent. per ann.* of the principal, and if not resident twenty weeks in the year, to pay 10 *per cent. per ann.* of the principal; and on paying 5 *per cent.* only to produce a certificate of two ministers of adjoining parishes of his residence; and when the buildings are completed he is to insure them against fire; on death or avoidance the annual payments to be in proportion between the late and present incumbent. *Ibid.*

If the living is worth 100*l.* *per ann.* or more, and has no house, or a ruinous one, and the incumbent is not resident for 20 weeks in any year, the ordinary may (if the incumbent neglects to make application for the purposes aforesaid) with the consent of the patron, procure a plan and estimate, and proceed to mortgage, in such manner as the parson is directed by this act. *Ibid.*

All money recovered or received from the former incumbent's representatives, for dilapidations, to go in improvements, and where buildings are necessary, the ordinary, patron, and incumbent may purchase a house within one mile of the church, and land not above two acres for each 100*l.* *per ann.* and the money may be raised by the sale of the glebe or tithes, by joint consent. *Ibid.*

Governors of queen Anne's bounty may lend 100*l.* to each living under 50*l.* *per ann.* (to promote this act) interest free; and if above 50*l.* *per ann.* may lend two years value on interest at four *per cent.* and the universities of Oxford or Cambridge, being patrons, may advance money for the purposes of the act, interest free; and if the patron is a minor, idiot, lunatic, or feme covert, the guardian, committee, or husband, may act, and it shall be binding. *Ibid.*

All writings under this act are to be free from the stamp-duty. If a corporation be patron, all acts by them to be under their common seal; where the rector or vicar nominates to a chapel or perpetual cure, his patron to consent. Disputes as to residence to be settled by the ordinary; and the person laying out the money may be allowed 5 *per cent.* for so doing. *Ibid.*

If the crown be patron, and the living above 20*l.* *per ann.* in the king's books, the first lord of the treasury is to consent; under 20*l.* *per ann.* the lord chancellor, and in the duchy of Lancaster the chancellor thereof. *Ibid.*

If an archbishop, bishop, or ecclesiastical corporation, sole or aggregate, be lord of the manor, they may grant the waste in perpetuity to build on, leaving sufficient for the commoners, with the consent of the lessees. *Ibid.*

By 21 *Geo.* 3. *c.* 66. the incumbent of every living, whereof the glebes, tithes, and other profits have been or shall be mortgaged for the purposes of the above act, shall pay to the mortgagee, beside interest, 5 *per cent.* *per ann.* of the principal, if resident, or 10 *per cent.* if non-resident.

DILATORY PLEAS, are such as are put in merely for delay, as coverture, misnomer, and the like, and there may be a demurrer to a dilatory plea, or issue may be taken on the fact, if false. If the plea is true in fact, and good in law, and is in abatement, the plaintiff must enter up judgment of *cassetur billa* before he commences a new suit. If the plea is adjudged ill, on demurrer, there must be a *respondeas ouster*, and defendant must plead another plea. If issue in fact, is taken, and found by the jury, for plaintiff, in case, &c. they assess the damages, in debt, the judgment for plaintiff is final, &c. And the truth of a dilatory plea must be verified by affidavit of the fact, by stat. 4 *Ann. c.* 16. *s.* 11.

DILIGIATUS, outlawed, *i. e. de lege ejectus.* *Cowel. Blount.*

DILLIGROUT, was a tenure in serjeanty, by which lands were held of the king, by the service of finding dilligrout, *i. e. pottage*, at the coronation of the king. *Cowel. Blount.*

DIMIDIETAS, is used in our records for a moiety, or one half. *Ibid.*

DIMINUTION, (*diminutio*) is where the plaintiff or defendant in a writ of error alleges to the court that part of the record is omitted and remains in the inferior court not certified; whereupon he prays that it may be certified by *certiorari*. *Co. Ent.* 232, 242.

DIMISSORY LETTERS, (*literæ dimissoriæ*) are such as are used where a candidate for holy orders has a title in one diocese, and is to be ordained in another: the proper diocesan sends his letters dimissory directed to some other ordaining bishop, giving leave that the bearer may be ordained, and have such a cure within his district. *Cowel. Blount.*

DIOCESE, (*diœcesis*) signifies the circuit of every bishop's jurisdiction. For this realm hath two sorts of divisions; one into shires or counties, in respect to the temporal state; and another into dioceses, in regard to the ecclesiastical state. *Co. Lit.* 94. And the kingdom is said to be divided in its ecclesiastical jurisdiction into two provinces of Canterbury and York; each of which provinces is divided into dioceses, and every diocese into archdeaconries, and archdeaconries into parishes, &c. *Wood's Inst.* 2.

DISABILITY, (*disabilitas*) is where a person is disabled, or made incapable to inherit any lands, or do such acts which otherwise he might. And this disability is either by the *common law* as in the cases of *attainder* of treason or felony, working corruption of blood; *lunacy* or *ideocy*, *infancy*, *coverture*, and *alienage*, or by statute as in the case of officers not taking the oaths, who are incapable to hold offices, and many other cases. *Terms de Ley.* 4 *Rep.* 123, 4. 5 *Rep.* 21. 6 *Rep.* 43. 11 *Rep.* 77. *Stat.* 12 & 13 *W.* 3. *c.* 2. 1 *Geo.* 2. *stat.* 2. *c.* 4.

In equity, if a plaintiff is not entitled to sue by reason of any personal disability, which is apparent on his bill, the defendant may demur, therefore if an infant or a married woman, an ideot or a lunatic exhibit a bill, if they appear on the face of it to be thus incapable of instituting a suit alone, and no next friend or committee is named in the bill, the defendant may demur, but if the incapacity does not appear upon the face of the bill, the defendant must take advantage of it by plea. *Mitf.* 135.

This objection extends to the whole bill, and advantage may be taken of it, as well in the case of a bill for discovery merely, as in the case of a bill for relief: for the defendant in a bill for a discovery merely, being always entitled to costs after a full answer as a matter of course would be materially injured by being compelled to answer a bill exhibited by persons whose property is not in their own disposal, and who are therefore incapable of paying the costs. *Ibid.* 136.

In a plea of disability to the person of the plaintiff for matters not appearing on the face of the bill, it may be shewn that he is disabled to sue being, 1st, outlawed; or 2d, excommunicated, or 3d, a popish rescusant convict; or 4th, attainted in a *præmunire*, or of treason or felony; or 5th, an alien, or it may be shewn; 6th, that the the plaintiff is incapable of insituting the suit alone. *Mitf.* 185.

A plea of this kind is in the nature of a plea in abatement of the suit. *Ibid.*

1. A person outlawed is disabled from suing in a court of justice, and if a bill is filed in his name, the defendant may plead the outlawry, which whilst it remains in force, will delay the proceeding. The record of the outlawry, or the *capias* thereupon, must be pleaded *sub pede sigilli*, and is usually annexed to the plea: a plea of outlawry, in a suit for the same duty or thing for which relief is sought by the bill, is insufficient according to the rule of law, and shall be disallowed of course, as put in for delay, otherwise a plea of outlawry is always a good plea, so long as the outlawry remains in force; but if that is reversed, the plaintiff upon payment of costs, may sue out fresh process against the defendant, and compel him to answer the bill. Outlawry, in a plaintiff, executor or administrator cannot be pleaded, for he sues in *auter droit*; it is equally insufficient, if alleged in disability of a person named in the bill, as the next friend of an infant, plaintiff, or in an information as a relater. *Mitf.* 186.

2. The defendant may plead that the plaintiff is excommunicated, which must be certified by the ordinary; either by letters patent containing a positive affirmation, that the plaintiff stands excommunicated, and for what; or by letters testimonial reciting *quod scrutatis registeriis invenitur*, either of those certificates must be *sub sigillo*, and so pleaded. Excommunication is a good plea to an executor or administrator, though they sue in *auter droit*; but not to the next friend of an infant. This, like the plea of outlawry, ceases to be a bar, when the disability is removed; and therefore, the plaintiff purchasing letters of absolution, may, as at law, sue out fresh process, and compel the defendant to answer the bill. *Mitf.* 186, 7.

3. By stat. 3 *Jac.* 1. *c.* 5. *s.* 11. every popish recusant convict is in many cases disabled to sue in the same manner as a person excommunicated: the instances of a plea of conviction of recusancy, have probably been rare, as no traces of any occur in the books of reports, nor does the form of a plea appear in the books of practice: if advantage was attempted to be taken of this statute, the court would probably require the same averments to support the plea, as are necessary to a plea of the same nature at law: this plea also ceases to be a bar, if the plaintiff, by conforming, removes the disability. *Mitf.* 187.

4. A plea, that the plaintiff is disabled from suing, being attainted, is equally rare, it would probably be likewise judged with the same strictness, as if it was a plea at law. *Mitf.* 187.

5. There is little more to be found in the books upon the subject of a plea, that the plaintiff is an alien: an alien, who is not an alien enemy, is under no disability of suing for any personal demand, and an alien enemy may sue under some circumstances. A plea has been put in to a bill filed by an alien infidel, not of the Christian faith, and was attempted to be supported, upon the ground, that the plaintiff was upon a cross bill incapable of being examined upon oath: the plea was overruled without argument. *Mitf.* 188.

6. If a bill is filed in the name of any person incapable *alone* of insituting a suit; as an infant, a married woman, or an ideot or lunatic so found by inquisition, the defendant may plead the infancy, the coverture, or the inquisition of ideocy or lunacy in abatement of the suit. *Mitf.* 188.

DISADVOCARE, to deny, or not acknowledge a thing. *Cowel. Blount.*

DISAGREEMENT, will make a nullity of a thing, that had essence before. *Co. Lit.* 380.

DISALT, according to Littleton, is to disable a person. *Lit.* tit. *Dis.*

DISBOSCATIO, a turning wood ground into arable or pasture. *Cowel. Blount.*

DISCARCARE, (from *dis* and *cargo*) is to unlade a ship or vessel by taking out the cargo or goods. *Ibid.*

DISCEIT, a writ or action for fraud and deceit. See *Deceit.*

DISCENT, (Lat. *descendus*, Fr. *discent*). Discent or hereditary succession; is the order or means whereby lands or tenements devolve upon any man from his ancestors; and this is either by common law, custom, or statute.

Discent at common law is lineal, or collateral: lineal is a discent downward in a right line, from the grandfather to the father, the father to the son, son to the grandson, and so on, and the lineal heir shall first inherit. Collateral, is a discent which springeth out of the side of the whole blood, as another branch thereof; such as the grandfather's brother, father's brother, and so downward. *Co. Lit.* 10, 11. Therefore, if a man purchaseth lands in fee-simple, and dies without issue, for default of the right line, he which is next of kin in the collateral line of the whole blood, though never so remote, comes in by discent as heir to him; for there is a next of kin by right of representation, and by right of propinquity or nearness of blood. *Lit.* 2. 1 *Vent.* 415. 3 *Rep.* 40.

To have land in fee simple by discent, a person must be heir of the whole blood; he is to be the next, and most worthy of blood, to the ancestor; and he ought to be heir to him that was last actually seised. Where ands descend to the son from the father, and he enters on the lands, and dies seised thereof, without having any issue, this land will descend to the heirs of the part of the father, who are of the whole blood; and if there are none such, the land shall escheat: so where lands descend on the part of the mother. *Lit. sect.* 4. *Co. Lit.* 13. And there is a maxim in law, that where lands descend on the part of the father, the heirs of the mother shall never inherit; and when lands descend on the part of the mother, the heirs of the father shall never inherit. *Co. Lit.* 14. But if there has been a fine and render of lands, claimed by a party, as heir at law, *ex parte materna*, this will alter the quality of the estate; so that it shall descend to the heir *ex parte paterna*. 6 *Rep.* 63. *Carthew* 141.

Also if a man seised of land, as heir of the part of his mother, make a feoffment, and take back an estate to him and his heirs; this, as a purchase, alters the discent, and if he die without issue, the heir of the part of the father shall inherit it. *Co. Lit.* 12. There is a difference between discents from father and mother to their children, and discents between brothers and sisters; for a son or a daughter need be only of the blood of either the father or mother, which hath the inheritance, to inherit them: though the brothers and sisters must be of the same father and mother, to inherit one another. *Noy* 68.

If a man hath issue two sons by divers wives, the younger brother of the half blood shall not have land purchased by the elder brother, on his dying without issue; but the elder brother's uncle or next cousin shall have it. *Co. Lit.* 14. The elder brother of the whole blood shall have land by discent, purchased by a middle or younger brother, if such die without issue; (for as to discents between brethren, the eldest is the most worthy of blood to inherit to them as well as to the father). And if there be no brother or sister, the uncle shall have it as heir, and not the father: and yet it may afterwards come to the father, as heir to the uncle; likewise if the father hath issue another son or daughter, after the discent to the uncle, that issue may enter upon the uncle, and hold the estate. *Lit.* 3. 3 *Rep.* 40.

The next and most worthy of blood are the male and all descendants from him, before the females; and the female on the part of the father, before the male or female of the part of the mother: and the eldest brother, and his posterity, shall have lands in fee-simple before any younger brother. *Ibid.*

Also a sister of the whole blood shall be preferred, and taken before the younger brother, which is of the half blood; but such a younger brother, though he may not be heir to a brother, for want of the whole blood, yet he may be heir to his father, or his uncle. *Co. Lit.* 14. 3 *Rep.* 41.

All the descendants from a person, who by our laws might have been heir to another, hold the same right as that common root from whom they are derived: so that the son, or grandchild, whether son or daughter of the eldest son, takes before the youngest son; and a son or grandchild of the eldest brother before the youngest brother: and so it is through all degrees of discents; by representation, the proximity is transferred from the root to the branches, and gives them the same preference, as next and worthiest of blood. *Hale's Hist. L.* 237.

The great grandchild of the elder brother, whether it be a son or a daughter, shall here be preferred as the heir before the younger brother; for though a female be less worthy than the male, yet she stands in right of representation of the eldest brother, who was more worthy than the younger. *Hale's Hist. L.* 237.

As to being heir to him that was last seised: if tenant in fee-simple hath a son and a daughter by one woman or venter, and a son by another venter, and dies seised, and the eldest son dies without issue, before actual seisin, the younger brother as heir to the father shall have the estate; but if the elder brother had entered on the lands, the sister would have it as heir to him. *Co. Lit.* 11, 15. *Lit.* 8.

None can inherit any lands as heir, but only the blood of the first purchaser; as if the father make a purchase, the blood of the mother shall not have the estate: but if a son purchases, and there is no heir on the side of the father, the land shall go to the heirs on the side of the mother; for they are of the blood of the son of the first purchaser, and he hath the blood of both father and mother. *Lit.* 4. *Co. Lit.* 12.

So that there is a difference where the son purchaseth lands in fee-simple, and where he cometh to them by discent. Land thus purchased may go to the heirs of the father and mother of the purchaser; unless it be once attached in the heir of the part of the father, for then the heirs of the mother cannot have it, because they are not of the blood of him who was last seised. 49 *E.* 3. 12. *Finch.* 119. Where, for want of heirs of a purchaser, of the part of his father, or when such heir had not entered, the lands descend to the line of the mother; there the heirs of the mother of her father's side, shall take in succession, before her heirs of the part of her mother. *Hale's Hist. L.* 247. *Plowd.* 444. The discent of lands is particularly and very judiciously treated of by Mr. Justice Blackstone, in his Commentaries. 2 V. 201, &c.

The law takes no notice of the disability of the father in case of discent, but only of the immediate relation of brothers and sisters, as to their estates; so that the inability of the father doth not hinder the discent between them: for example, a man had issue a son and a daughter, and was attainted of treason, and died; the son purchased lands and died without issue; and it was adjudged that, notwithstanding the attainder of the father, the daughter shall take by discent from her brother, because the discent between them was immediate, and the law doth not regard the disability of the father. 4 *Leon.* 5. 1 *Nels. Abr.* 645.

If there be father and son, and the son is attainted of treason or felony in the father's life time, and yet out-live his father, the land by discent shall not come to such son, nor any of his issue; but if he die before the father, it will descend to his other children. 4 *Rep.* 31, 124. And where a person seised of lands, hath issue two daughters, if one of them commits felony, after the father's death, both daughters being alive, a moiety shall descend to one daughter, and the other shall escheat. *Co. Lit.* 163.

Inheritances may descend but not ascend: and in the right line, children inherit their ancestors without limitation; but the ancestors may not take from their children, for the father can never come to the lands which his son hath purchased, by lineal ascent; though he may by collateral ascent, where the son's lands come to the uncle, and then to the father. In the collateral line, the uncle inherits the nephew, and the nephew the uncle. *Lit.* 3. 3 *Rep.* 40. *Vaugh.* 244.

In fine, *lands and tenements in fee-simple* DESCEND, first, *to the eldest son as heir, and to his issue; the sons first, in order of birth; and for want of sons, to all the daughters equally, for where there are females in equal degree, they all inherit as one heir, and as coparceners;* secondly, *if the eldest son hath no issue, then to his next eldest brother of the whole blood, and his heirs, and for want of a brother, to his sister or sisters of the whole blood, and her and their issue;* thirdly, *if there be no brother or sister, to the uncle and his issue; and for want of an uncle, to an aunt or aunts, and her and their issue;* fourthly, *thence to the father;* fifthly, *thence to the half;* and sixthly, *for want of uncle, father, and half blood, to the next of kin in the collateral line.* *Wood's Inst.* 218. 2 *Black. Com.* 201.

DISCENT *of lands* in fee-simple by custom, are of several kinds, sometimes to all the sons, or to all the brothers, when one brother dieth without issue, as in *gavel* kind: sometimes to the youngest, as in *borough* English: sometimes to his eldest daughter, or to the youngest as is the case in respect to some customary or copyhold lands. *Dr. & St. Di.* 1. *c.* 10. *Lit.* 210, 211. 1 *Inst.* 110. b. 140. a. and b, 175, b.

DISCENT *by statute.* Discents of estates in *fee-tail*, are by the stat. of *Westm.* 2 and 13 *Ed.* 1. *c.* 1., to be according to the manner of the settlement or limitation.

DISCENT OF CROWN LANDS. All the lands whereof the king is seised *in jure coronæ*, shall *secundum jus coronæ* attend upon and follow the crown; so that to whomsoever the crown descends, these lands and possessions descend also. *Plowd.* 247. *Co. Lit.* 15.

The dignity of the crown of England, for want of heirs male, is descendable immediately to the eldest daughter, and her posterity; and so it has been declared by act of parliament. *Stat.* 25 *H.* 8. *cap.* 22.

DISCENT OF DIGNITIES. A dignity differs from common inheritances, and goes not according to the rules of the common law; for it descends to the half blood, and there is no copartnership in it, but the eldest takes the whole. *Co. Lit.* 27. The dignity of peerage is personal, annexed to the blood, and so inseparable that it cannot be transferred to any person, or surrendered even to the crown; it can move neither forward nor backward, but only downward to posterity; and nothing but corruption of blood, as if the ancestor be attainted of treason or felony, can hinder the discent to the right heir. *Lex Constitutionis, p.* 85.

DISCHARGE, on writs and process, &c. is where a man confined by some legal writ or authority, doth that which by law he is required to do; whereupon he is released or discharged from the matter for which he was confined. 1 *Lil. Abr.* 470.

DISCLAIMER, (*disclamium*, from the Fr. *clamer*, with the privative *dis*) is a plea containing an express denial, or renouncing of a thing. *Terms de Ley.*

And by stat. 21 *Jac.* 1. *cap.* 16. *s.* 5. in all actions of trespass *quare clausum fregit*, wherein the defendant shall disclaim any title to the land, and the trespass be by negligence or involuntary, the defendant shall be admitted to plead a disclaimer, and that the trespass was by negligence or involuntary, and a tender of sufficient amends before the action brought; and if the issue be found for the defendant, or the plaintiff be nonsuited, the plaintiff shall be barred from the said action, and all suits concerning the same.

Also in chancery, a defendant may disclaim all right or title to the matter in demand by the plaintiff's bill, or by any part of it: but a disclaimer can hardly be put in alone; for if the defendant has been made a party by mistake, having never had any interest in the matter or question, yet as he may have had an interest which he may have parted with, the plaintiff may require an answer sufficient to answer whether that is the fact or not; and if in truth it is so, an answer seems necessary to enable the plaintiff to make the proper party instead of the defendant disclaiming: the form of a disclaimer alone, seems to be simply an assertion, that the defendant disclaims all right and title to the matter in demand, but the forms given in the books are all of an answer and disclaimer. *Mitf.* 253.

If the defendant disclaims, the court will in general, dismiss the bill as against him, with costs: but it is said, that if the plaintiff shews probable cause for exhibiting the bill, he may pray a decree against the defendant, upon the ground of the disclaimer. *Prec. Reg.* 141. *Atk.* 582. And where the defendant disclaims, the plaintiff is not to reply. 2 *Br. P. C.* *Mitf.* 254.

A defendant may demur to one part of a bill, plead to another, answer to another, and *disclaim* as to another: but all these defences must clearly refer to separate and distinct parts of the bill: for the defendant cannot *by answer claim, what by disclaimer he has declared he has no right to:* and if a disclaimer and answer are inconsistent, the matter will be taken most strongly against the defendant upon the disclaimer. *Mitf.* 254.

DISCONTINUANCE, (*discontinuatio*, derived from the Fr. *discontinuer*, i. e. *cessare*) signifies an interruption or breaking off; and is twofold, discontinuance of possession, and discontinuance in pleading. *Co. Lit.* 325. *F. N. B.* 191.

A discontinuance of *estate* may be five ways, *viz.* by feoffment, fine, recovery, release, and confirmation with warranty. 1 *Rep.* 44. But an exchange will not make a discontinuance; as if tenant in tail exchanges land with another, that is not any discontinuance, by reason no livery is requisite thereon. 2 *Danv.* 57. And it is the same of a bargain and sale, &c. And an alteration of such things as lie in grant, and not in livery, works no discontinuance; for such grant does no wrong either to the issue in tail, or him in reversion or remainder, because nothing passeth but during the life of the particular tenant, which is lawful. *Co. Lit.* 332.

DISCONTINUANCE OF PLEA, is where divers things should be pleaded to, and some are omitted; this is a discontinuance. 1 *Nels. Abr.* 660, 661.

DISCONTINUANCE OF PROCESS, is when the opportunity of prosecution is lost for that time; or the plaintiff is dismissed the court, &c. And every suit, whether civil or criminal, and every process therein, ought to be properly continued from day to day, &c. from its commencement to its conclusion; and the suffering any default or gap herein, is called a discontinuance: the continuance of the suit by improper process, or by giving the party an illegal day, is properly a miscontinuance. 2 *Hawk.* 298.

But by stat. 32 *H.* 8. *cap.* 30. All discontinuances, miscontinuances and negligences therein, of plaintiff or defendant, are cured after verdict.

DISCOVERT, is used in the law for a woman unmarried or widow, one not within the bonds of matrimony. *Law Fr. Dict. Cowel. Blount.*

DISCOVERY, *bill of.* A course of proceeding in the courts of equity for the discovery of facts, resting in the knowledge of a defendant: or of deeds or writings or other things in his custody or power, and seeking no relief in consequence of the discovery. *Mitf.* 52.

This bill is commonly used in aid of the jurisdiction of some other court, as to enable the plaintiff to prosecute or defend an action at law, or proceeding before the king in council, or any other legal proceeding of a nature merely civil, before a jurisdiction which cannot compel a discovery on oath; except that the court has in some instances refused to give this aid to the jurisdiction of inferior courts. A bill of this nature must state the matter touching which a discovery is sought, the interest of the plaintiff and defendant in the subject, and the right of the first to require the discovery from the other. *Mitf.* 52.

The courts of equity will not, however, entertain a bill for a discovery to aid the action of a common informer, though the statute under which he may sue (as under the statutes against gaming for the recovering back of monies lost at play) may allow of a bill for a discovery, and direct that the defendant shall not demur thereto: for this the court will intend to be for the benefit of a party grieved, and not for the furtherance of the views of a common informer, contrary to the positive rule of law, that no man is compellable to criminate himself. *Holloway q. t.* v. *Ogden, reported in Mr. Anstruther's Exchequer Reports,* 1803, 4.

DISCRETION, (*discretio*) when any thing is left to any person to be done according to his discretion, the law intends it must be done with sound discretion, and according to law: and the court of *B. R.* hath a power to redress things that are otherwise done, notwithstanding they are left to the discretion of those that do them. 1 *Lil. Abr.* 477.

DISFRANCHISE, is to take away one's freedom or privilege: it is the contrary to enfranchise. And corporations have power to disfranchise members, for doing any thing against their oaths; but not for contempts, &c. 11 *Rep.* 98.

DISHERISON, is an old word which signifies as much as disinheriting: mentioned in the stat. 20 *Ed.* 1. and 8 *R.* 2.

DISHERITOR, one that disinheriteth, or puts another out of his inheritance. *Cowel. Blount.*

DISMES, (*decimæ*) signify tithes. *Comyn's Dig.* Also the tenths of all spiritual livings given to the prince, which is called a perpetual dism. *Stat.* 2 & 3 *Ed.* 3. *cap.* 35. See *Tithes.*

DISPARAGEMENT, matching an heir in marriage under his degree, or against decency. *Co. Lit.* 107.

DISPAUPER. When a person by reason of his poverty, is admitted to sue *in forma pauperis*; and afterwards, the privilege is taken from him, he is said to be dispaupered. See *Forma Pauperis.*

DISPENSATION. By 25 *H.* 8. *cap.* 21.

"the archbishop of Canterbury has power "of dispensing in any case wherein *dispensations* (not contrary to the law of God) were "formerly granted by the see of Rome; and "may grant *dispensations* to the king, as well "as to his subjects: but such dispensations "shall not be granted out of the realm, &c. "And during the vacancy of the see of Canterbury, the guardian of the spiritualities may grant dispensations."

The archbishop of Canterbury grants dispensations, not only in his own province, but in the province of York; and the archbishop of York, and other bishops, dispense as they were wont to do, by the common law and custom of the realm. *Wood's Inst.* 26. And every bishop of common right has the power of institution into benefices, and of dispensing in common cases, &c. *Ibid.* 505.

DISPENSATIONS OF THE KING. If a dispensation by the archbishop of Canterbury, is to be in extraordinary matters, or in a case that is new, the king and his counsel are to be consulted: and it ought to be confirmed under the broad seal. The king's authority to grant dispensations remains as it did at common law; notwithstanding the 25 *H.* 8. *c.* 21. *Cro. Eliz.* 542, 601. The dispensation of the king, &c. makes a thing prohibited, lawful to be done by him who hath it: but *malum in se* will not admit of a dispensation. *March Rep.* 213. Where the subject hath an immediate interest in an act of parliament, the king cannot dispense with it; but where the king is intrusted with the management thereof, and the subject interested by way of consequence only, he may. *March* 214, 216. This must be where the king is, by the act itself, empowered to dispense with it. When an offence wrongs none but the king; or if the suit is only the king's for the breach of a penal law, that is not to the damage of a third person, the king may dispense: but in case the suit is the king's, for the benefit of another, he cannot. *Vaugh.* 334, 339, 344, &c.

DISPENSATION BY NON OBSTANTE. Formerly if any statute tended to restrain some prerogative incident to the person of the king; by a clause in grants of *non obstante*, he might dispense with it. 2 *Hawk.* 390. But by 1 *W. & M. sess.* 2. *cap.* 2. no dispensation by *non obstante*, of, or to any statute, or any part thereof, shall be allowed, but the same shall be held void, and of none effect, except a dispensation be allowed in such statute.

DISPERSONARE, is to scandalize or disparage. *Blount.*

DISSIGNARE, to break open a seal. *Ibid.*

DISSEISIN, (from the Fr. *dissaisin*) is the unlawful dispossessing a man of his right. As where a person enters into lands or tenements, and his entry is not lawful, and keeps him that hath the estate from the possession thereof. *Bract. lib.* 4. *c.* 3. And disseisin is of two sorts; either single disseisin, committed without force of arms; or disseisin by force, but this latter is more properly deforcement. *Brit. cap.* 42, 43. See *Assise of Novel Disseisin* and *Entry.*

DISSEISOR, is he that disseiseth or puts another out of his land, without order of law: and a disseisee is he that is so put out. 4 *H.* 4. 1 *E.* 5, 8. *Stat.* 20 *H.* 3. *c.* 3.

DISSENTERS, are non-conformists who secede from the church, and the service and worship thereof. But by 1 *Will. & Mar. c.* 18. the statutes of Q. Eliz. and K. James I. concerning the discipline of the church, are not to extend to Protestant dissenters: but the persons dissenting, are to subscribe the declaration of 30 *Car.* 2. *c.* 1. and take the oaths, or the declaration of fidelity, &c. *But they must not hold their meetings, till their place of worship is certified to the bishop, &c. or to the justices at their quarter sessions, and registered there; also they are not to keep the doors of their meeting-houses locked, &c.* And if any person disturb them in their worship, on conviction at the sessions, he shall forfeit 20*l.*

DISTILLERS. See EXCISE.

DISTRESS, (*districtio*) in the most general sense, is any thing which is taken and distrained for rent behind, or in arrear. But by the common law, besides distresses for rent, there is a distress for homage, fealty, or any services; for fines and amercements; and for damage-feasant, &c. And there are likewise distresses in actions compulsory to cause a man to appear in court: as upon a *distringas* after a *clausum fregit*, &c. *Co. Lit.* 57, 205.

The law of distresses is of great use and consequence, it will therefore be fit to consider *first*, for what injuries a distress may be taken; *secondly*, what things may be distrained; and, *thirdly*, the manner of taking, disposing of, and avoiding distresses.

I. A distress, *districtio*, is the taking of a personal chattel out of the possession of the wrong doer into the custody of the party injured to procure a satisfaction for the wrong committed. 1st, The usual injury, for which a distress may be taken is that of non-payment of rent. And distresses were incident by the common law to every rent-service, and by particular reservation to rent-charges also; but not to rent-seck, till the statute 4 *Geo.* 2. *c.* 28. extended the same remedy to all rents alike, and thereby in effect abolished all material distinctions between them. So that it is now an universal principle, that a distress may be taken for any kind of rent in arrear; the detaining whereof beyond the day of payment is an injury to him that is entitled to receive it. 2dly, For neglecting to do suit to the lord's court (*Bro. Abr. tit. Distress,* 15.) or other certain personal service (*Co. Lit.* 46.), the lord may distrain, of common right. 3dly, For amercements in a court-leet, a distress may be had of common right, but not for the amercements in a court-baron, without a special prescription to warrant it. (*Brownl.* 36.) 4thly, Another injury, for which distresses may be taken, is where a man finds beasts of a stranger wandering on his grounds, *damage-feasant;* that is, doing him hurt or damage, by treading down his grass, or the like; in which case the owner of the soil may distrein them, till satisfaction be made him for the injury he has thereby sustained. 5thly, and lastly, for several duties and penalties inflicted by special acts of parliament, (as for assessments made by commissioners of sewers (*Stat.* 7 *Ann. c.* 10.) or for the relief of the poor) (*Stat.* 43 *Eliz. c.* 3.) remedy by distress and sale is given; and such distresses (4 *Burr.* 589.) are partly analogous to the antient distress at common law, as being repleviable, and the like; but more resembling the common law process of execution, by seizing and selling the goods of the debtor under a writ of *fieri facias.* 3 *Black. Com.* 6, 7.

II. As to the things which may be distrained, or taken in distress, it is a general rule, that all chattels personal are liable to be distrained, unless particularly protected or exempted. Instead, therefore, of mentioning what things are distrainable, it will be easier to recount those which are not so, with the reason of their particular exemptions (*Co. Lit.* 47.) And, 1st, as every thing which is distrained is presumed to be the property of the wrong doer, it will follow that such things, wherein no man can have an absolute and valuable property (as dogs, cats, rabbits, and all animals *feræ naturæ*) cannot be distrained. Yet if deer (which are *feræ naturæ*) are kept in a private inclosure for the purpose of sale or profit, this so far changes their nature by reducing them to a kind of stock or merchandize, that they may be distrained for rent. 2dly. Whatever is in the personal use or occupation of any man, is for the time privileged and protected from any distress; as an axe with which a man is cutting wood, or a horse while a man is riding him. But horses, drawing a cart, may (cart and all) be distrained for rent-arrere; also it was formerly held, 1 *Sid.* 940. that if a horse, with a man riding him, was found *damage-feasant,* or trespassing in another's grounds, the horse notwithstanding his rider, might be distreined and led away to the pound, but this hath been since held not to be law. 6 *Ter. Rep.* 138. 3dly. Valuable things in the way of trade shall not be liable to distress. As a horse standing in a smith's shop to be shoed, or in a common inn; or cloth at a taylor's house; or corn sent to a mill, or a market. For all these are protected and privileged for the benefit of trade; and are supposed in common presumption not to belong to the owner of the house, but to his customers. But, generally speaking, whatever goods and chattels the landlord finds upon the premises, *whether they in fact belong to the tenant or a stranger,* are distrainable by him for rent: for otherwise a door would be open to infinite frauds upon the landlord; and the stranger has his remedy over by action on the case against the tenant, if by the tenant's default, the chattels are distrained, so that he cannot render them when called upon. With regard to a stranger's beasts which are found on the tenant's land, the following distinctions are however taken. If they are put in by consent of the owner of the beasts, they are distrainable immediately afterwards for rent arrere by the landlord, (*Cro. Eliz.* 549.) So also, if the stranger's cattle break the fences, and commit a trespass by coming on the land, they are distrainable immediately by the lessor for his tenant's rent, as a punishment to the owner of the beasts for the wrong committed through his negligence, (*Co. Litt.* 47.) But if the lands were not sufficiently fenced so as to keep out cattle, the landlord cannot distrain them, till they have been *levant* and *couchant* (*levantes et cuchantes*) on the land; that is, have been long enough there to have laid down and rose up to feed; which in general is held to be one night at least: and then the law presumes, that the owner may have notice whither his cattle have strayed, and it is his own negligence not to have taken them away. Yet, if the lessor, or his tenant were bound to repair the fences, and did not, and thereby the cattle escaped into their grounds without the negligence or default of the owner; in this case, though the cattle may have been *levant* and *couchant,* yet they are not distrainable for rent, till actual notice is given to the owner, that they are there, and he neglects to remove them, (*Lutw.* 1580.): for the law will not suffer the landlord to take advantage of his own or his tenant's wrong. 4thly. There are also other things privileged by the antient common law; as a man's tools and utensils of his trade, the axe of a carpenter, the books of a scholar, and the like: which are said to be privileged for the sake of the public, because the taking them away would disable the owner from serving the commonwealth in his station. So, beasts of the plough, *averia carucæ,* and sheep, are privileged from distresses at common law, (*Stat.* 51 *H.* 3. *st.* 4. *de districtione scaccarii*); while goods or other sort of beasts, which Bracton calls *catalla otiosa,* may be distrained. But, as beasts of the plough may be taken in execution for debt, so they may be for distresses by statute, which partakes of the nature of executions, (4 *Burr.* 589.) And perhaps the true reason, why these and the tools of a man's trade were privileged at the common law, was because the distress was then merely intended to compel the payment of the rent, and not as a satisfaction for its non-payment: and therefore, to deprive the party of the instruments and means of paying it, would counteract the very end of the distress (4 *Burr.* 588.) 5thly. Nothing shall be distrained for rent, which may not be rendered again in as good plight as when it was distrained: for which reason milk, fruit, victuals, and the like, cannot be distrained; a distress at common law being only in the nature of a pledge or security, to be restored in the same plight when the debt is paid. So, antiently, sheaves or shocks of corn could not be distrained, because some damage must needs accrue in their removal: but a cart loaded with corn might; as that could be safely restored. But now by statute 2 *W. & M. c.* 5. corn in sheaves or cocks, or loose in the straw, or hay in barns or ricks, or otherwise, may be distrained as well as other chattels. 6thly. Lastly, things fixed to the freehold may not be distrained; as caldrons, windows, doors, and chimney-pieces: for they savour of the realty. For this reason also, corn growing, could not be distrained; till the statute 11 *Geo.* 2. *c.* 19. empowered landlords to distrain corn, grass, or other products of the earth, and to cut and gather them when ripe. 3 *Black. Com.* 8, 9, 10.

How distresses may be taken, disposed of, or avoided.] Distresses formerly were looked upon in no other light than as a mere pledge or security, for payment of rent or other duties, or satisfaction for damage done. And so the law still continues with regard to distresses of beasts taken *damage-feasant*, and for other causes, not altered by act of parliament; over which the distrainor has no other power than to retain them till satisfaction is made. But, *distresses for rent arrere* being found by the legislature to be the shortest and most effectual method of compelling the payment of such rent, many beneficial laws for this purpose have been made in the present century, which have much altered the common law, as laid down in our antient writers. 3 *Black. Com.* 10.

In the first place then, all distresses must by the common law, be made *on the premises*, and by day, unless in the case of *damage-feasant;* an exception being there allowed, lest the beasts should escape before they are taken (*Co. Litt.* 142.) And when a person intends to make a distress, he must, by himself or his bailiff, enter on the demised premises: formerly during the continuance of the lease, but now (*Stat.* 8 *Ann. c.* 14.) he may distrain within six months after the determination of such lease whereon rent is due during the tenant's possession. If the lessor does not find *sufficient distress on the premises*, formerly he could resort no where else; and therefore tenants, who were knavish, made a practice to convey away their goods and stock fraudulently from the house or lands demised, in order to cheat their landlords. But now (by *stat.* 8 *Ann. c.* 14. 11 *Geo.* 2. *c.* 19.) the landlord may distrain any goods of his tenant, carried off the premises clandestinely, wherever he finds them, within thirty days after, *unless they have been* bona fide *sold for a valuable consideration:* and all persons privy to, or assisting in, such fraudulent conveyance, forfeit double the value to the landlord. *The landlord may also distrain the beasts of his tenant, feeding upon any commons or wastes, appendant or appurtenant to the demised premises.* The landlord might not formerly break open a house, to make a distress, for that is a breach of the peace. But when he was in the house, it was held that he might break open an inner door (*Co. Litt.* 161. *Comberb.* 17.): and now by *Stat.* 11 *Geo.* 2. *c.* 19. he may, by the assistance of the peace officer of the parish, break open in the day time any place, locked up to prevent a distress; oath being first made, in case it be a dwelling-house, of a reasonable ground to suspect that goods are concealed therein. 3 *Black. Com.* 11.

Where a man is intitled to distrain for an entire duty, he ought to distrain for the whole at once; and not for part at one time, and part at another. (2 *Lutw.* 1532.) But if he distrains for the whole, and there is not sufficient on the premises, or he happens to mistake in the value of the thing distrained, and so takes an insufficient distress, he may take a second distress to complete his remedy. (*Cro. Eliz.* 13. *stat.* 17 *Car.* 2. *c.* 7. 4 *Burr.* 59.)

Distresses must be proportioned to the thing distrained for. By the statute of Malbridge, 52 *Hen.* 3. *c.* 4. if any man takes a great or unreasonable distress, for rent-arrere, he shall be heavily amerced for the same. As if (2 *Inst.* 107.) the landlord distrains two oxen for twelve pence rent; the taking of both is an unreasonable distress; but if there were no other distress nearer the value to be found, he might reasonably have distrained one of them. But for homage, fealty, or suit, as also for parliamentary wages, it is said that no distress can be excessive. (*Bro. Abr. t. assise.* 291. *prerogative,* 98.) For as these distresses cannot be sold, the owner, upon making satisfaction, may have his chattels again. The remedy for excessive distresses is by a special action on the statute of Marlbridge; for an action of trespass is not maintainable upon this account, it being no injury at the common law. 1 *Vent.* 104. *Fitzgibb.* 85. 4 *Burr.* 590. 3 *Black. Com.* 12.

When the distress is thus taken, the next consideration is, the disposal of it. For which purpose the things distrained, must in the first place be carried to some pound, and there impounded by the taker. But, in their way thither, they may be rescued by the owner, in case the distress was taken without cause, or contrary to law: as if no rent be due; if they were taken, not on the premises, but upon the highway, or the like; in these cases, the tenant may lawfully make rescue. (*Co. Litt.* 160, 161.) But if they be once impounded, even though taken without any cause, the owner may not break the pound and take them out; for they are then in the custody of the law. *Co. Lit.* 160, 161. 3 *Black. Com.* 12.

A pound (*parcus*, which signifies any inclosure) is either pound-overt, that is, open over head; or pound-covert, that is close. By the statute 1 & 2 *P. & M. c.* 12. no distress of cattle can be driven out of the hundred where it is taken, unless to a pound-overt within the same shire; and within three miles of the place wherein it was taken. This is for the benefit of the tenants, that they may know where to find and replevy the distress. And by statute 11 *Geo.* 2. *c.* 19. which was made for the benefit of landlords, *any person distraining for rent may impound the distress taken upon any part of the same for securing of such distress.* If a live distress, of animals, be impounded in a common pound-overt, the owner must take notice of it at his peril; but if in any special pound-overt, so constituted for this particular purpose, the distrainor must give notice to the owner; and, in both these cases, the owner and not the distrainor, is bound to provide the beasts with food and necessaries. But if they be put in a pound-covert, as in a stable or the like, the landlord or distrainor must feed and sustain them (*Co. Litt.* 47.) A distress of household goods, or other dead chattels, which are liable to be stolen or damaged by weather, ought to be impounded in a pound-covert, else the distrainor must answer for the consequences. 3 *Black.* 13.

When impounded, the goods were formerly, as was before observed, only in the nature of a pledge or security to compel the performance of satisfaction; and upon this account it hath been held (*Cro. Jac.* 148.) that the distrainor is not at liberty to work or use a distrained beast. And thus the law still continues with regard to beasts taken damage-feasant, and distresses for suit or services; which must remain impounded, till the owner makes satisfaction, or contests the right of distraining, by replevying the chattels. And as a distress is at common law only in nature of a security for the rent or damages done, a replevin answers the same end to the distrainor as the distress itself: since the party replevying gives security to return the distress, if the right be determined against him. 3 *Black.* 13, 14.

A distress for a debt due to the crown, unless paid within forty days, was always saleable at the common law (*Bro. Abr. t. distress*, 71.) And for an amercement imposed at a court-leet, the lord might also sell the distress (8 *Rep.* 41.); partly because, being the king's court of record, its process partakes of the royal prerogative (*Bro. Ibid.* 12 *Mod.* 330): but principally because it is in the nature of an execution to levy a legal debt. 3 *Black.* 14.

By 2 *Will. & Mar. c.* 5. where *a distress is taken it may be replevied within five days after taken, and if the tenant and owner of the goods do not* within five days, (*that is*, five days inclusive, 1 *Hen. Black.* 13.) *after the day* on which the same shall be taken, and notice given, and of the cause, left at the dwelling house, &c. replevy the same according to law; then the person distraining, may, with the under sheriff of the county, or constable of the place, &c. (who are required to be assisting) cause the goods to be appraised by two sworn appraisers, and sold to satisfy the rent, &c. leaving the overplus in the constable's hands for the use of the owner.

And by 11 *Geo.* 2. *c.* 19. distresses made for rent justly due, shall not be unlawful, nor distrainers, trespassers *ab initio*, for any irregularity in the disposition thereof; but the parties grieved to have satisfaction for special damage in an action on the case, &c. But no tenant shall recover by such action, if tender of amends hath been made before the action brought. And in all actions of trespass, or on the case, relating to the entry, distress, or sale, made by landlords for rents, the defendants may plead the general issue, and if the plaintiffs become non-suit, &c. shall recover double costs of suit.

Incidental to a distress, is the right of the party whose goods are distrained to replevy (*replegiare*) that is, to take back the pledge, upon giving to the sheriff good security to try the right of taking the distress in a suit at law, and if that be determined against him to return the cattle or goods once more to the hands of the distrainor. See *Replevin.*

DISTRESS OF THE KING. The king may distrain for rent-service, or fee-farm, in all the lands of the tenant wheresoever they be; not only on lands held of himself, but of others: where his tenant is in actual possession, and the land manured with his own beasts, &c. 2 *Inst.* 132. 2 *Danv. Abr.* 643.

DISTRESS OF A TOWN. If a town be assessed to a certain sum, a distress may be taken in any part, subject to the whole duty. 2 *Danv.* 643.

DISTRIBUTION *of intestates' estates according to custom.*] The statute of distribution (which see under title *Administrator*) expressly excepts and reserves the custom of the city of LONDON, of the province of YORK, and of all OTHER PLACES HAVING PECULIAR CUSTOMS OF DISTRIBUTING INTESTATES' EFFECTS. So that, though in those places the restraint of devising is removed by the stautes 4 & 5 *Wil. & Mar. c.* 2. explained by 2 & 3 *Ann. c.* 5. for *York*, 7 & 8 *Wil.* 3. *c.* 38. for *Wales*, and 11 *Geo.* 1. *c.* 18. for *London*, whereby it is enacted, that persons within those districts, and liable to those customs, may if they think proper, dispose of *all their personal estates by will*; and the claims of the widow, children and other regulations, to the contrary are barred: YET their *antient customs e*-

main in full force, with respect to the estates of intestates.

In the first place, therefore, we may observe, that in the city of London, *Ld. Raym.* 1329. and province of York, 2 *Burn. Eccl. Law*, 746. as well as in the kingdom of Scotland, *Ibid.* 782. and probably also in Wales, (concerning which there is little to be gathered, but from the statute 7 & 8 *W.* 3. *c.* 38.) the effects of the intestate, after payment of his debts, are in general divided according to the antient universal doctrine of the *pars rationabilis.* If the deceased leaves a widow and children, his substance (deducting for the widow's apparel and the furniture of her bed-chamber, which in London is called the widow's chamber) is divided into three parts; one of which belongs to the widow, another to the children, and the third to the administrator: if only a widow, or only children, they shall respectively, in either case, take one moiety, and the administrator the other, 1 *P. Wms.* 341. *Salk.* 246.; if neither widow nor child, the administrator shall have the whole, 2 *Show.* 175. And this portion, of dead man's part, the administrator was accustomed to apply to his own use, 2 *Freem.* 85. 1 *Vern.* 133. till the statute 1 *Jac.* 2. *c.* 17. declared that the same should be subject to the statute of distribution. So that if a man dies worth 1800*l.* personal estate, leaving a widow and two children, this estate shall be divided into eighteen parts; whereof the widow shall have eight, six by the custom, and two by the statute; and each of the children five, three by the custom and two by the statute: if he leaves a widow and one child, she shall still have eight parts, as before; and the child shall have ten, six by the custom and four by the statute: if he leaves a widow and no child, the widow shall have three fourths of the whole, two by the custom and one by the statute; and the remaining fourth shall go by the statute to the next of kin. It is also to be observed that if the wife be provided for, by a jointure before marriage, in bar of her customary part, it puts her in a state of non-entity, with regard to the custom only, 2 *Vern.* 665. 3 *P. Wms.* 16.; but she shall be entitled to her share of the dead man's part under the statute of distributions, unless barred by special agreement, 1 *Vern.* 15. 2 *Chanc. Rep.* 252. And if any of the children are advanced by the father in his life time with any sum of money (not amounting to their full proportionable part) they shall bring that portion into hotchpot with the rest of the brothers and sisters, but not with the widow, before they are entitled to any benefit under the custom, 2 *Freem.* 279. 1 *Equ. Cas. Abr.* 155. 2 *P. Wms.* 526.: but, if they are fully advanced, the custom entitles them to no further dividend, 2 *P. Wms.* 527.

Thus far in the main the customs of London and of York agree; but, besides certain other less material variations, there are two principal points in which they considerably differ. One is, that in London, the share of the children (or orphanage part) is not fully vested in them till the age of twenty-one, before which they cannot dispose of it by testament, 2 *Vern.* 558.: and, if they die under that age, whether sole or married, their share shall survive to the other children; but after the age of twenty-one, it is free from any orphanage custom, and in case of intestacy, shall fall under the statute of distributions, *Prec. Chanc.* 537. The other, that in the province of York, the heir at common law, who inherits any land either in fee or in tail, is excluded from any filial portion or reasonable part, 2 *Burn.* 754. But, notwithstanding these provincial variations, the customs appear to be substantially one and the same. 2 *Black.* 519.

DISTRICTIONE SCACCARII, a statute so called. 51 *H.* 3. *stat.* 4.

DISTRICT, (*districtus*) a territory, or place of jurisdiction.

DISTRINGAS, is a writ directed to the sheriff, or other officer, commanding him to distrain a man for a debt to the king, &c. or for his appearance at a day therein affixed. *F. N. B.* 138.

DISTRINGAS JURATORES, is a compulsory writ issued from *B. R.* and directed to the sheriff, commanding him to have the bodies of the jurors at a day appointed, or to distrain; and return issues on their lands and goods for non-appearance. 1 *Lil. Abr.* 483. And the writ of *distringas jur'* ought to be delivered to the sheriff so timely, that he may warn the jury to appear four days before the writ is returnable, if the jurors live within forty miles of the place of trial; and eight days if they live further off. *Ibid.* 484.

And a *distringas* in the latter case, is the usual process where a defendant neglects to appear upon a summons under a *clausum fregit* in C. B. or a *venire* in the *Exchequer.*

DIVIDEND *of Bankrupts' Effects.* See BANKRUPTS.

DIVIDEND IN THE EXCHEQUER, is taken for one part of an indenture. 10 *Ed.* 1. *c.* 11. *Cowel. Blount.*

DIVIDEND IN THE UNIVERSITY, is that part or share which every one of the fellows do justly and equally divide among themselves of their annual stipend. *Ibid.*

DIVISA, hath various significations: sometimes it is used for a devise, award or decree: sometimes for devise of a portion or parcel of lands, &c. by will: and sometimes it is taken for the bounds or limits of division of a parish or farm, &c. As *divisas perambulare*, to walk the bounds of a parish; in which sense it has been extended to the divisions between counties, and given name to towns, as to the Devises, a town in Wiltshire, situate on the confines of the West Saxon and Mercian kingdoms. *Leg. H.* 2. *cap.* 9. *Leg. Inæ, c.* 44. *Leg. H.* 1. *c.* 57. *Cowel.*

DIVIL ON THE NECK. A tormenting engine made of iron, straightening and winching the neck of a man with his legs together; formerly in use among the persecuting papists. *Cowel. Blount.*

DIVORCE, (*divortium a divertendo*) is a separation of two, *de facto* married together, made by law: it is a judgment spiritual; and therefore, if there be occasion, it ought to be reversed in the spiritual court. *Co. Lit.* 335.

The usual divorces are only of two kinds, *i. e.* A MENSA ET THORO, from bed and board; and A VINCULO MATRIMONII, from the very bond of marriage.—A divorce *a mensa & thoro* dissolveth not the marriage; for the cause of it is subsequent to the marriage, and supposes the marriage to be lawful: and this divorce may be by reason of adultery in either of the parties, for cruelty or the like. *Co. Lit.* 235. 3 *Inst.* 89. 7 *Rep.* 43.—A divorce *a vinculo matrimonii*, absolutely dissolves the marriage, and makes it void from the beginning, the cause of it being precedent to the marriage; as præcontract with some other person, consanguinity or affinity, within the levitical degrees, impotency, impuberty, &c. On this divorce, dower is gone; and if by reason of præ-contract, consanguinity, or affinity; the children begotten between them are bastards. *Co. Lit.* 335. 2 *Inst.* 93, 687.

Also by 26 *Geo.* 2. *c.* 33. marriages by licence, without consent of parents or guardians, where either of the parties, not being a widower or widow, shall be *under age*, shall be null and void.

DIURNALIS, signifies as much land as can be ploughed in a day, with an ox; in some authors, it is written *diuturna*. *Blount.*

DOCKET, or DOGGET, a record in the courts containing an entry of judgments: thus when rolls of judgments are brought in, they are docketted, *i. e.* entered on the docket of that term.

DOCTRINES, illegal. See SEDITION.

DOGS. By 10 *Geo.* 3. *c.* 18. persons stealing dogs from the owner or person intrusted therewith, or selling, buying, receiving, or detaining dogs, knowing the same to be stolen, and convicted on the oath of one witness before two justices, shall pay not more than 30*l.* nor less than 20*l.* for the first offence, with charges, and on non-payment may be committed for twelve months, and not less than six.

For the second offence to pay 50*l.* and not less than 30*l.* with charges, one moiety to the informer and the other to the poor, and on non-payment, may be committed for eighteen months, and not less than twelve, and to be publicly whipped in three days. *Ibid.*

Search may be made for dogs and skins stolen, and the person in whose custody found liable to the same penalties; appeal lies to the quarter sessions, where costs may be given, but no *certiorari*. *Ibid.*

DOG-DAYS, (*dies caniculares*) are the hottest time of the year, by reason the sun is then in Leo: they are reckoned 64 in all, *a tertio idus Julii usque in idus Septembris. Cowel. Blount.*

DOG-DRAW, is a manifest deprehension of an offender against venison in a forest, when he is found drawing after a deer by the scent of a hound led in his hand; or where a person hath wounded a deer, or wild beast, by shooting at him, or otherwise, and is caught with a dog drawing after him to receive the same. *Manwood, par.* 2. *cap.* 8.

DOGGER, a light ship or vessel, as a Dutch dogger. &c. thus *dogger-fish* are fish brought in those ships; and *dogger-men*, fishermen that belong to *dogger-ships*. *Cowel. Blount.*

DOITKIN, or doit, was a base coin of small value, prohibited by the stat. 3 *H.* 5. *c.* 1.

DO LAW, (*facere legem*) is the same with to make law. Stat 23 *H.* 8. *c.* 14.

DOLE, (*dola*) a Sax. word signifying as much as *pars* or *portio* in the Latin; and anciently where a meadow was divided into several shares it was called a dole meadow. *Cowel. Blount.*

DOLEFISH, seems to be the share of fish which the fishermen, yearly employed in the North seas, do customarily receive for their allowance. *Ibid.* 35 *H.* 8. *c.* 7.

DOLG-BOTE, (Sax.) a recompense or amends for a scar or wound. *Cowel. Blount.*

DOLLAR, a piece of foreign coin going for about 4*s.* 6*d.* *Lex Mercat.*

DOM-BOT, (Sax.) signifies *liber judicialis*, as appears by the laws of king *Ed.* 1. This, it is conjectured, was a book of statutes of the English Saxons, wherein the laws of the ancient Saxon kings were contained. *Leg. Inæ. c.* 29. See *Dome-book*. *Cowel. Blount.*

DOME, or DOOM, (from the Sax. *dom*) a judgment, sentence, or decree.

DOME-BOOK, or *liber judicialis*, was a book (now lost) composed under the direction of Alfred, for the general use of the whole kingdom, containing the local customs of the several provinces of the kingdom. 1 *Black. Com.* 64, 65. 4, 404. and see also *Dom-boc*.

DOMESDAY, (*liber judicialis, vel censualis Angliæ*) is a most ancient record, made in the time of William the conqueror, and new remaining in the Exchequer, fair and legible, consisting of two volumes, a greater and a less; the greater containing a survey of all the lands in England, except the counties of Northumberland, Cumberland, Westmorland, Durham, and part of Lancashire, which it is said were never surveyed, and except Essex, Suffolk, and Norfolk, which three last are comprehended in the lesser volume. There is also a third book, which differs from the others in form more than matter, made by the command of the same king. And there is a fourth book kept in the exchequer which is called domesday; and, though a very large volume, is only an abridgment of the others. Likewise a fifth book is kept in the remembrancer's office in the exchequer, which has the name of domesday, and is the very same with the fourth before mentioned..

Domesday was begun by five justices, assigned for that purpose in each county, in the year 1081, and finished *anno* 1086. And it is generally known, that the question whether lands are ancient demesne, or not, is to be decided by the domesday of *Will.* 1. from whence there is no appeal.

DOMES-MEN, judges, or men appointed to doom, and determine suits and controversies. *Cowel. Blount.*

DOMICELLI. The domicelli were the better sort of servants in monasteries. *Ibid.*

DOMIGERIUM, danger, or perhaps more properly, power over another; *sub domigerio alicujus vel manu esse. Bract. lib.* 4. *tr.* 1. *cap.* 19. *Cowel. Blount.*

DOMINA, (*dame*) a title given to honourable women, who anciently in their own right of inheritance held a barony. *Paroch. Antiq.*

DOMINICA IN RAMIS PALMARUM, Palm-Sunday. *Anno* 23 *Ed.* 1.

DOMINIUM, signifies right, or regal power. *Paroch. Antiq.* 498.

DOMINUS. This word prefixed to a man's name, in ancient times usually denoted him a knight, or a clergyman; and sometimes a gentleman, not a knight, especially a lord of a manor. *Cowel. Blount.*

DOMO REPARANDA, is a writ that lies for one against his neighbour by the fall of whose house he fears a damage and injury to his own. *Reg. Orig.* 153.

DOMUS CONVERSORUM. See *Conversos.*

DOMUS DEI, the hospital of St. Julian in Southampton, so called. *Mon. Ang. tom.* 2. 440.

DONATIO MORTIS CAUSA, a death-bed disposition of property, so called, *viz.* when a person in his last sickness, apprehending his dissolution near, delivers or causes to be delivered to another the possession of any personal goods, (under which have been included bonds, and bills drawn by the deceased upon his banker) to keep in case of his decease. This gift, if the donor dies, needs not the assent of his executor; yet it shall not prevail against creditors; and is accompanied with this implied trust, that if the donor lives the property thereof shall revert to himself, being only given in contemplation of death, or *mortis causa. Prec. Chan.* 269. 1 *P. Wms.* 406. 411. 3 *P. Wms.* 357. 2 *Black. Com.* 514.

DONATIVE, (*donativum*) is a benefice merely given and collated by the patron to a man, without either presentation to, or institution by, the ordinary, or induction by his order. *F. N. B.* 35.

DONIS, Statute de, the stat. of Westm. 2. *viz.* 13 *Ed.* 1. *c.* 1, called the stat. *de donis conditionalibus.* This statute revives, in some sort, the ancient feudal restraints which were originally laid on alienations, by enacting that from thenceforth *the will of the donor be observed; and that the tenements so given (to a man and the heirs of his body) should at all events go to the issue, if there were any, or if none should revert to the donor.* 2 *Black. Com.* 112. Tenant in fee-tail is by virtue of this statute. *Lit. sec.* 3. But he may bar the entail by fine, and also the remainders and reversions expectant thereon, by recovery.

DONOR and DONEE. Donor is he who gives lands or tenements to another in tail, &c. And the person to whom given is the donee.

DORTURE, (*dormitorium*) is the common room or chamber where all the friars, or religious of one convent slept and laid all night. *Cowel. Blount.*

DOSSALE, a word used for hangings or tapestry. *Ibid.*

DOTE ASSIGNANDA, was a writ that laid for a widow, where it was found by office that the king's tenant was seised of lands in fee, or fee-tail at the day of his death, and that he held of the king in chief, &c. In which case the widow came into the chancery, and there made oath that she would not marry without the king's leave; whereupon she had this writ to the escheator, to assign her dower, &c. But it was usual to make the assignment of the dower in the chancery, and to award a writ to the escheator to deliver the lands assigned unto her. Stat. 15 *Ed.* 4. *cap.* 4. *Reg. Orig.* 297. *F. N. B.* 263. See *Dower.*

DOTE UNDE NIHIL HABET, is a writ of dower, that lies for the widow against the tenant of land whereof her husband in his life-time was solely seised in fee-simple or fee-tail, and of which she is dowable. *F. N. B.* 147.

DOTIS ADMENSURATIONE. See *Admeasurement of dower.*

DOUBLE PLEA, (*duplex placitum*) is where a defendant alleges for himself two several matters in bar of the plaintiff's action, when one of them is sufficient, which shall not be admitted. *Kitch.* 223. 18 *Ed.* 4. 17. *Hob.* 197. *Jenk. Cent.* 75.

For all pleas ought to be single, that the jury may not be troubled and perplexed with too many things at once. *Smith's Rep. Angl. lib.* 2, *c.* 13.

But by stat. 4 *Ann. c.* 16. *sect.* 4, it shall be lawful for any defendant or tenant in any action or suit, or for any plaintiff in replevin, in any court of record, with the leave of the same court, to plead as many several matters thereto as he shall think necessary for his defence: that is, in so many separate and distinct pleas, and where there are more pleas than one. By virtue of this statute defendant is said to plead double, by leave of the court.

After a judge's order for time to plead, pleading issuably, the court on motion will give defendant leave to plead double, pleading issuable pleas, and taking short notice of trial. Notes in *C. B.* 244.

But after a defendant has pleaded a single plea he cannot have leave to plead double. *Ibid.* 245.

DOUBLE QUARREL, (*duplex querela*) is a complaint made by any clerk, or other, to the archbishop of the province, against an inferior ordinary, for delaying or refusing to do justice in some cause ecclesiastical, as to give sentence, institute a clerk, &c. and seems to be termed a double quarrel, because it is most commonly made against both the judge and him at whose suit justice is denied or delayed: the effect whereof is, that the archbishop, taking notice of the delay, directs his letters under his authentical seal to all clerks of his province, commanding them to admonish the ordinary within a certain number of days, to do the justice required, or otherwise to appear before him or his official, and there allege the cause of his delay; and to signify to the ordinary, that if he neither perform the thing enjoined, nor appear and show cause against it, he himself, in his court of audience, will forthwith proceed to do the justice that is due. *Cowel. Blount.*

DOUBLES, (Fr.) signify as much as letters patent. Stat. 14 *H.* 6. *c.* 6. *Ibid.*

DOZEN PEERS, were twelve peers assigned at the instance of the barons in the reign of king *Hen.* 3. to be privy-councillors to the king, or rather conservators of the kingdom. *Ibid.*

DOVER CASTLE. The constable of Dover castle shall not hold plea of any foreign county within the castle gates, except it concern the keeping of the castle; nor shall he distrain the inhabitants of the ports to plead elsewhere, or otherwise than as they ought, according to the charters, &c. Stat. 28 *Ed.* 1. *c.* 7.

DOW, to give or endow, from the Latin word *do. Cowel. Blount.*

DOWAGER, (*dota a dotissa*) a widow endowed; applied to the widows of princes, dukes, earls, and other great personages. *Ibid.*

DOWAGER, (queen) is the widow of the king, and as such enjoys most of the privileges belonging to her as queen consort. But it is not high treason to conspire her death, or violate her chastity, because the succession to the crown is not thereby endangered. But no man can marry her without special license from the king, on pain of forfeiting his lands and goods. 2 *Inst.* 18. See *Riley's Plac. Parl.* 672. 1 *Black. Com.* 224.

DOWER, (*dotarium*) is the portion which a widow has of the lands of her husband after his decease, for the sustenance of herself, and education of her children. 1 *Inst.* 30.

And at this day dower is only of two sorts, that is to say, 1st, by the common law; 2ndly, by custom.

1. *Dower by the common law;* which is a third part of such lands or tenements whereof the husband was solely seised in fee-simple or fee-tail during the coverture; and this the widow is to enjoy during her life. *Co. Lit.* 30.

2. *Dower by custom;* which is that part of the husband's estate to which the widow is entitled after the death of her husband by the custom of any manor or place, so long as she lives sole and chaste; and this is more than one third part, for in some places she shall have half the land, as by gavelkind; and in divers manors the widow shall have the whole during her life, which is called her free-bench; but as custom may enlarge, so it may abridge dower to a fourth part. *Co. Lit.* 33.

And by *Magna Charta*, 9 *Hen.* 3. *c.* 7, a widow shall immediately after her husband's death have her marriage inheritance, and *remain in his chief house* 40 *days*, within which time dower is to be asigned her of the third part of all his lands, &c.

But a woman entitled to dower cannot enter till it be assigned to her, and set out either by the heir, tertenant, or sheriff in certainty. 1 *Rol. Abr.* 681. *Dyer* 343. *Plowd.* 529. *Bro.* 16. *Co. Lit.* 34 *b.* 37. *a, b.*

And none can assign dower but those who have a freehold, or against whom a writ of dower lies; therefore a tenant by statute merchant, statute staple, or elegit, or lessee for years, cannot assign dower, for none of these have an estate large enough to answer the plaintiff's demand. *Perk.* 403, 404. *Co. Lit.* 35. *Bro.* 63, 94. 1 *Rol. Abr.* 681, 6 *Co.* 57.

Bar of Dower. If a wife levies a fine with her husband, she bars herself of her dower: and if a common recovery be had against the husband and wife, of the husband's lands, it shall bar the wife of her dower. 2 *Rep.* 74. *Plowd.* 514. Where a woman releases her right to him in reversion, her dower may be extinguished. 8 *Rep.* 151. If a wife commits treason or felony; or *if she elope from her husband,* and *live with the adulterer willingly,* without being reconciled to the husband, she shall lose and forfeit her dower; but if the husband be reconciled to her, and she lives with him again, she shall be endowed. 2 *Inst.* 453. *Dyer* 106. And if after elopement of the wife, her husband and she demean themselves as husband and wife, it is evidence of reconciliation. *Dyer* 196. If a man grants his wife with her goods to another, and the wife by virtue of the grant lives with the grantee during the life of the husband, this shall forfeit her dower; for she lived in adultery, notwithstanding the grant. *Co. Lit.* 135. 2 *Danv.* 662. 2 *Inst.* 435.

When a jointure is made of lands after marriage, the wife may wave it, and demand her dower: and though during the coverture the husband and wife levy a fine thereof, yet this is no bar to her dower of any other lands of her husband, because the jointure being made after the marriage, she had election after the death of the husband to refuse it, and claim dower, and not before, and then the fine levied of the jointure before her time for election of dower was come can be no bar for electing of dower when it is come. 1 *Bulst.* 173. 1 *Leon.* 285. *Dyer.* 358.

If a woman takes a lease for life of her husband's lands after his death, she shall have no dower, because she cannot demand it against herself; and if she takes a lease for years only, yet she shall not sue to have dower during these years, because it was her own act to suspend the fruit and effect of her dower during that time. *Perk.* 350. *F. N. B.* 149. *Mo. pl.* 403.

If the husband levy a fine with proclamation of his lands, and dies, his wife is bound to make her claim within five years after his death, otherwise she shall be barred of her dower; for though her title of dower was not consummate at the time of the fine levied, yet it being initiate by the marriage and seisin of the husband, the fine begins to work upon it presently after the husband's death; and if she does not claim it within five years after she shall be barred. 2 *Co.* 93. 10 *Co.* 49. 99. 4 *Inst.* 216. *Hob.* 265. *Mo. pl.* 154. 879. *Dyer* 224. 13 *Co.* 20.

DOWL and DEAL, a division. Hence comes the word dealing. So the stones which are laid to the boundaries of lands are called dowle-stones, *i. e.* such as divide the lands. *Cowel. Blount.*

DOWRY, (*dos mulieris*) was in ancient time applied to that which the wife brings her husband in marriage, otherwise called *maritagium*, or marriage-goods: but these are termed more properly goods given in marriage, and the marriage portion. *Co. Lit.* 31.

DOWRY-BILL. Among the Jews the bridegroom at the time of marriage gave his wife a dowry-bill. *Cowel. Blount.*

DOZEIN, a territory or jurisdiction, mentioned in the statute of *View and Frankpledge.* 18 *Ed.* 2. See *Deciners.* *Cowel. Blount.*

DRACO REGIS, the standard, ensign, or military colours borne in war by our ancient kings, having the figure of a dragon painted on them. *Ibid.*

DRAGIUM, Drag; a coarser sort of bread, corn: or a kind of malt, made of oats mixed with barley. *Ibid.*

DRAGS, seem to be floating pieces of timber so joined together, that by swimming on the water they may bear a burden or load of other things down a river. 6 *H.* 6. *c.* 15. *Ibid.*

DRANA, a drain or water-course; sometimes written *drecca*. *Ibid.*

DRAW-GERE, signifies any harness belonging to cart-horses, for drawing a waggon, or other carriage. *Paroch. Antiq. p.* 549. *Cowel. Blount.*

DRAW-LATCHES, were thieves and robbers: *Lambert* in his *Eiren. lib.* 1, *c.* 6, calls them thieves, wasters, and roberdsmen: the two last words are grown out of use. They are mentioned in 5 *E.* 3. *c.* 14, and 7 *R.* 2. *c.* 5. *Cowel. Blount.*

DREDGERMEN, are fishers for oysters, &c. *Stat.* 2 *Geo.* 2. *c.* 19.

DREIT-DREIT, or Droit, are words signifying formerly a double right, *viz.* of possession, and of property or interest. *Bract. lib.* 4. *cap.* 27. *Co. Lit.* 266.

DRENCHED, (from the Germ.) an old word, used where a person was overcome. *Cowel. Blount.*

DRENCHES, or DRENGES, (*drengi*) were tenants *in capite*, and such as at the coming of Will. the Conqueror were put out of their estates, and afterwards restored thereunto on their making it appear that they were owners thereof, and neither *in auxilio*, or *consilio*, against him. *Spelm. Cowel. Blount.*

Hence *Drengage*, (*drengagium*) is the tenure by which the drenches or drenges held their lands. *Ibid.*

DRIFT OF THE FOREST, (*agitatio animalium in foresta*) is a view or examination of what cattle are in the forest, that it may be known whether it be surcharged or not; and whose the beasts are, and whether they are commonable, &c. These drifts are made at certain times in the year by the officers of the forest, when all the cattle of the forest are driven into some pound, or place enclosed, for the purposes aforementioned, and to the end it may be discovered whether any cattle of strangers be there which ought not to common. *Manw. par.* 2, *c.* 15. *Stat.* 32 *Hen.* 8, *c.* 13. 4 *Inst.* 309.

DRINKLEAN, in some records *potura drinklean*, was a contribution of tenants, in the time of the Saxons, towards a potation, or ale, provided to entertain the lord, or his steward. *Cowel. Blount.*

DROFDENE, signified, with our Saxon ancestors, a grove, or woody place, where cattle were kept, and the keeper of them was called drofman. *Domesday.* *Cowel. Blount.*

DROFLAND, or DRYFLAND, another Saxon word, signifying a tribute or yearly payment made by some tenants to the king, or their landlords, for driving their cattle through a manor to fairs or markets. *Cowel, Blount.*

DROIT, right, is the highest writ of all other real writs whatsoever, and hath the greatest respect and the most assured and final judgment; and therefore is called a writ of right, and in the old books *droit*. *Co. Lit.* 158. and there are divers of these writs used in our law, such as the *droit de advowson*; *droit de dower*; *droit de garde*; *droit patent*; *droit rationabili parte*; *droit sur disclaimer*. *Booth* on *Real Actions*.

DROMONES, DROMOS, DROMUNDA, high ships of great burden, but afterwards those which we now call men of war. *Cowel. Blount.*

DROVERS, those who buy cattle in one place to sell in another. 5 *Eliz. c.* 12. 1 *Car.* 1, *c.* 1.

DRUGGERIA, a place of drugs, or drugster's shop. And druggists and their wares. Vide *Coffee*.

DRUNKENNESS, is an offence for which a man may be punished in the ecclesiastical court, as well as by justices of peace by statute. And he who is guilty of any crime through his own voluntary drunkenness, shall be punished for it as if he had been sober. *Co. Lit.* 247. 1 *Hawk. P. C.* 2.

And equity will not relieve against a bond, &c. given by a man when drunk, unless the drunkenness is occasioned through the management or contrivance of him to whom it is given. 3 *P. Will.* 130.

By 1 *Jac.* 1. *c.* 9, alehouse-keepers permitting townsmen to sit tippling are liable to 10*s.* penalty, and on non-payment to be imprisoned till paid; and persons tippling therein are to forfeit 3*s.* 4*d.* or sit in the stocks 4 hours.

By 4 *Jac.* 1. *c.* 5, persons convicted of drunkenness are to forfeit 5*s.* or be put in the stocks 6 hours.

If convicted a second time to be bound over to their good behaviour; but the prosecution must be within 6 months. *Ibid.*

By 7 *Jac.* 1, *c.* 10, an alehonse-keeper, convicted under either of the two last acts is disabled to keep an alehouse for three years.

By 21 *Jac.* 1. *c.* 7, one witness, or the party's own confession, shall be sufficient; and the oath of the party confessing shall convict others.

By 1 *Car.* 1. *c.* 14, alehouse-keepers permitting any person whatsoever to sit tippling shall incur the penalty of 1 *Jac.* 1. *c.* 9. Vintners keeping inns or victualling-houses to be also liable.

DRY EXCHANGE, (*cambium siccum*) a term invented in former times for the disguising and covering of usury, in which something was pretended to pass on both sides, whereas in truth nothing passed but on one side, in which respect it was called dry. 3 *Hen.* 7, *c.* 5, *Cowel. Blount.*

DRY RENT, a rent reserved without clause of distress.

DUCES TECUM, is a writ commanding a person to appear at a certain day in the court of chancery, and to bring with him some writings, evidences, or other things which the court would view. *Reg. Orig.* So a subpœna with a clause *duces tecum*, is often sued out at common law, to compel witnesses to produce, on trials at *Nisi prius*, deeds, bonds, bills, notes, books, or memorandums, in their custody or power, and which relate to the issue in question. But as this clause is of modern introduction, and not justified by the form in the *register*, and the practice interferes with the jurisdiction of the courts of equity to enforce the production of such things by a bill for a discovery, it was at first doubted, in the case of *Amey* v. *Long*, whether the party is upon such a subpœna obliged to produce what is thereby required. But after solemn argument, and time taken by the court to consider, LORD *Ellenborough*, CHIEF JUSTICE, delivered the unanimous opinion of the judges, that the writ of *duces tecum*, is a writ of compulsory obligation on a witness to produce the papers in his possession thereby demanded, having no lawful or reasonable excuse for not producing the same, of the validity of which excuse, the court is to decide, and not the witness. *Ea. Ter.* 48 *Geo.* 3. 9 *East's Rep.* 473.

DUCES TECUM LICET LANGUIDUS, a writ, now in disuse, and anciently directed to the sheriff upon a return that he cannot bring his prisoner without danger of death, he being *adeo languidus*, in which case the court grants a *habeas corpus* in the nature of a *duces tecum licet languidus*. *Book. Entr.*

DUCKING-STOOL. See *Castigatory*.

DUES, ecclesiastical. The non-payment of ecclesiastical dues to the clergy, as pensions, mortuaries, compositions, offerings, and whatsoever falls under the denomination of surplice-fees for marriage, or other ministerial offices of the church. 3 *Black. Com.* 90. are cognizable in the spiritual court, which makes decrees for their actual payment.

But by 7 and 8 *Will.* 3, *c.* 6, all offerings, oblations, and obventions, not exceeding the value of 40*s.* may be recovered in a summary way before two justices of the peace.

DUEL, (*Duellum*) in our ancient law, is a fight between persons in a doubtful case for the trial of the truth. *Fleta.* But this kind of duel is disused, and what we now call a duel is a fighting between two, upon some quarrel precedent; wherein, if a person is killed, both the principal and his seconds are guilty of murder, whether the seconds fight or not. *H. P. C.* 47. 51. 1 *Hawk.* 82.

And where two persons in cool blood meet and fight upon a precedent quarrel, and one of them is killed, the other is guilty of murder, and cannot excuse himself by alleging that he was first struck by the deceased, or that he had declined to meet him, was prevailed on to do it by his importunity, or that it was not his intent to kill, but only to vindicate his reputation, &c. 1 *Hawk. P. C.* 81.

And whenever it appears that one who kills another in a duel, or fighting on a sudden quarrel, was master of his temper at the time, he is guilty of murder; as if after the quarrel he fall into another discourse, and talk calmly thereon, or the like.

It is also a very high offence to challenge another, either by word or letter, to fight a duel, or to be the messenger of such a challenge, or even barely to endeavour to provoke another to send a challenge, or to fight, or by dispersing letters for that purpose, full of reflection, &c. And persons convicted thereof may be fined, imprisoned, and bound to their good behaviour. 1 *Sid.* 186. 3 *Inst.* 158. 1 *Hawk. P. C.* 135, 138.

DUKE, (Lat. *dux*, Fr. *duc*, *a ducendo*) signified, among the ancient Romans, *ductorem exercitus*, such as led their armies; since which they were called *duces*, and were governors of provinces, &c. In England the title of duke is the next dignity to the prince of Wales; and the first duke we had in England was Edward the Black Prince, who was created duke of Cornwall in the 11th year of king *Ed.* 3. 1 *Black. Com.* 307, 408.

DUM FUIT INFRA ÆTATEM, is where an infant makes a feoffment of his lands; when he comes of full age he may have this writ to recover those lands and tenements which were so aliened; and within age he may enter into the land and take it back again, and by his entry he shall be remitted to his ancestor's right. *New N. B.* 426.

DUM NON FUIT COMPOS MENTIS, a writ that lies where a man that is not of sound memory aliens any lands or tenements, then he shall have this writ against the alienee. And he shall allege that he was not of sane memory, but being visited with infirmity, lost his discretion for a time, so as not to be capable of making a grant, &c. *New Nat. Br.* 449.

DUN, down, in which termination it hath varied into *don*, signifies a mountain or high open place; so that the names of thos, towns which end in dun, or don, as Ashdone &c. were either built on hills, or near them in open places; hence *dunsetts* are those who dwell on hills or mountains, and *dunum* and *duna*, a down or hill. *Cowel. Blount.*

DUODENA, a jury of twelve men. *Ibid.*

DUODENA MANU, (*jurare duodecima manu*) twelve witnesses to purge a criminal of an offence. 3 *Black. Com.* 343.

DUPLEX QUERELA, a process ecclesiastical. See *Double Quarrel.*

DUPLICATE, anciently signified the second letters patent, granted by the lord chancellor, in a case wherein he had before done the same, which were therefore thought void. *Cromp. Jurisd. fol.* 215. But in more common acceptation it signifies a copy or transcript of any deed, writing, or account.

DUPLICITY, in pleading. Every plea must be simple, entire, connected, and confined to one single point: it must never be entangled with a variety of distinct independent answers to the same matter, which must require as many different replies, and introduce a multitude of issues upon one and the same point. 3 *Black. Com.* 311. See DOUBLE PLEA.

DURANTE ABSENTIA, administration. An administration granted when the executor is out of the realm, to continue in force until his return. *Cowel. Blount.*

DURANTE MINORE ÆTATE, administration. An infant cannot act as executor until seventeen, during which minority this administration is granted. *Ibid.*

DURDEN, a thicket of wood in a valley. *Ib.*

DURESS, (*Duritia*) is where one is wrongfully imprisoned or restrained of his liberty contrary to law, till he seals a bond or other deed to another; or threatened to be killed, wounded, or beaten if he doth not do it: and a bond or deed so obtained is void in law. And if one under a just fear of being imprisoned, killed, &c. enters into a bond to him that threatens him, it is *duress per minas*; and may be pleaded to avoid the bond: but it must be a threatening of life or member, or of imprisonment; and not of battery only; or to take away goods, &c. *Co. Lit.* 162, 253. 2 *Inst.* 483.

And a warrant of attorney given by a man in custody to confess judgment, no attorney on his part being present, is by the rules of the court void. 2 *Lill. Abr.* 682.

DURHAM. See COUNTIES PALATINE.

DURSLEY, signifies blows without wounding or bloodshed, *vulgo* dry blows. *Blount.*

DUSTY FATTS, dusty foots, pedlars or traders who have no settled habitation, and they have their name from their feet being covered with *dust*, by their continual travelling. See *Piepoudre Court.*

DUTCHY COURT OF LANCASTER, is a court of the Dutchy chamber of Lancaster held at Westminster before the chancellor, for matters concerning the lands and franchises of the dutchy. And the proceedings in this court are by English bill, as in chancery. 4 *Inst.* 204.

This special jurisdiction, is a thing very distinct from the county palatine, and comprizes much territory which lies at a vast distance from it, as particularly a very large district within the city of Westminster. But the courts of chancery and exchequer, on he equity side have a concurrent jurisdiction with this court. 4 *Inst.* 206. 1 *Chanc. Rep.* 55. *Toth.* 145. *Hardr.* 171. 3 *Black. Com.* 78.

DUTIES of persons. Allegiance is the duty of the people, protection the duty of the magistrate; yet they are reciprocally the rights, as well as duties of each other. Allegiance is the right of the magistrate, and protection the right of the people. 1 *Black. Com.* 123.

DUTY. Any thing that is known to be due by law, and thereby recoverable, is a duty before it is recovered, because the party interested in the same has power to recover it. 1 *Lill.* 495.

DWELLING-HOUSE. A man may assemble people together lawfully (at least if they do not exceed eleven) without danger of raising a riot, or unlawful assembly, in order to protect and defend his house, which he is not permitted to do in any other case. 1 *Hal. P. C.* 547. 4 *Black. Com.* 224.

DWINED, signifies any thing consumed, whence comes the word dwindle. *Cowel. Blount.*

DYKE-REED, or REEVE, an officer who has the care and oversight of the dykes and drains in fenny countries; as of Dieping fens, &c. See 16 and 17 *Car.* 2, *c.* 11.

DYRGE, or DIRGE, a mournful laudatory song over the dead (from the Teutonic *dyrke, laudare*, to praise and extol) and hence *dyrenum*, a ditty or song. *Cowel. Blount.*

E

EABALUS, (from the Sax. *eale, cervisia, et hus, domus,*) an alehouse. *Cowel. Blount.*

EALHORDA, the privilege of assising and selling ale and beer. *Ibid.*

EALDERMAN, (or *ealdorman*) among the Saxons was as much as earl with the Danes. *Cambd. Brit.* 107. Also an elder, senator, &c. *Ealdermen* or *aldermen*, are now those that are associated to the mayor or chief officer in the common council of a city or borough town. *Stat.* 24 *H.* 8, *c.* 13. 1 *Black. Com.* 398.

EARL. (Sax. *eorle*, Lat. *comes*) This it is said was a great title among the Saxons, and is the most ancient of the English peerage, there being no title of honour used by our present nobility that was likewise in use by the Saxons except this of earl. *Verstegan* derives this word from the Dutch *ear*, i. e. honour, and *ethel*, which signifies noble. *Cowel.*

Their place is now next to a marquis, and before a viscount. See *Countee.*

EARNEST, money paid in part of a larger sum, or part of the goods delivered on any contract, &c. which being done by way of earnest, the property of the goods is absolutely bound by it, and the buyer may recover the goods by action, as well as the vendor may the price of them. And by 29 *Car.* 2. *c.* 3, no contract for sale of goods to the value of 10*l.* or more, to be valid unless such earnest is made or given. 2 *Black. Com.* 447, 448.

EASEMENT, *Aisiamentum*, from the Fr. *Aise*, (*i. e. commoditas*) is defined to be a service or convenience, which one neighbour has of another, by charter or prescription, without profit, as a way through his land, a sink, watercourse, or the like. *Kitch.* 105. *Cro. Jac.* 170. 3 *Leon.* 254. 3 *Mod.* 294. *Lil. Abr.* 496.

EASTER, is the feast of the Passover.

EASTINTUS, (Sax. *east-tyne*) is an easterly coast or country; also the east street, east side of a river, or the like. *Cowel. Blount.*

EAST-INDIA COMPANY. A corporation styled by 6 *Ann. c.* 17. *s.* 13. "*The united Company of Merchants of England trading to the East Indies,*" that is, according to 9 & 10 *Will.* 3. *c.* 44. *s.* 61. trading "in, to, and from, the East Indies in the countries and parts of Asia and Africa, and in, to, and from the islands, ports, havens, cities, creeks, towns, and places of Asia, Africa, and America, or any of them beyond the Cape of Good Hope to the Straights of Magellan, where any trade or traffic of merchandize is, or may be used or had, and to and from every of them.

After the discovery of the passage by sea, to the peninsula of India, at about the close of the 15th century, several attempts were made by private individuals to open a trade in that part of the world: but these proving unsuccessful, Q. Eliz. by a charter, dated Dec. 31, 1600, established an incorporated company under the name of *The London East India Company.*"

This company on an accidental failure in the payment of a small duty imposed on their capital stock, (4 & 5 *W. & M. c.* 15. *s.* 10, 12.) forfeited their charter: but afterwards in the same year, the crown revived their powers and exclusive privileges by a new charter. However, by stat. 9 & 10 *W.* 3. *c.* 44. two new companies were established, and the subscribers to a loan of 2,000,000 for carrying on the then war, were incorporated into a *general society*, with liberty for each individual member to trade to India within the exclusive limits of the said company to the extent of his share of this loan, and power was granted to such of the subscribers as should choose to convert their subscriptions into a joint-stock, to do so, and they were to be incorporated by a separate charter, by the name of "*The English East-India Company.*"

The old company to whose prejudice these two new corporations were to be erected, became subscribers for a very large proportion of the loan of two millions, and *united* with the English company in 1702, which union was afterwards confirmed by parliament, by stat. 6 *Ann. c.* 17. and the separate traders of *the general society*, whose subscription to the loan amounted to only 2700*l.* at the time of the union, soon afterwards joined *the united company.*

This is a brief account of the rise and progressive establishment of the present East-India Company, whose concerns are now regulated by divers statutes, too numerous and diffuse to be inserted in this work.

EAVES-DROPPERS, persons that listen under walls or windows, or the eaves of a house, to hearken after discourse, and thereupon to frame slanderous and mischievous tales, are a common nuisance, and presentable at the court-leet, or are indictable at the sessions, and punishable by fine and finding sureties for good behaviour. *Kitch. of Courts*, 20. 1 *Hawk. P. C.* 132. 4 *Black. Com.* 169.

EBDOMADARIUS. An ebdomary was an officer appointed weekly in cathedral churches, to supervise the regular performance of divine service, and prescribe the particular duties of each person attending in the choir, as to reading, singing, praying, &c. *Cowel. Blount.*

EBEREMORTH or EBEREMORS, (Sax.) bare, or downright murder. *Leg. H.* 1. *c.* 12. *Cowel. Blount.* Hence also *Eberemurder*, (*apertum murdrum*) *Spelm.*

ECCLESIA, (Lat.) a church; but in law proceedings it intends a parsonage. *F. N. B.* 32. 2 *Inst.* 363.

ECCLESIÆ SCULPTURA. The image or sculpture of a church in ancient times, which was often cut out or cast in plate or other metal, and preserved as a religious treasure or relique, and to perpetuate the memory of some famous churches. *Mon. Ang.* tom. 3, p. 309.

ECCLESIASTICAL, belonging to or set apart for the church; as distinguished from civil or secular with regard to the world.

ECCLESIASTICAL CORPORATIONS, were erected in the furtherance of religion, and perpetuating the rights of the church. 1 *Black. Com.* 470. See *Corporation.*

ECCLESIASTICAL COURTS, are various, as the archdeacon's, the consistory, the court of arches, of peculiars, the prerogative, and the great court of appeal of all ecclesiastical causes, *viz.* the court in delegates, appointed by the king's commission, under his great seal, &c. 3 *Black. Com.* 61. See *Courts Ecclesiastical.*

ECCLESIASTICAL JURISDICTION and LAW. See *Canon*, and *Courts Ecclesiastical.*

ECCLESIASTICAL PERSONS, (*ecclesiastici*) are churchmen whose functions consist in performing the service and keeping up the discipline of the church. *Cowel. Blount.* See *Clergy.*

EDESTIA, from *ædes*, used for buildings. *Ibid.*

EDIA, aid, or help: according to Du Fresne, but according to Cowel, ease.

EDICT, (*edictum*) an ordinance or command; a statute. *Cowel. Blount.*

EDUCATION *of children.* See Parent and Child.

EEL-FARES, a fry or brood of eels. See 25 *H.* 8.

EFFORCIALITER, is used for military force. *Cowel. Blount.*

EFFRACTORES, (Lat.) breakers applied to burglars, that break open houses to steal. *Ibid.*

EFTERS, (Sax.) ways, walks or hedges *Blount.*

EFFUSIO SANGUINIS, the mulct, fine, or penalty imposed by the old English laws for the shedding of blood, which the king granted to many lords of manors. *Ibid.*

EGYPTIANS, (*Egyptiani*) outlandish persons calling themselves *Egyptians* or *Gypsies*, from a strange kind of commonwealth among themselves of wandering impostors and jugglers, who were first taken notice of in Germany, about the beginning of the fifteenth century, and have since spread themselves all over Europe. 4 *Black.* 165.

Munster, who is followed and relied upon by Spelman, fixes the time of their first appearance to the year 1417 under passports, real or pretended, from the emperor *Sigismund*, king of Hungary, and pope *Pius* II, (who died A. D. 1464.) mentions them in his history, as thieves and vagabonds, then wandering with their families over Europe, under the name of *Zigari*, whom he supposes to have migrated from the country of the *Zigi*, which nearly answers to the modern Circassia. 4 *Black.* 165.

In the compass of a few years, they gained such a number of idle proselytes (who imitated their language and complexion, and betook themselves to the same arts of chiromancy, begging, and pilfering) that they became troublesome and even formidable to most of the states of Europe; hence they were expelled from France in the year 1560, and from Spain 1591, and the government in England took the alarm much earlier: for in 1530, they are described by stat. 22 *H.* 8. *c.* 10. as "outlandish people, "calling themselves Egyptians, using no "craft nor feat of merchandize, who have "come into this realm, and gone from shire "to shire, and place to place in great company, and used great subtel and crafty "means to deceive the people, bearing them "in hand, that they by palmistry, could "tell men's and women's fortunes; and so "many times by craft and subtelty have "deceived the people of their money, and "also have committed many heinous felonies and robberies." Wherefore they are directed to avoid the realm, and not to return, under pain of imprisoment and forfeiture of their goods and chattels, and upon their trials for any felony which they may have committed, they shall not be entitled to a jury *de medietate linguæ*, and afterwards it was enacted by *stat.* 1 & 2 *Phil. & Mar. c.* 4. and 5 *Eliz. c.* 20. that if any such persons were imported into this kingdom, the importer was to forfeit 40*l.* and if the Egyptians themselves remained one month in this kingdom, or if any person being fourteen years old, whether natural born subject or stranger, which had been seen or found in the fellowship of such Egyptians, or which had disguised him or herself, should remain in the same one month, at one or several times, it was made *felony* without *benefit of clergy*: and Sir Matthew Hale informs us, that at one Suffolk assizes, no less than 13 Gypsies were executed upon these statutes a few years before the restoration. 4 *Black.* 166. 1 *Hale, P. C.* 671.

But the felonies created by these very severe statutes have been lately repealed by stat. 23 *Geo.* 3. *c.* 51. And Gypsies are now only punishable under the vagrant act. 17 *Geo.* 2. *c.* 5. which declares, that *all such gypsies shall be deemed rogues and vagabonds.* See title VAGRANT.

EIA, (from the Sax. *eig.*) signifies an island. *Cowel. Blount.*

EJECTA, a woman ravished or deflowered; or cast forth from the virtuous. *Ejectus,* a whoremonger. *Blount.*

EJECTIONE CUSTODIÆ, (*ejectment de garde*) is a writ which anciently lay against him that casteth out the guardian from any land during the minority of the heir. *Reg. Orig.* 162. *F. N. B.* 139.

EJECTIONE FIRMÆ, or EJECTMENT. A writ *de ejectione firmæ,* or action of trespass in ejectment, lieth, where lands or tenements are let for a term of years; and afterwards the lessor, reversioner, remainderman, or any stranger, doth eject or oust the lessee of his term (*F. N. B.* 220.) In this case he shall have this writ of *ejection,* to call the defendant to answer for entering on the lands so demised to the plaintiff for a term, that is not yet expired, and ejecting him. And by this writ the plaintiff shall recover back his term, or the remainder of it, with damages. 3 *Black.* 199.

Since the disuse of real actions, this mixed proceeding is become the common method of trying the title to lands or tenements. It is therefore proper to detail with some degree of minuteness, its history, the manner of its process, and the principles whereon it is grounded.

The writ of covenant, for breach of the contract contained in the lease for years, was antiently the only specific remedy for recovering against the lessor a term from which he had ejected his lessee, together with damages for the ouster. But if the lessee was ejected by a stranger, claiming under a title superior to that of the lessor, or by a grantee of the reversion, (who might at any time by a common recovery have destroyed the term) though the lessee might still maintain an action of covenant against the lessor for non-performance of his contract or lease, yet he could not by any means recover the term itself. If the ouster was committed by a mere stranger, without any title to the land, the lessor might indeed by a real action recover possession of the freehold, but the lessee had no other remedy against the ejector but in damages, by a writ *de ejectione firmæ,* for the trespass committed in ejecting him from his farm. But afterwards, when the courts of equity began to oblige the ejector to make a specific restitution of the land to the party immediately injured, the courts of law also adopted the same method of doing complete justice; and, in the prosecution of a writ of ejectment, introduced a species of remedy, not warranted by the original writ, nor prayed by the declaration (which go only for damages merely, and are silent as to any restitution) *viz.* a judgment to recover the term, and a writ of possession thereupon. This method seems to have been settled as early as the reign of Edward VI: though it hath been said to have first begun under Henry VII because it probably was then first applied to its present principal use, that of trying the title to the land. 3 *Black.* 200, 1.

This remedy by ejectment *is in its original, an action brought by one who hath a lease for years, to repair the injury done him by dispossession.* In order therefore to convert it into a method of trying titles to the freehold, it is first necessary that the claimant do take possession of the lands, to empower him to constitute a lessee for years, that may be capable of receiving this injury of dispossession. For it would be an offence, called in our law maintenance, to convey a title to another, when the grantor is not in possession of the land: and indeed it was doubted at first, whether this occasional possession, taken merely for the purpose of conveying the title, excused the lessor from the legal guilt of maintenance. When therefore a person, who hath right of entry into lands, determines to acquire that possession, which is wrongfully withheld by the present tenant, he makes (as by law he may) a formal entry on the premises; and being so in possession of the soil, he there, upon the land, seals and delivers a lease for years to some third person or lessee: and, having thus given him entry, leaves him in possession of the premises. This lessee is to stay upon the land, till the prior tenant, or he who had the previous possession, enters thereon afresh and ousts him; or till some other person (either by accident or by agreement before hand) comes upon the land, and turns him out or ejects him. For this injury, the lessee is entitled to his action of ejectment against the tenant, or this casual ejector, whichever it was that ousted him, to recover back his term and damages. But where this action is brought against such a casual ejector as is before mentioned, and not against the very tenant in possession, the court will not suffer the tenant to lose his possession without any opportunity to defend it. Wherefore it is a standing rule, that no plaintiff shall proceed in ejectment to recover lands against a casual ejector, without notice given to the tenant in possession (if any there be) and making him a defendant, if he pleases. And, in order to maintain the action, the plaintiff must, in case of any defence, make out four points before the court; *viz.* title, lease, entry, and ouster. First, he must shew a good title in his lessor, which brings the matter of right entirely before the court; then, that the lessor, being seised by virtue of such title, did make him the lease for the present term; thirdly, that he, the lessee or plaintiff, did enter or take possession in consequence of such lease; and then, lastly, that the defendant ousted or ejected him. Whereupon he shall, in consequence, have a writ of possession, which the sheriff is to execute by delivering him the undisturbed and peaceable possession of his term. 3 *Black.* 201, 2.

This was the regular method of bringing an action of ejectment, in which the title of the lessor comes collaterally and incidentally before the court, in order to shew theinjury done to the lessee by this ouster. And at this day the same method must be still continued in due form and strictness, save only as to the notice to the tenant, whenever the possession is vacant, or there is no actual occupant of the premises; and also in some other cases. But as much trouble and formality were found to attend the actual making of the lease, entry, and ouster, a new and more easy method of trying titles by writ of ejectment, where there is any actual tenant or occupier of the premises in dispute, was invented somewhat more than a century ago, by the lord chief justice Rolle, who then sat in the court of upper bench; so called during the exile of king Charles the second. This new method entirely depends upon a string of legal fictions: no actual lease is made, no actual entry by the plaintiff, no actual ouster by the defendant; but all are merely ideal, for the sole purpose of trying the title. To this end, in the proceedings a lease for a term of years is stated to have been made, by him who claims title, to the plaintiff who brings the action; as by John Rogers to Richard Smith; which plaintiff ought to be some real person, and not merely an ideal fictitious one who has no existence, as is frequently, though unwarrantably practised (6 *Mod.* 309): it is also stated, that Smith, the lessee, entered; and that the defendant William Stiles, who is called the casual ejector, ousted him; for which ouster he brings this action. As soon as this action is brought, and the complaint fully stated in the declaration, Stiles, the casual ejector, or defendant, sends a written notice to the tenant in possession of the lands, as George Saunders, informing him of the action brought by Richard Smith, and transmitting him a copy of the declaration; withal assuring him, that he, Stiles the defendant, has no title at all to the premises, and shall make no defence; and therefore advising the tenant to appear in court and defend his own title: otherwise he, the casual ejector, will suffer judgment to be had against him; and thereby the actual tenant Saunders will inevitably be turned out of possession. On receipt of this friendly caution, if the tenant in possession does not within a limited time apply to the court, to be admitted a defendant in the stead of Stiles, he is supposed to have no right at all; and, upon judgment being had against Stiles, the casual ejector, Saunders the real tenant will be turned out of possession by the sheriff. 3 *Black.* 203.

But, if the tenant in possession applies to be made a defendant, it is allowed him upon this condition, that he enter into a rule of court to confess, at the trial of the cause, three of the four requisites for the maintenance of the plaitnff's action, *viz.* the lease of Rogers the lessor, the entry of Smith the plaintiff, and his ouster by Saunders himself, now made the defendant instead of Stiles: which requisites, as they are wholly fictitious, should the defendant put the plaintiff to prove, he must of course be nonsuited for want of evidence; but by such stipulated confession of lease, entry, and ouster, the trial will now stand upon the merits of the title only. This done, the declaration is altered by inserting the name of George Saunders instead of William Stiles, and the cause goes down to trial under the name of Smith (the plaintiff) on the demise of Rogers, (the lessor) against Saunders, the new defendant. And therein the lessor of the plaintiff is bound to make out a clear title, otherwise his fictitious lessee cannot obtain judgment to have possession of the land for the term supposed to be granted. But, if the lessor makes out his title in a satisfactory manner, then judgment and a writ of possession shall go for Richard Smith the nominal plaintiff, who by this trial has proved the right of John Rogers his supposed lessor. Yet, to prevent fraudulent recoveries of the possession, by collusion with the tenant of the land, all tenants are obliged by stat. 11 *Geo.* 2. *c.* 19. on pain of forfeiting three years rent, to give notice to their landlords, when served with any declaration in ejectment: and any landlord may, by leave of the court, be made a co-defendant to the action; which indeed he had a right to demand, long before the provision of this statute (7 *Mod.* 70. *Salk.* 257): in like manner as (previous to the statute of *Westm.* 2. *c.* 3.) if in a real action, the tenant of the freehold made default, the remainder-man or reversioner had a right to come in and defend the possession; lest, if judgment were had against the tenant, the estate of those behind should be turned to a naked right (*Bracton, l.* 5. *c.* 10. *sect.* 14.) But if the new defendant fails to appear at the trial, and to confess lease, entry, and ouster, the plaintiff Smith must indeed be there nonsuited, for want of proving those requisites; but judgment will in the end be entered against the casual ejector Stiles: for the condition on which Saunders was admitted a defendant is broken, and therefore the plaintiff is put again in the same situation as if he never had appeared at all; the consequence of which would have been, that judgment would have been entered for the plaintiff, and the sheriff, by virtue of a writ for that purpose, would have turned out Saunders, and delivered possession to Smith. The same process therefore as would have been had, provided no conditional rule had been ever made, must now be pursued as soon as the condition is broken. But execution shall be stayed, if any landlord after the default of his tenant applies to be made a defendant, and enters into the usual rule, to confess lease, entry, and ouster (11 *Geo.* 2. *c.* 19.) 3 *Black.* 205.

The damages recovered in these actions, though formerly their only intent, are now usually (since the title has been considered as the principal question) very small and inadequate; amounting commonly to one shilling, or some other trivial sum. In order therefore to complete the remedy, when the possession has been long detained from him that has right, an action of trespass also lies, after a recovery in ejectment, to recover the mesne profits which the tenant in possession has wrongfully received. Which action may be brought in the name of either the nominal plaintiff in the ejectment, or his lessor, against the tenant in possession; whether he be made party to the ejectment, or suffers judgment to go by default. 3 *Black.* 205.

Such is the modern way of obliquely bringing in question the title to lands and tenements, in order to try it in this collateral manner; a method which is now universally adopted in almost every case. It is founded on the same principle as the antient writs of assise, being calculated to try the mere possessory title to an estate; and hath succeeded to those real actions, as being infinitely more convenient for attaining the ends of justice; because, the form of the proceedings being intirely fictitious, it is wholly in the power of the court to direct the application of that fiction, so as to prevent fraud and chicane, and eviscerate the very truth of the title. The writ of ejectment, and its nominal parties (as was resolved by all the judges) are "judicially to be considered as "the fictitious form of an action, really "brought by the lessor of the plaintiff "against the tenant in possession: invent"ed, under the control and power of the "court, for the advancement of justice in "many respects; and to force the parties "to go to trial on the merits, without being "intangled in the nicety of pleadings on "either side." 3 *Black.* 206.

But a writ of ejectment is not an adequate means to try the title of all estates; for on those things whereon an entry cannot in fact be made, no entry shall be supposed by any fiction of the parties. Therefore an ejectment will not lie of an advowson, a rent, a common, or other incorporeal hereditament; except for tithes in the hands of lay appropriators, by the express purview of statute 32 *Hen.* 8. *c.* 7. which doctrine hath since been extended by analogy to tithes in the hands of the clergy; nor will it lie in such cases, where the entry of him that hath right is taken away by discent, discontinuance, twenty years dispossession, or otherwise. 3 *Black.* 206.

This action of ejectment is, however, rendered a very easy and expeditious remedy to landlords, whose tenants are in arrear, by statute 4 *Geo.* 2. *c.* 28. which enacts, that every landlord, who hath by his lease a right of re-entry in case of non-payment of rent, when half a year's rent is due, and no sufficient distress is to be had, may serve a declaration in ejectment on his tenant, or fix the same upon some notorious part of the premises, which shall be valid, without any formal re-entry or previous demand of rent. And a recovery in such ejectment shall be final and conclusive, both in law and equity, unless the rent and all costs be paid or tendered within six calendar months afterwards. 3 *Black.* 206.

The writ of *quare ejecit infra terminum* lieth, by the antient law, where the wrong doer or ejector is not himself in possession of the lands, but another who claims under him. As where a man leaseth lands to another for years, and, after, the lessor or reversioner entereth, and maketh a feoffment in fee, or for life, of the same lands to a stranger: now the lessee cannot bring a writ of *ejectione firmæ* or ejectment against the feoffee; because he did not eject him, but the reversioner: neither can he have any such action to recover his term against the reversioner, who did oust him; because he is not now in possession. And upon that account this writ was devised, upon the equity of the statute *Westm.* 2. *c.* 24, as in a case where no adequate remedy was already provided. And the action is brought against the feoffee for deforcing, or keeping out, the original lessee during the continuance of his term: and herein, as in the ejectment, the plaintiff shall recover so much of the term as remains, and also damages for that portion of it whereof he has been unjustly deprived. But since the introduction of fictitious ousters, whereby the title may be tried against any tenant in possession (by what means soever he acquired it) this action is fallen into disuse. 3 *Black.* 207.

EJECTUM, *ejectus maris, quod e mari ejicitur*: jet, jetsom, wreck, &c. See *Wreck.*

EIGNE, (Fr. *aisne*) eldest or first-born; thus bastard *eigne* is the elder son of a woman, born out of wedlock; and *mulier puisne, quasi melior* the younger son afterwards born in marriage.

EINECIA, (Fr. *aisne*, i e. *primogenitus*) signifies eldership. *Cowel. Blount.*

EIRE, or EYRE, (Fr. *eire*, i. e. *iter*) justices in eyre, *justiciarii itinerantes*, were appointed by the great council of the realm, A. D. 1176, 22 *H.* 2, with a delegated power from the king's great court, or *aula regia*, and they made their circuit round the kingdom once in seven years for the purpose of trying causes. They were afterwards directed by *Mag. Char.* to be sent into every county once a year, to take or try certain actions or assises, the most difficult of which they were directed to adjourn into the court of common pleas, to be there determined; and from these the present justices of assise have originated. 3 *Black.* 57.

ELECTION, (*electio*) is when a man is left to his own free will to take or do one thing or another which he pleases. And if it be of several things, he who is the first agent, and ought to do the first act, shall have the election. *Co. Lit.* 144.

As if I give to you one of my horses in my stable, there you shall have the election, for you shall be the first agent by taking or seizure of one of them. *Co. Lit.* 145.

Where the election creates the interest nothing passes till election, and if no election can be made, no interest will arise. *Hob.* 174. Also if the election is given to several persons, there the first election made by any of the persons shall stand. *Co. Lit.* 145. 2 *Rep.* 36.

If a man has an election to do one of two things, and he cannot by any default of a stranger, or of himself, or the obligee, or by the act of God, do the one, he must at his peril do the other. 1 *Lil. Abr.* 506.

Where the law allows a man two actions to recover his right, it is at his election to bring which he pleases; and when a man's act may work two ways, both arising of his interest, he hath election given him to use it either way. *Dyer* 20. 2 *Roll. Abr.* 787.

If a person hath election to pay or perform one of two things at a day, and he do neither of them at that day, his election is gone. 2 *Rep.* 37.

In some cases where one has cause of suit he may sue one person or another at his election, for there is an election of persons as well as of things. *Dyer* 204, 207.

ELECTION OF A CLERK OF STATUTE-MERCHANT. A writ anciently laid for the choice of a clerk assigned to take bonds called statutes-merchant, granted out of the chancery, upon suggestion that the clerk formerly assigned was gone to dwell at another place, or under some impediment to attend the duty of his office, or had not lands sufficient to answer his transgressions, if he should act amiss, &c. *F. N. B.* 164.

ELECTION OF ECCLESIASTICAL PERSONS. By 9 *Ed.* 2, *c.* 14, there is to be a free election for the dignities of the church. And by 31 *Eliz. c.* 6, none shall disturb any person from making free election, on pain of great forfeiture. If any persons that have a voice in elections, take any reward for an election in any church, college, school, &c. the election shall be void: and if any of such societies resign their places to others for reward, they incur a forfeiture of double the sum; and the party giving it, and the party taking it, is incapable of such place.

ELECTION OF MEMBERS OF PARLIAMENT. See *Parliament.*

ELECTION OF A VERDEROR OF THE FOREST (*electione viridariorum forestæ*). For the choice of a verderor, where any of the verderors of the forest were dead, or removed from their office, &c. a writ was directed to the sheriff, and the verderors were to be elected by the freeholders of the county, in the same manner as coroners. *New Nat. Br.* 366. *Cowel. Blount.*

ELEEMOSYNÆ, the possessions belonging to the churches. *Blount.*

ELEEMOSYNA REGIS, or *eleemosyna aratri*, a penny ordered by king *Æthelred* to be paid for every plough in England, towards the support of the poor: and so called because it was first appointed by the king. *Leg. Æthelred, cap.* 1. *Cowel. Blount.*

ELEEMOSYNARIA, the place in a religious house, where the common alms were reposited, and thence by the almoner distributed to the poor. *Ibid.*

ELEEMOSYNARIUS, the almoner or peculiar officer who received *eleemosynary*, rents and gifts, and in due method distributed them to pious and charitable uses. *Ibid.*

ELEEMOSYNARY CORPORATIONS, are corporate bodies appointed over hospitals, &c. constituted for the perpetual distribution of the free alms, or bounty of the founder o fthem. 1 *Black. Com.* 471.

ELEGIT, (from the words in it, *elegit sibi liberar*) is a writ of execution that lies for him who hath recovered debt or damages, or, upon a recognizance in any court against one not able in his goods to satisfy the same; directed to the sheriff, commanding him to make delivery of a moiety of the party's land, and all his goods, beasts of the plough excepted. And the creditor shall hold the said moiety of the land so delivered unto him, until his whole debt and damages are paid and satisfied; and during that term he is tenant by elegit. *Reg. Orig.* 299. *Co. Lit* 289. See title *Execution.*

ELF-ARROWS, were flint-stones sharpened on each side in shape of arrow-heads, made use of in war by the ancient Britons. *Cowel. Blount.*

ELISORS. If the sheriff be not an indifferent person, as if he be a party in the suit, or be related, either by blood or affinity, to either of the parties, he is not then trusted to return a jury; but the *venire* shall be directed to the coroners, who in this, as in many other instances, are the substitutes of the sheriff, to execute process when he is deemed an improper person: if any exception lies to the coroners, the *venire* shall be directed to two clerks of the court, or two persons of the county, named by the court, and sworn, *and these two, who are called elisors* or electors, shall indifferently name the jury, and their return is final. 3 *Black.* 355.

ELKE, a kind of yew to make bows of. 32 *H.* 8. *cap.* 9. Also the name of the wild beast somewhat like a deer. *Cowel. Blount.*

ELOINE, (from the Fr. *esloisner*) to remove or send a great way off: and by 13 *Ed.* 1. *c.* 15. If such as are within age be eloined, so that they cannot come to sue personally, their next friends shall be admitted to sue for them.

ELONGATA, a return to the sheriff that cattle are not to be found, or removed, so that he cannot make deliverance, &c. in replevin. 2 *Lil. Abr.* 454, 458. 3 *Black.* 129. 149.

ELOPEMENT, (derived from the Belg. E, *viz. matrimonio* & loopen, *currere*) is where a married woman of her own accord goes away and departs from her husband, and lives with an adulterer. And in this case her husband is not obliged to allow her any alimony, nor shall he be chargeable for necessaries for her. And where the same is notorious, whoever gives her credit, doth it at his peril: but on elopement, the putting a wife in the Gazette, or other news-paper is no legal notice to persons in general not to trust her; though personal notice to particular persons given by the husband, will be good not to be chargeable to them. 1 *Rol.* 350. 1 *Vent.* 42. Also by *Stat.* 13 *Ed.* 1. *c.* 34, if the wife goes away from the husband, and tarrieth with the adulterer, without returning and being reconciled to her husband, she forfeits her dower.

Also an action lies against the adulterer for carrying away another person's wife.

ELY, is only a royal franchise, and not a county palatine, though sometimes erroneously called so. 1 *Black. Com.* 118. 3 *Ib.* 78.

EMBARGO, a prohibition upon shipping, not to go out of any port. *Cowel. Blount.* 1 *Black.* 270.

EMBASSADORS. See *Ambassadors.*

EMBLEMENTS, (from the Fr. *emblavence de bled*, viz. corn sprung or put up above ground) signifies properly the profits of sown land: but is sometimes used more largely for any products that arise naturally from the ground, as grass, fruit, and other crops. 5 *Rep.* 116.

A tenant for life, or his representatives, shall not be prejudiced by any sudden determination of his estate, because such a determination is contingent and uncertain; therefore if a tenant for his own life sows the lands and dies before harvest, his executors shall have the *emblements*, or profits of the crop, and not the lessor or reversioner: for the estate was determined by the *act of God;* and it is a maxim of the law that *actus Dei nemini facit injuriam*: the representatives, therefore, of the tenant for life shall have the emblements to compensate for the labour and expense of tilling, manuring, and sowing the lands; and also for the encouragement of husbandry, which being a public benefit, tending to the increase and plenty of provisions, ought to have the utmost security and privilege that the law can give it. *Co. Lit.* 55. 2 *Black.* 122. *Cro. Eliz.* 463. 2 *Danv. Abr.* 765.

Also if a man be tenant for the life of another, and *cestui que vie*, or he on whose life the land is held, dies after the corn sown, the tenant *pur autre vie* shall have the emblements. *Ibid.*

The same is also the rule if a life estate be determined by the act of law: therefore if a lease be made to husband and wife during coverture (which gives them a determinable estate for life) and the husband sows the land, and afterwards they are divorced *a vinculo matrimonii*, the husband shall have the emblements in this case, for the sentence of divorce is the act of law. *Ibid.*

But if an estate for life be determined by the *tenant's own act*, (as by surrender to the lessor before severance, forfeiture for waste committed, or, if a tenant during widowhood thinks proper to marry, in these and similar cases, the tenants having thus determined the estate by their own acts, shall not be entitled to the emblements. 1 *Lil. Abr.* 511. 2 *Black.* 122, 3.

The doctrine of emblements extends not only to corn sown, but to roots planted, or other annual artificial profits; but it is otherwise of fruit trees, grass, and the like, which are not planted annually at the expense and labour of the tenant, but are either a permanent or natural profit of the earth. *Co. Lit.* 55, 56. 1 *Rol. Abr.* 728. For when a man plants a tree he cannot be presumed to plant it in contemplation of any present profit, but merely with a prospect of its being useful to himself in future, and to future successions of tenants. 2 *Black.* 123.

The advantages also of emblements are particularly extended to the parochial clergy by stat. 28 *Hen.* 8, *c.* 12, which *enables an incumbent to bequeath by will the corn and grain growing upon the glebe land:* for all persons who are presented to any ecclesiastical benefice, or to any civil office, are considered as tenants for their own lives, unless the contrary be expressed in the form of donation. 2 *Black.* 123, 4.

With regard to emblements, or the profits of lands sown by tenant for years, there is this difference between him and tenant for life, that where the term of tenant for years depends upon a certainty, as if he holds from Midsummer for ten years, and in the last year he sows a crop of corn, and it is not ripe and cut before Midsummer, the end of his term, the landlord shall have it; for the tenant knew the expiration of his term, and therefore it was his own folly to sow what he never could reap the profits of. *Lit. s.* 68. 2 *Black.* 144, 5.

But where the lease for years depends upon an uncertainty, as upon the death of the lessor, being himself only tenant for life, or being a husband seised in right of his wife, or if the term of years be determinable upon a life or lives, in all these cases the estate for years not being certainly to expire at a time foreknown, but merely by the act of God, the tenant or his executors shall be entitled thereto: but it is not so if it determine by the act of the party himself: as if tenant for years does any thing that amounts to a forfeiture, in which case the emblements shall go to the lessor, and not to the lessee, who hath determined his estate by his own default. *Ibid.*

These emblements are distinct from the real estate in the land, and subject to many, though not all, the incidents attending personal chattels; but they are not the subject of larceny until severed. 2 *Black.* 403.

If husband and wife are jointenants, though the husband sow the land with corn, and dies before ripe, the wife and not his executors shall have the corn, she being the surviving jointenant. *Co. Lit.* 199.

So if a widow is endowed with lands sown, she shall have the emblements, and not the heir. 2 *Inst.* 81. And a tenant in dower may dispose of corn sown on the ground; or it may go to her executors, if she die before severance. 2 *Inst.* 80, 81.

If tenant by statute-merchant sows the land, and before severance a casual profit happens, by which he is satisfied, yet he shall have the corn. *Co. Lit.* 55. Also if lands sown are delivered in execution, the person to whom delivered shall have the corn on the ground. 2 *Leon.* 54.

A person seised in fee of land dies, having a daughter, and his wife *privement ensient* with a son; the daughter enters and sows the land, and before severance of the corn, the son is born; in this case the daughter shall have the corn, her estate being lawful, and defeated by the act of God; and it is for the public good that the land should be sown. *Co. Lit.* 55.

A man seised in fee-simple sows land, and then devises the land by will, and dies before severance; the devisee shall have the corn; and not the devisor's executors. *Winch* 52. *Cro. Eliz.* 61. But if he dies without will, it goes to the executor, and not the heir. 10 *Ed.* 4. 1. *b.* 21 *H.* 6. 30. *a.* 37 *H.* 6. 35. *b.*

Where there is a right to emblements, ingress, egress and regress are allowed by law, to enter, cut and carry them away, when the estate is determined, &c. 1 *Inst.* 56.

EMBLERS DE GENTS, (Fr.) a stealing from the people. *Cowel. Blount.*

EMBRACEOR, (Fr. *embrasour*) is one who, when a matter is in trial between party and party, (not being counsel or attorney in the cause) comes to the bar with one of the parties, having received some reward so to do, and speaks in the case; or privately labours the jury, or stands in the court to survey and overlook them, whereby they are awed or influenced, or put in fear or doubt of the matter. *Co. Lit.* 369. *Hob.* 294. 1 *Saund.* 391. So if the party himself instruct a juror, or promise any reward for his appearance, then the party is likewise an embraceor. And a juror may be guilty of embracery, where he by indirect practices gets himself sworn on the tales, to serve on one side. 1 *Lil.* 513.

EMBRACERY, is the act or offence of embraceors, and to attempt to influence a jury, or any way incline them to be more favourable to the one side than the other, by promises, threatenings, money, treats, or the like, whether the jurors upon whom any such attempt is made, give any verdict or not, or whether the verdict pass on his side or not, this is embracery. *Co. Lit.* 369. *Noy's Rep.* 102. 4 *Black.* 140.

The punishment for the person embracing is by fine and imprisonment; and for the juror so embraced, if it be by taking money, the punishment is by divers statutes of the reign of *Ed.* 3, perpetual infamy, imprisonment for one year, and forfeiture of tenfold the value. 4 *Black.* 140.

EMBRING DAYS, (from embers, *cineres*) so called either because our ancestors when they fasted sat in ashes, or strewed them on their heads, are of great antiquity in the church: they are observed on Wednesday,

Friday, and Saturday next after *quadragesima* Sunday, (or the first Sunday in Lent) after Whitsunday, Holyrood day in September, and St. Lucy's day, about the middle of December; hence in our calendar these weeks are called Ember weeks.

EMBROIDERY. See *Manufactures*.

EMENDALS, (*emenda*) an old word, used in the accounts of the Inner Temple, where so much in emendals at the foot of an account signifies the balance thereof. *Cowel. Blount.*

EMENDARE, *emendam solvere*, to make amends for any crime or trespass committed. *Ibid.*

EMENDATIO, the power of amending and correcting abuses, according to stated rules and measures. *Ibid.*

EMPANNEL a jury, *ponere in assisis et juratis, &c.* See *Juries*.

EMPEROR, (*imperator*) the highest ruler of large kingdoms; a title anciently given to renowned and victorious generals. This title was formerly belonging to the kings of England, as appears by a charter of king *Edgar*, viz. *ego Edgarus Anglorum Basileus, omniumque regum insularum oceani quæ Britanniam circumjacent, &c. imperator et dominus.* *Cowel. Blount.*

EMPHYTENSIS. By the civil law if a tenant who held lands upon payment of rent or services, or as they call it *jure emphytentiro*, neglected to pay or perform them *per totum triennium*, he might be ejected from such *emphytentic* lands. *Cod.* 466, 22. 3 *Black.* 232.

ENBREVER, (Fr.) to write down in short. *Britton* 56.

ENCHESON, a French word, signifying the cause or reason wherefore any thing is done. Stat. 5 *Ed.* 3. *c.* 3. *Cowel. Blount.*

ENDEAVOUR. According to the common law where one who has the use of his reason endeavours to commit felony, &c. he may be punished as for a misdemeanor, and fined and imprisoned. 3 *Inst.* 68, 69, 161. 11 *Rep.* 98.

And now by stat. 7 *Geo.* 2, *c.* 21, it is made felony (transportable for 7 years) unlawfully and maliciously to assault another with any offensive weapon, or instrument, or by menace, or by other forcible or violent manner to demand any money or goods with a felonious intent to rob.

ENDOWMENT, signifies the bestowing or assuring of dower on a woman, but sometimes the settling a provision upon a parson, or building of a church or chapel, and the severing a sufficient portion of tithes, &c. for the vicar, towards his perpetual maintenance, when the benefice is appropriated. Stat. 15 *R.* 2, *c.* 6. 4 *H.* 4, *c.* 12.

ENEMY, (*inimicus*) is an alien or foreigner who under the authority of his own government acts in a hostile manner towards any other nation; and whether such persons act by themselves or in company with traitors, they cannot be punished as traitors, but shall be dealt with by martial law. *H. P. C.* 10, 15. 1 *Hawk.* 35. 1 *Black.* 257.

But the subjects of a foreign prince coming into England, and living under the protection of the king, if they take up arms against the government, may be punished as traitors, not as alien enemies. 1 *Hawk. ibid.* for such unauthorized volunteers in violence are not ranked among open enemies, but are treated like pirates and robbers, according to the rule of the civil law, *hostes hi sunt qui nobis aut quibus nos publice bellum decrevimus: cæteri latrones aut prædones sunt.* 1 *Black.* 257.

ENFRANCHISE, (Fr. *enfranchir*) to make free, or incorporate a man in any society, &c. *Cowel. Blount.*

ENFRANCHISEMENT, (Fr. *franchise*, i. e. *libertas*) signifies the act of incorporation whereby a person is incorporated into any society or body politic, and made partaker of those liberties, that appertain to the corporation. When a man is enfranchised into the freedom of any city or borough he hath a freehold in his freedom during life. 11 *Rep.* 91.

ENGLECERY, or ENGLESCHIRE, (*Engleceria*) an old word signifying the being an Englishman. *Cowel. Blount.*

ENGLISH. Pleas, records, bonds, and proceedings in courts of justice, are to be in English. 4 *Geo.* 2, *c.* 26. And see 5 *Geo.* 2, *c.* 27. 6 *Geo.* 2, *c.* 14.

ENGRAVINGS. By 8 *Geo.* 2, *c.* 13, persons who shall design, engrave, etch, or work in mezzotinto or chiaro obscuro, any historical or other prints, shall have the sole right of printing and publishing the same for fourteen years, so as the proprietor's name is affixed to each print.

Printsellers or others pirating or copying the same, are to forfeit the plates, and also five shillings for every copy found in their custody, if prosecuted within three months, half the penalty to the king, and half to the informer; but this act does not extend to purchasers of plates from the original proprietors. *Ibid.*

By 7 *Geo.* 3, *c.* 38, the original inventors, designers, or engravers of historical or other prints, and such who shall cause prints to be done from works of their own invention, and also such as shall engrave any print taken from any picture, drawing, model, or sculpture, are entitled to the benefit and protection of the above act; and those who shall engrave or import for sale copies of such prints, are liable to the like penalties, with costs, so as prosecuted within six months.

The right intended to be secured by this and the above act is extended, and vested in the proprietors for the term of twenty-eigh years from publication. *Ibid.*

By 17 *Geo.* 3, *c.* 57, if any engraver shall, within the above term, engrave or etch any print, without the consent of the proprietor, he shall be liable to an action for damages and double costs.

ENGROSSING, is the getting into one's possession, or buying up large quantities of corn, or other dead victuals, with intent to sell them again, this must of course be injurious to the public, by putting it in the power of one or two rich men to raise the price of provisions at their own discretion. And so the total engrossing of any other commodity with intent to sell it at an unreasonable price, is an offence indictable and finable at the common law. And the general punishment for such offence by the common law (all the statutes concerning them having been repealed) is, as in other misdemeanors, discretionary fine and imprisonment. 4 *Black.* 158, 9.

ENHANCE, to raise the price of goods or merchandise. *Cowel. Blount.*

ENPLEET, anciently used for implead. *Ibid.*

ENQUIRY, WRIT OF. Where a defendant suffers judgment to go against him by default, that is, by neglecting to put in any plea to the plaintiff's declaration: in such case, if the damages to be recovered, are uncertain, the judgment is *interlocutory*, and not final, and a writ issues to the sheriff to summon a jury to enquire what damages the plaintiff hath sustained, and when this is returned, with the inquisition thereon taken, final judgment is entered, and execution sued out. But if default be made in any action where the specific thing sued for, is to be recovered, as in detinue, or debt for a sum or thing certain, there the judgment is final and absolute in the first instance, and there is no necessity for any writ of enquiry.

ENROLMENT. Deeds were enrolled at common law for their preservation, though not to pass any estate. *Style.* 370. But now by the stat. 27 *Hen.* 8, *c.* 10, and 27 *Hen.* 8. c. 16, no deed of bargain and sale is effectual to pass any estate of inheritance, unless the same is enrolled in one of the courts at Westminster, or in the county where the lands lie, with the *custos rotulorum*, within six months after the date. The 5 *Eliz. c.* 26, also authorizes the courts in the counties-palatine to enrol bargains and sales in like manner. Also the 5 *Ann. c.* 18, authorizes the registrars of the west riding, and 6 *Ann.* c. 35, *s.* 16, the registrars of the east riding of Yorkshire, to make like enrolments.

ENSIENT, or ENSEINT, is the being with child. *Law Fr. Dict. Ibid.*

ENSIENTURE, of any woman condemned for a crime, is no ground to stay judgment, but it may be afterwards alleged against execution. 2 *Hale's Hist. P. C.* 413.

ENTAIL, (Fr. *entaille*, i. e. *incisus*) is a fee entailed, *viz.* abridged, limited, and tied to certain conditions, at the will of the donor; where lands are given to or settled on others. See *Fee* and *Tail.*

ENTERPLEADER, (*enterplaider*, Fr. *interplacitare*, Lat.) signifies to discuss or try a point incidentally happening as it were between, before the principal cause can be determined. And *enterpleader* is allowed, that the defendant may not be charged to two severally, where no default is in him; as if one brings detinue against the defendant upon a bailment of goods, and another against him upon a trover, there shall be *enterpleader* to ascertain who has right to his action. 2 *Danv. Abr.* 779.

Formerly the head enterpleader made a great title in the law, but the bill of interpleader in courts of equity (which see under the head BILL in EQUITY) having been found most convenient, it is unnecessary to enlarge upon the subject in this place.

ENTIERTIE, (from the Fr. *entierete*, entireness) is a contradistinction in our books to moiety, denoting the whole. *Cowel. Blount.*

Thus if there be a devise to husband and wife, and to their heirs and assigns for ever, they take by entireties, and not by moieties; and it being uncertain until the death of one, in whom the whole entirety will vest, the husband alone cannot by his own conveyance divest the estate of the wife. 5 *Ter. Rep.* 652.

ENTIRE TENANCY, contrary to several tenancy, and signifying a sole possession in one man, whereas the other is a joint or common possession in more. *Brook. Cowel. Blount.*

ENTRY, (*ingressus*, Fr. *entrée*, i. e. *introitus*) signifies the taking possession of lands or tenements, where a man hath title of entry, and it is also used for a writ of possession. This entry into lands is where any man enters into or takes possession of any lands, &c. in his proper person; and is an actual entry when made by a man's self, or by attorney, by warrant from him that has the right; or it is an entry in law, for a continual claim is an entry implied by law, and has the same force with it. *Lit. sec.* 419.

Where a stranger who has no right hath taken possession of lands, in this case the *legal* owner may make a formal but peaceable entry thereon, declaring that thereby he takes possession; which notorious act of ownership is equivalent to a feodal investiture by the lord; or he may enter on any part of it in the same county, declaring it to be in the name of the whole, but if it lies in different counties he must make different entries; for the notoriety of such entry or claim to the *pares* or freeholders of Westmorland, is not any notoriety to the *pares* or freeholders of Sussex. Also if there be two disseisors the party disseised must make his entry on both: or if one disseisor has conveyed the lands with livery to two distinct feoffees, entry must be made on both: for as their seisin is distinct, so also must be the act which devests that seisin. If the claimant be deterred from entering by menaces or bodily fear, he may make claim as near to the estate as he can, with the like forms and solemnities, which claim is in force for a year and a day only. And therefore this claim, if it be repeated once in the space of every year and day (which is called continual claim), has the same effect with, and in all respects amounts to, a legal entry. Such an entry gives a man seisin, or puts him into immediate possession that hath right of entry on the estate, and thereby makes him complete owner, and capable of conveying it from himself either by descent or purchase. 3 *Black.* 175.

This remedy by entry takes place in three only of the five species of ouster, *viz.* abatement, intrusion, and disseisin: for, as in these the original entry of the wrongdoer was unlawful, they may therefore be remedied by the mere entry of him who hath right. But, upon a discontinuance or deforcement, the owner of the estate cannot enter, but is driven to his action: for herein the original entry being lawful, and thereby an apparent right of possession being gained, the law will not suffer that right to be overthrown by the mere act or entry of the claimant. *Ibid.*

On the other hand, in case of abatement, intrusion, or disseisin, where entries are generally lawful, this right of entry may be tolled, that is, taken away, by descent. Descents, which take away entries, are when any one, seised by any means whatsoever of the inheritance of a corporeal hereditament, dies, whereby the same descends to his heir: in this case, however feeble the right of the ancestor might be, the entry of any other person, who claims title to the freehold is taken away; and he cannot recover possession against the heir by this summary method, but is driven to his action to gain a legal seisin of the estate. And this, first, because the heir comes to the estate by act of law, and not by his own act; the law therefore protects his title, and will not suffer his possession to be devested, till the claimant has proved a better right. Secondly, because the heir may not suddenly know the true state of his title, and therefore the law, which is ever indulgent to heirs, takes away the entry of such claimant as neglected to enter on the ancestor, who was well able to defend his title, and leaves the claimant only the remedy of a formal action against the heir. Thirdly, this was admirably adapted to the military spirit of the feodal tenures, and tended to make the feudatory bold in war, since his children could not by any mere entry of another, be dispossessed of the lands whereof he died seised. And, lastly, it is agreeable to the dictates of reason and the general principles of law. 3 *Black.* 176.

For, in every complete title to lands there are two things necessary, the possession or seisin, and the right or property therein, or, as it is expressed in Fleta, the *juris et seisinæ conjunctio.* Now, if the possession be severed from the property, if A has the *jus proprietatis*, and B by some unlawful means has gained possession of the lands, this is an injury to A, for which the law gives a remedy, by putting him in possession, but does it by different means according to the circumstances of the case. Thus, as B, who was himself the wrongdoer, and hath obtained the possession by either fraud or force, hath only a bare or naked possession, without any shadow of right; A, therefore, who hath both the right of property and the right of possession, may put an end to his title at once, by the summary method of entry. But if B, the wrongdoer, dies seised of the lands, then B's heir advances one step farther towards a good title: he hath not only a bare possession, but also an apparent *jus possessionis*, or right of possession: for the law presumes that the possession, which is transmitted from the ancestor to the heir, is a rightful possession until the contrary be shown; and therefore the mere entry of A is not allowed to evict the heir of B, but A is driven to his action at law to remove the possession of the heir, though his entry alone would have dispossessed the ancestor. 3 *Black.* 176, 177.

So that in general it appears, that no man can recover possession by mere entry on lands which another hath by descent. Yet this rule hath some exceptions; wherein those reasons cease upon which the general doctrine is grounded, especially if the claimant were under any legal disabilities during the life of the ancestor, either of infancy, coverture, imprisonment, insanity, or being out of the realm: in all which cases there is no neglect or laches in the claimant, and therefore no descent shall bar, or take away his entry. And this title of taking away entries by descent, is still farther narrowed by the statute 32 *Hen.* 8. *c.* 33, which enacts, that if any person disseises or turns another out of possession, no descent to the heir of the disseisor shall take away the entry of him that has right to the land, unless the disseisor had peaceable possession five years next after the disseisin. But the statute extendeth not to any feoffee or donee of the disseisor, mediate or immediate; because such a one by the genuine feodal constitutions always came into the tenure solemnly and with the lord's concurrence, by actual delivery of seisin or open and public investiture. On the other hand, it is enacted by the statute of limitations, 21 *Jac.* 1. c. 16, that no entry shall be made by any man upon lands, unless twenty years after his right shall accrue. And by statute 4 & 5 *Ann.* c. 16, no entry shall be of force to satisfy the said statute of limitations, or to avoid a fine levied of lands, unless an action be thereupon commenced within one year after, and prosecuted with effect. 3 *Black.* 177, 8.

Upon an ouster, by the discontinuance of tenant in tail, we have said that no remedy by mere entry is allowed; but that, when tenant in tail alienes the lands entailed, this takes away the entry of the issue in tail, and drives him to his action at law to recover the possession. For, as in the former cases the law will not suppose, without proof, that the ancestor of him in possession acquired the estate by wrong; and therefore, after five years peaceable possession, and a descent cast, will not suffer the possession of the heir to be disturbed by mere entry without action; so here, the law will not suppose the discontinuor to have aliened the estate without power so to do, and therefore leaves the heir in tail to his action at law, and permits not his entry to be lawful. Besides, the alienee, who came into possession by a lawful conveyance, which was at least good for the life of the alienor, hath not only a bare possession, but also an apparent right of possession; which is not allowed to be devested by the mere entry of the claimant, but continues in force till a better right be shown and recognized by a legal determination. And something also, perhaps, in framing this rule of law, may be allowed to the inclination of the courts of justice, to go as far as they could in making estates-tail alienable, by declaring such alienations to be voidable only, and not absolutely void. 3 *Black.* 178.

In case of deforcements also, where the deforciant had originally a lawful possession of the land, but now detains it wrongfully, he still continues to have the presumptive *prima facie* evidence of right, that is, possession lawfully gained: which possession shall not be overturned by the mere entry of another, but only by the demandant's showing a better right in a course of law. 3 *Black.* 178, 9.

This remedy by entry must be pursued, according to the statute 5 *Ric.* 2, stat. 1. *c.* 8, in a peaceable and easy manner, and not with force or strong hand. For if one turns or keeps another out of possession forcibly, this is an injury of both a civil and a criminal nature. The civil is remedied by immediate restitution, which puts the ancient possessor in *statu quo*: the criminal injury, or public wrong, by breach of the king's peace, is punished by fine to the king. For by the stat. 8 *Hen.* 6. *c.* 9, upon complaint made to any justice of the peace of a forcible entry, with strong hand, on lands or tenements, or a forcible detainer after a peaceable entry, he shall try the truth of the complaint by jury, and, upon force found, shall restore the possession to the party so put out; and in such case, or if any alienation be made to defraud the possessor of his right (which is declared to be absolutely void) the offender shall forfeit for the force found treble damages to the party grieved, and make fine and ransom to the king. But this does not extend to such as endeavour to keep possession *manu forti*, after three years peaceable enjoyment of either themselves, their ancestors, or those under whom they claim, by a subsequent clause of the same stat. enforced by stat. 31 *Eliz.* *c.* 11. *Ibid.* See *Forcible Entry.*

ENTRY, WRITS OF. The ancient writs of entry were of four degrees:

I. The first a writ of entry *sur disseisin*, for the disseisee against a disseisor, upon a disseisin done by himself, and was called a writ of entry in the nature of an assise:

II. A writ of entry *sur disseisin in le per*, for the heir by discent, who is said to be in the *per*, as he comes in by his ancestor; and so it is if a disseisor make a feoffment in fee, gift in tail, &c. the feoffee and donee are in the *per* by the disseisor.

III. A writ of entry *sur disseisin in le per & cui*, where the feoffee of a disseisor makes a feoffment over to another, when the disseisee shall have this writ of entry *sur disseisin, &c.* of the lands in which such other had no right of entry but by the feoffee of the disseisor, to whom the disseisor demised the same, who unjustly and without judgment disseised the demandant:

IV. A writ of *entry sur disseisin in le post*, which lieth when after a disseisin the land is removed from hand to hand beyond the degrees, in case of a more remote seisin, whereunto the other three degrees do not extend. *Co. Lit.* 238.

The writ of *entry in le post* is so called, because the words of the writ are, *Post disseisinam quam B. injuste & sine judicio fecit*, &c. And the words, *in le per*, *in le per & cui*, and *in le post*, signified nothing but divers forms of this writ, applied to the case whereupon it was brought. *F. N. B.* 193.

ENTRY AD COMMUNEM LEGEM, an ancient writ of entry which laid where tenant for term of life, or for term of another's life, or by the curtesy, &c. aliened and died, when he in the reversion had this writ against whomsoever was in possession of the land. *New Nat. Br.* 461. *Cowel. Blount.*

ENTRY AD TERMINUM QUI PRETERIIT, a writ of entry brought against a tenant for years, who held over his term, and thereby kept out the lessor. *New Nat. Br.* 447, 448. But an ejectment is now the usual course of proceeding to recover the possession.

ENTRY IN CASU CONSIMILI. See *Casu Consimili.*

ENTRY IN CASU PROVISO. See *Casu Proviso.*

ENTRY SINE ASSENSU CAPITALI, a writ of entry that laid where a bishop, abbot, &c. aliened lands or tenements of the church, without the assent of the chapter or convent. *F. N. B.* 195. *Cowel. Blount.*

ENURE, signifies in the law to take place

or be available; and is as much as *effectum*, as for example; a release made to tenant for life, shall enure, and be of force and effec to him in the reversion. *Ibid. Co. Lit.* 193. *a. b.* 273.

EODORBRICE, (from the Sax. *eodor*, a hedge, and brice, *ruptura*) hedge-breaking. *Cowel. Blount.*

EORLE, Sax. for earl. See *Earl. Ibid.*

EPIMENIA, expenses or gifts. *Cowel. Blount.*

EPIPHANY, the day when the star appeared to the wise men at Christ's nativity, generally called Twelfth-day. *Ibid.*

EPISCOPALIA, synodals, or other customary payments from the clergy to their bishop or diocesan; formerly collected by the rural deans, and by them transmitted to the bishop. *Ibid.*

EPISCOPUS PUERORUM. A custom in former times in some places, (long since abolished) for some lay person, at a particular festival, to put on the garments of a bishop, and in them exercise episcopal jurisdiction, and do several ludicrous actions, for which reason he was called bishop of the boys. *Mon. Ang. tom.* 3. *pag.* 169. *Cowel. Blount.*

EQUALITY, It is a maxim in Equity that "equality is equity." *Fran. Max.* 9. And at common law if a charge is made upon one, and divers ought to bear it, he shall have relief against the rest. 2 *Rep.* 25. Also under a power to give an estate, or bequeath monies to younger children, in such proportions as the party shall think fit, the party executing such power must give to each an *equal* or at least a *substantial* share, and not an *illusory*, nominal, or trifling one, unless good reason be given for doing otherwise. *Prec. Canc.* 256.

EQUES AURATUS, (Lat.) a knight, because anciently none but knights were allowed to beautify and gild their armour with gold. 4 *Inst.* 5. *Cowel. Blount.*

EQUITY (*æquitas, quasi equalitas*). Equity, in its true and genuine meaning, is the soul and spirit of all law, and is synonimous to justice. But the terms of a court of equity and a court of law, as contrasted to each other, are apt to confound and mislead us: as if the one judged without equity, and the other was not bound by any law: whereas every illustration to be met with, which now draws a line between the two jurisdictions, by setting law and equity in opposition to each other, will be found either totally erroneous, or erroneous to a certain degree. 3 *Black.* 429.

1. Thus, in the first place it is said, that it is the business of a court of equity in England *to abate the rigour* of the common law. But no such power is contended for. Hard was the case of bond-creditors, whose debtor devised away his real estate; rigorous and unjust the rule, which put the devisee in a better condition than the heir: yet a court of equity had no power to interpose. Hard is the common law still subsisting, that land devised, or descending to the heir, shall not be liable to simple contract debts of the ancestor or devisor, although the money was laid out in purchasing the very land *, and that the father shall never immediately succeed as heir to the real estate of the son, but a court of equity can give no relief; though in both these instances the artificial reason of the law, arising from feodal principles, has long ago entirely ceased. The like may be observed of the descent of lands to a remote relation of the whole blood, or even their escheat to the lord in preference to the owner's half-brother, and of the total stop to all justice, by causing the parol to demur, whenever an infant is sued as heir or is party to a real action. In all such cases of positive law, the courts of equity, as well as the courts of law, must say with Ulpian, *hoc quidem perquam durum est, sed ita lex scripta est.* 3 *Black.* 429.

2. It is said that a court of equity determines according to the spirit of the rule, and not according to the strictness of the letter. But so also does a court of law. Both, for instance, are equally bound, and equally profess, to interpret statutes according to the true intent of the legislator. In general laws all cases cannot be foreseen; or, if foreseen, cannot be expressed: some will arise that will fall within the meaning, though not within the words of the legislator, and others, which may fall within the letter, may be contrary to his meaning, though not expressly excepted. These cases, thus out of the letter, are often said to be within the equity, of an act of parliament; and so cases within the letter are frequently out of the equity. Here by equity we mean nothing but the sound interpretation of the law; though the words of the law itself may be too general, too special, or otherwise inaccurate or defective. These then are the cases which, as Grotius says, '*lex non exacte definit, sed arbitrio boni viri permittit,*' in order to find out the true sense and meaning of the law-giver, from every other topic of construction. But there is not a single rule of interpreting laws, whether equitably or strictly, that is not equally used by the judges in the courts both of law and equity: the construction must in both be the same; or, if they differ, it is only as one court of law may also happen to differ from another. Each endeavours to fix and adopt the true sense of the law in question; neither can enlarge, diminish, or alter, that sense in a single tittle. 3 *Black.* 430.

3. Again, it has been said that fraud, accident, and trust, are the proper and peculiar

* But *trader's* are now placed, in this respect, on a different footing; for by 47 *Geo.* 3. *sess.* 2, *c.* 84, *when a trader shall* die entitled to any estate, or interest in real estates, the same shall be assets.

objects of a court of equity. But every kind of fraud is equally cognizable, and equally adverted to, in a court of law; and some frauds are only cognizable there, as frauds in obtaining a devise of lands, which are always sent out of the equity courts to be there determined. Many accidents are also supplied in a court of law, as, loss of deeds, mistakes in receipts or accounts, wrong payments, deaths, which make it impossible to perform a condition literally, and a multitude of other contingencies: and many cannot be relieved even in a court of equity; as if by accident a recovery is ill suffered, a devise ill executed, a contingent remainder destroyed, or a power of leasing omitted in a family settlement. A technical trust, indeed, created by the limitation of a second use, was forced into the courts of equity, in the manner formerly mentioned: and this species of trusts, extended by inference and construction, has ever since remained as a kind of *peculium* in those courts. But there are other trusts, which are cognizable in a court of law, as deposits, and all manner of bailments, and especially that implied contract, so highly beneficial and useful, of having undertaken to account for money received to another's use, which is the ground of an action on the case, almost as universally remedial as a bill in equity. 3 *Black.* 431.

4. Once more; it has been said that a court of equity is not bound by rules or precedents, but acts from the opinion of the judge, founded on the circumstances of every particular case: whereas the system of our courts of equity is a laboured, connected system, governed by established rules, and bound down by precedents, from which they do not depart, although the reason of some of them may perhaps be liable to objection. Thus, the refusing a wife her dower in a trust-estate, yet allowing the husband his curtesy; the holding the penalty of a bond to be merely a security for the debt and interest, yet considering it sometimes as the debt itself, so that the interest shall not exceed that penalty; the distinguishing between a mortgage at 5 *per cent.* with a clause of reduction to four, if the interest be regularly paid, and a mortgage at 4 *per cent.* with a clause of enlargement to five, if the payment of the interest be deferred; so that the former shall be deemed a conscientious, the latter an unrighteous bargain: all these and other cases that might be instanced, are plainly rules of a positive law, supported only by the reverence that is shown, and generally very properly shown, to a series of former determinations; that the rule of property may be uniform and steady. Nay, sometimes a precedent is so strictly followed that a particular judgment, founded upon special circumstances, gives rise to a general rule. 3 *Black.* 432.

In short, if a court of equity in England did really act, as a very ingenious writer in the other part of the island supposes it (from theory) to do, it would rise above all law, either common or statute, and be a most arbitrary legislator in every particular case. No wonder he is so often mistaken: Grotius or Puffendorff, or any other of the great masters of jurisprudence, would have been as little able to discover, by their own light, the system of a court of equity in England, as the system of a court of law, especially as the notions beforementioned, of the character, power, and practice of a court of equity, were formerly adopted and propagated (though not with approbation of the thing) by our principal antiquarians and lawyers, Spelman, Coke, Lambard, and Selden, and even the great Bacon himself. But this was in the infancy of our courts of equity, before their jurisdiction was settled, and where the chancellors themselves, partly from their ignorance of law (being frequently bishops or statesmen) partly from ambition and lust of power (encouraged by the arbitrary principles of the age they lived in) but principally from the narrow and unjust decisions of the courts of law, had arrogated to themselves such unlimited authority as hath totally been disclaimed by their successors for now above a century past. The decrees of a court of equity were then rather in the nature of awards formed on the sudden *pro re nata* with more probity of intention than knowledge of the subject; founded on no settled principles, as being never designed, and therefore never used, for precedents. But the systems of jurisprudence, in our courts both of law and equity, are now equally artificial systems, founded on the same principles of justice and positive law, but varied by different usages in the forms and mode of their proceedings; the one being originally derived (though much reformed and improved) from the feodal customs, as they prevailed in different ages in the Saxon and Norman judicatures; the other (but with equal improvements) from the imperial and pontifical formularies introduced by their clerical chancellors. 3 *Black.* 433.

The suggestion indeed of every bill to give jurisdiction to the courts of equity (copied from those early times) is, that the complainant hath no remedy at the common law: but he who should from thence conclude that no case is judged of in equity where there might have been relief at law, and at the same time casts his eye on the extent and variety of the cases in our equity-reports, must think the law a dead letter indeed. The rules of property, rules of evidence, and rules of interpretation in both courts are, or should be exactly the same; both ought to adopt the best, or must cease to be courts of justice. Formerly some causes, which now no longer exist, might occasion a different rule to be followed in one court from what was afterwards adopted in the other, as founded in the nature and reason of the thing: but the instant these causes ceased the measure of substantial justice ought to have been the same in both. Thus the penalty of a bond, originally contrived to evade the absurdity of those monkish constitutions which prohibited taking interest for money, was therefore very pardonably considered as the real debt in the courts of law, when the debtor neglected to perform his agreement for the return of the loan with interest: for the judges could not, as the law then stood, give judgment that the interest should be specifically paid. But when afterwards the taking of interest became legal, as the necessary companion of commerce, nay after the stat. of 37 *Hen.* 8, c. 9, had declared the debt or loan itself to be "the just and true interest" for which the obligation was given, their narrow-minded successors still adhered wilfully and technically to the letter of the ancient precedents, and refused to consider the payment of principal, interest, and costs, as a full satisfaction of the bond. At the same time more liberal men, who sat in the courts of equity, construed the instrument according to its "just and true intent," as merely a security for the loan: in which light it was certainly understood by the parties, at least after these determinations; and therefore this construction should have been universally received. So in mortgages, being only a landed as the other is a personal security for the money lent, the payment of principal, interest, and costs ought at any time, before judgment executed, to have saved the forfeiture in a court of law, as well as in a court of equity. And the inconvenience, as well as injustice, of putting different constructions in different courts upon one and the same transaction, obliged the parliament at length to interfere, and to direct by the statutes 4 & 5 *Ann.* c. 16. and 7 *Geo.* 2. c. 20, that, in the cases of bonds and mortgages, what had long been the practice of the courts of equity should also for the future be followed in the courts of law. 3 *Black.* 434.

Again; neither a court of equity nor of law can vary men's wills or agreements (in other words) make wills or agreements for them. Both are to understand them truly, and therefore both of them uniformly. One court ought not to extend, nor the other abridge, a lawful provision deliberately settled by the parties, contrary to its just intent. A court of equity, no more than a court of law can relieve against a penalty in the nature of stated damages; as a rent of 5*l.* an acre for ploughing up ancient meadow: nor against a lapse of time, where the time is material to the contract; as in covenants for renewal of leases. Both courts will equitably construe, but neither pretend to controul or change a lawful stipulation or engagement. 3 *Black.* 435.

The rules of decision are in both courts equally opposite to the subjects of which they take cognizance. Where the subject matter is such as requires to be determined *secundum æquum et bonum*, as generally upon actions on the case, the judgments of the courts of law are guided by the most liberal equity. In matters of positive right, both courts must submit to and follow those ancient and invariable maxims '*quæ relicta sunt et tradicta.*' Both follow the law of nations, and collect it from history and the most approved authors of all countries, where the question is the object of that law: as in case of the privileges of embassadors, hostages, or ransom-bills. In mercantile transactions they follow the marine law, and argue from the usages and authorities received in all maritime countries. Where they exercise concurrent jurisdiction, they both follow the law of the proper *forum*: in matters originally of ecclesiastical cognizance they both equally adopt the canon or imperial law, according to the nature of the subject; and, if a question came before either, which was properly the object of a foreign municipal law, they would both receive information what is the rule of the country, and would both decide accordingly. 3 *Black.* 436.

Such then being the parity of law and reason which governs both species of courts, wherein (it may be asked) does their essential difference consist? it principally consists in the different modes of administering justice in each; in the mode of proof, the mode of trial, and the mode of relief. Upon these, and upon two other accidental grounds of jurisdiction, which were formerly driven into those courts by narrow decisions of the courts of law, *viz.* the true constructions of securities for money lent, and the form and effect of a trust or second use; upon these main pillars hath been gradually erected that structure of jurisprudence which prevails in our courts of equity, and is inwardly bottomed upon the same substantial foundations as the legal system; however different they may appear in their outward form, from the different tastes of their architects. 3 *Black. Com.* 436.

EQUITY OF REDEMPTION, where money is due on mortgage, and not paid at the day appointed, the mortgagee may enter and take possession, without any possibility *at law*, of being afterwards evicted by the mortgagor: but here the courts of equity interpose, and though a mortgage be thus forfeited, and the estate absolutely vested in the mortgagee at the common law, yet they will consider the real value of the tenements compared with the sum borrowed, and if the estate be of greater value than the sum lent thereon, they will allow the mortgagor at any reasonable time to recall or redeem his estate, paying to the mortgagee his principal, interest, and expences: for otherwise, in strictness of law, an estate worth 1000*l.* might be forfeited for non-payment of 100*l.* or a less sum: this reasonable advantage allowed to mortgagors, is called the EQUITY OF REDEMPTION: and it is this which enables a mortgagor to call on the mortgagee, who has possession of his estate, to deliver it back and account for the rents and profits received on payment of his whole debt and interest. 2 *Black.* 158. 2 *Vent.* 364.

But in general, *if the mortgagee has been 20 years in possession*, the courts of equity, in conformity with the statute of limitations which restricts the time of bringing ejectments, will not permit the mortgagor to redeem, unless during part of the time the mortgagor has been an infant, or a married woman, or unless the mortgagee admits he holds the estate as a mortgage; or he has kept accounts upon it, and treated it as redeemable within 20 years; or there are some other special circumstances which form an exception to the general rule. *Eq. Ca. Abr.* 313. 2 *Bro.* 399. 2 *Ves. Jun.* 83. And where two different estates are mortgaged by the owner to the same person, one cannot be redeemed without the other. *Amb.* 733.

EQUIVALENT, commissioners were appointed by statute to examine and state the debts due to Scotland on the union by way of equivalent. 1 *Geo.* 1. *c.* 27. 5 *Geo.* 1. *c.* 20.

EQUUS COOPERTUS, a horse equipped with saddle and furniture. *Cowel. Blount.*

ERIACH. By the Irish Brehon law, in case of murder, the brehon or judge compounded between the murderer and the friends of the deceased who prosecuted, by causing the malefactor to give unto them, or to the child or wife of him that was slain, a recompence, which was called an eriach. 4 *Black.* 309.

ERMINS, (from the Fr. *ermine*) a fur used in robes of state. *Cowel. Blount.*

ERN, (from the Sax. *ern*, *locus secretus*) places ending in *ern*, signify a melancholy situation. *Ibid.*

ERNES, loose scattered ears of corn, left on the ground, after binding or cocking, derived from the Teutonic, *ernde*, harvest; *ernden*, to cut or mow corn: hence to *ern* is in some places to glean. *Kennett's Gloss. Cowel. Blount.*

ERRANT, (*itinerant*). See *Eyre.*

ERRATICUM, a waif, or stray. *Cowel. Blount.*

ERROR, (Fr. *erreur*) signifies something wrong in pleading or process, &c. whereupon a writ is brought for remedy thereof, called a writ of error, in Lat. *de errore corrigendo.* And a writ of error is a writ which issues out of chancery, and lies where any one is grieved by the proceedings and judgment in any court of record, having power to hold plea of debt, or trespass above 40*s.* for to amend error in a base court not of *record*, a writ of false judgment lies. *Finch. L.* 484. And where they are in a summary way, or in a new course different from the common law, the remedy on an erroneous judgment is by *certiorari.* 1 *Salk.* 263. *Bac. Abr. tit. Er.*

A writ of error is a commission to judges of a superior court, by which they are authorised to examine the record upon which a judgment was given in an inferior court, and on such examination to affirm or reverse the same according to law. *Jenk. Rep.* 25. 2 *Inst.* 40. *Yelv.* 202. *Rep. Temp. Hardw. per Annaly.* 340.

The writ of error only lies upon matter of law arising upon the face of the proceedings; so that no evidence is required to substantiate or support it: and there is no method of reversing an error in the determination of facts, but by an attaint, or a new trial, to correct the mistakes of the former verdict. 3 *Black.* 405, 6.

Formerly the suitors were much perplexed by writs of error brought upon very slight and trivial grounds, as misspellings and other mistakes of the clerks, all which might be amended at the common law, while all the proceedings were in paper (4 *Burr.* 1099.); for they were then considered as only in *fieri*, and therefore subject to the controul of the courts. But, when once the record was made up, it was formerly held, that by the common law no amendment could be permitted, unless within the very term in which the judicial act so recorded was done: for during the term the record is in the breast of the court; but afterwards it admitted of no alteration (*Co. Litt.* 260.) But now the courts are become more liberal; and, where justice requires it, will allow of amendments at any time while the suit is depending, notwithstanding the record be made up, and the term be past. For they at present consider the proceedings as in *fieri*, till judgment is given; and therefore that, till then, they have power to permit amendments by the common law: but when judgment is once given and enrolled, no amendment is permitted in any subsequent term (*Stat.* 11 *Hen.* 4. *c.* 3.) Mistakes are also effectually helped by the statutes of amendment and jeofails: so called, because when a pleader perceives any slip in the form of his proceedings, and acknowledges such error (*jeo faile*) he is at liberty by those statutes to amend it; which amendment is seldom actually made, but the benefit of the acts is attained by the courts overlooking the exception (*Stra.* 1011.) By these statutes all trifling exceptions are so thoroughly guarded against, that writs of error cannot now be maintained, but for some material mistake assigned. 3 *Black.* 406.

The following is the substance of the several acts here referred to.

By 14 *Ed.* 3. *stat.* 1. *c.* 6. errors in record, owing to the misprision of clerks, of a letter, or syllable, may be amended, as well after judgment given, as before. Also 9 *Hen.* 5. c. 4.

But by 4 *Hen.* 6. c. 3. such acts are not to extend to Wales, or outlawries.

By 8 *Hen.* 6. *c.* 12. no record shall be reversed for error assigned by reason of rasing, interlineation, addition, or diminution.

The judges may reform all defects in any record, process, writ, or return, (appeals, indictments of treason, or felony, and outlawries thereupon excepted) and variance between a record and the certificate shall be amended by the judges. *Ibid.* and 8 *Hen.* 6. *c.* 15.

No judgment shall be reversed, for a variation from the exemplification, where the record is exemplified or inrolled. *Ibid.*

By 32 *Hen.* 8. *c.* 30. after verdict, judgment shall be given, notwithstanding any mispleading, jeofail, misjoining of issue, or want of warrant of attorney.

By 18 *Eliz. c.* 14. after verdict, judgment shall not be stayed for default in form, variance, or want of form, in any writ, count, return of sheriff, or for want of any warrant of attorney.

But this does not extend to information on any penal statute, nor to appeals, indictments, or presentments of felony and murder.

By 21 *Jac.* 1. *c.* 13. after verdict no judgment shall be stayed or reversed for variance in form between the writ and the declaration, or want of averment for the life of parties, or that the venire was awarded to a wrong officer, or that the sheriff's name is not to the return, or that the plaintiff being an infant did appear by attorney, if the verdict passed for him.

This does not extend to appeals, indictments, or informations.

By 16 & 17 *Car.* 2. *c.* 8. after verdict, judgment shall not be stayed or reversed for default in form, want of pledges, or want of alleging profert, &c. not being against the right of the suit. Nor shall the death of either party between the verdict and judgment, be alleged for error, so as such judgment be entered within two terms after the verdict.

But this likewise does not extend to appeals, indictments or informations.

By 4 & 5 *Ann. c.* 16. after demurrer joined, judgment shall be given on the very right, without regarding defect in any writ, return, pleading, or process though taken to be substance, so as sufficient matter appear, unless the party demurs specially. And all the acts shall extend to judgments by confession or default.

By 5 *Geo.* 1. *c.* 13. writs of error varying from the record may be amended; except in criminal matters.

And by the 10 & 11 *W.* 3. *cap.* 14. it is enacted, "that no fine or common recovery, nor judgment in any real or personal action, shall be reversed or avoided for any error or defect therein, unless the writ of error, or suit for the reversing such fine, recovery or judgment be commenced or brought, and prosecuted with effect, within twenty years after such fine levied, or such recovery suffered, or judgment signed or entered of record." Saving the rights of infants, femecoverts, persons *non compos*, in prison, or beyond sea.

He that brings writ of error, to reverse a judgment in a superior court, in all cases after a verdict, or in any action of debt, upon bond for payment of money only, or on a contract, must put in good sureties to prosecute his writ of error with effect, and pay the debt and damages if judgment be affirmed: but inferior courts, as well upon verdicts as other judgments, by default, or on demurrer, &c. have their writs of error allowed without putting in bail, they being omitted in the statute. 3 *Jac.* 1. *cap.* 8. If bail be not put in, on the writ of error brought upon a judgment in the courts at Westminster, in those cases where bail is required, the writ of error is no *supersedeas* to the execution; though such writ is in being, until a *nolle prosequi* is entered, or judgment affirmed, &c. And it is the same where insufficient bail is given, on rule to put in better bail, or justify those put in, which if the plaintiff doth not do, execution is ordered upon the judgment, with a *non obstante* to the writ of error, &c. *Mich.* 9 *W.* 3. *B. R.*

The court will not let the plaintiff in error quash his own writ of error; though they may grant leave to discontinue it. 5 *Mod.* 67. If a verdict is for a defendant in error, and judgment is affirmed, costs are allowed by stat. 3 *Hen.* 7. *c.* 10. *occasione dilationis executionis.* And by 4 & 5 *Ann. c.* 16. Upon quashing writs of error, for defect or variance from the record, &c. the defendant is to have costs as if judgment were affirmed.

A writ of error lies from the inferior courts of record in England into the king's bench, and not into the common pleas. It likewise may be brought from the common pleas at Westminster to the king's bench; and from the king's bench the cause is removeable to the house of lords. From proceedings on the law side of the exchequer a writ of error lies into the court of exchequer chamber before the lord chancellor, lord treasurer, and the judges of the court of king's bench and common pleat: and from thence it lies to the house of peers. From proceedings in the king's bench, in debt, detinue, covenant, account, case, ejectment, or trespass originally begun therein (except where the king is party) it lies to the exchequer chamber, before the justices of the common pleas, and barons of the exchequer; and from thence also to the house of lords: but where the proceedings in the king's bench, are commenced by original writ, sued out of chancery, this takes the case out of the general rule laid down by the statute; so that the writ of error then lies, without any intermediate stage of appeal, directly to the house of lords, the dernier resort for the ultimate decision of every civil action. Each court of appeal, in their respective stages, may, upon hearing the matter of law in which the error is assigned, reverse or affirm the judgment of the inferior courts; but none of them are final, save only the house of peers, to whose judicial decisions all other tribunals must therefore submit and conform their own. 3 *Black.* 410.

ERTHMIOTUM, a meeting of the neighbourhood to compromise differences among themselves, customary in former days. *Cowel. Blount.*

ESBRANCATURA, (from the Fr. *esbrancher*) cutting off branches or boughs in forests, &c. *Ibid.*

ESCALDARE, to scald: *escaldare porcos,* was one of our ancient tenures in serjeanty, within the counties of Essex and Hertford. *Ibid.*

ESCAMBIO, (derived from the Span. *cambier*, to change) was a licence granted to make over a bill of exchange to another beyond the sea, under stat. 5 *Ric.* 2. *c.* 2. *Ibid.*

ESCAPE, (*escapium*, from the Fr. *eschapper*, i. e. *effugere*) to fly from.

ESCAPE *in civil cases.*] Wherever a sheriff or other officer hath a person in custody by virtue of an authority from a court which hath jurisdiction over the matter, the suffering such person to go at large is an escape, but if the court has no jurisdiction of the matter, then all is void, and consequently the officer not punishable for suffering a person taken upon such void authority to escape. *Moor* 274. *Dyer* 66. 175, 306. *Poph.* 203. 1 *Leon.* 30. 5 *Co.* 64. 8 *Co.* 141, *b. Cro. Jac.* 280, 289. 2 *Bulst.* 64, 237. 256.

The sheriff cannot be charged with an escape before he had the party in actual custody by a legal authority; and therefore if an officer, having a warrant to arrest a man, see him shut up in a house, and challenge him as his prisoner, but never actually have him in his custody, and the party get free, the officer cannot be charged with an escape. *Bro. Escape,* 22.

Every person in prison by process of law is to be kept *in salva & arcta custodia,* in order to compel them the more speedily to pay their debts, and make satisfaction to their creditors. *Plowd.* 36. 3 *Co.* 44. 2 *Inst.* 381. 1 *Rol. Abr.* 806.

Persons in the King's Bench and Fleet prisons are to be actually detained within the said prisons; and if they escape action of debt lies against the warden, &c. 1 *R.* 2. *c.* 12. But now the marshal or warden grant the liberty of the rules to such as they think proper, (not criminally charged) on proper security. Keepers of those prisons suffering prisoners either upon contempt or mesne process, or in execution, to be out of the rules (except on rule of court, &c.) is an escape; and persons conniving at an escape shall forfeit 500*l.* &c. by 8 & 9 *W.* 3. *c.* 27. And by this statute, where any prisoner in execution escapes, the creditor may have any other new execution against him.

By *Stat.* 5 *Ann.* *c.* 9, if any person in custody, for not performing any decree in Chancery, &c. escape, the party for whom the money is decreed may have the same remedy against the sheriff as if the prisoner had been in custody on execution. A prisoner in execution should not be allowed to go out of gaol; for if he goes out, though he returns again, even though he go out with the gaoler, it is an escape. 3 *Rep.* 43, 44. 2 *Inst.* 260. 381.

But it has been adjudged no escape on mesne process to let a prisoner go, where the sheriff has a prisoner in custody, if it be before the return of the writ: for it is sufficient on mesne process if the officer have the party at the return of the writ, &c. *Moor* 299. 1 *Salk.* 401. 2 *Nels.* 739, 740.

And an escape in one place is an escape in all places; for a prisoner being once escaped, and at large, it shall be intended he is confined to no place, and so the action is transitory, and may be laid in any county. 1 *Lil. Abr.* 537.

On a judgment against two, and both in execution, if the sheriff suffer one to escape he shall be answerable for the whole debt, though he has one of them still in custody. 1 *Rol. Abr.* 810.

And by 8 & 9 *Wil.* 3, *cap.* 27, if the marshal or warden, or their deputies, or keeper of any prison, shall, after one day's notice in writing, refuse to show any prisoner committed in execution to the creditor at whose suit such prisoner was committed, or to his attorney, every such refusal shall be adjudged to be an escape in law.

In civil actions the sheriff is to answer for the escape of his bailiff by action on the case. *Cro. Eliz.* 623, 625. 1 *Danv. Abr.* 183. See also *Cro. Jac.* 419. *Dyer* 241. See *Ni. Pri.* 59, 60.

Where one has the custody of a *gaol of freehold or inheritance,* and commits it to another person, who is insufficient the superior is answerable for all escapes suffered by his inferior; but if the inferior be sufficient, the action should be brought against him, and not against the superior. 9 *Co.* 98. 2 *Jon.* 60. 2 *Lev* 158. 1 *Vent.* 314. 2 *Mod* 119. 4 *Rep.* 98.

But by 8 & 9 *W.* 3, *cap.* 27. the marshal of the King's Bench and warden of the Fleet shall be answerable for their deputies, and for all forfeitures, escapes, and other misdemeanors in their office by such deputies permitted, &c. and the profits and inheritances of the said offices shall be sequestered, &c. to make satisfaction. *s.* 11.

And an action of escape will lie against the marshal or warden for an escape upon mesne process though the prisoner returns the same day, and the plaintiff afterward proceeds to final judgment against him. 2 *Wils. Rep.* 294.

An action of escape will not lie against the executor or administrator of a sheriff, &c. for an escape, because it was personal, and *actio personalis moritur cum persona:* but it is otherwise if there be a judgment recovered against the sheriff before he died. *Dyer* 322.

If a sheriff suffer a prisoner voluntarily to go at large, the sheriff cannot retake him even upon fresh suit; and if he does, the prisoner may have an action of trespass against him. *Car.* 212. 3 *Rep.* 32. but his creditors may. 1 *Vent.* 4. 269. 3 *Salk.* 160. 8 and 9 *Will.* 3, *c.* 27.

However if the plaintiff himself permit the prisoner to escape he cannot afterwards retake him; and if the body and goods, &c. of a conusor are taken in execution upon a statute-merchant, if the conusee agree that he shall go at large, it is a discharge of the whole execution, and the conusor shall have the lands again: it is otherwise if the sheriff had permitted him to escape; the execution on the lands would not be discharged. 2 *Nels. Abr.* 737.

If the marshal of the King's Bench, or warden of the Fleet, or any other who has the keeping of prisons in fee, suffer a voluntary escape, it is a forfeiture of the office. 3 *Mod.* 146. *Carter* 212. And there is likewise a further penalty of 500*l.* added by 8 and 9 *W.* 3, *c.* 27.

There is this difference between an escape on *mesne* process and execution; if the sheriff arrest a person on *mesne* process, and he is rescued by *J. S.* he may return the rescue, and such return is good, and no action of escape lies against him after such return; but the court will issue process against such rescuer, or fine him; for in this case, though the sheriff may, yet he is not obliged to raise the *posse comitatus.* 1 *Rol. Abr.* 807. 1 *Jon.* 207. 1 *Rol. Rep.* 388. 3 *Lev.* 46.

But after judgment on a *capias ad satisfaciendum* the sheriff cannot return a rescue, for in such case the sheriff is obliged to raise the *posse comitatus,* if needful, and therefore, if he return a rescue, an action of escape lies, or a new *capias,* for the return of an ineffectual execution is as none. 1 *Rol. Abr.* 807. *Cro. Car.* 240. 255. 8 *Co.* 42. See *Ni. Pri.* 59, 60, and 6 *Rep.* 51. *Cro. Eliz.* 868.

If the prison takes fire, by means whereof the prisoners escape, this shall excuse the sheriff, and he may well plead it. 1 *Rol. Abr.* 808.

So if the prison is broke by the king's enemies, this shall excuse the sheriff, for he can have no remedy over against them. 4 *Co.* 84. 1 *Rol. Abr.* 808.

But if the prison was broke by rebels and traitors, the king's subjects, this shall not excuse him, for he may have his remedy over against these. *Ibid.* †

And by the 8 and 9 *W.* 3, *cap.* 27, no retaking on fresh pursuit shall be given in evidence unless the same be specially pleaded, and oath made that the prisoner did, without his consent, privity, or knowledge, make such escape, which, if false, the defendant shall forfeit 500*l.* *sec.* 6.

Escape in criminal cases.] An escape of a person arrested upon criminal process, by eluding the vigilance of his keepers, before he is put in hold, is an offence against public justice, and the party himself is punishable by fine and imprisonment. 2 *Hawk. P. C.* 122. But the officer permitting such escape, either by negligence or connivance, is much more culpable than the prisoner; the natural desire of liberty pleading strongly in his behalf, though he ought in strictness of law to submit himself quietly to custody till cleared by the due course of law. 4 *Black.* 129. Officers, therefore, who after arrest *negligently* permit a felon to escape are also punishable by fine. 1 *Hale P. C.* 600. But *voluntary* escapes by consent and connivance of the officer, are a much more serious offence; for it is generally agreed that such escapes amount to the same kind of offence, and are punishable in the same degree, as the offence of which the prisoner is guilty, and for which he is in custody, whether treason, felony, or trespass; and this whether he were actually committed to gaol, or only under a bare arrest. 1 *Hale P. C.* 590. 2 *Hawk. P. C.* 134. But the officer cannot be thus punished till the original offender hath actually received judgment, or been attainted upon verdict, confession, or outlawry, of the crime for which he was so committed or arrested, otherwise it might happen that the officer might be punished for treason or felony, and the person arrested and escaping might turn out to be an innocent man. 2 *Black.* 129. But before the conviction of the principal party the officer thus neglecting his duty may be fined and imprisoned for a misdemeanor. 1 *Hale's P. C.* 588, 589. 2 *Hawk. P. C.* 134, 135.

---

† And upon this principle, after the Riots in the year 1780, it was found necessary to pass an act to indemnify the different gaolers from the escapes which were occasioned by the demolition of their prisons by the rioters.

And by 16 *Geo.* 2, *c.* 31, it is enacted, that "persons who any ways assist a prisoner, "committed for treason, or felony, to at- "tempt his escape from any gaol, shall be "adjudged guilty of felony, and be trans- "ported; and if the prisoner be committed "for any other crime, or upon process for "a debt of 100*l.* &c. the offenders are lia- "ble to fine and imprisonment.

"And where any person conveys any "arms, instrument or disguise, to a pri- "soner in gaol for felony, &c. or for his use, "in order to an escape, it is likewise felony "and transportation. Also if one assist any "prisoner to escape from any constable, or "other officer or person in whose custody he "is by virtue of a warrant of commitment "for felony, it is declared to be the like "offence." *Ibid.*

ESCAPE-WARRANT. If any person committed or charged in custody in the King's Bench or Fleet prisons in execution, or on mesne process, &c. go at large, on oath thereof before a judge of the court where the action was brought, an escape-warrant shall be granted, directed to all sheriffs, &c. throughout England, to retake the prisoner, and commit him to gaol where taken, there to remain till the debt is satisfied: and a person may be taken on a Sunday upon an escape-warrant, stat. 1 *Ann. c.* 6. And the judges of the respective courts may grant warrants, upon oath to be made before persons commissioned by them to take affidavits in the country, (such oath being first filed) as they might do upon oath made before themselves. 5 *Ann. c.* 9.

ESCAPIO QUIETUS, he that by charter is *quietus de escapio*, is delivered from that punishment which by the laws of the forest lieth upon those whose beasts escape and are found within the land where forbidden. *Cromp. Jurisd.* 196. *Cowel. Blount.*

ESCAPIUM, what comes by chance or accident. *Cowel. Blount.*

ESCEPPA, a scepp, or measure of corn. *Ibid.*

ESCHEAT, (*eschaeta*, from the Fr. *escheoir*, i. e. *accidere*, *chance* or *accident*) signifies any lands or tenements that casually fall to a lord within his manor, by some unforeseen contingency, as by forfeiture, or by the death of his tenant, leaving no heir general or special; in which case the land naturally results back, by a kind of reversion, to the *original grantor*, or lord of the fee. *Co. Lit.* 23. *F. N. B.* 144.

But before the lord enters the homage jury of the lord's court ought to present it. 2 *Inst.* 36.

In our law escheats were of two sorts:

I. Regal—Those forfeitures which belong to our kings by the ancient rights and prerogative of the crown, upon the defect of heirs to succeed to the inheritance.

II. Feodal, which accrue to every lord of the fee, as well as the king, by reason of his seigniory, under the king's grant. 3 *Inst.* 111. 1 *Black.* 302.

The law of escheats is founded upon this single principle, that the blood of the person last seised in fee-simple is, by some means or other utterly extinct and gone: and since none can inherit his estate but such as are of his blood and consanguinity, it follows as a regular consequence that when such blood is extinct, the inheritance itself must fail; the land must become what the feodal writers denominate *feodum apertum*; and must result back again to the lord of the fee, by whom, or by those whose estate he hath, it was given. 2 *Black.* 244.

Escheats are frequently divided into, 1st, those *propter defectum sanguinis*, and 2ndly, those *propter delictum tenentis*; the *one* sort, if the tenant *dies without heirs*; the *other*, if his blood be *attainted*. *Co. Lit.* 13. 90. But both these species may well be comprehended under the first denomination only; for he that is *attainted* suffers an extinction of his blood (*see title* Attainder) as well as he that dies without relations; the inheritable quality is expunged in one instance, and expires in another. 2 *Black.* 245.

But a saving against the corruption of blood in a statute concerning felony doth by consequence save the land to the heir, so as not to escheat; because the escheat to the lord for felony is only *pro defectu tenentis*, occasioned by the corruption of blood; but a saving against the corruption of blood, in a statute concerning treason, does not save the land to the heir; for in treason the land goes to the king by way of immediate forfeiture. 3 *Inst.* 47. 1 *Salk.* 85.

The first three cases, wherein inheritable blood is wanting, are, 1st, where the tenant dies without any relations on the part of any of his ancestors: 2ndly, where he dies without any relations on the part of those ancestors from whom his estate descended. 3dly, where he dies without any relations of the whole blood. In two of these cases the blood of the first purchaser, is, *certainly*; in the other, it is, *probably*, at an end: and therefore in all of them the law directs that the land shall escheat to the lord of the fee; for the lord would be manifestly prejudiced, if contrary to the inherent condition, tacitly annexed to all feuds, any person should be suffered to succeed to the lands who is not of the blood of the first feudatory, to whom, for his personal merit, the estate is supposed to have been granted. *Co. Lit.* 7, 8. 2 *Black.* 248.

But if an estate be limited, or devised to a trustee, and the *cestui que trust* becomes *attainted*, or *dies without heirs*, in neither of such cases do the lands escheat; for there is no want of a legal tenant, and therefore the trustee shall hold them for his own benefit. *Hard.* 495, 496. 1 *Rol. Abr.* 816. (b.) *pl.* 2. *Cro. Jac.* 513. 1 *Inst.* 268. (b.) *Burgess* v. *Wheate*, 1 *Black. Rep.* 123. *Williams* v. *Ld. Lonsdale*. 3 *Vez.* jun. 752.

ESCHEAT, *writ of.* A writ of escheat is in the nature of a writ of right, and lies where the tenant having an estate in fee-simple in any lands or tenements holden of a superior lord, dies without heir; in which case the lord brings this writ against him that is in possession of the lands after the death of his tenant, and shall thereby recover the same in lieu of his services. *F. N. B.* 144. 3 *Black.* 194.

ESCHEATOR, (*eschaetor*) was an officer appointed by the lord treasurer, &c. in every county, to make inquests of titles by escheat; which inquests were to be taken by good and lawful men of the county, impanelled by the sheriff. 14 *Ed.* 3. *c.* 8. 34 *Ed.* 3. *c.* 13. 8 *Hen.* 6, *c.* 16.

ESCHECCUM, a jury or inquisition. *Cowel. Blount.*

ESCHIPARE, to build or equip. *Ibid.*

ESCROW, is a deed delivered to a third person, to hold until some future condition is performed by the grantee, and then to be delivered to him. 2 *Rol. Abr.* 25, 26 *Co. Lit.* 31. This delivery signifies, in fact, a delivery as a scroll or writing, which is not to take effect as a deed till the condition be performed, when it becomes a deed to all intents and purposes. *Co. Lit.* 36. 2 *Black.* 307.

ESCUAGE, (*scutagium*, from the *Fr. escu*, a shield) a kind of knight-service, called service of the shield, whereby the tenant was bound to follow his lord into the wars at his own charge. Also it has been sometimes taken as a compensation, taken for actual service. *Co. Lit.* 68. 2 *Black.* 74.

ESCURARE, to scour or cleanse. *Cowel. Blount.*

ESGLISE, (Fr.) a church, and a considerable title in the old law books. See *Com. Dig. tit. Esglise.*

ESINGÆ, the kings of Kent, so called from the first king *Ochta*, who was surnamed *Ese*: he was grandfather of king *Ethelbert*. *Cowel. Blount.*

ESKECTORES, (from the Fr. *escher*) robbers or destroyers of other men's lands and fortunes. *Ibid.*

ESKIPPER, (Fr.) to ship, and eskipped is used for shipped. *Cromp. Jur. Cur.*

ESKIPPAMENTUM, skippage, tackle, or ship-furniture. *Cowel. Blount.*

ESKIPPESON, shipping or passage by sea. *Ibid.*

ESNECY, (*æsnecia, dignitas primogeniti*) is a private prerogative allowed to the eldest coparcener, where an estate is descended to daughters for want of heir male, to choose first after the inheritance is divided. *Fleta, lib.* 5. *c.* 10. *Ibid.*

ESPERONS, spurs, *esperons de or*, gilt spurs. *Cowel. Blount.* 7 *Co. Rep.* 13.

ESPERVARIUS, (Fr. *espervier*) a sparrow-hawk. *Cowel. Blount.*

ESPLEES, (*expletiæ*, from *expleo*) are the products or profits which ground or land yield, as the hay of the meadows, the herbage of the pasture, corn of the arable; rent and services, &c. And in all writs of right the demandant ought to allege in his count, that he or his ancestors took the esplees of the thing in demand; otherwise the pleading will not be good. *Terms de Ley.*

ESPOUSALS, (*sponsalia*) the contract or mutual promise between a man and a woman to marry each other. *Wood's Inst.* 57.

ESQUIRE, called *escuier* in French, and *scutifer* or *armiger*, (*i. e.* armour-bearer) in Latin, was originally he who, attending a knight in the time of war, did carry his shield. *Cowel. Blount.*

Esquires and gentlemen are confounded together by sir *Ed. Coke*, who observes that every esquire is a gentleman, and a gentleman is defined to be one *qui arma gerit*, who bears coat-armour, the grant of which adds gentility to a man's family; in like manner as civil nobility among the Romans was founded in the *jus imaginum*, or having the image of one ancestor at least who had borne some curule office: it is indeed a matter unsettled what constitutes the distinction, or who is a real esquire; for it is not an estate, however large, that confers this rank upon its owner. *Camden*, who was himself an herald, distinguishes them most accurately, and he reckons up four sorts of them; 1st, the eldest sons of knights, and their eldest sons in perpetual succession. 2ndly, the eldest sons of younger sons of peers, and their eldest sons in like perpetual succession; both which species of esquires sir Henry Spelman intitles *armigeri natalitii.* 3dly, esquires created by the king's letters patent, or other investiture (long since disused) and their eldest sons. 4thly, esquires by virtue of their offices, as sheriffs, justices of the peace, and others, who bear any office of trust under the crown, and who are styled esquires in the king's commission: to these may be added the esquires of the knights of the bath, each of whom constitutes three at his installation: and all foreign, nay *Scotch* and *Irish* peers, not sitting in parliament; for not only these, but the eldest sons of peers of Great Britain, though frequently titular lords by courtesy, are only esquires in the law, and must be so named in all legal proceedings. 2 *Inst.* 658. 667. 668. *Spelm.* 47. 1 *Black.* 405.

Barristers are also esquires; and the court of common pleas refused to hear an affidavit read because a barrister named in it was not called an esquire. 1 *Wils.* 244.

ESSENDI QUIETUM DE TOLONIO.

A writ to be quit of toll lies for citizens and burgesses of any city or town that by charter or prescription ought to be exempted from toll. *Reg. Orig.* 258.

ESLISORS, or ELISORS, are persons appointed by a court of law, to whom a writ of *venire facias* is directed to empanel a jury, on challenge to the sheriff and coroners, who return the writ in their own names, with a panel of the jurors names. 15 *Ed.* 4. 24. *pl.* 4. 3 *Black.* 355.

ESSOIN, (*essonium*, Fr. *essoine*) signifies an excuse for him that is summoned to appear and answer to an action, or to perform suit to a court baron, &c. by reason of sickness and infirmity, or other just cause of absence. It is a kind of imparlance, or craving of a longer time, that lies in real, personal, and mixed actions; and the plaintiff as well as the defendant shall be essoined to save his default. *Co. Lit.* 131.

ESSOIN DAY OF THE TERM. The first return in every term, is, properly speaking, the first day in that term; and thereon the courts are opened according to ancient form to take essoigns, or excuses for such as do not appear according to the summons of the writ: wherefore this is usually called the essoign day of the term. But as the person summoned hath three days grace beyond the return of the writ in which to make his appearance, and if he appears on the fourth day inclusive, the *quarto die post*, it is sufficient; the courts do not sit on the essoign day for dispatch of business. 3 *Black. Com.* 278.

ESSOIN DE MALO VILLÆ, when the defendant was in court the first day, but gone without pleading, and being afterwards surprised by sickness, &c. and could not attend, he might send two essoigners openly to protest in court that he was detained by sickness in such a vill. *Cowel. Blount.*

ESSOINS AND PROFFERS, words used in stat. 38 *Hen.* 8. *c.* 21. See *Profer.*

ESTABLISHMENT OF DOWER, is the assurance or settlement of dower made to the wife by the husband, on marriage. *Britt. cap.* 102, 103. *Cowel. Blount.*

ESTACHE, (from the Fr. *eastacher*, to fasten) a bridge, or stank of stone and timber. *Cowel. Blount.*

ESTANDARD, or STANDARD, an ensign for horsemen in war. *Ibid.*

ESTATE (Fr. *estat.* Lat. *Jus*). An estate in *lands, tenements* and *hereditaments*, signifies such interest as the tenant hath therein; so that if a man grants *all his estate* in *D*, to *A*, and his heirs, every thing that he can possibly grant shall pass thereby: it is called in Latin *status*, it signifying the condition or circumstance in which the owner stands with regard to his property. *Co. Lit.* 345. 2 *Black.* 103.

These estates are acquired divers ways, *viz.* by discent from a father to the son, &c. Conveyance, or grant from one man to another; by gift or purchase, deed or will: and a fee-simple is the largest estate that can be in law. 1 *Lil.* 541.

Estates personal include all sorts of things *moveable*, which may attend a man's person wherever he goes, and therefore, being only the objects of the law while they remain under the limits of its jurisdiction, and being also of a perishable quality are not esteemed of so high a nature, nor paid so much regard to by the law as things which are in their nature more permanent and immoveable, as land and houses, and the profits issuing therefrom: and the property in chattels *personal* may be either in possession, which is where a man hath not only the right to enjoy, but hath the actual enjoyment of the thing: or else it is *in action*; as where a man hath only a bare right, and not any occupation or enjoyment; and as this bare right may be recovered by a suit or action at law, the thing so recoverable is called a *thing*, or *chose* in *action*: thus money due on a bond, bill, note, or simple contract, is *a chose* in action, because it remains to be recovered at law, and reduced into actual possession.

ESTOPPEL, (from the Fr. *estouper*, i. e. *oppilare, obstipare*) is an impediment or bar of an action arising from a man's own act, or where he is forbidden by law to speak against his own deed; for by his act or acceptance he may be estopped to allege or speak the truth. *F. N. B.* 142. *Co. Lit.* 352.

And therefore on a deed, all the parties thereto are at law estopped to say any thing against what is contained in it, and are not permitted to aver or prove any thing in contradiction to what they have once so solemnly and deliberately avowed. And parties and privies are bound by estoppel. *Lit.* 58. *Co. Lit.* 352. 4 *Rep.* 53.

ESTOVERS, (from *estoffe*, or *estouver*, Fr.) is generally used in the law for allowances of wood made to tenants, comprehending house-bote, hedge-bote, and plough-bote, for repairs, &c. *Cowel. Blount.*

These *botes* or *estovers* must be reasonable ones, and such any tenant or lessee may take off the land let or demised to him, without waiting for any leave, assignment, or appointment of the lessor, unless he be restrained by special covenant to the contrary. *Co. Lit.* 41.

This word hath also been taken for sustenance as *Bracton* uses it, *i. e.* for that sustenance, or allowance, which a man committed for felony is to have out of his lands or goods for himself and his family during his imprisonment. *Bract. lib.* 3. *tract.* 2. *cap.* 18.

ESTOVERIIS HABENDIS, *writ de.* The alimony or allowance granted by the ecclesiastical court to the wife on a divorce *a mensa et thoro*, is also called her *estovers*, and if the husband refuses to pay, there is, besides the ordinary process of excommunication, a writ at common law *de estoveriis habendis*, to recover it. 1 *Lev.* 6.

ESTRAY, (*extrahura*, from the old Fr. *estrayeur*) is any beast that is not wild, found within a manor or lordship, and owned by no man. In which case if it be cried and proclaimed according to law in the two next market-towns on two market-days, and is not claimed by the owner within a year and a day, it belongs to the lord of the liberty. *Brit. cap.* 17. If the beast stray to another lordship within the year, after it hath been an estray, the first lord cannot retake it, for, until the year and day be past, and proclamation made as aforesaid, he hath no property; and therefore the possession of the second lord is good against him. *Wood's Inst.* 213. *Cro. Eliz.* 716. If the cattle were never proclaimed, the owner may take them at any time. And where a beast is proclaimed as the law directs, if the owner claims it in a year and a day, he shall have it again; *but must pay the lord for keeping.* 1 *Rol. Abr.* 879. *Finch.* 177.

But if any other person finds and takes care of another's property, not being entitled to it as an estray, the owner may recover it or its value without being obliged to pay the expenses of its keeping. 2 *Black. Rep.* 1117. 2 *Hen. Black.* 254.

ESTREAT (*extractum*). If the condition of any recognizance be broken, such recognizance becomes forfeited, or absolute, and being *estreated* or extracted (taken out from among the other records) and sent up to the exchequer, the party and his sureties having now become the king's absolute debtors, are sued for the several sums in which they are respectively bound; *estreat* therefore signifies the true copy or note of such original record, and of the fines imposed on the rolls of court, which remain to be levied by exchequer process.

ESTRECIATUS, streightened. *Cowel. Blount.*

ESTREPE, (Fr. *estropier*) to make spoil in lands to the damage of another, as of the reversioner, &c. *Ibid.*

ESTREPEMENT, (*estrepamentum*) from the Fr. *estropier*, *mutilare*, or from the Lat. *extirpare*) is an old French word, signifying the same as *waste* or extirpation, as where any spoil is made by tenant for life upon any lands or woods to the prejudice of him in reversion; and also signifies to make land barren by continual ploughing. *Cowel. Blount.* 3 *Black.* 225.

And the writ of estrepement lay after judgment obtained in a real action, and before possession was delivered by the sheriff, to stop any waste which the defendant might be tempted to commit in lands which were determined to be no longer his. But as in some cases the demandant may be justly apprehensive that the tenant may make waste or estrepement pending the suit, well knowing the weakness of his title; therefore the statute of Gloucester (6 *Ed.* 1. *c.* 13) gave another writ of estrepement *pendente placito*, commanding the sheriff firmly to inhibit the tenant, *faciat wastum vel estrepementum pendente placito dicto indiscusso*; and by virtue of either of these writs the sheriff may resist them that do, or offer to do, waste; and if otherwise he cannot prevent them, he may lawfully imprison the wasters, or make a warrant to others to imprison them, or, if necessity require, he may take the *posse comitatus* to his assistance. 2 *Inst.* 328. *Reg.* 47. 5 *Rep.* 115. 3 *Black.* 225, 6.

Besides this preventative redress at common law the courts of equity, upon a bill filed therein, complaining of intended, or actual waste and destruction, will immediately on the filing of such bill, and before the service of the defendant with a subpœna thereon, upon an *ex parte* motion, and affidavit verifying all the facts alleged in the bill, grant an injunction, or order, to restrain the defendant from committing waste until he shall have put in his answer, and the court shall thereupon make further order; and this is now become the most convenient mode of staying waste.

ETHELING or ÆTHELING, (*Sax.*) signifies noble, and among the English Saxons it was the title of the prince, or the king's eldest son. *Cowel. Blount.*

EVASION, (*evasio*) is a subtle endeavouring to set aside truth, or to escape the punishment of the law, which will not be endured. Thus if a person says to another that he will not strike him, but will give him a pot of ale to strike first and accordingly he strikes, the returning of it is punishable; and if the person first striking be killed, it is murder; for no man shall evade the justice of the law by such a pretence to cover his malice. 1 *H. P. C.* 81.

EVENINGS. Anciently signified the delivery at *even* or night of a certain portion of grass or corn, &c. to a customary tenant, who performed the service of cutting, mowing, or reaping for his lord, and which were given to him as a gratuity or encouragement. *Kennet's Gloss.*

EVESDROPPERS, are such persons as stand under the eves or walls, or windows of a house, by night or day, to hearken after news, and carry it to others, and thereby cause strife and contention in the neighbourhood. *Terms de Ley.* And by the *stat. Westm.* 1. *c.* 33, they may be punished, either in the court-leet by way of presentment, and fine, or at the quarter-sessions by indictment, and binding to good behaviour. *Kitch.* 11.

EVICTION, (from *evinco* to overcome) is a recovery of land, &c. by law 10 *Rep.* 128. And where lands taken on extent are evicted, or recovered by better title, the plaintiff shall have a new execution. 4 *Rep.* 66. If a widow is evicted of her dower or thirds she shall be endowed in the other lands of the heir. 2 *Danv. Abr.* 670. And if on an exchange of lands either party is evicted of the lands given in exchange, he may enter on his own lands. 4 *Rep.* 121.

EVIDENCE, (*evidentia*) is used in the law for some proof, by testimony of men on oath, or by writings or records, and it is called evidence because thereby the point in issue in a cause to be tried, is to be made evident to the jury. *Co. Lit.* 283. And it demonstrates, makes clear, or ascertains the truth of the very fact or point in issue, either on the one side or the other; and no evidence ought to be admitted to any other point. 3 *Black.* 367.

Therefore upon an action of debt, when the defendant denies his bond by the plea of *non est factum*, and the issue is, whether it be the defendant's deed or no; he cannot give a release of this bond in evidence, for that does not destroy the bond, and therefore does not prove the issue which he has chosen to rely upon, *viz.* that the bond has no existence. 3 *Black.* 367.

General maxims relating to evidence]. Evidence in the trial by jury is of two kinds, either that which is given in proof, or that which the jury may receive by their own private knowledge. The former, or proofs, (to which in common speech the name of evidence is usually confined) are either written, or parol, that is, by word of mouth. Written proofs, or evidence, are, 1. Records, and, 2. Antient deeds of thirty years standing, which prove themselves; but, 3. Modern deeds, and 4. Other writings, must be attested and verified by parol evidence of witnesses. And the one general rule that runs through all the doctrine of trials is this, that the best evidence the nature of the case will admit of shall always be required if possible to be had; but, if not possible, then the next best evidence that can be had shall be allowed. For if it be found that there is any better evidence existing than is produced, the very not producing it is a presumption that it would have detected some falsehood that at present is concealed. Thus, in order to prove a lease for years, nothing else shall be admitted but the very deed of lease itself, if in being; but if that be positively proved to be burnt or destroyed (not relying on any loose negative as that it cannot be found, or the like) then an attested copy may be produced; or parol evidence be given of its contents. So no evidence of a discourse with another will be admitted, but the man himself must be produced; yet in some cases (as in proof of any general customs, or matters of common tradition or repute) the court admit of hearsay evidence, or an account of what persons deceased have declared in their life-time: but such evidence will not be received of any particular facts. So too, books of account, or shop-books, are not allowed of themselves to be given in evidence, for the owner; but a servant who made the entry may have recourse to them to refresh his memory; and, if such servant (who was accustomed to make those entries) be dead, and his hand be proved, the book may be read in evidence: for, as tradesmen are often under a necessity of giving credit without any note or writing, this is therefore, when accompanied with such other collateral proofs of fairness and regularity, the best evidence that can then be produced. However, this dangerous species of evidence is not carried so far in England as abroad; where a man's own books of accounts, by a distortion of the civil law (which seems to have meant the same thing as is practised with us), with the suppletory oath of the merchant, amount at all times to full proof. But as this kind of evidence, even thus regulated, would be much too hard upon the buyer at any long distance of time, the statute 7 *Jac.* I. c. 12, (the penners of which seem to have imagined that the books of themselves were evidence at common law) confines this species of proof to such transactions as have happened within one year before the action brought; unless between merchant and merchant in the usual intercourse of trade. For accounts of so recent a date, if erroneous, may more easily be unravelled and adjusted. 3 *Black.* 368, 369.

With regard to parol evidence, or witnesses, it must first be remembered, that there is a process to bring them in by writ of *subpœna ad testificandum*; which commands them, laying aside all pretences and excuses, to appear at the trial on pain of 100*l.* to be forfeited to the king; to which the stat. 5 *Eliz.* c. 9, has added a penalty of 10*l.* to the party aggrieved, and damages equivalent to the loss sustained by want of his evidence. But no witness, unless his reasonable expences be tendered him, is bound to appear at all; nor, if he appears, is he bound to give evidence till such charges are actually paid him, except he resides within the bills of mortality, and is summoned to give evidence within the same. This compulsory process, to bring in unwilling witnesses, and the additional terrors of an attachment in case of disobedience, are of excellent use in the thorough investigation of truth: and upon the same principle, in the Athenian courts, the witnesses who were summoned to attend the trial had their choice of three things; either to swear to the truth of the fact in question, to deny or abjure it, or else to pay a fine of a thousand drachmas. 3 *Black.* 370.

All witnesses that have the use of their reason, are to be received and examined, except such as are infamous *, or such as are interested in the event of the cause †. All others are competent witnesses; though the jury, from other circumstances, will judge of their credibility. Infamous persons are such as may be challenged as jurors, *propter delictum*; and therefore never shall be admitted to give evidence to inform that jury, with whom they were too scandalous to associate. Interested witnesses may be examined upon a *voir dire*, if suspected to be secretly concerned in the event; or their interest may be proved in court. Which last is the only method of supporting an objection to the former class; for no man is to be examined to prove his own infamy. And no counsel, attorney, or other person, intrusted with the secrets of the cause by the party himself, shall be compelled, or perhaps allowed, to give evidence of such conversation or matters of privacy, as came to his knowledge by virtue of such trust and confidence: but he may be examined as to mere matters of fact, as the execution of a deed, or the like, which might have come to his knowledge without being intrusted in the cause. *Ibid.*

One witness (if credible) is sufficient evidence to a jury of any single fact; though undoubtedly the concurrence of two ‡ or more corroborates the proof. Yet our law considers that there are many transactions to which only one person is privy; and therefore does not always demand the testimony of two, as the civil law universally requires. "*Unius responsio testis omnino non audiatur.*" To extricate itself out of which absurdity, the modern practice of the civil law courts has plunged itself into another. For as they do not allow a less number than two witnesses to be *plena probatio*, they call the testimony of one, though ever so clear and positive, *semi plena probatio* only, on which no sentence can be founded. To make up therefore the necessary complement of witnesses, when they have one only to any single fact, they admit the party himself (plaintiff or defendant) to be examined in his own behalf: and administer to him what is called the suppletory oath; and, if his evidence happens to be in his own favour, this immediately converts the half proof into a whole one. By this ingenious device, satisfying at once the forms of the Roman law, and acknowledging the superior reasonableness of the law of England: which permits one witness to be sufficient where no more are to be had; and, to avoid all temptations of perjury, lays it down as an invariable rule, that *nemo testis esse debet in propriâ causa.* 3 *Black.* 371.

Positive proof is always required, where from the nature of the case it appears it might possibly have been had. But, next to positive proof, circumstantial evidence, or the doctrine of presumption, must take place; for when the fact itself cannot be demonstratively evinced, that which comes nearest to the proof of the fact is the proof of such circumstances which either necessarily or usually, attend such facts; and these are called presumptions, which are only to be relied upon till the contrary be actually proved. *Stabitur præsumptione donec probetur in contrarium.* Violent presumption is many times equal to full proof: for there those circumstances appear, which necessarily attend the fact. As if a landlord sues for rent due at Michaelmas 1754, and the tenant cannot prove the payment, but produces an acquittance for rent due at a subsequent time, in full of all demands, this is a violent presumption of his having paid the former rent, and is equivalent to full proof; for though the actual payment is not proved, yet the acquittance in full of all demands is proved, which could not be without such payment; and it therefore induces so forcible a presumption, that no proof shall be admitted to the contrary. Probable presumption, arising from such circumstances as usually attend the fact, hath also its due weight: as if, in a suit for rent due 1754, the tenant proves the payment of the rent due in 1755; this will prevail to exonerate the tenant, unless it be clearly shewn that the rent of 1754 was retained for some special reason, or that there was some fraud or mistake: for otherwise it will be presumed to have been paid before that in 1755, as it is most usual to receive first the rents of longest standing. Light or rash presumptions have no weight or validity at all. 3 *Black.* 371, 2.

The oath administered to the witness is not only that what he deposes shall be true, but that he shall also depose the whole truth: so that he is not to conceal any part of what he knows, whether interrogated particularly to that point or not. 3 *Black.* 372.

And by 46 *Geo.* 3. *c.* 37, it is declared that a witness cannot by law refuse to answer, on the ground, that it may subject him to a suit for debt.

And all this evidence is to be given in open

* By 31 *Geo.* 3. *c.* 35, persons convicted of *petty larceny* are rendered competent witnesses.

† Parishioners may be witnesses on summary convictions, although the penalty or part be given to the poor, where such penalty does not exceed 20*l.*

‡ And in our courts of equity, if a defendant by his answer denies the truth of any of the allegations contained in the bill, *two* witnesses must be produced to contradict the answer.

court, in the presence of the parties, their attornies, the counsel, and all by-standers; and before the judge and jury: each party having liberty to except to its competency, which exceptions are publicly stated, and by the judge are openly and publicly allowed or disallowed, in the face of the country; which must curb any secret bias or partiality that might arise in his own breast. And if, either in his directions or decisions, he misstates the law by ignorance, inadvertence, or design, the counsel on either side may require him publicly to seal a bill of exceptions; stating the point wherein he is supposed to err: and this he is obliged to seal by statute Westm. 2. 13 *Edw.* I. c, 31, or, if he refuses so to do, the party may have a compulsory writ against him, commanding him to seal it, if the fact alleged be truly stated: and if he returns, that the fact is untruly stated, when the case is otherwise, an action will lie against him for making a false return. This bill of exceptions is in the nature of an appeal; examinable, not in the court out of which the record issues for the trial at *nisi prius*, but in the next immediate superior court, upon a writ of error, after judgment given in the court below. But a demurrer to evidence shall be determined by the court out of which the record is sent. This happens, where a record or other matter is produced in evidence concerning the legal consequences of which there arises a doubt in law; in which case the adverse party may, if he pleases, demur to the whole evidence; which admits the truth of every fact that has been alleged, but denies the sufficiency of them all in point of law to maintain or overthrow the issue: which draws the question of law from the cognizance of the jury, to be decided (as it ought) by the court. But neither these demurrers to evidence, nor the bills of exceptions, are at present so much in use as formerly; since the more frequent extension of the discretionary powers of the court in granting a new trial, which is now very commonly had for the misdirection of the judge at *nisi prius*, or the mistake of the jury. 3 *Black.* 373.

This open examination of witnesses *viva voce*, in the presence of all mankind, is much more conducive to the clearing up of truth, than the private and secret examination taken down in writing before an officer, or his clerk, in the ecclesiastical courts, and all others that have borrowed their practice from the civil law: where a witness may frequently depose that in private, which he will be ashamed to testify in a public and solemn tribunal. There an artful or careless scribe may make a witness speak what he never meant, by dressing up his depositions in his own forms and language; but he is here at liberty to correct and explain his meaning, if misunderstood, which he can never do after a written deposition is once taken. Besides, the occasional questions of the judge, the jury, and the counsel, propounded to the witnesses on a sudden, will sift out the truth much better than a formal set of interrogatories previously penned and settled: and the confronting of adverse witnesses is another opportunity of obtaining a clear discovery, which can never be had upon any other method of trial. Nor is the presence of the judge, during the examination, a matter of small importance; for, besides the respect and awe with which his presence will naturally inspire the witness, he is able by use and experience to keep the evidence from wandering from the point in issue. In short, by this method of examination, and this only, the persons who are to decide upon the evidence have an opportunity of observing the quality, age, education, understanding, behaviour, and inclinations of the witness; in which points all persons must appear alike, when their depositions are reduced to writing, and read to the judge, in the absence of those who made them: and yet as much may be frequently collected from the manner in which the evidence is delivered, as from the matter of it. These are a few of the advantages attending this, the English, way of giving testimony, *ore tenus*. Which was also indeed familiar among the antient Romans, as may be collected from Quinctilian; who lays down (*Inst. Ora. l.* 5. *c.* 7.) very good instructions for examining and cross-examining witnesses *viva voce*. And this, or somewhat like it, was continued as low as the time of Hadrian; but the civil law, as it is now modelled, rejects all public examination of witnesses. 3 *Black.* 373, 4.

As to such evidence as the jury may have in their own consciences, by their private knowledge of facts, it was an antient doctrine, that this had as much right to sway their judgment as the written or parol evidence which is delivered in court. And therefore it hath been often held, that though no proofs be produced on either side, yet the jury might bring in a verdict. For the oath of the jurors, to find according to their evidence, was construed to be, to do it according to the best of their own knowledge. Which construction was probably made out of tenderness to juries; that they might escape the heavy penalties of an attaint, in case they could show, by any additional proof, that their verdict was agreeable to the truth, though not according to the evidence produced: with which additional proof the law presumed they were privately acquainted, though it did not appear in court. But this doctrine was gradually exploded, when attaints began to be disused, and new trials introduced in their stead. For it is quite incompatible with the grounds upon which such new trials are every day awarded, *viz.*

that the verdict was given without, or contrary to evidence. And therefore, together with new trials, the practice seems to have been first introduced, which now universally obtains, that if a juror knows any thing of the matter in issue, he may be sworn as a witness, and give his evidence publicly in court. 3 *Black*. 375.

Evidence in criminal matters.] The doctrine of evidence upon pleas of the crown is, in most respects, the same as that upon civil actions. There are however a few leading points, wherein, by several statutes and resolutions, a difference is made between civil and criminal evidence. 4 *Black*. 356.

First, in all cases of high treason, petit treason, and misprision of treason, by statutes 1 *Edw*. VI. c. 12, and 5 & 6 *Edw*. VI. c. 11. *two lawful witnesses* are required to convict a prisoner; unless he shall willingly and without violence confess the same.

By statute 1 & 2 *Ph*. & *Mar*. c. 10, a farther exception is made as to treasons in counterfeiting the king's seals or signatures, and treasons concerning coin current within this realm; and more particularly by c. 11, the offences of importing counterfeit foreign money current in this kingdom, and impairing, counterfeiting, or forging any current coin.

The statutes 8 & 9 *W*. III. c. 25, and 15 & 16 *Geo*. II. c. 28, in their subsequent extensions of this species of treason do also provide, that the offenders may be indicted, arraigned, tried, convicted, and attainted, by the like evidence, and in such manner and form, as may be had and used against offenders for counterfeiting the king's money.

But by statute 7 *W*. III. c. 3, in prosecutions for those treasons to which that act extends, the same rule (of requiring two witnesses) is again enforced; with this addition, that the confession of the prisoner, which shall countervail the necessity of such proof, must be in open court. In the construction of which act it hath been holden, that a confession of the prisoner, taken out of court, before a magistrate or person having competent authority to take it, and proved by two witnesses, is sufficient to convict him of treason. But hasty unguarded confessions, made to persons having no such authority, ought not to be admitted as evidence, under this statute. And indeed, even in cases of felony at the common law, they are the weakest and most suspicious of all testimony; ever liable to be obtained by artifice, false hopes, promises of favour, or menaces; seldom remembered accurately or reported with due precision; and incapable in their nature of being disproved by other negative evidence. By the same statute 7 *W*. III. it is declared that both witnesses must be to the same overt act of treason, or one to one overt act, and the other to another overt act, of the same species of treason, and not of distinct heads or kinds, and no evidence shall be admitted to prove any overt act not expressly laid in the indictment. And therefore in sir John Fenwick's case, in king William's time, where there was but one witness, an act of parliament was made on purpose to attaint him of treason, and he was executed. But in almost every other accusation one positive witness is sufficient. Baron Montesquieu lays it down for a rule, that those laws which condemn a man to death in any case on the deposition of a single witness, are fatal to liberty: and he adds this reason, that the witness who affirms, and the accused who denies, make an equal balance; there is a necessity therefore to call in a third man to incline the scale. But this seems to be carrying matters too far: for there are some crimes, in which the very privacy of their nature excludes the possibility of having more than one witness; must these therefore escape unpunished? Neither indeed is the bare denial of the person accused equivalent to the positive oath of a disinterested witness. In cases of indictments for perjury, this doctrine is better founded; and there our law adopts it: for one witness is not allowed to convict a man indicted for perjury, because then there is only one oath against another. In cases of treason also there is the accused's oath of allegiance, to counterpoise the information of a single witness; and that may perhaps be one reason why the law requires a double testimony to convict him: though the principal reason, undoubtedly, is to secure the subject from being sacrificed to fictitious conspiracies, which have been the engines of profligate and crafty politicians in all ages. 4 *Black*. 356, 7.

Secondly, though from the reversal of colonel Sidney's attainder by act of parliament in 1689 it may be collected, that the mere similitude of hand-writing in two papers shown to a jury, without other concurrent testimony, is no evidence that both were written by the same person; yet undoubtedly the testimony of witnesses well acquainted with the party's hand, that they believe the paper in question to have been written by him, is evidence to be left to a jury. 4 *Black*. 358.

Thirdly, all presumptive evidence of felony should be admitted cautiously; for the law holds, that it is better that ten guilty persons escape, than that one innocent suffer. And sir Matthew Hale in particular lays down two rules most prudent and necessary to be observed: 1. Never to convict a man for stealing the goods of a person unknown, merely because he will give no account how he came by them, unless an actual felony be proved of such goods: and, 2. Never to convict any person of murder or manslaughter, till at least the body be found dead, on account of two instances he mentions, where persons were executed for the murder of others, who were then alive, but missing. 4 *Black.* 358.

Lastly, it was an ancient and commonly received practice, (derived from the civil law, and which also to this day obtains in the kingdom of France) that as counsel was not allowed to any prisoner accused of a capital crime, so neither should he be suffered to exculpate himself by the testimony of any witnesses. And therefore it deserves to be remembered to the honour of Mary I. (whose early sentiments, till her marriage with Philip of Spain, seem to have been humane and generous,) that when she appointed sir Richard Morgan chief justice of the common pleas, she enjoined him, "that "notwithstanding the old error, which did "not admit any witness to speak, or any "other matter to be heard, in favour of the "adversary, her majesty being party; her "highness's pleasure was, that whatsoever "could be brought in favour of the subject "should be admitted to be heard: and "moreover, that the justices should not "persuade themselves to sit in judgment "otherwise for her highness than for her "subject." Afterwards, in one particular instance (when embezzling the queen's military stores was made felony by statute 31 *Eliz. c.* 4.) it was provided that any person impeached for such felony, "should be "received and admitted to make any lawful proof that he could, by lawful wit"ness or otherwise, for his discharge and "defence:" and in general the courts grew so heartily ashamed of a doctrine so unreasonable and oppressive, that a practice was gradually introduced of examining witnesses for the prisoner, but not upon oath: the consequence of which still was, that the jury gave less credit to the prisoner's evidence, than to that produced by the crown. Sir Edward Coke protests very strongly against this tyrannical practice; declaring that he never read in any act of parliament, book-case, or record, that in criminal cases the party accused should not have witnesses sworn for him, and therefore there was not so much as *scintilla juris* against it. And the house of commons were so sensible of this absurdity, that in the bill for abolishing hostilities between England and Scotland, when felonies committed by Englishmen in Scotland were ordered to be tried in one of the three northern counties, they insisted on a clause, and carried it against the efforts of both the crown and the house of lords, against the practice of the courts in England, and the express law of Scotland, "that in all such trials for the better disco"very of the truth, and the better infor"mation of the consciences of the jury and "justices, there shall be allowed to the "party arraigned the benefit of such credi"ble witnesses, to be examined upon oath "as can be produced for his clearing and "justification." At length by the statute 7 *Wil.* 3, c. 3, the same measure of justice was established throughout all the realm, in cases of treason within the act; and it was afterwards finally declared by statute 1 *Ann. st.* 2, *c.* 9, that in all cases of treason and felony all witnesses for the prisoner should be examined upon oath, in like manner as the witnesses against him. 4 *Black.* 360.

EWAGE, (*ewagium*) is the same with *aquage*, toll paid for water-passage. *Cowel. Blount.*

EWBRICE, (Sax. *ew*, i. e. *conjugium*, and *bryce*, *fractio*) adultery or marriage breaking. *Ibid.*

EWE, (*euva*) a German word signifying law; it is mentioned in *Leg. W.* 1.

EXACTION, a wrong done by an officer, by taking a reward or fee for that which the law allows not. And the difference between exaction and extortion is this: extortion is where an officer extorts *more than his due*, when something is due to him; and exaction is, when he wrests a fee or reward, *where none is due;* for which the offender is to be fined and imprisoned, and render to the party twice as much as the money he so takes. *Co. Lit.* 368. 10 *Rep.* 100. 32 *Geo.* 2. *c.* 28.

EXACTOR REGIS, the king's exactor or collector. *Cowel. Blount.*

EXAMINATION IN CHANCERY. The examination of witnesses in chancery, is done by taking their depositions in writing according to the manner of the civil law upon *interrogatories*, or questions in writing formed for that purpose.

For the purpose of examining witnesses in or within 20 miles of London, there is an examiner's office appointed; but for evidence who live in the country; a commission to examine witnesses, is usually granted to four commissioners, two named of each side, or any three or two of them to take the depositions there, and if the witnesses reside beyond sea, a commission may be had to examine them there upon their own oaths, and if foreigners, upon the oaths of skilful interpreters.

——— OF BANKRUPT. See *Bankrupts.*

——— OF PRISONERS. By stat. 1 & 2 *P. & M. c.* 13. and 2 & 3 *P. & M. c.* 10. justices of peace are to examine felons apprehended, and witnesses, before the felon is committed; and the accusers must be bound over to appear and give evidence at the next assises, &c. to which the examinations are to be certified.

——— OF WITNESSES. See *Evidence.*

———, TRIAL BY. See *Trial.*

EXANNUAL ROLL. In the old way of exhibiting sheriffs accounts, the illeviable fines and desperate debts were transcribed into a roll under this name; which was yearly read, to see what might be gotten. *Hale's Sher. Acco.* 67.

EXCAMBIATORS, a word used antiently for exchangers of land, supposed to be such as we now call brokers, that deal upon the Exchange between merchants. *Cowel. Blount.*

EXCEPTION, (*exceptio*). In *law* proceedings, is a matter pleaded and alleged in bar to the action: and in equity, it is what is alleged against the sufficiency of an answer, the master's reports, &c.

EXCEPTION TO EVIDENCE, &c. See *Bill of Exceptions.*

EXCEPTION IN DEEDS, is a saving out of the deed of a particular thing out of a general one, as a room out of an house, a ground out of a manor, timber out of land, or the like. *Co. Lit.* 47. 1 *Lev.* 287. *Cro. El.* 244.

EXCHANGE, (*excambium* or *cambium*) the king's exchange, is the place appointed by the king for exchange of plate or bullion for the king's coin, &c. of which there is now only one, *viz.* the Mint in the Tower.

EXCHANGE *among merchants*] is a commerce of money, or a bartering or exchanging of the money of one city or country for that of another. *Lex Mercatoria*, or *Merch. Comp.* 98.

At London, all exchanges are made upon the pound sterling of 20*s.* Spain and Italy, &c. upon the ducat; and at Florence, Venice, and other places in the Streights by the dollar and florin. See *Bill of Exchange*, and *Lex Mercatoria.*

EXCHANGES OF GOODS AND MERCHANDISE, were the original and natural way of commerce, precedent to buying; for there was no buying till money was invented; though in exchanging, both parties are as buyers and sellers, and both equally warrant. 3 *Salk.* 157.

EXCHANGE OF LANDS. A deed of exchange is a mutual grant of equal interests, the one in consideration of the other. The word "exchange" is so individually requisite and appropriated by law to this case, that it cannot be supplied by any other word or expressed by any circumlocution, *Co. Litt.* 50, 51. The estates exchanged must be equal in quantity, *Litt. s.* 64, 65.; not of value, for that is immaterial, but of interest; as fee-simple for fee-simple, a lease for twenty years for a lease for twenty years, and the like. And the exchange may be of things that lie either in grant or in livery, *Co. Litt.* 51. But no livery of seisin, even in exchanges of freehold, is necessary to perfect the conveyance, *Litt. s.* 62.; for each party stands in the place of the other and occupies his right, and each of them hath already had corporal possession of his own land. But entry must be made on both sides; for, if either party die before entry, the exchange is void, for want of sufficient notoriety, *Co. Litt.* 50. And so also, if two parsons, by consent of patron and ordinary, exchange their preferments; and the one is presented, instituted, and inducted, and the other is presented, and instituted, but dies before induction, the former shall not keep his new benefice, because the exchange was not completed, and therefore he shall return back to his own. *Perk. s.* 288. For if, after an exchange of lands or other hereditaments, either party be evicted of those which were taken by him in exchange, through defect of the other's title; he shall return back to the possession of his own, by virtue of the implied warranty contained in all exchanges. *Co. Lit.* 174.

EXCHANGE OF CHURCH LIVINGS. Parsons some times exchange their churches, and resign them into the bishop's hands. *Wood's Inst.* 284.

By the 31 *El. c.* 6. if any incumbent shall corruptly resign or exchange, or corruptly take for resigning or exchanging, directly or indirectly, any pension, money, or other benefit; as well the giver as the taker, shall lose double the value; half to the queen, and half to him that shall sue. *s.* 8.

If two parsons by one instrument agree to exchange their benefices, and in order thereto to resign them into the hands of the ordinary, such exchange being executed on both parts, is good; and each may enjoy the other's living: but the patrons must present them again to each living; and if they refuse to do it, or the ordinary will not admit them respectively, then the exchange is not executed; and in such case either clerk may return to his former living, even though one of them should be admitted, instituted and inducted to the benefice of the other; which is expressed in the exchange itself. 2 *Co. Rep.* 74. *Rol. Abr.* 814.

EXCHANGEORS, were those that returned money by bills of exchange. See *Excambiators.* 5 *R.* 2. *c.* 2.

EXCHEQUER, (*scaccarium*, from the Fr. *eschequier*, i. e. *abacus*, *tabula lusoria*, or from the Germ. *schatz*, viz. *thesaurus*) The court of exchequer is a court of *law* and a court of equity also. It is a very antient court of record, set up by William the conqueror (*Lamb. Archeion.* 24.) as a part of the *aula regia* (*Madox. Hist. Exch.* 109.) though regulated and reduced to its present order by king Edward I. (*Spelm. Guil. I. in cod. leg. vet. apud Wilkins.*); and intended principally to order the revenues of the crown, and to recover the king's debts and duties (4 *Inst.* 103—116.) It is called the exchequer, *scaccarium*, from the chequed cloth, resembling a chess-board, which covers the table there; and on which, when certain of the king's accounts are made up, the sums are marked and scored with counters. It consists of two divisions: the receipt of the exchequer, which manages the royal revenue, and with which these commentaries have no concern; and the court or judicial part of it, which is again subdivided into a court of equity and a court of common law. 3 *Black.* 44.

The court of equity is held in the exchequer chamber before the lord treasurer, the chancellor of the exchequer, the chief baron, and three *puisne* ones. These Mr. Selden conjectures (*Tit. Hon.* 2, 5, 16.) to have antiently been made out of such as were barons of the kingdom or parliamentary barons; and thence to have derived their name; which conjecture receives great strength from Bracton's explanation of magna carta, *c.* 14. which directs that the earls and barons be amerced by their peers; that is, says he, by the barons of the exchequer (*l.* 3. *tr.* 2. *c.* 1. *s.* 3.) The primary and original business of this court is to call the king's debtors to account by bill filed by the attorney-general; and to recover any lands, tenements, or hereditaments, any goods, chattels, or other profits or benefits, belonging to the crown. So that by their original constitution the jurisdiction of the courts of common pleas, king's bench, and exchequer, was entirely separate and distinct; the common pleas being intended to decide all controversies between subject and subject; the king's bench to correct all crimes and misdemesnors that amount to a breach of the peace, the king being there plaintiff, as such offences are in open derogation of the *jura regalia* of his crown; and the exchequer to adjust and recover his revenue, wherein the king also is plaintiff, as the withholding and non-payment thereof is an injury to his *jura fiscalia*. But, as by a fiction almost all sorts of civil actions are now allowed to be brought in the king's bench; in like manner by another fiction all kinds of personal suits may be prosecuted in the court of exchequer. For as all the officers and ministers of this court have, like those of other superior courts, the privilege of suing and being sued only in their own court; so also the king's debtors, and farmers, and all accomptants of the exchequer are privileged to sue and implead all manner of persons in the same court of equity, that they themselves are called into. They have likewise privilege to sue and implead one another, or any stranger, in the same kind of common law actions (where the personalty only is concerned) as are prosecuted in the court of common pleas. 3 *Black.* 45.

This gives original to the common law part of their jurisdiction, which was established merely for the benefit of the king's accomptants, and is exercised by the barons only of the exchequer, and not the treasurer or chancellor. The writ upon which all proceedings here are grounded is called a *quo minus:* in which the plaintiff suggests that he is the king's farmer or debtor, and that the defendant hath done him the injury or damage complained of; *quo minus sufficiens existit*, by which he is the less able to pay the king his debt or rent. And these suits are expressly directed, by what is called the statute of Rutland (10 *Edw.* 1. *c.* 11.), to be confined to such matters only as specially concern the king or his ministers of the exchequer. And by the *articuli super cartas* (28 *Edw.* 1. *c.* 4.) it is enacted, that no common pleas be thenceforth holden in the exchequer, contrary to the form of the great charter. But now by the suggestion of privilege, any person may be admitted to sue in the exchequer as well as the king's accomptant. The surmise, of being debtor to the king, is therefore become matter of form and mere words of course, and the court is open to all the nation equally. The same holds with regard to the equity side of the court; for there any person may file a bill against another upon a bare suggestion that he is the king's accomptant; but whether he is so or not, is never controverted. In this court, on the equity side, the clergy have long used to exhibit their bills for the non-payment of tithes; in which case the surmise of being the king's debtor is no fiction, they being bound to pay him their first fruits, and annual tenths. But the chancery has of late years obtained a large share in this business. *Ibid.* 46.

An appeal from the equity side of this court lies immediately to the house of peers; but from the common law side, in pursuance of the statute 31 *Ed.* 3. *c.* 12. a writ of error must be first brought into the court of exchequer chamber. And from their determination there lies, in the *dernier resort*, a writ of error to the house of lords. *Ibid.*

The court of exchequer chamber, is one that hath no original jurisdiction, but is only a court of appeal, to correct the errors of other jurisdictions. This was first erected by statute 31 *Ed.* 3. *c.* 12. to determine causes upon writs of error from the common law side of the court of exchequer. And to that end it consists of the lord treasurer, the lord chancellor, and the justices of the king's bench and common pleas. In imitation of which, a second court of exchequer chamber was erected by statute 27 *Eliz.* *c.* 8. consisting of the justices of the common pleas, and the barons of the exchequer; before whom writs of error may be brought to reverse judgments in certain suits originally begun in the court of king's bench. Into the court also of exchequer chamber, (which then consists of all the judges of the three superior courts, and now and then the lord chancellor also) are sometimes adjourned from the other courts such causes as the judges upon argument find to be of great weight and difficulty, before any judgment is given upon them in the court below. 4 *Inst.* 119. 4 *Bulst.* 146. 3 *Black.* 56.

From all the branches of this court of exchequer chamber, a writ of error lies to the house of peers. 3 *Black.* 56.

The court of exchequer is governed by the chancellor of the exchequer, the lord chief baron, and three other barons, who are the sovereign auditors of England, and the judges of the court. There also sits in this court a *puisne* baron, who administers the oath of all high-sheriffs, under-sheriffs, bailiffs, auditors, receivers, collectors, controllers, surveyors, and searchers of all the customs in England.

The chancellor or under treasurer hath the custody of the seal of this court. The king's attorney general is made privy to all manner of pleas that are not ordinary and of course, which rise upon the process of the court; and he puts into court in his own name, informations of concealments of customs, seizures, &c. And also for intrusions, wastes and incroachments upon any of the king's lands; or upon penal statutes, forfeitures, &c.

The remembrancers keep the records of the court betwixt the king and his subjects, and enter the rules and orders there made: one is called the king's remembrancer, and the other the lord treasurer's remembrancer: the remembrancer for the king hath all manner of informations upon penal statutes used in his office only; and he calls to account, in open court, all the great accountants of the crown, collectors of customs, &c. he makes out writs of privilege, enters judgments of pleas; and all matters upon English bill are remaining in his office.

The remembrancer for the lord treasurer makes out all the estreats; he sets down in his book the debts of all sheriffs, and takes their foreign accounts; and issues out writs and process in many cases, &c. And these remembrancers have several attornies to do business under them; who by statute are not to issue out of the remembrancer's office, any writs upon supposition, but upon just grounds, &c. 1 *Jac.* 1. *c.* 26.

There are two chamberlains that keep the keys of the treasury, where the records lie, with the book of Domesday, &c. They may sit in court if they please, but not intermeddle with any thing; unless it be relating to the sheriffs, in the pricking whereof they have a vote. And besides the chamberlains, there is a clerk of the pipe, in whose custody are conveyed out of the king's and treasurer's remembrancer, &c. as water through a pipe, all accounts and debts due to the king.

The controller of the pipe; who is said to be the chancellor of the exchequer. The clerk of the estreats, who receives the estreats from the remembrancer's office, and writes them out to be served for the king, &c. The foreign opposer, who opposes or makes a charge on all sheriffs, &c of their green wax, *i. e.* fines, issues, amerciaments, recognisance, &c. certified in estreats annexed to the writ, under the seal in green wax, and delivereth the same to the clerk of the estreats to be put in process. The auditors, that take the accounts of the king's receivers, collectors, &c. and perfect them. The four tellers, whose business to receive and pay all money is well known. The clerk of the pells, from his parchment rolls, called *pellis receptorum.* The clerk of the nihils, who makes a roll of such sums as the sheriff upon process returns nihil, &c. The clerk of the pleas, in whose office all officers and privileged persons are to sue and be sued; and here are divers under clerks employed in suits commenced or depending in this court. There is a clerk of the summons; under chamberlains of the exchequer; secondaries in the offices of the remembrancers; secondaries of the pipe: the usher of the exchequer, marshal, &c.

EXCHEQUER BILLS. By 48 *Geo.* 3. *c.* 1. (an act for regulating the issuing and paying of exchequer bills), the powers given by this act to the commissioners of the treasury may be executed by three of them, *s.* 1, and exchequer bills shall issue in such form as they think convenient; but the auditor, or some person authorized by him, shall sign the bills. *s.* 2.

The bills are to be numbered arithmetically, *s.* 3, but the course of payment is to be as the commissioners find convenient. *s.* 4.

The interest due on bills, which shall be payable in part of the revenue, shall be paid to the parties; but after they get into the hands of receivers or collectors, the interest shall from that time cease. *s.* 5.

When such bills are paid in at the exchequer, the parties are to write their names and the date thereon. *s.* 6.

The treasury are to direct cheques, indents, and counterfoils, *s.* 7; but bills defaced are to be exchanged. *s.* 8.

Persons forging any exchequer bill, or any indorsement, shall be guilty of felony without clergy. *s.* 9.

Paymasters, comptrollers, and other officers, are to be appointed for payment of bills, *s.* 10, which paymasters are to be liable to the controul of the treasury, *s.* 11; the commissioners whereof are to settle salaries and rewards, *s.* 12, and contract with persons to circulate bills, *s.* 13, and the governor and directors of the bank are not disabled from being members of parliament by reason of such contracts, *s.* 14; the rates payable to the contractors to be paid out of the money applicable to that purpose. *s.* 15.

No fees to be taken at the exchequer, *s.* 16, nor interest on any less sum than 1*d.* to be paid. *s.* 17.

Bills lost or destroyed to be paid, on proof of the casualty, before the barons of the exchequer. *s.* 18.

But bills discharged are not to be cancelled. *s.* 19.

EXCISE, (from the Belg. *acciisse, tributum*) The excise duty is an inland imposition, paid sometimes upon the consumption of the commodity, or frequently upon the retail sale, which is the last stage before the consumption. This is the most œconomical way of taxing the subject: the charges of levying, collecting, and managing the excise duties being considerably less in proportion than in other branches of the revenue. It also renders the commodity cheaper to the consumer, than charging it with customs to the same amount would do; because generally paid in a much later stage of it. The frauds that might be committed in this branch of the revenue, unless a strict watch is kept, make it necessary, wherever it is established, to give the officers a power of entering and searching the entered houses of such as deal in exciseable commodities, at any hour of the day, and, in many cases, of the night likewise. And the proceedings in case of transgressions are so summary and sudden, that a man may be convicted in two days time in the penalty of many thousand pounds by two commissioners or justices of the peace, without trial by jury, according to the ordinary course of the common law.* 1 *Black.* 318.

The original establishment of the excise, was in 1643, and its progress was gradual; being at first laid upon those persons and commodities, where it was supposed the hardship would be least perceivable, *viz.* the makers and vendors of beer, ale, cyder, and perry, and the pretended champions of liberty boldly and openly declared, "the "impost of excise to be the most easy and in- "different levy that could be laid upon the "people." *Com. Jour.* 17 *May* 1643. *Dug.* 120. *Scobel.* 453. Upon king Charles's return, it having then been long established and its produce well known, some part of it was given to the crown, in 12 *Car.* II. by way of purchase for the feodal tenures and other oppressive parts of the hereditary revenue. But, from its first original to the present time, its very name has been odious. It has nevertheless been imposed on abundance of other commodities in the reigns of king William III. and every succeeding prince, to support the expences of the country. Thus brandies and other spirits are now excised at the distillery, wine in the hands of the importer, tobacco and snuff in the hands of the manufacturer, printed silks and linens, at the printer's; starch and hair powder, at the maker's; gold and silver wire, at the wiredrawer's; plate in the hands of the vendor, who pays yearly for a licence to sell it; lands and goods sold by auction, for which a pound-rate is payable by the auctioneer, who also is charged with an annual duty for his licence. To these we may add coffee, tea, and cocoa, for which the duty is paid by the retailer; all artificial wines, commonly called sweets; paper and pasteboard, first when made, and again if stained or printed; malt as before-mentioned; vinegars; and the manufacture of glass; bricks for all which the duty is paid by the manufacturer; hops, for which the person that gathers them is answerable; candles and soap, which are paid for at the maker's; malt liquors brewed for sale, which are excised at the brewery; cyder and perry, at the vendor's; and leather and skins, at the tanner's; salt at the works. 1 *Black.* 320.

The acts relating to each particular article of excise are too voluminous to be in this work: but the following is a summary of the most general statutes relative to the Excise.] By 12. *Car.* 2. *c.* 23. no person shall intermeddle in the excise until he has taken oath to execute the same faithfully, which is to be certified at the next quarter-sessions. Also 15 *Car.* 2. *c.* 11. 10 *Ann.* *c.* 19. and *c.* 36.

All parts within the weekly bills of mortality shall be under the head office. The king shall appoint commissioners and all officers. The excise offices shall be kept open from eight in the morning till twelve at noon, and from two till five in the afternoon; and the monies collected shall be paid into the exchequer. 12 *Car.* 2.

By 15 *Car.* 2. *c.* 11. no commissioner or other officer of excise shall farm the revenue thereof; nor shall they act as justices of peace in matters touching the excise.

Officers shall attend in market towns touching receipts and duties of excise, on pain of 10*l.* *Ibid.*

Gaugers shall take no bribes to make false returns, on forfeiture of 10*l.* and the person bribing forfeit the same. *Ibid.*

Foreign liquors imported shall be duly entered; on pain of forfeiture. *Ibid.*

Upon appeals in excise cases the duty shall be deposited. Complaints shall be determined in the proper counties; the commissioners shall take no fees; on pain of 10*s.* for each offence. Two justices may determine matters on this act: and the penalties shall go one third to the king, one third to the poor, and the other third to the informer. *Ibid.*

Appeals in town must be within two

---

* It is certainly an evil that a fair dealer cannot have the benefit of any secret improvement in the management of his trade or manufactory; yet, perhaps it is more than an equivalent to the public at large, that, by the survey of the excise, the commodity is preserved from many shameful adulterations, as experience has fully proved since wine was made subject to the excise laws. 1 *Black.* 318. n. by *Chris.*

months, in the country within four. *Ibid.*

By 16 & 17 *Car.* 2. c. 4. farmers of excise shall have like authority as the commissioners of excise.

By 22 & 23 *Car.* 2. c. 5. justices of peace, and commissioners may mitigate the fines, so as the same be not made less than double the duty, besides costs.

By 1 *Will. & Mar. stat.* 1. c. 24. offices shall be kept at Holyhead, Newborough, and Lanerchtinth in Anglesey, as well as at Beaumaris.

Commissioners of excise, or clerks taking money of any person other than the king, shall forfeit their office, and be incapable of any office in the revenue. *Ibid.*

By 7 *Will.* 3. c. 30. the commissioners and justices may summon witnesses, and if they refuse to appear, or give evidence, they forfeit 10*l.*

Inferior officers of excise, and salt, shall continue in their offices, notwithstanding the death or removal of any of the commissioners. *Ibid.*

By 6 *Geo.* 1. c. 21. any person obstructing an officer of excise in relation to the duties forfeits 10*l.*

By 11 *Geo.* 1. c. 30. officers of excise may go on board ships to search for brandy, or other exciseable liquors, in like manner as officers of the customs.

Excise officer, by special warrant, may search any place for brandy or the like fraudulently hid, and any person obstructing, forfeits 100*l.* *Ibid.*

Any person taking out a permit, and not sending away the commodities in the time limited, or not returning the permit, forfeits treble the value of the goods; and if there does not appear a sufficient decrease to answer the removal, the officer may seize a like quantity: any person taking a permit for removal, without direction of a person, from whose stock the commodities are to be removed, forfeits 50*l.* *Ibid.*

Constable refusing to go with an excise officer shall forfeit 20*l.* *Ibid.*

On question, whether the person be an excise officer, proof shall be admitted that he was reputed such, without producing the commission. *Ibid.*

Any person attempting to corrupt an officer of excise in his duty, shall forfeit 500*l.* half to the king and half to the poor. *Ibid.*

By 12 *Geo.* 1. c. 28. no officer of excise shall be subject to penalty, for not leaving a copy of the charge, unless demanded in writing.

By 1 *Geo.* 2. *stat.* 2. c. 16. complaints may be determined by, and adjudications executed by warrant of, three commissioners.

By 18 *Geo.* 2. c. 26. any entry made by dealers in exciseable goods shall not be deemed a legal entry, unless made in the name of the real owner, and the person acting as visible owner shall be deemed the real owner, and liable as such to the duties and penalties, and all goods found in places of trade shall be liable.

Offences against the excise laws may be prosecuted out of the jurisdiction wherein they were committed. *Ibid.*

By 32 *Geo.* 2. c. 17. in all cases relating to the excise, summons directed to the party by his right, or assumed name, or left at his usual place of residence, shall be deemed legal notice, except where particular directions shall be enacted for summoning or condemning.

By 33 *Geo.* 2. c. 9. officers of excise may seize all vessels liable to be forfeited by former laws, and proceed to condemnation in like manner as officers of the customs.

By 5 *Geo.* 3. c. 43. all powers by 18 *Geo.* 2. c. 26. shall be executed against persons offending against the excise laws.

Commissioners of excise may appoint persons (in the absence of the collector) to administer oaths to exporters, and to grant certificates of duty paid.

By 6 *Geo.* 3. c. 47. the six months allowed by 15 *Geo.* 2. c. 26. for payment of excise duties on warehoused rum, are enlarged to twelve months.

By 9 *Geo.* 3. c. 6. excise officers may seize horses and carriages removing foreign spirits and goods, duties unpaid, like as custom-house officers may, and proceed by the excise laws, or by action, plaint, or information, &c.

By 10 *Geo.* 3. c. 44. traders using false scales or weights, in weighing stock, to defraud the revenue, shall forfeit 100*l.* but not to be punished under this and other acts for the same offence; a moiety to the king, and the other to the informer.

By 19 *Geo.* 3. c. 69. all druggists, grocers, chandlers, coffee or chocolate house-keepers, and dealers in coffee, tea, cocoa nuts, and makers of chocolate, shall put over their doors these words, *Dealer in Coffee, Tea, or Chocolate*, on pain of 200*l.* and all importers, and dealers in foreign brandy, arrack, rum, spirits or strong waters, shall put on some conspicuous part of their house these words, *Importer of* or *Dealer in Foreign Spirituous Liquors*, on penalty of 50*l.*

Any dealer buying where the words are not up, penalty of 100*l.* but not for buying goods warehoused, according to 10 *Geo.* 1. c. 10. or at the East India company's sales, or sold for insurers for salvage, or prize teas, or spirituous liquors on board ships, or on quays, by the first purchaser, or of rum warehoused according to 15 & 16 *Geo.* 2. c. 25. or arrack in the East India company's warehouses, nor foreign spirituous liquors, or if sold by insurers. *Ibid.*

Putting up the words not having entered the place at the excise office, penalty 50*l.* and persons, not dealers, buying where the words are not (except as before) penalty 10*l.* and any smuggler selling goods, and informing against the buyer in twenty days (and before information laid against himself) indemnified. *Ibid.*

By 21 *Geo.* 3. *c.* 55. officers in their permits for removing exciseable goods, are to express the time they shall be in force, and not removing such goods agreeable to the permits, incurs the penalties of 2 *Geo.* 1. and forfeiture of the goods; but in case of unavoidable delay in delivering such goods, the same shall not be forfeited.

By 22 *Geo.* 3. *c.* 68. persons counterfeiting any permit for removal of exciseable goods, or who shall knowingly publish or use any such permit, shall forfeit 200*l.*

By 23 *Geo.* 3. *c.* 70. the commissioners of excise are to provide moulds for making of paper to be used for permits, with the words *excise office* visible in the substance of such paper; and no permits shall be granted on any other paper.

All persons who shall make any mould for making such paper as aforesaid, or assist in making such paper, unless appointed by the commissioners of excise, shall suffer death as felons. *Ibid.*

Persons counterfeiting permits, or giving or receiving any false permit, or altering any granted by the proper officer, shall forfeit 500*l.* *Ibid.*

Excise officers delivering out paper for permits improperly, or granting false permits, are guilty of felony, and may be transported for seven years. *Ibid.*

Upon every action entered in any court of record for the penalty of 500*l.* a *capias* shall issue, and the defendant shall give bail for his appearance, and also to pay the penalty. *Ibid.*

Officers of excise shall not be sued for executing their office, until after a month's notice of the offence. Officers may tender amends, and if sufficient, a verdict shall be given for the defendant, who shall be intitled to costs. *Ibid.*

No evidence of the cause of action shall be produced, except what is contained in the notice; and the defendant may pay money into court. *Ibid.*

Claimers of goods seized shall prove payment of the duties, and persons obstructing officers in executing this act shall forfeit 100*l.* *Ibid.*

By 25 *Geo.* 3. *c.* 74. silks, callicoes, linens or stuffs printed, painted or dyed in England, and candles, leather, soap, hops, paper, paste-board, mill-board, scale-board, paper printed, painted, or stained, starch, gold or silver wire, and bricks or tiles for which the duties are paid, may be exported, giving the excise officer notice before packing up the same, and persons opening them after packed, except the excise officer, shall forfeit 20*l.*

If such goods shall not be packed agreeable to notice, a fresh one shall be given. *Ibid.*

Exporters shall give security for the shipping thereof, and not to reland the same, whereupon they shall receive a certificate from the officer, and have the drawback. *Ib.*

Officers attending the shipping such commodities may examine them; and goods landed, after giving security for obtaining the drawback, shall be forfeited. *Ibid.*

By 26 *Geo.* 3. *c.* 77. persons using any art to deceive officers in taking the weight or account of stock shall forfeit 100*l.*

Persons having in possession British spirits, soap, or candles, for which the duties have not been paid, forfeit the same and treble the value, which shall be estimated at the price of the best articles of the sort. *Ibid.*

Proof may be admitted of officers being authorised to act, without producing their particular appointments. *Ibid.*

Actions for penalties shall be filed in the name of the attorney-general, or of an officer of the customs or excise, or else be void, and the attorney-general may enter a *noli prosequi* in any action for fines. *Ibid.*

Persons assaulting excise or custom officers, or attempting to rescue prohibited goods, shall be bound with two sureties, to appear to informations, and refusing to become bound, shall be imprisoned. *Ibid.*

By 27 *Geo.* 3. *c.* 31. within thirty days after report of any vessel bringing French calicoes, muslins, linen, stuff, fustian, velvet, velveret, dimity or figured stuffs (except dyed of one colour) or French beer, ale, or mum; entry of the goods shall be made with the collector of excise, and the duties paid, on penalty of their being forfeited.

If the goods are landed before the duties are paid, they are forfeited, and the persons aiding therein, or receiving them, forfeit treble their value. *Ibid.*

Commissioners of the excise shall provide frames to denote the measure of French calicoes, and the like stuffs, which are to be marked with such frames, and with a stamp, to denote the payment of the duty. *Ibid.*

Persons fraudulently counterfeiting such frames, or having calicoes or the like marked therewith, in their custody, knowingly, shall forfeit 100*l.* *Ibid.*

Persons fraudulently counterfeiting stamps shall suffer death, and persons selling calicoes, or the like, with counterfeit stamps, shall be liable to the same punishment. *Ibid.*

On oath of a credible person, the houses of persons suspected to have in their possession calicoes, or the like, unstamped, may be searched, and if found in any place, except shipped for exportation, they are forfeited, and also 100*l.* *Ibid.*

Officers of excise may administer the necessary oaths on the exportation of goods entitled to drawbacks or bounties. *Ibid.*

By 28 *Geo.* 3. *c.* 37. if any trader shall,

in weighing his stock, use false scales and weights, the same shall be forfeited, and may be seized by an officer.

All exciseable goods and utensils in the custody of makers shall be subject to the amount of duty due from the proprietors, and also to all penalties incurred by makers.

By 32 *Geo.* 3. *c.* 10. if any person against whom a body warrant is granted shall remove out of the jurisdiction where convicted, it may be indorsed by the commissioners of excise, or any justices of the peace where the offender shall be.

By 35 *Geo.* 3, *c.* 31. commissioners of excise in Scotland may reward their officers as the commissioners of excise in England are authorised. *s.* 2.

By 35 *Geo.* 3. *c.* 96. where persons committed under 26 *Geo.* 3. *c.* 77. are detained for want of bail, the prosecutor may cause a copy of the indictment to be delivered, with notice that unless an appearance is entered in a limited time, an appearance and the plea of not guilty will be entered, which may accordingly be done; and if, on trial, the defendant shall be acquitted, the judge may order his discharge.

By 38 *Geo.* 3. *c.* 54. officers of excise accepting counterfeited certificates, or giving improper credit in excise books, that undue drawbacks may be obtained, shall be guilty of felony, and transported according to 24 *Geo.* 3. *stat.* 2. *c.* 56.—*s.* 8.

Persons counterfeiting excise debentures, or making use of them, shall be guilty of felony without clergy. *s.* 9.

By 41 *Geo.* 3. (u. k.) *c.* 91. persons forging certificates required to be granted under 38 *Geo.* 3. *c.* 54. by officers of excise, or knowingly giving or receiving false certificates, shall be guilty of felony, and transported for seven years. *s.* 5.

Seizures made by commanders of ships of war, under 26 *Geo.* 3. *c.* 40. *s.* 27. (see *Customs*), of goods liable to excise duty, may be lodged in any of his majesty's warehouses of excise in Great Britain, under the care of the proper officer. *s.* 6.

Commissioners of excise in cases of goods lost in the exportation to Ireland, Guernsey, or Jersey, which are entitled to bounty or drawback on landing, may order debentures to be made out for payment, on being satisfied that the goods were lost. *s.* 7.

By 46 *Geo.* 3. *c.* 112. the stat. 26 *Geo.* 3. *c.* 77. *s.* 13. directing that prosecutions in courts of record for penalties relating to the customs or excise shall be prosecuted in the name of the attorney-general, or some officer of such revenues, shall extend to all proceedings for excise penalties before commissioners of excise, or justices of peace. *s.* 1.

Persons taking false oaths in any case where an oath is required by the excise laws, shall be liable to the pains of perjury. *s.* 3.

By 47 *Geo.* 3. *sess.* 2. *c.* 30. the commissioners, on evidence that the forfeiture arose without any design of fraud may restore any seizures upon such terms and conditions as they may deem proper.

By 49 *Geo.* 3, *c.* 81, where any *vessels* would, if found, be liable to forfeiture for want of entry, or notice, or for being private or concealed, all the utensils used in any private or unentered place where any such vessel shall be found, shall be forfeited. *s.* 8.

EXCLUSA, EXCLUSAGIUM, a sluice for the carrying off of water; and the payment to the lord for the benefit of such a sluice. *Cowel. Blount.*

EXCLUSION, Bill of. A bill by which parliament, about the latter end of the reign of Charles II. attempted to exercise the right of altering and limiting the succession to the crown, by setting aside the king's brother and presumptive heir, the duke of York, from the succession, on the ground of his being a papist: this bill which raised a considerable ferment in the public mind at that time, after passing the house of commons, was rejected in the house of lords, the king having previously in the most open manner declared, that it never should receive the royal assent.

EXCOMMENGEMENT, law French, signifying excommunication.

EXCOMMUNICATION, (*excommunicatio*) an ecclesiastical censure, by which a person is excluded from the communion of the church, and from the company of the faithful. *Bac. Abr.* tit. *Ex.*

This excommunication is generally for contempt in not appearing, or not obeying a decree, &c. And in other respects the causes of it are many; as for matters of heresy, refusing to receive the sacrament, or to come to church; incontinency, adultery, simony, &c. *Ibid.*

By the common law an excommunicated person is disabled to do any act that is required to be done by one that is *probus et legalis homo*. He cannot serve upon juries, cannot be a witness in any court; and, which is the worst of all, cannot bring an action, either real or personal, to recover lands or money due to him. *Litt. sect.* 201. Nor is this the whole; for if, within forty days after the sentence has been published in the church, the offender does not submit and abide by the sentence of the spiritual court, the bishop may certify such contempt to the king in chancery: upon which there issues out a writ to the sheriff of the county, called, from the bishop's certificate, a *significavit*, or, from its effect, a writ *de excommunicato capiendo*: and the sheriff shall thereupon take the offender, and imprison him in the county gaol, till he is reconciled to the church, and such reconciliation certified by the bishop; upon which another writ, *de excommunicato deliberendo*, issues out of chancery to deliver and release him. *F. N. B.* 62.

EXCOMMUNICATO CAPIENDO, is a writ directed to the sheriff for apprehending him who stands obstinately excommunicated forty days; for the contempt of such a person not seeking absolution, being certified or signified into the chancery, this writ issues for the imprisoning him without bail or mainprize until he conforms. *F. N. B* 62.

EXCOMMUNICATO DELIBERANDO, is a writ to the sheriff for delivery of an excommunicated person out of prison, upon certificate from the ordinary of his conformity to the ecclesiastical jurisdiction. *Fitz. N B.* 39. *Reg. Orig.* 67.

EXCOMMUNICATO RECIPIENDO, is a writ whereby persons excommunicated being for their obstinacy committed to prison, and unlawfully delivered before they have given caution to obey the authority of the church, are commanded to be sought after and imprisoned again. *Reg. Orig.* 67.

EXCUSABLE HOMICIDE. See *Homicide.*

EXECUTED CONTRACT. A contract is said to be *executed* if A agrees to change horses with B, and they do it immediately, in which case the possession and the right are transferred together; or it may be *executory*, as if they agree to change next week; here the right only vests, and their reciprocal property in each other's horse is not in possession but in action; for a contract *executed*, which differs nothing from a grant, conveys *a chose in possession*, a contract *executory* being only a *chose in action.* 2 *Black.* 442.

EXECUTED ESTATE. Estates in *possession* are called *estates executed*, because a present interest passes to and resides in the tenant, not depending on any subsequent circumstance or contingency, as in the case of estates executory. 2 *Black.* 163.

EXECUTED FINE. The fine *sur cognizance de droit comme ceo*, &c. conveys a clear and absolute freehold, and gives the cognizee a seisin in law, without any actual livery; and it is therefore called a *fine executed*, whereas the other fines are but executory. 2 *Black.* 352.

EXECUTED REMAINDER. Remainders *executed*, or vested remainders, are such as pass a positive and indefeasible interest to the party, to be enjoyed *in futuro.* See *Remainder.*

EXECUTION AT LAW. The *execution* of the judgment of the court after the decision of a suit, is enforced by writ in divers ways, according to the nature of the action upon which it is founded, and of the judgment which is had or recovered. 3 *Black.* 412.

Thus if the plaintiff recovers in an *action real*, or mixed, whereby the seisin or possession of land is awarded to him, the writ of execution shall be an *habere facias seisinam*, or *writ of possession* of a *chattel interest*: these are writs directed to the sheriff of the county, commanding him to give actual possession to the plaintiff of the land so recovered; in the execution of which the sheriff may take the *posse comitatus*, or power of the county, and may justify breaking open doors, if the possession be not quietly delivered: but if it be peaceably yielded up, the delivery of a twig, a turf, or the ring of the door, in the name of seisin, is sufficient execution of the writ. *Ibid.*

Upon a presentation to a benefice recovered in a *quare impedit*, or assise of *darrein presentment*, the execution is by a writ of *de clerico admittendo*, directed, not to the sheriff, but to the bishop or archbishop, and requiring him to admit and institute the clerk of the plaintiff. *Ibid.*

In other actions, where the judgment, is that something in special be done or rendered by the defendant, then in order to presentment the execution is by a writ *de clerico admittendo*, directed, not to the sheriff, but to the bishop or his metropolitan, requiring them to admit and institute the clerk of the plaintiff. 3 *Blach.* 413.

In other actions where the judgment is, that something in special be done or rendered by the defendant, then, in order to compel him so to do, and to see the judgment executed, a special writ of execution issues to the sheriff according to the nature of the case. As upon an assise or *quod permittat prosternere* for a nuisance, where one part of the judgment is *quod amoveatur*, a writ goes to the sheriff to abate it at the charge of the party, which likewise issues even in case of an indictment. *Ibid.*

Upon a replevin, the writ of execution is the writ *de retorno habendo*; and, if the distress be eloigned, the defendant shall have a *capias in withernam*, but, on the plaintiff's tendering the damages and submitting to a fine, the process in *withernam* shall be stayed. In detinue, after judgment, the plaintiff shall have a distringas, to compel the defendant to deliver the goods, by repeated distresses of his chattels; or else a *scire facias* against any third person in whose hands they may happen to be, to show cause why they should not be delivered: and, if the defendant still continues obstinate, the sheriff shall summon an inquest to ascertain the plaintiff's damages, which shall be levied (like other damages) by seisure of the person or goods of the defendant. So that, after all, in replevin and detinue, (the only actions for recovering specific possession of personal chattels) if the wrongdoer be very perverse, he cannot be compelled to a restitution of the identical thing taken or detained; but he still has his election, to deliver the goods, or their value: an imperfection in the law, that results from the nature of personal property, which is easily concealed or conveyed out of the reach of justice, and not, like land and other real property, always amesnable to the magistrate. *Ibid.*

Executions in actions where money only is recovered, as a debt or damages, (and not any specific chattel) are of five sorts: either against the body of the defendant; or against his goods and chattels; or against his goods and the profits of his lands; or against his goods and the posesssion of his lands; or against all three, his body, lands, and goods. 3 *Black.* 414.

1. The first of these species of execution is by writ of *capias ad satisfaciendum*, which distinguishes it from the former *capias ad respondendum*, which lies to compel an appearance at the beginning of a suit. And, properly speaking, this cannot be sued out against any but such as were liable to be taken upon the former *capias*. The intent of it is to imprison the body of the debtor till satisfaction be made for the debt, costs, and damages: it therefore doth not lie against any privileged persons, peers, or members of parliament, nor against executors or administrators, nor against such other persons as could not be originally held to bail. And sir Edw. Coke also gives us a singular instance where a defendant in 14 *Ed.* 3, was discharged from a *capias* because he was of so advanced an age, *quod pœnam imprisonamenti subire non potest.* If an action be brought against a husband and wife, for the debt of the wife, when sole, and the plaintiff recovers judgment, the *capias* shall issue to take both the husband and wife in execution; but if the action was originally brought against herself, when sole, and pending the suit she marries, the *capias* shall be awarded against her only, and not against her husband. Yet if judgment be recovered against a husband and wife for the contract, nay even for the personal misbehaviour of the wife during her coverture, the *capias* shall issue against the husband only, which is one of the greatest privileges of English wives. *Ibid.*

The writ of *capias ad satisfaciendum* is an execution of the highest nature, in as much as it deprives a man of his liberty till he makes the satisfaction awarded; and therefore, when a man is once taken in execution upon this writ, no other process can be sued out against his lands or goods. Only, by statute 21 *Jac.* 1. c. 24, if the defendant dies, while charged in execution upon this writ, the plaintiff may, after his death, sue out new executions against his lands, goods, or chattels. The writ is directed to the sheriff, commanding him to take the body of the defendant, and have him at Westminster, on a day therein named, to make the plaintiff satisfaction for his demand; and if he does not then make satisfaction he must remain in custody till he does. This writ may be sued out, as may all other executory process, for costs, against a plaintiff as well as a defendant, when judgment is had against him. 3 *Black.* 415.

When a defendant is once in custody upon this process he is to be kept in *arcta et salva custodia*: and if he be afterwards seen at large it is an escape; and the plaintiff may have an action thereupon against the sheriff for his whole debt. For though, upon arrests, and what is called *mesne* process, being such as intervenes between the commencement and end of a suit, the sheriff, till the statute 8 & 9 *W.* 3. *c.* 27, might have indulged the defendant as he pleased, so as he produced him in court to answer the plaintiff at the teturn of the writ: yet, upon a taking in execution, he could never give any indulgence; for, in that case, confinement is the whole of the debtor's punishment, and of the satisfaction made to the creditor.—Escapes are either voluntary, or negligent. Voluntary are such as are by the express consent of the keeper, after which he can never retake his prisoner again, (though the plaintiff may retake him at any time) but the sheriff must answer for the debt. Negligent escapes are where the prisoner escapes without his keeper's knowledge or consent; and then upon fresh pursuit the defendant may be retaken, and the sheriff shall be excused, if he has him again before any action brought against himself for the escape. A rescue of a prisoner in execution, either going to gaol or in gaol, or a breach of prison, will not excuse the sheriff from being guilty of and answering for the escape; for he ought to have sufficient force to keep him, seeing he may command the power of the county. But by statute, commonly called *the lords acts*, if a defendant, charged in execution for any debt less than 100*l.* will surrender all his effects to his creditors, (except his apparel, bedding, and tools of his trade, not amounting in the whole to the value of 10*l.*) and will make oath of his punctual compliance with the statute, the prisoner may be discharged, unless the creditor insists on detaining him; in which case he shall allow him 3*s.* 6*d.* *per* week, to be paid on the first day of every week, and on failure of regular payment the prisoner shall be discharged. Yet the creditor may, at any future time, have execution against the lands and goods of the defendant, though never more against his person. And, on the other hand, the creditors may, as in case of bankruptcy, compel (under pain of transportation for seven years) such debtor charged in execution for any debt under 100*l.* to make a discovery and surrender of all his effects for their benefit; whereupon he is also entitled to the like discharge of his person. 3 *Black.* 415, 416.

If a *capias ad satisfaciendum* is sued out,

and a *non est inventus* is returned thereon, the plaintiff may sue out a process against the bail, if any were given: who, originally stipulated in this triple alternative that the defendant should, if condemned in the suit, satisfy the plaintiff his debt and costs; or, that he should surrender himself a prisoner; or, that they would pay it for him: as therefore the two former branches of the alternative are neither of them complied with, the latter must immediately take place. In order to which a writ of *scire facias* may be sued out against the bail, commanding them to show cause why the plaintiff should not have execution against them for his debt and damages; and on such writ, if they show no sufficient cause, or the defendant does not surrender himself on the day of return, or of showing cause (for afterwards is not sufficient) the plaintiff may have judgment against the bail, and take out a writ of *capias ad satisfaciendum,* or other process of execution against them. 3 *Black.* 417.

2. The next species of execution is against the goods and chattels of the defendant, and is called a writ of *fieri facias,* from the words in it, where the sheriff is commanded, *quod fieri faciat de bonis,* that he cause to be made of the goods and chattels of the defendant the sum or debt recovered. This lies as well against privileged persons, peers, &c. as other common persons, and against executors or administrators with regard to the goods of the deceased. The sheriff may not break open any outer doors to execute either this or the former writ, but must enter peaceably, and may then break open any inner door belonging to the defendant, in order to take the goods. And he may sell the goods and chattels (even an estate for years, which is a chattel real) of the defendant, till he has raised enough to satisfy the judgment and costs, first paying the landlord of the premises upon which the goods are found, the arrears of rent then due, not exceeding one year's rent in the whole. If part only of the debt be levied on a *fieri facias,* the plaintiff may have a *capias ad satisfaciendum* for the residue. *Ibid.*

A third species of execution is by writ of *levari facias,* which affects a man's goods and the profits of his lands, by commanding the sheriff to levy the plaintiff's debt on the lands and goods of the defendant, whereby the sheriff may seize all his goods, and receive the rents and profits of his lands, till satisfaction be made to the plaintiff. Little use is now made of this writ, the remedy by *elegit,* which takes possession of the lands themselves, being much more effectual. And of this species is a writ of execution proper only to ecclesiastics, which is given when the sheriff, upon a common writ of execution sued, returns that the defendant is a beneficed clerk, not having any lay-fees. In this case a writ goes to the bishop of the diocese, in the nature of a *levari,* or *fieri facias,* to levy the debt and damages *de bonis ecclesiasticis,* which are not to be touched by lay hands; and thereupon the bishop sends out a sequestration of the profits of the clerk's benefice, directed to the churchwardens, to collect the same, and pay them to the plaintiff, till the full sum be raised. 3 *Black.* 418.

4. The fourth species of execution is by the writ of *elegit,* which is a judicial writ given by the stat. Westm. 2. 13 *Ed.* 1. *c.* 18, either upon a judgment for a debt, or damages, or upon the forfeiture of a recognizance taken in the king's court. By the common law a man could only have satisfaction of goods, chattels, and the present profits of lands by the two last-mentioned writs of *fieri facias* or *levari facias,* but not the possession of the lands themselves, which was a natural consequence of the feodal principles, which prohibited the alienation, and of course the encumbering of the fief with the debts of the owner. And, when the restriction of alienation began to wear away, the consequence still continued; and no creditor could take the possession of lands, but only levy the growing profits; so that if the defendant aliened his lands the plaintiff was ousted of his remedy. The statute therefore granted this writ, (called an *elegit,* because it is in the choice or election of the plaintiff whether he will sue out this writ, or one of the former) by which the defendant's goods and chattels are not sold, but only appraised, and all of them (except oxen and beasts of the plough) are delivered to the plaintiff, at such reasonable appraisement and price, in part of satisfaction of his debt. If the goods are not sufficient, then the moiety, or one half of his freehold lands, whether held in his own name, or by any other in trust, for him, are also to be delivered to the plaintiff, to hold till out of the rents and profits thereof the debt be levied, or till the defendant's interest be expired; as, till the death of the defendant, if he be tenant for life or in tail. During this period the plaintiff is called tenant by *elegit.* Till this statute, by the ancient common law, lands were not liable to be charged with, or seized for, debts; because by this means the connection between lord and tenant might be destroyed, fraudulent alienations might be made, and the services be transferred to be performed by a stranger, provided the tenant incurred a large debt sufficient to cover the land. And therefore, even by this statute, only one half was, and now is, subject to execution; that out of the remainder sufficient might be left for the lord to distrain upon for his services. And upon the same feodal principle copyhold lands are at this day not liable to be taken in execution upon a judgment. But in case of a debt to the king it appears by *Magna*

Charta, *c.* 8, that it was allowed by the common law for him to take possession of the lands till the debt was paid: for he being the grand superior, and ultimate proprietor of all landed estates, might seize the lands into his own hands if any thing was owing from the vassal; and could not be said to be defrauded of his services, when the ouster of the vassal proceeded from hie own command. This execution, or seizing of lands by *elegit*, is of so high a nature that after it the body of the defendant cannot be taken; but if execution can only be had of the goods, because there are no lands, and such goods are not sufficient to pay the debt, a *capias ad satisfaciendum* may then be had after the *elegit*, for such *elegit* is in this case no more in effect than a *fieri facias*. So that body and goods may be taken in execution, or land and goods; but not body and land too, upon any judgment between subject and subject in the course of the common law. But,

5. Upon some prosecutions given by statute, as in the case of recognizances or debts acknowledged on statutes-merchant, or statutes-staple, (pursuant to the statutes 13 *Edw.* 1. de *mercatoribus*, and 27 *Edw.* 3, *c.* 9) upon forfeiture of these, the body, lands, &c. to be appraised to their full extended value, before the sheriff delivers them to the plaintiff, that it may be certainly known how soon the debt will be satisfied. And by statute 33 *Hen.* 8. *c.* 39, all obligations made to the king shall have the same force, and of consequence the same remedy to recover them, as a statute-staple; though indeed, before this statute, the king was entitled to sue out execution against the body, lands, and goods of his accountant or debtor. And his debt shall, in suing out execution, be preferred to that of every other creditor who has not obtained judgment before the king commenced his suit. The king's judgment also affects all lands which the king's debtor has at or after the time of contracting his debt, or which any of his officers mentioned in the stat. 13 *Eliz.* *c.* 4, has, at or after the time of his entering on the office; so that if such officer of the crown aliens for a valuable consideration, the land shall be liable to the king's debt, even in the hands of a *bonâ fide* purchaser, though the debt due to the king was contracted by the vender many years after the alienation. Whereas judgments between subject and subject relates, even at common law, no farther back than the first day of the term in which they were recovered, in respect of the lands of the debtor, and did not bind his goods and chattels, but from the date of the writ of execution. And now, by the statute of frauds, 29 *Car.* 2, *c.* 3, the judgment shall not bind the land in the hands of a *bonâ fide* purchaser, but only from the time of actually signing the same, nor the goods in the hands of a stranger, or a purchaser, *Skin.* 257, but only from the actual delivery of the writ to the sheriff. 3 *Black.* 418--421.

These are the methods which the law of England has pointed out for the execution of judgments; and when the plaintiff's demand is satisfied, either by the voluntary payment of the defendant, or by this compulsory process, or otherwise, satisfaction ought to be entered on the record, that the defendant may not be liable to be afterwards harassed a second time on the same account. But all these writs of execution must be sued out within a year and a day after the judgment is entered, otherwise the court concludes *primâ facie* that the judgment is satified and extinct; yet however it will grant a writ of *scire facias* in pursuance of Stat. Westm. 2, 13 Edw. 1, c. 45, for the defendant to show cause why the judgment should not be revived, and execution had against him; to which the defendant may plead such matter as he has to allege, in order to show why process of execution should not be issued; or the plaintiff may still bring an action of debt, founded on this dormant judgment, which was the only method of revival allowed by the common law. *Co. Lit.* 290. 3 *Black.* 421.

Execution from inferior courts.] By 19 *Geo.* 3, *c.* 70, when final judgment is obtained in *an inferior court*, on affidavit thereof in a court of record at Westminster, and that execution has been sued out, and that the defendant is not to be found within the jurisdiction of such inferior court, the judgment may be removed, and execution sued in the court above. *s.* 1.

No execution for less than 10*l.* in an inferior court shall be stayed, or a writ of error, or suspersedeas allowed, unless the defendant, with two sureties, give a recognizance in double the above sum, to prosecute such writ of error with effect, and pay the debt and costs, if the judgment be affirmed. *s.* 5.

For the poundage on executions see Poundage.

EXECUTION IN EQUITY. Writs of *execution* of orders and decrees in the courts of equity are made out by the clerks in court, and after service thereof upon the party personally, by delivery to and leaving with him a true copy of the writ of execution, showing the original writ under seal at the time of service; the performance of such orders and decrees may be enforced by a commitment of the person under an attachment for his contempt in non-performance, or by a sequestration of his estates.

EXECUTION for the king's debt, or prerogative execution, is always preferred before any other executions. 7 *Rep.* 20.

EXECUTION OF CRIMINALS. This,

in all cases, as well capital as otherwise, must be performed by the legal officer, the sheriff or his deputy; whose warrant for so doing was anciently by precept under the hand and seal of the judge, as it is still practised in the court of the lord high steward, upon the execution of a peer. 2 *Hal. P. C.* 409. though, in the court of the peers in parliament it is done by writ from the king. *Finch L.* 478. However, in general, in case of life, the judge may command execution to be done without any writ. And now the usage is, for the judge to sign the calendar, or list of all the prisoners names, with their separate judgments in the margin, which is left with the sheriff. Thus for a capital felony, it is written opposite to the prisoner's name "let him be "hanged by the neck;" formerly, in the days of Latin and abbreviation, *Staundf. P. C.* 182, "*sus. per. col.*" for "*suspen-* "*datur per collum.*" And this is the only warrant that the sheriff has for so material an act as taking away the life of another. 5 *Mod.* 22.

In this, however, though it be true that a marginal note of a calendar, signed by the judge, is the only warrant that the sheriff has for the execution of a convict, yet it is made with great caution and solemnity. At the end of the assizes the clerk of assize makes out in writing four lists of all the prisoners, with separate columns, containing their crimes, verdicts, and sentences, leaving a blank column, in which, if the judge has reason to vary the course of the law, he writes opposite the names of the capital convicts, to be reprieved, respited, transported, &c.—These four calendars, being first carefully compared together by the judge and the clerk of assize, are signed by them, and one is given to the sheriff, one to the gaoler, and the judge and the clerk of assize each keep another. If the sheriff receives afterwards no special order from the judge, he executes the judgment of the law in the usual manner, agreeably to the directions of his calendar. In every county this important subject is settled with great deliberation by the judge and the clerk of assize, before the judge leaves the assize-town; but probably in different counties, with some slight variation, as in Lancashire no calendar is left with the gaoler, but one is sent to the secretary of state. 4 *Black. Com.* 404. *n.* 1, by *Christian.*

If the judge thinks it proper to reprieve a capital convict, he sends a memorial or certificate to the king's most excellent majesty, directed to the secretary of state's office, stating that, from favourable circumstances appearing at the trial, he recommends him to his majesty's mercy, and to a pardon upon condition of transportation, or some slight punishment. This recommendation is always attended to. *Ibid.*

The sheriff upon receipt of his warrant is to do execution within a convenient time; which in the country is also left at large. In London a more solemn exactness is used, both as to the warrant of execution, and the time of executing thereof: for the recorder, after reporting to the king in person the case of the several prisoners, and receiving his royal pleasure, that the law must take its course, issues his warrant to the sheriffs; directing them to do execution on the day and at the place assigned. And, in the court of king's bench, if the prisoner be tried at the bar, or brought there by *habeas corpus* a rule is made for his execution; either specifying the time and place, or leaving it to the discretion of the sheriff. And, throughout the kingdom, by statute 25 *Geo.* 2. *c.* 37, it is enacted that, in case of murder, the judge shall in his sentence direct execution to be performed on the next day but one after sentence passed. But, otherwise, the time and place of execution are by law no part of the judgment.

The sheriff cannot alter the manner of the execution by substituting one death for another, without being guilty of felony himself, 2 *Hawk. P. C.* 463. It is held also by sir Edward Coke, 3 *Inst.* 52, and sir Matthew Hale, 2 *Hale's Pl. C.* 412, that even the king cannot change the punishment of the law, by altering the hanging or burning into beheading; though, when beheading is part of the sentence, the king may remit the rest. And, notwithstanding some examples to the contrary, sir Edward Coke stoutly mantains, that "*judicandum* "*est legibus, non exemplis.*" But others have thought, *Fost.* 270. *F. N. B.* 244. h. 19 *Rym. Fœd.* 284, and more justly, that this prerogative, being founded in mercy, and immemorially exercised by the crown, is part of the common law. For hitherto, in every instance, all these exchanges have been for more merciful kinds of death; and how far this may also fall within the king's power of granting conditional pardons, (*viz.* by remitting a severe kind of death, on condition that the criminal submits to a milder,) is a matter that may bear consideration. It is observable, that when lord Strafford was executed for the popish plot in the reign of king Charles the Second, the then sheriffs of London, having received the king's writ for beheading him, petitioned the house of lords for a command or order from their lordships, how the said judgment should be executed: for he being prosecuted by impeachment, they entertained a notion (which is said to have been countenanced by lord Russel) that the king could not pardon any part of the sentence. 2 *Hume's Hist. of G. B.* 328. The lords resolved, *Lords Journ.* 21 *Dec.* 1680, that the scruples of the sheriffs were unnecessary, and declared, that the king's writ ought to be obeyed. Disappointed of raising a flame in that assembly, they immediately signified, *Com. Journ.* 21 *Dec.* 1680, to the house of commons by one of the members, that they were not satisfied as to the power of the said writ. That house took two days to consider of it; and then, 23 *Dec.* 1680, sullenly resolved, that the house was content that the sheriff do execute lord Strafford by severing his head from his body. It is further related, that when afterwards the same lord Russel was condemned for high treason upon indictment, the king, while he remitted the ignominious part of the sentence, observed, "that his lordship would "now find he was possessed of that prero-"gative, which in the case of lord Strafford "he had denied him, 2 *Hume* 360." One can hardly determine (at this distance from those turbulent times) which most to disapprove of, the indecent and sanguinary zeal of the subject, or the cool and cruel sarcasm of the sovereign. 4 *Black.* 405.

To conclude: it is clear, that if, upon judgment to be hanged by the neck till he is dead, the criminal be not thoroughly killed, but revives, the sheriff must hang him again. 2 *Hal. P. C.* 412. 2 *Hawk. P. C.* 462. For the former hanging was no execution of the sentence; and, if a false tenderness were to be indulged in such cases, a multitude of collusions might ensue. Nay even while abjurations were in force, such a criminal so reviving was not allowed to take sanctuary and abjure the realm; but his flying to sanctuary was held an escape in the officer. *Fitzh. Abr. tit. corone,* 335. *Finch L.* 467. 4 *Black.* 326. 406.

EXECUTION OF STATUTES. The court of Star Chamber, erected in the reign of *Hen.* 7, was said to be for the execution of Statutes, &c. *Stat.* 3 *H.* 7, *c.* 1.

EXECUTIONE FACIENDA, a writ commanding execution of a judgment, and diversly used. *Reg. Orig.*

EXECUTIONE FACIENDA IN WITHERNAMIUM, a writ that lies for taking his cattle who has conveyed the cattle of another out of the county, so that the sheriff cannot replevy them. *Reg. Orig.* 82.

EXECUTIONE JUDICII, is a writ directed to the judge of an inferior court to do execution upon a judgment therein, or to return some reasonable cause wherefore he delays the execution. *F. N. B.* 20. If execution be not done on the first writ, an *alias* shall issue, and a *pluries* with this clause *vel causam nobis significes quare,* &c. And if upon this writ execution is not done, or some reasonable cause returned why it is delayed, the party shall have an attachment against him who ought to have done the execution, returnable in *B. R.* or *C. B. New Nat. Br.* 43.

EXECUTION *of Devises.* See WILLS.

EXECUTION *of Uses.* See USES.

EXECUTIVE POWER. The supreme executive power of these kingdoms is vested by our laws in a single person, the king, or queen, for the time being. 1 *Black.* 190.

The executive power, in this state, hath a right to a negative, in parliament, *i. e.* to refuse assent to any acts offered, or otherwise the other two branches of the legislative power would or might become despotic. *Montes. Lib.* 12. *chap.* 6.

EXECUTOR, (*Lat.*) is one that is appointed by a man's last will and testament, to have the execution thereof after his decease, and the disposing of all the testator's substance according to the tenor of the will: like the *hæres designatus* or *testamentarius* in the civil law. *Terms de Ley.* And all persons are capable of being executors that are capable of making wills, and many others besides, as femes covert, and infants, nay even infants unborn, or in *ventre sa mere,* may be made executors. *West Symb.* p. 1. § 635. But no infant can act as such till the age of seventeen years, till which time administration must be granted to some other, *durante minore ætate. Went. Off. Ex. c.* 18, in like manner as it may be granted *durante absentia,* or *pendente lite,* when the executor is out of the realm, 1 *Lutw.* 342, or when a suit is commenced in the ecclesiastical court touching the validity of the will. 2 *P. Wil.* 589, 590. This appointment of an executor is essential to the making of a will, *Went. c.* 1. *Plowd.* 281. And it may be performed either by express words, or such as strongly imply the same. But if the testator makes an incomplete will, without naming any executors, or if he names incapable persons, or if the executors named refuse to act, in any of these cases the ordinary must grant administration *cum testamento annexo,* 1 *Rol. Abr.* 907. *Comb.* 20, to some other person, and then the duty of the administrator, as also when he is constituted only *durante minore ætate,* &c. of another, is very little different from that of an executor. And this was law so early as the reign of *Hen.* 2. *Glanv. l.* 7. *c.* 6.

It is laid down as a general rule, that if a creditor makes his debtor executor, it is an extinguishment of the debt, for he cannot sue himself. 1 *Rol. Abr.* 920, 1. 5 *Co.* 30. *Offic. of Ex.* 30. *Godolph.* 30. But still in equity the executor's debt is assets, with respect to creditors, if the residue of the testator's estate is not sufficient; because it is extinguished not by release, but in the way of legacy. 8 *Rep.* 136. 2 *Rol. Abr.* 920.

And if a person dies intestate, and the ordinary commits administration to a debtor, the debt is not thereby extinguished, for he comes into the administration by the act of law, whereas the other is the act of the party. *5 Co.* 136. 1 *Salk.* 306. *Offic. of Ex.* 31.

And if a person indebted to another makes his creditor or debtor his executor; or if such creditor obtains letters of administration to his debtor, he may retain sufficient to pay himself before any other creditor whose debts are of equal degree. 1 *Rol. Abr.* 922. *Plowd.* 543. 3 *Black. Com.* 18.

An executor may be appointed either by express words, or words that amount to a direct appointment. *Wood's Inst.* 320.

If there is no executor there is properly no will; and where there is no will there can be no executor; but this is understood of goods, for where lands in fee are devised this is good, though no executor be named, executors having nothing to do with land, which is not testamentary but by act of parliament. *Offic. Exec.* 3, 4. *Finch.* 167. And where a testator has omitted to appoint an executor the ordinary will grant an administration, with the will annexed. *Perk.* 485. 1 *Rep.* 113.

The interest vested in the executor by the will of the deceased, may be continued and kept alive by the will of the same executor, so that the executor of A's executor is to all intents and purposes the executor and representative of A himself, *Stat.* 25 *Edw.* 3. *st.* 5. *c.* 5. 1 *Leon.* 275, But the executor of A's administrator, or the administrator of A's executor, is not the representative of A. (*Bro. Abr. tit. Administrator,* 7.) For the power of an executor is founded upon the special confidence and actual appointment of the deceased; and such executor is therefore allowed to transmit that power to another, in whom he has equal confidence: but the administrator of A is merely the officer of the ordinary, prescribed to him by act of parliament, in whom the deceased has reposed no trust at all: and therefore on the death of that officer it results back to the ordinary to appoint another. And, with regard to the administrator of A's executor, he has clearly no privity or relation to A; being only commissioned to administer the effects of the intestate executor, and not of the original testator. Wherefore in both these cases, and whenever the course of representation from executor to executor is interrupted by any one administration, it is necessary for the ordinary to commit administration afresh, of the goods of the deceased not administered by the former executor or administrator. And this administrator, *de bonis non,* is the only legal representative of the deceased in matters of personal property. *Styl.* 225. But he may, as well as an original administrator, have only a limited or special administration committed to his care, *viz.* of certain specific effects, such as a term of years and the like; the rest being committed to others. 1 *Rol. Abr.* 908. *Godolph. p.* 2. *c.* 30. *Salk.* 36.

The office and duty in general are very much the same in both executors and administrators; excepting, first, that the executor is bound to perform a will, which an administrator is not, unless where a testament is annexed to his administration, and then he differs still less from an executor: and, secondly, that an executor may do many acts before he proves the will. *Wentw. ch.* 3. Thus he may commence an action, but he cannot declare in the action before probate; for when he declares he must produce in court the letters testamentary. And he may release or pay a debt; may assent to a legacy, and be sued before probate; and do other acts, which seem to be fully enumerated in 1 *Salk.* 299, and *Com. Dig. Admin.* B. 9. But an administrator may do nothing till letters of administration are issued; for the former derives his power from the will, and not from the probate, *Comyns,* 151. The latter owes his entirely to the appointment of the ordinary.

The power and duty of a rightful executor or administrator.] 1. He must bury the deceased in a manner suitable to the estate which he leaves behind him. Necessary funeral expenses are allowed previous to all other debts and charges; but if the executor or administrator be extravagant it is a species of devastation or waste of the substance of the deceased, and shall only be prejudicial to himself, and not to the creditors or legatees of the deceased. *Salk.* 196. *Godolph.* p. 2. c. 26, *sec.* 2.

2. The executor or the administrator *durante minore ætate,* or *durante absentia,* or *cum testamento annexo,* must prove the will of the deceased, which is done either in common form, which is only upon his own oath before the ordinary, or his surrogate, or *per testes,* in more solemn form of law, in case the validity of the will be disputed. *Godolph. p.* 1. *c.* 20. *sec.* 4. When the will is so proved the original must be deposited in the registry of the ordinary, and a copy thereof on parchment is made out under the seal of the ordinary, and delivered to the executor or administrator, together with a certificate of its having been proved before him: all which together is usually styled the probate. In defect of any will, the person entitled to be administrator must also at this period take out letters of administration under the seal of the ordinary; whereby an executorial power to collect and administer, that is, dispose of the goods of the deceased, is vested in him: and he must, by statute 22 & 23 *Car.* 2. *c.* 10, enter into a bond with sureties faithfully to execute his trust. If all the goods of the deceased lie within the same jurisdiction, a probate before the ordinary,

or an administration granted by him, are the only proper ones: but if the deceased had *bona notabilia*, or chattels to the value of a hundred shillings, in two distinct dioceses or jurisdictions, then the will must be proved, or administration taken out, before the metropolitan of the province, by way of special prerogative, 4 *Inst.* 335, whence the courts where the validity of such wills is tried, and the offices where they are registered, are called the prerogative courts, and the prerogative offices, of the provinces of Canterbury and York. Lyndewode, who flourished in the beginning of the fifteenth century, and was official to archbishop Chichele, interprets these hundred shillings to signify *solidos legales*; of which he tells us seventy-two amounted to a pound of gold, which in his time was valued at fifty nobles or 16*l.* 13*s.* 4*d.* He therefore computes, *Provinc. l.* 3. *t.* 13. *c. item. v. centum. &c. statutum v. laicis*, that the hundred shillings, which constitute *bona notabilia*, were then equal in current money to 23*l.* 3*s.* 0¼*d.* This will account for what is said in our ancient books, that *bona notabilia* in the diocese of London (4 *Inst.* 335. *Godolph. p.* 2. *c.* 22.), and indeed every where else (*Plowd.* 281.), were of the value of ten pounds by composition: for, if we pursue the calculations of Lyndewode to their full extent, and consider that a pound of gold is now almost equal in value to an hundred and fifty nobles, we shall extend the present amount of *bona notabilia* to nearly 70*l.* But the makers of the canons of 1603 understood this antient rule to be meant of the shillings current in the reign of James I, and have therefore directed (*Can.* 92.) that five pounds shall for the future be the standard of *bona notabilia*, so as to make the probate fall within the archiepiscopal prerogative. Which prerogative (properly understood) is grounded upon this reasonable foundation: that, as the bishops were themselves originally the administrators to all intestates in their own diocese, and as the present administrators are in effect no other than their officers or substitutes, it was impossible for the bishops, or those who acted under them, to collect any goods of the deceased, other than such as lay within their own dioceses, beyond which their episcopal authority extends not. But it would be extremely troublesome, if as many administrations were to be granted, as there are dioceses within which the deceased had *bona notabilia*; besides the uncertainty which creditors and legatees would be at, in case different administrators were appointed, to ascertain the fund out of which their demands are to be paid. A prerogative is therefore very prudently vested in the metropolitan of each province, to make in such cases one administration serve for all. This accounts very satisfactorily for the reason of taking out administration to intestates, that have large and diffusive property, in the prerogative court: and the probate of wills naturally follows, as was before observed, the power of granting administrations; in order to satisfy the ordinary that the deceased has, in a legal manner, by appointing his own executor, excluded him and his officers from the privilege of administering the effects. 2 *Black.* 509.

3. The executor or administrator is to make an inventory of all the goods and chattels, whether in possession or action, of the deceased; which he is to deliver in to the ordinary upon oath, if thereunto lawfully required. 21 *Hen.* 8. *c.* 5.

4. He is to collect all the goods and chattels so inventoried; and to that end he has very large powers and interests conferred on him by law; being the representative of the deceased, (*Co. Litt.* 209.) and having the same property in his goods as the principal had when living, and the same remedies to recover them. And if there be two or more executors, a sale or release by one of them shall be good against all the rest (*Dyer* 23,); but in case of administrators it is otherwise (1 *Atk.* 460.) Whatever is so recovered, that is of a saleable nature and may be converted into ready money, is called *assets* in the hands of the executor or administrator, (*Finch.* 119.) that is sufficient or enough, (from the French *assez*) to make him chargeable to a creditor or legatee, so far as such goods and chattels extend. Whatever assets so come to his hands he may convert into ready money, to answer the demands that may be made upon him. And the goods of a testator, in the possession of the executor, cannot be taken in execution of a judgment in an action brought against the executor in his own right. 4 *T. R.* 621.

5. The executor or administrator must pay the debts of the deceased. In payment of debts he must observe the rules of priority; otherwise, on deficiency of assets, if he pay those of a lower degree first, he must answer those of a higher out of his own estate. And, *first*, he may pay all funeral charges, and the expence of proving the will, and the like. *Secondly*, debts due to the king on record or specialty (1 *And.* 129.) *Thirdly*, such debts as are by particular statutes to be preferred to all others; as the forfeitures for not burying in woollen, (*stat.* 30 *Car.* 2. *c.* 3.) money due upon poors rates (*stat.* 17 *Geo.* 2. *c.* 38.), for letters to the post office (*stat.* 9 *Ann. c.* 10.), and some others. *Fourthly*, debts of records; as judgments, (docquetted according to the statute 4 & 5 *W. & M. c.* 20.) statutes and recognizances (4 *Rep.* 60. *Cro. Car.* 363.) debts under a decree of a court of equity. 3 *P. Wms.* 401. *Fifthly*, debts due on special contracts; as for rent, (for which the lessor has often a better remedy in his own hands, by distraining,) or upon bonds, covenants, and the like, under seal, (*Wentw. ch.* 12) And

a court of equity will order voluntary bonds or other special contracts, without consideration, to be postponed to simple contract debts. 3 *P. Wms.* 222. *Lastly*, debts on simple contract, *viz.* upon notes unsealed, and verbal promises. Among these simple contracts, servants wages are by some (1 *Roll. Abr.* 927.) with reason preferred to any other: and so stood the antient law, according to Bracton (*l.* 2. *c.* 26.) and Fleta (*l.* 2. *c.* 56. *s.* 10.), who reckon among the first debts to be paid, *servitia servientium et stipendia famulorum.* Among debts of equal degree, the executor or administrator is allowed to pay himself first, by retaining in his hands so much as his debt amounts to (10 *Mod.* 496.) But an executor of his own wrong is not allowed to retain: for that would tend to encourage creditors to strive who should first take possession of the goods of the deceased; and would besides be taking advantage of his own wrong, which is contrary to the rule of law (5 *Rep.* 30.) Also, if no suit is commenced against him, the executor may pay any one creditor in equal degree his whole debt, though he has nothing left for the rest: for, without a suit commenced, the executor has no legal notice of the debt (*Dyer* 32. 2 *Leon.* 60.)

After a suit is commenced, the executor or administrator may still give a preference to other creditors of the same degree, by confessing a judgment to them for the real amount of their debts. 1 *P. Wms.* 295. But after a bill is filed by a creditor for a discovery of assets and payment of his debt, the executor or administrator may not pay another creditor of equal degree without confessing a judgment. 3 *P. Wms.* 401.

The course of administration, or payment of the debts according to their priority, applies only to legal estates; but as natural equity requires that all the creditors of the testator should be paid equally, when therefore the testator leaves his real estate to trustees or to executors, who thus become trustees, for the payment of his debts, these are called equitable assets, because a court of equity will order all the creditors to be paid *pari passu*, or an equal share out of this fund. 1 *Bro.* 138. 2 *Atk.* 50.

And even where specialty creditors have received part of their debts out of the personal estate, a court of equity will restrain them from receiving any part of the equitable fund, till all the other creditors are paid an equal proportion of their debts. 3 *P. Wms.* 322.

The personal estate is said to be the natural fund, for the payment of debts, yet it will be exonerated if the testator leaves by his will sufficient real property for the payment of his debts, provided it is the manifest intention that the personal estate shall be exonerated, and that the real estate shall be alone applied to that purpose. 1 *Bro.* 462. 2 *Bro.* 60.

If lands descend to the heir charged by the testator with his debts, there it shall be liable to all his debts, although it shall be considered as legal assets, and they shall be paid according to their priority. 2 *Atk.* 290. 1 *P. Wms.* 430. The equity of redemption of lands, mortgaged in fee, is equitable assets; for the creditors can have no relief from it, but in a court of equity. 2 *Atk.* 290.

Actions by and against executors.] The law subjects the executors to every person's claim and action, which he had against the testator, except as to a trespass, *vi et armis, &c.* committed by the testator; for which reason the executor is said to be the testator's assignee, and to represent the person of the testator: but for *personal wrongs* done by the testator to the person, or goods, &c. of another, the executor doth not represent him; because personal actions die with the person. *Co. Lit.* 209. 9 *Rep.* 89.

One executor cannot regularly sue another at law; but he may have relief in equity: in the eye of the law all are but as one executor; and most acts done by, or to any of them, are esteemed acts done by, or to all of them. 1 *Rol. Abr.* 918.

Special bail is not required of executors, &c. in any action brought for the testator's debt: and executors, or administrators are not liable to costs, where they sue in right of the testator. *Hut.* 69. *Cro. Eliz.* 503. *Yelv.* 168. *Dal.* 96. *Bend. pl.* 28. 2 *Rol.* 87. *Com. Dig.* 2 *V.* 439.

And if an executor brings a writ of error, though the judgment is affirmed, he shall not pay any costs; because as he is executor, it is *in auter droit:* also an executor shall not put in bail on a writ of error, *causa supra. Mich.* 5 *W. & M.* And the reason that executors are excused from paying costs, is their being presumed to have no knowledge of the affairs of the testator; yet they shall pay costs for not going on to trial, or where the cause of action arises to the executor himself, &c. 1 *Salk.* 207. 3 *Salk.* 106.

If on a *scire facias* against an executor, the sheriff return a *devastavit;* the plaintiff shall have judgment and execution *de bonis propriis* of the defendant: and if *nulla bona* be returned, he may have either a *capias ad satisfaciend.* or an *elegit.* 2 *Nels.* 791. *Dyer* 185. But one executor shall not be charged with a *devastavit* made by his companion; for the act of one shall charge the other no further than the goods of the testator in his hands amount to. *Cro. Eliz.* 318.

EXECUTOR DE SON TORT, or *executor of his own wrong*, is he that takes upon him the office of an executor by intrusion, not being so constituted by the testator; or, for want thereof, appointed by the ordinary to administer. *Dyer* 166. And if an executor of his own wrong takes upon himself the office of an executor without a lawful authority, he is chargeable to the rightful executor, and to all the creditors of the testator, and likewise to the legatees, so far as the goods amount unto which he wrongfully possessed: and such an executor is made by any act of acquisition, transferring or possessing himself of any of the estate or goods of the deceased; but not by acts of necessity, piety, or charity, as by locking up the goods, or burying the corpse of the deceased. 2 *Nels. Abr.* 793.

And by statute, persons obtaining any goods or debts of an intestate by fraud, or procuring administration to be granted to a stranger, &c. are chargeable as executors in their own wrong, to the value of the goods or debts, &c. and executors and administrators of executors in their own wrong, shall be liable to pay the debts of the testator; in like manner as their testator or intestate. 43 *Eliz. cap.* 8. 30 *Car.* 2. *cap.* 7.

An executor of his own wrong may be sued as executor; and he shall be sued for legacies, as well as a rightful executor. *Noy* 13. But he cannot maintain any suit or action himself, because he cannot produce any will to justify it: and the execution shall be awarded for the whole debt, though he meddled with a thing of very small value. *Noy* 69.

He cannot plead that he never was executor, nor administered as such; for it is not material whether he have assets or no, but to prove that he has administered any thing is enough: for this false plea will make him chargeable with the debt: whereas if he had not pleaded falsely, he would have been liable for no more than the value of the goods of the deceased. *Style* 120.

Such a one cannot retain for his own debt, against another creditor. 5 *Rep.* 31. But if afterwards administration is granted him, he may by virtue thereof retain goods for his own debt. 5 *Rep.* 30.

And an executor *de son tort* shall be allowed in equity, all such payments which a rightful executor ought to have paid. 2 *Chanc. Rep.* 33.

EXECUTORY, is where an estate in fee created by deed or fine is to be afterwards executed by entry, livery, writ, &c. And leases for years, rents, annuities, conditions, &c. are called inheritances executory. *Wood's Inst.* 293. Estates executed are when they pass presently to the person to whom conveyed, without any after-act. 2 *Inst.* 513.

EXECUTORY DEVISE, is where a future interest is devised, that vests not at the death of the testator, but depends on some contingency which must happen before it can vest. 1 *Eq. Cas. Abr.* 186.

It differs from a remainder in three very material points: 1. That it needs not any particular estate to support it. 2. That by it a fee-simple, or other less estate, may be limited after a fee-simple. 3. That by this means a remainder may be limited of a chattel interest, after a particular estate for life created in the same. 2 *Black.* 172.

1. The first case happens when a man devises a future estate to arise upon a contingency; and, till that contingency happens, does not dispose of the fee-simple, but leaves it to descend to his heir at law. As if one devises land to a feme-sole and her heirs, upon her day of marriage: here is in effect a contingent remainder without any particular estate to support it; a freehold commencing *in futuro.* This limitation, though it would be void in a deed, yet it is good in a will, by way of executory devise, (1 *Sid.* 153.) For, since by a devise, a freehold may pass without corporal tradition or livery of seisin, (as it must do, if it passes at all,) therefore it may commence *in futuro*; because the principal reason why it cannot commence *in futuro* in other cases, is the necessity of actual seisin, which always operates *in præsenti.* And, since it may thus commence *in futuro,* there is no need of a particular estate to support it; the only use of which is to make the remainder, by its unity with the particular estate, a present interest. And hence also it follows, that such an executory devise, not being a present interest, cannot be barred by a recovery, suffered before it commences. (*Cro. Jac.* 593.)

2. By executory devise a fee, or other less estate, may be limited after a fee. And this happens where a devisor devises his whole estate in fee, but limits a remainder thereon to commence on a future contingency. As if a man devises land to A. and his heirs; but, if he dies before the age of twenty-one, then to B. and his heirs: this remainder, though void in a deed, is good by way of executory devise (2 *Mod.* 289.) But, in both these species of executory devises, the contingencies ought to be such as may happen within a reasonable time; as within one or more life or lives in being, or within a moderate term of years; for courts of justice will not indulge even wills, so as to create a perpetuity, which the law abhors (12 *Mod.* 287. 1 *Vern.* 164.): because by perpetuities, (or the settlement of an interest, which shall go in the succession prescribed, without any power of alienation, *Salk.* 229.), estates are made incapable of answering those ends of social commerce, and providing for the sudden contingencies of private life, for which property was at first established. The utmost length that has been hitherto allowed for the contingency of an executory devise of either kind to happen in, is that of a life or lives in being, and one and twenty years afterwards. As where lands are devised to such unborn son of a feme-covert, as shall first attain the age of twenty-one and his heirs; the utmost length of time that can happen before the estate can vest, is the life of the mother and the subse-

quent infancy of her son: and this hath been decreed to be a good executory devise. *Fort.* 232.

And lord Kenyon has explained the whole doctrine of executory devises in the following words: "The rules respecting executory devises have conformed to the rules laid down in the construction of legal limitations, and the courts have said, that the estate shall not be unalienable by executory devises for a longer term than is allowed by the limitations of a common law conveyance. In marriage settlements the estate may be limited to the first and other sons of the marriage, in tail; and until the person to whom the first remainder is limited is of age, the estate is unalienable. In conformity to that rule the courts have said, so far we will allow executory devises to be good. To support this position, I could refer to many decisions; but it is sufficient to refer to the duke of Norfolk's case, in which all the learning on this head was gone into; and from that time to the present, every judge has acquiesced in that decision. It is an established rule that an executory devise is good, if it must necessarily happen within a life or lives in being, and twenty-one years, and the fraction of another year, allowing for the time of gestation."—See *Long* v. *Blackall*, 7 *T. R.* 100. In which case it was also determined that a child *en ventre sa mere* was to be considered as a child born, and therefore that an estate might be devised to it for life, and after its death to its issue in tail.

So in *Doe* v. *Clarke*, 2 *Hen. Black.* 399. a testator had devised his estate to such children as should be living at the time of his death; and the court of common pleas determined that a posthumous child came under that description.

A devise therefore to the youngest son of A, whether A is born, or *en ventre sa mere*, at the death of the testator, when that youngest son attains the age of twenty-one will be good, but if it were limited a day after that period, it would be null and void:

The subject of executory devises has undergone much learned investigation, in determining the validity of the will of Peter Thelluson, Esq. an eminent merchant in the city of London.

That gentleman had three sons, to whom he bequeathed some inconsiderable pecuniary legacies; but which, he observed, with their own great success, would be sufficient to procure them comfort; but the rest of his immense property, consisting of lands of the annual value of 4,500*l.* and 600,000*l.* in personal property, he devised to trustees, nearly to the following effect; *viz.* in trust that they should receive the rents, interest, and profits, and dispose of them for the purpose of accumulating, during the lives of his three sons, and the lives of all their sons who should be living at the time of his death, or who should be born within due time afterwards, and during the lives and life of the survivors or survivor of them; and then he directs, that after the decease of the survivor of such persons, the accumulated fund should be divided into three shares, and that one share should be conveyed to the eldest male lineal descendant of each of his three sons; and upon the failure of such a descendant, that share to go to the descendants of the other sons; and upon failure of all such male descendants, he devises all the accumulated property to be applied to the use of the sinking fund. At the time of his death his three sons were living, they had four sons living, and two other twin sons were born soon afterwards, who of course were then *en ventre sa mere*. It was calculated that at the death of the survivor of these nine persons, the accumulated fund would probably amount to above nineteen million sterling:

This extraordinary will did not originate from any dissatisfaction which the testator's family had ever occasioned, though he was resolved that none of his descendants, who were born, or were in embryo at the time of his death, should ever enjoy any part of this property:

The chancellor, lord Loughborough, lord Alvanley, then master of the rolls, and the judges, Buller and Lawrence, after hearing counsel for several days, were unanimously and clearly of opinion that the period of accumulation in this case was not more extensive than what had been established in former cases, and that it was within the prescribed limit and boundary of executory devises, as these nine lives were wearing out together, like so many candles burning at once; that this property was rendered unalienable only during one life, that of the survivor of the nine; and therefore they held themselves compelled by the force of authorities to decide in favour of the validity of this will. 4 *Vesey*, jun. 227.

But to prevent similar instances of vanity, illiberality, and folly in future, the 39 & 40 *Geo.* 3. *c.* 98. was passed, by which the power of settling and devising property for the purpose of accumulation is restrained in general to twenty-one years after the death of the grantor or the testator. It enacts that no person shall, by any deed, will, or by any other mode, settle or dispose of any real or personal property, so that the rents or profits may be wholly or partially accumulated for a longer term than the life of the grantor, or the term of twenty-one years after the death of the grantor or the testator, or the minority of any person who shall be living, or *en ventre sa mere*, at the death of the grantor or the testator, or during the minority only of such person as would for the time being, if of full age, be entitled to the rents and produce so directed to be accumulated;

and where any accumulation is directed otherwise, such direction shall be void, and the rents and profits, during the time that the property is directed to be accumulated contrary to this act, shall go to such person as would have been entitled thereto, if no such accumulation had been directed; provided that this act shall not extend to any provision for the payment of debts, or for raising portions for children, or to any direction touching the produce of woods or timber.

3. By executory devise a term of years may be given to one man for his life, and afterwards limited over in remainder to another, which could not be done by deed: for by law the first grant of it, to a man for life, was a total disposition of the whole term; a life estate being esteemed of a higher and larger nature than any term of years, (8 *Rep.* 95.) And, at first, the courts were tender, even in the case of a will, of restraining the devisee for life from aliening the term; but only held, that in case he died without exerting that act of ownership, the remainder over should then take place (*Bro. tit. chatteles*, 23. *Dyer* 74.) for the restraint of the power of alienation, especially in very long terms, was introducing a species of perpetuity. But, soon afterwards, it was held, (*Dyer* 358. 8 *Rep.* 96.) that the devisee for life hath no power of aliening the term, so as to bar the remainder-man: yet, in order to prevent the danger of perpetuities, it was settled, (1 *Sid.* 451.) that though such remainders may be limited to as many persons successively as the devisor thinks proper, yet they must all be *in esse* during the life of the first devisee; for then all the candles are lighted and are consuming together, and the ultimate remainder is in reality only to that remainder-man who happens to survive the rest: and it was also settled, that such remainder may not be limited to take effect, unless upon such contingency as must happen (if at all) during the life of the first devisee, (*Skinn.* 341. 3 *P. Wms.* 258.)

It has long been fully settled that a term for years, or any chattel interest, may be given by an executory devise to an unborn child of a person in existence, when it attains the age of twenty-one; and that the limits of executory devises of real and personal property are precisely the same. *Fearne*, 320. It is very common to bequeath chattel interests to A and his issue, and if he dies without issue, to B. It seems now to be determined, that where the words are such as would have given A an estate-tail in real property, in personal property the subsequent limitations are void, and A has the absolute interest: but if it appears from any clause or circumstance in the will, that the testator intended to give it over only in case A had no issue living at the time of his death, upon that event the subsequent limitation will be good as an executory devise. See *Fearne*, 371. and cases referred to in 3 *Coxe's P. Wms.* 262.

EXEMPLIFICATION OF LETTERS PATENT, is a copy or transcript of letters patent, made from the inrolment thereof, and sealed with the great seal of England, which exemplifications may be shewn or pleaded, as the letters patent themselves. 6 *R.* 2. *c.* 4. 3 & 4 *Ed.* 6. *c.* 4. and 13 *Eliz.* *c.* 6. 5 *Rep.* 53.

EXEMPLIFICATIONE, is a writ granted for the exemplification of an original record. *Reg. Orig.* 290.

EXEMPTION, (*exemptio*) signifies a privilege to be free from service or appearance; as knights, clergymen, &c. are exempted to appear at the county-court by statute; and peers from being put upon inquests. 6 *Rep.* 23. Persons seventy years of age, apothecaries, &c. are also exempted by law from serving on juries: and justices of peace, attorneys, &c. from parish offices. 2 *Inst.* 247. There is also an exemption from tolls, &c. by the king's letters patent: and a writ of exemption, or of ease, to be quit of serving on juries, and all public service. *Shep. Epitom.* 1049.

EXERCITUALE, was anciently used for a heriot; being paid only in arms and military accoutrements. *Cowel. Blount.*

EXFREDIARE, (from the Sax. *frede*, *frith*, *peace*, and *frithian*) to break the peace, or commit open violence. *Ibid.*

EX GRAVI QUERELA, is a writ that anciently lay for him to whom any lands or tenements in fee were devised by will, (within any city, town or borough, wherein lands were deviseable by custom) and the heir of the devisor entered and detained them from him. *Reg. Orig.* 244. *Old Nat. Br.* 87.

EXHENIUM, or EXENNIUM, a gift or present, and more properly a new year's gift. *Cowel. Blount.*

EXHIBIT, (*exhibitum*) where a deed, or other writing in a suit in chancery, or bankruptcy is exhibited to be proved by witnesses, and the examiner or commissioners certify on the back of it, that the deed or writing was shewed to the witness, to prove it at the time of his examination, and by him sworn to; this is called an exhibit.

EXHIBITIO, an allowance for meat and drink, customary among the religious appropriators of churches, who usually made it to the depending vicar: the benefactions settled for the maintaining of scholars in the universities, not depending on the foundation, are also at this day called exhibitions. *Cowel. Blount.*

EXIGENDARIES OF THE COMMON PLEAS, (*exigendarii de banco communi*) are otherwise called exigenters, by stat. 10 *H.* 6. *c.* 4.

EXIGENT, (*exigendo*) is a writ that lies where the defendant in *an action personal* cannot be found, nor any thing of his within the county, whereby to be attached or distrained; and is directed to the sheriff, to proclaim and call him five county court days, one after another, charging him to appear upon pain of outlawry: it is called exigent, because it exacteth the party, *i. e.* requires his appearance or forth-coming to answer the law; and if he come not at the last day's proclamation, he is said to be *quinquies exactus*, and is outlawed. *Cromp. Juris.* 188.

The writ of exigent also lies *on an indictment of felony*, where the party indicted cannot be found: and upon suing out an exigent for a criminal matter before conviction, there shall be a writ of proclamation, &c. 3 *Inst.* 31. 4 & 5 *W. & M.* c. 22. See *Outlawry*.

EXIGENTER, (*exigendarius*) an officer of the court of common pleas; of which there are four in number: they make all exigents and proclamations, in actions where process of outlawry doth lie. *Cowel. Blount.*

EXIGI FACIAS, the exigent is so called. 3 *Black. Com.* 283.

EXILE, a banishment or driving out of a person. *Lit. Dict.* And this exile is either by restraint, when the government forbids a man, and makes it penal to return; or it is voluntary, where he leaves his country upon disgust, but may come back at pleasure. 2 *Lev.* 191.

EXILIUM, signifies a spoiling: or the injury done to tenants, by altering their tenure, ejecting them, &c. and Fleta distinguishes between *vastum, destructio*, and *exilium*; for he tells us that *vastum* and *destructio* are almost the same, and are properly applied to houses, gardens or woods; but *exilium* is when tenants are enfranchised, and afterwards unlawfully turned out of their tenements. *Cowel. Blount.*

EXITUS, issue, or off-spring: and applied to the issues or yearly rents and profits of lands. *Ibid.*

EXLEGALITUS, is he who is prosecuted as an outlaw. *Ibid.*

EX MERO MOTU, words used in the king's charters and letters patent, to signify that he grants them of his own will and motion, without petition or suggestion of any other: which words shall be taken most strongly against the king, 1 *Co. Rep.* 451.

EX OFFICIO, an act done in execution of the power which a person has by virtue of an office, to do in certain cases, and without being applied to: thus a justice of peace may not only grant surety of the peace, at the complaint or request of any person, but he may demand and take it *ex officio* at discretion, &c. *Dalt.* 270.

EX OFFICIO INFORMATIONS, are informations at the suit of the king, filed by the attorney-general, as by virtue of his office, without applying to the court wherein filed, for leave, or giving the defendant any opportunity of shewing cause why it should not be filed.

EXONERATIONE SECTÆ, was a writ that lay for the king's ward, to be free from all suit to the county-court, hundred court, leet, &c. during wardship. *F. N. B.* 158. *Cowel. Blount.*

EXONERATIONE SECTÆ AD CURIAM BARON. A writ of the same nature, sued by the guardian of the king's ward, and directed to the sheriff or stewards of the court, that they do not distrain him, &c. for not doing suit of court. *New Nat. Br.* 352. *Cowel. Blount.*

EX PARTE, partly, or of the one part; as a commission *ex parte* in chancery, which is a commission taken out and executed by one side or party only, on the other party's neglecting or refusing to join. *Cowel. Blount.*

EX PARTE TALIS, is a writ that lies for a bailiff or receiver, who having auditors assigned to take his account, cannot obtain of them reasonable allowance, but is cast into prison: and the course in this case is to sue this writ out of the chancery, directed to the sheriff to take four mainpernors to bring his body before the barons of the exchequer at a certain day, and to warn the lord to appear at the same time. *F. N. B.* 129.

EXPECTANT, having relation to or depending upon; and this word is used in the law with fee, as fee-expectant.

EXPECTANCY, *estates in*, are of two sorts; one created by the act of the parties, called a remainder; the other by act of law, called a reversion. 2 *Black. Com.* 163. See title *Remainder, Reversion.*

EXPEDITATE, (*expeditare*) in the laws of the forest, signifies to cut out the ball of the dog's fore-feet, for the preservation of the king's game: but the ball of the foot of a mastiff is not to be taken out, but the three claws of the fore-foot on the right side are to be cut off by the skin. *Cromp. Jurisd.* 152. *Manwood, cap.* 16.

EXPEDITATÆ ARBORES, trees rooted up or cut down to the roots. *Fleta, lib.* 2. *c.* 41. *Cowel. Blount.*

EXPENCES OF PROSECUTION. On a conviction (or even upon an acquittal where there was a reasonable ground to prosecute, and in fact a *bona fide* prosecution,) for any grand or petit larceny or other felony, the reasonable expences of prosecution, and also, if the prosecutor be poor, a compensation for his trouble and loss of time, are by stats. 25 *Geo.* 2. *c.* 36. and 18 *Geo.* 3. *c.* 19. to be allowed him out of the county stock, if he petitions the judge for that purpose, and by stat. 27 *Geo.* 2. *c.* 3. explained by the same stat. 18 *Geo.* 3. *c.* 19. all persons appearing upon recognizance, or subpœna to give evidence, whether any indictment be preferred or not, and as well without conviction as with it, are entitled to be paid their charges, with a further allowance (if poor) for their trouble and loss of time.

But the costs cannot be allowed the prosecutor out of the county rates in any case for a misdemeanor.

EXPENCES OF WITNESSES. See *Evidence.*

EXPENDITORS, are the persons appointed by commissioners of sewers to pay, disburse or expend the money collected by the tax for the repairs of sewers, &c. when paid into their hands by the collectors, on the reparations, amendments, and reformations ordered by the commissioners, for which they are to render accounts when thereunto required. *Laws of Sewers*, 87, 88.

EXPENSÆ LITIS, costs of suit allowed a plaintiff or defendant recovering in his action. See *Costs.*

EXPENSIS MILITUM NON LEVANDIS, &c. is an ancient writ to prohibit the sheriff from levying any allowance for knights of the shire, upon those that hold lands in ancient demesne. *Reg. Orig.* 261. For there is a writ *de expensis militum levandis*, for levying expences for knights of the parliament, &c. *Reg. Orig.* 191. *Cowel. Blount.*

EXPLEES, the rents or profits of an estate, &c. See *Esplees.*

EXPLORATOR, a scout: also a huntsman or chaser. *Cowel. Blount.*

EXPORTATION, is the shipping or carrying out goods, wares, and the merchandize of England for other countries; mentioned in the statutes relating to the customs.

EXPOSITION OF DEEDS. Deeds are to be expounded according to the apparent intent; and be reasonable and equal, &c. *Co. Lit.* 313.

EX POST FACTO, is a term used in the law, signifying something done after the time when it should have been done: thus an act done, or estate granted, may be made good by matter *ex post facto*, that was not so at first, by election, &c. As sometimes a thing well done at first, may afterwards become ill. 5 *Rep.* 22. 8 *Rep.* 146.

EXTEND, (*extendere*) is to value the lands or tenements of one bound by a statute, who hath forfeited his bond, at such an indifferent rate, as by the yearly rent the creditor may in time be paid his debt. *F. N. B. Cowel. Blount.*

EXTENDI FACIAS, a writ of extent, whereby the value of lands is commanded to be made and levied, &c. *Reg. Orig.*

EXTENT, (*extenta*) signifies a writ or commission to the sheriff for the valuing of lands or tenements; and sometimes the act of the sheriff or other commissioners upon this writ. *Bro.* 313. *Stat.* 16 & 17 *Car.* 2. *cap.* 5. *Cowel. Blount.* See also title *Execution.*

EXTINGUISHMENT, (from *extinguo*) signifies a consolidation: for example, if a man hath a yearly rent out of lands, and afterwards purchases the lands whereout it ariseth, so that he hath as good an estate in the land as the rent, now both the property and rent are consolidated or united in one possessor; and therefore the rent is said to be extinguished. Also where a person has a lease for years, and afterwards buys the property; this is a consolidation of the property and fruits, and is an extinguishment of the lease: but if a man have an estate in land but for life or years, and hath a higher estate as a fee-simple in the rent; the rent is not extinguished, but in suspence for a time; for after the term, the rent shall revive. *Terms de Ley.*

EXTINGUISHMENT OF COMMON. By purchasing lands wherein a person hath common appendant, the common is extinguished. *Cro. Eliz.* 594. A commoner releases his common in one acre, it is an extinguishment of the whole common. *Show. Rep.* 350. And where a person hath common of vicinage, if he incloses any part of the land, all the common is extinct. 1 *Brownl.* 174.

But if one hath common appendant in a great waste, belonging to his tenant, and the lord improve part of the waste leaving sufficient; if he after make a feoffment to the commoner of the land improved, this will be no extinguishment. *Dyer* 339. *Hob.* 172. A commoner aliens part of his land, to which the common doth belong; the common is not extinct, but shall be divided. 2 *Shep. Abr.* 152. Vide *Common.*

EXTINGUISHMENT OF COPYHOLD. Any act of the copyholder's, which denotes his intention to hold no longer of his lord, and amounts to a determination of his will, is an extinguishment of his copyhold. *Hutt.* 81. *Cro. Eliz.* 21. 1 *Jon.* 41. As if a copyholder in fee accepts a lease for years of the same land from the lord, or the lord leases to another, and the copyholder accepts an assignment from the lessee. *Moor* 184. 2 *Co.* 16. *b.* *Godb.* 11, 101.

So if a copyholder bargains and sells his copyhold to the lessee for years of the manor, or if he joins with his lord in a feoffment of the manor, his copyhold is extinct. *Hutt.* 65. 1 *Jon.* 41. *S. C. Godb.* 11.

And so it is if a copyholder accepts to hold of his lord, by any less estate than he has in the grounds, this is an extinguishment. 1 *And.* 199. *Latch.* 213.

EXTINGUISHMENT OF DEBT. If feme sole debtee take the debtor to husband, or if there be two joint obligors in a bond, and the obligee marries one of them; or in case a person is bound to a feme sole and another, and she takes the obligor to husband; in these cases, the debt will be extinguished. 8 *Rep.* 136. And if a debtor makes the debtee his executor, or him and another executor, and they take the executorship upon them; or if the debtee makes his debtor executor, &c. it is an extinguishment of the debt, and it shall never revive. *Plowd.* 184. 1 *Salk.* 304. But in the latter case the debt is in equity in favor of creditors, if the residue of the testator's estate is not sufficient. 8 *Rep.* 136. 2 *Rol. Abr.* 920.

It is agreed as a general rule, that a creditor's accepting a higher security than he had before, is an extinguishment of the first debt; as if a creditor by simple contract accepts an obligation, this extinguishes the simple contract debt. 1 *Rol. Abr.* 470, 471, 604. 6 *Co.* 44.

So if a man accepts a bond for a legacy, he cannot after sue for his legacy in the spiritual court; for by the deed the legacy is extinct, and it is become a mere debt at common law. *Yelv.* 38.

So if a bond creditor obtains judgment on the bond, or has judgment acknowledged to him, he cannot afterwards bring an action on the bond; for the debt is drowned in the judgment, which is a security of a higher nature than the bond. 6 *Co.* 44. *b.*

But the accepting a security of an inferior nature is by no means an extinguishment of the first debt; as if a bond be given in satisfaction of a judgment. *Cro. Jac.* 579. 2 *Brownl.* 29. *Cro. Jac.* 649, 650.

Also the accepting a security of equal degree is no extinguishment of the first debt; as where an obligee has a second bond given to him; for one deed cannot determine the duty upon another. *Cro. Eliz.* 304, 716, 727. 1 *Brownl.* 74. *Lit. Rep.* 58. *Cro. Car.* 86.

By release of part of a debt due on bond, the whole is gone, and the obligation extinguished. *Bro. Contract.* 80. 1 *And.* 235.

EXTINGUISHMENT OF LIBERTIES. As to liberties and franchises granted by the king, sometimes they may be extinguished, and sometimes they shall not. *Moor* 474. When the king grants any privileges, liberties or franchises, which were in his own hands, as parcel of the flowers of the crown; such as *bona felonum, fugitivorum & utlagatorum*, waifs, strays, deodand, wreck on the sea, &c. if they come to the crown again, they are drowned and extinct in the crown, and the king is seised of them *jure coronæ:* but if liberties of fairs, markets, or other franchises, and jurisdictions, be erected and created by the king, they will not be extinguished, nor their appendances severed from the possessions. 9 *Rep.* 25. A man has liberties by prescription, if he takes letters patent of them, the prescription will be gone and extinct; for things of a higher determine those of a lower nature. 2 *H.* 7. 5.

EXTINGUISHMENT OF SERVICES. The lord purchases or accepts parcel of the tenancy, out of which an entire service is to be paid or done: by this the whole service will be extinct: but if the service be *pro bono publico*, then no part of it shall be extinguished; and homage and fealty are not subject to extinguishment, by the lord's purchasing part of the land. 6 *Rep.* 1, 105. *Co. Lit.* 149. If the lord and another person do purchase the lands, whereout he is to have services, they are extinct: also by severance of the services, a manor may be extinguished. *Co. Lit.* 147. 1 *And.* 257.

EXTINGUISHMENT OF WAYS. If a man hath a way as appendant, and after purchases the land wherein this way is, the way is extinct. *Terms de Ley.* Though a way of necessity to market, or church, or to arable land, &c. is not extinguished by purchase of ground, or unity of possession. 11 *H.* 7. 25. *Co. Lit.* 155.

EXTIRPATIONE, is a judicial writ, either before or after judgment, that lies against a person who when a verdict is found against him for land, &c. doth maliciously overthrow any house, or extirpate any trees upon it. *Reg. Jud.* 13. 56. *Cowel. Blount.*

EXTOCARE, to grub up lands, and reduce them to arable or meadow. *Mon. Ang. tom.* 2. *p.* 71. *Cowel. Blount.*

EXTORTION, (*extorsio*, from *extorqueo*, to wrest away) is an abuse of public justice, and consists in any officer's taking by colour of his office, from any one any money, or thing of value, where none at all is due, or not so much is due, or before it is due. *Co. Lit.* 368. 10 *Rep.* 102. 1 *Hawk. P. C.* 170.

And extortion in a large sense, is taken for any oppression by power or pretence of right. 1 *Hawk. P. C.* 170.

This offence by the common law is severely punished on indictment by fine and imprisonment, and removal of officers from the offices wherein committed. 4 *Black.* 141.

EXTRACTA CURIÆ, the issues or profits of holding a court arising from the customary fees, &c. *Paroch. Antiq.* 572. *Cowel. Blount.*

EXTRACTS *of writings or records*, are the short contents thereof.

EXTRA-JUDICIAL, any act done or judgment given, out of the ordinary course of the law, in a case, not then before the court, or in a cause wherein the judge has not jurisdiction, is perused *extrajudicial.*

EXTRA-PAROCHIAL, signifies to be out of the bounds or limits of a parish; which extra-parochial places are privileged and exempt from the duties of a parish. Thus extra-parochial lands signify lands newly left by the sea, not taken into any parish.

EXTRAVAGANTS, are certain constitutions of popes, so called, because they are *extra corpus canonicum gratiani, sive extra decretorum libros vagantur.* *Du Cange.* 1 *Black.* 82.

EXTUMÆ, reliques in churches and tombs. *Cartular. Abbat. Glaston. MS. f.* 15. *Cowel. Blount.*

EXUPERARE, to overcome; and it sometimes signifies to apprehend or take, as, exuperare *vivum vel mortuum*. *Leg. Edm. c.* 2. *Cowel. Blount.*

EY, *insula*, an island: and where the names of places end in *ey*, it denotes them an island. As Ramsey, Sheppy, Hersey, &c. *Ibid.*

EYE, putting out. See *Mayhem.*

EYERY *of hawks.* See *Aery.*

EYRE. See *Eire*, and *Justices in Eyre.*

F

F, was a letter wherewith felons, &c. were branded and marked with a hot iron, on their being admitted to the benefit of clergy. *Stat.* 4 *H.* 7. *c.* 13. But this is abolished by *stats.* 4 *Geo.* 1. *c.* 11. 6 *Geo.* 1. *c.* 23. and 19 *Geo.* 3. *c.* 74. See *Clergy.*

FABRICK-LANDS, lands given towards the rebuilding or repairing of cathedral and other churches. *Cowel. Blount,*

FACTA ARMORUM, feats of arms, justs, tornaments, &c. *Ibid.*

FACTO, in fact; as where any thing is actually done, &c. thus in *stat.* 1 *Ed.* 4. *c.* 1. the three Henrys are stiled *nuper de facto, et non de jure, reges Angliæ.*

FACTOR, the agent of a trader or manufacturer, constituted by letter or power of attorney, and if the principal give the factor a general commission to act for the best, he may do for him as he thinks fit; but otherwise he may not. *Lex Mercat.* 151.

A bare commission to a factor to sell and dispose of merchandize, is not a sufficient power for the factor to entrust any person, or to give a further day of payment than the day of the sale of the goods. 1 *Bulst.* 102.

If a factor buys goods on account of his principal, where he is used so to do, the contract of the factor shall oblige the principal to a performance of the bargain. But where goods are bought or exchanged without orders, it is at the merchant's curtesy whether he will accept of them or turn them on the factor's hands. *Lex Mer.* 154,5. *Goldsb.* 137.

Goods remitted to a factor ought to be carefully preserved; and he is accountable for all lawful goods which shall come to his hands. 4 *Rep.* 83. (See also title *Bailment.*)

If the factor has orders from his principal not to sell any goods but in such a manner, and he breaks those orders, he is liable to the loss or damage that shall be received thereby. *Lex Mercat.* 154, 155.

When a factor has bought or sold goods pursuant to orders, he is immediately to give advice of it to his principal; and where a factor has made a considerable profit for his principal, he must take due care in the disposition of the same; for without commission, or particular orders, he is answerable. *Ibid.* A factor shall suffer for not-observing orders; and no factor acting for another man's account in merchandize, can justify receding from the orders of his principal, though there may be a probability of advantage by it: and if he make any composition with creditors without orders, he shall answer it to his principal. *Ibid.*

Factors ought to observe the contents of all letters from their principals, or written to them by their order. A merchant is answerable in action upon the case for the deceits of his factor, in selling goods abroad: and as somebody must be a loser by such deceit, it is more reasonable that he who employs, and puts confidence in the deceiver, should lose, than a stranger. 1 *Salk.* 289.

Though a factor has power to sell, and thereby bind his principal, yet he cannot bind or affect the property of the goods by *pledging them* as a security for his own debt, though there is the formality of a bill of parcels and a receipt. *Stran.* 1178.

Factors are also liable to the statutes concerning bankrupts. 5 *Geo.* 2. *c.* 30. *s.* 39.

And where a factor sells the goods of his principal, on credit, without mentioning the name of his principal, and the factor becomes bankrupt, before payment, the assignees shall not receive the money, but the principal.

Also if one employs a factor, and entrusts him with the disposal of merchandize, and the factor receives the money, and dies indebted, to debts of a higher nature, and it appears by evidence, that this money was vested in other goods, and remains unpaid, those goods shall be taken as part of the merchant's estate, and not the factor's; but if the factor have the money it shall be looked upon as the factor's estate. 1 *Salk.* 160.

Also, if a person employs a factor to sell goods, who sells them on credit, and before the money is paid dies indebted more than his assets will pay, this money shall be paid to the principal merchant, and not to the factor's administrator, but thereout must be deducted what was due for commission: for a factor is in nature only of a trustee for his principal. 2 *Vern.* 638.

FACTORAGE, the allowance or commission paid to a factor. See *Del Credere.*

FACTUM, a man's own fact, act, or deed.

FACULTY, *(facultas)* a privilege granted to a man by favour and indulgence, to do that which by law he ought not to do. For granting of these there is a court under the archbishop of Canterbury, called the court of the faculties, and the chief officer thereof the master of the faculties, who has power by stat. 25 *Hen.* 8, *cap.* 21, to grant dispensations, as to marry persons without the banns first asked, (and every diocesan may make the like grants) to ordain a deacon under age, for a son to succeed the father in his benefice, one to have two or more benefices incompatible, &c. And in this court are registered the certificates of bishops and noblemen granted to their chaplains to qualify them for pluralities and non-residence. 4 *Inst.* 337.

FASTING-MEN, vassals, or according to *Cowel* pledges or bondsmen, who, by the custom of the Saxons were fast bound to answer for one another's peaceable behaviour. *Cowel. Blount.*

FAG, a knot or excrescence in cloth, stat. 4 *Ed.* 4, *c.* 1. Thus the fag-end signifies that end of a piece of cloth or linen where the weaver ends his piece, and works up the worst part of his materials. *Ibid.*

FAGOT, a badge worn in the times of popery by persons who had recanted and abjured what the then powers adjudged heresy. *Ibid.*

FAIDA, malice or deadly feud. *Leg. H.* 1, *c.* 88.

FAILURE OF RECORD, is where an action is brought against a man who alleges in his plea matter of record in bar of the action, and avers to prove it by the record, but the plaintiff saith *Nul tiel record,* i. e. denies there is any such record: upon which the defendant has a day given him by the court to bring it in, and if he fails to do it, then he is said to fail of his record, and the plaintiff shall have judgment to recover. *Terms de Ley.*

FAINT-ACTION (Fr. *feinte*). A feigned action; such, that although the words of the writ are true, yet for certain causes the plaintiff hath no title to recover thereby; but a false action is properly where the words of the writ are false. *Co. Lit.* 361.

FAINT-PLEADER, is a fraudulent, false or collusory manner of pleading to the deceit of a third person. Stat. 3 *Ed.* 1, *c.* 19.

FAIR-PLEADER. See *Beaupleader.*

FAIR, a greater sort of market, instituted for the convenience of trade and commerce, and that merchants and traders may be furnished with such commodities as they want, at a particular place, without that trouble and loss of time which must necessarily attend travelling about from place to place; and as this is a matter of universal concern to the commonwealth, no person can claim a fair or market unless it be by grant from the king, or by long and immemorial usage and prescription, which pre-supposes such a grant. 2 *Inst.* 220. 3 *Mod.* 123. 1 *Black.* 273.

The limitation of these public resorts to such time and such place as may be most convenient for the neighbourhood, forms a part of the king's prerogative. 1 *Black.* 273.

And therefore, if any person sets up any such fair or market, without the king's authority, a *quo warranto* lies against him; and the persons who frequent such fair, &c. may be punished by fine to the king. 3 *Mod.* 127.

Also it seems, that, if the king grants a patent for holding a fair or market, without a writ of *ad quod damnum* executed and returned, the same may be repealed by *scire facias*; for though such fairs and markets are a benefit to the commonwealth, yet too great a number of them may become nuisances to the public, as well as a detriment to those who have more ancient grants. 3 *Lev.* 222.

Fairs are generally kept once or twice in the year; and it has been observed that fairs were first occasioned by the resort of people to the feast of dedication, and therefore in most places the fairs by old custom are on the same day with the wake or festival of that saint to whom the church was dedicated; and for the same reason kept in the church-yard, till it was enacted by 13 *Ed.* 1, *stat.* 2, *c.* 6, that no fairs or markets shall be kept in church-yards. 2 *Inst.* 221. *Blount.*

The court of *pie-poudre* is a court incident to every fair, &c. of which the steward of him who owns or has the toll of the market, is the judge. And it is instituted to administer justice for all contracts made, and injuries done, in that identical fair or market, and not in any preceding one. 3 *Black.* 32. But by the stat. 2 *Ed.* 3, *cap.* 15. Fairs are not to be kept longer than they ought by the lords thereof, on pain of their being seized into the king's hands until such lords have paid a fine for the offence; and proclamation is to be made how long fairs are to continue: also no merchant shall sell any goods or merchandise at a fair after the time of the fair is ended, under the penalty of forfeiting double the value of the goods sold, one fourth part thereof to the prosecutor, and the rest to the king. 5 *Ed.* 3. *c.* 5. Any citizen of London may carry his goods or merchandise to any fair or market in England at his pleasure. See 3 *Hen.* 7. *c.* 9.

It is also clearly agreed that if a person has a right to a fair or market, and another erects a fair or market so near his that it becomes a nuisance to his fair, &c. that for this detriment and injury done to him an action on the case lies; for it is implied in the king's grant that it should be no prejudice to another. 2 *Rol. Abr.* 140. 3 *Black.* 218.

But in order to make this out to be a nuisance it is necessary, 1st, that my market or fair be the elder, otherwise the nuisance lies at my own door. 2. That the market be erected within the third part of 20 miles from mine; for Sir Matthew Hale construes the *dieta*, or reasonable day's journey, mentioned by *Bracton*, *lib.* 3, *c.* 16, indeed as it is usually understood, not only in our own law, 2 *Inst.* 367, but also in the civil, *Ff.* 2, 11. 1, from which we probably borrowed it. So that if the new market be not within seven miles of the old one it is no nuisance, for it is held reasonable that every man should have a market within one third of a day's journey from his own house; that the day being divided into three parts he may spend one part in going, another in returning, and the third in transacting his necessary business there. 3 *Black.* 219.

If such market or fair be on the same day with mine it is *primâ facie* a nuisance to mine, and there needs no proof of it, for the law will intend it to be so: but if it be on any *other* day it may be a nuisance, though whether it is so or not cannot be intended or presumed, but must be in fact proved to the jury. *Ibid.*

Also if a man have a fair or market, and a stranger disturbs those who are coming to buy or sell there, by which he loses his toll, or receives some prejudice in the profits arising from his fair, &c. an action on the case lies. 1 *Rol. Abr.* 106. 2 *Vent.* 26, 28. So if upon a sale in a fair a stranger disturbs the lord in taking the toll, an action upon the case lies for this. 1 *Rol. Abr.* 106.

The king is the sole judge where fairs and markets ought to be kept. 3 *Mod.* 123. And if no place be limited for keeping a fair by the king's grant, the grantees may keep it where they please, or rather where they can most conveniently; and if it be so limited they may keep it in what part of such place they will. 3 *Mod.* 108.

The owners of fairs are to take care that every thing be sold according to just weight and measure, who for that and other purposes may appoint a clerk of the fair or market, who may take his reasonable and just fees. See 4 *Inst.* 274. *Moor* 523. 1 *Salk.* 327.

Fairs and markets are such franchises as may be forfeited if held contrary to the charter, by disuser, and by extorting fees not justly due. 2 *Inst.* 220. *Finch* 164. 3 *Mod.* 108.

The interest of the owners arises chiefly from tolls, which toll is a reasonable sum due upon sale of things tollable, or for stallage, pickage, or the like. 2 *Inst.* 222. 2 *Jon.* 207.

But this is not incident to a fair or market without special grant; for where it is not granted such a fair or market is accounted a free fair or market. 2 *Inst.* 220. *Cro. Eliz.* 559.

No toll shall be paid for any thing brought to the fair or market before the same is sold, unless it be by custom time out of mind, and upon such sale the toll is to be paid by the buyer, and therefore *Coke* says, that a fair or market by prescription is better than one by grant. 2 *Inst.* 221.

And by *West.* 1, *cap.* 31, "Touching them that take outrageous toll, contrary to the common custom of the realm in market towns, it is provided, that if any do so in the king's town which is let in fee-farm, the king shall seize into his own hand the franchise of the market; and if it be another's town, and the same be done by the lord of the town, the king shall do in like manner; and if it be done by a bailiff, or any mean officer, without the commandment of his lord, he shall restore to the plaintiff as much more, for the outrageous taking as he had of him, if he carried away his toll, and shall have 40 days imprisonment."

But where by custom a toll is due upon the sale of any goods in a fair or market, and he who ought to pay it refuses, an action on the case lies against him. 1 *Rol. Abr.* 103, 104, 106.

Some persons however are exempt from payment of toll, and if the king or any of his progenitors have granted to any to be discharged of toll, either generally or specially, this grant is good to discharge him of all tolls to the king's own fairs or markets, and of the tolls, which, together with any fair or market have been granted after such grant of discharge; but cannot discharge tolls formerly due to subjects either by grant or prescription. 2 *Inst.* 221.

Also the king himself shall not pay toll

for any of his goods; and if any be taken it is punishable within the statute *Westm.* 1, *cap.* 31. 2 *Inst.* 221. So tenants in ancient demesne are free and quit from all manner of tolls in fairs and markets, whether such tenants hold in fee, or for life, years, or at will. 2 *Inst.* 221. 4 *Inst.* 269. 1 *Rol. Abr.* 321.

But this privilege does not extend to him who is a merchant, and gets his living by buying and selling, but is annexed to the person in respect of the land, and to those things which grow and are the produce of the land. *F. N. B.* 228. 2 *Leon.* 191. *Cro. Eliz.* 227. 2 *Inst.* 221. 1 *Rol. Abr.* 321, 322.

FAIT, *(factum)* a deed or writing, lawfully executed. *Cowel. Blount.*

FAIT ENROLLE, (*Fr.*) a deed of bargain and sale, enrolled, &c.

FAITOURS, (*Fr.*) evil doers, or idle livers, from *faitardise*, a kind of sleepy disease, proceeding from too much sluggishness; and in 7 *Ric.* 2, *c.* 5, it seems to be synonymous with vagabonds. *Terms de Ley.*

FALANG, a jacket or close coat. *Cowel. Blount.*

FALCATURA, one day's mowing of grass; a customary service to the lord by his inferior tenants. *Kennet's Gloss. Cowel. Blount.*

FALCO, a falcon. *Cowel. Blount.*

FALDA, a sheepfold. *Ibid.*

FALDAGE, (*faldagium*) a privilege which several lords anciently reserved to themselves, of setting up folds for sheep in any fields within their manors, for the better manurance of the same, not only with their own but their tenants sheep. *Cowel. Blount.*

FALDÆCURSUS, a sheep-walk, or feed for sheep. 2 *Vent.* 139.

FALDFEY, FALD-FEE, a fee or rent formerly paid by some customary tenants for liberty to fold their sheep upon their own land. *Cowel. Blount.*

FALDISTOR, (*Sax.*) the highest seat of a bishop, enclosed round with a lettice. *Ibid.*

FALDWORTH, a person of age, that he may be reckoned of some decennary. *Ibid.*

FALERÆ, (Lat. *phaleræ*) the tackle and furniture of a cart or wain. *Ibid.*

FALESIA, a great rock, bank, or hill by the sea side. *Ibid.*

FALLOW-LAND, land ploughed up, and left for a time unsown, with a view to the improvement of the soil, and the better fitting it for the sowing of grain therein.

FALLUM, a sort of land, as appears by the *Monasticon Anglicanum.* —— *De duobus acris & viginti fallis in, &c.* *Mon.* tom. 2. 425. *Cowel. Blount.*

FALMOTUM, or falkmote, the same with folkmote. *Ibid.*

FALSE ACTION. If one man hold another to bail without a reasonable cause, an action upon the case will lie for the vexation and injury. But if he dies pending the suit, the law giveth no remedy in this case, because the truth or falsehood of the matter cannot appear before it is tried. *Jenk. Cent.* 161. See *Faint-Action.*

FALSE CLAIM, by the forest laws is where a man claims more than is his due, and is amerced and punished for the same. *Manwood, cap.* 25. *num.* 3.

FALSE FORM, in proceedings at law, is aided by a verdict, &c. 1 *Keb.* 734, 876.

FALSE IMPRISONMENT, *(falsum imprisonamentum)* is a trespass committed against a person, by arresting and imprisoning him without just cause, contrary to law: or where a man is unlawfully detained without legal process. And if a person be any way unlawfully detained, it is false imprisonment; and considerable damages are recoverable in these actions. *Co. Lit.* 124.

FALSE JUDGMENT, (*Falsum Judicium*) is a writ that lieth where false judgment is given in the county-court, court baron, or other courts not of record. *F. N. B.* 17, 18.

FALSE LATIN. Before the stat. which directs that all law proceedings shall be in English, if a Latin word was significant though not good Latin, yet an indictment, declaration, or fine, should not be made void by it: but if the word was not Latin, nor allowed by the law, and it were in a material point, it made the whole vicious. 5 *Rep.* 121. 2 *Nels.* 830. Vide *Latin.*

FALSE NEWS. Spreading false news, to make discord between the king and nobility, or concerning any great man of the realm, is punished by common law, with fine and imprisonment, which is confirmed by statutes *Westm.* 1. 3 *Ed.* 1. *c.* 34. 2 *Ric.* 2. *stat.* 1. *c.* 5. And 12 *Ric.* 2. *c.* 11. 2 *Inst.* 226. 3 *Inst.* 198.

FALSE OATH. See *Perjury.*

FALSE PLEA. Where a plea is found false by a verdict at law, the judgment is final, and a plaintiff in a suit in equity shall have the same advantage; and shall have all the same consequences there as follow on a false plea at law to all intents. 2 *Chanc. Cases* 201.

FALSE RETURN, on a false return by a mayor, or other officer to a mandamus, or by a sheriff, to a writ, a special action on the case will lie. 3 *Black.* 111, 163.

FALSE TOKENS. See *Cheats* and *Swindlers.*

FALSE VERDICT, a writ of attaint lieth, to inquire whether a jury of twelve men have given a false verdict; that so the judgment following thereupon may be reversed. It is allowed in almost every action except in a writ of right. 1 *Ed.* 3, *c.* 6. 5 *Ed.* 3. *c.* 7. 28 *Ed.* 3. *c.* 8. 34 *Ed.* 3. *c.* 7. 9 *Ric.* 2. *c.* 3. 3 *Black.* 403. But this has long since fallen into disuse. See *Attaint.*

FALSI CRIMEN, See *Forgery.*

FALSIFY, to prove a thing to be false. *Perk.* 383.

FALSIFYING AN ATTAINDER. Judgments, with their several connected consequences, of attainder, forfeiture, and corruption of blood, may be set aside, 1st. By falsifying or reversing the judgment, or 2ndly, by reprieve or pardon, the first of which it is only necessary to treat of in this place.

A judgment may be falsified, reversed, or avoided, in the first place, without a writ of error, for matters foreign to or *dehors* the record, that is, not apparent upon the face of it: so that they cannot be assigned for error in the superior court, which can only judge from what appears in the record itself; and therefore, if the whole record be not certified, or not truly certified, by the inferior court, the party injured thereby (in both civil and criminal cases) may allege a diminution of the record, and cause it to be rectified. Thus, if any judgment whatever be given by persons, who had no good commission to proceed against the person condemned, it is void, and may be falsified by shewing the special matter, without writ of error. As, where a commission issues to A and B, and twelve others, or any two of them, of which A or B shall be one, to take and try indictments; and any of the other twelve proceed without the interposition or presence of either A, or B: in this case all proceedings, trials, convictions, and judgments are void for want of a proper authority in the commissioners, and may be falsified upon bare inspection without the trouble of a writ of error. 2 *Hawk. P. C.* 459. It being a high misdemeanor in the judges so proceeding, and little (if any thing) short of murder in them all, in case the person so attainted be executed and suffer death. So likewise if a man purchases land of another; and afterwards the vendor is, either by outlawry or his own confession, convicted and attainted of treason or felony previous to the sale or alienation; whereby such land becomes liable to forfeiture or escheat: now, upon any trial the purchaser is at liberty, without bringing any writ of error, to falsify not only the time of the felony or treason supposed, but the very point of the felony or treason itself; and is not concluded by the confession or the outlawry of the vendor; though the vendor himself is concluded, and not suffered now to deny the fact, which he has by confession or flight acknowledged.—But if such attainder of the vendor was by verdict, on the oath of his peers, the alienee cannot be received to falsify or contradict the fact of the crime committed; though he is at liberty to prove a mistake in time, or that the offence was committed after the alienation, and not before. 3 *Inst.* 231. 1 *Hale's P. C.* 361. 4 *Black.* 390.

Secondly, a judgment may be reversed by writ of error, which lies from all inferior criminal jurisdictions to the court of king's bench, and from the king's bench to the house of peers; and may be brought for notorious mistakes in the judgment or other parts of the record: as where a man is found guilty of perjury and receives the judgment of felony, or for other less palpable errors; such as any irregularity, omission, or want of form in the process of outlawry, or proclamations; the want of a proper addition to the defendant's name, according to the statute of additions: for not properly naming the sheriff or other officer of the court, or not duly describing where his county court was held; for laying an offence, committed in the time of the late king, to be done against the peace of the present; and for many other similar causes, which (though allowed out of tenderness to life and liberty) are not much to the credit or advancement of the national justice. These writs of error, to reverse judgments in case of misdemeanors, are not to be allowed of course, but on sufficient probable cause shewn to the attorney-general; and then they are understood to be grantable of common right, and *ex debito justitiæ.* But writs of error to reverse attainders in capital cases are only allowed *ex gratia*; and not without express warrant under the king's sign manual, or at least by the consent of the attorney-general. 1 *Vern.* 170. 175. These therefore can rarely be brought by the party himself, especially where he is attainted for an offence against the state: but they may be brought by his heir, or executor, after his death, in more favourable times, which may be some consolation to his family. 4 *Black.* 391.

Lastly, the easier and more effectual way is to reverse the attainder by act of parliament. This may and has been frequently done, upon motives of compassion, or perhaps from the zeal of the times, after a sudden revolution in the government, without examining too closely into the truth or validity of the errors assigned. And sometimes, though the crime be universally acknowledged and confessed, yet the merits of the criminal's family shall after his death obtain restitution in blood, honours, and estate, or some or one of them, by act of parliament, which, so far as it extends, has all the effect of reversing the attainder, without casting any reflections upon the justice of the preceding sentence. 4 *Black.* 392. And this has lately been done with respect to the forfeited estates in Scotland, by statute 24 *Geo.* 3, *c.* 57.

The effect of falsifying, or reversing, an

outlawry is, that the party shall be in the same plight as if he had appeared upon the *capias*; and if it be before the plea pleaded he shall be put to plead to the indictment; if after conviction he shall receive the sentence of the law: for all the other proceedings, except only the process of outlawry for his non-appearance, remain good and effectual as before: but when judgment pronounced upon conviction is falsified or reversed, all former proceedings are absolutely set aside, and the party stands as if he had never been at all accused, restored in his credit, his capacity, his blood, and his estates; with regard to which last, though they be granted away by the crown, yet the owner may enter upon the grantee with as little ceremony as he might enter upon a disseisor. 2 *Hawk. P. C.* 462.

But he still remains subject to another prosecution for the same offence: for the first being erroneous he never was in jeopardy thereby. 4 *Black.* 392.

FALSIFYING A RECOVERY. Issue in tail may falsify a recovery suffered by tenants for life, &c. And it has been held that a person may falsify a recovery had by the issue in tail, where an estate tail is before bound by a fine. 2 *Nels. Abr.* 831. But where there is tenant for life, remainder in tail, and reversion in fee, tenant for life suffers a common recovery, in which he in remainder is vouched, and the uses declared to him, who had the remainder in tail; adjudged, that by the recovery all remainders and reversions are barred, and that they could not falsify this recovery. 10 *Rep.* 43.

He in reversion suffered a common recovery, and declared the uses; his heir shall not falsify it by pleading that his father had nothing at the time of the recovery, because he is estopped to say he is not tenant to the *præcipe*. *Godb.* 189. An infant brought an assise in B. R. pending which action the tenant brought an assise against the infant in C. B. for the same land, and had judgment by default, which he pleaded in bar to the assise brought by the infant; who set forth all this matter in his replication, and that the demandant at the time of the second writ brought was tenant of the land, and prayed that he might falsify this recovery; and it was held that he might, because he could not have writ of error, or attaint. *Godb.* 271. *Cro. Eliz.* 284. It has been determined, that a recovery is not so firm, but it may be falsified in point of recovery of the thing itself, between the same parties. *Ibid.*

FALSIFYING A VERDICT. Where in any real action there is a verdict against tenant in tail the issue can never falsify such verdict in the point directly tried; but only in a special manner, as by saying that some evidence was omitted, &c. 2 *Ld. Raym.* 1050.

FALSONARIUS, a forger. *Hoveden* 424. *Cowel. Blount.*

FALSO RETURNO BREVIUM, is a writ that lies against the sheriff who has execution of process for false returning of writs. *Reg. Jud.* 43.

FAMILIA, signifies all the servants belonging to a particular master; but in another sense it is taken for a portion of land sufficient to maintain one family. It is sometimes mentioned by our writers to be a hide of land, which is also called a manse, and sometimes *carucata*, or a plough-land. *Cowel Blount.*

FANATICS, are persons pretending to be inspired; a reproachful name applied to all sectaries and factious dissenters from the church of England.

FANATIO, (*mensis fanationis*) the fawning season, or fence-months in forests. *Cowel. Blount.*

FARANDMAN, (Sax.) a traveller or merchant stranger. *Ibid.*

FARDEL OF LAND, (*fardelle terræ*) is generally accounted the fourth part of a yard-land, but according to *Noy*, (in his Complete Lawyer, p. 57) it is an eighth part only, for there he says that two fardels of land make a nook, and four nooks a yard-land. *Ibid.*

FARDING-DEAL, (*quadrantata terræ*) is the fourth part of an acre. *Ibid.*

FARE, (Sax.) the money paid for a voyage, or passage by water, or personal carriage by land.

FARINAGIUM, toll of meal or flour. *Cowel. Blount.*

FARLEU, money paid by tenants in the west of England in lieu of a heriot. *Cowel. Blount.*

FARLINGARII, whoremongers and adulterers.

FARM, or FERM, according to *Blackstone*, who cites *Spelm.* 229. *Farm* or *Feorme* is an old Saxon word, signifying provisions, and it came to be used instead of rent or render, because anciently the greater part of rents were reserved in provisions, in corn, in poultry, and the like, till the use of money became more frequent; so that *firmarius* was one who held his lands upon payment of a rent or *feorme*. 2 *Black.* 317.

But at present, by a gradual departure from the original sense, the word *farm* is brought to signify the very estate or lands so held upon farm or rent. *Ibid.*

Thus at this day it signifies a messuage and land taken by lease or from year to year, under a certain yearly rent, payable by the tenant. *Ter. de Ley.* It is a collective word, consisting of divers things gathered into one, as a messuage, land, meadow, pasture, wood, common, &c. And the reason of it may also be in respect of the firm or sure hold the tenants thereof have above tenants at will. *Plowd.* 195. See LEASE.

FARMER, is he that tenants a farm, or is lessee thereof. *Terms de Ley.*

FARTHING, was the fourth part of a Saxon penny, as it is now of the English penny. *Cowel. Blount.*

FARTHING OF GOLD, (*quasi* fourth thing) a coin used in ancient times, containing in value the fourth part of a Noble. *Ibid.*

FARTHING OF LAND, seems to differ from Farding-deal; for it is a large quantity of land. *Ibid.*

FARUNDEL of land, the same with farding-deal. *Ibid.*

FASTUS, (Fr. *Faisseau)* a fagot of wood. *Ibid.*

FAST-DAYS, are days of fasting and humiliation, appointed to be observed by public authority. And by 12 *Car.* 2. *c.* 14, the 30th of January is ordained to be a day of fasting and repentance, for the murder of king Charles 1. Other days of fasting are not fixed, but occasionally appointed by the king's proclamation. 1 *Hawk. P. C.* 8. See *Embring Days.*

FASTERMANS, among the Saxons were pledges. *Cowel Blount.*

FAT, or WATE, a vessel used by maltsters and brewers, and by others for the making of salt at Droitwich. *Ibid.*

FATUA MULIER, a whore. *Ibid.*

FAUSETUM, a faucet, musical pipe or flute. *Ibid.*

FAUTORS, are favourers or supporters of others; abettors of crimes, &c. *Ibid.*

FEAL. The tenants by knight service did swear to their lords to be feal and leal, *i. e.* to be faithful and loyal. *Ibid.*

FEALTY, *(fidelitas)* Fr. *(feaulté,* i. e. *fides)* signifies an oath taken at the admittance of every tenant, to be true to the lord of whom he holds his land. *Smith de Repub. Ang. lib.* 3, *c.* 8. *Co. Lit.* 93.

FEASTS, anniversary times of feasting and thanksgiving, as Christmas, Easter, Whitsuntide, &c. The four feasts which our laws especially take notice of, are the feasts of the annunciation of the blessed Virgin Mary, of the nativity of St. John the Baptist, of St. Michael the Archangel, and of St. Thomas the Apostle; (or in lieu of the last, the birth of our Lord Christ,) on which quarterly days rent on leases is usually reserved to be paid.

FEE, *(Feodum,* or *Feudum)* is applied to all those lands and tenements which are held by perpetual right.

And this estate in fee is commonly divided into fee absolute, otherwise called fee-simple: and fee conditional, termed otherwise fee-tail.

Fee-simple, *(feodum simplex)* is where a man hath lands or tenements, to hold to him and *his heirs* for ever: fee-tail is an estate whereof one is seised, with limitation to him and *the heirs of his body.* *Lit.* 14, 16.

And to have fee-simple implies that it is without limitation to what heirs, but to heirs generally. 4 *Inst.* 206.

FEE EXPECTANT. *(Feudum Expectativum.)* See *Expectant.*

FEE-FARM, *(feudi ferma)* is where the lord, upon creation of the tenancy, reserves to himself and his heirs, either the rent for which it was before let to farm, or was reasonably worth, or at least a fourth part of the value; without homage, fealty, or other services, beyond what are especially comprised in the feoffment. 2 *Inst.* 44.— And Lord Coke says, fee-farm rents may be one half, a third, or fourth part of the value. *Co. Lit.* 143. It is the nature of fee-farm, that if the rent be behind and unpaid for the space of two years, then the feoffor or his heirs may bring an action to recover the lands, &c. *Brit. cap.* 66. *num.* 4. 10 *Ann. c.* 18. *sec.* 4. 30 *Geo.* 2. *c.* 3. *sec.* 5.

FEE-FARM RENTS OF THE CROWN. Are *rents* remaining in the kings of England from *their ancient demesnes,* many of which were alienated in the reigns of *Car.* 2, under stat. 22 *Car.* 2. *c.* 6, and stat. 22 & 23 *Car.* 2. *c.* 24.

FEES, are certain perquisites allowed to officers who have to do with the administration of justice, as a recompence for their labour and trouble; and these are either ascertained by acts of parliament, or established by ancient usage, which gives them an equal sanction with an act of parliament. *Bac. Abr. tit. Fees.*

All fees allowed by acts of parliament become established fees; and the several officers entitled to them may maintain action of debt for them. 2 *Inst.* 210. All such fees as have been allowed by the courts of justice to their officers, as a recompence for their labour and attendance, are established fees; and the parties cannot be deprived of them without an act of parliament. *Co. Lit.* 368. *Prec. Chan.* 551.

But where a fee is due by custom, such custom, like all others, must be reasonable. *Hob.* 175. 1 *Rol. Abr.* 557, 559.

And it is extortion for any officer to take more for executing his office, than is allowed by act of parliament, or is the known and settled fee in such case. 10 *Co.* 102. *a.* *Co. Lit.* 368.

Also it is extortion for any officer to take his fee before it is due: and the party may bring an action against him for not doing his duty, or may pay him his fees, and then indict him for extortion. *Co. Lit.* 368. 10 *Co.* 102. *a.* 1 *Salk.* 330. *Stran.* 814. 1262.

FEES *of Attornies.* Action on the case

nes for an attorney for his fees, against him that retained him in his cause. And attornies are not to be dismissed by their clients, till their fees are paid. 1 *Lil.* 142. But attornies are not to demand more than their just fees, nor to be allowed fees to counsel without tickets, &c. *Stat.* 3 *Jac.* 1. c. 7.

FEES TO COUNSEL. A counsellor can maintain no action for his fees, which are given not as a salary, or hire, but as a mere gratuity (*quiddam honorium non mercenarium*) which a barrister cannot demand without doing wrong to his reputation. *Davis* 22, 23.

And by 3 *Jac.* 1. c. 7, attornies or solicitors shall not be allowed fees to counsel without they produce the signatures of the counsel for the same.

FEIGNED ACTION. See *Faint Action.*

FEIGNED ISSUE. If, in a suit of equity, any matter of fact is strongly contested, the court usually directs the matter to be tried by a jury, especially such important facts as the validity of a will, or whether A. is the heir at law to B. or the existence of a *modus decimandi*, or real and immemorial composition for tithes.—But as a jury cannot be summoned to attend a court of equity, the fact is usually directed to be in the court of King's Bench, or at the assises, upon a feigned issue. For this purpose, a feigned action is brought, wherein the pretended plaintiff declares that he laid a wager of 5*l.* with the defendant, that A. was heir at law to B. then he avers that he is so; and brings his action for the 5*l.* The defendant allows the wager, but avers that A. is not the heir to B. and thereupon that issue is joined, which is directed out of Chancery to be tried: and thus, the verdict of the jurors at law determines the fact in the court of equity. 3 *Black.* 452. And a feigned issue cannot be tried without such directions; for if any one bring a feigned action at law in order to obtain the opinion of the court, it is *a contempt*, and the court will after trial stay the proceedings. 4 *Ter. Rep.* 402.

FELAGUS, (*quasi fide cum eo ligatus*) a companion, but particularly a friend, who was bound in the decennary for the good behaviour of another. *Cowel. Blount.*

FELD, a Saxon word, signifying field; and in its compound it signifies wild, as feld honey, is wild honey, &c. *Ibid.*

FELE HOMAGERS, from the Sax. *fai*, i. e. *fides*, were faithful subjects. *Ibid.*

FELO DE SE. When a person with deliberation and direct purpose kills himself, by hanging, drowning, shooting, stabbing, &c. this is *felo de se*; if he be of the age of discretion, *i. e.* 14, and *compos mentis.* 3 *Inst.* 44. *Dalt. ch.* 145.

A *felo de se* shall forfeit all his goods and chattels real and personal; but not until it is lawfully found of record by the return upon oath of twelve men, before the coroner *super visum corporis*, that he is *felo de se.* 3 *Inst.* 55. 1 *Lev.* 8. But the lands of inheritance of a *felo de se* are not forfeited, by reason he was not attainted in his life-time: nor is such a person's wife barred of dower, or his blood corrupted. 1 *Hawk.* 68.

FELONS GOODS. The stat. *de prærogativa regis*, 17 *Ed.* 2. c. 1, grants to the king, among other things, the goods of felons and fugitives.

FELONY (Lat. *felonia*), seems to be derived from the Greek φηλωμα or φηλωσις a capital crime; hence the party committing such crime is termed a FELON.

Felony was anciently every capital crime perpetrated with an evil intention. And all capital offences by the common law, came generally under the title of felony; and could not be expressed by any word but *felonice*; which must even at this day of necessity be laid in an indictment of felony. *Co. Lit.* 391. And the bare intention to commit a felony is so very criminal, that at the common law it was punishable as felony, where it missed of its effect through some accident; and as our law now is, the party may be severely fined for such an intention. 1 *Hawk. P. C.* 65.

Felony is either by the common law, or by statute: felony by the common law is against the life of a man, as murder, manslaughter, *felo de se, se defendendo*, &c. Against a man's goods, such as larceny and robbery: Against his habitation, as burglary, arson, or house-burning, and against public justice, as breach of prison. 3 *Inst.* 31. Piracy, robbery, or murder, upon the sea, are felonies punishable by the civil law; and likewise by statute.

Of felonies in general there are two sorts, one of which, for the first offence, is allowed clergy, and another that is not; but clergy is granted where it is not expressly taken away by statute. *Staundf. lib.* 1.

The punishment of a person for felony is 1st, To lose his life. 2ndly, To lose his blood, as to his ancestry, and so as to have neither heir nor posterity. 3dly, To lose his goods. 4thly, To lose his lands; and the king shall have *annum, diem & vastum*, to the intent that his wife and children be cast out of the house, his house pulled down, and all that he had for his comfort or delight destroyed. 4 *Rep.* 124.

Private persons may arrest felons by their own authority, or by warrant from a justice of peace: and every private person is bound to assist an officer to take felons, &c. 2 *Hawk.* 75.

FELONIES by statute, are very numerous, and of these the following will be found to be an accurate summary.

—— *Accessaries.*] By 23 *Hen.* 8. c. 1, made

perpetual by 32 *Hen.* 8. *c.* 3, accessaries before the fact in petit treason, murder, burglary ; robbery in dwelling houses, churches, or in or near highways, burning houses or barns wherein any corn or grain shall be, felony *without benefit of clergy.*

By 37 *Eliz. c.* 12, an accessary to an horse-stealer, before or after such felony, felony *without benefit of clergy.*

By 39 *Eliz. c.* 9, accessaries before the offence, in stealing women who are heirs apparent, or have lands, felony *without benefit of clergy.*

By 21 *Jac.* 1. *c.* 26, accessaries before the fact in procuring any fine, recovery, deed indented, statute, recognizance, bail or judgment, in the name of another not privy thereto, felony without *benefit of clergy.*

By 22 & 23 *Car.* 2, *c.* 1, accessaries before the fact in malicious maiming, felons *without benefit of clergy.*

By 3 & 4 *Will. & Mar. c.* 9, accessaries before the fact in burglary or in robbing any dwelling-house, shop, or warehouse, felony *without benefit of clergy.*

By 3 & 4 *Will. & Mar. c.* 9, buyers of stolen goods knowing the same, shall be deemed accessaries to such felony, after the fact.

And by 5 *Ann. c.* 31, buyers or receivers of stolen goods shall be deemed accessaries, *without benefit of clergy.*

By 10 & 11 *Will.* 3. *c.* 23, accessaries before the fact in robberies in shops, warehouses, coach-houses, or stables, felons, *without benefit of clergy.*

By 11 & 12 *Will.* 3. *c.* 7, persons setting forth, or assisting any pirate, or after the piracy committed, concealing such pirate, shall be deemed accessaries, and shall be tried and suffer as the principals, made perpetual by 6 *Geo.* 1. *c.* 19.

And by 8 *Geo.* 1. *c.* 24, persons declared accessaries to piracy by 11 & 12 *Will.* 3, *c.* 7, shall be deemed principals *without benefit of clergy.*

By 2 *Geo.* 2, *c.* 25, made perpetual by 9 *Geo.* 2. *c.* 18, accessaries to forgery of any deed, will, bond, bill of exchange, promissory note, indorsement, acquittance, or receipt, felons *without benefit of clergy.*

By 7 *Geo.* 2, *c.* 22, accessaries to forging or altering the acceptance of bills of exchange, or the number or sums of any accountable receipt, or any warrant or order for payment of money, or delivery of goods, felons *without benefit of clergy.*

By 14 *Geo.* 2, *c.* 6, and 15 *Geo.* 2, *c.* 34, accessaries before the fact in stealing sheep, felons *without benefit of clergy.*

By 18 *Geo.* 2. *c.* 27, accessaries before the fact in stealing linen, fustian, calico, cloth, or cloth woven, out of any bleaching grounds, felons *without benefit of clergy.*

By 24 *Geo.* 2. *c.* 45, accessaries before the fact in stealing goods, of the value of 40*s.* on board any vessel, or upon any quay, adjacent to any navigable river, felons *without benefit of clergy.*

By 29 *Geo.* 2. *c.* 30, buyers or receivers of lead, iron, copper, brass, or bell metal, knowing the same to be stolen, may be convicted and *transported for seven years,* although the principal felon has not been convicted ; felon convicting the receiver pardoned.

By 31 *Geo.* 2. *c.* 23, procuring London bridge, or any works belonging thereto, to be burnt or destroyed, felony *without benefit of clergy.*

—— *Aliens.*] By 43 *Geo.* 3. *c.* 155. *sec.* 39, aliens returning from transportation for life, felons *without clergy.*

—— *Arson.*] See *Black Act. Burning. Shooting.*

—— *Bail.*] By 21 *Jac.* 1. *c.* 26, acknowledging bail in the name of another not privy thereto, shall be felony *without benefit of clergy.*

By 4 *Will. & Mar. c.* 4, personating bail before commissioners in the country, (or in the court of common pleas in *Lancashire,* 34 *Geo.* 3. *c.* 46. *s.* 5.) is felony.

—— *Bank of England.*] By 15 *Geo.* 2. *c.* 13, any officer or servant of the company who shall secrete, embezzle, or run away with any note, bill, dividend warrant, bond, deed, or security for money, shall be deemed guilty of felony, *without benefit of clergy.*

By 13 *Geo.* 3. *c.* 79, making, using, procuring or assisting in making or using, or knowingly having in custody any frame, mould, or instrument, for making paper, with the words, Bank of England, visible in the substance of such paper, or procuring the same, felony *without benefit of clergy.*

By 33 *Geo.* 3. *c.* 30, persons making, or assisting in making, any transfer of stock in any other names than the owners, forging or assisting in the forging of transfers, or making, or assisting in making false entries in the books of the bank, shall be guilty of felony *without clergy. s.* 1, 2, 3.

Persons making out any false dividend warrants shall be guilty of felony, and transported *for fourteen years. s.* 4.

By 35 *Geo.* 3. *c.* 66, persons forging or altering receipts or debentures, in respect of the Irish annuities, transferrable by this act at the Bank of England, to be guilty of felony *without clergy. s.* 3.

Persons forging letters of attorney to transfer such stock, or personating the proprietors, felony *without clergy. s.* 4.

Persons forging dividend warrants thereof felony *without clergy. s.* 5.

Officers of the Bank embezzling notes, or other securities deposited in consequence of this act, felony *without clergy. s.* 6.

Persons making transfers in any but names of the proprietors, felony *without clergy. s.* 7.

Persons forging transfers, felony *without clergy. s.* 8.

Persons making false entry in the books at the bank, felony *without clergy*. s. 9.

Clerks of the bank making out false dividend warrants under this act, to be transported *for seven years*. s. 10.

By 37 *Geo*. 3. *c*. 46, persons forging or altering receipts or debentures, in respect of the Irish annuities, transferable at the bank of England, to be guilty of felony *without benefit of clergy*. s. 3.

Persons forging letters of attorney, or personating proprietors, to be guilty of felony *without benefit of clergy*. s. 4.

Persons forging or uttering forged dividend warrants, to be guilty of felony *without benefit of clergy*. s. 5.

Officers of the bank embezzling notes or dividend warrants, to be guilty of felony *without clergy*. s. 6.

Persons making transfers in other than proprietors names, to be guilty of felony *without benefit of clergy*. s. 7.

Persons forging or uttering forged transfers, to be guilty of felony *without benefit of clergy*. s. 8.

Persons making false entries in the books of the bank, to be guilty of felony *without clergy*. s. 9.

Officers of the bank making out false dividend warrants, to be *transported for seven years*. s. 10.

By 45 *Geo*. 3. *c*. 89, forging or uttering bank notes, dividend warrants, or the like, is felony *without clergy*. s. 2.

If any person, not authorised by the bank, shall use or have any frame for making paper with curved bar lines, or sums in words appearing in the substance of the paper, or make use of or sell such paper, or cause the sum of any bank note so to appear in the paper, or assist in so doing, such offenders shall be adjudged felons, and *transported for fourteen years*. s. 3.

But this is not to restrain the issue of bills with the amount expressed in guineas, or pounds sterling, in figures in the paper. s. 4.

Nor to restrain persons from making or using paper with devices in the nature of watermarks, not resembling the watermarks used by the bank. s. 5.

Persons knowingly receiving or having forged bank notes, or blank bank notes, shall be adjudged felons, and *transported for fourteen years*. s. 6.

Persons engraving on any bank note, blank bank note, or part thereof, or using any such plate, or any device for making or printing any such bank note, without the authority of the bank, having any such plate, or uttering any such blank bank note, or part of bank note, shall be adjudged felons, and *transported for fourteen years*. s. 7.

The act extends to the whole of Great Britain. s. 8.

Counterfeiting dollars or tokens of the bank of England or Ireland, felony *within clergy*. 44 *Geo*. 3. *c*. 71. s. 1—3. 45 *Geo*. 3. *c*. 42. s. 1.

—— *Bankers*.] By 41 *Geo*. 3. (u. k.) *c*. 57, if any person shall make or use any frame or mould for making paper, with the name or firm of any bankers appearing in the substance of the paper, without a written authority for that purpose, or shall make or vend such paper, or cause such name or firm to appear in the substance of the paper, whereon the same shall be written or printed, he shall be imprisoned, for the first offence, for not exceeding two years, nor less than six months; and for the second, *transported for seven years*. s. 1.

Any person who shall, without authority, engrave any bill or note of any banker, or use any plate so engraved, or any device for making or printing such bill or note, or shall knowingly have the same in his custody, or shall utter such bill or note, shall be liable to the like punishment. s. 2.

If any person shall engrave on any plate any subscriptions subjoined to any bill or note of any person or banking company, payable to bearer on demand, or have in his possession any such plate, he shall, for the first offence, be imprisoned for not exceeding three years, nor less than twelve months; and for the second, *transported for seven years*. s. 3.

—— *Bankrupt*.] By 5 *Geo*. 2. *c*. 30, bankrupt not surrendering within forty-two days notice, and conforming to the statutes, or embezzling goods to the value of 20*l*. is guilty of felony *without benefit of clergy*.

—— *Bigamy*.] By 1 *Jac*. 1. *c*. 11, persons, unless divorced, or married within age of consent, marrying a second husband or wife, the former being living, and not absent for seven years, are guilty of *felony*.

And by 35 *Geo*. 3. *c*. 67, persons convicted, under the above stat. of 1 *Jac*. 1. *c*. 11, in England, of bigamy, are made subject to the penalties inflicted for larceny, and returning before the expiration of the term for which they are transported, to be guilty of felony *without clergy*, and may be tried in the county where convicted or found at large.

—— *Black Act*.] By 9 *Geo*. 1. *c*. 22, made perpetual by 31 *Geo*. 2. *c*. 42, persons disguised, and appearing in arms in any forest, park, warren, or like place, and killing or stealing deer, fish, or the like, or breaking down the head of any fish pond, maliciously wounding any cattle, destroying any trees planted in any avenue there, or setting fire to any house, barn, or the like, or shooting at any persons, or sending letters without a name, demanding money, or rescuing such offenders, or procuring others to join in any such unlawful act, shall be deemed felons *without benefit of clergy*. See also *Shooting*.

——*Buggery*.] By 25 *Hen*. 8. *c*. 6. 32 *Hen*. 8.

c. 3. 2 and 3 *Ed.* 6. *c.* 9, and 1 *Mar. c.* 1, revived and made perpetual by 5 *Eliz. c.* 17, buggery with man or beast is felony *without benefit of clergy*. These acts extend to women as well as men.

——*Burglary.*] By 1 *Ed.* 6, *c.* 12, *no person shall have his clergy* who is indicted for burglary, and on his trial stands mute, or challenges above twenty persons: also 25 *Hen.* 8, *c.* 3, 28 *Hen.* 8, *c.* 1, 32 *Hen.* 8. *c.* 3. and 5 & 6 *Ed.* 6, *c.* 10.

Or is attainted where the goods were carried which were stolen in another county. *Ibid.*

By 5 & 6 *Ed.* 6, *c.* 9, and 18 *Eliz. c.* 7, persons committing burglary, the owner being in another part of the house, or asleep, or in a tent or booth in a fair or market, shall *not have benefit of clergy.*

By 12 *Ann.* stat. 1, *c.* 7, entering into a house without breaking it, or being there committing felony, and breaking it in the night to get out, shall be burglary.

——*Burning.*] By 23 *Hen.* 1, *c.* 1, persons wilfully burning any dwelling-house, or barn, wherein any grain or corn shall be, *shall not have benefit of clergy.*

By 43 *Eliz. c.* 13, burning of barns, or stacks of corn, in Cumberland, Northumberland, Westmorland, and the bishopric of Durham, shall be felony *without benefit of clergy.*

The 22 & 23 *Car.* 2. *c.* 7, makes it felony to burn any ricks of corn, hay, or barns; houses, buildings, or kilns, in the night time; but *the convict may elect to be transported.*

By 1 *Geo.* 1. *stat.* 2. *c.* 48, the malicious burning any wood, underwood, or coppice, *is made felony.* See also *Shooting.*

—— *Cattle.*] By 22 & 23 *Car.* 2. *c.* 27, maliciously killing any horses, sheep, or other cattle, in the night time, shall be felony; but *the convict may elect to be transported.* See also "*Sheep.*"

—— *Challenge of jurors.*] One indicted for felony, without benefit of clergy, challenging above the number of twenty peremptorily, *shall lose his clergy*, as if convicted. 25 *Hen.* 8. *c.* 3. 5 & 6 *Ed.* 6. *c.* 10. 4 & 5 *Phil. & Mar. c.* 4. 3 & 4 *Will. & Mar. c.* 9. 1 *Ann. stat.* 2. *c.* 9.

—— *Clothes spoiling.*] By 6 *Geo.* 1. *c.* 23. assaulting any person in the streets or highways, with intent to tear or spoil their clothes, shall be felony, and the offender may be transported *for seven years.*

—— *Cloth.*] By 22 *Car.* 2. *c.* 5. stealing cloth from the tenter in the night-time, felony *without benefit of clergy.*

By 15 *Geo.* 2. *c.* 27. stealing or taking away cloth from the tenter, felony, and *transportation for seven years* for the third offence.

——*Coals.*] By 10 *Geo.* 2. *c.* 32. made perpetual by 31 *Geo.* 2. *c.* 42. setting a mine, pit, or delph of coals on fire, felony *without benefit of clergy.*

—— *Corn.*] By 11 *Geo.* 2. *c.* 22. using violence to hinder the exportation of corn, is, for the *second offence*, made *felony*; or destroying granaries, or corn therein: and *returning from transportation* for such offence within the seven years, shall be felony *without benefit of clergy.*

By 36 *Geo.* 3. *c.* 9. persons convicted a *second time* of hindering the buying of corn, or seizing it in its progress from place to place, or who shall destroy storehouses or carry corn away therefrom unlawfully, shall be *transported for seven years. s.* 2.

—— *Customs.*] By 6 *Geo.* 1. *c.* 21. eight or more hindering officers of the customs in execution of their office, shall be *transported*; and returning before the expiration of the term, is felony *without benefit of clergy.*

By 8 *Geo.* 1. *c.* 18. persons passing with foreign goods, landed without entry, and being more than five, and resisting officers of the customs, shall be *transported*; and returning within the term, is felony, *without benefit of clergy.*

By 9 *Geo.* 2. *c.* 35. and 18 *Geo.* 2. *c.* 20. persons liable to be transported for offences against the customs, committing the like, after claiming the benefit of these acts for indemnifying, are guilty of felony *without benefit of clergy.*

Three or more persons assembling armed, to assist in running goods, shall be *transported*; and returning within the term, felony *without benefit of clergy.* 9 *Geo.* 2. *c.* 35.

Two or more persons found passing together, within five miles from a navigable river, or the sea coasts, with horse or carriage, laden with more than six pounds of tea, or five gallons of brandy, the duties unpaid, and bearing offensive arms, are to be deemed runners of foreign goods, *and be transported*; if they return within the term, it is felony *without benefit of clergy. Ibid.*

Any person or persons forcibly obstructing any officer of the customs on board any ship or vessel, in execution of his office, to be transported; and returning within the term, felony *without benefit of clergy. Ibid.*

By 19 *Geo.* 2. *c.* 34. armed persons, to the number of three, assembled to assist in the illegal exporting or running of goods, or appearing in disguise with such goods, or resisting officers in execution of their duty, guilty of felony *without benefit of clergy.*

Any person concealing others who stand charged with such offence, after the time appointed for their surrender, shall be transported; and returning within the term, felony *without benefit of clergy. Ibid.*

By 43 *Geo.* 3. *c.* 157. the last act of 19 *Geo.* 2. *c.* 34. is made perpetual, and offences may be tried in any county, but corruption of blood, loss of dower, and forfeiture of lands are saved.

By 45 *Geo.* 3. *c.* 121. persons assaulting or resisting officers of the army, navy, customs, or excise, in execution of this act, shall be guilty of felony, and transported *for seven years.* s. 11.

And shooting at any ship, vessel, or boat, or any such officer, or any persons assisting them, within 100 leagues of the coast, or shooting at, maiming, or wounding them, whether attempting to go on board, or being aboard, or returning, or otherwise acting in their duty, shall be guilty of felony *without clergy. Ibid.*

By 46 *Geo.* 3. *c.* 87. running goods in company with five, or armed within twenty miles of the coast in Ireland, felony *without clergy.* s. 5.

By 46 *Geo.* 3. *c.* 106. concealing smugglers in Ireland, felony *within clergy. Ibid.*

By 48 *Geo.* 3. *c.* 84. persons sailing in any vessel on the enemy's coast, or under her batteries, or vessels of war, with intent to take on board spirits, tea, tobacco, or snuff, shall be guilty of felony, and may be *transported for seven years.* s. 9.

—— *Damages wilful.*] Destroying works, *viz.* breaking down or cutting up of dikes in marsh land in Norfolk and Cambridge, felony. 22 *H.* 8. *c.* 4.

Burning or destroying Fulham bridge, felony *without clergy.* 12 *Geo.* 1. *c.* 36.

Maliciously breaking down the bank of any river, or any sea bank, felony *without clergy.* 6 *Geo.* 2. *c.* 37. made perpetual by 31 *Geo.* 2. *c.* 42.

Destroying Westminster bridge, felony *without clergy.* 9 *Geo.* 2. *c.* 29.

Burning the engines for draining the fens in the Isle of Ely, the second offence felony. 11 *Geo.* 2. *c.* 34. 14 *Geo.* 2. *c.* 24. 21 *Geo.* 2. *c.* 18.

Destroying Walton bridge, felony. 20 *Geo.* 2. *c.* 22.

Setting fire to, or destroying any of the works for draining the fens in Whittlesea, in the Isle of Ely, to be transported. 22 *Geo.* 2. *c.* 19.

Damaging Hampton Court bridge, felony. 23 *Geo.* 2. *c.* 37.

Destroying Ribble bridge, felony. 24 *Geo.* 2. *c.* 36.

Maliciously destroying or damaging any of the works for draining Bedford Level, felony *without clergy.* 27 *Geo.* 2. *c.* 19.

Destroying the bridge at Sandwich, felony. 28 *Geo.* 2. *c.* 55.

Destroying or damaging the works at London bridge, or any of the works, felony. 29 *Geo.* 2. *c.* 40. and *without clergy* by 31 *Geo.* 2. *c.* 20.

Destroying Wye bridge, felony. 29 *Geo.* 2. *c.* 73.

Destroying or damaging Blackfriars bridge, felony. 29 *Geo.* 2. *c.* 86.

Destroying or damaging the bridge at Jeremy's Ferry, felony. 30 *Geo.* 2. *c.* 59.

Destroying the bridge at Old Brentford, felony. 30 *Geo.* 2. *c.* 63. 31 *Geo.* 2. *c.* 46.

Destroying the bridge across the Trent, at Wilden's Ferry. 31 *Geo.* 2. *c.* 59.

Damaging banks, floodgates, or works of rivers made navigable by act of parliament, transportation for seven years. 4 *Geo.* 3. *c.* 12.

By 28 *Geo.* 3. *c.* 55. persons entering by force to destroy goods in the frame, or destroying the same, or damaging any frame or utensil, or breaking any machinery in any mill used in preparing wool or cotton for that manufactory, are guilty of felony, and may be transported for not more than fourteen, nor less than seven, years.

Destroying works for draining marsh lands in Cartley and Hassingham, in Norfolk, transportation for seven years, or punishment as in cases of petty larceny. 39 & 40 *Geo.* 3. *c.* v.

Setting fire to the works or vessels in the West India docks, felony without clergy. 39 *Geo.* 3. *c.* lxix. s. 104.

And persons otherwise wilfully damaging the same, may be fined and imprisoned, or transported. *Ibid.*

Persons destroying the works of the canal from Gravesend to the Medway, guilty of felony, and to be punished as for petty larceny. 39 & 40 *Geo.* 3. *c.* xxiii.

Persons setting fire to the works or vessels in the basins of the London Docks, to be guilty of felony *without clergy.* 39 & 40 *Geo.* 3. *c.* xlvii. s. 95.

And damaging the same by other means, punishable by fine, imprisonment, or transportation. *Ibid.*

Destroying works for draining lands in the parish of Hickling, in Norfolk, felony, and transportation for seven years. 41 *Geo.* 3. (u. k.) *c.* cxxi. s. 70.

Destroying the works of the Surry canal, felony, and to be punished as such, or mitigated to petty larceny. 41 *Geo.* 3. (u. k.) *c.* xxxi. s. 75.

Damaging, destroying, or stealing any part of the Wandsworth railway, felony, or payment of double damages, or imprisonment. 41 *Geo.* 3. (u. k.) *c.* xxxiii. s. 71.

Destroying the works for draining lands in North Wotton, and other places in the county of Somerset, felony, and to be punished as in cases of petty larceny. 41 *Geo.* 3. (u. k.) *c.* lxxii. s. 49.

Destroying the works for draining lands in the Isle of Ely, Cambridgeshire, felony, and transportation for seven years. 41 *Geo.* 3. (u. k.) *c.* lxxiii. s. 33.

Destroying the works for draining lands in

Potter Heigham, in Norfolk, petty larceny. 41 *Geo.* 3. (u. k.) *c.* lxxvi. *s.* 33.

Destroying the works for draining lands in the moors in the county of Salop, felony, and to be punished as petty larceny. 41 *Geo.* 3. (u. k.) *c.* lxxvi. *s.* 22.

Destroying the works for draining lands in Crowland, in Lincolnshire, felony, and to be punished as such. 41 *Geo.* 3. (u. k.) *c.* cxvi. *s.* 42.

Destroying the works for draining lands in Deeping and other places in Lincolnshire, felony, and to be punished as such. 41 *Geo.* 3. *c.* cxxxviii. *s.* 103.

Destroying the works for draining lands in the east fens in Lincolnshire, felony; and to be punished as such, or mitigated to fine and imprisonment. 41 *Geo.* 3. (u. k.) *c.* cxxxv. *s.* 61.

Destroying the works for draining lands in certain townships in the county of Nottingham, felony, 36 *Geo.* 3. *c.* 99. but this is repealed, and the party is to be punished as for a misdemeanor. 41 *Geo.* 3. (u. k.) *c.* cxxxvi. *s.* 21.

Destroying the works in Lipsorn bay, Plymouth, to be punished as felony, subject to mitigation as petty larceny. 42 *Geo.* 3. *c.* 32. *s.* 46.

Destroying the works of Stoke river and Brandon, in Norfolk and Suffolk, felony, subject to mitigation as petty larceny. 42 *Geo.* 3. *c.* xxiv. *s.* 46.

Destroying the works for draining lands in Wookey, and other places in Somersetshire, felony, subject to mitigation as petty larceny. 42 *Geo.* 3. *c.* lviii. *s.* 45.

Destroying the works on the inclosure of lands at Cutlfield and Sutton in Norfolk, felony, or to be punished as petty larceny. 42 *Geo.* 3. *c.* lxxiv. *s.* 53.

Destroying the works of the Croydon railway, felony, or to be punished as for petty larceny, or fine and imprisonment. 43 *Geo.* 3. *c.* xxxv. *s.* 82.

Destroying the bridge at Loftsome Ferry, in Yorkshire, felony, or punishment as for petty larceny. 43 *Geo.* 3. *c.* xlix. *s.* 47.

Destroying the works of Alloa harbour, felony, or punishment as for petty larceny. 43 *Geo.* 3. *c.* lv. *s.* 19.

Destroying the works of the pier or quay at Torquay in Devon, felony, or punishment as for petty larceny. 43 *Geo.* 3. *c.* lxxxviii.

Destroying the works of the Tavistock canal, felony, or punishment as for petty larceny. 43 *Geo.* 3. *c.* cxxx.

Destroying Ravensborne bridge, felony, or punishment as for petty larceny. 43 *Geo.* 3. *c.* cxxxi. *s.* 17.

Destroying the works of the Bristol Dock company, felony, and to be fined, imprisoned, or transported, at the discretion of the court. 44 *Geo.* 3. *local.*

Destroying the works of the Caledonian canal, felony, or by lesser punishment, or fine. 44 *Geo.* 3. *c.* 62. *s.* 68.

Destroying the works for draining the forest of Ramsey and Bury in Huntingdon. 44 *Geo.* 3. *c.* xx.

Destroying the works erected for draining the lands in Winterton, and East and West Somerton, in Norfolk, felony, and to be punished as petit larceny. 45 *Geo.* 3. *c.* viii. *s.* 47.

Attempting to destroy ships, lighters, or boats, or cutting cables by ballast men on the Thames, felony, and transportation for seven years, or fine and imprisonment for not exceeding two years. 45 *Geo.* 3. *c.* xcviii. *s.* 33.

Destroying the works erected for draining lands in Selby, and other parishes in the west riding of York, felony, and to be punished as such, or by fine and imprisonment. 45 *Geo.* 3. *c.* cv. *s.* 58.

Destroying the works of the South London waterworks, felony, and to be punished as petit larceny; or otherwise, on being convicted before one justice, to forfeit double damages and costs; or such offender may be committed for not exceeding four calendar months. 45 *Geo.* 3. *c.* cxix.

By 46 *Geo.* 3. *c.* xxxv. persons purchasing articles stolen from any ship or vessel in the Bristol docks, shall be punished by transportation for not exceeding fourteen years, or by fine and imprisonment, or whipping. *s.* 32.

By 46 *Geo.* 3. *c.* xcv. every person who shall wilfully and maliciously destroy any bank, engine, bridge, floodgate, tunnel, or sluice, or any of the works set up for draining and preserving fen lands in the south level, part of Bedford level, between Brandon river and Sams cut drain, shall be guilty of felony, and transported for seven years, or punished as in cases of petit larceny. *s.* 65.

And by 46 *Geo.* 3. *c.* cvii. (30 *Geo.* 2. *c.* 35. repealed), persons doing the like as to works set up for inclosing and draining lands in the Honor Manor, and parish of Wormegay, in the county of Norfolk, to be guilty of felony, and punished as felons, or otherwise suffer as in cases of petit larceny. *s.* 54.

By 48 *Geo.* 3. *c.* 72. breaking down inclosures in the forest of Dean, or new forest Hants, third offence, felony, and transportation for seven years.

By 48 *Geo.* 3. *c.* 130. persons cutting away or defacing buoy ropes or marks belonging to any ship within the jurisdiction of the cinque ports, to be guilty of felony, and transported for not more than fourteen years. *s.* 6.

All wrecked merchandize and ship stores within such jurisdiction, if sold, or marks defaced by the salvers, they, the salvers, to be adjudged guilty of felony. *s.* 8. But punishment not fixed.

Pilots or boatmen advising masters of ships within the jurisdiction, whether in distress or not, to cut their cables or buoy ropes, to be guilty of felony, and transported for not exceeding fourteen years. *s.* 12.

See also other titles.

—— *Deeds.*] By 21 *Jac.* 1. *c.* 26. acknowledging any deed inrolled in the name of another not privy thereto, felony *without benefit of clergy.*

—— *Escape.*] By 16 *Geo.* 2. *c.* 31. assisting a prisoner to escape who was committed for treason or felony, *shall be deemed felony;* and if so committed for petty larceny, a misdemeanor.

—— *Fines.*] By 21 *Jac.* 1. *c.* 26. acknowledging any fine in another's name, not privy thereto, felony *without benefit of clergy.*

—— *Fish.*] By 5 *Geo.* 3. *c.* 14. persons, convicted within six months after the offence of stealing, or destroying fish in fish ponds, shall be *transported for seven years.*

—— *Foreign States.*] By 3 *Jac.* 1. *c.* 4. any subject that shall go out of the realm to serve any foreign prince, not having before taken the oath of obedience, shall be a *felon.*

—— *Foreign Bills, Notes, and Copper Monies.*] By 43 *Geo.* 3. *c.* 139. persons forging foreign bills of exchange, or notes, or uttering the same, guilty of felony, and to be *transported for not exceeding fourteen years.* *s.* 1.

No person shall engrave plates for foreign bills or notes, nor print them without a written authority, on pain, for the first offence, to be punished as for a misdemeanor, by imprisonment for not exceeding six months, or to be fined or whipped, and for the second offence by *fourteen years transportation.* *s.* 2.

But this is not to alter the laws in force against forgery. *Ibid.*

Persons counterfeiting foreign copper coin, for the first offence to be punished as for a misdemeanor, and for the second by *seven years transportation.* *s.* 3.

—— *Forgery.*] By 5 *Eliz. c.* 14. forging any deed, or writing, sealed court roll, or will in writing, whereby another's freehold may be troubled, shall pay double costs, be set upon the pillory, have both ears cut off, nostrils slit, forfeit profits of lands, and be imprisoned for life.

Forging any deed or writing, whereby lease or annuity, or any obligation, acquittance, release, or discharge of debt shall be made, shall pay double costs, be set upon the pillory, have one ear cut off, and be imprisoned for one year. *Ibid.*

The plaintiff may release his damages, but not the penalties; and the second offence is felony *within benefit of clergy.* *Ibid.*

By 39 *Eliz. c.* 17. any person wandering as a soldier or mariner, forging a testimonial of justice of peace, felony *without benefit of clergy.*

By 8 & 9 *Will.* 3. *c.* 20. 11 *Geo.* 1. *c.* 9. and 15 *Geo.* 2. *c.* 13. it is made felony *without benefit of clergy* to forge the common seal of the bank, or any bank note, or to alter or rase any indorsement thereon.

By 9 *Ann. c.* 11. 5 *Geo.* 1. *c.* 2. and 38 *Geo.* 3. *c.* 54. *s.* 10. the forging any mark or stamp upon leather, hides, or the like, to defraud of the duties, is felony *without benefit of clergy.*

By 9 *Ann. c.* 21. forging the common seal of the South-sea company, or any bond, obligation, receipts, warrants, or indorsements thereon, is made felony *without benefit of clergy.* Also 6 *Geo.* 1. *c.* 4. & *c.* 11. and 12 *Geo.* 1. *c.* 32.

By 10 *Ann. c.* 19. forging any mark or stamp upon linens or calicoes, to defraud of the duties; felony *without clergy.* The same also by 4 *Geo.* 3. *c.* 37.

By 12 *Ann. c.* 2. and 5 *Geo.* 1. *c.* 3. forging or counterfeiting lottery orders, or the hand of any person to such orders, or altering the number or principal sum; felony *without clergy.* Also 6 *Geo.* 3. *c.* 30. 8 *Geo.* 3. *c.* 31.

By 5 *Geo.* 1. *c.* 14. forging debentures, felony *without clergy.*

By 6 *Geo.* 1. *c.* 18. 31 *Geo.* 2. *c.* 22. and 4 *Geo.* 3. *c.* 37. forging the common seal, or any policy of the Royal Exchange, or London assurance companies; felony *without clergy.*

By 8 *Geo.* 1. *c.* 22. and 31 *Geo.* 2. *c.* 22. forging any letter of attorney, or authority to transfer stock, or receive dividends, or counterfeiting names, or personating of proprietors of shares; felony *without clergy.* The same also by 4 *Geo.* 3. *c.* 25.

By 9 *Geo.* 1. *c.* 12. and 9 *Geo.* 2. *c.* 34. forging any order, assignment thereof, or discharge to the exchequer, for the annuities due thereon, or personating the proprietor; felony *without clergy.*

By 12 *Geo.* 1. *c.* 32. forging the hand of the accountant general, the register, the clerk of the report office, or any cashier of the bank, to obtain any money belonging to the suitors in chancery, or forging any East India or South Sea bond, felony *without clergy.*

By 2 *Geo.* 2. *c.* 25. perpetuated by 9 *Geo.* 2. *c.* 18. forging any deed, will, bond, bill of exchange, promissory note for payment of money, indorsement, or acquittance, felony *without clergy.*

By 4 *Geo.* 2. *c.* 18. forging any Mediterranean passes, felony *without clergy.*

By 7 *Geo.* 2. *c.* 22. forging or altering any acceptance of bills of exchange, or the number or sum of any accountable receipt, or any warrant or order for payment of money, delivery of goods, or the like, felony *without clergy.*

By 8 *Geo.* 2. *c.* 6. forging any entry of bargainor's acknowledgment in bargain and sale, in the registry for the North Riding in the county of York, or any memorial, the second offence, felony *without clergy*.

By 26 *Geo.* 2. *c.* 33. forging any entry in the register relating to any marriage, or forging licence of marriage, felony *without clergy*.

By 31 *Geo.* 2. *c.* 32. forging the stamp used for marking plate, or being in possession of such forged stamp, felony *without clergy*.

By 32 *Geo.* 2. *c.* 14. forging the hand of the receiver of the pre-fines, felony *without clergy*.

By 9 *Geo.* 3. *c.* 30. forging seaman's tickets, to obtain wages, prize-money, or the like, felony *without clergy*.

By 13 *Geo.* 3. *c.* 56. forging the stamp or seal of the commissioners of excise, provided, renewed, or altered by this act, or counterfeiting or resembling the impression thereof, on any goods chargeable by 10 *Ann. c.* 19. 12 *Ann. c.* 9. 3 *Geo.* 1. *c.* 9. or 6 *Geo.* 1. *c.* 14. to defraud the king, felony *without clergy*.

By 13 *Geo.* 3. *c.* 59. counterfeiting or altering the marks on gold or silver plate, *transportation for seven years*.

By 14 *Geo.* 3. *c.* 72. counterfeiting stamps or seals on printed cottons or linens, or selling such, felony *without clergy*.

By 18 *Geo.* 3. *c.* 18. forging the acceptance of a bill of exchange, or number or principal sum in any accountable receipt for note, bill, or other security for money, or warrant, or order for payment of money, in order to defraud any corporation, or uttering such, felony *without clergy*.

Forgery of stamps directed to be used for bills, notes, or receipts, felony *without benefit of clergy*. 31 *Geo.* 3. *c.* 25. *s.* 29.

Forgery of tickets for seamen's wages, felony *without benefit of clergy*. 32 *Geo.* 3. *c.* 33. *s.* 23.

Forgery of certificates or checks to obtain letters of administration, or probate to seamen or marines, felony *without benefit of clergy*. 32 *Geo.* 3. *c.* 34. 49 *Geo.* 3. *c.* 108.

Forgery of certificates or orders under the act relating to the redemption of the public debt, felony *without clergy*. 32 *Geo.* 3. *c.* 55. *s.* 9.

Forgery of certificates for the payment of seamen's wages in Ireland, felony *without clergy*. 32 *Geo.* 3. *c.* 67. *s.* 12.

Forgery of the seal of the Royal Exchange assurance for granting annuities, felony *without clergy*. 33 *Geo.* 3. *c.* 14.

Forgery of orders for the payment of seamen's allotments of a portion of their wages, felony *without clergy*. 35 *Geo.* 3. *c.* 28. *s.* 30.

Forgery of debentures, annuity bonds, letters of attorney, or personating others to receive the dividends on the imperial loan, felony *without benefit of clergy*. 35 *Geo.* 3. *c.* 93. *s.* 7.

Forgery of orders for the pay of naval officers, felony *without clergy*. 35 *Geo.* 3. *c.* 94. *s.* 34.

Forgery of stamps or seals used for starch or hair powder, felony *without clergy*. 36 *Geo.* 3. *c.* 6. *s.* 13.

Forgery of stamps for the linings of hats, felony *without clergy*. 36 *Geo.* 3. *c.* 125. *s.* 19.

Forgery of the names of witnesses to instruments for the transfer or receipt of dividends of stock at the bank, or of the South Sea, or the East India company's stocks, to be guilty of *felony and transported for seven years*, or suffer such lesser punishment as the court may award. 37 *Geo.* 3. *c.* 122.

Forgery of debentures required relating to the duties of excise, felony *without clergy*. 38 *Geo.* 3. *c.* 54. *s.* 9.

Forgery of stamps provided to denote payment of the duty on tanned leather, as enacted by 9 *Ann. c.* 11. 10 *Ann. c.* 26. and 5 *Geo.* 1. *c.* 2. to remain felony *without clergy*. 38 *Geo.* 3. *c.* 54. *s.* 10.

Forgery of the Globe Insurance company's seal, felony *without benefit of clergy*. 39 *Geo.* 3. *c.* lxxxiii.

Forgery of excise certificates or debentures, under 38 *Geo.* 3. *c.* 54. for exportation of tea to Ireland, *felony and transportation for seven years*. 41 *Geo.* 3. (u. k.) *c.* 91. *s.* 5.

Forging contracts for the redemption of the land tax, felony *without clergy*. 42 *Geo.* 3. *c.* 116. *s.* 194.

Forgery of Irish franks, third offence, felony *within clergy*. 43 *Geo.* 3. *c.* 28. *s.* 22.

Personating pensioners on the Greenwich chest, felony *without clergy*. 43 *Geo.* 3. *c.* 119. *s.* 17.

By 45 *Geo.* 3. *c.* 89. persons forging deeds, or wills, or securities, receipts or orders for money, or uttering any such with intent to defraud any person or corporation, shall be guilty of felony *without benefit of clergy*.

Forging of drafts of public officers, felony *without clergy*. 46 *Geo.* 3. *c.* 45. *s.* 9. *cap.* 75. *s.* 8. *cap.* 76. *s.* 9. *cap.* 83. *s.* 9. *cap.* 142. *s.* 14. *cap.* 150. *s.* 10. 49 *Geo.* 3. *c.* 113. *s.* 12.

Forgery of certificates for soldiers pensions, felony *within clergy*. 46 *Geo.* 3. *c.* 69. *s.* 9.

Forging certificates of orders of council for quarantine, felony *without clergy*. 46 *Geo.* 3. *c.* 98. *s.* 8.

By 46 *Geo.* 3. *c.* 150. forging the name or hand-writing of the receiver general of the customs, or supervisor of his accounts to any draft on the bank of England, felony *without clergy*. *s.* 10.

By 47 *Geo.* 3. *sess.* 2. *c.* 36. counterfeiting any certificate, copy of sentence of condemnation, or receipt, under this act, for abolishing the slave trade, felony *without clergy*. *s.* 12.

By 47 *Geo.* 3. *sess.* 2. *c.* 25. personating half-pay officers, or widows, entitled under the compassionate list, felony *within clergy, and transportation for fourteen years.* *s.* 7.

Forging or counterfeiting the names or hand-writing of officers or widows entitled to half pay, pensions, or allowances, under the compassionate list, felony *within clergy, and transportation for fourteen years.* *s.* 8.

By 47 *Geo.* 3. *sess.* 2. *c.* 30. persons counterfeiting stamps on any cover, or wrapper, or label, affixed to any ream or quantity of paper, guilty of felony *within clergy, and to be transported for seven years.* *s.* 13.

By 47 *Geo.* 3. *sess.* 2. *c.* 59. forging the name of any person authorised by the receiver-general, and approved of by the post-master general, to receive and pay monies at the bank, felony *without clergy.* *s.* 3.

By 48 *Geo.* 3. *c.* 1. forging exchequer bills, or any indorsement thereon, felony *without clergy.* *s.* 9.

By 48 *Geo.* 3. *c.* 142. *s* 27. and 49 *Geo.* 3. *c.* 64. *s.* 3. forging any instruments under the act authorising the commissioners for the reduction of the national debt to grant life annuities, felony *without clergy.*

Personating the widows of officers of the navy in order to receive, under this act, their pensions; or forging bills, certificates, vouchers, or receipts, in relation to such pensions, *transportation* for not exceeding fourteen years. 49 *Geo.* 3. *c.* 35. *s.* 9, 10.

Personating officers of the royal marines, in order to receive, under this act, their allowances on the compassionate list, or half-pay, or forging bills, certificates, vouchers, or receipts, in relation thereto, *transportation* for not exceeding fourteen years. 49 *Geo.* 3. *c.* 45. *s.* 10, 11.

Persons counterfeiting the excise marks on paper, or having paper in their possession with such counterfeited marks, shall be adjudged felons, and *transported* for seven years. 49 *Geo.* 3. *c.* 81.

Forging of *stamps*, by all the stamp acts, felony *without clergy.*

——*Hawks.*] By 34 *Ed.* 3. *c.* 22. every person who finds an hawk, or falcon, shall bring the same to the sheriff, who shall make proclamation, and return it to the owner; and by 37 *Ed.* 3. *c.* 19. stealing any hawk and carrying the same away contrary thereto, shall be *felony.*

——*Hops.*] By 6 *Geo.* 2. *c.* 37. made perpetual by 31 *Geo.* 2. *c.* 42. maliciously cutting hop binds, growing on poles, in any plantation of hops, felony *without clergy.*

——*Horses.*] By 37 *Hen.* 8. *c.* 8. 1 *Ed.* 6. *c.* 12. and 2 & 3 *Ed.* 6. *c.* 43. stealing any horse, gelding, mare, or foal, felony *without clergy.*

——*Hunting.*] By 1 *Hen.* 7. *c.* 7. unlawful hunting in the night, with disguises, is *felony.* See also *Black Act.*

——*Judgments.*] By 21 *Jac.* 1. *c.* 26. acknowledging any judgment, recognizance, statute, or recovery, in the name of any other person not privy thereto, felony *without clergy.*

—— *Lead, Pewter, Iron, and Copper.*] By 4 *Geo.* 2. *c.* 32. stealing any iron bars, or lead fixed to any houses, or fences belonging thereto; felony, and the offender may be *transported for seven years.*

By 21 *Geo.* 3. *c.* 68. all persons who shall steal, or remove with intent to steal, any copper, brass, bell metal, utensil, or fixture, being fixed to any dwelling-house, out house, or in any garden, yard, orchard, or out-let, or any iron rails, shall be deemed guilty of felony, and may be *transported for seven years;* and all persons assisting in such stealing; or who shall buy such goods, knowing them to be stolen, shall be liable to the same punishments.

Every person who shall buy or receive any pewter pot, or other pewter, knowing the same to be stolen, shall, on conviction, be *transported, as a felon, for seven years,* or may be kept to hard labour, not more than three years, nor less than one, and within that time be publicly whipped. *Ibid.* *c.* 69.

—— *Lead Mines.*] By 25 *Geo.* 2. *c.* 10. entering any mines of black lead, with intent to steal, shall be deemed felony, and *the offender shall be transported.* Returning before the time, felony *without* clergy.

The receivers of lead, knowing the same to be so unlawfully taken, shall be deemed *guilty of felony.* *Ibid.*

——*Letters threatening.*] By 27 *Geo.* 2. *c.* 15. persons convicted of sending letters, without any name, or with a fictitious name, threatening, or of rescuing persons in custody for such offences, are guilty of felony *without clergy.*

—— *Linen.*] By 18 *Geo.* 2. *c.* 27. stealing any linen, fustian, calico, cotton, cloth, or cloth mixed with cotton or linen yarn, or any thread, linen or cotton yarn, tape, incle, filleting, laces or any other linen, fustian or cotton goods, laid to be printed or bleached in any bleaching ground, or aiding, or hiring another to commit such offence; felony *without* clergy: but the court may order such offenders to be *transported for fourteen years;* and if they break gaol or return, they are to suffer death.

By 4 *Geo.* 3. *c.* 37. breaking or entering by force into any place, with intent to steal, cut, or destroy, any linen belonging to any manufactory, felony *without clergy.*

—— *Maiming.*] By 5 *Hen.* 4. *c.* 5. cutting the tongue, or putting out the eyes of people, of malice prepense, shall be felony.

By 22 & 23 *Car.* 2. *c.* 1. unlawfully disabling the tongue, slitting the nose, or the like, of malice forethought, by lying in wait, and with intention to maim; felony *without clergy*. See also *Shooting*.

——*Marriage*.] By 26 *Geo*. 2. *c*. 33. persons convicted of solemnizing matrimony in any other place than a church, or public chapel, or without banns or licence, unless by special licence, guilty of felony, and shall be *transported for fourteen years*.

——*Money*.] By 17 *Ed*. 3. *stat*. 1. bringing false and ill money into the realm, and officers assenting thereto, or suffering silver money to be exported, shall be *felony*.

By 8 & 9 *Wil*. 3. *c*. 26. blanching copper for sale, or mixing it with silver, or taking or paying any counterfeit milled money, shall be *felony*.

By 15 *Geo*. 2. *c*. 28. uttering false money knowingly, for the third offence, shall be felony *without clergy*.

Uttering false money twice within ten days, or having other false money in his custody, being once convicted, the second offence, shall be felony *without clergy*. *Ibid*.

By 37 *Geo*. 3. *c* 126. counterfeiting foreign gold or silver coin, felony and *transportation for seven years*, tendering in payment such counterfeit foreign gold or silver coin, third offenee, felony *without clergy*. See also *Bank*.

——*Murder*.] By 12 *Hen*. 7. *c*. 7. no lay person, purposely killing his master, *shall be admitted to his clergy*.

No person found guilty of petty treason, wilful murder, poisoning, or the like, shall have *benefit of clergy*. 23 *Hen*. 8. *c*. 1. 25 *Hen*. 8. *c*. 3. 28 *Hen*. 8. *c*. 1. 32 *Hen*. 8. *c*. 3. and 1 *Ed*. 6. *c*. 12.

——*Mute*.] Every person, who being arraigned of murder, robbery, or felony, shall stand mute, or will not answer directly, shall lose his clergy, as if he had been found guilty. 25 *Hen*. 8. *c*. 3. 1 *Ed*. 6. *c*. 12. 5 & 6 *Ed*. 6. *c*. 10. 4 & 5 *Phil*. & *Mar*. *c*. 4. 3 & 4 *W*. & *Mar*. *c*. 9. and 1 *Ann*. *stat*. 2. *c*. 9.

By 12 *Geo*. 3. *c*. 20. standing mute on arraignment for felony, or piracy, to be convicted, and have the same judgment and execution, as if found guilty by verdict or confession.

——*Mutiny*.] By 22 & 23 *Car*. 2. *c*. 11. any officer wilfully destroying the ship, or mariners laying violent hands on their commander, to hinder him from fighting in defence of his ship and the goods, shall be guilty of *felony*.

By 2 & 3 *Ann*. *c*. 20. any officer or soldier beyond, or upon the sea, raising any mutiny, or resisting his officer, is *guilty of felony*.

By 37 *Geo*. 3. *c*. 70. (in force for seven years from 1 August, 1807, 47 *Geo*. 3. *sess*. 1. *c*. 15.) any person who shall attempt to seduce any sailor or soldier from his duty, or incite him to traitorous or mutinous practices, shall be guilty of felony *without benefit of clergy*, and whether committed at sea, or within Great Britain, may be tried before any court of oyer and terminer; but persons tried for offences against this act are not to be tried again for the same as high treason or misprision thereof.

——*Northern borders*.] By 43 *Eliz*. *c*. 13. carrying away or detaining any person against his will, assenting or aiding therein, or receiving, or giving of black mail in Cumberland, Northumberland, and Durham, for protection against burning stacks of corn, shall be felony *without benefit of clergy*.

By 18 *Car*. 2. *c*. 3. *clergy is taken away* from notorious thieves and spoil-takers in Cumberland and Northumberland, or otherwise, the judges may cause them to be *transported*.

——*Oaths*.] By 37 *Geo*. 3. *c*. 123. persons administering unlawful oaths, or taking them voluntarily, shall be guilty of felony, and *transported for seven years*: and persons compelled to take such oaths are not justified, unless they declare the same within four days. *s*. 1, 2.

Persons aiding at taking such oaths, or causing them to be administered, though not present, to be deemed principals. *s*. 3.

——*Outlawry*.] Persons outlawed for felony, without benefit of clery, *shall not have their clergy*. 1 *Ed*. 6. *c*. 12. 4 & 5 *Ph*. & *M*. *c*. 4. 8 *Eliz*. *c*. 4. 18 *Eliz*. *c*. 7. 22 *Car*. 2. *c*. 5. and 3 & 4 *Will*. 3. *c*. 9.

——*Oyster beds*.] By 48 *Geo*. 3. *c*. 144. persons stealing oysters or oyster brood from oyster beds (not having or claiming to have a right to take the same, *s*. 2.) shall be guilty of felony, *and may be transported for seven years*, or imprisoned and kept to hard labour for three years. *s*. 1.

——*Perjury*.] By 2 *Geo*. 2. *c*. 25. persons convicted of wilful perjury, breaking prison, or returning from transportation before the time, are guilty of felony *without clergy*.

——*Personating others*.] See *Bail*, *Fines*, *Forgery*.

——*Pick-pocket*.] The 8 *Eliz*. *c*. 4. making the taking from the person of another, privily without his knowledge, any money or goods, felony *without clergy*, *is repealed*, by 48 *Geo*. 3. *c*. 129.

And by the same act, 48 *Geo*. 3. *c*. 129. persons feloniously stealing from the person of another, whether privily or not, but without force or putting in fear, and those present aiding and abetting *may be transported for life*, *or not less than seven years*, or if the court think fit, be imprisoned only, or imprisoned and kept to hard labour for not exceeding three years.

——*Piracy*.] Piracy shall be tried and punished as felony *without benefit of clergy*. 11 & 12 *Will*. 3. *c*. 7. 4 *Geo*. 1. *c*. 11. 6 *Geo*. 1. *c*. 19. 8 *Geo*. 1. *c*. 24. and 18 *Geo*. 2. *c*. 30.

By 11 & 12 *Will*. 3. *c*. 7. commander or mariner who shall betray his trust or turn pirate, or person laying violent hands on commander, shall be adjudged a pirate and felon, *and shall suffer death.*

By 8 *Geo.* 1. *c.* 24. trading with pirates, furnishing them with stores, or corresponding with them, shall be adjudged piracy, and felony *without clergy.*

——*Plague.*] By 1 *Jac.* 1. *c.* 31. any person infected with the plague, and commanded to keep house, wilfully going abroad, is *guilty of felony.*

——*Plate-glass company.*] By 38 *Geo.* 3. *c.* xvii. forging the seal of the British plate glass company is felony, and persons stealing or destroying glass materials or tools, are also *guilty of felony,* and may be transported for seven years, or suffer such lesser punishment as the court may award. *s.* 23, 24.

——*Popish Priests and Recusants.*] By 27 *Eliz. c.* 2. receiving or aiding any popish priest, or jesuit, shall be felony *without clergy.*

By 35 *Eliz. c.* 1. and *c.* 2. popish recusants refusing to abjure the realm, not departing within the time appointed, or returning without licence, are guilty of felony *without benefit of clergy.* But see general title *Papists.*

——*Post-office.*] By 42 *Geo.* 3. *c.* 81. secreting letters containing any securities, or procuring or receiving the same, felony *without clergy. s.* 1, 2.

——*Prisons.*] By 1 *Ed.* 2. *stat.* 2. prison-breaker shall not have judgment of life or member for breaking prison only, unless the cause for which he was imprisoned required such judgment, if he had been convicted.

By 14 *Ed.* 3. *c.* 10. the keeper of a prison causing any prisoner to become an appellor by duress, *guilty of felony.*

By 16 *Geo.* 2. *c.* 31. assisting any prisoner to escape, who was imprisoned for felony, except petty larceny, shall be felony, and may be *transported for seven years.*

By 18 *Geo.* 2. *c.* 27. and 25 *Geo.* 2. *c.* 10. person convicted of stealing, and sentenced to transportation, voluntarily breaking prison, guilty of felony *without clergy.*

——*Privy Councillors.*] By 3 *Hen.* 7. *c.* 14. any servant in the cheque roll of the king's household, conspiring to destroy the king, or any person sworn to his council, shall be judged *guilty of felony.*

By 9 *Ann. c.* 16. attempting to kill, or assaulting a privy councillor, in the execution of his office, shall be felony *without clergy.*

——*Process.*] By 9 *Geo.* 1. *c.* 28. persons in any disguise opposing the execution of legal process in the Mint, or any other pretended privileged place, are *guilty of felony.*

By 11 *Geo.* 1. *c.* 22. resisting officers in execution of legal process in Wapping, Stepney, or other place, shall be *felony and transportation.*

——*Quarantine.*] By 45 *Geo.* 3. *c.* 10. disobedience to orders of quarantine, felony *without clergy. s.* 23.

——*Rape.*] By 13 *Ed.* 1. *stat.* 1. *c.* 34. it shall be *felony* to commit a rape.

By 18 *Eliz. c.* 7. persons found guilty or outlawed for a felonious rape, *shall have no benefit of clergy.*

Knowing a woman child carnally, under the age of ten years, felony *without clergy. Ibid.*

——*Record.*] By 8 *Hen.* 6. *c.* 12. embezzling of a record, whereby any judgment shall be reversed, shall be judged *felony.*

——*Rescue.*] By 1 *Hen.* 7. *c.* 7. rescuing offenders in hunting in parks in the night or disguised, shall be *felony.*

By 6 *Geo.* 1. *c.* 23. rescuing felons delivered to contractors for transportation, felony *without clergy.*

By 25 *Geo.* 2. *c.* 37. rescuing one committed for, or found guilty of murder, or in going to, or during execution; felony *without clergy.*

Rescuing the body of a murderer after execution, is felony and *transportation for seven years,* and returning within the term subject to punishment of unlawful returning from transportation. *Ibid.*

——*Riots.*] By 1 *Geo.* 1. *stat.* 2. *c.* 5. twelve persons or more assembled unlawfully, not dispersing in an hour after commanded by one justice of peace, shall be adjudged felons *without clergy.*

Persons riotously pulling down any church, building for religious worship, dwelling house, or out-house, shall be adjudged felons *without clergy. Ibid.*

Persons obstructing the making the proclamation shall be adjudged felons *without clergy.*

——*Robbery.*] Robbing churches or chapels, robbing persons in their dwelling-houses, or in or near the highways, felony *without benefit of clergy.* 23 *Hen.* 8. *c.* 1. 25 *Hen.* 8. *c.* 3. 1 *Ed.* 6. *c.* 12. 5 & 6 *Ed.* 6. *c.* 9. and *c.* 10.

By 5 & 6 *Ed.* 6. *c.* 9. robbing any person in a booth or tent, in any fair or market, felony *without benefit of clergy.*

By 39 *Eliz. c.* 15. robbery in any dwelling-house or out-house in the day time, to the value of five shillings, although no person be therein at the time, felony *without clergy.*

By 3 & 4 *Will. & Mar. c.* 9. and 6 & 7 *Will.* 3. *c.* 14. robbing any dwelling-house, shop, or warehouse, to the value of 5*s.*, felony *without benefit of clergy.*

Persons stealing furniture, let with any lodging, shall be adjudged guilty of *larceny and felony.* 3 & 4 *Will. & Mar. c.* 9.

By 10 & 11 *Will.* 3. *c.* 23. robbing any shop, warehouse, coach house or stable, to the value of five shillings, felony *without clergy.*

By 12 *Ann. stat.* 1. *c.* 7. stealing to the value of 40*s.* in any dwelling-house or out-house, though the same be not broken, felony *without clergy*: but this does not extend to apprentices under fifteen years of age.

By 2 *Geo.* 2. *c.* 25. and 31 *Geo.* 2. *c.* 22. stealing or taking by robbery any exchequer orders, tallies, or other orders intitling any other person to any annuity or share in any parliamentary fund, or any exchequer bills, bank notes, South Sea bonds, East India bonds, dividend warrants of the bank, South Sea company, East India company, or any other company, society, or corporation, bills of exchange, navy bills or debentures, Goldsmith's notes, other bonds, warrants, promissory notes, being the property of any other person or corporation, notwithstanding the same may be deemed a chose in action, shall be deemed felony *without benefit of clergy*, in the same manner as if the robbery had been of goods of like value.

By 7 *Geo.* 2. *c.* 21. persons convicted of assaulting others with offensive weapons, with intent to rob, shall be adjudged guilty of felony, *and transported for seven years.* Returning before the term is felony *without clergy.*

——*Rogues.*] By 17 *Geo.* 2. *c.* 5. incorrigible rogues breaking or escaping out of the house of correction, where they were ordered to be detained, or offending again, are guilty of felony, and may be *transported for not exceeding seven years.*

——*Sea and Seamen.*] By 28 *Hen.* 8. *c.* 15. for treasons, robberies, felonies, murders, and confederacies done upon the sea, the offenders *shall not have benefit of clergy.*

By 5 *Eliz. c.* 5. mariners taking prest or wages to serve the queen's majesty, and departing without licence, are guilty of *felony.*

By 31 *Geo.* 2. *c.* 10. and 9 *Geo.* 3. *c.* 30. personating an officer or seaman supposed to have wages due to him, or his executor, or forging letters of attorney, tickets or wills, or making false oath to obtain probate, wages or the like, belonging to such person, shall be felony *without clergy.*

By 33 *Geo.* 3. *c.* 67. made perpetual by 41 *Geo.* 3. *c.* 19. *s.* 4. seamen or others riotously assembled, who shall forcibly prevent the loading, unloading, or sailing of vessels, or who shall forcibly prevent others from working, to be *transported for not more than fourteen nor less than seven years,* for the second offence. *s.* 3.

Seamen or others wilfully setting fire to ships, *felony without clergy.* *s.* 5.

And destroying or damaging them by any other means, to be *transported for not more than fourteen, nor less than seven, years.* *s.* 6. See also *Forgery.*

——*Seditious meetings.*] If twelve or more persons assembled shall continue together one hour after being required by a justice to disperse, felony *without clergy.* 36 *Geo.* 3. *c.* 8. *s.* 4, 6, 7.

Obstructing magistrates in the execution of their duty, felony *without clergy.* *s.* 10.

Persons convicted by indictment of being members of corresponding or other seditious societies, *may be transported for seven years.* 39 *Geo.* 3. *c.* 79. *s.* 8.

——*Servants.*] By 33 *Hen.* 6. *c.* 1. servants riotously despoiling their master's goods after his death, and not appearing on proclamation, shall be *attainted of felony.*

By 21 *Hen.* 8. *c.* 7. made perpetual by 5 *Eliz. c.* 10. servant withdrawing himself with money or goods delivered to him to keep by his master, to the value of 40*s.* or above, shall be adjudged *guilty of felony.* But by 12 *Ann. stat.* 1. *c.* 7. this act is not to extend to any apprentice, or one within eighteen years of age.

By 12 *Geo.* 1. *c.* 34. assaulting a master woolcomber, or master weaver concerned in the woollen manufactures, for not submitting to illegal bye-laws, *felony and transportation for seven years.*

By 24 *Geo.* 2. *c.* 11. officer or servant of the South Sea company, embezzling any security, money, or effects of the company intrusted with him, guilty of felony *without clergy.*

By 39 *Geo.* 3. *c.* 85. servants or clerks receiving any money or other effects received on their master's account, and fraudulently embezzling or secreting any part thereof, shall be deemed to have feloniously stolen the same; and such offenders and their abettors shall on conviction, be liable to be *transported for not exceeding fourteen years.*

——*Sheep.*] By 14 *Geo.* 2. *c.* 6. and 15 *Geo.* 2. *c.* 34. stealing one or more sheep, or any bull, cow, ox, steer, bullock, heifer, calf or lamb, or killing one or more sheep, or other such cattle, with a felonious intent to steal the carcase, or any part thereof, felony *without clergy.*

——*Ships.*] By 43 *Geo.* 3. *c.* 113. persons wilfully casting away, burning or otherwise destroying any ship or vessel, or who shall in any wise, counsel, direct, or procure the same to be done, shall be guilty of felony *without benefit of clergy.* *c.* 2. See also *Wreck.*

——*Shooting, stabbing, administering poison, or setting fire to places.*] By 43 *Geo.* 3. *c.* 58. persons in England or Ireland who shall maliciously shoot at, or shall stab or cut with intent to murder, rob, or maim any of his majesty's subjects, or to prevent arrests of culprits; or shall administer poison or other noxious and destructive thing, with intent to murder, or cause the miscarriage of any woman quick with child, or who shall wilfully set fire to any house, barn, granary, hops-oast, malt-house, stable, coach-house, out-house, mill, warehouse, or shop, whether in his own possession or of any other, shall be guilty of felony *without benefit of clergy.*

——*Soldiers.*] By 18 *Hen.* 6. *c.* 19. 7 *Hen.* 7. *c.* 1. 2 & 3 *Ed.* 6. *c.* 2. and 4 & 5 *Phil.* & *Mar. c.* 3 a soldier retained to serve the king in his wars, leaving his captain without licence, shall be adjudged *guilty of felony.*

By 39 *Eliz. c.* 17. soldiers and mariners, wandering without testimonial, or counterfeiting one, are guilty of felony *without clergy.*

Such offenders may be placed by the sessions in the service of a freeholder, for a year, and departing within the year, shall be *felony without clergy. Ibid.*

By 9 *Geo.* 2. *c.* 30. enlisting or procuring any of his majesty's subjects to enlist, as a soldier in foreign service, without licence of his majesty, felony *without clergy;* such offences may be tried in any county in England. But persons inveigled so as to list themselves, making a discovery in fourteen days to a justice, are indemnified.

By 29 *Geo.* 2. *c.* 17. subjects of the crown of Great Britain, accepting commissions, being officers or soldiers in the service of the French king, or remaining therein, without leave from his majesty, or contracting to enlist, felony *without clergy.*

By 46 *Geo.* 3. *c.* 69. personating soldiers entitled to pensions, felony *without clergy.* See also *Mutiny.*

——*Spirits.*] By 11 *Geo.* 2. *c.* 26. and 24 *Geo.* 2. *c.* 40. rescuing offenders against the acts concerning spirituous liquors, or assaulting informers against such offenders, is felony *and transportation for seven years.*

—— *Stealing.*] By 12 *Ann. stat.* 1. *c.* 7. persons stealing to the value of 40*s.* in a dwelling-house, though the same be not broken, or any persons therein, felony *without benefit of clergy;* but this does not extend to apprentices under fifteen.

By 24 *Geo.* 2. *c.* 45. stealing goods to the value of 40*s.* on board any vessel, in any navigable river, or upon any wharf, or quay adjacent, is felony *without clergy.*

——*Stolen Goods.*] By 4 *Geo.* 1. *c.* 11. and 6 *Geo.* 1. *c.* 23. persons taking rewards for helping to stolen goods, unless they cause the felon to be brought to trial, and give evidence against him, shall be deemed *guilty of such felony.*

By 18 *Geo.* 2. *c.* 27. buyers or receivers of linen, fustian, or cotton stolen from a bleaching croft, are guilty of felony *without benefit of clergy.*

Purchasing stolen goods from on board vessels using the Bristol docks, felony *within clergy.* 46 *Geo.* 3. *c.* xxxv. *s.* 32.

——*Stores.*] By 31 *Eliz. c.* 4. embezzling stores provided for soldiers, mariners, and the like persons to the value of 20*s.* shall be felony *without benefit of clergy.* 12 *Car.* 2. *c.* 3. and 1 *Geo* 1. *stat.* 2. *c.* 25.

By 12 *Geo.* 3. *c.* 24. burning the king's ships built or building, dock-yards, magazines, materials, navy or victualling stores, or aiding therein, shall be *felony without clergy,* and offending out of the realm, the trial may be in any county within the same.

——*Transportation.*] By 4 *Geo.* 1. *c.* 11. 6 *Geo.* 1. *c.* 23. and 16 *Geo.* 2. *c.* 15. persons convicted of offences, within the benefit of clergy, except receivers and buyers of stolen goods, *shall be sent to the plantations for seven years,* the court before whom convicted to contract for their transportation. Persons convicted of offences for which they are excluded the benefit of clergy, and also receivers and buyers of stolen goods may be transported for fourteen years, and the persons contracting for their transportation, shall have property in their service.

Returning before the expiration of the term is felony *without benefit of clergy:* service of the term, shall have the effect of a pardon. *Ibid.* and also 18 *Geo.* 2. *c.* 27. and 25 *Geo.* 2. *c.* 10.

By 8 *Geo.* 3. *c.* 15. offenders convicted of a crime subject to death, and pardoned on condition of transportation, if found at large within the time, are guilty of felony *without benefit of clergy.*

By 39 & 40 *Geo.* 3. *c.* 79. persons transported by the courts in India to New South Wales, coming into Great Britain or Ireland, felony *without clergy.*

—— *Trees.*] By 6 *Geo.* 3. *c.* 36. lopping, topping, cutting down, barking, burning, or spoiling, or carrying away in the night, any oak, beech, ash, elm, fir, chesnut, or asp, or other timber tree, or digging up any roots, shrubs, or plants of 5*s.* value, in inclosed ground, *transportation for seven years;* and aiders and receivers are liable to the same penalty.

—— *Turnpikes and Locks.*] By 8 *Geo.* 2. *c.* 20. made perpetual by 27 *Geo.* 2. *c.* 16. maliciously destroying locks, sluices, or floodgates, erected by authority of parliament, or rescuing persons in custody for such offences, is felony *without benefit of clergy.*

By 13 *Geo.* 3. *c.* 84. the malicious destroying of any turnpike gates, houses, or weighing engines, or rescuing persons in custody for such offences, is felony *and transportation for seven years.*

——*Watermen.*] By 1 *Geo.* 2. *c.* 31. where a greater number is taken into any boat, than respectively allowed by act of parliament, if any be drowned, the waterman is *guilty of felony.*

——*Women.*] By 3 *Hen.* 7. *c.* 2. unlawfully carrying away a woman against her will, that hath lands or goods, or is heir apparent, shall be felony; and by 39 *Eliz. c.* 9. *without benefit of clergy.*

——*Wool.*] By 28 *Geo.* 3. *c.* 38. if any person shall be obstructed in seizing sheep, wool, &c. intended to be exported, or carrying on board any vessel contrary to this act, the offenders and all persons attempting to rescue the same, shall be *transported for seven years,* and returning before is felony *without clergy.*

——*Wreck.*] By 12 *Ann. stat.* 2. *c.* 18. making or assisting in making any hole in any vessel in distress, or in stealing the pump, or wilfully doing any thing, tending to the immediate loss of such vessel, is felony *without clergy.*

By 26 *Geo.* 2. *c.* 19. persons convicted of plundering shipwrecked goods, or of obstructing the escape of any person from a wreck, or of putting out false lights, with intention to injure, are guilty of felony *without clergy.*

Where goods of small value shall be stolen, without any circumstances of cruelty, the offender may be indicted for petty larceny. *Ibid.*

On oath before a magistrate of the plunder, theft, or breaking a ship, the clerk of the peace shall prosecute the offenders; and persons convicted of assaulting any magistrate, or any officer, in the salvage of any vessel or goods, shall be *transported for seven years. Ibid.*

By 49 *Geo.* 3. *c.* 122. persons cutting away or defacing any buoy, buoy rope, or mark, whether the ship is in distress or not, shall be guilty of *felony* and transported *for not exceeding seven years,* or imprisoned. *s.* 12.

Persons *purchasing* any anchors, cables, or goods, or merchandize, taken up, weighed, swept for, or taken possession of, whether the ship was in distress or not, if the directions of this act be not complied with, shall be deemed guilty of receiving stolen goods knowingly, and suffer as for a misdemeanor, or be *transported* for seven years. *s.* 13.

Pilots, hovellers, boatmen, and others, selling or disposing of any such anchors or cables in foreign countries, are guilty of felony, and may be transported for seven years. *s.* 14.

FEME COVERT, a married woman. *Cowel. Blount.*

FEME SOLE, (Fr.) a woman that is unmarried. 1 *Rol. Abr.* 351. See Baron *and* Feme.

FENCE, is a hedge, ditch, or other inclosure of land for the better manurance and improvement of the same. And where a hedge and ditch join together, in whose ground or side the hedge is, to the owner of that land belongs the keeping of the same hedge or fence, and the ditch adjoining to it on the other side, in repair and scoured. *Par. Offic.* 188. And an action on the case or trespass lies, for not repairing of fences, whereby cattle come into the ground of another, and do damage. 1 *Salk.* 335.

FENCE-MONTH, (*mensis prohibitionis,* or *mensis ventitus*) is a month wherein female deer in forests, &c. do fawn, and therefore it is unlawful to hunt in forests during that time; which begins fifteen days before Midsummer, and ends fifteen days after it, being in all thirty days. *Manw. part* 2. *cap.* 13.

FENGELD, (Sax.) a tax or imposition, exacted for the repelling of enemies. *Cowel. Blount.*

FENS, *(paludes)* are low marshy grounds, or lakes for water.

FEOD or FEUD, is defined to be a right which a vassal hath in lands, or some immoveable thing of his lord's, to use the same, and take the profits thereof hereditarily; rendering unto the lord such feodal duties and services as belong to military tenure, &c. and the property of the soil always remaining to the lord. *Spelm. of Tenures, cap.* 1.

FEODAL, *(feodalis, vel feudalis)* of or belonging to the fee. *Cowel. Blount.*

FEODALITY, fealty paid to the lord by his feodal tenant. *Ibid.*

FEODARY, or FEUDARY, *(feudatarius)* an officer of the court of wards, appointed by the master of that court, by virtue of the statutes 32 *Hen.* 8. *cap.* 26. now wholly taken away by statute 12 *Car.* 2. *cap.* 24. *Ibid.*

FEODATARY, sometimes called *homager,* was the tenant who held his estate by feodal service. *Ibid.*

FEODUM. See Feud.

FEODUM MILITIS, a knight's fee: *feodum laicum,* a lay fee, or land held in fee of a lay lord. *Ibid.*

FEOFFMENT, (*feoffamentum,* from the Gothic word *feudum,* and signifies *donationem feudi*) is a gift or grant of any manors, messuages, lands or tenements, to another in fee, to him and his heirs for ever, by the delivery of seisin and possession of the thing given or granted; and in every feoffment, the giver or grantor is called the feoffor, and he that receives by virtue thereof, is the feoffee. And the proper difference between a feoffor and a donor, is, that the one gives in fee-simple, the other in fee-tail. *Litt. lib.* 1. *cap.* 6. The deed of feoffment is our most ancient conveyance of lands; for at common law, the usual conveyance was by feoffment, to which livery and seisin was necessary, the possession being thereby given to the feoffee. *Co. Lit.* 9, 49. And a feoffment, though of late not much used, in some respects excels the conveyance by fine and recovery; it clearing all disseisins, abatements, intrusions, and other wrongful estates, which no other conveyance doth: and by reason that it is so solemnly and publicly made, it has been of all other conveyances the most observed. *West. Symb.* 235. *Plowd.* 554.

It is made by these words, have *enfeoffed, given, granted,* &c. but by the mere words of the deed, the feoffment is by no means perfected, for there must be *livery and seisin,* without which, the feoffee has but a mere estate at will. 1 *Inst.* 207. *Lit.* 39, 66.

This livery of seisin is no other than the pure *feodal* investiture, or delivery of corporeal possession of the land or tenement, and is necessary to be made upon every grant of an estate of freehold in *hereditaments corporeal*, whether of inheritance or for life only. But in hereditaments *incorporeal* it is impossible to be made, for they are not the object of the senses, and, therefore things *incorporeal* pass by deed only: neither is it necessary in leases for years or other chattel interest. 1 *Inst.* 9. *a.* 49. *a.* 5 *Rep.* 84. 2 *Black.* 311, 313.

Livery of seisin is either in deed, or in law. First, Livery in deed is thus performed. The feoffor, lessor, or his attorney, together with the feoffee, lessee, or his attorney, (for this may as effectually be done, by deputy or attorney, as by the principals themselves in person,) come to the land, or, to the house; and there, in the presence of witnesses, declare the contents of the feoffment or lease, on which livery is to be made. And then the feoffor, if it be of land, doth deliver to the feoffee, all other persons being out of the ground, a clod or turf, or a twig or bough there growing, with words to this effect; "I deliver these to you in the name of seisin of all the lands and tenements contained in this deed." But if it be of a house, the feoffor must take the ring, or latch of the door, the house being quite empty, and deliver it to the feoffee in the same form; and then the feoffee must enter alone, and shut to the door, and then open it, and let in the others (*Co. Litt.* 48. *West. Symb.* 251.) If the conveyance or feoffment be of divers lands, lying scattered in one and the same county, then in the feoffor's possession, livery of seisin, of any parcel, in the name of the rest, sufficeth for all (*Litt. s.* 414.); but if they be in several counties, there must be as many liveries as there are counties. For, if the title to these lands comes to be disputed, there must be as many trials as there are counties, and the jury of one county are no judges of the notoriety of a fact in another. 2 *Black.* 315.

Also, if the lands be out on lease, though all lie in the same county, there must be as many liveries as there are tenants: because no livery can be made in this case, but by the consent of the particular tenant; and the consent of one will not bind the rest (*Dyer* 18.) And in all these cases it is prudent, and usual, to endorse the livery of seisin on the back of the deed, specifying the manner, place, and time of making it; together with the names of the witnesses. 2 *Black.* 316.

Secondly. Livery in law is, where the same is not made on the land, but in sight of it only; the feoffor saying to the feoffee, "I give you yonder land, enter, and take possession." Here, if the feoffee enters during the life of the feoffor, it is a good livery, but not otherwise; unless he dares not enter, through fear of his life or bodily harm: and then his continual claim, made yearly, in due form of law, as near as possible to the lands (*Litt. s.* 421, &c.), will suffice without an entry (*Co. Litt.* 48.) This livery in law cannot, however, be given or received by attorney, but only by the parties themselves. (*Co. Litt.* 52.)

FERÆ NATURÆ, beasts and birds that are *of a wild nature*, in opposition to the tame; such as hares, foxes, wild geese, and the like, and wherein no man can claim a property, are deemed to be *feræ naturæ*. *Cowel. Blount.*

And of these no man can commit felony, unless they are so confined that the owner can take them whenever he pleases; or if they are not confined, unless they are reduced to tameness and known by the thief to be so. 1 *Hawk. b.* 1. *c.* 33. *s.* 26.

FERDFARE, (from the Sax. *fyrd* and *fare iter*) *significat quietantium eundi in exercitum.* *Fleta, lib.* 1. *c.* 47. *Cowel. Blount.*

FERDWIT, (Sax. *ferd exercitus*, & *wite pœna*) was used for being quit of manslaughter, committed in the army. *Fleta, lib.* 1. It is rather a fine imposed on persons for not going forth in a military expedition; to which duty all persons, who held land, were of necessity obliged: and a neglect or omission of this common service to the public, was punished with a pecuniary mulct called the *ferdwite*. *Cowel. Blount.*

FERIAL DAYS, (*dies feriales, feriæ*) according to the Latin holy days; but in the stat. 27 *H.* 6. *c.* 5. taken for working days. *Cowel. Blount.*

FERLINGATA TERRÆ, a quarter or fourth part of a yard-land. *Ibid.*

FERM, (*firma*) a house and land let by lease. See *Farm.*

FERMARY, (from the Sax. *feorme, victus*) is an hospital; and we read of friers of the firmary. *Cowel. Blount.*

FERMISONA, the winter season of killing deer; as *tempus pinguedinis* is the summer season. *Ibid.*

FERNIGO, a piece of waste ground where fern grows. *Ibid.*

FERRAMENTUM, *ferramenta*, the iron tools or instruments of a mill. *Ibid.*

FERRANDUS, an iron collar, particularly applied to horses, which we at this time call an iron gray. *Ibid.*

FERRY. A liberty by prescription of the king's grant, to have a boat for passage upon a river, for carriage of horses and men for reasonable toll: it is usually to cross a large river, and is no more than a common highway. *Terms de Ley.* 3 *Mod. Rep.* 294.

A ferry is in respect of the landing-place, and not of the water, for the water may be free to any one, but the landing place is the property of the owner of the soil, and in every ferry, the land on both sides of the water ought to belong to the owner of the ferry, or otherwise he cannot land on the other part. *Savill* 11.

FERSPEKEN, to speak suddenly. *Cowel. Blount.*

FESTA IN CAPPIS, were some grand holy-days, on which the whole choirs and cathedrals wore caps. *Ibid.*

FESTINGMEN, the Sax. *festinman* signifies a surety or pledge; and to be free of *festingmen*, was probably to be free of frank-pledge, and not bound for any man's forth-coming, who should transgress the law. *Ibid.*

FESTING-PENNY, earnest given to servants when hired or retained in service. *Ibid.*

FESTUM, a feat, i. e. *festum S. Michaelis*, the feast of St. Michael, &c. *Ibid.*

FESTUM STULTORUM, the feast of fools. See *Caput Anni.*

FEUD, (*feida*) in the German *guerram*, Lat. *bellum;* and according to Lambard, *capitales inimicitias*, and *feud deadly* in Scotland is a combination of kindred for revenging the death of any of their blood against the killer and all his race; or any other great enemy.

FEUDAL and FEUDARY. See *Feudal* and *Feodary.*

FEUDBOTE, the recompense for engaging in a feud, and the damages consequent; in ancient times, when the kindred engaged in their kinsman's quarrel. *Cowel. Blount.*

FEUDS, (*feoda*) Estates in lands were originally at will, and then they were called *munera;* afterwards they were for life, and then they were termed *beneficia*, and for that reason the livings of clergymen are so called at this day; and afterwards they were made hereditary, when they were called *feoda*, and in our law fee-simple. *Rel. Spel.* 9. And feuds are called by various names according to their respective natures, as

Feudum antiquum, a feud descending to a son, from his ancestors. 2 *Black.* 212. 221.

Feudum apertum, a feud resulting back again to the lord of the fee, where the blood of the person last seised in fee-simple, is utterly extinct and gone. 2 *Black.* 245.

Feudum honorarium, (and *Feudum individuum*) an honorary feud, or title of nobility, not of a divisible nature, and descendible to the eldest son, in exclusion of all the rest. 2 *Black.* 56, 7. 215.

Feudum improprium, an improper or derivative feud; and *feoda impropria* are all such feuds as do not fall within the description of *feoda propria.* 2 *Black.* 58.

Feudum maternum, a feud descending to the son from the mother. 2 *Black.* 212, 243.

Feudum novum, a feud newly acquired by the son, to which in ancient times only the descendants from his body could succeed, by the known maxim of the early feodal constitutions. 2 *Black.* 212, 221.

Feudum novum, held *ut antiquum*: descendible in the same manner as a *feudum novum. Ibid.*

Feudum paternum, a feud descendible from father to son, &c. 2 *Black.* 243.

Feudum proprium, a proper feud, distinguished from an improper, which are the two grand and general divisions. 2 *Black.* 58.

FIAT, signifies the order or warrant of some judge for making out and allowing certain processes, &c.

FIAT JUSTITIA. On a petition to the king, for his warrant to bring a writ of error in parliament, he writes on the top of the petition *fiat justitia*, and then the writ of error is made out, &c. And when the king is petitioned to redress a wrong, he indorses upon the petition, Let right be done the party. *Dyer* 385. *Stamf. Prerog. Reg.* 22.

FICTION OF LAW, (*Fictio juris*) is allowed for the furtherance of justice in several cases: but it must be framed according to the rules of law; not what is imaginable in the conceptions of man; and there ought to be equity and possibility in every legal fiction. Thus the seisin of the conusee in a FINE is but a fiction in our law, it being an invented form of conveyance only. Also a COMMON RECOVERY is *fictio juris*, a formal act or device by consent, to bar estates tail, remainders, &c. And so is THE LESSOR of the plaintiff in ejectment.

By fiction of law, also a bond made beyond sea, or personal injury done there, may be pleaded to be made in the place where made, or done, as at *Calcutta* in the East Indies with a viz. to wit, at Islington in the county of Middlesex, &c. to try the same here; without which it cannot be done.

FICTITIOUS PLAINTIFF. Suing another in the name of a *fictitious* plaintiff, either one not in being at all, or one who is ignorant of the suit, is considered as an offence of great malignity and audaciousness. This offence, if committed in any of the king's superior courts, is left, as a high contempt, to be punished at their discretion; but in courts of a lower degree, where the crime is equally pernicious, but the authority of the judges not equally extensive, it is directed by stat. 8 *Eliz.* c. 2, to be punished by six months imprisonment, and treble damages to the party injured. 4 *Black.* 134.

FIDEI COMMISSUM. This in the civil law was very similar in its nature to that of our uses and trusts: it was usually created by will, and was the disposal of an inheritance to *one in confidence that he should convey it*, or dispose of the profits *at the will of an other*, and *Inst.* 2, *tit.* 23. 2 *Black.* 327.

FIDEM MENTIRI, is when a tenant does not keep that fealty which he has sworn to the lord. *Leg. H.* 1. *c.* 53.

FIEF, which we call fee, is in other countries the contrary to chattels, and in Germany certain districts or territories are called fiefs, where there are fiefs of the empire. 2 *Black.* 45.

FIERI FACIAS, is a judicial writ, given by the statute of *Westm.* 2, 13 *Ed.* 1, that lies where judgment is had for debt, or damages recovered in the King's courts, by which writ the sheriff is commanded to levy the debt and damages of the goods and chattels of the defendant, &c. *Old. Nat. Br.* 152.

It is so called because the words of the writ directed to the sheriff are "*Quod fieri facias de bonis & catallis*, &c." *Co. Lit.* 290. *b.* See EXECUTION.

FIFTEENTHS were temporary aids anciently issuing out of personal property, and granted to the king by parliament. Originally the amount of these taxes was uncertain, being levied by assessments, new made at every fresh grant of the Commons; but it was at length reduced to a certainty in the 8th year of *Ed.* 3, when by virtue of the king's commission new taxations were made of every township, borough and city in the kingdom, and recorded in the Exchequer: after which, when of late years the Commons granted the king a fifteenth, every parish in England immediately knew their proportion of it, viz. the same identical sum that was assessed by the same aid in 8 *Ed.* 3, and then raised it by a rate among themselves, and returned it into the exchequer. 1 *Black.* 308.

FIGHTING AND QUARRELING. See *Assault.*

FIGHTWITE, (Sax.) a mulct for fighting, or making a quarrel to the disturbance of the peace. *Cowel. Blount.*

FIGURES. The year of the reign of the king is enough; and the stat. 6 *Geo.* 2, *c.* 14, allows the expressing numbers by figures in all writs, &c. pleadings, rules, orders and indictments, in courts of justice, as have been commonly used in the said courts.

FILACER, or FILIZER, (*filizarius*, from the Lat. *filum*) is an officer of the court of common pleas, called by this name, because he files those writs whereon he makes out process. He enters all appearances and special bails, and by an order of court 14 *Jac.* 1, his proceedings are limited to all matters before appearance, and the prothonotaries to all after.

FILE, (*filacium*) a thread, string, or wire, upon which writs and other exhibits in courts and offices are fastened or filed for the more safe keeping and ready turning to the same. A file is a record of the court; and the filing of process of a court, makes it a record of it. 1 *Lil.* 112.

FIELD-ALE or FILKDALE; a kind of drinking in the field, by bailiffs of hundreds at the expence of the inhabitants, long since prohibited. *Bract.* 4 *Inst.* 307.

FILIAL PORTION, the *pars rationabilis*, or reasonable part of an intestate's effects.

FILICETUM, signifies a ferny ground. *Co. Lit.* 4. *Cowel. Blount.*

FILIOLUS, a little son, also a godson. *Cowel. Blount.*

FILUM AQUÆ, is the thread or middle of the stream which divides counties, townships, parishes, manors, liberties, or the like; and in general the owners of the soil on each side are entitled to the soil, *co-operta aqua*, and the right of fishing, *usque ad medium filum aquæ.*

FINAL DECREE. See EQUITY.

FINAL JUDGMENT. See INQUIRY, *writ of.*

FINDERS, the same with those now called searchers, for the discovery of goods imported or exported, without custom.

FINE, (*finis*) is a final agreement, or, conveyance upon record, for the settling and assuring of lands and tenements acknowledged in the king's courts by the cognizor to be the right of the cognizee.

And it is sometimes said to be a feoffment of record, *Co. Lit.* 50, though it might, as *Blackstone* very justly observes, with more accuracy be called an acknowledgment of a feoffment on record: by which is to be understood, that it has the same force and effect with a feoffment, in the conveying and assuring of lands: though it is one of those methods of transferring estates of freehold by the common law, in which livery of seisin is not necessary to be actually given; the supposition and acknowledgment thereof in a court of record, however fictitious, inducing an equal notoriety. But, more particularly, a fine may be described to be an amicable composition or agreement of a suit, either actual or fictitious, by leave of the king or his justices; whereby the lands in question become, or are acknowleged to be, the right of one of the parties. *Co. Lit.* 129. In its original it was founded on an actual suit, commenced at law for recovery of the possession of land or other hereditaments; and the possession thus gained by such composition was found to be so sure and effectual that fictitious actions were, and continue to be, every day commenced for the sake of obtaining the same security. 2 *Black.* 348.

A fine is so called because it puts an end, not only to the suit thus commenced, but also to all other suits and controversies concerning the same matter. 2 *Rol. Abr.* 13. And is of equal antiquity with the first rudiments of the law itself. *Glanv. l.* 8. *c.* 1. *Bract. l.* 5. *t.* 5. *c.* 28. *Plowd.* 369. 2 *Black.* 348.

The manner in which they are to be levied, or carried on according to *Stat.* 18 *Ed.* 1, *de modo levandi fines*, is as follows:

1. The party, to whom the land is to be conveyed or assured, commences an action or suit at law against the other, generally an action of covenant, by suing out a writ of *præcipe*, called a writ of covenant: the foundation of which is a supposed agreement or covenant, that the one shall convey the lands to the other; on the breach of which agreement the action is brought.—On this writ there is due to the king, by antient prerogative, a primer or pre-fine or a noble for every five marks of land sued for; that is, one tenth of the annual value. 2 *Inst.* 511. The suit being thus commenced, then follows,

2. The *licentia concordandi*, or leave to agree the suit. For, as soon as the action is brought, the defendant, knowing himself to be in the wrong, is supposed to make overtures of peace and accommodation to the plaintiff. Who, accepting them, but having, upon suing out the writ, given pledges to prosecute his suit, which he endangers if he now deserts it without licence, he therefore applies to the court for leave to make the matter up. This leave is readily granted, but for it, there is also another fine due to the king by his prerogative, which is an antient revenue of the crown, and is called the king's silver, or sometimes the post fine, with respect to the primer or pre-fine before mentioned. And it is as much as the pre-fine, and half as much more, or ten shillings for every five marks of land; that is, three twentieths of the supposed annual value. 5 *Rep.* 39. 2 *Inst.* 511. *Stat.* 32 *Geo.* 2. *c.* 14. 2 *Black.* 349.

3. Next comes the concord, or agreement itself, after leave obtained from the court; which is usually an acknowledgment from the deforciants (or those who keep the other out of possession) that the lands in question are the right of the complainant. And from this acknowledgment, or recognition of right, the party levying the fine is called the cognizor, and he to whom it is levied the cognizee. This acknowledgment must be made either openly in the court of common pleas, or before the lord chief justice of that court; or else before one of the judges of that court, or two or more commissioners in the country, empowered by a special authority called a writ of *dedimus potestatem*; which judges and commissioners are bound by statute 18 *Edw.* 1, *st.* 4. to take care that the cognizors be of full age, sound memory, and out of prison. If there be any feme covert among the cognizors, she is privately examined whether she does it willingly and freely, or by compulsion of her husband. 2 *Black.* 350.

By these acts all the essential parts of a fine are completed: and, if the cognizor dies the next moment after the fine is acknowledged, provided it be subsequent to the day on which the writ is made returnable, *Comb.* 71, still the fine shall be carried on in all its remaining parts, of which the next is,

4. The note of the fine; which is only an abstract of the writ of covenant, and the concord; naming the parties, the parcels of land, and the agreement. This must be enrolled of record in the proper office, by direction of the statute 5 *Hen.* 4. *c.* 14. *Ibid.*

5. The fifth part is the foot of the fine, or conclusion of it: which includes the whole matter, reciting the parties, day, year, and place, and before whom it was acknowledged or levied. Of this there are indentures made, or engrossed, at the chirographer's office, and delivered to the cognizor and the cognizee; usually beginning thus, "*hæc est finalis concordia*, this is "the final agreement," and then reciting the whole proceeding at length. And thus the fine is completely levied at common law.

By several statutes still more solemnities are superadded, in order to render the fine more universally public, and less liable to be levied by fraud or covin. And, first, by 27 *Ed.* 1. *c.* 1, the note of the fine shall be openly read in the court of common pleas, at two several days in one week, and during such reading all pleas shall cease. By 5 *Hen.* 4. *c.* 14, and 23 *Eliz. c.* 3, all the proceedings on fines, either at the time of acknowledgment, or previous, or subsequent thereto, shall be enrolled of record in the court of common pleas. By 1 *Ric.* 3. *c.* 7, confirmed and enforced by 4 *Hen.* 7. *c.* 24, the fine, after engrossment, shall be openly read and proclaimed in court (during which all pleas shall cease) sixteen times; *viz.* four times in the term in which it is made, and four times in each of the three succeeding terms; which is reduced to once in each term by 31 *Eliz. c.* 2, and these proclamations are indorsed on the back of the record. It is also enacted by 23 *Eliz. c.* 3, that the chirographer of fines shall every term write out a table of the fines levied in each county in that term, and shall affix them in some open part of the court of common pleas all the next term: and shall also deliver the contents of such table to the sheriff of every county, who shall at the next assizes fix the same in some open place in the court, for the more public notoriety of the fine. 2 *Black.* 352.

2. Fines, thus levied, are of four kinds. 1. What in our law French is called a fine "SUR COGNIZANCE DE DROIT, COME CEO QUE "IL AD DE SON DONE," or, a fine upon acknowledgment of the right of the cognizee, as that which he hath of the gift of the cognizor. This is the best and surest kind of fine; for thereby the deforciant, in order

to keep his covenant with the plaintiff, of conveying to him the lands in question, and at the same time to avoid the formality of an actual feoffment and livery, acknowledges in court a former feoffment, or gift in possession, to have been made by him to the plaintiff. This fine is therefore said to be a feoffment of record; the livery, thus acknowledged in court, being equivalent to an actual livery: so that this assurance is rather a confession of a former conveyance, than a conveyance now originally made; for the deforciant, or cognizor, acknowledges, *cognoscit*, the right to be in the plaintiff, or cognizee, as that which he hath *de son done*, of the proper gift of himself, the cognizor. 2. A fine "SUR COGNIZANCE DE DROIT TANTUM," or, upon acknowledgement of the right merely; not with the circumstance of a preceding gift from the cognizor. This is commonly used to pass a reversionary interest, which is in the cognizor. For of such reversions there can be no feoffment, or donation with livery, supposed; as the possession during the particular estate belongs to a third person. *Moor.* 629. It is worded in this manner: "that the cognizor "acknowledges the right to be in the cogni-"zee; and grants for himself and his heirs, "that the reversion, after the particular "estate determines, shall go to the cogni-"zee." 3. A fine "SUR CONCESSIT" is where the cognizor, in order to make an end of disputes, though he acknowledges no precedent right, yet grants to the cognizee an estate *de novo*, usually for life or years, by way of supposed composition. And this may be done reserving a rent, or the like: for it operates as a new grant. *West. Symb. p.* 2. 95. 4. A fine, "SUR DONE, GRANT, ET RENDER," is a double fine, comprehending the fine *sur cognizance de droit come ceo*, &c. and the fine *sur concessit*: and may be used to create particular limitations of estate: whereas the fine *sur cognizance de droit come ceo*, &c. conveys nothing but an absolute estate, either of inheritance or at least of freehold. *Salk.* 340. In this last species of fine, the cognizee, after the right is acknowledged to be in him, grants back again, or renders to the cognizor, or perhaps to a stranger, some other estate in the premises. But, in general, the first species of fine, *sur cognizance de droit come ceo*, &c. is the most used, as it conveys a clean and absolute freehold, and gives the cognizee a seisin in law, without any actual livery; and is therefore called a fine, executed, whereas the others are but executory. 2 *Black.* 352.

The force and effect of a fine.]—These principally depend, at this day, on the common law, and the two statutes, 4 *Hen.* 7. *c.* 24, and 32 *Hen.* 8. *c.* 36. The antient common law, with respect to this point, is very forcibly declared by the statute 18 *Edw.* 3, in these words: "And the reason "why such solemnity is required in the "passing of a fine, is this; because the "fine is so high a bar, and of so great "force, and of a nature so powerful in it-"self, that it precludes not only those "which are parties and privies to the fine, "and their heirs, but all other persons in "the world, who are of full age, out of "prison, of sound memory, and within "the four seas, the day of the fine levied; "unless they put in their claim on the "foot, *Lit. s.* 441, of the fine within a year "and a day." But this doctrine, of barring the right by non-claim, was abolished for a time by a statute made in 34 *Edw.* 3. *c.* 16, which admitted persons to claim, and falsify a fine, at any indefinite distance: whereby, as sir Edward Coke observes, 2 *Inst.* 518, great contention arose, and few men were sure of their possessions, till the parliament held 4 *Hen.* 7. *c.* 24, reformed that mischief, and excellently moderated between the latitude given by the statute and the rigour of the common law. For the statute, then made, restored the doctrine of non-claim; but extended the time of claim. So that now, by that statute, the right of all strangers whatsoever is bound, unless they make claim, by way of action or lawful entry, not within one year and a day, as by the common law, but within five years after proclamations made: except feme-coverts, infants, prisoners, persons beyond the seas, and such as are not of sane mind; who have five years allowed to them and their heirs, after the death of their husbands, their attaining full age, recovering their liberty, returning into England, or being restored to their right mind. 2 *Black.* 354.

And this is the chief use and excellence of a fine, that it confirms and secures a suspicious title, and puts an end to all litigation after five years. Other conveyances and assurances admit an entry to be made upon the estate within twenty years, and in some instances, the right to be disputed in a real action for sixty years afterwards. *Harg. Co. Lit.* 121. *a. n.* 1.

It seems to have been the intention of that politic prince, king *Henry* 7, to have covertly by this statute extended fines to have been a bar of estates-tail, in order to unfetter the more easily the estates of his powerful nobility, and lay them more open to alienations; being well aware that power will always accompany property. But doubts having arisen whether they could, by mere implication, be adjudged a sufficient bar, (which they were expressly declared not to be by the statute *de donis*,) the statute 32 *Hen.* 8. *c.* 36, was thereupon made; which removes all difficulties, by declaring that a fine levied by any person of full age, to whom or to whose ancestors lands have been entailed, shall be a perpetual bar to them and their heirs claiming by force of such entail; unless the fine be levied by a woman after the death of her husband, of lands which were, by the gift of him or his ancestors, assigned to her in tail for her jointure, see stat. 11 *Hen.* 7, *c.* 20; or unless it be of lands entailed by act of parliament or letters patent, and whereof the reversion belongs to the crown. 2 *Black.* 355.

From this view of the common law, regulated by these statutes, it appears that a fine is a solemn conveyance on record from the cognizor to the cognizee, and that the persons bound by a fine are parties, privies, and strangers. *Ibid.*

The parties are either the cognizors or cognizees, and these are immediately concluded by the fine, and barred of any latent right they might have, even though under the legal impediment of coverture. And indeed, as this is almost the only act that a feme covert, or married woman, is permitted by law to do, (and that because she is privately examined as to her voluntary consent, which removes the general suspicion of compulsion by her husband,) it is therefore the usual and almost the only safe method, whereby she can join in the sale, settlement, or encumbrance, of any estate. *Ibid.*

Thus a wife may join her husband in either a fine or recovery to convey her own estate and inheritance, or an estate settled upon her by her husband as her jointure, or to convey the husband's estates discharged of dower. 1 *Cru.* 99. 2 *Cru.* 143. *Pig.* 123. But if a jointress after her husband's death levies a fine, or suffers a recovery without the consent of the heir, or the next person entitled to an estate of inheritance, the fine or recovery is void, and is also a forfeiture of her estate. 11 *Hen.* 7. *c.* 20. *Pig.* 75.

Privies to a fine are such as are any way related to the parties who levy the fine, and claim under them by any right of blood, or other right of representation; such as are the heirs general of the cognizor, the issue in tail since the statute of Henry the eighth, the vendee, the devisee, and all others who must make title by the persons who levied the fine. For the act of the ancestor shall bind the heir, and the act of the principal his substitute, or such as claim under any conveyance made by him subsequent to the fine so levied. 3 *Rep.* 83. 2 *Black.* 355.

Strangers to a fine are all other persons in the world, except only parties and privies. And these are also bound by a fine, unless within five years after proclamations made, they interpose their claim; provided they are under no legal impediments, and have then a present interest in the estate. The impediments, as hath before been said, are coverture, infancy, imprisonment, insanity, and absence beyond sea; and persons, who are thus incapacitated to prosecute their rights, have five years allowed them to put in their claims after such impediments are removed. Persons also that have not a present but a future interest only, as those in remainder or reversion, have five years allowed them to claim in, from the time that such right accrues. *Co. Lit.* 372. And if within that time they neglect to claim, or (by stat. 4 *Ann. c.* 16.) if they do not bring an action to try the right, within one year after making such claim, and prosecute the same with effect, all persons whatsoever are barred of whatever right they may have, by force of the statute of non-claim. 2 *Black.* 356.

But in order to make a fine of any avail at all, it is necessary that the parties should have some interest or estate in the lands to be affected by it; else it were possible that two strangers, by a mere confederacy, might without any risk, defraud the owners by levying fines of their lands; for if the attempt be discovered they can be no sufferers but must only remain in *statu quo*; whereas if a tenant for life levies a fine, it is an absolute forfeiture of his estate to the remainder-man or reversioner, *Co. Lit.* 251. if claimed in proper time. It is not therefore to be supposed that such tenants will frequently run so great a hazard; but if they do, and the claim is not duly made within five years after their respective terms expire, 2 *Lev.* 52, the estate is for ever barred by it. Yet where a stranger, whose presumption cannot be thus punished, officiously interferes in an estate which in no wise belongs to him, his fine is of no effect, and may at any time be set aside (unless by such as are parties or privies thereunto,) *Hob.* 334, by pleading that "*partes finis nihil habuerunt.*" And, even if a tenant for years, who hath only a chattel interest, and no freehold in the land, levies a fine, it operates nothing, but is liable to be defeated by the same plea, 5 *Rep.* 123. *Hardr.* 401. Wherefore, when a lessee for years is disposed to levy a fine, *it is usual for him to make a feoffment first,* to displace the estate of the reversioner, and create a new freehold by disseisin. *Hard.* 402. 2 *Lev.* 52. This conveyance, or assurance by fine, not only like other conveyances, binds the grantor himself, and his heirs, but also all mankind, whether concerned in the transfer or no, if they fail to put in their claims within the time allotted by law. 2 *Black.* 357.

And it is not necessary to be in possession of the freehold in order to levy a fine; but if any one entitled to the inheritance, or to a remainder in tail, levies a fine, it will bar his issue and all heirs who derive their title through him, *Hob.* 333. But a fine by tenant in tail does not affect subsequent remainders, but it creates a base or qualified fee, determinable upon the failure of the issue of the person to whom the estate was granted in tail; upon which event the remainder-man may enter. If tenant in tail, with an immediate reversion in fee, levies a fine, the base fee merges in the reversion, which will become liable to all the incumbrances of the ancestors, from whom the estate-tail descended; as judgments, recognizances, and such leases as are void with respect to the issue in tail. 5 *T. R.* 108. 1 *Cru.* 274. And a recovery suffered by any tenant in tail lets in all the incumbrances created by himself, which were defeasible by the issue in tail, and after the recovery they will follow the lands in the hands of a *bona fide* purchasor. *Pig.* 120. 2 *Cru.* 287.

—— Fine also signifies a sum of money paid for the grant of lands, &c. by lease, or on the admission to a copyhold interest. Fine also signifies that pecuniary imposition or punishment which may be levied or inflicted, for an offence committed against the king and his laws.

FINE ADNULLANDO LEVATO TENEMENTO QUOD FUIT DE ANTIQUO DOMINICO, a writ anciently directed to the justices of C. B. for disannulling a fine levied of lands in antient demesne, to the prejudice of the lord. *Reg. Orig.* 15. *Cowel. Blount.*

FINES FOR ALIENATIONS, were fines paid to the king by his tenant in chief, for licence to alien their lands according to the stat. 1 *Ed.* 3. *c.* 12. taken away by stat. 12 *Car.* 2. *c.* 24.

FINES LE ROY, are all fines to the king. *New Nat. Br.* 212.

FINE NON CAPIENDO PRO PULCHRE PLACITANDO, a writ anciently used to inhibit officers of courts to take fines for fair pleadings. *Reg. Orig.* 179. *Cowel. Blount.*

FINE CAPIENDO PRO TERRIS, &c. A writ anciently lying where a person upon conviction of any offence by jury, hath his lands and goods taken into the king's hand, and his body is committed to prison; to be remitted his imprisonment, and have his lands and goods re-delivered him, on obtaining favour for a sum of money, &c. *Reg. Orig. fol.* 142. *Cowel. Blount.*

FINE PRO REDISSEISINA CAPIENDA, is a writ that lies for the release of one imprisoned for a *redisseisin*, on payment of a reasonable fine. *Reg. Orig.* 222. *et Ibid.*

FINE FORCE, is where a person is forced to do that which he can no ways help; so that it seems to signify an absolute necessity or constraint not avoidable. *Old Nat. Br.* 68. *Stat.* 35 *H.* 8. *c.* 12. *et Cowel. Blount.*

FINIRE, to fine, or pay a fine upon composition and making satisfaction. *Cowel. Blount.*

FINITIO, death, so called; because *vita finitur morte.* *Cowel. Blount.*

FIRDERINGA, a preparation to go into the army. *Leg. H.* 1. *Cowel. Blount.*

FIRE, negligence of. By stat. 6 *Ann. c.* 31. any servant negligently setting fire to a house or out-house, shall forfeit 100*l.* or be sent to the house of correction for eighteen months.

FIREBARE, (Sax.) a beacon or high tower by the sea-side, wherein are continual lights, either to direct sailors in the night, or to give warning of the approach of an enemy. *Cowel. Blount.*

FIREBOTE, fuel for firing for necessary use, allowed by law, to tenants out of the lands, &c. granted them. See *Estovers. Cowel. Blount.*

FIRMA, victuals or provisions; also rent, &c. *Cowel. Blount.*

FIRMA ALBA, rent of lands let to farm paid in silver, not in provision for the lord's house. See *Alba Firma.*

FIRMA NOCTIS, was a custom or tribute paid towards the entertainment of the king for one night, or the value of it. *Cowel. Blount.*

FIRMAM REGIS, anciently *pro villa regia, seu regis manerio. Spelm. Cowel. Blount.*

FIRMATIO, *firmationis tempus.* Doe season, as opposed to buck season. *Cowel. Blount.*

FIRMURA. Liberty to scour and repair the mill dam, and carry away the soil, &c. *Ib.*

FIRE-ORDEAL. See *Ordeal.*

FIRE-WORKS. No person whatsoever shall make, sell, &c. squibbs, rockets, serpents, &c. or cases, moulds, &c. for making such squibbs, and every such offence shall be adjudged a common nuisance. 9 & 10 *Will.* 3. *c.* 7.

Persons throwing or firing squibbs, &c. or suffering them, &c. to be thrown or fired from their houses incur a penalty of 20*s.* Likewise persons throwing, casting or firing, or aiding or assisting in the throwing, casting or firing of any squibbs, rockets, serpents, or other fire-works, in or into any public street, house, shop, river, highway, road or passage, incur the like penalty of 20*s.* and on non-payment may be committed to the house of correction for one month. But officers of the ordnance may order the making of fire-works, and the Artillery Company of London, or other like society may use them in the exercise of arms. Stat. 9 & 10 *Wil.* 3. *c.* 7.

FIRST-FRUITS, (*primitiæ*) are the profits payable to the king after avoidance of every spiritual living for the first year, according to the valuation thereof in the king's books.

These were originally a part of the papal usurpations over the clergy of this kingdom. But in the reign of Henry VIII. when the papal power was abolished, and the king was declared the head of the church of England, this revenue was annexed to the crown; by stat. 26 *Hen.* 8. *c.* 3. (confirmed by stat. 1 *Eliz. c.* 4.) and a new *valor bene-*

ficiorum was then made, by which the clergy are at present rated.

This stat. of 26 *Hen.* 8. *c.* 3. enacted, that commissioners should be appointed in every diocese, who should certify the value of every ecclesiastical benefice and preferment in the respective dioceses; and according to this valuation, the first-fruits and tenths were to be collected and paid in future. *This valor beneficiorum is what is commonly called the king's books;* a transcript of which is given in Ecton's *Thesaurus*, and Bacon's *Liber Regis.*

By these last-mentioned statutes all vicarages under ten pounds a year, and all rectories under ten marks, are discharged from the payment of first-fruits: and if, in such livings as continue chargeable with this payment, the incumbent lives but half a year, he shall pay only one quarter of his first-fruits; if but one whole year, then half of them; if a year and a half, three quarters; and if two years, then the whole; and not otherwise.* Likewise by the statute 27 *Hen.* 8. *c.* 8. no tenths are to be paid for the first year, for then the first-fruits are due: and by other statutes of queen Anne, in the fifth and sixth years of her reign, if a benefice be under fifty pounds *per annum* clear yearly value, it shall be discharged of the payment of first-fruits and tenths.

These tenths and first-fruits were entirely remitted by queen Anne; but, in a spirit of the truest equity, applied as the superfluities of the larger benefices to make up the deficiencies of the smaller. For to this end she granted her royal charter, which was confirmed by the stat. 2 *Ann. c.* 11. *whereby all the revenue of first-fruits and tenths is* vested in trustees for ever, to form a perpetual fund for the augmentation of poor livings. This is usually called QUEEN ANNE'S BOUNTY. In augmentation of which, in the session of parliament *anno* 49 *Geo.* 3. a sum of 100,000*l.* was voted. See stat. 49 *Geo.* 3. *c.* 128.

These trustees were erected into a corporation, and have authority to make rules and orders for the distribution of this fund. The principal rules they have established are, that the sum to be allowed for each augmentation, shall be 200*l.* to be laid out in land, which shall be annexed for ever to the living; and they shall make this donation, first, to all livings not exceeding 10*l.* a year; then to all livings not above 20*l.*; and so in order, whilst any remain under 50*l.* a year. But when any private benefactor will advance 200*l.* the trustees will give another 200*l.* for the advancement of any living not above 45*l.* a year, though it should not belong to that class of livings which they are then augmenting. 2 *Burn Ec. L.* 260.

FISH and FISHING. By 13 *Ed.* 1. *c.* 47. the waters of Humber, Ouse, Trent, Dun, Air, Derwent, Wherfe, Nid, Yore, Swale, Teese, Tine, and all others where salmon are taken, shall be in defence from Lady-day to Martinmas, young salmon shall not be taken by unlawful nets, nor at mill pools, from the midst of April to St. John the Baptist, the first trespass shall be punished by burning the nets, &c. the second a quarter of a year's imprisonment, and the third a year's imprisonment.

By 13 *Ric.* 2. *c.* 19. young salmons shall not be taken from the middle of April till the 24th of June, nor shall any nets be used to destroy or take the fry or breed of any fish. And the Lone, Wyre, Mersey, Ribble, and waters in Lancashire, shall be in defence as to salmons from Michaelmas to the Purification: on the pains in 13 *Ed.* 1. *c.* 47.

By 17 *Ric.* 2. *c.* 9. the justices of the peace in the country shall be conservators of these acts.

By 1 *Eliz. c.* 17. persons using any net or engine to destroy the fry of fish, or taking salmons or trouts out of season, or salmon shorter than sixteen inches, trout eight, pike ten, barbel twelve; shall forfeit 20*s.* the fish and nets.

None shall fish with any net in any river, but only where the mesh shall be two inches and an half broad, angling excepted; on the like pain; but smelts, loaches, minnows, bull-heads, gudgeons, or eels may be taken in the usual nets, lepes, or other engines, so that no other fish be taken. *Ibid.*

The admiral, mayor of London, and other conservators may determine offences, stewards of leets are to charge the jury to enquire of offences under this act; on pain of 40*s.* and if they conceal any, the penalty is 20*s.* each. *Ibid.*

By 1 *Jac.* 1. *c.* 23. fishermen in the counties of Somerset, Devon, and Cornwall, may enter on the grounds of others, to direct the fishers, and draw fish on shore, and on action brought for the same, may plead the general issue, and recover.

By 13 & 14 *Car.* 2. *c.* 28. from the first of June to the last of November, no person shall fish on the coast of Devon and Cornwall, with drift nets, unless at one league and an half from the shore, on forfeiture thereof, and one month's imprisonment.

Any partner purloining, or taking away any pilchard fish without leave, shall pay treble value, and be sent to the house of correction for three months. And idle or suspicious persons flocking about any pilchard craft, not departing on warning, shall pay five shillings, or be set in the stocks for five hours. *Ibid.*

* The archbishops and bishops have four years allowed for the payment, and shall pay one quarter every year, if they live so long upon the bishoprick; but other dignitaries in the church pay theirs in the same manner as rectors and vicars.

By 10 & 11 *Will.* 3. *c.* 24. mackerel may be sold on Sundays.

By 4 & 5 *Ann. c.* 21. the 4 & 5 *Will. & Mar. c.* 23. for preserving the salmon, and also 13 *Ed.* 1. *c.* 47. shall be put into execution in Southampton and Wilts, and no young salmon shall be destroyed by nets.

Overseers of this act shall be assigned by the justices, who shall enquire after offenders, who are to forfeit not more than 5*l.* nor less than 20*s.* for the first offence, and double for every other.

No person, qualified or not, shall take salmon, until after the 11th of November, (except the owners of such fisheries, by 1 *Geo.* 1. *stat.* 2. *c.* 18.) *Ibid.*

Owners of meadow grounds shall let salmon, got into the dykes, pass into the main rivers again. Owners of mills shall keep open one scuttle in the waste hatch, for the salmon to pass and re-pass and not use nets. Eel pots shall have racks before them. No sea trouts shall be taken in the rivers. None shall keep nets, or the like, other than allowed by 4 *Will. & Mar.* c. 23. and this act shall only extend to Southampton and Wilts. *Ibid.*

By 1 *Geo.* 1. *c.* 18. no unsizable fish shall be offered to sale, namely, bret and turbot, less than sixteen inches long, brill fourteen, codling twelve, plaice eight, and flounders seven, on forfeiture of the same, and 40*s.* *Ibid.*

Owners of fisheries in the counties of Southampton and Wilts, may take salmon from 11th November, to 1 August; but not after 1 August till 12 November following. *Ibid.*

None shall destroy any fry of salmon, nor take any salmon in the Severn, Dee, Teame, Were, Tees, Ribble, Mersey, Dun, Air, Ouse, Swale, Calder, Wharfe, Eure, Derwent, and Trent, between the last day of July and the 12th November, nor after, with unlawful nets, on pain of 5*l.* *Ibid.*

No salmon shall be sent from the said rivers to London, less than six pounds weight each, on forfeiture of the same, and 5*l.*

By 9 *Geo.* 2. *c.* 33. no person shall kill lobsters on the coast of Scotland, between 1 June and 1 September yearly, on pain of 5*l.* *Ibid.*

By 23 *Geo.* 2. *c.* 26. liberty is given to take salmon in the river Ribble, between 1 January and 15 September yearly.

By 15 *Geo.* 3. *c.* 46. no salmon shall be taken in Tweed river between 10th October and 10th January yearly, on penalty of not more than 10*l.* nor less than 40*s.*

And the 37 *Geo.* 3. *c.* 48. gives additional powers to justices of the peace to enforce this act.

By 37 *Geo.* 3. *c.* 95. so much of 1 *Geo.* 1. *c.* 18. as restrains the taking of salmon in the rivers in Southampton and Wilts are repealed, and salmon may be taken between January 1, and September 12; but persons taking such fish between September 12, and January 1, shall be subject to the penalties of 4 *Ann. c.* 21. and persons taking the spawn or fry between 10 March and 30 May, are to forfeit 10*s.* for every quantity taken. Overseers are to be appointed to preserve the fish, and occupiers of mills are to keep their scuttles and hatches open from 11th November to 11th July.

By 43 *Geo.* 3. *c.* lxi. notwithstanding 13 *Ed.* 1. *c.* 47. and 13 *Ric.* 2. *c.* 19. the legal owners of the fisheries in the rivers Teign, Dart, and Plym, in Devon, may take salmon with legal nets in the Teign from 4th March to 4th December, and in the Dart and Plym from 15th February to 15th November, but no bouges or sea trout shall be taken between 29th September and 2d February, nor shall there be any fishing on a Sunday.

By 45 *Geo.* 3. *c.* xxxiii. notwithstanding stat. *Westm.* 1. 13 *Ed.* 1. *stat.* 1. *c.* 47. and stat. 13 *Ric.* 2. *stat.* 1. *c.* 19. it shall be lawful for the legal owners of rivers and waters in Carmarthenshire to take salmon and its species with legal nets between 1st April and 1st November in every year. *s.* 1.

And taking them illegally, or at improper times of the year, is a penalty of not exceeding 10*l.* nor less than 20*s.* recoverable before a justice of peace. *s.* 3.

By 46 *Geo.* 3. *c.* xix. notwithstanding 13 *Ed.* 1. *st.* 1. *c.* 47. and 13 *Ric.* 2. *st.* 1. *c.* 19. the owners and proprietors, and persons lawfully entitled, may take salmon in Milford harbour, and the waters communicating therewith, with legal nets, from 30th April to 1st November, yearly. *s.* 1.

Penalty on persons taking salmon at other times of the year, or purloining or injuring the same with spears or the like, 10*l.* for the first offence, and 20*l.* for the second, *s.* 2. Penalty on taking soles under eight inches long, 40*s.* *s.* 4. Penalty on taking oysters between 30th August and 1st October 10*l.* first offence, and 20*l.* second offence, *s.* 5. Persons found taking, or using engines, refusing to discover themselves, may be seized. *s.* 6.

If any offender shall escape out of the jurisdiction, any justice may indorse the warrant of apprehension or distress, which shall be executed accordingly where the offender or his goods shall be. *s.* 13.

Fishing in private waters.] By 31 *Hen.* 8. *c.* 2. fishing in any pond, moat, or stew, in the day time, without the owner's consent, shall suffer three months imprisonment.

By 9 *Geo.* 1. *c.* 22. to appear with faces blacked or otherwise disguised to steal fish, or to procure by gift or promise of reward, any person to join them in such unlawful act, is felony *without* benefit of clergy.

Also by 5 *Geo.* 3. *c.* 14. the penalty of transportation for 7 years is inflicted on persons stealing or taking fish in any water within a park, paddock, garden, orchard, or yard, and a forfeiture of 5*l.* to the owner of the fishery is made payable by persons taking or destroying (*or attempting to destroy*) any fish in any river, or other water, within any inclosed ground being private property.

FISH-ROYAL, are whale and sturgeon, which the king is entitled to when either thrown on shore or caught near the coasts. *Plowd.* 315. 1 *Black.* 290.

FISHERY, COMMON OF, or COMMON OF PISCARY, is a liberty of fishing in another man's water. 2 *Black.* 34.

FISHERY FREE, is an exclusive right of fishing in a public stream or river: this is a royal franchise, and must be at least as old as the reign of Henry II. no such franchise being grantable by the express provision of *magna charta,* c. 16.

It differs from a common of piscary, in that the free fishery is an exclusive right, the common of piscary is not so, and therefore in a free fishery, a man has a property in the fish before they are caught, in a common of piscary not till afterwards. 2 *Black.* 39.

FISHERY, SEVERAL. He who claims a several fishery, must be, or at least derive his right from, the owner of the soil, which in a free fishery is not requisite. 2 *Black.* 39.

And a subject may have by prescription a right to a several fishery in an arm of the sea. 4 *Ter. Rep.* 437.

And where the lord of the manor hath the soil on both sides the river, it is good evidence that he hath a right of fishing, and it puts the proof upon him who claims *liberam piscariam;* and where the soil belongs to the owners of the land on each side of a private river, each hath a several right of fishery *ad medium filum aquæ.*

FISHERIES, several statutes have been made to regulate the different sea fisheries, and the following is an accurate summary thereof:

——— THE BRITISH FISHERY.] By 31 *Ed.* 3. *stat.* 1. c. 1. no herring shall be bought or sold in the sea till the fishers come into haven, and the ship's cable be drawn to land.

By 3 *Ed.* 3. *st.* 2. *c.* 2. the fishers shall be free to sell their herrings and fish, at the fair of *Great Yarmouth:* there shall be no forestalling: the barons of the cinque ports shall govern the fair there: the hundred of herrings shall be six score, the last 10,000.

By 31 *Ed.* 3. *st.* 1. *c.* 3. the chancellor and treasurer may make orders for the buying and selling stock fish of St. Botolph and salmon of Berwick.

By 31 *Ed.* 3. *st.* 3. *c.* 1. doggers and load ships of Blackney haven shall discharge their fish there.

By 31 *Ed.* 3. *st.* 3. *c.* 1. and 35 *Ed.* 3. the price of dogger fish, and the like, shall be assessed at the beginning of Blackney fair; fish shall not be kept secret to be sold by retail: none shall buy fishing hooks or the like in Norfolk but owners, masters, and mariners of fishing ships, and herrings shall be sold free, and to the first comer.

By 22 *Ed.* 4. *c.* 2. salmons shall be well packed, and the vessel contain, if a butt, eighty-four gallons, and so in proportion, on pain of 6*s.* 8*d.*

The barrel of herrings shall be thirty-two gallons, on pain of 3*s.* 4*d.* the barrel of eels forty-two gallons, on pain of 20*s.* and if mixed, 10*s.* *Ibid.*

Chief officers of cities and boroughs shall appoint searchers to search and guage fish vessels, *Ibid.* who are by 11 *Hen.* 7. *c.* 23. to be paid certain fees for so doing.

By 5 *Eliz.* *c.* 5. no price shall be set or toll taken of sea fish imported if catched by English subjects; but the town of Kingston upon Hull may take 2*s.* 4*d.* for every last of herrings from non-freemen.

By 3 *Jac.* 1. *c.* 12. making any new wear along the sea shore, or within five miles of any haven, or destroying the fry of any fish, is a penalty of 10*l.* and fishing with a drag net under three inches mesh shall forfeit the same, and 10*s.* a time; but this is not to extend to nets of a less mesh for taking herrings, pilchards, and sprats only.

By 15 *Car.* 2. *c.* 7. herrings shall be well packed, and able packers shall be appointed, and sworn by the chief magistrates of towns, on pain of 100*l.*

By 1 *Geo.* 1. *c.* 18. the meshes of nets shall be three inches and an half from knot to knot, nor shall any knot be put behind another, on forfeiture thereof, and 20*l.* except for catching herrings or the like.

By 29 *Geo.* 2. *c.* 23. all inhabitants of Great Britain may freely buy from fishermen and cure white fish in any of the seas or rivers in Scotland or Ireland thereto belonging, and persons obstructing the fishery, or taking any gratuity for liberty of fishing, forfeit 100*l.*

Staves of herring barrels in Scotland, (except those used in the white herring fishery, 30 *Geo.* 2. *c.* 30.) to be half an inch thick throughout, on pain of seizure.

By 30 *Geo.* 2. *c.* 30. such nets may be used in the white herring fishery as are best adapted thereto, so as the like quantity may be carried on board each buss.

Persons employed in the white herring fisheries to have free use of all ports, shores, and the like, below high water mark, and a hundred yards above, on any waste grounds for landing and drying nets, and persons obstructing such use, forfeit 100*l.* *Ibid.*

But this is not to exempt vessels employed in the fisheries from payment of lawful duties in piers or harbours lawfully made. *Ibid.*

By 26 *Geo.* 3. *c.* 81. lastly continued by 39 *Geo.* 3. *c.* 100. (and revived and further continued till March 25, 1809, by 48 *Geo.* 3.

c. 86.) an annual bounty of 20*s.* per ton is granted for seven years, to owners of ships of fifteen tons and upwards, employed in the white herring fishery.

Vessels entitled to the bounty must be decked vessels, built in Great Britain after January 1, 1780, must have on board barrelled, twelve bushels of salt for every last of fish such vessel can hold, and also 250 square yards of netting for every ton, buss measurement, with the customary equipment; not less than five men for the first fifteen tons, and one more for every five after; and so equipt shall clear out of some British port between 1st June and 1st October, and proceed to the fishery, and there continue three months, unless they return sooner with a full cargo of fish. *Ibid.*

No vessel shall be intitled to the bounty, unless it proceeds on the fishery directly from the port to which it belongs. Officers of the customs shall examine vessels and certify particulars to the commissioners. Oath shall be made of the vessel's being to proceed immediately on the fishery, and security given for the faithful conduct of the crew, which is to entitle them to licences for the voyage. *Ibid.*

Officers of the customs, on the return of a ship, shall certify her condition, and oath shall be made, that she has answered to the terms required, which certificate, with the licence, shall be transmitted to the commissioners, who are to order the bounty to be paid by the receiver general. *Ibid.*

Vessels returning with less than the proper number of men, or without a full cargo, shall not be intitled to the bounty. *Ibid.*

There shall be paid for every barrel of herrings, twice packed, and completely cured, landed from a buss, intitled to the bounty of 20*s.* per ton, a bounty of 4*s.* but if the quantity imported exceeds the proportion of two and one half barrels to a ton, only 1*s.* per barrel above that proportion. And the quantity shall be computed while in the state of sea steeks, four barrels of which are to be deemed equal to three of herrings twice packed. *Ibid.*

To boats not intitled to the bounty of 20*s.* per ton, a bounty of 1*s.* per barrel shall be paid. (See Excise, head *Salt.*) Casks containing herrings intitled to bounty, shall be branded. *Ibid.*

The bounties of 4*s.* and 1*s.* per barrel shall be paid as the bounty of 20*s.* per ton. *Ibid.*

To vessels employed in the Deep Sea fishery, additional premiums shall be paid, *viz.* for the greatest quantity of herrings imported in one vessel, between June 1st, and November 31st, *eighty guineas*; for the next greatest quantity *sixty*; for the next *forty*; and for the next *twenty*. *Ibid.*

The duties on fish caught and cured for home consumption shall cease.

If after October 1st, 1786, fish be packed in casks, not branded with the curers names, it shall be forfeited. After June 1st, 1787, the staves of barrels, in which white herrings are packed for exportation, must be half an inch thick, and full bound, or forfeited. *Ibid.*

Persons who have served as seamen or fishermen seven years in the fisheries, shall be intitled to the privileges granted by 22 *Geo.* 2. *c.* 44. which enables mariners and soldiers to exercise trades. *Ibid.*

Fish cured with British salt may be exported from one port to another in the united kingdom, for home consumption. *Ibid.*

Fish may be carried from one port to another in Britain, for exportation, on oath being made, that they were caught in Britain, and cured with home salt. *Ibid.*

Fish so brought coastways for exportation, shall be intitled to the bounties, and shall be subject to the regulations thereof. *Ibid.*

Bounties on exportation of fish carried from England to Scotland, shall be paid by the customs in England, and from Scotland to England in Scotland; on debenture from the officer at the port of exportation. *Ibid.*

Entry shall be made at the port of shipping, of the quantity, and where cured. Officers of the customs shall grant certificate of such entry, which is to be delivered by the master, previous to his landing the fish, on penalty of forfeiture thereof. *Ibid.*

Salt for the curing of fish, taken in the herring season, for home consumption, as well as for curing fish for exportation, may be taken duty free, on entering at the next salt office the quantity, and weighing the same in the presence of an officer, and swearing to the quantity, and that it is intended for curing fish. Entry shall be made at the port of shipping such salt, and bond given; and like entry shall be made at the intended port of relanding it. Officers of the customs shall deliver certificate of entry, which is to cancel the bond. And salt carried coastways, contrary to this act, shall be forfeited, with double its value, besides the duties. *Ibid.*

Salt may henceforward be delivered into the custody of the proprietor on his own bond. Credit shall be given on the back of the bond, for the quantity of salt accounted for; and bonds are exempted from the stamp duties. *Ibid.*

Officers accepting fees shall forfeit treble the value, and be discharged. *Ibid.*

The bounty per barrel shall be paid to the inhabitants of the isle of Man, for herrings caught and cured by them according to the terms of this act; and on exportation thereof they shall be allowed the bounties, to be paid if exported from the isle of Man, as the bounty per barrel is payable there; and if from Great Britain, as the bounty on exportation from thence, and under the like regulations. *Ibid.*

The penalties on officers taking fees shall

extend to the fisheries of the isle of Man. *Ibid.*

Commissioners of customs may add to the salaries of officers, in consideration of the abolition of fees. Persons counterfeiting certificates shall be punished as forgers; and taking false oaths are guilty of perjury. *Ibid.*

If officers suspect fresh fish to have been imported into London, contrary to 1 *Geo.* 1. *c.* 18. 9 *Geo.* 2. *c.* 33. and this act, two justices may summon the parties and determine the complaint. *Ibid.*

By 27 *Geo.* 3. *c.* 10. that part of the clause of the last act which restricts the bounty of 20*s.* per ton, to decked vessels, is repealed, and the said bounty extended to all vessels whatever, built in Great Britain, and employed in the said fishery, agreeable to the said act.

No vessel shall be deemed to have a full cargo, if under the proportion of four barrels of herrings once packed, or three twice packed, for every ton burthen. *Ibid.*

Decked vessels of not less than fifteen tons, shall be intitled to the bounties, if they take in one year the proportion of six barrels of herrings, when cured, for every ton burthen, though they may not have been fitted out with the quantity of salt required by the act. *Ibid.*

An account of the quantity of herrings delivered from vessels not fitted out agreeable to the said act, shall be taken at the port of delivery, and no more than fifty such vessels fitted out in one year from the same port, shall be intitled to the bounty of 20*s.* per ton, which shall be paid to the fifty vessels that shall have taken the greatest quantity, if more than that number should be fitted out. *Ibid.*

By 35 *Geo.* 3. *c.* 56. herrings, or cod, ling, hake, and salmon, sprinkled with salt on landing, may be carried coastways in bulk free of duty; but the cocquet must express that no bounty has been paid on such fish. *s.* 4.

The act in Scotland of 3d session of 1st parliament of queen Anne, relating to ungutted herrings found in casks, is repealed. *s.* 5.

And arrestments in Scotland, in order to attach the bounty in the hands of the commissioners of customs, must specify the names of the vessels. *s.* 6.

By 48 *Geo.* 3. *c.* 110. from and after 1st June, 1809, a bounty of 3*l.* per ton, is to be paid annually to the owners of busses employed in the Deep Sea British white herring fishery, and if a hired buss be employed, the person hiring the same shall be intitled to the bounty as if he were owner. *s.* 1.

No vessel shall be deemed to be so employed unless the nets be attached to the vessel while set, and shall be shot from and hauled back without the use of a small boat, the vessel not being at anchor while they are shot, set, or hauled in, nor unless the herrings taken receive their first cure on board. *s.* 2.

A bounty of two shillings per barrel is to be paid on white herrings taken and cured in the British fishery. *s.* 3.

The admiralty are to appoint a commissioned officer of the navy to be superintendant for the season of the Deep Sea British white herring fishery, at Brassy Sound in Shetland, the place of rendezvous, who is to arrive there before 15th of June. *s.* 8.

The treasury are to appoint officers of the fishery at the places where herrings are caught, the vessels discharge their cargoes, and also at the port of exportation, to overlook the curing, and take proper accounts; which persons must be coopers, skilful in curing and packing herrings. Which officers are to obey the orders of the commissioners for the British fisheries in Scotland. *s.* 10.

No net is to be used that has a mesh of less than one inch from knot to knot. *s.* 12.

Busses to be entitled to the bounty on the tonnage, must have in new barrels sixteen bushels of salt, at least, for every cask of herrings, and as many more new barrels as the vessel can contain, together with 300 square yards of netting for every ton, and the usual materials, and to be manned with ten men, if the vessel shall not exceed 60 tons; if she shall exceed sixty and be under seventy tons, with eleven men; and if of 70 tons or upwards, then with one man more for every ten tons, two of which men may be foreigners, but ships exceeding 100 tons need not have on board more salt, netting, or men than a vessel of 100 tons, nor more than five hundred barrels, nor is the full complement of men required to be on board until arrival at the place of rendezvous. *s.* 13.

The busses must proceed to Brassy Sound before 22d June in each year, and not cast their nets till the 24th, from which day they shall continue to fish on the coast of Great Britain or Ireland till 15th September following, unless they have before that day taken the requisite quantity. *s.* 14.

To obtain the tonnage bounty, the owners must enter the vessel according to her registry, with the particulars of her outfit at the port from whence she is fitted out, to be verified on oath; the owners, or their agent, shall also give bond, with one or more sureties, for fair dealing on the voyage; which done, the proper officer of the fishery is to give the master a licence to proceed on the voyage, and the busses are to be examined at the place of rendezvous. *s.* 15, 16.

The herrings taken every day are to be distinguished by a mark on the barrels in which they are cured. *s.* 17.

Herrings may be transhipped out of one buss into another vessel, previous to 16th of July. *s.* 18.

A buss not arriving at the rendezvous, or not beginning to fish at the time prescribed, is not to lose the benefit of the tonnage bounty, if it be proved that she was prevented by stress of weather. *s*. 19.

The tonnage bounty is not to be paid unless the full number of men were on board during the whole voyage, unless diminished by death, sickness, or actual desertion, *s*. 20, and the master shall keep a regular journal. *s*. 21.

The superintendant on vessel's return, to examine the same, and if there has been any thing culpable on his report, the commissioners of the fishery are to enquire into the same. *s*. 22, 23.

The officer of the fishery at each port is to attend the landing of the herrings and salt, and take an account thereof, and certify the same, who is also to transmit the licence, master's oath, and such certificate to the commissioners of the fishery, who are to give excise debentures for payment of the tonnage bounty; but in case of any omission being made in the journal, the commissioners may make an abatement of the bounty; but no bounty is to be paid at any port other than where there is an officer of the fishery. *s*. 24, 25, 26.

Mariners employed in this fishery are exempt from being impressed. *s*. 27.

Owners of busses entitled to the tonnage bounty are to pay the crew 2*s*. per barrel on the herrings taken and cured by them. *s*. 28.

And there shall be allowed an additional bounty of 1*l*. per ton for the first thirty busses fitted out for, and employed in this fishery, and which shall be entitled to the bounty of 3*l*. per ton. *s*. 31.

Vessels not fitted out for the tonnage bounty, but carrying out salt and stores for the fishery, are to be duly entered, and masters are to keep an account of the quantity cured on board vessels or boats cleared out with salt, which vessels arriving from the fisheries laden with herrings cured with salt carried out in a different vessel are subject to particular regulations, and if landed contrary thereto are to be forfeited. *s*. 31, 32, 33, 34.

Curers having salt stored at the fishery may cure herrings therewith, under certain regulations. *s*. 35.

The bounty of 2*s*. per barrel on white herrings shall not be paid for herrings not taken after 1st June, nor if of a bad quality, or broken, or if not originally gutted, or which were cured in bulk, or otherwise than in barrels, or which having been cured in barrels shall afterwards be laid in bulk, or which shall not be repacked, or being packed, and in all respects well cured, nor unless of certain weights. *s*. 36, 37.

And herrings of such description which are not entitled to the bounty of 2*s*. per barrel produced to the officer in order to obtain the bounty, are to be forfeited. *s*. 38.

White herrings repacked, going coastwise for exportation, to be accompanied with a certificate that they were not repacked before the lapse of fifteen days from the day when first cured. *s*. 39.

White herrings shall not be exported unless packed in barrels of half an inch in thickness at the bulge, or for any foreign port in Europe, unless bound with sixteen hoops of wood or iron, or for any port out of Europe, unless in a new barrel, and with one iron hoop at each end, and subject to other regulations, on pain of forfeiture. *s*. 40, 41.

No coast sufferance, or cocket, or landing sufferance from the customs, shall be required for salt, nets, or materials for the herring fishery, or herrings, salt, or materials from thence. *s*. 42.

Herrings may be cured and packed in half barrels, of sixteen gallons each, two of which shall be equal to one barrel, and be entitled to bounty. *s*. 45.

Boats employed in the herring fishery are to have the name of the place to which they belong, and name of the owners painted thereon, on pain of forfeiture. *s*. 46.

Officers of the fishery may enter warehouses and storehouses of fish-curers by day or by night (but if at night with a constable,) to search. *s*. 47.

Persons wilfully making false oaths, guilty of perjury, *s*. 49; persons fraudulently branding barrels of herrings with marks appointed to be branded by the officers, or falsifying documents, are to forfeit not exceeding 50*l*. or be imprisoned not exceeding six months, and forfeit the barrels and implements, *s*. 50; if the marks are altered or effaced, the barrel, with the herrings, shall be forfeited. *s*. 51.

This act does not repeal the salt act of 38 *Geo*. 3. *c*. 89.—*s*. 51.

And persons resisting the officers of the fishery, are to forfeit 50*l*.

Officers taking any fees other than their salaries, are to forfeit 100*l*. and be incapacitated. *s*. 54.

The commissioners may allow premiums or bounties, in such proportion as they think fit, for fishing herrings in boats exceeding fifteen tons in Scotland, to be paid by the commissioners of excise there, provided the said premiums do not exceed in the whole, in one year, 3000*l*. *s*. 55.

The act to continue until 1st June, 1813. *s*. 61.

Greenland.] By 25 *Car*. 2. *c*. 7. all persons may freely trade into and from Greenland, and those seas, and may take and import whales, oil, and blubber, and may have harponeers, as well as English mariners.

But no English ship shall have the benefit of this act, unless such vessel did proceed from England, or Wales, or Berwick, and was victualled there.

By 4 & 5 *Will*. & *Mar*. *c*. 17. certain persons were incorporated by the name of *The*

Greenland Company, enabled to buy lands and to trade to Greenland.

By 10 *Will.* 3. *c.* 25. the Greenland company may import oil, blubber, and whale fish, custom free.

By 1 *Ann. c.* 16. any person who will adventure to Greenland for whale fishing, shall have all privileges granted to the Greenland company, and no harpooner shall be impressed.

By 26 *Geo.* 3. *c.* 41. (till March 25, 1810, 48 *Geo.* 3. *c.* 20.) British ships going on the whale fishery, must be visited by an officer of the customs, who shall certify the admeasurement to the commissioners. If such certificate proves the ship is fit for the voyage, and if oath is made of the intention to proceed forthwith there, and to import the whale fins, &c. into Great Britain, the commissioners, on security given, may licence the ship.

Ships of 200 tons burthen must have forty fishing lines, forty harpoon irons, four boats, with seven men, including an harpooner, a steersman, and a line manager to each boat, making twenty-eight men, besides a master and surgeon, with six months provision; and larger ships are to have an increase of six men, one boat, ten lines, and ten harpoons for every fifty tons more, with proportionable provisions; and such ships must have one apprentice, and one green man for every thirty-five tons, to be reckoned with the above number of men. *Ibid.*

The officers of the customs, on return of the ship to Great Britain, shall make a report of her condition, and oath shall be made of her not having deviated from the conditions on which the certificate was granted, which documents shall be transmitted to the commissioners, who shall order a bounty of 30*s.* per ton. *Ibid.*

No person shall be entitled to the bounty, unless the ship sails from the port of survey before April 10th, yearly, and continues fishing till August 10th following, unless laden with thirty tons of oil, or blubber in proportion of three to two tons thereof, and one ton and an half of whale fins, if in ships of 300 tons; and so in proportion if of greater or less burthen; or unless forced by unavoidable accident to depart sooner, which shall be verified on oath, and transmitted with the other documents to the commissioners of the customs. *Ibid.*

If a ship ready for sailing by April 10th, is by unavoidable necessity prevented from sailing till April 25th, the bounty may be paid; and the bounties may be paid out of any monies in the hands of the receiver general. *Ibid.*

Ships of 150 tons burthen are entitled to the bounty; but no ship shall be entitled to a larger bounty than for 400 tons, and only for five years from December 25th 1786, and if not employed in the fishery before that day, not longer than for 300 tons. *Ibid.*

Ships of more than 400 tons, or 300 tons, need not be fitted out but as of those burthens to entitle them to the bounty; and no bounty shall be allowed to any ship where a log-book has not been properly kept, which shall be delivered to the collector of the customs, before whom the contents shall be verified on oath. *Ibid.*

If a ship of war is met at sea, the log-book must be produced to the captain, who must make therein a memorandum of the production, and it must likewise be produced to the British consul at any foreign port. *Ibid.*

Ships fitted out from Ireland, agreeable to the regulations of this act, shall be entitled to the bounty. *Ibid.*

The owners may insure the bounty, in case of the loss of the ship. Whale fins may be imported in British ships, duty free; but not unless oath is made that the cargo was caught by the crews of such ships. Persons granting or using false certificates, forfeit 500*l.* *Ibid.*

No harpooner, line manager, or steerer, shall be impressed, but may, when unemployed therein, sail in the colliery trade, on giving security to return the next season; and common seamen shall in like manner be protected, till the end of the season after entry. *Ibid.*

The Greenland seas and Davis's Streights shall be deemed to extend to the latitude of 59° 30′ north, and no farther. *Ibid.*

The commissioners of the customs shall lay before parliament, annually, the amount of the number of ships employed. *Ibid.*

By 29 *Geo.* 3. *c.* 53. any master permitting an apprentice indentured pursuant to 26 *Geo.* 3. *c.* 41. 26 *Geo.* 3. *c.* 50. and 28 *Geo.* 3. *c.* 20. to quit his service before the expiration of his term, shall forfeit 50*l.* unless such apprentice be discharged before a magistrate, or turned over to another master in the said fisheries.

No premium shall be paid under the acts, unless the names of the ships on board which apprentices are bound to serve be inserted in the indentures.

By 39 & 40 *Geo.* 3. *c.* 51. on return of any vessel from the Greenland and Davis's Streights, the blubber may be boiled into oil, and be admitted to entry.

By 46 *Geo.* 3. *c.* 9. (until the signature of preliminary articles of peace, *s.* 2), vessels not provided with the full complement of men at the port of clearance, may proceed to any of the ports in the Forth of Clyde, or in Lough Ryan, or to Lerwick, or Kirkwall, and complete them, who may be landed on their return: but certificates are required of the men taken on board, and oath ..t the men proceeded on the fishery, to entitle the vessel to bounty. *s.* 1.

By 48 *Geo.* 3. *c.* 20. the act 26 *Geo.* 3. *c.* 41. and so much of 29 *Geo.* 3. *c.* 53. as relates to the Greenland seas, and Davis's

Streights, are further continued till March 25th 1810. *s.* 1.

Newfoundland Fishery.] By 2 & 3 *Ed.* 6. *c.* 6. the admiralty shall not exact any fees from fishermen from the voyage to Iceland, Newfoundland, or elsewhere, on pain of treble damages.

By 15 *Car.* 2. *c.* 7. no vessel shall go on a fishing voyage for Iceland and Westmona until the 10th of March, on forfeiture of the ship.

By 15 *Car.* 2. *c.* 16, no toll shall be levied in Newfoundland for any fish of English catching, nor any net cast near any harbour in Newfoundland to take the spawn of poor John, or the like, except for taking of bait only, on forfeiture.

None shall destroy any house, or stage, or utensils of fishing in Newfoundland or Greenland, on pain of double the value. *Ibid.*

By 10 & 11 *Will.* 3. *c.* 25. all the king's subjects shall have free trade to Newfoundland, and no alien shall bait or fish there; none shall throw any annoyance into harbours, or destroy any stage there.

The first fishing ship, entering the harbour in the fishing season, shall be admiral for that time, the second vice-admiral, and so on, and shall see the rules in this act executed. *Ibid.*

Persons possessed of several places shall make their election which to abide in, and give their resolution to any after-comer, in forty-eight hours after demand, and, in case of difference, admirals shall proportion the place. *Ibid.*

No fisherman, or inhabitant of Newfoundland, shall possess any stage until all fishing ships be provided, except they have built them themselves. *Ibid.*

Bye-boat keepers shall not meddle with house or stage belonging to any fishing ships: they shall carry two fresh men in six, and the inhabitants shall employ them; the master of a fishing ship shall carry one fresh man in five, and make oath thereof, and have every fifth man a green man. *Ibid.*

Marks of boats or train vats shall not be obliterated without the owner's consent: standing trees shall not be rinded, nor woods fired, necessary fuel excepted; sayns shall not be annoyed, nor nets, baits, or the like stolen. *Ibid.*

Robberies and capital crimes in Newfoundland may be tried in England. Admirals shall keep a journal, and deliver a copy thereof to the privy council: they shall determine differences between the fishers and inhabitants, with power to appeal to the king's officers. *Ibid.*

The inhabitants shall observe the Lord's day, and not sell any liquors thereon. *Ibid.*

By 26 *Geo.* 3. *c.* 26. certain bounties were granted to ships employed in the Newfoundland fishery, and the same were lastly continued by 41 *Geo.* 3. (u. k.) *c.* 97. and are now expired.

By 41 *Geo.* 3. *c.* 77. salted salmon or codfish may be imported from Newfoundland or the coast of Labrador by British subjects, and shall on certain conditions be allowed a bounty of 3*s.* per quintal or cwt. and such fish may be exported without repayment of the bounty.

By 48 *Geo.* 3. *c.* 20. so much of 43 *Geo.* 3. *c.* 68. as relates to the admission to entry of oil or blubber from Newfoundland is further continued till March 25th 1810. *s.* 2.

And the act 47 *Geo.* 3. *c.* 24. is also continued till March 25th 1810. *s.* 3.

Oyster Fisheries.] The 2 *Geo.* 2. *c.* 19. was made for regulating, well-ordering, and improving the oyster fishery in the river Medway, under the authority of the mayor and citizens of Rochester.

By 31 *Geo.* 3. *c.* 51. persons unlawfully catching oysters or brood within the limits of any fishery, may be prosecuted at the sessions, and punished by fine and imprisonment: but the act is not to extend to the taking of floating fish. *s.* 1, 2.

Justices may issue warrants for apprehending offenders, and, for want of sureties, may commit them till the quarter-sessions. *s.* 3.

Persons found taking, or using engines for taking oysters or brood, refusing to discover themselves, may be seized. *s.* 4.

But no justice is to commit, or require a security from, any person, without a recognizance is entered into to prosecute. *s.* 5.

And persons may be discharged from confinement upon entering into a recognizance of 20*l.* *s.* 6.

This act is not to affect any act in force respecting any particular oyster fishery, or to preclude a prosecution at the common law. *s.* 7, 8.

By 48 *Geo.* 3. *c.* 144. persons stealing oysters or oyster brood from oyster beds shall be guilty of felony, and may be transported for seven years, or imprisoned, and kept to hard labour for three years; but this is not to affect persons claiming a right to take the same away from such oyster beds. *s.* 1, 2.

The parish need not be named in the indictment, and where the county cannot be ascertained, the offence may be stated to be in the county in which the indictment shall be prepared, being within the actual county, or the adjoining county, and justices for towns may act as justices for counties in execution of this act. *s.* 3, 4.

Southern Whale Fishery.] By 48 *Geo.* 3. *c.* 124. premiums are granted to ships fitted out for the Southern whale fishery.

For eight of such ships fitted out between 1st January and 31st December 1809, and between 1st January and 31st December in each of the two succeeding years, which shall sail to the southward of the equator, and there fish, and which shall return before the 1st December in the subsequent year, there shall be paid to each of the eight ships which shall first arrive with the greatest quantity, and not less than twenty tons of oil, or head matter, 300*l.*

And for the four other ships which shall be fitted out, and sail by the aforesaid time, to the southward of 36° of south latitude, and shall there fish and not return until after fourteen calendar months from the day on which they cleared out, but before 31st Dec. in the second year, there shall be paid 400*l.* to each of such ships arriving with the greatest quantity, not less than twenty tons.

And for ten other ships, which shall be fitted out, and sail by the aforesaid time, and shall double Cape Horn, or pass the Streights of Magellan, or double the Cape of Good Hope, and carry on the fishing for four months to the eastward of 105° of east longitude from London, and not return till after the expiration of sixteen months, but before the 31st of Dec. in the second year, there shall be paid to one which shall first arrive with the greatest quantity, not being less than thirty tons, 600*l.* and to each of the other nine ships, with the greatest quantity, not less than thirty tons, 500*l.*

Apprentices who shall not have completed two voyages, and whose age shall not exceed twenty-one years, shall not be impressed, and they shall have special protections granted by the admiralty. *s.* 5.

Ships returning to ports in Ireland are entitled to the same benefits. *s.* 6.

By 35 *Geo.* 3. *c.* 92. the master and three-fourths of the crew of ships fitted out for the Southern whale fishery shall be British subjects; or, if cleared out from Great Britain, foreign protestants, intending to settle in Britain, and taking the oaths. *s.* 7.

No premium to be paid unless there is an apprentice indentured for three years, on board, for every fifty tons burthen. *s.* 8.

Penalty of 50*l.* on masters suffering apprentices to quit their services before the expiration of the term; and no premium is to be allowed, unless the names of vessels in which apprentices are to serve are inserted in indentures. *s.* 9.

Apprentices are to be considered as such for the voyage, though their indentures expire during it. *s.* 10.

No premium to be allowed unless a log-book be regularly kept, and delivered to the collector of the customs at the port of arrival, and verified on oath. *s.* 11.

The log-book to be produced to the captain of any ship of war that may be met with at sea, who shall make therein a memorandum of the protection, and to the British consul at any foreign port for the like purpose. *s.* 12.

Oath to be made that the cargo is the produce of creatures killed by the ship's crew. *s.* 13.

Persons taking part of the cargo of other vessels for the purpose of obtaining the premium, forfeit 500*l.* one moiety to the informer, if information be given within a month after report at the custom-house; and when information has been given, the owners are to pay money due to the masters to the collectors of the customs, and if paid otherwise, to be accountable for the same. *s.* 14.

Produce of whales caught to the northward of the equator, or to the northward of 56° of south latitude, of the quantity to be entitled to the premium. *s.* 15.

Commissioners of the customs may order payment of premiums; but no premium to be paid unless claimed within two months after the crew being mustered inwards. *s.* 16, 17.

Ships are permitted to sail to the east of the Cape of Good Hope, and west of Cape Horn, not sailing to the northward of the equator, nor making more than 51° of east longitude, or 180° west from London, and ships so sailing are to take a licence from the East India company. *s.* 18, 19, 20, 21.

Ships sailing out of their limits, or having improper merchandise on board, liable to the penalties of trading to the East Indies without licence; and if any thing be done contrary to this act, the owners of the ships are not to be entitled to a future licence from the company. *s.* 22, 23.

Ships touching at St. Helena may be examined, and unlicensed goods seized. And certificates are to be delivered to the secretary of the East India company, that no produce of the East Indies has been imported, to entitle to a premium. *s.* 24, 25.

Ships sailing within the limits of the South Sea company must have a licence from the company. *s.* 26.

Ships may be furnished with arms and ammunition, on licence from the admiralty. *s.* 27, 28.

No ship entitled to more than one premium the same season. *s.* 29.

No premium to be allowed for vessels unless certified to have been visited on clearing out, and on their return, not unless registered. *s.* 30, 31.

If water be mixed with oil or matter imported, it shall be forfeited, as well as the claim to the bounty, and in case of dispute, the owner is to prove the purity of the oil. *s.* 32.

The quantity of oil and head matter imported to be ascertained by the officer of the customs, and certified to the commissioners. *s.* 33.

No harpooners, line managers, or boat steerers to be impressed. *s.* 34.

Whale boats are not liable to seizure, of whatever built, if used only in the fishery. *s.* 35.

Persons granting false certificates, to forfeit 500*l.* and be incapacitated, and persons counterfeiting, or using counterfeit certificates knowingly, forfeit 500*l.* *s.* 39.

The penalties are recoverable according to the law of customs. *s.* 40.

By 42 *Geo.* 3. *c.* 77. British-built ships may pass through the Streights of Magellan, or round Cape Horn, and carry on the fisheries in the Pacific Ocean, without licence from the East India or South Sea companies.

And by 43 *Geo.* 3. *c.* 90. having passed 180 degrees of west latitude, may sail to the northward as far as 10 degrees of south latitude, but not further, until they have sailed with 51 degrees of east latitude.

By 43 *Geo.* 3. *c.* 90. ships fitted out, and licensed conformably to 38 *Geo.* 3. *c.* 57. and sailing to the eastward of the Cape of Good Hope, for carrying on the fishing, may sail to the northward as far as 10 degrees of south latitude, but no further northward until they have passed 115 degrees of east latitude, and then to 1 degree north latitude, and no further until they have passed to the eastward of 180 degrees of east latitude.

FISHGARTH, a dam or wear in a river, made for the taking of fish. *Cowel. Blount.*

FLACO, a place covered with standing water. *Ibid.*

FLECTA, a feathered or fledged arrow. *Ibid.*

FLEDWITE or FLIGHTWITE, (from the Sax. *flyth fuga, et wite, mulcta*) in ancient law signifies a discharge from amerciaments, where a person having been a fugitive, comes to the peace of our lord the king of his own accord, or with licence. *Rastal. Cowel. Blount.*

FLEET, (Sax. *fleot,* i. e. *flota,* a place of running-water, where the tide or float comes up) a prison in London, so called from a river or ditch that was formerly there, on the side whereof it stood. To this prison men amenable to the courts of chancery, common pleas, and exchequer, are liable to be committed for defaults or contempts.

FLEM, *flema,* (from the Sax. *flean,* to kill or slay) was anciently considered an outlaw. *Cowel. Blount.*

FLEMENEFRIT, FLEMENESTRINTHE, FLYMENAFRYNTHE, the receiving or relieving of a fugitive or outlaw. *Ibid.*

FLEMESWITE, (Sax.) *habere catalla fugitivorum.* *Fleta, lib.* 1. *c.* 47.

FLIGHERS, masts for ships. *Cowel. Blount.*

FLIGHT, implies guilt: and in felony, if found by the jury, incurs a forfeiture of goods: but the return of flight by the present administration of our code of criminal jurisprudence is not required.

FLOOD-MARK, *high-water mark.* The mark which the sea makes on the shore, at flowing water and the highest tide.

FLORENCE, an ancient piece of English gold coin, made current at six shillings each. *Cowel, Blount.*

FLORIN, a foreign coin, in Spain 4*s.* 4*d*, Germany, 3*s.* 4*d.* and Holland 2*s.* *Ibid.*

FLOTA NAVIUM, a fleet of ships. *Ibid.*

FLOTAGES, are such things as by accident swim on the top of great rivers; the word is sometimes used in the commissions of water bailiffs. *Ibid.*

FLOTSAM, is where a ship is sunk or cast away, and the goods are found floating upon the sea. 5 *Rep.* 106. The king, or the lord of the manor as his grantee, shall have *flotsam,* if the owners of the goods are not known; but not otherwise. *F. N. B.* 122. And where the proprietor of the goods may be known, they have a year and a day to claim *flotsam.* 1 *Keb.* 657. See title *Wreck.*

FOCAGE, (*focagium*) the same with house-bote or fire-bote. *Cowel. Blount.*

FOCAL, a right of taking wood for firing, *Ibid.*

FODER, (Sax. *foda,* i. e. *alimentum*) any kind of sustenance for horses, or other cattle: and in feudal times it was the prerogative of the prince, to be provided with corn and other meat for his horses, by his subjects, in his wars or other expeditions. *Cowel. Blount.*

FODERTORIUM, provision or fodder, to be paid by custom to the king's purveyor. *Ibid.*

FOENUS NAUTICUM. Where money was lent to a merchant to be employed in a beneficial trade, with condition to be repaid, with extraordinary interest, in case such a voyage was safely performed, the agreement was sometimes called *foenus nauticum,* sometimes *usura maritima.* But as this gave an opening for usurious and gaming contracts, 19 *Geo.* 2. *c.* 37. enacts, that all money lent on bottomry or at *respondentia,* on vessels bound to or from the East Indies, shall be expressly lent, only upon the ship or merchandize; the lender to have the benefit of salvage, &c. 2 *Black.* 459.

FOESA, (Fr. *foisson*) grass, herbage. *Cowel. Blount.*

FOGAGE, (*fogagium*) fog or after-grass, springing after the summer month.

FOITERERS, vagabonds. See *Faitours.*

FOLC-LANDS, (Sax.) copyhold lands so called in the time of the Saxons, as charter lands were called boc-lands. *Kitch.* 174. Folkland was *terra vulgi* or *popularis* the land of the vulgar people, who had no certain estate therein, but held the same under the rents and services accustomed or agreed, at the will only of their lord, and it was therefore not put in writing, but accounted *prædium rusticum & ignobile.* *Spelm. of Feuds, cap.* 5.

FOLC-MOTE or FOLKMOTE, (Sax. *folgemot,* i. e. *conventus populi*) is compounded of *folk, populus,* and *mote,* or *gemote, convenire*; and signified originally, a general assembly of the people to consider of, and order matters of the commonwealth. *Leg. Edw.*

Confess. cap. 35. And according to Spelman, the folcmcte was a sort of annual parliament, or convention of the bishops, thanes, aldermen, and freemen, upon every May-day yearly: where the laymen were sworn to defend one another, and to the king, and to preserve the laws of the kingdom, and then consulted of the common safety. But Dr. Brady infers from the laws of our Saxon kings, that it was an inferior court, held before the king's reeve or steward, every month to do folk right, or compose smaller differences, from whence there lay appeal to the superior courts. *Brady's Gloss. p.* 48. Squire seems to think the folcmote, not distinct from the shiremote, or common general meeting of the county. See his *Angl. Sax. Gov.* 155. *n. Cowel. Blount.*

FOLDAGE and FOLD-COURSE, a liberty to fold sheep, &c. *Cowel. Blount.* See *Faldage* and *Faldfee.*

FOLGARII, menial servants. *Ibid.*

FOOL, a natural, one so from the time of his birth. *Ibid.*

FOOT *of a fine.* See FINE.

FOOTGELD, (from the Sax. *fot, pes, et geldan, solvere,*) is as much as *pedis redemptio,* and signifies an amercement for not cutting out and expeditating the balls of great dogs feet in the forest: and to be quit of footgeld is a privilege to keep dogs within the forest unlawed, without punishment. *Manwood, par.* 1. *p.* 86. *Cowel. Blount.*

FORAGE, (Fr. *fourage*) hay and straw for horses, particularly for the use of horse in an army. *Cowel, Blount.*

FORAGIUM, straw when the corn is thrashed out. *Ibid.*

FORBALK, (*forbalka*) lying forward or next the highway. *Ibid.*

FORBARRE, is to bar or deprive one of a thing for ever. *Ibid.*

FORBATUDUS, when the aggressor in combat was slain, he was termed *forbatudus. Cowel. Blount.*

FORBISHER OF ARMOUR, (*forbator*) *si quis forbator arma alicujus susceperit, ad purgandam, &c. LL. Aluredi, MS. c.* 22. *Cowel. Blount.*

FORCE, (*vis*) an offence, by which violence is used to things or persons. *West. Symbol. pa.* 2. *sec.* 65. There is also a force implied in law; as every trespass, rescous, or disseisin, implieth it. *Co. Lit.* 257. All force is against the law; and it is lawful to repel force by force: and there is a law maxim, *quod alias bonum et justum est, si per vim vel fraudem petatur, malum et injustum est.* 3 *Rep.* 78.

FORCIBLE ENTRY AND DETAINER. The first is a violent actual entry into houses or lands: and forcible detainer is a withholding by violence, and with strong hand, of the possession of land, &c. whereby he who hath right of entry is barred or hindered. *Lamb.* 135. *Cromp.* 70. *Keilw.* 92.

And by 5 *R.* 2. *stat.* 1. *c.* 8. 15 *R.* 2. *c.* 2. 8 *H.* 6. *c.* 9. *s.* 2. none shall enter into any lands or tenements, but where entry is given by law, and in a peaceable manner, though they have title of entry, on pain of imprisonment, &c. And when a forcible entry is committed, justices of peace are impowered to view the place, and inquire of the force by a jury summoned by the sheriff of the county; and cause the tenements to be seized and restored, and imprison the offenders till they pay a fine.

If a justice of peace come to view a force in a house, and they refuse to let him in; this of itself will make forcible detainer in all cases; but it must be upon complaint made. The justices of peace are not to inquire into the title of either party: and there shall be no restitution upon an indictment of forcible entry or detainer, where the defendant hath been in quiet possession for three years together without interruption, next before the day of the indictment found, and his estate in the land not ended; which may be alleged in stay of restitution, and restitution is to be stayed till that be tried, if the other will traverse the same, &c. *Dalt.* 312. *Stat.* 31 *Eliz. c.* 11.

The remedy may be, 1. by action. For an action lies upon stat. 15 *R.* 2. *c.* 2. against him who makes a forcible entry. So, upon stat. 8 *H.* 6. *c.* 9. against him who makes a forcible entry, or detainer.

2dly. *By justices of peace upon view.* For by the several statutes of 15 *Ric.* 2. *c.* 2. 8 *Hen.* 6. *c.* 9. 31 *Eliz. c.* 11. and 21 *Jac.* 1. *c.* 15. upon any forcible entry, or forcible detainer after peaceable entry, into any lands, or benefices of the church, one or more justices of the peace, taking sufficient power of the county, may go to the place, and there record the force upon his own view, as in case of riots; and upon such conviction may commit the offender to gaol, till he makes fine and ransom to the king. And moreover the justice or justices have power to summon a jury, to try the forcible entry or detainer complained of: and, if the same be found by that jury, then, besides the fine on the offender, the justices shall make restitution by the sheriff of the possession, without inquiring into the merits of the title; for the force is the only thing to be tried, punished, and remedied by them: and the same may be done by indictment at the general sessions. But this provision does not extend to such as endeavour to maintain possession by force, where they themselves, or their ancestors, have been in the peaceable enjoyment of the lands and tenements, for three years immediately preceding. And holding over by force, where the tenant's title was under a lease now expired, is said to be a forcible detainer. (*Cro. Jac.* 199.)

FORCIBLE MARRIAGE. This is a force against the parents; and an information will lie for seducing a young man or woman from their parents, against their consent, in order to marry them. *Cro. Car.* 557. *Raym.* 473. 4 *Black.* 208.

And by 3 *H.* 7. *c.* 2. "if any persons shall "take away any woman having lands or "goods, or that is heir apparent to her an-"cestor, by force, and against her will, and "marry or defile her, the takers, procurers, "abettors, and receivers of the woman taken "away against her will, and knowing the "same, shall be deemed principal felons."

In the construction of this statute, it hath been determined, 1. That the indictment must allege that the taking was for lucre, for such are the words of the statute. 2. In order to shew this, it must appear that the woman has substance either real or personal, or is an heir apparent. 3. It must appear that she was taken away against her will. 4. It must also appear, that she was afterwards married, or defiled. And though possibly the marriage or defilement might be by her subsequent consent, being won thereunto by flatteries after the taking, yet this is felony, if the first taking were against her will: and so *vice versa*, if the woman be originally taken away by her own consent, yet if she afterwards refuse to continue with the offender, and be forced against her will, she may, from that time, as properly be said to be taken against her will, as if she never had given any consent at all; for till the force was put upon her, she was in her own power. It is held that a woman, thus taken away and married, may be sworn and give evidence against the offender, though he is her husband *de facto*, contrary to the general rule of law; because he is no husband *de jure*, in case the actual marriage was also against her will. In cases indeed where the actual marriage is good, by the consent of the inveigled woman obtained after her forcible abduction, sir Matthew Hale seems to question how far her evidence should be allowed: but other authorities seem to agree, that it should even then be admitted; esteeming it absurd, that the offender should thus take advantage of his own wrong, and that the very act of marriage, which is a principal ingredient of his crime, should (by a forced construction of law) be made to stop the mouth of the most material witness against him. 1 *Hawk. P. C.* 110. 1 *Hal. P. C.* 660. 1 *Hawk. P. C.* 109. 1 *Hal. P. C.* 660. 1 *Hawk. P. C.* 110. 1 *Hal. P. C.* 661. *Cro. Car.* 488. 3 *Keb.* 193. *State Trials*, *V.* 455. 4 *Black.* 208.

An inferior degree of the same kind of offence, but not attended with force, is punished by the statute 4 & 5 *Ph. & Mar. c.* 8. which enacts, that if any person, above the age of fourteen, unlawfully shall convey or take away any woman child unmarried, (which is held to extend to bastards as well as to legitimate children,) within the age of sixteen years, from the possession and against the will of the father, mother, guardians, or governors, he shall be imprisoned two years, or fined at the discretion of the justices; and if he deflowers such maid or woman child, or without the consent of parents contracts matrimony with her, he shall be imprisoned five years, or fined at the discretion of the justices, and she shall forfeit all her lands to her next of kin, during the life of her said husband.* So that as these stolen marriages, under the age of sixteen, were usually upon mercenary views, this act, besides punishing the seducer, wisely removed the temptation. But this latter part of the act is now rendered almost useless, by provisions of a very different kind, which make the marriage totally void, in the statute 26 *Geo.* 2. *c.* 33. 4 *Black.* 209.

FORD, (*forda*) a shallow place in a river. *Cowel. Blount.*

FORDOL, (from the Sax. *fore*, before, and *dæle*, a part or portion) signifies a butt or head-land, shooting upon other bounds. *Ib.*

FORECHEAPUM, *præemption*, from the Sax. *fore*, *ante*, and *ceapean*, i. e. *nundinari*, *emere*. *Ibid.*

FORECLOSED, shut out or excluded, as the barring the equity of redemption on mortgages, &c. 2 *Inst.* 298. 2 *Black.* 159. See *Mortgage*,

FOREGOERS. The king's purveyors were so called from their going before to provide for his household. *Cowel. Blount.*

FOREIGN, (Fr. *foraign*, Lat. *forinsecus*, *extraneus*) strange or outlandish, of another country: and in our law, not agreeable to the purpose or matter in hand. *Kitch.* 126.

FOREIGN ANSWER. An answer not triable in the county where it is made. *L.* 3.

FOREIGN ATTACHMENT, is an attachment of foreigners goods, found within a liberty or city, for the satisfaction of some citizen to whom the foreigner is indebted; or of money in the hands of another person, due to him against whom an action of debt is brought, &c. *Cowel. Blount.* See *Attachment.*

FOREIGN COURT. At Leominster there is the borough and the foreign court; which last is within the jurisdiction of the manor, but not within the liberty of the bailiff of the borough: so there is a foreign court of the honour of Gloucester, and some other places. *Cowel. Blount.*

FOREIGN KINGDOM, is a kingdom

---

* It has been decided in the court of exchequer, that she forfeits her lands only during the life of her husband. *Amb.* 73. Though the more natural construction of the statute seems to be, that the next heir shall retain them during the life of the wife, even after the death of the husband. 1 *Brown.* 23.

under the dominion of a foreign prince. 3 *Inst.* 48. One Hutchinson killed Mr. Colson abroad in Portugal, for which he was tried there and acquitted, the exemplifications of which acquittal he produced under the great seal of that kingdom; and the king being willing he should be tried here, referred it to the judges, who all agreed, that the party being already acquitted by the laws of Portugal, could not be tried again for the same fact here. 3 *Keb.* 785.

Where a bond is given, or contract made in a foreign kingdom, it may be tried in the king's bench, and laid to be done in any place in England. *Hob.* 11. 2 *Bulst.* 322.

FOREIGN OPPOSER, or APPOSER. See *Exchequer.*

FOREIGN PLANTATIONS. See *Plantations.*

FOREIGN PLEA, is a plea in objection to a judge, where he is refused as incompetent to try the matter in question, because it arises out of his jurisdiction. *Kitch.* 75. See title *Abatement.*

FOREIGN SERVICE, is that whereby a mesne lord holds of another, without the compass of his own fee: or that which the tenant performs either to his own lord, or to the lord paramount out of the fee. *Kitch.* 299.

FOREIGNERS. Though made denizens or naturalized here are disabled to bear offices in the government, to be of the privy council, members of parliament, &c. by the acts of settlement of the crown. 12 *W.* 3. *c.* 2. 1 *Geo.* 1. *c.* 4. See *Aliens.*

FOREJUDGER, (*forejudicatio*) a judgment whereby a person is deprived or put by the thing in question. *Bract. lib.* 4. To be forejudged the court, is when an officer or attorney of any court is expelled the same for some offence; or for not appearing to an action, on a bill filed against him, &c. and if the attorney appears not in four days, then the bill is entered upon a roll of that term, and carried to the clerk of the warrants and inrolments; and he thereupon strikes such attorney out of the roll of attornies, when he stands unprivileged, and may be arrested as any other person, &c. *Practis. Solic.* 322. *Attorn. Compan.* 182, 183.

But an attorney forejudged, may be restored, on clearing himself from his contumacy in not appearing when he was called, and on making satisfaction to the plaintiff; and then a judge will make an order to the clerk of the warrants, to replace him in the proper roll of attornies: and there are instances of restoring attornies forejudged, upon payment of a small fine. *Ibid. Rastal* 96. See *Attornies* and *Stamps.*

FORESCHOKE, (*derelictum*) forsaken; when a man doth not pursue the course appointed by law to recover lands seized by the lord for want of services, he doth in presumption of law disavow or forsake all the right he hath to the same; and then such lands shall be called foreschoke. *Cowel. Blount.*

FOREST, (*foresta, saltus*) signifies a great or vast wood; *locus sylvestris & saltuosus.* And according to Blackstone, forests are waste grounds belonging to the king; replenished with all manner of beasts of chase or venary; which are under the king's protection, for the sake of his royal recreation, and delight: and to that end, and for the preservation of the king's game, there are particular laws, privileges, courts and offices belonging to the king's forests. 1 *Black.* 288. But a forest in the hands of a subject is properly nothing more than a *chase*, being subject to the common law *only*, and not to the forest laws. 2 *Black.* 38.

FORESTAGIUM, some duty payable to the king's forestors, as chiminage, or such like. *Cowel. Blount.*

FORESTAL, (*forestallamentum*, from the Sax. *fore*, i. e. *via & stal*) signifies to intercept on the highways. *Spelm.* And, in our law, forestalling is the buying or bargaining for any corn, cattle, or other merchandize, by the way as they come to fairs or markets to be sold, before they are brought thither; to the intent to sell the same again, at a higher and dearer price. And all endeavours to inhance the common price of any victuals or merchandize, and practices which have an apparent tendency thereto, whether by spreading false rumours, or buying things in a market before the accustomed hour, or by buying and selling again the same thing in the same market, &c. are highly criminal by the common law; and all such offences anciently came under this general appellation of forestalling. 3 *Inst.* 195, 196. And so jealous is the common law of practices of this nature, which are a general inconvenience and prejudice to the people, and very oppressive to the poorer sort, that it will not suffer corn to be sold in the sheaf before thrashed; for by such sale the market is in effect forestalled. 3 *Inst.* 197. *H. P. C.* 152. By the common law, persons guilty of forestalling, upon an indictment found, are liable to fine and imprisonment, answerable to the heinousness of their offence. 1 *Hawk.* 235.

FORESTALLER, is a person guilty of any of the acts before described, as acts of forestalling.

FORETOOTH, striking out the foretooth is a mayhem. 4 *Black.* 206.

FORFANG or FORFENG, (from the Sax. *fore, ante & fangen, prendere*) the taking of provision from any one in fairs or markets, before the king's purveyors were served with necessaries for his majesty. *Cowel. Blount.*

FORFEITURE, as generally defined by Blackstone, is a punishment annexed by law to some illegal act or negligence in the owner of lands, tenements, or hereditaments: whereby he loses all his interest therein, and they go to the party injured as a recompence for the wrong, which either he alone, or the public together with himself hath sustained. 2 *Black.* 267.

But forfeiture *for crimes and misdemeanors*, (of which it is alone intended to speak in this place) may be incurred, not only in respect to lands and hereditaments, but also in respect to goods and chattels in the following instances: 1. the offences which induce a forfeiture of *lands and tenements* to the crown, or its grantee are principally the following six: 1. *Treason*; 2. *Felony*; 3. *Misprision of Treason*; 4. *Præmunire*; 5. Drawing a weapon on a judge or striking any one in the presence of the king's principal courts of justice; 6. Popish recusancy. 2 *Black.* 268.

I. Forfeiture by attainder in high treason; a man forfeits to the king all his lands and tenements of inheritance, whether fee-simple or fee-tail, and all his rights of entry on lands and tenements, which he had at the time of the offence committed, or at any time afterwards, to be for ever vested in the crown: and also the profits of all lands and tenements, which he had in his own right for life or years, so long as such interest shall subsist. This forfeiture relates backwards to the time of the treason committed: so as to avoid all intermediate sales and incumbrances, but not those before the fact: and therefore a wife's jointure is not forfeitable for the treason of her husband; because settled upon her previous to the treason committed. But her dower is forfeited by the express provision of statute 5 & 6 *Ed.* 6. *c.* 11. And yet the husband shall be tenant by the curtesy of the wife's lands, if the wife be attainted of treason; for that is not prohibited by the statute. But, though after attainder the forfeiture relates back to the time of the treason committed, yet it does not take effect unless an attainder be had, of which it is one of the fruits: and therefore if a traitor dies before judgment pronounced, or is killed in open rebellion, or is hanged by martial law, it works no forfeiture of his lands: for he never was attainted of treason. But if the chief justice of the king's bench (the supreme coroner of all England) in person, upon the view of the body of one killed in open rebellion, records it and returns the record into his own court, both lands and goods shall be forfeited. *Co. Litt.* 392. 3 *Inst.* 19. 1 *Hal. P. C.* 240. 2 *Hawk. P. C.* 448. 3 *Inst.* 211. 1 *Hal. P. C.* 359. *Co. Litt.* 13. 4 *Rep.* 57. 4 *Black.* 301.

The natural justice of forfeiture or confiscation of property, for treason, is founded on this consideration: that he who hath thus violated the fundamental principles of government, and broken his part of the original contract between king and people, hath abandoned his connections with society; and hath no longer any right to those advantages, which before belonged to him purely as a member of the community: among which social advantages the right of transferring or transmitting property to others is one of the chief. Such forfeitures, moreover, whereby his posterity must suffer as well as himself, with help to restrain a man, not only by the sense of his duty, and dread of personal punishment, but also by his passions and natural affections; and will interest every dependent and relation he has, to keep him from offending. 4 *Black.* 382.

With us in England, forfeiture of lands and tenements to the crown for treason is by no means derived from the feodal policy, but was antecedent to the establishment of that system in this island; being transmitted from our Saxon ancestors, and forming a part of the antient Scandinavian constitution. But in certain treasons relating to the coin, rather a species of the *crimen falsi*, than the *crimen læsæ majestatis*, it is provided by some of the modern statutes (*stat.* 5 *Eliz.* *c.* 11. 18 *Eliz.* *c.* 1.) which constitute the offence, that it shall work no forfeiture of lands, save only for the life of the offender; and by all, that it shall not deprive the wife of her dower (*Ibid.* 8 & 9 *Will.* 3. *c.* 26. 15 & 16 *Geo.* 2. *c.* 28.) And, in order to abolish such hereditary punishment entirely, it was enacted by statute 7 *Ann.* *c.* 21. that after the decease of the late pretender, no attainder for treason should extend to the disinheriting of any heir, nor to the prejudice of any person, other than the traitor himself. By which, the law of forfeitures for high treason would by this time have been at an end, had not a subsequent statute intervened. 4 *Black.* 383.

For by the 39 *Geo.* 3. *c.* 93. the clause in the 7 *Ann.* *c.* 21. and that in the 17 *Geo.* 2. *c.* 39. limiting the periods when forfeiture for treason should be abolished, are repealed. So the law of forfeiture in cases of high treason is now the same as it was by the common law, or as it stood prior to the seventh year of the reign of queen Anne.

In petit treason and felony, the offender also forfeits all his chattel interests absolutely, and the profits of all estates of freehold during life; and after his death, all his lands and tenements in fee-simple (but not those in tail) to the crown, for a very short period of time: for the king shall have them for a year and a day, and may commit therein what waste he pleases; which is called the king's year, day, and waste (2 *Inst.* 37.) Formerly the king had only a liberty of committing waste on the lands of felons, by pulling down their houses, extirpating their gardens, ploughing their meadows, and cutting down their woods. But this tending greatly to the prejudice of the public, it was agreed in the reign of Henry the first, in this kingdom, that the king should have the profits of the land for one year and a day, in lieu of the destruction he was otherwise at liberty to commit (*Mirr. c. 4. s. 16. Fleta, l. 1. c. 8.*): and therefore magna charta (9 *Hen. 3. c. 22.*) provides, that the king shall only hold such lands for a year and a day, and then restore them to the lord of the fee; without any mention made of waste. But the statute 17 *Edw. 2. de prærogativa regis* seems to suppose, that the king shall have his year, day, and waste: and not the year and day instead of waste. Which sir Edward Coke (and the author of the Mirror before him) very justly look upon as an encroachment, though a very antient one, of the royal prerogative (*Mirr. c. 5. s. 2. 2 Inst. 37.*) This year, day, and waste are now usually compounded for; but otherwise they regularly belong to the crown; and, after their expiration, the land would naturally have descended to the heir, (as in gavelkind tenure it still does,) did not its feodal quality intercept such descent, and give it by way of escheat to the lord. These forfeitures for felony do also arise only upon attainder: and therefore a *felo de se* forfeits no lands of inheritance or freehold, for he never is attainted as a felon (3 *Inst. 55.*) They likewise relate back to the time of the offence committed, as well as forfeitures for treason; so as to avoid all intermediate charges and conveyances. This may be hard upon such as have unwarily engaged with the offender: but the cruelty and reproach must lie on the part, not of the law, but of the criminal; who has thus knowingly and dishonestly involved others in his own calamities. 4 *Black.* 386.

These are all the forfeitures of real estates, created by the common law, as consequential upon attainders by judgment of death or outlawry. The particular forfeitures created by the statutes of *præmunire* and others are rather a part of the judgment and penalty, inflicted by the respective statutes, than consequences of such judgment; as in treason and felony they are. But a part of the forfeiture of real estates, *viz.* the forfeiture of the profits of lands during life: extends to two instances, besides those already spoken of; 1. misprision of treason (*Ibid.* 218.), and 2. striking in Westminster-hall, or drawing a weapon upon a judge there, sitting in the king's courts of justice. *Ibid.*

II. The forfeiture of goods and chattels accrues in every one of the higher kinds of offence: in high treason or misprision thereof, petit treason, felonies of all sorts whether clergyable or not, self-murder, or felony *de se*, petit larciny, standing mute, and the above-mentioned offences of striking, &c. in Westminster-hall. For flight also, on an accusation of treason, felony, or even petit larciny, whether the party be found guilty or acquitted, if the jury find the flight, the party shall forfeit his goods and chattels: for the very flight is an offence, carrying with it a strong presumption of guilt, and is at least an endeavour to elude and stifle the course of justice prescribed by the law. Bu the jury very seldom find the flight (*Staundf. P. C.* 183, *b.*): forfeiture being looked upon, since the vast increase of personal property of late years, as too large a penalty for an offence, to which a man is prompted by the natural love of liberty. 4 *Black.* 386, 7.

There is a remarkable difference or two between the forfeiture of lands, and of goods and chattels. 1st. Lands are forfeited upon attainder, and not before: goods and chattels are forfeited by conviction. Because in many of the cases where goods are forfeited, there never is any attainder; which happens only where judgment of death or outlawry is given: therefore in those cases the forfeiture must be upon conviction, or not at all; and being necessarily upon conviction in those, it is so ordered in all other cases, for the law loves uniformity. 2. In outlawries for treason or felony, lands are forfeited only by the judgment: but the goods and chattels are forfeited by a man's being first put in the *exigent*, without staying till he is *quinto exactus*, or finally outlawed; for the secreting himself so long from justice, is construed a flight in law (3 *Inst.* 232.) 3. The forfeiture of lands has relation to the time of the fact committed, so as to avoid all subsequent sales and incumbrances: but the forfeiture of goods and chattels has no relation backwards; so that those only which a man has at the time of conviction shall be forfeited. Therefore a traitor or felon may *bona fide* sell any of his chattels, real or personal, for the sustenance of himself and family between the fact and conviction (2 *Hawk. P. C.* 454.): for personal property is of so fluctuating a nature, that it passes through many hands in a short time; and no buyer could be safe, if he were liable to return the goods which he had fairly bought, provided any of the prior vendors had committed a treason or felony. Yet if they be collusively and not *bona fide* parted with, merely to defraud the crown, the law (and particularly the statute 13 *Eliz. c. 5.*) will reach them; for they are all the while truly and substantially the goods of the offender: and as he, if acquitted, might recover them himself, as not parted with for a good consideration; so in case he happens to be convicted, the law will recover them for the king. 4 *Black.* 387, 8.

FORFEITURE OF MARRIAGE, (*forisfactura maritagii,*) was a writ which lay against him, who, holding by knight's-service, and being under age, and unmarried, refused her whom the lord offered him without his disparagement, and married another. *F. N. B. fol.* 141. *Rep. Orig. fol.* 163.

FORGAVEL, (*forgabulum*) a small reserved rent in money, or quit-rent. *Cowel. Blount.*

FORGE, (*forgia*) a smith's forge, to melt and work iron. *Ibid.*

FORGERY, (from the Fr. *forger*, i. e. *ac-*

cudere, fabricare, to beat on an anvil, forge or form) and in law it signifies where a person fraudulently makes and publishes false writings, to the prejudice of another man's right: and forgery is either at COMMON LAW, or by STATUTE. But there can be no forgery where none can be prejudiced by it but the person doing it. 1 *Salk.* 375.

Forgery by the common law extends to false and fraudulent making or altering of a deed or writing, whether it be matter of record, or any other writing, deed, or will. 3 *Inst.* 169. 1 *Rol. Abr.* 65.

And according to Blackstone, 4 *Com.* 247, 8. it is defined to be *the fraudulent making or alteration of a writing to the prejudice of another man's right,* for which the offender may suffer fine, imprisonment, and pillory, and also by a variety of statutes, a more exemplary punishment. For which see article *Forgery,* under head FELONY.

A person convicted of forgery, and adjudged to the pillory, &c. whereby he becomes infamous, is not allowed to be a witness; but it is a good exception to his evidence. *Hawk. P. C.* 432. And one convicted of this crime, may be challenged on a jury, so as to be incapable to serve as a juror; and it hath been holden, that exceptions to persons found guilty of perjury or forgery, as well as felony, &c. are not salved by a pardon. 2 *Hawk.* 417. The court of *B. R.* will not ordinarily, at the prayer of the dependant, grant a *certiorari* for a removal of an indictment of forgery, &c. 1 *Sid.* 54.

By a late act, forging or counterfeiting any deed, will, bond, bill of exchange, note or acquittance for money, or any indorsement or assignment of a bill, &c. with intent to defraud any person, or publishing such false deed, &c. to be true, knowingly, the offenders shall be guilty of felony, and suffer death as felons; but not to work corruption of blood, &c. Stat. 2 *Geo.* 2. *c.* 25. Vide 7 *Geo.* 2. *c.* 22.

As to forging of exchequer and bank bills, lottery tickets, letters of attorney to transfer stock, &c. But for the several species of this offence, see title *Forgery* under title *Felonies* in the table to the quarto edition of the *Statutes,* or the octavo *Index*: and 4 *Black. Com.* 245.

FORINSECUS, outward, or on the outside. *Cowel. Blount.*

FORINSECUM MANERIUM, the manor as to that part of it which lies without the town, and not included within the liberties of it. *Ibid.*

FORINSECUM SERVITIUM, the payment of extraordinary aid, opposed to *intrinsecum servitium,* which was the common and ordinary duties, within the lord's court. *Kennet's Gloss. Cowel. Blount.* See *Foreign Service.*

FORISBANNITUS, banished. *Ibid.*

FORISFAMILIARI. When a son accepts of his father's part of lands, in the life-time of the father, and is contented with it; he is said to be *forisfamiliari,* and cannot claim any more. *Cowel. Blount.*

FORLAND, (*forlandum*) lands extending further or lying before the rest; also a *promontory. Ibid.*

FORLER-LAND, was land in the bishoprick of Hereford granted or leased *dum episcopus in episcopatu steterit,* so as the successor might have the same for his present revenue: this custom has been long since disused, and the land thus formerly granted is now let by lease as other lands, though it still retains the name by which it was anciently known. *Butterfield's Surv.* 56.

FORM, is required in all law proceedings, otherwise the law would be no art; but it ought not to be used to ensnare or intrap. *Hob.* 232. And the formal part of the law or method of proceeding, cannot be altered but by parliament: for, if once those outlets were demolished, there would be an inlet to all manner of innovation in the body of the law itself. 1 *Black.* 142.

FORMA PAUPERIS, a suit in *forma pauperis* is allowed to any person who has just cause of suit, and is so poor, that he cannot bear the usual charges of suing at law, or in equity: in this case, upon his making oath that he is not worth 5*l.* except the matter in question, his debts being paid, and bringing a certificate from some barrister, that he hath cause of suit, the judge admits him to sue in *forma pauperis,* i. e. without paying any fees to counsellor, attorney or clerk: for by stat. 11 *H.* 7. *c.* 12. "*poor persons having cause of action or suits, shall have original writs, counsel and attornies, assigned them gratis.*"

' To proceed *in forma pauperis* in chancery after the bill is filed, an affidavit must be made that the plaintiff is not worth 5*l.* in lands, tenements, goods or chattels, his wearing apparel and the matters of the suit excepted; and then a petition is drawn up and presented to the lord chancellor or master of the rolls, praying to be admitted *in forma pauperis,* and to have counsel, &c. assigned him, who are neither to take fees, nor make any contract or agreement for recompence, on pain of punishment; and no counsellor or attorney assigned shall refuse to proceed, without shewing good cause to the lord chancellor, &c. *Pract. Sol.* 24. If a cause goes against a pauper, or a plaintiff *in forma pauperis* be nonsuit, he shall not pay costs to the defendant, but shall suffer such punishment in his person as the court shall award. 23 *H.* 8. *c.* 15. 1 *Lil. Abr.* 634. 2 *Sid.* 261. Paupers using delays to vex their adversaries; or being proved to be vexatious persons, and having many frivolous suits depending, will be dispaupered by the court; for the law doth not assist them to do injury to others. 1 *Lill.* 633. 3 *Black.* 400.

FORMEDON, (*breve de forma donationis*) is a writ that lieth for him who hath right to lands or tenements by virtue of any intail, growing from the stat. *Westm.* 2. *c.* 2. It is a writ of right for recovery of land; and is of three kinds, *viz.* in descender, remainder, and reverter.

Formedon in descender lies where tenant in tail enfeoffs a stranger, or is disseised and dieth, the heir shall have this writ to recover the land.

Formedon in remainder lies where one gives land in tail, and for default of issue the remainder to another in tail, &c. If the tenant in tail die without issue, and a stranger abates and enters into the land, he in remainder shall have this writ.

Formedon in the reverter lieth where land is intailed to certain persons and their issue, with remainder over for want of issue, and on the remainders failing to revert to the donor and his heirs; now if tenant in tail dies without leaving any issue, and likewise he in remainder, then the donor or his heirs, to whom the reversion comes, shall have this writ for recovery of the estate, in case it be aliened, &c. *Reg. Orig.* 238,242. *F.N.B.* 111.

But by stat. 21 *Jac.* 1. *c.* 16. *formedons must be brought within* twenty years *after the cause of action accrued.*

The writ of formedon has fallen into disuse, the trying titles by *ejectione firmæ* having supplied its place, and being an easier manner. 3 *Black.* 191.

FORMELLA, a weight of about seventy pounds. *Cowel. Blount.*

FORNAGIUM, *furnagium*, (Fr. *fournage*) the fee taken by a lord of his tenant, bound to bake in the lord's common oven, or for a permission to use their own; in ancient times usual in the northern parts of England. *Ibid.*

FORNICATION, (*fornicatio*, from the Fornices in Rome, where lewd women prostituted themselves for money) is the act of incontinency in single persons; for if either party is married, it is adultery. The spiritual court hath cognizance of this offence. 2 *Inst.* 488. 4 *Black.* 64.

FORPRISE, (*forprisum*) an exception or reservation, thus in leases and conveyances, excepted and forprised is an usual expression. *Thorn. anno.*

FORSES, (*catatudæ*) water-falls. *Cowel. Blount.*

FORSPEAKER, an attorney or advocate in a cause. *Ibid.*

FORTIA, power, dominion or jurisdiction. *Ibid.*

FORTIORI, *à fortiori*, is used thus in argument, "if it be *so* in a feoffment passing a new right, *much more* is it for the restitution of an ancient right, &c." *Co. Lit.* 253, 260.

FORTILICE and FORTILITY, (*fortellescum*) a fortified place, bulwark, or castle. *Cowel. Blount.*

FORTLET, (Fr.) a place or fort of some strength; or rather a little fort, *Old Nat. Br.* 45.

FORTS and CASTLES, the stat. 13 *Car.* 2. *c.* 6. extends to forts and other places of strength within the realm; the sole prerogative as well of erecting, as manning and governing of which belongs to the king, in his capacity of general of the kingdom. 2 *Inst.* 30. 1 *Black.* 263.

FORTUNA, treasure-trove. *Cowel. Blount.*

FORTUNE-TELLERS. See *Vagrants.*

FORTUNIUM, a tournament or fighting with spears; or an appeal to fortune therein. *Cowel. Blount.*

FORTY-DAYS-COURT. The court of attachment or woodmote, held before the verderors of the forest once in every forty days, to inquire concerning all offenders against vert and venison. 3 *Black.* 71.

FOSSA, a ditch full of water; wherein women committing felony were drowned: it has been likewise used for a grave, in ancient writings. *Cowel. Blount.* See *Furca.*

FOSSATUM, (Lat.) is a ditch, or place fenced round with a ditch or trench; also it is taken for the obligations of citizens to repair the city ditches. *Kennet's Gloss. Cowel. Blount.*

FOSSEWAY, (from *fossus*, digged) was anciently one of the four principal highways in England, leading through the kingdom, which had its name from its being supposed to be dug and made passable by the Romans, and having a ditch upon one side. *Cowel. Blount.*

FOSTERLEAN, (Sax.) nuptial gift, which we call a jointure or stipend for the maintenance of the wife. *Ibid.*

FOTHER or FODDER, (from the Teuton. *fuder*) is a weight of lead containing eight pigs, and every pig one and twenty stone and a half; that is about a ton or common cart load: among the plumbers in London it is nineteen hundred and a half; and at the mines it is two and twenty hundred weight and a half. *Skene. Cowel. Blount.*

FOVEA, a place for burial of the dead. *Cowel. Blount.*

FOUNDATION, the founding and building of a college, hospital, or other public institution, is called *foundatio, quasi foundatio* or *fundamenti locatio. Co. Lit.* 10.

Persons seised of estates in fee-simple, may erect and found hospitals for the poor, by deed inrolled in chancery, &c. which shall be incorporated, and subject to such visitors as the founder shall appoint, &c. Stat. 39 *Eliz. c.* 5. By 7 & 8 *W.* 3. *c.* 37. The crown may grant licence to alien in mortmain. By 9 *Geo.* 2. *c.* 36. Gifts in mortmain by will, &c. are restrained, but there are exceptions with respect to universities and royal colleges. See *College*. 1 *Black. Com.* 480.

FOUNDER OF METAL, (from the Fr. *foundre*, to melt or pour) the person that melts metal, and makes any thing of it by pouring or casting it into a mould. *Cowel. Blount.*

FOURCHER, (Fr. *fourchir*) signifies a putting off, or delaying of an action. *Terms de Ley. Stat. Westm.* 1. *c.* 42. 6 *Ed.* 1. *c.* 10. 23 *Hen.* 6. *c.* 2. 2 *Inst.* 250.

FRACTION. The law makes no fraction of a day; thus if any offence be committed, in case of murder, or the like, *the year and day* shall be computed from the beginning of the day on which the wound was given, and not from the precise minute or hour. 2 *Hawk.* 163. *Co. Litt.* 255.

And in presumption of law, when a thing is to be done upon one day, all that day is allowed to do it in, and when done, it shall be taken to be done the first instant of the day, for the avoiding of fractions in time, which the law admits not of, but in case of necessity. *Sti.* 119. *Mo.* 137.

Thus if A. be born on the 3d day of September, and on the 2d day of September, twenty-one years afterwards, he makes his will, this is a good will, for the law will make no fraction of a day, and by consequence he is of age. 2 *Salk.* 625.

FRACTITIUM, is made use of for arable land. *Cowel. Blount. Ibid.*

FRACTURA NAVIUM, wreck of shipping at sea. *Ibid.*

FRAMPOLE FENCES, are such fences as the tenants in the manor of Writtle in Essex, set up against the lord's demesnes; and they are intitled to the wood growing on those fences, and as many poles as they can reach from the top of the ditch with the helve of an axe, towards the reparation of their fences. *Ibid.*

FRANCHILANUS, (Fr. *franchi*, i. e. free) a freeman. *Ibid.*

FRANCHISE and LIBERTY, are used as synonymous terms: and their definition is, *a royal* privilege, or branch of the king's prerogative, subsisting in the hands of a subject. Being therefore derived from the crown, they must arise from the king's grant; or, in some cases, may be held by prescription, which, as has frequently been said, pre-supposes a grant. The kinds of them are various, and almost infinite: I will here briefly touch upon some of the principal; premising only, that they may be vested in either natural persons or bodies politic; in one man, or in many; but the same identical franchise, that has before been granted to one, cannot be bestowed on another, for that would prejudice the former grant (2 *Roll. Abr.* 191. *Keilw.* 196.)

To be a county palatine is a franchise, vested in a number of persons. It is likewise a franchise for a number of persons to be incorporated, and subsist as a body politic; with a power to maintain perpetual succession and do other corporate acts: and each individual member of such corporation is also said to have a franchise or freedom. Other franchises are, to hold a court leet; to have a manor or lordship; or, at least, to have a lordship paramount: to have waifs, wrecks, estrays, treasure-trove, royal fish, forfeitures, and deodands: to have a court of one's own, or liberty of holding pleas; and trying causes: to have the cognizance of pleas: which is a still greater liberty, being an exclusive right, so that no other court shall try causes arising within that jurisdiction: to have a bailiwick, or liberty exempt from the sheriff of the county; wherein the grantee only, and his officers are to execute all process: to have a fair or market: with the right of taking toll, either there or at any other public places, as at bridges, wharfs, or the like; which tolls must have a reasonable cause of commencement, (as in consideration of repairs, or the like,) else the franchise is illegal and void (2 *Inst.* 220.): or, lastly, to have a forest, chase, park, warren, or fishery, endowed with privileges of royalty. 2 *Black.* 37, 8.

FRANCIGENÆ, was the general appellation of all foreigners. *Cowel. Blount.* See *Englecery*.

FRANCLAINE, according to ancient authors, a freeman or gentleman. *Ibid.*

FRANK, a French gold coin, worth about a French shilling; but in computation was twenty sols, which is a livre, and ten pence in our money. *Ibid.*

FRANKALMOIGN. Tenure in frankalmoign, *in libera eleemosyna*, or free alms, is that whereby a religious corporation, aggregate or sole, holds lands of the donor to them and their successors for ever (*Litt. s.* 133.) The service which they were bound to render for these lands was not certainly defined: but only in general to pray for the souls of the donor and his heirs, dead or alive; and therefore they did no fealty, (which is incident to all other services but this, *Ibid.* 131.) because this divine service was of a higher and more exalted nature (*Ibid.* 135.) This is the tenure by which almost all the antient monasteries and religious houses held their lands; and by which the parochial clergy, and very many ecclesiastical and eleemosynary foundations, hold them at this day (*Bracton, l.* 4. *tr.* 1. *c.* 28. *s.* 1.); the nature of the service being upon the reformation altered, and made conformable to the purer doctrines of the church of England. It was an old Saxon tenure; and continued under the Norman revolution, through the great respect that was shewn to religion and religious men in antient times. Which is also the reason that tenants in frankalmoign were discharged of all other services, except the *trinoda necessitas*, of repairing the highways, building castles, and repelling invasions, (*Seld. Jan.* 14. 2.) just as the Druids among the ancient Britons had *omnium rerum immunitatem* (*Cæs. de bel. Gal. l.* 6, *c.* 13.). And even at present this is a tenure of a nature very distinct from all others, being not in the least feodal, but merely spiritual. For if the service be neglected, the law gives no remedy by distress or otherwise to the lord of whom the lands are holden, but merely a complaint to the ordinary or visitor to correct it (*Litt. s.* 136.). Wherein it materially differs from what was called tenure by divine service, in which the tenants were obliged to do some special divine services in certain, as to sing so many masses, to distribute such a sum in alms, and the like, which being expressly defined and prescribed could with no kind of propriety be called free-alms, especially as for this, if unperformed, the lord might distrain without any complaint to the visitor, (*Litt. s.* 137). All such donations are indeed now out of use; for since the statute of *quia emptores*, 18 *Ed.* 1, none but the king can give lands to be holden by this tenure, (*Litt.* 140). So that it is only mentioned because frankalmoign is excepted by name in the stat. of *Cha.* 2, and therefore subsists in many instances at this day. 2 *Black.* 100, 101.

FRANK-CHASE, is a liberty of free chase, by which all persons that have lands within the compass thereof are prohibited to cut down any wood, &c. without the view of the forester, though it be in their own demesnes. *Cromp. Juris.* 187.

FRANKED-LETTERS. See *Post-Office.*

FRANK-FEE, was where freehold lands were held exempted from all services, but not from homage, they were termed frank-free. *Reg. Orig.* 12. *F. N. B.* 161. And the author of the Terms of the Law defines a free-fee to be a tenure pleadable at the common law, and not an ancient demesne. *Fachineus, lib.* 7. *c.* 39. *Cowel. Blount.*

FRANK-FERM, when lands or tenements were changed in the nature of the fee by feoffment, &c. out of knights service, for certain yearly services, they were called *frank-ferm. Britton, c.* 66. See *Fee-farm.*

FRANK LAW, (*libera lex*) is applied to the benefit of the free and common law of the land. *Cromp. Juris.* 156. *Lib. Assis.* 59. See *Conspiracy.*

FRANK-MARRIAGE, (*liberum maritagium*) was where a man seised of land in fee-simple gave it to another with his daughter, sister, &c. in marriage, to hold to them and their heirs. It was a tenure in special tail. *Litt.* 17. *West. Symb. par.* 1. *lib.* 2. *s.* 303. *Cowel. Blount.*

These gifts were common in former times, but are now disused. 2 *Nels. Abr.* 888.

FRANK-PLEDGE, (*Franci plegium*, from the Fr. *Franc*, i. e. *liber*, and pledge, *fidejussor*, a pledge or surety for the behaviour of freemen) it was the ancient custom of this kingdom that for the preservation of the public peace, every freeborn man at the age of fourteen, (religious persons, clerks, &c. excepted) should give security for his truth towards the king and his subjects, or be committed to prison; whereupon a certain number of neighbours usually became bound for one another, to see each man of their pledge forthcoming at all times, or to answer the transgression done by any gone away: and whenever any one offended it was forthwith inquired in what pledge he was, and then those of that pledge either produced the offender within 31 days, or satisfied for his offence. This was called frank-pledge; and this custom was so kept, that the sheriffs at every county-court, did from time to time take the oaths of young persons as they grew to fourteen years of age, and see that they were settled in one decennary or other; whereby this branch of the sheriff's authority was called *visus franci plegii*, or view of frank-pledge. 4 *Inst.* 78.

FRANK-TENEMENT, a possession of freehold lands and tenements. *Cowel. Blount.*

FRASSETUM, a wood or woody ground, where ashes grow. *Co. Litt.* 4. *Cowel. Blount.*

FRATERIA, a fraternity, brotherhood, or society. *Ibid.*

FRATERNITIES, of places in respect to a trade or mystery. *Ibid.* See *Corporation.*

FRATER NUTRICIUS, a bastard brother. *Ibid.*

FRATRES CONJURATI, sworn brothers or companions, and those were so called who were sworn to defend the king against his enemies. *Ibid.*

FRATRES PYES, certain friars, wearing black and white garments. *Ibid.*

FRATRIAGIUM, a younger brother's inheritance. *Bract. lib.* 2. *c.* 35. *Cowel. Blount.*

FRAUD, (*Fraus*) is defined to be a *deceit* in grants and conveyances of lands, and bargains and sales of goods, &c. to the damage of another person. *Bacon's Abr.* 3. *tit. fraud.*

And fraud, covin, collusion, and deceit, are often used as synonimous words, and in whatever shape or form they appear, are always deemed odious in the eye of the law. *Ibid.*

And it is a general rule, that without the express provision of any act of parliament, all deceitful practices in defrauding or endeavouring to defraud another of his known right, by means of some artful device, contrary to the plain rules of common honesty, are condemned by the common law, and punishable according to the heinousness of the offence. *Co. Lit.* 3. *b. Dyer.* 295.

As to frauds in contracts and dealings, the common law subjects the wrong-doer to an action on the case for the recovery of a compensation in damages, or an indictment, or information. 1 *Rol. Abr.* 90. *Cro. Jac.* 474.

And all frauds and deceits for which there is no remedy by the ordinary course of law are properly cognizable in equity, which matters of fraud are one of the chief branches to which the jurisdiction of the courts of equity was originally confined. 4 *Inst.* 84.

The following is a summary of the statutes against frauds and fraudulent conveyances.

By 1 *Ric.* 2. *c.* 9, a feoffment of lands or gift of goods by fraud, or for maintenance, shall be void; and actions may be maintained against such feoffors as take the profits. Also 4 *Hen.* 4. *c.* 7, and 11 *Hen.* 6. *c.* 3.

By 3 *Hen.* 7. *c.* 4, all deeds of gift of goods and chattels to the use of the person who made the same, to the intent to defraud creditors, shall be void.

By 13 *Eliz. c.* 5, all fraudulent conveyances, bonds, and deeds, made to defraud or hinder creditors, shall be void; and parties and privies shall forfeit one year's value of lands, and the whole value of goods; and so much money as shall be mentioned in such bonds. But common recoveries shall be good, and the act shall not extend to voucher in formedon, or to purchasers for a valuable consideration.

By 27 *Eliz. c.* 4, conveyances made to defraud a purchaser, against such purchaser only, shall be void; and parties justifying the conveyance as made *bona fide*, shall forfeit one year's value of the lands, and be imprisoned half a year. Where lands are conveyed with clause of revocation, and afterwards sold for valuable consideration, the first conveyance shall be void against the vendee. But mortgages made *bona fide*, are not impeached. And statutes merchant shall be entered in six months, and for searching the same, the fee is 2*d.* a term.

By 29 *Car.* 2. *c.* 3, called the statute of frauds, parol leases of freehold shall have the force of estates at will only, except leases not exceeding three years, whereon the rent reserved amounts to two thirds of the improved value.

No action shall be brought upon any special promise to charge an executor or administrator to answer damages out of his own estate, or to charge any defendant for the debt of another, or upon any agreement on consideration of marriage, or upon any contract for lands or any interest therein, or upon any agreement that is not to be performed within one year, unless the agreement, or memorandum thereof, be in writing signed by the party. *Ibid.*

No contract for sale of goods for ten pounds or more, shall be good, except the buyer accept part of the same, or give earnest, or some memorandum be made. *Ibid.*

By 3 & 4 *W. & M. c.* 14, wills of lands shall be deemed, only as against bond creditors, to be fraudulent. And they may sue the devisee and the heir of the obligor, jointly, and such devisee shall be chargeable for a false plea, as an heir.

Devises for raising younger childrens portions, pursuant to marriage contract, shall be good. *Ibid.*

If the heir or devisee aliens before action brought, he shall still be liable to the value of the land. *Ibid.* See also CHEATS.

FRAUS LEGIS. If a person having no manner of title to a house, procure an affidavit of the service of a declaration in ejectment, and thereupon gets judgment; and by virtue of a writ of *hab. fac. possessionem* turns the owner out of possession of the house, *and seises and converts the goods therein to his own use*, he may be punished as constructively guilty of felony in respect to the goods, because he used the process of the law with a felonious purpose, in *fraudem legis*, to get possession of the chattels. *Raym.* 276. *Sid.* 254.

This however must be left under all the circumstances of the case, as in the case of *Semple*, and many others *quo animo* the possession obtained.

FRAXINETUM, a wood of ash trees. *Cowel. Blount.*

FREDUM, was a composition made by a criminal, to be freed from prosecution, of which the third part was paid into the exchequer. 1 *Robertson's Hist. Emp. C.* V. 300.

FREDWIT, a liberty to hold courts, and take up amerciaments, &c. *Cowel. Blount.*

FREE-BENCH, (*francus bancus*, i. e. *fedes libera*) is that estate in copyhold lands which the wife hath on the death of her husband for her dower, to hold so long as she lives sole and continent. *Kitch.* 102. 2 *Black.* 122.

FREE-BOOTER, a person who fights without pay, in hopes of getting some booty. *Cowel. Blount.*

FREEBORD, (*francbordus*) is ground claimed in some places more or less, beyond, or without the fence; and it is said to contain two feet and a half. *Ibid.*

FREE-BOROUGH-MEN, were such great men as did not engage like the frank-pledge men for their decennier. *Ibid.*

FREE-CHAPEL, (*libera capella*) a chapel exempt from the jurisdiction of the diocesan. *Ibid.*

FREEHOLD, (*liberum tenementum*) is that land or tenement which a man holds in fee-simple, fee-tail, or for term of life. *Bract. lib.* 2. *c.* 9. Freehold is also extended to offices, which a man holds either in fee, or during life; but those who hold land upon an execution of a statute-merchant, or by elegit, are not freeholders, only as freeholders for their time, till they have received the profits of the land to the value of their debt. *Reg. Judic.* 68, 73. A lease for ninety-nine years, &c. determinable upon a life or lives is not a lease for life to make a freehold, but a lease for years, or chattel determinable upon a life or lives; and an estate for one thousand years is not a freehold, or of so high a nature as an estate for life. *Co. Lit.* 6. He that hath an estate for the term of *his own life*, or the life of another, hath a freehold, and no other of a less estate, though they of a greater estate have a freehold, as tenant in fee, &c. *Lit.* 57.

The following is a summary of the doctrine respecting an estate of freehold, as set forth in the excellent commentaries of the learned Blackstone.

An estate of freehold, *liberum tenementum*, or franktenement, seems to be any estate of inheritance, or for life, in either a corporeal or incorporeal hereditament, existing in, or arising from, real property of free tenure, that is, now, of all which is not copyhold. Such estate, therefore, and no other, as requires actual possession of the land is, legally speaking, freehold, which actual possession can by the course of the common law be only given by the ceremony called livery of seisin, which is the same as the feodal investiture. And from these principles we may extract this description of a freehold; that it is such an estate in lands as is conveyed by livery of seisin, or in tenements of an incorporeal nature, by what is equivalent thereto. And accordingly it is laid down by Littleton, *s.* 59, that where a freehold shall pass, it behoveth to have livery of seisin. As therefore estates of inheritance and estates for life could not by common law be conveyed without livery of seisin, these are properly estates of freehold; and, as no other estates were conveyed with the same solemnity, therefore no others are properly freehold estates. 2 *Black.* 104.

Estates of freehold (thus understood) are either estates of inheritance, or estates not of inheritance. The former are again divided into inheritances absolute or fee-simple, and inheritances limited, one species of which we usually call fee-tail. *Ibid.*

1. Tenant in fee-simple (or, as he is frequently styled, tenant in fee) is he that hath lands, tenements, or hereditaments, to hold to him and his heirs for ever generally, absolutely, and simply; without mentioning what heirs, but referring that to his own pleasure, or to the disposition of the law. The true meaning of the word fee (*feodum*) is the same with that of feud or fief, and in its original sense it is taken in contradistinction to *allodium*, which latter the writers on this subject define to be every man's own land, which he possesses merely in his own right, without owing any rent or service to any superior. This is property in its highest degree, and the owner thereof hath *absolutum et directum dominium*, and therefore is said to be seised thereof absolutely *in dominico suo*, in his own demesne. But *feodum*, or fee, is that which is held of some superior, on condition of rendering him service, in which superior the ultimate property of the land resides. And therefore sir Henry Spelman defines a feud or fee to be the right which the vassal or tenant hath in lands, to use the same, and take the profits thereof to him and his heirs, rendering to the lord his due services; the mere allodial property of the soil always remaining in the lord. This allodial property no subject in England has; it being a received, and now undeniable, principle in the law, that all the lands in England are holden mediately or immediately of the king. The king therefore only hath *absolutum et directum dominium*: but all subjects lands are in the nature of feodum or fee; whether derived to them by descent from their ancestors, or purchased for a valuable consideration; for they cannot come to any man by either of those ways, unless accompanied with those feodal clogs, which were laid upon the first feudatory when it was originally granted. A subject therefore hath only the usufruct, and not the absolute property of the soil; or, as sir Edward Coke expresses it, he hath *dominium utile*, but not *dominium directum*. And hence it is that in the most solemn acts of law we express the strongest and highest estate that any subject can have, by these words, "he "is seised thereof in his demesne, as of "fee." It is a man's demesne, *dominicum*, or property, since it belongs to him and his heirs for ever: yet this *dominicum*, property, or demesne, is strictly not absolute or allodial, but qualified or feodal: it is his demesne, as of fee; that is, it is not purely and simply his own, since it is held of a superior lord, in whom the ultimate property resides. 2 *Black.* 104, 5.

This is the primary sense and acceptation of the word fee. But (as sir Martin Wright very justly observes) the doctrine, "that all lands are holden," having been for so many ages a fixed and undeniable axiom, our English lawyers do very rarely (of late years especially) use the word fee in this its primary original sense, in contradistinction to allodium or absolute property, with which they have no concern; but generally use it to express the continuance or quantity of estate. A fee therefore, in general, signifies an estate of inheritance being the highest and most extensive interest that a man can have in a feud: and when the term is used simply, without any other adjunct, or has the adjunct of simple annexed to it, (as a fee, or a fee-simple,) it is used in contradistinction to a fee conditional at the common law, or a fee-tail by the statute; importing an absolute inheritance, clear of any condition, limitation, or restrictions to particular heirs, but descendible to the heirs general, whether male or female, lineal or collateral. And in no other sense than this is the king said to be seised in fee, he being the feudatory of no man. *Co. Lit.* 1.

Taking therefore fee in this its secondary sense, as a state of inheritance, it is applicable to, and may be had in, any kind of hereditaments either corporeal or incorporeal, *feodum est quod quis tenet sibi et hæredibus suis, sive sit tenementum, sive reditus,* &c. *Flet. l.* 5, *c.* 5, *s.* 7. But there is this distinction between the two species of hereditaments; that, of a corporeal inheritance, a man shall be said to be seised in his demesne, as of fee; of an incorporeal one, he shall only be said to be seised as of fee, and not in his demesne. *Lit. s.* 10. For, as incorporeal hereditaments are in their nature collateral to and issue out of lands and houses, their owner hath no property, *dominicum,* or demesne, in the thing itself, but hath only something derived out of it, resembling the servitudes, or services, of the civil law. *Servitus est jus, quo res mea alterius rei vel persona servit. Ff.* 8. 1. 1. The *dominicum* or property is frequently in one man, while the appendage or service is in another. Thus Gaius may be seised as of fee of a way leading over the land, of which Titius is seised in his demesne as of fee. 2 *Black.* 105, 106.

The fee-simple or inheritance of lands and tenements is generally vested and resides in some person or other; though divers inferior estates may be carved out of it. As if one grants a lease for twenty-one years, or for one or two lives, the fee-simple remains vested in him and his heirs; and after the determination of those years or lives, the land reverts to the grantor or his heirs, who shall hold it again in fee simple. Yet sometimes the fee may be in abeyance, that is (as the word signifies) in expectation, remembrance, and contemplation in law; there being no person in *esse,* in whom it can vest and abide: though the law considers it as always potentially existing, and ready to vest whenever a proper owner appears. Thus, in a grant to John for life, and afterwards to the heirs of Richard, the inheritance is plainly neither granted to John nor Richard, nor can it vest in the heirs of Richard till his death, for *nemo est hæres viventis*: it remains therefore in waiting or abeyance, during the life of Richard. *Co. Litt.* 342. This is likewise always the case of a parson of a church, who hath only an estate therein for the term of his life; and the inheritance remains in abeyance. *Litt. s.* 646. And not only the fee, but the freehold also, may be in abeyance; as, when a parson dies, the freehold of his glebe is in abeyance until a successor be named, and then it vests in the successor. *Litt. s.* 647. 2 *Black.* 107. But see head ABEYANCE.

The word "heirs" is necessary in the grant or donation, in order to make a fee, or inheritance. For if land be given to a man for ever, or to him and his assigns for ever, this vests in him but an estate for life. *Ibid. s.* 1. This very great nicety about the insertion of the word "heirs" in all feoffments and grants, in order to vest a fee, is plainly a relic of the feodal strictness: by which it was required that the form of the donation should be punctually pursued; or that, as Craig, (*l.* 1, *t.* 9, *s.* 17,) expresses it in the words of Baldus, "*donationes sint stricti juris* "*ne quis plus donasse præsumatur quam* "*in donatione expresserit.*" And therefore, as the personal abilities of the donee were originally supposed to be the only inducements to the gift, the donee's estate in the land extended only to his own person, and subsisted no longer than his life; unless the donor, by an express provision in the grant, gave it a longer continuance, and extended it also to his heirs: but this rule is now softened by many exceptions. *Co. Lit.* 9, 10. 2 *Black.* 108.

For, 1. It does not extend to devises by will; in which, as they were introduced at the time when the feodal rigour was apace wearing out, a more liberal construction is allowed; and therefore by a devise to a man for ever, or to one and his assigns for ever, or to one in fee-simple, the devisee hath an estate of inheritance; for the intention of the devisor is sufficiently plain from the words of perpetuity annexed; though he hath omitted the legal words of inheritance. But if the devise be to a man and his assigns, without annexing words of perpetuity, there the devisee shall take only an estate for life; for it does not appear that the devisor intended any more. 2 *Black* 118. But it is not necessary to use any words of perpetuity in a devise, in order to give a fee-simple, where it appears to be the intention of the testator to dispose of all his interest in an estate, and that is implied from the word estate alone; as if a testator gives to Richard his estate or estates in or at Dale, though neither heirs, assigns, or any other word is annexed to Richard's name, yet he takes an estate in fee-simple. 1 *T. R.* 411. 2 *T. R.* 656. So also where lands are given to Richard charged with the payment of a specific sum, and which is not to be raised out of the rents and profits, such a devise without words of perpetuity will carry a fee-simple; for otherwise the devisee might be a loser by dying before he was repaid the sum charged upon the estate. *Hargr. Co. Litt.* 9. *b.* 3 *T. R.* 356. 8 *T. R.* 1.

And where an estate is given generally

without words being added, which would create a fee or an estate tail, and it is charged with the payment of annuities, the devisee takes a fee, but that is not the case where an estate tail is given to the devisee. *5 T. R.* 335.

But where a testator leaves all his hereditaments to A, A takes only an estate for life, *5 T. R.* 558. A fee also will not pass by general introductory words in a will, by which the testator declares his intention to dispose of all his estate both real and personal, if there is not afterwards in the will some specific devise for that purpose. But where such subsequent devise is in some degree ambiguous, then the introductory words may have some effect, as indicative of the intention of the testator. *5 T. R.* 13. *6 T. R.* 610.

2. Neither does this rule extend to fines or recoveries considered as a species of conveyance; for thereby an estate in fee passes by act and operation of law without the word "heirs," as it does also for particular reasons by certain other methods of conveyance, which have relation to a former grant or estate wherein the word "heirs" was expressed. *Co. Lit.* 9. 3. In creations of nobility by writ, the peer so created hath an inheritance in his title, without expressing the word "heirs;" for heirship is implied in the creation, unless it be otherwise specially provided: but in creations by patent, which are *stricti juris*, the word "heirs" must be inserted, otherwise there is no inheritance. 4. In grants of lands to sole corporations and their successors, the word "successors" supplies the place of "heirs;" for as heirs take from the ancestor, so doth the successor from the predecessor. Nay, in a grant to a bishop, or other sole spiritual corporation, in frankalmoign the word "frankalmoign" supplies the place of "successors" (as the word "successors" supplies the place of "heirs) *ex vi termini*; and in all these cases a fee-simple vests in such sole corporation. But in a grant of lands to a corporation aggregate, the word "successors" is not necessary, though usually inserted: for, albeit such simple grant be strictly only an estate for life, yet as that corporation never dies, such estate for life is perpetual, or equivalent to a fee-simple, and therefore the law allows it to be one. 5. Lastly, in the case of the king, a fee-simple will vest in him, without the word "heirs" or "successors" in the grant; partly from prerogative royal, and partly from a reason similar to the last, because the king in judgment of law never dies. But the general rule is that the word "heirs" is necessary to create an estate of inheritance. *2 Black.* 108, 9.

II. Limited fees, or such estates of inheritance as are clogged and confined with conditions, or qualifications, of any sort, are of two sorts. 1st. Qualified, or base fees: and 2. Fees conditional, so called at the common law; and afterwards fees-tail, in consequence of the statute *de donis*, for which see *Base Fee, Qualified,* and *Tenant in Tail.*

FREEHOLDERS, are such as hold any freehold estate.

FREEMAN (*liber homo*). The distinction of a freeman from a vassal; under the feudal policy *liber homo*, was commonly opposed to *vassus*, or *vassallus*, the former denoting an allodial proprietor, the latter one who held of a superior. *Cowel. Blount.*

The title of freeman is also given to any one admitted to the freedom of a corporate town, or of any other corporate body, consisting, among other members, of those called freemen.

FREIGHT, (Fr. *fret*) signifies the money paid for carriage of goods by sea, or in a larger sense it is taken for the cargo or burthen of the ship. *Lex Mercat.*

FRENCH. King *William* I, called the conqueror, being a native of Normandy in France, caused the laws of this realm, in his time, to be written and pleaded in the French language. *3 Rep.* 17. But by the Stat. 37 *Ed.* 3, *c.* 15, all pleas that are *pleaded in any of the king's* courts, shall be pleaded in the English tongue; though appeals were still to be arraigned, and the plea of the defendant read in French in the same manner as anciently. *2 Hawk. P. C.* 308. *Sed vide* stat. 4 *Geo.* 2. *c.* 26, by which all pleadings were directed to be in English.

FRENCHMAN, heretofore a term for every stranger or outlandishman. *Bract. lib.* 3. *tract.* 2. *c.* 15. See *Francigenæ.*

FRENDWITE, comes from the Saxon *freond*, i. e. *amicus*, and wite, *mulcta*, and is a mulct exacted of him who harboured his outlawed friend. *Cowel. Blount. Fleta lib.* 1. *c.* 7.

FRESCA, fresh water, or rain, and land floods.

FRESH DISSEISIN, (*frisca disseisina*, from the Fr. *fraiz*, i. e. *recens et disseisir*, viz. *possessione ejicere*) signified that disseisin which a man might formerly seek to defeat of himself, and by his own power, without resorting to the king, or the law; as where it was not above fifteen days old, or of some other short continuance. *Britt. c.* 5. *Cowel. Blount.*

FRESH FINE, is that which was levied within a year past: it is mentioned in the statute of *Westm.* 2, 13 *Ed.* 1. *c.* 45.

FRESH FORCE, (*frisca fortia*) is a force newly done in any city, borough, &c. And before ejectments were introduced, if a person were disseised of any lands or tenements within such a city, or borough, he who had a right to the land, by the usage and custom of the said city, &c. might bring his assise, or bill of fresh force, within forty days after the force committed; and recover the lands. *F. N. B.* 7. *Old Nat. Br.* 4.

FRESH SUIT, or *Pursuit*, (*recens insecutio*) is such a present and earnest following of an offender, where a robbery is committed, as never ceases from the time of the offence done or discovered, until he be apprehended. Vide "*Hundred*" and "*Hue and Cry*." And the benefit of a pursuit of a felon is, that the party pursuing shall have his goods restored to him; which otherwise are forfeited to the king. *Staundf. Pl. Cor. lib.* 3. *cap.* 10 and 12. It has been anciently holden, that to make a fresh suit, the party ought to make hue and cry with all convenient speed, and to have taken the offender himself, &c. But at this day, if the party hath been guilty of no gross negligence, but hath used all reasonable care in inquiring after, pursuing, and apprehending the felon, he shall be allowed to have made sufficient fresh suit. 2 *Hawk. P. C.* 169. Also it is said, that the judging of fresh suit is in the discretion of the court, though it ought to be found by the jury; and the justices may, if they think fit, award restitution without making any inquisition concerning the same. *Ibid.* 169, 171.

Where a gaoler immediately pursues a felon, or other prisoner, escaping from prison, it is fresh suit, to excuse the gaoler: and if a lord follow his distress into another's ground, on its being driven off the premises, this is called fresh suit: so where a tenant pursues his cattle that escape or stray into another man's lands, &c. Fresh suit may be either within the view, or without; as to which the law makes some difference: and it has been said, that fresh suit may continue for seven years. 3 *Rep. S. P. C.*

FRETUM BRITANNICUM, in ancient writings used for the streights between Dover and Calais. *Cowel. Blount.*

FRETTUM and FRECTUM, the freight of a ship, or freight-money. *Ibid.*

FRIBURGH, *alias* FRITHBURGH, (*frideburgum*, from the Sax. *frid*, i. e. *pax*, & *borge*, *fidejussor*) is the same with frank-pledge; the one being in the time of the Saxons, and the other since the conquest. *Bracton, lib.* 3. *tract.* 2. *c.* 10. *Lambard, fol.* 143. *Fleta, lib.* 1. *cap.* 47.

FRIDSTOLL and FRITHSTOW, (Sax. *frid*, *pax*, & *stol*, *sedes*) a seat, chair, or place of peace, an immunity granted to the church. And there were many such in England; but the most famous was at Beverly, which had this inscription: *hæc sedes lapidea freedstoll dicitur*, i. e. *pacis cathedra, ad quam reus fugiendo perveniens, omnimodam habet securitatem*. *Camd. Cowel. Blount.*

FRIENDLESS MAN, the old Saxon word for him whom we call an outlaw; because he was denied all help of friends after certain days. *Bract. lib.* 3. *tract.* 2. *c.* 12. See *Frendwite.*

FRIER, (Lat. *frater*. Fr. *frere*) the name of an order of religious persons, of which there were four principal branches, *viz.* 1. Minors, Grey Friers, or Franciscans. 2. Augustines. 3. Dominicans, or Black Friers, 4. White Friers, or Carmelites; of which the rest descended. 4 *H.* 7. *cap.* 17. *Lyndewood de Relig. Domibus, c.* 1. *Cowel. Blount.*

FRIER-OBSERVANT, (*frater observans*) a branch of the Franciscan friers. *Ibid.*

FRILING, FREOLING, (from the Sax. *freoh*, *liber* & *ling*, *progenies*) signifies a man that is free. *Ibid.*

FRIPERER, (Fr. *fripier*, i. e. *interpolator*) one that scours and furbishes up old clothes to sell again; a kind of broker. *Ibid.*

FRISCUS, uncultivated ground. *Ibid.*

FRIFT, a term among merchants for selling goods upon credit. *Ibid.*

FRITH, (Sax.) a wood, from *frid*, i. e. *pax*; for the English Saxons held woods to be sacred, and therefore made them sanctuaries. Sir Edward Coke expounds it a plain between woods, or a lawn. *Co. Lit.* 5. Cambden in his Britan. useth it for an arm of the sea, or a streight, between two lands, from the word *fretum*. *Cowel. Blount.*

FRITHBRECH, (*pacis violatio*) the breaking of the peace. *Ibid.*

FRITHGEAR, (from the Sax. *frith* or *frid*, *pax* & *gear*, *annus*) the year of jubilee, or of meeting for peace and friendship. *Ibid.*

FRITHGILD, is the same which we now call a Guildhall; or a company or fraternity. *Ibid.*

FRITHMAN, one belonging to such fraternity or company. *Ibid.*

FRITHMOTE, is mentioned in the records of the county palatine of Chester: *per Frithmote J. Stanley, ar, clamat capere annuatim de villa de Olton, &c.* *Cowel. Blount.*

FRITHSOKE, FRITHSOKEN, surety of defence, or liberty of having *frank pledge*. *Cowel. Blount.*

FRODMORTEL, *rectius* FREOMORTEL, (from the Sax. *freo*, free, and *morthdel*, *homicidium*) an immunity for committing manslaughter.

FRUIT, *stealing of*. See *Felony* and *Trespass*.

FRUMGYLD, (Sax.) is the first payment made to the kindred of a person slain, towards the recompence of his murder. *Cowel. Blount.*

FRUMSTOL, the chief seat or mansion-house; by some the homestal. *Ibid.*

FRUSCA TERRÆ, waste and desart lands. *Ibid.*

FRUSTURA, (from the Fr. *froissure*) a breaking down; also a ploughing or breaking up. *Ibid.*

FRUSTRUM TERRÆ, a small piece or parcel of land. *Ibid.*

FRUTECTUM, a place where shrubs, or tall herbs do grow. *Ibid.*

FUAGE, an imposition of *fuage* was laid in the reign of Edward III. by Edward the Black Prince upon the subjects of a dukedom, of *Acquitain*, of 12*d.* for every fire. *Rot. Parl.* 25 *Ed.* 3. And it is probable, that the hearth-money imposed by *Car.* 2. originated from hence.

FUEL. By an antient statute, if any person shall sell billet-wood or faggots for fuel under the assise, &c. on presentment thereof upon oath by six persons sworn by a justice of peace, the party may be set on the pillory in the next market town, with a faggot, &c. bound to some part of his body. For the assise of fuel, stat. 7 *Ed*, 6. *c.* 7. and 43 *Eliz. c.* 14. None are to buy fuel but such as will burn it, or retail it to those who do; on pain to forfeit the treble value; also no person may alter any mark or assise of fuel, on the like forfeiture. *Stat. Ibid.* See *Billets.*

FUER, (Fr. *fuir*, Lat. *lugere*) is twofold, *fuer in fait*, or *in facto*, when a man doth apparently and corporally fly; and *fuer in ley*, *in lege*, when being called in the county court he appeareth not, which is flight in the interpretation of the law. *Staundf. Pl. Cor. lib.* 3. *c.* 22.

FUGA CATALLORUM, a drove of cattle: *fugatores carrucarum*, waggoners who drive oxen, without beating or goading. *Fleta, lib.* 2. *c.* 78. *Cowel. Blount.*

FUGACIA, a chase, being all one with *chasea*; and *fugatio*, hunting, or the privilege to hunt. *Cowel. Blount.*

FUGAM FECIT, is where it is found by inquisition, that a person fled for felony, &c. And if flight and felony be found on an indictment for felony, or before the coroner, where a murder is committed, the offender shall forfeit all his goods, and the issues of his lands, till he is acquitted or pardoned. 3 *Inst.* 218. *Hawk. P. C.* 27. 2 *Hawk. P. C.* 450. See *Forfeiture.*

FUGITIVES GOODS, (*bona fugitivorum*) are the proper goods of him that flies upon felony, which after the flight lawfully found on record, do belong to the king or lord of the manor, as grantee thereof. 5 *Rep.* 109.

FUGITIVES OVER SEA. To depart this realm over the sea, without the king's licence, except it be great men and merchants, and the king's soldiers, incurs forfeiture of goods: and masters of ships, &c. carrying such persons beyond sea, shall forfeit their vessels; also if any searcher of any port negligently suffer any persons to pass, he shall be imprisoned, &c. 9 *Ed.* 3. *c.* 10. 5 *R.* 2. *c.* 2. See *Manufactures.*

FUGITIO, *pro fuga*. *Cowel. Blount.*

FULL-AGE. The ages of male and female are different, for different purposes. A male at twelve may take the oath of allegiance; at fourteen may consent, or disagree, to marriage, may choose his guardian, and, if his discretion be actually proved, may make a testament of his personal estate; at seventeen may be an executor; and at twenty-one is at his own disposal, and alien his lands, goods and chattels: a female at seven may be betrothed or given in marriage; at nine is entitled to dower; at twelve is at years of maturity, and therefore may consent or disagree to marriage, and, if proved to have sufficient discretion, may bequeath her personal estate; at fourteen is at years of legal discretion, and may choose a guardian; at seventeen may be executrix; and at twenty-one may dispose of herself and her lands. 1 *Black. Com.* 463.

FULLUM AQUÆ, a fleam or stream of water, such as comes from a mill. *Cowel. Blount.*

FUMAGE, (*fumagium*) dung for soil, or a manuring of land with dung, also sometimes used for smoke-money, a customary payment for every house that had a chimney. *Domesday.* 1 *Black.* 323.

FUMADOES, are pilchards garbaged and salted, then hung in the smoke, and pressed. *Cowel. Blount.*

FUNDITORES, pioneers. *Ibid.*

FUNDS. After the revolution (*not perhaps correctly termed happy and glorious from its present consequences*) had introduced a new system of foreign politics with respect to our new connections with Europe; the expences of the nation, therefore, not only in settling a new establishment, *founded in positive disseisin*, but in maintaining long wars, as principals, on the continent, for the security of the Dutch barrier, reducing the French monarchy, settling the Spanish succession, supporting the house of Austria, maintaining the liberties of the Germanic body, and other purposes, increased to an unusual degree: insomuch that it was not thought advisable to raise all the expences of any one year by taxes to be levied within that year, lest the unaccustomed weight of them should create murmurs among the people.* It was therefore *the policy of the times to anticipate the revenues of their posterity, by borrowing immense sums for the current service of the state*, and to lay no more taxes upon the subject than would suffice to pay the annual interest of the sums so borrowed: by this means converting the principal debt into a new species of property, transferrable from one man to another at any time and in any quantity. This policy of the English parliament laid the foundation of what is called the national debt: for a few long annuities created in the reign of Charles II. will hardly

* Happy for us and our posterity would it have been, if this system ultimately adopted by the immortal Pitt, had then been taken up and acted on.

deserve that name. And the example then set by the partizans of *Will.* 3. has been so closely followed during the long wars in the reign of queen Anne, and since, that the capital of the funded national debt amounted at the close of the sessions 49 *Geo.* 3. to a most enormous sum in the aggregate, redeemable by the same authority that imposed the same; which, if at any time it can pay off the capital, will abolish those taxes which are raised to discharge the interest.

The produce of the several taxes were originally separate and distinct funds; being securities for the sums advanced on each several tax, and for them only. But at last it became necessary to avoid confusion, as they multiplied yearly, to consolidate the whole, and accordingly

By 27 *Geo.* 3. *c.* 13. the whole of the duties of customs, excise, and stamps, and the several duties on hackney coaches, and chairs, hawkers, and pedlars, with the assessed taxes were first carried to one fund, directed to be called THE CONSOLIDATED FUND.

Since this act various new duties have been imposed, and all the acts imposing the same, contain clauses, directing that the monies arising therefrom and paid into the exchequer, (not otherways appropriated) shall be carried to the said consolidated fund.

And by the said act of 27. *Geo.* 3. *c.* 13. and all subsequent acts whereby monies have been raised by annuities, it is directed that all such annuities so due from the public, shall be payable out of the said consolidated fund at the times and in manner as the said annuities become due.

Whenever the consolidated fund shall be insufficient to pay the annuities, the treasury may make good the deficiency out of the supplies for that year, which shall be replaced out of any future surplus of the fund. 27 *Geo.* 3. *c.* 13.

Also by 26 *Geo.* 3. *c.* 31. commissioners were appointed for the reduction of the national debt, and it was enacted that 250,000*l.* shall be set apart quarterly out of the surplusses of the sinking fund; and in case of a deficiency in the said surplusses, the same shall be carried on as a charge, on the subsequent quarters.

Surplusses remaining (after former incumbrances are provided for) shall be applied in payment of former deficiencies, and of so much of the quarterly sum of 250,000*l.* as they will extend to pay. *Ibid.*

Deficiencies at the end of any year shall be made good out of the supplies granted the same year *Ibid.*

The monies set apart quarterly, shall be paid into the bank: and shall be applied in reducing the national debt. Officers of the exchequer are not to issue the produce of the sinking fund, before payment of the 250,000*l.* quarterly, and the redeemed stock shall be transferred to the commissioners, and the dividends shall be received by the bank, and placed to the commissioners' account. *Ibid.*

When any stock shall be placed to the account of the commissioners, no money shall be issued for the management thereof. And monies placed to the account of the commissioners shall be applied in redemption of annuities at or above par. *Ibid.*

The commissioners are impowered, if they shall think expedient, to subscribe towards any public loan; and the speaker of the house of commons, the chancellor of the exchequer, the master of the rolls, the accountant general in chancery, and the governor and deputy governor of the bank, for the time being respectively, shall be commissioners, who are to appoint clerks, and officers. *Ibid.*

The bank shall pay such money vested in the commissioners, as shall be ordered by them, and shall make up their accounts with them annually, which shall be laid before the parliament annually. *Ibid.*

Commissioners are to lay an account of their proceedings before parliament; and before the commissioners for auditing the public accounts. *Ibid.*

Forging any certificate made by virtue of this act is felony *without* clergy. *s.* 21.

The cashiers of the bank shall give security: and the treasury may discharge incidental charges of executing this act. *s.* 22.

By 27 *Geo.* 3. *c.* 13. from July 5th 1787, the sum of 250,000*l.* directed by 26 *Geo.* 3. *c.* 31. to be set apart at the exchequer quarterly, shall be set apart out of the consolidated fund, and the provisions of that act shall continue in force. *Ibid.*

From May 10th, 1787, all monies reserved for payment of annuities on lives, which shall not have been claimed for three years prior to January 5th 1787, or which shall thereafter not be claimed for three years, shall be placed to the account of the commissioners for reducing the national debt. *Ibid.*

The exchequer shall transmit, by April 5th annually, an account of annuities fallen in by death, or unclaimed for three years, to the treasury, who are to cause the same to be placed to the account of the said commissioners. *Ibid.*

But if any claimants of annuities so appropriated shall thereafter appear, they are to be paid out of any money applicable for the payment of annuities. *Ibid.*

By 32 *Geo.* 3. *c.* 55. the exchequer shall keep a separate account of the interest of new loans, and if provision be not made for paying them off within forty-five years, an additional sum equal to one hundredth part of the stock, to be issued from the exchequer quarterly, and placed to the account of the commissioners. *s.* 3.

And if such loans be raised by annuities

for any term longer than forty-five years, one-hundredth part of such as may be expected to be then out-standing shall be issued: the computation of such value is to be made under the direction of the commissioners, and copies delivered to the speaker; and the speaker is to certify to the treasury and exchequer the amount of the additional sum to be issued. *s.* 4.

Sums to be issued under this act to be issued in the order the loans have taken place. *s.* 5.

Whenever there remains not money of the consolidated fund to pay the further sum to be issued in consequence of any new loan, the deficiency shall be made good, as directed by 26 *Geo.* 3. *c.* 91. *s.* 6.

Any deficiency in the quarterly payments, which may arise at the end of the year, shall be made good out of any supplies granted for the current or any preceding year. *s.* 7.

Monies placed to the account of the commissioners to be applied in the purchase of such redeemable annuities as shall be at or above par according to 26 *Geo.* 3. and the stock redeemed to be transferred to their account, and the dividends to be placed thereto: but sums placed to their account in consequence of any new loan to be kept separate. *s.* 8.

Persons counterfeiting certificates, guilty of felony without clergy. *s.* 9.

Subsequent to the passing the act for the redemption of the public debt, an additional annual sum of 200,000*l. has, under the authority of several acts, annually passed for that purpose, been issued from the exchequer over and above the quarterly sum of* 250,000*l.*

And by 42 *Geo.* 3. *c.* 71. it is enacted, that the said sum of 200,000*l.* heretofore annually issued shall be a permanent charge, and paid quarterly out of the British consolidated fund to the bank for the commissioners. *s.* 4.

The money placed to the account of the commissioners under this and the former acts shall accumulate, and be applied in redemption of the public annuities, until the whole shall be paid off, within forty-five years from their respective creation. *s.* 5.

By 48 *Geo.* 3. *c.* 142. the commissioners for the reduction of the national debt, are empowered to accept transfers of stock in the 3*l.* per cent consols, or reduced bank annuities, for the purchase of life annuities, for a single life, or the life of a nominee; or the lives of two nominees; in doing which, the party may name himself; but the nominees must not be under thirty-five, and previously to the transfer, the parties are to produce certificates or good proof of the age of the nominees. *s.* 1—5.

The purchasers of life annuities on single lives, upon the transfer of stock in manner directed by the act, are to be entitled to the annuities as specified in the schedule D, and the purchasers of life annuities, on the continuance of two lives, are to be entitled to the annuities specified in schedule E. *s.* 7, 8, 9.

Annuitants may make further purchases on the lives of original nominees without fresh certificates; but the annuities on the life of one nominee are not to exceed 1000*l.* nor for two nominees 1500*l.* *s.* 12—14.

Persons appointed by the commissioners, for reducing the national debt, may accept stock from the purchasers, the dividends whereof shall be afterwards received, and constitute a part of the sinking fund. *s.* 14.

The annuities are to be payable half yearly, at the same days as the stock transferred, and on the death of a single life, or the survivor of two lives, after the last half-yearly payment, one quarter's annuity is to be paid to the personal representative, at the next half-yearly dividend. *s.* 15.

To prevent frauds in the receipt of annuities, certificates must be produced from the minister of the parish, or, in his absence, the churchwardens and overseers, or from some justice, of the existence of the life of the nominee, with an affidavit or affirmation annexed of the identity of the party, upon production whereof at the bank, the annuity shall be payable. *s.* 18.

And certificates of the death of a single or surviving nominee must be also produced, to enable the personal representative to receive the quarterly share. *s.* 19.

These life annuities are transferrable, and are to be free from taxes, except such as dividends of consols and reduced annuities are liable to, and shall be deemed personal estate. *s.* 20, 21.

Penalty on producing false certificates and affidavits, or receiving annuities after the deaths of nominees, 500*l.* *s.* 22, 23.

Annuities ceasing to revert to the sinking fund. *s.* 24.

The certificates, transfers of stock, and life annuities are to be exempt from stamp duties. *s.* 25.

Persons making false affidavits, guilty of perjury. *s.* 26.

Persons forging registers, certificates, names of witnesses thereto, or the certificate of any judge, baron, justice, or magistrate, or any certificates of the commissioners or cashier, or clerk to the bank, or the names of persons in any transfer, or any receipt, or letter of attorney, or who shall personate the nominee, or shall utter any such forged certificate, or instrument as aforesaid, shall be guilty of felony without clergy. *s.* 28.

Penalties may be recovered in the name of the attorney-general at Westminster, or in Dublin, in the court of exchequer, and in Scotland in the name of the advocate-general, to be applied to the sinking fund; but the commissioners may give the informer one half. *s.* 29.

By 49 *Geo.* 3. *c.* 64. the commissioners for the reduction of the national debt, may grant under the last act (48 *Geo.* 3. *c.* 142.) annuities of an annual amount for the life of any one nominee, or of the lives of two nominees, and of the life of the longer liver of them, so as the same do not exceed 3000*l.* per ann.

FUNERAL CHARGES. In strictness no funeral expences are allowable *against a creditor*, except for the coffin, ringing the bell, parson, clerk, and bearers fees; but not for pall or ornaments; *per Holt.* 1 *Salk.* 296. *Trin.* 5 *W.* & *M. B. R. Shelton's case.* Ten pounds is enough to be allowed for the funeral of one in debt; *per Holt.* Baron Powell in his circuit would allow but 11*s.* 6*d.* as all the necessary charge. *Comb.* 342. *Trin.* 7 *W. B. R. Anon.* But 5*l.* and no more is now the usual sum that is allowed in case of an insolvent. *Salk.* 196. *Bull. N. P.*

FURCA and FOSSA (*i. e.* the gallows and the pit) in ancient privileges granted by our kings, it signified a jurisdiction of punishing felons; that is, men by hanging, and women by drowning. *Cowel. Blount.*

FURCARE AD TASSUM, to pitch corn with a fork in loading a waggon, or in making a rick or mow. *Ibid.*

FURCUM ET FLAGELLUM, the meanest of all servile tenures, when the bondman was at the disposal of his lord for life and limb. *Ibid.*

FURIGELDUM, a mulct paid for the theft. *Ibid.*

FURLONG, is a quantity of ground containing generally forty poles or perches in length, every pole being sixteen feet and a half; eight of which furlongs make a mile: it is otherwise the eighth part of an acre of land in quantity. Stat. 35 *Ed.* 1. *c.* 6. In the former acceptation, the Romans call it *stadium;* and in the latter *jugerum.* Also the word furlong hath been sometimes used for a piece of land of more or less acres.

FURNAGE, (*furnagium*). See *Formagium.*

FURNARIUS, is used for a baker, who keeps an oven; and *furniare* signifies to bake or put any thing in the oven. *Mat. Paris. Anno* 1258. *Cowel. Blount.*

FURR, (*furrura*, from the Fr. *fourer*, i. e. *pelliculare*) is the coat or covering of a beast. *Ibid.*

FURST ET FONDONG, (Sax.) time to advise, or to take counsel. *Ibid.*

FURTUM, theft, or robbery of any kind. *Lit. Dict.*

FUSTIANS. See *London* and *Manufactures.*

FUSTICK, wood brought from Barbadoes, Jamaica, &c. used by dyers.

FYRDERINGA, (from the Sax. *firderung*, i. e. *expeditionis apparatus*) a going out to war, or a military expedition at the king's command; not going upon which when summoned, was punished by fine at the king's pleasure. *Leg. H.* 1. *c.* 10. Blount calls it an expedition; or a fault or trespass for not going upon the same. *Cowel. Blount.*

FYRTHING or FYRDUNG, a military expedition. *Ibid.*

G

GABBLE, (*blatero, garrio*) to babble and talk idly. *Cowel. Blount.*

GABEL, (*gabella, gablum, gablagium*) a tax, and hath been variously used; as for a rent, custom, service, &c. And where it was a payment of rent, those who paid it were termed *gablatores. Domesday. Co. Litt.* 213. When the word *gabel* was formerly mentioned, without any addition to it, it signified the tax on salt, though afterwards it was applied to all other taxes. *Cowel. Blount.*

GABLE-END, (*gabulum*) the head or extreme part of a house or building. *Ibid.*

GABULUS DENARIORUM, rent paid in money. *Ibid.*

GAFOLD-GILD, (Sax.) payment of tribute or custom; sometimes usury. *Ibid.*

GAFOLD-LAND, or GAFUL-LAND, (*terra censualis*) land liable to taxes; and rented or let for rent. *Ibid.*

GAGE, (Fr. Lat. *vadium*) signifies as much as to pawn or pledge. *Glanv. lib.* 10. *c.* 6. Gage deliverance is a security put in on suing out replevins, that he will re-deliver the distress upon the plaintiff's praying the same. *Kitch.* 145. And in original writs it runs, "put by gage and safe pledges A. B. the defendant," &c. 3 *Black.* 280.

GAGE, *estates in.* Estates held in *vadio*, in *gage* or pledge, are of two kinds, *vivum vadium* or living pledge: that is, to hold the estate till by the receipt of the rents and profits, the principal sum borrowed on the security of the estate is repaid: the other estate in gage or pledge is, *mortuum vadium*, a dead pledge or mortgage.

GAGER DE LEY. See *Wager of Law.*

GAINAGE, (*gainagium*, i. e. *plaustri apparatus*, Fr. *gaignage*, viz. *lucrum*) the gain or profit of tilled or planted land, raised by cultivating it. *Bract. lib.* 1. *c.* 9. *Old Nat. Br.* 117. *Cowel. Blount.*

GAINERY, (Fr. *gaignerie*) tillage, or the profit arising from it, or of the beasts employed therein. *Ibid.*

GALEA, a galley or swift sailing ship, *Cowel. Blount.*

GALETTI, were Welchmen. *Ibid.*

GALLIGASKINS, wide hose or breeches, from their use by the Gascoigns. *Ibid.*

GALLIHALPENCE, a kind of coin, which with *suskins* and *doitkins*, were forbidden by the stat. 3 *H.* 5. *c.* 1.

GALLIMAWFRY, a meal of coarse victuals, given to galley slaves. *Cowel. Blount.*

GALLIVOLATIUM, (from *gallus*, a cock) a cock shoot or cock-glade. *Ibid.*

GALOCHES, (Fr.) a kind of shoe, worn by the Gauls in dirty weather. *Ibid.*

GAMBA, GAMBERIA, GAMBRIA, (Fr. *jambiere*) military boots or defence for the legs. *Ibid.*

GAMBEYSON, (*gambezonum*) a horseman's coat used in war, which covered the legs: or rather a quilted coat, to put under the armour, to make it set easy. *Fleta, lib.* 1. *c.* 24.

GAME, (*aucupia*, from *anceps*, *aucupis*, i. e. *avium captio*) birds or prey got by fowling and hunting.

There are five wild beasts of venary that are called beasts of forest; and they are the *hart*, the *hind*, the *hare*, the *boar* and the *wolf*. *Antiq. Brit.* 43. *Manwood* 91.

So there are five wild beasts that are called beasts of chase, and they are the *buck*, the *doe*, the *fox*, the *martron**, and the *roe*. *Antiq. Brit.* 43. *Manwood* 91.

And the beasts and fowls of warren are only these, the *hare*, the *coney*, the *pheasant*, and the *partridge*†. *Manwood* 94.

In these, and the like wild animals, generally known by the denomination of GAME, no person can have a property, unless they be tamed, or reclaimed; and as property is the power that a man hath over any other things for his own use, and the ability that he has to apply it to the sustentation of his being; when the power ceases, his property is lost; and by consequence an animal of this kind, which after my seizure escapes into the wild common of nature, and asserts its own liberty by its swiftness, is no more mine than any creature in the Indies, because I have it no longer in my power or disposal. *Bacon's Abr.* tit. *Game.*

But by immediate manucaption, or taking them or killing them a property may be acquired in them; for in these cases they belong to such person in the same manner as any other chattels, and cannot be taken from him, since the first seizure and caption was sufficient to vest the property of them in him. 7 *Co.* 16. *b.* *Bacon's Abr.* tit. *Game.*

So by taking and taming them they belong to the owner, as do all other tame animals‡, so long as they continue in this condition, that is, as long as they can be considered to have the mind of returning to their masters; for while they appear to be in this state, they are plainly the owner's, and ought not to be violated (and an action will lie against any man that detains them from the owner, or unlawfully destroys them, 2 *Black. Com.* 325.) but when they forsake the houses and habitations of men, and betake themselves to the woods, they are then the property of any man. *Ibid.*

And another way of gaining property in them is by inclosure, and then the beasts must be understood to be mine, as the profits of the soil itself are, and they can no more be taken and carried off than any other profits of the land; and therefore if inclosed deer in a park or paddock comes in a field or warren, they become so my own that no man ought to kill or take them away: now since in this case it is the inclosure only that re-

* A large kind of weazel, whose fur is valuable. *Johnson.*

† In *Co. Lit.* 233, it is said that there be both beasts and fowls of the warren: beasts, as *hares*, *conies*, *roes*; fowls of two sorts, *terestres* or land fowls, and *aquatiles* or water fowls; and that the land fowl are of two sorts; *silvestres*, or such as inhabit the woods, and *campestres*, or such as are to be found in the field; *campestres*, as partridge, quail, rail, &c. *silvestres*, as pheasant, wood-cock, &c. but it rather seems, from Manwood and the authorities which he has cited, that there are only two beasts and two fowls of warren, as above stated.

‡ Such as horses, cows, sheep, hens, chickens, peacocks, and other domestic fowls, and dogs; for these do not fly the dominion of mankind; and therefore the owner hath the same kind of property in them as he hath in all other inanimate chattels, and for the violation thereof may bring an action of trespass. *Bacon's Abr.* tit. *Game.*

tains them, (for take away the inclosure and they are in their natural liberty,) therefore the party is said to have as much right thereto as he hath to any other profits there inclosed, and a distinct and independent right in every animal. *Ibid.*

Thus all such creatures as are *feræ naturæ*, being the property of no one, it follows, that by the law of nature, every man from the prince to the peasant, has an equal right of pursuing and taking them, to his own use, 2 *Black.* 411.

But from the very end and constitution of society, this natural right, as well as many others belonging to man as an individual, may be restrained by positive laws enacted for reasons of state, as for the supposed benefit of the community; this restriction may be either with respect to the place in which this right may, or may not be exercised; with respect to the animals that are the subject of this right; or with respect to the persons allowed or forbidden to exercise it. 2 *Black. Com.* 411.

And in consequence of this authority, we find that the municipal laws of many nations have exerted such power of restraint, have in general forbidden the entering on another man's grounds, for any cause, without the owner's leave; have extended their protection to such particular animals as are usually the objects of pursuit; and have invested the prerogative of hunting and taking such animals, in the sovereign of the state only, and such as he shall authorise. 2 *Black. Com.* 411.

Many reasons have concurred for making these constitutions; 1st, For the encouragement of agriculture and improvement of lands, by giving every man an exclusive dominion over his own soil. 2dly, For the preservation of the several species of these animals, which would soon be extirpated by a general liberty. And 3dly, For prevention of idleness and dissipation in husbandmen, artificers, and other persons of lower rank, which would be the unavoidable consequence of universal licence. 2 *Black. Com.* 411.

But before we proceed to consider the particulars of these civil prohibitions in this country, it will be proper to shew their rise and origin.

In England, hunting has ever been esteemed a most princely diversion and exercise, the whole island was replenished with all sorts of game in the times of the Britons, who lived in a wild and pastoral manner, without inclosing or improving their grounds, and derived much of their subsistence from the chase, which they all enjoyed in common. But when husbandry took place under the Saxon government, and lands began to be cultivated, improved, and inclosed, the beasts naturally fled into the woody and desert tracts; which were called the forests; and having never been disposed of in the first distribution of lands, were therefore held to belong to the crown: these were filled with great plenty of game, which our royal sportsmen reserved for their own diversion, on pain of a pecuniary forfeiture, for such as interfered with their sovereign. But every freeholder had the full liberty of sporting upon his own territories, provided he abstained from the king's forests. 3 *Black. Com.* 411.

However, upon the Norman conquest, a new doctrine took place; and the right of pursuing and taking all beasts of chase or venary, and such other animals as were accounted game, was then held to belong to the king, or to such only as were authorised under him; and this as well upon the principles of the feodal law, that the king is the ultimate proprietor of all the lands in the kingdom, they being all held of him as the chief lord, or lord paramount of the fee; and that therefore he has the right of the universal soil to enter thereon, and to chace and take such creatures at his pleasure: as also upon another maxim of the common law, that these animals are *bona vacantia*, and having no other owner, belong to the king by his prerogative. As therefore, the former reason was held to vest in the king a right to pursue and take them any where, the latter was supposed to give the king, and such as he should authorise, a sole and exclusive right. 2 *Black.* 415.

This right, thus newly vested in the crown, was exerted with the utmost rigour; and after the time of the Norman establishment, not only in the antient forests, but in the new ones which the conqueror made, by laying together vast tracts of country, depopulated for that purpose, and reserved solely for the king's royal diversion, in which were exercised the most horrid tyrannies and oppressions under colour of forest law, for the sake of preserving the beasts of chase; to kill any of which within the limits of the forest, was as penal as the death of a man; and in pursuance of the same principle, king John laid a total interdict upon the winged as well as the four-footed creation. 2 *Black. Com.* 416.

The cruel and insupportable hardships which these forest laws created to the subject, occasioned our ancestors to be as zealous for their reformation, as for the relaxation of the feodal rigours, and the other exactions introduced by the Norman family; and accordingly the immunities of *charta de foresta* were as warmly contended for, and extorted from the king, with as much difficulty as those of *magna charta* itself. *Ibid.*

By this charter confirmed in parliament, 9 *Hen.* 3. many forests were disafforested, or stripped of their oppressive privileges: and regulations were made in the regimen of such as remained; particularly killing the king's deer was made no longer a capital offence, but only punished by a fine, imprisonment, or abjuration of the realm. And by a variety of subsequent statutes together with the long acquiescence of the crown, without exerting the forest laws, this prerogative is now become no longer a grievance to the subject. *Ibid.*

But as the king reserved to himself the forests for his own exclusive diversion, so he granted out from time to time other tracts of lands to his subjects under the name of *chases* or *parks*, or gave them licence to make such in their own grounds; which indeed are smaller forests, in the hands of a subject, but not governed by the forest laws: and by the common law, no person is at liberty to take or kill any beasts of chase but such as hath an ancient chase, or park; unless they be also beasts of prey. *Ibid.*

For the common law warrants the hunting of ravenous beasts of prey on another's ground, such as foxes, wolves, badgers, and the like, because the destroying of them is looked upon as a public benefit; so that the party in pursuing those through the grounds of another is subject to no action whatsoever; but it hath been resolved, that the hunting and killing such noxious animals must be done in the ordinary and usual manner, and that therefore the digging and breaking the ground to unearth them or searching for, or unbagging a fox, for the purpose of the pleasure of hunting, and not actually for the purpose of killing and destroying such noxious animals is unlawful, and the owner of the ground may maintain an action of tres-pass. *Poph.* 162. *Latch.* 119. *Cro. Jac.* 321. 2 *Bulst.* 60.

As to all inferior species of game, called beasts and fowls of warren, the liberty of taking or killing them is another franchise or royalty, derived likewise from the crown, and called free warren, a word which signifies preservation or custody. 2 *Black. Com.* 217.

The principal intention of granting to any one these franchises or liberties, was in order to protect the game, by giving the grantee a sole and exclusive power of killing it himself, provided he prevented other persons. *Ibid.*

And no man, but he who has a chase or free warren, by grant from the crown, or prescription, which supposes one, can justify hunting or sporting upon another man's soil; nor indeed, in thorough strictness of common law, either in hunting or sporting at all. *Ibid.*

But it is not lawful for any man to make any chase, park, or free warren, in his own freehold or elsewhere, to keep in it any wild beasts, or birds of forest, chase, park, or warren, without the king's grant or warrant so to do, and if any man do, he is to be punished in a *quo warranto*, and the franchise to be seized into the king's hands. *Manwood* 56. *Co. Ent.* 561.

But the prosecution must be in the name of the attorney-general, because it is of a private nature; and therefore proper to be prosecuted only in the name of the attorney-general, by information, if his majesty thinks fit. 2 *Ld. Raym.* 1409. 1 *Str.* 637. *Cas. B. R. Temp. Hard.* 261.

From what has been before set forth, it is clear (however novel the doctrine may be, to such as call themselves qualified sportsmen) that the sole right of taking and destroying game belongs exclusively to the king. 2 *Black. Com.* 417.

This appears as well from the preceding historical deduction, as because he may grant to his subjects an exclusive right of taking them, which he could not do unless such a right was first inherent in himself. *Ibid.*

And hence it will follow, that no person whatsoever, but he who hath such derivative right from the crown, is by common law entitled to take or kill any beasts of chase, or other game whatsoever. *Ibid.*

It is true, that by the acquiescence of the crown, the frequent grants of free warren in ancient times, and the introduction of new penalties of late years, by certain statutes for preserving the game, this exclusive prerogative of the king is little known or considered; every man that is exempted from these modern penalties looking upon himself as at liberty to do what he pleases with the game: whereas the contrary is strictly true, that no man however qualified he may vulgarly be esteemed, has a right to encroach on the royal prerogative by the killing of game, unless he can show a particular grant of free warren; or a prescription, which presumes a grant; or some authority under an act of parliament.* 2 *Black. Com.* 417, 418.

The truth of the matter is, that these game laws do indeed qualify no one, except a gamekeeper, to kill game: but only to save the trouble and formal process of an action, by the person injured, who perhaps too might remit the offence, these statutes inflict additional penalties, to be recovered either in a regular or summary way by any of the king's subjects, from certain persons of inferior rank, who may be found offending in this particular. 2 *Black. Com.* 418.

But it does not follow, that persons excused from these additional penalties are therefore authorized to kill game; the circumstance of having 100*l. per ann.* and the rest, are not properly qualifications, but exemptions. And these persons, so exempted from the penalties of the game statutes, are not only liable to actions of trespass by the owners of the lands; but also if they kill game within the limits of any royal franchise, they are liable to the actions of such who

* Of which the only instance is that of a game-keeper, who under 5 *Ann. c.* 14, (hereafter set forth) is expressly authorized to kill game for the use of the lord or lady of the manor.

may have the right of chase or free-warren therein. *Ibid.*

Upon the whole it appears, that the king by his prerogative, and such persons as have, under his authority, the royal franchise of chase, park, or free-warren, are the only persons who may acquire any property, however fugitive and transitory, in these animals *feræ naturæ*, while living; which is said to be vested in them, *propter privilegium*. 2. *Black. Com.* 419.

And it must also be remembered, that such persons as may thus lawfully hunt *ratione privilegii*, have only a qualified property in these animals; it not being absolute or permanent, but lasting only so long as the creatures remain within the limits of each respective franchise or liberty, and ceasing the instant they voluntarily pass out of it. *Ib.*

But if a man starts any game within his own grounds, and follows it into another's and kills it there, the property remains in himself, and this is grounded on reason and natural justice; for the property consists in the possession, which possession commences by the finding it in his own liberty, and is continued by the immediate pursuit. *Manw.* 389. 11 *Mod.* 75. *Puff. L. N.* 64. *c.* 6. 2 *Black. Com.* 419.

But it is said in Manwood, that if a man flies his hawk at a pheasant in his own ground, and the hawk pursues the pheasant into another's warren, which is a privileged place for fowls of warren, and kills it there, the owner of the hawk cannot justify entering the warren, and taking the pheasant, but it shall belong to the owner of the warren, and that the law is the same in the cases of all wild beasts of the forest and chase. *Manw.* 389.

And so if a stranger starts game in one man's chase or free-warren, and hunts it into another liberty, the property continues in the owner of the chase or warren; and the warrener or keeper may pursue them and retake them, for the chase or warren is a public establishment, to look after and preserve the game; wherein there are officers established by authority to have an eye over the game, and to keep it within the boundaries, so that the property is not altered by driving it out of the inclosures, unless it be also out of the pursuit of the officers; for as long as he that is intrusted doth pursue it, it is not in its natural liberty, but is still belonging to the chase or warren. 2 *Black. Com.* 419. 2 *Bacon's Abr.* 613.

So if a man starts game on another's private grounds and kills it there, the property belongs to and may be seized by him on whose ground it was killed, because it was also started there, this property arising *ratione soli*. 2 *Black. Com.* 419. 1 *Ld. Raym.* 251. 2 *Bac. Abr.* 613.

But if after being started there, it is killed in the grounds of a third person, the property belongs not to the owner of the first ground, because the property is local; nor yet to the owner of the second, because it was not started in his soil; but it vests in the person who started and killed it, though guilty of a trespass against both owners. 7 *Mod. Com.* 218. 1 *Ld. Raym.* 251. 2 *Bac. Abr.* 613. 2 *Black. Com.* 419.

Acts for the preservation of Game.

—— *Destroying game out of season.*] By 9 *Ann. c.* 25. if any person (between the first of June and the first of October yearly, 10 *Geo.* 2. *c.* 32.) shall by hays, tunnels or other nets, drive and take any wild-duck, teal, widgeon, or other water-fowl, in any fens, lakes, broad-waters, or other places of resort for wild-fowl in the moulting season, such person being thereof convicted, before one justice of peace, by the oath of one witness, shall, for every water-fowl so taken, forfeit 5*s.* one moiety to the informer, and the other moiety to the poor of the parish; the same to be levied by distress and sale of goods, by warrant of the justice before whom the offender shall be convicted; and for want of distress the offender shall be committed to the house of correction for any time not exceeding one month, nor less than fourteen days, there to be whipt and kept to hard labour; and the justice shall order such hays, nets, or tunnels, that were used in driving and taking the said wild-fowl, to be seized, and destroyed in the presence of such justice. *s.* 4.

By 39 *Geo.* 3. *c.* 34. no person shall, upon any pretence whatsoever, take, kill, destroy, carry, sell, buy, or have in his possession or use any partridge, between 1st Feb. and 1st Sept. in any year. *s.* 3.

And by 2 *Geo.* 3. *c.* 19. no person shall, upon any pretence whatsoever, kill, destroy, carry, sell, buy, or have in his possession any pheasant between 1st Feb. and 1st Oct. in any year.* *s.* 1.

Nothing in this act shall extend to any pheasant taken in season, and kept in any mew or breeding place. *s.* 2.

---

* It was by 7 *Jac.* 1. *c.* 11. enacted, that every person which shall hawk at, destroy or kill, any pheasants or partridges, with hawks or dogs, by colour of hawking, between the first of July and the last of August, being accused within six months, and the offence being proved by confession, or by oath of two witnesses, before two justices, shall be by the justices committed to the common gaol for one month, unless he pay to the churchwardens or overseers for the use of the poor 40*s.* for every such hawking, and 20*s.* for every pheasant or partridge, which he, his hawk or dog shall take, kill, or destroy, contrary to this statute. *s.* 2, 5.

But this act seems to be virtually repealed and superseded by the above general restriction in the act 2 *Geo.* 3. *c.* 19.

If any person shall transgress this act, and shall be lawfully convicted thereof by the oath of one or more credible witnesses, every such person shall, for every partridge or pheasant so taken, killed, destroyed, carried, sold, bought or found in his possession, contrary to this act, forfeit five pounds to the person who shall inform: and any person may sue for the five pounds, with full costs, in any court of record at Westminster. 2 *Geo.* 3. *c.* 19. *s.* 2. 39 *Geo.* 3. *c.* 34. *s.* 3.

By 13 *Geo.* 3. *c.* 55, no person shall kill, destroy, carry, sell, buy, or have in his possession, any heath-fowl, commonly called black-game; between 10th Dec. and 20th Aug. nor any grouse, commonly called red-game, between 10th Dec. and 12th Aug. nor any bustard, between 1st Mar. and 1st Sep. in any year, upon pain to forfeit for the first offence, not exceeding twenty, nor less than ten pounds; and for the second and every subsequent offence, not exceeding thirty, nor less than twenty pounds. *s.* 2.

And by 43 *Geo.* 3. *c.* 102. persons taking or killing in the New Forest in the county of Southampton any black-game, between Dec. 10th and Sept. 1st, shall be liable to the forfeitures imposed by the above act of 13 *Geo.* 3. *c.* 55.

—— *Destroying game in the night time.*] By 23 *Eliz.* *c.* 10. no person of what estate, degree, or condition soever, shall take or destroy any pheasants or partridges with nets, snares, gins, engines, rowsting, lowing or other devices, in the night, upon pain of forfeiture for every pheasant 20*s.* and for every partridge 10*s.* which forfeitures, if he do not pay within ten days after conviction, then to have one month's imprisonment; and besides such forfeiture or imprisonment, to put in bond with sureties for two years, that he shall not take or destroy any partridges or pheasants contrary to this act, the bond to be taken by some justice of peace; the one half of which forfeitures to be to the chief lords of the liberties or manors, and the other moiety to such as will sue for the same, in any court of record, or at the assizes, sessions, or leet. *s.* 2, 5.

Unless such lord shall dispense with or procure any such taking or destroying, in which case his half shall be to the poor of the parish, and be levied or recovered by any of the churchwardens. *s.* 3.

By 9 *Ann.* *c.* 25. if any person whatsoever shall take or kill any hare, pheasant, partridge, moor, heath game, or grouse, in the night-time, he shall, on conviction, before one justice, on oath of one witness, forfeit 5*l.*; half to the informer, and half to the poor, by distress; and for want of distress to be sent to the house of correction for three months for the first offence, and for every other offence four months. *s.* 3.

And by 13 *Geo.* 3. *c.* 80. it is further enacted, that if any person shall kill, take, or destroy any hare, pheasant, partridge, moor game, or heath game, or use any gun, dog, snare, net, or other engine, with intent to kill, take, or destroy, any hare, &c. in the night, *viz.* between seven o'clock at night and six in the morning, from 12th October to 12th February, and between nine o'clock at night and four in the morning, from 12th February to 12th October; such person being convicted thereof, upon the oath of one witness, before one justice, shall forfeit for the first offence, not exceeding twenty nor less than ten pounds; and for the second, not exceeding thirty, nor less than twenty pounds. *s.* 1.

And if it shall appear, that such offender hath already been convicted of a first and second offence against this act; then such justice shall commit such offender to the common gaol, there to remain till the next general quarter sessions, unless such offender shall have entered into a recognizance, with two securities, to appear at such session, to be tried by indictment for the offence; and also shall bind over the informer to prosecute the offender by indictment, and the general or quarter sessions shall direct the said indictment to be tried; and if upon such indictment such offender shall be convicted, he shall forfeit and pay in court 50*l.*: and in case he shall neglect or refuse to pay the 50*l.* he shall be committed to the common gaol, for not less than six nor more than twelve calendar months, unless such penalty be sooner paid: and such offender shall, if the justices think proper, be once publicly whipped at the expiration of such commitment, in the town or place where such gaol shall be, between twelve and one in the day. *s.* 1.

And by 4 & 5 *Will.* & *Mar.* *c.* 23. all lords of manors, or any persons authorized by them as game-keepers, may within their royalties resist offenders in the night-time, in the same manner, and be equally indemnified, as if such fact had been committed within any ancient chase, park, or warren. *s.* 4.

That is to say, according to stat. *de malefact. in parc.* 21 *Edw.* 1. *stat.* 2.—whereby it is ordained, that if any forester, parker, or warrener, find any trespasser wandering within his liberty, intending to do damage therein, and that after hue and cry made to him to stand unto the peace will not yield himself, but doth continue and execute his malice, and disobeying the king's peace, doth flee or defend himself with force and arms, although such foresters, &c. or their company, do kill any offender so found, they shall not be arraigned, nor lose life or limb, or suffer punishment. *s.* 1.

—— *Destroying game on a Sunday, or Christmas day.*] By 13 *Geo.* 3. *c.* 80. if any person shall, upon a Sunday, or on Christmas day, in the day-time, take, kill, or destroy any hare, pheasant, partridge, heath-game, or moor-game, or shall upon a Sunday or Christmas day, use any gun, dog, net, or engine for taking, killing, or destroying thereof, such person convicted in the manner prescribed by this act*, shall be subject to the like forfeitures, as are by this act inflicted for destroying game in the night. *s.* 6.

—— *Tracing hares in the snow.*] By 14 & 15 *Hen.* 8. *c.* 10. no person of what estate, degree, or condition they be, shall trace and kill any hare in the snow: and the justices of peace at every sessions, and stewards of leets, shall have power to inquire of such offenders; and after such inquisitions found, the justices of peace and stewards for every hare so killed shall cess upon every such offender 6*s.* 8*d.* to be forfeited to the king, if found by the justices of peace, and to the lord of the leet if found in the leet.

And by 1 *Jac.* 1. *c.* 27. every person which shall trace, or course any hares in the snow, shall, on conviction before two justices, by confession or oath of two witnesses, be committed to gaol for three months, unless he pay to the churchwardens for the use of the poor 20*s.* for every hare which he shall take or destroy, or after one month after his commitment, become bound by recognizance with two sureties in 20*l.* a piece before two justices, not to offend in like manner; the recognizance to be returned to the next sessions. *s.* 2.

—— *Taking hares in gins.*] By 1 *Jac.* 1. *c.* 27. every person who shall at any time take or destroy any hares with hare-pipes, cords, or with any such instruments, or other engines, shall on conviction before two justices, by confession or oath of two witnesses, be committed to gaol for three months, unless he pay to the churchwardens for the use of the poor 20*s.* for every hare which he shall take or destroy, or after one month after his commitment, become bound by recognizance with two sureties in 20*l.* a piece, before two justices, not to offend in like manner; the recognizance to be returned to the next sessions. *s.* 2.

And by 22 & 23 *Car.* 3. *c.* 25. *s.* 6. if any person shall be found setting or using any snares, hare-pipes, or other like engines, and shall thereof be convicted by confession, or oath of one witness, before one justice, in one month after the offence, he shall give to the party injured such satisfaction, and in such time, as the justice shall appoint, and shall pay down presently to the overseers for the use of the poor such sum, not exceeding 10*s.* as the justice shall appoint, and if such offender do not make such satisfaction, and pay such sum to the poor, the justice shall commit him to the house of correction, for not exceeding one month.

—— *Destroying the eggs of the winged game.*] By 25 *Hen.* 8. *c.* 11. from the first of March to the last of June yearly, no person shall withdraw, take, destroy, or convey, any eggs of wild-fowl from or in any nest where they shall be laid, upon pain of imprisonment for one year, and to forfeit for every egg of any crane or bustard 20*d.* and for every egg of bittour, heron, or shovelard, 8*d.* and for every egg of mallard, teal, or other wild-fowl, 1*d.* the one moiety to the king, and the other half to him that will sue for the same; and all justices of peace shall have power to enquire, hear, and determine the same. *s.* 5.

But this act shall not extend to any persons that will destroy crows, choughs, ravens, and boscards, or their eggs, or any fowl or their eggs, not used to be eaten. *s.* 6.

By 1 *Jac.* 1. *c.* 27. every person who shall take the eggs of any pheasant or partridge out of the nest, or willingly break, spoil, or destroy the same in the nest, shall on conviction before two justices, by confession, or oath of two witnesses, be committed to gaol for three months, unless he pay upon conviction to the churchwardens for the use of the poor 20*s.* for every egg; or after one month after his commitment, become bound by recognizance with two sureties, before two justices, in 20*l.* each, not to offend again in like manner; the recognizance to be returned to the next sessions. *s.* 2.

—— *Buying or selling game.*] By 1 *Jac.* 1. *c.* 27. every person which shall sell, or buy to sell again, any deer, hare, partridge, or pheasant (except partridges and pheasants reared in house, or brought from beyond sea), shall on conviction at the assizes or quarter sessions, or before two justices out of sessions, forfeit for every deer 40*s.* for every hare 10*s.* and for every partridge 10*s.* and for every pheasant 20*s.* of which forfeitures the one moiety shall be to him that will sue, and the other moiety to the poor of the parish where the offence shall be committed. *s.* 4, 5.

And by 5 *Ann.* *c.* 14. if any higler, chapman, carrier, inn-keeper, victualler or alehouse keeper, shall have in his custody any hare, pheasant, partridge, moor, heath-game or grouse, or shall buy, sell, or offer to sell any hare, &c. unless such game in the hands of such carrier be sent up by persons qualified to kill the game, (or if any person whatsoever, whether qualified or not, shall sell, expose, or offer to sell, any hare, pheasant, partridge, moor, heath-game or grouse, 28 *Geo.* 2. *c.* 12. *s.* 1.); he shall be carried before some justice of peace, and upon view, or upon the oath of one witness, shall be convicted, and shall forfeit for every hare, &c. 5*l.*; one half to the informer, and the other half to the poor of the parish; to be levied by distress and sale of goods, by warrant of the justice before whom such

* For which see the preceding section.

offender shall be convicted; and for want of sufficient distress to be committed to the house of correction, for the first offence, for three months, and for every other offence four months; provided such conviction be within three months after such offence. *s.* 2.

And by 9 *Ann. c.* 25. if any hare, pheasant, partridge, moor, heath-game or grouse, shall be found in the shop, house, or possession of (any poulterer, salesman, fishmonger, cook or pastry cook, 28 *Geo.* 2. *c.* 12. *s.* 2.), or of any person not qualified in his own right to kill game, or entitled thereto under some person so qualified, the same shall be adjudged an exposing thereof to sale. *s.* 3.

And any justice of the peace, and lord within his manor, may take away to his own use any such hare, pheasant, partridge, moor, heath-game or grouse, or any other game, from any such higler, chapmen, inn-keeper, victualler, or carrier, or any other person not qualified, which shall be found in his custody or possession. 5 *Ann. c.* 14. *s.* 4.

And any person that shall destroy, sell or buy any hare, &c. and shall within three months make discovery of any higler, &c. that hath bought or sold, or offered to buy or sell, or had in their possession, any hare, &c. so as any one shall be convicted, such discoverer shall be discharged of the penalties, and shall receive the same benefit as any other informer. *s.* 3.

—— *Hawking or hunting with spaniels in standing corn.*] By 23 *Eliz. c.* 10. no person shall hawk, or with his spaniels hunt, in any ground where corn shall grow (except it be in his own ground) at such time as any eared or codded corn shall be standing upon the same, nor before such corn shall be shocked, cocked, hilled or copped; upon pain of forfeiture for every time that he shall so hawk or hunt (without the consent of the owner of the corn) to the owner of the said corn 40*s.* to be levied or recovered in any court of record, or at the assizes, sessions, or leet. *s.* 4, 5.

—— *Hawking.*) By 34 *Ed.* 3. *c.* 22. every person who findeth a faulcon, tercelet, laner, or laneret, or other hawk that is lost, shall presently bring the same to the sheriff; and the sheriff shall make proclamation in all the good towns in the country, that he hath such a hawk in his custody, and if he is challenged, the owner shall pay the costs, and have the hawk: but if none within four months challenge it, the sheriff shall have the hawk, making gree to him that did take him, if he be a simple man: and if he be a gentleman and of estate to have the hawk, then the sheriff shall re-deliver to him the hawk, taking of him reasonable costs for the time that he had him in his custody.

And by 37 *Ed.* 3. *c.* 19. if any steal any hawk, and the same carry away, not doing the ordinance aforesaid, it shall be done of him as of him that stealeth a horse or other thing—that is, it shall be felony; but the offender shall have the benefit of his clergy: for at the time of the making of this act, he that had stolen a horse should have had his clergy. 3 *Inst.* 98.

No man shall bear any hawk of the breed of England, called a nyesse, goshawk, tassel, laner, laneret or faulcon, upon pain of forfeiture of his hawk to the king; and if he bring any from beyond sea, he shall bring a certificate under the customer's seal of the port where he landed, upon the same pain; and the person that bringeth such hawk to the king, shall have reward of the king or the hawk for his labour. 11 *Hen.* 7. *c.* 17.

And no man shall take any ayre, faulcon, goshawk, tassel, or laner or lanerets, in their warren, or woods, or in other place, nor purposely drive them out of their coverts accustomed to breed in, to cause them to go to other coverts to breed, nor slay them for any hurt by them done, but suffer them to pass at their liberties; upon pain of 10*l.* the one half to the party that will sue by action, by examination before the justices of peace, information, or otherwise, and the other half to the king. 11 *Hen.* 7. *c.* 17.

Also no person of what condition or degree he be, shall take or cause to be taken, on his own ground or any other man's, the eggs of any falcon, goshawks, or laners, out of the nests, upon pain of imprisonment of a year and a day, and fine at the king's will, the one half to the king, and the other half to the owner of the ground where the eggs were taken; and the justices may hear and determine such matter, as well by inquisition as information and proofs. 11 *Hen.* 7. *c.* 17.

And it is further enacted, by 5 *Eliz. c.* 21. *s.* 3. that if any persons shall take away any hawks or their eggs, by any means unlawfully out of the woods or grounds of any person, and be thereof convicted at the assizes or sessions, on indictment, bill or information, at the suit of the king or of the party, he shall be imprisoned three months and shall pay treble damages; and after the three months expired, shall find sureties for his good abearing for seven years, or remain in prison till he doth it.

—— *Burning grig, ling, heath, furze, goss or fern.*] For preserving the red and black game of grouse, called heath-cocks, or heath-polts, it is by 4 & 5 *Will. & Mar. c.* 23. enacted that no person on any mountains, hills, heaths, moors, forests, chases, or other wastes, shall burn, between the second of February and 24th of June, any grig, ling, heath, furze, goss, or fern, upon pain that the offender shall be committed to the house of correction, for any time not exceeding one month, and not less than ten days, there to be whipt and kept to hard labour. *s.* 11.

As this act gives no direction how such of-

fenders shall be convicted; it seems that the party guilty of disobedience thereto can only be proceeded against by indictment.

—— *Persons qualified to kill game.*] The laws made for the preservation of the different sorts of game, and to which all persons, of whatsoever rank, estate, or degree they may be, are subject, have been distinctly stated. It is therefore intended in this place, to shew what penalties inferior persons, not qualified by the laws of this realm, to keep or use dogs or instruments for the destruction of game, are liable to, for keeping or using the same: in doing this, it will be necessary to set down, in progressive order, the statutes which appear to be in force at the present day respecting such offenders; and in the next place, give a summary view of the points determined on the construction of those statutes.

By 22 & 23 *Car.* 2. *c.* 25. every person not having lands and tenements, or some other estate of inheritance, in his own or his wife's right, of the clear yearly value of 100*l.* or for term of life, or a lease or leases, of ninety-nine years, or for any longer term, of the clear yearly value of 150*l.* other than the son and heir apparent of an esquire, or other person of higher degree, and the owners and keepers of forests, parks, chases or warrens, being stocked with deer or conies for their necessary use, (in respect of the said forests, parks, chases or warrens), are hereby declared to be persons by the laws of this realm not allowed to have or keep for themselves or any other persons, guns, bows, greyhounds, setting dogs, ferrets, coney dogs, lurchers, hays, nets, lowbells, hare-pipes, gins, snares, or other engines for the taking and killing of conies, hares, pheasants, partridges, or other game, but shall be prohibited to have, keep, or use the same. *s.* 3.

And by 5 *Ann.* *c.* 14. if any person not so qualified shall keep or use any greyhounds, setting dogs, hays, lurchers, tunnels, or any other engines to kill and destroy the game, and shall be thereof convicted upon the oath of one witness, by the justice of peace where such offence is committed, the person so convicted shall forfeit 5*l.*; one half to the informer, and the other half to the poor of the parish, to be levied by distress and sale of goods, by warrant of such justice; and for want of distress, the offender shall be sent to the house of correction, for three months for the first offence, and for every other offence, four months. *s.* 4.

And it shall be lawful for any justices of the peace, within their respective counties, ridings, cities, towns corporate or liberty, and the lords and ladies of manors within the said manors, to take away any hare, or other game, and likewise such dogs, nets, or other engines, which shall be in the custody of any persons not qualified to keep the same, to their own use. *s.* 4.

And game-keepers or any other persons thereunto authorized by warrant under the hand and seal of any justices of peace, may in the day-time search the houses or other places of any such persons prohibited by this act to keep or use the same, as upon good ground shall be suspected to have in their custody any guns, bows, greyhounds, setting-dogs, ferrets, coney-dogs, or other dogs, to destroy hares or conies, hays, tramels, or other nets, lowbells, hare-pipes, snares, or other engines aforesaid, and the same to seize and keep, for the use of the lord, of the manor, or otherwise to cut in pieces or destroy, as things prohibited. 22 & 23 *Car.* 2. *c.* 25. *s.* 2.

And by 1 *Jac.* 1. *c.* 27. every person which shall shoot at, kill or destroy, with any gun, cross-bow, stone-bow, or long-bow, any pheasant, partridge, pigeon, heron, mallard, duck, teal, widgeon, grouse, heath-cock, moor-game, or any such fowl; and the same offence is proved by the confession of the party, or by the testimony of two witnesses upon oath, before two justices where the offence shall be committed or the party apprehended, shall be by the said justices committed to the common gaol for three months, unless the offender forthwith upon conviction pay to the churchwardens where the offence shall be committed or the party apprehended, to the use of the poor, 20*s.* for every pheasant, partridge, pigeon, heron, mallard, duck, teal, widgeon, grouse, heath-cock, moor-game, or any such fowl; and for every hare which such person so offending and convicted, shall take or willingly destroy; or after one month after commitment, together with two sureties, become bound by recognizance in 20*l.* a piece to the king, with condition that he shall not shoot at, kill, take or destroy, any of the said game by the means aforesaid; which recognizance shall be taken by any two justices, and returned to the next quarter sessions. *s.* 2.

And by 7 *Jac.* 1. *c.* 11. every person which shall take, kill, or destroy, any pheasant or partridge, with setting-dogs and nets, or with any nets, snares or engines, and the same offence proved by confession of the party, or by the testimony of one witness upon oath, before two justices where the offence shall be committed or the party apprehended, shall be by the said justices committed to the common gaol, there to remain three months, unless he pay to the churchwardens or overseers of the parish where the offence shall be committed, 20*s.* for every pheasant or partridge which such person shall take, kill, or destroy, contrary to this statute, and become bound by recognizance in 20*l.* to his majesty, with condition that he shall not any at time thereafter, take, kill, or destroy, any pheasant or partridge; which recognizance shall be taken by any one justice, and shall be returned to the next quarter sessions, to remain of record. *s.* 8.

And by 4 & 5 *Will.* & *Mar.* *c.* 23. every

constable, headborough and tythingman, being authorized by one justice of peace, shall enter into and search the houses of suspected persons not qualified; and in case any hare, partridge, pheasant, pigeon, fish, fowl or other game*, shall be found, the offender shall be carried before some justice of peace; and if such person do not give a good account how he came by such game, or shall not in convenient time, to be set by the justice, produce the party of whom he bought the same, or some credible person to depose upon oath such sale thereof, shall be convicted by the justice of such offence, and shall forfeit for every hare, partridge, fish, or other game, any sum not under 5*s.* and not exceeding 20*s.* to be ascertained by the justice; one moiety thereof to the informer, and the other moiety to the poor of the parish where the offence was committed, to be levied by distress and sale of goods, by warrant of the justice; and for want of distress, the offender shall be committed to the house of correction, for any time not exceeding one month, and not less than ten days, there to be whipt and kept to hard labour. *s.* 3.

And if any person produced, shall not before the justice give evidence of his innocence as aforesaid, he shall be convicted in the same manner as the person first charged, and so from person to person, until the first offender be discovered. *s.* 3.

And by the 49th section of the *annual mutiny act*, if any officer or soldier shall, without leave of the lord of the manor, under his hand and seal, take, kill or destroy, any hare, coney, pheasant, partridge, pigeon, or any other sort of fowls, poultry, or fish, or his majesty's game; and, upon complaint thereof, shall be upon oath of one witness convicted before any justice, every officer so offending, shall forfeit 5*l.* to the poor of the place, and every officer commanding in chief upon the place, for every such offence committed by any soldier under his command, shall forfeit 20*s.* in like manner; and if upon conviction by the justices and demand by the constable or overseers, such officer shall not within two days pay the penalties, he shall forfeit his commission.

Upon these statutes, the qualification is properly reducible to the six following distinctions, *viz.*

1st, Every person having lands or tenements, or some other estate of inheritance of the clear yearly value of 100*l.*

2dly, Or for term of life, or lease or leases for ninety-nine years, or any longer terms of the clear yearly value of 150*l.*

And hereon it has been decided, that an estate of the value of 150*l.* per ann. holden by the defendant in his own right; under a lease for ninety-nine years to trustees, if the defendant and others should so long live, is a sufficient qualification to kill game under the statute. *Earl Ferrers* v. *Hilton*, *Ea.* 40 *Geo.* 3. 8 *Ter. Rep.* 506.

A life estate of less than 150*l.* per ann. is not a qualification to kill game, the words, *or for term of life*, being necessarily connected with and carried over to the last member of the sentence; and consequently according to grammatical construction, a tenant for life must have an estate to the amount of 150*l.* per ann. to qualify him to kill game. *Caldecot's cas.* 188.

And it seems that a vicar, in respect of his church, has not an estate of inheritance in him, but an estate for life only. *Ibid.*

3dly, The son and heir apparent of an esquire, or other person of higher degree.

In the table of precedence, the heralds next below knights and their sons, and above esquire, rank colonels, serjeants at law, and doctors in the three learned professions. 1 *Black. Com.* 405.

An esquire or other person of higher degree, as such, is not qualified under this act, though the son of an esquire or the son of any other person of higher degree is. 1 *Ter. Rep.* 41.

4thly, The owner or keeper of any forest, park, chase, or warren.

5thly, The lord of any manor or royalty.

6thly, The game-keeper of any lord or lady of a manor, provided he be a person qualified, or truly a servant to such lord or lady, or immediately employed and appointed to take and kill the game for the sole use and immediate benefit of such lord or lady.

Every person having lands or tenements, or some other estate of inheritance of the clear yearly value of 100*l.*] It seems that an equitable as well as a legal estate gives a qualification under the game laws, but the clear value of the necessary estate means the value, clear at least of all mortgages or incumbrances created by the owner, or those under whom he claims.

The words of the statute 5 *Ann. c.* 14. are in the disjunctive, *viz.* keep or use any greyhounds, setting-dogs, hays, lurchers, tunnels, or any other engines to kill and destroy the game; the offences are therefore distinct and several, and a conviction either for the keeping, or for using of any of the dogs of the kinds enumerated, will be good. 1 *Strange* settled 496. *Caldecot* 175.

It has been a question, whether a gun is such an engine as is within the statute; and it seems now to be fully settled, that it is not an instrument, the bare keeping of which is penal, because it differs from nets and dogs which can only be kept for an ill purpose: the bare keeping whereof is not enough to be shown, because it may be kept for the defence of a house or some other lawful purpose;

* *Or other game.*] This act extends only to game, and not to rabbits kept in a private warren. 1 *Ld. Raym.* 151.

but it must be also shown that it was used for the destruction of the game. 1 *Sess. Cas.* 93. *Cas.* 88. 2 *Str.* 1098.

The penalty of 5*l.* is given for the keeping or using dogs or engines, and not for the game destroyed; therefore, although a person kill ever so many hares in one day, he can be convicted in but one penalty for that day. 10 *Mod.* 96. *Corn. Rep.* 274.

And where several persons commit the offence in company, and they are joined in the same conviction, the justice can only convict them in one penalty. 1 *Ter. Rep.* 809.

It seems also, that the justice ought not to convict an unqualified person, if he acts in company with, and under the permission of one that is qualified. *Loft.* 173.

Trespassing on grounds, qualified or not.] It is a trespass at common law, for any man to hunt on another's ground; and the owner of the soil may maintain his action of trespass for the same.

But if the party is qualified to kill game, and the damage found be under 40*s.* he shall in such case pay no more costs than damages by 22 & 23 *Car.* 2. *c.* 9.

But for preventing wilful and malicious trespasses, it is enacted by 8 & 9 *Will.* 3. *c.* 11. *s.* 4. that in all actions of trespass in any of the courts of record at Westminster, wherein at the trial of the cause, it shall appear, and be certified by the judge, under his hand, on the back of the record, that the trespass upon which any defendant shall be found guilty was wilful and malicious, the plaintiff shall recover not only his damages, but his full costs of suit.

Under this statute therefore, if the owner of the land expressly forewarns another not to come thereon, he will in an action for trespass subsequent thereto, be entitled to full costs, notwithstanding the damages recovered may be under 40*s.*

For every trespass is wilful, when the defendant has notice and is especially forewarned not to come on the land; as every trespass is malicious, though the damage may not amount to 40*s.* where the intent of the defendant plainly appears to be to harass and distress the plaintiff. 3 *Black. Com.* 214.

And if a general notice be given to all persons not to trespass on certain lands, and another hunts over a close belonging to the party giving such notice, the judge on the trial of an action for trespass is bound under the stat. 8 & 9 *Will.* 3. *c.* 11. *s.* 4. to certify that it was wilful and malicious, in order to entitle the plaintiff to his full costs, notwithstanding it appear on the trial that the defendant was anxious to avoid trespassing on the ground, and that he made frequent inquiries respecting the plaintiff's boundaries. *Reynolds* v. *Edwards, Mic. Ter.* 35 *Geo.* 3. 6 *Ter. Rep.* 11.

And as great mischiefs do ensue by inferior tradesmen, apprentices, and other dissolute persons, neglecting their trades and employments, who follow hunting, fishing, and other game, to the ruin of themselves and damage of their neighbours, it is enacted by 4 & 5 *Will. & Mar. c.* 23. *s.* 10. that if any inferior tradesman, apprentice, or other dissolute person, shall hunt, hawk, fish, or fowl (unless in company with the master of such apprentice duly qualified) such persons shall be subject to the penalties, and may be sued for their wilful trespass in coming on any person's land, and if found guilty, the plaintiff shall recover full costs. *s.* 10.

Upon this statute it has been adjudged, that if a person be an inferior tradesman, as a clothier for instance, it matters not what qualification he may have in point of estate; but if he be guilty of such trespass, he shall be liable to pay full costs. 3 *Black.* 215.

—— *General penalties under the game laws, and how recoverable.*] By 8 *Geo.* 1. *c.* 19. where any person shall for any offence against any law now in being, for preservation of the game, be liable to pay any pecuniary penalty upon conviction before any justice of peace, it shall be lawful for any other person, either to proceed to recover the said penalty by information before a justice, or to sue for the same in any court of record. *s.* 1.

And by 2 *Geo.* 3. *c.* 19. it shall be lawful for such person, to sue for and recover the whole penalty for his own use, by action of debt, or on the case, bill, plaint, or information, in any court of record at Westminster, and if he recovers, he shall have double costs; and no part of the penalty, recovered in any such suit, shall be paid to the use of the poor. *s.* 5.

But no such action shall be brought but within six [*lunar*] months after the matter is done. *s.* 6.

And no offender shall be prosecuted for the same offence, both by the way prescribed by this law and by the way prescribed by any of the former laws: and in case of any second prosecution, the person so doubly prosecuted may plead in defence the former prosecution pending, or the conviction or judgment thereupon. 8 *Geo.* 1. *c.* 19.

—— *For the duty on certificates for killing of game.* See head Taxes.

GAME-KEEPERS, are those who have the care of keeping and preserving of the game, being appointed thereto by lords of manors, &c.

And by 22 & 23 *Car.* 2. *c.* 25. all lords of manors or other royalties, not under the degree of an esquire, may by writing under their hands and seals, authorize game-keepers within their manors or royalties, who may take and seize all such guns, bows, greyhounds, setting-dogs, lurchers, or other dogs to kill hares or conies, ferrets, trammels, lowbells, hays, or other nets, hare-pipes, snares or other engines for the taking and killing of conies, hares, pheasants, partridges, or other game as within the precincts of such manors, shall be used by any persons by this act prohibited to keep or use the same. *s.* 2.

And by 5 *Ann. c.* 14. it shall be lawful for any lord or lady of a manor, by writing under hand and seal, to empower game-keepers, upon the manor, to kill hare, pheasant, partridge or other game. *s.* 4.

But if the game-keeper shall, under colour of the said power, kill or take the same, and afterwards dispose thereof* without the consent or knowledge of the lord or lady, and shall be thereof convicted upon the complaint of such lord or lady, and upon oath of one witness before any one justice of peace, such game-keeper shall be committed to the house of correction for three months, and kept to hard labour. *s.* 4.

And by 9 *Ann. c.* 25. no lord or lady of a manor shall make above one game-keeper within one manor, with power to kill game; and the name of such person shall be entered with the clerk of the peace; such entry to be made and viewed without fee, and a certificate thereof to be granted by the clerk of the peace, upon payment of 1*s.*

And in case any other game-keeper, whose name shall not be entered as aforesaid, (who shall not be otherwise qualified to kill game,) shall kill any hare, pheasant, partridge, moor, heath-game, or grouse, he shall on conviction before one justice, on oath of one witness, forfeit for every offence, 5*l.* half to the informer, and half to the poor by distress: for want of distress to be sent to the house of correction for three months for the first offence, and for every other offence four months.

And by 3 *Geo.* 1. *c.* 11. no lord or lady of a manor shall appoint any person to be a game-keeper with power to kill game, unless such person be qualified by the laws of this realm so to do, or unless such person be truly a servant to the said lord or lady, or immediately employed to kill the game for the sole use of such lord or lady:

And no such lord or lady shall authorize or qualify any person, not qualified by the laws of this realm so to do, to take or kill any hare, pheasant, partridge, or other game whatsoever, or to keep or use any greyhound, setting dogs, hayes, lurchers, guns, tunnels, or any other engine, to kill and destroy the game. *Ibid.*

And any person whatsoever, not qualified by the laws so to do, or not being truly and properly a servant of any lord or lady of a manor, or not immediately employed and appointed to take and kill the game for the sole use or immediate benefit of the said lord or lady, who under colour or pretence of any power or authority, deputation, or qualification to him granted by any lord or lady of a manor, shall take or kill any hare, pheasant, partridge, or other game whatsoever, or shall keep or use any greyhounds, setting dogs, hayes, lurchers, guns, tunnels, or any other engine to kill and destroy the game, being thereof legally convicted shall, for every such offence, incur the penalty of 5*l.* as aforesaid. *Ibid.*

But by 48 *Geo.* 3. *c.* 93. so much of the above act of 3 *Geo.* 1. *c.* 11. as relates to the appointment of game-keepers is repealed. And lords of manors may appoint any person, whether acting as a game-keeper or not, or whether retained and paid for as a servant, or whether qualified or not to kill game for his use, or the use of any other person, who shall have the same rights as if appointed to kill game for the use of the lord of the manor; and shall not be liable to the duty on stewards.

A lord of a hundred or wapentake is not a lord of a royalty, within the meaning of the act: and he cannot as such grant a deputation to a game-keeper. 1 *Doug.* 28.

Although a game-keeper is restricted from killing game out of the limits of the manor for which he is appointed, yet he may keep dogs or engines for the destruction of the game in any place. 2 *Wils.* 287.

GAMING, or speculating on the hazard of winning or losing money by any play, sport, or divertisement, is a vice to restrain which divers statutes have been passed; and *gaming*, in general acceptation, is always taken in *mitiori sensu*, to be an offence.

To restrain this pernicious vice it was by the statute 33 *Hen.* 8, *c.* 9, enacted that justices of the peace, and head officers in corporations, shall have power to enter houses suspected of unlawful games, and to arrest and imprison the gamesters, till they give security not to play for the future. Also the persons keeping unlawful gaming-houses may be committed by a justice until they find sureties not to keep such houses, who shall forfeit 40*s.* and the gamesters 6*s.* 8*d.* each time; and if the king license the keeping of gaming-houses it is against law, and void.

No artificer, apprentice, labourer, or servant, shall play at tables, tennis, dice, cards, bowls, cogetting in the fields, slide, shift, shove-groat, cloyish, cayles, half-bowl, and coyting, out of Christmas time, on pain of 20*s.* for every offence; and at Christmas they are to play in their master's house, or presence; but any nobleman or gentlemen having 100*l.* *per ann.* estate may license his servants or family to play within the precincts of his house, or garden, at cards, dice, tables, or other games, as well

* But no person whatsoever, whether qualified or not, can now sell game. See section *Destroying game out of season.*

among themselves, as others repairing thither. *Ibid.*

By 16 *Car.* 2, *c.* 7, if any person, of what degree soever, shall by fraud, deceit, or unlawful device in playing at cards, dice, tables, bowls, cock-fighting, horse-races, foot races, or other games or pastimes, or bearing a share in the stakes, betting, &c. win any money or valuable thing, he shall forfeit treble the value, one moiety to the crown, and the other to the party grieved, prosecution being in six months; in default whereof the last-mentioned moiety is to go to such other person as will prosecute within one year, &c.

By stat. 9 *Ann. cap.* 14, all notes, bills, bonds, judgments, mortgages, or other securities given for money won by playing at cards, dice, tables, tennis, bowls, or other games, or by betting on the sides of such as play at any of those games, or for repayment of any money knowingly lent for such gaming or betting, shall be void: and where lands are granted by such mortgages or securities they shall go to the next person who ought to have the same as if the grantor were actually dead, and the grants had been made to the person so entitled after the death of the person so encumbering the same. If any person playing at cards, dice, or other game, or betting, shall lose the value of 10*l.* at one time, to one or more persons, and shall pay the money, he may recover the money lost by action of debt within three months * afterwards; and if the loser do not sue, any other person may do it, and recover the same, and treble the value, with costs, one moiety to the prosecutor, and the other to the poor; and the person prosecuted shall answer upon oath, and not demur on preferring a bill to discover what sums he has won.

A bill in equity may be filed to discover the consideration of a promissory note or other security alleged to be given for money lost at play, to have it delivered up. 3 *Anst.* 684. But if money be lent to game with, it may be recovered back as money lent, though the bond, note, or other security given for it is void. 1 *Burr.* 1077.

Persons by fraud or ill practice in playing at cards or dice, or by bearing a share in the stakes, &c. or by betting, winning any sum above 10*l.* shall forfeit five times the value of the thing won, and suffer such infamous and corporal punishment, as in cases of wilful perjury, being convicted thereof on indictment or information; and the penalty shall be recovered by action, by such person as will sue for the same.—And if any one shall assault and beat, or challenge to fight any other person, on account of money won by gaming, upon conviction thereof, he shall forfeit all his goods, and suffer imprisonment for two years. *Ibid.*

Also by this statute, any two or more justices of peace, may cause such persons to be brought before them as they suspect to have no visible estates, &c. to maintain them; and if they do not make it appear that the principal part of their expences is got by other means than gaming, the justices shall require securities for their good behaviour for a twelvemonth; and in default of such security, commit them to prison until they find it: And playing or betting during the time, to the value of 20*s.* shall be deemed a breach of good behaviour, and a forfeiture of their recognisances. *Ibid.*

By 2 *Geo.* 2, *c.* 28, *s.* 9, where it shall be proved before any justice of peace, that any person hath used unlawful games contrary to the statute 33 *Hen.* 8. *c.* 9, the justice may commit such offender to prison, till he enter into a recognizance that he shall not from thenceforth, at any time to come, play at any unlawful game. And by 12 *Geo.* 2. *c.* 28, for better preventing excessive and deceitful gaming, the ace of hearts, faro, basset, and hazard, are declared to be lotteries by cards or dice; and persons setting up these games are liable to the penalty of 200*l.* And every person who shall be an adventurer, or play or stake therein, forfeits 50*l.* Likewise the sale of any house, plate, &c. in the way of lottery by cards, &c. is adjudged void, and the things to be forfeited to any person that will sue for the same. And by 13 *Geo.* 2. *c.* 19. The game of passage, and all other games with one or more dice, or any thing in that nature, having figures or numbers thereon, (back-gammon and games now played with those tables only excepted) shall be deemed games or lotteries by dice, within the 12 *Geo.* 2. *c.* 28. And such as keep any office or table for the said game, &c. or play thereat, are subject to the penalties in that act.

By 18 *Geo.* 2, *cap.* 34, playing at, or keeping any house or place for playing at the game of roulet, otherwise roly-poly, or any other game with cards or dice already prohibited, incurs the penalties in stat. 12 *Geo.* 2. *c.* 28. Persons losing 10*l.* and paying the same, may sue the winner, and recover the same,

---

* This restriction as to a demurrer applies only to where the bill is filed for a discovery on the part of the loser, or party aggrieved, and not to cases where there is an action by a common informer after the expiration of the three months, and such informer files a bill against the winner for a discovery of the money lost, it being contrary to the rules of the courts of equity to aid *qui tam* actions; and in such a case the defendant may consequently demur for want of equity. *Holloway, qui tam,* v. *Ogden, Ed. MSS.*

with costs. And on a bill in equity the court may decree the same to be paid. The persons who have jurisdiction to determine informations on the statutes against gaming may summon witnesses, who on refusing to appear and give evidence shall forfeit 50*l.* No privilege of parliament shall be allowed on prosecution for keeping a gaming-house.

Persons losing 10*l.* at one time, or 20*l.* in twenty-four hours, may be indicted and fined five times the value; and such offenders discovering others shall be discharged.

By 5 *Geo.* 2, *c.* 30, no bankrupt shall have any benefit under the acts relating to bankrupts who shall have lost at gaming 5*l.* in one day, or 100*l.* in one year before he became bankrupt. *s.* 12.

And by 30 *Geo.* 2, *c.* 24, persons licensed to sell liquors permitting (see 33 *Hen.* 8, *c.* 9, *supra*) journeymen, labourers, servants and apprentices to game in their houses, shall forfeit 40*s.* for the first offence, and for every subsequent offence 10*l.*

On complaint of such persons gaming in public houses, justices of peace are to issue warrants for apprehending them, who upon conviction forfeit not exceeding 20*s.* nor less than 5*s.* otherwise they shall be committed; and inhabitants of parishes may be witnesses.

These are the chief statutes against gaming in general. For other subjects of legislative restriction, see articles Horse-Races, Little Goes, and Lotteries.

But notwithstanding these restraining statutes, it seems that by the common law the playing at cards, with dice, or at any game not *expressly prohibited,* when practised innocently, and as a *mere recreation,* without any mad desire of winning or losing, is not at all unlawful, nor punishable as any offence whatsoever. 2 *Vent.* 175. 5 *Mod.* 13. *Salk.* 100. *pl.* 10.

However, common gaming-houses are common nuisances in the eye of the law, not only because they are great temptations to idleness, but as they draw together great numbers of disorderly persons to the disturbance of the neighbourhood. 1 *Hawk. P. C.* 198.

GANG-DAYS. See *Rogation-Week.*

GAOL DELIVERY, Commission of, is one of the commissions under which the judges sit at the assises, and empowers them to try and deliver every prisoner who shall be in the gaol when the judges arrive at the circuit town, wherever or before whomsoever indicted, or for whatever crime committed.

GAOL, is a prison, a strong place, or house for keeping of debtors, or criminal offenders against the laws. *Bac. Abr.*

And all prisons and gaols belong to the king, although the subject may have the custody or keeping of them. 2 *Inst.* 100.

And to this purpose by 5 *Hen.* 4, *cap.* 10, (which is only declaratory of the common law, 2 *Inst.* 73,) it is enacted that "none "shall be imprisoned by any justice of the "peace, but only in the common gaol, sav- "ing to lords and others, who have gaols, "their franchises in this case."

So by 11 & 12 *Wil.* 3, *c.* 10, all murderers and felons shall be imprisoned in the common gaol, and the sheriffs shall have the keeping of the gaol.

But the court of King's Bench may commit to any prison in the kingdom which they shall think most proper, and the offender so committed or condemned to imprisonment cannot be removed or bailed by any other court. *Moor* 666. *pl.* 913. 1 *Sid.* 145.

And by 14 *Ed.* 3, *st.* 1, *c.* 10, the sheriffs shall have the custody of the gaols, as before that time they were wont to have, (*meaning the county gaols*) and shall put in under keepers for whom they will answer. But by 22 & 23 *Car.* 2, *c.* 20, felons and prisoners for debt shall not be lodged together, but kept separate and in distinct rooms; and any one offending against any part of this act shall forfeit his office and treble damages to the party grieved.

GAOLER. A gaoler is the master or governor of a prison, and as such is considered as an officer relating to the administration of justice, and is so far under the protection of the law, that if a person threatens him for keeping a prisoner in safe custody, he may be indicted, and fined and imprisoned for it. 2 *Roll. Abr.* 76. And if in repelling force he commit homicide, it will be justifiable; and on the contrary if he is himself killed it will be murder in the party or parties slaying him.

By the 3 *Geo.* 1. *cap.* 15, none shall purchase the office of gaoler, or any other office pertaining to the high sheriff, under pain of 500*l.*

GARB, (*garba,* from the Fr. *garbe,* alias *gerbe,* i. e. *fascis*) a bundle or sheaf of corn. *Chart. Forest. c.* 7. *Cowel. Blount.*

GARBLE, to sever the dross and dust from spice, drugs, &c. thereby purifying and cleansing the good from the bad. *Ibid.*

GARBLER OF SPICES, an officer of antiquity in the city of London, who may enter into any shop, warehouse, &c. to view and search drugs and spices, and garble and make clean the same, or see that it be done. 21 *Jac.* 1, *c.* 19.

GARCIO, (Fr. *garcon*) a groom or servant. *Cowel. Blount.*

GARCIONES, servants who followed the camp. *Ibid.*

GARD, GARDIAN, &c. See *Guardian.*

GARDEBRACHE, (Fr. *gardebrace*) an armour or vambrace for the arm. *Charta k. Hen.* 5. *Cowel. Blount.*

GARDENS. *Robbing of.* See *Trespass.*

GARDEROBE, (*Garderoba*) a closet or small apartment, for hanging up clothes, being the same with wardrobe. 2 *Inst.* 255.

GARDIA, used by the feudists for *custodia. Lib. Feud.* 1. *Cowel. Blount.*

GARE, a coarse wool, full of staring hairs, such as grow about the shanks of sheep. 31 *Ed.* 3. *cap.* 8.

GARLANDA, a chaplet, coronet, or garland. *Mat. Paris. Cowel. Blount.*

GARNESTURA, victuals, arms, and other implements of war, necessary for the defence of a town or castle. *Mat. Paris. Ann.* 1250. *Cowel. Blount.*

GARNISH, to garnish the heir, signifies in law to warn the heir. *Stat.* 27 *Eliz. cap.* 3.

GARNISHMENT, (Fr. *Garnement*, from *Garnir*, i. e. *instruere*) in a legal sense intends a warning given to one for his appearance, for the better furnishing of the cause and court. *Cromp. Juris.* 211. *F. N. B.* 106.

GARNISHEE, is a third person or party in whose hands money is attached within the liberties of the city of London, by process out of the sheriff's court; so called, because he hath had garnishment or warning not to pay the money to the defendant, but to appear and answer to the plaintiff creditor's suit. *Cowel. Blount.* Vide *Attachment.*

GARNISTURE, a furnishing or providing. *Ibid.*

GARSUMMUNE, *Gersuma*, or *Gersoma*, a fine or amerciament. *Ibid.*

GARTER, Knight of, the first personal dignity after the peerage of the realm is a *knight* of the order of St. Ge rge, or of the Garter, first instituted by *Ed.* 3, A. D. 1344. *Seld. tit. Hen.* 2, 5, 41.

GARTH, from the *ancient British* word, a little back-side or close in the North of England, *gardd* signifying garden.

GARTHMAN. As there are fishgarths or wears for catching of fish, so there are garthmen. See 17 *R.* 2. *cap.* 9. The word is derived from the Scottish gart, which signifies enforced, or compelled; and fish are forced by the wear to pass in at a loop where they are taken.

GASTALDUS, a governor of the country, whose office was only temporary, and who had jurisdiction over the common people. *Cowel. Blount.*

GATE, at the end of the names of places, signifies a way or path. *Ibid.*

GAVEL, (Sax. *gafel*) tribute, toll, custom or yearly revenue. *Ibid.* See *Gabel.*

GAVELET, (*gaveletum*) was an ancient and special kind of *cessavit* used in Kent, where the custom of gavelkind yet prevails, whereby a tenant, if he withheld his rents and services due to the lord, was to forfeit his land when no distress could be found, or the tenant within a year and a day did not come and pay his rent. *Fitz. Cess.* 60. *Terms de Ley.*

Hence *gaveletum* was as much as to say to cease, or to let to pay the rent. *Cowel. Blount.*

GAVELET IN LONDON, (*breve de gaveleto* in London, *pro reddilu ibidem, quia tenementa fuerunt indistringibilia*) a writ anciently used in the hustings of London, 10 *Ed.* 2, under which the parties, tenant and demandant, appear by *scire facias*, to show cause why the one should not have his tenement again on payment of his rent, or the other recover the lands, on default thereof. *Practic. Solic.* 419.

GAVELGELD, the payment of tribute or toll. *Mon. Ang. tom.* 3. *Cowel. Blount.*

GAVELKIND, supposed by Lambard, to be compounded of three Saxon words, gyfe, eal, kyn, *omnibus cognatione proximis data, quasi* give all kind, that is to each child his part; it signifies a tenure or custom, annexed and belonging to lands in Kent, not disgaveled by stat. whereby the lands of the father are equally divided at his death among all his sons; or the land of the brother among all the brethren if he have no issue of his own. *Lit.* 210.

All the lands in England, it is said, were of the nature of gavelkind before the Conquest, and descended to all the issue equally, but after the Conquest (as it is called) when knight-service was introduced, the descent was restrained to the eldest son for the preservation of the tenure. (*Lamb.* 167. 3 *Salk.* 129. 3 *Bac.* by *Gwil.* 360.) How this property was held unimpaired in tenure by the people of Kent is uncertain, but the distinguishing properties of this tenure, which also prevails in some other counties, are various, some of the principal are these: 1. The tenant is of age sufficient to aliene his estate by feoffment at the age of fifteen (*Lamb. Peramb.* 614). 2. The estate does not escheat in case of an attainder and execution for felony, their maxim being "the "father to the bough, the son to the plough." (*Lamb.* 634.) 3. In most places he had a power of devising lands by will, before the statute for that purpose was made (*F. N. B.* 198. *Cro. Car.* 561.). 4. The lands descend not to the eldest, youngest, or any one son only, but to all the sons together (*Litt. s.* 210.), which was indeed anciently the most usual course of descent all over England (*Glanvil. l.* 7. *c.* 3.), though in particular places particular customs prevailed. These among other properties distinguished this tenure in a most remarkable manner: and yet it is said to be only a species of a socage tenure, modified by the custom of the country; the lands being holden by suit of court and fealty, which is a service in its nature certain. (*Wright.* 211.) Wherefore, by a charter of king John, (*Spelm. cod. vet. leg.* 355.) Hubert archbishop of Canterbury was authorized to exchange the gavelkind tenures holden of the see of Canterbury into tenures by knight's-service; and by statute 31 *Hen.* 8. *c.* 3, for disgavelling the lands of divers lords and gentlemen in the county of Kent, they are directed to be descendible for the future like other lands, which were never holden *by service of socage*,

GAVELMAN, a tenant liable to tribute. *Cowel. Blount.*

GAVELMED, an ancient duty or work of mowing grass, or cutting of meadow land, required by the lord. *Ibid.*

GAVELCESTER, (Sax.) *Sextarius Vectigalis*, an ancient measure of rent-ale. *Ibid.*

GAVEL-WERK, (Sax.) was either *manu et persona opera*, by the hands and person of the tenant, or *carropera*, by his carts or carriages. *Ibid.*

GAUGETUM, a gauge or gauging, done by the gauger; and the true English gauge is mentioned. *Rot. Parl.* 35. *Ed.* 1. *Ibid.*

GAUGER, (*gaugeator*, Fr. *ganchir*, i. e. *in gyrum torquere*) an officer anciently appointed by the king, to examine all tuns, pipes, hogsheads, barrels, &c. containing customable articles.

GEASPECIA. In a charter of the privileges of Newcastle upon Tyne, renewed *anno* 30 *Eliz.* we find *sturgiones, porpecias*, i. e. (*porpoises*) *delphinos*, geaspecias, (viz. *grampois*,) &c. *Cowel. Blount.*

GEBURSCIP, (*geburscipa*) neighbourhood or adjoining district. *Leg. Edw. Confess. cap.* 1. *Ibid.*

GEBURUS, a country inhabitant of the same gebureship, or village; from the Sax. gebure, a carl, ploughman, or farmer. *Cowel. Ibid.*

GELD, (*geldum*) *mulcta compensatio delicti & pretium rei*, a mulct or fine, according to our ancient laws; thus *wergeld* was used for the value or price of a man slain; and *orfgeld* of a beast.

GELDABLE, (*geldabilis*) signified liable to pay tax or tribute.

GEMOTE, (Sax. *i. e. conventus*,) an assembly.

GENERAL ISSUE, is what is termed the general plea in an action at law, and it traverses, thwarts, and denies at once the whole declaration without offering any special matter whereby to evade it. As in trespass, either *vi et armis*, on the case, *non culpabilis*, not guilty—in debt upon contract, *nil debet*, he owes nothing—in debt on bond, *non est factum*, it is not his deed—on an *assumpsit*, *non assumpsit*, he made no such promise: or, in real actions, *nul tort*, no wrong done—*nul disseisin*, no disseisin; and in a writ of right the *mise*, or issue, is that the tenant has more right to hold than the demandant has to demand. These pleas are called the general issue, because by importing an absolute and general denial of what is alleged in the declaration they amount at once to an issue, by which a fact is affirmed on one side and denied on the other.

GENERALE, anciently the single commons or ordinary mess of students in the universities or inns of courts.

GENERATIO. On the splitting and dividing of ancient religious houses into different bodies, the sectarians were anciently classed under the denomination *generatio*.

GENTLEMAN (*generosus*). Under the denomination of gentlemen are comprised all above yeomen, who, according to the best heraldists, are those without any title bear a coat of arms, or whose ancestors have been freemen; and by the coat that a gentleman giveth he is known to be or not descended from those of his name that lived several hundred years since. *Jacob* as edited by *Morgan*.

GENTLEWOMAN, (*generosa*) is a good addition; and if a gentlewoman be named spinster it is said to be cause of abatement. 2 *Inst.* 668.

GENU, a generation. *Cowel. Blount.*

GENUS, (Latin) the general stock, extraction. *Cowel. Blount.*

GEORGE NOBLE, a piece of gold, current at six shillings and eight-pence, in the reign of king *Hen.* 8. *Lownds's Ess.* upon Coins, p. 41.

GESTU ET FAMA, an ancient writ where a person's good behaviour was impeached, now out of use. *Lamb. Eiren. lib.* 4. *cap.* 14. *Cowel. Blount.* See *Good Abearance.*

GEWINEDA, (Sax.) was used for the public convention of the people, to decide a cause: *et pax quam aldermanus regis in quinque burgorum gewineda dabit emendatur.* 12 *libris. LL. Æthelred. cap.* 1. *Cowel. Blount.*

GEWITNESSA, the giving of evidence. *Leg. Ethel. cap.* 1. *apud Brompton.*

GIFT. Gifts, or grants of chattels personal, are the act of transferring the right and the possession of them, whereby one man renounces, and another man immediately acquires, all title and interest therein, which may be done either in writing, or by word of mouth, attested by sufficient evidence, of which the delivery of possession is the strongest and most essential. But this conveyance, when merely voluntary, is somewhat suspicious, and is usually construed to be fraudulent, if creditors or others become sufferers thereby. And, particularly by stat. 3 *Hen.* 7. c. 4, all deeds of gift of goods made in trust for the use of the donor shall be void; because otherwise persons might be tempted to commit treason or felony, without danger of forfeiture, and the creditors of the donor might also be defrauded of their rights. And by statute 13 *Eliz.* c. 5, every grant or gift of chattels as well as lands, with an intent to defraud creditors or others, shall be void as against such persons to whom such fraud would be prejudicial; but as against the grantor himself shall stand good and effectual; and all persons partakers in or privy to such fraudulent grants shall forfeit the whole value of the goods, one moiety to the king, and another moiety to the party aggrieved; and also on conviction shall suffer imprisonment for half a year. *Perk. s.* 57. 3 *Rep.* 82. 2 *Black.* 441.

A true and proper gift or grant is always

accompanied with delivery of seisin, and takes effect immediately: as if A gives to B 100*l*. or a flock of sheep, and puts him in possession of them directly, it is then a gift executed in the donee; and it is not in the donor's power to retract it, though he did it without any consideration or recompense: unless it be prejudicial to creditors; or the donor were under any legal incapacity, as infancy, coverture, duress, or the like; or if he were drawn in, circumvented, or imposed upon by false pretences, ebriety or surprise. But if the gift does not take effect by delivery of immediate possession, it is then not properly a gift, but a contract: and this a man cannot be compelled to perform but upon good and sufficient consideration. *Jenk.* 109. 2 *Black.* 441.

If a man sells goods and still continues in possession as visible owner, the sale is fraudulent, and void against creditors. 2 *T. R.* 596. But the sale or mortgage of a ship at sea is valid if the grand bill of sale be delivered to the vendee or mortgagee, and he takes possession the first opportunity after the ship arrives in port. 1 *T. R.* 462.

The conveyance by GIFT (*donatio*) is properly applied to the creation of an estate tail, as feoffment is to that of an estate in fee, and lease to that of an estate for life or years. It differs in nothing from a feoffment but in the nature of the estate passing by it, for the operative words of conveyance in this case are *do* or *dedi*. *West. Symb.* 256. And gifts in tail are equally imperfect without livery of seisin, as feoffments in fee-simple. *Lit. s.* 59. And this is the only distinction that *Littleton* seems to take when he says, (*s.* 57,) "it is to be understood that there is feoffor and feoffee, *donor* and *donee*, lessor and lessee, *viz.* feoffor, as applied to a feoffment in fee-simple, *donor*, to a *gift* in tail, and lessor to a lease for life, or for years, or at will." 2 *Black.* 316. But gifts and grants which relate to the transferring of incorporeal hereditaments are said to be alike in nature, and therefore very frequently confounded. *Wood's Inst.* 260.

GIFTA AQUÆ, the stream of water to a mill. *Cowel. Blount.*

GIGMILLS, a kind of fulling-mills for fulling and burling of woollen cloth.

GILD, a fraternity or company.

GILDA MERCATORIA, a mercantile meeting or assembly. 10 *Rep.* 30. 1 *Rol. Abr.* 513. 1 *Black.* 473.

GISARMS, or GUISARMES, an halbert or hand-ax. *Cowel. Blount.*

GIST OF ACTION, (from the Fr. *gist*,) is the particular point on which the action lies; the very ground and foundation thereof, without which it is not maintainable. 5 *Mod. Rep.* 305.

GLADIOLUM, a little sword, or dagger; also a kind of sedge. *Mat. Paris.* 1206. *Cowel. Blount.*

GLADIUS. *Jus gladii*, is mentioned in our Latin authors, and the Norman laws, and it signifies a supreme jurisdiction. *Camd.* And it is said that from hence at the creation of an earl he is *gladio succinctus*, to signify that he had a jurisdiction over the county of which he was made earl. *Ibid.*

GLAIRE, (*Fr.*) a sword, lance, or horseman's staff. Gleyre was one of the weapons allowed the contending parties in a trial by combat. *Orig. Jurisd.* 79.

GLASS-MEN, are reckoned amongst wandering rogues and vagrants, by the old statutes. 39 *Eliz. c.* 17, and 1 *Jac.* 1. *c.* 7. *Cowel. Blount.*

GLAVEA, an hand-dart. *Blount.*

GLEANING. It was formerly considered that by the common law and custom of England, the poor are allowed to enter and glean upon another's ground, after the harvest, without being guilty of trespass; (*Gilb. Ev.* 253. *Trials per Pais c.* 15. *p.* 438.) 3 *Black. Com.* 212, 213.

But in a recent case in the court of common pleas it has been decided (*Gould, J.* dis.) that a right to glean in the harvest field cannot be claimed by any person at common law; and to set it up as a common law right would be opening a tempting door to fraud and idleness, the point having never been recognized by any judicial determinations. 1 *Hen. Black. Rep.* 51. 63.

GLEBE, (*gleba*) is church-land; and most commonly taken for the land belonging to a parish church, besides the tithes. *Wood's Inst.* 163.

GLEBARIÆ, turfs dug out of the ground. *Cowel. Blount.*

GLISCYWA, an old Saxon word for a fraternity. *Ibid.*

GLOMERELLS, commissaries appointed to determine differences between scholars of a school or university, and the townsmen of the place.

GLOVE-SILVER, money customarily given to servants to buy them gloves, as an encouragement for their labours. Glove money has been also applied to extraordinary rewards given to officers of courts, &c. It is now given on the circuits, by the barristers, to the judge's crier. *Cowel. Blount.*

GLYN, a valley, according to the book of *Domesday*. *Ibid.*

GO. This word is sometimes used in a special signification, as to go without day, is to be dismissed the court; so in old phrase, to go to God. *Broke. Kitch.* 190.

GOATS, no man may common goats within the forest without especial warrant. *Cowel. Blount.*

GOD-BOTE, (Sax.) an ecclesiastical or church fine, paid for crimes and offences committed against God. *Ibid.*

GOD-GILD, that which is offered to God, or his service. Sax. *Ibid.*

GOD AND RELIGION, offences against. See APOSTACY and HERESY.

GOLDA, a mine, according to *Blount.*

GOLD and SILVER LACE. See MANUFACTURER.

GOLDSMITHS. See *Manufacturers.*

GOLDWIT, or GOLDWICH, supposed to be a golden mulct; in the records of the Tower there is mention of *consuetudo vocata* Goldwith *vel* Goldwich. *Cowel. Blount.*

GOLIARDUS, is a jester or buffoon, mentioned in *Matt. Paris.* 1229. *Cowel. Blount.*

GOOD ABEARANCE, (*Bonus Gestus*) This security consists in being bound with one or more sureties in a recognizance or obligation to the king, entered on record, and taken in some court, or by some judicial officer, whereby the parties acknowledge themselves to be indebted to the crown in the sum required (for instance 1000*l.*) on condition to be void and of none effect if the party shall appear in court on such a day, and in the mean time shall keep the peace, either generally towards the king, and all his liege people, or particularly also with regard to the person who craves the security: or, if it be for the good behaviour, then on condition that he shall demean and behave himself well, (or be of good behaviour,) either generally or specially, for the time therein limited, as for one or more years, or for life. This recognizance, if taken by a justice of the peace, must be certified to the next sessions, in pursuance of the statute 3 *Hen.* 7. *c.* 1, and if the condition of such recognizance be broken, by any breach of the peace in the one case, or any misbehaviour in the other, the recognizance becomes forfeited or absolute; and being estreated or extracted (taken out from among the other records) and sent up to the exchequer, the party and his sureties having now become the king's absolute debtors, are sued for the several sums in which they are respectively bound. 4 *Black.* 253.

Any justices of the peace, by virtue of their commission, or those who are *ex officio* conservators of the peace, may demand such security according to their own discretion; or it may be granted at the request of any subject, upon due cause shewn, provided such demandant be under the king's protection; for which reason it has been formerly doubted, whether jews, pagans, or persons convicted of a præmunire, were entitled thereto. (1 *Hawk. P. C.* 126.) Or, if the justice is averse to act, it may be granted by a mandatory writ, called a supplicavit, issuing out of the court of king's bench or chancery; which will compel the justice to act, as a ministerial and not as a judicial officer: and he must make a return to such writ, specifying his compliance, under his hand and seal. (*F. N. B.* 80. 2 *P. Wms.* 202.) But this writ is seldom used: for, when application is made to the superior courts, they usually take the recognizances there, under the directions of the statute 21 *Jac.* 1. *c.* 8. And indeed a peer or peeress cannot be bound over in any other place, than the courts of king's bench or chancery: though a justice of the peace has a power to require sureties of any other person being *compos mentis* and under the degree of nobility, whether he be a fellow justice or other magistrate, or whether he be merely a private man. (1 *Hawk. P. C.* 127.) Wives may demand it against their husbands, or husbands, if necessary, against their wives. (2 *Stra.* 1207.) But feme coverts, and infants under age, ought to find security by their friends only, and not to be bound themselves; for they are incapable of engaging themselves to answer any debt, which is the nature of these recognizances or acknowledgments. 4 *Black.* 254.

A recognizance may be discharged either by the demise of the king, to whom the recognizance is made, or by the death of the principal party bound thereby, if not before forfeited; or by order of the court to which such recognizance is certified by the justices, (as the quarter-sessions, assises, or king's bench,) if they see sufficient cause: or in case he at whose request it was granted, if granted upon a private account, will release it, or does not make his appearance to pray that it may be continued. 1 *Hawk. P. C.* 129.

Thus far what has been said is applicable to both species of recognizances for the peace and for the good behaviour, *de pace, et legalitate, tuenda,* as expressed in the laws of k. Edw. But as these two species of securities are in some respects different, especially as to the cause of granting, or the means of forfeiting them, they must now be considered separately; FIRST, for what cause such a recognizance, with sureties for the peace, is grantable, and then how it may be forfeited. 4 *Black.* 254.

1. Any justice of the peace may *ex officio,* bind all those to keep the peace who in his presence make any affray, or threaten to kill or beat another, or contend together with hot and angry words; or go about with unusual weapons or attendance, to the terror of the people; and all such as he knows to be common barrators, and such as are brought before him by the constable for a breach of the peace in his presence; and all such persons as having been before bound to the peace, have broken it and forfeited their recognizances. Also, wherever any private man hath just cause to fear that another will burn his house, or do him a corporal injury, by killing, imprisoning, or beating him: or that he will procure others so to do; he may demand surety of the peace against such person; and every justice of the peace is bound to grant it,

if he who demands it will make oath, that he is actually under fear of death or bodily harm; and will show that he has just cause to be so, by reason of the other's menaces, attempts, or having lain in wait for him; and will also further swear, that he does not require such surety out of malice or for mere vexation. This is called swearing the peace against another: and, if the party does not find such sureties, as the justice in his discretion shall require, he may immediately be committed till he does. 1 *Hawk. P. C.* 126, 127, 128.

2. Such recognizance for keeping the peace, when given, may be forfeited by any actual violence, or even an assault, or menace, to the person of him who demanded it, if it be a special recognizance, or if the recognizance be general, by any unlawful action whatsoever, that either is or tends to a breach of the peace, or more particularly by any one of the many species of offences which are crimes against the public peace, such as tumultuous assemblies, and the like, or by any private violence committed against any of his majesty's subjects. But a bare trespass upon the lands or goods of another, which is a ground for a civil action, unless accompanied with a wilful breach of the peace, is no forfeiture of the recognizance. 2 *Hawk.* 131. Neither are mere reproachful words, as calling a man knave or liar, any breach of the peace so as to forfeit one's recognizance, (being looked upon to be merely the effect of unmeaning heat and passion,) unless they amount to a challenge to fight. 2 *Hawk.* 130. 4 *Black.* 255.

The species of recognizance with sureties for the good abearance, or good behaviour, includes security for the peace, and somewhat more. *Lamb. Eiren. lib.* 4, *c.* 2.

First, the justices are empowered by the statute 34 *Edw.* 3. c. 1, to bind over to the good behaviour towards the king and his people, all them that be not of good fame, wherever they be found; to the intent that the people be not troubled nor endamaged, nor the peace diminished, nor merchants and others, passing by the highways of the realm, be disturbed nor put in the peril which may happen by such offenders. Under the general words of this expression, "that be not of good fame," it is holden that a man may be bound to his good behaviour for causes of scandal, *contra bonos mores*, as well as *contra pacem*; as, for haunting bawdy-houses with women of bad fame, or for keeping such women in his own house; or for words tending to scandalise the government, or in abuse of the officers of justice, especially in the execution of their office. Thus, also a justice may bind over all night-walkers, eaves-droppers, such as keep suspicious company, or are reported to be pilferers, or robbers; such as sleep in the day, and wake in the night; common drunkards, whoremasters; the putative fathers of bastards; cheats; idle vagabonds, and other persons, whose misbehaviour may reasonably bring them within the general words of the statute, as persons not of good fame: an expression, it must be owned, of so great a latitude, as leaves much to be determined by the discretion of the magistrate himself. But, if he commits a man for want of sureties, he must express the cause thereof with convenient certainty; and take care that such cause be a good one. 1 *Hawk. P. C.* 132. 4 *Black.* 256.

2. A recognizance for the good behaviour may be forfeited by all the same means, as one for the security of the peace may be; and also by some others. As, by going armed with unusual attendance, to the terror of the people; by speaking words tending to sedition, or by committing any of those acts of misbehaviour which the recognizance was intended to prevent, but not by barely giving fresh cause of suspicion of that which perhaps never may happen. 1 *Hawk. P. C.* 133. For though it is just to compel suspected persons to give security to the public against misbehaviour that is apprehended, yet it would be hard upon such suspicion, without the proof of any actual crime, to punish them by a forfeiture of their recognizance. 4 *Black.* 257.

GOOD BEHAVIOUR, surety for the good behaviour is surety for the peace, and differs very little from good abearing.

GOOD CONSIDERATION. A deed must be founded upon good and sufficient consideration. Not upon an usurious contract, (*Stat.* 13 *Eliz. c.* 8,) nor upon fraud or collusion, either to deceive purchasers *bona fide*, (*Stat.* 27 *Eliz. c.* 4,) or just and lawful creditors; (*Stat.* 13 *Eliz. c.* 5,) any of which bad considerations will vacate the deed, and subject such persons, as put the same in ure to forfeitures, and often to imprisonment. A deed also, or other grant, made without any consideration, is, as it were, of no effect; for it is construed to enure, or to be effectual, only to the use of the grantor himself*.

* This seems to be only true of a bargain and sale: for "herein it is said to differ "from a gift, that this may be without any "consideration or cause at all; and that "hath always some meritorious cause mov-"ing it, and cannot be without it."—*Shep. Touch.* 221. But otherwise a voluntary conveyance is good both in law and equity. *Tr. of Eq. b.* 1. *c.* 5. *s.* 2. And if after a voluntary grant of lands, the party make another conveyance of them for a valuable consideration, the first grant is not void with regard to this purchaser under the 27 *Eliz. c.* 4. For there must be some

(*Perk. s.* 535.) The consideration may be either a good or a valuable one. A good consideration is such as, that of blood, or of natural love and affection, when a man grants an estate to a near relation; being founded on motives of generosity, prudence, and natural duty; a valuable consideration is such as money, marriage, or the like which the law esteems an equivalent given for the grant; (3 *Rep.* 83,) and is therefore founded in motives of justice. And deeds upon good consideration only, are considered as merely voluntary, and are frequently set aside in favour of creditors, and *bona fide* purchasers. 2 *Black.* 296.

GOODS AND CHATTELS, (*bona et catalla*) the personal estate and effects of any one.

GOOLE (Fr. *goulet*), a breach in a sea bank or wall, or a passage worn by the flux and reflux of the sea. 16 & 17 *Car.* 2, *c.* 11. *Cowel. Blount.*

GORCE (from the Fr. *gort*) a wear; but according to *Coke* from *gurges*, a deep pit of water, called a *gors*, or gulf. And by stat. 25 *Ed.* 3, *c.* 4, it is ordained that all gorces, mills, wears, &c. levied and set up, whereby the king's ships and boats are disturbed and cannot pass in any river, shall be utterly pulled down, without being renewed. *Co. Lit.* 5.

GORE, a narrow slip of ground. *Paroch. Antiq.* 393.

GOTE, (Saxon *geotan*, i. e. *fundere*) a ditch, sluice or gutter, mentioned in the 23 *Hen.* 8. *c.* 5. *Cowel. Blount.*

GOVERNMENT. The political writers of antiquity will not allow more than three regular forms of government:

I. When the sovereign power is lodged in an aggregate assembly consisting of all the free members of a community, which is called a DEMOCRACY:

II. When it is lodged in a council, composed of select members, and then it is styled an ARISTOCRACY:

III. When it is intrusted in the hands of a single person, and then it takes the name of a MONARCHY.

All other species of government, they say, are either corruptions of, or reducible to, these three. 1 *Black.* 48.

By the sovereign power, is meant the power of making of laws; for wherever that power resides, all others must conform to, and be directed by it, whatever appearance the outward form and administration of the government may put on. For it is at any time in the option of the legislature to alter that form and administration by a new edict or rule, and to put the execution of the laws into whatever hands it pleases; by constituting one, or a few, or many executive magistrates: and all the other powers of the state must obey the legislative power in the discharge of their several functions, or else the constitution is at an end.

In a *democracy*, where the right of making laws resides in the people at large, public virtue, or goodness of intention, is according to *Blackstone*, more likely to be found, than in either of the other qualities of government, for although popular assemblies are frequently foolish in their contrivance, and weak in their execution; yet they generally mean to do the thing that is right and just, and have always a degree of patriotism or public spirit. 1 *Black.* 49.

This, with all deference to the opinion of the late learned commentator, is an hypothesis not supported by historical facts: the annals of the world, from the most early period of time, down to the present, show that in all *republics* there have been constantly great diversities and distraction of opinion in their councils, and too frequently private and personal animosities introduced into their deliberations; added to which it is seen that too often in these popular assemblies the majority of the legislators are led away from acts of sound state policy by the specious rhetoric and eloquence of a few factious and interested demagogues; it does not therefore seem perfectly clear that this eulogy on, and marked preference to a democratic form of government by the learned commentator can be well supported; for the happiness and welfare of a nation must solely depend on the virtue, integrity, and sound policy of those to whom the powers of legislation are committed; and it appears to be going too far to insinuate that an aristocracy or a monarchy cannot be wholly virtuous and incorrupt.

In *aristocracies*, Blackstone observes, there is more wisdom to be found* than in the other frames of government, being composed, or intended to be composed, of the most experienced citizens; but *there* is less ho-

---

circumstance of fraud to vacate the first conveyance, the want of consideration alone not being sufficient. *Cowp.* 705.

But if a person is indebted at the time of making a voluntary grant, or becomes so soon afterwards, it will be considered fraudulent and void with respect to creditors under the 13 *Eliz. c.* 5.

And, if a person makes a voluntary grant, and afterwards becomes bankrupt, whether he was indebted or not at the time, it will be void by 1 *Jac.* 1, *c.* 15, and the estate granted may be conveyed by the commissioners to the assignees for the benefit of the creditors. 1 *Atk.* 93. See FRAUDS.

---

* How can this intellectual superiority be admitted to prevail in aristocratic more than in popular or democratic assemblies?

nesty than in a republic *, and less strength than in a monarchy. 1 *Black*. 49.

A *monarchy* is indeed the most powerful of any, for by the entire conjunction of the legislative and executive powers all the sinews of government are knit together and united in the hands of the prince; but then there is imminent danger of his employing that strength to improvident or oppressive purposes †. 1 *Black.* 49.

These three species of governments, as Blackstone observes, have all of them their several perfections and imperfections. *Democracies* are usually the best calculated to direct the end of a law; *aristocracies* to invent the means by which that end shall be obtained; and *monarchies* to carry those means into execution. 1 *Black.* 50.

Happily for us of this island, (according to the opinion of *Cicero*, "*esse optime constitutam* " *rempublicam, quæ ex tribus generibus illis,* " *regali, optimo, et populari, sit modice con-* " *fusa*," (a mixed government, founded out of them all, and partaking of the advantages of each) which Tacitus treated as a visionary whim, and one that if effected could never be lasting or secure, " *Cunctus na-* " *tiones et urbes populus aut primores aut singuli* " *regunt: delecta ex his et constituta reipub-* " *licæ forma laudari facilius quam evenire, vel* " *si evenit, haud diuturna esse potest.*" *Ann. lib.* 4, the British constitution must long continue a standing exception to the truth of this observation. 1 *Black.* 59.

With us the legislature of the kingdom is intrusted to three distinct powers, entirely independent of each other; FIRST, the king; SECONDLY, the lords spiritual and temporal, which is an aristocratical assembly of persons selected for their piety, their birth, their wisdom, their valour, or their property; and, THIRDLY, the house of commons, freely chosen by the people from among themselves, which makes it a kind of democracy; as this aggregate body, actuated by different springs, and attentive to different interests, composes the British parliament, and has the supreme disposal of every thing, there can no inconvenience be attempted by either of the three branches but will be withstood by one of the other two; each branch being armed with a negative power sufficient to repel any innovation which it shall think inexpedient or dangerous. 2 *Black.* 57.

Here then is lodged the sovereignty of the British constitution, and lodged as beneficially as is possible for society. For in no other shape could we be so certain of finding the three great qualities of government so well and so happily united. If the supreme power were lodged in any one of the three branches separately, we must be exposed to the inconveniencies of either absolute monarchy, aristocracy, or democracy; and so want two of the three principal ingredients of good policy, either virtue, wisdom, or power. If it were lodged in any two of the branches; for instance, in the king and house of lords; our laws might be providently made, and well executed, but they might not always have the good of the people in view: if lodged in the king and commons, we should want that circumspection and mediatory caution, which the wisdom of the peers is to afford: if the supreme rights of legislature were lodged in the two houses only, and the king had no negative upon their proceedings, they might be tempted to encroach upon the royal prerogative, or perhaps to abolish the kingly office, and thereby weaken (if not totally destroy) the strength of the executive power. But the constitutional government of this island is so admirably tempered and compounded, that nothing can endanger or hurt it but destroying the equilibrium of power between one branch of the legislature and the rest. For if ever it should happen that the independence of any one of the three should be lost, or that it should become subservient to the views of either of the other two, there would soon be an end of our constitution. The legislature would be changed from that, which (upon the supposition of an original contract, either actual or implied) is presumed to have been originally set up by the general consent and fundamental act of the society; and such a change, however effected, is at once an entire dissolution of the bands of government; and the people are thereby reduced to a state of anarchy, with liberty to constitute to themselves a new legislative power. 1 *Black.* 51, 52.

GOVERNMENT, CONTEMPT AGAINST. Contempts and misprisions against the king's *person* and government may be by speaking or writing against them, cursing or wishing him ill; giving out scandalous stories concerning him, or doing any thing that may tend to lessen him in the esteem of his subjects, may weaken his government, or may raise jealousies between him and his people. It has been also held an offence of this species to drink to the pious memory of a traitor; or for a clergyman to absolve persons at the gallows who then persist in the treasons for which they die, these being acts which impliedly encourage rebellion. 4 *Black.* 123.

For this species of contempt a man may not only be fined and imprisoned, but suf-

* This is nothing more than a broad and unsupported assertion; for surely it behoves every government in order to preserve its existence, to be at least as honest as a republic.

† This is a proposition too clear to be denied.

fer the pillory, or other infamous corporal punishment. 1 *Hawk. P. C.* 62.

GRACE. Acts of parliament for a general and free pardon are called acts of grace.

GRADUATES, (*graduati*) scholars who have taken degrees in an university. 1 *H.* 6. *c.* 3. *Cowel. Blount.*

GRAFFER, (Fr. *greffier*, i. e. *Scriba*, a notary or scrivener, used in the stat. 5 *H.* 8. *c.* 1. *Ibid.*

GRAFFIO, GRAVIO, a landgrave, or earl. *Ibid.*

GRAFFIUM, a writing-book, register, or cartulary of deeds and evidences. *Ibid.*

GRAIL, (*gradale*, or *graduale*) a gradual, or book, containing some of the offices of the Roman church. *Ibid.*

GRAIN, the twenty-fourth part of a penny weight, also any kind of corn sown on the ground. *Ibid.*

GRAND ASSISE, a peculiar species of trial by jury, giving the tenant or defendant in a writ of right his election or choice of the form of a trial by *battle* or by a jury. 3 *Black.* 341.

GRAND CAPE, is a writ on plea of land, where the tenant makes default in appearance at the day given, for the king to take the land into his hands, &c. See *Cape Magnum. Cowel. Blount.*

GRAND DAYS, are those days in the Terms which are solemnly kept in the Inns of Court and Chancery, *i. e.* Candlemas day in Hilary term, Ascension day in Easter term, St. John the Baptist day in Trinity term, and all Saints day in Michaelmas term; which days are *Dies non Juridici*, or no days in court.

GRAND DISTRESS, in real actions lies in two cases, either when the tenant or defendant is attached, and does not appear, but makes default; or where the tenant has once appeared, and after makes default. *Cowel. Blount.*

GRAND JURY. For the purpose of receiving indictments, or written accusations of one or more persons, for crimes or misdemeanors, which may be preferred to a grand jury, the sheriff of every county is bound to return to *every session of the peace*, and every commission of *oyer and terminer*, and of *general gaol delivery*, twenty-four good and lawful men of the county, some out of every hundred, to inquire, present, do, and execute all those things which on the part of our lord the king shall then and there be commanded them (4 *Black.* 301). They ought to be freeholders, but to what amount is uncertain; which seems to be *casus omissus*, and as proper to be supplied by the legislature as the qualifications of the petit jury; which were formerly equally vague and uncertain, but are now settled by several acts of parliament. However, they are usually gentlemen of the best figure in the county. As many as appear upon this panel are sworn upon the grand jury, to the amount of twelve at least, and not more than twenty-three, that twelve may be a majority.

This grand jury are previously instructed in the articles of their inquiry by a charge from the judge who presides upon the bench. They then withdraw to sit and receive indictments, which are preferred to them in the name of the king, but at the suit of any private prosecutor; and they are only to hear evidence on behalf of the prosecution; for the finding of an indictment is only in the nature of an inquiry or accusation, which is afterwards to be tried and determined; and the grand jury are only to inquire upon their oaths, whether there be sufficient cause to call upon the party to answer it. A grand jury however ought to be thoroughly persuaded of the truth of an indictment, so far as their evidence goes, and not to rest satisfied merely with remote probabilities, a doctrine that might be applied to very oppressive purposes. 4 *Black.* 302.

And the grand jury ought never to be assisted by the depositions taken before the magistrate, except where these depositions can be read in evidence to the petit jury. *Denby's Case, Leach,* 580.

The grand jury are sworn to inquire only for the body of the county, *pro corpore comitatus*, and therefore they cannot regularly inquire of a fact done out of that county for which they are sworn, unless particularly enabled by act of parliament. 4 *Black.* 302.

When the grand jury have heard the evidence, if they think it a groundless accusation, they used formerly to endorse on the back of the bill, "*ignoramus*;" or, we know nothing of it; intimating, that though the facts might possibly be true, that truth did not appear to them: but now, they assert in English, more absolutely "not a true bill;" or (which is the better way) "not found," and then the party is discharged without further answer. But a fresh bill may afterwards be preferred to a subsequent grand jury. If they are satisfied of the truth of the accusation, they then endorse upon it, "a true bill;" anciently, "*billa vera*." The indictment is then said to be found, and the party stands indicted. But to find a bill there must at least twelve of the jury agree; for so tender is the law of England of the lives of the subjects that no man can be convicted at the suit of the king of any capital offence unless by the unanimous voice of twenty-four of his equals and neighbours, that is, by twelve at least of the grand jury, in the first place assenting to the accusation; and afterwards by the whole petit jury of twelve more, finding him guilty upon his trial. But if twelve of the grand jury assent, it is a good presentment, though some of the rest disagree. (2 *Hal. P. C.* 161.) And the indictment, when so found, is publicly delivered into court. 4 *Black.* 305.

A grand juror disclosing to any one indicted, the evidence that appeared against him, is guilty of a high misprision, and liable to be fined and imprisoned. 1 *Hawk. P. C.* 59. 4 *Black.* 126, 299.

GRAND SERJEANTRY, (i.e. *per magnum servitium*) a tenure whereby the tenant was bound instead of serving the king generally in his wars, to do some special honorary service to the king in person; as to carry his banner, his sword, or the like; or to be his butler, champion, or other office at his coronation. *Lit. s.* 153.

It was in most other respects like knight service, only he was not bound to pay aid or escuage. 2 *Inst. Ibid. s.* 158. 2 *Inst.* 233. and when tenant by knight service, paid five pounds for a relief on every knight's fee; tenant by grand serjeantry paid one year's value of his land, were it much or less. *Lit. s.* 158, 154.

Tenants by *cornage*, which was to wind a horn when the Scots or other enemies entered the land, in order to warn the king's subjects, was (like other services of the same nature) a species of grand serjeantry. 4 *Inst.* 192. But this tenure, with all others of a military nature, have been long since abolished by stat. 12 *Car.* 2. *c.* 24.

GRANGE, (*grangea*, Latin, from *granium*) a great farm which hath barns, stables, stalls, and other places, laid up for agricultural purposes.

GRANGEARIUS, was the person who had the care of such a farm or place. *Fleta, lib.* 2. *cap.* 8. *Cowel. Blount.*

GRANT, (*concessio*) signifies, in the common law, a conveyance in writing of incorporeal hereditaments not lying in livery, and which cannot pass by word only; as of reversions, advowsons in gross, tithes, rents, services, common in gross, &c. *Co. Lit.* 172. 3 *Rep.* 63. These, therefore, pass merely by the delivery of the deed; and he that granteth is termed the *grantor;* he to whom the grant is made, is the *grantee. West. Symb.* 234. And in seignories or reversions of lands, such grant, together with the attornment of the tenant (while attornments were necessary) were held to be of equal notoriety with, and therefore equivalent to a feoffment, and livery of lands in immediate possession: it therefore differs but little from a feoffment, except in its subject matter, for the operative words used therein, commonly used are *dedi et concessi*, "have given and granted." 2 *Black.* 317.

GRANTS OF THE KING. The king's grants are matters of public record. These grants whether of lands, honours, liberties, functions, or aught besides are contained in charters, or letters patent, that is of our letters *literæ patentes:* literally so called, because they are not sealed up, but exposed to public view with the great seal pendant at the bottom; and are usually directed or addressed by the king to all his subjects at large, and therein they differ from certain other grants of the king, sealed also with his great seal, but directed to particular persons, and for particular purposes, which therefore not being proper for inspection, are closed up and sealed on the outside, and are thereupon called writs *ecore* (*litteræ clausæ*) and are recorded in the *close rolls* in the same manner as the others are in the patent rolls. 2 *Black.* 346.

Grants or letters patent must first pass by bill: which is prepared by the attorney and solicitor general, in consequence of a warrant from the crown; and is then signed at the top, with the king's own sign manual, and sealed with his privy signet, which is always in the custody of the principal secretary of state; and then sometimes it immediately passes under the great seal, in which case the patent is subscribed in these words, "*per ipsum regem*," by the king himself. 9 *Rep.* 18. Otherwise the course is to carry an extract of the bill to the keeper of the privy seal, who makes out a writ or warrant thereupon to the chancery, so that the sign manual is the warrant to the privy seal, and the privy seal is the warrant to the great seal; and in this last case the patent is subscribed, "*per breve de privato sigillo*," by writ of privy seal. 9 *Rep.* 18.

But there are some grants which only pass through certain offices, as the admiralty or treasury, in consequence of a sign manual, without the confirmation of either the signet, the great, or the privy seal. 2 *Black.* 346.

The manner of granting by the king does not more differ from that by a subject, than the construction of his grants when made. 1. A grant made by the king, at the suit of the grantee, shall be taken most beneficially for the king, and against the party, whereas the grant of a subject is construed most strongly against the grantor. Wherefore it is usual to insert in the king's grants, that they are made, not at the suit of the grantee, but "*ex speciali gratia, certa scientia, et mero motu regis;*" and then they have a more liberal construction. 1 *Finch. L.* 100. 10 *Rep.* 112. 2. A subject's grant shall be construed to include many things, besides what are expressed, if necessary for the operation of the grant. Therefore, in a private grant of the profits of land for one year, free ingress, egress, and regress, to cut and carry away those profits, are also inclusively granted. *Co. Litt.* 56. And if a feoffment of land was made by a lord to his villein, this operated as a manumission. *Litt.* § 206. For he was otherwise unable to hold it. But the king's grant shall not enure to any other intent, than that which is precisely expressed in the grant. As, if he grants land to an alien, it operates nothing; for such grant shall not also enure to make him a denizen, that so he may be capable of taking by grant. (*Bro. Abr. tit. Patent.* 62. *Finch. L.* 110). 3. When it appears, from the face of the grant, that the king is mistaken or deceived, either in matter of fact or matter of law, as in case of false suggestion, misinformation, or misrecital of former grants; or if his own title to the thing granted be different from what he supposes, or if the grant be informal, or if he grants an estate contrary to the rules of law; in any of these cases the grant is absolutely void. *Freem.* 172. For instance, if the king grants lands to one and his heirs male, this is merely void; for it shall not be an estate tail, because there want words of procreation, to ascertain the body out of which the heirs shall issue, neither is it a fee-simple as in common grants it would be; because it may reasonably be supposed, that the king meant to give no more than an estate tail: *Finch* 101, 102. The grantee is therefore (if any thing) nothing more than tenant at will. (*Bro. Abr. tit. Estates,* 34, *tit. Patents,* 104. *Dyer.* 270. *Dav.* 45).

GRANTS, used for grandees. *Cowel. Blount.*

GRASS-HEARTH, the grasing or turning up the earth with a plough, an ancient term. *Cowel. Blount.*

GRABA, a little wood or grove. *Ibid.*

GRABARE ET GRABATIO, an accusation or impeachment. *Ibid.*

GRAVE. The names of places ending with grave come from the Sax. graf, a wood, thicket, den or cave. *Ibid.*

GRAZIER, (*Pecuarius*) one who occupies land for the purpose of feeding cattle.

GREAT COUNCIL, the parliament of England was annually held under the several names of *Mychel Synothe* great council, *Miehel Gemotte* or great meeting, and now frequently *within a gemotte* or the meeting of wise men.

GREAT SEAL. See *Chancery or Interfaction.*

GREE, (Fre. Gre. i. e. good liking, allowance). *Cowel. Blount.*

GREEN CLOTH, of the king's household, so termed from the green cloth on the table: is a court of justice composed of the lord steward, treasurer of the household, comptroller, and other officers; to which is committed the government and oversight of the king's court, and the keeping of the peace within the verge, &c. *Cowel. Blount.*

GREENHEW or GREENHUE, is all one with vert in forests, &c. *Ibid.*

GREEN SILVER. An ancient rent of one half-penny payable by custom within the manor of Writtel, in the county of Essex, by the tenant whose fore-door opens to Greenbury. *Cowel. Blount.*

GREEN-WAX. Estreats delivered to the sheriffs of the Exchequer, under the seal of that court made in green-wax. *Cowel. Blount.*

GREGORIAN CODE, a collection of civil institutes compiled by Gregorius. 1 *Black.* 81.

GREVE, (Sax. *Gerefa*) *Præceptus* same as Reve an officer, of power and authority, signifying in boroughs as much as *comes, vicecomes.* Vide *Cowel. Blount.*

GRILS, a kind of small fish.

GRITH, a Saxon word signifying peace. *Terms de Ley.*

GRITHPRECHE, (Sax. *Grythbryce,* i. e. *Pacis fractio*) breach of the peace. *Cowel. Blount.*

GRITHSTOLE, (Sax. *sedes pacis*) a place of sanctuary. *Ibid.*

GRONNA, A deep pit, or bituminous place where turfs are dug to burn. *Hoved.* 438. *Mon. Ang. Tom.* 1. *p.* 243. *Cowel. Blount.*

GROOM, a servant in some inferior place in stables, but there is amongst the king's household, the groom of the stole, &c. which is a great officer of the king's household, whose precinct is properly the king's bed-chamber; where the lord chamberlain hath nothing to do, and stole signifies a robe of honour. *Lex Constitutionis, p.* 182. *Cowel. Blount.*

GROOM PORTER, an officer or superintendant over the royal gaming-tables. *Ibid.*

GROSS, (*Grossus*) in gross, absolute, intire, not depending on one another, for which see *Advowson in gross, and Common in gross.*

GROSSE BOIS, (Fr. *Gros bois,* i. e. great wood) by the common law or custom reputed timber. 2 *Inst.* 642.

GROSS WEIGHT, the whole weight of goods or merchandize, dust and dross mixed with them, and of the chest, bag, &c. out of which tare and tret are allowed. *Merchant's Dict.*

GROT, (Fr.) A den, cave, or hollow place in the ground, also a shady wood place, with springs of water. *Cowel. Blount.*

GROUNDAGE, A custom or tribute paid for the standing of a ship in a port. *Ibid.*

GROUSE, red and black heath-game. See *Game.*

GROWME. An engine anciently used to stretch woollen cloth after it is woven.

GROWTH-HALFPENNY, an ancient rate so called and paid in some places for the tithe of every fat beast, ox, or other unfruitful cattle. *Clayton's Rep.* 92; *Cowel. Blount.*

GRUARII, (From the Fr. *Gruyer*) the principal officers of the forest in general. *Ibid.*

GUARD, (Fr. *Garde,* Lat. *Custodia*) A custody or care of defence.

GUARDIAN AND WARD, the guardian is a temporary parent of the ward, for so long time as the ward is an infant, or under age.

Of the several species of guardians, the first are guardians by nature, viz. the father and (in some cases) the mother of the child. For if an estate be left to an infant, the father is by common law the guardian, and must account to his child for the profits. (*Co. Litt.* 88). But an executor is not justified in paying to the father a legacy left to the child; and if he pays it to the father, and the father becomes insolvent, he may be compelled to pay it over again. (1 *P. Wms.* 285. *Co. Litt.* 88). And, with regard to daughters, it seems by construction of the statute, 4 & 5 *Ph.* & *Mar.* c. 8. that the father might by deed or will assign a guardian to any woman child under the age of sixteen; and, if none be so assigned, the mother shall in this case be guardian. (3 *Rep.* 39). There are also guardians for nurture, (*Co. Litt.* 88); which are, of course the father or mother, till the infant attains the age of fourteen years, (*Moor.* 738. 3 *Rep.* 38); and in default of father or mother, the ordinary usually assigns some discreet person to take care of the infant's personal estate, and to provide for his maintenance and education. (2 *Jones* 90. 2 *Lev.* 163). Next are guardians in socage, who are also called guardians by the common law. These take place only when the minor is entitled to some estate in lands, and then by the common law the guardianship devolves upon his next of kin, to whom the inheritance cannot possibly descend; as where the estate descended from his father, in this case his uncle by the mother's side, cannot possibly inherit this estate, and therefore shall be the guardian. (*Litt.* § 123). For the law judges it improper to trust the person of an infant in his hands, who may by possibility become heir to him; that there may be no temptation nor even suspicion of temptation for him to abuse his trust. *Nunquam custodia alicujus de jure alicui remanet, de quo habeatur suspicio, quod possit vel velit aliquod jus in ipsa haereditate clamare. Glanv. l.* 7, *c.* 11.

These guardians in socage, like those for nurture, continued only till the minor is fourteen years of age; for, then in both cases, he is presumed to have discretion, so far as to choose his own guardian. This he may do, unless one be appointed by the father, by virtue of the statute 12 *Car.* 2. c. 24, which considering the imbecility of judgment in children of the age of fourteen, and the abolition of guardianship in chivalry (which lasted till the age of twenty-one), enacts, that any father, under age or of full age, may by deed or will dispose of the custody of his child, either born or unborn, to any person except a popish recusant, either in possession or reversion, till such child attains the age of one and twenty years.* These are called guardians by statute, or testamentary guardians. There are also special guardians by custom of London, and other places, (*Co. Litt.* 88), but they are particular exceptions, and do not fall under the general law. 1 *Black.* 462.

The power and reciprocal duty of a guardian and ward are the same *pro tempore*, as that of a father and child; added to which that the guardian, when the ward comes of age, is bound to give him an account of all that he has transacted on his behalf, and must answer for all losses by his wilful default or negligence. In order therefore to prevent disagreeable contests with young gentlemen, it has become a practice for many guardians of large estates especially, to indemnify themselves by applying to the court of chancery, acting under its direction, and accounting annually before the officers of that court. For the lord chancellor is, by right derived from the crown, the general and supreme guardian of all infants, as well as idiots and lunatics; that is, of all such persons as have not discretion enough to manage their own concerns. In case therefore any guardian abuses his trust, the court will check and punish him; nay sometimes will proceed to the removal of him, and appoint another in his stead. (1 *Sid.* 424. 1 *P. Will.* 703. 1 *Black.* 462).

As to the ward or person within age, for whose assistance and support these guardians are constituted by law; or who it is that is said to be within age. The ages of male and female are different for different purposes. A male at twelve years old may take the oath of allegiance; at fourteen is at years of discretion, and therefore may consent or disagree to marriage, may choose his guardian, and if his discretion be actually proved, may make his testament of his personal estate; at seventeen may be an executor; and at twenty-one is at his own disposal, and may alien his lands, goods, and chattels. A female also

---

* By this statute, the father may dispose of the guardianship of any child unmarried under the age of twenty-one, by deed or will executed in the presence of two or more witnesses, till such child attains the age of twenty-one, or for any less time. And the guardian so appointed has the tuition of the ward, and the management of his estate and property.

A father cannot appoint guardians under this statute to a natural child; but where he has named guardians by his will to an illegitimate child, the court of chancery will appoint the same persons guardians without any reference to a master for his approbation. 2 *Bro.* 583.

at seven years of age may be betrothed, or given in marriage; at nine is entitled to dower; at twelve, is at years of maturity and therefore may consent or disagree to marriage; and, if proved to have sufficient discretion may bequeath her personal estate; at fourteen is at years of legal discretion, and may choose a guardian; at seventeen may be executrix, and at twenty-one may dispose of herself and her lands. So that full age in male or female is twenty-one years, which age is completed on the day preceding the anniversary of a person's birth, who till that time is an infant, and so stiled in law. 1 *Black.* 462,3.

And if an infant be born on the 1st of January, he is of age to do any legal act on the morning of the last day of December, though he may not have lived twenty-one years by nearly forty-eight hours; for in law there is no fraction of a day, and if the birth was on the first second of one day, and the act on the last second of the other, then twenty-one years would be complete; and in the law it is the same whether a thing be done upon one moment of the day or on another. *Christian's N. on* 1 *Black.* 463,4.

It is here also proper to notice that upon the abolition of the court of wards, the care which the crown was bound to take as guardian of its unprovided for infant tenants, was totally extinguished in every feodal view, but resulted to the king in his court of chancery, together with the general protection of all other infants in the kingdom. 3 *Black.* 426.

When therefore a fatherless child has no other guardian, the court of chancery hath a right to appoint one, and from all proceedings relative thereto, an appeal lies to the house of lords. *Ibid.*

The court of exchequer can only appoint a guardian *ad litem* to manage the defence of the infant, if a suit be commenced against him, a power which is incident to every court of justice: but when the interest of a minor comes before the court judicially in the progress of a cause, or upon a bill for that purpose filed, either tribunal will indiscriminately take care of the property. 3 *Black.* 427.

GUARDIAN DE L'ESTEMARY, is the guardian or warden of the Stannaries, or mines in Cornwall. *Cowel. Blount.*

GUARDIANS DE L'EGLIS, church-wardens. *Ibid.*

GUARDIANS OF THE PEACE, those that have the keeping of the peace, as justices, &c. *Ibid.*

GUARDIAN OF THE CINQUE PORTS, a magistrate that hath peculiar jurisdiction within the ports or havens, commonly called the Cinque Ports. *Ibid.*

GUARDIAN OF THE SPIRITUALTIES, the person to whom the spiritual jurisdiction of any diocese is committed, during the vacancy of the see, is called by this name. *Cowel. Blount.*

GUERNSEY. See *Jersey.*

GUEST, (Sax. *gest*, Fr. *gist*, a stage of rest in a journey) a lodger or stranger in an inn, is protected in the possession of his property while he remains there as the guest, and the inn-keeper is liable to make good any loss that may happen thereto, also an action lies against an innkeeper refusing a guest lodging, &c. having room.

GUIDAGE, (*guidagium*) an old legal word, signifying that which was given for safe conduct through a strange land, or unknown country. *Cowel. Blount.*

GUILD, (from the Sax. *guildan*, to pay) a fraternity or company, because every one was gildare, *i. e.* to pay something towards the charge and support of the company. *Cowel. Blount.*

GUILD-HALL, the chief hall of the city of London, for the meeting of the lord mayor and commonalty of the city. The chief halls or places of meeting for the transaction of public business in other cities and in boroughs, are also in general denominated *guild-halls.*

GUILDHELDA TEUTONICORUM. The fraternity of easterling merchants in London, called the still-yard. 22 *Hen.* 8. *cap.* 8. *Cowel. Blount.*

GUILD-RENTS, rents payable to the crown, by any guild or fraternity; or which formerly belonged to religious guilds, and came to the crown at the general dissolution of monasteries. *Ibid.*

GUILDER, a foreign coin.

GULE OF AUGUST, (*gula augusti*, alias *goule de August*) is the day of St. Peter *ad* Vincula, celebrated on the 1st of August, and called the gule of August, from the Lat. *gula*, a throat, and from the supposed miraculous cure of a tribune's daughter that had a disease in her throat, by seeing and kissing the chains that St. Peter was chained with under Nero. *Durand's Rationale Divinorum, lib.* 7. *cap.* 19. *F. N. B.* 62. *Plowd.* 316. *Stat. Westm.* 2. *cap.* 30. 27 *Ed.* 3.

GUNS. See *Game.*

GUNPOWDER. By 16 *Car.* 1. *c.* 21. all subjects may make and sell gunpowder, and to obtain an exclusive patent for the sole making or importation of gunpowder or arms, or to hinder others from importing them, is also a *præmunire* by 16 *Car.* *c.* 21. and 1 *Jac.* 2. *c.* 28.

But in general, it seems that erecting powder-mills or keeping magazines near a town, is a nuisance at common law, punishable by indictment or information. 2 *Stra.* 1169.

And to regulate the manufacture, conveyance, and keeping of this inflammable and dangerous commodity, an act has been passed, 12 *Geo.* 3. *c.* 61. in which it is enacted, that no new mill for gunpowder shall be erected without licence from the quarter sessions, and no pestle mill to be used, nor more than 40lb. of gunpowder to be made at a time under a single pair of stones, except at *Battle, Crowhurst, Siddlecomb and Brede* in *Sussex*, on pain of 2*s.* per 1lb. *s.* 1—5; nor more than 40lbs. to be dried at a time, *s.* 6.; no more than necessary kept in drying houses, and sufficient magazines of brick or stone to be appointed by the quarter sessions at a distance of fifty yards from the mills, on penalty of 25*s* a month. *s.* 7.

No dealer to keep more than 200lbs. at a time; nor any person not a dealer, more than 50lbs. in London or Westminster, or within three miles thereof, or within any other city, borough or market town, or one mile thereof, or within two miles of the king's palaces or magazines, or half a mile of any parish church, on pain of 2*s.* per lb. except in licensed mills, or to the amount of 800lbs. for the use of collieries and mines within 200 yards of them, *s.* 12, 13, 14, 15, 16; not more than twenty-five barrels to be conveyed by land, nor above 200 by water, unless going beyond sea or coastwise, each to contain not more than 100lbs. *s.* 17.; justices of peace may search mills, houses, carriages, &c. *s.* 23.

No ship (except in the king's service) is to have more than 25lbs. of gunpowder above Blackwall, on penalty of 2*s.* per lb. for all above, and the Trinity House officers may seize unlawful quantities, *s.* 24, 25.; and penalties may be recovered on prosecution within fourteen days. *s.* 26, 7.

The act does not extend to mills on the king's lands, or his storehouses, or the magazines at *Barking, Creekmouth,* and *Erith Level,* or those at *Liverpool* and *Bristol,* nor to powder carrying by the order of the Board of Ordnance, expressing the quantity and time, or with forces on their march, or militia, and any quantity may be carried in close decked-vessels below Blackwall. *s,* 29, 30.

GURGITES, is used as a Latin word for weares. See *Gorce.*

GUTI and GOTTI, Engl. *Goths,* called sometimes *Jutæ,* and by the Romans *Getæ,* is derived from the old word *jet,* which signifies a giant: they were one of those three nations or people who left Germany, and came to inhabit this island. *Leg. Edw. Confess. cap.* 35. *Cowel. Blount.*

GUTTERA, a gutter or spout to convey the water from the leads and roofs of houses. *Ibid.*

GWADR-MERCHED, is a British word, which signifies a payment or fine, made to the lords of some manors, upon the marriage of their tenants daughters; or otherwise on their committing incontinency. *Ibid.*

GWALSTOW, (Sax.) a place of execution. *Ibid.*

GYLPUT, the name of a court held every three weeks, in the liberty or hundred of Pathbew in the county of Warwick. *Ibid.*

GYLTWITE, a compensation or amends for trespass *Ibid.*

GYPSIES. See *Egyptians.*

GYROVAGI, wandering monks, who, pretending great piety, left their own cloisters, and visited others. *Cowel. Blount.*

H

HABEAS CORPORA JURATORUM, is a writ in C. B. for the bringing up a jury on the *venire facias,* for the trial of any cause brought to issue. *Old Nat. Br.* 157. And the *habeas corpora juratorum* in the court of C. B. serves for the same purpose as the *distringas jurator* in B. R. It commands the sheriff to have the jurors before the judges at such a day, to pass on the trial of certain parties, in such a cause, &c. *Practis. Solic.* 308, 309.

HABEAS CORPUS. Wherever a person is restrained of his liberty by being confined in a common gaol or by a private person, whether it be for a criminal or civil cause, he may regularly, by *habeas corpus* have his body and cause removed to some superior jurisdiction, which hath authority to examine the legality of such commitment, and on the return thereof, either bail, discharge or remand the prisoner. *Vaughan* 136. Bushel's case.

And it is at this day the most usual remedy to be relieved against a wrongful imprisonment. 3 *Bac. Abr.* tit. *Hab. Corp.* (A.)

The writs of *habeas corpus* are as follows:

I. The writ of *habeas corpus* AD SUBJICIENDUM, is that which issues in criminal cases, and is deemed a prerogative writ, which the king may issue to any place, as he has a right to be informed of the condition of the prisoner, and for what reasons he is confined: it is also in regard to the subject, the great and efficacious writ, in all manner of illegal confinement, and is directed to the person detaining another, commanding him to produce the body of the prisoner, with the day and cause of his caption and detention, *ad faciendum, subjiciendum, et recipiendum*, to do, submit to, and receive, whatsoever the judge or court awarding such writ shall consider in that behalf. This is a high prerogative writ, and therefore by the common law issues out of the court of king's bench, not only in term-time, but also during the vacation, by a *fiat* from the chief justice or any other of the judges, and runs into all parts of the king's dominions: for the king is at all times intitled to have an account, why the liberty of any of his subjects is restrained wherever that restraint may be inflicted.

If it issues in vacation, it is usually returnable before the judge himself who awarded it, and he proceeds by himself thereon; unless the term should intervene, and then it may be returned in court. Indeed, if the party were privileged in the courts of common pleas and exchequer, as being an officer or suitor of the court, an *habeas corpus ad subjiciendum* might also have been awarded from thence: and, if the cause of imprisonment were palpably illegal, they might have discharged him; but, if he were committed for any criminal matter, they could only have remanded him, or taken bail for his appearance in the court of king's bench (*Carter* 221. 2 *Jon.* 13.); which occasioned the common pleas to discountenance such applications. It hath also been said, and by very respectable authorities (4 *Inst.* 182. 2 *Hal. P. C.* 147.), that the like *habeas corpus* may issue out of the court of chancery in vacation; but, upon the famous application to lord Nottingham by Jenks, notwithstanding the most diligent searches, no precedent could be found where the chancellor (*L. Nott. MSS. Rep.* July 1676) had issued such a writ in vacation, and therefore his lordship refused it. 3 *Black.* 131, 2.

In the court of king's bench it was, and is still, necessary to apply for it by motion to the court (2 *Mod.* 306. 1 *Lev.* 1.), as in the case of all other prerogative writs (*certiorari, prohibition, mandamus*, &c.) which do not issue as of mere course, without shewing some probable cause why the extraordinary power of the crown is called in to the party's assistance. For, as was argued by lord chief justice Vaughan (*Bushel's case.* 2 *Jon.* 13.) "it is granted on motion, because it cannot be had of course; and there is therefore, no necessity to grant it; for the court ought to be satisfied that the party hath a probable cause to be delivered." And this seems the more reasonable, because (when once granted) the person to whom it is directed can return no satisfactory excuse for not bringing up the body of the prisoner. (*Cro. Jac.* 543.) So that, if it issued of mere course, without shewing to the court or judge some reasonable ground for awarding it, a traitor or felon under sentence of death, a soldier or mariner in the king's service, a wife, a child, a relation, or a domestic, confined for insanity, or other prudential reasons, might obtain a temporary enlargement by suing out an *habeas corpus*, though sure to be remanded as soon as brought up to the court. And therefore sir Edward Coke, when chief justice, did not scruple in 13 *Jac.* 1. to deny a *habeas corpus* to one confined by the court of admiralty for piracy; there appearing, upon his own shewing, sufficient grounds to confine him (3 *Bulstr.* 27. See also 2 *Roll. Rep.* 138.) On the other hand, if a probable ground be shewn, that the party is imprisoned without just cause (2 *Inst.* 615.), and therefore hath a right to be delivered, the writ of *habeas corpus* is then a writ of right, which "may not be denied, but ought to be granted to every man that is committed, or detained in prison, or otherwise restrained, though it be by the command of the king, the privy council, or any other (*Com. Journ.* Apr. 1628.)" 3 *Black.* 133.

The personal liberty of the subject is a natural inherent right, which cannot be surrendered or forfeited, unless by the commission of some great and atrocious crime, nor ought to be abridged in any case without the special permission of law. This doctrine is co-eval with the first rudiments of the English constitution; and handed down to us from our Saxon ancestors, notwithstanding all their struggles with the Danes, and the violence of the Norman conquest: asserted afterwards and confirmed by the conqueror himself and his descendants: and though sometimes a little impaired by the ferocity of the times, and the occasional despotism of jealous or usurping princes, yet established on the firmest basis by the provisions of *magna charta*, and a long succession of statutes enacted under Edward III. To assert an absolute exemption from imprisonment in all cases, is inconsistent with every idea of law and political society; and, in the end, would destroy all civil liberty, by rendering its protection impossible: but the glory of the English law consists in clearly defining the times, the causes, and the extent, when, wherefore, and to what degree, the imprisonment of the subject may be lawful. This induces an absolute necessity of expressing upon every commitment the reason for which it is made: that the court upon an *habeas corpus* may examine into its validity; and, according to the circumstances of the case, may discharge, admit to bail, or remand the prisoner. 3 *Black.* 133.

And yet, early in the reign of Cha. I. the court of king's bench, relying on some arbitrary precedents, (and those perhaps misunderstood) determined (*State Tr. vii.* 136.) that they could not upon an *habeas corpus* either bail or deliver a prisoner, though committed without any cause assigned, in case he was committed by the special command of the king, or by the lords of the privy council. This drew on a parliamentary inquiry, and produced the petition of right, 3 *Car.* 1. which recites this illegal judgment, and enacts, that no freeman hereafter shall be so imprisoned or detained. But when, in the following year, Mr. Selden and others were committed by the lords of the council, in pursuance of his majesty's special command, under a general charge of "notable contempts, and stirring up sedition against the king and government," the judges delayed for two terms (including also the long vacation) to deliver an opinion how far such a charge was bailable. And, when at length they agreed that it was, they however annexed a condition of finding sureties for the good behaviour, which still protracted their imprisonment; the chief justice, sir Nicholas Hyde, at the same time declaring (*State Tr. vii* 240.), that "if they were again remanded for that cause, perhaps the court would not afterwards grant a *habeas corpus*, being already made acquainted with the cause of the imprisonment." But this was heard with indignation and astonishment by every lawyer present; according to Mr. Selden's own account of the matter, whose resentment was not cooled at the distance of four-and-twenty years. *Mare Clausum ed.* 1653. 3 *Black.* 134.

These pitiful evasions gave rise to the statute 16 *Car.* 1. *c.* 10. *sect.* 8. whereby it was enacted, that if any person be committed by the king himself in person, or by his privy council, or by any of the members thereof, he shall have granted unto him, without any delay upon any pretence whatsoever, a writ of *habeas corpus*, upon demand or motion made to the court of king's bench or common pleas; who shall thereupon, within three court days after the return is made, examine and determine the legality of such commitment; and do what to justice shall appertain, in delivering, bailing, or remanding such prisoner. Yet still in the case of Jenks, before alluded to, who in 1676 was committed by the king in council for a turbulent speech at Guildhall (*State Tr. vii.* 471.), new shifts and devices were made use of to prevent his enlargement by law; the chief justice (as well as the chancellor) declining to award a writ of *habeas corpus ad subjiciendum* in vacation, though at last he thought proper to award the usual writs *ad deliberandum, &c.* whereby the prisoner was discharged at the Old Bailey. Other abuses had also crept into daily practice, which had in some measure defeated the benefit of this great constitutional remedy. The party imprisoning was at liberty to delay his obedience to the first writ, and might wait till a second and a third, called an *alias* and a *pluries*, were issued, before he produced the party; and many other vexatious shifts were practised to detain state-prisoners in custody. But whoever will attentively consider the English history, may observe, that the flagrant abuse of any power, by the crown or its ministers, has always been productive of a struggle; which either discovers the exercise of that power to be contrary to law, or (if legal) restrains it for the future. This was the case in the present instance. The oppression of an obscure individual gave birth to the famous *habeas corpus* act, 31 *Car.* 2. *c.* 2. which is frequently considered as another *magna carta* of the kingdom; and, by consequence, has also in subsequent times reduced the method of proceeding on these writs (though not within the reach of that statute, but issuing merely at the common law) to the true standard of law and liberty.

The statute itself enacts, 1. That the writ shall be returned and the prisoner brought up, within a limited time, according to the distance, not exceeding in any case twenty days. 2. That such writs shall be indorsed, as granted in pursuance of this act, and signed by the person awarding them. 3. That on complaint and request in writing by or on behalf of any person committed and charged with any crime (unless committed for treason or felony expressed in the warrant, or for suspicion of the same, or as accessary thereto before the fact, or convicted or charged in execution by legal process) the lord chancellor, or any of the twelve judges, in vacation, upon viewing a copy of the warrant, or affidavit that a copy is denied, shall (unless the party has neglected for two terms to apply to any court for his enlargement) award a *habeas corpus* for such prisoner, returnable immediately before himself or any other of the judges: and upon the return made shall discharge the party, if bailable, upon giving security to appear and answer to the accusation in the proper court of judicature. 4. That officers and keepers neglecting to make due returns, or not delivering to the prisoner or his agent within six hours after demand a copy of the warrant of commitment, or shifting the custody of a prisoner from one to another, without sufficient reason or authority (specified in the act) shall for the first offence forfeit 100*l.* and for the second offence 200*l.* to the party grieved, and be disabled to hold his office. 5. That no person, once delivered by *habeas corpus*, shall be re-committed for the same offence, on penalty of 500*l.* 6. That every person committed for treason or felony shall, if he requires it the first week of the next term, or the first day of the next session of *oyer* and *terminer*, be indicted in that term or session, or else admitted to bail; unless the king's witnesses cannot be produced at that time: and if acquitted, or if not indicted and tried in the second term or session, he shall be discharged from his imprisonment for such imputed offence: but that no person, after the assizes shall be opened for the county in which he is detained, shall be removed by *habeas corpus*, till after the assizes are ended; but shall be left to the justice of the judges of assize. 7. That any such prisoner may move for and obtain his *habeas corpus*, as well out of the chancery or exchequer, as out of the king's bench or common pleas; and the lord chancellor, or judges denying the same, on sight of the warrant or oath that the same is refused, forfeit severally to the party grieved, the sum of 500*l.* 8. That this writ of *habeas corpus* shall run into the counties palatine, cinque ports, and other privileged places, and the islands of Jersey and Guernsey. 9. That no inhabitant of England (except persons contracting, or convicts praying to be transported; or having committed some capital offence in the place to which they are sent) shall be sent prisoner to Scotland, Ireland, Jersey, Guernsey, or any places beyond the seas, within or without the king's dominions: on pain that the party committing, his advisers, aiders, and assistants, shall forfeit to the party grieved a sum not less than 500*l.* to be recovered with treble costs; shall be disabled to bear any office of trust or profit; shall incur the penalties of *præmunire*; and shall be incapable of the king's pardon.

This is the substance of that great and important statute: which extends only to the case of commitments for such criminal charge, as can produce no inconvenience to public justice by a temporary enlargement of the prisoner; all other cases of unjust imprisonment being left to the *habeas corpus* at common law. But even upon writs at the common law it is now expected by the court, agreeable to antient precedents (4 *Burr.* 856), and the spirit of the act of parliament, that the writ should be immediately obeyed, without waiting for any *alias* or *pluries*; otherwise an attachment will issue. By which admirable regulations, judicial as well as parliamentary, the remedy is now complete for removing the injury of unjust and illegal confinement. A remedy the more necessary, because the oppression does not always arise from the ill-nature, but sometimes from the mere inattention of government. For it frequently happens in foreign countries, (and has happened in England during temporary suspensions of the statute) that persons apprehended upon suspicion have suffered long imprisonment, merely because they were forgotten. 3 *Black.* 138.

II. The common writ of *habeas corpus ad faciendum et recipiendum*, issues out of any of the courts at Westminster-hall, when a person is sued in some inferior jurisdiction, and is desirous to remove the action into the superior court, commanding the inferior judges to produce the body of the defendant, together with the day and cause of his caption and detainer, (whence the writ is frequently denominated an *habeas corpus cum causa*) to do and receive whatsoever the king's court shall consider in that behalf. This is a writ grantable of common right, without any motion in court (2 *Mod.* 306), and it instantly supersedes all proceedings in the court below. But, in order to prevent the surreptitious discharge of prisoners, it is ordered by statute 1 & 2 *Phil. & Mar. c.* 13. that no *habeas corpus* shall issue to remove any prisoner out of any goal, unless signed by some judge of the court out of which it is awarded. And, to avoid vexatious delays by removal of frivolous causes, it is enacted by statute 21 *Jac.* 1. *c.* 23. that, where the judge of an inferior court of record is a barrister of three years standing, no cause shall be removed from thence by *habeas corpus*, or other writ, after issue or demurrer deliberately joined: that no cause, if once remanded to the inferior court by writ of *procedendo*, or otherwise, shall ever afterwards be again removed: and that no cause shall be removed at all, if the debt or damages laid in the declaration do not amount to the sum of 5*l.* But an expedient (*Bohun instit. legal.* 85. *edit.* 1708.) having been found out to elude the latter branch of the statute, by procuring a nominal plaintiff to bring another action for five pounds or upwards (and then by the course of the court the *habeas corpus* removed both actions together), it is therefore enacted by stat. 12 *Geo.* 1. *c.* 29. *s.* 3. that the inferior court may proceed in such actions as are under the value of 5*l.* notwithstanding other actions may be brought against the same defendant to a greater account.

And by 19 *Geo.* 3. *c.* 70. *s.* 6. no cause where the cause of action shall not amount to 10*l.* or upwards, shall be removed or removable into any superior court by any writ of *habeas corpus* or otherwise: unless the defendant shall enter into a recognizance to the plaintiff in the inferior court, with two sufficient sureties, in double the sum demanded for the payment of the debt and costs, in case judgment shall pass against him. The *habeas corpus ad faciendum & recipiendum* issues only in civil cases, and in this case the body is to be removed by *habeas corpus*, but the proceedings are by *certiorari.* 3 *Bac. Abr.* 2.

III. There is likewise a writ of *habeas cor-*

pus ad respondendum, where a person is confined in gaol, for a cause of action accruing within some inferior court; and a third person hath also a cause of action against him; in which case he may have this writ in order to charge him in such superior court; for inferior courts being tied down to causes arising within their own jurisdiction, the party would be without remedy, unless allowed to sue him in another court; but it seems, that regularly a person confined in B. R. cannot be removed to the C. B. by this writ, nor *vice versa*; for in these cases there can be no defect of justice, as these courts have conusance as well of local, as transitory actions. *Dyer* 197. *a.* 249. *pl.* 84, 296, 307. 1 *Mod.* 235. *Style Pract. Regis.* 330.

IV. There are also, beside these, other writs of *habeas corpus*, as a *habeas corpus ad deliberandum & recipiendum*, which lies to remove a person to the proper place or county, where he committed some criminal offence. 3 *New. Abr.* 2, 3.

V. There is also a writ of *habeas corpus ad satisfaciendum* after a judgment; and on this writ the attorney for the plaintiff must endorse the number roll of the judgment on the back of the writ. *Style Regist.* 331.

VI. *Habeas corpus* upon a *cepi*, where the party is taken in execution in the court below. So upon an attachment out of chancery, and a *cepi corpus* returned by the sheriff, the next step is a *habeas corpus*; for the sheriff having executed the command of the writ of attachment by taking the body, he cannot carry him out of the county without the king's writ.

VII. There is also a writ of *habeas corpus ad testificand'*, which is to remove a person in confinement, in order to give his testimony in some court of justice; for which vide *Style* 119, 126, 230. 3 *Keb.* 51. *Comb.* 17, 48.

And by 43 *Geo.* 3. *c.* 140. any judge at the courts of Westminster may award a writ of *habeas corpus* for bringing up prisoners for trial or examination upon courts martial, commissioners of bankrupts, commissioners for auditing the public accounts, or other commissioners acting under any commission or warrant from the king.

Of these several writs the most usual in practice are, 1. the *habeas corpus ad subjiciendum*: and 2. the *habeas corpus ad faciendum & recipiendum*.

HABENDUM ET TENENDUM, (to have and to hold) is an essential part of every deed or conveyance, and the office of the *habendum* is properly to determine what estate or interest is granted by the deed: though this may be performed, and sometimes is performed in the premises. In which case the *habendum* may lessen, enlarge, explain, or qualify, but not totally contradict or be repugnant to, the estate granted in the premises. As if a grant be "to A. and the "heirs of his body," in the premises, *habendum* "to him and his heirs for ever," or *vice versa*; here A has an estate-tail, and a fee-simple expectant thereon (*Co. Litt.* 21. 2 *Roll Rep.* 19, 23. *Cro. Jac.* 476.) But, had it been in the premises "to him and his "heirs," *habendum* "to him for life," the *habendum* would be utterly void (2 *Rep.* 23. 8 *Rep.* 56.); for an estate of inheritance is vested in him before the *habendum* comes, and shall not afterwards be taken away, or devested by it. The *tenendum* "and to "hold," is now of very little use, and is only kept in by custom. It was formerly used to signify the tenure, by which the estate granted was to be holden; viz. "*tenendum* "*per servitium militare, in burgagio, in libero* "*socagio, &c.*" But, all these being now reduced to free and common socage, the tenure is never specified. Before the statute of *quia emptores*, 18 *Edw.* 1. it was also sometimes used to denote the lord of whom the land should be holden: but that statute directing all future purchasors to hold, not of the immediate grantor, but of the chief lord of the fee, this use of the *tenendum* hath been also antiquated; though for a long time after we find it mentioned in ancient charters, that the tenements shall be holden *de capitalibus dominis feodi*; but as this expressed nothing more than the statute had already provided for, it gradually grew out of use.

HABENTIA, riches. *Cowel. Blount.*

HABERDASHERS, persons who sell small wares, as hats, ribbands, and the like. *Bailey*, 8 *Eliz. c.* 7.

HABERE FACIAS POSSESSIONEM, a judicial writ that lies where one hath recovered a term for years in action of *ejectione firmæ*, to put him into possession. *F. N. B.* 167. See *Execute.*

HABERE FACIAS SEISINAM, a writ directed to the sheriff, to give seisin of a freehold estate recovered in the king's courts, by *ejectione firmæ*, or other action. *Old Nat. Br.* 154.

HABERE FACIAS VISUM, a writ anciently used in real actions, as in *formedon*, &c. where a view was required to be taken. *Reg. Jud.* 26, 28, &c. *F. N. B.*

HABERGEON, (from the Germ. *hals, collum, & bergen, tegere*) an helmet which covered the head and shoulders. *Blount.*

HABERJECTS, (*haubergetæ*) a sort of cloths of a mixed colour. *Ibid.*

HABILIMENTS OF WAR, apparel, armour, utensils, provisions and all warlike stores. 3 *Eliz. cap.* 4.

HABLE, (Fr.) signifies a sea-port town; this word is used in 27 *H.* 6. *cap.* 3.

HACHIA, a hack, pick, or instrument for digging. *Placit.* 2 *Ed.* 3. *Cowel. Blount.*

HACKNEY COACHES AND CHAIRS. See *London.*

HADBOTE, (Sax.) a recompence or amends for violence offered to persons in holy orders. *Sax. Dict. Cowel. Blount.*

HADE OF LAND, (*hada terræ*) is a small quantity of land. *Ibid.*

HADERUNGA, respect or distinction of persons. *Ibid.*

HADGONEL, (Sax.) a tax or mulct. *Ibid.*

HÆREDE ABDUCTO, a writ that antiently lay for the lord, who having by right the wardship of his tenant under age, could not come by his body, the same being carried away by another person. *Old Nat. Br.* 93.

HÆREDE DELIVERANDO ALII, QUI HABET CUSTODIAM TERRÆ, a writ directed to the sheriff to require one that had the body of him who was a ward to another, to deliver him to the person whose ward he was, by reason of his land. *Reg. Orig.* 161.

HÆREDE RAPTO, a writ also on Ravishment of Ward. *Reg. Orig.* 163. *Cowel. Blount.*

HÆREDIPETA, the next heir to lands.

HÆREDITAS JACENS. See *Occupancy.*

HÆRETICO COMBURENDO, a writ said to be co-eval with the common law, 4 *Black.* 46. that lay against an heretic, who having been convicted of heresy by the bishop, and abjured it, afterwards fell into the same again, or some other, and was thereupon delivered over to the secular power. *F. N. B.* 69.

HAFNE, (Danish) a haven or port. *Cowel. Blount.*

HAGA, (Sax. *mansio*) a house in a city or borough. *Ibid.*

HAGIA, a hedge, (Sax. *hæg*, melted into hay, whence *haia*) *Mon. Angl. Tom.* 2. *p.* 273.

HAIA, also an hedge: sometimes taken for a park, &c. enclosed. *Bract. lib.* 2. *c.* 40. And *haiement* is used for a hedge-fence. *Rot. Inq.* 36 *Ed.* 3.

HAKE, a fish dried and salted; hence the proverb in Kent, *as dry as a hake. Paroch. Antiq.* 575. *Spelm.*

HAKETON, a military coat of defence. *Cowel. Blount.*

HALF-BLOOD, the children of the same parents under different intermarriages, are deemed to be of the half-blood; for the relative rights of those, see titles *Administrator* and *Heir.*

HALFENDEAR, the moiety, or one half of a thing; as *fardingeal* is a quarter, or fourth part of an acre of land, &c. *Cowel. Blount.*

HALF-MARK, (*dimidia markæ*) is a noble, or six shillings and eight pence in money. *Ibid.*

HALF-SEAL, is what is used in the chancery, for sealing of commissions to delegates, upon any appeal to the court of delegates, either in ecclesiastical or marine causes. *Ibid.*

HALF-TONGUE, (*medietas linguæ*) as to pleas and trials of foreigners. *Ibid.*

HALKE, (from the Sax. *heale*, i. e. *angulus*) an hole; seeking in every halke, &c. *Ibid.*

HALL, (Lat. *halla*, Sax. *heall*) a mansion-house or habitation. *Ibid.*

HALL, or COMMON-HALL. There is a common-hall for electing a mayor, sheriffs, and other officers of the city of London, assembled at Guild-hall by the lord mayor. *Ord.* 7 *W.* 3.

HALLAGE, toll paid for goods or merchandize vended in a hall. *Cowel. Blount.*

HALLAMAS, the day of All Hallows or All Saints, Nov. 1. *Ibid.*

HALLAMSHIRE, a part of the county of York, in which Sheffield stands. *Ibid.*

HALLMOTE or HALIMOTE, (Sax. *heall*, i. e. *aula*, & *gemote*, *conventus*) was that court among the Saxons, which we now call a court baron. *Ibid.*

HALYMOTE, an holy or ecclesiastical court. *Ibid.*

HALYWERCFOLK, *holyworkfolk*, or people who enjoyed lands by the service of repairing or defending a church or sepulchre. *Ibid.*

HAM, a Saxon word, used for a place of dwelling; a village or town: hence Nottingham, Buckingham, &c. *Ibid.*

HAMBLING, or HAMELING OF DOGS, the ancient term used by foresters for expeditating. *Manwood* et *ibid.*

HAMESECKEN. Burglary or nocturnal house-breaking, was by our antient law called *hamesecken*, as it is in Scotland to this day. 4 *Black.* 223.

HAMLET, and HAMEL, or HAMPSEL, (from the Sax. *ham*, i. e. *domus*, and Germ. *let*, *membrum*) a little village, or part of a village or parish. *Cowel. Blount.*

HAMFARE, breach of the peace in a house. *Ibid.*

HAMSOKEN, (Sax. *hamsocen*) the liberty or privilege of a man's own house; also a franchise granted to lords of manors, whereby they hold pleas, and take cognizance of the breach and violation of that immunity. *Ibid.*

HANAPER OFFICE. One of the offices so called, belonging to the court of chancery. Writs relating to the business of the subject and their returns, were, according to the simplicity of antient times, originally kept in an hamper, *in hanaperio*; and the others, relating to such matters wherein the crown is immediately, or mediately concerned, were preserved in a little sack or bag, *in parva baga*; and thence hath arisen the distinction of the hanaper office, and petty bag office, which both belong to the common law court in chancery. 3 *Black. Com.* 49.

HANDBOROW, a surety or manual pledge. *Cowel. Blount.*

HAND-HABEND, a thief caught in the very fact. *Ibid.*

HAND IN AND OUT, is the name of an unlawful game, now disused and prohibited by 17 *Ed.* 4. *c.* 2. *Ibid.*

HANDFUL, in measuring, is four inches by the standard. *Anno* 33 *H.* 8. *c.* 5. *Ibid.*

HANDGRITH, (from the Sax. *hond, manus,* and *grith, pax*) peace or protection given by the king with his own hand. *Ibid.*

HAND-GUN, an engine to destroy game. See *Game.*

HANDY-WARP, a kind of cloth. *Cowel. Blount.*

HANGING, is the punishment inflicted for a capital offence by hanging the culprit by the neck till dead; and if upon judgment to be hanged by the neck till he is dead, the criminal be not thoroughly killed, but revives, the sheriff must hang him again, for the former hanging was no execution of the sentence, and if a false tenderness were to be indulged in such cases, a multitude of collusions might ensue. 4 *Black.* 376, 405, 6.

HANIG, a term for customary labour to be done and performed. *Cowel. Blount.*

HANKWIT *alias* HANGWITE, (from the Sax. *hangan,* i. e. *suspendere, & wite mulcta*) a liberty granted to a person, whereby he is quit of a felon, or thief hanged without judgment; or escaped out of custody. *Cowel. Blount.*

HANPER or HANAPER, (*haniperium*) the hanaper of the chancery. See *Hanaper.*

HANSE, an old Gothick word; signifies a society of merchants, for the good usage and safe passage of merchandize from one kingdom to another; hence the Hans Towns.

HANS TOWNS. Towards the middle of the thirteenth century, the nations around the Baltic were extremely barbarous, and infested that sea with their piracies; this obliged the cities of Lubeck and Hamburgh, soon after they began to open some trade with those people, to enter into a league of mutual defence. They derived such advantages from this union, that other towns acceded to their confederacy, and in a short time eighty of the most considerable cities scattered through those vast countries which stretch from the bottom of the Baltic to Cologne on the Rhine, joined in the famous Hanseatic league, which became so formidable, that its alliance was courted, and its enmity dreaded by the greatest monarchs. The members of this powerful association formed the first systematic plan of commerce, known in the middle ages, and conducted it by common laws enacted in their general assemblies.

HANTELODE, an arrest. *Cowel. Blount.*

HAP, (Fr. *happer,* i. e. *rapere,* to catch) is of the same signification with us as in the French; as to hap the rent, is where partition being made between two parceners, and more land allowed to one than the other, she that has most of the land charges it to the other, and she haps the rent, whereon assise is brought, &c. This word is used by Littleton, where a person happeth the possession of a deed poll. *Lit. s.* 8.

HAQUE, a little hand-gun. 33 *H.* 8. *c.* 6. and 2 & 3 *Ed.* 6. *cap.* 14.

HAQUEBUT, a bigger sort of hand-gun than the haque; from the Teuton. *haeck buyse.* 2 & 3 *Ed.* 6. *c.* 14. and 4 & 5 *Ph. & Mar. c.* 2.

HARATIUM, (from the Fr. *haras*) a race of horses and mares, kept for breed; in some parts of England termed, a stud of mares, &c. *Spelm. Gloss. Cowel. Blount.*

HARBINGER, an officer of the king's house, &c. *Ibid.*

HARBOURS and HAVENS. By 1 *Eliz. c.* 11. and 13 & 14 *Car.* 2. *c.* 11. *s.* 14. the crown is enabled by commission to ascertain the limits of all ports, and to assign proper wharfs and quays in each port, for the exclusive landing and loading of merchandize.

And by 46 *Geo.* 3. *c.* 153. no pier, quay, wharf, jetty breast, or embankment, shall be erected in or near to any public harbour, without giving one month's notice to the admiralty, on pain of 200*l.* to be recovered by action or information.

HARES. See *Game.*

HARLOTS. See *Disorderly Houses.*

HARNESS, (Fr. *harnisch*) warlike instruments. *Cowel. Blount.*

HARO, HARRON, an outcry after felons and malefactors. *Cowel. Blount.*

HARPING-IRONS, are iron instruments for the striking and taking of whales.

HARRIERS, (*harecti canes*) small hounds, between the fox and beagle tribe, for hunting the hare.

HART, a stag, or male deer of the forest five years old compleat. *Manwood, par.* 2. *cap.* 4.

HASTA PORCI, a shield of brawn. *Cowel. Blount.*

HATCHES, dams made to prevent water issuing. And from a hatch, gate, or door, some houses situate on the highway, near a common gate, are called hatches.

HAUTHONER, (*homo loricatus*) a man armed with a coat of mail. *Cowel. Blount.*

HAW, a small parcel of land so called in Kent. *Ibid.*

HAWGH or HOWGH, a green plot in a valley, as used in the north of England. *Ibid.*

HAWKS. See *Game.*

HAWKERS and PEDLARS. By 29 *Geo.* 3. *c.* 26. the following yearly duties shall be paid, *viz.* for every hawker 4*l.* and a further duty of 4*l.* for every horse or other beast of burthen. *Ibid.*

Every hawker selling goods by auction, shall forfeit 50*l.* *Ibid.*

Duty to be paid on taking out a licence,

and the persons applying for licences, shall produce a certificate of good character from the minister and two householders of the place where they reside. *Ibid.*

Hawkers shall mark their packs, "Licensed Hawker" with the number of his licence; and unlicensed persons so marking their packs, shall forfeit 10*l*. *Ibid.*

Hawkers selling smuggled goods, &c. shall forfeit their licences, and be incapable of haying a new licence ever after. *Ibid.*

Hawkers trading without such licence, or contrary thereto, or refusing to produce, or not having their licences to produce, shall forfeit 10*l*. Persons forging licences, or travelling with them, shall forfeit 100*l*. Persons lending licences, or trading with lent licences, shall forfeit 40*l*. each, and the lender his licence, and be incapable of a new one. Persons trading without licence or refusing to produce it, may be seized and carried before a magistrate, who may convict, &c. Peace officers neglecting their duty, shall forfeit 10*l*. *Ibid.*

No hawker shall expose any goods to sale in a city or market town, or within two miles thereof, on penalty of 10*l*. except on market or fair days. Hawkers vending goods in any city or town contrary to this act, shall be liable to the like penalties as unlicensed hawkers. *Ibid.*

Hawkers who were licensed on May 1, 1789, may set up any business where they are resident inhabitants, though not brought up thereto. *Ibid.*

No wholesale trader in English lace, in woollen, linen, silk, cotton, or mixed goods, or any other kind of British goods, shall be deemed a hawker. *Ibid.*

This act does not extend to the selling of newspapers, fish, fruits, or victuals, nor to the real workers or makers of British goods selling the same, nor to any travelling tinker, cooper, glazier, plumber, or harness-mender. *Ibid.*

Penalties above 20*l*. are to be recovered in the courts at Westminster; under before one justice, in which case an appeal is allowed to the quarter sessions. The penalties go, half to the crown and half to the informer. *Ibid.*

Witnesses neglecting or refusing to appear before a justice, on summons, are to forfeit 10*l*. *Ibid.*

By 35 *Geo.* 3. *c.* 91. the penalty inflicted by 29 *Geo.* 3. *c.* 26. on hawkers trading without a licence, or not producing it, may be levied by distress, and sale of the goods, and in the mean time, and until payment, the offender may be committed. *s.* 1.

HAY, *haya*, Fr. *haye*, a hedge or inclosure; also a net to take game. See *Haia*.

HAY-BOTE, a liberty to take thorns and other wood, to make and repair hedges, gates, fences, &c. either by tenant for life or years: it is also said to be wood, for the making of rakes and forks, with which men in summer make hay. 2 *Black.* 35.

HAYWARD, (from the Fr. *haye*, i. e. *sepes*, & *garde*, *custodia*) is an officer appointed in the lord's court: who is to look to the fields, and impound cattle that do trespass therein; to inspect that no pound breaches be made, and if any be, to present them at the leet, &c. *Kitch.* 46.

HAZARD, an unlawful game at dice. See *Gaming*.

HEADBOROW, or HEADBOROUGH, (from the Sax. *head*, *caput*, & *borge*, *fidejussor*) the head of the frank-pledge in boroughs; and as he was called headborow, so he was also stiled borowhead, borsholder, thirdborough, tithingman, &c. according to the usage and diversity of speech in several places. *Lamb.* These headborows were the chief of the ten pledges; the other nine being denominated handborows, or inferior pledges: headborows are now a kind of constables. 1 *Black.* 114, 115.

HEADLAND, is the upper part of ground left for the turning of the plough; whence the headway. *Paroch. Antiq.* 587. *Cowel. Blount.*

HEAD-PENCE, an exaction of a certain sum heretofore collected by the sheriff of Northumberland; abolished by stat. 23 *H.* 6. *c.* 7. *Cowel. Blount.*

HEAD-SILVER, paid to lords of leets, &c. See *Common Fine*.

HEALFANG or HALSFANG, is compounded of two Saxon words, *hals*, i. e. *collum*, and *fang*, *capere*, and signifies that punishment, *qua alicui collum stringatur*, (*collestrigium*). Sometimes it is taken for a pecuniary mulct, to commute for standing in the pillory; payable to the king or chief lord. *Leg. H.* 1. *cap.* 11. *Cowel. Blount.*

HEALTH, (*injuries to*) injuries affecting a man's health, are where by any unwholesome practices of another, a man sustains any apparent damage in his vigour or constitution. As by selling him bad provisions or wine; (1 *Rol. Abr.* 90.) by the exercise of a noisome trade, which infects the air in his neighbourhood; (9 *Rep.* 57. *Hutt.* 135.) or by the neglect, or unskilful management of his physician, surgeon or apothecary. For it hath been solemnly resolved, that *mala praxis* is a great misdemeanor and offence at common law, whether it be for curiosity and experiment, or by neglect; because it breaks the trust which the party had placed in his physician, and tends to his destruction. *Ld. Raym.* 214. These are wrongs or injuries unaccompanied by force, for which there is a remedy in damages, by special action of trespass on the case. 3 *Black.* 122.

HEARTH-MONEY, a tax, long since abolished. See *Chimney-money*.

HEBBER-MEN, fishermen, or poachers below London Bridge, who fish for whitings, smelts, &c. commonly at ebbing water, mentioned in one of the articles of the Thames jury, at the court of the conservator of the river Thames, printed *anno* 1632. *Cowel. Blount.*

HEBBING-WEARS, wears or engines made or laid at ebbing water. *Ibid.*

HEBDOMAS, (Lat.) a week. *Ibid.*

HEBDOMADIUS, the week's man, canon or prebendary in the cathedral church, who hath the care of the choir, and the officers belonging to it, for his own week. *Reg. Episc. Hereford. MS. Cowel. Blount.*

HECK, the name of an engine to take fish in the river Ouse. 23 *H.* 8. *c.* 18. *Cowel. Blount.*

HECCAGIUM, rent paid to the lord of the fee for liberty to use the engines called hecks. *Ibid.*

HEDA, a small haven, wharf, or landing place. *Domesd. Cowel. Blount.*

HEDAGIUM, toll or customary duties paid at the hith or wharf, for the landing goods, &c. from which exemption was granted by the king to some particular persons and societies. *Cartular. Abbat. de Radinges, MS. f.* 7. *Cowel. Blount.*

HEDGE-BOTE, is necessary stuff to make hedges, which the lessee may of common right take. 2 *Black.* 35. See *Estovers.*

HEDGE-BREAKERS. See *Trespass.*

HEGIRA, a term in chronology, signifying the *epocha*, or account of time used by the Arabians and Turks; who begin their accounts from the day that Mahomet was forced to make his escape from the city of Mecca, which was on Friday, July 16, A. D. 622.

HEIR, (*hæres, ab hæreditate*) an heir saith my *Lord Coke*, in the legal understanding of the common law, is he *ex justis nuptiis procreatus*, who succeeds by descent to the lands, tenements and hereditaments, being an estate of inheritance. *Co. Lit.* 7. *b.* 3 *Co.* 12. *b.* And in general, without the word *heir*, no fee-simple can be created. *Co. Lit.* 9.

The several kinds of heirs are,

1. *Heir apparent;* 2. *heir general;* 3. *heir special;* 4. *heir by custom;* 5. *heir by devise,* called *hæres factus.*

1. Although no person can be *heir* until the death of his ancestor, according to the rule *nemo est hæres viventis,* yet in common parlance, he who stands nearest in degree of kindred to the ancestor, is called in his life time *heir apparent. Co. Litt.* 8. *a.*

2 *Heir general.* The heir general, or *heir at common law* is he who after his father or ancestor's death hath a right to, and is introduced into, all his lands, tenements and hereditaments. But he must be of the whole blood, not a bastard, alien, or the like. 3 *Bac. Abr. Gw. Ed.* 450.

The heir at law is bound by his ancestor's alienations and dispositions; and also by his covenants and obligations, so far as he has assets. *Ibid.* 451.

Also if the ancestor agrees to convey or sell lands, and receives part of the purchase money, but dies before a conveyance is executed, and a bill is brought against the heir, he will be decreed to convey, and the money shall go to the executor, especially if there are more debts due than the testator's personal estate is sufficient to pay. 2 *Vern.* 215. *Abr. Eq.* 265.

But in such case, the agreement must be by *deed under seal,* for the inheritance cannot be aliened or in any wise charged or incumbered by the ancestor, except it be by deed under seal.

And as the heir must otherwise be entitled by *descent*, the most ancient title by which lands can be acquired, it is a rule in law, that if a man devise lands to one who is his heir at law, the devise is void, and that the devisee and heir shall take by descent. *Dyer.* 54, 126. *Style* 148. 1 *Nels. Abr.* 645. 3 *Lev.* 127. 2 *Danv.* 557. 1 *Lil.* 593. 1 *Salk.* 241.

3. *Special heir,* or *issue in tail.* The issue in tail claims *performam doni*, and as the statute *de donis* preserves the estate to him, his ancestor cannot grant or alien, nor make any rightful estate of freehold to another, but for term of his own life. *Lit. sect.* 613. 3 *Bac. Abr. Gw. Ed.* 452.

4. *Heir by custom.* A custom in particular places varying the rules of descent at common law is good; such as the custom of gavel-kind, by which all the sons shall inherit, and make but one heir to their ancestor. *Co. Litt.* 140. Or *borough-english,* where the youngest son succeeds to the inheritance. 1 *Mod.* 102.

5. *Heir by devise,* or *hæres factus,* is only a devisee of lands, being made so by the will of the testator, and has no other right or interest than the will gives him. 3 *Co.* 42. *a.* 3 *Bac. Abr. Gw. Ed.* 452.

Where the ancestor binds himself and his heirs in an obligation, the obligee may sue his heir or executor, or administrator at his election, and may have execution of the land descended to the heir; for the common law having allowed the action of debt against the heir, he could have no benefit by the action unless he were permitted to have execution of the lands which descended to the heir. *Plowd.* 441. 3 *Co.* 12. *a. Cro. Jac.* 458.

But the body of the heir is protected, for it would be most unreasonable to subject the heir to the payment of his ancestor's debts, any further than the value of the assets descended. *Dyer.* 81, *pl.* 62.

By the common law if the heir *before an action brought* against him had aliened the assets, the obligor was without any remedy: but if he only aliened *pending the writ*, the lands which he had by descent at the time of the original purchased, were liable *Co. Litt.* 102. 3 *Bac. Abr. Gw. Ed.* 459.

But to prevent the wrong and injury to

creditors by alienation of the lands descended, by stat. 3 and 4 *Will. & Mar.* c. 14, made perpetual by 6 & 7 *Will.* 3. *c.* 14, "if the "heir aliens before action brought, he "shall be liable to the value of the land." s. 5, 7.

Also if, before this statute, the ancestor had devised away the lands, a creditor by specialty had no remedy either against the heir or devisee. *Abr. Eq.* 149, but now by the said statute 3 & 4 *Will. & Mar. c.* 14, "creditors by *specialty* may have an action "of debt against the heir, and the devisee "of the debtor jointly, who shall be charge-"able for a false plea." *s.* 3, 6.

Also by 47 *Geo.* 3. *sess.* 2. *c.* 84, when "any trader within the meaning of the "bankrupt laws, shall die entitled to any "estate or interest in real estates, the same "shall be assets to be administered in equity "by the heir or devisee for the payment "of all his debts; but creditors by specialty "in which heirs are bound shall be first "paid." *s.* 1.

—— *What shall be assets.*] Whenever the ancestor binds himself and his heirs all his *lands of freehold* which descend in fee-simple, are *assets by descent*, and shall be liable as far as they extend to answer the ancestor's obligations. 3 *Bac. Abr. Gw. Ed.* 467.

But if a *copyhold* descends to the heir, this shall not be assets, because it is an inheritance created by custom. 4 *Co.* 22. *a.*

A reversion after a lease for *years* made by the ancestor is present assets, and so is a reversion expectant on the determination of an estate for life. 3 *Bac. Abr. Gw. Ed.* 468.

But a reversion in fee expectant upon an *estate tail* is not assets, because it is in the power of the tenant in tail to dock and bar it at his pleasure. *Ibid.*

By the statute of frauds and perjuries, (29 *Car.* 2. *c.* 3), "if lands *pur autre vie* come "to the heir by special occupancy they "shall be chargeable in his hands as assets "by descent; and if there be no special "occupant, shall go to the executors or "administrators of the party that had the "estate, and be assets in their hands." *s.* 12.

Also by the said statute, "when lands "are settled in trust, and descend in fee "to the heir of *cestui que trust*, the same "shall be assets in the same manner as "lands in possession, but no heir shall by "reason thereof become chargeable of his "own estate." *s.* 10, 11.

An equity of redemption of an inheritance is also assets in the hands of the heir. 3 *Bac. Abr. Gw. Ed.* 469.

But the personal estate of the ancestor shall in all cases be *primarily* applied in the discharge of his personal debts, and this although such personal debts be also secured by *mortgage*, and whether there be a bond or covenant for payment or not. 3 *Bac. Abr. Gw. Ed.* 85.

For the personal estate of the ancestor has had the benefit of the debt contracted, and the heir at law may therefore call upon the personal representatives in equity to pay the specialty and mortgage of the deceased in the first instance in preference to his other personal debts. 1 *Ch. Cas.* 74. 2 *Ch. Cas.* 5. 2 *Salk.* 449. 1 *Vern.* 37.

Goods and chattels annexed to the freehold go to the heir, and not to the executor or administrator, as the glass in a window, doors, locks, keys, bolts, coppers, furnaces, pictures, and glass used instead of wainscoat, mill-stones, and the like. *Off. Ex.* 86. 4 *Co.* 64. *Com. Dig.* tit. *Ex. c.* 4. 2 *Vern.* 508. 2 *Ch. Cas.* 156, 160. *a.*

HEIRESS, a *female heir*, and where there are several female children, they all take jointly, and are called *co-heirs* or *co-heiresses*, and it is the same where there is an only sister, or several sisters taking by inheritance from a deceased brother or sister. See *Parceners.*

—— *Stealing of.*] See *Forcible Marriage.*

HEIR-LOOMS are such goods and personal chattels, as contrary to the nature of chattels, shall go by special custom to the heir along with the inheritance, and not to the executor of the last proprietor. The termination loom, is of Saxon original; in which language it signifies a limb or member, (*Spelm. Gloss.* 277;) so that an heir-loom is nothing else, but a limb or member of the inheritance. They are generally such things as cannot be taken away without damaging or dismembering the freehold: otherwise the general rule is, that no chattel interest whatsoever shall go to the heir, notwithstanding it be expressly limited to a man and his heirs, but shall vest in the executor. *Co. Litt.* 388. Or if any chattel be given to a man and the heirs of his body, he takes the entire and absolute interest in it: it is true indeed, that there have been many fruitless attempts to make pictures, plate, books, and household furniture, descend to the heir with a family mansion; yet where they are left to be enjoyed as heir-looms by the persons who shall respectively be in possession of a certain house, or to descend as heir-looms as far as courts of law and equity will admit, the absolute interest of them, subject to the life interests of those who have life estates in the real property, will vest in that person who is entitled to the first estate tail or estate of inheritance, and upon his death that interest will pass to his personal representative. 1 *Bro.* 274. 3 *Bro.* 101.

But deer in a real authorized park, fishes in a pond, doves in a dove-house, &c. though in themselves personal chattels, yet they are so annexed to and so necessary to the well being of the inheritance, that they shall accompany the land wherever it vests, by either descent or purchase. (*Co. Litt.* 8.) For this reason also it is, that the antient jewels of the crown are held to be heir-looms, (*Co. Litt.* 18); for they are necessary to maintain the state, and support the dignity of the sovereign for the time being. Charters likewise, and deeds, court-rolls, and other evidences of the land, together with the chests in which they are contained, shall pass together with the land to the heir, in the nature of heir-looms, and shall not go to the executor. (*Bro. Abr. tit. chatteles.* 18). By special custom, also in some places, carriages, utensils, and other household implements, may be heir-looms, *Co. Litt.* 18, 185). But such custom must be strictly proved; on the other hand, by almost general custom whatever is strongly affixed to the freehold or inheritance, and cannot be severed from thence without violence or damage, "*quod ab aedibus non facile revellitur,*" (*Spelm. Gloss.* 277); is become a member of the inheritance, and shall thereupon pass to the heir; as chimney pieces, pumps, old fixed or dormant tables, benches, and the like. (12 *Mod.* 520).

HELPING TO STOLEN GOODS. By 4 *Geo.* I. *c.* 11, whoever shall take a reward under the pretence of helping any one to stolen goods, shall suffer as the felon who stole them: unless he causes such felon to be apprehended and brought to trial, and also gives evidence against him.

HELSING, a brass coin among the Saxons equivalent to our halfpenny. *Cowel. Blount.*

HELM, (Sax.) The bar by which the rudder of a ship or vessel is governed. Also the head of a still or alembic, because it is something like an *helmet*, an head piece or covering of armour for the head, hence in ancient times according to Crowe, *helm* sometimes called *halm* also signified thatch or straw, the common covering of tenements.

HOLOWE WALL, the holl-wall or end wall. *Cowel. Blount.*

HEMP. By 33 *Hen.* 8. *c.* 17, hemp or flax shall not be watered in any running stream or common pond under pain of 40s.

By 15 *Car.* 2. *c.* 15, any person, native or foreigner, may freely exercise the trade of dressing and using hemp, flax, or make tapestry hangings, twine, nets or cordage, and after three years shall have the privilege of natural born subjects.

HENCHMAN, according to *Cowel* and *Blount* seems to have been a running footman attendant upon persons of honour or worship.

HENED PENNY, a customary payment of money instead of hens at Christmas. *Cowel. Blount.*

HENEWARD, a duty to the king in Cambridgeshire. *Ibid.*

HENGHEN, (Sax. *hengen*) a prison, gaol, or house of correction. *Cowel. Blount.*

HENGWITE. See *Hangwite.*

HEERDFESTE. The master of a family. *Cowel. Blount.*

HEORDPENNY. See *Peter pence.*

HEPTARCHY, (Sax.) The kingdom of England was formerly, under the Saxons, divided into an heptarchy, consisting of seven independent kingdoms peopled and governed by different clans and colonies; these were all reduced into one kingdom, by Egbert king of the West Saxons in the year 827 or 828, Egbert is therefore stiled the first king of England.

HERALD, (*heraulà*, *heralt*, Fr. *heraldo*, Span. *herold*, Teut). An officer at arms; Verstegan derives it from *here*, Sax. an army, and *held* a champion, Teut. but *Minservus* takes it from *hierholden* to put an end to, because they are sent to bring wars to an end, and to proclaim future peace. It is the duty of this officer to denounce war, to proclaim peace, or to be employed by the king in martial messages; they are judges and examiners of gentlemen's coats of arms, and conservators of genealogies, and they marshal the solemnities at the coronation of kings, and funerals of princes and other great men. *Cowel. Blount.*

The chief of these are called *kings at arms*, of which garter is the principal, first instituted by Henry V. to attend the knights of the garter, and marshal the funerals of the nobility, *Clarencieux* or *Clarentius* first ordained by Ed. VI. to marshal the funerals of the lesser nobility, knights and esquires throughout the realm, south of the Trent is the second; and *Norroy* quasi *North Roy*, to do the like on the north side of the Trent is the third. *Ibid.*

Besides the *kings at arms* there are eight inferior heralds, viz. York, Lancaster, Chester, Windsor, Richmond, Somerset, Hanover, Gloucester; and to the superior and inferior heralds, are added four others called *Marshals* or *Pursuivants* at arms who succeed the heralds who die, and they are *blue mantle*, *rouge cross*, *red dragon*, and *portcullis*. *Ibid.*

The ancient heralds have been made a corporation or college under the earl marshal of England. 3 *Black.* 105.

HERBAGE, the green pasture and natural produce or the earth, from which cattle are sustained.

HERBAGIUM ANTERIUS, the first crop of grass of hay in opposition to latter math or after grass. *Cowel. Blount.*

HERBERRY or HERBURY, an inn. *Ibid.*

HERBINGER or HARBINGER, (*herberger*, Teut.) an officer of the court, who provides lodgings in a prince's progress; also an innkeeper. *Cowel. Blount. Bailey.*—Hence *herbergagium*, lodgings to receive guests in the way of hospitality; *herbergatus*, spent in an inn; and *herbergare* to harbour, to entertain. *Cowel.*

HERCE, (*hercia*) an harrow, *Fleta. lib.* 2. *c.* 77, also a candlestick in the shape of a harrow, containing many candles anciently placed at the head of a *cenotaph.* *Cowel. Blount.* Hence also *herciare* from the French *hercer* to harrow. 4 *Inst*, 270.

HERDWICH or HERDWIT, a grange or place for cattle and husbandry. *Cowel. Blount.*

HERDWERCH, HEORDWERCH, herdsman's work, or customary labours done by shepherds, herdsmen, and other inferior tenants at the will of their lord. *Ibid.*

HEREBANNUM, (Sax. *here* exercitus & *ban.* ædictum *mulcta*) a mulct for not going armed into the field when called forth. *Spelm. Cowel. Blount.*

HEREBOTE, (Sax. *here* exercitus and *bode* a messenger) the king's edict commanding his subjects into the field. *Ibid.*

HEREDITAMENTS. An hereditament is of the largest and most comprehensive expression, for it includes not only lands and tenements, but whatsoever may be inherited, be it corporeal or incorporeal, real, personal, or mixed. Thus an heir-loom, or implement of furniture which by custom descends to the heir, together with an house, is neither land nor tenement, but a mere moveable; yet, being inheritable, is comprized under the general word hereditament: and so a condition, the benefit of which may descend to a man from his ancestor, is also an hereditament. 1 *Inst.* 4. 3 *Rep.* 4. 2 *Black.* 17.

Hereditaments are of two kinds, corporeal and incorporeal. Corporeal consist of such as affect the senses: such as may be seen and handled by the body; incorporeal are not the object of sensation, can neither be seen nor handled, are creatures of the mind, and exist only in contemplation. 2 *Black.* 17.

Corporeal hereditaments consist wholly of substantial and permanent objects; all which may be comprehended under the general denomination of land only. For land, says sir Edward Coke, 1 *Inst.* 4; comprehendeth in its legal signification any ground, soil, or earth whatsoever; as arable, meadows, pastures, woods, moors, waters, marshes, furzes, and heath. It legally includeth also all castles, houses, and other buildings: for they consist, saith he, of two things; *land* which is the foundation and structure thereupon: so that, if I convey the land or ground, the structure or building passeth therewith. It is observable that water is here mentioned as a species of land, which may seem a kind of solecism; but such is the language of the law, and therefore I cannot bring an action to recover possession of a pool or other piece of water by the name of water only, either by calculating its capacity, as for so many cubical yards; or by superficial measure, for twenty acres of water: or by general description, as for a pond, a watercourse, or a rivulet; but I must bring my action for the land that lies at the bottom, and must call it twenty acres of land covered with water, *Brownl.* 142. For water is a moveable wandering thing, and must of necessity continue common by the law of nature; so that I can only have a temporary, transient, usufructuary, property therein: wherefore, if a body of water runs out of my pond into another man's, I have no right to reclaim it. But the land, which that water covers, is permanent, fixed, and immoveable; and therefore in this I may have a certain substantial property, of which the law will take notice, and not of the other. 2 *Black.* 18.

Land hath also, in its legal signification, an indefinite extent, upwards as well as downwards. *Cujus est solum, ejus est usque ad coelum*, is the maxim of the law, upwards; therefore no man may erect any building, or the like, to overhang another's land: and downwards, whatever is in a direct line, between the surface of any land, and the center of the earth, belongs to the owner of the surface; as is every day's experience in the mining countries: so that the word "land" includes not only the face of the earth, but every thing under it or over it. And therefore, if a man grants all his lands, he grants thereby all his mines of metal and other fossils, his woods, his waters, and his houses, as well as his fields and meadows. Not but the particular names of the things are equally sufficient to pass them, except in the instance of water, by a grant of which, nothing passes but a right of fishing; but the capital distinction is this, that by the name of a castle, messuage, toft, croft, or the like, nothing else will pass, except what falls with the utmost propriety under the term made use of, but by the name of land, which is *nomen generalissimum*, every thing terrestrial will pass. *Co. Litt.* 4. *Ibid.* 4, 5, 6. 2 *Black.* 19. So also by the name of a castle, one or more manors may be conveyed; and *é converso* by the name of a manor, a castle may pass. 1 *Inst.* 5. 2 *Inst.* 31.

——— *Incorporeal hereditament* is a right issuing out of a thing corporate (whether real or personal) or concerning or annexed to, or exercisable within, the same. (*Co. Litt.* 19, 20). It is not the thing corporeal itself, which may consist in lands, houses, jewels, or the like; but something collateral thereto, as a rent issuing out of those lands or houses, or an office relating to those jewels. In short, as the logicians speak, corporeal hereditaments are the substance, which may be always seen, always handled, incorporeal hereditaments are but a sort of accidents, which inhere in and are supported by that substance; and may belong, or not belong to it, without any visible alteration therein. Their existence is merely in idea and abstracted contemplation, though their effects and profits may be frequently objects of our bodily senses. And indeed, if we would fix a clear notion of an incorporeal hereditament, we must be careful not to confound together the profits produced, and the thing or hereditament which produces them. An annuity, for instance, is an incorporeal hereditament, for though the money, which is the fruit or product of this annuity, is doubtless of a corporeal nature, yet the annuity itself, which produces that money, is a thing invisible, has only a mental existence, and cannot be delivered over from hand to hand. So tithes, if we consider the produce of them as the tenth sheaf or tenth lamb, seem to be completely corporeal; yet they are indeed incorporeal hereditaments; for they, being merely a contingent springing right collateral to and issuing out of lands, can never be the object of sense; that casual share of the annual increase is not till severed, capable of being shewn to the eye, nor of being delivered into bodily possession. 2 *Black.* 20.

These incorporeal hereditaments are principally of ten sorts; 1. *Advowsons;* 2. *Tithes;* 3. *Commons;* 4. *Ways;* 5. *Offices;* 6. *Dignities;* 7. *Franchises;* 8. *Corodies,* or *Pensions;* 9. *Annuities;* and 10. *Rents,* which see under their proper titles.

HEREDITARY RIGHT. See *Heir*.—TO THE CROWN. See *King*.

HEREDITARY REVENUE. See *King*.

HEREFARE, (Sax.) a military expedition or going to warfare. *Cowel. Blount.*

HEREGILD, (Sax.) a tribute or tax levied for the maintenance of an army. *Ibid.*

HERELLUS, a sort of little fish, either the minow or gudgeon. *Ibid.*

HEREMITORIUM, a solitary place of retirement for hermits. *Ibid.*

HERENACH, an archdeacon. *Ibid.*

HEREMENES or HERETEAMS, one who followed an army of rebels. *Ibid.*

HERESLITA, or HERESSA, or HERESSIZ, (Sax. from *here exercitus* and *sliten*, to depart, 4 *Co. Inst.* 128.) a hired soldier that departed without licence. *Cowel. Blount.*

HERESY, (*hæresis*) is an offence, which consists not in a total denial of Christianity, but of some of its essential doctrines, publicly and obstinately avowed; being defined by sir Matthew Hale, "*sententia rerum divinarum humano sensu excogitata, palam docta et pertinaciter defensa* (1 *Hal. P. C.* 384.)" And here it must also be acknowledged that particular modes of belief or unbelief, not tending to overturn christianity itself, or to sap the foundations of morality, are by no means the object of coercion by the civil magistrate. What doctrines shall therefore be adjudged heresy, was left by our old constitution to the determination of the ecclesiastical judge, who had herein a most arbitrary latitude allowed him. For the general definition of an heretic given by Lyndewood (*cap. de haereticis*), extends to the smallest deviations from the doctrines of holy church, "*haereticus est qui dubitat de fide catholica, et qui negligit servare ea, quæ Romana ecclesia statuit, seu servare decreverat.*" Or, as the statute 2 *Hen.* 4. *c.* 15. expresses it in English, "teachers of erroneous opinions, contrary to the faith and blessed determinations of the holy church." Very contrary this to the usage of the first general councils, which defined all heretical doctrines with the utmost precision and exactness. And what ought to have alleviated the punishment, the uncertainty of the crime, seems to have enhanced it in those days of blind zeal and pious cruelty. It is true that the sanctimonious hypocrisy of the canonists went at first no farther than enjoining penance, excommunication, and ecclesiastical deprivation, for heresy; though afterwards they proceeded boldly to imprisonment by the ordinary, and confiscation of goods *in pios usus.* But in the mean time they had prevailed upon the weakness of bigoted princes, to make the civil power subservient to their purposes, by making heresy not only a temporal, but even a capital offence: the Romish ecclesiastics determining, without appeal, whatever they pleased to be heresy, and shifting off to the secular arm the odium and drudgery of executions; with which they themselves were too tender and delicate to intermeddle. Nay, they pretended to intercede and pray, on behalf of the convicted heretic, *ut citra mortis periculum sententia circa eum moderetur* (*Decretal. l.* 5. *t.* 40. *c.* 27.): well knowing at the same time that they were delivering the unhappy victim to certain death. Hence the capital punishments inflicted on the antient Donatists and Manicheans by the emperors, Theodosius and Justinian (*Cod. l.* 1. *tit.* 5.): hence also the constitution of the emperor Frederic mentioned by Lyndewode (*c. de hæreticis*), adjudging all persons without distinction to be burnt with fire, who were convicted of heresy by the ecclesiastical judge. The same emperor, in another constitution (*Cod.* 1. 5. 4.), ordained that if any temporal lord, when admonished by the church, should neglect to clear his territories of heretics within a year, it should be lawful for good catholics to seize and occupy the lands, and utterly to exterminate the heretical possessors. And upon this foundation was built that arbitrary power, so long claimed and so fatally exerted by the pope, of disposing even of the kingdoms of refractory princes to more dutiful sons of the church. The immediate event of this constitution was something singular, and may serve to illustrate at once the gratitude of the holy see, and the just punishment of the royal bigot; for upon the authority of this very constitution, the pope afterwards expelled this very emperor Frederic from his kingdom of Sicily, and gave it to Charles of Anjou (*Baldus in Cod.* 1. 5. 4.) 4 *Black.* 45, 6.

Christianity being thus deformed by the demon of persecution upon the continent, we cannot expect that our own island should be entirely free from the same scourge. And therefore we find among our antient precedents (*F. N. B.* 269.) a writ *de hæretico comburendo*, which is thought by some to be as antient as the common law itself. However, it appears from thence, that the conviction of heresy by the common law was not in any petty ecclesiastical court, but before the archbishop himself in a provincial synod; and that the delinquent was delivered over to the king to do as he should please with him: so that the crown had a control over the spiritual power, and might pardon the convict by issuing no process against him; the writ *de hæretico comburendo* being not a writ of course, but issuing only by the special direction of the king in council (1 *Hal. P. C.* 395.) 4 *Black.* 46.

But in the reign of Henry the fourth, when the eyes of the christian world began to open, and the seeds of the protestant religion (though under the opprobrious name of lollardy*) took root in the kingdom; the clergy taking advantage from the king's dubious title to demand an increase of their own power, obtained an act of parliament (2 *Hen.* 4. *c.* 15.), which sharpened the edge of persecution to its utmost keenness. For, by that statute, the diocesan alone, without the intervention of a synod, might convict of heretical tenets; and unless the convict abjured his opinions, or if after abjuration he relapsed, the sheriff was bound *ex officio*, if required by the bishop, to commit the unhappy victim to the flames, without waiting for the consent of the crown. By the statute 2 *Hen.* 5. *c.* 7. lollardy was also made a temporal offence, and indictable in the king's courts; which did not thereby gain an exclusive, but only a concurrent jurisdiction with the bishop's consistory. 4 *Black.* 47.

Afterwards, when the final reformation of religion began to advance, the power of the ecclesiastics was somewhat moderated: for though what heresy is, was not then precisely defined, yet we are told in some points what it is not: the statute 25 *Hen.* 8. *c.* 14. declaring, that offences against the see of Rome are not heresy; and the ordinary being thereby restrained from proceeding in any case upon mere suspicion; that is, unless the party be accused by two credible witnesses, or an indictment of heresy be first previously found in the king's courts of common law. And yet the spirit of persecution was not then abated, but only diverted into a lay channel. For in six years afterwards, by statute 31 *Hen.* 8. *c.* 14. the bloody law of the six articles was made, which established the six most contested points of popery, transubstantiation, communion in one kind, the celibacy of the clergy, monastic vows, the sacrifice of the mass, and auricular confession; which points were "determined and resolved by the most godly study, pain, and travail of his majesty: for which his most humble and obedient subjects, the lords spiritual and temporal, and the commons, in parliament assembled, did render and give unto his highness their most high and hearty thanks," but did also enact and declare all oppugness of the first to be heretics, and to be burnt with fire; and of the five last to be felons, and to suffer death. The same statute established a new and mixed jurisdiction of clergy and laity for the trial and conviction of heretics; the reigning prince being then equally intent on destroying the supremacy of the bishops of Rome, and establishing all other their corruptions of the christian religion. 4 *Black.* 48.

After various repeals and revivals of these sanguinary laws in the two succeeding reigns, we come to the reign of queen Elizabeth; when the reformation was finally established with temper and decency, unsullied with party rancour, or personal caprice and resentment. And we find by statute 1 *Eliz.* *c.* 1. *all former statutes relating to heresy are repealed, which leaves the jurisdiction of heresy as it stood at common law*; *viz.* as to the infliction of common censures, in the ecclesiastical courts; and in case of burning the heretic, in the provincial synod only (5 *Rep.* 23. 12 *Rep.* 56, 92.) Sir Matthew Hale is indeed of a different opinion, and holds that such power resided in the diocesan also, though he agrees, that in either case the writ *de hæretico comburendo* was not demandable of common right, but grantable or otherwise merely at the king's discretion. (1 *Hal. P. C.* 405.) But the principal point now gained was, that by this statute a boundary is for the first time set to what shall be accounted heresy; nothing for the future being to be so determined, but only such tenets, which have been heretofore so declared, 1. By the words of the canonical scriptures: 2. By the first four general councils, or such others as have only used the words of the holy scriptures; or, 3. Which shall hereafter be so declared by the parliament, with the assent of the clergy in convocation. Thus was heresy reduced to a

* So called not from *lolium* or tares (an etymology, which was afterwards devised in order to justify the burning of them; *Matth.* *xiii.* 30.) but from one Walter Lolhard, a German reformer, A. D. 1315. *Mod. Un. Hist.* xxvi. 13, *Spelm. Gloss.* 731.

greater certainty than before; though it might not have been the worse to have defined it in terms still more precise and particular: as a man continued still liable to be burnt, for what perhaps he did not understand to be heresy, till the ecclesiastical judge so interpreted the words of the canonical scriptures. 4 *Black.* 48.

For the writ *de hæretico comburendo* remained still in force; and we have instances of its being put in execution upon two Anabaptists in the seventeenth of Elizabeth, and two Arians in the ninth of James the first. But it was totally abolished, and heresy again subjected only to ecclesiastical correction *pro salute animæ*, by virtue of the statute 29 *Car.* 2. *c.* 9. Thus in one and the same reign, our lands were delivered from the slavery of military tenures; our bodies from arbitrary imprisonment by the *habeas corpus* act; and our minds from the tyranny of superstitious bigotry, by demolishing this last badge of persecution in the English law. *Ibid.*

Every thing is therefore as it should be, with respect to the spiritual cognizance, and spiritual punishment, of heresy; unless perhaps that the crime ought to be more strictly defined, and no persecution permitted, even in the ecclesiastical courts, till the tenets in question are by proper authority previously declared to be heretical. Under these restrictions, it seems necessary for the support of the national religion, that the officers of the church should have power to censure heretics; yet not to harass them with temporal penalties, much less to exterminate or destroy them. The legislature, however, hath thought it proper, that the civil magistrate should again intepose, with regard to one species of heresy, very prevalent in modern times; for by statute 9 & 10 *W.* 3. *c.* 32. if any person educated in the christian religion, or professing the same, shall by writing, printing, teaching, or advised speaking, deny any one of the persons of the holy trinity to be God, or maintain that there are more Gods than one, he shall undergo the same penalties and incapacities, as are inflicted on apostacy, by the same statute. 4 *Black.* 48, 9. See *Apostacy.*

HERETABLE JURISDICTIONS. The feodal grievance of these jurisdictions in Scotland, is removed by stat. 20 *Geo.* 2. *c.* 43. 2 *Black.* 77.

HERETICK, (*hæreticus*). See *Heresy.*

HERETICO COMBURENDO. See *Heresy.*

HERETOCHE, (from the Sax. *here, exercitus*, and *togen, ducere*) the general of an army; a leader or commander of military forces. *Cowel. Blount.*

HERETOCHIAS, a leader or commander of military forces. *Cowel. Blount.* 1 *Black.* 397, 409. 4 *Black.* 413.

HERETUM, a court or yard for drawing up the guards or military tenure, which usually attended our prelates and nobility. *Ibid.*

HERGRIPA, (Sax. *hær, capillus*, and *grypan, capere*) pulling by the hair. *Ibid.*

HERIGALDS, a sort of garment so called. *Ibid.*

HERIOT. (*heriotum*) Heriots, according to *Blackstone*, originated from a Danish custom, and are a render of the best beast, goods, piece of plate, or the like, (as the custom may be) to the lord on the death of the tenant. 2 *Black.* 97.

These heriots are usually divided into two sorts, *heriot-service*, and *heriot-custom.* I. *Heriot-service*, are such as are due upon a special reservation in a grant or lease of lands, and therefore amount to little more than a mere rent (2 *Saund.* 166.) II. *Heriot-custom* arise upon no special reservation whatsoever, but depend merely upon immemorial usage and custom (*Co. Cop. s.* 24.) Of these therefore, we are here principally to speak: and they are defined to be a customary tribute of goods and chattels, payable to the lord of the fee on the decease of the owner of the land. 2 *Black.* 422.

The first establishment, if not introduction, of compulsory heriots into England, was by the Danes: and we find in the laws of king Canute (*c.* 69.) the several heregeates or heriots specified, which were then exacted by the king on the death of divers of his subjects, according to their respective dignities; from the highest eorle down to the most inferior thegne or landholder. These, for the most part, consisted in arms, horses, and habiliments of war; which the word itself, according to sir Henry Spelman (*of feuds, c.* 18.) signifies. These were delivered up to the sovereign on the death of the vassal, who could no longer use them, to be put into other hands for the service and defence of the country. And upon the plan of this Danish establishment did William the conqueror fashion his law of reliefs; when he ascertained the precise relief to be taken of every tenant in chivalry, and, contrary to the feodal custom and the usage of his own duchy of Normandy, required arms and implements of war to be paid instead of money. (*LL. Guil. Conq. c.* 22, 23, 24.) 2 *Black.* 423.

The Danish compulsive heriots being thus transmuted into reliefs, underwent the same several vicissitudes as the feodal tenures, and in soccage estates do frequently remain to this day in the shape of a double rent payable at the death of the tenant: the heriots which now continue among us, and preserve that name, seeming rather to be of Saxon parentage, and at first to have been merely discretionary (*Lambard Peramb. of Kent*, 492.) These are now for the most part confined to copyhold tenures, and are due by custom only, which is the life of all estates by copy; and perhaps are the only instance where custom has favoured the lord. For this payment was originally a voluntary donation, or gratuitous legacy of the tenant; perhaps in acknowledgment of his having been raised a degree above villenage, when all his goods and chattels were quite at the mercy of the lord; and custom, which has on the one hand confirmed the tenant's interest in exclusion of the lord's will, and has on the other hand established this discretional piece of gratitude into a permanent duty. An heriot may also appertain to free land, that is held by service and suit of court; in which case it is most commonly a copyhold enfranchised, whereupon the heriot is still due by custom. Bracton (*l.* 2. *c.* 36. *s.* 9.) speaks of heriots as frequently due on the death of both species of tenants: "*est quidem alia præstatio quæ nominatur heriettum; ubi tenens, liber vel servus, in morte sua dominum suum, de quo tenuerit, respicit de meliori averio suo, vel de secundo meliori, secundum diversam locorum consuetudinem.*" And this he adds, "*magis sit de gratia quam de jure;*" in which Fleta (*l.* 3. *c.* 18.) and Britton (*c.* 69.) agree: thereby plainly intimating the original of this custom to have been merely voluntary, as a legacy from the tenant; though now the immemorial usage has established it as of right in the lord.

This heriot is sometimes the best live beast, or *averium*, which the tenant dies possessed of, (which is particularly denominated the villein's relief in the twenty-ninth law of king William the conqueror,) sometimes the best inanimate thing, under which a jewel or piece of plate may be included: but it is always a personal chattel, which, immediately on the death of the tenant who was the owner of it, being ascertained by the option of the lord (*Hob.* 60.), becomes vested in him as his property; and is no charge upon the lands, but merely on the goods and chattels. The tenant must be the owner of it, else it cannot be due; and therefore on the death of a feme-covert no heriot can be taken; for she can have no ownership in things personal. (*Keilw.* 84. 4 *Leon.* 239.) In some places there is a customary composition in money, as ten or twenty shillings in lieu of a heriot, by which the lord and tenant are both bound, if it be an indisputably antient custom; but a new composition of this sort will not bind the representatives of either party; for that amounts to the creation of a new custom, which is now impossible. (*Co. Cop. s.* 31.)

HERISCHILD, military service or knight's fee: from the Sax. *here*, an army, and *scyld*, *scutum*. *Cowel. Blount.*

HERISHIT, laying down of arms: from the Sax. *here*, *exercitus*, and *slitan*, *scissura*. *Ibid.*

HERISCINDIUM, a division of household goods. *Ibid.*

HERISTALL, a castle; from the Sax *here*, an army, and *stall*, *statio*. *Ibid.*

HERMAPHRODITE, (*hermaphroditus*) a person that partakes in some respects of the sexes of both man and woman. *Lit. Dict.* And as *hermaphrodites* partake of both sexes, they may give or grant lands, or inherit as heirs to any, and shall take according to the prevailing sex. *Co. Lit.* 2, 7.

HERMER, among the Saxons was a great lord: from the Sax. *hera*, i. e. *major*, and *mære*, *dominus*. *Cowel. Blount.*

HERMINUS, (*mus ponticus*) a mouse, of whose skins we have *ermine*. *Ibid.*

HERMITAGE, (*hermitagium*) the habitation of a hermit, a solitary place.

HERMITORIUM, the chapel or place of prayer, belonging to an hermitage. *Ibid.*

HERNESEUS, herons. *Ibid.*

HERNESSUM, anciently used for the tackle or furniture of a ship. It is also called *hernasium*, from the Teuton. *harnas*, English *harness*, and signified any sort of furniture of a house, implements of trade, or rigging of a ship. *Cowel.*

HEROUDES, the same with heralds.

HERRINGS. See *Fisheries.*

HERRING SILVER. Seems to have been a composition in money, for the custom of paying such a number of herrings, for the provision of a religious house, &c. *Cowel. Blount.*

HESIA, an easement. *Ibid.*

HESTA or HESTHA, a little loaf of bread. *Ibid.*

HESTCORN. It is mentioned in *Mon. Ang. tom.* 2. *p.* 367. that king Athelstan in his return from the North after a victory, went to Beverley, where he gave to God, &c. *Quasdam avenas, vulgariter dictas hestcorne, percipiendas de dominiis & ecclesiis in illis partibus, quas, &c. Ibid.*

HESTHA, a capon or young cockerill.

HEUVELBORTH, (from the Sax. *healf*, i. e. *dimidium*, *et borgh*, *debitor vel fidejussor*) a surety for debt. *Ibid.*

HEXAM and HEXAMSHIRE, anciently *hagustald*, was a county of itself, and likewise a bishoprick, endowed with great privileges: but by the stat. 14 *Eliz. c.* 13. it is enacted, that Hexham and Hexhamshire, shall be within and accounted part of the county of Northumberland. 4 *Inst.* 22.

HEYBOTE. See *Haybote.*

HEYLOED, a customary load or burden laid upon the inferior tenants for mending or repairing the heys or hedges. *Cowel. Blount.*

HEYMECTUS, a net for catching conies; a hay-net. *Ibid.*

HIDAGE, (*hidagium*) an extraordinary tax, payable to the king for every hide of land. Sometimes the word hidage was used for the being quit of that tax, which was also called hidegild. *Cowel. Blount.* 1 *Black.* 316.

HIDE AND GAIN, anciently signified arable land. *Co. Lit.* 85. *b.* See *Gainage.*

HIDELANDS, (Sax. *hydelander.*) *Terræ ad hydam seu tectum pertinentes.*

HIDE OF LAND, (Sax. *hyde-lands*, from *hyden, tegere.*) A plough-land, it is said to be of 900 acres, as much as will maintain a family. Crompton, in his *Jurisdict. fo.* 222. says, a hide of land contains one hundred acres, and eight hides make a knight's fee. But sir Edward Coke holds, that a knight's fee, a hide or plough-land, a yard-land, or an oxgang of land, do not contain any certain number of acres. *Lit. fol.* 69. One thing is, however, clear, that the distribution of England by hides of land is very ancient. *Spelman. Camb. Brit. fol.* 156. *Cowel. Blount.*

HIDEL, signifies a place of protection or sanctuary. 1 *Hen.* 7. *c.* 6. *Cowel.*

HIDGILD, (*in LL. Canuti R.*) *exponitur pretium redemptionis aut manumissionis servi.* From the Sax. *hide*, i. e. the skin; and *geld*, *pretium*, i. e. the fine by which servants redeemed their skin, *i. e.* redeemed it from being whipped, which was the punishment for servants; *vel hidgildum*, i. e. let him pay for his skin; by which payment he is to be excused from whipping. *Cowel.*

HIERLOOM. See *Heirloom.*

HIGH COMMISSION COURT. The court of the king's high commission in causes ecclesiastical, was erected and united to the regal power (4 *Inst.* 324.) by virtue of the statute 1 *Eliz. c.* 1. instead of a larger jurisdiction which had before been exercised under the pope's authority. It was intended to vindicate the dignity and peace of the church, by reforming, ordering, and correcting the ecclesiastical state and persons, and all manner of errors, heresies, schisms, abuses, offences, contempts, and enormities. Under the shelter of which very general words, means were found in that and the two succeeding reigns, to vest in the high commissioners extraordinary and almost despotic powers of fining and imprisoning; which they exerted much beyond the degree of the offence itself, and frequently over offences by no means of spiritual cognizance. For these reasons this court was justly abolished by stat. 16 *Car.* 1. *c.* 11. And the weak and illegal attempt that was made to revive it, during the reign of king James the second, served only to hasten that infatuated prince's ruin. 3 *Black.* 67.

HIGH CONSTABLE OF ENGLAND. The lord high constable of England was to regulate all manner of chivalry, tilts, tournaments, and feats of arms, which were performed on horseback: this great office of lord high constable hath been disused in England, except only upon great and solemn occasions, as the king's coronation, or the like, ever since the attainder of Stafford, duke of Buckingham, under king Henry VIII.; and from hence it is said that the lower order of constables originated. 1 *Black.* 355. See *Constable.*

HIGH MISDEMEANORS. See *Impeachment, Misprisions.*

HIGH TREASON. See *Treason.*

HIGHWAYS. (*via regia*) It is said that there are three kinds of ways: *first*, a footway, which is called in Latin *iter.* *Secondly*, a pack and prime way, which is both a horse and foot way, and called in Latin *actus.* *Thirdly*, a cartway, called in Latin *via* or *aditus*, which contains the other two, as well as a cartway. *Co. Lit.* 56.

And it seems that any of the said ways, which is common to all the king's subjects, whether it leads directly to a market town, or only from town to town, may properly be called a highway, and that any such cartway may be called the king's highway; and that a river common to all men, may also be called a highway; and that nuisances in any of the said ways are punishable by indictment, for otherwise they would not be punished at all, inasmuch as it seems to be certain, that it is not punishable by action, because if one man might bring his action in respect of the possibility of the damage which he might receive from it, all other men might do the like, which would introduce a multiplicity of actions. 1 *Hawk. c.* 76. *s.* 1.

And it hath been holden, that if there be a highway in an open field, and the people have used, time out of mind, when the ways are bad, to go by outlets on the land adjoining, such outlets are parcel of the way, for the king's subjects ought to have a good passage*, and the good passage is the way, and not the beaten track only; from whence it follows, that if such outlets be sown with corn, and the beaten track be founderous, the king's subjects may justify going upon the corn. 1 *Rol. Abr.* 390. *Comyn's Dig.* tit. *Chimin* (A 1.) *Cro. Car.* 366. 4 *Vin. Abr.* 502. 1 *Hawk. c.* 76. *s.* 2.

But in regard to private ways there is a difference; for although they may be rendered impassable, either by want of repair, or by the overflowing of a river; yet it seems that those who have the right of way cannot justify going over the adjoining land, unless they are entitled to a way generally over the river; for if the grant be not of a way generally over the land, or the owner be bound, either by prescription or his own agreement, to repair, or provide against the overflowing of the land, but of a precise specific way, it authorizes the use of a particular line only, and does not give a right to go either on the right or the left. 2 *Doug.* 8vo. *ed.* 748.

A way to a parish-church, or to the common fields of a town, or perhaps to a village which terminates there, and is for the benefit

---

* For highways are for the public service; and if the usual track is impassable, it is for the general good that people should be entitled to pass in another line. 2 *Doug.* 647.

of the particular inhabitants, of such parish, house or village only, may be called a private way, but not a highway, because it belongeth not to all the king's subjects, but only to some particular persons, each of which, as it seems, may have an action on the case for a nuisance thereon. 1 *Hawk. c.* 76. *s.* 1.

So a private way may be from a meadow, or close to a street, or to an highway; or from one part of a close, across the ground of another, to another part of the same land. *Comyn's Dig.* tit. *Chimin* (D 1).

And a private way may be claimed by prescription, reservation, or grant, or for necessity. 6 *Mod. Rep.* 3.

By prescription, as where a man can shew no other right than that he, and those under whom he claims, have immemorially used to enjoy it.

By reservation or grant, as if A grants, that B shall have a way through such a close. *Comyn's Dig.* tit. *Chimin* (D 3).

By necessity; as where a man has land surrounded by the lands of another, in such case he shall have a way through the land of the other, for the necessity. *Mod. Cas.* 3.

So if a man has title to a wreck, he has a right to have a way over the land of another where the wreck lies, to take it of necessity. 6 *Mod. Rep.* 149.

The grantee of a way has power to amend it as incident to the grant. *Godb.* 53. 1 *Sand.* 323.

But if a man grants a way through his close to another, the grantor is not bound to keep it in repair, if it be foundrous. 1 *Sand.* 322.

For by common law, those who have the use and benefit of the way ought to repair it. 2 *Doug.* 8*vo. ed.* 748.

And if the commissioners under an inclosure act set out a private road for the use of the inhabitants of nine different parishes, directing the inhabitants of six of those parishes to keep it in repair, no indictment can be supported against the latter for not repairing it, for the known rule is that those matters only that concern the public are the subject of an indictment, and it having been in this case described to be a private road, the court held that it neither concerned the public, nor could be taken to be of a public nature, but merely concerned the individual who had a right to use it, and the circumstance of its having been set out under a public act of parliament did not make it an indictable offence. 8 *Ter. Rep.* 634.

Also if an act for dividing and enclosing certain lands enacts, that the public roads to be set out by the commissioners, shall be repaired in such manner as other public roads are by law to be repaired, and that the private roads shall be repaired by such person or persons as they shall award; the commissioners have no authority to impose on the parish at large, the burden of repairing any of the private roads set out in pursuance of the act, but only on those individuals for whose benefit they are made. 8 *Ter. Rep.* 20.

But if a man be bound, either by prescription or his own agreement, to repair, he ought; and if the way become impassable, in such case a passenger may break the fence, and go out of the way, but as near to the same as he possibly can, in order to avoid the bad way. 6 *Mod. Rep.* 163. 1 *Salk.* 358. *Jones*, 296. 2 *Doug.* 8*vo. ed.* 745.

But if the owner of the adjoining land be not so bound, no one can justify going over his ground, although the way be rendered impassable. 2 *Doug.* 8*vo. ed.* 748.

If a common way to church, vill, or the like, be out of repair, he who ought to repair it may be indicted for it. 6 *Mod. Rep.* 163.

And if he be convicted upon the indictment, the court will not set the fine till the justices of peace certify that it is well repaired. 6 *Mod. Rep.* 163.

And if he be fined before the way be repaired, yet a *distringas in infinitum*, shall afterwards go against the party, till the sheriff certify, that the way is in good repair. 1 *Salk.* 359. 6 *Mod. Rep.* 163.

But those who are bound to repair, are not obliged to put it in better condition than has been time out of mind, but as it has been usually at the best. 1 *Salk.* 359.

And if one grants me a way, and afterwards digs trenches in it to my hindrance, I may fill them up again: but if a way which a man has, becomes not passable, or becomes very bad, by the owner of the land tearing it up with his carts, so that the same be filled with water; yet he who has the way cannot dig the ground to let out the water; for he has no interest in the soil. *Godb.* 52, 53.

But in such case he may have his action upon the case against the wrong doer. *Lut.* 111. 3 *Lev.* 266. 1 *Vent.* 275. 2 *Vent.* 186.

So if a man hath a private way without a gate, and a gate is hung up, an action lies upon the case; for he has not his way as he had before. *Litt.* 267.

Or he who has such right of way, may justify the breaking of the gate so erected, through which he could not pass. 3 *Lev.* 92. 2 *Mod.* 66. 1 *Burrows* 266.

Though every highway is said to be the king's, yet this must be understood so as that in every highway, the king and his subjects may pass and repass at their pleasure. 1 *Rol. Abr.* 392. 4 *Viner* 515.

But the freehold, and all the profits belong to the lord of the soil; or to the owner of the lands on both sides the way. 1 *Rol. Abr.* 392. 4 *Vin.* 515.

And so do all the trees upon it, and mines under it, and which may be extremely valuable. 1 *Burrows* 143.

And the lord or owner of the soil may maintain an action of trespass for digging the ground. 1 *Rol. Abr.* 392. 4 *Vin. Abr.* 515. 2 *Strange* 1004.

But the lord of a rape within which there are ten hundreds, may prescribe to have all the trees growing within any highway within his rape, though the manor or soil adjoining belongs to another; for usage to take the trees is a good badge of ownership. 1 *Rol. Abr.* 392. 4 *Vin.* 515.

And in a modern case it is reported, that lord Mansfield said, where no person claims the property of the lands on either side of the highway, the presumption is in favour of the lord of the manor; but if the highway goes through the property of others, the presumption is in favour of the owner of the land on each side, but in either case the presumption only stands till the contrary be proved. *Anonymous Cas.* M. 13 *Geo.* 3. *Lofl's Rep.* 358.

And if a man make a street upon his own ground, it is a dedication to the public, so far as the public has occasion for it, *viz.* for a right of passage only; but it is not to be understood as a transfer of the absolute property in the soil: the owner may therefore have his action of trespass for any encroachment on the soil. 2 *Strange* 1004.

And the owner of the soil may bring an ejectment for the land, subject, however, to the servitude or easement of a passage over it, as the king's highway. 1 *Burrows* 143.

By the common law, an ancient highway cannot be changed without the king's licence first obtained upon a writ of *ad quod damnum*, and an inquisition thereon found by a jury that such a change will not be prejudicial to the public. 1 *Hawk. c.* 76. *s* 3.

And it seems, that it is not necessary for the sheriff to give formal notice of the execution of the writ; it is sufficient if the jury be summoned impartially, and the inquisition be taken in a fair and open manner. *Ex parte Vennor, Hil.* 1754. 3 *Atkyns* 766.

But this inquisition being a proceeding *ex-parte*, it is traversable: that is, the party grieved may traverse or deny the matter of fact found by the inquisition, and put it in a course of trial, by the common law process of the court of chancery.

And if the party traverse the inquisition, and issue be taken thereon and a verdict found, he cannot apply to the court of chancery upon a suggestion of surprize, and a fraudulent and clandestine execution of the writ, for the traverse is a waiver of any objection in that respect. 3 *Atkyns* 770.

But this course of proceeding by way of traverse being both expensive and dilatory, a more speedy remedy is given by 13 *Geo.* 3. c. 78. by allowing an appeal to the justices of the peace in such cases.

For it is enacted by that statute, *sec.* 19, that it shall be lawful for any person injured or aggrieved by the inclosure of any road or highway, by virtue of any inquisition taken, upon any writ of *ad quod damnum*, to appeal to the next general quarter sessions, giving ten days notice to the party interested, if there be time for that purpose; if not, to the next sessions after: and the determination of such sessions shall be final.

Though the appeal is directed to the next quarter sessions, yet the justices may adjourn the quarter sessions itself to another day, or they may adjourn the particular matter to a subsequent sessions. And this appeal was thought, by lord Hardwicke, to be a waiver to any objection of surprize, or mal-execution of the writ: because the statute has put the justices in the room of the traverse, upon which, as has been before observed, no such objection could be taken. 3 *Atkyns* 770.

It is also certain, that the highway may be changed by the act of God; and therefore it hath been holden, that if a water which has been an ancient highway, by degrees changes its course, and goes over different ground from that wherein it used to run; yet the highway continues in the new channel in the same manner as in the old. 1 *Hawk. c.* 76. *s.* 4.

Of common right, the general charge of repairing all highways lies on the occupiers of the lands in the parish wherein they are, unless by prescription they can throw the burthen on particular persons by reason of their tenure. 1 *Hawk. c.* 76. *s.* 5. 4 *Burrows Rep.* 2511, 5 *Burrows Rep.* 2702. 2 *Term Rep.* 111

And as the repair of the highway lies of common right upon the whole parish; the indictment, notwithstanding the parish lies part in one county and the rest in another, must be preferred against the whole parish, and must be laid in that county where the ruinous road lies.

Also as the inhabitants of a parish are bound to repair all highways within their boundaries, they cannot be discharged from such liability by any agreement with others. 3 *East's Rep.* 86.

It is also said that the tenants of the land adjoining the highway are bound to scour their ditches. 1 *Hawk. c.* 76. *s.* 5.

And it is certain, that particular persons may be burthened with the general charge of repairing the highway in two cases; first, in respect of an inclosure of the land wherein it lies, and secondly, in respect of a prescription. 1 *Hawk. c.* 76. *s.* 5.

First. A particular person may be bound to repair an highway in respect of an inclosure, as where the owner of lands not inclosed, next adjoining to the highway, incloses his lands on both sides thereof *, in which

---

* This he may lawfully do, of his own authority, but he is bound to leave sufficient space and room for the road, and he is obliged to repair it so long as he continues his inclosure. 1 *Burrows* 465.

case he is bound to make a perfect good way, and shall not be excused for making it as good as it was at the time of the inclosure, if it were then any way defective; because, before the inclosure, the people used, when the way was bad, to go for their better passage over the fields adjoining out of the common track; which liberty is taken away by the inclosure. 1 *Hawk. c.* 76. *s.* 6.

And if the way is not sufficient, any passenger may break down the inclosure, and go over the land and justify it, till a sufficient way is made. 3 *Salk.* 182.

And it hath been holden, that if one inclose land on one side which hath been anciently inclosed on the other side, he ought to repair all the way, but if there be not such an ancient inclosure of the other side, he ought to repair but half that way. 1 *Siderfin* 464. 1 *Hawk. c.* 76. *s.* 7.

And so if one person makes an hedge on one side of the way, and another person makes an hedge on the other side of the way, they shall be chargeable to the repair thereof by moieties. 1 *Sider.* 464.

But it seems that a man is bound to repair a highway in respect of an inclosure, no longer than whilst it continues; for if he lays it open again as it was before, he shall be freed from the charge of repairing it. 1 *Siderfin.* 464. 1 *Hawk. c.* 76. *s.* 7. 4 *Burrows Rep.* 465.

And if he alter or change the road by the legal course of a writ of *ad quod damnum*, he is not obliged to repair the new road, unless the jury impose such a condition upon him; for if they do not, the repair of the road stands just as it did before: even though it was at first open, and should be directed by the jury to be inclosed. 1 *Burrows* 465.

For when a new road is made in pursuance of such writ, and inquisition thereupon found, it is incumbent on the parishioners to keep it in repair; because being discharged from the repairing the old road, no new burthen is laid upon them: their labour is only transferred from one place to another. 3 *Atk.* 766.

But if the new road lies in another parish, then the person who sued out the writ, and his heirs, ought not only to make it, but to keep it in repair; because the parishioners of such other parish gaining no benefit from the old road being taken away, it would be imposing a new charge upon them, for which they enjoyed no compensation. *Ibid.*

And a private act of parliament for inclosing common fields or other lands, which vests a power in commissioners to set out new roads by their award, is equally strong, as to these consequences as a writ of *ad quod damnum;* therefore, unless it is otherwise directed in the act, the repair of such new roads clearly stands as it did before, and must by operation of law, fall on the parish or township; and this is but reasonable; for if the person to whom an allotment was made near the highway, was to be obliged to repair, it might make a vast difference in the value of the lands respectively allotted to each person: for one person's allotment might perhaps run along very far by the side of the highway, and another person's allotment not lie at all near it. 1 *Burrows* 465.

But if the inhabitants of a township, bound by prescription to repair the roads within the township, be expressly exempted by the provisions of a road act, from the charge of repairing new roads to be made within the township; then the charge must necessarily fall on the rest of the parish. *The K.* v. *Sheffield, Mic.* 28 *Geo.* 3. 2 *Term Rep.* 106.

However, if an indictment for non-repair of a highway within certain limits, charge a corporation with a prescriptive liability to repair all common highways, within such limits, except such as ought to be repaired according to the form of the several statutes in such case made, it must also contain an averment that the highway in question is not within any of the exceptions; for the circumstance of a statute being public, does not take away the necessity of such averment. 3 *East's Rep.* 86.

And if the trustees under a road act, turn a road through an inclosure, and make the fences at their own expence, and repair them for several years, they cannot be compelled to continue such repairs, unless there be a special provision in the act to that effect. 3 *Term Rep.* 232.

Secondly, A particular person may be bound to repair a highway in respect of a prescription. 1 *Hawk. c.* 76. *s.* 8.

And it is said, that a corporation aggregate, may be compelled to do it by force of a general prescription, that it ought, and hath used to do it, without shewing that it used to do so in respect of the tenure of certain lands, or for any other consideration, because such a corporation in judgment of law never dies; and therefore, if it were ever bound to such a duty, it must needs continue to be always so; neither is it any plea, that such corporation have always done it out of charity; for what it hath always done, it shall be presumed to have been always bound to do. 1 *Hawk. c.* 76. *s.* 8.

But it is said, that a person cannot be charged with such a duty by a general prescription from what his ancestors have done, because no one is bound to do what his ancestors have done, unless it be for some special reason, as the having lands descended from such ancestors, which are holden by such like service: yet it seems, that an indictment charging a tenant in fee-simple, with having used of right to repair such a way by reason of the tenure of his land, is certain enough, without adding that his ancestors or those whose estate he hath, have always so done; for that is implied, in saying, that he has always used to do it, by reason of his tenure. 1 *Hawk. c.* 76. *s.* 8.

But the indictment must set forth where those lands lie. 2 *Hale's Hist.* 181.

And it seems certain, that, whether a particular person be bound to repair a highway by inclosure or prescription; yet the parish cannot take advantage of it, upon the plea of not guilty to an indictment against them for not repairing it, but ought to set forth their discharge in a special plea. 1 *Hawk. c.* 76. *s.* 9.

And it is not enough to allege generally, that a particular division or district, from the time whereof the memory of man is not, to the contrary, ought to repair and amend, when and so often as it shall be necessary: for the inhabitants of the parish at large being bound by common law and of common right to repair highways, it must be expressly shewn why the inhabitants of a particular division or district are obliged to repair. 5 *Burrows* 2702. 2 *Term Rep.* 513.

It therefore must be shewn that they have immemorially repaired, and have used and been accustomed, and of right ought, to repair and amend. 5 *Burrows* 2702.

This being the general law of the land in relation to highways, the stat. 13 *Geo.* 3. c. 78. was passed for the more readily enforcing the reparation thereof.

This act has been amended by subsequent acts, and the whole are too voluminous to be noticed in this work, except in the following particulars.

Statute duty.] By 34 *Geo.* 3. *c.* 74. the surveyor, together with the inhabitants and occupiers of lands, tenements, woods, tithes, and hereditaments, shall, at proper seasons, in every year, use their endeavours for the repair of the highways, and shall be chargeable thereto as followeth: that is to say,

Every person keeping a waggon, cart, wain, plough, or tumbrel, and three or more horses or beasts of draught used to draw the same, shall be deemed to keep a team, draught, or plough, and be liable to perform statute duty with the same, in the parish, township, or place where he resides, and shall six days in every year, (if so many days be found necessary,) to be computed from Michaelmas to Michaelmas, send on every day, and at every place, to be appointed by the surveyor, for amending the highways in such parish, township, or place, one wain, cart, or carriage, furnished after the custom of the country with oxen, horses, or other cattle, and all other necessaries fit to carry things for that purpose, and also two able men with the same: which duty so performed, shall excuse every such person from his duty in such parish, township, or place, in respect of all lands, tenements, goods, tithes, or hereditaments, not exceeding the annual value of 50*l.* which he shall occupy therein. *s.* 4.

Every person keeping such team, draught, or plough, and occupying in the same parish, township, or place, lands, tenements, woods, tithes, or hereditaments of the yearly value of 50*l.* over and beyond the said yearly value of 50*l.* in respect whereof such team duty shall be performed;—and every such person occupying lands, tenements, woods, tithes, or hereditaments, of the yearly value of 50*l.* in any other parish, township, or place, besides that wherein he resides;—and every other person, not keeping a team, draught, or plough, but occupying lands, tenements, woods, tithes, or hereditaments of the yearly value of 50*l.* in any parish, township, or place:—shall find and send one wain, cart, or carriage, furnished with not less than three horses, or four oxen and one horse, or two oxen and two horses, and two able men to each wain, cart, or carriage: and in like manner for every 50*l.* a year respectively, which every such person shall further occupy in any parish, township, or place respectively: such wains, carts, or carriages to be employed by the surveyor in repairing the highways within the parish, township, or place where such estate lies. *Ibid.*

Every person who shall not keep a team, draught, or plough, but shall occupy such estate under the yearly value of 50*l.* in the parish, township, or place where he resides, or in any other parish, township, or place;—and every person keeping a team, draught, or plough, and occupying such estate under the yearly value of 50*l.* in any other parish, township, or place than that wherein he resides;—shall respectively contribute to the repair of the highways, and pay to the surveyor, in lieu of such duty, the sums following; *viz.* for every 20*s.* of the annual value of such lands, tenements, woods, tithes, or hereditaments, one penny for every day's statute duty; and in like manner shall pay one penny for every 20*s.* of the annual value of such estate which he shall occupy in any such parish, township, or place respectively, above the annual value of 50*l.* and less than 100*l.*; and so for every 20*s.* that each progressive and intermediate annual value of 20*s.* which he shall so occupy, shall fall short of the further increase of 50*l.* in every parish, township, or place where such lands, tenements, woods, tithes, and hereditaments shall respectively lie, for every day's statute duty so to be required as aforesaid. *Ibid.*

Provided, that no person keeping such team, draught, or plough, and performing duty with the same as aforesaid, in the parish, township, or place where he resides, and not occupying lands, tenements, woods, tithes, or hereditaments within the same, of the yearly value of 30*l.* shall be obliged to send more than one labourer, with such team, draught, or plough. *Ibid.*

All which said several sums shall be considered as compositions, and shall be paid to the surveyor, at the time the compositions are to be paid under the authority of the act, or within ten days after; or in default of such payments, the surveyor shall apply to a justice acting for such district, who shall summon such defaulter to appear at some special or petty sessions to be holden for such district, at which two justices, at the least, shall be present, to shew cause why he refused or neglected to pay; and in default of appearance, or if on appearance he shall not make it appear to the satisfaction of such justices, that he is poor and indigent, and as such an object deserving relief; such money shall be levied by distress, in like manner as the forfeitures for neglect of statute duty. Provided, that when the justices shall discharge any poor person from payment of such rate or composition money, such person shall, at the same time, be discharged from any expences in consequence thereof. *Ibid.*

Every person who shall not keep a team, draught, or plough, but shall keep one or more cart or carts, and one or two horses or beasts of draught only, used to draw in each of such carts upon the highways, shall be obliged to perform his statute duty for the like number of days, with such cart or carts, and horse or horses, or beasts of draught, and one labourer to attend each cart; or to pay for the lands, tenements, woods, tithes, and hereditaments, which he shall occupy, according to the rate herein-after mentioned, at the option of the surveyor. *s.* 2.

Every person who shall keep a coach, post-chaise, chair, or other wheel carriage, and not keep a team, draught, or plough, nor occupy 50*l.* a-year in the parish, township, or place where he resides, shall pay to the surveyor 1*s.* in respect of every such day's statute duty, for every horse which he shall draw in any such carriage; or shall pay according to the value of the lands, tenements, or hereditaments which he shall occupy, at the option of the surveyor. *Ibid.*

And if the teams, draughts, or ploughs, or any of them, shall not be thought needful by the surveyor, on any of the said days; then every such person who should have sent any such team, draught, or plough according to the directions aforesaid, shall, according to the notice given to him by the surveyor, send unto the said work, for every one so spared, three able men; or pay 4*s.* 6*d.* in lieu thereof, at the option of the surveyor. *Ibid.*

And where the employment for teams is of such sort, that two horses will be sufficient for one cart, or where a stand cart with one horse shall be necessary, the surveyor may call upon any person liable to send a team, draught, or plough, according to this act, who keeps one or more cart or carts, and three or more horses, to send such cart or carts, horse or horses, to perform his statute duty, as the surveyor shall find most convenient; and he shall allow every such stand cart and one horse as half a team, and every cart and two horses as two thirds of a team. And if a waggon shall be found necessary for any particular business, the surveyor may require the duty, or any part thereof, to be performed with such waggon by any person who keeps one. Which directions of the surveyor shall be observed, or the person liable to perform such duty shall forfeit such sum as the duty so required of him shall bear, in proportion to the forfeiture hereby inflicted for every neglect in performing duty with a team, draught, or plough. 13 *Geo.* 3. *c.* 78. *s.* 36.

But by 42 *Geo.* 3. *c.* 90. no serjeant, corporal, or drummer of the militia, nor any private man, from the time of his inrolment until his discharge, shall be obliged to perform any highway duty, commonly called statute work. *s.* 174.

The surveyor shall give to, or cause to be left at the abode of every person liable to perform such duty, four days notice at least, of the day, hour, and place, upon which each of the day's duty shall be to be performed. 13 *Geo.* 3. *c.* 78. *s.* 37.

And all persons shall have and bring with them such shovels, spades, picks, mattocks, and other tools, as are useful. *s.* 37. 34 *Geo.* 3. *c.* 74. *s.* 2.

And all the said persons and carriages shall diligently perform the work to which they shall be appointed by such surveyor for eight hours in every day, within such parish, or in getting materials in and from any other parish, to be employed in the repair of the highways of the parish, for which they shall perform duty. *Ibid.*

And if any person sending a team, shall not send a sufficient labourer besides the driver (except as before mentioned) or if any such labourer or driver, or any other labourer, or the driver of any cart, shall refuse to work, during the time above mentioned, according to the direction of the surveyor; or if any driver shall refuse to carry proper loads, it shall be lawful for such surveyor to discharge such team, cart, or labourer, and to recover from the owner the forfeiture which such person would have incurred, in case no such team, &c. had been sent. *Ibid.*

And every person making default in finding and sending such wain, cart, or carriage, furnished as aforesaid, and such able men with the same, as herein required, or in performing the said duty in manner by this act directed, shall, for every default, forfeit 10*s.*—For every default in sending a cart with one horse and one man, 3*s.*—and for not sending a cart with two horses and one man, 5*s.* And every person making default in sending such labourer, and every person making default in performing such labour at the time and place, and in manner directed by this act, or in paying composition-money for the same, shall, for every such neglect, forfeit 1*s.* 6*d.* all which forfeitures shall be applied for the use of the highways within the parish. 13 *Geo.* 3. *c.* 78. *s.* 37.

And the surveyor shall equally demand such duty from every person liable, without favour. *s.* 37.

And if in any parish, it shall not be necessary to call forth the whole duty in any year, it shall be abated in proportion amongst all persons liable. *s.* 37.

By 44 *Geo.* 3. *c.* 52. any persons liable to perform statute duty, by sending one or more teams, draughts, or ploughs, with men, horses, or oxen, in manner mentioned in the 34 *Geo.* 3. *c.* 74. may compound for the same, if they shall think fit, by paying to the surveyor of the highways, at the time, and in the manner mentioned in the 13 *Geo.* 3. such sums of money as the justices for the limits wherein the parish, township, or place for which the said duty is liable to be performed, is situate, or the major part of them, at their special session to be held in the first week after Michaelmas quarter session in every year, shall adjudge and declare to be reasonable, not exceeding 12*s.* nor less than 3*s.* for each team, draught, or plough, for each day; and in default of their adjudging and declaring the same, 6*s.* for and in lieu of every day's duty for each team, draught, or plough; and for each cart with two horses or beasts of draught, not exceeding 8*s.* nor less than 3*s.* and in default of their adjudging and declaring the same, the sum of 4*s.* and for each cart with one horse or beast of draught, not exceeding 6*s.* nor less than 2*s.* and in default of their adjudging and declaring the same, the sum of 3*s.* *s.* 2.

"And, whereas it may frequently happen, "that persons wholly gaining their liveli- "hood by the wages of daily labour, and "occupying rateable tenements within a pa- "rish, by reason of age, sickness, a numer- "ous family, or misfortune, may be in poor "and indigent circumstances, and it may "be expedient in certain cases to discharge "such persons from all rates, assessments, "or compositions whatsoever;" It is therefore enacted, that on the application of any poor and indigent person to be discharged from the rate or composition, made to any two justices at any special or petty sessions, held for the limits wherein such poor and indigent person shall reside, the said justices (having first given notice to the surveyor to appear on the part of the parish) shall inquire and examine into the situation and circumstances of the person making such application; and if it shall appear to the satisfaction of such justices that such person is really poor and indigent, and a deserving object of such relief, the said justices may exempt such poor and indigent person from the payment of all rates, assessments, or compositions whatsoever. 34 *Geo.* 3. *c.* 74. *s.* 5.

But if it appear to the justices, at their special sessions, to be held in the week next after Michaelmas quarter sessions, or at any other special or petty sessions, held within the limits of any parish, at which two or more justices shall be present, that, from the directions before given for performing and compounding the statute duty, there will be difficulty in procuring the necessary carriage, or a sufficient number of labourers for the repair of the highways, in any particular parish, within their limits, without paying high prices for the same; it shall be lawful for such justices to order the team duty hereby required, or so much thereof as they think fit, to be performed in kind, within every parish, &c. except in respect of such teams as belong to persons who do not occupy lands, &c. of the annual value of 30*l.* within the same; and also to order all such persons as shall gain their living by the wages of daily labour, or such part of them as they shall think fit, to perform six days labour upon such highways in kind, either by themselves or others, in case so many days duty shall be required, upon being paid for such labour the usual wages given to labourers in such parish. 34 *Geo.* 3. *c.* 74. *s.* 6.

But if part of such teams or labourers only are required, it shall be directed by the said order of the justices in some given proportion, as one half, third, or fourth part thereof; and the surveyor shall, in that case, at a public vestry for such parish, put the names of all persons liable to send such teams, into one hat or box, and the names of all persons liable to perform such labour into another hat or box, and some inhabitant then present shall draw out such number from each as shall be equal to the proportion ordered by the justices, and the persons drawn, shall perform such duty in kind for that year, and if such order shall be made or continued in the subsequent year, the same method shall be observed, but the names drawn in the preceding year shall not be put into such hat or box; and in every succeeding year, such method shall be observed by such surveyor, so as to render the duty to be performed in kind equal amongst the persons liable thereto; which order of the justices, so far as the same shall be extended, shall supersede the power or liberty of compounding, and shall be binding, and shall continue in force until discharged or varied by the justices at some subsequent special sessions for the highways within such limit, to be held in the week after Michaelmas quarter sessions. *s.* 6.

And if any person shall keep a team, and shall not occupy lands, &c. of 30*l.* per ann. in the parish where he shall reside, but shall in part maintain his horses and beasts of draught used in such team upon lands in adjacent parishes, it shall be lawful for the justices, at some special sessions, to mitigate the duty or composition, as they think just. 13 *Geo.* 3. *c.* 78. *s.* 40.

—— *Nuisance to the highway.*] There is no doubt that all injuries whatsoever to any highway, as by digging a ditch, or making a hedge over thwart it, or laying logs of timber in it, or by doing any other act, which will render it less commodious to the king's people, are public nuisances at common law. *Kitch.* 34, 35.

Also it seems to be clear, that it is no excuse for one who lays such logs in the highway, that he only laid them here and there, so that the people might have a passage by windings and turnings through the logs: yet it is said to be no nuisance for the inhabitants of a town to unlade billits, &c. in the street before their houses, by reason of the necessity of the case, unless they suffer them to continue there an unreasonable time, after they are unloaded. 2 *Rol. Abr.* 137, 265. 1 *Hawk. c.* 76. *s.* 49.

A gate erected in a highway is also a common nuisance, because it interrupts the people in that free and open passage which they before enjoyed and were entitled to; but where such gate has continued time out of mind, it shall be intended, that it was set out at first by consent, on a composition with the owner of the land on the laying out the road, in which case the people had never any right to a freer passage than what they still enjoy. 1 *Hawk. c.* 75. *s.* 9.

Also it seems clear, that it is a like nuisance to suffer the ditches adjoining to a highway to be foul, by reason whereof it is impaired, or to suffer the boughs of trees growing near the highway to hang over the road, in such a manner as thereby to incommode the passage. 1 *Hawk. c.* 76. *s.* 50.

And not only all the above-mentioned nuisances, which are such at common law, are esteemed also nuisances by statute; but there is one particular nuisance which is made such by the statute, and doth not seem to be taken notice of at common law, and that is the drawing of a travelling carriage with a greater number of horses than the statute permits. 1 *Hawk. c.* 76. *s.* 51.

It is said that one convicted of a nuisance done to the king's highway, may be commanded by the judgment to remove the nuisance at his own costs. 1 *Hawk. c.* 75. *s.* 14.

Also it seems to be certain, that at common law, any one may pull down or otherwise destroy a common nuisance, as a new gate, or even a new house erected in a highway, (that is, he may take down and remove the materials, but not convert them to his own use, 1 *Hawk. c.* 76. *s.* 61.); for if one whose estate is, or may be prejudiced by a private nuisance actually erected, as a house hanging over his ground, or stopping his lights, may justify the entering into another's ground, and pulling down and destroying such a nuisance, whether it were erected before or since he came to the estate, it cannot but follow much more that any one may lawfully destroy a common nuisance. 1 *Hawk. c.* 75. *s.* 12. *c.* 76. *s.* 61.

HIGHWAY ROBBERY. Open and violent larceny from the person, or robbery, the *rapina* of the civilians, is the felonious and forcible taking from the person of another of goods or money to any value, by violence, or putting him in fear. (1 *Hawk. P. C.* 95.) But 1st, There must be a taking, otherwise it is no robbery. And a mere attempt to rob, though held to be felony so late as Henry the Fourth's time, (1 *Hale's P. C.* 532) was afterwards taken to be only a misdemeanor, and punishable with fine and imprisonment, till the statute 7 *Geo.* 2. *c.* 21, which makes it a felony (transportable for seven years) unlawfully and maliciously to assault another, with any offensive weapon or instrument; or by menaces, or by other forcible or violent manner, to demand any money or goods; *with a felonious intent to rob.* If the thief, having once taken a purse, returns it, still it is a robbery; and so it is whether the taking be strictly from the person of another, or in his presence only: as, where a robber by menaces and violence puts a man in fear, and drives away his sheep or his cattle before his face. (1 *Hal. P. C.* 533.) But if the taking be not either directly from his person, or in his presence, it is no robbery. (*Comyns*, 478. *Stra.* 1015.) 2ndly, It is immaterial of what value the thing taken is; a penny as well as a pound thus forcibly extorted makes a robbery. (1 *Hawk. P. C.* 97.) 3. Lastly, the taking must be by force, or a previous putting in fear, which makes the violation of the person more atrocious than privately stealing. For, according to the maxim of the civil law, (*Ff.* 4. 2. 14. *s.* 12,) "*qui vi rapuit, fur improbior esse videtur,*" this previous violence, or putting in fear, is the criterion that distinguishes robbery from other larcenies. For if one privately steals sixpence from the person of another, and afterwards keeps it by putting him in fear, this is no robbery, for the fear is subsequent, (1 *Hal. P. C.* 534.) neither is it capital, as privately stealing, being under the value of twelvepence. Not that it is indeed necessary, though usual, to lay in the indictment that the robbery was committed by putting in fear, it is sufficient if laid to be done by violence. (*Trin.* 3 *Ann.* by all the judges.) And when it is laid to be done by putting in fear, this does not imply any great degree of terror or affright in the party robbed; it is enough that so much force, or threatening by word or gesture, be used, as might create an apprehension of danger, or induce a man to part with his property without or against his consent. (*Fost.* 128.) And Mr. J. Ashhurst is reported to have thus expressed himself in delivering the opinion of the judges in Willan's case, *Leach.* 232: "The true definition of robbery is "the stealing, or taking from the person, "or in the presence of another, property of "any amount, with such a degree of force "or terror as to induce the party unwillingly "to part with his property, and whether the "terror arises from real or expected vio- "lence to the person, or from a sense of in- "jury to the character, the law makes no "kind of difference, for to most men the "idea of losing their fame and reputation "is equally if not more terrific than the "dread of personal injury. The principal "ingredient in robbery is a man's being "forced to part with his property; and the "judges are unanimously of opinion that "upon the principles of law, and the au- "thority of former decisions, a threat to "accuse a man of having committed the "greatest of all crimes is a sufficient force "to constitute the crime of robbery by "putting in fear"

This distinction has been frequently admitted by the judges in prosecutions for robbery, *viz.* that if any thing is snatched suddenly from the head, hand, or person of any one without any struggle on the part of the owner, or without any evidence of force or violence being exerted by the thief, it does not amount to robbery. But if any thing is broken or torn in consequence of the sudden seizure, it would be evidence of such force as would constitute a robbery; as where part of a lady's hair was torn away by snatching a diamond pin from her head, and an ear was torn by pulling off an ear-ring, each of these cases was determined to be a robbery. *Leach.* 238.

So if a man be knocked down without previous warning, and stripped of his property while senseless, though strictly he cannot be said to be put in fear, yet this is undoubtedly a robbery. Or if a person with a sword drawn begs an alms, and I give it him through mistrust and apprehension of violence, this is a felonious robbery. (1 *Hawk. P. C.* 96.) Also if under a pretence of sale a man forcibly extorts money from another neither shall this subterfuge avail him. But it is doubted whether the forcing a higler, or other chapman to sell his wares, and giving him the full value of them, amounts to so heinous a crime as robbery. 4 *Black.* 243, 4.

This species of larceny is debarred of the benefit of clergy by stat. 23 *Hen.* 8, *c.* 1. and other subsequent statutes; not indeed in general, but only when committed in a dwelling-house, or in or near the king's highway. A robbery therefore in a distant field, or foot-path, was not punished with death, (1 *Hal. P. C.* 535.) but was open to the benefit of clergy, till the stat. 3 & 4 *Wil. & M. c.* 9, which takes away clergy from both principals and accessories before the fact, in robbery, wheresoever committed.

And by the 5 *Geo.* 3. *c.* 25, and 7 *Geo.* 3. *c.* 50, If any person shall rob any mail, in which letters are sent by the post, of any letter, packet, bag or mail of letters, such offender shall be guilty of felony, without benefit of clergy; but the indictments for mail robberies are generally drawn as for common highway robberies by taking a portmanteau, or a bag of a certain value from the person intrusted with the carriage of the letters.

A reward of 40*l.* is given for the apprehending and taking of a highwayman, to be paid within a month after conviction, by the sheriff of the county, &c. Stat. 4 & 5 *W. & M. c.* 8.

HIGLER, a person who carries from door to door, and sells by retail, small articles of provisions, &c.

HIIS TESTIBUS, words anciently added in deeds, after the *In cujus rei testimonium*; but this clause of *hiis testibus* has been disused since *Hen.* 8. *Co. Lit.* 6. *Cowel. Blount.*

HINDENI HOMINES, (from the Sax. *Hindenc*, i. e. *Societas*) a society of men: In the time of the Saxons, all men were ranked into three classes, and valued, as to satisfaction for injuries, &c. according to the class they were in; the highest were valued at twelve hundred shillings, and were called Twelf-hindmen: the middle class at six hundred shillings, and called Sex-hindmen; and the lowest, at ten pounds or two hundred shillings, called Twy-hindmen: their wives were termed *Hindas. Brompt. Leg. Alfred. cap.* 12, 30, 31. *Cowel. Blount.*

HINE, (Sax.) a servant in husbandry. *Ibid.*

HINEFARE, (Sax. *hine*, a servant, and *fare*, a going or passage) the loss or departure of a servant from his master. *Ibid.*

HINEGELD, *significat quietantiam transgressionis illatæ in servum transgredientem. Ibid.*

HIRCISCUNDA, is the division of an inheritance among heirs. *Ibid.*

HIRD, *domestica vel intrinseca familia. Ibid.*

HIREMAN, a subject, from the Sax. *Hiran*, i. e. *Obedire*, to obey: or it may be one who serves in the king's hall, to guard him; from *hird, aula*, and man, *homo. Du Fresne. Cowel. Blount.*

HIRING. A contract by which a qualified property may be transferred to the hirer. Hiring is always for a price, stipend, or recompence. By this contract the possession and a transient property is transferred for a particular time or use, on condition and agreement to restore the goods, &c. so hired, as soon as the time is expired or use performed; together with the price or stipend, either expressly agreed on by the parties, or left to be implied by law according to the value of the service. 2 *Black*. 453.

HIRST or HURST, a little wood. *Domesday*.

HITHE. See *Hythe*.

HLAFORDSOCNA, the Lord's protection; from the Sax. Halford, *dominus*, and *socn*, *libertas*. *Cowel*.

HLASOCNER, the benefit of the law. *Ibid*.

HLOTH, an unlawful company, from seven to thirty-five, cleared by a mulct, called *hlothbota*. *Cowel*.

HLOTHBOTE, Sax. hloth, *turma*, and bote, *compensatio*, a mulct set on him who was in a riot. *Ibid*.

HOAST-MEN, an antient gild, or fraternity at Newcastle upon Tyne, who dealt in sea-coal. *Ibid*.

HOBLERS or HOBILERS, (*Hobellarii*) were light horse-men; or certain tenants bound by their tenure to maintain a little light horse, for giving notice of any invasion made by enemies, or such like peril towards the sea side. *Cowel*.

HOCCUS SALTIS, seems to have been a hoke, hole or lesser pit of salt. *Ibid*.

HOCKETTOR, or HOCQUETEUR, an old French word for a knight of the post, a decayed man, a basket carrier. *Ibid*.

HOCK-TUESDAY-MONEY, a duty formerly given to the landlord that his tenants and bondmen might solemnise that day on which the English mastered the Danes, being the second Tuesday after Easter week. *Cowel*.

HOGA, HOGIUM, HOCH (from the Germ. *hoogh*, *altus*), a mountain or hill. *Ibid*.

HOGASTER (*hogastrum*), a little hog; also a young sheep. *Ibid*.

HOGENHINE, (Sax.) was one that came guest-wise to an inn or house, and lying there the third night was accounted as, and became, one of the family. *Ibid*.

HOGGACIUS, HOGGASTER, a sheep of the second year. And in many, especially the northern parts of England, sheep after they lose the name of lambs are called hogs, as in Kent, tags. *Cowel*.

HOGSHEAD, a vessel containing in liquid measure 63 gallons, being half a pipe, and the fourth part of a tun. 1 *Ric*. 3. *c*. 3.

HOGGUS, HOGIETUS, a hog or swine, beyond the growth of a pig. *Cowel*.

HOGS. The keeping of hogs in any city or market-town is indictable as a public nuisance. *Salk*. 460. 4 *Black*. 167.

HOKE-DAY, otherwise Hock-Tuesday, (*dies martis, quam quindenam Paschæ vocant*) in ancient times rents were reserved payable thereon; and so called because on that day the women in merriment stopped the ways with ropes, and pulled the passengers to them, desiring something to be laid out in pious uses. *Cowel*.

HOLDES, (from the Sax. *hold*, i. e. *summus præpositus*) bailiffs of a town or city.

HOLDING OVER. By stat. 4 *Geo*. 2. *c*. 28, in case any tenant for life or years, or other person claiming under or by collusion with such tenant, shall wilfully hold over after the determination of the term, and demand made and notice in writing given, by him to whom the remainder or reversion of the premises shall belong, for delivering the possession thereof: such person, so holding over or keeping the other out of possession, shall pay for the time he detains the lands, at the rate of double their yearly value. And, by stat. 11 *Geo*. 2. *c*. 19, in case any tenant, having power to determine his lease shall give notice of his intention to quit the premises, and shall not deliver up the possession at the time contained in such notice, he shall thenceforth pay double the former rent for such time as he continues in possession.

Where a tenant has a lease for a term certain, and holds over after the expiration of it, it is not necessary for the landlord to give him any notice to quit in order to recover possession by ejectment. (1 *Term Rep*. 53. 162.) But if the landlord afterwards receives rent, or does any act by which he proves his assent to the continuance of the tenant, this turns the estate at sufferance into a tenancy from year to year, The notice by 4 *Geo*. 2, *c*. 28, may be given at any time previous to the end of the term, (*Black. Rep*. 1075.) or afterwards, though the double value can only be recovered from the delivery of the notice, and demand of possession. The double value may be recovered though it is not mentioned in the notice to quit. (1 *T. R*. 53.) The notice by the landlord must be in writing, but that by the tenant, under 11 *Geo*. 2, *c*. 19, may be by parol. (3 *Burr*. 1603.) The double value can only be recovered by action of debt, but the double rent may be recovered by distress, or otherwise, like single rent. (1 *Black*. 535.) No length of time is necessary to the validity of these notices under the statutes, to entitle the landlord to double value.

And if the tenant hold over after the expiration of his term, or after the end of the year, when he has had a proper notice to quit, the landlord may turn his cattle upon the premises, but without force, and the cattle cannot be distrained as damage feasant by the tenant. 7 *Term Rep*. 431.

HOLIDAYS. No holidays whatever shall

be permitted or allowed to be kept at the London or other *Wet-docks*, or at any of the *Custom-houses*, or at the chief or any other office of Excise, except *Christmas day*, and *Good Friday*, general *Fasts*, and *Thanksgiving days*, and the anniversaries of the *Restoration* of *Charles* 2, and of the *Coronation* of his Majesty, and the *Birth-days* of their Majesties and the *Prince* of *Wales*. 46 *Geo.* 3, c. 82. 47 *Geo.* 3, *stat.* 1, *c.* 51. 48 *Geo.* 3, *c.* 126. 49 *Geo.* 3, *c.* 66.

And by 39 & 40 *Geo.* 3, *c.* 42, for the better observance of Good Friday, when bills or notes become due on that day they shall be payable on the day before.

The fifth of November is to be kept as a day of thanksgiving, 3 *Jac.* 1, *c.* 1. The 29th of May is to be an anniversary thanksgiving, 12 *Car.* 2. *c.* 14. The 30th of January to be kept as an anniversary day of humiliation, 12 *Car.* 2, *c.* 30, *sec.* 1. The 2d of September to be annually kept as a fast in London, 19 *Car.* 2, *c.* 3, *sec.* 28.

HOLM, (Sax. *hulmus*, *insulas amnica*) an isle or fenny gronnd, or a river-island. A place surrounded with water; as the Flatholmes and Stepholmes in the Severn near Bristol; but if it is not near the water it may then signify a hilly place, holm in Saxon being a hill or cliff. *Cowel.*

HOLT, (Sax.) a wood, wherefore the names of towns beginning or ending with holt, as Buckholt, &c. denote that formerly there was great plenty of wood at those places. *Ibid.*

HOLYHEAD, Rock-salt may be used in its salt-works, 6 *Ann.* c. 12, *sec.* 2.

HOMAGE, (*homagium*) is a French word, derived from *homo*. *Co. Lit.* 64. On the original grants of lands and tenements by way of fee under the feudal system, the lord not only obliged his tenants to certain services, but the vassal or tenant also usually did homage to his lord, openly and humbly kneeling, being ungirt, uncovered, and holding up his hands both together between those of the lord, who sat before him; and there professing, that "he did "become his man, from that day forth, "of life and limb and earthly honour:" and then he received a kiss from his lord. (*Lit. s.* 85.) Which ceremony was denominated *homagium*, or manhood, by the feudists, from the stated form of words, *devenio vester homo*. *Britton, c.* 68. 2 *Black.* 53.

——— HOMAGE AUNCESTREL.] If a man and his ancestors had immemorially holden lands of another, and his ancestors by the service of homage, this was called *homage auncestral*, and the lord was bound to warranty. *Lit. sec.* 143.

——— HOMAGE LIEGE.] Under the feudal system every owner of lands held them in subjection to some superior or lord, from whom or whose ancestors the tenant or vassal had received them; and there was a mutual trust or confidence subsisting between the lord and vassal, that the lord should protect the vassal in the enjoyment of the territory he had granted him, and on the other hand, that the vassal should be faithful to the lord, and defend him against all his enemies. This obligation on the part of the vassal was called his *fidelitas*, or fealty; and an oath of fealty was required by the feudal law to be taken by all tenants to their landlord, which is couched in almost the same terms as our ancient oath of allegiance, (2 *Feud.* 5, 6, 7) except that in the usual oath of fealty there was frequently a saving or exception of the faith due to a superior lord by name, under whom the landlord himself was perhaps only a tenant or vassal. (1 *Black.* 367.) But when the acknowledgment was made to the absolute superior himself, who was vassal to no man, it was no longer called the oath of fealty, but the oath of allegiance, and therein the tenant swore to bear faith to his sovereign lord, in opposition to all men, without any saving or exeption: "*contra omnes homines fidelitatem fecit.*" (2 *Feud.* 99.) Land held by this exalted species of fealty was called *feudium ligium*, a liege fee; the vassals *homines ligii*, or liege men; and the sovereign their *dominus ligius*, or liege lord. And when sovereign princes did homage to each other for lands held under their respective sovereignties, a distinction was always made between simple homage, which was only an acknowledgment of tenure, (7 *Rep. Calvin's Case*, 7.) and liege homage, which included the fealty before mentioned, and the services consequent upon it. Thus when our Edward 3, in 1329, did homage to Philip 6th of France for his ducal dominions on that continent, it was warmly disputed of what species the homage was to be, whether liege or simple homage. (2 *Cart.* 401. *Mod. Un. Hist.* 23. 420.) But with us in England, it becoming a settled principle of tenure, that all lands in the kingdom are holden of the king as their sovereign and lord paramount, no oath but that of fealty could ever be taken to inferior lords, and the oath of allegiance was necessarily confined to the person of the king alone. *Ibid.*

HOMAGE JURY, is a jury in a court-baron, consisting of tenants that do homage to the lord of the fee; and these by the feodists are called *pares curiæ*: they inquire and make presentments of defaults and deaths of tenants, assess fines, admittances, and surrenders, in the Lord's court, &c. *Kitch.*

And if the number of suitors should so fail as not to leave sufficient to make a jury or homage, that is, two tenants at the least, the manor itself is lost. 2 *Black.* 91.

HOMAGER, one that does or is bound to do homage to another. *Cowel.*

HOMAGIO RESPECTUANDO, a writ to the escheator, commanding him to deliver seisin of lands to the heir of the king's tenant, notwithstanding his homage not done. *F. N. B.* 269. And the heir at full age was to do homage to the king, or agree with him for respiting the same. *New Nat. Br.* 563. *Cowel.*

HOMAGIUM REDDERE, to renounce homage, when the vassal made a solemn declaration of disowning and defying his lord. For which there was a set form prescribed by the feudatory laws. *Cowel.*

HOMESOKEN, HOMSOKEN, or HAMSOKEN, and HAMSOCA, (from the Sax. *ham, domus,* and *socnæ, immunitas*). In ancient times some men had an immunity from amercement for entering houses violently, and without license. *Cowel.*

Homesoken is also the privilege or freedom which every man has in his house, and he who invades that freedom is properly said *facere homesoken,* perhaps what we now call burglary. *Ibid.*

HOMESTALL, a mansion-house, or seat in the country. *Bailey.*

HOMICIDE, (*homicidium*) is the killing of any human creature, and is of three kinds, 1st, *justifiable,* 2dly, *excusable,* and 3dly, *felonious.*

I. ———— Justifiable.] *Justifiable homicide* has no share of guilt at all, and is of divers kinds.

1. Such as is owing to some unavoidable necessity, without any will, intention, or desire, and without any inadvertence or negligence, in the party killing; and therefore without any shadow of blame. As, for instance, by virtue of such an office as obliges one, in the execution of public justice, to put a malefactor to death, who hath forfeited his life by the laws and verdict of his country. This is an act of necessity, and even of civil duty; and therefore not only justifiable, but commendable, where the law requires it. But the law must require it, otherwise it is not justifiable: therefore wantonly to kill the greatest of malefactors, a felon or a traitor, attainted or outlawed, deliberately, uncompelled, and extrajudicially, is murder.—(1 *Hal. P. C.* 497.) And further, if judgment of death be given by a judge not authorized by lawful commission, and execution is done accordingly, the judge is guilty of murder (1 *Hawk. P. C.* 70. 1 *Hal. P. C.* 497). And upon this account sir Matthew Hale himself, though he accepted the place of a judge of the common pleas under Cromwell's government, (since it is necessary to decide the disputes of civil property in the worst of times,) yet declined to sit on the crown side at the assises, and try prisoners; having very strong objections to the legality of the usurper's commission, (*Burnet in his life,*) a distinction perhaps rather too refined; since the punishment of crimes is at least as necessary to society, as maintaining the boundaries of property. Also such judgment, when legal, must be executed by the proper officer, or his appointed deputy; for no one else is required by law to do it, which requisition it is that justifies the homicide. If another person doth it of his own head, it is held to be murder: (1 *Hal. P. C.* 501. 1 *Hawk. P. C.* 70,) even though it be the judge himself. (*Dalt. Just. c.* 150.) It must further be executed, *servato juris ordine*: it must pursue the sentence of the court. If an officer beheads one who is adjudged to be hanged, or *vice versa,* it is murder. (*Finch. L.* 31. 3 *Inst.* 52. 1 *Hal. P. C.* 501.) For he is merely ministerial, and therefore only justified when he acts under the authority and compulsion of the law: but, if a sheriff changes one kind of death for another, he then acts by his own authority, which extends not to the commission of homicide, and besides, this licence might occasion a very gross abuse of his power. The king indeed may remit part of a sentence; as in the case of treason, all but the beheading: but this is no change, no introduction of a new punishment; and in the case of felony, where the judgment is to be hanged, the king (it hath been said) cannot legally order even a peer to be beheaded. 3 *Inst.* 52. 212. 4 *Black.* 179.

2. Homicide, committed for the advancement of public justice, is by *permission* of the law justifiable in the following cases. 1. Where an officer, in the execution of his office, either in a civil or criminal case, kills a person that assaults and resists him. (1 *Hal. P. C.* 494. 1 *Hawk. P. C.* 71.) 2. If an officer, or any private person, attempts to take a man charged with felony, and is resisted, and in the endeavour to take him kills him. (1 *Hal. P. C.* 494.) 3. In case of a riot, or rebellious assembly the officers endeavouring to disperse the mob are justifiable in killing them, both at common law, (1 *Hal. P. C.* 495. 1 *Hawk. P. C.* 161,) and by the riot act, 1 *Geo.* 1. *c.* 5. 4. Where the prisoners in a gaol, or going to gaol, assault the gaoler or officer, and he in his defence kills any of them, it is justifiable, for the sake of preventing an escape. (1 *Hal. P. C.* 496.) 5. If trespassers in forests, parks, chases, or warrens, will not surrender themselves to the keepers, they may be slain by virtue of the statute 21 *Edw.* 1, *st.* 2, *de malefactoribus in parcis,* and 3 & 4 *W. & M. c.* 10.—But, in all these cases, there must be an apparent necessity on the officer's side; *viz.* that the party could not be arrested or apprehended, the riot could not be sup-

pressed, the prisoners could not be kept in hold, the deer-stealers could not but escape, unless such homicide were committed; otherwise without such absolute necessity it is not justifiable. 6. If the champions in a trial by battle killed either of them the other, such homicide was justifiable, and was imputed to the just judgment of God, who was thereby presumed to have decided in favour of the truth. (1 *Hawk. P. C.* 71.) 4 *Black.* 179, 180.

3. In the next place, such homicide as is committed for the prevention *of any forcible and atrocious* crime, is justifiable by the law of nature; (*Puff. L. of N. l.* 2. *c.* 5,) and also by the law of England, as it stood so early as the time of Bracton, (*fol.* 155.) and as it is since declared in statute 24 *Hen.* 8. *c.* 5, if any person attempts a robbery or murder of another, or attempts to break open a house in the night time, (which extends also to an attempt to burn it,) (1 *Hal. P. C.* 488,) and shall be killed in such attempt, the slayer shall be acquitted and discharged. This reaches not to any crime unaccompanied with force, as picking of pockets; or to the breaking open of any house in the day time, unless it carries with it an attempt of robbery also. 4 *Black.* 179, 180.

The English law likewise justifies a woman, killing one who attempts to ravish her: (*Bac. Elem.* 34. 1 *Hawk. P. C.* 71,) and so, too, the husband or father may justify killing a man, who attempts a rape upon his wife or daughter; but not if he takes them in adultery by consent, for the one is forcible and felonious, but not the other. (1 *Hal. P. C.* 485, 486.) And *Blackstone* does not doubt but the forcibly attempting a crime of a still more detestable nature, may be equally resisted by the death of the unnatural aggressor. For the one uniform principle that runs through our own, and all other laws, seems to be this; that where a crime, in itself capital, is endeavoured to be committed by force, it is lawful to repel that force by the death of the party attempting. 4 *Black.* 180.

In these instances of justifiable homicide the slayer is in no kind of fault whatsoever, not even in the minutest degree; and is therefore to be totally acquitted and discharged, with commendation rather than blame. 4 *Black.* 181.

II. ———— Excusable homicide imports some fault, some error, or omission, so trivial however, that the law excuses it from the guilt of felony, though in strictness it judges it deserving of some little degree of punishment; and is of two sorts, either *per infortunium*, by misadventure, or *se defendendo*, upon a principle of self-preservation. We will first see wherein these two species of homicide are distinct, and then wherein they agree.

1. *Homicide per infortunium*, or misadventure, is where a man, doing a lawful act, without any intention of hurt, unfortunately kills another; as where a man is at work with a hatchet, and the head thereof flies off and kills a stander-by; or where a person qualified to keep a gun is shooting at a mark, and undesignedly kills a man, (1 *Hawk. P. C.* 73, 74.) for the act is lawful, and the effect is merely accidental. So where a parent is moderately correcting his child, a master his apprentice, or scholar, or an officer punishing a criminal, and happens to occasion his death, it is only misadventure, for the act of correction was lawful; but if it exceeds the bounds of moderation, either in the manner, the instrument, or the quantity of punishment, and death ensues, it is manslaughter at least, and in some cases (according to circumstances) murder, (1 *Hal. P. C.* 473, 474.) for the act of immoderate correction is unlawful. 4 *Black.* 181, 182.

But a tilt or tournament, the martial diversion of our ancestors, was however an unlawful act, and so are boxing and sword-playing, the succeeding amusement of their posterity; and therefore if a knight in the former case, or a gladiator in the latter, be killed, such killing is felony of manslaughter. But if the king command, or permit such diversion, it is said to be only misadventure, for then the act is lawful. (1 *Hal. P. C.* 473. 1 *Hawk. P. C.* 74.) Likewise to whip another's horse, whereby he runs over a child and kills him, is held to be accidental in the rider, for he has done nothing unlawful, but manslaughter in the person who whipped him, for the act was a trespass, and at best a piece of idleness, of inevitably dangerous consequence. (*Hawk. P. C.* 73.) And in general, if death ensues in consequence of an idle, dangerous, and unlawful sport, as shooting, or casting stones in a town, or the barbarous diversion of cock-throwing, in these and similar cases the slayer is guilty of manslaughter, and not misadventure only, for these are unlawful acts. *Ibid.* 74. 1 *Hal. P. C.* 472. *Fost.* 261. 4 *Black.* 182, 3.

———— 2. *Homicide* in *self-defence*, or *se defendendo*, upon a sudden affray, is also excusable rather than justifiable, by the English law. This species of self-defence must be distinguished from that now just mentioned, as calculated to hinder the perpetration of a capital crime; which is not only a matter of excuse, but of justification. But the self-defence which we are now speaking of is that whereby a man may protect himself from an assault, or the like, in the course of a sudden broil or quarrel, by killing him who assaults him. And this is what the law expresses by the word chance-medley, or (as some rather choose to write it) chaud-medley, the former of which in its etymology signifies a casual affray, the latter an affray in the heat of blood or passion; both of them of pretty much the same import, but the former is in common speech too often erroneously applied to any manner of homicide by misadventure, whereas it appears by the stat. 24 *Hen.* 8, *c.* 5, and our ancient books, (*Staundf. P. C.* 16,) that it is properly applied to such killing as happens in self-defence upon a sudden rencounter. (3 *Inst.* 55, 57. *Fost.* 275, 276.) This right of natural defence does not imply a right of attacking, for instead of attacking one another for injuries past or impending, men need only have recourse to the proper tribunals of justice. They cannot therefore legally exercise this right of preventive defence but in sudden and violent cases, when certain and immediate suffering would be the consequence of waiting for the assistance of the law. Wherefore to excuse homicide by the plea of self-defence it must appear that the slayer had no other possible (or at least probable) means of escaping from his assailant. 4 *Black.* 183, 4.

It is frequently difficult to distinguish this species of homicide (upon chance-medly in self-defence) from that of manslaughter, in the proper, legal sense of the word.—(3 *Inst.* 55.) But the true criterion between them seems to be this, when both parties are actually combating at the time when the mortal stroke is given, the slayer is then guilty of manslaughter; but if the slayer hath not begun to fight or (having begun) endeavours to decline any further struggle, and afterwards being closely pressed by his antagonist, kills him to avoid his own destruction, this is homicide excusable by self-defence: (*Fost.* 277.) For which reason the law requires that the person who kills another in his own defence should have retreated as far as he conveniently or safely can, to avoid the violence of the assault, before he turns upon his assailant, and that not fictitiously, or in order to watch his opportunity, but from a real tenderness of shedding his brother's blood. And though it may be cowardice in time of war between two independent nations to fly from an enemy, yet between two fellow subjects the law countenances no such point of honour; because the king and his courts are the *vindices injuriarum*, and will give to the party wronged all the satisfaction he deserves. (1 *Hal. P. C.* 481, 483.) The party assaulted must therefore fly as far as he conveniently can, either by reason of some wall, ditch, or other impediment, or as far as the fierceness of the assault will permit him: (1 *Hal. P. C.* 483.) for it may be so fierce as not to allow him to yield a step, without manifest danger of his life, or enormous bodily harm; and then in his defence he may kill his assailant instantly. And this is the doctrine of universal justice, (*Puff. b.* 2. *c.* 5. *s.* 13,) as well as of the municipal law. 4 *Black.* 184.

And, as the manner of the defence, so also is the time to be considered; for if the person assaulted does not fall upon the aggressor till the affray is over, or when he is running away, this is revenge, and not defence. Neither under the colour of self-defence will the law permit a man to screen himself from the guilt of deliberate murder: for if two persons, A and B, agree to fight a duel, and A gives the first onset, and B retreats as far as he safely can, and then kills A, this is murder, because of the previous malice and concerted design. (1 *Hal. P. C.* 479.) But if A upon a sudden quarrel assaults B first, and upon B's returning the assault A really and *bona fide* flies, and being driven to the wall turns again upon B and kills him, this may be *se defendendo* according to some of our writers, (1 *Hal. P. C.* 482.) though others (1 *Hawk. P. C.* 75.) have thought this opinion too favourable, in as much as the necessity to which he is at last reduced originally arose from his own fault. Under this excuse of self-defence the principal civil and natural relations are comprehended; therefore master and servant, parent and child, husband and wife, killing an assailant in the necessary defence of each other, respectively, are excused; the act of the relation assisting being construed the same as the act of the party himself. 1 *Hal. P. C.* 484. 4 *Black.* 185, 6.

There is one species of homicide *se defendendo*, where the party slain is equally innocent as he who occasions his death; and yet this homicide is also excusable from the great universal principle of self-preservation, which prompts every man to save his own life preferable to that of another, where one of them must inevitably perish. As, among others, in that case mentioned by lord Bacon, (*Elem. c.* 5. 1 *Hawk. P. C.* 73.) where two persons being shipwrecked, and getting on the same plank, but finding it not able to save them both, one of them thrusts the other from it, whereby he is drowned. He who thus preserves his own life at the expense of another man's is excusable through unavoidable necessity, and the principle of self-defence; since their both remaining on the same weak plank is a mutual though innocent attempt upon, and an endangering of, each other's life. *Ibid.*

These two species of homicide, by *misadventure* and *self-defence*, agree in their blame and punishment: for the law sets so high a value upon the life of a man, that it always intends some misbehaviour in the person who takes it away, unless by the command or express permission of the law. In the case of *misadventure* it presumes neligence, or at least a want of sufficient caution in him who was so unfortunate as to commit it; who therefore is not altogether faultless. (1 *Hawk. P. C.* 72.) And as to the necessity which excuses a man who kills another *se defendendo*, lord Bacon (*Elem. c.* 5.) intitles it *necessitas culpabilis*, and thereby distinguishes it from the former necessity of killing a thief or a malefactor. For the law intends that the quarrel or assault arose from some unknown wrong, or some provocation, either in word or deed; and since in quarrels both parties may be, and usually are, in some fault; and it scarcely can be tried who was originally in the wrong; the law will not hold the survivor entirely guiltless. But it is clear in the other case that where I kill a thief that breaks into my house, the original default can never be upon my side. The law besides may have a further view, to make the crime of homicide more odious, and to caution men how they venture to kill another upon their own private judgment, by ordaining that he who slays his neighbour, without an express warrant from the law so to do, shall in no case be absolutely free from guilt. 4 *Black.* 185, 186.

The penalty inflicted by our laws is said by sir Edward Coke to have been anciently no less than death, (2 *Inst.* 148. 315.) which however is with reason denied by later and more accurate writers. (1 *Hal. P. C.* 425. 1 *Hawk. P. C.* 75. *Fost.* 282, &c.) It seems rather to have consisted in a forfeiture, some say of all the goods and chattels, others of only part of them by way of fine or *weregild*; (*Fost.* 287.) which was probably disposed of, as in France, *in pios usus*, according to the humane superstition of the times, for the benefit of his soul who was thus suddenly sent to his account, with all his imperfections on his head. But that reason having long ceased, and the penalty (especially if a total forfeiture) growing more severe than was intended, in proportion as personal property has become more considerable, the delinquent has now, and has had, as early as our records will reach, (*Fost.* 283.) a pardon and writ of restitution of his goods as a matter of course and right, only paying for suing out the same. (2 *Hawk. P. C.* 381.) And indeed to prevent this expense, in cases where the death has notoriously happened by misadventure, or in self-defence, the judges will usually permit (if not direct) a general verdict of acquittal. *Fost.* 288.

And where the homicide does not amount to murder or manslaughter it is now the universal practice to direct an acquittal. 4 *Black.* 188.

III. ———— Felonious Homicide is the killing of a human creature of any age or sex, without justification or excuse; and it may be done either by killing one's self, or another.

1. Self-murder. The law of England has ranked this among the highest crimes, making it a peculiar species of felony, *a felony committed on one's self*: and this admits of accessories before the fact, as well as other felonies; for if one persuades another to kill himself, and he does so, the adviser is guilty of murder. (*Keilw.* 136.) A *felo de se*, therefore, is he that deliberately puts an end to his own existence, or commits any unlawful malicious act, the consequence of which is his own death; as if attempting to kill another he runs upon his antagonist's sword, or shooting at another the gun bursts and kills himself. (1 *Hawk. P. C.* 68. 1 *Hal. P. C.* 413.) The party must be of years of discretion, and in his senses, else it is no crime. But this excuse ought not to be strained to that length to which our coroners juries are apt to carry it, *viz.* that the very act of suicide is an evidence of insanity; as if every man who acts contrary to reason had no reason at all: for the same argument would prove every other criminal *non compos*, as well as the self-murderer. The law very rationally judges that every melancholy or hypochondriac fit does not deprive a man of the capacity of discerning right from wrong, which is necessary to form a legal excuse. And therefore if a real lunatic kills himself in a lucid interval he is a *felo de se* as much as another man. 1 *Hal. P. C.* 412. 4 *Black.* 189.

The laws for this offence of self-murder can only inflict a punishment upon what the *felo de se* has left behind him, his reputation and fortune; on the former by *an ignominious burial* in the highway, with a stake driven through his body; on the latter by a forfeiture of all his *goods and chattels* to the king. And it is observable that this forfeiture has relation to the time of the act done in the felon's lifetime, which was the cause of his death. As if husband and wife be possessed jointly of a term of years in land, and the husband drowns himself, the land shall be forfeited to the king, and the wife shall not have it by survivorship. For by the act of casting himself into the water he forfeits the term, which gives a title to the king prior to the wife's title by survivorship, which could not accrue till the instant of her husband's death. (*Finch. L.* 216.) And though the letter of the law herein borders a little upon severity, yet it is some alleviation that the power of mitigation is left in the breast of the sovereign, who upon this, as on all other occasions, is reminded by the oath of his office to execute judgment in mercy. 4 *Black.* 189, 190.

2. Manslaughter is the unlawful killing of another, without malice, either express or implied, which may be either voluntarily, upon a sudden heat, or involuntarily, but in the commission of some unlawful act.

And hence it follows that in manslaughter there can be no accessaries before the fact, because it must be done without premeditation. 4 *Black.* 190, 191.

As to the first, or voluntary branch, if upon a sudden quarrel two persons fight, and one of them kills the other, this is manslaughter; and so it is if they upon such an occasion go out and fight in a field; for this is one continued act of passion, (1 *Hawk. P. C.* 82.) and the law pays that regard to human frailty as not to put a hasty and deliberate act upon the same footing with regard to guilt. So also if a man be greatly provoked, as by pulling his nose, or other great indignity, and immediately kills the aggressor, though this is not excusable *se defendendo*, since there is no absolute necessity for doing it to preserve himself; yet neither is it murder, for there is no previous malice; but it is manslaughter. (*Kelyng.* 135.) But in this, and in every other case of homicide, upon provocation, if there be a sufficient cooling-time for passion to subside and reason to interpose, and the person so provoked afterwards kills the other, this is deliberate revenge and not heat of blood, and accordingly amounts to murder. (*Fost.* 296.) So if a man takes another in the act of adultery with his wife, and kills him directly upon the spot; yet it is not absolutely ranked in the class of justifiable homicide, as in case of a forcible rape, but it is manslaughter. (1 *Hal. P. C.* 486.) It is however the lowest degree of it; and therefore in such a case the court directed the burning in the hand to be gently inflicted, because there could not be a greater provocation. (Sir *T. Raym.* 212.) Manslaughter therefore on a sudden provocation differs from excusable homicide *se defendendo* in this, that in one case there is an apparent necessity, for self-preservation, to kill the aggressor; in the other no necessity at all, being only a sudden act of revenge. 4 *Black.* 191, 192.

The second branch, or involuntary manslaughter, differs also from homicide excusable by misadventure in this, that misadventure always happens in consequence of a lawful act, but this species of manslaughter in consequence of an unlawful one. As if two persons play at sword and buckler, unless by the king's command, and one of them kills the other, this is manslaughter; because the original act was unlawful, but it is not murder, for the one had no intent to do the other any personal mischief (3 *Inst.* 56.) So where a person does an act, lawful in itself, but in an unlawful manner, and without due caution and circumspection: as when a workman flings down a stone or piece of timber into the street, and kills a man; this may be either misadventure, manslaughter, or murder, according to the circumstances under which the original act was done: if it were in a country village, where few passengers are, and he calls out to all people to have a care, it is misadventure only; but if it were in London or any populous town, where people are continually passing, it is manslaughter, though he gives loud warning (*Kel.* 40.); and murder, if he knows of their passing, and gives no warning at all, for then it is malice against all mankind (3 *Inst.* 57.) And, in general, when an involuntary killing happens, in consequence of an unlawful act, it will be either murder or manslaughter according to the nature of the act which occasioned it. If it be in prosecution of a felonious intent, or in its consequences naturally tended to bloodshed, it will be murder; but, if no more was intended than a mere civil trespass, it will only amount to manslaughter (*Foster* 258. 1 *Hawk. P. C.* 84.) 4 *Black.* 192, 3.

The crime of manslaughter amounts to felony, but is within the benefit of clergy; and the offender was formerly burnt in the hand*, and he forfeits all his goods and chattels. *Ibid.*

But there was one species of manslaughter, which was punished as murder, the benefit of clergy being taken away from it by statute; namely, the offence of mortally stabbing another, though done upon sudden provocation. For by stat. 1 *Jac.* 1. *c.* 8. it is enacted, that if any one thrusts or stabs another, not then having a weapon drawn, or who hath not then first stricken the party stabbing, so that he dies thereof within six months after, the offender shall have the benefit of clergy, though he did it not of malice aforethought. But this statute which was made on account of the frequent quarrels and stabbings with short daggers, between the Scotch and the English, at the accession of James the first (*Ld. Raym.* 140.); and, being therefore of a temporary nature, ought to have expired with the mischief which it meant to remedy, has been recently altered by stat. 43 *Geo.* 3. *c.* 58. whereby stabbing in general is made a capital offence.†

Wilful Murder. Murder is defined, or rather described, by sir Edward Coke to be, "when a person of sound memory and discretion, unlawfully killeth any reasonable creature in being, and under the king's peace,

---

* But by 19 *Geo.* 3. *c.* 74. instead of burning in the hand, the court may, if they think fit, impose a moderate pecuniary fine, and this shall have the same legal effect and consequences as burning in the hand.

† By 43 *Geo.* 3. *c.* 58. persons in England or Ireland who shall stab or cut with intent to *murder*, *rob*, or *maim* any of his majesty's subjects, or to prevent arrests of culprits, shall be guilty of felony without benefit of clergy.

with malice aforethought, either express or implied." 3 *Inst.* 47.

First, it must be committed by a person of sound memory and discretion, for lunatics or infants, as was formerly observed, (see *Age.*) are incapable of committing any crime, unless in such cases where they shew a consciousness of doing wrong, and of course a discretion, or discernment, between good and evil. 4 *Black.* 195.

Next, it happens when a person of such sound discretion unlawfully killeth. The unlawfulness arises from the killing without warrant or excuse: and there must also be an actual killing to constitute murder: for a bare assault with intent to kill, is only a great misdemeanor. (1 *Hal. P.C.* 425). The killing may be by poisoning, striking, starving, drowning, and a thousand other forms of death, by which human nature may be overcome. And if a person be indicted for one species of killing, as by poisoning, the bare administration of which alone is now felony without clergy, 43 *Geo.* 3. *c.* 58, he cannot be convicted by evidence of a totally different species of death, as by shooting with a pistol or starving. But where they only differ in circumstance, as if a wound be alleged to be given with a sword, and it proves to have arisen from a staff, an axe, or a hatchet, this difference is immaterial. There was also, by the ancient common law, one species of killing held to be murder, which may be dubious at this day, as there hath not been an instance wherein it has been held to be murder for many ages past. 1 *Fost.* 132; that is by bearing false witness against another, with an express premeditated design to take away his life, so as the innocent person be condemned and executed, (*Mirror, c.* 1. § 9. *Brit. c.* 2. *Bracton. l.* 3. *c.* 4.) And Lord Coke says expressly, "it is not holden for murder at this day." 3 *Inst.* 48; for though there is no doubt but this is equally murder *in foro conscientiæ* as killing with a sword; yet few honest witnesses would venture to give evidence against a prisoner tried for his life, if thereby they made themselves liable to be prosecuted as murderers. 4 *Black.* 196,7.

If a man however does such an act, of which the probable consequence may be, and eventually is death; such killing may be murder, although no stroke be struck by himself, and no killing may be primarily intended; as was the case of the unnatural son, who exposed his sick father to the air, against his will, by reason whereof he died, (1 *Hawk. P. C.* 78); of the harlot, who laid her child under leaves in an orchard, where a kite struck it and killed it, (1 *Hal. P. C.* 432); and of the parish officers, who shifted a child from parish to parish, till it died for want of care and sustenance. (*Palm.* 545). If a master refuses his apprentice necessary food or sustenance, or treats him with such continued harshness and severity as his death is occasioned thereby, the law will imply malice, and the offence will be murder. *Leach.* 127. So also, if a man hath a beast that is used to do mischief; and he knowing it suffers it to go abroad, and it kills a man, even this is manslaughter in the owner; but if he had purposely turned it loose, though barely to frighten people, and make what is called sport, it is with us as much murder as if he had incited a bear or dog to worry them, (*Ibid.* 431). If a physician or surgeon gives his patient a potion or plaister to cure him, which contrary to expectation kills him, this is neither murder nor manslaughter, but misadventure; and he shall not be punished criminally, however liable he might formerly have been to a civil action for neglect or ignorance, (*Mirr. c.* 4. § 16. 3 *Black.* 122): but it hath been holden, that if it be not a regular physician or surgeon, who administers the medicine or performs the operation, it is manslaughter at the least, (*Britt. c.* 5. 4 *Inst.* 251.) Yet sir Matthew Hale very justly questions the law of this determination, (1 *Hal. P. C.* 430.) In order also to make the killing murder, it is requisite that the party die within a year and a day after the stroke received, or cause of death administered, in the computation of which the whole day upon which the hurt was done, shall be reckoned the first. 1 *Hawk. P. C.* 79. 4 *Black.* 196,7.

Farther, the person killed must be "a reasonable creature in being, and under the king's peace," at the time of the killing. Therefore to kill an alien, a jew, or an outlaw, who are all under the king's peace and protection, is as much murder as to kill the most regular born Englishman; except he be an alien enemy in time and course of war, (3 *Inst.* 50. 1 *Hal. P. C.* 433). To kill a child in its mother's womb is not strictly speaking murder, and until a recent statute only a great misprision, but it is now enacted by 43 *Geo.* 3. *c.* 58. that if any person shall administer poison or other noxious or destructive thing with intent to cause the miscarriage of any woman quick with child, they shall be guilty of felony without clergy.

And persons administering medicines to women, though *not quick with child,* to procure miscarriage, are guilty of felony, and to be punished by fine, imprisonment, the pillory, or public or private whipping, or to be transported for not exceeding fourteen years. *s.* 2.

And before the above statute if the child was born alive, and died by reason of the potion or bruises it received in the womb, it was the better opinion that it was murder in such as administered or gave them, (3 *Inst.* 50.

1 *Hawk. P. C.* 80, but see 1 *Hal. P. C.* 433). There was also one case where it was difficult to prove the child's being born alive; namely, in the case of the murder of bastard children by the unnatural mother, and it was therefore enacted by statute 21 *Jac.* 1. *c.* 27, that if any woman be delivered of a child, which if born alive should by law be a bastard; and endeavoured privately to conceal its death, by burying the child or the like, the mother so offending was to suffer death as in the case of murder, unless she could prove by one witness at least that the child was actually born dead. This statute has however been recently repealed, and it is enacted by statute 43 *Geo.* 3. *c.* 58, that the trials of women for murder of bastards shall proceed as in other cases of murder, s. 3, and that women acquitted of such murder, may, where the jury find that the mother concealed her pregnancy, be imprisoned for not exceeding two years.

Lastly, the killing must be committed with malice aforethought, to make it the crime of murder. This is the grand criterion which now distinguishes murder from other killing: and this malice prepense, *malitia præcogitata*, is not so properly spite or malevolence to the deceased in particular, as any evil design in general, the dictate of a wicked, depraved, and malignant heart, (*Foster*, 256); and it may be either express or implied in law. Express malice is when one, with a sedate deliberate mind and formed design, doth kill another: which formed design is evidenced by external circumstances discovering that inward intention; as laying in wait, antecedent menaces, former grudges, and concerted schemes to do him some bodily harm (1 *Hal. P.C.* 451.) This takes in the case of deliberate duelling, where both parties meet avowedly with an intent to murder. Also, if even upon a sudden provocation one beats another in a cruel and unusual manner, so that he dies, though he did not intend his death, yet he is guilty of murder by express malice; that is, by an express evil design, the genuine sense of *malitia.* As when a park-keeper tied a boy, that was stealing wood, to a horse's tail, and dragged him along the park; when a master corrected his servant with an iron bar; and a schoolmaster stamped on his scholar's belly; so that each of the sufferers died; these were justly held to be murders, because the correction being excessive, and such as could not proceed but from a bad heart, it was equivalent to a deliberate act of slaughter (1 *Hal. P. C.* 454, 473, 474.) Neither shall he be guilty of a less crime, who kills another in consequence of such a wilful act, as shews him to be an enemy to all mankind in general; as going deliberately, and with an intent to do mischief (*Ld. Raym.* 143.), upon a horse used to strike, or coolly discharging a gun among a multitude of people (1 *Hawk. P. C.* 74.) So if a man resolves to kill the next man he meets, and does kill him, it is murder, although he knew him not; for this is universal malice. And, if two or more come together to do an unlawful act against the king's peace, of which the probable consequence might be bloodshed, as to beat a man, to commit a riot, or to rob a park: and one of them kills a man; it is murder in them all, because of the unlawful act, the *malitia præcogitata*, or evil intended before-hand (*Ibid.* 84.) 4 *Black. Com.* 199, 200.

Also in many cases where no malice is expressed, the law will imply it: as, where a man wilfully poisons another, in such a deliberate act the law presumes malice, though no particular enmity can be proved (1 *Hal. P. C.* 455.) And if a man kills another suddenly, without any, or without a considerable provocation, the law implies malice; for no person, unless of an abandoned heart, would be guilty of such an act, upon a slight or no apparent cause. *Ibid.*

And no affront, by words or gestures only, is a sufficient provocation, so as to excuse or extenuate such acts of violence as manifestly endanger the life of another (1 *Hawk. P. C.* 82. 1 *Hal. P. C.* 455, 456.) But if the person so provoked had unfortunately killed the other, by beating him in such a manner as shewed only an intent to chastise and not to kill him, the law so far considers the provocation of contumelious behaviour, as to adjudge it only manslaughter, and not murder (*Fost.* 291.) In like manner, if one kills an officer of justice, either civil or criminal, in the execution of his duty, or any of his assistants endeavouring to conserve the peace, or any private person endeavouring to suppress an affray or apprehend a felon, knowing his authority or the intention with which he interposes, the law will imply malice, and the killer shall be guilty of murder (1 *Hal. P. C.* 457. *Foster*, 308, &c.) And if one intends to do another felony, and undesignedly kills a man, this is also murder (1 *Hal. P. C.* 465.) Thus if one shoots at A and misses him, but kills B, this is murder; because of the previous felonious intent, which the law transfers from one to the other. The same is the case where one lays poison for A; and B, against whom the prisoner had no malicious intent, takes it, and it kills him; this is likewise murder (*Ibid.* 466.) So also, if one gives a woman with child a medicine to procure abortion, and it operates so violently as to kill the woman, this is murder in the person who gave it (*Ibid.* 429.) It were endless to go through all the cases of homicide, which have been adjudged either expressly, or impliedly, malicious: these therefore, may suffice as a specimen; and we may take it for a general rule, that all homicide is malicious, and of course amounts to murder, unless where justified by the command or permission of the law; excused on the account of accident or self-preservation; or alleviated into manslaughter, by being either the involuntary consequence of some act, not strictly lawful, or (if voluntary) occasioned by some sudden and sufficiently violent provocation. And all these circumstances of justification, excuse, or alleviation, it is incumbent upon the prisoner to make out, to the satisfaction of the court and jury: the latter of whom are to decide whether the circumstances alledged are proved to have actually existed; the former, how far they extend to take away or mitigate the guilt. For all homicide is presumed to be malicious, until the contrary appeareth upon evidence (*Fost.* 255.) 4 *Black.* 200, 1.

——— The punishment of murder, and that of manslaughter, were formerly one and the same; both having the benefit of clergy: so that none but unlearned persons, who least knew the guilt of it, were put to death for this enormous crime (1 *Hal. P. C.* 450.) But now, by stat. 23 *Hen.* 8. *c.* 1. 1 *Edw.* 6. *c.* 12. 4 & 5 *Ph. & Mar. c.* 4. the benefit of clergy is taken away from murderers through malice prepense, their abettors, procurers, and counsellors. And it is now enacted by stat. 25 *Geo.* 2. *c.* 37. "that the judge, before whom any person is found guilty of wilful murder, shall pronounce sentence immediately after conviction, unless he sees cause to postpone it; and shall, in passing sentence, direct him to be executed on the next day but one, (unless the same shall be Sunday, and then on the Monday following) and that his body be delivered to the surgeons to be dissected and anatomized (*Fost.* 107.): and that the judge may direct his body to be afterwards hung in chains*, but in no wise to be buried without dissection. And, during the short but awful interval between sentence and execution, the prisoner shall be kept alone, and sustained with only bread and water. But a power is allowed to the judge upon good and sufficient cause to respite the execution, and relax the other restraints of this act.

Parricide, or the murder of one's parents or children, is in our English laws treated no otherwise than as simple murder, unless the child was also the servant of his parent (1 *Hal. P. C.* 380.) *Fos.* 107, 324, 336.

——— Petit treason, according to the stat. 25 *Edw.* 3. *c.* 2. may happen three ways: by a servant killing his master, a wife her husband, or an ecclesiastical person (either secular or regular) his superior, to whom he owes faith and obedience. A servant who kills his master whom he has left, upon a grudge conceived against him during his service, is guilty of petit treason: for the traiterous intention was hatched while the relation subsisted between them; and this is only an execution of that intention (1 *Hawk. P. C.* 89. 1 *Hal. P. C.* 380.) So if a wife be divorced *a mensa et thoro*, still the *vinculum matrimonii* subsists; and if she kills such divorced husband, she is a traitress (1 *Hal. P. C.* 381.) And a clergyman is understood to owe canonical obedience to the bishop who ordained him, to him in whose diocese he is beneficed, and also to the metropolitan of such suffragan or diocesan bishop: and therefore to kill any of these is petit treason. (*Ibid.*)

As to the rest, whatever has been said, or remains to be observed hereafter, with respect to wilful murder, is also applicable to the crime of petit treason, which is no other than murder in its most odious degree: except that the trial shall be as in cases of high treason, before the improvements therein made by the statutes of William III. (*Fost.* 337.) But a person indicted for petit treason, may be acquitted thereof, and found guilty of manslaughter or murder (*Foster*, 106. 1 *Hal. P. C.* 378. 2 *Hal. P. C.* 184.): and in such case two witnesses are not necessary, as in case of petit treason they are; for it has been determined, that a person indicted for petit treason, may upon the evidence of *one witness* be convicted of murder, though acquitted of the petit treason, *Radbourne's case, Leach* 363. which crime is also distinguished from murder in its punishment. 4 *Black.* 203.

The punishment of petit treason, in a man, is to be drawn and hanged, and in a woman, it was formerly, to be drawn and burnt (1 *Hal. P. C.* 382. 3 *Inst.* 311.) Persons guilty of petit treason, were first debarred the benefit of clergy, by stat. 12 *Hen.* 7. *c.* 7. which has been since extended to their aiders, abettors, and counsellors, by statutes 23 *Hen.* 8. *c.* 1. and 4 & 5 *P. & M. c.* 4.

But by 30 *Geo.* 3. *c.* 48. women shall no longer be sentenced to be burnt; but in all cases of high and petit treason, they shall be condemned to be drawn and hanged; and in petit treason, they shall be subject besides to the same judgment with regard to dissection, and the time of execution as is directed by 25 *Geo.* 2. *c.* 37. in cases of murder,—this is a legislative confirmation of the opinion of the majority of the judges, who soon after the passing of 25 *Geo.* 2. *c.* 37. agreed, that in the case of men convicted of petit treason, the judgment introduced by that statute should be added to the common law judgment for petit treason. *Fost.* 107.

HOMINATIO. The mustering of men; also the doing of homage. *Cowel. Blount.*

* The judge, if he thinks it advisable, may afterwards direct the hanging in chains, by a special order to the sheriff; but it does not form any part of the judgment. *Fost.* 107.

HOMINE CAPTO IN WITHERNAMIUM, a writ that anciently lay to take him that had taken any bondman or woman and led them out of the country, so that he or she could not be replevied according to law. *Reg. Orig. fol.* 79. *Cowel. Blount.*

HOMINE ELIGENDO AD CUSTODIENDAM PECIAM SIGILLI PRO MERCATORIBUS EDITI, a writ directed to a corporation, for the choice of a new person to keep one part of the seal appointed for statutes merchant, when a former was dead, according to the statute of *Acton Burnel. Reg. Orig.* 178. *Cowel. Blount.*

HOMINE REPLEGIANDO, a writ that anciently lay to bail a man out of prison, if bailable, *F. N. B. fol.* 6. *Reg. Orig. fol.* 77. now seldom used, as the cause of the party being in custody, may be enquired into, and bail accepted, if bailable, or the person discharged without bail, if unlawfully imprisoned, by the more efficacious writ of *habeas corpus*.

HOMINES, feudatory tenants, who claimed a privilege of having their causes and persons tried only in the court of their lord. *Cowel. Blount.*

HOMIPLAGIUM, maiming a man. *Ibid.*

HOMO. Includes both man and woman, in a large or general understanding. 2 *Inst.* 45.

HOMSTALE, a home-stall, or mansion-house. *Cowel. Blount.*

HOND-HABEND, (from the Sax. *hond*, hand, and *habens*, having) manifest theft, when one is apprehended with the *mainor* or *mainover*, *i. e.* the thing stolen in his hand. *Bract. lib.* 3. *tract.* 2. *cap.* 8. *Cowel. Blount.*

HONEY. All vessels of honey are to be marked with the initial letters of the name of the owner, on pain of 6*s.* 8*d.* and be of such a content, as follows: the barrel 32 gallons, the kilderkin 16 gallons, and the firkin 8 gallons, on pain of 5*s.* for every gallon wanting; and if any honey sold, be corrupted with any deceitful mixture, the seller shall forfeit the honey, &c. *Stat.* 23 *Eliz. c.* 8.

HONORARY FEUDS. Titles of nobility when first introduced, were called *honorary feuds*, and were not of a divisible nature; but could only be inherited by the eldest son. *Feud.* 2. *t.* 55. *Wright* 32.

HONORIS PROPTER RESPECTUM, is one of the challenges to the polls of the jurors, as if a lord of parliament be impannelled on a jury, he may be challenged by either party, or he may challenge himself. 3 *Black.* 361.

HONOUR. A man may claim an honour by grant, or by prescription. But the king at this day cannot make an honour by grant, without an act of parliament. *R.* 1 *Bul.* 195, 196. *Co. Lit.* 108.*a.*

There are within the realm 80 honours, *viz.* the honour of Aquila, Arundel, Abergavenny, Boloine, Berkhamstead, Beaulieu, Barnard's Castle, Bullingbroke, Barstable, Bononia, Brecknock, Brember, Bedford, Clare, Crovecure, Clun, Christchurch, Cockermouth, Cormayls, Candicut, Carisbrook, Clifford-Castle, Chester, Carmarthen, and Cardigan, Dudley, and Dover-Castle, Eyre, and Egremond.

The honour of East and West Greenwich, Gloucester, Grentmesnil, Gower, Haganet, Huntingdon, Heveningham, Hawenden-Castle, Hertford, and Halton, Lancaster, Lincoln, Leicester, Lovetot, Hinckley, and Kington, and Falkingham.

The honour of Montgomery, Mowbray, Middleham, and Maidstone, Nottingham, Newelhn, Oakhampton, and Oxford.

The honour of Plimpton, Peverel, Pickering, Raleigh, Richard's Castle, Skipton, Stafford, Strigal, Tickhil, Tremanton, Totness, Theony, Tamworth.

The honour of Wigmore, Wallingford, Windsor, Wormgay, Whirwelton, Werk, Whitchurch, and Warwick, Webley, and Tutbury.

By the statute of 31 *Hen.* 8. *c.* 5. Hampton Court is made an honour.

So, by the stat. 33 *H.* 8. *c.* 37, 38. Ampthill, and Grafton. And by the stat. 37 *H.* 8. *c.* 18. Westminster, Kingston on Hull, St. Osyth, and Donnington-Castle.

HONOUR, *Court of.* The court *military*, or court of *chivalry*, is held before the earl marshal of England. 2 *Hawk. P. C.* 11.

The jurisdiction of which is declared by statute 13 *Ric.* 2. *c.* 2. to be this; "that it "hath cognizance of contracts touching "*deeds of arms and of war, out of the realm,* "and also of things which touch *war within* "*the realm, which cannot be determined or* "*discussed by the common law;* together with "other usages and customs to the same "matters appertaining." So that wherever the common law can give redress, this court hath no jurisdiction; which has thrown it entirely out of use as to the matter of contracts, all such being usually cognizable in the courts of Westminster-hall, if not directly, at least by fiction of law: for if a contract be made at Gibraltar, the plaintiff may lay it as made at *Gibraltar to wit,* at *Northampton,* &c.; for the locality, or place of making it, is of no consequence with regard to the validity of the contract. 3 *Black.* 103.

But the words, "*other usages and customs,*" support the claim of this court, 1. To give relief to such of the nobility and gentry as think themselves aggrieved in matters of honour; and 2. To keep up the distinction of degrees and quality. Whence it follows, that the civil jurisdiction of this court of chivalry, is principally in two points; the redressing injuries of honour, and correcting encroachments in matters of coat-armour, precedency, and other distinctions of families. *Ibid.*

As a court of honour, it is to give satisfaction to all such as are aggrieved in that point; a point of a nature so nice and delicate, that its wrongs and injuries escape the notice of the common law, and yet are fit to be redressed somewhere. Such, for instance, as calling a man coward, or giving him the lie; for which, as they are productive of no immediate damage to his person or property, no actions will lie in the courts at Westminster; and yet they are such injuries as will prompt every man of spirit to demand some honourable amends, which by the antient law of the land, was appointed to be given in the court of chivalry (*Year book*, 37 *Hen.* 6. *Selden of duels*, *c.* 10. *Hal. Hist. C. L.* 37.) But modern resolutions have determined, that how much soever such a jurisdiction may be expedient, yet no action for words will lie at present therein (*Salk.* 553. 7 *Mod.* 125. 2 *Hawk. P. C.* 11) And it hath always been most clearly holden (*Hal. Hist. C. L.* 37.), that as this court cannot meddle with any thing determinable by the common law, it therefore can give no pecuniary satisfaction or damages; inasmuch as the quantity and determination thereof is ever of common law cognizance. And therefore, this court of chivalry can at most order reparation in point of honour; as, to compel the defendant *mendacium sibi ipsi imponere*, or to take the lie that he has given, upon himself, or to make such other submission as the laws of honour may require (1 *Roll. Abr.* 128.) Neither can this court, as to the point of reparation in honour, hold plea of any such word, or thing, wherein the party is relieved by the courts of the common law. As if a man gives another a blow, or calls him thief or murderer; for in both these cases, the common law has pointed out his proper remedy by action. 3 *Black.* 104.

As to the other point of its civil jurisdiction, the redressing of encroachments and usurpations in matters of heraldry and coat-armour; it is the business of this court, according to sir Matthew Hale, to adjust the right of armorial ensigns, bearings, crests, supporters, pennons, &c. and also rights of place or precedence, where the king's patent or act of parliament (which cannot be over-ruled by this court) have not already determined it. 3 *Black.* 105.

The proceedings in this court are by petition, in a summary way; and the trial not by a jury of twelve men, but by witnesses or by combat (*Co. Lit.* 261.) But as it cannot imprison, not being a court of record, and as by the resolution of the superior courts, it is now confined to so narrow and restrained a jurisdiction, it has fallen into contempt and disuse. The marshalling of coat-armour, which was formerly the pride and study of all the best families in the kingdom, is now greatly disregarded; and has fallen into the hands of certain officers and attendants upon this court, called heralds, who consider it only as a matter of lucre, and not of justice: whereby such falsity and confusion have crept into their records, (which ought to be the standing evidence of families, descents, and coat-armour,) that, though formerly some credit has been paid to their testimony, now even their common seal will not be received as evidence in any court of justice in the kingdom (*Roll. Abr.* 686. 2 *Jon.* 224.) But their original visitation-books, compiled when progresses were solemnly and regularly made into every part of the kingdom, to inquire into the state of families, and to register such marriages and descents as were verified to them upon oath, are allowed to be good evidence of pedigrees (*Comb.* 63.) And it is much to be wished, that this practice of visitation at certain periods were revived; for the failure of inquisitions *post mortem*, by the abolition of military tenures, combined with the negligence of the heralds in omitting their usual progresses, has rendered the proof of a modern descent, for the recovery of an estate or succession to a title of honour, more difficult than that of an antient. This will be indeed remedied for the future, with respect to claims of peerage, by a late standing order (11 *May* 1767) of the house of lords: directing the heralds to take exact accounts, and preserve regular entries of all peers and peeresses of England, and their respective descendants; and that an exact pedigree of each peer and his family shall, on the day of his first admission, be delivered to the house by garter, the principal king at arms. But the general inconvenience affecting more private successions, still continues without a remedy. 3 *Black.* 105, 106.

HONOUR OF A PEER. A peer sitting in judgment, gives not his verdict upon oath like an ordinary juryman, but upon his honour. 2 *Inst.* 42. He answers also to bills in equity, upon his honour, and not upon his oath. 2 *Pere Wms.* 146. But when he is examined as a witness, either in civil or criminal cases, he must be sworn. *Salk.* 512. So also, if he is examined as a witness in the high court of parliament, he must be sworn as was done in the case of the bishop of Oxford in the impeachment of lord *Macclesfield* and lord *Stormont*, on that of *Warren Hastings*: for the respect which the law shews to the honour of a peer, does not extend so far as to overturn a settled maxim, that, *in judicio non creditur nisi juratis*. *Cro. Car.* 64.

The honour of a peer is, however, so highly regarded by the law, that it is much more penal to spread false reports of them, and certain other great officers of the realm: scandal against them, being called by the name of *scandalum magnatum*, and subjected to peculiar punishments by the antient statutes of 3 *Ed.* 1. *c.* 34. 2 *Ric.* 2. *st.* 2. *c.* 5. 12 *Ric.* 2. *c.* 11. which see under title SCANDALUM MAGNATUM.

HONOUR or DIGNITY. The king is, by the constitution, entrusted with the sole power of conferring dignities and honours, in confidence that he will bestow them upon none, but such as deserve them: and therefore, all degrees of nobility, of knighthood and other titles, are received by immediate grant from the crown: either expressed in writing, by writs of letters patent; as in the creation of peers and baronets; or by corporeal investiture, as in the creation of a simple knight. 1 *Black.* 271, 2.

HONOUR or SEIGNORY. In the early times of our legal constitution, the king's greater barons, who had a large extent of territory held under the crown, granted out frequently smaller manors to be holden of themselves, which do therefore now continue to be held under a superior lord, who is called in such cases, *the lord paramount* over all those manors, and his *seignory* is frequently termed an *honour*, not a manor, especially if it hath belonged to an antient feodal baron, or hath been at any time in the hands of the crown. 2 *Black.* 91. 1 *Buls.* 197. 2 *Rol.* 72. *l.* 48. *Co. Lit.* 108. a. 2 *Rol.* 72. *l.* 45.

HONTFONGENETHEF, a thief taken *hond-habend*, *i. e.* having the thing stolen in his hand. *Cowel.*

HOPCON, signifies a valley; so do *hope*, *hawgh*, and *howgh*. *Cowel.*

HOPS. By 6 *Geo.* 2. *c.* 37. *sect.* 6. unlawfully and maliciously cutting hop-binds is made felony without benefit of clergy.

HORA AURORÆ, the morning bell, anciently called the four o'clock bell, contradistinguished from the eight o'clock bell, or the bell in the evening, called *ignitegium* or *coverfeu*. *Cowel.*

HORDERA, (from the Sax. *hord*, *thesaurus*) a treasurer: hence *hord* or *hoard*. *Ibid.*

HORDERIUM, a hoard, a treasury, or repository. *Ibid.*

HORDEUM PALMATE, that sort of barley which is called *beer*. *Ibid.*

HORNEBEAME POLLENGERS, trees so called, that have been usually lopped, and are about twenty years growth, and therefore not titheable. *Plowden*, 407. *Cowel.*

HORNEGELD, (from the Sax. *horn*, *cornu*, and *geld*, *solutio*) signifying a tax within a forest, to be paid for horned beasts. *Cromp. Jurisd.* 197. *Cowel.*

HORN WITH HORN, or HORN UNDER HORN. The promiscuous feeding of bulls and cows, or all horned beasts, that are allowed to run together upon the same common. *Cowel.*

HORNAGIUM, supposed to be the same with *horngeld*. *Ibid.*

HORNERS, no stranger was to buy any English horns gathered or growing in London, or within twenty-four miles thereof, by the stat. 4 *Ed.* 4. *c.* 8. And no one may sell English horns unwrought to any stranger, or send them beyond sea, on pain of forfeiting double value: the wardens of horners in London may search all wares, &c. 7 *Jac.* 1. *cap.* 14.

HORS DE SON FEE, (Fr. *i. e.* out of his fee) is an exception to avoid an action brought for rent or services, &c. issuing out of land, by him that pretends to be the lord; for if the defendant can prove that the land is without the compass of his fee, the action falls. *Broke. Cowel.*

HORSES, BREED OF. By 27 *Hen.* 8. *c.* 6. persons having inheritance or freehold in a park, and a mile about, shall keep two mares apt to bear foal thirteen hands high, on pain of 40*s.* a month: and they are not to suffer them to be leaped by horses under fourteen hands high, on pain of 40*s.* But this does not extend to Westmoreland, Cumberland, Northumberland, or Durham.

By 32 *Hen.* 8. *c.* 13. stone-horses put into commons, being above two years old, shall be fifteen hands high; and those of less size may be seized by any person for his own use; refusing to be present at the measuring, is a penalty of 40*s.* Commons shall be driven yearly at Michaelmas, or within fifteen days after, on pain of 40*s.* and putting diseased horses into commons is a forfeiture of 10*s.* But by 8 *Eliz.* *c.* 8. stoned horses of thirteen hands high may be put in the commons and fens in Cambridgeshire, Huntingdonshire, Lincolnshire, and Norfolk. And by 21 *Jac.* 1. *c.* 28. the act is not to extend to Cornwall.

HORSES, EXPORTATION OF. By 11 *Hen.* 7. *c.* 13, no horse shall be exported without the king's licence, nor mare above the value of 6*s.* 8*d.*

By 1 *Ed.* 6. *c.* 5. no horse or mare shall be exported without the king's licence, on forfeiture thereof, and of 40*l.*: and no mare shall be exported exceeding 10*s.* in price.

Although the above acts remain on the face of the Statute Book, they have long since fallen into total disuse and non-observance, particularly as subsequent acts, from 22 *Car.* 2. down to the present time, allow of the exportation of horses, mares, or geldings of British breeding, at an export duty, *viz.* by 49 *Geo.* 3. *c.* 98. of 2*l.* 2*s.* each.

HORSES FOR KING'S SERVICE. None shall take the horse of any person to serve the king without the owner's consent, or sufficient warrant, on pain of imprisonment, &c. *Stat.* 20 *R.* 2. *c.* 5. See *Mutiny Act.*

HORSES HIRED, action of trespass on the case lies for abusing a horse hired, by immoderate riding, &c. 1 *Mod.* 210.

HORSE RACES. By stat. 13 *Geo.* 2.

c. 19. to prevent the multiplicity of horse-races (a too prevalent mode of gaming) no plates or matches under 50*l* value shall be run, under a penalty of 200*l*. to be paid by the owner of each horse running, and 100*l*. on such as advertise the plate.

By 18 *Geo*. 2. *c*. 34. horses may run any match for the real value of 50*l*. at any weights and at any place whatsoever; but the race must be begun and ended in one day. 13 *Geo*. 2. *c*. 19.

But although such horse races according to the statutes, are lawful, yet it has been determined that they are games within the stat. of 9 *Ann*. *c*. 1. (see GAMING,) and that of consequence wagers above 10*l*. upon a horse race, though the race itself be allowed by statute, are illegal. 2 *Black. Rep*. 706. A wager for less than 10*l*. upon an illegal horse race, is also void and illegal. 4 *Ter. Rep*. 1. So a race against time, or to travel a certain distance with a chaise and pair, within a certain time have been held to be games within the statute of gaming. 2 *Wils*. 36. 6 *Ter. Rep*. 499.

HORSES, SALE OF. The property in horses is not easily altered by sale, without the express consent of the owner, 2 *Inst*. 719. for a purchaser gains no property in a horse that has been stolen, unless it be bought in a fair or market overt, according to the directions of the *stats*. 2 *Phil. & Mar*. *c*. 7. and 31 *Eliz*. *c*. 12.

By 2 & 3 *Phil. & Mar*. *c*. 7. all horses shall be sold in the open place appointed in a fair or market from ten o'clock till sunset; shall be tolled in the presence of the parties, and their names and places of abode shall be registered in a book by the toll taker, which is to be given to the owner of such fair or market within a day after, on pain of 40*s*. in every case.

And the owner's property in a horse stolen shall not be altered by sale in a fair, unless the horse continued an hour therein, and was registered, for which the buyer is to pay 1*d*. *Ibid*.

And stolen horses sold contrary hereto, may be seized by the owner, and justices of peace may determine offences. *Ibid*.

By 31 *Eliz*. *c*. 12. sellers of horses in fairs or markets must be known to the toll taker, or some other person who will testify his knowledge of him, which is to be entered in a book, and sale made otherwise shall be void.

The owner of a horse stolen, notwithstanding such sale, may redeem the same, upon payment or tender of the price within six months after stolen. *Ibid*.

And by 26 *Geo*. 3. *c*. 71. every person keeping a place for slaughtering horses, geldings, mares, mules, asses, bulls, oxen, cows, heifers, sheep, hogs, goats, or other cattle not killed for butcher's meat, shall take out a licence at the quarter sessions; but must produce a certificate from the parish where he resides, testifying his ability, and the representatives of such licensed person, after his death, may act under such licence till the next sessions.

Persons licensed shall affix to their houses, "licensed for slaughtering horses, pursuant to an act passed in the 26th year of his majesty king George the Third." *Ibid*.

Six hours previous notice shall be sent, when horses or cattle are intended to be slaughtered, to the inspector, who is to take an account of the beasts, and none shall be slaughtered but in the day time. *Ibid*.

An account shall be kept by the owners of slaughtering-houses, of the owners of the cattle, which may be inspected. *Ibid*.

Inspectors are to be chosen annually by the parishioners; they are to enter in a book a particular account of all cattle slaughtered, for each of which entries they are to be paid 6*d*. by the slaughterman; and persons searching are to pay 6*d*. a time. They are to affix over their doors their names, and the words, "inspector of houses and places for slaughtering horses." If the inspector suspects any animal to be stolen, he may prohibit the killing it eight days, and in the mean time he is to describe and advertise it twice publicly; the expences whereof are to be paid by the slaughterman. *Ibid*.

Inspectors may visit slaughtering-houses at all times; if at night, with a constable. *Ibid*.

Persons bringing cattle refusing to give an account of themselves, may be carried before a justice, who may, on suspecting such persons, commit them. *Ibid*.

Persons slaughtering horses or cattle without licence, are guilty of felony and may be transported. *Ibid*.

Persons destroying hides shall be deemed guilty of a misdemeanor, and may be corporally punished. *Ibid*.

Persons making false entries shall be liable to a penalty of 20*l*. and not less than 10*l*. and persons lending houses for the purpose of slaughtering, unlicensed, incur a like penalty. *Ibid*.

This act is not to extend to curriers, fellmongers, tanners or dealers in hides, or persons killing distempered or aged cattle for the hides or for dogs meat; but such persons or collar-makers, or farriers killing sound horses, shall be liable to a penalty of 20*l*. and not less than 10*l*. *Ibid*.

Inspectors books are to be produced at the quarter sessions, witnesses refusing to attend the justices, are to forfeit 10*l*. and parishioners shall be deemed competent ones. *Ibid*.

HOSTILERS, (Fr. *hosteliers*) inn-keepers. *Blount*.

HOSPES GENERALIS, a great chamberlain. *Ibid*.

HOSPITALLERS, (*hospitalarii*) were the knights of a religious order, so called, because they built an hospital at Jerusalem, wherein pilgrims were received. Their chief abode is now in Malta, and they are now called knights of Malta. All the lands and goods of these knights here in England were given to the king, by 32 *Hen.* 8. *c.* 34. *Cowel. Blount.*

HOSPITALS, are eleemosynary foundations constituted for the perpetual distribution of the free alms or bounty of the founders for the maintenance of the poor sick and impotent.

And by stat. 39 *Eliz. c.* 5. any person seised of an estate in fee-simple, may by deed inrolled in chancery erect and found an hospital for the sustenance and relief of the poor, to continue for ever; and place such heads, &c. therein, as he shall think fit: and such hospital shall be incorporated, and subject to such visitors, &c. as the founder shall nominate; also such corporations have power to take and purchase lands not exceeding 200*l.* per ann. so as the same be not holden of the king, &c. and to make leases for twenty-one years, reserving the accustomed yearly rent: but no hospital is to be erected unless upon the foundation it be endowed with lands or hereditaments of the clear yearly value of 10*l.* per annum.

By 39 *Eliz. c.* 6. and 43 *Eliz. c.* 4. commissions may be awarded to certain persons to enquire of lands or goods given to hospitals; and the lord chancellor is empowered to issue commissions to commissioners for enquiring by a jury, of all grants, abuses, breaches of trust, &c. of lands given to charitable uses, who may make orders and decrees concerning the same, and the due application thereof; and the commissioners are to decree that recompence be made for fraud and breaches of trust, &c. so as their orders and decrees be certified into the chancery; and the lord chancellor shall take order for the execution of the said judgments and decrees, and after certificate may examine into, annul, or alter them agreeable to equity, on just complaint: but this does not extend to lands given to any college or hall in the universities, &c. nor to any hospital over which special governors are appointed by the founders; and it shall not be prejudicial to the jurisdiction of the bishop or ordinary, as to his power of inquiry into and reforming abuses of hospitals, by virtue of the stat. 2 *Hen.* 5. *c.* 1, &c.

These commissioners may order houses to be repaired, by those who receive the rents; see that the lands be let at the utmost rent; and on any tenant's committing waste, by cutting down and sale of timber, they may decree satisfaction, and that the lease shall be void. *Hil.* 11 *Car.* Where money is kept back, and not paid, or paid where it should not, they have power to order the payment of it to the right use: and if money is detained in the hands of executors, &c. any great length of time, they may decree the money to be paid with damages for detaining it. *Duke, Read.* 123. 4 *Rep.* 104.

HOSPITIUM, the same with procuration, or visitation-money. *Cowel. Blount.*

HOSTAGIUM, the same with *hospitium. Ibid.*

HOSTELAGIUM, a right to have lodging and entertainment; reserved by lords in the houses of their tenants. *Ibid.*

HOSTELER, (*hostellarius*) from the Fr. *hosteler*, i. e. *hospes*, an inn-keeper. *Ibid.*

HOSTLERS, inn-keepers. *Ibid.*

HOSTERIUM, a hoe. *Ibid.*

HOSTIA, host bread, or consecrated wafers in the Holy Eucharist. *Ibid.*

HOSTILARIUS, an hospitaller. *Ibid.*

HOSTILIARIA, HOSPITULARIA, a place or room in religious houses, allotted to the use of receiving guests and strangers, for the care of which there was a peculiar officer appointed, called *hostillarius*, and *hospitalarius*. *Ibid.*

HOSTRICUS, (*austercus*, from the Lat. *astur*, a goshawk). *Ibid.*

HOTCHPOT, (a commixture) and in a metaphorical legal sense, is a blending or mixing of lands given in marriage, with other lands in fee falling by descent: as if a man seised of thirty acres of land in fee, hath issue only two daughters, and he gives with one of them ten acres in marriage to the man that marries her; and dies seised of the other twenty acres: now she that is thus married, to gain her share of the rest of the land, must put her part given in marriage in hotchpot, *i. e.* she must refuse to take the sole profits thereof, and cause her land to be mingled with the other; so that an equal division may be made of the whole between her and her sister, as if none had been given to her; and thus for her ten acres she shall have fifteen, otherwise her sister will have the twenty acres of which her father died seised. *Lit.* 55. *Co. Lit. lib.* 3. *cap.* 12.

And there is a bringing of money into hotchpot, upon the clauses and within the intent of the act of parliament for distribution of intestate's estates, 22 & 23 *Car.* 2. *c.* 10. *stat.* 2. Where a certain sum is to be raised, and paid to a daughter for her portion, by a marriage settlement; this has been decreed to be an advancement by the father in his life-time, within the meaning of the statute, though future and contingent; and if the daughter would have any further share of her father's personal estate, she must bring this money into hotchpot; and shall not have both the one and the other. *Abr. Cas. Eq.* 253. See 2 *Vern.* 638.

HOVEL, (*mandra*) a place wherein husbandmen set their ploughs and carts out of the rain or sun. *Cowel. Blount.*

HOUR, (*hora*) a certain space of time of sixty minutes, twenty-four of which make the natural day. And it is not material at what hour of the day one is born, as there can be no fraction of a day. *Co. Lit.* 135. See *Fractions.*

HOUSAGE, a fee paid for housing goods by a carrier, or at a wharf or key, &c. *Shep. Epit.* 1725. *Cowel.*

HOUSE, (*domus*) a place of dwelling or habitation; and the dwelling house of every man, is as it were, his castle; therefore if thieves come to a man's house to rob or kill him, and the owner or his servant kill the thieves in defending him and his house, that is not felony, nor shall he forfeit any thing. 2 *Inst.* 316. And the doors of a house may not be broke open, unless it be for treason or felony, &c. *H. P. C.* 137. *Plowd.* 5. 5 *Rep.* 91. But when the door is once open, the sheriff may enter and make execution at the suit of any subject, either of body or goods; though while the door is shut, he cannot break it to execute process at the suit of a subject. And the house, although it is a castle for the owner himself and his family and his own goods, &c. yet it is no protection for a stranger flying thither, or the goods of such a one, to prevent lawful execution; and therefore in such case, after request to enter, and denial, the sheriff may break the house. 5 *Rep.* 91. *a.* to 93. *a. Lee* v. *Gansell, Cowp. Rep.* 1.

Also commissioners of bankruptcy cannot break open a house to search for the bankrupt's goods, unless it be in the house of the bankrupt. 2 *Show.* 247.

But upon recovery in any real action or ejectment, the sheriff may break the house and deliver seisin, &c. to the plaintiff, the writ being *habere facias seisinam* or *possessionem*; and after judgment, it is not the house of the defendant in right and judgment of law.

Also, in all cases where the king is party, the sheriff (if no door be open) may, after notice and request, break the party's house to take him, or to execute other process of the king, if he cannot otherwise enter. See also *Execution, Felonies* and *Taxes.*

HOUSEBOLD and HAYBOLD, the same as *houseboot* and *hedgeboot. Cowel.*

HOUSEBOTE, a compound of *house* and *bote, i. e. compensatio,* signifies estovers, or an allowance of necessary timber out of the lord's wood, for the repairing and support of a house or tenement. And this belongs of common right to any lessee for years or for life: but if he take more than is needful, he may be punished by an action of waste. *Cowel.*

HOUSE BREAKING, or HOUSE-ROBBING. See *Felony.*

HOUSE-BURNING. See *Arson, Burning.*

HOUSE OF CORRECTION. The house of correction is, after conviction, chiefly for the punishing of idle and disorderly persons; parents of bastard children, beggars, servants running away; trespassers, rogues, vagabonds, &c. 2 *Bulst.* 351. *Sid.* 281.

In every county there shall be a house of correction built at the charge of the county, with conveniences for the setting of people to work, or every justice of peace shall forfeit 5*l.*, and the justices in sessions are to appoint governors of such house of correction, with salaries, which are to be paid quarterly out of the county stock: these governors are to set the persons sent on work, and moderately correct them, by whipping, &c. and to yield a true account every quarter sessions of persons committed to their custody; and if they suffer any to escape, or neglect their duty, the justices may fine them. 7 *Jac.* 1. *c.* 4. and 14 *Geo.* 2. *c.* 33.

And by 6 *Geo.* 1. *c.* 19. vagrants and other criminal offenders, and persons charged with small offences, may for such offences or for want of sureties, be committed either to the common gaol or *house of correction*, as the justices in their judgment shall think proper.

By 14 *Geo.* 2. *c.* 33. and 17 *Geo.* 2. *c.* 5. upon presentment of the grand jury, the justices at sessions may build, or purchase land for building, or enlarge, buy, or hire fit houses of correction. And the justices are to take care that the houses of correction be provided with proper materials for relieving, employing, and correcting persons sent to the same: and two justices shall visit the same twice or oftener in a year, and examine into the estate and management thereof, and report the same at the sessions. The governor misbehaving, may be fined or turned out, at the discretion of the justices. Offenders liable to be sent to the house of correction, where the time and manner of their punishment is not expressly limited by law, may be committed until the next sessions, or until discharged by due course of law. See also *Prisons.*

HOUSE TAX. See *Taxes.*

HOUSEHOLDER, (*pater-familias*) the occupier of a house. *Cowel. Blount.*

HREDIGE, readily or quickly. *Cowel. Blount.*

HUDEGELD. Where a villain or servant had committed any trespass, for which he deserved whipping or corporal punishment, when he bought off his penalty with money, the price of exemption from such chastisement, was called *hudgeld*, or *hidegeld*; money given to save his hide. *Cowel. Blount.*

HUE AND CRY. An hue (from *huer*, to shout; and cry, *hutesium et clamor*) is the old common law process of pursuing, with horn and with voice, all felons, and such as have dangerously wounded another (*Bracton, l.* 3. *tr.* 2. *c.* 1. *s.* 1. *Mirr. c.* 2. *s.* 6.) It is also mentioned by statute *Westm.* 1. 3 *Ed.* 1. *c.* 9. and 4 *Ed.* 1. *de officio coronatoris.* But the principal statute, relative to this matter, is that of Winchester, 13 *Ed.* 1. *c.* 1. *and* 4. which directs, that from thenceforth "every "country shall be so well kept, that imme-"diately upon robberies and felonies com-"mitted, fresh suit shall be made from town "to town, and from county to county; and "that hue and cry shall be raised upon the "felons, and they that keep the town shall "follow with hue and cry, with all the town "and towns near; and so hue and cry shall "be made from town to town, until they be "taken and delivered to the sheriff. And, "that such hue and cry may more effectu-"ally be made, the hundred is bound by the "same statute, c. 3. to answer for all rob-"beries therein committed, unless they take "the felon; which is the foundation of an ac-"tion against the hundred, in case of any loss "by robbery." By statute 27 *Eliz.* *c.* 13. "no hue and cry is sufficient unless made "with both horsemen and footmen." And by statute 8 *Geo.* 2. *c.* 16. "the constable "or like officer, refusing or neglecting to "make hue and cry, forfeits 5*l.* half to the "king and half to him that sues within six "months, to be recovered with full costs; "and the whole vill or district is still in "strictness liable to be amerced, according "to the law of Alfred, if any felony be com-"mitted therein and the felon escapes." Hue and cry (2 *Hal. P. C.* 100, 104.) may be raised either by a precept of a justice of the peace, or by a peace officer, or by any private man that knows of a felony. The party raising it must acquaint the constable of the vill with all the circumstances which he knows of the felony, and the person of the felon; and thereupon the constable is to search his own town, and raise all the neighbouring vills, and make pursuit with horse and foot; and in the prosecution of such hue and cry the constable and his attendants have the same powers, protection, and indemnification, as if acting under the warrant of a justice of the peace. But if a man wantonly or maliciously raises an hue and cry, without cause, he shall be severely punished as a disturber of the public peace. 1 *Hawk. P. C.* 75.

By 29 *Car.* 2. *c.* 7. the hundred shall not be answerable when persons who travel on the Lord's day, are robbed. And by 22 *Geo.* 2. *c.* 24. no person shall recover in any action on the statutes of hue and cry, more than 200*l.* unless at the time of the robbery there be two present to attest the truth thereof. And by the *land tax acts,* the receivers general shall not sue the county for a robbery, unless there were three persons in company carrying the money.

Also the party robbed shall give notice thereof to the inhabitants of some town, and be examined within twenty days before a justice, whether he knew any of the offenders. 27 *Eliz. c.* 13. *s.* 11. 8 *Geo.* 2. *c.* 16.

Also no person shall sue the hundred in case of robbery, without first giving notice to a constable describing the felon, and publishing the same in the London gazette, within twenty days after the robbery. 8 *Geo.* 2. *c.* 16. *s.* 1.

And before any action is commenced, the party shall go before the filazer or other officer of the court, and give bond with two sureties to the high constable, in a penalty of 100*l.* to answer costs. 8 *Geo.* 2. *c.* 16. *s.* 2.

And no action shall be brought against the hundred, except it be commenced within six months. *Ibid. s.* 14.

No process is to be served against the hundred, &c. for a robbery committed, but on the high constable, who shall give notice of it in one of the principal market towns, &c. and then enter an appearance, and defend the action. *Ibid. s.* 4.

In actions against the hundred, the inhabitants may be witnesses for such hundred. *s.* 15.

By 27 *Eliz. c.* 13. where any one of the malefactors shall be apprehended, the hundred shall not be chargeable. *s.* 8.

Nor shall the hundred be chargeable, if any of the felons be apprehended in forty days after notice in the gazette. 8 *Geo.* 2. *c.* 16. *s.* 3.

And persons apprehending such felons within such time, so that the hundred be indemnified, are on proof thereof before two justices to have a reward of 10*l.* from the hundred. *s.* 4.

By the stat. 8 *Geo.* 2. *c.* 16. and 22 *Geo.* 2. *c.* 46. *s.* 4. after judgment against the hundred, no process shall be served on the high constable or any inhabitant, but the sheriff on receipt of the writ of execution shall shew it to two justices of the peace in or near the hundred, who shall speedily cause an assessment to be levied pursuant to the stat. 27 *Eliz. c.* 13. and also for the necessary expences of the high constable above the costs and damages recovered, or which, on notice from the two justices, he shall give an account and proof on oath to their satisfaction, having first caused his attorney's bill to be taxed. And the sheriff shall pay the money levied to the parties without fee.

And the like assessment shall be in case the plaintiff be nonsuit, discontinue, or have a verdict or judgment on demurrer against him, if by insolvency of the plaintiff or his sureties, he cannot be reimbursed on the bond of 100*l.* penalty; and the money levied shall be paid to the justices for the high constable in ten days after it is levied. And the justices may limit a time not exceeding thirty days for levying such assessment; and the officer appointed refusing or neglecting to levy and pay the money, &c. in such time, forfeits double the sum.

HUIFFIER, an usher of a court, or in the king's palace, &c. *Cowel. Blount.*

HUISSERIUM or UFFERS, ships to transport horses. *Cowel. Blount.*

HULKA, a hulk or small vessel. *Cowel. Blount.*

HULLUS, a hill. *Ibid.*

HUMAGIUM, a moist place. *Ibid.*

HUMBER. See *Fish.*

HUNDRED, (*hundredum centuria*) a well known division of the counties; first ordained by king Alfred, who divided the different counties into hundreds, for better government, an institution brought from Germany: for there *centa*, or *centena*, is a jurisdiction over an hundred towns. 1 *Black.* 115.

And the *centeni* were the principal inhabitants of a district composed of different villages, originally in number *an hundred*, but afterwards only called by that name. 3 *Black.* 33.

The word *hundredum* is also sometimes taken for an immunity or privilege, whereby a man is quit of money or customs due to the hundreds. *Cowel.* See *Hue and Cry, and other titles.*

HUNDRED-COURT, is a large court-baron, being held for all the inhabitants of a particular hundred instead of a manor. The free suitors are here the judges, and the steward the registrar, as in the case of a court-baron. It is not a court of record, and it resembles a court-baron in all points, except that in point of territory it is of a greater jurisdiction. 3 *Black.* 34.

This it is said by *Coke*, 2 *Inst.* 71. was derived out of the county-court for the ease of the people, that they might have justice done to them at their own doors, without any charge or loss of time. But according to Blackstone, its institution was probably co-eval with that of hundreds themselves, introduced, though not invented, by Alfred, being derived from the policy of the ancient Germans. 1 *Black. Introd.* s. 4. 3 *Black.* 34. 4 *Black.* 408.

This hundred-court, as causes are equally liable to be removed from hence, as from the common court-baron, and by the same writs, and may also be received by writ of false judgment, is therefore fallen into total disuse with regard to the trial of actions. 3 *Black.* 35.

HUNDREDORS, (*hundredarii*) the *centeni* or hundredors, are persons serving on juries, or fit to be impannelled thereon for trials, dwelling within the hundred where the land in question lies. *Stat.* 35 *H.* 8. *c.* 6.

Hundredor also signifies him that hath the jurisdiction of the hundred, and is in some places applied to the bailiff of an hundred. 13 *Ed.* 1. *c.* 38. 9 *Ed.* 2. 2 *Ed.* 3. *Horn's Mirror, lib.* 1.

HUNDRED-LAGH, (Sax. *laga, lex*) the hundred court. *Manwood, par.* 1. *pag.* 1.

HUNDRED-PENNY, was collected by the sheriff or lord of the hundred, *in oneris sui subsidium.* *Camd.* 223.

HUNDRED-SETENA, dwellers or inhabitants of a hundred. *Cowel. Blount.*

HUNGER. Hunger will not justify stealing food, to relieve a present necessity. 1 *Hal. P. C.* 54. 4 *Black.* 31.

HUNTING. See *Deer* and *Game.*

HURDLE, a sledge or hurdle used to draw traitors to execution. 4 *Black.* 92, 377.

HURDERFERST, (Sax. *hyred, familia*, and *fæest, firmus*) a domestic, or one of the family. *Cowel. Blount.*

HURRERS. The cappers and hat-makers of London were formerly one company of the haberdashers, called by this name. *Stow's Surv. Lond.* 312.

HURST, HYRST, HERST, (Sax. *hyrst*) a wood or grove of trees. *Cowel. Blount.*

HURST-CASTLE, so called, because situated near the woods. *Ibid.*

HURTARDUS, HURTUS, a ram or wether, a male sheep. *Ibid.*

HUS AND HANT, words used in ancient pleadings, *offert domino regi hus & hant in plegio ad standum recto.* 4 *Inst.* 72.

HUSBAND AND WIFE. See *Baron* and *Feme.*

HUSBANDRY and HUSBANDMAN. See *Commons, Sheep, Labourers, Servants, and other proper titles.*

HUSBREÇE, (Sax. *hus*, a house, and *brice*, a breaking) the offence which we now call burglary. *Blount.*

HUSCARLE, a menial servant. *Cowel. Blount.*

HUSCANS, (Fr. *hauseau*) a sort of boot, or buskin made of coarse cloth, and worn over the stockings. 4 *Ed.* 4. *c.* 7. *Cowel.*

HUSFASTNE, (Sax. *hus*, i. e. *domus* and *fæest, fixus*) is he that holdeth house and land. *Cowel. Blount.*

HUSGABLE, (*husgablum*) house-rent, or some tax or tribute laid upon houses. *Ibid.*

HUSSELING-PEOPLE, communicants, (from the Sax. *hussel*) which signifies the holy sacrament. *Ibid.*

HUSTINGS, (*hustingum*, from the Sax. *hustinge*, i. e. *concilium*, or *curia*) is a court held before the lord mayor, recorder, and sheriffs of London, and is the principal and supreme court of the city. To this court a writ of error lies from judgment in the sheriff's court, and from thence to justices appointed by the king's commission, who used to sit in the church of *St. Martin le grand. Fitz. N. B.* 32. And from the judgment of these justices, a writ of error lies immediately to the house of lords. 3 *Black.* 80.

HUTESIUM, a hue and cry. *Cowel.*

HUTISAN, an exaction. *Terras quietas ab omni hutilan & omni alia exactione.* *Ibid.*

HYBERNAGIUM, the season for sowing winter corn, wheat, and rye, between Michaelmas and Christmas: as *tremagium* is the season for sowing the summer corn, barley, oats, &c. in the spring of the year. *Ibid.*

HYDE OF LAND, and HYDEGELD. See *Hide* and *Hidage*.

HYPOTHECA, in the civil law, was where the possession of the thing pledged remained with the debtor. 2 *Black*. 159.

HYPOTHECATIO, (Lat. *hypotheca*, a pledge) is the pledging or pawning of a ship for necessaries. Thus if a ship be at sea and spring a leak or be otherwise in danger of being lost, or the voyage defeated for want of provisions or other necessaries, in these cases of extremity, the master may pledge or hypothecate the ship and goods or either of them for such necessaries as are wanting, which power is impliedly given him, in constituting him master, and which he may exercise rather than that the ship should be lost, or the voyage defeated. *Roll. Abr*. 53. *Hob*. 11. *Moor* 918.

But the master can only hypothecate where the calamity or want of necessaries happened after the ship had put to sea. *Molloy* 214. 6 *Mod*. 70.

And the master cannot hypothecate the ship or goods for any debt of his own, nor in any case but for the preservation of the ship, and completing her voyage. *Molloy* 213.

And although the power of *hypothecation* be necessary for the navigation, without which masters could not get credit abroad, yet a master cannot make the owner *personally* liable by any contract of his: but only the ship and cargo by way of hypothecation. 6 *Mod*. 79. 2 *Sider*. 161. And therefore the admiralty court hath jurisdiction herein, so far as to subject the ship, but cannot proceed against the person otherwise than is necessary to make him a party towards the condemnation of the ship. *Molloy* 214. 6 *Mod*. 70.

HYTH, a port or little haven; also a wharf, &c. *Cowel*. *Blount*. See *Hith*.

I

JACENS HÆREDITAS, an estate in abeyance. *Cowel*.

JACK: armour anciently worn by horsemen in war, made of plates of iron fastened together; also called *lorica*, because at first it was made with leather. *Cowel*.

JACTITATION OF MARRIAGE. One of the first and principal matrimonial causes, is *causa jactitationis matrimonii*: as, when one of the parties boasts or gives out that he or she is married to the other, whereby a common reputation of their marriage may ensue. On this ground the party injured may libel the other in the spiritual court; and, unless the defendant undertakes and makes out a proof of the actual marriage, he or she is enjoined perpetual silence upon that head: which is the only remedy the ecclesiastical court can give for this injury. 3 *Black*. 93.

JACTIVUS, (Lat.) he that loseth by default. *Cowel*.

JAMAICA, an American island taken from the Spaniards in the year 1655. See *Plantations*.

JAMBEAUX, leg-armour, from *jambe*, *tibia*. *Blount*.

JAMPNUM, furze or gorse, and gorsy ground. *Cowel*. *Blount*.

JANNUM, or JAUN, heath, whins, or furze. *Ibid*.

JACQUES, small money. *Ibid*.

JAR, (Span. *jarro*) an earthen pot. *Ibid*.

JARROCK, (mentioned in stat. 1 *R*. 3, *c*. 8.) a kind of cork, or other ingredient, which this statute prohibits dyers to use in dying cloth. *Ibid*.

JAUN, (Fr. *jaune*) yellow colour, is used for furze or gorze. *Cowel*. *Blount*.

IBERNAGIUM, *hibernagium*, *ybernagium*, season for sowing winter corn. *Ibid*.

ICENI, the people of Suffolk, Norfolk, Cambridgeshire, and Huntingdonshire. *Ib*.

ICH DIEN, (from the German) is the motto belonging to the arms of the prince of Wales, signifying *I serve*; it was formerly the motto of John, king of Bohemia, slain in the battle of Cressy, by Edward the Black Prince; and taken up by him to shew his subjection to his father king Edward III. *Ib*.

ICONA, (*iconia*) a figure or representation of a thing. *Ibid*.

ICTUS ORBUS, a maim, bruise, or swelling; any hurt without cutting the skin and shedding of blood, which was called *plaga*. *Bracton, lib.* 2. *tr. cap.* 5, *and* 24. *Cowel.*

IDENTITATE NOMINIS, a writ that lay for him who was taken and arrested in any personal action, and committed to prison for another man of the same name; in such case he may have this writ directed to the sheriff, which is in nature of a commission to inquire whether he be the same person against whom the action was brought; and if not, then to discharge him. *Reg. Orig.* 194. *F. N. B.* 267.

IDENTITY OF PERSON. Where a person convicted of, or outlawed for, a criminal offence, being asked what he hath to alledge why execution should not be awarded against him, if he pleads diversity of person, *viz.* that *he is not the same as was* attainted; a jury shall be impannelled to try this collateral issue, *viz.* the *identity of the person*; and not whether guilty or innocent for that he has beeh tried before. This trial is *instanter*, and no time allowed the prisoner for defence, or producing of witnesses, unless he will make oath, that he is not the person attainted: neither shall any peremptory challenge of the jury be allowed the prisoner. 1 *Sid.* 72. *Fost.* 42, 46. 1 *Lev.* 61. 4 *Black. Com.* 395, 6.

IDEOTS AND LUNATICS. An *ideot* (Lat. *illiteratus, imperitus,* and in our law *non compos mentis*) is a fool or madman from his nativity, and one who never has any lucid intervals; an ideot or not, being a question of fact, must be tried by jury or inspection. *Dyer* 25. *Moor* 4. *pl.* 11. *Bro. Ideots. F. N. B.* 233.

One made such by sickness, which my lord Hale calls *dementia accidentalis vel adventitia*, is such a madness as excuseth in criminal cases. 1 *Hale's Hist. P. C.* 30.

A *lunatic*, from the great influence which the moon has in all disorders of the brain, is also *dementia accidentalis vel adventitia*; and is intitled to the same indulgence as to his acts, and stands in the same degree with one whose disorder is fixed and permanent. 4 *Co.* 125. *Co. Lit.* 247. 1 *Hale's Hist. P. C.* 31.

If one go mad by drunkenness, which is called *dementia effectata*; yet this madness, though contracted by the vice and will of the party, if it becomes an habitual and fixed phrenzy, it puts the man in the same condition as if the same was contracted involuntarily at first. *Plowd.* 19. *a.* *Crom. Inst.* 29. *a.* *Co. Lit.* 247. 1 *Hale's Hist. P. C.* 32.

But he who is guilty of any crime whatsoever through his voluntary drunkenness, shall be punished for it as much as if he had been sober. See *Homicide*.

Therefore, the prevailing distinction in law is between *ideocy* and *lunacy*; the first *a fatuity a nativitate, vel dementia naturalis*, which excuseth the party as to his acts, and intitles the king to the receipt of the rents and profits of his estate during his life, without being obliged to render any account for the same; the other accidental or adventitious madness, which, whether permanent and fixed, or with lucid intervals, goes under the general name of lunacy, and equally excuseth with ideocy, as to acts done during the phrenzy; but herein they differ, that in the latter case, the king is only a trustee for the lunatic, and accountable to him, if he happens to be restored to his understanding, or to his representatives if it happen otherwise. *Bac. Abr.* 4 *Co.* 125. *a.*

The trial of ideocy, madness, or lunacy in civil cases, and in order to the commitment or custody of the person and his estate, which belongs to the king, as mentioned above, is by writ or commission to the sheriff or escheator, or particular commissioners both by their own inspection and by inquisition to enquire and return their inquisition into the chancery; and thereupon a grant or commitment of the party and his estate ensues; and in case the party or his friends find themselves injured by the finding him a lunatic or ideot, a special writ may issue to bring the party before the chancellor, or before the king, to be inspected; and if, on examination, it appear the party is no ideot, the whole commission and office shall be discharged without any traverse or *monstrans de droit*. 4 *Co.* 126. 9 *Co.* 31. *a.*

Also the party found an ideot or lunatic may traverse the inquisition, as may any other person having a title to the land. *Skin.* 178.

The king as *parens patriæ* hath the protection of all those who, by reason of their imbecility and want of understanding, are incapable of taking care of themselves. *Staund. Prærog. cap.* 9. *fol.* 33. 2 *Inst.* 14. 4 *Co.* 126. *a.* *Dyer* 25.

And by stat. *de prærogativa regis*, or 17 *Ed.* 2. *cap.* 9. it is enacted, that the king shall have the custody of the lands of natural fools, taking the profits of them, without waste or destruction, and shall find them their necessaries, of whose fees soever the lands be holden; and after the death of such ideots, he shall render it to the right heirs, so that such ideots shall not alien, nor their heirs be disinherited.

And by *cap.* 10. of the said statute, "the king shall provide when any (that before time hath had his wit and memory) happen to fail of his wit, and there are many *per lucida intervalla*, that their lands and tenements shall be safely kept without waste and destruction, and that they and their household should live and be maintained competently with the profits of the same, and the residue, besides their sustentation, shall be kept to their use, to be delivered unto them when they come to right mind: so that such lands and tenements shall in no wise be aliened, and the king shall take nothing to his own use; and if the party die in such estate, then the residue shall be distributed for his soul, by the advice of the ordinary."

And by 17 *Geo.* 2. *c.* 5. it shall be lawful for two justices, where a lunatic or mad person shall be found, by warrant to the constables, churchwardens and overseers of the parish, to cause such person to be apprehended and kept safely locked up in such place, as such justices shall direct; and (if such justices find it necessary) to be there chained, if the settlement of such person shall be in any parish, within such county; and if such settlement shall not be there, then such person shall be sent to the place of his last settlement, and shall be kept safely locked up or chained, as aforesaid; and the charges shall be paid by order of two justices, out of the estate of such person, if such person hath an estate over and above what shall be sufficient to maintain his wife and children; and if he hath not, then the charges shall be paid by such ways as the poor are to be provided for."

But by 14 *Geo.* 3. *c.* 49. made perpetual by 26 *Geo.* 3 *c.* 91. confining more than one lunatic in any one house, without licence, shall forfeit 500*l.*

Five fellows of the college of physicians, or licentiates, shall be commissioners to grant licences within seven miles of London, on 5*s.* stamps, one for each house annually; but no commissioner to keep such house, on penalty of 50*l.* *Ibid.* to *s.* 10.

Commissioners to visit licensed houses, and refusing them admittance, forfeiture of the licence; commissioners to be paid each, on every inspection, 1*l.* 1*s.*; keepers to give to the commissioners' secretary an account of admission of patients (except paupers) in three days, within seven miles of London, and admitting without an order, to forfeit 100*l.* *Ibid.* to *s.* 21.

Quarter sessions to licence houses more than seven miles from London annually; if keeping ten lunatics, to pay 10*l.*; if above, 15*l.*; and only one house for each licence: and justices, with a physician, to visit licensed houses; and keepers to give notice of admission of patients in fourteen days, on forfeiture of 100*l.* and to give a recognizance of 100*l.* on each licence. *Ibid.* to *s.* 28.

The lord chancellor, and two chief justices may order commissioners, or justices, to inspect licensed houses, and report the state thereof, and may inspect registers, and examine parties, but not to extend to public hospitals. *Ibid.* to *s.* 30.

Not to give greater power than is allowed by law. *Ibid.* *s.* 31.

By 48 *Geo.* 3. *c.* 96. the justices, at their general quarter sessions, may give notices respecting the erecting lunatic asylums, for the better care and maintenance of lunatics being paupers and criminals, which asylums are to be erected at the expence of the county or counties uniting, in the manner prescribed by the act; such expence to be paid out of, and charged on, the county rates. *s.* 9—16.

And so soon as any lunatic asylum so erected, shall be declared by the visiting justices to be fit for the reception of lunatics, and the same shall be published three times in the county paper, the justices may issue their warrants for the committal of dangerous lunatics to such places. *s.* 17.

Any overseer neglecting to give information of any lunatic pauper to a justice of the peace, is to forfeit not exceeding 10*l.* nor less than 40*s.*

On the committal of lunatics under the vagrant act of 17 *Geo.* 2. *c.* 5. if there be a lunatic asylum established, the warrant shall direct such lunatic to be confined in such asylum, and not elsewhere: or if there be no such asylum, the justice may order the lunatic to be confined in a licensed madhouse. *s.* 19.

Where the legal settlement of lunatics cannot be discovered, the justices shall direct that they shall be sent to the lunatic asylum, or some other place of confinement. *s.* 20.

But no lunatic asylum shall be liable to the reception of lunatics chargeable to any city, town, or place, which is exempt from the county rates. *s.* 21.

Persons having lunatics in their care, at such asylums, suffering them to go at large without an order from two justices, are to forfeit not exceeding 10*l.* nor less than 40*s.* *s.* 23.

The buildings are to be exempted from the window duty. *s.* 26.

When persons charged with murder are found to be insane and ordered to be confined, according to 39 & 40 *Geo.* 3. *c.* 94. two justices are to enquire into their settlement, and make an order on the parish for their maintenance. *s.* 27.

An ideot, or person *non compos*, may inherit or purchase. *Co. Lit.* 2. 2 *Vent.* 203.

Also if an ideot or lunatic marry, and die, his wife shall be endowed. *Co. Lit.* 31. *a.* 4 *Co.* 124, 5.

So a lunatic shall be tenant by the curtesy, and though a woman, being a lunatic, kill her husband, yet she shall be endowed, because this cannot be felony in her, who was deprived of her understanding by the act of God. *Perk.* 365.

But ideots and lunatics are incapable of being executors or administrators. *Godolph.* 86.

And therefore, if an executor become *non compos*, the spiritual court may commit administration to another. 1 *Salk.* 36.

Also he who incites a madman to do

murder, or other crime, is a principal offender, and as much punishable as if he had done it himself. *Keilw.* 53. *Dalt. cap.* 95. 1 *Hawk. P. C.* 2.

But by 39 & 40 *Geo.* 3. *c.* 94. the jury, in case of any person charged with treason, murder, or felony, proving to be insane, shall declare whether he was acquitted by them on account of insanity, and the court shall order him to be kept in custody till his majesty's pleasure be known; and his majesty may give an order for the safe custody of such insane person. *s.* 1.

Insane persons indicted for any offence, and found to be insane by a jury, to be impannelled on their arraignment, shall be ordered by the court to be kept in custody till his majesty's pleasure be known. *s.* 2.

Persons committed by any justice, on account of being dangerous and insane, shall not be bailed, except by two justices (one qu.), or by the quarter sessions, or one of the judges. *s.* 3.

The privy council, or one of the secretaries of state, may cause persons appearing to be insane, and endeavouring to gain admittance to his majesty, to be kept in custody till the insanity of such persons be enquired into; and such persons may be committed, and discharged if on an enquiry by a jury, or a commission in the nature of a writ *de lunatico inquirendo,* he be returned sane. *s.* 4.

Acts done by ideots and lunatics in a court of record, as fines and recoveries, and the uses declared on them, and recognizances, they are good, and can neither be avoided by themselves nor their representatives; for it is to be presumed, that had they been under these disabilities, the judges would not have admitted them to make these acknowledgments. 4 *Co.* 124. 2 *And.* 145. *Co. Lit.* 247. 2 *Inst.* 483. *Bro.* tit. *Fines* 75. 2 *And.* 193.

As to acts done by them not of record, they are distinguished into void and voidable. 4 *Co.* 124, 5. *Beverley's case, Bro.* tit. *Fail* 62. *F. N. B.* 202. *Cro. Eliz.* 398.

But if parceners of non-sane memory make partition, unless it be equal, it shall only bind the parties themselves, but not their issue. *Co. Lit.* 166. *a.*

The contracts of ideots and lunatics, after office found and the party legally committed, are also void; and the *non compos* restored to his legal right, at the suit of his committee. 4 *Co.* 125.

Ideots and lunatics, during their lunacy, and persons grown childish by extreme age, are incapable of making any will or testament. *Swinb.* 71. *Godolph. Orph. Leg.* 25.

But if a lunatic, in a lucid interval, make a will, it shall not stand good. *Swinb.* 72. *Godolph.* 25. *Dyer* 203. 8 *Co.* 147.

And if a person of sound memory makes his will, and afterwards becomes *non compos,* this is no revocation of the will. *Godolph.* 26. 4 *Co.* 126. 1 *Vern.* 105.

And by stat. 4 *Geo.* 2. *cap.* 10. any person being ideot, lunatic, or *non compos mentis,* or the committee of such person may, by direction of the lord chancellor, upon the petition of the person for whom such ideot, lunatic or *non compos mentis,* shall be seised or possessed in trust, or of the mortgagor, to convey and assure lands in such manner as the chancellor shall by such order direct.

And by 11 *Geo.* 3. *c.* 20. the guardians or committees of lunatics, are enabled, by order of the lord chancellor, to accept of surrenders of leases, and to grant new ones.

By 43 *Geo.* 3. *c.* 75. the lord chancellor of the united kingdom and of Ireland, being entrusted with the persons and estates of lunatics, may order the freehold and leasehold estates of such person to be sold, or charged by mortgage, for raising money for the payment of their debts; and the surplus to be applied as the estate would have been applicable to. *s.* 1, 2.

The power of leasing of lands belonging to lunatics, having only a limited estate therein, may be executed by the committee of the estate of such person, under the directions of the chancellor. *s.* 3.

When lunatics are seised of freehold or copyhold estates, in fee or in tail, and an absolute interest in leasehold estates, the chancellor may direct the committee of the estate to make leases thereof. *s.* 4.

The acts of the committee, under this act, shall be binding. *s.* 5.

But the act shall not subject estates of lunatics to debts, otherwise than they are now subject by law, but shall be applied only for the benefit of lunatics. *s.* 6.

When an ideot doth sue or defend he shall not appear by guardian, prochein amy, or attorney, but he must be ever in proper person. *Co. Lit.* 135. *b.* *F. N. B.* 27. 2 *Inst.* 390.

But it is otherwise of him who becomes *non compos mentis;* for he shall appear by guardian, if within age, or by attorney if of full age. 4 *Co.* 124. *b.* *Palm.* 520. *et vid.* 2 *Saund.* 335.

And if a trespass be committed in the lands of a lunatic who is legally committed, the committee cannot bring an action of trespass; but this must be brought in the name of the lunatic. 2 *Sid.* 125.

And if a lunatic be sued, he must have a committee assigned to him to defend the suit. 1 *Vern.* 106.

IDEOTA INQUIRENDO VEL EXAMINANDO, a writ to examine whether a person be an ideot. *F. N. B.* 232. *Reg. Orig.* 267. 9 *Rep.* 31.

IDES, (*idus*) with the ancient Romans, were eight days in every month, so called; being the eight days immediately after the Nones. In the months of March, May, July and October, these eight days begin at the eighth day of the month, and continue to the fifteenth day: in other months, they begin at the sixth day, and last to the thirteenth. But it is observable, that only the last day is called *ides*, the first of these days is the eighth *ides*, the second day the seventh, the third day the sixth, *i. e.* the eighth, seventh, or sixth day before the *ides;* and so it is of the rest of the days; wherefore when we speak of the *ides* of any month in general, it is to be taken for the fifteenth or thirteenth of the month mentioned. See *Calends.*

IDLENESS. Idle and disorderly persons are liable to be imprisoned in the house of correction for one month. 17 *Geo.* 2. *c.* 5. See *Vagrants.*

IDONEUM SE FACERE, IDONEARE SE, to purge himself by oath of a crime of which he is accused. *Cowel. Blount.*

IDUMANUS FLUVIUS, Black-water in Essex. *Ibid.*

JEJUNUM, (*purgatio per jejunium*) mentioned in *Leg. Canuti, cap.* 7. viz. *cum sociis se purget vel jejunum ineat, si opus est, et applicetur ad cornsned, et fiat voluntas Dei. Ibid.*

JEMAN, sometimes used for yeomen. *Cowel.*

JEOFAILE, (from the Fr. *j'ay faillè*, i. e. *ego lapsus sum*) signifies an oversight in pleading or other law proceedings. *Terms de Ley.*

The statutes of jeofails help errors and defects by mispleading in records, process, misprisions of clerks, &c. and are inserted under head *Error.*

JERSEY, *Guernsey, Sark, Alderney*, and their appendages were parcel of the duchy of Normandy, and were united to the crown of England by the first princes of the Norman line; they are governed by their own laws, which are for the most part the ducal customs of Normandy, being collected in an ancient book of great authority, entitled *le grand Coustumier.* The king's writ or process from the courts of Westminster is there of no force, but his commission is; they are not bound by common acts of our parliament, unless particularly named; all causes are originally determined by their own officers, the bailiffs and jurats of the island, but an appeal lies from them to the king and council in the last resort. 4 *Inst.* 280. 1 *Black.* 106.

JESSE, a large brass candlestick, with many sconces, hanging down in the middle of a church or choir. *Cowel. Blount.*

JETSAM, JETZON, and JOTSON, (from the Fr. *jetter, ejicire*) is any thing thrown out of a ship, being in the danger of wreck, and by the waves driven to the shore. 5 *Co. Rep.* 103. 1 *Black.* 292. 3 *Black.* 106.

JESUITS, the society of Jesuits, a monastic order first instituted by *Ignatio Loyola*, a Biscayan gentleman. See *Papists.*

JEWS, (*Judæi*) in former times the Jews were subject to many hardships, and were considered to be here, by an implied licence only, being under a proclamation of banishment: which case was similar to a determination of letters of safe conduct to an alien enemy, who was here by virtue of such letters before, &c. *Arg.* 2 *Show.* 371. in *East India Company* v. *Sands.*

But these hardships are now removed, and Jews, whether natural born subjects or not, participate equally with others in the just and benign administration of the British laws: there is, however, one corrective statute to which these persons are liable, *viz.* 1 *Ann. st.* 1. *c.* 30. which ordains, that if Jewish parents refuse to allow their Protestant children a fitting maintenance suitable to the fortune of the parent, the lord chancellor on complaint, may make such order therein, as he shall see proper.

IFUNGIA, the finest white bread, formerly called cocked bread. *Cowel.*

IGNIS JUDICIUM, purgation by fire. *Ibid.*

IGNORAMUS, (*i. e.* we are ignorant) the return of the grand jury on a bill of indictment, when they reject the evidence as too weak or defective to put the party on trial. 3 *Inst.* 30.

IGNORANCE, (*ignorantia*) which is want of knowledge of the law, shall not excuse any man from the penalty of it. *Doct. et Stud.* 1. 46.

IKENILD-STREET, is one of the four famous ways that the Romans made in England, called *Stratum Icenorum*, because it took beginning *ab Icenis*, which were the people that inhabited Norfolk, Suffolk and Cambridgeshire. *Camb. Brit. f.* 343. *Leg. Edw. Conf. c.* 12. See *Watling Street.*

ILET, by contraction *ight*, signifies a little island. *Blount.*

ILLEVIABLE, a debt or duty that cannot or ought not to be levied. *Cowel. Blount.*

ILLITERATE. If an illiterate man seal a deed falsely read to him, it will be void. 2 *Rep.* 3, 11. *Moor* 148. 11 *Rep.* 28. 11 *Rep.* 27. *b. Piggot's case.*

ILLUMINARE, to illuminate, to draw in gold and colours the initial letters, and the occasional pictures in manuscript books. Those persons who particularly practised this art, were called *illuminatores*, hence our limners.

ILLUSORY. If a father by will directs the mother to leave or apply a sum of money to or for the benefit of children in such shares and proportions as she may think fit: she must leave to each, a *substantial* legacy, not a small and trifling sum, otherwise the bequest will be deemed *illusory*, and set aside in equity.

IMAGES. See *Papists.*

IMAGINING, (or *compassing*, &c.) THE KING'S DEATH. See *Treason.*

IMBARGO, (Span. in Lat. *navium detentio*) is a stop, stay, or arrest upon ships or merchandize, by public authority. *Carth.* 297. *Cowel. Blount.*

IMBASING OF MONEY, (from *adultero*, to corrupt or mingle) signifies to mix specie with an allay below the standard of sterling; which the king by his prerogative may do, and yet keep it up to the same value as before: inhancing of it, is when it is raised to a higher rate, by proclamation. 1 *Hale's Hist. P. C.* 192.

IMBEZZLE, to steal, pilfer, or purloin. See *Felony*.

IMBRACERY. See *Embracery*.

IMBROCUS, a brook, a gut, a water-passage. *Cowel. Blount.*

IMMUNITIES. Immunity from all tolls, &c. are granted by charter.

IMPALARE, is to put in a pound. *Cowel. Blount.*

IMPANEL, (*impanellare juratis*) signifies the writing and entering into a parchment schedule by the sheriff, the names of a jury summoned to appear for the performance of such public service as juries are employed in. *Impanulare* was sometimes a privilege granted, that a person should not be impanelled or returned upon a jury. *Non ponatur nec impanuletur in aliquibus juratis*, &c. *Paroch. Antiq.* 657. *Cowel. Blount.*

IMPARLANCE, (*interlocutio, vel licentia interloquendi*) from the Fr. *parler*, to speak, is in the common law, the time granted by the court to a defendant to consider or advise what answer he shall make to the action of the plaintiff: being a continuance of the cause till another day, or a longer time given by the court.

IMPARSONEE, a parson *imparsonee, persona impersonata*, is he that is inducted, and in possession of a benefice. *Cowel.*

IMPEACHMENT, (from the Lat. *impetere.*) An impeachment before the lords by the commons of Great Britain, in parliament, is a prosecution of the already known and established law, and has been frequently put in practice, being a presentment to the most high and supreme court of criminal jurisdiction by the most solemn grand inquest of the whole kingdom (1 *Hal. P. C.* 150.) A commoner cannot, however, be impeached before the lords for any capital offence, but only for high misdemesnors: a peer may be impeached for any crime. And they usually (in case of an impeachment of a peer for treason) address the crown to appoint a lord high steward, for the greater dignity and regularity of their proceedings; which high steward was formerly elected by the peers themselves, though he was generally commissioned by the king (1 *Hale P. C.* 350.); but it hath of late years been strenuously maintained (*Lord's Journ.* 12 *May*, 1679. *Com. Journ.* 15 *May*, 1679. *Fost*, 142, &c.), that the appointment of an high steward in such cases is not indispensably necessary, but that the house may proceed without one.

The articles of impeachment are a kind of bills of indictment, found by the house of commons, and afterwards tried by the lords; who are in cases of misdemesnors considered not only as their own peers, but as the peers of the whole nation. This is a custom derived to us from the constitution of the antient Germans; who in their great councils sometimes tried capital accusations relating to the public: "*licet apud consilium accusare quoque, et discrimen capitis intendere* (*Tacit. de mor. Germ.* 12.)" And it has a peculiar propriety in the English constitution; which has much improved upon the antient model imported hither from the continent. For, though in general the union of the legislative and judicial powers ought to be most carefully avoided, yet it may happen that a subject, intrusted with the administration of public affairs, may infringe the rights of the people, and be guilty of such crimes, as the ordinary magistrate either dares not or cannot punish. Of these, the representatives of the people, or house of commons, cannot properly judge; because their constituents are the parties injured: and can therefore only impeach. But before what court shall this impeachment be tried? Not before the ordinary tribunals, which would naturally be swayed by the authority of so powerful an accuser. Reason therefore will suggest, that this branch of the legislature, which represents the people, must bring its charge before the other branch, which consists of the nobility, who have neither the same interests, nor the same passions as popular assemblies (*Montesq. Sp. L.* xi. 6.) This is a vast superiority, which the constitution of this island enjoys, over those of the Grecian or Roman republics; where the people were at the same time both judges and accusers. It is proper, that the nobility should judge, to insure justice to the accused; as it is proper that the people should accuse, to insure justice to the commonwealth. And therefore, among other extraordinary circumstances attending the authority of this court, there is one of a very singular nature, which was insisted on by the house of commons in the case of the earl of Danby in the reign of Charles II. (*Com. Journ.* 5 *May*, 1679); and it is now enacted by statute 12 & 13 *W.* 3. *c.* 2. that no pardon under the great seal shall be pleadable to an impeachment by the commons of Great Britain in parliament.

And in the impeachment of Warren Hastings, Esq. it was confidently advanced, that the lords are not bound to observe the same rules of evidence in an impeachment, as are admitted in criminal trials in the inferior courts. The high reputation of those, who strenuously maintained this doctrine, induced Professor Christian to endeavour to prove, that it was not only contrary to all precedent and authority, but repugnant to the first and great principles both of the English law and constitution, in a pamphlet, intitled "A

Dissertation, shewing that the house of lords in cases of judicature are bound by precisely the same rules of evidence, as are observed by all other courts." 4 *Black.* 261.

IMPEACHMENT OF WASTE, (*impetitio vasti*, from the Fr. *empeschement*, i. e. *impedimentum*) signifies a restraint from committing of waste upon lands; but he that holds without impeachment of waste, may make waste without being impeached for it; that is, without being sued for it, so that it is not wanton, such as demolishing of houses, or cutting down ornamental tress and shrubs. 11 *Rep.* 82. *b.* Bills in equity are also often filed to stay waste, on which an injunction will be readily granted *ex parte*, where a proper case is made out. See *Waste.*

IMPECHIARE, (French *empecher*, Latin *impetere*) to impeach, to accuse and prosecute, for felony or treason. *Cowel. Blount.*

IMPEDIATUS, *expeditatus*,*impediati canes*, dogs lamed and disabled from doing mischief in the forests, and purlieus. *Cowel.*

IMPEDIENS, a defendant, or deforciant. *Cowel.*

IMPEDIMENTS IN LAW, are those persons within age, under coverture, *non compos mentis*, in prison, beyond sea, &c. whose rights after the impediments removed, are reserved in cases of fines levied, &c. See *Limitation.*

IMPERIALE, a sort of very fine cloth. *Cowel.*

IMPESCATUS, impeached or accused. *Ibid.*

IMPETITIO, accusation or impeachment. *Ibid.*

IMPETRATION, (*impetratio*) signifies an obtaining any thing by request and prayer. *Ibid.*

IMPIERMENT, is used for impairing or prejudicing. *Ibid.*

IMPLEAD, to sue or prosecute by course of law. *Ibid.*

IMPLEMENTS, (from the Lat. *impleo*, to fill up) things necessary in any trade or mystery, without which the work cannot be performed; also the furniture of an house, as all household goods, implements, &c. And implements of household are tables, presses, cupboards, bed-steads, wainscot, and the like. *Terms de Ley.*

IMPLICATION, is where the law doth imply something that is not declared between parties in their deeds and agreements: and when our law giveth any thing to a man, it impliedly giveth whatsoever is necessary for the enjoying the same. *Moor* 123.

But no implication shall be allowed against an express estate, limited by express words, to drown the same. *Salk.* 266.

IMPORTATION, (*importatio*) is where goods and merchandize are brought into this kingdom from other nations. See *Customs.*

IMPOSSIBILITY. A thing which is impossible in law, is all one with a thing impossible in nature: and if any thing in a bond or deed is impossible at the time of its execution to be done, or afterwards becomes impossible by the act of God, such deed, &c. is void. 2 *Co. Rep.* 74. 2 *Black.* 156.

IMPOST, (from the Lat. *impono*) in strictness signifieth the tax received for merchandise brought into any haven from foreign nations. 31 *Eliz.* 5. And is in some sort distinguished from custom, the profit made of wares shipped out; yet they are frequently confounded. *Cowel.*

IMPOSTORS, (*religious*) those who falsely pretend an extraordinary commission from heaven; or terrify and abuse the people with false denunciations of judgments, are punishable by the temporal courts with fine, imprisonment, and infamous corporal punishment. 1 *Hawk. P. C.* 7. 4 *Black.* 62.

IMPOTENCY, is a sufficient ground by the ecclesiastical law, to avoid marriage; but the marriage is not void *ab initio*, but voidable only by sentence of separation, but to be actually made during the life of the parties. 1 *Black.* 434, 435.

IMPOTENTIÆ, *property ratione.* A qualified property may subsist with relation to animals *feræ naturæ*, *ratione impotentiæ*, on account of their own inability. As when hawks, herons, or other birds build in my trees, or conies or other creatures make their nests or burrows in my land, and have young ones there; I have a qualified property in those young ones, till such time as they can fly or run away, and then my property expires, but till then, it is in some cases trespass, and in others felony, for a stranger to take them away. 7 *Rep.* 17. *Lamb. Eiren.* 274. For here, as the owner of the land has it in his power to do what he pleases with them, the law therefore vests a property in him of the young ones in the same manner as it does of the old ones, if re-claimed or confined: for these cannot through weakness any more than the others through restraint use their natural liberty and forsake him. 2 *Black.* 394.

IMPRESSING SEAMEN. The power of impressing men for the sea service by the king's commission, has been a matter of some dispute, and submitted to with great reluctance; though it hath very clearly and learnedly been shewn by sir Michael Foster, (*Rep.* 154. *Broadfoot's case*) that the practice of impressing, and granting powers to the admiralty for that purpose, is of very antient date, and hath been uniformly continued by a regular series of precedents to the present time: hence he concludes it to be part of the common law. The difficulty arises from this, that no statute has expressly declared this power to be in the crown, though many of them very strongly imply it. The stat. 2 *Ric.* 2. *c.* 4. speaks of mariners being arrested and retained for the king's service, as of a thing well known, and practised without dispute; and provides a remedy against their running away. By a later statute, (2 & 3 *Ph. & M. c.* 16.) if any waterman, who uses the river Thames, shall hide himself during the execution of any commission of pressing for the king's service, he is liable to heavy penalties By another, (5 *Eliz. c.* 5.) no fisherman shall be taken by the queen's commission to serve as a mariner; but the commission shall be first brought to two justices of the peace, inhabiting near the sea-coast where the mariners are to be taken, to the intent, that the justices may chuse out, and return such a number of able-bodied men, as in the commission are contained, to serve her majesty. And, by others (7 & 8 *W.* 3. *c.* 21. 2 *Ann. c.* 6. 4 & 5 *Ann. c.* 19. 13 *Geo.* 2. *c.* 17, &c.) especial protections are allowed to seamen in particular circumstances, to prevent them from being impressed. All which do most evidently imply a power of impressing to reside somewhere; and, if any where, it must from the spirit of our constitution, as well as from the frequent mention of the king's commission, reside in the crown alone. 1 *Black.* 418, 419.

This method of impressing is only defensible from public necessity, to which all private considerations must give way. 1 *Black.* 419.

And the legality of pressing is now so fully established, that it will not now admit of a doubt in any court of justice. In the case of the King *v.* Jubbs, lord Mansfield says, "the "power of pressing is founded upon imme- "morial usage, allowed for ages. If it be "so founded and allowed for ages, it can have "no ground to stand upon, nor can it be "vindicated or justified by any reason, but "the safety of the state. And the practice "is deduced from that trite maxim of the "constitutional law of England, 'that pri- "vate mischief had better be submitted to, "than public detriment and inconvenience "should ensue.' And though it be a legal "power, it may, like many others, be abus- "ed in the exercise of it." *Cowp.* 517. In that case, the defendant was brought up by *habeas corpus,* upon the ground that he was entitled to an exemption; but the court held, that the exemption was not made out, and he was remanded to the ship from which he had been brought.

Lord Kenyon has also declared in a similar case, that the right of pressing is founded on the common law, and extends to all persons exercising employments in the seafaring line. Any exemptions, therefore, which such persons may claim, must depend upon the positive provisions of statutes. 5 *T. R.* 276.

IMPREST-MONEY, is money paid on inlisting soldiers. *Cowel. Blount.*

IMPRETIABILIS, invaluable. *Ibid.*

IMPRIMERY, (Fr.) a print, or impression; and the art of printing, also a printing-house. *Ibid.*

IMPRISTI, those who side with, or take the part of another, either in his defence or otherwise. *Ibid.*

IMPRISONMENT, (*imprisionamentum*) is the restraint of a man's liberty under the custody of another; and extends not only to a gaol, but to a house, stocks, or where a man is held in the street, &c. for in all these cases the party so restrained is said to be a prisoner, so long as he hath not his liberty freely to go about his business, as at other times. *Co. Lit.* 253.

And the law so much discourages unlawful confinement, that if a man is under duress of imprisonment; a compulsion by an illegal restraint of liberty, until he seals a bond or the like; he may allege this duress, and avoid the extorted bond. But if a man be lawfully imprisoned, and either to procure his discharge, or on any other fair account, seals a bond or a deed, this is not by duress of imprisonment, and he is not at liberty to avoid it (2 *Inst.* 482.)

To make imprisonment lawful, it must either be by process from the courts of judicature, or by warrant from some legal officer having authority to commit to prison; which warrant must be in writing, under the hand and seal of the magistrate, and express the causes of the commitment, in order to be examined into (if necessary) upon a *habeas corpus.* If there be no cause expressed, the gaoler is not bound to detain the prisoner. For the law judges in this respect, saith sir Edward Coke, like Festus the Roman governor; that it is unreasonable to send a prisoner, and not to signify withal the crimes alleged against him. (*Ibid.* 52, 53.)

The satisfactory remedy for this injury of false imprisonment, is by an action of trespass *vi et armis,* usually called an action of *false* imprisonment, which is generally and almost unavoidably accompanied with a charge of assault and battery also; and therein the party shall recover damages for the injury he has received; and also the defendant is, as for all other injuries committed with force, or *vi et armis,* liable to pay a fine to the king for the violation of the public peace. 3 *Black.* 137.

And the law of England regards, asserts, and preserves the personal liberty of individuals. This personal liberty consists in the power of loco-motion, of changing situation, or removing one's person to whatsoever place one's own inclination may direct; without imprisonment or restraint, unless by due course of law; and is a right strictly natural, which the laws of England have never abridged without sufficient cause; and, in this kingdom it cannot ever be abridged at the mere discretion of the magistrate, without the explicit permission of the laws. For the language of the great charter (*c.* 29.) is, that no freeman shall be taken or imprisoned, but by the lawful judgment of his equals, or by the law of the land. And many subsequent old statutes, (5 *Ed.* 3. *c.* 9. 25 *Ed.* 3. *st.* 5. *c.* 4. 28 *Ed.* 3. *c.* 3.) expressly direct, that no man shall be taken or imprisoned by suggestion or petition to the king or his council, unless it be by legal indictment, or the process of the common law. By the petition of right, 3 *Car.* 1. it is enacted, that no freeman shall be imprisoned or detained without cause shewn, to which he may make answer according to law. By 16 *Car.* 1. *c.* 10. if any person be restrained of his liberty by order or decree of any illegal court, or by command of the king's majesty in person, or by warrant of the council board, or any of the privy council; he shall, upon demand of his council, have a writ of *habeas corpus*, to bring his body before the court of king's bench or common pleas; who shall determine whether the cause of his commitment be just, and thereupon do as to justice shall appertain. And by 31 *Car.* 2. *c.* 2 commonly called the *habeas corpus act*, the methods of obtaining this writ are so plainly pointed out and enforced, that, so long as this statute remains unimpeached, no subject of England can be long detained in prison, except in those cases in which the law requires and justifies such detainer. And, lest this act should be evaded by demanding unreasonable bail, or sureties for the prisoner's appearance, it is declared by 1 *W. & M. st.* 2. *c.* 2. that excessive bail ought not to be required.

Of great importance to the public is the preservation of this personal liberty: for if once it were left in the power of any, the highest, magistrate to imprison arbitrarily whomever he or his officers thought proper, (as in France it is daily practised,) there would soon be an end of all other rights and immunities. Some have thought, that unjust attacks, even upon life or property, at the arbitrary will of the magistrate, are less dangerous to the commonwealth, than such as are made upon the personal liberty of the subject. To bereave a man of life, or by violence to confiscate his estate, without accusation or trial, would be so gross and notorious an act of despotism, as must at once convey the alarm of tyranny throughout the whole kingdom: but confinement of the person, by secretly hurrying him to gaol, where his sufferings are unknown or forgotten, is a less public, a less striking, and therefore a more dangerous engine of arbitrary government. And yet sometimes, when the state is in real danger, even this may be a necessary measure. But the happiness of our constitution is, that it is not left to the executive power to determine when the danger of the state is so great, as to render this measure expedient: for it is the parliament only, or legislative power, that, whenever it sees proper, can authorize the crown, by suspending the *habeas corpus* act for a short and limited time, to imprison suspected persons without giving any reason for so doing. But this is only done in cases of extreme emergency; and in these, the nation parts with its liberty for a while, in order to preserve it for ever. 1 *Black.* 135, 6.

IMPROPER FEUDS. See *Deadly Feud.*

IMPROPRIATION. When a benefice ecclesiastical is in the hands of a layman, it is called an *impropriation;* and appropriation when in the hands of a bishop, college, or religious house, though sometimes they are confounded. 1 *Black. Com.* 386.

This appropriation may be severed, and the church become disappropriate, two ways: as, first, if the patron or appropriator presents a clerk, who is instituted and inducted to the parsonage: for the incumbent so instituted and inducted, is to all intents and purposes complete parson; and the appropriation, being once severed, can never be re-united again, unless by a repetition of the same solemnities (*Co. Litt.* 46.) And, when the clerk so presented* is distinct from the vicar, the rectory thus vested in him, becomes, what is called a *sine-cure;* because he hath no cure of souls, having a vicar under him to whom that cure is committed.† Also, if the corporation which has the appropriation is dissolved, the parsonage becomes disappropriate at common law; because the perpetuity of person is gone, which is necessary to support the appropriation. (2 *Burn. eccl. law*, 347.)

IMPROVEMENT. See *Approvement.*

IMPRUIARE, to improve land. *Cowel. Blount.*

IMPRUIAMENTUM, the improvement of lands. *Ibid.*

IN AUTER DROIT, in another's right; as executors, administrators, and trustees are.

INBLAURA, profit or product of ground. *Cowel. Blount.*

INBORH AND OUTBORH, (Sax.) The ingress and egress of those who travelled to and fro between England and Scotland. *Cowel. Blount.*

INCASTELLARE, to reduce a thing to serve instead of a castle. *Ibid.*

IN CASU CONSIMILI. See *Casu Consimili.*

IN CASU PROVISO. See *Casu Proviso.*

---

* That is, if the appropriator or impropriator should, either by design or mistake, present his clerk to the parsonage, it is held, that the vicarage will ever afterwards be dissolved, and the incumbent will be entitled to all the tithes and dues of the church as rector. *Wats.* c. 17. 2 *R. Ab.* 338.

† Wherever a rector and vicar are presented and instituted to the same benefice, the rector is excused all duty, and has what is properly called a sinecure. But where there is only one incumbent, the benefice is not in law, a sinecure, though there should be neither a church nor any inhabitants within the parish. *Ibid.*

INCAUSTUM, or ENCAUSTUM, ink. *Cowel. Blount.*

INCENDIARIES. See *Arson.*

INCEPTION. The commencement of a right or title, which may have its *inception* in the life of another, though it does not vest till the death of the party tenant for life.

Thus, institution gives inception to a lay fee, so that if a caveat be entered after to prevent induction, a prohibition shall be granted. 2 *Rol.* 294. *Prohibition* (M) *pl.* 14.

INCERTAINTY, is where a thing is so ambiguously set down, that one cannot tell how to understand it. 5 *Rep.* 121. *Plowd.* 25.

In law proceedings, incertainty will make them void. *Plowd.* 84. 3 *Mod.* 121. So also incertainty in deeds renders them void. *Plowd.* 6. 273. 6 *Rep.* 20. 2 *Bulst.* 180. 9 *Rep.*

INCEST. In the year 1650, when the ruling powers found it for their interest to put on the semblance of a very extraordinary strictness and purity of morals, incest and wilful adultery were made capital crimes. But at the restoration, when men, from an abhorrence of the hypocrisy of the late times, fell into a contrary extreme, of licentiousness, it was not thought proper to renew a law of such unfashionable rigour. And these offences have been ever since left to the feeble coercion of the spiritual court, according to the rules of the canon law. 4 *Black. Com.* 64.

INCHANTMENT. By 9 *Geo.* 2. *c.* 5. no prosecution shall be carried on against any person for conjuration, witchcraft, sorcery, or inchantment. But persons pretending to use withcraft, or tell fortunes, are still punishable as rogues and vagabonds under the *Vagrant act*, 17 *Geo.* 2. *c.* 5.

INCHANTER, (*incantator*) described to be one who by charms conjures the devil; so called because their charms were in verse. 3 *Inst.* 44.

INCHANTRESS, (*incantatrix*) a woman who useth charms and incantations. *Ibid.*

INCHARTARE, to give or grant any thing by an instrument in writing. *Cowel. Blount.*

INCH OF CANDLE, a mode of selling goods by merchants in the following manner, *viz.* when the goods are exposed to sale, a small piece of wax-candle, about an inch long, is burning, and the last bidder when the candle goes out, is intitled to the lot or parcel so exposed.

INCIDENT, (*incidens*) is a thing necessarily depending upon, appertaining to, or following another that is more worthy or principal; such as a court-baron, which is inseparably incident to a manor, and the like. *Kitch.* 36. *Co. Lit.* 151.

INCLAUDARE, signifies to fetter a horse. *Cowel. Blount.*

INCLAUSA, a home-close, or inclosure near the house. *Ibid.*

INCLOSURES. By 41 *Geo.* 3. (u. k.) *c.* 119. no person shall act as a commissioner under any future inclosure act (except by signing notice of the first meeting, and administering the oath,) until he shall have taken an oath to act without favour or affection, and the oaths and appointments of new commissioners shall be enrolled with the award, and a copy shall be evidence. *s.* 1.

Commissioners declining to act, shall give notice to the others, and no commissioner shall purchase lands within the parish, where inclosures are made, for five years after their award. *s.* 2.

Commissioners shall inquire into the boundaries of parishes, and if not sufficiently ascertained, they shall fix them, giving previous notice of their intention so to do; and the commissioners shall cause a description of the boundaries to be delivered to the churchwardens and overseers of the respective parishes; and lords of manors, and persons dissatisfied, may appeal to the quarter sessions, whose decision shall be final. *s.* 3.

A survey, admeasurement, plan, and valuation of the lands to be inclosed, shall be made and kept by the commissioners, which shall be verified by the persons making them, and proprietors may inspect admeasurements and plans, and take copies. *s.* 4.

Until the division shall be completed, the lands may be entered by the commissioners, or any persons they may appoint, to make surveys; but maps made at the time of passing the acts, may be used, without making new ones, if the commissioners shall think fit. *s.* 5.

Claimants of common, in lands to be inclosed, shall deliver to the commissioners, schedules of the particulars, or shall be excluded, which claims may be inspected and copies taken; and objections to claims shall be delivered at or before the meeting appointed for that purpose, or shall not be received, except for special cause. *s.* 6.

Commissioners are not hereby authorised to determine disputes touching titles to lands; but shall assign the allotments to the persons in actual seizin or possession, and disputes as to title shall not delay inclosures. *s.* 7.

The commissioners, before making any allotment, shall appoint public carriage roads, and prepare a map thereof, to be deposited with their clerk, and give notice thereof, and appoint a meeting, at which if any person shall object, the commissioners, with a justice of the division, shall determine the matter: and where commissioners may be empowered to stop up any old road, it shall not be done, without the order of two justices, subject to appeal to quarter sessions. *s.* 8.

Carriage roads shall be fenced on both sides, according to the direction of the commissioners; and no person shall erect any gate across any road, or plant any trees on the sides, at less than fifty yards distance. *s.* 9.

Commissioners shall appoint surveyors, whose salary, and the expence of making the road (above the statute duty), shall be raised as other expences, and paid before the execution of the award. *Ibid.*

The surveyors shall be subject to the controul of the justices, and shall account to them for monies received.—Justices may levy rates. Surveyors neglecting to complete the roads, within a limited time, shall forfeit 20*l.* and the inhabitants shall not be chargeable (except to statute duty) until the roads are declared to be completed at a special sessions. *Ibid.*

The commissioners shall appoint private roads, footways, ditches, drains, watering-places, quarries, bridge-gates, fences, and marks. *s.* 10.

The grass and herbage on roads shall belong to the proprietors of the lands adjoining, and all roads which shall not be set out shall be allotted and inclosed; but no turnpike-road shall be altered without the consent of the trustees. *s.* 11.

Commissioners in making allotments shall have due regard to the situation of the houses, as well as the quantity and quality of land. *s.* 12.

Commissioners may direct small allotments to be laid together, and ring fenced and stocked, and depastured in common by the proprietors. *s.* 13.

Allotments shall be in full compensation for all rights in the lands, which shall cease on notice from the commissioners, affixed on the church door. *s.* 14.

Commissioners may exchange allotments, messuages, lands, and the like, with the consent of the proprietors, or if belonging to churches, with the consent of the bishop and of the patron. *s.* 15.

Commissioners may make allotments in severalty to joint tenants, or tenants in common. *s.* 16.

Persons shall accept their allotments within two calendar months after the award, or forfeit their right. *s.* 17.

Guardians, trustees, and committees may accept for incapacitated persons, and tenants for life shall accept of allotments. *s.* 18.

And their non-acceptance shall not prejudice the rights of the *cestui que trusts*, who shall accept within twelve months after their inability is removed. *Ibid.*

Before execution of the award, allotments may be ditched and inclosed, with the consent of the commissioners. *s.* 19.

Timber and other trees and bushes shall be allotted with the lands whereon they stand, the parties paying to the owners such sums as the commissioners shall direct; but in case of neglect, the owners may cut them down, and take them away. *s.* 20.

Where money is to be paid for lands, and which ought to be laid out in other purchases, to be settled to the same uses, the commissioners may thereout defray a proportion of the expence of passing the act, and putting it in execution; and if the surplus amounts to 200*l.* it shall as soon as may be, be laid out in other purchases, and in the mean time be paid into the bank, and applied under the direction of the court of chancery. *s.* 21.

If such money be less than 200*l.* and upwards of 20*l.* it shall, at the option of the person entitled to the rents, be paid into the bank, or to two trustees, to be approved of by the commissioners, for the same purposes. *s.* 22.

If less than 20*l.* it shall be applied to the use of the persons entitled to the rents of the lands. *s.* 23.

If any person does not accept, inclose, and fence in his allotment as the commissioners shall direct, they may cause it to be inclosed and fenced, and let and receive the rents until the expences are satisfied, or they may charge them upon the proprietor. *s.* 24.

During seven years after fencing the allotments, the fences may be erected on the outside of the ditches, and the materials carried away by the proprietors. *s.* 25.

No standing fences or hedges shall be destroyed till the execution of the award, without the consent of the commissioners; and if assigned as a boundary fence, shall be left uncut, the persons entitled to the allotments making compensation thereof. *s.* 26.

Where the boundary of any common fields shall be fenced by any mound, the proprietors of adjoining allotments shall not be compelled to fence them, but such boundaries shall be maintained by the proprietors as before, or as the commissioners may appoint. *s.* 27.

Persons destroying fences put up under the authority of any act, shall forfeit 5*l.* and the proprietor or occupier of the lands may give evidence. *s.* 28.

When the expences of obtaining and carrying any act into execution shall be paid by the proprietors, the commissioners may on neglect, cause the same to be levied by distress, or may take possession of the allotments, and receive the rents till satisfied. *s.* 29.

Guardians, trustees, committees, and tenants for life, or in tail, may charge allotments with expences, if not exceeding 5*l.* per acre, and if persons in possession shall advance the money, the commissioners may mortgage the lands to them for reimbursement. *s.* 30.

The commissioners may deduct from allotments for charity or school lands, what shall be deemed equal to the proportionable share of the expences, and allot the same to persons undertaking to pay. *s.* 31.

When the expences of obtaining and carrying any act into execution shall be to be paid by sale of part of the lands, the commissioners shall set out and sell a part, and the purchasers shall immediately make a deposit, which shall be forfeited if the purchase money be not duly paid. *s.* 32.

Commissioners may summon witnesses, and if they neglect to attend, or refuse to be examined, they are to forfeit not more than 10*l.* nor less than 5*l.*; but no witness shall be obliged to travel above eight miles. *s.* 33, 34.

After allotment, the commissioners shall draw up their award, which shall be read and executed at a meeting of the proprietors, and proclaimed the next Sunday in the church, and then considered as complete. *s.* 35.

The award shall be inrolled in one of the courts at Westminster, or with the clerk of the peace of the county, and may be inspected and copies obtained—the award and copies shall be legal evidence, and the award binding on all parties interested—and the commissioners may annex maps to the award, which shall be deemed part thereof. *Ibid.*

The commissioners shall keep accounts of all monies, which may be inspected at their clerk's office gratis, on pain of his forfeiting not more than 10*l.* nor less than 5*l.* *s.* 36.

Monies raised shall be deposited as directed by a majority in value of the proprietors, and not issued without an order from the commissioners. *s.* 37.

The rector or vicar, with the consent of the bishop of the diocese, and of the patron of the living, may lease allotments for twenty-one years, at a rack rent. *s.* 38.

Penalties are recoverable before one justice by distress, and are to be applied according to the directions of the commissioners. *s.* 39.

The rights of lords of manors, the king, and others, except so far as they are affected hereby, are saved. *s.* 40, 41.

Two justices may take affidavits of the notices required having been given, *s.* 42.—Persons taking false oaths to be deemed guilty of perjury. *s.* 43.

The act is binding in all cases, except where other provisions are made. *s.* 44.

INCOMPATIBLE, when certain acts are contradictory to each other, they cannot both stand, being incompatible; as for instance, it is incompatible by the statutes to hold two benefices with cure, if of a certain value in the king's books without a dispensation.

INCONTINENCY, (*incontinentia*) this is a crime punishable in the ecclesiastical courts by canonical censures, such as where parties live together in a state of fornication or adultery, and the like. And incontinency by bigamy, or having more wives than one; rapes of women; sodomy, or buggery; getting bastards, &c. is punishable by different statutes. See *Felony.*

INCOPOLITUS, a proctor or vicar. *Cowel. Blount.*

INCORPORATION. The king's consent is absolutely necessary to the erection of any corporation, either implied or expressly given. The king's implied consent is to be found in corporations which exist by force of the common law, to which our former kings are supposed to have given their concurrence; common law being nothing else but custom, arising from the universal agreement of the whole community. The king's consent is also presumed as to all corporations by prescription, such as the city of London, and many others, which have existed time out of memory; and therefore are looked upon in law to be well created. The methods by which the king's consent is expressly given, are either by act of parliament or by charter. But the immediate creative act is usually performed by the king alone, in virtue of his royal prerogative, *i. e.* by charter. 2 *Inst.* 330. 10 *Rep.* 29, 30. 1 *Rol. Abr.* 512, 513. 8 *Rep.* 114. 1 *Black.* 472, 3.

INCORPOREAL HEREDITAMENTS. An incorporeal hereditament is a right issuing out of a thing corporeal, (whether real or personal) or concerning, or annexed to, or exercisable within the same. *Co. Lit.* 19, 20. See *Hereditaments.*

INCREMENTUM, increase or improvement; to which was opposed *decrementum* or abatement. *Paroch. Antiq.* 164. *Cowel. Blount.*

INCROACHMENT, signifies an unlawful gaining upon the right or possession of another man. 9 *Rep.* 33. See *Encroachment.*

INCUMBENT, (Lat. *incumbo*, to strictly mind) is a clerk who is resident on his benefice with cure; and is so called, because he does or ought to bend all his study to the discharge of the cure of the church to which he belongs. *Co. Lit.* 119.

INCUMBRANCE. See *Mortgage.*

INCURRAMENTUM, the incurring or being subject to a penalty, fine, or amercement. *Cowel. Blount.*

INDEBITATUS ASSUMPSIT, is an action so called from the words used in the declaration, "that *he the defendant being so indebted, undertook and promised to pay,*" and it is brought to recover in damages, the amount of the debt or demand; upon the trial of which action, the jury will, according to the nature of the evidence, allow to the plaintiff either the whole of the damages, or any less sum.

INDECIMABLE, (*indecimabilis*) not tithable, or by law liable to pay tithe. 2 *Inst.* 490.

INDEFEISIBLE, or INDEFEASIBLE, that which cannot be defeated or made void.

INDEFEASIBLE RIGHT TO THE THRONE. The doctrine of hereditary right does by no means imply an indefeasible right to the throne. It is unquestionably in the breast of the supreme legislative authority of this kingdom, the king and both houses of parliament, to defeat this hereditary right; and, by particular entails, limitations and provisions, to exclude the immediate heir, and vest the inheritance in any one else. This is strictly consonant to our laws and constitution; as may be gathered from the expression so frequently used in our Statute Book, of "the king's majesty, his heirs and successors." In which we may observe, that as the word "heirs," necessarily implies an inheritance or hereditary right, generally subsisting in the royal person; so the word "successors," distinctly taken, must imply that this inheritance may sometimes be broken through; or, that there may be a successor, without being the heir of the king. 1 *Black.* 195.

This is a doctrine perfectly reasonable, for in case the heir apparent should be an ideot, a lunatic, or otherwise incapable of reigning, it is necessary that such a power should be lodged somewhere; but the inheritance and regal dignity would be very precarious indeed, if this power were expressly and avowedly lodged in the hands of the people, only to be exerted whenever prejudice, caprice, or discontent, should happen to take the lead: consequently it can no where be so properly lodged as in the two houses of parliament, by and with the consent of the reigning king; and therefore, in the king, lords and commons in parliament assembled, our laws have expressly lodged it. 1 *Black.* 195.

INDEFENSUS, one that is impleaded, and refuseth to make answer.

INDEMNITY, *acts of*, occasionally pass to indemnify persons from penalties who have neglected certain acts, as taking the oaths, delivering in qualifications, &c.

INDENTURE, (*indentura*) is a writing containing some contract, agreement or conveyance between two or more persons, being indented at the top answerable to another part, which hath the same contents. *Co. Lit.* 229.

INDIA COMPANY. See *East India Company.*

INDICAVIT, is a writ of prohibition that lies for a patron of a church, whose clerk is sued in the spiritual court by another clerk for tithes, which amount to a fourth part of the profits of the advowson; in which case the suit belongs to the king's courts, by stat. *Westm.* 2. *c.* 5. *Reg. Orig.* 35. *Old Nat. Br.* 31.

This writ may be also purchased by the parson sued; and is directed as well unto the judge of the court, as unto the party plaintiff, that they do not proceed, &c. *New Nat. Brev.* 66, 101.

INDICTED, (*indictatus*) when the grand jury have found a true bill against any one accused by bill preferred to them at the king's suit, for some offence indictable, he is said to be indicted thereof.

INDICTION, (*indictio, ab indicendo*) formerly the space of fifteen years, by which computation, charters and public writings were dated. And by this account of time, each year increased one till it came to fifteen; and then returned again, making first, second indiction, &c. as *dat. apud Chippenham,* 18 *die Aprilis, indictione nona, anno Dom.* 1266. *Cowel. Blount.*

INDICTMENT, (*indictio, indictamentum,* from the Fr. *enditer,* i. e. *deferre nomen alicujus indicare*) is a bill of complaint or accusation drawn up in form of law, and exhibited for some offence criminal or penal, to a grand jury; upon whose oath it may be found to be true. *Lamb. lib.* 4. *cap.* 5.

But although a bill of indictment may be preferred to a grand jury upon oath, they are not bound to find the bill, if they find cause to the contrary; and they must either find the whole bill to be true, or reject it, and not find specially for part, &c. 2 *Hawk. P. C.* 210.

An indictment is the king's suit; for which reason the party who prosecutes, is a good witness to prove it. 2 *Hawk.* 210.

After a person is indicted for felony, the sheriff is commanded to attach his body by a *capias;* and on return of a *non est inventus,* a second *capias* shall be granted, and the sheriff is to seize the offender's chattels, &c. And if on that writ a *non est inventus* is returned, an *exigent* shall be awarded, and the chattels be forfeited, &c. 25 *Ed.* 3. *stat.* 5. *c.* 2.

Upon indictments at the sessions, the magistrates on certificate of the bill being found, will issue what is termed a bench warrant, upon which the party may be apprehended. But if he come in voluntarily, and put in bail, the justices will grant a *supersedeas* to such warrant: and if he do not put in such bail, but is apprehended, he must remain in custody, and give the prosecutor *forty-eight hours* notice of bail before he can be discharged.

Also by 48 *Geo.* 3. *c.* 58. whenever any person shall be charged with any offence for which he may be prosecuted by indictment or information in B. R. *not being treason* or *felony,* on affidavit thereof or certificate of an indictment or information filed, one of the judges may cause the party to be held to bail, and the prosecutor may deliver a copy of the indictment or information to the party, and unless he plead within eight days enter an appearance and plead not guilty for him, and proceed to trial. *s.* 1.

When a person is convicted upon an indictment for trespass or misdemeanor, he is to appear in court, on judgment pronounced; and the court having set a fine upon him, will commit him in execution, &c. 2 *Lil. Abr.* 41.

But in trifling misdemeanors, assaults, &c. the court will on motion, (the clerk in court engaging to pay any fine set,) dispense with the personal appearance of a defendant.

INDICTOR, is he that indicteth; and *indictee*, the party indicted.

INDISTANTER, signifies without delay. *Cowel.*

INDIVISUM, that which two or more hold in common without partition. *Ibid.*

INDOLIS, a studious young man. *Ibid.*

INDOMIT, law French for boisterous and ungovernable. *Law Fr. Dict.*

INDORSEMENT, (*indorsamentum*) any thing written on the back of a deed. *West. Symb. par.* 2. *sect.* 157. And the indorsement and deed shall stand. *Moor* 679. There is also an indorsement of bills or notes. See *Bills of Exchange.*

INDOWMENT. See *Endowment.*

INDUCEMENT, the motive or incitement to a thing: thus the ground of the action is inducement, as a promise in consideration of forbearing a debt till such a day, is good without shewing how due. *Cro. Jac.* 548. 2 *Mod.* 70.

INDUCTION, (*inductio*, i. e. leading into) is the giving a parson possession of his church, and is the *investiture* of the temporal part of the benefice, as institution is of the *spiritual*. This induction is done in the following manner: after the bishop hath granted *institution*, he issues his mandate to the archdeacon to induct the clerk, who usually issues out a precept to other clergymen to perform it for him; and then one of the clergymen so commissioned, takes the parson to be inducted by the hand, lays it on the key of the church, and pronounces these words; *by virtue of this commission, I induct you into the real and actual possession of the rectory of, &c. with all its appurtenances*, and puts the parson into actual possession. *Countr. Pars.* 21, 22. *Pars. Counsel.* 8.

This induction is a temporal act; and if the archdeacon refuse to induct a parson, or to grant a commission to others to do it, action on the case lies against him, on which damages shall be recovered; he may likewise be compelled, by sentence in the ecclesiastical court, to induct the clerk, and shall answer the contempt. 12 *Rep.* 128.

INDULGENCIES *of the Romish church.* See PAPISTS, &c.

INDUSTRIAM, property PER. A qualified property may subsist in animals *feræ naturæ per industriam hominis:* by a man's reclaiming and making them tame by art, industry, and management; or by confining them within his own immediate power that they cannot escape, and use their natural liberty: such as deer in a park, hares or rabbits in an inclosed warren, doves in a dove-house; pheasants, partridges, or other birds mewed up, and fish in private ponds: but these are no longer the property of a man, than while they continue in his keeping or actual possession, for if at any time they regain their natural liberty, his property instantly ceases. 2 *Black.* 392.

IN ESSE, any thing in being; distinguished from *in posse;* as, a thing that is not, but by *possibility* may come into being, such as an unborn child.

INEWARDUS, (*inwardus*) a guard, a watchman, one set to keep watch and ward. *Cowel. Blount.*

INFALISTATUS. Mr. Selden supposes this to be made out of the French word *falize*, which is fine sand by the water side, or a bank of the sea. And in this sand or bank, it seems that executions for felony at Dover were made. *Mon. Angl. tom.* 2. *p.* 165. *b.*

INFAMY, which extends to forgery, perjury, conspiracy, gross cheats, &c. disables a witness, or juror; but a pardon of crimes restores a person's credit to make him a good evidence. 2 *Hawk. P. C.* 432, 433.

INFANGTHEF, INFANGENETHEOF, (from the Sax. *fang* or *fangen*, i. e. *capere*, and *theof, fur*) a privilege or liberty granted unto lords of certain manors, to judge any thief taken within their fee. *Bract. lib.* 3. *c.* 35. But these franchises of *infangthef* or *outfangthef*, to be heard and determined in court-barons, are antiquated, and long since gone. 2 *Inst.* 31.

INFANT, (*infans*) a person under twenty-one years of age, whose acts are in many cases either void or voidable. *Co. Lit. lib.* 1. *cap.* 21.

But if one is born on the 1st of January, he is of age to do any legal act on the morning of the last day of December, though he may not have lived twenty-one years by nearly forty-eight hours; the reason assigned is, that in law there is no fraction of a day: and if the birth were on the first second of one day, and the act on the last second of the other, then twenty-one years would be complete; and in the law it is the same whether a thing is done upon one moment of the day or on another. *Christian's Note* on 1 *Black.* 463.

Infants have various privileges, and various disabilities: but their very disabilities are privileges, in order to secure them from hurting themselves by their own improvident acts. An infant cannot be sued but under the protection, and joining the name, of his guardian; for he is to defend him against all attacks as well by law as otherwise (*Co. Lit.* 135.): but he may sue either by his guardian, or *prochein amy*, his next friend who is not his guardian. This *prochein amy* may be any person who will undertake the infant's cause; and it frequently happens, that an infant, by his *prochein amy*, institutes a suit in equity against a fraudulent guardian. In criminal cases, an infant of the age of fourteen years may be capitally punished for any capital offence (1 *Hal. P. C.* 25.); but under the age of seven he cannot. The period between seven and fourteen is subject to much uncertainty: for the infant shall, generally speaking, be judged *prima facie* innocent; yet if he was *doli capax*, and could discern between good and evil at the time of the offence committed, he may be convicted, and undergo judgment and execution of death, though he had not attained to years of puberty or discretion (*Ibid.* 26.) And sir Matthew Hale gives us two instances, one of a girl of thirteen, who was burned for killing her mistress; another of a boy still younger, that had killed his companion and hid himself, who was hanged; for it appeared by his hiding that he knew he had done wrong, and could discern between good and evil: and in such cases the maxim of law is, that *malitia supplet ætatem.* So also, in much more modern times, a boy of ten years old, who was guilty of a heinous murder, was held a proper subject for capital punishment, by the opinion of all the judges. *Foster* 72.

With regard to estates and civil property, an infant hath many privileges: thus an infant may wave a purchase or conveyance when he comes to full age: or, if he does not then actually agree to it, his heirs may wave it after him. And, in general, an infant shall lose nothing by non-claim, or neglect of demanding his right; nor shall any other laches or negligence be imputed to an infant, except in some very particular cases. *Co. Lit.* 2. 1 *Black.* 464.

It is generally true, that an infant can neither alien his lands, nor do any legal act, nor make a deed, nor indeed any manner of contract, that will bind him. But still to all these rules there are some exceptions: part of which are mentioned in reckoning up the different capacities which they assume at different ages, under the title Age; and there are others, a few of which it may not be improper to recite, as a general specimen of the whole. And, first, it is true, that infants cannot alien their estates: but infant trustees, or mortgagees, are enabled to convey, under the direction of the court of chancery or exchequer, or other courts of equity, the estates they hold in trust or mortgage, to such person as the court shall appoint (*Stat.* 7 *Ann. c.* 19. 4 *Geo.* 3. *c.* 16.) Also it is generally true, that an infant can do no legal act: yet, an infant, who has an advowson, may present to the benefice when it becomes void (*Co. Lit.* 172.) For the law in this case dispenses with one rule, in order to maintain others of far greater consequence: it permits an infant to present a clerk (who, if unfit, may be rejected by the bishop) rather than either suffer the church to be unserved till he comes of age, or permit the infant to be debarred of his right by lapse to the bishop. An infant may also purchase lands, but his purchase is incomplete: for, when he comes to age, he may either agree or disagree to it, as he thinks prudent or proper, without alleging any reason; and so may his heirs after him, if he dies without having completed his agreement (*Ibid.* 2.) as hath been before observed. It is further generally true, that an infant under twenty-one, can make no deed but what is afterwards voidable; yet in some cases (*Stat.* 5 *Eliz. c.* 4. 43 *Eliz. c.* 2. *Cro. Car.* 179.) he may bind himself apprentice by deed indented or indentures, for seven years; and (*Stat.* 12 *Car.* 2. *c.* 24.) he may by deed or will, appoint a guardian to his children, if he has any. Lastly, it is generally true, that an infant can make no other contract that will bind him: yet he may bind himself to pay for his necessary meat, drink, apparel, physic, and such other necessaries; and likewise for his good teaching and instruction, whereby he may profit himself afterwards. *Co. Lit.* 172.

But it has been held that an infant is not liable to repay money lent to him, although he should lay it out in necessaries. 1 *Salk.* 386. Nor is he bound to pay for goods bought to trade with, *Bull. N. P.* 154. But debts contracted during infancy are a good consideration to support a promise made to pay them, when a person is of full age. Also infancy may be given in evidence as upon the general issue, or it may be pleaded. *Bull.* 152.

And where the defendant pleads infancy, and the plaintiff replies that the defendant confirmed the promise or contract when he was of age, the plaintiff need only prove the promise, and the defendant must discharge himself by proof of the infancy. 1 *T. R.* 648.

INFANCY OF CORPORATIONS. The king cannot be an infant by our law. (1 *Inst.* 43.) And he shall never avoid his grants, &c. in respect of infancy; for he cannot be a minor, being as king a body politic. (2 *Danv. Abr.* 767.) So the acts of a mayor and commonalty shall not be avoided by reason of infancy of the mayor. *Cro. Car.* 557.

INFEODATION OF TITHES, the granting of tithes to mere laymen. 2 *Black. Com.* 27.

INFERIOR COURTS. The courts of judicature of this kingdom are divided into a general division of superior and inferior. The courts at Westminster are the superior, and in general have (especially the courts of King's Bench and Common Pleas) superintendance over the inferior. All other courts are deemed inferior.

INFIDELS, (*infideles*) those who may not be witnesses by refusal to take an oath on the Old or New Testament. (1 *Inst.* 6.

2 *Hawk. P. C.* 434.) may nevertheless be sworn according to the ceremonies of their own religion. Therefore Turks, Mahometans, and Gentoos, may be sworn on oath after the manner of their own accustomed rites and particular modes of belief.

INFINITY OF ACTIONS are not allowed by the law; therefore, although one subject may have his action against another for a *private* nuisance, yet he may not have it for *a common nuisance*; for if he might, then every man would have it, and so the actions would be infinite, &c. 2 *Co. Inst.* 56. 9 *Rep.* 113.

INFIRMARY, (*infirmarius*) he who had the care of the apartments allotted for infirm or sick persons in monasteries was called *infirmarius*. *Cowel. Blount.*

IN FORMA PAUPERIS. See *Forma Pauperis.*

INFORMATIONS. Informations are of two sorts; first those which are partly at the suit of the king, and partly at that of a subject; and secondly, such as are only in the name of the king. The former are usually brought upon penal statutes, which inflict a penalty upon conviction of the offender, one part to the use of the king, and another to the use of the informer; and are a sort of *qui tam* actions, only carried on by a criminal instead of a civil process; upon which it is to be observed that by the stat. 31 *Eliz.* c. 5, "No prosecution upon any penal "statute, the suit and benefit whereof are "limited in part to the king, and in part "to the prosecutor, can be brought by any "common informer after one year is expir-"ed since the commission of the offence, "nor on behalf of the crown after the lapse "of two years longer, nor where the for-"feiture is originally given only to the "king can such prosecution be had after "the expiration of two years from the "commission of the offence."

The informations that are exhibited in the name of the king alone are also of two kinds, first, those which are truly and properly his own suits, and filed *ex officio* by his own immediate officer, the attorney general: Secondly, those in which, though the king is the nominal prosecutor, yet it is at the relation of some private person or common informer; and they are filed by the king's coroner and attorney in the court of King's Bench, usually called the master of the crown-office, who is for this purpose the standing officer of the public.—The objects of the king's own prosecutions, filed *ex officio* by his own attorney-general, are properly such enormous misdemeanors, as peculiarly tend to disturb or endanger his government, or to molest or affront him in the regular discharge of his royal functions. For offences so high and dangerous, in the punishment or prevention of which a moment's delay would be fatal, the law has given to the crown the power of an immediate prosecution, without waiting for any previous application to any other tribunal; which power, thus necessary, not only to the ease and safety, but even to the very existence of the executive magistrate, was originally reserved in the great plan of the English constitution, wherein provision is wisely made for the due preservation of all its parts. The objects of the other species of informations, filed by the master of the crown-office upon the complaint or relation of a private subject, are any gross and notorious misdemeanors, riots, batteries, libels, and other immoralities of an atrocious kind (2 *Hawk. P. C.* 260.), not peculiarly tending to disturb the government, (for those are left to the care of the attorney-general) but which, on account of their magnitude or pernicious example, deserve the most public animadversion. And when an information is filed, either thus, or by the attorney-general *ex officio*, it must be tried by a petit jury of the county where the offence arises; after which, if the defendant be found guilty, the court must be resorted to for his punishment *.

---

* If an information, or an indictment for a misdemeanor removed into the court of King's Bench by certiorari, be not of such importance as to be tried at the bar of the court, it is sent down by writ of *nisi prius* into the county where the crime is charged to have been committed, and it is there tried either by a common or a special jury, like a record in a civil action, and if the defendant is found guilty, he must afterwards receive judgment from the court of King's Bench. But where an indictment for treason or felony is removed by *certiorari*, the law upon the subject seems to be fully stated by lord Hale in the two following sections. 2 *P. C.* 41.

"As to an indictment of felony or trea-"son removed out of the county by *certio-*"*rari*, and the party pleading, the record "is sent down by *nisi prius* to be tried, the "judges of *nisi prius* may upon that record "proceed to trial, and judgment, and "execution, as if they were justices of gaol-"delivery by virtue of the stat. of 14 *H.* 6, "*cap.* 1.

"But if there were any question upon "that statute, yet the stat. of 6 *H.* 8, *cap.* 6, "which extends to all justices and com-"missioners, as well those of gaol-deli-"very, as of the peace, enables the court "of King's Bench to send to them the very "record itself, and by special writ or man-"date to command them to proceed to trial "and judgment upon such issue joined; as "they may command the justices before

There can be no doubt but that this mode of prosecution, by information, (or suggestion,) filed on record by the king's attorney-general, or by his coroner or master of the crown-office in the court of King's Bench, is as ancient as the common law itself. (1 *Show.* 118.) For as the king was bound to prosecute, or at least to lend the sanction of his name to a prosecutor, whenever a grand jury informed him upon their oaths that there was a sufficient ground for instituting a criminal suit; so, when these his immediate officers were otherwise sufficiently assured that a man had committed a gross misdemeanor, either personally against the king or his government, or against the public peace and good order, they were at liberty, without waiting for any further intelligence, to convey that information to the court of King's Bench by a suggestion on record, and to carry on the prosecution in his majesty's name. But these informations (of every kind) are confined by the constitutional law to mere misdemeanors only; for, wherever any capital offence is charged, the same law requires that the accusation be warranted by the oath of twelve men, before the party shall be put to answer it. And as to those offences in which informations were allowed as well as indictments, so long as they were confined to this high and respectable jurisdiction, and were carried on in a legal and regular course in his majesty's court of King's Bench, the subject had no reason to complain. The same notice was given, the same process was issued, the same pleas were allowed, the same trial by jury was had, the same judgment was given by the same judges, as if the prosecution had originally been by indictment. But when the statute of 3 *Hen.* 7, *c.* 1, had extended the jurisdiction of the court of star-chamber, the members of which were the sole judges of the law, the fact, and the penalty; and when the statute 11 *Hen.* 7, *c.* 3, had permitted informations to be brought by any informer upon any penal statute, not extending to life or member, at the assises, or before the justices of the peace, who were to hear and determine the same according to their own discretion, then it was that the legal and orderly jurisdiction of the court of King's Bench fell into disuse and oblivion, and Empson and Dudley (the wicked instruments of king *Henry* 7,) by hunting out obsolete penalties, and this tyrannical mode of prosecution, with other oppressive devices, (1 *And.* 157) continually harassed the subject, and shamefully enriched the crown. The latter of these acts was soon indeed repealed by stat. 1 *Hen.* 8, *c.* 6, but the court of star-chamber continued in high vigour, and daily increasing its authority, for more than a century longer, till finally abolished by statute 16 *Car.* 1. *c.* 10.

Upon this dissolution the old common law authority (5 *Mod.* 464,) of the court of King's Bench, as the *custos morum* of the nation, being found necessary to reside somewhere for the peace and good government of the kingdom, was again revived in practice. (*Styl. Rep.* 217, 245. *Styl. pract. Reg. tit. information, page* 187. *Edit.* 1657. 2 *Sid.* 71. 1 *Sid.* 152.) And it is observable that in the same act of parliament which abolished the court of star-chamber, a conviction by information is expressly reckoned up as one of the legal modes of conviction of such persons as should offend a third time against the provisions of that statute (*Stat.* 16 *Car.* 1, *c.* 10, *sec.* 6). It is true, sir Mat. Hale, who presided in this court soon after the time of such revival, is said (5 *Mod.* 460,) to have been no friend to this method of prosecution; and if so, the reason of such his dislike was probably the ill use which the master of the crown-office then made of his authority, by permitting the subject to be harassed with vexatious informations whenever applied to by any malicious or revengeful prosecutor, rather than his doubt of their legality or propriety upon urgent occasions (1 *Saund.* 301. 1 *Sid.* 174). For the power of filing informations without any control then resided in the breast of the master, and being filed in the name of the king they subjected the prosecutor to no costs, though on trial they proved to be groundless. This oppressive use of them in the times preceding the Revolution, occasioned a struggle soon after the accession of king William (1 *W. & M.* 5 *Mod.* 459. *Comb.* 141. *Far.* 361. 1 *Show.* 106.) to procure a declaration of their illegality by the judgment of the court of King's Bench. But sir John Holt, who then presided there, and all the judges, were clearly of opinion that this proceeding was grounded on the common law, and could not be then impeached. And in a few years afterwards a more temperate remedy was applied in parliament by statute 4 & 5 *W. & M.* *c.* 18, which enacted, that the clerk of the crown shall not file any information without express direction from the court of King's Bench; and that every prosecutor permitted to promote such information shall give security by a recognizance of 20*l.* (which now seems to be too small a sum) to prosecute

---

" whom the indictment was taken to proceed to hear and determine the same if " no such issue were joined." See sir Miles Stapleton's case, *Raym.* 367.

If the treason or felony is to be tried at *nisi prius* under the 14 *Hen.* 6, *cap.* 1, then the court sends a transcript of the record, and not the record itself. 2 *Hal. P. C.* 3. 4 *Co.* 74.

the same with effect, and to pay costs to the defendant, in case he be acquitted thereon, unless the judge who tries the information shall certify there was reasonable cause for filing it; and, at all events, to pay costs, unless the information shall be tried within a year after issue joined. But there is a proviso in this act that it shall not extend to any other informations than those which are exhibited by the master of the crown-office, and consequently informations at the king's own suit, filed by his attorney-general, are no way restrained thereby. 4 *Black.* 311.

Where an information is given by statute, to be prosecuted at the assises, &c. the informer on filing his information must make oath before a judge, that the offence laid in the information was not committed in any other county than that mentioned in the information; and that he believes the offence was committed within a year next before the filing of the information. 21 *Jac.* 1. c. 4.

Offences created since the stat. 21 *Jac.* 1, *cap.* 4, are not within that statute to be prosecuted in the county where the fact was done; so that informations on subsequent penal statutes are not restrained thereby. 1 *Salk.* 373.

By the stat. 18 *Eliz. cap.* 5, informers are to exhibit their suits in proper person, by way of information, or original action; they are not to compound with the defendant without the consent of the court, on pain of 10*l.* penalty, pillory, and to be for ever disabled to sue on any penal statute. And if they discontinue, or are nonsuited, the court shall immediately assign costs to the defendant, but this statute, and the 21 *Jac.* 1, c. 4, do not extend to informations of officers, nor on the statutes of maintenance, champerty, concerning concealments of customs, &c. and it extends not to parties grieved, and those to whom any forfeiture is given in certain. *Ibid.*

And by 4 & 5 *Wil. & Mar.* c. 18, the clerk of the crown in the court of King's Bench shall not without express order given by the court file any information before he shall have taken, or have delivered to him, a recognizance from the person procuring such information, with the place of his abode, title, or profession, to be entered, to the person against whom such information is exhibited, in the penalty of 20*l.* that he will effectually prosecute, &c. and if the prosecutor shall not at his own costs, within one year after issue joined therein, procure the same to be tried, or if upon such trial a verdict pass for the defendant, or in case the informer procure a *nolle prosequi* to be entered, then the court of King's Bench may award the defendant costs, unless the judge shall at the trial in open court certify upon record there was reasonable cause for exhibiting such information; and in case the informer shall not within three months after the costs taxed, and demand made thereof, pay to the defendant the costs, then the defendant shall have the benefit of the recognizance.

But nothing in this act shall extend to any other information than such as shall be exhibited in the name of their majesties coroner, or attorney, in the court of King's Bench for the time being, commonly called the master of the crown-office.

Notwithstanding this last clause all informations, except these exhibited in the name of his majesty's attorney-general, remain as before by the common law. *Carth.* 503. 1 *Salk.* 376. *S. C.*

And it is to be observed that an informer upon a popular statute shall never have costs, if not given by statute, but the party grieved in an action on the statute shall, where a certain penalty is given. 2 *Hawk.* 273.

See also LIMITATIONS and QUO WARRANTO.

INFORMATION IN THE EXCHEQUER. An information on behalf of the crown, filed in the Exchequer by the king's attorney-general, is a method of suit for recovering money or other chattels, or for obtaining satisfaction in damages for any personal wrong committed in the lands or other possessions of the crown. (*Moor.* 375,) It differs from an information filed in the court of King's Bench, in that this is instituted to redress a private wrong, by which the property of the crown is affected, that is calculated to punish some public wrong, or heinous misdemeanor in the defendant. It is grounded on no writ under seal, but merely on the intimation of the king's officer the attorney-general, who "gives the court to understand and be "informed of" the matter in question; upon which the party is put to answer, and trial is had, as in suits between subject and subject. The most usual informations are those of intrusion and debt; intrusion, for any trespass committed on the lands of the crown (*Cro. Jac.* 212. 1 *Leon.* 48. *Savil.* 49), as by entering thereon without title, holding over after a lease is determined, taking the profits, cutting down timber, or the like; and debt, upon any contract for monies due to the king, or for any forfeiture due to the crown upon the breach of a penal statute. This is most commonly used to recover forfeitures occasioned by transgressing those laws which are enacted for the establishment and support of the revenue: others which regard mere matters of police, and public convenience, being usually left to be enforced by common informers in *qui tam* informations, or actions. But after the attorney-general has informed upon the breach of a penal law no other information can be received. (*Hard.* 201.) There is also an information *in rem*, when any goods are supposed to become the property of the crown, and no man appears to claim them, or to dispute the title of the king. As anciently in the case of treasure-trove, wrecks, waifs, and estrays, seized by the king's officer for his use. Upon such seizure an information was usually filed in the king's exchequer, and thereupon a proclamation was made for the owner (if any) to come in and claim the effects, and at the same time there issued a commission of appraisement to value the goods in the officer's hands, after the return of which, and a second proclamation had, if no claimant appeared, the goods were supposed derelict, and condemned to the use of the crown (*Gilb. Hist. of Exch. ch.* 13). And when in later times forfeitures of the goods themselves, as well as personal penalties on the parties, were inflicted by act of parliament for transgressions against the laws of the customs and excise, the same process was adopted in order to secure such forfeited goods to the public use, though the offender himself had escaped the reach of justice. 3 *Black.* 261.

INFORMATUS NON SUM, or *non sum informatus*, is the formal answer where an attorney is authorized by his client to let judgment pass in that form against him, on a warrant of attorney given for confessing judgment.

INFORMER, (*informator*) a person who informs against or prosecutes in the king's courts for an offence against any law, or penal statute.

INFORTIATUM one part of the digests of the civil law, according to Benedict, abbot of Peterborough, in the reign of Hen. 3. *Cowel. Blount.*

INFORTUNIUM, homicide. See Homicide.

INFUGARE, signifies to put to flight. *Cowel. Blount.*

INFULA, anciently the garment of a priest, like that which we now call a cassock; also a coif. *Ibid.*

INGE, a meadow or pasture, from the Sax. *ing*, *pratum.* *Ibid.*

INGENIUM, an instrument anciently used in war, *arte et ingenio confectum*; from whence, it is said, we derive the word engine. *Ibid.*

INGENUITAS, liberty given to a servant by manumission. *Ibid.*

INGENUITAS REGNI, *Ingenui, liberi et legales homines*, the freeholders and commonalty of the kingdom. *Ibid.*

INGRESS, EGRESS, AND REGRESS, words in leases of lands, to signify a free entry into, going forth of, and returning from, some part of the lands let; as to get in a crop of corn, &c. after the term expired. *Ibid.*

INGRESSU, a writ of entry, whereby a man seeks entry into lands or tenements. *Ibid.* See *Entry.*

INGRESSUS, the relief which the heir at full age paid to the head lord for entering upon the fee, or lands fallen by the death or forfeiture of the tenant, &c. *Cowel. Blount.*

INGROSSATOR MAGNI ROTULI. See *Clerk of the Pipe.*

INGROSSER, (*ingrossator*) is one who buys and sells any thing by wholesale; and whoever shall get into his hands by buying, contract, or promise, (other than by demise, grant or lease of lands,) any corn growing, or other corn or grain; butter, cheese, fish, or other thing whatsoever, within the realm of England, to the intent to sell the same again. All the statutes concerning this offence having been repealed by 12 *Geo.* 3, *c.* 71, the same now remains as before, viz. an offence indictable, for which as in other misdemeanors the party may be fined or imprisoned at the discretion of the court. *Cro. Car.* 232. 1 *Hawk. P. C.* 235.

INGROSSING OF DEEDS, is the writing thereof on paper or parchment.

INGROSSING OF A FINE, the making of the indentures by the chirographer, for delivery of them to the party to whom the fine is levied. *F. N. B.* 147.

INHABITANT, is a dweller or householder in any place, (2 *Inst.* 702,) and every one is deemed an *inhabitant* within the parish where he occupies land, although he may not be actually a resident within such parish, but elsewhere.

INHERITANCE, (*hæreditas*) is a perpetuity in lands or tenements to a man and his heirs. *Lit. sec.* 9. See Heir and Hereditaments.

INHIBITION, (*inhibitio*) is a writ to forbid a judge from further proceeding in a cause depending before him, being in nature of a prohibition. 9 *Ed.* 2, *c.* 1. 24 *Hen.* 8, *c.* 12. 15 *Car.* 2, *c.* 9. *F. N. B.* 39.

INHOC, or INHOKE, (from *in*, within, and *hoke*, a corner or nook) signifies any corner or part of a common field, ploughed up and sowed with oats, &c. and sometimes fenced in with a dry hedge, in that year wherein the rest of the same field lies fallow and common. *Cowel. Blount.*

INITIATE, tenant by the curtesy. As soon as a child is born the father begins to have a permanent interest in the land, and the child could not be in ward of the lord of the fee during the life of his father, who by the birth became one of the *pares curtis*, and was called "tenant by the curtesy initiate." And this estate being once vested in him by the birth of the child is not liable to be determined by the subsequent death or coming of age of the infant. 2 *Black. Com.* 127.

INJUNCTION, (*injunctio*) is a prohibition granted in divers cases; it is generally grounded upon an interlocutory order or decree out of the court of chancery or exchequer, on the equity side, to stay proceedings in courts of law; and sometimes it is issued to the spiritual courts. *West. Symb. sec.* 25.

When a bill in equity is filed, if an injunction be prayed therein, it may be had at various stages of the cause, according to the circumstances of the case. If the bill be to stay execution upon an oppressive judgment, and the defendant does not appear, or put in his answer within the stated time allowed by the rules of the court, an injunction will issue of course; and when the answer comes in the injunction can only be continued upon a sufficient ground appearing from the answer itself. But if an injunction be wanted to stay waste, or other injuries of an equally urgent nature, such as to stay the sale of a pirated copy of a book, or the like, then upon the filing of the bill, and a proper case supported by affidavits, the court will grant an injunction immediately *ex parte*, to continue till the defendant has put in his answer, and till the court shall make some further order concerning it: and when the answer comes in, whether it shall then be dissolved, or continue till the hearing of the cause, is determined by the court upon argument, drawn from considering the answer and affidavit together. *Bac. Abr.* and 14 *Vin. Abr.* tit. *Injunction.*

INJURY, (*injuria*) is a wrong or damage to a man's person or goods. And civil injuries are of two kinds, the one *without force* or violence, as slander, or breach of contract; the other coupled with *force* and violence, as batteries, or false imprisonment. *Finch L.* 184.

INLAGARE, to restore to the benefit of the law. *Cowel. Blount.*

INLAGATION, (*inlagatio*, from the Sax. *in lagiam*, i. e. *in lagare*) signifies a restitution of one outlawed to the protection of the law, and benefit of a subject. *Bract. lib.* 3, *tract.* 2, *c.* 14. *Leg. Canut. par.* 1, *c.* 2.

INLAGH, (*inlagatus, vel homo sub lege*,) is he who is of some frank-pledge, and not outlawed; the contrary to *utlagh. Bract. tract.* 2, *lib.* 3, *c.* 11.

INLAND, is said to be *terra dominicalis, pars manerii dominica, terra interior vel inclusa*; for that which was let to tenants was called outland. *Cowel. Blount.*

INLAND BILLS. See *Bills of Exchange.*

INLAND TRADE, a trade wholly managed at home, in one country. *Merc. Dict.*

INLANTAL, INLANTALE, demesne or inland, to which was opposed *delantal*, land tenanted or outlawed. *Cowel. Blount.*

INLEASED, from the Fr. *enlass*, entangled or ensnared. *Co. Inst.* 2 *par. fol.* 247.

INLEGIARE. When a delinquent had satisfied the law, and was again *rectus in curia*, he was said *se inlegiare. Cowel. Blount.*

INMATES, are those persons who are admitted to dwell with and in the house of another. *Kitch.* 45.

INNAMUM for NAMIUM, a pledge. *Innama non capiantur nisi per communem assensum. Du Cange.*

INNATURALITAS, unnatural usage. *Cowel. Blount.*

INNINGS, lands recovered from the sea. *Cowel. Blount.*

INNONIA, (from the Sax. *innan*, i. e. *intus*,) an enclosure. *Spelm. Gloss. Cowel.*

INNOTESCIMUS. This word and *vidimus* are all one; it signifies letters patent, so called, which are always of a charter of feoffment, or some other instrument, not of record, concluding *innotescimus per præsentes*, &c. *Cowel.*

INNOVATIONS, are thought dangerous by our laws; and the ancient judges of the law have ever suppressed them, lest the certainty of the common law should be disturbed. *Co. Lit.* 379. In the reign of king *Ed.* 3, the judges said "we will not change the law which always hath been used:" and in the time of k. *Hen.* 4, they declared "it would be better that it should be turned to a default than that the law should be changed, or any *innovation* made." *Ibid.* 303.

Many modern determinations have done honour to the judges of the present age; and though by some they may, for want of due consideration, be thought innovations, they certainly are not, but are only a more liberal construction of our common law, which will give relief, if properly construed, in most cases.

INNOXIARE, to purge one of a fault, and make him innocent. *Leg. Ethelred, c.* 10.

INNS OF COURT AND CHANCERY. After the court of common pleas, the grand tribunal for disputes of property, was fixed to be held in one certain spot, that the seat of ordinary justice might be permanent and notorious to all the nation, the professors of the municipal law, who before were dispersed about the kingdom, collected together and formed themselves into an aggregate body, whereby a society was established of persons who (as Spelman observes) addicting themselves wholly to the study of the laws of the land, and no longer considering it as a mere subordinate science for the amusement of leisure hours, soon raised those laws to that pitch of perfection which they suddenly attained under the auspices of our English Justinian, king *Edward* 1. *Spelm.* 334. *Dug. Orig. Jur.* 55. 1 *Black.* 23.

In consequence of this assemblage they naturally fell into a kind of collegiate order, and, being excluded from Oxford and Cambridge, found it necessary to establish a new university of their own. This they did by purchasing at various times certain houses (now called the inns of court and of chancery) between the city of Westminster, the place of holding the king's courts, and the city of London. Here exercises were performed, lectures read, and degrees were at length conferred in the common law, as at other universities in the canon and civil. The degrees were those of barristers (first styled apprentices †, from *apprendre*, to learn) who answered to our bachelors, as the state and degree of a serjeant, *servientis ad legem*, did to that of doctor. 1 *Black.* 23, 24.

The crown seems to have soon taken under its protection this infant seminary of common law; and the more effectually to foster and cherish it K. *Hen.* 3, in the 19th year of his reign issued out an order, directed to the mayor and sheriffs of London, commanding that no regent of any law-schools within that city should for the future teach law therein. (*Ne aliquis scholas regens de legibus in eadem civitate de cætera ibidem leges doceat.*) In order, as sir *Edward Coke* (2 *Inst. proem.*) understands it, by such restraint to collect all the common lawyers into the one public university then newly instituted in the suburbs. *Ibid.*

In this juridical university there are two sorts of collegiate houses, one called inns of chancery, in which the younger students of the law were usually placed; "learning "and studying," (says *Fortesc. c.* 49,) "the "originals, and as it were the elements of "the law; who profiting therein, as they "grew to ripeness, so were they admitted "into the greater inns of the same study, "called the inns of court."

But by degrees this custom has fallen into disuse; first, because the inns of chancery, being now almost totally filled by the inferior branches of the profession, are neither commodious nor proper for the resort of gentlemen of any rank or figure; and if gentlemen were to be entered at present in the inns of chancery with an intention of being called to the bar, their admission there would now be of no avail with regard to the time and attendance required by the inns of court.

These Inns of Court are, the Inner Temple, Middle Temple, Lincoln's Inn, and Gray's Inn, from which societies alone students are called to the bar. And the Inns of Chancery are, Clifford's Inn, Clement's Inn, Lion's Inn, New Inn, Furnival's Inn, Thavies' Inn, Staple's Inn, and Barnard's Inn. These are subordinate to the inns of court; the three first belong to the Inner Temple, the fourth to the Middle Temple, the two next to Lincoln's Inn, and the two last to Gray's Inn. *Dugd. Orig. Jur.* 320.

The inns of court are governed by masters, principals, benchers, stewards, and other proper officers; and the chief of them have chapels for divine service, and all of them public halls for exercises, readings, and arguments, which the students were formerly obliged to perform and attend for a competent number of years before admitted to speak at the bar, &c. These societies or colleges, nevertheless, are no corporations, nor have any judicial power over their members, but have certain orders among themselves, which by consent have the force of bye-laws. For light offences persons are only excommoned, or put out of commons; for greater they lose their chambers, and are expelled; and when expelled out of one society shall never be received by any of the others. *Fortescue.*

But the twelve judges sitting in Serjeants Inn-Hall exercise an appellant jurisdiction in all matters of controversy arising upon the rules or bye-laws of these societies, and to no other forum ought appeal to be made. *Hart's case*, at Serjeants' Inn, *anno* 1780, Ed. MS.

INNS AND INNKEEPERS. Common inns were instituted for the lodging and relief of travellers, and at common law any man might erect and keep an inn, or alehouse, to receive travellers; but now they are to be licensed, and give recognizances for keeping good order. See *Alehouses.*

If one who keeps a common inn refuses to receive a traveller as guest into his house, or to find him victuals, or lodging, upon his tendering a reasonable price for the same, having room, the innkeeper is liable to render damages in an action at the suit of the party grieved; and may also be indicted and fined at the suit of the king. And it is said he may be compelled by the constable of the town to receive and entertain such a person as his guest. 1 *Hawk. P. C.* 225.

An action on the case on an implied *assumpsit* will lie against the guest for things had, where the innkeeper is obliged by law to furnish him with meat, drink, &c. And when a guest calls for any thing at an inn the innkeeper may justify detaining a horse, or other thing, till he is paid his just reckoning. *Dyer* 30. *Mod. Cas. in L. & E.* 172.

And if a horse eat out as much as he is worth, the master of the inn, after a reasonable appraisement, may sell the horse and pay himself. (*Yelv.* 66.) But if one bring several horses to an inn, and afterwards takes them all away but one, the innkeeper may not sell this horse for payment of the debt for the others, but every horse is to be sold to satisfy what is due for his own meat; for the act of allowing the owner to take the others away implies that the

† Apprentices, or barristers, seem to have been first appointed by an ordinance of K. *Edw.* 1. in parliament, in the 20th year of his reign. *Spelm. Gloss.* 37. *Dugdale Orig. Jurid.* 55.

innkeeper, as to those, gave his guest personal credit. 1 *Bulst.* 207. 217.

If any theft be committed on a guest while lodging in an inn, by any servant of the inn, or by any other person, (not the guest's servant or companion) the inn-keeper is answerable in an action on the case: But if the guest be not a traveller, but one of the same town, the master of the inn is not chargeable for his servant's theft; and if a man is robbed in a private tavern, the master is not chargeable. 8 *Rep.* 32, 33. And although the guest deliver not his goods to the inn-keeper to keep, &c. if they be stolen while he is a guest, as where finding that he cannot be lodged he requires to rest while he takes some refreshment, he shall be charged. 2 *Shep. Abr.* 334. 5 *Ter.Rep.* 273.

INNUENDO, (from *innuo*, to nod, or beckon with the hand to one) is a word used in declarations and law pleadings to ascertain a person or thing which was named before, as to say he (*innuendo*, that is *meaning* the plaintiff) did so and so, when there was mention before of another person. 4 *Rep.* 17.

INOFFICIOUS TESTAMENT. The Romans were used to set aside testaments as being *inefficiosa*, deficient in natural duty, if they disinherited or totally passed by, without assigning a true and sufficient reason, any of the children of the testator.

But if the child had any legacy, though ever so small, it was a proof that the testator had not lost his memory or his reason, which otherwise the law presumed, but was then supposed to have acted thus for some substantial cause; and in such case no *querela inefficiosi testamenti* was allowed. Hence probably has arisen that groundless vulgar error, of the necessity of leaving the heir a shilling, or some other express legacy, in order to disinherit him effectually; whereas the law of England makes no such constrained suppositions of forgetfulness or insanity; and therefore, though the heir or next of kin be totally omitted, it admits no *querela inefficiosi* to set aside such a testament.

INOPERATIO, is one of the legal excuses to exempt a man from appearing in court on the days in which all pleadings are to cease, or *in diebus non juridicis.* *Cowel. Blount.*

INORDINATUS, anciently taken for one who died intestate. *Ibid.*

INPENNY AND OUTPENNY, Money paid by the custom of some manors on the alienation of tenants, &c. *Ibid.*

INPRISI, adherents or accomplices.

INQUEST, (*inquisitio*) is an inquisition of jurors in causes civil and criminal, on proof made of the fact on either side, when it is referred to their trial, being empannelled by the sheriff, coroner, or other proper officer for that purpose. *Staundf. P. C. lib.* 3. *c.* 12.

INQUIRENDO. An authority given in general to some person, or persons, to inquire into something for the king's advantage. *Reg.* 72.

INQUISITION, OR INQUEST OF OFFICE, is an inquiry made by the king's officer, his sheriff, coroner, or escheator, *virtute officii*, or by writ to them sent for that purpose, or by commissioners specially appointed, concerning any matter that entitles the king to the possession of lands or tenements, goods or chattels. (*Finch. L.* 323, 4, 5.) This is done by a jury of no determinate number; being either twelve, or less, or more. As, to inquire, whether the king's tenant for life died seised, whereby the reversion accrues to the king: whether A, who held immediately of the crown, died without heirs; in which case the lands belong to the king by escheat: whether B be attainted of treason; whereby his estate is forfeited to the crown: whether C, who has purchased lands, be an alien; which is another cause of forfeiture: whether D be an idiot *a nativitate*; and therefore, together with his lands, appertains to the custody of the king: and other questions of like import, concerning both the circumstances of the tenant, and the value or identity of the lands. These inquests of office were more frequently in practice than at present, during the continuance of the military tenures amongst us: when, upon the death of every one of the king's tenants, an inquest of office was held, called an INQUISITIO POST MORTEM, to enquire of what lands he died seised, who was his heir, and of what age, in order to entitle the king to his marriage, wardship, relief, primer-seisin, or other advantages, as the circumstances of the case might turn out. To superintend and regulate these inquiries the court of wards and liveries was instituted by statute 32 *Hen.* 8. *c.* 46, which was abolished at the restoration of king Charles the second, together with the oppressive tenures upon which it was founded. 3 *Blac.* 258.

With regard to other matters, the inquests of office still remain in force, and are taken upon proper occasions; being extended not only to lands, but also to goods and chattels personal, as in the case of wreck, treasure-trove, and the like; and especially as to forfeitures for offences. For every jury which tries a man for treason or felony, every coroner's inquest that sits upon a *felo de se*, or one killed by chancemedley, is, not only with regard to chattels, but also as to real interests, in all respects an inquest of office: and if they find the treason or felony, or even the flight of the party accused (though innocent) the king is thereupon, by virtue of this office found, entitled to have his forfeitures; and also, in the case of chancemedley, he or his grantees are entitled to such things, by way of deodand, as have moved to the death of the party. *Ibid.* 259.

These inquests of office were devised by law, as an authentic means to give the king his right, by solemn matter of record; without which he in general can neither take, nor part from, any thing. (*Finch. L.* 82.) For it is a part of the liberties of England, and greatly for the safety of the subject, that the king may not enter upon or seize any man's possessions upon bare surmises, without the intervention of a jury. (*Gilb. Hist. Exch.* 132. *Hob.* 347.) It is however particularly enacted by the statute 33 *Hen.* 8. *c.* 20, that in case of attainder for high treason, the king shall have the forfeiture instantly, without any inquisition of office, and, as the king hath no title at all to any property of this sort before office found, therefore by the statute 18 *Hen.* 6. *c.* 6, it was enacted, that all letters patent or grants of lands and tenements before office found, or returned into the exchequer, shall be void. And, by the bill of rights at the Revolution, 1 *W. & M. st.* 2. *c.* 2, it is declared, that all grants and promises of fines and forfeitures of particular persons before conviction (which is here the inquest of office) are illegal and void, which indeed was the law of the land in the reign of Edward the third. 2 *Inst.* 48.

With regard to real property, if an office be found for the king it puts him in immediate possession without the trouble of a formal entry, provided a subject in the like case would have had a right to enter; and the king shall receive all the mesne or intermediate profits from the time that his title accrued: (*Finch. L.* 325, 326.) As, on the other hand, by the *articuli super cartas* (28 *Ed.* 1, *st.* 3, *c.* 19), if the king's escheator or sheriff seize lands into the king's hand without cause, upon taking them out of the king's hand again, the party shall have the mesne profits restored to him. 3 *Black.* 260.

In order to avoid the possession of the crown acquired by the finding of such office, the subject may not only have his petition of right, which discloses new facts not found by the office, and his *monstrans de droit*, which relies on the facts as found, but also he may (for the most part) traverse or deny the matter of fact itself, and put it in a course of trial by the common law process of the court of chancery; yet still, in some special cases, he has no remedy left but a mere petition of right. (*Finch. L.* 324.) These traverses, as well as the *monstrans de droit*, were greatly enlarged and regulated for the benefit of the subject by the statutes before mentioned, and others. (*Stat.* 34 *Ed.* 3, *c.* 13. 36 *Ed.* 3, *c.* 13. 2 and 3 *Ed.* 6, *c.* 8.) And in the traverses thus given by statute, which came in the place of the old petition of right, the party traversing is considered as the plaintiff, (Law of *nisi prius*, 202) and must therefore make out his own title, as well as impeach that of the crown, and then shall have judgment *quod manus domini regis amoveantur, &c. Ibid.*

INQUISITORS, (*inquisitores*) are sheriffs, coroners, or the like, who have power to inquire in certain cases; and inquirors, or inquisitors, are included under the name of *ministri*. 2 *Inst.* 211.

INROLMENT, (*irrotulatio*) is the registering, or entering in the rolls of the Chancery, King's Bench, Common Pleas, or Exchequer, or by the clerk of the peace in the records of the quarter sessions, of any lawful act, as a statute or recognizance acknowledged, a deed of bargain and sale of lands, &c. 2 *Lil. Abr.* 69.

INSCRIPTIONES, were written instruments by which any thing was granted. *Cowel.*

INSECTATOR, a prosecutor or adversary at law. *Ibid.*

INSERVIRE, to reduce persons to servitude. *Ibid.*

INSETENA, (Sax.) an inditch. *Ibid.*

INSIDIÆ, the same with *vigiliæ* or *excubiæ*. *Ibid.*

INSIDIATORES VIARUM, are waylayers; which words are not to be put in indictments, appeals, &c. by stat. *H.* 4. *c.* 2.

INSIGNIA, ensigns or arms. *Cowel. Blount.*

INSILIUM, evil advice or counsel. *Insiliarus* an evil counsellor. *Ibid.*

INSIMUL COMPUTASSET, a writ or action of account, which lies not for things certain but only for things uncertain. *Bro. Acc.* 81. Also, in *assumpsit*, a count is often added to the declaration, called an *insimul computasset*, that is, setting forth that an account was stated, wherein defendant was found indebted to the plaintiff in so much, and being so indebted, he the defendant undertook and promised to pay the sum found in arrear.

INSIMUL TENUIT, one species of the writ of *formedon*, brought against a stranger by a coparcener on the possession of the ancestor, &c. See *Formedon*.

INSINUATION, (*insinuatio*) is a creeping into a man's mind or favour covertly. *Cowel. Blount.*

INSOLVENT. Where a trustee is insolvent, the court of chancery will compel him to give security before he shall enter upon the trust. *Carth.* 458.

INSOLVENT DEBTORS. See EXECUTION.

INSPECTION. Trial by inspection or examination, is when for the greater expedition of a cause, in some point or issue, being either the principal question, or arising collaterally out of it, but being evidently the object of sense, the judges of the court, upon the testimony of their own senses, shall decide the point in dispute. 3 *Black. Com.* 331, 332. See *Age, Infancy, Trial.*

INSPEXIMUS, a word used in letters patent giving name to them, being the same with exemplification, and called *inspeximus*, because it begins *rex omnibus*, *&c.* *Inspeximus irrotulamentum quarund.* *Cowel. Blount.*

INSTALLMENT, a settlement, establishing, or sure placing in; as installment into dignities. *Ibid.*

In ecclesiastical promotions, where the freehold passes to the person promoted, corporal possession is required, to vest the property completely in the new proprietor, who, according to the distinction of the canonists, acquires the *jus ad rem*, or inchoate and imperfect right, by nomination and institution; but not the *jus in re*, or complete and full right, unless by corporal possession. Therefore in dignities possession is given by installment; in rectories and vicarages by induction, without which no temporal rights accrue to the minister, though every ecclesiastical power is vested in him by institution. 2 *Black. Com.* 312.

Installments also signify times appointed for payment of different portions of a sum of money, at stated times.

INSTANT, (Lat. *instans, instanter*) in law *eo instante*, the very instant a fact is done. And in our law, things which are to be done in an instant, have in consideration of law a priority of time in them. *Plowd.* 258 *b.* *Co. Lit.* 185. *b.* and *Vin. Abr.* tit. *Instant*, *A. pl.* 2.

INSTANTER, (Lat.) instantly or presently. And a trial instanter is where a prisoner between attainder and execution, pleads that he is not the same that was attainted. In such case a jury is to be impannelled to try this collateral issue, *viz.* the identity of his person, and in such collateral issue, the trial shall be instanter. 4 *Black.* 389.

INSTAURUM, used in ancient deeds for a stock of cattle. *Cowel. Blount.*

INSTIRPARE, to plant or establish. *Ibid.*

INSTITUTION, (*institutio*) is when the bishop says to a clerk, who is presented to a church living, *instituo te rectorem talis ecclesiæ, cum cura animarum, & accipe curam tuam & meam.* If the bishop upon examination finds the clerk presented capable of the benefice, he admits and institutes him; an institution may be granted either by the bishop under his episcopal seal; or it may be done by the bishop's vicar general, chancellor, or commissary; and if granted by the vicar general, or any other substitute; their acts are taken to be the acts of the bishop: also the instrument or letters testimonial of institution may be granted by the bishop, though he is not in his diocese; to which some witnesses should subscribe their names. 1 *Inst.* 344. *Clergym. Law.* 109. The bishop, by institution, transfers the cure of souls to the clerk; and if he refuseth to grant institution, the party may have his remedy in the court of audience of the archbishop, by *duplex querela*, *&c.* for institution is properly cognizable in the ecclesiastical court: where institution is granted, and suspected to be void for want of title in the patron, &c. a super-institution hath been sometimes granted to another, to try the title of the present incumbent by ejectment. 2 *Rol. Abr.* 220. 4 *Rep.* 79.

Taking a reward for institution incurs a forfeiture of double value of one year's profit of the benefice, and makes the living void. *Stat.* 31 *Eliz. c.* 6. On institution, the clerk hath a right to enter on the parsonage house and glebe, and take the tithes; but he cannot grant, let, or do any act to charge them, till he is inducted into the living; he is complete parson as to the spiritualty, by institution; but not as to the temporalty, &c. By the institution he is only admitted *ad officium*, to pray and preach; and is not entitled *ad beneficium*, until formal induction. *Plowd.* 528. Vide INDUCTION.

INSUPER, is used by auditors in their accounts in the exchequer; as when so much is charged upon a person as due on his account, they say so much remains insuper to such an accountant. *Cowel. Blount.*

INSURANCE or ASSURANCE, signifies a security given, in consideration of a sum of money paid in hand of so much per cent. to an assurer or insurer, to indemnify the insured from such losses as shall be specified in the policy, or instrument of assurance, subscribed by the insurer or insurers for that purpose. *Dict. Tr.* and *Com.* 135.

A policy of insurance is, therefore, a contract between A and B, that upon A's paying a premium equivalent to the hazard run, B will indemnify or insure him against a particular event. This is founded upon one of the same principles as the doctrine of interest upon loans, that of hazard; but not that of inconvenience. For if I insure a ship to the Levant, and back again, at five per cent., here I calculate the chance that she performs her voyage to be twenty to one against her being lost: and, if she be lost, I lose 100*l.* and get 5*l.* Now this is much the same as if I lend the merchant whose whole fortunes are embarked in this vessel, 100*l.* at the rate of eight per cent. For by a loan I should be immediately out of possession of my money, the inconvenience of which we have supposed equal to three per cent.: if therefore I had actually lent him 100*l.* I must have added 3*l.* on the score of inconvenience, to the 5*l.* allowed for the hazard, which together would have made 8*l.* But, as upon an insurance, I am never out of possession of my money till the loss actually happens, nothing is therein allowed upon the principle of inconvenience, but all upon the principle of hazard. Thus, too, in a loan, if the chance of repayment depend upon the borrower's life, it is frequent (besides the usual rate of interest) for the borrower to have his life insured till the time of repayment; for which he is loaded with an additional premium, suited to his age and constitution. Thus, if Sempronius has only an annuity for his life, and would borrow 100*l.* of Titius for a year; the inconvenience and general hazard of this loan, we have seen, are equivalent to 5*l.* which is therefore the legal interest: but there is also a special hazard in this case; for if Sempronius dies within the year, Titius must lose the whole of his 100*l.* Suppose this chance to be as one to ten: it will follow, that the extraordinary hazard is worth 10*l.* more, and therefore, that the reasonable rate of interest in this case would be fifteen per cent. But this the law, to avoid abuses, will not permit to be taken; Sempronius therefore gives Titius the lender only 5*l.* the legal interest; but applies to Gaius an insurer, and gives him the other 10*l.* to indemnify Titius against the extraordinary hazard. And in this manner, may any extraordinary or particular hazard be provided against, which the established rate of interest will not reach; that being calculated by the state to answer only the ordinary and general hazard, together with the lender's inconvenience in parting with his specie for the time. 2 *Black.* 459.

Insurance is, however, in effect nothing more than a wager, for the underwriter, who insures at five per cent. receives five pounds to return one hundred upon the contingency of a certain event; and it is precisely the same in its consequences, as if he had betted a wager of 95*l.* to five, or nineteen to one, that the ship arrives safe, or that a certain event does not happen. So where a life is insured for a year at ten per cent.; that is, where ten pounds are received to pay one hundred, if a certain person dies within a year; this insurance is in effect precisely the same as a wager of nine to one, that the person, whose life is insured, lives a year. It is not surprising then, that insurance should have become so prevalent and pernicious a mode of gaming, that the legislature was obliged to repress it, and to confine it within those limits, within which it is beneficial or absolutely necessary to the security of commerce. The writers on mercantile law, with that natural partiality which authors feel for their subjects, have amused themselves by endeavouring to discover what country could first claim the honour of the invention of insurance. But it is a contract far too simple, and too obvious to the understandings of mankind, however uncultivated, to be dignified by the name of invention. Yet its progress and refinements would be a necessary consequence of the extension of commerce, and the gradual improvement in the science of law. *Ibid. N.* by *Chris.*

However, to prevent these insurances from being turned into a mischievous kind of gaming, it is enacted by stat. 14 *Geo.* 3. *c.* 48. that no insurance shall be made on lives, or on any other event, wherein the party insured hath no interest; that in all policies, the name of such interested party shall be inserted; and nothing more shall be recovered thereon than the amount of the interest of the insured.

This does not, however, extend to marine insurances, which were provided for by a prior law of their own: which being founded on equitable principles, chiefly resulting from the special circumstances of each case, cannot be easily reduced to any general heads in mere elementary institutes. Thus much, however, may be said; that, being contracts, the very essence of which consists in observing the purest good faith and integrity, they are vacated by any the least shadow of fraud or undue concealment: and, on the other hand, being much for the benefit and extension of trade, by distributing the loss or gain among a number of adventurers, they are greatly encouraged and protected both by common law and acts of parliament (*Ib.* 460.) As the contract of insurance is therefore founded upon the purest principles of morality and abstract justice, it is necessary that the contracting parties should have perfectly equal knowledge or ignorance of every material circumstance respecting the thing insured. If on either side there is any misrepresentation or *allegatio falsi*, or concealment or *suppressio veri*, which would in any degree affect the premium, or the terms of the engagement, the contract is fraudulent and absolutely void. *Park's Ins.* c. x.

Also as a practice had obtained of insuring large sums without having any property on board, which were called insurances, interest or no interest, and also of insuring the same goods several times over; both of which were a species of gaming, without any advantage to commerce, and were denominated wagering policies: it is therefore enacted by stat. 10 *Geo.* 2. *c.* 37. that all insurances, interest or no interest, or without farther proof of interest than the policy itself, or by way of gaming or wagering, or without benefit of salvage to the insurer, (all of which had the same pernicious tendency) shall be totally null and void, except upon privateers, or upon ships or merchandize from the Spanish and Portuguese dominions, for reasons sufficiently obvious; and that no re-assurance shall be lawful, except the former insurer shall be insolvent, a bankrupt, or dead: and lastly, that, in the East India trade, the lender of money on bottomry, or at *respondentia*, shall alone have a right to be insured for the money lent, and the borrower shall (in case of a loss) recover no more upon any insurance than the surplus of his property, above the value of his bottomry, or *respondentia* bond.

This statute does not extend to foreign ships, upon which, as before the statute, there may still be insurances, interest or no interest. These were not included in the act, on account of the difficulty of bringing witnesses from abroad to prove the interest. *Doug.* 302. But where there is an interest on board, the owner by a valued policy, in which the value of the goods is agreed upon and fixed between the parties, may insure far beyond the extent of the real value. For the excess of the insurance is held not to be within the statute, unless it should appear, that the interest is so small as to be a mere evasion of the act, and a pretence for gaming. In an open policy, where no value is fixed, the prime cost of the goods must be proved. 2 *Burr.* 1170.

A re-assurance is the contract, which an insurer, who wishes to be indemnified against the risk he has taken upon himself, makes with another person, by giving him a premium to re-assure to him the same event, which he himself has insured. Re-assurances are prohibited by the statute 19 *Geo.* 2. *c.* 37. both upon foreign and English ships, unless the assurer is insolvent, a bankrupt, or dead, in which cases he, his assignee, or personal representative, may make a re-assurance, which must be expressly mentioned as a re-assurance in the policy. 2 *T. R.* 161.

The object of prohibiting re-assurance, was to prevent idle gaming speculations, by persons endeavouring to obtain a high premium for insurance, and then to secure themselves by getting the same risk insured at a lower rate. The learned judge seems to have mistaken a double insurance for a re-assurance: a double insurance is where the owner insures his goods twice or several times over, with different underwriters, which he may lawfully do; by which means he increases his security, and though he cannot recover more than a single satisfaction for his loss, yet he may bring his action against any one of the underwriters, and compel him to pay the whole extent of the interest insured, and this underwriter may afterwards recover from each of the rest a rateable satisfaction or apportionment of the sum which he has been obliged to pay to the assured. *Park.* 280.

Formerly a *court of policies of assurance* was yearly instituted by the lord chancellor for deciding questions on policies of assurance within London, which court *when subsisting* was erected in pursuance of stat. 43 *Eliz. c.* 12. which recites the immemorial usage of policies of assurance "by means "whereof it comes to pass upon the loss or "perishing of any ship, there followeth not the "undoing of any man, but the loss lighteth "rather easily upon many than heavy upon "few, and rather upon them that adventure not, "than upon those that do adventure; where- "by all merchants, especially those of the "younger sort, are allured to venture more "willingly and more freely: and that hereto- "fore such assurers had used to stand so just- "ly and precisely upon their credits, as few "or no controversies had arisen thereupon; "and if any had grown, the same had from "time to time been ended and ordered by "certain grave and discreet merchants ap- "pointed by the lord mayor of the city of "London; as men by reason of their expe- "rience fittest to understand and speedily "decide those causes:" but that of late years divers persons had withdrawn themselves from that course of arbitration, and had driven the assured to bring separate actions at law against each assurer: it therefore enables the lord chancellor yearly to grant a standing commission to the judge of the admiralty, the recorder of London, two doctors of the civil law, two common lawyers, and eight merchants; any three of which, one being a civilian or a barrister, are thereby, and by the statute 13 & 14 *Car.* 2. *c.* 23. empowered to determine in a summary way all causes concerning policies of insurance in London, with an appeal (by way of bill) to the court of chancery. But the jurisdiction being somewhat defective, as extending only to London, and to no other assurances but those on merchandize (*Styl.* 166.), and to suits brought by the assured only, and not by the insurers (1 *Show.* 396.), no such commission has of late years issued: but insurance causes are now usually determined by the verdict of a jury of merchants, and the opinion of the judges in case of any legal doubts; whereby the decision is more speedy, satisfactory, and final: though it is to be wished, (as *Blackstone* justly observes) that some of the parliamentary powers invested in these commissioners, especially for the examination of witnesses, either beyond the seas, or speedily going out of the kingdom (*Stat.* 13 & 14 *Car.* 2. *c.* 22. *sect.* 3 & 4.), could at present be adopted by the courts of Westminster-hall, without requiring the consent of parties. 3 *Black.* 74.

INTAKERS, were a kind of thieves in the northern parts of England, so called, because they did take in and receive such booties as their confederates the outpartners brought to them from the borders of Scotland. 9 *H.* 5. *cap.* 7. *Cowel. Blount.*

INTASSARE. See *Tassum.*

INTENDMENT OF LAW, (*intellectus legis*) the understanding, intention and true meaning of law. *Co. Lit.* 78.

Sometimes a thing is necessarily intended by what precedes or follows it; and where an indifferent construction may have two intendments, the rule is to take it most strongly against the plaintiff. *Show.* 162.

INTENDMENT OF CRIMES. In antient times felonious attempts, intending the death of another, were adjudged felony; for the will was taken for the fact. *Bract.* 1. *E.* 3. But at this day the law does not generally punish intendments to do ill, if the intent be not executed, except in case of treason, where intention proved by circumstances shall be punished as if put in execution. 2 *Inst.* 108.

INTENT or INTENTION. The words of deeds shall be construed according to the intent of the parties, and not otherwise; but the intent shall be destroyed where it does not agree with the law. *Pl. C.* 160. *b.* 162. *b.*

And common usage and reputation frequently govern the matter, and direct the intention of the parties; as upon sale of a barrel of beer the barrel itself is not sold, though upon sale of a hogshead of wine it is otherwise. *Savil.* 124.

INTENSIONE, a writ that anciently laid against him who entered into lands after the death of a tenant in dower or for life, &c. and held him out in reversion or remainder. *F. N. B.* 203.

INTER CANEM ET LUPUM, words formerly used in appeals to signify the crime being done in the twilight. *Cowel. Blount.*

INTERCOMMONING, is where the commons of two manors lie together, and the inhabitants of both have time out of mind depastured their cattle promiscuously in each. *Ibid.*

INTERDICTION, (*interdictio* and *interdictum*) has the same signification in the common, as it hath in the canon law, and was a general excommunication of a whole country or province: such as the excommunication by the pope, *anno* 1208, of King John, and all his adherents, *et totam terram Anglicanam supposuit interdicto;* this began the first Sunday after Easter, and continued six years and one month; during all which time nothing was done in the churches besides baptism and confessions of dying people. *Cowel. Blount.*

INTERDICTUM, an injunction in either of our courts of equity to quiet the possession of lands, to stay waste, or to stop proceedings at law, is in the nature of the *interdictum* of the civil law, which was a prohibition or injunction of the prætor, or an order for the possession of a thing in dispute, made by the magistrate *per interdictum repetere possessionem suam.* 3 *Black.* 442.

INTERDICTED OF WATER AND FIRE, persons anciently banished for a crime, were said to be *interdicted,* by the judgment in which order was given, that no man should receive them into his house, but deny them *fire and water,* the two necessary elements of life, which amounted as it were to a civil death. *Cowel. Blount.*

INTEREST, (*interesse*). In legal understanding an interest extends to estates, rights and titles, that a man hath in, or out of lands, so as by grant of his whole interest in such land, a reversion therein as well as possession in fee-simple shall pass. *Co. Lit.* 345.

INTEREST OF MONEY. See *Usury.*

INTEREST ON BANKRUPT'S DEBTS. The usual rule is, that all interest on debts carrying interest shall cease, from the time of issuing the commission. *Atk.* 244. Yet, in case of a surplus left after payment of every debt, such interest shall again revive, and be chargeable on the bankrupt, or his representatives. 1 *Atk.* 244.

And in case of a surplus, the chancellor will not order it to be returned to the bankrupt till he has discharged the interest up to the time on all debts bearing interest, and satisfied all other equitable claims upon the fund. 2 *Vez. Jun.* 303.

Bills and notes in which interest is not named, carry interest only between the protest and the date of the commission. 2 *Black. N.* by *Chris.* 488.

INTEREST ON LEGACIES. In case of a vested legacy, due immediately, and charged on land, on money in the funds, which yield an immediate profit, interest shall be payable thereon from the testator's death; but if charged only on the personal estate, which cannot be immediately got in, it shall carry interest only from the end of the year after the death of the testator. 2 *P. Wms.* 26, 27.

INTERESTED WITNESS. Interested witnesses may be examined upon a *voir dire,* if suspected to be secretly concerned in the event, or their interest may be proved in court. 3 *Black.* 370.

INTERLINEATION *in a deed.* A deed may be avoided by matter *ex post facto,* as by erasure, interlining, or other alteration in any material part; unless a memorandum be made thereof at the time of the execution and attestation. 11 *Rep.* 27.

INTERLOCUTORY DECREE *in equity,* is an intermediate decree or decretal order made upon the hearing of a cause, and when it is necessary to direct an issue at law, or a reference to the master, in which cases the *final* decree is not made until after the trial of the issue or the coming in of the master's report.

INTERLOCUTORY JUDGMENT *at law,* is such as is given in the middle of a cause, upon some plea, or on default, which is only intermediate, and does not finally determine or complete the suit. As judgment for the plaintiff in abatement, of *respondeat ouster,* i. e. that defendant shall answer over, or farther, plead in chief, or put in a more substantial plea. But the interlocutory judgments, most usually spoken of, are those incompleat judgments, whereby the right of the plaintiff is indeed established, but the quantum of damages sustained by him is not ascertained, which is the province of a jury. In such case a writ of inquiry issues to the sheriff, who summons a jury, enquires of the damages, and returns to the court the inquisition so taken, whereupon the plaintiff's attorney taxes costs, and signs final judgment. 3 *Black.* 396, 7.

INTERLOCUTORY ORDER, (*ordo interlocutorius*) is an order made in the progress of a cause upon some incidental matter, which happens between the beginning and end of it; as an order for an injunction, &c.

INTERLOPERS, persons who intercept the trade of a company of merchants. *Merc. Dict.*

INTERPLEADER. See *Bill in Equity*, and *Enterpleader*.

INTER-REGNUM. There cannot be an *interregnum* in this country, by the policy of the constitution, for the right of sovereignty is fully vested in the successor, by the very descent of the crown. 1 *Black.* 196, 249.

INTERROGATORIES IN EQUITY, are particular questions reduced into writing, and demanded of witnesses brought in to be examined in a cause in courts of equity.

They are to be pertinent, and only to the points necessary, and either drawn or perused by counsel, and be signed by them: if they are leading, *viz.* such as these, *did you not do or see such a thing, &c.* the depositions on them will be suppressed; for they should be drawn, *did you see, or did you not see, &c.* without leaning to either side; and not only where they point more to one side of the question than the other; but if they are too particular, they will likewise be suppressed: the commissioners, &c. who examine witnesses on interrogatories, must examine to one interrogatory only at a time; they are to hold the witnesses to every point interrogated; and take what comes from them on their examination, without asking any idle questions, or putting down any impertinent answers not relating to the interrogatories, &c.

For the purpose of examining witnesses in or near London, there is an examiner's office; but, for evidence who live in the country, a commission to examine witnesses is usually granted to four commissioners, two named of each side, or any three or two of them, to take the depositions there. And if the witnesses reside beyond sea, a commission may be had to examine them there, upon their own oaths, and (if foreigners) upon the oaths of skilful interpreters.

The commissioners are sworn to take the examinations truly and without partiality, and not to divulge them till published in the court of chancery; and their clerks are also sworn to secresy. The witnesses are compellable by process of *subpœna*, as in the courts of common law, to appear and submit to examination. And when their depositions are taken, they are transmitted to the court with the commission annexed, sealed up under their respective seals, by some person receiving the same from one of the commissioners, who is willing to take charge thereof to town, which person must make oath at the time of the delivery thereof to the proper officer, that the packet was received from the commissioners, and hath not been opened.

INTERROGATORIES *at law*: one of the defects of the trial by jury, is the want of powers to examine witnesses abroad, and to receive their depositions in writing, where the witnesses reside, and especially when the cause of action arises in a foreign country. To which may be added the power of examining witnesses that are aged, or going abroad, upon interrogatories *de bene esse*; to be read in evidence if the trial should be deferred till after their death or departure, but otherwise to be totally suppressed. For though these defects are frequently removed by mutual consent, if the parties are open and candid, and consent to a commission, yet the compelling parties to submit to such a course, has never yet been directly adopted as the rule of practice in a court of law, although in a case of obvious hardship (if the party does not resort to a court of equity for a discovery) the court may indirectly relieve by from time to time ordering the trial to be postponed, on the ground of the absence of material witnesses, till the parties consent to a commission.

INTERROGATORIES *upon an attachment for contempt*. If a contempt be committed in the face of the court, the offender may be instantly apprehended and imprisoned, at the discretion of the judges (*Staundf. P. C.* 73. *b.*), without any farther proof of examination. But in matters that arise at a distance, and of which the court cannot have so perfect a knowledge, unless by the confession of the party or the testimony of others, if the judges upon affidavit see sufficient ground to suspect that a contempt has been committed, they either make a rule on the suspected party *to shew cause why an attachment should not issue against him* (*Styl.* 277.); or, in very flagrant instances of contempt, the attachment issues in the first instance (*Salk.* 84. *Stra.* 185, 564.); as it also does if no sufficient cause be shewn to discharge, and thereupon the court confirms and makes absolute the original rule. This process of attachment is merely intended to bring the party into court: and, when there, he must either stand committed, or put in bail, in order to answer upon oath to such interrogatories as shall be administered to him, for the better information of the court with respect to the circumstances of the contempt. These interrogatories are in the nature of a charge or accusation, and must by the course of the court be exhibited within the first four days (6 *Mod.* 73.): and if any of the interrogatories are improper, the defendant may refuse to answer, and move the court to have them struck out (*Stra.* 444.) If the party can clear himself upon oath, he is discharged; but, if perjured, may be prosecuted for the perjury (6 *Mod.* 73.) If he confesses the contempt, the court will proceed to correct him by fine, or imprisonment, or both, and sometimes by a corporal or infamous punishment (*Cro. Car.* 146.) If the contempt be of such a nature, that, when the fact is once acknowledged, the court can receive no farther information by interrogatories, than it is already possessed of, (as in the case of a *rescous, the King* v. *Elkins, M.* 8 *Geo.* 3. *B. R.*) the defendant may be admitted to make such simple acknowledgment, and receive his judgment, without answering to any interrogatories, but if he wilfully and obstinately refuses to answer, or answers in an evasive manner, he is then clearly guilty of a high and repeated contempt, to be punished at the discretion of the court. And although the defendant acknowledges all the facts charged against him, yet it is the practice of the court to compel him to answer interrogatories, unless they are waived by the prosecutor. 5 *T. R.* 362.

An attachment sometimes issues against a person supposed guilty of some contempt to the court whence the process goes forth, to bring him in; and when there, he is to stand committed, or put in bail to answer interrogatories upon oath. But, where a contempt is committed in the presence of a witness, it should seem more rational, and is certainly more congenial with the principles of the constitution to indict the party, and give him the benefit of a legal trial, by his peers.

If it is in a court where the practice is to grant a rule to shew cause why an attachment should not issue for a contempt, &c. if there appears to the court a sufficient ground to make the rule absolute, a subsequent examination on interrogatories seems needless.

And it is, perhaps, only giving the party an opportunity of committing perjury to exculpate himself, when he comes to reconsider his situation and the consequences that may ensue, if the report of the officer should be ultimately against him.

If a contempt is committed in the face of the court, and a commitment ensues, an examination upon interrogatories is unnecessary.

INTESTATE, is one who dies without having made a will respecting the disposal of his real or personal property.

INTESTATE'S ESTATES, are the goods and chattels of persons dying intestate. See *Administrator*, and *Distribution of Intestates Estates.*

INTOL ET UTTOL, toll or custom paid for things imported and exported. *Cowel. Blount.*

INTRARE MARISCUM, to drain low ground, and by dikes, walls, &c. take in and reduce it to herbage or pasture; hence the word *innings*. *Ibid.*

INTRUSION, (*intrusio*) is when the ancestor dies seised of any estate of inheritance, expectant upon an estate for life, and then tenant for life dies, between whose death and entry of the heir, a stranger intrudes. *Co. Lit.* 227.

This entry and interposition of the stranger differ from an abatement, in this; that an abatement is always to the prejudice of the heir, or immediate devisee; an *intrusion* is always to the prejudice of him in remainder or reversion. For example, if A dies seised of lands in fee-simple, and, before the entry of B his heir, C enters thereon, this is an abatement; but if A be tenant for life, with remainder to B in fee-simple, and, after the death of A, C enters, this is an intrusion. Also if A be tenant for life on lease from B, or his ancestors, or be tenant by the curtesy, or in dower, the reversion being vested in B; and after the death of A, C enters and keeps B out of possession, this is likewise an intrusion. So that an intrusion is always immediately consequent upon the determination of a particular estate; an abatement is always consequent upon the descent or devise of an estate in fee-simple. And in either case the injury is equally great to him whose possession is defeated by this unlawful occupancy. 3 *Black.* 169.

INTRUSION DE GARD, a writ that lay where the infant within age entered into his lands, and held out his lord. *Old Nat. Br.* 90. See also *Information in Exchequer.*

INTRUSIONE, is the writ brought against an intruder; by him that hath fee-simple, &c. *New Nat. Br.* 453.

INVADIARE, to engage or mortgage lands. *Cowel.*

INVADIATIONES, mortgages or pledges. *Ibid.*

INVADIATUS, was when one had been accused of some crime, which being not fully proved, he was put *sub debita fidejussione. Ibid.*

INVASIONES, in the inquisition of serjeancies and knights fees, *anno* 12 and 13 of king John, there are some titles called *invasiones; et invasiones super regem. Ibid.*

INVENTIONES, used in antient charters for treasure-trove, money or goods found by any person, and not challenged by the owner; which, by the common law is due to the king, who grants the privilege or benefit, to some particular subjects. *Ibid.*

INVENTORY, (*inventorium*) is a list or schedule containing a true description of all the goods and chattels of a person deceased at the time of his death, with their value appraised by indifferent persons; which every executor or administrator ought to exhibit to the bishop or ordinary at such time as he shall appoint. 21 *Hen.* 8. *c.* 5. See ADMINISTRATOR, *and* MARSHALLING OF ASSETS.

IN VENTRE SA MERE, (Fr.) in the mother's belly. Infant *in ventre sa mere*, is where a woman is with child at the time of her husband's death; which child, if he had been born, would have been heir to the land of the husband: and this is sometimes privily, and sometimes open and visible, 1 *Shep. Abr.* 142. And in all cases, where a daughter or female comes into land by discent; there the son born after, shall oust her and have the land. 3 *Rep.* 61. *Plowd.* 375. But if the daughter and female heir cometh to land in nature of a purchaser; as on a will of lands given to J. S. and his heirs, and he hath a daughter when the devisor dies, his wife being then with child of a son; in this case the daughter shall enjoy the land, and not the after-born son. 3 *Rep.* 61. 5 *Ed.* 4. 6. 9 *H.* 7. 24.

INVERITARE, to verify or make proof of a thing. *Leg. Inæ, c.* 16. *Cowel. Blount.*

INVEST and INVESTITURE, (from the Fr. *investir*) signifies to give possession: a giving livery of seisin or possession of lands, has succeeded in the place of the antient feodal *investiture*, whereby, while feuds were precarious, the vassal, on the discent of lands, was formerly admitted in the lords court (as is still the practice in Scotland), and there received his seisin, in the nature of a renewal of his ancestors grant in the presence of the feodal peers: till at length, when the right of succession became indefesible, entry on any part of the lands within the county, (which, if disputed, was afterwards to be tried by those peers) or other notorious possession was admitted as equivalent to the formal grant of seizin, and made the tenant capable of transferring this his estate by discent. 2 *Black.* 23, 53, 208, 311.

INVITATORIA ET VENITARIUM, those hymns and psalms that were sung in the church to invite the people to prayer. *Cowel. Blount.*

INVOICE. A particular account of merchandise, with its value, custom and charges, &c. sent by a merchant to his factor or correspondent. 12 *Car.* 2. *c.* 34.

INVOLUNTARY MANSLAUGHTER. See HOMICIDE.

INURE, signifies to take effect, as the pardon enureth, the deed enureth. *Staund. Prær.* 40. See *Enure.*

JOBBER, one who lives by buying and selling of cattle. There are also stock-jobbers, who buy and sell stocks for other persons. See *Brokers.*

JOCALIA, (Fr. *joyaux*) jewels; derived from the Lat. *jocus, joculus,* and *jocula*, which comprehend every thing that delighteth. Jewels are part of the wife's paraphernalia, but she shall not be intitled thereto on the death of the husband, unless they are suitable to her quality, and the husband leaves assets to pay debts, &c. 1 *Roll. Abr.* 911.

JOCARI, to contend with pikes. *Cowel.*

JOCARIUS, a jester, the king's jester. *Ibid.*

JOCELET, (Sax.) a little farm or manor; in some parts of Kent, a *yoklet*, as requiring but a small yoke of oxen to till it. *Sax. Dict. Cowel.*

JOCUS PARTITUS. It is so called when two proposals are made, and a man hath liberty to choose which he will. *Cowel.*

JOINDER IN ACTION, is the coupling or joining of two in a suit or action against another. *F. N. B.* 118, 201, 221. As where two joint owners of a sum of money are robbed upon the highway, they are to join in one action against the hundred. *Latch.* 127. *Dyer* 307. So where the suit will survive to the wife, she must join in the action. *Wils. par.* 1. *p.* 224. and see *ibid. par.* 2. *fol.* 423.

So also, though one partner acts in trade, where there are many partners, actions are to be brought against all the partners jointly for his acts. 1 *Salk.* 292. But if one man calls two other men thieves, they shall not join in an action against him; for one joint action will not lie for, or against several persons for speaking the same words. 1 *Danv.* 5. *Palm.* 313.

But on a joint trespass, the plaintiff may declare severally, 2 *Salk.* 454. or jointly. *Style* 153. 10 *Rep.* 66.

Also tenants in common cannot join in an action against their lessee; but it is otherwise in the case of coparceners or jointenants, *Moor* 34.

JOINDER OF COUNTIES. There can be no joinder of counties for the finding of an indictment, where a wound is given in one county, and the party die in another: for by stat. 2 & 3 *Ed.* 6. *c.* 24. the whole may be tried either on indictment or appeal, in the county wherein the death is.

JOINDER IN DEMURRER. When there is a demurrer averring the pleading insufficient in law, to answer the end proposed by it, the opposite party avers it to be sufficient, which is called a joinder in demurrer, and then the parties are at issue in point of law.

JOINDER IN BATTLE, the form, on a writ of right, was as follows: *AND that such is his right, he is prepared to prove by the body of his freeman, Henry Broughton by name, who is present here in court ready to prove the same by his body or in what manner soever the court of the lord the king shall consider that he ought to prove; and if any mischance should befal the said Henry, (which God defend) he is ready to prove the same by another man, who, &c. And hereupon it is demanded of the said George and Henry, whether they are ready to make battle, as they before have waged it: who say that they are.*

JOINDER OF ISSUE. Joinder of an issue in fact, is when a party denies the fact pleaded by his antagonist, who has tendered the issue thus, "and this he prays may be inquired of by the country," or "and of this he puts himself upon the country," the party denying the fact, may immediately subjoin, "and the said A. B. doth the like," which done, the issue is said to be joined. 3 *Black.* 315. 4 *Black.* 334.

JOINT ACTIONS. In personal actions, several wrongs may be joined in one writ; but actions founded upon a tort, and on a contract, cannot be joined, for they require different pleas and different process. 1 *Keb.* 847. 1 *Vent.* 366.

JOINT AND SEVERAL. An interest cannot be granted jointly and severally; as if a man grants *proximam advocationem*, or makes a lease for years, to two jointly and severally, those words severally are void, and they are joint-tenants. 5 *Rep.* 19. *Mich.* 29 & 30 *Eliz. Slingsby's case.*

JOINT EXECUTORS, are accounted in law but as one person, and acts done by any of them shall be taken to be the acts of every one of them; for they all represent the testator. 2 *Nels. Abr.* 1026.

JOINT FINES. If a whole vill is to be fined, a joint fine may be laid, and it will be good for the necessity of it; but in other cases, fines for offences are to be severally imposed on each particular offender, and not jointly upon all of them. 1 *Rol. Rep.* 33. 11 *Rep.* 42. *Dyer.* 211.

JOINT INDICTMENTS. If the offences of several persons arise from a joint criminal act, an indictment or information may charge the defendants jointly. 1 *Ventr.* 302. 2 *Hawk. P. C.* 240.

JOINT-TENANCY. The king cannot be joint-tenant with any person, because none can be equal with him. 1 *Inst.* 1. *Finch.* 83. and 2 *Black.* 409. Also a corporation cannot be jointly seised of any estate with another. 2 *Lev.* 12.

And the essential difference between joint-tenants and tenants in common is, that joint-tenants have the lands by one joint title, and in one right, and tenants in common by several titles, or by one title and by several rights; this is the reason, says L. Coke, that joint-tenants have one joint freehold, and tenants in common have several freeholds, though this property is common to them both, *viz.* that their occupation is undivided, and neither of them knoweth his part in severalty. *Co. Lit.* 189. *a.*

JOINT-TENANTS, (*simul tenentes* or *qui conjunctim tenent*) are those who come to, and hold lands or tenements jointly by one title; and these joint-tenants must jointly plead, and be jointly sued. *Lit.* 277, 280. 1 *Inst.* 180.

This estate in joint-tenancy is sometimes an estate in jointure, which word as well as the other, signifies an union or conjunction of interest; though in common speech the term jointure is now usually confined to that joint estate, which by virtue of the statute 27 *Hen.* 8. *c.* 10, is frequently vested in the husband and wife before marriage, as a full satisfaction and bar of the woman's dower. 2 *Black.* 137.

In respect to an estate in joint-tenancy, it is to be observed,

1. The creation of an estate in joint-tenancy depends on the wording of the deed or devise, by which the tenants claim title; for this estate can only arise by purchase or grant, that is, by the act of the parties, and never by the mere act of law. Now if an estate be given to a plurality of persons, without adding any restrictive, exclusive, or explanatory words, as if an estate be granted to A and B, and their heirs, this makes them immediately joint-tenants in fee of the lands: for the law interprets the grant so as to make all parts of it take effect, which can only be done by creating an equal estate in them both. As therefore the grantor has thus united their names, the law gives them a thorough union in all other respects. For,

2. The properties of a joint estate are derived from its unity, which is four-fold; the unity of interest, the unity of title, the unity of time, and the unity of possession; or in other words, joint-tenants have one and the same interest, accruing by one and the same conveyance, commencing at one and the same time, and held by one and the same undivided possession.

First, they must have one and the same interest. One joint-tenant cannot be entitled to one period of duration or quantity of interest in lands, and the other to a different; one cannot be tenant for life, and the other for years; one cannot be tenant in fee, and the other in tail. (*Co. Litt.* 188.) But if land be limited to A and B for their lives, this makes them joint-tenants of the freehold; if to A and B and their heirs, it makes them joint-tenants of the inheritance. (*Litt. s.* 277.) If land be granted to A and B for their lives, and to the heirs of A, here A and B are joint-tenants of the freehold during their respective lives, and A has the remainder of the fee in severalty; or if land be given to A and B, and the heirs of the body of A, here both have a joint estate for life, and A has a several remainder in tail (*Ibid. sec.* 285). Secondly, joint-tenants must also have an unity of title; their estate must be created by one and the same act, whether legal or illegal; as by one and the same grant, or by one and the same disseisin. (*Ibid. sec.* 278.) Joint-tenancy cannot arise by descent or act of law, but merely by purchase, or acquisition by the act of the party; and, unless that act be one and the same, the two tenants would have different titles; and if they had different titles, one might prove good, and the other bad, which would absolutely destroy the jointure. Thirdly, there must also be an unity of time; their estates must be vested at one and the same period, as well as by one and the same title: As in case of a present estate made to A or B, or a remainder in fee to A and B after a particular estate; in either case A and B are joint-tenants of this present estate, or this vested remainder. But if after a lease for life the remainder be limited to the heirs of A and B, and during the continuance of the particular estate A dies, which vests the remainder of one moiety in his heir, and then B dies, whereby the other moiety becomes vested in the heir of B, now A's heir and B's heir are not joint-tenants of this remainder, but tenants in common; for one moiety vested at one time, and the other moiety vested at another. (*Co. Lit.* 188.) Yet where a feoffment was made to the use of a man, and such wife as he should afterwards marry, for term of their lives, and he afterwards married, in this case it seems to have been held that the husband and wife had a joint estate, though vested at different times: (*Dyer* 340. 1 *Rep.* 101.) because the use of the wife's estate was in abeyance, and dormant till the intermarriage, and being then awakened had relation back, and took effect from the original time of creation. Lastly, in joint-tenancy there must be an unity of possession. Joint-tenants are said to be seised *per my et per tout*, by the half or moiety, and by all; that is, they each of them have the entire possession, as well of every parcel as of the whole. (*Lit. sec.* 288. 5 *Rep.* 10.) They have not, one of them a seisin of one half or moiety, and the other of the other moiety; neither can one be exclusively seised of one acre, and his companion of another, but each has an undivided moiety of the whole, and not the whole of an undivided moiety. (*Bract. l.* 5, *tr.* 5, *c.* 26.) And therefore, if an estate in fee be given to a man and his wife, they are neither properly joint-tenants, nor tenants in common; for husband and wife being considered as one person in law, they cannot take the estate by moieties, but both are seised of the entirety, *per tout et non per my*; the consequence of which is that neither the husband nor the wife can dispose of any part without the assent of the other, but the whole must remain to the survivor. *Litt. sec.* 665. *Co. Litt.* 187. *Bro. Abr. t. cui in vita*, 8. 2 *Vern.* 120. 2 *Lev.* 39.

And if a grant is made of a joint estate to husband and wife, and a third person, the husband and wife shall have one moiety, and the third person the other moiety, in the same manner as if it had been granted only to two persons. So if the grant is to husband and wife and two others, the husband and wife take one third in joint-tenancy. *Litt. sec.* 291.

Upon these principles of a thorough and intimate union of interest and possession depend many other consequences and incidents to the joint-tenant's estate. If two joint-tenants let a verbal lease of their land, reserving rent to be paid to one of them, it shall enure to both, in respect of the joint reversion. (*Co. Litt.* 214.) If their lessee surrenders his lease to one of them, it shall also enure to both, because of the privity, or relation of their estate. (*Ibid.* 192.) On the same reason, livery of seisin, made to one joint-tenant, shall enure to both of them, (*Ibid.* 49,) and the entry, or re-entry, of one joint-tenant is as effectual in law as if it were the act of both. (*Ibid.* 319. 364.) In all actions also relating to their joint estate, one joint-tenant cannot sue or be sued without joining the other. (*Ibid.* 195.) But if two or more joint-tenants be seised of an advowson, and they present different clerks, the bishop may refuse to admit either, because neither joint-tenant has a several right of patronage, but each is seised of the whole; and if they do not both agree within six months the right of presentation shall lapse. But the ordinary may, if he pleases, admit a clerk presented by either, for the good of the church, that divine service may be regularly performed; which is no more than he otherwise would be entitled to do, in case their disagreement continued, so as to incur a lapse: and if the clerk of one joint-tenant be so admitted, this shall keep up the title in both of them, in respect of the privity and union of their estate. (*Ibid.* 185.) Upon the same ground it is held that one joint-tenant cannot have an action against another for trespass in respect of his land, (3 *Levinz* 262.) for each has an equal right to enter on any part of it. But one joint-tenant is not capable by himself to do any act which may tend to defeat or injure the estate of the other, as to let leases, or to grant copyholds; (1 *Leon.* 234.) and if any waste be done which tends to the destruction of the inheritance, one joint-tenant may have an action of waste against the other, by construction of the stat. *Westm.* 2, *c.* 22, (2 *Inst.* 403). So, too, though at common law no action of account lay for one joint-tenant against another, unless he had constituted him his bailiff or receiver; (*Co. Lit.* 200,) yet now by the stat. 4 *Ann. c.* 16, joint-tenants may have actions of account against each other for receiving more than their due share of the profits of the tenements held in joint-tenancy.

This action is now, perhaps, never brought; but the practice is to apply to a court of equity to compel an account, which is also the jurisdiction generally resorted to, in order to obtain a partition between joint-tenants, parceners, and tenants in common. 3 *Com. Dig. Chanc.* 6. and 4. *E. Mitf.* 109.

From the same principle also arises the remaining grand incident of joint estates, *viz.* the doctrine of survivorship, by which, when two or more persons are seised of a joint estate of inheritance for their own lives, or *pur auter vie*, or are jointly possessed of any chattel interest, the entire tenancy upon the decease of any of them remains to the survivors, and at length to the last survivor; and he shall be entitled to the whole estate whatever it be, whether an inheritance, or a common freehold only, or even a less estate, (*Litt. sec.* 280, 281.) This is the natural and regular consequence of the union and entirety of their interest. The interest of two joint-tenants is not only equal or similar, but also is one and the same. One has not originally a distinct moiety from the other, but if by any subsequent act (as by alienation or forfeiture of either) the interest becomes separate and distinct, the joint-tenancy instantly ceases. But while it continues, each of two joint-tenants has a concurrent interest in the whole, and therefore on the death of his companion, the sole interest in the whole remains to the survivor. For the interest which the survivor originally had is clearly not divested by the death of his companion; and no other person can now claim to have a joint estate with him, for no one can now have an interest in the whole, accruing by the same title, and taking effect at the same time with his own; neither can any one claim a separate interest in any part of the tenements, for that would be to deprive the survivor of the right which he has in all and every part. As, therefore, the survivor's original interest in the whole still remains, and as no one can now be admitted, either jointly or severally, to any share with him therein, it follows that his own interest must now be entire and several, and that he shall alone be entitled to the whole estate, (whatever it be) that was created by the original grant.

This right of survivorship is called by our ancient authors (*Bracton, l.* 4, *tr.* 3, *c.* 9, *sec.* 3. *Fleta, l.* 3, *c.* 4.) the *jus accrescendi*, because the right, upon the death of one joint-tenant, accumulates and increases to the survivors, or, as they themselves express it, "*pars illa communis accrescit superstitibus, de persona in personam, usque ad ultimam superstitem.*" And this *jus accrescendi* ought to be mutual, which is one reason why neither the king, (*Co. Litt.* 190. *Finch. L.* 83.) nor any corporation, (2 *Lev.* 12.) can be a joint-tenant with a private person. For here is no mutuality: the private person has not even the remotest chance of being seised of the entirety by benefit of survivorship, for the king and the corporation can never die.

But lord *Coke* says expressly, "there may be joint-tenants though there be not equal benefit of survivorship; as if a man let lands to A and B during the life of A, if B die A shall have all by survivorship; but if A die B shall have nothing." *Co. Litt.* 181. The mutuality of survivorship does not therefore appear to be the reason why a corporation cannot be a joint-tenant with a private person, for two corporations cannot be joint-tenants together, but whenever a joint estate is granted to them they take as tenants in common. *Co. Litt.* 190.

There is also no survivorship of a capital, or a stock in trade, among merchants and traders, for this would be ruinous to the family of the deceased partner; and it is a legal maxim *jus accrescendi inter mercatores pro beneficio commercii locum non habet. Co. Litt.* 182.

3. We are lastly to inquire how an estate in joint-tenancy may be severed and destroyed. And this may be done by destroying any of its constituent unities: 1. That of time, which respects only the original commencement of the joint-estate, cannot indeed (being now past) be affected by any subsequent transactions. But, 2. The joint-tenant's estate may be destroyed, without any alienation, by merely disuniting their possession. For joint-tenants being seised *per my et per tout*, every thing that tends to narrow that interest, so that they shall not be seised throughout the whole, and throughout every part, is a severance or destruction of the jointure. And therefore, if two joint-tenants agree to part their lands, and hold them in severalty, they are no longer joint-tenants: for they have now no joint-interest in the whole, but only a several interest respectively in the several parts. And for that reason also, the right of survivorship is by such separation destroyed. (*Co. Litt.* 188, 193.) By common law all the joint-tenants might agree to make partition of the lands, but one of them could not compel the other so to do; (*Litt. sec.* 290.) for this being an estate originally created by the act and agreement of the parties, the law would not permit any one or more of them to destroy the united possession without a similar universal consent. But now by the statutes 31 *Hen.* 8, *c.* 1, and 32 *Hen.* 8, *c.* 32, joint-tenants, either of inheritances, or other less estates, are compellable by writ of partition to divide their lands. (*Ff.* 12. 6. 26. *sec.* 4.) 3. The jointure may be destroyed by destroying the unity of title: as if one joint-tenant aliens and conveys his estate to a third person; here the joint-tenancy is severed, and turned into tenancy in common; (*Litt. sec.* 292.) for the grantee and the remaining joint-tenant hold by different titles, (one derived from the original, the other from the subsequent, grantor,) though till partition made the unity of possession continues. But a devise of one's share by will is no severance of the jointure: for no testament takes effect till after the death of the testator, and by such death the right of

the survivor (which accrued at the original creation of the estate, and has therefore a priority to the other, *jus accrescendi præfertur ultimæ voluntati.* *Co. Litt.* 185.) is already vested (*Litt. sec.* 287) *.

4. It may also be destroyed by destroying the unity of interest. And therefore, if there be two joint-tenants for life, and the inheritance is purchased by or descends upon either, it is a severance of the jointure, (*Cro. Eliz.* 470.); though, if an estate is originally limited to two for life, and after to the heirs of one of them, the freehold shall remain in jointure, without merging in the inheritance, because, being created by one and the some conveyance, they are not separate estates, (which is requisite in order to a merger,) but branches of one entire estate. (2 *Rep.* 60. *Co. Lit.* 182.) In like manner, if a joint-tenant in fee makes a lease for life of his share, this defeats the jointure (*Litt. sec.* 302, 303,); for it destroys the unity both of title and of interest. And, whenever or by whatever means the jointure ceases, or is severed, the right of survivorship, or *jus accrescendi*, the same instant ceases with it. (*Co. Lit.* 188.) Yet if one of three joint-tenants aliens his share, the two remaining tenants still hold their parts by joint-tenancy and survivorship (*Litt. sec.* 294.); and if one of three joint-tenants releases his share to one of his companions, though the joint-tenancy is destroyed with regard to that part, yet the two remaining parts are still held in jointure (*Ibid.* 304.); for they still preserve their original constituent unities. But when by any act or event different interests are created in the several parts of the estate, or they are held by different titles, or if merely the possession is separated, so that the tenants have no longer these four indispensable properties, a sameness of interest, and undivided possession, a title vesting at one and the same time, and by one and the same act or grant, the jointure is instantly dissolved.

In general it is advantageous for the joint-tenants to dissolve the jointure, since thereby the right of survivorship is taken away, and each may transmit his own part to his own heirs. Sometimes, however, it is disadvantageous to dissolve the joint estate; as if there be joint-tenants for life, and they make partition, this dissolves the jointure; and though before they each of them had an estate in the whole for their own lives and the life of their companion, now they have an estate in a moiety, only for their own lives merely, and on the death of either the reversioner shall enter on his moiety (1 *Jones* 55.) And therefore, if there be two joint-tenants for life, and one grants away his part for the life of his companion, it is a forfeiture (4 *Leon.* 237.): for in the first place, by the severance of the jointure, he has given himself in his own moiety, only an estate for his own life; and then he grants the same land for the life of another: which grant, by a tenant for his own life merely, is a forfeiture of his estate (*Co. Litt.* 252); for it is creating an estate, which may, by possibility last longer than that which he is legally entitled to. 2 *Black.* c. 12.

——— Joint-tenants *in things personal.*] Things personal may belong to their owners, not only in severalty, but also in joint-tenancy, and in common, as well as real estates. They cannot indeed, be vested in coparcenary; because they do not descend from the ancestor to the heir, which is necessary to constitute coparceners. But if a horse, or other personal chattel, be given to two or more, absolutely, they are joint tenants hereof; and, unless the jointure be severed, the same doctrine of survivorship shall take place as in estates of lands and tenements (*Litt. s.* 282. 1 *Vern.* 482.) And, in like manner, if the jointure be severed, as by either of them selling his share, the vendee and the remaining part-owner shall be tenants in common, without any *jus accrescendi* or survivorship (*Lit. s.* 321.) So also, if 100*l.* be given by will to two or more, equally to be divided between them, this makes them tenants in common (1 *Eq. Cas. Abr.* 292.); as the same words would have done in regard to real estates.

So also, residuary legatees and executors are joint tenants, unless the testator uses some expression which converts their interest into a tenancy in common; and if one dies before a division or severance of the surplus, the whole that is undivided will pass to the survivor or survivors. 2 *P. Wms.* 113. 3 *Bro.* 455.

But, for the encouragement of husbandry and trade, it is held that a stock on a farm, though occupied jointly, and also a stock used in a joint undertaking, by way of partnership in trade, shall always be considered as common and not as joint property, and there shall be no survivorship therein (1 *Vern.* 217. *Co. Lit.* 182.

JOINTURE. A jointure, which, strictly speaking, signifies a joint estate, limited to

* If a will is made by a joint-tenant of real property, devising his interest in the premises, and after the execution of the will there is a partition of the estate, the testator's share cannot pass by the devise, unless there is a republication of the will subsequent to the partition. 3 *Burr.* 1488.

For a joint-tenant is not enabled to devise his estate by the statute of wills 32 *Hen.* 8, *c.* 1, explained by 34 and 35 *Hen.* 8, *c.* 5, as tenants in common and coparceners. But if a tenant in common devises his estate a subsequent partition is not a revocation of the will. 3 *P. Wms.* 169.

both husband and wife, and in common acceptation extends also to a sole estate, limited to the wife only, is thus defined by sir Edward Coke (1 *Inst.* 36.); "a competent "livelihood of freehold for the wife, of lands "and tenements; to take effect, in profit or "possession, presently after the death of "the husband; for the life of the wife at "least."

This description is framed with the purview of the statute 27 *Hen.* 8. c. 10. commonly called the statute of uses; before the making of which statute, the greatest part of the land of England was conveyed to uses; the property or possession of the soil being vested in one man, and the use, or profits thereof, in another; whose directions, with regard to the disposition thereof, the former was in conscience obliged to follow, and might be compelled by a court of equity to observe. Now, though a husband had the use of lands in absolute fee-simple, yet the wife was not entitled to any dower therein; he not being seised thereof: wherefore it became usual, on marriage, to settle by express deed some special estate to the use of the husband and his wife, for their lives, in joint-tenancy, or jointure; which settlement would be a provision for the wife in case she survived her husband. At length the statute of uses ordained, that such as had the use of lands, should, to all intents and purposes, be reputed and taken to be absolutely seised and possessed of the soil itself. In consequence of which legal seisin, all wives would have become dowable of such lands as were held to the use of their husbands, and also entitled at the same time to any special lands that might be settled in jointure: had not the same statute provided, that upon making such an estate in jointure to the wife before marriage, she shall be for ever precluded from her dower. (4 *Rep.* 1, 2.) But then these four requisites must be punctually observed; 1. The jointure must take effect immediately on the death of the husband. 2. It must be for her own life at least, and not *per auter vie*, for any term of years, or other smaller estate. 3. It must be made to herself, and no other in trust for her. 4. It must be made, and so in the deed particularly expressed to be, in satisfaction of her whole dower, and not of any particular part of it,* or it may be averred to be. 4 *Rep.* 3.

If the jointure be made to her after marriage, she has her election after her husband's death, as in dower *ad ostium ecclesiæ*, and may either accept it, or refuse it and betake herself to her dower at common law; for she was not capable of consenting to it during coverture. And where a devise is expressed to be given in lieu and satisfaction of dower, or where that is the clear and manifest intention of the testator, the wife shall not have both, but shall have her choice. *Harg. Co. Litt.* 36. *b.* And if, by any fraud or accident, a jointure made before marriage proves to be on a bad title, and the jointress is evicted, or turned out of possession, she shall then (by the provisions of the same statute) have her dower *pro tanto* at the common law.

It has been determined, that if a woman, who is under age at the time of marriage, agrees to a jointure and settlement in bar of her dower, and her distributive share of her husband's personal property, in case he dies intestate, she cannot afterwards waive it; but is as much bound, as if she were of age at the time of marriage. Lord Northington had decreed the contrary; but his decree was upon both points reversed. *Drury* v. *Drury*, 4 *Brown's P. C.* 570.

There are some advantages attending tenants in dower that do not extend to jointresses; and so *vice versa*, jointresses are in some respects more privileged than tenants in dower. Tenant in dower by the old common law is subject to no tolls or taxes; and hers is almost the only estate on which, when derived from the king's debtor, the king cannot distrein for his debt; if contracted during the coverture (*Co. Lit.* 31. *a.* *F. N. B.* 150.) But, on the other hand, a widow may enter at once, without any formal process, on her jointure land; as she also might have done on dower *ad ostium ecclesiæ*, which a jointure in many points resembles; and the resemblance was still greater, while that species of dower continued in its primitive state: whereas no small trouble, and a very tedious method of proceeding, is necessary to compel a legal assignment of dower (*Co. Litt.* 36.) And, what is more, though dower be forfeited by the treason of her husband, yet lands settled in jointure remain unimpeached to the widow (*Ibid.* 37.) Wherefore sir Edward Coke very justly gives it the preference, as being more sure and safe to the widow, than even dower *ad ostium ecclesiæ*, the most eligible species of any. *Co. Lit.* 37.

And a jointure is not forfeited by the adultery of the wife, as dower is; and the court of chancery will decree against the husband a performance of marriage articles, though he alleges and proves that his wife lives separate from him in adultery. *Cox's P. Wms.* 277. *vol.* 3.

JOINTRESS, is she who hath an estate settled on her by the husband, to hold during her life, if she survive him. 17 *H.* 8. *c.* 10. 1 *Inst.* 46. See *Jointure.*

JOUR, (Fr.) a day, used in heads of our law; *touts jours* for ever. *Law Fr. Dict.*

---

* An assurance was made to a woman, to the intent it should be for her jointure, but it was not so expressed in the deed. And the opinion of the court was, that it might be averred that it was for a jointure, and that such averment was traversable. *Owen*, 33. But a trust estate, or an agreement to settle lands as a jointure, is a good equitable jointure in bar of dower.

JOURNAL, a day-book or diary of transactions. *Cowel.*

JOURNALS OF PARLIAMENT, are not records, but remembrances, and have been of no long continuance. *Hob. Rep.* 109.

JOURNCHOPPERS, were regrators of yarn, which formerly perhaps was called *journ*, mentioned in 8 *H.* 6. *c.* 5. *Cowel.*

JOURNEYMAN, (from the Fr. *journée*, *i. e.* a day, or day's work) properly one who works with another by the day; though extended by 5 *Eliz. c.* 4. to those also who covenant to work with others in their trades by the year. See *Combinations*, *Labourers*, *Manufactures* and *Servants*.

JOURNEYS ACCOUNTS, (*dietæ computatæ*) is a term in law thus understood: if a writ abates by the death of the plaintiff or defendant, or for false Latin, want of form, &c. the plaintiff shall have a new writ by journeys accounts, *i. e.* within as little time as he possibly can after the abatement of the first writ; and this second writ shall be a continuance of the cause, as if the first writ had not abated. *Terms de Ley.*

IPSO FACTO, by the deed itself: and many things are in the law considered to be *ipso facto* void: as where the same person obtains two or more preferments in the church with cure, not qualified by dispensation, &c. the first living is void *ipso facto*, *viz.* without any declaratory sentence, and the patron may present to it. *Dyer* 275.

IRE AD LARGUM, to go at large, to escape, or be set at liberty. *Blount.*

IRELAND. Ireland, until the late union, was a distinct kingdom; and up to 22 & 23 *Geo.* 3. a dependent subordinate kingdom under the crown of Great Britain.

Anciently it was only entitled the dominion or lordship of Ireland (*Stat. Hiberniæ*, 14 *Hen.* 3.), and the king's stile was no other than *dominus Hiberniæ*, lord of Ireland, till the title of king was conferred upon him and his successors by a statute passed in Ireland expressly for that purpose, and it was made treason for any inhabitant of Ireland to deny it. 33 *Hen.* 8. *c.* 1. *Irish Stat.*

The inhabitants of Ireland are, for the most part descended from the English, who planted it as a kind of colony, after the conquest of it by king Henry the second; and the laws of England were then received and sworn to by the Irish nation, assembled at the council of Lismore. *Pryn. on* 4 *Inst.* 249.

At the time of this conquest, the Irish were governed by what they call the Brehon law, so stiled from the Irish name of the judges, who were denominated Brehons (4 *Inst.* 358.) But king John, in the twelfth year of his reign, went into Ireland, and carried over with him many able sages of the law; and there by his letters patent, in right of the dominion of conquest, is said to have ordained and established, that Ireland should be governed by the laws of England (*Vaugh.* 294. 2 *Pryn. Rec.* 85. 7 *Rep.* 23.): which letters patent, sir Edward Coke (1 *Inst.* 141.) apprehends to have been there confirmed in parliament. But to this ordinance, many of the Irish were averse to conform, and still stuck to their Brehon law: so that both Henry the third (*A. R.* 30. 1 *Rym. Feod.* 442.) and Edward the first (*An. R.* 5. 3 *Pryn. Rec.* 1218.) were obliged to renew the injunction; and at length, in a parliament holden at Kilkenny, 40 *Edw.* 3. under Lionel, duke of Clarence, and then lieutenant of Ireland, the Brehon law was formally abolished, it being unanimously declared to be indeed no law, but a lewd custom crept in of later times. And yet, even in the reign of queen Elizabeth, the wild natives still kept and preserved their Brehon law; which is described (*Edm. Spenser, p.* 1513.) to have been "a rule of right unwritten, but delivered by tradition from one to another, in which oftentimes there appeared great shew of equity in determining the right between party and party, but in many things repugnant quite both to God's laws and man's. The latter part of this character is alone ascribed to it, by the laws before-cited of Edward the first and his grandson.

But as Ireland was a distinct dominion, and had parliaments of its own, it is to be observed, that though the immemorial customs, or common law, of England were made the rule of justice in Ireland also, yet no acts of the English parliament extended into that kingdom; unless it were specially named, or included under general words, such as, "within any of the king's dominions." And this is particularly expressed, and the reason given in the year books (20 *Hen.* 6. 8. 2 *Ric.* 3. 12.): "a tax granted by the parliament of England shall not bind those of Ireland, because they are not summoned to our parliament;" and again, "Ireland hath a parliament of its own, and maketh and altereth laws; and our statutes do not bind them, because they do not send knights to our parliament: but their persons are the king's subjects, like as the inhabitants of Calais, Gascoigne, and Guienne, while they continued under the king's subjection." The general run of laws, enacted by the superior state, are supposed to be calculated for its own internal government, and do not extend to its distant dependent countries, which, bearing no part in the legislature, are not therefore in its ordinary and daily contemplation. But, when the sovereign legislative power sees it necessary to extend its care to any of its subordinate dominions, and mentions them expressly by name, or includes them under general words, there can be no doubt but then they are bound by its laws. *Year Book*, 1 *Hen.* 7. 3. 7 *Rep.* 22. *Calvin's case.*

The original method of passing statutes in

Ireland, was nearly the same as in England, the chief governor holding parliaments at his pleasure, which enacted such laws as they thought proper (*Irish Stat.* 11 *Eliz. st.* 3. *c.* 8.) But an ill use being made of this liberty, particularly by lord Gormanstown, deputy-lieutenant in the reign of Edward IV. (*Irish Stat.* 10 *Hen.* 7. *c.* 23.) a set of statutes were there enacted in the 10 *Hen.* 7. (sir Edward Poynings being then lord deputy, whence they are called Poynings' laws) one of which (*cap.* 4. expounded by 3 & 4 *Ph. & Mar. c.* 4.), in order to restrain the power as well of the deputy as the Irish parliament, provided, 1. That before any parliament be summoned, or holden, the chief governor and council of Ireland should certify to the king under the great seal of Ireland, the considerations and causes thereof, and the articles of the acts proposed to be passed therein. 2. That after the king, in his council of England, should have considered, approved, or altered the said acts or any of them, and certified them back under the great seal of England, and should have given licence to summon and hold a parliament, then the same should be summoned and held; and therein the said acts so certified, and no other should be proposed, received, or rejected (4 *Inst.* 353.) But as this precluded any law from being proposed, but such as were pre-conceived before the parliament was in being, which occasioned many inconveniences, and made frequent dissolutions necessary, it was provided by the statute of Philip and Mary, before-cited, that any new propositions might be certified to England in the usual forms, even after the summons and during the session of parliament. By this means, however, there was nothing left to the parliament in Ireland, but a bare negative or power of rejecting, not of proposing or altering, any law. But the usage, till the independence of Ireland in 1782, 3, was, for bills to be framed in either house, under the denomination of "heads for a bill or bills:" and in that shape they were offered to the consideration of the lord lieutenant and privy council: who, upon such parliamentary intimation, or otherwise upon the application of private persons, received and transmitted such heads, or rejected them without any transmission, to England.

But the Irish nation being excluded from the benefit of the English statutes, were deprived of many good and profitable laws, made for the improvement of the common law: and the measure of justice in both kingdoms becoming thence no longer uniform, it was therefore enacted, by another of Poynings' laws (*cap.* 22), that all acts of parliament, before made in England, should be of force within the realm of Ireland (4 *Inst.* 351.) But, by the same rule, that no laws made in England, between king John's time and Poynings' law, were then binding in Ireland, it followed that no acts of the English parliament made since the 10 *Hen.* 7. could bind the people of Ireland, unless specially named or included under general words (12 *R. p.* 112.)

But this state of dependence being almost forgotten, and ready to be disputed by the Irish nation, it became necessary to declare how that matter really stood: and therefore by stat. (6 *Geo.* 1. *c.* 5.) it was declared, that the kingdom of Ireland ought to be subordinate to, and dependent upon, the imperial crown of Great Britain, as being inseparably united thereto: and that the king's majesty, with the consent of the lords and commons of Great Britain in parliament, hath power to make laws to bind the people of Ireland.

The laws of Ireland thus communicated with those of England; and it was by the same stat. 6 *Geo.* 1. *c.* 5. expressly declared, that the peers of Ireland have no jurisdiction to affirm or reverse judgments or decrees whatsoever. So that from that time up to 1782-3, the ultimate resort from the courts of justice in Ireland was, as in Wales, to those in England: a writ of error in nature of an appeal lying from the king's bench in Ireland to the king's bench in England, as the appeal from the chancery in Ireland lay immediately to the house of lords here.

But this subjection of the people of Ireland having occasioned much popular discontent in that country, the act 22 *Geo.* 3. *c.* 53. repealed the statute of *Geo.* 1. However, as the statute of *Geo.* 1. was thought to be merely declaratory of the former law, the repeal of it could produce no further operation than to render the law in some degree less clear than that statute had made it. Therefore, to produce the intended effect, it required another statute, which was passed in the 23 *Geo.* 3. *c.* 28. which expressly declared, that in all cases whatever, the people of Ireland should be bound only by laws enacted by his majesty and the parliament of that kingdom; and that no appeal or writ of error from any court in Ireland should for the future be brought into any of the courts in England.

Since these last acts, the great and important event of AN UNION between GREAT BRITAIN and IRELAND, hath taken place.

The manner in which this happy consolidation of the national rights and interests of both countries, was brought about, appear from the *stat.* 39 & 40 *Geo.* 3. *c.* 77. which is in substance, as follows:

In pursuance of his majesty's most gracious recommendation to the two houses of parliament in Great Britain and Ireland respectively, to consider of such measures as might best tend to strengthen and consolidate the connection between the two kingdoms, the two houses of parliament in each country resolved, that, in order to promote and secure the essential interests of Great Britain and Ireland, and to consolidate the strength, power, and resources of the British empire, it was adviseable to concur in such measures as should best tend to unite the two kingdoms into one kingdom, on such terms and conditions as should be established by the acts of the respective parliaments in the two countries. And, in furtherance of that resolution, the two houses of each parliament agreed upon eight articles, which, by an address of the respective houses of parliament, were laid before his majesty for his consideration; and his majesty having approved of the same, and having recommended it to his parliaments in Great Britain and Ireland to give full effect to them, they were ratified by an act passed in the parliament of Great Britain on the 2d of July 1800.

Art. I. That the kingdoms of Great Britain and Ireland shall, on the first day of January 1801, and for ever after, be united into one kingdom, by the name of The United Kingdom of Great Britain and Ireland; and that the royal style and titles of the imperial crown, and the ensigns, armorial flags, and banners, shall be such as should be appointed by his majesty's royal proclamation.

Art. II. That the succession to the imperial crown shall continue settled in the same manner as the succession to the crown of Great Britain and Ireland stood before limited.

Art. III. That there shall be one parliament, stiled, The Parliament of the United Kingdom of Great Britain and Ireland.

Art. IV. That four lords spiritual of Ireland, by rotation of sessions, and twenty-eight lords temporal of Ireland, elected for life by the peers of Ireland, shall sit in the house of lords: and one hundred commoners, two for each county, two for the city of Dublin, and two for the city of Cork, one for Trinity College, and one for each of the thirty-one most considerable cities and boroughs, shall be the number to sit in the house of commons on the part of Ireland.

That questions respecting the rotation or election of the spiritual or temporal peers shall be decided by the house of lords, and in the case of an equality of votes in the election of a temporal peer, the clerk of the parliament shall determine the election by drawing one of the names from a glass.

That a peer of Ireland, not elected one of the twenty-eight, may sit in the house of commons; but whilst he continues a member of the house of commons, he shall not be entitled to the privilege of peerage, nor capable of being elected one of the twenty-eight, nor of voting at such election, and he shall be sued and indicted for any offence as a commoner.

That as often as three of the peerages of Ireland, existing at the time of the Union, shall become extinct, the king may create one peer of Ireland; and when the peers of Ireland are reduced to one hundred by extinction, or otherwise, exclusive of those who shall hold any peerage of Great Britain subsisting at the time of the union, or created of the united kingdom since the union, the king may then create one peer of Ireland for every peerage that becomes extinct, or as often as any of them is created a peer of the united kingdom, so that the king may always keep up the number of one hundred Irish peers, over and above those who have an hereditary seat in the house of lords.

That questions respecting the election of the members of the house of commons returned for Ireland, shall be tried in the same manner, as questions respecting the elections for places in Great Britain, subject to such particular regulations as the parliament afterwards shall deem expedient.

That the qualifications by property of the representatives in Ireland, shall be the same respectively as those for counties, cities, and boroughs in England, unless some other provision be afterwards made.

Until an act shall be passed in the parliament of the united kingdom, providing in what cases persons holding offices and places of profit under the crown of Ireland, shall be incapable of sitting in the house of commons, not more than twenty such persons shall be capable of sitting; and if more than twenty such persons shall be returned from Ireland, then the seats of those above twenty shall be vacated, who have last accepted their offices or places.

That all the lords of parliament on the part of Ireland, spiritual and temporal, sitting in the house of lords, shall have the same rights and privileges respectively as the peers of Great Britain; and that all the lords spiritual and temporal of Ireland shall have rank and precedency next and immediately after all the persons holding peerages of the like order and degree in Great Britain, subsisting at the time of the union; and that all peerages hereafter created of Ireland, or of the united kingdom, of the same degree, shall have precedency according to the dates of their creations; and that all the peers of Ireland, except those who are members of the house of commons, shall have all the privileges of peers as fully as the peers of Great Britain, the right and privileges of sitting in the house of lords, and upon the trial of peers only excepted.

Art. V. That the churches of England and Ireland be united into one protestant episcopal church, to be called, The United Church of England and Ireland; that the doctrine and worship shall be the same; and that the continuance and preservation of the united church as the established church of England and Ireland, shall be deemed an essential and fundamental part of the union; and that, in like manner, the church of Scotland shall remain the same as is now established by law, and by the acts of union of England and Scotland.

Art. VI. The subjects of Great Britain and Ireland, shall be entitled to the same privileges with regard to trade and navigation, and also in respect of all treaties with foreign powers.

That all prohibitions and bounties upon the importation of merchandize from one country to the other shall cease.

But that the importation of certain articles therein enumerated, shall be subject to such countervailing duties as are specified in the act.

Art. VII. The sinking funds, and the interest of the national debt, of each country, shall be defrayed by each separately. And, for the space of twenty years, after the union, the contribution of Great Britain and Ireland towards the public expenditure in each year, shall be in the proportion of fifteen to two, subject to future regulations.

Art. VIII. All the laws and courts of each kingdom shall remain the same as they are now established, subject to such alterations by the united parliament, as circumstances may require; but that all writs of error and appeals shall be decided by the house of lords of the united kingdom, except appeals from the court of admiralty in Ireland, which shall be decided by a court of delegates, appointed by the court of chancery in Ireland.

The statute then recites an act passed in the parliament of Ireland, by which the rotation of the four spiritual lords for each sessions is fixed; and it also directs the time and mode of electing the twenty-eight temporal peers for life; and it provides that sixty-four county members, two for each county, two for the city of Dublin, two for the city of Cork, one for Trinity College, Dublin, and one for each of thirty-one cities and towns which are there specified, which are the only places in Ireland to be represented in future. One of the two members of each of those places, was chosen by lot, unless the other withdrew his name to sit in the first parliament, but at the next elections, one member only will be returned.

IRON. By 4 *Geo.* 2. *c.* 32. to steal or sever, with intent to steal any iron, fixed to a house, or in any court or garden, thereunto belonging, is made felony, liable to transportation for seven years.

IRONS, *to secure prisoners.* Imprisonment (before trial) is only for safe custody, and not for punishment: therefore, in the dubious interval between the commitment and trial, a prisoner ought to be used with the utmost humanity; and neither be loaded with needless fetters, or subjected to other hardships than such as are absolutely requisite for the purpose of confinement only: though what are so requisite, must too often be left to the discretion of the gauler. 4 *Black.* 300.

Yet the law will not justify them in fettering a prisoner, unless he is unruly, or has attempted an escape. 2 *Inst.* 381. 3 *Inst.* 34. *Fleta, lib.* 1. *c.* 26.

And when the prisoner is called to the bar, he must be brought without irons, or any manner of shackles or bonds; unless there be evident danger of an escape, and then he may be secured with irons. *Bract. lib.* 3. *de coron. c.* 18. *sect.* 3. *Mir. c.* 5. *sect.* 1, 54. *Fleta, lib.* 1. *c.* 31. *sect.* 1. *Brit. c.* 5. *Staundf. P. C.* 78. 3 *Inst.* 34. *Kel.* 10. 2 *Hal. P. C.* 219. 2 *Hawk. P. C.* 308.

IRONY. In libels, makes them as properly libels as what is expressed in direct terms. *Hob.* 215. 1 *Hawk.* 193, 194. See *Libel.*

IRREGULARITY, (*irregularitas*) signifies disorder, or going out of rule: and in the canon law, it is used for an impediment to the taking holy orders; as where a man is base born, notoriously defamed of any crime, maimed, or much deformed in body, &c. *Cowel.*

IRREPLEVIABLE or IRREPLEVISABLE, that which neither may, nor ought to be replevied or delivered on sureties. 13 *Ed.* 1. *c.* 2. But it is against the nature of a distress for rent, to be irreplevisable. 1 *Inst.* 145. *Cowel.*

ISINGLASS, a kind of fish glue, brought from Iceland, used by some persons in the adulterating of wine: formerly prohibited by stat. 12 *Car.* 2. *cap.* 25.

ISLAND or ISLE, (*insula*) is land inclosed in, and environed with the sea or fresh water.

And according to the *civil law,* an island in the sea, that has no owner, by the law of nations, belongs to him that first finds it. *Justin. Inst. lib.* 2.

But by the law of England, if an island arise in the middle of a river, it belongs in common to those who have lands on each side thereof; but if it be nearer to one bank than the other, it belongs only to him who is proprietor of the nearest shore: which is agreeable to, and probably copied from, the civil law (*Inst.* 2. 1, 22.) Yet this seems only to be reasonable, where the soil of the river is equally divided between the owners of the opposite shores: for if the whole soil is the freehold of any one man, as it usually is, whenever a several fishery is claimed (*Salk.* 637.), there it seems just (and so is the constant practice) that the eyotts or little islands, arising in any part of the river, shall be the property of him who owneth the piscary and the soil. However, in case a new island rise in the sea, though the civil law gives it to the first occupant (*Inst.* 2. 1, 18.), yet ours gives it to the king. *Bract.*

l. 2. *c.* 2. *Callis of Sewers*, 22. See also *Alluvions.*

ISLE OF MAN. See *Man.*

ISLET, a small island.

ISSUABLE TERMS. Hilary and Trinity terms are usually called issuable terms, from the making up of the issues therein, for the trial of causes out of *Middlesex* and *London.*

ISSUE, (*exitus*, from the Fr. *issuer*, i. e. *emanare*) hath divers significations in law; sometimes it is taken for the children begotten between a man and his wife, sometimes for profits growing from amerciaments and fines; sometimes for the profits of lands and tenements: but it generally signifies the point of matter, issuing out of the allegations and pleas of the plaintiff and defendant in a cause, to be tried by a jury of twelve men. 1 *Inst.* 126. 11 *Rep.* 10.

The issues upon matter of fact, are, whether the fact is true or false, which are triable by a jury only, and they are either *general* or *special.*

General, when it is left to the jury to try whether the defendant hath done any such thing as the plaintiff lays to his charge; as when he pleads *non assumpsit* on the contract, or not guilty on a tort.

Special, when some special matter, or material point alledged by the defendant in his defence, is to be tried; as a justification of the right of assault upon the ground that the first assault, was committed by the plaintiff, or in an action for slanderous words, that the facts justify the slanderous words.

If the plaintiff does not proceed to try the issue after joined, in such time as he ought by the course of the court, the defendant may give him a rule to enter it; which if he does not, he shall be nonsuit, &c. 2 *Lil.* 84.

ISSUES ON SHERIFFS, are for neglects and defaults, by amercement and fine to the king, levied out of the issues and profits of their lands: and double or treble issues may be laid on a sheriff for not returning writs, &c. But they may be taken off before estreated into the exchequer, by rule of court, on good reason shewn. 2 *Lil. Abr.* 89. Issues also may be levied on jurors for non-appearance. 35 *Hen.* 8. *cap.* 6. See 1 *Keb.* 475.

ITINERANT, (*itinerans*) travelling or taking a journey: and those were anciently called *justices itinerant*, who were sent with commission into divers counties to hear causes. 3 *Black.* 59. 4 *Black.* 411, 422.

The king's courts were formerly itinerant, being kept in the king's palace, and removing with his household. The common pleas is now fixed by *magna charta*; but though the court of king's bench is constantly held in Westminster-hall, yet there is nothing but custom to fix it there, as it is supposed to be before the king, and if actually so must be itinerant. *Ibid.*

ITINERARY, (*itinerarium*) a commentary concerning things fallen out in journies. *Law Lat. Dict.*

JUBILEE, (*annus jubilæus*) an ancient solemn but happy time of festival at Rome, when the pope gives his blessing and remission of sins. It was first instituted by Boniface the 8th, in 1300, who granted a plenary indulgence and remission of sins to all who should visit the churches of St. Peter and St. Paul at Rome in that year, and stay there fifteen days; and this he ordered to be observed once in every hundred years; which pope Clement the 6th reduced to fifty years, anno 1350, and to be held upon the day of circumcision of our Saviour: and Urban the 4th, in the year 1389, ordained it to be kept every thirty-three years, that being the age of our Saviour: after which, pope Sixtus the 6th, reduced it to twenty-five years. In imitation of the grand jubilee of Rome, the monks of Christ-Church in Canterbury, every fiftieth year invited great concourse of people to come thither, and visit the tomb of Thomas Becket. And king Edward III. in the fiftieth year of his age, which was 1362, caused his birth day to be observed at court, in the name of a jubilee, giving pardons, privileges, and other civil indulgencies. *Cowel. Blount.*

JUBILÆUS, signified afterwards a man one hundred years old, and likewise a possession or prescription for fifty years. *Ibid.*

JUDAISM, (*judaismus*). See *Jews.*

Judaismus is also taken for the mansion or dwelling-place of the Jews in any town; as *Wigorniam cepit et intrarit, et judaismum evertit. Rishangor, p.* 668. And it sometimes signifies usury: as, *empta fuit grangia, &c. domus obligata in magnis debitis in judaismo. Mon.* 1 *tom. p.* 834.

JUDGER. In Cheshire, to be a judger of a town, is to serve on the jury there. *Leicester's Hist. Antiq.* 302.

JUDGES. Although it is probable, and almost certain, that in very early times, before our constitution arrived at its full perfection, our kings in person often heard and determined causes between party and party. Yet at present, by the long and uniform usage of many ages, our kings have delegated their whole judicial power to the judges of their several courts; which are the grand depositaries of the fundamental laws of the kingdom, and have gained a known and stated jurisdiction, regulated by certain and established rules, which the crown itself cannot now alter but by act of parliament (2 *Hawk. P. C.* 2.) And, in order to maintain both the dignity and independence of the judges in the superior courts, it is enacted by the statute 13 *W.* 3. *c.* 2. that their commissions shall be made (not, as formerly, *durante bene placito*, but) *quamdiu bene se gesserint*, and their salaries ascertained and established; but that it may be lawful to remove them on the address of both houses of parliament. And now, by the noble improvements of that law in the statute of 1 *Geo.* 3. *c.* 23. enacted at the earnest recommendation of the king himself from the throne, the judges are continued in their offices during their good behaviour, notwithstanding any demise of the crown, which was formerly held (*Ld. Raym.* 747.) immediately to vacate their seats, and their full salaries were absolutely secured to them during the continuance of their commissions; his majesty having been pleased to declare, that "he looked upon the independence and uprightness of the judges, "as essential to the impartial administration "of justice; as one of the best securities of "the rights and liberties of his subjects; and "as most conducive to the honour of the "crown (*Com. Journ.* 3 *Mar.* 1761.)"

When his majesty was pleased to make this memorable declaration, he introduced it by observing; that "upon "granting new commissions to the judges, "the present state of their offices fell naturally under consideration. In consequence "of the late act, passed in the reign of my "late glorious predecessor William the third, "for settling the succession to the crown in "my family, their commissions have been "made during their good behaviour; but "notwithstanding that wise provision, their "offices have determined upon the demise of "the crown, or at the expiration of six "months afterwards, in every instance of "that nature which has happened."

JUDGMENT, (*judicium, quasi juris dictum.*) Judgments are the sentence of the law, pronounced by the court upon the matter contained in the record; and are of four sorts.

First, where the facts are confessed by the parties, and the law determined by the court; as in case of judgment upon *demurrer:*

Secondly, where the law is admitted by the parties, and the facts disputed; as in case of judgment on a verdict:

Thirdly, where both the fact and the law arising thereon are admitted by the defendant, which is the case of judgments by confession or default:

Or, lastly, where the plaintiff is convinced that either fact, or law, or both, are insufficient to support his action, and therefore abandons or withdraws his prosecution; which is the case in judgments upon a *nonsuit* or *retraxit.* 3 *Black.* 395.

The judgment, though pronounced or awarded by the judges, is not their determination or sentence, but the determination and sentence of the law. It is the conclusion, that naturally and regularly follows from the premises of law and fact, which stand thus: against him, who hath rode over my corn, I may recover damages by law; and as A hath rode over my corn; therefore I shall recover damages against A. If the major proposition be denied, this is a demurrer in law: if the minor, it is then an issue of fact: but if both be confessed (or determined) to be right, the conclusion or judgment of the court cannot but follow. Which judgment or conclusion depends not therefore on the arbitrary caprice of the judge, but on the settled and invariable principles of justice. The judgment, in short, is the remedy prescribed by law, for the redress of injuries; and the suit or action is the vehicle or means of administering it. What that remedy may be, is indeed the result of deliberation and study to point out, and therefore the style of the judgment is, not that it is decreed or resolved by the court, for then the judgment might appear to be their own; but, "it is considered," *consideratum est per curiam,* that the plaintiff do recover his damages, his debt, his possession, and the like: which implies that the judgment is none of their own; but the act of law, pronounced and declared by the court, after due deliberation and inquiry. 3 *Black.* 396.

All these species of judgments are either interlocutory or final. Interlocutory judgments are such as are given in the middle of a cause, upon some plea, proceeding, or default, which is only intermediate, and does not finally determine or complete the suit. Of this nature are all judgments for the plaintiff upon pleas in abatement of the suit or action: in which it is considered by the court, that the defendant do answer over, *respondeat ouster;* that is, put in a more substantial plea (2 *Saund.* 30.) It is easy to observe, that the judgment here given is not final, but merely interlocutory; for there are afterwards farther proceedings to be had, when the defendant hath put in a better answer. *Ibid.*

But the interlocutory judgments, most usually spoken of, are those incomplete judgments, whereby the right of the plaintiff is indeed established, but the quantum of damages sustained by him is not ascertained: which is a matter that cannot be done without the intervention of a jury. As by the old Gothic constitution the cause was not completely finished, till the *nembda* or jurors were called in "*ad executionem decretorum* "*judicii, ad æstimationem pretii, damni, lucri,* &c. (*Stiernhook de jure Goth. l.* 1. "*c.* 4.)" This can only happen where the plaintiff recovers; for when judgment is given for the defendant it is always complete as well as final. And this happens, in the first place, where the defendant suffers judgment to go against him by default, or *nihil dicit;* as if he puts in no plea at all to the plaintiff's declaration; by confession or *cognovit actionem,* where he acknowledges the plaintiff's demand to be just: or by *non sum informatus*, when the defendant's attorney declares he has no instructions to say any thing in answer to the plaintiff, or in defence of his client; which is a species of judgment by default. If these, or any of them, happen in actions where the specific thing sued for is recovered, as in actions of detinue or debt for a sum or thing certain, the judgment is final and absolutely complete. And therefore it is very usual, in order to strengthen a bond-creditor's security, for the debtor to execute a warrant of attorney to any one, empowering him to confess a judgment by either of the ways just now mentioned (by *nihil dicit*, *cognovit actionem*, or *non sum informatus*) in an action of debt to be brought by the creditor for the specific sum due: which judgment, when confessed, is absolutely complete and binding. But, where damages are to be recovered, a jury must be called in to assess them, unless the defendant, to save charges, will confess the whole damages laid in the declaration: otherwise the entry of the judgment is, "that the plaintiff ought to "recover his damages, (indefinitely) but, "because the court know not what damages "the said plaintiff hath sustained, therefore "the sheriff is commanded, that by the oaths "of twelve honest and lawful men he inquire "into the said damages, and return such "inquisition (when taken) into court." This process is called a writ of inquiry: in the execution of which, the sheriff sits as judge, and tries by a jury, subject to nearly the same law and conditions as the trial by jury at *nisi prius*, what damages the plaintiff hath really sustained; and when their verdict is given, which must assess some damages (but to what amount they please) the sheriff returns the inquisition into court, which is entered upon the roll in manner of a *postea*; and thereupon it is considered, that the plaintiff do recover the exact sum of the damages so assessed. In like manner, when a demurrer is determined for the plaintiff upon an action wherein damages are recovered, the judgment is also incomplete, till a writ of inquiry is awarded to assess damages, and returned; after which the judgment is completely entered. *Ibid.*

Final judgments are such as at once put an end to the action, by declaring that the plaintiff has either entitled himself, or has not, to recover the remedy he sues for. In which case, if the judgment be for the plaintiff; it is also considered that the defendant be either amerced, for his wilful delay of justice in not immediately obeying the king's writ by rendering the plaintiff his due (5 *Rep.* 49.); or be taken up, *capiatur*, to pay a fine to the king, in case of any forcible injury. Though now by statute 5 & 6 *W. & M. c.* 12. no writ of *capias* shall issue for this fine, but the plaintiff shall pay 6*s.* 8*d.* and be allowed it against the defendant among his other costs. And therefore, in judgments in the court of common pleas, they enter that the fine is remitted, and in the court of king's bench, they now take no notice of any fine or *capias* at all (*Salk.* 54. *Carth.* 390.) But if judgment be for the defendant, then it is considered, that the plaintiff and his pledges of prosecuting be (nominally) amerced for his false suit, and that the defendant may go without a day *eat sine die*, that is, without any farther continuance or adjournment; the king's writ, commanding his attendance, being now fully satisfied, and his innocence publicly cleared.

JUDGMENT IN CRIMINAL CASES. When upon *a capital charge* the jury have brought in their verdict guilty, in the presence of the prisoner, he is either immediately, or at a convenient time soon after, asked by the court, if he has any thing to offer why *judgment* should not be awarded against him. And in case the defendant be found guilty of *a misdemeanor*, (the trial of which may, and does usually, happen in his absence, after he has once appeared,) a *capias* is awarded and issued to bring him in to receive his judgment; and if he absconds he may be prosecuted even to outlawry. But whenever he appears in person, upon either a capital or inferior conviction, he may at this period, as well as at his arraignment, offer any exceptions to the indictment, in arrest or stay of judgment; as for want of sufficient certainty in setting forth either the time, the place, or the offence. And if the objections be valid the whole proceedings shall be set aside, but the party may be indicted again (4 *Rep.* 45.) And we may take notice, 1. That none of the statutes of jeofails for amendment of errors extend to indictments or proceedings in criminal cases; and therefore a defective indictment is not aided by a verdict, as defective pleadings in civil cases are. 2. That, in favour of life, great strictness has at all times been observed in every point of an indictment. Sir Matthew Hale indeed complains "that this "strictness is grown to be a blemish and "inconvenience in the law, and the administration thereof; for that more of"fenders escape by the over-easy ear given "to exceptions on indictments than by their "own innocence." (2 *Hal. P. C.* 193.) And yet no man was more tender of life than this truly excellent judge. 4 *Black.* 375.

A pardon also, may be pleaded in arrest of judgment; and it has the same advantage when pleaded here as when pleaded upon arraignment, *viz.* the saving the attainder, and of course the corruption of blood, which nothing can restore but parliament, when a pardon is not pleaded till after sentence. And certainly upon all accounts, when a man hath obtained a pardon he is in the right to plead it as soon as possible. *Ibid.*

Praying the benefit of clergy may also be ranked among the motions in arrest of judgment. *Ibid.*

If all these resources fail the court must pronounce that judgment which the law has annexed to the crime. Of these some are capital, which extend to the life of the offender, and consist generally in being hanged by the neck till dead; though in very atrocious crimes other circumstances of terror, pain, or disgrace, are superadded, as in treasons of all kinds, being drawn or dragged to the place of execution; in high treason affecting the king's person or government, embowelling alive, beheading, and quartering, and in murder, a public dissection. And in case of any treason committed by a female, the judgment was formerly to be burned alive; but this is now altered by 30 *Geo.* 3, *c.* 48, and such offender is to be punished as for murder.

The humanity of the English nation has, however, authorized by a tacit consent, an almost general mitigation of such part of these judgments as savours of torture or cruelty; a sledge or hurdle being usually allowed to such traitors as are condemned to be drawn; and there being very few instances (and those accidental or by negligence) of any persons being embowelled or burned, till previously deprived of sensation by strangling.

In *præmunire*, the party offending is to be out of the king's protection, and his body to remain in prison during the king's pleasure, &c. And for misprision of felony, fine and imprisonment is inflicted. 2 *Hawk.* 443, 444.

For crimes and misdemeanors of an infamous nature, perjury, or forgery at common law, gross cheats, conspiracy, keeping bawdy-houses, &c. the judgments are *discretionary in the court*, by fine, pillory, whipping, &c. 2 *Hawk.* 445.

JUDGMENT ARRESTED, in civil and criminal cases. See *Arrest of Judgment.*

JUDGMENT OR TRIAL BY THE HOLY CROSS, was a trial in ecclesiastical cases, anciently in use among the Saxons. *Cowel. Blount.*

JUDICATORES TERRARUM, are persons in the county palatine of Chester, who on a writ of error out of Chancery, are to consider of the judgment given there, and reform it; and if they do not, and it be found erroneous, they forfeit 100*l.* to the king, by the custom. *Dyer* 348. *Jenk. Cent.* 71.

JUDICES FISCALES, Empson and Dudley, who were employed by *Hen.* 7, for taking the benefit of penal statutes, and were put to death by *Hen.* 8, were so called. *Cowel.*

JUDICIAL decisions, opinions or determinations, are of three kinds. *Hale's Hist. c.* 2, 68, 69.

1st, They are either such as have their reasons singly in the laws and customs of this kingdom, as who shall succeed as heir to the ancestor, or the like.

Or 2dly, They are such decisions, as by way of deduction and illation upon those laws are formed or deduced; as for the purpose, whether of an estate thus or thus limited the wife shall be endowed.

3dly, Or they are such as seem to have no other guide but the common reason of the thing, unless the same point has been formerly decided, as in the exposition of the intention of clauses in deeds, wills, covenants, &c. where the very sense of the words, and their positions and relations, give a rational account of the meaning of the parties.

An extra-judicial opinion given in or out of court is no more than the *dictum* or saying of him who gives it, nor can be taken for his opinion, unless every thing spoken at pleasure must pass as the speaker's opinion. *Vaugh.* 382.

So an opinion given in court is not necessary to the judgment given of record, but that it might have been as well given if no such or a contrary opinion had been broached, is no judicial opinion, nor more than a *gratis dictum. Ibid.*

JUDICIAL POWER. By the long and uniform usage of many ages our kings have delegated their whole judicial power to the judges of their several courts, which are the grand depository of the fundamental laws of the kingdom, and have gained a known and stated jurisdiction, regulated by certain and established rules, which the crown itself cannot alter but by act of parliament. 1 *Black.* 267. 2 *Hawk. P. C.* 2.

And there is great propriety in separating the judicial from the legislative and executive power of the state. *Montesquieu L'Esprit des Loix, Liv.* 11, *c.* 6, *fol.* 208.

JUDICIAL WRITS. The *capias* and all other subsequent to the original writ, not issuing out of chancery, but from the court into which the original was returnable, and being grounded on what has passed in that court in consequence of the sheriff's return, are called judicial, not original writs; they issue under the private seal of that court, and not under the great seal of England, and are tested, not in the king's name, but in that of the chief justice only. 3 *Black. Com.* 282.

JUDICIUM DEI, the judgment of God, so our ancestors called those now prohibited trials of ordeal, and its several kinds. *Cowel.*

JUDICIUM PARIUM, a trial by a man's equals, *i. e.* peers by peers, commoners by commoners. See JURY.

JUG, a watery place. *Cowel. Blount.*

JUGULATOR, a cut-throat, or murderer. *Ibid.*

JUGUM TERRÆ, a yoke of land, containing half a plough-land. *Gale* 700.

JUNCARE, to strew rushes, as was of old the accommodating the parochial church, and even the bed-chambers of princes. *Ibid.*

JUNCARIA, or JONCARIA, (from *juncus*, Lat. a rush,) is a place or soil wherein rushes grow. *Ibid.*

JUNCTUM JUNCTA, a measure of salt. *Ibid.*

JURA REGALIA. See *Regalia.*

JURATS, (*jurati*) are in nature of aldermen, for the government of many corporations.

JURE DIVINO, right to the throne, a doctrine long since exploded, and now universally denied. 1 *Black.* 191.

JURE DIVINO, right to tithes. The title of the clergy to tithes does not stand upon any divine right, though such right certainly commenced, and as certainly ceased, with the Jewish Theocracy. Yet an honourable and competent maintenance for the ministers of the gospel is undoubtedly *jure divino*, whatever the particular mode of that maintenance may be. 2 *Black.* 25.

JURIDICAL DAYS, (*dies juridici*) days in court, on which the law was administered. *Cowel.*

JURISDICTION, (*jurisdictio*) is an authority or power to do justice in causes of complaint.

Thus the courts and judges at Westminster have jurisdiction all over England, and are not restrained to any county or place; but all other courts are confined to their particular jurisdictions, which if they exceed, whatever they do is erroneous. 2 *Lill. Abr.* 120.

JURIS UTRUM, is a writ which laid for the parson of a church whose predecessor had alienated the lands and tenements thereof. *F. N. B.* 48.

JURNALE, the journal or diary of accounts in a religious house. *Cowel. Blount.*

JURNEDUM, a journey, or one day's travelling. *Cowel. Blount.*

JUROR, (*jurator*) is one of those persons who are sworn on a jury.

JURY (*jurata*, Lat. *jurare*, to swear). The subject of the trial by jury, called also the trial *per pais*, or by the country, the great bulwark of every Englishman's liberties is secured to him by the great charter, 9 *Hen.* 3. *c.* 29: "*Nullus liber homo capiatur*, vel *imprisonetur* "*aut exulet, aut aliquæ, alio modo destruatur*, "*nisi per legalem judicium parium suorum* "VEL *per legem terræ*;" a trial that has been used time out of mind in this nation, and seems to have been coeval with the first civil government thereof. Some authors have endeavoured to trace the origin of juries up as high as the Britons themselves, the first inhabitants of our island; but certain it is, that they were in use among the earliest Saxon colonies, their institution being ascribed by bishop Nicolson (*De jure Saxonum*, *p.* 12,) to Woden himself, their great legislator and captain. Hence it is, that we may find traces of juries in the laws of all those nations which adopted the feodal system, as in Germany, France, and Italy, who had all of them a tribunal composed of twelve good men and true, "*boni* "*homines*," usually the vassals or tenants of the lord, being the equals or peers of the parties litigant; and as the lord's vassals judged each other in the lord's courts, so the king's vassals, or the lords themselves, judged each other in the king's court. (*Sp. L. b.* 30, *c.* 18. *Capital. Lud. pit. A. D.* 819, *c.* 2.) In England we find actual mention of them so early as the laws of Ethelred, and that not as a new invention (*Wilk. LL. Angl. Sax.* 117). Stiernhook (*De jure Sueonum. l.* 1, *c.* 4,) ascribes the invention of the jury, which in the Teutonic language is denominated *nembda*, to Regner, king of Sweden and Denmark, who was cotemporary with our king Egbert. Just as we are apt to impute the invention of this, and some other pieces of juridical polity, to the superior genius of Alfred the great; to whom, on account of his having done much, it is usual to attribute every thing; and as the tradition of ancient Greece placed to the account of their one Hercules whatever achievement was performed superior to the ordinary prowess of mankind. Whereas the truth seems to be, that this tribunal was universally established among all the northern nations, and so interwoven in their very constitution, that the earliest accounts of the one give us also some traces of the other. Its establishment, however, and use, in this island, of what date soever it be, though for a time greatly impaired and shaken by the introduction of the Norman trial by battle, was always so highly esteemed and valued by the people, that no conquest, no change of government, could ever prevail to abolish it. In *Magna Charta* it is more than once insisted on as the principal bulwark of our liberties; but especially by c. 29, that no freeman shall be hurt in either his person or property, "*nisi per legale* "*judicium parium suorum vel legem terræ.*" A privilege which is couched in almost the same words with those of the emperor Conrad 200 years before (*LL. Longob. l.* 3, *t.* 8, *l.* 4,) "*nemo beneficium suum perdat*, "*nisi secundum consuetudinem antecessorum* "*nostrorum et per judicium parium suorum.*" And it was ever esteemed in all countries a privilege of the highest and most beneficial nature. 3 *Black.* 350.

Trials by jury in civil causes are of two kinds, extraordinary and ordinary. 3 *Black.* 351.

The first species of extraordinary trial by jury is that of the grand assise, which was instituted by king *Hen.* 2, in parliament, by way of alternative offered to the choice of the tenant or defendant in a writ of right, instead of the barbarous and unchristian custom of duelling. For this purpose a writ *de magna assisa eligenda* is directed to the sheriff, (*F. N. B.* 4,) to return four knights, who are to elect and choose twelve others to be joined with them, in the manner mentioned by *Glanvil,* (*l.* 2, *c.* 11—21.) who having probably advised the measure itself, is more than usually copious in describing it; and these all together form the grand assise, or great jury which is to try the matter of right, and must consist of sixteen jurors. *Finch L.* 412. 1 *Leon.* 303.

Another species of extraordinary juries is the jury to try an attaint, which is a process commenced against a former jury for bringing in a false verdict. This jury is to consist of twenty-four of the best men in the county, who are called the grand jury in the attaint, to distinguish them from the first, or petit-jury, and these are to hear and try the goodness of the former verdict.

With regard to the ordinary trial by jury in civil cases the order and course of the proceedings are as follow:

When an issue is joined by these words, "and this the said A prays may be inquired of by the country," or, "and of this he puts himself upon the country, and the said B does the like," the court awards a writ of *venire facias* upon the roll or record, commanding the sheriff "that he cause to come here on such a day twelve free and lawful men, *liberos et legales homines,* of the body of his county, by whom the truth of the matter may be better known, and who are neither of kin to the aforesaid A, nor the aforesaid B, to recognize the truth of the issue between the said parties." And such writ is accordingly issued to the sheriff.

Thus the cause stands ready for a trial at the bar of the court itself: for all trials were there anciently had, in actions which were there first commenced; which never happened but in matters of weight and consequence, all trifling suits being ended in the court-baron, hundred, or county-courts; and all causes of great importance or difficulty are still usually retained upon motion, to be tried at the bar in the superior courts. But when the usage began, to bring actions of any trifling value in the courts of Westminster-hall, it was found to be an intolerable burthen to compel the parties, witnesses, and jurors, to come from Westmorland perhaps, or Cornwall, to try an action of assault at Westminster. Therefore the legislature took into consideration, that the king's justices came usually twice in the year into the several counties, *ad capiendas assisas,* to take or try writs of assise, of *mort d' ancestor, novel disseisin, nuisance,* and the like. The form of which writs was that they commanded the sheriff to summon an assise or jury, and go to view the land in question; and then to have the said jury ready at the next coming of the justices of assise (together with the parties (to recognize and determine the disseisin, or other injury complained of. As therefore these judges were ready in the country to administer justice in real actions of assise, the legislature thought proper to refer other matters in issue to be also determined before them, whether of a mixed or personal kind. And therefore it was enacted by statute *Westm.* 2. 13 *Edw.* 1, c. 30, that a clause of *nisi prius* should be inserted in all the aforesaid writs of *venire facias;* that is, "that the sheriff should cause the jurors to come to Westminster (or wherever the king's courts should be held) on such a day in Easter and Michaelmas terms, *nisi prius,* unless before that day the justices assigned to take assises shall come into his said county." By virtue of which the sheriff returned his jurors to the court of the justices of assise, which was sure to be held in the vacation before Easter and Michaelmas terms, and there the trial was had. 3 *Black.* 353.

An inconvenience attended this remedy; principally because as the sheriff made no return of the jury to the court at Westminster the parties were ignorant who they were till they came upon the trial, and therefore were not ready with their challenges or exceptions. For this reason, by the stat. 42 *Edw.* 3, *c.* 11, the method of trials by *nisi prius* was altered; and it was enacted that no inquest, except of assise and gaol delivery, should be taken by writ of *nisi prius* till after the sheriff had returned the names of the jurors to the court above. So that now the clause of *nisi prius* is left out of the writ of *venire facias,* which is the sheriff's warrant to warn the jury, and is inserted in another part of the proceedings. *Ibid.*

For now the course is to make the sheriff's *venire* returnable on the last return of the same term wherein issue is joined, *viz.* Hilary or Trinity terms, which from the making up of the issues therein are usually called issuable terms. And he returns the names of the jurors in a panel (a little pane, or oblong piece of parchment) annexed to the writ. This jury is not summoned, and therefore, not appearing at the day must unavoidably make default. For which reason a compulsive process is now awarded against the jurors, called in the Common Pleas a writ of *habeas corpora juratorum,* and in the King's Bench a *distringas,* commanding the sheriff to have their bodies, or to distrain them by their lands and goods, that they may appear upon the day appointed. The entry, therefore, on the roll or record is, "that the jury is respited "through defect of the jurors till the first "day of the next term, then to appear at "Westminster, unless before that time, *viz.* "on Wednesday the fourth of March, the "justices of our lord the king, appointed "to take assises in that county, shall have "come to Oxford, that is, to the place "assigned for holding the assises. There-"fore the sheriff is commanded to have "their bodies at Westminster on the said "first day of next term, or before the "said justices of assise, if before that "time they come to Oxford, *viz.* on the "fourth of March aforesaid." And, as the judges are sure to come and open the circuit commissions on the day mentioned in the writ, the sheriff returns and summons this jury to appear at the assises, and there the trial is had before the justices of assise and *nisi prius*, among whom are usually two of the judges of the courts at Westminster, the whole kingdom being divided into six circuits for this purpose. And thus we may observe that the trial of common issues at *nisi prius* was in its original only a collateral incident to the original business of the justices of assise, though now by the various revolutions of practice it is become their principal employment, hardly any thing remaining in use of the real assises but the name. 3 *Black.* 354.

If the sheriff be not an indifferent person, as if he be a party in the suit, or be related by either blood or affinity to either of the parties, he is not then trusted to return the jury, but the *venire* shall be directed to the coroners, who in this, as in many other instances, are the substitutes of the sheriff, to execute process when he is deemed an improper person. If any exception lies to the coroners the *venire* shall be directed to two clerks of the court, or two persons of the county named by the court, and sworn (*Fortesc. de Laud. LL. c.* 25). And these two, who are called elisors, or electors, shall indifferently name the jury, and their return is final. *Ibid.*

In these first preparatory stages of the trial this constitution is admirably adapted and framed for the investigation of truth, beyond any other method of trial in the world.

For, first the person returning the jurors is a man of some fortune and consequence; that so he may be not only the less tempted to commit wilful errors, but likewise be responsible for the faults of either himself or his officers: and he is also bound by the obligation of an oath faithfully to execute his duty.

Next, as to the time of their return; the panel is returned to the court upon the original *venire*, and the jury are to be summoned and brought in many weeks afterwards to the trial, whereby the parties may have notice of the jurors, and of their sufficiency or insufficiency, characters, connections, and relations, that so they may be challenged upon just cause, while at the same time by means of the compulsory process (of distringas or *habeas corpora*) the cause is not like to be retarded through defect of jurors.

Thirdly, as to the place of their appearance, which in causes of weight and consequence is at the bar of the court, but in ordinary cases at the assise held in the county where the cause of action arises, and the witnesses and jurors live, a provision most excellently calculated for the saving of expense to the parties. For though the preparation of the causes in point of pleading is transacted at Westminster, whereby the order and uniformity of proceeding is preserved throughout the kingdom, and multiplicity of forms is prevented; yet this is no great charge or trouble, one attorney being able to transact the business of forty clients. But the troublesome and most expensive attendance is that of jurors and witnesses at the trial, which therefore is brought home to them in the country where most of them inhabit.

Fourthly, the persons before whom they are to appear, and before whom the trial is to be held, are the judges of the superior court, if it be a trial at bar; or the judges of assise, delegated from the courts at Westminster by the king, if the trial be held in the country; persons whose learning and dignity secure their jurisdiction from contempt, and the novelty and very parade of whose appearance have no small influence upon the multitude. The very point of their being strangers in the county is of infinite service in preventing those factions and parties, which would intrude in every cause of moment were it tried only before persons resident on the spot, as justices of the peace, and the like. And, as this constitution prevents party and faction from intermingling in the trial of right, so it keeps both the rule and the administration of the laws uniform.

These justices, though thus varied and shifted at every assises, are all sworn to the same laws, have had the same education, have pursued the same studies, converse and consult together, communicate their decisions and resolutions, and preside in those courts, which are mutually connected, and their judgments blended together, as they are interchangeably courts of appeal or advice to each other. And hence their administration of justice and conduct of trials are consonant and uniform, whereby that confusion and contrariety are avoided which would naturally arise from a variety of uncommunicating judges, or from any provincial establishment. 3 *Black.* 356.

As to the assises here spoken of.

When the general day of trial is fixed, the plaintiff or his attorney must bring down the record to the assises, and enter it with the proper officer, in order to its being called on in course. If it be not so entered it cannot be tried; therefore it is in the plaintiff's breast to delay any trial by not carrying down the record; unless the defendant, being fearful of such neglect in the plaintiff, and willing to discharge himself from the action, will himself undertake to bring on the trial, giving proper notice to the plaintiff. Which proceeding is called the trial by proviso, by reason of the clause then inserted in the sheriff's *venire*, *viz.* "proviso, provided, that if two writs "come to your hands, (that is, one from "the plaintiff and another from the de-"fendant) you shall execute only one of "them." But this practice begins to be disused since the stat. 14 *Geo.* 2, *c.* 17, which enacts, that if, after issue joined, the cause is not carried down to be tried according to the course of the court, the plaintiff shall be esteemed to be nonsuited, and judgment shall be given for the defendant as in case of a nonsuit. In case the plaintiff intends to try the cause he is bound to give the defendant (if he lives within 40 miles of London) eight days notice of trial, and if he lives at a greater distance, then fourteen days notice, in order to prevent surprise; and if the plaintiff then changes his mind, and does not countermand the notice six days before the trial, he shall be liable to pay costs to the defendant for not proceeding to trial, by the same last-mentioned statute. The defendant, however, or plaintiff, may upon good cause shown to the court above, as upon absence or sickness of a material witness, obtain leave upon motion to defer the trial of the cause till the next assises. 3 *Black.* 357.

When the cause is called on in court the record is then handed to the judge, to peruse, and observe the pleadings, and what issues the parties are to maintain and prove, while the jury is called and sworn. To this end the sheriff returns his compulsive process, the writ of *habeas corpora*, or distringas, with the panel of jurors annexed, to the judge's officer in court. The jurors contained in the panel are either special or common jurors. Special juries were originally introduced in trials at bar, when the causes were of too great nicety for the discussion of ordinary freeholders, or where the sheriff was suspected of partiality, though not upon such apparent cause as to warrant an exception to him. He is in such cases, upon motion in court, and a rule granted thereupon, to attend the prothonotary, or other proper officer, with his freeholders book, and the officer is to take indifferently forty-eight of the principal freeholders in the presence of the attornies on both sides; who are each of them to strike off twelve, and the remaining twenty-four are returned upon the panel. By the stat. 3 *Geo.* 2, *c.* 25, either party is entitled upon motion to have a special jury struck upon the trial of any issue, as well at the assises as at bar; he paying the extraordinary expence, unless the judge will certify (in pursuance of the stat. 24 *Geo.* 2, *c.* 18,) that the cause required such special jury. 3 *Black.* 358.

A common jury is one returned by the sheriff according to the directions of the stat. 3 *Geo.* 2, *c.* 25, which appoints that the sheriff shall not return a separate panel for every separate cause, as formerly, but one and the same panel for every cause to be tried at the same assises, containing not less than 48, nor more than 72, jurors; and that their names, being written on tickets, shall be put into a box or glass; and when each cause is called, twelve of these persons whose names shall be first drawn out of the box, shall be sworn upon the jury, unless absent, challenged, or excused; and unless a previous view of the lands, or tenements, or other matters in question, shall have been thought necessary by the court: in which case six or more of the jurors returned, to be agreed on by the parties, or named by a judge, or other proper officer of the court, shall be appointed to take such view, and then such of the jury as have appeared upon the view, if any, (4 *Burr.* 252) shall be sworn on the inquest previous to any other jurors. These acts are well calculated to restrain any suspicion of partiality in the sheriff, or any tampering with the jurors when returned. *Ibid.*

When the jurors are called, and appear, they shall be sworn, unless challenged. See *Challenges.*

And if by means of challenges, or other cause, a sufficient number of unexceptionable jurors do not appear at the trial, either party may pray a *tales*, which tales is a supply of such men as are summoned upon the first panel, in order to make up the deficiency.

When the jurors are sworn the opening counsel briefly informs them of the names of the parties, the nature of the action, the declaration, the plea, replication, and other proceedings, and lastly, upon what point the issue is joined. The nature of the case, and the evidence intended to be produced, are then next laid before them by the leading counsel on the same side; and when their evidence is gone through, the counsel on the other side opens the adverse case, and supports it by evidence; and then the party which began is heard by way of reply; but if no evidence is gone into on the part of the defendant, the counsel for the plaintiff can make no reply.

When the evidence is gone through on both sides, the judge, in the presence of the parties, the counsel, and all others, sums up the whole to the jury, omitting all superfluous circumstances, observing wherein the main question and principal issue lies, stating what evidence has been given to support it, with such remarks as he thinks necessary for their direction, and giving them his opinion in matters of law arising upon that evidence. 3 *Black.* 375.

The jury, after the proofs are summed up, unless the case be very clear, withdraw from the bar to consider of their verdict; and in order to avoid intemperance and causeless delay, are to be kept without meat, drink, fire, or candle, unless by permission of the judge, till they are all unanimously agreed. But if our juries eat or drink at all, or have any eatables about them, without consent of the court, and before verdict, it is fineable; and if they do so at his charge for whom they afterwards find, it will set aside the verdict. Also if they speak with either of the parties or their agents, after they are gone from the bar, or if they receive any fresh evidence in private, or if to prevent disputes they cast lots for whom they shall find, any of these circumstances will entirely vitiate the verdict. And it has been held that if the jurors do not agree in their verdict before the judges are about to leave the town, (though they are not to be threatened or imprisoned, *Mirr. c.* 4, *sec.* 24) the judges are not bound to wait for them, but may carry them round the circuit from town to town in a cart (*Lib. Ass. fol.* 40, *pl.* 11). This necessity of a total unanimity seems to be peculiar to our own constitution, (see *Barrington on the Statutes,* 17, 18, 19,) for at least in the *nembda* or jury of the ancient Goths there was required, even in criminal cases, only the consent of the major part, and in case of an equality, the defendant was held to be acquitted. *Stiernh. l.* 1, *c.* 4.

When they are all unanimously agreed the jury return to the bar, and before they deliver their verdict the plaintiff is bound to appear in court, by himself, attorney, or counsel, in order to answer the amercement to which by the old law he is liable, in case he fails in his suit, as a punishment for his false claim to be amerced, or *à mercie,* that is, to be at the king's mercy with regard to the fine to be imposed; *in misericordia domini regis pro falso clamore suo.* This amercement is disused, but the form still continues; and if the plaintiff does not appear no verdict can be given, but the plaintiff is said to be nonsuit, *non sequitur clamorem suum.* Therefore it is usual for a plaintiff, when he or his counsel perceive that he has not given evidence sufficient to maintain his issue, to be voluntarily nonsuited, or withdraw himself; whereupon the crier is ordered to call the plaintiff, and if neither he, nor any body for him, appears, he is nonsuited, the jurors are discharged, the action is at an end, and the defendant shall recover his costs.

The reason of this practice is, that a nonsuit is more eligible for the plaintiff than a verdict against him; for after a nonsuit, which is only a default, he may commence the same suit again for the same cause of action; but after a verdict had, and judgment consequent thereupon, he is for ever barred from attacking the defendant upon the same ground of complaint. But in case the plaintiff appears the jury by their foreman deliver in their verdict.

When the jury have delivered in their verdict, and it is recorded in court, they are then discharged; and so ends the trial by jury, a trial which, besides the other vast advantages in its progress, is also as expeditious and cheap as it is convenient, equitable, and certain; for a commission out of chancery, or the civil law courts, for examining witnesses in one cause, will frequently last as long, and of course be full as expensive, as the trial of an hundred issues at *nisi prius;* and yet the fact cannot be determined by such commissioners at all; no, not till the depositions are published and read at the hearing of the cause in court. *Black.* 379.

Upon these accounts the trial by jury has been and ever will be looked upon as the glory of the English law. It is the most transcendent privilege which any subject can enjoy or wish for, that he cannot be affected either in his property, his liberty, or his person, but by the unanimous consent of twelve of his neighbours and equals. A constitution that has under Providence secured the just liberties of this nation for a long succession of ages. *Ibid.*

JURROCK, a kind of cork, mentioned in 1 *Ric.* 3, *c.* 8. *Cowel.*

JUS, law or right, authority and rule. *Lit. Dict. Cowel.*

JUS ACCRESCENDI, the right of survivorship between joint-tenants. *Lit.* 280, 1 *Inst.* 180.

JUS AD REM, an inchoate and imperfect right, such as a parson promoted to a living acquires by nomination and institution. 2 *Black.* 312.

JUS ANGLORUM. The laws and customs of the West Saxons in the time of the Heptarchy, by which the people were for a long time governed, and which were preferred before all others, were termed *Jus Anglorum.* *Cowel.*

JUS CORONÆ, the right of the crown, and it is part of the law of England, though it differs in many things from the general law relating to the subject. 1 *Inst.* 15.

JUS CURIALITATIS ANGLIÆ. See *Curtesy.*

JUS DUPLICATUM, is where a man has the possession as well as property of any thing. *Bract. lib.* 4, *tract.* 4, *c.* 4.

JUS GENTIUM, is the law by which nations in general are governed. *Selden.*

JUS HABENDI ET RETINENDI, right to have and retain the profits, tithes, and offerings, &c. of a rectory or parsonage. *Cowel.*

JUS HÆREDITATIS, the right or law of inheritance. *Cowel.*

JUS IN RE, complete and full right, such as a parson acquires on promotion to a living, who after nomination and institution has corporal possession delivered to him, for till such delivery of corporal possession he had only *jus in rem.* 2 *Black.* 312.

JUS PATRONATUS, is a commission granted by the bishop to some persons to inquire who is the rightful patron of a church. If two patrons present their clerks, the bishop shall determine who shall be admitted by right of patronage, &c. on commission of inquiry of six clergymen, and six laymen, living near to the church, who are to inquire on articles as a jury, Whether the church is void: who presented last: who is the rightful patron, &c. 5 *Rep.* 102. 1 *Inst.* 116.

JUS POSSESSIONIS, a right of seisin or possession; and a parson has a right to the possession of the church and glebe, for he has the freehold, and is to receive the profits to his own use. *Pars. Law,* 188.

JUS PRESENTATIONIS, the right of the patron of presenting his clerk unto the ordinary to be admitted, instituted and inducted into a church. *Ibid.*

JUS RECUPERANDI, INTRANDI, &c. A right of recovering and entering lands, &c. *Cowel.*

JUSTA, a certain measure of liquor, *quasi justa mensura,* as much as was sufficient to drink at once. *Cowel.*

JUSTS, (Fr. *jousta,* i. e. *decursus*) were exercises between martial men and persons of honour, with spears, on horseback, and different from tournaments, which were military contentions, and consisted of many men in troops, whereas jousts were usually between two men singly.

JUSTICE, *(justicia)* the rendering to every one his due, or the act of doing what is right and just. *Johnson.*

And by *Mag. Chart.* 9 *Hen.* 3, *c.* 29, justice and right shall not be sold, denied, or delayed. Also right shall be done to all without respect. Stat. *West.* 1. 3 *Edw.* 1, *c.* 1. Justice shall not be delayed for any command under the great seal, &c. 2 *Ed.* 3, *c.* 8. 14 *Ed.* 3, *stat.* 1, *c.* 14. 11 *Ric.* 2, *c.* 10. See *Black. Com.* 1 v. 141, 265. 3 v. 109. 4 v. 123, 179.

JUSTICE, *(justiciarius)* signifies an officer deputed by the king to administer justice, and do right by way of judgment, and is called justice, because in ancient time the Latin word for him was *justitia,* and for that he has his authority by deputation, and not *jure magistratus. Glanv. lib.* 2, *c.* 6. See JUDGES.

JUSTICE OF THE FOREST, *(justiciarius forestæ)* is also a lord by his office, and hears and determines all offences within the forest, committed against vert or venison: of these there are two, whereof one has jurisdiction over all forests on this side Trent, the other of all beyond it. *Charta de Foresta, anno* 9 *Hen.* 3. *Cambd. Brit.* p. 214. The court where this justice sits and determines is called " The justice-seat of the Forest;" held once in every three years. *Manwood, cap.* 24. He is also called justice in eyre of the forest. 33 *Hen.* 8, *c.* 35.

JUSTICE OF THE HUNDRED. *(Justiciarius hundredi) Erat ipse hundredi dominus, qui et centurio et centenarius, hundredique aldermannus appellatus est. Spelm. Cowel.*

JUSTISEMENTS, from *justitia,* all things belonging to justice. *Cowel.* Also the effects of the execution of justice or of jurisdiction. *Co.* on *Westm.* 1, *fol.* 225.

JUSTICES OF ASSISE, *(justiciarii ad capiendas assisas)* were such as were wont by special commission to be sent, as occasion was offered, into this or that county, to take assises for the ease of the subjects; for as these actions pass always by jury, many men could not without damage and charge be brought to London, therefore justices for this purpose, by commission particularly authorized, were sent to them.

These commissions *ad capiendas assisas,* have of late years been settled and executed only in Lent, and the long vacation, (called now the Lent and Summer assises) when the justices, and other learned lawyers, may be at leisure to attend those controversies. By these means, the justices of both benches being worthily accounted the fittest of all others, and their assistants, were employed in these affairs. But no justice of either bench, or any other, might heretofore be justice of assise in his own county, or in the county where he was *born* or *inhabited. Anno* 8 *R.* 2. *c.* 2, and 33 *Hen.* 8. *c.* 24.

However, by 12 *Geo.* 2, *c.* 27, the judges may act as justices of *oyer and terminer,* or *gaol delivery,* notwithstanding they were *born* or *inhabitant* in that county without being liable to any penalty.

And by 49 *Geo.* 3, *c.* 91, notwithstanding

8 *Ric.* 2. *c.* 2. and 33 *Hen.* 8. *c.* 24. justices of either bench, or barons of the exchequer, or other persons appointed justices of assise may exercise the office in any county, though they were *born* or do *inhabit* therein.

JUSTICES OF BOTH BENCHES, are the judges of the courts of king's bench and common pleas.

JUSTICES IN EYRE, (*justiciarii itinerantes.*) These in ancient time, were sent with commission into divers counties to hear such causes especially, as were termed *pleas of the crown.* They differed from the justices of oyer and terminer, because they were sent upon one or few special causes, and to one place; whereas the justices in eyre were sent through the provinces and counties of the land, with more indefinite and general commission. *Bracton, lib.* 3. *c.* 11, 12, 13. and *Britton, cap.* 2.

JUSTICES OF GAOL DELIVERY, (*justiciarii ad gaolus deliberandas*) are those who are sent with commission, to hear and determine all causes appertaining to such, who for any offence are cast into gaol. *Cowel.* See *Assizes.*

JUSTICES OF THE JEWS, (*justiciarii ad custodiam Judæorum assignati,*) king Richard I. after his return out of the Holy Land, *anno* 1194, appointed particular justices, laws, and orders, for preventing the frauds, and regulating the contracts and usury of the Jews. *Cowel. Blount.*

JUSTICES OF LABOURERS, were justices heretofore appointed to redress the frowardness of labouring men, who would either be idle, or have unreasonable wages. 21 *Ed.* 3. *c.* 1. 25 *Ed.* 3. *c.* 8. and 31 *Ed.* 1. *c.* 6. *Cowel.*

JUSTICES OF NISI PRIUS, are all one at this time with *justices of assise*; the common adjournment of a cause to put it off to such a day, being *nisi prius justiciarii venerint ad eas partes ad capiendas assisas*; and upon this clause of adjournment, they are called *justices of nisi prius,* as well as justices of assise. *Cowel.*

JUSTICES OF OYER AND TERMINER, (*justiciarii ad audiendum & terminandum*) justices deputed upon some special or extraordinary occasions. And Fitzherbert in his *Nat. Brev.* saith, that the commission *d'oyer and terminer* is directed to certain persons upon any great riot, insurrections, heinous misdemeanors, or trespasses committed. 2 *Ed.* 3. *c.* 2. See *F. N. B. f.* 110.

JUSTICES OF THE PAVILION, (*justiciarii pavilionis*) are judges of a pie-powder court, of a most transcendant jurisdiction, held under the bishop of Winchester at a fair on St. Giles's Hill, near that city.

JUSTICES OF THE PEACE, (*justiciarii ad pacem*) are those who are appointed by the king's commission to keep the peace of the county where they dwell; of whom some of the greater quality are of the quorum, because business of importance may not be dispatched without the presence of them, or one of them.

The general commission of the peace, began by stat. 1 *Ed.* 3. though before that time, there were particular commissions of peace to certain men, in certain places; though not throughout England.

The power of constituting them is only in the king; though they are generally made at the discretion of the lord chancellor or lord keeper, by the king's leave; and the king may appoint in every county in England and Wales, as many as he shall think fit. 1 *Inst.* 174, 175.

These justices possess both at common law and by different statutes vast powers, and are particularly protected in the execution of the duties of their office by the following statutes:

By stat. 24 *Geo.* 2. *c.* 44. no writ shall be sued out against any justice of peace, for any thing done by him in the execution of his office, until a notice in writing shall be delivered to him one month before the suing out of the same, containing the cause of action, &c. within which month he may tender amends, and if the tender be found sufficient, he shall have a verdict. No such plaintiff shall recover against the justice, unless such notice shall be proved at the trial.

If the justice shall neglect to make such tender, or shall make an insufficient tender, he may, before issue joined, pay into court such sum as he shall think fit.

Where an action is against a justice and constable, if there be a verdict against the justice, and the constable be acquitted, the plaintiff shall recover such costs against the justice, so as to include the costs the plaintiff shall be obliged to pay to the constable. If plaintiff in any such action shall recover against a justice, and the judge shall certify that the injury was wilfully and maliciously done, the plaintiff shall recover double costs.

No action shall be brought against a justice for any thing done in the execution of his office, unless commenced within six months after the act committed.

And by stat. 26 *Geo.* 2. *c.* 27. no action lies against the justice, who backs or indorses a warrant, but only against the justice who granted it.

Also by 43 *Geo.* 3. *c.* 141. in actions against justices of the peace for any conviction or levying any penalty; the plaintiff, besides any penalty levied, shall recover only 2*d.* damages, unless malice and want of probable cause be expressly alleged, nor shall the penalty be recovered if the plaintiff be proved to have been guilty of the offence.

JUSTICES OF PEACE WITHIN LIBERTIES, (*justiciarii ad pacem infra libertates*) are such in cities, and other corporate towns, as the others are of the county.

But if the king grant to a corporation, that the mayor and recorder, &c. shall be justices of peace within the city; if there be no words of exclusion, justices of the county have concurrent jurisdiction with them; and the king, notwithstanding his charter, may grant a commission of the peace specially in that city or county. 2 *Hale's Hist. P. C.* 47.

JUSTICES OF TRAIL-BASTON, were justices appointed by king Edward I. during his absence in the Scotch and French wars. They were so stiled, says Holingshead, of trailing or drawing the staff of justice; or for their summary proceeding, according to sir Edward Coke, who tells us, they were in a manner justices in eyre; and it is said, they had a baston, or staff delivered to them as the badge of their office, so that whoever was brought before them was *traile ad baston, traditus ad baculum:* whereupon they had the name of *justices de trail-baston*, or *justiciarii ad trabendum offendentes ad baculum vel baston*. Their office was to make inquisition through the kingdom on all officers and others, touching extortion, bribery, and such like grievances; of intruders into other men's lands, barretors, robbers, and breakers of the peace, and divers other offenders; by means of which inquisitions, some were punished with death, many by ransom, and the rest flying the realm, the land was quieted, and the king gained great riches towards the support of his wars. *Mat. Westm. anno* 1305. A commission of *trail-baston* was granted to Roger de Grey, and others his associates, in the reign of king *Edw.* 3. *Spelm. Gloss.*

JUSTICE SEAT, is the highest court that is held in a forest, and is always held before the lord chief justice in eyre of the forest, upon warning forty days before; and there fines are set for offences, and judgments given, &c. *Manwood, cap.* 24.

JUSTICIAR, or JUSTICIER, (Fr. *justicier*) a justice, or *justicier*. The whole jurisdiction of which is now distributed among the several courts of Westminster-hall. 2 *Hawk. P. C.* 6.

JUSTICIATUS, judicature, prerogative. *Cowel.*

JUSTICIES. The sheriff cannot hold plea of debt in his county-court, except for sums under 40*s*. *F. N. B.* 117. *Kitch.* 74.

But by a writ of *justicies*, which is a writ directed to and empowering the sheriff for the sake of dispatch, to do the same justice in his county court, as might otherwise be had at Westminster; he may hold plea in his county court of many real actions, and of all personal actions to any amount.

JUSTIFIABLE HOMICIDE. See *Homicide*.

JUSTIFICATION, (*justificatio*) is a maintaining or shewing good reason in court why one did speak or write such a thing which he is called to answer. *Broke.* And pleas in justification are to set forth some special matter whereby the party justifies what he hath done. *Shep. Epit.* 1041. 3 *Salk.* 218. 2 *Mod.* 70. 2 *Nels. Abr.* 1067. *Cro. Eliz.* 667. 5 *Rep.* 85. 3 *Black. Com.* 306.

JUSTIFICATORS, (*justificatores*) are a kind of compurgators, or those that by oath justify the innocence, or oaths of others; as in the case of waging of law. *Cowel. Blount.*

JUSTIFYING BAIL. If a man is arrested and puts in bail, the defendant's attorney may except against the bail, as being, in his opinion, insufficient. In such case, the bail (or other bail in their place) must justify themselves in court, or before a commissioner (for taking bail) in the country, by swearing themselves house-keepers, and each of them to be worth double the sum for which they are bail, after payment of all their debts. *Harrison. Tidd. Sellon.*

JUSTITIA, was anciently used for a judge, and sometimes for a statute, law, or ordinance.

It is also often taken for jurisdiction, or the office of a judge. And the *justitiarius* was formerly called *justitia, i. e.* a judge. *Cowel. Blount.*

JUSTITIAS FACERE, is to hold plea of any thing. *Ibid.*

JUSTITIUM, a ceasing from the prosecution of law, and exercising justice in places judicial. *Ibid.*

K

KAIA, a key or wharf. *Spelm. Cowel.*

KAIAGIUM. The toll-money paid for loading or unloading goods at a key or wharf. *Ibid.*

KALENDÆ, rural chapters or conventions of the rural deans and parochial clergy, so called because formerly held on the kalends, or first day of every month. *Ibid.*

KALENDAR MONTH, consists of thirty or thirty-one days, (except February, which hath but eight and twenty, and in leap year nine and twenty) according to the kalendar; twelve of which months make a year. Stat. 16 *Car.* 2. *c.* 7. 24 *Geo.* 2. *c.* 23. 25 *Geo.* 2. *c.* 30.

KALENDS, the beginning of a month, &c. See *Calends.*

KANTREF, one hundred towns, which the Welsh call *cwmmwd*, and signifies *provincia* or *regio*, and consisteth of twelve manors or circuits, and two townships. *Cowel. Blount.*

KARITE, CARITE, the religious called their best conventual drink, or their strong beer, by this name. *Cowel.*

KARLE, (Sax.) a man, and with any addition a servant or clown; a domestic servant. *Cowel.*

KARRATA FŒNI, a cart-load of hay. *Cowel.*

KAY. See *Key.*

KEBBARS, (or *Cullers*) the refuse of sheep drawn out of a flock. *Cowel.*

KEELAGE, (*killagium*) a privilege to demand money for the bottom of ships resting in a port or harbour. *Cowel.*

KEELMEN, mariners, seamen, &c. employed in the North on the collieries.

KEELS, to carry coals, &c.

KEEP. A strong tower or hold in the middle of any castle or fortification, something of the nature of that which is called a citadel. *Cowel.*

KEEPER OF THE FOREST, (*custos forestæ*) or chief warden of the forest, hath the principal government over all officers within the forest; and warns them to appear at the court of justice seat, on a general summons from the lord chief justice in eyre. *Manwood, par.* 1. *p.* 156.

KEEPER OF THE GREAT SEAL, (*custos magni sigilli*) is a lord by his office, stiled lord keeper of the great seal of England, and is of the king's privy council.

The lord keeper of the great seal, by statute 5 *Eliz. c.* 18. hath the same place, authority, pre-eminence, jurisdiction and execution of laws, as the lord chancellor of England hath, and he is constituted *per traditionem magni sigilli, &c.* and by taking his oath. 4 *Inst.* 87.

The lord chancellor, or lord keeper, is superior, in point of precedency, to every temporal lord. 3 *Black.* 71.

KEEPER OF THE PRIVY SEAL, (*custos privati sigilli*) is that officer through whose hands all charters, pardons, &c. pass, signed by the king, before they come to the great seal. 4 *Inst.* 55.

KEEPER OF THE TOUCH, 12 *Hen.* 6. 14. seems to be that officer in the king's mint, at this day called the Master of the Assay. *Cowel.* See *Mint.*

KENNETS, a sort of coarse Welsh cloth, mentioned in 3 *Hen.* 8. *c.* 6. *Cowel.*

KERHERE, signifies a custom to have a cart-way; or a commutation for the customary duty for carriage of the lord's goods. *Cowel.*

KERNALLARE DOMUM, (from Lat. *crena*, a notch) to build a house formerly with a wall or tower, kernelled with crannies or notches, for the better convenience of shooting arrows, and making other defence. *Cowel. Blount.*

KERNELLATUS, fortified or embatteled. *Ibid.*

KERNES, idle persons, vagabonds. *Ord. Hiber.* 31 *Ed.* 3. *m.* 11, 12. *Ibid.*

KEVERE, a cover or vessel used in a dairy house for milk or whey. *Ibid.*

KEY, (*kaia & caya*, Sax. *leg*, Teut. *kay*) sometimes *quay*, from the Fr. *quai*, a wharf to land or ship goods or wares at. *Cowel.*

KEYAGE, (*kaiagium*) the money or toll paid for loading or unloading wares at a key or wharf. *Ibid.*

KEYLES, or KEELS, (*ciuli* or *ciules*) a kind of long-boats of great antiquity, mentioned in stat. 23 *Hen.* 8. *c.* 18. *Spelm. Cowel.*

KEYING, five fells, or pelts, or sheepskins with their wool on them. *Cowel.*

KEYUS, KEYS, a guardian, warden, or keeper. And in the Isle of Man, the twenty-four chief commoners, who are, as it were, conservators of the liberties of the people, are called keys of the island. *Ibid.* See Man, Isle of.

KICHELL. It was an old custom for godfathers and godmothers, every time their god-children asked them blessing, to give them a cake; which was called a god's kichell. *Cowel.*

KIDDER, a badger, or carrier of corn, dead victual, or other merchandize, up and down to sell. 5 *Eliz. c.* 12. 13 *Eliz. cap.* 25.

KIDDLE, KIDEL, or KEDEL, (*kidellus*) a dam, or open wear in a river, with a loop or narrow cut in it, accommodated for the laying of wheels or other engines to catch fish. 2 *Inst. fol.* 438. *Cowel.*

KIDNAPPING, is the forcible abduction or stealing away of a man, woman, or child, from their own country, and sending them into another. This is unquestionably a very heinous crime, as it robs the king of his subjects, banishes a man from his country, and may in its consequences, be productive of the most cruel and disagreeable hardships; and therefore, the common law of England has punished it with fine, imprisonment, and pillory (*Raym.* 474. 2 *Show.* 221. *Skin.* 47. *Comb.* 10.) And also the statute 11 & 12 *W.* 3. *c.* 7. though principally intended against pirates, has a clause that extends to prevent the leaving of such persons abroad, as are thus kidnapped or spirited away; by enacting, that "if any captain of a merchant vessel shall (during his being abroad) force any person on shore, or wilfully leave him behind, or refuse to bring home all such men as he carried out, if able and desirous to return, he shall suffer three months imprisonment."

Also where a child is stolen for the sake of its cloaths, it is the same species of felony, as if the cloaths were stolen without the child. But it cannot be considered a felony, where a child is stolen, and not deprived of its cloaths. This crime would in general, be an aggravated species of false imprisonment; but without referring it to that class of offences, stealing a child from its parents, is an act so shocking and horrid, that it would be considered the highest misdemeanor, punishable by fine, imprisonment, and pillory, upon the same principle on which it was decided to be a misdemeanor to steal a dead body from a grave. *Chr. N.* 4 *Black.* 218, 219.

KILDERKIN, the eighth part of an hogshead.

KILKETH, an ancient servile payment made by tenants in husbandry. *Cowel.*

KILLAGIUM, keelage. *Cowel.*

KILLING. See *Homicide.*

KILLYTH-STALLION, is where lords of manors were bound by custom to provide a stallion for the use of their tenants mares. *Spelman's Gloss. Cowel.*

KILTH, *ac omnes annuales redditus de quadam consuetudine in, &c. vocat'.* kilth. *Pat.* 7 *Eliz. Cowel.*

KINDRED, are persons of kin or related to each other. And there are three degrees of these in our law; one in the right line descending, another in the right line ascending, and the third in the collateral line.

Lineal consanguinity is that which subsists between persons, of whom one is *descended in a direct line* from the other, as between John Stiles and his father, grandfather, great-grandfather, and so upwards in *the direct ascending line;* or between John Stiles and his son, grandson, great-grandson, and so downwards in the *direct descending line.* Every generation, in this lineal direct consanguinity, constitutes a different degree, reckoning either upwards or downwards: the father of John Stiles is related to him in the first degree, and so likewise is his son; his grandsire and grandson in the second; his great-grandsire and great-grandson in the third. This is the only natural way of reckoning the degrees in the direct line, and therefore universally obtains, as well in the civil (*Ff.* 38. 10. 10.) and canon (*Decretal, l.* 4. *tit.* 14.), as in the common law (*Co. Litt.* 23.)

The doctrine of lineal consanguinity is sufficiently plain and obvious; but it is at the first view astonishing to consider the number of lineal ancestors which every man has, within no very great number of degrees; and so many different bloods is a man said to contain in his veins, as he hath lineal ancestors. Of these he hath two in the first ascending degree, his own parents; he hath four in the second, the parents of his father and the parents of his mother; he hath eight in the third, the parents of his two grandfathers and two grandmothers; and by the same rule of progression, he hath an hundred and twenty-eight in the seventh; a thousand and twenty-four in the tenth; and at the twentieth degree, or the distance of twenty generations, every man hath above a million of ancestors, as common arithmetic will demonstrate.* 2 *Black.* 202.

---

* This will seem surprising to those who are unacquainted with the increasing power of progressive numbers: but is palpably evident from the following table of a geometrical progressing, in which the first term is 2, and the denominator also 2: or, to speak more intelligibly, it is evident, for that each of us has two ancestors in the first degree; the number of whom is doubled at every remove, because each of our ancestors has also two immediate ancestors of his own.

Lineal Degrees.	*Number of Ancestors.*
1	2
2	4
3	8
4	16
5	32
6	64
7	128
8	256
9	512
10	1024
11	2048
12	4096

Collateral kindred answers to the same description: collateral relations agreeing with the lineal in this, that they descend from the same stock or ancestor; but differing in this, that they do not descend one from the other. Collateral kinsmen, are such then as lineally spring from one and the same ancestor, who is the stirps, or root, the stipes, trunk, or common-stock, from whence these relations are branched out. As if John Stiles hath two sons, who have each a numerous issue; both these issues are lineally descended from John Stiles as their common ancestor; and they are collateral kinsmen to each other, because they are all descended from this common ancestor, and all have a portion of his blood in their veins, which denominates them *consanguineos*. 2 *Black.* 205.

Lineal Degrees.	*Number of Ancestors.*
13	8192
14	16384
15	32768
16	65536
17	131072
18	262144
19	524288
20	1048576

A shorter method of finding the number of ancestors at any even degree, is by squaring the number of ancestors at half that number of degrees. Thus 16 (the number of ancestors at four degrees) is the square of 4, the number of ancestors at two; 256 is the square of 16; 65536 of 256; and the number of ancestors at 40 degrees would be the square of 1048576, or upwards of a million millions.

The method of computing these degrees in the canon law (*Decretal.* 4. 14. 3 & 9.), which our law has adopted (*Co. Litt.* 23.), is as follows. We begin at the common ancestor, and reckon downwards; and in whatsoever degree the two persons, or the most remote of them, is distant from the common ancestor, that is the degree in which they are related to each other. 2 *Black.* 206.

The nature and degrees of kindred will be better understood from the following table:

TABLE OF CONSANGUINITY.

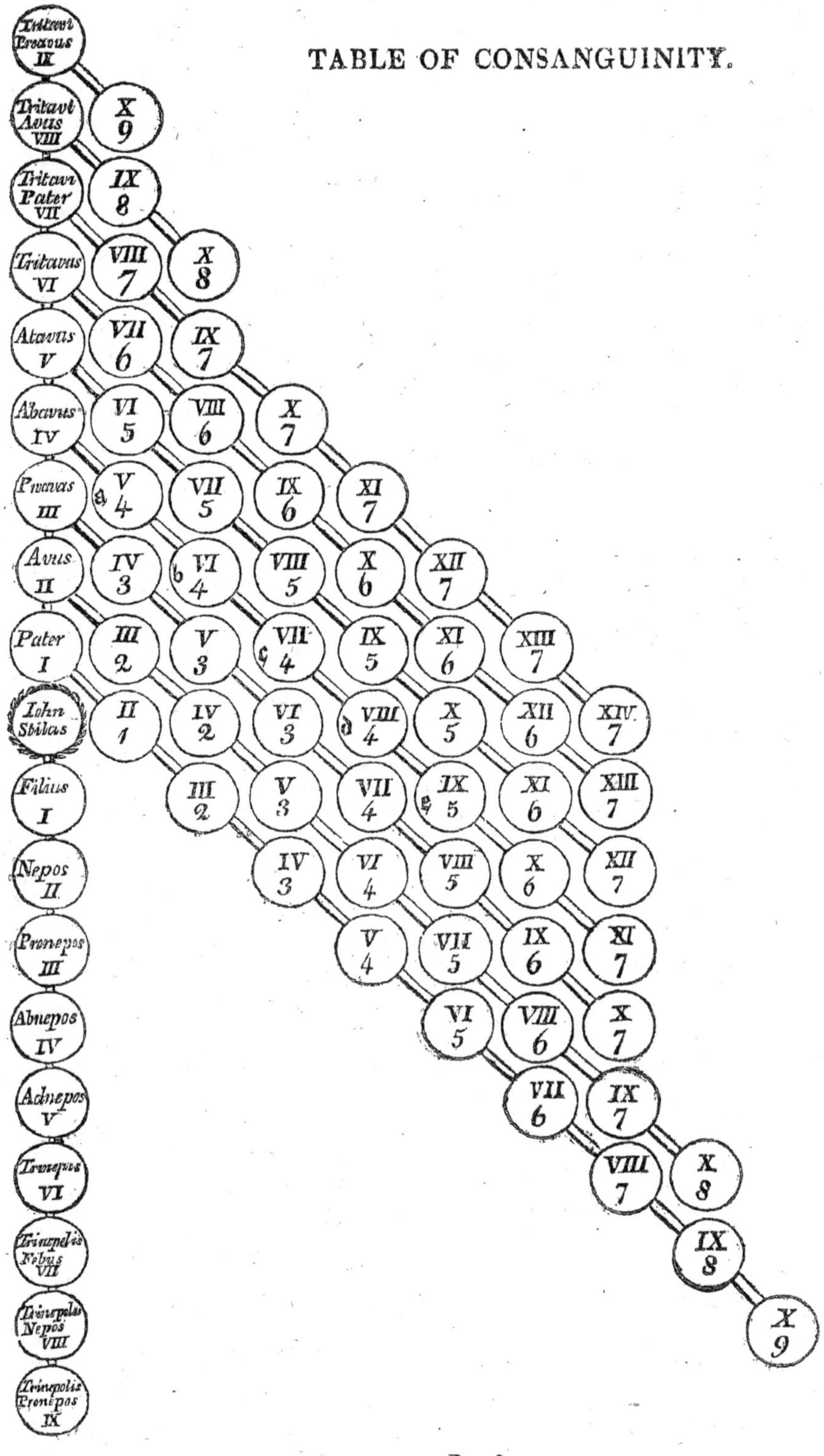

KING, (from the Sax. *Cyning*, or *Coning*, a cunning or wise man,) is a monarch or potentate, that has the highest power and rule in the land. *Bract. lib.* 1, *c.* 8.

And the supreme executive power of these kingdoms is vested by our laws in a single person, the king or queen; for it matters not to which sex the crown descends, but the person entitled to it, whether male or female, is immediately invested with all the ensigns, rights, and prerogatives of sovereign power, as is declared by stat. 1 *Marlb. st.* 3, *c.* 1.

The executive power of the English nation being vested in a single person, by the general consent of the people, the evidence of which general consent is long and immemorial usage, it became necessary to the freedom and peace of the state, that a rule should be laid down, uniform, universal, and permanent; in order to mark out with precision, who is that single person, to whom are committed (in subservience to the law of the land) the care and protection of the community; and to whom, in return, the duty and allegiance of every individual are due. 1 *Black.* 190.

And according to *Blackstone* the grand fundamental maxim upon which the *jus coronæ*, or right of succession to the throne of these kingdoms, depends, is this: "that the crown is by common "law and constitutional custom, hereditary; and this in a manner peculiar to "itself: but that the right of inheritance "may from time to time be changed or "limited by act of parliament; under "which limitation the crown still continues hereditary."

First, it is in general hereditary, or descendible to the next heir on the death or demise of the last proprietor.

All regal governments must be either hereditary or elective; and as there is no instance wherein the crown of England has ever been asserted to be elective, except by the regicides at the infamous and unparalleled trial of k. Charles I. it must of consequence be hereditary. Yet this must not be intended to be a *jure divino* title to the throne: such a title may be allowed to have subsisted under the theocratic establishments of the children of Israel. But though the founders of our English monarchy might, perhaps, if they had thought proper, have made it an elective monarchy, yet they rather chose to establish originally a succession by inheritance. This has been acquiesced in by general consent, and ripened by degrees into common law; the very same title that every private man has to his own estate. Lands are not naturally descendible any more than thrones: but the law has thought proper, for the benefit and peace of the public, to establish hereditary succession in the one as well as the other. 1 *Black.* 192.

Secondly, it is hereditary in a manner peculiar to itself.

As to the particular mode of inheritance, it in general corresponds with the feodal path of descents, chalked out by the common law in the succession to landed estates, yet with one or two material exceptions. Like estates, the crown will descend lineally to the issue of the reigning monarch. As in common descents the preference of males to females, and the right of primogeniture among the males, are strictly adhered to. But among the females the crown descends by right of primogeniture to the eldest daughter only, and her issue, and not, as in common inheritances, to all the daughters at once; the evident necessity of a sole succession to the throne having occasioned the royal law of descents to depart from the common law in this respect; and therefore queen Mary on the death of her brother succeeded to the crown alone, and not in partnership with her sister Elizabeth. Again: the doctrine of representation prevails in the descent of the crown as it does in other inheritances, whereby the lineal descendants of any person deceased stand in the same place as their ancestor, if living, would have done. Lastly, on failure of lineal descendants the crown goes to the next collateral relations of the late king, provided they are lineally descended from the blood royal, that is, from that royal stock which originally acquired the crown. But herein there is no objection (as in the case of common descents) to the succession of a brother, an uncle, or other collateral relation of the half blood, that is, where the relationship proceeds not from the same couple of ancestors (which constitutes a kinsman of the whole blood) but from a single ancestor only; as when two persons are derived from the same father, and not from the same mother, or *vice versa*; provided only, that the one ancestor from whom both are descended be that from whose veins the blood royal is communicated to each.

Thirdly, this inheritance is subject to limitation by parliament.

The doctrine of hereditary right does by no means imply an indefeasible right to the throne, for it is in the breast of the supreme legislative authority of this kingdom, *the king and both houses of parliament*, to defeat this hereditary right; and, by particular entails, limitations, and provisions, to exclude the immediate heir, and vest the inheritance in any one else. This is strictly consonant to our laws and constitution, as may be gathered from the expression so frequently used in our statute-book, of "the king's majesty, his heirs and successors;" in which we may observe, that as the word "heirs" necessarily implies an inheritance or hereditary right, generally subsisting in the royal person, so the word "successors," distinctly taken, must imply that this inheritance may sometimes be broken through, or that there may be a successor, without being the heir, of the king. And this is so extremely reasonable, that without such a power, lodged somewhere, our polity would be very defective. For if the heir apparent should be a lunatic, an idiot, or otherwise incapable of reigning: miserable would be the condition of the nation if he were also incapable of being set aside. It is therefore necessary that this power should be lodged somewhere; and yet the inheritance, and regal dignity, would be very precarious indeed if this power were expressly and avowedly lodged in the hands of the subjects only, to be exerted whenever prejudice, caprice, or discontent should happen to take the lead. Consequently it can no where be so properly lodged as in the two houses of parliament, by and with the consent of the reigning king, who it is not to be supposed will agree to any thing improperly prejudicial to the rights of his own descendants. And therefore in the king, lords, and commons, in parliament assembled, our laws have expressly lodged it. 1 *Black.* 195, 196.

Fourthly, however the crown may be limited or transferred, it still retains its descendible quality, and becomes hereditary in the wearer of it. Hence in our law the king is said never to die, in his political capacity, though, in common with other men, he is subject to mortality in his natural; for immediately upon the natural death of the king, the kingly office survives in his successor.—For the right of the crown vests, *eo instanti,* upon his heir; either the *hæres natus,* if the course of descent remains unimpeached, or the *hæres factus,* if the inheritance be under any particular settlement. So that there can be no *inter-regnum,* but, as sir Matthew Hale (1 *Hist. P. C.* 61,) observes, the right of sovereignty is fully invested in the successor by the very descent of the crown. (1 *Hist. P. C.* 61.)

Thus the statutes passed in the first year after the restoration of *Car.* 2, are always called the acts of the twelfth year of his reign; and all the other legal proceedings of that reign are reckoned from the year 1648, and not from 1660. And therefore, however acquired, it becomes in him absolutely hereditary, unless by the rules of the limitation it is otherwise ordered and determined. In the same manner as landed estates are by the law hereditary, or descendible to the heirs of the owner; but still there exists a power by which the property of those lands may be transferred to another person. If this transfer be made simply and absolutely the lands will be hereditary in the new owner, and descend to his heir at law; but if the transfer be clogged with any limitations, conditions, or entails, the lands must descend in that channel, so limited and prescribed, and no other. 1 *Black.* 196.

The first instance in point of time wherein the parliament has asserted or exercised this right of altering and limiting the succession to the crown since the reigns of *Hen.* 4, *Hen.* 7, *Hen.* 8, 2. *Mary,* and 2. *Eliz.* in which that right had been before exercised, is the famous bill of exclusion, which raised such a ferment in the latter end of the reign of *Cha.* 2. The purport of this bill was to have set aside the king's brother and presumptive heir, the duke of York, from the succession, on the score of his being a papist; it passed the house of commons, but was rejected by the lords, the king having also declared beforehand that he never would be brought to consent to it. And from this transaction we may collect two things, first, that the crown was universally acknowledged to be hereditary, and the inheritance indefeasible, unless by parliament, else it had been needless to prefer such a bill. Secondly, that the parliament had a power to have defeated the inheritance, else such a bill had been ineffectual. The commons acknowledged the hereditary right then subsisting, and the lords did not dispute the power, but merely the propriety of an exclusion. However, as the bill took no effect, king *James* II. succeeded to the throne of his ancestors, and might have enjoyed it during the remainder of his life but for his own infatuated conduct, which (with other concurring circumstances) brought on the Revolution in 1688. 1 *Black.* 210.

The ground upon which that memorable event proceeded was an entirely new case in politics, which had never before happened in our history, the abdication of the reigning monarch, and the vacancy of the throne thereupon. It was not a defeasance of the right of succession, and a new limitation of the crown, by the king and both houses of parliament; it was the act of the nation alone, upon a conviction that there was no king in being. For in a full assembly of the lords and commons, met in a convention upon the supposition of this vacancy, both houses (Comm. Journ. 7 Feb. 1688,) came to this resolution, "That *K. James* 2, "having endeavoured to subvert the constitution of the kingdom, by breaking "the original contract between the king "and people, and by the advice of jesuits, "and other wicked persons, having violated "the fundamental laws, and having withdrawn himself out of this kingdom, has "abdicated the government, and that the "throne is thereby vacant." Thus ended at once, by this sudden and unexpected vacancy of the throne, the old line of succession. This abdication did not only affect the person of the king himself, but also all his heirs, and rendered the throne absolutely and completely vacant. 1 *Black.* 210.

It is worthy of observation that the convention in this their judgment avoided with great wisdom the wild extremes into which the visionary theories of some zealous republicans would have led them. They held that this misconduct of *James* amounted to an endeavour to subvert the constitution, and not to an actual subversion, or total dissolution, of the government, which would have reduced the society almost to a state of nature; would have levelled all distinctions of honour, rank, offices, and property; would have annihilated the sovereign power, and in consequence have repealed all positive laws; and would have left the people at liberty to have erected a new system of state upon a new foundation of polity. They therefore very prudently voted it to amount to no more than an abdication of the government, and a consequent vacancy of the throne; whereby the government was allowed to subsist, though the executive magistrate was gone, and the kingly office to remain, though king James was no longer king. (*Law of forfeit.* 118, 119.) And thus the constitution was kept entire; which upon every sound principle of government must otherwise have fallen to pieces had so principal and constituent a part as the royal authority been abolished, or even suspended.

The vacancy of the throne being once established, the rest that was then done followed almost of course. For if *the throne be at any time vacant, (which may happen by other means besides that of abdication, as if all the blood-royal should fail, without any successor appointed by parliament,) if a vacancy by any means whatsoever should happen,* the right of disposing of this vacancy seems naturally to result from the lords and commons, the trustees and representatives of the nation. For there are no other hands in which it can so properly be intrusted; and there is a necessity of its being intrusted somewhere, else the whole frame of government must be dissolved and perish.

The preamble to the bill of rights expressly declares, that "the lords spiritual and temporal, and commons, assembled at Westminster lawfully, fully and freely represent all the estates of the people of this realm." The lords are not less the trustees and guardians of their country, than the members of the house of commons. And it was justly said, when the royal prerogatives were suspended during his majesty's illness, "that the two houses of parliament were the organs by which the people expressed their will."

The lords and commons having therefore determined this main fundamental article, that there was a vacancy of the throne, they proceeded to fill up that vacancy in such manner as they judged the most proper: and this was done by their declaration of 12 *Feb.* 1688, (*Com. Journ.* 12 *Feb.* 1688) in the following manner: "That *William* and *Mary*, prince and princess of Orange, be, and be declared, king and queen, to hold the crown and royal dignity during their lives, and the life of the survivor of them; and that the sole and full exercise of the regal power be only in and executed by the said prince of Orange, in the names of the said prince and princess during their joint lives, and after their deceases the said crown and royal dignity to be to the heirs of the body of the said princess; and for default of such issue to the princess Anne of Denmark, and the heirs of her body; and for default of such issue to the heirs of the body of the said prince of Orange."

They thus settled the crown, first on king *William*, and queen *Mary*, king *James*'s eldest daughter, for their joint lives; then on the survivor of them, and then on the issue of queen Mary: upon failure of such issue it was limited to the princess Anne, king *James*'s second daughter, and her issue; and lastly, on failure of that, to the issue of king *William*, who was the grandson of *Charles* 1, and nephew as well as son-in-law to *James* 2, being the son of Mary his eldest sister. This settlement included all the protestant posterity of *Charles* 1, except such other issue as *James* might at any time have, which was totally omitted through fear of a popish succession. And this order of succession took effect accordingly.

These three princes, therefore, *William*, queen *Mary*, and queen *Anne*, did not take the crown by hereditary right or descent, but by way of donation, or purchase, as the lawyers call it, by which they mean any method of acquiring an estate otherwise than by descent. The new settlement did not merely consist in excluding *James*, and the person pretending to be the prince of Wales, and then suffering the crown to descend in the old hereditary channel: for the usual course of descent was in some instances broken through; and yet the convention still kept it in their eye, and paid a great, though not total, regard to it. If no abdication had happened, and king James had left no other issue than his two daughters queen Mary and queen Anne, it would have stood thus: queen Mary and her issue; queen Anne and her issue; king William and his issue. Therefore these princes were successively in possession of the crown by a title different from the usual course of descent.

Towards the end of king William's reign, when all hopes of any surviving issue from any of these princes died with the duke of Gloucester, the king and parliament again exerted their power of limiting and appointing the succession, in order to prevent another vacancy of the throne, which must have ensued upon their deaths, as no further provision was made at the Revolution than for the issue of queen Mary, queen Anne, and king William. The parliament had previously by the stat. of 1 *Will. & Mar. st.* 2, c. 2, enacted, that "every person who "should be *reconciled* to, or *hold communion* "with, the see of Rome, should profess "the popish religion, or should marry a "papist, should be excluded and for ever "incapable to inherit, possess, or enjoy "the crown; and that in such case the "people should be absolved from their allegiance, and the crown should descend "to such persons, being protestants, as "would have inherited the same, in case "the person so reconciled, holding communion, professing, or marrying, were "naturally dead." To act therefore consistently with themselves, and at the same time pay as much regard to the old hereditary line as their former resolutions would admit, they turned their attention to the princess Sophia, electress and duchess dowager of Hanover. For, upon the impending extinction of the protestant posterity of Charles the first, the old law of regal descent directed them to recur to the descendants of James the first; and the princess Sophia, being the youngest daughter of Elizabeth queen of Bohemia, who was the daughter of James the first, was the nearest of the ancient blood royal, who was not incapacitated by professing the popish religion. On her therefore, and the heirs of her body, being protestants, the remainder of the crown, expectant on the death of king William and queen Anne without issue, was settled by stat. 12 & 13 *W.* 3. c. 2. And at the same time it was enacted, that "whosoever should hereafter come to the "possession of the crown should join in "the communion of the church of England "as by law established."

These several actual limitations, from the time of Henry 4 to the present, clearly prove the power of the king and parliament to new-model or alter the succession. And it is now made highly penal to dispute it: for by the stat. 6 *Ann. c.* 7, it is enacted, that *if any person maliciously, advisedly, and directly, shall maintain, by writing or printing, that the kings of this realm with the authority of parliament are not able to make laws to bind the crown and the descent thereof, he shall be guilty of high treason; or if he maintains the same by only preaching, teaching, or advised speaking, he shall incur the penalties of a præmunire.*

The princess Sophia dying before queen Anne, the inheritance thus limited descended on her son and heir king George the first; and, having on the death of the queen taken effect in his person, from him it descended to his late majesty king George the second; and from him to his grandson and heir, his present majesty, king George the third.

Hence it is easy to collect, that the title to the crown is at present hereditary, though not quite so absolutely hereditary as formerly: and the common stock or ancestor, from whom the descent must be derived, is also different. Formerly the common stock was king Egbert; then William the conqueror; afterwards in James the first's time the two common stocks united, and so continued till the vacancy of the throne in 1688: now it is the princess Sophia, in whom the inheritance was vested by the new king and parliament. Formerly the descent was absolute, and the crown went to the next heir without any restriction: but now, upon the new settlement, the inheritance is conditional; being limited to such heirs only, of the body of the princess Sophia, as are protestant members of the church of England, and are married to none but protestants. 1 *Black.* 217.

KING, ACTS RELATING TO.] By 26 *Hen.* 8, *c.* 1, the king shall be deemed the only supreme head on earth of the church of England.

By 1 *Mar. stat* 3. *c.* 1, the kingly office may be exercised by male or female.

By 1 *Eliz. c.* 1, foreign authority was abolished, and ecclesiastical jurisdiction annexed to the crown; and maintenance of foreign authority is for the first offence forfeiture of goods and chattels, or a year's imprisonment, for the second a *præmunire*, and the third high treason.

By 1 *Ann. stat.* 1. *c.* 7, no grant of crown lands shall be made unless for 31 years, or three lives, the tenant to be punishable for waste, and the ancient rent reserved.

But grants of repairing or building leases may be in like manner of such tenements for fifty years, or three lives. *Ibid.*

No grant of office shall cease on the demise of the sovereign, but continue for six months after, unless avoided by the successor, nor shall any writ, plea, or process, be discontinued thereby. *Ibid. c.* 8.

No commission of assise, oyer and terminer, writs of admittance, *si non omnis*, assistance, or commission of the peace, shall be determined by the sovereign's death, but continue for six months after, unless avoided by the successor; nor shall any writs or process be discontinued thereby; and this act is to extend to Ireland, Jersey, Guernsey, and America. *Ibid.*

By 6 *Ann. c.* 7, the privy council, and places of the great officers of state, shall not be dissolved by the death of the sovereign, but continue for six months, unless sooner discharged.

The great seal, and other public seals in being, shall continue to be the respective seals of the successor until order to the contrary. *Ibid.*

By 2 *Geo.* 3. *c.* 1, the king may grant an annuity of 100,000*l. per ann.* to the queen, to commence at his demise, payable quarterly out of the hereditary and other revenues carried to the aggregate fund, and in case of deficiency, to be made good in preference to all future charges thereon.

By 5 *Geo.* 3. *c.* 27, the king may appoint a guardian to his successor, if the crown descends to any of his children under eighteen years of age. See *Regent.*

By 15 *Geo.* 3. *c.* 53. Buckingham House was settled on the queen in lieu of Somerset House, to be called the queen's royal palace.

By 18 *Geo.* 3. *c.* 31, an annuity of 60,000*l.* is settled on the bishop of Osnaburgh, and his five next brothers, and the survivor of them, to commence on the king's demise, payable quarterly tax free, out of the hereditary duties (now part of the consolidated fund, 27 *Geo.* 3. *c.* 13,) but none of them to have more than 15,000*l. per ann.* each.

An annuity of 30,000*l.* to the king's five eldest daughters, and the survivor of them, in the same manner, and upon the death or marriage of any one with a portion of 40,000*l.* her share to go to the others; and if a second die, or marry with a like portion, her share to go to the other three; and if a third die, or marry with a like portion, the other two to have 20,000*l. per ann.* and if either of them die or marry, the other to have 12,000*l. per ann.* which is to cease on her death or marriage. *Ibid.*

By 22 *Geo.* 3. *c.* 82, the following offices were suppressed. The office of secretary of state for the colonies; the board of trade and plantations; the lords of police in Scotland; the board of works; the principal officers of the great wardrobe, and of the jewel office; the treasurer of the chamber: the cofferer of the household; the six clerks of the board of green cloth; the paymaster of the pensions; the offices of master of the harriers and fox hounds, and of the stag hounds.

Any similar office hereafter established shall be deemed a new office. The court of verge, with all its lawful jurisdictions and powers, is preserved. His majesty's buildings and gardens shall be under the direction of a surveyor or comptroller, to be appointed by his majesty. *Ibid.*

Estimates of new buildings or repairs exceeding 1000*l.* must be laid before the lord chamberlain, and by him referred to the treasury, who are to authorize the execution thereof. *Ibid.*

The treasury before payment for any such works may order the same to be surveyed. Where expences shall be under 1000*l.* vouchers shall be produced to the lord chamberlain. Clerks and workmen in the royal palaces shall be paid monthly; and no new works in his majesty's parks or gardens above 500*l.* shall be undertaken without an order from his majesty. *Ibid.*

Furniture, plate, and moveables, shall be under the management of the lord chamberlain. *Ibid.*

Work formerly under the direction of the great wardrobe shall be executed by the surveyor of the buildings; and the business heretofore done by the board of trade shall be executed by a committee of the privy council. *Ibid.*

No pensions above 300*l. per ann.* to one person, nor more than 600*l. per ann.* in the whole shall be granted in one year; lists whereof are to be delivered to parliament in 20 days after the beginning of each session, till the pension list is reduced to 90,000*l.* and then it is not to exceed 5000*l.* more; nor shall any pensions be then granted to one person of more than 1200*l. per ann.* unless to the royal family, or on a parliamentary address. *Ibid.*

This is not to extend to persons who have served the crown in foreign courts, if they have no other place. *Ibid.*

All pensions on the civil list shall be paid at the exchequer; but the treasurer may with the king's consent take away from the private list the names and pensions of persons therein entered, and he may return into the exchequer any pension, without the name of the pensioner, on swearing that it is not for a member of the house of commons, or to corrupt elections, which pension shall be paid to his order; but when any secret pension shall continue in the list more than five years, oath of the party's life shall be made. *Ibid.*

The payment of home secret service money is restricted to 10,000*l. per ann.* and foreign secret service money is to be sent to the minister or commander abroad, who shall account for such money within a year after their arrival in Great Britain, and swear to the disposition thereof; the secretaries of state making payment of any such secret service money shall be sworn as to the disposal thereof. No stated sum shall be allowed for secret service money to the secretaries of state, but the same shall be annexed to their salaries. Sums issued for any special service shall be entered in a book. Grants of royal bounty more than once in eight years shall be deemed *pensions.* The payments of the civil list revenues shall be divided into regular classes. No pension shall be paid out of course. Salaries in arrear for two years shall be extinguished. Fees payable shall be disposed of by the treasury. Books shall be kept for the charges of each class. *Ibid.*

By 25 *Geo.* 3, *c.* 61, all bounties already given by his majesty to persons in low and indigent circumstances, or which shall hereafter be given, may continue to be paid by the lord steward, the lord chamberlain, the master of the horse, the master of the robes, and the lords of the treasury.

By 32 *Geo.* 3, *c.* 13, the king may grant to the duke and duchess of York annuities not exceeding 18,000*l.* and 8000*l.* to the duchess, to commence from the decease of the duke.

By 35 *Geo.* 3, *c.* 130, his majesty was authorized to grant to the princess of Wales an annuity of 50,000*l.* from the decease of the prince, payable quarterly out of the revenues, for the support of the household, to be free from taxes, paid without fee, and be in bar of dower.

By 39 *Geo.* 3, *c.* 30, his majesty was enabled to settle on the five royal princesses Augusta, Elizabeth, Mary, Sophia, and Amelia, instead of the annuity mentioned in 18 *Geo.* 3, *c.* 31, an annuity of 30,000*l.* to commence from the demise of his majesty, and to be payable out of that part of the hereditary revenues of the crown, as by 27 *Geo.* 3, *c.* 13, were made part of the consolidated fund; and on the marriage of any one or more of the princesses, with portions of 40,000*l.* each, the whole annuity to go to the remaining unmarried princesses.

By 39 and 40 *Geo.* 3, *c.* 88, none of the provisions in stat. 1 *Ann. st.* 1, *c.* 7, *s.* 5. 1 *Geo.* 3, *c.* 1, *s.* 3, or 34 *Geo.* 3, *c.* 75, relating to crown lands, shall from the time of the king's birth extend to estates purchased out of monies from the privy purse, or not appropriated to any public service, nor to lands coming to his majesty, his heirs, or successors, from any person not being kings or queens of the realm. *s.* 1.

Copyholds or leaseholds so purchased, or to be purchased, to be vested in trustees for the crown. *s.* 2, 3.

His majesty, his heirs, and successors, may sell or devise such estates, in like manner as his subjects may like estates belonging to them: and trustees shall convey such etates as the crown shall direct. *s.* 4.

If no disposition of such estates be made by the crown, or a disposition be made which shall not exhaust the whole, the estate undisposed of shall descend as if this act had not been made, subject to the provisions herein contained, and the restrictions of the said acts as to such as are freeholds. *s.* 5.

Estates so vested in the crown, or in its trustees, shall be subject to all taxes, and taxes charged upon such estates shall be paid out of the privy purse. *s.* 6, 7.

Her present majesty, or any queen of the realm, during the joint lives of their majesties, by deed, or by will, may dispose of estates purchased by, or in trust for, or that may vest in her majesty, or in trust for her, and also bequeath all her chattels and personal estate as if she were sole. *s.* 8, 9.

But this act is not to enable her majesty or any queen consort, to dispose of any palace or lands belonging to the king, in right of the crown, vested in her for life; or to make any grant but such as she might make if sole. *s.* 9.

Monies for the privy purse, or not appropriated to any public service, or effects which shall not come to the crown, shall be deemed personal estate, and subject to disposition by will, or writing under the sign-manual, and shall be liable to all debts payable out of the privy-purse—in default of such disposition such personal estate shall go as before this act was made. *s.* 10.

Any will made by his majesty before this act shall be valid. *s.* 11.

And the crown may by warrants under the sign-manual direct the execution of any trusts to which lands becoming vested by escheat would have been liable, in case they had not escheated, and restore such lands, or reward persons discovering such escheats. *s.* 12.

By 42 *Geo.* 3, *c.* 48, his majesty was authorized to grant to the duke of Sussex and the duke of Cambridge annuities of 12,000*l.* each, payable quarterly out of the consolidated fund.

By 43 *Geo.* 3, *c.* 26, his majesty was authorized to grant to the prince of Wales an annuity of 60,000*l.* payable quarterly out of the consolidated fund.

By 46 *Geo.* 3, *c.* 145, his majesty may by his sign-manual grant the following annuities, *viz.* to the dukes of Clarence, Kent, Cumberland, Sussex, and Cambridge, 6000*l.* each during pleasure; to the princess Charlotte of Wales 7000*l.* during the life of the king and prince of Wales; to the duchess dowager of Gloucester 4000*l.* during pleasure; to the duke of Gloucester 14,000*l.* during pleasure, in lieu of 8000*l.* under 18 *Geo.* 3, *c.* 31; and to the princess Sophia of Gloucester 5000*l.* during pleasure, in lieu of 4000*l.* by the same act; and 2000*l.* additional after the death of the duchess of Gloucester, all payable quarterly at the exchequer out of the consolidated fund. *s.* 1, 2.

By 47 *Geo.* 3, *sess.* 1, *c.* 39, the annuities charged by 46 *Geo.* 3, *c.* 145, on the consolidated fund to the duke of Gloucester, and the princess Sophia of Gloucester, shall be payable during their lives. *s.* 1.

And all annuities granted to the other branches of the royal family under 18 *Geo.* 3, *c.* 31, shall be payable during their respective lives. *s.* 2.

By 47 *Geo.* 3, *sess.* 2, *c.* 24, in amendment of 39 *Geo.* 3, *c.* 88, in cases where his majesty shall become entitled to freehold or copyhold premises by forfeiture, he may direct the execution of any trusts or purposes wherein they may have been directed to be applied, and may make grants thereof.

By 47 *Geo.* 3, *sess.* 2, *c.* 45, his majesty is enabled to grant to her majesty the queen a capital messuage, called Frogmore, and divers lands and hereditaments, in the parishes of New Windsor and Old Windsor, in the county of Berks, and a piece of land in Wyrothsbury, in the county of Bucks, for a term of 99 years, if her majesty and the princesses, her five younger daughters, or any of them, shall so long live, for and in lieu of her majesty's present term and interests therein, and also to make exchanges.

By 48 *Geo.* 3, *c.* 59, his majesty was enabled to settle an annuity of 10,000*l.* on the duchess of Brunswick Wolfenbuttle. And by 50 *Geo.* 3. *c.* . an annuity of 7,000*l.* on the duke of Brunswick.

KING's COUNSEL. His majesty's counsel learned in the law are usually selected from barristers, and serjeants at law, the two principal of whom are called his attorney and solicitor-general. These king's council, who are now the sworn servants of the crown, with a standing salary, answer in some measure to the advocates of the revenue, *advocati fisci*, among the Romans: for they must not be employed in any cause against the crown without special license.

A custom has also of late years prevailed of granting letters patent of precedence to such barristers as the crown thinks proper to honour with that mark of distinction; whereby they are entitled to such rank and pre-audience (see *Pre-audience*) as are assigned in their respective patents; sometimes next after the king's attorney-general, but usually next after his majesty's counsel then being. These (as well as the queen's attorney and solicitor-general, *Seld. tit. hon.* 1. 6, 7,) rank promiscuously with the king's counsel, and together with them sit within the bar of their respective courts, but receive no salaries, and are not sworn, and therefore are at liberty to be retained in causes against the crown.

KING's GRANTS. The king's grants are matters of public record: for the king's excellency is so high in the law that no freehold may be given to the king, nor derived from him, but by matter of record. And to this end a variety of offices are erected, communicating in a regular subordination one with another, through which all the king's grants must pass, and be transcribed and inrolled, that the same may be narrowly inspected by his officers, who will inform him if any thing contained therein is improper, or unlawful to be granted. These grants, whether of lands, honours, liberties, franchises, or aught besides, are contained in charters, or letters patent, that is, open letters, *literæ patentes*, so called because they are not sealed up, but exposed to open view, with the great seal pendent at the bottom, and are usually directed or addressed by the king to all his subjects at large; and therein they differ from certain other letters of the king, sealed also with his great seal, but directed to particular persons, and for particular purposes; which, therefore, not being proper for public inspection, are closed up, and sealed on the outside, and are thereupon called writs close, *literæ clausæ*, and are recorded in the close rolls, in the same manner as the others are in the patent rolls. 2 *Black.* 346.

KING's HOUSEHOLD. See statute 22 *Geo.* 3, *c.* 82, under head *King, acts relating to*, and *King's Revenue.*

KING's PALACE. The limits of the king's palace at Westminster extend from Charing Cross to Westminster Hall, and shall have such privileges as the ancient palaces. Stat. 28 *Hen.* 8. See *Misprisions. Palaces.*

KING's REVENUE. The king's revenue is either ordinary or extraordinary; 1st. The ORDINARY REVENUE is such as has either subsisted time out of mind in the crown, or else has been granted by parliament by way of purchase or exchange for such of the king's inherent hereditary revenues as were found inconvenient to the subject. 2ndly, The EXTRAORDINARY REVENUE consists of those taxes authorized by parliament to be raised and levied upon the subject, which are now carried to and compose what is called the consolidated fund, for which see title *Funds.*

As to the ordinary revenue of the crown great part thereof will appear to consist of what lords of manors and other subjects look upon to be their own absolute inherent rights, because they are and have been vested in them and their ancestors for ages, though in reality originally derived from the grants of our ancient kings. 1 *Black.* 281.

1st. The first of the king's ordinary revenues is of an ecclesiastical kind, viz. the custody of the temporalities of bishops till such time as a successor is appointed, with power of taking to himself all the intermediate profits, without any account to the successor, and with the right of presenting (which the crown very frequently exercises) to such benefices and other preferments as fall within the time of vacation. Stat. 17 *Edw.* 2, *c.* 14. *F. N. B.* 32.

This revenue of the king, which was formerly very considerable, is now by a customary indulgence almost reduced to nothing; for at present, as soon as the new bishop is consecrated and confirmed, he usually receives the restitution of his temporalities quite entire, and untouched, from the king *; and at the same time does

* But queen Elizabeth kept the see of Ely vacant 19 years, in order to retain the revenue. 4 *Strype*, 351.

homage to his sovereign; and then, and not sooner, he has a fee-simple in his bishopric, and may maintain an action for the profits. *Co. Litt.* 67. 341.

2. The king is entitled to a corody, as the law calls it, out of every bishopric, that is, to send one of his chaplains to be maintained by the bishop or to have a pension allowed him till the bishop, promote him to a benefice. *F. N. B.* 230. This is now fallen into total disuse, though sir Matthew Hale says that it is due of common right, and that no prescription will discharge it. *Notes on F. N. B. above cited.*

3. The king also is entitled to all the tithes arising in extra-parochial places. 2 *Inst.* 647.

4. The next branch consists in the first-fruits and tenths of all spiritual preferments in the kingdom. See *First-fruits.*

These were originally a part of the papal usurpations over the clergy of this kingdom, but in the reign of Henry 8, when the papal power was abolished, and the king was declared the head of the church of England, this revenue was annexed to the crown by stat. 26 *Hen.* 8, *c.* 3, (confirmed by stat. 1 *Eliz. c.* 4,) and a new *valor beneficiorum* was then made, by which the clergy are at present rated.

This stat. of 26 *Hen.* 8. *c.* 3, enacted that commissioners should be appointed in every diocese, who should certify the value of every ecclesiastical benefice and preferment in the respective dioceses; and according to this valuation, the first-fruits and tenths were to be collected and paid in future. *This valor beneficiorum is what is commonly called* the *king's books*; a transcript of which is given in Ecton's Thesaurus, and Bacon's Liber Regis.

5. The next branch of the king's ordinary revenue consists in the rents and profits of the demesne lands of the crown.

6. The advantages which used to arise to the king from the profits of his military tenures, to which most lands in the kingdom were subject till the statute 12 *Car.* 2, *c.* 24, which in great measure abolished them all, was also one of the ordinary branches of the royal revenue.

7. A seventh branch also formerly arose from wine licenses; or the rents payable to the crown by such persons as were licensed to sell wine by retail throughout England, except in a few privileged places. But this revenue was abolished by the stat. 30 *Geo.* 2, *c.* 19, and an annual sum of upwards of 7000*l.* *per annum*, issuing out of the stamp duties settled on the crown in its stead.

8. An eighth branch of the king's ordinary revenue is usually reckoned to consist in the profits arising from his forests. 1 *Jones*, 267—298.

9. The profits arising from the king's ordinary courts of justice make a ninth branch of his revenue. And these consist not only in fines imposed upon offenders, forfeitures of recognizances, and amercements levied upon defaulters, but also in certain fees due to the crown in a variety of legal matters, as for setting the great seal to charters, original writs, and other forensic proceedings, and for permitting fines to be levied of lands in order to bar entails, or otherwise to ensure their title. These in process of time have been almost all granted out to private persons, or else appropriated to certain particular uses; so that though our law proceedings are still loaded with their payment, very little of them is now returned into the king's exchequer, for a part of whose royal maintenance they were originally intended. All future grants of them, however, by the stat. 1 *Ann. st.* 1. *c.* 7, are to endure for no longer time than the prince's life who grants them.

10. A tenth branch of the king's ordinary revenue, said to be grounded on the consideration of his guarding and protecting the seas from pirates and robbers, is the right to royal fish, which are whale and sturgeon; and these, when either thrown ashore, or caught near the coast, are the property of the king on account of their superior excellence. And this right being the prerogatives of the kings of Denmark and dukes of Normandy, is expressly claimed and allowed in the statute *de prærogativa regis.* (*Plowd.* 315. *Stiernh. de jure Sueonum, lib.* 2, *c.* 8. *Gr. coustom. cap.* 17. 17 *Edw.* 2, *c.* 11.) And the most ancient treatises of law now extant make mention of it, though they seem to have made a distinction between whale and sturgeon.—*Bracton. l.* 3. *c.* 3. *Britton. c.* 17. *Fleta. l.* 1. *c.* 45 & 46. *Memorand. Scacch. H.* 24 *Edw.* 1. 37, prefixed to Maynard's year book of Edward 2.

11. Another maritime revenue, and founded partly upon the same reason, is that of shipwrecks, which are also declared to be the king's property by the same prerogative stat. 17 *Edw.* 2, *c.* 11, and were so, long before, at the common law, upon general principles of policy and convenience; for if every person was permitted to carry home what he found upon the sea-coast, the true owner would stand a very poor chance of recovering back his property: therefore, for the benefit of the owner, the law places it in the custody of the sheriff or a public officer of the crown, where it will be preserved safely and honestly, and to whom the owner is directed to make inquiries for the property he has lost.—And at a time when a rightful claimant is despaired of, it is very properly applied to the augmentation of the public revenue.

12. A twelfth branch of the royal revenue, the right to mines, has its original from the king's prerogative of coinage, in order to

supply him with materials; and therefore those mines, which are properly royal, and to which the king is entitled when found, are only those of silver and gold. 2 *Inst.* 577. *Plowd.* 336.

13. To the same original may in part be referred the revenue of treasure-trove, (derived from the French word, *trover*, to find) called in Latin *thesaurus inventus*, which is where any money or coin, gold, silver, plate, or bullion, is found hidden in the earth, or other private place, the owner thereof being unknown; in which case the treasure belongs to the king: but if he that hid it be known, or afterwards found out, the owner and not the king is entitled to it. 3 *Inst.* 132. *Dalt. of Sheriffs*, c. 16.

14. Waifs, *bona waviata*, are goods stolen, and waived or thrown away by the thief in his flight, for fear of being apprehended. These are given to the king by the law, as a punishment upon the owner for not himself pursuing the felon, and taking away his goods from him; and therefore if the party robbed do his diligence immediately to follow and apprehend the thief, (which is called making fresh suit,) or do convict him afterwards, or procure evidence to convict him, he shall have his goods again. *Cro. Eliz.* 694. *Finch. L.* 212.

15. Estrays are such valuable animals as are found wandering in any manor or lordship, and no man knoweth the owner of them, in which case the law gives them to the king as the general owner and lord paramount of the soil, in recompense for the damage which they may have done therein, and they now most commonly belong to the lord of the manor by special grant from the crown.

16. The next branch of the king's ordinary revenue consists in forfeitures of lands and goods for offences and deodands.

17. Another branch of the king's ordinary revenue arises from escheats of lands, which happen upon the defect of heirs to succeed to the inheritance; whereupon they in general revert to and vest in the king, who is esteemed, in the eye of the law, the original proprietor of all the lands in the kingdom.

18. The last branch of the king's ordinary revenue, consists in the custody of idiots. For which see *Idiots* and *Lunatics*.

This is a short view of the king's ordinary revenue, or the proper patrimony of the crown; which was very large formerly, and capable of being increased to a magnitude truly formidable. But this hereditary land revenue, by a series of improvident management, is sunk almost to nothing; and the casual profits arising from the other branches of the *census regalis*, are likewise almost all of them alienated from the crown. In order to supply the deficiencies of which, we are now obliged to have recourse to new methods of raising money, unknown to our early ancestors; which methods constitute the king's EXTRAORDINARY REVENUE. For, the public patrimony being got into the hands of private subjects, it is but reasonable that private contributions should supply the public service. Individuals being, in common reason, bound to contribute a portion of their private gains, in order to support that government, and reward that magistracy, which protects them in the enjoyment of their respective properties; who, when properly taxed, contribute only some part of their property, in order to enjoy the rest. 1 *Black.* 307.

These taxes, which are raised upon the subject, and compose the king's *extraordinary revenue*, are carried to and form what is called the consolidated fund.

This revenue is subject to the payment of the interest of the public debt and other national charges. But, before any part of the fund can be applied to such purposes, it stands mortgaged by parliament to raise an annual sum for the maintenance of the king's household and the *civil list*. For his present majesty having, soon after his accession, spontaneously signified his consent, that his own hereditary revenues might be so disposed of, as might best conduce to the utility and satisfaction of the public; and having graciously accepted the limited sum of 800,000*l.* *per annum* for the support of his civil list; the said hereditary and other revenues (thus amounting to one million or more) were carried into and made a part of what was at that time called the aggregate fund, since converted into *the consolidated fund**, and that fund was charged (*stat.* 1 *Geo.* 3. *c.* 1.) with the payment of the whole annuity to the crown of 800,000*l.* which being found insufficient, was increased in 1777 by 17 *Geo.* 3. *c.* 21. to 900,000*l.* *per annum*, since which, a further sum of 60,000*l.* has been added to the civil list, by 44 *Geo.* 3. *c.* 80. Hereby the revenues themselves, being put under the same care and management as the other branches of the public patrimony, produce more and are better collected than heretofore; and the public thereby gain near 100,000*l.* *per annum* by the disinterested conduct of his majesty.†

The expences defrayed by the civil list are those that in any shape relate to civil government; as, the expences of the royal

---

* By 27 *Geo.* 3. *c.* 13. the 800,000*l.* by 1 *Geo.* 3. *c.* 1. and 100,000*l.* by 17 *Geo.* 3. *c.* 21. payable out of the *aggregate* fund, shall be paid out of the *consolidated* fund.

† The revenue of the commnowealth under *Cromwell*, was upwards of 1,500,000*l.* which is a striking instance to prove, that the burdens of the people are not necessarily lightened by a change in the government. 2 *Sinc. Hist. Rev.* xiv.

household; the revenues allotted to the judges, previous to the year 1758; all salaries to officers of state, and every of the king's servants; the appointments to foreign embassadors; the maintenance of the queen and royal family; the king's private expences, or privy purse; and other very numerous outgoings, as secret service money, pensions, and other bounties: which sometimes have so far exceeded the revenues appointed for that purpose, that application has been made to parliament to discharge the debts contracted on the civil list.

And by 44 *Geo.* 3. *c.* 80 for the prevention of the accumulation of debt on the civil list in future, an account of the accumulation of arrears in any of the classes of the civil list, shall be laid before parliament within one month after the same shall have arisen *if sitting:* or if not within the first 14 days of the next session.

KINGELD, escuage or loyal aid. *Cowel. Blount.*

KING OF HERALDS, *rex heraldorum.* See *Herald* and *Garter.*

KING OF THE MINSTRELS, at Tutbury *in com. Staff.* His power and privileges appears by a charter of Rich. II. confirmed by Hen. VI. in the 21st year of his reign, to be to licence trumpeters and other minstrels. *Cowel. Blount.*

KING'S BENCH, (*bancus regius*) from the Sax. *banca*, a bench or form.

The court of king's bench is so called because the king used formerly to sit there in person (4 *Inst.* 73.), (the stile of the court still being *coram ipso rege*) is the supreme court of common law in the kingdom; consisting of a chief justice and three *puisne* justices, who are by their offices, the sovereign conservators of the peace and supreme coroners of the land. Yet, though the king himself used to sit in this court, and still is supposed so to do; he did not, neither by law is he empowered (*Dial. de Scacch. l.* 1. *c.* 4. 4 *Burr.* 851.) to determine any cause or motion, but by the mouth of his judges, to whom he hath committed his whole judicial authority (4 *Inst.* 71.)

This court (which as we have said) is the remnant of the *aula regia*, is not, nor can be, from the very nature and constitution of it, fixed to any certain place, but may follow the king's court wherever it goes; for which reason all process issuing out of this court in the king's name is returnable "*ubicunque fuerimus in Anglia.*" It hath, indeed, for some centuries past, usually sate at Westminster, being an antient palace of the crown; but might remove with the king to York or Exeter, if he thought proper to command it. And we find that, after Edward I. had conquered Scotland, it actually sate at Roxburgh (*M.* 20. 21 *Edw.* 1. *Hale's Hist. C. L.* 200.) And this moveable quality, as well as its dignity and power, are fully expressed by Bracton, when he says that the justices of this court are "*capitales, generales, perpetui, et* "*majores; a latere regis residentes; qui om-* "*nium aliorum corrigere tenentur injurias et* "*errores* (*l.* 3. *c.* 10.)" And it is moreover especially provided in the *articuli super cartas* (28 *Edw.* 1. *c.* 5.) that the king's chancellor, and the justices of his bench shall follow him, so that he may have at all times near unto him some that be learned in the laws.

The jurisdiction of this court is very high and transcendent. It keeps all inferior jurisdictions within the bounds of their authority, and may either remove their proceedings to be determined here, or prohibit their progress below. It superintends all civil corporations in the kingdom. It commands magistrates and others to do what their duty requires, in every case where there is no other specific remedy. It protects the liberty of the subject, by speedy and summary interposition. It takes cognizance both of criminal and civil causes; the former in what is called the crown-side or crown-office; the latter in the plea-side of the court. The jurisdiction of the crown-side is confined to pleas of the crown. But on the plea-side, or civil branch, it hath an original jurisdiction and cognizance of all trespasses, and other injuries, alleged to be committed *vi et armis:* which, being a breach of the peace, savour of a criminal nature, although the action is brought for a civil remedy; and for which the defendant ought, in strictness, to pay a fine to the king, as well as damages to the injured party (*Finch. l.* 198.) This court might likewise, upon the division of the *aula regia*, have originally held plea of any other civil action whatsoever, (excepting actions real, which are now very seldom in use) provided the defendant was an officer of the court; or in the custody of the marshall, or prison-keeper of this court, for a breach of the peace or any other offence (4 *Inst.* 71.) In process of time, by a fiction, this court began to hold plea of all personal actions whatsoever, and has continued to do so for ages (*Ibid.* 72.): it being surmised, that the defendant is arrested for a supposed trespass, which he never has in reality committed; and being thus in the custody of the marshal of this court, the plaintiff is at liberty to proceed against him for any other personal injury: which surmise, of being in the marshal's custody, the defendant is not at liberty to dispute. And these fictions of law, though at first they may startle the student, he will find upon farther consideration to be highly beneficial and useful: especially as this maxim is ever invariably observed, that no fiction shall extend to work an injury; its proper operation being to prevent a mischief, or remedy an inconvenience, that might result from the general rule of law (3 *Rep.* 30. 2 *Roll. Rep.* 502.) So true is it, that *in factione juris semper subsistit æquitas* (11 *Rep.* 51. *Co. Litt.* 150.) In the present case, it gives the suitor his choice of more than one tribunal, before which he may institute his action, and prevents the circuity and delay of justice, by allowing that suit to be originally, and in the first instance, commenced in this court, which after a determination in another, might ultimately be brought before it on a writ of error. For this court is likewise a court of appeal, into which may be removed by writ of error, all determinations of the court of common pleá, and of all inferior courts of record in England. Yet even this so high and honourable court is not the *dernier resort* of the subject; for if he be not satisfied with any determination here, he may remove it by writ of error into the house of lords, or the court of exchequer chamber, as the case may happen, according to the nature of the suit, and the manner in which it has been prosecuted.

KING'S SILVER. See *Fines.*

KING'S SWANHERD, *prædictorum fuerit.* No fowl can be a stray, but a swan. 4 *Inst. fol.* 280.

KINTAL, is a certain weight of merchandise, most commonly of one hundred pounds. *Plowden, fol.* 3. *Cowel. Blount.*

KINTLIDGE, a ship's ballast. *Cowel.*

KIPE, (from the Sax. *cypa*) a basket or engine made of osiers, broad at one end, and narrower by degrees, used in Oxfordshire and other parts, for taking of fish. *Ibid.*

KIPPER-TIME. No salmon shall be taken between Gravesend and Henley upon Thames in kipper-time, *viz.* between the Invention of the Cross, (3 May) and the Epiphany. *Rot. Parl.* 50 *Edw.* 3. *Cowel.* But see *Fish.*

KIRBY'S QUEST, an ancient record remaining with the remembrancer of the exchequer; so called from its being the inquest of John de Kirby, treasurer to king Edw. I. *Cowel.*

KIRK-MOTE, a synod; and sometimes taken for a meeting in the church or vestry. *Cowel. Blount.*

KNAVE, an old Saxon word, which at first, signified a boy; Sax. *cnapa*, hence a knave child, *i. e.* a boy distinguished from a girl; afterwards it was taken for a servant boy, and at length for any servant man: also it was applied to a minister or officer, that bore the weapon or shield of his superior, as *scild knapa*, whom the Latins called *armiger*, and the French *escuyer.* 14 *Ed.* 3. *c.* 3. And it was sometimes of old made use of as a titular addition; as *Johannes C. filius Willielmi C. de Derby*, knave, &c. 22 *Hen.* 7. *c.* 36. The word is now perverted to the hardest meaning, *viz.* a false and deceitful fellow. And Wickliff in his old translation, *Exod.* 1. xvi. if it be a knave-child, *i. e.* a son or male child. In the vision of Piers Plowman, cokes and her knaves *cryden hotes pyes, hote, i. e.* cooks and their boys, or skullions. *Cowel.*

KNIGHT, (Sax. *cynt*, Lat. *miles*, and *eques auratus*, from the gilt spurs he usually wore, and thence called anciently knights of the spur: the Italians term them *cavalieri*, the French *chevaliers*, the Germans *ruyters*, the Spaniards *cavallaro's*, &c.) In its original sense, it properly signified a servant; *but there is now but one instance here where it is taken in that sense*, and that is KNIGHT OF A SHIRE, who properly *serves in parliament* for such a county.

In all other instances, it signifies one who bears arms, who, for his virtue and martial prowess, is by the king, or one having his authority, exalted above the rank of gentleman to a higher degree of dignity. *Cowel. Blount.* 2 *Black.* 69. 4 *Black.* 432.

KNIGHTEN-GYLD, was a gyld in London, consisting of nineteen knights, which king Edgar founded, giving them a portion of void ground lying without the walls of the city, now called Portsoken-ward. *Stow. Cowel.*

KNIGHTHOOD. Formerly when the heir came of full age, provided he held a knight's fee, he was to receive the order of knighthood, and was compellable to take it upon him, or else to pay a fine to the king. 2 *Black.* 69.

But this being considered in the reign of Charles I. as a great grievance, the stat. 16 *Car.* 1. *c.* 20. was passed, whereby it was enacted, "that none shall be compelled to take knighthood."

KNIGHTS BACHELORS, is the most ancient, though the lowest order of knighthood amongst us; for we have an instance of king Alfred's conferring this order on his son Athelstan. *Wil. Malms. lib.* 2. 1 *Black.* 404.

KNIGHTS BANERET, (*milites vexillarii*) are made only in the time of war, and is a high honour: and though knighthood is commonly given for some personal merit, which therefore dies with the person; yet John Coupland, for his valiant service performed against the Scots, had the honour of baneret conferred on him and his heirs for ever, by patent. 29 *Ed.* 3. See *Baneret.*

KNIGHTS OF THE BATH, (*milites balnei*) have their name from their bathing the night before their creation. This order of knights was introduced by king Henry IV. and revived by king George the first in the year 1725; who erected the same into a regular military order for ever, by the name and title of The Order of the Bath, to consist of thirty-seven knights, besides the sovereign. They have each three honorary esquires; and they now wear a red ribband across their shoulders; have a prelate of the order, who is the bishop of Rochester, several heralds, and other officers. *Black.* 404.

KNIGHTS OF THE CHAMBER, (*milites cameræ*) seem to be such knights bachelors as are made in time of peace, because knighted in the king's chamber, and not in the field. 1 *Black. Com.* 404.

KNIGHTS OF THE GARTER, (*equites garterii*, or *periscelidis*) are an order of knights, founded by king Edward III. who after he had obtained many notable victories, for furnishing this honourable order, made choice in his own realm, and all Europe, of twenty-five the most excellent and renowned persons for virtue and honour, and ordained himself and his successors kings of England, to be the sovereign thereof, and the rest to be fellows and brethren, bestowing this dignity on them, and giving them a blue garter, decked with gold, pearl, and precious stones, and a buckle of gold, to wear daily upon the left leg only, a kirtle, crown, cloak, chaperon, a collar, and other magnificent apparel, both of stuff and fashion; exquisite and heroical to wear at high feasts, as to so high and princely an order was meet. *Smith's Repub. Ang. lib.* 1. *cap.* 20. And, according to Camden and others, this order was instituted upon king Edward the Third's having great success in a battle, wherein the king's garter was used for a token: and it is the first personal dignity after the nobility.

It is also said, that the king in the height of his glory, the kings of France and Scotland being both prisoners in the Tower of London at one time, first erected this order, *anno* 1350, from the Countess of Salisbury's dropping her garter, in a dance before his majesty, which the king taking up, and seeing some of his nobles smile, he said, *honi soit qui mal y pense*, interpreted, evil (or shame) be to him that evil thinketh, which has ever since been the motto of the garter.

Charles I. as an addition to the splendor, ordered all the knights companions to wear on their upper garment, the cross incircled with the garter and motto. This honorable society is dedicated to St. George; and they are a college or corporation, having a great seal, &c.

The site of the college is the royal castle of Windsor, with the chapel of St. George, and the chapter-house in the castle, for their solemnity on St. George's day, and at their feasts and installations. Besides, the king their sovereign, and twenty-five companions, knights of the garter, they have a dean and canons, &c. and twenty-six poor knights, that have no other subsistence but the allowance of this house, which is given them in respect of their daily prayer to the honour of God and St, George; and these are vulgarly called poor knights of Windsor.

There are also certain officers belonging to the order; as prelate of the garter, which office is inherent to the bishop of Winchester, for the time being; the chancellor of the Garter who is the bishop of Sarum; register, always dean of Windsor; the principal king at arms, called garter, to manage and marshal their solemnities, and the usher of the garter, being likewise usher of the black rod.

A knight of the garter wears daily abroad, a blue garter decked with gold, pearl, and precious stones on the left leg; and in all places of assembly, upon his coat on the left side of his breast, a star of silver embroidery; and the picture of St. George, enamelled upon gold and beset with diamonds, at the end of a blue ribbon that crosses the body from the left shoulder; and when dressed in his robes, a mantle collar of S S. &c.

KNIGHTS COURT, is a court baron, or honour-court, held twice a year under the bishop of Hereford, at his palace there, wherein those who are lords of manors, and their tenants, holding by knight's service of the honour of that bishoprick, are suitors; which court is mentioned in Butterfield's *Surv. fol.* 244. If the suitor appears not at it, he pays 2*s*. suit-silver for respite of homage. *Cowel.*

KNIGHT'S-FEE, (*feodum militare*) is so much inheritance, as is sufficient yearly to maintain a knight with convenient revenue; which, in Henry the Third's days, was 15*l*. *Cam. Britan. pag.* 111. But sir Thomas Smith (in his *Repub. Angl. lib.* 1. *cap.* 18.) rates it at 40*l*. and by the statute for knights, 1 *Ed.* 2. *cap.* 1. such as had 20*l*. per ann. in fee, or for life, might be compelled to be knights; which statute is repealed by 17 *Car.* 1. *cap.* 20. Stow, in his *Annals, p.* 285. says, there were found in England, at the time of the conqueror, 60,211 knights-fees, according to others, 60,215; whereof the religious houses, before their suppression, were possessed of 28,015. *Oct. carucatæ terræ faciunt feodum unius militis. Mon. Angl. pag.* 2. *fol.* 825. *a.* of this you may read more in Selden's Title of Honour, *fol.* 691, and Bracton, *lib.* 5. *tract.* 1. *cap.* 2. See *Coke on Lit. fol.* 69. *a.* A knight's-fee contained twelve plow-lands. 2 *Inst. fol.* 596. or 680 acres. *Virgata terra continet* 24 *acras*, 4 *virgatæ terræ* make an hide, and five hides make a knight's-fee, whose relief is five pounds. *Cowel.* See 1 *Black.* 405, 409. 2 *Black.* 62.

KNIGHTS OF ST. JOHN OF JERUSALEM, (*milites sancti Johannis Hierosolymitani*) were an order of knighthood, that began about the year 1120. They had their denomination from John the charitable patriarch of Alexandria, though vowed to St. John the Baptist their patron. *Fern.* 127. They had their primary abode in Jerusalem, and then in the isle of Rhodes, until they were expelled thence by the Turks, *anno* 1523. Since which time, their chief seat is in the Isle of Malta. They live after the order of friers. They had in England one general prior that had the government of the whole order within England and Scotland. *Reg. Orig. fol.* 20. and was the first prior in England, and sate in the house of lords. But towards the end of Henry the Eighth's days, they in England and Ireland, being found to adhere to the pope too much against the king, were suppressed, and their lands and goods given to the king, by the 32 *Hen.* 8. *c.* 24.

KNIGHT OF MALTA. See *last article*.

KNIGHT MARSHAL, (*mareschallus hospitii regis*) an officer of the king's house, having jurisdiction and cognizance of transgressions within the king's house, and verge of it; as also of contracts made within the same house, whereto one of the house is a party. See *Marshalsea*.

KNIGHTS OF RHODES. Knights of St. John of Jerusalem.

KNIGHTS OF ST. PATRICK, an illustrious order of knighthood instituted by his majesty *K. Geo.* III. 5 Feb. 1783, to consist of the sovereign, grand master, the lord lieutenant of Ireland for the time being, a prince of the blood royal, and thirteen knights.

KNIGHTS SERVICE, (*servitium militare*) a tenure whereby lands were held of the king; which drew after it homage, and service in war, escuage, wardship, marriage, &c. taken away by stat. 12 *Car.* 2. *cap.* 24.

KNIGHTS OF THE SHIRE, (*milites comitatus*) are two knights or gentlemen of worth, chosen on the king's writ, *in pleno comitatu*, by the freeholders of every county that can dispend 40*s.* a year; to represent them in the house of commons; but now *notabiles armigeri* may be chosen. 1 *Hen.* 5. *c.* 1. 10 *Hen.* 6. *c.* 2. 23 *Hen.* 6. *c.* 6. Their expences were formerly to be borne by the county, at the rate of 4*s. per diem*, during their sitting in parliament, by 35 *Hen.* 8. *c.* 11. And as to their qualifications, they are to have 600*l. per ann.* freehold estate.

KNIGHTS TEMPLARS, (*milites templarii*) were a religious order of knights, instituted in the year 1119, and so called, because they dwelt in part of the buildings belonging to the Temple at Jerusalem, and not far from the Sepulchre of *Jesus Christ*. They entertained Christian strangers and pilgrims, and in their armour, led them through the Holy Land, to view the sacred monuments of Christianity, without danger from infidels. This order was far spread in Christendom, particularly here in England, where it flourished in the time of Henry II. And had in every nation, a particular governor or master, but at length, some of them at Jerusalem falling away to the Saracens from Christianity, the whole order was suppressed by *Clemens quintus, anno* 1307. And their substance given partly to the knights of St. John of Jerusalem, and partly to other religious. *Cassan. de Gloria Mundi, par.* 9. These knights at first, wore a white garment; and afterwards, in the pontificate of pope Eugenius, it was ordained that they should wear a red cross: in ancient records, they were also called *fratres Militiæ Templi solomonis. Mon. Angl. tom.* 2. *p.* 554.

KNIGHTS OF THE THISTLE, an honourable order of Scotch knighthood, the knights whereof wear a green ribbon over their shoulders, and are otherwise honourably distinguished.

KNOPA, knob, nob, bosse, or knot.

KNOWN-MEN. The Lollards in England, called heretics, for opposing the church of Rome before the reformation, went commonly under the name of known-men. *Cowel. Blount.*

KYLYW, some liquid thing; and in the North, used for a kind of liquid victuals. *Ibid.*

KYSTE, (Sax.) a coffin or chest for burial of the dead. *Ibid.*

KYTH, used for kin or kindred. *Cognatus. Ibid.*

L

LAAS, (*laqueus à lax*, i. e. *fraus*) a net, gin, or snare. *Cowel. Blount.*

LABEL, (*appendix lemniscus*) is a narrow slip of paper or parchment, affixed to a deed, writing or writ, hanging at or out of the same; and an appending seal is called a label. *Ibid.*

LABINA, watery land. *Ibid.*

LABORARIIS, was an ancient writ against persons refusing to serve and do labour, who had no means of living; or against such as, having served in the winter, refused to serve in the summer. *Reg. Orig.* 189. *Cowel. Blount.*

LABOUR, is the foundation of property, and bodily labour bestowed upon any subject which before lay in common to all men, and subject to first occupancy, is universally allowed to give the fairest and most reasonable title to an exclusive property therein. 2 *Black*. 5.

LABOURERS. A species of servants who are only hired by the day or the week, and do not live *intra moenia*, as part of the family; concerning whom, the stat. 5 *Eliz.* c. 4. and some others, have made many very good regulations; 1. Directing that all persons who have no visible effects may be compelled to work: 2. Defining how long they must continue at work in summer and in winter: 3. Punishing such as leave or desert their work: 4. Empowering the justices at sessions, or the sheriff of the county, to settle their wages: 5. Inflicting penalties on such as either give, or exact, more wages than are so settled.

By 5 *Eliz. c.* 4. no person shall be hired or taken into service for less time than a year, in the mysteries or arts of a taylor, shoemaker, tanner, pewterer, baker, brewer, glover, cutler, smith, farrier, currier, sadler, spurrier, turner, capper, hatmaker, bowyer, fletcher, arrow-head makers, butchers, cooks, or millers.

Persons unmarried, and persons under thirty years of age, brought up in any of the said arts, may be compelled to serve. *Ibid.*

No person shall put away such servant, nor shall any servant depart from his master before the end of the time, unless for reasonable cause, to be determined by a magistrate. *Ibid.*

No such servant shall depart, or be put away at the end of his term, without one quarter's warning before given, the one to the other. *Ibid.*

Persons between the age of twelve years and sixty, not being apprentices, nor lawfully retained in any employment, nor worth 10*l.* may be compelled to serve by the year in husbandry. *Ibid.*

No such retained persons shall depart out of the parish after the time expired, without a testimonial of their liberty to serve elsewhere, nor shall they be retained without shewing such testimonial, on pain of 5*l.* on the master hiring, and imprisonment and whipping as a vagabond, on the servant not having the same, or forging one. *Ibid.*

Labourers, artificers, and others, shall continue at work during the proper hours, and not depart before it be finished, upon pain of imprisonment, and 5*l.* *Ibid.*

The wages of labourers, artificers, and servants, shall be assessed by the chief magistrates every year, on pain of 10*l.* and proclamation shall be made of the rates of the wages; and any master or labourer giving or taking more wages than allowed, shall be imprisoned, and the master moreover forfeit 5*l.* *Ibid.*

Every retainer contrary to this statute, shall be void. *Ibid.*

Servant assaulting his master, mistress, or overseers, shall be imprisoned a year, or less. *Ibid.*

Artificers may be compelled to work in hay time and harvest, and if they refuse, they may be imprisoned in the stocks two days and one night. *Ibid.*

Persons unemployed, may go into other shires for work in harvest time, bringing a testimonial. *Ibid.*

Women may be compelled to serve that be above twelve, and under forty years old, unmarried and forth of service *Ibid.*

This act does not extend to London or Norwich. The justices of the peace shall assemble twice in the year, for due execution of this statute, and shall be allowed 5*s.* a day out of the penalties thereof. *Ibid.*

Justices of peace may grant writs of *capias* against such servants as depart from their masters, and go into other shires. *Ibid.*

By 1 *Jac.* 1. *c.* 6. labourers, weavers, spinsters, and workmens' wages, may be rated by the justices, by the year, day, week, or month, or by the great, whereof proclamation is to be made by the sheriff in the county. And clothiers or others not paying the wages rated, shall forfeit to the workmen ten shillings. But no clothier, being a justice of peace, shall rate any wages in that branch of business.

By 20 *Geo.* 2. *c.* 19. differences between masters and servants in husbandry, artificers, handicrafts, miners, colliers, keelmen, pitmen, glassmen, potters, and other labourers, shall be determined by a justice of peace, who is to examine upon oath, and to make order for payment of wages, not exceeding the sum of ten pounds, with regard to servants, and not exceeding five pounds, with respect to the other persons, and on nonpayment to be levied by distress.

Justices to hear master's complaint on oath, and to punish the offender by commitment, abatement of wages, or dismission; also to hear such servant's complaint on oath, and to summon the master, and, on satisfactory proof, to discharge the servant. *Ibid.*

This act was not to extend to the stannaries in Devon and Cornwall. *Ibid.* But this exclusion by the 27 *Geo.* 2. *c.* 6. was repealed without prejudice to the stannary courts.

And the 31 *Geo.* 2. *c.* 11. extended the act to all servants employed in husbandry, though hired for less time than a year.

See also *Combinations, Manufactures* and *Servants.*

LACE. See *Manufactures.*

LACERTA, a word signifying a fathom. *Domesday.*

LACHES, (from the Fr. *lascher;* i. e. *laxare*, or *lasche, ignavus*) in our law signifies slackness or negligence. *Lit.* 136. *Co. Lit.* 146.

LACTA, a defect in the weight of money, whence the word lack. *Cowel. Blount.*

LADA, had divers significations, 1st, from the Sax. *lathian*, to convene or assemble, and was taken for a *lath*, or court of justice. 2dly, purgation by trial, from *ladian*. 3dly, a *lade*, or course of water: a broad way. *Spelm. Gloss. Mon. Angl. tom.* 1. *p.* 854. *Cowel.*

LADE, Lode, *i. e.* the mouth of a river, from the Sax. *ladian*, *purgare*, hence *Cricklade*, *Lechlade*, &c. *Cowel.*

LAEDORIUM, reproach. *Camd. cap.* 14. *Cowel.*

LÆSÆ MAJESTATIS CRIMEN, a crime amongst the Romans, equivalent to what we call high treason. Lat. *altaproditio.*

LÆSIONE FIDEI, suits *pro.* The clergy so early as the reign of king Stephen attempted to turn their ecclesiastical courts into courts of equity, by entertaining suits *pro læsione fidei*, as a spiritual offence against conscience, in case of non-payment of debts, or any breach of civil contracts. But they were checked by the constitutions of *Clarendon*, 10 *Hen.* 2, *c.* 15. 3 *Black.* 52.

LAFORDSWICK, (Sax. *hlaford*, i. e. *dominus*, and *swic*, *proditio*,) a betraying one's lord or master. *Cowel. Blount.*

LAGA, (*lex*,) the law. Hence *Saxonlage. Ibid.*

LAGAN, Goods sunk in the sea, from the Sax. *liggan cubare*, when mariners in danger of shipwreck cast goods out of the ship, and because they know they are heavy, and sink, fasten a buoy or cork to them, that they may find and have them again. If the ship be lost, these goods are called *lagan*, and so long as they continue upon the sea belong to the lord admiral; but if they are cast away upon the land they are then a wreck, and belong to the lord entitled to the same. 5 *Co. Rep.* 106. At first *lagan* was that right which the chief lord of the fee had to take goods cast on shore by the violence of the sea, &c. *Bract. lib.* 3. *c.* 2. See Wreck.

LAGEDAYUM, *Laghday*, a law-day, or time of open court. *Cowel. Blount.*

LAGEMAN. (*legamannus*) *Homo habens legem*, or *homo legalis seu legitimus*, what we now call good men of the jury. *Blount.*

LAGEN, (*lagena*) *Fleta*, *lib.* 2, *cap.* 8, 9. In ancient times it was a measure of six *sextarii*. Hence, perhaps, our flagon. *Charta* 2 *Edw.* 3, *m.* 25, *n.* 82. *Cowel. Blount.*

LAGHDAY, or *lahday*, a time of open court: Law-day. *Ibid.*

LAGHSLITE, LAGSLITE, LAHSLITE, (Sax. *lag*, leg, and slite, *ruptio*,) a breaking or transgressing of the law; sometimes the punishment inflicted for so doing. *Ibid.*

LAGON. See *Lagan.*

LAIA, a broad way in a wood; the same with *lada. Ibid.*

LAIRWITE, LECHERWITE, and LEGERGELDUM, (from the Sax. *legan*, i. e. *concumbere*, and *wite*, *mulcta*.) The privilege of punishing adultery and fornication anciently belonged to the lords of some manors, in reference to their tenants. *Fleta*, *lib.* 1, *c.* 47. 4 *Inst.* 206.

LAITY. The *lay* part of his majesty's subjects are such of the people as are not comprehended under the denomination of clergy.

LAMMAS-DAY, the first of August, so called *quasi* Lamb-mass, on which day the tenants that held land of the cathedral church of York, (which is dedicated to St. Peter *ad vincula*) were bound by their tenure to bring a live lamb into the church at high mass. It is otherwise said to come from the Sax. *hlaffmæsse*, viz. *loaf mass*, as on that day the English made an offering of bread made with new wheat. *Cowel.*

LANCASTER, was erected into a county palatine *anno* 50 *Ed.* 3, and granted by the king to his son John for life, that he should have *jura regalia*, and a kingly power to pardon treasons, outlawries, &c. and make justices of peace and assise within the said county, and all processes and indictments to be in his name; but these royalties were abridged by the statute 27 *Hen.* 8, *c.* 24, though still all writs are witnessed in the name of the owner thereof, and all forfeitures for treason by the common law accrue to them; (4 *Inst.* 205.) and the dukes of Lancaster hold them, but not as counties palatine, for they had not *jura regalia* over those lands, (2 *Lutw.* 1236. 3 *Salk.* 110, 111.) The stat. 37 *Hen.* 8, *c.* 16, annexes lands to the duchy of Lancaster for the enlargement of it. Fines levied before the justices of assise of Lancaster of lands in the county palatine, shall be of equal force with those acknowledged before the justices in the common pleas. (37 *Hen.* 8, *c.* 19.) And process against an outlawed person in the county of Lancaster is to be directed to the chancellor of the duchy, who shall thereupon issue like writs to the sheriff, &c. (5 & 6 *Ed.* 6. 26.) The stat. 17 *Car.* 2, concerning causes of replevin shall be of force in the court of common pleas for the county palatine of Lancaster (19 *Car.* 2, 5.) By the stat. 17 *Geo.* 2, *c.* 7, the chancellor or vice-chancellor may by commission empower persons to take affidavits in any cause, &c. depending in the chancery or courts of session, in any plea whatsoever, civil or criminal. 1 *Black.* 116. 3 *Black.* 78.

LANCETI, *agricolæ quidam, sed ignotæ speciei. Spelm. Cowel.*

LAND, (*terræ*) signifies generally not only arable ground, meadow, pasture, woods, moors, waters, &c. but also messuages and houses; for in conveying the land the buildings pass with it. *Co. Lit.* 4. 19. *Doct. et Stud.* 8. 1 *Vent.* 260. *Co. Lit. lib.* 1, *cap.* 2, *sec.* 14. *Co.* 9 *Rep.* 2 *Black.* 7, 16, 17.

LANDA, a lawn, or open field without wood. *Cowel.*

LANDBOC, (from the Sax. *land* and *boc*, *liber*) a charter or deed, whereby land was held. *Spelm. Gloss.* *Cowel.*

LANDCHEAP, (Sax. *land ceap*, from *ceapan*, to buy and sell) an ancient customary fine, paid at every alienation of land lying within some manor, or liberty of a borough. *Cowel.*

LANDEA, a ditch in marshy lands to carry water into the sea. *Ibid.*

LANDEFRICUS, (*lanfricus*) the lord of the soil, or the landlord. *Ibid.*

LANDEGANDMAN, one of the inferior tenants of a manor. *Ibid.*

LAND-GABLE, a tax or rent issuing out out of land. *Ibid.*

This *landgavel* or *langable* in the register of *Domesday* was a quit-rent for the site of a house, or the land whereon it stood, the same with what we now call ground-rent. *Ibid.*

LANDIMERS, *Agrimensores*, measurers of land, so called of old; hence meers. *Ibid.*

LANDIRECTA. In the Saxon times the duties which were laid on all who held lands were termed *trinoda necessitas*, viz. expedition, *burghbote* and *brigbote*, which duties the Saxons did not call *servitia*, because they were not feodal, arising from the condition of the owners, but *landirecta*, rights that charged the very land whoever possessed it. *Spelman of Feuds.* *Cowel.*

LANDLORD, is he of whom lands or tenements are holden. *Co. Lit.* 57. 205.

LAND-MAN, *terricola*, the terre-tenant. *Cowel.*

LAND-TAX. The ancient mode of charging lands by *scutage*, *hydage*, and *talliage*, was to all intents and purposes a land-tax; and the assessments were sometimes expressly called so. (Com. Journ. 26 Jun. 9 Dec. 1678.) But the land-tax as it now stands was first introduced in the reign of k. William 3, because in the year 1692 a new assessment or valuation of estates was made throughout the kingdom. And the method of raising it, is by charging a particular sum upon each county, according to the valuation given in, A. D. 1692: and this sum is assessed and raised upon individuals (their personal estates, as well as real, being liable thereto) by commissioners appointed from time to time by act of parliament, being the principal landholders of the county, and their officers.

The land tax up to the year 1798, was an annual tax: but by 38 *Geo.* 3, *c.* 60, after reciting "that it may materially conduce to "strengthening and supporting the public "credit, and to augmenting the nation's re"sources at this important conjuncture, that "the duty now payable for one year on land "should be made perpetual, but subject to "redemption and purchase on transferring "to the commissioners for the reduction of "the national debt a certain proportion of "capital stock, in manner therein stated," —it was enacted, that the land tax shall be raised and paid yearly to his majesty and his heirs FOR EVER, subject to redemption under certain rules and conditions. This act was afterwards amended by several other acts, all of which were repealed, and the provisions consolidated and amended by the statute 42 *Geo.* 3. *c.* 116. The consideration for redemption shall (generally speaking) be so much capital stock of the three pounds *per centum* consolidated annuities, or the three pounds *per centum* reduced annuities, as will yield a dividend exceeding the amount of the land tax redeemed by one tenth part thereof. This stock may be transferred by the purchaser all at once, or by instalments, and in certain cases, the redemption may be made by payments in money.

The regulations of this statute are far too numerous to be detailed at large.

The provisions, however, which are contained in this stat. of 42 *Geo.* 3 *c.* 116. as amended by subsequent acts, are in substance as follows:

1. *Commissioners for redemption and sale of the land tax.*]—By 42 *Geo.* 3, *c.* 116. his majesty may appoint commissioners of the land tax to be commissioners for selling the land tax, who are to be sworn, and they may examine and receive information on oath from persons desirous of advancing or purchasing any land tax, or relating to persons entitled in remainder, and may require inspection of any deeds relating to persons claiming preference, and they may receive affidavits made in or out of Great Britain, and two of the commissioners may contract for the redemption of the land tax, according to the assessment made under 38 *Geo.* 3, *c.* 5, for the year the contract shall be entered into. *s.* 5—8.

But his majesty is to appoint members of the privy council to be commissioners for regulating sales by corporations or tenants of the crown, two of whom may act, being sworn, which commissioners may require information and receive depositions as to sales, and employ a secretary, and the sales by corporations and tenants of the crown shall be made under the directions of such commissioners, two of whom shall be made parties. *s.* 72—76.

And such commissioners shall adjust all questions between corporations and their lessees, as to enfranchisement of lands. *s.* 84.

And by 46 *Geo.* 3, *c.* 133, the commissioners appointed under 42 *Geo.* 3. *c.* 116. *s.* 72, may exonerate small livings and charitable institutions from the land tax without any consideration, provided the annual amount in the whole doth not exceed 6000l. *s.* 2.

But incumbents of such livings and trustees of such charities, shall transmit statements of the income of such living or charity, and certificates of the amount of l. and tax within six months after 22d July, 1806, or six months further, if the commissioners think fit to extend the time, *s.* 3; and the commissioners may by indorsement on the certificate of land tax, declare the lands exonerated, *s.* 4; which certificates of exoneration shall be registered gratis, *s.* 5; and the proceedings of the commissioners are to be laid before parliament before the end of the year 1809. *s.* 6.

II. *Parties empowered to contract.*]—By 42 *Geo.* 3. *c.* 116, corporations and trustees for public purposes, are empowered to contract. *s.* 9.

Corporations or trustees for public purposes, are empowered to sell or mortgage lands, or grant rent charges to redeem land tax, but no such sale or mortgage shall be made but for redeeming the land tax. *s.* 69.

When the reversion of lands holden under corporations by lease for lives, shall be purchased by the person beneficially entitled to the profits, but not having the absolute interest, they shall be bound to renew, at their own charge, the interests under the lease, and the reversion shall, under the directions of the said commissioners, be chargeable with the money advanced and interest, and settled by them, but where the immediate estates are charged with such payment, the persons entitled to the rents shall be chargeable with interest, and the commissioners may direct an application to chancery for obtaining its directions, as to the mode of settlement of the reversion or equity of redemption. *s.* 85.

Corporations may purchase of their lessees the land tax redeemed by them, and may sell lands for that purpose as in the first instance; or if money shall be in the Bank, from sales previously made, it may be applied in such purchase. *s.* 86.

All persons interested, are empowered to contract, except tenants at rack rent, or tenants for years, or at will, or tenants of crown lands, or the duchy of *Lancaster* or *Cornwall.* *s.* 10.

And the surveyor general of the land revenues of the crown, with the consent of the treasury; receiver general of the duchy of *Lancaster*, with consent of the chancellor; and surveyor-general of the duchy of *Cornwall*, are empowered to agree for the redemption of the land tax within their respective surveys. *s.* 131.

His majesty may appoint persons, to ascertain the land tax on crown lands, within the survey of the exchequer, a report of which shall be sent to the treasury. *s.* 132.

Surveyor general of the land revenues may contract for sale of crown lands, to redeem the land tax; and the money shall be paid into the bank and laid out in 3*l.* per cent. consols. *s.* 133.

But such contracts shall be made by special warrant of the treasury. *s.* 134.

The chancellor and council of the duchy of Lancaster, may appoint persons to ascertain the land tax on crown lands within their survey, to be reported to them. *s.* 135.

Surveyor general shall give certificate of contracts to purchasers of crown lands, on production of which the bank shall receive the consideration, and give a receipt, which with the certificate, shall be enrolled with the auditor of the land revenue, or clerk of the peace, which shall complete the purchase. *s.* 136.

The expence of surveys may be paid out of the purchase money. *s.* 137.

Chancellor of the duchy of Lancaster may sell lands to redeem the land tax, and the purchase money shall be paid to the receiver-general of the duchy. *s.* 139.

The treasurer and chancellor of the duchy of Lancaster respectively may, from the produce of sales, transfer to commissioners for the national debt the stock necessary to redeem land tax on crown lands. *s.* 140.

Crown lands shall thereupon be exonerated from the land tax, and the amount considered as rent from lessees and under lessees. *s.* 141.

The prince of *Wales* may appoint persons to ascertain the land tax on lands of the duchy of *Cornwall*, to be reported to his council, and a copy sent to the surveyor-general of the duchy, which surveyor-general may contract for the sale of lands to redeem the land tax, and the purchase money shall be paid into the bank, but such contracts are to be by special warrants. *s.* 142—144.

The bank shall open an account with the duchy of *Cornwall*, and the surveyor-general shall give purchasers of lands a certificate of contracts, on which the bank shall give receipts, which, with the certificates, shall be inrolled with the auditor of the duchy. *s.* 145.

Contracts with the crown and duchy of *Cornwall*, if not certified and enrolled, and money paid within 40 days, shall be void, unless the surveyors-general order the certificate to be enrolled, *nunc pro tunc.* *s.* 146.

Money paid into the Bank on account of the duchy shall be invested in the 3*l. per cents.* in the name of the duke of *Cornwall*, and the dividends be paid to the receiver of the duchy. *s.* 147.

The prince's council may transfer stock

to the commissioners for the reduction of the national debt, for the redemption of the land tax, and the lands of the duchy shall thereupon be exonerated from land tax, which shall be considered as rent payable by the lessees. *s.* 148, 149.

Where lessees of crown lands within the survey of the exchequer, may have improperly proceeded to redeem the land tax, the treasury may re-transfer to them the amount of any consideration, whereupon his majesty shall be entitled to land tax, and the parties shall acknowledge the transfer, which shall be registered as a contract, stamp duty free, but such lessees may receive the land tax up to the preceding quarter. *s.* 150.

Any one or more co-parceners or joint tenants may contract for redemption of their own proportion, and the proportion of others refusing, on three months notice, *s.* 11. [See also *s.* 93, under sec. 4 of this title.]

Where one or more co-parceners shall redeem their land tax, their allotments shall be exonerated immediately on partition. *s.* 39.

Where a co-parcener redeems his own proportion of the land tax and the proportions of others, their lands shall be chargeable to him for their proportions. *s.* 124.

Canal companies, and other works of public utility, are empowered to contract, or proprietors for their proportions of the land tax, as well in the tolls as on the lands. *s.* 12.

And they may redeem by calls under the respective acts by which they are authorised to raise money. *s.* 49.

Shares in water-works, insurance offices, lights, stock in king's printing-office, companies of merchants in London, and the bank, are empowered to contract. *s.* 13.

Committees, trustees, and guardians, are empowered to contract for those for whom they act. *s.* 14.

And they may sell lands for that purpose; but such sales shall be made in England under the authority of the commissioners for the place where the lands lie, and one month's previous notice of such sale shall be given to the commissioners with a schedule of the particulars. *s.* 53, 54, 55.

And the guardians of infants and trustees of married women, may transfer stock standing in the names of such infants, or femes covert, or jointly with themselves for redemption of the land tax. *s.* 128.

Governors of queen Anne's bounty may contract, where incumbents have not. *s.* 15.

And they may apply money in redeeming land tax on livings, and purchasing rent charges granted by incumbents under former acts. *s.* 44.

Trustees for poor clergy may contract, *s.* 16, and lay out trust money in redeeming land tax on livings. *s.* 45.

And the governors of charity for clergymens widows and orphans may sell lands with the consent of the special commissioners. *s.* 77.

And the governors of queen *Anne's* bounty and other trustees for poor clergy so empowered to redeem land tax, may purchase land tax, which shall issue as a fee farm out of the lands, and be annexed to the livings, and accept from others land tax so purchased. *s.* 161.

Colleges and other patrons of livings, may contract where incumbents have not redeemed. *s.* 17.

And they may redeem the land tax on livings belonging to them by sale of any of their lands, and shall be entitled to an equivalent rent-charge out of the living, unless they declare otherwise at the time of presentation. *s.* 78.

And by 45 *Geo.* 3, *c.* 77, the incumbent for the time being may purchase an assignment of the land tax redeemed, by the patron or former incumbent, for the benefit of the living, by sale or mortgage under the regulations of the acts, after which the land tax shall become merged, and the money arising by such sale need not be paid into the Bank, but shall be paid to the assignor. *s.* 1.

III. *Property applicable to the redemption.*] —By 42 *Geo.* 3. *c.* 116. personal property directed to be laid out in the purchase of lands in trust for any corporation or charitable institution, may be applied with the consent of the commissioners, (and of the court, under whose control it may be) in redemption of land tax. *s.* 41.

Trust property may be applied in redemption of land tax on settled lands, and the land tax so redeemed with trust property shall merge in the lands, and when the trust property is insufficient the deficiency may be supplied under this act. *s.* 42, 43.

Land tax on land settled for the benefit of any parish may be redeemed out of the poor or church rates, with the approbation of two justices. *s.* 46.

Such land tax may be redeemed by trust property, and the lands shall be charged with an annuity equal to the trust property so applied, with the like consent of justices. *s.* 47.

Donations to hospitals and charitable institutions may be applied in redemption of land tax. *s.* 48.

And money may be bequeathed to redeem land tax for charitable uses. *s.* 50.

Gifts of land tax redeemed, or purchased for augmentation of livings, shall be valid. *s.* 102.

Where money from sale of lands belonging to corporations, shall be insufficient to redeem the whole land tax, the Bank may receive the deficiency from them. *s.* 87.

Trust property may be laid out by corporations in purchase of land tax, as well as redemption, under s. 41 and 42, and the amount as a fee farm rent shall be settled subject to the same trusts. s. 159.

IV. *Raising money for redemption.*]—By 42 *Geo.* 3, *c.* 116, for redeeming land tax on lands belonging to individuals, the persons in possession, but not having the absolute estate, and persons beneficially entitled to rents, except tenants at rack rent and crown tenants, (see s. 71.) may sell part of such lands, or may mortgage the same, or grant any rent charge to the amount of the land tax, but no such sale shall be made but for redeeming land tax. s. 51.

But tenants for lives or years on fine, may not sell without the consent of the reversioners. s. 57.

Corporations may also sell or mortgage lands, or grant rent-charges to redeem land tax, and they may also enfranchise copyholds for that purpose. s. 69, 70.

Ecclesiastical rectors may redeem land tax on vicarages, by sale of part of the rectorial glebe, and the incumbent of the rectory shall be entitled to an equivalent rent-charge out of the vicarage. s. 122.

Where individuals or corporations have redeemed land tax by advance of money, or contracted for assignment, they may raise money as they might have done in the first instance. s. 91.

Money arising from lands sold for reimbursing sums advanced shall, under the order of the commissioners, be paid to the persons entitled, and the remainder into the Bank. s. 104.

Where any person having an estate, other than of inheritance, shall redeem the land tax with his own property, the estate shall be chargeable with the amount of the consideration and interest, equivalent to the land tax redeemed: reversioners shall be liable to interest only from coming into possession, and reversioners redeeming shall be entitled to such yearly equivalent, until the estate vest in them. s. 123.

Where purchasers die, without completing contracts, the instalments shall be paid out of the assets, and if deficient the contract may be sold, but if the person who shall be come into possession shall be desirous of taking the contract, it may be assigned to him, whether there are assets or not, and the assignees shall complete contracts on the original terms, but the time for payment of instalments may be enlarged by the court of exchequer, or commissioners of taxes. s. 166.

Where trusts, mortgages, or incumbrances, equally affect the whole of lands, part whereof shall be proposed to be sold, the court of chancery in *England*, or session in *Scotland*, may order such part to be conveyed to the purchaser discharged from such trusts. s. 58.

When such sale shall be by auction, ten days previous notice shall be given; when by private contract, an estimate of the value shall be made. s. 59.

Owners of manors in *England*, not being corporations, (see s. 70,) may enfranchise copyholds to redeem land tax. s. 60.

Possessors of lands granted under the crown, or any act of parliament, wherein his majesty hath any estate (except tenants for life, years, or from year to year, or during pleasure,) may sell or enfranchise lands for redeeming land tax. s. 71.

Timber may be cut down and sold by consent of court of chancery or session for redemption, which shall merge in the lands, unless otherwise ordered. s. 67.

Tenants in tail in *England*, may convey by deed enrolled, s. 52, and in *Scotland*, heirs of entail in possession, their tutors and like persons, may sell for redeeming the land tax, under the authority of the court of session; and money borrowed by such heirs on heritable security under the like authority of the court. s. 61, 62.

Owners of fee farm rents may bar the entail by deed enrolled. s. 157.

Where lands are sold at various times, situate in different counties, certificates of former sales shall be granted and produced, and parties may be examined on oath by commissioners. s. 56.

The whole of a farm which cannot be eligibly divided, may be sold, and the surplus disposed of by the court, as under s. 101, 102, and the expences of such sales to be ascertained by the court, may be defrayed out of the purchase money, and such sales shall be by public auction, under articles of sale settled by the court, and the price shall be paid to a trustee, and by him into the Bank. s. 63, 64, 65.

And such sales shall be as valid as if the estate had been unencumbered, saving to the mortgagee his principal and interest. s. 66.

In all cases the whole of lands usually occupied together may be sold, where they cannot be divided without loss. s. 90.

But no more of an estate, except as last-mentioned, shall be sold, nor more money raised than the commissioners shall think necessary for redeeming land tax and paying expenses. s. 95.

Surplus of stock, if any, after transferring sufficient to redeem the land tax from lands in *England*, shall be invested in the name of the accountant-general, and applied by order of chancery for the benefit of parties entitled to the lands. s. 100.

In Scotland such surplus stock shall be sold, and the produce placed in one of the public banks, and applied in like manner by authority of the court of session. s. 101.

But if the surplus do not exceed 200*l.* stock, the same shall be transferred to a trustee without application to the courts. *s.* 102.

And surplus stock, or monies arising from sales for redeeming land tax, may be applied in purchasing land tax as a fee farm rent. *s.* 160.

When any certificate shall be produced for entering into contract for redemption, by a money consideration, the clerk to the commissioners for redemption shall transmit to the tax-office and receiver-general, the amount of land tax proposed to be redeemed, and the terms whereupon the treasury may direct money to be advanced to the commissioners for reducing the national debt, to be applied in purchasing stock to complete contracts. *s.* 37.

And where purchase money is to be paid within the year, and at not more than six instalments, the treasury may, after payment of the first advance, procure money for the immediate completion of the contract. *s.* 106.

Purchasers receiving such advance shall enter into bonds (exempt from duty) to the king for repayment with interest. *s.* 107.

On failure of payment of principal or interest, the treasury or other lenders shall issue certificates to the proper officers of the crown, requiring them to proceed against such defaulters for the sum due, which shall be inserted in the writ, and the money, when recovered, paid into the bank, and no *scire facias* is necessary. *s.* 108.

But on payment, the purchaser's bond shall be delivered up: process may issue against the lands purchased: and persons receiving such advance shall be considered as having completed their contracts. *s.* 110—112.

No duty is payable on sales under this act by auction. *s.* 113.

V. *Proceedings on redemption and sale.*]—By 42 *Geo.* 3. *c.* 116, corporations and persons before described, shall have the preference till June 24, 1803; and corporations, trustees, and persons in possession (except tenants for years or lives on a fine) shall be preferred to those in reversion, till Dec. 25, 1802; and those in reversion to all, having no interest, till said 24th June, 1803. *s.* 18, 19.

After June 24, 1803, parties entitled to preference may redeem on the same terms, except as to periods of transfer, (see *s.* 25) if no other offer shall have been made, (see *s.* 157) and if parties interested give notice of their intent to redeem, the land tax shall not be sold to others for three months; and if parties in possession, viz. those receiving the rack rent give such notice, they shall be preferred to parties in reversion. *s.* 20.

Where corporations shall treat for sale of lands held under demise from them, and obtain a certificate from two commissioners appointed under the great seal, they may, during the period specified therein, be preferred to the beneficial lessees, on producing such certificate to commissioners of sale under this act. *s.* 21.

Parties claiming preference shall produce a description of the property to two commissioners of the land tax, who shall settle and certify the amount of the land tax, which certificate shall be produced to and examined by the commissioners for redemption, who may agree with the parties for the redemption of the land tax. *s.* 30.

Where the commissioners for redemption have copies of assessments of land tax transmitted to them, they may contract with the parties, although they do not produce certificates of the amount; but the description of the estate, and also a copy of the assessment, shall be transmitted to the commissioners, and inserted in the certificate of contract. *s.* 32.

Clerks to the land tax commissioners, when required by the commissioners for redemption, or whenever any alteration shall be made in the assessment, shall transmit copies of such assessment or alteration on pain of 30*l.* *s.* 33.

The consideration for redemption shall be so much stock in the 3*l. per cents.* as will produce a dividend exceeding the amount of the land tax redeemed by one 10th. *s.* 22.

The bank shall transmit weekly accounts of the price of the 3*l.* per cent. consols, or 3*l.* per cent. reduced, respectively to the commissioners for taxes, who shall publish in the Gazette, and transmit to the receiver-general an account of the price, to regulate the considerations for the redemption of land tax in money. *s.* 24.

[And the consideration for such redemption is to be settled according to certain tables set forth in 43 *Geo.* 3. *c.* 51.]

Where the land tax to be redeemed in any place, for which separate commissioners are appointed, shall not exceed 25*l.* per. ann. the consideration may be paid in money to the receiver-general in England, or collector in Scotland. *s.* 23.

The consideration in money may be paid at once, or by instalments, not exceeding eight, payable in two years, according to the price of stock. *s.* 27.

The whole or part of such consideration may be paid in advance, on notice to the receiver-general, who shall transmit to the tax-office an account of such intended payments, which shall be made according to the price of stock ascertained in the week preceding. *s.* 28.

On making the next and subsequent instalments, interest shall be paid, but interests shall cease on payments in advance. *s.* 39.

On production of certificate of contract,

and transfer of the consideration in stock, the cashier of the bank shall indorse a receipt on the certificate of contract, and on a money consideration, the receiver-general shall, on payment, indorse the receipt on the certificate. *s.* 38.

Where lands are sold or are charged for not more than 500*l.* and the consideration for redemption is in money, it may be paid to the receiver-general, and the surplus to a trustee. *s.* 103.

[Where the consideration for the redemption of the land tax by corporations and others entitled to preference, shall be in stock, the same may be transferred to the commissioners for reducing the national debt within sixteen years, by four equal instalments in each year. 46 *Geo.* 3. *c.* 133. *s.* 1.]

When any stock is transferred to the commissioners for the national debt, the dividends thereon shall cease. *s.* 186.

No contracts for redemption under this act, or the amount of the land tax redeemed, shall be any way affected by any appeal from assessment of land tax. *s.* 129.

But if land tax contracted for, shall have been fraudulently reduced within three years, before completion of the contract, it may be altered on appeal within one year. *s.* 130.

Where tythes free from rent or the like have not been, or not distinctly, assessed to the land tax, the commissioners of the land tax may adjust the proportions, and on their certificate the commissioners for redemption may contract; as may also the commissioners for redemption on application to them. *s.* 35, 36.

Mines shall not pass by conveyance of land sold, nor advowsons though appendant to the land. *s.* 80.

Land tax redeemed by bishops, and other ecclesiastical corporations, shall be considered as an additional yearly rent on all demises. *s.* 88.

As shall also land tax redeemed by corporations and charitable institutions on copyhold lands or on lease. *s.* 89.

When land tax on lands (except of bishops), let on beneficial leases, shall be redeemed by sale of part, the unsold parts shall be chargeable to such corporations, with an equivalent rent charge. *s.* 118.

And the interest, or rent charge, shall be payable at the periods when the land tax was. *s.* 125.

Where a tenant is bound to pay land tax, the amount of it, if redeemed by the person entitled to the rent, shall be payable as rent. *s.* 126.

And where the land tax shall be purchased by a tenant not bound to pay it, he may retain the amount out of the rent. *s.* 156.

Money arising from sale shall be paid, except otherwise directed, (see *s.* 95, 91, 104.) into the bank, to the account of the commissioners for the national debt, and invested in 3*l.* per cents. and on the cashier's receipt the land tax shall be redeemed, as if stock had been transferred by the parties. *s.* 98.

Purchase money may be agreed to be paid by instalments into the bank, and purchasers shall be liable to all penalties on default. *s.* 105.

When money is not paid into the bank, but invested in 3*l.* per cents. commissioners for the national debt, shall accept the transfer thereof, and grant a certificate, on the production of which at the bank a receipt shall be given. *s.* 117.

When money has been improperly paid into the bank, the commissioners under the great seal, or commissioners for taxes, may order the money to be repaid, or stock purchased therewith, to be retransferred. *s.* 121.

When stock has been improperly transferred, or money paid to the bank for interest, such stock may be re-transferred on certificate from the tax-office; which may also direct receivers-general to re-pay monies improperly paid. *s.* 171.

When stock shall be re-transferred, the dividends shall be issued, and payable, as if there had been no transfer to the commissioners for the national debt. *s.* 172.

Deeds shall be inrolled in England in one of the courts at Westminster, the counties palatine, or great sessions, within six months, and in Scotland, according to the law of Scotland; but when the consideration does not exceed 200*l.* with the registrar of land tax contracts, and on payment of money and enrolment, the deeds shall be valid. *s.* 114.

And proof of execution of the deeds by the commissioners, shall be evidence, that every thing required was rightly done. *s.* 120.

Contracts shall be registered, and three duplicates made of the amount of land tax redeemed, one for the receiver-general of the county, another for the commissioners of land tax, and another for the king's remembrancer. *s.* 164.

And copies of the registers shall be good evidence of the contracts. *s.* 165.

Where the whole of the land tax shall not before June 24, 1803, be redeemed by parties entitled to preference, the commissioners may contract with any other persons for sale of the part remaining unsold. *s.* 151.

And the consideration for the purchase of such land tax, shall not be less in stock or money than for redemption by parties entitled to preference, transferrable at once, or within one year, by not more than four instalments. *s.* 153.

Persons desirous of purchasing, shall produce to the commissioners of the land tax a statement of the amount of the land tax, which amount the commissioners shall ascertain and certify, and on producing such certificate to the commissioners for executing this act, (who may amend the same) they shall cause notice of the offer to be fixed on the church door for 14 days, and if within that time no offer higher by 1*l.* per cent. shall be made, they may contract for sale, but if such higher offer shall be made, the commissioners shall contract with the party making it, and upon production of the contract at the Bank, and transferring the stock over to the receiver-general, and payment of the consideration, the party shall be entitled to certificates, and on registry of the contract and certificate (see *s.* 38, 164), the lands shall be exonerated from the land tax, and the purchaser entitled to a fee farm rent out of the lands, equal to the land tax redeemed. *s.* 154.

On the desire of the person beneficially interested in the lands, the commissioners may order the whole fee farm rent to be paid out of any part of the lands, equal in annual value to three times the rent, and such part shall be separately described in the contract. *s.* 155.

On default of fulfilling contracts, the land tax shall revive, and the defaulter shall be subject to a penalty not exceeding 1-16th of the consideration. *s.* 167.

Where the penalty on default has not been prosecuted for, the commissioners for the national debt may recover the amount out of any instalments made, and retransfer the remainder. *s.* 170.

Collectors of the land tax in Scotland are to give security for paying to the receiver-general the monies received by such collectors. *s.* 174—176.

When lands of corporations or charitable institutions shall be sold which are subject to any charge, the commissioners shall direct how the same shall be paid in future—so, when part of lands usually demised together, are liable to an ancient rent. *s.* 82, 83.

When any allowance shall be made out of any fee farm rent or other rents, in respect to the land tax, they may be sold, subject to such allowance. *s.* 92.

Grantees of rent charges may recover the same as rents. *s.* 116.

Persons redeeming land tax on lands subject to any fee farm rent, may continue to deduct the proportion of land tax on such fee farm rent. *s.* 127.

Prior mortgages shall not be affected by mortgages under this act, except as to interest, and shall have preference to redeem the land tax. *s.* 114.

But no reversioner is liable to payment of more than one year's arrear of interest on such mortgages. *s.* 115.

Commissioners shall not vacate seats in parliament; nor shall the office of a commissioner be deemed a place of profit under his majesty. *s.* 185.

The investing of money in purchase of land tax under the act 39 *Geo.* 3. *c.* lxxxiii. enabling his majesty to incorporate the Globe Company, and the said company's charter shall be regulated by this act. *s.* 198.

Persons claiming to vote for members of parliament for lands, the land tax whereon has been redeemed, shall be entitled to vote on proving such redemption. *s.* 200.

Penalties to the parties aggrieved, may be sued for in the courts of record with costs; and other penalties exceeding 50*l.* within six months: half to the king, and half to the informer, but the attorney-general, in the latter case, may stay proceeding where there was no fraud. *s.* 189.

Penalties not exceeding 50*l.* are recoverable before two justices. *s.* 190—192.

Persons swearing falsely to be guilty of perjury, *s.* 193—and forging any contract, agreement, certificate, or receipt, is felony without clergy. *s.* 194.

LAND-TENANT, is he that possesses land let, or hath it in his manual occupation.

LANGEMANNI, lords of manors. 1 *Inst.* 5.

LANGEOLUM, an under garment made of wool, formerly worn by the monks, which reached down to their knees; so called because *lanea fil.* *Cowel.*

LANIS DE CRESCENTIA WALLIÆ TRADUCENDIS ABSQUE CUSTUMA, &c. an ancient writ that lay to the customer of a port, to permit one to pass wool without paying custom, he having paid it before in Wales. *Cowel. Blount.*

LANTERIUM, the lantern, *cupolo*, or top of a steeple. *Ibid.*

LANO NIGER, base coin, formerly current in this kingdom. *Ibid.*

LAPIS MARMORIUS, a marble stone about twelve foot long and three foot broad, placed at the upper end of Westminster-hall, where was likewise a marble chair erected on the middle thereof, in which our kings anciently sat at their coronation dinner, and at other times, the lord chancellor. Over this marble table are now erected the courts of chancery and king's bench. *Orig. Jurid.* 37. *Cowel. Blount.*

LAPIS PACIS, the same with *osculum pacis.* *Ibid.*

LAPSE, (*lapsus*) is a slip or omission of a patron to present to a church, within six months after it becomes void; in which case we say, that benefice is in lapse or lapsed. 13 *Eliz.* *c.* 12. And lapse is defined to be a species of forfeiture, whereby the right of presentation to a church accrues to the ordinary by neglect of the patron, to present, to the metropolitan by neglect of the ordinary, and to the king by neglect of the metropolitan. For it being for the interest of religion, and the good of the public, that the church should be provided with an officiating minister, the law has therefore given this right of lapse, in order to quicken the patron; who might otherwise, by suffering the church to remain vacant, avoid paying his ecclesiastical dues, and frustrate the pious intentions of his ancestors. This right of lapse was first established about the time (though not by the authority, 2 *Roll. Abr.* 336. *pl.* 10.) of the council of Lateran (*Bracton, l.* 4. *tr.* 2. *c.* 3.), which was in the reign of our Henry the second, when the bishops first began to exercise universally the right of institution to churches (2 *Black. Com.* 23.) And therefore, where there is no right of institution, there is no right of lapse: so that no donative can lapse to the ordinary (*Bro. Abr. tit. Quar. Imped.* 3 *Cro. Jac.* 518.), unless it hath been augmented by the queen's bounty (*St.* 1 *Geo.* 1. *st.* 2. *c.* 10.) But no right of lapse can accrue, when the original presentation is in the crown (*stat.* 17 *Edw.* 2. *c.* 8. 2 *Inst.* 273.)

If a right of lapse accrues to the bishop and he dies, or is translated before he avails himself of it, the right of presentation to the lapsed benefice does not pass to the king, like the vacant patronage of the see, but to the guardian of the spiritualties. *Gibs.* 770.

The term, in which the title to present by lapse accrues from the one to the other successively, is six calendar months (6 *Rep.* 62. *Regist.* 42.), (following in this case the computation of the church, and not the usual one of the common law,) and this exclusive of the day of the avoidance. (2 *Inst.* 361.) But, if the bishop be both patron and ordinary, he shall not have a double time allowed him to collate in (*Gibs. Cod.* 769.); for the forfeiture accrues by law, whenever the negligence has continued six months in the same person. And also, if the bishop doth not collate his own clerk immediately to the living, and the patron presents, though after the six months are lapsed, yet his presentation is good, and the bishop is bound to institute the patron's clerk (2 *Inst.* 273.) For as the law only gives the bishop this title by lapse, to punish the patron's negligence, there is no reason that, if the bishop himself be guilty of equal or greater negligence, the patron should be deprived of his turn. If the bishop suffer presentation to lapse to the metropolitan, the patron also has the same advantage if he presents before the archbishop has filled up the benefice; and that for the same reason. Yet the ordinary cannot, after lapse to the metropolitan, collate his own clerk to the prejudice of the archbishop (2 *Roll. Abr.* 368.) For he had no permanent right and interest in the advowson, as the patron hath, but merely a temporary one; which having neglected to make use of during the time, he cannot afterwards retrieve it. But if the presentation lapses to the king, prerogative here intervenes and makes a difference; and the patron shall never recover his right till the king has satisfied his turn by presentation: for *nullum tempus occurrit regi* (*Dr. & St. d.* 2. *c.* 36. *Cro. Car.* 355.) And therefore it may seem, as if the church might continue void for ever, unless the king shall be pleased to present; and a patron thereby be absolutely defeated of his advowson. But to prevent this inconvenience, the law has lodged a power in the patron's hands, of as it were compelling the king to present. For if, during the delay of the crown, the patron himself presents, and his clerk is instituted, the king indeed by presenting another, may turn out the patron's clerk; or, after induction, may remove him by *quare impedit:* but if he does not, and the patron's clerk dies incumbent, or is canonically deprived, the king hath lost his right, which was only to the next or first presentation (7 *Rep.* 28. *Cro. Eliz.* 44.)

In case the benefice becomes void by death, or cession through plurality of benefices, there the patron is bound to take notice of the vacancy at his own peril; for these are matters of equal notoriety to the patron and ordinary: but in case of a vacancy by resignation, or canonical deprivation, or if a clerk presented be refused for insufficiency, these being matters of which the bishop alone is presumed to be cognizant, here the law requires him to give notice thereof to the patron, otherwise he can take no advantage by way of lapse (4 *Rep.* 75. 2 *Inst.* 632.) Neither shall any lapse thereby accrue to the metropolitan or to the king; for it is universally true, that neither the archbishop or the king shall ever present by lapse, but where the immediate ordinary might have collated by lapse, within the six months, and hath exceeded his time: for the first step or beginning faileth, *et quod non habet principium, non habet finem* (*Co. Litt.* 344, 345.) If the bishop refuse or neglect to examine and admit the patron's clerk, without good reason assigned or notice given, he is stiled a disturber by the law, and shall not have any title to present by lapse; for no man shall take advantage of his own wrong (2 *Roll. Abr.* 369.) Also, if the right of presentation be litigious or contested, and an action be brought against the bishop to try the title, no lapse shall incur till the question of right be decided. (*Co. Lit.* 344.)

LAPSED-LEGACY. A legacy will lapse and fall into the undisposed part of a testator's personal estate, if the legatee dies before the testator, or the period when the legacy is to vest, or become payable.

LARCINY, (Fr. *larrecin*, Lat. *latrocinium*) Larciny, or theft, by contraction for latrociny, *latrocinium*, is distinguished by the law into two sorts; the one called simple larciny, or plain theft unaccompanied with any other atrocious circumstance; and mixed or compound larciny, which also includes in it the aggravation of a taking from one's house or person.

Simple larciny, when it is the stealing of

goods *above the value of twelvepence*, is called grand larciny; when of goods to that value, or *under*, is petit larciny.

Simple larciny then is "*the felonious taking, and carrying away, of the personal goods of another.*"

And it must be a taking without the consent of the owner. Therefore no delivery of the goods from the owner to the offender, upon trust, can ground a larciny. But if a horse, or a carriage or the like be hired, and never returned, if the jury are of opinion from the circumstances, that the persons to whom they were delivered, intended at the time of hiring never to restore them, or that the intention to steal them or convert them to their own use existed in their minds at the time they gained possession, they are guilty of felony. *Pear's case*, and *Major Semple's case*, *Leach.* 189, 327. And it is now generally held, that if the possession of property is obtained by any contrivance *animo furandi*, as by pretending to find a valuable ring, cutting cards, or laying wagers, or by undertaking to exchange a note into cash, or gold into silver, it amounts to felony. *Leach*, 206, 226, 239.

But where the sale of a horse or any other article is complete, and possession is delivered to the buyer, who rides away with the horse, or carries off the article, without paying for it, no felony is committed. For the property, as well as possession, is in that case parted with, and the owner is defrauded not of the horse or article, but only of its price, and he has remedy by an action to recover it. *Leach*, 528.

Also it has been decided, that if a parcel is left by accident in a hackney coach, and the coachman instead of restoring it to the owner, opens it and embezzles part of its contents, he is guilty of larciny. *Leach*, 320.

And there must not only be a taking, but a carrying away; *cepit et asportavit* was the old law-Latin.

2. A bare removal from the place in which he found the goods, though the thief does not quite make off with them, is a sufficient asportation, or carrying away. As if a man be leading another's horse out of a close, and be apprehended in the fact; or if a guest, stealing goods out of an inn, has removed them from his chamber down stairs; these have been adjudged sufficient carryings away, to constitute a larciny (3 *Inst.* 108, 109.) Or, if a thief intending to steal plate, takes it out of a chest in which it was, and lays it down upon the floor, but is surprized before he can make his escape with it; this is larciny (1 *Hawk. P. C.* 93.)

Thus where a man snatched an earring from a lady's ear, and afterwards dropped it in her hair, it was held a sufficient carrying away to constitute a robbery. *Leach*, 264. The removal of a parcel from one end of a waggon to the other, with an intent to steal, amounted to a larciny. *Ibid.* 204.) But where a bale of goods was raised and placed upon its end in a perpendicular posture, this was thought not to be a sufficient carrying away, there not being a complete removal from the space it before occupied. *Ibid.* And where a man was stopped and ordered by the prisoner to put down upon the ground a parcel, which he was carrying, but which the prisoner did not afterwards take up, this was held not a sufficient asportation to complete the crime of robbery. *Ibid.* 266.

3. This taking and carrying away, must also be felonious; that is, done *animo furandi*: or, as the civil law expresses it, *lucri causa* (*Inst.* 4. 1. 1.) This requisite, besides excusing those who labour under incapacities of mind or will, indemnifies also mere trespassers, and other petty offenders. As if a servant takes his master's horse, without his knowledge, and brings him home again: if a neighbour takes another's plough, that is left in the field, and uses it upon his own land, and then returns it: if, under colour of arrear of rent, where none is due, I distrein another's cattle, or seise them: all these are misdemesnors and trespasses, but no felonies (1 *Hal. P. C.* 509.) The ordinary discovery of a felonious intent, is where the party doth it clandestinely; or, being charged with the fact, denies it. But this is by no means the only criterion of criminality: for in cases that may amount to larciny, the variety of circumstances is so great, and the complications thereof so mingled, that it is impossible to recount all those, which may evidence a felonious intent, or *animum furandi*: wherefore they must be left to the due and attentive consideration of the court and jury. 4 *Black.* 232.

4. This felonious taking and carrying away must be of the personal goods of another: for if they are things real, or savour of the realty, larciny at the common law cannot be committed of them. Lands, tenements, and hereditaments (either corporeal or incorporeal) cannot in their nature be taken and carried away. And of things likewise that adhere to the freehold, as corn, grass, trees, and the like, or lead upon a house, no larciny could be committed by the rules of the common law; but the severance of them was, and in many things is still, merely a trespass which depended on a subtilty in the legal notions of our ancestors. These things were parcel of the real estate; and therefore, while they continued so, could not by any possibility, be the subject of theft, being absolutely fixed and immoveable. (2 *Black. Com.* 16.) And if they were severed by violence, so as to be changed into moveables; and at the same time, by one and the same continued act, carried off by the person who severed them; they could never be said to be taken from the proprietor, in this their newly acquired state of mobility,

(which is essential to the nature of larciny,) being never, as such, in the actual or constructive possession of any one, but of him who committed the trespass. He could not, in strictness, be said to have taken what at that time were the personal goods of another, since the very act of taking was what turned them into personal goods. But if the thief severs them at one time, whereby the trespass is completed, and they are converted into personal chattels, in the constructive possession of him on whose soil they are left or laid; and come again at another time, when they are so turned into personalty, and takes them away; it is larciny: and so it is, if the owner, or any one else, has severed them. But by several *statutes*, the stealing of certain things affixed to, or considered as part of the realty, is felony. See *Felony*.

Larciny also cannot be committed of such animals, in which there is no property either absolute or qualified; as of beasts that are *feræ naturæ*, and unreclaimed, such as deer, hares, and conies, in a forest, chace, or warren; fish, in an open river, or pond; or wild fowls at their natural liberty (1 *Hal. P. C.* 511. *Fost.* 366.) But if they are reclaimed or confined, and may serve for food, it is otherwise, even at common law: for of deer so inclosed in a park, that they may be taken at pleasure, fish in a trunk, and pheasants or partridges in a mew, larciny may be committed (1 *Hawk. P. C.* 94. 1 *Hal. P. C.* 511.)

Notwithstanding, however, that no larciny can be committed, unless there be some property in the thing taken, and an owner; yet, if the owner be unknown, provided there be a property, it is larciny to steal it; and an indictment will lie, for the goods of a person unknown (1 *Hal. P. C.* 512.) This is the case of stealing a shroud out of a grave; which is the property of those, whoever they were, that buried the deceased: but stealing the corpse itself, which has no owner, (though a matter of great indecency) is no felony, unless some of the graveclothes be stolen with it (2 *Black.* 429.)

The inferior species of theft, or petit larciny, is only punished by imprisonment or whipping at common law (3 *Inst.* 218), or, by statute 4 *Geo.* 1. *c.* 11. by transportation for seven years. But the punishment of grand larciny, or the stealing above the value of twelvepence, (which sum was the standard in the time of king Athelstan, eight hundred years ago,) is at common law regularly death. Which, considering the great intermediate alteration (2 *Black.* 509.) in the price or denomination of money, is undoubtedly a very rigorous constitution; and made sir Henry Spelman (above a century since) when money was at twice its present rate, complain, that while every thing else was risen in its nominal value, and become dearer, the life of man had continually grown cheaper (*Gloss.* 350.) It is true, that the mercy of juries will often make them strain a point, and bring in larciny to be under the value of twelvepence, when it is really of much greater value:* but this, though evidently justifiable and proper, when it only reduces the present nominal value of money to the antient standard (2 *Inst.* 189.), is otherwise a kind of pious perjury, and does not at all excuse our common law in this respect from the imputation of severity, but rather strongly confesses the charge. It is likewise true, that by the merciful extensions of the benefit of clergy by our modern statute law, a person who commits a simple larciny to the value of thirteenpence or thirteen hundred pounds, though guilty of a capital offence, shall be excused the pains of death: but this is only for the first offence. And in many cases of simple larciny, the benefit of clergy is taken away by statute: as from horsestealing in the principals, and accessories both before and after the fact (*stat.* 1 *Edw.* 6. *c.* 12. 2 & 3 *Edw.* 6. *c.* 33. 31 *Eliz. c.* 12.); theft by great and notorious thieves in Northumberland and Cumberland (*stat.* 18 *Car.* 2. *c.* 3.); taking woollen cloth from off the tenters (*stat.* 22 *Car.* 2. *c.* 5.), or linens, fustians, calicoes, or cotton goods, from the place of manufacture (*stat.* 18 *Geo.* 2. *c.* 27.); (which extends, in the last case, to aiders, assisters, procurers, buyers, and receivers;) feloniously driving away, or otherwise stealing one or more sheep or other cattle specified in the acts, or killing them with intent to steal the whole or any part of the carcase (*stat.* 14 *Geo.* 2. *c.* 6. 15 *Geo.* 2. *c.* 34. 1 *Black.* 88.), or aiding or assisting therein; thefts on navigable rivers above the value of forty shillings (*stat.* 24 *Geo.* 2. *c.* 45.), or being present, aiding, and assisting thereat; plundering vessels in distress, or that have suffered shipwreck (*stat.* 12 *Ann. st.* 2. *c.* 18. 26 *Geo.* 2. *c.* 19.); stealing letters sent by post (*stat.* 7 *Geo.* 3. *c.* 50.); and also stealing deer, fish, hares, and conies under the peculiar circumstances mentioned in the Waltham black act (*stat.* 9 *Geo.* 1. *c.* 22.)

Mixed, or compound larciny is such as has all the properties of the former, but is accompanied with either one, or both, of the aggravations of a taking from one's house or person.

1st. Larciny from the house, though it seems to have a higher degree of guilt than simple larciny, yet is not at all distinguish-

---

* In a prosecution for a simple larciny, in general, it is not very material to the prisoner, whether he is convicted of grand or petty larciny, as the court can transport for both. But upon a second conviction for grand larciny, he may be deprived of the benefit of clergy.

ed from the other at common law (1 *Hawk. P. C.* 98.): unless where it is accompanied with the circumstance of breaking the house by night; and then it falls under the description of burglary. But now, by several acts of parliament, the benefit of clergy is taken from larcinies committed in an house in almost every instance, *viz.* First, in larcinies above the value of twelvepence committed, 1. In a church or chapel, with or without violence, or breaking the same (*stat.* 23 *Hen.* 8. *c.* 1. 1 *Edw.* 6. *c.* 12. 1 *Hal. P. C.* 518.): 2. In a booth or tent in a market or fair, in the day time or in the night, by violence or breaking the same; the owner or some of his family being therein (*stat.* 5 & 6 *Edw.* 6. *c.* 9. 1 *Hal. P. C.* 522.): 3. By robbing a dwelling-house in the day time (which robbing implies a breaking) any person being therein (*stat.* 3 & 4 *W. & M. c.* 9.): 4. In a dwelling-house by day or by night, without breaking the same, any person being therein and put in fear (*Ibid.*); which amounts in law to a robbery: and in both these last cases, the accessory before the fact is also excluded from his clergy. Secondly, in larcinies to the value of five shillings, committed, 1. By breaking any dwelling-house, or any outhouse, shop, or warehouse thereunto belonging in the day time, although no person be therein (*stat.* 39 *Eliz. c.* 15.); which also now extends to aiders, abettors, and accessories before the fact (*stat.* 3 & 4 *W. & M. c.* 9.): 2. By privately stealing goods, wares, or merchandize in any shop, warehouse, coachhouse or stable, by day or by night (see *Foster.* 78. *Bar.* 379.); though the same be not broken open, and though no person be therein (*stat.* 10 & 11 *W.* 3. *c.* 23.): which likewise extends to such as assist, hire, or command the offence to be committed.* Lastly, in larcinies to the value of forty shillings in a dwelling-house, or its outhouses, although the same be not broken, and whether any person be therein or no; unless committed against their masters by apprentices under the age of fifteen (*stat.* 12 *Ann. st.* 1. *c.* 7.) This also extends to those, who aid or assist in the commission of any such offence.†

2. Larciny from the person is either by privately stealing, or by open and violent assault, which is usually called robbery.

The offence of privately stealing from a man's person, as by picking his pocket or the like, privily without his knowledge, was debarred of the benefit of clergy, by statute 8 *Eliz. c.* 4. But this severe statute has been repealed by 48 *Geo.* 3. *c.* 129. by which it is enacted, that persons feloniously stealing from the person of another, whether *privily* or not, *but without force or putting in fear*, and those present aiding and abetting, may be transported for life, or not less than seven years, or if the court think fit, be imprisoned only, or imprisoned and kept to hard labour for not exceeding three years.

Open and violent larciny from the person, or robbery, the *rapina* of the civilians, is the felonious and forcible taking from the person of another, of goods or money to any value, by violence or putting him in fear (1 *Hawk. P. C.* 95.), but there must be a taking, otherwise it is no robbery. See *Highway Robbery.*

LARDARIUM, the larder, or place where the lard and meat were kept. *Cowel. Blount.*

LARDERARIUS REGIS, the king's larderer, or clerk of the kitchen. *Ibid.*

---

* It has been held, that privately stealing money to the amount of five shillings, is not within the statute 10 & 11 *W.* 3. *c.* 23. Shops and warehouses when they are used merely as repositories of goods, and not as places of sale, are not within the act, and consequently a prisoner cannot be convicted of privately stealing in a shop an article, which is not exposed there for sale, but which happens to be left there to be repaired, or for some other similar purpose. And with regard to coach-houses and stables, the articles must be such as are generally deposited there. *Fost.* 78. *Leach,* 43, 235, 248, 274.—In prosecutions under this statute, it is held not to be privately stealing if any person whatever see or perceive the theft at the time it is committed. And where there are several shopmen employed in a shop, they must appear at the trial to prove they did not perceive the theft, or the judge will direct the jury to presume that the stealing was not done privately.

† A person cannot be convicted capitally for stealing to the value of 40*s.* in his own house, nor a wife in her husband's house. *Leach,* 277. Upon an indictment for burglariously breaking and entering a dwelling-house, and stealing therein property to the value of 40*s.* the prisoner may be acquitted of the breaking, and be capitally convicted of stealing in the dwelling-house. *Ibid,* 83.

If property is stolen immediately from the person of any one in a house, it is not within this statute, the judges having determined, that the statute was made to protect such property as might be deposited in the house, and not that which was on the person of the party. *Campbell's* and *Owen's cases, Leach,* 642, 652.

Stealing bank notes to the amount of 40*s.* in a dwelling-house, is a capital crime under this statute; the 2 *Geo.* 2. *c.* 25. having made the stealing of bank notes and other choses in action therein mentioned, a felony of the same nature, as stealing other property of the value of the money due upon the note. *Dean's case, Leach,* 798.

LARDING MONEY. In the manor of Bradford, the tenants pay to their lord a small yearly rent by this name; which is said to be for liberty to feed their hogs with the mast of the lord's woods, the fat of a hog being called lard; or it may be a commutation for some customary service of carrying salt or meat to the lord's larder. Called *lardarium* in old charters; and *decimam lardarii de haga*. *Ibid.*

LARONS, (Fr.) thieves. *Ibid.*

LASLATINUS, an assassin or murderer. *Ibid.*

LAST, (Sax. *hlæstan*, i. e. *onus*, Fr. *lest*) denotes a burden in general, and particularly a certain weight or measure of fish, corn, wool, leather, pitch, &c. As a last of white herrings, is twelve barrels, of red herrings, twenty cades or thousand, and of pilchards, ten thousand; of corn, ten quarters, and in some parts of England twenty-one quarters; of wool, twelve sacks; of leather, twenty dickers, or ten score; of hides or skins, twelve dozen; of pitch, tar, or ashes, fourteen barrels; of gunpowder, twenty-four firkins, weighing a hundred pound each, &c. 32 *Hen.* 8. *cap.* 14. 1 *Jac.* 1. *cap.* 33. 15 *Car.* 1. *cap.* 7.

LAST, in the marshes of Kent: a court held by the twenty-four jurats, and summoned by the bailiffs; wherein orders are made to lay and levy taxes, impose penalties, &c. for the preservation of the said marshes. *Cowel.*

LASTAGE, (*lastagium*) a custom, according to Rastal, exacted in some fairs and markets, to carry things bought where one will. But it is taken for the ballast or lading of a ship. *Stat.* 21 *R.* 2. *cap.* 18. And lastage, says another author, is properly that custom which is paid for wares sold by the last; as herrings, pitch, &c. *Cowel.*

LASTAGE AND BALASTAGE. See *Harbours* and *London.*

LAST HEIR, (*ultimus hæres*) is he to whom land comes by escheat for want of lawful heirs, that is, in the case of copyhold estates, the lord of whom they hold, but in other cases of freehold, the king. *Bract. lib.* 7. *cap.* 17.

LATERA, sides-men, companions, assistants. *Cowel.*

LATERARE, to lie side ways, in opposition to laying end-ways; used in the description of lands. *Ibid.*

LATHE, LETH, (*læslum*, *leda*, Sax. *læthe*) is a great part of a county, containing three or four hundreds, or wapentakes; as it is used in Kent and Sussex. *Ibid.*

LATHREVE, LEIDGREVE or TRITHINGREVE, was an officer under the Saxon government, who had authority over a third part of the county; and whose territory was therefore called Trithing, otherwise a Leid or Leithen, in which manner the county of Kent is still divided; and the Rapes in Sussex seem to answer the same. *Cowel. Blount.*

LATIMER, is used by sir Edward Coke for an interpreter. 2 *Inst.* 515. But according to Cambden and Cowell, the word is mistaken, and should be *latiner*, because heretofore, he that understood Latin, which in the time of the Romans was the prevailing language, might be a good interpreter. *Camb. Britan.* 598. *Cowel.*

LATIN. There are three sorts of Latin, 1. Good Latin, allowed by grammarians and lawyers. 2. False or incongruous Latin, which in times past would abate original writs; though not make void any judicial writ, declaration, or plea, &c. And 3. words of art, known only to the sages of the law, and not to grammarians, called lawyers Latin. 1 *Lil. Abr.* 146, 147. But now all law proceedings are to be in English. 4 *Geo.* 2. *c.* 26

LATINARIUS, an interpreter of Latin, or *latiner*. 2 *Co. Inst.* 515.

LATITAT, is a writ which issues into all counties, except Middlesex, whereby all men are originally called to answer in personal actions in the king's bench, having its name upon a supposition, that the defendant doth lurk and lie hid, and cannot be found in the county of Middlesex, to be taken by bill, the usual process against parties residing there, but is gone into some other county, to the sheriff of which this writ is directed, to apprehend him there. *F. N. B.* 78. *Terms de Ley.*

The original of it is this: in ancient time, while the king's bench was moveable, when any man was sued, a writ was sent forth to the sheriff of the county where the court was resident, called a bill of Middlesex, to take him; and if the sheriff returned *non est inventus*, then a second writ was sued out, that had these words, *cum testatum est quod Latitat, &c.* and thereby the sheriff was commanded to attach the party in any other place, where he might be found.

LATRO, (*latrocinium*) he who had the sole jurisdiction *de latrone* in a particular place. See *Infangthef. Cowel.*

LATTA, a lath. *Cowel.*

LAVATORIUM, a laundry, or place to wash in, applied to such a place in the porch or entrance of cathedral churches, where the priest and other officiating members were obliged to wash their hands before they proceeded to divine service. *Ibid.*

LAVERBREAD, in the county of Glamorgan and some other parts of Wales, they used to make a sort of food of a sea plant, the oyster green, or sea liver-wort; and this they call *laverbread*. *Ibid.*

LAVINA, for *Labina*, watry land. *Ibid.*

LAUDARE, to advise or persuade. *Ibid.*

LAUDUM, an arbitrament or award. *Ibid.*

LAUNCEGAYS, a kind of offensive weapons now disused, and prohibited by stat. 7 *R.* 2. *c.* 13. *Ibid.*

LAUND or LAWND, (*landa*) an open field, without wood. *Blount.*

LAURELS, pieces of gold coined in 1619, with the king's head laureated; the twenty-shilling pieces whereof were marked with XX. The ten-shillings X. and the five-shilling piece with V. *Cowel. Blount.*

LAW, (in Sax. *lag*, Lat. *lex*, from *lego* or *legendo*, choosing, or rather *à ligando* binding). Law, in its most general and comprehensive sense, signifies a *rule of action;* and denotes those rules by which man is commanded to make use of his faculties in the general regulation of his behaviour. 1 *Black.* 58.

And *municipal* or *civil* law is, the rule by which particular districts, communities, or nations are governed; being thus defined by Justinian, "*jus civile est quod quisque sibi* "*populus constituit.*" It is called municipal law, in compliance with common speech; for, though strictly that expression denotes the particular customs of one single *municipium* or free town, yet it may with sufficient propriety be applied to any one state or nation, which is governed by the same laws and customs. 1 *Black.* 58-60.

Municipal law, thus understood, is properly defined to be "*a rule of civil conduct* "*prescribed by the supreme power in a state,* "*commanding what is right, and prohibiting* "*what is wrong.*" *Ibid.*

And it is a rule: not a transient sudden order from a superior to or concerning a particular person; but something permanent, uniform, and universal.

And it is called a rule, to distinguish it from a compact or agreement; for a compact is a promise proceeding from us, law is a command directed to us. The language of a compact is, "I will, or will not, do "this;" that of law is, "thou shalt, or "shalt not, do it."

The municipal law of England, or *the rule of civil conduct* prescribed to the inhabitants of this kingdom, may be divided into two kinds: the *lex non scripta,* the unwritten or common law; and the *lex scripta,* the written, or statute law. 1 *Black.* 63.

The *lex non scripta,* or unwritten law, includes not only general customs, or the common law properly so called; but also the particular customs of certain parts of the kingdom; and likewise those particular laws, that are by custom observed only in certain courts and jurisdictions. *Ibid.*

As to the *leges non scriptæ, viz.* the unwritten or common law, these are properly distinguishable into three kinds: 1. General customs; which are the universal rule of the whole kingdom, and form the common law, in its stricter and more usual signification. 2. Particular customs: which for the most part affect only the inhabitants of particular districts. 3. Certain particular laws; which by custom are adopted and used by some particular courts, of pretty general and extensive jurisdiction. 1 *Black.* 67.

I. As to general customs, or the common law, properly so called; this is that law, by which proceedings and determinations in the king's ordinary courts of justice are guided and directed. This, for the most part, settles the course in which lands descend by inheritance; the manner and form of acquiring and transferring property; the solemnities and obligation of contracts; the rules of expounding wills, deeds, and acts of parliament; the respective remedies of civil injuries; the several species of temporal offences, with the manner and degree of punishment; and an infinite number of minuter particulars, which diffuse themselves as extensively as the ordinary distribution of common justice requires. Thus, for example, that there shall be four superior courts of record, the chancery, the king's bench, the common pleas, and the exchequer;—that the eldest son alone is heir to his ancestor;—that property may be acquired and transferred by writing;—that a deed is of no validity unless sealed and delivered;—that wills shall be construed more favourably, and deeds more strictly;—that money lent upon bond is recoverable by action of debt;—that breaking the public peace is an offence, and punishable by fine and imprisonment;—all these are doctrines that are not set down in any written statute or ordinance, but depend merely upon immemorial usage, that is, upon common law, for their support. *Ibid.* 68.

II. The second branch of the unwritten laws of England are particular customs, or laws which affect only the inhabitants of particular districts.

These particular customs, or some of them, are without doubt, the remains of that multitude of local customs before-mentioned, out of which the common law, as it now stands, was collected at first by king Alfred, and afterwards by king Edgar and Edward the confessor: each district mutually sacrificing some of its own special usages, in order that the whole kingdom might enjoy the benefit of one uniform and universal system of laws. But for reasons that have been now long forgotten, particular counties, cities, towns, manors, and lordships, were very early indulged with the privilege of abiding by their own customs, in contradistinction to the rest of the nation at large: which privilege is confirmed to them by several acts of parliament. (*Mag. Cart.* 9 *Hen.* 3. *c.* 9. 1 *Edw.* 3. *st.* 2. *c.* 9. 14 *Edw.* 3. *st.* 1. *c.* 1. and 2 *Hen.* 4. *c.* 1. 1 *Black.* 74.

Such is the custom of gavelkind in Kent and some other parts of the kingdom (though perhaps it was also general till the Norman conquest) which ordains, among other things, that not the eldest son only of the father shall succeed to his inheritance, but all the sons alike: and that, though the ancestor be attainted and hanged, yet the heir shall succeed to his estate, without any escheat to the lord.—Such is the custom that prevails in divers antient boroughs, and therefore called borough-english, that the youngest son shall inherit the estate, in preference to all his elder brothers.—Such is the custom in other boroughs, that a widow shall be entitled, for her dower, to all her husband's lands; whereas at the common law she shall be endowed of one third part only.--Such also are the special and particular customs of manors, of which every one has more or less, and which bind all the copyhold and customary tenants that hold of the said manors.—Such likewise is the custom of holding divers inferior courts, with power of trying causes, in cities and trading towns, the right of holding which, when no royal grant can be shewn, depends entirely upon immemorial and established usage.—Such, lastly, are many particular customs within the city of London, with regard to trade, apprentices, widows, orphans, and a variety of other matters. All these are contrary to the general law of the land, and are good only by special usage; though the customs of London are also confirmed by act of parliament. (8 *Rep.* 126. *Cro. Car.* 347.)

To this head may most properly be referred a particular system of customs used only among one set of the king's subjects, called the custom of merchants, or *lex mercatoria*: which however different from the general rules of the common law, is yet ingrafted into it, and made a part of it; being allowed, for the benefit of trade, to be of the utmost validity in all commercial transactions: for it is a maxim of law, that "*cuilibet in suâ* "*arte credendum est.*" (*Winch.* 24.)

The *lex mercatoria*, or the custom of merchants, like the *lex et consuetudo parliamenti*, describes only a great division of the law of England. The laws relating to bills of exchange, insurance, and all mercantile contracts, are as much the general law of the land, as the laws relating to marriage or murder. But the expression has frequently led merchants to suppose, that all their new fashions and devices immediately become the law of the land: a notion which, perhaps, has been too much encouraged by the courts. Merchants ought to take their law from the courts, and not the courts from merchants: and when the law is found inconvenient for the purposes of extended commerce, application ought to be made to parliament for redress. This is agreeable to the opinion of Mr. justice Foster, who maintains, that "the "custom of merchants is the general law of "the kingdom," and therefore ought not to "be left to a jury after it has been settled "by judicial determinations." 2 *Bur.* 1226.

III. The third branch of them are those peculiar laws which by custom are adopted and used only in certain peculiar courts and jurisdictions. These are THE CIVIL and CANON laws.

By the CIVIL LAW, absolutely taken, is generally understood the civil or municipal law of the Roman empire, as comprised in the institutes, the code, and the digest of the emperor Justinian, and the novel constitutions of himself and some of his successors.

This consists of, 1. The institutes, which contain the elements or first principles of the Roman law, in four books. 2. The digests, or pandects, in fifty books, containing the opinions and writings of eminent lawyers, digested in a systematical method. 3. A new code, or collection of imperial constitutions, in twelve books; the lapse of a whole century having rendered the former code, of Theodosius, imperfect. 4. The novels or new constitutions, posterior in time to the other books, and amounting to a supplement to the code; containing new decrees of successive emperors, as new questions happened to arise. These form the body of the Roman law, or *corpus juris civilis*, as published about the time of Justinian; which, however, fell soon into neglect and oblivion, till about the year 1130, when a copy of the digests was found at Amalfi in Italy: which accident, concurring with the policy of the Roman ecclesiastics, suddenly gave new vogue and authority to the civil law, introduced it into several nations, and occasioned that mighty inundation of voluminous comments, with which this system of law, more than any other, is now loaded. 1 *Black.* 81.

The CANON LAW is a body of Roman ecclesiastical law, relative to such matters as that church either has or pretends to have, the proper jurisdiction over. This is compiled from the opinions of the antient Latin fathers, the decrees of general councils, and the decretal epistles and bulls of the holy see. All which lay in the same disorder and confusion as the Roman civil law: till, about the year 1151, one Gratian, an Italian monk, animated by the discovery of Justinian's pandects, reduced the ecclesiastical constitutions also into some method, in three books; which he entitled *concordia discordantium canonum*, but which are generally known by the name of *decretum Gratiani*. These reached as low as the time of pope Alexander III. The subsequent papal decrees, to the pontificate of Gregory IX. were published in much the same method under the auspices of that pope, about the year 1230, in five books; entitled *decretalia Gregorii noni*. A sixth book was added by Boniface VIII. about the year 1298, which is called *sextus decretalium*. The Clementine constitutions, or decrees of Clement V. were in like manner authenticated in 1317 by his successor John XXII.; who also published twenty constitutions of his own, called the *extravagantes Joannis*: all which in some measure answer to the novels of the civil law. To these have been since added some decrees of later popes, in five books, called *extravagantes communes*. And all these together, Gratian's decree, Gregory's decretals, the sixth decretal, the Clementine constitutions, and the extravagants of John and his successors, form the *corpus juris canonici*, or body of the Roman canon law.

Besides these pontifical collections, which during the times of popery, were received as authentic in this island, as well as in other parts of Christendom; there is also a kind of national canon law, composed of legatine and provincial constitutions, and adapted only to the exigencies of this church and kingdom. The legatine constitutions were ecclesiastical laws, enacted in national synods, held under the cardinals Otho and Othobon, legates from pope Gregory IX. and pope Clement IV., in the reign of king Henry III., about the years 1220 and 1268. The provincial constitutions are principally the decrees of provincial synods, held under divers archbishops of Canterbury, from Stephen Langton in the reign of Henry III. to Henry Chichele in the reign of Henry V.; and adopted also by the province of York in the reign of Henry VI. At the dawn of the reformation, in the reign of king Henry VIII. it was enacted in parliament, that a review should be had of the canon law; and, till such review should be made, all canons, constitutions, ordinances, and synodals provincial, being then already made, and not repugnant to the law of the land or the king's prerogative, should still be used and executed. And, as no such review has yet been perfected, upon this statute now depends the authority of the canon law in England.

The LEGES SCRIPTÆ, the *written laws of the kingdom*; are statutes, acts, or edicts, made by the king's majesty, by and with the advice and consent of the lords spiritual and temporal and commons in parliament assembled. The oldest of these now extant, and printed in our statute books, is the famous *magna charta*, as confirmed in parliament 9 *Hen.* 3.: though doubtless there were many acts before that time, the records of which are now lost, and the determinations of them perhaps at present currently received for the maxims of the old common law. 1 *Black.* 84.

Of these statutes there are several kinds: and they are either *general* or *special*, *public* or *private*. A *general or public act* is an universal rule, that regards the whole community: and of this, the courts of law are bound to take notice judicially and *ex officio*; without the statute being particularly pleaded, or formally set forth by the party who claims an advantage under it. *Special or private acts* are rather exceptions than rules, being those which only operate upon particular persons, and private concerns. And of these (which are not promulgated with the same notoriety as the former) the judges are not bound to take notice, unless they be formally shewn and pleaded.

Statutes also are either DECLARATORY of the common law, or REMEDIAL of some defects therein. *Declaratory*, where the old custom of the kingdom is almost fallen into disuse, or become disputable; in which case the parliament has thought proper, *in perpetuum rei testimonium*, and for avoiding all doubts and difficulties, to declare what the common law is and ever hath been. *Remedial statutes* are those which are made to supply such defects, and abridge such superfluities, in the common law, as arise either from the general imperfection of all human laws, from change of time and circumstances, from the mistakes and unadvised determinations of unlearned (or even learned) judges, or from any other cause whatsoever. And this being done, either by enlarging the common law where it was too narrow and circumscribed, or by restraining it where it was too lax and luxuriant, hath occasioned another subordinate division of *remedial* acts of parliament into enlarging and restraining statutes. Thus clipping the current coin of the kingdom was an offence not sufficiently guarded against by the common law: therefore it was thought expedient by statute 5 *Eliz.* c. 11. to make it high treason, which it was not at the common law; so that this was an enlarging statute. At common law also, spiritual corporations might lease out their estates for any term of years, till prevented by the statute of 13 *Eliz.* (see *Leases*) this was therefore a restraining statute.

These are the several grounds of the laws of England: over and above which, equity is also frequently called in to assist, to moderate, and to explain them. For, (besides the liberality of sentiment with which our common law judges interpret acts of parliament, and such rules of the unwritten law as are not of a positive kind) there are also peculiar courts of equity established for the benefit of the subject; to detect latent frauds and concealments, which the process of the courts of law is not adapted to reach; to enforce the execution of such matters of trust and confidence, as are binding in conscience, though not cognizable in a court of law; to deliver from such dangers as are owing to misfortune or oversight; and to give a more specific relief, and more adapted to the circumstances of the case, than can always be obtained by the generality of the rules of the positive or common law. 1 *Black.* 91.

This is the business of our courts of equity, which, however, are only conversant in matters of property. For *the freedom of our constitution will not permit, that in criminal cases a power should be lodged in any judge, to construe the law otherwise than according to the letter.* This caution, while it admirably protects the public liberty, can never bear hard upon individuals. *A man cannot suffer* MORE *punishment than the law assigns, but he may suffer* LESS. The laws cannot be strained by partiality to inflict a penalty beyond what the letter will warrant; but, in cases where the letter induces any apparent hardship, the crown has the power to pardon.

LAW OF ARMS, (*lex armorum*) is a kind of law among all nations, that in case of a solemn war, the prince that conquers, gains a right of dominion, as well as property over the things and persons he has subdued; and it is for this reason, because both parties have appealed to the highest tribunal that can be, *viz.* the trial by arms and war; wherein the Great judge and Sovereign of the world, in a more especial manner, seems to decide the controversy. *Hale's Hist. L.* 73, 74.

Common things concerning arms and war, are under the cognisance of the constable and marshal of England. 13 *R.* 2.

LAW-BOOKS. Books written upon the subject of the law, such as the Year Books; Treatises on distinct branches of law, Abridgments, and books of Reports, many of which are highly valued as authoritative.

LAW-DAY, (*lagedayum*) called also view of frank-pledge, or court-leet, was any day of open court; and commonly used for the courts of a county or hundred. *Cowel.*

LAWING OF DOGS, was the cutting off several claws of the fore-feet of dogs in the forest. 3 *Black.* 72.

LAWLESS-COURT, a court held on Kingshill at Rochford in Essex, on Wednesday morning next after Michaelmas day yearly, at cock-crowing; at which court, they whispered, and had no candle, nor any pen and ink, but a coal: and he that owed suit or service there, and appeared not, forfeited double his rent: this court is mentioned by Cambden, who says, that this servile attendance was imposed on the tenants, for conspiring at the like unseasonable time to raise a commotion. *Camd. Britan.* 441. It belongs to the honour of Raleigh, and is called lawless, because held at an unlawful hour; or *quia dicta sine lege*. *Cowel. Blount.*

LAWLESS MAN, (*ex lex*) is an outlaw. *Ibid.*

LAW OF MARQUE, (from the Germ. *march,* i. e. *limes*) is where they that are driven to it, do take the shipping and goods of that people of whom they have received wrong, and cannot get ordinary justice in another territory, when they can take them within their own bounds and precincts. *Ibid.* See *Marque* and *Prerogative*.

LAW MERCHANT, (*lex mercatoria*) is a special law differing from the common law of England, proper to merchants, and part of the law of the realm. See *Law*.

LAW PROCEEDINGS, of all kinds, as writs, processes, pleadings, &c. are to be in the English language, from the 25th March 1733. 4 *Geo.* 2. *c.* 26. 5 *Geo.* 2. *c.* 27.

LAW SPIRITUAL, (*lex spiritualis*) is the ecclesiastical law, allowed by our laws where it is not against the common law, nor the statutes and customs of the kingdom. *Co. Lit.* 344.

LAW OF THE STAPLE, is the same with law merchant. *Cowel.*

LAWYER, (*legista, legisperitus, jurisconsultus*) by the Saxons called *lahman*, is a counsellor, or one learned in the law. *Cowel.*

LAY-CORPORATIONS, are of two sorts, civil and eleemosynary. The civil are such as are erected for a variety of temporal purposes. The eleemosynary sort are such as are constituted for the perpetual distribution of the free alms, or bounty, of the founder of them, to such persons as he hath directed. 1 *Black.* 470, 471.

LAY INVESTITURE OF BISHOPS. By stat. 25 *Hen.* 8, *c.* 20, it is enacted that at every future avoidance of a bishopric "the king may send the dean and chapter his usual license to proceed to election, "which is always to be accompanied with "a letter missive from the king, containing "the name of the person whom he would "have them elect; and if the dean and "chapter delay their election above twelve "days, the nomination shall devolve to the "king, who may by letters patent appoint "such person as he pleases." This election or nomination, if it be of a bishop, must be signified by the king's letters patent to the archbishop of the province; if it be of an archbishop, to the other archbishop and two bishops, or to four bishops, requiring them to confirm, invest, and consecrate the person so elected, which they are bound to perform immediately, without any application to the see of Rome. *After which the bishop elect shall sue to the king for his temporalties, shall make oath to the king and none other, and shall take restitution of his secular possessions out of the king's hands only.* 1 *Black.* 379, 380.

LAY-FEE, (*feodum laicum*) lands held in fee of a lay-lord, by the common services to which military tenure was subject, as distinguished from the ecclesiastical holding in frankalmoigne, discharged from those burdens. *Kennet's Gloss. Cowel.*

LAYMAN, is one that is not of the clergy. See *Laity*.

LAYSTALL, (Sax.) a place to lay dung or soil in. *Cowel. Blount.*

LAZARETS, places where quarantine is to be performed by persons coming from infected countries. See *Plague. Quarantine.*

LAZZI. The Saxons divided the people

of the land into three ranks, the first they called *edhilinghi*, which were such as are now nobility; the second were termed *frilingi*, from *friling*, signifying that he was born a freeman, or of parents not subject to any servitude, which are the present gentry; and the third and last were called *lazzi*, as born to labour, and being of a more servile state than our servants, because they could not depart from their service without the leave of the lord, but were fixed to the land where born, and in the nature of slaves; hence the word *lazzi*, or *lazy*, signifies those of a servile condition. *Nithardus de Saxonibus*, *lib.* 24. *Cowel. Blount.*

LEA OF YARN, a quantity of yarn at Kidderminster, containing 200 threads on a reel four yards about. 22 & 23 *Car.* 2, *c.* 8.

LEAD, stealing of lead affixed to a house, &c. is transportation for seven years. 4 *Geo.* 2, *c.* 32.

LEAGUE, is an agreement between princes: Also a measure of way at sea, or an extent of land, containing three miles in most countries abroad. The *solemn league* and *covenant* was a seditious conspiracy invented in Scotland; voted illegal by parliament, and provisions made against it by stat. 14 *Car.* 2, *c.* 4.

LEAK, or LECHE, (from the Sax. *leccian*, to let out water) in the bishopric of Durham is used for a gutter; so in Yorkshire any slough or watery hole upon the road is called by this name; and hence the water-tub to put ashes in to make lee for washing of clothes, is in some parts of England termed a leche. *Cowel.*

LEAKAGE, an allowance to merchants out of the duties of customs, and excise. *Merch. Dict.*

LEAP, a net, engine, or wheel, made of twigs, to catch fish in. 4 & 5 *Wil.* & *Mar.* *c.* 23.

LEAP YEAR, every fourth year, having one day more than other years. The day increasing in the leap year, and the day before, shall be accounted for one day. 21 *Hen.* 3.

LEASE. A lease is properly a conveyance of any lands or tenements (usually in consideration of rent, or other annual recompense,) made for life, for years, or at will, but always for a less time than the lessor hath in the premises; for if it be for *the whole* interest it is more properly an assignment than a lease. 2 *Black.* 317.

The usual words of operation in it are *demise*, *grant*, and to farm let. By this conveyance an estate for life, for years, or at will, may be created, either in corporeal or incorporeal hereditaments; though livery of seisin is indeed incident and necessary to one species of leases, *viz.* leases for life of corporeal hereditaments, but no other.

By the common law all persons seised of any estate might let leases to endure so long as their own interest lasted, but no longer. Therefore *tenant in fee-simple* might let leases of any duration; for he hath the whole interest: but *tenant in tail*, or *tenant for life*, could make no leases which should bind the issue in tail, or reversioner: nor could a husband, seised *jure uxoris*, make a firm or valid lease for any longer term than the joint lives of himself and his wife, for then his interest expired. Yet some tenants for life, where the fee-simple was in abeyance, might (with the concurrence of such as had the guardianship of the fee) make leases of equal duration with those granted by tenants in fee-simple, such as parsons and vicars with consent of the patron and ordinary. (*Co. Litt.* 44.) So also bishops, and deans, and such other sole ecclesiastical corporations as are seised of the fee-simple of lands in their corporate right, might, with the concurrence and confirmation of such persons as the law requires, have made leases for years, or for life, estates in tail, or in fee, without any limitation or control. And corporations aggregate might have made what estates they pleased, without the confirmation of any other person whatsoever. Whereas now, by several statutes, this power where it was unreasonable, and might be made an ill use of, is restrained: and where in the other cases the restraint by the common law seemed too hard, it is in some measure removed. The former statutes are called the RESTRAINING, the latter the ENABLING statute.

FIRST, the enabling statute, 32 *Hen.* 8, *c.* 28, empowers three manner of persons to make leases, to endure for three lives, or 21 years, which could not do so before. 1st, *tenant in tail* may by such leases bind his issue in tail, but not those in remainder or reversion. 2dly, *a husband seised in right of his wife, in fee-simple or fee-tail*, provided the wife joins in such lease, may bind her and her heirs thereby. *Lastly*, all persons *seised of an estate of fee-simple in right of their churches*, which extends not to parsons and vicars, may (without the concurrence of any other person) bind their successors: but then there must many requisites be observed, which the statute specifies, otherwise such leases are not binding. (*Co. Lit.* 44.) 1. The lease must be by indenture, and not by deed poll, or by parol. 2. It must begin from the making, or day of making, and not at any greater distance of time *. 3. If there be any old lease

* By various acts of parliament, and also frequently by private settlements, a power is

in being, it must be first absolutely surrendered, or be within a year of expiring. 4. It must be either for twenty-one years, or three lives, and not for both. 5. It must not exceed the term of three lives, or twenty-one years, but may be for a shorter term. 6. It must be of corporeal hereditaments, and not of such things as lie merely in grant; for no rent can be reserved thereout by the common law, as the lessor cannot resort to them to distrein *. 7. It must be of lands and tenements most commonly letten for twenty years past; so that if they had been let for above half the time (or eleven years out of the twenty) either for life, or for years, at will, or by copy of court roll, it is sufficient. 8. The most usual and customary feorm or rent, for twenty years past, must be reserved yearly on such lease. 9. Such leases must not be made without impeachment of waste. These are the guards, imposed by the statute (which was avowedly made for the security of farmers and the consequent improvement of tillage) to prevent unreasonable abuses, in prejudice of the issue, the wife, or the successor, of the reasonable indulgence here given.

Next follows, in order of time, the disabling or restraining statute, 1 *Eliz. c.* 19.) (made entirely for the benefit of the sucessor) which enacts, that all grants by archbishops and bishops, (which include even those confirmed by the dean and chapter; the which, however long or unreasonable, were good at common law,) other than for the term of one-and-twenty years, or three lives from the making, or without reserving the usual rent, shall be void. Concurrent leases, if confirmed by the dean and chapter, are held to be within the exception of this statute, and therefore valid; provided they do not exceed (together with the lease in being) the term permitted by the act (*Co. Lit.* 45). But by a saving expressly made, this statute of 1 *Eliz.* did not extend to grants made by any bishop to the crown; by which means queen Elizabeth procured many fair possessions to be made over to her by the prelates, either for her own use, or with intent to be granted out again to her favourites, whom she thus gratified without any expense to herself. To prevent which for the future, the stat. 1 *Jac.* 1, c. 3, extends the prohibition to grants and leases made to the king as well as to any of his subjects. 11 *Rep.* 71.

Next comes the stat. 13 *Eliz. c.* 10, explained and enforced by the statutes 14 *Eliz. c.* 11 and 14. 18 *Eliz. c.* 11, and 43 *Eliz. c.* 29, which extend the restrictions laid by the last-mentioned stat. on bishops, to certain other inferior corporations, both sole and aggregate. From laying all which together we may collect, that all colleges, cathedrals, and other ecclesiastical, or eleemosynary corporations, and all parsons and vicars, are restrained from making any leases of their lands, unless under the following regulations: 1. They must not exceed 21 years, or three lives, from the making. 2. The accustomed rent, or more, must be yearly reserved thereon. 3. Houses in corporations, or market-towns, may be let for forty years, provided they be not the mansion-houses of the lessors, nor have above ten acres of ground belonging to them, and provided the lessee be bound to keep them in repair: and they may also be aliened in fee-simple for lands of equal value in recompence. 4. Where there is an old lease in being, no concurrent lease shall be made, unless where the old one will expire within three years. 5. No lease (by the equity of the statute) shall be made without impeachment of waste. (*Co. Litt.* 45.) 6. All bonds and covenants tending to frustrate the provisions of the statutes of 13 & 18 *Eliz.* shall be void.

Concerning these restrictive statutes there are two observations to be made. First, that they do not by any construction, enable any persons to make such leases as they were by common law disabled to make. Therefore a parson, or vicar, though he is restrained from making longer leases than for twenty-one years or three lives, even with the consent of patron and ordinary, yet is not enabled to make any lease at all, so as to bind his successor, without

---

granted of making leases in possession, but not in reversion, for a certain term; the object being that the estate may not be incumbered by the act of the party beyond a specific time. Yet persons, who had this limited power of making leases in possession only, had frequently demised the premises to hold *from the day of the date*; and the court in several instances had determined that the words *from the day of the date* excluded the day of making the deed; and that of consequence these were leases in reversion, and void: But this question having been brought again before lord Mansfield and the court of king's bench, that learned lord proved, with his usual ability, that *from the day* might either be inclusive or exclusive of the day; and therefore that it ought to be construed so as to effectuate these important deeds, and not to destroy them. Pugh *v.* Duke of Leeds, *Cowp.* 714.

* But now by the stat. 5 *Geo.* 3, *c.* 17, a lease of tithes or other incorporeal hereditaments, alone, may be granted by any bishop or any such ecclesiastical or eleemosynary corporation, and the successor shall be entitled to recover the rent by an action of debt, which (in case of a freehold lease) he could not have brought at the common law.

obtaining such consent (*Co. Lit.* 44). Secondly, that though leases contrary to these acts are declared void, yet they are good against the *lessor* during his life, if he be a sole corporation; and are also good against an aggregate corporation, so long as the head of it lives, who is presumed to be the most concerned in interest. For the act was intended for the benefit of the successor only; and no man shall make an advantage of his own wrong. *Ibid.* 45.

There is yet another restriction with regard to college leases, by statute 18 *Eliz.* c. 6, which directs, that one third of the old rent, then paid, should for the future be reserved in wheat or malt, reserving a quarter of wheat for each 6*s.* 8*d.* or a quarter of malt for every 5*s.*; or that the lessees should pay for the same according to the price that wheat and malt should be sold for in the market next adjoining to the respective colleges, on the market-day before the rent becomes due. This is said (*Strype's Annals of Eliz.*) to have been an invention of lord treasurer Burleigh, and sir Thomas Smith, then principal secretary of state, who observing how greatly the value of money had sunk, and the price of all provisions risen, by the quantity of bullion imported from the new found Indies, (which effects were likely to increase to a greater degree,) devised this method for upholding the revenues of colleges. Their foresight and penetration has in this respect been very apparent: for, though the rent so reserved in corn was at first but one third of the old rent, or half of what was still reserved in money, yet now the proportion is nearly inverted; and the money arising from corn rents is, *communibus annis*, almost double to the rents reserved in money *.

* The price of a quarter of wheat being at present near 50*s.* and the colleges receiving a quarter of wheat, or its value, for every 13*s.* 4*d.* which they are paid in money, it follows that the corn rent will be in proportion to the money rent nearly as four to one.

But both these rents united are very far from the present value. Colleges therefore, in order to obtain the full value of the term, take a fine upon the renewal of their leases. It was a great object to colleges to restrain those in possession from making long leases, and impoverishing their successors by receiving the whole value of the lease by a fine at the commencement of the term.

The corn rent has made the old rent approach in some degree nearer to its present value; otherwise it should seem the principal advantage of a corn rent is to secure the lessor from the effect of a sudden scarcity of corn.

The leases of beneficed clergymen are further restrained, in case of their non-residence, by statutes 13 *Eliz.* c. 20. 14 *Eliz.* c. 11. 18 *Eliz.* c. 11, and 43 *Eliz.* c. 9, which direct, that if any beneficed clergyman be absent from his cure above fourscore days in any one year, he shall not only forfeit one year's profit of his benefice, to be distributed among the poor of the parish, but that all leases made by him, of the profits of such benefice, and all covenants and agreements of like nature, shall cease and be void:† except in the case of licensed pluralists, who are allowed to demise the living on which they are non-resident to their curates only, provided such curates do not absent themselves above 40 days in any one year. If the curate leases over, the lease will become void by his absence, but not by the absence of the incumbent. *Gibs.* 740. See *Residence.*

LEASES OF THE KING. See *King*, and *King's Grants.*

LEASE *and* RELEASE, CONVEYANCE BY, is a mode of transferring the possession, and right or interest in lands or tenements to another.

This conveyance by lease and release was first invented by serj. Moore, soon after the statute of uses, and is now the most common of any, and therefore not to be shaken; though very great lawyers (as, particularly, Mr. *Noy*, attorney-gen. to *Cha.* I. formerly doubted its validity, 2 *Mod.* 252.) It is thus contrived: a lease, or rather bargain and sale, upon some pecuniary consideration, for one year, is made by the tenant of the freehold to the lessee or bargainee. Now this, without any enrolment, makes the bargainor stand seised to the use of the bargainee, and vests in the bargainee the *use* of the term for a year; and then the statute immediately annexes the *possession*. He therefore being thus in possession, is capable of receiving a release of the freehold and reversion; which must be made to a tenant in possession: and, accordingly, the next day, a release is granted to him. This is held to supply the place of livery of seisin: and so a conveyance by lease and release is said to amount to a feoffment. *Co. Litt.* 270. *Cro. Jac.* 604.

LEAT, a mill-leat, corruptly milleat. A

† In a late case it was determined where an incumbent had leased his rectory, and had been afterwards absent for more than 80 days in a year, that his tenant could not maintain an ejectment against a stranger who had got into possession without any right or title whatever. 2 *T. R.* 749.

But where the lease is void by non-residence the tenant in possession may maintain an action of trespass against a wrong-doer. 1 *East*, 244.

trench to convey water to or from a mill. *Cowel. Blount.*

LEATHER. There are several statutes relating to leather, which see under titles *London*, and *Manufactures.*

LECCATOR, a debauched person, *lecher*, or whoremaster, *Cowel. Blount.*

LECHERWITE, a fine on adulterers and fornicators. *Ibid.*

LECTISTERNIUM, a bed, sometimes all that belongs to a bed. *Ibid.*

LECTRINUM, is taken for a pulpit. *Ibid.*

LECTURER (*Prælector*), a reader of lectures; and in London and other cities there are *lecturers* who are assistants to the *rectors* of churches in preaching, &c. chosen by the vestry, or chief inhabitants of the parish, and are usually the afternoon preachers: The law requires, that they should have the approbation and admission of the ordinary; and they are, at the time of their admission, to subscribe to the thirty-nine articles of religion, &c, required by the 13 & 14 *Car.* 2, *c.* 4. They are to be licensed by the bishop, as other ministers, and a man cannot be a *lecturer* without a license from the bishop or archbishop; but the power of a bishop, &c. is only as to the qualification and fitness of the person, and not as to the right of the *lectureship*; for if a bishop determine in favour of a *lecturer*, a *prohibition* may be granted to try the right. *Mich.* 12 *W.* 3, *B. R.* If *lecturers* preach in the week days, they must read the common Prayer for the day when they first preach, and declare their assent to that book; they are likewise to do the same the first *lecture* day in every month so long as they continue *lecturers*, or they shall be disabled to preach till they conform to the same: and if they preach before such conformity, they may be committed to prison for three months, by warrant of two *justices of peace*, granted on the certificate of the ordinary. 13 & 14 *Car.* 2. *c.* 4. *Rights Clerg.* 388.

Where lectures are to be preached or read in any cathedral or collegiate church, if the lecturer openly, at the time aforesaid, declare his assent to all things in the book of Common Prayer, it shall be sufficient; and university sermons or lectures are excepted out of the act concerning lectures. There are lectures founded by the donations of pious persons, the lecturers whereof are appointed by the founders; without any interposition or consent of rectors of churches, &c. though with the leave and approbation of the bishop; such as that of lady Moier at St. Paul's, &c. But such are not entitled to the pulpit without the consent of the rector, or vicar, in whom the freehold of the church is. *Cases B. R.* 420, 433. See *Regius Professor.*

LECTURNIUM, (*lectorium*) the desk or reading place in churches, *Cowel.*

LEDGRAVE, the chief man of the lathe or lethe. *Ibid.*

LEDO, (*ledona*) the rising water or increase of the sea. *Ibid.*

LEET. The court-leet or view of frankpledge is a court of record, held once in the year and not oftener (*Mirror, c.* 1. *s.* 10. 4 *Inst.* 261. 2 *Hawk. P. C.* 72.), within a particular hundred, lordship, or manor, before the steward of the leet: being the king's court granted by charter to the lords of those hundreds or manors. Its original intent was to view the frankpledges, that is, the freemen within the liberty; who, according to the institution of the great Alfred, were all mutually pledges for the good behaviour of each other. Besides this, the preservation of the peace, and the chastisement of divers minute offences against the public good, are the objects both of the court-leet, and the sheriff's tourn: which have exactly the same jurisdiction, one being only a larger species of the other; extending over more territory, but not over more causes. All freeholders within the precinct are obliged to attend them, and all persons commorant therein; which commorancy consists in usually lying there: a regulation, which owes its original to the laws of king Canute (*part* 2. *c.* 19.) But persons under twelve and above sixty years old, peers, clergymen, women, and the king's tenants in ancient demesne, are excused from attendance there: all others being bound to appear upon the jury, if required, and make their due presentments. It was also antiently the custom to summon all the king's subjects, as they respectively grew to years of discretion and strength, to come to the court-leet, and there take the oath of allegiance to the king. The other general business of the leet and tourn, was to present by jury all crimes whatsoever that happened within their jurisdiction; and not only to present, but also to punish, all trivial misdemesnors, as all trivial debts were recoverable in the court-baron, and county-court: justice, in these minuter matters of both kinds, being brought home to the doors of every man by our antient constitution: as in the Gothic constitution, the *hæreda*, which answered to our court leet, "*de omnibus quidem cognoscit, non tamen* "*de omnibus judicat* (*Stiernh, de jur. Goth,* "*l.* 1. *c.* 2.)"

The objects of their jurisdiction are, therefore, unavoidably very numerous: being such as in some degree, either less or more, affect the public weal, or good governance of the district in which they arise; from common nusances and other material offences against the king's peace and public trade, down to eavesdropping, waifs, and irregularities in public commons, But both the tourn and the leet have been for a long time in a declining way: a circumstance, owing in part to the discharge granted by the statute of Malbridge, 52 *Hen.* 3. *c.* 10. to all prelates, peers, and clergymen, from their attendance upon these courts; which occasioned them to grow into disrepute. And hence it is that their business hath for the most part gradually devolved upon the quarter sessions: which it is particularly directed to do in some cases by statute 1 *Ed.* 4. *c.* 2.

LEETS or LEITS, meetings appointed for the nomination or elections of officers. *Spots. Hist. Chu. Scotl.*

LEGA ET LACTA. Anciently the allay of money was so called. *Cowel. Blount.*

LEGABILIS, signifies what is not entailed as hereditary; but may be bequeathed by legacy in a last will and testament. *Ibid.*

LEGACY. (*legatum*) A legacy is a bequest, or gift, of goods and chattels by testament; and the person to whom it was given, is stiled the legatee: which every person is capable of being, unless particularly disabled by the common law or statutes, as traitors, papists, and some others. This bequest transfers an inchoate property to the legatee; but the legacy is not perfect without the assent of the executor: for if I have a general or pecuniary legacy of 100*l.* or a specific one of a piece of plate, I cannot in either case take it without the consent of the executor (*Co. Litt.* 111. *Aleyn.* 39.)* For in him all the chattels are vested; and it is his business first of all to see whether there is a sufficient fund left to pay the debts of the testator: the rule of equity being, that a man must be just, before he is permitted to be generous. (*Bract. l.* 2. *c.* 26.) And in case of a deficiency of assets, all the general legacies must abate proportionably, in order to pay the debts: but a specific legacy (of a piece of plate, a horse, or the like) is not to abate at all, or allow any thing by way of abatement, unless there be not sufficient without it (2 *Vern.* 111.) Upon the same principle, if the legatees have been paid their legacies, they are afterwards bound to refund a rateable part, in case debts come in, more than sufficient to exhaust the *residuum* after the legacies paid (*Ibid.* 205.) And this law is as old as Bracton and Fleta, who tell us, "*si plura* "*sint debita, vel plus legatum fuerit, ad quæ* "*catalla defuncti non sufficiant, fiat ubique de*-"*falcatio, excepto regis privilegio.*" (*Bract. l.* 2. *c.* 26. *Flet. l.* 2. *c.* 47. *s.* 11.)

If the legatee dies before the testator, the legacy is a lost or lapsed legacy, and shall sink into the *residuum.* And if a contingent legacy be left to any one; as when he shall attain, or if he attains the age of twenty-one, and he dies before that time, it is a lapsed legacy (*Dyer* 59. 1 *Eq. Cas. Abr.* 295.) But a legacy to one, to be paid *when* he attains, or *at* the age of twenty-one years, is a vested legacy; an interest which commences *in præsenti,* although it be *solvendum in futuro.* And, if the legatee dies before that age, his representatives shall receive it out of the testator's personal estate, at the same time that it would have become payable, in case the legatee had lived.† But if such legacies be charged upon a real estate, in both cases they shall lapse for the benefit of the heir (2 *P. Wms.* 601.); for, with regard to devises affecting lands, the ecclesiastical court hath no concurrent jurisdiction.‡ And,

---

* In *Decks* v. *Strutt,* 5 *T. R.* 690, it was determined, that *no action can be maintained in a court of law to recover a legacy,* though it had before been decided, that an action of assumpsit might have been brought against an executor in his own right, if *in consideration of assets in his possession* he had promised to pay the legatee the legacy. *Cowp.* 284, 289.

But if the executor assents, an action at law may be maintained for a specific legacy, as for a lease or any other chattel. 3 *East,* 120.

† But where a legacy is given to another, in case the first legatee dies under twenty-one or a certain age, the legacy must be paid upon the death of the infant. And where it is not given over to another, if it bears interest, his representative shall be entitled to it immediately; but if the interest allowed by the testator is less than the interest allowed by a court of equity, the executor of the testator, shall be entitled to the difference until the first legatee would have arrived at the age prescribed by the testator. 2 *P. Wms.* 478. 1 *Bro.* 105.

A bequest of a residue or fund to all the children of A, to be paid when they shall attain the age of twenty-one, must be divided among those only who are in existence, when the eldest attains that age. 3 *Bro.* 404.

Where a legacy was given to the eldest child of A upon the death of B, A had at the death of B only illegitimate children, but had afterwards a legitimate child, it was held that neither could take, the first not legally answering the description, and the second not existing when the legacy was to vest. 6 *Ves. jun.* 43.

‡ It is generally true, that both portions created by deed or will, and legacies which are to be raised out of real property, and to be paid upon a future day, shall never be raised if the person to whom they are given dies before the day of payment. But legacies and portions in a will shall be raised, if the time of payment is postponed on account of the circumstances of the testator's estate, and not on account of the circumstances of the legatee; or where it is the apparent intention of the testator, notwithstanding the death of the legatee prior to the time specified. If the portions are to be raised out of

the land, and no time is limited, although in case of a vested legacy, due immediately, and charged on land, or money in the funds, which yield an immediate profit, interest shall be payable thereon from the testator's death; but if charged only on the personal estate, which cannot be immediately got in, it shall carry interest only from the end of the year after the death of the testator (2 *P. Wms*. 26, 27.) And a pecuniary legacy given by a parent to a legitimate child, shall carry interest from the death of the testator; otherwise the child might perish within the year for want of maintenance. 1 *Ves*. 310.

Besides these formal legacies, contained in a man's will and testament, there is also permitted another death-bed disposition of property, which is called a donation *causa mortis*. And that is, when a person in his last sickness, apprehending his dissolution near, delivers or causes to be delivered to another the possession of any personal goods, (under which have been included bonds, and bills drawn by the deceased upon his banker,) to keep in case of his decease; but not of other promissory notes or bills of exchange, these being choses in action which cannot pass. 3 *P. Wms*. 357. and 2 *Ves*. 431. This gift, if the donor dies, needs not the assent of his executor; yet it shall not prevail against creditors; and is accompanied with this implied trust, that, if the donor lives, the property thereof shall revert to himself, being only given in contemplation of death, or *mortis causa* (*Prec. Chanc*. 269. 1 *P. Wms*. 406, 441. 3 *P. Wms*. 357.)

For the substraction, withholding, or detaining of legacies, (which is most apparently injurious, by depriving the legatees of that right with which the laws of the land, and the will of the deceased have invested them) the spiritual court administers redress, by compelling the executor to pay them. But in this last case, the courts of equity also exercise a concurrent jurisdiction with the ecclesiastical courts, as incident to some other species of relief prayed by the complainant: as to compel the executor to account for the testator's effects, or assent to the legacy, or the like. For, as it is beneath the dignity of the king's courts to be merely ancillary to other inferior jurisdictions, the cause, when once brought there, receives there also its full determination. 3 *Black*. 98.

LEGALIS HOMO, one who stands *rectus in curia*, not outlawed, excommunicated, or infamous. *Cowel. Blount. Hawkins.*

LEGALIS MONETA ANGLIÆ, lawful money of England, is gold or silver money coined or made current here by the king's authority. 1 *Inst*. 207.

LEGATARY, (*legatarius*) the person to whom any thing is bequeathed; a legatee.

LEGATE, (*legatus*) an ambassador or *nuncio* from the people. And the popes of Rome had formerly in England, the archbishops of Canterbury their *legatus natus*; and, upon extraordinary occasions, sent over *legatus a latere*. *Cowel. Blount.*

LEGATEE or LEGATORY, the person to whom a legacy is bequeathed.

LEGATUM, in the ecclesiastic sense, a legacy given to the church or accustomed mortuary. *Cowel.*

LEGEM FACERE, to make law, or oath. *Ibid.*

LEGERGILD. (*legergildum*) See *Lecherwite* and *Lairwite*.

LEGIOSUS, litigious, and so subjected to a course of law. *Cowel.*

LEGISLATURE. The parliament, consisting of king, lords, and commons: in which the supreme and absolute power of the state is vested by our invaluable constitution.

LEGITIMATION, (*legitimatio*) a making lawful or legitimate: thus naturalization, &c. makes a foreigner a lawful subject of the state. *Cowel.*

LEIPA, a departure from service. *Cowel.*

LEIRWIT, (*mulcta adulteriorum*. *Fleta, lib.* 1. *cap*. 7.) is used for a liberty, whereby a lord challengeth the penalty of one that lieth unlawfully with his bond-woman. *Ibid.*

LENDING. See *Usury*.

LENT, (from the Germ. *lentz*, i. e. *ver*, the spring fast) is a time for fasting for forty days, next before Easter.

LEP AND LACE, (*leppe & lasse*) is a custom in the manner of Writtel in the county of Essex, that every cart which goes over Greenbury within that manor (except it be the cart of a nobleman) shall pay 4*d*. to the lord. This Greenbury is conceived to have been antiently a market-place; on which account this privilege was granted. *Blount.*

LEPA, a measure which contained the third part of two bushels: hence a seed-leap. *Cowel.*

LEPORARIUS, a greyhound for the hare. *Ibid.*

LEPORIUM, a place where hares were kept together. *Ibid.*

LEPROSO AMOVENDO, an ancient writ that lay to remove a leper or lazer, who thrusts himself into the company of his neighbours in any parish, either in the church, or at other public meetings, to their annoyance. *Reg. Orig*. 237. *New Nat. Br*. 521.

LE ROY LE VEUT, words by which the royal assent is signified by the clerk of the parliament to public bills; and to a private bill the king's answer is, *soi fait comme il est desire*.

LE ROY SE AVISERA, by these words

---

cases upon the subject are contradictory, it seems they shall sink into the estate, if the children die before they are wanted. See the cases upon this subject fully collected in 2 *Cox's P. Wms*. 612. and *Harg. Co. Litt.* 237.

to a bill, presented to the king by his houses of parliament, are understood his denial of that bill. By this means, the indecency of a positive refusal to give the royal assent to a bill passed by the lords and commons is avoided.

LESCHEWES, trees fallen by chance, or windfalls. *Broke's Abr.* 341.

LESIA, a leash of greyhounds, now restrained to the number of three, but formerly more. *Spelm.*

LESPEGEND, (Sax. *les pegen*) *baro minor, hominibus quos Angli lespegend, nun capant Dani vero* young men *vocant, &c.* *Constitut. Canut. de Foresta, Art.* 2.

LESSA, a legacy; from this word also lease is derived. *Cowel.*

LESSOR AND LESSEE, the parties to a lease. See *Landlord and Tenant.*

LESTAGE, the same as lastage.

LESTAGEFRY, lestage-free, exempt from the duty of paying ballast money. *Cowel.*

LESWES, or LELVES, used in Domesday, to signify pastures. *Ibid.*

LETARE JERUSALEM, the customary oblations made on Midlent Sunday, when the proper hymn was *Lætare Jerusalem,* &c. by the inhabitants within a diocese to the mother cathedral church. From the ancient custom of processions at that time, began the practice, which is still retained in many parts of England, of mothering, or going to visit parents, distributing cakes, or making feasts on Midlent Sunday. *Ibid.*

LETTERS, *threatening.* See *Felony.*

LETTER MISSIVE FOR ELECTING A BISHOP. A letter from the king to the dean and chapter containing the name of the person whom he would have them elect. 1 *Black.* 379.

LETTER MISSIVE IN CHANCERY. If a peer is a defendant in the court of chancery, the lord chancellor sends a letter missive to him to request his appearance, together with a copy of the bill; if he neglects to appear, then he may be served with a *subpœna;* if he continues still in contempt, a *sequestration* issues out immediately against his lands and goods, without any of the mesne process of attachments, &c. which are directed only against the person, therefore cannot affect a lord of parliament. The same process issues against a member of the house of commons, except that the lord chancellor doth not send him any letter missive. 3 *Black.* 445. See *Privilege.*

LETTERS OF ABSOLUTION, (*litera absolutoriæ*) were such in former times, when an abbot released any of his brethren *ab omni subjectione & obedientia,* from his order, and made them capable of entering into some other.

LETTERS OF ATTORNEY, (*litera attornati*) is a writing, authorising an attorney to do any lawful act in the stead of another: as to give seisin of lands; receive debts, or sue a third person, &c. and these may be either general or special. But the authority must be strictly pursued. *Plowd.* 475. *Preced. Chanc.* 125. 2 *Vern.* 391.

LETTERS CLAUS, (*literæ clausæ*) close letters, opposed to letters patent; being commonly sealed up with the king's signet or privy seal; whereas the letters patent are left open and sealed with the broad seal.

LETTER OF CREDIT, is where a merchant or correspondent writes a letter to another, requesting him to credit the bearer with a certain sum of money. *Merc. Dict.*

LETTERS OF EXCHANGE, (*literæ cambii*) *Reg. Orig.* 194. See *Bills of Exchange.*

LETTER OF LICENCE, an instrument or writing made by creditors to a man giving him longer time for the payment of his debts, and protecting him from arrests in going about his affairs.

LETTERS OF MARQUE. See *Marque* and *Reprisal.*

LETTERS PATENT, (*literæ patentes*) sometimes called *letters overt,* are writings of the king sealed with the great seal of England, whereby a person is enabled to do or enjoy that which otherwise he could not; and so called, because they are open with the seal affixed, and ready to be shewn for confirmation of the authority thereby given. 2 *Black.* 346.

LETTERS OF SAFE CONDUCT. See *Safe Conduct.*

LEVANT AND COUCHANT, a law term for cattle that have been so long in the ground of another, that they have lain down and are risen again to feed.

LEVANUM, (from the Lat. *levare,* to make lighter) is leavened bread. *Cowel.*

LEVARE FOENUM, to make hay, or properly to cast it into wind-rows, in order *ad tassandum,* to cock it up. *Ibid.*

LEVARI FACIAS, a writ directed to the sheriff for levying a sum of money upon a man's lands and tenements, goods and chattels. *Reg. Orig.* 298. For which see *Execution.*

LEUCA, is a measure of land, consisting of 1500 paces. Ingulphus tells us, it is 2000 paces, *pag.* 910. In the *Monastic.* 1 *tom. p.* 313. it is 480 perches.

LEUCATA, is a space of ground, as much as a mile contains. *De bosco, &c. continente unam leucatam in latitudine et dimidium in longitudine.* *Monast.* 1 *tom. p.* 768. And so it seems to be used in a charter of William the Conqueror to Battle Abbey. *Cowel.*

LEVELLUS, a level, even or upon the level. *Ibid.*

LEVITICAL DEGREES, the degrees of kindred prohibited by the *levitical law* from intermarrying with each other, are set forth in the Book of Common Prayer.

LEVY, (*levare*) to collect, or exact; as to levy money, sometimes to erect, or cast up; as to levy a ditch, &c. And to levy a fine of land, is the usual term.

LEVYING MONEY WITHOUT CONSENT OF PARLIAMENT. No subject of England can be constrained to pay any aids or taxes, even for the defence of the realm or the support of government, but such as are imposed by his own consent, or that of his representatives in parliament. 1 *Black.* 140.

LEVYING WAR AGAINST THE KING. See *Treason*.

LEWDNESS, is punishable by our law by fine, imprisonment, and pillory, or either. 4 *Black.* 64.

LEX, a law for the government of mankind in society. See *Law*.

LEX AMISSA, or *legem amittere, viz.* one who is an infamous, perjured, or outlawed person. *Bracton, lib.* 4. *cap.* 19. *par.* 2.

LEX APOSTA, or LEGEM APOSTATARE, is to do a thing contrary to law. *Cowel.*

LEX BREHONIA, the Brehon or Irish law. See *Ireland*.

LEX BRETOISE, the law of the ancient Britons, or Marches of Wales. *Cowel.*

LEX DERAISNIA. *Deraisnia est lex quædam in Normannia constituta, per quam in simplicibus querelis insecutus factum, quod à parte adversa ei objicitur, se non fecisse declarat.* And it is the proof of a thing, which one denies to be done by him, where another affirms it; defeating the assertion of his adversary, and shewing it to be against reason or probability. *Ibid.*

LEX HOSTILIA DE FURTIS, a law amongst the Romans, by which it was provided that a prosecution for the theft of goods belonging to a person unknown, might be carried on without the intervention of the owner. *Gravin. l.* 3. *s.* 6.

LEX JUDICIALIS, is properly *purgatio per judicium ferri. Cowel.*

LEX SACRAMENTALIS, *purgatio per sacramentum. Ibid.*

LEX TALIONIS, is *juris positivi*; and the *talionis* among the Jews, were converted into pecuniary estimates, so that the price of an eye, &c. lost was allowed to the person injured. 1 *Hale's Hist. P. C.* 12. 4 *Black.* 12.

LEX TERRÆ, the law and custom of the land. See *Law*.

LEX WALLENSICA, the British law or law of Wales. See *Wales*.

LEY, or LEYS, the French word for law. *Cowel. Blount.*

LEY, LEE, LAY, whether in the beginning or end of names of places, signifies an open field, or large pasture. *Cowel.*

LEY-GAGER, (1 *Car.* 1. *cap.* 3.) wager of law. See *Wager of Law*.

LIBEL, (*libellus*) signifies literally a little book.

With regard to libels in general, there are, as in many other cases two remedies; one by *indictment*, and another by *action*. The former for the public offence; inasmuch as every libel has a tendency to break the peace, or provoke others to break it: which offence is the same whether the matter contained be true or false; and therefore, the defendant, on an indictment for publishing a libel, is not allowed to alledge the truth of it by way of justification (5 *Rep.* 125.) But in the remedy by action on the case, which is to repair the party in damages for the injury done him, the defendant may, as for words spoken, justify the truth of the facts, and shew that the plaintiff has received no injury at all (11 *Mod.* 99.) The same rule holds in every particular with regard to libels by writing or printing, and the civil actions consequent thereupon, as in regard to words spoken, (see *Slander;*) but as to signs or pictures, it seems necessary always to shew, by proper *innuendoes* and averments of the defendant's meaning, the import and application of the scandal, and that some special damage has followed; otherwise it cannot appear, that such libel by picture was understood to be levelled at the plaintiff, or that it was attended with any actionable consequences.

These *libels* (*libelli famosi*) taken in their largest and most extensive sense, signify any writings, pictures, or the like, of an immoral or illegal tendency; they are malicious defamations of any person, and especially a magistrate, made public by either printing, writing, signs, or pictures, in order to provoke him to wrath, or expose him to public hatred, contempt and ridicule (1 *Hawk. P. C.* 193.) The direct tendency of these libels is the breach of the public peace, by stirring up the objects of them to revenge, and perhaps to bloodshed. The communication of a libel to any one person is a publication in the eye of the law (*Moor.* 813.); and therefore, the sending an abusive private letter to a man, is as much a libel as if it were openly printed, for it equally tends to a breach of the peace (2 *Brown.* 151. 12 *Rep.* 35. *Hob.* 215. *Poph.* 139. 1 *Hawk. P. C.* 195.) For the same reason it is immaterial with respect to the essence of a libel, whether the matter of it be true or false (*Moor.* 627. 5 *Rep.* 125. 11 *Mod.* 99.); since the provocation, and not the falsity, is the thing to be punished criminally:* though, doubtless, the falsehood of it may aggravate its guilt, and enhance its punishment. For though in a civil action, the truth of the accusation may be pleaded in bar of the suit; yet, in a criminal prosecution, the tendency which all libels have to create animosities, and to disturb the public peace, is the whole that the

* Consequently an information or an indictment need not state, that the libel is false, or that the offence was committed by force and arms. 7 *T. R.* 4.

law considers. And therefore in such prosecutions, the only points to be enquired into are, first, the making or publishing of the book or writing; and, secondly, whether the matter be criminal: and, if both these points are against the defendant, the offence against the public is complete.

But, though it has been held for more than two centuries, that *the truth of a libel** is no justification in *a criminal prosecution*, yet in many instances it is considered an extenuation of the offence; and the court of king's bench has laid down this general rule, *viz.* that it will not grant an information for a libel, unless the prosecutor, who applies for it, makes an affidavit, asserting directly and pointedly, that he is innocent of the charge imputed to him. But this rule may be dispensed with, if the person libelled resides abroad, or if the imputations of the libel are general and indefinite, or if it is a charge against the prosecutor for language which he has held in parliament. *Doug.* 271, 372.

A person may be punished for a libel reflecting on the memory and character of the dead, but it must be alleged, and proved to the satisfaction of the jury, that the author intended by the publication to bring dishonour and contempt on the relations and descendants of the deceased. 4 *T. R.* 261.

And it is not a libel to publish a correct copy of the reports or resolutions of the two houses of parliament, or a true account of the proceedings of a court of justice. "For "though (as Mr. Justice Lawrence has well "observed) the publication of such proceed-"ings may be to the disadvantage of the "particular individual concerned, yet it is "of vast importance to the public that the "proceedings of courts of justice should be "universally known. The general advan-"tage to the country in having these pro-"ceedings made public, more than coun-"terbalances the inconveniences to the pri-"vate persons, whose conduct may be the "subject of such proceedings." *R.* v. *Wright*, 8 *T. R.* 293.

It had frequently been determined by the court of king's bench, that the only questions for the consideration of the jury, in *criminal prosecutions* for libels, were the fact of publication, and the truth of the innuendos, that is, the truth of the meaning and sense of the passages of the libel, as stated and averred in the record, and that the judge or courtalone were competent to determine whether the subject of the publication was or was not a libel. 3 *T. R.* 428. But the legality of this doctrine having been much controverted, the 32 *Geo.* 3. *c.* 60. was passed, intituled, *An act to remove doubts respecting the functions of juries in cases of libels.* And it declares and enacts, that on every trial of an indictment or information for a libel, the jury may give a general verdict of guilty, or not guilty, upon the whole matter in issue, and shall not be required or directed by the judge to find the defendant guilty, merely on the proof of the publication of the paper charged to be a libel, and of the sense ascribed to it in the record. But the statute provides, that the judge may give his opinion to the jury respecting the matter in issue, and the jury may at their discretion, as in other cases, find a special verdict, and the defendant, if convicted, may move the court as before the statute, in arrest of judgment.

The sale of the libel by a servant in a shop, is *prima facie* evidence of publication in a prosecution against the master, and is sufficient for conviction, unless contradicted by contrary evidence, shewing that he was not privy, nor in any degree assenting to it. *Ibid.* and 5 *Burr.* 2686.

When a person is brought to receive judgment for a libel, his conduct, subsequent to his conviction, may be taken into consideration, either by way of aggravation or mitigation of the punishment. 3 *T. R.* 432. Accordingly when Johnson the bookseller was brought up for judgment for having published a seditious libel, the attorney-general produced an affidavit that the defendant after his conviction, had published the same libel in the Analytical Review. *M. T.* 1798.

LIBERA, a livery or delivery of so much grass or corn to a customary tenant, who cuts down or prepares the said grass or corn, and receives some part or small portion of it as a reward or gratuity. *Cowel.*

LIBERA BATELLA, signifies a free boat.

LIBERA CHASEA HABENDA, was a judicial writ granted to a person for a free chase belonging to his manor; after proof made by inquiry of a jury, that the same of right belonged to him. *Reg. Orig.* 36.

LIBERAM LEGUM. On trial by battel, if either champion proved *recreant*, i. e. yielded and pronounced the word *craven*, he was condemned as a *recreant*, *amittere liberam legem*, that is, to become infamous, and not be accounted *liber et legalis homo*, being supposed by the event to be proved forsworn, and therefore never to be put upon a jury, or admitted as a witness in any cause. 3 *Black.* 340, 341.

LIBERA PISCARIA, a free fishery. 2 *Salk.* 637. See *Fish* and *Fisheries*.

LIBER CAURUS, a free bull. *Cowel*, *Blount.*

LIBERA WARA. See *Wara.*

* And as truth is a greater provocation than falsehood to an irritable mind, and has the greater tendency to produce a breach of the peace from the preclusion of any redress by a civil action which might be had in the case of a falsehood, the doctrine of *the greater the truth, the greater the libel* upon a criminal prosecution, is certainly well founded.

LIBERATE, a writ that lies for the payment of a yearly pension or sum of money granted under the great seal, and directed to the treasurer and chamberlains of the exchequer, &c. for that purpose. In another sense, it is a writ to the sheriff of a county, for the delivery of possession of lands and goods extended, or taken upon the forfeiture of a recognizance. Also a writ issuing out of the chancery directed to a gaoler for delivery of a prisoner that hath put in bail for his appearance. *F. N. B.* 132. 4 *Inst.* 116. This writ is most commonly used for delivery of goods, &c. on an extent; and by the extent the conusee of a recognizance hath not any absolute interest in the goods, until the *liberate* 2 *Lil.* 169. See *Extent.*

LIBERATIO, is taken for money, meat, drink, clothes, &c. yearly given and delivered by the lord to his domestic servants. *Blount.*

LIBERTAS ECCLESIASTICA. Church liberty, or ecclesiastical immunities. *Cowel.*

LIBERTATE PROBANDA, an ancient writ that lay for such as being demanded for villeins offered to prove themselves free; directed to the sheriff that he should take security of them for the proving of their freedom before the justices of assise, and that in the mean time they should be unmolested. *F. N. B.* 77.

LIBERTATIVUS ALLOCANDIS, a writ lying for a citizen or burgess, impleaded contrary to his liberty, to have his privilege allowed. *Reg. Orig.* 262.

LIBERTATIBUS EXIGENDIS IN ITINERE, an ancient writ whereby the king commands the justices in eyre to admit of an attorney for the defence of another man's liberty. *Reg. Orig.* 19.

LIBERTIES or FRANCHISES. These are synonymous terms, and their definition is, a royal privilege, or branch of the king's prerogative, subsisting in the hands of a subject. The kinds of them are various, and almost infinite. 2 *Black.* 37. *Bracton.*

LIBERTY TO HOLD PLEAS, signifies to have a court of one's own; and to hold it before a mayor, bailiff, &c. See *Franchise.*

LIBERTIES AND RIGHTS. The absolute rights of man, considered as a free agent, endowed with discernment to know good from evil, and with power of choosing those measures which appear to him to be most desirable, are usually summed up in one general appellation, and denominated the natural liberty of mankind. This natural liberty consists properly in a power of acting as one thinks fit, without any restraint or control, unless by the law of nature; being a right inherent in us by birth, and one of the gifts of God to man at his creation, when he endued him with the faculty of free-will. But every man, when he enters into society, gives up a part of his natural liberty, as the price of so valuable a purchase; and, in consideration of receiving the advantages of mutual commerce, obliges himself to conform to those laws, which the community has thought proper to establish. And this species of legal obedience and conformity is infinitely more desirable than that wild and savage liberty which is sacrificed to obtain it. For no man, that considers a moment, would wish to retain the absolute and uncontrolled power of doing whatever he pleases: the consequence of which is, that every other man would have the same power; and then there would be no security to individuals in any of the enjoyments of life. 1 *Black.* 125.

Political or civil liberty, is therefore no other than natural liberty so far restrained by human laws (and no farther) as is necessary and expedient for the general advantage of the public (*Inst.* 1. 3. 1.) Hence we may collect that the law, which restrains a man from doing mischief to his fellow-citizens, though it diminishes the natural, increases the civil liberty of mankind; but that every wanton and causeless restraint of the will of the subject, whether practised by a monarch, a nobility, or a popular assembly, is a degree of tyranny: nay, that even laws themselves, whether made with or without our consent, if they regulate and constrain our conduct in matters of mere indifference, without any good end in view, are regulations destructive of liberty: whereas, if any public advantage can arise from observing such precepts, the control of our private inclinations, in one or two particular points, will conduce to preserve our general freedom in others of more importance; by supporting that state of society, which alone can secure our independence. So that the laws, when prudently framed, are by no means subversive but rather introductive of liberty; for (as Mr. Locke has well observed, *Locke. on Gov. p.* 2. *s.* 57.) where there is no law there is no freedom. But then, on the other hand, that constitution or frame of government, that system of laws, is alone calculated to maintain civil liberty, which leaves the subject entire master of his own conduct, except in those points wherein the public good requires some direction or restraint.

The idea and practice of this political or civil liberty flourish in their highest vigour in these kingdoms, where it falls little short of perfection, and can only be lost or destroyed by the folly or demerits of its owner: the legislature, and of course the laws of England, being peculiarly adapted to the preservation of this inestimable blessing even in the meanest subject.

However, to excite discontent, and to stir up rebellion against all good order and peaceful government, a proposition has lately been industriously propagated, *viz.* that ALL MEN ARE BY NATURE EQUAL. If this subject is considered even for a moment, the very reverse will appear to be the truth, and that ALL MEN ARE BY NATURE UNEQUAL. For though children come into the world equally helpless, yet in a few years, as soon as their bodies acquire vigour, and their minds and passions are expanded and developed, we perceive an infinite difference in their natural powers, capacities, and propensities; and this inequality is still further increased by the instruction which they happen to receive. *Chris. n. ed. Black.* 407.

Independent of any positive regulations, the unequal industry and virtues of men must necessarily create unequal rights. But it is said that *all men are equal because they have an equal right to justice,* or to the possession of their rights. This is a self-evident truth, which no one ever denied, and it amounts to nothing more than to the identical proposition, that all men have equal rights to their rights; for when different men have perfect and absolute rights to unequal things, they are certainly equal with regard to the perfection of their rights, or the justice that is due to their respective claims. This is the only sense in which equality can be applied to mankind. *In the most perfect republic that can be conceived in theory, the proposition is false and mischievous;* the father and child, the master and servant, the judge and prisoner, the general and common soldier, the representative and constituent, must be eternally unequal, and have unequal rights. *Ibid.*

And where every office is elective, the most virtuous and the best qualified to discharge the duties of any office, have rights and claims superior to others. *Ibid.*

In this happy country, the son of the lowest peasant may rise by his merit and abilities to the highest stations in the church, law, army, navy, and in every department of the state. *Ib.* The doctrine, that all men are, or ought to be, equal, is little less contrary to nature, and destructive of their happiness, than the invention of *Procrustes,* who attempted to make men equal by stretching the limbs of some, and lopping off those of others. *Ibid.*

But the experiment, concludes the learned annotator, has been tried on the continent, and the result has hitherto been (an awful warning to the world) a rapid succession of assassinations, judicial murders, proscriptions, and usurpation. *Ibid.*

But to return; these absolute rights of every Englishman, (which, taken in a political and extensive sense, are usually called their liberties,) as they are founded on nature and reason, so they are coëval with our form of government; though subject at times to fluctuate and change; their establishment (excellent as it is) being still human. At some times we have seen them depressed by overbearing and tyrannical princes; at others so luxuriant as even to tend to anarchy, a worse state than tyranny itself, as any government is better than none at all. But the vigour of our free-constitution has always delivered the nation from these embarrassments: and, as soon as the convulsions consequent on the struggle have been over, the balance of our rights and liberties has settled to its proper level; and their fundamental articles have been from time to time asserted in parliament, as often as they were thought to be in danger. 1 *Black.* 127.

FIRST, by the great charter of liberties, *magna charta,* 9 *Hen.* 3. *cap.* 29. no freeman shall be taken and imprisoned, or disseised of his freehold, or of his liberties or free-customs, or be outlawed, banished, or otherwise destroyed; nor shall the king pass upon him, but by the lawful judgment of his peers, or by the law of the land. The king shall sell to none, or deny or delay to none, right or justice. See 25 *Ed.* 3. *st.* 5. *cap.* 4. and 42 *Ed.* 3. *cap.* 3.

Stat. *confirm. chart.* 25 *Ed.* 1. *cap.* 2. if any judgment be given contrary to the great charters, it shall be undone and holden for nought.

Stat. 2 *Ed.* 3. *cap.* 8. it shall not be commanded by the great seal or the little seal, to disturb or delay common right; and though such commandments come, the justices shall not cease to do right.

Stat. 5 *Ed.* 3. *cap.* 9. no man shall be attached by any accusation, nor forjudged of life or limb, nor shall his lands or goods be seised into the king's hands against the great charter and the law of the land.

Stat. 25 *Ed.* 3. *st.* 5. *cap.* 4. none shall be taken by petition or suggestion made to the king or his council, unless it be by indictment of lawful people of the neighbourhood, or by process made by writ original at the common law. And none shall be put out of his franchises or freehold, unless he be duly brought to answer, and forejudged by course of law; and if any thing be done to the contrary, it shall be redressed and holden for none.

Stat. 42 *Ed.* 3. *cap.* 3. no man shall be put to answer, without presentment before justices, or matter of record of due process, or writ original, according to the ancient law of the land. And if any thing be done to the contrary, it shall be void in law, and held for error.

By 3 *Car.* 1. *c.* 1. THE PETITION OF RIGHT, levying of money without consent of parliament, molesting the subject on that account, compelling them to receive soldiers and commissions of martial law, are declared to be contrary to the lawful liberties of the subject.

L

By 16 *Car.* 1. *c.* 10. the court of star-chamber and all its powers were abolished.

AND LASTLY by the important BILL OF RIGHTS. Stat. 1 *Wil. & Mar. st.* 2. *cap.* 2. *sect.* 1. whereas the lords spiritual and temporal, and commons assembled at Westminster, representing all the estates of the people of this realm, did upon the 13th of February 1688, present unto their majesties, then prince and princess of Orange, a declation, containing that,

The said lords spiritual and temporal, and commons, being assembled in a full and free representation of this nation, for the vindicating their ancient rights and liberties, declare,

That the pretended power of suspending of laws, or the execution of laws, by regal authority, without consent of parliament, is illegal;

That the pretended power of dispensing with laws, or the execution of laws, by regal authority, as it hath been assumed and exercised of late, is illegal;

That the commission for erecting the late court of commissioners for ecclesiastical causes, and all other commissions and courts of like nature, are illegal and pernicious;

That levying money for or to the use of the crown, by pretence of prerogative, without grant of parliament, for longer time, or in other manner than the same is or shall be granted, is illegal;

That it is the right of the subjects to petition the king, and all commitments and prosecutions for such petitioning, are illegal;

That the raising or keeping a standing army within the kingdom in time of peace, unless it be with consent of parliament, is against law;

That the subjects which are protestants may have arms for their defence suitable to their conditions, and as allowed by law;

That election of members of parliament ought to be free;

That the freedom of speech, and debates or proceedings in parliament, ought not to be impeached or questioned in any court or place out of parliament;

That excessive bail ought not to be required, nor excessive fines imposed, nor cruel and unusual punishments inflicted;

That jurors ought to be duly impannelled and returned, and jurors which pass upon men in trials for high treason ought to be freeholders;

That all grants and promises of fines and forfeitures of particular persons before conviction, are illegal and void;

And for redress of all grievances, and for the amending, strengthening and preserving of the laws, parliaments ought to be held frequently.

And they do claim, demand, and INSIST UPON all and singular the premises, as their UNDOUBTED RIGHTS AND LIBERTIES; and that no declarations, judgments, doings, or proceedings, to the prejudice of the people in any of the said premises, ought in any wise to be drawn hereafter into consequence or example;

Sect. 6. All and singular the rights and liberties asserted and claimed in the said declaration are the true, ancient and indubitable RIGHTS and LIBERTIES of the people of this kingdom, and so shall be esteemed, allowed, adjudged, and taken to be; and all the particulars aforesaid shall be firmly holden as they are expressed in the said declaration; and all officers shall serve their majesties according to the same in all times to come.

Sect. 12. No dispensation by *non obstante* of any statute shall be allowed, except a dispensation be allowed of in such statute; and except in such cases as shall be specially provided for during this session of parliament.

Sect. 13. No charter granted before the 23d of October 1689, shall be invalidated by this act, but shall remain of the same force as if this act had never been made.

Also by stats. 12 & 13 *Wil.* 3. *cap.* 2. *c.* 10. 6 *Ann. c.* 7. 1 *Geo.* 1. *st.* 2. *c.* 56. 15 *Geo.* 2. *c.* 22. 22 *Geo.* 3. *c.* 41. it is amongst other things enacted, that no person who has an office or place of profit under the king, or receives a pension from the crown, or is a contractor, shall be capable of serving as a member of the house of commons.

But by 6 *Ann. c.* 7. the acceptance of an office, by a member, only vacating his seat, and he may be re-elected, if the electors think proper.

LIBERTY OF THE PRESS. Factious demagogues have ever exclaimed against the prosecutions for libels in matter of political controversy as endangering the liberty of the press; but although in all instances *blasphemous, immoral, treasonable, schismatical, seditious* or *scandalous* libels, are punished by the English law, some with a greater, others with a less degree of severity: yet by this, the LIBERTY OF THE PRESS, properly understood, is by no means infringed or violated. *The liberty of the press* is indeed essential to the nature of a free state, *but this liberty consists in laying no previous restraints upon publications,* not as foolishly imagined in *a freedom from all censure for criminal matter when once published.* 1 *Black.* 152.

For every freeman has, according to the law of England, an undoubted right to lay what sentiments he pleases before the public: to *forbid,* to *prohibit this,* is to destroy the freedom of the press: *but if he publishes what is improper, mischievous,* or *illegal,* he must take the consequence of his own temerity. *Ibid.*

To subject the press to the restrictive power of a licenser, as was formerly done, both before and since the revolution,* is to

---

* The art of printing, soon after its intro-

subject all freedom of sentiment to the prejudices of one man, and make him the arbitrary and infallible judge of all controverted points in learning, religion, and government. But to punish (as the law does at present) any dangerous or offensive writings, which, when published, shall on a fair and impartial trial be adjudged of a pernicious tendency, is necessary for the preservation of peace and good order, of government and religion, the only solid foundations of civil liberty. Thus the will of individuals is still left free; the abuse only of that free will is the object of legal punishment. Neither is any restraint hereby laid upon freedom of thought or inquiry: liberty of private sentiment is still left; the disseminating, or making public, of bad sentiments, destructive of the ends of society, is the crime which society corrects. A man (says a fine writer on this subject) may be allowed to keep poisons in his closet, but not publicly to vend them as cordials. And to this we may add, that the only plausible argument heretofore used for the restraining the just freedom of the press, "that it was necessary to "prevent the daily abuse of it," will entirely lose its force, when it is shewn (by a seasonable exertion of the laws) that the press cannot be abused to any bad purpose, without incurring a suitable punishment: whereas it never can be used to any good one, when under the controul of an inspector. So true will it be found, that to censure the licentiousness, is to maintain the liberty of the press. 4 *Black.* 153.

---

duction, was looked upon (as well in England as in other countries) as merely a matter of state, and subject to the coërcion of the crown. It was therefore regulated with us by the king's proclamations, prohibitions, charters of privilege and of licence, and finally by the decrees of the court of star-chamber; which limited the number of printers, and of presses which each should employ, and prohibited new publications, unless previously approved by proper licensers. On the demolition of this odious jurisdiction in 1641, the long parliament of Charles I. after their rupture with that prince, assumed the same powers as the star-chamber exercised with respect to the licensing of books: and in 1643, 1647, 1749, and 1652, (*Scobell.* i. 44. 134. ii. 88. 230.) issued their ordinances for that purpose, founded principally on the star-chamber decree of 1637. In 1662 was passed the statute 13 & 14 *Car.* 2. *c.* 33, which (with some few alterations) was copied from the parliamentary ordinances. This act expired in 1679, but was revived by statute 1 *Jac.* 2. *c.* 17. and continued till 1692. It was then continued for two years longer by statute 4 *W. & M. c.* 24. but though frequent attempts were made by the government to revive it, in the subsequent part of that reign (*Com. Journ.* 11 Feb. 1694. 26 Nov. 1695. 22 Oct. 1696. 9 Feb. 1697. 31 Jan. 1698.), yet the parliament resisted it so strongly, that it finally expired, and the press became properly free in 1694, and has ever since so continued.—But see *Printers.*

LIBLACUM, the manner of bewitching any person; also a barbarous sacrifice. *Leg. Athelstan*, 6. *Cowel.*

LIBRÆ ARSÆ PENSATÆ ET AD NUMERUM. They sometimes took their money at the Exchequer *ad numerum*, by tale, in the current coin upon consent; but sometimes they rejected the common coin by tale, and would melt it down to take it by weight when purified from the dross and too great alloy; for which purpose they had in those times always a fire ready in the Exchequer to burn the money, and then weigh it. *Cowell.*

LIBRA PENSA, a pound of money in weight, when it was usual in former days not only to tell the money but to weigh it. *Ibid.*

LIBRARY. Where a library is erected in any parish, it shall be preserved for the uses directed by the founder: and incumbents and ministers of parishes, are to give security therefore and make catalogues of the books. None of the books shall be alienable, without consent of the bishop, and then only where there is a duplicate of such books: if any book shall be taken away and detained, a justice's warrant may be issued to search for and restore the same: also action of trover may be brought in the name of the proper ordinary. And bishops have power to make rules and orders concerning libraries, appoint persons to view their condition, and inquire of the state of them in their visitation. Stat. 7 *Ann. c.* 14.

LIBRATÆ TERRÆ, contains four oxgangs, and every oxgang thirteen acres. *Skene.* With us it is so much land as is yearly worth 20*s.* *Cowel. Blount.*

LICENSE, (*licentia*) is a power or authority given to a man to do some lawful act; and is a personal liberty to the party to whom given, which cannot be transferred over, though it may be made to a man and his assigns. 12 *Hen.* 7, 25. And there may be a parol license, as well as by deed in writing. 2 *Nels. Abr.* 1123.

LICENSE TO ALIEN IN MORTMAIN. See *Mortmain.*

LICENSE TO ARISE, (*licentia surgendi*) was a liberty or space of time given by the court to a tenant to arise out of his bed, who was essoigned *de malo lecti*, in a real action; it was also the writ thereupon. *Bracton, lib.* 5. *Fleta, lib.* 6, *c.* 10.

LICENSE TO FOUND A CHURCH, granted by the king. See *Church.*

LICENSE TO GO TO ELECTION OF BISHOPS. See *Conge d'elire.*

LICENSE OF MARRIAGE. Bishops have power to grant licenses for the marrying of persons; and parsons marrying any person without publishing the banns of matrimony, or without license, incur a forfeiture of 100*l.* and are to be suspended 3 years. 6 & 7 *Wil.* 3, *c.* 6. See *Marriage.*

LICENSE TO ERECT A PARK OR WARREN. See *Park* and *Warren.*

LICENTIA CONCORDANDI, the license for which the king's silver is paid on passing a fine. See *Fines.*

LICENTIA COGNENDI, an imparlance.

LICENTIA SURGENDI, the writ whereby the tenant essoigned *de malo lecti,* obtained liberty to rise. See *License* to *arise.*

LICENTIA TRANSFRETANDI, was a writ or warrant directed to the keeper of any sea-port, commanding him to let such persons pass over sea who had obtained the king's license thereunto. *Reg. Orig.* 193.

LIDFERD LAW, *i. e.* to hang a man first, and judge him afterwards. *Cowel.*

LIEGE, (*ligeus*) is used for liege-lord, and sometimes for liege-man: liege-lord is he that acknowledges no superior; and liege-man is he who owes allegiance to his liege-lord. The king's subjects are called liege-people, because they owe and are bound to pay allegiance to him. Stat. 8 *Hen.* 6, *c.* 10. 14 *Hen.* 8, *c.* 2. *Cowel. Blount.*

LIEGES AND LIEGE-PEOPLE, (*ligati*) the king's subjects. Stat. 8 *Hen.* 6, *c.* 10. 14 *Hen.* 8, *c.* 2. *Cowel.*

LIEN, a specific charge on the *personalty* or *realty:* a personal lien is such as bond, covenant, or contract; and a real lien, a judgment, statute, or recognizance, which oblige and affect the land. *Terms de Ley.*

LIEU, instead, or in place of another thing. 2 *Shep. Abr.* 359.

LIEU CONUS, in law proceedings, signified a castle, manor, or other notorious place, well known and generally taken notice of by those that dwelt about it. 2 *Lil. Abr.* 641. 2 *Cro.* 574. 2 *Mod. Rep.* 48, 49.

LIEUTENANT, (*locum tenens*) is the king's deputy, or he that exercises the king's or any other's place, and represents his person, as the lieutenant of Ireland. Stat. 4 *Hen.* 4, *c.* 6, and 2 & 3 *Ed.* 6, *c.* 2. The lieutenant of the Ordnance, 39 *Eliz. c.* 7, and the lieutenant of the Tower, an officer under the constable, &c. county *lieutenants,* and deputy *lieutenants.* The word lieutenant is also used for a military officer, next in command to the captain.

LIFE, is the immediate gift of God, a right inherent by nature in every individual, and under the peculiar protection of the law. *Wood's Inst.* 11. See *Homicide.*

LIFE ESTATE. Estates for life, expressly created by deed or grant (which alone are properly conventional), are, 1. Where a lease is made of lands or tenements to a man, to hold for the term of his own life, or for that of any other person, or for more lives than one; in any of which cases he is styled tenant for life, only when he holds the estate by the life of another he is usually called tenant *pur auter vie.* These estates for life are, like inheritances, of a feodal nature, and they are given or conferred by the same feodal rites and solemnities, the same investiture or livery of seisin, as fees themselves are, and they are held by fealty, if demanded, and such conventional rents and services as the lord or lessor, and his tenant or lessee, have agreed on. *Lit. s.* 56.

Estates for life may be created, not only by the express words before mentioned, but also by a general grant, without defining or limiting any specific estate. As, if one grants to A. B. the manor of Dale, this makes him tenant for life. (*Co. Litt.* 42.) For though, as there are no words of inheritance, or *heirs,* mentioned in the grant, it cannot be construed to be a fee; it shall however be construed to be as large an estate as the words of the donation will bear, and therefore an estate for life. Also such a grant at large, or a grant for term of life generally, shall be construed to be an estate for the life *of the grantee,* (*Ibid.*) in case the grantor hath authority to make such a grant: for an estate for a man's own life is more beneficial and of a higher nature than for any other life; and the rule of law is, that all grants are to be taken most strongly against the grantor (*Ibid.* 36), unless in the case of the king.

Such estates for life will, generally speaking, endure as long as the life for which they are granted: but there are some estates for life which may determine upon future contingencies, before the life, for which they are created, expires. As, if an estate be granted to a woman during her widowhood, or to a man until he be promoted to a benefice; in these, and similar cases, whenever the contingency happens, when the widow marries, or when the grantee obtains a benefice, the respective estates are absolutely determined and gone. (*Co. Litt.* 42. 3 *Rep.* 20.) Yet, while they subsist, they are reckoned estates for life; because, the time for which they will endure being uncertain, they may by possibility last for life, if the contingencies upon which they are to determine do not sooner happen. And, moreover, in case an estate be granted to a man for his life, generally, it may also determine by his *civil* death: as if he enters into a monastery, whereby he is dead in law (2 *Rep.* 48. *Co. Litt.* 132); for which reason in conveyances the grant is usually made "for the term of a man's *natural* life;" which can only determine by his *natural* death. *Ibid.*

The *incidents* to an estate for life are principally the following; which are applicable not only to that species of tenants for life, which are expressly created by deed, but also to those, which are created by act and operation of law.

1. Every tenant for life, unless restrained by covenant or agreement, may of common right take upon the land demised to him reasonable *estovers*, or *botes* (*Co. Lit.* 41,); for he hath a right to the full enjoyment and use of the land, and all its profits, during his estate therein. But he is not permitted to cut down timber or do other waste upon the premises (*Ibid.* 53.) : for the destruction of such things as are not the temporary profits of the tenement, is not necessary for the tenant's complete enjoyment of his estate ; but tends to the permanent and lasting loss of the person entitled to the inheritance. *Co. Litt.* 41. 53, 55.

But tenant for life, *without impeachment of waste*, has full power to cut timber as if he had an estate of inheritance, and is in the same manner entitled to the timber if owned by others. 1 *Ter. Rep.* 56. *Harg. Co. Lit.* but he cannot commit *wilful spoil* and *devastation*, as by pulling down houses, or destroying ornamental trees. 2 *Vern.* 738. 1 *Bro.* 166. 3 *Bro.* 549. 6 *Vez. Jun.* 107.

2. Tenant for life, or his representatives shall not be prejudiced by any sudden determination of his estate, because such a determination is contingent and uncertain. (*Co. Lit.* 55.) Therefore if a tenant for his own life sows the lands, and dies before harvest, his executors shall have the *emblements*, or profits of the crop : for the estate was determined by the *act of God* ; and it is a maxim in the law, that *actus Dei nemini facit injuriam*. *Co. Litt.* 55.

3. A third incident to estates for life relates to the under-tenants or lessees. For they have the *same* and in some instances *greater* indulgences than their lessors, the original tenants for life.

THE SAME ; for the law of estovers and emblements, with regard to the tenant for life, is also law with regard to his under-tenant, who represents him and stands in his place (*Co. Litt.* 55.) : and GREATER ; for in those cases where tenant for life shall not have the emblements, because the estate determines by his own act, the exception shall not reach his lessee who is a third person. As in the case of a woman who holds *durante viduitate* ; her taking husband is her own act, and therefore deprives her of the emblements : but if she leases her estate to an under-tenant, who sows the land, and she then marries, this her act shall not deprive the tenant of his emblements, who is a stranger and could not prevent her. *Cro. Eliz.* 461. 1 *Roll. Abr.* 727. The lessees of tenants for life had also at the common law another most unreasonable advantage ; for, at the death of their lessors, the tenants for life, these under-tenants might if they pleased quit the premises, and pay no rent to any body for the occupation of the land since the last quarter day, or other day assigned for payment of rent. (10 *Rep.* 127.) To remedy which it is now enacted, (by Stat. 11 *Geo.* 2. *c.* 19. *sec.* 15,) that the executors or administrators of tenant for life, on whose death any lease determined, shall recover of the lessee a rateable proportion of rent, from the last day of payment to the death of such lessor.

This act is confined to the death of the landlord, who holds for his own life ; and therefore, it seems if tenant *pur autre vie* leases, and the *cestui que vie* dies, the lessee is not compellable to pay any rent from the last day of payment before the death of *cestui que vie*. 10 *Rep.* 128.

LIFE-RENT, a rent which a man receives for term of life, or for sustentation of it. *Skene.*

LIGEANCE, LIGEANCY, (*ligeantia*) is such a duty or fealty as no man may owe or bear to more than one lord ; and therefore it is used for that duty and allegiance which every good subject owes to his liege lord the king. *Co. Lit.* 129.

LIGHTERMEN, persons employed in the carrying of goods to and from ships, in barges or lighters on the river Thames. *Cowel.*

LIGHT-HOUSE, a building erected near the sea shore, wherein a fire, or large and strong light, is kept in the night-time, for direction to ships at sea. 1 *Black.* 264.

LIGHTS, stopping. If a man erect a house or other building so near to mine that it stops up my ancient lights and windows, this is a private nuisance, for which an action will lie (9 *Rep.* 58) ; but in this case it is necessary that the windows be *ancient* : that is, have subsisted there time out of mind ; otherwise there is no injury done ; for he has as much right to build a new edifice upon his ground *usque ad cœlum*, as I have upon mine ; since every man may do what he pleases upon the upright or perpendicular of his own soil ; and it was my folly to build so near another's ground. *Cro. Eliz.* 118. *Salk.* 459.

LIGNAGIUM, the right which a man had to cut fuel in woods ; sometimes a tribute, or payment due for the same. *Cowel.*

LIGNAMINA, timber fit for building. *Du Fresne.*

LIGULA, a copy or transcript of a court-roll, or deed. *Cowel.*

LIGURITOR, a flatterer, sometimes a glutton. *Ibid.*

LIMBS. The limbs as well as the life of a man are of such high value, in the estimation of the law of England, that it pardons even homicide, if committed *se defendendo*, or in order to preserve them. 1 *Black. Com.* 130.

LIMITATION, (*limitatio*) is a certain time assigned by statute, within which an action must be brought.

1. *In real actions.*] By 32 *Hen.* 8, *c.* 2,

it is enacted, "That no person shall from thenceforth sue, have or maintain any *writ of right*, or make any prescription, title or claim to or for any manors, lands, tenements, rents, annuities, commons, pensions, portions, corodies, or other hereditaments, of the possession of his or their ancestor or predecessor, and declare and allege any further seisin or possession of his ancestor or predecessor, but only of the seisin or possession of his ancestor or predecessor which hath been or now is, or shall be seised of the said manors, lands, tenements, rents, annuities, commons, pensions, portions, corodies, or other hereditaments, within three-score years next before the teste of the same writ, or next before the said prescription, title or claim so hereafter to be sued, commenced, brought, made or had. *s.* 1.

"That no manner of person shall sue, have or maintain any *assise of mort d'ancestor*, cosenage, ayle, writ of entry upon disseisin, done to any of his ancestors or predecessors, or any manors, lands, tenements or other hereditaments, of any further seisin or possession of his or their ancestor or predecessor, but only of the seisin or possession of his or their ancestor or predecessor, which was or hereafter shall be seised of the same manors, lands, tenements, or other hereditaments, within fifty years next before the teste of the original of the same writ hereafter to be brought. *s.* 2.

"That no person shall sue, have or maintain any *action* for any manors, lands, tenements, or other hereditaments, of or *upon his or their own seisin* or possession therein, above thirty years next before the teste of the original of the same writ hereafter to be brought. *s.* 3.

"That no person shall hereafter make any *avowry or cognizance* for any rent, suit or service, and allege any seisin of any rent, suit, or service, in the same avowry or cognizance in the possession of any other, whose estate he shall pretend or claim to have, above fifty years next before the making of the said avowry or cognizance." *s.* 4.

It is further enacted by the said st. par. 5. "That all formedons in reverter, formedons in remainder, and *scire facias* upon *fines* of any manors, lands, tenements, or other hereditaments, at any time hereafter to be sued, shall be sued and taken within fifty years next after the title and cause of action fallen, and at no time after the fifty years past.

By 1 *Mar.* c. 5, it is enacted, "That the 32 *Hen.* 8, *c.* 2, shall not extend to any writ of right of advowson, *quare impedit*, or assise of darrein presentment, nor *jus patronatus*, nor to any writ of right of ward, writ of ravishment of ward for the wardship of the body, or for the wardship of any castles, honours, manors, lands, tenements or hereditaments holden by knights service, but that such suits may be brought as before the making of the said act.

By the 21 *Jac.* 1, *c.* 16, for quieting mens estates, and avoiding of suits, it is enacted, "that all *writs of formedon* in descender, formedon in remainder, and formedon in reverter, at any time hereafter to be sued or brought of or for any manors, lands, tenements or hereditaments, whereunto any person or persons now hath or have any title, or cause to have or pursue any such writ, shall be sued and taken within twenty years next after the end of this present session of parliament; and after the said 20 years expired, no person or persons, or any of their heirs, shall have or maintain any such writ of or for any of the said manors, lands, tenements or hereditaments; and that all writs of formedon in descender, formedon in remainder, formedon in reverter, of any manors, lands, tenements or other hereditaments whatsoever, at any time hereafter to be sued or brought by occasion or means of any title, or cause hereafter happening, shall be sued, and taken within 20 years next after the title and cause of action first descended or fallen, and at no time after the said 20 years; and that no person or persons that now hath any *right or title of entry* into any manors, lands, tenements or hereditaments, now held from him or them, shall thereinto enter, but within 20 years next after the end of this present session of parliament, or within 20 years next after any other title of entry accrued; and that no person or persons shall at any time hereafter make any entry into any lands, tenements or hereditaments, but within 20 years next after his or their right or title, which shall hereafter first descend or accrue to the same; and in default thereof such persons so *not entering*, and their heirs, shall be utterly excluded, and disabled from such entry after to be made, any former law," &c.

Provided, that "if any person be entitled to "such writs, or that hath such right or "title of entry, shall be, at the time of "the said right or title first descended, ac- "crued, come or fallen, within the age of "21 years, feme covert, *non compos mentis*, "imprisoned, or beyond the seas, then such "person and his and their heirs shall, notwith- "standing the said 20 years be expired, bring "his action, or make his entry, as he might "have done before this act, so as such "person or his heirs shall within 10 years "next after his full age, discoverture, "coming of sound mind, enlargement out "of prison, or coming into this realm, or "death, take benefit of and sue forth the "same, and at no time after the said 10 "years." *s.* 2.

Also by 9 *Geo.* 3, *c.* 16, the crown is in

like manner as a subject now disabled to sue for lands (except liberties or franchises) where the right has not first accrued within 60 years before the suit: and the subject is secured in the free enjoyment against the crown, and all others claiming by grant or on suggestion of concealment, if no judgment within 60 years before the suit.

2. *In penal actions.* By the 31 *Eliz. c.* 5, *par.* 5, it is enacted, "That all actions, suits, bills, indictments or informations, which shall be brought for any forfeiture upon any statute penal, made or to be made, whereby the forfeiture is or shall be limited to the crown, shall be brought within two years after the offence; and that all actions, suits, bills or informations, which shall be brought for any forfeiture upon any penal statute, made or to be made, except the statutes of tillage, the benefit and suit whereof is or shall be by the said statute limited to the queen, her heirs or successors, and to any other that shall prosecute in that behalf, shall be brought by any person that may lawfully sue for the same within one year next after the offence committed; and in default of such pursuit that then the same shall be brought for the queen's majesty, her heirs or successors, any time within the two years after that year ended. Where a shorter time is limited by any penal statute, the prosecution must be that time."

And the 18 *Eliz. c.* 5, requires a memorandum of the day of exhibiting an information, and 21 *Jac.* 1, *c.* 4, an oath from the informer.

3. *In personal actions and suits.* By the 21 *Jac.* 1, *c.* 16, it is enacted, That "all "actions on the case for words shall be "commenced and sued within two years "*next after* the words spoken, and not "after."

And by 27 *Geo.* 3, *c.* 44, "suits in eccle-"siastical courts for *defamatory* words shall "be commenced within 6 *months.*"

By the 21 *Jac.* 1. *c.* 16, it is also enacted, "that all actions of trespass, of assault, "battery, wounding, imprisonment, or any "of them, shall be commenced and sued "within 4 years *next after* the cause of "such actions or suits, and not after."

Also by 27 *Geo.* 3. *c.* 44, "for fornica-"tion, or incontinence, or for striking or "brawling in any church or church-yard, "*within* 8 *months*, and there shall be no "prosecution for fornication after the par-"ties have intermarried."

By 21 *Jac.* 1, *c.* 16, it is also enacted, that "all actions of trespass *quare clausum* "*fregit*, all actions of trespass, detinue, ac-"tion *sur trover* and replevin for taking "away of goods and chattels, all actions of "account, other than such accounts as con-"cern the trade of merchandize between "merchant and merchant, their factors or "servants, all actions on the case, (other "than for slander) all actions of debt "grounded upon any lending or contract "without specialty, all actions of debt for "arrearages of rent within six years, *next* "*after* the cause of action."

Provision is made for femes covert, persons that are *non-compos*, imprisoned, or beyond sea, in case they bring the action within the same time after the disability removed.

4. *On writs of error.* By 10 & 11 *Will.* 3, *c.* 14, no fine, recovery, or judgment, shall be reversed unless a writ of error be brought within 20 years after obtained, but persons disabled by infancy, or otherwise, shall bring such writ of error within five years after the disability is removed.

LIMITATION OF THE CROWN. See *King.*

LIMITATION OF ESTATE. A limitation of estate, which Littleton denominates also a condition in law, is when an estate is so expressly confined and limited by the words of its creation, that it cannot endure for any longer time, than till the contingency happens, upon which the estate is to fail, this is denominated a limitation; as when land is granted to a man so long as he is parson of Dale, or while he continues unmarried, or until out of the rents and profits he shall have made 500*l.* and the like; in such case the estate determines as soon as the contingency happens (when he ceases to be parson, marries a wife, or has received the 500*l*), and the next subsequent estate, which depends upon such determination, becomes immediately vested, without any act to be done by him who is next in expectancy. *Lit. s.* 380. 1 *Inst.* 234. 10 *Rep.* 41, 42.

LIMOGIA, signifies enamelled. *Cowel. Blount.*

LINARIUM, a flax plat, where flax is sown. *Ibid.*

LINDESFERN, formerly a bishop's see, now Holy Island. *Ibid.*

LINEAL CONSANGUINITY. See *Consanguinity.*

LINEAL DESCENT. The descent of estates, from ancestor to heir, *i. e.* from one to another, in a right line, for estates cannot lineally ascend. 2 *Black.* 210.

LINEAL DESCENT OF THE CROWN. The crown lineally descends, unless otherwise settled by parliament. 1 *Black.* 194.

LINEAL WARRANTY. See *Warranty.*

LINEN. See *Felony* and *Manufactures.*

LITERA, (from the Fr. *litiere*, or *lictiere*, Lat. *lectum*) was anciently used for straw for a bed, even the king's; hence litter is now in use in stables among horses. *Cowel.*

LITERATURA, *ad literaturam ponere*, signifies to put children out to school, anciently denied to those parents who were servile tenants, without the consent of the lord. *Ibid.*

LITERÆ *ad faciendum attornatum pro secta faciend. Reg. Orig.* 192.

LITERÆ, *canonici ad exercendam jurisdictionem loco suo. Ibid.* 305.

LITERÆ, *per quas dominus remittit curiam suam Regi. Ibid.* 4.

LITERÆ, *de requestu. Ibid.* 129.

LITERÆ SOLUTORIÆ, were magical characters supposed to be of such power that it was impossible for any one to bind those persons who carried these about them. *Bede, lib.* 4, *c.* 22. *Cowel.*

LITERARY PROPERTY, the property that the author, or his assignee, hath in the copy of any work. See *Authors. Books.*

LITH OF PICKERING, the liberty, or a member of Pickering in the county of York. *Cowel.*

LITIGATOR, (Lat.) a party pleading, that contends or litigates a suit at law. *Lit. Dict.*

LITIGIOUS. The litigiousness of a church is where several persons have, or pretend to several titles to the patronage, and present several clerks to the ordinary; it excuses him from refusing to admit any of them, till a trial of the right by *jure patronatus*, or otherwise. *Jenk. Cent.* 11.

LITTLE GOES. See *Lotteries.*

LITTERA, as *tres carectas litteræ*, three cart-loads of straw or litter. *Cowel.*

LITTLETON, a famous lawyer in the time of king *Ed.* 4. *Staundf. Prær. c.* 21. *fol.* 72.

LIVERY, (Fr. *livre*, i. e. *insigne gestamen*, or *liverer*, i. e. *tradere*) hath three significations: 1st. it is used for a suit of clothes, cloak, gown, hat, &c. which a nobleman or gentleman gives to his servants or followers, mentioned in 1 *Ric.* 2, *c.* 7, and other statutes.

2dly, Livery signifies a delivery of possession to those tenants who held of the king *in capite*, or knights service; as the king by his prerogative hath *primer* seisin of all lands and tenements so holden of him. *Staundf. Prærog.* 12.

3dly, Livery was the writ which laid for the heir of age to obtain the possession or seisin of his lands at the king's hands. *F. N. B.* 155. But by the statute 12 *Car.* 2, *c.* 24, all wardships are taken away,

LIVERY OF SEISIN, (*liberatio seisinæ*) is a delivery of possession of lands, tenements and hereditaments, unto one that hath a right to the same; being a ceremony in the common law used in the conveyance of lands, &c. where an estate of fee-simple, fee-tail, or other freehold passes. *Bract. lib.*2, *cap.* 18. *West. Symb. por.* 1. *lib.* 2. And it is a testimonial of the willing departing of him who makes the livery, from the thing whereof the livery is made, and of the willing acceptance of the other party receiving the livery, first invented that the common people might have knowledge of the passing or alteration of estates from man to man, and thereby be better able to try in whom the right of possession of lands and tenements were, if the same should be contested, and they should be empanelled on juries, or otherwise have to do concerning the same. *Ibid.*

Of livery of seisin there are two kinds, 1st. a livery in deed; and 2dly, livery in law.

1. Livery in deed is when the feoffor takes the ring of the door, &c. and delivers the same to the feoffee, in the name of seisin of the whole. 1 *Inst.* 48. 6 *Rep.* 26. *Wood's Inst.* 237.

2. Livery in law is when the feoffor himself, being in view of the house or land, says to the feoffee, after delivery of the deed, "I give to you yonder land, &c. to you and your heirs; go into the same, and take possession accordingly." 1 *Inst.* 48, 52. 181. 3 *Rep.* 26.

But no person ought to be in the house, or upon the land, when livery is made, but the feoffor and feoffee. *Cro. Eliz.* 321. *Dalis. Rep.* 94.

Livery and seisin is necessary in a feoffment of leases for life or lives, or more properly speaking, years determinable upon a life or lives *, or a lease for years, remainder to another for life, in tail or in fee, particularly in the latter, for without livery and seisin nothing passes to him in remainder. *Lit.* 60. 1 *Inst.* 49. *Wood's Inst.* 238. 4 *Leon.* 67. 2 *Rol. Rep.* 109. *Moor* 14. 5 *Rep.* 91. 1 *Inst.* 52.

But since the introduction of the conveyance by lease and release, bargain and sale by deed inrolled, exchange, &c. by which a freehold passes without livery, (1 *Inst.* 49,) livery and seisin is not so commonly used as formerly. 29 *Car.* 2, *c.* 3. 2 *Black.* 311.

LIVERY AND OUSTER LE MAIN, is where, by inquest before the escheator, it was found that nothing was held of the king, then he was immediately commanded by writ to put from his hands the lands taken into the king's hands. Stat. 29 *Ed.* 1. 28 *Ed.* 3, *c.* 4. Vide *Ouster le Main.*

LIVERYMEN OF LONDON. In the companies of London liverymen are chosen out of the freemen, and rank next to the court of assistants, or the master and wardens.

LOBBE, a large kind of North-sea fish. *Cowel.*

LOCAL, (*localis*) tied or annexed to a certain place. Real actions, such as ejectments, and others touching the freehold or realty, are local, and to be brought in the

* A lease for life or lives only being void for uncertainty.

county where the lands lie; but a personal action, as of trespass or battery, &c. is transitory, not local, and it is not material that the action should be tried, or laid in the same county where the fact was done. *Kitch.* 230. See *Venue.*

LOCKMAN. In the Isle of Man the lockman is an officer to execute the orders of the governor, much like our under-sheriff. *King's Isle of Man*, 26.

LOCKS ON RIVERS. For the offence of destroying any lock or sluice on any navigable river, see *Felony.*

LOCULUS, signifies a coffin. *Cowel.*

LOCUS IN QUO, the place where any thing is alleged to be done in pleadings, &c. 1 *Salk.* 94.

LOCUS PARTITUS, a division made between two towns or counties. *Cowel.*

LOCUTORIUM. The monks and other religious in monasteries, after they had dined in their common hall, had a withdrawing room, where they met and talked together among themselves, which room for that sociable use and conversation, they called *locutorium, à loquendo*, as we call such a place in our houses parlour, from the Fr. *parler*; and they had another room which was called *locutorium forinsecum*, where they might talk with laymen. *Walsing.* 257. *Cowel.*

LODE-MANAGE, is the hire of a pilot for conducting a vessel from one place to another. *Cowel.*

LODE-MEREGE, mentioned in the laws of Oleron, is expounded to be the skill or art of navigation. *Cowel.*

LODE-SHIP, a kind of fishing vessel. See 31 *Ed.* 3, *c.* 2.

LODGERS AND LODGINGS. Stealing furniture from lodgings, see *Felony.*

LOGATING, an unlawful game, mentioned in 33 *Hen.* 1, *c.* 9, now disused. See title *Games.*

LOGIA, a little house, lodge or cottage. *Cowel. Blount.*

LOITH, or LOYCH-FISH, a large North-sea fish. 31 *Ed.* 3, *st.* 3, *c.* 2.

LOLLARDS, so called from one *Walter Lollard*, a German, at the head of them, who lived about the year 1315. They were certain heretics, (in the opinion of those times) that abounded here in England in the reigns of king *Edw.* 3, and *Hen.* 5, whereof Wickliff was the chief in this nation. *Stow's Annals*, 425. And their intent was to subvert the Christian faith, the law of God, the church, and the realm. 2 *Hen.* 5, *c.* 7; but this stat. was repealed by 1 *Ed.* 6, *c.* 12. 3 *Inst.* 41.

LOLLARDY, the doctrine and opinion of the Lollards. 1 & 2 *Phil. & Mar.* *c.* 6. 4 *Black. Com.* 47.

LONDON, the metropolis of that part of the united kingdom, called *England*, formerly called *Augusta*, has been built above 3000 years, and flourished for 1500 years. *Stow.*

It is divided into 26 wards, over each of which there is an alderman, and is governed by a lord mayor, who is chosen yearly, and presented to the king, or in his absence to his justices, or the barons of the Exchequer at Westminster. *Chart.* k. *Hen.* 3.

The lord mayor of London for the time being is chief justice of gaol delivery, escheator within the liberties, and bailiff of the river Thames, He is a high officer in the city, having all courts for distribution of justice under his jurisdiction, *viz.* the court of hustings, sheriffs court, mayor's court, court of common council, &c. 2 *Inst.* 330.

The local privileges of the city of London are too numerous to be set forth, but the following is an accurate summary of the statutes relating to this vast city, and its domestic polity.

In general.] By Mag. Chart. 9 *Hen.* 3, *c.* 9. and 14 *Ed.* 3, *st.* 1. *c.* 1. the liberties of the city of London are confirmed.

By 13 *Ed.* 1, *stat.* 5, it is commanded that no person be found walking the streets of London with sword and buckler after curfew, unless great lords, or persons known, with lights. No tavern shall be open after curfew. No school of fencing and buckler shall be kept in London on 40 days imprisonment. Evil doers imprisoned shall not be delivered by the sheriff, but by award of the mayor and aldermen. No stranger shall keep inns in the city. Ministers in the city shall not be punished for imprisoning offenders, unless done for malice, and not for keeping the peace.

By 10 *Edw.* 2, *stat.* 1. lords of rents in London may recover them in the hustings by a writ of gavelet, and on default the lands in demesne.

By 28 *Edw.* 3, *c.* 10, misprision of the mayor, sheriffs, and aldermen of London, in not redressing errors, shall be tried by inquest of neighbouring counties, and they shall be fined 1000 marks for the first offence, 2000 for the second, and for the third forfeit the franchise.

But by 1 *Hen.* 4, *c.* 15, the penalties inflicted by the last act shall hereafter be according to the discretion of the justices.

By 1 *Hen.* 4, *c.* 10, merchants of London shall be as free to pack their cloths as other merchants.

By 3 *Hen.* 7, *c.* 9, citizens and freemen of London may carry their wares to any fair or market, and any bye-law to the contrary shall be void.

By 35 *Hen.* 8, *c.* 10, the mayor and commonalty of London may enter lands to lay and amend water-pipes, making recompense to the owner; not to withdraw any water that is brought to any person's house; shall pay to the bishop of Westminster a pound of pepper yearly as an acknowledgment for fetching water from Hampstead heath; but they are not to meddle with the enclosed spring at the foot of the heath.

By 3 *Jac.* 1, *c.* 18, and 4 *Jac.* 1, *c.* 12, the lord mayor and commonalty of London were empowered to lay out ground for making a trench for the new river, making recompense to the owners of ground. Also 12 *Geo.* 2, *c.* 32.

By 7 *Jac.* 1, *c.* 9, the corporation of Chelsea College were enabled to cut a drain out of the river Lee, at Hackney, to convey water to London in pipes.

By 2 *Will. & Mar.* stat. 1, *c.* 8, the judgment in *quo warranto* was reversed, and the corporation of London restored to all its rights and privileges.

By 8 *Geo.* 1, *c.* 26, the commissioners of Chelsea water-works were incorporated, saving the rights of the New-River company.

By 6 *Geo.* 2, *c.* 22, the lord mayor and citizens of London were empowered to fill up part of Fleet Ditch, and the inheritance of the ground was vested in them.

By 29 *Geo.* 2, *c.* 40, the mayor and common council were empowered to purchase and remove buildings, to improve, widen, and enlarge the passage over and through London bridge.

——— *Aldermen.*] By 17 *Ric.* 2, *c.* 11, the aldermen shall not be elected yearly, but remain until put out for just cause.

——— *Attaint.*] By 11 *Hen.* 7, *c.* 21, attaint may be sued by bill in the hustings of London, upon any false verdict given in any of the courts of that city. If the petty jury be attainted, judgment shall be given against the defendant as at common law, and against the jury, to forfeit each of them 20*l.* If a debt be recovered in the first action, and that verdict be found false, the plaintiff shall have restitution, but if the verdict be affirmed, the plaintiff shall be imprisoned and fined.

By 37 *Hen.* 8, *c.* 5, persons worth 400 marks in goods may be impanelled in attaints in London, and attaints in London shall be tried there only.

——— *Bakers.*] By 34 *Geo.* 3, *c.* 61, no baker in London, or within 12 miles thereof, shall work on Sunday, except as hereinafter mentioned, on penalty of 10*s.* to be levied by distress and sale on complaint made within 6 days, to be paid over to the churchwardens and overseers of the parish. *s.* 1, 3, 4.

But bakers may sell bread, and bake meat, puddings, or pies, only between 9 in the forenoon, and 1 in the afternoon, so as the party carry the same to and from the place where they are baked. *s.* 2.

By 48 *Geo.* 3, *c.* lxx, so much of 31 *Geo.* 2, (see general title *Bread*) as relates to the weighing of bread, and punishing of persons for deficiency of weight within the weekly bills of mortality, and within 10 miles of the Royal Exchange, except as hereafter, is repealed. *s.* 1.

And if any person within such limits shall make, send out, sell, or expose to sale, any bread deficient in weight, the justice before whom any information shall be given on oath, and any peace-officer, under a warrant, may enter the premises in the daytime to search for and try all bread baked within 24 hours, and which may be weighed by the bushel, or in any larger or smaller quantity; and if any deficiency shall be found in its due weight in the average of the whole weight, to be proved on oath before such justice, then the offender shall forfeit not exceeding 5*s.* nor less than 1*s.* per ounce, and in proportion for less than an ounce; and all loaves so deficient shall be seized, unless it be proved that the deficiency arose from unavoidable accident. *s.* 1.

Bakers of bread are to keep scales and weights in their shops, that buyers may weigh if they think fit, on pain of not exceeding 20*s.* nor less than 5*s.* *s.* 2, 3.

No master or journeyman baker within London or 12 miles of the city, shall on the Lord's day make or bake bread, rolls, or cakes of any sort, or on any part of that day, except between 9 and 1, sell or expose to sale any bread, rolls, or cakes, or bake or deliver any meat, pudding, pie, tart or victuals, except as hereinafter-mentioned, or in any manner exercise the business of a baker, except in setting sponge for the next day, and any person offending or making any sale or delivery hereby allowed, otherwise than within his bake-house or shop, shall on conviction, either upon view of the justice, or oath, forfeit for the first offence 10*s.* the second, 20*s.* and for every subsequent offence 40*s.* together with costs, and also an allowance to the prosecutor, for loss of time, of 3*s.* per day; the residue to be paid to the justice within 7 days, transmitted by him to the churchwardens and overseers, and if the whole be not paid within 14 days, the same may be levied by distress; and for want of sufficient, the offender is to be committed, for the first offence, to the house of correction for 7 days; a second, for 14 days, and for any subsequent one, for 1 month. *s.* 5.

But bakers within the limits aforesaid may deliver to their customers bakings until half past one. *Ibid.*

The rights of the city of London, the bakers company, Westminster, Southwark, and courts leet, are saved. *s.* 6.

——— *Ballastage.*] By 45 *Geo.* 3, *c.* xcviii, the acts 6 *Geo.* 2, *c.* 29, and 32 *Geo.* 2, *c.* 16, are repealed. *s.* 1. And the sole right of supplying with ballast, all ships and vessels that shall pass and repass in the river

Thames between London bridge and the main, and of raising gravel, sand, and soil of the Thames, for that purpose, is vested in the corporation of the Trinity house. *s.* 2.

Persons supplying or taking ballast, except for the corporation, to forfeit 10*l.* *s.* 2, 3.

But king's ships are allowed to take sea ballast or any other ballast. *s.* 4.

Land ballast may be shipped eastward of Woolwich, on paying one penny per ton to the corporation; ballast-men are to be subject to bye-laws to be made by the corporation, but the rights of the corporation of London are saved. *s.* 37—41.

Ballast-men wilfully and maliciously attempting to destroy ships, lighters, or boats, or cutting cables, are guilty of felony, and to be transported for 7 years; or fined and imprisoned for not exceeding 2 years. *s.* 33.

——— *Bargain and Sale.*] By 33 *Geo.* 2. *c.* 30. bargains and sales of land, in London, enrolled in the hustings of the city, by virtue of the act for widening the streets, shall have the operation of a fine or recovery.

——— *Blackwell Hall.*] By 4 & 5 *Phil. & Mar. cap.* 5. cloth sealed shall not be searched in Blackwell Hall market during the time of such market.

By 39 *Eliz. c.* 20, northern cloths brought to London for sale shall be brought to Blackwell Hall to be searched dry, and out of market time, upon pain of 40*s.* for not carrying them there, and 5*l.* for searching them during the market.

By 8 and 9 *Will.* 3, *c.* 9, the public market of Blackwell Hall shall be held every Thursday, Friday, and Saturday. Factors selling cloth out of the market to forfeit 5*l.* Hall-keepers, clerks, and master porters, not keeping weekly registers of cloths bought and sold, to forfeit likewise 10*l.* Factors selling cloth in trust, and not transmitting to the owners the buyer's note for the money, in 12 days, liable to forfeit double the value. Buyers neglecting to give such note, on request, within 8 days, to forfeit 20*s.* for every cloth sold; and if the cloth is not returned within 8 days, the same to be deemed as approved by the buyer. All contracts allowing longer time void.

By 1 *Geo.* 1, *stat.* 2, *c.* 15, a table 30 yards in length, with an inch to each, shall be provided in Blackwell Hall, for measuring Medly broad cloth.

The buyer shall give notice to the seller when the cloth is to be wetted, and if he does not attend, the buyer may proceed to prove the cloth, and the keeper of Blackwell Hall shall measure the same, and his certificate thereof shall be the rule of payment to the buyer, and a conviction of the party offending. *Ibid.*

None but the owner of the cloth unsatisfied, shall sue the factor for not demanding notes pursuant to 8 & 9 *W.* 3, and the prosecutions must be in 12 months after the offence.

——— *Bowyers.*] By 8 *Eliz. c.* 10, every bowyer in London shall keep 50 bows of elm, witch, hazel, or ash, on pain of 10*s.* a bow.

——— *Brokers.*] By 13 *Ed.* 1. *stat.* 5, no brokers shall be in London but those who are admitted and sworn by the mayor and aldermen.

By 1 *Jac.* 1. *c.* 21, no pawn or sale to a broker in London, or within 2 miles thereof, shall alter the property of goods wrongfully taken; and broker on demand shall manifest what goods are come to his hands, on forfeiture of double the value.

By 6 *Ann. c.* 16, brokers in London are to pay 40*s.* to the chamberlain of London on their admittance, and also 40*s.* yearly, on pain of 25*l.* to the corporation for acting without.

——— *Buildings.*] By 11 *Geo.* 3, *c.* 26, the corporation may grant licenses to the owners of leases, whereof 35 years or upwards are to come, of houses adjoining to the late Bridewell Dock, to build, but not to others.

By 14 *Geo.* 3, *c.* 78, all buildings whatsoever, heretofore built, or to be built hereafter within London and Westminster, and bills of mortality, the parishes of St. Mary-le-bone, Paddington, Pancras, and Chelsea, shall be divided into the seven rates following, that is to say, churches, chapels, meeting-houses, or places of public worship; still-houses, brew-houses, soap-houses, houses for melting tallow, dying, sugar-houses, turpentine-houses, founderies of brass or iron, chymical glass-houses of all dimensions, warehouses and other buildings, not dwelling-houses (except of the 5th, 6th, or 7th rate) not exceeding three stories above ground, exclusive of rooms in the roof, of the height of 31 feet above ground, to the top of the blocking course; and dwelling-houses above the value of 850*l.* and above 9 squares of building of 100 superficial feet each, on the ground floor, shall be the first rate. *s.* 1.—4.

External walls, of the first rate, shall be at the foundation $2\frac{1}{2}$ bricks, or 1 foot $9\frac{1}{2}$ inches thick, and decrease on each side $2\frac{1}{2}$ inches to the top of the footing of the wall, which is to be 9 inches high, and 2 bricks, or $17\frac{1}{2}$ inches thick, to the under side of the one-pair-of-stairs floor; from thence $1\frac{1}{4}$ brick thick, or 13 inches, to the under side of the plate under the roof; from thence 1 brick, or $8\frac{1}{2}$ inches thick, to the under side of the blocking-course, except walls of stone of 14 inches thick below the ground-floor, and 9 inches above, and except recesses arched, and at the back 1 brick, or $8\frac{1}{2}$ inches thick. *Ibid.*

Party walls of the first rate shall be $3\frac{1}{2}$ bricks, or 2 feet $6\frac{1}{2}$ inches thick at the foundation, and decreasing on each side $4\frac{1}{2}$ inches to the top of the footing, 1 foot high, and below the pavement of the cellar story two inches; the wall shall be from the top of the footing 2½ bricks, or 1 foot 9½ inches thick, to the under side of the ground-floor, and thence 2 bricks, or 17½ inches thick to the under side of the floor of the rooms in the roof of the highest adjoining building, and thence 1½ brick, or 13 inches to the top. *Ibid.*

2. Warehouses, stables, and other buildings, not a dwelling-house, (except of the 1st, 5th, 6th, and 7th rates) exceeding two stories, and not more than three stories above ground, exclusive of rooms in the roof, or of the height of 22 feet, and not so high as 31 feet from the ground to the top of the coping; and dwelling-houses above 300*l.* value, and not more than 850*l.* and exceeding 5 squares, and not more than 9 squares of building, shall be the second rate of building. *s.* 5—7.

External walls of the second rate shall be at the foundation 2 bricks, or 17½ inches thick, and decreasing on each side 2¼ inches to the top of the footing, which is to be 9 inches high, and below the cellar floor 2 inches; and from the top of the footing 1½ brick, or 13 inches thick, to the under side of the one-pair-of-stairs floor; from thence 1 brick, or 8½ inches thick, to the under side of the coping, except walls of stone above ground 9 inches thick, and recesses arched, and at the back 1 brick, or 8½ inches thick. *Ibid.*

Party walls of the second rate shall be at the foundation 3½ bricks, or 2 feet 6½ inches thick, and from thence decreasing on each side 4½ inches to the top of the footing, 9 inches high, and under the cellar floor 2 inches; and from thence 2½ bricks, or 1 foot 9½ inches thick to the under side of the ground-floor; and thence 2 bricks, or 17½ inches thick to the under side of the two-pair-of-stairs floor; and thence 1½ brick, or 13 inches thick to the top of the party wall. *Ibid.*

3. Warehouses, stables, and other buildings, not dwelling-houses (except of the 1st, 5th, 6th, and 7th rates) exceeding 1 story, and not more than 2 above ground, besides rooms in the roof, or 13 feet, and not more than 22 feet high from the ground to the coping, and dwelling-houses of the value of 150*l.* and not more than 300*l.* and exceeding 3 squares and an half, and not more than 5 squares, shall be the third rate of building. *s.* 8.

External walls of the 3rd rate shall be at the foundation 2 bricks, or 17½ inches thick, and thence regularly decreasing on both sides 2¼ inches to the top of the footing, 6 inches high, 2 below the floor of the cellar story, and from the top of the footing, 1½ brick, or 13 inches thick, to the under side of the ground-floor, and thence 1 brick, or 8½ inches to the under side of the coping. *s.* 9.

Party walls of the 3rd rate shall be at the foundation 3 bricks, or 26 inches thick, and from thence regularly decreasing on each side 4½ inches to the top of the footing, 9 inches high, and 2 inches below the floor of the cellar story, and from the top of the footing 2 bricks, or 17½ inches thick, to the under side of the ground-floor, and from thence 1½ brick, or 13 inches thick, to the top of the wall. *s.* 10.

4. Warehouses, stables, and other buildings, not dwelling-houses (except of the 1st, 5th, 6th, and 7th rates) not exceeding one story above ground, exclusive of rooms in the roof, and not more than 13 feet high from the ground to the top of the coping, and dwelling-houses not more than 150*l.* value, and not exceeding 3½ squares of building, shall be the fourth rate of building. *s.* 11.

External walls of the 4th rate shall be at the foundation 2 bricks, or 17½ inches thick, and thence decreasing on each side 2¼ inches, to the top of the footing, 6 inches, and 2 inches below the floor of the cellar story, and from thence 1½ brick, or 13 inches thick, to the under side of the ground-floor, and from thence 1 brick, or 8½ inches thick, to the under side of the coping. *s.* 12.

Party walls of the 4th rate shall be two bricks, or 17½ inches thick at the foundation, from thence gradually decreasing on each side 2¼ inches to the top of the footing, 9 inches high, and 2 inches below the cellar floor, and from the top of the footing 1½ brick, or 13 inches thick, to the under side of the ground floor, and from thence 1 brick, or 8½ inches thick, to the top of the wall. *s.* 13.

All houses of the 1st, 2d, 3d, or 4th rate, contiguous to other buildings, shall have party walls between them, to extend to the outward surfaces of each, and those and all chimnies and chimney shafts shall be of brick or stone, or both together (except timber, wood, lead, or iron, laid in as after directed, and except piling, bridging or planking, necessary for foundation) and such party walls shall be topped with stone, tile, or brick, and of the dimensions before directed, and one half on the ground of each house, for which purpose workmen may enter the ground of the other house, and all party walls above four stories high shall be built as of the 1st rate, and those of the fourth rate houses, four stories high, as if of the 3d rate. *s.* 14, 15.

Internal inclosures for separating buildings of the 1st, 2d, 3d, and 4th rate, shall be of brick or stone, or artificial stone or stucco, or all together (except timber, wood, lead, or iron work, laid in as after directed), and except necessary piling, bridging, or planking for foundation, and in ascertaining the rates, to estimate the value as if of good materials, and to take the squares of the level of the entrance, and an appeal allowed to the quarter sessions. *s.* 16, 17.

5. Dwelling-houses, warehouses, stables, and other buildings (except buildings not being dwelling-houses, and of the 1st rate) at the distance of 4 feet, and not 8 feet from any public road, street, or cause-way, and detached from any other building, not in the same possession, 16 feet at least and not 30 feet, or connected only by a fence-wall, shall be of the 5th rate, and may be built of any dimensions. *s.* 18.

6. Dwelling-houses, warehouses, stables, and other buildings (except such buildings not being dwelling-houses, and of the 1st rate) which are 8 feet from any public road, street, or causeway, and detached from any other building, not in the same possession, 30 feet, or connected only by a fence-wall, shall be of the 6th rate, and may be built of any dimensions, or of any materials. *s.* 19.

7. Crane-houses on wharfs or quays, shambles, wind or water mills, and all buildings out of London and Westminster, and liberties, and used for workshops, or drying places for tanners, fell-mongers, glue-makers, size-makers, calico-printers, whitsters, whiting-makers, curriers, leather-dressers, buckram stiffners, oil-cloth painters, wool staplers, throwsters, parchment and paper-makers, so long as used for those purposes, shall be of the 7th rate, and may be built of any dimensions; external enclosures of crane-houses shall be of stone, brick, slate, tile, oak, elm, steel, iron, or brass; but other buildings of the said rate may be of any materials, so that they be not covered with pitch, tar, or other inflammable composition, and not used for other purposes. *s.* 20, 21.

Detached offices, or if only connected by fence-walls, to be deemed of the rate such office would be of, if the same did not appertain to any other building, and old sound party walls to remain; if the adjoining building is rebuilt without making use of such wall, the owner of the other part shall have only one half of such old wall and ground when pulled down; if party walls are not of the thickness aforesaid, to be condemned as ruinous; and also if it shall have any timber through it, to be cut off, so as not to leave six inches of brick-work. *s.* 22, 23.

Timber partitions to remain till one of the adjoining houses be taken down, or condemned as ruinous, and no longer; and external walls not to become party walls, unless of the height and thickness and of such materials as before directed. *s.* 24, 25.

Party walls to be 18 inches above the buildings adjoining, and no recesses therein (except for chimnies, flues, girders, and beams, and ends of piers, as after) so as to reduce such wall under the thickness required; nor openings (except for communication between different stacks of warehouses, or between stables, and to have iron doors, and except necessary passages on the ground-floors, which shall be arched over with brick or stone, 13 inches thick in every building of the 1st and 2d rate, and 8½ inches thick in every building of the 3d and 4th rate, and if there is a cellar under, to be all arched in the same manner.) *s.* 26.

No timber to be in party walls (except bonds, templets, and chains, and the ends of girders, beams, and the like), and to have 8½ inches of solid brick-work between the ends and sides of every piece of timber, except opposite to other timbers, and then no part of such timbers to approach nearer than 4 inches to the centre of the said wall. Party walls not to be cut, except 9 inches from the front or back wall, to the centre of such party wall, for the purpose of inserting the end of such new front or back wall; and if a breast-summer and story-posts, 14 inches, and the same may be 4 inches wide in the cellar story, and 2 inches wide in the ground-story, or may cut the wall for railing of stone-stairs or landings, or timbers for wood stairs, not nearer than 8½ inches to a chimney, or 4 inches to the timbers of the next house, and may cut recesses for inserting the walls, not more than 15 inches wide, nor 4 inches deep, and not nearer than 10 feet to any other recess, and to make good all damages. *s.* 27, 28.

Chimnies shall be 13 inches thick in the cellar story, and 8½ inches in every other story, and if against another chimney in party wall of the 1st rate, 8½ inches, and of the 2d, 3d, and 4th rate, 6½ inches, and no flue opposite another in party walls (except 2 inehes from the centre), and the breast to be 8½ inches thick in the cellar story, and 4 in the other stories; and all withs to be brick or stone, and ½ brick thick; the bricks, backs, and withs, to be pargetted within and without (except next to vacant ground) and then marked (except fronts), but chimnies may be placed in party walls, if desired by the owner of the adjoining house, on notice, which shall be deemed making use of such party wall, and the builder to pay a proportionate part of the expense thereof, with costs. *s.* 29, 30.

When buildings are mixed property the party wall shall be of the highest rate of building adjoining, with party arches of 1½ brick, or 13 inches thick in the 1st and 2d rates, and 1 brick, or 8½ inches thick in the 3d and 4th rates, between them, but not to extend to inns of court or chancery (except party walls of stair-cases). *s.* 31, 32.

Where owners are under any disability to contract or agree, a jury shall determine the expense of rebuilding; and sessions may give judgment thereon, which is to be final; and in 14 days workmen may enter, and if interrupted the penalty is 10*l.* and builders are to be paid expenses according to the verdict. *s.* 33.

Old decayed party walls or arches may be pulled down on 3 months notice, as specified in this act, and surveyors to be appointed to view them; if the major part condemn them as ruinous, they are to certify the same, and the owner may appeal to sessions, whose judgment is to be final; if of the 1st, 2d, or 3d rates, to give three months notice of pulling down, or the same if wooden partitions; and the expense to be paid by the owner of the improved rent, and till payment the property of the wall vested in the builder: new walls to pay a moiety of building, and old also, for pulling down, removing furniture, and shoring, but not for clearing away rubbish, and the expense to be estimated at 7*l.* 15*s.* per rod, deducting 1*l.* 8*s.* per rod for the materials (if any) of the old wall, and 2*d.* per cube foot for materials (if any) of old timber partition; and in 10 days after built an account to be delivered of the expenses, and if not paid in 21 days may be recovered by action; if the plaintiff gives three months notice of such action, and recovers, he shall have double costs. *s.* 38—41.

Party walls to be of the thickness required for the highest rate of building adjoining, and may be raised above the other building, but if used by the other side to be paid for: party fence-walls may be likewise raised, but not to be used as party walls, unless of sufficient thickness, though either side may take it down and build a party wall: and if the other side use it, to contribute, and the first builder not to lose his right of the soil, if the party wall is not half on each ground. *s.* 42, 43, 44.

If the fore and back front be rebuilt as low as the one-pair-of-stairs floor, in five years from each other, the party walls to be subject to the regulations of this act; and chimnies, not in party walls of the 1st rate, to be 13 inches in the cellar story, to 12 inches above the mantle, and if of other rates, 8½ inches (except built against a wall, and then it may be half a brick thinner); and the backs of chimnies of the 2d, 3d, and 4th rates, and not in party walls, to be 8½ inches thick from the hearth to the mantle (except against a wall, and then half a brick thinner); and no timber over the opening of any chimney to support it, but brick, stone, or iron; and no timber under the hearth nearer than 18 inches, and to have slabs of tile, stone, marble, or iron, 18 inches broad; and no wood in the brick-work of any oven, stove, copper, still, boiler, or furnace, within two feet of the inside, nor of any chimney nearer than 9 inches to the opening, or 5 inches to the flue; nor wood to the front of chimnies except fastened by iron nails, not more than 3 inches in the wall, or nearer than 4 inches of the inside; and no chimney to be erected on timber-work, except below the foundation, and on brick or stone corbels, or iron shores. *s.* 45.

External walls to be of brick, stone, artificial stone, lead, copper, tin, slate, tile, or iron, or mixed, except necessary piling for foundation and templets, chains, and bond-timbers, and except doors, windows, and the frames thereof set in recesses, 4 inches from the front, and except breast-summers, and stallboards for shops in the ground story only; story posts to be 2 inches in party walls, and of oak or stone, and 12 inches square; and flats, gutters, and roofs, of the first five rates, and all turrets, are to be covered with glass, copper, lead, tin, slate, tile, or artificial stone, except doors and windows. *s.* 46, 47.

External decorations to be of brick, stone, burnt clay, or artificial stone, and also covered ways the same; and no water to drip into the streets, except from porticoes and entrances, but to be conveyed by pipes or trunks to the ground; no bow windows to project beyond the line of buildings (except decorations, shop windows, and stall-boards) in streets 30 feet wide, not more than 10 inches; in lesser streets 5 inches; and no cornice more than 18 inches in streets of 30 feet; and 13 inches in lesser streets: and materials of bow-windows and projections to be the same as external walls; but this is not to affect the commissioners of paving, or sewers, in London. *s.* 49, 50.

Old external walls may be repaired with the same materials as before, but if rebuilt to conform to this act; and no bow-window or projection to be rebuilt, unless originally built with the house, and in a line with the street; no stack of warehouses to be above 35 squares, or any communication through party walls, unless by stone door-cases, and iron doors, and no timber within 18 inches, no stables more than 25 squares, and the like doors. *s.* 51—54.

Buildings of the first 4 rates (except inns of court and chancery, Royal Exchange, companies halls, warehouses and dwelling-houses, under 25*l.* per annum rent) converted into two distinct tenures, to be deemed separate buildings, and to have party walls; but warehouses under 35 squares, and stables under 25 squares, may be divided. *s.* 55, 56, 57.

Buildings of the 5th and 6th rates, in distinct tenures, and not at requisite distances, deemed nuisances; and no funnel for smoke to be next the street in front of the first four rates, and not nearer than 14 inches of timber, nor any brick funnel to extend beyond the line of the street: every building contrary to this act is declared a common nuisance, and the builder may be bound to demolish the same in convenient time, if convicted in three months after being built: the lord mayor and justices may respectively order irregular buildings to be taken down, and materials sold to defray the expense. *s.* 59, 60, 61.

The lord mayor and aldermen, and justices in session, may respectively appoint surveyors, who are to be sworn, and leave notice of their place of abode with the clerk of the peace, and to whom notice is to be given 24 hours before the beginning of any building, who is to survey the same, and to be paid by the builder:

For 1st rate new building -	3	10	0
Alteration - - - -	1	15	0
2d rate new building -	3	3	0
Alteration - - - -	1	10	0
3d rate new building -	2	10	0
Alteration - - - -	1	5	0
4th rate new building -	2	2	0
Alteration - - - -	1	1	0
5th rate new building -	1	10	0
Alteration - - - -	0	15	0
6th rate new building -	1	1	0
Alteration - - - -	0	10	6
7th rate new building -	0	10	6
Alteration - - - -	0	5	0

which may be levied by distress on the master workman, with costs, and on default of notice, treble satisfaction to the surveyor, and 20*l.* penalty. *s.* 63, 64.

Surveyor is to give information of irregular buildings, and the lord mayor and justices are to order the same to be demolished or amended, and 50*s.* penalty on the workman, or to be committed, not more than 3 months, nor under one. Houses and buildings are to be surveyed in 14 days after finished, and the surveyor in 14 days more to make oath, which is to be filed, that such house or building is duly built: and the builder neglecting to have the same done, forfeits 10*l.* and if not done in a month after conviction, he is to forfeit 10*l.* more, and so *toties quoties* every month; but the surveyor misbehaving shall be discharged, and incapable of acting again. *s.* 65—68.

Not to extend to the king's palaces. *s.* 69.

When buildings are presented as ruinous, a hoard is to be put up; if owners on notice neglect to take down the same, the court of lord mayor and aldermen, or churchwardens and overseers of the poor (out of the city), may order the same to be taken down, and the materials to be sold to pay the expense, and the surplus to be paid to the owner, if demanded in 6 years, and if deficient the owner or occupier is to make it good, and the landlord is to allow the tenant what is so paid. *s.* 70—71.

Fire engines and ladder shall be kept in known places, and the parish officers shall place on mains of water-works, stop-blocks, and fire-cocks, and shall mark the house near, and keep keys there; the fire-cocks to be kept in repair by the parish, and the plugs by the owners of the water-works; and if changed the same; and engines and ladders shall be kept in every parish, on penalty of 10*l.* on the officers, to be levied by distress. In case of fire, the turn-cock whose water comes first shall have 10*s.* paid by the parish officers. First engine 1*l.* 10*s.* second engine 1*l.* and third engine 10*s.* to be paid by the same; but no reward without the approbation of an alderman, or two common-council-men in London, and a justice out. Where officers pay rewards for fires in chimnies only, or first beginning there, they are to be reimbursed by the occupier, as the mayor or justice shall direct, who may examine the parties, or others, on oath, and if not paid in fourteen days may be levied by distress. United parishes shall be deemed one, and parishes may have more than one engine, under the like regulations. Rewards to be paid out of the poors rate. *s.* 76—81.

Watermen belonging to insurance offices shall not be impressed; and directors of insurance offices may, on request of any person interested in houses burnt, or on suspicion of fraud in the insurer, cause the money insured to be laid out in rebuilding, unless the party in sixty days, give security to lay out the same, or that the money be disposed of with the approbation of the directors. *s.* 82, 83.

Servants carelessly firing houses shall forfeit 100*l.* or be imprisoned eighteen months. *s.* 84.

Constables and beadles on notice shall repair to fires, and may seize misdoers. No action shall be brought against a person where the fire accidentally begins. (This clause extended to every part of England) And distress for penalties is not unlawful for want of form, but the party aggrieved may recover special damages; and the plaintiff shall not recover, if amends are tendered before action, or money is paid into court before issue joined. *s.* 85—88.

Irregular buildings erected since 12 *Geo.* 3, shall be made secure, and altered, though no prosecution, by order of the lord mayor and aldermen, or quarter-sessions, filed: and the same shall be reformed in nine months, on penalty of 50*l.* and the like every nine months till done. *s.* 93—100.

Prosecutions are not to be removed by certiorari, but appeal lies to the quarter-sessions, who may give costs, and the appellant shall give security for the same. *Ibid.*

Parishioners may be witnesses. Penalties may be sued for in 6 months, and actions against persons acting under the act in 3 months, and they may plead the general issue, and have treble costs. *Ibid.*

By 25 *Geo.* 3, *c.* 77, no person, either in

London, or in any other part of England, shall distil or boil any turpentine or tar, or draw any oil of turpentine or rosin, by distilling turpentine, or drawing any oil of tar or pitch, by distilling or boiling tar, or boil any oil and turpentine, or oil and tar together, above ten gallons at one time, in any place which is not 75 feet distant from any other building, on penalty of 100*l.* and treble costs.

But this is not to prevent shipwrights, barge-builders, and such persons, from boiling or mixing oil, and other things, to pay ships, barges, and the like. *Ibid.*

The 27 *Geo.* 3, *c.* 48, reciting, that the *East India* company are possessed of, and building warehouses exceeding 35 squares, and that it is expedient that the said company should be allowed to continue their present warehouses, and build others, freed from the regulations in 14 *Geo.* 3, *c.* 78, enacts, that the warehouses of the said company shall be freed from the regulations of the said act.

——— *Butchers.*] By 4 *Hen.* 7, *c.* 3, butchers shall not kill beasts within the walls of London, or in any walled town, or in Cambridge. See also *Leather.*

——— *Carts.*] By 1 *Geo.* 1, *stat.* 2, *c.* 57, no carter, drayman, carman, waggoner, or other person, shall within the bills of mortality, ride on his cart, dray, car, or waggon, not having some person on foot to guide the same, on forfeiture of 10*s.*; in default of payment he is to be sent to the house of correction for three days. But this act does not take away the power of the mayor of London, or the governors of Christ's hospital.

By 18 *Geo.* 2, *c.* 33, carts, cars, or drays in London, may be drawn by three horses, and the name of the owner is to be placed thereon, and numbered, and registered with the commissioners for hackney coaches, under penalty of 40*s.* Using more than three horses is a forfeiture of the extra ones to the seizer.

Cart wheels, being full six inches broad, may be bound with iron, without rose-headed nails. *Ibid.*

By 24 *Geo.* 2, *c.* 43, the penalty on a carter for riding on his cart, within the bills of mortality, is extended to within ten miles thereof. *s.* 8, 9.

By 30 *Geo.* 2, *c.* 22, justices of the city may annually assess the rates of carriage of goods, and make rules for regulating carts and drivers, and for payment of their fare, and may annex reasonable penalties on breach of such rules: they may also alter and amend the same, or make new orders, but such rules must be printed and published. *s* 3.

By 30 *Geo.* 2, *c.* 28, empty carts, obstructing the streets or highways, except while they are loading, forfeit a sum not exceeding 20*s.* *s.* 5, 7, 8.

No carts shall ply for hire in the streets leading to Westminster bridge. *s.* 6.

Every cart carrying goods for hire, shall be deemed a common stage, and have the owner's name thereon. *s.* 13.

By 7 *Geo.* 3. *c.* 44, any person may search the register of carts, cars, and drays, kept by the commissioners of hackney coaches, on paying 4*d.* See also 33 *Geo.* 3. *c.* 75. under article *Paving*, infra.

——— *Cattle.*] By 31 *Geo.* 2. *c.* 40, salesmen, or others employed to buy or sell cattle for others, are not to buy or sell on their own account, other than for provision in their own family, on penalty of forfeiting double the value.

By 14 *Geo.* 3, *c.* 87, and 21 *Geo.* 3, *c.* 67, any peace officer may secure persons driving cattle through the streets of London in an improper manner. If the party be convicted before a justice he shall forfeit from 5*s.* to 20*s.* to the prosecutor, or be committed to the house of correction for one month.

Persons not being drivers of cattle, who shall pelt them with stones, or set dogs at them without leave, may be taken before a justice, and shall be subject to the same penalties. *Ibid.*

Offender to pay the forfeit though the informer should neglect to attend. *Ibid.*

The court of aldermen may make orders for regulating drivers of cattle within London and Westminster, and impose fines, not more than 40*s.* but the time for keeping Smithfield market open shall not be shortened. *Ibid.*

Any justice within the bills of mortality may determine complaints of offences against any rules to be made by the court of aldermen, and if the party be convicted, may fine him. Offender not paying the penalty may be committed to the house of correction. *Ibid.*

Offenders who refuse to discover their names and places of abode shall be committed to the common gaol. And an abstract of the penalties contained in this act, and of all rules to be made by the court of aldermen, shall be printed, and posted up in the streets. *Ibid.*

Warrants may be executed on offenders, or their goods, out of the jurisdiction wherein they were granted. Prosecutions to be commenced in 14 days. Appeal lies to the quarter sessions, giving 14 days notice. Proceedings not to be quashed for want of form, nor removable by certiorari. *Ibid.*

——— *Coals.*] By 16 & 17 *Car.* 2, *c.* 2, all coals brought into the Thames shall contain 36 bushels to the chaldron, to be heaped; the hundred to weigh 112*lb.* Selling contrary hereto is a forfeiture of the coals, and double the value thereof.

The lord mayor of London, and the justices of peace, may set the rates on retail ing them; and retailers refusing to sell at such rates, they may authorize persons, taking a constable, to enter by force, and make sale at the rates appointed.

By 9 *Ann. c.* 28, crimps, husbands, agents, or factors, for ship-masters, importing coals at London, vending coals to their own agents, in trust for themselves, are to forfeit 50*l.*

By 3 *Geo.* 2, *c.* 26, dealers in coals may use their own lighters on the river Thames; the lighters are to be entered, marked, and subject to the rules of the watermens company.

Buyers of coals for sale acting as crimps, and masters employing them, are to forfeit 200*l.* each. *Ibid.*

To further enforce the last act 9 *Ann. c.* 28, persons receiving gratuities for contracts from fitters, coal-owners, or masters of ships, and selling one sort of coals for another, shall forfeit 500*l.* but coal owners may employ fitters and crimps, not being lightermen or coal-dealers. *Ibid.*

Masters of vessels refusing to give yearly accounts to the owners forfeit 100*l.*

Coal sacks shall be sealed and marked with white paint at Guildhall, London, or at the exchequer, in Westminster. Consumers of coals may, for their own use, have such sacks as they think proper. *Ibid.*

By 4 *Geo.* 2, *c.* 30, a penalty of 100*l.* is inflicted on masters of coal ships keeping turn in delivering coals in the Thames.

Cocquets are to be delivered by the master within four days after the arrival of the ship at Gravesend, on penalty of 50*l.* *Ibid.*

By 11 *Geo.* 2, *c.* 15, buyers and sellers of coals at Billingsgate, or within the bills of mortality, shall sign all contracts made between them in the factor or crimp's book. See 47 *Geo.* 3, *c.* 68. *s.* 29.

By 7 *Geo.* 3, *c.* 37, a duty of 6*d.* per chaldron, and 6*d.* per ton, on coals imported into London, established by 5 & 6 *Will. & Mar. c.* 10, is continued for 46 years, from the 29th of Sept. 1785, for completing Blackfriars bridge, redeeming the tolls of London bridge, rebuilding Newgate, repairing the Royal Exchange, and embanking part of the north side of the river Thames, and then for paving the streets of Westminster and Southwark, to pay the orphans debt by 1803, and to do the other works by Michaelmas 1831. Further continued by 44 *Geo.* 3, *c.* 27, until the 5th of July 1837, to complete the improvements at Snowhill and Temple-bar.

By 10 *Geo.* 3, *c.* 53, coal undertakers are not to take reward for employing heavers, on penalty of 5*l.*

Victuallers are not to be undertakers on penalty of 5*l.* Persons discharging coal ships to be paid 1*s.* 6*d.* per score, subject to alteration by the court of lord mayor and aldermen; the money to be paid to the foreman of the gang in current coin. *Ibid.*

Leaving any ship before discharged punishable as servants in husbandry, except where otherwise directed; and the foreman may stop 6*d.* per pound till the charges of passing this act are paid. *Ibid.*

By 47 *Geo.* 3, *sess.* 2, *c.* 68, the coal exchange shall be a free, open, and public market, and held every Monday, Wednesday, and Friday, from twelve at noon until two in the afternoon. *s.* 18, 19.

When coals are sold by weight, 112*lbs.* shall be deemed to be 1 *cwt.* and 20 hundred 1 ton. *s.* 23.

Masters of ships are to give an account of the coals in their ships within 24 hours after their arrival at Blackwall, and not before; and the clerk of the market is to register the same: and delivering false accounts, or making false entries, is a penalty of 50*l.* *s.* 24.

The said accounts are to be affixed in the market, on pain of 20*l.* on the clerk for default. *s.* 25.

Coals are to be sold in the market and during market hours only, on pain of 100*l.* *s.* 26.

But coals loaded and freighted on board any ships for government, may be unloaded and delivered without being put up to sale in the market, provided the ship-master first send to the clerk of the market a copy of the fitter's certificate, together with an affidavit stating the coals to have been so loaded and freighted. *s.* 27.

The sales of coals (see 11 *Geo.* 2. *c.* 15.) shall be entered by the factor or crimp with the clerk of the market, on pain of 100*l.* but persons may sell their own coals without the intervention of a factor or crimp. *s.* 29.

Coals may be purchased in the market in quantities of not less than 21 chaldrons. *s.* 31.

If any vender of coals shall knowingly sell one sort of coals for a sort which they really are not, within 25 miles from the Royal Exchange, he shall forfeit 20*l.* per chaldron, up to and not exceeding 25 chaldrons for the same offence.

No meter is to be appointed to a ship until part of the coals are sold: but coal ships damaged may be unloaded without waiting for a ship meter: and meters may appoint an assistant out of the fellowship porters. *s.* 34—36.

Meters and coalheavers, if unnecessarily detained on board a ship, are entitled to detention money; and money paid by the ship-master or owner for any detention occasioned by the default of the coal-buyer, is to be repaid by the coal-buyer, and enforced by one justice, who may levy the same by distress, or in default of payment commit for not exceeding 6 calendar months. *s.* 37, 38.

Coal-buyers, are not to be liable to detention-money for the day on which the meter is appointed, unless the meter attend on that day at his request. *s.* 39.

Coal-buyers, or master or owner respectively, may appeal to sessions against the decision of the justice. *s.* 40.

Ship-masters are not to bring actions against coal-buyers to recover money paid for detention. *s.* 41.

No person shall follow the trade of a coal undertaker, without a license from the court of aldermen, on pain of 10*l.* and the lord mayor or sitting alderman may suspend, and court of aldermen may erase the name of any coal undertaker misconducting himself; and acting after suspension or erasure is a penalty of 100*l.* wholly to the informer. *s.* 42, 43.

Victuallers are not to act as coal undertakers, or supply implements of any kind, on pain of 10*l.* *s.* 45.

Shovels and other implements for the unloading of coal ships, shall be provided by the ship-master; and any other person except a licensed coal undertaker or ship-master letting the same out to hire, shall forfeit 10*l.* *s.* 46.

Coal undertakers are to receive from the ship-masters 1*d.* per chaldron, and coalheavers 3*s.* for every 20 chaldrons delivered, as their pay or wages. *s.* 47.

But the court of aldermen may increase such wages, when reasonable; and those who take or pay more, are to forfeit 10*l.* *s.* 48.

The wages of coalheavers shall be paid in money, and not in coals, goods, meat, drink, lodging, or apparel, on pain of 10*l.* nor at any alehouse, on pain of 20*l.* *s.* 49, 50.

Undertakers shall, during the time of the ship's delivery, advance to coalheavers requesting the same, between five and seven in the evening, one half of the wages then earned. *s.* 51.

Undertakers are, before seven o'clock of the next evening after each ship's delivery, to pay the coalheavers in full, on pain of 20*l.* *s.* 52, 53.

Undertakers are not to give, nor masters to take, any reward for giving any preference to any particular gang of coalheavers, on pain of 20*l.* *s.* 54.

Ship meters are to give certificates of the coals delivered into each lighter, on pain of 10*l.* and lightermen are to deliver such certificates to the wharfingers, on pain of 20*l.* *s.* 55, 56.

Ship meters are to keep accounts of the coals delivered by them, and deliver the same to the clerk of the market, to be open for inspection; and the clerk of the market refusing to receive the same, or to let them be inspected, shall forfeit not exceeding 20*l.* *s.* 57.

Preventing the vat from being filled, according to the directions of the meter, is a penalty not exceeding 20*l.* The spout or stage for shooting coals from ships, shall be provided by the master or owner, 5 feet 6 wide at the top, 4 feet 6 at the bottom, and 10 inches high at the sides, on pain of 10*l.* *s.* 58, 59.

When a cargo of coals is sold to different buyers, the same shall be delivered, in the turns settled between the parties, within one hour after the close of the market. *s.* 60.

Lightermen may carry on partnership with coal dealers. *s.* 61.

Not less than 5 chaldrons and 1 vat, or some multiple of that quantity, shall be delivered into any barge or room of a barge, on pain of 20*l.* But coals may be loaded in bulk. *s.* 62, 63.

Meter is not to deliver coals into open barges, or into rooms of barges having coals in them before, except into empty rooms, on pain of 20*l.* *s.* 64, 65.

And in case barges have the clearance of a ship on board, coals of the same sort may be put therein, on the production of the certificate from the former ship. *s.* 66.

Penalty on ship meters for delivering certificates without measuring the coals, 20*l.* *s.* 67.

Penalty on giving gifts to ship meters (except the sums specified in the schedule for wages and allowances), which are not to be deemed gifts, 100*l.* *s.* 68.

Coals by the vat may be remeasured on notice within one hour after delivery into the craft, and the meter is liable to certain penalties for deficiencies; ship meters may also be suspended from their offices if convicted of any penalty for delivering false measure. *s.* 69, 70.

When the coals are remeasured by desire of the vender, and the meter shall be found not to have incurred any penalty, the owner of the lighter shall have a compensation from the vender for the detention of his lighter, to be settled by a justice and levied by distress; or in default of payment, commitment for not exceeding three calendar months. *s.* 71.

The principal land meters already appointed for WESTMINSTER *shall continue in their office.* s. 72.

The principal land meters already appointed for LONDON *and between* TOWER DOCK *and* LIMEHOUSE-HOLE, *shall continue in their office.* s. 73.

But upon the death of any one of the present three principal meters for London, the number shall be reduced to two: and upon any vacancy happening hereafter, the court of common council shall have the appointment of the principal meters for London. *s.* 73.

The principal meters already nominated for SURREY *shall continue.* s. 74.

His majesty shall appoint principal land

coal meters for Westminster upon any vacancy. *s.* 75.

And the principal land coal meters for Westminster are punishable by the justices for neglect, by a penalty not exceeding 20*l.* and costs. *s.* 76.

Labouring coal meters for Westminster are subject to the controul of the justices, on complaints, to be heard in a summary way. *s.* 77.

Land coal meters for the city of London are subject to the lord mayor and aldermen. *s.* 78.

The common council are to appoint the labouring land coal meters for London, who are not to be less than 45 in number, but the principal meters for London may suspend labouring meters, provided they report the cause of such suspension to the lord mayor or court of aldermen within seven days. *s.* 79, 80.

The principal and labouring meters for Surrey are subject to the controul of the quarter sessions. *s.* 81.

After the death of the survivor of the present principal meters for Surrey, the churchwardens of the different parishes shall have the election and appointment of the principal meters, and the principal meters may be re-elected when the times expire. *s.* 82, 83.

All the principal meter's offices shall be kept open every day, Sundays, Good-fridays, and Christmas, and fast days, only excepted, from 25th March to 29th September, from 5 till 9, and from 29th September to 25th March, from 6 to 6, on pain of 20*l.* *s.* 84.

The principal meters for Westminster and Surrey are to appoint a sufficient number of labouring meters for their respective districts, who are to be sworn before a justice to act truly. *s.* 86, 87.

Labouring meters are to attend at their stations during the same hours as the principal offices are open, and are to attend at wharfs and places on notice, on pain of 5*l.* *s.* 83.

The principal meters for Westminster are to pay not less than 20*s.* per week wages to each of their labouring meters, on pain of 20*l.* *s* 89.

Principal meters for Surrey are also to pay not less than 20*s.* per week wages to each of their labouring meters who shall serve at any station between Nine-Elms and Dock-Head both inclusive. *s.* 90.

Coal meters are not be interested in the sale of coals, on pain of 100*l.* on the principal, and 50*l.* on a deputy or labouring meter, and disability. *s.* 91.

The land coal meter may demand from a wharfinger a sight of the ship's certificate to be inspected, and when the coals are delivered from the craft, countersigned '*Delivered;*' and if the wharfinger refuse to produce the same, he shall forfeit 5*l.* and the meter countersigning the certificate without first inspecting it and satisfying himself that the coals are of the sort described, shall also forfeit 5*l.* *s.* 92.

Coals sold by pool measure are to be loaded in sacks in the presence of one of the labouring meters, who may measure sacks, and direct the whole of any room to be entirely emptied and sent away, and if obstructed the penalty is 5*l.* *s.* 93.

The vender of pool measure coals, when sent by a waggon or cart, shall send a man with a ticket in the form prescribed by the act, on pain of 10*l.* and if the driver neglect to deliver the same to the purchaser or his servant, he shall forfeit 10*l.* *s.* 94.

The principal meter is to receive from the vendor for inspecting coals sold by pool measure 1*s.* for every 5 chaldrons and 1 vat. *s.* 95.

But purchasers of coals sold by pool measure may have the same delivered without the intervention of a meter, provided it be not at a wharf or meter's station. *s.* 96.

Purchasers of coals sent by water may have the same remeasured within two hours in case fraud is suspected, on notice to one of the offices, and the expences of remeasurement are to be paid, if the deficiency amount to 1 bushel, by the vender, and if not to 1 bushel, by the purchaser. *s.* 98.

But coals sold by pool measure are not to be measured by the bushel without the desire of the purchaser. *s.* 99.

Coals sold by wharf measure shall be measured in the presence of a land coal meter; and the meter suffering wharf measure coals to be sent out without being measured, as by this act is directed, is a penalty of 10*l.* *s.* 100, 101.

The coal meter's offices are to take 6*d.* per chaldron for wharf measure coals, and a meter's ticket, descriptive thereof, is to be sent with such coals, and the carman is to deliver the same to the purchaser or his servant; and the penalty on the meter for not giving such ticket is 10*l.* and on the carman for not delivering the same to the purchaser, 40*s.* *s.* 102.

Wharfingers giving bribes to meters, forfeit 20*l.* and meters receiving bribes or delivering false tickets 10*l.* with forfeiture of office. *s.* 103, 4.

Penalty on a vendor for not delivering a meter's ticket with wharf coals 10*l.* *s.* 105.

Sacks used within the limits shall be made of linen and marked with white paint at Guildhall or the exchequer office at Westminster, and measure in the inside 4 feet 2 inches at least in length, by 2 feet 1 in breadth; and the penalty for using sacks not so marked or of less dimensions, is not exceeding 40*s.* nor less than 20*s.* per sack; but coals delivered by gang labourers need not be put into such sacks. *s.* 107.

Meters permitting sacks of less dimensions to be used, are to forfeit 5*l.* *s.* 108.

No bushel shall be used but that described in 12 *Ann. c.* 17. and 36 of such bushels heaped shall be a chaldron; and vender using any other bushels, or diminishing the same, shall forfeit 20*l.* and if his servant shall use any other bushel, or diminish the same, he shall be committed to hard labour in the house of correction for not exceeding three calendar months. *s.* 109.

Measures of a smaller measure used within the limits are to bear the same proportion and be stamped, and venders using others shall forfeit 10*l.* *s.* 110.

Venders of coals sold as wharf measure, if dissatisfied, may have them remeasured, paying to the meter's office 6*d.* per chaldron; and if there is an excess of 2 bushels in any chaldron remeasured, the meter shall forfeit 40*s.* *s.* 111.

The carman is to carry a bushel measure in his cart, on pain of 10*l.* and on the vender 20*l.* but this does not extend to purchasers carting the coals themselves. *s.* 112.

Venders are to deliver tickets of coals sold by wharf measure, containing the particulars of the number of sacks and quantity of the coals to the carman, who is to deliver the same to the purchaser; and if the vender do not deliver such ticket to the carman, he is to forfeit 20*l.* and the carman not delivering to the purchaser forfeits 10*l.* *s.* 113.

The carman may be required to measure one sack gratis in such cart, and if the carman drive coals away without measuring the sack, he shall forfeit not exceeding 20*l.* nor less than 5*l.* *s.* 114, 115.

Coals sent by land carriage are to be remeasured if desired by the purchaser, and the carman is to remain till they are remeasured, and not drive the coals away, on pain of not exceeding 10*l.* *s.* 116.

But the purchaser is to send notice to the meter's office if he is desirous of having the coals remeasured; and the purchaser may at his option either have the contents of each sack separately remeasured, or else the contents of all the sacks sent taken together, paying to the meter's office for the attendance of the meter 6*d.* per sack. *s.* 117.

And if in remeasurement it shall appear, that any separate sack contains not 3 bushels, the vender shall forfeit 40*s.*; and if there is a deficiency in the whole, the forfeiture is 5*l.* per bushel, and of the coals for the use of the poor. *Ibid.*

Meters, in case of any coals sold for wharf measure proving deficient on such remeasurement, are to forfeit 20*s.* per bushel, and the coal porters 2*s.* 6*d.* *Ibid.*

But if such coals shall be sold for pool measure, then the vender for a deficiency exceeding 4 and not 10 bushels in 5 chaldrons and 1 vat, shall forfeit 40*s.* per bushel; and if the deficiency exceed 10 bushels, 5*l.* *Ibid.*

But no remeasurement is to take place after more than one sack shall have been shot. *Ibid.*

The meter, in case of coals sold for pool measure, proving deficient upon remeasurement, shall forfeit, for more than 4 bushels in 5 chaldrons and 1 vat, 20*s.* per bushel. *s.* 118.

If, on remeasurement, the deficiency on the whole quantity shall amount to, or exceed, 1 bushel, the vender is to repay to the purchaser the expences of remeasurement; and if one fourth of the number of sacks do not contain 3 bushels each, the vender shall repay the expences; but if the number shall not amount to one fourth, then the purchaser is to bear the expence. *s.* 119.

Principal meters, not sending a labouring meter to measure the coals, after notice, to forfeit not exceeding 10*l.* *s.* 120.

The carman is to be paid 3*d.* per hour for every hour when stopt for the purpose of having coals remeasured. *s.* 121.

Coals sold by weight shall be sold or weighed by the cwt. of 112lbs. and 20 cwt. shall be deemed 1 ton; and the same shall be weighed and loaded in the presence of one of the labouring land meters, for which 6*s.* per ton is to be paid to the meter's office. *s.* 122.

The vender is to send a ticket with all coals sold by weight, to be delivered by the carman to the purchaser, and the vender, not sending such ticket, shall forfeit 20*l.* and the carman, not delivering the same, shall also forfeit 20*l.* *s.* 123.

But coals may be sold either by weight, or by the chaldron or bushel, half bushel, peck, or half peck, of aliquot parts. *s.* 124.

Principal meters for London are to produce, upon oath, before the common council, their accounts of metage money received by them, and to pay the same into the city chamber, by which it is to be applied in payment of the principal and labouring meters, and all expences of the London meter's office. *s.* 125, 6.

Wallsend, Temples Walls, and Hebburn Main, Heaton Main, Biggs Main, South Hebburn, Willington, Killingsworth, and Percy Main coals, may be mixed together, and sold by the name of *best coals mixed*; and Harly, Blythe, and Coupens Main coals may be mixed together, and sold by either of those names. *s.* 127, 8.

Clearings of coal barges, when reduced to 5 chaldrons wharf measure, may be heaped up and mixed together in any warehouse; but the same shall be sold by wharf measure, and described in the vender's tickets as *coals of different sorts mixed.* Venders making default herein are to forfeit not exceeding 50*l.* *s.* 128, 9.

And no other coals are to be mixed, within the limits of the act, on pain of 20*l.* *s.* 130.

And nothing herein shall prevent coalsheds, or warehouses where coals are sold in quantities not exceeding half a chaldron, from mixing coals, so as they be sold for mixed coals. *s.* 132.

The court of aldermen may make bye-laws to regulate the coal market, to be approved by one of the judges, and printed and published. *s.* 134—145.

Fines and forfeitures, not exceeding 20*l.* to be recovered before a justice of the peace; and penalties above 20*l.* in any of the courts at Westminster. *s.* 146—153.

The act commenced 4th October, 1807 (see *s.* 155.) *and is permanent.*

——— *Constables.*] By 26 *Geo.* 2. *c.* 25. and 31 *Geo.* 2. *c.* 17. eighty constables are to be appointed yearly at a court-leet for the city and liberty of Westminster.

High constable of Westminster shall obey the orders of the court-leet, and petty constables are to be assisting, on pain of being amerced not exceeding 40*s.* but persons aged are exempted from serving as constables or as leet jurymen in Westminster. 31 *Geo.* 2. *c.* 17.

——— *Coopers.*] By 23 *Hen.* 8. *c.* 4. and 31 *Eliz.* *c.* 8. the wardens of the mystery of coopers' shall search, mark, and guage, all vessels in London, and such as are brought from beyond the sea for ale and beer; and one halfpenny for other vessels, and the vessels may be detained till the fee is paid.

The said wardens shall come to the brewers' houses to guage vessels; but such as shall be filled with ale or beer, and directly exported, are exempt. 31 *Eliz.* *c.* 8.

——— *Court of Requests.*] By 3 *Jac.* 1. *c.* 15. citizens and freemen of London having debts under 40*s.* may cause the debtor to be summoned to the court of requests at Guildhall; and the debt there shall be summarily determined. Debtors refusing to appear, or pay, shall be imprisoned; but this shall not extend to debts for rent, or on real contracts.

The 14 *Geo.* 2. *c.* 10. extends the above act to all persons inhabiting the city.

By 23 *Geo.* 2. *c.* 27. and 24 *Geo.* 2. *c.* 42. the like in Westminster.

By 23 *Geo.* 2. *c.* 30. the like in the Tower Hamlets.

By 23 *Geo.* 2. *c.* 33. the like also in the county court of Middlesex.

By 39 & 40 *Geo.* 3. *c.* civ. so much of 3 *Jac.* 1. *c.* 15. and 14 *Geo.* 2. *c.* 10. as restrains the jurisdiction of the court of requests of the city to debts not exceeding 40*s.* shall be repealed. *s.* 1.

And a court of three of the commissioners shall have jurisdiction over debts not exceeding 40*s.* and seven shall have jurisdiction over debts not exceeding 5*l.* *s.* 2.

Debtors are to be summoned before commissioners, who may make such order therein, between the parties, as they shall see just; and orders and proceedings shall be registered. *s.* 5.

Where a debt shall be due from two partners, summoning one shall be sufficient. *s.* 6.

Beadles of the court shall summon witnesses, who if they refuse to give evidence shall forfeit 40*s.* and in default of payment may be committed for not exceeding one month; the penalty to go to the poor of the parish where the offender dwells. *s.* 7.

Persons giving false evidence, shall be punished as for perjury. *s.* 8.

Debts due by persons under age for necessaries, may be recovered: servants, though under age, may recover wages; and attorneys are subject to the processes of the court. *s.* 9, 10.

But this act does not extend to any debt where the title of premises may come in question, or to any specialty debt, or any debt concerning testament or matrimony, or any ecclesiastical matter, though it shall not exceed 5*l.* *s.* 11.

Verdicts in the superior courts, for debts which were recoverable in this court, are not to entitle to costs; and if a verdict be given for the defendant, and the judge certify that the debt ought to have been sued for in the court of requests, he shall have double costs. *s.* 12.

Nothing herein is to prevent persons from recovering rents by distress. *s.* 13.

The statute of limitations may be pleaded. *s.* 14.

Debtors are to be imprisoned for non-payment no longer than as follows, *viz.* where the debt, exclusive of costs, does not exceed 20*s.* twenty days; not exceeding 40*s.* forty days; not exceeding 3*l.* sixty days; not exceeding 5*l.* one hundred days: but the time of imprisonment shall extend separately and successively to each execution. *s.* 16.

The act 25 *Geo.* 3. *c.* 45. (see this act *infra*), as far as it respects the discharge of imprisoned persons without payment of fees, is extended to this act. *s.* 17.

By 46 *Geo.* 3. *c.* lxxxvii. the jurisdiction of the court for the recovery of small debts within the borough of Southwark, and certain parishes connected therewith, by 22 *Geo.* 2. *c.* 47. and 32 *Geo.* 2. *c.* 6. whereby debts under 40*s.* may be recovered in the court of conscience in Southwark, is extended, and three commissioners may determine debts not exceeding 40*s.* and five commissioners not exceeding 5*l.* *s.* 1, 2.

On verdicts in inferior courts, for debts recoverable under this act, the plaintiff shall not have costs; and on verdict for the defendant, and certificate of the judge, he shall have double costs. *s.* 13.

But persons may distrain or bring actions for rent, though it do not exceed 5*l.* *s.* 14.; and persons may sue in the palace court for sums above 40*s.* *s.* 24.: the rights of the city of London are also secured. *s.* 25.

By 46 *Geo.* 3. *c.* lxxxviii. the jurisdiction

of the court for the recovery of small debts within the western division of the hundred of Brixton in Surrey, under 31 *Geo.* 2. *c.* 23. is in like manner extended to 5*l.* *s.* 11. and the regulations of 26 *Geo.* 3. *c.* 38. are extended to this act. *s.* 19.

By 19 *Geo.* 3. *c.* 68. commissioners of the Tower Hamlets may purchase ground and build a court house, and grant annuities; may take cognizance of debts for rent under 40*s.* if the complainant hath been in possession twelve months; and no recovery of rent in the said court shall be given in evidence in support of a title, nor shall this act extend to prevent a distress or action for rent.

If the defendant does not appear, judgment may be given in his absence, but he must have a day to shew cause. No victualler to act as a commissioner, nor is this act to extend to the liberty of the Tower within. *Ibid.*

By 25 *Geo.* 3. *c.* 45. debtors committed to prison by courts of conscience in London, Middlesex, or Southwark, for a debt of 20*s.* or under, shall not be confined more than twenty days, and not exceeding 40*s.* for more than forty days.

Such prisoners are to be discharged without paying gaol fees: and gaolers demanding or taking fees shall forfeit 5*l.* Two justices may determine offences against this act, levy the penalties by distress, or on non-payment commit the offender for two months. *Ibid.*

Courts of conscience are not to issue process against both body and goods of the same party; and no commissioner shall act unless he has a real estate of 20*l.* *per ann.* or a personal estate of 500*l.* on pain of 20*l.* *Ibid.*

——— *Customs.*] By 1 *Ann. stat.* 1. *c.* 26. no cocquet shall be required of masters of hoys carrying corn or other goods on the Thames, whereon no duty is payable on exportation, but the same may be conveyed by transire, for which the officers shall not take more than 3*s.* 4*d.*

When there are not 50 quarters of corn, or 50 bags of hops in such vessels, the officers shall not take more than 1*s.* 8½*d.* *Ibid.*

Certificates on bonds transmitted into the exchequer shall be indorsed on the back of the bond on pain of treble damages and costs. But this act does not take away any tolls payable to the city of London, or the ports of Sandwich or Ipswich. *Ibid.*

——— *Disseisin.*] By 6 *Ed.* 1. *c.* 14. on disseisin in London damages shall be recovered with the freehold, and the disseisors shall be amerced before two barons of the exchequer, who shall once a year come into the city to do it.

——— *Dyers.*] By 23 *Geo.* 3. *c.* 15. dyers in London, or within ten miles thereof, shall be subject to the examination of the dyers' company, who are to appoint searchers; which searchers may enter dyers' houses to examine and take samples of cloths, bays, or the like, to be dyed black or blue; opposing them is a penalty of 10*l.* and in case the dyers' company neglect to appoint searchers, the quarter sessions may appoint them.

——— *Elections.*] By 11 *Geo.* 1. *c.* 18. at all elections by the liverymen of London, and at the wardmotes, a convenient number of clerks shall be appointed by the presiding officer to take the poll; none shall be polled before sworn, that he is a freeman of London, and has not polled before.

If a poll be demanded, the presiding officer, on pain of 200*l.* shall begin at the same day, or the next day, and finish within seven days. If a scrutiny be demanded upon the declaration, scrutineers shall not exceed six on each side; to begin within ten days, and finish within fifteen. *Ibid.*

A true list shall be given of the voters disallowed, to any of the candidates desiring the same; and the mayor is to issue precepts to the city companies to bring in lists of their livery within three days. *Ibid.*

The election of aldermen and common councilmen shall be by freemen paying 30*s.* a year scot and lot, and paying 10*l.* *per ann.* rent, and partners in trade, or two inhabiting one house, may vote, each paying 10*l.* *per ann.* rent. *Ibid.*

Persons exempted from scot and lot, by act of parliament, charter, or privilege, may vote. Complainants about assessments may appeal to the mayor and aldermen. But none shall vote at elections who have not been upon the livery twelve months; nor shall they vote if they have received back their livery fines, or been excused paying the rates and taxes within two years. *Ibid.*

——— *Estates personal.*] By 11 *Geo.* 1. *c.* 18. freemen of London may dispose of their personal estates as they think fit, notwithstanding any custom to the contrary, unless they have made a marriage agreement that their personal estates shall be subject to the custom, or die intestate.

——— *Fireworks.*] By 9 & 10 *Will.* 3. *c.* 7. the artillery company of London may use any sorts of fireworks in the exercise of arms, as before the making this act. (*See general title* Fireworks.

——— *Fire.*] By 6 *Ann.* *c.* 31. churchwardens of each parish within the bills of mortality shall fix stop-blocks of wood, or fire-cocks, on the mains and pipes of any waterwork; shall fix a mark on the front of the opposite house. Every parish shall keep one large engine, one hand-engine, and one leather pipe, on pain of 10*l.* Gratuities shall be paid to turncocks, engine-keepers, and others first assisting to extinguish any fire.

Watermen belonging to insurance offices shall be free from impressing. *Ibid.*

Servants who through negligence fire any

house shall forfeit 100*l.* or be sent to the workhouse for eighteen months. *Ibid.*

On breaking out of any fire, all constables and beadles shall give their utmost assistance; and no action shall be prosecuted against any person in whose house any fire accidentally begins, excepting any agreement between landlord and tenant.

By 7 *Ann. c.* 17. the vestries may order more engines than one to be kept in a parish. A key and pipe shall be left at the house where there is a notice of a fire-plug. The parish officers may assess rates for maintaining the engines, to be levied as poor rates, but subject to the like appeal.

In case of removal of mains or pipes, the like stock-blocks shall be fixed, and the key removed to the house where the fire-pipe is. *Ibid.*

Not above ten gallons of turpentine shall be boiled or distilled at one time in any place contiguous to other buildings (except in houses already built in Southwark,) on forfeiture of 100*l.* and treble costs. *Ibid.* (See *Buildings.*)

——— *Fish.*] By 17 *Ric.* 2. *c.* 9. the mayor of London shall have the conservation of the statutes for preserving fish in the Thames to Staines and Medway.

By 2 *Hen.* 6. *c.* 15. he that fastens any nets, trunks, or the like, across the Thames, or other rivers, all night, shall forfeit 5*l.* every time.

By 39 *Eliz. c.* 10. the ordinances of the company of fishmongers in London to restrain the taking, selling, or buying of fish, shall be void: but

By 43 *Eliz. c.* 9. such clause was repealed, and they shall not restrain fishermen in taking, selling, or buying salted fish or herrings, being wholesome and sweet.

By 10 & 11 *Will.* 3. *c.* 24. Billingsgate market shall be free and open every day (except Sunday), for all sorts of fish.

No fisherman shall pay any other toll than as follows, *viz.* for every vessel with salt fish 8*d. per* day for groundage, and 20*d. per* voyage; for every lobster boat or vessel with sea-fish 2*d. per* day for groundage, and 13*d. per* voyage; and for every oyster boat 2*d.* a day for groundage, a halfpenny *per* bushel for metage, and 13*d.* a voyage. *Ibid.*

Fish bought at Billingsgate may be sold elsewhere. No person shall demand toll or sample of sea-fish contrary to 5 *Eliz. c.* 15. (see title *Fish,*) on pain of 10*l.* *Ibid.*

Fish shall not be bought there to be divided into shares, and afterwards retailed, or on behalf of other fishmongers, on pain of 20*l.* nor shall lobsters under eight inches be bought, on pain of 1*s.* each. *Ibid.*

By 9 *Ann. c.* 26. the court of assistants of the fishermen's company may make byelaws, to be approved by the court of aldermen of London, and the water-bailiff is to be one of the wardens of the company.

No spawn shall be killed, nor fish caught out of season, nor salmon taken between the 24th August and 11th November, and the lord mayor may order stakes to be fixed in the Thames to preserve the fry. *Ibid.*

No fish shall be sold more than once within Billingsgate market; and none shall sell fish in the said market, or within 150 yards thereof, except free fishmongers, fishermen, importers, and the like. *Ibid.*

The said company shall pay the water-bailiff 30*l.* a year. No fish shall be sold in Billingsgate before three in the morning from Lady-day to Michaelmas, and five from Michaelmas to Lady-day. The offenders against this act are to forfeit not more than 10*l.* nor less than 5*s.* but it does not prejudice the authorities of the city of London, nor extend to fishermen in the Cinque Ports. *Ibid.*

By 22 *Geo.* 2. *c.* 49. fishermen forfeit the cargo for not selling the same within eight days after their arrival on the coast between North Yarmouth and Dover. *s.* 12.

By 29 *Geo.* 2. *c.* 39. fishing-vessels employed for the supply of London and Westminster markets, breaking bulk, or vending their fish, before their arrival in the river, or not entering their vessel, or not selling their fish within eight days, to forfeit vessel and cargo of fish. *s.* 1.

Twelve days are allowed for the sale of lobsters; and fishing vessels may remove their cargoes before their arrival at the Nore, so as not to make sale thereof. *s.* 2, 3.

Peter boats employed for serving towns near the banks of the river, may dispose of their fish as heretofore. *s.* 4.

The trustees of the market shall appoint inspectors of the fishing vessels, who are authorised to examine: 10*l.* penalty on persons on board not giving him the information he wants, or obstructing him in his office. *Ibid.*

Warrants of distress on fishing-vessels or cargoes may be executed in any part of the rivers Medway or Thames, between the Nore and the city of Westminster. *Ibid.*

By 30 *Geo.* 2. *c.* 21. the court of mayor and aldermen of London are impowered to make and enforce regulations of fishermen and dredgermen in the Thames and Medway.

The court may examine fishermen touching the fishery of the Thames and Medway; fishermen refusing, forfeit 40*s.* for the benefit of Greenwich hospital. *Ibid.*

The water-bailiff may enter into fishermen's boats, and seize all prohibited fish and nets. *Ibid.*

Fishermen are not liable to take out licences, or to pay any gratuity for liberty of fishing. *Ibid.*

By 2 *Geo.* 3. *c.* 15. any person, though not a fishmonger, may buy at any market, sea-coast, or river, any fish in season, and sizeable, and may sell the same again in any fish or flesh market, Covent-Garden market and its precincts excepted.

Such fish not to be resold by the first purchaser before brought to London or Westminster, or where consigned, under penalty of 20*l.* *Ibid.*

And to be conveyed to the places consigned, without being liable to be stopped, and exposed to sale on the way. *Ibid.*

Carriages employed in the service are to carry fish only, and to be marked on the outside, *fish machine only*; and are to be entered at the office for licensing hackney coaches, paying 1*s.* for the registering; and numbered, on penalty of 40*s.*; and are not liable to be deemed common-stage waggons. *Ibid.*

They shall be permitted to travel with four horses in pairs, or with one horse, or three horses in length, though with narrow wheels; and shall only pay the like toll as post-chaises drawn by a like number of horses; and may travel on Sundays and holidays: and neither carriages nor horses, if returning empty, shall be liable to toll: and if any game, or other thing besides fish, and the necessary implements of carriages, be put therein for conveyance, the person putting in the same shall forfeit 5*l.*; and if the driver shall take up, or suffer any passenger, game, or other thing, to be carried therein, he shall forfeit 40*s.* or be imprisoned one month. *Ibid.*

If bulk shall be broke of any fish carriage consigned for London markets before brought within the bills of mortality, or sale made of the fish before they are exposed in the markets, the offender shall forfeit 10*l.* *Ibid.*

The fish, after brought up, is to be sorted, and exposed to sale in market next morning (Sundays excepted); and till so exposed no part thereof is to be sold by retail on pain of 10*l.* but mackarel may be sold on Sundays. *Ibid.*

Persons contracting for buying up fish, other than salmon and lobsters, before the same shall be first brought to market, and exposed to sale there, forfeit 50*l.* and the contract is void. *Ibid.*

No contract for British salmon and lobsters shall be in force longer than one year. *Ibid.*

No person may employ or be employed in buying at the markets, fish brought there for sale, to be afterwards divided amongst fishmongers, or others, to be sold; nor may any person buy in the said markets any fish, but what shall be for his own sale or use, on pain of 20*l.* *Ibid.*

No salesman or other person may refuse to sell, or agree not to sell to or for any particular person's use, any fish exposed to sale at a public market, on pain of 20*l.* *Ibid.*

All fish of the respective sorts specified, brought for sale to the London markets, shall be openly sold at the first hand, in the lots prescribed, and every lot is to consist of one sort of fish only. *Ibid.*

The species of fish, and number allowed to be sold in each lot at Billingsgate, or other markets, are by 42 *Geo.* 3. *c.* lxxxviii. as follows, *viz.*

	IN ONE LOT.
Fresh salmon, not exceeding	12
Sturgeon	2
Fresh cod	10
Skait	6
Pike	10
Turbot	12
Bret	10
Bril	10
Pearl	10
Kingston	5
Ling	5
Doreys	5
Half-fresh cod	16
Quarter-fresh cod	24
Mullets	10
Cole-fish	5
Salmon and other trout	12
Small cod	48
Small pike	24
Large haddock	12
Small haddock	48
Perch above 6 inches long	24
Carp, gurnet, tench, and sea-bass	24
Thornbacks	8
Large soals, in pair	12
Small soals, in do.	24
Mackarel, whitings, pouts, plaice, dabs, herrings, pilchards, garb-fish, flounders, and maids, not exceeding	120
Small smelts	520
Large smelts	104
Eels (unless in a single fish)	30lbs. in one lot.
Large lobsters and crabs	20
Small lobsters and crabs	40

But fish may be sold in smaller quantities, or by the single fish; and fishmongers refusing to sell smaller lots, or a single fish, are to forfeit 20*l.* recoverable before an alderman or the recorder, by distress and sale, or imprisonment for two months, on a prosecution within three months, 42 *Geo.* 3. *c.* lxxxviii. *s.* 4, 5, 6.

Before any fish be sold at the first hand in the said markets, an account of the sorts and quantities to be set up at the fish stand, the number of flounders, plaice, and dabs excepted; and also of mackarel, maids, herrings, and pilchards: and if any other fish of the sorts mentioned, be brought for sale before the market of the day is over, they are likewise to be added to the account, before they are exposed to sale; and the said accounts are to be kept up till the fish are sold, or the market over, on pain of 5*l.*; or if any person, before such time, shall take down, or alter the accounts put up, or cause the same to be done, he forfeits 40*s.* 2 *Geo.* 3. *c.* 15.

No fisherman, after the arrival of his vessel from fishing, may destroy, or cast away any fish, not being unsound, remaining unsold after the market is over, on pain of imprisonment for not more than two months, nor less than one week. *Ibid.*

The following persons are exempted from being impressed, *viz.* 1st, masters of fishing vessels, having one or more apprentices therein under sixteen years of age, bound for five years; 2dly, all such apprentices, not exceeding four to every master or owner of vessels of thirty tons or more, and two to every vessel under thirty tons, during their apprenticeship, and till the age of twenty years, continuing in the business of fishing only; 3dly, one mariner, besides the master and apprentices, to every fishing vessel of ten tons burthen or upwards, employed on the sea coast, during his continuance in such service; 4thly, any landman entering, and employed on board for two years, if he so long continue in the service. *Ibid.*

On affidavit being made before some justice, and laid before the admiralty, that the persons therein named and described come within some or one of the above descriptions (inserting the particulars), the admiralty shall thereupon, unless they suspect the truth of such affidavit (which in such case they are to enquire into), grant, without fee, a separate protection to each person, which being produced shall discharge him from any impress; and if any officer refuses his discharge, or takes away the protection, he forfeits 20*l.* to the party, if not an apprentice, and if an apprentice, to the master. *Ibid.*

Masters, or owners of fishing vessels, knowingly harbouring a deserter from the king's service, forfeit 20*l.* *Ibid.*

Justices may determine offences under this act, and levy the penalties by distress if not paid in twenty-four hours, or for want of distress, on prosecutor's application (except in the case of a driver of a fish carriage), the offender may be committed for two months. *Ibid.*

Prosecutions to be within three months; and one moiety of the penalties goes to the informer, and the other to Greenwich hospital. *Ibid.*

This act is extended to the parish of St. Mary-la-bonne in Middlesex. *Ibid.*

The prohibitory clauses in this act against contracts are not to extend to those made with regard to salt or dried fish, or oysters, carp, or tench. *Ibid.*

By 30 *Geo.* 3. *c.* 54. the estate and property of the trustees of Westminster fish market, under 22 *Geo.* 2. *c.* 49. 29 *Geo.* 2. *c.* 39. and 33 *Geo.* 2. *c.* 27. were vested in the marine society.

By 36 *Geo.* 3. *c.* 118. so much of 2 *Geo.* 3. *c.* 15. as restrains the sale of fish by retail at Billingsgate is repealed, and the sale of fish by retail at Billingsgate is authorised: the court of common council also are to have the same jurisdiction over the said retail market, as over the other public markets of the city.

And by 42 *Geo.* 3. *c.* lxxxviii. they may in like manner regulate the sale of fish by wholesale.

By 42 *Geo.* 3. *c.* 19. notwithstanding 29 *Geo.* 2. *c.* 39. and 22 *Geo.* 2. *c.* 49. the sale of eels by owners of vessels within 28 days after their arrival at the Nore, shall be as good a sale as if made within 8 days, the time limited by the said acts.

——— *Frame-work Knitters.*] By 7 & 8 *Will.* 3. *c.* 20. to prevent exportation, the masters and wardens of the company of frame knitters, London, shall have notice of the selling or removing of stocking frames.

——— *Fuel.*] The 7 *Ed.* 6. *c.* 7. and 43 *Eliz.* *c.* 14. direct the size of talwood billets, and faggots, to be sold in London and elsewhere; and by the first of these acts none shall buy fuel but such as will burn, or retail the same.

By 9 *Ann.* *c.* 15. billets exposed to sale on any wharf shall be assised, cut, and marked, according to their casts, and each contain in length 3 feet and 4 inches, on forfeiture thereof to the poor; but proprietors of trees may mark or not mark their billets as they please for private use.

By 10 *Ann.* *c.* 6. the laws directing the assise of fuel shall not extend to billet made of beech wood. But beech wood billet shall net be sold by retail in London or Westminster, unless by weight, or assized according to former usage.

——— *Fustians.*] By 11 *Hen.* 7. *c.* 27. and 39 *Eliz.* *c.* 13. no deceitful practices shall be used upon any fustian, but only the broad sheers, on pain of 20*s.*; and the lord mayor of London or the clothworkers' company may enter and search the occupiers of fustians.

——— *Goldsmiths.*] By 6 & 7 *Will.* 3. *c.* 17. the wardens of the goldsmith's company, with two of the assistants, within the bills of mortality, may search houses for bullion; and the person in whose possession bullion is found, not proving it to be neither coin nor clippings melted, shall be imprisoned six months.

By 12 *Geo.* 2. *c.* 26. the goldsmith's company may take for assaying and marking plate as follows: for gold watch-cases or boxes and hooks for watch-chains 10*d.* each: gold buckles 5*d.* each: gold snuff-boxes 15*d.* each: wrought gold of 30 ounces or under 2*s.* 6*d.*; from 30 to 50 ounces 3*s.* 9*d.* and so in proportion; and 15*d.* for each piece of wrought gold not amounting to 15*d.* by such rates.

For every parcel of wrought silver weighing four pounds troy 5*d.* if above, a diet of ten grains per pound shall be taken; for every sword hilt *5d.* snuff-box 3¾*d.*, a pair of spurs 3¾*d.*, watch-case 2½*d.*, knife or fork haft 1¼*d.*, pair of buckles ½*d.*, dozen tea spoons 3¾*d.*, belt buckles, locks, runners, and pendants, 2½*d.* each; orange strainers, or graters, 1¼*d.* each; dram cups ¼*d.* dozen of seals 3¾*d.*, salt cellar 1¼*d.*, clasps ¾*d.* a pair, buttons 3¾*d.* the dozen.

The company, on persons refusing to pay such prices, may refuse to assay the plate. And the assay office shall be kept open from seven till nine in the morning. *Ibid.*

——— *Hackney coaches and chairs.*] By 9 *Ann. c.* 23, the crown, under the great seal, may nominate five commissioners.

And such commissioners may licence 800 coaches, by 9 *Ann. c.* 23.; 200 more by 11 *Geo.* 3. *c.* 24.; and 100 more by 42 *Geo.* 3. *c.* 78. TOTAL 110.

And the said commissioners are also to licence 200 chairs, 9 *Ann. c.* 23.; 100 more by 10 *Ann. c.* 19.; and 100 more by 12 *Geo.* 1. *c.* 12. TOTAL 400.

And by 9 *Ann. c.* 23. and 11 *Geo.* 3. *c.* 24. upon each hackney coach licence there shall be received (to be paid monthly by 24 *Geo.* 3. *c.* 27.) the weekly rent or sum of 5*s.* and by 24 *Geo.* 3. *c.* 27. an additional 5*s.* TOTAL per week 10*s.*

And by 9 *Ann. c.* 23. upon every chair licence there shall be reserved the yearly sum of 10*s.* to be paid quarterly.

Driving a coach without a licence is a penalty of 5*l.* and for carrying a chair without one 40*s.* *Ibid.*

The commissioners may make bye-laws, to bind the renters keeping and driving of hackney coaches and chairs, which must be approved of by the lord chancellor, the two chief justices, and chief baron, or any three of them. *Ibid.*

And the commissioners are to licence antient coachmen and chairmen, or their widows, in preference to others; and on misbehaviour they may revoke such licence, or inflict a penalty not exceeding 3*l.* which if not paid the offender is to be committed to the house of correction for 30 days. *Ibid.*

Every coach and chair is to have a mark on each side, and altering the same is a penalty of 5*l.* *Ibid.*

And no horse is to be used with a hackney coach which shall be under 14 hands high. *Ibid.*

——— *Hackney coach fares.*] By 48 *Geo.* 3. *c.* 87. the following rates of fares are allowed to be taken.

ACCORDING TO DISTANCE.

Not exceeding	*s.*	*d.*
one mile	1	0
one mile and half	1	6
two miles	2	0
two miles and half	3	0
three miles	3	6
three miles and half	4	0
four miles	4	6

ACCORDING TO DISTANCE.

Not exceeding	*s.*	*d.*
four miles and half	5	6
five miles	6	0
five miles and half	6	6
six miles	7	0
six miles and half	8	0
seven miles	8	6
seven miles and half	9	0
eight miles	9	6
eight miles and half	10	6
nine miles	11	0
nine miles and half	11	6
ten miles	12	0
ten miles and half	13	0
eleven miles	13	6
eleven miles and half	14	0
twelve miles	15	0

and so on at the rate of 6*d.* for every half mile, and an additional 6*d.* for every two miles completed.

ACCORDING TO TIME.

Not exceeding	*s.*	*d.*
30 minutes	1	0
45 minutes	1	6
one hour	2	0
one hour 20 minutes	3	0
one hour 40 minutes	4	0
two hours	5	0
two hours 20 minutes	6	0
two hours 40 minutes	7	0
three hours	8	0
three hours 20 minutes	9	0
three hours 40 minutes	10	0
four hours	11	0

and for any further time 6*d.* for every 15 minutes.

The fares are to be taken by the hour or mile only, and not by the day. *s.* 2.

Hackney coaches are obliged to go on the turnpike or lighted roads, a distance not exceeding two miles and a half after sunset, 39 & 40 *Geo.* 3. *c.* 47. which sunset hours are, after eight between Lady-day and Michaelmas, and after five between Michaelmas and Lady-day, 48 *Geo.* 3. *c.* 87. *s.* 3.: and coaches taken after those hours are entitled to the full fare back to the end of the carriage-way pavement, or if hired at a stand beyond such pavement, to the full fare back to such stand, or the next carriage-way pavement, at the option of the party. *s.* 4.

And coaches hired to go into the country, in the day time are to have for their return empty, for ten miles 5*s.* eight miles 4*s.* six miles 3*s.* and for four miles 2*s.* but there is no allowance for less than four miles.

Coaches are not compellable to take more than four adults in the inside and a servant out; but if the coachmen agree to take more, the fare will be 1*s.* for each extra person, and if taken into the country, 1*s.* for going, and 1*s.* for returning. *s.* 6.

Persons taking coaches to Vauxhall, or other places of public resort, to be kept in waiting, are to pay to the coachman a reasonable deposit, to be accounted for when the coach is discharged. *s.* 7.

Coachman refusing to go on, or exacting more than his fare, to forfeit as under former acts. *s.* 11.

——— *Fares of Sedan Chairs.*] By 7 *Geo.* 3. *c.* 44, the following rates of fares are allowed to be taken by licensed hackney chairs, *viz.* for one mile 1*s.* one mile and four furlongs 1*s.* 6*d.* for every four furlongs farther 6*d.* *By the time,* the first hour 1*s* 6*d.* and for every half hour after 6*d.* *Ibid.*

By 9 *Ann. c.* 23. the drivers of coaches, and carriers of chairs, on demanding more than the fare, or giving abusive language, are to forfeit not more than 5*l.* and in default of the payment they are to be sent to the house of correction for seven days.

By 1 *Geo.* 1, *c.* 57, coachmen refusing to go at, or extorting more than their fare, are to forfeit not more than 3*l.* nor less than 10*s.*

None but licensed persons shall ply or drive, on forfeiture of 5*l.*; and mourning coaches shall not be driven to funerals except they have a number, or be gentlemen's coaches attending the master, under the like forfeiture. *Ibid.*

Aldermen in London may inflict the like penalties as the commissioners. *Ibid.*

By 4 *Geo.* 3, *c.* 36, justices of peace of Kent and Essex may execute the laws relating to hackney coaches in their respective jurisdictions.

By 7 *Geo.* 3, *c.* 44, hackney coaches let out for hire by way of a job, by the day, or for a less time, contrary to 9 *Ann. c.* 23, are liable to the penalty, though no hiring is proved.

Hackney coaches plying for hire are liable to go, at seasonable times, any where within 10 miles from London or Westminster. *Ibid.*

Offenders liable to be committed by any of the laws relating to licensing hackney coaches and chairs may be committed either to prison, or to Bridewell, and kept to hard labour, and receive the correction of the house. *Ibid.*

Hackney coaches are liable to do the like work on Sundays as on any other day of the week.

By 10 *Geo.* 3, *c.* 44, the commissioners may commit offenders immediately to Bridewell, or the house of correction, for 1 month. Licensed person refusing to appear upon summons forfeit 20*s.* and refusing to appear, with his renter, on third summons, commissioners may determine the complaint and inflict the due penalty. *Ibid.*

Not only commissioners, but also justices, may determine offences, and inflict punishments, as directed by 9 *Ann.* *Ibid.*

The king's share of all penalties is to be sent to the receiver-general of those duties by the person levying the same, within 10 days, on penalty of 10*l.* *Ibid.*

By 11 *Geo.* 3, *c.* 28, all squares, buildings, and streets, in the parishes of St. Mary-le-bone, St. George, Hanover-square, St. George the Martyr, Queen-square, and St. George, Bloomsbury, and all burying grounds within five miles of London and Westminster, belonging to any parish there, shall be under the jurisdiction of the commissioners of hackney coaches.

The commissioners are to order check strings to every hackney coach, and every hackney coachman plying without such, shall forfeit 5*s.* *Ibid.*

By 11 *Geo.* 3. *c.* 29, only ten hackney coaches shall stand between Freeman's-court, and the east end of Cornhill, and five from Bucklersbury to King-street, and to be twenty feet asunder, and at other places to be 8 feet asunder, and room to be left for waggons, on penalty of 20*s.* and hackney coaches shall be registered at Guildhall.

By 12 *Geo.* 3. *c.* 49, the act 7 *Geo.* 3. *c.* 44, shall extend to all coaches licensed, and plying within the bills of mortality, and the suburbs of London and Westminster.

Stage coaches, though numbered, having a writing denoting their being stages, are not compellable to carry fares out of the course of the stage. *Ibid.*

By 24 *Geo.* 3, *c.* 27, if owners of hackney coaches neglect to appear before the commissioners upon the third summons, their licenses may be revoked.

Any person driving a mourning coach or hearse, within 5 miles of Temple-bar, without a number properly fixed thereon, may be summoned before the commissioners, and fined 5*l.* *Ibid.*

No person shall drive any cart, dray, or like carriage, within 5 miles of Temple-bar, or in the bills of mortality, except the owner shall have entered his name and place of abode at the hackney-coach office, and shall affix his name and the number of the carriage on some conspicuous part thereof, on pain of such forfeitures and penalties as are inflicted on such drivers within London, Westminster, Southwark, and streets within the bills. *Ibid.*

By 32 *Geo.* 3, *c.* 47, hackney coachmen are compellable to go any distance within 10 miles from London or Westminster, if they have time to return by or before sunset, or the fare shall undertake to return. s. 1.

And they shall be compellable on every day, and at any hour of the night (unless they shall have been out 12 hours, or have other reasonable excuse), to go upon all turnpike roads, any where within two miles and a half from the ends of the carriage-way pavement.

By 33 *Geo.* 3, *s.* 75, not more than two coaches are to stand at the west gate of St. Paul's, and not more than two immediately westward of Dean's-gate, on pain of 20*s*.

By 33 *Geo.* 3, *c.* 75, on complaint made to any justice of the peace of the city of London, against any master or driver of any hackney coach residing out of the city, such justice may summon the party, and after 3 days notice, by service of the summons personally, or leaving the same at his abode, such justice on his appearance may hear the complaint and convict; but if the offender neglect to attend, the justice may issue a warrant for apprehending him, which being backed by some magistrate of the place where the offender may be found, and the justice, either upon the appearance of the offender on such summons, or upon his being brought before him, may convict such offender in like manner as if he had resided within the city, and on non-payment of the penalty may commit to Bridewell for not exceeding 20 days. *s.* 6.

By 39 & 40 *Geo.* 3, *c.* 47, the commissioners may appoint inspectors of hackney coaches and horses, and suspend the license of any person whose coach shall be defective or horses unfit; and may annul licenses if the inspectors are refused to examine coaches. *s.* 4.

Hackney coachmen, whose coaches are standing in the streets, although off the stand, are compellable to go with any person desirous of hiring them, and, in case of refusal, are liable to be fined, unless they prove they were hired at the time. *s.* 5.

If a coachman, summoned for such refusal, shall prove his having been hired, the commissioners may order the party to make him satisfaction for his loss of time. *s.* 6.

The commissioners may require persons licensed to keep hackney coaches, to enter in their office the names and residence of their drivers, to whom they may grant leave to drive, and revoke or suspend the same, as also the licenses for keeping hackney coaches, of persons who shall omit to enter the names of their drivers, or suffer any person not entered to drive. *s.* 7.

Persons attending as watermen to hackney coachmen not authorized by the commissioners to be liable to the penalty inflicted by the commissioners bye-laws. *s.* 8.

The commissioners may make rules for regulating hackney coachmen, and watermen attending them, and annex penalties for breach thereof. *s.* 9.

No person shall carry persons for hire in a sedan chair (unless hired for a day), within the weekly bills of mortality, without a license, on penalty of 40*s*. *s.* 10.

In case of arrears of license-rent, the license may be revoked, and the arrears levied either upon the owner or renter. *s.* 12.

By 48 *Geo.* 3, *c.* 87, hackney coaches are not to ply for promiscuous passengers when returning from the country on pain of not exceeding 3*l.* nor less than 20*s.* but this is not to prevent their taking up regular fares. *s.* 5.

Numbered stage coaches are not to take up passengers in the streets to be set down again in any of the paved streets, on pain of not exceeding 3*l.* nor less than 20*s.* or if, being the owner, he shall offend a second time the license is to be forfeited; but the penalty is not incurred if the party shall have previously taken his place for the country at a booking-house, and paid the whole fare. *s.* 9.

Not more than two booking-houses are to be kept, *viz.* one in town, and the other in the country, on pain of not exceeding 40*s.* nor less than 20*s.* *s.* 10.

Coachmen improperly summoned are to have from the party a compensation not exceeding 5*s.* nor less than 3*s.* *s.* 8.

Hay and Straw.] By 8 *Wil.* 3, *c.* 17, every cart load of hay standing to be sold in the Haymarket, shall pay 3*d.* and every cart load of straw 1*d.* towards the paving the streets, and the same may be levied by distress and sale by warrant from a justice; but if the hay or straw is not sold, it may stand there the next time without payment.

By 36 *Geo.* 3. *c.* 88, within London, Westminster, the weekly bills of mortality, or 30 miles thereof, no hay or straw shall be sold except in trusses, on pain of 20*s.* *s.* 2.

Each truss of hay sold between 31st August and 1st June following, shall weigh 56lbs. and between 1st June and 31st August, being new hay of that year's growth, 60lbs. or old 56lbs. and each truss of straw shall weigh 36lbs. and every load of hay or straw shall contain 36 trusses. *s.* 3.

Persons selling trusses of less weight are to forfeit for hay not exceeding 5*s.* nor less than 2*s.* 6*d.* per truss, and for straw 1*s.* but this is not to extend to a deficient truss in a quantity sold to the same person, if the whole amount to the average weight. *s.* 3.

Persons selling new for old hay are to forfeit 2*s.* 6*d.* per truss. Hay or straw are to be of one quality; and persons mixing the same, forfeit not exceeding 5*s.* nor less than 2*s.* 6*d.* per truss for hay, and 1*s.* for straw. *s.* 4, 5.

Persons selling hay with bands exceeding 5lbs. weight forfeit 1*s.* and 1*s.* more for every pound above the five. *s.* 6.

Persons binding hay or straw in trusses lighter than as above, shall forfeit 6*d.* per truss. *s.* 7.

Salesmen buying and selling on their own account hay or straw, or grass for hay, to forfeit not exceeding 5*l.* nor less than 50*s.* *s.* 8.

Salesmen within seven days to send to the owner an account of the place, time, and price of hay or straw sold, and of the purchaser, on pain of not exceeding 20*s.* nor less than 10*s.* *s.* 9.

A register is to be kept in markets for entering sales of hay and straw, which shall be open for inspection; and sellers not making due or making untrue entries, or the clerk refusing the inspection of the register on payment of the fee (1*d.*) shall forfeit not exceeding 5*l.* nor less than 10*s.* *s.* 10.

The act does not extend to hay or straw delivered on special contract. *s.* 11.

Clerk or toll-gatherer buying or selling hay or straw shall forfeit for hay per truss, 2*s.* 6*d.* straw, 1*s.* *s.* 12.

Scales and weights are to be kept at the clerk of the market's office, and at the parish watch-house; and constables are to be the hay weighers. Buyers of hay or straw may cause it to be weighed on delivery, in the presence of the seller or his servant, and if on such weighing the buyer or seller be dissatisfied, the same shall be weighed by the nearest hay-weigher; and if the clerk, toll-gatherer, churchwarden, or overseer, omit to provide scales and weights, or neglect to weigh hay or straw, they shall respectively forfeit not exceeding 5*l.* nor less than 10*s.* *s.* 13.

No penalty is to be incurred for selling hay or straw not weight, or of a bad quality, unless weighed at or before the delivery. *s.* 14.

The markets for hay and straw within the limits aforesaid shall end at three in the afternoon of every market-day between Lady-day and Michaelmas, and at two between Michaelmas and Lady-day, notices whereof shall be given by ringing of a bell; and persons selling after such hours shall forfeit for every truss of hay, 6*d.* and of straw, 3*d.*; and persons letting their carts stand, from Lady-day to Michaelmas, after five, and from Michaelmas to Lady-day, after three, shall forfeit not exceeding 20*s.* nor less than 5*s.* *s.* 16.

Persons permitting horses drawing hay or straw carrying to be sold within the limits to remain in a market 15 minutes during market-hours, shall forfeit not exceeding 20*s.* nor less than 5*s.* *s.* 17.

Persons buying and selling again hay and straw conveying to be sold within the limits of the act, or buying in a market-place to sell it again therein, shall forfeit 5*s.*; but this is not to extend to persons selling by retail on their own premises in less quantities than five trusses. *s.* 18.

Persons employed to buy, charging more than actually paid, shall forfeit 5*s.* per truss; delivering other than the commodity sold 5*s.* per truss. *s.* 19, 20

Persons fraudulently increasing the weight of hay or straw by water, sand, earth, or other things, or mixing the same therewith, shall forfeit, for hay, 10*s.* per truss, straw, 1*s.* *s.* 21.

Persons delivering less than the number of trusses sold, and drivers secreting, keeping back, or withholding, to forfeit 5*l.* per truss, and in default of immediate payment, to be committed to hard labour for not exceeding three months, nor less than one. *s.* 22.

Not bringing hay or straw exposed and not sold, but lodged, to the market-place on the ensuing market-day by 11 o'clock, is a penalty of not exceeding 5*l.* nor less than 40*s.* *s.* 23.

Persons giving or receiving false receipts of the price of hay or straw sold, shall forfeit not exceeding 10*l.* nor less than 5*l.* on complaint within 6 months, and the informer shall be indemnified from all penalties incurred by himself. *s.* 24.

Prosecutions (except where otherwise provided) to be within 14 days; the forfeitures are recoverable before one justice by distress, and for want thereof offenders may be committed for not exceeding 3 months, nor less than 14 days. *s.* 25, 26.

Salesmen convicted of offences may exhibit complaint against his employer before a justice, who may award satisfaction, and levy the same by distress; but the complaint must be made within 14 days, and if adjudged frivolous the justice may award costs to the employer.

——— *Hides.*] See *Leather.*

——— *Horners.*] By 4 *Ed.* 4, *c.* 8, and 7 *Jac.* 1, *c.* 14, no alien shall buy English horns unwrought, within 24 miles of London, on forfeiture of double value; and the mayor and wardens of the horners company may search the same.

——— *Insurance.*] By 43 *Eliz. c.* 12, the lord chancellor may award commissions for determining causes on policies of assurances, to the judge of the admiralty, the recorder, two doctors of civil law, two barristers, and eight merchants; from whose determinations an appeal lies by bill to the lord chancellor, on depositing the money awarded; and the commissioners are not to act till they have taken an oath before the lord mayor to do justice.

And by 13 and 14 *Car.* 2, *c.* 23, three commissioners may act, but they are not to proceed against both person and goods for the same debt.

——— *Juries.*] By 7 *Hen.* 7. *c.* 5, *riens deins le gard* shall be no challenge upon any issue to be tried in London.

By 11 *Hen.* 7. *c.* 21, no man shall be impannelled on any jury in London, unless he have in lands, goods, or chattels, to the value of 40 marks.

By 4 *Hen.* 8. *c.* 3, the sheriffs of London may return pannels of jurors in suits depending triable in London, of such as are worth a hundred marks in goods.

By 7 *Will.* 3. *c.* 32, the inhabitants of Westminster are exempted from serving on juries for the Middlesex sessions.

By 3 *Geo.* 2. *c.* 25, jurors in London shall be householders within the city, and have tenements or personal estate to the value of 100*l.*

By 29 *Geo.* 2. *c.* 19, persons summoned to serve on juries in London or any other town corporate, or franchise, not attending, shall forfeit not more than 40*s.* nor less than 20*s.* unless the court be satisfied with the cause of absence; such fine leviable by distress and sale.

—— *Leather.*] By 5 & 6 *Ed.* 6, *c.* 15, no sadler, girdler, cordwainer, or other artificer, who cuts leather in London, shall curry it at his house.

By 1 *Mar. stat.* 3, *c.* 8, the curriers of London and the suburbs thereof, shall use their own stuff.

By 13 and 14 *Car.* 2, *c.* 7, (see this act under the title *Manufactures, s. Leather*) the cordwainers, sadlers, girdlers, and curriers companies in London, may search and seize leather or hides intended to be transported; and in other places the officers of customs, or chief magistrates.

Leadenhall market shall be kept on a Tuesday. *Ibid.*

By 1 *Will.* & *Mar.* *c.* 33, all hides, skins, or tanned leather, shaved or liquored, shall be subject to the view, search, and seizure of the master and wardens of the said companies; but the master and wardens of the curriers company are not empowered to view, search, or seize any leather, hide, or skin, unless curried in London, by some members of their own company, nor in any place but an open market, or in the shops or warehouses of such curriers.

By 48 *Geo.* 3. *c.* lxxi, persons flaying hides and skins in London, Westminster, Southwark, or within 15 miles of the Royal Exchange, shall be subject to this act. *s.* 2.

Seven butchers named in this act, and their successors, together with seven persons to be annually appointed by the butchers company, seven by the curriers company, and seven by the cordwainers company, shall be commissioners for putting this act in execution, which commissioners are to be sworn to act impartially; and no act of theirs is to be valid unless at a meeting to be held in pursuance of this act, consisting of not less than five, the chairman of which is to have the casting vote, and vacancies are to be filled up in the first seven commissioners from time to time as they happen by a fresh nomination, by the remaining or surviving commissioners. *s.* 3, 13—19.

If the owner of any hide shall wilfully, negligently, or carelessly, gash any hide or skin, he shall forfeit not exceeding 2*s.* 6*d.* nor less than 6*d.* for the raw hide or skin of every ox, bull, cow, heifer, steer, stirk, or calf; not exceeding 1*s.* 6*d.* nor less than 6*d.* for every horse hide; not exceeding 3*s.* nor less than 3*d.* for every hog or pig skin; and ½*d.* for every sheep or lamb skin: but the penalties are not to be inflicted for unavoidable damage. *s.* 20, 21.

All hides and calf skins within 5 miles of the *Royal Exchange* shall be brought to *Leadenhall*; and sheep and lamb skins either to Woods-close, to the Borough, or Whitechapel markets; to be inspected, on pain of not exceeding 5*l.* nor less than 2*s.* *s.* 22, 23.

And places and hours of inspection are to be appointed for places beyond 5 miles from the *Royal Exchange*, within 3 months after 27th May, 1808; but nevertheless, butchers at any place within 15 miles, may bring their hides and skins to *Leadenhall*, or the other markets, on giving notice to the inspector of the district. *s.* 24.

Eight inspectors are to be annually appointed for Leadenhall—4 by the 7 commissioners, before named, in conjunction with the 7 nominees of the butchers' company, 2 by the 7 curriers, and the other 2 by the 7 cordwainers; 2 inspectors are also to be appointed for Woods-close—1 by the 7 commissioners and 7 butchers, and the other by the 7 curriers and 7 cordwainers; 2 are also to be appointed for the Borough, and 2 for the Whitechapel markets: and the commissioners have power to increase the number of inspectors, and make regulations for their attendance. *s.* 25, 26.

The inspectors are to be sworn before the lord mayor or an alderman, to act without favour, and they may take for inspecting the hide of every beast ½*d.* the skin of every calf, hog, or pig, ¼*d.* and for every score of sheep or lamb skins 3*d.*; but the commissioners may, if they see fit, increase the inspector's fees, not exceeding for beasts 1*d.* calves hogs, or pigs, ½*d.* and for the skin of every sheep or lamb, not exceeding ¼*d.* *s.* 27, 28, 29.

Persons imitating the inspector's mark, shall forfeit not exceeding 5*l.* *s.* 30.

Hours of the inspectors attendance on the market days, shall be at Leadenhall from 6 in the morning until 5 in the evening from 25th March to 29th September, and from 7 till 4 from 30th September to 24th March, and at the other markets for such hours as the commissioners may appoint. *s.* 31.

Inspectors are to provide stamps for marking hides and skins near the tail with the letter S if sound, and D if damaged; and if the penalty or fee be not paid, the inspector may seize the hide and sell it, unless notice of appeal be given to appeal to 2 arbitrators, who are to be appointed by the commissioners on the 1st Monday in June in every year, whose decision is to be final; and the party against whom such appeal shall be determined, shall pay not exceeding 5*s.* nor less than 2*s.* 6*d.* and if the arbitrators differ, they are to call in a third person, and the decision of such arbitrators and third person, or two of them, shall be conclusive, and the arbitrators are to attend on market days from the hour of 1 till the close of the market. *s.* 31, 35.

Arbitrators may also be appointed for the sheep-skin markets if found necessary. *s.* 36.

And if inspectors or arbitrators die, others are to be appointed in their room by the commissioners. *s.* 37.

The fees at each of the markets shall be weekly put together in one sum, together with one half of the fines for negligently gashing, and the remaining half with the whole of all other fines, shall be paid by the inspectors to the treasurers to be appointed by the commissioners. *s.* 40, 41.

The monies received by the treasurers shall be applied in payment of the expenses of carrying the act into execution; and the commissioners may direct such rewards as they think fit to be paid to working butchers for taking off hides and skins whole: and the surplus of the monies received by the treasurer shall be paid as follows: ¼th to the butchers company, ¼th to the curriers, ¼th to the cordwainers, to be applied to the use of the poor of the companies; and ¼th to the first-mentioned commissioners, to be applied to the use of the poor of the butchers who are not free of the company. *s.* 42.

Persons impeding inspectors, are to be liable to not exceeding 5*l.* nor less than 10*s.*; inspectors taking and persons offering bribes, are to forfeit not exceeding 20*s.* Salesmen are to give an account to their employers of fines imposed, on pain of 5*l.*; and workmen or servants gashing hides or skins are liable to repay one half of the fines to their principal. *s.* 43, 46.

Sellers of unstamped hides or skins within 5 miles of the Royal Exchange, and persons buying such, except in a public market, are to forfeit not exceeding 20*s.* nor less than 5*s.* for every hide; not exceeding 5*s.* nor less than 1*s.* for every calf, hog, or pig skin; and not exceeding 1*s.* nor less than 6*d.* for every sheep or lamb skin. *s.* 48.

The penalties may be recovered before 1 justice, and levied by distress; and for want thereof to be committed for not exceeding 1 month: but an appeal is allowed to the sessions, and every information must be laid within 7 days.

See also *Excise* and *Manufactures.*

——— *Mayor.*] By 24 *Geo.* 2. *c.*48, the presenting and swearing the mayors of London at Westminster shall be on the 9th of November yearly, unless it fall on a Sunday, and then the day following.

By 25 *Geo.* 2. *c.* 30, the annual admission and swearing the mayor of London at the Guildhall to be on the 8th of November.

——— *Malt.*] By 17 *Ric.* 2. *c.* 4, malt made in the counties of Huntingdon, Cambridge, Northampton, and Bedford, and brought to victual London, shall be well sifted, so that the buyers may have eight bushels of clean malt for the quarter.

——— *Merchants*] By 25 *Ed.* 3, *stat.* 4, *c.* 2, merchants, aliens or others, may buy and sell without disturbance in gross, or by retail, at their will, in London, or other cities or places.

By 7 *Hen.* 4, *c.* 9, all merchandises may be sold in gross, in London, to all subjects, as well as to the citizens.

By 12 *Hen.* 7, *c.* 6, merchants may resort to the marts in Flanders, Holland, Zealand, and other places adjoining, without any exactions of the fraternity of Londoners.

——— *Middlesex County Rate.*] By 37 *Geo.* 3, *c.* 65, the justices are empowered to make an equal county rate according to the annual value of estates in each parish, from returns to be annually made upon oath by the churchwardens and overseers of the different parishes at every Michaelmas sessions; and if they neglect to make such annual returns, the sessions may fine such churchwardens and overseers in not exceeding 100*l.* to be levied by the high constables in the same manner as under 12 *Geo.* 2, *c.* 29, relating to the county rates. *s.* 1, 4.

In cases where returns are neglected to be made, the sessions may make a rate according to an estimate of the fair annual value; from which rate the churchwardens and overseers may, if they think fit, appeal to the next general or general quarter-sessions. *s.* 5, 6.

A general power of appeal is also given, and the sessions are to allow constables their expences.

——— *Militia.*] By 36 *Geo.* 3. *c.* 92. the commissioners of lieutenancy for *the city of London* may arm, array, and exercise, the militia, and appoint officers, who shall have the same rank as the other militia forces; and such commissions shall not be vacated by the revocation of the power of the commissioners. *s.* 3, 4.

Officers are to possess the same qualification as for cities which are counties of themselves (see *Militia*), and are to take the oaths and subscribe a declaration as to their qualifications; and no bankrupt or person who has not paid 20*s.* in the pound shall be an officer. *s.* 5.

The establishment of the militia shall be

1200 men, and the commissions are to be inserted in the Gazette. *s.* 6.

Officers acting without being qualified, or without delivering in a description of their qualifications, are to forfeit 100*l.*; and acting after having become bankrupt or not paid 20*s.* in the pound is a like penalty, half to the king, and half to the informer, and the proof of qualification shall lie on the party. *s.* 8.

Two courts of lieutenancy are to be held in each year, *viz.* one on the third Wednesday in January, and the other on the third Wednesday in June. *s.* 9.

The men to be provided shall be furnished by the wards in the following proportions. *s.* 10.

The East Regiment.

By the wards of	Aldgate	60
	Bassishaw	12
	Billingsgate	41
	Bishopsgate within	44
	Bishopsgate without	50
	Bridge	26
	Broad street	50
	Candlewick	20
	Coleman-street	36
	Cornhill	36
	Dowgate	27
	Langbourn	67
	Lime-street	20
	Portsoken	45
	Tower	66

West Regiment.

By the wards of	Aldersgate within	18
	Aldersgate without	21
	Bread street	24
	Castle Baynard	44
	Cheap	44
	Cordwainer	22
	Cripplegate within	44
	Cripplegate without	36
	Farringdon within	84
	Farringdon without	192
	Queenhithe	21
	Vintry	23
	Walbrook	27

The commissioners may issue precepts to the aldermen and common council of the wards, to cause the men to be raised, to whom they may give 10*l.* bounty, and they are to appoint a court to receive the returns of men provided. The aldermen are to desire the ward officers to give notice to the persons provided, to attend at the court, and on their appearance they are to be sworn to serve, and enrolled for five years; and the ward officers and constables guilty of default are to forfeit not exceeding 40*s.* *s.* 11.

In case of deficiency of men, the commissioners are to issue their precepts to the aldermen and common council to provide men, or pay 10*l.* for each man wanting; and if they neglect to do so, or if the men be not approved, the ward is to be charged with 10*l.* for each, to be applied by the commissioners in providing the men, and the surplus monies are to be applied as part of the regimental stock. *s.* 12.

The aldermen and common council are to make a rate in the different wards to defray the expences of raising the men: but an appeal may be made against the rates to the court of mayor and aldermen, and the rates may be levied by distress. *s.* 13, 14, 15.

But no distress is to be made out of the limits of the city, unless the warrant be backed by a magistrate of the place. *s.* 15.

The penalty for not making the distress, not backing the warrants, or not acting in aid in making the distress, is not exceeding 40*s.* *s.* 16.

Householders serving in their own right are exempted from the rate. *s.* 17.

Aldermen and common council to be the ward assessors, and to appoint collectors with an allowance. *s.* 18.

And if they neglect to provide men or pay for them, or levy rates, the commissioners may levy and apply such rates, and may call for the last assessment to the land tax from the clerk, who shall produce it and give copies, on penalty of 20*l.* *s.* 19.

Commissioners are to appoint an adjutant to each regiment, who, if from the army, shall preserve his rank, and may hold a subaltern's commission, and have brevet rank of captain without the requisite qualification. *s.* 20.

A surgeon, quarter-master, and regimental clerk, are to be appointed, but neither of them shall be a captain of a company, except that the regimental clerk may be captain-lieutenant. *s.* 21.

The pay of the adjutants, regimental clerks, quarter-masters, serjeant-majors, and other non-commissions, shall be the same as the regular militia forces, and for this purpose the commissioners may make civil appointments. *s.* 22.

The pay of the militia is to be issued to the treasurer in like manner as by the receiver-general of the land tax for the county militia. *s.* 23.

The regimental clerks are to give security as in other regiments, and pay balances to the treasurer; and all costs of suit shall be recoverable as by the general militia act. *Ibid.*

Officers on half-pay serving as subalterns, may continue to receive the same on the usual oath. *s.* 24.

There shall be three serjeants, three corporals, and two drummers, to each company, with the addition of one drummer to each of the flank companies; and the serjeants, corporals, and drummers, when not in actual service, shall be clothed once in two years, and be sworn to serve until discharged. *s.* 25.

The colonel of each regiment may appoint a serjeant-major and drum-major; and non-commissioned officers and drummers having received pay, are compellable to serve, to live within one mile, and shall not be publicans. *Ibid.*

The colonel may discharge non-commissioned officers and drummers, and the captain may fill up vacancies. *s.* 26.

Officers may keep musicians as extra drummers, paying the expence. *s.* 27.

The militia shall be exercised twenty-eight successive days annually, and be subject to the mutiny act. *s.* 28.

Notice of the time and place of exercise to be affixed on the church doors, and lists of the men enrolled are to be sent by the clerk to the colonel. *s.* 29.

Adjutants, serjeants, corporals, and drummers, shall be subject to the mutiny act, and the colonel may direct the holding of courts martial when the regiment is embodied, for their trial for previous offences. *s.* 30.

The arms, accoutrements, and clothing, shall be kept where the commissioners shall appoint, and the privates are to be clothed once in five years when not embodied. *s.* 32.

The pay of the militia shall be the same as in the regular militia, and the men may be put under stoppages. *s.* 33.

And the militia in lieu of quarters shall be allowed 1*s.* 9*d. per* week for each man, in addition to the pay to provide quarters; but the serjeants, corporals, and drummers, not residing within the limited distance of one mile, are not entitled to the allowance. *s.* 34.

The commissioners are to appoint treasurers and clerks, and an account of the trophy tax is to be delivered annually to the corporation before a new rate is made. *s.* 35.

And security is to be taken from the treasurer and clerks. *s.* 36.

In case of invasion or danger thereof, or rebellion, or insurrection, his majesty may order the militia to be embodied, subject to the mutiny laws. *s.* 37.

And his majesty within 12 months may draw out the militia, and when drawn out to be entitled to the same pay as other regiments of foot, and the non-commissioned officers and privates to Chelsea hospital. *s.* 38, 39.

When drawn out, his majesty may put one regiment under the command of general officers, to be led to the distance of 12 miles. *s.* 40.

The commissioners may appoint an agent. *s.* 41. The militia men to be subject to the general militia act, as far as relates to penalties for not attending annual exercise, for deserting, and the like; and maimed militia men, having served, may set up trade in any part of Great Britain. *s.* 42.

The militia when disembodied, are liable only to the orders they were subjected to before drawn out. *s.* 43.

The commissioners may order the militia, when not embodied, to be trained and reviewed, and to be kept in readiness to be put under the orders of the lord-mayor or magistrates, who may call the whole, or part out, for the suppression of riots, in which case a court of lieutenancy is to be summoned, to whom the reasons for so doing are to be reported. *s.* 46, 47.

If a sufficient number of commissioners to make a court shall not attend, a fresh summons shall be issued. *s.* 47.

Militia men not appearing when called out by the lord-mayor or magistrates, if a serjeant, corporal, drummer, or fifer, for two hours, 40*s.* four hours, 5*l.* and if not in six hours, to be deemed deserters; privates receiving pay, not appearing for two hours are to forfeit 20*s.* for four hours 50*s.* and if not within six hours to be deemed deserters; privates not receiving pay, not appearing at the time and place appointed, shall forfeit 10*s.* not within twelve hours 20*s.* and if not within twenty-four hours to be deemed deserters. *s.* 48.

The aldermen and common council are to divide the quota of men amongst the parishes, and specify for which each serves, that the parish officers may be resorted to for defraying the expences of their families. *s.* 49.

The allowances to families of militia men (see 39 *Geo.* 3. *c.* 82. *infra*) shall not compel them to be sent to workhouses, nor deprive the husbands of their legal settlement or right to vote for members of parliament. *s.* 53.

Adjutants are to have the same allowances as in other regiments: serjeants may receive their allowance on the establishment of Chelsea; and non-commissioned officers and drummers are entitled to the benefit of Chelsea hospital. *s.* 54.

Acceptance of commissions shall not vacate seats in parliament, and officers are not liable to serve the office of sheriff. *s.* 55.

Militia men who are voters are not punishable for going to elections. *s.* 56.

A state of the regiment when called out to annual exercise, is to be returned to the commissioners by the commanding officer, on pain of 100*l.* *s.* 57.

No serjeants, corporals, drummers, or fifers, are compellable to serve as peace or parish officers or in the navy. *s.* 58.

The act 24 *Geo.* 2. *c.* 44. to render justices safe in the execution of their offices, to extend to the mayor, aldermen, and other officers. *s.* 59.

No officer of the city militia shall sit on any court martial upon other than the militia forces; nor any officer, other than of the militia forces, sit on any offender in the city militia. *s.* 60.

The act is not to prejudice the rights of the city; and the militia is to enjoy all the rights of the antient trained bands. *s.* 61.

Fines exceeding 20*l.* are recoverable in the courts at Westminster, and under 20*l.* before the mayor or magistrate, in a summary way. *s.* 62, 63.

By 39 *Geo.* 3. *c.* 82. if deserters or absentees be not taken, or do not return, in three months, the commissioners of lieutenancy shall provide other men out of the trophy tax; and deserters, if taken, shall be compelled to serve. *s.* 3.

The commissioners shall provide out of the trophy tax, men to serve instead of those promoted. *s.* 4.

A serjeant-major, and a quarter-master-serjeant, shall be added to each regiment. *s.* 5.

Non-commissioned officers may be reduced to privates for not exceeding fifteen calendar months, and afterwards, if not regularly re-appointed, to be discharged. *s.* 6.

The pay, clothing, and incidental expences, of the militia to be paid by the commissioners out of the annual levy of 4666l. 13*s.* 4*d.* for the month's tax, as hath been usual since 13 & 14 *Car.* 2. *c.* 3.; and collectors of the month's tax neglecting their duty, may be fined not exceeding 20*l.* *s.* 7, 8.

If non-commissioned officers, drummers, or fifers, when ordered to march, leave families behind them, they shall be relieved by the parish officers out of the poor rates; and if the family does not belong to the parish, the treasurer to the commissioners shall reimburse the allowance to such parish. *s.* 10.

And the treasurer is to be reimbursed by the parish to which the men are allotted, 36 *Geo.* 3. *c.* 92. *s.* 51.

Families of men not residing within London, or three miles thereof, not entitled to relief; and of men hereafter enrolled, only for one child born previous to the enrolment. *s.* 11.

The commissioners, forty days before the time of service of any man is expired, shall issue a precept for providing another man in his room. *s.* 12.

Parish officers refusing to pay money ordered at the sessions, shall be liable as under the former act, for refusing to pay money under an order of a justice, *viz.* 10*l.* see 36 *Geo.* 3. *c.* 92. *s.* 52.; but if they feel aggrieved they may appeal to the next sessions. *s.* 13.

If the treasurer to the commissioners shall refuse to reimburse the parish officers' money, paid to any families not belonging to the parish, he shall forfeit not exceeding 10*l.* *s.* 14.

By 37 *Geo.* 3. *c.* 25. the constable of the Tower, and lieutenant of the Tower Hamlets, may arm and exercise the militia of the hamlets according to 26 *Geo.* 3. *c.* 107. [*general militia act*, since repealed, see *Militia*], the provisions of which shall extend to them and the 13 & 14 *Car.* 2. *c.* 3. so far as repugnant to this act, is not to be applied to the Tower Hamlets. *s.* 1.

The men, in the whole amounting to 1120, shall be raised in the following proportions: *s.* 2.

Parish of Whitechapel	132
——— Christchurch	78
——— Norton Falgate	31
——— Old Artillery	11
——— Shoreditch	155
——— Hackney	84
——— Bethnal-green	122
——— Mile-end N. T.	22
——— Mile-end O. T.	57
——— Bromley	6
——— Stratford	22
——— Poplar and Blackwall	26
——— St. Ann	26
——— Ratcliffe	44
——— Shadwell	71
——— St. George	110
——— St. John	45
——— East Smithfield	45
——— St. Catherine	11
——— Tower without	5
——— Minories	8
——— Welclose	9

The constable is to appoint a clerk and messenger, and officers who have been approved by the king. *s.* 3.

The residents in the hamlets, and peace officers, are subject to the like duties as in the counties at large. *s.* 5.

When embodied, his majesty may put one regiment under the command of general officers, to be led to a distance of twelve miles, for repelling invasion or tumult. *s.* 6.

The constable and lieutenancy are to continue to raise trophy money, and the qualification of officers shall be as follows: deputy lieutenants 100*l.* *per annum*, or heir to 200*l.*; colonel of 300*l.* *per annum*, or heir to 600*l.*; lieutenant-colonel, or major-commandant, of 200*l.* *per annum*, or heir to 400*l.*; major, or captain, of 100*l.* *per annum*, or heir to 200*l.*; lieutenant of 30*l.* *per annum*, or personal estate of 600*l.* value, or real and personal together of 1000*l.* value; an ensign of 15*l.* or heir to 30*l.* *per annum*, or possessed of personal estate to the amount of 400*l.* *s.* 8.

Estates granted for twenty years, of equal value to those required for qualifications, sufficient. *s.* 9.

No rank superior to a lieutenant to be given till the qualification be delivered to the clerk of the peace. *s.* 10.

The clerk of the peace is to enter qualifications in a roll, and insert the dates of commissions in the Gazette; and the deputy lieutenants and officers are, within six months, to take the oaths of allegiance, supremacy, and abjuration. *s.* 11.

Unqualified persons acting, or not delivering in their qualifications, are to forfeit 50*l.* half to the king, and half to the informer. *s.* 12.

Prosecutions are to be heard and determined by the general quarter sessions for the Tower liberties. *s.* 13.

Peace officers are to obey the orders of the justices of the said liberties;—justices may act though they are deputy lieutenants or officers—and an appeal lies to the sessions, within three months, giving ten days' notice. *s.* 14—16.

And by 37 *Geo.* 3. *c.* 85. his majesty was authorized to draw out and embody the said militia.

——— *Nuisance.*] By 12 *Ric.* 2. *c.* 13. none shall cause any annoyance in London or other cities or towns, by casting dung or filth in ditches, rivers, or waters, and if they do they shall be punished at the discretion of the chancellor.

——— *Oil.*] By 3 *Hen.* 8. *c.* 18. the mayor of London, with the master and wardens of the tallow-chandlers, may search and see that oils put to sale be not mixed or defective; and may destroy defective oil, and imprison offenders. Chief magistrates in other cities and towns have like power.

——— *Orphans fund.*] By 5 & 6 *Will.* & *Mar. c.* 10. the lands, markets, fairs, and aqueducts, belonging to the city of London (except such as belong to hospitals, and are liable to the repairs of London bridge), are chargeable for ever with 8000*l.* *per annum,* to be appropriated for a perpetual fund for the orphans and other creditors of the city.

Towards such fund the common council may assess 2000*l.* yearly upon the personal estates of inhabitants, and distrain for the same; and all profits on lighting the streets shall be applied to such uses. *Ibid.*

Every apprentice shall pay 2*s.* 6*d.* on his binding, and 5*s.* on his freedom, into the hands of the warden of the company; 4*s.* per ton was granted on all wine imported at London for the increase of the fund; and likewise a duty on coals of 4*d.* per metage, and 6*d.* per chaldron, and 6*d.* per ton, which duty on coals, by 7 *Geo.* 3. *c.* 37. was connued for forty-six years, from the 29th of September, 1785, for completing Blackfriars bridge, redeeming the tolls of London bridge, rebuilding Newgate, repairing the Royal Exchange, and embanking part of the north side of the river Thames; and then for paving the streets of Westminster and Southwark.

The fund shall be applied for payment of debts due to orphans and creditors, by interest, after the rate of 4*l.* per cent for ever; for which the orphans and creditors shall acknowledge satisfaction, 5 & 6 *Will.* & *Mar.* *c.* 10.

Books of receipts and disbursements shall be kept by the chamberlain, which are to be audited yearly, allowing the auditors 20*s.* for every 1000*l.* therein; and the chamberlain or others misapplying the money shall forfeit treble the sum. *Ibid.*

The chamberlain and common serjeant shall give a note of what is owing to orphans and creditors, which debts are transferrable. *Ibid.*

No persons are compellable to pay orphans' money into the chamber. Corporation lands are liable if the city misapply the money: all fines shall be levied to the above abuses, and are not dischargeable by pardon. *Ibid.*

Orphans, hereafter, may have the benefit of the provision in this act, on paying to the chamberlain any sum of money, who is therewith to pay off any other orphan so much, and to admit the orphan who has paid in the monies to the benefit of such share. *Ibid.*

This act is not to extend to the New River, Shadwell, or London bridge waterworks.

——— *Oyer and Terminer, and Gaol Delivery.*] By 25 *Geo.* 3. *c.* 18. the session of gaol delivery of Newgate for Middlesex, shall not be discontinued by the sitting of the court of king's bench.

And by 32 *Geo.* 3. *c.* 48. the session of the peace and of oyer and terminer for Middlesex, is not to be discontinued by the sitting of the court of king's bench.

——— *Painters.*] By 1 *Jac.* 1. *c.* 20. no plasterer shall use the art of painter-stainer in London, unless he has served seven years to a painter as an apprentice, on pain of 5*l.*

No painter shall take above 16*d.* by the day for laying any flat colour. *Ibid.*

——— *Paving, Lighting, and Cleansing.*] By 2 *Geo.* 3. *c.* 21. for paving, lighting, and cleansing, within the city and liberty of Westminster, the parish of St. Giles, in the fields, St. George, Bloomsbury, St. Andrew, Holborn, in the county of Middlesex, the liberties of the Rolls and the Savoy, and that part of the duchy of Lancaster which lies in the county of Middlesex, certain commissioners were appointed, to have 300*l.* per annum, or 10,000*l.* qualification; and acting without, 100*l.* penalty: they are to appoint clerks, treasurers, receivers, surveyors, and other officers, who receiving any fees but their salaries, or being concerned in any contract, are disqualified, and forfeit 100*l.*

Three commissioners may order the squares, streets, or lanes, being thoroughfares, to be paved, altered, cleansed, and lighted; and five may contract for so doing, giving fourteen days' notice for proposals. *Ibid.*

Contractors for cleansing the streets may, by leave of two justices, lodge the dirt, for the accommodation of country carts, in vacant places. *Ibid.*

The property of all materials vested in the commissioners, and persons wilfully damaging the same, forfeit, for the first offence, not more than 40*s.* nor less than 10*s.* and for every other offence, not more than 3*l.* nor less than 20*s.* or, on non-payment, imprisonment for not more than two months, nor less than ten days. *Ibid.*

Pavements taken up by the water companies, or the commissioners of sewers, are to be relaid at their expence. *Ibid.*

The streets are not to be altered without the consent of five commissioners, on pain of 5*l.* *Ibid.*

Laying ashes or other annoyances in the street before the scavenger comes to carry away the same, is a penalty of 5*s.* for the first offence, 10*s.* for the second, and 20*s.* for every other. *Ibid.*

Obstruction, nuisance, or incroachment by carriages, timber, or other things, may be removed by the commissioners' order at the offender's expence, besides a penalty on him of 40*s.* *Ibid.*

A rate, not exceeding 1*s.* 6*d.* in the pound, shall be made on all houses, by five or more commissioners, half yearly, or oftener, for defraying the expence of paving, lighting, and cleansing; to be ascertained by the poor rates, for which purpose the commissioners may inspect such books. *Ibid.*

Houses let in tenements are chargeable, and the rates to be paid by the owners, and levied on the occupiers. *Ibid.*

Tenants are to pay the rates, and deduct a proportionable part out of their rent. *Ibid.*

Public buildings, and vacant ground, are chargeable; and the rates may be levied by distress and sale, if not paid in ten days. *Ibid.*

By 3 *Geo.* 3. *c.* 23. in Westminster and the aforesaid places, all signs and annoyances may be removed, and the same shall be placed in the front of the houses only, on pain of 5*l.*

The commissioners may order the streets to be watered, and the names of squares and streets to be affixed on corner houses, defacing which is a penalty of 40*s.* *Ibid.*

By 4 *Geo.* 3. *c.* 39. in the like places running, drawing, or driving, any wheel, sledge, wheel-barrow, or other carriage, on any of the foot pavements, is for the first offence 10*s.* for the second 20*s.* and for every other 40*s.*

Any quantity of coals, not exceeding one chaldron, with the ingrain, may be carried at one load, without being liable to any penalty. *Ibid.*

[*The foregoing acts were enlarged by* 5 *Geo.* 3. *c.* 50. 6 *Geo.* 3. *c.* 54. *and* 11 *Geo.* 3. *c.* 22.]

By 11 *Geo.* 3. *c.* 29. the corporation of London may appoint commissioners of sewers and pavements, whereof the recorder and common serjeant shall be two; and not less than seven to act, who may employ nonfreemen, and give other directions; and the property of sewers and pavements vested in the city.

The rates are not to exceed 1*s.* 6*d.* in the pound on inhabitants; and landlords may compound for rents under 10*l.* per annum, but not to be under half the rate; and lessees of markets to pay rates, or may compound, and so may the owners of large warehouses or workshops; empty houses to pay half tax, and wharfs two thirds of the poor rates; with several directions to prevent nuisances. *Ibid.*

Churches and public buildings, (except St. Paul's) to pay 4*d.* per square yard, and void spaces, and dead walls, 6*d.* per yard run; and the pavement surrounding St. Paul's, 2240 square yards, to pay 1*s.* 3*d.* per yard per ann. and tenants of hospitals to pay rates. *Ibid.*

	£.	s.	d.
Inner Temple to pay *per ann.*	2	2	0
Middle Temple - -	6	6	0
Serjeant's Inn, Chancery-lane	10	0	0
Staple Inn - -	14	0	0
Furnival's Inn - -	20	0	0
Bernard's Inn - -	6	0	0
Clifford's Inn - -	2	2	0

Rates for repairing sewers 4*d.* per pound, to be paid by the occupier, and deducted out of the rents: freemen not paying rates not to vote at elections, and the money to be paid into the chamber of London. *Ibid.*

Night-carts to work only between eleven at night and five in the morning. *Ibid.*

The commissioners may borrow on annuities tax free, and assignable, not more than 40,000*l.* at 8*l. per cent.* or if the life be above sixty, at 10*l. per cent.* and, on death, may sell other annuities in lieu thereof, so that the whole purchase money doth not exceed 175,000*l.* at a time. *Ibid.*

Capital felony to forge certificates relating hereto; and this act to extend to the parts of Holborn, the Minories, and Aldersgate-street, within the bars (supposing them to be out of the liberties of the city), and the courts and alleys communicating therewith, and the inhabitants are to pay the rates; but not to extend to the liberty of St. Martin-le-grand, belonging to the dean and chapter of Westminster. *Ibid.*

The commissioners of sewers to have power to act out of the city, and may take for paving the streets the same tolls (see *Toll*) as by 8 *Geo.* 3. *c.* 21. (*which is hereby repealed*), at the same gates, or at others erected by them near thereto, and may lease or compound the tolls; but none to pay more than once a day. *Ibid.*

By 33 *Geo.* 3. *c.* 75. the commissioners of paving under 11 *Geo.* 3. *c.* 29. not residing within the city or liberties, are to leave with the principal clerk a notice of some place where the summons may be left. *s.* 1.

No person shall without license of the commissioners alter the form of the streets, lanes, squares, yards, courts, alleys, passages, or places, or in any way encroach thereupon, or break up the pavement, on pain of *5l.* over and above the expenses of restoring the same, to be recovered by action within six months, in the name of the clerk to the commissioners. *s.* 2.

Persons placing bars, chains, or other obstacles, across such streets or places, to forfeit in like manner *5l.* *s.* 3.

If any person but the contractor for cleansing shall, under any pretence, take away ashes, any person may seize the party, with his horses, carts, and carriages, and convey him before some justice, before whom he may be convicted in not exceeding 40*s.* nor less than 20*s.* one moiety to the person seizing, and the other moiety to the city chamber, and if not immediately paid, the justice may send the articles seized to the Green-yard, to be there appraised and sold to pay the same, rendering the overplus; and in default of payment, or if seizure insufficient, the offender to be committed for not exceeding two calendar months, nor less than one. *s.* 4.

But owners of dust may remove the same for their own use. *s.* 5.

If the person taking away the ashes cannot be apprehended the owner of the horses and carts to be subject to the penalty. *s.* 6.

Collectors of the rates may on non-payment for seven days distrain, having a warrant from three commissioners. *s.* 7.

Houses let out in lodgings to be assessed on the landlord; and any of the occupiers of whom the rate is demanded, to pay or be subject to distress, and the landlord is to be answerable for the deficiency of the distress. *s.* 8, 19.

Butchers are not to hang meat beyond the story posts of their shops, on pain of 20*s.* *s.* 20.

Drivers of carts and carriages (except in cases of horses going a-breast, and single-horse carts with reins) shall hold in his hand a rope or strap to lead the shaft horse, on pain of 5*s.* for first offence, 10*s.* for the second, and 20*s.* for every subsequent offence. *s.* 11.

Persons neglecting to attend the summons of commissioners to forfeit 20*s.* and witnesses neglecting or refusing to appear, or appearing refusing to give evidence, to forfeit 20*s.* *s.* 12, 13.

And serving the summons personally, or leaving it at the parties' abode, sufficient. *s.* 14.

Penalties may be recovered before any justice by distress and sale, one moiety to the informer, and the other to the city chamber; and in default the party may be committed to one of the compters, or to Bridewell, for not exceeding three months, nor less than one. Warrants of distress may be backed, and penalties may be mitigated, but not to less than one half. *s.* 17, 18.

Drivers of waggons or carts with two or more horses, or other beasts of draught, riding on either of such horses, to forfeit 10*s.* for the first offence, 20*s.* for the second, 40*s.* for every other offence, or be committed to one of the compters, or to Bridewell, for not exceeding twenty, nor less than seven days.

Penalties on persons obstructing the collectors or their officers, first offence 5*s.* second 20*s.* and every other offence *5l.* *s.* 21.

Constables neglecting or refusing to assist in case of any distress being taken, to forfeit 20*s.* *s.* 22.

Monies in the hands of collectors dying or becoming bankrupt, or insolvent, to be paid in preference, and in case of non-payment within one month, may be recovered by action in the name of the clerk. *s.* 25.

Inhabitants may be witnesses, and persons aggrieved may appeal to the quarter-sessions. *s.* 27, 28.

———*Pharmacy and Surgery.*] By 3 *Hen.* 8, *c.* 11, no person within the city of London, or seven miles thereof, shall exercise as a physician or surgeon, except examined and approved, on forfeiture of *5l.* a month.

A physician or surgeon out of the precinct of London, seven miles, shall be approved by the bishop of the diocese, on like pain, but the rights of the universities are saved. *Ibid.*

By 5 *Hen.* 8, *c.* 6, the surgeons of London shall be exempt from bearing armour, parish offices, and inquests.

By 14 & 15 *Hen.* 8, *c.* 5, the king's charter for incorporating the college of physicians of London is confirmed; they are to choose a president, and have perpetual succession, a common seal, and ability to purchase lands and make ordinances. Eight of the chiefs of the college shall be called elects, who from amongst themselves are to choose a president yearly.

Physicians through England shall be examined by the president of the college, and three of the elects; graduates of the universities excepted. *Ibid.*

By 32 *Hen.* 8, *c.* 40, the president, commons, and fellows of physicians in London, are exempted from ward and parish offices.

Four physicians shall be chosen by the college to search apothecaries wares; and, in company with the warden of the mystery of apothecaries, they may destroy defective wares. Apothecaries refusing to be searched forfeit *5l.* and physicians to act, 40*s.* *Ibid.*

Any of the physicians in London may practice surgery. *Ibid.*

By 32 *Hen.* 8. *c.* 42, the barbers and surgeons of London were united and incorporated, and exempted from bearing arms, or serving on inquests or offices.

The masters and governors of the surgeons

of London may take yearly four condemned felons for anatomies. *Ibid.*

Barbers in and within 1 mile of London shall not use surgery or let blood, drawing of teeth except; and surgeons shall not be barbers. Surgeons shall have a sign at their doors. *Ibid.*

No one shall be a barber in London unless free of the company. *Ibid.*

Barbers and surgeons shall pay scot and lot; and any person may retain a surgeon or a barber in his house as a servant. *Ibid.*

By 34 & 35 *Hen.* 8. *c.* 8, any subject of the king having knowledge of the nature of herbs, may minister to any outward sore, wound, or disease.

By 1 *Mar. sess.* 2. *c.* 9, the president of the college of physicians may commit offenders to any prison within London except the Tower.

By 6 *Will.* 3, *c.* 4, apothecaries free of the company in London, practising there, or within 7 miles thereof, are exempted from the offices of constable, scavenger, or overseer, or any other parish, ward, or leet offices, and from serving on juries, producing a testimonial of their freedom.

Apothecaries in other parts, brought up in such art, or having served an apprenticeship of 7 years, shall also be exempted. *Ibid.*

By 18 *Geo.* 2, *c.* 15, the union of surgeons and barbers of London was dissolved, and the surgeons of London were made a separate corporation, with power to enjoy the same privileges as by former acts or grants.

Candidates to serve as surgeons in the army and navy shall be examined by the surgeons company. *Ibid.*

By 25 *Geo.* 2, *c.* 37, the bodies of murderers, convicted and executed in London or Middlesex, shall be delivered to Surgeons Hall; and in any other county to such surgeon as the judge shall direct.

The 14 *Geo.* 3. *c.* 49, regulates the keeping of madhouses, and is noticed under title *Lunatics.*

——— *Police Offices.*] By 2 *Geo.* 3. *c.* 28, persons using, living, or navigating bumboats on the Thames, unless entered at the office of the Trinity-house, unlawfully receiving goods, stores, or the like, from vessels in the river, may be convicted before a justice of peace of a misdemeanor, and forfeit the boat.

By 39 & 40 *Geo.* 3, *c.* 87, his majesty may cause a public office to be established at or near Wapping New stairs, and appoint 3 special justices for determining complaints of offences committed on the river Thames. *s.* 1.

One of whom shall attend every day from 10 until 8, and 2 from 11 till 1, and from 6 until 8. *s.* 2.

An account of the fees taken at the office is to be delivered monthly to the receiver, and the amount paid to him. *s.* 3.

All penalties (except to informers and parties aggrieved) received at this office shall be paid to the receiver. *s.* 4.

His majesty, by the advice of his privy council, may direct salaries to be paid to the justices. *s.* 5.

The salary to each to be 400*l.* clear, and the whole expence of the office not to exceed 8000*l.* *Ibid.*

His majesty may appoint a receiver of all fees at such salary as his majesty shall appoint, and to possess the same powers as the receiver under the other police act (see 42 *Geo.* 3, *c.* 76. *infra*); and if the monies applicable by the receiver shall not amount to 8000*l.* the deficiency shall be supplied out of the consolidated fund, and if they exceed he shall pay the surplus into the Exchequer. *s.* 6.

The justices may employ a sufficient number of sworn constables, and may suspend or dismiss them; and also any number of men not exceeding 30, under the name of Thames police surveyors, for inspecting the conduct of the constables and persons employed in and about ships and vessels on the river. *s.* 7, 8.

But the court of assistants of the Trinity-house may dismiss such constables or surveyors. *s.* 9.

The receiver is to pay the constables and surveyors such salaries as the justices shall appoint with the approbation of the Secretary of State. *s.* 10.

The inspectors may at all times by day or night enter every ship, hoy, barge, lighter, boat, or other vessel (not in his majesty's service), in the river, to inspect the conduct of the constables and all other persons on board, for providing against fire, preserving peace, preventing felonies or misdemeanors, or detecting offenders. *s.* 11.

Suspected persons and reputed thieves, frequenting the river and the quays and warehouses adjoining, with a felonious intent, may be apprehended by the constables or surveyors, and conveyed before the special justices, or any other justice, and if it shall appear that there is just ground to suspect such was their intent, they shall be deemed rogues and vagabonds within the meaning of 17 *Geo.* 2, *c.* 5; but persons thinking themselves aggrieved may appeal to the quarter sessions; if the conviction be affirmed, the justices may proceed against the offender as if he had been committed until the sessions; but persons convicted are not liable to any other punishment than imprisonment not exceeding 6 months. *s.* 12.

Persons damaging boats belonging to the justices are to forfeit not exceeding 15*l.* or be imprisoned for not exceeding 3 months. *s.* 13.

Persons breaking packages with an intent

that the contents may be spilled, to forfeit not exceeding 40*s.* nor less than 10*s.* to be paid on conviction, or be committed for not exceeding one calendar month. *s.* 14.

Persons letting fall any articles for the purpose of preventing the seizure or discovery of any unlawfully obtained, guilty of a misdemeanor; and if any of apparent value shall be let fall from any ship, into any boat, or from any boat or wharf, without the privity of the owner, the boat may be seized, and every person therein, or any suspected person near, conveyed before the special justice or justices of the jurisdiction, and if not made appear that it did not proceed from a fraudulent design, the parties shall be deemed guilty. *s.* 15.

If on information on oath it shall appear to the justices that there is reasonable cause for suspecting that any part of the cargo of any vessel, or any of his majesty's stores, have been unlawfully obtained, and are concealed, they, or any justices in their jurisdictions, may cause the place to be searched by day or by night, and by force, if necessary; and if any are found, and it be not made appear by what lawful means they came deposited, the person in whose house found, and the persons appearing to have been privy to the depositing, shall be deemed guilty of a misdemeanor. *s.* 16. See 2 *Geo.* 3, *c.* 28.

Every person who to prevent any articles from being seized, on suspicion of being stolen, or being produced in evidence, shall frame any false bill of parcels, shall be adjudged guilty of a misdemeanor, and may be advertised. *s.* 17.

When the production of the party from whom any goods have been bought, would, under 2 *Geo.* 3, *c.* 28, *s.* 6, 7, exempt any person from being adjudged guilty of a misdemeanor, such production shall not be deemed sufficient, unless the account given be satisfactory to the justice, who otherwise may examine all purchasers, and adjudge the party guilty of a misdemeanor. *s.* 18.

Misdemeanors under this act are punishable, first, by a penalty not exceeding 5*l.* nor less than 20*s.* or by imprisonment not exceeding eight weeks nor less than two; or secondly, by a penalty from 40*s.* to 10*s.* coupled with imprisonment from four weeks to one; and if penalty be not paid or secured, the offender may be committed for not exceeding 8 weeks; and the penalties are to go either wholly to the informer, or be distributed to such as shall have contributed to the conviction, and the informer may be an evidence. *s.* 19.

Complaints of offences declared misdemeanors, or for which pecuniary penalties are appointed, shall be heard and determined either by the special justices at their office, or by any justice in his jurisdiction; if in London by the lord mayor or aldermen. *s.* 20.

Misdemeanors under 2 *Geo.* 3, *c.* 28, *s.* 16, may be punished either under that act or under this. *s.* 21.

Persons guilty of offences under 2 *Geo.* 3, *c.* 28, *s.* 12 (See *Felony*), are punishable by transportation for 14 years, shall plead to indictments without having time to traverse. *s.* 22.

Nothing herein to deprive the city magistrates of any of their rights. *s.* 23.

The act shall continue in force until 25th March 1807. *s.* 26. But it is further continued by 47 *Geo.* 3, *sess.* 1, *c.* 37, *infra.*

By 43 *Geo.* 3, *c.* 115, coffee, tea, and all other exciseable articles, stopped under 2 *Geo.* 3, *c.* 28, and 39 and 40 *Geo.* 3, *c.* 87, by reason of forfeiture, shall be conveyed to the Excise office within 24 hours. *s.* 1.

And such articles being stopped on suspicion of being stolen, shall be deposited in the office of the Thames police till produced at the trial; but notice of such detention shall be given to the Excise office within 24 hours; and after trial the goods shall be conveyed to the Excise office. *s.* 2—4.

If such goods shall not be conveyed to the Excise office in manner hereby required, they may be seized, and persons making default are to forfeit 20*l.* and for obstructing the officers 200*l.* to be recovered as Excise penalties. *s.* 5—7.

By 47 *Geo.* 3, *sess.* 1, *c.* 37, the acts 39 and 40 *Geo.* 3, *c.* 87, and so much of 42 *Geo.* 3, *c.* 76, *infra*, as amend the same, are continued until 25th March, 1814. *s.* 1.

The Thames police surveyors may enter ships, hoys, barges, lighters, boats, or other vessels, on suspicion of felony having been committed, or being about to be committed. *s.* 2.

Boats forfeited may be destroyed, or restored, or sold, at the discretion of the justices. *s.* 3.

The magistrates are empowered to settle disputes relating to wages between captains and owners of ships, wharfs, or quays, and their labourers, *s.* 4, whose orders shall be final. *s.* 5.

Persons destroying or damaging any boat belonging to the justices, to forfeit 30*l.* instead of 15*l.* under the first-mentioned act. *s.* 6.

And all forfeitures for injuring packages may be recovered before one justice of the peace. *s.* 7.

All penalties in the first act as to framing fraudulent bills of parcels, are extended to persons knowingly producing the same. *s.* 8.

One justice may convict under the first act, and the offenders may be severally adjudged to different fines, and different periods of imprisonment. *s.* 9.

The jurisdiction of the justices not to extend to the city of London, or the suburbs and liberties thereof, or any vessel between the Tower and the western extremity of the Temple adjoining Essex-street. *s.* 10.

The jurisdiction of the corporation of London over Southwark not affected. *s.* 11.

Penalties under 39 *Geo.* 3. *c.* 69, for rendering more commodious the port of London, not affected. *s.* 12.

Privileges of the Trinity, and of St. Clement's, Deptford Strond, not affected. *s.* 13.

By 42 *Geo.* 3, *c.* 76, the former acts of 32 *Geo.* 2, *c.* 53, and 36 *Geo.* 3, *c.* 75, as to the Middlesex and Surrey police offices, are repealed. *s.* 1.

The seven public offices now established, and the justices acting therein, shall be continued. *s.* 2.

His majesty may appoint justices to fill up vacancies; and one of such justices shall attend at each of such offices every day from ten in the morning until eight in the evening, and two shall attend together from twelve till three, and from six till eight, but the attendance of one may be supplied by any other justice. *s.* 3.

No justice shall take any fees but at such public offices, on pain of 100*l.* except fees for licensing alehouses, or fees taken at the public office in Bow-street. *s.* 4.

An account of the fees taken at the seven offices shall be delivered monthly to the receiver, and the amount of fees paid to him, and all penalties (except to informers, and parties aggrieved) received at such public offices, shall be paid to the receiver; and if such fees and penalties are not accounted for, the receiver may sue for the same in any court of record at Westminster. *s.* 5, 6, 7.

The receiver may sue for money left in the hands of deceased receivers, and recover from their representatives. *s.* 8.

His majesty may in council order salaries of 500*l.* per ann. each to the justices, but the whole expences are not to exceed 18,000*l.* *s.* 9.

The present receiver is to continue in office, and in case of death or resignation his majesty may appoint another. *s.* 10.

The duty of the receiver is to pay all salaries, expences, and charges, out of his receipts; and he is to account on oath to the Treasury; and have an allowance of 400*l.* per annum for his trouble, to be made good, if the monies received by him are deficient, out of the consolidated fund. *s.* 10, 11.

His majesty in council may alter the situation of the offices. *s.* 12.

Acts directed to be done by the nearest justice, may be done by a justice of the next police office. *s.* 13.

The justices are rendered incapable of sitting in parliament. *s.* 14.

And no justice, receiver, or constable, under this act shall interfere in elections of members, on penalty of 100*l.* except in discharge of their duty. *s.* 15.

The justices may employ not exceeding 8 constables in each office, and dismiss such as they think fit. *s.* 16.

The receiver shall pay the constables (47 *Geo.* 3. *sess.* 2. *c.* 42.) 18*s.* a week and extraordinary expenses. *s.* 17.

Constables may apprehend any suspicious person frequenting places of public resort, and streets or highways, and carry him before a justice, and if it appear upon oath that he is a person of evil fame and a reputed thief, he shall be deemed a rogue and vagabond within 17 *Geo.* 2. *c.* 25, and no certiorari is allowed; but such persons thinking themselves aggrieved may appeal to the sessions, where, if the conviction be affirmed, the justices may proceed as if the party had been committed to the house of correction till the next sessions, but the punishment shall not exceed six months' imprisonment. *s.* 18.

The jurisdictions of London and Southwark, and of the dean or high steward of Westminster, are saved. *s.* 19, 20.

Instead of 400*l.* allowed by 39 & 40 *Geo.* 3. *c.* 87. *s.* 5, to each of the Thames police magistrates, 500*l.* shall be paid, but the whole expence of that office shall not exceed 8000*l.* per annum.

By 47 *Geo.* 3. *sess.* 2. *c.* 42, the act 42 *Geo.* 3. *c.* 76, is continued until 1st June, 1810, *s.* 1.; and 18*s.* per week shall be paid to the constables in lieu of 16*s.* *s.* 2.

——— *Poor.*] By 13 & 14 *Car.* 2. *c.* 12, there shall be one or more corporations or workhouses in London, Westminster, and the bills of mortality; the lord-mayor shall be president, with fifty-two assistants, chosen by the common council, who are to choose subordinate officers; and in Westminster the lord chancellor is to appoint the president and assistants, and approve of the officers.

The president and governors, or two of them, may apprehend beggars and vagrants, and cause them to be kept and set to work in the said workhouses. *Ibid.*

If they want money for the above purposes the common council in London, and the burgesses and justices in Westminster, and within the bills, may tax the inhabitants, and levy the same by distress. *Ibid.*

The president and governors may make bye-laws; and all sheriffs and officers shall assist the corporations. *Ibid.*

By 22 & 23 *Car.* 2, *c.* 18, officers of the above corporations shall account quarterly, and no assessment shall be made on any of the parishes after September 29, 1675. But the powers in London are not hereby vacated.

By 2 *Geo.* 3, *c.* 22, and 7 *Geo.* 3, *c.* 39, a regular, uniform, and annual register of all parish poor infants shall be kept within the bills of mortality, according to the forms in these acts.

By 7 *Geo.* 3, *c.* 39, in the several parishes within the bills of mortality children born in, or received into, any workhouse or parish-house there, are to be nursed and taken care of as follows, viz. those under six years of age are to be sent into the country three miles off; those under two years, not suckled by the mother, not less than five miles off; and those above two and under six, not less than three miles off.

Weekly rates to be paid for their nursing and maintaining till apprenticed, or returned to the workhouse, *viz.* until six years old 2*s.* 6*d.* a week, afterwards 2*s.*; and nurses may, for their care, have an annual reward of 10*s.*: clothing to be furnished, and all other incidental expences defrayed, by the parish, and separate accounts to be kept thereof. *Ibid.*

Five guardians of the parish poor children to be chosen out of each parish. Where any shall refuse to act, or shall resign, or die, a further choice to be made. *Ibid.*

Guardians to remain in office three years. *Ibid.*

Churchwardens and overseers, disqualified from being elected guardians, who are to visit the children, make enquiries, and report evils to the churchwardens, who are to redress the same, or, on their default, the guardians may. *Ibid.*

A meeting of the guardians to be summoned every six weeks, two to make a quorum, with power, singly or jointly, to call in the churchwardens or overseers. *Ibid.*

Parish poor children, under six years of age, may be sent to the Foundling hospital, upon such terms as shall be agreed on; the charge to be defrayed out of the poor rates; and if not duly paid, any justice may summon the overseers, and compel them to pay. *Ibid.*

The death, discharge, or apprenticeship of and child, to be certified to the vestry clerk of the parish. *Ibid.*

Hospital account to be kept with each parish distinct. *Ibid.*

Parish children and foundlings to be apprenticed for not more than seven years, or till twenty-one years of age. Apprentice-fee not to be less than 4*l.* 2*s.* and 40*s.* to be paid in seven weeks, and the remainder in three years, after the indentures are executed. *Ibid.*

An annual list to be made out by each parish of the children apprenticed, and delivered to the company of parish clerks; abstracts thereof to be printed, and delivered to each parish, commencing January 1st, and ending December 31st. *Ibid.*

General expences, not otherwise provided for, to be paid out of the poor rates, and parish officers or others neglecting their duty forfeit 5*l.* *Ibid.* See general title *Poor.*

——— *Porterage.*] By 39 *Geo.* 3. *c.* lviii. no person shall charge within London and Westminster, Southwark and the suburbs thereof, and other parts not exceeding half a mile from the end of the carriage pavements, for the porterage of parcels not exceeding 56lb. more than as follows: for not exceeding one quarter of a mile 3*d.* exceeding a quarter and not half a mile 4*d.* exceeding half mile and not one mile 6*d.* exceeding one mile but not one and a half 8*d.* and for any greater distance than one mile and a half, but not exceeding two miles 10*d.* and so in proportion 3*d.* for every further distance not exceeding half a mile. *s.* 1.

Tickets shall be made out at the inns and given to the porters, and by them delivered with the parcels; and any innkeeper not making out such tickets, to forfeit not exceeding 40*s.* nor less than 5*s.*; and porters not delivering or defacing the same, 40*s.* or porters overcharging, 20*s.* *s.* 3.

Parcels brought by coaches, shall be delivered within six hours, on pain of not exceeding 20*s.* nor less than 10*s.* *s.* 4.

Parcels brought by waggons shall be delivered within 24 hours, on a like penalty. *s.* 5.

Parcels directed to be left till called for, shall be delivered to persons to whom the same shall be directed, on payment of the carriage and 2*d.* for warehouse-room, on like penalty. *s.* 6.

Parcels if not sent for till the expiration of one week, 1*d.* more for warehouse-room may be charged. *s.* 7.

Parcels not directed to be left till called for, shall be delivered in like manner on demand, under a like penalty. *s.* 8.

Misbehaviour of porters may be punished by a justice, by a fine not exceeding 20*s.* nor less than 5*s.* *s.* 9.

The rates of porterage may be recovered before a justice, who may levy the same and costs of distress. *s.* 10.

Information must be laid within 14 days, *s.* 11. and no porter is to be employed contrary to the usage of the city of London. *s.* 10, 11.

The penalties may be recovered before one justice; witnesses not attending, to forfeit not more than 40*s.* nor less than 20*s.* and refusing to give evidence, may be committed for 14 days; appeal is allowed to the sessions, and the penalties go half to the informer, and half to the poor. *s.* 12—17.

——— *Privileged Places.*] By 8 & 9 *Will.* 3. *c.* 27. the sheriffs of London and Middlesex, and the bailiff of Southwark, shall take the *posse comitatus*, and arrest persons in any pretended privileged places, in London, Middlesex, or the Borough, on pain of 100*l.* and opposing officers in executing process there, rescuing, or concealing rescuers, is by 9 *Geo.* 1. *c.* 28. and 11 *Geo.* 1. *c.* 22. made felony and transportation for seven years, and returning within that time is felony without clergy.

Justices of peace, on affidavit of a person's residing in the Mint, or other privileged place, and owing a debt of above 50*l.* may issue their warrants to the sheriff to raise the *posse comitatus*, to execute process; and such sheriff shall so do on pain of 200*l.* 9 *Geo.* 1. *c.* 28. 11 *Geo.* 1. *c.* 22.

Persons apprehending offenders under this act shall have a reward of 40*l.* from the sheriff of Surrey, and if killed in so doing, the executor or administrator is to have the same. *Ibid.*

——— *Recoveries.*] By 6 *Ed.* 1. *c.* 11. the mayor and bailiffs of London, on challenge by termor before judgment, may enquire if recovery had against him in reversion was by collusion or not, and if found that it was, the termor shall enjoy his term.

If a man impleaded in London vouches a foreigner to warranty, execution shall be awarded in value on the warranty. *Ibid.* *c.* 12. and 9 *Ed.* 1.

——— *Recusants.*] By 3 *Jac.* 1. *c.* 5. recusants shall depart from London and ten miles thereof, within ten days after conviction, on pain of 100*l.* But see general title *Papists.*

——— *Savoy.*] By 12 *Geo.* 3. *c.* 42. the high German church and the low German church, and the church-yards and burying-grounds thereto belonging, and the buildings used as barracks, and two houses in the Friary, used by the officers, shall be under the survey of the exchequer; and the rest of the precinct of the Savoy, under the duchy of Lancaster.

——— *Scavage.*] By 19 *Hen.* 7. *c.* 8. disturbing any merchant by taking scavage shall forfeit 20*l.* saving to the city of London their rights hereto, to be determined by the king and council.

——— *Silk.*] By 13 & 14 *Car.* 2. *c.* 15. every person using the trade of silk throwing in London and Westminster, shall enter himself of the company of silk-throwers, and be subject to their laws, orders, and regulations.

Freemen may employ natives to turn the mill, tie threads, and double or wind silk, as before. *Ibid.*

By 20 *Car.* 2. *c.* 6. bye-laws of the commonalty of silk-throwers, restraining the number of mills, spindles, or other utensils to be employed, or to confine any freeman of the company to take less than three apprentices at a time, are declared void.

By 13 *Geo.* 3. *c.* 68. the wages of silk manufacturers shall be settled in London by the lord mayor, recorder, and aldermen; in Middlesex, by the justices; and in Westminster and the Tower hamlets by the general quarter sessions; and their order shall be published in two newspapers three times, at the expence of the persons applying; and giving or taking more or less wages than allowed thereby, to forfeit, masters 50*l.* and journeymen 40*s.*

Justices may summon witnesses, and commit them, for not attending; and masters employing men out of the limits to elude the act, to forfeit 50*l.* but not to extend to the wages of foremen; and no silk weaver to have more than two apprentices at one time, on penalty of 20*l.* *Ibid.*

By 32 *Geo.* 3. *c.* 44. the wages of journeymen weavers in any manufacture of silk mixed with other materials are to be settled as directed by 13 *Geo.* 3. *c.* 68. with regard to silk weavers. *s.* 1.

Persons buying, receiving, or taking in pawn, any silk from those who are employed to work up any silk manufacture, knowing them to be so employed, may be convicted at the sessions of a misdemeanor, and fined, imprisoned, or whipped, as also persons selling or pawning silk, knowing the same to have been purloined. *s.* 4, 5.

——— *Southwark.*] By 28 *Geo.* 2. *c.* 9. no market shall be held, nor stalls erected, nor coaches ply, or stand, in the high street of Southwark.

By 28 *Geo.* 2. *c.* 23. and 30 *Geo.* 2. *c.* 31, the inhabitants of Saint Saviour, Southwark, may hold a market, not interfering with the high-street, in a convenient place called the triangle. See also *Courts of Requests.*

——— *Spices.*] By 6 *Ann.* *c.* 16. the lord mayor, aldermen, and common council, may appoint a garbler to garble spices, drugs, and wares, garbleable within London, who is to be recompensed as they appoint.

——— *Still-yard.*] By 19 *Hen.* 7. *c.* 23. all statutes made in derogation of the merchants in the still-yard were repealed; but this was not to prejudice the liberties of London.

——— *Streets.*] By 6 *Geo.* 1. *c.* 23. the streets of the cities of London, Westminster, and other places, shall be deemed highways, to entitle persons apprehending and convicting robbers to receive the reward.

By 32 *Geo.* 2. *c.* 16. laying rubbish, ashes, or soil in any of the streets or common ways in London, Westminster, or the suburbs thereof, or sweeping or throwing the same into the kennels, is a penalty of 10*s.*; but none are liable to forfeit for sweeping before their houses immediately after snow, thaw, or rain.

Lessees, and occupiers of laystalls, shall inspect the streets and common passages, and give information of offenders; and on performing their duty therein, may ship annually as ballast from any laystalls in London 2000 tons of soil. *Ibid.*

——— *Sunday Tolls.*] The 6 *Geo.* 3. *c.* 24. for paving the streets in Southwark, grants Sunday tolls to be taken at Symond's-corner, Blackman-street; Newington Butts, the new road, end of Kent-street, Saint

George's church, Star-corner, Dock-head, and Folly bridge, as follows:

	£.	s.	d.
For a coach and six horses -	0	0	10
Ditto with four - -	0	0	8
With three or two -	0	0	6
With one - -	0	0	3
Horse not drawing -	0	0	1

By 8 *Geo.* 3. *c.* 21. for paving the streets n London, the like Sunday tolls shall be taken at the following turnpikes, *viz.* Mile-end, Bethnall Green, Hackney, Kingsland, Ball's Pond, Holloway, St. John's-street, Goswell-street, and the City-road, all in Middlesex.

By 5 *Geo.* 3. *c.* 13. and 26 *Geo.* 3. *c.* 102. for paving the streets of the city and liberty of Westminster, and parts adjacent, a street toll on Sundays, as before, shall be paid at the following turnpike gates, *viz.* that near Westminster-bridge in Surrey, nearest St. James's Park at Pimlico, at Kensington, nearest the entrance into Hyde Park, that at Hyde Park corner, the several gates at Tyburn, those near St. Mary-la-bonne, at Portland-street, at the Green Man, on the road from Paddington to Islington, on the said road eastward of Tottenham-court, at Tottenham-court, on the northern road, and that nearest the end of Gray's-inn-lane.

And by 49 *Geo.* 3. *c.* 171. (*local act*) the same tolls are authorised to be taken on Sundays at Blackfriars-bridge.

——— *Taylors.*] By 7 *Geo.* 1. *stat.* 1. *c.* 13. all contracts between journeymen taylors in London and Westminster, or within five miles thereof, for advancing their wages, or lessening their hours of work, are declared illegal and void; making such agreement, to be sent to the house of correction for two months.

By 8 *Geo.* 3. *c.* 17. journeymen taylors shall work from six in the morning till seven at night, at 2*s.* 7½*d.* a day, except during one month on a general mourning, and then at 5*s.* 1½*d.* a day.

Masters giving, or journeymen taking, more wages than hereby allowed, shall be sent to the house of correction, for not more than two months, nor less than fourteen days; and justices may call witnesses before them, on suspicion that the above regulation is broken through. *Ibid.*

The general sessions in London may alter the wages and hours, and make regulations in future, according to circumstances. *Ibid.*

This act is not to extend to taylor's foremen, or men working over hours, at 6*d.* per hour in general mournings, and 3*d.* an hour at other times. *Ibid.*

Masters employing men out of the limits, to evade the act, shall forfeit 500*l.* and persons aggrieved may appeal to the quarter sessions. *Ibid.*

Journeymen taylors refusing to work at the wages allowed, or departing before the work is finished, may be sent to the house of correction for two months; and their wages may be recovered before a justice. 7 *Geo.* 1.

——— *Thames.*] By 4 *Hen.* 7. *c.* 15. the lord mayor of London shall have like conservation in creeks and breaches, ebbing and flowing out of the river Thames, as touching unlawful engines and annoyances.

By 21 *Hen.* 8. *c.* 18. annoying the Thames, or digging to make shelps, or casting rubbish therein, or undermining the banks, is a forfeiture of 5*l.*

Persons taking, for ballast, any gravel or sand, but off the shelps between Greenhithe and Richmond, shall be imprisoned and forfeit 5*l.* but any one may take ballast from such shelps. *Ibid.*

By 13 *Eliz.* *c.* 18. the city of London, by a new cut, were empowered to make the river Lee navigable from Ware.

By 3 *Jac.* 1. *c.* 14. ditches, sewers, streams, and watercourses, falling into the Thames, within two miles of London, shall be subject to the commission of sewers.

The 11 *Geo.* 3. *c.* 34. embanked the Thames opposite Durham-yard, Salisbury-street, Cecil street, and Beaufort-buildings, and the city of London and dean and chapter of Westminster were at liberty to try their right.

For improving and completing the navigation of the Thames from London to Cricklade, in Wiltshire, *c.* 45. repealed as to the commissioners and their authority. 14 *Geo.* 3. *c.* 91.

By 14 *Geo.* 3. *c.* 91. no towing-paths shall be through gardens, orchards, yards, parks, paddocks, inclosed lawns, or planted avenues, without the consent of the owner; and the committee may fix the price of carriage, and hire of horses; and taking more, penalty of 20*l.*; and no vessel shall moor in Taplow mill stream.

By 15 *Geo.* 3. *c.* 11. on the river Thames, vessels shall draw three feet of water from May 1st to November 1st, and three feet eight inches the rest of the year; and to have metal marks instead of white lines; and when the water is above the high mark, the gates to be opened; and no lock-owner to be a commissioner.

By 17 *Geo.* 3. *c.* 18. the city may purchase the tolls for navigating the Thames westward from London bridge in their liberty, and in lieu thereof, may take per ton—

	£.	s.	d.
To Strand on the Green or Brentford - -	0	0	0½
To Isleworth or Richmond -	0	0	1
To Twickenham or Teddington	0	0	1½
To Kingston or Hampton Wick	0	0	2
To Ditton, Hampton-court, Moulsey, or Hampton-town -	0	0	2½

	£.	s.	d.
To Sunbury, Walton, Hawford, Shepperton, or Weybridge	0	0	3
To Chertsey or Laleham -	0	0	3½
And to Staines and above -	0	0	4

Nothing for vessels under three tons, or pleasure-boats; and may borrow 15,000*l.* on the tolls, on annuities for lives of forty-five, at 8*l.* per cent. and of sixty at 10*l.* per cent. *Ibid.*

——— *Tithes.*] By 37 *Hen.* 8. *c.* 12. tithes shall be paid in London, according to the decree made by the archbishop, quarterly, after the rate of 2*s.* 9*d.* for every 20*s.* yearly rent, and 2*d.* for each of the family for their four offering days yearly.

Where less than 2*s.* 9*d.* in the 20*s.* rent hath been paid for tithes, in such places, they shall still pay only after that rate. *Ibid.*

But by 22 & 23 *Car.* 2. *c.* 15. the tithes of the several parishes in London were ascertained at certain yearly sums, to be paid quarterly, to be levied by warrant of the lord mayor, the lord chancellor, or two barons of the exchequer; and no court to hold plea of the same; but the warden and minor canons of St. Paul's, parson and proprietors of St. Gregory, were to enjoy all tithes as formerly.

And finally, by 44 *Geo.* 3. *c.* lxxxix. the annual tithes of the parishes within the city of London were settled to be as follows:

	£.	s.	d.
Allhallows, Lombard-street	200	0	0
St. Bartholomew, Exchange	200	0	0
St. Bride's - -	200	0	0
St. Bennet Fink - -	200	0	0
St. Michael, Crooked-lane	200	0	0
St. Dionis back church -	200	0	0
St. Dunstan in the east -	333	6	8
St. James's, Garlick Hythe -	200	0	0
St. Michael, Cornhill -	233	6	8
St. Michael, Bassishaw -	220	18	4
St. Mary, Aldermanbury -	250	0	0
St. Martin, Ludgate -	266	13	4
St. Peter, Cornhill -	200	0	0
St. Stephen, Coleman-street	200	0	0
St. Sepulchre - -	333	6	8
Allhallows, Bread-street, and St. John - -	233	6	8
Allhallows, the great and less	333	6	8
St. Alban's, Wood-street, and St. Oliver - -	283	6	8
St. Ann and St. Agnes, and St. John Zachary -	233	6	8
St. Augustin and St. Faith	286	13	4
St. Andrew, Wardrobe, and St. Ann, Blackfriars -	233	6	8
St. Antholin and St. John the Baptist - -	200	0	0
St. Bennet, Grace-church-street, and St. Leonard, East Cheap	233	6	8
St. Bennet and St. Peter, Paul's wharf - -	200	0	0
Christ Church and St. Leonard Foster - -	333	6	8
St. Edmund and St. Nicholas	300	0	0
St. George Botolph and St. Bidulph - -	300	0	0
St. Lawrence Jury, and St. Magdalen - -	200	0	0
St. Margaret, and St. Christopher, Lothbury -	366	13	4
St. Magnus and St. Margaret	283	6	8
St. Michael Royal and St. Martin Vintry - -	233	6	8
St. Matthew, Friday-street, and St. Peter -	250	0	0
St. Margaret Pattens and St. Gabriel - -	200	0	0
St. Mary at Hill and St. Andrew	333	6	8
St. Mary Woolnoth, and St. Mary Woolchurch -	266	13	4
St. Clement East Cheap, and St. Martin - -	233	6	8
St. Mary Abchurch and St. Lawrence - -	200	0	0
St. Mary, Aldermanbury, and St. Thomas - -	250	0	0
St. Mary-la-bonne -	333	6	8
St. Mildred, Poultry, and St. Mary Colechurch -	283	6	8
St. Michael, Wood-street, and St. Mary - -	200	0	0
St. Mildred, Bread-street	216	13	4
St. Michael, Queenhythe	266	13	4
St. Magdalen, Old-fish-street	200	0	0
St. Mary Somerset and St. Mary Mounthaw - -	200	0	0
St. Nicholas Coleby -	216	13	4
St. Olave Jewry - -	200	0	0
St. Stephen Walbrook -	200	0	0
St. Swithin - -	233	6	8
St. Michael Vedast, Foster-lane	266	13	4

which sums of money are to be the annual maintenance (over and above glebes and perquisites, gifts and bequests) of the parsons, vicars, and curates. *s.* 2.

Power to make assessments on houses and other buildings before 21st August, 1804, was granted to the aldermen and common council and churchwardens in each ward, *s.* 3, appeal to the lord mayor and court of aldermen allowed against assessments, *s.* 4. and the assessments may be altered every seven years. *s.* 5.

Four transcripts of which are to be made, and one deposited with the town clerk, another with the bishop of London, a third with the vestry, and the fourth with the incumbent, *s.* 6.

The said sums are payable quarterly on 25th December, 25th March, 24th June, and 29th September, every year. *s.* 7.

The powers of the act 22 & 23 *Car.* 2. and the powers of this act, vested in the lord mayor and aldermen, may, on their default, be exercised by the barons of the exchequer, who may issue their warrants, authorising persons to make the assessment and levy the same by distress and sale. *s.* 18.

But no ecclesiastical court shall hold cognizance in respect of any monies payable by this act. *s.* 19.

——— *Victuallers.*] By 31 *Ed.* 3. *stat.* 1. *c.* 10. the mayor and aldermen of London may reform the defaults of victuallers there, and all men may bring and sell victuals freely. Also 7 *Rich.* 2. *c.* 11.

By 6 *Rich.* 2. *c.* 10. alien friends may import victuals into London and elsewhere, and sell in gross or by retail.

By 1 *Hen.* 4. *c.* 17. the last act shall be duly executed, notwithstanding the patent to the fishmongers' company.

——— *Voucher.*] By 6 *Ed.* 1. *c.* 12. one impleaded in London, who vouches a foreigner to warranty, shall have execution from the justices.

——— *Wager of law.*] By 38 *Ed.* 3. *stat.* 1. *c.* 5. any man may wage his law against a Londoner's papers.

——— *Watermen*] By 2 & 3 *Phil. & Mar. c.* 16. eight watermen shall be chosen by the court of aldermen of London, for overseers to keep good order among the rest. Two watermen shall not ply in one boat, but where one of them hath exercised the profession two years, and been allowed by the overseers under the known seal, on pain of being sent to the compter for one month; and a single man, not retained as an apprentice or servant one year at least, shall not use the profession, on the like pain.

The mayor, aldermen, and justices, may, on complaint of the rulers, hear and determine offences against this act. *Ibid.*

Wherries shall be twelve feet and a half long, and four feet and a half broad in the midship, or be liable to forfeiture. *Ibid.*

Watermen absconding in the time of pressing shall be imprisoned when they return, and watermen's names shall be registered by the overseers. *Ibid.*

Western barges shall retain no single person but by the year on pain of 40*s.* *Ibid.*

The fares of watermen shall be assessed by the court of aldermen, and approved by two of the privy council. And overseers being negligent, or refusing the office, shall forfeit 5*l.* *Ibid.*

By 8 *Eliz. c.* 13. mariners licensed by the Trinity-house, may ply as watermen on the Thames.

By 1 *Jac.* 1. *c.* 16. watermen shall not retain any servant as hath not been apprentice to a waterman five years; and no apprentice under eighteen years of age, or for less than seven years, on pain of 10*l.*; but watermen's sons at the age of sixteen may carry passengers from place to place.

The rulers of the company shall every 1st September and 1st March, read their orders in the hall, on pain of 6*l.* 13*s.* 4*d.* *Ibid.*

By 11 & 12 *Will.* 3. *c.* 13. lightermen on the Thames, between Gravesend and Windsor, shall be of the society of watermen and wherrymen, who are hereby made a company.

The lord mayor and court of aldermen shall elect eight of the best watermen, and three of the best lightermen, yearly, to be overseers and rulers. The watermen shall choose assistants, not exceeding sixty, nor less than forty, and the lightermen nine, at the principal stairs, for preserving good government. Auditors of accounts are to be appointed; and the rulers, auditors, and assistants, may make rules to be observed under penalties. *Ibid.*

The lord mayor and aldermen, and justices of peace, on complaint of the overseers, may hear and determine offences. *Ibid.*

The rulers may appoint forty watermen to work on Sundays between Vauxhall and Limehouse, for carrying passengers across the river, at 1*d.* each, to be paid to the rulers, to the use of decayed watermen, their widows and children, allowing the watermen for their labour. *Ibid.*

By 4 & 5 *Ann. c.* 13. the 1 *Jac.* 1. *c.* 16. restraining the taking apprentices under eighteen and sixteen years of age, is repealed, and the lord mayor and aldermen may review and amend the bye-laws of the watermen's company.

By 2 *Geo.* 2. *c.* 26. no waterman on the river Thames shall take an apprentice, unless he be a housekeeper, or have some known place of abode, to be registered with the clerk of the company, on pain of 10*l.* and the apprentices may be turned over to other masters on neglect herein.

An apprentice shall not have the sole care of a boat till sixteen years of age, if a waterman's son; and if not, not till seventeen years of age; on pain of 10*l.* from the master. *Ibid.*

None but freemen shall work any boat, except fishermen and ballastmen, persons navigating western barges, mill boats, chalk hoys, wood lighters, dung boats, and gardeners' boats, on pain of 10*l.* *Ibid.*

Owners of quays betwixt Hermitage bridge and London bridge may use their lighters as heretofore. *Ibid.*

And by 4 *Geo.* 2. *c.* 24. ferry boats, flat bottomed boats, and barges, navigated from Kingston or Windsor, are exempted from the penalties. *Ibid.*

By 10 *Geo.* 2. *c.* 31. no apprentice shall be taken under fourteen years of age, nor above twenty, for seven years at least, by indentures enrolled; and not more than two apprentices at one time, the first to have served four years when the second is taken. The penalty hereon is 10*l.*

Nor shall the master or mistress take an apprentice unless they have a known place of habitation, and lodge the apprentice there, on pain of 10*l.* *Ibid.*

Owners of twelve barges or boats may

take two apprentices, and of twenty, four. *Ibid.*

No person working any tilt boat, or row barge, shall take in above thirty-seven passengers, and three by the way; nor in any other boat above eight passengers, and two by the way; on forfeiture of 5*l.* for the first offence, and 10*l.* for the second: and if any person be drowned, where a greater number is taken in, the waterman shall be guilty of felony, and may be transported. *Ibid.*

Tilt boats used between London bridge and Gravesend shall be fifteen tons, and not under, and other boats three tons, on pain of 10*l.* *Ibid.*

No Gravesend boats with close decks, or bails nailed down, shall be navigated, tilt boats excepted, on pain of 10*l.* *Ibid.*

Watermen losing their tide from Billingsgate to Gravesend, or back, the passengers shall be discharged from paying. *Ibid.*

The rulers of the watermen's company shall appoint two officers to attend at Billingsgate at high water, and at Gravesend at the first flood, who shall ring the tide bell; and if the watermen do not put off they shall forfeit 5*l.* *Ibid.*

The watermen's company not setting up such bells, or appointing persons to ring them, shall forfeit 50*l.* and the persons appointed neglecting to ring them, forfeit 40*s.* *Ibid.*

By 34 *Geo.* 3. *c.* 65. so much of 2 & 3 *Phil. & Mar.* *c.* 16. as subjects persons taking more than their fare to penalties, repealed. *s.* 1.

The court of mayor and aldermen of London are empowered to make rules for regulating the conduct and demeanor of watermen, wherrymen, and lightermen, upon the river Thames; which rules are to be approved and allowed by one or more of the judges, who may allow or alter the same. *s.* 2.

Copy of intended alterations and new rules to be sent to the watermen's company thirty days before allowed by the judges, and the company may submit their objections. *s.* 3.

The rules are to be printed and published. *s.* 4.

Power vested in the lord mayor, aldermen, and justices, to summon and apprehend watermen, and examine witnesses upon oath, and punish offenders by fine and imprisonment; but constables are not to take watermen out of boats or craft until moored, and notice hereof to be inserted in the warrant. *s.* 5, 6.

Power to summon parties on refusal of payment of fares, and apprehend them on non-appearance, and examine witnesses upon oath, and order payment. *s.* 7.

Persons refusing to pay fares, or to give their names and residence, or giving fictitious names or places of abode, shall forfeit not exceeding 5*l.* and may be summoned for the same, and also the loss of time and costs of the waterman. *s.* 8.

Overseers or rulers of the watermen's company to hear and determine complaints between waterman and waterman. *s.* 9.

Apprentices are to serve, in addition to the seven years for which they are bound, the space of time they shall be respectively imprisoned. *s.* 11.

The mayor, aldermen, and justices, may administer oaths, and on complaint may proceed to convict offenders, and apply within one month after levied, the whole thereof to the poor freemen and widows of the company, rewarding the informer with not exceeding one half thereof; but persons injured may appeal to the quarter sessions, from whence there is no *certiorari.* *s.* 12, 13, 14, 15.

But the prosecution must be commenced within six days. *s.* 16.

The act 24 *Geo.* 2. *c.* 44. for protecting justices, shall extend to justices and others acting under this act: notice to be given to peace officer before commencing suit against him: tender of amends may be made by him and pleaded in bar: if none or insufficient tender has been made, the plaintiff upon a verdict to recover. *s.* 18.

The act not to abridge the late duke of Richmond's right of holding a court at Gravesend, called *Curia Cursus Aquæ*, nor to lessen the liberties of the inhabitants of Gravesend, relating to the ferry from Gravesend to London, nor to abridge the powers of the master of the Trinity-house in licensing mariners, nor to affect the present laws, unless hereby expressly repealed. *s.* 19—21.

But persons convicted under this act not to be otherwise punished, and offenders not to be twice punished for the same offence. *s.* 22, 23.

——— *Weights and Measures.*] By 11 *Hen.* 6. *c.* 8. the mayor of London shall have power to execute the statutes touching weights and measures, and shall be sworn so to do.

The 1 *Ann. stat,* 1. *c.* 15. does not extend to sealed measures allowed by the fruiterer's company in London. See title *Weights and Measures*, post.

By 31 *Geo.* 2. *c.* 17. weights and measures within the city and liberty of Westminster shall be sized, sealed, and marked; otherwise may be destroyed as unlawful, and the owners amerced, not exceeding 40*s.* See general title.

——— *Westminster.*] By 7 & 8 *Will.* 3. *c.* 32. inhabitants of Westminster are exempted from serving on juries at the sessions of the peace for the county of Middlesex.

By 23 *Geo.* 2. *c.* 14. commissioners were to appoint a proper place for a market at Westminster, in lieu of the ancient market place.

By 29 *Geo.* 2. *c.* 25. eighty constables shall be appointed yearly for the city and liberty of Westminster out of the several parishes,

Leet jury to present fit persons out of each parish to serve as constables. Leet jury to continue in office one year. *Ibid.*

Fine of 40*s.* on persons summoned refusing to execute the office of jurymen. *Ibid.*

Persons refusing to attend, or serve as constables, to forfeit 8*l.* *Ibid.*

None may serve as high constable for more than three years together; refusing to serve the office forfeits 20*l.* *Ibid.*

A jury shall be summoned twice a year to enquire of and remove annoyances. *Ibid.* and 31 *Geo.* 2. *c.* 17.

By 31 *Geo.* 2. *c.* 17. repairs of pavements in Westminster, and removal of annoyances belonging to churches and public buildings, shall be done by the churchwardens; if belonging to markets, by the proprietors.

——— *Wine.*] By 6 *Ed.* 1. *c.* 15. the mayor and bailiffs of London shall enquire of wines sold against the assize.

By 26 *Geo.* 2. *c.* 12. no wine exceeding ten gallons, imported into the outports, shall be brought to London, or within twenty miles of the Royal Exchange, without paying the London duty and certificate. See titles *Importation, &c. Excise, &c. Wine.*

——— *Wood.*] By 23 *Eliz.* *c.* 5. no wood or underwood, growing within twenty-two miles of London, shall be employed for fuel for iron-works, on pain of 40*s.* a load: and no new iron-works shall be built within twenty-two miles of London, fourteen of the Thames, nor within four miles of the Downs, or Romsey, Winchelsea, Hastings, or Rye, on pain of 100*l.*

LONGELLUS, a coverlet. *Cowel.*

LONGITUDE of a place, in geography, is an arch of the equator intercepted between the first meridian, and the meridian passing through the proposed place, which is always equal to the angle at the pole, formed by the first meridian, and the meridian of the place. *Cowel.*

The first meridian may be placed at pleasure, passing through any place, as London, Paris, Teneriffe, &c. but with us it is generally fixed at London; and the degrees of longitude counted from it, will be either east, or west, according as they lie on the east or west side of that meridian. *Ibid.*

In other words, to explain the subject in a familiar manner, to those wholly unacquainted with it, as by the latitude we learn the distance north or south, so by knowing the longitude, we know the distance from any given place, east or west; allowing for the difference of a degree of longitude at the *equator* (or middle of the globe) and at the arctic circle, &c. *Ibid.*

The longitude is, as before described, in other words, the distance of a place, east or west, from that imaginary line drawn from north to south, through a place fixed on for that purpose, and called the first meridian, *i. e.* the meridian or boundary from whence we reckon, east or west, so that by ascertaining the latitude and longitude of a place, its situation on the natural or artificial globe, with respect to all other places, is known. *Ibid.*

For the discovery of the longitude at sea the following acts have been passed:

The 12 *Ann. sess.* 2. *c.* 85. and several subsequent acts, appointed commissioners of longitude to determine rewards to be given to persons making useful discoveries.

But 14 *Geo.* 3. *c.* 66. repealed all such acts (except as to the appointment of commissioners), and directed certain rewards to be given to discoverers of the longitude.

The first discoverer of a method to find the longitude, if by a time-keeper not yet discovered, shall receive 5000*l.* if it determines the same to one degree of a circle; 7,500*l.* if it determines to two thirds of that distance; and 10,000*l.* if it determines the same to one half of a degree. *Ibid.*

And if by means of improved solar and lunar tables, the discoverers shall have 5000*l.* if they shew the exact distance of the moon from the sun and stars, within fifteen seconds of a degree, answering to about seven minutes of longitude, allowing half a degree for errors of observation. *Ibid.*

The commissioners are to receive proposals for discovering the longitude, and certify the same, with the names of the authors, to the commissioners of the navy. *Ibid.*

Persons making useful discoveries shall receive less rewards, agreeably to the judgment of the commissioners, so as the sums do not exceed 5000*l.* and no person is to receive more for discoveries than the greatest sum hereby provided. *Ibid.*

The commissioners may administer oaths for carrying the act into execution. *Ibid.*

By 30 *Geo.* 3. *c.* 14. the secretaries of the admiralty are to be commissioners of the longitude. *s.* 3.

By 43 *Geo.* 3. *c.* 118. five commissioners of longitude may construct nautical almanacs (the president of the Royal Society and the royal astronomer being two); and grant licences for printing and publishing them, which being signed by such five commissioners, is valid. *s.* 1, 2.

The penalties of 20*l.* for each pirated copy, shall be sued for by the secretary of the commissioners. *s.* 3.

The commissioners shall certify the amount of debts incurred by them to the commissioners of the navy, who shall make out bills for their discharge. *s.* 4.

The commissioners shall certify to the navy-board, the fitness of trying experiments for discovery of the longitude; and also whether in their judgment any person is entitled to a less reward than under 14 *Geo.* 3. *c.* 68. for improvements; and the treasurer is to pay the bills made out by the navy board. *s.* 5.

But all such rewards shall not exceed

5000*l.*—rewards not exceeding 1000*l.* shall be certified by the longitude commissioners to the navy-board; and if above 1000*l.* the same must be certified by the first lord of the admiralty, the first commissioner of the navy, the president of the Royal Society, the royal astronomer, and the comptroller of the navy. *s.* 6, 7.

But by 46 *Geo.* 3. *c.* 77. the commissioners of longitude, are to certify the probability of success, of any proposal for discovering the longitude, to the commissioners of the navy, who are to order rewards to such persons, so as the sums paid exceed not 5000*l.* *s.* 1, 2.

LOQUELA, an imparlance. *Cowel. Blount.*

LORD, (*dominus*) is a word or title of honour, such as lords of parliament, and peers of the realm: by *courtesy*, as the eldest sons of peers, or lord chief justice, lord of the manor, lord paramount, and lord mesne, very lord, &c. *Ibid.*

LORD HIGH ADMIRAL. See *Admiral.*

LORD IN GROSS, *F. N. B. fol.* 3, is he that is lord, having no manor, as the king in respect of his crown. *Ibid. fol.* 5, and *fol.* 8.

LORD OF A MANOR. See *Copyhold.*

LORD AND VASSAL. In the time of feodal tenures the grantor of land was called the proprietor, or lord, being the person who retained the dominion, or ultimate property of the feud or fee: and the grantee, who had only the use of possession, according to the term of the grant, was styled the feudatory or vassal, another name for the tenant or holder of the lands. 2 *Black.* 53.

LORDS OF THE MARCHES. See *Wales.*

LORIMERS, (Fr. *lormiers*, from the Lat. *lorum*) is one of the companies of London, that make bits for bridles, spurs, and such like small iron ware, mentioned in stat. 1 *Ric.* 2, *c.* 12.

LOSINGA, a flatterer, or sycophant. *Cowel.*

LOT, a contribution, or duty. *Ibid.*

LOT, or LOTH, the thirteenth dish of lead in the mines of Derbyshire, which belongs to the king. *Ibid.*

LOTHERWITE, or LEYERWIT, was a liberty or privilege to take amends of him that defiled a bond-woman without license. *Cowel.*

LOTTERIES. By 10 & 11 *Will.* 3. *c.* 7. lotteries are declared public nuisances, and patents for the same void and against law.

Any person keeping a lottery to draw or throw at by lots, dice, cards, or otherwise, shall forfeit 500*l.* and any person who shall play, throw, or draw at such lottery, shall forfeit 20*l.* *Ibid.*

By 9 *Ann.* *c.* 6. magistrates and peace officers are to suppress such lotteries; and any person publishing schemes to draw, shall forfeit 100*l.*

By 10 *Ann.* *c.* 26. persons setting up offices for insurances on marriages, births, and christenings, under the denomination of sale of goods, for the improvement of small sums, shall forfeit 500*l.* and printers advertising the same shall forfeit 100*l.*

By 5 *Geo.* 1. *c.* 9. selling chances of any ticket in any public lottery, not having the original ticket, shall incur the forfeitures inflicted on private lotteries, and 100*l.* more.

By 8 *Geo.* 1. *c.* 2. persons setting up offices for sale of houses, lands, goods, or other things, by way of lottery, shall forfeit 500*l.* besides the other penalties; and the contributors to such sales shall forfeit double the sum contributed.

By 9 *Geo.* 1. *c.* 19. and 6 *Geo.* 2. *c.* 35. persons publishing, selling, or delivering tickets in any foreign lottery, shall forfeit 200*l.* over and above the penalties in former acts.

By 12 *Geo.* 2. *c.* 28. sales of houses, lands, or goods, by lottery or chance, shall be void, and the lands and goods forfeited.

Not to extend to any games in palaces where the king resides; nor to affect right to any lands held by partition, by lots. *Ibid.*

By 42 *Geo.* 3. *c.* 119. all games or lotteries called LITTLE GOES, are declared public nuisances. *s.* 1.

Persons keeping any office or place for any game or lottery, called a little go, or any other lottery not authorized by law, shall forfeit 500*l.* and be deemed rogues and vagabonds, within the meaning of 17 *Geo.* 2. *c.* 5.; and offenders not proceeded against for the penalty, shall be punishable as rogues and vagabonds. *s.* 2, 3.

Justices, on information of suspected places, may authorize persons to break open doors of places (but if at night, with a peace officer) where such offences are committed and apprehend the offenders; and persons obstructing the officers in the execution of their duty, shall be deemed offenders against the law, and, on conviction, fined, imprisoned, and publicly whipped; and persons, though not discovered in such places, who may employ others in the transaction, shall be deemed rogues and vagabonds. *s.* 4.

No person shall agree to pay money or deliver goods on any event relative to such game or lottery, or publish any proposal, on pain of 100*l.* *s.* 5.

Offenders may be apprehended on the spot by any one, and carried before a justice, who shall, on the penalty not being paid, commit them for six months, or till payment, without appeal; and one third of the penalty is to go to the king, one third to the informer, and one third to the person apprehending. *s.* 6.

The regulations of the acts 22 Geo. 3. c. 47. *and* 27 Geo. 3. c. 11. *respecting* STATE LOTTERIES, *have been repealed; and the provisions relating to such lotteries now depend on the clauses contained in the act, which annu-*

ally passes on the establishment of a State Lottery: the most material of which in the last, are the following:

No persons are to take down the numbers at the drawing, unless they be employed as clerks to the managers, or licensed so to do by the commissioners of stamps, who are to grant such licences only on account of licensed offices; and if any person unlicensed shall take down or publish the numbers drawn, he shall forfeit 5*l.* and on complaint thereof, the magistrates of London, or any justice, may grant warrants for apprehending the offenders: or persons in the actual commission of the offence may be apprehended by any person, and carried before a magistrate, who may commit the offender for not exceeding fourteen, nor less than five days, if the penalty be not paid, which penalty is to go between the informer and the constable apprehending the party; and persons summoned as witnesses not appearing are to forfeit 50*l.*: but the penalties may be mitigated, not less than one half besides costs, and the conviction is not removeable by *certiorari*. *s.* 21—24.

Persons before dealing in lottery tickets shall take out a stamp licence either in Great Britain or Ireland, and pay 50*l.* over and above all other duties as brokers or otherwise, which licence is to continue in force till the expiration of the drawing of the lotteries. *s.* 25, 26.

No licence is to be granted for any lottery office within the universities of Oxford and Cambridge. *s.* 27.

Licensed persons are to deposit and divide in shares thirty tickets in each of the lotteries, or the licence shall be void. *s.* 28.

Persons sharing tickets contrary to their licence, are to forfeit 100*l.* *s.* 29.

Persons to whom licences are granted, are to give security by bond in 1000*l.* to observe the provisions of the act. *s.* 30.

Upon death, the personal representatives may be authorized to carry on the business for the residue of the term of the licences. *s.* 31.

And persons convicted of offences, whether on a prosecution on the bond, or as rogues and vagabonds, shall forfeit their licence. *s.* 32.

Persons counterfeiting licences, or using such as are counterfeit, shall forfeit 500*l.* *s.* 33.

No chances of any tickets for any less time than the whole time of drawing shall be sold, or insurance made for or against the drawing of any ticket; nor shall any person publish any proposal for such purpose, on penalty of 50*l.* and if he be not licensed, he shall also be deemed a rogue and vagabond, and punished as such. *s.* 34.

If any person shall sell any shares divided otherwise than into halves, quarters, eighths, and sixteenths, he shall forfeit 50*l.* and be also deemed a rogue and vagabond. *s.* 35.

Persons counterfeiting shares, or selling the same, to be guilty of felony. *s.* 39.

Tickets intended to be sold in shares, are to be deposited with the commissioners of stamps, who are to stamp the shares, on payment to the receiver-general of 2*d.* for each share; and persons selling shares otherwise than on stamped paper, are to forfeit 50*l.* and be deemed rogues and vagabonds. *s.* 40—45.

Tickets, so deposited, shall continue in the hands of the receiver-general until three days after drawn, if not entitled to a greater prize than 50*l.* or until the expiration of fourteen days after drawn, if entitled to a greater prize than 50*l.* *s.* 46.

On complaint, on oath, of offences against the act, whereby the parties may be liable to punishment as rogues and vagabonds, the justices may authorize constables and others to break open doors; and persons discovered, in such places, carrying on illegal transactions, are to be punished as rogues and vagabonds; and if any person obstruct the officers, the justices, on conviction, may order the offender to be fined, imprisoned, and publicly whipped: and all persons employing or aiding others to carry on such illegal transactions, are to be deemed rogues and vagabonds. *s.* 52.

Penalties (not otherwise directed) may be recovered in the courts of exchequer in England, Scotland, and Ireland, in the name of the attorney-general, or advocate-general if in Scotland, and not in any other person's name. *s.* 54.

And in every such suit the offender may be held to bail, specifying in the copies the amount of the penalty, and so as the bail required exceed not 500*l.*; but when the amount of the penalty is not inserted in the writ, the defendant is only to be served with a copy. *s.* 54, 55.

Two justices may commit offenders, adjudged rogues and vagabonds, to the house of correction for not exceeding six calendar months, nor less than one, and until the final drawing of the lottery in which the offence shall be committed, which proceedings are not removeable by *certiorari*. *s.* 56.

LOURCURDUS, a ram, or bell-wether. *Cowel.*

LURGULARY, is the casting any corrupt or poisonous thing into the water, which was *lowrgulary*, and felony; and some think it a corruption of burglary. *Ibid.*

LOWBELLERS, (Sax. *low*, which signified a flame of fire) are such persons as go out in the night-time with a light and a bell, by the sight and noise whereof birds sitting upon the ground become stupefied, and so are covered and taken with a net. *Ibid.*

LOWBOTE, a recompense for the death of a man killed in a tumult, or, as we say, by the mob. *Ibid.*

LUDI DE REGE ET REGINA, playing at cards, so called because there are kings and queens in the pack. *Ibid.*

LUMINARE, a lamp or candle, set burning on the altar of any church or chapel, for the maintenance whereof lands and rent-charges were frequently given to parish churches, &c. *Kennet's Gloss.*

LUNATIC, a person who is sometimes of good and sound memory and understanding, and sometimes not. 1 *Inst.* 247. 3 *Inst.* 46. *H.P. C.* 10.43. 1 *Hawk. P. C.* 2. 43. *Plowd.* 19. *Keyl.* 53. See *Ideots* and *Lunatics.*

LUNDA, a weight formerly used here. *Cowel. Blount.*

LUNDRESS, a sterling silver penny, which had its name from being coined only at London, and not at the country mints. *Lownd's Essay on Coin*, p. 17.

LUPANATRIX, a bawd or strumpet. 3 *Inst.* 206.

LUPINUM CAPUT GERERE, (*to carry a wolf's head*) signified to be outlawed, and have the head exposed, like a wolf's, with a reward to him who should bring it in. *Plac. Coron.* 4. *Cowel.*

LUPLICETUM, (Lat.) a hop-garden, or place where hops grow. 1 *Inst.* 4.

LUSHBURGHS, or LUXENBURGHS, was a base sort of foreign coin, made of the likeness of English money, and brought into England *anno Ed.* 3. *Cowel. Blount.*

LUXURY. There were formerly various laws to restrain excess in apparel, all repealed by stat. 1 *Jac.* 1, *c.* 25.

LYEF-YELD, LEF-SILVER, a small fine or pecuniary composition, paid by the customary tenant, to the lord for leave to plough or sow. *Cowel.*

LYMPUTTA, a lime-pit. *Ibid.*

LYNDEWODE, a doctor both of the civil and canon laws, and dean of the arches. Ambassador for *Hen.* 5, into Portugal, *anno* 1422. *Ibid.*

M

M, the letter with which persons convicted of manslaughter were formerly marked on the brawn of the left thumb. 4 *Hen.* 7. *c.* 13.

MAC, amongst the Irish and Scotch, signifies a son, *filius.*

MACE-GRIEFE, or MACE-GREFFS, (*Machecarii*) such as willingly buy and sell stolen flesh, knowing the same to be stolen, *Britt. cap.* 29. *Cromp. Just.* 193. *Leg. Inæ. cap.* 20.

MACECARIA, MACHEKUNA, (*Macella*) the flesh-market, or shambles. *Cowel.*

MACHECARIUS, a butcher. *Cowel.*

MACHECOLLARE, or MACHECOULARE, (from the Fr. *Maschecoulis*) to make a warlike device, especially over the gate of a castle, resembling a grate, through which scalding water, or offensive things may be thrown on pioneers or assailants. 1 *Inst.* 5, *a.*

MACIO, a mason. *Cowel.*

MACKAREL, may be sold on Sunday. 10 & 11 *Wil.* 3, *c.* 24.

MADDER. By 31 *Geo.* 2, *c.* 12, persons convicted of stealing or destroying any madder-roots, are for the first offence, to make such satisfaction for the damages as the justices of peace shall appoint, and pay a fine, not exceeding 10*s.* and for the second offence be imprisoned three months.

MAD-HOUSES. See *Ideots* and *Lunatics.*

MADNING-MONEY, old Roman coins, found about Dunstable. *Cowel.*

MADRIGALS, country songs. *Cowel.*

MAEREMIUM, (from the Fr. *meresme*) any sort of timber fit for building. *Ibid.*

MAGBOTE, or MÆGBOTE, (from the Sax. *Mæg*, i. e. *cognatus*, and *bote*, *compensatio*) a compensation for the slaying or murder of one's kinsman, in ancient times, when corporal punishments for murder, &c. were sometimes commuted into pecuniary fines, if the friends and relations of the party killed were so satisfied. *Leg. Canuti*, *c.* 2.

MAGIC, (*Magia, necromantia*) witchcraft and sorcery. See *Conjuration. Vagrants.*

MAGISTER. This title, often found in

old writings, signified that the person to whom attributed had attained some degree of eminency *in scientia aliqua, præfertim literaria;* and formerly those who are now called doctors were termed *magistri*. *Cowel.*

MAGISTRATE, (*Magistratus*) a ruler. See *Justice of the Peace*.

MAGNA ASSISA ELIGENDA, is a writ directed to the sheriff, to summon four lawful knights before the justices of assise, there upon their oaths to choose 12 knights of the vicinage, to pass upon the great assise, between A. B. plaintiff, and C. D. defendant, &c. *Reg. Orig.* 8.

MAGNA CHARTA, the great charter of liberties granted in the ninth year of king *Hen.* 3. See *Liberties* and *Rights*.

MAGNA PRECARIA, a great or general reap-day. *Cowel. Blount.*

MAGNUM CENTUM, the great hundred, or six score. *Ibid.*

MAGNUS PORTUS, the town and port of Portsmouth. *Ibid.*

MAHOMERIA, the temple of Mahomet. *Ibid.*

MAIDS. See *Abduction*.

MAIDEN ASSISES. When no person is condemned to die at a circuit-town, it is termed a maiden assise.

MAIDEN RENTS, a noble paid by every tenant in the manor of Builth, in Com. Radnor, at their marriage; anciently given to the lord for his omitting the custom of Marcheta, whereby he was to have the first night's lodging with his tenant's wife; but it was more probably a fine for a licence to marry a daughter. *Cowel. Blount.*

MAIGNAGIUM, (Fr. *maignen*, i. e. *faber ærarius*) a brazier's shop, though some say it signifies a house. *Ibid.*

MAIHEM, or MAYHEM, (*maihemium*, from the Fr. *mehaigne*, i. e. *membri mutilationem*) signifies a maim, wound, or corporal hurt, by which a man loses the use of any member, that is or might be of any defence to him: As, if a man's skull be broke, or any bone broken in any other part of the body; a foot, hand, finger, or joint of a foot, or any member be cut off, if by any wound the sinews be made to shrink; or where any one is castrated; or if an eye be put out, any fore-tooth broke. &c. *Glanv. lib.* 4, *cap.* 7. *Bract. lib.* 3, *tract.* 2. *Britton, cap.* 25. *S. P. C. lib.* 1, *cap.* 41. See *Assault*, *Battery*, and *Felony*.

MAII INDUCTIO, an ancient custom for the priest and people of country villages to go in procession to some adjoining wood on a May-day morning, and return in a kind of triumph, with a may-pole boughs, flowers, garlands, and other tokens of the spring. This May-game, or rejoicing at the coming of the spring, was for a long time observed, and still is in some parts of England; but there was thought to be so much heathen vanity in it that it was condemned and prohibited within the diocese of Lincoln by bishop Grosthead. *Cowel. Blount.*

MAIL, (*macula*) a coat of mail, so called from the Fr. *maille*, which signifies a square figure, or the hole of a net. *Ibid.*

MAILE, anciently a kind of money; and silver halfpence were termed mailes. 9 *H.* 5. See *Northern Borders*.

MAIMING. See *Maihem*.

MAINAD, a false oath, or perjury. *Cowel. Blount.*

MAINE-PORT, (*in manu portatum*) was a small tribute, commonly of loaves of bread, which in some places the parishioners paid to the rector of their church, in recompense for certain tithes. *Cowel.*

MAINOVRE, (from the Fr. *main*, i. e. *manus*, and *ouvrer*, *operari*) handy work, or some trespass committed by a man's hand. *Ibid.*

MAINOUR, MANOUR, or MEINOUR, (from the F. *manier*, i. e. *manu tractare*) in a legal sense denotes the thing that a thief taken away, or stealeth: As to be taken with the *mainour*, (*Pl. Cor. fol.* 179) is to be taken with the thing stolen about him; or as if it were in his hand. *Ibid.*

MAINPERNABLE, that may be let to bail. See *Bail*.

MAINPERNORS, (*manucaptores*) are those persons to whom a man is delivered out of custody or prison, on their becoming bound for his appearing. See *Bail*.

MAINPRISE, (*manucaptio*, from the Fr. *main*, i. e. *manus*, and *pris*, *captus*) signifies in our law the taking or receiving of a person into friendly custody who otherwise might be committed to prison, upon security given that he shall be forth-coming at a time and place assigned; as to let one to mainprise is to commit him to those that undertake he shall appear at a day appointed. *Old Nat. Br.* 42. *F. N. B.* 249. And there is this difference between mainprise and bail: he that is mainprised is said to be at large, after the day he is set to mainprise, until the day of his appearance; but where a man is let to bail by any judge, &c. until a certain day, there he is always accounted by the law to be in their ward for the time; and they may, if they will, keep him in prison, so that he that is so bailed shall not be said to be at large, or at his own liberty. *Manwood.* p. 167.

But a man under mainprise is supposed to go at large, under no possibility of being confined by his sureties or mainpernors, as in case of bail. 4 *Inst.* 179.

MAINSWORN, in the North of England, is taken for as much as forsworn. *Brownl.* 4. *Cowel.*

MAINTAINORS, are those that maintain or second a cause depending between others, by disbursing money, or making friends, for either party, or the like, not being interested in the suit, or attornies employed therein. Stat. 19 *Hen.* 7, *c.* 14.

MAINTENANCE, (*manutenentia*) signifies the unlawful upholding of a cause or person.

Maintenance is an offence that bears a near relation to BARRATRY, (*which see*) being an officious intermeddling in a suit that no way belongs to one, by maintaining or assisting either party with money, or otherwise, to prosecute or defend it; (*Hawk. P. C.* 249) a practice that was greatly encouraged by the first introduction of uses. (*Doct. & Stud.* 203.) This is an offence against public justice, as it keeps alive strife and contention, and perverts the remedial process of the law into an engine of oppression. And therefore by the Roman law it was a species of the *crimen falsi* to enter into any confederacy, or do any act to support another's lawsuit, by money, witnesses, or patronage (*Ff.* 48, 10, 20). A man may however maintain the suit of his near kinsman, servant, or poor neighbour, out of charity and compassion, with impunity. Otherwise the punishment by the common law is fine and imprisonment (1 *Hawk. P. C.* 255); and by the stat. 32 *Hen.* 8, *c.* 9, a forfeiture of 10*l.* See also *Buying and Selling pretended Titles*, and *Champerty*.

MAJORITY. The only method of determining the acts of many is by a majority; and the act of a majority, however, or when collected, is the act of the whole.

MAIOR, a mayor, does not come from the Lat. *major*, but from an old English word *maier*, i. e. *potestas*. *Cowel.*

MAISNADA, signifies a family, *quasi mansionata*. *Ibid.*

MAISON DE DIEU, a monastery, hospital, or alms-house. *Cowel. Blount.*

MAISURA, a house or mansion; a farm; from the Fr. *maison*. *Ibid.*

MAJUS JUS, is a writ or law proceeding in some customary manors, in order to a trial of right of land. *Ibid.*

MAKE, (*facere*) signifies to perform or execute, as to make his law, is to perform that law which he hath formerly bound himself to; that is, to clear himself of an action commenced against him by his oath, and the oaths of his neighbours. *Old Nat. Brev.* 161. *Kitchen*, 192. See *Wager of Law.*

MAKE SERVICES AND CUSTOMS, signifies nothing but to perform them. *Old Nat. Brev.* 14.

MALA, a male, or port-mail, a bag to carry letters. *Ibid. Cowel.*

MALA IN SE, are acts unlawful and bad in themselves, as theft, murder, perjury, and the like.

MALANDRINUS, a thief, or pirate. *Cowel. Blount.*

MALA PROHIBITA, offences become so by positive, written, restrictive rules of law, without reference to their moral guilt, by the interference of the legislature by statute: these are contradistinguished from *mala in se*, which are clearly restricted and punished in all civilized countries as by our common law, on principles of sound reason.

MALBERGE, *mons placiti*, a hill where the people assembled at a court, like our assises, which by the Scotch and Irish are called parley-hills. *Du Cange. Cowel.*

MALE-CREDITUS, one of bad credit, suspected, and not to be trusted. *Ibid.*

MALEDICTION, (*maledictio*) a curse, which was anciently annexed to donations of lands, made to churches and religious houses. *Ibid.*

MALEFEASANCE, (from the Fr. *malfaire*, i. e. to offend) is a doing of evil, or transgressing. 2 *Cro.* 266.

MALESWORN, in the North, signifies as much as forsworn. *Brownl. Rep.* 4. *Hobart's Rep.* 8.

MALETENT, is interpreted to be a toll for every sack of wool by statute. *Ibid.*

MALICE. See *Homicide. Murder.*

MALICIOUS MISCHIEF. See *Felony. Trespass.*

MALIGNARE, the same as to maim any one. *Cowel. Blount.*

MALIGNUS, i. e. *diabolus: pro dolor, hunc pepulit propria de sede malignus. Ibid.*

MALO GRATO, the doing a thing unwillingly.

MALT-MULNA, a quern, or malt-mill. *Cowel. Blount.*

MALT-SHOT, malt-scot, some payment for making malt. *Ibid.*

MALVEILLES, (from the Fr. *malvoillance*) is used in our ancient records for crimes and misdemeanors, or malicious practices. *Ibid.*

MALVEISA, a warlike engine to batter and beat down walls. *Ibid.*

MALVEISIN, (Fr. *mauvaise voisin, malus vicinus*) an ill neighbour. *Ibid.*

MALVEIS PROCURORS, such as used to pack juries. *Ibid.*

MALUM IN SE. See *Mala in se.*

MAN (ISLE OF). The isle of Man is a distinct territory from England, and is not governed by our laws; neither doth any act of parliament extend to it, unless it be particularly named therein, and then an act of parliament is binding there (4 *Inst.* 284. 2 *And.* 116). It was formerly a subordinate feudatory kingdom, subject to the kings of Norway; then to king John and Henry III. of England; afterward to the kings of Scotland, and then again to the crown of England; and at length we find king Henry IV. claiming the island by right of conquest, and disposing of it to the earl of Northumberland, upon whose attainder it was granted (by the name of the lordship of Man) to sir John de Stanley by letters patent, 7 Henry IV. (*Selden. tit. Hon.* 1, 3.) In his lineal descendants it continued for eight generations, till the death of Ferdinando earl of Derby, A. D. 1594, when a controversy arose concerning the inheritance thereof, between his daughters and sir William his surviving brother; upon which, and a doubt that was started concerning the validity of the original patent (*Camd. Eliz. ann.* 1594), the island was seized into the queen's hands, and afterwards various grants were made of it by king James I. all which being expired or surrendered, it was granted afresh, in 7 Jac. I. to William earl of Derby, and the heirs male of his body, with remainder to his heirs general, which grant was the next year confirmed by act of parliament, with a restraint of the power of alienation by the said earl and his issue male. On the death of James earl of Derby, 1735, the male line of earl William failing, the duke of Atholl succeeded to the island as heir general by a female branch. In the mean time, though the title of king had long been disused, the earls of Derby, as lords of Man, had maintained a sort of royal authority therein, by assenting or dissenting to laws, and exercising an appellate jurisdiction: yet, though no English writ, or process from the courts of Westminster, was of any authority in Man, an appeal laid from a decree of the lord of the island to the king of Great Britain in council (1 *P. Wms.* 329). But the distinct jurisdiction of this little subordinate royalty being found inconvenient for the purposes of public justice, and for the revenue, (it affording a commodious asylum for debtors, outlaws, and smugglers,) authority was given to the Treasury by statute 12 *Geo.* 1, *c.* 28, to purchase the interest of the then proprietors for the use of the crown, which purchase was at length completed in the year 1765, and confirmed by statutes 5 *Geo.* 3, *c.* 26, called the vesting act, and 39, called the regulating act; whereby the whole island, and all its dependencies, so granted as aforesaid, (except the landed property of the Atholl family, their manorial rights and emoluments, and the patronage of the bishopric *, and other ecclesiastical benefices) are unalienably vested in the crown, and subjected to the regulations of the British excise and customs.

MANA, signified formerly an old woman. *Cowel. Blount.*

MANAGIUM, (from the Fr. *manage*, a dwelling or inhabiting) a mansion-house, or dwelling-place. *Ibid.*

MANBOTE, (Sax.) a compensation or recompense for homicide; particularly due to the lord for killing his man or vassal. *Ibid.*

MANCA, was a square piece of gold coin, commonly valued at thirty pence, and *mancusa* was as much as a mark of silver, having its name from *manu-cusa*, being coined with the hand. *Leg. Canut. Spel. Cowel. Blount.*

MANCH, is sixty shekels of silver, or seven pounds and ten shillings; and one hundred shekels of gold, of seventy-five pounds. *Merch. Dict. Cowel.*

MANCIPLE, (*manseps*) a clerk of the kitchen, or caterer; and an officer in the Inner Temple was anciently so called, who is now the steward there, this officer still remains in colleges, in the universities. *Cowel.*

MANDAMUS, a writ of mandamus is, in general, a command issuing in the king's name from the court of king's bench, and directed to any person, corporation, or inferior court of judicature, within the king's dominions, requiring them to do some particular therein specified, which appertains to their office and duty, and which the court of king's bench has previously determined, or at least supposes, to be consonant to right and justice. It is a high prerogative writ, of a most extensively remedial nature, and may be issued in some cases where the injured party has also another more tedious method of redress, as in the case of admission or restitution to an office; but it issues in all cases where the party hath a right to have any thing done, and hath no other specific means of compelling its performance. A mandamus therefore lies to compel the admission or restoration of the party applying, to any office or franchise of a public nature, whether spiritual or temporal; to academical degrees; to the use of a meeting-house, &c. It lies for the production, inspection, or delivery of public books and papers; for the surrender of the regalia of a corporation; to oblige bodies corporate to affix their common seal; to compel the holding of a court; and for an infinite number of other purposes, which it is impossible to recite minutely. But it may suffice to remark, that it issues to the judges of any inferior court, commanding them to do justice according to the powers of their office, whenever the same is delayed. For it is the peculiar business of the court of king's bench to superintend all other inferior tribunals, and therein to enforce the due exercise of those judicial or ministerial powers with which the crown or legislature have invested them; and this, not only by restraining their excesses, but also by quickening their negligence, and obviating their denial of justice. A mandamus may therefore be had to the courts of the city of London to enter up judgment (*Raym.* 214); to the spiritual courts to grant an administra-

* The bishopric of Man, or Sodor, or Sodor and Man, was formerly within the province of Canterbury, but annexed to that of York by stat. 33 *Hen.* 8, *c.* 31.

tion, to swear a churchwarden, and the like. This writ is grounded on a suggestion, by the oath of the party injured, of his own right, and the denial of justice below; whereupon, in order more fully to satisfy the court that there is a probable ground for such interposition, a rule is made, (except in some general cases, where the probable ground is manifest,) directing the party complained of to show cause why a writ of mandamus should not issue: and if he shows no sufficient cause the writ itself is issued, at first in the alternative, either to do thus, or signify some reason to the contrary; to which a return or answer must be made at a certain day. And if the inferior judge, or other person to whom the writ is directed, returns or signifies an insufficient reason, then there issues, in the second place, a peremptory mandamus to do the thing absolutely, to which no other return will be admitted, but a certificate of perfect obedience and due execution of the writ. If the inferior judge or other person makes no return, or fails in his respect and obedience, he is punishable for his contempt by attachment. But, if he, at the first, returns a sufficient cause although it should be false in fact, the court of king's bench will not try the truth of the fact upon affidavits; but will for the present believe him, and proceed no farther on the mandamus. But then the party injured may have an action against him for his false return, and (if found to be false by the jury) shall recover damages equivalent to the injury sustained; together with a peremptory mandamus to the defendant to do his duty. 3 *Black.* 110. *Com. Dig. tit. Man.*

Mandamus was also a writ that laid after the year and day, where in the mean time the writ, called *diem clausit extremum*, had not been sent out to the escheator, on the death of the king's tenant *in capite*, &c. And was likewise a writ or charge to the sheriff to take into the hands of the king all the lands and tenements of the king's widow-tenant, who against her oath married without his consent. *F. N. B.* 253. *Reg. Orig.* 195. See *F. N. B.* 561. *Dyer.* 209. *pl.* 19, 248. *pl.* 81. *Lamb.* 36. See also *Corporations*, and *Quo Warranto*.

MANDATARY, (*mandatarius*) is he to whom a command or charge is given. *Cowel.*

MANDATE, (*mandatum*) Is a commandment judicial of the king, or his justices, to have any thing done for the dispatch of justice, of which there is great diversity. *Reg. Judic.* And we read of the bishop's mandate to the sheriff, &c. Stat. 31 *Eliz. c.* 9. A mandate may be issued by the King's Bench to swear a churchwarden, or parish clerk, &c. when refused to be sworn by the bishop's minister. *March. Rep.* 22, 101. But see *Mandamus.*

MANDATI DIES, (*Mandie* or Maunday Thursday) The day before *Good Friday*, when is commemorated and practised the command of our Saviour, in washing the feet of the poor, &c. And our Kings of England, to show their humility, long executed the ancient custom on that day, of washing the feet of poor men, in number equal to the years of their reign, and giving them shoes, stockings and money. *Cowel.*

MANDATO PANES, loaves of bread given to the poor upon Maunday Thursday. *Ibid.*

MANENTES, was anciently used for tenentes or tenants. *Ibid.*

MANGONARE, to buy in the market. *Ibid.*

MANGONELLUS, a warlike instrument made to cast small stones against the walls of a castle. *Cowel.*

MANHOOD. See *Age.*

MANIPULUS, was an handkerchief which priests always had in their left hands. *Blount.*

MANNER, (from the Fr. *manier*, or *mainer*, i. e. *manu tractare*,) to be taken with the manner, is where a thief having stolen any thing, is taken with the same about him, as it were in his hands; which is called *flagrante delicto*. *S. P. C.* 179. *H. P. C.* 201. *S. P. C.* 28. 2 *Hawk. P. C.* 211.

MANNING, (*manopera*) a day's work of a man, and in ancient deeds there was sometimes reserved so much rent, and so many mannings. *Cowel.*

MANNIRE, was where one was cited to appear in court, and stand to judgment there, and different from *bannire*; for though both of them signify a citation, one is by the adverse party, and the other by the judge. *Leg. Hen.* 1, *c.* 10. *Du Cange. Cowel.*

MANNOPUS, (*manopera*) goods taken in the hands of an apprehended thief. *Cowel.*

MANNUS, a horse, a pad, or saddle-horse. *Cowel.*

MANOR, (*manerium*) seems to be derived of the Fr. *manoir*, *habitatio*, or rather from *manendo*, of abiding there, because the lord did usually reside there.

Manors are in substance as antient as the Saxon constitution, though perhaps differing a little, in some immaterial circumstances, from those that exist at this day. *Co. Cop. s.* 2. & 10.

A manor therefore seems to have been a district of ground, held by lords or great personages; who kept in their own hands so much land as was necessary for the use of their families, which were called *terræ dominicales*, or *demense* lands; being occupied by the lord, or *dominus manerii*, and his servants. The other, or *tenemental*, lands they distributed among their tenants: which from the different modes of tenure were distinguished by two different names. First, book-land, or charter land, which was held by deed under certain rents, and free-services, and in effect differed nothing from free socage lands (*Co. Cop. s.* 3.), and from hence have arisen most of the freehold tenants who hold of particular manors, and owe suit and service to the same. The other species was called folk-land, which was held by no assurance in writing, but distributed among the common folk or people at the pleasure of the lord, and resumed at his discretion. The residue of the manor being uncultivated, was termed the lord's waste, and served for public roads, and for common of pasture to the lord and his tenants. Manors were formerly called baronies, as they still are lordships: and each lord or baron was empowered to hold a domestic court, called the court-baron, for redressing misdemeanors and nusances within the manor, and for settling disputes of property among the tenants. This court is an inseparable ingredient of every manor; and if the number of suitors should so fail as not to leave sufficient to make a jury or homage, that is, two tenants at the least, the manor itself is lost. *Kitch. fo.* 4. *Brac. lib.* 4, *c.* 31. *Co. Lit.* 58.

MANSE, (*mansa*) an habitation, or farm and land. *Spelm. Cowel.*

MANSER, a bastard. *Cowel.*

MANSION, (*mansio a manendo*) the lord's chief dwelling-house within his fee, otherwise called the capital messuage, or manor-place. *Skene.*

And it is taken in law for the dwelling of another. 3 *Co. Inst.* 64.

MANSLAUGHTER, (*homicidium*, from the Sax. *manslyte*) See *Homicide.*

MANSTEALING or KIDNAPPING. See *Abduction.*

MANSUM CAPITALE, the manor-house. *Cowel.*

MANSURA and MASURA, *mansiones vel habitacula villicorum. Ibid.*

MANSUS, anciently a farm. *Ibid.*

MANSUS PRESBYTERI, the manse or house of residence of the parish priest; being the parsonage or vicarage-house. *Par. Antiq.* 431.

MANTHEOF, (from the Lat. *mannus*, a nag, and Sax. *theoff*, i. e. a thief) signified, anciently, an horse-stealer. *Cowel.*

MANTILE, is a long robe; from the Fr. word *manteau*, mentioned in the stat. 24 *H.* 8. *c.* 13.

MANUALIA BENEFICIA, were the daily distributions of meat and drink to the canons and other members of cathedral churches, for their present subsistence. *Ibid.*

MANUALIS OBEDIENTIA, used for sworn obedience, or submission upon oath. *Ibid.*

MANUCAPTIO, a writ that lay for a man taken on suspicion of felony, &c. who could not be admitted to bail by the sheriff, or others having power to let to mainprise. *F. N. B.* 249.

MANUAL, (*manualis*) signifies what is employed or used by the hand, and whereof a present profit may be made: as such a thing in the manual occupation of one, is where it is actually used or employed by him. *Staundf. Prerog.* 54.

MANUFACTURES, are commodities produced by the work of the hand; as cloth, and the like. *Merch. Dict.*

And the following is a summary of the acts relating to manufactures and manufactories:

——— *General Provisions in different Manufactures.*] By 1 *Ann. stat.* 2. *c.* 18. (made perpetual by 9 *Ann. c.* 30.) and 13 *Geo.* 2. *c.* 8. persons employed in the woollen, linen, fustian, cotton, or iron manufactures, embezzling the same, shall forfeit double damages, or be imprisoned till satisfaction made, which, if not done, they are to be publicly whipped; and persons buying or receiving such goods embezzled, are liable to the like punishment.

Labourers and workmen shall be paid in money; and all wool to be wrought, shall be delivered out by just weight, on pain of double damages. *Ibid.*

Two justices may determine offences against this act, with liberty of appeal to the quarter sessions. *Ibid.*

By 5 *Geo.* 1. *c.* 27. persons convicted within twelve months of contracting with, or enticing, any artificer in wool, iron, steel, brass, or other metal, clock-maker, watch-maker, or other artificer, to go into a foreign country, shall be fined not more than 100*l.* for the first offence, and be imprisoned for three months; and for the second offence, shall be fined discretionally, and be imprisoned for twelve months.

Any such artificer going into a foreign country, there to exercise his trade, and not returning in six months after warning given him by the ambassador, shall be incapable of being an executor, or taking any legacy or devise, and shall forfeit all his lands and goods, and be deemed an alien. *Ibid.*

Any justice of peace may, on complaint of any offence against this act, apprehend the offender, and bind him to appear at the assizes or sessions: if he refuses, he may be committed; and persons convicted shall give security not to depart the kingdom, or be committed. *Ibid.*

Such offences in Scotland may be determined in the court of justiciary, or the circuits. *Ibid.*

By 13 *Geo.* 2. *c.* 8. and 22 *Geo.* 2. *c.* 27. manufacturers shall complete the work in which they were hired, or be sent to the house of correction.

Persons convicted of buying or receiving materials from workmen in manufactories, to forfeit 20*l.* for the first offence, and on non-payment to be committed and whipped;

and on subsequent offence to forfeit 40*l.* *Ibid.*

By 22 *Geo.* 2. *c.* 27. workmen not returning the materials not used in manufacturing, to suffer the punishment for embezzling.

The provisions in 12 *Geo.* 1. *c.* 34. (see the title *Woollen*) to prevent combinations of workmen in the woollen manufactures, are extended to persons employed as hatters, dyers, hotpressers, or in the manufactures of silk, mohair, fur, hemp, flax, linen, cotton, fustian, iron, or leather. *Ibid.*

By 23 *Geo.* 2. *c.* 13. persons convicted of seducing artificers in the manufactures of Great Britain or Ireland, out of the dominions of Great Britain, shall forfeit 500*l.* and be imprisoned twelve months; and for a second offence, shall forfeit 1000*l.* and be imprisoned for two years.

Persons exporting utensils of the woollen and silk manufactures, shall forfeit the tools and 200*l.* *Ibid.*

By 14 *Geo.* 3. *c.* 71. for exporting tools and utensils used in the cotton, linen, woollen or silk manufactures (*wool cards of 4s. and spinners' cards of 1s. 6d. value excepted,* 26 *Geo.* 3. *c.* 76.), is a forfeiture of the goods, and penalty of 200*l.* one half to the king, and the other to the prosecutor (to be levied by distress, and the offender to be committed for a month, 15 *Geo.* 3. *c.* 14.

Manufacturers of wool or linen shall be allowed a drawback of so much as is paid on home-made soap, for all soap used by them, whether imported or made in this kingdom. *c.* 73.

The 17 *Geo.* 3. *c.* 56. altered the punishment of 22 *Geo.* 2. of workmen in the woollen, hat, linen, fustian, cotton, iron, leather, fur, hemp, flax, mohair, and silk manufactures, for embezzling materials, and for receiving the same, or not performing their engagements; and two justices may grant a warrant to search for embezzled materials.

The punishment, under this act, for the first offence, is a penalty of not more than 40*l.* nor less than 20*l.* or commitment and whipping; and for a second offence from 50*l.* to 100*l.* or commitment and whipping.

——— *Buttons.*] By 4 & 5 *W.* & *M.* *c.* 10. foreign buttons made of hair, or other foreign buttons, shall not be imported, upon pain of forfeiting the same, and also 100*l.* Selling such buttons is a forfeiture of 50*l.*

By 10 *W.* 3. *c.* 2. buttons shall not be made, sold, or set upon any cloths, if formed out of cloth, serge, drugget, freeze, camlet, stuffs, or wood, under the penalty of 40*s.* per dozen.

By 8 *Ann.* *c.* 6. tailors or others, making, setting on, selling, or binding on any clothes, buttons, or button-holes, make of serge or other stuff, incur a penalty of 5*l.* per dozen.

By 4 *Geo.* 1. *c.* 7. no tailor shall make, sell, or set on any buttons or button-holes, made of cloth, serge, or the like, on any clothes whatsoever, on penalty of 40*s.* per dozen, if prosecuted within three months.

Persons dwelling in gaols are liable to the penalties for offending. *Ibid.*

Such clothes exposed to sale may be seized; and tailors causing their servants to make clothes contrary hereto, shall be subject to the penalties. *Ibid.*

By 7 *Geo.* 1. *c.* 12. no person shall wear, on any clothes, buttons made of cloth, or as above, on penalty of 40*s* per dozen, to be convicted before one justice, within a month.

Clothes made of velvet are excepted out of the acts.

By 36 *Geo.* 3. *c.* 60. persons putting false marks on gilt or plated buttons, shall forfeit the same, and 5*l.* for not exceeding twelve dozen, and at the rate of 1*l.* for every further twelve dozen. *s.* 1.

No marks are to be used but such as truly express the real quality of the buttons, on a like forfeiture and penalty. *s.* 2.

None shall mark any other than the words *gilt* or *plated* upon metal buttons, on pain of forfeiture thereof, with 5*l.* for any quantity exceeding one dozen, 5*l.* for not exceeding twelve dozen, and 1*l.* for every further dozen. *s.* 3.

But persons may mark the words *double gilt* and *treble gilt* upon metal buttons, if they are in fact so. *s.* 4.

If any person shall make out a false invoice, expressing other than the real quality of the buttons, he shall forfeit 20*l.* *s.* 5.

Persons mixing buttons of different qualities, are to forfeit the same and 5*l.* for every quantity not exceeding twelve dozen, and 1*l.* for every further twelve dozen *s.* 6.

The penalties are recoverable before two justices; but the same may be mitigated, so as not to be reduced to less than half, or where they shall be less than 40*l.* below 20*l.*; or the said penalties may be recovered by action. *s.* 8—14.

But the information or action must be laid or brought within three calendar months, *s.* 15; and the penalties go, one half to the poor, and the other to the informer, *s.* 17; and parishioners may be witnesses, *s.* 16; and any justice may, by warrant, cause the buttons to be seized and produced in evidence, and afterwards destroyed. *s.* 14.

Persons disclosing by whose order any thing punishable under this act was done, shall not be liable to any penalty for doing it, *s.* 18. Manufacturers are also not liable, if they prove that they ordered the gilder to conform to the act, *s.* 19. The act does not extend to buttons of mixed metals, or Bath or white metal buttons, inlaid with steel, or set in shells. *s.* 20.

——— *Clocks and Watches.*] By 9 & 10 *W.* 3. *c.* 28. no case or dial plate, for clock or watch, shall be exported without the movement, nor made up without engraving the maker's name, on forfeiture thereof, and also 20*l.*

By 27 *Geo.* 2. *c.* 7. persons employed in the manufacturing of clocks and watches, pawning, embezzling, or making away with any of the materials, shall forfeit 20*l.* for the first offence, and, on non-payment thereof, be imprisoned fourteen days; and if the penalty is not paid within two days before the expiration of that time, the offender is to be publicly whipped: for the second, and every subsequent offence, the penalty is 40*l.* and imprisonment for not more than three months, nor less than one; and if such penalty is not paid within seven days before the expiration of such imprisonment, the offender is in like manner to be publicly whipped.

Persons buying, receiving, or taking by way of gift, pawn, or exchange, any such goods or materials, knowing them to be purloined, are subject to the same penalties. *Ibid.*

——— *Cotton.*] By 13 *Geo.* 2. *c.* 8. persons employed in that manufacture, embezzling the same, shall forfeit double the value; and justices of the peace may punish them and the receivers, and may hear and determine concerning the wages and frauds of workmen.

By 4 *Geo.* 2. *c.* 16. and 18 *Geo.* 2. *c.* 27. stealing cotton to the value of 10*s.* from whitening grounds, is felony without clergy, or the judge may order transportation.

By 39 & 40 *Geo.* 3. *c.* 90. in cases of difference between masters and workmen, in the cotton manufacture in England, which cannot be mutually adjusted, the matter in dispute may be referred to arbitration. *s.* 1.

Parties or witnesses refusing to attend arbitrators, and, after being brought before a justice, refusing to give evidence, may be committed to the house of correction till they submit. *Ibid.*

And by 44 *Geo.* 3. *c.* 87. where the parties agree to abide the determination of a justice, the matter in dispute may be finally determined by him: if the parties do not so agree, the justice shall summon the party complained of, and appoint arbitrators, not less than four, nor more than six, one half of them masters or foremen, and the other half weavers; out of which masters, the masters or foremen shall choose one, and out of the weavers, the weavers shall choose another; and such referrees shall hear and examine the parties and their witnesses, and determine such dispute in two days. *s.* 2.

But by 39 & 40 *Geo.* 3. *c.* 90. the time of making the award may be extended by the parties, *s.* 2; submission and award may be drawn on unstamped paper, *s.* 3; and each party have a copy. *s.* 4.

By 44 *Geo.* 3. *c.* 87. persons complaining, not attending, shall lose the benefit of the act. *s.* 3.

And on arbitrators refusing to act, the justice may name others. *s.* 4.

Arbitrators not agreeing, and refusing to go before the justice, the dispute shall be determined by him. *s.* 5.

One arbitrator may make the award, if the other does not attend. *s.* 6.

Complaints are to be made within three days; and complaints respecting bad warps or utensils, are to be setttled near the place of work, *s.* 7, 8. Penalty on refusing to fulfil the award, 10*l.* *s.* 9.

The whole by 39 & 40 *Geo.* 3. *c.* 90. to be recovered before one justice, and leviable by distress and sale, or in default to be committed for not more than three nor less than two months; but an appeal lies to the quarter sessions, and there is no *certiorari*. *s.* 5—7.

Justices who are cotton manufacturers not to act. *s.* 10.

By 44 *Geo.* 3. *c.* 87. tickets stating the quantity of materials shall be given out with the work; and duplicate of the ticket shall be kept by the master; and a penalty of not exceeding 40*s.* nor less than 20*s.* to be incurred for not giving such ticket, to be recovered as above, without appeal. *s.* 10, 11, 12.

Complaints may be made against agents or partners: where masters become bankrupts, assignees shall be liable; and complaints of married women and infants, may be made by husbands and parents. *s.* 13, 14, 15.

The costs of the proceedings shall be settled by arbitrators or justices; and the following fees are payable, *viz.* to the clerk of the justice, 6*d.*; and for each summons, oath, or order, 6*d.*; for every warrant and conviction, 1*s.*; to the constable for service of summons or order, 6*d.*; for warrant of distress, 1*s.* 6*d.*; for holding distress *per* day 4*d.* for every mile he travels. *s.* 16, 17.

——— *Gloves.*] By 6 *Geo.* 3. *c.* 19. foreign leather gloves and mits imported, shall be forfeited, and the importer, vender, retailer, or concealer, shall forfeit 200*l.* besides, with double costs.

Such goods under the value of 20*l.* may be proceeded against before two justices, and if condemned they are to be sold for exportation only. *Ibid.*

In case of doubt, whether such goods are of foreign manufacture, the proof shall lie on the possessor, but the possessor (not importing or concealing the same) discovering the vender, is discharged from the penalty and forfeiture, and from giving proof. *Ibid.*

A moiety of the penalty goes to the king, the other to the officer seizing; and if he neglects for one month to sue for any penalty, any other person may sue for and recover the same in like manner. *Ibid.*

The wearers of such goods are not subject

to any penalty, forfeiture, or proof, on that account. *Ibid.*

By 25 *Geo.* 3. *c.* 55. the above act shall extend to all foreign leather cut, or prepared, in order to be made into gloves or mits, and called shapes or tranks.

——— *Hats.*] By 17 *Geo.* 3. *c.* 55. every master hatter shall employ one journeyman for each apprentice, or be disabled to take two apprentices.

Journeymen combining as mentioned in 22 *Geo.* 2. *c.* 27. (see title *Woollen*), and convicted, must, before any appeal allowed, give a recognizance. *Ibid.*

Attending combination, or soliciting others so to do, or contributing thereto, penalty three months' imprisonment. *Ibid.*

No hat-maker shall act as a justice under this act; and not to repeal 22 *Geo.* 2. *c.* 27. *Ibid.*

By 24 *Geo.* 3. *c.* 21. no person shall export any British hare-skins, hare-wool, or coney-wool, or undressed coney-skins, or load any horse or cart therewith, in order to export the same, on forfeiture thereof, besides a penalty of 500*l.* on the owner or exporter, and 40*l.* on the master and mariners.

No person shall stain or dye any British hare-skins or coney-skins, on forfeiture thereof, with the machines, and also 20*l.* *Ibid.*

——— *Iron and Steel.*] By 25 *Geo.* 3. *c.* 67. no person shall put on board any vessel for exportation, "any hand stamps, "doghead stamps, pulley stamps, stamps "of all sorts, hammers and anvils, or screws "for stamps, iron rods for stamps, presses "of all sorts in iron, steel, or other metal, "cutting-out presses, beds and punches "used therewith; piercing presses, and beds "and punches used therewith iron or "steel dies to be used in stamps or presses; "rollers of cast iron, wrought iron, or steel, "for rolling of metal, and frames for the same; flasks or casting moulds, and boards "used therewith; lathes of all sorts, whole "or in parts; lathe strings, polishing "brushes, scoring or shading engines, "presses for horn buttons, dies for horn "buttons, sheers for cutting of metal, rolled "steel, rolled metal, with silver thereon, "parts of buttons unfinished, engines for "chasing, stocks for casting buckles, buttons, and rings; cast iron anvils and hammers for forging mills for iron and copper; "rollers, slitters, beds, pillars, and frames "for slitting mills; die-sinking tools, engines for button shanks, laps, drilling engines, tools for pinching of glass; engines "for covering of whips; polishing brushes; "bars of metal covered with gold or silver; "iron or steel screw plates, pins, and stocks "for making screws, or any other tool or "thing which now is or hereafter shall be "used in the iron or steel manufactures," on penalty of forfeiture thereof; and if the offender shall not give a satisfactory account before the magistrate, he shall be bound to appear at the next assizes, or be committed for trial, and on conviction shall forfeit 200*l.* and be imprisoned twelve months.

Officers of the customs shall seize such articles laid or intended to be laid on board any outward-bound vessel, and the same shall be sold, and go half to the king and half to the officer. *Ibid.*

Masters of vessels permitting such things to be put on board, shall forfeit 200*l.* and be incapacitated. *Ibid.*

Officers of customs taking any entry outwards, for such articles, shall forfeit 200*l.* and be incapacitated. *Ibid.*

Any person having in possession any such things with intent to export the same, a magistrate may issue his warrant for seizing thereof, and bringing such person before him; and if he shall not give a satisfactory account thereof, such things may be detained, and the possessor bound over to appear at the next assizes, or he may be committed for trial; and if convicted, shall forfeit 200*l.* and be imprisoned twelve months. *Ibid.*

Persons enticing artificers in the iron or steel manufactures, to leave this kingdom, except to Ireland, shall forfeit for the first offence 500*l.* and may be imprisoned twelve months; and for the second, or other offence, they shall forfeit 1000*l.* and be imprisoned two years. *Ibid.*

But prosecutions hereon must be commenced within twelve months.

But by 26 *Geo.* 3. *c.* 89. from July 10, 1786, such tools used in the iron and steel manufactures may be exported, as might have been before passing the above act, except, "rollers, plain, grooved, or of other "form, of cast iron, wrought iron, or steel, "for the rolling of iron or metals; and "frames, beds, pillars, screws, pinions, and "tools thereof; rollers, slitters, frames, beds, "pillars and screws for slitting mills; presses of all sorts used with a screw above 1½ "inch in diameter, or any parts of these articles, or any model thereof, or any part "thereof, and engines for casting or boring "canon or artillery, or any model thereof; "hand stamps, dog-head stamps, pulley "stamps, hammers, and anvils for stamps; "cutting-out presses, their beds and punches; scoring or shading engines; presses "and dies for horn buttons; rolled metal, "with silver thereon; unfinished parts of "buttons; engines for chasing stocks for "casting buckles, buttons and rings; die-sinking tools; engines to make button "shanks; laps, tools for pinching glass, "engines for covering whips, bars of metal "covered with gold or silver, and blood "stones rough or finished."

No person shall have in possession, with intent to export (except to Ireland), "any "wire moulds for making paper; wheels "made of metal, stone, or wood, for rough-

" ing, cutting, polishing, and engraving " glass; purcellas, pincers, sheers, and pipes " used in blowing glass; potters' wheels and " potters' lathes, for plain, round, and en- " gine turning tools, used by sadlers, har- " ness-makers, and bridle-makers, *viz.* can- " tle strainers, side strainers, point strain- " ers, creasing irons, screw creasers, wheel " irons, seat irons, pricking irons, bolstering " irons, clams, head snives." And the above act, as far as relates to exporters of articles therein enumerated, shall extend to exporters of articles specified in this act. *Ibid.*

This act was made perpetual by 35 *Geo.* 3. *c.* 38.

——— *Lace.*] By 13 & 14 *Car.* 2. *c.* 13. foreign bone-lace, cut-work, embroidery, fringe, band, strings, buttons, or needle work made of thread or silk, shall not be imported or sold.

By 11 *W.* 3. *c.* 3. English bone-lace may be exported, custom free, to Scotland, Ireland, or the plantations.

By 5 *Ann. c.* 17. the 13 & 14 *Car.* 2. and all other acts restraining the importation, or selling of foreign lace, are repealed, as to thread-lace made in the Spanish Low Countries, or any other place not within the kingdom of France. But 27 *Geo.* 3. *c.* 13. allows the importation of bone-lace from France.

By 4 *Geo.* 1. *c.* 6. no maker or wholesale trader in English bone-lace, and selling the same by wholesale, shall be deemed a hawker and pedlar; but such persons may go from house to house to their customers who sell again.

By 19 *Geo.* 3. *c.* 49, all persons who shall employ any lace manufacturers, or shall purchace lace of them, shall pay them in money, and not with goods, or by way of truck, on penalty of 10*l.* to be levied by distress, and in default thereof to be imprisoned for six months.

Lace-makers may recover money due to them for lace sold, or for making thereof, before justices of peace: but persons aggrieved may appeal to the quarter sessions on giving fourteen days notice. *Ibid.*

By 46 *Geo.* 3. *c.* 81. foreign thread lace is subjected to a large duty on importation, in order to encourage the British lace manufacture (see title *Importation*); and the act directs that all foreign thread lace shall be sealed at one end of every piece, and shall not be imported in parcels of less than 12 yards, unless worth 2*l.* per yard, on pain of forfeiture thereof, and the same may be seized. *s.* 3.

Two justices may grant such warrants, on oath that there is reason to suspect the concealment of foreign lace, which has not paid the duty. *s.* 9.

And foreign thread lace found in any shop or warehouse, or other place upon land, not so sealed, shall be forfeited, and the person to whom the same shall belong, or in whose possession the same may be found, shall forfeit for the first offence 50*l.* and if the value exceed 50*l.* double the value; and upon a second conviction before two justices, double the sum forfeited on the first conviction; and for a third conviction, treble; one moiety to the king, and the other to the officer of customs. *s.* 10.

The penalty for counterfeiting the seals, is felony without clergy. *s.* 11.

Persons selling or offering any such thread lace, or having the same in their possession, with a counterfeit seal, shall forfeit 100*l.* half to the king and half to the officer of customs. *s.* 11.

Proof of lace not being foreign shall lie on the party. *s.* 12.

The commissioners of customs may alter their seals. *s.* 22.

And the penalties above 50*l.* are recoverable in the courts of record in Westminster, with costs, half to the king and half to the informer; and penalties not exceeding 50*l.* are recoverable before two justices; and if witnesses refuse to attend the latter, they are subject to a penalty of 10*l.* or two month's imprisonment. *s.* 23, 24, 25. See also *Stamps.*

——— *Leather.*] By 27 *Hen.* 8. *c.* 14. leather curried to be exported, shall be packed and told by a man appointed and sworn thereto.

No person having a tan-house shall export any manner of leather tanned or untanned. *Ibid.*

Captains of ships and masters of vessels going to Ireland, Dantzick, Norway, and the Straits, excepted. *Ibid.*

Hides untanned of beasts killed in Wales may be exported. *Ibid.*

Q. *Whether this act continued in force after the expiration of the old subsidy?*

By 5 & 6 *Ed.* 6. *c.* 15. tanned leather shall not be bought or engrossed to sell again, but by cordwainers, sadlers, girdlers, and other artificers, who may sell their necks, wombs, and shreds; but persons having licence to transport tanned leather, may buy so much as they are allowed to transport.

By 1 *Mar. sess.* 3. *c.* 8. curriers, shoemakers, girdlers, sadlers, budget makers, and all other artificers, may buy leather, but not convey the same beyond sea. Curriers are not to curry hides for shoemakers between St. James's day and March 25, unless the same have been twice dipped in the pan, upon pain of forfeiting the same; leather is to be curried within five days in summer, and within ten days in winter, upon pain of 10*s.* per hide; but this does not bind the currier to dress any leather which he cannot.

Repealed, and 5 *Ed.* 6. *c.* 15. revived by 1 *Eliz. c.* 8. which is repealed by 5 *Eliz. c.* 8. and 1 *Jac.* 1. *c.* 22. Quere, *therefore which is in force?*

By 5 *Eliz. c.* 22. no person shall take

the wool off any sheep skin or lamb skin, or buy the skin of any buck, doe, or the like, unless to make leather or parchment, on pain of 2*s.* 6*d.* a skin.

None shall export sheep skins, or the skin of any stag or the like, on pain of forfeiture, and 2*s.* 6*d.* per skin. *Ibid.*

But by 8 *Eliz. c.* 14. tawed leather made of sheep skins may be exported.

By 18 *Eliz. c.* 9. shipping any leather, tallow, or raw hides, with intent to be exported, forfeits ship and goods, and treble value.

Q. *If in force?*

By 1 *Jac.* 1. *c.* 22. extended by 24 *Geo.* 3. *c.* 19. to every part of Great Britain, no butcher shall gash or cut any hide, upon pain of twenty-pence *per* hide; and he shall not water any hide, except in June, July, and August, or sell any one that is rotten, on pain of 3*s.* 4*d.*

No butcher shall be a tanner; nor shall any other person be a tanner except apprentices or hired servants in that mystery by the space of seven years, or the son or daughter of a tanner. *Ibid.*

No tanner shall be a shoemaker, currier, butcher, or other leather cutter. No persons shall buy rough hides, or calves skins, but such as may use tanning of leather, nor forestal, nor buy any hide, other than in open fair or market, unless such person as killed the same beast. *Ibid.*

None may buy tanned leather unwrought but those who work the same into made wares, who may buy the same at Leadenhall. *Ibid.*

Sadlers and girdlers may sell their necks and shreds. *Ibid.*

No persons shall let any hide be over-lined, or put the same into tan fats before the lime be well soaken; they shall use in tanning only ash-bark, oak-bark, tap-wort, malt, meal, lime, culver-dung or hen-dung; leather shall not lie wet in any frost, until frozen; it shall not be parched by fire or summer sun; sole leathers shall lie in the woozes a year, upper leather nine months; rotten hides are not to be tanned; hides are to be well worked in the woozes, and no leather, worked contrary hereto, shall be sold. *Ibid.*

Tanners are not to raise with any mixture, any hide, to be converted into sole leathers unless the same be fit. *Ibid.*

Sale of tanned leather, red and unwrought, except in markets, is a forfeiture thereof, and also 6*s.* 8*d. per* hide, and 3*s.* 4*d.* for every dozen of calves skins, or sheep skins. *Ibid.*

Leather not sufficiently tanned or dried, shall not be exposed to sale. *Ibid.*

Leather shall not be put to take unkind heat, upon pain to forfeit 10*l.* and stand in the pillory three market days. *Ibid.*

There shall be no regrating or ingrossing of oaken bark; and oaken trees to be barked, shall not be felled, but between the first day of April and the last day of June. *Ibid.*

Persons shall curry leather only in their own houses, they shall not curry leather, except it be well tanned, nor any hide, which is not dry after their wet season, when they shall not use any stale or false stuff. They shall curry outer sole leather with hard tallow only, and with as much of that as it will take, upper leather with fresh stuff, and thoroughly liquored; they shall not burn or scald any hide or leather in currying, nor shave any leather too thin, nor gash or hurt any leather, upon pain of forfeiting 6*s.* 8*d.*, and the value of every skin or hide, and for gashing double the sum injured. *Ibid.*

A currier shall not be a tanner, shoemaker, butcher, or leather-cutter, upon pain of 6*s.* 8*d. per* hide. Curriers shall curry leather brought to them by the cutter, if he brings stuff for liquoring the same, within eight days in summer, and sixteen in winter, upon pain of 10*s. per* hide. *Ibid.*

Curried leather shall be searched and sealed, by the wardens of the curriers, or the persons by them appointed, upon pain of 6*s.* 8*d. per* hide. *Ibid.*

No shoemaker shall make any shoes, boots, or the like, but of leather well and truly tanned and curried, and sewed with good thread, well waxed and refined, and the stitches hard drawn, with hand leathers, nor shall he put in any leather made of a sheep skin, bull-hide, or horse-hide, or sell any wares on a Sunday. *Ibid.*

The mayors, bailiffs, and other head-officers, in places out of London, shall yearly upon pain of 40*l.* half to the crown and half to the informer, appoint eight persons to search and seal all tanned leather, which, if insufficient, is to be seized. *Ibid.*

They are also, within six days after such seizure, to appoint six indifferent persons, to try and determine the goodness of such leather, upon pain of 5*l.* *Ibid.*

The forfeiture of a sealer or searcher neglecting to do his duty, is 40*s.*, taking of bribes, 20*l.*, and refusing to act 10*l.* *Ibid.*

No person shall buy any leather before it is searched, sealed, and registered, upon pain of forfeiting the same. *Ibid.*

Forfeited wares shall not be sold to him that will sell them again; upon pain of 3*s.* 4*d. per* parcel. *Ibid.*

The authority of the officers of Oxford and Cambridge for search of leather is saved. *Ibid.*

The hides of ox, deer, calf, steer, cow, bull, goats, and sheep, being tanned and tawed, and every salt hide, shall be deemed leather. *Ibid.*

Dry cutting and frizing of leather shall be construed currying after the Spanish manner;

and all artificers, except shoemakers, may use the same. *Ibid.*

This act shall extend to Wales, to all intents and purposes. *Ibid.*

Customers or other officers suffering leather to be exported without seizing or disclosing it, forfeit for the first offence 100*l.*; for the second their office: making a false certificate of the arrival of leather, is a forfeiture of 100*l.* *Ibid.*

This act shall not extend to Scottish hides brought to Berwick. *Ibid.*

By 3 *Jac.* 1. *c.* 9. none but artizan-skinners shall dress or export black coney skins.

No merchant shall buy any coney skins or lamb skins, called morkins, under the number of 1000 black coney skins, or 3000 grey coney skins, or 2000 lamb skins, nor utter the same again in small quantities, unless to the artizan skinner. *Ibid.*

No skinner shall take any to be his journeyman, unless he has served seven years as an apprentice therein. *Ibid.*

By 4 *Jac.* 1. *c.* 6. there shall be no penalty for housing or selling sheep skins unsealed; and no tanned leather shall be sold by weight.

By 13 & 14 *Car.* 2. *c.* 7. no hides tanned or untanned of any ox, bull, cow, or calf, shall be exported, on pain of 500*l.*

But leather made into boots, shoes, or slippers, may be exported. *Ibid.*

Tanners shaving of leather shall forfeit the same. *Ibid.*

Leather for necessary use of ships in voyages, not exceeding six raw and three tanned hides, may be shipped. *Ibid.*

By 1 *Wil. & Mar. c.* 33. red tanned leather duly sealed and searched, and bought in an open fair or market, may be sold again in the buyer's shop.

Leather hides and skins may be bought and sold by weight, notwithstanding any act to the contrary. *Ibid.*

By 12 *Geo.* 2. *c.* 25. all persons who deal in leather, may bring all sorts of tanned leather curried or uncurried, in any open fair or market, being duly sealed; and may cut and sell the same in their open shops in any quantities.

But this does not licence any persons unqualified, to exercise the trade of shoemaker or cobler. *Ibid.*

Curriers neglecting to curry any leather within sixteen days, between 28th September and 25th March, and within eight days during the remainder of the year, shall forfeit 5*l.* on conviction before a magistrate. *Ibid.*

By 13 *Geo.* 2. *c.* 8. persons employed in manufacturing leather, who shall embezzle the same, shall forfeit double damages for the first offence, and quadruple damages after.

They shall be paid their wages in money, and not by any goods, and complaints are to be heard by two justices. *Ibid.*

They shall perform the business in which they are retained, and leaving it before completed, may be committed to the house of correction. *Ibid.*

This act to extend to Scotland. *Ibid.*

By 34 *Geo.* 3. *c.* 68. nothing in any act shall prevent Samuel Ashton or his assigns from tanning hides and skins in the manner mentioned in his letters patent.

By 39 *Geo.* 3. *c.* 54. so much of 2 *Jac.* 1. *c.* 22. as prohibits the buying hides of beasts slaughtered for the service of the navy, and not afterwards tanning or tawing them, or the buying of raw hides otherwise than in open market, is repealed. *s.* 4.

By 39 & 40 *Geo.* 3. *c.* 66. so much of 2 *Jac.* 1. *c.* 22. as prohibited the use of horse hides in shoes, and the like; and so much of the same act, and 9 *Ann.* *c.* 11. as related to the gashing of hides; were repealed. *s.* 1.

Mayors and head officers, or two justices of towns, are to appoint proper places and times for examining raw hides, and proper persons to be inspectors. *s.* 2.

If six or more manufacturers of leather, shall recommend to the persons authorized to appoint inspectors, two proper persons to be appointed, when one inspector shall be necessary, or four when two shall be requisite; then one or two of them, as the case may require, shall be appointed; and on complaint of misconduct or neglect in any inspector, he may be discharged, and another appointed in his room. *s.* 3.

If any person shall wilfully or carelessly injure any hide, so as to render it less valuable for making leather, and shall be convicted thereof before one justice, he shall pay not exceeding 10*s.* and not less than 1*s.* for the raw hide of every ox or like beast; not exceeding 5*s.* nor less than 6*d.* for the hide of every calf; not exceeding 5*s.* nor less than 1*s.* for the hide of every horse; and not exceeding 6*d.* nor less than 3*d.* for the hide of every hog, pig, sheep, or lamb. *s.* 4.

Inspectors are to be sworn, by those who appoint them, to act faithfully; and they are to examine and mark raw hides, and take for the hide of every ox, or like beast, or horse, 1*d.*; calf, hog, or pig skin, ½*d.*: and for every sheep, or lamb skin, ¼*d.*; and if any person, other than the inspector, shall mark any raw hide, he shall forfeit 20*l.* *s.* 5.

Inspectors may impose penalties, not exceeding half of the highest imposed by this act, for wilfully or carelessly cutting of hides without their being adjudged by a magistrate, subject to the determination of arbitrators. *s.* 6.

If any inspector shall deem any person liable to more than such half amount, he shall proceed for recovery thereof by information before a magistrate. *s.* 7.

The whole penalty to be paid to the inspector who shall impose or inform for it. *s.* 8.

Inspectors are to provide stamps for marking hides; and if penalty or fee for marking hides be not paid, any inspector may seize and sell them, unless notice be given of having the matter decided by arbitrators. *s.* 9.

If any person within any district where an inspector has been appointed, shall neglect to bring any raw hides to the proper place to be marked, or shall remove therefrom any that shall not have been marked, he shall be liable to a penalty not exceeding 5*l.* nor less than 40*s.* for each skin. *s.* 10.

If any person shall give notice to the inspector of his intention to carry his raw hides to any other place for inspection, for not less than a month, he may so do. *s.* 11.

In case of dispute whether hides have been injured, the magistrate shall summon five persons engaged in the working of leather, three of whom may finally determine the same: such persons are to take an oath to do equal justice, and the party against whom the decision shall be given shall pay all expences; to be ascertained by the magistrates. *s.* 12.

Persons summoned not attending, to forfeit 40*s.* *s.* 13.

And the penalties are to go half to the informer, and half to carry the act into execution. *s.* 14.

The act does not extend to London, Westminster, Southwark, or any place within 15 miles of the Royal Exchange. *s.* 15.

The penalties are recoverable before one magistrate by distress and sale; and for default of distress, the offender to suffer not exceeding one month's imprisonment. *s.* 16.

Persons aggrived by any judgment, when the penalty exceeds 10*s.* may appeal to the sessions; and no *certiorari* is allowed; and information for offences must be laid within three days after the offence. *s.* 17, 18.

By 41 *Geo.* 3. u. k. *c.* 53. mayors and others authorized by 39 & 40 *Geo.* 3. *c.* 66. may appoint proper places for examining raw hides, whether they shall be within cities or towns or not. *s.* 1.

So much of *s.* 3. & 14. of the above act as requires the recommendation of inspectors, and the approbation of the distribution of penalties to be by six tanners, is repealed; and from August 1, 1801, shoemakers, sadlers, or persons working or dealing in leather, may be joined with the tanners for those purposes. *s.* 2.

No recommendation of any inspector, nor approbation in regard to penalties, shall be good, unless three tanners, curriers, or manufacturers, join therein. *s.* 3.

Fines imposed by *s.* 4, of 39 & 40 *Geo.* 3. for wilfully or carelessly cutting raw hides or skins, shall not exceed for ox or like beast 5*s.* calf 2*s.* 6*d.* or horse 2*s.* 6*d.* *s.* 4.

And persons are not liable to penalty for flaying of hides not more than two inches below the knee. *s.* 5.

Raw hides shall be brought for examination within ten days from being flayed, under the penalty imposed by *s.* 10. of the above act. *s.* 6.

The whole of the penalty given by *s.* 8. of the said act shall be distributed, one half to the inspector, and the other half for better carrying the act into execution; and the inspector may receive a further reward out of the other half. *s.* 8.

Information for gashing raw hides shall be made within three days, and for other offences within fourteen days. *s.* 9. See *s.* 18. *of act.*

The former act and this (but see title *London*) shall extend to all raw hides flayed in Great Britain, found within the several districts, whether flayed within them or not. *s.* 9.

Magistrates may summon witnesses, though they shall not be within their jurisdiction; and witnesses not appearing shall forfeit 40*s.* but they are not obliged to travel more than six miles. *s.* 10.

By 48 *Geo.* 3. *c.* 60. no tanner shall by himself, or any other, use the trade of a shoemaker, currier, leather-cutter, or other artificer cutting or working of leather, upon pain of forfeiting every hide and skin by him wrought or tanned during the time, or the value thereof to be recovered by action, together with costs of trial. *s.* 7.

See also *London.*

——— *Linen.*] By 28 *Hen.* 8. *c.* 4. the contents of every piece of dowlas and lockeram shall be set upon the cloth, on pain of forfeiture.

By 1 *Eliz.* *c.* 12. linen cloth deceitfully stretched or used shall be forfeited, the offender imprisoned a month, and fined at the discretion of the justices.

By 29 *Geo.* 2. *c.* 15. altered by 10 *Geo.* 3. *c.* 38. and continued by 48 *Geo.* 3. *c.* 23. *s.* 3. until March 25, 1811, the following bounties are payable on exportation.

	£.	s.	d.
Linens twenty-five inches broad, made of hemp or flax, in Great Britain, Ireland, or the Isle of Man, and exported to Spain, Portugal, Gibraltar, or America, under the value of 5*d.* per yard - - - - -	0	0	0½
Value 5*d.* and under 6*d.* per yard - - - -	0	0	1
Value 6*d.* and under 1*s.* 6*d.* per yard - - - - -	0	0	1½
British checked or striped linen 7*d.* and not exceeding 1*s.* 6*d.* per yard - - - -	0	0	0½

	£.	s.	d.
For every yard of diaper, huckaback, sheeting, and other species of linen, upwards of one yard English in breadth, and not exceeding 1s. 6d. the square yard - - - -	0	0	1½

Any person affixing stamps on foreign linen, in imitation of the stamp used for that of Scotland or Ireland, or counterfeiting stamps on British or Irish linen, to forfeit 5*l.* for each piece: and for exposing such linens to sale knowingly, to forfeit such linens. 17 *Geo.* 2. *c.* 30. and 18 *Geo.* 2. *c.* 24.

British or Irish linens entered for exportation to receive the bounties at undervalue, fraudulently, to be forfeited, one half to the king, the other half to the informer. 17 *Geo.* 2. *c.* 31. 18 *Geo.* 2. *c.* 25. and 29 *Geo.* 2. *c.* 15.

Stamp masters to be sworn; no linens to be stamped before sworn to be of the manufacture of Scotland or Ireland. 18 *Geo.* 2. *c.* 24, and 29 *Geo.* 2. *c.* 15.

And by the same act no bounty shall be paid on exportation of such linens, before they are marked, numbered, and stamped.

By 18 *Geo.* 2. *c.* 27. whoever shall steal any linen, laid to be printed, bleached, or the like, or aid or hire another to commit such offence, shall be guilty of felony, and suffer death; and the court may order such offenders to be transported for fourteen years.

By 26 *Geo.* 2. *c.* 20. after the expiration of the bounties on exportation of British and Irish coarse linens, the annual sum of 3000*l.* shall be paid for nine years out of the duties in Scotland, for encouraging manufactures of linen in the Highlands.

By 19 *Geo.* 3. *c.* 27. the same bounty shall be allowed on the exportation of Irish linens the property of persons residing in Ireland, as on those the property of persons residing in America.

By 22 *Geo.* 3. *c.* 40. persons entering any house by force, with intent to cut or destroy any linen or cotton manufactures, or tools used therein, shall be deemed guilty of felony without benefit of clergy.

By 22 *Geo.* 3. *c.* 60. persons enticing workmen employed in printing calicoes, cottons, muslins, and linens, or in making blocks, plates, or implements used in such manufactory, to leave the kingdom, shall for the first offence forfeit 500*l.* and be imprisoned twelve months; and for the second offence 1000*l.* and be imprisoned two years: but prosecutions must be commenced within twelve months.

Exporting, or attempting to export, any blocks, plates, or implements, used in the said manufactory, is a forfeiture thereof, and of 500*l.* *Ibid.*

Officers of customs or excise may seize such blocks, plates, and implements, as shall be attempted to be exported: and captains or masters, who shall permit the same to be put on board their vessels, shall forfeit 100*l.* and if a king's officer, besides the penalty shall be disabled. *Ibid.*

Officers who shall take any entry outward for exporting any of the said articles, shall forfeit 10*l.* and be disabled. *Ibid.*

By 23 *Geo.* 3. *c.* 77. continued by 48 *Geo.* 3. *c.* 23. till March, 1810, the manufacturers of flax and cotton shall make oath before a proper officer, of the quantities of soap and starch consumed by them in each respective manufacture; and the collector, out of the money in his hands of the duty on soap, shall pay to such manufacturers a drawback on all soap so used, at the rate of three farthings per lb. (except it is used to whiten new linen for sale), and out of the money in his hands of the duties on starch, a drawback of three half pence per lb. on all starch so used (except for starch used for finishing linen for sale, and then threepence per lb.); and if the collector shall not have money sufficient in hand, he is to certify the same to the commissioners, who are to pay the same.

The manufacturer, or his chief workman, shall produce an account, upon oath, of the soap and starch used by him in his manufactory in the preceding year; and shall keep also a weekly account, to be produced to the officer on demand; and where there is a superintending owner and an overseer, each shall produce his accounts on oath before the collector. *Ibid.*

The importation duties on brimstone and saltpetre consumed in making oil of vitriol, shall be repaid; but manufacturers of flax and cotton, and makers of oil of vitriol, shall enter their names and places of abode with the collectors of excise and customs. *Ibid.*

Officers taking of manufacturers any fees, except 6*d.* for writing each oath, shall forfeit treble damages with costs. *Ibid.*

Manufacturers swearing falsely in the oaths before mentioned, shall forfeit 100*l.*; and for the second offence shall suffer as in cases of corrupt perjury. *Ibid.*

If any manufacturer, or his workman, keeping the account of the weekly consumption of soap and starch, shall swear falsely, he shall be committed for six months; and for a second offence, suffer as in cases of corrupt perjury. *Ibid.*

By 27 *Geo.* 3. *c.* 38. made perpetual by 34 *Geo.* 3. *c.* 23. the proprietor of any original pattern for printing linens, shall have the sole right of printing it for three months from first publication, 34 *Geo.* 3. *c.* 23.; and whoever shall within that period print the same, shall be liable to an action for damages: but any person purchasing plates from the proprietors may print therefrom.

——— *Paper.*] By 36 *Geo.* 3. *c.* 111. all contracts between journeymen papermakers, for advancing their wages, lessening their hours of work, or the like, are declared void; and journeymen paper-makers and others entering into such contracts, are to be committed to the house of correction, to hard labour, for not exceeding two calendar months. *s.* 1, 2.

Vat men, if required by the master, shall be half an hour about each post, twenty of which shall be a day's work; and the day-worker, if required by the master, shall work twelve hours per day, with an interval of an hour for refreshments. *s.* 3.

Journeymen taking more wages, or entering into combinations to raise wages, or persons seducing or hindering them from working, are, on conviction, to be committed to hard labour for not exceeding two months. *s.* 4.

If any person shall attend or solicit any journeyman paper-maker to attend any unlawful meeting, or shall subscribe or pay any sum of money to support the same, he may, on conviction, be committed for two months. *s.* 5.

Offenders against this act may be admitted evidence, and shall be indemnified against penalties. *s.* 6.

Any justice may, on complaint, summon offenders, and hear, determine, and commit. *s.* 7.

——— *Shoes.*] By 9 *Geo.* 1. *c.* 27. on due proof of a journeyman's purloining boots, shoes, slippers, or any other wares, or any materials for making the same, a justice may convict him, and award satisfaction for damage sustained, which may be levied by distress, and in default thereof he is to be whipped. The second offence is imprisonment for one month, or not less than fourteen days. Confederates by buying, receiving, or taking in pawn, such articles, are liable to the same punishment.

Justices of peace, upon information, on oath, may issue warrants to search for such goods, and cause them to be restored to the owners. *Ibid.*

Persons suffering themselves to be employed by a new master, before the shoes, boots, or other work, delivered by a former is done, shall be sent to the house of correction. *Ibid.*

But the party aggrieved by order of such justices, may appeal to the next sessions. *Ibid.* See also *Leather.*

——— *Silk.*] By 19 *Hen.* 7. *c.* 27. no silk wrought by itself or with any other stuff out of the realm, in ribbons, girdles, corses, kauls, corses of tissues or point, shall be imported, on forfeiture thereof; other silks, as well wrought as raw or unwrought, may be imported.

By 13 & 14 *Car.* 2. *c.* 15. none shall use the art of a silk thrower, unless he has served an apprenticeship of seven years, on pain of 40*s.* a month.

Persons embezzling any silk delivered to be wrought up, and also buyers and receivers, on conviction before a justice, shall make satisfaction, and on failure, be set in the stocks. *Ibid.*

By 2 *Will.* & *Mar. sess.* 1. *c.* 9. no thrown silk shall be imported, except of the produce of Italy, Sicily, or Naples, and in vessels navigated according to the act of navigation.

By 6 *Ann. c.* 19. clandestine importers of wrought silks, or silks mixed with gold or silver, shall forfeit 200*l.*; sellers and concealers forfeit 100*l.*; and the siks forfeited shall be sold at the custom house.

By 8 *Geo.* 1. *c.* 15. continued by 43 *Geo.* 3. *c.* 29. till June 24, 1808, and from thence to the end of the next session, exporters of ribbons and stuffs made in Great Britain of silk only, shall have an allowance of 3*s.* for every pound weight; of silk mixed with gold or silver 4*s.*; for every pound weight of silk stockings, gloves, fringes, laces, or sewing silk, 1*s.* 3*d.* per lb.; of stuffs of silk or grogram yarn, 8*d.* per lb.; of silk and cotton, 1*s.* per lb.; of silk and worsted 6*d.* per lb. (*Additional bounties are allowed by* 24 Geo. 3. c. 49.)

But there shall be no allowances for such manufactures mixed with gold or silver at the edges only. *Ibid.*

By 9 *Geo.* 1. *c.* 8. there shall be no allowances on exportation of such manufactures mixed with silk, unless two thirds of the warps at least be silk.

By 1 *Geo.* 2. *c.* 17. the securities given on exportation, where certificates cannot be obtained, may be discharged on the oath of the master.

There shall be no allowance on exportation of stuffs mixed with silk, unless the silk mixed in the warp be apparent to view, and double the value of the bounty. *Ibid.*

By 23 *Geo.* 2. *c.* 20. raw silk of the growth of the British colonies in America, may be imported duty free, so that the vessels be lawfully navigated, and entry made.

By 23 *Geo.* 2. *c.* 34. raw silk of the growth or produce of Persia purchased in Russia, may be imported into this kingdom from any port or place belonging to the empire of Russia.

By 26 *Geo.* 2. *c.* 21. foreign silks, velvets, and the like, imported, shall be sealed before delivery from the custom-house at the end of the piece; notice to be given by the exporter, and found without seals, may be seized.

By *Geo.* 3. *c.* 21. foreign ribbons, laces, and girdles, imported, may be seized by any person; importer to forfeit also 100*l.* and persons assisting 50*l.*

By 5 *Geo.* 3. *c.* 48. foreign manufactured silk stockings, mits, and gloves, imported, may be seized, and the importer and vender to forfeit the goods, and also 200*l.* with costs.

After condemnation, may be publicly sold for exportation to foreign parts, on security so to do; and if a doubt as to the place of manufacture, the proof to lie on the defendant; and the person in whose custody the goods are found, on discovering the seller, excused the penalty; and the wearer thereof not liable to penalty. *Ibid.*

The penalty in the last act for importing foreign ribbons, laces, and girdles, increased to 200*l.* with costs; and not to be burnt, but publicly sold for exportation to foreign parts, on security as above: and if officer neglects to sue for the penalty one month after condemnation, any other may recover the same. *Ibid.*

By 6 *Geo.* 3. *c.* 28. made perpetual by 48 *Geo.* 3. *c.* 22. *s.* 3. foreign wrought silks or velvets imported, are forfeited, and also 100*l.* with costs, and to be sold as above; but not to extend to silks and velvets made and imported from the East Indies, or to silk crapes and tiffanies made in Italy.

By 6 *Geo.* 3. *c.* 40. silk goods to be exported to Africa, may be removed from one part of Great Britain to another, on security.

By 11 *Geo.* 3. *c.* 41. raw silk and mohair yarn imported from the Streights, or Levant, shall be deemed as if imported from the Grand Seignor's dominions, and aired according to 26 *Geo.* 2. *c.* 18.

By 22 *Geo.* 3. *c.* 40. persons entering by force into any house with intent to cut or destroy any woollen goods, or tools used in manufacturing thereof, or any silk goods, or tools used in manufacturing thereof, shall be deemed guilty of felony without benefit of clergy.

By 24 *Geo.* 3. *c.* 49. from March 1, 1785, additional bounties shall be allowed on exportation of the following articles of British manufactures, *viz.*

Silk ribbons and stuffs, 2*s.* per lb.; silks and ribbons mixed with gold or silver, 2*s.* 8*d.* per lb.; silk stockings, gloves, fringes, laces, stitching or sewing silk, 1*s.* 9*d.* per lb.; stuffs of silk and grogram, 6*d.* per lb.; of silk and cotton 8*d.* per lb.; and of silk and worsted, 4*d.* per lb. *Ibid.*

And by 25 *Geo.* 3. *c.* 69. a like bounty shall in like manner be allowed upon the exportation of silk gauzes.

And by 46 *Geo.* 3. *c.* 110. until six months after the ratification of a definitive treaty of peace, there shall be allowed an additional bounty on the amount of the allowances under 8 *Geo.* 1. *c.* 15. of 33*l.* 6*s.* 8*d.* per cent.

——— *Stockings.*] By 6 *Geo.* 3. *c.* 29. all frame-work knitted pieces, and stockings (those made of silk excepted), containing three or more threads, are to be marked with the same number of oilet holes, and no more, but may use any materials or number of threads for the welt, and within three inches of the top. Not duly marking their goods, is a forfeiture thereof, and of 5*l.*; journeymen or servants not making such goods on their own account, excepted; who are liable to forfeit not exceeding 40*s.* nor less than 5*s.* unless they may make it appear that they acted according to the directions of the master; in which case they are exempted.

Persons who shall sell or expose to sale any such goods, not being duly and truly marked, forfeit 5*l.* per piece, and the goods; except they discover the vender, so as he shall be convicted, and become liable to the penalty; in which case they are exempted. *Ibid.*

The rights of the frame-work-knitters' company are saved. *Ibid.*

By 28 *Geo.* 3. *c.* 55. frame-work-knitters not delivering within fourteen days after notice, any stocking-frame to the person of whom it was hired, shall, before a justice, forfeit 20*s.* to the poor, and if not paid within six days, they may be committed for not more than three months, nor less than one.

Persons hiring stocking-frames, selling the same, shall, on conviction on indictment, be imprisoned for not less than three, nor more than twelve months; and persons receiving the same shall be liable to the same punishment. *Ibid.*

Persons entering by force to destroy goods in the frame, or destroying the same, or damaging any frame used in the hosiery or framework knitted manufactory, or breaking any machinery contained in any mill used in preparing of wool or cotton for that manufactory, is felony, and transportation for not more than fourteen, nor less than seven, years. *Ibid.*

——— *Thread.*] By 28 *Geo.* 3. *c.* 17. the reel used in making up ounce or nun's thread shall be one yard or thirty-six inches in circumference: and using a less reel is forfeiture thereof, and of 5*l.* to the prosecutor.

All ounce thread made in Great Britain shall be made up in hanks, ounces, quarters, and pounds, avoirdupois weight; the hank to contain thirty threads or rounds of the reel of the same quality and fineness; the ounce a particular number of such hanks entire, the quarter four such ounces, and the pound four such quarters; and the cover of each pound or smaller package shall be marked with a stamp, denoting it to be ounce thread, specifying the number of hanks in each ounce, and the manufacturer's name: reeling, or making up thread otherwise, or selling or offering to sell the same, is a forfeiture thereof, and of 10*l.* for each lb. to the prosecutor; but the act does not extend to thread of forty threads in the hank made prior to June 1, 1788. *Ibid.*

Counterfeiting the stamps, or stamping with one, or selling or offering to sell with a counterfeit stamp, is a penalty of 10*l.* to the person whose stamp is counterfeited, and the thread and stamps to be destroyed. *Ibid.*

The penalties are recoverable before two

justices, who may mitigate a moiety thereof; and if the penalties are not paid, the offender may be committed for three months: witnesses are liable to 5*l.* for not attending on summons. *Ibid.*

The *onus probandi* that the thread is of foreign manufacture shall lie on the owner. *Ib.*

——— *Woollen Cloth.*] By 11 *Ed.* 3. *c.* 3. none shall import into England, Ireland, Wales, or Scotland, any foreign cloths, on pain of forfeiture.

But foreign cloth workers may come, and shall have sufficient franchises, *cap.* 5.

By 27 *Ed.* 3. *stat.* 1. *c.* 4. there shall be no forfeiture for defect of assize, but there shall be an allowance made to the buyer, for so much as it wants thereof.

By 50 *Ed.* 3. *c.* 7. and 7 *Ed.* 4. *c.* 3. woollen cloths shall not be exported before fulled.

By 3 *Hen.* 7. *c.* 11. no woollen cloth shall be transported, before it is barbed, rowed, and shorn, except vesses, rays, sailing cloths, and others, under 40*s.*

By 3 *Hen.* 8. *c.* 7. vesses, rays, sailing and other cloths, at four marks or less, may be exported unbarbed.

By 8 *Eliz. c.* 6. for every nine cloths unwrought, exported by licence, one cloth shall be wrought, of like sort, length, breadth, and goodness, on pain of 10*l.*

No Kentish or Suffolk cloth shall be exported unwrought by any licence, on pain of 40*s.* *Ibid.*

By 12 *Car.* 2. *c.* 22. bays, called four and fifties, sixties, sixty-eights, eighties, and hundred bays, within the town of Colchester, shall be carried to the Dutch bay hall, and there searched and allowed.

By 22 & 23 *Car.* 2. *c.* 8. all clothes and stuffs woven at Kidderminster, shall be under the regulation of the president, wardens, and assistants, of the weavers there.

By 6 *Ann. c.* 8. white broad cloth intended to be exported, being shipped before duty paid, is a forfeiture thereof. And any person may export white woollen cloth made in Great Britain.

By 11 *Geo.* 1. *c.* 24. broad cloth in the West Riding of York, whether a half or a whole cloth, shall be five quarters and a half broad, and the half cloth shall not exceed in length twenty-four yards, nor the whole cloth forty-eight yards, on pain of forfeiting for every inch wanting in breadth, and for every yard exceeding in length, 20*s.*

Such broad cloth shall be measured at the fulling mill: the mill-man is to be sworn, and shall affix a seal of lead to the cloth, denoting the length and breadth, for which he is to be paid 2*d.* for a whole cloth, and 1*d.* for a half cloth; a moiety whereof is to be paid to the county treasurer, towards the salaries of the searchers under this act; but if the cloth be damaged in measuring, it may be measured again. *Ibid.*

Mill-man neglecting his duty, and persons forging or defacing the seals, shall forfeit 5*l.*: the buyer may wet the cloths, and measure the same, which, if deficient, is a forfeiture of the sixth part thereof by the seller, who is to be repaid by the mill-man. *Ibid.*

The mill-man is to affix new seals, and the measures are to be paid by the buyer, 6*d.* for every cloth measured. *Ibid.*

Merchant may return defective cloth to the clothier, who is to repay the money. *Ibid.*

Clothier shall affix his mark on his cloths, on pain of 5*l.*; and persons cutting out or altering the seals or marks, before sale, shall likewise forfeit 5*l.* *Ibid.*

Persons stretching cloth, over the measures in the seals, shall forfeit for every half yard more than one in length of a half cloth, and more than two in a whole cloth, and for every inch above one in a quarter in breadth, over-stretched, 20*s.*

Cloths shall be dressed in all parts alike, and the worker shall fix at the end his mark in lead, on pain of 5*l.* *Ibid.*

The lengths of yards shall be numbered on the tenters, on pain of 5*l.* *Ibid.*

The West Riding quarter sessions shall yearly, at Easter, choose searchers, conversant in the trade, to inspect the mills, who are to be sworn to execute the office truly. *Ibid.*

They may enter the houses, grounds, and warehouses, of clothiers, to search for frauds; and if refused, the penalty is 10*l.*; on discovery of frauds the owner shall forfeit 5*l.* *Ibid.*

Searchers acting against their oaths, forfeit 20*l.* They shall not examine cloths packed for exportation, but by warrant from a justice on an information laid, which, if groundless, the informer shall pay 5*s.* per cloth to the merchant. *Ibid.*

Cloth dresser, stretching the merchant's cloths, or altering the seals, shall repay the merchant the penalties; and cards with wire shall not be used in dressing cloth, on pain of 50*l.*

By 7 *Geo.* 2. *c.* 25. made perpetual by 14 *Geo.* 2. *c.* 35. owners of fulling mills, in the West Riding of York, shall stamp on a leaden seal, the true length and breadth of every broad cloth before it be carried from the mill, on penalty of 20*s.* for each offence.

Buyers suspecting the quantity, may put the cloth in water four hours, and cause the same to be measured by a sworn searcher, who is to make information on oath, of defective cloth, in five days after the admeasurement, on penalty of 20*s.* *Ibid.*

The seller in five days after notice, may examine the cloth complained of, and if refused by the buyer, the prosecution shall cease. *Ibid.*

There shall be no greater penalty than 10*s.* for the first inch, 15*s.* for the second, and 20*s.* for the rest, in cloth defective in breadth. And no penalties shall be incurred for white cloths, after put into hot water to be dyed. *Ibid.*

Stretching cloths more than one yard in every length of twenty yards, and one inch in every quarter of a yard in breadth, above the quantity marked, is a forfeiture of 10*s.* for every quarter of a yard in length, and 20*s.* for every inch in breadth. *Ibid.* and 5 *Geo.* 3. *c.* 51.

By 11 *Geo.* 2. *c.* 28. makers of narrow woollen cloth, in the West Riding of York, shall set the initial letters of their names at the head of every piece of cloth (except white kerseys and half ticks); and the same shall be measured and sealed at the fulling mill, on pain of 20*s.* by the maker, and 5*l.* by the mill-man.

Justices at quarter sessions are to appoint yearly, at Easter, searchers, conversant in the making of narrow cloths, who are to have salaries allowed, and be sworn to act truly; and in case of death or sickness, others are to be appointed. *Ibid.*

Cloths stamped wrong, shall be restamped, on penalty of 5*s.* and makers may stretch one inch in every yard in length, and two inches in every three quarters of a yard in breadth; but if that proportion is exceeded, the penalty is for the first half yard in length, or inch in breadth, 10*s.* and for the next 20*s.* *Ibid.*

A sum not above 3*d.* shall be paid to such persons as the justices appoint, by every maker for each cloth, before carried to the fulling mill, to pay the salaries of the searchers: and the mill-man, or persons appointed to receive the same, may detain the cloth till the money be paid. *Ibid.*

Prosecutions must be commenced against the mill-man or searchers within eight days, or against clothiers and dealers in cloth within one month, after the offence. *Ibid.*

Makers may make narrow cloth (except as before) of what length and breadth they think fit. *Ibid.*

Cloths made in the West Riding of York, and milled in adjacent counties, shall, before dry, be brought to the nearest mill-man in the said Riding, to be measured and marked. *Ibid.*

The 5 *Geo.* 3. *c.* 51. repealed 11 *Geo.* 1. *c.* 24. 7 *Geo.* 2. *c.* 25. and 14 *Geo.* 2. *c.* 35. relating to cloth made in the West Riding of Yorkshire. And the justices are to appoint searchers and measurers, and the maker shall pay for measuring and sealing,

	s.	*d.*
For whole cloth thirty-five yards long	0	6
If more than thirty yards - -	0	4
And less - - - - - - -	0	3

and not to take cloths from the mill till measured and stamped. The cloths shall be sealed before they are put on the tenters; and the justices are to appoint inspectors of fulling mills, who are to visit mills and tenter grounds.

Inspectors, if they find cloths falsely stamped by the measurer, above two inches in breadth, and one yard in length, are to complain to a magistrate, who shall convict the offender in the penalty of 10*s.*: the inspectors may also enter shops where they shall suspect any undue stamped or stretched cloths, and if found, the offenders are to forfeit not more than 5*l.* nor less than 10*s.*; but they are not to inspect cloth packed for exportation. *Ibid.*

Where false seals are found, the inspector is to fix new seals, which are to be the rule of payment for the cloths; and the treasurer of the county, to whom the fees for searching are to be paid, for the purpose of paying the searchers and inspectors thereout such salaries as shall be allowed them at the Easter sessions, shall deduct the forfeitures out of the inspector's salaries. *Ibid.*

Persons charged with frauds may examine the cloths, and if refused, all prosecutions shall be void. Clothiers shall weave their names and places of abode in the heads of their cloth, on pain of 20*s.*; and defacing or counterfeiting seals, before the cloth is taken from the tenters, is a forfeiture of not more than 5*l.* nor less than 40*s.* *Ibid.*

There shall be paid for milling long cloths, for every yard above fifty-eight yards 1½*d.* above the usual price; and justices shall settle disputes between clothiers and millers. *Ibid.*

By 6 *Geo.* 3. *c.* 23. merchants may have cloths made wet and remeasured by an inspector; and if of less quantity than the seal denotes, the searcher shall forfeit—

For every inch in breadth, or half-yard in length, defective, 5*s.*

And for every other inch in breadth, or half-yard in length, deficient, 10*s.*

One moiety, deducting costs, to the informer, and the other to the treasurer of the West Riding.

False seals found, inspectors to put new ones, and the seller to forfeit double the deficiency, or take his cloth back, and pay expences. *Ibid.*

Inspector for sale stamping shall forfeit—

For the first inch in breadth, or half-yard in length, deficient, 1*l.* and if two inches in breadth, or one yard in length, deficient, to lose his office. If the inspector suspects fraud in the maker, he may wet and measure cloth. *Ibid.*

Power given to the sessions repealed; over-stretching cloths to forfeit, for the first half-yard in length, or inch in breadth, 5*s.* and every other quarter of a yard in length, and inch in breadth, 10*s.*

To extend to all cloths made in the West Riding of Yorkshire, except narrow cloths described by 11 *Geo.* 2. *c.* 28. and blankets and striped duffel'd blankets. *Ibid.*

And by STAT. 49 *Geo.* 3. *c.* 109. whereby the ancient statutes relating to the manufacture of *woollen cloths* were repealed; it is

ENACTED, that "persons who have served an "apprenticeship to any branch of the woollen "manufacture, and their wives and families "may set up and exercise any trade in any "place in Great Britain, but such persons "may be obliged by two justices to swear "as to their place of last settlement: an "attested copy of which oath is sufficient, "if summoned a second time. But the pri- "vileges of the city of London and two uni- "versities are saved."

MANUMISSION, (*Manumissio*) was the freeing a villein or slave out of bondage. 2 *Black.* 94, 347.

MANU OPERA, stolen goods taken upon a thief, apprehended in the fact. *Cowel.*

MANUOPERA, cattle or any implements used to work in husbandry. *Fleta.*

MANUPASTUS, signifies a domestic. *Erat culpabilis tanquam de manupasto. Leg. Hen.* 1. *cap.* 66.

MANUPES, a foot of full and legal measure. *Cowel.*

MANURE, (*colo, melioro*) to till, plough, or manure land. *Lit. Dict.*

MANUS, was anciently used for an oath, and for him that took it as a compurgator. If a person swore alone, it was *propria manu et unica.* The use of this word came probably from its being required at a person's hands, to justify himself; or from laying the hand upon the New Testament, on taking the oath. *Cowel. Blount.*

MANUS MEDIAE ET INFIMAE HOMINES, men of a mean condition, of the lowest degree. *Ibid.*

MANUTENENTIA, is a writ used in case of maintenance. *Reg. Orig. fol.* 182 & 189.

MANWORTH, the price or value of a man's life, or head; paid to the lord in satisfaction for killing him. *Cowel.*

MAPS AND PRINTS, See *Books* and *Prints.*

MARA, a mere, lake, or great pond, that cannot be drawn dry. *Paroch. Antiq.* 418. *Cowel.*

MARCA, a certain quantity of money. See *Mark.*

MARCATU, the rent of a mark by the year, anciently reserved in leases, &c. *Cowel. Blount.*

MARCH, earldom of, grants of its lands are to be under the great seal. 4 *Hen.* 7. *c.* 14.

MARCHERS, or LORDS MARCHERS, were those noblemen that lived on the Marches of Wales or Scotland; who in times past (according to Camden) had their laws, and *potestatem vitæ*, &c. like petty kings; which are abolished by *stat.* 27 *H.* 8. *c.* 26. and 1 *Ed.* 6. *c.* 10.

MARCHES, (*marchia*, from the Germ. *march, i. e. limes*, or from the Fr. *marque, viz. Signum*, being the notorious distinction between two countries, or territories) are the limits between England and Wales, or between us and Scotland. 14 *Car.* 1. *Cro. Car.* 384.

MARCHET, (*marchetum*) *consuetudo pecuniaria, in mancipiorum filiabus maritandis. Bract. lib.* 2. *cap.* 8. This custom, with some variation is observed in some parts of England and Wales, as also in Scotland, and the isle of Guernsey: and in the manor of Dinevor, in the county of Carmarthen, where every tenant at the marriage of his daughter pays ten shillings to the lord, which in the British language is called *Gwabr Merched, i. e.* a maid's fee. The custom for the lord to lie the first night with the bride of his tenant was very common in Scotland, and the north of England: but it was abrogated by Malcolm the Third, at the instance of his queen; and instead thereof a mark was paid to the lord by the bridegroom; from whence it is denominated *mercheta mulieris.* 2 *Black.* 83.

MARCHIARE, to adjoin to, or border upon. *Cowel.*

MARCULUS, a hammer, a mallet. *Ibid.*

MARES, See *Horses.*

MARESCHAL, See *Marshall.*

MARETUM, (Fr. *maret*, a fen or marsh) signifies marshy ground, overflowed by the sea or great rivers. *Co. Lit.* 5.

MARINER, (*Manerarius*) a mariner or seaman: and *marinariorum capitaneus* was the admiral or warden of the ports. *Cowel. Blount.*

The mariners of a ship are accountable to the master; the master to the owners; and the owners to the merchant, for all damages by negligence or otherwise. *Lex. Mercat.* or *Merch. Compan.* 66.

If a mariner be hired, and he deserts the service before the voyage is ended, by the law marine, and by the common law, he shall lose his wages: and if a ship is lost by tempest, &c. the mariners lose their wages, as well as the owners their freight; and this is to oblige them to use their utmost endeavours to preserve the ship. *Leg. Oleron.* 1 *Sid.* 179.

Where a mariner is wounded in the service of a ship, he is to be provided for, at the charge of the ship; and if his illness is very violent, he shall be left ashore with necessary accommodations, and the ship is not to stay for him; if he recovers, he is entitled to his full wages, deducting what the master expended for him. *Leg. Ol. c.* 7.

The common law hath jurisdiction for wages due to mariners individually, and in the admiralty they may all join. 1 *Vent.* 146.

MARINE FORCES, the marine forces while on shore are regulated and subjected to martial law, by an act which annually passes for that purpose.

MARISCUS, a marshy or fenny ground. *Cowel.*

MARITAGIO AMISSO PER DEFALTAM, a writ for the tenant in frank marriage to recover lands, &c. whereof he was deforced by another. *Reg. fol.* 171.

MARITAGIUM, that portion which is given with a daughter in marriage. *Glanvil. Lib.* 2. *c.* 18.

Maritagium, also signified the authority or power which the lord or guardian in chivalry had of disposing of his infant ward in matrimony without disparagement or inequality, which if the infants refused, was a forfeiture of the value of the marriage, *valorem maritagii. Lit. s.* 110.

MARITAGIUM HABERE, to have the free disposal of an heiress in marriage, a favour granted by the kings of England, while they had the custody of all wards or heirs in minority. *Cowel.*

MARITIME, (*maritimus*) sea affairs: any thing belonging to the sea. *Ibid.*

MARITIMA ANGLIÆ, the profit and emolument arising to the king from the sea, which anciently was collected by sheriffs; but it was afterwards granted to the lord admiral. *Ibid.*

MARK, (*marca*, Sax. *mearc*) the mark of silver was thirteen shillings and four-pence. *Stow's Annal.* 32.

MARK TO DEEDS, if a party be blind or illiterate, the deed previous to its execution, must be read to him and explained, and if he be unable to subscribe his name, he must set his mark thereto, which is usually done by a cross.

MARK TO GOODS, is what ascertains the property or goodness thereof, &c. And if one man shall use the mark of another, to the intent to do him damage, and he is actually damaged thereby, an action upon the case with a *per quod* lieth. 2 *Cro.* 471.

MARKET, (*mercatus* from *mercando*, buying and selling) is the liberty by grant or prescription, whereby a town is enabled to set up and open shops, &c. at a certain place therein for buying and selling, and better provision of such victuals as the subject wanteth; it is less than a fair, and usually kept once or twice a week. *Bract. lib.* 2. *cap.* 24. 1 *Inst.* 220.

MARKETZELD, or MARKETGELD, signifies toll of the market. *Cowel. Blount.*

MARLE, (*marla*, from the Sax. *margel*, i. e. *medulla*) otherwise called *malin*, is a kind of earth or mineral; which in divers counties of this kingdom is used to fertilize land. 17 *Ed.* 4. *cap.* 4. *Cowel.*

MARLERIUM or MARLETUM, a marle pit. *Cowel.*

MARQUE and REPRISAL, *letters of.* Persons formerly aggrieved by spoliations at sea during a truce, were entitled to letters of *marque* and *reprisal* on application to the king, who could grant the same by virtue of his prerogative. See *Prerogative.*

But this manner of granting letters of marque has long been disused, and according to the statute 4 *Hen.* 5. *c.* 7. could only be granted to persons actually aggrieved.

If, during a war, a subject without any commission from the king take an enemy's ship, the prize will not be the property of the captor, but will be one of the droits of admiralty, and belong to the king, or his grantee the admiral. *Carth.* 399. 2 *Wood.* 443. Therefore, to encourage merchants and others to fit out privateers or armed ships in time of war, by various acts of parliament, the lord high admiral, or the commissioners of the admiralty, are empowered to grant commissions to the owners of such ships; and the prizes captured, shall be divided according to a contract, entered into between the owners and the captain and crew of the privateer. But the owners, before the commission is granted, shall give security to the admiralty to make compensation for any violation of treaties between those powers with whom the nation is at peace. And by 24 *Geo.* 3. *c.* 47, they shall also give security that such armed ship shall not be employed in smuggling. These commissions in the statutes, and upon all occasions, are now called letters of marque. 29 *Geo.* 2. *c.* 34. 19 *Geo.* 3. *c.* 67. *Molloy, c.* 3, *s.* 8. However the lords of the admiralty have sometimes this authority by a proclamation from the king in council, as was the case in December 1780, to empower them to grant letters of marque to seize the ships of the enemy.

MARQUESS, or MARQUIS, (*marchio*) is now a title of honour before an earl and next to a duke; a marquis is created by patent.

MARRIAGE, (*maritagium*) is a civil and religious contract, whereby a man is joined and united to a woman, for the ends of procreation; but our law considers marriage in no other light than as a civil contract; the holiness of the marriage state is left entirely to the ecclesiastical law; the temporal courts not having jurisdiction to consider unlawful marriage as a sin, but merely as a civil inconvenience, the punishment therefore or annulling of incestuous or other unscriptural marriages, is the province of the spiritual courts; which act *pro salute animæ. Salk.* 121.

Marriage, therefore, considered in a *civil* light, is treated by our law like all other contracts; allowing it to be good and valid in all cases where the parties, at the time of making it, were, in the first place, willing to contract. *Secondly*, able to contract, and lastly *actually* did contract in the proper forms and solemnities required by law.

1st, They must be *willing* to contract. "*Consensus non concubitus, facit nuptias,*" is the maxim of the civil law in this case (*Ff.* 50, 17. 30): and it is adopted by the common lawyers (*Co. Litt.* 33).

2dly, They must be *able* to contract. In general, all persons are able to contract themselves in marriage, unless they labour under some particular disabilities, and incapacities. Now these disabilities are of two sorts: such as are canonical, and therefore sufficient by the ecclesiastical laws to avoid the marriage in the spiritual court; but these in our law only make the marriage voidable, and not *ipso facto* void, until sentence of nullity be obtained. Of this nature are *precontract, consanguinity,* or *relation* by blood; and *affinity,* or *relation* by marriage; and some particular corporal infirmities. These canonical disabilities are either grounded, upon the express words of the divine law, or are consequences plainly deducible from thence; it therefore being sinful in the persons who labour under them, to attempt to contract matrimony together, they are properly the object of the ecclesiastical magistrate's coercion; in order to separate the offenders, and inflict penance for the offence *pro salute animarum.* But such marriages not being void *ab initio,* but voidable only by sentence of separation, they are esteemed valid to all civil purposes, unless such separation is actually made, during the life of the parties. For, after the death of either of them, the courts of common law will not suffer the spiritual courts to declare such marriages to have been void; because such declaration cannot now tend to the reformation of the parties (*Co. Litt.* 33). And therefore where a man had married his first wife's sister, and after her death the bishop's court was proceeding to annul the marriage and bastardize the issue, the court of king's bench granted a prohibition *quoad hoc;* but permitted them to proceed to punish the husband for incest *(Salk.* 548.) These canonical disabilities being entirely the province of the ecclesiastical courts, our books are perfectly silent concerning them. But there are a few statutes which serve as directories to those courts, of which it will be proper to take notice. By statute 32 *Hen.* 8. *c.* 38, it is declared, that all persons may lawfully marry, but such as are prohibited by God's law;* and that all marriages contracted by lawful persons in the face of the church, and consummate with bodily knowledge, and fruit of children, shall be indissoluble. And (because in the times of popery a great variety of degrees of kindred were made impediments to marriage, which impediments might however be bought off for money) it is declared by the same statute, that nothing (God's law excepted) shall impeach any marriage, but within the levitical degrees;† the farthest of which is that between uncle and niece (*Gilb. Rep.* 158). By the same statute all impediments arising from pre-contracts to other persons, were abolished and declared of none effect, unless they had been consummated with bodily knowledge: in which case the canon law holds such contract to be a marriage *de facto.* But this branch of the statute was repealed by statute 2 & 3 *Edw.* 6. *c.* 23. How far the act of 26 *Geo.* 2. *c.* 33, (which prohibits all suits in ecclesiastical courts to compel a marriage, in consequence of any contract) may collaterally extend to revive this clause of *H.* VIII.'s statute, and abolish the impediment of precontract is uncertain.‡

The other sort of disabilities are those

---

* In this statute the prohibitions by God's law are not specified; but in the 25 *Hen.* 8. *c.* 22, and 28 *Hen.* 8. *c.* 7, the prohibited degrees are particularized, which see in the book of common prayer.

† The prohibited degrees are all which are under the 4th degree of the civil law, excepting in the ascending and descending line, and by the course of nature it is scarcely a possible case that any one should ever marry his issue in the 4th degree; but between collaterals it is universally true, that all who are in the 4th or any higher degree are permitted to marry; as first cousins are in the 4th degree, and therefore may marry, and nephew and great aunt, or niece and great uncle, are also in the 4th degree, and may intermarry; and though a man may not marry his grand-mother, it is certainly true that he may marry her sister. *Gibs. Cod.* 413.

The same degrees by affinity are prohibited. Affinity always arises by the marriage of one of the parties so related; as a husband is related by affinity to all the *consanguinei* of his wife; and *vice versâ* the wife to the husband's *consanguinei*: for the husband and wife being considered one flesh, those who are related to the one by blood, are related to the other by affinity. *Gibs. Cod.* 412.

Therefore a man after his wife's death cannot marry her sister, aunt, or niece. But the *consanguinei* of the husband are not at all related to the *consanguinei* of the wife. Hence two brothers may marry two sisters, or father and son a mother and daughter; or if a brother and sister marry two persons not related, and the brother and sister die, the widow and widower may intermarry; for though I am related to my wife's brother by affinity, I am not so to my wife's brother's wife, whom if circumstances would admit, it would not be unlawful for me to marry. *Ibid.*

‡ A contract *per verba de præsenti tempore* used to be considered in the ecclesiastical courts *ipso matrimonium,* and if either party had afterwards married, this, as a second marriage, would have been annulled in the spiritual courts, and the first con-

which are created or at least enforced by the *municipal* laws.

1. The first of these legal disabilities is a prior marriage, or having another husband or wife living; in which case, besides the penalties consequent upon it as a felony, the second marriage is to all intents and purposes void (*Bro. Abr. tit. Bastardy, pl.* 8.)

2. The next legal disability is want of age. This is sufficient to avoid all other contracts, on account of the imbecility of judgment in the parties contracting; *a fortiori* therefore it ought to avoid this, the most important contract of any. Therefore if a boy under fourteen, or a girl under twelve years of age, marries, this marriage is only inchoate and imperfect; and when either of them comes to the age of consent aforesaid, they may disagree and declare the marriage void, without any divorce or sentence in the spiritual court. This is founded on the civil law (*Leon. Constit.* 109). But the canon law pays a greater regard to the constitution than the age of the parties (*Decretal. l.* 4. *tit.* 2. *qu.* 3); for if they are *habiles ad matrimonium*, it is a good marriage, whatever their age may be. And in our law it is so far a marriage, that, if at the age of consent they agree to continue together, they need not be married again (*Co. Litt.* 79). If the husband be of years of discretion, and the wife under twelve, when she comes to years of discretion he may disagree as well as she may: for in contracts the obligation must be mutual; both must be bound, or neither; and so it is, *vice versa*, when the wife is of years of discretion, and the husband under (*Ibid*).

3. Another incapacity arises from want of consent of parents or guardians. By the common law, if the parties themselves were of the age of consent, there wanted no other concurrence to make the marriage valid: and this was agreeable to the canon law. But by several statutes (6 & 7 *Will.* 3. *c.* 6. 7 & 8 *W.* 3. *c.* 35. 10 *Ann. c.* 19), penalties of 100l. are laid on every clergyman who marries a couple without publication of banns (which may give notice to parents or guardians) or without a licence, to obtain which the consent of parents or guardians must be sworn to. And by the 26 *Geo.* 2. *c.* 33. *s.* 7, if any clergyman shall marry a couple out of a church or a public chapel, where banns had been usually published before 1754, unless by special licence from the archbishop: or shall marry them without a licence, or publication of banns; he shall be guilty of felony, and shall be transported for 14 years. And there have been instances of convictions for this offence. And by the stat. 4 & 5 *Ph.* and *M. c.* 8, whosoever marries any woman child under the age of sixteen years without consent of parents or guardians, shall be subject to fine, or five years imprisonment: and her estate during the husband's life shall go to, and be enjoyed by the next heir. The construction of the statute seems to be, that it shall also go to the next heir during the life of the wife, even after the death of the husband. 1 *Brown. Ch. Rep.* 23. But the contrary has been decided in the Exchequer. *Amb.* 73. The civil law indeed required the consent of the parent or tutor at all ages; unless the children were emancipated, or out of the parents power, (*Ff.* 23, 2, 2. & 18), and if such consent from the father was wanting, the marriage was null, and the children illegitimate (*Ff.* 1. 5. 11), but the consent of the mother or guardians, if unreasonably withheld, might be redressed and supplied by the judge, or the president of the province (*Cod.*5. 4. 1. & 20); and if the father was *non compos*, a similar remedy was given (*Inst.* 1. 10. 1), and it has lately been thought proper to introduce somewhat of the same policy into our laws by statute 26 *Geo.* 2. *c.* 33, whereby it is enacted that all marriages celebrated by licence (for banns suppose notice) where either of the parties is under 21, (not being a widow or widower, who are supposed emancipated,) without the consent of the father, or, if he be not living of the mother or guardian,* shall be absolutely void. A like provision is made as in the civil law, where the mother or guardian is *non compos*, beyond sea, or unreasonably froward, to dispense with such consent at the discretion of the lord chancellor: but no provision is made, in case the father should labour under any mental or other incapacity.

Much may be, and much has been said, both for and against this innovation upon our antient laws and constitution. On the one hand, *it prevents the clandestine marriage of minors*, which are often a terrible inconvenience to those private families wherein they happen. *On the other hand*, restraints upon marriages, especially among the lower class, are evidently detrimental to the public, by hindering the increase of the people;

---

tract enforced. 4 *Co.* 29. But as this pre-engagement can no longer be carried into effect as a marriage, we may now be assured that it will never more be an impediment to a subsequent marriage actually solemnized and consummated. 1 *Black.* 435, 6. n. 3.

* That is the party under age marrying by licence, if a minor, and not having been married before, must have the consent of a father, if living; if he be dead, of a guardian of his *person*, *lawfully appointed*; if there be no such guardian, then of the mother if she is unmarried; if there be no mother unmarried, then of a guardian appointed by the court of chancery.

and to religion and morality, by encouraging licentiousness and debauchery among the single of both sexes, and thereby destroying one end of society and government, which is *concubitu prohibere vago.* 1 *Black.* 438.

4. A fourth incapacity is want of reason; without a competent share of which, as no other, so neither can the matrimonial contract be valid (1 *Roll. Abr.* 357). It was formerly adjudged, that the issue of an idiot was legitimate, and consequently that his marriage was valid. And the stat. 15 *Geo.* 2. *c.* 30. has provided that the marriage of lunatics and persons under phrenzies (if found lunatics under a commission, or committed to the care of trustees by any act of parliament) before they are declared of sound mind by the lord chancellor or the majority of such trustees, shall be totally void.

Lastly, the parties must not only be willing and able to contract, but actually must contract themselves in due form of law, to make it a good civil marriage. Any contract made, *per verba de præsenti,* or in words of the present tense, and in case of cohabitation *per verba de futuro* also, between persons able to contract, was before the late act deemed a valid marriage to many purposes; and the parties might be compelled in the spiritual courts to celebrate it *in facie ecclesiæ.* But these verbal contracts are now of no force, to compel a future marriage (*stat.* 26 *Geo.* 2. *c.* 33.) Neither is any marriage at present valid, that is not celebrated in some parish church or public chapel, unless by dispensation from the archbishop of Canterbury. For the marriage act, 26 *Geo.* 2. *c.* 33. requires, that the marriage shall be celebrated in some parish church or public chapel, where banns had been usually published; *i. e.* before the 25th of March 1754. But as there have been many marriages solemnized in chapels since erected, which are therefore defective, acts of parliament have been passed, to legalize all marriages celebrated in such churches or chapels, since the passing of the marriage act, up to 23d Aug. 1808. See 21 *Geo.* 3. *c.* 53. 44 *Geo.* 3. *c.* 77. 48 *Geo.* 3. *c.* 127. And in the chapel of Voylas, in Denbighshire, banns may be published and marriages solemnized, notwithstanding the marriage act. See 44 *Geo.* 3. *c.* lxxxviii. It must also be preceded by publication of banns, or by licence from the spiritual judge. Many other formalities are likewise prescribed by the act; the neglect of which, though penal, does not invalidate the marriage. It is held to be also essential to a marriage, that it be performed by a person in orders (*Salk.* 119.); though the intervention of a priest to solemnize this contract is merely *juris positivi,* and not *juris naturalis aut divini:* it being said that pope Innocent the third was the first who ordained the celebration of marriage in the church (*Moor.* 170.); before which it was totally a civil contract. And, in the times of the grand rebellion, all marriages were performed by the justices of the peace; and these marriages were declared valid, without any fresh solemnization, by statute 12 *Car.* 2. *c.* 33. But, as the law now stands, we may upon the whole collect, that no marriage by the temporal law is *ipso facto void,* that is celebrated by a person in orders, in a parish church or public chapel (or elsewhere, by special dispensation)—in pursuance of banns or a licence,—between single persons,—consenting,—of sound mind,—and of the age of twenty-one years;—or of the age of fourteen in males and twelve in females, with consent of parents or guardians, or without it, in case of widowhood. And no marriage is voidable by the ecclesiastical law, after the death of either of the parties, nor during their lives, unless for the canonical impediments of pre-contract, if that indeed still exists; of consanguinity; and of affinity, or corporal imbecility, subsisting previous to the marriage.

By marriage with a woman, the husband is intitled to all her estate real and personal; and the effects of marriage are, that the husband and wife are accounted one person, and he hath power over her person as well as estate. 1 *Inst.* 357.

As to the real estate the interest of the husband is only for her life, unless he has issue by her born alive that might inherit, and then he will be tenant by the curtesy, for his own life, if he survive her.

But in *chattel* interests, the sole and absolute property vests in her husband, to be disposed of at his pleasure if he chooses to take possession of them; but unless he reduces them to possession by exercising some act of ownership upon them, no property vests in him, but they shall remain to the wife or to her representatives after the coverture is determined; and if he assigns her choses in action for a valuable consideration in her life time, and she survives, she is bound only to her amount of the consideration, and the residue survives to her. 1 *Atk.* 207. *Cox's P. Wms.* 380. But if the husband before marriage makes a settlement upon the wife in consideration of the wife's fortune, the representative of the husband will be entitled to all her things in action. 3 *Peere Wms.* 199. But if it is in consideration of part of the estate only, the residue not reduced into possession will survive to the wife: and where there is a settlement made equivalent to the wife's fortune, though no mention be made of her personal estate, the husband's representative will be entitled to the whole. *Butler's note to Co. Lit.* 352. If the husband cannot recover the things in action of his wife but by the assistance of a court of equity, the court, upon the principle that he who seeks equity must do equity, will not assist him in recovering the property, unless he either has made a previous provision for her, or agrees to do it out of the estate prayed for; or unless the wife appears personally in court, and consents to the property being given to him. 2 *Ves*. 669. But the court will not direct the fortune in all cases to be paid to the husband, though the wife appears to consent, where no previous provision whatever is made upon her. 2 *Ves*. 579. Lord Thurlow has declared that he did not find it any where decided, that if the husband makes an actual assignment by contract for a valuable consideration, the assignee should be bound to make any provision for the wife out of the property assigned; but that a court of equity has much greater consideration for the assignment actually made by contract, than for an assignment by mere operation of law; for as to the latter, his lordship declared it to be his opinion, that when the equitable interest of the wife was transferred to the creditor of the husband by mere operation of law, (as in the case of an assignee under a commission of bankrupt,) he stood exactly in the place of the husband, and was subject precisely to the same equity in respect of the wife. *Cox's P. Wms*. 459. And it is determined, the wife shall have the same relief, under a general assignment by the husband of his estate for the benefit of his creditors. 4 *Bro*. 139. An assignee of a bankrupt in such cases generally allows the wife one half. 3 *Ves. jun*. 620.

The courts of equity at present are not inclined to make any distinction between an assignee by contract and an assignee by operation of law; but perhaps they would compel the former to make the same provision for the wife as the latter. 4 *Bro*. 326. 2 *Ves. jun*. 608.

But if the wife's fortune is paid to the husband, or he can receive it without applying to a court of equity, then it can give no relief to the wife. 2 *Atk*. 420. *But. Co. Litt*. 351. 1 *Fonb. Tr. Eq*. 304.

There is therefore a very considerable difference in the acquisition of this species of property by the husband, according to the subject-matter; *viz*. whether it be a chattel *real*, or a chattel *personal*: and, of chattels personal, whether it be in *possession*, or in *action* only. A chattel real vests in the husband, not absolutely, but *sub modo*. As, in case of a lease for years, the husband shall receive all the rents and profits of it, and may, if he pleases, sell, surrender, or dispose of it during the coverture (*Co. Litt*. 46.): if he be outlawed or attainted, it shall be forfeited to the king (*Plowd*. 263.); it is liable to execution for his debts (*Co. Litt*. 351.): and, if he survives his wife, it is to all intents and purposes his own (*Ibid*. 300.) Yet, if he has made no disposition thereof in his lifetime, and dies before his wife, he cannot dispose of it by will (*Poph*. 5. *Co. Litt*. 351.): for, the husband having made no alteration in the property during his life, it never was transferred from the wife; but after his death she shall remain in her antient possession, and it shall not go to his executors. So it is also of chattels personal (or choses) in action: as debts upon bonds, contracts, and the like: these the husband may have if he pleases; that is, if he reduces them into possession by receiving or recovering them at law. And, upon such receipt or recovery, they are absolutely and entirely his own; and shall go to his executors or administrators, or as he shall bequeath them by will, and shall not revest in the wife. But, if he dies before he has recovered or reduced them into possession, so that at his death they still continue choses in action, they shall survive to the wife; for the husband never exerted the power he had of obtaining an exclusive property in them (*Co. Litt*. 351.) And so, if an estray comes into the wife's franchise, and the husband seizes it, it is absolutely his property: but if he dies without seizing it, his executors are not at liberty to seize it, but the wife or her heirs (*Ibid*.); for the husband never exerted the right he had, which right determined with the coverture. Thus, in both these species of property the law is the same, in case the wife survives the husband; but, in case the husband survives the wife, the law is very different with respect to chattels real and choses in action: for he shall have the chattel real by survivorship, but not the chose in action (3 *Mod*. 186.); except in the case of arrears of rent, due to the wife before her coverture, which in case of her death are given to the husband by statute 32 *Hen*. 8. *c*. 37. And the reason for the general law is this: that the husband is in absolute possession of the chattel real during the coverture, by a kind of joint-tenancy with his wife; wherefore the law will not wrest it out of his hands, and give it to her representatives; though, in case he had died first, it would have survived to the wife, unless he thought proper in his life time to alter the possession. But a chose in action shall not survive to him, because he never was in possession of it at all, during the coverture; and the only method he had to gain possession of it, was by suing in his wife's right; but as, after her death, he cannot (as husband) bring an action in her right, because they are no longer one and the same person in law, therefore he can never (as such) recover the possession. But he still will be entitled to be her administrator; and may, in that capacity, recover such things in action as became due to her before or during the coverture. 2 *Black*. 434.

And by 29 *Car*. 2. *c*. 3. *s*. 25. the husband shall have administration of all his wife's personal estate, which he did not reduce into his possession before her death, and shall retain it to his own use: and if he dies before administration is granted to him, or he has recovered his wife's property, the right to it passes to his personal representative, and not to the wife's next of kin. 1 *P. Wms.* 378. *But. Co. Litt.* 351.

Thus, and upon these reasons, stands the law between husband and wife, with regard to chattels real and choses in action: but, as to chattels personal (or choses) in possession, which the wife hath in her own right, as ready money, jewels, household goods, and the like, the husband hath therein an immediate and absolute property, devolved to him by the marriage, not only potentially but in fact, which never can again revest in the wife or her representatives. *Co. Litt.* 351.

And, as the husband may thus generally acquire a property in all the personal substance of the wife, so in one particular instance, the wife may acquire a property in some of her husband's goods; which shall remain to her after his death, and not go to his executors. These are called her paraphernalia; which is a term borrowed from the civil law (*Ff.* 23. 3. 9. § 3.), and is derived from the Greek language, signifying something over and above her dower. Our law uses it to signify the apparel and ornaments of the wife, suitable to her rank and degree; and therefore even the jewels of a peeress, usually worn by her, have been held to be paraphernalia (*Moor* 213). These she becomes entitled to at the death of her husband, over and above her jointure or dower, and preferably to all other representatives (*Cro. Car.* 343. 1 *Roll. Abr.* 911. 2 *Leon.* 166.) Neither can the husband devise by his will such ornaments and jewels of his wife; though during his life perhaps he hath the power (if unkindly inclined to exert it) to sell them or give them away (*Noy's Max.* c. 49. *Grahme* v. *Ld. Londonderry*, 24 Nov. 1746. *Canc.*). But if she continues in the use of them till his death, she shall afterwards retain them against his executors and administrators, and all other persons, except creditors, where there is a deficiency of assets (1 *P. Wms.* 730). And her necessary apparel is protected even against the claim of creditors, *Noy's Max. c.* 49.

The husband may dispose absolutely of his wife's jewels or other paraphernalia in his lifetime (3 *Atk.* 394). And although after his death they are liable to his debts, if his personal estate is exhausted, yet the widow may recover from the heir, the amount of what she is obliged to pay, in consequence of her husband's specialty creditors, out of her paraphernalia. 1 *P. Wms.* 730.

Marriage is dissolved by the natural death of the husband or wife, or by divorce; and where a marriage is dissolved by the death of the husband, dower, &c. survives to the wife, where no settlement is made of the husband's lands, &c. See *Adultery*, *Baron and Feme*, *Divorce*, and *Elopement*.

MARROW, a lawyer of great account in Henry VIIth's days. *Lamb. Eirenarch, lib.* 1. *cap.* 10.

MARSHAL, (*marescallus*) is a French word, signifying as much as *tribunus militum*, with the ancient Romans; and *marescallus* may also come from the German *marschalk*, i. e. *equitum magister*, which Hotoman in his feuds under *verb. Marchallus* derives from the old word *march*, which signifies a horse; and others make it of the Sax. *mar*, i. e. *equus et scalch, præfectus*. *Cowel.*

With us there are several officers of this name; the chief whereof is the earl marshal of England, stat. 1 *Hen.* 4. *c.* 7, and 13 *R.* 2. *c.* 2, whose office consists especially in matter of war and arms, as well in this kingdom as in other countries; this office is very ancient, having formerly greater power annexed to it than now; it has been long hereditary in the family of the duke of Norfolk. *Ibid.*

The next is the marshal of the king's house, otherwise called knight marshal; his authority is exercised in the king's palace, in hearing and determining all pleas of the crown, and suits between those of the king's house and other persons within the verge, and punishing faults committed there, 18 *Ed.* 3, *c.* 7. 21 *Ed.* 3, *stat.* 2, *c.* 6, and 2 *H.* 4. *c.* 13. *Cromp. Jurisd.* 192.

There are other inferior officers called marshals, as marshal of the King's Bench, *Stat.* 5 *Ed.* 3, *c.* 8, who hath the custody of the prison called the King's Bench Prison, in Southwark. *Cowel.*

There is also a marshal of the Exchequer, to whom that court commits the custody of the king's debtors, for securing the debts; he likewise assigns sheriffs, customers and collectors, their auditors, before whom they shall account. *Stat.* 51 *Hen.* 3, 5.

MARSHALLING OF ASSETS, is the distributive appropriation, by an executor or administrator, of the personal estate of the deceased; for the payment and satisfaction of his debts, according to their legal priorities, the order of which is set forth under title *Executor.*

MARSHALSEA (*marescallia*). The court of the lord steward of the king's household, or (in his absence) of the treasurer, comptroller, and steward of the marshalsea, (4 *Inst.* 133. 2 *Hal. P.C.* 7.) was erected by stat. 33 *Hen.* 8, *c.* 12, with a jurisdiction to inquire of, hear, and determine, all treasons, misprisions of treason, murders, manslaughters, bloodshed, and other malicious strikings, whereby blood shall be shed in, or within the limits, (that is, within 200 feet from the gate,) of any of the palaces and houses of the king, or any other house where the royal person shall abide. The proceedings are also by jury, both a grand

and a petit one, as at common law, taken out of the officers and sworn servants of the king's household. The form and solemnity of the process, particularly with regard to the execution of the sentence for cutting off the hand, which is part of the punishment for shedding blood in the king's court, are very minutely set forth in the said stat. of 33 *Hen.* 8, and the several officers of the servants of the household in and about such execution are described, from the serjeant of the wood-yard, who furnishes the chopping-block, to the serjeant farrier, who brings hot irons to sear the stump.

The court of the marshalsea, and the palace court at Westminster, though two distinct courts, are frequently confounded together. The former was originally holden before the steward and marshal of the king's house, and was instituted to administer justice between the king's domestic servants, that they might not be drawn into other courts, and thereby the king lose their service (1 *Bulst.* 211). It was formerly held in, though not a part of, the *aula regis* (*Flet. lib.* 2, *c.* 2), and when that was subdivided remained a distinct jurisdiction, holding plea of all trespasses committed within the verge of the court, where only one of the parties, is in the king's domestic service, (in which case the inquest shall be taken by a jury of the country) and of all debts, contracts, and covenants, where both of the contracting parties belong to the royal household, and then the inquest shall be composed of men of the household only (*Artic. sup. cart.* 28 *Ed.* 1, *c.* 3. Stat. 5 *Ed.* 3, *c.* 2. 10 *Ed.* 3, *st.* 2, *c.* 2). By the statute of 13 *Ric.* 2, *st.* 1, *c.* 3, (in affirmance of the common law, 2 *Inst.* 548,) the verge of the court in this respect extends for 12 miles round the king's place of residence *. And as this tribunal was never subject to the jurisdiction of the chief justiciary no writ of error lay from it (though a court of record) to the King's Bench, but only to parliament (1 *Bulstr.* 211. 10 *Rep.* 79), till the statutes of 5 *Ed.* 3, *c.* 2, and 10 *Ed.* 3, *st.* 2, *c.* 3, which allowed such writ of error before the king in his place. But this court being ambulatory, and obliged to follow the king in all his progresses, so that by the removal of the household actions were frequently discontinued (*F. N. B.* 241. 2 *Inst.* 548), and doubts having arisen as to the extent of his jurisdiction, (1 *Bulst.* 208.) king Charles the First, in the sixth year of his reign by his letters patent, erected a new court of record, called the *curia palatii*, or palace court, to be held before the steward of the household and knight marshal, and the steward of the court, or his deputy; with jurisdiction to hold plea of all manner of personal actions whatsoever, which shall arise between any parties within 12 miles of his majesty's palace at Whitehall (1 *Sid.* 180. *Salk.* 439.) The court is now held once a week, together with the antient court of marshalsea, in the borough of Southwark. and a writ of error lies from thence to the court of King's Bench. But, if the cause is of any considerable consequence, it is usually removed on its first commencement, together with the custody of the defendant, either into the king's bench, or common pleas, by a writ of *habeas corpus cum causa*: (see *Habeas Corpus*) and the inferior business of the court hath of late years been much reduced, by the new courts of conscience erected in the environs of London. 3 *Black.* 76.

* By the ancient Saxon constitution the *pax regia*, or privilege of the king's palace, extended from his palace-gate to the distance of 3 miles, 3 furlongs, 3 acres, 9 feet, 9 palms, and 9 barley-corns; as appears from a fragment of the *textus Roffensis* cited in Dr. Hickes's *Dissertat. epistol.* 114.

MART, a great fair for buying and selling goods, holden every year. 2 *Inst.* 221.

MARTIAL LAW, is the law of war, which is built upon no settled principles, but is entirely arbitrary in its decisions, and is, as sir Matthew Hale observes (*Hist. C. L. c.* 2,) in truth and reality, no law, but something indulged rather than allowed as a law. The necessity of order and discipline in an army is the only thing which can give it countenance; and therefore it ought not to be permitted in time of peace, when the king's courts are open for all persons to receive justice according to the laws of the land. And it is laid down (3 *Inst.* 52), that if a lieutenant, or other, that hath commission of martial authority, doth in time of peace hang or otherwise execute any man by colour of martial law, this is murder, for it is against *Magna Charta, cap.* 29.

The petition of right (3 *Car.* 1, and stat. 31 *Car.* 2, *c.* 1,) also enact, that no soldier shall be quartered on the subject without his own consent; and that no commission shall issue to proceed within this land according to martial law. But by the annual *mutiny acts*, a standing army is now allowed, subject within itself to martial law and certain articles of war.

MARTILAGIUM, for *martyrilogium.* Monast. *tom.* 2, *p.* 322.

MARTYROLOGY, (*martyrologium*) a book of martyrs, containing the lives, &c. of those men who died for their religion. *Cowel.*

MASAGIUM, anciently used for *messuagium*, a messuage. *Cowel. Blount.*

MASKS. Formerly there was a penalty on selling or keeping visor-masks. 3 *Hen.* 8, *c.* 9.

MASS. See *Papists.*

MASSER, or MASS-PRIEST, a priest that says mass. *Blount.*

MAST, (*glans, pessona*) the acorns and nuts of the oak, or other large tree. *Cowel.*

MASTER AND SERVANT

MASTER, (*magister*) signifies in general a governor, teacher, &c. and also in many cases an officer.

MASTER and SERVANT. The relation between a master and a servant, from the superiority and power which it creates on the one hand, and duty, subjection, and, as it were, allegiance on the other, is, in many instances, applicable to other relations, which are in a superior and subordinate degree; such as lord and bailiff, principal and attorney, owners and masters of ships, merchants and factors, and all others having authority to enforce obedience to their orders, from those whose duty it is to obey them, and whose acts, being conformable to their duty and office, are esteemed the acts of their principals. But the *servants* here to be considered in the relationship of *master* and *servant* are, 1st, *menial* servants, so called from being *intra mœnia*, or domestics. 1 *Black.* 423.

As to what a master or servant may respectively do: by reason of the relationship between them, it is observable, the master may *maintain*, that is, abet and assist his servant, in any action at law against a stranger, whereas, in general, it is an offence against public justice to encourage suits and animosities, by helping to bear the expense of them, and is called in law, maintenance. 2 *Rol. Abr.* 115.

A master also may bring an action against any man for beating or maiming his servant, but in such case he must assign, as a special reason for so doing, his own damage by the loss of his service, *per quod servitium amisit*; and this loss must be proved upon the trial (9 *Rep.* 113).

A master likewise may justify an assault in defence of his servant, and a servant in defence of his master: the master, because he has an interest in his servant, not to be deprived of his service; the servant, because it is part of his duty, for which he receives his wages, to stand by and defend his master. (2 *Roll. Abr.* 546).

Also if any person do hire or retain my servant, being in my service, for which the servant departeth from me, and goeth to serve the other, I may have an action for damages against both the new master and the servant, or either of them; but if the new master did not know that he is my servant no action lies, unless he afterwards refuse to restore him upon information and demand. The reason and foundation, upon which all this doctrine is built, seem to be the property, that every man has in the service of his domestics, acquired, by the contract of hiring, and purchased by giving them wages. *F. N. B.* 167, 168.

As for those things which a servant may do on behalf of his master, they seem all to proceed upon this principle, that the master is answerable for the act of his servant, if done by his command, either expressly given, or implied: *nam qui facit per alium, facit per se* (4 *Inst.* 109).

Therefore, if the servant commit a trespass by the command or encouragement of his master, the master shall be guilty of it, though the servant is not thereby excused, for he is only to obey his master in matters that are honest and lawful. If an innkeeper's servants rob his guests the master is bound to restitution; but it has been long established law, that the innkeeper is bound to restitution if the guest is robbed in his house by any person whatever, unless it should appear that he was robbed by his own servant, or by a companion whom he brought with him. 8 *Co.* 33.

And where an innkeeper had refused to take the charge of the goods, because his house was full, yet he was held liable for the loss, the owner having stopt as a guest, and the goods being stolen during his stay: (5 *T. R.* 273.) for as there is a confidence reposed in him, that he will take care to provide honest servants, his negligence is a kind of implied consent to the robbery; *nam, qui non prohibit, cùm prohibere possit, jubet*, (*Noy's Max. c.* 43.)

So likewise if the drawer at a tavern sells a man bad wine, whereby his health is injured, he may bring an action against the master; for although the master did not expressly order the servant to sell it to that person in particular, yet his permitting him to draw, and sell it at all, is impliedly a general command. 1 *Roll. Abr.* 95.

In the same manner, whatever a servant is permitted to do, in the usual course of his business, is equivalent to a general command. If I pay money to a banker's servant, the banker is answerable for it: If I pay it to a clergyman's or physician's servant, whose usual business it is not to receive money for his master, and he embezzles it, I must pay it over again. If a steward lets a lease of a farm without the owner's knowledge, the owner must stand to the bargain, for this is the steward's business. A wife, a friend, a relation, that use to transact business for a man, are *quoad hoc* his servants; and the principal must answer for their conduct; for the law implies, that they act under a general command; and without such a doctrine as this no mutual intercourse between man and man could subsist, with any tolerable convenience. If I usually deal with a tradesman by myself, or constantly pay him ready money, I am not answerable for what my servant takes up upon trust; for here is no implied order to the tradesman to trust my servant; but if I usually send him upon trust, or sometimes on trust, and sometimes with ready money, I am answerable for all he takes up, for the tradesman cannot possibly distinguish when he comes by my order, and when upon his own authority. *Doct. & Stud. d.* 2, *c.* 42. *Noy's Max. c.* 44.

And if I once pay for what my servant has bought upon trust, without expressing any disapprobation of it, it is equivalent to a direction to trust him in future; and I shall be answerable for all he takes up, upon credit, till an express order is given to the tradesman, not to give him further credit. *Christian's* 1 *Black.* 430.

If a servant, lastly, by his negligence does any damage to a stranger, the master shall answer for his neglect: as if a smith's servant lames a horse, while he is shoeing him, an action lies against the master, and not against the servant. But in these cases the damage must be done, while he is actually employed in the master's service; otherwise the servant shall answer for his own misbehaviour. Upon this principle, by the common law, (*Noy's Max. c.* 44,) if a servant kept his master's fire negligently, so that his neighbour's house was burned down thereby, an action lay against the master; because this negligence happened in his service: otherwise, if the servant, going along the street with a torch, by negligence sets fire to a house; for there he is not in his master's immediate service; and must himself answer the damage personally. But now the common law is, in the former case, altered by statute 6 *Anne, c.* 3, which ordains that no action shall be maintained against any, in whose house or chamber any fire shall accidentally begin; for their own loss is sufficient punishment for their own or their servant's carelessness. But if such fire happens through negligence of any servant, (whose loss is commonly very little) such servant shall forfeit 100*l.* to be distributed among the sufferers; and in default of payment shall be committed to some workhouse, and there kept to hard labour for 18 months.

A master is, lastly, chargeable if any of his family lays or casts any thing out of his house into the street or common highway, to the damage of any individual, or the common nuisance of his majesty's liege people; for the master has the superintendance and charge of all his household. And this also agrees with the civil law, which holds that the *pater familias*, in this and similar cases, "*ob alterius culpam tenetur, sive servi, sive liberi.*" *Noy's Max. c.* 44. *Ff.* 9. 3. 1. *Inst.* 4, 5, 1.

The law which obliges masters to answer for the negligence and unskilfulness of their servants, though oftentimes severe upon an innocent person, is founded upon principles of public policy, in order to induce masters to be careful in the choice of their servants, upon whom both their own security and that of others so greatly depends. And to prevent masters from being imposed upon in the characters of their servants, it is enacted by 32 *Geo.* 3, *c.* 56, that if any person shall give a false character of a servant, or a false account of his former service; or if any servant shall give such false account, or shall bring a false character, or shall alter a certificate of a character, he shall, upon conviction before a justice of the peace, forfeit 20*l.* with 10*s.* costs. The informer is a competent witness. But if any servant will inform against an accomplice he shall be acquitted.

MASTER OF THE ARMOURY, (*magister armorum et armaturæ regis*) an officer who had the care of his majesty's arms and armoury. *Stat.* 39 *Eliz. c.* 7.

MASTER OF THE CEREMONIES, (*magister admissionum*) is one who receives and conducts ambassadors and other great persons to audience of the king, &c. instituted by *Jac.* 1. *Cowel.*

MASTER OF, or, IN CHANCERY, (*magister cancellariæ*). In the chancery there are masters, who are assistants to the lord chancellor or lord keeper, and master of the rolls: of these there are some ordinary, and some extraordinary; the masters in ordinary are 12 in number, of whom the master of the Rolls is chief; and some sit in court every day during term, and have referred to them interlocutory orders for stating accounts, computing damages, and the like; they also administer oaths, take affidavits, and acknowledgments of deeds and recognizances. The extraordinary masters are appointed to act in the country, in the several counties of England, beyond ten miles distance from London, by taking affidavits, recognizances, acknowledgments of deeds, &c. for the ease of the suitors of the court.

MASTER OF THE COURT OF WARDS AND LIVERIES, was the chief officer of that *court*, now abolished by stat. 12 *Car.* 2, *c.* 24.

MASTER OF THE FACULTIES, (*Magister facultatum*) an officer under the archbishop of Canterbury, to grant licences and dispensations, &c. *Cowel.*

MASTER OF THE HORSE, is he who hath the ordering and government of the king's stables; and of all horses, racers, and breeds of horses belonging to his majesty: the office is of high account, and always bestowed upon some great nobleman. He is the third great officer of the king's household; being next to the lord steward, and lord chamberlain. *Ibid.*

MASTER OF THE JEWEL OFFICE, an officer of the king's household, having the charge of all plate used for the king or queen's table, or by any great officer at court; and also of all the royal plate remaining in the Tower of London, and of chains and jewels not fixed to any garment. 39 *Eliz. c.* 7.

MASTER OF THE HOUSEHOLD, (*Magister Hospitii Regis*) otherwise called grand master of the king's houshold, now styled lord steward of the houshold. 32 *H.* 8.—And under him there is a principal officer still called master of the household, who surveys the accounts, and has great authority. *Cowel.*

MASTER OF THE KING'S MUSTERS, was a martial officer in the king's armies, to see that the forces were complete, well armed and trained. *Ibid.*

MASTER OF THE MINT, an officer who receives the silver of the goldsmiths, and pays them for it, and oversees every thing belonging to the Mint; he is at this day called warden of the Mint; there is also an *assay*-master in the Mint. *Ibid.*

MASTER OF THE ORDNANCE, a great officer, to whose care all the king's ordnance and artillery is committed. 39 *Eliz. c.* 7.

MASTER OF THE POSTS. An officer of the king's court, who had the appointing, placing, and displacing of all such through England as provided post-horses for the speedy passing of the king's messages, letters, packets, and other business, since the establishment of the Post-office discontinued. *Cowel.*

MASTER OF THE REVELS, an officer to regulate the diversions of dancing and masking, used in the palaces of the king, inns of court, &c. and in the king's court is under the lord chamberlain.

MASTER OF THE ROLLS, (*magister rotulorum*) an assistant to the lord chancellor in the high court of chancery, and in his absence hears causes there, and also at the chapel of the Rolls, and makes orders and decrees. *Cromp. Jurisd.* 41. *Ibid.*

MASTER OF THE TEMPLE. The founder of the order of the Knights Templars, and his successors were called *magni templi magistri*, and probably from hence he was the spiritual guide and director of the Temple; as the chief minister of the Temple church in London is now called master of the Temple. *Dugd. Warw.* 706.

MASTER OF THE WARDROBE, (*magister garderobe*) is a considerable officer at court, who has the charge and custody of all former kings and queens ancient robes remaining in the Tower of London; and all hangings, bedding, &c. for the king's houses; he has also the charge and delivering out of all velvet or scarlet cloth allowed for liveries, &c. The lord chamberlain has the oversight of the officers of the wardrobe. *Cowel.*

MASTINUS, a great dog, called a mastiff. *Cowel. Blount.*

MASURA, an old decayed house. *Ibid.*

MASURA TERRÆ. *Sunt in eisdem masuris 60 domus plus quam ante fuerunt. Domesday. Cowel.*

MATERIA, a great beam, or timber proper for building. *Cowel.*

MATERIA PRIMA. In the time of sir Tho. More the definition which the philosophers currently gave of their *materia prima*, the ground-work of all natural knowledge, was, that it is "*neque quid, neque quantum,* "*neque quale, neque aliquid eorum quibus ens* "*determinatur;*" or its subsequent explanation by Hadrian Heereboord, who assures us that "*materia prima non est corpus, neque* "*per formam corporeitatis, neque per simplicem essentiam: est tamen ens, et quidem* "*substantia, licet incompleta; habetque ac-* "*tum ex se entitativum, et simul est poten-* "*tia subjectiva.*" *Philosoph. natural. c.* 1, *sec.* 28, &c. 3 *Black.* 322.

MATRICULA, a register; hence to be entered in the register of the universities is to be matriculated. *Ibid.*

MATRIMONIUM, is sometimes taken for the inheritance descending to a man *ex parte matris. Cowel. Blount.*

MATRIMONY. See *Marriage.*

MATRIMONIAL CAUSES, or injuries respecting the rights of marriage, are a branch of the ecclesiastical jurisdiction.

MATRIX ECCLESIA, the mother church, and is either a cathedral, or a parochial church, with respect to the chapels depending on it. *Leg. Hen.* 1, *c.* 19.

MATRONS, JURY OF. When a widow feigns herself with child, in order to exclude the next heir, and a supposititious birth is suspected to be intended, then upon the writ *de ventre inspiciendo*, a jury of women is to be empanelled to try the question, whether with child or not. *Cro. Eliz.* 566.

Also where a woman is capitally convicted, and pleads her pregnancy, though this is no cause to stay judgment, yet it is to respite the execution till she be delivered:

In case this plea be made, in stay of execution, the judge must direct a jury of twelve matrons, or discreet women, to inquire the fact; and if they bring in their verdict *quick with child*, (for barely *with child*, unless it be alive in the womb, is not sufficient) execution shall be staid generally, till the next session, and so from session to session, till either she is delivered, or proves by the course of nature, not to have been with child at all. 1 *Hal. P. C.* 369.

MATTER IN DEED, and MATTER IN RECORD, are often mentioned in law proceedings, and differ thus: The first seems to be nothing else, but some truth or matter of fact, to be proved by some specialty, and not by any record; and the latter is that which may be proved by some record. *Old Nat. Brev.* 19. *Kitch.* 216.

MAUGRE, (from the Fr. *mal*, and *gre*, i. e. *animo iniquo*) signifies as much as to say with an unwilling mind, or in despite of another. *Lit. sec.* 672.

MAUM, a soft brittle stone. *Cowel. Blount.*

MAUND, a kind of great basket or hamper, containing eight bales, or two fats: *Ibid.*

MAUNDY THURSDAY, the Thursday before Easter. See *Mandati Dies.*

MAUPIGYRNUM, an old sort of broth or pottage. *Cowel.*

MAXIMS IN LAW. Maxims are the foundations of the law, and conclusions of reason, so perfect, that they ought not to be impugned or disputed, but always admitted: yet they may, by reason, be conferred and compared, the one with the other, though they do not vary; or it may be discussed by reason, which thing is nearest the maxim, and the mean, between the maxim, and which is not; but the maxims can never be impeached or impugned, but ought always to be observed, and held as firm principles and authorities of themselves. *Pl. C.* 27. *b.*

These maxims are principles and authorities, and part of the general customs or common law of the land, and are of the same strength, as acts of parliament, when the judges have determined what is a maxim, which belongs to the judges, and not a jury. *Terms de Ley. Doct. & Stud. Dial.* 1, c. 8.

Maxims of the law are holden for law, and all other cases that may be applied to them shall be taken for granted. 1 *Inst.* 11, 67.

The maxims in our books are many and various, and too numerous to be inserted here.

MAY-DAY. See *Maii Inductio.*

MAYHEM. See *Maihem.*

MAYOR, (*præfectis urbis*, anciently *meyr*, comes from the Brit. *miret*, i. e. *custodire*, or, from the old English word *maier*, viz. *potestas*, and not from the Lat. *major*) is the chief governor or magistrate of a city or town, as the mayor of London, the mayor of Southampton, &c. See *Corporations. Justices. Mandamus. Quo Warranto.*

MEAL-RENTS, certain rents heretofore paid in meal by the tenants of the honour of Clun, to make meat for the lord's hounds, now payable in money. *Cowel. Blount.*

MEALS, the shelves of land, or banks on the sea-coasts of Norfolk, called meals, and males. *Ibid.*

MEAN, (*medius*) the middle between two extremes, and that, either in time or dignity. In time it is the interim betwixt one act and another, and applied to mean profits of lands, between a disseisin and recovery, &c. As to dignity there is a lord mean, or *mesne*, that holds intermediately of another lord. *F. N. B.* 135. 13 *Ed.* 1, *c.* 9. 7 *Hen.* 4, 12. 15 *Hen.* 6. *New Nat. Brev.* 330. *Stat. West.* 2, *c.* 9. 14 *Ed.* 3. *Cowel. Blount.*

MEASE, (*messuagium*) a messuage or dwelling-house. *Kitch.* 139. *F. N. B.* 2. *Stat. Hibern.* 14 *Hen.* 3, and 21 *Hen.* 8, 13. Also a measure of herrings, containing 500, from the half of 1000, being called *mease* or *mese*. *Merch. Dict. Cowel.*

MEASON-DUE, in French *Maison de Dieu*, Lat. *Domus Dei*, a house of God; a monastery, religious house, or hospital. 2 & 3 *Phil. & Mar. c.* 23. 39 *Eliz.* 5, and 15 *Car.* 2, 7.

MEASURE, (*mensura*) is a certain quantity or proportion of any thing sold. See *Weights* and *Measures.*

MEDERIA, was a mead-house, or place where mead or metheglin was made. *Cartular. Abb. Glast. M. S.* 29.

MEDFEE, a bribe or reward, or compensation where things exchanged were not of equal value. *Cowel.*

MEDIÆ ET INFIMÆ MANUS HOMINES, men of a mean and base condition, of the lower sort. *Blount.*

MEDIANUS, a word used for middle-size, a man of middle fortune. *Cowel. Blount.*

MEDIATORS OF QUESTIONS, were six persons authorized by statute, who, upon any question arising among merchants, relating to unmercatable wool, or undue packing, &c. might before the mayor and officers of the staple, upon their oath, certify and settle the same, to whose order and determination therein, the parties concerned were to give entire credence, and submit. 27 *Ed.* 3, *stat.* 2, *c.* 24.

MEDIETAS LINGUA, or, *medietate linguæ, jure de*, signifies a jury or inquest empanelled, whereof the one half consists of natives, and the other of *aliens*, and is used in pleas wherein the one party is an alien. He that will have the advantage of trial *per medietatem linguæ* must pray it, for he cannot have the benefit of it by way of challenge. *S. P. C.* 158. 3 *Inst.* 127. Also in petit treason, murder and felony, *medietes linguæ* is allowed; but for high treason, an alien shall be tried by the common law, and not *per medietatem linguæ*. *H. P. C.* 261.—And a grand jury ought not to be *de medietate linguæ*, in any case. *Wood's Inst.* 263.

MEDIO ACQUIETANDO, a judicial writ to distrain a lord for the acquitting of a mean lord from a rent, which he formerly acknowledged in court not to belong to him. *Reg. Judic.* 129. See *Mean.*

MEDITERRANEAN, is that which passeth through the midst of the earth; hence the sea which stretcheth itself from West to East, dividing Europe, Asia, and Africa, is called the Mediterranean Sea. And the counterfeiting of Mediterranean passes for ships to the coast of Barbary, &c. or the seal of the Admiralty office to such passes is felony without benefit of clergy. *Stat.* 4 *Geo.* 2, *c.* 18.

MEDLEFE, (from the *Fr. mesler*, quarrelling or brawling. *Bract. lib.* 3. *tract.* 2, *c.* 35.

MEDLETA, a sudden scolding at and beating one another. *Bract. lib.* 3, *c.* 35.

MEDSYPP, a harvest-supper, or entertainment given to the labourers at harvest-home. *Cowel. Blount.*

MEER, (*merus*) though an adjective, is used as a substantive, to signify mere right. *Old Nat. Brev.* 2.

MEIGNE, the same with *maisnada. Cowel.*

MEINY, (Fr. *mesnia*) the king's *meiny*, the king's family, or household servants. *Ibid.*

MELDFEOTH, (Sax.) was the recompense, due and given to him, who made discovery of any breach of penal laws, committed by another person, called the promoter or informer's fee. *Leg. Inæ, cap.* 20. *Cowel.*

MELIUS INQUIRENDUM, was a writ that laid for a second inquiry where a partial dealing was suspected; and particularly of what lands or tenements a man died seised, on finding an office for the king. *F. N. B.* 255.

MEMBERS OF PARLIAMENT, the representatives of the people in the house of commons, elected and deputed in the place of the people, to repeal old and useless laws, make new ones, and grant money when requisite, for the service of government. 1 *Black.* 153.

MEMORIES, are some kind of remembrances or obsequies for the dead, in injunctions to the clergy. 1 *Ed.* 6.

MEMORY, (*time of*) by the law, commences from the reign of Richard I. and any custom may be destroyed, by evidence, of its non-existence, in any part of the long period from his days to the present. 2 *Black.* 31.

MENACES. A menace alone (except in the case of sending a threatening letter, and the like, provided against by statute) without a consequent inconvenience, makes no real injury; but to complete the wrong there must be both together. *Finch.* 202.

MENAGIUM, a family, mentioned in *Trivet's Chronicle, p.* 677, and in *Walsingham, p.* 66.

MENDLEFE, quarrels, scuffling or brawling. *Cowel.*

MENIALS, (from *mœnia*) the walls of a castle, house, or other place; hence *menial* servants are those who live under their lord or master's roof.

MENSA, all patrimony, or goods and necessaries for livelihood. *Cowel.*

MENSA ET THORO. See *Divorce.*

MENSALIA, such parsonages or spiritual livings as were united to the tables of religious houses, and called mensal benefices among the canonists. *Cowel. Blount.*

MENSURA, a bushel of corn, &c. *Ibid.*

MENSURA REGALIS, the king's standard measure kept in the Exchequer. *Ibid.*

MER, or MERE, words which begin or end with those syllables signify fenny places. *Ibid.*

MERA NOCTIS, midnight. *Ibid.*

MERCEN LAGE. The *mercen lage*, or Mercian laws, were observed in many of the *midland counties*, and those bordering on the principality of Wales, the retreat of the ancient Britons, and therefore very probably intermixed with the British or Druidical customs. *Cowel.*

MERCENNARIUS, a hireling or servant. *Ibid.*

MERCHANT, (*mercator*) is one who buys and trades in any thing. *Lex Mer.* 23.

The law of England, as a commercial country, pays a very particular regard to foreign merchants in innumerable instances. By *Magna Charta, c.* 30, it is provided, that all merchants (unless publicly prohibited beforehand) shall have safe conduct to depart from, to come into, to tarry in, and to go through England, for the exercise of merchandise, without any unreasonable imposts, except in time of war; and, if a war breaks out between us and their country, they shall be attached (if in England) without harm of body or goods, till the king or his chief justiciary be informed how our merchants are treated in the land with which we are at war; and if ours be secure in that land they shall be secure in ours. *Ibid.*

The custom of merchants is part of the common law of this kingdom, of which the judges ought to take notice; and if any doubt arise about the custom, they may send for merchants to know the custom. *Per Hobart,* Ch. J. *Winch.* 24.

The *Lex Mercatoria* is allowed, for the benefit of trade, to be of the utmost validity in all commercial transactions, for it is a maxim of law, that "*cui libet in sua arte credendum est.*" 1 *Black.* 75. *Bac. Abr. tit. Merchants.*

MERCHENLAGE (*Merciorum lex*). See *Mercen Lage.*

MERCHET, (*merchetum*) a fine or composition anciently paid by inferior tenants to the lord, for liberty to dispose of their daughters in marriage. See *Marchet, Maritagium.*

MERCIA, used in many places for amerciament. *Cowel. Blount.*

MERCIMONIATUS ANGLIÆ, was of old time used for the impost of England upon merchandise. *Ibid.*

MERCY, the arbitrament of the king or judge, in punishing offences, not directly censured by the law. 11 *H.* 6. *c.* 2. *Cowel. Blount.*

MERE RIGHT. The mere right of property, the *jus proprietatis*, without either possession or even the right of possession, is frequently spoken of in our books, under the name of the *mere right, jus merum;* and the estate of the owner is in such cases said to be totally devested, and put to a right (*Co. Lit.* 345.) A person in this situation may have the true ultimate property of the lands in himself: but by the intervention of certain circumstances, either by his own negligence, the solemn act of his ancestor, or the determination of a court of justice, the presumptive evidence of that right is strongly in favour of his antagonist; who has thereby obtained the absolute right of possession. As, in the first place, if a person disseised, or turned out of possession of his estate, neglects to pursue his remedy within the time limited by law: by this means the disseisor or his heirs, gain the actual right of possession: for the law presumes that either he had a good right originally, in virtue of which he entered on the lands in question, or that, since such his entry, he has procured a sufficient title; and, therefore, after so long an acquiescence, the law will not suffer his possession to be disturbed without enquiring into the absolute right of property. Yet, still, if the person disseised or his heir hath the true right of property remaining in himself, his estate is indeed said to be turned into a mere right: but, by proving such his better right, he may at length recover the lands. Again, if a tenant in tail discontinues his estate-tail, by alienating the lands, to a stranger in fee, and dies; here the issue in tail hath no right of possession, independent of the right of property: for the law presumes, *prima facie*, that the ancestor would not disinherit, or attempt to disinherit, his heir, unless he had power so to do; and therefore, as the ancestor had in himself the right of possession, and has transferred the same to a stranger, the law will not permit that possession, now to be disturbed, unless by shewing the absolute right of property to reside in another person. The heir therefore in this case has only a mere right, and must be strictly held to the proof of it, in order to recover the lands. Lastly, if by accident, neglect, or otherwise, judgment is given for either party in any possessory action, (that is such wherein the right of possession only, and not that of property, is contested,) and the other party hath indeed in himself the right of property, this is now turned to a mere right; and upon proof thereof in a subsequent action, denominated a writ of right, he shall recover his seisin of the lands. 2 *Black.* 1.

Thus, if a disseisor turns me out of possession of my lands, he thereby gains a mere naked possession, and I still retain the right of possession, and right of property. If the disseisor dies, and the lands descend to his son, the son gains an apparent right of possession; but I still retain the actual right both of possession and property. If I acquiesce for thirty years, without bringing any action to recover possession of the lands, the son gains the actual right of possession, and I retain nothing out the mere right of property. *Ibid.*

And even this right of property will fail, or at least will be without a remedy, unless I pursue it within the space of sixty years.

And if a man has only in him the right of either possession or property, he cannot convey it to any other, lest precluded titles might be granted to great men; whereby justice might be trodden down and the weak oppressed. *Co. Lit.* 214. See *Buying and Selling pretended Titles.—Limitation.*

MERGER, is where a lesser estate in lands, &c. is drowned in the greater; as if the fee comes to tenant for years or life, lesser estates are merged in the fee: but an estate-tail cannot be merged in an estate in fee; for no estate in tail can be extinct, by the accession of a greater estate to it. 2 *Rep.* 60, 61. 2 *Plowd.* 418. *Cro. Car.* 275.

MERSCUM, a lake. *Cowel.*

MERSE-WARE, (Sax. *incola paludum*) the inhabitants of Romney Marsh in Kent. *Cowel.*

MERTLAGE, a corruption of, or a law-French word for martyrology. A church kalendar or rubic. *Cowel.*

MESNALTY, (*medieta*) signifies the right of the mesne as the mesnalty is extinct. *Old Nat. Br.* 44.

MESNE, (*medius*) intermediate, signifies him who is a lord of a manor, and so hath tenants holding of him; yet himself holds of a superior lord. *Cowel.*

MESNE PROFITS. As the damages recovered in ejectment are now usually (since the title has been considered as the principal question) very small and inadequate; amounting commonly to one shilling, or some other trivial sum. To complete the remedy, when the possession has been long detained from him that has right, an action of trespass also lies, after a recovery in ejectment, to recover the MESNE PROFITS, that is, the actual value or rent which ought to have been paid. Which action may be brought in the name of either the nominal plaintiff in the ejectment, or his lessor, against the tenant in possession; whether he be made party to the ejectment, or suffers judgment to go by default. 3 *Black.* 205.

MESSARIUS, (from *messis*) the chief servant in husbandry, or harvest-time, now called a bailiff in some places. *Mon. Angl. tom.* 2. *p.* 832. *Fleta, lib.* 2. *c.* 75. *Cowel.*

MESSENGER, is a carrier of messages, particularly employed by the secretaries of state, &c. 1 *Salk.* 347. 2 *Hawk. P. C.* 118. *Skin.* 599.

MESSENGERS OF THE EXCHEQUER, are officers attending that court; they are four in number, and in nature of pursuivants to the lord treasurer. *Cowel.*

There are also MESSENGERS to the serjeant at arms in chancery; and MESSENGERS to the commissioners of bankrupts.

MESSE THANE, signifies a priest. The Saxons called every man *thane*, who was above the common rank; so *messe thane* was he who said mass; and *worules thane* was a secular man of quality. *Cowel.*

MESSINA, reaping-time, harvest. *Id. ib.*

MESSUAGE, (*messuagium*) is properly a dwelling-house, with some adjacent land assigned to the use thereof. *West. Symb.* tit. *Fines, sect.* 26. *Bract. lib.* 5. *cap.* 28. *Plowd.* 169, 170. *Co. Lit. cap.* 8.

MESTILO, *mesline*, or rather *mescellane*, that is, wheat and rye mingled together. *Cowel. Blount.*

METECORN, a measure or portion of corn, given out by the lord to customary tenants, as a reward and encouragement for their duties of labour. *Ibid.*

METEGAVEL, (Sax. *cibi gablum, seu vectigal*) a tribute, or rent paid in victuals. *Ibid.*

METHEGLIN, (*Brit. meddiglin*) an old British drink made of honey, still in repute in England. *Ibid.*

METTESHEP, METTENSCHEP, was an acknowledgment paid in a certain measure of corn; or a fine or penalty imposed on tenants, for their defaults in not doing their customary services, of cutting the lord's corn. *Paroch. Antiq.* 495. *Cowel. Blount.*

MEUM ET TUUM, Latin words used in law, for the proper guides of right. *Ibid.*

MEYA, a mey or mow of corn, as anciently used. *Blount. Ten.* 130.

MICEL-GEMOTES, MICEL-SYNODS, the great councils in the Saxon times of king and noblemen, were called *witiena-gemotes*, and after *micel-synods* and *micel-gemotes*, i. e. great and general assemblies. *Cowel.* 1 *Black. Com.* 147.

MICHEL SYNOTH, same with *michel-gemote*, or *micel-gemote*. 1 *Black. Com.* 147.

MIDDLESEX, BILL OF. The usual method of proceeding in the court of king's bench without any original, is by a peculiar species of process entitled A Bill of Middlesex; so entitled, because the court now sits in that county; for if it sat in Kent, it would then be a bill of Kent. This bill of Middlesex must be served on the defendant by the sheriff, if he finds him in that county: but, if he returns "*non est inventus*," then there issues out a writ of *latitat* to the sheriff of another county, as Berks; which is similar to the *testatum capias* in the common pleas, and recites the bill of Middlesex and the proceedings thereon, and that it is testified that the defendant "*latitat et discurrit*" lurks and wanders about in Berks; and therefore commands the sheriff to take him, and have his body in court on the day of the return. See *Latitat.*

MILE, (*milliare*) the distance or length of ground described to contain eight furlongs, every furlong being forty poles, and every pole sixteen foot and a half. Stat. 35 *Eliz. c.* 6.

MILES, a knight. *Mat. West. p.* 118. *Cowel.*

MILITARE, to be knighted. *Ibid.*

MILITARY CAUSES, are by statute 13 *R.* 2. *c.* 2. declared to be such as relate to contracts touching deeds of arms and war, as well out of the realm, as within it, which cannot be determined or discussed by the common law; together with other usages and customs to the same appertaining.

Under the words "other usages and customs," are comprehended, 1. Grievances in matters of honour; 2. The distinction of degrees and quality; or, matters of coat-armour, precedency, and other distinctions of families. 3 *Black.* 103.

MILITARY COURTS, the only court of this kind known to, and established by, the permanent laws of the land, is the court of chivalry, formerly held before the lord high constable, and earl marshal of England jointly. See *Chivalry.*

MILITARY FEUDS. See *Feuds.*

MILITARY OFFENCES. These are defined by our annual acts for punishing mutiny and desertion, and the articles of war.

MILITARY POWER OF THE CROWN. The king is considered as the generalissimo, or first in military command within the kingdom. See title *Prerogative.*

MILITARY STATE, includes the whole of the soldiery; or, such persons as are peculiarly appointed among the rest of the people, for the safeguard and defence of the realm. 1 *Black.* 408.

MILITARY TENURES, were abolished by stat. 12 *Car.* 2. *c.* 4.

MILITARY TESTAMENT. Soldiers in actual military service may make nuncupative wills, and dispose of their goods, wages, and other personal chattels without those forms, solemnities, and expences, which the law requires in other cases. 29 *Car.* 2. *c.* 3. 5 *Will.* 3. *c.* 21. *s.* 6.

MILITIA. (Lat.) King Alfred first settled a national militia in this kingdom, and by his prudent discipline made all the subjects of his dominion soldiers: but we are unfortunately left in the dark as to the particulars of this his so celebrated regulation. 1 *Black.* 409.

In consequence thereof, all the lands in the kingdom, were divided, into what were called knight's fees, in number above sixty thousand; and for every knight's fee a knight or soldier, *miles*, was bound to attend the king in his wars, for forty days in a year, in which space of time, before war was reduced to a science, the campaign was generally finished, and a kingdom either conquered or victorious. By this means the king had, without any expense, an army of sixty thousand men always ready at his command, until the feodal system was abolished at the restoration, by statute 12 *Car.* 2. *c.* 24.

After, the restoration of king Charles the second, in consequence of the military tenures being then abolished, it was thought proper to ascertain the power of the militia, to recognize the sole right of the crown, to govern and command them, and to put the whole into a more regular method of military subordination (13 *Car.* 2. *c.* 6. 14 *Car.* 2. *c.* 3. 15 *Car.* 2. *c.* 4.): and the order, in which the militia now stands by law, is principally built upon the statutes, which were then enacted. And all prior acts, relating to the militia, having been repealed in 1802, the chief regulations by which it is now governed, depend on the stat. 42 *Geo.* 3. *c.* 90. and several subsequent acts—the qualifications of the officers—and quotas are as follows:

By 42 *Geo.* 3. *c.* 90. his majesty shall appoint lieutenants of counties, who shall call out the militia yearly, and appoint deputy lieutenants and officers, to be approved by his majesty, who are to rank as youngest of the same rank of officers in the regulars. *s.* 2.

Three deputy lieutenants may act when the lieutenant is out of the kingdom. Commissions shall not be vacated by the removal or vacating of the commission of the lieutenant. And each county lieutenant shall have the chief command of the militia of his county, and shall appoint twenty deputies. *s.* 3, 4, 5.

Deputy lieutenants, except in Cumberland, Huntingdon, Monmouth, Westmorland, Ely, or Wales, must have 200*l.* per ann. or be heir to 400*l.*—colonel 1000*l.* per ann. or heir to 2000*l.* per ann.—lieutenant-colonel 600*l.* per ann. or heir to 1200*l.*—major 400*l.* per ann. or heir to 800*l.*—captain 200*l.* per ann. or heir to 400*l.* per ann. or the youngest son of a person worth 600*l.* per ann.—lieutenant 50*l.* per ann. or 1000*l.* personal estate, or real and personal value 2000*l.* or heir to 100*l.* per ann. or the son of a person worth 2000*l.* personal estate, or 3000*l.* real and personal—and an ensign 20*l.* per ann. or 500*l.* personal estate, or 1000*l.* real and personal, or the son of a person having 50*l.* per ann. or 1000*l.* personal estate, or 1500*l.* real and personal estate, and one moiety of such qualifications for deputy lieutenants, lieutenant-colonels, majors, and captains, shall be situate within the county. *s.* 6.

A deputy lieutenant, in the excepted counties, must have 150*l.* per ann. or be heir to 300*l.* per ann.—a colonel 600*l.* per ann. or heir to 1200*l.* per ann.—a lieutenant, or major-commandant, 400*l.* per ann. or heir to 800*l.* per ann.—a major 200*l.* per ann. or heir to 400*l.* per ann.—a captain 150*l.* per ann. or heir to 300*l.* per ann.—a lieutenant 30*l.* per ann. or 600*l.* personal estate, or 1200*l.* real and personal estate, or heir to 60*l.* per ann. or a person having 1200*l.* personal estate, or 2400*l.* real and personal—and an ensign 20*l.* per ann. or 300*l.* personal estate, or 600*l.* real and personal, or heir to one having 30*l.* per ann. or 600*l.* personal estate, or 1200*l.* real and personal; and one moiety (except for lieutenants or ensigns) must be in the county. *s.* 7.

Deputy lieutenants in Ely must have 150*l.* per ann. or be heirs to 300*l.* per ann.—a captain 100*l.* per ann. or heir to 200*l.* per ann. or son of one having 300*l.* per ann.—a lieutenant 30*l.* per ann. or personal estate of 600*l.* or son of one having 60*l.* per ann. or 1200*l.* personal estate—and an ensign 20*l.* per ann. or 300*l.* personal estate, or son of one having 30*l.* per ann. or 600*l.* personal estate, half, except as aforesaid, in the Isle of Ely. *s.* 8.

Cities and places that are counties within themselves are liable to this act; and every deputy lieutenant must have 150*l.* per ann. or a personal estate alone, or that with a real one, of 3000*l.* amount: every field officer 300*l.* per ann. or a personal estate alone, or jointly with a real one, 5000*l.* amount—a captain 150*l.* per ann. or a personal estate alone, or jointly with a real one, of 2500*l.*—a lieutenant 30*l.* per ann. or a personal estate alone, of 750*l.*—and an ensign 20*l.* per ann. or a personal estate alone, of 400*l.* half, except as aforesaid, within such city or town. *s.* 9.

The immediate reversion in leases on lives of 300*l.* per ann. shall be deemed equal to a qualification as herein before specified of 100*l.* per ann. and so proportionally. *s.* 10.

Estates granted for twenty years, of an annual value equal to the value of the estates, herein required for qualification, shall be deemed good. *s.* 11.

No commission superior to a lieutenant shall be granted till the qualification is delivered in to the clerk of the peace, and transmitted to the county lieutenant. *s.* 12.

Qualifications shall be inserted in the Gazette; and lists shall be annually laid, by the secretary of state, before parliament: and deputy lieutenants and officers are to take the oaths within six months after appointment; and persons acting who are unqualified, or who have not delivered in their qualifications, forfeit 200*l.* if a deputy lieutenant, colonel, lieutenant-colonel, major; and if a captain, 100*l.*; one moiety to the informer; but peers, or their heirs apparent, may act though not qualified. *s.* 13, 14.

His majesty may at any time signify his pleasure to the county lieutenant to displace all or any of the deputy lieutenants and officers of the militia, which the lieutenant shall do, and appoint others. *s.* 17.

County lieutenants and deputies may appoint clerks for their meetings; and the following number of men [total 40,963] shall be raised in each county respectively. *s.* 18, 19.

For the county of	Bedford	317
———	Berks	561
———	Bucks	599
———	Cambridge	481
———	Chester and city	885
———	Cornwall	647
———	Cumberland	615
———	Derby	939
———	Devon and Exeter	1512
———	Dorset and Poole	411
———	Durham	492
———	Essex	1244
———	Gloucester city, and Bristol	1163
———	Hereford	520
———	Hertford	480
———	Huntingdon	159
———	Kent and Canterbury	1296
———	Lancaster	2439
———	Leicester	643
———	Lincoln and city	1368
———	Middlesex (except the Tower Hamlets)	3038
———	Monmouth	280
———	Norfolk and Norwich	1209
———	Northampton	724
———	Northumberland, Newcastle, and Berwick	649
———	Nottingham and Town	564
———	Oxford	603
———	Rutland	83
———	Salop	991
———	Somerset	1556
———	Southampton and Town	850
———	Stafford and Lichfield	1133
———	Suffolk	1042
———	Surrey	1336
———	Sussex	803
———	Warwick and Coventry	853
———	Westmorland	243
———	Worcester and city	616
———	Wilts	917
———	York, the West riding and city	2429
The North Riding		911
The East Riding and Kingston upon Hull		564
For the county of	Anglesea	123
———	Brecknock	204
———	Cardigan	244
———	Carmarthen and Borough	405
———	Carnarvon	128
———	Denbigh	344
———	Flint	201
———	Glamorgan	403
———	Merioneth	121
———	Montgomery	279
———	Pembroke and Haverfordwest	201
———	Radnor	140

Such numbers shall continue the quotas until June 25, 1805, and afterwards the numbers shall be appointed by the privy council. *s.* 20.

Constables shall make out yearly lists of the names of men between eighteen and fory-five, and affix a copy to the church-door with notice of the meeting for appeals, and return another copy to the deputy lieutenants. *s.* 28.

An appeal therefrom is allowed to the subdivision meetings, whose determination shall be final. *s.* 29.

Persons, endeavouring to prevail on constables, to make false returns, are to forfeit 50*l.* and for refusing to tell their names 10*l.* *s.* 31.

At the second subdivision meeting, *deputy lieutenants* shall appoint the number of men for each parish, and order notice thereof, and of the next meeting, at which they *shall cause the persons to be ballotted for and appoint another meeting*, when the persons chosen shall attend, be sworn in, and enrolled for five years. *s.* 41.

But such persons may produce substitutes, who, if approved, shall be inrolled and sworn in. *Ibid.*

Volunteers may be received, with the consent of the inhabitants, of any place, and a rate established for paying them bounties, not exceeding 6*l.* each; but persons having served by themselves, or substitutes, are not liable to the rates, and the same may be appealed against. *s.* 42.

Peers—commissioned officers in the forces, castles, or forts—officers on half pay—non-commissioned officers or privates in the forces—commissioned officer serving, or who has served four years in the militia—members of the universities—clergymen, licensed teachers, whose grant of worship was licensed for twelve months before the annual meeting in October—constables and peace officers—articled clerks and apprentices—seamen—persons mustered in the dock yards at the Tower—Woolwich—the gun wharfs at Portsmouth—the powder mills—freemen of the watermen's company—poor men who have more than one child born in wedlock, are not liable to serve or find a substitute; nor shall any person who shall have served personally, or found a substitute, be liable until, by rotation, it comes to his turn. *s.* 43.

MILL, (*molendinum*) is a house or engine to grind corn, and either a water-mill, wind-mill, horse-mill, hand-mill, or the like. And besides corn and grist mills, there are paper-mills, fulling or tucking-mills, iron-mills, oil-mills, &c. 2 *Inst.* 621. The toll shall be taken according to the strength of the water, *ordin. pro pistor. incerti temp. Art. cler'.* 9 *Ed.* 2. *st.* 1. *c.* 5.

And by 36 *Geo.* 3. *c.* 85. a balance and weights are to be kept in every corn mill which may be examined by the persons appointed under 35 *Geo.* 3. *c.* 102. (see *Weights and Measures*), on penalty of 20*s.* *s.* 1.

Millers are to weigh corn, if required, before and after ground, on pain of 40*s.* *s.* 2.

Millers are to deliver the whole produce of corn when ground, if required, allowing for waste and toll, on penalty of 1*s.* per bushel for the deficiency and treble the value. *s.* 3.

The toll is to be deducted from corn before it is put into the mill. *s.* 4.

No corn, but money, shall be taken for the toll, on pain of 5*l.* except where the party has no money. *s.* 5.

But this is not to extend to ancient mills, where a right to take toll has been established by custom and law. *s.* 5.

Millers are to put up in their mills, a table of prices, on penalty of 20*s.* *s.* 6.

The act does not extend to private mills. *s.* 7. And the penalties are recoverable before one justice, who, for want of distress, may commit for one month.

MILLEATE, (mentioned in stat. 7 *Jac.* 1. *cap.* 19.) a trench to convey water to or from a mill.

MILLET, (*milium*) a small grain so termed from its multitude. *Cowel.*

MINA, a corn measure of different quantity, according to the things measured by it: and *minage* was a toll or duty paid for selling corn by this measure. *Cowel. Blount.*

MINARE, to mine or dig mines. *Ibid.*

MINATOR CARUCAE, a ploughman. *Ibid.*

MINERAL, is any thing that grows in mines, and contains metals. *Ibid.*

MINERAL COURTS, (*curiæ minerales*) are peculiar courts for regulating the concerns of lead mines; as stannary courts are for tin. See *Berghmote. Ibid.*

MINES, (*mineræ*) quarries or places whereout any thing is dug; they contain the hidden treasures of the earth. The king by his prerogative hath all mines of gold and silver to make money; and where gold and silver mines is of the greater value; they are called royal mines. *Plowd.* But by statute, no mine of copper or tin shall be adjudged a royal mine, though silver be extracted. 1 *W. & M. c.* 30. And persons having mines of copper, tin, lead, &c. shall enjoy the same, although claimed to be royal mines; but the king may have the ore, (except in Devon and Cornwall) paying to the owners of the mines, within thirty days after it shall be raised, and before removed, 16*l.* per tun for copper ore, washed and made merchantable; for lead ore, 9*l.* per tun; tin or iron, 40*s.* &c. Stat. 5 *W. & M. c.* 6. If a man hath lands where there are some mines open and others not, and he lets the land with the mines therein, for life or years, the lessee may dig in the open mines only, which is sufficient to satisfy the words in the lease; and hath no power to dig the mines unopened: but if there be no open mine, and the lease is made of the lands, together with all mines therein, there the lessee may dig for mines and enjoy the benefit thereof; otherwise those words would be void. 1 *Inst.* 54. 5 *Rep.* 12. 2 *Lev.* 184. To dig mines is waste, where lessees are not authorised by their leases; though a mine is not properly so called till it is opened; being but a vein of iron or coals, &c. before. 1 *Inst.* 54. v. 2 *Mod.* 193.

If any person maliciously set on fire any mine, or pit of coal, he shall suffer death as a felon, by stat. 10 *Geo.* 2. *c.* 32. And damaging such mines, or any coal-works, by conveying water therein, or obstructing sewers from draining them, &c. shall forfeit treble damages. 13 *Geo.* 2. *c.* 21. 24 *Geo.* 2. *c.* 57.

Entering mines of black lead with intent to steal, is felony. 25 *Geo.* 2. *c.* 10. See *Felony.*

And lastly, by 39 & 40 *Geo.* 3. *c.* 87. if any person shall pull down or fill up any air-way, or damage any road leading to or from any mine, or not having a right shall dig any mineral lying in any waste, he shall be deemed guilty of a misdemeanor, and may be imprisoned six months. *s.* 1.

But the act is not to extend to any damage done under ground by owners of adjoining mines in working the same. *s.* 2.

If any collier or miner shall work any coal or ore, different to his agreement, or contrary to the directions of the owner, or shall refuse to fulfil his engagement, he shall, on conviction before one justice, forfeit not exceeding 40*s.* and on non-payment may be imprisoned for not exceeding six months. *s.* 3.

If any collier or miner shall stack any coal or ore, in a fraudulent manner, to defraud his employer, or shall remove any iron stone to defraud his fellow-workmen, he may be imprisoned not exceeding three months. *s.* 4.

If any person shall steal any coal or materials, not more than 5*s.* value, from any place belonging to any manufacturer, or coal dealer, or out of any boat or carriage, or shall damage any carriage used for carrying coals, or damage any tools used for cutting coal or minerals, not exceeding 5*s.* value, he shall be liable to not exceeding 10*s.* or one month's imprisonment, for the first offence, 20*s.* or three months, for the second, and 40*s.* or six months, for the third and every other offence. *s.* 5.

The penalties go half to the informer, and half to the poor of the parish: the evidence of the parishioners shall be good; but prosecutions must be begun within nine months, and persons aggrieved may appeal to the quarter sessions (except in orders of commitment), and there is no *certiorari* allowed. *s.* 6, 7, 8, 9, 10.

Mines, in another signification, are caves or trenches dug under ground, whereby to undermine the walls of a city or fortification.

MINIMENTS, or MUNIMENTS, (*mu-*

nimenta, from *munio*, to defend) are the evidence and writings concerning a man's possession or inheritance, whereby he is enabled to defend the title of his estate. *Terms de Ley*. Stat. 5 *R*. 2. *c*. 8. and 35 *H*. 6. *c*. 37.

MINISTERS, disturbing them in the execution of their office, see *Church* and *Dissenters*.

MINISTRI REGIS, judges of the realm; as well as those who have ministerial offices in the government. 2 *Inst*. 208.

MINOR, one under age. See *Age—Infant*.

MINORES, *friars minorites*, of the order of St. Francis, that had no prior; they washed each other's feet, and increased very much in the year 1207. *Mat. West.*

MINSTREL, (*ministrellus et menestrullus*, from the Fr. *menestrier*) a musician, fidler, or piper. By stat. 39 *Eliz. c*. 4. fidlers are declared to be rogues, yet there is a proviso therein, exempting those in Cheshire licensed by Dutton of Dutton. *Cowel.* 2 *Black*. 96.

MINT, (*officina monetaria, monetarium*) is the place where the king's money is coined; which is at present and long hath been in the Tower of London.

The officers belonging to the mint are now the following, *viz*. the warden, who is the chief of the rest, and is by his office to receive the silver and bullion of the goldsmiths to be coined, and take care thereof, and he hath the overseeing of all the other offices. The master worker receives the silver from the warden, and causes it to be melted, when he delivers it to the moniers, and taketh it from them again after made into money. The comptroller, who is to see that the money be made to the just assise, and controul the officers, if the money be not made as it ought. The master of the assay, who weigheth the silver, and examineth whether it be according to the standard. The auditor takes account of the silver, &c. The surveyor of the melting, who is to see the silver cast out, and that it be not altered after the assay master hath made trial of it, and it is delivered to the melters. The clerk of the irons, who seeth that the irons be clean and fit for working. The graver, whose office is to engrave the stamps for the money. The melters, who melt the bullion, &c. The blanchers do anneal and cleanse the money. The moniers, who are some to shear the money, others to forge and beat it broad, some to round and some to stamp or coin it. The provost to provide for all the monies, and oversee them, &c. *Cowel.*

MINT, a pretended place of privilege from arrests in Southwark, near the King's Bench, put down by statute 9 *Geo*. 1. *c*. 28. See *Privileged Places*.

MINUERE, to let blood; *minutio*, blood-letting. *Cowel.*

MINURE TITHES, (*minutæ sive minores decimæ*) small tithes, such as usually belong to the vicar, as of wool, lambs, pigs, butter, cheese, herbs, seeds, eggs, honey, wax, &c. 2 *Inst*. 649.

MIRACULA, a superstitious sport or play, practised by the popish clergy for gain and deceit; prohibited by bishop Grosthead in the diocese of Lincoln. *Cowel.*

MIS: this syllable added to another word signifies some fault or defect; as, misprision. *Cowel.*

MISA, a compact or agreement, a form of peace, or compromise. *Id. ib.*

MISADVENTURE, (Fr. *misadventure*, i. e. *infortunium*) the killing a man, partly by chance. *S. P. C. lib*. 1. *c*. 8. See *Homicide*.

MISCASTING or MISCOMPUTING, formerly an *assumpsit* to pay 12*l*. if the jury found a promise to pay 7*l*. the judgment was reversed; because it was a miscasting or miscomputing not the same *assumpsit*. *Dyer* 219. b. *Marg. pl*. 11.

MISCHIEF, MALICIOUS. Malicious mischief, or damage; is an injury done to private property from a spirit of wantonness or black and diabolical revenge; and although this is in general only a trespass at common law, yet in many instances it is made penal in the highest degree by divers statutes.—Thus by stat. 22 *Hen*. 8. *c*. 11. perversely and maliciously to cut down or destroy the powdike, in the fens of Norfolk and Ely, is felony. —For this and other statutes relating to malicious mischief, see *Felony, Damages wilful*.

MISCOGNISANT, ignorant or not knowing.

MISCONTINUANCE, signifies the same with discontinuance. *Kitch*. 231.

MISDEMESNOR, or MISDEMEANOR. This word in the laws of England, signifies a crime.—Every crime is a misdemeanor, yet the law hath made a distinction between crimes of an higher and a lower nature, the latter being denominated misdemeanors, the former felonies, &c.

A crime or misdemeanor, is therefore an act committed or omitted, in violation of a public law, either forbidding or commanding it. This general definition comprehends both crimes and misdemeanors; which, properly speaking, are mere synonymous terms; though in common usage, the word "crimes," is made to denote such offences as are of a deeper and more atrocious dye; while smaller faults, and omissions of less consequence, are comprised under the gentle name of "misdemeanors." 4 *Black*. 3, 5.

MISE, (a French word, written in Latin *missum*, and sometimes *misa*) is a law term signifying expences, and it is so commonly used in the entries of judgments, in personal actions; as when the plaintiff recovers, that *recuperet damna sua* to such a value, and *pro misis et custagiis*, for costs and charges so much, &c. This word hath also another signification in the use made of it by law; which is where it is taken for a word of art, appropriated to a writ of right, so called because both parties have put themselves upon the mere right, to be tried upon the grand assise, so that what in all other actions is called an issue, in a writ of writ is termed a mise; but if in the writ of right, a collateral point be tried, there it is called an issue. To join the mise upon the meer right, is as much as to say, to join the mise upon the clear right, *i. e.* to join upon this point, which hath the more right, the tenant or demandant. 1 *Inst.* 294. 37 *Ed.* 3. *c.* 16.

MISE-MONEY, was money given by way of contract or composition to purchase any liberty, &c. *Blount. Ten.* 162.

MISES, taxes or tallages, &c. An honorary gift or customary present, from the people of Wales to every new king and prince of Wales, anciently given in cattle, wine and corn, afterwards in money, 5000*l.* or more, was denominated a mise: so was the tribute or fine of 3000 marks, paid by the inhabitants of the county palatine of Chester, at the change of every owner of the said earldoms for enjoying their liberties. And at Chester they have a *mise-book*, wherein every town and village in the county is rated what to pay towards the mise. And mise is sometimes corruptly used for mease, in law French *mees*, a messuage; as a mise place in some manors is such a messuage or tenement as answers the lord a heriot at the death of its owner. 2 *Inst.* 528.

MISELLI, leprous persons. *Cowel.*

MISERERE, *nobis domine*, the psalm of mercy.

MISERICORDA, is in law, used for an arbitrary or discretionary amerciament imposed for an offence; and where the plaintiff or defendant in any action is amerced, the entry is *ideo in misericordia, &c. Bract. lib.* 4. *tract.* 5 *cap.* 6. *Kitch.* 78. So called because it ought to be but small, and rather less than the offence, according to *magna charta, c.* 14. Sometimes *misericordia* is to be quit of all manner of amerciaments. *Cromp. Jurisd.* 196.

MISERICORDIA *in cibis & potu*, exceedings, or over-commons, or any gratuitous portion of meat and drink given to the religious above their ordinary allowance. *Cowel. Blount.*

MISERICORDIA COMMUNIS, is when a fine is set on the whole county, or hundred. *Ibid.*

MISEVENIRE, to succeed ill; as, where a man is accused of a crime, and fails in his defence, or purgation. *Ibid.*

MISFEASANCE, a misdeed or trespass. *Cro. Car.* 498.

MISFEASOR, a trespasser. 2 *Inst.* 200.

MISFORTUNE, or CHANCE, a deficiency of the will, or committing of an unlawful act, by misfortune or chance, and not by design. 4 *Black.* 26. See *Homicide.*

MISKENNING, (*miskenninga*) is derived from *mis*, and Sax. *cennan*, i.e. *citare*, and signifies a varying or changing one's speech in court. *Leg. H.* 1. *c.* 12. *Iniqua vel injusta in jus votatio; inconstanter loqui in curia, vel inviare.* Cowel.

MISKERING, to be quit of amerciaments, *hoc est quietus esse pro querelis coram quibuscunque in transumptione probata.* The same as *Abishersing*, which see.

MISNOMER, (compounded of the Fr. *mes*, signifying amiss, and *nomer*, i. e. *nominare*) is the using one name for another, a misnaming. 11 *Rep.* 20, 21. *Ld. Raym.* 304. *Hob.* 125. *Poph.* 57. 2 *Lil. Abr.* 199. 2 *Cro.* 67, 425. 1 *Leon.* 146. 1 *Rol. Abr.* 135. 1 *And.* 211. See *Abatement* and *Addition.*

MISPLEADING, if in pleading, any thing be omitted, that is essential to the action or defence, as if the plaintiff does not merely state his title in a defective manner, but sets forth a title that is wholly defective in itself, or if to an action of debt (*i. e.* on bond, contract, &c.) the defendant pleads *not guilty* instead of *nil debet*, these cannot be cured by a verdict for the plaintiff, in the first case, or for the defendant in the second. *Salk.* 365. *Cro. Eliz.* 778. 3 *Black.* 394.

But if a declaration or plea omits to state some particular circumstance, without proving of which, at the trial, it is impossible to support the action or defence, this omission shall be aided by a verdict. As if, in an action of trespass, the declaration doth not allege that the trespass was committed *on any certain day* (*Carth.* 389.); or if the defendant justifies, by prescribing for a right of common for his cattle, and does not plead that his cattle were *levant* and *couchant* on the land (*Cro. Jac.* 44.); though either of these defects might be good cause to demur to the declaration or plea, yet if the adverse party omits to take advantage of such omission in due time, but takes issue, and has a verdict against him, these exceptions cannot, after verdict, be moved, in arrest of judgment.

MISPRISION, (*misprisio contemptus*). Misprisions (a term derived from the old French *mespris*, a neglect or contempt) are, in the acceptation of our law, generally understood to be all such high offences as are under the degree of capital, but nearly bordering thereon; and it is said, that a misprision is contained in every treason and felony whatsoever; and that, if the king so please, the offender may be proceeded against for the misprision only (*Yearb. Ric.* 3. 10. *Staundf. P. C.* 37. *Kel.* 71. 1 *Hal. P. C.* 374. 1 *Hawk. P. C.* 55, 56.) Misprisions are generally divided into two sorts: negative, which consist in the concealment of something which ought to be revealed; and positive, which consist in the commission of something which ought not to be done.

I. Of the first or negative kind, is what is called misprision of treason; consisting in the bare knowledge and concealment of treason, without any degree of assent thereto. See *Treason.*

Misprision of felony is also the concealment of a felony which a man knows, but never assented to; for if he assented, this makes him either principal or accessory.

There is also another species of negative misprisions: namely, the concealing of treasure-trove, which belongs to the king or his grantees by prerogative royal: the concealment of which was formerly punishable by death (*Glanv. l.* 1, *c.* 2); but now only by fine and imprisonment (3 *Inst.* 133).

II. Misprisions, which are merely positive, are generally denominated contempts or high misdemesnors; of which

1. The first and principal is the mal-administration of such high officers, as are in public trust and employment. This is usually punished by the method of parliamentary impeachment: wherein such penalties short of death, are inflicted, as to the wisdom of the house of peers shall seem proper; consisting usually of banishment, imprisonment, fines, or perpetual disability. See *Impeachment.*

2. Contempts against the king's prerogative. As, by refusing to assist him for the good of the public; either in his councils, by advice, if called upon; or in his wars, by personal service for the defence of the realm against a rebellion or invasion (1 *Hawk. P. C.* 59). Under which class may be ranked the neglecting to join the *posse comitatus,* or power of the county, being thereunto required by the sheriff or justices, according to the statute 2 *Hen.* 5. *c.* 8, which is a duty incumbent upon all that are fifteen years of age, under the degree of nobility, and able to travel (*Lamb. Eir.* 315). Contempts against the prerogative may also be, by preferring the interests of a foreign potentate to those of our own, or doing or receiving any thing that may create an undue influence, in favour of such extrinsic power; as, by taking a pension from any foreign prince without the consent of the king (3 *Inst.* 144). Or, by disobeying the king's lawful commands, whether by writs issuing out of his courts of justice, or by a summons to attend his privy council, or by letters from the king to a subject commanding him to return from beyond the seas, (for disobedience to which his lands shall be seised till he does return, and himself afterwards punished), or by his writ of *ne exeat regnum,* or proclamation, commanding the subject to stay at home. Disobedience to any of these commands is a high misprision and contempt; and so, lastly, is disobedience to any act of parliament, where no particular penalty is assigned; for then it is punishable like the rest of these contempts, by fine and imprisonment, at the discretion of the king's courts of justice (1 *Hawk. P. C.* 60).

3. Contempts and misprisions against the king's person and government, may be by speaking or writing against them, cursing or wishing him ill, giving out scandalous stories concerning him, or doing any thing that may tend to lessen him in the esteem of his subjects, may weaken his government, or, may raise jealousies between him and his people. It has been also held an offence of this species to drink to the pious memory of a traitor: or for a clergyman to absolve persons at the gallows, who there persist in the treasons for which they die: these being acts which impliedly encourage rebellion. And for this species of contempt a man may not only be fined and imprisoned, but suffer the pillory or other infamous corporal punishment (*Ibid*): in like manner as, in the antient German empire, such persons as endeavoured to sow sedition, and disturb the public tranquillity, were condemned to become the objects of public notoriety and derision, by carrying a dog upon their shoulders from one great town to another. The emperors Otho I. and Frederic Barbarossa inflicted this punishment on noblemen of the highest rank (*Mod. Un. Hist.* xxix. 28. 119).

4. Contempts against the king's title, not amounting to treason or *præmunire,* are the denial of his right to the crown in common and unadvised discourse; for, if it be by advisedly speaking, it amounts to *præmunire.* (see *Præmunire.*) This heedless species of contempt is however punished by our law with fine and imprisonment. Likewise if any person shall in any wise hold, affirm, or maintain, that the common laws of this realm not altered by parliament, ought not to direct the right of the crown of England; this is a misdemesnor, by statute 13 *Eliz. c.* 1, and punishable with forfeiture of goods and chattels. A contempt may also arise from refusing or neglecting to take the oaths, appointed by statute for the better securing the government; and yet acting in a public office, place of trust, or other capacity, for which the said oaths are required to be taken; *viz.* those of allegiance, supremacy, and abjuration; which must be taken within six calendar months after admission. The penalties for this contempt inflicted by stat. 1 *Geo.* 1. *st.*2.*c.* 13, are very little, if any thing, short of those of a *præmunire*: being an incapacity to hold the said offices, or any other; to prosecute any suit, to be guardian or executor, to take any legacy or deed of gift; and to vote at any election for members of parliament: and after conviction the offender shall also forfeit 500*l.* to him or them that will sue for the same. Members on the foundation of any college in the two universities, who by this statute are bound to take the oaths, must also register a certificate thereof in the college register, within one month after; otherwise, if the electors do not remove him, and elect another within twelve months or after, the king may nominate a person to succeed him by his great seal or sign manual. Be-

sides thus taking the oaths for offices, any two justices of the peace may by the same statute summon, and tender the oaths to any person whom they shall suspect to be disaffected; and every person refusing the same, who is properly called a non-juror, shall be adjudged a popish recusant convict, and subject to the same penalties. See *Oaths*.

5. Contempts against the king's palaces or courts of justice have been always looked upon as high misprisions: and by the antient law, before the conquest, fighting in the king's palace or before the king's judges was punished with death (3 *Inst.* 140. *LL. Alured. cap.* 7 & 34). And at present, by statute 33 *Hen.* 8. *c.* 12, malicious striking in the king's palace, wherein his royal person resides, whereby blood is drawn, is punishable by perpetual imprisonment, and fine at the king's pleasure; and also with loss of the offender's right hand, the solemn execution of which sentence is prescribed in the statute at length.

But striking in the king's superior courts of justice, in Westminster-hall, or at the assises, is made still more penal than even in the king's palace. The reason seems to be, that those courts being antiently held in the king's palace, and before the king himself, striking there included the former contempt against the king's palace, and something more; *viz.* the disturbance of public justice. For this reason, by the antient common law before the conquest (*LL. Inae. c.* 6. *LL. Canut. c.* 56. *LL. Alured. c.* 7), striking in the king's courts of justice, or drawing a sword therein, was a capital felony: and our modern law retains so much of the antient severity as only to exchange the loss of life for the loss of the offending limb. Therefore a stroke or blow in such a court of justice, whether blood be drawn or not, or even assaulting a judge sitting in the court, by drawing a weapon, without any blow struck, is punishable with the loss of the right hand, imprisonment for life, and forfeiture of goods and chattels, and of the profits of his lands during life (*Staund. P. C.* 38. 3 *Inst.* 140, 141). A rescue also of a prisoner from any of the said courts, without striking a blow, is punished with perpetual imprisonment, and forfeiture of goods, and of the profits of lands during life (1 *Hawk. P. C.* 57), being looked upon as an offence of the same nature with the last; but only, as no blow is actually given, the amputation of the hand is excused. For the like reason an affray, or riot, near the said courts, but out of their actual view is punished only with fine and imprisonment (*Cro. Car.* 373).

Not only such as are guilty of an actual violence, but of threatening or reproachful words to any judge sitting in the courts, are guilty of a high misprision, and have been punished with large fines, imprisonment, and corporal punishment (*Ibid.* 503). And, even in the inferior courts of the king, an affray, or contemptuous behaviour, is punishable with a fine by the judges there sitting, as by the steward in a court-leet, or the like (1 *Hawk. P. C.* 58).

Likewise all such, as are guilty of any injurious treatment to those who are immediately under the protection of a court of justice, are punishable by fine and imprisonment: as if a man assaults or threatens his adversary for suing him, a counsellor or attorney for being employed against him, a juror for his verdict, or a gaoler or other ministerial officer for keeping him in custody and properly executing his duty (3 *Inst.* 141, 142): which offences, when they proceeded farther than bare threats, were punished in the Gothic constitutions with exile and forfeiture of goods (*Stiernh. de jure Goth. l.* 3. *c.* 3).

Lastly, to endeavour to dissuade a witness from giving evidence; to disclose an examination before the privy council; or, to advise a prisoner to stand mute (all of which are impediments of justice), are high misprisions, and contempts of the king's courts, and punishable by fine and imprisonment. And antiently it was held, that if one of the grand jury disclosed to any person indicted the evidence that appeared against him, he was thereby made accessory to the offence, if felony; and in treason, a principal. And at this day, it is agreed, that he is guilty of a high misprision (*See Bar.* 212. 27 *Ass. pl.* 44. *s.* 4. *fol.* 138), and liable to be fined and imprisoned (1 *Hawk. P. C.* 59).

MISPRISIONS OF CLERKS, relate to their neglects in writing, or keeping records; and here misprision signifies a mistaking. 14 *Ed.* 3. *c.* 6.

MISRECITAL, in an immaterial point, shall not avoid a grant. *Cart.* 149.

MISSA, the mass, at first used for the dismission or sending away of the people: hence it came to signify the whole church service or Common Prayer; but more particularly the communion service, and the office of the sacrament, after those who did not receive it were dismissed. *Litt. Dict.*

MISSAL, *messale*, the mass-book, containing all things to be daily said in the mass. *Cowel. Blount.*

MISSATICUS, a messenger. *Ibid.*

MISSÆ PRESBYTER, signifies a priest in orders. *Ibid.*

MISSURA, singing the *Nunc Dimittis*, and performing other ceremonies to recommend and dismiss a dying person. *Ibid.*

MISSURIUM, a dish for serving up meat to a table: hence a *messe*, or portion of any diet. *Ibid.*

MISTAKE, ignorance or mistake is a defect of the will: as when a man intending to do a lawful act, does that which is unlawful. 4 *Black. Com.* 27.

MISTERIUM. See *Ministerium*.

MIS-TRIAL, a false or erroneous trial;

where it is in a wrong county, &c. 3 *Cro.* 284. And consent of parties cannot help such a trial, when past. *Hob.* 5. See *Trial.*

MISUSER, is an abuse of any liberty or benefit; as he shall make fine for his misuser. *Old Nat. Br.* 149. By misuser, a charter of a corporation may be forfeited: so also an office, &c. 1 *Black.* 153.

MITRED ABBOTS, were those governors of religious houses, who obtained from the pope the privilege of wearing the mitre, ring, gloves, and crosier of a bishop. *Cowel.*

MITTA, (from the Sax. *mitten, mensura*) an ancient Saxon measure; its quantity doth not certainly appear, but it is said to be a measure of ten bushels. *Cowel. Blount.*

MITTENDO MANUSCRIPTUM PEDIS FINIS, was a judicial writ directed to the treasurer and chamberlains of the exchequer, to search for, and transmit, the foot of a fine, acknowledged before justices in eyre, into the common pleas, &c. *Reg. Orig.* 14.

MITTER LE DROIT, is the passing a right: as if a man be disseised, and releaseth to his disseisor all his right; hereby the disseisor acquires a new right, which changes the quality of his estate, and renders that lawful which before was tortious or wrongful (*Litt. s.* 466.)

MITTER LE ESTATE, is the passing an estate, as when one of two coparceners releaseth all her right to the other, this passeth the fee-simple of the whole (*Co. Litt.* 273.) And in both these cases there must be a privity of estate between the relessor and relessee (*Ibid.* 272, 273.); that is, one of their estates must be so related to the other, as to make but one and the same estate in law.

MITTIMUS, a writ for removing and transferring of records from one court to another; as out of the king's bench into the exchequer, and sometimes by *certiorari* into the chancery, and from thence into another court: but the lord chancellor may deliver such record with his own hand. Stat. 5 *R.* 2. *c.* 15. 28 & 29 *H.* 8. *Dyer* 29, 32. *Mittimus* is also a precept in writing, under the hand and seal of a justice of peace, directed to the gaoler, for the receiving and safe keeping of an offender until he is delivered by law. 2 *Inst.* 590.

MITTRE A LARGE, is generally to set or put at liberty. *Cowel. Blount.*

MIXED ACTIONS, suits partaking of the nature of real and personal, wherein some real property is demanded, and also personal damages for a wrong sustained. See *Ejectment.*

MIXED LARCENY, or *compound larceny.* See *Larceny.*

MIXED TITHES, are those of cheese, milk, and young beasts, &c. 2 *Inst.* 649.

MIXTILIO. See *Mestilo.*

MIXTUM, sometimes signifies a breakfast, but always a certain quantity of bread and wine. *Cowel.*

MODELS. By 38 *Geo.* 3. *c.* 71. the sole right and property of making models or casts, shall be vested in the original proprietor for fourteen years; and persons making copies of any model or cast, without the written consent of the proprietor, may be prosecuted for damages by a special action on the case, except such persons who shall purchase the same of the original proprietor; but the action must be commenced within six calendar months after discovery of the offence.

MODERATA MISERICORDIA, a writ (founded on *magna charta*) which lays for him who was amerced in a court not of record, for any transgression, beyond the quality or quantity of the offence: directed to the lord of the court or his bailiff, commanding them to take a moderate amerciament of the parties. *New Nat. Br.* 167.

MODIATIO, was a certain duty paid for every tierce of wine. *Mon. Angl. tom.* 2. *p.* 994.

MODIUS, a measure, usually a bushel.

MODIUS TERRÆ VEL AGRI. This phrase probably signified the same quantity of ground as with the Romans, *viz.* one hundred feet long, and as many broad. *Cowel. Blount.*

MODO ET FORMA, are words of art in law pleadings, &c. and particularly used in the answer of a defendant, whereby he denies to have done the thing laid to his charge, *modo & forma declarata.* *Kitch.* 232.

MODUS DECIMANDI. There may be a discharge from the payment of *tithes* by custom or prescription; that is, where time out of mind such persons or such lands have been, either partially or totally, discharged from the payment of tithes. And this immemorial usage is binding upon all parties; as it is in its nature an evidence of universal consent and acquiescence, and with reason supposes a real composition to have been formerly made. This custom or prescription is either *de modo decimandi*, or *de non decimando.* 2 *Rep.* 47. 2 *Inst.* 490, 657, 659. 13 *Rep.* 152. *Hob.* 40. 1 *Rol. Abr.* 651. 1 *Cro.* 276, 446.

A MODUS DECIMANDI, commonly called by the simple name of a MODUS only, is where there is by custom a particular manner of tithing allowed, different from the general law of taking tithes in kind, which are the actual tenth part of the annual increase. This is sometimes a pecuniary compensation, as twopence an acre for the tithe of land: sometimes it is a compensation in work and labour, as that the parson shall have only the twelfth cock of hay, and not the tenth, in consideration of the owner's making it for him: sometimes, in lieu of a large quantity of crude or imperfect tithe, the parson shall have a less quantity, when arrived to greater maturity, as a couple of fowls in lieu of the eggs; and the like. Any means, in short, whereby the general law of tithing is altered, and a new method of taking them is introduced, is called a *modus decimandi*, or a special manner of tithing. 2 *Black.* 29.

To make a good and sufficient *modus*, the following rules must be observed. 1. It must be certain and invariable (1 *Keb.* 602.), for payment of different sums will prove it to be no *modus*, that is, no original real composition; because that must have been one and the same, from its first original to the present time (1 *Keble* 602.) 2. The thing given, in lieu of tithes, must be beneficial to the parson, and not for the emolument of third persons only: thus a *modus*, to repair the church in lieu of tithes, is not good, because that is an advantage to the parish only; but to repair the chancel is a good *modus*, for that is an advantage to the parson (1 *Roll. Abr.* 649.) 3. It must be something different from the thing compounded for: one load of hay, in lieu of all tithe hay, is no good *modus*: for no parson would *bona fide* make a composition to receive less than his due in the same species of tithe: and therefore the law will not suppose it possible for such composition to have existed (1 *Lev.* 179.) 4. One cannot be discharged from payment of one species of tithe, by paying a *modus* for another. Thus a *modus* of 1*d.* for every milch cow will discharge the tithe of milch kine, but not of barren cattle: for tithe is, of common right, due for both; and therefore a *modus* for one, shall never be a discharge for the other (*Cro. Eliz.* 446. *Salk.* 657.) 5. The recompense must be in its nature as durable as the tithes discharged by it; that is, an inheritance certain: and therefore a *modus* that every inhabitant of a house, shall pay 4*d.* a year, in lieu of the owner's tithes, is no good *modus*; for possibly the house may not be inhabited, and then the recompense will be lost (2 *P. Wms.* 462.) 6. The *modus* must not be too large, which is called a rank *modus*: as if the real value of the tithes be 60*l.* per annum. and a *modus* is suggested of 40*l.* this *modus* will not be established; though one of 40*s.* might have been valid (11 *Mod.* 60.) Indeed, properly speaking, the doctrine of rankness in a *modus*, is a mere rule of evidence, drawn from the improbability of the fact, and not a rule of law (*Pyke* v. *Dowling*, *Hil.* 19 *Geo.* 3. *C. B.*) For, in these cases of prescriptive or customary *modus's*, it is supposed that an original real composition was anciently made; which being lost by length of time, the immemorial usage is admitted as evidence to shew that it once did exist, and that from thence such usage was derived. Now time of memory hath been long ago ascertained by the law to commence from the beginning of the reign of Richard the first; and any custom may be destroyed by evidence of its non-existence in any part of the long period from that time to the present; wherefore, as this real composition is supposed to have been an equitable contract, or the full value of the tithes, at the time of making it, if the *modus* set up is so rank and large, as that it beyond dispute exceeds the value of the tithes in the time of Richard the first, this *modus* is (in point of evidence) *felo de se* and destroys itself. For, as it would be destroyed by any direct evidence to prove its non-existence at any time since that æra, so also it is destroyed by carrying in itself this internal evidence of a much later original (2 *Inst.* 238, 239.)

To constitute a good *modus*, it seems necessary that it should be such as would have been a certain, fair, and reasonable equivalent or composition for the tithes in kind, before the year 1189; and therefore no *modus* for hops, turkies, or other things introduced into England since that time can be good. *Bunb.* 307.

The question of rankness, or rather *modus* or no *modus*, is a question of fact, which courts of equity will send to a jury, unless the grossness of the *modus* is so obvious as to preclude the necessity of it. 2 *Bro.* 163. 1 *Bl. R.* 420. 2 *Bl. R.* 1257.

But in a suit brought to establish a *modus* they seldom decide upon the question of rankness without a reference to a jury.

A prescription *de non decimando* is a claim to be entirely discharged of tithes, and to pay no compensation in lieu of them. Thus the king by his prerogative is discharged from all tithes (*Cro. Eliz.* 511.) So a vicar shall pay no tithes to the rector, nor the rector to the vicar, for *ecclesia decimas non solvit ecclesiæ* (*Cro. Eliz.* 479, 511. *Sav.* 3. *Moor.* 910.) But these personal privileges (not arising from or being annexed to the land) are personally confined to both the king and the clergy; for their tenant or lessee shall pay tithes, though in their own occupation their lands are not generally titheable (*Cro. Eliz.* 479.) But it seems to be determined that the king's tenant for years, or at will, is not liable to pay tithes, on account of the dignity of the king, who cannot be presumed to have leisure or occasion to cultivate his own lands. *Com. Dig. Dism. E.* 7. 2 *Woodd.* 100. And, generally speaking, it is an established rule, that, in lay hands, *modus de non decimando non valet* (*Ibid.* 511.) But spiritual persons or corporations, as monasteries, abbots, bishops, and the like, were always capable of having their lands totally discharged of tithes by various ways (*Hob.* 309. *Cro. Jac.* 308.); as, 1. By real composition: 2. By the pope's bull of exemption: 3. By unity of possession; as when the rectory of a parish, and lands in the same parish, both belonged to a religious house, those lands were discharged of tithes by this unity of possession: 4. By prescription; having never been liable to tithes, by being always in spiritual hands: 5. By virtue of their order; as the knights templars, cistercians, and others, whose lands were privileged by the pope with a discharge of tithes (2 *Rep.* 44. *Seld. tith. c.* 15. *s.* 2.) Though upon the dissolution of abbeys by Henry VIII. most of these exemptions from tithes would have fallen with them, and the lands become titheable again: had they not been supported and upheld by the statute 31 *Hen.* 8. *c.* 13. which enacts, that all persons who should come to the possession of the lands of any abbey then dissolved, should hold them free and discharged of tithes, in as large and ample a manner as the abbeys themselves formerly held them. This provision is peculiar to that statute, and therefore all the lands belonging to the lesser monasteries, dissolved by the 27 *Hen.* 8. *c.* 28. are now liable to pay tithes. *Com. Dig. Dism. R.* 7. And from this original have sprung all the lands, which, being in lay hands, do at present claim to be tithe-free: for, if a man can shew his lands to have been such abbey-lands, and also immemorially discharged of tithes by any of the means before mentioned, this is now a good prescription *de non decimando.* But he must shew both these requisites: for abbey lands, without a special ground of discharge, are not discharged of course; neither will any prescription *de non decimando* avail in total discharge of tithes, unless it relates to such abbey lands. 2 *Rep.* 44. *Selden tith. c.* 13. *s.* 2.

Posterior usage is evidence of the antecedent, and has always been allowed so in cases of this nature; for what other evidence can be had? *Ld. Hardw.* 2 *Atk.* 137.

It has been argued in the court of exchequer, that a grant of the tithes might be presumed from a lay-impropriator; but the court held that there was no distinction between a spiritual and a lay rector, and that no grant could be presumed, which would amount to a prescription *de non decimando.* 3 *Anstr.* 702.

Custom is what gives a right to a whole county, city, town or parish, and must be common to all within the limits, where it is averred to be. 1 *Roll. Abr.* 653. *Count Parf. Comp.* 159.

Prescription is that which gives a right to some particular person, with respect to some particular house, farm, &c. And the ecclesiastical laws allow forty years to make a good custom and prescription; but, by the common law, it must be beyond the memory of man. *Ibid.*

MOEDIA, in the Teutonic language, signifies the secret killing of another.

MOIETY, (*medietas*, Fr. *moitie*, i. e. *coæqua vel media pars*) is the half of any thing; and to hold by moieties, is mentioned in our books, in case of jointenants, &c. *Lit.* 125.

MOLENDINUM, a mill of divers kinds. See *Mill.*

MOLENDUM, corn sent to a mill, a grist. *Cowel. Blount.*

MOLITURA, the toll or multure paid for grinding corn at a mill, and sometimes called *molta. Ibid.*

MOLLITER MANUS IMPOSUIT. Several justifications in trespass, i. e. actions of assault, are called by this name, from the words gently laid his hands upon him used in the plea, as where the defendant justifies an assault by shewing that the plaintiff was unlawfully in the house of the defendant, making a disturbance, and being requested to cease such disturbance, and depart, he refused and continued therein, making such disturbance, he, the defendant, gently laid his hands on the plaintiff, and removed him out of the house. So in various other instances, as for separating two persons, fighting, in order to preserve the peace, so in the legal exercise of an office, &c. 3 *Black.* 121.

MOLMAN, a man subject to do service; applied to the servants of a monastery. *Cowel. Blount.*

MOLMUTIAN, or MOLMUTIN LAWS. Were the laws of *Dunvallo Molmutius*, sixteenth king of the Britons, who began his reign above four hundred years before the birth of our Saviour, and were famous in this land till the time of William the Conqueror. This king was the first who published laws in Britain; and his laws, (with those of queen Mercia,) were translated by Gildas out of the British into the Latin tongue. *Usher's Primord.* 126.

MOLNEDA, MULNEDA, a mill-pool or pond. *Cowel. Blount.*

MOLTA, the duty or toll paid to the lord, by his vassals, to grind corn at his mill. *Ibid.*

MONARCHY. That form of government, where the sovereign power is entrusted in the hands of a single person. See *King.*

MONASTERIES and *abbeys*, were dissolved by 27 *H.* 8. *c.* 28.

MONETAGIUM, signified a certain tribute paid by tenants to their lord every third year, that he should not change the money which he had coined, formerly when it was lawful for great men to coin money current in their territories; but not of silver and gold. *Cowel. Blount.*

MONEY, (*moneta*) is that metal, be it gold or silver, which receives authority by the prince's impress to be current; for as wax is not a seal without a print, so metal is not money without the impression. *Co. Litt.* 207. 1 *Hale's Hist. P. H.* 188.

It belongs to the king only, to put a value, as well as the impression on money; which being done, the money is current for so much as the king hath limited. 2 *Inst.* 575.

MONGER, a little sea vessel which fishermen use. 13 *Eliz. c.* 11. And when a word ends with *monger*, as ironmonger, &c. it signifies merchant, from the Sax. *manger*, i. e. *mercator. Cowel. Blount.*

MONIERS, or MONEYERS, *monetarii*, are ministers of the mint, who make and coin the king's money. *Reg. Orig.* 262. and 1 *Ed.* 6. 15. *Ibid.*

MONK, (*monachus*) from the Gr. Μόνος, *solus qui soli*, i. e. *separati ab aliorum consortio vivant*, because the first monks lived alone in the wilderness. Monks upon their profession or entering into a religious society, solemnly renounced all secular concerns, and were therefore accounted *civiliter mortuus*. *Cowel.*

MONKERY, the profession of a monk. *Cowel.*

MONKS CLOTHES, made of a certain kind of coarse cloth. *Ibid.*

MONOPOLY, (from Μόνος *unus* & πωλέω *vendo*) is an allowance of the king by his grant, commission, or otherwise, to any person or persons, for the sole buying, selling, making, working, or using of any thing, by which other persons are restrained of any freedom or liberty that they had before, or hindered in their lawful trade. 3 *Inst.* 181.

But by 21 *Jac.* 1. *c.* 3. all monopolies, grants, letters patent, and licence for the sole buying, selling, and making of goods and manufactures, are declared void, *except* PATENTS *for fourteen years, for the sole working or making any new invented manufacture*; and persons grieved by putting them in use, shall recover treble damages and double costs, by action on the statute; and delaying such action before judgment, by colour of any order, warrant, &c. or delaying execution after, incurs a *præmunire*: but this does not extend to any grant or privilege granted by act of parliament; nor to any grant or charter to corporations, or cities, &c. or to grants to companies or societies of merchants, for enlargement of trade; or to inventors of new manufactures, who have patents for the term of fourteen years; grants or privileges for printing; or making gunpowder, casting ordnance, &c.

Upon this statute it has been adjudged, that a manufacture must be substantially new, and not barely an additional improvement of any old one to be within the statute; it must be such as none other used at the granting the letters patent; and an old manufacture in use before, cannot be prohibited in any grant of the sole use of any such new invention. 3 *Inst.* 184.

MONSTER, one who hath not human shape, and yet is born in lawful wedlock: and such may not purchase or retain lands; but a person may be an heir to his ancestor's lands, though he be deformed in some part of his body. *Co. Lit.* 7.

A monster shewn for money is a misdemeanor. 2 *Chan. Ca.* 110. *Trin.* 34 *Car.* 2. *Harring* v. *Walrond.* This was the case of a monstrous child which was embalmed to be kept for shew, but was ordered by the lord chancellor to be buried in a week. *Ibid.*

MONSTRANS DE DROIT, is a shewing right, and was a writ out of chancery to be restored to lands and tenements that were a man's in right, though by some office found to be in the possession of one lately dead; by which office the king would be intitled to the said lands, &c. *Cowel. Blount.*

MONSTRANS DE FAITS ON RECORDS, shewing of deeds or records is thus; upon an action, he that pleads the deed or record, or declares upon it, ought to shew the same: and the other against whom such deed or record is pleaded, may demand oyer of the same. *Cowel.*

MONSTRAVERUNT, a writ which lay for tenants in ancient demesne, who held land by free charter, when they were distrained to do unto their lords other services and customs than they or their ancestors used to do: also it lay where such tenants were distrained for the payment of toll, &c. contrary to their liberty, which they did or should enjoy. *F. N. B.* 14 4 *Inst.* 269.

MONSTRUM, the box in which relics were kept. Is also what we call corruptly mustering soldiers. *Cowel,*

MONTH, or MONETH, Sax. MONATH, (*mensis à mensione, lunæ cursis*) signifies the time the sun goes through one sign of the zodiac, and the moon through all twelve; properly the time from the new moon to its change, or the course or period of the moon, whence it is called month from the moon. *Lit. Dict.* A month is a space of time containing by the week twenty-eight days; by the kalendar sometimes thirty, and sometimes thirty-one days: and Julius Cæsar divided the year into twelve months, each month into four weeks, and each week into seven days. The month by the common law is but twenty-eight days; and in case of a condition for rent, the month shall be computed at twenty-eight days; so in the case of inrolment of deeds, and generally in all cases where a statute speaks of months without specifying *calendar* months: but where the statute accounteth by the year, half year, or quarter of a year, then it is to be reckoned according to the kalendar. 1 *Inst.* 135. 6 *Rep.* 62. *Cro. Jac.* 167.

A twelvemonth in the singular number includes the whole year, according to the kalendar: but twelve months, six months, &c. in the plural number shall be accounted after twenty-eight days to every month. 6 *Rep.* 61. *Cro. Jac.* 141. *Wood's Inst.* 433.

MONUMENT, an heir may bring an action against one that injures the monument, &c. of his ancestor: and the coffin and shroud of a deceased person belong to the executors or administrators; but the deac body belongeth to none. 3 *Inst.* 202, 203.

MOORS, in the Isle of Man, are those who summon the courts for the several sheadings; they are the lords bailiffs, and every moor has the like office with our bailiff of the hundred. *King's Descrip. Isle of Man. Cowel.*

MOOT, (from the Sax. *motian*, *placitare*, to treat or handle) a term well understood in the inns of court, and signifies the exercise, or arguing of cases, which young barristers and students anciently performed at certain times, the better to enable them for the practice and defence of clients causes. The place where moot-cases were argued, was anciently called the Moot-hall: and in the inns of court there was a bailiff of the moot yearly chosen by the benchers, to appoint the mootmen for the inns of chancery; and keep accounts of the performance of excises, both there and in the house. *Orig. Jur.* 212.

MOOTA CANUM, a pack of dogs. *Cowel.*

MOOTMEN, those who argued the reader's cases, called moot-cases, in the inns of chancery, in the term-time, and in vacations. *Orig. Jur.* 212.

MORA, a moor, or barren and unprofitable ground. 1 *Inst.* 5. Also a heath. *Fleta, lib.* 2. *cap.* 71.

MORA MUSSA, a watery or boggy moor; *morossa* is used in the same sense. *Cowel. Blount.*

MORATUR IN LEGE, is the same with *demoratur*, and signifies as much as he demurs. *Co. Lit.* 71. See *Demurrer.*

MORETUM, a sort of brown cloth, with which caps were formerly made. *Cowel. Blount.*

MORGANGIA, (from the Sax. *morgen*, the morning, and *gifan*, to give) the gift on the wedding day, what we now call dowry money, or that gift the husband presents to his wife on the wedding day. *Du Cange. Cowel.*

MORIAM, (Fr. *morion*, i. e. *cassis*) a head piece. *Ibid.*

MORINA, MURRAIN; an infectious distemper in cattle. *Morina* also signifies the wool of sick sheep, and those dead with the *murrain*. *Fleta, lib.* 2. *c.* 79. *par.* 6.

MORLING, or MORTLING, signifies that wool which is taken from the skin of dead sheep, whether being killed or dying of the rot. 4 *Ed.* 4. *c.* 2 & 3. 27 *H.* 6. *c.* 2. 3 *Jac.* 1. *c.* 18. 14 *Car.* 2. *c.* 88. See *Shorling.*

MOROSUS. See *Mora.*

MORSELLUM TERRÆ, a small parcel or bit of land. *Cowel. Blount.*

MORSELLUS TERRÆ, a small parcel of land. *Ibid.*

MORTARIUM, a light or taper set in churches to burn over the graves or shrines of the dead.

MORT-DANCESTOR, a writ now seldom used. See *Assise of Mort-Dancestor.*

MORTGAGE, (*mortgagium*, *vel mortuum vadium*) is compounded of two French words, viz. *mort*, i. e. *mors*, and *gage*, i. e. *pignus*, and signifies a pawn of land or tenement, or any thing immoveable, laid or bound for money borrowed, to be the creditor's for ever, if the money be not paid at the day agreed upon; and the creditor holding land and tenement upon this bargain, he is called tenant in mortgage.

In this case the land, which is so put in pledge, is by law, in case of non-payment at the time limited, for ever dead and gone from the mortgagor; and the mortgagee's estate in the lands is then no longer conditional, but absolute. But, so long as it continues conditional, that is, between the time of lending the money, and the time allotted for payment, the mortgagee is called tenant in mortgage (*Litt. s.* 332.) But as it was formerly a doubt, whether, by taking such estate in fee, it did not become liable to the wife's dower, and other incumbrances, of the mortgagee, (though that doubt has been long ago over-ruled by our courts of equity,) it therefore became usual to grant only a long term of years by way of mortgage; with condition to be void on re-payment of the mortgage-money: which course has been since pretty generally continued, principally because on the death of the mortgagee such term becomes vested in his personal representatives, who alone are entitled in equity to receive the money lent, of whatever nature the mortgage may happen to be. (*Litt. s.* 357. *Cro. Car.* 191. *Hardr.* 466.)

As soon as the estate is created, the mortgagee may immediately enter on the lands; but is liable to be dispossessed, upon performance of the condition by payment of the mortgage-money at the day limited. And therefore the usual way is to agree, that the mortgagor shall hold the land till the day assigned for payment; when, in case of failure, whereby the estate becomes absolute, the mortgagee may enter upon it and take possession, without any possibility at law, of being afterwards evicted by the mortgagor, to whom the land is now for ever dead. But here again the courts of equity interpose; and, though a mortgage be thus forfeited, and the estate absolutely vested in the mortgagee at the common law, yet they will consider the real value of the tenements compared with the sum borrowed. And, if the estate be of greater value than the sum lent thereon, they will allow the mortgagor at any reasonable time to recall or redeem his estate; paying to the mortgagee his principal, interest, and expences: for otherwise, in strictness of law, an estate worth 1000*l.* might be forfeited for non-payment of 100*l.* or a less sum (*Hard.* 465. 1 *Vern.* 182, 193) But in general, if the mortgagee has been twenty years in possession, the court of chancery, in conformity to the time of bringing an ejectment, will not permit the mortgagor to redeem, unless during part of the time the mortgagor has been an infant or a married woman; or unless the mortgagee admits he holds the estate as a mortgage; or he has kept accounts upon it and treated it as redeemable within twenty years; or there is some other special circumstance, which forms an exception to the general rule. *Eq. Ca.*

Abr. 313. 2 *Bro.* 399. 2 *Ves. jun.* 83. And where two different estates are mortgaged by the owner to the same person, one cannot be redeemed without the other. *Amb.* 733. This reasonable advantage, allowed to mortgagors, is called the EQUITY OF REDEMPTION: and this enables a mortgagor to call on the mortgagee, who has possession of his estate, to deliver it back and account for the rents and profits received, on payment of his whole debt and interest; thereby turning the *mortuum* into a kind of *vivum vadium*. But, on the other hand, the mortgagee may either compel the sale of the estate, in order to get the whole of his money immediately; or else call upon the mortgagor to redeem his estate presently, or in default thereof, to be for ever foreclosed from redeeming the same; that is, to lose his equity of redemption without possibility of recall. And also, in some cases of fraudulent mortgages, the fraudulent mortgagor forfeits all equity of redemption whatsoever. By the 4 & 5 *W. & M.* if any person mortgages his estate, and does not previously inform the mortgagee in writing of a prior mortgage, or of any judgment or incumbrance which he has voluntarily brought upon the estate, the mortgagee shall hold the estate as an absolute purchaser free from the equity of redemption of the mortgagor. It is not however usual for mortgagees to take possession of the mortgaged estate, unless where the security is precarious, or small; or where the mortgagor neglects even the payment of interest: when the mortgagee is frequently obliged to bring an ejectment, and take the land into his own hands in the nature of a pledge (*Inst. l.* 4. *t.* 6. *s.* 7.) But, by statute, 7 *Geo.* 2. *c.* 20. after payment or tender by the mortgagor of principal, interest, and costs, the mortgagee can maintain no ejectment; but may be compelled to re-assign his securities.

The mortgagee is not, however, obliged to bring an ejectment to recover the rents and profits of the estate, for it has been determined that where there is a tenant in possession, by a lease prior to the mortgage, the mortgagee may at any time give him notice to pay the rent to him; and he may distrain for all the rent which is due at the time of the notice, and also for all that accrues afterwards. For the *mortgagor* has no interest in the premises, but by the mere indulgence of the mortgagee; he has not even the estate of a tenant at will, for it is held he may be prevented from carrying away the emblements, or the crops which he himself has sown. *Moss* v. *Gallimore*, *Doug.* 266.

MORTGAGOR, is he who mortgages or pawns the lands; and he to whom the mortgage is made is called the *mortgagee*.

MORTH, murder; Sax. *morth*, death. *Morthlaga*, a murderer or manslayer. *Morthlage*, homicide or murder, &c.

MORTIIVUS, dead of the rot, applied to sheep and lambs. *Mon.* 2 *tom. p.* 114.

MORTMAIN, (*manus, mortua*, compounded of two French words, *mort*, i. e. *mors*, & *maine*, i. e. *manus*) signifies an alienation of lands and tenements to any guild, corporation or fraternity, and their successors, as bishops, parsons, vicars, &c. In MORTMAIN *mortua manu*, into a *dead hand*, as it were never to revert to the donor, or any temporal or common use. *Magna Charta, cap.* 36. 7 *Ed. cap.* 3. The statute of *Mortmain*, and 18 *Ed.* 3. *cap.* 3. and 15 *Ric.* 2. *cap.* 5.

By the common law any man might dispose of his lands to any other private man at his own discretion, especially when the feodal restraints of alienation were worn away. Yet in consequence of these it was always, and is still, necessary for corporations to have a licence in mortmain from the crown, to enable them to purchase lands; for as the king is the ultimate lord of every fee, he ought not, unless by his own consent, to lose his privilege of escheats and other feodal profits, by the vesting of lands in tenants that can never be attainted or die. *F. N. B.* 121.

The foundation of all the statutes of mortmain was *magna charta*. By the 9 *H.* 3. *c.* 36. it is declared, "that it shall not be lawful for any to give his lands to any religious house, and to take the same land again to hold of the same house, &c. upon pain that the gift shall be void, and the land shall accrue to the lord of the fee."

But ecclesiastical persons found means to creep out of the statute, by purchasing lands holden of themselves, or by making leases for a long term of years, &c. wherefore by 7 *Ed.* 1. commonly called the STATUTE OF MORTMAIN, or *de religiosis*, "no persons religious, " or others whatsoever, shall buy or sell any " lands or tenements, or under the colour " of any gift or lease, or by reason of any " other title, receive the same, or by any " other craft shall appropriate lands in any " wise to come into mortmain, on pain of " forfeiture; and within a year after the " alienation, the lord of the fee may enter; " and if he do not, then the next immediate " lord, from time to time may enter in a " half year; and for default of all the lords " entering, the king shall have the lands so " alienated for ever, and may enfeoff others " by certain services, &c."

As this statute extended only to gifts, alienations, &c. made between ecclesiastics and others, they found out an evasion also of this statute; for pretending a title to the land, which they meant to gain, they brought a feigned action against the tenant of the land, and he by consent and collusion was to make default, and thereupon they recovered the land, and entered by judgment of law: so that the STAT. *Westm.* 2. 13 *Ed.* 1. *c.* 32. was thought necessary; by which "it is to " be inquired by the country whether the " demandant had a just title to the land; " and if so, then he shall recover seisin;

"but if otherwise, the lord of the fee shall "enter, &c."

And by 34 *Ed.* 1. "lands shall not be aliënated in mortmain, where there are mean "lords, without their consent declared under "hand and seal; nor shall any thing pass "where the donor reserves nothing to him"self."

Notwithstanding all these statutes, ecclesiastical persons (not being able to get lands, by purchase, gift, lease, or recovery) procured lands to be conveyed by feoffment, or in other manner, to divers persons and their heirs, to the use of them and their successors, whereby they took the profits. 2 *Inst.* 75. To bar this, the STAT. 15 *R.* 2. *c.* 5. was made, which statute enacts, "that no "feoffment, &c. of any lands and tene"ments, advowsons or other possessions, to "the use of any spiritual persons, or where"of they shall take the profits, shall be made "without licence of the king, and of the "lords, &c. upon pain of forfeiture."

And as the statutes had been eluded by purchasing large tracts of land, adjoining to churches, and consecrating them by the name of church-yards, such "subtile imagination "is also declared to be within the compass "of the statutes of mortmain. And civil or "lay corporations, as well as ecclesiastical, "are also declared to be within the mischief, "and of course within the remedy provided "by those salutary laws." And, lastly, as during the times of popery lands were frequently given to superstitious uses, though not to any corporate bodies; or were made liable in the hands of heirs and devisees to the charge of obits, chaunteries, and the like, which were equally pernicious in a well-governed state as actual alienations in mortmain; therefore, at the dawn of the reformation, the statute 23 *Hen.* 8. *c.* 10. declares, that *all future grants of lands for any of the purposes aforesaid, if granted for any longer term than twenty years, shall be void.*

But, during all this time, it was in the power of the crown, by granting a licence of mortmain, to remit the forfeiture, so far as related to its own rights; and to enable any spiritual or other corporation to purchase and hold any lands or tenements in perpetuity; which prerogative is declared and confirmed by the statute 18 *Edw.* 3. *st.* 3. *c.* 3. But, as doubts were conceived at the time of the revolution how far such licence was valid (2 *Hawk. P. C.* 391.), since the king had no power to dispense with the statutes of mortmain by a clause of *non obstante*, which was the usual course, though it seems to have been unnecessary (*Co. Lit.* 99.). and as, by the gradual declension of mesne signiories through the long operation of the statute of *quia emptores*, the rights of intermediate lords were reduced to a very small compass; it was therefore provided by the statute 7 & 8 *W.* 3. *c.* 37. that *the crown for the future at its own discretion may grant licences to aliene or take in mortmain, of whomsoever the tenements may be holden.*

After the dissolution of monasteries under Henry VIII. though the policy of the next popish successor affected to grant a security to the possessors of abbey lands, yet, in order to regain so much of them as either the zeal or timidity of their owners might induce them to part with, the statutes of mortmain were suspended for twenty years by the statute 1 & 2 *P. & M. c.* 8. and, during that time, any lands or tenements were allowed to be granted to any spiritual corporation without any licence whatsoever. And, long afterwards, for a much better purpose, the augmentation of poor livings, it was enacted by the stat. 17 *Car.* 2. *c.* 3. that appropriators may annex the great tithes to the vicarages; and that all benefices under 100*l.* per ann. may be augmented by the purchase of lands without licence of mortmain in either case; and the like provision hath been since made, in favour of the governors of queen Anne's bounty (*stat.* 2 & 3 *Ann. c.* 11.) It hath also been held (1 *Rep.* 24.), that the statute 23 *Hen.* 8. before-mentioned, did not extend to any thing but superstitious uses; and that therefore *a man may give lands for the maintenance of a school, an hospital, or any other charitable uses.* But as it was apprehended, from recent experience, that persons on their death-beds might make large and improvident dispositions even for these good purposes, and defeat the political ends of the statutes of mortmain; it is therefore enacted by the statute 9 *Geo.* 2. *c.* 36. that *no lands or tenements, or money to be laid out thereon, shall be given for or charged with any charitable uses whatsoever, unless by deed indented, executed in the presence of two witnesses twelve calendar months before the death of the donor, and enrolled in the court of chancery within six months after its execution,* (except stocks in the public funds, which may be transferred within six months previous to the donor's death,) *and unless such gift be made to take effect immediately, and be without power of revocation: and that all other gifts shall be void.** The two universities, their colleges, and the scholars upon the foundation

* Lord Hardwicke has declared, since this last mortmain act, that "there is no "restriction whatsoever upon any one, from "leaving a sum of money by will, or any "other personal estate, to charitable uses; "provided it be to be continued as a per"sonalty, and the executors or trustees are "not obliged, or under a necessity of laying "it out in land, by virtue of any direction "of the testator for that purpose." 2 *Burn. Ec.* 509. tit. *Mortm.*

Money left to repair parsonage houses, or to build upon land already in mortmain, is of the colleges of Eton, Winchester, and Westminster, are excepted out of this act; but such exemption was granted with this proviso, that no college shall be at liberty to purchase more advowsons, than are equal in number to one moiety of the fellows or students,* upon the respective foundations.

MORTUARIES (*mortuarium, mortarium*) are a sort of ecclesiastical heriots, being a customary gift claimed by and due to the minister in very many parishes on the death of his parishioners. A kind of expiation and amends to the clergy for the personal tithes, and other ecclesiastical duties, which the laity in their lifetime might have neglected or forgotten to pay. 2 *Black.* 525.

It was antiently usual in this kingdom to bring the mortuary to church along with the corpse when it came to be buried; and thence it is sometimes called a *corse present:* a term which bespeaks it to have been once a voluntary donation (*Selden. Hist. of Tithes, c.* 10.) This custom still varies in different places, not only as the mortuary to be paid, but the person to whom it is payable. In Wales a mortuary or corse-present was due upon the death of every clergyman to the bishop of the diocese; till abolished, upon a recompence given to the bishop, by the statute 12 *Ann. st.* 2. *c.* 6. And in the archdeaconry of Chester, a custom also prevailed, that the bishop, who is also archdeacon, should have, at the death of every clergyman dying therein, his best horse or mare, bridle, saddle, and spurs, his best gown or cloak, hat, upper garment under his gown, and tippet, and also his best signet or ring (*Cro. Car.* 237.) But by statute 28 *Geo.* 2. *c.* 6. this mortuary is directed to cease, and the act has settled upon the bishop an equivalent in its room. The king's claim to many goods, on the death of all prelates in England, seems to be of the same nature: though sir Edward Coke apprehends, that this is a duty due upon death and not a mortuary: a distinction which seems to be without a difference. For not only the king's ecclesiastical character, as supreme ordinary, but also the species of the goods claimed, which bear so near a resemblance to those in the archdeaconry of Chester, which was an acknowledged mortuary, puts the matter out of dispute. The king, according to the record vouched by sir Edward Coke, is entitled to six things; the bishop's best horse or palfrey, with his furniture: his cloak, or gown, and tippet: his cup and cover: his bason and ewer: his gold ring: and lastly, his *muta canum*, his mew or kennel of hounds, as was mentioned. 2 *Inst.* 491.

MORTUARIUM, hath been sometimes used in a civil as well as ecclesiastical sense, being payable to the lord of the fee.

MORTUO VADIO, *estate in.* See *Mortgage.*

MOSS-TROOPERS, a rebellious sort of people in the North of England, that lived by robbery and rapine. The counties of Northumberland and Cumberland, were charged with a yearly sum, and a command of men to be appointed by justices of the peace, to apprehend and suppress them. *Stat.* 4 *Jac.* 1. *c.* 1. 13 & 14 *Car.* 2. *c.* 22. 30 *Car.* 2. *c.* 2. 6 *Geo.* 2. *c.* 37. See *Felony* and *Northern Borders.*

MOTE, (*mota*, Sax. *gemote, curia, placitum, conventus*) as *Mota de Hereford*, i. e. *curia vel placita comitatus de Hereford.* Hence Burgemote, *curia vel conventus burgi*; Swainmote, *curia vel conventus ministorum, scil. foresta, &c.* From this also we draw our word mote and moot, to plead. The Scots say, to mute, as the Mute-hill at Scone, i. e. *Mons placiti de Scona. Cowel.*

We commonly apply the word *moot* to that arguing of cases used by young students in the inns of court and chancery.

Mote also signifies a standing pool of water to keep fish in.

It likewise signifies a great ditch encompassing a castle or dwelling-house.

MOTE-BELL, or MOT-BELL, the bell so called, which was used by the English Saxons to call people together to the court. *Cowel. Blount.*

MOTEER, a customary service or payment at the mote or court of the lord. *Ibid.*

MOTHERING *Sunday*, a custom formerly prevailed of visiting parents on Midlent Sunday. *Cowel.*

MOTIBILIS, one that may be removed or displaced, or rather a vagrant. *Fleta, lib.* 6. *c.* 6.

MOTION IN COURT, is an occasional application to the court by the parties or their counsel, in order to obtain some rule or order of court, which becomes necessary in the progress of a cause; and it is usually grounded upon an affidavit, (the perfect tense of the verb *affido*) being a voluntary oath before some judge or officer of the court, to evince the truth of certain facts upon which the motion is grounded.

MOVEABLES. All sorts of things moveable are included under the name of things

---

held not to be within the statute. 1 *Bro.* 444. But a legacy to the corporation of queen Anne's bounty is void: as by the rules of the corporation it must be laid out in land. 1 *Bro.* 13.

The bequest of personalty to establish a school has been held to be good; as it was not necessary to purchase land to give effect to the testator's design, for the master might teach in his own house or in the church. 4 *T. R.* 526.

* That is, of one moiety of the students in those colleges, in which there are no persons stiled fellows. The advowsons annexed to headships are not to be computed. *S.* 5.

personal, or are personal estate, *i. e.* all those things which may attend a man's person wherever he goes. 3 *Black.* 384.

MOULT, is an old English word for a mow of corn, or hay; *mullo fœni, &c. Par. Antiq.* 401.

MOUNTEBANKS, are public nusances, and may be indicted and fined. 1 *Hawk. P. C.* 198. See *Gaming*, and *Lotteries.*

MOWNTEE, an alarm or outcry, to mount and make some speedy expedition. *Cowel. Blount.*

MUFFULÆ, winter gloves made of ramskins. *Ibid.*

MULCT, (*mulcta*) a fine of money set upon one, for some fault or misdemeanor. *Ibid.*

MULIER, as used in our law, seems to be a word corrupted from *melior*, or the Fr. *meliour;* and signifies the lawful issue, born in wedlock, (though begotten before) preferred before an elder brother born out of matrimony. 9 *Hen.* 6. *c.* 11. *Smith's Repub. Angl. lib.* 3. *c.* 6. But by Glanvil, the lawful issue are said to be *mulier*, not from *melior*, but because begotten *e muliere* not *ex concubina;* for he calls such issue *filios mulieratos*, opposing them to be bastards. *Glanv. lib.* 7. *c.* 1.

If a man hath a son by a woman, before marriage, which is a bastard and unlawful, and after he marries the mother of the bastard, and they have another son, this second son is *mulier* and lawful, and shall be heir to his father, but the other cannot be heir to any man; and they are distinguished in our old books with this addition: *bastard eigne*, and *mulier puisne. Co. Lit.* 170, 243. See *Eigne.*

MULIERTY, the being or condition of a *mulier*, or lawful issue. *Co. Lit.* 352. b.

MULLONES FŒNII, cocks or ricks of hay; now a mow of hay or corn. *Cowel. Blount.*

MULMUTIN LAWS. See *Molmution Laws.*

MULNEDA, a place to build a watermill. *Cowel. Blount.*

MULTA, or MULTURA EPISCOPI, is derived from the Latin word *mulcta*, for that it was a fine given to the king, that the bishop might have power to make his last will and testament, and to have the probate of other men's, and the granting administrations. 2 *Inst.* 491.

MULTIPLICATION OF GOLD AND SILVER, was prohibited and declared to be felony by statute, 5 *Hen.* 4. *c.* 4. Which statute was made on a presumption that persons skilful in chymistry, could multiply or augment these metals, by changing other metals into gold or silver: repealed by 1 *W.* & *M. c.* 30. *Dyer* 88. 1 *Hawk. P. C.* 47.

MULTITUDE, (*multitudo*) according to some authors must be ten persons or more: but sir Edward Coke says, he could never find it restrained by the common law to any certain number. *Co. Lit.* 257. See *Riots.*

MULTO FORTIORI, or A MINORI AD MAJUS, is an argument often used by Littleton, and is framed thus: if it be so in a feoffment passing a new right, much more it is for the restitution of an ancient right, &c. *Co. Lit.* 253, 260. a. See *Fortiori.*

MULTO, MUTILO, MULTO, MUTO, MUTTO, a mutton or sheep, or rather a wether, *quia testiculis mutilati. Cowel. Blount.*

MULTONES AURI, pieces of gold money imprest with an *Agnus Dei*, a sheep or lamb on the one side, and from that figure called *multones. Ibid.*

MULTURE, (*molitura vel multura*) the toll that the miller takes for grinding corn. *Cowel.*

MUMMING, (from the Tuton. *mummen*, to mimick) antick diversions in the Christmas holidays, to get money and good chear. *Ibid.*

Mummers, are those who now display diversions at fairs.

MUNDBRECH, (is derived from the Sax. *mund*, i. e. *munitio, defensio,* & *brice, fractio*) according to some an infringement of privilege; though of later times it was expounded *clausarum fractionem*, a breach of mounds. *Ibid.*

MUNDE, is peace, and *mundebrece*, a breach of it. *Ibid.*

MUNDEBURDE, (*mundeburdum*, from the Sax. *mund*, i. e. *tutela*, and *bord* or *borh*, i. e. *fidejussor. Defensionis vel patrocinii fidejussio* & *stipulatio*) a receiving into favour and protection. *Ibid.*

MUNICIPAL LAW, is a rule: not a transient sudden order from a superior to or concerning a particular person, but something permanent, uniform and universal. 1 *Black.* 44. See *Law.*

MUNIMENT-HOUSE, (*munimen*) in cathedral and collegiate churches, castles, colleges, or such, is a house or little room of strength, purposely made for keeping the seal, evidences, charters, &c. of such church, colleges, &c. such evidences being called muniments, corruptly miniments, from *munio*, to defend; because inheritances and possessions are defended by them. 3 *Inst.* 170.

MUNIMENTS, (*munimenta.*) See *Miniments.*

MUNIMINA, the grants or charters of kings to churches. *Blount.*

MUNUS ECCLESIASTICUM, the consecrated bread, out of which a little piece is taken for a communicant. *Cowel. Blount.*

MURAGE, (*muragium*) a reasonable toll to be taken of every cart and horse coming laden through a city or town, for the building or repairing the public walls thereof, due either by grant or prescription: it seems to be a liberty granted to a town by the king, for the collecting of money towards walling the same. 3 *Ed.* 1. *c.* 30. 2 *Inst.* 222. *Cowel. Blount.*

MURALE, the city wall. *Ibid.*

MURATIO, a town or borough, surrounded with walls. *Ibid.*

MURDER, (*murdrum*, from the Sax. *morth*, whence (as it is said) comes the barbarous Latin *mordrum*, & *murdrum*; in Fr. *meudre*, though the word *mardrare*, evidently comes from the Latin *morti dare*) is a word in use long before the reign of king Canutus, which some would have to signify a violent death; and sometimes the Saxons expressed it by *morthdæd* & *morthweorce*, a deadly work. But the Sax. *morth*, relates generally to *mors*.

And this word *murdrum*, according to 3 *Black* 321. was necessarily framed to express a particular offence, since no other word in being was sufficient to express the intention of the criminal; or *quo animo* the act was perpetrated. See *Homicide*.

MURORUM OPERATIO, the service of work and labour done by inhabitants and adjoining tenants in building or repairing the walls of a city or castle. *Cowel. Blount.*

MUSICIANS. See *Minstrels*.

MUSSA, (Lat.) a moss or marsh ground; also a place where sedge grows; a place over-run with moss. *Cowel. Blount.*

MUSTER, (from the Fr. *moustre*) is to shew men, and their arms, that are soldiers, and inrol them in a book. *Terms de Ley.*

MUTA CANUM, (Fr. *meute de caiens*) signifies a kennel of hounds, in ancient records. *Ibid.*

MUTARE, to mew up hawks in the time of their molting or casting their plumes. *Ibid.*

And hence the *mews* (*Muta Regia*) near Charing-Cross, London, now the king's stables, was formerly the falconry or place for the king's hawks. *Ibid.*

MUTATORIUS, change of apparel. *Ibid.*

MUTATUS ACCIPITER, a mewed hawk. *Ibid.*

MUTE, (*muins*) one dumb, who cannot or refuses to speak. And by our law a prisoner is said to stand mute, when, being arraigned for treason or felony, he either, 1. Makes no answer at all: or, 2. Answers foreign to the purpose, or with such matter as is not allowable; and will not answer otherwise: or, 3. Upon having pleaded not guilty, refuses to put himself upon the country (2 *Hal. P.C.* 316) If he says nothing, the court ought *ex officio* to impannel a jury to enquire whether he stands obstinately mute, or whether he be dumb *ex visitatione Dei*. If the latter appears to be the case, the judges of the court (who are to be of counsel for the prisoner, and to see that he hath law and justice) shall proceed to the trial, and examine all points as if he had pleaded not guilty (2 *Hawk. P. C.* 327.) But whether judgment of death can be given against such a prisoner, who hath never pleaded, and can say nothing in arrest of judgment, is a point yet undetermined (2 *Hal. P. C.* 317.)

If he be found to be obstinately mute, (which a prisoner hath been held to be, that hath cut out his own tongue, 3 *Inst.* 178.), then, if it be on an indictment of high treason, it hath been clearly settled, that standing mute is an equivalent to a conviction, and he shall receive the same judgment and execution (2 *Hawk. P. C.* 329. 2 *Hal. P. C.* 317.) And as in this the highest crime, so also in the lowest species of felony, *viz.* in petit larciny, and in all misdemesnors, standing mute hath always been equivalent to conviction. But upon appeals or indictments for other felonies, or petit treason, the prisoner was not, by the antient law, looked upon as convicted, so as to receive judgment for the felony; but should, for his obstinacy, have received the terrible sentence of *penance* or *peine*, (which, as was probably nothing more than a corrupted abbreviation of *prisone*) *forte et dure*.

Before this was pronounced the prisoner had not only *trina admonitio*, but also a respite of a few hours, and the sentence was distinctly read to him, that he might know his danger (2 *Hal. P. C.* 320.): and, after all, if he continued obstinate, and his offence was clergyable, he had the benefit of his clergy allowed him, even though he was too stubborn to pray it (2 *Hal. P. C.* 321. 2 *Hawk. P. C.* 332.) But if no other means could prevail, and the prisoner (when charged with a capital felony) continued stubbornly mute, the judgment was then given against him, without any distinction of sex or degree.

The English judgment of penance for standing mute was as follows: that the prisoner be remanded to the prison from whence he came; and put into a low, dark chamber; and there be laid on his back, on the bare floor, naked, unless where decency forbids; that there be placed upon his body as great a weight of iron as he could bear, and more: that he have no sustenance, save only on the first day, three morsels of the worst bread; and, on the second day, three draughts of standing water, that should be nearest to the prison door; and in this situation this should be alternately his daily diet, till he died, or (as antiently the judgment ran) till he answered (2 *Hale's P. C.* 319. 2 *Hawk. P. C.* 329. *Britton. c.* 4. & 22. *Flet. l.* 1. *c.* 34. *s.* 33.)

And it appears, by a record of 31 *Edw.* 3. that the prisoner might then possibly subsist for forty days under this lingering punishment (6 *Raym.* 13.)

The law was, that by standing mute, and suffering this heavy penance, the judgment, and of course the corruption of the blood and escheat of the lands, were saved in felony and petit treason, though not the forfeiture of goods; and therefore this lingering punishment was probably introduced, in order to extort a plea: without which it was held that no judgment of death could be given, and so the lord lost his escheat. But in high treason, as standing mute is an equivalent to a conviction, the same judgment, the same corruption of blood, and the same forfeitures always attended it, as in other cases of conviction (*Year B.* 8 *Hen.* 4. 1. 2 *Hawk. P. C.* 331.)

And now to the honour of our laws, it hath been enacted by statute 12 *Geo.* 3. *c.* 20. that *every person who, being arraigned for felony or piracy, shall stand mute or not answer directly to the offence, shall be convicted of the same; and the same judgment and execution (with all their consequences in every respect) shall be thereupon awarded, as if the person had been convicted by verdict or confession of the crime.*

However, two instances have occurred since the passing of this statute, of persons who refused to plead, and who in consequence were condemned and executed. One was at the Old Bailey, for murder, in 1777; the other was for burglary, at the summer assises at Wells, in 1792. *Chris. N.* on 4 *Black.* 329.

And to advise a prisoner to stand mute, is an high misprision, a contempt of the king's court, and punishable by fine and imprisonment. See *Misprision.*

MUTILATION, is the depriving a man of any member. And the law pardons even homicide, if committed *se defendendo,* in order to preserve even a member. 1 *Black.* 130. It renders void any deed executed through fear of mayhem, *ibid.* And among the defensive members, considered as such, by the common law, are reckoned not only arms and legs, but a finger, an eye, and a foretooth, and also some others. *Finch. L.* 204. 1 *Hawk. P. C.* 111. The same remedial action of trespass *vi et armis* lies also to recover damages for this injury, an injury, (which when wilful) no motive can justify but necessary self-preservation. If the ear be cut off, treble damages are given by the stat. 37 *H.* 8. *c.* 6. though this is not mayhem or mutilation at common law. And here it may not be improperly observed, that exclusive of the civil remedy, an indictment may be brought; and frequently both are accordingly prosecuted; the one at the suit of the crown for the crime against the public; the other at the suit of the party injured, to make him a reparation in damages. 3 *Black. Com.* 121. See also *Felony.*

MUTINY ACT. An act that passes annually for the regulation of the army.

MUTUAL DEBTS. Mutual debts, though of different natures, may be set against each other. 2 *Geo.* 2. *c.* 22. 8 *Geo.* 2. *c.* 24.

MUTUAL PROMISE, is where one man promises to pay money to another, and he in consideration thereof promises to do a certain act, &c. Such promises are binding, as well on one side as the other; if both made at the same time. *Hob.* 88. 1 *Salk.* 21.

MUTUATUS. If a man oweth another 10*l.* and hath a note for the same, without seal, action of debt lies upon a *mutuatus;* but in this there may be a wager of law, which there may not be in an action upon the case, on an implied promise of payment, &c. *Comp. Attorn.* 6. 111.

MUTUO, in a legal understanding, signifies to borrow or to lend. 2 *Sand.* 291.

MUTUS ET MURDUS, a person dumb and deaf. 2 *Cro.* 105.

MYSTERY, (*misterium,* from the Fr. *meistier,* i. e. *ars, artificium*) an art, trade or occupation. *Cowel. Blount.*

N

NAB, (*nappa,* Swedish) to nab, or catch unexpectedly. *Litt. Dict. Cowel.*

NACELLA, a skiff or boat. *Cowel. Blount.*

NACKA, NACTA, a small ship, yacht, or transport vessel. *Ibid.*

NAM, or NAAM, (*namium,* from the Sax. *niman,* i. e. *capere*) signified the taking or distraining another man's moveable goods. *Horn's Mirror, lib.* 2. *Spelm. Glos. Cowel. Blount.*

NAMATION, (*namation*) a taking or distraining. *Ibid.*

NAME, (*nomea*, Fr. *nosme*, or *nom*) by which any person is known or called. See *Abatement, Addition, Misnomer.*

NAMIUM VETITUM, an unjust taking the cattle of another, and driving them to an unlawful place, pretending damage done by them. *Cowel. Blount.*

NAPPERA, (from the Ital. *naperia*, i. e. *linteamina domestica*) linen cloth, or household linen. *Ibid.*

NARR, an abbreviation of *narratio*, used to signify a declaration in a cause. *Ibid.*

NARRATOR, (Lat.) a pleader or reporter: and formerly *serviens narrator* was a serjeant at law. *Ibid.*

NASSE or NESSE, (from the Sax. *Næse*, i. e. *Promontorium*) the name of the port or haven of Orford in Suffolk. *Ibid.*

NATALE, the state and condition of a man. *Ibid.*

NATHWYTE, seems to be derived from the Sax. *nath*, i. e. lewdness; and to signify the same with *lairwite*. *Ibid.*

NATIONAL DEBT, the money owing by government, for which it pays interest, and which forms our national funds. See *Funds.*

NATIVI DE STIPITE. In the survey of the duchy of Cornwall, there is mention of *nativi de stipite*, and *nativi conventionarii*; the first were villeins or bondmen, by birth or stock; the other by contract or agreement. *LL. Hen.* 1. *cap.* 76. *Bract. lib.* 4. *c.* 21, 22.

NATIVITY, (*nativitas*) birth, or the being born in a place. *Cowel. Blount.*

NATIVO HABENDO, a writ that lay to the sheriff for a lord who claimed inheritance in any villein, when his villein was run away, for the apprehending and restoring him to the lord: and the sheriff might seize the villein, and deliver him unto his lord, if he confessed his villeinage; but if he alledged that he was a freeman, then the sheriff ought not to seize him, but the lord was to sue forth a *pone* to remove the plea before the justices of C. B. &c. And if the villein purchased a writ *de libertate probanda* before the lord had taken out the *pone*, it was a *supersedeas* to the lord, that he proceeded not on the writ of *nativo habendo*. *Reg. Orig.* 7, 8. *F. N. B.* 77. *New Nat. Brev.* 171, 172.

NATIVUS. He who was born a servant, and so differed from him who suffered himself to be sold, of which servants there were three sorts, bondmen, natives, and villains. *Ibid.*

NATURAL AFFECTION, (*naturalis affectio*) is a good consideration in a deed; and if one, without expressing any consideration, covenant to stand seised to the use of his wife, child, or brother, &c. Here the naming them to be of kin, implies the consideration of natural affection, whereupon such use will arise. *Cart.* 138. See *Consideration.*

NATURAL BORN SUBJECTS, are such as are born within the dominions of the crown of England; that is, within the ligeance, or, as it is generally called, the allegiance of the king.

NATURALIZATION, (*naturalizatio*) is where a person who is an alien, is made the king's natural subject.

By the stat. 12 *W.* 3. *c.* 2. which was passed from a jealousy of king William's partiality to foreigners, naturalization cannot be performed but by act of parliament: for by this an alien is put in exactly the same state as if he had been born in the king's ligeance; except only that he is incapable, as well as a denizen, of being a member of the privy council, or parliament, holding offices, grants, &c. And by stat. 1 *Geo.* 1. *c.* 4. no bill for naturalization can be received in either house of parliament, without such disabling clause in it: nor by stat. 14 *Geo.* 3. *c.* 84. without a clause disabling the person from obtaining any immunity in trade thereby, in any foreign country; unless he shall have resided in Great Britain for seven years next after the commencement of the session in which he is naturalized. Neither by stat. 7 *Jac.* 1. *c.* 2. can any person be naturalized or restored in blood, unless he hath received the sacrament of the Lord's supper within one month before the bringing in of the bill; and unless he also takes the oaths of allegiance and supremacy in the presence of parliament. But these provisions have been usually dispensed with by special acts of parliament, previous to bills of naturalization of any foreign princes or princesses (stat. 4 *Ann.* c. 1. 7 *Geo.* 2. *c.* 3. 9 *Geo.* 2. *c.* 24. 4 *Geo.* 3. *c.* 4.)

NATURÆ PUDENDA, privities. *Cowel. Blount.*

NAVAGIUM, a duty incumbent on tenants to carry their lord's goods in a ship. *Ibid.*

NAVAL, signifies any thing belonging to the sea, or maritime affairs. *Merch. Dict.*

NAVAL STORES. See *Stores.*

NAUFRAGE, a sea term for shipwreck. *Merch. Dict.*

NAVIGABLE RIVERS. See *Felony.*

NAVIGATION, is the art of sailing at sea. And a *navigator* is one who understands navigation.

NAVIS ECCLESIÆ, the nave or body of the church. *Cowel. Blount.*

NAVIS, NAVICULA, a small dish to hold frankincense before put into the *thuribulum*, censer or smoking pot. *Cowel. Blount.*

NAVITHALAMUS, a ship or barge used for pleasure. *Ibid.*

NAVY, signifies the fleet or shipping of a

prince or state; or an armament at sea. *Ibid.*

And for the regulation of the British navy, the stat. 22 *Geo.* 2, *c.* 33, contains the articles and orders following:

1. Officers are to cause public worship, according to the liturgy of the church of England, to be solemnly performed in their ships, and take care that prayers and preaching by the chaplains be performed diligently, and that the Lord's day be observed.

2. Persons guilty of profane oaths, cursing, drunkenness, uncleanness, &c. to be punished as a court-martial shall think fit.

3. If any person shall give or hold intelligence to or with an enemy without leave, he shall suffer death.

4. If any letter or message from an enemy be conveyed to any in the fleet, and he shall not in 12 hours acquaint his superior officer with it, or if the superior officer, being acquainted therewith, shall not reveal it to the commander in chief, the offender shall suffer death, or such punishment as a court-martial shall impose.

5. Spies and persons endeavouring to corrupt any one in the fleet shall suffer death, or such punishment as a court-martial shall impose.

6. No person shall relieve an enemy with money, victuals, or ammunition, on like penalty.

7. All papers taken on board a prize shall be sent to the court of Admiralty, &c. on penalty of forfeiting the share of the prize, and such punishment as a court-martial shall impose.

8. No person shall take out of any prize any money or goods, unless for better securing the same, or for the necessary use of any of his majesty's ships, before the prize shall be condemned, upon penalty of forfeiting his share, and such punishment as shall be imposed by a court-martial.

9. No person on board a prize shall be stripped of his clothes, pillaged, beaten, or ill treated, upon pain of such punishment as a court-martial shall impose.

10. Every commander, who upon signal or order of fight, or sight of any ship which it may be his duty to engage, or who upon likelihood of engagement shall not make necessary preparations for fight, and encourage the inferior officers and men to fight, shall suffer death, or such punishment as a court-martial shall deem him to deserve. And if any person shall treacherously or cowardly yield or cry for quarter, he shall suffer death.

11. Every person who shall not obey the orders of his superior officer in time of action, to the best of his power, shall suffer death, or such punishment as a court-martial shall deem him to deserve.

12. Every person who in time of action shall withdraw or keep back, or not come into the fight, or do his utmost to take or destroy any ship which it shall be his duty to engage, and to assist every ship of his majesty or his allies, which it shall be his duty to assist, shall suffer death, or such punishment as a court-martial shall deem him to deserve. 19 *Geo.* 3, *c.* 17.

13. Every person who through cowardice, &c. shall forbear to pursue the chase of any enemy, &c. or shall not assist or relieve a known friend in view to the utmost of his power, shall suffer death, or such punishment as a court-martial shall deem him to deserve. *Ibid.*

14. If any person shall delay or discourage any action or service commanded, upon pretence of arrears of wages, or otherwise, he shall suffer death, or such punishment as a court-martial shall deem him to deserve.

15. Every person who shall desert to the enemy, or run away with any ship, ordnance, &c. to the weakening of the service, or yield up the same cowardly or treacherously to the enemy, shall suffer death.

16. Every person who shall desert, or entice others so to do, shall suffer death, or such punishment as a court-martial shall think fit. If any commanding officer shall receive a deserter, after discovering him to be such, and shall not with speed give notice to the captain of the ship to which he belongs, or if the ship is at a considerable distance, to the secretary of the admiralty, or commander in chief, he shall be cashiered.

17. Officers and seamen of ships appointed for convoy of merchants ships, or of any other, shall diligently attend upon that charge according to their instructions; and whosoever shall not faithfully perform their duty, and defend the ships in their convoy, or refuse to fight in their defence, or run away cowardly, and submit the ships in their convoy to hazard, or exact any reward for convoying any ship, or misuse the master or mariners, shall make reparation of damages, as the court of admiralty shall adjudge; and be punished criminally by death, or other punishment, as shall be adjudged by a court martial.

18. If any officer shall receive or permit to be received on board any goods or merchandise, other than for the sole use of the ship, except gold, silver, or jewels, and except goods belonging to any ship which may be shipwrecked, or in danger thereof, in order to the preserving them for the owners, and except goods ordered to be received by the lord high admiral, &c. he shall be cashiered, and rendered incapable of further service.

19. Any person making or endeavouring to make any mutinous assembly shall suffer death. Any person uttering words of sedition or mutiny shall suffer death, or such punishment as a court-martial shall deem him to deserve. If any officer, mariner, or soldier, in or belonging to the fleet, shall

behave himself with contempt to his superior officer, being in the execution of his office, he shall be punished according to the nature of his offence by the judgment of a court-martial.

20. Any person concealing any traitorous or mutinous practice or design, shall suffer death, or such punishment as a court martial shall think fit. Any person concealing any traitorous or mutinous words, or any words, practice, or design, tending to the hinderance of the service, and not forthwith revealing the same to the commanding officer, or being present at any mutiny or sedition, shall not use his utmost endeavours to suppress the same, shall be punished as a court-martial shall think he deserves.

21. Any person finding cause of complaint of the unwholesomeness of victuals, or upon other just ground, he shall quietly make the same known to his superior, who, as far as he is able, shall cause the same to be presently remedied; and no person upon any such or other pretence shall attempt to stir up any disturbance, upon pain of such punishment as a court-martial shall think fit to inflict.

22. Any person striking any his superior officer, or drawing or offering to draw or lift up any weapon against him, being in the execution of his office, shall suffer death. And any person presuming to quarrel with any his superior officer, being in the execution of his office, or disobeying any lawful command of any his superior officer, shall suffer death, or such other punishment as shall be inflicted upon him by a court-martial.

23. Any person quarrelling or fighting with any other person in the fleet, or using reproachful or provoking speeches or gestures, shall suffer such punishment as a court-martial shall impose.

24. There shall be no wasteful expense or embezzlement of any powder, shot, &c. upon penalty of such punishment as by a court-martial shall be found just.

25. Every person burning or setting fire to any magazine, or store of powder, shot, &c. or furniture thereunto belonging, not then appertaining to an enemy, shall suffer death.

26. Care is to be taken that through wilfulness or negligence no ship be stranded, run upon the rocks or sands, or split or hazarded, upon pain of death, or such punishment as a court-martial shall deem the offence to deserve.

27. No person shall sleep upon his watch, or negligently perform his duty, or forsake his station, upon pain of death, or such punishment as, &c.

28. Murder,

29. And buggery or sodomy, shall be punished with death.

30. Robbery shall be punished with death, or otherwise as a court-martial shall find meet.

31. Every person knowingly making or signing, or commanding, counselling, or procuring the making or signing, any false muster, shall be cashiered, and rendered incapable of further employment.

32. Provost-marshal refusing to apprehend or receive any criminal, or suffering him to escape, shall suffer such punishment as a court-martial shall deem him to deserve. And all others shall do their endeavours to detect and apprehend all offenders, upon pain of being punished by a court-martial.

33. If any flag-officer, captain, commander or lieutenant, shall behave in a scandalous, infamous, cruel, oppressive, or fraudulent manner, unbecoming his character, he shall be dismissed.

34. Every person in actual service and full pay guilty of mutiny, desertion, or disobedience, in any part of his majesty's dominions on shore, when in actual service relative to the fleet, shall be liable to be tried by a court-martial, and suffer the like punishment as if the offence had been committed at sea.

35. Every person in actual service and full pay committing upon shore, in any place out of his majesty's dominions, any crime punishable by these articles, shall be liable to be tried and punished as if the crime had been committed at sea.

36. All other crimes not capital, not mentioned in this act, shall be punished according to the laws and customs used at sea.

No person to be imprisoned for longer than two years.—Courts-martial not to try any offence (except the 5th, 34th, and 35th articles) not committed upon the main sea, or in great rivers beneath the bridges, or in any haven, &c. within the jurisdiction of the Admiralty, or by persons in actual service and full pay, except such persons and offences as in the 5th article—nor to try a land-officer or soldier on board a transport ship.

The lord high admiral, &c. may grant commissions to any officer commanding in chief any fleet, &c. to call courts-martial, consisting of commanders and captains. And if the commander in chief shall die, or be removed, the officer next in command may call courts-martial. No commander in chief of a fleet, &c. of more than five ships, shall preside at an court-martial in foreign parts, but the officer next in command shall preside.

If a commander in chief shall detach any part of his fleet, &c. he may empower the chief commander of the detachment to hold courts-martial during the separate service.

If five or more ships shall meet in foreign parts, the senior officer may hold courts-martial, and preside thereat.

Where it is improper for the officer next to the commander in chief to hold or preside at a court-martial, the third officer in command may be empowered to preside at or hold a court-martial.

No court martial shall consist of more than thirteen, nor less than five, persons.

Where there shall not be less than three, and yet not so many as five of the degree of a port captain or superior rank, the officer who is to preside may call to his assistance as many commanders under the degree of a port captain, as, together with the port captains, shall make up the number of five, to hold the court martial.

After trial begun, no member of a court martial shall go on shore, until sentence, except in case of sickness, upon pain of being cashiered.

Proceedings shall not be delayed, if a sufficient number remain to compose the court, which shall sit from day to day (except Sunday) till sentence be given.

Nor shall the proceedings of courts martial be delayed by the absence of any members, if enough remain to make a court, but no member shall be absent except on some extraordinary occasion. 19 Geo. 3. c. 17. s. 1, 2.

The judge advocate and all officers constituting a court martial shall be upon oath.

Persons refusing to give evidence may be imprisoned.

Sentence of death within the Narrow Seas (except in case of mutiny) shall not be put in execution till a report be made to the lord high admiral, &c.

Sentence of death beyond the Narrow Seas, shall not be put in execution but by order of the commander-in-chief of the fleet, &c.

Sentence of death in any squadron, detached from the fleet, shall not be put in execution (except in case of mutiny) but by order of the commander of the fleet, or lord high admiral, &c.

And sentence of death passed in a court martial, held by the senior officer of five or more ships met in foreign parts (except in case of mutiny) shall not be put in execution but by order of the lord high admiral, &c.

The powers given by the said articles shall remain in force with respect to crews of ships wrecked, lost, or destroyed, until they be discharged or removed into another ship, or a court martial shall be held to inquire of the causes of the loss of the ship. And if upon inquiry it shall appear, that all or any of the officers and seamen did their utmost to save the ship, and behaved obediently to their superior officers, their pay shall go on: as also shall the pay of officers and seamen taken by the enemy, having done their best to defend the ship, and behaved obediently. If any officer shall receive any goods on board, contrary to the 18th article, he shall further forfeit the value of such goods, or 500*l.* at the election of the informer; one moiety to the informer, the other to Greenwich Hospital.

NE ADMITTAS, a writ directed to the bishop for the plaintiff or defendant, where a *quare impedit* or assise of *darrein presentment* is depending, when either party fears that the bishop will admit the other's clerk during the suit between them: it ought to be brought within six calendar months after the avoidance, before the bishop may present by lapse; for it is in vain to sue out this writ when the title to present is devolved unto the bishop. *Reg. Orig.* 31. *F. N. B.* 37.

NEAT, or NET, the weight of a pure commodity alone, without the cask, bag, dross, &c. *Merch. Dict.*

NECESSITY. The law charges no man with default where the act is compulsory, and not voluntary, and where there is not a consent and election; therefore if there be an impossibility for a man to do otherwise, or so great a perturbation of the judgment and reason, as in presumption of law he cannot overcome, such necessity carries a privilege in itself. *Bac. Elem.* 25. See *Homicide.*

NE EXEAT REGNO, is a writ to restrain a person from going out of the kingdom without the king's licence. *F. N. B.* 85. It may be directed to the sheriff to make the party find surety, that he will not depart the realm; and on his refusal, to commit him to prison: or it may be directed to the party himself; and if he then goes, he may be fined. 2 *Inst.* 178. And this writ is granted on a suit being commenced in chancery, when the plaintiff fears the defendant will fly to some other country, and thereby avoid the equity of the court; which hath been sometimes practised: when thus granted, the party must give bond to the master of the rolls in the penalty of 1000*l.* or some other large sum, for yielding obedience to it; or satisfy the court by answer, affidavit, or otherwise, that he hath no design of leaving the kingdom, and give security therefore.

But from the *court of exchequer*, no such writ issues, but only an order in the nature of the writ *ne exeat regno.*

NEGATIVE, is a proposition by which something is denied. *Ploud.* 206. b. 207. a.

A negative cannot be proved or testified by witnesses, only an affirmative. 2 *Inst.* 662. But though a negative is incapable of being proved directly, yet indirectly it is otherwise: for in case one accuses B. to have been at York, and there had committed a certain fact, in proof of which he produces several witnesses; here B. cannot prove that he was not at York, against positive evidence that he was; but shall be allowed to make out the negative by collateral testimony, that at that very time he was at Exeter, &c. in such a house and in such company. *Fortescue* 37.

NEGATIVE PREGNANT, (*negativa preg-*

nans) is a negative, implying also an affirmative: as if a man being impleaded to have done a thing on such a day, or in such a place, denieth that he did it *modo & forma declarata*, which implieth nevertheless, that in some sort he did it. *Dyer* 17. *num.* 95. and *Brook hoc titulo*, and *Kitchen* 232. and *Terms of the Law*.

A negative pregnant is a fault in pleading; and there must be a special demurrer to a negative pregnant plea, &c. for the court will intend every pleading to be good, till the contrary doth appear. 2 *Leon.* 248. *Bro. Issue join. pl.* 81. *Heath's Max.* 53. 2 *Lee* 199. *Cro. Jac.* 559, 560. *Lea* v. *Luthell*, 15 *Vin. Abr.* tit. *Neg. Preg.*

NEGGILDARE, signifies to claim kindred.

NEGLIGENCE, is where a person neglects or omits to do a thing which he is by law obliged to. And where one has goods of another to keep till such a time, and hath a certain recompence or reward for the keeping, he shall stand charged for injury by negligence, &c. But if he hath nothing for keeping them, he is not bound to answer. *Doct. & Stud.* 269. A man who finds another's goods, if they are after hurt by wilful negligence, it is held he is chargeable to the owner; though it is otherwise when they are lost by casualty, as in case they are laid in a house that is accidentally burnt, or if he deliver them to another to keep, who runs away with them, &c. *Ibid.* It is held if an accountant be robbed, and it is without his default and negligence, he shall not be answerable for the money. 1 *Inst.* 89. A right may be lost by negligence; as where an action is not brought in the time appointed by the statute of limitations, &c. 21 *Jac.* 1. *c.* 16. 2 *William's Rep.* 665. *Cowper* v. *Earl Cowper*. *Tot.* 76. *Kemp* v. *Palmer*. *Chanc. Rep.* 10. *Earl of Oxford's Case*. *Chan. Prec.* 583. *Ivey* v. *Gilbert*.

NEGRO. By the laws of the plantations in general, negro servants are saleable. But here in England, a man cannot have any property in his fellow creature; and therefore a Negro, after his arrival in England is immediately free. 11 *Str.* 340. *Lofft.* 1.

NEIF, (Fr. *naif*, i. e. *naturalis, nativa*) was a bondwoman or she villein. 2 *Black.* 93.

NEIFTY. There was an ancient writ called *writ of neifty*, whereby the lord claimed such a woman for his *neif*; now out of use. *Cowel. Blount.*

NEIGHBOUR, (*vicinus*) one who dwells near another. See *Vicinage*.

NE INJUSTE VEXES, a writ founded on *magna charta*, *c.* 10. that lies for a tenant distrained by his lord, for more services than he ought to perform; and was a prohibition to the lord not to distrain or vex his tenant. *Reg. Orig.* 4. *F. N. B.* 10. *New Br.* 22.

NEMINE CONTRADICENTE, words used to signify the unanimous consent of the members of either house of parliament, to a vote or resolution.

NE RECIPIATUR, a caveat against the receiving and setting down a cause to be tried, where the cause is not entered in due time.

NE VICECOMES, *colore Mandati Regis, quenquam amoveat a possessione ecclesiæ minus juste. Reg. Orig.* 61.

NEW ASSIGNMENT. In many actions the plaintiff, who hath alleged in his declaration a general wrong, may in his replication, after an evasive plea by the defendant, reduce that general wrong to a more particular certainty, by assigning the injury afresh with all its specific circumstances in such manner as clearly to ascertain and identify it, consistently with his general complaint; which is called a new or novel assignment. 3 *Black.* 310, 311.

NEWS. Persons reporting false news or tales, are punishable by statute 3 *Ed.* 1. *c.* 34. See *Scan. Mag.* 4 *Black.* 149.

NEWSPAPERS. By 38 *Geo.* 3. *c.* 78. no person shall print or publish a newspaper until an affidavit be delivered at the stamp office, specifying the names and abode of the printer, publisher, and the proprietors, if they do not exceed two, exclusive of the printer and publisher; and if they do, then of two proprietors and their proportional shares; and the description of the printing-house and title of the paper: and where the proprietors exceed two, the names of the two of the greatest proprietors, exclusive of the printer and publisher, shall be specified in the affidavit. *s.* 1—3.

An affidavit is to be made as often as the printers, publishers, or proprietors, named therein, or their respective abodes, shall be changed, or as often as the commissioners for stamps shall require. *s.* 4.

The affidavit shall be signed by the parties, and taken by a commissioner or officer specially appointed. *s.* 5.

Where the printers, publishers, and proprietors, required to be named in the affidavit, do not exceed four, the whole shall swear; and when they do not exceed that number, four are to swear and give notice to the parties not swearing, on pain of 50*l.* each. *s.* 6.

Persons printing, publishing, or vending a newspaper without such an affidavit, shall forfeit 100*l.*; and persons making false or imperfect affidavits, are liable to the penalties of perjury. *s.* 7, 8.

The affidavits are to be filed; and they, or certified copies, are to be admitted in all proceedings, civil or criminal, as evidence of the truth of their contents, against the persons swearing, and all mentioned therein, unless proved to the contrary; but if any person shall have delivered, previous to the publication of the paper to which the proceedings relate, an affidavit that he has ceased to be the printer, publisher, or proprietor, he shall not be so deemed after the delivery. *s.* 9.

In newspapers there shall be printed the names and abode of printers and publishers, on pain of 100*l.*; and proof, as before mentioned, that the party is the printer of the newspaper shall be sufficient, unless proved to the contrary. *s.* 10.

After production of the affidavit, or copy, and a paper entituled as therein mentioned, it shall not be necessary for a prosecutor for penalties under this act to prove the purchase of the paper. *s.* 11.

Service at the printing-house mentioned in the affidavit, shall be sufficient notice to all persons named therein; but if any person shall have delivered, previous to the publication of the party to which the proceedings relate, an affidavit that he has ceased to be printer, publisher, or proprietor, he shall be not so deemed after such delivery. *s.* 12.

Certified copies of such affidavits are to be delivered from the stamp office on payment of 1*s.* *s.* 13.

And copies of affidavits, so certified by the commissioners, or officers in whose custody they shall be, are to be sufficient evidence. *s.* 14.

Unauthorized persons giving certificates, forfeit 100*l.* *s.* 15.

Persons falsely certifying that affidavits were sworn to, or that false copies are true, shall forfeit 100*l.* *s.* 16.

A copy of every newspaper shall be delivered within six days of its publication to the commissioners of stamps, or their officer, on penalty of 100*l.* which paper is to be paid for by the commissioners, and may, within two years after publication, be produced as evidence in any proceeding, civil or criminal. *s.* 17.

Persons printing or publishing newspapers not duly stamped, are to forfeit 20*l.*; and persons taking or receiving a newspaper not duly stamped, are also to forfeit 20*l.* *s.* 18, 19.

Persons sending or procuring newspapers to be sent out of Great Britain, not duly stamped, forfeit 100*l.* *s.* 20.

The names and abode of proprietors out of Great Britain are to be specified in affidavits. *s.* 23.

Persons printing or publishing any seditious matter, under colour of its having been printed in a foreign paper, on conviction, shall be committed to prison for not exceeding twelve, nor less than six, months, and also subject to other punishment as for a high misdemeanor; and proof of its having been so previously printed is to lie on the defendant. *s.* 22.

And if such proof be made, the publication is to be deemed of the same nature as it would have been before this act. *s.* 25.

None but the commissioners of stamps, or their officer, shall supply paper stamped for printing newspapers, until the person so supplying has given security to deliver, once in six weeks, an account of the quantities and kind sold, on penalty of 100*l.* *s.* 26.

Persons concerned in printing or publishing newspapers, not legally stamped, are to be debtors to his majesty in the sum that would have accrued if duly stamped. *s.* 27.

To bills for the discovery of proprietors, printers, editors, or publishers, of newspapers, the defendants shall not demur, but shall make the discovery requisite. *s.* 28.

Penalties exceeding 20*l.* (except where otherwise provided) may be recovered in any court of record; and not exceeding 20*l.* before one justice, by distress, and in default the party may be committed for three months. *s.* 29—31.

NEW STILE. See *Calendar.*

NEW TRIAL. Judgments in civil cases, are often suspended by granting new trials. The causes of suspending the judgment by granting a new trial, are at present wholly extrinsic, arising from matter foreign to, or dehors the record. 3 *Black.* 387.

Of this sort are want of notice of trial; or any flagrant misbehaviour of the party prevailing towards the jury, which may have influenced their verdict; or any gross misbehaviour of the jury among themselves: also if it appears by the judge's report, certified to the court, that the jury have brought in a verdict without or contrary to evidence, so that he is reasonably dissatisfied therewith (*Law of Nisi Prius,* 303, 4.); or if they had given exorbitant damages; or if the judge himself has mis-directed the jury, so that they found an unjustifiable verdict; for these and other reasons of the like kind, it is the practice of the court to award a new, or second trial (*Comb.* 357.) But if two juries agree in the same or a similar verdict a third trial is seldom awarded: for the law will not readily suppose, that the verdict of any one subsequent jury can countervail the oaths of two preceding ones (6 *Mod.* 22. *Salk.* 649.)

NICOL, anciently used for Lincoln. *Cowel.*

NIDERLING, NIDERING, or NITHING, a vile base person, a sluggard. *Ibid.*

NIENT COMPRISE, an exception taken to a petition, because the thing desired was not contained in that deed or proceeding whereon the petition was founded: for example; one desires of the court wherein a recovery is had of lands, &c. to be put in possession of a house, formerly among the lands adjudged unto him; to which the adverse party pleads, that this is not to be granted, by reason this house is not comprised amongst the lands and houses for which he had judgment. *New Book Entries.*

NIENT CULPABLE, (*non culpabilis*) the plea of not guilty.

NIENT DEDIRE, to suffer judgment by default. *Cowel.*

NIGER LIBER, the Black Book or register in the exchequer. *Ibid.*

NIGHT, is when it is so dark, that the countenance of a man cannot be discerned. And what is reckoned night, and what day, for the purpose of convicting a man of burglary, is as follows: anciently the day was accounted to begin only at sun-rising, and to end immediately at sun-set; but the better opinion seems to be, that if there be daylight or *crepusculum* enough, begun or left, to discern a man's face withal, it is no burglary. But this does not extend to moonlight; for then many midnight burglaries would go unpunished: and besides, the malignity of the offence does not so properly arise from its being done in the dark, as at the dead of night; when all the creation, except beasts of prey, are at rest; when sleep has disarmed the owner, and rendered his castle defenceless. 3 *Inst.* 63. 1 *Hal. P. C.* 350. 1 *Hawk. P. C.* 101. 4 *Black.* 224.

NIGHTWALKERS, are such persons as sleep by day and walk by night, being oftentimes pilferers, or disturbers of the peace. 5 *Ed.* 3. *c.* 14. Constables are authorized by the common law to arrest nightwalkers and suspicious persons, &c. Watchmen may also arrest nightwalkers, and hold them until the morning: and it is said, that a private person may arrest any suspicious nightwalker, and detain him till he give a good account of himself. 2 *Hawk. P. C.* 61, 80. One may be bound to good behaviour for being a nightwalker; and common nightwalkers and haunters of bawdy-houses are to be indicted before justices of peace, &c. 1 *Hawk.* 132. 2 *Hawk.* 40. *Latch.* 173. *Poph.* 280. But it is held not lawful for a constable, &c. to take up any woman as a nightwalker, on bare suspicion only of being of ill fame; unless she be guilty of a breach of the peace, or some unlawful act, and ought to be found misdoing. *Holt's MS.* See 2 *Hale's Hist. P. C.* 89. 2 *Black.* 289.

NIHIL CAPIAT PER BREVE, or *per billam*, is the judgment given against the plaintiff in an action, either in bar of his action, or in abatement of his writ or bill, &c. *Co. Lit.* 363.

NIHIL, or NIL DEBET, is a common plea to an action of debt upon simple contract: but it is no plea in covenant or upon any specialty, for then the proper plea is *non est factum*; and if a defendant does not observe this distinction in pleading, his plea may be demurred to. 3 *Lev.* 170.

NIHIL, or NIL DICIT, is a failing by the defendant to put in an answer to the plaintiff's plea by the day assigned; which being omitted, judgment is had against him of course, as saying nothing, why it should not.

NIHIL, or NIL HABUIT IN TENEMENTIS, the plea of *nil habuit in tenementis*, is an estoppel; and the plaintiff cannot reply generally *quod habuit in tenementis, &c.* that for the replication he ought to shew what estate he had; but after verdict, it is good. *Cro. Jac.* 312.

NIHILS, or NICHILS, are issues which the sheriff that is opposed in the exchequer says, are nothing worth, and illeviable, for the insufficiency of the parties from whom due. *Practis. Excheq. pag.* 101. Accounts of *nihil* shall be put out of the exchequer. Stat. 5 *R.* 2. *c.* 13.

NISI PRIUS, is a commission to justices of *nisi prius*; so called from a judicial writ of *distringas*; whereby the sheriff is commanded to distrain the impannelled jury to appear at Westminster before the justices at a certain day in the following term, to try some cause, *nisi prius justic' domini regis ad assises capiend. venerint, viz.* unless the justices come before that day to such a place, &c. 2 *Inst.* 424. 4 *Inst.* 159.

NIVICOLINI BRITONES, is used for Welshmen; because in Carmarthenshire and other northern counties of Wales, they lived near high mountains covered with snow. *Cowel. Blount.*

NOBILITY, (*nobilitas*) signifies a nobleness of birth, generosity or greatness of mind, excellence of virtue: but nobility as here understood, compriseth all degrees of dignity above a baronet; and is derived from the king, who may grant it in fee, or for life. 1 *Black.* 157, 396.

NOBLE, an ancient kind of English money, in use in the reign of *Ed.* 3. of six shillings and eightpence value, or a third part of twenty shillings. *Merch. Dict.*

NOCTANTER, was the name of a writ, issuing out of chancery, returnable in the king's bench, given by statute *Westm.* 2. 13 *Ed.* 2. *c.* 46. By virtue of which statute, where any one having right to approve waste ground, &c. makes and erects a ditch or an hedge, and it is thrown down in the night time, and it cannot be known by a verdict of assise or a jury, by whom; or, if the neighbouring vills will not indict such as are guilty, they shall be distrained to make again the hedge or ditch at their own costs, and to answer damages. 2 *Inst.* 476.

The word noctanter is also necessary in an indictment of burglary, and it is insufficient without it. *Cro. Eliz.* 483. See *Trespass.*

NOCTES ET NOCTEM DE FIRMA. *Tot noctes de firma*, or *firma tot noctium*; or entertainment of meat and drink for so many nights. *Cowel. Blount.*

NODFYRS or NEDFRI, (Sax. *neod, obsequium & fry, ignis*) signified fires made in honour of the heathen deities. It is also said to come from the Saxon *neb*, that is necessary; and was used for the necessary fire. *Cowel. Blount.*

NOLLE PROSEQUI, is where a plaintiff in any action will proceed no further, and may be before or after verdict; though it is usually before: and it is then stronger against the plaintiff than a nonsuit, which is only a default in appearance; but this is a voluntary acknowledgment, that he hath no cause of action. 2 *Lil.* 218. 8 *Rep.* 58. *Cro. Jac.* 439. *Hob.* 180.

But a *nolle prosequi* does not amount to a *retraxit* or release, where there are more defendants. *Ld. Raym.* 599.

The king may also enter a *nolle prosequi* on an information; but it shall not stop the proceedings of the informer. 1 *Leon.* 119. And if an informer cause a *nolle prosequi* to be entered, the defendant shall have costs, &c. by stat. 4 & 5 *W. & M. c.* 18. Also the king may, by his attorney-general, enter a *nolle prosequi* on an indictment.

But the clerk of the crown cannot enter a *nolle prosequi* on an indictment, without leave of the attorney-general. *Ld. Raym.* 721.

NOMENCLATOR, one who opens the etymologies of names, interpreted Thesaurarius by Spelman. *Cowel.*

NOMINATION, (*nominatio*) is the power (by virtue of some manor or otherwise) of appointing a clerk to a patron of a benefice, by him to be presented to the ordinary. And the person who hath the nomination is in effect the patron of the church. *Plowd.* 529. *Moor* 47.

NOMINA VILLARUM. Edward II. sent his letters to every sheriff in England, requiring an exact account and return into the exchequer of the names of all the villages, and possessors thereof in every county, which being done accordingly, the returns of the sheriffs all joined together are called *nomina villarum*, still remaining in the exchequer. *Anno* 9 *Ed.* 2.

NOMINE PŒNÆ. If rent is reserved by the lease or agreement in writing, with a penalty, that is a *nomine pœnæ* on the non-payment of it at a certain day, and the rent be behind and unpaid, there must be an actual demand thereof made, before the grantee of the rent can distrain for it; the *nomine pœnæ* being of the same nature as the rent, and issuing out of the land out of which the rent doth issue. *Hob.* 82, 133. 2 *Nels. Abr.* 1182.

And when any sum *nomine pœnæ* is to be forfeited for non-payment of rent at the time, &c. the demand of the rent ought to be precisely at the day, in respect of the penalty: and debt will not lie on a *nomine pœnæ*, without a demand. 7 *Rep.* 28. *Cro. Eliz.* 383. *Style* 4. *Lutw.* 1156.

NON-ABILITY, is an exception taken against the plaintiff in a cause, upon some just ground, why he cannot commence any suit in law; as præmunire, outlawry, excommunication, &c. *F. N. B.* 35, 65. See *Abatement.*

NONÆ ET DECIMÆ, payments made to the church by those who were tenants of church farms. *Blount.*

NON-AGE, in general understanding is all the time of a person's being under the age of one-and-twenty. See *Age.*

NON-ASSUMPSIT, a plea in personal actions, whereby a man denies any promise made, &c. See *Assumpsit.*

NON ASSUMPSIT INFRA SEX ANNOS, is a plea where a defendant by virtue of the statute of limitations, 21 *Jac.* 1. *c.* 16. pleads that he did not undertake or promise within six years before the commencement of the action: which is the actual taking out of the plaintiff's writ. And the computation is to be made up to that day, though in vacation, and not to the teste of the writ.

NON-CLAIM, is an omission or neglect of one that claims not within the time limited by law, as within a year and a day, where continual claim ought to be made; or in five years after a fine levied, &c. By which a man may be barred of his right of entry. Stat. 4 *H.* 7. *c.* 24. 32 *H.* 8. *c.* 33.

NON COMPOS MENTIS, is where a person is not of sound mind, memory, and understanding. See *Ideots* and *Lunatics.*

NON-CONFORMISTS. Non-conformists are of two sorts. I. Such as absent themselves from divine worship in the established church, through total irreligion, and attend the service of no other persuasion. These by the statutes of 1 *Eliz. c.* 2. 23 *Eliz. c.* 1. and 3 *Jac.* 1. *c.* 4. forfeit one shilling to the poor every Lord's day they so absent themselves, and 20*l.* to the king if they continue such default for a month together. And if they keep any inmate, thus irreligiously disposed, in their houses, they forfeit 10*l.* per month.—II. The second species of non-conformists are those who offend through a mistaken or perverse zeal. Such were esteemed by our laws, enacted since the time of the reformation, to be papists and protestant dissenters: both of which were supposed to be equally schismatics in not communicating with the national church; with this difference, that the papists divided from it upon material, though erroneous, reasons; but many of the dissenters upon matters of indifference, or, in other words, upon no reason at all. Yet certainly our ancestors were mistaken in their plans of compulsion and intolerance. The sin of schism, as such, is by no means the object of temporal coërcion and punishment. If through weakness of intellect, through misdirected piety, through perverseness and acerbity of temper, or (which is often the case) through a prospect of secular advantage in herding with a party, men quarrel with the ecclesiastical establishment, the civil magistrate has nothing to do with it; unless their tenets and practice are such as threaten ruin or disturbance to the state. He is bound indeed to protect the established church: and, if this can be better effected, by admitting none but its genuine members to offices of trust and emolument, he is certainly at liberty so to do; the disposal of offices being matter of favour and discretion. But, this point being once secured, all persecution for diversity of opinions, however ridiculous or absurd they may be, is contrary to every principle of sound policy and civil freedom. The names and subordination of the clergy, the posture of devotion, the materials and colour of the minister's garment, the joining in a known or an unknown form of prayer, and other matters of the same kind, must be left to the option of every man's private judgment. 4 *Black*. 52.

With regard therefore to protestant dissenters, although the experience of their turbulent disposition in former times occasioned several disabilities and restrictions to be laid upon them by abundance of statutes (23 *Eliz*. *c*. 1. 29 *Eliz*. *c*. 6. 35 *Eliz*. *c*. 1. 22 *Car*. 2. *c*. 1.), yet at length the legislature, with a spirit of true magnanimity, extended that indulgence to these sectaries, which they themselves, when in power, had held to be countenancing schism, and denied to the church of England. (The ordinance of 1645 inflicted imprisonment for a year on the third offence, and pecuniary penalties on the former two, in case of using the book of common prayer not only in a place of public worship, but also in any private family.) The penalties are conditionally suspended by the statute 1 *W*. & *M*. *st*. 1. *c*. 18. "for exempting their majesties' "protestant subjects, dissenting from the "church of England, from the penalties of "certain laws," commonly called the toleration act; which is confirmed by statute 10 *Ann*. *c*. 2. and declares that neither the laws above-mentioned, nor the statutes 1 *Eliz*. *c*. 2. *s*. 14. 3 *Jac*. 1. *c*. 4, 5. nor any other penal laws made against popish recusants (except the test acts) shall extend to any dissenters, other than papists and such as deny the trinity: provided, 1. that they take the oaths of allegiance and supremacy (or make a similar affirmation, being quakers, *stat*. 8 *Geo*. 1. *c*. 6.) and subscribe the declaration against popery; 2. that they repair to some congregation certified to and registered in the court of the bishop or archdeacon, or at the county sessions; 3. that the doors of such meeting-house shall be unlocked, unbarred, and unbolted; in default of which the persons meeting there are still liable to all the penalties of the former acts. Dissenting teachers, in order to be exempted from the penalties of the statutes 13 & 14 *Car*. 2. *c*. 4. 15 *Car*. 2. *c*. 6. 17 *Car*. 2. *c*. 2. and 22 *Car*. 2. *c*. 1. are also to subscribe the articles of religion mentioned in the statute 13 *Eliz*. *c*. 12. (which only concern the confession of the true christian faith, and the doctrine of the sacraments) with an express exception of those relating to the government and powers of the church, and to infant baptism; or if they scruple subscribing the same, shall make and subscribe the declaration prescribed by statute 19 *Geo*. 3. *c*. 44. professing themselves to be christians and protestants, and that they believe the scriptures to contain the revealed will of God, and to be the rule of doctrine and practice. Thus, though the crime of non-conformity is by no means universally abrogated, it is suspended and ceases to exist with regard to these protestant dissenters, during their compliance with the conditions imposed by these acts: and, under these conditions, all persons, who will approve themselves no papists or oppugners of the trinity, are left at full liberty to act as their consciences shall direct them, in the matter of religious worship. And if any person shall wilfully, maliciously, or contemptuously disturb any congregation, assembled in any church or permitted meeting-house, or shall misuse any preacher or teacher there, he shall (by virtue of the same statute 1 *W*. & *M*.) be bound over to the sessions of the peace, and forfeit twenty pounds. But by statute 5 *Geo*. 1. *c*. 4. no mayor or principal magistrate, must appear at any dissenting meeting with the ensigns of his office, on pain of disability to hold that or any other office: the legislature judging it a matter of propriety, that a mode of worship, set up in opposition to the national, when allowed to be exercised in peace, should be exercised also with decency, gratitude, and humility. Dissenters also who subscribe the declaration of the act 19 *Geo*. 3. are excepted, (unless in the case of endowed schools and colleges) from the penalties of the statutes 13 & 14 *Car*. 2. *c*. 4. and 17 *Car*. 1. *c*. 2. which prohibit upon pain of fine and imprisonment all persons from teaching school unless they are licensed by the ordinary, and subscribe a declaration of conformity to the liturgy of the church, and reverently frequent divine service established by the laws of the kingdom. See also *Papists*.

NON CULPABILIS, the plea of not guilty to any action of trespass, or tort, or to an indictment, &c.

NON DAMNIFICATUS, is a plea to an action of debt upon a bond, with condition to save the plaintiff harmless. 2 *Lil*. *Abr*. 224.

NON DECIMANDO. A custom or prescription: *de non decimando* is to be discharged of all tithes, &c. See *Modus Decimandi*.

NON DISTRINGENDO, a writ not to distrain. *Cowel*. *Blount*.

NONES, (*nonæ*) of every month is, the seventh day of March, May, July, and October; and the fifth day of all the other month. *Ibid*. See *Ides*.

NON EST CULPABILIS, or *non cul.* is the general plea to an action of trespass, whereby the defendant absolutely denies the fact charged on him by the plaintiff. And as the plea of *non culp.* is the general answer in actions of trespass, being actions criminal, civilly prosecuted; so it is likewise in all actions criminally followed, either at the suit of the king or any other, where the defendant denies the crime for which he is brought to trial. *S. P. C. lib.* 2. *c.* 63.

NON EST FACTUM, a plea where an action is brought upon a bond, or any other deed, and the defendant denieth that to be his deed whereon he is impleaded. *Broke.* See *Nil Debet.*

NON EST INVENTUS, the sheriff's return to a writ, when the defendant is not to be found in his bailiwick. *Shep. Epit.* 1129.

NONFEASANCE. An offence of omission of what ought to be done; as in not coming to church, &c. But nonfeasance will not make a man a trespasser, &c. 1 *Hawk.* 13. *Hob.* 251. 8 *Rep.* 146.

NON IMPLACITANDO ALIQUEM DE LIBERO TENEMENTO SINE BREVI, a writ to prohibit bailiffs, &c. from distraining or impleading any man touching his freehold, without the king's writ. *Reg. Orig.* 171.

NON INTROMITTENDO, QUANDO BREVE PRÆCIPE IN CAPITE SUBDOLE IMPETRATUR, was a writ directed to the justices of the bench, or in eyre, commanding them not to give one, who had, under colour of intitling the king to land, &c. as holding of him *in capite*, deceitfully obtained the writ called *præcipe in capite*, any benefit thereof, but to put him to his writ of right. *Reg. Orig.* 4.

NONJURORS, are persons who refuse to take the oaths to government, who are liable to certain penalties. See stat. 1 *Geo.* 1. *c.* 55. and *Oaths.*

NON MERCHANDIZANDO VICTUALI, a writ to justices of assise to inquire whether the magistrates of such a town sold victuals in gross, or by retail, during the time of their being in office, which was contrary to an ancient statute; and to punish them if they did. *Reg. Orig.* 184.

NON MOLESTANDO, a writ that lies for a person who is molested contrary to the king's protection granted him. *Reg. of Writs* 184.

NON OBSTANTE, (*notwithstanding*) was a clause frequent in statutes and letters patent, and was a licence from the king to do a thing which at the common law might be lawfully done; but being restrained by act of parliament, could not be done without such licence. *Vaugh.* 347. *Plowd.* 501.

But the doctrine of *non obstante's*, which sets the prerogative above the laws, was effectually demolished by the bill of rights at the revolution, and abdicated at Westminster-hall when king James abdicated the kingdom. 1 *Black.* 342.

NON OMITTAS, is a writ directed to the sheriff, where the bailiff of a liberty or franchise hath the return of writs within his sheriffwick, for the sheriff to enter into the franchise and execute the king's process himself, or by his officer. *F. N. B.* 68, 74. 2 *Inst.* 453.

NON PLEVIN, (*non plevina*) is defined to be *defalta post defaltam*; but by stat. 9 *Ed.* 3. *c.* 2. it was enacted, that none should lose his land, because of *non-plevin*, i. e. where the land was not replevied in due time.

NON PONENDIS IN ASSISIS ET JURATIS, a writ granted for freeing and discharging persons from serving on assises and juries; and when one had a charter of exemption, he might sue the sheriff for returning him. 2 *Inst.* 127, 447. *Cowel. Blount.*

NON PROCEDENDO AD ASSISAM REGE INCONSULTO, a writ to stop the trial of a cause appertaining to one who is in the king's service, &c. until the king's pleasure be farther known. *Reg. Orig.* 220.

NON PROS, or NON PROSEQUITUR. If a plaintiff in an action, doth not declare against the defendant within reasonable time, a rule may be entered against him by the defendant's attorney to declare; and thereupon a *non pros*, &c. *Practic. Solic.* 222. See *Nolle Prosequi*, and *Nonsuit.*

NON RESIDENCE, is applied to those spiritual persons who are not resident, but wilfully absent themselves.

And by 43 *Geo.* 3. *c.* 84. and 43 *Geo.* 3. *c.* 109. every spiritual person who shall, without such sufficient cause as by 21 *Hen.* 8. 13. 25 *Hen.* 8. *c.* 16. 28 *Hen.* 8. *c.* 13. and 33 *Hen.* 8. *c.* 28. would exempt such spiritual person from the pains for non-residence, and who shall not have a licence for the purpose, according to this act, wilfully absent himself for three months together in one year, and reside at any other place, except at any other benefice, shall, when such absence shall exceed three and not exceeding six, months, forfeit one-third of the value of the benefice (deducting therefrom all outgoings, except the curate's stipend); if the absence exceed six and not eight months, one-half: if it exceed eight months, two-thirds; and if it be for the whole year, three-fourths; to be recovered in any court of record, with costs, and the whole to go to the informer; but no parsonage that hath a vicar endowed shall be deemed a benefice. *s.* 12.

And the court in which any action shall be depending may require the diocesan to certify the reputed annual value of benefices. *s.* 13.

No person having resided a year without absence for more than three months shall be commenced before he has so resided. *s.* 14.

Persons exempted by the acts mentioned in *s.* 12, the chaplain of the house of commons, the clerk of his majesty's closet and deputy, the chaplains of the army, navy, artillery, garrisons, and dock-yard, British factories, or household of ambassadors, spiritual persons belonging to ecclesiastical courts, or cathedral or collegiate churches or chapels royal, or the military or naval hospitals or asylums, the readers in the inns of court, tutors or chaplains in the universities, or Eaton or Winchester college, or Westminster school, shall be exempted. *s.* 15.

No penalty shall be levied personally, where it can be recovered by sequestration of the benefice in three years. *s.* 17.

Bishops in England may grant licences for non-residence, on oath before a surrogate, of actual necessity, in the following cases, *viz.* in case of actual illness or infirmity in himself—the want of a suitable place of residence in the same parish—having a small benefice, and serving as a curate elsewhere—any master or usher of any endowed school—masters or preachers of hospitals, or incorporated charitable foundation—persons holding any endowed lectureship, chapelry, or preachership—librarians of the British Museum—for which licence, a fee of 10*s.*, inclusive of the stamps, may be taken, and persons aggrieved by refusal of licences may appeal to the archbishop, the party appealing giving security for the expences thereof. *s.* 19.

In cases not enumerated bishops may grant licences, and assign salaries to curates employed; but the reasons for granting them shall be transmitted to the archbishop for examination and allowance. *s.* 20.

Licences shall not be void by the death or removal of the grantor, unless revoked by the successor. *Ibid.*

Archbishops, in their respective dioceses, may grant licences. *Ibid.*

Fees may be ordered to be paid by appellants, and the costs may be recovered by sequestration. *Ibid.*

Licences may be revoked, and none are to be in force for more than two years. *s.* 21.

Copies of licences or revocations shall be filed in the registry of the diocese, and a list kept for inspection; and copies of licences or revocations shall be transmitted to the churchwardens, and publicly read at the first visitation. *s.* 22.

A list of licences confirmed by the archbishop, or granted in his own diocese, shall be annually transmitted to his majesty in council, who may revoke the same; but between the grant and revocation of a licence it shall be deemed valid. *s.* 23, 24.

On or before March 25, annually, a return shall be made to his majesty in council of every benefice, and of the person who shall not have resided, and every non-resident by exemption, without licence, shall, within six weeks after Jan. 1, yearly, notify the nature of it to the diocesan; a duplicate whereof may be delivered to the registrar to be filed, and his certificate shall be evidence of its being made. *s.* 25.

Persons neglecting to make notifications shall not be entitled to exemption. *s.* 26.

Licences may be pleaded in bar of actions, and in case of nonsuit the defendant shall have costs. *s.* 27.

Licences may be granted while a see is vacant, or the prelate absented, by those who exercise his functions. *s.* 28.

The act shall not prevent ecclesiastical censures for non-residence without licence; but no censure for non-residence, not exceeding three months in one year, shall be put in force, nor any proceedings to be admitted, except at the suit of the bishop or archdeacon. *s.* 29.

If any unlicensed person does not sufficiently reside, the bishop may issue a monition to reside: returns shall be made to monitions, and, if required, upon oath: where returns shall not be made, or not be satisfactory, the bishop may order residence, and if disobeyed, may sequester the profits of the benefice, and direct the application thereof; but an appeal against sequestrations may be made to the archbishop, the appellant giving security for the expences thereof. *s.* 30.

Persons who shall return to residence on monition shall pay the costs. *s.* 31.

If any person returning to residence on monition, shall, before six months thereafter, absent himself, the bishop may, without monition, sequester the profits of the benefice. *s.* 32.

If a clerk shall continue under sequestration three years, or incur three years sequestration within that period, the benefice shall be void. *s.* 33.

Contracts for letting houses in which any spiritual persons shall, by order of the bishop, be required to reside, shall be void; and persons holding possession after the time appointed, shall be subject to a penalty of 48*s.* per day, and no spiritual person shall be liable to any penalty for non-residence while the tenant shall continue to occupy. *s.* 34, 35.

If any action be brought for non-residence before issuing a monition, a sum sufficient to satisfy the penalty and costs shall be retained out of the profits of the benefice; but if at the time of filling any monition no action shall have been commenced, none shall be afterwards brought. *s.* 36.

No oath relating to residence shall be required of any vicar. *s.* 37.

The act extends to all dignities, prebends, benefices, curacies, and chapelries. *s.* 38.

Archbishop, bishop, and archdeacon, within whose respective province, diocese, or jurisdiction, any benefice exempt shall be locally situate, shall have the same powers as if such benefice were not exempt; and when any such benefice shall be situate in more than one province, or between the limits of two, the archbishop or bishop to whose cathedral the parish church shall be nearest, shall have the like powers: and all peculiars shall be subject to the archbishop or bishop to whom they belong. *s.* 39.

The act shall not affect his majesty's prerogative in granting dispensations, nor clerks retained in his service under 9 *Ed.* 2. *c.* 8. *s.* 40.

No archbishop or bishop shall be liable to the penalties of non-residence. *s.* 41.

NON RESIDENTIA PRO CLERICIS REGIS, was a writ directed to the bishop, charging him not to molest a clerk employed in the king's service, by reason of his non-residence; in which case he is to be discharged. *Reg. Orig.* 58.

NON SANE MEMORY, (*non sanæ memoriæ.*) See *Ideots* and *Lunatics*. *Non compos Mentis.*

NONSENSE. Where a matter set forth is grammatically right, but absurd in the sense and unintelligible, some words cannot be rejected to make sense of the rest, but must be taken as they are. 1 *Salk.* 324. See *Mistake.*

NON SOLVENDO PECUNIAM, AD QUAM CLERICUS MULCTATUR PRO NON RESIDENTIA, a writ prohibiting an ordinary to take a pecuniary mulct, imposed upon a clerk of the king's for non-residence. *Reg. of Writs, fol.* 59.

NON-SUIT, (*non est prosecutus, &c.*) is a renunciation of the suit by the plaintiff or demandant. *Cowel.*

Thus where plaintiff is demanded and doth not appear, he is said to be non-suit; this usually happens, where upon trial, and when the jury are ready to give their verdict, the plaintiff discovers some error or defect in the proceedings, or is unable to prove a material point, &c. and thereupon the plaintiff may be demanded, (as he must be) his default is recorded, and the entry is *in misericordia quia non prosecutus est breve suum;* upon which defendant recovers his costs against him; but this arising from some supposed neglect or oversight, the plaintiff, except in some particular cases, is not barred from commencing a new action upon paying the costs. *Cro. Jac.* 213. 2 *Leon.* 177. 4 *Mod.* 86. 2 *Salk.* 456.

But a non-suit is no peremptory bar; but the plaintiff may, notwithstanding, commence any new action of the same or like nature, upon paying the costs of the first action. *Ibid.*

NON SUM INFORMATUS, is a formal answer made of course by an attorney, who is not instructed or informed to say any thing material in defence of his client; by which he is deemed to leave it undefended, and so judgment passeth against his client.

NON-TENURE, is a plea in bar to a real action, by saying, that he (the defendant) holdeth not the land mentioned in the plaintiff's count or declaration, or at least some part thereof. 25 *Ed.* 3. *c.* 16. 1 *Mod. Rep.* 250.

NON-TERM, (*non terminus*) is the vacation between term and term; formerly called the time or days of the king's peace. *Lamb. Archa.* 126.

NON-USER, of offices concerning the public, is cause of forfeiture. 9 *Rep.* 50. And if one have a franchise, and do not use it, he shall forfeit the same; which likewise may be lost by default, as well as non-user. Stat. 3 *Ed.* 2. *c.* 9. See *Office.*

NOOK OF LAND, (*nocata terræ*) about twelve acres and a half of land; but the quantity is generally uncertain.

NORROY quasi NORTH ROY, the Northern king at arms, mentioned in 14 *Car.* 2. *c.* 33. See *Herald.*

NORTHERN BORDERS. See *Felony.*

NORTH WALES. See *Wales.*

NOSE, slitting or cutting it off. See *Felony.*

NOTARY, (*notarius*) is a person (usually a scrivener) who takes notes, or makes a short draught of contracts, obligations, or other writings and instruments. Stat. 27 *Ed.* 3. *c.* 1. But now a public notary, is he who publicly attests deeds or writings, to make them authentic in another country; but principally in business relating to merchants: they make protests of foreign bills of exchange, &c. And noting a bill is the notary's going as witness, to take notice of a merchant's refusal to accept or pay the same. *Merch. Dict.*

By 41 *Geo.* 3. u. k. *c.* 79. no person in England shall act as a public notary unless duly admitted. *s.* 1.

No person shall be admitted a notary unless he shall have served as an apprentice to a notary or scrivener for seven years; and if bound after August 1, 1801, unless affidavit of the execution of the contract be made and filed in the proper court; and such affidavit shall be produced on the admission of the party bound as a notary, and the master of the faculties office shall be the place for taking and filling the same. *s.* 2—5.

The officer filing such affidavits shall enter the substance in a book, and take as a fee 5*s.* which book may be searched for 1*s.* *s.* 6.

No public notary shall have any apprentice but while he shall actually practise; and the apprentice shall be actually employed seven years in the business. *s.* 6, 7.

If any master shall die or leave off practice, or any apprentice shall be legally discharged, the apprentice may serve the residue of the seven years with another master, and an affidavit of such second contract shall be filed. *s.* 8.

Before admission, apprentices shall file affidavits that they have really served seven years. *s.* 9.

If any notary shall act or permit his name to be used for the profit of any person not entitled to act as a notary, he shall be struck off the roll on a summary application to the court of faculties. *s.* 10.

Persons acting as notaries for reward, without being admitted, shall forfeit 50*l.* *s.* 11.

Persons applying for a faculty to become notaries within the jurisdiction of the company of scriveners in London, shall previously take their freedom of the company. *s.* 12.

The act shall not extend to proctors, secretaries to bishops, or persons acting under government, except proctors being also notaries. *s.* 14.

The penalties may be recovered at Westminster by the party suing, with full costs. *s.* 16.

NOTE OF A FINE, is a brief of the fine made by the chirographer, before it is ingrossed. *West. Symb. par.* 2.

NOTES PROMISSORY. See *Bill of Exchange.*

NOT GUILTY, is the general issue or plea of the defendant in any action for a tort, wrong or injury, such as trespass, and the like; but not on a promise: the proper plea in which is *non assumpsit.* *Palm.* 393.

NOTICE, is the making something known that a man was or might be ignorant of before: and the party who gives the same shall have the benefit thereof. *Co. Lit.* 309.

Notice is required to be given in many cases by law, to justify proceedings where any thing is to be done or demanded, &c. But none is bound by law to give notice to another person of that which such other may otherwise inform himself, or ought to take notice, except such notice is directed by act of parliament.

A notice may not be pleaded upon issue joined; and in all writs of inquiry of damages, as well in real as personal actions, notice of trial and execution of such writs must be given to the other party to the suit. And want of notice is cause to set aside the judgment.

A month's notice is also to be given to a justice of the peace, before commencement of an action against him for any thing done in the execution of his office. 24 *Geo.* 2, *c.* 44.

NOVALE, signifies land newly ploughed or converted into tillage, that without memory of man had not been tilled; and sometimes it is taken for ground which hath been ploughed for two years, and afterwards lies fallow for one year, or that which lies fallow every other year; it is called *novale,* because the earth *novâ culturâ proscinditur.* *Cowel. Blount.*

NOVA OBLATA, mentioned in *Claus.* 12 *Ed.* 1, *m.* 7. See *Oblata.*

NOVEL ASSIGNMENT, (*nova assignatio*) is an assignment of time, place, or such like, in action of trespass, otherwise than as it was before assigned; or where it is more particularly in a declaration than in a writ, &c. (*Bro. Tres.* 122.) And if the defendant justifies in a place where no trespass was done, then the plaintiff is to assign the close where, to which the defendant is to plead, &c. *Terms de Ley.* See *New Assignment.*

NOVEL DISSEISIN (*nova disseisina*). See *Assise of Novel Disseisin.*

NOVELLÆ, those constitutions of the civil law which were made after the publication of the Theodosian code, were called *novellæ* by the emperors who ordained them, but some writers call the Julian edition only by that name. *Blount.* 1 *Black.* 81.

NUCES COLLIGERE, to gather hazel nuts, which was formerly one of the works or services imposed by lords upon their inferior tenants. *Paroch. Antiq.* 495.

NUDE CONTRACT, (*nudum pactum*) is a bare naked contract without a consideration. And where there is a want of consideration no action will lie for *ex nudo.*

NUDE MATTER, naked matter, a bare allegation of a thing done, &c. *Cowel.*

NUDUM PACTUM. A consideration of some sort or other is so absolutely necessary to the forming of a contract, that a *nudum pactum,* or agreement to do or pay any thing on one side, without any compensation on the other, is totally void in law; and a man cannot be compelled to perform it. 2 *Black.* 445.

NUL DISSEISIN, plea of, is a plea in real actions, of no disseisin, and is one species of the general issue. 3 *Black.* 305.

NUL TIEL RECORD, is the plea of a plaintiff, that there is no such record, on the defendant's alleging matter of record, such as a *judgment* recovered, in bar of the plaintiff's action.

NUL TORT, plea of, a plea in a real action, *i. e.* of no wrong done, and is a species of the general issue. 3 *Black.* 305.

NULLUM ARBITRIUM, the usual plea of the defendant prosecuted on an arbitration bond, for not abiding by an award.

NULLITY, is where a thing is null and void, or of no force. *Litt. Dict.*

NUMERUM. *Civitas Cant. Reddit.* 24 *l.* *ad numerum,* i. e. by number or tale, as we call it. *Domesday. Cowel.*

NUMMATA, signifies the price of any thing, generally by money, as *denariata* doth the price of a thing, by computation of pence, and *librata* by computation of pounds. *Cowel. Blount.*

NUMMATA, TERRÆ, is the same with *denariatus terræ*, and thought to contain an acre. *Cowel. Blount.*

NUMMUS, a piece of money or coin among the Romans. *Ibid.*

NUN, (*nunna*) a consecrated virgin or woman, who by vow hath bound herself to a single and chaste life, in some place, or company of other women, separated from the world, and devoted to the service of God by prayer and fasting, and such like holy exercises. *Ibid.*

NUNCIUS, a nuncio, or messenger, servant, &c. And the pope's nuncio was *legatus pontificis. Ibid.*

NUNCUPATIVE WILL, (*testamentum nuncupatum*) is a will by word of mouth: It is a verbal declaration of the testator's mind before a sufficient number of witnesses, which being reduced into writing either before or after the death of the testator, is good to dispose of his personal estate, but not his lands. (2 *Nels. Abr.* 1191.) Before the 29 *Car.* 2, *c.* 3, it was necessary, not only to put a nuncupative will in writing, but to prove it likewise by witnesses in the spiritual court, and to have it under the seal of the ordinary, until which it hath been decreed in equity that such will was not pleadable against an administrator. 1 *Chan. Rep.* 122.

The statute of frauds, 29 *Car.* 2, *c.* 3, hath laid them under many restrictions, except when made by mariners at sea, and soldiers in actual service. As to all other persons it enacts, 1. That no written will shall be revoked or altered by a subsequent nuncupative one, except the same be in the life-time of the testator reduced to writing, and read over to him, and approved; and unless the same be proved to have been so done by the oaths of three witnesses at least, who by statute 4 & 5 *Ann. c.* 16, must be such as are admissible upon trials at common law. 2. That no nuncupative will shall in any wise be good where the estate bequeathed exceeds 30*l.* unless proved by three such witnesses present at the making thereof, (the Roman law requiring seven, *Inst.* 2. 10. 4,) and unless they or some of them were specially required to bear witness thereto by the testator himself; and unless it was made in his last sickness, in his own habitation or dwelling-house, or where he had been previously resident ten days at the least, except he be surprised with sickness on a journey, or from home, and dies without returning to his dwelling. 3. That no nuncupative will shall be proved by the witnesses after six months from the making, unless it were put in writing within six days. Nor shall it be proved till fourteen days after the death of the testator, nor till process hath first issued to call in the widow, or next of kin, to contest it, if they think proper. Thus hath the legislature provided against any frauds in setting up nuncupative wills, by so numerous a train of requisites, that the thing itself has fallen into disuse; and is hardly ever heard of, but in the only instance where favour ought to be shown to it, when the testator is surprised by sudden and violent sickness. The testamentary words must be spoken with an intent to bequeath, not any loose idle discourse in his illness; for he must require the bystanders to bear witness of such his intention: the will must be made at home, or among his family or friends, unless by unavoidable accident, to prevent impositions from strangers: it must be in his last sickness, for if he recovers he may alter his dispositions, and have time to make a written will: it must not be proved at too long a distance from the testator's death, lest the words should escape the memory of the witnesses; nor yet too hastily, and without notice, lest the family of the testator should be put to inconvenience, or surprised. 2 *Black.* 500.

NUPER OBIIT, is a writ that lies for a sister or co-heir, deforced by her coparcener of land or tenements, whereof their father, brother, or any other common ancestor, died seised of an estate in fee-simple; for if one sister deforce another of land held in fee-tail, her sister and co-heir shall have a formedon against her, &c. and not a *nuper obiit*; and where the ancestor being once seised, died not seised of the possession, but the reversion, in such a case a writ of *rationabili parte* lies. *Reg. Orig.* 226. *F. N. B.* 197. *Terms de Ley.*

NURTURE, GUARDIAN FOR. There are guardians to infants, for nurture, which are, of course, the father or mother, till the infant attains the age of 14 years; and in default of father or mother the ordinary usually assigns some proper person. *Co. Lit.* 88. *Moor* 738. 3 *Rep.* 38. 2 *Jones* 90. 2 *Lev.* 163. 1 *Black.* 461.

NUSANCE, (*nocumentum*, from the Fr. *nuire*, i. e. *nocere*) Common nusances are of a species of offences against the public order and economical regimen of the state; being either the doing of a thing to the annoyance of all the king's subjects, or the neglecting to do a thing which the common good requires. (1 *Hawk. P. C.* 197.) Common nusances are such inconvenient or troublesome offences, as annoy the whole community in general, and not merely some particular person; and therefore are indictable only, and not actionable; as it would be unreasonable to multiply suits, by giving every man a separate right of action, for what damnifies him in common only with the rest of his fellow subjects. Of this nature are, 1. Annoyances in highways, bridges, and public rivers, by rendering the same inconvenient or dangerous to pass: either positively, by actual obstructions; or negatively, by want of reparations. For both of these, the person so obstructing, or such individuals as are bound to repair and cleanse them, or (in default of these last) the parish at large, may be indicted, distreined to repair and amend them, and in some cases fined. And a presentment thereof made by a judge of assise, &c. or a justice of the peace, shall be in all respects equivalent to an indictment (stat. 7 *Geo.* 3. *c.* 42.) Where there is an house erected, or an inclosure made, upon any part of the king's demesnes, or of an highway, or common street, or public water, or such like public things, it is properly called a *purpresture* (*Co. Litt.* 277.) 2. All those kinds of nusances, (such as offensive trades and manufactures,) which when injurious to a private man are actionable, are, when detrimental to the public, punishable by public prosecution, and subject to fine according to the quantity of the misdemeanor: and particularly the keeping of hogs in any city or market town is indictable as a public nusance (*Salk.* 460.) 3. All disorderly inns or ale-houses, bawdy-houses, gaming-houses, stage-plays unlicensed, booths and stages for rope-dancers, mountebanks, and the like, are public nusances, and may upon indictment be suppressed and fined (1 *Hawk. P. C.* 198, 225.)* Inns, in particular, being intended for the lodging and receipt of travellers, may be indicted, suppressed, and the inn-keepers fined, if they refuse to entertain a traveller without a very sufficient cause: for thus to frustrate the end of their institution is held to be disorderly behaviour (1 *Hawk. P. C.* 225.) Thus too the hospitable laws of Norway punish, in the severest degree, such inn keepers as refuse to furnish accommodations at a just and reasonable price (*Stiernh. de jure Sueon. l.* 2. *c.* 9.) 4. By statute 10 & 11 *W.* 3. *c.* 17. all lotteries are declared to be public nusances, and all grants, patents, or licences for the same to be contrary to law. But, as state-lotteries have, for many years past, been found a ready mode for raising the supply, an act was made, 19 *Geo.* 3. *c.* 21. to licence and regulate the keepers of such lottery-offices.† 5. The making and selling of fire-works and squibs, or throwing them about in any street, is, on account of the danger that may ensue to any thatched or timber buildings, declared to be a common nusance, by statute 9 & 10 *W.* 3. *c.* 7. and therefore is punishable by fine.‡ And to this head we may refer (though not declared a common nusance) the making, keeping, or carriage, of too large a quantity of gunpowder at one time, or in one place or vehicle; which is prohibited by statute 12 *Geo.* 3. *c.* 61. under heavy penalties and forfeiture. 6. Eaves-droppers, or such as listen under walls and windows or the eaves of a house, to hearken after discourse, and thereupon to frame slanderous and mischievous tales, are a common nusance and presentable at the court-leet (*Kitch. of courts* 20.): or are indictable at the sessions, and punishable by fine and finding sureties for their good behaviour (*Ib.* 1 *Hawk. P. C.* 132.) 7. Lastly, a common scold, *communis rixatrix*, (for our law-Latin confines it to the feminine gender) is a public nusance to her neighbourhood. For which offence she may be indicted (6 *Mod.* 213.); and, if convicted, shall (1 *Hawk. P. C.* 198, 200.) be sentenced to be placed in a certain engine of correction called the trebucket, castigatory, or cucking stool, which in the Saxon language is said to signify the scolding stool; though now it is frequently corrupted into ducking stool, because the residue of the judgment is, that, when she is so placed therein, she shall be plunged in the water for her punishment (3 *Inst.* 219)

Private nusances may be defined, any thing done to the hurt or annoyance of the lands, tenements, or hereditaments of another (*Finch. L.* 188.)

First, such nusances as may affect a man's corporeal hereditaments, and then those that may damage such as are incorporeal.

1. If a man builds a house so close to mine that his roof overhangs my roof, and throws the water off his roof upon mine, this is a nusance, for which an action will lie. (*F. N. B.* 184.) Likewise to erect a house or other building so near to mine, that it stops up my antient lights and windows, is a nusance of a similar nature. (9 *Rep.* 58.) But in this latter case it is necessary that the windows be *ancient*, that is, have subsisted there time out of mind; otherwise there is no injury done. For he hath as much right to build a new edifice upon his ground as I have upon mine: since every man may do what he pleases upon the upright or perpendicular of his own soil; and it was my folly to build so near another's ground.

---

* How stage-players are to be licensed, see the 28 *Geo.* 3. *c.* 30. under *Theatres.*

† State lotteries are now regulated by acts which pass annually.

‡ And if any person shall make or sell any squibs, rockets, or fire-works, he shall forfeit upon conviction before a magistrate, 5*l.* one half to the informer, and the other half to the poor. And if any person shall throw or fire them in any house, street, or highway, he shall forfeit 20*s.* in like manner. 9 & 10 *W.* 3. *c.* 7.

(*Cro. Eliz.* 118. *Salk.* 459.) Also, if a person keeps his hogs, or other noisome animals, so near the house of another that the stench of them incommodes him, and makes the air unwholesome, this is an injurious nuisance, as it tends to deprive him of the use and benefit of his house (9 *Rep.* 58.) A like injury is, if one's neighbour sets up and exercises any offensive trade: as a tanner, tallow-chandler, or the like: for though these are lawful and necessary trades, yet they should be exercised in remote places; for the rule is, " *sic utere tuo, ut alienum* " *non lædas* :" this therefore is an actionable nuisance (*Cro. Car.* 510). Thus nuisances which affect a man's dwelling may be reduced to these three, 1. Over-hanging it; which is also a species of trespass, for *cujus est solum ejus est usque ad cœlum.* 2. Stopping ancient lights; and 3. Corrupting the air with noisome smells; for light and air are two indispensable requisites to every dwelling. But depriving one of a mere matter of pleasure, as of a fine prospect, by building a wall, or the like; this as it abridges nothing really convenient or necessary, is no injury to the sufferer, and is therefore not an actionable nusance. (9 *Rep.* 58.)

2. If one erects a smelting-house for lead so near the land of another, that the vapour and smoke kills his corn and grass, and damages his cattle therein, this is held to be a nusance. (1 *Roll. Abr.* 89.) And by consequence it follows, that if one does any other act, in itself lawful, which yet being done in that place necessarily tends to the damage of another's property, it is a nusance; for it is incumbent on him to find some other place to do that act, where it will be less offensive. So also, if my neighbour ought to scour a ditch, and does not, whereby my land is overflowed, this is an actionable nuisance (*Hale on F. N. B.* 427).

With regard to *other* corporeal hereditaments: it is a nusance to stop or divert water that uses to run to another's meadow or mill; (*F. N. B.* 184.) to corrupt or poison a water-course, by erecting a dye-house or a lime-pit for the use of trade, in the upper part of the stream; (9 *Rep.* 59. 2 *Roll. Abr.* 141.) or in short to do any act therein, that in its consequences must necessarily tend to the prejudice of one's neighbour. So closely does the law of England enforce that excellent rule of gospel-morality, of " doing to others, as we would they should do unto ourselves."

3. If I have a way, annexed to my estate, across another's land, and he obstructs me in the use of it, either by totally stopping it, or putting logs across it or ploughing over it, it is a nusance: for in the first case I cannot enjoy my right at all, and in the latter I cannot enjoy it so commodiously as I ought. (*F. N. B.* 183. 2 *Roll. Abr.* 140.) Also, if I am entitled to hold a fair or market, and another person sets up a fair or market so near mine that it does me a prejudice, it is a nusance to the freehold which I have in my market or fair. (*F. N. B.* 184. 2 *Roll. Abr.* 140.) But in order to make this out to be a nusance it is necessary, 1. That my market or fair be the elder, otherwise the nusance lies at my own door. 2. That the market be erected within the third part of twenty miles from mine: for Sir Matthew Hale (*Hale on F. N. B.* 184,) construes the *dieta*, or reasonable day's journey, mentioned by Bracton (*l.* 3, *c.* 16), to be 20 miles; as indeed it is usually understood, not only in our own law (2 *Inst.* 367), but also in the civil law (*Ff*, 2. 11. 1.), from which we probably borrowed it. So that if the new market be not within seven miles of the old one it is no nusance; for it is held reasonable that every man should have a market within one third of a day's journey from his own home, that the day being divided into three parts he may spend one part in going, another in returning, and the third in transacting his necessary business there. If such market or fair be on the same day with mine, it is *prima facie* a nusance to mine, and there needs no proof of it, but the law will intend it to be so: but if it be on any other day, it *may be* a nusance; though whether it is so or not, cannot be intended or presumed, but I must make proof of it to the jury. If a ferry is erected on a river, so near another antient ferry as to draw away its custom, it is a nusance to the owner of the old one. For where there is a ferry by prescription, the owner is bound to keep it always in repair and readiness, for the ease of all the king's subjects; otherwise he may be grievously amerced (2 *Roll. Abr.* 140.): it would be therefore extremely hard if a new ferry were suffered to share his profits, which does not also share his burthen. But where the reason ceases the law also ceases with it; therefore it is no nusance to erect a mill so near mine, as to draw away the custom, unless the miller also intercepts the water. Neither is it a nusance to set up any trade, or a school, in neighbourhood or rivalship with another; for by such emulation the public are like to be gainers; and if the new mill or school occasion a damage to the old one it is *damnum absque injuria.* *Hale on F. N. B.* 184.

The remedy which the law has given for this injury of nusance is as follows: 1st, No action lies for a public or common nusance, but an indictment only: because the damage being common to all the king's subjects, no one can assign his particular proportion of it; or, if he could, it would be extremely hard, if every subject in the kingdom were allowed to harass the offender with separate actions. For this reason no person, natural or corporate, can have an action for a public nusance, or punish it, but only the king in his public capacity of supreme governor, and *pater-familias* of the kingdom (*Vaugh.* 341, 342.). Yet this rule admits of one exception, where a private person suffers some extraordinary damage beyond the rest of the king's subjects, by a public nusance, in which case he shall have a private satisfaction by action. As if, by means of a ditch dug across a public way, which is a common nusance, a man or his horse suffer any injury by falling therein, there, for this particular damage, which is not common to others, the party shall have his action (*Co. Litt.* 56. 5 *Rep.* 73.) Also if a man hath abated or removed a nusance which offended him, in this case he is entitled to no action; for he had choice of two remedies; either without suit, by abating it himself, by his own mere act and authority; or by suit, in which he may both recover damages, and remove it by the aid of the law: but, having made his election of one remedy he is totally precluded from the other. 9 *Rep.* 55.

The remedies for private nuisances by suit are, 1. By action on the case for damages; in which the party injured shall only recover a satisfaction for the injury sustained, but cannot thereby remove the nusance. Indeed every continuance of a nusance is held to be a fresh one (2 *Leon.* pl. 129. *Cro. Eliz.* 402.); and therefore a fresh action will lie, and very exemplary damages will probably be given, if after one verdict against him the defendant has the hardiness to continue it. Yet the founders of the law of England did not rely upon probabilities merely in order to give relief to the injured. They have therefore provided two other actions, the assise of nusance, and the writ of *quod permittat prosternere*, which not only give the plaintiff satisfaction for his injury past, but also strike at the root and remove the cause itself, the nusance that occasioned the injury. These two actions however can only be brought by the tenant of the freehold, so that a lessee for years is confined to his action upon the case. 9 *Rep.* 55.

NUTRIMENTUM, nourishment, particularly applied to breeding of cattle. *Paroch. Antiq.* 401. *Cowel. Blount.*

NYAS (*Nidarius accipiter*) a hawk, or bird of prey. *Litt. Dict.* See *Game.*

O

O is an adverb of exclamation, calling, or interjection of sorrow.

OATH, (Sax. *Eoth*, Lat. *Juramentum*) is an affirmation or denial of any thing before one or more persons who have authority to administer an oath, and is the calling of God, or the Almighty Creator, according to the faith of the party. 3 *Inst.* 165.

The oaths allowed by our law are, 1st, Oaths upon the book of the holy evangelists; 2dly, upon the Pentateuch, or Old Testament, by Jews; 3dly, oaths taken according to the rules of faith amongst those who do not profess the Christian religion; (see *Infidels*,) but the *affirmation* of a Quaker, being an *affirmation only*, and not an *oath*, is not received in criminal cases; but is only permitted in *civil* cases by stat. 7 & 8 *Will.* 3, *c.* 34. Nor can such affirmation be administered to them as jurors.

OATH is a solemn calling or appealing to Almighty God as a witness of the truth of what we affirm or deny, in the presence of those who are duly authorized to administer it to us; and it is called corporal, because in taking it the party is obliged to lay his hands on, and kiss the holy gospel. 3 *Co. Inst.* 165.

It seems to be a high contempt at the common law to refuse to take the oath of allegiance to the king, which all laymen above the age of twelve years are bound to take at the torn or court-leet. 1 *Hawk. c.* 24. *s.* 3. *Co. Lit.* 68.

For allegiance is the tie, or *ligamen*, which binds the subjects to the king, in return for that protection which the king affords the subjects, and it is founded in reason, and the nature of government. 1 *Black. Com.* 366.

And surely, saith Hawkins, nothing can be more unreasonable than to deny the king, whose government we are happy under, all proper assurances of our fidelity to him: for how can we expect to enjoy the privileges of subjects from one to whom we refuse to acknowledge ourselves subjects, or hope for protection from one, whom we provoke to esteem us as his enemies, or blame that government for treating us as malcontents, to which we give so just a cause to suspect our fidelity? If we consult the law of God, that will tell us, that the powers that be are ordained of God. If we will hear the voice of reason that will convince us, that not only the peace and safety of the community, but also our own preservation requires us to pay a dutiful obedience to those who govern us: and can we, adds the learned author, think it unlawful to engage ourselves to do what it is our duty to do? 1 *Hawk. c.* 24. *s.* 3.

But besides this express engagement, the law also holds that there is an implied, original and virtual allegiance, owing from every subject to his sovereign, antecedently to any express promise, and although the subject never swore any faith or allegiance in form. For as the king, by the very descent of the crown, is fully invested with all the rights, and bound to all the duties of sovereignty, before his coronation; so the subject is bound to his prince by an intrinsic allegiance, before the superinduction of those outward bonds of oath, homage and fealty, which were only instituted to remind the subject of this his previous duty, and for the better securing its performance. 1 *Black. Com.* 368,369.

The formal profession therefore, or oath of subjection, is nothing more than a declaration in words of what was before implied in law. 1 *Black. Com.* 869.

For as sir Ed. Coke very justly observes, all subjects are equally bounden to their allegiance, as if they had taken the oath; because it is written by the finger of the law in their hearts, and the taking of the corporal oath is but an outward declaration of the same. 2 *Inst.* 121.

And sir William Blackstone adds, the sanction of an oath, it is true, in case of violation of duty, makes the guilt still more accumulated, by superadding perjury to treason: but it does not increase the civil obligation to loyalty; it only strengthens the social tie by uniting it with that of religion. 1 *Black. Com.* 369.

This oath of allegiance, or rather the allegiance itself, is held to be applicable not only to the political capacity of the king, or regal office, but to his natural person and blood royal: and the same principle of personal attachment, and affectionate loyalty, which induced our forefathers, would doubtless, if occasion required, induce their sons to hazard all that is dear to them, life, fortune, and family, in defence and support of their liege lord and sovereign. 1 *Black. Com.* 371.

The oath of allegiance, as administered for upwards of six hundred years, contained a promise, "to be true and faithful to the "king and his heirs, and truth and faith to "bear of life and limb and terrene honour, "and not to know or hear of any ill or da-"mage intended him, without defending "him therefrom." Upon which sir Matthew Hale makes this remark, that it was short and plain, not entangled with long and intricate clauses or declarations, and yet is comprehensive of the whole duty from the subject to his sovereign. 1 *Black. Com.* 368.

But at the revolution, the terms of this oath being thought perhaps to favour too much the notion of non-resistance, the present form was introduced by the convention parliament, and finally settled in the first year of the reign of *Geo.* 1. 1 *Black. Com.* 368.

For by stat. 1 *Geo.* 1. *c.* 13. *s.* 2. it is enacted, that the form of the oath of allegiance shall be as follows:

"I *A. B.* do sincerely promise and swear, "that I will be faithful, and bear true alle-"giance to his majesty king George.—So "help me God."

This oath, it is observed by sir William Blackstone, is more general and indeterminate than the former; the subject only promising "that he will be faithful and bear "true allegiance to the king," without mentioning "his heirs," or specifying in the least wherein that allegiance consists. However the oath of abjuration, afterwards introduced in the reign of *Will.* 3, and finally altered and settled in the sixth year of his present majesty, very amply supplies the loose and general texture of the oath of allegiance. 1 *Black. Com.* 368.

It is also enacted, by the aforesaid statute of 1 *Geo.* 1. *c.* 13. *s.* 2, that the form of the oath of supremacy shall be as follows:

"I *A. B.* do swear that I do from my "heart abhor, detest and abjure as impious "and heretical, that damnable doctrine and "position, that princes excommunicated or "deprived by the pope, or any authority of "the see of Rome, may be deposed or mur-"dered by their subjects, or any other "whatsoever; and I do declare, that no "foreign prince, person, prelate, state or "potentate, hath or ought to have any ju-"risdiction, power, superiority, pre-emi-"nence, or authority, ecclesiastical or "spiritual, within this realm.—So help me "God."

And by 6 *Geo.* 3. *c.* 53. *s.* 1, the oath of abjuration shall be administered in the form hereinafter prescribed; (that is to say),

"I *A. B.* do truly and sincerely acknowledge, profess, testify, and declare, in my conscience, before God and the world, that our sovereign lord king George is lawful and rightful king of this realm, and all other his majesty's dominions and countries thereunto belonging. And I do solemnly and sincerely declare that I do believe in my conscience, that not any of the descendants of the person who pretended to be prince of Wales, during the life of the late king James the second, and, since his decease pretended to be, and took upon himself the style and title of king of England, by the name of James the third, or of Scotland, by the name of James the eighth, or the style and title of king of Great Britain, hath any right or title whatsoever to the crown of this realm, or any other the dominions thereunto belonging: and I do renounce, refuse, and abjure, any allegiance or obedience to any of them. And I do swear, that I will bear faith and true allegiance to his majesty king George, and him will defend to the utmost of my power against all traitorous conspiracies and attempts whatsoever, which shall be made against his person, crown, or dignity. And I will do my utmost endeavour to disclose and make known to his majesty, and his successors, all treasons and traitorous conspiracies which I shall know to be against him or any of them. And I do faithfully promise, to the utmost of my power, to support, maintain, and defend, the succession of the crown against the descendants of the said James, and against all other persons whatsoever, which succession, by an act, entitled, 'an act for the further limitation of the crown, and better securing the rights and liberties of the subject,' is, and stands limited to the princess Sophia, electress and duchess dowager of Hanover, and the heirs of her body being protestants. And all these things I do plainly and sincerely acknowledge and swear, according to these express words by me spoken, and according to the plain common sense and understanding of the same words, without any equivocation, mental evasion, or secret reservation whatsoever. And I do make this recognition, acknowledgment, abjuration, renunciation, and promise, heartily, willingly, and truly, upon the true faith of a christian.—So help me God."

Having stated the form of the respective oaths of allegiance, supremacy, and abjuration, it will be proper in the next place to consider—1st, the offence of refusing the oaths of allegiance and supremacy.—2dly, the offence of refusing the oath of abjuration. —3dly, how such oaths may be tendered to suspected persons, by two justices of peace.

First, *As to the offence of refusing the oaths of allegiance and supremacy.*] It is enacted by 1 *Will.* and *Mar. st.* 1. *c.* 8, that every person who shall neglect to take the oaths of allegiance and supremacy sha'l incur the penalties of former statutes. *s.* 3.

That is to say, by 5 *Eliz. c.* 1, commissioners may be appointed by the lord chancellor to tender the same to such persons as by their commissions they shall be authorised to tender the same unto. *s.* 7.

And if any person appointed by such commissioners to take the said oaths, shall refuse to take the same on tender thereof, he shall incur a *præmunire*. *s.* 8.

And all persons having authority to tender the said oaths shall, in forty days after such refusal, if the term be open, and if not, then on the first day of the term next after the said forty days, make certificate of the names, places and degrees of the persons refusing, into the King's Bench, upon pain of 100*l.* to the king: and the sheriff of the county wherein the said court shall sit, shall impannel a jury, who shall inquire of such refusals in such manner as if they had happened in the same county. *s.* 9.

May impannel a jury, who shall inquire.] But it hath been resolved that the trial must be by a jury of the county, wherein the oaths were refused; for the statute only authorizes an indictment by a jury of the county wherein the court sits. *Dyer*, 234. 1 *Hawk. c.* 19. *s.* 35.

Also by 7 *Jac.* 1. *c.* 6, it shall be lawful for any of the privy council, and every bishop in his diocese, to require any baron or baroness of the age of eighteen years, or above, to take the said oaths—and for any two justices of peace (one of whom shall be of the quorum) to require any person of the age of eighteen years, under the degree of a baron or baroness, to take the same:—

And if any person of or above the said age and degree shall be presented or convicted for not coming to church, or not receiving the communion, before the ordinary or other having lawful power to take such presentment, three of the privy council, whereof the lord chancellor, lord treasurer, lord privy seal, or principal secretary to be one, shall require such person to take the said oaths.

And if any other person of the said age, and under the said degree, shall be presented or convicted for not coming to church or receiving the sacrament, or if the minister, constable, and churchwardens, or any two of them, shall complain to any justice of peace, near adjoining to the place where any person complained of shall dwell, and the said justice shall find cause of suspicion, any justice shall require such person to take the oaths. *s.* 26.

Any justice shall require such person to take the oaths.] In the construction hereof it hath been resolved, that the justices may send their warrant to bring the bodies of such persons before them, but that they cannot authorize the constables to break open the doors to take them. 12 *Co. Rep.* 130, 131. 1 *Hawk. c.* 19. *s.* 40.

And if any person of the age of eighteen years shall refuse to take the oaths, being duly tendered, the persons authorized may commit the offender to the common gaol until the next assizes or quarter-sessions, where the oaths shall be again required; and if the party shall again refuse to take them, every person so refusing shall incur the penalty of *præmunire*, except women covert, who shall be only committed to prison till they do take the same. 7 *Jac.* 1. *c.* 6. *s.*26.

May commit the offender.] In the construction hereof it hath been holden, that the persons authorized to tender the oaths, may commit the party refusing though he be a lord of parliament, for the power to commit extends to all persons whatsoever. 12 *Co. Rep.* 131.

And moreover, every person refusing to take the oaths as above, shall be disabled to execute any public place of judicature, or bear any other office (being no office of inheritance or ministerial function), within England, or to practise the law, or physic, or surgery, or the art of an apothecary, or any liberal science for gain, until he shall receive the oaths. 7 *Jac.* 1. *c.* 6. *s.* 27.

It is also enacted, by 1 *Will.* and *Mar. s.*1. *c.* 8. that if any person shall refuse to take the said oaths, being tendered to them by persons lawfully authorized to tender the same, the persons tendering shall commit the persons refusing to the common gaol or house of correction for three months, unless such offender shall pay down to the person tendering, such sum, not exceeding 40*s.* as he shall require such offender to pay; which money shall be paid to the church-wardens or overseers for the relief of the poor of the parish where such offender did last inhabit;—and if at the end of three months the person so refusing shall again refuse to take the oaths when lawfully tendered, the person tendering shall commit the person refusing to the common gaol or house of correction for six months, unless such person pay down to the persons tendering, such sum, not exceeding 10*l.* nor under 5*l.* as they shall require for his second refusal, to be disposed in manner aforesaid; and unless such offender become bound with two sureties, with condition to be of good behaviour, and to appear at the next assize, or gaol delivery: at which assizes or gaol delivery the oaths shall be again tendered by the justices; and if the offender then refuse to take the same, he shall be incapable of any office civil or military, and shall be bound to good behaviour until he take the same; and in case such person shall refuse also to make the declaration against popery in 30 *Car.* 2. *st.* 2. *c.* 1, such person shall suffer all penalties as a popish recusant convict. *s.* 9.

And moreover, by 7 & 8 *Will.* 3. *c.* 27, every person who shall refuse to take the oaths when tendered by persons lawfully authorised, or who shall neglect to appear when summoned in order to have the oaths tendered, shall, until he take the oaths, be liable to the penalties inflicted upon popish recusants convict; and the persons tendering the oaths shall upon every such refusal or default of appearance, record the names and places of abode of the persons refusing or not appearing, with the time of such tender or default, and certify the record to the justices of assize of *oyer* and *terminer*, or gaol delivery, at their next session, who shall certify the same into the exchequer. *s.* 1.

But the penalties to be incurred by any persons as popish recusants convict by this act for not taking the oaths, may be pardoned by the king under the privy seal. *s.* 15.

And no person who shall refuse to take the oaths (which oaths and subscription, the sheriff or chief officer taking the poll at any election of members to serve in parliament, at the request of any one of the candidates, are required to administer) shall be admitted to give any vote for the election of any knight, citizen, burgess, or baron, to serve in parliament. *s.* 19.

Hawkins says, it seems to be the intention of the above statute of *Will.* & *Mar.* to give the government an election to proceed either in the mild method therein prescribed, or the more severe one appointed by former laws, according to the circumstances of the case, and quality of the offender. 1 *Hawk. c.* 24. *s.* 5.

Secondly, as to the offence of refusing the oath of abjuration, it is by 13 *Will.* 3. *c.* 6. (which first introduced that oath) enacted, that it shall be lawful for any person authorised to administer the oaths appointed by 1 *Wil.* & *Mar. st.* 1. *c.* 8, to tender the oath of abjuration to any person; and if any person to whom the oath shall be tendered, shall neglect to take the same, the person tendering the oath shall certify the refusal to the next quarter-sessions; and the refusal shall be recorded, and certified by the clerk of the peace into the Chancery or King's Bench. *s.* 13.

And it was further enacted by 6 *Anne, c.* 14, that it shall be lawful for any two justices of peace (one of whom shall be of the quorum) or any other persons appointed by the crown by order of privy council, or by commission under the great seal, to summon all such persons as they shall suspect to be dangerous or disaffected, and tender the oath of abjuration, and at the next quarter-sessions certify the names and places of abode of all persons refusing to take the oath, to be certified by the clerk of the peace into the King's Bench; and if the person certified shall not within the next term or sessions appear in the Chancery or King's Bench, and take the oath, and enter his so doing upon the certificate returned, he shall be adjudged a popish recusant convict, and undergo the penalties as such. *s.* 7.

Thirdly, how such oaths may be tendered to suspected persons by two justices.] By 1 *Geo.* 1. *st.* 2. *c.* 13, it shall be lawful for two justices of the peace, or any other person or persons who shall be by his majesty for that purpose specially appointed, by order in privy council, or by commission under the great seal, to administer and tender the oaths of allegiance, supremacy, and abjuration, to any person or persons whatsoever, whom they shall suspect to be dangerous or disaffected to his majesty or his government; and if any person to whom the said oaths shall be so tendered, shall neglect or refuse to take the same, such justices, or persons aforesaid, shall certify the refusal to the next quarter-sessions; and the said refusal shall be recorded amongst the rolls of that sessions, and shall be from thence certified by the clerk of the peace into the court of Chancery or King's Bench, there to be recorded in a roll there to be kept for that purpose only; and every person so neglecting or refusing to take the oaths, shall be adjudged from the time of his neglect or refusal, a popish recusant convict, and as such to forfeit and be proceeded against. *s.* 10.

And to the intent that no person may avoid taking the several oaths above-mentioned, upon any pretence whatsoever, it is further enacted, that it shall be lawful for two justices of peace, or any other persons specially appointed as aforesaid, by writing under their hands and seals, to summon any person to appear before them to take the said oaths; which summons shall be served upon such person, or left at his usual place of abode, with one of the family there; and if such person shall not appear according to such summons, then, upon proof upon oath of the serving of the said summons, such justices, or persons, are to certify the same to the next general quarter-sessions, there to be entered upon the rolls of the sessions; and if such person so summoned shall not appear and take the said oaths at the said general quarter-sessions, the names of the persons so certified being publicly read at the first meeting of the said sessions, such person shall be adjudged a popish recusant convict, and as such, to forfeit and be proceeded against as if he had actually refused to take the said oaths; and the same shall be from thence certified by the clerk of the peace into the court of Chancery or King's Bench, there to be recorded in a roll to be kept for that purpose only. *s.* 11.

But any persons who shall become popish recusants convict, and shall afterwards take the oaths, shall be discharged from such conviction. 1 *Geo.* 1. *st.* 2. *c.* 13. *s.* 26.

And it seems that the oaths ought to be read, or offered to be read to the party, otherwise he cannot be said to refuse them. *Read. on the stat. tit. Oath.*

OATHS UNLAWFUL. See *Seditious Societies.*

OATHS VOLUNTARY. The law takes no notice of any perjury but such as is committed in some court of justice having power to administer an oath; or before some magistrate or proper officer, invested *by statute* with a similar authority in some proceedings relative to a civil suit, or a criminal prosecution, for it esteems *all other oaths unnecessary at least*, and therefore will not punish the breach of them, for which reason *no magistrate or officer of any court is justifiable in taking a voluntary affidavit in any extra judicial matter, as is now too frequent in many trivial cases*, since it is more than possible, as *Blackstone*, (4 *Com.* 137.) elegantly and feelingly observes, that by such idle oaths a man may frequently in *foro conscientiæ* incur the guilt, and at the same time evade the temporal penalties of perjury.

Professor *Christian*, in a note on this part of Blackstone's Commentaries, truly observes, that where an oath is required by an act of parliament, but not in a judicial proceeding, the breach of that oath does not seem to amount to perjury, unless the statute enacts, that such oath, when false, shall be perjury, or shall subject the offender to the penalties of perjury.

OATHS IN PARLIAMENT. The House of Peers, as the supreme court of judicature in this country, has a general authority to administer oaths.

But the House of Commons, not participating in the judicature of parliament, has no power to administer an oath, except in those particular instances, in which that power is granted to them by express acts of parliament, such as in the case of a controverted election.

OBEDIENTIA, in the canon law is used for an office, or the administration of it: whereupon the word *obedientialis*, in the provincial constitutions, is taken for officers under their superiors. *Can. Law*, *c.* 1.

OBIT, (*Lat.*) a funeral solemnity or office for the dead, commonly performed when the corpse lay in the church uninterred, 2 *Cro.* 51. *Dyer* 313. The anniversary of any person's death was called the *obit*. The tenure of obit or chantry lands is taken away and extinct, by 1 *Ed.* 6. *c.* 14. and 15 *Car.* 2. *c.* 9.

OBJURGATRICES, scolds or unquiet women, punished with the cucking-stool. *Cowel. Blount.*

OBLATA, gifts or offerings made to the king by any of his subjects. *Ibid.*

OBLATIONS, (*oblationes.*) Formerly there were several sorts of oblations, viz. *ob-*

lationes altaris, which the priest had for saying mass; *oblationes defunctorum*, which were given by the last wills and testaments of persons dying to the church; *oblationes mortuorum*, or *funerales*, given at burials; *oblationes pœnitentium*, which were given by persons penitent; and *oblationes pentecostales*, *&c.* *Ibid.*

OBLIGATION, (*obligatio*) is a bond whereby a man binds himself and *his* heirs, executors, and administrators in a penalty, with a condition subjoined or under-written, for payment of money, performance of covenants, or the like. (*Co. Lit.* 172.) Obligations may also be by matter of record: as statutes and recognizances, to which there are sometimes added defeasances, like the condition of an obligation. 2 *Shep. Abr.* 475.

OBLIGOR, is he who enters into a bond or obligation, and obligee, the person to whom it is entered into.

OBOLATA TERRÆ, according to some accounts, half an acre of land; others half a perch. *Spelm. Gloss. Cowel.*

OBSTRUCTING PROCESS, is an offence against public justice. This is at all times an offence of a very high and presumptuous nature; but more particularly so, when it is an obstruction of an arrest upon criminal process. And it hath been holden, that the party opposing such arrest becomes thereby *particeps criminis:* that is, an accessory in felony, and a principal in high treason, (2 *Hawk. P. C.* 121). Formerly one of the greatest obstructions to public justice, both of the civil and criminal kind, was the multitude of pretended privileged places, where indigent persons assembled together to shelter themselves from justice, (especially in London and Southwark), under the pretext of their having been ancient palaces of the crown, or the like (such as *White-Friers*, and its environs; the *Savoy*; and the *Mint* in Southwark): all of which sanctuaries for iniquity are now demolished, and the opposing of any process therein is made highly penal, by the statutes 8 and 9 *Will.* 3. *c.* 27. 9 *Geo.* 1. *c.* 28. and 11 *Geo.* 1, *c.* 22. which enact, that persons opposing the execution of any process in such pretended privileged places within the bills of mortality, or abusing any officer in his endeavours to execute his duty therein, so that he receives bodily hurt, shall be guilty of felony, and transported for seven years: and persons in disguise, joining in or abetting any riot or tumult on such account, or opposing any process, or assaulting and abusing any officer executing, or for having executed the same, shall be felons without benefit of clergy.

OBVENTIONS, (*obventiones*) are offerings or tithes; oblations, obventions, and offerings are generally the same thing. *Cowel. Blount.*

OCCASIO, a tribute which the lord imposed on his vassals or tenants; *propter occasiones bellorum vel aliarum necessitatum. Fleta, lib.* 1. *c.* 24.

OCCASIONARI, charged or loaded with payments, or occasional penalties. *Fleta, lib.* 1. *c.* 24. *par.* 7.

OCCASIONES, *assarts*, i. e. harrowing or breaking clods. *Lib. Niger Scac. par.* 1. *c.* 13.

OCCUPANT, (*occupans*) is he who first gets possession of a thing. An island in the sea, precious stones on the sea shore, and treasure discovered in a ground, that has no particular owner, by the law of nations belong to him who finds them, and gets the first occupation of them. 2 *Black.* 3, 8, 258, 400.

OCCUPATION, (*occupatio.*) Use or tenure; such as in the tenure or *occupation* of such a man. Also it is used for a trade or mystery.

OCCUPAVIT, a writ that lay for him who was ejected out of his freehold in time of war; as the writ *novel disseisin* for one *disseised* in time of peace. *Hengham.*

OCTAVE, the eighth day after feast inclusive. See *Utas.*

ODHAL RIGHT. ODH *proprietas*, and ALL *totum.* The ODHAL *right* in Norway and other northern countries. *Mac Doual. Inst. par.* 2. Here by the transposition of these northern syllables, ALLHODH, will give us the true etymology of the *allodium*, or absolute property of the feudists. 2 *Black.* 45. *n.*

ODIO ET ATIA, a writ antiently called *breve de bono, et malo*, directed to the sheriff to enquire whether a man committed to prison upon suspicion of murder, were committed on just cause of suspicion, or only upon *malice* and *ill will*: and if upon inquisition found not guilty then there was another writ to the sheriff to bail him. *Reg. Orig.* 133. *Bract. lib.* 31. *cap.* 20. *Stat.* 3 *Ed.* 1. *cap.* 11. Now taken away by *stat.* 28 *Ed.* 3. *cap.* 9. *S. P. C.* 77. 2 *Inst.* 42. 9 *Rep.* 506. See *Habeas Corpus.*

OECONOMUS, an advocate or defender. *Cowel. Blount.*

OECONOMICUS, the executor of a last will and testament. *Ibid.*

OFFENCE, *(delictum)* an act *committed against* a law, or *omitted* where the law requires it, and punishable by it. *West. Symb.*

OFFERINGS, are reckoned among personal tithes, payable by custom to the parson or vicar of the parish, either occasionally, as at sacraments, marriages, christenings, churching of women, burials, &c. or at constant times, as at Easter, Christmas, &c. *Cowel. Blount.*

The four offering-days are Christmas, Easter, Whitsuntide, and the feast of the dedication of the parish-church. *Gibs.* 739.

OFFERINGS OF THE KING. All offerings made at the holy altar by the king and queen, are distributed amongst the poor, by the dean of the chapel. There are twelve days in the year, called offering days, as to these offerings, viz. Christmas, Easter, Whitsunday, All Saints, New Year's day, Twelfth day, Candlemas, Annunciation, Ascension, Trinity Sunday, St. John Baptist, and Michaelmas day: all which are high festivals. *Lex Constitution*. 184.

OFFERTORIUM, a piece of silk, or fine linen, to receive and wrap up the offerings or occasional oblations in the church. *Cowel. Blount.*

OFFICE, (*officium*) signifies that function by virtue whereof a man hath some employment in the affairs of another, as of the king, or of another person. *Cowel.*

And according to *Blackstone*, 2. *Com*. 36. Offices are a right to exercise a public or private employment, and to take the fees and emoluments thereunto belonging, are also incorporeal hereditaments; whether public, as those of magistrates; or private, as of bailiffs, receivers, and the like. For a man may have an estate in them, either to him and his heirs, or for life, or for a term of years, or during pleasure only: save only that offices of public trust cannot be granted for a term of years, especially if they concern the administration of justice, for then they might perhaps vest in executors or administrators, (9 *Rep*. 37). Neither can any judicial office be granted in reversion: because though the grantee may be able to perform it at the time of the grant, yet before the office falls he may become unable and insufficient: but ministerial offices may be so granted, (11 *Rep*. 4); for those may be executed by deputy. Also, by statute 5 and 6 *Edw*. 6. *c*. 16. no public office (a few only excepted) shall be sold, under pain of disability to dispose of or hold it. For the law presumes that he, who buys an office, will by bribery, extortion, or other unlawful means, make his purchase good, to the manifest detriment of the public. And if two offices are incompatible, by the acceptance of the latter, the first is relinquished and vacant, even if it should be a superior office. 2 *T. R.* 81.

And by 49 *Geo*. 3. *c*. 126. the statute 5 and 6 *Ed*. 6. *c*. 16. is extended to Scotland and Ireland, and to all offices in the gift of the crown, or of any office appointed by the crown, and all commissions, civil, naval, or military, and to all places and employments, and to all deputations to any such departments, or under the appointment of the treasury, secretary of state, admiralty, ordnance, commander in chief, secretary at war, paymaster-general, commissioners of India, of the excise, treasurer of the navy, commissioners of the navy, victualling transports, commissary-general, store-keeper-general, and also the principal officers of any other public departments of his majesty's government in any part of the united kingdom, or the dominions or plantations thereof, *s*. 1. And when the right of appointment under the former, or th s act, shall be forfeited, the same shall go to his majesty. *s*. 2.

Persons buying or selling offices, or receiving or paying money or rewards for offices, shall be guilty of a misdemeanor. *s*. 3.

Persons receiving or paying money for soliciting offices, and entering into any negociations or pretended negociations relating thereto, shall be also guilty of a misdemeanour. *s*. 4.

Persons opening or advertising houses for transacting business, relating to the sale of offices, also guilty of a misdemeanour. *s*. 5.

And persons advertising or publishing the names of brokers, or agents, shall forfeit 50*l*. with full costs to the informer, in any court of record. *s*. 6.

But this act is not to extend to the purchase or sale of commissions, for the regulated prices or authorized regimental agents, acting in such cases according to regulation, without fee or reward. *s*. 7.

Officers in the army giving more than the regulated prices or paying agents for negociating, are to forfeit their commissions and be cashiered, their commission to be sold, and half of the produce when not exceeding 500*l*. to go to the informer, and exceeding it according to his Majesty's regulations in that behalf to be made. *s*. 8.

But this act is not to extend to offices, excepted in former acts, nor to securities or transactions under legal securities, in respect of offices legally saleable. *s*. 9. Nor to lawful deputations, where the payment of the principal or deputy is out of the fees. *s*. 10. Nor does the act extend to annual payments out of the fees of any office, to any person formerly holding such office. *s*. 11.

Offenders in Scotland may be fined and imprisoned, or by one or both of such punishments. *s*. 13.

Offences committed abroad, shall be tried in the court of King's Bench. *s*. 14.

OFFICE FOUND, is where an inquisition is made to the king's use, of any thing by virtue of his office who inquireth, and it is found by the inquisition. *Staundford's Prerog. pag*. 60. To *traverse an office*, is to traverse an inquisition taken of *office*: and to return an *office*, is to return that which is found by virtue of the *office*. *Kitch*. 177. And if any *office* be wrongfully found, those who are grieved, may be relieved by a traverse, or *Monstrans de Droit*, by pleading or petition: For every *office* is in nature of a declaration, to which any man may plead, and either deny or confess, &c. *Plowd*. 448. *Bro*. 506.

OFFICIAL, (*officialis*) the minister of or attendant upon a magistrate. And in the canon law, one to whom any bishop generally commits the charge of his spiritual jurisdiction; and there is in every diocese *officialis principalis*, whom the law styles chancellor; and the rest, if there are more, are termed *officialis foranei*, i. e. *commissaries*. *Wood's Inst.* 30, 505.

OFFICIARIIS NON FACIENDIS VEL AMOVENDIS, a writ directed to the magistrates of a corporation, requiring them not to make such a man an officer, or to put one out of the office he hath, until inquiry is made of his manners, &c. *Reg. Orig.* 126.

OFFICIO, OATH EX. By *stat.* 13 *Car.* 2. *c.* 12, it is enacted, that it shall not be lawful for any bishop or ecclesiastical judge, to tender or administer to any person whatsoever, the oath usually called the oath EX OFFICIO, or any other oath whereby he may be compelled to confess, accuse, or purge himself of any criminal matter or thing, whereby he may be liable to any censure or punishment.

OLD JEWRY, (*Vetus Judaismus*) the place or street where the Jews lived in London. *Cowel.*

OLERON LAWS, (*Uliarenses Leges*) are the laws of King Rich. 1. relating to maritime affairs, so called, because made by him when he was at Oleron; which is an island lying in the bay of Aquitain, at the mouth of the river Charent, and now belongs to the French king. *Co. Lit.* 260.

OLYMPIAD, (*Olympias*) an account of time among the Greeks, consisting of four complete years, having its names from the olympic games, which were kept every fourth year, in honour of Jupiter Olympius, near the city of Olympia: The first Olympiad began in the year 3938 of the Julian period, 505 years after the taking of Troy, 776 before the birth of Christ, and 24 years before the founding of Rome. Æthelred, king of the English Saxons, computed his reign by Olympiads. *Spelm.*

OMER, a measure made use of by the Jews, of three pints and a half. *Merch. Dict.*

OMISSIONS, are placed among crimes and offences; and omission to hold a court-leet, or not swearing officers therein, &c. are causes of forfeiture. 2 *Hawk. P. C.* 73. Omissions in law proceedings render them vicious and defective, as want of warrants of attorney entered, &c. 1 *Keb.* 204, 222.

ONCUNNE, (Sax. *Oncunnen*) signifies as much as accused, *Accusatus. Leg. Alfred. c.* 29. *Cowel.*

ONERANDO PRO RATA PORTIONIS, a writ that lay for a jointenant, or tenant in common, who was distrained for more rent than his proportion of the land came to. *Reg. Orig.* 182.

O. NI, is the course of the exchequer, that as soon as the sheriff enters into and makes up his account for issues, amerciaments, and mean profits, to mark upon each head, *O. Ni.* which denotes *oneratur, nisi habeat sufficientem exonerationem*, and presently he becomes the king's debtor; and a *debet* is set upon his head; whereupon the parties *paravaile* become debtors to the sheriff, and are discharged against the king, &c. 4 *Inst.* 116.

ONUS EPISCOPALE, customary payments from the clergy to their diocesan bishop, of Synodals, Pentecostals, &c. *Cowel.*

ONUS IMPORTANDI, the charge or burden of importing merchandise, *Ibid.*

ONUS PROBANDI, *i. e.* the burden of proving. 14 *Car.* 2. *c.* 11.

OPEN LAW, (*lex manifesta*) is the making of law, which bailiffs may not put men to, upon the bare assertion, except they have witnesses to prove the truth of it. *Mag. Chart. c.* 21.

OPEN THEFT, (Sax. *Opentheof*) is a theft that is manifest. *Leg. Hen. c.* 13.

OPEN-TIDE, *i. e.* when corn is carried out of the common fields. *Brit.*

OPERARII, tenants who had some little portions of land by the duty of performing many bodily labours and servile works for their lord, being no other than the *servi bondmen*. *Cowel.*

OPERATIO, one day's work. *Ibid.*

OPPOSER, an officer belonging to the green wax in the Exchequer. *Ibid.*

OPPRESSION, in a private sense, is the trampling upon or bearing down one, on pretence of law, which is unjust: but where the law is known and clear, though it be unequitable, the judges must determine according to that. *Vaugh.* 37.

OPTION. When a new suffragan bishop is consecrated, the *archbishop* of the province by a customary prerogative claims the collation of the first vacant dignity or benefice in that see, at his own choice; which is called his *option*. *Cowel.*

OPTIONAL WRIT, a *præcipe* is an *optional* writ, i.e. it is in the alternative, commanding the defendant to do the thing required, or shew the reason wherefore he hath not done it. There is another species of original writs called *peremptory*, or a *si fecerit te securum*, from the words of the writ, which directs the sheriff to cause the defendant to appear in court, without any option given him, provided the plaintiff gives the sheriff security effectually to prosecute his claim. 3 *Black.* 274.

ORA. A Saxon coin, valued at sixteen pence, and sometimes according to variation of the standard at twenty pence.

ORANDO PRO REGE ET REGNO, an ancient writ, common in the time of king *Edw.* 3. *Cowel.*

ORARIUM, the hem, or border of a garment. *Cowel.*

ORBIS, *Anglice*, a *bonney*, a swelling or knot in the flesh, caused by a blow. *Bract. lib.* 3.

ORCHARDS AND GARDENS, robbing them, or destroying trees in them. See *Trespass.*

ORCHEL, or ORCHAL, a kind of cork, or rather a kind of stone like alum, which dyers use in their colours.

ORDEAL, or ORDAL, (*ordalium*) a kind

of purgation practised in ancient times, and in the canon law called *purgatio vulgaris*. There were of this two sorts, one by *fire*, another by *water*. *Cowel.*

Anciently, when an offender being arraigned, pleaded not guilty, he might choose whether he would put himself for trial upon God and the country, by twelve men, as at this day, or upon God only; and then it was called the judgment of God, presuming that he would deliver the innocent. *Terms de Ley.* 9 *Rep.* 32.

This trial was two ways, one by *water*, and another by *fire:* the *water ordeal* was performed either in hot or cold; in cold water the parties suspected were adjudged innocent, if their bodies were not borne up by the water contrary to the course of nature; in hot water, they were to put their bare arms or legs into scalding water, which if they brought out without hurt, they were taken to be innocent of the crime.

Those that were tried by the *fire ordeal*, passed bare-footed and blind-fold over nine hot glowing plough-shares; or were to carry burning irons in their hands, usually of one pound weight, which was called *simple ordeal*; or of two pounds, which was *duplex*; or of three pounds weight, which was *triplex ordalium*; and accordingly as they escaped, they were judged innocent or nocent, acquitted or condemned: this fire *ordeal* was for freemen, and persons of better condition; and the water *ordeal* for bondmen and rustics. *Glanv. lib.* 4. *c.* 1.

ORDEFFE, or ORDELFE, (*effossio metalli*, derived from the Saxon *ore*, *metallum*, and *delfan effodere*) a liberty, whereby a man claims the *ore* found in his own ground, or more properly, the *ore* lying *under* ground: also a *delfe* of coal, is coal lying in veins under ground, before it is dug up. *Cowel.*

ORDELS, *oaths* and *ordels*, privileges granted in old charters, meaning the right of administering oaths, and adjudging *ordeal* trials, within a precinct or liberty. *Cowel.*

ORDERS. *Orders* of the *Court of Chancery* are, either of course or otherwise, obtained on the petition or motion of one of the parties in a cause, or of some other interested in or affected by it; and they are sometimes made on a full hearing of the matter, sometimes by consent of parties.

Orders of the King's Bench and Common Pleas, are rules made by the court in causes there depending; and when they are drawn up and entered, they become *orders* of the court. 2 *Lil.* 261.

Orders of Justices of the Peace. Justices of peace at the quarter sessions may rectify defects of form in *orders*, &c. upon appeals, and then shall determine the matters according to the merits of the case; and no *orders* shall be removed into *B.R.* without entering into recognizance of 50*l.* to prosecute with effect, &c. otherwise the justices to confirm their *order*, by *stat.* 5 *Geo.* 2. *c.* 19; and by the stat. 26 *Geo.* 2. *c.* 27. No *order* of justices shall be set aside for not inserting that one of them is of the *quorum*. See *Poor.*

ORDINALE, a book which contains the manner of performing divine *offices*. *Cowel.*

ORDINANCE, (*ordinatio*) is a law, decree, or statute, variously used. *Lit. Dict. Cowel.*

ORDINANCE OF THE FOREST, (*ordinatio forestæ*) is a statute made touching matters and causes of the *forest*, anno 34 Ed. 1. *Cowel. Blount.*

ORDINANCE OF PARLIAMENT, is said to be the same with *act of parliament*; but originally there was this difference between them; that an *ordinance* was but a temporary act, by way of prohibition, which the commons might alter or amend at their pleasure; and an act of parliament is a perpetual law not to be altered but by king, lords, and commons. *Rot. Parl.* 37 *Ed.* 3. *Prynne's Animadver. on* 4 *Inst.* 13.

ORDINARY, (*ordinarius*) is a *civil law* term, for any judge who hath authority to take cognizance of causes in his own right, and not by deputation. *Co. Lit.* 344. *Stat. Westm.* 2. 13 *Ed.* 1. *cap.* 19.

This name is applied to a *bishop* who hath original jurisdiction; and an *archbishop* is the *ordinary* of the whole province, to visit and receive appeals from inferior jurisdictions, &c. 2 *Inst.* 398. 9 *Rep.* 41. *Wood's Inst.* 25. The word *ordinary* is also used for every *commissary* or official of the bishop, or other ecclesiastical judge, having judicial power: thus an *archdeacon* is an *ordinary*; and *ordinaries* may grant administration of intestate's estates, &c. *Stat.* 31 *Ed.* 3. *c.* 11. 9 *Rep.* 36.

ORDINARY OF NEWGATE, is one who is attendant in *ordinary* upon condemned malefactors in that prison, to prepare them for death; and he records the behaviour of such persons. *Cowel.*

ORDINATIONE CONTRA SERVIENTES, a writ that lays against a servant, for leaving his master contrary to the statute. *Reg. Orig.* 189.

ORDINATION OF CLERGY. By common law, a deacon, of any age, might be instituted and inducted to a parsonage or vicarage: but it was ordained by statute 13 *Eliz. c.* 12. that no person under twenty-three years of age, and in deacon's orders, should be presented to any benefice with cure; and if he were not ordained priest within one year after his induction, he should be *ipso facto* deprived; and now, by statute 13 & 14 Car. II. *c.* 4. no person is capable to be admitted to any benefice, unless he hath been first ordained a priest; and then he is, in the language of the law, a clerk in orders. But if he obtains orders, or a licence to preach, by money or corrupt practices (which seems to be the true, though not the common, notion of simony) the person giving such orders forfeits 40*l.* and the person receiving, 10*l.* and is incapable of any ecclesiastical preferment for seven years afterwards.

Any clerk may be presented to a parsonage or vicarage; that is, the patron, to whom the advowson of the church belongs, may offer his clerk to the bishop of the diocese to be instituted. Of advowsons, or the right of presentation, being a species of private property, we have already treated in another part of this dictionary, (see *Advowson*). But when a clerk is presented, the bishop may refuse him upon many accounts. As, 1. If the patron is excommunicated, and remains in contempt forty days. Or, 2. If the clerk be unfit: which unfitness is of several kinds. First, with regard to his person: as if he be a bastard, an outlaw, an excommunicate, an alien, under age, or the like.—Next, with regard to his faith or morals. By 24 *Geo.* 3. *c.* 35. the bishop of London, or any other bishop by him appointed, may admit aliens to the order of deacon or priest, without their taking the oaths of allegiance.

But persons so ordained, shall not exercise their office in his majesty's dominions, and the name and country of the person ordained shall be inserted in the letters testimonial. *Ibid.*

By 26 *Geo.* 3. *c.* 84. the archbishop of Canterbury or York, with such other bishops as they shall think fit to assist, may consecrate subjects of foreign states, bishops, without the king's licence for the election, or requiring them to take the usual oaths; but not without first obtaining his majesty's royal licence for performing the consecration.

No persons so consecrated, shall thereby be enabled to exercise their offices in his majesty's dominions. *Ibid.*

Certificates of consecration shall be given by the archbishops. *Ibid.*

By 44 *Geo.* 3. *c.* 43. none shall be admitted *deacon* before twenty-three, nor *priest* before twenty-four; nor be capable of holding a benefice: but no title by lapse shall accrue, without six months notice, from the ordinary to the patron: but the *right* of granting faculties by the archbishop of Canterbury or Armagh, is saved.

ORDINES. A general chapter, or other solemn convention of the religious of such a particular order. *Paroch. Antiq. p.* 576.

ORDINES MAJORES ET MINORES. The holy orders of priest, deacon, and subdeacon, any of which did qualify for presentation and admission to an ecclesiastical dignity or cure, were called *ordines majores;* and the inferior orders of chanter, psalmist, ostiary, reader, exorcist and acolyte, were called *ordines minores. Cowel.*

ORDINUM FUGITIVI, signified those of the religious who deserted their houses, and throwing off the habits, renounced their particular *order*, in contempt of their oath and other obligations. *Paroch. Antiq.* 388.

ORDO, that rule which the *monks* were obliged to observe. *Cowel. Blount.*

ORDO ALBUS, the White Friars, or Augustines; the Cistercians also wore white. *Ibid.*

ORDO NIGER, were the Black Friars. *Ibid.*

ORFGILD, or CHEAPGELD, (from the Saxon, *orf, pecus,* and *gild, solutio vel redemptio,*) a delivery or restitution of *cattle.* Also, a restitution made by the hundred, or county, for any wrong done by one who was in pledge. *Arch. pag.* 125, or, rather a penalty for taking away cattle. *Ibid.*

ORFRAIES, (*aurifrisium*) a sort of *cloth of gold*, frizzled or embroidered, formerly made and used in England, worn by our kings and nobility; and the clothes of the king's guards were called *orfraies*, because adorned with such works of gold. *Ibid.*

ORGALLOUS, from the French *orgueil, pride*, high-minded. 4 *Inst.* 89.

ORGEYS, (mentioned in stat. 32 *E.* 2. *st.* 3. *c.* 3.) Is the greatest sort of North-sea fish, (for the statute says they are greater than lob-fish) which we now call *organling*, corruptly from *Orkney-ling*, because the best are near that island. *Cowel.*

ORGILD, (*sine compensatione*) without recompence; as where no satisfaction was to be made for the death of a man killed, so that he was judged lawfully slain. *Spelm.*

ORIGINAL. The *original*, or *original* WRIT, is the bringing, or foundation of a suit in the King's superior courts of law at Westminster. When a *person* hath received an injury and seeks that redress which the law has given for the injury, he is thereupon to make application or suit to the crown for that specific remedy which he is advised to pursue. As, for money due on bond, an action of *debt*: for goods detained without force, an action of *detinue* or *trover*: or, if taken with force, an action of *trespass vi et armis*: or to try the title of lands, a *writ of entry*, or action of trespass in *ejectment*; or, for any consequential injury received, a special action *on the case*. To this end he is to sue out, or purchase by paying the stated fees, an *original* or original writ, from the court of chancery, which is the *officina justitiae*, the shop or mint of justice, wherein all the king's writs are framed. It is a mandatory letter from the king in parchment, sealed with his great seal (*Finch L.* 237.) and directed to the sheriff of the county wherein the injury is committed or supposed so to be, requiring him to command the wrong-doer or party accused, either to do justice to the complainant, or else to appear in court, and answer the accusation against him. Whatever the sheriff does in pursuance of this writ, he must *return* or certify to the court of common pleas, together with the writ itself: which is the foundation of the jurisdiction of that court, being the king's warrant for the judges to proceed to the determination of the cause. For it was a maxim introduced by the Normans, that there should be no proceedings in common pleas before the king's justices without his original writ; because they held it unfit that those justices, being only the substitutes of the crown, should take cognizance of any thing but what was thus expressly referred to their judgment. (*Flet. l.* 2. *c.* 34.)

Original writs are either *optional* or *peremptory*; or, in the language of our law, they are either a *praecipe*, or a *si te fecerit securum*. (*Finch. L.* 257.) The *praecipe* is in the alternative, commanding the defendant to do the thing required, or shew the reason wherefore he hath not done it. The use of this writ is where something certain is demanded by the plaintiff, which is in the power of the defendant himself to perform; as, to restore the possession of land, to pay a certain liquidated debt, to perform a specific covenant, to render an account, and the like: in all which cases the writ is drawn up in the form of a *praecipe* or command, to do thus, or shew cause to the contrary; giving the defendant his choice, to redress the injury or stand the suit. The other species of original writs is called a *si fecerit te securum*, from the words of the writ; which directs the sheriff to cause the defendant to appear in court, without any option given him, provided the plaintiff gives the sheriff security effectually to prosecute his claim. This writ is in use where nothing is specifically demanded, but only a satisfaction in general; to obtain which, and minister complete redress, the intervention of some judicature is necessary. Such are writs of trespass, or on the case, wherein no debt or other specific thing is sued for in certain, but only damages to be assessed by a jury. For this end the defendant is immediately called upon to appear in court, provided the plaintiff gives good security of prosecuting his claim. Both species of writs are *teste'd*, or witnessed, in the king's own name; "witness ourself at "Westminster," or wherever the chancery may be held. 3 *Black*. 274.

The security here spoken of, to be given by the plaintiff for prosecuting his claim, is common to both writs, though it gives denomination only to the latter. The whole of it is at present become a mere matter of form; and John Doe and Richard Roe are always returned as the standing pledges for this purpose. The antient use of them was to answer for the plaintiff; who, in case he brought an action without cause, or failed in the prosecution of it when brought, was liable to an amercement from the crown for raising a false accusation; and so the form of the judgment still is. (*Finch.L.* 189, 252.)

The day on which the defendant is ordered to appear in court, and on which the sheriff is to bring in the writ, and report how far he has obeyed it, is called the *return* of the writ; it being then returned by him to the king's justices at Westminster. And it is always made returnable at the distance of at least fifteen days from the date or *teste*, that the defendant may have time to come up to Westminster, even from the most remote parts of the kingdom, and upon some day in one of the four *terms*, in which the court sits for the dispatch of business.

ORIGINALIA. In the treasurer's remembrancer's office in the Exchequer, the transcripts, &c. sent thither out of the chancery are called by this name, and distinguished from *recorda*; which contain the judgments and pleadings in suits tried before the barons. *Cowel.*

ORPED. Some *orped* knight, *i.e.* a knight whose clothes shone with gold. *Blount.*

ORPHAN, (*orphanus*) is a fatherless child; and in the city of London there is a *court of record* established for the care and government of *orphans*. 4 Inst. 248. See *Distribution*.

ORTELLI, (*Fr.*) is a forest word, and signifies the claws of a dog's foot. *Kitch. Cowel.*

ORTOLAGIUM, a garden plot or *hortilage*. *Mon. Angl. tom.* 1. *Cowel.*

ORYAL, (*oriolum*) a room, or cloister, in a monastery, priory, &c. whence it is presumed that *Oriel* or *Oryel* college in Oxford took name. *Matt. Paris, in vit. Abb. St. Alban. Cowel.*

OSCULUM PACIS. A custom formerly of the church, that in the celebration of the mass, after the priest had spoke these words, viz. *pax domini vobiscum*, the people kissed each other, which was called *osculum pacis*. *Cowel.*

OSMONDS, a kind of iron ore, anciently brought into England. *Stat.* 32 *H.* 8. *cap.* 14.

OSTENSIO, a tribute paid by merchants for leave to expose their goods for sale in markets.

OSWALD'S LAW, (*lex Oswaldi*) the law by which was understood the ejecting *married priests*, and introducing monks into churches, by Oswald bishop of Worcester, about the year 964. *Cowel.*

OSWALD'S LAW HUNDRED, an ancient hundred in Worcestershire, so called from bishop Oswald who obtained it of king Edgar, to be given to St. Mary's church in Worcester; it is exempt from the jurisdiction of the sheriff, and comprehends 300 hides of land. *Camb. Brit.*

OTHO, a deacon-cardinal of St. Nicholas, *in carcere Tulliano*, a legate for the people here in England, 22 *H.* 3. *Cowel. Blount.*

OTHOBONUS, a deacon-cardinal of St. Adrian, and the pope's legate here in England, 15 *H.* 3. His constitutions, together with those of Otho, are (some of them at least) in use at this day, in our ecclesiastical courts. *Ibid.*

OUCH, a collar of gold, or such like ornament, worn by women about their necks. 24 *H.* 8. *c.* 13.

OVER, (Sax. *ofer*, ripa) in the beginning

or ending of the names of places, signifies a situation near the bank of some river; as St. Maryover in Southwark, Andover in Hampshire, &c. *Cowel. Blount.*

OVERCYTED, (from the Sax. *ofer*, i.e. super, and *cythan*, offendere) used where a person was convicted of any crime; that it is found upon the offender. *Ibid.*

OVERHERNISSA, contumacy, or contempt of court. *Ibid.*

OVERSAMESSA, an ancient fine before the statute for *hue* and *cry*, laid upon those, who, hearing of a murder or robbery, did not pursue the malefactor. 3 *Inst.* 116.

OVERSEERS OF THE POOR. See *Poor*.

OVERT, (*Fr.*) is used for *overture*, an opening, also a proposal. *Law Fr. Dict.*

OVERT-ACT, (*opertum factum*) an open act, capable by law of being manifestly proved. 3 *Inst.* 12. See *Treason*.

OVERT MARKET, an open market.

OVERT-WORD, is an open plain word, not to be mistaken. *Stat.* 1 *Mar. Sess.* 2, 3.

OVRES, (*Fr.*) acts, deeds, or works: and *ovrages*, or *ouvrages*, are days works. 8 *Rep.* 131.

OURLOP, the *leirwite* or fine paid to the lord by the inferior tenant, when his daughter was corrupted or debauched. *Cowel.*

OUSTED, (from the Fr. *ouster*, to put out) one removed or put out of possession. 3 *Cro.* 349.

OUSTER LE MAIN, (*amovere manum*) a livery of land out of the king's hand, or a judgment given in chancery, for him that sued a *monstrans de droit*; that the king's *hands be amoved*, whereupon an *amoveas manum* was awarded to the escheator, to restore the land. *Staundf. Prærog. cap.* 24. 28 *Ed.* 1. *cap.* 19. *F.N.B.* 256. 25 *Hen.* 8. *cap.* 22. But *ouster le mains*, &c. are taken away by *stat.* 12 *Car.* 2. *cap.* 24.

OUSTER LE MER, (*oultre*, i.e. ultra, & *le mer*, mere) *beyond the seas*. *Cowel. Blount.*

OUTFANGTHEF, (from the Sax. *ut*, i.e. extra, *fang*, captus, and *theof*, fur) a liberty or privilege, used in the ancient common law, whereby a lord was enabled to call any man dwelling in his manor, and taken for felony in another place out of his fee, to judgment in his own court. *Rastal. Cowel. Blount.*

OUTHEST, the same as *outhorn*; which was a calling men *out* to the army, by the sound of an *horn*. *Ibid.*

OUT-HOUSES, are those belonging and adjoining to dwelling houses. See *Felony*.

OUTLAND. The Saxon Thanes divided their hereditary lands into *inland*, such as lay nearest their dwelling, which they kept to their own use; and *outland*, which lay beyond the demeans, and was granted out to tenants, at the will of the lord, like copyhold estates. *Spelm. de Feud. cap.* 5.

OUTLAW, Sax. *utlaghe*, Lat. *utlagatus*, one deprived of the benefit of the law, and out of the king's protection. *Fleta, lib.* 1. *cap.* 47. 1 *Inst.* 128. But a woman cannot be an *outlaw*, because women are not sworn to the king as men are, to be ever *within* law; therefore they are said to be *waived*, as not regarded but forsaken of the law. *F. N. B.* 160. *Co. Lit.* 122.

OUTLAWRY, (*utlagaria*), is a punishment inflicted for a contempt, in refusing to be amenable to the justice of that court which hath authority to call him before them; and as this is a crime of the highest nature, being an act of rebellion against that state or community of which he is a member, so it subjects the party to forfeitures and disabilities; for he loseth his *liberam legem*, is out of the king's protection, &c. *Co. Lit.* 128. *Doct. and Stud. dial.* 2. *cap.* 3. 1 *Roll. Abr.* 802.

But as to forfeitures for refusing to appear, the law distinguishes between *outlawries* in CAPITAL cases, and those of an *inferior* nature; for as to *outlawries* in treason and felony, the law interprets the party's absence *a sufficient evidence of his guilt*, and without requiring further proof, accounts him *guilty of the fact*, on which ensues corruption of blood, and forfeiture of his estate, real and personal. *Co. Lit.* 128. 3 *Inst.* 161.

But *outlawry* in PERSONAL ACTIONS does not occasion the party to be looked on as guilty of the fact, nor does it occasion an entire forfeiture of his real estate, yet it is very fatal and penal in its consequences; for hereby he is restrained of his liberty, if he can be found, forfeits his goods and chattels, and the profits of his lands, *while the outlawry remains in force*. *Plow.* 541. 9 *H.* 6, 20. *b.* *Show. Parl. Ca.* 73.

Anciently *outlawry* was looked upon as so horrid a crime, that *any one might as lawfully kill a person outlawed as he might a wolf*, or *other noxious animal*; but now no man is intitled to kill an *outlaw* wantonly or wilfully; but in so doing is guilty of murder, (1 *Hal. P.C.* 497.) unless it happens in the endeavour to apprehend him. *Bracton, fol.* 125.

Also from the heinousness of the offence the sheriff may, on a *capias utlagatum*, break open the house of the person outlawed; for it would be unreasonable, that the protection allowed in other cases, should extend to him who is declared a contemner and violater of the law; therefore the seizing him as an outlaw, implies the liberty of entering and seizing him wherever he lies hid. 2 *Hale's Hist. P. C.* 202. 9 *Co.* 91. 1 *Buls.* 146. *Cro. Eliz.* 908. *Moor* 606, 668. *Yelv.* 28. *Cro. Car.* 537. 4 *Leon.* 41. 2 *Jon.* 233.

An outlawry in PERSONAL ACTIONS may be reversed by the defendant's appearing personally in court; and in the King's Bench without any personal appearance; so that he appears by attorney, according to the STAT. 4 and 5 *W.* & *M. c.* 18. by which it is enacted, that "no person who shall be outlawed in the "court of *B. R.* for any cause whatsoever, "(*treason* and *felony* only excepted) shall be "compelled to appear in person in the said "court to reverse such outlawry, but may "appear *by attorney* and reverse the same "without bail in all cases, (except where "special bail shall be ordered by the said "court.)"

And any plausible cause, however slight, will in general be sufficient to reverse, it being considered only as a process to compel an appearance: but then the defendant must pay full costs, and put the plaintiff in the same condition as if he had appeared before the writ of *exigi facias* awarded. 3 *Black.* 284.

After an outlawry of *treason* or *felony* is *reversed*, the party shall be put to plead to the indictment, for that still remains good, and he may be tried at the King's Bench bar; or the record may be remitted into the country, if it were removed into the King's Bench by *certiorari*, with a command to the justices below, to proceed by the statute of 6 *Hen.* 6. *cap.* 1. *Cro. Jac.* 646. *Cro. Car.* 365. 3 *Mod.* 42. 6 *Mod.* 115. 2 *Hale's Hist. P.C.* 209.

So if a man be outlawed by process in an information, and comes in and reverses the outlawry, he must plead *instanter* to the information. 1 *Salk.* 371. *Rex* v. *Hill*, 5 *Mod.* 141. S.P.

A person shall, after outlawry reversed, be restored to his law, and be of ability to sue. *Co. Litt.* 288. *b.*

OUTPARTERS, (mentioned in stat. 9 *H.* 5. *st.* 1. *c.* 7.) A kind of thieves in Riddesdale, that stole cattle or other things without that liberty. *Cowel.*

OUTRIDERS, bailiffs errant anciently employed by the sheriffs, or their deputies, to ride to the farthest place of their counties or hundreds, with the more speed to summon such as they thought good to their county or hundred courts. 14 *E.* 3. *st.* 1. c. 9.

OWEL, (*L. Fr.*) signifieth equal. *Cowel. Blount.*

OWELTY, (*Owelty of services*) was where there was lord, mesne, and tenant, and the tenant held of the mesne by the same service that the mesne holds over of the lord above him. *F. N. B.* 136. And owelty is equality of services. *Co. Lit.* 169.

OWLERS, persons that carry wool to the sea side by night, in order to be shipped off contrary to law, prohibited by 28 *Geo.* 3. *c.* 38.

OWLING, is an offence so called from its being usually carried on in the night, and is the offence of transporting wool or sheep out of this kingdom, to the detriment of its staple manufacture. See 28 *Geo.* 3. *c.* 38.

OXFILD, a restitution made by a hundred or county, of any wrong done by one that was within the same. *Lamb. Archaion.* 125.

OXGANG, (from *ox*, i. e. *bos*, and *gang*, or gate, *iter*) commonly taken for fifteen acres of land, or as much as one *ox* can plough in a year.

OYER, anciently used for what we now call assises. *Anno* 13 *Ed.* 1.

OYER OF A DEED, where a man brings an action of debt upon a bond, deed, or other written testament, and defendant may pray that he may hear the bond, &c. wherewith he is charged read to him, which shall be allowed him. 2 *Lil. Abr.* 266.

For defendants in the times of ancient simplicity were supposed incapable to read it themselves. And therefore on craving *oyer*, the whole is entered *verbatim* upon the record, and the defendant may take advantage of any condition or other part of it, not stated in the plaintiff's declaration. 3 *Black.* 299.

OYER DE RECORD, (*audire recordum*) is a petition made in court, that the judges, for better proof-sake, will hear or look upon any record. 2 *Lutw.* 1641. *Doct. Plac.* 270, 2.

Thus if the defendant pleads another action depending for the same cause, in the same court, the plaintiff may pray *oyer* of the record, being in the same court; and if there is no *oyer* of the record, the plaintiff may sign judgment by default, the plea being as no plea. *Ld. Raym.* 347. *Keilw.* 95, 96. *Carth.* 453. 3 *Salk.* 119.

OYER AND TERMINER, (Fr. *Ouir & Terminer*, Lat. *Audiendo & Terminando*) a commission directed to the judges, and other gentlemen of the county to which it is issued, by virtue whereof they have power to hear and determine treasons, and all manner of felonies and trespasses. *Cromp. Jurisd.* 121. 2 *Inst.* 419. 4 *Inst.* 152. It is the first and largest of the five commissions, by which our judges of assise sit in their several circuits: and is general, for trying all offenders and offences, or special, to try only particular persons, or offences: when any sudden insurrection, or trespass is committed, which requires speedy reformation, in which case a special commission is immediately granted. 4 *Inst.* 162. *Westm.* 2. 13 *Ed.* 1. *c.* 29. *F. N. B.* 110.

O YES, (from the Fr. *oyez*, i. e. *Audite*, hear ye) is the usual proclamation to enjoin silence and attention.

OYSTER-FISHERY, See *Fishery.*

OZE, or oozy ground, (*Solum uliginosum*) moist, wet, and marshy land. *Lit. Dict.*

P

PAGE, (*paagium.*) See *Passagium.*

PACABILIS, payable, or passable. *Cowel.*

PACARE, to pay, as *tolnetum pacare* is to pay toll. *Ibid.*

PACE, (*passus*) a step in going, containing two feet and an half, the distance from the heel of the hinder foot to the toe of the fore foot; and there is a pace of five feet, which contains two steps, a thousand whereof make a mile; but this is called *passus major. Ibid.*

PACEATUR. *Leg. Inæ, cap.* 45: Let him be free, or discharged, for the time to come. *Ibid.*

PACIFICATION, (*pacificatio*) a peace-making, quieting, or appeasing; relating to war. *Ibid.*

PACK OF WOOL, a horse-load, of 17 stone and two pounds, or 240 pounds weight. *Merch. Dict. Fleta, lib.* 2, *c.* 12. *Cowel.*

PACKAGE, ancient rates payable to the corporation of London and other places, for all goods and merchandises packed, casked, piped, barrelled, or any wise repelled, in order to be transported to parts beyond the seas, although the mayor and commonalty, or their officers, do not pack the said goods when they are ready, and upon reasonable request and proper notice given. See 43 *Geo.* 3, *c.* 68, *s.* 1.

PACKING WHITES, an ancient kind of cloth so called. See 1 *Ric.* 3, *c.* 8.

PACT (*Fr.*) a contract or agreement. *Cowel.*

PAGUS, used in ancient records, and meaning a county.

PAIN (or PEINE) FORT ET DURE, (Lat. *pœna fortis & dura*, Fr. *peine forte et dure*) a special punishment, formerly inflicted on those, who being arraigned of felony refused to put themselves on the ordinary trial, but stubbornly stood mute. It was vulgarly called pressing to death. *Stat. West.* 1, *c.* 12. See *Mute.*

PAINS AND PENALTIES. Acts of parliament to attaint particular persons of treason or felony, or to inflict pains and penalties beyond or contrary to the common law, to serve a special purpose, are new laws, made *pro re natâ*, and by no means an execution of such as are already in being. 3 *Black.* 256.

Thus in the 9 *Geo.* 1, pains and penalties were inflicted on the bishop of Rochester, Kelly, and others, for being concerned in Layer's conspiracy, and these were condemned by parliament for want of such evidence as is strictly required in the common law courts. 9 *Geo.* 1, *c.* 16, 17.

PAIS, a county; thus a trial *in pais* is a trial by the *county*, i. e. by a jury, and not *per recordum.*

PAISSO, pasnage, or liberty for hogs to run in forests or woods to feed on mast. *Mon. Angl. tom.* 1. *p.* 682. See *Passune.*

PALACE COURT. See *Marshalsea.*

PALAGIUM, a duty anciently paid to lords of manors for exporting and importing vessels of wine in any of their ports. *Cowel.*

PALATINE. CHESTER, DURHAM, and LANCASTER, are called counties palatine. The two former are such by prescription, or immemorial custom; or at least as old as the Norman conquest (*Seld. tit. hon.* 2. 5. 8.): the latter was created by king *Edw.* 3, in favour of Henry Plantagenet, first earl and then duke of Lancaster; (*Pat.* 25 *Edw.* 3, *p.* 1. *m.* 18. *Seld. ibid. Sandford's Gen. Hist.* 112. 4 *Inst.* 204.) whose heiress being married to John of Gant the king's son, the franchise was greatly enlarged and confirmed in parliament, (*Cart.* 36 *Edw.* 3, *n.* 9.) to honour John of Gant himself, whom, on the death of his father-in-law, the king had also created duke of Lancaster. (*Pat.* 51 *Edw.* 3, *m.* 33. *Plowd.* 215. 7 *Rym.* 138.) Counties palatine are so called *a palatio*, because the owners thereof, the earl of Chester, the bishop of Durham, and the duke of Lancaster, had in those counties *jura regalia*, as fully as the king hath in his palace; *regalem potestatem in omnibus*, as Bracton expresses it (*l.* 3. *c.* 8, § 4.). They might pardon treasons, murders, and felonies; they appointed all judges and justices of the peace; all writs and indictments ran in their names as in other counties in the king's; and all offences were said to be done against their peace, and not, as in other places, *contra pacem domini regis.* (4 *Inst.* 204.) And indeed by the ancient law, in all peculiar jurisdictions, offences were said to be done against his peace in whose court they were tried: in a court-leet, *contra pacem domini*; in the court of a corporation, *contra pacem ballivorum*; in the sheriff's court or tourn, *contra pacem vice-comitis.* (*Seld. in Heng. magn. c.* 2.) These palatine privileges (so similar to the regal independent jurisdictions usurped by the great barons on the continent, during the weak and infant state of the first feudal kingdoms in Europe) were in all probability originally granted to the counties of Chester and Durham, because they bordered upon inimical countries, Wales and Scotland: in order that the inhabitants, having justice administered at home, might not be obliged to go out of the county, and leave it open to the enemy's incursions; and that the owners, being encouraged by so large an authority, might be the more watchful in its defence. And upon this account also there were formerly two other counties palatine, Pembrokeshire and Hexhamshire; the latter now united with Northumberland; but these were abolished by parliament, the former in 27 *Hen.* 8, the latter in 14 *Eliz.* And in 27 *Hen.* 8, likewise, the powers before mentioned of owners of counties palatine were abridged; the reason for their continuance in a manner ceasing, though still all writs are witnessed in their names, and all forfeitures for treason by the common law accrue to them. 4 *Inst.* 205.

Of these three, the county of Durham is now the only one remaining in the hands of a subject. For the earldom of Chester, as Camden testifies, was united to the crown by Henry 3, and has ever since given title to the king's eldest son. And the county palatine, or duchy, of Lancaster, was the property of Henry Bolingbroke, the son of John of Gant, at the time when he wrested the crown from king Richard 2, and assumed the title of king Henry 4. But he was too prudent to suffer this to be united to the crown; lest if he lost one, he should lose the other also. For, as Plowden (215.) and sir Edw. Coke (4 *Inst.* 205.) observe, "he knew he had the duchy of "Lancaster by sure and indefeasible title, "but that his title to the crown was not so "assured: for that after the decease of "Richard 2, the right of the crown was in "the heir of Lionel duke of Clarence, second "son of Edward 3; John of Gant, father to "this Henry 4, being but the fourth son." And therefore he procured an act of parliament, in the first year of his reign, ordaining that the duchy of Lancaster, and all other his hereditary estates, with all their royalties and franchises, should remain to him and his heirs for ever, and should remain, descend, be administered and governed in like manner as if he never had attained the regal dignity: and thus they descended to his son and grandson, Henry 5, and Henry 6, many new territories and privileges being annexed to the duchy by the former. (*Parl.* 2 *Hen.* 5, *n.* 30. 3 *Hen.* 5, *n.* 15.) Henry 6 being attainted in 1 *Edw.* 4, this duchy was declared in parliament to have become forfeited to the crown (1 *Vent.* 155.), and at the same time an act was made to incorporate the duchy of Lancaster, to continue the county palatine (which might otherwise have determined by the attainder) and to make the same parcel of the duchy: and further, to vest the whole in king *Edw.* 4, and his heirs, kings of England, for ever; but under a separate guiding and governance from the other inheritances of the crown. And in 1 *Hen.* 7, another act was made, to resume such part of the duchy lands as had been dismembered from it in the reign of Ed. 4, and to vest the inheritance of the whole in the king and his heirs for ever, as amply and largely, and in like manner, form, and condition, separate from the crown of England and possession of the same, as the three Henries and Ed. 4, or any of them, had and held the same. (1 *Black.* 118.) But the isle of Ely is not a county palatine, though sometimes erroneously called so, but only a royal franchise; the bishop having by grant of king *Hen.* 1, *jura regalia*, within the isle of Ely, whereby he exercises a jurisdiction over all causes, as well criminal as civil. 4 *Inst.* 220. 1 *Black.* 119.

PALES. See *Trespass.*

PALFREY, *(palfredus, palafredus, palefredus, palifredus,)* one of the better sort of horses used by noblemen or others for state. See *Co.* on *Lit.* 149. *Cowel.*

PALICEA, a parkpale. *Cowel.*

PALINGMAN, (mentioned in stat. 22 *Ed.* 4, *c.* 23, and 11 *Hen.* 7, *c.* 23,) a merchant denizen, one born within the English pale. *Cowel.*

PALIA, a canopy; also an altar-cloth. *Cowel. Blount.*

PALLIO COOPERIRE. It was anciently a custom where children were born out of wedlock, and their parents afterwards intermarried, that those children, together with the father and mother, stood under a cloth extended while the marriage was solemnizing, which was in the nature of adoption; and by such custom the children were taken to be legitimate: but such children were never legitimate in this country at common law, though the clergy wanted to have a law pass to render them legitimate. *Cowel.*

PALLIUM, an ancient garment made of white wool. *Cowel.*

PALLS, the pontifical vesture made of lambs-wool, in breadth not exceeding three fingers, cut round that they might cover the shoulders, given or sent by the Pope to archbishops and metropolitans, and upon extraordinary occasions to other bishops. *Cowel.*

PALMESTRY, a kind of divination practised by looking upon the lines and marks of the hands and fingers, being a deceitful art used by Egyptians. See *Vagrants.*

PANDECTS, are the books of the civil law, compiled by Justinian; mentioned in the historians of this nation. *Bede, c.* 5. 1 *Black. Com.* 17, 81.

PANDOXATRIX, an ale-wife, who both brews and sells ale and beer; from *pandoxatorium*, a brewhouse. *Cowel.*

PANEL, *(panella, pannellum)* a panel, or pane of parchment, containing the names of such jurors as the sheriff returns to pass upon any trial. *Kitch.* 226. *Reg. Orig.* 223.

PANETIA, a pantry, or place to set up cold victuals. *Cowel.*

PANIS ARMIGERORUM, the bread distributed to servants. *Mon.* 1., *p.* 420. *Cowel.*

PANIS VISUS, coarse bread. *Id. ib.*

PANIS, called *blackwhytlof*, bread of a middle sort, between white and brown. *Cowel.*

PANIS MILITARIS, hard biscuit, brown George, camp bread, coarse and black. *Ibid.*

PANNAGE, or PAWNAGE, (*pannagium*, Fr. *pasnage*) is that food which the swine feed upon in the woods, as mast of beech, acorns, &c. *Ibid.*

PANNUS, a garment made with skins. *Cowel.*

PAPER. See *Manufactures.*

PAPER BOOKS, are issues at law, &c. upon special pleadings, which paper books are to be delivered to the judges with the names of the counsellors who signed those pleas. 2 *Lill. Abr.* 268.

PAPER-OFFICE, is an ancient office within the palace of Whitehall, wherein all the public papers, writings, matters of state and council, letters, intelligences, negotiations of the king's ministers abroad, and generally all the papers and dispatches that pass through the offices of the two principal secretaries of state, are lodged and transmitted, and there remain disposed in the way of library. *Cowel.*

PAPISTS, are those who profess the popish religion in this kingdom: and since the Reformation there have been many statutes concerning them. Thus

By 3 *Car.* 1, *c.* 3, in case any person under the obedience of the king shall go or send any child, or other person, beyond the seas, to the intent to be trained up in any abbey, popish university, or school, or house of Jesuits, or in any private popish family, and shall be there by any popish person instructed in the popish religion, to profess the same, or shall send any money or other thing under the name of alms, towards the relief of any abbey or religious house, every person so sending, and every person sent, being convicted upon any information or indictment, shall be disabled to sue any action in law, or suit in equity, or to be committee of any ward, or executor or administrator to any person, or capable of any legacy, or deed of gift, or to bear any office, and shall forfeit all his goods and chattels, and all his lands during life. *s.* 1.

No person sent as aforesaid, that shall within six months after his return conform to the church of England, and receive the sacrament, shall incur the penalties. *s.* 2.

Offences against this statute may be inquired, heard and determined, before the justices of the King's Bench, or justices of assise, or gaol delivery, or of *oyer* and *terminer*, of such counties where the offenders did last dwell, or whence they departed out of this kingdom, or where they were taken. *s.* 3.

If any person so sent shall after his return conform to the church of England, and receive the sacrament, he shall have his lands restored. *s.* 4.

By 30 *Car.* 2, *st.* 2, no peer shall vote or make his proxy in the house of peers, or sit there during any debate; nor shall any member of the house of commons vote in the house, or sit there during any debate, after their speaker is chosen; until such peer or member shall first take the oaths of allegiance and supremacy, and subscribe and repeat this declaration following:

"I A. B. do solemnly and sincerely, in "the presence of God, profess, testify and "declare, that I do believe, that in the sa-"crament of the Lord's supper there is not "any transubstantiation of the elements of "bread and wine into the body and blood of "Christ at or after the consecration thereof "by any person whatsoever, and that the "invocation or adoration of the Virgin "Mary, or any other saint, and the sacri-"fice of the mass, as they are now used "in the church of Rome, are superstitious "and idolatrous. And I do solemnly, in "the presence of God, profess, testify and "declare, that I do make this declaration, "and every part thereof, in the plain and "ordinary sense of the words read unto me, "as they are commonly understood by Eng-"lish protestants, without any evasion, "equivocation, or mental reservation what-"soever, and without any dispensation al-"ready granted me for this purpose by the "pope, or any other authority or person "whatsoever, or without any hope of any "such dispensation from any person or au-"thority whatsoever, or without thinking that "I am or can be, acquitted before God or "man, or absolved of this declaration, or any "part thereof, although the pope, or any "other person or persons, or power what-"soever, should dispense with or annul the "same, or declare that it was null and void "from the beginning."

Which oaths and declaration shall be made betwixt nine in the morning and four in the afternoon, by every such peer, at the table in the middle of the house, and while a full house of peers is there with the speaker in his place; and by every member of the house of commons at the table in the middle of the house, and while a full house of commons is there sitting with their speaker in his chair; and the same shall be done in either house in like order, as each house is called over. *s.* 2.

Every peer of this realm and of the kingdom of Scotland, or of Ireland, being of the age of 21 years, not having taken the said oaths, and made the declaration, and every member of the house of commons, not having taken the oaths, and made the declaration, and every person convicted of popish recusancy, who shall come advisedly into or remain in the presence of the king or queen, or shall come into the house where they reside, shall incur the penalties in this act, unless such peer, member, or person convicted, do in the next term take the oaths and make the declaration in chancery between nine and twelve in the forenoon. *s.* 3.

If any peer of this realm, or member of the house of commons, shall offend in any of the cases aforesaid, such peer and member shall be adjudged a popish recusant convict, and shall be disabled to hold any office or place of profit or trust, civil or military, in England or Ireland, Wales or Berwick, or in any of his majesty's islands or plantations, and shall be disabled to sit or vote in parliament, or make a proxy in the house of peers, or to sue in law or equity, or to be guardian of any child, or executor or administrator of any person, or capable of any legacy, or deed of gift, and shall forfeit for every wilful offence 500*l.* to be recovered by him that shall sue for the same in any of his majesty's courts at Westminster. *s.* 4.

It shall be lawful for the house of peers and house of commons to order the members to take the oaths, and make the declaration; and if any peer shall, contrary to such order, presume to sit without taking the oaths, &c. such peer shall be disabled to sit in the house, and give any voice by proxy or otherwise, during that parliament. And if any member of the house of commons shall, contrary to such order, presume to sit without taking the oaths, &c. such member shall be disabled to sit in the house of commons, or give any voice during that parliament. *s.* 5.

Where any member of the house of commons shall by this act be disabled to sit or vote, a new writ shall issue by warrant from the speaker, for the election of a new member to serve in the place of such member so disabled. *s.* 6.

During the time of taking the said oaths, &c. all other matters in the said houses of parliament shall cease; and the oaths, declaration and subscription, with a schedule of the names of the persons who shall by this act take the same, shall be filed in parchment rolls by the clerk of the house of lords, and the clerk of the house of commons; and none of the peers or members shall pay to any such clerk above 12*d.* for the entry of his taking the oaths, which rolls the clerks are without fee to show to any person desiring the same. *s.* 9.

This act shall not prejudice any person for coming into the presence of the king or queen, who have a licence so to do by warrant of six privy counsellors, by order of council, upon urgent occasion therein to be expressed; so as such licence exceed not ten days, and be first filed in the petty bag for any body to view without fee; and no person to be licenced for above thirty days in one year. *s.* 10.

If any offender, contrary to this act, shall take the oaths, &c. in chancery, such person shall be discharged of all penalties of this act, so as such discharge extend not to restore such person to any office, nor to any other office, till after one year, nor to discharge the forfeiture of 500*l.* *s.* 11.

By 1 *Will. & Mar. st.* 1, *c.* 9, it is required that the lord mayor of London, and every justice of peace of London and Westminster, and Southwark, and of Middlesex, Surry, Kent, and Sussex, [Essex by 1 *Will. & Mar. c.* 17,] cause to be arrested and brought before him every person (not being a merchant foreigner within the said cities, or ten miles of the same) reputed to be a papist, and tender him the declaration in 30 *Car.* 2, *st.* 2, and in case such person refuse to make the declaration, and shall after such refusal continue within the said cities, or ten miles distance from the same, he shall suffer as a popish recusant convict. *s.* 2.

Every justice of peace shall certify every subscription before him taken, and the name of every person refusing, into the King's Bench, the next term, or at the next quarter session; and if the person so refusing, and certified, shall not within the next term or sessions appear in the King's Bench or sessions, where such certificate shall be returned, and make the declaration, and indorse his so doing upon the certificate, he shall be adjudged a popish recusant convict. *s.* 3.

Nothing in this act shall relate to any foreigner that shall be menial servant to any ambassador or public agent. *s.* 5.

By 1 *Will. & Mar. c.* 15, it shall be lawful for any two justices of peace to tender to any person known or suspected to be a papist, the declaration in 30 *Car.* 2, *st.* 2, and if such person shall not make the said declaration, or shall forbear to appear before the justices, upon notice to him given or left at his place of abode, by any person authorized by warrant of the two justices, such person shall be subject to the penalties in this act. *s.* 2.

The justices shall certify the name and place of abode of every person who shall refuse to make the declaration, or to appear before them, as also of every person who shall make the declaration, at the next quarter-sessions to be recorded. *s.* 3.

No papist or reputed papist refusing or making default as aforesaid, shall have any arms, gunpowder, or ammunition, other than such necessary weapons as shall be allowed him by order of the quarter-sessions for the defence of his house or person. And any two justices by warrant may authorize any persons in the day time, with the constable, tithingman or headborough, to search for arms and ammunition which shall be in the custody of any such papist or reputed papist, and seize the same for the use of their majesties, which justices shall at the next quarter-sessions deliver the arms and ammunition in open court. *s.* 4.

Every papist or reputed papist, who shall not within ten days after such refusal or default as aforesaid deliver to some of the justices of peace all arms or ammunition, which he shall have, or shall hinder any person authorized by two justices to search for and seize the same, such person shall be committed to gaol by warrant of two justices, for three months; and shall also forfeit the arms, and treble the value of them, to their majesties, to be appraised by the justices at the next quarter-sessions. *s.* 5.

Every person who shall be privy to the concealing the arms or ammunition of any person so refusing or making default, or shall hinder any person authorized in searching for and seizing the same, shall be committed to gaol by two justices for three months, and forfeit treble the value of the arms to their majesties. *s.* 6.

If any person shall discover any concealed arms, &c. belonging to any refusing or making default as aforesaid, so as the same may be seized, the justices upon delivery of the same at the quarter-sessions shall by order of sessions allow him a sum of money amounting to the value of the arms, &c. to be assessed by the sessions, and levied by distress and sale of the goods of the person offending. *s.* 7.

If any person, who shall have refused or made default as aforesaid, shall desire to submit, and present himself before the justices at the quarter-sessions, and shall in open court make the declaration, and take the oaths in 1 *Will. & Mar. st.* 1, *c.* 1, viz. of allegiance and supremacy, he shall be discharged of all disabilities and forfeitures. *s.* 8.

No papist, or reputed papist, refusing or making default as aforesaid, shall have any horse above the value of 5*l.* and any two justices of the peace by warrant may authorize any person, with the assistance of the constable, tithingman, or headborough, to search for and seize for the use of their majesties all such horses, which are declared to be forfeited. *s.* 9.

If any person shall be assisting in the concealing any such horse belonging to any papist, or reputed so, refusing or making default as aforesaid, such person shall be committed to prison as aforesaid for three months, and shall forfeit to their majesties treble the value of such horses, to be settled as aforesaid. *s.* 10.

By 1 *Will & Mar. c.* 17, the powers by 1 *Will. & Mar. st.* 1, *c.* 9, given to the justices of peace of Sussex are declared to extend to the justices of peace of the county of Essex. *s.* 2.

By 1 *Will. & Mar. c.* 26, every person who shall refuse to make the declaration mentioned in 1 *Will. & Mar. st.* 1. *c.* 15, or shall refuse to appear for the making thereof, and shall thereupon have his name certified and recorded at the quarter-sessions, shall be disabled to make presentation, donation, or grant of avoidance, of any ecclesiastical living, as fully as if he were a popish recusant convict [See *Recusants*]; and the chancellor and scholars of the university of Oxford and of Cambridge shall have the presentation in the respective limits in the act 3 *Jac.* 1, *c.* 5, *s.* 2.

Where any persons are seised or possessed of any advowson of any ecclesiastical living, free school, or hospital, in trust for any papist or popish recusant, such persons shall be disabled to present, or to grant any avoidance; and the respective universities shall have the presentations; and in case any trustee or mortgagee, or grantee of any avoidance, present any person to such ecclesiastical living, &c. without giving notice of the avoidance in writing to the vice-chancellor of the university, to whom the presentation shall belong, within three months after the avoidance, he shall forfeit 500*l.* to the repective universities, to be recovered in any of their majesties courts of record. *s.* 3 & 4.

The universities shall not present to any ecclesiastical living any person as shall then have any other benefice with cure; and if any such presentation shall be, the same shall be void. *s.* 5.

If any person so presented to any benefice with cure shall be absent above sixty days in one year, the benefice shall become void. *s.* 6.

If any such person shall present himself before the justices at the quarter-sessions where his name was recorded, and make the declaration, and take the oaths of supremacy and allegiance, he shall be discharged of the disability. *s.* 7.

By 11 & 12 *Will.* 3, *c.* 4, the 100*l.* mentioned in 3 *Jac.* 1. *c.* 5, [See *Recusants*,] shall be to the sole use of him who shall discover and convict any person so offending. *s.* 6.

If any parent, in order to the compelling his protestant child to change his religion, shall refuse to allow such child a fitting maintenance, upon complaint, it shall be lawful for the lord chancellor to make such order therein as shall be agreeable to this act. *s.* 7.

By 12 *Ann. st.* 2, *c.* 14, every papist, or person making profession of the popish religion, and every child, not being a protestant, under the age of 21 years, of every such papist, &c. and every mortgagee, or trustee for any papist, &c. or such child, shall be disabled to present to any ecclesiastical living, school, hospital, or donative, or to grant any avoidance; and every such presentation and grant, and every admission, institution, and induction thereupon, shall be void; and the universities of Oxford and of Cambridge shall respectively have the presentation in the respective limits in the act 3 *Jac.* 1, *c.* 5, *s.* 1.

When any presentation shall be brought to any ordinary from any person who shall be reputed to be, or whom such ordinary shall have cause to suspect to be, a papist, or trustee of any person making profession of the popish religion, it shall be lawful for such ordinary to tender to such person, if present, the declaration against transubstantiation in 25 *Car.* 2, *c.* 2, "Recusants;" and in case such person be absent, the ordinary shall, by notice in writing to be left, at the place of habitation of such person, appoint when and where such person shall appear before such ordinary, or persons authorized under his seal of office; and upon appearance, the ordinary shall tender the declaration to the person making such presentation; and in case such person refuse to make such declaration, or to appear, such presentation shall be void; and such ordinary shall within ten days send a certificate under his seal of office of such neglect or refusal to the vice-chancellor of that university, to whom such presentation would belong; and it shall be lawful for such university to present. *s.* 2.

When the presentation shall be brought to any ordinary, he is required, before he give institution, to examine the person presented, upon oath, whether to the best of his knowledge and belief, the person who made such presentation be the true patron, or be not trustee for papists, or the children of such, or any other person; and if such person presented shall not answer directly, such presentation shall be void. *s.* 3.

It shall be lawful for the respective universities to whom the presentation should belong, and their clerks, to exhibit their bill in equity against such persons presenting, and such as they have reason to believe to be the *cestui que* trust, or any other who they have cause to suspect may be able to make any discovery of secret trusts, to which bill the defendants shall answer; and in case they neglect to answer, the bill shall be taken *pro confesso*; provided that every person having fully answered, and not knowing of any such trust for a papist, or other person disabled, shall be entitled to his costs to be taxed. *s.* 4.

It shall be lawful for the court where any *quare impedit* shall be depending, at the instance of either of the universities, by motion, to make any rule, requiring satisfaction upon the oath of such patron and his clerk who shall contest the right of the university, by examination in court, or by commission, or by affidavit, as the court shall find proper; and in case it shall appear that the patron is but a trustee for other persons, then the patron and his clerk shall discover who such persons are, and where they live, and upon their refusal to make such discovery they shall be punished as persons guilty of a contempt; and in case such patron or his clerk shall discover the person for whom the patron is a trustee, the court, upon motion, shall make a rule, that the person for whom the patron is a trustee shall, in court, or before commissioners, make the declaration against transubstantiation, and likewise give such further satisfaction upon oath touching the trust, as the court shall think fit; and such person required to make the declaration, and neglecting so to do, shall be esteemed a popish recusant convict in respect of such presentation. *s.* 5.

The answer of such patrons, and the person for whom they are intrusted, and their clerk, and their examinations and affidavits taken by order of court, or by any ordinary, or the commissioners, as aforesaid (which examinations shall be reduced into writing, and signed by the party examined), shall be evidence against such patron and his clerk. *s.* 6.

Provided that no such bill, nor any discovery to be made by any answer thereto, or to any examination as aforesaid, shall be made use of to subject any person making such discovery, or not answering such bill, to any penalty other than the loss of the presentation. *s.* 7.

In case of any such bill of discovery exhibited by either of the universities, or their presentee, no lapse shall incur, nor plenarty be a bar, till after three months from the time that the answer shall be put in, or the bill be taken *pro confesso*, or the prosecution deserted, provided such bill be exhibited before any lapse incurred. *s.* 8.

The universities are entitled to sue any writ of *quare impedit*, by the name of chancellor and scholars of the universities of Oxford and Cambridge respectively, or by their proper names of incorporation, at their election. *s.* 9.

In case of any trust for a papist discovered by answer to such bill, or such examination as aforesaid, it shall be lawful for the court to enforce the producing of the deeds relating to the trusts. *s.* 10.

Nothing herein before shall extend to *Scotland*. *s.* 11. See *Scotland*.

By 1 *Geo.* 1, *c.* 55, all persons having

any estate in lands in England, Wales, or Berwick, who shall be a popish recusant, or papist, or educated in the popish religion, or whose parent shall be a papist, shall within six months after they attain the age of 21 years, take the oaths appointed by 1 *Geo.* 1, c. 13, and repeat the declaration in 30 *Car.* 2, *st.* 2, in the chancery, common pleas, king's bench, or exchequer, or at the quarter-sessions, where such lands, &c. lie, between nine and twelve in the forenoon: or shall within six months after they shall come into the possession of the profits of any lands, &c. register their names and lands, and who are the possessors thereof, and what interest they have in the same, and the yearly rent reserved, if the same are let, and if upon lease, by whom such lease was made, and what fine was paid for such lease, in a parchment roll, to be kept by the clerk of the peace; and every person whose name and estate ought to be registered, is to take care that his name be subscribed to such registry in the presence of two justices of peace in open sessions, or by his lawful attorney authorised under hand and seal; two of the witnesses to which letter of attorney shall make proof of such execution on oath at the quarter-sessions, and two of the justices shall subscribe their names to such entry, and in default thereof each of the justices present shall forfeit 20*l.* to the king. And the clerks of the peace are to keep rolls, and register the names of all who shall come to be registered, or who shall send any writing to such clerk desiring him to register their names; and shall also register the estate of such persons, provided they pay the fees appointed, and apply to enter such registry ten days before the sessions where the entries are to be subscribed; which books, &c. they shall carry to the quarter-sessions, that all those whose names shall be registered, or their attornies, may come to the quarter-sessions, and subscribe the names of the persons registered; and such clerk, &c. shall also keep alphabetical tables of their names, and of the places where the lands lie, and shall keep all such warrants of attorney on a file, and enter such warrants on record, and shall have for such registering and entry 3*d.* for every 200 words, and 4*d.* for every search; and such clerk is to give copies of such registers subscribed to every person desiring the same, and tendering the fees; and shall suffer such persons to examine the same with the rolls, and shall take 3*d.* for every 200 words in such copy; and if any clerk of the peace shall neglect to do any thing hereby appointed, and be convicted, he shall forfeit his office. And if any person required to take the oaths, &c. or register his name and estate, shall neither take the said oaths, &c. nor register, he shall forfeit the inheritance of all such lands, &c. not registered, or fraudulently registered, of which he, or any in trust for him, was seised at the time of such default, and the full value of the inheritance of all such lands whereof he was not seised in fee-simple; two thirds to the king, and the other to such person, being a protestant, as will sue for the same in any the courts at Westminster, or in chancery. And the person suing in chancery shall be entitled to such discoveries as if he were a purchaser of the estate sued for, to which bill the defendant shall answer; and the person suing for such real estate may bring an ejectment upon his own demise; and if it shall appear on trial that the estate sued for is the estate of the person neglecting to register, and the defendant shall not make it appear that he took the oaths, and repeated the declaration, or that he registered his name and the estate sued for, a verdict shall be for the lessor of the plaintiff, and the lessor of the plaintiff shall have costs; and by such judgment two third parts of the lands recovered shall be vested in the king, and the other third in the lessor of the plaintiff. *s.* 1.

In case such person making default, or committing fraud in registering, shall before suit brought, for a valuable consideration convey or encumber any such lands, &c. the person so purchasing, &c. not knowing the offender to be within this act, shall not be prejudiced; but the offender shall forfeit the value of the lands, &c. *s.* 3.

This act shall not compel any person to register, &c. till he or his trustees have been seised, and have notice thereof, or possessed, or in receipt of the rents, for six months. *s.* 4.

Nor shall it compel any person to register lands, &c. whereof he shall be only farmer at a rack-rent, or which he shall hold by lease, whereon two thirds of the yearly value are reserved. *s.* 5.

Nor shall it prejudice any protestant or other creditor who hath any charge on any real estate, but the person making default shall forfeit the value of such charge; one third to the person who will sue, the other two thirds to the crown. *s.* 6.

By 3 *Geo.* 1, *c.* 18, no suit for any forfeiture contained in the foregoing act for refusing to register, or for any fraud in such registry shall be commenced after two years after the offence committed. *s.* 2.

Where any lands or entire farms lie in more counties than one, the registering in the county where the mansion-house doth lie, taking notice that the same extend to such other county, shall be a sufficient register. *s.* 3.

No sale for a full consideration by reputed owners, or persons in possession of the rents and profits to be made only for the benefit of protestants, shall be avoided for any of the disabilities in 11 & 12 *Will.* 3, *c.* 4, or in 1 *Jac.* 1, *c.* 4, [See *Recusants*], or other acts made against papists, unless the person entitled to take advantage of such disability shall have recovered, &c. or given notice of his claim to such purchaser, or before the contract for such sale shall have claimed by reason of such disability, and have entered his claim at the sessions of the peace, and with due diligence pursued his remedy. *s.* 4.

The clause in 11 & 12 *W.* 3, *c.* 4, by which papists are disabled from purchasing, shall not be hereby altered. *s.* 5.

No manors, lands, tenements, hereditaments, or interest therein, or rent or profit thereof, shall pass from any papist by any deed or will, except such deed within six months after date, and such will within six months after the testator's death, be inrolled in one of the courts of record at Westminster, or in the county where such manors, &c. lie, by the *custos rotulorum* and two justices and the clerks of the peace, or two of them, whereof the clerk of the peace to be one. *s.* 6. And by 21 *Geo.* 3. *c.* 51, the deputy clerk of the peace shall have the like power as the clerk of the peace.

By 11 *Geo.* 2, *c.* 17, every person, being reputed owner, or in possession of, any lands or hereditaments, who having been a papist, or educated in the popish religion, hath conformed, or shall conform to and profess the protestant religion, and take the oaths of allegiance, supremacy and abjuration, and subscribe the declaration in 30 *Car.* 2, *st.* 2, (which shall be recorded in one of his majesty's courts at Westminster, or quarter-sessions); and all persons being protestants claiming under such persons conforming and not for the benefit of any papist, shall hold and enjoy such lands, &c. freed from the disabilities incurred by such owners, or by any other persons through whom the title shall be derived, unless the person entitled to take advantage of such disability shall recover such lands, &c. by judgment or decree in some suit to be commenced six calendar months at least before the making of such record, and to be prosecuted with diligence. *s.* 1.

This act shall not prejudice the right of any person entitled to take advantage of such disability, who now is in possession, or shall have, precedent to the making of such record, been in possession, of such lands, &c. two calendar months. *s.* 2.

If any such person conforming shall return to the popish religion, such person shall for ever afterwards be disabled from having any benefit of this act, and shall be liable to the same disabilities as if he had not taken the oaths, &c. *s.* 3.

Nothing in this act shall prejudice the right of any person entitled to any remainder or reversion, in case such person shall pursue his right by suit to be commenced within twelve calendar months after the estate on which such remainder or reversion depends shall be determined, or within twelve calendar months after the 29th of September 1738, if such precedent estate be already determined by the death of any persons whose deaths have been concealed from the person entitled, by reason of their having been buried beyond the seas or in a private manner, and shall prosecute such suit with diligence. *s.* 4.

Every grant of any advowson of any ecclesiastical living, school, hospital or donative, and every grant of any avoidance thereof, by any papist or person making profession of the popish religion, or any mortgagee or person intrusted for any papist, &c. shall be void, unless such grant shall be made *bona fide*, and for a full consideration, to a protestant purchaser, and only for the benefit of protestants; and such grantee shall be deemed a trustee for a papist, and they and their presentees shall be compelled to make such discovery relating to such grants and presentations, as by the act 12 *Ann. st.* 2, *c.* 14, are directed; and every devise to be made by any papist of any such advowson, &c. with intent to secure the benefit thereof to the heirs or family of such papist, shall be void; and such devisees, and persons claiming under such devisees, and their presentees, shall be compelled to discover whether such devises were not made with the said intent. *s.* 5.

By 18 *Geo.* 3, *c.* 60, so much of 11 & 12 *Will.* 3, *c.* 4, as relates to the apprehending or prosecuting popish bishops, priests, or jesuits, or that subjects them, or papists keeping school, or educating or boarding youth in the realm, to perpetual imprisonment, or that disables papists to inherit, or take by devise or limitation, any estate, and gives the same to the next of kin, being a protestant, and so much of the same act as disables papists to purchase, and makes void all estates therein, was repealed. *s.* 1.

Every person having or claiming any lands, &c. under titles not hitherto litigated, shall enjoy the same as if the said act had not been made. *s.* 2.

Nothing herein shall affect any action now depending, which shall be prosecuted with effect, and without delay. *s.* 3.

Nothing herein shall extend to any person but such who shall within six calendar months after the passing of this act, or of accruing of his title, being of the age of 21 years, or who being under the age of 21 years shall within six months after he shall attain the age of 21 years, or being of unsound mind, or in prison, or beyond the seas, then within six months after such disability removed, take and subscribe an oath in the following words:

"I, A. B. do sincerely promise and swear "that I will be faithful, and bear true allegiance to his majesty king George the "Third, and him will defend to the utmost "of my power against all conspiracies and "attempts whatever, which shall be made "against his person, crown, or dignity. "And I will do my utmost endeavour to dis-"close and make known to his majesty, his "heirs and successors, all treasons and trai-"torous conspiracies, which may be formed "against him or them: and I do faithfully "promise to maintain, support, and de-"fend, to the utmost of my power, the "succession of the crown in his majesty's "family, against any person or persons "whatsoever: hereby utterly renouncing "and abjuring any obedience, or allegiance "unto the person taking upon himself the "style and title of prince of Wales, in the "life-time of his father, and who since his "death, is said to have assumed the style "and title of king of Great Britain, by the "name of Charles the third, and to any "other person claiming or pretending a "right to the crown of these realms: and I do "swear, that I do reject and detest, as an "unchristian and impious position, that it "is lawful to murder or destroy any person "or persons whatsoever, for or under pre-"tence of their being heretics; and also "that unchristian and impious principle, "that no faith is to be kept with heretics. "I further declare, that it is no article of "my faith, and I do renounce, reject, and "abjure the opinion, that princes excom-"municated by the pope and council, or by "any authority of the see of Rome, or by "any authority whatsoever, may be depos-"ed or murdered by their subjects or any "person whatsoever: and I do declare, that "I do not believe that the pope of Rome, or "any other foreign prince, prelate, state, "or potentate, hath, or ought to have, any "temporal or civil jurisdiction, power, su-"periority, or pre-eminence, directly or "indirectly, within this realm. And I do "solemnly, in the presence of God, profess, "testify, and declare, that I do make this "declaration, and every part thereof, in "the plain and ordinary sense of the words "of the oath, without any evasion, equivoca-"tion, or mental reservation whatever, and "without any dispensation already granted "by the pope, or any authority of the see of "Rome, or any person whatever, and with-"out thinking that I am or can be acquit-"ted before God or man, or absolved of "this declaration, or any part thereof, al-"though the pope, or any other persons or "authority whatsoever, shall dispense with "or annul the same, or declare that it was "null or void."

Which oath the court of chancery, or any court of record at Westminster, the courts of great sessions within Wales, and county palatine of Chester, the courts of chancery or common pleas within the counties palatine of Lancaster and Durham, or any court of general or quarter sessions in England or Wales may administer, and they are to administer the same accordingly; of the taking and subscribing of which oaths a register shall be kept in manner prescribed by the laws requiring oaths from persons taking offices and employments. *s.* 4.

Nothing in this act shall extend to any popish bishop, priest, jesuit, or schoolmaster, who shall not have taken and subscribed the above oath in the above words, before he shall have been apprehended, or any prosecution commenced against him. *s.* 5.

By 29 *Geo.* 3, *c.* 36, every deed and will made since the 29th of September 1717, to pass any hereditaments from any person professing the popish religion, though not enrolled, shall be good, provided the same be enrolled on or before the 1st of December 1789, in such manner as by the 3 *Geo.* 1, *c.* 18, is directed. *s.* 1.

Nothing herein shall make good any such deed, will, or lease, of the want of enrolment whereof advantage shall have been taken, on or before 1st January 1789. *s.* 2.

No purchase made for full consideration of any hereditaments, by any protestant for the benefit of protestants, shall be impeached by reason that any deed or will through which the title thereto is derived hath not been enrolled, so as no advantage was taken of [*the want of* *] enrolment thereof before such purchase was made, and so as no decree or judgment hath been obtained for want of the enrolment of such deeds or wills. *s.* 3.

Nothing herein shall make good any grant, lease, or mortgage of the advowson, or right of presentation to any benefice, prebend, or ecclesiastical living, school, hospital, or donative, or any avoidance thereof, made by any papist in trust for any papist, whether such trust hath been declared in writing or not. *s.* 4.

PAR, is a term in exchange of money, and is defined to be a certain number of pieces of the coin of one country, containing in them an equal quantity of silver to that of another number of pieces of the coin of some other country. *Lock's Cons. of Money*, 18.

PARACIUM, the tenure that is between parceners, *viz.* that which the youngest oweth to the eldest. *Domesday.*

PARAGE, (*paragium*) equality of name, blood, or dignity; but more especially of land, in the partition of an inheritance between coheirs: hence to disparage, and disparagement. *Co. Lit.* 166.

PARAGIUM, the equal condition betwixt two parties, to be contracted in marriage. *Cowel.*

---

* Not in the act.

PARAMOUNT, (Fr. *per*, and *monter*, *ascendere*) the highest lord of the fee. *F.N.B.* 135. Thus the king is chief lord, or lord paramount of all the lands in the kingdom. So where there is a lord mesne, who holds of a superior under certain services, this superior lord is lord paramount. *Co. Lit.* 1.

PARAPHARNALIA, or PARAPHERNALIA, from the Greek παρὰ, *Præter*, and φερνὴ, *dos*,) are those goods which a wife challengeth over and above her dower or jointure, after her husband's death; as furniture for her chamber, wearing apparel, and jewels, which are not to be put into the inventory of her husband. A wife, after the death of her husband, may claim her *paraphernalia* or necessary apparel for her body, and cloth given her to make a garment, &c. besides her dower; so that the husband cannot give them away by will: but she shall not have excessive apparel, beyond her rank. 2 *Black.* 435. See *Marriage*.

PARASITUS, a domestic servant. *Cowel. Blount.*

PARAVAIL, (*per-availe*) the lowest tenant of the fee, or he who is immediate tenant to one who holds over of another; and he is called tenant *paravail*, because it is presumed he hath profit and avail by the land. *F. N. B.* 135. 2 *Inst.* 296. 9 *Rep. Coney's Case.* 2 *Black. Com.* 60.

PARCELLA TERRÆ, a piece or parcel of land.

PARCEL-MAKERS, two officers in the Exchequer, who make the parcels of the escheators accounts, wherein they charge them with every thing they have levied for the king's use, within the time of their being in office, and deliver the same to the auditors, to make up their accounts therewith. *Pract. Excheq.* 99.

PARCENERS, (*quasi* parcellers, i. e. *rem in parcellas dividentes*) are of two sorts, *viz.* according to the course of the common law, and according to custom.

An estate held in coparcenary is therefore, where lands of inheritance descend from the ancestor to two or more persons. It *arises* either by COMMON LAW or particular CUSTOM. By common law: as where a person seised in fee-simple or in fee-tail dies, and his next heirs are two or more females, his daughters, sisters, aunts, cousins, or their representatives; in this case they shall all inherit: and these coheirs are then called coparceners, or for brevity, parceners only (*Litt. sec.* 241, 242). Parceners by particular custom are where lands descend, as in gavelkind, to all the males in equal degree, as sons, brothers, uncles, &c. (*Ibid. s.* 265.) And, in either of these cases, all the parceners put together make but one heir; and have but one estate among them. *Co. Litt.* 163.

The properties of parceners are in some respects like those of joint-tenants; they having the same unities of interest, title, and possession. They may sue and be sued jointly for matters relating to their own lands (*Ibid.* 164): and the entry of one of them shall in some cases enure as the entry of them all (*Ibid.* 188. 243). They cannot have an action of trespass against each other, but herein they differ from joint tenants, that they are also excluded from maintaining an action of waste (2 *Inst.* 403); for coparceners could at all times put a stop to any waste by writ of partition, but till the statute of Henry the eighth joint-tenants had no such power. Parceners also differ materially from joint-tenants in four other points: 1. They always claim by descent, whereas joint-tenants always claim by purchase. Therefore if two sisters purchase lands, to hold to them and their heirs, they are not parceners, but joint-tenants (*Litt. sec.* 254), and hence it likewise follows, that no lands can be held in coparcenary, but estates of inheritance which are of a descendible nature; whereas not only estates in fee and in tail, but for life or years, may be held in joint-tenancy. 2. There is no unity of time necessary to an estate in coparcenary. For if a man hath two daughters, to whom his estate descends in coparcenary, and one dies before the other; the surviving daughter and the heir of the other, or, when both are dead, their two heirs, are still parceners (*Co. Litt.* 164. 174.); the estates vesting in each of them at different times, though it be the same quantity of interest, and held by the same title. 3. Parceners, though they have an unity have not an entirety, of interest. They are properly entitled each to the whole of a distinct moiety (*Ibid.* 163, 164.) and of course there is no *jus accrescendi*, or survivorship between them: for each part descends severally to their respective heirs, though the unity of possession continues. And as long as the lands continue in a course of descent, and united in possession, so long are the tenants therein, whether male or female, called parceners. But if the possession be once severed by partition, they are no longer parceners, but tenants in severalty; or if one parcener aliens her share, though no partition be made, then are the lands no longer held in coparcenary, but in common. *Litt. sec.* 309.

Parceners are so called, saith Littleton (*sec.* 241), because they may be constrained to make partition. And he mentions many methods of making it (*sec.* 243 to 264.), four of which are by consent, and one by compulsion. The first is, where they agree to divide the lands into equal parts in severalty, and that each shall have such a determinate part. The second is, when they agree to chuse some friend to make partition for them, and then the sisters shall choose each of them her part according to seniority of age; or otherwise, as shall be agreed. The privilege of seniority is in this case personal; for if the eldest sister be dead, her issue shall not choose first but the next sister. But, if an advowson descend in coparcenary, and the sisters cannot agree in the presentation, the eldest and her issue, nay her husband, or her assigns, shall present alone, before the younger (*Co. Litt.* 166. 3 *Rep.* 22). * And the reason given is, that the former privilege, of priority in choice upon a division, arises from an act of her own, the agreement to make partition, and therefore is merely personal; the latter of presenting to the living, arises from the act of the law, and is annexed not only to her person, but to her estate also. A third method of partition is, where the eldest divides, and then she shall choose last; for the rule of law is, *cujus est divisio, alterius est electio.* The fourth method is, where the sisters agree to cast lots for their shares. And these are the methods by consent. That by compulsion is, where one or more sue out a writ of partition against the others; whereupon the sheriff shall go to the lands, and make partition thereof by the verdict of a jury there impanneled, and assign to each of the parceners her part in severalty †.

And by stat. 8 & 9 *Wil.* 3, *c*, 31, if the high sheriff by reason of distance, &c. cannot be present at the execution of any judgment in partition, then the under sheriff, in the presence of two justices of peace of the county, shall proceed to the execution of the writ, by inquisition, and the high sheriff is to make the return, &c. *Ibid.* When the partition is made and returned, the persons who were tenants of the lands, or any part thereof, before divided, shall continue tenants of the lands they held, to the respective owners, under such conditions and rents as before: and no plea in abatement shall be admitted or received in any suit of partition; nor shall the same be abated by the death of any tenant, &c. *Ibid.*

But there are some things which are in their nature impartible: the mansion-house, common of estovers, common of piscary uncertain, or any other common without stint, shall not be divided, but the eldest sister, if she pleases, shall have them, and make the others a reasonable satisfaction in other parts of the inheritance: or if that cannot be, then they shall have the profits of the thing by turns, in the same manner as they take the advowson. *Co. Litt.* 164, 165.

There is yet another consideration attending the estate in coparcenary: that if one of the daughters has had an estate given with her in frankmarriage by her ancestor, (which was a species of estates-tail, freely given by a relation for advancement of his kinswoman in marriage,) in this case, if lands descend from the same ancestor to her and her sisters in fee-simple, she or her heirs shall have no share of them, unless they will agree to divide the lands so given in frankmarriage in equal proportion with the rest of the lands descending (*Bracton. l.* 2. *c.* 34. *Litt. sec.* 266 to 273). This mode of division was known in the law of the Lombards (*l.* 2. *t.* 14. *c.* 15); which directs the woman so preferred in marriage, and claiming her share of the inheritance, *mittere in confusum cum sororibus, quantum pater aut frater ei dederit, quando ambulaverit ad maritum.* With us it is denominated bringing those lands into *hotchpot* (*Britton. c.* 72), which term is here explained in the words of Littleton (*sec.* 267): "it seemeth that this word, "*hotchpot*, is in English a pudding; for "in a pudding is not commonly put one "thing alone, but one thing with other "things together." By this housewifely metaphor our ancestors meant to inform us (*Litt. sec.* 268) that the lands, both those given in frankmarriage and those descending in fee-simple, should be mixed and blended together, and then divided in equal portions among all the daughters. But this was left to the choice of the donee in frankmarriage: and if she did not choose to put her lands into hotchpot she was presumed to be sufficiently provided for, and the rest of the inheritance was divided among the other sisters. The law of hotchpot took place then only when the other lands descending from the ancestor were fee-simple; for if they descended in tail, the donee in frankmarriage was entitled to her share without bringing her lands so given into hotchpot (*Litt. sec.* 274). And the reason is, because lands descending in fee-simple are distributed by the policy of law, for the maintenance of all the daughters; and if one has a sufficient provision out of the same inheritance, equal to the rest, it is not reasonable that she should have more; but lands, descending in tail are not distributed by the operation of the law, but by the designation of the giver, *per formam doni*; it matters not therefore how unequal this distribution may be. Also no lands but such as are given in frankmarriage shall be brought into hotch-

* It has been doubted whether the grantee of the eldest sister shall have the first and sole presentation after her death. *Harg. Co. Litt.* 166. But it was expressly determined in favour of such a grantee in 1 *Ves.* 340.

† Another, and the most usual, mode of compulsion is by a decree of a court of equity.

pot; for no others are looked upon in law as given for the advancement of the woman, or by way of marriage-portion (*Litt.* 275). And therefore as gifts in frankmarriage are fallen into disuse, it would have been unnecessary to have mentioned the law of hotchpot, had not this method of division been revived and copied by the statute for distribution of personal estates.

The estate in coparcenary may be dissolved, either by partition, which disunites the possession; by alienation of one parcener, which disunites the title, and may disunite the interest, or by the whole at last descending to and vesting in one single person, which brings it to an estate in severalty.

PARCENARY, is the holding of lands jointly by parceners, when the common inheritance is not divided. *Lit.* 56.

PARCO FRACTO, a writ which laid against him who violently broke a pound, and took out beasts from thence, which for some trespass done, &c. were lawfully impounded (*Reg. Orig.* 166). Damages were recoverable on this writ, and the party might be punished as for a pound-breach in the court-leet. 1 *Inst.* 47. *F. N. B.* 100.

PARDON, (*pardonatio*, *venia*) is the remitting or forgiving of an offence committed against the king. *Staundf. Pl. Cor.* 47.

This high prerogative of pardoning offences is inseparably incident to the crown, and is intrusted to the king upon a special confidence, that he will spare those only whose case, could it have been foreseen, the law itself may be presumed willing to have excepted out of its general rules, which the wisdom of man cannot possibly make so perfect as to suit every particular case. 1 *Show.* 284.

Under this head it will be proper to consider, 1. The object of pardon: 2. The manner of pardoning: 3. The method of allowing a pardon: 4. The effect of such pardon when allowed.

I. *What offences may be pardoned.*] First, the king may pardon all offences merely against the crown, or the public; excepting, 1. That, to preserve the liberty of the subject, the committing any man to prison out of the realm, is by the *habeas corpus* act, 31 *Car.* 2, *c.* 2, made a *præmunire*, unpardonable even by the king. Nor, 2, can the king pardon, where private justice is principally concerned in the prosecution of offenders: "*non potest rex gratiam facere cum injuria et* "*damno aliorum*," (3 *Inst.* 236). Therefore in appeals of all kinds (which are the suit, not of the king, but of the party injured) the prosecutor may release, but the king cannot pardon (*Ibid.* 237). Neither can he pardon a common nuisance, while it remains unredressed, or so as to prevent an abatement of it; though afterwards he may remit the fine: because though the prosecution is vested in the king to avoid multiplicity of suits, yet (during its continuance) this offence savours more of the nature of a *private* injury to each individual in the neighbourhood, than of a public wrong (2 *Hawk. P. C.* 391). Neither, lastly, can the king pardon an offence against a popular or penal statute, after information brought: for thereby the informer hath acquired a private property in his part of the penalty. 3 *Inst.* 338.

There is also a restriction of a peculiar nature, that affects the prerogative of pardoning, in case of parliamentary impeachments; *viz.* that the king's pardon cannot be pleaded to any such impeachment, so as to impede the inquiry, and stop the prosecution of great and notorious offenders. Therefore, when in the reign of Cha. 2, the earl of Danby was impeached by the house of commons of high treason, and other misdemeanors, and pleaded the king's pardon in bar of the same, the commons alleged (*Com. Journ.* 28 *Apr.* 1679) "that there "was no precedent that ever any pardon "was granted to any person impeached by "the commons of high treason, or other high "crimes, depending the impeachment;" and thereupon resolved (*Com. Journ.* 5 *May*, 1679), "that the pardon so pleaded was "illegal and void, and ought not to be al- "lowed in bar of the impeachment of the "commons of England:" for which resolution they assigned (*Com. Journ.* 26 *May*, 1679) this reason to the house of lords, "that the setting up a pardon to be a bar of "an impeachment defeats the whole use "and effect of impeachments: for should "this point be admitted, or stand doubted, "it would totally discourage the exhibiting "any for the future; whereby the chief "institution for the preservation of the go- "vernment would be destroyed." Soon after the Revolution the commons renewed the same claim, and voted (*Com. Journ.* 6 *June* 1689) "that a pardon is not plead- "able in bar of an impeachment." And at length it was enacted by the Act of Settlement, 12 & 13 *Will.* 3, *c.* 2, "that no par- "don under the great seal of England shall "be pleadable to an impeachment by the "commons in parliament." But after the impeachment has been solemnly heard and determined it is not understood that the king's royal grace is further restrained or abridged: for after the impeachment and attainder of the six rebel lords in 1715, three of them were from time to time reprieved by the crown, and at length received the benefit of the king's most gracious pardon.

Also after the lords have delivered their sentence of guilty, the commons have the power of pardoning the impeached convict, by refusing to demand judgment against him, for no judgment can be pronounced by the lords till it is demanded by the commons. Lord Macclesfield was found guilty without a dissenting voice in the house of Lords; but when the question was afterwards proposed in the house of Commons 'That this house will demand judgment of the lords against Thomas earl of Macclesfield,' it occasioned a warm debate, but (the previous question being first moved) it was carried in the affirmative by a majority of 136 voices against 65. (*Com. Journ.* 27 May 1725. 6 *H. St. Tr.* 762.) In the impeachment of Warren Hastings, esq. it was decided, after much serious and learned investigation and discussion, by a very great majority in each house of parliament, that an impeachment was not abated by a dissolution of the parliament, though almost all the legal characters of each house voted in the minorities.

II. *As to the manner of pardoning.*] 1. First, it must be under the great seal. A warrant under the privy seal, or sign manual, though it may be a sufficient authority to admit the party to bail, in order to plead the king's pardon, when obtained in proper form, yet is not of itself a complete irrevocable pardon (5 *Sta. Tr.* 166. 173). 2. Next, it is a general rule that wherever it may reasonably be presumed the king is deceived, the pardon is void (2 *Hawk. P. C.* 383). Therefore any suppression of truth, or suggestion of falsehood, in a charter of pardon will vitiate the whole; for the king was misinformed (3 *Inst.* 238). 3. General words have also a very imperfect effect in pardons. A pardon of all felonies will not pardon a conviction or attainder of felony; (for it is presumed the king knew not of those proceedings,) but the conviction or attainder must be particularly mentioned, (2 *Hawk. P. C.* 383), and a pardon of felonies will not include piracy (1 *Hawk. P. C.* 99), for that is no felony punishable at the common law. 4. It is also enacted by statute 13 *Ric.* 2, *st.* 2, *c.* 1, that no pardon for treason, murder, or rape, shall be allowed, unless the offence be particularly specified therein; and particularly in murder it shall be expressed whether it was committed by lying in wait, assault, or malice prepense. Upon which sir Edward Coke observes (3 *Inst.* 236), that it was not the intention of the parliament that the king should ever pardon murder under these aggravations; and therefore they prudently laid the pardon under these restrictions, because they did not conceive it possible that the king would ever excuse an offence by name, which was attended with such high aggravations. And it is remarkable enough that there is no precedent of a pardon in the register for any other homicide than that which happens *se defendendo* or *per infortunium*, to which two species the king's pardon was expressly confined by the statutes 2 *Ed.* 3, *c.* 2, and 14 *Ed.* 3, *c.* 15, which declare that no pardon of homicide shall be granted but only where the king may do it by the oath of his crown; that is to say, where a man slayeth another in his own defence, or by misfortune. But the statute of Richard the second, before-mentioned, enlarges by implication the royal power, provided the king is not deceived in the intended object of his mercy. And therefore pardons of murder were always granted with a *non obstante* of the statute of king Richard, till the time of the revolution; when the doctrine of *non obstantes* ceasing, it was doubted whether murder could be pardoned generally: but it was determined by the court of king's bench (*Salk.* 499.) that the king may pardon on an indictment of murder, as well as a subject may discharge an appeal. Under these and a few other restrictions, it is a general rule, that a pardon shall be taken most beneficially for the subject, and most strongly against the king.

A pardon may also be conditional, that is, the king may extend his mercy upon what terms he pleases; and may annex to his bounty a condition either precedent or subsequent, on the performance whereof the validity of the pardon will depend; and this by the common law (2 *Hawk. P. C.* 394). Which prerogative is daily exerted in the pardon of felons, on condition of being confined to hard labour for a stated time, or of transportation to some foreign country for life, or for a term of years; such transportation or banishment * being allowable and warranted by the *habeas corpus* act, 31 *Car.* 2, *c.* 2, § 14, and both the imprisonment and transportation rendered more easy and effectual by statutes 8 *Geo.* 3, *c.* 15, and 19 *Geo.* 3, *c.* 74, and still further by 24 *Geo.* 3, *c.* 56, and 31 *Geo.* 3, *c.* 46.

III. *The manner of allowing pardons.*] We may observe, that a pardon by act of parliament is more beneficial than by the king's charter; for a man is not bound to plead it, but the court must *ex officio* take notice of it (*Fost.* 43.); neither can he lose the benefit of it by his own laches or negligence, as he may of the king's charter of pardon (2 *Hawk. P. C.* 397). The king's charter of pardon must be specially pleaded, and that at a proper time; for if a man is indicted, and has a pardon in his pocket, and afterwards puts himself upon his trial by pleading the general issue, he has waved the benefit of such pardon (2 *Hawk. P. C.* 396). But,

---

* Transportation is said (*Bar.* 252) to have been first inflicted as a punishment by stat. 39 *Eliz.* *c.* 4.

if a man avails himself thereof, as soon as by course of law he may, a pardon may either be pleaded upon arraignment, or in arrest of judgment, or in the present stage of proceedings, in bar of execution. Antiently, by statute 10 *Edw.* 3, *c.* 2, no pardon of felony could be allowed, unless the party found sureties for the good behaviour before the sheriff and coroners of the county (*Salk.* 499). But that statute is repealed by the statute 5 & 6 *W.* & *M.* *c.* 13, which, instead thereof gives the judges of the court a discretionary power to bind the criminal, pleading such pardon, to his good behaviour, with two sureties, for any term not exceeding seven years.

IV. *The effect of such pardon* by the king, is to make the offender a new man; to acquit him of all corporal penalties and forfeitures annexed to that offence for which he obtains his pardon; and not so much to restore his former, as to give him a new, credit and capacity. But nothing can restore or purify the blood when once corrupted, if the pardon be not allowed till after attainder, but the high and transcendant power of parliament. Yet if a person attainted receives the king's pardon, and afterwards hath a son, that son may be heir to his father, because the father being made a new man might transmit new inheritable blood; though, had he been born before the pardon, he could never have inherited at all. So a son born after the attainder may inherit, if he has no elder brother living born before the attainder, otherwise the land will escheat *pro defectu hæredis.* 1 *H. P. C.* 358.

PARDONERS, persons who carried about the pope's indulgences, and sold them to any who would buy them. *Stat.* 22 *Hen.* 8. *Cowel.*

PARENT, (*parens*) a father or mother, but generally applied to the father. *Wood's Inst.* 63.

The most universal relation in nature is that between parent and child, and consists of, 1st, The legal duties of parents to their legitimate children. 2dly, Their power over them. 3dly, The duties of such children to their parents.

I. The duties of parents consist in three particulars, 1st, their maintenance; 2dly, their protection; and, 3dly, their education.

1. The duty of parents to provide for the maintenance of their children is a principle of natural law; an obligation laid on them not only by nature herself, but by their own proper act in bringing them into the world; for they would be in the highest manner injurious to their issue if they only gave their children life that they might afterwards see them perish. By begetting them therefore they have entered into a voluntary obligation to endeavour, as far as in them lies, that the life which they have bestowed shall be supported and preserved. And thus the children will have a perfect right of receiving maintenance from their parents. *Puffendorf* 4, *c.* 11. *Montesquieu*, *b.* 23, *c.* 2.

This natural duty is enforced by our laws, it being an admitted principle of law (*Raym.* 500), that there is an obligation on every man to provide for those descended from his loins; and the manner, in which this obligation shall be performed, is pointed out by the stat. 43 *Eliz.* *c.* 2, which enacts that the father and mother, grandfather and grandmother, of poor impotent persons, shall maintain them at their own charges, if of sufficient ability, according as the quarter session shall direct. That is, they may respectively be compelled to allow each other 20*s.* a month, or 13*l.* a year; but that is the greatest allowance which a son can be obliged to make an aged parent, or a father a legitimate child, by our law.

Any two justices may make this order of allowance, which is in fact in aid of the parish to which the indigent person belongs. The relation, on whom the order is made, may appeal to the justices in sessions, who, upon evidence, and the consideration of the circumstances and ability of the party, can reduce the allowance, or discharge the order.

And if a parent runs away (*Stat.* 5 *Geo.* 1. *c.* 8), and leaves his children, the churchwardens and overseers of the parish shall seize his rents, goods, and chattels, and dispose of them toward their relief.

By the interpretations which the courts of law formerly made upon these statutes, if a mother or grandmother marries again, and was before such second marriage of sufficient ability to keep the child, the husband shall be charged to maintain it (*Styles.* 283. 2 *Bulstr.* 346): for this being a debt of hers, when single, shall like others extend to charge the husband. But it has lately been decided that the authorities here relied upon by the learned commentator never were law; and that a husband is not bound, even whilst his wife is alive, to support her parents, or her children, by a former husband, or any other relation; for the statute 43 *Eliz.* *c.* 2, extends only to relations by blood (4 *T. R.* 118.) But at her death, the relation being dissolved, the husband is under no further obligation.

But in general no person is bound to provide a maintenance for his issne, unless where the children are impotent and unable to work, either through infancy, disease, or accident; and then is only obliged to find them with necessaries, the penalty on refusal being no more than 20*s.* a month. For the policy of our laws, which are ever watchful to promote industry, did not mean to compel a father to maintain his idle and lazy children in ease and indolence: but thought it unjust to oblige the parent, against his will, to provide them with superfluities, and other indulgences of fortune; imagining they might trust to the impulse of nature, if the children were deserving of such favours. Yet, as nothing is so apt to stifle the calls of nature as religious bigotry, it is enacted (stat. 11 & 12 *W.* 3, *c.* 4), that if any popish parent shall refuse to allow his protestant child a fitting maintenance, with a view to compel him to change his religion, the lord chancellor shall by order of court constrain him to do what is just and reasonable. But this did not extend to persons of another religion, of no less bitterness and bigotry than the popish; and therefore in the very next year we find an instance of a Jew of immense riches, whose only daughter, having embraced christianity, he turned her out of doors; and on her application for relief it was held she was entitled to none, not because she was the daughter of a Jew, but because the order did not state that she was poor, or likely to become chargeable to the parish. But this gave occasion (*Com. Journ.* 18 *Feb.* 12 *Mar.* 1701) to another statute (1 *Ann. st.* 1, *c.* 30), which ordains, that if Jewish parents refuse to allow their protestant children a fitting maintenance, suitable to the fortune of the parent, the lord chancellor on complaint may make such order therein as he shall see proper.

Our law has made no provision to prevent the disinheriting of children by will, leaving every man's property in his own disposal, upon a principle of liberty in this as well as every other action; though perhaps it had not been amiss if the parent had been bound to leave them at the least a necessary subsistence. Indeed, among persons of any rank or fortune, a competence is generally provided for younger children, and the bulk of the estate settled upon the eldest by the marriage-articles. Heirs also, and children, are favourites of our courts of justice, and cannot be dis-inherited by any dubious or ambiguous words, there being required the utmost certainty of the testator's intentions to take away the right of an heir. 1 *Lev.* 130. 1 *Black.* 449.

2. From the duty of maintenance we may easily pass to that of protection, which is also a natural duty, but rather permitted than enjoined by any municipal laws: nature, in this respect, working so strongly as to need rather a check than a spur. A parent may, by our laws, maintain and uphold his children in their law-suits, without being guilty of the legal crime of maintaining quarrels (2 *Inst.* 564). A parent may also justify an assault and battery in defence of the persons of his children (1 *Hawk. P. C.* 131): nay, where a man's son was beaten by another boy, and the father went near a mile to find him, and there revenged his son's quarrel by beating the other boy, of which beating he afterwards unfortunately died, it was not held to be murder, but manslaughter merely (*Cro. Jac.* 296. 1 *Hawk. P.C.* 83). Such indulgence does the law show to the frailty of human nature, and the workings of parental affection. 1 *Black.* 450.

3. The last duty of parents to their children is that of giving them an education suitable to their station in life, a duty pointed out by reason, and of far the greatest importance of any: for, as Puffendorf very well observes (*Law of Na. b.* 6. *c.* 2, *s.* 12), it is not easy to imagine or allow that a parent has conferred any considerable benefit upon his child by bringing him into the world, if he afterwards entirely neglects his culture and education, and suffers him to grow up like a mere beast, to lead a life useless to others, and shameful to himself. Yet the municipal laws of most countries seem to be defective in this point, by not constraining the parent to bestow a proper education upon his children. Perhaps they thought it punishment enough to leave the parent, who neglects the instruction of his family, to labour under those griefs and inconveniences which his family, so uninstructed, will be sure to bring upon him. Our laws, though their defects in this particular cannot be denied, have in one instance made a wise provision for breeding up the rising generation, since the poor and laborious part of the community, when past the age of nurture, are taken out of the hands of their parents by the statutes for apprenticing poor children, and are placed out by the public in such a manner as may render their abilities, in their several stations, of the greatest advantage to the commonwealth. The rich indeed are left at their own option whether they will breed up their children to be ornaments or disgraces to their family; yet in one case, that of religion, they are under peculiar restrictions: for it is provided, (*stat.* 1 *Jac.* 1, *c.* 4, and 3 *Jac.* 1, *c.* 5,) that if any person sends any child under his government beyond the seas, either to prevent its good education in England, or in order to enter into or reside in any popish college, or to be instructed, persuaded, or strengthened in the popish religion, in such case, beside the disabilities incurred by the child so sent, the parent or person sending shall forfeit 100*l.* which (*stat.* 11 & 12 *Wil.* 3, *c.* 4) shall go to the sole use and benefit of him that shall discover the offence. And (*stat.* 3 *Car.* 1. *c.* 2) if any parent, or other, shall send or convey any person beyond sea, to enter into, or be resident in, or trained up in, any priory, abbey, nunnery, popish university, college, or school, or house of jesuits, or priests,

or in any private popish family, in order to be instructed, persuaded, or confirmed in the popish religion; or shall contribute any thing towards their maintenance when abroad by any pretext whatever, the person both sending and sent shall be disabled to sue in law or equity, or to be executor or administrator to any person, or to enjoy any legacy or deed of gift, or to bear any office in the realm, and shall forfeit all his goods and chattels, and likewise all his real estate for life. But by the 31 *Geo.* 3, *c.* 32, no person professing the Roman catholic religion, who shall take and subscribe the oath required by that statute, shall be subject to the penalties in the statutes before mentioned.

II. The power of parents over their children is derived from the former consideration, their duty: this authority being given them, partly to enable the parent more effectually to perform his duty, and partly as a recompense for his care and trouble in the faithful discharge of it. 1 *Black.* 452.

The power of a parent by our English laws is sufficient to keep the child in order and obedience. He may lawfully correct his child, being under age, in a reasonable manner (1 *Hawk. P. C.* 130), for this is for the benefit of his education. The consent of the parent to the marriage of his child under age was also directed by our ancient law to be obtained, but now is absolutely necessary, for without it the contract is void (*Stat.* 26 *Geo.* 2, *c.* 33. See *Marriage*). And this also is another means which the law has put into the parent's hands, in order the better to discharge his duty; first, of protecting his children from the snares of artful and designing persons, and next, of settling them properly in life, by preventing the ill consequences of too early and precipitate marriages. A father has no other power over his son's estate than as his trustee or guardian; for though he may receive the profits during the child's minority, yet he must account for them when he comes of age. He may indeed have the benefit of his children's labour while they live with him, and are maintained by him; but this is no more than he is entitled to from his apprentices or servants. The legal power of a father over the persons of his children ceases at the age of 21, for they are then enfranchised by arriving at years of discretion, or that point which the law has established when the empire of the father, or other guardian, gives place to the empire of reason. Yet till that age arrives this empire of the father continues even after his death; for he may by his will appoint a guardian to his children.

III. The duties of children to their parents arise from a principle of natural justice and retribution. For to those, who gave us existence, we naturally owe subjection and obedience during our minority, and honour and reverence ever after: they who protected the weakness of our infancy are entitled to our protection in the infirmity of their age; they who by sustenance and education have enabled their offspring to prosper, ought in return to be supported by that offspring in case they stand in need of assistance. Upon this principle, by our law a child is equally justifiable in defending the person, or maintaining the cause or suit of a bad parent, as a good one; and is equally compellable (*stat.* 43 *Eliz. c.* 2,) if of sufficient ability, to maintain and provide for a wicked and unnatural progenitor, as for one who has shown the greatest tenderness and parental piety. 1 *Black.* 459.

PARENTELA, or DE PARENTELA SE TOLLERE, to renounce his kindred, which was done in open court before the judge, and in the presence of twelve men, who made oath that they believed it was done lawfully, and for a just cause. *Laws of H.* 1, *cap.* 88. *Cowel.*

PARES CURIÆ, *vel* CURTIS, the jury or homage of a court-baron for the trial of their fellow tenants.

PARISH, (*parochia*) the circuit of ground in which the people who belong to one church do inhabit.

PARISH CLERK. In every parish the parson, vicar, &c. hath a parish clerk under him, who is the lowest officer of the church. There were formerly clerks in orders, and their business was at first to officiate at the altar, for which they had a competent maintenance by offerings; but now they are laymen, and have certain fees with the parson, on christenings, marriages, burials, &c. besides wages for their maintenance. *Count. Pars. Compan.* 83, 84.

They are regarded by the common law, as persons who have freeholds in their offices; and therefore though they may be punished, yet they cannot be deprived, by ecclesiastical censures (1 *Black.* 395). They are generally appointed by the minister, unless there is a custom for the parishioners or churchwardens to choose them; in which case, if such custom appears, the court of *B. R.* will grant a *mandamus* to the archdeacon to swear him in, for the establishment of the custom turns it into a temporal or civil right. *Cro. Car.* 589, 1 *Black.* 395.

PARISHIONER, (*Parochianus*) is an inhabitant of or belonging to any parish, lawfully settled therein; and those who rent lands or tenements within a parish, though not actually inhabitant or resident therein, are, for the purpose of all parochial charges and burthens, considered to be parishioners.

PARK, (Lat. *parcus*, Fr. *parque*, i. e. *locus inclusus*) is a large quantity of ground inclosed and privileged for wild beasts of chase, by the king's grant or prescription. 1 *Inst.*

233. And according to Blackstone (2 *Com.* 38,) a park is an enclosed chase, extending only over a man's own grounds. The word park indeed properly signifies an enclosure; but yet it is not every field or common, which a gentleman pleases to surround with a wall or paling, and to stock with a herd of deer, that is thereby constituted a legal park: for the king's grant, or at least immemorial prescription, is necessary to make it so. (*Co. Lit.* 233. 2 *Inst.* 199. 11 *Rep.* 86.) Though now the difference between a real park, and such inclosed grounds, is in many respects not very material: only that it is unlawful at common law for any person to kill any beasts of park or chase, except such as possess these franchises of forest, chase or park.

To a park three things are required. 1. A grant thereof. 2. Inclosures by pale, wall or hedge. 3. Beasts of a park, such as the buck, doe, &c. And where all the deer are destroyed, it shall no more be accounted a park; for a park consists of vert, venison, and inclosure, and if it is determined in any of them, it is a total disparking. *Cro. Car.* 59, 60. See *Deer, Forest, Game.*

PARK BOTE, to be quit of inclosing a park, or any part thereof. 4 *Inst.* 308.

PARLIAMENT, (*Parliamentum*, from the Fr. *Parler*, i. e. *loqui*, & *ment*, *mens*, to speak the mind, sometimes called *Commune Concilium Regni Angliæ, Magnum Concilium, &c.*)

The original or first institution of parliaments is one of those matters which lie so far hidden in the dark ages of antiquity, that the tracing of it out is a thing equally difficult and uncertain. 1 *Black. Com.* 147.

For although it seems probable that there was in the most early periods something of the nature of a parliamentary assembly, yet it does not appear how such assemblies were constituted or composed.

It seems, however, to be generally agreed, that in the main, the constitution of parliament, as it now stands, was marked out so long ago as the seventeenth year of king John, *anno Dom.* 1215, in the great charter granted by that prince; wherein he promises to summon all archbishops, bishops, abbots, earls, and greater barons personally; and all other tenants in chief under the crown, by the sheriff and bailiffs, to meet at a certain place with forty days notice, to assess aids and scutages when necessary. 1 *Black. Com.* 149.

And this constitution has subsisted in fact, at least from the year 1266, *anno* 49 *Hen.* 3. there being still extant writs of that date to summon knights, citizens, and burgesses to parliament. 1 *Black. Com.* 149. *Simeon's L. Elect.* 3.

We shall therefore, without attempting to investigate with minuteness the rise and progress of parliamentary representation, which cannot be supposed to have been so matured at the above early period as to have existed in the same perfect manner as at this day, endeavour to shew wherein consists this constitution of parliament as it now stands.

I. Of what persons the parliament consists.
II. The manner and time of its assembling.
III. Elections—
 i. The qualifications of the electors.
 ii. The qualifications of the elected.
 iii. The proceedings at elections.
IV. Method of passing bills.
V. Privilege of parliament.
VI. The continuance, adjournment, prorogation, and dissolution of the parliament.

I. *Of what persons the parliament consists.*] In all tyrannical governments the supreme magistracy, or the right of both making and of enforcing the laws, is vested in one and the same man, or one and the same body of men; and wherever these two powers are united together, there can be no public liberty. The magistrate may enact tyrannical laws, and execute them in a tyrannical manner, since he is possessed, in quality of dispenser of justice, with all the power which he as legislator thinks proper to give himself. 1 *Black. Com.* 146.

But where the legislative and executive authority are in distinct hands, the former will take care not to entrust the latter with so large a power, as may tend to the subversion of its own independence, and therewith of the liberty of the subject. 1 *Black. Com.* 146.

With us, therefore, in England, this supreme power is divided into two branches; the one legislative, to wit, the parliament, consisting of king, lords, and commons; the other executive, consisting of the king alone. 1 *Black. Com.* 146.

And it is highly necessary, for preserving the balance of the constitution, that the executive power should be a branch, though not the whole of the legislative; for the total union of them, as before observed, would be productive of tyranny; and the total disjunction of them, for the present, would in the end produce the same effects, by causing that union against which he seems to provide. 1 *Black. Com.* 154.

In that case the legislature would soon become tyrannical by making continual encroachments, and gradually assuming to itself the rights of the executive power. 1 *Black. Com.* 154.

To hinder therefore any such encroachments, the king is himself a part of the parliament; and as this is the reason of his being so, very properly therefore the share of legislation, which the constitution has placed in the crown, consists in the power of rejecting, rather than resolving; this being sufficient to answer the end proposed: the crown has therefore not any power of doing wrong, but merely of preventing wrong from being done. 1 *Black. Com.* 154.

The crown cannot begin of itself any alterations in the present established law; but it may approve or disapprove of the alterations suggested and consented to by the two houses. The legislative thereof cannot abridge the executive power of any rights which it now has by law, without its own consent, since the law must perpetually stand as it now does, unless all the powers will agree to alter it. 1 *Black. Com.* 154.

And herein indeed consists the true excellence of the English government, that all the parts of it form a mutual check upon each other. In the legislature, the people are a check upon the nobility, and the nobility a check upon the people; by the mutual privilege of rejecting what the other has resolved: while the king is a check upon both, which preserves the executive power from encroachments. And this very executive power is again checked, and kept within due bounds by the two houses, through the privilege they have of inquiring into, impeaching, and punishing the conduct (not indeed of the king, which would destroy his constitutional independence, but which is more beneficial to the public) of his evil and pernicious counsellors. 1 *Black. Com.* 155.

Thus every branch of our civil policy supports, and is supported, regulates, and is regulated, by the rest; for the two houses naturally drawing into two directions of opposite interest, and the prerogative in another still different from them both, they mutually keep each other from exceeding their proper limits, while the whole is prevented from separation, and artificially connected together by the mixed nature of the crown, which is a part of the legislative, and the sole executive magistrate. Like three distinct powers in mechanics, they jointly impel the machine of government in a direction different from what either, acting by itself, would have done; but at the same time in a direction partaking of each, and formed out of all; a direction which constitutes the true line of the liberty and happiness of the community. 1 *Black. Com.* 155.

Of a constitution so wisely contrived, so strongly raised, and so highly finished, it is hard, saith sir William Blackstone, to speak with that praise, which is justly and severely its due; but he adds that its protection is a duty which we owe to ourselves who enjoy it; to our ancestors who transmitted it down; and to our posterity who will claim at our hands, this, the best birth-right and noblest inheritance of mankind. 4 *Black. Com.* 44.

The constituent parts of a parliament are therefore, the king, the lords of parliament, and the commons. *Co. Lit.* 109, *b.*

And the king and these estates together form the great corporation or body politic of the kingdom, of which the king is said to be *caput, principium, et finis.* 4 *Inst.* 1, 2, 3. 1 *Black. Com.* 153.

The lords of parliament (who sit together with the king in one house) are of two sorts, viz. spiritual and temporal. *Co. Lit.* 109. *b.*

The lords spiritual consist of two archbishops, and twenty-four bishops, who set in parliament by succession, in respect of their counties or baronies, parcel of their bishopricks. 4 *Inst.* 1, 45.

And when any parliament is holden, each of them is to have a writ of summons *ex debito justitiæ.* 4 *Inst.* 1.

But though these lords spiritual are in the eye of the law a distinct estate from the lords temporal, and are so distinguished in most of our acts of parliament, yet in practice they are usually blended together under the one name of the lords; they intermix in their votes, and the majority of such intermixture joins both estates; and from this want of a separate assembly, and separate negative of the prelates, some writers have argued very cogently, that the lords spiritual and temporal are now in reality only one estate, which is unquestionably true in every effectual sense, though the ancient distinction between them still nominally remains; for if a bill should pass their house there is no doubt of its validity, though every lord spiritual should vote against it; and on the other hand, it seems, according to Blackstone, that it would be equally good, if the lords temporal present were inferior to the bishops in number, and every one of those temporal lords gave his vote to reject the bill. 1 *Black. Com.* 156.

The lords temporal consist of all the peers of the realm, such as dukes, marquisses, earls, viscounts, and barons, who sit by reason of their dignities, which they hold by descent or creation: of these the number is indefinite, and may be increased at will by the power of the crown, and when any parliament is holden, each of them is to have a writ of summons *ex debito justitiæ*: there are also sixteen other peers, who, since the union of Scotland, sit by election, and represent the body of the Scots nobility. 4 *Inst.* 1. 1 *Black. Com.* 157.

The commons, which form the third estate of parliament, are chosen by force of the king's writ, which issues *ex debito justitiæ*; and they are divided into three parts, *viz.* into knights of shires or counties, citizens out of cities, and burgesses out of boroughs. *Co. Lit.* 109. b. 4 *Inst.* 1.

These compose the house of commons, and represent all the commons of England. 4 *Inst.* 1.

The number of English representatives is five hundred and thirteen, of Scots forty-five, and from Ireland one hundred, in all six hundred and fifty-eight; and every member, though chosen by one particular district, when elected and returned serves for the whole realm; for the end of his coming thither is not particular, but general; not barely to advantage his constituents, but the commonwealth; and therefore he is not bound to consult with, or take the advice of, his constituents upon any particular point, unless he himself thinks it proper or prudent to so do. 1 *Black. Com.* 159.

II. *The manner and time of its assembling.*] The parliament commences by the king's writ of summons by the advice of his privy council, agreeable to the rule established before the conquest, that all judicature proceeds from the king. 4 *Inst.* 4. 1 *Bac. Abr. tit. Court of Par.* (C)

This writ of summons issues out of chancery, at least forty days before the beginning of a parliament. 4 *Inst.* 4.

And every lord spiritual and temporal of full age, ought to have a distinct writ of summons *ex debito justitiæ*. 4 *Inst.* 1, 4.

But a first summons of a peer to parliament differs from an ordinary summons, because in the first summons he is called up by his proper christian and sirname, not having the name and title of dignity in him till he has sat; but after he has sat, the name of dignity becomes part of his name; but the writ of creation in all other things, is the same with the ordinary writ that calls him. *Co. Lit.* 16.

Also the judges of the realm, and barons of the exchequer of the coif, are summoned as assistants to, and attendants upon, the house of lords to advise and assist them when required, but not to have voices. 4 *Inst.* 4. 50. *Simeon's L. Elect.* 31.

So also are the attorney and solicitor general. 4 *Inst.* 4. *Comyns's Dig. tit. Par.* D. (18).

So also the masters in chancery were used to be summoned by writ as assistants to the house of lords, so late as in Lord Coke's time: but they now only attend of course, and have a place assigned to them in the house, and are not summoned. 4 *Inst.* 4. *Simeon's L. Elec.* 29.

And indeed the present summons of assistants by writ seems little more than a matter of form, kept alive for the sake of some official perquisite; for though writs of summons still issue to the attorney and solicitor general (on which there are fees of office amounting in all to about a guinea), no return is ever made; and yet like masters they attend the house of lords, and have places assigned to them. *Simeon's L. Elec.* 30.

A writ of summons must also be directed to every sheriff of every county in England and Wales, for the choice and election of knights, citizens, and burgesses, within each of their respective counties. 4 *Inst.* 6, 10. *Co. Lit.* 109. *b.*

So a writ of summons must issue out to the lord warden of the Cinque Ports, for the election of the barons for the same, who in law are burgesses; except for the election at Dover, where it is delivered to the constable of Dover. 4 *Inst.* 6. *Simeon's L. El.* 117, 118.

In the counties palatine, the writ issues to the chamberlain, his lieutenant or deputy, who makes his precept to the sheriff; and in that of Durham, it issues to the bishop or his chancellor, who in like manner makes his precept to the sheriff. 34 & 35 *H.* 8. *c.* 13. 25 *Car.* 2. *c.* 9. *Simeon's L. El.* 117.

These writs are original writs, and therefore cannot be enlarged, restrained, or varied, in any material point, but by act of parliament. 3 *Inst.* 10. *Simeon's L. El.* 21.

At the return of the writ, the parliament cannot begin but by the royal presence of the king, either in person or by representation; by representation two ways; either by a guardian of England, by letters patent under the great seal when the king is out of the realm; or by commission under the great seal of England, to certain lords of parliament, representing the person of the king, he being within the realm, in respect of some infirmity. 4 *Inst.* 6.

But if the king pleases that the parliament shall not begin at the day of the return of the writ of summons, a writ patent under the great seal tested before the day of the return, and directed to the lords spiritual and temporal, and knights, citizens, and burgesses, shall be read at the day of the return in the upper house before the lords, and other commons there assembled, whereby the parliament shall be prorogued to another day; and in such case the parliament does not begin till the day to which it is prorogued. 4 *Inst.* 7.

And every lord spiritual and temporal, and every knight, citizen, and burgess, shall upon summons come to the parliament, except he can reasonably and honestly excuse himself; or he shall be amerced, that is, respectively a lord by the lords, and one of the commons by the commons. 5 *Ric.* 2. *st.* 2. *c.* 4. 4 *Inst.* 43.

Also for departing without licence the lords may fine one of their body; and so of the house of commons. 4 *Inst.* 44.

III. *Elections.*] In a free state where the territories are small, and its citizens easily known, a part of the legislative power may be exercised by the people in their aggregate or collective capacity; but this will be highly inconvenient, when the public territory is extended to any considerable degree, and the number of citizens increased. It is therefore very wisely contrived in so large a state as ours, that the people should do that by their representatives, which it is impracticable to perform in person. 1 *Black. Com.* 158, 159.

But as it is of the utmost importance to regulate by whom, and in what manner the suffrages are to be given, the laws have very strictly guarded against the usurpation or abuse of this power, by many salutary provisions. 1 *Black. Com.* 170.

These, according to the order observed by Blackstone and other writers, may be reduced to these three points:—

i. The qualifications of the electors.

ii. The qualifications of the elected.

iii. The proceedings at elections.

i. *The qualifications of the electors.*] The qualifications of the electors may be considered, First, as they regard electors in general; Secondly, as they regard electors of knights of the shire in particular; Thirdly, as they regard electors of citizens and burgesses in particular.

First; *as to the qualifications of electors in general.*] No peer hath a right to vote at elections. *Comyn's Dig. tit. Peers Par.* (D. 10.)

And there is a resolution of the house of commons, that it is a high infringement of the liberties and privileges of the commons of Great Britain for any lord of parliament, or any lord lieutenant of a county, to concern themselves in the elections of members to serve for the commons in parliament. *Simeon's L. El.* 158.

Women, ideots, and madmen, are absolutely disqualified from the exercise of this privilege. *Simeon, L. El.* 50.

And no persons shall be admitted to vote under the age of twenty-one years. 7 & 8 *Will.* 3. *c.* 25. *s.* 8.

Aliens also can have no vote. *Simeon's L. El.* 50.

But denizens, from the time of denization, and naturalized persons, acquire this right, being then king's subjects, and, after their adoption, supposed as much interested in the choice of representatives, by whom their lives and property are to be bound, as the natives themselves. *Simeon's L. El.* 50.

No person convicted of wilful and corrupt perjury, or subornation of perjury, shall be capable of voting in any election of a member to serve in parliament. 2 *Geo.* 2. *c.* 24. *s.* 6.

No person who shall refuse to take the oaths of allegiance and supremacy, or abjuration, or in case he be a quaker, who shall refuse to take the declaration of fidelity, and affirm the effect of the oath of abjuration, the same being tendered by the sheriff or returning officer, who is to administer the same at the request of any candidate, shall be capable of voting at any election of any knight, citizen, burgess or baron. 7 & 8 *Will.* 3. *c.* 27. *s.* 19.

And by 22 *Geo.* 3. *c.* 41, no commissioner, collector, supervisor, gauger, or other officer or person whatsoever, concerned or employed in the excise, or any part thereof; nor any commissioner, collector, comptroller, searcher, or other officer or person whatsoever, concerned or employed in the customs, or any part thereof; nor any commissioner, officer, or other person concerned or employed in managing any of the duties on stamps; nor any person appointed by the commissioners for distributing of stamps; nor any commissioner, officer, or other person employed in managing any of the duties on salt; nor any surveyor, collector, comptroller, inspector, officer, or other person employed in collecting, managing, or receiving the duties on windows or houses; nor any postmaster, postmasters general, or their deputies, or any person employed under them in the revenue of the post-office, or any part thereof; nor any captain, master, or mate of any ship, packet, or other vessel, employed by the postmaster general in conveying the mail to and from foreign ports, shall be capable of giving his vote for the election of any knight of the shire, commissioner, citizen, burgess, or baron, to serve in parliament; and if any person, hereby made incapable of voting, shall nevertheless presume to give his vote, during the time he shall hold, or within twelve months after he shall cease to hold or execute any of the offices aforesaid, contrary to this act, such votes shall be void; and every person so offending shall forfeit 100*l.* one moiety to the informer, and the other to be immediately paid into the hands of the treasurer of the county, to be disposed of to such purposes as the next general quarter session shall think fit; to be recovered by any person that shall sue in any court of record at Westminster. *s.* 1.

But nothing in this act shall extend to any commissioner of the land tax, or officer acting under the appointment of such commissioners, for the purpose of assessing, collecting, or managing the land-tax; nor to any office held by letters patent for any estate of inheritance or freehold. *s.* 2, 3.

And no person shall be liable to any forfeiture, unless prosecution be commenced within twelve months. *s.* 5.

And no collector, supervisor, gauger, or other person employed in the collecting or managing the duties of excise; nor any commissioner, or collector, or other persons employed in collecting or managing the customs; nor the postmaster-general or his deputies, or any person employed under him in the revenue of the post-office, shall, by word, message, or writing, or in any other manner, endeavour to persuade any elector to give, or dissuade any elector from giving his vote, for the choice of any knight, citizen, burgess, or baron to serve in parliament, and every person offending therein shall forfeit 100*l.* one moiety to the informer, the other moiety to the poor of the parish, to be recovered by any person that shall sue for the same in any court at Westminster;

and every person convicted on any such suit, shall become disabled of bearing any office relative to the said duties or any other place under the king. 5 & 6 *Will. & Mar.* c. 20. s. 48. 12 & 13 *Will.* 3. c. 10. s. 91. 9 *Ann.* c. 10. s. 44.

Secondly; *as to the qualifications of electors of knights of the shire in particular.*] The first statute that requires a qualification of landed property is 8 *Hen.* 6, c. 7, and thereby every elector of a knight of the shire shall have land or tenement to the value of 40*s.* by the year at least above reprizes, and the sheriff shall have power to examine upon oath every such chooser how much he may expend by the year.

And by 10 *Hen.* 6. c. 2, the said 40*s.* a year shall be freehold.

Also by 18 *Geo.* 2. c. 18, no person shall vote in any such election, without having a freehold estate in the county for which he votes, of the yearly value of 40*s.* over and above all rents and charges, payable out of the same. *s.* 5.

But no public or parliamentary tax, county, church, or parish rate, or any other tax to be assessed upon any county or division, shall be deemed any charge, payable out of any freehold estate, within the meaning of this act. *s.* 6.

And as certain persons who held their estate by copy of court roll, pretended, notwithstanding the above acts, that they had a right to vote, it is expressly enacted by 31 *Geo.* 2. c. 14, that no person who holds his estate by copy of court roll, shall be intitled thereby to vote at the election of any knight of a shire; and if he do, such vote shall be void; and every person so voting shall forfeit to any candidate, for whom such vote shall not have been given, and who shall first sue for the same, 50*l.* to be recovered, with costs, by action, to be brought within nine months in any court of record at Westminster, wherein the proof shall lie on the defendant. *s.* 1, 3.

But according to *Comyns*, if a man has a freehold in ancient demesne, he may elect. *Comyn's Dig. tit. Par.* (D. 10.)

And although it is laid down generally by lord *Coke* that freeholders in ancient demesne have no right to vote, yet Mr. *Simeon* says, that the practice for a great many years, seems to have been agreeable to what is laid down by *Comyns*; and he observes, that *Blackstone*, in his accurate and learned treatise upon the right of copyholders to vote, does not exclude freeholders in ancient demesne from the exercise of that franchise; and the above act of parliament, which was framed on his doctrine, declares the incapacity in those only who hold their estates by copy of court roll; but he very justly adds, that the difficulty of these cases arises from the nice discrimination between customary freeholds, which are not held by copy of court roll, and estates which are so held. See *Simeon's L. El.* 82, 83.

No person shall have any vote in electing members for any trust estate, or mortgage, unless such trustee, or mortgagee, be in actual possession or receipt of the rents; but the mortgagor or *cestui que trust* in possession may vote for the estate. 7 & 8 *Will.* 3. c. 25. s. 7.

And all conveyances of any hereditaments, in order to multiply votes, or to split the interest in any houses or lands among several persons, to enable them to vote at elections of members, are declared to be void, and no more than one voice shall be admitted for one and the same house or tenement. 7 & 8 *Will.* 3. c. 25. s. 7.

But the fraudulent erection of freeholds, for the purpose of giving votes, having increased, notwithstanding the last mentioned act, the legislature was again obliged to interpose, and it was accordingly enacted by 10 *Ann.* c. 23, that all conveyances to qualify persons for voting, shall be against those who executed the same, free and absolute, and discharged of all trusts, conditions, and other defeasances; and all bonds, covenants, or other securities for the defeating or recovering the same shall be void. *s.* 1.

And every person who shall make such conveyance, or being privy to such purposes, shall prepare the same, and every person, who by colour thereof shall give any vote, at any election of knights of a shire, shall forfeit 40*l.* to any one who shall sue for the same, to be recovered with costs in any court at Westminster. 10 *Ann.* c. 23. s. 1.

And no person shall vote for a knight of the shire, without having been in the actual possession of the estate for which he votes, or in the receipt of the rents and profits thereof for his own use above twelve calendar months, unless the same came to him within the time aforesaid, by descent, marriage, marriage settlement, devise, or promotion to any benefice in a church, or by promotion to any office, on pain, if he vote contrary hereto, to forfeit to any candidate, for whom such vote shall not have been given, 40*l.* to be recovered, with costs by action of debt in any court at Westminster, within nine calendar months, and the proof shall lie on the defendant. 18 *Geo.* 2. c. 18. s. 5, 14.

Also no person shall vote more than once at the same election, under the like penalty, except that in this case the proof is not on the defendant. 18 *Geo.* 2. c. 18. s. 5, 14.

By 20 *Geo.* 3. c. 17, no person shall vote for electing of any knight of the shire to serve in parliament within England or Wales, (or for any member to serve in parliament for the borough of Cricklade in Wilts. 22 *Geo.* 3. c. 21.) in respect of any messuages, lands, or tenements, which have not for six months next before such election been charged towards a land tax (in case such aid be then granted), "in the name of the "person who shall claim to vote at such "election, or in the name of his tenant "actually occupying the same as tenant" of the owner thereof. *s.* 1.

But this act, with respect to such rating and assessing, shall not extend to annuities or fee farm rents (duly registered) issuing out of any premises, rated as aforesaid; nor shall the same extend to any person who became entitled by descent, marriage, marriage settlement, devise, or promotion to any benefice in a church, or by promotion to an office, within twelve months next before such election; but such person shall be entitled to vote, if the premises have been within two years before rated to the land tax, in the name of the person through whom such person shall derive his title; or in the name of some predecessor, within two years before such election, or in the name of the tenant actually occupying. *s.* 2.

And the commissioners of the land tax, at their meetings for appointing assessors, shall cause to be delivered to each of the assessors, a printed form of an assessment, as follows: *s.* 3.

Form of Assessment.

County of N— *to wit. For the parish of—in the said county.* } An assessment made in pursuance of an act of parliament passed in the ———— year of his Majesty's reign, for granting an aid to his Majesty by a land tax, to be raised in Great Britain, for the service of the year one thousand eight hundred and ————

Names of proprietors.	Names of occupiers.	Sums assessed.
A. B. ——	Himself ——	———
A. B. ——	C. D. ——	———
E. F. ——	C. D. ——	———
C. D. ——	G. H. ——	———
I. K. and L. M. ——	N. O. ——	———
P. Q. ——	R. S. and T. U. ——	———

Signed this ———— day of ———— 18— by us ————

A. B. }
C. D. } Assessors.

And if any person shall occupy any premises belonging to different owners, the same shall be distinctly rated in such assessments, that the proportion of the land tax to be paid by each owner may be ascertained. *s.* 3.

And the said assessors are to make their assessments according to the said form; and shall make three duplicates thereof; and shall (fourteen days before such assessment shall be delivered to the commissioners cause one of the duplicates, or a fair copy thereof, to be stuck up upon one of the doors of the church or chapel of the place for which such assessment shall be made; but in case such assessment shall be made for an extra parochial or other place, where there is no church or chapel, then such assessment shall be stuck up upon one of the doors of the church or chapel next adjoining. *s.* 3.

"But as doubts had arisen whether if "the above form was not strictly pursued, "the suffrage of the party claiming to vote "would be admissible;" it is enacted by another statute that nothing in this act of 20 *Geo.* 3. *c.* 17, shall extend to prevent any person from voting for any premises assessed, for six months next before such election, towards a land tax, in the name of the person claiming to vote, or if they have come by descent, marriage, marriage settlement, devise, or promotion to any office, within twelve months before such election, if they have been within two years before assessed to the land tax; in the name of the predecessor of such person claiming to vote, although the name of the tenant actually occupying such premises shall not be inserted in such assessment according to the above form. See 30 *Geo.* 3. *c.* 35. *s.* 1.

Neither shall the said act prevent any person from voting for any premises, assessed, for six months next before such election, in the name of a tenant actually occupying the same, although the name of the person claiming to vote, or the person through whom he derives his title, or his predecessor, shall not be inserted in the assessment, according to the said form. 30 *Geo.* 3. *c.* 35. *s.* 2.

And the said duplicates shall be delivered to the land tax commissioners, at their meeting for the receipt of assessments. 20 *Geo.* 3. *c.* 17. *s.* 4.

And if the name of any owner entitled to vote, shall not appear in such assessment, such person may appeal to the commissioners, giving notice thereof in writing to one of the assessors; and the commissioners, on cause shewn, shall amend the duplicates. 20 *Geo.* 3. *c.* 17. *s.* 3.

And any person dissatisfied, by any determination of the commissioners, may appeal to the next general quarter sessions, giving ten days notice to one of the commissioners, signing the duplicate, and also to one of the assessors; and such sessions are, upon examination upon oath, to hear and determine such appeal, and to amend such assessments where necessary; and also to award costs; and by warrant to levy the same by distress and sale, rendering the overplus, after deducting the charges. 20 *Geo.* 3. *c.* 17 *s.* 10.

And if the commissioners or sessions upon appeal, find it requisite to insert the names of any person omitted, such person shall be deemed to be rated, as effectually as if the name had been originally inserted. 20 *Geo.* 3. *c.* 17. *s.* 11.

And the commissioners are to cause one of the duplicates so amended (after sealed and signed by them, or three of them) to be returned to the assessors; and such assessors are to deliver such duplicate, so amended, within ten days of the receipt thereof, to one of the chief constables of the hundred, taking his receipt for the same; and such chief constable is to deliver such duplicate upon oath, without any alteration, at the next general quarter sessions, in open court, the first day of such sessions, to the clerk of the peace, to be by him filed amongst the records. 20 *Geo.* 3. *c.* 17. *s.* 3.

And if any assessor shall neglect to deliver such duplicate so amended, to such chief constable, or if such chief constable neglect to deliver the same to such clerk of the peace, or shall wilfully alter or deface such duplicate, he shall forfeit 5*l.* 20 *Geo.* 3. *c.* 17. *s.* 4.

And at the Michaelmas sessions in every year, the clerk of the peace or his deputy shall, before the conclusion of such sessions, examine whether the duplicates of all the assessments for the county shall have been delivered for that year; and if it shall appear that any have not been delivered, then he shall report the same to the court, and the court shall immediately impose the said fine of 5*l.* upon such chief constables; and the said clerk of the peace shall give to such chief constables immediate notice of such fine; and if the same is not immediately paid, the justices in quarter sessions shall, by order of the court, issue a warrant of distress for the recovery thereof, directed to the constable of the parish where such chief constable shall live; and such warrant shall be delivered by the clerk of the peace, to such constable, who shall levy such fine by distress and sale, rendering the overplus after deducting the charges. 20 *Geo.* 3. *c.* 17. *s.* 5.

But if such chief constable shall voluntarily make oath at such sessions, that such duplicate was not delivered by the assessor, then the said fine shall be put upon such assessor or assessors; and the justices in quarter sessions shall, by order of court, issue a warrant of distress for the recovery thereof, directed to the petty constable, or such other person as they shall think proper; and also shall, by order of court, require the chief constables, or one of them, to give notice to such assessor, that such fines have been set; and such chief constables are to serve such notices upon such assessors within fourteen days after such sessions; and if such assessors shall not deliver such duplicate, or the chief constable's receipt for the same, to the clerk of the peace, or his deputy, within ten days after being served with such notice, then the said clerk of the peace shall deliver such warrant of distress against the assessor or assessors, to the person to whom the same shall be directed, who is to levy the said fine by distress and sale, rendering the overplus after deducting the charges. 20 *Geo.* 3. *c.* 17. *s.* 6.

But if such assessor shall within ten days after such notice, produce to the clerk of the peace, or his deputy, the receipt of such chief constable for such duplicate, then such clerk of the peace shall deliver the warrants against such chief constables, or such of them who shall have signed such receipt, to the proper constable to whom the same shall be directed, that the same may be executed as aforesaid, and the warrant for levying the fine upon such assessors shall not be executed. 20 *Geo.* 3. *c.* 17. *s.* 7.

And the fines imposed upon such chief constables and assessors shall, after recovered, be paid to the treasurer of the county, to be applied as part of the county stock. 20 *Geo.* 3. *c.* 17. *s.* 8.

And whenever any assessment shall not have been made by the assessor and returned to the chief constable, and by the chief constable to the clerk of the peace, by the neglect of any person concerned therein, the justices at quarter sessions, or two justices out of sessions, may order such assessment forthwith to be made in manner aforesaid. 20 *Geo.* 3. *c.* 17. *s.* 9.

And it shall be lawful for all persons to inspect the duplicates in the hands of such clerk of the peace, or his deputy, paying for every search 1*s.*; and the clerk of the peace is, upon demand, to deliver a true copy of all such duplicates, or of such part of which a copy shall be demanded, to any person who shall demand the same, signed by him or his deputy, for which copy he shall be paid at the rate of sixpence for every three hundred words or figures; which said duplicates, and also a true copy of them signed as aforesaid, and also the duplicate of any assessment in the possession of the commissioners of land tax, or the receiver general, or a copy of the said duplicates signed by such commissioners, and purporting the same to be a true copy, shall be admitted as legal evidence. 20 *Geo.* 3. *c.* 17. *s.* 13.

And such clerk of the peace, or his deputy, shall, upon reasonable notice, attend at every election of a knight of the shire, with the original duplicates, at the request of any candidate; such candidate paying him a satisfaction for such attendance, at the rate of two guineas per day, together with an allowance of 1*s.* 6*d.* a mile for his journey, from his place of abode, to and from the place of election. 20 *Geo.* 3. *c.* 17. *s.* 14.

And after issuing any writ or precept for such election, the clerk of the peace, or his deputy, shall attend gratis, from day to day, from nine in the forenoon to three in the afternoon in each day, at the place where the records of the county are kept, from the time of the delivery of such notice, to the day immediately preceding the day of election, for the purpose of receiving applications for the inspection of such duplicates, and for making copies of them. 20 *Geo.* 3. *c.* 17. *s.* 15.

And if any clerk of the peace, or his deputy, shall neglect or refuse to permit such duplicates to be inspected, or to deliver any copy thereof, or attend where the records are kept, or at any county election, with such duplicates, he shall forfeit 500*l.* to the party aggrieved, provided such action is brought within two months; and if no action is brought within the said time, then to any person who shall sue for the same within twelve months. 20 *Geo.* 3. *c.* 17. *s.* 16.

The said penalty to be recovered with full costs, in any court at Westminster. 20 *Geo.* 3. *c.* 17. *s.* 18.

And he shall also forfeit his office, the same to be absolutely void upon being convicted; and he shall be rendered incapable of being again appointed a clerk of the peace, or deputy, or of acting as such in any county, riding or division whatsoever. 20 *Geo.* 3. *c.* 17. *s.* 16.

And final judgment upon any verdict obtained against such clerk, or deputy, for the recovery of such forfeiture, shall be deemed a sufficient conviction, without any other prosecution whatsoever; and immediately after such judgment, the said office shall be absolutely void. 20 *Geo.* 3. *c.* 17. *s.* 17.

As some nice questions had been raised upon the husband's right of voting in right of his wife's dower before actual assignment, which in little freeholds is scarce ever done; it is also enacted by the said 20 *Geo.* 3. *c.* 17, that where any woman, the widow of a person tenant in fee or in tail, shall be entitled to dower, out of the freehold estate of which her husband died seized, and shall intermarry with a second husband, such second husband shall be entitled to vote in respect of such dower, if such dower shall be of the clear yearly value of 40*s.* although the same has not been set out by metes or bounds, if such husband shall be in the actual receipt of the profits of such dower, and the estate from whence the same issues is rated to the land tax in the name of the actual owner. *s.* 12.

The stat. 7 & 8 *Will.* 3. *c.* 25. *s.* 7, to prevent the splitting of freeholds extends to freeholders in cities and towns, counties of themselves. *Simeon's L. El.* 64.

And by 13 *Geo.* 2. *c.* 20, the provisions and penalties of the stat. 10 *Ann.* *c.* 23, against fraudulent conveyances are expressly extended to freeholders, and freeholds in cities and towns, counties of themselves.

Also by 19 *Geo.* 2. *c.* 28, no person shall vote for a member to serve for a city or town, which is a county of itself, in right of any freehold messuages, lands or tenements, of the yearly value of 40*s.* which have not been charged or assessed to the land tax twelve calendar months before such election, with an exception of persons voting in right of any rents, messuages, or seats belonging to any offices which have not been usually assessed to the land tax: and it is further provided, that the acting commissioners of the land tax for the time being, or any three or more of them, at their meetings, shall sign and seal one other duplicate of the copies of the assessment or assessments, to be delivered by them to the assessors after all appeals determined; and shall deliver, or cause the same to be delivered to the persons officiating as clerks of the peace within the districts of the said cities and towns, being counties of themselves, to be by them kept among the records of the sessions; to which all persons may resort and inspect the same, paying sixpence, and the said persons officiating as clerks of the peace, or their deputies, shall give copies of the said duplicates or any part thereof to any person who shall require the same, paying after the rate of sixpence for every three hundred words. *s.* 3.

By 3 *Geo.* 3. *c.* 24, no person shall vote for any knight of a shire, citizen, or burgess for England, in respect of any annuity or rent charge issuing out of freehold lands or tenements, unless a certificate upon oath be entered with the clerk of the peace or town clerk, twelve months before the first day of the election. *s.* 1.

And no person shall vote in respect of such annuity or rent charge which shall come by descent, marriage, marriage settlement, devise, or presentation to a benefice in church, or promotion to an office within twelve calendar months next before such election, unless a certificate upon oath, or affirmation if a quaker, shall have been entered with the clerk of the peace, town clerk or other officer as aforesaid, before the first day of such election. *s.* 2.

And the form of such certificate is directed to be as follows. *s.* 1, 2.

"I, A B, of —— am really and *bona* "*fide* seized of an annuity or rent charge, "for my own use and benefit, of the clear "yearly value of forty shillings, above all "rents and charges payable out of the "same, wholly issuing out of freehold lands, "tenements or hereditaments, belonging to "C. D. of ——— situate, lying, and being "in the parish, township, or place, or in the "parishes, townships, or places of E, in the "county of ———, without any trust, "agreement, matter, or thing to the con- "trary notwithstanding; and I, or the per- "son or persons under whom I claim, was "or were seised of the said annuity or rent "charge, before the first day of June, one "thousand seven hundred and sixty-three "[or in the case of the same coming by "descent, marriage, or the like, say, And "I became seised of the said annuity or "rent charge on the ——— day of ——— "last past by descent, (or otherwise as the "case may happen)]."

And no person shall vote in respect of any such annuity or rent charge to be granted after the said first day of June, 1763, unless a memorial of the grant shall have been registered with the clerk of the peace, town clerk, or other public officer, having the custody of the records, where the premises out of which such annuity or rent charge issues, shall be twelve calendar months at least before the first day of such election:

Which memorial shall be wrote on parchment, and directed to such clerk of the peace, town clerk, or other public officer, and shall be under the hand and seal of the grantor, and attested by two witnesses, one whereof to be one of the witnesses to the execution; which witness shall upon oath before such clerk prove the sealing and delivering of such grant, and the signing and sealing of such memorial:

Which memorial shall contain the day and year of the date, and the names, additions, and abodes of the parties and witnesses, and all the premises out of which the annuity or rent charge issues, and the place where they lie:

And such grant shall, at the time of entering such memorial, be produced to such clerk, who shall thereon indorse a certificate, in which shall be mentioned the day and year on which such memorial shall be so entered. *s.* 3.

And no person shall vote by reason of any assignment of such annuity or rent charge, without like certificate, entry, and memorial of such grant and assignment as in case of an original grant. *s.* 4.

And the clerk of the peace or other officer shall keep a book for entering such certificate and memorial, and shall be allowed for the entry of every certificate 1*s.*; and of every memorial 2 .; and for every search 1*s.* and every person may inspect the certificates, memorials, and entries; and the clerk of the peace or other officer is to give copies thereof to any persons requiring the same, and paying for such copy if it contains no more than two hundred words 6*d.* and so on in proportion. *s.* 5.

And such clerks of the peace or officers may administer an oath when required, and true copies of the certificate and memorials attested by the clerk of the peace or other officer, shall be legal evidence. *s.* 5.

But a memorial of such grant or assignment as shall be executed in any place not within forty miles of the office of the clerk of the peace or other officer aforesaid, shall be registered by him, in case an affidavit sworn, or affirmation made before one of the judges of Westminster-hall, or a master in chancery, ordinary or extraordinary, be brought with such memorial, wherein one of the witnesses to the grant shall swear that he saw the same executed. *s.* 6.

And the clerk of the peace, or other officer aforesaid, shall, upon notice, attend at any election with the book of such entries as aforesaid, at the request of any candidate, he making satisfaction for such attendance. *s.* 7.

And any clerk of the peace, or officer aforesaid, guilty of any wilful neglect, misdemeanor or fraudulent practice, contrary to this act, shall forfeit 100*l.* to the person who shall sue for the same within twelve months in any court of record at Westminster. *s.* 8, 9.

In the construction of the above act, it has been determined by a committee of the house of commons, that a person who was entitled to a salary of 20*l.* a year issuing out of the great tithes of the parish, had a right to vote, although he had not registered it as an annuity; and the same committee held unanimously, that neither reserved nor fee farm rents need be registered, as not being within the meaning of the act. *Simeon's L. El.* 67.

Thirdly; *as to the qualifications of electors of citizens and burgesses in particular.*] The right and qualification of voters in cities, towns, and boroughs, is various, depending intirely on the several charters, customs, and constitutions of the respective places, as have prevailed in them time immemorial. 1 *Black. Com.* 174.

These general rights may be ranked under three divisions: 1st. the right by tenure, which includes the burgage tenures; 2dly. right by charter, which includes all cases where the right of voting is in a body corporate; and 3dly. right popular, which last class comprehends all the other rights of voting. *Simeon's L. El.* 94.

1. It is part of the constitution of England, that burgage tenure boroughs shall elect members to serve in parliament: and such right of election is a privilege annexed to the burgage land, and is a real privilege. 6 *Mod. Rep.* 51, 52. 2 *Lord Raym.* 951.

And this real privilege cannot be lost though the tenements are destroyed, so long as the evidence of the right remains. *Simeon's L. El.* 94, 95.

2. The corporate right of election is prescribed by charters, which are mostly existing. *Simeon's L. El.* 97.

3. Under the third class of rights popular, are included every species of right not falling within the other two. The most general and largest right of this kind is that which is comprehended under the words commonalty, populacy, or potwallers, which mean much the same. *Simeon's L. El.* 100.

Respecting these rights infinite disputes have arisen, and it was enacted by 2 *Geo.* 2. *c.* 24, that all votes shall be deemed legal which should be so declared by the last determination in the house of commons, which determination concerning any city, borough, or place, was to be final to all intents and purposes. *s.* 4.

But this clause has been since repealed by the statute 28 *Geo.* 3. *c.* 52. *s.* 31, so far as it relates to any determination to be made in the house of commons, subsequent to that act, and the power of finally concluding the right by determination is now transferred to and vested in the select committees of the house of commons, for it is by that act enacted, that the report of the select committee respecting the right of election, or respecting the right of appointing the returning officer, shall be entered in the journals of the house, and notice thereof sent by the speaker to the sheriff or returning officer; a true copy of which notice shall by such officer be affixed to the doors of the county hall or town hall, or of the parish church nearest to the place where such election has usually been held; and such notice shall also be inserted, by order of the speaker, in the next London Gazette. 28 *Geo.* 3. *c.* 52. *s.* 25.

But any person may within twelve months after the day on which such report shall be made to the house, or within fourteen days after the commencement of the next session, petition the house to be admitted to oppose that right which shall have been deemed valid in the judgment of such committee. *s.* 26.

And if no such petition shall be presented within the time above limited, the judgment of such committee shall be conclusive in all subsequent elections for that place, to which the same shall relate. *s.* 27.

Alms received within a year before the election is held a disqualification at common law. *Simeon's L. El.* 88.

For this dependent situation, and want of the common necessaries of life, renders it probable that the party voting will not exercise a free choice. *Simeon's L. El.* 88.

But this, though laid down as a general position, must be confined to elections for citizens and burgesses only; as freeholders qualified within the statutes, at the time of election, claim their privilege by statute law, which has made no exception. *Simeon's L. El.* 88, 89.

So persons claiming a right to vote by a burgage tenure in their possession at the election, are not, as it should seem, disqualified by the receipt of alms within the year, unless alms-men are excepted by usage, or the last determination. *Simeon's L. El.* 89.

And the word *alms*, in this case, seems to be understood to be *parish relief*. *See Simeon's L. El.* 91.

For where there is a charitable foundation, in which the members have a permanent interest, as in the case of Chelsea and Greenwich pensioners, and the like; this does not disable them from voting, for it is their estate. *See Simeon's L. El.* 91.

Also, where the right of election is large enough to comprehend certificate persons, and there is no special usage to the contrary, such persons have a right to vote; for though they are not parishioners, they are not paupers, and may be very substantial persons. *Simeon's L. El.* 93.

By 3 *Geo.* 3. *c.* 15, (which is to be read at the time of election by the returning officer, openly, where the right of election is in the whole or in part, in freemen, immediately after the reading of the act for preventing bribery), no person claiming to vote as a freeman, at any election for any city, town, port or borough, where such voter's right is as a freeman only, shall be admitted to vote, unless he shall have been admitted to the freedom twelve months before the first day of election: and if he vote contrary hereto, he shall forfeit 100*l.* to him who shall inform, to be recovered, with costs, in any court at Westminster, within one year; and the vote given shall be void. *s.* 1, 5, 6, 7.

But nothing herein shall extend to any person entitled to freedom by birth, marriage, or servitude, nor to the cities of London or Norwich. *s.* 2. 8.

And if any mayor, or other officer of any corporation, or other person whatsoever, shall wilfully antedate, or cause to be antedated, any admission, he shall forfeit 500*l.* to him who shall inform, to be recovered as above. *s.* 3.

And the mayor, or any other officer of any corporation, having the custody of the records, shall, upon the demand of any candidate, or his agent, or two freemen, on the payment of one shilling, permit them between nine in the morning and three in the afternoon, at any time before, and within one month after the election, to inspect the books and papers wherein admissions are entered, and have copies thereof, paying a reasonable charge for writing the same; and such books and papers shall, if demanded by such candidate, be produced by such officer at the election, and be referred to in case of dispute; and if such officer shall refuse or neglect to do what is above required, he shall in every case forfeit 100*l.* to him who shall inform to be recovered as aforesaid. *s.* 4.

By 26 *Geo.* 3. *c.* 100, no person shall vote for any city or borough, as "an inhabitant "paying scot and lot, or as an inhabitant "householder, housekeeper, and pot-waller "legally settled, or as an inhabitant house-"holder, housekeeper, and potwaller, or as "an inhabitant-householder resiant, or as "an inhabitant of such city or borough," unless he shall have been actually an inhabitant paying scot and lot, &c. within such city or borough six months previous to the day of election; and if any person shall vote contrary to this act, his vote shall be void, and he shall forfeit to any person who shall sue, 20*l.* to be recovered by action of debt, at Westminster; and in such action the proof of inhabitancy shall lie upon the person against whom the same shall be brought. *s.* 1.

But nothing in this act shall extend to any person acquiring the possession of any house by descent, marriage, or marriage settlement, or promotion to any office or benefice. *s.* 1.

And it shall relate only to those persons who claim to exercise the franchise of voting as inhabitants paying scot and lot, or as inhabitants, householders, housekeepers, and potwallers legally settled, or as inhabitants, householders, housekeepers, and potwallers, or as inhabitants householders resiants, or as inhabitants within such cities or boroughs, and shall not extend to any other persons who claim to vote by any other title. *s.* 2.

II. *The qualifications of the elected.*] There are some persons who are disqualified and incapable of being elected to that trust, which is the most important, both in its nature and consequences, that can be conferred by subjects upon a fellow citizen in a free country—a voice in the legislation to lay down the rules by which the life, liberty, and the property of the subject is regulated and controuled. *Simeon's L. El.* 23.

And there are some disqualifications which are *general,* as arising from a principle acknowledge by the common law of the land, and are implied, though they are not expressed in the parliamentary writ. There are also disqualifications which are *special*; but which having been introduced, or arisen from circumstances subsequent to the formation of the parliamentary writ, have not been literally made exceptions within it. *Simeon's L. El.* 23.

Of the first kind is that disqualification, which is grounded on the supposed want of discretion or imbecility. *Simeon's L. El.* 24.

Thus infants and women are ineligible. 4 *Inst.* 47. *Simeon's L. El.* 24.

Persons deaf and dumb are said to be ineligible, and ideots and madmen seem to be clearly so; as having no judgment, and therefore incapable of executing the trust. *Simeon's L. El.* 24.

Aliens also, as being ignorant of the laws and customs of the realm, and unable or unlikely to promote the interest of the state, to which they are not naturally allied, were always ineligible. 4 *Inst.* 47. *Simeon's L. El.* 24.

So though they are made denizens, which gives them in most other respects the rights of subjects from the date of the patent of denization, yet such grant does not make them eligible to parliament. 4 *Inst.* 47. *Simeon's L. El.* 24.

Persons naturalized by act of parliament, though unfit to be trusted, yet by the fiction of naturalization, being made completely, in all respects, citizens of the state from their birth, were formerly capable of being elected. 4 *Inst.* 47. *Simeon's L. El.* 24.

But by 12 & 13 *Will.* 3. *c.* 2, no person born out of the kingdoms of England, Scotland, or Ireland, or the dominions thereunto belonging (although he be naturalized), shall be capable to be a member of either house of parliament. *s.* 3.

And by 1 *Geo.* 1. *st.* 2. *c.* 4, no person shall hereafter be naturalized, unless in the bill there be a clause or particular words inserted, to declare that such person shall not thereby be enabled to be a member of either house of parliament, nor shall any bill be received in either house of parliament, without such clause. *c.* 2.

A man attainted for treason or felony cannot be elected. 4 *Inst.* 47.

But outlawry in civil suits does not render the person outlawed ineligible. *Simeon's L. El.* 25, 26.

Peers of parliament, who compose a distinct and separate part of the constitution, are, and always were ineligible, and incapable of sitting in the house of commons. *Simeon's L. El.* 26, 27.

The judges of the King's Bench, Common Pleas, and barons of the Exchequer also, being summoned as assistants to, and attendants upon the house of lords to advise and assist them when required, and being also one of the executive parts of the constitution, are ineligible to the house of commons. 4 *Inst.* 47. *Whitel.* 70. *Simeon's L. El.* 27.

But any who have a judicial place in the duchy court, or other court, ecclesiastical or civil, are eligible. 4 *Inst.* 47.

And the master of the rolls is not considered as a judge, and therefore there is no doubt but that he is perfectly eligible. *Simeon's L. El.* 27.

It seems also certain that, at the present day, the attorney-general, and solicitor general, and also masters in chancery, are eligible. *Simeon's L. El.* 28, 29, 30.

Sheriffs of counties, and mayors and bailiffs of boroughs are not eligible in their respective jurisdictions, as being returning officers. 1 *Black. Com.* 175.

Neither is a sheriff eligible to a borough, within the county of which he is sheriff at the time of election. *Simeon's L. El.* 43.

But sheriffs of one county are eligible to be knights of another. 1 *Black. Com.* 175.

Also the sheriff of a county is eligible for a town, which is a county of itself, though lying within the district of which he is sheriff. *Simeon's L. El.* 43.

And any other under the degree of a baron may be elected knight, citizen, or burgess. 4 *Inst.* 47.

Such as a knight banneret, or the heir apparent of a peer. 4 *Inst.* 47. *Comyns's Dig tit. Par.* (D. 9.).

Also, although the eldest sons of Scots peers have been by a great number of resolutions formerly declared incapable of sitting in the house of commons, yet they are now deemed eligible, except for places in Scotland. *Simeon's L. El.* 31.

No papist shall sit in either house of parliament. 30 *Car.* 2. *st.* 2. *c.* 1.

And every person chosen, before he can take his seat as a member of the house, must take the oaths of supremacy, allegiance, and abjuration, and subscribe the declarations against popery. 30 *Car.* 2. *st.* 2. 1 *Geo.* 1. *st.* 2. *c.* 13. *s.* 1, 16, 17.

It does not appear to be clearly settled, whether prisoners in execution for debt, or persons abroad, are ineligible. *Simeon's L. El.* 31.

But ambassadors, ministers, officers in the army or navy, or others being abroad at the time of election upon national affairs, are clearly eligible. Upon a contrary doctrine, the most meritorious might be excluded from that trust, which of all others they would be most able to perform, and might best deserve. *Par. Deb.* 1620. vol. i. p. 40, 50. *Simeon's L. El.* 32.

Also persons to be elected members of the house of commons must not be of the clergy, for they are represented in convocation. 4 *Inst.* 47. 1 *Black. Com.* 175.

And it has been recently declared in positive and express terms by a modern statute, THAT no person having been ordained a priest or deacon, or being a minister of the church of Scotland, shall be capable of being elected to serve in parliament, as a member of the house of commons. *See* 41 *Geo.* 3. *sess.* 2. *c.* 63. *s.* 1.

And if any such person shall be elected, such election and return shall be void. *s.* 2.

And if any person being elected shall after his election be ordained to the office of priest, or deacon, or become a minister of the church of Scotland, then the seat of such person shall immediately become void. *s.* 2.

And if such person shall in any of the aforesaid cases presume to sit or vote he shall forfeit 500*l.* for every day to any person who shall sue for the same, in any of the courts at Westminster, within twelve calendar months. *s.* 1, 3.

And every person against whom any such penalty shall be recovered shall be from thenceforth incapable of taking, holding, or enjoying any benefice, living or promotion ecclesiastical, or any office of honour or profit under his majesty. *s.* 2.

And proof of the celebration of divine service according to the rites of the church of England or of the church of Scotland, in any church or chapel consecrated or set apart for public worship, shall be *prima facie* evidence. *s.* 4.

There is another disqualification for a limited time, as it creates an ineligibility either to a county, city, or borough during the time it lasts, which cannot be beyond the period of one parliament; that is, where a person is declared by a solemn resolution of the house of commons to be incapable of sitting as a member thereof during that parliament. *Simeon's L. El.* 35.

The exercise of this power of removing a member by a vote of the house of commons seems grounded on continued usage, which is called the law of parliament. *Ibid.*

And such a power seems naturally, and even necessarily to belong to all aggregate bodies; they cannot exist honourably, and fulfil the object of their creation without it. The use, however, of this power should be regulated by the strictest justice; for if once the violence of party is let loose upon an object, and a representative of the people is discharged of the trust conferred upon by his constituents without good cause, the representative body assumes a power of controul over the constituent body, inconsistent with the freedom of election. *Ibid.*

Any crime which renders a man infamous has been made a ground, sometimes of actual and express expulsion;—sometimes, which amounts to the same, clothed only in gentler terms, of being discharged from sitting as a member of that house. *Ibid.*

Thus bribery before, as well as since the *stat.* of king *William*, has been held a sufficient reason for expulsion; so a breach of trust in an office of the state, or corruption in that office, has been resolved a good cause; and a conviction for an obscene and blasphemous libel, followed by a judgment of the King's Bench, of fine and imprisonment, and actual execution under it, have been determined sufficient to call forth this mark of censure from the house. *Simeon's L. El.* 36.

But it seems necessary for the house to follow up its resolution of expulsion, by an actual declaration of the party expelled being incapable of sitting as a member, to make him actually ineligible. *Ibid.*

Any person already a member of parliament, after he is returned, is ineligible for any other place, unless he vacates his former seat. *Ibid.*

But persons elected before they are returned, are eligible, and frequently are elected for other places also, and they cannot make their election till fourteen days after their return. *Simeon's L. El.* 38.

It has been held also that a petitioner, depending his petition in parliament, may be chosen for another place. *Ibid.*

The acceptance of almost any public office of emolument under government, will also by various acts of parliament since the revolution, render the acceptor ineligible. *Ibid.*

For by 5 *Will. & Mar. c.* 7, no member of the house of commons shall be concerned, or any other in trust for him, in the collecting or managing any of THE DUTIES ON SALT. *s.* 57.

And by 11 & 12 *Will.* 3. *c.* 2, no member of the house of commons shall be capable of being a commissioner, or farmer of THE DUTY OF EXCISE, or a commissioner for appeals concerning the said duty, or controuling or auditing the account of the said duty, or of holding in his name, or in trust for his use, any office or employment touching the farming, collecting, or managing the said duty. *s.* 150.

Also by 12 & 13 *Will.* 3. *c.* 10, no member of the house of commons shall be capable of being a commissioner or farmer of the CUSTOMS, or of holding or enjoying in his own name, or in trust for him, any place or employment touching the farming, collecting, or managing the customs. *s.* 89.

And if any member shall enjoy or execute such place or employment, such person is declared *incapable of sitting or voting* in such parliament. *s.* 90.

Also no register or deputy register for the east or north riding of Yorkshire, or for Middlesex, shall be capable of being chosen a member of parliament. 2 & 3 *Ann. c.* 4. *s.* 22. 6 *Ann. c.* 35. *s.* 32. 7 *Ann. c.* 20. *s.* 21. 8 *Geo.* 2. *c.* 6. *s.* 37.

Also by 6 *Ann. c.* 7, no person who shall have in his own name or in trust for him, any new office or place of profit under the crown which since the 25th of October, 1705, have been created, or hereafter shall have been created,—nor any person who shall be a commissioner or sub-commissioner of prizes,—secretary or receiver of prizes,—nor any comptroller of the accompts of the army,—nor any commissioner of the transports,—nor any commissioner of the sick and wounded,—nor any agent for any regiment,—nor any commissioner for wine licences,—nor any governor or deputy governor of the plantations,—nor any commissioner of the navy employed in the out ports,—nor any person having "any pension from the "crown during pleasure, shall be capa-"ble of being elected, or of sitting or vot-"ing as a member of the house of commons." *s.* 25.

"And if any person chosen a member of "the house of commons, shall accept of any "office of profit from the crown, his elec-"tion shall be void, and a new writ shall "issue for a new election; but such person "shall be capable of being again elected." *s.* 27.

But nothing herein shall extend to any member of the house of commons, being an officer in the army or navy, who shall receive any new commission in the army or navy.

And if any person hereby disabled to sit or vote in parliament shall be returned, such election and return are declared to be void: and if any person so disabled shall sit or vote as a member, he shall forfeit 500*l.* to be recovered by such as shall sue. *s.* 29.

Also by 1 *Geo.* 1. *c.* 56, no person having "any pension from the crown for any "term of years," either in his own name, or in trust for him, shall be capable of being elected a member of any house of commons. *s.* 1.

And if any person who shall have such pension shall presume to sit or vote, he shall forfeit 20*l.* for every day in which he shall sit or vote there, to him who shall sue for the same in any of the courts at Westminster, with costs. *s.* 2.

Also by 7 *Geo.* 2. *c.* 16, no judge of the court of session, or justiciary, or baron of the court of Exchequer in Scotland, shall be capable of being elected a member of the house of commons. *s.* 4.

And by 32 *Geo.* 3. *c.* 53, no justices of the peace appointed under that act to officiate at the seven police offices thereby established in and near the metropolis shall, during their continuance in such appointment, be capable of being elected, or of sitting as members of the house of commons. *s.* 13.

Also by 15 *Geo.* 2. *c.* 22, no person who shall be a commissioner of the revenue in Ireland,—or commissioner of the navy or victualling offices,—nor any deputies or clerks in any of the said offices,—or in any of the several offices of the lord high treasurer, or the commissioners of the treasury,—or of the auditor of the receipt of his majesty's exchequer, or of the tellers of the exchequer, or of the chancellor of the exchequer, or of the lord high admiral, or the commissioners of the admiralty,—or of the paymasters of the army—or of the navy,—or of his majesty's principal secretaries of state,—or of the commissioners of the salt,—or of the stamps,—or of appeals,—or of wine licences,—or of hackney coaches,—or of hawkers and pedlars, nor any person having an office, civil or military, within the island of Minorca, or in Gibraltar, other than officers having commission in any regiment there only, shall be capable of being elected, or of sitting or voting as a member of the house of commons. *s.* 1.

And if any person thereby disabled shall be returnedas a member to serve in parliament, such election and return are hereby declared void. And if any person disabled by this act to be elected, shall presume tosit or vote as a member in the house of commons, he shall forfeit 20*l.* with costs, for every day in which he shall sit or vote in the said house, to such persons who shall sue for the same in any court at Westminster, and shall from thenceforth be incapable of taking or holding any office of honour or profit under his majesty. *s.* 2.

"But nothing in this act shall exclude the "treasurer or comptroller of the navy, the "secretaries of the treasury, the secretary "to the chancellor of the Exchequer, or se-"cretaries of the Admiralty, the under se-"cretary to any of the principal secretaries "of state, or the deputy paymaster of the "army, or any person having any office or "employment for life, or for so long as he "shall behave himself well in his office." *s.* 3.

Also by 22 *Geo.* 3. *c.* 45, any person who shall, directly or indirectly, himself, or by any person in trust for him, or for his use, or on his account, undertake, execute, hold, or enjoy, in the whole or in part, any contract, agreement, or commission, made or entered into with the commissioners of the treasury, or of the navy or victualling office, or with the master general or board of ordnance, or with any of such commissioners, or with any other person on account of the public service; or shall knowingly furnish, in pursuance of such agreement, any money to be remitted abroad, or any wares to be used in the service of the public, shall be incapable of being elected, or of sitting or voting as a member of the house of commons, during the time he shall enjoy such contract, or any share thereof, or any benefit arising from the same. *s.* 1.

And if any member shall enter into any such contract as aforesaid, his seat shall be void. *s.* 2.

And if any person hereby disabled to sit or vote shall nevertheless be returned, such election and return are void; and if any person incapable to be elected shall presume to sit or vote, he shall forfeit 500*l.* with costs for every day, to any person who shall sue within twelve months, and also from thenceforth be incapable of holding any contract, or any share thereof, or benefit from the same. *s.* 9, 11.

Also in every contract, &c. there shall be inserted an express condition, that no member of the house of commons be admitted to any share, or to any benefit therefrom; and in case any person who shall enter into the same, shall admit any member to any share thereof, or to receive any benefit thereby, he shall forfeit 500*l.* to be recovered, with costs, by any person who shall sue for the same within twelve months. *s.* 10, 11.

But nothing herein shall extend to any contract, agreement, or commission, by any incorporated trading company, nor to any company now established and consisting of more than ten persons, where it is for the general benefit of such company. *s.* 3.

By 41 *Geo.* 3. *sess.* 2. *c.* 52. [*in pursuance of the stat.* 39 & 40 *Geo.* 3. *c.* 67. *for the union of the kingdoms of Great Britain and Ireland,*] it is enacted, that from and after 20th June, 1801, all persons disabled from or incapable of being elected, or sitting and voting in the house of commons of any parliament of Great Britain, shall be disabled from being elected, or sitting and voting in the house of commons of *any parliament of the united kingdom,* for any county, stewarty, city, borough, cinque port, town, or place in Great Britain. *s.* 1.

And all persons disabled from or incapable of being elected, or sitting and voting in the house of commons of any parliament of Ireland, shall be disabled from being elected, or sitting and voting in the house of commons of *any parliament of the united kingdom,* for any county, city, borough, town, or place in Ireland. *s.* 2.

But nothing in this act shall enable persons, heretofore disabled by any act of the parliament of Great Britain, to sit or vote in the united parliament as knights, citizens, or burgesses for any county, city, borough, town or place in Ireland; nor enable persons heretofore disabled by any acts of the parliament of Ireland, to sit or vote in the said united parliament, as knights, citizens, or burgesses, for any county, stewartry, city, borough, cinque port, town, or place in Great Britain. *s.* 3.

And no person who shall by himself, or deputy, or any other in trust for him, or for his benefit, take, hold, or execute, any of the offices herein-after mentioned, in Ireland, shall be capable of being elected a member of, or of sitting or voting in any parliament of the united kingdom; viz.—No commissioners of customs, excise, or stamps, or who shall be concerned, directly or indirectly, in the farming, collecting, or managing, any of the duties, (except the commissioners of the treasury, and their secretary), nor any commissioner for determining appeals concerning the duties of customs, excise, or stamps, or for controlling or auditing the account of the said duties (except the auditor general of the exchequer): nor any commissioner of imprest accounts:—nor any agent for any regiment:—nor any person who shall, directly or indirectly, himself, or by any person whatsoever in trust for him, or for his use, or on his account, undertake, execute, hold, or enjoy, in the whole, or in part, any *contract, agreement, or commission,* under the commissioners of the treasury in Ireland, or with any other persons whomsoever, on account of the public service in Ireland; or who shall furnish, in pursuance of any such agreement, contract, or commission, any money to be remitted abroad, or any wares, or merchandize, to be used in the service of the public (except persons who shall be members of any incorporated trading company, consisting of more than ten persons, as to contracts entered into by such company in its corporate capacity:)--nor any deputies or clerks in any of the offices following; that is to say, the office of lord high treasurer, or the commissioners of the treasury (except the secretary of the treasury); or of the auditor of the receipt of the exchequer, or of the tellers of the exchequer (except the secretary of the chancellor); or of the commissioners of stamps, or of the commissioners of appeals.

And no person who shall have in his own name, or in the name of any person in trust for him or his benefit, any office or place of profit, by the nomination, or by any appointment subject to the approbation of the lord lieutenant or chief governor of Ireland, created after the act of the parliament of Ireland 33 *Geo.* 3. *c.* 41. "for securing "the freedom and the independence of the "house of commons," shall be capable of being elected, or of sitting or voting in the house of commons of any parliament of the united kingdom. *s.* 5.

And if any person hereby disabled, shall nevertheless be elected, such election or return are declared to be void; and if any person so elected, and disabled, shall presume to sit or vote, such person shall incur such pains, penalties, and forfeitures, as are inflicted by the several acts of parliament heretofore passed in Great Britain or Ireland; and if such person shall be disabled by the having, holding, or accepting of any office, in this act particularized, then such person shall forfeit 500*l.* for every day, to be recovered by such person as shall sue for the same in any court of record in any part of the united kingdom. *s.* 6.

But nothing in this act shall exclude any person having any office for life, or for so long as he shall behave himself well (except the commissioners of imprest accounts, and persons concerned in the managing, collecting, or farming of any duties). *s.* 8.

And if any person being chosen a member of the house of commons shall accept of any office of profit whatever, immediately from the crown, or by the nomination, or by any other appointment, subject to the approbation of the lord lieutenant or chief governor of Ireland, his seat shall thereupon become vacant, and a writ issued for a new election; but such person (if he is not incapacitated by any thing herein-before contained), shall be capable of being again elected. *s.* 9.

Also by 43 *Geo.* 3, *c.* 25, all the officers belonging to the excise, customs, stamps, and post-office in Ireland, are rendered incapable of voting in any election of members to serve in parliament for Ireland.

Formerly it was required that all members should be inhabitants of the places for which they were chosen; but this having been long disregarded, was at length entirely repealed by *stat.* 14 *Geo.* 3. *c.* 58. 1 *Black. Com.* 175.

Knights of the shire were also required to be actual knights, or such notable esquires and gentlemen as had estates sufficient to be knights, and by no means of the degree of yeomen. 1 *Black. Com.* 176.

But no particular rank or quality was necessary for citizens and burgesses. *Simeon's L. El.* 48.

It is, however, now enacted, by 9 *Ann.* *c.* 5, that no person shall be capable to sit or vote as a member of the house of commons for any county, city, borough, or cinque port, who shall not have an estate, freehold or copyhold, for his own life, or some greater estate in law or equity for his own benefit, in lands or hereditaments, over and above what will clear all incumbrances that may affect the same, of the respective annual value hereafter limited, viz. the annual value of 600*l.* for every knight of a shire,—and of 300*l.* for every citizen, burgess, or baron of the cinque ports; and if any person who shall be elected or returned, shall not at the time of such election and return be seised of, or entitled to, such estate, such election and return shall be void. *s.* 1.

But nothing in this act shall make the eldest son, or heir apparent of any peer, or of any person qualified to serve as knight of a shire, incapable of being elected. *s.* 2.

Nor shall this act extend to either of the universities. *s.* 3.

And no person shall be qualified within the meaning of this act, by virtue of any mortgage, whereof the equity of redemption is in any other, unless the mortgagee shall have been in possession seven years before his election. *s.* 4.

Also every person (except as aforesaid) who shall appear as a candidate, or be proposed to be elected, shall upon reasonable request (at the time of such election, or before the day prefixed in the writ of summons) by any other candidate, or by any two persons having a right to vote at such election, take an oath to the effect following:

"I, *A B*, do swear, that I truly and *bona* "*fide* have such an estate in law or equity, "to and for my own use and benefit, of or "in lands, tenements, or hereditaments "(over and above what will satisfy and clear "all incumbrances that may affect the "same), of the annual value of 600*l.* above "reprizes, as doth qualify me to be elected "and returned to serve as a member for the "county of ——— according to the

" tenor and true meaning of the act of par-
" liament in that behalf; and that my said " lands, tenements, or hereditaments, are " lying or being within the parish, township, " or precinct, of ——— or, in the several " parishes, townships, or precincts, of —— " ——— in the county of ——— or, in " the several counties of ——— (as the " case may be)."

And in case such candidate is to serve for any city, borough, or cinque port, then the oath shall relate only to the value of 300*l.* *per annum.* *s.* 5.

And the oaths aforesaid may be administered by the sheriff, or under-sheriff, or by the mayor, bailiff, or other officer, who shall take the poll, or make the return, or by any two justices of the peace; and they who shall administer the oaths, are to certify the taking thereof into the Chancery, or Queen's Bench, within three months, under the penalty of 100*l.*: one moiety to the queen, and the other to such as will sue, to be recovered with costs in any court at Westminster; and if any of the candidates shall refuse to take the oath, the election and return shall be void. *s.* 6.

But no fee shall be taken for administering such oath, or making or filing the certificate, except 1*s.* for administering the oath, and 2*s.* for making the certificate, and 2*s.* for filing the same, under the penalty of 20*l.* to be recovered as aforesaid. *s.* 7.

Also by 33 *Geo.* 2. *c.* 20, every person (except the eldest son or heir apparent of any peer, or of any person qualified to serve as knight of a shire, or the members of either of the universities, *s.* 3.) who shall be elected a member, shall, before he presumes to vote in the house of commons, or sit there during any debate, after the speaker is chosen, deliver in to the clerk of the house, at the table in the middle of the house, and whilst the house is there duly sitting, with their speaker in the chair, an account, signed by such member, containing the names of the parishes, townships, or precincts, and of the counties in which the lands or hereditaments lie, whereby he makes out his qualification, declaring the same to be of the annual value of 600*l.* above reprizes, if a knight of the shire; and of the annual value of 300*l.* above reprizes, if a citizen, burgess or baron; and shall at the same time take and subscribe the following oath: viz.

" I, *A B*, do swear, that I truly and *bona* " *fide* have such an estate in law or equity, " and of such value, to and for my own use " and benefit, of or in lands, tenements, or " hereditaments, over and above what will " satisfy and clear all incumbrances that " may affect the same, as doth qualify me " to be elected and returned to serve as a " member for the place I am returned for, " according to the tenor and true meaning " of the acts of parliament in that behalf; " and that such lands, tenements, or here- " ditaments, do lie as described in the paper " or account signed by me, and now deli- " vered to the clerk of the house of com- " mons. So help me God."

And the house of commons is to administer the said oath and subscription immediately after the party shall have taken the oaths of allegiance, supremacy, and abjuration, at the table. And the said oath and subscription shall be entered in a parchment roll, to be provided by the clerk of the house of commons; and the accounts so signed and delivered to the said clerk shall be filed and kept by him. *s.* 1.

And if any person presume to sit or vote as a member, before he has delivered in such account, and taken such oath, or shall not be qualified according to 9 *Ann.* *c.* 5, and this act; his election shall be void, and a new writ shall be issued to elect another member. *s.* 2.

Subject to the foregoing restrictions and disqualifications, every subject of the realm is eligible of common right, even against their inclination. 1 *Black. Com.* 177. *Simeon's L. El.* 49.

And after their election, they cannot renounce their return, but must serve in the trust conferred upon them, it being a trust not for their own, but for the public benefit. *Simeon's L. El.* 49.

And for the same reason it is, that the king cannot grant to a subject an exemption from serving as a representative of the people. *Simeon's L. El.* 49.

iii. *The proceedings at elections.*] It has been before shewn, that *upon the summons of a new parliament* a warrant issues signed by the king, and addressed to the lord chancellor or keeper of the great seal, directing him upon the receipt thereof, to cause such and so many writs to be made and sealed, under the great seal, as has been used and accustomed. *Simeon's L. El.* 114.

And when any new parliament shall be summoned, there shall be forty days between the *teste* and return of the writ. 7 & 8 *Wil.* 3. *c.* 25. *s.* 1.

But the issuing of the writ by the chancellor is only *upon the first summons of the parliament*; for if a vacancy happens *after the first day of sitting*, the house, whether it be actually sitting or not, at the time of such vacancy, has the sole power of ordering such writ to issue. 2 *Grey's Deb.* 6. *Simeon's L. El.* 115.

And in order the better to supply any vacancies that may happen *during a prorogation or an adjournment*, and that the full number of members may be present at its meeting, it is enacted by 24 *Geo.* 3. *c.* 26, that the speaker may issue his warrant to the clerk of the crown to make out a new writ for electing a member of the house of commons, *in the room of any member who shall die or become a peer*, either during the recess, or previous thereto, as soon as he shall receive notice by a certificate thereof, under the hands of two members; but he is to cause notice of receiving of such certificate, to be inserted in the London Gazette, the publisher whereof is to give a receipt for the same, and the speaker is not to issue his warrant until fourteen days after such insertion. *s.* 2, 3, 9.

Also nothing herein shall enable the speaker to issue such warrant, unless the return of the writ by which the member deceased or become a peer was elected, shall have been brought into the office of the clerk of the crown fifteen days before the end of the last sitting of the house; nor unless the application be made so long before their next meeting, that the writ for election may be issued before the day of such next meeting, nor in case such application be made with respect to any seat vacated by any member against whose election and return a petition was depending, at the time of prorogation or adjournment. *s.* 4.

And to prevent the inconveniences that may arise from the death of the speaker, or by his seat becoming vacant, or by his absence out of the realm, the speaker is to authorize not more than seven, nor less than three members of the house of commons to execute the powers given to him by this act; and when such number shall be reduced to less than three, a new appointment shall be made; but such persons are only to act, in the case of there being no speaker, or one that is out of the realm, and only while they are members of the house; and the said appointment is to be entered in the journals of the house, and published in the Gazette. *s.* 5, 6, 7, 8.

As the messenger of the great seal is responsible for the due delivery of the writ, any one may have *the carriage* of it to whom he chuses to entrust it. *Simeon's L. El.* 117.

But as to *the due delivery* thereof, it is expressly enacted by 7 & 8 *Wil.* 3. *c.* 25, that as well upon the calling of any new parliament, as upon a vacancy in parliament time, the writ *shall be delivered* to the proper officer to whom the execution thereof doth belong, and to no other person. *s.* 4.

And every such officer upon the receipt of the writ shall endorse thereon the day that he received the same, and forthwith make out the precept to each borough, town corporate, or place within his jurisdiction; and within three days (or if it be for the cinque ports within six days, 10 & 11 *Will.* 3. *c.* 7. *s.* 2.) after receipt of the writ deliver such precept to the proper officer of every such borough, town corporate, or place, and to no other person; and such officer upon the back of the precept shall endorse the day of the receipt thereof, in the presence of the party from whom he received such precept, and shall forthwith cause public notice to be given of the time and place of election, and shall proceed to election thereupon within eight days after his receipt of the precept, and give four days notice at least of the day appointed for the election. 7 & 8 *Wil.* 3. *c.* 25. *s.* 1.

And in a city or town being a county of itself, the sheriff, or under sheriff, or such person as he shall depute, shall forthwith on receipt of the writ, give public notice of the time and place of election, and proceed to election thereupon within eight days next after the receipt of the writ, and give three days notice thereof at least, exclusive of the day of receipt of the writ and of the day of election. 19 *Geo.* 2. *c.* 28. *s.* 7.

And he shall allow a cheque-book for every poll-book for each candidate, to be kept by their inspectors at the place of taking the poll. *s.* 6.

Upon every election of any knight of the shire, the sheriff shall, within two days after the receipt of the writ, cause proclamation to be made, at the place where the ensuing election ought by law to be holden, of a special county court to be there holden *for the purpose of such election only*, on any day, Sunday excepted, not later from the day of making such proclamation than the sixteenth day, nor sooner than the tenth day, and shall proceed in such election at such special county court in the same manner as if the said election was to be held at a county court, or an adjournment thereof, according to the laws then in being. 25 *Geo.* 3. *c.* 84. *s.* 4.

Provided that the usual county court for all other purposes, or any adjournment thereof, may be held and proceeded in by the sheriff, in the same manner, and at the same times and places as if the writ for the election of a knight of the shire had not been received. *Ibid.*

And all notices to be given of the time and place of any election for members to serve in parliament, shall be publicly given at the usual place or places within the hours of eight o'clock in the forenoon and four o'clock in the afternoon, from 25th October to 25th of March inclusive, and within the hours of eight o'clock in the forenoon, and six o'clock in the afternoon, from 25th of March to 25th October inclusive, and not otherwise: and no notice shall be valid for any purposes whatsoever, which shall not be published in manner aforesaid. 33 *Geo.* 3. *c.* 64.

And upon every election of any knight of the shire, the sheriff shall hold his county court for the election at the most public and usual place of election, and where the same has most usually been for forty years. 7 & 8 *Will.* 3. *c.* 25. *s.* 3.

And the sheriff shall not adjourn such county court to any other place without the consent of the candidates. *s.* 5.

But it shall be lawful for the sheriff of the county of Southampton, after any poll for the said county shall have closed at Winchester, and which shall always be closed within fifteen days at most, to adjourn the poll to Newport in the Isle of Wight, in case the same shall be required by one of the candidates, so that such adjourned poll shall commence within four days from the close of the poll at Winchester, and shall not continue longer than three days. 25 *Geo.* 3. *c.* 84. *s.* 16.

The writ having been delivered to the sheriff as before directed, and notice of the time and place of election given in manner aforesaid, the sheriff must by stat. 23 *Hen.* 6. *c.* 14. *s.* 2, under the penalty of 100*l.* to the king, and 100*l.* to him who will sue against him, his executors or administrators, with costs, proceed to the election of every knight of the shire betwixt the hours of eight and eleven in the forenoon, and in case the election be not determined on a view, the sheriff, if required, must take the poll.

And where a poll is demanded, the same shall commence on the day on which such demand is made, or upon the next day at farthest (unless it be Sunday, and then on the day after), and shall be duly and regularly proceeded in from day to day (Sundays excepted) until the same be finished; but so as not to continue more than fifteen days at most (Sundays excepted), and if the same shall continue for fifteen days, then to be finally closed before the hour of three in the afternoon. 25 *Geo.* 3. *c.* 84. *s.* 1.

And every returning officer, unless prevented by some unavoidable accident, shall cause the said poll to be kept open for seven hours at least in each day, between eight in the morning and eight at night. *s.* 3.

And for the better taking of the poll, the sheriff or under sheriff, with such others as shall be deputed by him, shall forthwith proceed to take the poll. 7 & 8 *Will.* 3. *c.* 25. *s.* 3.

And such sheriff or under sheriff, or such as he shall depute, shall appoint such number of clerks as he shall think fit for taking the poll in his presence. *Ibid.*

And he shall also appoint for each candidate, such one person as shall be nominated by each candidate, to be inspectors of every clerk. *Ibid.*

And in order to facilitate the poll, and to prevent confusion, it is enacted by 18 *Geo.* 2. *c.* 18, that the sheriff, or in his absence the under sheriff, or such as he shall depute, shall erect at the expence of the candidates, such number of booths or places for taking the poll, as any of the candidates shall, three days before the commencement of the poll desire, so as the same do not exceed the number of hundreds or like divisions, and not exceeding in the whole the number of fifteen; and shall affix on the most public part of each, the name of the hundred for which such booth is designed. *s.* 7.

And shall make out a list for each booth of the several towns, parishes, and hamlets, wholly or in part within such hundred; and shall upon request deliver a copy thereof to any of the candidates or their agents, taking for each copy 2*s.* and no more. *Ibid.*

And no person shall be admitted to vote for any freehold estate sworn to be at some parish or place not mentioned in the list so made out for such booth, unless such estate lie in some place not mentioned in any of the lists. *s.* 8.

And the sheriff or under sheriff, or such as he shall depute, shall also appoint a clerk or clerks at each booth to take the poll, who shall at the expence of the candidates be paid, not exceeding one guinea per day each clerk. *s.* 7.

And he shall at every such election allow a cheque book for every poll book for each candidate, to be kept by their respective inspectors, at every place where the poll shall be taken. *s.* 9.

As it is essential to the very being of parliament, that elections should be absolutely free, all undue influences upon the electors are illegal and strongly prohibited. 1 *Black. Com.* 179.

Thus it is commanded by the stat. 3 *Ed.* 1. c. 5, upon great forfeiture, that no man *by force of arms, nor by malice or menacing*, shall disturb any to make free election.

And by stat. 1 *Will.* & *Mar. sess.* 2. *c.* 2, it is declared that elections of members of parliament ought to be free.

Also by 8 *Geo.* 2. *c.* 30, on notice of an election either in counties or boroughs, the secretary at war shall send orders for the removal of all soldiers quartered in the place, to the distance of two miles, one day at least before the election, and not to return till one day after the poll is ended; but this is not to extend to the guards, nor to any castle or fortified place where a garrison is usually kept; nor to any officer or soldier having right to vote at such election.

Likewise if there be riots, it will be a good ground to avoid the election, and the principal rioters, if duly criminated, will be committed by the house. 1 *Black. Com.* 179. *Simeon's L. El.* 158.

And the lord wardens of the cinque ports having claimed, as of right, a power of nominating to each of the cinque ports of the two ancient towns and their members, one person whom they ought to elect as a baron or member of parliament; it was by 2 *Will.* & *Mar. st.* 1. c. 7, *s.* 1. expressly declared that *all such nominations are contrary to law and void.*

It has also been declared by vote of the house of commons, as has been before observed, that no lord of parliament or lord lieutenant of a county hath any right to interfere in the election of commoners.

And by the several statutes herein before noticed, if any officer of the excise, customs, stamps, or post office, presume to intermeddle in elections by persuading any voter, or dissuading him, he forfeits 100*l.* and is disabled to hold any office.

Thus, saith sir William Blackstone, are the electors of one branch of the legislature secured from any undue influence from either of the other two, and from all external violence and compulsion; but the greatest danger is that in which themselves co-operate by the infamous practice of bribery and corruption, to prevent which the following statutes have been made. 1 *Black. Com.* 179.

By 7 *Will.* 3. *c.* 4, no person to be elected to serve in parliament for any place after the *teste* of the writ of summons, or after the ordering of the writs of election upon the calling of any parliament, or after such place becomes vacant in time of parliament, shall before his election give or allow to any person having voice in such election, any money, meat, drink, entertainment or provision, or make any present, gift, reward, or entertainment, or any promise, agreement, obligation, or engagement, to give or allow any money, meat, drink, provision, present, reward or entertainments, to or for any such person in particular, or to such place in general, in order to be elected. *s.* 1.

And every person so giving, presenting, or allowing, making, promising or engaging, doing, acting, or proceeding, shall be disabled upon such election to serve in parliament for such place. *s.* 2.

And by 2 *Geo.* 2. *c.* 24, which is required to be read by the returning officer immediately after the reading of the writ; if any person who shall claim a right to vote in any election for members to serve for the commons in parliament, shall receive any money or other reward, or agree for any money, gift, office, or employment, or other reward, to give his vote, or to forbear to give his vote, in any such election; or if any person shall by any gift or reward, or by any promise or security for any gift or reward, corrupt or procure any person to give his vote, or to forbear to give his vote; the offender shall forfeit 500*l.* to be recovered with costs. *s.* 7.

And any person offending in the said cases, after judgment obtained against him in any action, or being otherwise lawfully convicted, shall be for ever disabled to vote in any election of members to serve in parliament: and shall be for ever disabled to hold or enjoy any office or franchise, as a member of any city, borough, or cinque port. *s.* 7.

Bribery however was, and still remains an offence at common law, punishable by indictment or information, and there are several instances where this mode of prosecution has been adopted. 3 *Burrow's Rep.* 1338. *Simeon's L. El.* 160.

And it has been said that the above statutory incapacities attach upon a common law conviction. *Simeon's L. El.* 160.

Undue influence being thus guarded against, the election is to be proceeded to, and to this purpose it is enacted by the said stat. 2 *Geo.* 2. *c.* 24, that every sheriff, or other returning officer, shall, immediately after reading the writ or precept for the election, take and subscribe the following oath, *viz.*

"I, *A B*, do solemnly swear, that I have "not directly or indirectly received any sum "or sums of money, office, place or employ-"ment, gratuity or reward, or any bond, "bill or note, or any promise or gratuity "whatsoever, either by myself, or any other "person to my use, or benefit, or advantage, "for making any return of the present elec-"tion of members to serve in parliament; "and that I will return such person (*or* per-"sons) as shall to the best of my judgment "appear to me to have the majority of legal "votes."

Which oath *any justice of peace* of the county, city, corporation or borough, where the election shall be made, or in his absence any three of the electors, are required to administer; and the oath shall be entered among the records of the sessions. *s.* 3.

And by 25 *Geo.* 3. *c.* 84, at every election every person whom the returning officer shall retain to act as a clerk in taking the poll, shall, before beginning to take such poll, be sworn by such returning officer "truly and "indifferently to take the poll, and to set "down the name of each voter, and his addi-"tion, and place of abode, and for whom he "shall poll; and to poll no person who is "not sworn or put to his affirmation," where by statute required, which oath, of such poll clerk, the returning officer is to administer. *s.* 7.

By 42 *Geo.* 3. *c.* 62, when a poll shall be demanded at any election for any county, city, borough, or other place in England or Wales, or for the town of Berwick-upon-Tweed, the returning officer after such poll shall be demanded, shall, at the instance and request in writing of any candidate, under his hand, immediately after such request, and before he shall proceed in taking the poll, appoint two or more persons at different places, and separate from the place where the poll shall be taken to administer all the oaths, and take the declarations and affirmations now required to be taken and made by voters, and to certify the names of the electors who shall take such oaths and make such declarations and affirmations in the manner prescribed by 34 *Geo.* 3. *c.* 73, hereinafter mentioned, and the persons appointed as aforesaid shall have full power to administer such oaths and take such declarations and affirmations. *s.* 1.

But the oath or affirmation required by 2 *Geo.* 2. *c.* 24, shall be taken or made by every freeholder, citizen, freeman, burgess or person at the poll, and immediately before he is admitted to poll at such election, in the manner prescribed by the said act, in case the same shall be demanded by either of the candidates or any two of the electors. 43 *Geo.* 3. *c.* 74.

And every person so appointed shall immediately after appointment, and before he shall act, take the following oath: 42 *Geo.* 3. *c.* 62.

" I do swear, that I will faithfully and " impartially administer the oaths, and take " the declarations and affirmations, now re- " quired by law to be taken or made by " voters at elections for members to serve " in parliament, to and from such persons " as shall lawfully apply to me in that be- " half, in order to qualify themselves to vote " at this election; and that I will, on being " thereunto requested, fairly and truly give " to every such person, or any of them, who " shall take such oaths, or make such de- " clarations or affirmations, respectively, " or any of them, before me, a certificate " thereof; and that I will not give such cer- " tificate to any person before he shall have " taken such oath or oaths, or made such " declaration or declarations, affirmation " or affirmations respectively, as shall be " mentioned in such certificate, before me " and in my presence."

Which oath the returning officer, or his deputy, is to administer. *s.* 1.

And if the number of persons so appointed shall be insufficient, the returuing officer may, at the like instance of any of the candidates, appoint a further number at any time during the poll. 34 *Geo.* 3. *c.* 73. *s.* 4.

And the returning officer shall appoint a proper place for every person so appointed, to execute his duty, to which place the electors may have free access, without interrupting the poll, and so as to enable the persons appointed to act separately, without interfering with each other; and each of the places appointed shall be open, and attended by the person appointed, during all such times as the poll shall be kept open, and continue at least eight hours in every day, between eight in the morning and eight in the evening, until the final close of the poll; and the said oaths and declarations or affirmations shall be administered to as many of the electors, being ready, and desiring to take the same, as can conveniently take the same together, not exceeding twelve at one time; and the returning officer shall find, provide, and deliver to each person so appointed, a sufficient number of printed forms of the declaration of fidelity required to be made and subscribed by quakers, one of which shall be filled up with the name of, and subscribed by, the person desiring to make and subscribe the declaration of fidelity: and the returning officer shall also find, provide, and deliver to each person so appointed, a sufficient number of printed certificates, agreeable to the form after directed, to be filled up, and delivered to each elector. *s.* 5.

And in case any of the candidates shall, three days before any election, give notice in writing to the returning officer to provide such places, then the same shall be provided, so as to be ready before the day of election; and in case there shall not be a sufficient number of fit places at the town or place where the election shall be had, then the returning officer shall cause such booths or temporary erections to be made, as shall be necessary, the expence of which booths, and of the said printed forms, and also the allowance to be made to the persons appointed to administer the said oaths, &c. for their trouble and attendance, not exceeding 1*l.* 1*s.* a-day to every of them, for each day, shall be defrayed and repaid by the candidates, in equal proportions, to be recovered by the returning officer in any court of record. *s.* 6.

And the electors may apply to the persons appointed as aforesaid before voting, who shall administer the oaths, &c. and give certificates thereof in the following form:

" A. B [*naming the person taking the oath*] " of [*naming the place of such person's abode,* " *and his addition or occupation*] has taken the " oath [*or oaths*] of [*naming the said oath or* " *oaths so administered*] before me this —— " —— day of ——."

Or if a quaker:

" *A. B.* [*naming the person subscribing or* " *affirming*] of [*naming the place of such per-* " *son's abode, and his addition or occupation*] " has made and subscribed the declaration " of fidelity, and affirmed the effect of the " oath of abjuration [*or if only one of those* " *acts has been done, then naming such one* " *act only*] before me this ———— day " of ————."

And every such voter, to whom such certificate shall be given, shall, on producing the same to the returning officer, or person taking the poll, be permitted to poll. *s.* 2.

Persons offering to vote without producing such certificate, being required to take the said oaths, shall immediately withdraw, and take the same before one of the persons appointed as aforesaid. *s.* 3.

By 2 *Geo.* 2. *c.* 24, upon every election for any member to serve for the commons in parliament, every freeholder, citizen, freeman, burgess, or person having a right to vote, shall, before he is admitted to poll, take the following oath (or being a quaker make the solemn affirmation), in case the same be demanded by either of the candidates, or any two electors, *viz.*

" I *A. B.* do swear (*or being a quaker*, do " solemnly affirm) I have not received or " had, by myself, or any person whatsoever " in trust for me, for my use and benefit, " directly or indirectly, any sum or sums of " money, office, place or employment, gift " or reward, or any promise or security " for any money, office, employment or " gift, in order to give my vote at this elec-

"tion; and that I have not been polled at "this election."

Which oath the officer taking the poll is to administer *gratis*, on pain to forfeit 50*l.* to the person that shall sue. And no person shall be admitted to poll until he has taken the oath, if demanded, before the returning officer, or others legally deputed by him. *s.* 1.

And if any sheriff, or other returning officer, shall admit any person to be polled without such oaths, if demanded, he shall forfeit 100*l.* with costs; and if any person shall vote without having first taken the oath, if demanded, he shall incur the same penalty. *s.* 2.

Also by 18 *Geo.* 2. *c.* 18, upon every election of any knight of the shire to serve in parliament, every freeholder, before he is admitted to poll, shall, if required by any of the candidates, or any person having a right to vote, first take the oath (or being a quaker the affirmation) following, *viz.*

"You shall swear *(or being a quaker*, solemnly affirm) that you are a freeholder "in the county of ———— and have a "freehold estate consisting of——(*specifying* "*the nature thereof; and if it consists in mes-* "*suages, lands or tythes, in whose occupation* "*the same are; and if in rent, the names of* "*the owners or possessors of the tenements out* "*of which such rent is issuing, or of some of* "*them)*, lying or being at ———— in the "county of ———— of the clear yearly "value of forty shillings, over and above all "rents and charges payable out of, or in "respect of the same; and that you have "been in the actual possession or receipt "of the rents and profits thereof, for your "own use, above twelve calendar months, "or that the same came to you, within the "time aforesaid, by descent, marriage, "marriage settlement, devise, or promo- "tion to a benefice in a church, or by promo- "tion to an office; and that such freehold "estate has not been granted or made, to "you fraudulently, on purpose to qualify "you to give your vote; and that the place "of your abode is at ———— in———— "and that you are twenty-one years of age, "as you believe, and that you have not "been polled before at this election."

Which oath (or affirmation) the sheriff, under sheriff, or such sworn clerk as shall be by him appointed for taking the poll, is to administer. And in case any person taking the said oath or affirmation, shall thereby commit wilful perjury, and be convicted; and if any person do corruptly procure or suborn any person to take the said oath or affirmation in order to be polled, whereby he shall commit such wilful perjury, and shall be convicted; they for every such offence shall incur such penalties as are inflicted by 5 *Eliz. c.* 9. & 2 *Geo.* 2. *c.* 25, on persons guilty of perjury. *s.* 1.

And the sheriffs and clerks shall enter not only the place of his freehold, but also the place of his abode, as he shall declare the same at the time of giving his vote; and shall enter *jurat* against the name of every such voter who hath taken the oath. 10 *Ann. c.* 23. *s.* 5.

And the above act of 10 *Geo.* 2. is extended by stat. 19 *Geo.* 2. *c.* 28, *to cities and towns that are counties of themselves*, where every person has a right to vote in respect of any freehold estate of 40*s.* a year.

And although from the various and disputed rights of voting in several cities, boroughs and other places, a positive oath of qualification cannot be required from the electors, yet as unqualified persons may be deterred from polling at such elections, under fictitious names or otherwise, by requiring from electors previously to their polling the oath or affirmation hereinafter mentioned: IT IS ENACTED by 25 *Geo.* 3. *c.* 84, that upon every election of members of parliament, in all cases where no oath or affirmation of qualification, other than those against bribery, or of allegiance, supremacy and abjuration, can now by law be required, every person claiming to give his vote at such election, shall, if required by any candidate, or any person having a right to vote, before he is admitted to poll, take the oath, or being a quaker affirm as follows:

"I do swear [*or being a quaker* do affirm] "that my name is *A.B.* and that I am [*spe-* "*cifying the addition, profession or trade*] and "that the place of my abode is at ———— "in the county of ———— [*and if it is* "*a town consisting of more streets than one*, "*specifying what street*], and that I have not "before polled at this election, and that I "verily believe myself to be of the full age "of twenty-one years."

Which oath or affirmation the returning officer and his deputies, and poll clerks, are to administer. *s.* 5.

The poll being ended, and the numbers cast up, if the returning officer is perfectly satisfied without a scrutiny, he declares the election according to the majority of votes; and when the poll is once declared and acknowledged, the election is complete. *Simeon's L. El.* 132. 135.

The poll being thus taken, closed and declared, the returning officer must make his return of the persons duly chosen according to the mode prescribed by the writ, and statutes relating thereto. *Simeon's L. El.* 136.

That is to say, the returning officer in boroughs is to return his precept to the sheriff, with the persons elected by the majority: and the sheriff is to return the whole, together with the writ for the county, and the knights elected thereupon, to the clerk of the crown in Chancery. 1 *Black. Com.* 180, 181.

And to this purpose it is enacted, that the returning officer at every election for members to serve for any county, city, borough or other place, shall immediately after the final close of the poll, or on the day next after, truly, fairly, and publicly declare, the names of the persons who have the majority of votes, and shall forthwith make a return of such persons; unless the returning officer, upon a scrutiny being demanded by any candidate, or any two electors, shall deem it necessary to grant the same; in which case he shall proceed thereon, but so as that in all cases of a general election, every returning officer having the return of the writ, shall cause a return of the member to be filed in the crown office, on or before the day on which such writ is returnable. and every other returning officer acting under a precept or mandate, shall make a return of the member in obedience thereto, six days before the day of the return of the writ; and so that in case of any election upon a writ issued during a session or prorogation of parliament, and a scrutiny being granted as aforesaid, then that a return shall be made within thirty days after the close of the poll, or sooner if the same can be done. 25 *Geo.* 3. *c.* 84. *s.* 1.

And whenever a scrutiny shall be granted as aforesaid, and there shall be more parties than one; the returning officer shall decide alternately on the votes given for the different candidates who shall be parties to such scrutiny, or against whom the same shall be carried on *s.* 2.

And it shall be lawful for such returning officers, if they see cause during the continuance of any scrutiny, to administer an oath to any person *consenting to take the same,* touching the right of any person having voted at such election, or touching any other matter material towards carrying on such scrutiny. *s.* 6.

And if any person taking an oath or affirmation before any returning officer, shall commit wilful perjury, or if any person shall suborn any other person to take any such oath or affirmation, whereby he shall commit perjury, he shall incur such pains as are inflicted in 5 *Eliz. c.* 9. and 2 *Geo.* 2 *c.* 25, on persons guilty of wilful perjury. *s.* 8.

But nothing in this act shall affect, alter, or regulate the election for any place where particular regulations, touching the duration of polls and scrutinies, are enacted by statute. *s.* 9.

And by 7 & 8 *Will.* 3. *c.* 25, every sheriff, under-sheriff, mayor, bailiff, and other officer, to whom the execution of any writ or precept shall belong for electing members, shall forthwith deliver to such as shall desire the same a copy of the poll, paying a reasonable charge for writing the same, on pain to forfeit to every party grieved 500*l.* to be recovered by him or his administrators with costs. *s.* 6.

And as to the form of the return, it is enacted, that after the election, the names of the persons chosen, whether present or absent, shall be written in an indenture under the seals of the choosers, and tacked to the writ, *which indenture so sealed and tacked, shall be holden for the sheriff's return* to the said writ for the knights of the shires. 7 *Hen.* 4. *c.* 15.

And the certificate of the election is required to be the same both in county and borough elections, that is, by indentures under under the seals of the electors, and of the returning officer, who seals a counterpart thereof. *Simeon's L. El.* 137.

And in order the more particularly to enforce a regularity in the making of such return, and to prevent negligent, false, and double returns, various statutes have been enacted from time to time, and some of them at an early period. *Simeon's L. El.* 139, 140.

Thus by 5 *Ric.* 2. *st.* 2. *c.* 4, if a sheriff be negligent in making his return, or leave out of his return any city or borough bound, or of old wont to come to parliament, he shall be amerced, or otherwise punished as was accustomed in times past.

Also by 7 *Hen.* 4. *c.* 15, the sheriff is commanded, that he do certify the election made, at the day and place in the writ contained.

And by 11 *Hen.* 4. *c.* 1, justices of assize may inquire of returns made to writs of parliament, and if found by inquest that the return is contrary to the stat. 7 *Hen.* 4. *c.* 15, the sheriff shall incur 100*l.* to the king.

And by 10 & 11 *Will.* 3. *c.* 7, the sheriff or other officer having the execution and return of any writ for the choice of a member, shall on or before the day that any parliament shall be called, and with all convenient expedition, not exceeding fourteen days after election, make return of the same to the clerk of the crown in Chancery, to be filed; and he shall pay to the clerk of the crown the ancient fees of 4*s.* for every knight of the shire, and 2*s.* for every citizen, burgess, or baron of the cinque ports, and have allowance thereof in his account. *s.* 1.

And every sheriff or other officer, who shall not make the returns according to this act, shall forfeit 500*l.* one moiety to his majesty, and the other moiety to him shall sue for the same in any of his majesty's courts at Westminster. *s.* 3.

As to *false returns,* the stat. 23 *Hen.* 6. *c.* 14, "after reciting that the sheriff often "returned citizens and burgesses not duly "chosen, and sometimes such as were not "returned by the mayor or other returning "officer; and sometimes embezzled the "writ, making no precept, ENACTS," that if any sheriff shall make a return contrary to that or any other statute for elections, he shall incur the penalty of *st.* 8 *Hen.* 6. *c.* 7, viz. 100*l.* to the king, and a year's imprisonment without bail, and also pay to every person chosen and not duly returned 100*l.* to be recovered with costs in debt against the sheriff, his executors or administrators, by the party grieved, if he sue in three months after the beginning of the parliament, or in his default by any that will sue. *s.* 1.

And if any mayor or bailiff return to the sheriff any not duly chosen, he shall forfeit 40*l.* to the king, and 40*l.* to every person chosen and not returned, to be recovered as above. *Ibid.*

Moreover by stat. 7 & 8 *Will.* 3. *c.* 7, *all false returns*, wilfully made, are declared to be against law; and in case any person shall return any member to serve in parliament for any place contrary to the last determination in the house of commons of the right of election in such place, such return shall be deemed to be a false return. *s.* 1.

And every person who shall be duly elected to serve for any place, on such false return, may sue the officers and persons making or procuring the same, or any of them, and shall recover double damages with costs, on action brought within two years. *s.* 2.

And in order to prevent the evil of *double returns* it was by the same stat. 7 & 8 *Will.* 3. *c.* 7. enacted, that if any officer shall wilfully, falsely, and maliciously, return more persons than are required to be chosen by the writ or precept, the like remedy may be had against him, and the parties that willingly procure the same, by the party grieved. *s.* 3.

And it is enacted by 25 *Geo.* 3. *c.* 84, that if upon any writ issued for election of members, no return shall be made to the same on or before the day on which such writ is made returnable;—or if a writ shall have been issued during any session or prorogation, and no return shall be made to the same 52 days after the day on which such writ bears date;—or if the return made in either of such cases shall not be a return of members, according to the requisition thereof, but contain special matters only concerning such election,—it shall be lawful for any person, having a right to vote at such election, or claiming to have had a right to be returned, as duly elected thereat, who shall think himself aggrieved, to petition the house of commons concerning the same; and upon such petition being presented, a day and hour shall be appointed for taking the same into consideration, and notice thereof in writing shall be forthwith given by the speaker to the petitioners, and to the returning officer, accompanied with an order to them to attend the house at the time appointed, according to 10 *Geo.* 3. *c.* 16, and 11 *Geo.* 3. *c.* 42. for regulating the trial of controverted elections; which committee shall try "whether any, and "which of the persons named in such petition ought to have been returned, or whether a new writ ought to issue;" which determination shall be final; and the house being informed thereof by the chairman of the select committee, shall order the same to be entered on their journals, and give directions for ordering a return to be made, or for altering the return, if made, or for issuing a new writ, or for carrying the said determination into execution. *s.* 10.

And the rules, prescribed by the said acts, shall be in full force with respect to select committees appointed by virtue of this act. *s.* 11.

And if the returning officer cannot be found, to be served with the notice or order before mentioned, or being served, shall not appear by himself, counsel or agents, at the day appointed for taking such petition into consideration, the house may authorise any person to appear in the stead of him; and in case there shall be more petitions than one presented, complaining of such return, or omission of a return, on distinct interests, or different grounds, the house shall determine from the nature of the case, whether the returning officer, or person appearing in the stead of him, shall, together with such petitioners, be entitled to strike off from the list of members drawn by lot, as directed by 11 *Geo.* 3, in the case where there shall be more than two parties before the house, or whether such list shall be reduced by the parties, severally presenting the said petitions only. *s.* 12.

And if any sheriff, or other returning officer who shall preside at any election, shall wilfully act contrary to this act, such person shall be liable to be prosecuted within one year after the fact, or six months after the conclusion of any proceedings in the house of commons, by information or indictment in the King's Bench, or at any court of *oyer* and *terminer*, great sessions, or gaol delivery, in which no *noli prosequi* or *cesset processus* shall be granted. *s.* 13.

And if any sheriff or returning officer shall wilfully delay, neglect or refuse duly to return any person who ought to be returned, such person may, in case it shall be determined by a select committee, appointed as before directed, that such person was entitled to have been returned, sue the sheriff or officer, and shall recover double the damages he shall sustain, together with costs. *s.* 14.

All contracts and securities given to procure any return of any member shall be adjudged void; and whoever makes such contract or security, or any gift or reward, to procure such false or double return, shall forfeit 300*l.* one third part to his majesty, another third part to the poor of the county or place concerned, and one third part to the informer with costs, to be recovered on action brought within two years. 7 & 8 *Will.* 3. *c.* 7. *s.* 4.

By stat. 7 & 8 *Will.* 3. *c.* 25, neither the sheriff or his under-sheriff, nor the mayor, bailiff, constable, port-reeve, or other officer, of any borough or town, to whom the execution of any writ or precept for electing doth belong, shall pay or take any fee for the making out, receipt, delivery, return, or execution, of any such writ or precept, on pain to forfeit 500*l.* to the party grieved, to be recovered by him or his administrators, with costs. *s.* 2.

Lastly, by 10 *Ann. c.* 23, the sheriff, or returning officer, shall, within 20 days after such election, deliver over upon oath (which oath the two next justices of the peace, one of the *quorum*, are to administer) unto the clerk of the peace, all the poll books of such elections, without any alteration, and in such counties where there are more than one clerk of the peace, the original poll-books to one of such clerks of the peace, and attested copies thereof to the rest, to be kept among the records of the peace. *s.* 5.

IV. *Method of passing bills.*] An act of parliament must have the consent of the lords, the commons, and the royal assent of the king, and whatsoever passeth in parliament by this threefold consent, hath the force of an act of parliament. 4 *Inst.* 25. 2 *Inst.* 157.

And in each house the act of the majority binds the whole, and this majority is declared by votes openly and publicly given. 1 *Black. Com.* 181, 182.

In the house of lords, the lords give their voices from the puisne lord in due order, by the word of *content* or *not content.* 4 *Inst.* 34.

The commons give their voices upon the question by *yea* or *no*; and if it be doubtful, and neither party yield, two are appointed to number them, one for the *yea's*, another for the *no's*, the *yea's* going out and the *no's* sitting; and thereof report is made to the house: at a committee, though it be of the whole house, the *yea's* go on one side of the house, and the *no's* on the other, whereby it will easily appear which is the greatest number. 4 *Inst.* 35.

For the dispatch of business each house of parliament has its speaker. The speaker of the house of lords, whose office it is to preside there, and manage the formality of business, is the lord chancellor, or keeper of the king's great seal, or any other appointed by the king's commission; and if none be so appointed, the house of lords (it is said) may elect:—the speaker of the house of commons is chosen by the house; but must be approved by the king. And herein the usage of the two houses differs, that the speaker of the house of commons cannot give his opinion or argue any question in the house; but the speaker of the house of lords if a lord of parliament may. 1 *Black. Com.* 181.

To the passing of a bill, the assent of the knights, citizens, and burgesses must be in person, but the lords may give their votes by proxy; and the reason hereof is, that the barons did always sit in parliament in their own right, as part of the *pares curtis* of the king; and therefore as they were allowed to serve by proxy in the wars, so they had leave to make their proxies in parliament; but the commons coming only as representing the *barones minores*, and the socage tenants in the county, and citizens and burgesses, as representing the men of their cities and boroughs, they could not constitute proxies, because they themselves were but proxies and representatives of others, and therefore could not constitute a proxy in their place. 4 *Inst.* 12.

To bring a bill into the house, if the relief sought by it is of a private nature, it is first necessary to prefer a petition; which must be presented by a member, and usually sets forth the grievance desired to be remedied. This petition (when founded on facts that may be in their nature disputed) is referred to a committee of members, who examine the matter alledged, and accordingly report it to the house, and then (or otherwise upon the mere petition) leave is given to bring in the bill. In public matters the bill is brought in upon motion made to the house, without any petition at all. 1 *Black. Com.* 182. *Comyns's Dig. tit. Par.* (g. 10).

Formerly all bills were drawn in the form of petitions, which were entered upon the parliament rolls, with the king's answer thereunto subjoined; not in any settled form of words, but as the circumstances of the case required; and at the end of each parliament the judge drew them into the form of a statute, which was entered on *the statute rolls.* In the reign of Henry V. to prevent mistakes and abuses, the statutes were drawn up by the judges before the end of the parliament; and in the reign of Henry VI. bills in the form of acts, according to the modern custom, were first introduced. 2 *Black. Com.* 182.

The persons directed to bring in the bill, present it in a competent time to the house, drawn out on paper, with a multitude of blanks or void spaces, where any thing occurs that is dubious, or necessary to be settled by the parliament itself; such especially as the precise date of times, the nature and quantity of penalties, or of any sums of money to be raised; being indeed only the skeleton of the bill. 1 *Black. Com.* 182.

In the house of lords, if the bill begins there, it is, when of a private nature, referred to two of the judges, to examine and report the state of the facts alledged, to see that all necessary parties consent, and to settle all points of technical propriety. 1 *Black. Com.* 182.

This is read a first time, and at a convenient distance a second time; and after each reading the speaker opens to the house the substance of the bill, and puts the question, whether it shall proceed any farther. The introduction of the bill may be originally opposed, as the bill itself may at either of the readings; and if the opposition succeeds, the bill must be dropped for that session: as it must also, if opposed with success in any of the subsequent stages. 1 *Black. Com.* 183.

After the second meeting it is committed, that is, referred to a committee; which is either selected by the house in matters of small importance, or else, upon a bill of consequence, the house resolves itself into a committee of the whole house. 1 *Black. Com.* 183.

A committee of the whole house is composed of every member; and to form it, the speaker quits the chair (another member being appointed chairman), and may sit and debate as a private member. 1 *Black. Com.* 183.

In these committees the bill is debated clause by clause, amendments made, the blanks filled up, and sometimes the bill entirely new modelled. 1 *Black. Com.* 183.

After it has gone through the committee, the chairman reports it to the house with such amendments as the committee have made; and then the house reconsiders the whole bill again, and the question is repeatedly put upon every clause and amendment. 1 *Black. Com.* 183.

When the house hath agreed or disagreed to the amendments of the committee, and sometimes added new amendments of its own, the bill is then ordered to be engrossed, or written in a strong gross hand, on one or more long rolls of parchment sewed together. 1 *Black. Com.* 183.

When this is finished, it is read a third time, and amendments are sometimes then made to it; and if a new clause be added, it is done by tacking a separate piece of parchment on the bill, which is called a rider. 1 *Black. Com.* 183.

The speaker then again opens the contents; and holding it up in his hands, puts the question whether the bill shall pass. If this is agreed to, the title to it is then settled; which used to be a general one for all the acts passed in the session, till in the first year of Henry VIII. distinct titles were introduced for each chapter. 1 *Black. Com.* 183.

After this one of the members is directed to carry it to the lords, and desire their concurrence; who attended by several more, carries it to the bar of the house of peers, and then delivers it to their speaker, who comes down from his wool-sack to receive it. 1 *Black. Com.* 183, 184.

It there passes through the same forms as in the other house, except engrossing, which is already done; and, if rejected, no more notice is taken, but it passes *sub silentio*, to prevent unbecoming altercations. 1 *Black. Com.* 184.

But if it is agreed to, the lords send a message by two masters in Chancery (or upon matters of high dignity or importance, by two of the judges), that they have agreed to the same: and the bill remains with the lords, if they have made no amendment to it; but if any amendments are made, such amendments are sent down with the bill to receive the concurrence of the commons. 1 *Black. Com.* 184.

If the commons disagree to the amendments, a conference usually follows between members deputed from each house; who for the most part settle and adjust the difference: but if both houses remain inflexible, the bill is dropped. 1 *Black. Com.* 184.

If the commons agree to the amendments, the bill is sent back to the lords by one of the members, with a message to acquaint them therewith. 1 *Black. Com.* 184.

The same forms are observed *mutatis mutandis*, when the bill begins in the house of lords. 1 *Black. Com.* 184.

But when an act of grace or pardon is passed, it is first signed by his majesty, and then read once only in each of the houses, without any new engrossing or amendment. 1 *Black. Com.* 184.

And when both houses have done with any bill, it is always deposited in the house of peers, to wait the royal assent, except in the case of a bill of supply, which after receiving the concurrence of the lords, is sent back to the house of commons. 1 *Black. Com.* 184.

The royal assent may be given two ways; first, in person when the king comes to the house of peers, in his crown and royal robes, and sending for the commons to the bar, the titles of all the bills that have passed both houses are read; and the king's answer is declared by the clerk of the parliament in Norman French; that is to say, if the king consents to a public bill, the clerk usually declares, *le roy le veut*, "the king wills it so to "be;" if to a private bill, *soit fait, comme il est desiré*, "be it as it is desired;" if the king refuses his assent, it is in the gentle language of *le roy s' avisera*, "the king will advise upon it." When a bill of supply is passed, it is carried up and presented to the king by the speaker of the house of commons, and the royal assent is thus expressed, *le roy remercie ses loyal subjects, accepte lour benevolence, et aussi le veut*, "the king thanks his loyal subjects, accepts their benevolence, and wills it so to be." In case of an act of grace, which originally proceeds from the crown, and has the royal assent in the first stage of it, the clerk of the parliament thus pronounces the gratitude of the subject: *les prelats, seigneurs, et commons, en ce present parliament assembles, au nom de touts vous autre subjects, remercient tres humblement votre majeste, et prient a Dieu vous donner en sante bone vie et longue*, "the prelates, lords, and commons in this present parliament assembled, in the name of all your other subjects most humbly thank your majesty, and pray to God to grant you in health and wealth long to live." Secondly, by stat 33 *Hen. 8. c.* 21, the king may give his assent by letters patent under his great seal, signed with his hand, and notified in his absence to both houses assembled together in the high house; for it is by that statute declared, that the king's royal assent by his letters patent under his great seal, and signed with his hand, and notified in his absence to the lords and commons, is and ever was of as good strength, as though the king had been present, and assented publicly to the same, and shall hereafter be taken for effectual. 1 *Black. Com.* 185.

This statute or act is placed among the records of the kingdom, there needing no formal promulgation to give it the force of a law; because every man in England is, in judgment of law, party to the making of an act of parliament, being present thereat by representation. 1 *Black. Com.* 185.

However, a copy thereof is usually printed at the king's press for the information of the whole land. 1 *Black. Com.* 185.

Formerly every statute began to have effect, unless a particular time for its commencement was therein mentioned, from the first day of that session of parliament in which it was made. 1 *Rol. Abr.* 465. 4 *Inst.* 25, 27. *Hob.* 309. *Sid.* 310.

But it is now enacted by 33 *Geo.* 3. *c.* 13, that the clerk of parliament shall endorse in English, on every act immediately after the title, the day, month, and year, when the same shall have passed and received the royal assent, which indorsement shall be part of such act, and the date of its commencement, where no other commencement shall be provided.

V. *Privileges of parliament.*] The privileges of parliament are very large and indefinite, and were principally established in order to protect its members, not only from being molested by their fellow subjects, but also more especially from being oppressed by the power of the crown. 1 *Black. Com.* 163, 164.

Some of the more notorious privileges of the members of either house, are privilege of speech, of person, of their domestics, and of their lands and goods. 1 *Black. Com.* 164.

1. By 1 *Will. & Mar. sess.* 2. *c.* 2, it is declared that freedom of speech, and debates or proceedings in parliament, ought not to be impeached or questioned in any court or place out of parliament.

And this freedom of speech is particularly demanded of the king in person, by the speaker of the house of commons, at the opening of every new parliament. 1 *Black. Com.* 164.

2. By the common law, a member of parliament shall have the privilege of parliament, not only for himself and his servants, to be free from arrest, subpœna, citation, and the like; but also for his horses and goods to be free from distresses. 4 *Inst.* 24, 25.

But privilege of parliament doth not extend to high treason, felony, breach (or surety) of the peace, or any indictable offence whatsoever. 4 *Inst.* 25. 1 *Black. Com.* 166.

For all crimes are treated by the law as *against the peace;* and instances have not been wanting wherein privileged persons have been convicted of misdemeanours, and committed, or prosecuted to outlawry, even in the middle of a session, which proceeding has afterwards received the sanction and approbation of parliament. 1 *Black. Com.* 166.

Also peers of the realm, whether spiritual or temporal, are punishable by attachment for contempts against the king's court in many instances; as for rescuing a person arrested by due course of law; for proceeding in a cause against the king's writ of prohibition; for disobeying other writs, wherein the king's prerogative or the liberty of the subject are nearly concerned; such as for refusing obedience to a writ of *habeas corpus;* and for other contempts which are of an enormous nature. 2 *Hawk. c.* 22. *s.* 33. 1 *Burr. Rep.* 634.

This privilege of the person in civil causes, in a peer (by the privilege of peerage) is for ever sacred and inviolable; and in a commoner (by the privilege of parliament) for forty days after every prorogation, and for forty days before the next appointed meeting; which is now in effect as long as the parliament subsists, it seldom being prorogued for more than fourscore days at a time. 1 *Black. Com.* 165.

But by 10 *Geo.* 3. *c.* 50, any person may, *at any time,* commence and prosecute any action or suit, in any court of record, or court of equity, or of admiralty, and in all causes matrimonial and testamentary, in any court having cognizance of causes matrimonial and testamentary, against any peer or lord of parliament of Great Britain, or any of the knights, citizens, and burgesses, and the commissioners for shires and burghs of the house of commons of Great Britain, or against their menial or other servants, or any other persons entitled to the privilege of parliament of Great Britain, and no such action, suit, or other process or proceedings thereupon, shall be impeached, stayed, or delayed, under colour of any privilege of parliament.

"Provided that this shall *not* subject the "person of any of the knights, citizens, and "burgesses, or the commissioners of shires "and burghs of the house of commons of "Great Britain, to be arrested or imprisoned "upon any such suit or proceedings." *s.* 2.

And the plaintiff may prosecute at law by summons, and distress infinite, or by original bill and summons, attachment, and distress infinite, until the defendant shall enter a common appearance, or file common bail. 12 & 13 *Will.* 3. *c.* 3. *s.* 2. 11 *Geo.* 2. *c.* 24. *s.* 2.

And the court out of which the writ (*distringas*) proceeds, may order the issues levied to be sold, and the money arising thereby to be applied to pay costs to the plaintiff, and the surplus to be retained until the defendant shall have appeared, or other purpose of the writ be answered. 10 *Geo.* 3. *c.* 50. *s.* 3.

And when the purpose of the writ is answered, the said issues shall be returned:

or, if sold, what shall remain shall be repaid to the party distrained upon. *s.* 4.

But as the mode of proceeding by distringas is extremely dilatory and expensive, it is now enacted by 45 *Geo.* 3. *c.* 124, that the plaintiff upon affidavit of the personal service of the summons may enter an appearance for the defendant, and proceed as if such defendant had entered his appearance. *s.* 3.

And in equity the plaintiff may proceed by letter or subpœna; and after service thereof, may for want of appearance or answer, or non-performance of an order or decree, or for breach thereof, sequester the real and personal estate of the party, but not arrest his body. 12 & 13 *Will.* 3. *c.* 3. *s.* 2. 11 *Geo.* 2. *c.* 24. *s.* 2.

But as some persons have stood out to the return of such process of sequestration, and the same is not sufficient to enforce an appearance, it is enacted by 45 *Geo.* 3. *c.* 124, that the court upon producing the return of such sequestration may, on motion or other application of the plaintiff, appoint a clerk in court to enter an appearance for the defendant, and if after appearance, no answer shall be put in within the time allowed by the rules of the court, then the plaintiff may apply for an order that the bill may be taken *pro confesso.*

And the court shall make an order that such bill shall be taken *pro confesso*, unless the defendant within eight days shew cause to the contrary, and such bills in equity, &c. so taken *pro confesso*, shall be taken and read in evidence.

Also obedience may be enforced to any rule of the King's Bench, Common Pleas, or Exchequer, against any person entitled to privilege of parliament, by distress infinite. 10 *Geo.* 3. *c.* 50. *s.* 5.

Likewise for the benefit of commerce it is provided by 4 *Geo.* 3. *c.* 33, that the petitioning creditors, on affidavit of the debt, and that they verily believe that the debtor is a trader within the statutes of bankruptcy, may issue out a summons, or an original bill and summons, and serve him with a copy thereof; and if he shall not, within two months after service, pay the debt, or enter into bond to pay such sum as shall be recovered with costs, he shall be adjudged a bankrupt from the time of service of the summons, and the creditors may proceed against him as against other bankrupts; provided that this shall not extend to subject any person entitled to privilege to be arrested during the time of such privilege, except in cases made felony by any of the statutes of bankruptcy.

And by 45 *Geo.* 3. *c.* 124, when any summons or original bill and summons shall be sued out against any person deemed a merchant, banker, broker, factor, scrivener or trader within the description of the acts relating to bankrupts having privilege of parliament, and such affidavit of the debt duly made and filed, and such trader shall enter into such bond; every such trader shall also within two months after such personal service of such summons, cause an appearance to be entered to such action, and on default thereof, he shall be accounted a bankrupt from the time of the service of such summons, and any creditor may sue out a commission. *s.* 1.

And where any decree or order shall have been pronounced in the court of chancery or exchequer, or any order made in the matter of bankruptcy, or in the matter of any lunacy against any trader having privilege of parliament, *thereby ordering such person to pay any money*, and the person so ordered shall disobey such order, the same having been duly sued, it shall be lawful for the party to apply to the court to fix a peremptory day for the payment, and if such trader being personally served with such order, at least eight days before the day therein appointed for payment, shall neglect or omit to pay the same, then such person shall be deemed a bankrupt from the time of the service of such last mentioned order, and any creditor may sue out a commission. *s.* 7.

But nothing in this act shall extend to subject any person entitled to privilege of parliament to be arrested, restrained or imprisoned during the term of such privilege. *s.* 8.

VI. *The continuance, adjournment, prorogation, and dissolution of parliament.*] In order to prevent the great and continued expences of frequent elections, and the violent heats and animosities consequent thereupon, and for the peace and security of the government, it was enacted by 1 *Geo.* 1. *st.* 2. *c.* 38, that the then present parliament, and all parliaments that should at any time thereafter be called, assembled or held, should and might respectively have continuance for seven years and no longer, to be accounted from the day on which by the writ of summons the parliament is appointed to meet, unless sooner dissolved by his majesty, his heirs, or successors.

Thus the parliament must expire, or die a natural death at the end of every seventh year, if not sooner dissolved by the royal prerogative. 1 *Black. Com.* 189.

For, as the king has the sole right of convening the parliament, so also it is a branch of the royal prerogative, that he may (*whenever he pleases*) prorogue the parliament for a time, or put a final period to its existence. 1 *Black. Com.* 188.

A parliament may also be dissolved by the demise of the crown. This dissolution formerly happened immediately upon the death of the reigning sovereign; for he being considered in law as the head of the parliament, that falling, the whole body was held to be extinct. 1 *Black. Com.* 188.

But the calling a new parliament immediately upon the inauguration of the successor being found inconvenient, and dangers being apprehended from having no parliament in being, in case of a disputed succession, this inconvenience is now provided against by statute. 1 *Black. Com.* 188.

For it is enacted, by 37 *Geo.* 3. *c.* 127, that in case of the demise of his majesty, subsequent to the dissolution or expiration of a parliament, and before the day appointed by the writs of summons for assembling a new parliament, then the last preceding parliament shall immediately convene and sit at Westminster, and be a parliament, to continue for six months, and no longer, as if the same parliament had not been dissolved or expired, but subject to be sooner prorogued or dissolved by the person to whom the crown shall come. *s.* 3.

And in case of the demise of his majesty's heir or successor within the said six months, and before the same shall have been dissolved, or after the same shall have been dissolved, and before a new parliament shall have met, then the said last preceding parliament shall immediately convene and sit, and continue to be a parliament for six months longer, to be computed from such last demise, but subject to be sooner prorogued or dissolved by the person who shall succeed to the crown, and so often as any such demise shall happen before a new parliament shall have met. *s.* 4.

And in case of the demise of his majesty, on the day appointed by the writs of summons for assembling a new parliament, or at any time after such day, and before such new parliament shall have met, and sat, such new parliament shall, immediately after such demise, convene and sit at Westminster, and be a parliament, to continue for six months, but subject to be sooner prorogued or dissolved. *s.* 5.

An *adjournment* is no more than a continuance of the session from one day to another, as the word signifies; and this is done by the authority of each house separately every day: and sometimes for a fortnight or a month together, as at Christmas or Easter, or upon other particular occasions, but the adjournment of one house is no adjournment of the other. 1 *Black. Com.* 186.

It hath also been usual, when his majesty hath signified his pleasure that both or either of the houses should adjourn themselves to a certain day, to obey the king's pleasure so signified, and to adjourn accordingly; otherwise, besides the indecorum of a refusal, a prorogation would assuredly follow, which would often be very inconvenient to both public and private business; for *prorogation* puts an end to the session; and then such bills as are only begun and not perfected, must be resumed *de novo*, if at all, in a subsequent session; whereas, after an adjournment, all things continue in the same state as at the time of the adjournment made, and may be proceeded on without any fresh commencement. 1 *Black. Com.* 186, 187.

By 39 & 40 *Geo.* 3. *c.* 14, in all cases where both houses of parliament shall stand adjourned for more than fourteen days from the day of the date of the proclamation hereinafter mentioned, it shall be lawful for his majesty to issue his proclamation, with the advice of his privy council, thereby declaring that the said parliament shall meet on a day not less than fourteen days from the day of the date of such proclamation, and the parliament shall thereupon stand adjourned to the day and place declared in such proclamation, notwithstanding any previous adjournment to any longer day. *s.* 1.

All the orders which shall have been made by either house, and appointed for the day to which such house shall have been adjourned, or to any day subsequent thereto, other than any order that shall have been specially appointed for particular days by either house, and declared to be so fixed notwithstanding any meeting of parliament under this act, and also except any order made under the provisions of any act, shall be deemed to have been appointed for the day on which the parliament shall meet in pursuance of such proclamation. *s.* 2.

A *prorogation* is the continuance of the parliament from one session to another, as an adjournment is a continuation of the session from day to day; this is done by the royal authority, expressed either by the lord chancellor in his majesty's presence, or by commission from the crown, or frequently by proclamation. Both houses are necessarily prorogued at the same time, it not being a prorogation of the house of lords or commons, but of the parliament. The session is never understood to be at an end until a prorogation; though *unless some act be passed, or some judgment given* in parliament, it is in truth no session at all, but a *convention*. 1 *Black. Com.* 187. 4 *Inst.* 38.

And by 37 *Geo.* 3. *c.* 127, whenever his majesty shall, with the advice of the privy council, issue his proclamation giving notice that parliament shall meet for the dispatch of business, on any day not less than 14 days from the date of such proclamation, the same shall be a sufficient notice to all persons, and the parliament shall thereby stand prorogued to the day and place therein declared, notwithstanding any previous prorogation to any longer day. *s.* 1.

PARLIAMENTUM DIABOLICUM, a parliament held at Coventry, 38 *Hen.* 6, wherein Edward earl of March, (afterwards king,) and many of the chief nobility were attainted, but the acts then made were annulled by the succeeding parliament. *Hollingsh. Chron.*

PARLIAMENTUM INDOCTUM, a parliament 6 *Hen.* 4. whereunto by special precept to the sheriffs in their several counties, no lawyer, or other person skilled in the law was to come; therefore it was so termed. 1 *Black.* 176.

PARLIAMENTUM INSANUM, a parliament assembled at Oxford, *anno* 41 *Hen.* 3, so styled from the madness of their proceedings; and because the lords came with armed men to it, and contentions grew very high between the king, lords, and commons, whereby many extraordinary things were done. 4 *Inst.*

PARLIAMENTUM RELIGIOSUM. In most convents they had a common room, into which the brethren withdrew for conversation; and the conference there had was termed *parliamentum*. *Mat. Par.*

PAROL. By stat. 29 *Car.* 2. *cap.* 3, all leases, estates, interests of freehold, or terms of years, or any uncertain interest in or out of lands, &c. not put in writing, and signed by the parties, or their agents authorised by writing, shall have no greater effect than as estates at will; except leases not exceeding three years, whereof the rent shall be two thirds of the full value.

No such estates or interests, not being copyhold or customary interest, shall be assigned, granted, or surrendered, unless by deed or note in writing, signed (*ut supra*) or by operation of law. No action shall be brought to charge an executor on a special promise to answer damages out of his own estate, or to charge the defendant upon any promise to answer for the debt or miscarriage of another, or upon an agreement or consideration of marriage, or on any contract of sale of lands, &c. or any interest concerning them, or on any agreement not to be performed within a year after the making, unless such agreement, or some note thereof, be in writing, signed by the party to be charged, or some other by him authorized.

All devises of lands or tenements shall be in writing, and signed by the party devising, or some other in his presence, and by his direction, and subscribed in his presence by three or four witnesses, or else shall be void.

No such devises in writing shall be revocable otherwise than by writing or burning, tearing, or cancelling the same by the testator, or in his presence, and by his consent.

All declarations or creations of trusts shall be made by some writing, signed by the party, or by his last will in writing, or else be void.

Assignments of trust shall be in writing, signed by the party granting or assigning by such last will, or else shall be of no effect.

Trusts resulting by implication of law, or transferred or extinguished by act of law, shall be as if this statute had not been made.

No contract for the sale of any goods for 10*l.* or upwards, shall be good, except the buyer actually receive part of them, or give something in earnest, or some note thereof in writing be made and signed by the parties to be charged, or their agents.

No will in writing of any personal estate shall be repealed by words only, except the same be in the life of the testator committed to writing, and read to him, and allowed by him, and that be proved by three witnesses.

PAROL ARREST, any justice of peace may by word of mouth authorize any one to arrest another who is guilty of a breach of the peace in his presence, &c. *Dalt.* 117.

PAROL, DEMUR OF, is a privilege allowed an infant who is sued concerning lands which came to him by descent; and the court thereupon will give judgment, *quod loquela predicta remaneat quousque* the infant comes to the age of 21 years. And where the age is granted on parol demurrer the writ doth not abate, but the plea is put *sine die*, until the infant is of full age, and then there shall be a re-summons. 2 *Lill. Abr.* 280. 2 *Inst.* 258. *Rast. Entr.* 363.

PAROL EVIDENCE. See *Evidence.*

PAROL, or PLEADINGS, are the mutual altercations between the plaintiff and defendant; which at present are set down and delivered into the proper office in writing, though formerly they were usually put in by their counsel *ore tenus*, or *viva voce*, in court, and then minuted down by the chief clerks, or prothonotaries; whence in our old law French the pleadings are frequently denominated the *parol*. 3 *Black.* 293.

PARRICIDE, (*patricida*) is properly he who kills his father, and may be applied to him who kills his mother. *Law Lat. Dict.* See *Homicide.*

PARSON (*persona ecclesiæ*), is one that hath full possession of all the rights of a parochial church. He is called parson, *persona*, because by his person the church, which is an invisible body, is represented; and he is in himself a body corporate, in order to protect and defend the rights of the church (which he personates) by a perpetual succession (*Co. Litt.* 300.) He is sometimes called the rector, or governor, of the church: but the appellation of parson (however it may be deprecated by familiar, clownish, and indiscriminate use) is the most legal, most beneficial, and most honourable title that a parish priest can enjoy; because such a one, (sir Edward Coke observes,) and he only, is said *vicem seu personam ecclesiæ gerere*. A parson has, during his life, the freehold in himself of the parsonage house, the glebe, the tithes, and other dues. But these are sometimes appropriated; that is to say, the benefice is perpetually annexed to some spiritual corporation, either sole or aggregate, being the patron of the living; which the law esteems equally capable of providing for the service of the church, as any single private clergyman. See *Appropriation*.

PARSON IMPARSONEE, (*persona impersonata*) is he who is in possession of a church, be it presentative or impropriate, and with whom the church is full. *Co. Lit.* 300.

PARSONAGE, (*personatus, personagium*) is sometimes taken for a dignitary in a church, and sometimes for the benefice itself. *Cowel.*

But generally the parsonage, or rectory, is a parish church, endowed with a house, glebe, tithes, &c. *Pars. Coun.* 190. *Hugh's Pars. Law* 188.

PARSON MORTAL. The rector instituted and inducted, for his own life, was called *persona mortalis*; and any collegiate or conventual body, to whom the church was for ever appropriated, were termed *persona immortalis. Cartular. Rading. M S. fol.* 182.

PARTES FINIS NIHIL HABUERUNT, is an exception taken against a fine levied, *viz.* that the cognizors had not estate or interest in the tenement. 3 *Rep.* 88. *The case of Fines.*

PARTICIPATIO, the charity so called, by which the poor were made *participes* of other mens goods. 2 *Monast.* 321. *Cowel.*

PARTIES, are those who are named in a deed of fine, as parties to it; as those who levy the fine, and to whom the fine is levied; so they who make any deed, and they to whom it is made, are called parties to the deed. *Cowel.*

PARTICULAR ESTATE, is that estate and interest which is vested in any one precedent to the remainder or reversion invested thereon.

PARTITION, (*partitio*) is dividing land descended by the common law, or custom, among coheirs or parceners. In Kent, where the land is of gavelkind nature, they call their partition shifting, from the Saxon *shiftan*, to divide. In Latin it is called *hercissere.* Partition also may be made by joint-tenants, or tenants in common, by deed, or writ. 31 *H.* 8. 1. 32 *H.* 8. 32. See *Joint-tenants. Parceners.*

PARTITIONE FACIENDA, a writ that laid for those who held lands or tenements *pro indiviso*, and would sever to every one his part, against those who refused to join in partition, as copartners, tenants in gavelkind, &c. *Old Nat. Brev.* 142. *F. N. B.* 61.

PARTNERS. Where two or more persons agree to come in share and share alike, or in any other proportion, to any trade or bargain, these are partners in trade.

Partners are joint-tenants in all the stock and partnership effects, and they are so not only of the particular stock in being at the time of entering into the partnership, but they continue joint-tenants throughout, whatever changes may take place in the course of trade; for if it were otherwise it would be impossible to carry on partnership trade. 1 *Vez.* 242.

Hence assignees under a commission of bankrupt against one partner can only be tenants in common of an undivided share, subject to all the rights of the other partner: and if a creditor of one partner takes out execution against the partnership effects, he can only have the undivided share of his debtor, and must take it in the same manner the debtor himself had it, and subject to the rights of the other partner. *Cowper* 449.

But in this case the sheriff must seize all, because the moieties are undivided; for if he seize but a moiety, and sell that, the other will have a right to a moiety of that moiety; therefore he must seize the whole, and sell a moiety thereof undivided, and the vendee will be tenant in common with the other partner. *Salk.* 392. *Show.* 173. *Comb.* 217.

The whole of this doctrine seems to arise out of the very principle upon which partnership is founded, namely, probable profit, and the risk of loss, the advantages or disadvantages of which cannot in common justice be confined to one side only, but must be reciprocal throughout. 12 *Mod.* 446.

But in order to constitute a copartnership, and to make a person liable as a partner, there must be an agreement between him and the ostensible person to share *in all risks of profit or loss*, or he must have permitted him to use his credit, and *to hold him out* as jointly liable with himself. *Doug.* 371.

But although partners are joint tenants, yet there is no right of survivorship between them, and therefore there is no necessity to provide in the copartnership deed against survivorship, it being a maxim of the common law, *jus accrescendi inter mercatores locum non habet*; and this is for the benefit of commerce, that the fruits of each person's labour and industry should go to his executors or administrators for the benefit of his children and family. *Vin.* 217.

PART OWNERS, are those who are concerned in ship matters, and have joint shares therein. And when there are part-owners of a ship, the majority may fit her out, without consent of the rest; and if they do, such majority run all hazard, and are to partake of the profits. *Show.* 13, 30.

PARVISE (*parvisa, parvisus, non à parvus, adj. sed à Gal. le parvis*) an afternoon's exercise, or moot for the instruction of young students, bearing the same name originally with the *parvisiæ* at Oxford. *Seld.* 56.

PASCHA CLAUSUM, the octaves of Easter, or Low Sunday, which closes that solemnity. *Cowel.*

PASCHA FLORIDUM, the Sunday before Easter, called Palm Sunday. *Ibid.*

PASCHAL RENTS, rents or yearly tributes paid by the clergy to the bishop or archdeacon, at their Easter visitations. *Ibid.*

PASCUA, a meadow or pasture ground. *Ibid.*

PASCUAGE, (*pascuagium*, Fr. *pascage*) the grazing or pasturing of cattle.

PASNAGE, pathnage in woods, &c. See *Pannage.*

PASSAGE, (*passagium*,) is properly over water, as way is over land; it relates to the sea and great rivers, and is a French word, signifying *transitum.* *Cowel.*

Also *passagio* is a writ directed to the keepers of the ports to permit a man to pass over sea, who has the king's leave. *Reg. Orig.* 193.

PASSAGIUM REGIS, a voyage or expedition to the Holy Land. *Cowel.*

PASSATOR, he who has the interest or command of the passage of a river, or the lord to whom a duty is paid for passage. *Cowel.*

PASSPORT, (from the French *passar, transire*, and *port, portus*, a haven.) It signifies a licence, for the safe passage of any man from one place to another. 1 *Black.* 260.

PASSIAGIARIUS, a ferry-man. *Cowel. Blount.*

PASTITIUM, a pasture field. *Ibid.*

PASTORAL STAFF. The form of it was straight, which signified *rectum regimen.* All the top part of it was crooked, and the other part sharp: The crooked signified, that the bishop presided over the people; and the sharp signified, to punish the stubborn. *Ibid.*

PASTURE, is generally any place where cattle may feed; and feeding for cattle is called pasture, wherefore feeding grounds are called common of pasture: But common of pasture is properly a right of putting beasts to pasture in another man's soil, and in this there is an interest of the lord and of the tenant. *Wood's Inst.* 196, 197. For in those waste grounds, which are usually called commons, the property of the soil is generally in the lord of the manor; as in common fields it is in the particular tenants. And common of pasture is either appendant, appurtenant, because of vicinage, or in gross. 2 *Black.* 32.

PASTUS, the same with procuration, or the provision which tenants were bound to make for their lords at certain times, or as often as they made a progress to their lands: this in many places was turned into money. *Cowel.*

PATENTEE, one to whom the king grants his letters patent. 7 *Ed.* 6. *c.* 3.

PATENTS. See *King. Monopolies. Peers. Precedence.*

PATRIA, the country; but in law the men or jury of the neighbourhood. *Cowel.* 3 *Black.* 349.

PATRIMONY, an hereditary estate, or right descended from ancestors. *Cowel.*

PATRINUS, a godfather, and *matrina*, a godmother.

PATRITIUS, an honour conferred on men of the first quality in the time of the English-Saxon kings. *Cowel. Blount.*

PATRON (*patronus*). He who has the right of advowson is called the patron of the church. For, when lords of manors first built churches on their own demesnes, and appointed the tithes of those manors to be paid to the officiating ministers, which before were given to the clergy in common, (from whence arose the division of parishes) the lord, who thus built a church, and endowed it with glebe or land, had of common right a power annexed of nominating such minister as he pleased (provided he were canonically qualified) to officiate in that church, of which he was the founder, endower, maintainer, or, in one word, the patron. 2 *Black.* 21. See *Advowson. Parson. Presentation,* &c. And 3 *Black.* 242.

PAVAGE, (*Pavagium*) money paid towards paving the streets or highways.—*Cowel. Blount.*

PAUPER, a poor man. Thus we have a term in law, to sue *in forma pauperis.*

It is said, that if a pauper gives notice of trial, and does not proceed, he shall be dispaupered. 1 *Salk.* 506.

But notwithstanding the stat. 23 *Hen.* 8, *c.* 15, whereby it is provided "That whoever sues *in forma pauperis* shall not pay costs, but shall suffer such other punishment as the court shall think fit," if he be dispaupered or nonsuited, the usual practice is to tax the costs, and for non-payment to order him to be whipped. 2 *Salk.* 506. *Stile* 386. See *Forma Pauperis.*

And paupers or such as will swear themselves not worth five pounds, are, by statute 11 *Hen.* 8, *c.* 12, to have original writs and *subpœnas gratis*, and counsel and attorney assigned them without fee; and are excused from paying costs, when plaintiffs, by the statute 23 *Hen.* 8, *c.* 15, but shall suffer other punishment at the discretion of the judges. And it was formerly usual to give such paupers, if nonsuited, their election either to be whipped or pay the costs (1 *Sid.* 261. 7 *Mod.* 114); though that practice is now disused (*Salk.* 506). It seems however agreed, that a pauper may recover costs, though he pays none; for the counsel and clerks are bound to give their labour to him, but not to his antagonist (1 *Equ. Cas. Abr.* 125).

PAWN, (*pignus*) a pledge or gage for

payment of money lent. (*Lit. Dict.*) The party who pawns goods, hath a general property in them; they cannot be forfeited by the party who hath them in pawn for any offence of his, nor be taken in execution for his debt; neither may they otherwise be put in execution, till the debt for which they are pawned is satisfied. *Lit. Rep.* 332.

He who borrows money on a pawn, is to have the pledge again when he repays it, or he may have action for the detainer; and his tender of the money revests the special property. (2 *Cro.* 244.) And where a broker or pawnee refuses (upon tender of the money) to redeliver the goods in pawn, he may be indicted; because, being secretly pawned, it may be impossible to prove a delivery for want of witnesses, if trover should be brought for them. (3 *Salk.* 268.) Also if goods are lost, after the tender of the money, the pawnee is liable to make them good to the owner; for after tender he is a wrongful detainer. But if they are lost before a tender, it is otherwise; for the pawnee is not liable, if his care of keeping them was exact; and the law requires nothing of him, but only that he should use an ordinary care in keeping the goods, that they may be restored on payment of the money for which they were deposited; and in such case if the goods are lost, the pawnee hath still his remedy against the pawner for the money lent. 2 *Salk.* 522. 3 *Salk.* 268. See *Bailment.*

But a factor cannot pawn the goods of his principal, nor can he to whom goods are delivered for safe custody pawn them. (*Strange* 1178. 1187.) Also there can be no market-overt for pawning, for the purpose of changing property stolen or embezzled. *Ibid.*

PAWNBROKERS. By 43 *Geo.* 3, *c.* 69, pawnbrokers trading in gold or silver plate are to take out an excise license, and pay a duty of 5*l.* 15*s.* *per annum*; and also by 44 *Geo.* 3, *c.* 48, within the bills of mortality, an annual stamp duty of 10*l.* elsewhere 5*l.*

By 39 &40 *Geo.* 3, *c.* 99, pawnbrokers are allowed to take the following rates for profit, *viz.*

For every pledge not exceeding 2*s.* 6*d.* one halfpenny, for any time it shall remain in pawn, not exceeding one month; and the same for every other month, including the current month in which such pledge shall be redeemed, although such month shall not be expired.

For every pledge upon which there shall have been lent 5*s.* one penny; 7*s.* 6*d.* one penny halfpenny; 10*s.* two pence; 12*s.* 6*d.* two pence halfpenny; 15*s.* three pence; 17*s.* 6*d.* three pence halfpenny; and 1*l.* four pence, and so on, and in proportion for not exceeding 40*s.*; exceeding 40*s.* and not 42*s.* eight pence; exceeding 42*s.* and not 10*l.* three pence, and no more, for every 20*s.*

The pawnbroker may take for any pledge above 2*s.* 6*d.* and not more than 40*s.* after the rate of 4*d.* for the loan of 20*s.* per month. *s.* 3.

But parties may redeem within seven days after the end of the first month, without paying any thing extra for the seven days, or within fourteen days, upon paying for one month and a half: but parties applying to redeem after the fourteen days must pay for the second month; and the like regulations are observable in every subsequent month when application shall be made to redeem. *s.* 5.

And pawnbrokers are to give farthings in exchange. *s.* 4.

Pawns shall be entered in books, with a description of the goods, the money lent, the date and the name and place of abode of the person pawning; and the pawnbrokers shall give to the person pawning a note describing the goods, the money lent, the date, the name and place of abode of the person pawning, with the name and place of abode of the pawnbroker; which note shall be given gratis if the sum lent is under 5*s.* but where the money lent is 5*s.* and under 10*s.* the pawnbroker may take a halfpenny for the same; for 10*s.* and under 20*s.* one penny; 20*s.* and under 5*l.* two pence; 5*l.* or more, four pence; upon the production of which notes the pawnbrokers shall deliver up the goods pawned. *s.* 6.

The interest taken shall be indorsed on the duplicates of pledges redeemed, and kept by the pawnbrokers for one year. *s.* 7.

Persons unlawfully pawning goods, not being authorised by the owner, shall forfeit not exceeding 5*l.* nor less than 20*s.* and the full value of the goods; and on default of payment, may be committed to hard labour for not more than three months, and if the penalties are not paid within three days before the expiration of the imprisonment, the party may, upon the application of the prosecutor be whipped: the penalties go to the party injured; but if he will not accept the same, to the poor. *s.* 8.

Persons forging, or counterfeiting notes, or not giving an account of themselves, on offering to pawn or redeem goods, may be seized and carried before a justice, who, on conviction, may send the offender to the house of correction for not more than three months. *s.* 9.

Persons not giving a good account of themselves on offering to pawn goods, may be detained and taken before a magistrate to be examined, and committed to be dealt with according to law, when necessary, or otherwise, for not exceeding three months. *s.* 10.

Persons buying or taking in pledge unfinished goods, or linen or apparel intrusted to others to wash or mend, shall forfeit double the sum lent, and restore the goods; and peace officers, under a warrant may search for such things, which if found, are to be restored to the owner. *s.* 11, 12.

Where goods are unlawfully pawned the pawnbroker shall restore them; the party may have a search warrant, and if found, the justice may direct them to be restored. *s.* 13.

Where a pawnbroker will not deliver up goods to the pawner upon production of a note, and tender of the principal and interest within a year, or one year and three months, as the case is, the justice may upon proof thereof convict the pawnbroker, and send him to prison without bail, there to remain till he deliver up the goods, or make such compensation as the justice thinks fit. *s.* 14.

Persons producing notes or memorandums shall be deemed the owners; and where notes or memorandums are lost, the pawnbroker shall deliver a copy, with the form of an affidavit, according to the case, taking for such copy and form of an affidavit, where the goods pawned do not exceed 5*s.* one halfpenny; exceeding 5*s.* and not 10*s.* one penny; and if above 10*s.* according to the rates payable for the original notes: which affidavit, being made before a justice, shall authenticate the same, and the pawnbroker shall thereupon permit the pawner to redeem. *s.* 15.

Pawned goods shall be deemed forfeited at the end of one year, and shall be sold by public auction, where the goods are pawned for more than 10*s.* and not above 10*l.* and the auctioneer shall expose the same to view, publish catalogues, and advertise the time and place of sale, with the name of the pawnbroker, in some newspaper two days before the sale; but on notice in writing in the presence of a witness, from persons having goods in pledge not to sell, three months further shall be allowed beyond the year for redemption. *s.* 17—19.

But pictures, prints, books, bronzes, statues, busts, carvings, in ivory and marble, cameos, intaglios, musical, mathematical, and philosophical instruments, and china, shall only be sold four times in the year; *viz.* on the first Monday and following days in January, April, July, and October, in each year, and to be regularly advertised, on pain of not exceeding 5*l.* nor less than 40*s.* *s.* 20.

An account of sales of pledges above 10*s.* shall be entered by the pawnbrokers in a book, and the overplus paid to the owner of the goods pawned or sold, on pain of 10*l.* and treble the sum lent. *s.* 20.

Pawnbrokers shall not purchase, or agree to purchase, any goods whilst they are in their custody, in pledge, except at auction; nor shall they take pawns from persons appearing to be under twelve years of age, or intoxicated with liquor; nor shall they purchase, or take in pawn, the notes of other pawnbrokers; nor shall they buy any goods before eight in the forenoon, or after seven in the evening; nor receive pawns before eight in the forenoon or after eight in the evening, between Michaelmas and Lady-day, or before seven in the morning, or after nine in the evening, during the remainder of the year, Saturday evenings, and the evenings preceding Good Friday and Christmas-day excepted. *s.* 21.

Pawnbrokers shall place in view the table of profits, and the price of notes. *s.* 22.

Pawnbrokers' names and business shall be placed over the door, on penalty of 10*l.* for every shop so used, for one week, without; to be levied by distress and sale, and in default thereof, the party may be imprisoned for not more than three months, nor less than fourteen days. *s.* 23.

Pawnbrokers selling goods before the limited time, or injuring them, shall make such satisfaction as the justice shall award, on penalty of 10*l.*. *s.* 24.

Pawnbrokers shall produce their books when necessary, on penalty of not exceeding 10*l.* nor less than 5*l.*; and pawnbrokers offending against this act, in neglecting to keep books, or make entries, shall forfeit not exceeding 10*l.* and for every other offence, where no forfeiture is provided, not less than 40*s.* nor more than 5*l.* *s.* 25, 26.

All forfeitures are to be recovered before any justice, so that prosecutions be commenced within twelve months. *s.* 27.

The churchwardens and overseers nominated by a justice, are obliged to prosecute, and any inhabitant may be a witness. *s.* 28—31.

This act is not to extend to persons lending money at 5*l.* *per cent.* without further profit. *s.* 30.

It extends to the executors and administrators of pawnbrokers, *s.* 31. and an appeal from the justice's conviction lies to the sessions, *s.* 35; and no person convicted of fraud or obtaining money under false pretences, or any felony, shall be allowed to prosecute. *s.* 36.

PAYMENT of money before the day appointed, is in law payment at the day, (5 *Rep.* 117.) but payment of a lesser sum in satisfaction of a greater, cannot be a satisfaction for the whole, unless the payment be before the day. (4 *Mod.* 89.) And upon the plea of *solvit ad diem* it is good evidence to prove payment at any time after the day, and before action brought; and payment, although after the day, may be pleaded to any action of debt, upon bill, bond, or judgment, or *scire facias* upon a judgment. 2 *Lil. Abr.* 287.

PAYMENT OF MONEY INTO COURT, is a species of confession of the right of action. It is for the most part necessary upon pleading a tender, and is itself a kind of tender to the plaintiff; by paying into the hands of the proper officer of the court as much as the defendant acknowledges to be due, together with the costs hitherto incurred, in order to prevent the expence of any farther proceedings. This may be done upon motion, for leave to pay the money into court. If, after the money paid in, the plaintiff proceeds in his suit, it is at his own peril: for, if he does not prove more due than is so paid into court, he shall be nonsuited, and pay the defendant costs; but he shall still have the money so paid in, for that the defendant has acknowledged to be his due. So if a defendant pleads a set-off, he must pay the remaining balance into court. 3 *Black.* 304.

PEACE, (*Pax*) in a legal sense intends a quiet behaviour toward the king and his subjects. And if any man is in danger from another, and makes oath of it before a justice of peace, he shall be secured by good bond, which is called *binding to the peace*. *Lamb. Eiren. lib.* 2. *cap.* 2. 77. *Cromp. Just. of Peace*, 118, 129.

PEACE OF GOD AND THE CHURCH, (*Pax Dei & Ecclesiæ*) was anciently used for that cessation which the king's subjects had from trouble and suit of law between the terms. *Cowel.* See *King* and *Prerogative*.

PECIA, a small piece or small quantity of ground. *Cowel. Blount.*

PECTORALE, is the same with that garment called *rationale*, which the high priest in the old law wore on his shoulders, as a sign of perfection. *Ibid.*

PECTORAL, from the Lat. *pectus*, armour for the breast, a breast-plate or *petrel*, for a horse. *Ibid.*

PECULIAR, (Fr. *peculier*, i. e. private) a particular parish or church, that hath jurisdiction within itself, and power to grant administration or probate of wills, &c. exempt from the ordinary.

The *Court of Peculiars* of the archbishop of Canterbury, is a branch of, and annexed to the Court of Arches, and hath a particular jurisdiction in the city of London, and over all those parishes in other dioceses, &c. within his province, these are exempt from the ordinary's jurisdiction, and subject to the metropolitan only. 4 *Inst.* 338.

For where a man dies, leaving goods in several *peculiars*, the archbishop is to grant administration or probate. *Sid.* 90. 5 *Mod.* 239. 16 *Vin. Abr.* tit. *Peculiars*.

And by stat. 25 *Hen.* 8. *c.* 19, an application from this court to the Court of Delegates under the king's commission from the court of Chancery.

PECUNIA, properly money, but anciently used for cattle, and sometimes for other goods as well as money. *Cowel.*

PECUNIA SEPULCHRALIS, (*LL. Canuti*, 102.) money anciently paid to the priest at the opening of the grave for the good of the departed soul.

PECUNIARY CAUSES, cognizable in the ecclesiastical courts, are such arise either from the withholding tithes and other ecclesiastical dues, or the doing or neglecting some act relating to the church, whereby damage accrues to the plaintiff; towards obtaining a satisfaction for which he is permitted to institute a suit in the spiritual court. For the principal of these causes, See 3 *Black.* 88.

PECUNIARY LEGACY. See *Legacy*.

PEDAGE, (*pedagium*) money given for the passing by foot or horse through a country. *Spelm. Cowel. Blount.*

PEDALE, a foot cloth, or piece of tapestry laid on the ground to tread on for greater state and ceremony. *Ingulph. pag.* 41.

PEDIS ABSCISSIO, cutting off the foot, was a punishment of criminals, inflicted here, instead of death. *Leg. Wil. Con.* 1. *cap.* 7. *Ingul.* 856. *Fleta, lib.* 1. *c.* 38. *Bracton, lib.* 3. *cap.* 32. *Cowel.*

PEDONES, foot soldiers. *Cowel. Blount.*

PEDLAR, one who travels from place to place on foot, selling small wares. See *Hawkers*.

PEER, or PIER, (*Pera*, Fr. *pierre, saxum, quod e saxis fieri solebat*), a mole or rampart made to resist the force of the sea, or great rivers, for the better security of ships that lie at harbour in any haven, such as the peer of Dover and the like. Hence the duty or imposition for maintenance of a sea peer is called *Peerage*.

PEERAGE, the dignity of the lords or peers of the realm.

PEERS, (*Pares*) signify in law, those who are empannelled in an inquest upon a man, for convicting or clearing him of any offence; the reason is, because the custom of the realm is, to try every man in such case by his peers or equals. *Westm.* 1. *cap.* 6. *Mag. Car. c.* 29.

PEERS OF FEES. The word *peer* denoted originally one of the same rank; afterwards it was used for the vassals or tenants of the same lord, who were obliged to serve and attend him in his courts, being equal in function: these were termed *peers of fees*, because holding fees of the lord, or because their business in court was to sit and judge under their lord, of disputes arising on fees; but if there were too many in one lordship, the lord usually chose twelve, who had the title of *peers*, by way of distinction, from whence it is said we derive our common juries, and other *peers*. *Cowel.*

PEERS OF THE REALM, (*Pares, regni proceres*) *S. P. C. lib.* 3. The peers of the realm are by their birth hereditary counsellors of the crown, and may be called together by the king to impart their advice in all matters of importance to the realm, either in time of parliament, or which hath been their principal use, when there is no parliament in being. *Co. Lit.* 110.

Accordingly, Bracton speaking of the nobility of his time, says they might probably be called *consules, a consulendo; reges enim tales sibi associant ad consulendum* (*Brac. L.* 1. *c.* 8), and in our law books it is laid down that peers are created for two reasons: 1, *ad consulendum*, 2, *ad defendendum regem*, on which account the law gives them certain great and high privileges, such as freedom from arrests, and others which will be noticed hereafter, because it intends that they are always assisting the king with their counsel for the commonwealth, or keeping the realm in safety by their prowess and valour. 7 *Rep.* 34. 9 *Rep.* 49. 12 *Rep.* 96. 1 *Black.* 227.

When a lord is newly created he is introduced into the house of peers by two lords of the same form in their robes, Garter king at arms going before, and his lordship is to present his writ of summons, &c. to the lord chancellor; which being read, he is conducted to his place: and lords by descent, where nobility comes down from the ancestor, and is enjoyed by right of blood, are introduced with the same ceremony, the presenting of the writ excepted. *Lex Constitution.* 79.

Though dignities of peerage are granted from the crown, yet they cannot be surrendered to the crown, except it be in order to new and greater honours. *Lex Constit.* 85, 86, 87.

All peers of the realm are looked upon as the king's hereditary counsellors, and may be called together by the king to impart their advice in all matters of importance to the realm, either in time of parliament, or, which hath been their principal use, when there is no parliament in being. *Co. Litt.* 110. *Bract. l.* 1. *c.* 8.

Instances of conventions of the peers, to advise the king, have been in former times very frequent, though now fallen into disuse, by reason of the more regular meetings of parliament. Many instances of this kind of meeting are to be found under our ancient kings; though the former method of convoking them had been so long left off, that when Charles 1, in 1640, issued out writs under the great seal to call a great council of all the peers of England to meet and attend his majesty at York, previous to the meeting of the long parliament, the earl of Clarendon mentions it as a new invention, not before heard of, that is, as he explains himself, so old, that it had not been practised in some hundreds of years. But, though there had not so long before been an instance, nor has there been any since, of assembling them in so solemn a manner, yet, in cases of emergency our princes have at several times thought proper to call for and consult as many of the nobility as could easily be got together, as was particularly the case with king James 2, after the landing of the prince of Orange, and with the prince of Orange himself before he called that convention parliament which afterwards called him to the throne. 1 *Black.* 228.

Besides this general meeting it is usually looked upon to be the right of each particular peer of the realm to demand an audience of the king, and to lay before him, with decency and respect, such matters as he shall judge of importance to the public. 4 *Inst.* 53. See 2 *Black. Com.* 227, 228, 229.

1. A DUKE, though he be with us, in respect of his title of nobility, inferior in point of antiquity * to many others, yet is superior to all of them in rank; his being the first title of dignity after the royal family. (*Camden Britan. tit. ordines.*) And Dr. Henry, in his History of England, informs us, that "about a year before Edw. 3 assumed the title of king of France, he introduced *a new order* of nobility, to inflame the military ardour and ambition of his earls and barons, by creating his eldest son prince Edward DUKE of Cornwall, which was done with great solemnity in full parliament at Westminster, March 17, A. D. 1337." 8 *Hen. Hist.* 135.

However, in the reign of queen Elizabeth, A. D. 1572, the whole order became utterly extinct; but it was revived about fifty years afterwards by her successor, who was remarkably prodigal of honours, in the person of George Villiers duke of Buckingham. *Camd. Brit. tit. ordines. Spel. Gloss.* 191.

2. A marquis, *marchio*, is the next degree of nobility. His office formerly was (for dignity and duty were never separated by our ancestors) to guard the frontiers and limits of the kingdom; which were called the marches, from the Teutonic word, *marche*, a limit: such as, in particular, were the marches of Wales and Scotland, while each continued to be an enemy's country. The persons, who had command there, were called lords marchers, or marquisses; whose authority was abolished by stat. 27 Hen. 8, c. 27, though the title had long before been made a mere ensign of honour; Robert Vere, earl of Oxford, being created marquis of Dublin, by Richard 2 in the eighth year of his reign. 2 *Inst.* 5. 1 *Black.* 397.

3. An earl is a title of nobility so ancient, that its original cannot clearly be traced out. Thus much seems tolerably certain: that

* At the time of the conquest the temporal nobility consisted only of earls and barons.

among the Saxons they are called ealdormen, *quasi* elder men, signifying the same as senior or senator among the Romans; and also schiremen, because they had each of them the civil government of a several division or shire. On the irruption of the Danes, they changed the name to eorles, which, according to Camden (*Britan. tit. ordines*) signified the same in their language. In Latin they are called *comites* (a title first used in the empire) from being the king's attendants; "*a societate nomen sumpserunt,* "*reges enim tales sibi associant.*" (*Bract. l.* 1, *c.* 8. *Flet. l.* 1. *c.* 5.) After the Norman conquest they were for some time called counts or countees, from the French; but they did not long retain that name themselves, though their shires are from thence called counties to this day. The name of earls or *comites* is now become a mere title, they having nothing to do with the government of the county; which, as has been more than once observed, is now entirely devolved on the sheriff, the earl's deputy, or vice-comes. In writs and commissions, and other formal instruments, the king, when he mentions any peer of the degree of an earl, usually styles him, "trusty and well "beloved cousin:" an appellation as ancient as the reign of Henry 4; who being either by his wife, his mother, or his sisters, actually related or allied to every earl then in the kingdom, artfully and constantly acknowledged that connection in all his letters and other public acts: from whence the usage has descended to his successors, though the reason has long ago failed.

4. The name of vice-comes or viscount was afterwards made use of as an arbitrary title of honour, without any shadow of office pertaining to it, by Henry the sixth; when, in the eighteenth year of his reign, he created John Beaumont a peer, by the name of viscount Beaumont, which was the first instance of the kind. 2 *Inst.* 5.

5. A baron's is the most general and universal title of nobility; for originally every one of the peers of superior rank had also a barony annexed to his other titles (2 *Inst.* 5, 6.) But it hath sometimes happened that, when an antient baron hath been raised to a new degree of peerage, in the course of a few generations the two titles have descended differently; one perhaps to the male descendants, the other to the heirs general; whereby the earldom or other superior title hath subsisted without a barony: and there are also modern instances, where earls and viscounts have been created without annexing a barony to their other honours: so that now the rule doth not hold universally, that all peers are barons. The original and antiquity of baronies have occasioned great inquiries among our English antiquaries. The most probable opinion seems to be, that they were the same with our present lords of manors; to which the name of court baron (which is the lord's court, and incident to every manor) gives some countenance. It may be collected from king John's *Magna Charta,* (*cap.* 14,) that originally all lords of manors, or barons, that held of the king *in capite,* had seats in the great council or parliament: till about the reign of that prince the conflux of them became so large and troublesome, that the king was obliged to divide them, and summon only the greater barons in person, leaving the small ones to be summoned by the sheriff, and (as it is said) to sit by representation in another house; which gave rise to the separation of the two houses of parliament. *Gilb. Hist. of Exch. c.* 3. *Seld. tit. of Hon.* 2, 5, 21.

Peers how created.] The right of peerage seems to have been originally territorial; that is, annexed to lands, honours, castles, manors, and the like, the proprietors and possessors of which were (in right of those estates) allowed to be peers of the realm, and were summoned to parliament to do suit and service to their sovereign: and, when the land was alienated, the dignity passed with it as appendant. Thus the bishops still sit in the house of lords in right of succession to certain antient baronies annexed, or supposed to be annexed, to their episcopal lands (*Glan. l.* 7. *c.* 1,) and thus, in 11 Hen. 6, the possession of the castle of Arundel was adjudged to confer an earldom on its possessor (*Seld. tit. of hon. b,* 2. *c.* 9, *s.* 5.) But afterwards, when alienations grew to be frequent, the dignity of peerage was confined to the lineage of the party ennobled, and instead of territorial became personal. Actual proof of a tenure by barony became no longer necessary to constitute a lord of parliament; but the record of the writ of summons to him or his ancestors was admitted as a sufficient evidence of the tenure.

Peers are now created either by writ, or by patent: for those who claim by prescription must suppose either a writ or patent made to their ancestors; though by length of time it is lost. The creation by writ, or the king's letter, is a summons to attend the house of peers, by the style and title of that barony, which the king is pleased to confer: that by patent is a royal grant to a subject of any dignity and degree of peerage. The creation by writ is the more ancient way; but a man is not ennobled thereby, unless he actually take his seat in the house of lords; and some are of opinion that there must be at least two writs of summons, and a sitting in two distinct parliaments, to evidence an hereditary barony, (*Whitelocke of parl.* ch. 114.) and therefore the most usual, because the surest, way is to grant the dignity by patent, which enures to a man and his heirs according to the limitations thereof, though he never himself makes use of it (*Co. Litt.* 16). Yet it is frequent to call up the eldest son of a peer to the house of lords by writ of summons, in the name of his father's barony, because in that case there is no danger of his children losing the nobility in case he never takes his seat, for they will succeed to their grandfather *. Creation by writ has also one advantage over that by patent: for a person created by writ holds the dignity to him and his heirs, without any words to that purport in the writ †; but in letters patent there must be words to direct the inheritance, else the dignity enures only to the grantee for life (*Co. Litt.* 9, 16). For a man or woman may be created noble for their own lives, and the dignity not descend to their heirs at all, or descend only to some particular heirs: as where a peerage is limited to a man, and the heirs male of his body by Elizabeth his present lady, and not to such heirs by any former or future wife.

Let us next take a view of a few of the principal incidents attending the nobility, exclusive of their capacity as members of parliament, and as hereditary counsellors of the crown; both of which we have before considered. And first we must observe that in criminal cases a nobleman shall be tried by his peers ‡. The great are always obnoxious to popular envy: were they to be judged by the people they might be in danger from the prejudice of their judges, and would moreover be deprived of the privilege of the meanest subjects, that of being tried by their equals, which is secured to all the realm by *magna charta*, c. 29. It is said that this does not extend to bishops, who, though they are lords of parliament, and sit there by virtue of their baronies, which they hold *jure ecclesiæ*, yet are not ennobled in blood, and consequently not peers with the nobility (3 *Inst.* 30, 31.) As to peeresses, there was no precedent for their trial when accused of treason or felony, till after Eleanor duchess of Gloucester, wife to the lord protector, was accused of treason and found guilty of witchcraft, in an ecclesistical synod, through the intrigues of cardinal Beaufort. This very extraordinary trial gave occasion to a special stat. 20 *H.* 6. *c.* 9, which declares (*Moor.* 769. 2 *Inst.* 50. *Staund. P.C.* 152. 6 *Rep.* 52) the law to be, that peeresses, either in their own right or by marriage, shall be tried before the same judicature as other peers of the realm. If a woman, noble in her own right, marries a commoner, she still remains noble ||, and shall be tried by her peers; but if she be only noble by marriage, then by a second marriage with a commoner she loses her dignity; for as by marriage it is gained, by marriage it is also lost ¶ (*Dyer* 79. *Co. Litt.* 16). Yet if a duchess dowager marries a baron she continues a duchess still; for all the nobility are *pares*, and therefore it is no degradation (2 *Inst.* 50). A peer, or peeress (either in her own right or by marriage,) cannot be arrested in civil cases (*Finch. L. L.* 355. 1 *Vent.* 298): and they have also many peculiar privileges annexed to their peerage in the course of judicial proceedings. A peer, sitting in judgment, gives not his verdict upon oath, like an ordinary juryman, but upon his honour (2 *Inst.* 49.) he answers also to bills in chancery upon his honour, and not upon his oath (1 *P.*

---

* And where the father's barony is limited by patent to him and the heirs male of his body, and his eldest son is called up to the house of lords by writ with the title of this barony, the writ in this case will not create a fee or a general estate tail, so as to make a female capable of inheriting the title, but upon the death of the father the two titles unite, or become one and the same. Case of the claim to the barony of Sidney of Penshurst disallowed. *Dom. Proc.* 17 *June* 1782.

† Though this is the authority of lord Coke, it is now understood to be erroneous; a creation by writ does not confer a fee-simple in the title, but only an estate-tail general; for every claimant of the title must be descended from the person first ennobled. 1 *Woodd.* 37.

‡ A nobleman is tried by his peers only in treason and felony, and misprision of the same; but in all misdemeanors, as libels, riots, perjury, conspiracies, &c. he is tried like a commoner by a jury. 3 *Inst.* 30. 2 *Hawk.* 424.

|| But she communicates no rank or title to her husband. *Harg. Co. Litt.* 326. *b.* There have been claims, and these are supported by authorities, by a husband after issue to assume the title of his wife's dignity, and after her death to retain the same as tenant by the courtesy; but from Mr. Hargrave's statement of this subject, in *Co. Litt.* 29. *b.* n. 1, there is no probability that such a claim would now be allowed.

¶ Yet she is commonly called and addressed by the style and title which she bore before her second marriage, but this is only by courtesy; as the daughters of dukes, marquisses, and earls are usually addressed by the title of lady, though in law they are commoners. In a writ of partition brought by Ralph Haward and lady Ann Powes his wife, the court held that it was a misnomer, and that it ought to have been by Ralph Haward and Ann Haward his wife, late wife of lord Powes deceased. *Dyer* 79.

Wms. 146); but when he is examined as a witness either in civil or criminal cases, he must be sworn (*Salk.* 512) *: for the respect which the law shows to the honour of a peer, does not extend so far as to overturn a settled maxim, that *in judicio non creditur nisi juratis* (*Cro. Car.* 64). The honour of peers is however so highly tendered by the law that it is much more penal to spread false reports of them and certain other great officers of the realm, than of other men; scandal against them being called by the peculiar name of *scandalum magnatum,* and subjected to peculiar punishments by divers ancient statutes. 3 *Edw.* 1, *c.* 34. 2 *Ric.* 2, *st.* 1, *c.* 5. 12 *Ric.* 2. *c.* 11. See *Scandalum Magnatum.*

A peer cannot lose his nobility but by death or attainder, nor degraded except by act of parliament. 12 *Rep.* 107. 12 *Mod.* 36.

PEERESS. See *Peers. Creation. Descent,* and *Marriage.*

PELA, a peel, pile or fort. *Cowel.*

PELES, issues arising from or out of a thing. *Ibid.*

PELF, and PELFRE (*pelfra*). In time of war the earl marshal is to have of preys and booties all the gelded beasts, except hogs, &c. which is called pelfre. *Ibid.*

PELLAGE, the ancient custom or duty paid for skins of leather. *Ibid.*

PENE FORT ET DURE. See *Mute.*

PELLICIA, a pilch, *tunica vel indumentum pelliceum*; *hinc super pelliceum,* a surpilch, or surplice. *Spelman. Cowel.*

PELLIPARIUS, (*Pat.* 15 *Edw.* 3, *p.* 2, *m.* 45.) a leather-seller or skinner. *Cowel.*

PELLOTA, (Fr. *Pelote*) the ball of the foot. 4 *Inst.* 308.

PELT-WOOL, wool pulled off the skin, or pelt of dead sheep. 8 *Hen.* 6, *cap.* 22. *Cowel.*

PEN, a high mountain. *Camd. Britan.*

PENAL LAWS. Penal statutes are to be construed strictly, and not extended by equity; but the words may be interpreted beneficially, according to the intent of the legislators. 1 *Inst.* 54, 268. See *Conviction.*

PENALTY OF BONDS. If a man brings an action of debt upon a bond he shall recover the whole penalty, because in debt the judgment must be according to the demand, and the demand is to be for the whole penalty.

But by the stat. 8 & 9 *W.* 3, *c.* 11, *s.* 8, in actions on bonds *for performance of covenants,* the plaintiff may assign as many breaches as he pleases, and jury may assess damages. Defendant paying the damages, execution may be stayed, but the judgment to remain, to answer any further breach, and plaintiff may have *sci. fac.* against the defendant.

And by the statute 4 & 5 *Ann. c.* 16, in the case of a bond conditioned *for the payment of money,* the defendant upon bringing the principal, interest, and costs, into court shall be discharged of the penalty. *s.* 13.

PENANCE, an ecclesiastical punishment, which affects the body of the penitent; by which he is obliged to give a public satisfaction to the church, for the scandal he hath given by his evil example.

In the case of incest, or incontinency, the sinner is usually enjoined to do a public penance in the cathedral or parish church, or public market bare legged and bare headed in a white sheet, and to make an open confession of his crime in a prescribed form of words.

So in smaller faults, a public satisfaction or penance as the judge shall decree, is to be made before the minister, churchwardens, or some of the parishioners, respect being bad to the quality of the offence, as in the case of defamation, or laying violent hands on a minister, or the like. *God. Append.* 18. *Wood's Inst.* 507. Penance may be changed into a sum of money to be applied to pious uses called *commuting.* 3 *Inst.* 150. 4 *Inst.* 336. 4 *Black.* 105. 217, 272. 361.

PENANCE, at common law, where a person stands mute. See *Mute.*

PENDENTE LITE. See *Administration.*

PENERARIUS, an ensign-bearer. *Cowel.*

PENITENTIARY HOUSES. By the stat. 19 *Geo.* 3, *c.* 74, all offenders liable to transportation may in lieu thereof, at the discretion of the judges, be employed, if males (except in the case of petty larceny.) in hard labour for the benefit of some public navigation; or, whether males or females, may in all cases be confined to hard labour in certain PENITENTIARY HOUSES, to be erected by virtue of the said act, for the several terms therein specified, but in no case exceeding seven years; with a power of subsequent mitigation, and even of reward, in case of their good behaviour. But if they escape and are re-taken, for the first time an addition of three years is made to the term of their confinement; and a second escape is felony without benefit of clergy.

In forming the plan of these penitentiary houses, the principal objects have been, by sobriety, cleanliness, and medical assistance, by a regular series of labour, by solitary confinement during the intervals of work, and by due religious instruction, to preserve and amend the health of the unhappy offenders, to inure them to habits of industry, to guard them from pernicious company, to accustom them to serious re-

* If he is examined as a witness in the high court of parliament he must be sworn. The bishop of Oxford was sworn in the impeachment of lord Macclesfield, and lord Mansfield (then lord Stormont) in that of Mr. Hastings.

flection, and to teach them both the principles and practice of every christian and moral duty. And if the whole of this plan be properly executed, and its defects be timely supplied, there is reason to hope that such a reformation may be effected in the lower classes of mankind, and such a gradual scale of punishment be affixed to all gradations of guilt, as may in time supersede the necessity of capital punishment, except for very atrocious crimes. 4 *Black.* 371.

PENNY WEIGHT. As every pound contained 12 ounces, each ounce was formerly divided into 20 parts, called penny-weights; and though the penny-weight be altered, yet the denomination still continues. Every penny-weight is subdivided into 24 grains. *Cowel.*

PENON, (mentioned in stat. 11 *Ric.* *c.* 1,) is a standard, banner, or ensign, carried in war. *Cowel.*

PENSA SALIS, *Casei*, &c. A wey of salt, or cheese, containing 256 pounds. *Cowel.*

PENSAM, *ad pensam*, the ancient way of paying into the Exchequer as much money for a pound sterling, as weighed twelve ounces troy. *Lowndes* 4.

PENSION, (Fr. *pension*,) a salary or allowance made by the crown to any one for meritorious services performed, or other good cause. And to receive a pension from a foreign prince or state, without leave of our king, has been held to be criminal, because it may incline a man to prefer the interest of such foreign prince to that of his own country. 1 *Hawk. P. C.* 58.

Persons having pensions from the crown during pleasure, or for term of years, are declared incapable of being elected or sitting as members of parliament, &c. by statute 6 *Ann.* *c.* 7. 1 *Geo.* 1, *c.* 56. See *Parliament.*

PENSION OF CHURCHES, are certain sums of money paid to clergymen in lieu of tithes.

PENSIONS OF THE INNS OF COURTS, are annual payments of each member to the houses. And also that which in the two Temples is called a parliament, and in Lincoln's Inn a council, in Gray's Inn is termed a pension, being usually an assembly of the benchers to consult of the affairs of the society.

PENSIONERS, (*pensionarii*) are *a band of gentlemen* so called, who attend as a guard on the king's person: They were instituted *anno* 1539, and have an allowance of fifty pounds a year, to maintain themselves and two horses for the king's service. *Stow's Annals* 973.

PENSION-WRIT. When a pension writ is once issued, none sued thereby in any inns of court, shall be discharged or permitted to come into commons, till all duties be paid. Order in Gray's Inn, wherein it seems to be a peremptory order against such of the society as are in arrear for pensions and other duties. *Cowel.*

PENTECOSTALS, (*pentecostalia*) were certain pious oblations made at the feast of pentecost, by parishioners to their priest, and sometimes by inferior churches or parishes, to the principal mother church. *Cowel.*

PENY, (Sax. *penig*) was our ancient current silver. 2 *Inst.* 575.

PERAMBULATION, (*perambulatio*) a travelling through, or over; as perambulation of the forest is the surveying or walking about the forest, and the utmost limits of it, by justices, or other officers thereto assigned, to set down and preserve the metes and bounds thereof. 17 *Car.* *c.* 16. 20 *Car.* 2, *c.* 3. 4 *Inst.* 30.

So perambulation of parishes is to be made by the minister, churchwardens and parishioners, by going round the same once a year, in or about Ascension week; and the parishioners may well justify going over any man's land in their perambulation, according to usage; and it is said may abate all nusances in their way. *Cro. Eliz.* 441.

There is also a perambulation of manors; and a writ *perambulatione facienda*, which lies where any encroachments have been made by a neighbouring lord, &c. Also a commission may be granted to other persons to make perambulation, and to certify the same in the Chancery, or the Common Pleas, &c. And this commission is issued to make perambulation of towns, counties, &c. *New Nat. Br.* 206.

PERCA, for pertica, a perch of land. *Cowel.*

PERCAPTURA, a place in a river made up with banks, &c. for the better preserving and taking fish. *Paroch. Antiq.* 120. *Cowel.*

PERCH, is a rod or pole of sixteen feet and a half in length, whereof forty in length and four in breadth, make an acre of ground. *Cromp. Jurisd.* 222.

PER CUI ET POST, writs of entry so called. See *Entry.*

PER MY ET PER TOUT. Jointenants are said to be seised *per my et per tout*, by the half or moiety, and by all; that is, they each of them have the entire possession, as well of every parcel as of the whole. They have not one of them a seisin of one half or moiety, and the other of the other moiety; neither can one be exclusively seised of one acre, and his companion of another; but each has an undivided moiety of the whole, and not the whole of an undivided moiety. 2 *Black.* 182.

PER QUOD, are words made use of by a plaintiff in his declaration in the averring of particular damage to have happened, without which his action would not have been maintainable. As in slander, to say that such a clergyman is a bastard, he cannot for this bring any action against me, unless he can shew some special loss by it: in which case he may bring his action against me, for saying he was a bastard *per quod* he lost the presentation to such a living. 4 *Rep.* 17. 1 *Lev.* 248. 2 *Black.* 124.

PERDINGS, the dregs of the people, men of no substance. *Cowel.*

PERDONATIO UTLAGARIÆ, a pardon for a man outlawed, and who afterwards of his own accord surrendered. *Reg. Orig.* 28.

PEREMPTORY, (*peremptorius*, from the verb *perimere*, to cut off,) joined with a substantive, as a peremptory action or exception, signifies a final and determinate act, without hope of renewing or altering. *Nat. Brev.* 35, 38. 104. 108. *Idem*, 5, 11. *Cowel.*

PEREMPTORY CHALLENGE, in criminal cases, or at least in capital ones, there is, *in favorem vitæ*, allowed to the prisoner an arbitrary and capricious species of challenge to a certain number of jurors, without showing any cause, that is to the number of 35, being under the number of three full juries, which is called a peremptory challenge. 4 *Black.* 353. See *Mute.*

PEREMPTORY MANDAMUS. If the inferior judge or other person to whom a writ of mandamus is directed, returns or signifies an insufficient reason, then there issues a peremptory mandamus, to do the thing absolutely; to which no other return will be admitted, but a certificate of perfect obedience and due execution of the writ. 3 *Black.* 111. 265.

PEREMPTORY WRIT, a species of original writ, called a *si fecerit te securum*, from the words of the writ; which directs the sheriff to cause the defendant to appear in court, without any option given him, provided the plaintiff gives the sheriff security effectually to prosecute his claim. This writ is in use where nothing is specifically demanded, but only a satisfaction in general; to obtain which, and minister complete redress, the intervention of some judicature is necessary. 3 *Black.* 274.

PERFECTION OF THE KING. Besides the attribute of sovereignty, the law also ascribes to the king, in his political capacity, absolute perfection, as the fundamental maxim is that the king can do no wrong. *Plowd.* 487. 1 *Black.* 246. See *King.*

PERINDE VALERE, a term in the ecclesiastical law, signifying a dispensation granted to a clerk, who being defective in capacity for a benefice, or other ecclesiastical function, is *de facto* admitted to it; and it hath the appellation from the words, which make the faculty as effectual to the party dispensed with as if he had been actually capable of the thing for wh'ch he is dispensed with at the time of his admission. 25 *Hen.* 8, *c.* 21, it is called a writ. *Cowel.*

PERINDINARE, to stay, remain, or abide in a place. *Ibid.*

PERIPHRASIS. No periphrasis, or circumlocution, will supply words of art, which the law hath appropriated for the description of offences in indictment. *Cro. Eliz.* 535, 749. 2 *Hawk. P. C.* 224, 249.

PERJURY, (*perjurium est mendacium cum juramento firmatum.*) 3 *Inst.* 163.

The crime of wilful and corrupt perjury is defined by sir Edward Coke to be a crime committed when a lawful oath is administered, in some judicial proceeding, to a person who swears wilfully, absolutely, and falsely, in a matter material to the issue or point in question. 3 *Inst.* 164.

The law takes no notice of any perjury but such as is committed in some court of justice, having power to administer an oath; or before some magistrate or proper officer, invested with a similar authority, in some proceedings relative to a civil suit or a criminal prosecution: for it esteems all other oaths unnecessary at least, and therefore will not punish the breach of them*. For which reason it is much to be questioned, how far any magistrate is justifiable in taking a voluntary affidavit in any extrajudicial matter, as is now too frequent upon every petty occasion: since it is more than possible, that by such idle oaths a man may frequently *in foro conscientiæ*, incur the guilt, and at the same time evade the temporal penalties, of perjury. The perjury must also be corrupt (that is, committed *malo animo*) wilful, positive, and absolute; not upon surprize, or the like: it also must be in some point material to the question in dispute; for if it only be in some trifling collateral circumstance, to which no regard is paid, it is no more penal than in the vo-

* Where an oath is required by an act of parliament, but not in a judicial proceeding, the breach of that oath does not seem to amount to perjury, unless the statute enacts that such oath, when false, shall be perjury, or shall subject the offender to the penalties of perjury. *Christian's N.* 4 *Black.* 137.

It is remarkable that the house of commons have no power to administer an oath, except in those particular instances in which that power is granted to them by express acts of parliament. It is supposed that the reason they have never obtained the general authority of administering an oath, is owing to the jealousy of the upper house, which, by securing this privilege to itselfe prevents the commons from participating in the judicature of parliament. *Ibid.*

luntary extrajudicial oaths before mentioned *. Subornation of perjury is the offence of procuring another to take such a false oath, as constitutes perjury in the principal. The punishment of perjury and subornation, at common law, has been various. It was antiently death; afterwards banishment, or cutting out the tongue; then forfeiture of goods; and now it is fine and imprisonment, and never more to be capable of bearing testimony (3 *Inst.* 163). But the stat. 5 *Eliz.* c. 9, (if the offender be prosecuted thereon) inflicts the penalty of perpetual infamy, and a fine of 40*l.* on the suborner: and in default of payment, imprisonment for six months, and to stand with both ears nailed to the pillory. Perjury itself is thereby punished with six months imprisonment, perpetual infamy, and a fine of 20*l.* or to have both ears nailed to the pillory. But the prosecution is usually carried on for the offence at common law; especially as to the penalties before inflicted, the stat. 2 *Geo.* 2, *c.* 25, superadds a power, for the court to order the offender to be sent to the house of correction for a term not exceeding seven years, or to be transported for the same period; and makes it felony without benefit of clergy to return or escape within the time. 4 *Black.* 137.

PERMISSIVE WASTE. Waste is either voluntary, which is a crime of commission, as by pulling down a house; or it is permissive, which is a matter of omission only, as by suffering it to fall for want of necessary reparations. 2 *Black.* 281.

PERMIT, (from *permitto*) a license granted to remove goods liable to the custom duties, or excise.

PERMUTATIONE ARCHIDIACONATUS ET ECCLESIA EIDEM ANNEXÆ CUM ECCLESIA ET PRÆBENDA, a writ to an ordinary, commanding him to admit a clerk to a benefice, upon exchange made with another. *Reg. Orig.* 307.

PERNANCY, (from the Fr. *prendre*) signifies a taking or receiving; as tithes in pernancy are tithes taken or that may be taken in kind. 2 *Black.* 163.

PERNOR OF PROFITS, he who receives the profits of lands, &c. and is all one with *cestui que* use. *Ibid.*

PERPARS, a part of the inheritance.

PERPETUATING THE TESTIMONY OF WITNESSES. If witnesses to a disputable fact are old and infirm, it is usual to file a bill to perpetuate the testimony of those witnesses, although no suit is depending; for it may be, a man's antagonist only waits for the death of some of them to commence his suit. 3 *Black. Com.* 450.

PERPETUITY. A perpetuity is, where if all who have interest join, yet they cannot bar or pass the estate. But if by concurrence of all having interest the estate-tail may be barred, it is no perpetuity. *Ch. Cases,* 213.

A perpetuity is a thing odious in law, and destructive to the commonwealth; it would put a stop to the commerce, and prevent the circulation of the property of the kingdom. *Vern.* 164.

And any attempt to make a perpetual succession of estates for life is vain, and not practicable. 2 *Vern.* 738. See *Executory Devise.*

PERPETUITY OF THE KING. The law ascribes to the king, in his political capacity, an absolute immortality: for though the reigning monarch may die, yet the king survives still: and immediately upon the decease of the reigning prince in his natural capacity, his kingship or imperial dignity, by act of law, without any interregnum, or interval, is vested at once in his heir, who is, *eo instanti,* king to all intents and purposes. 2 *Black.* 249.

PER QUÆ SERVITIA, a judicial writ, issuing from the note of a fine, for the cognisee of a manor, seigniory, chief-rent, or other services, to compel him who was tenant of the land at the time of the note of the fine levied, to attorn unto him. *Old Nat. Brev.* 155.

PERQUISITE, (*perquisitum*) any thing got by industry, or purchased with money, different from that which descends from an ancestor; so used by *Bracton, lib.* 2, *cap.* 30. *n.* 3, and *lib.* 4, *cap.* 22.

PERQUISITES OF COURTS, profits which arise to lords of manors, from their court baron. *Perk.* 20, 21.

PER QUOD CONSORTIUM AMISIT, and per quod servitium *amisit,* are words necessary in declarations for trespass, &c. where a man's wife or servant is beaten, or taken from him, by which means he loses their service, &c. 2 *Lil. Abr.* 595, 596.

PERSONABLE, (*personabilis,*) signified as much as enabled to maintain plea in court: as for example the defendant was judged personable to maintain this action. *Old Nat. Brev.* 142. and in *Kitchen,* 214.

PERSONAL, (*personalis*) being joined with the substantives, things, goods or chattels, as things personal, goods personal, chattels personal; signifies any moveable thing, quick or dead. *West. Symbol. part* 2. *sec.* 58. *Cowel.*

PERSONAL ACTION, (*actio personalis*) Personal actions are such whereby a man claims a debt, or personal duty, or damages in lieu thereof; and, likewise, whereby a man claims a satisfaction in damages for

* A man may be indicted for perjury in swearing that he believes a fact to be true which he must know to be false. *Leach,* 270.

some injury done to his person or property. The former are said to be founded on contracts, the latter upon torts or wrongs: and they are the same which the civil law calls "*actiones in personam, quæ adversus eum intenduntur, qui ex contractu vel delicto obligatus est aliquid dare vel concedere.*" (*Inst.* 4, 6, 15.) Of the former nature are all actions upon debt or promises; of the latter, all actions for trespasses, nuisances, assaults, defamatory words, and the like. 3 *Black.* 117.

In actions merely personal, arising *ex delicto*, for wrongs actually done or committed by the defendant, as trespass, battery, and slander, the rule is that *actio personalis moritur cum persona* (4 *Inst.* 315.); and it never shall be revived either by or against the executors or other representatives. For neither the executors of the plaintiff have received, nor those of the defendant have committed, in their own personal capacity, any manner of wrong or injury. But in actions arising *ex contractu*, by breach of promise and the like, where the right descends to the representatives of the plaintiff, and those of the defendant have assets to answer the demand, though the suits shall abate by the death of the parties, yet they may be revived against or by the executors: (*Mar.* 14.) being indeed rather actions against the property than the person, in which the executors have now the same interest that their testator had before.

PERSONAL SECURITY. The right of personal security consists in a person's legal and uninterrupted enjoyment of his life, his limbs, his body, his health, and his reputation. 1 *Black.* 129.

PERSONAL TITHES, are tithes paid of such profits as come by the labour of a man's person, as buying and selling, gains of merchandise, and handicrafts, &c. 2 *Black.* 24.

PERSONALTY, (*personalitas*) signifies things personal, as contra-distinguished from the realty.

PERSONATE, to represent by a fictitious or assumed character, so as to pass for the person represented. *Johns.* See *Felony.*

PERSONS, are divided by law into either natural persons, or artificial. Natural persons are such as the God of Nature formed us; artificial are such as are created and devised by human laws for the purposes of society and government, which are called corporations or bodies politic. 1 *Black.* 123. 467.

PERTICATA TERRÆ, the fourth part of an acre. *Cowel.*

PERTICULAS, poor scholars of the Isle of Man.

PERVISE, the area in front of Westminster Hall, now called Palace Yard. *Cowel.*

PESA, *pensa, pisa,* a wey or weigh of cheese and wool, &c. containing 256 pounds. *Cowel.*

PESAGE, (*pesagium*) a custom or duty paid for weighing merchandise, or other goods, and hence *pesarius*, a weigher. *Cowel.*

PESSONA, mast of oaks, &c. or money taken for mast, or feeding hogs. *Ibid.*

PESSURABLE, PESTARBLE, or PESTARABLE WARES, seem to be such wares or merchandise as pester and take up much room in a ship. *Ibid.*

PETER-CORN. In some of the ancient registers of our bishops there is a grant thereof by the king. *Ibid.*

PETER-PENCE, (*denarii sancti Petri,*) called in the Saxon tongue *Romefeoh*, the fee of Rome, or due to Rome; a tribute to the pope, so called because collected on the day of St. Peter *ad Vincula*, and was a penny for every house. *Cowel.*

It was prohibited by *Edw.* 3, and by 25 *Hen.* 8, *c.* 21, but revived by 1 & 2 *P. & M.* *c.* 8, and was wholly abrogated 1 *Eliz. c.* 1. 4 *Black.* 106.

PETITION, (*petitio*) a supplication made by an inferior to a superior, and especially to one having jurisdiction. *S. P. C. c.* 15. *Standf. Prærog. c.* 22. 3 *Black.* 256.

By stat. 13 *Car.* 2, *st.* 1, *c.* 5, (which is still in force, and no wise repealed, (*Doug.* 592) the soliciting, labouring, or procuring the putting the hands or consent of above 20 persons to any petition, remonstrance, or address to the king, or both or either house of parliament, for alterations in church or state, unless by assent of three or more justices of peace of the county, or a majority of the grand jury at the assises or sessions, &c. or if in *London* by the mayor, aldermen, and common council, and repairing to the king or parliament to deliver such petition, with above the number of ten persons, is subject to a fine of 100*l.* and three months imprisonment, being proved by two witnesses within six months in the court of *B. R.* or at the assises, &c.

If what is required by this statute be observed, *care must be taken that petitions to the king contain nothing which may be interpreted to reflect on the administration;* for if they do, it may come under the denomination of a LIBEL: and it is remarkable that the petition of the city of London, for the sitting of a parliament was deemed libellous; because it suggested that the king's dissolving a late parliament was an obstruction of justice. *Read. Stat. Vol.* 4, 353.

To subscribe a petition to the king, to frighten him into a change of his measures, intimating that, if it be denied many thousands of his subjects will be discontented, &c. is included among the contempts against the king's person and government, tending to weaken the same, and punishable by fine and imprisonment. 1 *Hawk. P. C.* 60.

But if there should happen any uncommon

injury, or infringement of the rights of the subject, which the ordinary course of law is too defective to reach, there remains a right, appertaining to every individual, namely, the right of petitioning the king or either house of parliament for the redress of grievances. There are doubtless restrictions to this right, but, while they promote the spirit of peace they are no check upon that of liberty. Care only must be taken, lest, under the pretence of petitioning, the subject be guilty of any riot or tumult; to prevent which the stat. 13 *Car.* 2, *st.* 1, *c.* 5, above mentioned was enacted. 1 *Black.* 142.

But under these regulations, it is declared by the *stat.* 1 *W. & M. st.* 2, *c.* 2, that the subject hath a right to petition; and that all commitments and prosecutions for such petitioning are illegal.

PETITION IN CHANCERY, is a statement in writing addressed to the lord chancellor, or master of the rolls, showing some matter whereupon the petitioner prays some order of the court. *P. R. C.* 269.

But the master of the rolls is not to be petitioned for rehearings, but the chancellor; also the chancellor only is to be petitioned touching pleas, demurrers, or exceptions, or touching decrees or special orders made before the chancellor. *P. R. C.* 270. See 16 *Vin. Abr.* 337, 338.

PETITION OF RIGHT. See *Liberties* and *Rights.*

PETIT CAPE. See *Cape.*

PETIT LARCENY. See *Larceny.*

PETIT SERJEANTY, *parva serjeantia.* To hold by petit serjeanty was to hold lands or tenements of the king, yielding him a knife, a buckler, an arrow, a bow without a string, or other like service, at the will of the first feoffor, abolished by 12 *Car.* 2. *c.* 24.

PETIT SESSION. In both corporations and counties at large there is sometimes kept a special or petty sessions, by a few justices, for dispatching smaller business in the neighbourhood between the times of the general sessions, as for licensing alehouses, passing the accounts of parish officers, and the like, which petty sessions must be held by two justices at the least.

PETIT TREASON (*parva proditio*). See *Homicide.*

PETRA, a sort of weight which we now call a stone, but differing in many parts of England; in some places consisting of 16, in others of 14, 12, or 8 pounds. *Cowel.*

PETRARIA, a quarry of stones, or a great gun called petrard: often mentioned in both senses. *Cowel.*

PEWS, in a church, may descend by immemorial custom, without any ecclesiastical concurrence, from the ancestor to the heir, as appurtenant to an ancient messuage of inheritance. 3 *Inst.* 202. 12 *Rep.* 105.

For the right to sit in a particular pew in a church arises either from prescription as appurtenant to a messuage, or from a faculty or grant from the ordinary, for he has the disposition of all pews which are not claimed by prescription. *Gibs. Cod.* 221.

And in an action upon the case for a disturbance of the enjoyment of a pew, if the plaintiff claims it by prescription, he must state it in the declaration as *appurtenant to a messuage in the parish.* This prescription may be supported by an enjoyment for 36 years, and perhaps any time above 20 years. 1 *T. R.* 428. But where a pew was claimed as appurtenant to an ancient messuage, and it was proved that it had been so annexed for 30 years, but that it had no existence before that time, it was held this modern commencement defeated the prescriptive claim. 5 *T. R.* 296.

PHAROS, (from *Pharus*, a small island in the mouth of the Nile, wherein stood a high watch tower) a watch tower or seamark: and no man can erect a pharos, light-house, beacon, &c. without lawful warrant and authority. 3 *Inst.* 204.

PHYSICIANS. By 14 & 15 *Hen.* 8. *c.* 5, if any practise physic in the city of London, or within 7 miles of it, without licence of the college under their seal, he shall forfeit 5*l.* per month, half to the king and half to the college. Also persons practising physic in other parts of England, are to have letters testimonial from the president and 3 elects, unless they be graduate physicians of Oxford or Cambridge, &c.

The fees of a physician are honorary, and not demandable of right, consequently a physician cannot maintain an action for them. 4 *Ter. Rep.* 317.

PHILOSOPHER'S STONE. Henry 6 granted letters patent to certain persons, who undertook to find out the philosopher's stone, and to change other metals into gold, &c. to be free from the penalty of the *Stat.* 5 *Hen.* 4, made against the attempts of chymists of this nature. *Pat.* 34 *Hen.* 6. 3 *Inst.* 74.

PICARDS, boats of 15 tons or upwards, used on the Severn, 34 & 35 *Hen.* 8, *c.* 3. Also a fisher-boat. 13 *Eliz.* 11.

PICCAGE, (*piccagium*, from the Fr. *piquer*, i. e. *effodere*) is a sum of money paid for leave to break up ground to set up booths, stalls, or standings in fairs, payable to the lord or owner of the soil. *Palmer* 77. This stands upon the same footing as *Stallage*, which see.

PICLE, (*pictellum*) a small parcel of land enclosed with a hedge; a little close. In some parts of England it is called pightel. *Cowel.*

PIE-POUDRE COURT, (*curia pedis pulverizati*) from the Fr. *pied*, i. e. *pes*, and *poudreux*, i. e. *pulverulentus.* The lowest, and at the same time the most expeditious, court of justice known to the law of England is the court of *pie poudre, curia pedis pulverizati*: so called from the dusty feet of the suitors; or according to Sir Edward Coke (4 *Inst.* 272), because justice is there done as speedily as dust can fall from the foot. Upon the same principle that justice among the Jews was administered in the gate of the city (*Ruth, chap.* 4), that the proceedings might be the more speedy, as well as public. But the etymology given us by a learned modern writer (*Barrington's Observations on the Statutes*, 337), is much more ingenious and satisfactory; it being derived, according to him, from *pied puldreaux*, a pedlar in old French, and therefore signifying the court of such petty chapmen as resort to fairs or markets. It is a court of record, incident to every fair and market; of which the steward of him, who owns or has the toll of the market, is the judge. It was instituted to administer justice for all injuries done in that very fair or market, and not in any preceding one. So that the injury must be done, complained of, heard, and determined, within the compass of one and the same day. The court hath cognizance of all matters that can possibly arise within the precinct of that fair or market; and the plaintiff must make oath that the cause of an action arose there (*Stat.* 17 *Edw.* 4. *c.* 2). From this court a writ of error lies, in the nature of an appeal, to the courts at Westminster (*Cro. Eliz.* 774). The reason of its institution seems to have been to do justice expeditiously among the variety of persons, that resort from distant places to a fair or market: since it is probable that no other inferior court might be able to serve its process, or execute its judgments on both or perhaps either of the parties; and therefore, unless this court had been erected, the complaint must necessarily have resorted even in the first instance to some superior judicature. 3 *Black.* 32.

PIES, *freres pies*, monks, so called because they wore black and white garments, like magpies. *Cowel.*

PIETANTIA, a small portion of meat and drink, distributed to the members of some collegiate body, or other people, upon a high festival, or stated anniversary; hence

PIETANTIARIUS, the pittancer or officer who was to distribute the pittances. *Cowel.*

PIG OF LEAD. See *Fother*.

PIGHTLE OF LAND, a little close of land.

PIGEONS. By 2 *Geo.* 3, *c.* 29, any person who shall wilfully shoot at, with an intent to kill, or shall by any means whatever kill or take with a wilful intent to destroy any house-dove or pigeon belonging to other persons, shall forfeit on conviction 20*s.* to the prosecutor; and if not forthwith paid, the offender may be committed and kept to hard labour for any time not exceeding three months, nor less than one, unless the forfeiture be sooner paid. The owners of dove-cotes or other places built for the preservation or breeding of pigeons, and those appointed by them, excepted. Offender is liable only to one conviction for same offence; and prosecutions are to be commenced and carried on with effect within two months after the offence; and where persons suffer imprisonment, they are not liable afterwards to pay the penalty. But it seems that if *pigeons* come upon my land I may kill them, and the owner hath not any remedy. *Cro. Jac.* 492.

PIGEON-HOUSE. Formerly none but the lord of the manor, or the parson, might erect a pigeon-house; though it has been since held, that any freeholder may build a pigeon-house on his own ground. 5 *Rep.* 104. *Cro. Eliz.* 548. *Cro. Jac.* 382, 440.

PILA, that side of money which is called pile, because it is the side on which there was an impression of a church built on piles. *Fleta, lib.* 1. *c.* 39. *Cowel.*

PILETTUS, anciently used for an arrow, which had a round knob, a little above the head, to hinder it from going far into a mark; from the Lat. *pila*, which signifies generally any round thing like a ball. *Cowel.*

PILEUS SUPPORTATIONIS, a cap of maintenance. *Cowel.*

PILLORY, (*collistrigium, collum stringens; pilloria*, from the Fr. *pilleur*, i. e. *depeculator*, or *peluor*, derived from the Greek Πύλη, *Janua*, a door, because one standing on the pillory, puts his head, as it were through a door, and Οράω, *video*,) is an engine made of wood to punish offenders, by exposing them to public view. There is a statute of the pillory, 51 *H.* 3. And by statute, it is appointed for bakers, forestallers, and those who use false wieghts, perjury, forgery, &c. (3 *Inst.* 219.) Lords of leets are to have a pillory and tumbrel, or it will be cause of forfeiture of the leet; and a vill may be bound by prescription to provide a pillory, &c. 2 *Hawk. P. C.* 73.

PILOT, is one employed to conduct ships into roads and harbours, or over bars and sands. Also the steersman who stands at the helm, and manages the rudder.

By 43 *Geo.* 3, *c.* 152, the warden of the Cinque Ports, or his deputy, with assent of the court of Load Manage, shall make rules and orders for the regulation of pilots at Dover, Deal, and other ports, undertaking the navigation of vessels there, and on the coasts of France, Flanders, Holland, and the Baltic, which rules shall be printed; pilots refusing to obey such rules may be convicted by the lord warden or deputies; and the conviction shall be returned to the court of Load Manage, to which the party aggrieved may appeal. *s.* 1—3.

Pilots navigating vessels during their suspension, shall forfeit 10*l.* *s.* 4.

By 48 *Geo.* 3, *c.* 104, for the better regulation of pilots and the pilotage of vessels navigating the British seas, the corporation of Trinity-house of Deptford shall license fit persons, as pilots, to conduct all vessels within certain limits in the Thames and Medway, and none other shall act, and certain rates of pillotage are to be paid; which pilots are to pay, annually, three guineas to the corporation of Trinity-house, on pain of suspension. *s.* 1—4.

No person shall be licensed as a pilot, unless he has served either as a mate for three years, or commander of a square-rigged vessel for one year, or been employed as a pilot by the Trinity-house for seven years, or served an apprenticeship of five years to some licensed pilot vessel. *s.* 5.

Till a pilot has acted three years, he shall not take charge of a ship drawing more than fourteen feet water, on pain of 10*l.* and the like on the master. *s.* 6.

No Cinque Port pilot shall take charge of any ship till he has been admitted; on pain to forfeit, for the first offence, 10*l.*; the second, 20*l.*; and every other offence, 40*l.* *s.* 7.

A sufficient number of Cinque Port pilots shall constantly ply to take charge of ships coming from the westward; and upon making signals of fleets from the westward, all pilots shall prepare to go off, on pain to forfeit, for the first offence, 20*l.*; for the second, to be suspended for twelve months; and for the third offence, to forfeit his licence and be incapacitated. *s.* 10.

Masters of ships, coming from the westward, not having a Cinque Port pilot, shall display a signal for one, and facilitate his getting on board, under the same pain as for refusing to take one on board. *s.* 11.

Cinque Port pilots quitting ships before arrival at the place to which bound in the Thames or Medway, without the consent of the master, are to forfeit their pay, and be subject to such penalty as by this act, or any rules made by the corporations aforesaid by virtue thereof, shall be imposed on pilots quitting their ships before their arrival at the place of destination. *s.* 12.

Rules and regulations are to be made by the two corporations for the government of their respective pilots. *s.* 13—16.

Pilots shall qualify themselves to conduct, and shall conduct, ships into and out of Ramsgate, Dover, Sandwich, and Margate, harbours, on pain of forfeiting their pilotage, and such fine as may be imposed by the rules. *s.* 17—19.

Pilots suspended, or deprived of licence, are liable to the same penalty as for acting without a licence; and on suspension may appeal to the privy council. *s.* 23, 24.

No owner or master shall be answerable for any loss, nor owners of ships, or consignee of goods, prevented from receiving insurance, by reason of a pilot not being on board. *s.* 25.

The act is not to extend to ships belonging to the king, nor vessels not exceeding sixty tons. *s.* 27.

The act is not to prevent masters of ships, residing at Dover, Deal, or the Isle of Thanet, from piloting their own ships in the Thames or Medway. *s.* 30.

Licensed pilots may supersede those not licensed for the limits; and masters continuing unlicensed pilots, or those acting out of their limits, after a proper pilot shall have offered to take charge of the ship, are to forfeit not exceeding 50*l.* nor less than 20*l.* *s.* 31.

Masters of vessels bound to the river Thames, repairing to Stangate Creek, to pay full charges of pilotage during the quarantine; and pilots quitting ships at Standgate Creek before arrival at the place to which bound, are to forfeit their pay, and be liable to the penalty in the rules. *s.* 39.

A description of the pilot is to be indorsed on his licence, which shall be inspected by masters, who, if they suspect the party not to be the right person, they are to send a copy to the corporation granting the same. *s.* 40.

If any pilot shall keep a public-house, unless authorised by his corporation, or shall offend against the revenue laws, he shall be dismissed or suspended. *s.* 41.

No pilot shall act till his licence has been registered at the custom-house office near his residence, nor without having his licence in his custody, on pain to forfeit, for the first offence, not exceeding 30*l.* nor less than 10*l.* and for every other offence not exceeding 50*l.* nor less than 30*l.* *s.* 42.

On the death of the pilot, the licence is to be returned by his personal representative, to the corporation that granted it, on pain of not exceeding 20*l.* nor less than 40*s.* *s.* 43.

Pilot-boats, in the service of the corporations, shall be fitted, with the name and number of the principal pilot painted thereon; and if the name or number shall be hid by any one on board, the penalty is 20*l.* to be paid by the pilot; and boats not in the service of the corporations shall carry a flag to show she has a pilot. *s.* 45.

Penalty on carrying such flag without having such pilot on board, 100*l.* *s.* 46.

Pilots declining to take charge of vessels, or exacting more than due, getting drunk, or otherwise misbehaving, to forfeit not exceeding 100*l.* nor less than 10*l.* and be liable to be dismissed or suspended. *s.* 47.

Pilot employing, or requiring masters to employ, any boat, matter, or thing, beyond what is necessary, thereby to increase expence, to forfeit not exceeding 50*l.* nor less than 10*l.* and be liable to lose his licence, or be suspended. *s.* 48.

Any person whatever, under colour of pilotage, conducting any vessel into danger, or unnecessarily cutting cables or the like, is to forfeit not exceeding 100*l.* nor less than 10*l.* and being a pilot to be dismissed or suspended. *s.* 49.

Pilot-boats running before vessels not having a pilot on board are entitled to pilotage. *s.* 50.

No pilot shall be taken to sea without his consent, except in case of necessity, and then shall receive 10*s.* 6*d.* per day. *s.* 51.

Masters of vessels, piloted by any other than a licensed pilot, to forfeit double the amount of the pilotage, and 5*l.* for every 50 tons burthen of his vessel, except in the case of its being piloted by himself up and down channel, or in passing any part of the coast not being a port or place, to which any act or charter extends, or the case of no licensed pilot offering himself, or distress of weather.

Persons reporting to pilots a false account of the draught of water of vessels, to forfeit double the amount of the pilotage; and altering the marks, to denote such draught, te forfeit 500*l.* *s.* 56.

PIMP-TENURE.—Willielmus Hoppeshort, *tenet dimidiam vergatum terræ in* Rockampton *de Domino Rege, per servitium custodiendi sex demisellas, scil meretrices, ad usum Domini Regis.* 12 *Ed.* 1. viz. by *Pimp-Tenure. Blount's Ten.* 39.

PINNAS BIBERE, or *ad pinnas bibere*, a custom of drinking brought in by the Danes, which was to fix a pin in the side of the bowl, and to drink exactly to the pin. *Cowel.*

PIPE, (*pipa*) is a roll in the Exchequer, called the Great Roll; it is also a measure of wine, containing two hogsheads, or half a ton, that is, one hundred and twenty-six gallons. 1 *R.* 3. *c.* 3.

PIQUANT, a French word for sharp, made use of to express malice or rancour against any one. *Law Fr. Dict.*

PIRATES, (*Piratæ*) are common sea rovers, without any fixed place of residence, who acknowledge no sovereign and no law, and support themselves by pillage and depredations at sea. *Spelm. Cowel.*

The crime of piracy, or robbery and depredation upon the high seas, is an offence against the universal law of society; a pirate being, according to sir Edward Coke (3 *Inst.* 113,) *hostis humani generis.* As therefore he has renounced all the benefits of society and government, and has reduced himself afresh to the savage state of nature, by declaring war against all mankind, all mankind must declare war against him: so that every community hath a right, by the rule of self-defence, to inflict that punishment upon him, which every individual would in a state of nature have been otherwise entitled to do, for any invasion of his person or personal property.

By the ancient common law, piracy, if committed by a subject, was held to be a species of treason, being contrary to his natural allegiance; and by an alien to be felony only, but now, since the statute of treasons, 25 *Edw.* 3. *c.* 2, it is held to be only felony in a subject (*Ibid*). Formerly it was only cognisable by the admiralty courts, which proceed by the rules of the civil law (1 *Hawk. P. C.* 98). But, it being inconsistent with the liberties of the nation, that any man's life should be taken away, unless by the judgment of his peers, or the common law of the land, the statute 28 *Hen.* 8. c. 15. established a new jurisdiction for this purpose; which proceeds according to the course of the common law, and of which we shall say more hereafter.

The offence of piracy, by common law, consists in committing those acts of robbery and depredation upon the high seas, which, if committed upon land, would have amounted to felony there (1 *Hawk. P. C.* 100).

But, by statute some other offences are made piracy also: as, by stat. 11 & 12 *W.* 3. *c.* 7, if any natural born subject commits any act of hostility upon the high seas, against others of his majesty's subjects, under colour of a commission from any foreign power; this, though it would only be an act of war in an alien, shall be construed piracy in a subject. And further, any commander, or other seafaring person, betraying his trust, and running away with any ship, boat, ordnance, ammunition, or goods; or yielding them up voluntarily to a pirate; or conspiring to do these acts; or any person assaulting the commander of a vessel to hinder him from fighting in defence of his ship, or confining him, or making or endeavouring to make a revolt on board; shall, for each of these offences, be adjudged a pirate, felon, and robber, and shall suffer death, whether he be principal, or merely accessory by setting forth such pirates, or abetting them before the fact, or receiving or concealing them or their goods after it. And the stat. 4 *Geo.* 1, *c.* 11, expressly excludes the principals from the benefit of clergy. By the stat. 8 *Geo.* 1, *c.* 24, the trading with known pirates, or furnishing them with stores or ammunition, or fitting out any vessel for that purpose, or in any wise consulting, combining, confederating, or corresponding with them; or the forcibly boarding any merchant vessel, though without seizing or carrying her off, and destroying or throwing any of the goods over board, shall be deemed piracy: and such accessories to piracy as are described by the statute of king William are declared to be principal pirates, and all pirates convicted by virtue of this act are made felons without benefit of clergy. By the same statutes also, (to encourage the defence of merchant vessels against pirates,) the commanders or seamen wounded, and the widows of such seamen as are slain, in any piratical engagement, shall be entitled to a bounty, to be divided among them, not exceeding one fiftieth part of the value of the cargo on board: and such wounded seamen shall be entitled to the pension of Greenwich hospital, which no other seamen are, except only such as have served in a ship of war. And if the commander shall behave cowardly, by not defending the ship, if she carries guns or arms, or shall discharge the mariners from fighting, so that the ship falls into the hands of pirates, such commander shall forfeit all his wages, and suffer six months imprisonment. Lastly, by stat. 18 *Geo.* 2. *c.* 30, any natural born subject, or denizen, who in time of war shall commit hostilities at sea against any of his fellow-subjects, or shall assist an enemy on that element, is liable to be tried and convicted as a pirate.

PIRATES GOODS. In the patent to the admiral he has granted to him *bona piratar'*: but the proper goods of pirates only pass by this grant; and not piratical goods. So it is of a grant *de bonis felonum*, the grantee shall not have goods stolen, but the true and rightful owner. But the king shall have piratical goods, if the owner be not known. 10 *Rep.* 109. *Dyer* 269. *Jenk. Cent.* 325.

PISCARY, (*piscaria, vel privilegium piscandi*) is a right or liberty of fishing: and there are three sorts of piscaries, *libera piscaria*, or a *free fishery*, *separalis piscara*, or a *several fishery*, and *communis piscaria*, or *common of fishery*.

1. A *free fishery*. It is an exclusive right of fishing in a public river, and is considered as a royal franchise in all countries where the feodal polity has prevailed; and with us this franchise of *free fishery* must now be at least as old as the reign of *Hen.* 2.

2. A *several fishery*. He that has a several fishery must also be the owner of the soil, which in a free fishery is not requisite.

3. *Common of Piscary* is a liberty of fishing in another man's water, and differs from a *free fishery* in that the free fishery is an exclusive right, the common of piscary is not so; and therefore in a free fishery a man has property in the fish before they are caught; in a mmon of piscary not till afterwards.

PISCENARIUS, used in ancient records for a fishmonger. *Pat.* 1 *Edw.* 3, *part.* 3, *m.* 13.

PIT, is a hole wherein the Scots used to drown women thieves; and to say condemned to the pit is as when we say condemned to the gallows. *Skene.*

PITCHING-PENCE, money (commonly a penny) paid for pitching, or setting down every bag of corn, or pack of goods, in a fair or market. *Cowel.*

PITTANCE, (*pittancia modicum*) a little repast, or refection of fish or flesh, more than the common allowance. *Ibid.*

PLACARD, (Fr. *placuart*, Dutch *placcaert*) hath several significations: in France it is a bill, or paper posted up, a proclamation, a libel: in Holland it is an edict, or proclamation; also it signifies a writing of safe conduct; WITH US it is little used, but was mentioned as a license to shoot with a gun, or use certain games, &c. See stat. 2 & 3 *Ph. & Mar. c.* 7. 33 *Hen.* 8, *c.* 6.

PLACE, (*locus*) the place where a fact was committed must be alleged in appeals of death, indictments, &c. *Co. Lit.* 282. *Shep. Epit.* 700. See *Venue*.

PLACEMEN. No persons concerned in the management of any duties or taxes created since 1692, except the commissioners of the treasury, (5 & 6 *W. & M. c.* 7), nor any of the officers following, (11 & 12 *Will.* 3, *c.* 2,) (*viz.* commissioners of prizes, transports, sick and wounded, wine licences, navy, and victualling; secretaries or receivers of prizes; comptrollers of the army accounts; agents for regiments; governors of plantations and their deputies; officers of Minorca or Gibraltar; officers of the excise and customs; clerks or deputies in the several offices of the treasury, exchequer, navy, victualling, admiralty, pay of the army or navy, secretaries of state, salt, stamps, appeals, wine licences, hackney coaches, hawkers and pedlars,) nor any persons that hold any new office under the crown created since 1705 (*Stat.* 6 *Ann. c.* 7.) are capable of being elected or sitting as members *. 6. That no person having a pension under the crown during pleasure, or for any term of years, is capable of being elected or sitting (*stat.* 6 *Ann. c.* 7. 1 *Geo.* 1, *c.* 56). If any member accepts an office under the crown, except an officer in the army or navy accepting a new commission, his seat is void; but such member is capable of being re-elected. *Stat.* 6 *Ann. c.* 7.

---

* All the persons enumerated above are utterly incapable of sitting in the house of commons, whilst they continue in their respective situations; and amongst these are all persons who accept from the crown any office created since 1705. But by the 26th

PLA

PLACITA, pleas, or pleadings. Placita is a word used in the intituling of pleadings at law, as *pleas before our sovereign lord the king*, &c.

PLACITARE, *i. e. litigare et causas agere*, to plead; hence *placitator*, a pleader. *Cowel. Blount.*

PLAINT (Fr. *plainte*, Lat. *querela*). The first process in an inferior court is a plaint, which is in the nature of an original writ, because therein is briefly set forth the plaintiff's cause of action; and on this plaint there may issue a pone, till the return of a nihil, upon which a *capias* will lie against the body of the defendant. 2 *Lill. Abr.* 294.

Where a plaint is levied in an inferior court, the defendant must be first distrained for non-appearance, by something of small value; then, if he doth not appear, a further distress is to be taken to a greater value, and so on; if all his goods are distrained on the first distress, attachment may be issued out of *B. R.* against the officers, &c. *Ibid.* 3 *Black.* 273.

PLAINT in a superior court, is said to be the cause for which the plaintiff complains against the defendant; and for which he obtains the king's writ: For as the king denies his writ to none, if there be cause to grant it; so he grants not his writ to any, without there be cause alleged for it. 2 *Lill.* 294.

---

section of the same act, 6 Ann. c. 7, if any member shall accept of any office of profit from the crown, his election or seat becomes void, but he may be re-elected. This means an office of profit, which was in existence prior to 1705.

The office or trust of a member of parliament cannot be resigned, and every member is compellable to discharge the duties of it, unless he can shew such a cause, as the house in its discretion will think a sufficient excuse for his non-attendance upon a call of the house. The only way therefore of vacating a seat, is by accepting a situation, in consequence of which the law declares his seat vacant. So where members wish to vacate their seats and retire from parliament, it is now usual for the crown to grant them the office of the stewardship of the Chiltern Hundreds. Mr. Hatsell observes, that "the practice of accept-
"ing this nominal office, which began, he
"believes, only about the year 1750, has
"been now so long acquiesced in from its
"convenience to all parties, that it would
"be ridiculous to state any doubt about the
"legality of its proceedings; otherwise
"(he believes) it would be found very diffi-
"cult from the form of these appoint-
"ments, to shew that it is an office of pro-
"fit under the crown." 2 *Hats.* 41.

PLANCHIA, a plank of wood. *Cowel.*

PLANTATION, (*plantatio, colonia,*) is a place where people are sent to dwell; or to which a company of people voluntarily emigrate with the sanction of government. *Lit. Dict.*

Our plantations abroad are chiefly islands in America, the Leeward Islands, and at *New South Wales*. In settlements acquired by conquest the laws and customs by which the people were governed before the conquest bind them until new laws are given; for there is a necessity that the former shall be in force till the new are obtained. But if an uninhabited country be newly found out by English subjects, all the laws of the kingdom of England are immediately in force there. 2 *Salk.* 411. 3 *Mod.* 159. 4 *Mod.* 225, 226.

With respect to interior polity our colonies and plantations are properly of three sorts,

1. Provincial establishments:
2. Proprietary governments:
3. Charter governments.

But the form of government in most of them is borrowed from that of England. They have a governor named by the king, (or in some proprietary colonies by the proprietor) who is his representative or deputy. They have courts of justice of their own, from whose decisions an appeal lies to the king in council here in England. Their general assemblies, which are their house of commons, together with their council of state, being their upper house, with the concurrence of the king or his representative the governor, make laws suited to their own emergencies. But all laws, &c. in the plantations that are repugnant to any law made or to be made in this kingdom, are void, 1 *Black.* 106.

PLATE, a hoy, or small water-vessel. 13 *Eliz. cap.* 15. Also vessels, &c. of gold and silver. *Cowel. Blount.* See *Manufactures*.

PLAYHOUSE. Playhouses were originally instituted with a design of recommending virtue and exposing vice and folly; therefore are not in their own nature nusances: but a common playhouse may become a nusance, if it draw together such great numbers as to prove generally inconvenient to the places adjacent. 5 *Mod.* 142.

By 3 *Jac.* 1, *c.* 21, any person in a stage play or entertainment profanely using the name of God or the Trinity, shall forfeit 10*l.*

By 10 *Geo.* 2. *c.* 19, stage players acting for gain, in or within five miles of either of the universities, may be committed as rogues and vagabonds, by the vice chancellor,

By 10 *Geo.* 2. *c.* 28, persons acting plays in any place where they have not a legal settlement, for hire, gain, or reward, without royal authority, or licence from the lord chamberlain, shall be deemed rogues and vagabonds; and, whether they have a settlement or not, they are to forfeit 50*l.* but if they pay that sum, they are discharged of the other penalties.

No new plays, or additions to old ones, shall be acted unless a copy thereof be sent to the lord chamberlain fourteen days before. *Ibid.*

The lord chamberlain may prohibit the acting any play or part thereof; and persons acting the same before such copy be sent, or contrary to such prohibition, shall forfeit 50*l.* and their licence. *Ibid.*

No persons shall be authorised to act plays, by royal patent or licence from the lord chamberlain, but in the city and liberties of Westminster, or places of his majesty's residence. *Ibid.*

Plays acted in public houses shall be deemed performed for gain; and prosecutions must be within six months. *Ibid.*

By 25 *Geo.* 2. *c.* 36, made perpetual by 28 *Geo.* 2. *c.* 19, houses, gardens, or places, for public entertainment, music, dancing, or singing, within twenty miles of London, without a licence from the preceding Michaelmas quarter sessions, shall be deemed disorderly houses. Constables may seize persons found therein, and the persons keeping the same shall forfeit 100*l.*

Licensed places shall have an inscription over them declaratory thereof, and they are not to be opened before five in the evening: on breach of either of the conditions, the licence shall be revoked. *Ibid.*

Not to extend to the theatres royal, or performances licensed by the crown or the lord chamberlain. *Ibid.*

By 28 *Geo.* 3. *c.* 30, the justices in sessions on petition may license the performance of such plays as are performed at either of the patent theatres, or have been inspected by the chamberlain of the household, for not more than sixty days, to commence within the next six months, and to be within such four months as shall be specified in the licence, so as there be but one licence in use at the same time, the place be not within twenty miles of London, Westminster, or Edinburgh, or eight miles of any patent or licensed theatre, or ten miles of the royal residence, or of any place at which, within six months preceding, a licence under this act shall have been had, or within fourteen miles of either of the universities, or within two miles of the limits of any peculiar jurisdiction, and so also as no licence under this act shall have been at the same place within eight months before.

But no licence shall be granted to be exercised within any peculiar jurisdiction, unless with the consent of the majority of the justices acting for the same. *Ibid.*

Nor shall any such licence be granted within any town, &c. unless three weeks notice be given to the mayor or chief officer of the intended application. *Ibid.*

PLAYS AND GAMES. See *Gaming.*

PLEA (*placitum*). Pleas are divided into pleas of the crown, and common pleas; pleas of the crown are all suits in the king's name, for offences committed against his crown and dignity, and also against the peace. Common pleas are those that are agitated between common persons, in civil cases: and pleas may be further divided into as many branches as action; for they signify all one. *S. P. C. cap.* 1. 4 *Inst.* 10.

A plea to the action is that which goes to the merits of the cause or action, and is either a GENERAL, or a SPECIAL plea: A general plea in debt or contract is, he owes nothing: in debt on bond, it is not his deed, or he paid it at the day: in action of the case upon a promise, he did not promise: in trespass upon the case, not guilty: in covenant, performance of covenants, &c.

A special plea contains matter at large, concluding to the declaration or action; and special pleas in answer to the declaration are, PLEAS IN BAR, or in ABATEMENT; and every plea must be pleaded either in bar to the action, or in abatement of the writ or bill, upon which the action is framed, or it is but a discourse, and not a plea. *Finch* 362, 378. *Co. Lit.* 282, 372.

Special pleas are drawn up in form, setting forth the matter pleaded, &c. and must be signed by counsel. And when a defendant hath pleaded, the plaintiff answers the defendant's plea, which is called a replication; and the defendant answers the replication by rejoinder: which the plaintiff may answer by surrejoinder; and sometimes, (though seldom,) pleadings come to rebutter, in answer to surrejoinder, and surrebutter. *Co. Litt.* 303. See *Abatement. Bar*, and other titles.

PLEAS AT LAW, are at present set down and delivered into the proper office in writing, though formerly they were usually put in by their counsel *ore tenus*, or *viva voce*, in court, and then minuted down by the chief clerks, or prothonotaries; whence in our old law French, the pleadings are frequently denominated the *parol.* 3 *Black.* 293.

PLEAS OF THE SWORD, *placita ad gladium.* Ranulph, the third earl of Chester, in the second year of Henry the third, granted to his barons of Cheshire, an ample charter of liberties, *exceptis placitis ad gladium meum pertinentibus. Cowel. Blount.*

PLEBANIA, *plebanalis ecclesia*, a mother church, which has one or more subordinate chapels. *Ibid.*

PLEBANUS, a rural dean. *Ibid.*

PLEBISCITUM, a law or statute made by the joint consent of the people or commons without the senate. *Lit. Dict.* 1 *Black.* 80.

PLEDGE, (*plegius*, may be derived from the Fr. *pleige, fidejussor.)* See 4 *Inst.* 180.

When writs were delivered to the sheriff to be by him returned, he was obliged, before the return, to take pledges of prosecution, which, when the fines and amerciaments were considerable, were real and responsible persons, and answerable for those amercements. But they being now so inconsiderable, there are only formal pledges entered, *viz.* John Doe and Richard Roe. *Gilb. Hist. of C. B.* 6, 7.

PLEDGE, a *pledge* is he who undertakes, or is thereby for another: and therefore every bail and mainprize is, *stricte loquendo*, a pledge. 4 *Inst.* 180.

But a pledge is such as the demandant or plaintiff finds, where the writ says, *si quærcus fecerit te securum de clamore suo prosequendo*, for then the plaintiff was to find pledges for security of the king's amerciament, if the plaintiff be nonsuited. 4 *Inst.* 108.

PLEDGES OF GOODS. See *Bailment* and *Pawnbrokers.*

PLEDGERY or PLEGGERY, (Fr. *plegerie*, Lat. *plegiagium*) suretyship, an undertaking or answering for. *Cowel. Blount.*

PLEDGING, is where goods and chattels are delivered in security for money lent, and by such pledging the pawnee hath more than the naked possession in the nature of a bailment; for he hath the property and interest in the thing itself; and, by the better opinions, shall have a reasonable use of it, so that it be without damage to the thing pledged. *Doct. and Stud.* 130. 1 *Rol. Abr.* 338, 673. *Owen* 124. 2 *Salk.* 522. See *Bailment.*

PLEGIIS AD QUIETANDIS, a writ that lay for a surety, against him for whom he is surety, if he paid not the money at the day. *F. N. B.* 137.

PLENA FORISFACTURA, a forfeiture of all that one hath, &c. *Cowel.* See *Forfeiture.*

PLENA PROBATIO. See *Evidence.*

PLENARTY, is where a church is full of an incumbent, plenarty and vacation are direct contraries. *Staundf. Prærog. cap.* 8. *fol.* 32. *Westm.* 2. *cap.* 5. 6 *Rep.* 49.

And by the common law, where a person is presented, instituted and inducted to a church, the church is full, though the person presented be a layman; and shall not be void, but from the time of the deprivation of the incumbent for his incapacity. *Count. Pars. Compan.* 99. 3 *Black.* 243.

PLENE ADMINISTRAVIT, is a plea pleaded by an executor or administrator, that he hath administered the whole of the deceased's estate before the action brought.

PLENUM DOMINIUM, according to the Roman law was not said to subsist, unless where a man had both the *right* and the *corporeal* possession, which possession could not be acquired without both an actual intention to possess, and an actual seisin or entry into the premises, or part of them in the name of the whole. *Ff.* 41,2,3. *Cod.* 2, 3, 20.

PLIGHT, an old English word, signifying sometimes the estate with the habit, condition, and quality of the land. *Co. Lit.* 221. *b.*

PLONKETS, a kind of coarse woollen cloth, 1 *R.* 3. *c.* 8.

PLOW-ALMS, (*eleemosynæ aratrales*) 1*d.* anciently paid to the church for every plowland. *Cowel.*

PLOW-BOTE, a right of tenants to take wood to repair ploughs, carts and harrows; and for making rakes, forks, &c. 2 *Black.* 35.

PLOW-LAND, is the same with a hide of land.

PLOW-SILVER, money anciently paid by some tenants, in lieu of service to plough the lord's lands. *Cowel.*

PLURALITY, (*pluralitas*) is applied to such clergymen who have more benefices than one. And *plurality of livings*, is where the same person claims two or more spiritual preferments, with cure of souls; in which case the first is void *ipso facto*, and the patron may present to it, if the clerk be not qualified by dispensation, &c. for the law enjoins residence, and it is impossible that the same person can reside in two places at the same time. *Count. Pars. Comp.* 94. See *Dispensation*, *Ecclesiastical Persons*, and *Residence.*

PLURIES, is a writ that issues in the third place, after two former writs have been disobeyed; for first goes out the original writ or *capias*, which if it has not effect, then issues the *alias*; and if that also fails, then the *pluries*. *Old Nat. Br.* 33.

POCKET SHERIFFS. When the king appoints a person sheriff, who is not one of the three nominated by the judges in the exchequer, as he may do in the exercise of his prerogative, the person so appointed is called a pocket sheriff.

POCKET OF WOOL, a quantity of wool containing half a sack. 3 *Inst.* 96.

POISON. See *Boiling to Death* and *Homicide.*

POLE. See *Perch.*

POLEIN, a shoe, sharp or picked, and turned up at the toe. In the reign of *Ric.* 2. they were tied up to the knees with gold or silver chains: they were restrained in 4 *Ed.* 4. but not wholly laid aside till the reign of *Hen.* 8. *Cowel. Blount.*

POLICE, offences against, are all felonies, misdemeanors, breaches of the peace. See *London.*

POLICY OF ASSURANCE. See *Insurance.*

POLLARDS, or POLLENGERS, are such trees as have been usually cropped, therefore distinguished from timber-trees. *Plowd.* 469. *Cowel.*

POLL, (DEED) a deed made by one party only, is not indented, but polled or shaved quite even; and is therefore called a deed poll, or a single deed. 2 *Black.* 296.

POLLS, where one or more jurors are excepted against, it is called a challenge to the polls. *Co. Lit.* 156.

POLYGAMY, (*polygamia*) is where a man marries two or more wives together, or a woman has two or more husbands at the same time; when the body of the first wife or husband may be said to be injured by the second marriage, while either are living. 3 *Inst.* 88. *Wood's Inst.* 363. See *Bigamy* and *Felony*.

PONDUS, *poundage*, which duty, with that of tonnage, was anciently paid to the king according to the weight and measure of merchants goods. *Cowel.*

PONDUS REGIS, the standard weight appointed by our ancient kings, 35 *Ed.* 1. Now called troy weight, or *le roy weight.* Whereas the *aver de pois* was the fuller weight, with a declining scale. *Cowel.*

PONE, a writ whereby a cause depending in the county or other inferior court, is removed into the common pleas; and sometimes into the king's bench: as when a replevin is sued by writ out of chancery, &c. then if the plaintiff or defendant will remove that plea out of the county court into C. B. or K. B. it is done by *pone.* *F. N. B.* 4, 69. 2 *Inst.* 339. It also lies to remove actions of debt, and of detinue, writ of right, of nusance, &c. *New Nat. Br.* *Wood's Inst.* 570.

PONENDIS IN ASSISIS, a writ anciently granted by the statute of *Westm.* 2. *c.* 38. which statute shews what persons sheriffs ought to impanel upon assise and juries. *Reg. Orig.* 175. *F. N. B.* 165.

PONENDUM IN BALLIUM, a writ anciently issued, commanding that prisoner be bailed in cases bailable. *Reg. Orig.* 133.

PONENDUM SIGILLUM AD EXCEPTIONEM, a writ by which justices were formerly required to put their seals to exceptions, exhibited by defendant against the plaintiff's evidence, verdict or other proceedings before them, according to the statute *Westm.* 2. *Cowel.*

PONE PER VADIUM, a writ commanding the sheriff to take surety of one for his appearance at a day assigned. *Reg. Jud.*

PONTAGE, (*pontagium*) a contribution towards the maintenance, or re-edifying of bridges. *Westm.* 2. *c.* 25. It also signifies toll taken to this purpose of those who passed over bridges. 1 *Hen.* 8. *cap.* 9. 22 *Hen.* 8. *cap.* 5. and 39 *Eliz. cap.* 25. *Cowel.*

PONTIBUS REPARANDIS, a writ anciently directed to the sheriff, &c. requiring him to charge one or more, to repair a bridge, to whom it belongeth. *Reg. Orig.* 153.

POOR. Before the reformation there was no regular provision for the poor. For although it appears by the *Mirror*, *c.* 1. *s.* 3. that by the common law the poor were to be sustained by parsons, rectors of the church, and the parishioners, so that none of them die for default of sustenance; yet it seems, that they were in a great measure left to such relief as the humanity of their neighbours would afford them. 1 *Burrow's Rep.* 450, 451. 1 *Black. Com.* 359.

And in this respect there seemed to be a pious contention among our ancestors who should first bring their offering to the church; and the bishop, to whom the charge of souls was committed, was for that reason thought the fittest person to be intrusted with the administration of those oblations. *Shaw's Par. L. c.* 32. *s.* 3. 2 *Shaw's Jus.* 1.

By these and other superabundant offerings at altars, sepulchres, and shrines of martyrs, the church became extremely rich, and several monasteries, priories, religious houses, and hospitals, were by these means founded and plentifully endowed; at which were supported and fed a very numerous and idle poor, whose sustenance depended upon what was daily distributed in alms at the gates of such religious houses. *Shaw's Par. L. c.* 32. *s.* 4. 2 *Shaw's Jus.* 1. 1 *Black. Com.* 359. *Cowper's Rep.* 560.

But upon the total dissolution of these, the inconvenience of thus encouraging the poor in habits of indolence and beggary, was quickly felt throughout the kingdom; and abundance of statutes were made in the reign of Henry VIII. and his children, for providing for the poor and impotent, which, the preambles to some of them recite, had of late years greatly increased. 1 *Black. Com.* 360.

These poor were principally of two sorts, sick and impotent, and therefore unable to work; idle and sturdy, and therefore able, but not willing to exercise any honest employment. To provide in some measure for both of these in and about the metropolis, Edward the sixth founded three royal hospitals, Christ's and St. Thomas's, for the relief of the impotent through infancy or sickness; and Bridewell, for the punishment and employment of the vigorous and idle: but these were far from being sufficient for the care of the poor throughout the kingdom at large, and therefore, after many other fruitless experiments, by stat. 43 *Eliz. c.* 2. overseers of the poor were appointed in every parish. 1 *Black. Com.* 360.

From this statute the present system of poor laws hath arisen, which may be arranged in the following order:

1. Overseers of the poor; 2. Poor's rate; 3. Relief and ordering of the poor. 4.

Overseers accounts. 5. Indemnity of overseers in the due execution of their office. 6. Punishment of overseers for neglect of duty and for misbehaviour. 7. Relief, and ordering of the poor in incorporated districts.

I. *Appointment of Overseers.*

By 43 *Eliz.* c. 2. " the churchwardens and four, three, or two substantial householders, according to the greatness of the parish, to be nominated yearly in Easter week, or within one month after Easter, by two justices (1 qu.) near the parish, shall be called *overseers of the poor* of the same parish." *s.* 1.

And by 13 & 14 *Car.* 2. c. 12. (after reciting, that the inhabitants of Lancashire, Cheshire, Derbyshire, Yorkshire, Northumberland, the bishoprick of Durham, Cumberland, Westmoreland, and many other counties in England and Wales, by reason of the largeness of the parishes, cannot reap the benefit of the said act of 43 *Eliz.*) it is enacted, that " there shall be yearly chosen and appointed, according to the directions of 43 *Eliz.* c. 2. two or more overseers within every of the townships or villages respectively. *s.* 21.

" Also by 43 *Eliz.* c. 2. the mayors, bailiffs, or other head officers of every town corporate and city, shall have the same authority within their jurisdictions. And every alderman of London, within his ward, may do so much as is appointed to be done by justices. *s.* 8.

" And if any parish extend into more counties than one, or part be within any city or town corporate, and part without, then the justices shall deal only in so much of the parish as lieth within their liberties. *s.* 9.

" And if in any place there happen to be no nomination of overseers, every justice of peace, dwelling within the division, and every mayor or alderman, and head officer, of any city or place corporate, where such default shall happen, shall forfeit 5*l.* towards the relief of the poor, to be levied by warrant from the sessions." *s.* 10.

And by 17 *Geo.* 2. c. 38. " if any such overseer shall die, remove, or become insolvent, on oath thereof made, two justices may appoint another." *s.* 3.

By 43 *Eliz.* c. 2. If any persons shall find themselves grieved with any act done by the said justices, the justices, at their general quarter sessions, may take such order therein as to them shall be thought convenient, to conclude all parties. *s.* 6.

But by 17 *Geo.* 2. c. 38. *s.* 4. this appeal must be made to the next sessions.

II. *Poor's Rate.*

By 43 *Eliz.* c. 2. the churchwardens and overseers of every parish shall, with the consent of two justices, (1 qu.) raise weekly, or otherwise (by taxation of every inhabitant, parson, vicar, and other, and of every occupier of lands, houses, tithes impropiate, propriations of tithes, coal mines, or saleable underwoods in the parish, in such sums of money as they shall think fit,) a convenient stock of flax, hemp, wool, thread, iron, and other necessary ware and stuff, to set the poor on work; and also money for the relief of the lame, impotent, old, blind, and other, being poor and not able to work; and also for the putting out of poor children apprentices, and to do all other things concerning the premises. *s.* 1.

And the mayors, bailiffs, or other head officers of every town corporate and city, being justices of peace, shall have the same authority within their jurisdiction. *s.* 8.

Also by 13 & 14 *Car.* 2. c. 12. which authorizes justices to appoint separate overseers in places that cannot have the benefit of 43 *Eliz.* c. 2. " the justices of peace within the said counties shall have like powers to raise monies within every township or village. *s.* 22.

And by 17 *Geo.* 2. c. 38. overseers of the poor within every township or place where there are no churchwardens, shall execute all powers concerning the relief of the poor, as churchwardens and overseers may do. *s.* 15.

And by 17 *Geo.* 2. c. 3. the churchwardens and overseers shall give public notice in the church of every rate for the relief of the poor, allowed by the justices, the next Sunday after the same is allowed, and no rate shall be valid, so as to collect the same, unless such notice shall have been given. *s.* 1.

And by 17 *Geo.* 2. c. 38. copies of all rates made for the relief of the poor shall be entered in a book, and shall be produced at the general or quarter sessions, when any appeal is to be heard. *s* 13.

And if any churchwarden, overseer, or other officer, shall neglect so to do, he shall forfeit for the use of the poor not exceeding 5*l.* nor less than 20*s.* *s.* 4.

And by 17 *Geo.* 2. c. 3. the churchwardens and overseers shall permit every inhabitant to inspect such rate at all seasonable times, paying 1*s.* and shall upon demand give copies, paying 6*d.* for every twenty-four names. *s.* 2.

And if any churchwarden or overseer shall not permit the same, he shall forfeit 20*l.* to the party aggrieved. *s.* 3.

The statute 43 *Eliz* c. 2. authorizes the overseers, with the concurrence of the justices, to tax the inhabitants, weekly or otherwise, to the poor.

And by 17 *Geo.* 2. c. 38. where any person shall come into any premises from which any person assessed shall be removed, every person removing or coming in, shall pay the rate in proportion to their occupation, *s.* 12.

By 17 *Geo.* 2. c. 38. in case any person shall

neglect to pay to the overseers any sum that he shall be legally rated to, the succeeding overseers shall levy such arrears, and reimburse their predecessors all sums expended for the use of the poor, and allowed to be due to them in their accounts. *s.* 11.

By 43 *Eliz. c.* 2. if the justices perceive that the inhabitants of any parish are not able to levy among themselves a sufficient sum for the purposes aforesaid, then they shall rate any other of other parishes out of any parish within the hundred where the said parish is, to pay such sums to the churchwardens and overseers of the said poor parish for the said purposes, as the said justices shall think fit. *s.* 2.

And if the hundred shall not be thought by the justices able to relieve the said parishes, unable to provide for themselves, then the general quarter sessions shall rate any other of other parishes or out of any parish within the county for the purposes aforesaid. *s.* 3.

By 17 *Geo.* 2. *c.* 97. where there shall be any dispute in what parish waste and barren lands, and land formerly fen and marsh ground, or covered with water, heretofore improved or drained, or hereafter to be improved or drained, lie, and ought to be rated, the occupiers of such lands, houses built thereon, tenements, tythes arising therefrom, mines, and saleable underwoods therein, shall be rated to the poor, and all other parochial rates within such parish which lies nearest to such lands; and if on application to the officers to have such lands rated, any dispute shall arise, the justices at their next general quarter sessions may hear and determine the same on the appeal of any person interested. *s.* 1. 2.

By 43 *Eliz. c.* 2. the father and grandfather, and the mother and grandmother, and the children of every poor, old, blind, lame, and impotent person, or other poor person not able to work, being of a sufficient ability, shall, at their own charges, relieve and maintain every such poor person in that manner, and according to that rate, as by the justices at their general quarter sessions, shall be assessed, upon pain to forfeit 20*s.* to the use of the poor of the said parish, for every month which they shall fail therein. *s.* 7, 11.

Where persons run away from their places of abode, some men leaving their wives or children, and some mothers leaving children upon the charge of the parish, although such persons have some estates, by 5 *Geo.* I. *c.* 8., it shall be lawful for the churchwardens or overseers, where any wife or children shall be left chargeable to the parish, by warrant from any two justices, to seize so much of the goods, and receive so much of the annual rents of the husband, father, or mother, as such justices shall direct, for the discharge of the parish, which order being confirmed at the next quarter sessions, the justices there may make an order for the churchwardens or overseers to dispose of such goods and chattels by sale, and to receive the rents and profits of his or her lands and tenements, for the purposes aforesaid. *s.* 1.

And the churchwardens and overseers shall be accountable at the quarter sessions for the money. *s.* 2.

Also by 17 *Geo.* 2. *c.* 5. all persons who run away or leave their wives or children chargeable to the parish, shall be deemed rogues and vagabonds, and punished as such. *s.* 2.

Also all persons who threaten to run away and leave their wives or children chargeable to the parish, shall be deemed idle and disorderly persons, and kept to hard labour for not exceeding one month. *s.* 1.

And by the 32 *Geo.* 3. *c.* 45. if it be made appear to two justices, that any person doth not use proper means to get employment, or if he be able to work, by his neglect of work, or by spending his money in alehouses or places of bad repute, or in any other improper manner, shall not apply a proper proportion of the money he earns towards the maintenance of his wife and family, by which they or any of them become chargeable to their parish, he shall be deemed an idle and disorderly person. *s.* 8.

By 17 *Geo.* 2. c. 38. if any person shall be aggrieved by any assessment, or have any material objection thereto, he may appeal to the next general or quarter sessions, and the justices there are to receive such appeal and determine the same. *s.* 4.

And upon all appeals from rates, the justices (where they see just cause) shall amend the same in such manner only as shall be necessary for giving relief, without altering such rates with respect to other persons, but if upon an appeal from the whole rate, it shall be found necessary to quash the same, then they shall order the churchwardens and overseers to make a new equal rate. *s.* 6.

And by 41 *Geo.* 3. *sess.* 2. *c.* 23. all notices of appeal from or against any rate, or against the account of churchwardens and overseers, shall be in writing, and signed by the person or his attorney, and shall be delivered at the place of abode of the churchwardens and overseers. *s.* 4.

But with the consent of the overseers, and any other person interested, the sessions may proceed to hear such appeal, although no notice shall have been given in writing. *s.* 5.

And upon all appeals from any rate, the sessions shall, where they see just, amend such rate, either by inserting therein or striking out the name of any person, or by altering the sum therein charged on any person, or in any other manner which the court shall think necessary for giving such relief, and without wholly setting aside such rate.

Except the said court shall be of opinion that it is necessary for the purpose of giving relief to the person appealing, that the rate should be wholly quashed. *s.* 1.

But nevertheless, all sums of money by such rate charged may be levied in the same manner as if no appeal had been made against such rate, and all sums of money which any person shall so pay shall be deemed payments, on account of the next effective rate. *s.* 1.

And all sums at which any persons are rated may be levied, notwithstanding the person so rated, or any other, shall have given notice of appeal; but if any person rated shall give notice of appeal, then until the appeal shall have been heard, no proceedings shall be carried on to recover any greater sum than the sum at which he shall have been rated in the last effective rate. *s.* 2.

And in case the sessions shall, upon appeal, order any rate to be quashed, the said court may order any sum in such rate not to be paid. *s.* 3.

Also if any person shall appeal against any rate, because any other person is rated or is omitted therein, or because any other person is rated at any greater or less sum than the sum at which he ought to be rated therein, or for any other cause that may require any alteration to be made in such rate with respect to any other person; the person appealing shall give such notice of appeal, in writing, as before mentioned, not only to the churchwardens or overseers, but also to the other person so interested. *s.* 6.

If upon the hearing of any appeal, the court shall order the name of any person to be inserted, or the sum rated to be increased, the sum so ordered may be recovered in the same manner as if originally in such rate. *s.* 7.

If upon the hearing of any appeal, the sessions shall order the name of any person to be struck out, or the sum rated to be decreased; and if it be made appear that such person hath previously paid any sum in consequence of such rate, then the court shall order such sum to be repaid by the churchwardens and overseers, together with costs. *s.* 8.

It shall be lawful, as well for the present as subsequent churchwardens and overseers, or any of them, by warrant from two justices, (1 qu.) to levy the said sums, and all arrearages, of every one that shall refuse to contribute according as they shall be assessed, by distress and sale, 43 *Eliz. c.* 2. *s.* 4.

And the goods of any person assessed and refusing to pay, may be levied by warrant of distress, but if any person find himself aggrieved by such distress, he may appeal to the next general or quarter sessions. 17 *Geo.* 2. *c.* 38. *s.* 7.

In defect of such distress, such two justices may commit the party to the common gaol until payment, 43 *Eliz. c.* 2. *s.* 4.

And if any person shall neglect to pay any sum that he shall be rated to, the succeeding overseers are to levy such arrears, and out of the money so levied reimburse their predecessors all sums which they have expended for the use of the poor, and which are allowed to be due to them in their accounts. 17 *Geo.* 2. *c.* 38. *s.* 11.

And all justices may execute all acts, notwithstanding such justices are rated to any such rates. 26 *Geo.* 2. *c.* 18. *s.* 1, 2.

And when any such distress shall be made, the distress shall not be deemed unlawful, on account of any defect in the warrant. 17 *Geo.* 2. *c.* 38. *s.* 8.

But where the plaintiff recovers, he shall be paid his costs. *s.* 9.

And no plaintiff shall recover for any irregularity, if tender of amends hath been made by the party distraining before action. *s.* 10.

III. *Relief and ordering of the Poor.*

By 43 *Eliz. c.* 2. the churchwardens and overseers shall take order from time to time, with the consent of two justices (1 qu.) for setting to work the children of all such whose parents shall not be able to keep and maintain them; and for setting to work all such persons, married or unmarried, having no means to maintain them, and using no ordinary and daily trade: AND ALSO, to raise weekly or otherwise (by taxation as aforesaid) a convenient stock of flax, hemp, wool, thread, iron, and other necessary stuff, to set the poor on work: AND ALSO, competent sums for the necessary relief of the lame, impotent, old, blind, and such other among them being poor and not able to work: AND ALSO, for the putting out such children to be apprentices. *s.* 1.

And the said churchwardens and overseers shall meet together at least once every month in the church upon the Sunday in the afternoon after divine service, to consider of some good course to be taken, and of some meet order to be set down in the premises. *s.* 2.

The churchwardens and overseers may, with the consent of two justices, and when there is only one, with the assent of that one justice, set up any trade for the setting on work and relief of the poor. 3 *Car.* 1. *c.* 5. *s.* 22.

And the said justices shall send to the house of correction or common gaol, such as shall not employ themselves to work, and two justices to commit to prison the churchwardens and overseers which shall refuse to account. 43 *Eliz. c.* 2. *s.* 4.

And the churchwardens and overseers, by leave of the lord of the manor, may build on the waste at the charges of the parish, or of the hundred or county, houses of dwelling for the poor, which cottages shall not be used for any other habitation, but only for impotent and poor of the parish. *s.* 5.

And for the greater ease of parishes in the relief of the poor, it shall be lawful for the churchwardens and overseers, with the consent of the major part of the parishioners, to purchase or hire any house or houses and to contract with any person or persons for the keeping and employing the poor which shall desire to receive relief or collection; and there to keep and employ all such poor, and take the benefit of the work, labour, and service of such poor persons. 9 *Geo.* 1. *c.* 7. *s.* 4.

But by 36 *Geo.* 3. c. 23. it shall be lawful for the overseers, with the approbation of a majority of the parishioners, or of one justice, to pay collection and relief to any industrious poor person, at his or her home, under circumstances of temporary illness or distress, although such poor person shall refuse to be lodged, kept, and maintained within such house. *s.* 1.

And where any parish shall be too small to purchase or hire such house, two or more parishes, with the consent of the major part of the parishioners, and with the approbation of any justice, may unite in purchasing, hiring, or taking such house. 9 *Geo.* 1. *c.* 7. *s.* 4.

But no poor person or his apprentice, or child, shall acquire a settlement in the parish, or place to which they are removed by virtue of this act; but their settlement shall remain in such parish or place as it was before such removal. *s.* 4.

And by 30 *Geo.* 3. c. 49. it shall be lawful for any justice of peace, or any physician, surgeon, or apothecary, authorized by warrant under the hand and seal of such justice, or for the officiating clergyman of the parish, so authorized, to visit in the day time any parish workhouse, or house kept for the maintenance of the poor, to examine into the state of the poor people therein, and the food, clothing, and bedding, and the state of such house; and upon their report, the sessions, on hearing the parties, shall make such orders and regulations for the removing of any cause of complaint as to them shall seem meet. *s.* 1.

And in case the persons authorized as aforesaid shall find any of the poor afflicted with any infectious disease, or in want of immediate medical or other assistance, or of sufficient and proper food, or requiring separation or removal, then two justices shall make such order therein as they shall think proper, until the next sessions, who are to make such order for the further relief of the poor as to them shall seem meet. *s.* 2.

By 24 *Geo.* 2. c. 40. *s.* 13, 14, 15, no spirituous liquors shall be sold or used in any workhouse or house of entertainment of parish poor.

There shall be provided and kept in every parish a book, wherein the names of all persons who receive a collection shall be registered, with the day and year when they were first admitted to have relief, and the occasion which brought them under that necessity. 3 *Will. & Mar.* c. 11. *s.* 11.

And yearly in Easter week a new list shall be made and entered of such persons as they allow to receive collection. *s.* 11.

No other person shall be allowed to receive collection at the charge of the parish, but by authority of one justice, except in cases of pestilential diseases, plagues, or small-pox. *s.* 11.

But no justice shall order relief till oath be made before such justice of some matter which he shall judge to be a reasonable cause for such relief. 9 *Geo.* 1. *c.* 7. *s.* 1.

And the person whom such justice shall order to be relieved, shall be entered in the parish books, on forfeiture of 5*l.* *s.* 2.

And every such person as shall be upon the collection of any parish, and the wife and children of such person cohabiting in the same house (such child only excepted as shall be by the churchwardens and overseers permitted to live at home, in order to attend an impotent parent) shall upon the shoulder of the right sleeve of the uppermost garment, wear such a badge as is herein mentioned, *viz.* a large Roman P. with the first letter of the name of the parish cut in red or blue cloth, and if any such poor person shall neglect or refuse to wear such badge, any justice may punish such offender, either by ordering his allowance to be abridged, suspended, or withdrawn, or by committing such offender to the house of correction to be whipt, and kept to hard labour for not exceeding twenty-one days. 8 & 9. *Wil.* 3. c. 30. *s.* 2.

And by 9 *Geo.* 3. c. 37. if any churchwarden or overseer shall wilfully make any payment in base or counterfeit money, he shall forfeit not less than ten nor more than twenty shillings. *s.* 7.

IV. *Overseers Accounts.*

By 17 *Geo.* 2. c. 38. the churchwardens and overseers shall yearly, within fourteen days after other overseers shall be appointed, deliver in to such succeeding overseers a just account in writing, fairly entered in a book to be kept for that purpose, and signed by them, of all sums by them received, or rated and not received; and also of all goods, chattels, stock and materials in their hands, or in the hands of any of the poor to be wrought, and of all monies paid by such churchwardens and overseers so accounting, and of all other things concerning the said office. *s.* 1.

And shall also pay and deliver over all money, goods, and other things in their hands, to the succeeding overseers. *s.* 1.

And the said book shall be preserved by the churchwardens and overseers in some public or other place, in every parish: persons assessed may inspect the same at all seasonable times, paying 6*d.*; and shall, upon demand, have copies, at the rate of 6*d.* for every three hundred words. *s.* 1.

And if they shall refuse or neglect to make and yield up such account, or to pay and deliver over such money and things, two justices may commit them to the common gaol, until they shall account, or pay and yield up such monies and things. *s.* 2.

And if any overseer shall remove, he shall, before such removal, deliver over to some churchwarden or other overseer, his accounts, with all rates, books, papers, money, and other things, under the like penalties. *s.* 3.

If any overseer shall die before the expiration of his office, his executors or administrators shall, within forty days after, deliver over all things to some churchwarden or other overseer, and shall pay out of the assets all money remaining due, before any other debts are paid. *s.* 3.

And in case any person shall refuse or neglect to pay any sum that he shall be rated at, the succeeding overseers are to levy such arrears. *s.* 11.

By 17 *Geo.* 2. *c.* 38. if any person shall find himself aggrieved by, or have any material objection to such account, he may appeal to the next general or quarter sessions.

V. *Indemnity of Overseers in the due Execution of their Office.*

By 43 *Eliz. c.* 2. if any action of trespass or other suit shall be brought against any person for any thing done by authority of this act, the defendant may either plead *not guilty*, or make *avowry, cognizance*, or *justification* for the taking of the distresses, making of sale, or other thing done by virtue of this act, alleging that the thing, whereof the plaintiff complained, was done by authority of this act, without expressing any other matter. To which the plaintiff may reply, that the defendant did the act of his own wrong, without any such cause alleged by the said defendant. And after such issue tried for the defendant, or nonsuit of the plaintiff after appearance, the same defendant to recover treble damages, with his costs, and that to be assessed by the same jury, or writ to inquire of the damages. *s.* 19.

Also by 7 *Jac.* 1, *c* 5. if any action shall be brought against any justice of peace, mayor or bailiff of any city or town corporate, headborough or constable, (or against any churchwardens, or persons called *sworn men* executing the office of churchwarden, or any overseers of the poor, or others, which in their aid and assistance, or by their commandment, shall do any thing concerning their office, 21 *Jac.* 1. *c.* 12. *s.* 3, 5.) every such person may plead the general issue, not guilty, and give the special matter in evidence. And if the verdict shall pass with him, or the plaintiff become nonsuit, the judge before whom the matter shall be tried, shall by virtue of this act allow unto the defendant double costs."

And by 24 *Geo.* 2. *c.* 44. no action shall be brought against any constable, headborough, or other officer, or any person acting in his aid, for any thing done in obedience to any warrant of any justice of the peace, until demand hath been made or left at the usual place of his abode by the party, or his attorney, in writing, of the perusal and copy of such warrant, and no action shall be brought unless commenced within six calendar months. *s.* 6. 8.

VI. *Punishment of Overseers for neglect of duty and misbehaviour.*

By 43 *Eliz. c.* 2. the churchwardens and overseers being negligent in their office, or in the execution of the orders made by the justices, shall forfeit for every default 20*s.* to the use of the poor, and in default, two such justices may commit the offender to prison till the forfeitures be paid. *s.* 2. 11.

And by 17 *Geo.* 3. *c.* 38. if any churchwarden, overseer, or other officer, shall neglect to obey the directions of that act, where no penalty is provided, or act contrary thereto, he shall forfeit, for the use of the poor, not exceeding 5*l.* nor less than 20*s.* *s.* 14.

Also by 33 *Geo.* 3. *c.* 55. two justices, at any special or petty sessions, upon complaint upon oath of any neglect of duty, or of any disobedience of any lawful warrant, or order of any justice by any overseer or other parish officer, may impose upon conviction any reasonable fine, not exceeding 40*s.* but the party may appeal to the next general or quarter sessions. *s.* 1.

And by 3 *Will. & Mar. c.* 11. in all actions to be brought for recovery of any money mis-spent or taken by churchwardens or overseers of the poor to their own use, the evidence of the parishioners, other than such as receive alms, or pension, shall be admitted. *s.* 12.

VII. *Relief and ordering of the poor in incorporated districts.*

The poor in those districts are regulated by an act passed 22 Geo. 3. c. 8. but the provisions of the said *stat.* 22 *Geo.* 3. *c.* 83

are of considerable length: and from the consideration that they are not general, but strictly confined to such parishes only which may have united for the purpose of taking the benefit thereof, it is unnecessary in a work of this nature to go into any lengthened detail of such provisions for the settlement and removal of poor persons. See title *Settlement* and *Removals*.

POOR KNIGHTS OF WINDSOR. See *Knights*.

POPE. See *Papists*, *Recusants*, and *Roman Catholic Toleration*.

POST OFFICE. This owes its first legislative establishment to the parliament of 1643; for although there existed under the authority of the crown post-masters in much earlier times, yet their business was confined to the furnishing of post-horses to persons who were desirous to travel expeditiously, and to the dispatching of extraordinary packets upon special occasions. However, on March 21, 1649, the house of commons declared that the office of postmaster was and ought to be in the sole power and disposal of the parliament (*Com. Jour.*) and in 1657, a regular post-office was erected by the authority of the protector and his parliament upon nearly the same model as has been ever since adopted.

The preamble of the ordinance stated, that the establishing one general post-office, besides the benefit to commerce, and the convenience of conveying public dispatches, "will be the best means to discover and prevent many dangerous and wicked designs against the commonwealth."

And the policy of having the correspondence of the kingdom under the inspection of government is still continued; for, by a warrant from one of the principal secretaries of state, letters may be detained and opened; but if any person shall wilfully detain or open a letter delivered to the post-office without such authority, he shall forfeit 20*l*. and be incapable of having any future employment in the post-office, 9 *Ann.* c. 10. s. 40. It has however been decided, no person is subject to this penalty but those who are employed in the post-office. 5 *T. R.* 101.

After the restoration, a similar office, with some improvements, was established by statute 12 *Car. II.* c. 35. but the rates of letters, with the privilege of franking and receiving letters free, have been altered, and farther regulations added, by divers subsequent statutes.

Under these statutes a Roman Catholic peer is not entitled to send or receive letters free of postage, for it is the sitting in parliament that gives the right, not the peerage. Lord Petre *v.* Lord Auckland, postmaster-general. 2 *Bos. & Pul.* 139.

Also no action can be maintained against the postmaster-general for the loss of bills or articles sent in letters by the post. 1 *Ld. Raym.* 6. *Comyns* 100. And when an action was brought against Lord Despenser and Mr. Carteret, postmaster-general in 1778, to recover a bank-note of 100*l*. which had been sent by the post and was lost, Lord Mansfield delivered the opinion of the court, and proved, with much perspicuity and ability, that there was no resemblance, or analogy between the postmasters and a common carrier, and that no action for any loss in the post-office could be brought against any person by whose actual negligence the loss accrued, that this point seemed as fully established as if it had been declared by the full authority of parliament. *Cowp.* 754.

For this reason it is recommended by the secretary of the post-office, to cut bank-notes into halves, and to send one half at a time. This is the only safe mode of sending bank-notes, as the bank would never pay the holder of that half which had been fraudulently obtained.

Many attempts have been made by postmasters in country towns, to charge a halfpenny or a penny a letter upon delivery at the houses in the town above the parliamentary rates, under pretence that they were not obliged to carry the letters out of the office gratis; but it has been repeatedly decided, that such a demand is illegal, and that they are bound to deliver the letters to the inhabitants within the usual and established limits of the town, without any addition to the rate of postage. 5 *Burr.* 2709. 2 *Bl. Rep.* 906. *Cowp.* 182.

POST, (Writ of entry in.) It is given by the stat. of Marlbridge, 52 *Hen.* 3. c. 30, which provides, that when the number of alienations or descents exceeds the usual degrees, a new writ shall be allowed, without any mention of degrees at all, *viz.* that the tenant had no legal entry unless after. 3 *Black.* 182.

POST CONQUESTUM, words inserted in the king's title, by king *Edw.* 1. and constantly used in the time of *Edw.* 3. *Cowel.*

POST DIEM, is where a writ is returned after the day assigned. *Ibid.*

POST DISSEISIN, is a writ that lies for him who having recovered lands or tenement by *præcipe quod reddat*, on default or reddition, is again disseised by the former disseisor; then he shall have this writ and recover double damages, and the party shall be punished by imprisonment, &c. *Stat. Westm.* 3. c. 26. *Reg. Orig.* 208. *F. N. B.* 190.

POSTEA. Upon the trial of an issue of fact, if it be found for either plaintiff or defendant, or specially, or if the plaintiff makes default, or is nonsuit, or whatever, in short, is done subsequent to the joining of issue and awarding the trial, it is entered by indorsement on record, and is called a *postea*: The substance of which is, that *postea*, afterwards, the said plaintiff and defendant appeared, by their attornies, at the place of trial, and a jury being sworn, found such a verdict; or, that the plaintiff after the jury sworn made default, and did not prosecute his suit, or, as the case may happen. 3 *Black*. 386.

POSTERIORITY, (*posterioritas*) signifies the being or coming after, and is a word of comparison and relation in tenures, the correlative whereof is priority: as a man holding lands or tenements of two lords, holds of the ancienter lord by priority, and of his latter lord by posteriority. 2 *Inst*. 392.

POST-FINE, is a duty to the king for a fine acknowledged in his court, paid by the cognisee after the fine is fully passed, and it is so much, and half so much as was paid to the king for the *præfine*. 2 *Black*. 350.

POSTHUMOUS, is where a child is born after his father's death, &c. And posthumous children are enabled to take estates by remainder in settlements, as if born in their fathers' life-time, though no estate be limited to trustees to preserve them till they come in *esse*. 10 & 11 *W*. 3. *cap*. 16.

POST-MAN, in the exchequer. In the court of exchequer two of the most experienced barristers, called the post-man and the tub-man, (from the places in which they sit) have a precedence in motions. 2 *Black*. 28.

POSTNATUS, is a word that signifieth the second son, or one born afterwards; children of persons attainted of treason, born after the king's pardon, may inherit lands, though not those born before, &c. *Co. Litt*. 391.

POST-TERMINUM, is the return of a writ, not only after the return thereof, but after the term; on which the *custos brevium* takes 20*d*. It is also used for the fee so taken. *Cowel*.

POSTULATION, (*postulatio*) signifies a petition. And formerly, when a bishop was translated from one bishopric to another, he was not elected to the new see; for the canon law is *electus non potest elegi;* and the pretence was, that he was married to the first church, which marriage could not be dissolved but by the pope; thereupon he was petitioned, and consenting to the petition, the bishop was translated, and this was said to be by postulation; but being an usurpation, and against law, it was restrained by 16 *R*. 2. and 9 *H*. 4. *c*. 8. Since which, translations of bishops have been by election, and not by postulation. 1 *Jones*, 160. 1 *Salk*. 137.

POUND, (*parcus*, signifies any inclosure, a pound) is either pound-overt, that is, open over head; or pound-covert, that is close. By the statute 1 & 2 *P*. & *M*. c. 12. no distress of cattle can be driven out of the hundred where it is taken, unless to a pound-overt within the same shire, and within three miles of the place where it was taken. This is for the benefit of the tenants, that they may know where to find and replevy the distress. And by statute 11 *Geo*. 2. c. 13. which was made for the benefit of landlords, *any person distraining for rent may impound the distress taken upon any part of the same, for securing of such distress*. If a live distress of animals be impounded in a common pound-overt, the owner must take notice of it at his peril; but if in any special pound-overt, so constituted for this particular purpose, the distreinor must give notice to the owner; and in both these cases the owner, and not the distreinor, is bound to provide the beasts with food and necessaries; but if they be put in a pound-covert, as in a stable, or the like, the landlord or distreinor must feed and sustain them (*Co. Litt*. 47). A distress of household goods, or other dead chattels, which are liable to be stolen, or damaged by weather, ought to be impounded in a pound-covert, else the distreinor must answer for the consequences. 3 *Black* 13.

POUNDAGE. See *Sheriff*.

POUND-BREACH. If a distress be taken and impounded, though without just cause, the owner cannot break the pound, and take away the distress; if he doth, the party distrained may have his action, and retake the distress wherever he finds it: And for pound-breaches, &c. action of the case lies, whereon treble damages may be recovered. *Co. Lit*. 261. 2 *W*. & *M*. c. 5.

POUND IN MONEY, (from the Sax. *pund*, i. e. *pondus*) is twenty shillings. In the time of the Saxons it consisted of 240 pence, as it doth now: and 240 of those pence weighed a pound. *Lambard* 291.

POUR FAIRE PROCLAIMER, QUE NULL INJECT FIMES OU ORDURES EN FOSSES, OU RIVERS, PRES CITIES, &c. an ancient writ heretofore directed to the mayor or bailiff of a city or town, requiring them to make proclamation that none cast filth into places near such city or town, to the nuisance thereof; and if any be cast there already to remove the same. *Stat*. 12. *R*. 2. c. 13. F. N. B. 176.

POURPARTY, (*Propars, propartis, propartia*) contrary to *pro indiviso*: for to make pourparty is to divide the lands that fall to parceners, which before partition they hold jointly and *pro indiviso*. *Old Nat. Brev*. 11.

POURPRESTURE, (*pourprestura*, from the Fr. *pourpris*, an inclosure). *Pourpresture* is properly when a man takes any thing he ought not, whether it be in any jurisdiction land, or franchise; and generally when any thing is done to the nuisance of the king's tenants, See *Kitchen*, 10. *Manwood's Forest Laws, cap.* 10.—*Cromp. Juris.* 152.

POUR SEISIR TERRES LE FEME QUE TIENT EN DOWER, &c. was a writ whereby the king seised the land which the wife of his tenant who held *in capite* deceased, had for her dowry, if she married without his leave. *F. N. B.* 174.

POURSUIVANT, (from the Fr. *poursuivre*, i. e. *persequi*) signifies the king's messenger attending him, to be sent on any occasion or message; as for the apprehending a person accused or suspected of any offence: those employed in martial causes are called pursuivants at arms. 24 *H.* 8. 13. See *Herald*.

POURVEYANCE or PURVEYANCE. The profitable prerogative of purveyance and pre-emption, was a right enjoyed by the crown of buying up provisions and other necessaries, by the intervention of the king's purveyors, for the use of his royal household, at an appraised valuation, in preference to all others, and even without consent of the owner; and also of forcibly impressing the carriages and horses of the subject, to do the king's business on the public roads, in the conveyance of timber, baggage, and the like, however inconvenient to the proprietor, upon paying him a settled price. 3 *Inst.* 82. 1 *Black.* 297.

But by 12 *Car.* 2. c. 24. it is provided, "that no person by colour of buying or "making provision or purveyance shall "take any thing of any subject, without "the full and free consent of the owner, "obtained without menace or force," &c.

POURVEYOR or PURVEYOR, (*provisor*, derived from the Fr. *pourvoir*, i. e. *providere*) was the officer of the king or queen, or other great personage, to provide corn and other victuals for their house, restrained by stat. 12 *Car.* 2. c. 24.

POW-DIKE. To perversely and maliciously cut down or destroy the pow-dike, in the fens of Norfolk and Ely, is felony, by 22 *Hen.* 8. c. 11.

POWER is an authority which one man gives another to act for him; and is sometimes a reservation which a person makes in a conveyance for himself to do some acts, as to make leases, raise portions for younger children, and the like. 2 *Lill. Abr.* 339.

But a power must be pursued strictly; therefore if a man has power to make leases generally, this extends to make leases in possession only, and not in reversion, or to commence in *futuro*. 2 *Roll.* 261. c. 5. *Cro. Jac.* 318. *Yelv.* 222. *Roy.* 48. 1 *Ld. Raym.* 267. 2 *Salk.* 537. 1 *Lev.* 168. 6 *Co.* 33. *a.* *Mo.* 199. 1 *Leo.* 35. 3 *Leo.* 31. *Ray* 248. 1 *Leo.* 35. *Yelv.* 222. *Cro. Jac.* 318. *Mo.* 494. *Ray* 163. 1 *Sid.* 101. *Ca. Cha.* 18. *Com. Dig. til. Poier.*

POWER OF THE CROWN. See *King*.

POWER OF THE PARENT. See *Parent* and *Child*.

POYNING'S LAW. See *Ireland*.

PRACTICE is that course of conduct, which the professors and practitioners of the law pursue in the courts wherein they practice, and the law will sustain plain and fair practice, and not countenance fraud in proceedings, or suffer advantage to be taken therein. 2 *Lil.* 342.

The rules by which the proceedings in the courts of law and equity are to be carried on, are also denominated the practice of such courts.

PRÆCEPTORIES, (*præceptoriæ*) were a kind of benefices having their name from being possessed by the more eminent Templars, whom the chief master by his authority created and called *præceptores Templi*, of which *præceptores* there were sixteen. *Mon. Angl. tom.* 2. 543. *Cowel.*

PRÆCIPE. Original writs are either optional or *peremptory*, viz. either a *præcipe*, or a *si te fecerit securum*. The *præcipe* is in the alternative, commanding the defendant to do the thing required, or show the reason wherefore he hath not done it; that is, either to redress the injury or stand the suit. 3 *Black.* 274.

PRÆCIPE IN CAPITE, was a writ issuing out of the Chancery, for a tenant holding of the king *in capite*, viz. in chief, as of his crown. *Mag. Chart. cap.* 24. *Reg. Grig.* 3.

PRÆCIPE QUOD REDDAT, is the form of a writ which extends as well to a writ of right as to other writs of entry or possession, beginning *præcipe* A *quod reddat* B *unum messuagium*, &c. *Old Nat. Brev.* 13. See *Fines* and *Recoveries*.

PRÆCIPITIUM, was a punishment inflicted on criminals, by casting them from some high place. *Malms. lib.* 5. *p.* 155. *Cowel.*

PRÆDICT, *prædictus*, (Lat.) in English, aforesaid, is a word used in pleadings and deeds. *Hob.* 6.

PRÆFECTUS VILLÆ, is the same as *præpositus villæ*, i. e. the mayor of a town. *Leg. Ed. Confes. c.* 28. *Cowel.*

PRÆFINE, is that fine which, on suing out the writ of covenant on levying fines, is paid before the fine is passed. See *Fines*.

PRÆMIUM PUDICITIÆ, is a consideration given to a previously innocent and virtuous woman by the person who may have seduced her. And equity will enforce the payment of a bond given as *præmium pudicitiæ* to an innocent woman, whom the obligor hath seduced; for if a man misleads a previously virtuous woman, it is both reason and justice that he should make her a reparation. 2 *Peere Wms.* 432. *Eq. Ca. Abr.* 87. 3 *Br. P. C.* 445. *Cas. Temp. Talb.* 153.

So also if an annuity is granted by one to his housekeeper, with a bond for payment of it, and the bond is lost, equity will decree payment of the annuity; for service is a consideration, and no *turpis contractus* shall be presumed unless proved. *Abr. Eq.* 24. *p.* 7. 93. *p.* 5.

Also a bond given by the seducer as *præmium pudicitiæ* hath been holden good at law. *Turner* v. *Vaughan*, 2 *Wilts.* 339.

So where a provision has been made for her, by an ineffectual conveyance, equity will interpose in her behalf, both against the grantor himself and his representatives. 2 *Peere Wms.* 435. *Ambl.* 520.

But the courts of law and equity distinguish between these obligations for considerations past, and considerations in future; and therefore a voluntary bond given during cohabitation, to a woman *previously of a very loose life*, purporting to be in consideration of *cohabitation had*, (by which must be understood past and discontinued) between the obligor and obligee, was *after the death of the obligor* held to be good; and the bill filed by the personal representatives to have the bond delivered up, dismissed with costs. *Gray* v. *Matthias.* 5 *Vez.* jun. 286.

But these bonds being voluntary in their nature, they are postponed to simple contract debts in the marshalling of assets, and shall be chargeable on the real estates on a deficiency of personal assets. *Forrest* 148.

And where a court of equity is required to interpose, it is not only influenced by the above distinction of the consideration being past or future, but also by the character and situation of the parties to the contract; therefore if a man hath given a bond to his mistress, a common strumpet, and afterwards files a bill to be relieved against the same, it appears from the case of *Whaley* v. *Norton*, that if the bill charge such to have been her situation, equity will relieve against it. 1 *Vern.* 483. 1 *Fonbl.* 228.

So where a woman of good character went to live with the defendant, as a companion to his sister, *knowing him to be married*, and he having seduced her, and separated from his wife on the occasion, gave her a bond, as *præmium pudicitiæ*: on a bill filed to enforce the payment thereof, the same was dismissed, as arising *ex turpi causa.* 2 *Vez.* 160.

So where a man married a second wife, the first being living, and after a discovery of his former marriage gave the second wife a bond for 1000*l.* to induce her to stay with him, the court held the same to be void. So where the condition of the bond was that the parties should live together in a state of fornication. 3 *Peere Wms.* 339.

PRÆMUNIRE, is taken either for a writ so called, or for the offence whereon the writ is granted. The offence of *præmunire* is so called from the words of the writ preparatory to the prosecution thereof, "*præmunire* (a barbarous word for *præmoneri*) *facias A. B.*" cause A. B. to be forthwarned that he appear before us to answer the contempt wherewith he stands charged; which contempt is particularly recited in the preamble to the writ. *Old Na. Brev.* 101, *edit.* 1524. 4 *Black.* 183.

The nature and several species of *præmunire* depend upon divers statutes, all of which are noticed under their proper titles; and its punishment, according to such statutes, is thus shortly summed up by sir Edward Coke: (1 *Inst.* 129,) "*that, from the conviction, the defendant shall be out of the king's protection, and his lands and tenements, goods and chattels, forfeited to the king: and that his body shall remain in prison at the king's pleasure; or (as other authorities have it) during life.*" (1 *Bulst.* 199.) But the stat. 5. *Eliz.* c. 1. provides, that "it shall not be lawful to kill any person attainted in a *præmunire*, any law, statute, opinion, or exposition of law to the contrary notwithstanding."

PRÆPOSITUS-ECCLESIÆ, a churchreeve, or churchwarden. *Cowel.*

PRÆPOSITUS VILLÆ, sometimes is used for the constable of a town, or petit-constable. *Cromp. Jurisd.* 205.

PRAYER. See *Service* and *Sacraments.*

PRAYERS OF THE CHURCH. See *Common Prayer.*

PREACHING. Every beneficed preacher residing on his benefice, and having no lawful impediment, shall in his own cure, or some neighbouring church, preach one sermon every Sunday of the year. No person shall be permitted to preach in any church, but such as appear to be authorized thereto, by showing their licence; and churchwardens are to note in a book the names of all strange clergymen who preach in their parish; to which book every preacher is to subscribe his name, the day he preached, and the name of the bishop of whom he had licence to preach. *Can.* 44. 54. 49.

PREAMBLE, (*Procemium*, from the preposition *præ*, before, and *ambulo*, to walk; as to walk before). The beginning of an act is called the *preamble;* which is a key to the intent of the makers of the act, and the mischiefs which they would remedy by the same. *Cowel.*

PRE AUDIENCE. The *pre-audience* which usually obtains among the practisers in his majesty's courts is as follows:

1. The king's premier serjeant, (so constituted by special patent.) 2. The king's ancient serjeant, or the eldest among the king's serjeants. 3. The king's advocate-general. 4. The king's attorney-general. 5. The king's solicitor-general. 6. The

king's serjeants. 7. The king's counsel, with the queen's attorney and solicitor. 8. Serjeants at law. 9. The recorder of London. 10. Advocates of the civil law. 11. Barristers.

In the court of exchequer two of the most experienced barristers, called the postman and the tubman, (from the places in which they sit) have also a precedence in motions. 3 *Black.* 28.

PREBEND, (*præbenda*) is a portion which every prebendary of a cathedral church receives, in right of his place, for his maintenance; *canonica portio* is properly used for that share which every canon receiveth yearly out of the common stock of the church. *Dyer*, 221.

PREBENDARY, (*prebendarius*) is he who hath such a prebend. 3 *Rep.* 75.

PRECARIÆ, are days works which tenants of some manors were bound, by reason of their tenure, to do for their lord in harvest. *Cowel.*

PRECEDENCE. The rules of precedence in England are according to the following

Table of Precedence.

The king's children and grand-children.
——— brethren.
——— uncles.
——— nephews.
Archbishop of Canterbury.
Lord chancellor keeper, if a baron.
Archbishop of York.
Lord treasurer. } If barons
Lord president of the council. } If barons
Lord privy seal. } If barons
Lord great chamberlain. But see private stat. 1 Geo. 1. *c.* 3. } Above all peers of their own degree.
Lord high constable. }
Lord marshall. }
Lord admiral. }
Lord steward of the household. }
Lord chamberlain of the household. }
Dukes.
Marquisses.
Dukes eldest sons.
Earls.
Marquisses eldest sons.
Dukes younger sons.
Viscounts.
Earls eldest sons.
Marquisses younger sons.
Secretary of state, if a bishop.
Bishop of London.
——— Durham.
——— Winchester.
Bishops.
Secretary of state, if a baron.
Barons.
Speaker of the house of commons.
Lords commissioners of the great seal.
Viscounts eldest sons.
Earls younger sons.
Barons eldest sons.
Knights of the garter.
Privy councillors.
Chancellor of the exchequer.
Chancellor of the duchy.
Chief justice of the king's bench.
Master of the rolls.
Chief justice of the common pleas.
Chief baron of the exchequer.
Judges, and barons of the coif.
Knights bannerets, royal.
Viscounts younger sons.
Barons younger sons.
Baronets.
Knights bannerets.
Knights of the bath.
Knights bachelors.
Baronets eldest sons.
Knights eldest sons.
Baronets younger sons.
Knights younger sons.
Colonels.
Serjeants at law.
Doctors.
Esquires.
Gentlemen.
Yeomen.
Tradesmen.
Artificers.
Labourers.

Married women and widows are entitled to the same rank among each other as their husbands would respectively have borne between themselves, except such rank is merely professional or official; and unmarried women to the same rank as their eldest brothers would bear among men, during the lives of their fathers.

PRECEDENTS, are authorities to follow in determinations in courts of justice. 4 *Rep.* 93. *Cro. Eliz.* 65. 2 *Lil. Abr.* 344. *Vaugh.* 169. 382. 399. 429.

There are also *precedents* or *forms* for conveyances, and pleadings in the courts of law, which are to be followed, and are of great authority.

PRECE PARTIUM, is when a suit is continued by the prayer, assent, or agreement of both parties. *Cowel.*

PRECEPT, (*præceptum*) is a command in writing, by a justice of peace, or other officer, for bringing a person before him, or the like. The civilians use *mandatum* in this case. *Cowel.*

PRE-CONTRACT, (mentioned in stat. 2 & 3 *Ed.* 6. *c.* 23.) is a contract made before another contract, but hath relation especially to marriage. See *Marriage.*

PREDIAL TITHES, (*decimæ prædiales*) are those which are paid of things arising and growing from the ground only, as corn, hay, fruit of trees, and such like. 2 *Ed.* 6. 13. *Co. Inst.* 649. See *Tithes.*

PRE-EMPTION, (*præ-emptio*) signifies the first buying of a thing; and it was a privilege allowed the king's purveyor to have the choice and first buying of provisions for the king's house, taken away by 12 *Car.* 2. c. 24.

PREGNANCY (plea of). Where a woman is capitally convicted, and pleads her pregnancy, though this is no cause to stay the judgment, yet it is to respite the execution till she is delivered. See *Judgment.*

PREMISSES, are those parts of a deed which set forth the number of the parties, with their additions or titles, the recitals, if any, of such deeds, agreements, or matters of fact, as are necessary to explain the occasion of the present deed. *Co. Lit.* 21. 2 *Roll. Rep.* 19. 23. *Cro. Jac.* 476. 5 *Rep.* 55.

The parcels conveyed or charged by the deed, are also generally called the premisses.

PREMIUM, (*præmium*) the money the insured gives to the insurer for insuring the safe return of any ship or merchandise.

PRENDER, the power or right of taking a thing before it is offered; from the Fr. *prendre*, i. e. *accipere:* it lies in render, but not in prender. *Rep.* 1.

PRENDER DE BARON, signified literally to take an husband, and was used for an exception to disable a woman from pursuing an appeal of murder against one who killed her former husband. *S. P. C. lib.* 3. *c.* 59.

PREPENSED, (*prepensus*) forethought; as propensed malice is *malitia præcogitata*, which makes killing murder; and when a man is slain on a sudden quarrel, if there were malice prepensed formerly between the parties, it is murder; or, as it is called by the statute, prepensed murder, 12 *Hen.* 7. c. 7. 3 *Inst.* 51. See *Murder.*

PREROGATIVE, (from *præ*, *ante*, and *rogare*, to ask or demand) is a word of large extent, including all the rights which by law the king hath as chief of the commonwealth, and as intrusted with the execution of the laws. *Bac. Abr. tit. Pre.*

By the word prerogative is usually understood that special pre-eminence which the king hath over and above all other persons, and out of the ordinary course of the common law, in right of his regal dignity. It signifies, in its etymology, (from *præ* and *rogo*) something that is required or demanded before, or in preference to all others: and hence it follows that it must be, in its nature, singular and eccentrical; that it can only be applied to those rights and capacities which the king enjoys alone, in contradistinction to others, and not to those which he enjoys in common with any of his subjects: for if once any one prerogative of the crown could be held in common with the subject, it would cease to be prerogative any longer; and therefore Finch lays it down as a maxim, that the prerogative is that law in case of the king, which is law in no case of the subject. *Finch. L.* 85.

Prerogatives are either direct or incidental. The direct are such positive substantial parts of the royal character and authority, as are rooted in and spring from the king's political person, considered merely by itself, without reference to any other extrinsic circumstance; as, the right of sending embassadors, of creating peers, and of making war or peace. But such prerogatives as are incidental bear always a relation to something else, distinct from the king's person; and are indeed only exceptions in favour of the crown, to those general rules that are established for the rest of the community; such as, that no costs shall be recovered against the king; that the king can never be a joint-tenant; and that his debt shall be preferred before a debt to any of his subjects. 1 *Black.* 240.

PREROGATIVE COURT, (*curia prærogativa archiepiscopi Cantuariensis*) is the court wherein all wills are proved, and all administrations taken which belong to the archbishop by his prerogative; that is, in cases where the deceased had goods in divers diocesses of the value of 5*l.*; in which case the will must be proved, or the administration taken out, before the metropolitan of the province, by way of special prerogative; that is, either in the prerogative office of Canterbury or York. 2 *Black.* 508.

PRESBYTER, a priest, elder, or honourable person. *Isidore, lib.* 7.

PRESBYTERIUM, a presbytery, or that part of the church in which divine offices are performed, applied to the choir or chancel, because it was the place appropriated to the bishop, priests, and other clergy, while the laity were confined to the body of the church. *Mon. Ang. tom.* 1. *p.* 243.

PRESBYTERIAN, a sectarist, or dissenter from the church. 13 *Car.* 2. 4 *Black.* 53.

PRESCRIPTION, (*præscriptio*) is a title acquired by use and time, and allowed by law, as when a man claims any thing because he, his ancestors, or they whose estate he hath, have had or used it all the time whereof no memory is to the contrary; or it is where, for continuance of time, *ultra memoriam hominis*, a particular person hath a particular right against another. *Kitch.* 104. *Co. Lit.* 114. 4 *Rep.* 32.

But there is a great distinction between custom and prescription: 1st. That custom is properly a local usage, and not annexed to any person; such as a custom in the manor of Dale, that lands shall descend to the youngest son: 2d. That prescription is merely a personal usage; as, that Sempronius and his ancestors, or those whose estate he hath, have used, time out of mind, to have such an advantage or privilege. *Co. Litt.* 113.

PRESCRIPTIONS AGAINST ACTIONS AND STATUTES. See LIMITATION, *statutes of.*

PRESENCE. Sometimes the presence of a superior magistrate supersedes the power of an inferior. 9 *Rep.* 118.

PRESENTATION, (*presentatio*) is properly the act of a patron, offering his clerk to the bishop of the diocese, to be instituted in a church or benefice of his gift which is void. 2 *Lil. Abr.* 351. See *Advowson.*

PRESENTMENT OF COPYHOLD. See *Surrender of Copyholds.*

PRESENTEE, the clerk presented to a church by the patron. *Cowel.*

PRESENTMENT OF OFFENCES. A presentment, *generally* taken, is a very comprehensive term, including not only presentments properly so called, but also inquisitions of office, and indictments by a grand jury. But a presentment, *properly* speaking, is the notice taken by a grand jury of any offence from their own knowledge or observation, (*Lamb. Eirenarch. l.* 4. *c.* 5.) without any bill of indictment laid before them at the suit of the king, as the presentment of a nuisance, a libel, and the like; upon which the officer of the court must afterwards frame an indictment, before the party presented can be put to answer it. 2 *Inst.* 739.

PRESIDENT OF THE COUNCIL, is the fourth great officer of state: he is as ancient as the reign of king John; and hath sometimes been called *principalis consiliarius*, and other times *capitalis consiliarius.*

The office of president of the council was ever granted by letters patent under the great seal, *durante bene placito;* and this officer is to attend on the king, to propose business at the council table, and report to his Majesty the transactions there: also he may associate the lord chancellor, treasurer, and privy seal, at naming of sheriffs; and all other acts limited by any statute, to be done by them. 21 *H.* 8. c. 20. *Black.* 230.

PRESS, (liberty of). See *Libel, and Liberties, and Rights.*

PRESSING. See *Impressing Seamen.*

PRESSING TO DEATH. See *Mute.*

PREST, is used for a duty in money, to be paid by the sheriff on his account, in the exchequer, or for money left, or remaining in his hands. 2 & 3 *Ed.* 6. *cap.* 4.

PRESTATION-MONEY, (*præstatio*, a paying or performing) a sum of money paid by archdeacons yearly to their bishop *pro exteriore jurisdictione—ut sint quieti a* præstatione *muragii. Præstatio* was also anciently used for *purveyance. Cowie.*

PREST-MONEY, is so called from the French word *prest*, that is, *promptus expeditus*, for that it binds those who receive it, to be ready at all times appointed, being meant commonly of soldiers. 18 *H.* 6. 19. 7 *H.* 7. 1. 3. *H.* 8. 5. & 2 *Ed.* 6. 2.

PRESUMPTION, (*presumptio*) a supposition, opinion, or belief: next to *positive* proof, *circumstancial* evidence, or the doctrine of PRESUMPTIONS, must take place: for when the fact itself cannot be demonstratively evinced, that which comes nearest to the proof of the fact is the proof of such circumstances which either *necessarily*, or *usually*, attend such facts; and these are called presumptions, which are only to be relied upon till the contrary be actually proved. *Stabitur præsumptione donec probetur in contrarium* (*Co. Litt.* 373.); and *presumptions* are of three sorts: 1st. *Violent* presumption is many times equal to full proof, for there those circumstances appear, which *necessarily* attend the fact. As if a landlord sues for rent due at Michaelmas 1810, and the tenant cannot prove the payment, but produces an acquittance for rent due at a subsequent time, in full of all demands, this is a violent presumption of his having paid the former rent, and is equivalent to full proof; for though the actual payment is not proved, yet the acquittal in full of all demands is proved, which could not be without such payment; and it therefore induces so forcible a presumption, that no proof shall be admitted to the contrary. (*Co. Lit.* 6. *Gilb. Ev.* 161.) 2dly. *Probable* presumption, arising from such circumstances as *usually* attend the fact, hath also its due weight: as if, in a suit for rent due 1810, the tenant proves the payment of the rent due in 1811; this will prevail to exonerate the tenant, unless it be clearly shewn that the rent of 1810 was retained for some special reason, or that there was some fraud or mistake: for otherwise it will be presumed to have been paid before that in 1811, as it is most usual to receive first the rents of longest standing (*Lit.* 373.) *Light*, or rash, presumptions have no weight or validity at all. *Lit. lib.* 1. c. 1. § 1.

PRESUMPTIO, was anciently taken for intrusion, or the unlawful seizing of any thing. *Leg. Hen.* 1. *c.* 11.

PRESUMPTIVE EVIDENCE OF FELONY. See *Evidence.*

PRESUMPTIVE HEIRS, are such, who, if the ancestor should die immediately, would in the present circumstance of things be his heirs; but whose right of inheritance may be defeated by the contingency of some nearer heir being *born:* as a brother, or nephew, whose presumptive succession may be destroyed by the birth of a child; or a daughter, whose present hopes may be hereafter cut off by the birth of a son. Nay, even if the estate hath descended, by the death of the owner, to such brother, or nephew, or daughter; in the former case the estate shall be divested and taken away by the birth of a posthumous child; and, in the latter, it shall also be totally divested by the birth of a posthumous son. 2 *Black.* 208.

But besides the case of a posthumous child, if lands are given to a son, who dies, leaving a sister his heir; if the parents have, at any distance of time afterwards, another son, this son shall divest the descent upon the sister, and take the estate, as heir to his brother. So the same estate may be frequently divested by the subsequent birth of nearer presumptive heirs, before it fixes upon the nearest presumptive heir. As if an estate is given to an only child, who dies, it may descend to an aunt, who may be stripped of it by an after-born uncle, on whom a subsequent sister of the deceased may enter, and who will again be deprived of the estate by the birth of a brother; but every one has a right to retain the rents and profits which accrued whilst he was thus legally possessed of the inheritance. *Co. Litt.* 11. *Doct. & Stud.* 1 *Dial. c.* 7. *Harg. Co. Litt.* 11. 2 *Wils.* 526.

PRETENDED PRIVILEGED PLACES. See *Obstructing Process.*

PRETENDED TITLES. No one shall sell or purchase any *pretended* right or title to land, unless the vendor hath received the profits thereof for one whole year before such grant, or hath been in actual possession of the land, or of the reversion or remainder; on pain that both purchaser and vendor shall each forfeit the value of such land to the king and the prosecutor (32 *Hen.* 8. *c.* 9). This offence relates chiefly to the commencement of *civil* suits. 4 *Black.* 135.

PRETENDER AND HIS SONS. See *Treason.*

PRETENSED RIGHT, (*jus prætensum*) is where one is in possession of land, and another who is out of possession claims and sues for it; here the pretensed right or title is said to be in him who so *claims* and sues for the same. *Mod. Cas.* 302.

PRETIUM SEPULCHRI, those goods which accrue to the church when a corpse is buried. *Irish Can. lib.* 19. *c.* 6.

PRIDE-GAVEL, (from *prid.* the last syllable of *lamprid*, and *gavel*, a rent or tribute). In the manor of Rodeley in the county of Gloucester is a rent paid to the lord, by certain tenants, in duty and acknowledgment to him for the privilege of fishing for lampreys or lamprids in the river Severn. *Cowel.*

PRIESTS, in general signification, are any ministers of a church. See *Ecclesiastical Persons, Parsons, and Papists.*

PRIMAGE, is a duty at the water-side, due to the master and mariners of a *ship*; to the master for the use of his cables and ropes, to discharge the goods of the merchant; and to the mariners for loading and unloading in any port or haven; it is usually about 12*d.* per ton, or 6*d.* per pack or bale, according to custom. *Merch. Dict.*

PRIMER-FINE, on suing out the writ or *præcipe*, called a writ of covenant, there is due to the king, by ancient prerogative, a *primer fine*, or a noble for every five marks of land sued for; that is, one tenth of the annual value. 2 *Black.* 350.

PRIMICERIUS, the first of any degree of men; the nobility of England. *Mon.* 1 *tom. p.* 838.

PRIMIER SEISIN, (*prima seisina*) the first possession, or *seisin*, was heretofore used as a branch of the *king's prerogative*, whereby he had the first possession, that is, the entire profits for a year of all the lands and tenements, whereof his tenant (who held of him *in capite*) died *seised* in his demesne as of fee, his heir being then at full age, until he do homage, or, if under, until he were of age. (*Staundf. Prærog. cap.* 3. & *Bracton, lib.* 4. *tract.* 3. *c.* 1.) But all the charges arising by *primier seisins* are taken away by 12 *Car.* 2. *c.* 24.

PRIMIER SERJEANT, is the king's first serjeant at law.

PRIMO BENEFICIO, the first benefice in the king's gift, &c. See *Beneficio.*

PRIMOGENITURE, (*primogenitura*) the title of an elder brother in right of his birth: the reason of which, *Co.* upon *Lit.* says, is, *Qui prior est tempore, potior est jure.* *Cowell.* & *Leg. Alfred Dodd. Treat. Nobil.* 119. 1 *Black.* 194. 2 *Black.* 214. 4 *Black.* 414.

PRINCE, (*princeps*) is sometimes taken at large for the king himself; but more properly for the king's eldest son, who is called prince of Wales.

It is said by some writers, that the king's eldest son is prince of Wales by nativity; but the fact is not so, for he is born duke of Cornwall, and afterwards created prince of Wales, though from the day of his birth he is stiled prince of Wales, a title originally given by Edward I. And all his titles are, prince of Wales, duke of Cornwall, and earl of Chester. 1 *Black.* 223.

PRINCE OF WALES, Establishment of. By 35 *Geo.* 3. *c.* 115. when a separate establishment shall be made for any future heir apparent, his principal officer is to make out a plan of establishment, and all disbursements from the revenues are to be made by the treasurer, for which he shall be responsible: which plan may be altered. *s.* 1.

Treasurer to cause payments to be entered in a book, which his majesty's treasury is to inspect. *s.* 2.

Treasurer to cause an account of expences to be made out quarterly, which he is to examine and sign. *s.* 3.

Treasurer may by warrant pay the sums specified in quarterly accounts, and the arrears at the end of quarters shall be discharged. *s.* 4. 5.

The surplus at the end of quarters to be paid to the heir-apparent. *s.* 6.

Demands which shall accrue, after the first quarterly day of payment, to be delivered within ten days after the expiration of the quarter in which they accrued. *s.* 7.

No demand to be included in the account but which has accrued within the quarter preceding the audit, nor any paid. *Ibid.*

Demands not delivered within ten days after the expiration of the quarter in which they were incurred to be barred, and securities for such debts void. *Ibid.*

And officers neglecting to insert demands in quarterly accounts, liable to payment of them. *Ibid.*

No action to be brought against the heir-apparent, for any debt which shall accrue, after the first quarterly day of payment. *s.* 8.

For demands delivered in time limited, the creditors may sue within three months after delivery: the treasurer to be made defendant, and the judgment to be a charge on the heir-apparent's funds. *s.* 9.

Officer neglecting to prepare accounts, or to apply monies as settled by this act, or misapplying monies, to be liable to damages, which may be sued for in any court at Westminster. *s.* 10.

And by 35 *Geo.* 3. *c.* 129. *the same regulations are made for the management of the present prince of Wales's establishment, as are contained in the preceding act relating to the future princes of Wales.* *s.* 25 to 36.

PRINCIPAL, (*principalium*) is variously used in our law, as an heir-loom, &c. The word principal, was also sometimes used for a mortuary, or corse-present.

In Urchenfield, in the county of Hereford, certain principals, as the best beast, the best bed, the best table, &c. pass to the eldest child, and are not liable to partition. Also the chief person in some of the inns of Chancery is called principal of the house. *Cowell.*

PRINCIPAL AND ACCESSARY. The principal is the person who actually commits a crime; and the accessary he who is assisting in the doing thereof. 9 *Lill. Abr.* 355.

PRINCIPAL CHALLENGE, a species of challenge to jurors for suspicion or partiality; and takes place where the cause assigned carries with it *prima facie* evident marks of suspicion, either of malice or favour. See *Challenge.*

PRINCIPAL MONEY. See *Mortgage.*

PRINTERS. By 39 *Geo.* 3. *c.* 79. printers shall give a notice in writing to the clerk of the peace, of the number of their presses, who shall grant a certificate thereof and file the notice, and transmit an attested copy to the secretary of state. *s.* 23.

Persons keeping presses or types without notice, or using them in any place not expressed therein, to forfeit 20*l.* *Ibid.*

But this is not to extend to his majesty's printers, or the universities of *England.* *s.* 24.

Letter-founders and printing-press-makers shall give a notice in writing of the places where they carry on business, to the clerk of the peace, who shall grant a certificate thereof and file the notice, and transmit an attested copy to the secretary of state: and persons carrying on such businesses without giving such notices, are to forfeit 20*l.* *s.* 25.

An account is to be kept of types and printing-presses sold, and to whom: to be produced to any justice when required, on pain of 20*l.* *s.* 26.

The name and abode of the printer shall be printed on every paper or book; and printers omitting so to do, and persons dispersing papers without such name and place of abode, shall forfeit 20*l.* *s.* 27.

But this is not to extend to papers printed by authority of parliament. *s.* 28.

Printers shall keep a copy of every paper they print, and write therein the name and abode of their employer, on pain of 20*l.* for neglect, or refusing to produce the copy within six months. *s.* 29.

Any person in whose presence a printed paper shall be sold without the name and abode of the printer, may seize the party and convey him before a justice, to determine whether he hath offended against this act. *s.* 30.

This is not to extend to impressions of engravings, or the printing names and addresses, or the articles in which the party deals, or papers for the sale of estates or goods, nor to alter any provisions respecting newspapers. *s.* 31, 32.

A justice may empower a peace-officer to search for presses and types which he suspects to be illegally used, and to seize them and the printed papers found. *s.* 33.

Prosecutions for any penalty under this act (see also *Seditious Practices*) must be commenced within three months after the penalty incurred. *s.* 34.

Pecuniary penalties exceeding 20*l.* may be recovered in the superior courts with full costs; and not exceeding 20*l.* before any justice of the peace, who may levy the same by distress, and in default thereof, commit the party for not more than six nor less than three calendar months; and the penalties go one moiety to the plaintiff or informer and the other to his majesty. *s.* 35, 36.

See *Libel* and *Liberties*, and *Rights.*

PRINTS AND ENGRAVINGS. See *Engravings.*

PRIOR, was first in dignity next to the abbot or chief of a convent. 26 *H.* 8. *cap.* 2. 1 *Black.* 155.

PRIORS ALIENS *(priores alieni)*, certain religious men, born in *France* and *Normandy*, governors of religious houses erected for foreigners here in England, suppressed by Henry V. *Stow's Annals. Cowel.*

PRIORITY *(prioritas)*, is an antiquity of tenure, in comparison of another less ancient. *Old Nat. Br.* 94. See *Posteriority.*

PRIORITY OF SUIT. See *Administrators, Executors*, and *Mortgage.*

PRIORITY OF DEBTS. A *prior suit* depending may be pleaded in abatement of a *subsequent* action or prosecution for the same matter.

But there is no *priority* of time, in *judgments;* for the judgment first executed shall be first paid.

And if two informations be exhibited on the very same day for the same offence, they may mutually abate one another, because *there is no priority to attach the right of the suit in one informer, more than in the other.* It seems, that an information or bill the same day that they are filed, may be so far said to be depending before any process sued on them, that they may be pleaded in abatement. 2 *Hawk. P. C.* 275.

PRISAGE *(prisagium)*, was a right of *taking* two tons of wine from every ship, (English or foreign) importing into England twenty tons or more; one before, and one behind the mast: which by charter of Edward I. was exchanged into a duty of 2*s.* for every ton imported by merchant-strangers, and called butlerage, because paid to the king's butler. *Dav.* 8. 2 *Bulst.* 254. *Stat. Estr.* 16 *Edw.* 2. *Com. journ.* 27 *Apr.* 1689.

PRISE, or PRISE *(captio, præda*, from the Fr. *Prendre)* a capture from an enemy in time of war, the sale and distribution of which captures under the admiralty jurisdiction are provided for at the commencement of every war by special act of parliament.

PRISO, a prisoner taken in war. *Hoveden*, 541. *Cowel.*

PRISON *(prisona)* a place of confinement for the safe custody of persons, in order to their answering any action, civil or criminal prosecution, and upon conviction of a criminal offence, a prison is, in innumerable instances, by statute appointed to be a place of punishment as well as safe custody.

PRISON-BREAKING. Breach of prison by the offender himself, when committed for any cause, was felony at the common law, (1 *Hal. Pl.* 607), or even conspiring to break it *(Bruc. l.* 3. *c.* 349), but this severity is mitigated by the *stat. de frangentibus prisonam*, 1 *Ed.* II. which enacts, that "no person shall have judgment of life or member for breaking prison, unless committed for some capital offence;" so that to break prison and escape, when lawfully committed for any treason or felony remains still felony as at the common law; and to break prison (whether it be the county gaol, the stocks, or other usual place of severity) when lawfully confined upon any other inferior charge, is still punishable as a high misdemeanor by fine and imprisonment; for the statute, which ordains that such offence shall be no longer capital, never meant to exempt it entirely from every degree of punishment. 2 *Hawk. P. C.* 128.

PRISONER, *(Prisonarius*, Fr. *Prisonnier)*, one confined in prison, on an action, or commandment: and a man may be a prisoner on *matter of record*, or of *fact;* a prisoner on matter of record, is he who, being present in court, is by the court committed to prison; and the other is on an arrest, by the proper officer, for safe custody until bailed, or the like. *Staundf. P. C.* 34, 35.

But a prisoner at the suit of the king may not be charged in an action at the suit of the subject, without leave of the court on special motion. 1 *Lev.* 125. 146.

But a prisoner in custody for debt, charged with a felony, may be removed from the sheriff, warden, keeper, or marshal of the King's Bench, in whose custody he is by habeas corpus, before one of the judges. 1 *Wms. Jus.* 200.

PRIVATE ACTS OF PARLIAMENT are of late years become a very common mode of assurance. For it may sometimes happen, that by the ingenuity of some, and the blunders of other practitioners, an estate is most grievously entangled by a multitude of contingent remainders, resulting trusts, springing uses, executory devises, and the like artificial contrivances; so that it is out of the power of either the courts of law or equity to relieve the owner. Or it may sometimes happen, that by the strictness or omissions of family settlements, the tenant of the estate is abridged of some reasonable power, (as letting leases, making a jointure for a wife, or the like,) which power cannot be given him by the ordinary judges either in common law or equity. Or it may be necessary, in settling an estate, to secure it against the claims of infants or other persons under legal disabilities; who are not bound by any judgments or decrees of the ordinary courts of justice. In these, or other cases of the like kind, the transcendent power of parliament is called in, by a particular law, enacted for this very purpose, to unfetter an estate; to give its tenant reasonable powers; or to assure it to a purchaser, against the remote or latent claims of infants or disabled persons, by settling a proper equivalent in proportion to the interest so barred. 2 *Black.* 345.

Acts of this kind are however at present carried on, in both houses, with great deliberation and caution, particularly in the house of lords; they are usually referred to two judges to examine and report the facts alleged, and to settle all technical forms. Nothing also is done without the consent, expressly given, of all parties in being and capable of consent, that have the remotest interest in the matter: unless such consent shall appear to be perversely and without any reason withheld. And an equivalent in money or other estate is usually settled upon infants, or persons not *in esse*, or not of capacity to act for themselves, who are to be concluded by this act. And a general saving is constantly added, at the close of the bill, of the right and interest of all persons whatsoever; except those whose consent is so given or purchased, and who are therein particularly named: though it hath been holden, that, even if such saving be omitted, the act shall bind none but the parties. *Co.* 138. *Godb.* 171.

A law thus made, though it binds all parties to the bill, is yet looked upon rather as a private conveyance, than as the solemn act of the legislature. It is not therefore allowed to be a *public*, but merely a *private* statute; it is not printed or published among the other laws of the session; it hath been relieved against, when obtained upon fraudulent suggestions; it hath been holden to be void, if contrary to law and reason; and no judge or jury is bound to take notice of it, unless the same be specially set forth and pleaded to them. It remains however enrolled among the public records of the nation, to be for ever preserved as a perpetual testimony of the conveyance or assurance so made or established. *Richardson v. Hamilton, Canc.* 3. Jan 1733. M'Kenzie v. Stuart. *Dom. Proc.* 13 Mar. 1754. 4 *Rep.* 12.

PRIVATEERS. Private men of war, allowed during national hostilities under letters of marque and reprisal, the persons concerned in which administer at their own costs a part of the war, by fitting out these ships of force, and providing them with all military stores; and they have, instead of pay, leave to keep what they take from the enemy, under the regulations of the prize acts.

PRIVATION, (*privatio*), a taking away or withdrawing: most commonly applied to a bishop or rector, when by death; or other act, they are deprived of their preferments; it seems to be an abbreviation of the word *deprivation*. *Co. Lit.* 329.

PRIVEMENT ENSIENT, is where a woman is *with child* by her husband, but not *quick* with child. *Wood's Inst.* 662.

PRIVIES, (from the Fr. *Prive*, i. e. *familiaris*), are those who are partakers, or have an interest in any action or thing, or any relation to another: as every heir in tail is *privy* to recover the land entailed, &c. *Old Nat. Br.* 117.

There are five several kinds of *privies*, viz. *privies of blood*, such as *the heir* to the ancestor; *privies in representation*, as executors or administrators to the deceased; *privies in estate*, between donor and donee, lessor and lessee, &c. *Privies* in respect of *contract*; and *privies* on account of *estate* and *contract* together. 3 *Rep.* 23. 123. 4 *Rep.* 123. *Latch.* 260.

PRIVILEGE, (*privilegium*), is that exemption whereby a private man, or a particular corporation is exempted from the ordinary obligations of the law, and it is sometimes used in law for a place which hath some special immunity. *Kitchin*, 118.

Privilege is either *personal* or *real*: a *personal* privilege is, that which is granted to any person, either against or beyond the course of the common law: as, for example, a member of parliament may not be arrested, nor any of his servants.

Privilege real is that which is granted to a place, as to the *universities*, that none of either may be called to Westminster-Hall, on any contract made *within their own precincts*, or prosecuted in other courts. *Cowell.*

Privilege is therefore an exemption from some duty, burthen, or attendance, to which certain persons are entitled, from a supposition of law, that the stations they fill, or the offices they are engaged in, are such as require all their care; that therefore without this indulgence it would be impracticable to execute such offices to that advantage which the public good requires. *Bac. Abr. Tit. Priv.*

The officers, ministers, and clerks of the courts in Westminster-Hall are allowed particular privileges in respect of their necessary attendance on those courts; and they are regularly to sue and be sued in the courts *they respectively belong to.* 2 *Inst.* 551. 4 *Inst.* 71. *Vaugh.* 154. *Dyer* 377. *a. pl.* 30.

And an attorney, *so long as he remains on record* (and continues in practice), shall have his privilege. *Bro.* tit. *Attorney* 67. *Tit. Bill* 24. 1 *Vent.* 1.

And a serjeant at law, barrister, attorney, or other privileged person, whose attendance is necessary in Westminster-Hall, may lay his action in Middlesex, though the cause of action accrue in another county; and the *usual* affidavit will not change the venue. *Stil.* 460. *Moor* 64. 2 *Show.* 242.

So all peers, without distinction, are entitled to privilege; for they are equally obliged to attend the service of the public, and are always supposed amenable, and to have sufficient property to answer in suits brought against them, and on these grounds are not to be arrested or molested *in their persons*. And this privilege extends to bishops, members of the convocation, and members of the house of commons. 4 *Inst.* 24. *Stil.* 222. 253. *Dyer* 314. 1 *Mod.* 66. *Bro. Exig.* 3. *Moor* 767. *Scobel's Memorials* 88. 103. *Sir Simond D'Ewes's Journals* 41[illegible]. *Finch* 355. *Dyer* 60 *a.* in margin. *Noy* 102. *Moor* 78. *Staundf. P. C.* 38.

A peeress *by birth* is entitled to privilege; so of a peeress by marriage, and that as well during coverture as after. 2 *Inst.* 50. *Stil.* 222. 234. 252. 2 *Cha. Ca.* 224. *Co. Lit.* 16 6 *Co.* 53. *Dyer* 79.

And peers and members of parliament shall have privilege of parliament, not only for their *servants*, but for their horses, &c. or other goods distrainable. 4 *Inst.* 24.

But this privilege is restrained to *menial* servants, and others *necessarily* employed about their estates.

In all civil causes this privilege is regularly to be allowed; so that a peer, or member of the house of commons, is not to be arrested or molested in his person or estate. *Bro. Exigent.*

But privilege of parliament doth not extend to high treason, felony, breach of the peace, surety of the peace, or commitments for contempts under the warrant of the speaker of the house of commons. 4 *Inst.* 25. and *Burdett's Case*, 1811.

And privileged persons are punishable by attachment for contempts in many instances: as for rescuing a person arrested; for proceeding in a cause against the king's writ of prohibition; for discharging other writs, wherein the king's prerogative, or the liberty of the subject, are nearly concerned; and for other contempts which are of an enormous nature, such as libel and the like. 2 *Hawk. P. C.* 152. and the Cases of *Wilkes* and *Burdett.*

In *Jenkins*, the following privileges are laid down as belonging to peers: 1, they are entitled to a letter missive; 2, they have *a knight* to try an issue which concerns them; 3, they are not to be arrested for any personal action; 4, they are exempted from serving on juries; 5, to have no day of grace against them; 6, upon the trial of a peer for treason or felony, they try him on their honour *only*, not on oath; 7, when they pass through any of the king's forests *to attend the king*, on blowing a horn they may have a buck or doe, as the season of the year is; 8, they have power in their house to reverse judgments given in the King's Bench; 9, they have the benefit of clergy, though they cannot read; 10, they are not liable to find carriages for the king, when he removes from one place to another. *Jenk.* 107.

But by 13 *Will.* 3. c. 3. all persons may sue or proceed in any suit in the courts at Westminster, Admiralty, Court of Arches, Prerogative Court of Canterbury and York, and delegates in causes matrimonial and testamentary, and all courts of appeals against any *peer*, or *member* or *their servants*, immediately from the dissolution, prorogation, or adjournment for more than fourteen days, till the time of meeting or re-assembling, so as they arrest not the person privileged, but proceed by summons and distress infinite, or by ex parte bill, summons, and distress infinite, till common bail filed: so also by stat. 11 *Geo.* 2. c 24, in any court of record, Wales, or county palatine.

And by stat. 10 *Geo.* 3. c. 50. peers and members may be sued at *any time*, and the suit shall not be impeached or stayed by privilege, but the person is not to be imprisoned.

And by 45 *Geo* 3. c. 124. on process by summons against persons having the privilege of parliament, an appearance on default may be entered for the defendant. *s.* 3.

An appearance may also be put in for a defendant, having privilege of parliament, in courts of equity, on return of a process of sequestration. *s.* 4.

In default of answer to a bill in equity against persons having privilege of parliament, the bill be taken *pro confesso*. *s.* 5.

And such bill shall be read in evidence as an answer admitting the facts. *s.* 6.

And by 47 *Geo.* 3. *s.* 2. *c.* 40. when any bill of complaint shall be exhibited in any court of equity against any member of the house of commons, it shall not be necessary to leave a copy of the bill with the defendant, but proceed for want of appearance to sequestrate the estate.

By 12 & 13 *Will.* 3. *c.* 3. none stayed by privilege shall be barred by the statute of limitations.

By 4 *Geo.* 3. c. 33. the creditors of any merchant within the description of the laws relating to bankrupts, having privilege of parliament, may, upon affidavit made of the debt, and filed in any of the courts of Westminster, sue out a summons or ex parte bill against such debtor, and if he shall not within 2 months pay so much or compound for the debt, (or enter an appearance, 45 *Geo.* 3. c. 124. *s.* 1.) he shall be adjudged a bankrupt, and a commission may be accordingly sued out against him. *s.* 12.

And by 45 *Geo.* 3. c. 124, traders having privilege of parliament, disobeying the orders of the court of chancery or exchequer, and refusing to pay money according to the tenor thereof, shall be declared bankrupts. *s.* 7.

But persons entitled to privilege are not to be arrested except in cases made felony by the bankrupt laws. 4 *Geo.* 3. *c.* 33. *s.* 3. 45 *Geo.* 3. *c.* 124. *s.* 8.

There is also a privilege to the person of a man, to be free from arrest, in respect of his attendance upon the courts; as where a man has a subpoena, to attend the courts of justice at Westminster, and he be arrested during his attendance there, he shall upon his oath be discharged. 1 *Ch. R.* 217. 2 *Mod.* 182.

And all persons who have relation to a cause, which calls for their attendance in court, and who attend in the course of their cause, such as the parties thereto or the bail, though not compelled by process, are privileged from arrest, provided their attendance be not for any unfair purpose. 1 *Hen. Black.* 636.

But a man who attends the court without process, or necessity, to do a voluntary act there, shall not be privileged. *Salk.* 544.

And the party shall be protected *eundo et redeundo*, though he goes out of his way; and upon this principle, a party who had attended his cause all day in court, and in the evening went with his attorney and witnesses to a tavern in Palace Yard to dine, was held to be privileged from arrest *causâ redeundi.* 4 *Ed.* 4. 21 *a.* *Bro. Priv.* 4. 2 *Black. Rep.* 1113.

But an action for false imprisonment does not lie for such an arrest; it is a breach of the privilege of the court, for which an attachment will be granted. 2 *Black. Rep.* 1190. *Doug.* 675.

This privilege extends to bail returning from court, after a justification; to an attorney returning after attendance on a judge's summons; to a party attending a reference under a rule of nisi prius; to parties and witnesses attending in the inferior courts; and to a justice of peace, clerk of the peace, or other officer going to or returning from sessions. *Burnes*, 27. 378. 6 *Com. Dig.* 88. 1 *Brownl.* 15. *Raym.* 100. 1 *Lev.* 159. *Bro. Priv.* 35. *Crom. J.* 162.

So a person attending commissioners of bankrupt, or other commissioners under the great seal, under their summons, is not liable to arrest, 1 *Atk.* 54. But a person attending such commissioners without a summons, to do a voluntary act, such as to prove a debt before commissioners of bankrupt, is not privileged from arrest. 4 *Ter. Rep.* 377.

So if any one be arrested within a place having privilege, as in Westminster-Hall, *sedente curiâ*, or in the king's palace at Westminster, or other place where the king resides. 3 *Inst.* 141.

But this privilege from arrest only extends to arrests for debt, and not to criminal cases. 1 *Strange.* 530.

PRIVILEGED PLACES. See *Felony* and *Obstructing Process.*

PRIVILEGIUM CLERICALE. See *Benefit of Clergy.*

PRIVILEGIUM, PROPERTY *propter*. A man may have a qualified property in animals *feræ naturæ*, *propter privilegium*: that is, he may have the privilege of hunting, taking, and killing them, in exclusion of other persons. 3 *Black.* 394.

PRIVITY, (*Privitas.*) There are three sorts of privities, viz. Privity in *estate*, in *blood*, and in *law*.

Privies in *estate* are as joint tenants, baron and feme, donor and donee, lessor and lessee, &c.

Privies in *blood* are intended of privies in blood *inheritable*, and this is in three manners, viz. inheritable as *general heir*, or as *special heir*, or as *general and special heir*.

Privies in *law* are, when the law without blood or privity of estate casts the land on one, or makes his entry lawful, as lord by escheat, lord who enters for mortmain, lord of villain, &c. 8 *Rep.* 42 *b.* *Jo.* 32.

PRIVY, (derived from the French *Prive, familiaris*), signifies him who is partaker, or hath an interest in any action or thing; as *privies* of blood. *Old Nat. Brev.* 117, 147.

PRIVY COUNCIL. (*Consilium Regis, Privatum Consilium*), counsellors in the king's court or palace, for matters of state. 4 *Inst.* 53.

The principal council belonging to the king is his privy council, which is generally called, by way of eminence, *the council.* And this, according to Sir Edward Coke's description of it, (4 *Inst.* 53), is a noble, honourable, and reverend assembly, of the king and such as he wills to be of his privy council in the king's court or palace, and is at present of an indefinite number. No inconvenience arises from the extension of their numbers, as those only attend who are specially summoned for that particular occasion upon which their advice and assistance are required. The cabinet-council, as it is called, consists of those ministers of state who are more immediately honoured with his majesty's confidence, and who are summoned to consult upon the important and arduous discharge of the executive authority: their number and selection depend only upon the king's pleasure; and each member of that council receives a summons or message for every attendance.

There is also, and of antient time hath been, a president of the council, who has precedence next after the lord chancellor and lord treasurer. This office was never granted but by letters-patent under the great seal *durante beneplacito*, and is very antient; for John bishop of Norwich was president of the council *anno* 7 *regis Johannis. Dormivit tamen hoc officium regnante magna Elizabetha.* 4 *Inst.* 55.

Privy counsellors are *made* by the king's nomination, without either patent or grant; and, on taking the necessary oaths, they become immediately privy counsellors during the life of the king that chooses them, but subject to removal at his discretion. 1 *Black*. 230.

As to the *qualifications* of members to sit at this board: any natural born subject of England is capable of being a member of the privy council; taking the proper oaths for security of the government, and the test for security of the church. But, in order to prevent any persons under foreign attachments from insinuating themselves into this important trust, as happened in the reign of king William in many instances, it is enacted by the act of settlement, that no person born out of the dominions of the crown of England, unless born of English parents, even though naturalized by parliament, shall be capable of being of the privy council. Stat. 12 & 13 *Will*. 3. c. 2.

The *duty* of a privy counsellor appears from the oath of office, which consists of seven articles: 1, to advise the king according to the best of his cunning and discretion; 2, to advise for the king's honour and the good of the public, without partiality through affection, love, meed, doubt, or dread; 3, to keep the king's counsel secret; 4, to avoid corruption; 5, to help and strengthen the execution of what shall be there resolved; 6, to withstand all persons who would attempt the contrary; and lastly, in general, 7, to observe, keep, and do all that a good and true counsellor ought to do to his sovereign lord. 4 *Inst*. 54.

The *power* of the privy council is to inquire into all offences against the government, and to commit the offenders to safe custody, in order to take their trial in some of the courts of law. But their jurisdiction herein is only to inquire, and not to punish, and the persons committed by them are intitled to their *habeas corpus* by statute 16 *Car*. I. c. 10. as much as if committed by an ordinary justice of the peace. And, by the same statute, the court of starchamber and the court of requests, both of which consisted of privy counsellors, were dissolved; and it was declared illegal for them to take cognizance of any matter of property, belonging to the subjects of this kingdom. But, in plantation or admiralty causes, which arise out of the jurisdiction of this kingdom; and in matters of lunacy or idiocy (3 *P. Wms*. 108), being a special flower of the prerogative; with regard to these, although they may eventually involve questions of extensive property, the privy council continue to have cognizance, being the court of appeal in such cases: or, rather, the appeal lies to the king's majesty himself in council.* Whenever also a question arises between two provinces in America or elsewhere, as concerning the extent of their charters and the like, the king in his council exercises *original* jurisdiction therein, upon the principles of feodal sovereignty. And so likewise when any person claims an island or a province, in the nature of a feodal principality, by grant from the king or his ancestors, the determination of that right belongs to his majesty in council: as was the case of the earl of Derby with regard to the Isle of Man in the reign of queen Elizabeth, and the earl of Cardigan and others, as representatives of the Duke of Montague, with relation to the island of St. Vincent in 1764. But from all the dominions of the crown, excepting Great Britain and Ireland, an *appellate* jurisdiction (in the last resort) is vested in the same tribunal; which usually exercises its judicial authority in a committee of the whole privy council, who hear the allegations and proofs, and make their report to his majesty in council, by whom the judgment is finally given.†

The *privileges* of privy counsellors, as such (abstracted from their honorary precedence,) consist principally in the security which the law has given them against attempts and conspiracies to destroy their lives. For, by statute 3 *Hen*. 8. c. 14. if any of the king's servants, of his household, conspire or imagine to take away the life of a privy counsellor, it is felony, though nothing be done upon it. The reason of making this statute, Sir Edward Coke tells us, (3 *Inst*. 38), was because such a conspiracy was, just before this parliament, made by some of King Henry the Seventh's household servants, and great mischief was like to have ensued thereupon. This extends only to the king's menial servants. But the st. 9 *Ann*. c. 16. goes farther, and enacts, that *any person* that shall unlawfully attempt to kill, or shall unlawfully assault, and strike, or wound, any privy counsellor in the execution of his office, shall be a felon without benefit of clergy. This statute was made upon the daring attempt of the Sieur Guiscard, who stabbed Mr. Harley, afterwards earl of Oxford, with a penknife, when under examination for high crimes in a committee of the privy council. 1 *Black*. 232.

The *dissolution* of the privy council depends upon the king's pleasure; and he may, whenever he thinks proper, discharge any particular member, or the whole of it, and appoint another. By the common law also it was dissolved *ipso facto* by the king's demise, as deriving all its authority from

* This is, in fact, a court of justice, which must consist of at least three privy counsellors.

† The court of privy council cannot decree *in personam* in England, unless in certain criminal matters; and the court of chancery cannot decree *in rem* out of the kingdom. 1 *Ves*. 444.

him. But now, to prevent the inconveniencies of having no council in being at the accession of a new prince, it is enacted by statute 6 *Ann.* c. 7. that "the privy council shall continue for six months after the demise of the crown, unless sooner determined by the successor."

PRIVY SEAL, (*Privatum Sigillum,*) is a seal which the king useth to such grants or things as pass the great seal. 2 *Inst.* 554.

First, they pass the privy signet, then the privy seal, and lastly, the great seal of England; and the clerks of the privy signet office write out such grants, patents, &c. as pass the sign manual, which, being transcribed and sealed with the signet, is a warrant to the privy seal, as the privy seal is warrant to the great seal. *Wood's Inst.* 457.

PRIVY VERDICT. See *Verdict.*

PRIZES. See *Privateers.*

PRO, is a preposition, signifying for, or in respect of a thing; as *pro consilio,* &c. *Plowd.* 412. *Wood's Inst.* 231.

PROBATE, in the laws of Canutus, was used as signifying, to claim a thing as a man's own. *Leg. Canut.* c. 44.

PROBATE OF TESTAMENTS, (*probatio testamentorum*) is the exhibiting and proving wills and testaments before the ecclesiastical judge: and if all the deceased's goods, chattels, and debts owing to him, were in the same diocese, then the bishop of the diocese hath the probate of the testament; but if the goods and chattels were dispersed in divers dioceses, so that there were any thing out of the diocese where the party lived, to make what is called *bona notabilia,* to the value of 5*l.* then the archbishop of Canterbury, or York, is the ordinary to make probate by his prerogative. *Blount.*

PROBATOR, an accuser, or approver, or one who undertakes to prove a crime charged upon another. *Fleta, lib.* 2. *cap.* 52. *sec.* 42. 44.

PROCEDENDO, is a writ which lieth where an action is removed from an inferior to a superior court, as the chancery, king's bench, or common pleas, by *habeas corpus, certiorari,* or writ of privilege; to send down the cause to the court from whence removed, to proceed on it, it not appearing to the higher court that the suggestion is sufficiently proved. *F. N. B.* 153 5 *Rep.* 63. 21 *Jac.* 1, *cap.* 23.

This writ of *procedendo* is, called a *procedendo in loquela.* 1 *Black.* 353.

PROCEDENDO ON AID PRAYER. If a man pray in aid of the king, in a real action, and aid be granted, it shall be awarded that he sue to the king in chancery, and the justices in the common pleas shall stay until the writ of *procedendo de loquela* come to them: and if it appear to the judges by pleading, or shewing of the party, that the king hath interest in the land, or shall lose rent, &c. there the court ought to stay until they have from the king a *procedendo in loquela:* and then they may proceed in the plea, until they come to give judgment; when the justices ought not to proceed to judgment, without a writ for that purpose. *New Nat. B. R.* 342.

PROCEDENDO AD JUDICIUM, lies where the judges of any court delay the party, plaintiff or defendant, and will not give judgment in the cause, when they ought to do it. *Wood's Inst.* 570.

PROCESS, in *civil causes,* is the means of compelling a defendant to appear in court. This is sometimes called original process, being founded upon the original writ; and also to distinguish it from *mesne* or intermediate process, which issues, pending the suit, upon some collateral interlocutory matter, as to summon juries, witnesses, and the like (*Finch, L.* 436). *Mesne* process is also sometimes put in contradistinction to final process, or process of execution; and then it signifies all such process as intervenes between the beginning and end of a suit. 3 *Black.* 279.

PROCESS UPON AN INDICTMENT. The manner of issuing process, after indictment found, to bring in the accused to answer it, where the offender is not in custody, or hath not, in misdemesnors, been bound over to appear at the assises or sessions, is as follows:

The proper process *on an indictment for any petit misdemesnor, or on a penal statute,* is a writ of *venire facias,* which is in the nature of a summons, to cause the party to appear. And if by the return to such *venire* it appears that the party hath lands in the county whereby he may be distrained, then a *distress infinite* shall be issued from time to time till he appears. But if the sheriff returns that he hath no lands in his bailiwick, then (upon his non-appearance) a writ of *capias* shall issue, which commands the sheriff to take his body, and have him at the next assises; and if he cannot be taken upon the first *capias,* a second and a third shall issue, called an *alias,* and a *pluries capias.*

But, on *indictments for treason or felony,* a *capias* is the first process; and for treason or homicide, only one shall be allowed to issue, or two in the case of other felonies, by statute 25 *Edw.* 3. *c.* 14. though the usage is to issue only one in any felony; the provisions of this statute being in most cases found impracticable.

And so, in the case of misdemesnors, it is now the usual practice for any judge of the court of king's bench, upon certificate of an indictment found, to award a writ of *capias* immediately, in order to bring in the defendant. 4 *Black.* 318.

PROCESS, (obstructing the execution of). This is an offence against public justice, of a very high and presumptuous nature; but more particularly so, when it is an obstruction of an arrest upon criminal process. And it hath been holden, that the party opposing such arrest becomes thereby *particeps criminis*; that is, an accessary in felony, and a principal in treason. 4 *Black.* 129.

PROCESSION. In cathedral and conventual churches, the members had their stated processions, wherein they walked in their most ornamental habits, with music, singing hymns, and other suitable solemnity; and, in every parish, there was a customary annual procession of the parish priest, the patron of the church, with the chief flag, or holy banner, and the other parishioners, to take a circuit round the limits of the parish or manor, and pray for a blessing on the fruits of the earth; to which we owe our present custom of perambulation, which in most places is still called processioning, and going in procession, though we have lost the order and devotion, as well as pomp and superstition of it. *Cowell.*

PROCESSUM CONTINUANDO, a writ for the continuance of process, after the death of the chief justice, or other justices in the commission of oyer and terminer. *Reg. Orig.* 128.

PROCHEIN AMY, (*proximus amicus*) he who sues as the next friend to a child in his nonage. 2 *Inst.* 261.

If no guardian is appointed by the father, &c. of an infant, the course of the courts of law hath been used to allow one of the officers of the court to be *prochein amy* to the infant to sue (*Terms de Ley.* 2 *Lil. Abr.* 52). Or this *prochein amy* may in equity be any person who will undertake the infant's cause, and answer for costs. 1 *Black.* 463.

PROCHEIN AVOIDANCE, is nothing but a power to present a minister to a church when it shall become void: as when one hath presented a clerk to a church, and then grants the next avoidance to another. See *Avoidance.*

PROCLAMATION (*proclamatio*) is a notice publicly given of any thing, whereof the king thinks fit to advertise his subjects, and so it is used (7 *Rich.* 2. c. 6). And the subject is obliged, on pain of fine and imprisonment, to obey every proclamation legally made; and that though the thing prohibited were an offence before, for the proclamation is a circumstance which highly aggravates it; and on which alone the party disobeying may be punished. 12 *Co.* 74. *Hob.* 251.

PROCLAMATION OF COURTS, is used particularly in the beginning or calling of a court, and at the discharge or adjourning thereof, for the attendance of persons, and dispatch of business. 1 *Lev.* 63.

PROCLAMATION OF EXIGENTS. On awarding an exigent, in order to outlawry, a writ of proclamation issues to the sheriff of the county where the party dwells, to make three proclamations for defendant to yield himself, or be outlawed. *Stat.* 6 *Hen.* 8. c. 4. 31 *Eliz.* c. 3. 4. & 5. *Wil.* & *Mar.* c. 22. s. 4. 3 *Black.* 284. 314.

PROCLAMATION OF A FINE. When any fine of land is passed, proclamation is solemnly made thereof in the court of common pleas where levied, after ingrossing it; and transcripts are also sent to the justices of *assise*, and justices of the peace of the county in which the lands lie, to be openly proclaimed there. 1 *R.* 3. c. 7. 3 *Black. Com.* 352.

PROCLAMATION OF NUISANCES. By statute, proclamation is to be made against nuisances, and for the removal of them, &c. 12 *R.* 2. c. 13.

PROCLAMATION OF REBELLION, is a writ whereby a man not appearing upon a *subpœna*, or an attachment in the chancery, is deputed and declared a rebel, if he render not himself by a day assigned. See *Commission of Rebellion.* 3 *Black.* 444.

PROCLAMATION OF RECUSANTS. There is a proclamation of recusants, by which they shall be convicted, on non-appearance at the assises. 29 *Eliz.* c. 6. 3 *Jac.* 1. c. 4 & 5.

PRO CONFESSO, is where a bill is exhibited in chancery, to which defendant appears, and is afterwards in contempt for not answering; when the matter contained in the bill shall be taken as if it were confessed by defendant. *Terms de Ley.*

PROCTOR, (*procurator*) is he who undertakes to manage another man's cause, in any court of the civil or ecclesiastical law, for his fee. A proctor is not to practice, if a popish recusant (3 *Jac.* 1. c. 5). Nor to act as justice of peace. 5 *Geo.* 2. c. 18. 3 *Black.* 25.

PROCTORS OF THE CLERGY, (*procuratores cleri*) are those who are chosen and appointed to appear for cathedral or other collegiate churches; as also for the common clergy of every diocese, to sit in the convocation house in the time of parliament.

PROCONSULES, were those who were called justices in eyre, or *justiciarii errantes*, in England. *Cowell.*

PROCURATION MONEY. By 12 *Ann*, s. 2. c. 16. if any scrivener or broker shall take more than 5s. per cent. procuration money, or more than 12*d.* for making a bond, he shall forfeit 20*l.* with costs, and shall suffer imprisonment for half a year.

And by 17 *Geo.* 3. c. 26. if any person shall take more than 10s. per cent. for procuring any money to be advanced on any life annuity, he may be indicted as for a misdemeanor, and punished by fine and imprisonment.

PROCURATIONS, (*procurationes*) certain sums of money which parish priests pay yearly to the bishop or archdeacon, *ratione visitationis.*

These are also called proxies; and it is said there are three sorts of procurations or proxies; *ratione visitationis, consuetudinis, & pacti;* and that the first is of ecclesiastical cognisance, but the two last are triable at law. *Hardr.* 180.

There is also an indorsement of bills and notes by procuration; that is, as proxy for another.

PROCURATOR, is one who hath a charge committed to him by any person; in which general signification it hath been applied to a vicar or lieutenant, who acts instead of another; and we read of *procurator regni,* and *procurator reipublicæ,* which is a public magistrate: also proxies of lords in parliament are in our law books called *procuratores;* the bishops are sometimes termed *procuratores ecclesiarum;* and the advocates of religious houses, who were to solicit the interests, and plead the causes of the societies, were denominated *procuratores monasterii;* and from this word comes the common word proctor. It is likewise used for him who gathers the fruits of a benefice for another man; and procuracy for the writing or instrument whereby he is authorised. 3 *R.* 2. *c.* 3.

PROCURATORES ECCLESIÆ PAROCHIALIS, the churchwardens. *Par. Antiq.* 562.

PROCURATORIUM, the procuratory, or instrument by which any person or community did constitute or delegate their proctors, to represent them in any judicial court or cause. *Cowell.*

PRODES HOMINES, a title often given in our old books to the barons of the realm, or other military tenants. *Cowell.*

PRODITORIE, (*traitorously.*) A word necessary to indictments of treason. 2 *Hawk. P. C.* 224.

PROFANENESS, (*qu. procul à fano*) is a disrespect paid to the name of God, and to things and persons consecrated to him. *Wood's Inst.* 396. See *Blasphemy.*

PROFER, (*profrum, vel proferum,* from the Fr. *proferor,* i. e. *producere*) is the time appointed for the accounts of officers in the exchequer, which is twice in the year. *Stat.* 51. *H.* 3. *st.* 5.

If on the conclusion of the sheriff's accounts, and after allowances and discharges had by him, it appears that there is a surplusage, or that he is charged with more than he could receive, he hath his profers paid or allowed him agaim. *Hale's Sher. Account.* 52.

There is a writ, *De attornato vicecomitis pro profro faciendo. Reg. Orig.* 139. *Brit.* c. 28. and *Fleta, lib.* 1. c. 38.

PROFER THE HALF-MARK, that is to offer or tender the half-mark. See *Half-mark.*

PROFERT IN CURIA, is where the plaintiff in an action declares on a deed, or defendant pleads a deed, he must do it, with a *profert in curia:* that is, in these words: "And the said A. B. brings here into court the writing obligatory aforesaid, which testifies the debt aforesaid, in the form aforesaid, the date whereof is the day and year above-mentioned," to the end that the other party may, at his own charges, have a copy of it, and until then he is not obliged to answer it, but may demur. 2 *Lil. Abr.* 382.

PROFESSION, (*professio*) the entering into any religious order, &c. This entering into religion, whereby a man is shut up from all the common offices of life, is termed a civil death. 1 *Black.* 132, &c.

PROFITS. By a general devise of the profits of lands, the lands usually pass; unless there are other words to shew the intention of the testator to be otherwise. *Moor,* 753. 758. 2 *Nels. Abr.* 1051. *Dyer,* 210.

PROFITS OF COURTS. The profits arising from the king's ordinary courts of justice, make a branch of his revenue. And these consist not only in fines imposed upon offenders, forfeitures of recognizances, and amercements levied on defaulters; but also in certain fees due to the crown in a variety of legal matters, as, for setting the great seal to charters, original writs, and other forensic proceedings; and for permitting fines to be levied of lands, in order to bar entails, or otherwise to insure titles. 1 *Black.* 289. See *King's Revenue.*

PROHIBITION, (*prohibitio*) is a writ to forbid any court to proceed in any cause there depending, on suggestion that the cognizance thereof belongeth not to the court. *F. N. B.* 39.

But the awarding a prohibition is a matter discretionary; that is, that from the circumstances of the case, the superior courts are at liberty to exercise a legal discretion therein, but not an arbitrary one, in refusing prohibition, where in such like cases they have been granted, or where by law they ought to be granted. *Winch,* 78.

PROHIBITIO DE VASTO DIRECTA PARTI, a judicial writ usually directed to the tenant, prohibiting him from making waste on the land in controversy, during the suit. *Reg. Judic.* 21.

PRO INDIVISO, for undivided, is taken in law for a possession or occupation of lands or tenements belonging to two or more persons, whereof none knows his several portion, as coparceners before partition. *Bract. lib.* 5.

PROLES, (*Lat.*) in English progeny, are such issue as proceed from a lawful marriage; though, if the word be used at large, it may denote others. *Cowell.*

PROLOCUTOR OF THE CONVOCATION-HOUSE, (*prolocutor domus convocationis*) an officer chosen by ecclesiastical persons, publicly assembled in convocation by virtue of the king's writ at every parliament.

PROMISE, (*promissio*) is where, on a valuable consideration, persons bind themselves by words to perform such a thing as is agreed on; upon which an action may be brought: and a promise against a promise made at one and the same time, is a sufficient ground for an action. *Cro. Eliz.* 543. 703. 848.

But a consideration of some sort or other is so absolutely necessary to the forming of a promise or contract, that a *nudum pactum*, or agreement to do or pay any thing on one side, *without any compensation* on the other, is totally void in law: and a man cannot be compelled to perform it (*Dr. & St. d. 2. c. 24*). As if one man promises to give another 100*l.* here there is nothing contracted for or given on the one side, and therefore there is nothing binding on the other. And, however a man may or may not be bound to perform it, in honour or conscience, which the municipal laws do not take upon them to decide; certainly those municipal laws will not compel the execution of what he had no visible inducement to engage for: and therefore our law has adopted the maxim of the civil law, that *ex nudo pacto non oritur actio*. But any degree of reciprocity will prevent the pact from being nude: nay, even if the thing be founded on a prior moral obligation, (as a promise to pay a just debt, though barred by the statute of limitations) it is no longer *nudum pactum*,* And as this rule was principally established, to avoid the inconvenience that would arise from setting up mere verbal promises, for which no good reason could be assigned, it therefore does not hold in some cases, where such promise is authentically proved by written documents. For if a man enters into a voluntary bond, or gives a promissory note, he shall not be allowed to aver the want of a consideration in order to evade the payment: for every bond, from the solemnity of the instrument, and every note, from the subscription of the drawer, carries with it an internal evidence of a good consideration. Courts of justice will therefore support them both, as against the contractor himself; but not to the prejudice of creditors, or strangers to the contract. 2 *Black.* 446.

PROMISSORY NOTES, or notes of hand, are a plain and direct engagement in writing, to pay a sum specified at a time therein limited to a person therein named, or sometimes to his order, or often to the bearer at large. 2 *Black.* 467. See *Bill of Exchange.*

PROMOTERS, (*promotores*) are those who in popular and penal actions prosecute offenders, in their name and the king's, as informers do, having part of the fines or penalties for their reward. 3 *Inst.* 191.

PROMULGE A LAW, (*promulgare legem*) is to declare, publish, and proclaim a law to the people. 1 *Black.* 45.

PRONOTARY. See *Prothonotary.*

PROOF. See *Evidence and Witnesses.*

PRO PARTIBUS LIBERANDIS, an ancient writ for partition of lands between co-heirs. *Reg. Orig.* 316.

PROPERTY (*proprietas.*) One of the absolute rights inherent in every Englishman, is that of property: which consists in the free use, enjoyment, and disposal of all his acquisitions, without any controul or diminution, save only by the laws of the land. The original of private property is probably founded in nature: but certainly the modifications under which we at present find it, the method of conserving it in the present owner, and of translating it from man to man, are entirely derived from society; and are some of those civil advantages, in exchange for which every individual has resigned a part of his natural liberty. The laws of England are therefore, in point of honour and justice, extremely watchful in ascertaining and protecting this right. Upon this principle the great charter has declared that *no freeman shall be disseised or divested of his freehold, or of his liberties, or free customs, but by the judgment of his peers, or by the law of the land.* And by a variety of antient statutes it is enacted, that *no man's lands or goods shall be seised into the king's hands, against the great charter, and the law of the land; and that no man shall be disinherited, nor put out of his franchises or freehold, unless he be duly brought to answer, and*

* Where a man is under a moral obligation which no court of law or equity can enforce, and promises, the honesty and rectitude of the thing is a consideration. As if a man promise to pay a just debt, the recovery of which is barred by the statute of limitations; or if a man, after he comes of age, promise to pay a meritorious debt contracted during his minority, but not for necessaries; or if a bankrupt, in affluent circumstances after his certificate, promise to pay the whole of his debts; or if a man promise to perform a secret trust, or a trust void for want of being in writing by the statute of frauds. In such, and many other instances, though the promise gives a compulsory remedy where there was none before, either in law or equity, yet as the promise is only to do what an honest man ought to do, the ties of conscience upon an upright man are a sufficient consideration. (*Ld. Mansfield*, 1 *Cowp.* 290.) But if a bankrupt, after obtaining his certificate, promise to pay a prior debt when he is able, it has been held that this is a conditional promise, and that the plaintiff must prove the defendant's ability to pay. 2 *Hen. Bl.* 116.

be forejudged by course of law; and if any thing be done to the contrary, it shall be redressed, and holden for none. 1 *Black.* 139.

PROPRIETATE PROBANDA, is a writ to the sheriff to inquire of the property of goods distrained, when defendant claimeth property on a replevin sued; for the sheriff cannot proceed till that matter is decided by writ; and if it is found for plaintiff, then the sheriff is to make replevin; but if for defendant, he can proceed no further. *F. N. B.* 77. *Finch* 316. 450. *Co. Lit.* 145. *b.*

PRO RATA, is as much as *pro proportione*; as joint-tenants, &c. are to pay *pro rata*, i. e. in proportion to their estates. 16 *Car.* 2. c. 6.

PROROGUE, (*Prorogare*,) to prolong or put off to another day: thus, prorogation of parliament, and adjournment, were anciently used as synonymous; but of late there hath been a distinction, a prorogation making a session, and an adjournment only a continuance. 1 *Black.* 186.

PROTECTION, (*Protectio*,) is that benefit and safety which every subject hath by the king's laws; every man who is a loyal subject is in the king's protection; and in this sense to be out of the king's protection, is to be excluded the benefit of the law. 25 *Ed.* 3. c. 22.

PROTECTION OF AMBASSADORS. See *Ambassadors.*

PROTECTION OF CHILDREN. See *Parent and Child.*

PROTECTION OF PARLIAMENT. See *Privilege.*

PROTECTION OF THE COURTS. See *Privilege.*

PROTECTIONIBUS. The statute of allowing a challenge to be entered against a protection, &c. 33 *Ed.* 1. *st.* 1.

PROTEST, (*Protestaria*,) hath two applications; one by way of caution, to call witnesses (as it were) or openly affirm that he doth either not at all, or but conditionally, yield his consent to any act, or unto the proceeding of a judge in a court, wherein his jurisdiction is doubtful, or to answer on his oath further than by law he is bound. See *Plowden* 676. and *Reg. Orig.* 306.

There is also amongst mariners a protest made on oath before the chief magistrate or notary public of any distant part, of the damages and circumstances of delay during a ship's voyage.

There is also a protest on Bills of Exchange.

Each peer of the realm has also a right, by leave of the house, when a vote passes contrary to his sentiments, to enter his dissent on the journals of the house, with the reasons for such dissent; which is usually stiled his protest. 1 *Black.* 168.

PROTESTATION, (*Protestatio*,) is a defence or safeguard to the party who maketh it, from being concluded by the action he is about to do, that issue cannot be joined by it. *Plowd.* 276. whereof see *Reg. Orig.* 326.

It is a form of pleading when one does not directly affirm or deny any thing alleged by another, or which he himself alledgeth. *Cowell.* For it is frequently expedient to plead in such a manner, as to avoid any implied admission of a fact, which cannot with propriety or safety be positively affirmed or denied. And this may be done by what is called a protestation; whereby the party interposes an oblique allegation or denial of some fact, protesting (by the gerund, *protestando*) that such a matter does or does not exist; and at the same time avoiding a direct affirmation or denial. Sir Edward Coke hath defined a protestation (in the pithy dialect of that age) to be "an exclusion of a conclusion." For the use of it is, to save the party from being concluded with respect to some fact or circumstance, which cannot be directly affirmed or denied without falling into duplicity of pleading; and which yet, if he did not thus enter his protest, he might be deemed to have tacitly waived or admitted. Thus, if a defendant, by way of inducement to the point of his defence, alledges (among other matters) a particular mode of seisin or tenure, which the plaintiff is unwilling to admit, and yet desires to take issue on the principal point of the defence, he must deny the seisin or tenure by way of protestation, and then traverse the defensive matter. So, if an award be set forth by the plaintiff, and he can assign a breach in one part of it, (viz. the non-payment of a sum of money,) and yet is afraid to admit the performance of the rest of the award, or to aver in general a non-performance of any part of it, lest something should appear to have been performed; he may save to himself any advantage he might hereafter make of the general non-performance, by alledging that by protestation; and plead only the non-payment of the money.

PROTESTANT CHILDREN. The lord chancellor may make an order on Popish and Jewish parents refusing to allow their protestant children a maintenance. 11 & 12 *Will.* 3. c. 4. *sect.* 7. 1 *Ann. st.* 1, c.

PROTESTANT DISSENTERS. See *Dissenters.*

PROTESTANT SUCCESSION. See *King, Treason.*

PROTHONOTARY, (*Protonotarius, vel Primus Notarius*,) is a chief officer or clerk of the Common Pleas and King's Bench; and for the first court there are three prothonotaries, and the other hath but one. *Cowell.*

PROVINCE (*Provincia*,) the ecclesiastical division of England is primarily divided into two provinces, Canterbury and York;

a province is the circuit of an archbishop's jurisdiction, and each contains divers dioceses or sees of suffragan bishops.

PROVINCIAL, (*Provincialis,*) of or belonging to a province; also a chief governor of a religious order. *Cowell.*

PROVINCIAL GOVERNMENTS. See *Plantations.*

PROVISION, (*Provisio,*) is used with us as in the canon law for providing a bishop, or any other person, an ecclesiastical living. *Cowell.*

PROVISIONS. Acts to restrain the exorbitant abuse of arbitrary power made in the parliament at Oxford 1258. *Cowell.*

PROVISIONS (*selling unwholesome*) is an offence against public health. To prevent which, the statute 51 Hen. 3. st. 6. and the ordinance for bakers, c. 7. prohibit the sale of corrupted wine, contagious or unwholesome flesh, or flesh that is bought of a Jew; under pain of amercement for the first offence, pillory for the second, fine and imprisonment for the third, and abjuration of the town for the fourth. And by 12 *Car.* 2. c. 25. *s.* 11. any brewing or adulteration of wine is punished with the forfeiture of 100*l.* if done by the wholesale merchant; and 40*l.* if done by the vintner or retail trader. And the selling corrupt and unwholesome provisions is generally a misdemeanor, for which the party offending may at common law be indicted, fined, and imprisoned.

PROVISO, is a condition inserted in any deed, on the performance whereof the validity of the deed depends; or it is sometimes only a covenant, *secundum subjectam materiam.* 2 *Rep.* 70. 2 *Lill. Abr.* 399.

PROVISO, *Trial by.* When the general day for the trial of causes is fixed, the plaintiff or his attorney must bring down the record to the assises, and enter it with the proper officer, in order to its being called on in course. If it be not so entered, it cannot be tried; therefore it is in the plaintiff's breast to delay any trial by not carrying down the record: *unless the defendant, being fearful of such neglect in the plaintiff, and willing to discharge himself from the action, will himself undertake to bring on the trial, giving proper notice to the plaintiff.* Which proceeding is called the trial by proviso; by reason of the clause then inserted in the sheriff's venire, viz. "proviso, provided, that if two writs come to your hands, (that is, one from the plaintiff and another from the defendant,) you shall execute only one of them." But this practice begins to be disused, since the statute 14 Geo. II. c. 17. which enacts, that if, after issue joined, the cause is not carried down to be tried according to the course of the court, the plaintiff shall be esteemed to be nonsuited, and judgment shall be given for the defendant as in case of a nonsuit. In case the plaintiff intends to try the cause, he is bound to give the defendant (if he lives within forty miles of London) eight days notice of trial; and, if he lives at a greater distance, then fourteen days notice, in order to prevent surprize: and if the plaintiff then changes his mind, and does not countermand the notice six days before the trial, he shall be liable to pay costs to the defendant for not proceeding to trial, by the same last-mentioned statute. The defendant, however, or plaintiff, may, upon good cause shewn to the court above, as upon absence or sickness of a material witness, obtain leave upon motion to defer the trial of the cause till the next assises. 3 *Black* 357.

PROVISOR, was one who sued to the court of Rome for a provision, which offence was made a premunire. See *Præmunire.*

PROVISOR MONASTERII, the treasurer or steward of a religious house. *Cowell.*

PROVISOR VICTUALIUM. The king's purveyor. *Cowell.*

PROVOCATION. See *Homicide.*

PROVOST MARSHAL. An officer of the king's navy, who hath the charge of prisoners taken at sea. *Cowell.*

PROXIES, are persons appointed by others to represent them.

And every peer of the realm called to parliament, hath the privilege of constituting a proxy to vote for him in his absence on a lawful occasion; but such proxies are to be entered in person.

Proxies are also annual payments made by parochial clergy to the bishop, &c. on visitations. See *Procurations.*

PRYK, a kind of service or tenure; and according to Blount, an old-fashioned spur, with one point only, which the tenant, holding land by this tenure, was to find for the king. *Cowell. Blount.*

PUBERTY, (*Pubertas.*) The ripe age of fourteen in men and twelve in women, when they are fit for marriage.

PUBLICATION. When all the witnesses in a court of equity are examined, then, and not before, the depositions may be published, by a rule to pass publication; after which, and not before, they are open for the inspection of all the parties, and copies may be taken of them.

There is also a publication of a will, which is a solemnity requisite to the making thereof, by declaring it to be the last will of the testator, in the presence of such a number of witnesses. 3 *Nels. Abr.* 27.

PUBLIC ACT *of Parliament.* A general or a public act is an universal rule, that regards the whole community; and of this the courts of law are bound to take notice judicially and *ex officio*, without the statute being particularly pleaded, or formally set forth by the party who claims an advantage under it. 1 *Black.* 86.

PUERITIA. See *Puberty.*

PUIS DARREIN CONTINUANCE, is a plea of new matter pending an action. *post ultimam continuationem,* or since the last adjournment. *Cowell.* 3 *Black.* 316.

PUISNE, (F. *Puisne.*) Younger, puny, born after, junior. See *Mulier.* So the several judges and barons, not chiefs, are called puisne judges, puisne barons. *Cowell.* 3 *Black.* 40, 41, 44.

PULSATOR. The plaintiff or actor; and *pulsare* signifies to accuse any one. *Leg. Hen.* 1. c. 26.

PUNISHMENT, (*Pœna.*) The penalty for transgressing the law. The punishments of offences are many and various, adapted to the several degrees of crimes, and the countries wherein committed; such as beheading, hanging, imprisonment, fine, amercement, &c. 4 *Black.* 7.

PUR AUTER VIE, is where lands, &c. are held for another's life. 2 *Black.* 120. See *Occupant.*

PURCHASE, (*Acquisitum, perquisitum, purchasium,*) signifies the buying or acquisition of lands, or tenements, with money, or by deed or agreement; and not obtaining it by descent or hereditary right; and *conjunctum perquisitum* is where two or more persons join in the purchase. *Lit.* 12. *Reg. Orig.* 143.

One cometh in by purchase when he comes to lands by legal conveyance, and he hath a lawful estate: and a purchase is always intended by title, either from some consideration, or by gift; (for a gift is in law a purchase,) whereas descent from an ancestor cometh of course by act of law; also all contracts are comprehended under this word purchase. *Co. Lit.* 18. *Doct. and Stud.* c. 24.

Purchase, in opposition to descent, is taken largely; if an estate comes to a man from his ancestors without writing, that is a descent; but where a person takes any thing from an ancestor or others, by deed, will, or gift, and not as heir at law, that is a purchase. 2 *Lill. Abr.* 403.

When an estate doth originally vest in the heir, and never was nor could be in the ancestor, such heir shall take by way of purchase; but when the thing might have vested in his ancestor, though it be first in the heir, and not in him at all, the heir shall have it in nature of descent. 1 *Rep.* 95. 106.

PURGATION. See *Ordeal.*

PURIFICATIO BEATÆ MARIÆ VIRGINIS. The Purification of the Blessed Virgin Mary is one of the general returns of writs, viz. the third in Hilary term.

PURLIEU-MEN, are those who have ground within the purlieu, and being able to dispend forty shillings a year freehold; who, on these two points, are licensed to hunt in their own purlieus, observing what is required. *Mainw. For. Laws* 151, 157, 180, 186.

PURLUE, or PURLIEU, (from the Fr. *pur,* i. e. purus, and *lieu,* locus,) is all that ground near a forest, which being added to the ancient forests by king Hen. 2. Rich. 1. and king John, was afterwards disafforested and severed by the *Charta de Foresta,* and the perambulations and grants thereon by Hen. 3. so that it becomes *purlue,* viz. pure and free from the laws and ordinances of the forest. *Mainw. For. Laws. par.* 2. c. 20.

PURPARTY, (Fr. *pour part,* i. e. *pro parte,*) is that part or share of an estate, first held in common by parceners, which is by partition allotted to any of them. *Old Nat. Br.* 11. See *Pro indiviso.*

PURPRESTURE, (*Pourprestura,* from the Fr. *pourprist,* an inclosure,) is when any thing is done to the nuisance of the king's demesnes, or the highways, &c. by inclosure or buildings, endeavouring to make that private which ought to be public. *Glanv. lib.* 9. c. 11. *Co. Lit.* 38. 272. And when a man takes to himself, or incroaches any thing which he ought not, it is a purpresture. *Kitch.* 10. 2 *Inst.* 38. See *Pourpresture.*

PURSE. A certain quantity of money, containing 500 dollars, or 125*l.* in Turkey. *Merch. Dict.*

PURSUIVANT, (from the Fr. *Pursuivre,* i. e. *agere, pursequi,*) the king's messenger. See *Poursuivant.*

PURVEYANCE. A right formerly enjoyed by the crown of buying up provisions and other necessaries, by the intervention of the king's purveyors, for the use of his royal household, at an appraised valuation, in preference to all others, and even without consent of the owner; and also of forcibly impressing the carriages and horses of the subject, to do the king's business on the public roads, in the conveyance of timber, baggage, and the like, however inconvenient to the proprietor, upon paying him a settled price. 4 *Inst.* 273.

Purveyance is however now taken away by the statute 12 Car. 2. c. 24. s. 12.

PURVIEW, (Fr. *Pourveu,* a patent or grant,) is the body, or that part of an act of parliament which begins with, Be it enacted, &c. The statute 3 Hen. 7. stands upon a preamble and purview. 2 *Inst.* 403. 12 *Rep.* 20.

PUTAGE, (*Putagium, Fornicatio ex parte fœminæ, quod vox nulla Latina exprimit, quasi puttam agere:* from the Fr. *putain,* or the Italian *putta,* i. e. *meretrix*) fornication.

PUTATIVUS, Putative, reputed, or

commonly esteemed, in opposition to notorious and unquestionable. See *Bastard.*

PUTTING IN FEAR. See *Larceny* and *Robbery.*

PUTURA, (*q. Potura.*) A custom claimed by keepers in forests, and sometimes by bailiffs of hundreds, to take man's meat, horse meat, and dog's meat of the tenants and inhabitants within the perambulation of the forest, hundred, &c. turned into the payment of money by each tenant.

PYHER, or PYCAR. A small ship or herring boat. 31 *Ed.* 3. *c.* 2.

Q

QUADRAGESIMA. The fortieth part. Also the time of Lent, from our Saviour's forty day's fast. *Lit. Dict.*

And Quadragesima Sunday is the first Sunday in Lent, so called because about the fortieth day before Easter. *Blount.*

QUADRAGESIMALIA. In former days it was the custom for people to visit their mother church on Midlent-Sunday, and their offerings were then called Quadragesimalia. *Cowell. Blount.*

QUADRANS. A fourth part of a penny. *Ibid.*

QUADRANTATA TERRÆ. The fourth part of an acre. *Ibid.*

QUADRIVIUM. The centre of four ways, where four roads meet and cross each other. *Ibid.*

QUÆ EST EADEM. An averment in pleading, is used to supply the want of a traverse. 2 *Lil. Abr.* 405. 1 *Lev.* 241. *Lutw.* 1457.

QUÆ PLURA. A writ which lay where an inquisition had been taken by an escheator of lands, &c. that a man died seised of, and all the land was supposed not to be found by the office or inquisition; this writ was therefore to inquire of what other lands or tenements the party died seised; but it is now useless, since the taking away the court of *wards* and offices *post mortem.* 12 *Car.* 2. *c.* 24. *Reg. Orig.* 293.

QUÆRE, or QUERIE, is where any point of law, or matter in debate, is doubted, as not having sufficient authority to maintain it. 2. *Lil. Abr.* 406.

QUÆRENS NON INVENIT PLEGIUM. A return made by the sheriff, on a writ directed to him with this clause, viz. *Si A. fecerit B. securum de clamore suo prosequendo,* &c. *F. N. B.* 38.

QUÆ SERVITIA. See *Per quæ servitia.*

QUÆSTA. An indulgence or remission of penance exposed to sale by the Pope. *Cowell.*

QUÆSTUS. Is that which a man hath by purchase, as *hæreditas* is what he hath by descent. *Ibid.*

QUAKERS. A religious sect in civil causes, who, where an oath is required, are permitted to make a solemn affirmation or declaration, declaring in the presence of God the truth, &c. But they are not capable of being witnesses in a criminal cause. 7 & 8 W. 3. c. 34. Unless they are sworn like others, for an affirmation is not in its nature an oath.

Thus, on the affirmation of a Quaker, the court will not grant an attachment for non-performance of an award. 1 *Strange* 441. Nor security for the peace. *Ibid* 527. Nor a rule for an information. 2 *Strange* 856, 872, 946.

And by 22 *Geo.* 2. *c.* 46. *s.* 36. an affirmation shall be allowed in all cases except criminal, where by any act of parliament an oath is required, though no provision be therein contained for admitting a Quaker to make his affirmation.

If Quakers refuse to pay tithes or church rates, justices of peace are to levy them, with costs, when the arrears exceed not 10*l.* 7 & 8 *W.* 3. *c.* 34. *s.* 4. 1 *Geo.* 1. *c.* 6.

QUALE JUS. A judicial writ which was brought where a man of religion had judgment to recover land, before execution was made of the judgment; it went forth to the escheator between judgment and execution, to inquire whether the religious person had right to recover, or the judgment were obtained by collusion between the parties, to the intent that the lord might not be defrauded. *Reg. Judic.* 8, 16, 46. *Stat. Westm.* 2. c. 32.

QUALIFIED (or *base*) FEE. Is such a one as hath a qualification subjoined thereto, and which must be determined whenever the qualification annexed to it is at an end. As, in the case of a grant to *A.* and his heirs, tenants of the manor of Dale; in this instance, whenever the heirs of *A.* cease to be tenants of that manor, the grant is entirely defeated. So when Hen. 6. granted to John Talbot, lord of the manor of Kingstone-Lisle, in Berks, that he and his heirs, lords of the said manor, should be peers of the realm, by the title of Barons of Lisle. Here John Talbot had a base or qualified fee in that dignity; and the instant he or his heirs quitted the seigniory of this manor, the dignity was at an end. *Co. Lit.* 27. 2 *Black. Com.* 109.

This estate is a fee, because by possibility it may endure for ever in a man and his heirs; yet, as that duration depends on the concurrence of collateral circumstances, which qualify and debase the purity of the donation, it is therefore a qualified or base fee. 2 *Black. Com.* 109.

QUALIFIED PROPERTY. See *Bailment.*

QUAMDIU SE BENE GESSERIT. Is a clause often inserted in letters patent of the grant of offices, that the party shall hold the same so long as he behaves himself well. 4 *Inst.* 117.

QUANTUM MERUIT. A count in a declaration, averring, How much he has deserved.

And if a man retains any person to do work or other thing for him, although there be not any certain agreement, he shall pay for the same, on the *quantum meruit.* 3 *Black.* 161.

QUANTUM VALEBAT, is where goods and wares sold are delivered by a tradesman at no certain price, or to be paid for them, as much as they are worth in general; then *quantum valebat* lies.

QUARE CLAUSUM FREGIT. Before the statute 19 Hen. 7. s. 9. giving the process of *capias* in all actions on the case, a practice had been introduced of commencing the suit by bringing an original writ of trespass *quare clausum fregit,* for breaking the plaintiff's close, *vi et armis;* which, by the old common law, subjected the defendant's person to be arrested by writ of *capias:* and then afterwards, by connivance of the court, the plaintiff might proceed to prosecute for any other less forcible injury. This practice (through custom rather than necessity, and for saving some trouble and expence, in suing out a special original adapted to the particular injury) still continues in almost all cases, except in actions of debt. 3 *Black.* 281.

QUARE CUM. General words used in original writs, &c. See *Original.*

QUARE EJECIT INFRA TERMINUM, is a writ which lies for lessee, where he is cast out of his farm before his term is expired, against a feoffee of the lands, or the lessor who ejects him; and the effect of it is to recover his term again, and damages. *Reg. Orig.* 227. *F. N. B.* 197. *New Nat. Br.* 439. See *Ejectment.*

QUARE IMPEDIT, is a writ lying for him who hath purchased an advowson, against a person who disturbs him in his right of advowson by presenting a clerk thereto, when the church is void. *F. N. B.* 32. *Stat. Westm.* 2. c. 5.

QUARE INCUMBRAVIT. A writ which lieth against the bishop, who within six months after the vacation of a benefice, confers it on his clerk, whilst two others are contending at law for the right of presentation. *Reg. Orig.* 32.

QUARE NON ADMISIT, is a writ which lies against a bishop where a man hath recovered his advowson, or presentation in a writ of right of advowson, or in *quare impedit,* or other action, and the bishop refuses to admit his clerk, on pretence of lapse, &c. it is requisite in the writ to mention the recovery; and it is to be brought in the county where the refusal was. *F. N. B.* 47. 7 *Rep. Dyer* 40.

QUARE NON PERMITTIT, is mentioned as an ancient writ which lieth for one who hath a right to present to a church for a turn, against the proprietary. *Fleta, lib.* 5, *cap.* 6.

QUARENTINE, or QUARENTAINE, (*Quarentina,*) is a benefit allowed by law to the widow of a man dying seised of lands, whereby she may challenge to continue in his capital messuage, or chief mansion-house, (not being a castle,) by the space of forty days after his decease, in order to the assignment of her dower, &c. And if the heir, or any other, eject her, she may bring the writ *de quarentena habenda;* but the widow shall not have meat, drink, &c. though if there be no provision in the house, according to Fitzherbert, she may kill things for her provision. *Magna Charta,* c. 7. *Bract. lib.* 2. c. 40. *F. N. B.* 161. See 2 *Black. Com.* 135.

QUARENTINE, is also the term of forty days wherein any persons coming from foreign parts infected with the plague, are not permitted to land or come on shore, until so many days are expired. 4 *Black.* 162.

And by 45 *Geo.* 3. c. 10. vessels and goods coming from places adjudged by the king in council to be infected, or probably so, shall be liable to quarantine; and any goods or ships specified in any order of council, may be made subject to quarantine. s. 10. 11.

The privy council may make such orders as they shall think necessary upon emergency respecting ships or goods, and in case of infectious disease appearing in Great Britain, and for mitigating quarantine. s. 12.

Masters of ships liable to quarantine shall make signals on meeting other ships at sea, or being within four leagues of the United Kingdom or the islands aforesaid, on pain of 200*l.* s. 14.

Persons hoisting signals when not liable, shall forfeit 200*l.* s. 15.

Masters of vessels, on their arrival from foreign parts, shall give to the pilots an account of the places at which they shall have laden and touched, on pain of 200*l.* s. 16.

Pilots bringing ships liable to quarantine into places not appointed for their reception, are to forfeit 100*l.* s. 17.

For better ascertaining whether ships be actually infected, or the persons on board liable to orders of quarantine, the masters shall answer enquiries truly, on pain of 200*l.* s. 18.

Ships subject to quarantine arriving at any port, except that at which it ought to be performed, may be forced to repair to the appointed place. s. 19.

Masters of vessels having touched at infected places, omitting to disclose the same, or to hoist the prescribed signals, shall be guilty of felony without benefit of clergy. s. 20.

Commanders shall deliver up bills of health, manifests, and log-books, to the super-intendant of quarantine, on pain of 100*l.* s. 21.

Masters quitting vessels or permitting persons to quit them, or not conveying ships to the appointed places, are to forfeit 500*l.*; and persons coming in such vessels, or, going on board, quitting them before discharged, are to be imprisoned for six months, and forfeit 200*l.* s. 21.

No goods shall be landed from vessels having performed quarantine in a foreign lazaret, without notice to the officer of the customs, nor before directions from the privy council, on pain of 200*l.* s. 22.

Disobedience or refractory behaviour may be punished by force, in persons under or liable to quarantine, or persons having intercourse with them. s. 23.

And persons refusing to repair to the lazaret, shall be guilty of felony without clergy. *Ibid.*

Persons quitting ships liable to perform quarantine, may be seized and carried before a magistrate, to be detained until conveyed to some place for performance of quarantine. s. 24.

Officers embezzling goods performing quarantine or neglecting their duty, are to forfeit 100*l.* and be incapacitated. s. 26.

And permitting any person, ship, or goods, to depart without authority, or giving false certificates, or damaging goods, is felony without clergy. *Ibid.*

Persons not infected entering the lazaret, shall perform quarantine; and attempting to escape, may be compelled to return; and such person escaping shall be guilty of felony without clergy. s. 27.

After proof of performance of quarantine, and proper certificate to that effect, vessels or persons shall not be liable to further detention. s. 28.

Goods liable to perform quarantine shall be opened and aired as directed by order in council; proof of which shall be made before the officer of the customs, who shall grant certificates thereof, which shall entitle them to be discharged from further detention. s. 29.

Persons forging certificates, are guilty of felony without clergy. s. 30.

Persons landing goods from vessels liable to perform quarantine, or receiving them, are to forfeit not exceeding 500*l.* nor less than 100*l.* and persons secreting them from vessels performing quarantine, are guilty of felony without clergy. s. 31.

His majesty, in cases of infection, may prohibit vessels under twenty tons from sailing until bond be given by the master not to touch at places specified; and sailing without giving such security, is a forfeiture of the vessel and 20*l.* per man. s. 32.

Publication in the London Gazette of orders in council shall be sufficient notice. s. 33.

Penalties may be recovered in courts of record, one moiety to the informer and the other to the king; but such action must be prosecuted in the name of the attorney-general, or advocate in Scotland, or some officer of customs. s. 34, 35.

In prosecutions by officers of the customs, the attorney-general, or advocate, for sufficient cause, may stop proceedings. s. 36.

Persons authorized to take examinations may administer oaths; and persons swearing falsely or procuring others so to do, shall be punished as guilty of perjury. s. 37.

Offences not being felony, and offences not punished by a specific penalty, may be determined before two justices, who may fine not exceeding 50*l.* or imprison not exceeding three months. s. 38.

No attainder of felony shall work corruption of blood or forfeiture. s. 39.

Answers of persons having the charge of vessels shall be received in evidence so far as they relate to the places from which vessels came, or at which they touched; and the having been directed to perform quarantine, shall be received as evidence that vessels were liable thereto, unless proof be made to the contrary; and the being performing quarantine shall be proof of vessels being liable to perform it. *s.* 40.

On affidavit of indictment filed for offences under this act, a judge may cause the party to be apprehended, and if he refuses to become bound for his appearance, he may be committed to gaol. *s.* 41.

When persons are detained, the prosecutor may cause a copy of the indictment to be delivered to the party or the gaoler, with notice to appear and plead, or demur; and on failure, an appearance and plea of not guilty may be entered by the prosecutor, and the trial shall proceed. *s.* 41.

Defendant acquitted, may be discharged by the judge trying the offence. *s.* 41.

All offences against law of quarantine may be tried in any county. *s.* 42.

By 46 *Geo.* 3. *c.* 98. the signal to be used by ships having the plague, or coming from infected places, shall be, in the day time, a flag of yellow and black, and at night, two signal lanterns, one over the other, at mast-head. *s.* 1.

In addition to the particulars required by 45 *Geo.* 3. *c.* 10. the master shall deliver an account of the cargo to the pilot, on pain of 200*l.* *s.* 2.

And the pilot shall give notice to the master if any articles be on board liable to quarantine, on pain of 100*l.* and the commander shall hoist signals accordingly. *Ibid.*

The pilot or master not bringing-to, on request of the quarantine officer (see 45 *Geo.* 3 *c.* 10. *s.* 18.), shall forfeit 100*l.* *s.* 3.

Ships liable to quarantine solely by involuntary communication, shall not be liable to pay the quarantine duty. *s.* 4.

Proof and certificate of goods having been opened and aired under this act, allowed instead of the proof and certificate required by 45 *Geo.* 3. *c.* 10. *s.* 29. *s.* 5.

The privy council may order ships coming from America or the West Indies, when the yellow fever or other infectious disorder prevails there, to go to places to be appointed from time to time, without being liable to quarantine. *s.* 6.

Intercourse within limits of stations allotted for quarantine of ships without clean bills of health, may be prohibited by order in council, and persons guilty of disobedience forfeit 500*l.* *s.* 7.

Persons forging or uttering false certificates required by orders in council, is felony without benefit of clergy. *s.* 8.

Consuls may administer oaths; persons authorized to take examinations may administer oaths; and the pains of perjury inflicted for false oaths. *s.* 10.

QUARENTINE likewise signifies a quantity of ground, containing 40 perches. *Leg. Hen.* 1. *c.* 16.

QUARE OBSTRUXIT. A writ which lay for him, who, having a liberty to pass through his neighbour's ground, could not enjoy his right, because the owner has so obstructed it. *Fleta, lib.* 4. *c.* 26.

QUARREL, (*Querela, a querendo,*) extends not only to actions personal, but also to mixt, and the plaintiff in them is called *querens*, and in most of the writs it is said *queritur;* so that if a man release all quarrels, (a man's deed being taken most strongly against himself) yet it is as beneficial as all actions, for by it all actions real and personal are released. *Co. lib.* 8. 153. and *Co. Lit. lib.* 3. *c.* 8. *s.* 511.

QUARRELLING IN CHURCH OR CHURCH-YARD. See *Affrays.*

QUARTELOIS, were upper garments with coats of arms quartered on them, the old habit of English knights.—Walsing. in vit. Ed. 2. *Cowell.*

QUARTERIFARI. To be quartered, or cut into four quarters in execution. *Ibid.*

QUARTERIZATIO, is part of the punishment and execution of a traitor, by dividing his body into four quarters. *Ibid.*

QUARTER-SESSIONS. Is a general court held by the justices of peace in every county, once every quarter of a year, for matters touching the breach of the peace, &c.

And by stat. 2 *Hen.* 5. *c.* 4. they are appointed to be in the first week after Michaelmas day, the first week after the Epiphany, the first week after the close of Easter, and in the week after the translation of Saint Thomas à Becket, or the 7th of July.

QUARTO DIE POST, is the fourth day inclusive after the return of the writ, and if the defendant makes his appearance on this day, it is sufficient. 3 *Black.* 278.

QUASH *Quassare*, (from the French word *quasser*, i. e. *cassum facere.*) To overthrow or annul. *Bracton, lib.* 5. Such as, quash orders of sessions, presentments, indictments, &c. 2 *Lill. Abr.* 410. 2 *Hawk. P. C.* 258.

QUAYS. See *Ports.*

QUEEN, (Lat. *Regina*, Sax. *Cwen*, i. e. *Uxor*, a wife, *sed propter excellentiam*, the wife of the king.) In our law the queen of England is either queen regent, queen consort, or queen dowager. The queen regent, regnant, or sovereign, is she who holds the crown in her own right; as the first (and perhaps the second) queen Mary, queen Elizabeth, and queen Anne; and such a one has the same powers, prerogatives, rights, dignities, and duties, as if she had been a king. This is expressly declared by stat. 1 Mary 1. stat. 3. c. 1. But the queen consort is the wife of the reigning king; and she, by virtue of her marriage, is participant of divers prerogatives above other women. *Finch. L.* 86.

And, first, she is a public person, exempt and distinct from the king, and not, like other married women, so closely connected as to have lost all legal or separate existence so long as the marriage continues. For the queen is of ability to purchase lands, and to convey them, to make leases, to grant copyholds, and to do other acts of ownership, without the concurrence of her lord, which no other married woman can do (4 Rep. 23,) a privilege as old as the Saxon æra. She is also capable of taking a grant from the king, which no other wife is from her husband. The queen of England hath separate courts and offices distinct from the king's, not only in matters of ceremony, but even of law; and her attorney and solicitor-general are entitled to a place within the bar of his majesty's courts, together with the king's counsel. She may likewise sue and be sued alone, without joining her husband. She may also have a separate property in goods as well as lands, and has a right to dispose of them by will. In short, she is in all legal proceedings looked upon as a *feme sole*, and not as a *feme covert*; as a single, not as a married woman. For which the reason given by Sir Edward Coke is this: because the wisdom of the common law would not have the king (whose continual care and study is for the public, and *circa ardua regni*) to be troubled and disquieted on account of his wife's domestic affairs; and therefore it vests in the queen a power of transacting her own concerns, without the intervention of the king, as if she was an unmarried woman.

The queen hath also many exemptions, and minute prerogatives. For instance: she pays no toll, nor is she liable to any amercement in any court. But in general, unless where the law has expressly declared her exempted, she is upon the same footing with other subjects, being to all intents and purposes the king's subject, and not his equal, in like manner as in the imperial law.

The queen hath also some pecuniary advantages, which form her a distinct revenue: as, in the first place, she is entitled to an ancient perquisite called queen-gold, or *aurum reginæ*; which is a royal revenue, belonging to every queen consort during her marriage with the king, and due from every person who hath made a voluntary offering or fine to the king, amounting to ten marks or upwards, for and in consideration of any privileges, grants, licences, pardons, or other matter of royal favour conferred upon him by the king; and it is due in the proportion of one tenth part more, over and above the entire offering or fine made to the king; and becomes an actual debt of record to the queen's majesty by the mere recording of the fine. As, if an hundred marks of silver be given to the king for liberty to take in mortmain, or to have a fair, market, park, chase, or free warren: there the queen is entitled to ten marks in silver, or (what was formerly an equivalent denomination) to one mark in gold, by the name of queen-gold, or *aurum reginæ*. But no such payment is due for any aids or subsidies granted to the king in parliament or convocation; nor for fines imposed by courts on offenders, against their will; nor for voluntary presents to the king, without any consideration moving from him to the subject, nor for any sale or contract whereby the present revenues or possessions of the crown are granted away or diminished.

The collecting of this duty of queen-gold seems to have been much neglected after the accession of the Tudor family; and there being no queen consort afterwards till the accession of James I. a period of near sixty years, its very nature and quantity became then a matter of doubt; and being referred by the king to the chief justices and chief baron, their report of it was so very unfavourable that his consort queen Anne (though she claimed it) yet never thought proper to exact it.

Another ancient perquisite belonging to the queen consort, mentioned by all old writers, and therefore only worth notice, is this: that on the taking of a whale on the coasts, which is a royal fish, it shall be divided between the king and queen; the head only being the king's property, and the tail of it the queen's. *De sturgione observetur, quod rex illum habebit integrum: de balena vero sufficit, si rex habeat caput, et regina caudam.*

Though the queen is in all respects a subject, yet, in point of the security of her life and person, she is put on the same footing with the king. It is equally treason (by the statute 25 Edw. III.) to compass or imagine the death of our lady the king's companion, as of the king himself; and to violate, or defile the queen consort, amounts to the same high crime, as well in the person committing the fact, as in the queen herself, if consenting. 1 *Black.* 222. But the stat. 25 Edw. III. which makes it treason to violate the queen, does not extend to a queen-dowager. 2 *Inst.* 50.

Ann Boleyn was convicted of high treason in the court of the lord high steward. One of the charges against this unhappy queen was, that she had said, "that the king never had had her heart;" a declaration, if made, in which there was probably more truth than discretion; but this was adjudged to be a slander of her own issue, and therefore high treason, according to a statute which had been passed about two years before for her honour and protection. *Harg. St. Tr.* 11 vol. p. 10.

QUEEN-DOWAGER. See *Queen.*

QUEEN-GOLD, (*Aurum Reginæ,*) is a royal duty or revenue formerly belonging to every queen of England, during her marriage to the king. *Scac. p.* 43. 12 *Co. Rep.* 21. 22. See *Queen.*

QUE ESTATE, signifies, which estate; and is a plea, where a man entitling another to land, &c. saith, that the same estate such other had he has from him. *Broke* 175. *Co. Lit.* 121.

QUE EST EADEM. See *Quæ est eadem, &c.*

QUE EST LE MESME, (signifying *verbatim*, the same thing,) is a word of art, in actions of trespass, &c. for a direct justification of the very act complained of by plaintiff as a wrong. *Kitch.* 236.

QUEM REDDITUM REDDAT. A judicial writ which lay for him, to whom a rent-seck or rent-charge is granted, by fine levied in the king's court against the tenant of the land who refuseth to attorn to him, thereby to cause him to attorn. *Old Nat. Brev.* 126. *West, Symbol.* par. 2. tit. *Fines*, sect. 156.

QUERELA. An action preferred in any court of justice, in which the plaintiff was *querens* or complainant, and his brief complaint or declaration was *querela*, whence our *quarrel* against any person. *Cowell.*

QUIETUS ESSE A QUERELIS, was to be exempted from the customay fees paid to the king or lord of a court, for the purchase of liberty to prefer such an action. But more usually to be exempted from fines and amercements, imposed for common trespasses and faults. *Ibid.*

QUERELA CORAM REGE A CONCILIO DISCUTIENDA ET TERMINANDA. A writ whereby one was called to justify a complaint of a trespass made to the king himself, before the king and his council. *Reg. Orig.* 124.

QUERELA FRESCÆ FORTIÆ. See *Fresh Force.*

QUEST, QUESTUS, (*Questa.*) A quest or inquest, inquisition or inquiry on the oaths of an impannelled jury. *Cowell.*

QUESTION, or *Torture.* See *Torture.*

QUESTUS EST NOBIS. The form of a writ of nuisance against him to whom the house or other thing which occasioned the nuisance, was alienated; whereas, before the statute, this action lay only against him who first levied the thing to the annoyance of his neighbour. *Cowel.*

QUIA DOMINUS REMISIT CURIAM. Writ of right, to oust the lord of his jurisdiction, is restrained by Magna Charta, c. 24. 3 *Black.* 195.

QUIA EMPTORES. The stat. of Westm. 3. or *quia emptores*, 18 Ed. 1. c. 1, directs, that upon all sales or feoffments of land, the feoffee shall hold the same, not of his immediate feoffor, but of the chief lord of the fee, of whom such feoffor himself held it.

QUIA IMPROVIDO. A supersedeas granted in behalf of a clerk of the chancery sued against the privilege of that court in the common pleas, and pursued to the exigent, or in many other cases where a writ is erroneously sued. *Dyer* 33. *n.* 18.

QUICK WITH CHILD. See *Pregnancy.*

QUICK-SETS. See *Trespass.*

QUID JURIS CLAMAT. A judicial writ issuing out of the record of the fine, which remaineth with the Custos Brevium of the Common Pleas, before it be engrossed; and it lies for the grantee of a reversion or remainder, when the particular tenant will not attorn. *West. Symbol.* part 2. tit. *Fines*, sect. 118. *Reg. Judic.* 36, 57. See 18 *Vin. Abr.* 143.

QUID PRO QUO, signifieth something for somewhat; and is used in the law, for the giving one thing of value for another thing, being the mutual consideration and performance of both parties to a contract. *Kitch.* 184. See *Promise.*

QUIETANTIA, (*Acquietantia.*) See *Acquittance.*

QUIETARE, To quit, acquit or discharge, or save harmless. *Cowell.*

QUIETE CLAMARE, is to quit claim, or renounce all pretensions of right and title. *Ibid.*

QUIETUS, (freed or acquitted,) is a word made use of by the Clerk of the Pipe and Auditors in the Exchequer, in their discharges given to accountants; usually concluding with *abinde recessat quietus*, which is called a *quietus est*: a *quietus est* granted to the sheriff, will discharge him of all accounts due to the king. Stat. 21 Jac. 1. c. 5. And these *quietus's* are mentioned in the acts of general pardon. 12 *Car.* 2. c. 11. and 4 *Car.* 2. c. 21.

QUIETUS REDDITUS. See *Quit-Rent.*

QUINQUAGESIMA SUNDAY. Shrove Sunday, so named because it is about the fiftieth day before Easter. *Cowell.*

QUINQUE PORTUS. The Cinque Ports: which are, 1. Hastings; 2. Romney; 3. Hythe; 4. Dover; and 5. Sandwich. To the first, Winchelsea and Rye belong, which are reckoned as part, or members of the cinque ports. *Cowell.* See *Cinque Ports.*

QUINSTEME, or QUINZIME, (*Decima Quinta,*) is a French word, signifying a fifteenth; with us it was a tax, so called because it was raised after the fifteenth part of men's lands or goods. *Anno* 10 *Rich.* 2. *cap.* 1. and 7 *Hen.* 7. c. 5. See *Fifteenths.*

QUINTAL, (*Quintallus.*) A weight of lead, iron, and common metals, usually one hundred pounds, at six score per cent. *Cowell.*

QUINTANE, (*Quintena,*) was a Roman military sport or exercise, by men on horseback, formerly practised in this kingdom to try the agility of the country youth. *Cowell.*

QUINTO EXACT', (*Quintus exactus*, mentioned in the statute 31 Eliz. cap. 3.) is the last call of the defendant, who is sued to outlawry, where, if he appear not, he is by the judgment of the coroners returned outlawed; if a woman, waved. 4 *Black.* 283.

QUI TAM. Is where an information is exhibited (or action prosecuted) against any person on a penal statute, at suit of the king and the party who is informer; where the penalty, for breach of the statute, is to be divided between them, and the party informer prosecutes as well for the king as himself. *Finch*, 340.

QUIT-CLAIM, (*Quieta clamantia*,) is a release or acquitting of a man, for any action which the releasor hath, might, or may have against him. Also a quitting of one's claim or title. Bracton, lib. 5. tract. 5. c. 9. *Cowell.*

QUIT-RENT, (*Quietus Redditus*, *quasi* quit-rent,) is a certain small rent, payable by the tenants of manors in token of subjection, and by which the tenant goes quiet and free. In ancient records it is called white-rent, because paid in silver money, to distinguish it from rent corn, &c. 2 *Inst.* 19.

QUOAD HOC (*as to this*,) is often used in law pleadings and arguments, to signify, as to the thing named the law is so, &c. *Cowell.*

QUOD CLERICI BENEFICIATI DE CANCELLARIA, was a writ to exempt a clerk of the chancery from the contribution towards the proctors of the clergy in parliament. *Reg. Orig.* 261.

QUOD CLERICI NON ELIGANTUR IN OFFICIO BALLIVI, &c. is a writ which lies for a clerk, who, by reason of some land he hath, is made, or about to be made bailiff, beadle, reeve, or some such officer. See *Clerico infra sacros*, *&c.* *Reg. Orig.* 187. and *F. N. B.* 261.

QUOD CUM, in indictments, &c. As A. B. was indicted *quod cum* C. D. he had done such a thing; and this being by way of recital, and not positively, is not good. 2 *Hawk. P. C.* 227. 3 *Salk.* 188.

QUOD EI DEFORCEAT. A writ for tenant in tail, tenant in dower, by the curtesy, or for term of life, having lost their lands by default, against him who recovers, or his heir. *Reg. Orig.* 171. *Stat. Westm.* 2. c. 4.

QUOD PERMITTAT. A writ which lays against any person who erects a building, though on his own ground, so near to the house of another, that it hangs over, or becomes a nuisance to it. 2 *Lill. Abr.* 413.

Quod permittat lay also for the heir of him who was disseised of his common of pasture, against the heir of the disseisor, being dead. *Terms de Ley.*

QUOD PERMITTAT PROSTERNERE, was a writ in the nature of a writ of right: it was a writ commanding the defendant to permit the plaintiff to abate, *quod permittat prosternere*, the nuisance complained of; and, unless he so permitted to summon him to appear in court, and shew cause why he would not. And this writ lay as well for the alienee of the party first injured, as against the alienee of the party first injuring. And the plaintiff was to have judgment herein to abate the nuisance, and to recover damages against the defendant. But these actions of *quod permittat prosternere* are now out of use, and have given way to the action on the case. 2 *Inst.* 405. *F. N. B.* 104. 5 *Rep.* 100, 101. Yet, as therein it is not necessary that the freehold should be in the plaintiff and defendant respectively, as it must be in these real actions, but it is maintainable by one that hath possession only, against another that hath like possession, the process is therefore easier; and the effect will be much the same, unless a man has a very obstinate as well as an ill-natured neighbour, who had rather continue to pay damages than remove his nuisance; for in such case, recourse must at last be had to the old and sure remedies, which will effectually conquer the defendant's perverseness, by sending the sheriff with his *posse comitatus*, or power of the county to level it.

QUOD PERSONA NEC PREBENDARII, ETC. A writ which lay for spiritual persons, distrained in their spiritual possessions, for payment of a fifteenth with the rest of the parish. *F. N. B.* 176.

QUO JURE. A writ which lay for him who had land, wherein another challenged common of pasture time out of mind. And it was to compel him to shew by what title he challenged it. *F. N. B.* 128. *Reg. Orig.* 156.

QUO MINUS. A writ which lay for him who had a grant of house-bote and hay-bote in another man's woods, against the grantor, making such waste as the grantee could not enjoy his grant. *Old Nat. Br.* 148, and *Kitch.* 178.

This writ also lies for the king's accountant in the exchequer, against whom he hath any cause of personal action, suggesting that he is thereby made less able to pay the king's rent; and this surmise gives jurisdiction to the court of exchequer to hear and determine the cause of any other person. *Pract. Excheq.* 225.

QUORUM, (*Lat.*) often occurs in our statutes and commissions both of the peace and others, but particularly in commissions to justices of the peace; and a justice of the quorum is so called, from the words in the commission, *quorum* A. B. *unum esse volumus*: as where a commission is directed to five persons, whereof A. B. and C. D. to be two. In this case, A. B. and C. D.

are said to be of the quorum, and the rest cannot proceed without them. They are usually persons of greater quality or estates than the common commissioners. 3 Hen. 7. c. 3. 32 Hen. 8. c. 43. It is usual now to make almost every one (two or three excepted) of the quorum. 1 *Black.* 351.

QUORUM NOMINA. In the reign of Hen. 6. the king's collectors were allowed a writ of *quorum nomina*, and writ for suing out their *quietus*. *Chron. Angl.*

QUOTA. A tax to be levied in an equal manner. *Chart. Rich.* 2. *Cowell.*

QUO WARRANTO. A writ of quo warranto is in the nature of a writ of right for the king, against him who claims or usurps any office, franchise, or liberty, to inquire by what authority he supports his claim, in order to determine the right. *Finch.* L. 322. 2 *Inst.* 282. It lies also in case of non-user or long neglect of a franchise, or mis-user or abuse of it; being a writ commanding the defendant to shew by what warrant he exercises such a franchise, having never had any grant of it, or having forfeited it by neglect or abuse. This was originally returnable before the king's justices at Westminster. *Old Nat. Brev.* fol. 107. edit. 1534; but afterwards only before the justices in eyre, by virtue of the statutes of quo warranto, 6 Edw. 1. c. 1. And 18 Edw. 1. stat. 2. 2 *Inst.* 498. *Rast. Entr.* 540.; but since those justices have given place to the king's temporary commissioners of assise, the judges on the several circuits, this branch of the statutes hath lost its effect, 2 *Inst.* 498; and writs of quo warranto (if brought at all) must now be prosecuted and determined before the king's justices at Westminster. And in case of judgment for the defendant, he shall have an allowance of his franchise; but in case of judgment for the king, for that the party is intitled to no such franchise, or hath disused or abused it, the franchise is either seised into the king's hands, to be granted out again to whomever he shall please; or, if it be not such a franchise as may subsist in the hands of the crown, there is merely judgment of ouster, to turn out the party who usurped it. *Cro. Jac.* 259. 1 *Show.* 280.

The judgment on a writ of quo warranto (being in the nature of a writ of right) is final and conclusive even against the crown. 1 *Sid.* 86. 2 *Show.* 47. 12 *Mod.* 225.; which, together with the length of its process, probably occasioned that disuse into which it is now fallen, and introduced a more modern method of prosecution, by information filed in the court of king's bench by the attorney-general, in the nature of a writ of quo warranto, wherein the process is speedier, and the judgment not quite so decisive. This is properly a criminal method of prosecution, as well to punish the usurper by a fine for the usurpation of the franchise, as to oust him, or seise it for the crown; but hath long been applied to the mere purposes of trying the civil right, seising the franchise, or ousting the wrongful possessor, the fine being nominal only. 3 *Black.* 263.

And now, by virtue of the stat 9 Ann. c. 20. an information in nature of quo warranto is permitted to be brought with leave of the court, at the relation of any person desiring to prosecute the same (who is then styled the relator) against any person usurping, intruding into, or unlawfully holding any franchise or office in any city, borough, or town corporate; and this statute directs, that if the defendant be convicted, judgment of ouster, as well as a fine, may be given against him, and that the relator shall pay or receive costs according to the event of the suit.

Informations in the nature of a writ of quo warranto are regulated by stat. 9 *Ann.* c. 20. The modern information tends to the same purpose as the ancient writ, being generally made use of to try the civil rights of such franchises, though it is commenced in the same manner as other informations are, by leave of the court, or at the will of the attorney-general: being properly a criminal prosecution, in order to fine the defendant for his usurpation, as well as to oust him from his office, yet usually considered at present as merely a civil proceeding. And because an information in the nature of a quo warranto is considered merely as a civil proceeding, the court of king's bench will grant a new trial, though the verdict should have been given for the defendant. 2 *T. R.* 484.

R

RACK. An engine to extort confession from delinquents, but utterly unknown to the law of England. 4 *Black.* 329.

RACK-RENT. The full yearly value of the land. *Wood's Inst.* 185.

RACK-VINTAGE. A second vintage, or voyage made by our merchants for racked wines, i. e. wines drawn from the lees. *Cowell.*

RAGEMAN. A statute of justices assigned by Edw. I. to hear and determine complaints of injuries done throughout the realm, within the five years next before Michaelmas, in the fourth year of his reign. *Cowell.*

RAGLORIA. A word mentioned in the charter of Edw. III. whereby he made his eldest son Edward prince of Wales. Rhaglaw, among the Welsh, signifies *seneschalus, surlogutus, præpositus.* *Cowell.*

RAGLORIUS. A steward. *Ibid.*

RAGMAN'S ROLL, Ragimund's Roll, taken from the Scots by Edw. I. and re-delivered to them in the beginning of the reign of Edw. III. *Cowell.*

RAN, (A Saxon word,) signifies *aperta rapina*, open or public theft. *Lamb. Archai.* 125.

RANGE, from the French *ranger.* To order, dispose of. *Cowell.*

RANGER. A sworn officer of the forest. To walk daily through his charge, to see, hear, and inquire of trespasses in his bailiwick; to drive the beasts of the forest both of venary and chase out of the de-afforested into the forested lands; and to present all trespasses of the forest the next court holden for the forest. This ranger is made by the king's letters patent. *Cowell.*

RANSOM, (Fr. *Rançon*, i. e. *Redemptio.*) Is properly the sum paid for redeeming a captive or prisoner of war; and sometimes taken in our law for a sum of money paid for pardoning some great offence, and setting the offender at liberty who was under imprisonment. *Stat.* 1 *Hen.* 4. c. 7. 11 *Hen.* 6. c. 11.

Ransom differs from Amerciament, being a redemption of a corporal punishment due to any crime. *Lamb. Eiren.* 556.

And when any statute speaks of *fine* and *ransom*, it is holden that the ransom shall be treble the fine at least. *Dyer*, 232.

RAPE, (*Rapus vel Rapa.*) Is part of a county, signifying as much as a hundred, and oftentimes contains in it more hundreds than one. *Cowell.*

RAPE OF THE FOREST, (*Raptus Forestæ.*) Trespass committed in the forest by violence. *Ibid.*

RAPE OF WOMEN. Is an unlicensed and carnal knowledge of a woman by force and against her will—a ravishment of the body, and violent deflowering her, which is felony by the common and statute law. *Co. Lit.* 190.

By statute Westm. 2. c. 34. and by stat. 18 Eliz. c. 7. it is made felony without benefit of clergy; as is also the abominable wickedness of carnally knowing and abusing any woman child under the age of ten years: in which case the consent or non-consent is immaterial, as by reason of her tender years she is incapable of judgment and discretion.

A male infant under the age of fourteen years is presumed by law incapable to commit a rape, and therefore it seems cannot be found guilty of it; for, though in other felonies *malitia supplet ætatem*, yet, as to this particular species of felony, the law supposes an imbecility of body as well as mind. 1 *Hal. P. C.* 631.

The civil law seems to suppose a prostitute or common harlot incapable of any injuries of this kind (*Cod.* 9. 9. 22. *Ff.* 47. 2. 39.), not allowing any punishment for violating the chastity of her, who hath indeed no chastity at all, or at least hath no regard to it. But the law of England holds it to be felony to force even a concubine or harlot; because the woman may have forsaken that unlawful course of life.

As to the evidence upon an indictment of rape, it is to be observed, first, that the party ravished may give evidence upon oath, and is in law a competent witness; but the credibility of her testimony, and how far forth she is to be believed, must be left to the jury upon the circumstances of fact that concur in that testimony. For instance: if the witness be of good fame; if she presently discovered the offence, and made search for the offender; if the party accused fled for it; these and the like are concurring circumstances which give greater probability to her evidence. But, on the other side, if she be of evil fame, and stand unsupported by others; if she concealed the injury for any considerable time after she had opportunity to complain; if the place, where the fact was alleged to be committed, was where it was possible she might have been heard, and she made no outcry: these and the like circumstances carry a strong, but not conclusive presumption that her testimony is false or feigned. 4 *Black.* 213.

Moreover, if the rape be charged to be committed on an infant under twelve years of age, she may still be a competent witness, if she hath the sense and understanding to know the nature and obligations of an oath, or even to be sensible of the wickedness of telling a deliberate lie. Nay, though she hath not, it is thought by Sir Matthew Hale that she ought to be heard without oath, to give the court information; and others have held, that what the child told her mother, or other relations, may be given in evidence, since the nature of the case admits frequently of no better proof. But it is now settled, [Brazier's case, before the twelve judges, 19 Geo. 3,] that no hearsay evidence can be given of the declaration of a child who hath not capacity to be sworn, nor can such child be examined in court without oath: and that there is no determinate age at which the oath of a child ought either to be admitted or rejected. 4 *Black.* 214. See *Age.*

RAPINE, (*Rapina.*) To take a thing in private against the owner's will, is properly theft; but to take it openly, or by violence, is rapine. 4 *Black.* 241.

RAPTU HEREDIS. A writ for taking away an heir holding in socage; of which there were two sorts, one when the heir was married, the other when he was not. See *Reg. Orig.* 163.

RASE, (*Raseria.*) Seems to have been a measure of corn now disused. "Toll shall be taken by the rase, and not by the heap or cantel." *Ordinance for Bakers.*

RASURE of a deed, so as to alter it in a material part, without consent of the party bound by it, will make the same void, and if it be rased in the date, after delivery, it is said it goes through the whole. 5 *Rep.* 23. 119.

Rasure, is most suspicious when it is in a deed poll, that there is but one part of the deed, and it makes to the advantage of him to whom made. And where a deed by rasure, addition, or alteration becomes no deed, the defendant may plead *non est factum.* *Ibid.* 2 *Black. Com.* 2 *V.* 308.

RATE. A valuation of every man's estate, or the assessing and setting down how much every one shall pay or be charged with to any tax. *Stat.* 43 Edw. II. *Cowell.*

RATE-TITHE. Was when any sheep or other cattle were kept in a parish for less time than a year, the owner was to pay tithe for them *pro rata*, according to the custom of the place. *F. N. B.* 51.

RATIFICATION, (*Ratificatio.*) A ratifying or confirming: it is particularly used for the confirmation of a clerk in a prebend, &c. formerly conferred on him by the bishop, where the right of patronage is doubted or supposed to be in the king. *Reg. Orig.* 304.

RATIHABITIO. Confirmation, agreement, consent. *Cowell. Blount.*

RATIO. Properly signifies reason, but we take it mostly for an account, as *reddere rationem*, to give an account, and so it is frequently used. According to some, it is a cause or judgment therein; and *ponere ad rationem* is to cite one to appear in judgment. *Ibid.*

RATIONABILIS DIVISIO. A writ which lay when two lords, in divers towns, had seigniories joining together, for him who found his waste by little and little to have been encroached on, against the other who had encroached, thereby to rectify their bounds. *F. N. B.* 128. & *Reg. Orig.* 157. *Cowell. Blount.*

RATIONABILE ESTOVERIUM. Was alimony heretofore so called. (*Rot.* 7. *H.* 3.)

RATIONABILI PARTE. A writ of right for lands, &c. See *Recto de Rationabili parte.*

RATIONABILI PARTE BONORUM. A writ which lay for a wife after the death of her husband, against the executors of the husband denying her the third part of his goods after debts and funeral charges paid. *F. N. B.* 2. See *Intestate.*

RATIONALE. Was the same with pallium. *Cowell. Blount.*

RAVISHMENT, (Fr. *Ravissement*, i. e. *Direptio, raptio.*) See *Abduction* and *Rape.*

RAVISHMENT DE GARD. A writ which lay for the guardian by knight's service, or in socage, against a person who took from him the body of his ward. *F. N. B.* 140. But by 12 Car. 2. c. 24. this writ is taken away. 317.

RAY. Cloth never coloured or dyed. 17 *R.* 2. *cap.* 3. 11 *H.* 4. *cap.* 6. and 1 *R.* 3. cap. 8.

READING OF DEEDS. This is requisite for the making of a good deed, whenever any of the parties desire it; and if it be not done on his request, it is void as to him; if he can he should read it himself; if he be blind, or illiterate, another must read it to him; if it be read falsely, it will be void, at least for so much as is misread, unless it be agreed by collusion, that the deed shall be read false, on purpose to make it void, for in such case it shall bind the fraudulent party. 2 *Black.* 303. 2 *Rep.* 3. 9. 11 *Rep.* 27.

REAFFORESTED. Is where a forest which had been disafforested is again made forest, as the forest of Dean is by stat. 20 Car. 2. c. 3.

REAL ACTIONS. See *Ejectment.*

REALTY. Is an abstract of real, as distinguished from personalty. *Cowell.*

REASON. Is the very life of law, and what is contrary to it is unlawful. When the reason of the law once ceases, the law itself generally ceases, because reason is the foundation of all our laws. And if maxims of law admit of any difference, those are to be preferred which carry with them the more perfect and excellent reason. *Co. Lit.* 97. 183.

REASONABLE AID. Was a duty claimed by the lord of the fee of his tenant holding by knight's service, to marry his daughter, &c. *Stat. Westm.* 2. *c.* 24. 12 *Car.* 2. c. 14.

REASONABLE PART. By the common law, as it stood in the reign of Henry II. a man's goods were to be divided into three equal parts: of which, one went to his heirs or lineal descendants, another to his wife, and the third was at his own disposal; or, if he died without a wife, he might then dispose of one moiety, and the other went to his children; and so *e converso*, if he had no children the wife was entitled to one moiety, and he might bequeath the other; but if he died without either wife or issue, the whole was at his own disposal, (Bracton, l. 2. c. 26. Flet. l. 2. c. 57.) The shares of the wife and children are called their reasonable parts; and the writ *de rationabili parte bonorum* was given to recover them. *F. N. B.* 122.

REASSURANCE. See *Insurance.*

REATTACHMENT, (*Reattachiamentum.*) A second attachment of him who was formerly attached and dismissed the court without day, by the not coming of the justices, or some such casualty. *Broke Reg. Orig.* 35.

REBATE. Is an abating what the interest of money comes to, in consideration of prompt payment. *Merch. Dict.*

REBELLION, (*Rebellio.*) The taking up of arms traitorously against the king, whether by natural subjects, or others when once subdued; and the word rebel sometimes applies to him who wilfully breaks a law. *Stat.* 25 *Ed.* 3. c. 6. 1 *R.* 2. c. 6.

REBELLIOUS ASSEMBLY. See *Riots.*

REBELLION, COMMISSION OF. A *Process in Equity.*

REBUTTER, (from the Fr. *bouter*, i. e. *repellere*, to put back or bar.) Is the answer of the defendant to the plaintiff's surrejoinder: and the plaintiff's answer to the rebutter is called a surrebutter; but it is very rare the parties go so far in pleading. *Pract. Attorn.* edit. 1. 86.

Rebutter is also where a man by deed or fine grants to warranty any land or hereditament to another; and the person making the warranty or his heir, sues him to whom the warranty is made, or his heir or assignee, for the same thing; if he who is sued, plead the deed or fine with warranty, and pray judgment if the plaintiff shall be received to demand the thing, which he ought to warrant to the party, against the warranty in the deed, &c.; this is called a rebutter. *Terms de Ley.* *Co. Entr.* 284. *Co. Litt.* 365.

RECAPTION, (*Recaptio.*) Signifies the taking a second distress of one formerly distrained; and it is a writ to recover damages for him whose goods being distrained for rent, or service, &c. are distrained again for the same cause, pending the replevin. *F. N. B.* 71, 72. *Stat.* 47 *Ed.* 3. c. 7.

RECAPTION. Is also a species of remedy by the mere act of the party injured. As when any one hath deprived another of his property in goods or chattels personal, or wrongfully detains one's wife, child, or servant; in all which cases the owner of the goods, and the husband, parent, or master, may lawfully claim and retake them, wherever he happens to find them, so it be not in a riotous manner, or attended with a breach of the peace. 3 *Inst.* 134. *Hal. Annal.* s. 46.

RECEIPT. See *Resceit.*

RECEIVER, (*Receptor.*) Is commonly used in the civil part, for such as receive stolen goods, &c. And receiving a felon, and concealing him and his offence, makes a person accessary to the felony. 2 *Inst.* 183. *S. P. C.* 41. *H. P. C.* 218, 219. 2 *Hawk. P. C.* 122, 319, 320. See *Accessary* and *Stolen Goods.*

RECEIVER. There is also a receiver of rents belonging to the king or other personage, and receivers are appointed by the courts of equity. *Compt. Jurisd.* 18. See *Accompt.*

RECEIVER OF THE FINES. An officer who receives the money of all such as compound with the king on original writs sued out of chancery. *West. Symb. par.* 2. *sect.* 106. *Stat.* 1 *Ed.* 4. c. 1.

RECEIVER GENERAL OF THE DUTCHY OF LANCASTER. An officer of the dutchy court, who collects all the revenues, fines, forfeitures, and assessments within the dutchy. 39 *Eliz. cap.* 7.

RECITAL, (*Recitatio.*) Is the setting forth or making mention in a deed or writing of something which has been done before. 2 *Lill. Abr.* 416.

RECOGNITION, (*Recognitio.*) Signifies an acknowledgment, as in stat. 1 Jac. 1, whereby the parliament acknowledged the crown of England, on the death of Queen Elizabeth, rightfully to have descended to King James.

RECOGNITIONE ADNULLANDA PER VIM ET DURITIEM FACTA. A writ to the justices of C. B. for sending a record touching a recognizance, which the recognizor suggested was acknowledged by force and duress; that, if it so appear, the recognizance might be disannulled. *Reg. Orig.* 183.

RECOGNITORS, (*Recognitores.*) Are the jury impannelled on an assize, so called, because they acknowledge a disseisin by their verdict. *Bract. lib.* 5.

RECOGNIZANCE, (Fr. *Recognoissance*, i. e. *Recognitio Obligatio.*) A recognizance is an obligation of record, which a man enters into before some court of record or magistrate duly authorized, (Bro. Abr. tit. *Recognizance.* 24.) with condition to do some particular act; as to appear at the assises, to keep the peace, to pay a debt, or the like. It is in most respects like another bond: the difference being chiefly this; that the bond is the creation of a fresh debt or obligation *de novo*, the recognizance is an acknowledgment of a former debt upon record; the form whereof is, "that A. B. doth acknowledge to owe to our lord the king, to the plaintiff, to C. D. or the like, the sum of ten pounds, with condition to be void on performance of the thing stipulated; in which case the king, the plaintiff C. D. &c. is called the cognizee, "*is cui cognoscitur*;" as he that enters into the recognizance is called the cognizor, "*is qui cognoscit.*" This, being either certified to, or taken by the officer of some court, is witnessed only by the record of that court, and not by the party's seal; so that it is not in strict propriety a deed, though the effects of it are greater than a common obligation, being allowed a priority in point of payment, and binding the lands of the cognizor, from the time of enrolment on record. There are also other recognizances of a private kind, in nature of a statute staple, by virtue of the statute 23 Hen. 8, c. 6. See *Statute Merchant* and *Statute Staple*, and *Surety*.

RECORD, (*Recordum*, from the Lat. *Recordari*, to remember.) A memorial or authentic testimony in writing, contained in rolls of parchment, and preserved in a court of record. *Britton*, c. 27. *Co. Litt.* 260. 2 *Lill. Abr.* 418.

There are three kinds of records, viz. A judicial record, as an attainder, &c.; a ministerial record on oath, being an office or inquisition found: and a record made by conveyance and consent, as a fine, or a deed inrolled. 4 *Rep.* 54. 2 *Lill.* 421.

Records, being the rolls or memorials of the judges, import in themselves such incontroulable verity, that they admit of no proof or averment to the contrary, insomuch that they are to be tried only by themselves; for otherwise there would be no end of controversies. But during the term wherein any judicial act is done, the roll is alterable in that term, as the judges shall direct: when the term is past, then the record admitteth of no alteration, or proof that it is false in any instance. *Co. Litt.* 260. 4 *Rep.* 52.

Matter of record is therefore to be proved by the record itself, and not by evidence, because no issue can be joined on it to be tried by a jury like matters of fact; and the credit of a record is greater than the testimony of witnesses. *Hob.* 124.

RECORDARE FACIAS LOQUELAM, Is a writ directed to the sheriff to remove a cause depending in an inferior court, to the King's Bench or Common Pleas, and it is called a recordare, because it commands the sheriff to make a record of the proceedings in the county court, and then to send up the cause. *F. N. B.* 71. 2 *Inst.* 339.

RECORDER, (*Recordator.*) Is a person whom the mayor and other magistrates of any city or town corporate, (having jurisdiction, and a court of record within their precincts), by the king's grant, associate unto them for their better direction in matters of justice, and proceedings according to law: therefore he is generally a barrister or some other person experienced in the law. *Co. Lit.* 288.

RECOVERY, (*Recuperatio*, from the Fr. *recouvrer*, *recuperare*,) Signifies, in a legal acceptation, obtaining any thing by judgment or trial of law; and there is both a true recovery and feigned one.

A true recovery is an actual or real recovery, of any thing, or the value thereof, by judgment; as if a man sue for any land, or other thing moveable or immoveable, and have a verdict or judgment for him. *Cowell.*

A feigned recovery is a certain form or course set down by law to be observed, for the better assuring lands or tenements. *West. Sym. par.* 2. tit. *Recoveries*, *s.* 1.

This assurance, by matter of record, is called a common recovery, and was invented by the ecclesiastics to elude the statutes of mortmain; and afterwards encouraged by the finesse of the courts of law in 12 Edw. 4. in order to put an end to all fettered inheritances, and bar not only estates tail, but also all remainders and reversions expectant thereon.

I. *The nature of a common recovery.*] A common recovery is so far like a fine, that it is a suit or action, either actual or fictitious; and in it the lands are recovered against the tenant of the freehold; which recovery, being a supposed adjudication of the right, binds all persons, and vests a free and absolute fee-simple in the recoveror.

As, for instance, suppose David Edwards to be tenant of the freehold, and desirous to suffer a common recovery, in order to bar all entails, remainders, and reversions, and to convey the same in fee simple to Francis Golding. To effect this, Golding is to bring an action against him for the lands; and he accordingly sues out a writ, called a *præcipe quod reddat*, because those were its initial or most operative words, when the law proceedings were in Latin. In this writ the demandant Golding alleges that the defendant Edwards (here called the tenant) has no legal title to the land, but that he came into possession of it after one Hugh Hunt had turned the demandant out of it. The subsequent proceedings are made up into a record or recovery roll, in which the writ and commplaint of the demandant are first recited: whereupon the tenant appears, and calls upon one Jacob Morland, who is supposed, at the original purchase, to have warranted the title to the tenant; and thereupon he prays, that the said Jacob Morland may be called in to defend the title which he so warranted. This is called the voucher, vocatio, or calling of Jacob Morland to warranty; and Morland is called the vouchee. Upon this, Jacob Morland, the vouchee, appears, is impleaded, and defends the title. Whereupon Golding, the demandant, desires leave of the court to imparl, or confer with the vouchee in private; which is, as usual, allowed him. And soon afterwards the demandant, Golding, returns to court, but Morland the vouchee disappears, or makes default. Whereupon judgment is given for the demandant Golding, now called the recoveror, to recover the lands in question against the tenant Edwards, who is now the recoveree; and Edwards has judgment to recover of Jacob Morland lands of equal value, in recompense for the lands so warranted by him, and now lost by his default; which is agreeable to the doctrine of warranty, (see *Warranty.*) This is called the recompense, or recovery in value. But Jacob Morland having no lands of his own, being usually the cryer of the court, (who, from being frequently thus vouched, is called the common vouchee), it is plain that Edwards has only a nominal recompense for the land so recovered against him by Golding; which lands are now absolutely vested in the said recoveror by judgment of law, and seisin thereof is delivered by the sheriff of the county. So that this collusive recovery operates merely in the nature of a conveyance in fee-simple, from Edwards the tenant in tail, to Golding the purchasor.

The recovery, here described, is with a single voucher only; but sometimes it is with double, treble, or farther voucher, as the exigency of the case may require. And indeed it is now usual always to have a recovery with double voucher at the least: by first conveying an estate of freehold to any indifferent person, against whom the *præcipe* is brought; and then he vouches the tenant in tail, who vouches over the common vouchee. For, if a recovery be had immediately against tenant in tail, it bars only such estate in the premises of which he is then actually seised; whereas, if the recovery be had against any person, and the tenant in tail be vouched, it bars every latent right and interest which he may have in the lands recovered. If Edwards therefore be tenant of the freehold in possession, and John Barker be tenant in tail in remainder, here Edwards doth first vouch Barker, and then Barker vouches Jacob Morland the common vouchee, who is always the last person vouched, and always makes default; whereby the demandant Golding recovers the land against the tenant Edwards, and Edwards recovers a recompense of equal value against Barker the first vouchee, who recovers the like against Morland the common vouchee, against whom such ideal recovery in value is always ultimately awarded.

This supposed recompense in value is the reason why the issue in tail is held to be barred by a common recovery. For, if the recoveree should obtain a recompense in lands from the common vouchee, (which there is a possibility in contemplation of law, though a very improbable one, of his doing,) these lands would supply the place of those so recovered from him by collusion, and would descend to the issue in tail. This reason will also hold with equal force, as to most remainder-men and reversioners, to whom the possibility will remain and revert, as a full recompense for the reality, which they were otherwise entitled to. But it will not always hold, and therefore, as Pigot says, the judges have been even *astuti*, in inventing other reasons to maintain the authority of recoveries. And, in particular, it hath been said, that, though the estate-tail is gone from the recoveree, yet it is not destroyed, but only transferred; and still subsists, and will ever continue to subsist (by construction of law) in the recoveror, his heirs and assigns; and, as the estate-tail so continues to subsist for ever, the remainders or reversions expectant on the determination of such estate-tail can never take place. Thus fines and recoveries are now considered as mere forms of conveyances or common assurances, the theory and original principles of them being little regarded. They have been in use some hundreds of years, have gained ground by time, and we must now take them, as they really are, common assurances. 1 *Wils.* 73.

2. The force and effect of common recoveries appear therefore to be an absolute bar not only of all estates-tail, but of remainders and reversions expectant on the determination of such estates. So that *a tenant in tail may, by this method of assurance*, convey the lands held in tail to the recoveror, his heirs and assigns, absolutely free and discharged of all conditions and limitations in tail, and of all remainders and reversions. But, by statute 34 and 35 Hen. 8. c. 20, no recovery had against tenant in tail, of the king's gift, whereof the remainder or reversion is in the king, shall bar such estate-tail, or the remainder or rever-

sion of the crown. And by the statute 11 *Hen.* 7. *c.* 20. no woman, after her husband's death, shall suffer a recovery of lands settled on her by her husband, or settled on her husband and her by any of his ancestors. And by statute 14 *Eliz. c.* 8. no tenant for life, of any sort, can suffer a recovery, so as to bind them in remainder or reversion; for which reason, if there be tenant for life, with remainder in tail, and other remainders over, and the tenant for life is desirous to suffer a valid recovery; either he, or the tenant to the *præcipe* by him made, must vouch the remainder-man in tail, otherwise the recovery is void; but if he does vouch such remainder-man, and he appears and vouches the common vouchee, it is then good; for if a man be vouched, and appears, and suffers the recovery to be had against the tenant to the *præcipe*, it is as effectual to bar the estate-tail as if he himself were the recoveree.*

In all recoveries it is necessary that the recoveree, or tenant to the *præcipe*, as he is usually called, be actually seised of the freehold, else the recovery is void. For all actions, to recover the seisin of lands, must be brought against the actual tenant of the freehold, else the suit will lose its effect, since the freehold cannot be recovered of him who has it not; and though these recoveries are in themselves fabulous and fictitious, yet it is necessary that there be *actores fabulæ* properly qualified; but the nicety which was thought some years ago to be requisite in conveying the legal freehold, in order to make a good tenure to the *præcipe*, is removed by the provisions of the statute 14 *Geo.* 2. *c.* 20. which enacts, that "though the legal freehold be vested in lessees, yet those who are entitled to the next freehold estate in remainder or reversion, may make a good tenant to the *præcipe*, without any surrender of the leases;" that "the deed making a tenant to the writ of entry, shall be sufficient evidence of a recovery for purchasers after 20 years possession: and common recoveries, after 20 years, shall be deemed good, if it appear therein that there was a tenant to the writ, though no deed for making such tenant appear;" and that "a recovery shall be deemed good, though the deed for making the tenant be executed after the time of the judgment, so that it be executed before the end of the term."

* If a tenant in tail, to whom the estate has descended *ex parte materna*, suffers a recovery, and declares the uses to himself in fee, the estate will descend to an heir on the part of the mother, even if he had the reversion in fee from his father, and *vice versa*; but if he took the estate-tail by purchase, the new fee will descend to the heirs general (5 *T. R.* 104.) If then a person who has inherited an estate-tail from his mother, wishes to cut off the intail and to make the estate descendible to his heirs, on the part of the father, after the recovery, he ought to make a common conveyance to trustees, and to have the estate reconveyed back by them, by which means he will take the estate by purchase, which will then descend to his heirs general. *Christian.* 2 *Black.* 362.

A fine or recovery had of copyhold lands in the king's court may, if not duly reversed, alter the tenure of the lands, and convert them into frank fee; which is defined, in the old book of tenures, to be land pleadable at the common law; but upon an action in the case, in the nature of a writ of deceit, brought by the lord in the king's courts, such fine or recovery will be reversed, the lord will recover his jurisdiction, and the lands will be restored to their former state of copyhold. *Fitz. N. B.* 13.

RECOUPE, (from the Fr. *recouper*) signifies the keeping back or stopping something which is due, such as to default or discount (1 *Inst.*) If a rent-charge be issuing out of land, and paid by the tenant, he may recoupe the same. *Terms de Ley. Dyer* 2.

RECREANT, (*Fr.*) cowardly, faint-hearted. When trial by battle was in use, victory was obtained if either champion proved recreant; that is, yielded, and pronounced the horrible word *craven*, a word of disgrace and obloquy rather than of any determinate meaning: and a most horrible word it was to the vanquished champion, for as a punishment to him for forfeiting the land of his principal by pronouncing that word, he was condemned as a RECREANT, *amittere librum legem*; that was, to become infamous, and not be actual *liber et legalis homo*, being supposed by the event to be proved forsworn, and therefore never to be put upon a jury, or admitted as a witness in any cause. *Cowell. Blount.*

RECTA PRISA REGIS, the king's right to a prize, or taking of one butt or pipe of wine before, and another behind the mast, as a custom for every ship laden with wines. *Ibid.*

RECTITUDO, right or justice: sometimes it signifies legal dues, a tribute or payment. *Ibid.*

RECTO. See *Right.*

RECTO DE ADVOCATIONE ECCLESIÆ, a writ lying where a man hath right of advowson, and the parson of the church dying, a stranger presents his clerk to the church, the party who hath right not having brought his action of *quare impedit*, nor *darrein presentment*, but suffered the stranger to usurp on him: and it lieth only where an advowson is claimed in fee to him and his heirs. *F. N. B.* 30. 4 *Ed.* 3. *c.* 18.

RECTO DE CUSTODIA TERRÆ ET HÆREDIS, a writ which lay for him whose tenant, holding of him chivalry, died in nonage, against a stranger who entered on the land, and took the body of the heir. *F. N. B.* 139. *Reg. Orig.* 161.

RECTO DE DOTE, a writ of right of dower, which lies for a woman who has received part of her dower, and demands the residue against the heir of the husband, or his guardian. *F. N. B.* 7. 8. 147. *Co. Litt.* 32. 38.

RECTO DE DOTE UNDE NIHIL HABET, is a writ of right, which lies in case where the husband having divers lands or tenements, hath assured no dower to his wife, and she thereby is driven to sue for her thirds against the heir, or his guardian. *Old. Nat. Br.* 6. *Reg. Orig.* 170.

RECTO QUANDO DOMINUS REMISSIT, is a writ which lieth where lands or tenements in the seigniory of any lord, are in demand by a writ of right: if the lord in such case holdeth no court at the prayer of demandant or tenant, but sends to the king's court his writ to put the cause thither for that time, (saving to him at other times the right of his seigniory) then this writ shall issue out for the other party, and hath its name from the words therein contained. *F. N. B.* 16.

RECTO DE RATIONABILI PARTE, a writ of right lying between privies in blood, as brothers in gavel-kind, sisters, and other co-parceners, for land in fee-simple. *F. N. B.* 9.

In this writ the demand shall be of a certain portion of land, to hold in severalty. *Ibid.*

RECTO STAT IN CURIA, signifies to be acquitted or discharged in any court of law.

RECTO SUR DISCLAIMER, a writ which lies where the lord, in the court of common pleas, avows on his tenant, and the tenant disclaims to hold of him; on which disclaimer the lord shall have this writ; and if he avers and proves that the land is holden of him, he shall recover the land for ever. This writ is grounded on the statute of *Westm.* 2. c. 2. *N. Br.* 150.

RECTOR, (*Lat.*) a governor; and *rector ecclesiæ parochialis*, is he who hath the charge and cure of a parish church, and is one who hath a parsonage where there is a vicarage endowed. 1 *Black.* 384. See *Appropriation.*

RECTORIAL TITHES. The parson or rector hath for the most part the whole right to all the tithes and ecclesiastical dues in his parish.

RECTORY, (*rectoria*) is taken *pro integra ecclesia parochiali, cum omnibus suis juribus, prædiis, decimis aliisque pro ventuum speciebus* spelm. Also the word *rectoria* hath been often applied to the rector's mansion or parsonage-house. *Par. Antiq.* 549. See *Vicar.*

RECTUM, right; anciently it was used for a trial or accusation. *Bract. lib.* 3.

RECTUM *esse, ad rectum in curia domini*, is the same with *stare ad rectum*. *Leg. H.* 1. c. 43. See *infra.*

RECTUM *rogare*, is to petition the judge to do right. *Leg. Inæ.* c. 9.

RECTUM, *stare ad rectum*, to stand trial at law, or abide the justice of the court. *Hoved.* 655.

RECTUS IN CURIA, *i. e.* right in court, is he who stands at the bar, and no man objects any offence against him.—*Smith de Repub. Angl. lib.* 2. c. 3.

RECUSANTS. At the reformation, those were deemed recusants who disputed the authority of the crown in causes ecclesiastical, and denied the king's supremacy. See *Papists* and *Roman Catholics.*

RED, (Sax. *ræd*) is an old word signifying advice; and *redbana* is one who advised the death of another. *Cowell.* See *Dedbana.*

RED BOOK OF THE EXCHEQUER, (*liber rubens scaccarii*) is an ancient record, wherein are registered the names of those who held lands *per baroniam* in the time of Hen. 2. *Ryley*, 667. *Cowell.*

REDDENDUM, is the clause in a lease, whereby the rent is reserved to the lessor; and anciently corn, flesh, fish, and other victuals, were and still may be reserved on leases, as well as money. 2 *Rep.* 72. *Wood's Inst.* 226.

REDDIDIT SE, is a plea to an action of *scire facias* against *facias* bail; for where a man procures bail for himself to an action in any court at law, if the party bailed at any time before the return of the second *scire facias* against the bail, renders himself in discharge of his bail, they are thereby discharged, and may plead the same. 2 *Lill. Abr.* 430. *Cro. Jac.* 109.

REDDITARIUS, a renter; and *redditarium*, hath been used for a rental of a manor, or other estate. *Cowell.*

REDDITION, (*redditio*) a surrendering or restoring; being also a judicial acknowledgment that the thing in demand belongs to the demandant, and not to the person so surrendering. *Ibid.*

REDDITUS ASSISUS, is set or standing rent. *Ibid.* See *Assisus.*

RE-DELIVERY, is a yielding and delivery back of a thing; but if a person has committed a robbery, and stolen the goods of another, he cannot afterwards purge the offence by any re-delivery, or the like. *Co. Lit.* 69. *H. P. C.* 72.

REDEMISE, is a regranting of lands demised or leased for 99 years, or some long term, at a nominal rent, upon an actual reserved rent: an assurance formerly much in use for securing the payment of annuities.

REDEMPTION, (*redemptio*) a ransom or commutation; and by the old Saxon laws, a man convicted of a crime paid such a fine, according to the estimation of his head, *pro redemptione sua.* *Cowell.* See *Mortgage.*

REDISSEISSIN, (*redisseisina*) is a disseisin made by him, who once before was found and adjudged to have disseised the same man of his lands or tenements, for which there lies a special writ called a writ of redisseisin. *Old Nat. Br.* 106. *F. N. B.* 188.

REDRESS OF INJURIES. The more effectually to accomplish the redress of injuries, courts of justice are instituted in every civilized society, in order to protect the weak from the insults of the stronger, by expounding and enforcing those laws, by which rights are defined, and wrongs prohibited: this remedy is therefore principally to be sought by application to these courts of justice; that is, by civil suit or action. 3 *Black.* 2.

REDUBBERS, those that bought stolen cloth, and turned it into some other colour or fashion, that it might not be known again. *Britton*, c. 29. 3 *Inst.* 134.

RE-ENTRY, (from the Fr. *rentrer*, i. e. *rursus intrare*) is the resuming or retaking a possession, as if a man makes a lease of lands, &c. to another, he thereby quits the possession; and if he covenants with the lessee, that, for non-payment of rent at the day, it shall be lawful for him to re-enter; this is as much as if he conditioned to take again the land into his own hands, and to recover the possession by his own act, without assistance of the law. But words in a deed give no re-entry, if a clause of re-entry be not added. *Wood's Inst.* 140.

All persons who would re-enter on their tenants for non-payment of rent, are to make a demand of the rent on the day that it is due; and, to prevent the re-entry, tenants are to tender their rent, &c. 1 *Inst.* 201.

RE-EXCHANGE, is the like sum of money payable by the drawer of a bill of exchange which is returned protested, for the exchange of the sum mentioned in the bill back again to the place whence it was drawn. *Lex Mercat.* 98.

RE-EXTENT, is a second extent on lands or tenements, on complaint that the former was partially made, &c. *Broke*, 313.

REFARE, (from the Sax. *reaf*, or *ræfan*) to bereave, take away, or rob. *Leg. H.* 1. c. 83.

REFERENCE, is where a matter is referred by the court of chancery to a master; by the court of exchequer to the deputy remembrancer; and by the courts at law to the master, prothonotary, or secondary, to examine and report to the court. 2 *Lill. Abr.* 432. Or by the parties to some indifferent person. See *Award.*

REFERENCE TO WORDS, all those messuages, &c. late in the tenure of J. S. situate, &c. in the city of W. are words of reference by reason of the word (those), as well to the will as to the tenure of J. S. 18 *Vin. Abr.* 272.

REFENDARY, (*refendarius*) an officer in the time of the English Saxons here, of the same nature as masters of requests to the king; the refendaries being those who exhibited the petitions of the people to the king, and acquainted the judges with his commands; and we read of a *referendarius Angliæ. Spelm.*

REFORMATION OF RELIGION. See *Constitution.*

REFUNDING. Where money has been improperly paid, or paid by mistake, courts of equity will decree the parties to refund. 1 *Pere Wms.* 355. *Ver.* 466.

REFUSAL, is where one hath by law a right and power of having or doing something of advantage to him, and he refuseth it. An executor may refuse an executorship, but the refusal ought to be before the ordinary: for no man can be compelled to take on him the executorship, unless he hath intermeddled with the estate.

There is also a refusal of a clerk presented to a church, for illiterature, &c. And if a bishop once refuses a clerk for insufficiency, he cannot accept of him afterwards, if a new clerk is presented. 5 *Rep.* 58. *Cro. Eliz.* 27.

In trover, a demand of the goods, and refusal to deliver them, must be proved, &c. 10 *Rep.* 56. 1 *Danv. Abr.* 20.

REFUTANTIA, a discharge, or renouncing of all future claim. *Cowell.*

REGALE EPISCOPORUM, the temporal rights and privileges of a bishop. *Ibid.*

REGALES, the king's servants, or officers of Walsingham, anno 1291. *Cowell. Blount.*

REGAL FISHES, (mentioned in 1 *Eliz.* c. 5.) are whales and sturgeons; some add porpoises. *Cowell. Blount.*

REGALIA, (*dicuntur jura omnia ad fiscum spectantia*, saith Spelman) the royal rights of a king. See *King.*

REGALIA FACERE, is to do homage or fealty, when he is invested with the regalia. *Cowell.*

REGARD, (*regardum* and *rewardum*, Fr. *regard*, i. e. *aspectus*, *respectus*,) signifies generally special care; also affection and respect. It is also used in matters of the forest, for there is the office of REGARDER (*Crom. Jur.* 175. 199. See *Manwood, part* 1. 194 & 198.) who has the charge of the whole forest, that is, all the ground which is parcel of the forest; for there may be woods within the limits of the forest, that are no parcel thereof, and those are without the regard. *Manwood, part* 2. c. 7. *num.* 4. *anno* 20. *Car.* 2. *c.* 3.

There is also the COURT OF REGARD, or survey of dogs, which is to be holden every third year, for the lawing or expeditation of mastiffs, which is done by cutting off the claws of the forefeet, to prevent them from running after the deer. No other dogs but mastiffs are to be thus lawed or expeditated, for none other were permitted to be kept within the precincts of the forest, it being supposed that those only were necessary for the defence of a man's house. *Cast. de Forest*, c. 8. 4 *Inst.* 308.

REGARDANT, (Fr. seeing, marking, vigilant) as a villain regardant was called regardant to the manor, because he had the charge to do all base services within the same, and to see the same freed of all things that might annoy it. *Co. Lit.* 120.

REGE INCONSULTO, a writ issued from the king to the judges not to proceed in a cause which may prejudice the king, until he is advised. *Cowell. Moor*, 844. *Jenk. Cent.* 97.

REGENCY, (Fr. *regence*) the government or governors of a kingdom during the minority, mental incapacity, or absence of a prince; and, with us, if the throne should at any time become vacant, by abdication, or any other means whatsoever, as by the total failure of the blood royal, or the like, *the right of disposing of this vacancy results to the lords and commons*, who are the constitutional trustees and representatives of the nation, and fully and freely represent all the estates of the people of this realm; for the two houses of parliament are the organs by which the people express their will; the lords being as much the trustees and guardians of their country, as the members of the house of commons.

REGENT, (Fr. *regent*) one who governs a kingdom during the minority of a sovereign prince, or under one who is by absence, mental incapacity, or otherwise incapable of reigning.

REGIO ASSENSU, a writ whereby the king gives his royal assent to the election of a bishop. *Reg. Orig.* 294.

REGISTER, (*registrarius*) an officer who keeps a registry. *Cowell.*

REGISTER is the name of a book, wherein are entered most of the forms of writs, original and judicial, used at common law, called the register of writs. *Co. Lit.* 159.

It is the most ancient and highly venerable collection of legal forms, upon which *Fitzherbert's Natura Brevium* is a comment, and in which every man who is injured will be sure to find a method of relief, exactly adapted to his own case, described in the compass of a few lines, and yet without the omission of any material circumstance. 3 *Black.* 183.

REGISTER OF THE PARISH CHURCH (*registrum ecclesiæ parochialis*) is that wherein baptisms, marriages, and burials, are registered in each parish every year; it was instituted *anno* 13 *Hen.* 8. *Cowell. Blount.*

These parish registers are to be subscribed by the minister and churchwardens; and the names of the persons shall be transmitted yearly to the bishop, &c. *Ibid.*

REGISTRY, (*registrum*, from the old Fr. *gister*, i. e. *in lecto reponere*) is properly the same with repository, and the office books, and rolls wherein the proceedings of the chancery, or any spiritual court, are recorded, &c. are called by this name. *Ibid.*

REGISTRY OF DEEDS. By 2 *Ann*, c. 4. a memorial of all deeds, conveyances, wills, and the like, made in the EAST RIDING of Yorkshire, may be registered; and, if not, shall be deemed fraudulent, and void against subsequent purchasers.

The registrar shall keep an office at Wakefield, and be elected by ballotting of all the freeholders in the west riding of 100*l.* per ann. *Ibid.*

Memorials shall be registered on parchment, shall be numbered, dated, filed, and entered. *Ibid.*

This act extends not to copyhold estates, or leases at a rack-rent. *Ibid.*

A memorial of deeds, &c. made in London, or elsewhere, touching any lands in the west riding, may be registered on affidavit, and the registrar shall give a certificate. *Ibid.*

Persons forging or counterfeiting memorials or certificates, incur the penalties of 5 *Eliz.* c. 14. against forgers; and persons forswearing themselves before the registrar, the same penalties as in the courts at Westminster. *Ibid.*

Memorials of wills registered within six months after the death of a testator, if he dies in England; and three years after, if he dies beyond sea, shall be effectual. *Ibid.*

No member of parliament shall be chosen registrar; nor any registrar be capable of being chosen a member of parliament. *Ibid.*

By 5 *Ann*, c. 18. bargains and sales of lands in the WEST RIDING of Yorkshire, enrolled in the registrar's office at Wakefield, shall be good in law, as if enrolled at Westminster; the same to be on parchment, certified, and allowed.

No judgment, statute, or recognizance, shall affect lands in the west riding, but from the time that a memorial thereof be entered in the registrar's office. *Ibid.*

On certificate that money due on mortgage, judgment, statute, or recognizance, is paid, the registrar shall make an entry thereof. *Ibid.*

By 6 *Ann*, c. 35. a register-office, under like directions, is established for the east riding of Yorkshire, and the town of Kingston-upon-Hull; which office is directed to be held at Beverley. And the 8 *Geo.* 2. c. 6. establishes a like office for the north riding, to be held at such place as the justices of peace adjudge most central.

By 7 *Ann*, c. 20. all conveyances and wills that may affect any lands in Middlesex may be registered; and every conveyance or will shall be void against any after-purchaser, unless such memorial thereof be registered before that under which the subsequent purchaser claims.

The clerk of enrolment in chancery for Middlesex (the master of the king's bench office, by 25 *Geo.* 2. c. 4.) the clerk of the warrants in the common pleas, and the remembrancer, or his deputy, in the exchequer, shall be registrars; the office shall be kept near the inns of court; and the deputy shall be approved by the lord chancellor, who may make rules and orders. *Ibid.*

Memorials shall be on parchment attested, specifying the date, and effect of the deed, and a certificate indorsed shall be evidence; and the register shall be paged, numbered, and entered, in order of time. *Ibid.*

Memorials of wills shall be registered in six months after the death of a testator in Great Britain; if dying beyond sea, in three years. *Ibid.*

The registrar shall be allowed, for the entry of every memorial of 200 words, 1*s.*; and 6*d.* for every 100 words after. *Ibid.*

This act does not extend to *copyhold estates*, or *leases at a rack-rent*, or to any *chambers in the inns of court*. *Ibid.*

And no judgments, statutes, or recognizances, other than to the crown, shall bind lands in Middlesex, but from the time of memorial thereof registered. *Ibid.* 63.

The statutes were intended to give notice of incumbrances to purchasers, that they may not be defrauded; but if a man knows of an incumbrance, and will notwithstanding purchase, he is bound, though the incumbrance was not registered. 1 *Strange*, 664. 1 *Vez.* 64.

And the registry of an assignment, or mortgage of a lease, will not bar a subsequent purchaser, if the lease itself is not registered. 2 *Strange*, 1064.

REGISTRY OF SEAMEN. About the middle of king William's reign a scheme was set on foot (*Stat.* 7 & 8 *W.* 3. c. 21.) for a register of seamen, to the number of thirty thousand, for a constant and regular supply of the king's fleet, with great privileges to the registered men; and, on the other hand, heavy penalties in case of their non-appearance when called for: but this registry being judged to be ineffectual, as well as oppressive, was abolished by 9 *Ann*, c. 21.

A very judicious plan for supplying the navy with seamen, upon any emergency, without resorting to the expedient of impressing them, has however been laid before the editor of this dictionary by captain Patrick Holland, of North Shields, who was encouraged therein by the late lord Melville. The leading principle is to let the shipowners raise amongst themselves, upon bounties, the number of men wanted, according to the tonnage of their respective ships, and which they can on any emergency almost instantaneously do: to permit this would certainly not only encourage the increase of British seamen, who fly to neutrals to avoid the impress, but also keep down the war charges.

REGIUS PROFESSOR, a reader of lectures in the universities, founded by the king: king Hen. 8. was the founder of five lectures in each university of Oxford and Cambridge, viz. of divinity, Greek, Hebrew, law, and physic, the readers of which are called, in the university statutes, *regii professores*. *Cowell. Blount.*

REGNANT QUEEN. See *Queen*.

REGNI POPULI, a name given to the people of Surrey and Sussex, and on the sea-coasts of Hampshire. *Blount.*

REGNUM ECCLESIASTICUM. In some countries, formerly, the clergy held there was a double supreme power, or two kingdoms in every kingdom; the one a *regnum ecclesiasticum*, absolute and independent of any but the pope, over ecclesiastical men and causes, exempt from the secular magistrate; the other a *regnum seculare*, of the king or civil magistrate, which had subordination and subjection to the ecclesiastical kingdom; but these usurpations and absurdities were exterminated by Henry 8. 2 *Hale's Hist. P. C.* 324.

REGRATOR, (*regratarius*, Fr. *regrateur*) one who buys and sells any wares or victuals in the same market or fair: and regrators are, by stat. 5. c. 6. *Ed.* 6. c. 14. described to be those who buy or get into their hands, in fairs or markets, any grain, fish, butter, cheese, sheep, lambs, calves, swine, pigs, geese, capons, hens, chickens, pigeons, conies, or other dead victuals whatsoever, brought to a fair or market to be sold there, and do sell the same again in the same fair, market, or place, or in some other within four miles thereof. See *Forestaller*.

REGULARS, (*regulares*) such as professed to live under some certain rule: such as monks, or canon regulars, who were always to be under some rule of obedience. *Cowell.*

REGULUS, SUBREGULUS, words often mentioned in the councils of the English Saxons: the first signifies *comes*, the other *vicecomes;* but in many places they signify the same dignitary. *Cowell.*

REHABERE FACIAS SEISINAM, (*quando vicecomes liberavit seisinam de majore parte, quam deberet*) is a writ judicial, of which there is another of the same name and nature. *Reg. Judic.* 13. 51. 54. *Cowell. Blount.*

REHABILITATION, (*rehabilitatio*) a restoring to former ability; one of those exactions claimed by the pope, by his bull or brief, for re-enabling a spiritual person to exercise his function who had been disabled. *Cowell. Blount.*

REHEARING. If by a decree either party thinks himself aggrieved, he may petition the chancellor for a rehearing, whether it was heard before his lordship, or any of the judges sitting for him, or before the master of the rolls; for whoever may have heard the cause, it is the chancellor's decree, and must be signed by him before it is enrolled, (3 *Geo.* 2. *c.* 30.) which is done, of course, unless a rehearing be desired. Every petition for a rehearing must be signed by two counsel of character, usually such as have been concerned in the cause, certifying that they apprehend the cause is proper to be reheard. And upon the rehearing all the evidence taken in the cause, whether read before or not, is now admitted to be read: because it is the decree of the chancellor himself, who only now sits to hear reasons why it should not be enrolled and perfected; at which time all omissions of either evidence or argument may be supplied; but, after the decree is once signed and enrolled, it cannot be reheard or rectified but by bill of review, or by appeal to the house of lords. 3 *Black.* 453. *Gilb. Rep.* 151. 152.

REIF, (Sax. *refian*, i. e. *spoliare*) in our old law signifies robbery. *Ibid.*

REJOINDER, (*rejunctio*) is where the defendant in any action makes answer to the plaintiff's replication: and it is an exception or answer thereto. 2 *Lil. Abr.* 433.

RELATION, (*relatio*) is where, in consideration of law, two different times, or other things, are accounted as one; and by some act done, the thing subsequent is said to take effect by relation from the time preceding: as if one deliver a writing to another, to be delivered to a third person, as the deed of him who made it, when such third person hath paid a sum of money; now when the money is paid, and the writing delivered, this shall be taken as the deed of him who made and delivered it, at the time of its first delivery, to which it has relation; and so things relating to a time long before, shall be as if they were done at that time; such as an admission to a copyhold, under a previous surrender, the admission has relation back to the surrender. *Terms de Ley. Shep. Epit.* 837.

This device is to help acts in law, and make a thing take effect: but it must relate to the same thing, the same intent, and between the same parties only; and shall never be taken so as to operate wrongly, or lay a charge upon a person that is no party. *Co. Lit.* 190. 1 *Rep.* 99. *Plowd* 188.

RELATIONS, (private.) The three great relations in private life are, 1. That of master and servant, which is founded in convenience, whereby a man is directed to call in the assistance of others, where his own skill and labour will not be sufficient to answer the cares incumbent upon him. 2. That of husband and wife, which is founded in nature, but modified by civil society: the one directing man to continue and multiply his species; the other prescribing the manner in which that natural impulse must be confined and regulated. 3. That of parent and child, which is consequential to that of marriage, being its principal end and design: and it is by virtue of this relation that infants are protected, maintained, and educated; but since the parents, on whom this care is primarily incumbent, may be snatched away by death before they have completed their duty, the law has therefore provided a fourth relation; 4. That of guardian and ward, which is a kind of artificial parentage, in order to supply the deficiency, whenever it happens, of the natural. 1 *Black.* 422.

RELATIONS, (public) the most universal public relation by which men are connected together is that of government, namely, as governors and governed; or, in other words, as magistrates and people. 1 *Black.* 146.

RELATOR. Whenever it is necessary for the attorney-general, at the *relation* of some informant, to file an information in equity, *ex officio*, to have a charity properly established, or better regulated, the informer is called the relator.

RELEASE, (*relaxatio*) is an instrument whereby estates, or other things, are extinguished, conveyed, and transferred, abridged, or enlarged. *West Symbol. part* 1. *lib.* 2. *sect.* 509.

And it is a general rule in the construction of releases, that where there are general words only in a release, they shall be taken most strongly against the releasor; but where there is a particular recital in a deed, and then general words follow, the general words shall be qualified by the special words. 1 *Mod.* 99. 1 *Ld. Raym.* 235.

A release of all *claims* and *demands* is the best release to him to whom it is made; and Coke says, that the word DEMAND is the largest word in law except *claim;* and that a release of demands discharges all sorts of actions, rights and titles, conditions before or after breach, executions, appeals, rents of all kinds, covenants, annuities, contracts, recognizances, statutes, commons, &c. then immediately existing. *Litt. sect.* 508. 509. *Co. Litt.* 291. See also *Lease and Release.*

RELEGATION, (*relegatio*) a banishing, or sending away; as abjuration is forswearing the realm for ever, so relegation is banishment for a time only. *Co. Lit.* 133.

RELIEF, (*relevamen;* but, in domesday, *relevatio, relevium*) a certain sum of money which the tenant, holding by knight's service, grant serjeanty, or other tenure, (for which homage or legal service was due) and being at full age, at the death of his ancestor, paid unto his Lord at his entrance, *Mag. Char. cap.* 2. *Cowell. Blount.*

Reliefs had their origin while *feuds* were only life estates, for a *feudatory* or *beneficiary estate* in lands was at first granted only for life; and after death of the vassal it returned to the chief lord, for which reason it was called *feudum caducum*, viz. fallen to the lord by the death of the tenant; afterwards these feudatory estates being turned into inheritances by the connivance and assent of the chief lord, when the possessor of such an estate died, it was called *hæreditas caduca*, i. e. it was fallen to the chief lord, to whom the heir having paid a certain sum of money, he did then *relevare hæreditatem caducam* out of his hands; and the money thus paid was called a relief. 2 *Black.* 52. 64.

Relief was due upon socage tenure as upon tenures in chivalry, but the manner of entering it was very different; the relief on a knight's fee was 5*l.* or one quarter of the supposed value of the land; but a socage relief was one year's rent or render, payable by the tenant to the lord, be the same either great or small: and therefore Bracton will not allow this to be properly a relief, but *quædam præstatio loco relevii in recognitionem domini.* So too the *stat.* 23 *Edw.* 1. c. 1. declares, that a free sokeman shall give no relief, but shall double his rent after the death of his ancestor, according to that which he hath used to pay his lord, and shall not be grieved above measure. Reliefs in knight-service were only payable if the heir, at the death of his ancestor, was of full age; but in socage they were due even though the heir was under age, because the lord has no wardship over him. The statute of *Charles* 2. reserves the reliefs incident to socage tenures; and therefore, wherever lands in fee simple are holden by a rent, relief is still due of common right upon the death of a tenant. *Litt. s.* 126. *l.* 2. *c.* 37. *s.* 8. *Litt. s.* 127. 3 *Lev.* 145.

RELIGION, (*religio*). All blasphemies against God, as denying his being or providence, all profane scoffing at the holy scriptures, or exposing any part to contempt or ridicule, all impostures in religion, as falsely pretending to extraordinary commissions from God, and terrifying or abusing the people with false denunciations of judgments, &c. inasmuch as they tend to subvert all religion or morality, which are the foundation of government, are punishable by the temporal judges with fine and imprisonment, and also such corporal infamous punishment as to the court, in discretion, shall seem meet, according to the heinousness of the crime. 1 *Hawk. P. C.* 6. 7.

So also seditious words in derogation of the established religion are indictable, as tending to a breach of the peace. 1 *Hawk. P. C.* 7.

RELIGIOUS HOUSES, (*religiosæ domus*) houses set apart for pious uses, such as monasteries, churches, hospitals, and all other places where charity was extended to the relief of the poor and orphans, or for the use or exercise of religion. *Cowell. Blount.*

RELIGIOUS MEN, (*religiosi*) such as enter into some monastery or convent, there to live devoutly. *Ibid.*

RELIGIOUS ORDERS. See *Ordination.*

RELINQUISHMENT, is the abandonment or giving up a right or demand. *Style,* 175. *Dyer,* 66. 11 *Rep.* 59.

RELIQUES, (*reliquiæ*) are some remainders, such as the bones, &c. of saints, who are dead, preserved by persons living with great veneration, as sacred memorials of them: forbidden to be used or brought into England. *Jac.* 1. c. 26.

REMAINDER IN CHATTELS PERSONAL. By the rules of the ancient common law, there could be no future property, to take place in expectancy, created in personal goods and chattels; because, being things transitory, and by many accidents subject to be lost, destroyed, or otherwise impaired, and the exigencies of trade requiring also a frequent circulation thereof, it would occasion perpetual suits and quarrels, and put a stop to the freedom of commerce, if such limitations in remainder were generally tolerated and allowed. However, in last wills and testaments such limitations of personal goods and chattels, in remainder, after a bequest for life, were permitted, (1 *Equ. Cas. abr.* 360.) though originally that indulgence was only shewn when merely the use of the goods, and not the goods themselves, was given to the first legatee (*Mar.* 106.); the property being supposed to continue all the time in the executor of the devisor. But now that distinction is disregarded (2 *Freem.* 206.): and therefore if a man, either by deed or will, limits his books or furniture to A for life, with remainder over to B, this remainder is good. But where an estate-tail in things personal is given to the first or any subsequent possessor, it vests in him the total property, and no remainder over shall be permitted on such a limitation (*P. Wms.* 290.); for this, if allowed, would tend to a perpetuity, as the devisee or grantee in tail of a chattel has no method of barring the intail, and therefore the law vests in him at once the entire dominion of the goods. 3 *Black.* 397.

REMAINDER IN LANDS. An estate in remainder may be defined to be, an estate limited to take effect and be enjoyed after another estate is determined; as if a man seised in fee-simple granteth lands to A for twenty years, and, after the determination of the said term then to B, and his heirs for ever: here A is tenant for years, remainder to B in fee. In the first place an estate for years is created or carved out of the fee, and given to A; and the residue or remainder of it is given to B. But both these interests are in fact only one estate; the present term of years, and the remainder afterwards, when added together, being equal only to one estate in fee. They are indeed different parts, but they constitute only one whole: they are carved out of one and the same inheritance: they are both created, and may both subsist together; the one in possession, the other in expectancy. So if land be granted to A for twenty years, and after the determination of the said term to B for life; and after the determination of B's estate for life, it be limited to C and his heirs for ever: this makes A tenant for years, with remainder to B f r life, remainder over to C in fee. Now here the estate of inheritance undergoes a division into three portions; there is first A's estate for years carved out of it; and after that B's estate for life; and then the whole that remains is limited to C, and his heirs. And here also the first estate, and both the remainders, for life and in fee, are one estate only, being nothing but parts or portions of one entire inheritance: and if there were a hundred remainders, it would still be the same thing, upon a principle grounded in mathematical truth, that all the parts are equal, and no more than equal to the whole. And hence also it is easy to collect, that no remainder can be limited after the grant of an estate in fee-simple; because a fee-simple is the highest and largest estate that a subject is capable of enjoying; and he that is tenant in fee hath in him the whole of the estate: a remainder therefore, which is only a portion, or residuary part of the estate, cannot be reserved after the whole is disposed of. A particular estate, with all the remainders expectant thereon, is only one fee simple; as 40*l.* is part of 100*l.* and 60*l.* is the remainder of it: wherefore, after a fee-simple once vested, there can no more be a remainder limited thereon, than after the whole 100*l.* is appropriated there can be any residue subsisting.

The rules that are laid down by law to be observed in the creation of remainders, and the reasons upon which those rules are founded, are as follows:—

I. First, there must necessarily be some particular estate precedent to the estate in remainder; as, an estate for years to A, remainder to B for life; or, an estate for life to A, remainder to B in tail. This precedent estate is called the particular estate, as being only a small part, or *particula*, of the inheritance, the residue or remainder of which is granted over to another. The necessity of creating this preceding particular estate, in order to make a good remainder, arises from this plain reason, that remainder is a relative expression, and implies that some part of the thing is previously disposed of: for where the whole is conveyed at once, there cannot possibly exist a remainder; but the interest granted, whatever it be, will be an estate in possession.

An estate created to commence at a distant period of time, without any intervening estate, is therefore properly no remainder: it is the whole of the gift, and not a residuary part; and such future estates can only be made of chattel interests, which were considered in the light of mere contracts by the ancient law, to be executed either now or hereafter, as the contracting parties should agree; but an estate of freehold must be created to commence immediately: for it is an ancient rule of the common law, that an estate of freehold cannot be created to commence *in futuro;* but it ought to take effect presently either in possession or remainder: because, at common law, no freehold in lands could pass without livery of seisin, which must operate either immediately, or not at all. It would therefore be contradictory if an estate, which is not to commence till hereafter, could be granted by a conveyance which imports an immediate possession. Therefore, though a lease to A. for seven years, to commence from next Michaelmas, is good; yet a conveyance to B. of lands, to hold to him, and his heirs, for ever, from the end of three years next ensuing, is void. So that when it is intended to grant an estate of freehold, whereof the enjoyment shall be deferred till a future time, it is necessary to create a previous particular estate, which may subsist till that period of time is completed; and for the grantor to deliver immediate possession of the land to the tenant of this particular estate, which is construed to be giving possession to him in remainder, since his estate, and that of the particular tenant, are one and the same estate in law. As, where one leases to A. for three years, with remainder to B. in fee, and makes livery of seisin to A.; here by the livery the freehold is immediately created, and vested in B. during the continuance of A.'s term of years. The whole estate passes at once from the grantor to the grantees, and the remainder-man is seised of his remainder at the same time that the termor is possessed of his term. The enjoyment of it must indeed be deferred till hereafter; but it is to all intents and purposes an estate commencing *in præsenti*, though to be occupied and enjoyed *in futuro*.

As no remainder can be created without such a precedent particular estate, therefore the particular estate is said to support the remainder. But a lease at will is not held to be such a particular estate as will support a remainder over; for an estate at will is of a nature so slender and precarious, that it is not looked upon as a portion of the inheritance; and a portion must first be taken out of it, in order to constitute a remainder. Besides, if it be a freehold remainder, livery of seisin must be given at the time of its creation: and the entry of the grantor, to do this, determines the estate at will in the very instant in which it is made; or, if the remainder be a chattel interest, though perhaps the deed of creation might operate as a future contract, if the tenant for years be a party to it, yet it is void by way of remainder: for it is a separate independent contract, distinct from the precedent estate at will; and every remainder must be part of one and the same estate, out of which the preceding particular estate is taken. And hence it is generally true, that if the particular estate is void in its creation, or by any means is defeated afterwards, the remainder, supported thereby, shall be defeated also: as where the particular estate is an estate for the life of a person not *in esse*, or an estate for life upon condition, on breach of which condition the grantor enters and avoids the estate, in either of these cases the remainder over is void.

II. A second rule to be observed is this, that the remainder must commence or pass out of the grantor at the time of the creation of the particular estate; as, where there is an estate to A. for life, with remainder to B. in fee: here B.'s remainder in fee passes from the grantor at the same time that seisin is delivered to A. of his life estate in possession. And it is this, which induces the necessity at common law of livery of seisin being made on the particular estate, whenever a freehold remainder is created; for, if it be limited even on an estate for years, it is necessary that the lessee for years should have livery of seisin, in order to convey the freehold from and out of the grantor, otherwise the remainder is void. Not that the livery is necessary to strengthen the estate for years; but, as livery of the land is requisite to convey the freehold, and yet cannot be given to him in remainder without infringing the possession of the lessee for years, therefore the law allows such livery, made to the tenant of the particular estate, to relate and enure to him in remainder, as both are but one estate in law.

III. A third rule respecting remainders is this, that the remainder must vest in the grantee during the continuance of the particular estate, or *eo instanti* that it determines. As, if A. be tenant for life, remainder to B. in tail; here B.'s remainder is vested in him, at the creation of the particular estate to A. for life; or, if A. and B. be tenants for their joint lives, remainder to the survivor in fee; here, though during their joint lives the remainder is vested in neither, yet on the death of either of them the remainder vests instantly in the survivor, wherefore both these are good remainders. But, if an estate be limited to A. for life, remainder to the eldest son of B. in tail, and A. dies before B. hath any son; here the remainder will be void, for it did not vest in any one during the continuance, nor at the determination of the particular estate: and, even supposing that B. should afterwards have a son, he shall not take by this remainder; for, as it did not vest at or before the end of the particular estate, it never can vest at all, but is gone for ever. And this depends upon the principle before laid down, that the precedent particular estate, and the remainder, are one estate in law; they must therefore subsist and be *in esse* at one and the same instant of time, either during the continuance of the first estate, or at the very instant when that determines, so that no other estate can possibly come between them. For there can be no intervening estate between the particular estate, and the remainder supported thereby: the thing supported must fall to the ground, if once its support be severed from it.

It is upon these rules, but principally the last, that the doctrine of contingent remainders depends; for remainders are either vested or contingent. Vested remainders (or remainders executed, whereby a present interest passes to the party, though to be enjoyed *in futuro*) are where the estate is invariably fixed, to remain to a determinate person, after the particular estate is spent. As if A. be tenant for twenty years, remainder to B. in fee; here B.'s is a vested remainder, which nothing can defeat, or set aside.

Contingent, or executory remainders, (whereby no present interest passes) are where the estate in remainder is limited to take effect, either to a dubious and uncertain person, or upon a dubious and uncertain event; so that the particular estate may chance to be determined, and the remainder never take effect.

First, they may be limited to a dubious and uncertain person; as if A. be tenant for life, with remainder to B.'s eldest son (then unborn) in tail; this is a contingent remainder, for it is uncertain whether B. will have a son or no: but the instant that a son is born, the remainder is no longer contingent, but vested; though if A. had died before the contingency happened, that is, before B.'s son was born, the remainder would have been absolutely gone, for the particular estate was determined before the remainder could vest. Nay, by the strict rule of law, if A. were tenant for life, remainder to his own eldest son in tail, and A. died without issue born, but leaving his wife *enseint*, or big with child, and after his death a posthumous son was born, this son could not take the land by virtue of this remainder; for the particular estate determined before there was any person *in esse*, in whom the remainder could vest. But, to remedy this hardship, it is enacted by statute 10 & 11 *W.* 3. c. 16. that posthumous children shall be capable of taking in remainder, in the same manner as if they had been born in their father's lifetime: that is, the remainder is allowed to vest in them, while yet in their mother's womb.*

This species of contingent remainders to a person not in being, must, however, be limited to some one, that may by common possibility, or, *potentia propinqua*, be *in esse* at or before the particular estate determines. As if an estate be made to A. for life, remainder to the heirs of B.; now, if A. dies before B. the remainder is at an end, for during B.'s life he has no heir, *nemo est hæres viventis*: but if B. dies first, the remainder then immediately vests in his heir, who will be entitled to the land on the death of A. This is a good contingent remainder, for the possibility of B.'s dying before A. is *potentia propinqua*, and therefore allowed in law. But a remainder to the right heirs of B. (if there be no such person as B. *in esse*) is void; for here there must two contingencies happen: first, that such a person as B. shall be born; and, secondly, that he shall also die during the continuance of the particular estate, which make it *potentia remotissima*, a most improbable possibility. A remainder to a man's eldest son, who hath none (we have seen) is good, for by common possibility he may have one; but if it be limited in particular to his son John, or Richard, it is bad, if he have no son of that name; for it is too remote a possibility that he should not only have a son, but a son of a particular name. A limitation of a remainder to a bastard, before it is born, is not good; for though the law allows the possibility of having bastards, it presumes it to be a very remote and improbable contingency. Thus may a remainder be contingent, on account of the uncertainty of the person who is to take it.

A remainder may also be contingent, where the person to whom it is limited is fixed and certain, but the event upon which it is to take effect is vague and uncertain. As, where land is given to A. for life, and in case B. survives him, then with remainder to B. in fee: here B. is a certain person, but the remainder to him is a contingent remainder, depending upon a dubious event, the uncertainty of his surviving A. During the joint lives of A. and B. it is contingent; and if B. dies first, it never can vest in his heirs, but is for ever gone; but if A. dies first, the remainder to B. becomes vested.

Contingent remainders of either kind, if

---

* A father had devised an estate to his son for life, with a remainder to the first and other sons of the son in tail; the son died, leaving his wife pregnant, who was afterwards delivered of a son: the courts of common pleas and king's bench held clearly, that the grandson not being born at the expiration of the estate for life, was not entitled to take it; but the lords, moved by the hardship of the case, reversed the judgments of the courts below, contrary to the opinions of all the judges. (*Reeve v. Long*, 1 *Salk.* 227.) But the house of commons, in reproof of this assumption of legislative authority in the lords, immediately brought in the 10 & 11 *W.* 3. which passed into a statute. The statute only mentions marriages, and other settlements; and it is probable, that devises were designedly omitted to be expressed, from a delicacy that the authority of the judgment of the peers might not be too openly impeached, as the statute says, the posthumous son in this case shall take the estate as if born before the death of the father, he is entitled to the intermediate profits from the death of the father (3 *Atk.* 203), which is different from the case of a descent devested by the birth of a posthumous child.

they amount to a freehold, cannot be limited on an estate for years, or any other particular estate, less than a freehold. Thus if land be granted to A. for ten years, with remainder in fee to the right heirs of B. this remainder is void: but if granted to A. for life, with a like remainder, it is good; for, unless the freehold passes out of the grantor at the time when the remainder is created, such freehold remainder is void: it cannot pass out of him, without vesting somewhere; and in the case of a contingent remainder it must vest in the particular tenant, else it can vest nowhere: unless, therefore, the estate of such particular tenant be of a freehold nature, the freehold cannot vest in him, and consequently the remainder is void.

Contingent remainders may be defeated, by destroying or determining the particular estate upon which they depend, before the contingency happens whereby they become vested. Therefore when there is tenant for life, with divers remainders in contingency, he may, not only by his death but by alienation, surrender, or other methods, destroy and determine his own life estate, before any of those remainders vest; * the consequence of which is, that he utterly defeats them all. As, if there be tenant for life, with remainder to his eldest son unborn in tail, and the tenant for life, before any son is born, surrenders his life-estate, he by that means defeats the remainder in tail to his son: for his son not being *in esse*, when the particular estate determined, the remainder could not then vest; and, as it could not vest then, by the rules before laid down, it never can vest at all. In these cases, therefore, it is necessary to have trustees appointed to preserve the contingent remainders, in whom there is vested an estate in remainder for the life of the tenant for life, to commence when his estate determines. If, therefore, his estate for life determines otherwise than by his death, the estate of the trustees, for the residue of his natural life, will then take effect, and become a particular estate in possession, sufficient to support the remainders depending in contingency. This method is said to have been invented by Sir Orlando Bridgman, Sir Geoffrey Palmer, and other eminent counsel, who betook themselves to conveyancing during the time of the civil wars, in order thereby to secure in family settlements a provision for the future children of an intended marriage, who before were usually left at the mercy of the particular tenant for life: and when, after the restoration, those gentlemen came to fill the first offices of the law, they supported this invention within reasonable and proper bounds, and introduced it into general use. See *Moor*, 486. 2 *Roll. Abr.* 797. *pl.* 12. 2 *Sid.* 159. 2 *Chan. Rep.* 170.

In a grant of a fee-simple to A. it is necessary to give it to A. and his heirs; of a fee-tail, to A. and the heirs of his body; and that a grant to A. without any additional words, gives him only an estate for life. Hence the word heirs, in the first case, and the word heirs of the body in the second, are said to be words of limitation, because they limit or describe what interest A. takes by the grant, viz. in one case a fee-simple, in the other a fee-tail: and the heirs in both instances take no interest any farther than as the ancestor may permit the estate to descend to them. But if a remainder is granted, or estate devised to the heirs of A. where no estate of freehold is at the same time given to A. the heir of A. cannot take by descent from A.; but he takes by purchase, under the grant, in the same manner as if the estate had been given to him by his proper name. Here the word heirs is called a word of purchase. Having premised the distinction between words of limitation and words of purchase, it may be observed, that the much-talked-of rule in Shelly's case (1 *Co.* 104.) is this, viz. "when the ancestor, by any gift or conveyance, takes an estate of freehold, and in the same gift or conveyance an estate is limited, either mediately or immediately, to his heirs in fee or in tail, that always in such cases the heirs are words of limitation, and not words of purchase:" and the remainder is said to be executed in the ancestor, where there is no intermediate estate; or, vested, when an estate for life or in tail intervenes.

As if an estate be given to A. for life, and, after his death, to the heirs of his body; this remainder is executed in A. or it unites with his estate for life; and the effect is the same as if the estate had at once been given to A. and the heirs of his body; which expression limits an estate tail to A. and the issue have no indefeasible interest conveyed to them, but can only take by descent from A. So also if an estate be given to A. for life, with remainder

---

* But a conveyance of a greater estate than he has by bargain and sale, or by lease and release, is no forfeiture, and will not defeat a contingent remainder. 2 *Leo.* 60. 3 *Mod.* 151.

But the tenant for life may bar the contingent remainders by a feoffment, a fine, or a recovery. 1 *Co.* 66. *Cro. Eliz.* 630. 1 *Salk.* 224.

Where there is a tenant for life, with all the subsequent remainders contingent, and he suffers a recovery to the use of himself in fee, he has a right to this tortious fee against all persons but the heirs of the grantor or devisor. 1 *Salk.* 224.

to B. for life, or in tail, remainder to the heirs, or to the heirs of the body of A.; A. takes an estate for life, in this case, with a vested remainder in fee or in tail; and his heir, under this grant, can only take by descent at his death (*Fearne*, 21.) But when the estate for life, and the remainder in tail or in fee unite and coalesce, and heirs is a word of limitation, the two estates must be created by the same instrument, and must be either both legal, or both trust estates (*Doug*. 490. 2 *T. R*. 444.) But an appointment in pursuance of a power, when executed, is to be considered as if it had been inserted in the original deed by which the power of appointment was created (7 *T. R*. 347.) The rule with regard to the execution or coalition of such estates seems now to be the same in equitable as in legal estates (1 *Bro*. 206.) And in all these cases where a person has an estate tail, or a vested remainder in tail, he can cut off the expectations or inheritance of his issue, by a fine, or a recovery (*Doug*. 323.) In order, therefore, to secure a certain provision for children, the method was invented of granting the estate to the father for life, and, after his death, to his first and other sons in tail: for the words son or daughter were held to be words of purchase, and the remainder to them did not, like the remainder to heirs, unite with the prior estate of freehold. But if the son was unborn, the remainder was contingent, and might have been defeated by the alienation of the father by feoffment, fine, or recovery: to prevent this, it was necessary to interpose trustees, to whom the estate is given upon such a determination of the life-estate, and in whom it rests, till the contingent estate, if at all, comes into existence; and thus they are said to support and preserve the contingent remainders. This is called a strict settlement, and is the only mode (executory devises excepted) by which a certain and indefeasible provision can be secured to an unborn child. But in the case of articles or covenants before marriage, for making a settlement upon the husband and wife, and their offspring, if there be a limitation to the parents for life, with a remainder to the heirs of their bodies, the latter words were generally considered as words of purchase, and not of limitation; and a court of equity will decree the articles to be executed in strict settlement. (See *Fearne*, 124, and examples there cited.) It being the great object of such settlements to secure fortunes for the issue of the marriage, it would be useless to give the parents an estate tail, of which they would almost immediately have the absolute disposal. And therefore the courts of equity will decree the estate to be settled upon the parent or parents for life; and upon the determination of that estate by forfeiture, to trustees to support contingent remainders for their lives; and, after their decease, to the first and other sons successively in tail, with remainder to all the daughters in tail as tenants in common, with subsequent remainders or provisions, according to the occasions and intentions of the parties. In these strict settlements, the estate is unalienable till the first son attains the age of 21, who, if his father is dead, has then, as tenant in tail, full power over the estate; or, if his father is living, he then can bar his own issue by a fine, independent of the father (*Cruise*, 161.) But the father, and the son at that age, can cut off all the subsequent limitations, and dispose of the estate in any manner they please, by joining a common recovery. This is the origin of the vulgar error, that a tenant of an estate-tail must have the consent of his eldest son to enable him to cut off the intail; for that is necessary where the father has only a life-estate, and his eldest son has the remainder in tail. But there is no method whatever of securing an estate to the grandchildren of a person, who is without children at the time of the settlement, for the law will not permit a perpetuity; and lord Thurlow has defined a perpetuity to be "any extension of an estate beyond a life in being, and 21 years after." (2 *Bro*. 30.) Hence, where in a settlement the father has a power to appoint an estate to or amongst his children, he cannot afterwards give this to his children in strict settlement, or give any of his sons an estate for life, with a remainder in tail to his eldest son; for if he could do this, a perpetuity would be created by the original settlement. 2 *T. R*. 241. See *Executory Devise*.

REMAINDER, (formedon in). A formedon in the remainder lieth, where a man giveth lands to another for life or in tail, with remainder to a third person in tail or in fee; and he who hath the particular estate dieth, without issue inheritable, and a stranger intrudes upon him in remainder, and keeps him out of possession. In this case the remainder-man shall have his writ of formedon in the remainder, wherein the whole form of the gift is stated, and the happening of the event upon which the remainder depended. This writ is not given in express words by the statute *de donis*; but is founded upon the equity of the statute, and upon this maxim in law, that if any one hath a right to the land, he ought also to have an action to recover it.

A formedon in the reverter lieth, where there is a gift in tail, and afterwards by the death of the donee, or his heirs, without issue of his body, the reversion falls in upon the donor, his heirs or assigns; in such case the reversioner shall have this writ to recover the lands, wherein he shall suggest the gift, his own title to the reversion minutely derived from the donor, and the failure of issue upon his reversion takes place. This lay at common law, before the statute *de donis*, if the donee aliened before he had performed the condition of the gift, by having issue, and afterwards died without any.

REMANDING OF A CAUSE, is sending it back by a *procedendo* into the same court out of which it was called and sent for. *Marsh*, 106.

REMANENTES, (*remansi.*) Are words used to signify belonging to ——. *Cowell. Blanc.*

REMANET IN CUSTODIA. Entry of an action in the marshal's book, by *reman. custod.* where a man is actually in custody, is a good commencement of an action in B. R. 3 *Salk.* 150.

REMEDY, (*Remedium.*) The means given by law for recovery of a right or recompence; and there is a maxim, *Lex semper dabit remedium. Stud. Compan.* 177. 179. *Wood's Inst.*, 528, 529, 530.

REMEMBRANCERS, (*Rememoratores.*) Formerly called Clerks of the Remembrance, are officers of the exchequer, of which there are three: 1, The king's remembrancer; 2, The lord treasurer's remembrancer; and 3, The remembrancer of first-fruits.

The king's remembrancer enters into his office all recognizances taken before the barons for any of the king's debts, for appearances, &c. and he takes all bonds for such debts, and makes out process for breach of them; also he writes process against the collectors of customs, subsidies, excise, and other public payments for their accounts.

The treasurer's remembrancer issues out process of *fieri facias* and extents, for debts to the king; and against sheriffs, escheators, &c. not accounting; he takes the accounts of all sheriffs, and makes the record, whereby it appears whether sheriffs and other accountants pay their profers due at Easter and Michaelmas; and he makes another record, whether sheriffs and other accountants keep their days prefixed. There are also brought into his office all the accounts of customers, comptrollers, and accountants, to make entry thereof on record. All estreats of fines, issues, and amerciaments, set in any of the courts at Westminster, or at the assises or sessions, are certified into his office, and by him delivered to the clerk of the estreats to make out process on them; and he may issue process for discovery of tenures, and all such revenue as is due to the crown by reason thereof, &c.

The remembrancer of the First-Fruits office is to take all compositions, and bonds for payments of first-fruits and tenths; he makes process against all such persons as do not pay the same. *Stat.* 35 *Eliz. cap.* 5. 5 *R.* 2. c. 14.

REMITTER, (from the Lat. *remittere*, to restore or send back.) Remitter is where he, who hath the true property or *jus proprietatis* in lands, but is out of possession thereof, and hath no right to enter without recovering possession in an action, hath afterwards the freehold cast upon him by some subsequent, and of course, defective title. In this case he is remitted, or sent back, by operation of law, to his ancient and more certain title. The right of entry, which he hath gained by a bad title, shall be *ipso facto* annexed to his own inherent good one; and his defeasible estate shall be utterly defeated and annulled, by the instantaneous act of law, without his participation or consent. As if A. disseises B, that is, turns him out of possession, and dies leaving a son C.; hereby the estate descends to C. the son of A., and B. is barred from entering thereon till he proves his right in an action. Now, if afterwards C. the heir of the disseisor makes a lease for life to D., with remainder to B. the disseisee for life, and D. dies, hereby the remainder accrues to B., the disseisee; who thus gaining a new freehold by virtue of the remainder, which is a bad title, is by act of law remitted, or invested of his former and surer estate. For he hath hereby gained a new right of possession, to which the law immediately annexes his ancient right of property.

If the subsequent estate, or right of possession, be gained by a man's own act or consent, as by immediate purchase being of full age, he shall not be remitted; for the taking such subsequent estate was his own folly, and shall be looked upon as a waiver of his prior right. Therefore it is to be observed, that to every remitter there are regularly these incidents: an ancient right, and a new defeasible estate of freehold, uniting in one and the same person; which defeasible estate must be cast upon the tenant, not gained by his own act or folly. The reason given by Littleton, why this remedy, which operates silently and by the mere act of law, was allowed, is because otherwise he who hath right would be deprived of all remedy. For as he himself is the person in possession of the freehold, there is no other person against whom he can bring an action to establish his prior right. And for this cause the law doth adjudge him in by remitter, that is, in such plight as if he had lawfully recovered the same land by suit. For, as Lord Bacon observes, the benignity of the law is such, as when, to preserve the principles and grounds of law, it depriveth a man of his remedy without his own fault, it will rather put him in a better degree and condition than in a worse. *Nam quod remedio destituitur, ipsa re valet: si culpa absit.* But there shall be no remitter to a right, for which the party has no remedy by action: as if the issue in tail be barred by the fine or warranty of his ancestor, and the freehold is afterwards cast upon him, he shall not be remitted to his estate tail; for the operation of the remitter is exactly the same after the union of the two rights, as that of a real action would have been before it. As, therefore, the issue in tail could not by any action have recovered his ancient estate, he shall not recover it by remitter. *Moor* 115. 1 *And.* 286.

REMITTITUR. The entry in B. R. on a writ of error abating in the exchequer chamber, &c. is called by this name. See *Error.*

REMOVAL OF POOR. See *Settlements* and *Removals.*

REMOVER. Is where a suit or cause is removed out of one court into another: and for this there are divers writs and means. 11 *Rep.* 41.

RENANT, or rather *reniant*, i. e. *negans*, from the Fr. *renier*, *negare*, to deny or refuse. *Cowell.*

RENDER, (Fr. *rendre*, viz. *reddere.*) Signifies to yield, give again, or return, as in levying a double fine, is to grant and render back again the land, &c. to the cognisor. *West's Symb.*

RENOVANT, (from *renovo.*) To renew or make again: thus, a parson sued one for tithes, to be paid of things renovant, &c. *Cro. Jac.* 430.

RENT, (*redditus*, in Latin, from *redeundo*, because, as Fleta tells us, *Retroit & quotannis redit.* lib. 3. c. 14.) Signifies with us a sum of money, or other compensation or return issuing yearly out of lands or tenements corporal. *Plowden* 132. 138. 141. 2 *Black.* 41.

It must be a profit; yet there is no occasion for it to be, as it usually is, a sum of money, for spurs, capons, horses, corn, and other matters, may be rendered, and frequently are rendered by way of rent. It may also consist in services or manual operations: as, to plough so many acres of ground, to attend the king or the lord to the wars, and the like; which services in the eye of the law are profits. This profit must also be certain, or that which may be reduced to a certainty by either party. It must also issue yearly, though there is no occasion for it to issue every successive year, but it may be reserved every second, third, or fourth year; yet, as it is to be produced out of the profits of lands and tenements, as a recompence for being permitted to hold or enjoy them, it ought to be reserved yearly, because those profits do annually arise and are annually renewed. It must issue out of the thing granted, and not be part of the land or thing itself: wherein it differs from an exception in the grant, which is always of part of the thing granted. It must, lastly, issue out of lands and tenements corporeal; that is, from some inheritance whereunto the owner or grantee of the rent may have recourse to distrain. Therefore a rent cannot be reserved out of an advowson, a common, an office, a franchise, or the like. But a grant of such annuity or sum may operate as a personal contract, and oblige the grantor to pay the money reserved, or subject him to an action of debt, though it doth not affect the inheritance, and is no legal rent in contemplation of law.

There can be no doubt but the lessee of tithes, an advowson, or any incorporeal hereditament, would be liable to an action of debt for the rent agreed upon. And in 2 *Wood.* 69, where this passage is taken notice of, it is observed, that there are at common law three manner of rents, rent-service, rent-charge, and rent-seck. Rent-service is so called because it has some corporal service incident to it, as at the least fealty or the feodal oath of fidelity. For, if a tenant holds his lands by fealty, and ten shillings rent, or by the service of ploughing the lord's land, and five shillings rent, these pecuniary rents, being connected with personal services, are therefore called rent-service. And for these, in case they be behind, or arrere, at the day appointed, the lord may distrein of common right, without reserving any special power of distress, provided he hath in himself the reversion or future estate of the lands and tenements, after the lease or particular estate of the lessee or grantee is expired. A rent-charge is where the owner of the rent hath no future interest, or reversion expectant in the land: as where a man by deed maketh over to others his whole estate in fee simple, with a certain rent payable thereout, and adds to the deed a covenant or clause of distress, that if the rent be arrere, or behind, it shall be lawful to distrain for the same. In this case the land is liable to the distress, not of common right, but by virtue of the clause in the deed; and therefore it is called a rent-charge, because in this manner the land is charged with a distress for the payment of it. Rent-seck, *reditus siccus*, or barren rent, is in effect nothing more than a rent reserved by deed, but without any clause of distress.

There are also other species of rents, which are reducible to these three. Rents of assize are the certain established rents of the freeholders and ancient copyholders of a manor, which cannot be departed from or varied. Those of the freeholders are frequently called chief rents, *reditus capitales;* and both sorts are indifferently denominated quit-rents, *quieti reditus;* because thereby the tenant goes quit and free of all other services. When these payments were reserved in silver or white money, they were anciently called white-rents, or blanch-farms, *reditus albi*, in contradistinction to rents reserved in work, grain, or baser money, which were called *reditus nigri*, or black-mail. Rack-rent is only a rent of the full value of the tenement, or near it. A fee-farm rent is a rent-charge issuing out of an estate in fee, of at least one fourth of the value of the lands at the time of its reservation; for a grant of lands, reserving so considerable a rent, is indeed only letting lands to farm in fee simple instead of the usual methods for life or years.

These are the general divisions of rent, but the difference between them, in respect to the remedy for recovering them, is now totally abolished; and all persons may have the like remedy by distress for rents-seck, rents of assise, and chief rents, as in case of rents reserved upon lease, by stat. 4 Geo. 2, c. 28; that is, for such as had been paid for three years, within twenty years before the passing of that act, or for such as have been since created. 4 *Geo.* 2, *c.* 28. *s.* 5. *Doug.* 602.

Rent is regularly due and payable upon the land from whence it issues, if no particular place is mentioned in the reservation; but in case of the king, the payment must be either to his officers at the exchequer, or to his receiver in the country. And, strictly, the rent is demandable and payable before the time of sun-set of the day whereon it is reserved, though perhaps not absolutely due till midnight. If the lessor dies before sun-set on the day upon which the rent is demandable, it is clearly settled that the rent unpaid is due to his heir, and not to his executor; but if he dies after sun-set and before midnight, it seems to be the better opinion, that it shall go to the executor and not to the heir. 1 *P. Wms.* 178. See also *Distress*, *Ejectment*, *Replevin*.

In Scotland, this kind of small payment is called blanch-holding, or *reditus albæ firmæ*.

RENTAL, or RENT-ROLL. A roll wherein the rents of a manor are written and set down, by which the lord's bailiff collects the same. *Compl. Court Keep.* 475.

RENTS OF ASSISE. The certain rents of freeholders and ancient copyholders, so called because they were assised, and different from others which were uncertain, paid in corn, &c. 2 *Inst.* 19.

RENTS RESOLUTE. (*Redditus resoluti.*) Rents or tenths. Renewal of leases were anciently payable to the crown, from the lands of abbeys and religious houses; and which, after their dissolution, were still reserved, and made payable again to the crown. *Cowell.*

REPAIRS. A tenant for life or years may cut down timber-trees to make reparations, although he be not compelled thereto; as, where a house is ruinous at the time of the lease made, and the lessee suffers it to fall, he is not bound to rebuild it; and yet if he fell timber for reparations, he may justify the same. *Co. Lit.* 54.

And a lessee for years, whether there be an express covenant or not, is bound to repair, but a tenant at will is not.

REPARATIONE FACIENDA. A writ which lies in many cases; one whereof is, where there are tenants in common or joint tenants of a house, &c. which is fallen to decay, and one is willing to repair it, but the others are not. In this case the party willing to repair the same shall have this writ against the others. *F. N. B.* 127.

And if a man have a house adjoining to my house, and he suffer his house to lie in decay to the annoyance of my house, I may have a writ against him to repair his house. So, if a person have a passage over a bridge, and another ought to repair the bridge, who suffers it to fall to decay, &c. *New Nat. Br.* 281.

REPEAL, (from the Fr. *rappel*, i. e. *revocatio.*) Signifies the same with revoke; as, the repealing of a statute or will is the revoking or disannulling it. *Rastal. Style.* 241.

REPLEADER, (*Replacitare.*) Is to plead that again which was once pleaded before. *Broke.*

If, by the misconduct or inadvertence of the pleaders, the issue be joined on a fact totally immaterial, or insufficient to determine the right, so that the court upon the finding cannot know for whom judgment ought to be given; as if, on an action on the case in assumpsit against an executor, he pleads that he himself (instead of the testator) made no such promise; or if, in an action of debt on bond conditioned to pay money on or before a certain day, the defendant pleads payment on the day (which, if found for the plaintiff, would be inconclusive, as it might have been paid before; in these cases the court will, after verdict, award a repleader, *quod partes replacitent*, unless it appears from the whole record that nothing material can possibly be pleaded in any shape whatsoever, and then a repleader would be fruitless. And, whenever a repleader is granted, the pleadings must begin *de novo* at that stage of them, whether it be the plea, replication, or rejoinder, &c. wherein there appears to have been the first defect, or deviation from the regular course. *Ventr.* 196. *Stra.* 994. 3 *Black.* 395.

REPLEGIARE. Is to redeem a thing detained or taken by another, by putting in legal sureties. See *Replevin.*

REPLEGIARE DE AVERIIS. A writ brought by one whose cattle are distrained, or put in the pound on any cause by another person, on surety given to the sheriff to prosecute or answer the action at law. *F. N. B.* 68. *Reg. Orig. Stat.* 7 *H.* 8. c. 4.

REPLEVIN, (*Plevina* from *replegiare*, to deliver to the owner on pledges.)

The action of replevin is founded upon a distress taken wrongfully and without sufficient cause: being a redelivery of the pledge or thing taken in distress, to the owner, upon his giving security to try the right of distress, and to restore it if the right be adjudged against him (*Co. Lit.* 145.) And formerly, when the party distrained upon intended to dispute the right of the distress, he had no other process by the old common law than by a writ of replevin, *replegiari facias. F. N. B.* 68.; which issued out of chancery, commanding the sheriff to deliver the distress to the owner, and afterwards to do justice in respect of the matter in dispute in his own county court. But this being a tedious method of proceeding, the beasts or other goods were long detained from the owner, to his great loss and damage. 2 *Inst.* 139. For which reason the statute of Marlbridge (52 *Hen.* 3. c. 21.) directs, that (without suing a writ out of chancery) the sheriff, immediately upon complaint to him made, shall proceed to replevy the goods. And, for the greater ease of the parties, it is farther provided by statute 1 Ph. & Mar. c. 12. that the sheriff shall make at least four deputies in each county, for the sole purpose of making replevins. Upon application, therefore, either to the sheriff, or one of his said deputies, security is to be given, in pursuance of the stat. of Westm. 2. 13 *Edw.* 1. c. 2. 1, That the party replevying will pursue his action against the destrainor, for which purpose he puts in *plegios de prosequendo*, or pledges to prosecute; and 2, That if the right be determined against him, he will return the distress again; for which purpose he is also bound to find *plegios de retorno habendo*. Besides these pledges, which are merely discretionary in the sheriff, the statute 11 Geo. 2. c. 19. requires that the officer, granting a replevin on a distress for rent, shall take a bond, with two sureties in a sum of double the value of the goods distrained; which bond shall be assigned to the avowant, or person making cognizance, on request made to the sheriff; and, if forfeited, may be sued in the name of the assignee.

The sheriff, on receiving such security, is immediately, by his officers, to cause the chattels taken in distress to be restored into the possession of the party distrained upon, unless the distrainer claims a property in the goods so taken. For if by this method of distress the distrainer happens to come again into possession of his own property in goods which before he had lost, the law allows him to keep them, without any reference to the manner by which he thus has regained possession, being a kind of personal remitter. If, therefore, the distrainer claims any such property, the party replevying must sue out a writ *de proprietate probanda*, in which the sheriff is to try, by an inquest, in whom the property previous to the distress subsisted. (*Finch, L.* 316.) And if it be found to be in the distrainor, the sheriff can proceed no farther, but must return the claim of property to the court of king's bench or common pleas, to be there farther prosecuted, if thought advisable, and there finally determined. 3 *Black.* 148.

But if no claim of property be put in, or if, upon trial, the sheriff's inquest determines it against the distrainor, then the sheriff is to replevy the goods (making use of even force, if the distrainer makes resistance, 2 *Inst.* 193,) in case the goods be found within his county. But if the distress be carried out of the county, or concealed, then the sheriff may return that the goods, or beasts, are eloigned, *elongata*, carried to a distance, to places to him unknown; and thereupon the party replevying shall have a writ of *capias in withernam*, or *in vetito namio*, a term which signifies a second or reciprocal distress, in lieu of the first which was eloigned. It is therefore a command to the sheriff to take other goods of the distrainor, in lieu of the distress formerly taken and eloigned, or withheld from the owner. *F. N. B.* 69, 73. So that here is now distress against distress; one being taken to answer the other by way of reprisal and as a punishment for the illegal behaviour of the original distrainor. For which reason goods taken in withernam cannot be replevied, till the original distress is forthcoming. *Raym.* 475. 3 *Black. Com.* 149.

But, in common cases, the goods are delivered back to the party replevying, who is bound to bring his action of replevin; which may be prosecuted in the county court, be the distress of what value it may. 2 *Inst.* 139. But either party may remove it to the superior courts; the plaintiff at pleasure, the defendant upon reasonable cause, *F. N. B.* 69. 70. And also, if in the course of proceeding any right of freehold comes in question, the sheriff can proceed no farther, 2 *Finch. L.* 317.; so that it is usual to carry it up in the first instance to the courts of Westminster-hall. Upon this action brought, the distreinor, who is now the defendant, makes avowry; that is, he avows taking the distress in his own right, or the right of his wife, 2 *Saund.* 195: and sets forth the reason of it, as for rent arrere, damage done, or other cause;

or else, if he justifies in another's right, as his bailiff or servant, he is said to made cognizance; that is, he acknowledges the taking, but insists that such taking was legal, as he acted by the command of one who had a right to distrein; and on the truth and legal merits of this avowry or cognizance the cause is determined. If it be determined for the plaintiff, viz. that the distress was wrongfully taken; he has already got his goods back into his own possession, and shall keep them, and moreover recover damages, *F. N. B.* 69. But if the defendant prevails, and obtains judgment that the distress was legal, then he shall have a writ *de retorno habendo*, whereby the goods or chattels (which were distreined and then replevied) are returned again into his custody; to be sold, or otherwise disposed of, as if no replevin had been made. Or, in case of rent arrere, he may have a writ to inquire into the value of the distress by a jury, and shall recover the amount of it in damages, if less than the arrear of rent; or, if more, then so much as shall be equal to such arrear; and, if the distress be insufficient, he may take a farther distress or distresses, (*stat.* 17 *Car.* 2. c. 7.): but otherwise, if, pending a replevin for a former distress, a man distreins again for the same rent or service, then the party is not driven to his action of replevin, but shall have a writ of recaption, *F. N. B.* 71., and recover damages for the defendant's contempt of the process of law. 3 *Black. Com.* 150.

REPLEVY. Tenants having their goods taken as a distress for rent, are to replevy them in five days, or they may be appraised and sold, by *stat.* 2 *Wm. & Mar. sess.* 1. *c.* 5.

To replevy is also used for the bailing a man. *Stat. Westm.* 1. c. 11. See *Homine Replegiando.*

REPLEVISH. Signifies to let one to mainprise on surety. 3 *Edw.* 1. cap. 11.

REPLICATION, (*replicatio.*) Is an answer made by the plaintiff to the defendant's plea. And it is also that which the complainant puts in to a defendant's answer in the courts of equity. *West's Symb. par.* 2.

REPLICATION IN CRIMINAL CASES. When the prisoner hath pleaded not guilty, *non culpabilis*, or *nient culpable*, which was formerly used to be abbreviated upon the minutes, thus, "*non* (or *nient*) *cul*," the clerk of the assise, or clerk of the arraigns, on behalf of the crown, REPLIES, that the prisoner is guilty, and that he is ready to prove him so. This is done by two monosyllables in the same spirit of abbreviation, "*cul. prit.*" which signifies first that the prisoner is guilty, (*cul. culpable*, or *culpabilis*,) and then that the king is ready to prove him so; *prit*, *præsto sum*, or *paratus verificare*. This is therefore a replication on behalf of the king *viva voce* at the bar, which was formerly the course in all pleadings, as well in civil as in criminal causes.

REPORT, (from the Lat. *reportare.*) Is a public relation of cases judicially adjudged in courts of justice, with the reasons as delivered by the judges. *Co. Lit.* 293.

These reports are handed out to public view in the numerous volumes of reports which furnish the lawyer's library. These reports are histories of the several cases, with a short summary of the proceedings which are preserved at large in the record; the arguments on both sides, and the reasons the court gave for its judgment, taken down in short notes by persons present at the determination. And these serve as indexes to, and also to explain, the records; which always, in matters of consequence and nicety, the judges direct to be searched. 1 *Black.* 71.

There are likewise reports, when the court of chancery, or other court, refer the taking of accounts or making some inquiry to a master of chancery, or some other officer, whose certificate therein is called a report, on which the court makes an absolute order. *Pract. Solic.* 67.

REPOSITION OF THE FOREST, (*reposito forestæ*, i. e. a reputting to.) Was a statute whereby certain forest grounds being made purlieu on view, were by a second view put to the forest again. *Manw. par.* 1.

REPOSITORIUM, (*Lat.*) A storehouse or place wherein things are kept; also a warehouse. *Cro. Car.* 555.

REPRESENTATION, (*repræsentatio.*) Is a representing or standing in the place of another man. There is an heir by representation, where a father dies in the life of the grandfather, leaving a son, who shall inherit his grandfather's estate, before the father's brother, &c. *Bro. Abr.* 303. Also executors and administrators in the personal representations of the deceased, to collect and apply his assets. *Co. Lit.* 209.

REPRIEVE, (from the Fr. *repris*, though Blackstone takes it from *reprendre.*) Signifies to take back or suspend a prisoner from the execution and proceeding of law for that time. *Terms de Ley.* Every judge who hath power to order execution, hath power to grant a reprieve. *Kel.* 4. 2 *Hawk. P. C.* 463. *Wood's Inst.* 662.

REPRISAL, (*reprisale*, or *reprisalia.*) Is a species of remedy by the mere act of the party injured. This happens, when any one hath deprived another of his property in goods or chattels personal, or wrongfully detains one's wife, child, or servant; in which case the owner of the goods, and the husband, parent, or master, may lawfully claim and retake them, wherever he happens to find them, so it be not in a riotous manner, or attended with a breach of the peace. 3 *Inst.* 134. *Hal. Anal.* § 46. See also *Recaption* and *Letters of Marque.*

REPRISES, (Fr. *resumptions*, or a taking back.) Is used for deductions and payments out of a manor or lands, as rent-charges, annuities, &c. Therefore when we speak of the clear yearly value of a manor or estate or land, we say it is so much per annum besides all reprises. *Cowell.*

REPUBLICATION. See *Will.*

REPUGNANT, (*repugnans.*) Contrary to any thing said before: and repugnancy in deeds, grants, indictments, verdicts, &c. make them void. 3 *Nels.* 135. *Jenk. Cent.* 251. 256.

Thus, where an award was, that each should give the other a general release within four days after the award; proviso, that if either disliked the award within twenty days after made, and should pay to the other within the said twenty days ten shillings, that then the arbitrement should be void, the proviso was held repugnant. *Cro. Eliz.* 291.

REPUTATION, (*reputatio.*) That is not reputation which this or that man says, but that which generally hath been, and many men have said or thought. 1. *Leon.* 15. Land may be reputed parcel of a manor, though not really so. 1 *Ventr.* 51. 2 *Mod.* 69. 3 *Nels. Abr.* 137. And there is a parish and office in reputation, &c.

REPUTATION, or GOOD FAME. The security of reputation or good name from the arts of detraction and slander, is one of the rights to which every man is intitled, by reason and natural justice. Therefore, if a man maliciously and falsely utter any slander or false tale of another, which may either endanger him in law, by impeaching him of some heinous crime, as to say that a man hath poisoned another, or is perjured, *Finch. L.* 185; or which may exclude him from society, as to charge him with having an infectious disease; or which may impair or hurt his trade or livelihood, as to call a tradesman a bankrupt, a physician a quack, or a lawyer a knave, *Finch. L.* 186. This is such an offence, that the party may recover damages for the injury sustained, in an action upon the case.

Also a man's reputation may be affected by printed or written libels, pictures, signs, and the like, which set him in an odious and ridiculous light, and thereby diminish his reputation. For these there are two remedies, one by indictment, and another by action. The former for the public offence, inasmuch as every libel has a tendency to break the peace, or provoke others to break it; and it is immaterial whether the matter be true or false; and therefore the defendant, on an indictment for publishing a libel, is not allowed to alledge the truth of it by way of justification, 5 *Rep.* 125. But in the remedy by action on the case, which is to repair the party in damages for the injury done him, the defendant may, as for words spoken, justify the truth of the facts, and shew that the plaintiff has received no injury at all. 11 *Mod.* 99. As in regard to words spoken, (see *Scandal,*) the same rule holds with regard to libels by writing or printing, and the civil actions consequent thereupon; but as to signs or pictures, it seems necessary also to shew, by proper innuendoes and averments of the defendant's meaning, the import and application of the scandal, and that the same special damage has followed; otherwise it cannot appear, that such libel by picture was understood to be levelled at the plaintiff, or that it was attended with any actionable consequences.

A man's reputation may also be injured by preferring malicious indictments or prosecutions against him. For this, however, the law has given a very adequate remedy in damages, either by an action of conspiracy, which cannot be brought but against two at the least; or, which is the more usual way, by a special action on the case for a false and malicious prosecution. *F. N. B.* 116.

REQUEST. Where one is to do a collateral thing, agreed on making a contract, there ought to be a request to do it. 2 *Lill. Abr.* 464. *Cro. Eliz.* 74. 1 *Saund.* 33. 1 *Lev.* 289.

And if a debt or duty does not accrue on a promise, until request made, the statute of limitations runs from the time of the request only, and not from the time of the precedent promise. *Cro. Car.* 98.

And it must be where a thing is done on request, or reasonable request. *Dyer* 218. *Cro. Car.* 176. 3 *Nels. Abr.* 140. 142.

REQUESTS. See *Court of Requests.*

RERE COUNTY. Writs shall be delivered in the full, or rere county. *Stat.* 2 *Ed.* 3. *cap.* 5. Vide *Rier County.*

RERE FIEFS. In the Scotch law, inferior feudatories, who hold their lands under an obligation to make such returns in service, corn, cattle, or money, as might enable the chief feudatories to attend their military duties without distraction. *Wright* 30.

RESCEIT, (*Receptio.*) Is an admission or receiving of a third person to plead his right in a cause formerly commenced between two other persons; as where an action is brought against tenant for life or years, or any other particular tenant, and he makes default, in such case he in reversion may move that he may be received to defend his right, and to plead with demandant. *Cowell.*

Resceit is likewise applied to the admittance of a plea, where the controversy is between the same two persons. *Broke* 205. *Co. Lit.* 192. *Nels.* 3 *Abr.* 146.

RESCEIT OF HOMAGE, (*Receptis Homogii,*) The lord's receiving homage of his tenant, at his admission to the land. *Kitch.* 148.

RESCUE. Is the forcibly and knowingly freeing another from an arrest or imprisonment; and it is generally the same offence in the stranger so rescuing, as it would have been in a gaoler to have voluntarily permitted an escape. A rescue therefore of one apprehended for felony, is felony, for treason, treason; and for a misdemesnor, a misdemesnor also. But here likewise, as upon voluntary escapes, the principal must first be attainted or receive judgment before the rescuer can be punished: and for the same reason, because perhaps in fact it may turn out that there has been no offence committed. By statute 11 *Geo.* 2. c. 26, and 24 *Geo.* 2. c. 40, if five or more persons assemble to rescue any retailers of spirituous liquors, or to assault the informers against them, it is felony, and subject to transportation for seven years. By the statute 16 *Geo.* 2. c. 31. to convey to any prisoner in custody for treason or felony any arms, instruments of escape, or disguise, without the knowledge of the gaoler, though no escape be attempted, or any way to assist such prisoner to attempt an escape, though no escape be actually made, is felony, and subjects the offender to transportation for seven years: or if the prisoner be in custody for petit larceny or other inferior offence, or charged with a debt of 100*l.* it is then a misdemesnor, punishable with fine and imprisonment. And by several special statutes, (6 Geo. 1. c. 23, *transportation*; 9 Geo. 1. c. 22, *black act*; 8 Geo. 2. c. 20, *destroying turnpikes*; 19 Geo. 2. c. 34, *smuggling*; 25 Geo. 2, c. 37, *murder*; 27 Geo. 2. c. 15, *black act*) to rescue, or attempt to rescue any person committed for the offences enumerated in these acts, is felony without benefit of clergy; and to rescue, or attempt to rescue the body of a felon executed for murder, is single felony, and transportation for seven years; and even if any person be charged with any of the offences against the Black Act, 9 *Geo.* 1. c. 22. and being required by the order of the privy council to surrender himself, neglects so to do for forty days, both he and all that knowingly conceal, aid, abet, or succour him, are felons without benefit of clergy.

When goods are distrained, they are in the custody of the law; and the taking them back by force is looked upon as an atrocious injury, and denominated a *rescous;* for which the distreinor has a remedy in damages, either by writ of rescous, (*F. N. B.* 101.) in case they were going to the pound; or by writ *de parco fracto*, or pound breach, (*F. N. B.* 100), in case they were actually impounded. He may also at his option bring an action on the case for this injury; and shall therein, if the distress were taken for rent, recover treble damages. Stat. 2 *W. & M. sess.* 1. *c.* 5.

The term rescous is likewise applied to the forcible delivery of a defendant, when arrested, from the officer who is carrying him to prison. In which circumstances the plaintiff has a similar remedy by action on the case, or of rescous, 6 *Mod.* 211. Or, if the sheriff makes a return of such rescous to the court out of which the process issued, the rescuer will be punished by attachment *Cro. Jac.* 419. *Salk.* 586.

RESCUSSOR. The party who commits such a rescous. *Cro. Jac.* 419. *Cowell.*

RESEISER, (*Reseisire.*) Is retaking lands into the hands of the king, where a general livery or ouster le main was formerly misused, contrary to the order of law. *Staundf. Prærog.* 26. *Cowell.*

RESERVATION, (*Reservatio.*) Is where a man lets or parts with his land, but reserves a rent out of it. *Co. Lit.* 143.

A reservation is sometimes also a saving or exception of part of the thing granted, as of timber and other trees, mines of coal, lead, and the like. The proper place for a reservation is next after the limitation of the estate. *Co. Lit.* 47.

RESIANCE, (*Resiantia.*) Signifies a man's abode or continuance; hence comes the participle resiant, that is, continually dwelling or abiding in any place; and is all one with residence. *Old Nat. Br.* 85. *Kitch.* 33.

RESIANT-ROLLS, *i. e.* Rolls containing the resiants names of a tithing, &c. which are to be called over by the steward on holding courts leet. *Comp. Court. Keep.*

RESIDENCE, (*Residentia.*) One of the great duties incumbent on clergymen is, that they be resident on their livings; and on the first erecting parochial churches, every clergyman was obliged to reside on his benefice, for reading of prayers, preaching, &c. by the laws and canons of the church. 6 *Rep.* 21. *Cro. Eliz.* 580.

And by statute 21 *Hen.* 8. c. 13. persons wilfully absenting themselves from their benefices for one month together, or two months in the year, incur a penalty of five pounds to the king, and five pounds to any person that would sue for the same, except chaplains to the king, or others therein mentioned, during their attendance in the household of such as retain them; and also except all heads of houses, magistrates, and professors in the universities, and all students there under thirty years of age, residing there, *bona fide*, for study.

But by 43 *Geo.* 3. *c.* 84, and 43 *Geo.* 3. c. 109, the penalty for non-residence under 21 Hen. 8. c. 13. is repealed, and certain permanent regulations on the subject made. See *Ecclesiastical Persons* and *Non-residence.*

RESIDUARY LEGATEE. Is he to whom the residuum of the estate is left by will. 6 *Hen.* 7. 1 *Chan. Rep.* 238. *Show.* 26.

RESIDUE *of Intestate's Estates.* By the statute 22 and 23 *Car.* 2. c. 10. explained by 29 *Car.* 2. c. 30. it is enacted, that the surplusage of intestate's estates, (except of femes covert, which are left as at common law,) shall, after the expiration of one full year from the death of the intestate, be distributed in the following manner. One third shall go to the widow of the intestate, and the residue in equal proportions to his children, or if dead, to their representatives, that is, their lineal descendants: if there are no children or legal representatives subsisting, then a moiety shall go to the widow, and a moiety to the next of kindred in equal degree and their representatives: if no widow, the whole shall go to the children: if neither widow nor children, the whole shall be distributed among the next of kin in equal degree and their representatives: but no representatives are admitted, among collaterals, farther than the children of the intestate's brothers and sisters.

RESIGNATION, (*Resignatio.*) Is the yielding up of an ecclesiastical dignity or benefice; and every parson who resigns a benefice, must make the resignation to his superior; as an incumbent to the bishop, a bishop to the archbishop, and an archbishop to the king, as supreme ordinary; and a donative is to be resigned to the patron, not the ordinary, for in that case the clerk received his living immediately from the patron. 1 *Rep.* 137.

But if any incumbent corruptly resign his benefice, or take any reward for resigning the same, he shall forfeit double the value of the sum, &c. given, and the party giving it be incapable to hold the living. Stat. 31 *Eliz.* cap. 6. See also *Simony.*

RESIGNATION OF OFFICES. The declaring at an assembly of the corporation that he would hold the place of alderman no longer is a good resignation, especially since the corporation accepted it, and chose another in his place; but till such election he had power to waive his resignation, but not afterwards (2 *Salk.* 433.) And if a man can have no title to the profits of an office, without the admission or confirmation of a superior, there the resignation of that office must be to him. 3 *Nels. Abr.* 158.

RESORT, (*resortum*) the authority or jurisdiction of a court. Dernier resort, the last refuge. *Spelm. Cowell.*

RESPECTU COMPUTI VICECOMITIS HABENDO, a writ for respiting a sheriff's account, directed to the treasurer and barons of the exchequer. *Reg. Orig.* 139.

RESPITE, (*respectus*) a delay, forbearance, or continuation of time. *Glanvil. lib.* 12. c. 9. See *Reprieve.*

RESPITE OF HOMAGE, (*respectus homagii*) such as held in knight service and *in capite*, formerly paid into the exchequer every fifth term some small sum of money to be respited their homage, taken away by the stat. 12 *Car.* 2.

RESPITE OF JURY. See *Jury.*

RESPONDEAS, or RESPONDEAT OUSTER, is a judgment, to answer over to the merits of the cause, &c.; thus, if a demurrer is joined on plea to the jurisdiction, person, or writ, &c. and it be adjudged against defendant, it is a *respondeat ouster. Jenk. Cent.* 306. See *Judgment.*

RESPONDEAT SUPERIOR. If sheriffs of London are insufficient, the mayor and commonalty must answer for them; and *pur insufficience del bailiff d'un liberty, respondeat dominus libertates.* 4 *Inst.* 114. *Stat.* 44. *Ed.* 3. c. 13.

RESPONDENTIA. See *Bottomry.*

RESPONSALIS, (*qui responsum defert*) is he who appears and answers for another in court at a day assigned. *Glan. lib.* 12. c. 1. *Fleta. lib.* 6. c. 21.

RESTITUTION, (*restitutio*) is restoring any thing unjustly taken from another: it signifies also the setting him in possession of lands or tenements, who had been unlawfully disseised of them. *Cro. Just.* 144.

RESTITUTION OF CONJUGAL RIGHTS. The suit for restitution of conjugal rights is a matrimonial cause, which is brought whenever either the husband or wife is guilty of the injury of subtraction, or lives separate from the other without any sufficient reason; in which case the ecclesiastical jurisdiction will compel them to come together again, if either party be weak enough to desire it, contrary to the inclination of the other.

RESTITUTION OF STOLEN GOODS. On a conviction of larceny in particular, the prosecutor shall have restitution of his goods, by virtue of the statute 21 *Hen.* 8. c. 11; for by the common law there was no restitution of goods upon an indictment, because it is at the suit of the king only, and therefore the party was enforced to bring an appeal of robbery, in order to have his goods again. But, it being considered that the party, prosecuting the offender by indictment, deserves to the full as much encouragement as he who prosecutes by appeal, this statute was made, which enacts, that if any person be convicted of larceny by the evidence of the party robbed, he shall have full restitution of his money, goods, and chattels, or the value of them, out of the offender's goods, if he has any, by a writ to be granted by the justices. And the construction of this act having been in great measure conformable to the law of appeals, it has therefore in practice superseded the use of appeals of larceny. For instance: as formerly upon appeals, so now upon indictments of larceny, this writ of restitution shall reach the goods so stolen, notwithstanding the property of them is endeavoured to be altered by sale in market overt. And though this may seem somewhat hard upon the buyer, yet the rule of law is, that "*spoliatus debet, ante omnia, restitui;*" especially when he has used all the diligence in his power to convict the felon. And, since the case is reduced to this hard necessity, that either the owner or the buyer must suffer, the law prefers the right of the owner, who has done a meritorious act by pursuing a felon to condign punishment, to the right of the buyer, whose merit is only negative, that he has been guilty of no unfair transaction. And it is now usual for the court, upon the conviction of a felon, to order (without any writ) immediate restitution of such goods as are brought into court, to be made to the several prosecutors. Or else, secondly, without such writ of restitution, the party may peaceably retake his goods wherever he happens to find them (See *Recaption*) unless a new property be fairly acquired therein. Or, lastly, if the felon be convicted and pardoned, or be allowed his clergy, the party robbed may bring his action of trover against him for his goods, and recover a satisfaction in damages. But such action lies not before prosecution; for so felonies would be made up and healed; and also recaption is unlawful, if it be done with intention to smother or compound the larceny; it then becoming the heinous offence of theft-bote. 1 *Hal. P. C.* 546.

The owner of goods stolen, who has prosecuted the thief to conviction, cannot recover the value of his goods from a person who has purchased them, and sold them again, even with notice of the theft, before conviction. 2 *T. R.* 750.

And if the owner of goods loses them by a fraud, and not by a felony, and afterwards convicts the offender, he is not entitled to restitution, or to retain them, against a person, as a pawnbroker, who has fairly acquired a new right of property in them, 5 *T. R.* 175.

RESTITUTION ON AN INDICTMENT FOR A FORCIBLE ENTRY. An indictment lies for one joint-tenant against another for a forcible entry, and the court of king's bench hath power to award restitution, upon a removal of the indictment by *certiorari*. And per Hardwicke, C. J. there must be a writ of restitution, unless the defendant pleads in a reasonable time. *Rep. Temp. Hard.* 174. *Latch.* 172, 4 *Inst.* 176.

RE-RESTITUTION. A writ of restitution may be granted on motion, if the court see cause to grant it. And on quashing an indictment of forcible entry, the court of B. R. may grant a writ of re-restitution, &c. 2 *Lill. Abr.* 474.

RESTITUTIONE EXTRACTI AB ECCLESIA, a writ to restore a man to the church, which he had recovered for his sanctuary, being suspected of felony. *Reg. Orig.* 69.

RESTITUTIONE TEMPORALIUM, a writ directed to the sheriff to restore the temporalties, or barony of a bishopric to the bishop elected and confirmed. *F. N. B.* 169. 1 *Rol. Abr.* 880.

RESTRAINING STATUTE. See *Title, Statutes*.

RESULTING USE. Whenever the use limited by a deed expires, or cannot vest, it returns back to him who raised it, after such expiration, or during such impossibility, and is stiled a resulting use. As, if a man makes a feoffment to the use of his intended wife for life, with remainder to the use of her first-born son in tail: here, till he marries, the use results back to himself; after marriage, it is executed in the wife for life; and, if she dies without issue, the whole reversion results back to him in fee. *Bacon of Uses*, 350. 1 *Rep.* 120, 2 *Black*, 335. *Com. Dig. tit. Uses* (*K*, 7.)

But there must be an outstanding reversion; for where the whole fee or legal estate is devised away, and no residue left in the grantor, to commence in possession after the determination of the estate granted by him, there can be no resulting trust for the heir at law, (1 *Atk.* 621,) nor where the intention to disinherit the heir is manifest. 3 *Vez. Jun.* 210. *Bro. Ch. Cas.* 492.

RE-SUMMONS, (*resummonitio*) signifies a second summons, or calling a man to answer an action, where the first summons is defeated by any occasion. There is also a writ of re-summons, which issues after parol demurrer. *Cowell.*

RESUMPTION, (*resumptio*) the taking again into the king's hands such lands or tenements, &c. as before, on false suggestion, he had granted by letters patent to any man. *Broke*, 298.

RETAINER OF DEBTS. If a person indebted to another makes his creditor or debtor his executor, or if such creditor obtains letters of administration to his debtor; in these cases the law gives him a remedy for his debt, by allowing him to retain so much as will pay himself before any other creditors whose debts are of equal degree. 1 *Roll. Abr.* 992. *Plowd.* 543, 3 *Black*, 19.

RETAINER OF SERVANTS. The retaining a man's hired servant before his time is expired, is an illegal act; for every master has by his contract purchased, for a valuable consideration, the service of his domestics for a limited time, and the inveigling or hiring his servant, which induces a breach of this contract, is therefore an injury to the master, and for that injury the law has given him a remedy by a special action on the case: and he may also have an action against the servant for the non-performance of his agreement. But if a new master was not apprized of the former contract, no action lies against him, unless he refuses to restore the servant upon demand. *F. N. B.* 167. *Ibid. Winch.* 51.

RETAINING FEE, (*merces retinens*) is a fee given to any serjeant or barrister to retain him; that is, secure his services against the contrary party.

RETALIATION. The *lex talionis*, or law of retaliation, can never be in all cases an adequate or permanent rule of punishment. In general, the difference of persons, place, time, provocation, or other circumstances, may enhance or mitigate the offence; and in such cases retaliation can never be a proper measure of justice. If a nobleman strikes a peasant, all mankind will see, that if a court of justice awards a return of the blow, it is more than a just compensation. On the other hand, retaliation may, sometimes, be too easy a sentence; as, if a man maliciously should put out the remaining eye of him who had lost one before, it is too slight a punishment for the maimer to lose only one of his. Besides, there are very many crimes that will in no shape admit of these penalties, without manifest absurdity and wickedness. Theft cannot be punished by theft, defamation by defamation, forgery by forgery, adultery by adultery, and the like. It was, however, once attempted to introduce into England the law of retaliation, as a punishment for such only as preferred malicious accusations against others; it being enacted by stat. 37 *Edw.* 3. *c.* 18. that "such as preferred any suggestions to the King's great council should put in sureties of taliation;" that is, "to incur the same pain that the other should have had, in case the suggestion were found untrue. But, after one year's experience, this punishment of taliation was rejected, and imprisonment adopted in its stead. *Stat.* 38 *Edw.* 3. *c.* 9. 4 *Black.* 12. 14.

RETENEMENTUM, is a word used for detaining, withholding, or keeping back. *Cowell.*

RETINENTIA, a retinue, or persons retained to a prince or nobleman. *Pat.* 14. *R.* 2. *Cowell.*

RETORNO HABENDO. See *Replevin.*

RETRACTUS AQUÆ, the ebb or return of a tide. *Plac.* 30 *Edw.* 1. *Cowell.*

RETRAXIT, is where the plaintiff cometh in person in court where his action is brought, and saith he will not proceed in it, and this is a bar to that action for ever. And it must be always in person; for if it is by attorney it is error. 8 *Rep.* 58. 3 *Salk.* 245.

A retraxit differs from a nonsuit, in that one is negative, and the other positive: the nonsuit is a default and neglect of the plaintiff, and therefore he is allowed to begin his suit again, upon payment of costs; but a retraxit is an open and voluntary renunciation of his suit, in court, and by this he for ever loses his action. *Ibid.*

RETTE, (Fr.) a charge or accusation. *Stat. West.* 1. *c.* 2.

RETURN, (*returna*, or *retorna*, from the Fr. *retour*, i. e. *redditio*, *recursus*) is most commonly used for the return of writs, which is the certificate of the sheriff of what he hath done touching the execution of any writ directed to him, indorsed on the back of the writ, and delivered into the court whence the writ issued, at the day of the return thereof, in order to be filed. *Stat. Westm.* 2. *c.* 39. 2 *Lil. Abr.* 476.

If the sheriff doth not make a return of a writ, the court will amerce him: so if he makes an insufficient return; and if he makes a false return, the party grieved may have an action on the case against him. *Wood's Inst.* 71.

RETURN-DAYS, are days in term called by that name; or days in bank. See *Term.*

RETURNING FROM TRANSPORTATION, or being seen at large in Great Britain before the expiration of the term for which the offender was ordered to be transported, is a capital offence, and made felony, without benefit of clergy, in all cases, by statutes 4 *Geo.* 1. *c.* 11. 6 *Geo.* 1. *c.* 23. 16 *Geo.* 2. *c.* 15. and 18 *Geo.* 3. *c.* 15. as is also the assisting them to escape from such as are conveying them to the port of transportation. Previous to the 24th *Geo.* 3. *c.* 56. it was thought, that where a convict was pardoned upon condition of transporting himself for life, or a certain number of years, if he did not comply with that condition, he might be remitted to his original sentence, and in some cases that he was subject to no other punishment. But the statute 24 *Geo.* 3. *c.* 56. now includes every possible case by enacting, that "if any offender shall be ordered by the court to be transported, or shall agree to transport himself on certain conditions, either for life, or any number of years, and shall be afterwards at large before the expiration of the term, without lawful cause, in any part of Great Britain or Ireland, he shall, being lawfully convicted thereof, suffer death, without benefit of clergy."

RETURNO HABENDO. See *Replevin.*

RETURNUM AVERIORUM, a judicial writ, the same with *returno habendo. Reg. Judic.* 4.

RETURNUM IRREPLEGIABILE, is a writ judicial, directed to the sheriff for the final restitution or return of cattle to the owner when unjustly taken or distrained, and so found by verdict; and it is granted after a nonsuit in a second deliverance. *Reg. Judic.* 27. *Cowell.*

REVE, or GEREVE, (from the Saxon word *græfa, præfœctus.* Lambard's explication of Saxon words, verb *præfectus*) signifies with us the bailiff of a franchise or manor, especially in the western part of England.: hence *shire-reve* for sheriff. See *Kitchen*, 43. *Cowell.*

REVELACH, rebellion, from *revellare*, to rebel. *Cowell. Blount.*

REVELAND, (domesday-book). The lands here said to have been thane-land, in the time of Edw. 3. and after converted into reveland, seems to have been such land as being reverted to the king after the death of his thane, who had it for life, was not since granted out to any by the king, but rested in charge on the account of the reve or bailiff of the manor, who concealed the land from the auditor, and kept the profit of it, till the surveyors discovered the falsehood, and presented to the king that *furtim aufertur regi.* *Cowell. Blount.*

REVELS, sports of dancing and masking, formerly used in princes' courts, the inns of court, or other noblemen's houses, commonly performed by night; hence master of the revels. *Cowell.*

REVENUE, (Fr.) the yearly rent which accrues to any man from his lands and possessions, and the public revenue arising from customs, excise, stamps, and other taxes.

REVERSAL OF JUDGMENT, is the making it void for error. 2 *Lill. Abr.* 481.

The eldest judge of the court, or, in his absence, the next in seniority, always pronounces the reversal of an erroneous judgment openly in court, on the prayer of the party; but the judge only says, judgment affirmed, or judgment reversed, as the case happens. 2 *Lill.* 482.

REVERSION, (*reversio*, from *revertor*) signifies a returning again. 1 *Inst.* 142.

And an estate in reversion is the residue of an estate left in the grantor, to commence after the determination of some particular estate granted out by him. Sir Edward Coke describes a reversion to be the returning of land to the grantor, or his heirs, after the grant is over. As, if there be a gift in tail, the reversion of the fee is, without any special reservation, vested in the donor by act of law: and so also the reversion, after an estate for life, years, or at will, continues in the lessor; for the fee-simple of all lands must abide somewhere, and if he, who was before possessed of the whole, carves out of it any smaller estate, and grants it away, whatever is not so granted remains in him. A reversion is therefore never created by deed or writing, but arises from construction of law.

In order to assist such persons as have any estate in remainder, reversion, or expectancy, after the death of others, against fraudulent concealments of their deaths, it is enacted by the statute 6 *Ann*, c. 18. that all persons on whose lives any lands or tenements are holden, shall (upon application to the court of chancery, and order made thereupon) once in every year, if required, be produced to the court, or its commissioners; or, upon neglect or refusal, they shall be taken to be actually dead, and the person entitled to such expectant estate may enter upon and hold the lands and tenements, till the party shall appear to be living. *Ord. in Chan.* 69. 3 *Black.* 454.

REVERTER, (formedon in). See *Remainder.*

REVIEW, (bill of). A bill of review may be had upon apparent error in judgment, appearing on the face of the decree; or, by special leave of the court, upon oath made of the discovery of new matter or evidence, which could not possibly be had or used at the time when the decree passed. But no new evidence or matter then in the knowledge of the parties, and which might have been used before, shall be a sufficient ground for a bill of review. 3 *Black.* 454.

REVIEW, (commission of). A commission of review is a commission sometimes granted, in extraordinary cases, to revise the sentence of the court of delegates, when it is apprehended they have been led into a material error. This commission the king may grant, although the statutes 24 and 25 *Henry* 8, declare the sentence of the delegates definitive: because the pope, as supreme head by the canon law, used to grant such commission of review; and such authority, as the pope heretofore exerted, is now annexed to the crown, (4 *Inst.* 341.) by statutes 26 *Hen.* 8. c. 1. and 1 *Eliz.* c. 1. But it is not matter of right, which the subject may demand *ex debito justitiæ*, but merely a matter of favour, and which therefore is often denied; and the sum of 20*l.* must be deposited in court, on bringing this bill, as a security for costs and delay, if the matter be found against the party, &c. 3 *Black.* 67.

REVILING CHURCH ORDINANCES is a positive offence against religion, that affects the established church. See *Religion.*

REVIVAL OF PERSONS HANGED. If, on judgment to be hanged by the neck till dead, the criminal be not thoroughly killed, but revives, the sheriff must hang him again (2 *Hal. P. C.* 412. 2 *Hawk. P. C.* 463.) for the former hanging was no execution of the sentence unless he be dead. *Fitzh. Abr. t. corone*, 335. *Finch, L. A.* 67. 4 *Black.* 399.

REVIVING, a word metaphorically applied to rents and actions, and signifies renewing them after they are extinguished; such as the revival of a cause of action barred by the statute of limitations, by making a new promise.

REVIVOR, (bill of). When a bill hath been exhibited in equity against any one, and either party dies, a bill of revivor must be brought, praying the former proceedings to stand revived. See *Bill in Equity*.

REVOCATION, (*revocatio*) signifies the calling back of a thing granted; or a destroying or making void of some deed or instrument that had existence until the act of revocation made it void. 2 *Lil. Abr.* 485.

Letters of attorney, and other personal authorities, under seal, may be revoked by instruments of the same solemnity, viz. by deeds, under seal, by the persons giving the powers; and, as they are revocable in their nature, it has been adjudged that they may be revoked, though they are made irrevocable, (8 *Rep.* 82. *Wood's Inst.* 286) and there ought to be notice to the party; but if once the power be executed, a revocation after will come too late. *Dyer*, 210.

REVOCATIONE PARLIAMENTI, an ancient writ for recalling a parliament; and *anno* 5 *Ed.* 3. the parliament being summoned, was recalled by such writ before it met. *Pryn's Animad. on* 4 *Inst. fol.* 44.

REWARDS. In order to encourage the apprehending of certain felons, rewards and immunities are bestowed on such as bring them to justice, by divers acts of parliament. The statute 4 & 5 *W.* & *M.* c. 8. enacts, that such as apprehend a highwayman, and prosecute him to conviction, shall receive a reward of 40*l.* from the public; to be paid to them (or, if killed in the endeavour to take him, their executors) by the sheriff of the county; besides the horse, furniture, arms, money, and other goods taken upon the person of such robber; with a reservation of the right of any person from whom the same may have been stolen: to which the statute 8 *Geo.* 2. *c.* 16. superadds 10*l.* to be paid by the hundred indemnified by such taking. By statutes 6 & 7 *W.* 3. *c.* 17. and 15 *Geo.* 2. c. 28. persons apprehending and convicting any offender against those statutes, respecting the coinage, shall (in case the offence be treason or felony) receive a reward of 40*l.*; or 10*l.* if it only amount to counterfeiting the copper coin. By statute 10 & 11 *W.* 3. c. 23. any person apprehending and prosecuting to conviction a felon guilty of burglary, housebreaking, horsestealing, or private larceny, to the value of 5*s.* from any shop, warehouse, coach-house, or stable, shall be excused from all parish offices. And by statute 5 *Ann*, *c.* 31. any person so apprehending and prosecuting a burglar, or felonious housebreaker (or, if killed in the attempt, his executors), shall be entitled to a reward of 40*l.** By statute 6 *Geo.* 1. *c.* 23. persons discovering, apprehending, and prosecuting to conviction, any person taking reward for helping others to their stolen goods, shall be entitled to 40*l.* By statute 14 *Geo.* 2. c. 6. explained by 15 *Geo.* 2. c. 34. any person apprehending and prosecuting to conviction such as steal, or kill with intent to steal, any sheep or other cattle specified in the latter of the said acts, shall for every such conviction receive a reward of 10*l.* Lastly, by 16 *Geo.* 2. *c.* 15. and 8 *Geo.* 3. *c.* 15. persons discovering, apprehending, and convicting felons and others being found at large during the term for which they are ordered to be transported, shall receive a reward of 20*l.* The statutes 4 & 5 *W.* & *M.* c. 8. 6 & 7 *W.* 3. c. 17. and 5 *Ann*, c. 31. (together with 3 *Geo.* 1. c. 15. *s.* 4. which directs the method of re-imbursing the sheriffs) are extended to the county palatine of Durham, by statute 14 *Geo.* 3. *c.* 46. See *Approver*, *Accomplice*, *and Stolen Goods.*

REWEY, a term among clothiers, signifying cloth unevenly wrought, or full of rewes. 43 *Eliz.* c. 10.

RHANDIR, a part in the division of Wales, before the conquest: every township comprehended four gavels, and every gavel had four rhandirs, and four houses or tenements constituted every rhandir. *Cowell. Blount.*

RIAL, (from the Span. *reale*, i. e. royal money, because it is stamped with the king's effigies). Here, in England, a rial was a piece of gold coin, current for 10*s.* in the reign of king Henry 6. at which time there were half-rials passing for 5*s.* and quarter-rials, or rial farthings, going for 2*s.* 6*d.* In the beginning of queen Elizabeth's reign, golden rials were coined at 15*s.* a-piece; and 3 *Jac.* 1. there were

* If any person apprehends and prosecutes to conviction any of the felons described by 10 & 11 *W.* 3. *c.* 23. and 5 *Ann*, c. 31. he shall be entitled to a certificate from the judge, which will exempt him from all parish offices in the parish in which the felony was committed. And before it is used for that purpose it may be assigned, that is, sold once, and the assignee or buyer shall be privileged to the same exemption from it. This certificate of exemption, or Tyburn ticket, as it is sometimes called, is the only reward given to the prosecutors of horsestealers, and of felons, who steal to the value of 5*s.* privately from shops, warehouses, coach-houses, and stables.

rose-rials of gold at 30*s.* spur-rials at 15*s.* *Lownd's Essay on Coins, p.* 38. *Cowell.*

RIBAUD, (Fr. *ribauld, ribaldus*) a rogue, vagrant, whoremonger, or person given to all manner of wickedness. *Cowell.*

RICHMOND, (in Yorkshire). Spiritual persons in the archdeaconry of Richmond, shall not exact portions of the deceased's goods. 26 *Hen.* 8. c. 15.

RIDER ROLL, is a schedule, or small piece of parchment, often added to some part of a roll or record. *Cowell.*

RIDGE WASHED KERSEY, Kersey cloth made of fleece wool, washed only on the sheep's back. See *stat.* 35 *Eliz.* c. 10.

RIDING ARMED, with dangerous and unusual weapons, is an offence at common law. 4 *Inst.* 160. See *Affray.*

RIDING-CLERK, is one of the six clerks in Chancery, who in his turn, for one year, keeps the controulment books of all grants that pass the great seal. *Cowell. Blount.*

RIDINGS, are the names of the parts or divisions of Yorkshire, which are three, viz. East Riding, West Riding, and North Riding, mentioned in the stat. 22 *H.* 8. c. 5. And, in indictments for offences in that county, the town and the riding must be expressed, &c. (*West's Symb. p.* 2.) The word riding is a corruption from trithing. 1 *Black.* 116. See *Registry.*

RIENS ARREAR, a plea used in an action of debt for arrearages of account, whereby the defendant alledges that there is nothing in arrear. *Cowell. Blount.*

RIENS PASSE PER LE FAIT, signifies that nothing passes by the deed, and is the form of an exception taken in some cases to an action. *Ibid.*

RIENS PER DESCENT, is the plea of an heir, where he is sued for his ancestor's debt, that he hath no land from him by descent, or assets in his hands. 3 *Cro.* 151.

RIER COUNTY, (*retro comitatus*, from the Fr. *arrear*, i. e. posterior) is opposed to full and open county, and appears to be some public place, which the sheriff appoints for receipt of the king's money, after the end of his county court. 2 *Ed.* 3. c. 5. *Stat. Westm.* 2. c. 38. *Fleta, lib.* 2. c. 57. *Cowell. Blount.*

RIFFLARE, (from the Sax. *riefe, rapina*) is to take away any thing by force; from whence comes our English word rifle. *Leg. Hen.* 1. c. 57. *Cowell.*

RIFFLURA, a slight wound in the flesh. *Fleta. lib.* 1. c. 41. *Cowell.*

RIGHT, (*jus*) in general signification includes not only a right for which a writ of right lies, but also any title or claim, either by virtue of a condition, mortgage, or the like, for which no action is given by law, but only an entry. *Co. Lit. lib.* 3. c. 8. *s.* 445.

RIGHT CLOSE, writ of, (*secundum consuetudinem manerii*) is a writ which lies for the king's tenants in ancient demesne, and others of a similar nature, to try the right of their lands and tenements in the court of the lord exclusively. 3 *Black.* 195. See *Writ of Right.*

RIGHT IN COURT. See *Rectus in Curia.*

RIGHTS. See *Liberties and Rights.*

RINE, (Sax. *ryne*) a water course, or little stream, which rises high with floods. *Cowell.*

RINGA, a military girdle, (from the Sax. *ring*, i. e. *annulus, circulus*, because it was girt round the middle. *Ibid.*

RINGHEAD, an engine used in stretching of cloth. 43 *Eliz.* c. 10.

RINGILDRE, a kind of bailiff or serjeant; and such *rhingyl* signifies in Welsh. *Cowell.*

RIOT. A riot seems to be a tumultuous disturbance of the peace by three persons, or more, assembling together of their own authority, with an intent mutually to assist one another against any who shall oppose them, in the execution of some enterprize of a private nature, and afterwards actually executing the same in a violent turbulent manner, to the terror of the people, whether the act intended was of itself lawful or unlawful. *Hawk. P. C.* 155. c. 65. *s.* 1.

A RIOT seems to be, according to the general opinion, a disturbance of the peace by persons assembling together with an intent to do a thing which, if it be executed, will make them rioters, and actually making a motion towards the execution thereof; but, by some books, the notion of a riot is confined to such assemblies only as are occasioned by some grievance common to all the company, as the inclosure of land in which they all claim a right of common, &c. However, in as much as it generally agrees with a riot, as to all the rest of the above-mentioned particulars, requisite to constitute a riot, except only in this, that it may be a complete offence without the execution of the intended enterprize, it seems not to require any farther explication. *Hawk. P. C.* 158. c. 65. *s.* 8.

An unlawful assembly,* according to

---

* Nearly related to this head of riots, is the offence of tumultuous petitioning, which was carried to an enormous height in the times preceding the grand rebellion. Wherefore by the statute 13 *Car.* 2. *st.* 1. c. 5. it is enacted, that not more than twenty names shall be signed to any petition to the king, or either house of parliament, for any alteration of matters established by law in church or state, unless the contents thereof be previously approved, in the country, by three justices, or the majority of the grand jury at the assises or quarter-sessions; and, in London,

the common opinion, is a disturbance of the peace by persons barely assembling together, with an intention to do a thing, which, if it was executed, would make them rioters, but neither actually executing it, nor making a motion toward the execution of it; but this seems to be much too narrow a definition; for any meeting whatsoever of great numbers of people, with such circumstances of terror, as cannot but endanger the public peace, and raise fears and jealousies among the king's subjects, seems properly to be called an unlawful assembly; as where great numbers, complaining of a common grievance, meet together armed in a warlike manner, in order to consult together concerning the most proper means for the recovery of their interests; for no one can foresee what may be the event of such an assembly. *Hawk. P. C.* 158. *c.* 65. *s.* 9.

But if a man be menaced or threatened that if he comes to the house of *B.* or to *W.* that he shall be beat, he cannot make an assembly of people to assist him to go there, and this in safeguard of his person; for he need not go there, and he may have remedy by surety of the peace. 1 *Hawk.* c. 65. *s.* 10.

These offences are either felonious, or not felonious. The felonious offences are by virtue of the following statutes:—

1. The riotous assembling of twelve persons, or more, and not dispersing upon proclamation. This was first made high treason by statute 3 & 4 *Edw.* 6. *c.* 5. when the king was a minor, and a change in religion to be effected: but that statute was repealed by statute 1 *Mar. c.* 1. among the other treasons created since 25 *Edw.* 3. though the prohibition was in substance re-enacted, with an inferior degree of punishment, by statute 1 *Mar. st.* 2. *c.* 12. which made the same offence a single felony. These statutes specified and particularized the nature of the riots they were meant to suppress; as, for example, such as were set on foot with intention to offer violence to the privy council, or to change the laws of the kingdom, or for certain other specific purposes: in which cases, if the persons were commanded by proclamation to disperse, and they did not, it was by the statute of *Mary* made felony, but within the benefit of clergy; and also the act indemnified the peace-officers, and their assistants, if they killed any of the mob in endeavouring to suppress such riot. This was thought a necessary security in that sanguinary reign, when popery was intended to be re-established, which was like to produce great discontents: but at first it was made only for a year, and was afterwards continued for that queen's life. And by statute 1 *Elizabeth*, *c.* 16. when a reformation in religion was to be once more attempted, it was revived and continued during her life also, and then expired. From the accession of James the first to the death of queen Anne, it was never once thought expedient to revive it: but, in the first year of George the first, it was judged necessary, in order to support the execution of the act of settlement, to renew it, and at one stroke to make it perpetual, with large additions. For, whereas the former acts expressly defined and specified what should be accounted a riot: the statute 1 *Geo.* 1. *c.* 5. enacts, generally, that if any twelve persons are unlawfully assembled, to the disturbance of the peace, and any one justice of the peace, sheriff, under-sheriff, or mayor of a town, shall think proper to command them by proclamation, to disperse, if they contemn his orders, and continue together for one hour afterwards, such contempt shall be felony, without benefit of clergy. And farther, if the reading of the proclamation be by force opposed, or the reader be in any manner wilfully hindered from the reading of it, such opposers and hinderers are felons without benefit of clergy: and all persons to whom such proclamation ought to have been made, and knowing of such hinderance, and not dispersing, are felons, without benefit of clergy. There is the like indemnifying clause, in case any of the mob be unfortunately killed in the endeavour to disperse them, being copied from the act of queen Mary. And, by a subsequent clause of the new act, if any person, so riotously assembled, begin even before proclamation to pull down any church, chapel, meeting-house, dwelling-house, or out-houses, they shall be felons, without benefit of clergy. And, in another clause of the same act, persons injured by any buildings being demolished by a riotous assembly, may recover damages in an action against the hundred. And it was determined, after the riots in 1780, that the owners of houses might recover damages also for the destruction of furniture, or for any injury to their property done at the same

---

by the lord mayor, aldermen, and common-council, in common-council assembled:* and that no petition shall be delivered by a company of more than ten persons, on pain, in either case, of incurring a penalty not exceeding 100*l.* and three months imprisonment.

* It is only under this statute that the corporation of London, since the restoration, have usually taken the lead in petitions to parliament for the alteration of any established law; but it certainly does not warrant any petition from what is called the common-hall.

time that the buildings were demolished, or were in part pulled down. *Doug*. 673.

The punishment of unlawful assemblies, if to the number of twelve, we have just seen, may be capital, according to the circumstances that attend it; but, from the number of three to eleven, is by fine and imprisonment only. The same is the case in riots and routs by the common law; to which the pillory, in very enormous cases, has been sometimes superadded. And by the statute 13 *Hen*. 4. *c*. 7. any two justices, together with the sheriff or under-sheriff of the county, may come with the *posse comitatus*, if need be, and suppress any such riot, assembly, or rout, arrest the rioters, and record upon the spot the nature and circumstances of the whole transaction; which record alone shall be a sufficient conviction of the offenders. In the interpretation of which statute it hath been holden, that all persons, noblemen and others, except women, clergymen, persons decrepid, and infants under fifteen, are bound to attend the justices in suppressing a riot, upon pain of fine and imprisonment; and that any battery, wounding, or killing the rioters, that may happen in suppressing the riot, is justifiable. So that our ancient law, previous to the modern riot act, seems pretty well to have guarded against any violent breach of the public peace; especially as any riotous assembly on a public or general account, as to redress grievances or pull down all inclosures, and also resisting the king's forces, if sent to keep the peace, may amount to overt acts of high treason, by levying war against the king.

RIPARIA, (from *ripa*, a bank of a river) is a water running between the banks. *Magn. Chart. c*. 5. *Westm*. 2. *c*. 47. 2 *Inst*. 478.

RIPIERS, (*riparii, a fiscella, qua in devehendis piscibus utuntur, Anglice*, a rip). those that bring fish from the sea-coast to the inner parts of the land. *Cowell. Blount*.

RIPPERS, reapers, or cutters down of corn; and rip-towel was a gratuity or reward given to customary tenants when they had reaped their lord's corn. *Ibid*.

RIVAGIUM, (*rivage*, or *riverage*) a duty formerly paid to the king on some rivers for the passage of boats or vessels. *Ibid*.

RIVEARE. To have the liberty of a river for fishing and fowling. *Pat*. 2. *Ed*. 1. *Cowell. Blount*.

RIVERS. For annoyances in rivers, either positively by actual obstructions, or negatively, by want of reparations, the persons so obstructing, or such individuals as are bound to repair and cleanse them, or (in default of these last) the parish at large, may be indicted, and distrained to repair and amend them, and in some cases fined. 4 *Black*. 167.

And to pull down or destroy any lock, sluice, or floodgate, erected by authority of parliament on a navigable river, or rescuing any person in custody for the same, is made felony, without benefit of clergy, by 8 *Geo*. 2. *c*. 20.; and it may be inquired of and tried in any adjacent county, as if the fact had been therein committed.

By the statute 4 *Geo*. 3. *c*. 12. maliciously to damage or destroy any banks, sluices, or other works on such navigable river, to open the floodgates, or otherwise obstruct the navigation, is again made felony, punishable with transportation for seven years.

ROBA, a robe, coat, or garment; and those who *robas accipiebant* of another, are accounted of his family. *Walsingh*. 267. *Cowell. Blount*.

ROBBERY, (*robaria*). Robbery is a felony by the common law, committed by a violent assault upon the person of another, by putting him in fear, and taking from his person his money, or other goods of any value whatsoever. 3 *Inst*. 68. *c*. 16.

And this offence was called robbery, either because they bereaved the true man of some of his robes or garments, or because his money or goods were taken out of some part of his garment or robe about his person. *Co*. 3 *Inst*. c. 16. See *Highway Larceny, Hue-and-Cry, and Hundred*.

ROBBERS, (*Robatores*.) Are interpreted to be mighty thieves by Lambard in his Eiren. lib. 2. c. 6. *Cowell. Blount*.

ROBBERSMEN, or ROBERDSMEN. Were a sort of great thieves mentioned in the statutes 5 Edw. III. c. 14. and 7 R. II. c. 5. of whom Sir Edward Coke says, that Robin Hood lived in the reign of king Richard I. on the borders of England and Scotland, by robbery, burning of houses, rapine and spoil, &c. and that these Roberdsmen took name from him. 3 *Inst*. 197.

ROCHET. Is that linen garment which is worn by bishops, gathered at the wrists, and differs from a surplice, for that hath open sleeves hanging down, but a rochet hath close sleeves. *Lindewode*, lib. 3. tit. 27. *Cowell*.

ROD, (*Roda terræ*.) A measure of sixteen feet and a half long, otherwise called a perch. *Cowell*.

ROD-KNIGHTS, (from the Sax. *Rad*. i. e. *Equitatio & Cnys, Famulus, quasi Ministri Equitantes*.) Certain servitors who held their land by serving their lords on horseback. *Bract. lib*. 2. *c*. 35. *Cowell*.

ROGATION-WEEK, (*Dies Rogationum Robigalia*.) Is a time so called, because of the special devotion of prayer and fasting then enjoined by the church for a preparative to the remembrance of Christ's ascension. *Cowell.*

ROGUE, (*Fr.*) An idle sturdy beggar. See *Vagrants.*

ROGUS, (*Lat.*) A great fire, wherein dead bodies were burned; sometimes taken for a pile of wood. *Cowell.*

ROLL, (*Rotulus.*) Is a schedule of parchment that may be turned up with the hand in the form of a pipe, *Staundf. P. C.* 11; and on which all the pleadings, memorials, and acts of courts are entered and filed with the proper officer; after which they become records of the court. 2 *Lill. Abr.* 491.

ROLL OF COURT, (*Rotulus curiæ.*) The court-roll in a manor, wherein the names, rents, and services of the tenants were copied and inrolled. Per rotulum curiæ tenere, by copyhold. *Cowell. Blount.*

ROLLS OFFICE OF THE CHANCERY. There is an office called the Rolls Office in Chancery-lane, anciently called *Domus Conservorum*, which contains all the rolls and records of the high court of chancery, the master whereof is the second person in the chancery, &c. See *Master of the Rolls. Ibid.*

ROLLS OF THE EXCHEQUER, are of several kinds, as the great Wardrobe Roll, the Cofferer's Roll, the Subsidy Roll, &c. *Ibid.*

ROLLS OF PARLIAMENT. The manuscript registers of the proceedings of our old parliaments. *Ibid.*

ROLLS OF THE TEMPLE. In the two temples there was anciently a roll called the Calves-head Roll, wherein every bencher, barrister, and student, was taxed yearly at so much to the cook and other officers of the houses, in consideration of a dinner of calves heads provided in Easter term. *Orig. Jurid.* 199. *Cowell.*

ROMAN CATHOLICS. The Roman Catholics or Papists, might, as well as the Protestant Dissenters, be generally tolerated, provided their separation from the established church was founded only upon difference of opinion in religion, and their principles did not also extend to a subversion of the civil government. For if once they could be brought to renounce the supremacy of the Pope, they might quietly enjoy their seven sacraments, their purgatory, and auricular confession; their worship of reliques and images; nay, even their transubstantiation. But while they acknowledge a foreign ecclesiastical power superior to the sovereignty of the kingdom, they cannot complain if the laws of that kingdom will not treat them upon the footing of good subjects. 4 *Black.* 54.

The laws in force against the Papists, previous to 18 Geo. 3. c. 60, and 31 Geo. 3. c. 32. may be divided into three classes: first, persons professing popery; secondly, popish recusants convict; and thirdly, popish priests.

1. Persons professing the popish religion, besides the penalties for not frequenting their parish church, are disabled from taking their lands either by descent or purchase, after eighteen years of age, until they renounce their errors: they must, at the age of twenty-one, register their estates before acquired, and all future conveyances and wills relating to them; they are incapable of presenting to any advowson, or granting to any other person any avoidance of the same; they may not keep or teach any school under pain of perpetual imprisonment; and, if they willingly say or hear mass, they forfeit the one two hundred, the other one hundred marks, and each shall suffer a year's imprisonment. Thus much for persons, who, from the misfortune of family prejudices or otherwise, have conceived an unhappy attachment to the Romish church from their infancy, and publicly profess its errors. But if any evil industry is used to rivet these errors upon them, if any person sends another abroad to be educated in the popish religion, or to reside in any religious house abroad for that purpose, or contributes to their maintenance when there; both the sender, the sent, and the contributor, are disabled to sue in law or equity, to be executor or administrator to any person, to take any legacy or deed of gift, and to bear any office in the realm, and shall forfeit all their goods and chattels, and likewise all their real estate for life. And where these errors are also aggravated by apostacy or perversion, where a person is reconciled to the see of Rome, or procures others to be reconciled, the offence amounts to high treason.

2. Popish recusants, convicted in a court of law of not attending the service of the church of England, are subject to the following disabilities, penalties, and forfeitures, over and above those before mentioned. They are considered as persons excommunicated: they can hold no office or employment; they must not keep arms in their houses, but the same may be seized by the justices of the peace; they may not come within ten miles of London, on pain of 100*l.*; they can bring no action at law, or suit in equity; they are not permitted to travel above five miles from home, unless by licence, upon pain of forfeiting all their goods; and they may not come to court under pain of 100*l.* No marriage or burial of such recusant, or baptism of his child, shall be had otherwise than by the ministers of the church of England, under other severe penalties. A married woman, when recusant, shall forfeit two-thirds of her dower or jointure, may not be execu-

trix or administratrix to her husband, nor have any part of his goods; and during the coverture may be kept in prison, unless her husband redeems her at the rate of 10*l.* a month, or the third part of all his lands. And lastly, as a feme-covert recusant may be imprisoned, so all others must, within three months after conviction, either submit and renounce their errors, or, if required so to do by four justices, must abjure and renounce the realm: and if they do not depart, or if they return without the king's licence, they shall be guilty of felony, and suffer death as felons without benefit of clergy. There is also an inferior species of recusancy, (refusing to make the declaration against popery, enjoined by stat. 30 *Car.* 2. *st.* 2. when tendered by the proper magistrate,) which, if the party resides within ten miles of London, makes him an absolute recusant convict; or, if at a greater distance, suspends him from having any seat in parliament, keeping arms in his house, or any horse above the value of five pounds. This was till lately the state, by the laws now in being, of a lay papist.*

3. The remaining species or degree, viz. popish priests, are in a still more dangerous condition. For by statute 11 & 12 *W.* 3. *c.* 4. popish priests or bishops celebrating mass, or exercising any part of their functions in England, except in the houses of ambassadors, are liable to perpetual imprisonment. And by the statute 27 *Eliz.* c. 2. any popish priest, born in the dominions of the crown of England, who shall come over hither from beyond sea, (unless driven by stress of weather, and tarrying only a reasonable time (3 *Raym.* 377, *Latch.* 1.) or shall be in England without conforming and taking the oaths, is guilty of high treason; and all persons harbouring him are guilty of felony without the benefit of clergy.

These rigorous laws against Papists are rather to be accounted for from their history, and the urgency of the times which produced them, than to be approved (upon a cool review) as a standing system of law. The restless machinations of the Jesuits during the reign of Elizabeth, the turbulence and uneasiness of the Papists under the new religious establishment, and the boldness of their hopes and wishes for the succession of the Queen of Scots, obliged the parliament to counteract so dangerous a spirit by laws of a great, and then perhaps necessary severity. The powder treason, in the succeeding reign, struck a panic into James I. which operated in different ways: it occasioned the enacting of new laws against the Papists; but deterred him from putting them in execution. The intrigues of Queen Henrietta in the reign of Charles I., the prospect of a popish successor in that of Charles II., the assassination plot in the reign of King William, and the avowed claim of a popish pretender to the crown in that and subsequent reigns, will account for the extension of these penalties at those several periods of our history. But if a time should ever arrive, adds Blackstone, when all fears of a pretender shall have vanished, and the power and influence of the Pope shall become feeble, ridiculous, and despicable, not only in England, but in every kingdom of Europe, it probably would not then be amiss to review and soften these rigorous edicts.

This hath partly been done by statute 18 *Geo.* 3. *c.* 60. with regard to such papists as duly take the oath therein prescribed, of allegiance to his majesty, abjuration of the pretender, renunciation of the pope's civil power, and abhorrence of the doctrines of destroying and not keeping faith with heretics, and deposing or murdering princes excommunicated by authority of the see of Rome: in respect of whom only the statute of 11 & 12 *W.* 3. is repealed, so far as it disables them from purchasing or inheriting, or authorizes the apprehending or prosecuting the popish clergy, or subjects to perpetual imprisonment either them or any teachers of youth. Also by the statute 31 *Geo.* 3. *c.* 32. which may be called the toleration act of the Roman Catholics, all the severe and cruel restrictions and penalties above enumerated are removed from those Roman Catholics who are willing to comply with the requisitions of that statute, which are, that they must appear at some of the courts of Westminster, or at the quarter-sessions held for the county, city, or place where they shall reside, and shall make and subscribe a declaration, that they profess the Roman Catholic religion, and also an oath which is exactly similar to that required by 18 Geo. 3. c. 60. the substance of which is stated as above. On this declaration and oath being duly made by any Roman Catholic, the officer of the court shall grant him a certificate; and such officer shall yearly transmit to the privy council lists of all persons who have thus qualified themselves within the year in his respective court. The statute then provides that a Roman Catholic, thus qualified, shall not be prosecuted under any statute for not repairing to a parish church, nor shall he

---

* See a summary of the statutes :—Stat. 23 Eliz. c. 1. 27 Eliz. c. 2. 29 Eliz. c. 6. 35 Eliz. c. 2. 1 Jac. I. c. 4. 3 Jac. I. c. 4 & 5. 7 Jac. I. c. 6. 3 Car. I. c. 3. 25 Car. II. c. 2. 30 Car. II. st. 2. 1 W. & M. c. 9. 15. & 26. 11 & 12 W. III. c. 4. 12 Ann, st. 2. c. 14. 1 Geo. I. st. 2. c. 55. 3 Geo. I. c. 18. 11 Geo. II. c. 17. Under title *Papists.*

be prosecuted for being a papist, nor for attending or performing mass or other ceremonies of the church of Rome; provided that no place shall be allowed for an assembly to celebrate such worship until it is certified to the sessions; nor shall any minister officiate in it, until his name and description are recorded there. And no such place of assembly shall have its doors locked or barred during the time of meeting or divine worship.

And if any Roman Catholic whatever is elected constable, churchwarden, overseer, or into any parochial office, he may execute the same by a deputy, to be approved as if he were to act for himself as principal. But every minister, who has qualified, shall be exempt from serving upon juries, and from being elected into any parochial office. And all the laws for frequenting divine service on Sundays shall continue in force, except where persons attend some place of worship allowed by this statute, or the toleration act of the Dissenters, 1 *W. & M.*

Also if any person disturb a congregation allowed under this act, he shall, as for disturbing a dissenting meeting, be bound over to the next sessions, and upon conviction there shall forfeit 20*l.*

But no Roman Catholic minister shall officiate in any place of worship having a steeple and a bell, or at any funeral in a church or church-yard, or shall wear the habits of his order, except in a place allowed by this statute, or in a private house, where there shall not be more than five persons besides the family. This statute shall not exempt Roman Catholics from the payment of tithes, or other dues, to the church; nor shall it affect the statutes concerning marriages, or any law respecting the succession to the crown. No person, who has qualified, shall be prosecuted for instructing youth, except in an endowed school, or a school in one of the English universities; and except also, that no Roman Catholic schoolmaster shall receive into his school the child of any Protestant father; nor shall any Roman Catholic keep a school until his or her name be recorded as a teacher at the sessions.

But no religious order is to be established; and every endowment of a school or college by a Roman Catholic shall still be superstitious and unlawful. And no person henceforth shall be summoned to take the oath of supremacy, and the declaration against transubstantiation. Nor shall Roman Catholics, who have qualified, be removable from London and Westminster; neither shall any peer, who has qualified, be punishable for coming into the presence, or palace, of the king or queen. And no papists whatever shall be any longer obliged to register their names and estates, or enroll their deeds and wills. And every Roman Catholic, who has qualified, may be permitted to act as a barrister, attorney, and notary.

Roman Catholics, however, cannot sit in either house of parliament, because every member of parliament must take the oath of supremacy, and repeat and subscribe the declaration against transubstantiation. 1 *Black.* 162. Nor can they vote at elections for members for the house of commons, because, before they vote, they must take the oath of supremacy. *Ibid.* 180.

But the Roman Catholics in Ireland are permitted to vote at elections, though they cannot sit in either house of parliament.

ROMA-PEDITÆ. Pilgrims that travel to Rome on foot. *Matt. Paris*, anno 1250. *Cowell.*

ROME, CHURCH OF. Its incroachment of power here was suppressed by stat. 25 Hen. 8. c. 19. See *Papists* and *Præmunire.*

ROME-SCOT, (*Romefeoh vel Romcfee, Romepeny*, alias *denarius Sancti Petri & hearth-peny.*) An annual tribute of one penny from every family, paid yearly to Rome, at the feast of St. Peter ad Vincula, being the first of August, forbidden by Edward III. See *Præmunire.*

ROMNEY-MARSH. Is a large tract of land in the county of Kent, containing 24,000 acres; and is governed by certain ancient and equitable laws of sewers composed by Henry de Bathe, a venerable judge in the reign of king Henry 3; from which laws all commissioners of sewers in England may receive light and direction. 4 *Inst.* 276. The commissioners of sewers, in other parts of England, may act according to the laws and customs of Romney-marsh, or otherwise at their own discretion. 3 *Black. Com.* 74. But they are subject to the discretionary coercion of the court of King's Bench. *Ibid.*

ROOD, or *Holy Rood.* Signifies the Holy Cross. *Cowell.*

ROOD OF LAND, (*Rodata Terræ.*) Is the fourth part of an acre. Stat. 5 *Eliz.* c. 5. See *Rod.*

ROOTS, destroying of. See *Trespass.*

ROPE-DANCERS, &c. are public nuisances, and may, upon indictment, be suppressed and fined. 1 *Hawk. P.C.* 198. 225. See *Theatres.*

ROS. A kind of rushes, which some tenants were obliged, by their tenures, to furnish their lords. *Cowell.*

ROSETUM. A low watery place of reeds and rushes. *Ibid.*

ROSLAND. Heathy land, or ground full of ling; also watery and moorish land. 1 *Inst.* 5.

ROTHER-BEASTS. Oxen, cows, steers, heifers, and such like horned beasts. *Cowell.*

ROTULUS WINTONIÆ. Was an exact survey of all England, *per Comitatus, Centurias, & Decurias*, made by king Alfred, not unlike that of Domesday, because it was of old kept at Winchester among other records of the kingdom; but this roll time hath consumed. *Ingulph. Hist.* 516. *Cowell.*

ROUBLE. Coin in Muscovy, going for 10*s*. sterling. *Merch. Dict. Cowell.*

ROUT. See *Riot.*

ROYAL ASSENT, (*Regius assensus.*) Is that assent which the king gives to a thing formerly done by others, as to the election of a bishop by dean and chapter: which given, then he sends a special writ for the taking of fealty. *F. N. B.* 170. And to a bill passed in both houses of parliament, *Cromp. Jur.* fo. 8.; which assent in parliament being once given, the bill is indorsed with these words, *Le Roy le veult*, i. e. *It pleases the king.* But if he refuse to agree to it, then thus: *Le Roy avisera*, i. e. *The king will advise.* 1 *Black.* 154. 183.

ROYAL FAMILY. See *King.*

ROYALTIES, (*Regalitates.*) See *King.*

ROYNES. Streams, currents, or other usual passages of rivers and running waters. *Cowell.*

RUBRICKS, (*a rubro colore*, because anciently written in red letters) are constitutions of our church, founded upon the statutes of uniformity and public prayer, viz. 5 & 6 *Ed.* 6. c. 1. 1 *Eliz. c.* 2. 13 & 14 *Car.* 2. c. 2.

RUDMAS-DAY, (from the Sax. *Rode*, i. e. *Crux*, and mass-day, i. e. feast-day.) The feast of the Holy-Cross, of which there are two, viz. on the 3d of May, the invention of the cross, and the 14th of September, Holy Rood Day, or the Exaltation of the Cross. *Cowell.*

RULES OF COURT. Attornies are bound to observe the rules of the court, to avoid confusion; also the plaintiff and defendant in a cause are at their peril to take notice of the rules made in court touching the cause between them. 2 *Lill. Abr.* 492. 493.

RUMNEY-MARSH. King Henry the Third granted a charter to Rumney-marsh, in the county of Kent, impowering twenty-four men thereunto chosen to make distresses equally upon all those who have lands and tenements in the said marsh, to repair the walls and water-gates of the same, against the dangers of the sea. And there are several laws and customs observed in the said marsh, established by ordinance of justices thereto appointed, in the 42d year of king Henry 3. 16 Edw. 1. 33 Edw. 3. &c. See *Romney-marsh.*

RUMOURS. Spreading such as are false, is criminal and punishable by common law. 1 *Hawk. P. C.* 234. See *False News.*

RUNCARIA, (from *Runca.*) Land full of brambles and briars. 1 *Inst.* fol. 5. *a.*

RUNCILUS and RUNCINUS. Used in Domesday for a load-horse or a sumpter-horse, and sometimes for a cart-horse. *Cowell.*

RUNLET. Is a measure of wine, oil, &c. containing eighteen gallons and a half. 1 *R.* 3. c. 13.

RUNNERS OF FOREIGN GOODS. Who to be deemed so, and how punished. See 8 *Geo.* 1. c. 18. under *Customs.*

RUNNING *away with Women.* See *Forcible Marriage.*

RUPTARII. Were soldiers, or rather robbers, called also *rutarii*; and *rutta* was a company of robbers. Hence we derive the word rout and bankrupt. *Cowell.*

RUPTURA. Arable land, or ground broke up, as used in ancient charters. *Ibid.*

RURAL DEANS, are very ancient officers of the church, but almost grown out of use, though their deaneries still subsist as an ecclesiastical division of the diocese or archdeaconry: they seem to have been deputies of the bishop planted all round his diocese, the better to inspect the conduct of the parochial clergy, to inquire into and report dilapidations, and to examine the candidates for confirmation, and armed in minuter matters with an inferior degree of judicial and coercive authority. *Kennet's Par. Ant.* 633. *Gibs. Cod.* 972. 1550.

RURAL DEANRY. As every diocese is divided into archdeaconries, (of which there are sixty), so each archdeaconry is divided into rural deanries, which are the circuit of the archdeacon's and rural deans jurisdiction: and every deanry is divided into parishes. 1 *Black.* 111.

RUSCA. A tub or barrel of butter. *Cowell.*

RUSCATIA. The place where kneeholm or broom grows. *Co. Lit.* 5.

RUSTICI. The churls, clowns, or inferior country tenants, who held cottages and lands by the services of ploughing and other labours of agriculture for the lord. The land of such ignoble tenure was called by the Saxons Gafalland, as afterwards socage tenure, and was sometimes distinguished by the name of terra rusticorum. *Paroch. Antiq.* 136. *Cowell.*

RYDER. If a new clause is added to a bill upon its third reading, it is done by tacking a separate piece of parchment on the bill, which is called a ryder. *Noy* 84.

S

SABAIA. Poor small beer. *Lit. Dict.*

SABBATARIUS. A Sabbatarian, or Jew; of or belonging to the Sabbath. *Cowell.*

SABBATH. Profanation of the Lord's day, vulgarly, but improperly, called sabbath-breaking, is a ninth offence against God and religion, punished by the municipal law of England. For, besides the notorious indecency and scandal of permitting any secular business to be publicly transacted on that day, in a country professing christianity, and the corruption of morals which usually follows its profanation, the keeping one day in seven holy, as a time of relaxation and refreshment as well as for public worship, is of admirable service to a state, considered merely as a civil institution. It humanizes by the help of conversation and society the manners of the lower classes, which would otherwise degenerate into a sordid ferocity and savage selfishness of spirit; it enables the industrious workman to pursue his occupation in the ensuing week with health and cheerfulness; it imprints on the minds of the people that sense of their duty to God, so necessary to make them good citizens, but which yet would be worn out and defaced by an unremitted continuance of labour, without any stated times of recalling them to the worship of their Maker. And therefore the laws of king Athelstan (c. 24) forbad all merchandizing on the Lord's day, under very severe penalties. 4 *Black.* 62.

By the statute 27 Hen. VI. c. 5, no fair or market shall be held on the principal festivals, Good Friday, or any Sunday, (except the four Sundays in harvest,) on pain of forfeiting the goods exposed to sale.

And by the statute 1 Car. I. c. 1. "no person shall assemble out of their own parishes, for any sport whatsoever upon this day; nor, in their parishes, shall use any bull or bear baiting, interludes, plays, or other unlawful exercises or pastimes, on pain that every offender shall pay 3*s*. 4*d*. to the poor." This statute, however, does not prohibit, but rather impliedly allows, any innocent recreation or amusement within their respective parishes, even on the Lord's day, after divine service is over. 4 *Black.* 63.

But by 1 *Jac.* I. c. 22. no shoemaker shall shew, to the intent to put to sale any shoes, boots, buskins, startops, or pentofles, upon the Sunday, on pain of 3*s*. 4*d*. a pair, and the value thereof to be recovered at the assises, or sessions; one third to the king, one third to him who will sue, and one third to the town or vill. *s.* 28. c. 46. 50.

By 3 *Car.* I. c. 2. no carrier with horses or waggons, nor carman with carts, nor drover with cattle, shall travel upon the Lord's day, upon pain of 20*s*.; or if any butcher shall kill or sell, he shall forfeit 6*s*. 8*d*. to be recovered on the view of or before one justice, on the oaths of two witnesses or confession; to be levied by distress and sale, and go to the poor of the parish, rewarding the informer.

Also by 29 *Car.* 2. c. 17. no person shall do any worldly labour or work of their ordinary callings upon the Lord's day, works of necessity and charity excepted, on pain of 5*s*.

And no person shall publicly cry, shew forth, or expose to sale any wares, merchandizes, fruit, herbs, goods or chattels whatsoever upon the Lord's day, upon pain to forfeit the same goods. *s.* 1.

And no drover, post carrier, waggoner, butcher, or higgler, shall travel or come into their inn or lodging upon the Lord's day, upon pain to forfeit 20*s*. And no person shall travel upon the Lord's day with any boat, wherry, lighter, or barge, except upon extraordinary occasions to be allowed by some justice, (except 40 watermen on the Thames, 10 & 11 *Will.* 3. c. 24. s. 14.) upon pain to forfeit 20*s*. s. 2.; which penalties may be recovered on view or confession, or the oaths of two witnesses before one justice, who may levy the same by distress and sale, and for default set the offender in the stocks for two hours, and the penalties are to go to the poor, rewarding the informer in not exceeding one third part thereof. *s.* 2.

But this is not to prohibit the dressing of meat in families, or at inns, cook-shops, or victualling-houses, nor the crying of milk before 9 in the morning and after 4 in the afternoon, s. 3.; nor selling of mackarel before or after divine service, 10 & 11 *Will.* 3. c. 24. s. 14.; nor hackney-coaches, 9 *Ann.* c. 23.; nor any fish carriages passing on Sundays either laden or empty, 2 *Geo.* 3. 15. s. 7. And the prosecution under 29 *Car.* II. c. 7. must be within ten days. *s.* 4.

Persons exercising their calling on a

Sunday are only subject to one penalty; for the whole is but one offence, or one act of exercising, though continued the whole day. *Cowp.* 640.

Bakers were permitted to dress dinners on a Sunday, as a work of necessity. 5 *T. R.* 449. But by 34 Geo. III. c. 61. and 50 *Geo.* 3. c. 73. no master, mistress, journeyman, or other person exercising the trade of a baker, shall on Sunday make or bake any household or other bread, rolls, or cakes, or shall on any part of the said day, excepting between the hours of ten in the forenoon and half past one in the afternoon, on any pretence whatsoever, sell any bread, rolls, or cakes of any sort, or bake or deliver any meat, pudding, pie, tart, or victuals, at any time after half-past one of the clock in the afternoon; and no meat, pudding, pie, tart, or victuals shall be brought to or taken from the bakehouse during the time of divine service; and every person offending against the foregoing regulations, being convicted before any justice within two days, forfeits for the first offence five shillings, for the second ten shillings, for the third and every subsequent offence fifteen shillings, and pay the costs of the prosecution; which penalty, allowing thereout for loss of time to the prosecutor at the rate of 3*s.* per day, shall go to the poor of the parish; and in case of non-payment, the party is to be committed to the house of correction on a first offence for not exceeding seven days, on the second fourteen, and on the third or any subsequent offence twenty-one days.

The 21st *Geo.* 3. c. 49. was also passed to restrain an indecent practice, which had become very prevalent in London and Westminster. It enacts, that if any house, room, or place is opened upon a Sunday for any public entertainment, or for debating upon any subject whatever, to which persons are admitted by money or tickets, the keeper of it shall forfeit 200*l.* to any person who will prosecute, the manager or president 100*l.* and the receiver of the money or tickets 50*l.*; and every person advertising, or printing an advertisement of such a meeting, shall in like manner forfeit 50*l.* for every offence.

SABBATUM. The Sabbath, or day of rest; the seventh day from the creation. *Cowell.*

SABALLINÆ PELLES. Sable furs. *Ibid.*

SABULONARIUM. A gravel pit; or liberty to dig gravel and sand; also the money paid for the same. *Pet. Parl. temp. Edw.* III. *Cowell.*

SAC, (*Saca vel sacha.*) An ancient privilege which a lord of a manor claimed to have in his court, of holding plea in causes of trespass arising among his tenants, and of imposing fines and amercements touching the same. By some it is the amercement and forfeiture itself. *Rastal.*

SACA. In the Saxon, properly signifies as much as *causa* in Latin. Hence we still retain the expression, For whose sake, i. e. For whose cause, &c. *Cowell.*

SACABURH, or SACABERE. Is he that is robbed, or by theft deprived of his money or goods, and puts in surety to prosecute the felon with fresh suit. *Brit.* c. 15 & 29. *Bracton*, lib. 3. c. 32.

SACCINI. Monks so called, because they wore next their skins a garment of goat's hair; and saccus is applied to coarse cloth made of such hair. *Walsing. Cowell.*

SACCIS, (*Fratres de saccis.*) The sackcloth brethren, or the penitential order. *Cowell.*

SACCUS CUM BROCHIA. A service or tenure of finding a sack and a broach to the king, for the use of his army. *Bract.* lib. 2. c. 16. *Cowell.*

SACK OF WOOL. A quantity of twenty six stone of sheep's wool; and of cotton wool, from one hundred and a half to four hundred. Stat. 14 *Edw.* III. c. 2. *Cowell.*

SACRAMENT, (*Sacramentum.*) Is the most solemn act of worship amongst us, and by the Rubrick there must be three at the least to communicate. But the sacrament is not to be administered to such who refuse to be present at the prayers of the church, or to strangers; for a minister is not obliged to give it to any but those of his own parish; and the partakers of the Sacrament ought to signify their names to the curate at least a day before it is administered. *Can.* 27. *Count. Paris. Com.* 36, 37, 38.

By the statute, no person shall be chosen into any office of magistracy, or place of trust, &c. unless they receive the Sacrament according to the rites of the church of England, and deliver a certificate thereof to the court of King's Bench or quarter-sessions, under the hand of the minister, and prove it by witnesses. 13 & 14 *Car.* 2. c. 4. 25 *Car.* 2. c. 2. In every parish church the Sacrament is to be administered three times in the year, (whereof the feast of Easter to be one), and every layman is bound to receive it thrice every year, &c. In colleges and halls of the universities, the Sacraments are to be administered the first or second Sunday of every month; and in cathedral churches, upon all principal feast-days, *Canon* 21, 22, 23. The churchwardens, as well as the minister, are to take notice whether the parishioners come so often to the Sacrament as they ought, and on a churchwarden's presenting a man for not receiving the Sacrament, he may be libelled in the ecclesiastical court and excommunicated, &c. Reviling the Sacrament of the Lord's Supper is punishable by fine and imprisonment. 1 *Eliz.* c. 1.

SACRAMENTUM. Is used for an oath.

SACRAMENTUM ALTARIS. The sacrifice of the mass, or what is now called the Sacrament of the Lord's Supper. *Paroch. Antiq.* 488.

SACRAMENTUM DECISIONIS. See *Wager of Law*.

SACRILEGE, (*Sacrilegium.*) Is church larceny, or a taking of things out of a holy place; as where a person steals any vessels, ornaments, or goods of the church: and it is said to be a robbery of God, at least what is sacred to his service. 3 *Cro.* 153.

Common law distinguished this crime from other robberies: for it denied the benefit of the clergy to the offenders, which it did not do to other felons. But by statute it is put upon a footing with other felonies, by making it felony excluded of clergy, as most other felonies are. 2 *Inst.* 250.

All persons not in holy orders, who shall be indicted, whether in the same county where the fact was committed, or in a different country, of robbing any church, chapel, or other holy place, are excluded from their clergy by 23 *Hen.* 8. c. 1. 25 *Hen.* 8. c. 3. 5 & 6 *Ed.* 6. c. 10. And all persons in general are ousted of their clergy for the felonious taking of any goods out of any parish church, or other church or chapel, by 1 Ed. 6. c. 12. But the word robbing being always taken to carry with it some force, it seems no sacrilege is within these statutes, which is not accompanied with the actual breaking of a church, &c. *Kel.* 58. 69. *Dyer* 224. And the statute 23 Hen. 8. c. 1. is the only act which extends to accessaries to these robberies, except the offence amount to burglary, in which case accessaries before are ousted of clergy, by 3 & 4 *W. & M.* c. 9. 2 *Hawk. P. C.* 351.

SACRILEGE, Signifies also alienation to laymen and to profane or common purposes of what was given to religious persons and to pious uses. *Paroch. Antiq.* 390.

SACRISTA, (*Lat.*) A sexton, belonging to a church. *Cowell.*

SAFE-CONDUCT, (*Salvus conductus.*) Is a security given by the prince, under the great seal, to a stranger, for his safe-coming into and passing out of the realm. *Reg. Orig.* 25.

The violation of safe-conducts or passports, expressly granted by the king or his ambassadors to the subjects of a foreign power in time of mutual war; or committing acts of hostilities against such as are in amity, league, or truce with us, who are here under a general implied safe-conduct, are breaches of the public faith, without the preservation of which there can be no intercourse or commerce between one nation and another; and such offences may, according to the writers upon the law of nations, be a just ground of a national war, since it is not in the power of the foreign prince to cause justice to be done to his subjects by the very individual delinquent, but he must require it of the whole community. And as during the continuance of any safe-conduct, either express or implied, the foreigner is under the protection of the king and the law; and, more especially, as it is one of the articles of magna charta, that foreign merchants should be entitled to safe conduct and security throughout the kingdom; there is no question but that any violation of either the person or property of such foreigner may be punished by indictment in the name of the king, whose honour is more particularly engaged in supporting his own safe-conduct. And when this malicious rapacity was not confined to private individuals, but broke out into general hostilities, by the statute 2 Hen. V. st. 1. c. 6. breaking of truce and safe-conducts, or abetting and receiving the truce-breakers, was (in affirmance and support of the law of nations) declared to be high treason against the crown and dignity of the king; and conservators of truce and safe-conducts were appointed in every port, and empowered to hear and determine such treasons (when committed at sea) according to the ancient marine law then practised in the admiral's court; and, together with two men learned in the law of the land, to hear and determine according to that law the same treasons, when committed within the body of any county. Which statute, so far as made these offences amount to treason, was suspended by 14 Hen. VI. c. 8. and repealed by 20 Hen. VI. c. 11. but revived by 29 Hen. VI. c. 2. which gave the same powers to the lord chancellor, associated with either of the chief justices, as belonged to the conservators of truce and their assessors; and enacted, that notwithstanding the party be convicted of treason, the injured stranger should have restitution out of his effects, prior to any claim of the crown. And it is farther enacted by the statute 31 Hen. VI. c. 4. that if any of the king's subjects attempt or offend, upon the sea, or in any port within the king's obeysance, against any stranger in amity, league, or truce, or under safe-conduct; and especially by attaching his person, or spoiling, or robbing him of his goods; the lord chancellor, with any justices of either the king's bench or common pleas, may cause full restitution and amends to be made to the party injured.

SAFE-GUARD, (*Salva guardia.*) A protection of the king to one who is a stranger that fears violence from some of his subjects, for seeking his right by course of law. *Reg. Orig.* 26.

SAFE-PLEDGE, (*Salvus plegius.*) A surety given for a man's appearance at a day assigned. *Bracton, lib.* 4. *cap.* 2. *Cowell.*

SAGAMAN, (from the Sax. *Saga*, i. e.

Fabula.) Signifies a tale-teller, or secret accuser. *Leg. Hen.* 1. *cap.* 63. *Cowell.*

SAGIBARO, alias SACHBARO. Is the same that we now call justiciarius, a judge. *Leg. Inæ.* c. 6.

SAGITTA BARBATA. A bearded arrow. *Sancti Michaelis, &c.* *Blount.*

SAGITTARII. A sort of small ships or vessels, with oars. *Cowell. Blount*

ST. MARTIN LE GRAND, *Court of.* The chief of the several courts in London are the sheriffs courts, holden before their steward or judge; from which a writ of error lies to the court of hustings, before the mayor, recorder, and sheriffs; and from thence to justices appointed by the king's commission, who used to sit in the church of St. Martin le Grand, (*F. N. B.* 32.) and from the judgment of those justices a writ of error lies immediately to the house of lords. 3 *Black.* 80. *n.*

SAIO ET SAIONES, *Fori vel Magistratus Minister.* A tipstaff or serjeant at arms. *Cowell. Blount.*

SALARY, (*Salarium.*) Is a recompence or consideration made to a person for his pains and industry in another man's business. See *Taxes.*

SALE, (*Venditio.*) Sale or exchange is a translation of property from one man to another in consideration of some price or recompence in value, for there is no sale without a recompence; there must be a *quid pro quo.* *Noy's Max.* 42.

But with regard to the law of sales and exchanges, there is no difference, and both fall under the denomination of sales only.

Where the vendor hath in himself the property of the goods sold, he hath the liberty of disposing of them to whomever he pleases, at any time, and in any manner, unless judgment has been obtained against him for a debt or damages, and the writ of execution is actually delivered to the sheriff. For then, by the statute of frauds, 29 *Car.* II. c. 3. the sale shall be looked upon as fraudulent, and the property of the goods shall be bound to answer the debt from the time of delivering the writ. Formerly it was bound from the teste or issuing of the writ, 3 *Rep.* 171. 1 *Mod.* 188. and any subsequent sale was fraudulent; but the law was thus altered in favour of purchasers, though it still remains the same between the parties; and therefore, if a defendant dies after the awarding and before the delivery of the writ, his goods are bound by it in the hands of his executors.

If two writs are delivered to the sheriff on the same day, he is bound to execute the first which he receives; but if he levies and sells under the second, the sale to a vendee, without notice of the first, is irrevocable, and the sheriff makes himself answerable to both parties. 1 *Salk.* 320. 1 *T. R.* 729.

If a man agrees with another for goods at a certain price, he may not carry them away before he hath paid for them, for it is no sale without payment, unless the contrary be expressly agreed. And therefore, if the vendor says, the price of a beast is four pounds, and the vendee says he will give four pounds, the bargain is struck, and they neither of them are at liberty to be off, provided immediate possession be tendered by the other side. But if neither the money be paid, nor the goods delivered, nor tender made, nor any subsequent agreement be entered into, it is no contract, and the owner may dispose of the goods as he pleases. *Hob.* 41. *Noy's Max.* c. 42.

But if any part of the price is paid down, if it be but a penny, or any portion of the goods delivered by way of earnest, (which the civil law calls arrha, and interprets to be "emptionis-venditionis contractæ argumentum, *Inst.* 3. *tit.* 24,) the property of the goods is absolutely bound by it, and the vendee may recover the goods by action, as well as the vendor may the price of them, *Noy.* ibid.

But the property does not seem to be absolutely bound by the earnest; for Lord Holt has laid down the following rules, viz. "That notwithstanding the earnest, the money must be paid upon fetching away the goods, because no other time for payment is appointed; that earnest only binds the bargain, and gives the party a right to demand; but then a demand without the payment of the money is void; that after earnest given the vendor cannot sell the goods to another, without a default in the vendee; and therefore if the vendee does not come and pay, and take the goods, the vendor ought to go and request him; and then if he does not come and pay, and take away the goods in convenient time, the agreement is dissolved, and he is at liberty to sell them to any other person. 1 *Salk.* 113.

SALE OF DISTRESS. See *Distress.*

SALET. Is a head-piece (from the Fr. *Salut,* i. e. *Salus.*) A salet or scull of iron, &c. 20 *R.* 2. c. 1. 4 & 5 *P.* & *M.* *Cowell.*

SALICETUM. The soil where willows grow, or an osier bed. 1 *Inst.* 4.

SALINA. A salt-pit, or place wherein salt is made. *Cowell.*

SALIQUE LAW, (*Lex Salica.*) A law by which males only were to inherit. *Cowell. Blount.*

SALMON. See *Fisheries.*

SALMON-PIPE. An engine to catch salmons or such like fish. 25 *Hen.* 8. c. 7.

SALTATORIUM. Signifies a deer-leap. *Cowell. Blount.*

SALT. By 9 & 10 *Will.* 3. c. 6. no retailer shall sell salt otherwise than by weight, on pain of 5*l.* And by 38 *Geo.* 3. c. 89. s. 4. and 45 *Geo.* 3. c. 14. s. 4. sixty-five pounds avoirdupoise weight of rock salt shall be deemed a bushel, and fifty-six pounds of every other kind of salt.

The lord-mayor and aldermen of London, and the justices of the peace elsewhere, at their general sessions, may set the price of salt, and the prices so set are to be observed: and if any one sell at any higher price, or refuse to sell at the price set, he shall forfeit 20*l.* to be levied by distress by warrant of one justice, or otherwise be imprisoned till he pay, half to the king and half to the informer. 38 *Geo.* 3. c. 88. s. 143.

SALT-SILVER. One penny paid at the feast of St. Martin, by the tenants of some manors, as a commutation for the service of carrying their lord's salt from market to his larder. *Paroch. Antiq.* 496. *Cowell.*

SALTUS. A high thick wood or forest. *Cowell.*

SALVA-GARDA. A security given by the king to a stranger, fearing the violence of some of his subjects, for seeking his right by course of law. *Reg. Orig.* 26.

SALVAGE. Is an allowance made for saving of ships or goods from danger of seas, enemies, &c. *Merch. Dict.* See *Wreck.*

SALVAGIUS. Wild, savage; as *salvagius catus*, the wild cat. *Rot. Cart.* 1 *Job. Cowell.*

SALUTE, (*Salus.*) A coin made by Hen. V. after his conquest in France, whereon the arms of France and England were stamped and quartered. *Stowe's Chr.* 589. *Cowell. Blount.*

SANCTA. The relics of the saints; and *jurare super sancta* was to make oath on those relics. *Leg. Canut.* c. 57. *Cowell.*

SANCTION OF LAWS. Legislators have for the most part chosen to make the sanction of their laws rather vindicatory than remuneratory, or to consist rather in punishments than in actual particular rewards. 1 *Black.* 56.

And of all the parts of a law, the most effectual is the vindicatory. For it is but lost labour to say, "do this, or avoid that," unless we also declare, "this shall be the consequence of your non-compliance." We must therefore observe, that the main strength and force of a law consists in the penalty annexed to it. 1 *Black.* 57.

SANCTUARY, (*Sanctuarium.*) A place privileged for the safe-guard of offenders lives, being founded upon the law of mercy, and the great reverence and devotion which the prince bears to the place whereunto he grants such privilege. *Matt. West. Ann.* 187. *S. P. C.* lib. 2. cap. 38. *Fleta*, lib. 1. cap. 29.

Formerly, on indictments for felonies, a plea, now abrogated, viz. that of sanctuary (which was originally introduced and continued during the superstitious veneration that was paid to consecrated ground in the times of popery) was allowed. Thus if a person accused of any crime (except treason, wherein the crown, and sacrilege, wherein the church was too nearly concerned) had fled to any church or church-yard, and within forty days after went in sackcloth and confessed himself guilty before the coroner, and declared all the particular circumstances of the offence; and thereupon took the oath in that case provided, viz. that he abjured the realm, and would depart from thence forthwith at the port that should be assigned him, and would never return without leave from the king; he by this means saved his life, if he observed the conditions of the oath, by going with a cross in his hand, and with all convenient speed, to the port assigned, and embarking. For if, during this forty days privilege of sanctuary, or in his road to the sea-side, he was apprehended and arraigned in any court, for this felony he might plead the privilege of sanctuary, and had a right to be remanded, if taken out against his will. But by this abjuration his blood was attainted, and he forfeited all his goods and chattels. The immunity of these privileged places was very much abridged by the statutes 27 *Hen.* 8. c. 19. and 32 *Hen.* 8. c. 12. And now, by the statute 21 *Jac.* 1. c. 28. all privilege of sanctuary, and abjuration consequent thereupon, is utterly taken away and abolished.

SANDAL. A merchandise brought into England; and a kind of red bearded wheat. See 2 *R.* II. c. 1.

SAND-GAVEL. Is a payment due to the lord of the manor of Rodley, in the county of Gloucester, for liberty granted to the tenants to dig sand for their common use. *Tayl. Hist. Gavel.* 113. *Cowell.*

SANE MEMORY, *i. e.* Perfect and sound mind and memory to do any lawful acts, &c. See *Ideots.*

SANGUINEM EMERE. Was where villeins were bound to buy or redeem their blood or tenure, and make themselves freemen. *Cowell.*

SANGUIS. Is taken for that right or power which the chief lord of the fee had to judge and determine cases where blood was shed. *Mon. Angl.* tom. 1. p. 1021. *Ibid.*

SANG, and SANKE. Words used for blood. *Ibid.*

SARABARA. A covering for the head. *Ibid.*

SARCLIN-TIME, (from the Fr. *Sarcler*, Lat. *Sarclare.*) Is the time or season when husbandmen weed their corn. *Ibid.*

SARCULATURA. Weeding of corn. *Ibid.*

SARK. See *Guernsey*.

SARKELLUS. An unlawful net or engine for destroying fish. *Cowell*. *Blount*.

SARPLER OF WOOL, (*Serplera lanæ*, otherwise called a pocket.) Is half a sack. *Fleta*, lib. 2. c. 12. *Cowell*.

SART, or ASSART. A piece of woodland turned into arable. See *Assart*. *Cowell*.

SARUM, is intended for the city of Salisbury. It was a form of church service called *secundum usum Sarum*, and was composed by Osmond, the second bishop of Sarum, in the time of William the Conqueror. *Hollingshead*, p. 17. col. B. *Cowell*.

SASSE. Is a kind of wear with floodgates, most commonly in navigable and cut rivers, from the damming and shutting up and loosing the stream of water, as occasion requires, for the better passing of boats and barges. This in the west of England is called a lock, and in some places a sluice. *Cowell*. Stat. 16 & 17 *Car*. 2. c. 12.

SASSONS. The corruption of Saxons, a name of contempt formerly given to the English, while they affected to be called Angles; they are still so called by the Welch.

SATISFACTION. Is the giving of recompence for an injury done; or the payment of money due on bond, judgment, &c. In which last case, it must be entered on record. 2 *Lill. Abr*. 495.

SATURDAY'S STOP. A space of time from even-song on Saturday till sun-rising on Monday, in which it was not lawful to take salmon in Scotland and the northern parts of England. *Cowell*.

SAVER-DEFAULT. A law term, signifying to excuse: as when a man having made default by not appearing in court, &c. comes afterwards and alledges good cause for it, viz. imprisonment at the time, or the like. *Book Ent*. *Cowell*.

SANKEFIN, (Fr. from *Sang*: i. e. *Sanguis*, *Fin*, & *Finis*.) Is the determination or final end of the lineal race and descent of kindred. *Britton*, c. 119. *Cowell*.

SAURUS. A hawk of a year old. *Bract*. lib. 5. tract. 1. c. 2. par. 1. *Cowell*.

SAXON-LAGE, (*Saxon-laga*, *Lex Saxonum*.) The law of the West Saxons by which they were governed. See *Merchenlage*. 4 *Black*. 403, 4, 5.

SCABINI. A word used for wardens at Lynn, in Norfolk. *Cowell*.

SCALAM, *Ad scalam*. The old way of paying money into the exchequer. The sheriff, &c. is to make payment *ad scalam*, i. e. *solvere præter*, *quam libet numeratum librum sex denarios*. Stat. *W*. 1. And at that time sixpence superadded to the pound made up the full weight, and near the intrinsic value, and was told for the pound sterling. *Hale's Sher. Ac*. 21.

SCALE OF CRIMES AND PUNISHMENTS. Beccaria has ingeniously proposed, that in any state a scale of crimes should be found with a corresponding scale of punishments, descending from the greatest to the least; but Blackstone treats this as too romantic to be reduced to practice. *Bec*. c. 6. 1 *Black*. 17.

SCALINGA. A quarry or pit of stones, or rather slates, for covering houses. *Cowell*.

SCANDAL. An unfounded defamation, or words of abuse. *Rep. Temp. Hard*. 305. See *Defamation*, *Libel*, and *Reputation*.

SCANDAL IN EQUITY. If a bill in equity contain matter either scandalous or impertinent, the defendant may refuse to answer it, till such scandal or impertinence is expunged, which is done upon an order to refer it to one of the masters, if in chancery, or the deputy remembrancer in equity. The like is also done as to answers, and if the bill or answer is reported to be scandalous or impertinent, great costs are allowed as a punishment to the party, such as 50*l*. or 500*l*. *Pr. R*. 383. And scandal is the introduction of such language as is unbecoming the court to hear, or which is contrary to all good manners; also to charge any one with a crime not necessary to be set forth is scandal. Impertinence is setting forth something not necessary to be set forth, as being recitals and discussions not material. *Ibid*.

SCANDALUM MAGNATUM. Is the name of a statute, and also of a wrong done to any high personage of the land, as prelates, dukes, earls, barons, and other nobles; and also to the chancellor, treasurer, clerk of the privy seal, steward of the house, justice of one bench or other, and other great officers of the realm, by false news, or horrible or false messages, whereby debates and discords betwixt them and the commons, or any scandal to their persons might arise. *Cowell*.

The law on which an action is grounded for this is 2 *Rich*. II. st. 1. c. 5. which, after speaking of "devisors of false news and horrible lies of prelates, dukes, earls, barons, and other nobles and great men of the realm, and also of the chancellor, treasurer, clerk of the privy seal, steward of the king's house, justices of the one bench or of the other, and other great officers of the realm," ENACTS, "that none contrive or tell any false things of prelates, lords, and of others aforesaid, whereof discord or slander might rise within the realm, and he who doth the same shall be imprisoned till he have brought him forth that did speak the same." This statute is recited by 12 *R*. II. cap. 11. and thereby it is further provided, that the offender shall be punished by the advice of the council. 4 *Inst*. 51. 4 *Co*. 12. *b*.

Scandalum magnatum lies if a man speak against them any words which are actionable when spoken against a common person, and even though the words are not so certain as to maintain an action against a common person; for if they sound a slander, an action lies as if a man say, my lord P. sent after me to take my purse, though he do not say feloniously—that he is an unworthy man—no man considers him a dog—he bid me compound in robbery—cares not how he comes by goods, or the like. *Com. Dig.* tit. Acc. upon the case for Defamation.

SCANDAL. See *Slander*.

SCATINIA LEX, a law against buggery. *Cowell.*

SCAVAGE, SCEVAGE, or SCHEWAGE, (from the Sax. *scheawian*, i. e. *ostendere*) a kind of toll or custom, exacted by mayors, sheriffs, &c. of merchant strangers, for wares shewed or exposed to sale within their liberties, prohibited by the statute 19 *H.* 7. *c.* 7. But the city of London still retains this ancient custom. 49 *Geo.* 3. c. 98. *s.* 2.

SCAVALDUS, the officer who collected the scavage money, which was sometimes done with great extortion. *Cowell.*

SCAVENGERS, (from the Belg. *schaven*, to scrape or carry away) persons chosen in cities and corporate towns, to cleanse the streets, and carry the dirt and filth thereof away. These officers are still chosen, in some places, according to the local custom of the town; but in most places of consequence they are now appointed under the authority of some special act of parliament.

SCEAT, (Sax.) a small coin among the Saxons, equal to four farthings. *Cowell.*

SCEITHMAN, (Sax.) a pirate or thief. *Ibid.*

SCEPPA SALIS, an ancient measure of salt, the quantity now not known. *Ibid.*

SCEURUM, a barn or granary. *Ibid.*

SCHAFFA, a sheaf, as *schaffa sagittarum*, a sheaf of arrows. *Ibid.*

SCHARPENY, a small duty, or compensation. Some customary tenants were obliged to pen up their cattle at night in the pound or yard of the lord, for the benefit of their dung; or, if they did not so, they paid a small compensation called sharpenny or sharnpenny, i. e. dung penny, or money in lieu of dung. *Ibid.*

SCHAVALDUS, the officer who collected the scavage-money. *Cowell.*

SCHEDULE, is a little roll, or long piece of paper or parchment, in which are contained particulars of goods in a house let by lease. *Morg.*

Schedules are likewise frequently annexed to answers in a court of equity, containing an account of estates or effects, monies, debts, &c. received or disposed of, or expended by the person putting in the answer: and schedule is a term frequently used, instead of inventory.

SCHETES, formerly a term for usury. *Cowell.*

SCHILLA, a little bell, used in monasteries. *Ibid.*

SCHIRMAN, (Sax. *scir-man*) a sheriff. *LL. Inæ. Regis apud Brompton.* See *Shireman.*

SCHIRRENS-GELD, (*shire-geld*) was a tax paid to sheriffs for keeping the shire, or county court. *Cowell.*

SCHISM, (*schisma*) a rent or division in the church. *Black.* 52. 53.

SCHOOLMASTER. By our canons, no man shall teach in a public school, or private house, but such as is examined and allowed by the bishop, and of sober life, and all schoolmasters are to teach the catechism of the church in English or Latin, and bring their scholars to church, and afterwards examine them how they have benefited by sermons, &c. *Can.* 77. 79.

No person shall keep or maintain a schoolmaster who does not constantly go to church, or is not allowed by the ordinary, on pain of 10*l.* a month; and the schoolmaster shall be disabled, and suffer a year's imprisonment. (Stat. 23 *Eliz. c.* 1.) Recusants are not to be schoolmasters in any public grammar school, nor any other, unless the persons be licensed by the bishop, under the penalty of forfeiting 40*s.* a day. 1 *Jac.* 1. *c.* 4.

Every schoolmaster keeping any public or private school, and every tutor in any private family, shall subscribe the declaration, that he will conform to the liturgy of the church of England, as by law established, and be licensed by the ordinary, or he shall, for the first offence, suffer three months imprisonment; and for the second, and every other offence, be imprisoned three months, and forfeit 5*l.* to the king. 13 & 14 *Car.* 2. *s.* 4.

Persons keeping schools, without a licence from the bishop (except tutors in reading, writing, and arithmetic), shall be committed to the common gaol for three months, &c. 12 *Anne*, *s.* 2. *c.* 7.

Though the act of uniformity obliges schoolmasters only to assent to and subscribe the declaration, yet it adds, according to the laws and statutes of this realm, which presupposes some necessary qualification; and therefore a bishop may take time to inquire into the character of an elected schoolmaster, before he licences him. 2 *Strange*, 1023.

If any papist shall be convicted of keeping a school, or take upon him the education of youth, he shall be adjudged to perpetual imprisonment. 11 & 12 *W.* 3. *c.* 4.

But, by stat. 18 *Geo.* 3. *c.* 60. this act of 11 & 12 *W.* 3. *c.* 60. which subjects such teachers to perpetual imprisonment, is repealed, as to such persons who shall take the oaths therein prescribed. See *Papists.*

Also, by 19 *Geo. 3. c.* 44. "no dissenting minister, or other protestant dissenter, who shall take the oaths, and subscribe the declaration against popery, and the declaration that he is a protestant, shall be prosecuted for teaching and instructing youth as a tutor and schoolmaster; but this does not extend to colleges or endowed schools, unless founded since 1 *W. & M.* for the immediate use of protestant dissenters. *s.* 2.

And, finally, by 31 *Geo.* 3. *c.* 32. no person who has qualified shall be prosecuted for instructing youth, except in an endowed school, or a school at one of the English universities; and except also, that no roman catholic schoolmaster shall receive into his school the child of any protestant father; nor shall any roman catholic keep a school until his or her name be recorded as a teacher at sessions.

SCILICET, an adverb, signifying that is to say, or to wit, often used in law proceedings. It is not a direct and separate clause, but it is rather to usher in the sentence of another. *Hob.* 171. 172.

SCIRE FACIAS, is a writ judicial, most commonly to call a man to shew cause to the court whence it issues, why execution of a judgment passed should not be made out. *Old Nat. Brev. f.* 151.

Thus, in detinue, after judgment, the plaintiff shall have a distringas, to compel the defendant to deliver the goods, by repeated distresses of his chattels; or else a *scire facias* against any third person, in whose hands they may happen to be, to shew cause why they should not be delivered: and, if the defendant still continues obstinate, the sheriff shall summon an inquest to ascertain the plaintiff's damages, which shall be levied (like other damages) by seisure of the person or goods of the defendant.

So if a *capias ad satisfaciendum* is sued out against a defendant, on a judgment obtained, and a *non est inventus* is returned thereon, the plaintiff may sue out a process against the bail, if any were given: who stipulate in this triple alternative, that the defendant shall, if condemned in the suit, satisfy the plaintiff his debt and costs; or surrender himself a prisoner; or, that they will pay it for him: as, therefore, the two former branches of the alternative are neither of them complied with, the latter must immediately take place (*Lutw.* 1269. 1273.) In order to which a writ of *scire facias* may be sued out against the bail, commanding them to shew cause why the plaintiff should not have execution against them for his debt and damages: and on such writ, if they shew no sufficient cause, or the defendant does not surrender himself on the day of the return, or of shewing cause (for afterwards is not sufficient) the plaintiff may have judgment against the bail, and take out a writ of *capias ad satisfaciendum*, or other process of execution against them. 3 *Black.* 417.

All the different writs of execution must be sued out within a year and a day after the judgment is entered, otherwise the court concludes, *prima facie*, that the judgment is satisfied and extinct; yet, however, it will grant a writ of *scire facias* in pursuance of stat. *Westm.* 2. 13 *Edw.* 1. *c.* 45. for the defendant to shew cause why the judgment should not be revived, and execution had against him; to which the defendant may plead such matter as he has to alledge, in order to shew why process of execution should not be issued: or the plaintiff may still bring an action of debt, founded on this dormant judgment, which was the only method of revival allowed by the common law. *Co. Litt.* 290. 3 *Black.* 421.

On a *quare impedit*, and *ne admittas* sued out, if the bishop, after the receipt of the latter writ, admit any person, even though the patron's right may have been found in a *jure patronatus*, then the plaintiff, after he has obtained judgment in the *quare impedit*, may remove the incumbent, if the clerk of a stranger, by writ of *scire facias*. *Black.* 248.

So also a *scire facias* is deemed a judicial writ of execution; yet it is so far in nature of an original, that the defendant may plead to it, and is in that respect considered as an action. *Litt. s.* 505. *Co. Litt.* 290. *b.* 291. *a.* *F. N. B.* 267.

If one hath judgment in a *quare impedit*, and afterwards before execution the party is outlawed, the king may have a *sci. fa.* to execute the judgment, the king having privity enough in this case to have execution, because the thing, as it was in the plaintiff, vested in the king. *Cro. Eliz.* 44. 325. *Keilw.* 168. 169.

SCIRE FACIAS AD AUDIENDUM ERRORES, on writs of error. There are to be fifteen days between the teste and return of every *scire fac. ad audiend. error.* upon a writ of error returnable in *B. R.* And if on the return of two *nichils*, &c. the defendant in error doth not appear, it is not then with him as in case of a *sci. fac. quare execution. non*, &c. But the cause is to be set down to be heard by the court, and the plaintiff in error shall be held thereunto *ex parte*. 2 *Lil. Abr.* 499.

SCIRE FACIAS TO REPEAL LETTERS PATENT AND GRANTS. Where the crown hath unadvisedly granted any thing by letters patent, which ought not to be granted, or where the patentee hath done an act that amounts to a forfeiture of the grant, the remedy to repeal the patent is by writ of *scire facias* in Chancery. 3 *Black.* 248.

SCIRE FECI. Is the return of the sheriff, on a *scire facias*, that he hath caused notice to be given to the party, against whom the *scire facias* issued.

SCIREWYTE, the annual tax or prestation paid to the sheriff for holding the assizes or county courts. *Cowell.*

SCITE, (*situs*) the seat or situation of a building, or the ground whereon it stood. *Cowell.*

SCOLDS, are troublesome and angry women, who, by their brawling and wrangling amongst their neighbours, break the public peace, and increase discord. They are indictable in the sheriff's turn, and punished by the ducking-stool, &c. *Kitch.* 13.

SCOT AND LOT, (Sax. *sceat, pars,* and *llot,* i. e. *sors*). Whoever, though not by equal proportion, are assessed to any contribution, are generally said to pay scot and lot. *Cowell.*

SCOTAL or SCOTALE, was where any officer of a forest kept an alehouse within the forest, by colour of his office, caused people to come to his house, and there spend their money, for fear of his displeasure. *Cowell.*

SCOTTARE. Those tenants were called scottare, whose lands were subject to pay scot. *Mon. Ang. t.* 1. *p.* 875.

SCOTLAND. The kingdom of Scotland, notwithstanding the union of the crowns on the accession of James 6. to that of England, continued an entirely separate and distinct kingdom for above a century more, though an union had been long projected; which was judged to be the more easy to be done, as both kingdoms were anciently under the same government, and still retained a very great resemblance, though far from an identity, in their laws. By an act of parliament, 1 *Jac.* 1. c. 1. it is declared that these two mighty, famous, and ancient kingdoms, were formerly one. And sir Edward Coke observes, how marvellous a conformity there was, not only in the religion and language of the two nations, but also in their ancient laws, the descent of the crown, their parliaments, their titles of nobility, their officers of state and of justice, their writs, their customs, and even the language of their laws. Upon which account he supposes the common law of each to have been originally the same; especially as their most ancient and authentic book, called *regiam majestatem,* and containing the rules of their ancient common law, is extremely similar to that of Glanvil, which contains the principles of ours, as it stood in the reign of Henry 2. And the many diversities subsisting between the two laws at present, may be well enough accounted for, from a diversity of practice in two large and uncommunicating jurisdictions, and from the acts of two distinct and independent parliaments, which have in many points altered and abrogated the old common law of both kingdoms.

However, sir Edward Coke, and the politicians of that time, conceived great difficulties in carrying on the projected union; but these were at length overcome, and the great work was happily effected in 1707, by stat. 6 *Anne, c.* 8. when twenty-five articles of union were agreed to by the parliaments of both nations; the purport of the most considerable being as follows:

1. That on the 1st of May, 1707, and for ever after, the kingdoms of England and Scotland shall be united into one kingdom, by the name of Great Britain.

2. The succession to the monarchy of Great Britain shall be the same as was before settled with regard to that of England.

3. The united kingdom shall be represented by one parliament.

4. There shall be a communication of all rights and privileges between the subjects of both kingdoms, except where it is otherwise agreed.

9. When England raises 2,000,000*l.** by a land-tax, Scotland shall raise 48,000*l.*

16. 17. The standards of the coin, of weights, and of measures, shall be reduced to those of England, throughout the united kingdoms.

18. The laws relating to trade, customs, and the excise, shall be the same in Scotland as in England; but all the other laws of Scotland shall remain in force, though alterable by the parliament of Great Britain: yet with this caution, that laws relating to public policy are alterable at the discretion of the parliament; laws relating to private right are not to be altered but for the evident utility of the people of Scotland.

22. Sixteen peers are to be chosen to represent the peerage of Scotland in parliament, and 45 members to sit in the house of commons.

23. The 16 peers of Scotland shall have all privileges of parliament: and all peers of Scotland shall be peers of Great Britain, and rank next after those of the same degree at the time of the union, and shall have all privileges of peers, except sitting in the house of lords, and voting on the trial of a peer.

Since the union, the following orders have been made in the house of lords re-

---

* Accurately, 1,997,763*l.* 8*s.* 4½*d.* the sum raised by a land-tax of 4*s.* in the pound.

specting the peerage of Scotland. Queen Anne, in the seventh year of her reign, had created James, duke of Queensbury, duke of Dover, with remainder in tail to his second son. Under this article it was, upon the 21st of January, 1708-9, resolved by the lords, that a peer of Scotland claiming to sit in the house of peers by virtue of a patent, passed since the union, under the great seal of Great Britain, and who sits in the parliament of Great Britain, has no right to vote in the election of the 16 peers who are to represent the peers of Scotland in parliament.

And, in 1782, in the case of the duke of Hamilton, the judges were unanimously of opinion, that the peers of Scotland are not disabled from receiving, subsequently to the union, a patent of peerage of Great Britain, with all the privileges usually incident thereto.

These are the principal of the twenty-five articles of union, which are ratified and confirmed by stat. 5 *Ann*, c. 8. in which statute there are also two acts of parliament recited; the one of Scotland, whereby the church of Scotland, and also the four universities of that kingdom, are established for ever, and all succeeding sovereigns are to take an oath inviolably to maintain the same; the other of England, 5 *Ann*, c. 6. whereby the acts of uniformity of 13 *Eliz.* & 13 *Car.* 2. (except as the same had been altered by parliament at that time) and all other acts then in force for the preservation of the church of England, are declared perpetual; and it is stipulated, that every subsequent king and queen shall take an oath inviolably to maintain the same within England, Ireland, Wales, and the town of Berwick upon Tweed. And it is enacted, that these two acts "shall for ever be observed as fundamental and essential conditions of the union."

Upon these articles and act of union, it is to be observed, 1. That the two kingdoms are now so inseparably united, that nothing can ever disunite them again, except the mutual consent of both, or the successful resistance of either, upon apprehending an infringement of those points which, when they were separate and independent nations, it was mutually stipulated should be "fundamental and essential conditions of the union." * 2. That whatever else may be deemed "fundamental and essential conditions," the preservation of the two churches of England and Scotland, in the same state that they were in at the time of the union, and the maintenance of the acts of uniformity, which establish our common prayer, are expressly declared so to be. 3. That therefore any alteration in the constitution of either of those churches, or in the liturgy of the church of England (unless with the consent of the respective churches, collectively or representatively given), would be an infringement of these "fundamental and essential conditions," and greatly endanger the union. 4. That the municipal laws of Scotland are ordained to be still observed in that part of the island, unless altered by parliament; and, as the parliament has not yet thought proper, except in a few instances, to alter them, they still (with regard to the particulars unaltered) continue in full force. Wherefore the municipal or common laws of England are, generally speaking, of

* It may be justly doubted, whether even such an infringement (though a manifest breach of good faith, unless done upon the most pressing necessity), would of itself dissolve the union: for the bare idea of a state, without a power somewhere vested to alter every part of its laws, is the height of political absurdity. The truth seems to be, that in such an incorporate union (which is well distinguished by a very learned prelate from a federate alliance, where such an infringement would certainly rescind the compact) the two contracting states are totally annihilated, without any power of a revival; and a third arises from their conjunction, in which all the rights of sovereignty, and particularly that of legislation, must of necessity reside. (See *Warburton's Alliance*, 195.) But the wanton or imprudent exertion of this right would probably raise a very alarming ferment in the minds of individuals; and therefore it is hinted above that such an attempt might endanger (though by no means destroy) the union.

To illustrate this matter a little farther, an act of parliament to repeal or alter the act of uniformity in England, or to establish episcopacy in Scotland, would doubtless, in point of authority, be sufficiently valid and binding; and, notwithstanding such an act, the union would continue unbroken. Nay, each of these measures might be safely and honourably pursued, if respectively agreeable to the sentiments of the English church, or the kirk in Scotland. But it should seem neither prudent, nor perhaps consistent with good faith, to venture upon either of those steps, by a spontaneous exertion of the inherent powers of parliament, or at the instance of mere individuals. So sacred indeed are the laws above-mentioned (for protecting each church, and the English liturgy) esteemed, that in the regency acts both of 1751 and 1765 the regents are expressly disabled from assenting to the repeal or alteration of either these, or the act of settlement.

no force or validity in Scotland. 1 *Black.* 98.

But acts of parliament, in general, passed since the union, extend to Scotland; but where a statute is not applicable to Scotland, and where Scotland is not intended to be included, the method is to declare by proviso that it does not extend to Scotland, 3 *Burr.* 853.

SCOTS. Assessments by commissioners of sewers are so called. 3 *Black.* 74.

SCRIPTURE. All profane scoffing of the holy scripture, or exposing any part thereof to contempt and ridicule, is punished by fine and imprisonment. 1 *Hawk. P. C.* 7.

SCRIVENER. One who is employed or entrusted to draw up and engross deeds, conveyances, and securities for money.

SCUTAGE, (*scutagium*, Sax. *scildpenig*) was a tax or contribution, raised by those that held lands by knights' service, towards furnishing the king's army, at one, two, or three marks for every knight's fee. 1 *Black.* 309. 2 *Black.* 74.

SCUTAGIO HABENDO, a writ that anciently lay against tenants by knight-service, to serve in the wars, or send sufficient persons, or to pay a certain sum, &c. *F. N. B.* 83.

SCUTE, a French gold coin of 3*s.* 4*d.* in the reign of king Henry 5. *Cowell.*

SCUTELLA, (from *sutum*, Sax. *scutel*) a scuttle, any thing of a flat and broad shape, like a shield. *Ibid.*

SCUTELLA ELEEMOSYNARIA, an alms basket or scuttle. *Paroch. Antiq. Cowell.*

SCUTUM ARMORUM, a shield, or coat of arms. *Cowell.*

SCYLDWIT, (Sax.) a mulct for any fault; from the Saxon *scild.* i. e. *delictum*, and wite, *pœna.* *Leg. Hen.* 1. *Cowell.*

SCYRA, a fine imposed on such as neglected to attend the scyregemot court, which all tenants were bound to do. *Mon. Ang. t.* 1. *p.* 52. *Cowell.*

SCYRE-GEMOT, (Sax.) was a court held by the Saxons twice every year by the bishop of the diocese, and the earldorman, in shires that had earldormen; and by the bishop and sheriff, where the counties were committed to the sheriff, &c. wherein both the ecclesiastical and temporal laws were given in charge to the county. *Seld. Tit. Hon.* 628. *Cowell.*

SEA, (*mare.*) By statute the sea is to be open to all merchants (18 *Edw.* 3. *c.* 3.) The main sea, beneath the low-water-mark, and round England, is part of England, for there the admiral hath jurisdiction. 1 *Inst.* 260. 5 *Rep.* 207.

The seas which environ England are within the jurisdiction of the king of England. 1 *Roll. Abr.* 528. See *Admiralty.*

SEA-BANKS. By the statutes 6 *Geo.* 2. c. 37. and 10 *Geo.* 2. c. 32. it is made felony, without benefit of clergy, maliciously to cut down any river or sea-bank, whereby lands may be overflowed.

SEA-LAWS, are laws relating to the sea, as the laws of Oleron, &c. *Cowell.*

SEALER, (*sigillator*) is an officer in chancery, appointed by the lord chancellor, or lord keeper of the great seal of England, to seal the writs and instruments there made in his presence.

There is also a sealer of the writs issued by the other courts of law at Westminster; the profits of which office, formerly part of the king's ancient hereditary revenues, are now vested in the duke of Grafton, by alienation from the crown, in the reign of Charles 2.

SEALING DEEDS, is one of the requisites for making a good deed (2 *Black.* 305.) And, if a seal is broken, it will make the deed void (2 *Lev.* 220. *Cro. Eliz.* 408. 546.) But, in case the seal be broken by accident, though no action can be brought, yet relief may be had in equity. 2 *Bulst.* 246.

SEA-MARKS. The erection of beacons, light-houses, and sea-marks, is a branch of the royal prerogative. By 8 *Eliz.* c. 13. the corporation of the trinity-house are empowered to set up any beacons or sea-marks wherever they shall think them necessary; and if the owner of the land, or any other person, shall destroy them, or shall take down any steeple, tree, or other known sea-mark, he shall forfeit 100*l.*; or, in case of inability to pay it, he shall be *ipso facto* outlawed.

SEAMEN. Many laws have been made from time to time for the encouragement of the increase of British seamen; but the method of ordering seamen in the royal fleet, and keeping up a regular discipline there, is directed by certain express rules, articles, and orders, first enacted by the authority of parliament; but since new modelled and altered, after the peace of Aix la Chapelle, to remedy some defects, which were of fatal consequence in conducting the preceding war. See Stat. 22 *Geo.* 2. c. 23. amended by 19 *Geo.* 3. c. 17.

In these articles of the navy (see *Admiralty* and *Articles of the Navy*) almost every possible offence is set down, and the punishment thereof annexed: in which respect the seamen have much the advantage over their brethren in the land-service, whose articles of war are not enacted by parliament, but framed from time to time at the pleasure of the crown. 1 *Black.* 420.

With regard to the privileges conferred on sailors, they are pretty much the same with those conferred on soldiers; and by

31 *Geo.* 2. c. 10. no seamen aboard his majesty's ships can be arrested for any debt, unless the same be sworn to amount to at least 20*l*.

But as the statute excepts any criminal matter, it has been decided that he may be committed for refusing to indemnify the parish against a bastard child; or for disobeying an order of justices to pay a weekly allowance for it. 5 *T. R.* 156. 2 *T. R.* 270. See *Admiralty*, *Navy*, *Mariner*, and *Ships*.

SEAMEN'S WAGES. The recovery of seamen's wages is one of the objects of the admiralty jurisdiction, even though the contract be made for them upon the land. Yet the courts of common law have jurisdiction, and an action may be maintained for work and labour. 1 *Ventr.* 146. 2 *Black.* 107.

SEAN-FISH, fish taken with a large and long net, called a sean. Stat. 1 *Jac.* 1. c. 25.

SEARCHER, an officer of the customs, whose business it is to search and examine ships outward bound, if they have any prohibited or uncustomed goods on board. Stat. 12 *Car.* 2.

SEA-REEVE, *in villis maritimis est qui maritimam domini jurisdictionem curat, littus lustrat, & ejectum maris (quod* wreck *appellatur) domino colligit. Spelm.*

SEA-ROVERS, pirates and robbers at sea. Stat. 16 *Car.* 2. c. 6. See *Pirates*.

SECONDARY, *(secondarius)* an officer who is second, or next to the chief officer: as the secondaries to the prothonotaries of the courts of B. R. and C. B.; the secondary of the remembrancer in the exchequer; secondary of the compter, &c. 2 *Lill. Abr.* 506.

SECONDARY CONVEYANCES, are those which presuppose some other conveyance or precedent, and only serve to confirm, alter, restrain, restore, or transfer the interest granted by such original conveyance. 2 *Black.* 324.

SECONDARY USE. A use, though executed, may change from one to another by circumstances *ex post facto*; as, if *A.* makes a feoffment to the use of his intended wife and her eldest son, for their lives, upon the marriage the wife takes the whole use in severalty; and, upon the birth of a son, the use is executed jointly in them both. This is sometimes called a secondary, sometimes a shifting use. 2 *Black.* 334, 335.

SECOND DELIVERANCE, *(secunda deliberatione)* is a judicial writ that lies after a nonsuit of the plaintiff in replevin, and a *returno habendo* of the cattle replevied, adjudged to him that distrained them, commanding the sheriff to replevy the same cattle again, upon security given by the plaintiff in the replevin for the re-delivery of them, if the distress be justified. It is a second writ of replevin, &c. *F. N. B.* 68.

SECOND MARRIAGE, *(secundæ nuptiæ)* is when after the decease of one a man marries a second wife, which the law terms bigamus. *Cowell.*

SECOND SURCHARGE, (writ of). If after admeasurement of common, upon a writ of admeasurement of pasture, the same defendant surcharges the common again, the plaintiff may have this writ of second surcharge, *de secunda superoneratione*, which is given by the stat. *Westm.* 2. c. 13. *Ed.* 1. c. 8.; and thereby the sheriff is directed to inquire by a jury whether the defendant has in fact again surcharged the common, contrary to the tenure of the last admeasurement: and, if he has, he shall then forfeit to the king the supernumerary cattle put in, and shall also pay damages to the plaintiff. 2 *Black.* 239.

SECRETARIES OF STATE, so called, *ab epistolis & scriptis secretis.* The secretaries of state have an extraordinary trust, which renders them very considerable in the eyes of the king, and of the subject also, whose requests and petitions are for the most part lodged in their hands, to be represented to his Majesty, and to make dispatches thereupon, pursuant to his majesty's directions; they are privy counsellors, and a council is seldom or never held without the presence of one of them; they wait by turns, and one of these secretaries always attends the court, and by the king's warrant prepares all bills or letters for the king to sign, not being matter of law. And depending on them is the office called the paper office, which contains all the public writings of state, negociations, and dispatches, all matters of state and council, &c.; and they have the keeping of the king's seal, called the signet, because the king's private letters are signed with it.

The correspondence with all parts of Great Britain is managed by either of the secretaries, without distinction; but, in respect to foreign affairs, all nations which have intercourse of business with Great Britain, are divided into two provinces, the southern and the northern: of which the southern is under the senior, and the northern is under the junior secretary, &c. Our secretaries of state have power to commit persons for treason, and other offences against the state, as justices of peace all over England, and it is incident to their office (1 *Salk.* 347. *Wood's Inst.* 458.) And they are constantly named in the commissions of the peace for every county in England and Wales. 1 *Black.* 338.

But the secretary of state, as such, is not a conservator, or justice of the peace; nor is he, or the king's messengers in ordinary, acting under his warrant, within the meaning of the statute. 24 *Geo.* 2. *c.* 44. 2 *Wilson, p.* 2. *f.* 290. 291.

SECTA, or SUIT, *(a sequendo)* the witnesses or followers of the plaintiff. *Seld. in Fortesc. c.* 21. 3 *Black.* 295.

SECTA AD CURIAM, a writ that lies against him who refused to perform his suit either to the county or court-baron. *F. N. B. f.* 158.

SECTA AD JUSTITIAM FACIENDAM, a service which a man was bound to perform by his fee. *Bracton, l.* 2. *c.* 16. *n.* 6.

SECTA CURIÆ, suit and service done by tenants at the court of their lord. *Par. Antiq. p.* 320.

SECTA FACIENDA PER ILLAM QUÆ HABET ENICIAM PARTEM, a writ to compel the heir, who had the elder's part of the co-heirs, to perform service for all the coparceners. *Reg. Orig. f.* 177.

SECTA MOLENDINI, a writ which lies where a man by usage, time out of mind, &c. had ground his corn at the mill of a certain person, and afterwards went to another mill with his corn, thereby withdrawing his suit to the former: and this writ lies especially for the lord against his tenant, who holds of him to do suit at his mill. *Reg. Orig.* 153. *F. N. B.* 122.

SECTA REGALIS, a suit by which all persons were bound twice in a year to attend the sheriff's tourn; and was called regalis, because the sheriff's tourn was the king's leet wherein the people were to be obliged by oath to bear true allegiance to the king, &c. *Cowell.*

SECTA UNICA TANTUM FACIENDA PRO PLURIBUS HÆREDITATIBUS, a writ that lies for an heir who was distrained by the lord to do more suits than one, in respect of the land of divers heirs descended to him. *Reg. Orig.*

SECTIS NON FACIENDIS, a writ that lies for a woman who, for her dower, ought not to perform suit of court *(Reg. Orig. f.* 174.*)* It lay also for one in wardship to be freed of all suits of court during his wardship. *Reg. Orig. f.* 173.

SECUNDA SUPERONERATIONE PASTURÆ, a writ which lay where admeasurement of pasture had been made, and he that first surcharged the common did it a second time, notwithstanding the admeasurement. *Old Nat. Br.* 73.

SECURITATEM INVENIENDI QUOD SE NON DIVERTAT AD PARTES EXTERAS SINE LICENTIA REGIS, an ancient writ lying for the king against any of his subjects, to stay them from going out of this kingdom to foreign parts; the ground whereof is, that every man is bound to serve and defend the commonwealth, as the king shall think fit. *F. N. B.* 85. See *Ne exeat Regno.*

SECURITATIS PACIS, a writ that lay for one who was threatened death or bodily harm by another, against him which so threatened, and it issued out of Chancery, directed to the sheriff. *Reg. Orig.* 88.

SECURITY. See *Surety of the Peace.*

SE DEFENDENDO. See *Homicide.*

SEDITIOUS PRACTICES. The preamble of stat. 39 *Geo.* 3. *c.* 79. states, "Whereas a traitorous conspiracy has long been carried on, in conjunction with the persons from time to time exercising the powers of government in France, to overturn the laws, constitution, and government, and every existing establishment, civil and ecclesiastical, both in Great Britain and Ireland, and to dissolve the connection between the two kingdoms, so necessary to the security and prosperity of both: and whereas, in pursuance of such design, and in order to carry the same into effect, divers societies have been of late years instituted in this kingdom, and in the kingdom of Ireland, of a new and dangerous nature, inconsistent with public tranquillity, and with the existence of regular government, particularly certain societies calling themselves Societies of United Englishmen, United Scotchmen, United Britons, United Irishmen, and the London Corresponding Society. And whereas the members of many of such societies have taken unlawful oaths and engagements of fidelity and secrecy, and used secret signs, and appointed committees, secretaries, and other officers, in a secret manner; and many of such societies are composed of different divisions, branches, or parts, which communicate with each other by secretaries, delegates, or otherwise, and by means thereof maintain an influence over large bodies of men, and delude many ignorant and unwary persons into the commission of acts highly criminal;" it therefore enacts, that all these and other corresponding societies should be utterly suppressed and prohibited, as being unlawful combinations and confederacies.

And also every society of which the members shall, according to the rules of the society, be required to take an illegal oath, or an oath not authorised by law, or shall subscribe or assent to any test or declaration not required by law, or where the names of the members, or where the committees or presidents chosen are not known to the society at large; and every society which shall consist of different parts, either acting separately, or having separate presidents, or other officers, shall be deemed unlawful combinations and confederacies; and every person who shall become a member of such a society, or who shall correspond with them, or shall aid or support them with money, or otherwise, shall be guilty of an unlawful combination and confederacy.

This does not extend to a declaration subscribed to by a society, which declaration shall be approved by two justices, and afterwards confirmed at the quarter sessions, nor to persons who shall cease to act as members of such societies after the passing of the act, nor to established lodges of free-masons. But two members shall certify, and upon oath, that their society has been usually held as a lodge of free-masons, in conformity to the rules of free-masons in this kingdom; which certificate, and also an account of its place and times of meeting, and the names of all its members, shall be registered with the clerk of the peace; and the justices at the sessions, upon complaint made to them upon oath by any credible person, that such society is likely to be injurious to the public peace and good order, may direct that the meetings of such lodge be discontinued.

Persons offending against this statute may be proceeded against either in a summary way before one justice, or more, who may either fine the offender 20*l.* or imprison him three calendar months, or they may be prosecuted by indictment; and, upon conviction, the court may transport for seven years, or imprison for any time not exceeding two years.

The justices in a summary conviction may mitigate the punishment to one third. If any person shall permit the meeting of any illegal society in his house, he shall forfeit 5*l.* for the first offence, and for the second he shall be punishable as a member. And two justices, upon evidence on oath that any meeting has been held for a seditious purpose in a public-house, may declare the licence forfeited, and from the day of such declaration the licence is void and determined, and the owner of the house will be afterwards subject to penalties accordingly.

And because many places were open for lectures and debates of a seditious and immoral nature, and other places used for seditious and immoral purposes, under pretence of reading books, pamphlets, newspapers, or other publications, it is enacted, that all such places where, under any pretence, money shall be received for admission, shall be considered as disorderly houses, unless they are licensed for any time not more than one year by two justices; which licence may be revoked by the justices at the quarter sessions. Every alehouse shall be deemed licensed for reading publications; but upon evidence that publications of a seditious or immoral nature are usually distributed, in order to be read there, two justices may declare the licence void.

SEDUCTION OF WOMEN CHILDREN. By 4 & 5 *P.* & *M.* *c.* 8. if any person, above the age of 14, unlawfully shall convey or take away any woman child unmarried (which is held, *Stra.* 1162 to extend to bastards as well as to legitimate children), within the age of 16 years, from the possession, and against the will of the father, &c. he shall be imprisoned two years, or fined, at the discretion of the justices. 4 *Black.* 209. 210.

SEED-COD, (from the Sax. *sæd*, seed, and *codde*, a purse, or such like continent), is a basket or other vessel of wood, carried on one arm of the husbandman or sower of ground, to bear the seed or grain which he sows, and spreads abroad with the other hand. *Cowell.*

SEEDER, a seedsman, or one who sows the land. *Blount.*

SEIGNIOR, (Fr. *seignieur*, i. e. *dominus*) is, in general signification, as much as lord. *F. N. B.* 23. *Cowell.*

SEIGNIORAGE, a royalty or prerogative of the king, whereby he claims an allowance of gold and silver brought in the mass, to be exchanged for coin.

SEIGNIOR IN GROSS, seemeth to have been one that was a lord, but of no manor, and therefore could keep no court. *F. N. B. f.* 3. See next title.

SEIGNIORY, (*dominium*) borrowed from the French *seigneurie*, i. e. *dominatus*, *imperium*, *principatus*, and signifies with us a manor or lordship. *Kitchin*, 80.

SEISIN, (*seisina*, Fr. *seisine*) in the common law signifies possession. To seise is to take possession of a thing; and primer seisin is the first possession. *Co. Lit.* 152.

There is a seisin in deed or in fact, and a seisin in law; a seisin in deed is when an actual possession is taken; and seisin in law is where lands descend, and one hath not actually entered on them, but has a right to enter. 1 *Inst.* 31. *Perk.* 457. 458. 4 *Rep.* 9. 80. 1 *Danv. Abr.* 647.

SEISSINA HABENDA, (*quia rex habuit annum, diem & vastum*) is a writ that lies for delivery of seisin to the lord of lands or tenements, after the king in right of his prerogative hath had the year, day, and waste, on a felony committed, &c. *Reg. Orig.* 165.

SEISING OF HERIOTS, is the seising of the best beasts, &c. (where an heriot is due) on the death of the tenant. It is a species of self-remedy, not much unlike that of taking of cattle or goods in distress, only in the latter case they are seised as a pledge, in the former, as the property of the person for whom seised. 3 *Black.* 15.

SEIZURE OF GOODS FOR OFFENCES. No goods of a felon or other offender can be seised to the use of the king, before forfeited. 3 *Inst.* 103.

SEL, the bigness of a thing to which it

is added, as selwood is a great wood. *Cowell.*

SELDA, (from the Sax. *selde*, a seat, or stool) a shop, shed, or stall in a market; also a salt-pit. *Cowell. Co. Lit.* 4.

SELF-BANE, (Sax. *self-bana*) is where a man murders himself, called *felo de se. Cowell.*

SELF-DEFENCE. As to the defence of one's self, or the mutual and reciprocal defence of such as stand in the relations of husband and wife, parent and child, master and servant: if the party himself, or any of these his relations, be forcibly attacked in his person or property, it is lawful for him to repel force by force; and the breach of the peace which happens is chargeable upon him only who began the affray. 2 *Rol. Abr.* 546. 1 *Hawk. P. C.* 131. 3 *Black.* 3. See *Homicide.*

SELF-MURDER. The law hath ranked this among the highest crimes, making it a peculiar species of felony, a felony committed on one's self. See *Felo de se.*

SELF-PRESERVATION. Every creature has implanted in it by nature a strong desire of self-preservation: and by our ancient law, if a man stole victuals merely to satisfy his present hunger, being for the preservation of life, it was not felony; but the law is now otherwise, it being larceny. *Staundf. P. C.*

SELION OF LAND, (*selio terræ*, Fr. *seillon*) signifies a ridge of ground rising between two furrows. *Cromp. Jurisd.* 221.

SEME, (Sax. *seam*, i. e. *onus*) a horse-load, or eight bushels of corn. *Blount.*

SEMEBOLE, a pipe, or half a ton of wine. *Merch. Dict.*

SEMINARIES. See *Papists.*

SEMINIVERBIUS, a preacher or sower of words. *Pet. Blesen. Cowell.*

SENAGE, (*senagium*, from *senatus*, sometimes used for synod) is money paid for sinodals. *Cowell.*

SENATOR, (Lat.) a parliament-man. *Cowell.*

SENDAL, a kind of thin fine silk. *Stat.* 2 *R.* 2. *c.* 1.

SENESCHAL, (*senescallus*, derived from the Germ. *sein*, a house or place, and *schale*, an officer) is a steward, and signifies one who hath the dispensing of justice, in some particular cases: as the high seneschal, or steward of England; seneschal de la hotel de roy, steward of the king's household; seneschal, or steward of courts, &c. *Co. Lit.* 61. *Croke's Jurisd.* 102. *Kitch.* 83.

SENESCHALLO ET MARESHALLO *quod non teneant placita de libero tenemento*, a writ directed to the steward and marshal of England, inhibiting them to take cognisance of an action in their court that concerns freehold. *Reg. Orig.* 185, 191.

SENEUCIA, widowhood. If a widow, having dower after the death of her husband, shall marry *vel filium, vel filiam in seneucia peperit*, she shall forfeit and lose her dower in what place soever in Kent. *Tenen. in Gavel-kind. Plac. Trin.* 17. *E.* 3.

SENEY-DAYS, are play-days, or times of pleasure and diversion. *Cowell.*

SEPARIA, (*separaria*) several, or severed and divided from other ground. *Par. Antiq.* 336. *Cowell.*

SEPARATION, (*separatio*) is the living asunder of man and wife. See *Divorce.*

SEPTENNIAL ELECTIONS. The utmost extent of time that the same parliament was allowed to sit, by the stat. 6 *W. & M. c.* 2. was three years. But by the stat. 1 *Geo.* 1. *s.* 2. *c.* 38. (in order to prevent the great and continued expences of frequent elections, and the violent heats and animosities consequent thereupon, and for the peace and security of the government, then just recovering from the late rebellion) this term was prolonged to seven years.

SEPTUAGESIMA, the third Sunday before Quadragesima Sunday in Lent, and is called Septuagesima, because it is about the seventieth day before Easter; as Sexagesima and Quinquagesima, are thus denominated from their being, the one sixty, and the other fifty days before the same feast, days appointed by the church to acts of penance and mortification, preparatory to Lent. From Septuagesima Sunday, until the octaves after Easter, the solemnizing of marriage is forbidden by the canon law. *Cowell.*

SEPTUAGINT. The seventy interpreters of the bible, who were in truth seventy-two, viz. six out of every one of the twelve tribes. *Lit. Dict.*

SEPTUM, an enclosure so called, because it is encompassed *cum sepe & fossa*, with a hedge and a ditch, at least with a hedge; and it signifies any place paled in. *Cowell.*

SEPULCHRE, (*sepulchrum*) the place where any body lies buried; but a monument is set up for the memorial of the deceased, though the corpse lie not there. *Cowell.*

SEPULTURA, an offering made to the priest for the burial of a dead body. *Domesd.*

SEQUATUR SUB SUO PERICULO, a writ that lay where a summons *ad warrantizand'* was awarded, and the sheriff returned that the party had nothing whereby he might be summoned: upon which there issued an *alias* and a *pluries*, and if he came not in on the *pluries*, this writ issued. *Old Nat. Br.* 163.

SEQUELA CAUSÆ, the process and depending issue of a cause for trial. *Cowell.*

SEQUELA CURIÆ, is used for a suit of court. *Ibid.*

SEQUELA MOLENDINI, the owing suit to a particular mill, or being bound to grind corn in that place only; a duty and service laid upon many tenants. *Ibid.*

SEQUELA VILLANORUM, the retinue and appurtenances to the goods and chattels of villeins, which were at the absolute disposal of the lord.

SEQUENDUM ET PROSEQUENDUM, signify to follow a cause; as where a guardian is admitted *ad prosequend'* for an infant, &c. 1 *Vent.* 74.

SEQUESTER, (*sequestrare*) is a term used in the civil law for renouncing; as when a widow comes into court, and disclaims having any thing to do, or to intermeddle with her husband's estate, who is deceased, she is said to sequester. *Cowell.*

SEQUESTRATION, (*sequestratio*) signifies the separating or setting aside of a thing in controversy, from the possession of both the parties that contend for it; and it is two-fold, voluntary and necessary; voluntary, is that which is done by consent of each party; necessary, is what the judge of his authority doth, whether the party will or will not. *Fortescue, c.* 50. *Dyer*, 232, 256.

And there is a sequestration on a person's standing out all the processes of contempt in chancery, which is a commission usually directed to seven persons therein named, and impowering them to seize the defendant's real and personal estate into their hands (or it may be some particular part or parcel of his lands), and to receive and sequester the rents and profits thereof, until the defendant shall have answered the plaintiff's bill, or performed some other matter which has been ordered and decreed him by the court, for not doing whereof he is in contempt. *Curs. Canc.* 89.

This sequestration is grounded on the return of the serjeant at arms, wherein it is certified that the defendant had secreted himself; and therefore this process issues, and gives authority and power to the sequestrators (who are persons of the plaintiff's own naming), to enter upon and seize his (the defendant's) real and personal estate. *Cro. Eliz.* 651. 1 *Mod.* 259. 2 *Mod.* 256. 2 *Ch. Cas.* 44.

A sequestration is also a kind of execution for debt, in the case of a beneficed clerk, of the profits of the benefice, to be paid over to him that had the judgment, till the debt is satified (2 *Inst.* 472. 2 *Rol. Abr.* 474.) But the most usual sequestration of a benefice, is upon a vacancy, for the gathering up the fruits of the benefice to the use of the next incumbent; and the profits of the church, being in abeyance, are to be received by the churchwardens by appointment of the bishop, to make provision for the cure during the vacancy, &c. Stat. 28 *Hen.* 8. *c.* 11.

Sequestration is also the act of the ordinary, disposing of the goods of one that is dead, whose estate no man will meddle with. *Kennet's Gloss. Seq.*

SEQUESTRATION IN LONDON, Is made upon an action of debt, and the course of proceeding is thus: the action being entered, the officer goes to the shop or warehouse of the defendant, when there is nobody within, and takes a padlock and hangs it upon the door, &c. using these words, viz.: "I do sequester this warehouse, and the goods and merchandizes therein of the defendant in the action, to the use of the plaintiff, &c." and so puts on his seal, and makes return thereof at the Compter; then four court days being past, the next court after the plaintiff may have judgment to open the doors of the shop or warehouse, and to appraise the goods therein by a serjeant, who takes a bill of appraisement, having two freemen to appraise them, for which they are to be sworn at the next court holden for that Compter; and then the officer puts his hand to the bill of appraisement, and the court giveth judgment: though the defendant in the action may put in bail before satisfaction, and so dissolve the sequestration; and after satisfaction, may put in bail *ad disproband' debitum, &c.* *Pract. Soll.* 429.

SEQUESTRATION of the estates of peers and members of parliament, not appearing to actions. See *Parliament, Privilege.*

SEQUESTRO HABENDO. A writ judicial for the discharging a sequestration of the profits of a church benefice granted by the bishop at the king's command, thereby to compel the parson to appear at the suit of another; and the parson, upon his appearance, may have this writ for the release of the sequestration. *Reg. Judic.* 36. 3 *Black.* 418.

SEREMENT, (Fr.) An oath which is to be taken before a person who hath power to administer it, or shall be void. 2 *Keb.* 284.

SERJEANT, or SERGEANT, (Lat *Serviens.*) Is a word diversely used in our law, and applied to sundry offices and callings. First, a serjeant at law, (*serviens ad legem,*) otherwise called serjeant counter or of the coif, is the highest degree in the common law, as a doctor is in the civil law. To these serjeants, as men best learned and experienced in the law and practice of the courts, one court is severed to plead in, by themselves, which is that of the Common Pleas, where the common law of England is most strictly observed; yet they are not so limited as to be restrained from pleading in any other court, where the judges (who cannot be such till they have taken the degree of serjeant) call them brothers, and hear them with great respect; and of which one or more are stiled the king's serjeants, being commonly chosen out of the rest in respect of their great learning, to plead for the king in all his causes, especially upon indictments for treason, &c. Serjeants at law are made by the king's writ directed unto such as are called, commanding them to take upon them that degree by a certain day; and by the writ or patent of creation it appears that the honour of serjeant at law is a state and dignity of great respect. In conferring these degrees much ceremony is used, and the serjeants chosen hold a sumptuous feast, and make presents of gold rings to a considerable amount. *Fortescue*, c. 50. 3 *Cro*. 1. *Dyer* 72. 2 *Inst*. 213, 214.

By 39 Geo. 3. c. 113. his majesty, during the vacation while the office of chief justice or judge of the courts is vacant, may cause a writ to be issued out of the court of chancery to any barrister at law he shall think fit to appear in that court, and take upon himself the dignity of a serjeant at law; and such person shall, on taking the usual oaths, be, without further ceremony, deemed a serjeant at law: and his majesty may grant to that person the office of chief justice, chief baron, or judge or baron of the courts.

SERJEANTS AT ARMS. Their office is to attend the person of the king, to arrest persons of condition offending, and give attendance on the lord high steward of England, sitting in judgment on any traitor, &c. But there may not be above thirty serjeants at arms in the realm, who shall not oppress the people, on pain to lose their offices, and be fined, by the stat. 13 *R*. 2. c. 6. And two of them, by the king's allowance, do attend on the two houses of parliament. The office of him in the house of commons is, the keeping of the doors, and the execution of such commands touching the apprehension and taking into custody of any offender, as that house shall injoin him. Another of them attends on the lord chancellor in the chancery; and one on the lord treasurer of England: also one upon the lord mayor of London on extraordinary solemnities, &c. They are in the old books called Virgatories, because they carried silver rods gilt with gold, as they now do maces, before the king. Stat. 7 *Hen*. 7. c. 3. *Crompt. Jur*. 9. *Fleta*, lib. 2. c. 38. 3 *Black*. 444.

SERJEANTS. Of a more inferior kind are serjeants of the mace, whereof there is a great band in the city of London, and other corporate towns, that attend the mayor or other head officer, chiefly for matters of justice, &c. and to make arrests.

SERJEANTS OF THE HOUSEHOLD. Are officers who execute several functions within the king's household, mentioned in the stat. 33 *Hen*. 8. c. 12.

SERJEANTY, (*serjeantia*.) Signified in law a service, that could not be due from a tenant to any lord but to the king only; and this was either grand serjeanty, or petit. The first was a tenure, whereby one held his lands of the king by such services as he ought to do in person to the king at his coronation; and might also concern matters military, or services of honour in peace, as to be the king's butler, carver, &c. Petit serjeanty was where a man held lands of the king, to furnish him yearly with some small thing towards his wars, and in effect payable as rent. And though all tenures are turned into socage by 12 *Car*. 2. cap. 24. yet the honorary services of grand serjeanty still remain, being therein excepted. *Lit*. 153. 159. 1 *Inst*. 105. 108.

SERMONIUM was an interlude or historical play, acted by the inferior orders of the clergy, assisted by youths, in the body of the church, suitable to the solemnity of some high procession day; and before the improvements of the stage, these ruder sorts of performances were even a part of the unreformed religion. *Cowell*. *Blount*.

SERPLES. A mantle or upper coat, from the Lat. *superpellicium*. *Blount*.

SERVAGE, (mentioned in stat. 1. *Rich*. 2. c. 6.) Was when each tenant, besides payment of a certain rent, found one or more workmen for his lord's service.

SERVANTS. Are such as men of professions and trades employ under them to assist them in their particular callings; or such persons as others retain to perform the work and business of their families, which comprehends both men and women. And servants are menial, or not so: menial, from being *intra mœnia*, or domestics living within the walls of the house. *Wood's Inst*. 51.

The contract between them and their masters arises from the hiring. If the hiring be general without any particular time limited, the law construes it to be a hiring for a year; upon a principle of natural equity, that the servant shall serve, and the master maintain him, throughout all the revolutions of the respective seasons; as well when there is work to be done as when there is not: but the contract may be made for any larger or smaller term. All single men between twelve years old and sixty, and married ones under thirty years of age, and all single women between twelve and forty, not having any visible livelihood, are compellable by two justices to go out to service in husbandry or certain specific trades, for the promotion of honest industry: and no master can put away his servant, or servant leave his msster, after being so retained, either before or at the end of his term, without giving a quarter's warning, unless upon reasonable cause to be allowed by a justice of the peace. 5 *Eliz.* c. 4.

But it has been held that a master may turn away a servant for incontinence, or moral turpitude, for such misconduct produces a dissolution of the contract. *Cald.* 14.

And they may part by consent, or make a special bargain. The above statute relates only to servants employed in husbandry. It had been the practice for magistrates to exercise a jurisdiction over domestic servants, and it would be very useful to the public that they should possess such a jurisdiction, but it has lately been decided, that their authority, under 5 *Eliz.* c. 4. is confined to servants employed in husbandry. 6 *T. R.* 583.

By the common law, it was not larceny in any servant to run away with the goods committed to him to keep, but only a breach of civil trust. But by statute 33 Hen. VI. c. 1. the servants of persons deceased, accused of embezzling their master's goods, may by writ out of chancery (issued by the advice of the chief justices and chief baron, or any two of them) and proclamation made thereupon, be summoned to appear personally in the court of King's Bench, to answer their master's executors in any civil suit for such goods; and shall, on default of appearance, be attainted of felony. And by statute 21 *Hen.* 8. c. 7. if any servant embezzles his master's goods to the value of forty shillings, it is made felony, except in apprentices and servants under eighteen years old. But if he had not the possession, but only the care and oversight of the goods, as the butler of the plate, the shepherd of sheep, or the like, the embezzling of them is felony at common law. 1 *Hal. P. C.* 506.

And, to remove doubts which had existed respecting embezzlements by merchants' and bankers' clerks, it is enacted by 39 Geo. 3. c. 85. that if any servant or clerk shall, by virtue of his employment, receive any money, bills, or any valuable security, goods, or effects, in the name, or on the account of his master or employer, and shall afterwards embezzle any part of the same, he shall be deemed to have feloniously stolen the same, and shall be subject to transportation for any term not exceeding fourteen years.

By 6 *Ann.* c. 31. any servant negligently setting fire to a house or out-house, shall forfeit 100*l.* or be sent to the house of correction for eighteen months.

By 32 Geo. 3. c. 56. any person personating a master or mistress, or his or her executor, administrator, wife, relation, housekeeper, steward, agent, or servant, and, either personally or in writing, giving a false character to a servant; or asserting, that a servant has been hired for a period of time, or in a station; or was discharged at any other time, or had not been hired in any previous service, contrary to the fact; or any person offering him or herself as a servant, pretending to have served where he or she has not served, or with a false certificate, or who shall alter any certificate, or who, having been before in service, shall pretend not to have been in such service; shall, on conviction before two justices, forfeit 20*l.* half to the informer, and half to the parish; and the informer, though entitled to part of the penalty, is a competent witness. *s.* 1—7.

But parties aggrieved may appeal to the quarter sessions, where the matter may be finally determined; and the proceedings are not removable by certiorari. *s.* 10.

Persons not paying the penalty and 10*s.* for costs, or not giving notice of appeal, may be committed to the house of correction, and kept to hard labour, for not exceeding three months, nor less than one. *s.* 6. See *Master* and *Servant.*

SERVI. Bond men, or servile tenants.

SERVICE, (*Servitium.*) Is that duty which the tenant, by reason of his estate, oweth unto the lord.

Personal service is where something is to be done by the person of the tenant, as homage and fealty.

Annual and certain service is rent, suit of court to the lord, &c.

Accidental services, are heriots, reliefs, and the like. *Co. Copyhold* 22. *Co. Litt.* 222. 22 *E.* 4. 3.

As to feodal service, see *Feodal Service. Com.* 54. And as to heriot service, see *Heriot.*

SERVICE AND SACRAMENTS, See *Sacrament.*

SERVICE SECULAR. Worldly service, contrary to spiritual and ecclesiastical. 1 *Ed.* 4. c. 1.

SERVIENTIBUS. Certain writs touching servants and their masters, violating the statutes made against their abuses. *Reg. Orig.* 189, 190, 191.

SERVITIUM *Feodale et Prædiale.* Was not a personal service, but only by reason of the lands which were held in fee. *Bracton, lib.* 2. *c.* 16. *par.* 7.

SERVITIUM FORINSECUM. A service which did not belong to the chief lord, but to the king, because it was done *foris vel extra servitium quod fit domino capitali. Cowell.*

SERVITIUM INTRINSECUM. Service due to the chief lord alone from his tenants within his manor. *Bracton, lib.* 2. *Fleta, lib.* 3.

SERVITIUM LIBERUM. A service

to be done by feudatory tenants, who were called *liberi homines*, and distinguished from vassals, as was their service; for they were not bound to any of the base services of ploughing the lord's land, &c. but were to find a man and a horse, or go with the lord into the army, or to attend his court, &c. and sometimes it was called *servitium liberum armorum*. *Cowell. Blount.*

SERVITIUM REGALE. Royal service, or the prerogatives that within a royal manor belonged to the lord of it; which were generally reckoned to be the following, viz. power of judicature in matters of property, and of life and death in felonies and murders; right to waifs and estrays; minting of money; assise of bread and beer, and weights and measures. All which privileges, it is said, were annexed to some manors by grant from the king. *Paroch. Antiq.* 60.

SERVI TESTAMENTALES. Covenant servants. *Cowell.*

SERVITIIS ACQUIETANDIS. A writ judicial that lay for a man distrained for services to one, when he owed and performed them to another, for the acquittal of such services. *Reg. Judic.* 27.

SERVITOR, (*Servulus.*) A servingman; particularly applied to scholars in the colleges of the universities, who are upon the foundation. *Cowell. Blount.*

SERVITORS OF BILLS. Such servants or messengers of the marshal of the king's bench as were sent abroad with bills or writs to summon men to that court. 2 *H.* 4. c. 23. *Cowell.*

SESSEUR. The assessing or rating of wages. *Cowell.*

SESSION, (*Sessio.*) Is a sitting of justices in court upon their commission: as the Sessions of Oyer and Terminer, &c.

SESSION OF PARLIAMENT, (*Sessio Parliamenti.*) The sitting of the parliament; and the session of parliament continues till it be prorogued or dissolved, and breaks not off by adjournment. 4 *Inst.* 27.

SESSION, *Great, of Wales.* See *Wales.*

SESSION OF GAOL DELIVERY. A session held for delivering a gaol of the prisoners therein being.

SESSIONS OF THE PEACE. The court of general quarter sessions of the peace is a court that must be held in every county once in every quarter of a year. 4 *Inst.* 170. 2 *Hal. P. C.* 42. 2 *Hawk. P. C.* 32.; which, by statute 2 Hen. 5. c. 4. is appointed to be in the first week after Michaelmas day; the first week after the epiphany, the first week after the close of Easter, and in the week after the translation of St. Thomas the Martyr, or the 7th of July. It is held before two or more justices of the peace, one of which must be of the quorum. The jurisdiction of this court, by statute 34 *Edw.* 3. c. 1. extends to the trying and determining all felonies and trespasses whatsoever: though they seldom, if ever, try any greater offence than small felonies within the benefit of clergy; their commission providing, that if any case of difficulty arises, they shall not proceed to judgment, but in the presence of one of the justices of the courts of king's bench or common pleas, or one of the judges of assise. And therefore murders, and other capital felonies, are usually remitted for a more solemn trial to the assises. 4 *Black.* 270.

The sessions have jurisdiction over all misdemeanors, except forgery and perjury, by the common law; as these two offences were not considered to be breaches of the peace, which it was the chief object of the institution of the commission of the peace to preserve. The 5 *Eliz.* c. 9. however, gives the quarter-sessions expressly jurisdiction to try the perjuries specified in that statute. 2 *Hawk.* 40. 1 *East*, 173. 2 *East*, 18. See *Perjury.*

But they cannot try any new-created offence, without express power given them by the statute which creates it. 4 *Mod.* 379. *Salk.* 406. *Lord Raym.* 1144. There are, however, many offences, and particular matters, which by particular statutes belong properly to this jurisdiction, and ought to be prosecuted in this court: as, the smaller misdemeanors against the public or commonwealth, not amounting to felony; and especially offences relating to the game, highways, alehouses, bastard children, the settlement and provision for the poor, vagrants, servants' wages, apprentices, and popish recusants, see *Williams's Justice.* Some of these are proceeded upon by indictment, and others in a summary way by motion and order thereupon; which order may for the most part, unless guarded against by particular statutes, be removed into the court of king's bench, by writ of *certiorari facias*, and be there either quashed or confirmed. The records or rolls of the sessions are committed to the custody of a special officer denominated the *custos rotulorum*, who is always a justice of the quorum: and among them of the quorum (saith Lambard, lib. 4. c. 3.) a man for the most part especially picked out, either for wisdom, countenance, or credit. The nomination of the custos rotulorum (who is the principal civil officer in the county, as the lord lieutenant is the chief in military command) is by the king's sign manual: and to him the nomination of the clerk of the peace belongs, which office he is expressly forbidden to sell for money. Stat 37 *Hen.* 8. c. 1. 1 *W.* & *M.* stat. 1. c. 21. But the justices at the quarter-sessions, upon a complaint of his misconduct, may suspend or discharge him from his office. 1 *W.* c. 21. s. 6.

In most corporation towns there are quarter-sessions kept before justices of their own, within their respective limits, which have exactly the same authority as the general quarter-sessions of the county, except in a very few instances; one of the most considerable of which is the matter of appeals from orders of removal of the poor, which, though they be from the orders of corporation justices, must be to the sessions of the county, by statute 8 and 9 *W.* 3. c. 30. In both corporations and counties at large, there is sometimes kept a special or petty session, by a few justices, for dispatching smaller business in the neighbourhood between the times of the general sessions: as, for licensing alehouses, passing the accounts of the parish officers, and the like.

SESSIONS FOR ORDERING SERVANTS, called statute sessions, held by constables of hundreds, &c. 5 *Eliz.* c. 4. See *Statutum Sessionum.*

SESSIONS FOR WEIGHTS AND MEASURES. In London, four justices from among the mayor, recorder, and aldermen, (of which the mayor or recorder to be one) may hold a sessions to inquire into offences of selling by false weights and measures, contrary to the statutes; and to receive indictments, punish the offender, &c. *Char. K. Char. I.*

SET-OFF. A set-off against the demand of a plaintiff may be either by plea, or notice. In which case the defendant acknowledges the justice of the plaintiff's demand on the one hand; but, on the other, sets up a demand of his own, to counterbalance that of the plaintiff, either in the whole or in part. 2 *Geo.* 2. c. 22. and 8 *Geo.* 2. c. 24.

SETTLEMENTS AND REMOVALS. The Settlement of the Poor is as follows:

1. By Birth; for wherever a child is first known to be, that is always, *prima facie*, the place of settlement, until some other can be shewn (*Carth.* 433. *Comb.* 364. *Salk.* 485. 1 *Ld. Raym.* 567.) This is also generally the place of settlement of a bastard child; for a bastard having, in the eye of the law, no father, cannot be referred to his settlement as other children may (*Salk.* 427); but, in legitimate children, though the place of birth be *prima facie* the settlement, yet it is not conclusively so, for there are two settlements by parentage, being the settlement of one's father or mother: all legitimate children being really settled in the parish where their parents are settled, until they get a new settlement for themselves (*Salk.* 528. 2 *Ld. Raym.* 1473.)

If the parents acquire a new settlement, the children also follow, and belong to the last settlement of the father; or, after the death of the father, to the last settlement of the mother, whilst she is unmarried, till they are emancipated, or become independent of their father or mother's family; and, in that case, they have that settlement which their parent had at the time of emancipation.

This, it is true, is a very indefinite word; but lord Kenyon seems to have given as full and as just an explication of it as it will admit, in observing, that "the cases of emancipation have always been decided on the circumstances either of the son's being 21, or married, or having gained a settlement in his own right, or having contracted a relation, which was inconsistent with the idea of his being in a subordinate situation in his father's family." 3 *T. R.* 356. 8 *T. R.* 4791.

2. A new settlement may also be acquired several ways: as, By Marriage; for, a woman marrying a man that is settled in another parish, changes her own settlement, the law not permitting the separation of husband and wife (*Stra.* 544); but if the man has no settlement, her's is suspended during his life, if he remains in England, and is able to maintain her; but in his absence, or after his death, or during (perhaps) his inability, she may be removed to her old settlement. *Foley*, 249, 251, 252. *Burr. Sett. C.* 370.

In the absence, or after the death of the husband, in that case the wife and her children may be removed to her maiden settlement; but it seems fully determined that they cannot be separated or removed from the husband (*Burr. S. C.* 813. 1 *Stra.* 544.) The consequence is, that the whole family must be supported as casual poor in the parish where they may happen to want relief. In the removal of a wife or a widow it is sufficient, in the first instance, to prove her maiden settlement *Cald.* 39, 236.

3. The other methods of acquiring settlements in any parish, are all reducible to this one, of 40 days residence therein; but this 40 days residence (which is construed to be lodging or lying there) must not be by fraud or stealth, or, in any clandestine manner, but made notorious by one or other of the following concomitant circumstances:—

4. The next method therefore of gaining a settlement is by Forty Days Residence and Notice; for, if a stranger comes into a parish, and delivers notice in writing of his place of abode, and number of his family, to one of the overseers (which must be read in the church, and registered, and resides there unmolested for 40 days after such notice, he is legally settled thereby, according to stat. 13 & 14 *Car.* 2. c. 12. 1 *Jac.* 11, c. 17. 3 & 4 *W.* & *M.* c. 11; for the law presumes that such a one at the time of notice is not likely to become chargeable, else he would not venture to give it, or that in such case the parish would take care to remove him; but, by

the 35 *Geo.* 3. c. 101. it is enacted, that no person in future shall gain a settlement by such a notice.

There were also other circumstances equivalent to such notice; therefore, 5. Renting for a Year a tenement of the yearly value of 10*l.* and residing 40 days in the parish gained a settlement without notice (stat. 13 & 14 *Car.* 2. c. 12.) upon the principle of having substance enough to gain credit for such a house.

It is not necessary that the renting should be for a year. If a tenement, of the yearly value of 10*l.* be taken for two months, or 40 days only, it will be sufficient to give a settlement (*Burr. S. C.* 474.) Nor is it necessary there should be any house upon the premises; even a renting of the after-grass or pasture will be sufficient. 4 *T. R.* 348.

Also a person gains a settlement by residing in the parish in which part of the premises lie, but not by residing elsewhere. 2 *T. R.* 48.

And it need not be one entire tenement; for, if he takes one tenement in one parish, and another in a different parish, if together they are of the value of 10*l.* a year, he will gain a settlement by residing in either parish. The *value* only is material: it will be sufficient to give a settlement, if the enjoyment of the tenement is gratuitous, or if no rent is to be paid for it. 1 *T. R.* 458.

6. Being charged to and paying the Public Taxes and Levies of the Parish, excepting those for scavengers, highways (stat. 9 *Geo.* 1. c. 7.) and the duties on houses and windows (stat. 21 *Geo.* 2. c. 10. 18 *Geo.* 3. c. 26.) and by executing, when legally appointed, any public parochial office, for a whole year, in the parish, as church-warden, &c. are both of them equivalent to notice, and gain a settlement (stat. 3 & 4. *W.* &. *M.* c. 11.) if coupled with a residence of 40 days.

But by the 35 *Geo.* 3. c. 101. the payment of taxes for a tenement of less yearly value than 10*l.* will not give a settlement, so that this species of settlement is in effect abolished.

7. Being hired for a Year, when unmarried and childless, and serving a year in the same service, and a widower or widow, with children emancipated, is considered as childless, for such children cannot follow the settlements gained by their parents service. If an unmarried man is hired for a year, but before he enters upon the service, or during the service marries, he may gain a settlement (3 *T. R.* 382.) But this will not extend to the continuance in the service a second year, for he was married when this new contract was expressly or impliedly entered into (*Cald.* 54.) Hiring for any time certainly less than a year will not be sufficient; but from Whitsuntide to Whitsuntide is considered a year, though it will frequently happen to be a period less than 365 days. To gain a settlement as a servant there must be a hiring for a year, and a continued service for a year; but it is not necessary that the service should be subsequent to the hiring, for if there is a continued service for 11 months, or any other part of a year, by any number of modes of hirings, or with any difference of wages, and afterwards a hiring for a year, and a service to complete the year, a settlement is gained (*Cald.* 179.) There seemed to be great reason to think that the service, subsequent to the hiring for a year, should at least be 40 days; but it is now decided that that is not necessary (5 *T. R.* 98.) The settlement of a servant and an apprentice, is, where they last reside 40 days in their masters employ; and where they do not reside 40 days successively at one place, but alternately in two or more parishes, and more than 40 days upon the whole in each in the course of a year, the settlement is in that parish in which they slept the last night. *Doug.* 633.

8. Being bound an Apprentice, gives the servant and apprentice a settlement without notice (stat. 3 & 4 *W.* & *M.* c. 11.) in that place wherein they serve the last 40 days. This is meant to encourage application to trades, and going out to reputable services.

9. Lastly, the having an Estate of one's own, and residing thereon 40 days, however small the value may be, in case it be acquired by act of law, or of a third person, as by descent, gift, devise, &c. is a sufficient settlement (*Salk.* 524.); but if a man acquire it by his own act, as by purchase, in its popular sense, in consideration of money paid, then unless the consideration advanced *bona fide* be 30*l.* it is no settlement for any longer time than the person shall inhabit thereon (stat. 9 *Geo.* 1. c. 7.) He is in no case removable from his own property, but he shall not by any trifling or fraudulent purchase of his own acquire a permanent and lasting settlement.

All persons not so settled may be removed to their own parishes on complaint of the overseers, by two justices of the peace, if they shall adjudge them likely to become chargeable to the parish, into which they have intruded, unless they are in a way of getting a legal settlement, as by having hired a house of 10*l.* per annum, or living in an annual service, for then they are not removeable.

SETTLEMENT, *Act of.* See *Constitution*, *King*, *Liberties*, and *Rights*.

SEVERAL ACTION, is where two or more persons are severally charged in any action. *Cowell.*

SEVERAL COVENANT. A covenant by two or more severally, by which such are severally and separately bound. 5 *Rep.* 23.

SEVERAL FISHERY. A free fishery, or exclusive right of fishing in a public river, is a royal franchise; and is considered as such in all countries where the feodal polity has prevailed. 3 *Black.* 39.

SEVERAL INHERITANCE. An inheritance conveyed, so as to descend, or come to two or more persons severally by moieties, or in other purposes and proportions, &c. Vide *Inheritance.*

SEVERAL TAIL. Is that whereby land is given and entailed severally to two. *Co. Lit.*

SEVERAL TENANCY, (*Tenura separalis.*) A plea or exception taken to a writ that is laid against two persons as joint-tenants, who are several. *Bro.* 273.

SEVERALTY, *Estates in.* He that holds lands or tenements in severalty, or is sole tenant thereof, is he that holds them in his own right only, without any other person being joined or connected with him in point of interest, during his estate therein. 2 *Black.* 179.

SEVERANCE. Is the singling or severing of two or more joined in one writ or action, such as severance of the tenants in an assise. *Book Intr.* 81. 5 *Rep.* 97. *F. N. B.* 78. 10 *Rep.* 135. 6 *Rep.* 26.

SEVERANCE OF CORN. The cutting and carrying it from off the ground: and sometimes the setting out the tithes from the rest of the corn, is called severance. 2 *Cro.* 325.

SEVERANCE OF JOINT TENANCY. See *Joint-Tenant.*

SEVERITY OF PUNISHMENT. It is but reasonable among crimes of different natures those should be most severely punished which are the most destructive of the public safety and happiness. 4 *Black.* 16.

SEWARD. A Saxon word for him who guards the sea-coasts. It signifies *custos maris. Cowell.*

SEWER, (*Sewera.*) Is a fresh-water trench, or little river encompassed with banks on both sides, to carry the water into the sea, and thereby preserve the lands against inundations. *Cowell.*

SEWERS, COMMISSIONERS OF. The court of the commissioners of sewers is a temporary tribunal, erected by virtue of a commission under the great seal, which formerly used to be granted *pro re nata* at the pleasure of the crown. *F. N. B.* 113, but now at the discretion and nomination of the lord chancellor, lord treasurer, and chief justices, pursuant to the statute 23 Hen. 8. c. 5. Their jurisdiction is to overlook the repairs of sea-banks and sea-walls, and the cleansing rivers, public streams, ditches, and other conduits, whereby any waters are carried off: and is confined to such county or particular district as the commission shall expressly name. The commissioners are a court of record, and may fine and imprison for contempts, 1 *Sid.* 145.; and in the execution of their duty may proceed by jury, or upon their own view, and may take order for the removal of any annoyances, or the safe-guard and conservation of the sewers within their commission, either according to the laws and customs of Romney-Marsh, or otherwise, at their own discretion They may also, assess such rates or scots upon the owners of lands lying within the level drained, as they shall judge necessary; and if any person refuses to pay them, the commissioners may levy the same by distress of his goods and chattels: or they may, by statute 23 Hen. 8. c. 5, sell his freehold lands, (and by 7 Ann, c. 10, his copyhold also) in order to pay such scots or assessments: but their conduct is under the controul of the court of king's bench, which will prevent or punish any illegal or tyrannical proceedings. *Cro. Jac.* 336. It is clearly held, that this (as well as all other inferior jurisdictions) is subject to the discretionary coercion of his majesty's court of king's bench. 1 *Vent.* 66. *Salk.* 146.

Romney-marsh, in the county of Kent, a tract containing twenty-four thousand acres, is governed by certain ancient and equitable laws of sewers, composed by Henry de Bathe, a venerable judge in the reign of king Henry the Third; from which laws all commissioners of sewers in England may receive light and direction. 4 *Inst.* 276.

SEXAGESIMA SUNDAY. The sixtieth day before Easter. See *Septuagesima.*

SEXHINDENI, (*Sax.*) The middle Thanes, valued at 600 shillings. *Cowell.*

SEXTARY, (*Sextarius.*) Was an ancient measure, containing about our pint and a half. *Ibid.*

SEXTERY LANDS. Lands given to a church or religious house, for maintenance of the sexton or sacristan. *Ibid.*

SEXTONS. Parish clerks and sextons are regarded by the common law as persons who have freeholds in their offices: and therefore, though they may be punished, yet they cannot be deprived by ecclesiastical censures. 2 *Roll. Abr.* 234.

SHACKE. A custom in Norfolk to have common for hogs, from the end of harvest till seed-time, in all men's grounds without contradiction. *Co.* 7 *Rep. fol.* 5. Corbet's case. And in that country, *to go at shacke,* is as much as to go at large. *Cowell.*

SHARPING-CORN. A customary gift of corn, which, at every Christmas, the farmers in some parts of England give to their smith, for sharping their plough-irons, harrow tines, &c. *Blount.*

SHAW. A grove of trees, or a wood. 1 *Inst.* 4.

SHAWALDRES. By some chevaliers, but more probable soldiers. *Cowell.*

SHEADING. A riding, tithing, or division in the Isle of Man. *Cowell.*

SHEARMAN'S CRAFT. A craft or occupation used at Norwich; the artificers whereof do shear worsteds, fustians, and all woollen cloth. 19 *Hen.* 7. *c.* 17. 22 & 23 *Car.* 2.

SHEEP. By 3 *Hen.* 6. c. 2. none shall export any sheep, on pain of forfeiture.

By 25 *Hen.* 8. c. 13. no man shall have above 2000 sheep, on pain of 3*s.* 4*d.* for every extra one; but this does not extend to lambs under one year old, or sheep coming by executorship, or marriage, so as the number be reduced as above within one year, nor to sheep bequeathed by will to a child within age; and every person temporal may keep upon his inheritance as many sheep as he will.

Supernumerary sheep for the maintenance of the house may be kept; and six score of sheep shall be accounted a hundred. *Ibid.*

No man may take above two farms, unless he be resident in the parish, on pain of 3*s.* 4*d.* a week; and spiritual persons may keep as many sheep as they please on their own lands. *Ibid.*

By 14 *Geo.* 2. *c.* 6. stealing sheep (lamb, bullock, or other cattle, 15 *Geo.* 2. *c.* 34.), or part of the carcase, is made felony without benefit of clergy.

By 13 *Geo.* 3. *c.* 81. no rams shall be kept in the common fields between the 25th of August and the 25th of November.

By 38 *Geo.* 3. c. 65. if any person shall turn out upon any forest, wood, moor, marsh, heath, common, or other uninclosed land, any sheep or lambs having the mange, or having been within six months infected therewith, he shall forfeit not more than 10*l.* nor less than 20*s.* for each offence. *s.* 1.

The owner of every sheep or lamb so turned out shall cause them to be marked, on pain of not exceeding 2*s.* for each. *s.* 2.

Any person depasturing, or having a right to depasture, may apply to a justice, who may order sheep and lambs to be driven to the next pound, and there examined, and if found to have been depastured contrary to this act, may order them back to the place from whence taken, and award damages to the owner. *s.* 3.

But if they are found defective, he may order them to be detained, and marked S, and on demand to be delivered to the owner, who shall pay the expences and penalties. *s.* 4.

Persons destroying such marks, and the owners not renewing them, are to forfeit not more than 20*s.* nor less than 2*s.* for each. *s.* 5.

If the sheep or lambs be not demanded in five days after they are marked, they may be sold, and the produce paid to the overseers of the poor, and if not claimed in 12 months, applied in aid of the poor rate. *s.* 6.

The penalties may be levied by distress, on recovery thereof, before one justice; but persons aggrieved may appeal to sessions. *s.* 7-12. This act does not extend to Scotland. *s.* 13.

SHEEP-SILVER. A service turned into money, which was paid in respect that anciently the tenants used to wash the lord's sheep. *Cowell.*

SHEPWAY, *Court of.* This is a court held before the lord warden of the cinque ports, a writ of error lies from the mayor and jurats of each port, to the lord warden, in this court of Shepway, and from thence to the king's bench. 2 *Black.* 79.

SHERFEE. So the body of the lordship of Cardiff, in South Wales, is called, excluding the members of it. *Cowell.*

SHERIFF. The sheriff is an officer of very great antiquity in this kingdom, his name being derived from two Saxon words *scire, geretha*, the reeve, bailiff, or officer of the shire. He is called in Latin *vice-comes*, as being the deputy of the earl or *comes*; to whom the custody of the shire is said to have been committed at the first division of this kingdom into counties. But the earls, in process of time, by reason of their high employments and attendance on the king's person, not being able to transact the business of the county, were delivered of that burden, reserving to themselves the honour, but the labour was laid on the sheriff. So that now the sheriff does all the king's business in the county; and though he be still called vice-comes, yet he is entirely independent of, and not subject to the earl, the king, by his letters-patent, committing *custodiam comitatus* to the sheriff, and him alone. *Dalton of Sheriffs*, *c.* 1.

Sheriffs were formerly chosen by the inhabitants of the several counties. In confirmation of which it was ordained by statute 28 *Edw.* I. *c.* 8. that the people should have election of sheriffs in every shire, when the shrievalty is not of inheritance. For anciently in some counties the sheriffs were hereditary, as they were in Scotland till the statute 20 *Geo.* II. c. 43, and still continue in the county of Westmoreland to this day.* The city of London having also

---

* The earl of Thanet is hereditary sheriff of Westmoreland. This office may descend to, and be executed by a female; for

the inheritance of the shrievalty of Middlesex vested in their body by charter. 3 *Rep.* 72.*

The reason of these popular elections is assigned in the same statute, c. 13. "that the commons might chuse such as would not be a burden to them." And herein appears plainly a strong trace of the democratical part of our constitution, in which form of government it is an indispensable requisite that the people should chuse their own magistrates. *Montesq. Sp. L.* b. 2. c. 2.

This election was in all probability not absolutely vested in the commons, but required the royal approbation. For in the Gothic constitution, the judges of the county courts (which office is executed by our sheriff) were elected by the people, but confirmed by the king; and the form of their election was thus managed: the people, or *incolæ territorii*, chose twelve electors, and they nominated three persons, *ex quibus rex unum confirmabat. Stiern. de jure Goth. l.* 1. c. 3.

But with us in England these popular elections growing tumultuous, were put an end to by the statute 9 *Edw.* II. st. 2. which enacted, that "the sheriffs should from thenceforth be assigned by the chancellor, treasurer, and the judges," as being persons in whom the same trust might with confidence be reposed. By stat. 14 *Edw.* III. c. 7. 23 *Hen.* VI. c. 8. and 21 *Hen.* VIII. c. 20. "the chancellor, treasurer, president of the king's council, chief justices, and chief baron, are to make this election; and that on the morrow of All Souls in the exchequer." And the king's letters-patent, appointing the new sheriffs, used commonly to bear date the 6th day of November." *Stat.* 12 *Edw.* IV. c. 1.

The statute of Cambridge, 12 *Ric.* II. c. 2. ordains, that "the chancellor, treasurer, keeper of the privy seal, steward of the king's house, the king's chamberlain, clerk of the rolls, the justices of the one bench and the other, barons of the exchequer, and all other that shall be called to ordain, name, or make justices of the peace, sheriffs, and other officers of the king, shall be sworn to act indifferently, and to appoint no man that sueth either privily or openly to be put in office, but such only as they shall judge to be the best and most sufficient." And the custom now is, (and has been at least ever since the time of Fortescue, who was chief justice and chancellor to Henry the Sixth), that "all the judges, together with the other great officers and privy counsellors, meet in the exchequer on the morrow of All Souls yearly, (which day is now altered to the morrow of St. Martin by the last act for abbreviating Michaelmas term,) and then and there the judges propose three persons, to be reported (if approved of) to the king, who afterwards appoints one of them to be sheriff. *Fortes de L. L.* c. 24.

The following is the present mode of nominating sheriffs in the exchequer on the morrow of St. Martin:—The chancellor, chancellor of the exchequer, the judges, and several of the privy council assemble, and an officer of the court administers an oath to them in old French, that they will nominate no one from favour, partiality, or any improper motive. This done, the same officer having the list of the counties in alphabetical order, and of those who were nominated the year preceding, reads over the three names, and the last of the three he pronounces to be the present sheriff; but where there has been a pocket-sheriff, he reads the three names upon the list, and then declares who is the present sheriff. If any of the ministry or judges have an objection to any person named in the list, he then mentions it, and another gentleman is nominated in his room; if no objection be made, some one rises and says, "to the two gentlemen I know no objection, and I recommend *A. B.* esq. in the room of the present sheriff." *Chr. n.* 4. 1 *Black.* 341.

Another officer has a paper with a number of names given him by the clerk of assize for each county, which paper generally contains the names of the gentlemen upon the former list, and also of gentlemen who are likely to be nominated; and whilst the three are nominated, he prefixes 1, 2, or 3, to their names, according to the order in which they are placed; which, for greater certainty, he afterwards reads over twice. Several objections are made to gentlemen; some, perhaps, at their own request: such as, that they are abroad, that their estates are small and incumbered,

---

"Ann, countess of Pembroke, had the office of hereditary sheriff of Westmoreland, and exercised it in person. At the assises at Appleby she sat with the judges on the bench." *Harg. Co. Litt.* 326.

* The election of the sheriffs of London and Middlesex was granted to the citizens of London for ever in very ancient times, upon condition of their paying 300*l.* a year to the king's exchequer. In consequence of this grant, they have always elected two sheriffs, though these constitute together but one officer; and if one die, the other cannot act till another is elected. (4 *Bac. Abr.* 447.) In the year 1748, the corporation of London made a bye-law, imposing a fine of 600*l.* upon every person, who, being elected, should refuse to serve the office of sheriff; but protestant dissenters, who cannot qualify by taking the oaths, are not compellable to serve. 2 *Burn. E. L.* 185.

that they have no equipage, that they are practising barristers, or officers in the militia, &c. *Ibid.*

The new sheriff is generally appointed about the end of the following Hilary term; this extension of the time was, probably, in consequence of the 17 *Edw.* IV. c. 7. which enables the old sheriff to hold his office over Michaelmas and Hilary terms. *Ibid.*

But notwithstanding this is expressly recognized to be the law of the land, some writers have affirmed, that the king, by his prerogative, may name whom he pleases to be sheriff, whether chosen by the judges or no.—This is grounded on a very particular case in the 5th year of queen Elizabeth, when, by reason of the plague, there was no Michaelmas term kept at Westminster, so that the judges could not meet there *in crastino animarum* to nominate the sheriffs; whereupon the queen named them herself, without such previous assembly, appointing for the most part one of the two remaining in the last year's list. *Jenkins.* 229. *Dyer.* 225.

And the practice of occasionally naming what are called *pocket-sheriffs*,* by the sole authority of the crown, hath uniformly continued to the reign of his present majesty. 1 *Black.* 342.

Sheriffs, by virtue of several old statutes, are to continue in their office no longer than one year; and yet it hath been said (4 *Rep.* 32.) that a sheriff may be appointed *durante bene placito*, or during the king's pleasure; and so is the form of the royal writ (*Dalt. of Sheriffs*, 8.) Therefore, till a new sheriff be named, his office cannot be determined, unless by his own death, or the demise of the king; in which last case it was usual for the successor to send a new writ to the old sheriff; but now, by statute 1 *Ann, st.* 1. c. 8. all officers appointed by the preceding king may hold their offices for six months after the king's demise, unless sooner displaced by the successor. And by statute 1 *Ric.* 2. *c.* 11. no man that has served the office of sheriff for one year can be compelled to serve the same again within three years after.

The power and duty of the sheriff are either as a judge, as the keeper of the king's peace, as a ministerial officer of the superior courts of justice, or as the king's bailiff.

1. In his judicial capacity, he is to hear and determine all causes of forty shillings value and under, in his county court. He is likewise to decide the elections of knights of the shire, (subject to the controul of the house of commons,) of coroners, and of verderors; to judge of the qualification of voters, and to return such as he shall determine to be duly elected. *Dalt.* 7.

2. As the keeper of the king's peace, both by common law and special commission, he is the first man in the county, and superior in rank to any nobleman therein, during his office, 1 *Roll. Rep.* 237. He may apprehend, and commit to prison, all persons who break the peace, or attempt to break it; and may bind any one in a recognizance to keep the king's peace. He may, and is bound *ex officio* to pursue, and take all traitors, murderers, felons, and other misdoers, and commit them to gaol for safe custody. He is also to defend his country against any of the king's enemies when they come into the land: and for this purpose, as well as for keeping the peace and pursuing felons, he may command all the people of his county to attend him; which is called the *posse comitatus*, or power of the county. *Dalt.* c. 95.; and this summons every person above fifteen years old, and under the degree of a peer, is bound to attend upon warning (*Lamb. Eir.* 315), under pain of fine and imprisonment, 2 *Hen.* 5. c. 8. But though the sheriff is thus the principal conservator of the peace in his county, yet, by the express directions of the *Mag. Cart. c.* 17. he, together with the constable, coroner, and certain other officers of the king, are forbidden to hold any pleas of the crown, or, in other words, to try any criminal offence. For it would be highly unbecoming, that the executioners of justice should be also the judges; should impose, as well as levy, fines and amercements; should one day condemn a man to death, and personally execute him the next. Neither may he act as an ordinary justice of the peace during the time of his office, 1 *Mar. st.* 2. *c.* 8; for this would be equally inconsistent, he being in many respects the servant of the justices.

3. In his ministerial capacity the sheriff is bound to execute all process issuing from the king's courts of justice. In the commencement of civil causes, he is to serve the writ, to arrest, and to take bail; when the cause comes to trial, he must summon and return the jury; when it is determined, he must see the judgment of the court carried into execution. In criminal matters, he also arrests and imprisons, he returns the jury, he has the custody of the delinquent, and he executes the sentence of the court, though it extend to death itself. 1 *Black.* 344.

4. As the king's bailiff, it is his business to preserve the rights of the king within his bailiwick, for so his county is frequently

---

* When the king appoints a person sheriff, who is not one of the three nominated in the exchequer, he is called a pocket-sheriff; but there is no compulsory appointment of a pocket-sheriff. 2 *Inst.* 559. 1 *Black.* 342.

called in the writs; a word introduced by the princes of the Norman line, in imitation of the French, whose territory is divided into bailiwicks, as that of England into counties, *Fortesc. de L. L. c.* 24. He must seise to the king's use all lands devolved to the crown by attainder or escheat: must levy all fines and forfeitures; must seise and keep all waifs, wrecks, estrays, and the like, unless they be granted to some subject; and must also collect the king's rents within his bailiwick, if commanded by process from the exchequer. *Dalt. c.* 9.

To execute these various offices, the sheriff has under him many inferior officers: an under-sheriff, bailiffs, and gaolers, who must neither buy, sell, nor farm their offices, on forfeiture of 500*l*. *Stat.* 3 *Geo.* 1. c. 15.

The under-sheriff usually performs all the duties of the office, a very few only excepted, where the personal presence of the high-sheriff is necessary. But no under-sheriff shall abide in his office above one year, (*Stat.* 42 *Edw.* 3. *c.* 9.); and if he does, by statute 23 *Hen.* 6. *c.* 8. he forfeits 200*l*. a very large penalty in those early days. And no under-sheriff or sheriff's officer shall practise as an attorney during the time he continues in such office, (stat. 1 *Hen.* 5. *c.* 4.), for this would be a great inlet to partiality and oppression. But these salutary regulations are shamefully evaded, by practising in the names of other attorneys, and putting in sham deputies by way of nominal under-sheriffs; by reason of which, says Dalton, (of sheriffs, c. 115.) the under-sheriffs and bailiffs do grow so cunning in their several places, that they are able to deceive, and it may well be feared that many of them do deceive both the king, the high-sheriff, and the county.

The sheriff's officers are either bailiffs of hundreds, or special bailiffs. Bailiffs of hundreds are officers appointed over those respective districts by the sheriffs, to collect fines therein, to summon juries, to attend the judges and justices at the assises and quarter sessions; and also to execute writs and process in the several hundreds. But, as these are generally plain men, and not thoroughly skilful in this latter part of their office, that of serving writs, and making arrests and executions, it is now usual to join special bailiffs with them, who are generally mean persons, employed by the sheriffs on account only of their adroitness and dexterity in hunting and seizing their prey. The sheriff being answerable for the misdemeanors of these bailiffs, they are therefore usually bound in an obligation with sureties for the due execution of their office, and thence are called bound-bailiffs, which the common people have corrupted into a much more homely appellation. 1 *Black.* 345.

Gaolers are also the servants of the sheriff, and he must be responsible for their conduct. Their business is to keep safely all such persons as are committed to them by lawful warrant; and, if they suffer any such to escape, the sheriff shall answer it to the king, if it be a criminal matter; or, in a civil case, to the party injured. *Dalt.* c. 118. 4 *Rep.* 34. *c.* 4. 4 *Edw.* 3. *c.* 9. 5 *Edw.* 3. c. 4. And to this end the sheriff must have lands sufficient within the county to answer the king and his people. *Stat.* 6 *Edw.* 2. *st.* 2. 2 *Edw.* 3. 13 & 14 *Car.* 2. c. 21. *sect.* 7.

The vast expence which custom had introduced in serving the office of high-sheriff, was grown such a burthen to the subject, that it was enacted, by 13 and 14 *Car.* 2. c. 21. that no sheriff (except of London, Westmoreland, and towns which are counties of themselves) should keep any table at the assises, except for his own family, or give any presents to the judges or their servants, or have more than forty men in livery; yet, for the sake of safety and decency, he may not have less than twenty men in England and twelve in Wales, upon forfeiture, in any of these cases, of 200*l*. See also *Escape*, *Execution*, *Fieri facias*, &c.

SHERIFF'S COURT IN LONDON. The chief of the courts in London are the sheriff's courts, holden before their steward or judge. 3 *Black.* 80.

SHERIFF'S TOURN. See *Tourn* or *Turn*.

SHERIFFALTY, (*vicecomitatus.*) Is the sheriff-ship, or time of a man's being sheriff. *Cowell.*

SHERIFFWICK. The extent of a sheriff's authority. *Ibid.*

SHERIFF-GELD. A rent formerly paid by the sheriff; and it is prayed that the sheriff in his account may be discharged thereof. *Ibid.*

SHERIFF-TOOTH, seems to be a tenure by the service of providing entertainment for the sheriff at his county courts. *Ibid.*

SHEWING, (*monstratio.*) Is specially used to be quit of attachment in a court, in plaints shewed and not avowed. *Shep. Epitom.* 1130. *Cowell.*

SHIELD, (*scutum.*) An instrument of defence, (from the Sax. *scyldan*,) to cover, or the Greek σκυτος, a skin, anciently shields being made with skins. *Cowell. Blount.*

SHIFTING USE. See *Uses*.

SHILLING, (Sax. *scilling*, Lat. *solidus.*) Among the English Saxons passed but for 5*d.* afterwards it contained 16*d.* and often 20*d.* In the reign of King William 1. called the Conqueror, a shilling was of the same value as at this day. *Reg. H.* 1. *Domesday. Cowell.*

SHILWITE, *Est emenda pro transgressione facta in nativam, tam impregnando. Cowell. Blount.*

SHIP-MONEY, was an imposition charged upon the ports, towns, cities, boroughs, and counties of this realm, in the time of king Charles I. by writs commonly called ship-writs, under the great seal of England, in the year 1635 and 1636, for the providing and furnishing certain ships for the king's service, &c. which was declared to be contrary to the laws and statutes of this realm by the petition of right. Stat. 17 *Car.* 1. *c.* 14. 4 *Black.* 430.

SHIPPER, is a Dutch word, signifying the master of a ship, but used for any common seaman: a skipper. *Cowell. Blount.*

SHIPS. By 28 *Edw.* 3. *c.* 13. no ship, fraught towards England, shall be constrained to come to any port, or abide against the will of the merchants or masters, and they shall deliver their goods freely.

By 14 *Ric.* 2. *c.* 6. English merchants shall freight only in English ships, so that the owners take reasonable freight.

By 34 & 35 *Hen.* 8. c. 9. unlading of ballast in any haven or river running to a port, except on the land above high-water mark, is a forfeiture of 5*l.*

By 8 *Eliz. c.* 13. the corporation of the Trinity-House at Deptford Strond may erect beacons, marks, and signs for the sea, near the sea-coasts; and any person taking down a sea-mark, shall forfeit 100*l.* and not being worth so much, shall be deemed convict of outlawry.

By 12 *Car.* 2. *c.* 18. no goods shall be imported from the plantations but in English ships navigated by three-fourths English; and no one shall be a merchant or factor there, who is not a subject, naturalized, or made a free denizen, on forfeiture of all his goods.

No goods of the produce of Asia, Africa, or America, shall be imported, but in ships of England or Ireland, or the plantations, the master and mariners being three fourths English, on forfeiture of ship and goods. *Ibid.*

No goods of foreign growth or manufacture shall be imported in English ships, but only from the places of their said growth. *Ibid.*

No goods shall be carried from one port of England to another, in the vessel of any alien not denizened. *Ibid.*

By 22 & 23 *Car.* 2. *c.* 11. master of a ship of 200 tons, and 16 guns, delivering her up to any pirates without fighting, is rendered incapable of future command.

Master of a ship under 200 tons, and 16 guns, shall not yield to any pirate, not having at least his double number of guns, without fighting. *Ibid.*

Mariners or inferior officers refusing to fight and defend the ship, shall lose all wages due, and have six months' imprisonment and hard labour. *Ibid.*

Where the master is forced by the mariners to yield his ship, he shall not be liable; and mariners laying hands on the commander to hinder him from fighting in defence of his ship, shall suffer as felons. *Ibid.*

Officers or seamen wounded in defence of their ship, shall have reward from the owners, not exceeding 2*l.* per cent. amongst them. *Ibid.*

Merchant ship taking a ship that first assaulted them, shall have such share thereof as usual in privateers. *Ibid.*

Any officer or mariner wilfully destroying the ship, shall be guilty of felony. *Ibid.*

By 7 & 8 *Wil.* 3. *c.* 22, to prevent colouring foreign ships under English names, English-built ships, prizes, and foreign ships allowed, shall be registered and attested at the Custom-House; and ships' names changed shall be entered again, but this does not extend to open boats used on rivers.

By 7 *Geo.* 2. *c.* 15. owners of ships shall be liable only to forfeit the value of the ship and freight, for embezzlements committed without their knowledge.

If several proprietors suffer by such embezzlement, and the value of the ship be not sufficient to compensate their loss, their proportions shall be determined by average, and the freighters or owners may exhibit a bill for discovering the amount of such losses. *Ibid.*

Part owners exhibiting such bills, shall annex an affidavit to it, that they do not collude with the defendant. And this act is not to abridge the remedy at law against the master or mariners for embezzlements. *Ibid.*

By 19 *Geo.* 2. *c.* 22. masters throwing out ballast in any harbour, but upon dry land only, justices may issue warrants, and upon proof, fine them, not more than 5*l.* nor less than 50*s.*

Ships being stranded or sunk in an harbour, and permitted to remain there, the justices may summon the owner, and upon conviction, issue warrants for seizing and removing the ship. *Ibid.*

By 24 *Geo.* 2. *c.* 45. persons convicted of theft to the value of 40*s.* on board any ship or vessel, in any port, navigable river, or harbour, shall be excluded from benefit of clergy.

By 26 *Geo.* 2. *c.* 19. persons convicted of plundering shipwrecked goods, or of obstructing the escape of any person from a wreck, or of putting out false lights, shall suffer death without benefit of clergy.

By 9 *Geo.* 3. c. 39, ships (not belonging to the royal navy) stopping at, or fastening to, the king's moorings or hulks, or so as to bear against the king's ships, unless necessitated, shall forfeit 10*l.* per tide, one moiety to Greenwich hospital, the other to the prosecutor; and may be removed for not complying on notice.

By 13 *Geo.* 3. c. 26. no foreigner shall purchase any share in British ships without the consent of the owners of three-fourths in value.

13 *Geo.* 3. c. 74. Rule for ascertaining the tonnage of ships, viz. length in a straight line along the rabbet of the keel from the back of the main stern-post to a perpendicular line, from the fore part of the main stern-post, under the bowsprit, from which subtract three-fifths of the breadth, the remainder is the length of the keel to find the tonnage; and the breadth shall be taken from the outside plank, in the broadest place of the ship, above or below the main wales, exclusive of all doubling planks wrought on the sides of the ship, multiplying the length of the keel by the breadth so taken, and that product by half the breadth, and dividing the whole by 94, the quotient is the true contents of the tonnage.

By 22 *Geo.* 3. c. 25. vessels captured by an enemy shall not be ransomed. All contracts made, and securities given for the same, shall be void; and persons ransoming or contracting to ransom any ship or goods, shall forfeit 500*l.*

By 26 *Geo.* 3. c. 60. no ship built out of his majesty's dominions, except prizes, shall be entitled to the privileges of a British ship.

No ship rebuilt, or whose repairs exceed 15*s.* per ton, in a foreign port, shall be deemed British built, unless such repairs are necessary from extraordinary damages sustained on voyages: and the expences of repairs shall be certified, on arrival, to an officer of the customs. *Ibid.*

The provisions of 7 & 8 *Will.* 3. c. 22, shall be extended to vessels of fifteen tons and upwards, and certificates of registry obtained; and no registry shall be made but at the port to which a vessel belongs, except for prizes condemned at Guernsey, Jersey, or Man, unless authorized by the commissioners of customs. *Ibid.*

The port from and to which a a ship usually trades shall be deemed her port. No registry shall be required for any vessels belonging to the royal family: and no ship built in the United States of America, during the existence of any prohibitory acts, shall be entitled to be registered. *Ibid.*

No subject residing out of his majesty's dominions shall be entitled to be the owner of any ship authorized to be registered, except a member of a factory. *Ibid.*

The oath by *Will.* 3. required, is repealed, and another appointed to be taken before registry. *Ibid.*

Ships shall be examined before certificates are granted; and persons giving false descriptions, or making false registries of ships, forfeit 100*l.* *Ibid.*

Bond shall be given not to lend certificates, and to return them in case the ship is lost, or sold to a foreigner; and Mediterranean passes are to be delivered up with the certificates. *Ibid.*

Indorsements on certificates of registry shall specify the name and residence of the person to whom the property is transferred. Certificates shall be recited in all transfers of property; and the changes of masters of vessels shall be indorsed on certificates of registry.

No change shall be made in ships' names, which, and their ports, must be painted conspicuously on the vessels; and altering or defacing letters is a penalty of 100*l.* *Ibid.*

Persons applying for certificates in Great Britain, shall produce a particular account of the ships from the builders, and make oath to their identity. *Ibid.*

If certificates be lost, new ones shall be granted, according to 15 *Geo.* 2. c. 31, but security shall be given, on receiving fresh certificates, and oath made as hereinbefore directed; that is to say, the master shall make oath and give security that no illegal use shall be made of the first register, if found. 13 *Geo.* 2. c. 31.

Ships, if altered, must be registered anew, or be deemed foreign. The condemnation of prizes, and the particulars of the vessels, must be produced, to entitle to a certificate of registry; and prizes condemned in Guernsey, Jersey, or Man, must be registered at Southampton. 26 *Geo.* 3. c. 60. *Ibid.*

The sum, on oath, for which a prize sold in the colonies shall be subjoined to the certificate; and the certificate shall express in what part the ship was built. *Ibid.*

Ships already registered shall exchange their certificates for new ones; and others, now required to be registered, shall apply for certificates within a certain time after notice, to be given by the commissioners of customs, viz. in Great Britain, Guernsey, Jersey, or Man, within twelve months; in Africa or America, within eighteen months; and in Asia, within thirty months after notice; but certificates may be granted, where, from unavoidable necessity, application could not be made in time limited. *Ibid.*

Ships leaving port without certificates shall be forfeited. If ships be found without the port to which they belong without certificates, bond must be given that they shall be procured: and if square-rigged vessels cannot enter the ports to which they belong, certificates may be obtained, upon their being surveyed at the port where they touch. *Ibid.*

Certificates shall be numbered, and an account of them transmitted to the commissioners of customs by the officer, on penalty of 200*l.* and dismission. *Ibid.*

Certificates of registry shall be produced at every port, on penalty of 100*l.* *Ibid.*

Copies of certificates granted in Scotland shall be annually sent to the Custom-house in England; and there shall be paid on the first registry of ships built prior to May 1, 1786, in lieu of stamp duties, the following sums, viz. For a ship of fifteen tons, and not more than fifty, 1*s.* 6*d.*; above fifty, and not more than one hundred tons, 2*s.* 6*d.*; above one hundred, and not more than two hundred tons, 3*s.* 6*d.*; and all above two hundred tons, 5*s.* But the stamp duties shall continue to be paid on transfers of property. *Ibid.*

The privy council may order ships to be registered, to whom they have been granted or promised in consideration of their services, though not otherwise entitled thereto; and suits commenced in the colonies touching registers granted, such ships may be stopped till his majesty's pleasure be known. *Ibid.*

Any persons, by virtue of their office, required to act under this act, neglecting their duty, forfeit 500*l.* for the first offence, and for the second are incapacitated, and forfeit a like sum. *Ibid.*

Swearing falsely is perjury; and falsifying, or using false certificates, is a penalty of 500*l.* *Ibid.*

Ships of Ireland lawfully qualified and registered there, shall enjoy the privileges of British-built ships. *Ibid.*

By 26 *Geo.* 3. *c.* 86. owners of ships shall not be liable for any loss of goods shipped without their privity, further than the value of the vessel and the freight; nor for any occasional loss by fire; nor for loss of plate or jewels, unless, at the time of shipping, declaration be made of the value.

If the produce of the ship be insufficient to answer losses, it is to be proportionably divided among the losers; and freighters and owners of vessels may exhibit bills in equity for discovery of the amount of losses and value of vessels. *Ibid.*

This act is not to lessen the remedy against masters and mariners for embezzlement. *Ibid.*

By 27 *Geo.* 3. *c.* 12. no oath taken to acquire a temporary right as a citizen during residence in a foreign state, shall be deemed an oath of allegiance to such state. *Ibid.*

Instead of the oath required by 26 *Geo.* 3. *c.* 60. an oath, declaring to whom the vessel belongs, may be taken by the person properly authorized by the East-India company, or any other company or body corporate having ships. *Ibid.*

The commissioners of the customs, or the governors or commanders in chief of the islands, may permit the bond required, on obtaining a certificate of the registry of a vessel, to be executed wherever they think proper. *Ibid.*

Whenever the master of a vessel is changed, fresh security shall be given. *Ibid.*

Vessels not exceeding thirty tons burthen, and not having a fixed deck, may be employed in the fishery at Newfoundland, without being registered. *Ibid.*

Vessels built at Newfoundland, Quebec, Nova Scotia, and New Brunswick, for European owners, may be registered there, upon the ships' agents taking the requisite oath. But such ships, on their arrival in Europe, must be registered agreeable to 26 *Geo.* 3. *c.* 60. *Ibid.*

All vessels which, by 26 *Geo.* 3. *c.* 60. are declared not to be entitled to the privileges of a British-built ship, shall be deemed alien ships. *Ibid.*

By 28 *Geo.* 3. *c.* 34. on complaint on oath by the owner of a vessel, that the master has refused to deliver up the certificate of registry, granted according to 7 & 8 *Will.* 3. *c.* 22. and 26 *Geo.* 3. *c.* 60. before a justice, the master may be apprehended by warrant, and on proof of its not being lost, but maliciously detained, the master shall forfeit 100*l.* to be paid within two days, otherwise he is to be imprisoned for not less than six, or more than twelve months; the justice may grant a search warrant for the certificate, which, if found, is to be delivered to the owner; if not, the person who granted the first is to grant another.

By 34 *Geo.* 3. *c.* 68. after six months from the conclusion of the present war, no goods, wares, or merchandize, shall be imported into Great Britain, or Guernsey, Jersey, Alderney, Sark, or Man, nor any goods exported from thence, unless the master and three-fourths of the crew are British subjects; nor any such vessels, registered, to be otherwise navigated but as herein provided. *s.* 1—3.

No goods to be carried from one place to another in Great Britain or the said isles, nor any vessel to sail in ballast, nor to fish on the coasts, unless wholly manned with British subjects: but the commissioners of customs may authorize vessels to have foreign mariners to instruct British ones in fishing. *s.* 4.

The proportions of British mariners to continue so the whole voyage, unless reduced by death, sickness, or desertion; and the act is not to alter any regulations for which special provision has been made. s. 5.

None to be deemed British mariners but natural-born subjects, persons naturalized, denizens, or persons become subjects by conquest or cession of territory, and who shall have taken the oaths of allegiance. s. 6.

Foreign seamen serving three years in the navy in time of war, may be employed as masters; or British seamen, on certificate of their service. s. 7.

No person who has taken an oath of allegiance to any foreign state, except under the terms of some capitulation, to be qualified to be a master; or a British person disqualified, acting, to forfeit 10*l.* to be recovered before a justice. s. 8.

Vessels not to be forfeited, if the disqualification of persons was unknown to the owners. *Ibid.*

In America and the West Indies, and to the eastward of the Cape of Good Hope, negroes, lascars, and other natives, may be employed as heretofore. *Ibid.*

Goods imported contrary to this act to be forfeited with the vessels, and the same may be seized by any commissioned, warrant, or petty officer, or officer of customs; but on production of certificates of the necessity of engaging foreign mariners, no vessel to be detained; but the persons authorized to make seizures, to indorse the certificates for the consideration of the customs. s. 10—12.

After January 1, 1795, no transfer under 26 *Geo.* 3. *c.* 60. of any property in any vessel to be valid, unless made agreeably thereto; and a particular form of the indorsement on a change of property is prescribed. s. 14, 15.

If vessels be absent from the port to which they belong, when alteration in the property shall be made, the sale shall still be made as before directed. s. 16.

And particular regulations are made, for the transfer of property, where owners reside in any country not under the dominion of his majesty. s. 17.

Masters wilfully withholding their certificates of registry, (see 28 *Geo.* 3. *c.* 34.) to forfeit 100*l.* on conviction before a justice of the peace, or to be committed to gaol for not less than six nor more than 12 months. s. 18.

Justices are to certify the detainer of certificates, on which the registry may be made, *de novo*. s. 19.

Where property is transferred, no vessel to be registered *de novo* by the registrar, unless instrument of sale be produced; but the commissioners of customs may give directions for the registry. s. 20.

On alteration of property in vessels in the same port, (see 7 & 8 *Will.* 3. *c.* 22.) they may be registered *de novo*. s. 21.

On transfer of property to persons not subjects of his majesty, the masters are to proceed with the cargo, that may be legally taken on board, to some port of registry where the vessel may be registered *de novo*; and on failure of compliance, the vessels to be deemed foreign, and not entitled to the privileges of British vessels, unless the commissioners of customs think fit; and on transfer of property, vessels to be registered *de novo* within twelve months, if not on a voyage to the east of the Cape of Good Hope, or west of Cape Horn; and within two years if on a voyage to the east or west thereof. s. 22.

By 48 *Geo.* 3. *c.* 70. from October 1, 1808, no British-built vessel, captured by the enemy, shall afterwards be registered as a British vessel.

But by 49 *Geo.* 3. *c.* 41. notwithstanding the above act of 48 *Geo.* 3. *c.* 70. British-built ships, recaptured, may be registered and have the privilege of British ships.

See also *Customs, Excise, Importation, Seamen, Quarantine, Pilots.*

SHIPS, PASSENGERS. By 43 *Geo.* 3. *c.* 56. no master of any British vessel from any place in the united kingdom, shall carry to any parts beyond sea a greater number of persons than one for every two tons registered burthen of the part unladen, on pain of 50*l.* for each person, and the vessel shall be detained till the penalty be paid. s. 1, 2.

Vessels to North America shall have at least twelve weeks provisions and water; and the master for not distributing a daily allowance thereof, of not less than half a pound of meat, one pound and a half of bread or oatmeal, with a half-pint of molasses, and one gallon of water, for each person, shall forfeit 20*l.* for each omission, and demanding a clearance for vessels not properly stored, 50*l.* s. 3.

Before clearance a muster roll shall be delivered to the officer of customs; and delivering false musters is a penalty of 50*l.* per head. s. 4.

Officers of the customs, with a justice, shall muster the passengers and men before sailing, and may detain the vessel till bail be found for penalties incurred. *Ibid.*

No clearance shall be given until such muster; a certified copy whereof shall be delivered to the master, and the original preserved at the custom-house. *Ibid.*

Any passenger desirous of not proceeding on the voyage, may be taken out of the vessel by any justice, and set free from his engagement. s. 5.

No passenger shall be received on board at any place where an officer of the customs is not stationed, on pain of 500*l.* s. 6.

Vessels carrying fifty persons, shall be provided with a surgeon; and every surgeon shall have a medicine chest properly stored, on oath, on pain of 50*l.* *s.* 7, 8.

Bedding shall be once a day aired, and the vessel once a week fumigated, on pain of 20*l.* for each neglect. *s.* 9.

Master and surgeon shall give bond to keep journals during the voyage, and shall deliver them, on oath, to the officer at the port of arrival on return from the voyage; and the officer shall deliver to them copies, and transmit duplicates to the commissioners of customs; and masters or surgeons acting contrary hereto, forfeit 100*l.* *s.* 10.

Masters of foreign vessels shall not have on board more than one person for every five tons burthen, on pain of 50*l.* per head. *s.* 11.

The act does not extend to government vessels. *s.* 12.

Masters or others landing provisions or water, except in proportion to the persons landed, are to forfeit 200*l.* *s.* 13.

An abstract of the act shall be hung up in every custom-house, and a copy thereof, and of the muster-roll, in every vessel, on pain of 20*l.* *s.* 15.

Officers of ships of war and revenue cutters may call for muster rolls, and search ships at sea; and if the provisions of this act have not been complied with, may seize and send them to some port. *s.* 16.

Bond shall be given that vessels are seaworthy, and that passengers shall be duly delivered. *s.* 17.

Officers of the customs signing sufferances contrary to this act, are to forfeit 50*l.* *s.* 18.

Penalties may be recovered within three years in courts of record with double costs, half to the king and half to the informer. *s.* 19.

Persons taking false oaths incur the pains of perjury. *s.* 20.

And the act shall not alter the laws respecting artificers going to parts beyond the sea. *s.* 21.

But by 44 *Geo.* 3. *c.* 56. the act 43 *Geo.* 3. *c.* 56. shall not apply to vessels carrying passengers to or from the fishery at Newfoundland or the coast of Labrador.

SHIPS RIOTS. By 33 *Geo.* 3. *c.* 67. seamen, keelmen, ship-carpenters, or other persons riotously assembled, who shall forcibly prevent the loading or unloading or sailing of any vessels, being convicted at the quarter-sessions, shall be committed to hard labour for not exceeding twelve nor less than six calendar months: as also any such persons who shall forcibly prevent others from working. *s.* 1, 2.

Persons offending a second time, to be guilty of felony, and transported for not more than fourteen nor less than seven years. *s.* 3.

But nothing herein is to extend to matters done by the authority of his majesty. *s.* 4.

Seamen, keelmen, casters, ship-carpenters, or other persons, wilfully setting fire to any ship, to be guilty of felony without benefit of clergy. *s.* 5.

And destroying or damaging the same by any other means, to be transported for not more than fourteen nor less than seven years. *s.* 6.

Offences committed on the high seas, triable in any sessions for the trial of offences committed thereon. *s.* 7.

Prosecutions under this act to be commenced within one year. *s.* 8.

SHIRE, (*comitatus*, from the Sax. *scyre*, to part or divide), a well known part or portion of the kingdom, called also county.

SHIRE-CLERK. The person that keeps the county court. See *County Court.*

SHIRE-MAN, or SCYRE-MAN. Anciently the judge of the country, by whom trials for land, &c. were determined before the conquest. *Cowell.*

SHIREMOTE. An assembly of the county or shire at the assises, &c. *Ibid.*

SHOEMAKERS. See *Leather.*

SHOOTING. See *Felony* and *Game.*

SHOP, (*shopa*). A place where any thing is openly sold. *Cowell.*

SHOP-BOOKS. These are not allowed of themselves to be given in evidence for the owner; but a servant who made the entry may have recourse to them to refresh his memory. And if such servant (who was accustomed to make such entries) be dead, and his hand be proved, the book may be read in evidence. 3 *Black. Com.* 368.

SHOPLIFTERS, are those that steal goods privately out of shops, which being to the value of 5*s.* though no person be in the shop, is felony excluded clergy, by the 10 & 11 *W.* 3. *c.* 23.

SHORLING AND MORLING, are words to distinguish the fells of sheep: shorling being the fells after the fleeces are shorn off the sheep's back, and morling the fells flead off after they die or are killed.

SHORTFORD. An ancient custom of the city of Exeter, by which the lord of the fee, when he cannot be answered rent due to him out of his tenement, and no distress can be levied for the same, the tenement shall be adjudged to him to hold the same a year and a day. *Izack's Antiq. Exet.* 48. *Cowell. Blount.*

SHRIVED, or SHRIEVED, (from Sax. *scrifan.*) A penitent person confessed by a priest. *Cowell.*

SHROWD, *stealing of.* If any one in taking up a dead body steals the shroud, or other apparel, it will be felony; for the property thereof remains in the executor, or whoever was at the charge of the funeral. 3 *Inst.* 110. 12 *Rep.* 113. 1 *Hal. P. C.* 515.

SHRUBS, *destroying of.* See *Trespass.*

SI ACTIO, &c. Is the conclusion of a plea to the action, when the defendant demands judgment if the plaintiff ought to have his action, &c. *Cowell.*

SIB and SOM, (Sax.) i. e. *pax & concordia. Spelm. Cowell.*

SICA, SICHA. A ditch, from the Sax. *sic, lacuna. Cowell.*

SICH, (*sichetum* and *sikettus*,) Is a little current of water, which is dry in summer; a water furrow or gutter. *Ibid.*

SICIUS. A sort of money current among the old English, of the value of two-pence. *Ibid.*

SICUT ALIAS. Another writ like the former; it runs, *Præcipimus tibi sicut alias præcepim', &c.* 4 *Co. Rep.* 55.

SIDELINGS. Meers betwixt or on the sides of ridges of arable land. *Cowell.*

SIDESMEN, (*rectius* synodsmen.) Officers yearly chosen in great parishes, according to custom, to assist the churchwardens. They are called questmen, and take an oath for doing their duty; and are to present persons that do not resort to church on Sundays, and there continue during the whole time of divine service, &c. *Can.* 90. *Canon.* 117.

SI FECERIT TE SECURUM. A species of original writ, so called from the words of the writ, which directs the sheriff to cause the defendant to appear in court, without any option given him, provided the plaintiff gives the sheriff security effectually to prosecute his claim. 3 *Black.* 274.

SIGILLUM. A seal for the sealing of deeds and charters. *Cowell.*

SIGLA, (from the Sax. *segel.*) A sail, mentioned in the laws of king Ethelred, cap. 24. *Cowell.*

SIGNET. (Fr.) Is one of the king's seals, used in sealing his private letters, and all such grants as pass his majesty's hand by bill signed; which seal is always in the custody of the king's secretaries, and there are four clerks of the signet-office attending them. 2 *Inst.* 556. See *Privy Seal.*

SIGNIFICAVIT. A writ issuing out of the chancery, upon a certificate given by the ordinary of a man's standing excommunicate by the space of forty days, for the laying him up in prison till he submit himself to the authority of the church; and it is so called, because *significavit* is an emphatical word in the writ. *Reg. Orig.*

SIGNING of deeds and wills is necessary to make them binding: the signing a will by the testator is an essential circumstance, without which it is not a will; for this is expressly required by the stat. 29 *Car.* 2. 3. See *Will.*

SIGN-MANUAL. The subscription of the king at the top of grants or letters-patent, which first pass by bill, &c. 3 *Black.* 347. and by stat. 1 *Mar.* st. 2. c. 6. if any person shall falsely forge or counterfeit the sign-manual, privy signet, or privy seal, such offences shall be deemed high treason.

SIGNUM. A cross prefixed as a sign of assent and approbation to a charter or deed, used by the Saxons. See *Mark.*

SILENTARIUS, signifies one of the privy council; *silentium* was formerly taken for conventus privatus, *Matt. Paris, anno* 1171. According to Littleton, it is an usher, who seeth good rule and silence kept in court. *Litt. Dict. Cowell.*

SILK. See *Manufacturers.*

SILVA CÆDUA. Wood under twenty years growth, or coppice wood. 45 *Ed.* 3. c. 3.

SIMILITUDE OF HAND-WRITING. The mere similitude of hand-writing in two papers shewn to a jury, without other concurrent testimony, is no evidence that both were written by the same person. 2 *Hawk. P. C.* 431.

But the testimony of witnesses well acquainted with the party's hand, that they believe the paper in question to have been written by him is evidence to be left to a jury. 1 *Burr.* 644.

SIMNEL, or SIMNELL, (*siminellus, vel simnellus*). Mentioned in the assise of bread. The English simnel is *panis purior*, or the purest white bread. Stat. 51 *H.* 3. *st.* 1. *Ord. pro. pistor. incerti temp.* c. 1.

SIMONY, (*simonia, venditio rei sacræ*). Simony is the corrupt presentation of any one to an ecclesiastical benefice for money, gift, or reward. And by simony, the right of presentation to a living is forfeited and vested *pro hac vice* in the crown.

It is so called from the resemblance it is said to bear to the sin of Simon Magus, though the purchasing of holy orders seems to approach nearer to his offence. It was by the canon law a very grievous crime: and is so much the more odious, because, as sir Edward Coke observes, it is ever accompanied with perjury, for the presentee is sworn to have committed no simony (3 *Inst.* 156.) However, it was not an offence punishable in a criminal way at the common law, it being thought sufficient to leave the clerk to ecclesiastical censures (*Moor.* 564.) But as these did not affect the simoniacal patron, nor were efficacious enough to repel the notorious practice of the thing, divers acts of parliament have been made to restrain it by means of civil forfeitures.

By the statute 31 *Eliz.* c. 6. it is, for avoiding of simony, enacted, that if any patron, for any sum of money, reward, gift, profit, or benefit, or for any promise, agreement, grant, bond, covenant of, or for any sum of money, reward, gift, profit, or benefit, directly or indirectly, shall present or collate any person to an ecclesiastical benefice or dignity, such presentation shall be void, and the presentee be rendered incapable of ever enjoying the same benefice, and the crown shall present to it for that turn only. But if the presentee dies, without being convicted of such simony in his life-time, it is enacted by stat. 1 *W. & M.* c. 16. that the simoniacal contract shall not prejudice any other innocent patron, on pretence of lapse to the crown, or otherwise. Also by the stat. 12 *Ann*, *st*. 2. *c*. 12. if any person, for money or profit, shall procure in his own name, or the name of any other, the next presentation to any living ecclesiastical, and shall be presented thereupon, this is declared to be a simoniacal contract, and the party is subject to all the ecclesiastical penalties of simony, is disabled from holding the benefice, and the presentation devolves to the crown.

Upon these statutes many questions have arisen, with regard to what is, and what is not simony. And, among others, these points seem to be clearly settled: 1. That to purchase a presentation, the living being actually vacant, is open and notorious simony, this being expressly in the face of the statute (*Cro. Eliz.* 788. *Moor.* 914.) but lord Hardwicke was of opinion, that the sale of an advowson during a vacancy, is not within the statute of simony, as the sale of the next presentation is, but it is void by the common law (*Amb.* 268.) 2. That for a clerk to bargain for the next presentation, the incumbent being sick, and about to die, was simony, even before the statute of queen Anne (*Hob.* 165.) But it has been determined that the purchase of an advowson in fee, when the incumbent was upon his death-bed, without any privity of the clerk who was afterwards presented, was not simoniacal, and would not vacate the next presentation (2 *Black. Rep.* 1052.) However, by that statute, to purchase, either in his own name or another's, the next presentation, and be thereupon presented at any future time to the living, is direct and palpable simony. But, 3. It is held that for a father to purchase such a presentation, in order to provide for his son, is not simony, for the son is not concerned in the bargain, and the father is by nature bound to make a provision for him (*Cro. Eliz.* 686. *Moor.* 916.) 4. That if a simoniacal contract be made with the patron, the clerk not being privy thereto, the presentation for that turn shall indeed devolve to the crown, as a punishment of the guilty patron; but the clerk, who is innocent, does not incur any disability or forfeiture. 5. That bonds given to pay money to charitable uses, on receiving a presentation to a living, are not simoniacal, provided the patron or his relations be not benefited thereby; for this is no corrupt consideration, moving to the patron. 6. That bonds of resignation, in case of non-residence, or taking any other living, are not simoniacal, there being no corrupt consideration herein, but such only as is for the good of the public. So also bonds to resign, when the patron's son comes to canonical age, are legal, upon the reason before given, that the father is bound to provide for his son. 7. Lastly, general bonds to resign at the patron's request have been held to be legal, for they may possibly be given for one of the legal considerations before-mentioned; and where there is a possibility that a transaction may be fair, the law will not suppose it iniquitous without proof (*Cro. Car.* 180. *Stra.* 227.) But, if the party can prove the contract to have been a corrupt one, such proof will be admitted, in order to shew the bond simoniacal, and therefore void. Neither will the patron be suffered to make an ill use of such a general bond of resignation, as by extorting a composition for tithes, procuring an annuity for his relation, or by demanding a resignation wantonly or without good cause, such as is approved by the law; as, for the benefit of his own son, or on account of non-residence, plurality of livings, or gross immorality in the incumbent.

And, in the great case of the bishop of London *v.* Ffytche, it was determined by the house of lords, that a general bond of resignation is simoniacal and illegal. The circumstances of that case were briefly these: Mr. Ffytche, the patron, presented Mr. Eyre, his clerk, to the bishop of London, for institution. The bishop refused to admit the presentation, because Mr. Eyre had given a general bond of resignation; upon this Mr. Ffytche brought a *quare impedit* against the bishop, to which the bishop pleaded, that the presentation was simoniacal and void, by reason of the bond of resignation; and to this plea Mr. Ffytche demurred. From a series of judicial decisions, the court of common pleas thought themselves bound to determine in his favour, and that judgment was affirmed by the court of king's bench; but these judgments were afterwards reversed by the house of lords. The principal question was this, viz. whether such a bond was a reward, gift, profit, or benefit, to the patron, under the 31 *Eliz.* c. 6.; if it were so, the statute had declared the presentation to be simoniacal and void. 1 *Bro.* 286. *Cunningham's Law of Simony*, 52.

But, in a late case, where a bond was given to resign a rectory when the patron's son came of age, and before that time, to reside, and to keep the chancel and rectory-house in repair; as this case differed from the former, and it was understood that it was intended to carry it up to the house of lords, it was decided by the court of king's bench in favour of the bond, without an argument. 4 *T. R.* 395. & 78.

It has been decided, though with a difference of opinion, that a bond to resign a school or freehold office, at the request of the patron, is valid. 1 *East.* 391.

SIMPLE CONTRACT, (debt by.) Debts by simple contract are such, where the contract upon which the obligation arises is neither ascertained by matter of record, nor yet by deed or special instrument, but by mere oral evidence, the most simple of any; or by notes unsealed, which are capable of a more easy proof, and (therefore only) better, than a verbal promise. 3 *Black.* 465.

SIMPLE LARCENY. The felonious taking and carrying away of the personal goods of another. 3 *Black.* 230. See *Larceny.*

SIMPLEX, signifies simple, or single; as *charta simplex* is a deed-poll or single deed. *Cowell.*

SIMPLEX BENEFICIUM, a minor dignity in a cathedral or collegiate church, or any other ecclesiastical benefice opposed to a cure of souls; and which therefore is consistent with any parochial cure, without coming under the name of pluralities. *Ibid.*

SIMPLEX JUSTICIARIUS. This stile was anciently used for any puisne judge, that was not chief in any court. *Ibid.*

SIMUL CUM, are words used in indictments, and declarations of trespass against several persons, where some of them are known, and others not known: as the plaintiff declares against *A. B.* the defendant *simul cum,* i. e. together with *C. D. E. F.* and divers others unknown, for that they committed such a trespass, &c. 2 *Lil. Abr.* 469.

SINE ASSENSU CAPITALI, a writ that lies where a bishop, dean, prebendary, or master of an hospital, aliens the lands holden in right of his bishoprick, deanry, house, &c. without the assent of the chapter or fraternity; in which case his successor shall have this writ. *F. N. B.* 195. *New Nat. Br.* 432.

SINE-CURE, is where a rector of a parish hath a vicar under him endowed and charged with the cure, so that the rector is not obliged either to duty or residence (*Degg's Pars. Counc.* 195.) But where there is only one incumbent, and a church is fallen down, and the parish becomes destitute of parishioners, it is not in law a *sine-cure. Christ. in n.* 20. 1 *Black.* 385. 386. See *Appropriation.*

SINE DIE, i. e. without day. Before the act for turning the law into English, when judgment was given against the plaintiff in an action, he was said to be *in misericordia pro falso clamore suo;* and for that the defendant *eat inde sine die,* and the defendant was discharged, &c. 2 *Lil.* 220.

SINGLE BOND, *simplex obligatio,* a deed whereby the obligor obliges himself, his heirs, executors, and administrators, to pay a certain sum of money to another at a day appointed. 2 *Black.* 340.

SI NON OMNES, is a writ on association of justices, by which, if all in commission cannot meet at the day assigned, it is allowed that two or more of them may finish the business. *Reg. Orig.* 202. *F. N. B.* 111. 185.

SINKING FUND, is a provision made by parliament, consisting of surplusages of other funds, appropriated for paying the public debts of the nation. And by the 26 *Geo.* 3. *c.* 31. (see *Funds*) the parliament had the wisdom and firmness to vest unalienably in commissioners, the sum of 1,000,000*l.* annually for the reduction of the national debt; in which act every possible precaution was taken that could be devised, for preventing this fund from being diverted at any future time, and for carrying to the account of the commissioners, for the purposes of the act, the interest of such stock as should be purchased, and such temporary annuities as should fall in.

By that act it was provided, that when the whole sum, including the annual million, should amount to four millions, the dividends should no longer be paid upon the redeemed stock, and that the sinking fund should no longer accumulate.

By the 32 *Geo.* 3. *c.* 55. it was directed, that when the dividends amounted to 3,000,000*l.* exclusive of the annual grant, there should be no further accumulation.

And it was provided, that upon all future loans which were not to be paid off within 45 years, one per cent. should be annually appropriated for their reduction.

By the 33 *Geo.* 3. *c.* 22. an additional grant of 200,000*l.* was made for the same purpose, which has since been annually renewed.

The 42 *Geo.* 3. c. 71. repeals so much of the 26 *Geo.* 3. and 32 *Geo.* 3. as fixed a limit to the accumulation of the sinking fund, and consolidates the funds provided by each act, and states that by the accumulation of that joint fund the whole national debt may be redeemed in 45 years.

The wisdom of keeping this fund inviolable is striking; for during a peace it provides resources against the periods of war and difficulty, it supports public credit by keeping the funds steady and uniform, and even in the times of the greatest depression the country derives the benefit of the rapidity of their redemption.

The following was the state of this new sinking fund on the 1st of August, 1810:—

An account of the reduction of the national debt, from the 1st of August, 1786, to the 1st of August, 1810:—

Redeemed by the sinking fund - - - - -	£163,527,088
Transferred by land-tax redeemed - - -	23,576,480
Ditto by life annuities purchased - - - -	1,200,386
On account of Great Britain - - - - -	£188,303,954
Ditto of Ireland - -	7,132,030
Ditto of imperial loan -	1,070,173
Ditto of loan to Portugal -	43,618
Total - -	£196,542,775

And the sum to be expended in the ensuing quarter was 2,728,026*l.* 19*s.* 3½*d.*

SIPESSOCNA, what we now call a hundred. *Leg. Hen.* 1. c. 6. *Cowell.*

SI RECOGNOSCANT, a writ that, according to the old books, lies for a creditor against his debtor, who before the sheriff in the county court hath acknowledged to owe his creditor such a sum received of him. *Old Nat. Br.* 68.

SITE, of a messuage or manor-house, &c. See *Scite.*

SITHCUNDMAN, (Sax.) such a man as had the office to lead the men of a town or parish (*Leg. Inæ. c.* 56.) The chief officer within such a division, i. e. the high constable of the hundred. *Dugd. Antiq. Cowell.*

SITHESOCA, a Saxon word for franchise or liberty, a hundred. *Rot. Parl.* 16 *H.* 2. *Cowell.*

SIX CLERKS IN CHANCERY. These are officers in chancery of ancient continuance. They file all proceedings by bill and answer, and also issue some patents that pass the great seal, as pardons of men for chance-medley, patents for ambassadors, sheriffs patents, and some others: and all these matters are transacted by their under clerks, each of which has a seat in the office (in Chancery-lane), and whereof every six clerk has a certain number, usually about ten, besides two waiting clerks in each division; all which are accountable to their respective six clerks for the business they transact. These six clerks likewise sign all office copies in order to be read in court, and also certificates, and attend upon the court in term, by two at a time, at Westminster, and there read the pleadings. 1 *Har. Chan. Pract.* 25. 26.

SIXHINDI, were servants of the same nature with rod-knights, viz. bound to attend their lord wherever he went; but they were accounted among the English Saxons as freemen, because they had lands in fee, subject only to such tenure. *Leg. Inæ. c.* 26. *Cowell.* See *Hindeni.*

SIZEL, is where pieces of money are cut out from the flat bars of silver, after drawn through a mill, into the respective sizes or dimensions of the money to be made; the residue is called by this name, and is melted down again. *Lownd.* 96. *Cowell. Blount.*

SHARKALLA, an engine for catching of fish. 2 *Inst.* 38.

SKERDA, a scar or wound. *Bract. lib.* 3.

SKINS and SKINNERS. See *Leather.*

SKYVINAGE, the precincts of Calais. Stat. 27 *H.* 6, c. 2.

SLADES, (Sax. *slæd*) a long narrow piece or slip of ground. *Paroch. Antiq.* 465. *Cowell.*

SLANDER, is the defaming of a man in his reputation, profession, or livelihood. See *Reputation.*

SLAVES. There are no slaves in England: for a slave or negro, the instant he lands in England, becomes a freeman; that is, the law will protect him in the enjoyment of his person and his property. *Salk.* 666.

SLAVE TRADE. By 47 *Geo.* 3. *s.* 1. c. 36. from May 1, 1807, the slave trade shall be abolished; and penalty for trading in or purchasing slaves, 100*l.* for each slave. *s.* 1.

Vessels fitted out in this kingdom, or the colonies, for carrying on the slave trade, shall be forfeited. *s.* 2.

Persons prohibited from removing, as slaves, inhabitants of Africa, the West Indies, or America, from one place to another, or being concerned in receiving them; vessels employed on such removal to be forfeited, as also the property in the slaves; owners so employed to forfeit 100*l.* for each slave. *s.* 3.

Subjects of Africa, West Indies, or America, unlawfully carried away, and imported into any British colony as slaves, shall be forfeited to his majesty. *s.* 4.

Insurances on transactions concerning the slave trade not lawful; penalty 100*l.* and treble the amount of the premium. *s.* 5.

Slaves, natives of Africa, taken as prize during this or any other war, or seized as forfeitures, shall not be sold; but his majesty's officers, civil or military, may provide for them by enlisting them in his majesty's service, or binding them, whether of full age or not, as apprentices for 14 years. *s.* 7.

And a bounty shall be paid for such slaves to the captors, in the manner of head-money, not exceeding 40*l.* for every man, 30*l.* for every woman, or 10*l.* for every child not above 14 years old, delivered over to such officer as aforesaid. *s.* 8.

But certificates are to be produced by the captors to entitle them to bounty (*s.* 9.) and doubts of claim to bounty are to be determined by the judge of the admiralty. *s.* 10.

On condemnation of forfeitures of slaves for offences against this act, there shall be paid to the informer 13*l.* for every man, 10*l.* for every woman, and 3*l.* for every person under the age of 14, condemned, and delivered over in health; and also the like sums to the governor or commander in chief where such seizure shall have been made; but where such seizures shall be made at sea, the commander shall receive 20*l.* for every man, 15*l.* for every woman, and 5*l.* for every person under 14, to be distributed according to orders in council. *s.* 11.

Counterfeiting any certificate, copy of sentence of condemnation, or receipt, felony without benefit of clergy. *s.* 12.

Penalties and forfeitures to be recovered in any court of record or vice-admiralty, according to 4 *Geo.* 3. *c.* 15. *s.* 13. Seizures may be made by officers of customs and excise, or officers of ships of war (*s.* 14.) and offences may be enquired of, as if committed in Middlesex. *s.* 15.

His majesty may make regulations for disposal of negroes, after the expiration of their apprenticeship. *s.* 16.

And negroes, enlisted in his majesty's forces, are not entitled to the benefits of limited service, pensions, or allowances. *s.* 17.

Defendants may plead the general issue, and will be entitled to treble costs.

And by 47 *Geo.* 3. *s.* 2. *c.* 44. the dealing in slaves in the colony of Sierra Leone is prohibited. *s.* 4.

And by 51 *Geo.* 3. c. 23. Subjects or persons residing in the united kingdom, or any of the dominions belonging to his majesty, carrying on the slave trade, or any way engaged therein, shall be declared felons, and be transported for not exceeding fourteen years, or be kept to hard labour for not exceeding five nor less than three years, at the discretion of the court. *s.* 1.

Persons serving on board any ship, or underwriting any policy thereon, shall be guilty of a misdemeanor, and punished by imprisonment for not exceeding two years. *s.* 2.

And such persons shall not be deemed accessaries to felony. *s.* 3.

This act is not to prevent the removing of slaves from one British settlement to another, &c. nor prevent the transportation to foreign places of slaves that have been convicted of crimes. *s.* 4.

Governors and commanders in chief, and persons authorized by them, may seize vessels. *s.* 8.

And persons sailing in vessels, giving information of offences committed, are not liable to punishment. *s.* 9.

SLEDGE. A sledge or hurdle is generally allowed to draw offenders guilty of high treason to the gallows, to preserve them from the extreme torture of being dragged on the ground or pavement. 1 *Hal. P. C.* 82.

SLIPPA, a stirrup; and there was a tenure of land by holding the king's stirrup, in Cambridgeshire. *Cart.* 5. *Hen.* 7. *Cowell.*

SLOUGH-SILVER, a rent paid to the castle of Wigmore, in lieu of certain days work in harvest, reserved to the lord from his tenants. *Pat.* 43 *Eliz.* *Cowell.*

SLUICE, (*exclusa*) a frame to keep or let water out of a ground. By stat. 1 *Geo.* 2. *c.* 19. to destroy any sluice or lock on any navigable river, is made felony, to be punished with transportation for seven years.

SMAKA, a smack, or small light vessel. *Cowell.*

SMALL DEBTS, (courts for). By 27 *Geo.* 2. *c.* 16. all acts for erecting courts of conscience for recovery of small debts shall be deemed public acts.

By 26 *Geo.* 3. *c.* 38. debtors committed by courts of conscience for debts not exceeding 20*s.* shall not be imprisoned more than 20 days, and where the debt does not exceed 40*s.* not more than 40 days; but debtors found guilty of a fraudulent concealment of their effects, may be imprisoned for a longer term.

Debtors are to be discharged without paying gaol fees; and gaolers demanding the same forfeit 5*l.* *Ibid.*

Two justices may determine offences against this act within two months; and the penalties go half to the poor, and half to the informer. *Ibid.*

Process of courts of conscience shall not issue against the body and goods of the same person; and commissioners must be householders, and have 20*l.* per annum, or 500*l.* personal estate; acting without such qualification is a penalty of 20*l.* to the informer, if he sues within six months. *Ibid.*

SMALT, (Ital. *smalto*) that of which painters make their blue colouring. Stat. 21 *Jac.* 1. *c.* 3.

SMOAK-FARTHINGS, the pentecostals or customary oblations offered by the dispersed inhabitants within a diocese, when they made their procession to the mother cathedral church, came by degrees into a standing annual rent, called smoak-farthings. *Cowell.*

SMOKE-SILVER. Lands were holden in some places by the payment of the sum of 6*d.* yearly to the sheriff, called smoke-silver. *Pat.* 4. *Ed.* 6. Smoke-silver and smoke-penny are to be paid to the ministers of divers parishes, as a modus in lieu of tithe-wood: and in some manors, formerly belonging to religious houses, there is still paid, as appendant to the said manors, the ancient Peter pence, by the name of smoke-money. *Cowell.*

SMUGGLING is the offence of importing goods without paying the duties imposed thereon by the laws of the customs and excise. This is restrained by a great variety of statutes, which inflict pecuniary penalties and the seisure of the goods for clandestine smuggling; and affix the guilt of felony, with transportation for seven years, upon more open, daring, and avowed practices; for which see *Customs* and *Excise.*

SNOTTERING-SILVER. There was a custom in the village of Wylegh, that all the servile tenants should pay for their tenements a small duty called snottering silver, to the abbot of Colchester. *Placit.* 18 *Edw.* 1. *Cowell.*

SNUFF. Mixing it with fustick, yellow ebony, touchwood, logwood, red or guinea wood, braziletto or Jamaica wood, Nicaragua, Saunders, or any other wood, or any walnut tree, hop, sycamore, or other leaves, herbs or plants, incurs a penalty of 200*l.* by 29 *Geo.* 3. *c.* 68; and having any such materials in their possession is a forfeiture thereof, and of 50*l.* A very heavy duty is granted per pound on snuff imported from the Spanish West Indies, and 5*s.* for what is brought from Spain, by the Consolidated Act.

SOC, (Sax.) power, or liberty to minister justice and execute laws; also the circuit or territory wherein such power is exercised: hence soca is used for a seigniory or lordship, with the liberty of holding or keeping a court of his sockmen. *Bract. l.* 3. *Cowell.*

SOCAGE, (*socagium*, from the Fr. *soc.* that is *vomer*, a coulter or plough-share). Socage, in its most general and extensive signification, seems to denote a tenure by any certain and determinate service; and in this sense it is by our ancient writers constantly put in opposition to chivalry, or knight-service, where the render was precarious and uncertain. Thus (*Bracton, l.* 2. *c.* 16. *s.* 9.) if a man holds by a rent in money, without any escuage or serjeanty, *id tenementum dici potest socagium;* but if you add thereto any royal service, or escuage to any, the smallest amount, *illud dici poterit feodum militare.* So too the author of *Fleta, l.* 3. *c.* 14. *s.* 9. *ex donationibus, servitia militaria vel magnæ serjantiæ non continentibus, oritur nobis quoddam nomen generale, quod est socagium.* Littleton also, *s.* 117. defines it to be, where the tenant holds his tenement of the lord by any certain service, in lieu of all other services, so that they be not services of chivalry, or knight-service. And therefore afterwards (*s.* 118.) he tells us, that whatsoever is not tenure in chivalry is tenure in socage: in like manner as it is defined by *Finch, L.* 147, a tenure to be done out of war. The service must therefore be certain, in order to denominate it socage; as to hold by fealty and 20*s.* rent; or, by homage, fealty, and 20*s.* rent; or, by homage and fealty without rent; or, by fealty and certain corporal service, as ploughing the lord's land for three days; or, by fealty only, without any other service: for all these are tenures in socage (*Litt.* § 117, 118, 119.) And by the statute 12 *Car.* 2. c. 24. all tenures shall be adjudged and taken to be turned into free and common socage.

SOCAGERS, were those tenants whose tenure was called socage. *Cowell.*

SOCMANS or SOKEMANS, (*socmanni*) such tenants as hold their lands and tenements by socage tenure. *Kitchin,* 81. *Cowell.*

SOCMEN. The husbandmen among our Saxon ancestors were of two sorts: one that hired the lord's out-land or tenementary land, like our farmers; the other, that tilled and manured his inland or demeans (yielding *operam*, not *censum*, work, not rent) and were thereupon called his sockmen, or ploughmen. *Spel. of Feuds*, c. 7.

After the conquest they were taken to be those tenants who held of no servile tenure, but commonly paid their rent as a soke or sign of freedom to the lord, though they were sometimes obliged to customary duties for the service and honour of their lord. *Cowell.*

SOCNA, (Sax. *socne*) a privilege, liberty, or franchise. *Ibid.*

SOCOME, a custom grinding corn at the lord's mill. *Blount.*

SODOMY. See *Buggery.*

SOKE, SOC, SOK, SOCA, signify in general the liberty or privilege of tenants excused from customary burdens and impositions; sometimes the liberty of keeping court within his own soke or jurisdiction; sometimes it signified a payment or rent to the lord. *Cowell.*

SOKEMANS, and SOKEMANRIES. The former certain copyhold tenants so called, the latter their tenures. *Britton, c.* 66.

SOKE-REEVE, the lord's rent-gatherer in the soke or soken. *Fleta. Cowell.*

SOLARIUM, a sollar, upper room, garret, or loft. *Cowell.*

SOLDIERS. The military state of England includes the whole of the soldiery, or such persons as are peculiarly appointed among the rest of the people for the safeguard and defence of the realm (*Wood's Inst.* 45.) And a soldier (from the Ger. *sold*, or *sould*, signifying a stipend) is a man hired for pay to serve in war. *Wms. Jus. tit. Sol.*

In free states the profession of a soldier, taken singly, and merely as a profession, is justly an object of jealousy. In these, *Blackstone* observes, no man should take up arms but with a view to defend his country and its laws: he puts not off the citizen when he enters the camp; but it is because he is a citizen, and would wish to continue so, that he makes himself for a while a soldier (1 *Black.* 408.) The laws therefore and constitution of these kingdoms know no such state as that of a perpetual standing soldier, bred up to no other profession than that of war: and the statutes relating to the army are consequently but few.

To keep this body of troops in order, an annual act of parliament likewise passes, "to punish mutiny and desertion, and for the better payment of the army and their quarters." This regulates the manner in which they are to be dispersed among the several inn-keepers and victuallers throughout the kingdom, and establishes a law martial for their government. By this, among other things, it is enacted, that if any officer or soldier shall excite, or join any mutiny, or, knowing of it, shall not give notice to the commanding officer; or shall desert, or list in any other regiment, or sleep upon his post, or leave it before he is relieved, or hold correspondence with a rebel or enemy, or strike or use violence to his superior officer, or shall disobey his lawful commands, such offender shall suffer such punishment as a court-martial shall inflict, though it extend to death itself.

But as soldiers, by this annual act, are thus put in a worse condition than any other subjects, so by the humanity of our standing laws they are in some cases put in a much better. By statute 43 *Eliz. c.* 3. a weekly allowance is to be raised in every county for the relief of soldiers that are sick, hurt, and maimed: not forgetting the royal hospital at Chelsea, for such as are worn out in their duty. Officers and soldiers, that have been in the king's service, are by statutes, enacted at the close of a war, at liberty to use any trade or occupation they are fit for, in any town in the kingdom, (except the two universities) notwithstanding any statute, custom, or charter, to the contrary. And by the statute 42 *Geo.* 3. *c* 69. all officers, soldiers, and mariners, who have been employed in the king's service since 1784, and have not deserted, and their wives and children, may exercise any trade in any town in the kingdom, and shall not be removed till they are actually chargeable. The same privilege is extended to all officers and soldiers, who have served in the militia or the fencible regiments, and have been honourably discharged; but any two justices of the county or place may examine any such person with regard to his legal settlement, who shall make oath thereof; and the justices shall give such person an attested copy of his affidavit, which shall afterwards be admitted as evidence of such settlement.

And soldiers in actual military service may make nuncupative wills, and dispose of their goods, wages, and other personal chattels, without those forms, solemnities, and expences, which the law requires in other cases. Stat. 29 *Car.* 2. *c.* 3. 5 *W.* 3. *c.* 21. *s.* 6. See *Will.*

Besides which, it is now fully established, that both the full pay and half pay of an officer, or any person in a military or naval character, cannot in any instance be assigned before it is due; as the object of such pay is to enable those who receive it always to be ready to serve their country with that decency and dignity which their respective characters and stations require. 4 *T. R.* 258. *H. Bl.* 628. See *Army*, *Game*, *Poor*, and *Vagrants*.

SOLE CORPORATIONS. A corporation sole consists of one person only and his successors, in some particular station, who are incorporated by law, in order to give them some legal capacities and advantages, particularly that of perpetuity, which in their natural persons they could not have had. In this sense the king is a sole corporation; so is a bishop; so are some deans and prebendaries, distinct from their several chapters; and so is every parson and vicar. 1 *Black.* 469.

SOLET ET DEBET, words inserted in writs for recovery of rights, &c. *Cowell.*

SOLE TENANT, *(solus tenens)*, is he that holds land by his own right only, without any other joined; and if a man and his wife hold land for their lives, with remainder to their son for life, here the man dying, the lord shall not have an heriot, because he dies not sole tenant. *Kitch.* 134.

SOLICITOR, *(solicitator)* a person employed to follow and take care of suits depending in courts of law or equity. See *Attorney.*

SOLIDATUM, used in the neuter gender, is taken for that absolute right or property which a man hath in any thing. *Malmsb. lib.* 1.

SOLINUS TERRÆ, about 160 acres, and 7 *solini* are about 1120 acres, which is less than 17 *carucatæ*, for at the lowest *carucata terræ* is 100 acres. 1 *Inst.* 15. *Cowell.*

SOLLAR, *(solarium)* a garret or upper room, a loft. See *Solarium.*

SOLVENDO ESSE, is a term of art, signifying that a man hath wherewith to pay, or is a person solvent. *Cowell.*

SOLVERE PŒNAS, to pay the penalty, or undergo the punishment inflicted for offences. 3 *Salk.* 32.

SOLVIT AD DIEM, is a plea in action of debt on a bond, bill, &c. that the money was paid at the day limited. *Mod. Cas.* 22. 1 *Strange*, 652. See *Payment.*

SOLUTIONE FEODI MILITES PARLIAMENTI, and SOLUTIONE FEODI BURGENS. PARLIAMENTI, are writs whereby knights of the shire and burgesses may recover their allowance, if it be denied. Stat. 35 *H.* 8. c. 11.

SON ASSAULT DEMESNE, is a plea of justification in an action of assault and battery, stating that the plaintiff made the first assault, and what the defendant did was in his own defence. 2 *Lil. Abr.* 523.

SONTAGE, was a tax of 40*s.* laid upon every knight's fee. *Cowell.*

SORCERY, (*sortilegium*) witchcraft or divination by lots. By 9 *Geo.* 2. *c.* 5. no prosecution shall for the future be carried on against any person for conjuration, witchcraft, sorcery, or inchantment. But the misdemeanor of persons pretending to use witchcraft, tell fortunes, or discover stolen goods by skill in the occult sciences, shall be punished with a year's imprisonment, and standing four times in the pillory. 4 *Black.* 61.

SORS, in sums of money lent upon usury, the principal was anciently called sors, to distinguish it from the interest. *Cowell.*

SORUS ACCIPITER, is a sor or soar hawk. *Ibid.*

SOTHAIL, or SOTHALE, mistaken for scotale. *Bract. lib.* 3.

SOTHSAGA, or SOTHSAGE, an old word which signified history. *Cowell.*

SOVERAIGN, or SOVEREIGN, is a chief or supreme person, one highest of all, as a king. *Ibid.*

SOVEREIGN, a piece of gold coin current at 22*s.* in 1 *H.* 8. In 34 *H.* 8. sovereigns were coined at 20*s.* a-piece, and half sovereigns at 10*s.* But in 4 *Ed.* 6. the sovereign of gold passed for 24*s.*; and in 6 *Ed.* 6. at 30*s.* *Ibid.*

SOVEREIGN POWER, is the power of making laws. In our constitution the law ascribes to the king the attribute of sovereignty, but that is to be understood in a qualified sense, i. e. as supreme magistrate, not as sole legislator, the legislative power being vested in the king, lords, and commons, not in any one of the three estates alone. 1 *Black.* 49.

SOUL-SCOT. A mortuary is so called in the laws of *Canute*, c. 13. 2 *Black.* 425.

SOUND, is a narrow sea, as *mare Balticum*, the sound; and to sound, is to make trial how many fathom a sea is deep. *Mer. Dict.* *Cowell.*

SOUTH-SEA COMPANY, a company of merchants trading to the South Sea. They were incorporated, on lending the government ten millions of money. The corporation shall have the sole trade from the river Oroonoko, on the east side of America, to the southernmost part of Terra del Fuego, and from thence through the South Sea. And the company to be owners of all islands, ports, and places they can discover. Stat. 9 *Ann*, c. 21.

But by 47 *Geo.* 3. *s.* 1. c. 23. so much of 9 *Ann*, c. 21. as vests in the South Sea company the exclusive trade to and from certain limits of South America, in the possession of his majesty, is repealed.

SOWLEGROVE, an old name of the month of February, amongst the inhabitants of South Wales. *Cowell.*

SOWNE, (from the Fr. *souvenue*, i. e. remembered, is a word of art used in the exchequer, where estreats that sowne not, are those that the sheriff cannot levy, viz. such estreats and casualties as are not to be remembered, and run not in demand; and estreats that sowne, are such as he may gather and are leviable. 4 *Hen.* 5. c. 7. 4 *Inst.* 107.

SPADARIUS, (for spatharius) a sword-bearer. *Blount.*

SPATÆ PLACITUM, a court for the speedy execution of justice on military delinquents. *Cowell.*

SPATULARIA, is numbered among the holy vestments. *Ibid.*

SPEAKER. The lords and commons have two speakers: the one termed the lord speaker of the house of peers, and is most commonly the lord chancellor or lord keeper of the great seal of England; the other (being a member of the house of commons) is called the speaker of the house of commons. The duty of both consists in managing debates, putting questions, and thereby collecting the sense of the houses, the passing of bills, seeing the orders of each house observed, &c.

SPEAKING WITH PROSECUTOR. It is not uncommon when a person is convicted of a misdemeanor, which principally and more immediately affects some individual, as a battery, imprisonment, or the like, for the court to permit the defendant to speak with the prosecutor, before any judgment is pronounced; and, if the prosecutor declares himself satisfied, to inflict but a trivial punishment. 4 *Black.* 356, 357.

SPECIAL MATTER cannot be given in evidence in many cases, unless it is expressly pleaded, or the necessity of pleading the same specially is removed by the provision of some statute relating to the subject matter of the action.

SPECIALTY, (*specialitas*) a bond, bill, or such like instrument; a writing or deed, under the hand and seal of the parties. 2 *Black.* 465.

SPECIES. A relative term, expressing an idea which is comprised under some general one, called a genus; as, for instance, the action on the case we may call the genus, and of assumpsit, trover, &c. a species of that genus.

SPECIFIC LEGACY, is a bequest of any particular thing, as a piece of plate, a watch, a horse, or the like, and it cannot be taken by the devisee without the consent of the executor. *Co. Lit.* 111. *Aleyn* 39. See *Legacy.*

SPECIFIC PERFORMANCE. The want of a more specific remedy than can be obtained in the courts of law, gives a concurrent jurisdiction to a court of equity in a great variety of cases; as, for instance, in executory agreements, a court of equity will compel them to be carried into strict execution, unless where it is improper, or impossible, instead of giving damages for their non-performance. 1 *Eq. Cas. Abr.* 16.

SPECIEUM, the cell of a monk. *Cowell.*

SPIGURNEL, (*spigurnellus*) the sealer of the king's writs, from the Sax. *spicurran*, to shut up or inclose. *Cowell.*

SPINACIUM, a vessel called a pinnace. *Ibid.*

SPINDULÆ, three golden pins used about the archiepiscopal pall: hence *spindulatus* signified to be adorned with the pall. *Ibid.*

SPINSTER, an addition usually given to all unmarried women. *Dyer*, 46, 88. 2 *Co. Inst.* 668.

SPIRITING AWAY MEN AND CHILDREN. This offence is commonly called kidnapping. It is a very heinous crime, which the common law of England hath punished by fine, imprisonment, and pillory. *Raym.* 474. 2 *Show*, 221. *Skin.* 47. *Comb.* 10.

By statute 11 & 12 *W.* 3. *c.* 7. if any captain of a merchant vessel shall (during his being abroad) force any person on shore, or wilfully leave him behind, or refuse to bring home all such men as he carried out, if able and desirous to return, he shall suffer three months imprisonment.

SPIRITUAL CORPORATIONS. Spiritual or ecclesiastical corporations are where the members that compose it are entirely spiritual persons, such as bishops, and the like. 1 *Black.* 470.

SPIRITUAL COURTS have jurisdiction in causes matrimonial, and for probate of wills of goods, and granting administrations, and for tithes, where there is no modus; also in cases of defamation, as calling a woman whore, except in London, where calling a woman whore is actionable, whores being liable to be carted by the custom of the city. 3 *Black.* 61.

But, by 27 *Geo.* 3. *c.* 44. suits in ecclesiastical courts for defamatory words shall be commenced within 6 months: and for fornication or incontinence, or for striking or brawling in any church or church-yard within 8 months; and there shall be no prosecution for fornication after the parties have intermarried.

SPIRITUALTIES OF A BISHOP, are those profits which he receives as a bishop, and not as a baron of parliament; such as the duties of his visitation, prestation money, his benefit growing from ordinations and institutions of priests, the income of his jurisdiction, &c. *Staundf. P. C.* 132.

The archbishop of the province is guardian of spiritualties when a see is vacant, and hath the jurisdiction of courts, &c. 1 *Black.* 380.

SPITTLE-HOUSE, is a corruption from hospital, and signifies the same thing; or it may be taken from the Teuton. spital, and hospital or alms-house, mentioned in 15 *Car.* 2. *c.* 9.

SPOLIATION, (*spoliatio*) a writ or suit for the fruits of a church, or the church itself, to be sued in the spiritual court, and not in the temporal, that lies for one incumbent against another, where they both claim by one patron, and the right of patronage doth not come in question: as if a parson be created a bishop, and hath dispensation to hold his benefice, and afterwards the patron presents another incumbent, who is instituted and inducted; now, the bishop may have a spoliation in the spiritual court against the new incumbent, because they both claim by one patron, and the right of patronage doth not come in debate; and for that the other incumbent came to the possession of the benefice, by the course of the spiritual law, viz. by institution and induction; for otherwise, if he be not instituted and inducted, a spoliation lies not against him, but writ of trespass, or assise of novel disseisin. *F. N. B.* 36, 37.

SPONTE OBLATA, a free gift or present to the king, anciently so called. *Cowell.*

SPORTULA, signifies gifts and gratuities, forbidden to be received by the clergy. *Ibid.*

SPOUSALS, the betrothing of a man or woman before full marriage. *Ibid.*

SPOUSE-BREACH, is adultery opposed to simple fornication. *Ibid.*

SPRINGING USES, or CONTINGENT USES. They differ from an executory devise, in that there must be a person seised to such uses at the time when the contingency happens, else they can never be executed by the statute. 2 *Black.* 334.

SPULLERS OF YARN, are persons that work at the spole or wheel; or triers of yarn, to see that it be well spun, and fit for the loom. 1 *Mar. c.* 7. *Cowell.*

SPUR-ROYAL, (*spurareum aureum*) an ancient gold coin. *Cowell.*

SQUALLEY, a note of faultiness in the making of cloth. 43 *Eliz. c.* 10. *Cowell.*

SQUIBS. See *Fireworks.*

STABBING. See *Felony and Homicide.*

STABILIA, a writ called by that name, on a custom in Normandy, that where a man in power claimed lands in the possession of an inferior, he petitioned the prince that it might be put into his hands until the right was decided, whereupon he had this writ, *breve de stabilia.* *Cowell.*

STABILITIO VENATIONIS, the driving deer to a stand. *Ibid.*

STABLE-STAND, (*stabilis statio, vel stans in stabulo*) is where a man is found at his standing in the forest, with a cross or long bow bent, ready to shoot at any deer, or standing close by a tree, with greyhounds in a leash, ready to slip: and it is one of the four evidences or presumptions, whereby a person is convicted of intending to steal the king's deer in the forest: the other three are dog-draw, back-bear, and bloody-hand. *Manwood, p.* 2. c. 18.

STACK, a quantity of wood three feet long, as many feet broad, and twelve feet high. *Merch. Dict.* *Cowell.*

STADIUM, is accounted a furlong of land, which is the eighth part of a mile. *Domesday.* *Cowell.*

STAFF-HERDING, is the following of cattle within a forest: and where persons claim common in any forest, it must be inquired by the ministers whether they use staff-herding, for it is not allowable of common right; because by that means the deer, which would otherwise come and feed with the cattle, are frighted away, and the keeper or follower will drive the cattle into the best grounds, so that the deer shall only have their leavings: therefore if any man who hath right of common, under colour thereof use staff-herding, it is a cause of seizing his common till he pay a fine for the abuse. 1 *Jon. Rep.* 282.

STAGE COACHES. By 50 *G o.* 3. c. 48. any public stage coach drawn by four horses, shall be allowed to carry ten outside passengers, exclusive of the coachman, but including the guard, and one passenger and no more upon the box, and three of such passengers on the front of the roof, and the remaining six behind; and no such passengers shall be allowed to sit on the luggage, or that part of the roof allotted for the same; and all stage coaches drawn by two or three horses shall be allowed five outside passengers, exclusive of the coachman; and all long coaches or double-bodied coaches shall be permitted to carry eight outside passengers, and no more, exclusive of the coachman, but including the guard; but no child in the lap, or under seven years of age, shall be counted as one of such number, unless there be more than one; and if more than one, that two shall be accounted equal to one grown person; and no person paying as an outside passenger shall be permitted to sit as an inside passenger, unless with the consent of one of the inside passengers, and next to whom such outside passenger shall be placed: also, where such coach is of a construction peculiarly wide, and being so found shall be licensed for that purpose, four outside passengers, instead of three, shall be allowed to sit on the front, so that the number of outsides shall not exceed ten in all.

After the 1st of March, 1811, it shall not be lawful for any driver or proprietor of any coach to permit any luggage to be carried on the roof, or any person to go as an outside passenger on the outside of any such coach, the top of which shall be more than eight feet nine inches from the ground, or the bearing of which on the ground shall be less than four feet six inches from the centre of the track of the right or off wheel, to the centre of the track of the left or near wheel, under the penalty of 5*l.*

It shall not be lawful for any driver or proprietor to carry any luggage exceeding two feet in height on the roof of any coach drawn by four horses; and, if drawn by two or three, then not to exceed eighteen inches above the roof, on pain to forfeit 10*l.* for every inch above the spaces allowed; and, in default of payment, to be committed to gaol for two months; and all packages shall be so placed on the roof, as that no passenger shall sit thereon, under the penalty of 50*s.*; and the division on the top, allotted for luggage, shall be distinctly separated from the other part by some railing, or otherwise; and in case any driver or owner shall refuse to permit the carriage and luggage to be measured by any justice, constable, surveyor of the highway or turnpike road, inspector of coaches, or passenger, he shall forfeit the like penalty.

And in order to encourage the lowering of the present height of stage coaches, it is enacted, that it shall be lawful to carry any luggage on the roof of a greater height than two feet, provided such luggage be not a greater height from the ground, including the height of such coach, than ten feet nine inches.

In every stage coach licence there shall be specified the number of outside as well as inside passengers to be carried.

And all persons who shall be licensed (mail coaches excepted), shall paint, within six months after 9th June, 1810, on the outside of each door, or on some other conspicuous part, in legible characters of one inch in length, and in a different colour from the ground, and in words at length, the number of outside passengers which the licence shall specify, as well as the number of inside passengers, together with the names of the proprietors; or it shall be lawful for the commissioners to require, instead of such inscription, that a plate made of brass or other metal shall be fixed on the side of each coach, with the names of the proprietors, and a distinct number for each, to the end that the owners and drivers shall be known; and if any person shall be licensed to keep more than one coach, every one shall have several numbers; and if any person shall deface the number, figure, or mark, he shall forfeit 5*l.*; and if any person shall employ any such carriage without being licensed, or without having the words, and number, and name, painted on the outside, as herein directed, or shall at any time carry more outside passengers than specified in the licence, every person so offending shall forfeit 10*l.* for each outside passenger beyond the number, and double that sum if the driver be also owner or part owner.

The owners of stage coaches shall be liable to penalties in case drivers cannot be found; but if any such owner shall make out, to the satisfaction of the justice, that the offence was committed by the driver without his privity or knowledge, and that no profit, either directly or indirectly, has accrued, or could have accrued to such owner, such justice shall discharge the owner from such penalty, and levy the same upon the driver only, when found; who, on nonpayment, shall be committed to gaol for any time not exceeding six, nor less than three months.

The driver of any coach, mail coach, or other carriage, stopping at any place, where assistance can be procured, shall not quit his horses or the box until a proper person shall be employed to hold the horses or fore horses, and shall have actual hold of such horses; and such persons shall hold the same until the driver has returned to his box, or until the post-boy who rides one of the horses is again mounted, and has in his hands the reins; and if such driver shall neglect so to do, he shall be subject to a penalty of not less than 10*s.* nor more than 5*l.*; but this shall not extend to hackney coaches, drawn by two horses only.

In case the driver, or person acting as guard, shall, by intoxication or by negligence, or other misconduct (unavoidable accidents always excepted), endanger the safety of the passengers in their lives, their limbs, or their property, or shall not give due care to any other property with which such driver or guard may be entrusted; or if any driver of any mail coach, or any guard, shall loiter on the road, so as to retard the arrival of the mails at the next stage; or if the driver of any mail coach shall not in all possible cases convey such mails, at the speed of such a number of miles an hour, as are fixed by the post-master-general, unless the circumstances of the weather, or the badness of the roads, or the occurrence of any accident, prevent the same; or if any driver or guard of any such coach, mail coach, or other carriage, shall not duly account to his employers for all monies received by them, then the driver or guard shall forfeit not less than 5*l.* nor more than 10*l.* and shall return the money embezzled; and, in case of non-payment, be committed to gaol for any time not exceeding six, nor less than three months.

In case the driver or guard shall use abusive or insulting language to any passenger, or shall insist on and exact more than the sum to which he is entitled, then the driver or guard shall forfeit not less than 5*s.* nor more than 40*s.*; or, in case of non-payment, be committed to gaol for any time not exceeding one month, nor less than three days.

Any passenger may require toll collectors to count the number of passengers, and measure the height of the luggage; and if any driver shall refuse to stop, or to permit the collector to count the number of passengers, and ascertain the height of the luggage, then the driver shall forfeit 5*l.*; and shall, if more passengers shall have been carried, or the luggage shall exceed the height, forfeit double the penalty imposed by this act for such offence; one half to belong to the toll collector, and the other half to the passenger; and if any toll collector shall neglect or refuse to make such examination, he shall forfeit 5*l.*; and if any person shall endeavour to evade such examination, by descending from such coach previous to its reaching any turnpike gate, and re-ascending after it has passed such turnpike gate, he shall forfeit 10*l.*

If the coachman shall permit any other person, without the consent of a proprietor, or against the consent of the passengers, to drive, or shall quit the box without reasonable occasion (although the reins be left in the hands of the passenger on the box); or, if the coachman shall, by furiously driving, or by any negligence or misconduct overturn the carriage, or in any manner endanger the persons or property of the passengers, or the property of the owners (unavoidable accidents excepted), such coachman shall forfeit any sum not exceeding 10*l.*

If any guard shall fire off the arms, either while such coach is going on the road, or going through or standing in any town, otherwise than for the defence of such coach, such person shall forfeit 5*l.*

If any person shall receive any sum for conniving at any offence, he shall forfeit 50*l.*; and, in default of payment, be committed to any house of correction for any period not exceeding three, nor less than one month.

All stage coaches (long-bodied coaches

included,) carrying no parcels or luggage whatsoever, excepting in the inside, or in the front boot thereof, or in a boot behind, or under the body of such carriage; and where the top of each boot behind, when the coach is empty, is not more than six feet from the ground, having obtained a special licence for that purpose, and having the name of the owners, and the number of outside and inside passengers allowed painted thereon, shall be permitted to carry two outside passengers more than the number hereby limited.

Hackney coach stages are exempted from the operation of this act.

STAGE-PLAYS. See *Theatres.*

STAGIARIUS. A resident; and there is a distinction between *residentiarius* and *stagiarius*, for every canon installed to the privileges and profits of residence, was residentiarius; and while he actually kept such stated residence, he was stagiarius. Stagiari, to keep residence. Hence an old stager. *Cowell.*

STAGNES, (*stagna.*) Pools of standing water. 5 *Eliz. c.* 21. A pool consists of water and land; and therefore, by the name of *stagnum*, the water and land shall pass also. *Inst.* 5.

STAKE. It is part of the punishment of suicide to drive a stake through the body, see *Felo de se* and *Homicide.*

STAL-BOAT. A kind of fishing-boat, mentioned in 27 *Eliz. c.* 21.

STALKING. The going up gently step by step, to take game; and none shall stalk with bush or beast to any deer, except in his own forest or park, under the penalty of 10*l.* Stat. 19 *H.* 7. *c.* 11. See *Game.*

STALKERS. Certain fishing-nets. 13 *R.* 2. *c.* 20.

STALLAGE, (*stallagium*, from the Sax. *stal.* (i.e. *stabulum statio.*) Is a sum of money paid to the lord or owner of the soil for the liberty to erect stalls, or to remove a stall from one part of a fair to another. *Palm.* 77. This is payable, whether the goods are sold or not, and the owner of the soil is entitled to the same of common right, and is paid as a satisfaction for the use of the soil; trespass therefore will lie against any one who erects a stall within his diocese, but he cannot in such case distrain the goods as damage feasant. 1 *Wils.* 209. 115. 2 *Str.* 1938. 2 *Black. Rep.* 1116. 9 *Ld. Raym.* 1589.

STALLARIUS. Mentioned in historians, signifying *præfectus stabuli;* the same officer which we now call master of the horse. *Cowell.*

STAMPS. The stamp duties were first imposed in the early part of the reign of William the Third; but these and all the subsequent duties have been since repealed, and others imposed in lieu thereof; particularly by the stat. 55 *Geo.* 3. *c.* 184.

And if any person shall forge any stamp or die, or the impression thereof; or utter, or expose to sale any paper, &c. having such forged impression; or if any person shall get off any stamp that has been used, with intent to use the same on other paper, such person shall be guilty of felony without benefit of clergy. 55 *G.* 3. *c.* 184. *s.* 7.

The clauses in the stamp acts of most importance are the following:

By 44 *Geo.* 3. *c.* 98. no action at law, or information before justices of the peace, for penalties, shall, in future, be commenced but in the name of the attorney-general in England, or advocate for Scotland, or some officer of the stamp duties. *s.* 10.

And in any case where it shall appear to the commissioners upon oath or affirmation, that any instrument whatsoever, (except bills of exchange, promissory or other notes, drafts, orders, or receipts), hath been written on paper, not duly stamped either by accident or inadvertence, or from urgent necessity and without any intention to evade the duties, and such instrument shall be brought to be stamped within twelve months after the execution thereof, the commissioners may remit the penalty or any part thereof.

But by 35 *Geo.* 3. *c.* 55. *s.* 11. receipts may be stamped, if brought *within fourteen days after date*, on payment of a penalty of 5*l.* over and above the duty; and if brought *within one calendar month* on payment of a penalty of 10*l.* and the duty.

And by 37 *Geo.* 3. *c.* 136. the holder of any *bill, note, draft, or order*, stamped with a stamp of a different denomination than required, *if of equal or superior value* to the stamp required, may, *if produced before it be payable* be stamped on payment of the duty and 40*s.* penalty: but if produced *after payable* then on a penalty of 10*l.* *s.* 5, 6.

All fines shall go to his majesty. But the commissioners are to give such part as they think fit to any person who may inform or assist in the recovery. 44 *Geo.* 3. *c.* 98.

By 48 *Geo.* 3. *c.* 149, stamps appropriated to denote the duty charged upon any particular instrument, and bearing the name of such instrument on the face thereof, shall not be used for denoting any other duty of the same amount, or, if so used, the same shall be of no avail.

But by 55 *Geo.* 3. *c.* 184. in other cases, instruments having wrong stamps, but sufficient in value shall be valid.

By 48 *Geo.* 3. *c.* 149. In all conveyances the full consideration shall be truly set forth in words at length, and if the full consideration money shall not be truly expressed, the purchaser, and also the seller, shall forfeit 50*l.* and also be charged with the payment of five times the amount of the excess of duty which would have been payable in respect of the full consideration beyond the amount of duty actually paid. *s.* 22.

And if either of the parties give information, the party giving the information shall not only be indemnified, but also be rewarded out of the penalty, not exceeding one half; and any other person in like manner. *s.* 23.

And where the full consideration shall not be set forth, the purchaser may recover back from the seller so much as shall not be set forth, together with double costs. *s.* 24.

And if any attorney, solicitor, or other person, shall knowingly insert any other than the full consideration, he shall forfeit 500*l.* and being thereof convicted, shall also be from thenceforth disabled to practice; or, if done, in virtue of any public office, he shall also forfeit his office, and be thenceforth incapable of holding the same. *s.* 25.

But no one shall be liable to any penalty, disability, or forfeiture, unless the duty paid be less than would have been payable, if the full consideration had been truly set forth. *s.* 26.

Parties, on surrendering copyhold lands in court, are to deliver to the steward a note in writing, stating whether the surrender is for sale or not.

And until such note shall be delivered, the lord or lady, or steward, shall not take the proposed surrender, on pain of forfeiting 50*l.*; and where the surrender shall be upon a sale, if the steward neglect to insert the consideration upon the copy of court roll, in words at length, he shall forfeit 50*l.*; and, if upon sale, any person shall in the note state the surrender to be not upon a sale, he shall forfeit 100*l.*

And the lord or steward shall not inrol any surrender out of court, or deed, executed by commissioners of bankrupt, or under the powers contained in any will or act of parliament, or accept any presentment thereof, or admit any person under the same, unless such deed or surrender, or the memorandum of such surrender, shall be stamped with the duty charged thereon, on forfeiting the sum of 50*l.*

Penalty on lords and stewards of manors for taking surrenders, or granting admissions, &c. out of court, unless duly stamped, 50*l.*

Where the freedom of any city or company is obtained by servitude, the chamberlain, or other officer, is to enter the names of all persons bound or articled, with the names and abode of the masters, the apprentice fees, and date of the indentures, on forfeiture of 20*l.*: and the notice printed under all indentures is to be printed, on forfeiture of 10*l.* *Ibid.*

Public officers having in their custody any books or papers, which may tend to secure the stamp duties, or discover any frauds therein, are to permit the officer authorized to inspect, and take notes gratis, on penalty of 50*l.* *Ibid.*

Stamps spoiled, whether the instrument hath been executed or not, may, upon oath made thereof before the commissioners, be exchanged for new stamps, at the stamp office. 5 *Geo.* 3. *c.* 46.

And the commissioners in order to prevent any fraudulent claims, may make such rules *for regulating the method and limiting the time** for cancelling stamps, or allowing other stamps in lieu of such as have been damaged, as they shall find convenient. 44 *Geo.* 3. *c.* 98. *s.* 17.

Also by 50 *Geo.* 3. *c.* 35. the commissioners of stamps may give other stamps for such instruments as may have been *executed and signed* upon improper stamps, and also for all such as shall after executed and signed be rendered useless by some mistake, if application for relief be made within two calendar months after the date of the instrument. *s.* 14.

And where the commissioners have the power of allowing and cancelling stamps, and giving others of the same description, they may, if they see fit, give stamps of any denomination, and of equal value. *s.* 15.

And instruments on stamps of equal or greater value, though not of the proper denomination, shall be deemed valid, except where the stamps appropriated are marked with the name thereof, (*s.* 16.) that is to say, such as receipts, bills, notes, and some other instruments.

And by the last general stamp act, 55 *Geo.* 3. *c.* 184. the following important provisions have been made.

Bills and Notes.] If any person shall sign, accept or pay, any bill, draft, order or note liable to the duties, without being duly stamped, he shall forfeit 50*l.* *s.* 11.

If any person shall issue any bill, draft or order or note, which shall bear date subsequent to the day on which it shall be issued, so that it shall not in fact become payable in *two months* if after date, or in sixty days, if after sight, without the proper stamp in such case directed to be used, he shall forfeit 100*l.* *s.* 12.

And if any person shall issue any bill, draft or order payable to bearer, upon any banker, dated on any subsequent day, or which shall not specify the place where it issued, unless stamped as a bill of exchange, such person shall forfeit 100*l.* Persons receiving such drafts are also to forfeit 20*l.* and bankers paying the same shall not only forfeit 100*l.* but be disallowed the money paid in their accounts against the parties. *s.* 13.

* The time limited by the commissioners is in town, 6 months, and in the country 12 months.

Promissory notes payable to bearer on demand made out of Great Britain, shall not be negotiable, whether payable in Great Britain or not, unless duly stamped; and persons circulating the same are to forfeit 20*l*. for each; but this is not to extend to notes when made and payable only in Ireland. *s*. 29.

Annuities.] Releases and conveyances of annuities and rent-charges, on the repurchase thereof, are exempted from the *ad valorem* duty, and chargeable only with the ordinary duty on deeds.

Wills.] If any person shall take possession of, and in any manner administer any part of the personal estate and effects of the deceased, without obtaining probate or letters of administration, within six calendar months, such person shall forfeit 100*l*. and also 10*l*. per cent. on the amount of the stamp duty payable on such probate or administration. *s*. 37.

No ecclesiastical court shall grant probate or letters of administration without an affidavit, but which need not be stamped, that the estate and effects of the deceased, exclusive of trust property, but including of leaseholds, *and without deducting any thing for debts*, are under a certain amount, to the best of the deponent's knowledge, information and belief, in order that the proper duty may be paid, *s*. 38. and if the officer neglect to take such affidavit he shall forfeit 50*l*. *s*. 39.

Where any person shall have estimated the estate to be of greater value than it shall afterwards have proved to be, and shall have paid too high a duty; if such persons shall produce the probate or letters of administration to the commissioners of stamps within six calendar months with a particular inventory, and valuation verified on oath, the commissioners may cancel the stamp, and make an allowance, as in the cases of spoiled stamps; or *if the difference be considerable* repay the same in money, at their discretion. *s*. 40.

Where any person shall have paid too little duty, the commissioners on affidavit of the value, may cause the probate or administration to be duly stamped on payment of the full duty, and of the further penalty payable by law for stamping deeds after execution, without any deduction or allowance of the stamp duty originally paid; but if the application be made within six calender months after the true value shall be ascertained, and if it appear that it was in consequence of mistake or misapprehension, or not knowing some particular effects belonging to the deceased, the commissioners may remit the penalty, and cause the probate or administration to be stamped, on payment only of the sum wanting, *s*. 41. but in cases of administration on which too little duty has been paid at first, the commissioners shall not cause the same to be so stamped until the administrator shall have given full security to the ecclesiastical court to the full sum. *s*. 42.

If any executor or administrator shall not within six calendar months after discovery of the mistake, apply to the commissioners and pay what is wanting, he shall forfeit 100*l*. and pay 10*l*. per cent. on the amount wanting. *s*. 43.

The ecclesiastical court shall not call in and revoke any probate or letters of administration, on the ground of too high or too low a stamp duty having been paid, as heretofore; and if they so do, the commissioners shall not make any allowance whatsoever for the stamp duty. *s*. 44.

When in the case of letters of administration the proper stamp duty hath not been paid at first, and the administrator hath not been possessed of money sufficient *either of his own or of the deceased* to pay the requisite stamp duty; and where it may happen that executors or persons entitled to administration may *before probate or administration*, find the effects so circumstanced as not to be immediately got possession of, and may not have money sufficient *either of their own or of the deceased* to pay the duty, it shall be lawful for the commissioners on proof of the facts by affidavit to cause the probate or administration to be stamped, and to give credit for the duty, either upon payment of the penalty, or without, when too little duty has been paid, and either with or without the allowance of the duty already paid; upon security first given by the executor or administrator with two sureties in double the duty for payment within six calendar months, and interest at the rate of 10*l*. per cent. from the expiration of such period until payment, if any default be made therein, *s*. 45, but if at the expiration of such period it appear that effects have not been recovered, the commissioners may give further time, upon such conditions as they think expedient. *s*. 46.

But the probate or letters of administration so stamped on credit shall be deposited with the commissioners; subject nevertheless, to be produced in evidence by one of their officers at the expence of the executor or administrator as occasion shall require. *s*. 47.

The duty for which credit shall be given shall be a debt due to the crown, and paid by the executors or administrators in preference to any debt due from the estate of the deceased on pain of 500*l*. *s*. 41.

If before payment of the duty for which credit shall be given, it shall become necessary to take out letters of administration *de bonis non*, the commissioners may cause such administration to be stamped, in the same manner as if the duty had been paid, upon having the administration *de bonis non* deposited, and such further security as they think expedient. *s*. 49.

When it shall be proved by oath and vouch

ers that an executor or administrator hath paid debts to such an amount as would have occasioned a less stamp duty, the commissioners may return the difference if claimed within three years after the date of the probate or administration; or if prevented by proceedings at law, or in equity, the commissioners of the treasury may allow further time. *s.* 51.

Medicine duty.] Nothing in this, or any other act shall extend to charge with any stamp duties ginger and peppermint lozenges or any other article of confectionary unless vended as medicines, nor to compel the person vending the same to take out a licence. *s.* 54.

STAND, is a weight from two hundred and a half to three hundred of pitch. *Mer. Dict. Cowell.*

STANDARD. (from the Fr. *estandart, &c. signum. vexillum.*) In general signification, is an ensign in war; and it is used for the standing weight or measure of the king, because it standeth constant and immoveable. *Britton. c.* 30. See *Weights and Measures.*

STANDARDUS, True standard, or legal weight or measure. *Cowell.*

STANDEL. A young store oak-tree, which in time may make timber; and twelve such young trees are to be left standing in every acre of wood, at the felling thereof, by stat. 35 *Hen.* 8. *c.* 17.

STANDING-ARMY, not to be kept in time of peace, without consent of parliament. 1 *W.* & *M. s.* 2. *c.* 2.

The army is therefore only kept on foot by an annual act called the mutiny act: the last of which, 56 Geo. 3. c. 10. declares that it is judged necessary by his majesty, and this present parliament, that a body of forces should be continued for the safety of the united kingdom, the defence of the possessions of his majesty's crown, and the preservation of the balance of power in Europe, and that the whole number of such forces should consist of "one hundred and seventy-six thousand six hundred and fifteen effective officers and men," exclusive of his majesty's forces employed in the territorial possessions of the East India company, the foreign corps in British pay, and the embodied militia.

STANLAW. A word anciently used for a stony hill. *Doomsd. Cowell.*

STANNARIES, (*stannaria*, from the Lat. *stannum.*) Are the mines and works where tin metal is got and purified, as in Cornwall and Devonshire. *Cam. Brit.* 199.

The stannary courts in Devonshire and Cornwall, for the administration of justice among the tinners therein, are courts of record, but of a private and exclusive nature. They are held before the lord warden and his substitutes, in virtue of a privilege granted to the workers in the tin mines there, to sue and be sued in their own courts, that they may not be drawn from their business, which is highly profitable to the public, by attending their law-suits in other courts. 4 *Inst.* 232.

The privileges of the tinners are confirmed by a charter, 33 *Edw.* 1. and fully expounded by a private statute, 50 *Edw.* 3, which has since been explained by a public act, 16 *Car.* 1. *c.* 15. What relates to this article is only this: that all tinners and labourers in and about the stannaries, shall, during the time of their working therein, bona fide, be privileged from suits of any other courts, and be only impleaded in the stannary court in all matters, excepting pleas of land, life, and member. No writ of error lies from hence to any court in Westminster-hall, as was agreed by all the judges in 4th *Jac.* 1 4 *Inst.* 231. But an appeal lies from the steward of the court to the under-warden, and from him to the lord-warden, and thence to the privy council of the prince of Wales, as duke of Cornwall, 4 *Inst.* 230. when he hath had livery or investiture of the same. 3 *Bulstr.* 183. And from thence the appeal lies to the king himself in the last resort. *Doderidge Hist. of Cornw.* 94.

STANNARIUS. A pewterer or dealer in tin; of or belonging to tin. *Lit. Dict. Cowell.*

STAPLE, (*stapulum,*) comes from the Fr. estape, i. e. *fonum vinarium*, a market or staple for wines, which are the principal commodities of France; or rather from the Germ. *stapulen*, which signifieth to gather, or heap any thing together. In an old French book it is written, *a Calais estape de la Laine*, &c. i. e. the staple for wool. And with us it hath been a public mart appointed by law to be kept at the following places, viz. Westminster, York, Lincoln, Newcastle, Norwich, Canterbury, Chichester, Winchester, Exeter, Bristol, &c. A staple court was held at the wool staple in Westminster, the bounds whereof began at Temple-Bar, and reached to Tothill; in other cities and towns the bounds are within the wall; and where there are no walls, they extend through all the towns; and the court of the mayor of the staple is governed by the law merchant in a summary way, which is the law of the staple. 4 *Inst.* 934. See stat. 27 *Edw.* 3. *st.* 2. The staple goods of England are wool, woolfel, feather, lead, tin, cloth, butter, cheese, &c. as appears by the statute 14 *R.* 2. *c.* 1. though some allow only the five first; and yet of late staple goods are generally understood to be such as are vendible, of any kind, and not subject to perish. 1 *Blacks.* 314.

STAR, (*starrum*, a contraction from the Heb. *shetar*, a deed or contract.) Deeds, obligations, &c. were anciently called stars. 2 *Black.* 343. 4 *V.* 262.

STAR AND BENT. By 15 *Geo.* 2. c. 33. s. 6. persons cutting star or bent from the sand-hills on the north-west coasts, shall forfeit 20*s.* for the first offence, to be levied by distress; or in default, commitment for three months, and for the second or other offence, be committed to the house of correction for one year, and there be whipt and kept to hard labour. Persons in whose possession the same shall be found, shall be deemed the pullers, and punished as above for the first offences.

STAR-CHAMBER, (*camera stellata*, otherwise called *Chamber des estoylles.*) was a chamber at Westminster, so called, because at first the cieling thereof was adorned with images of gilded stars. And by 3 *Hen.* 7. *c.* 1. and 21 *Hen.* 8. *c.* 2. the chancellor, assisted by others there named, had power to punish routs, riots, forgeries, maintenances, embraceries, perjuries, and other such misdemeanors as were not sufficiently provided for by the common law, and for which the inferior judges were not so proper to give correction. But, by the stat. 16 *Car.* 1. c. 10. this court, of such indefinite powers, and all jurisdictions, power, and authority thereto belonging, have been abolished.

STATED DAMAGES. A court of equity cannot, any more than a court of law, relieve against a penalty, in the nature of stated or settled damages, by deed between the parties, as a rent of 5*l.* an acre for ploughing up ancient meadow. 2 *Atk.* 239. 4 *Burr.* 2228.

STATICS, (*statice*, *scientia ponderum.*) Knowledge of weights and measures, or the art of balancing or weighing in scales. *Merch. Dict.*

STATIONARIUS, (from *statio*, residence. The same as *stagiarius*, or a canon residentiary in a cathedral church. See *Stagiarius.*

STATUARIUM. A tomb adorned with statues. *Cowell.*

STATUS DE MANERIO. The state of a manor: all the tenants within the manor met in the court of their lord, to do their customary suit, and enjoy their right and usages; which was termed *omnis status de manerio. Paroch. Antiq.* 456.

STATUTE, (*statutum.*) A statute is a law enacted by the assent of the king, lords, and commons. These statutes are either declaratory of the common law, or remedial of some defects therein. Declaratory, where the old custom of the kingdom is almost fallen into disuse, or become disputable; in which case the parliament has thought proper, *in perpetuum rei testimonium*, and for avoiding all doubts and difficulties, to declare what the common law is and ever hath been. Remedial statutes are those which are made to supply such defects, and abridge such superfluities in the common law, as arise either from the general imperfection of all human laws, from change of time and circumstances, from the mistakes and unadvised determinations of unlearned, or even learned judges, or from any other cause whatsoever. And this being done, either by enlarging the common law where it was too narrow and circumscribed, or by restraining it where it was too lax and luxuriant, hath occasioned another subordinate division of remedial acts of parliament into enlarging and restraining statutes. Thus, clipping the current coin of the kingdom was an offence not sufficiently guarded against by the common law; therefore it was thought expedient, by statute 5 *Eliz. c.* 11. to make it high treason, which it was not at the common law; so that this was an enlarging statute. At common law also spiritual corporations might lease out their estates for any term of years, till prevented by the statute 13 *Eliz.* before-mentioned: this was therefore a restraining statute.

The rules to be observed with regard to the construction of statutes are principally these:

1. There are three points to be considered in the construction of all remedial statutes: the old law, the mischief, and the remedy: that is, 1, how the common law stood at the making of the act; 2, what the mischief was, for which the common law did not provide; and 3, what remedy the parliament hath provided to cure this mischief. And it is the business of the judges so to construe the act, as to suppress the mischief and advance the remedy. 3 *Rep.* 7. *Co. Litt.* 11. 42.

As, for instance, in the restraining statute of 13 *Eliz.* c. 10. By the common law, ecclesiastical corporations might let as long leases as they thought proper; the mischief was, that they let long and unreasonable leases, to the impoverishment of their successors: the remedy applied by the statute was by making void all leases by ecclesiastical bodies for longer terms than three lives, or twenty-one years. Now in the construction of this statute it is held, that leases, though for a longer time, if made by a bishop, are not void during the bishop's continuance in his see; or, if made by a dean and chapter, they are not void during the continuance of the dean: for the act was made for the benefit and protection of the successor, *Co. Litt.* 45. 3 *Rep.* 60. 10 *Rep.* 58. The mischief is therefore sufficiently suppressed by vacating them after the determination of the interest of the grantors; but the leases, during their continuance, being not within the mischief, are not within the remedy. 1 *Black.* 87.

2. A statute, which treats of things or persons of an inferior rank, cannot by any

general words be extended to those of a superior. Thus a statute, treating of "deans, prebendaries, parsons, vicars, and others having spiritual promotion," is held not to extend to bishops, though they have spiritual promotion; deans being the highest persons named, and bishops being of a still higher order. 2 *Rep.* 46.

3. Penal statutes must be construed strictly. Thus the statute 1 *Edw.* 6. c. 12. having enacted that those who are convicted of stealing horses should not have the benefit of clergy, the judges conceived that this did not extend to him that should steal but one horse, and therefore procured a new act for that purpose in the following year. 2 & 3 *Edw.* 6. *c.* 33. And, to come nearer our own times, by the statute 14 *Geo.* 2. c. 6. stealing sheep, or other cattle, was made felony without benefit of clergy. But these general words, "or other cattle," being looked upon as much too loose to create a capital offence, the act was held to extend to nothing but mere sheep. And therefore, in the next sessions, it was found necessary to make another statute, 15 *Geo.* 2. *c.* 34. extending the former to bulls, cows, oxen, steers, bullocks, heifers, calves, and lambs by name. But where statutes use the plural number, a single instance in such cases will be comprehended; thus the statute 2 *Geo.* 2. c. 25. *s.* 3. enacts, that it shall be felony to steal any bank-notes, and it has been adjudged to be felony to steal one bank-note. *Leach* 1. *Nassel's Case.*

4. Statutes against frauds, which are generally called remedial statutes, are to be liberally and beneficially expounded. This may seem a contradiction to the last rule; most statutes against frauds being in their consequences penal. But this difference is here to be taken: where the statute acts upon the offender, and inflicts a penalty, as the pillory or a fine, it is then to be taken strictly: but when the statute acts upon the offence, by setting aside the fraudulent transaction,* here it is to be construed liberally. Upon this footing the statute of 13 *Eliz.* c. 5. which avoids all gifts of goods, &c. made to defraud creditors and others, was held to extend by the general words to a gift made to defraud the queen of a forfeiture. 3 *Rep.* 82.

5. One part of a statute must be so construed by another, that the whole may (if possible) stand: *ut res magis valeat, quam pereat.* As if land be vested in the king and his heirs by act of parliament, saving the right of A; and A has at that time a lease of it for three years: here A shall hold it for his term of three years, and afterwards it shall go to the king. For this interpretation furnishes matter for every clause of the statute to work and operate upon. But,

6. A saving, totally repugnant to the body of the act, is void. If, therefore, an act of parliament vests land in the king and his heirs, saving the right of all persons whatsoever; or vests the land of A in the king, saving the right of A: in either of these cases the saving is totally repugnant to the body of the statute, and (if good) would render the statute of no effect or operation; and therefore the saving is void, and the land vests absolutely in the king. 1 *Rep.* 47.

7. Where the common law and a statute differ, the common law gives place to the statute; and an old statute gives place to a new one. And this upon a general principle of universal law, that "*leges posteriores priores contrarias abrogant.*" But this is to be understood only when the latter statute is couched in negative terms, or where its matter is so clearly repugnant, that it necessarily implies a negative. As if a former act says, that a juror upon such a trial shall have twenty pounds a-year; and a new statute afterwards enacts, that he shall have twenty marks: here the latter statute, though it does not express, yet necessarily implies a negative, and virtually repeals the former. For if twenty marks be made qualification sufficient, the former statute which requires twenty pounds is at an end, (*Jenk. Cent.* 2. 73.) But if both acts be merely affirmative, and the substance such that both may stand together, here the latter does not repeal the former, but they shall both have a concurrent efficacy. If by a former law an offence be indictable at the quarter-sessions, and a lat-

---

* And therefore it has been held, that the same words in a statute will bear different interpretations according to the nature of the suit or prosecution instituted upon them. As by the 9 *Ann.* c. 14. the statute against gaming; if any person shall lose at any time or sitting 10*l.* and shall pay it to the winner, he may recover it back within three months; and if the loser does not within that time, any other person may sue for it, and treble the value besides. So where an action was brought to recover back fourteen guineas, which had been won and paid after a continuance at play, except an interruption during dinner, the court held the statute was remedial, as far as it prevented the effects of gaming, without inflicting a penalty, and therefore, in this action, they considered it one time or sitting; but they said, if an action had been brought by a common informer for the penalty, they would have construed it strictly in favour of the defendant, and would have held, that the money had been lost at two sittings. 2 *Bl. Rep.* 1226.

ter law makes the same offence indictable at the assizes: here the jurisdiction of the sessions is not taken away, but both have a concurrent jurisdiction, and the offender may be prosecuted at either, unless the new statute subjoins express negative words, as, that the offence shall be indictable at the assizes, and not elsewhere. 11 *Rep*. 63.

8. If a statute, that repeals another, is itself repealed afterwards, the first statute is hereby revived, without any formal words for that purpose. So when the statutes of 26 and 35 *Hen*. 8. declaring the king to be the supreme head of the church, were repealed by a statute 1 and 2 *P*. & *M*. and this latter statute was afterwards repealed by an act of 1 *Eliz*. there needed not any express words of revival in queen Elizabeth's statute, but these acts of king Henry were impliedly and virtually revived. 4 *Inst*. 325.

9. Acts of parliament derogatory from the power of subsequent parliaments bind not. So that the statute 11 *Hen*. 7. c. 1. which directs that no person for assisting a king *de facto*, shall be attainted of treason by act of parliament or otherwise, is held to be good only as to common prosecutions for high treason; but will not restrain or clog any parliamentary attainder. Because the legislature, being in truth the sovereign power, is always of equal, always of absolute authority: it acknowledges no superior upon earth, which the prior legislature must have been, if its ordinances could bind a subsequent parliament. 4 *Inst*. 43.

10. Lastly, acts of parliament that are impossible to be performed are of no validity: and if there arise out of them collaterally any absurd consequences, manifestly contradictory to common reason, they are, with regard to those collateral consequences, void. But if the parliament will positively enact a thing to be done which is unreasonable, there is no power in the ordinary forms of the constitution that is vested with authority to control it; for, where the main object of a statute is unreasonable, if the judges were at liberty to reject it, it would be to set the judicial power above that of the legislature, which would be subversive of all government. But where some collateral matter arises out of the general words, and happens to be unreasonable, there the judges are in decency to conclude that this consequence was not foreseen by the parliament, and therefore they are at liberty to expound the statute by equity, and only *quoad hoc* disregard it. Thus, if an act of parliament gives a man power to try all causes that arise within his manor of D., yet, if a cause should arise in which he himself is party, the act is construed not to extend to that, because it is unreasonable that any man should determine his own quarrel. 3 *Rep* 118. But if we could conceive it possible for the parliament to enact, that he should try as well his own causes as those of other persons, there is no court that has power to defeat the intent of the legislature, when couched in such evident and express words, as leave no doubt whether it was the intent of the legislature or no. 1 *Black*. 91.

STATUTE OF FRAUDS. By stat. 29 *Car*. 2. c. 3. all leases, estates, interests of freehold, or terms of years, or any uncertain interest in lands created by livery and seisin only, or by parol, and not put in writing, and signed by the parties or their agents lawfully authorized, shall have the effect of estates at will only, any consideration for making any such parol leases or estates, or former usage to the contrary notwithstanding. *s*. 1.

Except leases not exceeding the term of three years, whereupon the rent reserved shall amount unto two third parts of the full value. *s*. 2.

Also, no leases, estates, or interests, either of freehold or terms of years, or any uncertain interest, not being copyhold or customary, shall be assigned, granted, or surrendered, unless it be by deed or note in writing, signed by the party or the agent thereunto authorized by writing or by act or by operation of law. *s*. 3.

No action shall be brought whereby to charge any executor or administrator, upon any special promise to answer damages out of his own estate, or whereby to charge the defendant upon any special promise to answer for the debt, default, or miscarriages of another person, or to charge any person upon any agreement made upon consideration of marriage, or upon any contract or sale of lands, tenements, or hereditaments, or any interest in or concerning them, or upon any agreement that is not to be performed within the space of one year from the making thereof, unless the agreement upon which such action shall be brought, or some memorandum or note thereof shall be in writing, signed by the party to be charged therewith, or some other person by him thereunto lawfully authorized. *s*. 4.

No contract for the sale of any goods, wares, and merchandizes, for the price of 10*l*. sterling or upwards, shall be allowed to be good, except the buyer shall accept part of the goods so sold, and actually receive the same, or give something in earnest to bind the bargain, or in part of payment; or that some note or memorandum, in writing, of the said bargain, be made and signed by the parties to be charged, or their agents thereunto lawfully authorized. s. 5. See also *Agreement*, *Frauds*, and *Wills*.

STATUTE-MERCHANT. A statute-merchant is a bond of record, acknowledged before the clerk of the statutes-merchant, and lord mayor of the city of London, or two merchants assigned for that purpose; and before the mayors of other cities and towns, or the bailiff of any borough, &c. sealed with the seal of the debtor and the king, upon condition, that if the obligor pays not the debt at the day, execution may be awarded against his body, lands, and goods, and the obligee shall hold the lands to him, his heirs and assigns, till the debt is levied. *Terms de Ley. Stat. Acton Burnel*, 11 *Ed.* 1. and *stat. de Mercatoribus*, 13 *Ed.* 1. *stat.* 3.

Statute-merchants were contrived for the security of merchants only, to provide a speedy remedy to recover their debts; but they were afterwards used by others who did not follow merchandize, and it has therefore become one of the common assurances of the kingdom. *Bridg.* 21. *Owen* 82.

STATUTE STAPLE. Is a bond of record, acknowledged before the mayor of the staple, in the presence of all or one of the constables; to this end, says the statute, there shall be a seal ordained, which shall be affixed to all obligations made on such recognizance acknowledged in the staple; this seal of the staple is the only seal the statute requires to attest this contract; but it is no more under the power or disposal of the mayor than that appointed by the statute-merchant; for though the statute appoints him the custody of it, yet it is in such a manner, that he cannot affix it to any obligation without their consent, it being to remain in the mayor's hands, under the security of their own seals. 2 *Rol. Abr.* 466. *Stat.* 27 *Edw.* 3. *c.* 9.

There is also a recognizance in nature of statute staple, which, as the words of the act declare, is the same with the former, only acknowledged under other persons; for, as the statute runs, the chief justices of the king's bench and common pleas, or in their absence, out of term, the mayor of the staple at Westminster, and the recorder of London jointly together, shall have power to take recognizances for payment of debt in the form set down in the statute; in this, as in the former cases, the king appoints a seal to attest the contract. 23 *Hen.* 8. *c.* 6. *Co. Lit.* 290. *a.* 4 *Inst.* 238. 2 *Rol. Abr.* 466. *Co. Ent.* 12.

But these recognizances both of the merchant and the staple, though sometimes referred to in argument, are now fallen into disuse, and the security by warrant of attorney taken in preference.

STATUTES MERCHANT AND STAPLE. He that is in possession of lands on a statute-merchant, or staple, is called tenant by statute-merchant, or statute staple, during the time of his possession. 27 *Ed.* 3. 2 *Black.* 160.

STATUTES OF A CORPORATION. An incident to a corporation as soon as it is duly erected, and which is annexed of course, is, to make bye-laws, or private statutes, for the better government of the corporation; which are binding upon themselves, unless contrary to the laws of the land, and then they are void. This is included by law in the very act of incorporation. 1 *Black.* 475.

STATUTO MERCATORIO. The writ for imprisoning him that had forfeited a statute-merchant bond until the debt was satisfied. *Reg. Orig.* 146. 148.

STATUTO STAPULÆ. A writ that lay to take the body to prison, and seize upon the lands and goods of one who had forfeited the bond called statute staple. *Reg. Orig.* 151.

STATUTUM DE LABORARIIS. An ancient writ for the apprehending of such labourers as refused to work according to statute. *Reg. Judic.* 27.

STATUTUM SESSIONUM. The statute sessions. A meeting in every hundred of constables and householders, by custom, for the ordering of servants, and debating of differences between the masters and servants, rating of servants wages, and the like. 5 *Eliz. cap.* 4.

STAURUM. Any store or standing stock of cattle, provision, &c. *Cowell.*

STEALING. Is the fraudulent taking away of another man's goods, with an intent to steal them, against or without the will of him whose goods they are. *Cowell.* See *Larceny*.

STEALING AN HEIRESS. See *Abduction.*

STEORESMAN. The same with the stiremannus, or sturemannus. *Cowell.*

STERLING, (*sterlingum.*) Money current within this kingdom. It took its name from this: that there was a pure coin stamped first in England by the Easterlings, or merchants of East Germany, by the command of king John; and Hoveden writes it esterling. *Lowndes* 14.

STEWARD, (*senescallus*, compounded of the Sax. *steda*, i. e. room, or stead and weard, a ward or keeper.) Is as much as to say a man appointed in my place or stead, and hath many applications, but always denotes an officer of chief account within his jurisdiction. The greatest of these officers is the lord high steward of England; the power of this officer being very great, of late the office of high steward of England hath not been granted to any one, only *pro hac vice*, either for the trial of a peer of the realm on an indictment for a capital offence; or for the determination of the pretensions of those who claim to hold by grand serjeanty, to do certain honourable services to the king at his coronation, &c. for both which purposes he holds a court, and proceeds according to the laws and customs of England; and he to whom this office is granted must be of nobility and a lord of parliament. 4 *Inst.* 58, 59. *Crompt. Jurisd.* 84. 13 *Hen.* 8. 11. 2 *Hawk. P. C.* 5. But when the special business for which he is appointed is once ended, his commission expires. *Lex Constitution*, 170.

There is a lord steward of the household, mentioned in stat. 24 *Hen.* 8. *cap.* 13. whose name was changed to that of great master of the household, anno 32 *Hen.* 8. But this statute was repealed by 1 *Mar. cap.* 4. and the office of lord steward of the household revived. He is the chief officer of the king's court, to whom is committed the care of the king's house; he has authority over all officers and servants of the household, except those belonging to the chapel, chamber, and stable; and the palace royal is exempted from all jurisdiction of any court but only of the lord steward, or, in his absence, of the treasurer and comptroller of the household, with the steward of the Marshalsea, who by virtue of their offices, without any commission, hear and determine all treasons, murders, felonies, breaches of the peace, &c. committed in the king's palace. Besides the treasurer and comptroller, the lord steward hath under him a cofferer, several clerks of the green cloth, &c. He attends the king's person at the beginning of parliaments, and is a white staff officer, which he breaks over the hearse on the death of the king, and thereby discharges all officers under him. *Fleta, lib.* 2. and *F. N. B.* 241. In the liberty of Westminster, an officer is chosen and appointed, called high steward, and there is a deputy steward of Westminster; and the word steward is of so great diversity, that in most corporations, and all houses of honour, an officer is found of this name and authority. 4 *Black. Com.* 258. 260.

STEWS, (from the Fr. *estuves*, i. e. *thermæ balneum.*) Are those places which were permitted in England to women of professed incontinency, and who for hire would prostitute themselves to all comers: so called, because dissolute persons are wont to prepare themselves for licentious acts by bathing. These stews were suppressed by king Henry 8, about the year 1546. *Cowell.*

STICA. A brass Saxon coin, of the value of half a farthing, four of them making a helfing. *Ibid.*

STICK OF EELS. A quantity or measure of twenty-five. A bind of eels contains ten sticks, and each stick twenty-five eels. *Stat. of Weights and Measures.*

STICKLER. An inferior officer who cuts wood within the king's parks of Clarendon. *Cowell.*

STILYARD, STEELYARD, otherwise called the Style-House, in the parish of Allhallows, in London, was by authority of parliament assigned to the merchants of the Hanse and Almaine, or Easterling merchants, to have their abode in for ever, with other tenements, rendering to the mayor of London a certain yearly rent. 14 *Ed.* 4. 19 *H.* 7. c. 32. and 22 *H.* 8. c. 8. 1 *Ed.* 6. c. 13.

STINT, *common without.* There are commons without stint, and which last all the year. By the statute of Merton, however, and other subsequent statutes, the lord of the manor may inclose so much of the waste as he pleases, for tillage or wood ground, provided he leaves common sufficient for such as are entitled thereto. 2 *Black.* 34.

STIPULA. Stubble left standing in the field after the corn is reaped and carried away. *Cowell.*

STIPULATION *in the Admiralty Courts.* The first process in these courts is frequently by arrest of the defendant's person; when they take recognizances or stipulation of certain fidejussors in the nature of bail, and, in case of default, may imprison both them and their principal. 3 *Black.* 108, 109.

STIREMANNUS, (*sturemannus*, Sax. *steor-man.*) A pilot of a ship, or steersman. *Cowell.*

STIRPES, distribution *per.* Under the statute of distributions it will sometimes happen that personal estates are divided *per capita*, and sometimes *per stirpes*; whereas the common law knows no other rule of succession but that *per stirpes* only. They are divided *per capita* to every man an equal share, when all the claimants claim in their own rights, as in equal degree of kindred, and not *jure representationis*, in the right of another person. As if the next of kin be the intestate's three brothers A. B. and C. here his estate is divided into three equal portions, and distributed *per capita*, one to each. But if one of these brothers (A.) had been dead, leaving three children and another (B.) leaving two, then the distribution must have been *per stirpes*, viz. one third to A.'s three children, another third to B.'s two children, and the remaining third to C. the surviving brother. Yet if C. had also been dead, without issue, then A.'s and B.'s five children being all in equal degree to the intestate, would take in their own rights *per capita*, viz. each of them one fifth part. *Prec. Chan.* 54. 2 *Black.* 517.

STIRPES, *succession in.* The lineal descendants, *in infinitum,* of any person deceased, shall represent their ancestor, that is, shall stand in the same place as the person himself would have done, had he been living. 2 *Black.* 217.

STOCK AND STOVEL. A forfeiture where any one is taken carrying *stipites & pabulum* out of the woods; for *stock* signifieth sticks, and *stovel* pabulum. *Cowell.*

STOCK or STOKE. Syllables added to the names of places, from the Sax. *Socce.* i. e. *stipe, truncus:* as Woodstock, Basingstoke. *Ibid.*

STOCK AND FAMILY. If lands were devised generally to a stock or family, it shall be understood of the heir principal of the house. *Hob.* 33.

STOCKJOBBERS. All stockjobbing not authorized by act of parliament, or by charter, or used by obsolete charters, shall be void, and the undertakings are declared nuisances. *Stat.* 6 *Geo.* 1. *c.* 18.

All *præmiums* to deliver or receive, accept or refuse, any public stock, or share therein, and contracts in nature of wagers, putts and refusals relating to the value of the stock, shall be void; and the *præmiums* returned, or may be recovered by action with double costs; and the persons entering into or executing any such contract, shall forfeit 500*l.* No money shall be given to compound any difference, for not delivering or transferring stock, or not performing contracts; but the whole money agreed is to be paid, and the stock transferred on pain of 100*l.* Persons buying, on refusal or neglect to transfer at the day, may buy the like quantity of stock of any other person, and recover the damage of the first contractor. And contracts for sale of any stock, where contractors are not actually possessed of or intitled unto the same, to be void; and the parties agreeing to sell, &c. incur a penalty of 500*l.* Brokers making agreements, &c. and doing contrary, are also liable to penalties. But this act not to hinder lending money on stocks, or contracts for redelivering or transferring thereon, so as no *præmium* be paid for the loan more than legal interest. Stat. 7 *Geo.* 2. *c.* 8. Made perpetual by 10 *Geo.* 2. c. 8. See *Brokers* and *Felony.*

STOCKS, (*cippus.*) A wooden engine to put the legs of offenders in, for the securing of disorderly persons, and by way of punishment in divers cases ordained by statute. And it is said that every vill within the precincts of a torn is indictable for not having a pair of stocks, and shall forfeit 5*l.* *Kitch.* 13.

STOCKLAND AND BONDLAND. In the manor of Wadhurst, in Sussex, there are two sorts of copyhold estates, viz. Stockland and Bondland, descendable by custom in several manors: as if a man be first admitted to stockland, and afterwards to bondland, and dies seised of both, his eldest son and heir shall inherit both estates; but if he be admitted first to bondland, and after to the other, and of these dieth seised, his youngest son shall inherit: and bondland held alone, descends to the youngest son. 2 *Leon.* 55.

STOLA. A garment formerly worn by priests, like unto those called hoods. And sometimes it is taken for the archiepiscopal pall. *Eadmer. cap.* 188. Also a vestment which matrons wore. *Cowell.*

STOLEN GOODS. By statute 4 *Geo.* 1. *c.* 11. whoever shall take a reward under the pretence of helping any one to stolen goods, shall suffer as the felon who stole them; unless he causes such principal felon to be apprehended and brought to trial, and also gives evidence against them.

By 6 *Geo.* 1. *c.* 23. persons prosecuting to conviction any person taking reward for helping to stolen goods, not having apprehended the felon, shall be entitled to a reward of 40*l.* *s.* 9, 10.

By 25 *Geo.* 2. *c.* 36. all persons advertising a reward, with no questions asked, for the return of things stolen or lost, or to pay the pawnbroker any money lent thereon, and the printer, shall respectively forfeit 50*l.*

By 29 *Geo.* 2. *c.* 30. buyers or receivers of lead, iron, copper, brass, bell-metal, or solder, knowing the same to be stolen, if convicted, shall be transported for fourteen years.

A justice may issue a search-warrant; and suspected persons found with any materials, in the night, may be apprehended by the parish officers or watchmen, and carried before two justices: the goods are to be advertised, and, till claimed, to be deposited in the hands of the churchwardens or overseers: if not claimed in thirty days they are to be sold, and the produce divided between the officer and the poor. *Ibid.*

Persons to whom such goods shall be offered for sale or pawn, shall, on suspicion, seize the offender and carry him before a justice, on pain of being deemed guilty of a misdemeanor, and forfeiting, for the first offence 20*s.* for the second 40*s.* and for every subsequent offence 4*l.* *Ibid.*

Persons having such stolen materials in their possession, and not accounting satisfactorily for the same, shall be guilty of a misdemeanor, and forfeit 40*s.* for the first offence, for the second 4*l.* and for every other 6*l.* *Ibid.*

Offenders convicting the buyers or receivers of such stolen materials are entitled to a pardon. *Ibid.*

The forfeitures go half to the poor, and half to the informer, to be levied by distress and sale; and for want thereof the party shall be imprisoned, for the first offence, one month; for the second, two months; and for every other offence, at the discretion of the sessions. *Ibid.*

By 22 *Geo.* 3. *c.* 58. every person buying or receiving stolen goods shall be deemed guilty of a misdemeanor, and prosecuted accordingly.

Justices may grant search-warrants to discover stolen goods; and persons in whose custody they are found shall be deemed guilty of a misdemeanor. *Ibid.*

Constables may apprehend persons suspected of having any stolen goods between sun-setting and sun-rising, and, on conviction, they may be imprisoned not more than six nor less than three months. *Ibid.*

Persons offering stolen goods to be pawned or sold, shall be taken before a justice; and persons, under fifteen years of age, charged with felony within clergy, discovering two receivers, shall be entitled to his majesty's pardon. *Ibid.*

But this act shall not repeal any former law for punishing such offenders. *Ibid.* See *Felony.*

STONE. A weight of fourteen pounds, used for weighing of wool. A stone of wax is eight pounds; and in London the stone of beef is no more. 11 *Hen.* 7. *c.* 4. *Cowell.*

STORES. By 9 and 10 *Will.* 3. *c.* 41. no warlike or naval stores, except for the king's use, shall be made with the king's marks, on forfeiture of the goods and 200*l.* with costs; and the like penalty is inflicted on persons in whose custody such stores are found, unless a certificate, under the hand of his majesty's commissioners, be produced.

Commissioners of the navy, ordnance, or victualling-office, may sell any of the stores so marked, and the buyer shall have a certificate thereof, expressing the quantities. *Ibid.*

But this is not to hinder any chief commander, at sea, from lending any of his majesty's stores to any merchant ship in distress, so they be restored; and the borrower is to have a certificate of the same. *Ibid.*

By 9 *Geo.* 1. *c.* 8. persons having timber marked with the broad arrow in their custody, or concealing the same, shall suffer according to 9 & 10 *Will.* 3. *c.* 41.

Naval stores and iron are prohibited to be exported, unless pre-emption be first offered to the commissioners of the navy. c. 35.

By 39 & 40 *Geo.* 3. *c.* 89. every person (not being a contractor) who shall sell or receive any new stores of war, or who shall conceal them, shall be deemed a receiver of stolen goods, and as such transported for fourteen years, unless he produces on the trial a certificate from the navy board, ordnance, or victualling. *s.* 1.

Persons in whose custody shall be found canvas or buntin, with a serpentine blue streak (not being charged to be new, or not more than one-third worn), and persons who shall be convicted of any offence contrary to 9 & 10 *Will.* 3. shall, besides the forfeiture thereby imposed, suffer corporal punishment; but the judge or justice may mitigate the penalty of 200*l.* as they see cause. *s.* 2.

Nothing herein, or in the act of *Will.* 3. shall exempt contractors or others, except so far as concerns naval stores, which shall not have been before delivered into the king's stores, unless they have been sold or returned by the commissioners. *s.* 3.

If any person shall deface any mark, denoting the property of the crown, in any stores, or shall employ any person so to do, he shall be guilty of felony, and transported for fourteen years. *s.* 4.

If any person convicted of any offence contrary to this act, for which he shall not have been transported, or contrary to the act of *Will.* 3. shall be convicted of a second offence, which would not, as the first, subject him to transportation, he shall be transported for fourteen years. *s.* 5.

Persons returning from transportation, under this act, shall suffer as felons without clergy. *s.* 6.

But the court may mitigate the punishment of transportation by pillory, whipping, fine, or imprisonment; and fines are to be applied, one half to the informer, and one half to the king. *s.* 7.

If any person shall discover to the navy, ordnance, or victualling boards, or apprehend any offender guilty of stealing or embezzling his majesty's stores, or of any offence against the act of *Will.* 3. or this, which shall not be prosecuted in a summary way, he shall, on conviction, receive a reward of 20*l.* over his share of the penalty, if not more than that sum. *s.* 8.

If any dispute shall arise as to the title to such reward, it shall be determined by any of the commissioners of the boards. *s.* 9.

Reward shall be paid on certificate from the officer of the court where the offender shall be tried, for which he may charge 5*s.* *s.* 10.

Any commissioner of the navy, ordnance, or victualling, or any justice of the peace, may grant warrants for searching places, when oath is made that there is reason to suspect king's stores are concealed (and if any stores or goods, marked as hereinbefore, or the act of *Will.* 3. mentioned, shall be found, the offender shall be dealt with according to law); and if upon such search, or any seizure of stores or goods marked as aforesaid, any not marked shall be found, suspected to belong to the king, and the party shall not give a satisfactory account thereof, they shall be forfeited, and he shall be deemed guilty of a misdemeanor. *s.* 11.

Persons deputed by the commissioners of the navy, ordnance, or victualling, may detain any craft in which may be suspected to be contained any articles stolen from his majesty's stores, and the parties, who shall be dealt with according to law respecting marked stores; and those not marked, suspected to belong to the crown, not satisfactorily accounted for, shall be forfeited, and the party deemed guilty of a misdemeanor, (see *s.* 11.); and if the person be convicted of stealing marked articles, or adjudged guilty of a misdemeanor with respect to unmarked ones, the craft in which found shall be forfeited. *s.* 12.

Persons, so deputed, may detain any craft, in which may be suspected to be contained any articles stolen from his majesty, and the parties, who shall be dealt with according to law, respecting marked stores; and those not marked, suspected to belong to his majesty, and not satisfactorily accounted for, shall be forfeited, and the party be deemed guilty of a misdemeanor. *s.* 12.

And if the person be convicted of stealing marked articles, or adjudged guilty of a misdemeanor, with respect to unmarked ones, the craft in which found shall be forfeited. *Ibid.*

Persons so deputed, or any police or peace officer, may apprehend persons suspected of having stolen articles, and may seize the articles, and convey them and the parties before a justice, and the like proceedings shall be had as with respect to stores found in any craft. *s.* 13.

Articles herein declared to be forfeited, on the parties not giving a satisfactory account of them, shall be returned into his majesty's stores, and applied for his use, unless proof be made within three months to the contrary. *s.* 14.

The commissioner or justice, by whom any craft shall be adjudged to be forfeited, shall issue his warrant to the officers of the customs for the sale thereof, who shall cause it and the furniture to be sold publicly; and the produce shall be paid to the commissioner or justice, and disposed of, one half to the seizer of the craft, and the other to the treasurer of the navy if naval stores, or the treasurer of the ordnance if ordnance stores. *s.* 15.

Persons guilty of misdemeanors, shall forfeit, for the first offence, 40*s.*; for the second, 5*l.*; for the third, 10*l.*; which may be levied by distress; to be applied, one half to the informer, and one half to the navy or ordnance board; and if distress cannot be found, the offender, who shall be kept in custody, shall be committed for three months. *s.* 16.

Adjudications in misdemeanors shall be certified to the next general or quarter sessions, and shall be final. *s.* 17.

Any commissioner of the navy, ordnance, or victualling, or justice of the peace, may determine any complaint against persons, not being contractors, for unlawfully selling or receiving stores not exceeding 20*s.* value, and may fine the offenders 10*l.* *s.* 18.

Which fine may be levied by distress, and applied, one half to the informer, and one half to the navy board, or ordnance; and if sufficient distress cannot be found, the offender may be committed to the common gaol, or, in lieu of the fine, may be kept to hard labour for three months: the commissioner or justice shall pay over the fines received within thirty days, or forfeit 50*l.*; and double costs by action, half to the king and half to the informer. *Ibid.*

The fine of 10*l.* may be mitigated to one half, besides expences. *s.* 19.

If in lieu of a fine the offender be imprisoned, the informer shall receive 5*l.* reward from the navy or ordnance board, upon production of a certificate from the commissioner or justices who convicted him. *s.* 20.

But no summary proceedings are to be had before any justice without the consent of the commissioners of the navy, ordnance, or victualling. *Ibid.*

Persons thinking themselves aggrieved by any judgment touching stores under the value of 20*s.* may appeal to the quarter-sessions; but no *certiorari.* *s.* 21, 22.

Witnesses neglecting to attend, shall forfeit 10*l.* *s.* 23.

Nothing herein shall prevent parties accused of selling or receiving stores under the value of 20*s.* from being prosecuted as receivers of stolen goods, so as offenders be not twice punished for the same offence. *s.* 24.

The commissioners may sell marked stores, and the buyers may keep them without incurring any penalty, on producing a certificate of their having bought them. *s.* 25.

Penalty for giving or publishing false certificates 200*l.* and corporal punishment (as under *s.* 2.), and penalty to go half to the king and half to the informer. *s.* 26.

If any person shall be sued for any seizure, and shall prove on the trial that the stores were marked, or if not marked might be suspected to belong to the king, or if the plaintiff shall not prove that he had a certificate, the defendant shall be acquitted. *s.* 27.

The commissioners shall have the benefit given to justices of the peace by 7 *Jac.* 1. c. 5. 21 *Jac.* 1. c. 12. and 24 *Geo.* 2. c. 44. and the peace officers acting under them, shall have the protection of the said acts. *s.* 28.

The act is to extend to Scotland, and the offenders there are to be tried according to the forms in trials for theft or reset of theft or in a summary way, according to the offence. *s.* 29—35.

If any person shall forswear himself, he shall be liable to the pains of wilful perjury. *s.* 36.

STOTARIUS, he who had the care of the stud or breed of young horses. *Leg. Alfred, c.* 9. *Cowell.*

STOTH, *Nativi de W. solvit quilibet pro filiabus suis Maritandis Gerson Domino, & Ourlop pro filiabus corruptis, & Stoth, & alia servitia, &c. Cowell.*

STOW, (Sax. i. e. *locus*) a place, and is often joined to other words; as Godstow is a place dedicated to God. *Ibid.*

STOWAGE, the room where goods are laid; or, it is the money paid for such places. *Ibid.*

STRAITS, a narrow sea, between two lands, or an arm of the sea. *Ibid.*

STRAND, (Sax.) any shore, or bank of a sea, or great river; hence the street in the west suburbs of London, which lay next the shore, or bank of the Thames, is called the Strand. *Ibid.*

STRANDED, (from the Sax. *strand*) is when a ship is by tempest or ill steerage run on ground, and so perishes. 17 *Car.* 1. c. 14. See *Ships* and *Wreck.*

STRANGER, (derived from the Fr. *estranger*, alienus) signifies generally, in our language, a man born out of the realm, or unknown. In the law it hath a special signification for him that is not privy to an act: as a stranger to a judgment, is he to whom a judgment doth not belong; and in this sense it is directly contrary to party or privy. *Old Nat. Br.* 128.

STRAY, or going astray of beasts and cattle. See *Estray.*

STREAM-WORKS, works in the Stannaries. 27 *H.* 8. c. 23.

STREEMAN, (Sax.) *robustus, vel potens vir. Cowell.*

STREETS. See *Felony* and *London.*

STREPITUS JUDICIALIS, the circumstances of noise and crowd, and other turbulent formalities at a process or trial in a public court of justice. *Cowell.*

STRETWARD, was an officer of the streets, like our surveyor of the highways, or rather a scavenger. *Ibid.*

STRIKING in the king's superior courts of justice, in Westminster hall, or at the assizes, subjects the offender to the loss of the right-hand, imprisonment for life, and forfeiture of goods and chattels, and of the profits of his lands during life. *Staundf. P. C.* 38. 3 *Inst.* 140, 141.

Maliciously striking in the king's palace, wherein his royal person resides, whereby blood is drawn, is punishable by perpetual imprisonment, and fine, at the king's pleasure, and also with loss of the offender's right-hand; the solemn execution of which sentence is described at length in the statute 33 *H.* 8. c. 12. 4 *Black.* 125, 273. See *Affrays, Church, Felony,* and *Palaces.*

STRIP, (*strepitus*) destruction, mutilation, from the Fr. *estropier. Cowell.*

STROND, an old Saxon word, signifying the same as strand. *Ibid.*

STRUMPET, (*meretrix*) a whore, harlot, or courtesan: heretofore used for an addition. *Ibid.*

STRYKE, the eighth part of a seam or quarter of corn, a stryke or bushel. *Ibid.*

STUD OF MARES, is a company of mares kept for breeding of colts: from the Sax. *stodmare*, i. e. *equa ad fœtum. Ib.*

STULTIFYING ONE'S SELF. It hath been said, that a *non compos* himself, though he be afterwards brought to a right mind, shall not be permitted to alledge his own insanity, in order to avoid his grant, for that no man shall be allowed to stultify himself, or plead his own disability; but late opinions, feeling the inconvenience of this rule, have in many points endeavoured to restrain it. *Comb.* 469. 3 *Mod.* 310, 311. 1 *Equ. Cas. Abr.* 279.

And it seems to be settled, that their acts are only binding, in case they be afterwards agreed to, when their imbecility ceases. 4 *Black.* 291, 292.

STURGEON. The king shall have sturgeon taken in the sea, or elsewhere within the realm, except in certain places privileged by the king. 17 *Ed.* 2. *s.* 1. c. 11.

STYLE, (*appello*) is to call, name, or intitle one; as the style of the king of England is George the third, by the grace of God, of the united kingdom of Great Britain and Ireland king.

There is an old and new style used in the dates of things abroad, the latter being eleven days before the former.

The new style was established by 24 *Geo.* 2. c. 23. And the opening of commons, and doing of other things depending on any moveable feast, must be according to this style. 25 *Geo.* 2. c. 30.

SUB-DEACON, an ancient officer in the church, made by the delivery of an empty platter and cup by the bishop, and of a pitcher, bason, and towel, by the archdeacon: his office was to wait on the deacon with the linen on which the body, &c. was consecrated, and to receive and carry away the plate with the offerings at sacraments, the cup with the wine and water in it, &c. *Cowell.*

SUBJECTION, (civil.) Civil subjection is the obligation whereby the inferior is constrained by the superior to act contrary to what his own reason and inclination would suggest. Obedience to the laws in being is undoubtedly a sufficient extenuation of civil guilt before the municipal tribunal. 4 *Black.* 28.

SUBJECTS, (*subditos*) are the members of the commonwealth under the king their head. *Wood's Inst.* 22.

SUBINFEUDATION, was where the inferiors, in imitation of their superiors, began to carve out and grant to others minuter estates than their own, to be held of themselves, and were so proceeding downwards, *in infinitum*, till the superior lords observed, that by this method of subinfeudation they lost all their feodal profits, of wardships, marriages, and escheats, which fell into the hands of the mesne or middle lords, who were the immediate superiors of the terretenant, or him who occupied the land. This occasioned the statute of *Westm.* 3. or *quia emptores*, 18 *Ed.* 1. to be made; which directs, that upon all sales or feoffments of lands, the feoffee shall hold the same, not of his immediate feoffor, but of the chief lord of the fee of whom such feoffor himself held it. And from hence it is held, that all manors existing at this day must have existed by immemorial prescription; or, at least, ever since the 18 *Ed.* 1. when the statute of *quia emptores* was made. 2 *Black.* 91, 92.

SUBJUGALIS, any beast carrying the yoke. *Cowell.*

SUBLEGERIUS, (from the Sax. *syblegger*, i. e. *incestus*) one who is guilty of incestuous incontinence. *Ibid.*

SUB-MARSHAL, an officer in the marshalsea, who is deputy to the chief marshal of the king's house, commonly called the knight marshal, and hath the custody of the prisoners there. He is otherwise termed under marshal. *Cromp. Juris.* 104.

SUBMISSION. See *Arbitrament.*

SUBNERVARE, to cut the sinews of the legs or thighs, to ham-string: and it was an old custom in England, *meretrices & impudicas mulieres subnervare. Cowell.*

SUBORNATION, (*subornatio*) a secret under-hand preparing, instructing, or bringing in a false witness; hence subornation of perjury is the preparing or corrupt alluring to perjury. See *Perjury.*

SUBPŒNA, is a writ whereby the party is called to appear at the day and place assigned, that is, under a penalty of 100*l.*; and it is the leading process in courts of equity, to oblige the defendant to appear and answer; and by 45 *Geo.* 3. c. 92. the service of a subpœna on parties or witnesses in any part of the united kingdom, shall be valid, to compel an appearance in any other part, the expences being tendered. *West. Symb. par.* 2. *Cromp. Jurisdict.* 33.

In this writ the 100*l.* penalty is inserted only *in terrorem*, being never levied; though if a witness, served with a subpœna, refuse to appear, on tender of his charges, the party injured thereby may recover 10*l.* damages, and other recompence by action of the case; 5 *Eliz.* c. 9, 12. or the court may issue an attachment for the contempt. 3 *Black.* 382.

SUBPŒNA AD TESTIFICANDUM, a writ or process, to bring in witnesses to give their testimony in any cause, not only in chancery but all other courts. If a witness, on being served with this process, does not appear, the court will issue an attachment against him; or a party, plaintiff or defendant, injured by his non-attendance, may maintain an action against the witness. 3 *Black.* 369.

SUBPŒNA DUCES TECUM. This is a writ or process of the same kind with the preceding subpœna, including a cause of requisition, for the witness to bring and produce books and papers in his hands, belonging to, or wherein the parties are interested, or tending to elucidate the matter in question. 3 *Black.* 382. See *Duces Tecum.*

SUBSCRIPTION OF WITNESSES. A will of lands must, by stat. 29 *Car.* 2. c. 3. *s.* 5. be attested or subscribed by three credible witnesses at least; in other conveyances, the actual subscription of the witnesses is not required by law, though it is prudent for them so to do. 2 *Black.* 378.

SUBSEQUENT CONDITIONS, are such, by the failure or non-performance of which an estate already vested may be defeated. 2 *Black.* 154.

SUBSEQUENT EVIDENCE. In attaint, he that brings the attaint can give no other evidence to the grand jury, than what was originally given to the petit. 3 *Black.* 403.

On a re-hearing in equity, all the evidence taken in the cause, whether read before or not, is admitted to be read; because it is the decree of the chancellor himself, who only now sits to hear reasons why the decree should not be enrolled and perfected; at which time all the omissions of either evidence or argument may be supplied. *Gill. Rep.* 151, 152. 3 *Black.* 454, 455.

SUBSIDY, (*subsidium*) an aid, tax, or tribute, granted to the king. *Jenk. Cent.* 208. *Dyer,* 165. *Lane,* 24. *Cro. Car.* 601.

SUBSTANCE. The substance of things is most to be regarded; and therefore our law doth prefer matter of substance before matters of circumstance. 36 *E.* 3. c. 15. 33 *H.* 6. c. 10. 21 *H.* 7. c. 24. 23 *Eliz.* c. 4.

SUBSTITUTE, (*substitutus*) one placed

under another person to transact some business, or perform some personal service. See *Attorney* and *Militia*.

SUBTRACTION OF CONJUGAL RIGHTS. This is when either husband or wife lives separate from the other without any sufficient reason; in which case the ecclesiastical jurisdiction (on a suit for restitution of conjugal rights) will compel them to come together again, if either party be weak enough to desire it, contrary to the inclination of the other. 3 *Black.* 94.

SUBTRACTION OF LEGACIES. This is the withholding or detaining of legacies; for this also the spiritual court administers redress, by compelling the executor to pay them. In this case the courts of equity exercise a concurrent jurisdiction with the ecclesiastical courts, to compel the executor to account; and the cause, when once brought there, receives there also its full determination. 3 *Black.* 98.

SUBTRACTION OF RENTS AND SERVICES, &c. This happens when any person, who owes any suit, duty, custom, rent, or service to another, withdraws or neglects to perform or pay it. 3 *Black.* 230.

SUBTRACTION OF TITHES. This is the withholding of tithes from the parson or vicar, whether the former be a clergyman or a lay appropriator. Stat. 27 *H.* 8. *c.* 20. 32 *H.* 8. *c.* 7. See *Tithes.*

SUBURBANI, are husbandmen. *Cowell. Blount.*

SUCCESSION AB INTESTATO. The statute of distributions bears some resemblance to the Roman law of successions *ab intestato.* 2 *Black.* 516.

SUCCESSION TO GOODS AND CHATTELS. The gaining a property in chattels, either personal or real, by succession, is, in strictness of law, only applicable to corporations aggregate of many, as dean and chapter, mayor and commonalty, master and fellows, and the like; in which one set of men may, by succeeding another set, acquire a property in all the goods, moveables, and other chattels of the corporation. 2 *Black.* 430.

SUCCESSOR, (Lat.) in corporations, is he that followeth or cometh in another's place; and sole corporations may take a fee-simple estate to them, and their successors, but not without the word successors. 4 *Rep.* 65. 1 *Inst.* 8, 46, 94. 4 *Inst.* 249. *Wood's Inst.* 111.

SUCCISSIONES ARBORUM, the cuttings and croppings of trees. *Cowell.*

SUFFERANCE. Tenant at sufferance, is he who holdeth over his term. *Terms de Ley.* 1 *Co. Inst.* 57.

SUFFERENTIA PACIS, a grant or sufferance of peace or truce. *Cowell.*

SUFFRAGAN, (*suffraganus, chorepiscopus, episcopi vicarius*) the vicar ordained by the bishop of the diocese to aid and assist him in his spiritual function; or one who supplieth the place instead of the bishop. And if any one exercise the jurisdiction of a suffragan, without the appointment of the bishop of the diocese, &c. he shall be guilty of a *præmunire.* 26 *Hen.* 8. *c.* 14.

SUGGESTION, (*suggestio*) the representing of a thing; thus suggestions are grounds to move for prohibitions to suits in the spiritual courts, &c. when they meddle with matters out of their jurisdictions. 2 *Lil. Abr.* 536.

So upon suggestion of the party, supported by an affidavit made of the matter suggested, the court may grant a rule for staying the proceedings upon the record. 2 *Lill.* 537. 1 *Plowd.* 76.

SUICIDE. See *Felo de se.*

SUIT, (*secta*, Fr. *suite*, i. e. *consecutio*, *sequela*) signifies a following another, but in divers senses. The first is a suit in law, and is divided into suit real and personal, which is all one with action real and personal. 2. Suit of court, an attendance which the tenant owes to the court of his lord. 3. Suit covenant, when a man hath covenanted to do suit in the lord's court. 4. Suit custom, where I and my ancestors owe suit time out of mind. 5. Suit is the following one in chase, as fresh suit: and this word is used for a petition made to the king, or any great personage. 3 *Black.* 295.

SUIT AND SERVICE. When the tenant had professed himself to be the man of his superior or lord; the next consideration was concerning the service, which, as such, he was bound to render for the land he held. This, in pure, proper, and original feuds, was only twofold: to follow, or do suit to the lord in his courts in time of peace; and in his armies, or warlike retinue, when necessity called him to the field. 2 *Black.* 54.

SUIT OF COURT, i. e. suit to the lord's court, is that service which the feudary tenant was bound to do at the lord's court; but all the lord's tenants were not bound to attend his courts, but only those to whom their estates were granted upon that condition. *Cowell.*

SUITS AT LAW, are to be prosecuted in certain times, limited by the statute 21 *Jac.* 1. *c.* 16. (See *Limitations.*) And persons desiring to end any suits or controversies, for which there is no remedy but by personal action, or bill in equity, may agree that their submission to the award of arbitrators shall be made a rule of court.

SUIT IN EQUITY. The first commencement is by preferring a bill in the stile of a petition, setting forth the circumstances of the case at length, as some fraud, trust, or hardship, and praying relief, and also process of subpœna against the defendant. The defendant is to answer, upon oath, to all the matter charged in the bill; or the defendant may plead and demur, or demur alone, as advised by counsel. If the defendant answers, and the plaintiff finds sufficient matter confessed in the defendant's answer to ground a decree upon, he may proceed to the hearing of the cause on bill and answer only. But, in that case, he must take the defendant's answer to be true in every point; otherwise the course is for the plaintiff to reply generally to the answer, averring his bill to be true, certain, and sufficient, and the defendant's answer to be directly the reverse, which he is ready to prove, as the court shall award; upon which the defendant rejoins, averring the like on his side, which is joining issue upon the facts in dispute. 3 *Black.* 442.

SUIT OF THE KING'S PEACE, is the pursuing a man for the breach of the peace. 6 *R.* 2. *c.* 1. 5 *H.* 4. *c.* 15.

SUIT-SILVER, a small sum paid in some manors to excuse the appearance of freeholders at the courts of their lords. *Cowell.*

SULCUSAQUÆ, a little brook, or stream of water. *Ibid.*

SULLERY, (from the Sax. *sulth*, i. e. *aratrum*) a plough-land. 1 *Inst.* 5.

SULLINGA, (*sullingata terræ*) is the same with swoling. *Cowell.*

SUMAGE, (*sumagium* & *summagium*) toll for carriage on horseback. *Cromp. Juris.* 191. *Cowell.*

SUMMARY, (*summarium*) a compendious abridgment.

SUMMARY CONVICTIONS, are such as are directed by act of parliament for the conviction of offenders, and the inflicting of certain penalties created by those acts of parliament. In these cases there is no intervention of a jury, but the party accused is acquitted or condemned by the suffrage of such person only, as the statute hath appointed for his judge. See *Conviction.*

SUMMER-HUS-SILVER, a payment to the lords of the wood in the wealds of Kent, who used to visit those places in summer-time, when their under-tenants were bound to prepare little summer-houses for their reception, or else pay a composition in money. *Cowell.*

SUMMONEAS, a judicial writ of great diversity, according to the divers cases wherein it is used. *Ibid.*

SUMMONERS, (*summonitores*) are petty officers that cite and warn men to appear in any court, and these ought to be *boni homines*, &c.; they are also called apparitors. *Fleta, l.* 4. *Cowell.*

SUMMONITORES SCACCARII, officers who assisted in collecting the king's revenues, by citing the defaulters therein into the court of exchequer. *Cowell.*

SUMMONS, (*summonitio*) is a writ to the sheriff, to warn him to appear at a day. 6 *Rep.* 54. 37 *H.* 6. *c.* 26.

SUMMONS AND SEVERANCE. Although this title is distinguished in the books by the name of summons and severance, yet the proper name is severance; for the summons is only a process, which must, in certain cases, issue before judgment of severance can be given. *Bar. Abr.*

Severance therefore is a judgment by which, where two or more are joined in an action, one or more of these is enabled to proceed in such action without the other or others. *Ibid.*

And to prevent inconvenience, the law has provided, that if any one, in whose name a joint action is commenced, does not appear, or after appearance makes default, the other may have judgment *ad sequendum solum*, or, in other words, a judgment of severance. *Hard.* 48. *Bro. Summ. and Selv. pl.* 4. 16. *F. N. B.* 128. 1 *Inst.* 139.

SUMMONS TO PARLIAMENT. See *Parliament.*

SUMMONS AD WARRANTIZANDUM, *summoneas ad warrantizand'*, the process whereby the vouchee in a common recovery is called. *Co. Lit.* 101.

SUMPTUARY LAWS, (*sumptuaria lex*, from *sumptuarius*, of or belonging to expences) are laws made to restrain excess in apparel, and prohibit costly clothes, of which heretofore we had many in England, but they are all repealed by 1 *Jac.* 1. 3 *Inst.* 199.

SUNDAY, (*dies dominicus*) is the Lord's day set apart for the service of God, to be kept religiously, and not be profaned. See *Sabbath.*

SUPERCARGO, a person employed by merchants to go a voyage, and oversee their cargo, and dispose of it to the best advantage. *Merch. Dict. Cowell.*

SUPER-INSTITUTION, (*super-institutio*) is one institution upon another; as where *A. B.* is admitted and instituted to a benefice upon one title, and *C. D.* is admitted and instituted on the title or presentment of another. 2 *Cro.* 463.

SUPER-JURARE, a term used in our ancient law, when a criminal endeavoured to excuse himself by his own oath, or the oath of one or two witnesses, and the crime objected against him was so plain and notorious, that he was convicted by the oaths of many more witnesses: this was called *super-jurare*. *Cowell.*

SUPERONERATIONE PASTURÆ, is a judicial writ that lies against him who is impleaded in the county-court for the surcharging or overburthening a common with his cattle, in a case where he was formerly impleaded for it, in the same court, and the cause is removed into one of the courts at Westminster. *Reg. Judic.*

SUPER PRÆROGATIVA REGIS, a writ which formerly lay against the king's tenant's widow for marrying without the king's licence. *F. N. B.* 174.

SUPERSEDEAS, a writ that lies in a great many cases; and signifies, in general, a command to stay some ordinary proceedings at law, on good cause shewn, which ought otherwise to proceed. *F. N. B.* 236.

SUPER STATUTO, 1 *Ed.* 3. *c.* 12, 13, is a writ that lay against the king's tenants holding in chief, who aliened the king's land without his licence. *F. N. B. f.* 175.

SUPER STATUTO *de Articulis Cleri*, *c.* 6. a writ that lay against the sheriff or other officer that distrained in the king's highway, or in the lands anciently belonging to the church. *F. N. B.* 173.

SUPER STATUTO *facto pour Seneschal & Marshal de Roy*, &c. a writ that lay against the steward or marshal, for holding plea in his court of freehold, or for trespass or contracts not made and arising within the king's household. *F. N. B.* 241.

SUPER STATUTO *versus Servantes & Laboratores*, a writ against him who kept servants departed out of their services contrary to law. *F. N. B.* 167.

SUPER STATUTO *de York*, *quo null serra viteller*, &c. is a writ lying against a person that uses victualling, either in gross or by retail, in a city or borough-town, during the time he is mayor, &c. *F. N. B.* 172.

SUPERSTITIOUS USES. No information can be brought in chancery, for such mistaken charters, as are given to the king by the statutes for suppressing superstitious uses; but the same must be determined in the court of exchequer, as a court of revenue. 3 *Black.* 428. See *Uses.*

SUPERVISOR, (Lat.) a surveyor or overseer: as supervisor (now surveyor) of the highways, of excise, and the like.

SUPPLEMENTAL BILL IN EQUITY. If a plaintiff hath replied to a defendant's answer, whereby the cause is at issue, and afterwards new matter arises, which did not exist before, he must set it forth by a supplemental bill. 3 *Black.* 448.

SUPPLETORY OATH. The civil law universally requires the testimony of two; and where there is only one witness, to make up the necessary complement of two, they admit the party himself (plaintiff or defendant) to be examined in his own behalf, and administer to him what is called the suppletory oath; and, if his evidence happens to be in his own favour, this immediately converts the half proof into a whole one. 3 *Black.* 270, 271.

SUPPLICAVIT, is a writ issuing out of chancery, for taking surety of the peace, when one is in danger of being hurt in his body by another; it is directed to the justices of peace and sheriff of the county, and is grounded upon the statute 1 *Ed.* 3. c. 16. which ordains, that certain persons shall be assigned by the chancellor to take care of the peace, &c. (*F. N. B.* 80, 81.) And if he, against whom the writ is sued, come into the chancery, and there find sureties that he will not do hurt or damage unto him that sueth the writ, he shall have a writ of supersedeas. *New Nat. Br.* 180.

To sue the writ of supplicavit, the party that desires it must go before one of the masters in chancery, and make oath that he does not desire the same through any malice, but for his own safety; upon which the master makes out a warrant, and the writ is made out by one of the clerks in the six clerks office; and when made, the supplicavit is to be delivered to the sheriff to have his warrant thereupon for arresting the party, &c.; and then, having sued out a certiorari, it is to be delivered to them that took bail thereon, and they are required to certify it, &c. *Pract. Solic.* 130.

SUPPLIES. Extraordinary grants to government, by parliament, to supply the exigencies of the state. 1 *Black.* 307.

SUPREMACY, signifies sovereign dominion, authority, and pre-eminence, the highest estate. And, by our ancient laws, this kingdom is an absolute empire and monarchy, consisting of one head, which is the king, and of a body politic, made up of many well agreeing members. And the kingly head of this politic body is furnished with prerogative and jurisdiction, to render justice and right to every part and member of this body, of what estate or degree soever, otherwise he would not be at the head of the whole. 5 *Co. Rep.* 8. See *Constitution*, *King*, and *Oaths*.

SURCHARGE, an over-charge, beyond what is just and right.

SURCHARGE OF COMMON. This is a disturbance of common of pasture, by any one, who hath right of common, putting more cattle therein than the pasture and herbage will sustain, or the party hath a right to do. This surcharging can, properly speaking, only happen where the common is appendant or appurtenant, and of course limitable by law; or where, when in gross, it is expressly limited and certain: for where a man hath common in gross, *sans nombre*, or without stint, he cannot be a surcharger. But even in this case there must be sufficient for the lord's own beasts; for the law will not suppose that, at the original grant of the common, the lord meant to exclude himself. The remedy for surcharging common, is by the lord's distraining the surplus number, or by his bringing trespass, or by action on the case, in which any commoner may be plaintiff. 3 *Black.* 237, 238.

SURCHARGE OF THE FOREST, (*superoneratio forestæ*) is where a commoner puts on more beasts in the forest than he has a right to. *Manwood, p.* 2. *c.* 14. *n.* 7. 3 *Inst. f.* 293.

SUR CUI IN VITA, a writ that lay for the heir of a woman, whose husband had aliened her land in fee, and she neglected to bring the writ *cui in vita* for recovery thereof: in this case her heir might bring this writ against the tenant after her decease. *F. N. B.* 193.

SURETY, is a general word which comprehends bail, mainprize, pledge, and caution; and it is required either by the common law or by statute. By the common law, upon a writ *ne exeat regno*; upon a *supplicavit* for the peace, and the like (2 *Inst.* 40, 41. 4 *Inst.* 180.) And by statute, upon default of good behaviour, (34 *Ed.* 3. *c.* 1.) and the like. 1 *Com. tit. B. in E.*

SURETY OF THE PEACE, (*securitas pacis*, so called, because the party, that was in fear, is thereby secured.) This security consists in being bound, with one or more sureties, in a recognizance or obligation to the king, entered on record, and taken in some court or by some judicial officer, whereby the parties acknowlege themselves to be indebted to the crown in the sum required, (for instance 100*l.*) with condition to be void and of none effect, if the party shall appear in court on such a day, and in the mean time shall keep the peace; either generally, towards the king, and all his liege people, or particularly also with regard to the person who craves the security; or, if it be for the good behaviour, then, on condition that he shall demean and behave himself well (or be of good behaviour), either generally or specially, for the time therein limited, as for one or more years, or for life. This recognizance, if taken by a justice of the peace, must be certified to the next sessions, in pursuance of the statute 3 *Hen.* 7. *c.* 1; and if the condition of such recognizance be broken by any breach of the peace in the one case, or any misbehaviour in the other, the recognizance becomes forfeited, or absolute; and being estreated, or extracted (taken out from among the other records), and sent up to the exchequer, the parties, and his sureties, having now become the king's absolute debtors, are sued for the several sums in which they are respectively bound.

SURGEON, (*chirurgus*) may be deduced from the *Fr. chirurgeon*, signifying him that dealeth in the mechanical part of physic, and the outward cures performed with the hand; and therefore is compounded of the two Greek words Χεὶρ, *manus*, Ἔργον, *opus*. *Cowell.* See *London*, article *Pharmacy*.

SUR LUI JUZ, i. e. upon his oath, according to ancient laws. *Leg. W. c.* 16.

SURMISE, something offered to a court to move it to grant a prohibition. *Audita querela*, or other writ grantable thereon. 2 *Cro.* 219, 501, 669. See *Suggestion*.

SURPLUSAGE, (Fr. *surplus*, Lat. *surplusagium*, *corollarium*) is a superfluity or addition more than needful, which sometimes is the cause that a writ abates; but in pleading many times it is absolutely void, and the residue of the plea shall stand good. *Broke. Plowd.* 63.

If a jury find the substance of the issue before them to be tried, other superfluous matter is but surplusage (6 *Rep.* 46.) And where a verdict or judgment is compleat, if there be any other matter repugnant or uncertain, it shall be rejected as surplusage. 3 *Nels.* 262. 2 *Hawk. P. C.* 441. 1 *Wils.* 238.

SURPLUSAGE OF ACCOUNTS, signifies a greater disbursement than the charge of the accountant amounts unto. In another sense, surplusage is the remainder or overplus of money left. *Litt. Dict.*

SURPLUS *of Intestates Effects.* See *Administrator, Intestates Effects*, and *Residue*.

SURREBUTTER, a second rebutter; or, more properly, it is the replication or answer of the plaintiff to the defendant's rebutter. 3 *Black.* 310.

SURREJOINDER, is a second defence of the plaintiff's declaration in a cause, and answers the rejoinder of the defendant. *West. symb. p.* 2. *Wood's Inst.* 586.

SURRENDER, (*sursum redditio*) is a deed or instrument, under seal, testifying that the particular tenant for life or years, of lands and tenements, doth yield up his estate to him that hath the immediate estate in remainder or reversion, that he may have the present possession thereof; and whereas the estate for life or years may merge or drown by the mutual agreement of the parties. *Co. Litt.* 337.

SURRENDER OF A BANKRUPT. The bankrupt, at the third meeting of the commissioners, at farthest, which must be on the 42d day after the advertisement in the Gazette, upon notice personally served upon him, or left at his usual place of abode, must surrender himself personally to the commissioners, and must thenceforth in all respects conform to the directions of the statutes of bankruptcy; or, in default thereof, shall be guilty of felony, without benefit of clergy, and shall suffer death, and his goods and estate shall be distributed among his creditors. 5 *Geo.* 2. *c.* 30.

SURRENDER OF COPYHOLDS, is the yielding up of the estate by the tenant into the hands of the lord, for such purposes as in the surrender are expressed. As, it may be, to the use and behoof of *A.* and his heirs; to the use of his own will, and the like. The process, in most manors, is, that the tenant comes to the steward, either in court (or, if custom permits, out of court), or else to two customary tenants of the same manor, provided there be also a custom to warrant it; and there, by delivering up a rod, a glove, or other symbol, as the custom directs, resigns into the hands of the lord, by the hands and acceptance of his said steward, or of the said two tenants, all his interest and title to the estate, in trust, to be again granted out by the lord to such persons, and for such uses as are named in the surrender, and the custom of the manor will warrant. If the surrender be made out of court, then, at the next or some subsequent court, the jury or homage must present and find it upon their oaths; which presentment is an information to the lord or his steward of what has been transacted out of court. Immediately upon such surrender in court, or upon presentment of a surrender made out of court, the lord, by his steward, grants the same land again to *cestuy que use* (who is sometimes, though rather improperly, called the surrenderee), to hold by the ancient rents and customary services, and thereupon admits him tenant to the copyhold, according to the form and effect of the surrender, which must be exactly pursued; and this is done by delivering up to the new tenant the rod, or glove, or the like, in the name, and as the symbol, of corporal seisin of the lands and tenements. Upon which admission he pays a fine to the lord, according to the custom of the manor, and takes the oath of fealty. 2 *Black.* 365.

This method of conveyance is so essential to the nature of a copyhold estate, that it cannot properly be transferred by any other assurance. No feoffment or grant has any operation thereupon. If I would exchange a copyhold estate with another, I cannot do it by an ordinary deed of exchange at the common law, but we must surrender to each other's use, and the lord will admit us accordingly. If I would devise a copyhold, I must surrender it to the use of my last will and testament; and in my will I must declare my intentions, and name a devisee, who will then be entitled to admission.* A fine or recovery had of copyhold lands in the king's court may indeed, if not duly reversed, alter the tenure of the lands, and convert them into frank fee, which is defined in the old book of tenures to be "land pleadable at the common law:" but upon an action on the case, in the nature of a writ of deceit, brought by the lord in the king's court, such fine or recovery will be reversed, the lord will recover his jurisdiction, and the lands will be restored to their former state of copyhold. *Co. Copyh. s.* 36. *Old Nat. Brev. t. briefe de recto clauso.* *F. N. B.* 12.

In this peculiar assurance, its several parts are—1. the surrender; 2. the presentment; and 3. the admittance.

1. A surrender by an admittance, subsequent whereto the conveyance is to receive its perfection and confirmation, is rather a manifestation of the alienor's intention, than a transfer of any interest in possession; for, till admittance of *cestui que use*, the lord taketh notice of the surrenderor as his tenant; and he shall receive the profits of the land to his own use, and shall discharge all services due to the lord. Yet the interest remains in him not absolutely, but *sub modo;* for he cannot pass away the land to any other, or make it subject to any other incumbrance than it was subject to at the time of the surrender. But no manner of legal interest is vested in the nominee before admittance. If he enters, he is a trespasser, and punishable in an action of trespass;* and if he surrenders

---

* Unless a surrender is made by the testator some time before his death to the use of his last will and testament, the devise of a copyhold is in general absolutely void, and the estate descends to the heir at law; but, in three instances, a court of equity will interfere, and will supply the defect of a surrender, viz. when copyholds are devised for the payment of debts, and in favour of a wife or younger children; yet a wife or younger children will not be relieved in equity, if the heir is disinherited or unprovided for. 1 *Atk.* 387. 3 *Bro.* 229. 1 *Cox's P. Wms.* 60.

But a wife will be relieved against an heir, who is not the child of the testator, or one who has an equal claim to his protection and bounty as his wife, though such heir be unprovided for, for the wife will be preferred, where there is not an equal moral obligation violated by giving her relief. 3 *Bro.* 229.

If both freehold and copyhold estates are devised for the payment of debts, the chancellor will not supply the defect of the surrender of the copyhold, unless the freehold is insufficient. 1 *Bro.* 273. 2 *Bro.* 325.

Equity will not assist a brother, grandchildren, or a natural child. 3 *Atk.* 189. 2 *Ves.* 582.

* The surrenderee would not now be

to the use of another, such surrender is merely void, and by no matter *ex post facto* can be confirmed; for though he be admitted in pursuance of the original surrender, and thereby acquires afterwards a sufficient and plenary interest as absolute owner, yet his second surrender previous to his own admittance is absolutely void *ab initio;* because at the time of such surrender he had but a possibility of an interest, and could therefore transfer nothing: and no subsequent admittance can make an act good, which was *ab initio* void. Yet, though upon the original surrender the nominee hath but a possibility, it is however such a possibility as may, whenever he pleases, be reduced to a certainty: for he cannot either by force or fraud be deprived or deluded of the effect and fruits of the surrender; but if the lord refuse to admit him, he is compellable to do it by a bill in chancery, or a mandamus, and the surrenderor can in nowise defeat his grant, his hands being for ever bound from disposing of the land in any other way, and his mouth for ever stopped from revoking or countermanding his own deliberate act. *Co. Copyh. s.* 39.

2. As to the presentment, that, by the general custom of manors, is to be made at the next court baron immediately after the surrender; but, by special custom, in some places, it will be good, though made at the second or other subsequent court. And it is to be brought into court by the same persons that took the surrender, and then to be presented by the homage; and, in all points material, must correspond with the true tenor of the surrender itself. And, therefore, if the surrender be conditional, and the presentment be absolute, both the surrender, presentment, and admittance thereupon, are wholly void: the surrender, as being never truly presented; the presentment, as being false; and the admittance, as being founded on such untrue presentment. If a man surrenders out of court, and dies before presentment, and presentment be made after his death, according to the custom, this is sufficient. So too, if *cestuy que use* dies before presentment, yet, upon presentment made after his death, his heir according to the custom shall be admitted. The same law is, if those, into whose hands the surrender is made, die before presentment; for, upon sufficient proof in court that such a surrender was made, the lord shall be compelled to admit accordingly. And if the steward, the tenants, or others into whose hands such surrender is made, refuse or neglect to bring it in to be presented, upon a petition preferred to the lord in his court baron, the party grieved shall find remedy. But if the lord will not do him right and justice, he may sue both the lord, and them that took the surrender, in chancery, and shall there find relief. *Co. Copyh.* § 40.

3. Admittance is the last stage, or perfection, of copyhold assurances. And this is of three sorts: first, an admittance upon a voluntary grant from the lord; secondly, an admittance upon surrender by the former tenant; and thirdly, an admittance upon a descent from the ancestor.

In admittances, even upon a voluntary grant from the lord, when copyhold lands have escheated or reverted to him, the lord is considered as an instrument. For though it is in his power to keep the lands in his own hands, or to dispose of them at his pleasure, by granting an absolute fee-simple, a freehold, or a chattel interest therein, and quite to change their nature from copyhold to socage tenure, so that he may well be reputed their absolute owner and lord; yet, if he will still continue to dispose of them as copyhold, he is bound to observe the ancient custom precisely in every point, and can neither in tenure nor estate introduce any kind of alteration, for that were to create a new copyhold, wherefore in this respect the law accounts him custom's instrument. For if a copyhold for life falls into the lord's hands by the tenant's death, though the lord may destroy the tenure and enfranchise the land, yet if he grants it out again by copy, he can neither add to nor diminish the ancient rent, nor make any the minutest variation in other respects; nor is the tenant's estate, so granted, subject to any charges or incumbrances by the lord.

Where a copyhold has been granted for lives, upon the death of one or more of the lives, the heir of the grantee cannot claim by custom a renewal of the grant for fresh lives upon the payment of a reasonable fine, i. e. a fine of two years value, as in the case of a copyhold of inheritance. No custom to renew a copyhold for lives is legal, unless the fine has been certain and unvaried, for copyholds grantable for lives only, if the fine is not certain, are like leases of freehold lands for lives, and renewable only upon the best terms the party can make. *Wharton v. King. Anst.* 659.

In admittances upon surrender of another, the lord is to no intent reputed as owner, but wholly as an instrument: and the tenant admitted shall likewise be subject to no charges or incumbrances of the lord; for his claim to the estate is solely

---

considered a trespasser; for it has been determined that he may recover in an ejectment against the surrenderor, upon a demise laid after the surrender, where there was an admittance of the nominee before trial. 1 *T. R.* 600.

under him that made the surrender. 4 *Rep.* 27. *Co. Litt.* 59.

And, as in admittances upon surrenders, so in admittances upon descents by the death of the ancestor, the lord is used as a mere instrument; and, as no manner of interest passes into him by the surrender or the death of his tenant, so no interest passes out of him by the act of admittance. And therefore neither in the one case nor the other, is any respect had to the quantity or quality of the lord's estate in the manor. For whether he be tenant in fee or for years, whether he be in possession by right or by wrong, it is not material, since the admittances made by him shall not be impeached on account of his title, because they are judicial, or rather ministerial acts, which every lord in possession is bound to perform.

Admittances, however, upon surrender, differ from admittances upon descent in this, that by surrender nothing is vested in *cestuy que use*, before admittance, no more than in voluntary admittances; but upon descent the heir is tenant by copy immediately upon the death of his ancestor: not indeed to all intents and purposes, for he cannot be sworn on the homage, nor maintain an action in the lord's court as tenant; but to most intents the law taketh notice of him as of a perfect tenant of the land instantly upon the death of his ancestor, especially where he is concerned with any stranger. He may enter into the land before admittance; may take the profits; punish any trespass done upon the ground; nay, upon satisfying the lord for his fine due upon the descent, may surrender into the hands of the lord to whatever use he pleases. And the heir having as complete a title without admittance as with it, against all the world but the lord, the court of king's bench will not grant a mandamus to compel the lord to admit him. 2 *T. R.* 197. For these reasons we may conclude, that the admittance of an heir is principally for the benefit of the lord, to entitle him to his fine, and not so much necessary for the strengthening and completing the heir's title. Hence indeed an observation might arise, that if the benefit, which the heir is to receive by the admittance, is not equal to the charges of the fine, he will never come in and be admitted to his copyhold in court; and so the lord may be defrauded of his fine. But to this we may reply in the words of Sir Edward Coke, "I assure myself, if it were in the election of the heir to be admitted or not to be admitted, he would be best contented without admittance; but the custom in every manor is in this point compulsory. For, either upon pain of forfeiture of their copyhold, or of incurring some great penalty, the heirs of copyholders are inforced, in every manor, to come into court and be admitted according to the custom, within a short time after notice given of their ancestor's decease." *Copyh.* §41.

But copyholds are not within the statute *de donis*, and cannot be intailed without a special custom within the manor; and where such a custom exists, there may also be a custom to bar the estate tail, by a recovery suffered in the lord's court; but if no such custom appears of barring by recovery, the intail may be barred by surrender, or otherwise it would amount to a perpetuity. 2 *Ves.* 601. Yet in some manors the custom of barring by one mode is co-existent with the custom of barring by the other. 2 *Bl. Rep.* 944.

SURRENDER OF LETTERS PATENT, AND OFFICES. A surrender may be made of letters-patent to the king, to the end he may grant the estate to whom he pleases, &c. and a second patent for years to the same person for the same thing is a surrender in law of the first patent. 10 *Rep.* 66.

SURROGATE, (*Surrogatus.*) Is one that is substituted or appointed in the room of another; as the bishop or chancellor's surrogate. *Cowell.*

SURSISE, (*Supersisa.*) A word especially used in the castle of Dover for penalties and forfeitures laid upon those that pay not the duties or rent of castle-ward, at their days limited. *Bract. lib.* 5. *Cowell.*

SURVEY. Is to measure, lay out, or particularly describe a manor, or estate in lands; and to ascertain not only the bounds and royalties thereof, but the tenure of the respective tenants, the rent and value of the same, &c. It is also understood to be a court; for on the falling of an estate to a new lord, consisting of manors, where there are tenants by lease, and copyholders, a court of survey is generally held; and sometimes at other times, to apprise the lord of the present terms and interests of the tenants, and as a direction on making further grants, as well as in order to improvements, &c. *Comp. Court Keep. Cowell.*

SURVEYOR, (compounded of two Fr. words, *sur.* i. e. *super*, and voir, *cernere.*) One that has the overseeing or care of lands or works. *Cowell.*

SURVEYOR OF THE KING'S EXCHANGE. An ancient officer belonging to the mint and coinage, mentioned in the statute 9 *H.* 5. c. 4. *Cowell.*

SURVEYOR GENERAL OF THE KING'S MANORS AND LANDS. *Cro. Jurisd.* 106.

SURVEYORS OF THE HIGHWAYS. Every parish is bound of common right to keep the high roads that go through it in good and sufficient repair; unless by reason of the tenure of lands, or otherwise, this care is consigned to some particular private person. As it was not (formerly) incumbent on any particular officer to call the parish together, and set them upon this work; therefore, by statute 2 & 3 *Ph.* & *M.* c. 8. surveyors of the highways were ordered to be chosen in every parish; but now they are constituted by two neighbouring justices out of such inhabitants or others as are described in stat. 13 *Geo.* 3. *c.* 78, and may have salaries alloted them for their trouble.

SURVEYOR *of the Navy.* An officer appointed over all stores, and to survey hulls and masts of ships, &c. *Chamberl. Cowell.*

SURVEYOR *of the King's Ordnance.* This officer surveys the ordnance and provisions of war, allows bills of debt, and keeps the checks on labourers works, &c. *Ibid.*

SURVEYORS *of the Wards and Liberties,* taken away with the courts of wards and liveries. 12 *Car.* 2. *c.* 24.

SURVIVOR, (from the Fr. *survivre,* and Lat. *supervivo.*) Is the longer liver of two joint tenants, or of any two persons joined in the right of a thing. He that remaineth alive after others be dead, &c. *Broke* 33. See *Joint-tenant.*

SUSANA TERRÆ, is said to be land worn out with ploughing. *Thorn. Cowell.*

SUSCEPTOR, (Lat.) An undertaker or godfather, also a receiver of tribute in the Roman provinces. *Litt. Dict. Cowell.*

SUSPENSE, (*suspensio.*) Is a temporal stop, or hanging up, as it were, of a man's right, for a time; and, in legal understanding, is taken to be when either the rent or land is so conveyed, not absolutely and finally, but for a time, after which the rent will be revived again; and it differs from extinguishment, which is when it dies or is gone for ever.

SUSPENSION. A censure, whereby ecclesiastical persons are forbidden to exercise their office, or take the profits of their benefices; or where they are prohibited for a certain time in both of them, in the whole, or in part. *Wood's Inst.* 510.

SUSPENSION *of the Habeas Corpus Act.* In cases of great emergency, the parliament can authorize the crown, by suspending the habeas corpus act for a short and limited time, to imprison suspected persons without giving any reason for so doing; for should the legislature think itself in danger by some secret conspiracy against the state, or by a correspondence with a foreign enemy, it is reasonable that it should have power to authorize the executive, for a short and limited time, to imprison suspected persons, who in that case lose their liberty only for a while, to preserve it for ever. 1 *Black.* 210.

SUS. PER COLL. On the trial of criminals, the usage is for the judge to sign the calendar, or list of all the prisoner's names, with their separate judgments in the margin, which is left with the sheriff. As for a capital felony, it is written opposite the prisoner's name, "hanged by the neck;" formerly in the days of Latin and abbreviation, "Sus. per coll." for *suspendatur per collum.* See *Execution.*

SUSPICION. A person may be taken up on suspicion, where a felony is done; but those who are imprisoned for a light suspicion of larceny or robbery, are bailable by statute 2 *Hawk. P. C.* 101. And the party being a private person, that takes up one on suspicion of felony, must do it of his own suspicion, not upon that of another; and he must have reasonable cause of it, &c. *Hale's Hist. P. C.* 78.

SUSPIRAL, (from the Lat. *suspirare,* i. e. *ducere suspiria.*) A spring of water, passing under ground towards a conduit or cistern. 35 *Hen.* 8. *cap.* 10.

SUTHDURE, (Sax.) i. e. the south door of a church, was the place where canonical purgation was performed, by the party accused coming to the south door of the church, and there, in the presence of the people, making oath that he was innocent. *Cowell.*

SWAN, (*Cygnus.*) Is a noble bird of game; and a person may prescribe to have game of swans within his manor, as well as a warren or park. 7 *Rep.* 17, 18. But no person may have a swan-mark, except he have lands of the yearly value of five marks, and unless it be by grant of the king, or his officers lawfully authorized, or by prescription. Stat. 22 *Edw.* 4. *c.* 6. Stealing swans marked and pinioned, or unmarked, if kept in a mote, pond, or private river, and reduced to tameness, is felony. *H. P. C.* 68. And he that steals the eggs of swans out of their nests, shall be imprisoned a year and a day, and be fined at the king's pleasure. 11 *Hen.* 7. *c.* 17. And no fowl can be a stray but a swan. 4 *Inst.* 280.

SWANHERD. The king's swanherd, *magister deductus cygnorum.* *Cowell.*

SWANIMOTE, or *Swainmote,* (*swainmotus,* from the Sax. *swang,* i. e. a country swain, and *gemote,* i. e. *conventus.*) Signifies a court touching matters of the forest, held by the charter of the forest thrice in the year, before the verderors as judges. *Cromp. Jurisd* 108. 3 *Hen.* 8. *c.* 18.

SWARF-MONEY, is mentioned among customs and services, and was one penny halfpenny paid before the rising of the sun; the party was to go three times about the cross, and lay down the swarf-money, and then take witness and lay it in the hole; and he was to look well that his witness did not deceive him; for if it were not so paid, he was to forfeit xxxs. and a white bull, due to the Catesbys in Lodbroke, and other places in Warwickshire.

SWATH, (Sax. *swatha.*) A swathe, or as in Kent, a sweath, and in some parts a sworth, is a straight row of cut grass or corn, as it lies after the scithe at the first mowing of it. *Cowell.*

SWEARING, (*Imprecatio.*) Is an offence against God and religion, and a sin of all others the most extravagant and unaccountable, as having no benefit or advantage attending it. And there are several good laws and statutes for punishing this crime.

By 21 *Jac.* I. *c.* 20. persons swearing or cursing, shall forfeit 12*d.* a time to the poor of the parish, and for want of distress, be set in the stocks three hours. Prosecution must be within twenty days; and the act is to be read in every church twice a year.

By 6 & 7 *Will.* & *Mar.* c. 11. and 19 *Geo.* 2. c. 21. servant, labourer, common soldier, or seaman, convicted of swearing, shall forfeit 1*s.*; every other person 2*s.*; the second offence double, and afterwards treble; for want of distress, to be set in the stocks one hour.

Every person of or above the degree of a gentleman, swearing, shall, in like manner, forfeit 5*s.* 19 *Geo.* 2. c. 21.

Profane swearers, in the hearing of any justice, shall be convicted without other proof. Constables shall seize persons profanely swearing, if unknown, and bring them before the next justice, who is to convict them on the officer's oath; and if they are known, information shall be made, whereupon the justice shall order the offender to appear, and the penalty shall be paid, or security given, or the offender committed for ten days to the house of correction. *Ibid.*

Common soldiers and sailors not paying the penalty, shall be set in the stocks for two hours. Justices not doing their duty, forfeit 5*l.* and constables 40*s.*; who, for want of distress, are to be committed for one month to the house of correction. All offenders are to pay all charges over and above the penalties, or be committed to the house of correction for six days extraordinary. *Ibid.*

The penalties go to the poor; the act to be read quarterly in all churches, on pain of 5*l.* and the fee to the justice's clerk is 1*s.* *Ibid.*

SWEARING THE PEACE. If any man hath just cause to fear that another will burn his house, or do him a corporal injury, by killing, imprisoning, or beating him, or that he will procure others so to do, he may demand sureties of the peace against such person. And every justice of the peace is bound to grant it, if he who demands it will make oath that he is actually under fear of death or bodily harm, and will shew that he has just cause to be so, by reason of the other's menaces, attempts, or having lain in wait for him; and will also farther swear, that he does not require such surety out of malice or for mere vexation. 1 *Hawk. P. C.* 127. This is called swearing the peace against another; and if the party does not find such sureties as the justice in his discretion shall require, he may be immediately committed till he does. *Ibid* 128. See *Surety of the Peace.*

SWEEPAGE, is the crop of hay got in a meadow, called also the swepe in some parts of England. *Co. Litt.* 4.

SWEETS. By 28 *Geo.* 3. *c.* 37. no person shall be entitled to sell wines or sweets for consumption in his own house, unless he shall also have obtained an ale licence.

SWEINMOTE, *Court of.* The court of Sweinmote is one of the forest courts, and is to be holden before the verderors as judges, by the steward of the sweinmote, thrice in every year, the sweins and freeholders within the forest composing the jury. The principal jurisdiction of this court is, first, to inquire into the oppressions and grievances committed by the officers of the forest: *de super-oneratione forestariorum, & aliorum ministrorum forestæ; & de eorum oppressionibus populo regis illatis.* And, secondly, to receive and try presentments certified from the court of attachment against offenders in vert and venison. Stat. 34 *Edw.* I. c. 1. And this court may not only inquire, but convict also, which conviction shall be certified to the court of justice-seat under the seals of the jury; for this court cannot proceed to judgment. 4 *Inst.* 289. 3 *Black.* 72. See *Swanimote.*

SWINDLERS. By 33 *Hen.* 8. *c.* 1. persons obtaining another's money, goods, or other things, by any false token or counterfeit letter, shall suffer imprisonment, pillory, or any corporal punishment, as the court, on conviction, shall adjudge.

And by 30 *Geo.* 2. *c.* 24. persons convicted of obtaining money or goods by false pretences, or of sending threatening letters in order to extort money or goods, may be punished by fine and imprisonment, or by pillory, whipping, or transportation. See *Cheats, Frauds.*

SWINE or HOGS shall not go unringed in woods. 35 *Hen.* 8. c. 17. s. 17.

SWOLING OF LAND. (*Solinga vel Swolinga Terræ*, in Sax. *Sulung*, from *Sul.*) *Aratrum*, (as to this day in the west country a plough is called a sul.) Is as much as one plough can till in a year. A hide of land; though some writers say it is an uncertain quantity. *Cowell.*

SWORN BROTHERS, (*fratres jurati.*) Persons who, by mutual oath, covenanted to share each other's fortune in any notable expedition. This practice gave occasion to our proverb of sworn brothers, or brethren in iniquity, because of their dividing plunder and spoil. *Cowell.*

SYLVA CÆDUA. Wood under twenty year's growth: coppice-wood. 2 *Inst.* 642.

SYMBOLUM. Is a symbol, or sign in the sacrament. *Cowell.*

SYNCOPARE. A word used in several ecclesiastical councils and synods, signifying to cut short or pronounce things so as not to be understood. *Ibid.*

SYNDICUS. An advocate or patron; a burgess or recorder of a town, &c. *Mat. Paris, anno* 1245.

SYNGRAPH, (*synographus.*) A deed, bond, or writing, under the hand and seal of all the parties; and it was the custom for both the debtor and creditor in writings obligatory to write their names and the sum borrowed on a piece of paper, with the word syngraphus in large letters in the middle; which being cut through, one part of the paper was delivered to each party, for their better security, &c. 2 *Black.* 206. See *Chirograph.*

SYNOD, (*synodus.*) A meeting or assembly of ecclesiastical persons concerning religion. 1 *Black.* 279.

SYNODALE. A tribute or payment in money, paid to the bishop or archdeacon, by the inferior clergy, at Easter visitation. *Cowell.*

SYNODALES TESTES. The urban and rural deans, whose office was to inform of and attest the disorders of the clergy and people in the episcopal synod, and for which a solemn oath was given them to make their presentments, &c.; afterwards by degrees devolved upon churchwardens. *Paroch. Antiq.* 649.

SYNONYMOUS. A thing of the same name, or of the like signification. *Johnson.*

T

PERSONS convicted of any felony, (except murder), and admitted to benefit of clergy, were formerly branded with a T. upon the brawn of the thumb. Stat. 4 *Hen.* 7. c. 13; but by 19 *Geo.* 3. c. 74. made perpetual by 39 *Geo.* 3. *c.* 75, the court may fine a felon liable to be burnt in the hand, or order him to be whipt; but this act does not take away the power to imprison.

TABACUM. *Herba ab insula* Tobaco, *ubi copiose provenit*; *qui primus eam ex* India *ad nos adduxit*, see *Tobacco.*

TABARD, TABARDER. The bachelor scholars on the foundation of Queen's College, Oxford, are called tabitars or tabarders, from a gown worn by them called a tabert, tabarr, or tabard. And tabert was anciently a short gown that reached not farther than the middle of the leg.

TABARDUM. A garment like a gown, and used for an herald's coat, but generally taken for the gown of ecclesiastics. *Cowell.*

TABELLION, (*Tabellio.*) A notary public or scrivener. *Ibid.*

TABLE-RENTS, (*redditus ad mensam.*) Rents paid to bishops and others, reserved and appropriated to their table or housekeeping. *Cowell.* See *Bord-land.*

TABLING OF FINES. A table for every county, containing the substance of fines passed; as the name of the county, town, or place, where the lands or tenements lie, the name of the demandant and deforceant, and of the particular lands, &c. mentioned in the fine. This is done by the chirographer, who, every day of the next term after the ingrossing of any such fine, who sets up these tables in an open place on the left hand side of the court of common pleas during its sitting: and he also delivers to the sheriff of each county, his under-sheriff, or deputy, fairly written in parchment, a perfect content of the table so made for that shire, in the term next before the assises, or between the term and assises, to be set up at the assises in an open place of that court, and continue there so long as the justices shall sit. And if either the chirographer or sheriff fail herein, they are liable to the penalty of 5*l.* *Stat.* 23 *Eliz.* c. 3.

TABULA. See *Ebdomadarius.*

TAC or TAK. A customary payment of tak and toll. *Blount's ten.* 155.

TACFREE, is used in old charters as an exemption from payments. *Cowell.*

TACTARE, for *Confirmare.* *Fleta, lib.* 2. c. 61. *Cowell.*

TAIL, (Fr. *taille*, from *tailler*, to cut or limit. Lat. *feodom talliatum.*) Is a limited fee, opposed to fee-simple: and it is that inheritance whereof a man is seised to him and some particular heirs, exclusive of others, as the heirs of his body begotten or to be begotten. And he that giveth the lands in tail is called the donor, and he to whom the gift is made, the donee. *Litt.* 18. See *Tenant in Tail*, *Tenant in Fee Simple.* 2 *Black.* 104.

TAINT, (Fr. *teinct.* i. e. *infectus*, *tinctus.*) A conviction, or a person convicted. See *Attaint.*

TAKING, *felonious.* See *Larceny.*

TAKING, *unlawful.* Whoever, either by fraud or force, dispossesses another of his goods or chattels, is guilty of a transgression against the laws of society. 3 *Bl.* 145.

TALE, or *Count.* The first of pleadings, or mutual altercations between the plaintiff and defendant, is the declaration, narratio, or count, anciently called the Tale, in which the plaintiff sets forth the cause of his complaint at length. 3 *Black.* 293.

TALENT. A weight of sixty-two pounds; also a sum of money among the Greeks of about 100*l.* value. *Merch. Dict.* *Cowell.*

TALES, is used in the law for a supply of men impannelled on a jury and not appearing, or on their appearance challenged as not indifferent; when the judge, upon motion, orders a supply to be made by the sheriff, &c. of one or more such persons present in court, equal in reputation to those that were impannelled, to make up a full jury, which he could do by the common law. 35 *Hen.* 8. c. 6. 2 & 3 *Ed.* 6. c. 32. 14 *Eliz.* c. 9. 7 & 8 *W.* 3. c. 32, &c.

Tales are of two sorts, i. e. *tales de circumstantibus*, and a *decem tales.* A *tales de circumstantibus* is where a full jury do not appear at the nisi prius; or so many are challenged that there is not a full jury; then, on the prayer of the plaintiff's council or attorney, the judge will grant this tales, which the sheriff returns immediately in court. A *decem tales* is when a full jury doth not appear at a trial at bar, and is a writ to the sheriff *apponere* decem tales. 10 *Rep.* 102. *Finch* 414. 2 *Roll. Abr.* 67.

TALES, is also the name of a book in the King's Bench office, of such persons as were admitted of the tales. 4 *Inst.* 93.

TALIONIS LEX. The law of retaliation. This can never be in all cases (indeed but in few) an adequate or permanent rule of punishment. In the case of murder the punishment is death. See *Lex Talionis.*

TALLAGE, (*Tallagium.*) from the Fr. *taille.* Is metaphorically used for a part or a share of a man's substance, carved out of the whole, paid by way of tribute, toll, or tax. *Cowell.* 2 *Inst.* 532. 1 *Black.* 310.

TALLAGERS. Tax or toll-gatherers. *Cowell.*

TALLAGIUM FACERE. To give up accounts in the exchequer, where the method of accounting is by talleys. *Cowell.*

TALLEY, (*Tallea*, Fr. *Taille*, Ital. *Tagliare*, i. e. *scindere.*) Is a stick cut in two parts, on each whereof is marked with notches, or otherwise, what is due between debtor and creditor; the ancient way of keeping all accounts, one part being kept by the creditor, the other by the debtor. Hence the tallier of the exchequer is now called the teller; and in the exchequer there is a talley court, where the two deputy chamberlains of the exchequer attend, and the talley cutter. *Lex Constitut.* 205. *Cowell.*

TALLIA. Every canon and prebendary in our old cathedral churches, had a stated allowance of provisions delivered to him *per modum talliæ.* Hence their commons in meat and drink were called tallia. *Ibid.*

TALLYMAN. A person that sells or lets goods, cloaths, or the like, to be paid for by so much per week. *Merch. Dict.*

TALWOOD, (*Talliatura.*) Fire-wood cleft and cut into billets of a certain length, otherwise written talywood and talshide in the ancient statutes. 34 & 35 *Hen.* 8. c. 3. 7 *Edw.* 6. c. 7. 43 *Eliz.* c. 14.

TAM QUAM, is in nature of a *qui tam*, being where a man prosecutes as well for the king as for himself, *tam pro domino rege*, *quam pro seipso*, on an information for breach of some penal law, whereby any penalty is given, one part to the king, the other, or another part, to the party that sues. 2 *Inst.* 118. *Cro. Eliz.* 655. *Cro. Jac.* 134. See *Information.*

TANGIER. An ancient city of Barbary, formerly part of the dominions of the crown of England, as Gibraltar is at present. Stat. 15 *Car.* 2. c. 7. 22 & 23 *Car.* 2. c. 26.

TANISTRY, seems to be derived from Thanis, and is a law or custom in some parts of Ireland, of which Sir John Davis says, that is, a man of ripe age is to be preferred before a child, as an uncle before a nephew, and the like. *Dav. Rep.* 28. *Antiq. Hibern. p.* 38. *Cowell.*

TANNARE. Is a word used for to dress or tan leather. *Cowell.*

TANNERS. See *Manufacturers.*

TANTAMOUNT, is where one thing doth amount to another, and then it is all one as if it was the same: as a lease and release amount to a feoffment; and licence to occupy land for years, to a lease for the term. 14 *Hen.* 8. *c.* 13. *Shep. Epit.* 1130.

TARE and TRET. The first is an allowance in merchandise, made to the buyer for the weight of the box, bag, or cask, wherein goods are packed. And the last is a consideration in the weight, for waste in emptying and reselling the goods by dust, dirt, or breaking. *Cowell.*

TARGET, (from the Lat. *Targus.*) A shield, originally made of leather, wrought out of the back of an ox. *Blount.*

TARGIA, (*Tarida.*) A ship of burden, called a tartan. *Cowell. Blount.*

TARIFF. Custom, duties, toll, or tribute payable upon merchandize exported and imported, are so called. 1 *Black.* 313.

TARPAULIN, or TARPAWLING. A tarred canvas to keep the weather out of ships; used also for a mariner, or drudge in a ship that does the vilest service. *Merc. Dict. Cowell.*

TARTARON. A sort of fine cloth or silk. *Stat.* 4 *Hen.* 8. *c.* 6.

TAS, (Fr.) Is a cock, heap, stack, or rick of hay or corn. *Law Fr. Dict. Cowell.*

TASSALE, for *Casula.* A priest's garment covering him over.

TASSUM, (from the Fr. *Tasser*, to pile up.) A mow of corn or hay. Tasser, to mow or heap up; and *ad tassum furcare* is to pitch to the mow. *Cowell.*

TATH. In the counties of Norfolk and Suffolk, the lords of manors claimed the privilege of having their tenants flocks or sheep brought at night upon their own demesne lands, there to be folded for the improvement of the ground; which liberty was called by the name of Tath. *Spelm. Cowell.*

TAVERN. See *Alehouses, Drunkenness, Inns,* and *Tippling.*

TAU. Signifies a cross. *Cowell.*

TAURI LIBERI LIBERTAS, in ancient charters, is used for a common bull; so called, because he is free and common to all the tenants within such a manor or liberty, &c. *Cowell. Blount.*

TAWERS. See *Leather* and *Manufacturers.*

TAX, (*Taxa*, from the Gr. Τάξις, i. e. *Ordo. Tributum.*) A tribute or imposition laid upon the subject. 4 *Inst.* 26. 33.

It is said, that in ancient times taxes were imposed by the king at his pleasure; but king Edward I. bound himself and his successors, in the 25th year of his reign, that from that time forward no tax should be laid upon the subject without the assent of the lords and commons in parliament. *Stat.* 25 *Edw.* 1. *c.* 5.

The taxes which are now raised upon the subject are the following: 1. The land-tax, where unredeemed; 2. The malt-tax; 3. The customs; 4. The excise; 5. Postages of letters; 6. The stamp-duties; 7. The assessed taxes and personal property tax; and 8. The hackney-coach and hawkers' licences.

TAXATIO BLADORUM. A tax or imposition laid upon corn. *Cowell.*

TAXATIO NORWICENSIS. The valuation of ecclesiastical benefices made through every diocese in England, on occasion of the Pope's granting to the king the tenth of all spirituals for three years. Which taxation was made by Walter, bishop of Norwich, delegated by the Pope to this office in 38 Hen. 3. and obtained till the 19th of Edw. 1. when a new taxation, advancing the value, was made by the bishops of Winchester and Lincoln. *Cowell.*

TAXERS. Two officers yearly chosen in Cambridge, to see the true gauge of all weights and measures; though the name took its rise from taxing or rating the rents of houses, which was anciently the duty of their offices.

TAYLORS. See *London*, art. *Taylors* and *Manufacturers.* Art. *Buttons.*

TEAM AND THEAME, (from the Sax. *Tyman*, i. e. *propagare*, to teem or bring forth.) A royalty or privilege granted by the king's charter to the lord of a manor, for the having, restraining, and judging of bondmen and villeins, with their children, goods, and chattels, in his court. *Glanvil. lib.* 5. *c.* 2.

TECHNICAL WORDS. In some cases particular words of art must be used, which are so appropriated by the law to express the precise idea which it entertains of the offence, that no other words, however synonymous they may seem, are capable of doing it. Thus, in treason, the facts must be laid to be done *treasonably, and against his allegiance*, else the indictment is void. In indictments for murder, it is necessary to say, that the party indicted *murdered*, not *killed* or *slew* the other. In all indictments for felonies, the adverb *feloniously* must be used; and for burglaries, *burglariously*; and all these to ascertain the intent. In rapes, the word *ravished* is necessary, and must not be expressed by any periphrasis; in order to render the crime certain. So in larcenies also, the words *feloniously took and carried away* are necessary to every indictment, for these only can express the very offence. 4 *Black.* 302.

TEDING-PENNY, *Tething-penny, Tithing-penny.* A small duty or payment to the sheriff from each tithing, towards the charge of keeping courts, for which some of the religious were exempted by charter from the king. *Chart. Hen.* 1. *Cowell.*

TEENAGE, (from the Sax. Tynan, to inclose or shut), is used in many parts of England for wood for fences and inclosures. *Ibid.*

TEINLAND, *Tainland*, or *Thainland.* The land of a thaine, or noble person. *Ibid.*

TELLER. Is a considerable officer of the exchequer, of which officers there are four, whose office is to receive all money due to the king, and to give the clerk of the pells a bill to charge him therewith. They also pay to all persons any money payable by the king, by warrant from the auditor of the receipt: and make weekly and yearly books of their receipts and payments, which they deliver to the lord treasurer. *Ibid.*

TELLIGRAPHIÆ, (from the Gr. τελος, *procul*, and γράφω, *scribo*, writing. Are written evidences of things far past. *Blount.*

TELWORK. Is that work or labour which the tenant was bound to do for his lord, for a certain number of days; from the Saxon *Tællan*, numerare, and *worc*, opus. *Thorn. Ann.* 1364. *Cowell.*

TEMENTALE, or TENMENTALE. A tax of two shillings upon every ploughland. *Hov. Hist. fo.* 419. *Cowell.*

TEMPLARS, (*Templarii.*) The Knights Templars were a religious order of knighthood, instituted about the year 1119, so called because they dwelt in part of the buildings belonging to the Temple at Jerusalem, and not far from the Sepulchre. They entertained christian strangers and pilgrims charitably, and in their armour led them through the Holy Land, to view the sacred monuments of christianity. This order was far spread, and particularly here in England. The Temples, which we now call the inns of court, were the places where they dwelt, and in the Middle Temple the king's treasure was kept. *Cowell.*

TEMPORALTIES OF BISHOPS are the revenues, lands, tenements, and lay-fees, belonging to bishops, as barons and lords of parliament, i. e. all things which a bishop hath by livery from the king, as manors, lands, tithes, and the like. 1 *Rol. Abr.* 881.

TEMPTATIO, or TENTATIO, is used in ancient records for a trial or proof. *Cowell.*

TEMPUS *Pessonis.* Mast time in the forest, which is from about Michaelmas to St. Martin's Day, November 11. *Ibid.*

TEMPUS *pinguedinis et firmationis.* The season of killing the buck and the doe. *Ibid.*

TENA. Coif, worn by ecclesiastics. *Ibid.*

TENANCIES. Houses or places for habitation, held of another. *Ibid.*

TENANT, (*Tenens*, from the Latin *tenere*, to hold.) Signifies one that holds or possesses lands or tenements by any kind of right, either in fee, for life, years, or at will. *Kitch. fol.* 160.

TENANTS IN COMMON. Are such as hold land for life or years, by several titles, or by one title and several rights; and as joint-tenants have one joint freehold, so tenants in common law have separate freeholds. 1 *Inst.* 188. 2 *Lill. A. Br.* 559.

TENANT TO THE PRÆCIPE. Is he against whom the writ of præcipe is to be brought in suing out a recovery. 3 *Keb.* See *Recoveries.*

TENANT IN TAIL. When a fee was restrained to some particular heirs exclusive of others, as to the heirs of a man's body, by which only his lineal descendants were admitted in exclusion of collateral heirs, or to the heirs male of his body, in exclusion both of collaterals and lineal females also. This was in common law called a conditional fee, by reason of the condition expressed or implied in the duration of it; so that if the donee died without such particular heirs, the reversion not being disposed of, the land would revert to the donor. *Fleta, c.* 3. §. 52. *Black.* 109.

For this was a condition annexed by law to all grants whatsoever; that, on failure of the heirs specified in the grant, the grant should be at an end, and the land returned to its ancient proprietor. *Plowd.* 241.

Now, with regard to the condition annexed to these fees by the common law, our ancestors held, that such a gift (to a man and the heirs of his body) was a gift upon condition that it should revert to the donor, if the donee had no heirs of his body; but, if he had, it should then remain to the donee. They therefore called it a fee-simple, on condition that he had issue.

And by the statute *de donis*, 13 *Ed.* 1. *c.* 1. it is enacted, that from "thenceforth the will of the donor be observed; and that the tenements so given (to a man and the heirs of his body) should at all events go to the issue, if there were any; or, if none, should revert to the donor."

Upon the construction of this act of parliament, the judges determined that the donee had no longer a conditional fee-simple, which became absolute and at his own disposal the instant any issue was born; but they divided the estate into two parts, leaving in the donee a new kind of particular estate, which they denominated a *fee-tail*; and vesting in the donor the ultimate fee-simple of the land, expectant on the failure of issue; which expectant estate is what we now call a reversion. 2 *Inst.* 335. And hence it is that Littleton tells us, that tenant in fee-tail is by virtue of the statute of Westminster the second. 2 *Inst.* 413.

An estate to a man and his heirs for another's life cannot be entailed: for this is strictly no estate of inheritance, (as will appear hereafter,) and therefore not within the statute *de donis*. 2 *Vern*. 225.

Neither can a copyhold estate be entailed by virtue of the statute, for that would tend to encroach upon and restrain the will of the lord: but, by the special custom of the manor, a copyhold may be limited to the heirs of the body, for here the custom ascertains and interprets the lord's will. 3 *Rep*. 8.

2. Estates tail are either general or special. Tail-general is where lands and tenements are given to one, and the heirs of his body begotten, which is called tail-general, because, how often soever such donee in tail be married, his issue in general by all and every such marriage, is, in successive order, capable of inheriting the estate-tail, *per formam doni*. *Litt. s*. 14, 15. Tenant in tail special is where the gift is restrained to certain heirs of the donee's body, and does not go to all of them in general. And this may happen several ways. *Ibid. s*. 16, 26, 27, 28, 29. As where lands and tenements are given to a man and the heirs of his body, on Mary his now wife to be begotten. Here no issue can inherit, but such special issue as is engendered between them two; not such as the husband may have by another wife, and therefore it is called special tail. And here we may observe, that the words of inheritance (to him and his heirs) give him an estate in fee; but they being heirs to be by him begotten, this makes it a fee-tail; and the person being also limited, on whom such heirs shall be begotten, (viz. Mary his present wife) this makes it a fee-tail special. 2 *Black*. 113.

3. There is still another species of entailed estates, now indeed grown out of use, yet still capable of subsisting in law, which are estates *in liberi maritagio*, or frankmarriage. These are defined to be, where tenements are given by one man to another, together with a wife, who is the daughter or cousin of the donor, to hold in frankmarriage. Now by such gift, though nothing but the word frankmarriage is expressed, the donees shall have the tenement to them, and the heirs of the two bodies begotten; that is, they are tenants in special tail. For this one word, frankmarriage, does *ex vi termini* not only create an inheritance, like the word frankalmoign, but likewise limits that inheritance, supplying not only words of descent, but of procreation also. Such donees in frankmarriage are liable to no service but fealty; for a rent reserved thereon is void, until the fourth degree of consanguinity be past between the issues of the donor and donee. *Litt. s*. 19, 20. 2 *Black*. 115.

4. The incidents to a tenancy in tail, under the statute Westm. 2. are chiefly these. 1. That a tenant in tail may commit waste on the estate-tail, by felling timber, pulling down houses, or the like, without being impeached, or called to account for the same. 2. That the wife of the tenant in tail shall have her dower, or thirds of the estate-tail. 3. That the husband of a female tenant in tail may be tenant by the curtesy of the estate-tail. 4. That an estate tail may be barred, or destroyed by a fine, by a common recovery, or by lineal warranty descending with assets to the heir. 2 *Black*. 115.

Also, by stat. 33 *Hen*. 8. *c*. 39. *s*. 75, all estates-tail are rendered liable to be charged for payment of debts due to the king by record or special contract. Also, by 21 *Jac*. 1. *c*. 19. they are subjected to be sold for the debts contracted by a bankrupt. And, by the construction put on the statute 43 *Eliz. c*. 4. an appointment (2 *Vern*. 453. *Chan. Prec*. 16.) by tenant in tail of the lands entailed, to a charitable use, is good without fine or recovery. And by the statutes for the redemption and sale of the land-tax, they may be sold for the redemption thereof.

TENANT IN TAIL, AFTER POSSIBILITY OF ISSUE EXTINCT. This happens where one is tenant in special tail, and a person, from whose body the issue was to spring, dies without issue; or, having left issue, that title becomes extinct: in either of these cases the surviving tenant in special tail becomes tenant in tail after possibility of issue extinct. As, where one has an estate to him and his heirs on the body of his present wife to be begotten, and the wife dies without issue: in this case the man has an estate-tail, which cannot possibly descend to any one; and therefore the law makes use of this long periphrasis, as absolutel necessary to give an adequate idea of his estate. For if it had called him barely tenant in fee-tail special, that would not have distinguished him from others; and besides, he has no longer an estate of inheritance, or, fee, for he can have no heirs capable of taking *per formam doni*. 1 *Roll. Rep*. 184. 11 *Rep*. 80. Had it called him tenant in tail without issue, this had only related to the present fact, and would not have excluded the possibility of future issue. Had he been stiled tenant in tail without possibility of issue, this would exclude time past as well as present, and he might under this description never have had any possibility of issue. No definition therefore could so exactly mark him out, as this of tenant in tail after possibility of issue extinct, which (with a precision peculiar to our own law) not only takes in the possibility of issue in tail which he once had, but also states that this possibility is now extinguished and gone. 2 *Black.* 124.

This estate must be created by the act of God, that is, by the death of that person out of whose body the issue was to spring; for no limitation, conveyance, or other human act can make it. For, if land be given to a man and his wife, and the heirs of their two bodies begotten, and they are divorced *a vinculo matrimonii*, they shall neither of them have this estate, but be barely tenants for life, notwithstanding the inheritance once vested in them. A possibility of issue is always supposed to exist, in law, unless extinguished by the death of the parties, even though the donees be each of them an hundred years old.

This estate is of an amphibious nature, partaking partly of an estate-tail, and partly of an estate for life. The tenant is, in truth, only tenant for life, but with many of the privileges of a tenant in tail; as, not to be punishable for waste, &c. * or he is tenant in tail, with many of the restrictions of a tenant for life; as, to forfeit his estate if he alienes it in fee-simple; whereas such alienation by tenant in tail, though voidable by the issue, is no forfeiture of the estate to the reversioner, who is not concerned in interest, till all possibility of issue be extinct. But, in general, the law looks upon this estate as equivalent to an estate for life only, and as such will permit this tenant to exchange his estate with a tenant for life; which exchange can only be made of estates that are equal in their nature.

TENDE, seems to signify as much as tender, or offer; it is mentioned in our old books, as to tend a traverse, an averment, or the like. *Britton*, c. 76. *Staundf. Prærog.* 16.

TENDER, (Fr. *Tendre.*) Is the offering of money, or any other thing in satisfaction, or circumspectly to endeavour the performance of a thing. *Terms de Ley*, 557.

To an action upon the case upon assumpsit, the defendant may plead matter in excuse, or discharge, as before, a general imparlance, he may plead a tender, and that he was always ready to pay. *Lut.* 226. 238. *Clift.* 203. *Willes*, 632.

And a tender of bank-notes is good, unless specially objected to on that account. 3 *T. Rep.* 534.

But by 38 *Geo.* 3. *c.* 1. no person, during the restriction on the bank from making payments in cash, shall be held to special bail, unless the usual affidavit adds that there has been no offer to pay in bank-notes, otherwise the same proceedings are to be had as where no affidavit is filed. *s.* 8.

And by 43 *Geo.* 3. *c.* 18. persons applying to be discharged, shall prove a tender in notes or in money.

Also by 38 *Geo.* 3. *c.* 1. if any person having offered to pay in bank-notes, cannot, by reason of this act, be held to special bail, the court may order him to deposit bank-notes to answer the demand; and if not done, he may be arrested and held to bail. *s.* 8.

So to debt upon bond, the defendant may plead a tender, and always ready. 2 *Mod. Ent.* 234. *Bro. V. M.* 213.

But where a tender is pleaded, the money must be brought into court; and if the plaintiff accept it, he cannot afterwards proceed for damages. 1 *Ld. Raym.* 639. *Salk.* 583. 2 *Ld. Raym.* 774. 2 *Cro.* 126.

And if a defendant bring money into court on a plea of tender, the plaintiff may take it out, though he reply that the tender was not made before action brought. 1 *Bos. and Pull.* 332.

So the defendant may plead a tender of the rent at a day, and always ready. 2 *Mod. Ent.* 236. *Lutw.* 367.

So the plaintiff may plead in bar of an avowry tender of amends. *Lutw.* 1232.

Also to an involuntary trespass the plaintiff may plead a tender of sufficient amends. 1 *Bro. Ent.* 332. *Tho. Ent.* 304.

And by the stat. 21 *Jac.* 1. c. 16. to trespass *quare clausum fregit*, the defendant disclaiming title to the land, and shewing it to be an involuntary trespass, may plead tender of amends at any time before action brought. So to a negligent trespass by escape of cattle, or the like, 2 *Rol.* 570. c. 20: but tender after action brought is too late. *Cro. Car.* 264. 1 *Rol.* 538. *l.* 3. And the tender must be of a sum certain.

But to a voluntary trespass, or trespass by mistake, as by putting cattle into a close, or the like, tender before action brought is no plea. 2 *Rol.* 570. *l.* 25. *Noy* 12. 3 *Lev.* 37. Nor can it be pleaded in trespass for taking goods. 1 *Str.* 549.

And by several modern statutes, particularly 11 *Geo.* 2. *c.* 19. in case of irregularity in the method of distraining, 24 *Geo.* 2. c. 24. in case of mistakes committed by justices of the peace; 28 *Geo.* 3. *c.* 37. in case of error by custom-house officers; and 23 *Geo.* 3. c. 70. in respect of mistakes by excise officers, the party may tender sufficient amends to the party injured, and it will be a bar of all actions, whether he thinks proper to accept them or not.

* But although he is not punishable if he cuts down trees, yet they are not his property, but will belong to the first person living at the time when they are cut, who has an estate of inheritance. *Harg. Co. Litt.* 27. *b.* 3 *P. Wms.* 240.

To a plea of tender of amends, the plaintiff may reply that the defendant did not tender, or that the amends were not sufficient. *Comyn's Dig. Plead.* 3 *m*, 36.

TENEMENT, (*Tenementum.*) Signifies properly a house or home-stall; but more largely it comprehends not only house, but all corporeal inheritances which are holden of another, and all inheritances issuing out of or exerciseable with the same. *Co. Lit.* 6. 19. 154. And it may be said to be any thing that is any way held or possessed; but being a word of a large and ambiguous meaning, and not so certain as messuage, therefore it is not fit to be used to express any thing which requires a particular description. 2 *Lill. Abr.* 566.

TENEMENTARY LAND. The outland of manors granted out to tenants by the Saxon thanes, under arbitrary rents and services. *Spelm. Cowell.*

TENEMENTIS LEGATIS. An ancient writ lying to the city of London, or any other corporation; (where the old custom was, that men might devise, by will, lands and tenements as well as goods and chattels) for the hearing and determining any controversy touching the same. *Reg. Orig.* 244. *Cowell.*

TENENDUM, is a clause in a deed wherein the tenure of the land is created and limited. The office of a tenendum in a deed, is to limit and appoint the tenure of the land which is held, and how, and of whom it is to be held. *Co. Lit.* 6. *a.* 2 *Inst.* 66, 67. 500, 501, 502, 505.

The tenendum most commonly and properly succeeds the *habendum*, and was usually in these words, *tenendum per servitium, &c.* But the *tenendum* seems now to be incorporated with the *habendum*; for we say, "to have and to hold," in which clause the estate is limited. 2 *Black.* 298.

TENENTIBUS IN ASSISA NON QUERENDIS. A writ that lay for him to whom a disseisor had alienated the land whereof he disseised another, that he be not molested in assise for the damages, if the disseisor have wherewith to satisfy them. *Reg. Orig.* 214.

TENHEDED, or TIENHEOFED. A Saxon word, signifying *Decanus, Caput vel Princeps Decaniæ sive Decuriæ. Leg. Edw. Conf.* c. 29.

TENMENTALE, (Sax. *Tienmantale,* i. e. *decem virorum numerus*) *Decennaria, Tithinga. Leg. Edw. Conf.* Also an ancient tax or tribute paid to the king. *Hoveden* 737.

TENOR, (Lat.) Of writs, records, and the like, is the substance or purport of them; or a transcript or copy. 2 *Hawk. P. C.* 295.

TENORE INDICTAMENTI MITTENDO. A writ whereby the record of an indictment, and the process thereupon, was called out of another court into the king's bench. *Reg. Orig.* 69.

TENORE PRÆSENTIUM. The tenor of these presents, is the matter contained therein or rather the intent and meaning thereof. *Cowell.*

TENTATUS PANIS. The essay or assay of bread. *Blount.*

TENTER. A stretcher or trier of cloth, used by dyers. *Cowell.*

TENTHS, (*Decimæ.*) Are the tenth part of the annual value of every spiritual benefice, being that yearly portion or tribute which all ecclesiastical livings pay to the king. They were annexed perpetually to the crown by stat. 26 *Hen.* 8. c. 3. *Eliz.* c. 4. And at last Q. Anne granted the same, with the first-fruits, towards the augmentation of the maintenance of poor clergymen. 1 *Anne*, c. 11.

TENTS. See *Felony.*

TENURE, (*Tenura,* from the Lat. *Tenere.*) Is the manner whereby lands or tenements are holden; or the service that the tenant owes to his lord. 1 *Inst.* 1. 93. And all the lands and tenements in England are holden either mediately or immediately of the king, and therefore he is *summus dominus supra omnes.* 2 *Inst.* 531.

Under the wor tenure is included every holding of an inheritance; and it sometimes denotes the duration of the tenant's estate: as if a man holds to himself and his heirs, it is called tenure in fee simple. At other times the tenure is coupled with words pointing out the instrument by which an inheritance is held. Thus, if the holding is by copy of court-roll, it is called tenure by copy of court-roll. At other times, this word is coupled with words that shew the principal service by which an inheritance is held: as where a man holds by knight's service, it is called tenure by knight's service. *Rol. Abr. title Tenure.*

Burgage tenure is where land is holden of the lord of the borough, at a certain rent. Grand serjeanty, a tenure of lands by honorary services at the king's coronation. *Ibid.*

Of the general ancient tenures, knight service, chivalry, escuage, petit-serjeanty, villenage, &c. are taken away by stat. 12 *Car.* 2. c. 24. The common tenures at this day are fee-simple, fee-tail, by the curtesy, in dower, for life and years, and copyhold tenure. 2 *Black.* 59.

TERM, (*Terminus.*). Signfies commonly the limitation of time or estate; as a lease for term of life, or years. *Bract. lib.* 2.

TERMINUM QUI PRETERIIT. Writ of entry *ad.* This is a writ for the reversioner, when the possession is withheld by the lessee or a stranger, after the determination of a lease for years. *F. N. B.* 201.

This writ is now disused, since the invention of ejectments. 3 *Black.* 183.

TERMOR, (*Tenens ex Termino.*) Is he that holds lands or tenements for term of years or life. *Litt.* 100.

TERMS. Are those spaces of time wherein the courts of justice are open, for all that complain of wrongs or injuries, and seek their rights by course of law or action, in order to their redress; and during which, the courts in Westminster-Hall sit and give judgments, &c. But the high court of parliament, the chancery, and inferior courts, do not observe the terms; only the court of king's bench, the common pleas, and exchequer, the highest courts at common law. Of these terms there are four in every year: viz, Hilary term, Easter term, Trinity term, and Michaelmas term.

The terms in Scotland are Martinmas, Candlemas, Whitsuntide, and Lammas. *Stat.* 6 *Anne*, c. 7.

TERMS OF THE LAW. are technical words and terms of art, particularly used in and adapted to the profession of the law. 2 *Hawk. P. C.* 239.

TERMS *for payment of Rent*, are the four quarterly feasts, upon which rent is usually paid. *Cowell.*

TERRA. In Domesday, is taken for arable land, and always so distinguished from the *Pratum*. *Cowell.*

TERRA AFFIRMATA. Land let to farm. *Cowell.*

TERRA *Boscalis.* Woody lands. *Ibid.*

TERRA *Culta.* Land that is tilled or manured. *Ibid.*

TERRA *debilis.* Weak or barren ground. *Ibid.*

TERRA *dominica vel indominicata.* The demesne land of a manor. *Ibid.*

TERRA *Excultabilis.* Such land as may be ploughed. *Ibid.*

TERRA *extendenda.* A writ directed to the escheator, willing him to enquire and find out the true yearly value of any land, by the oath of twelve men, and to certify the extent into the chancery. *Reg. of Writs*, 293.

TERRA *frusca.* Fresh land, or such as hath not been lately ploughed. *Cowell.*

TERRA *hydata.* Land subject to the payment of hydage. *Selden.*

TERRA *lucrabilis.* Land that may be gained from the sea, or inclosed out of a waste, to a particular use. *Cowell.*

TERRA *Normanorum.* In the beginning of Hen. 3. such land in England as had been lately held by some noble Norman, who, by adhering to the French king, or dauphin, had forfeited his estate in this kingdom, which by this means became an escheat to the crown, was called *Terra Normannorum*, and restored, or otherwise disposed at the king's pleasure. *Par. Antiq.* 197. *Cowell.*

TERRA *nova.* Land newly asserted and converted from wood ground to arable. *Cowell.*

TERRA PUTURA. Land in forests held by the tenure of furnishing man's meat, horse-meat, and the like, to the keepers therein. *Ibid.*

TERRA *fabulosa.* Gravelly or sandy ground. *Ibid.*

TERRA VESTITA. Land sown with corn. *Ibid.*

TERRA *mainabilis.* Tillable land. *Ibid.*

TERRA *marenuata.* Land that has the liberty of free warren. *Ibid.*

TERRÆ *Testementales.* Lands that were held free from feodal services, in allodio, in socage, descendible to all the sons, and therefore called gavel-kind, were deviseable by will, and thereupon called *terræ testamentales*, as the thane who possessed them was said to be *testamento dignus*. *Cowell.*

TERRAGE (*Terragium.*) Edward the Third granted to John of Gaunt, and Blanch his wife, for their lives, *quod sint quieti de thelonio, passagio, soccagio, lastagio, tallagio, caruagio, priscagio, pickagio,* & TERRAGIO, which seems to be an exemption *a precariis*, viz. boons of ploughing, reaping, &c. and perhaps from all land-taxes, or from money paid for digging and breaking the earth in fairs and markets. *Cowell.*

TERRAR, or *Terrier*, (*Terrarium, catalogus Terrarum.*) Is a land-roll, or survey of lands, either of a single person, or of a town; containing the quantity of acres, tenants names, and such like. *Ibid.*

TERRARIUS. A landholder, or one who possesses many farms of land. *Ibid.*

TERRARIUS *Cœnobialis.* An officer in religious houses, whose office was to keep a terrier of all their estates. *Ibid.*

TERRE-TENANT, *Tertenant*, (*Terræ Tenens.*) Is he who hath the actual possession of the land. *West. Symb. par.* 2. *Briton, cap.* 29. 3 *Rep.* 12. *Cro. Eliz.* 872. *Cro. Jac.* 506.

TERRIS, *Bonis et Catallis rehabendis post Purgationem.* A writ for a clerk to recover his lands, goods, and chattels, formerly seized, after he had cleared himself of the felony of which he was accused, and delivered to his ordinary to be purged. *Reg. Orig.* 68

TERRIS *et Catallis tentis ultra debitum levatum.* A judicial writ for the restoring of lands or goods to a debtor, that was distrained above the quantity of the debt. *Reg. Judic.* 38.

TERRIS *liberandis.* A writ which lay for a man convicted by attaint, to bring the record and process before the king, and take a fine for his imprisonment, and then to deliver him his lands and tenements again, and release him of the strip and waste. *Reg. Orig.* 232.

TERTIAN. A measure of 84 gallons, the third part of a tun. *Cowell.*

TEST ACTS. By 25 *Car.* 2. *c.* 2. commonly called the Test Act, all officers civil and military are to take the oaths and test; and if they neglect it, and execute any office within the words of that statute, being legally convicted thereof upon information, presentment, or indictment, in any of the courts at Westminster, or at the assises, they shall forfeit 500*l.* to be recovered by him who will sue for the same in any action of debt, &c. See *Oaths.*

TESTA *de Nevil.* An ancient record in the King's Remembrance Office in the Exchequer, containing an account of lands held in grand serjeanty, with fees and escheats to the king, &c. *Cowell.*

TESTAMENT, (*Testamentum.*) Is thus defined by Plowden, *Testamentum est testatio mentis*, a testament is a witness of the mind. It is *verbum simplex*, and therefore may be better defined, *Testamentum est ultimæ voluntatis justa sententia, de eo quod quis post mortem suam fieri vult, &c.* *Cowell.* See *Wills.*

TESTAMENTARY CAUSES. A species of causes belonging to the ecclesiastical jurisdiction. 3 *Black.* 95. which vide.

TESTAMENTARY GUARDIAN. By 12 *Car.* 2. *c.* 24. any father may, by deed or will, dispose of the custody of his child, either born or unborn, to any person, except a popish recusant, either in possession or reversion, until such child attains the age of one and twenty years; and the guardians so appointed are called guardians by statute or testamentary guardians. 1 *Black. Com.* 462.

TESTAMENTARY JURISDICTION *in Equity.* For want of a power of discovering, at law, what rests only in the private knowledge of the party, courts of equity have acquired a concurrent jurisdiction with every other court, in all matters of account. As incident to accounts, they take a concurrent cognizance of the administration of the personal assets, consequently of debts, legacies, the distribution of the residue, and the conduct of executors and administrators. 3 *Black.* 437.

TESTAMENTARY JURISDICTION IN SPIRITUAL COURTS, is principally exercised in the consistory courts of every diocesan bishop, and in the prerogative court of the metropolitan, originally; and in the arches court and court of delegates by way of appeal. It is divisible into three branches: the probate of wills, the granting of administration, and the suing for legacies. The two former of which, when no opposition is made, are granted merely *ex officio et debito justitiæ*, and are then the object of what is called the voluntary, and not the contentious jurisdiction. But when a caveat is entered against proving the will, or granting administration, and a suit thereupon follows, to determine either the validity of the testament, or who hath a right to the administration; this claim and obstruction by the adverse party, are an injury to the party entitled, and as such are remedied by the sentence of the spiritual court, either by establishing the will, or granting the administration.

TESTAMENTO ANNEXO, Administration *cum.* If a testator makes his will, without naming any executors, or if he names incapable persons, or if the executors named refuse to act; in any of these cases, the ordinary must grant administration *cum testamento annexo*, to some other person. 2 *Black.* 503.

TESTATOR, (Lat.) He that makes a testament or will.

TESTATUM, is a writ in personal actions, where the defendant cannot be arrested upon a capias in the county where the action is laid, but is returned *non est inventus* by the sheriff; then this writ shall be sent out into any other county where such person is thought to be, or to have wherewith to satisfy: and this is termed a *testatum*, by reason the sheriff hath testified that the defendant was not to be found in his bailiwick. *Kitch. Ret. Writs*, 287.

TESTE. A word generally used in the last part of all writs, wherein the date is contained, which begin with these words, *Teste meipso, &c.* if it be an original writ; or teste the lord chief justice, &c. if judicial. *Co. Lit.* 134.

TESTIMONIAL, is a certificate under the hand of a justice of peace, or some court, testifying some special matter, such as the place and time, when and where a soldier or mariner landed, and the place of his dwelling and birth unto which he is to pass. 39 *Eliz. cap.* 17.

TESTIMONIALS OF CLERGY, are necessary to be made by persons present, that a clergyman inducted to a benefice hath performed all things according to the act of uniformity; to evidence that the clerk hath complied with what the law requires on his institution and induction, which in some cases he shall be put to do. *Count Pars. Comp.* 24. 26.

TESTIMOIGNES, is French for witnesses, and *Testimoignage*, testimony. *Law Fr. Dict.*

TESTON, or *Testoon*, commonly called tester, a sort of money which among the French did bear the value of 18*d.* but being made of brass lightly gilt with silver, in the reign of King Henry the Eighth, it was reduced to 12*d.* and afterwards to 6*d.* *Lowndes's Ess. on Coins*, 22.

TEXTUS. A text or subject of a discourse, and is mentioned by several authors to signify the New Testament. *Cowell.*

TEXTUS *magni Altaris*, is mentioned in Domesday and Cartular S. Edmund. *Cowell.*

TEXTUS *Roffensis*. An ancient manuscript containing the rights, customs, and tenures of the church of Rochester, drawn up anno 1114. *Ibid.*

THAMES. See *London.*

THANAGE *of the King*, (*Thanagium Regis,*) signified a certain part of the king's land or property, whereof the ruler or governor was called thane. *Cowell.*

THANE, (from the Sax. Thenian, *ministrare,*) Was the title of those who attended the English Saxon kings in their courts, and who held their lands immediately of those kings. *Cowell. Spelm. cap.* 7.

THANE-LANDS. Such lands as were granted by charter of the Saxon kings to their thanes. *Cowell.*

THASCIA. A sum of money or tribute imposed by the Romans on the Britons, and their lands. *Leg. H.* 1. c. 78.

THEFT, (*Furtum.*) Is an unlawful felonious taking away of another man's moveable and personal goods, against the will of the owner. See *Larceny. Robbery.*

THEFT-BOTE, (from the Sax. *Theof*, i. e. *fur*, & bote, *compensatio.*) Is the receiving of a man's goods again from a thief, after stolen, or other amends not to prosecute the felon, and to the intent the thief may escape; which is an offence punishable with fine and imprisonment. *H. P. C.* 130.

THELONIUM, or *Breve effendi quieti de Thelonio.* A writ lying for the citizens of any city, or burgesses of any town, that have a charter or prescription to free them from toll, against the officers of any town or market, who would constrain them to pay toll of their merchandize contrary to their grant or prescription. *F. N. B. fol.* 226.

THELONMANNUS. The toll-man, or officer who receives toll. *Cowell.*

THELONIO *rationabili habendo pro dominis habentibus dominica Regis ad firmam.* A writ that lay for him that had of the king's demesne in fee-farm to recover reasonable toll of the king's tenants there, if his demesne had been accustomed to be tolled. *Reg. Orig. fol.* 87. *Cowell.*

THEMMAGIUM. A duty or acknowledgment paid by inferior tenants in respect of theme or team. *Ibid.*

THENICIUM. Hedge-rows, or dike-rows. *Ibid.*

THEODAN. In the degrees or distinctions of persons among the Saxons, the earl or prime lord was called thane, and the king's thane; and the husbandman or inferior tenant was called theodan, or under thane. *Cowell.*

THEOWES. The bondmen among our Saxons were called theowes and esnes, who were not counted members of the commonwealth, but parcels of their master's goods and substance. *Ibid.*

THESAURUS. Sometimes taken in old charters for thesaurarium, the treasury *Ibid.*

THETHINGA. A tithing: *tithingmannus*, a tithingman. *Sax.*

THEW, or THEOWE, (Sax.) Among the Saxons, a slave or captive. *Ibid.*

THINGS: In general, the chief part of every thing, is the beginning of it; but the end thereof, though it be last in the execution, is first in intention, and therefore favoured in law. 1 *Inst.* 298. 10 *Rep.* 25. Things which are more worthy, are ever preferred before those less worthy, and draw the others after them. *Plowd.* 169. 1 *Inst.* 44. But things may be destroyed by the same way or manner they were made. 2 *Rep.* 53. 6 *Rep.* 15. 2 *Black.* 1. 16. 384.

THINGUS. The same with Thanus; a nobleman, knight, or freeman. *Cromp. Jurisd.* 197.

THIRDBOROW. A constable. *Cowell.*

THIRDINGS, i. e. the third part of the corn growing on the ground, due to the lord for a heriot on the death of his tenant, within the manor of Turfat, in com. Hereford. *Blount. Ten.*

THIRD NIGHT AWN-HINDE, (*trium noctium hospes.*) By the laws of St. Edward the Confessor, if any man lay a third night in an inn, he was called a third night awn-hinde, for whom his host was answerable, if he committed an offence. *Bract. lib.* 3. *Cowell.*

THIRD-PENNY. See *Denarius Tertius Comitatus.*

THISTLE-TAKE. Was a custom within the manor of Halton, in Cheshire, that if, in driving beasts over the common, the driver permitted them to graze or take but a thistle, he must pay a halfpenny a beast to the lord of the fee. Also a tFiskerton, in Nottinghamshire, by ancient custom, if a native or a cottager killed a swine above a year old, he paid to the lord a penny which purchase of leave to kill a hog wa also called thistle-take. *Cowell.*

THOKES. Fish with broken bellie *Ibid.*

THORP, *Threp*, *Trop.* Either in the beginning or end of names of places, signifies a street or village, as Aldestrop, from the Sax. *Thorp*, *villa*, *vicus.* *Cowell.*

THRAVE OF CORN, (*Trava bladi*, from the Sax. *Threav*, i. e. a bundle, or the British *drefa*, i. e. twenty-four.) In most parts of England, consists of twenty-four sheaves, or four shocks, six sheaves to every shock. 2 *Hen.* 6. c. 2. Yet, in some counties, they reckon but twelve sheaves to the thrave. *Cowell.*

THREAD. See *Manufactures.*

THREATENING LETTERS. By 9 *Geo.* 1. c. 22. amended by 27 *Geo.* 2. c. 15. Knowingly to send any letter without a name, or with a fictitious name, demanding money, venison, or any other valuable thing, or threatening (without any demand) to kill or fire the house of any person, is made felony without benefit of clergy.

The words of these statutes are, "shall knowingly send," and therefore it has been determined, if the writer of a threatening letter delivers it himself, he is not guilty of felony. *Leach.* 351.

THREATS. Threats and menaces of bodily hurt, through fear of which a man's business is interrupted, is a species of injury to individuals. But a menace alone, without a consequent inconvenience, makes not the injury; but to complete the wrong, there must be both of them together. The remedy for this is in pecuniary damages, to be recovered by action of trespass *vi & armis.* 3 *Black.* 120. But where bodily harm is justly feared from any such menaces, surety of the peace may be obtained. See *Surety.*

THRENGUS. A vassal, but not of the lowest degree of those who held lands of the chief lord. *Spelm. Cowell.*

THRIMSA, (Sax. *Thrim,* three.) An old piece of money, or the third part of a shilling, being a German coin passing for four-pence. *Cowell.*

THRITHING, (*Thrithingum.*) A court consisting of three or four hundreds. 2 *Inst.* 99.

THROWING OF SILK. See *Manufacturers.*

THUDE WEALD, (Sax.) A wood-ward, or person that looked after the woods. *Cowell.*

THUMELUM. A thumb. *Ibid.*

THWERTNICK. A Saxon word: an old custom of giving entertainments to the sheriff for three nights. *Ibid.*

TICAL. A piece of money in China, of two pounds sixteen shillings and threepence value. *Mer. Dict.*

TIDESMEN. Officers of the custom-house, appointed to watch or attend upon ships, till the customs are paid; so called, because they go aboard the ships at their arrival in the Thames, and come up with the tide. *Cowell.*

TIERCE, (Fr. *Tiers,* i. e. a third.) A measure of wine, oil, and the like, containing the third part of a pipe of forty-two gallons. *Cowell.*

TIGH, (Sax. *Teag.*) A close or inclosure still used in Kent. *Ibid.*

TIBLA, (Sax.) Signifies an accusation in the laws of K. Canutus. *Cowell.*

TILES. See *Bricks.*

TILLAGE, (*Agricultura.*) Is of great account in law, as being very profitable to the commonwealth; and therefore arable land hath the preference before meadows, pastures, and all other ground whatsoever. And so careful is our law to preserve it, that a bond or condition to restrain tillage, or sowing of lands, &c. is void. 11 *Rep.* 53.

TILTING. Where one kills another in fighting at tilting, by the king's command, the accident is excusable; but if it be by tilting without the command of the king, or by parrying with naked swords, covered with buttons at the points, which cannot be used without manifest hazard of life, it will be felony of manslaughter. *H. P. C.* 31.

TIMBER. See *Trespass* and *Waste.*

TIMBERLODE. A service by which tenants were to carry timber felled from the woods to the lord's house. *Cowell.*

TIME and *Place.* Are to be set forth with certainty in a declaration. 5 *Mod.* 286.

If no certain time is implied by law for the doing of any thing, and there is no time agreed upon by the parties, then the law doth allow a convenient time to the party for the doing thereof, i. e. as much as shall be adjudged reasonable, without prejudice to the doer of it. 2 *Lill. Abr.* 572.

Regularly, there cannot be any fraction in a day, and therefore the proceedings were set aside, where it appeared the principal surrendered on the day, though after the return, of the scire facias. *Rep. Temp. Hardw. per Annaly,* 208.

TIME LIMITED. See *Limitation.*

TINEL LE ROY, (Fr.) The king's hall wherein his servants used to dine and sup. 13 *R.* 2. c. 3. *Cowell.*

TINEMAN, or TIENMAN. A petty officer in the forest, who had the nocturnal care of vert and venison, and other servile employments. *Cowell.*

TINET, (*Tinettum.*) is used in Monmouthshire and other places in or bordering on South Wales, for brush-wood and thorns, to make and repair hedges. In Monmouthshire, to tine a gap in a hedge is to fill it up with thorns, that cattle may not pass through it. *Chart.* 21 *Hen.* 6.

TINEWALD. The parliament or annual convention of the people of the Isle of Man. *Cowell.*

TINKERMEN. Those fishermen who destroyed the young fry on the river Thames, by nets and unlawful engines, till suppressed by the mayor and citizens of London. *Cowell.*

TINPENY. A tribute so called, usually paid for the liberty of digging in tin-mines, from the Sax. *Tinnen Stannus*, and Penig. *Denarius. Ibid.*

TIPSTAFFS. Officers appointed by the marshal of the king's bench, to attend upon the judges with a kind of rod or staff tipt with silver, who take into their custody all prisoners either committed or turned over by the judges at their chambers. *Cowell*

TITHES, (*Decimæ*, from the Sax. *Teotha.* i. e. tenth.) A certain part of the fruit, or lawful increase of the earth, beasts and men's labour, which in most places, and of most things, is the tenth part which, by the law, hath been given to incumbents, in recompence of their office. 11 *Co. Rep.* 13. *Dyer* 84.

Tithes are either prædial, personal, or mixt; and these are divided into great or small tithes.

1. The prædial tithes are such as arise from the land spontaneously, or by manurance; as tithe of corn, hay, wood, herbs, wine, flax, hops, and fruits; such as apples, pears, and the like.

2. Mixt tithes are such as arise from cattle and beasts receiving their nourishment upon the land; and are therefore due in respect of calves, lambs, kids, pigs, wool, milk, cheese, eggs, and the like.

3. Personal tithes are the tenth part of the clear gain which is raised from the personal labour of a man, his charges, and expences, according to his condition and degree, being deducted; but these are only payable in such places as had accustomably for forty years before the stat. 2 and 3 *Ed.* 6. c. 13, paid personal tithes.

And by that statute, neither day labourers are obliged to pay personal tithes, nor, according to 1 *Roll's Abridgment*, c. 646, fol. 25, husbandry servants, in respect of their wages.

4. Other ecclesiastical revenues, usually considered with tithes as part of the inheritance of the church, are oblations or obventions, pensions and mortuaries.

And they are either voluntary, or due by custom at a certain time—as upon marriage, baptism, purification of women, funerals, or the like.

And by the statute 2 and 3 *Ed.* 6. c. 13. all who by the laws and customs of the realm ought to pay offerings, shall yearly pay them at the four most usual days, or otherwise at Easter.

5. Great tithes are chiefly of wood, corn, or hay; and small tithes are in general, unless there has been an immemorial usage to the contrary, all other prædial tithes, besides corn, hay, and wood; and likewise those tithes which are mixed and personal.

6. Of the produce of the earth;—the tithes are to be set out and taken in manner following:

Wheat and rye, by the tenth shock, and by the tenth sheaf.

Barley and oats, by the tenth cock or shock, and also the tenth sheaf.

Beans, pease, tares, and all other pulse, by the tenth cock, heap, or bundle.

Stubble: wheat stubble, employed in purposes of husbandry and tillage of the lands of the farm on which it grew, yields no tithe, but if sold, or otherwise disposed of, then by the tenth of its value.

Hay, clover, and other artificial grasses; by the tenth grass cock after having been tedded from the swath: of the first mowing; and, also of the second mowing by the tenth cock, when made into hay.

After-mowth of grass; clover, or other artificial grasses: if eaten by barren and unprofitable stock, by an agistment tithe.

Hobbings of grass in pasture: by the tenth cock.

Seeds of clover, artificial grasses, and also turnip, cole, and rape seed; if grown for seed, by the tenth measure of the seed when threshed out; if sold, by the tenth of what it sold for.

Turnips; if pulled, by every tenth turnip or heap.

Turnips, rape and cole; if eaten, whether by profitable or unprofitable stock, by an agistment tithe; if sold, by the tenth of their value.

Barren lands; titheable when cultivated.

Flax, hemp, and madder.—The tithes thereof are ascertained at five shillings per acre, and so in proportion for small quantities.

Woad or woald; by the tenth heap or gathering.

Saffron; by a tenth when gathered, though only once in three years.

Hops; by a tenth part of the whole after picking; that is, after pulled from the bine.

Potatoes and other roots growing in fields: by a tenth of their produce when taken up.

Gardens; by a tenth of their produce.

Orchards; by a tenth of their produce, whether windfalls or gathered.

Nursery grounds. Their produce, whether fruits or plants, indigenous or exotic, if sold in the way of trade, by a tenth, or tenth of their value.

Timber-wood, or charcoal; that is, oak, ash, and elm, above twenty years' growth, yield no tithe, except when cut down and sold as fire-wood, or converted into charcoal.

Other wood. All other wood of any growth, by a tenth, according to the quantity cut down, whether sold or not, except in counties where timber wood is scarce, and any other wood is substituted, as beech and the like.

Osiers and willows; by the tenth bundle or pole, when cut.

Underwood. Underwood, coppice-wood, loppings and toppings of old bowlings, loppings and toppings of trees, reeds, and germins, cut from stumps of trees, though above twenty years growth, by a tenth of their quantity when cut.

Hedge-rows and gorse or furze; if sold, or not used upon the farm on which they grow, by every tenth kid or faggot.

7. Of Sheep. The tithes are to be taken in manner following:

Lambs; by every tenth lamb, to be taken away when able to live upon the same food the dam doth: and the tenth of the value of the odd numbers: if sold upon the fall, the tenth of what they sold for: bought in and put to ewes, by an agistment tithe, to be computed from the time of weaning, unless kept until clip day and clipped.

Ewes and lambs, sold or removed out of the parish before clip-day, by an agistment tithe, to be computed from the last clip-day.

Feeding sheep-shearlings or hogs bred or bought in; by an agistment tithe, if sold or removed before clip-day, to be computed from the last clip-day, but if bought in from that day, until sold or removed.

Sheep, bought in and kept until clip-day, by the tenth weight of their wool.

Sheep dying. Dying after clip-day of the rot, or otherwise, whether bought in or bred upon the farm, by an agistment tithe, to be computed from the last clip-day, if bred on the farm; but if bought in, from that time until they died.

Ewes removed out of the parish to lamb by the tenth lamb, according to the number of ewes, and by the tenth of the value for the odd numbers.

Ewes or other sheep removed out of the parish to be clipped; by the tenth fleece, according to the number of sheep removed, and by the tenth of the weight of the odd fleeces.

Wool; by the tenth weight at the time of clipping.

Belts and locks; by the tenth weight when washed and dried.

8. Of Beasts. The tithes are to be taken in manner following:

Calves; by the tenth if ten; to be taken at the time of weaning, and by a tenth of the value of all above or under ten; if one or more, and sold upon the fall, or fed for the butchers, by the tenth of the price sold for, and in the same manner for all above ten.

Calves reared for the plough or pail yield no tithe; but if sold or removed before they are worked or milked, by an agistment tithe, to be computed from the time they become yearlings, until sold or removed.

Working beasts yield no tithe while working, unless they work for hire or profit, or are employed in another parish than that in which the owner lives; then by an agistment tithe.

Beasts turned off to feed; by an agistment tithe, to be computed from the day turned off until sold or removed.

Cows sold before calving or dying, by an agistment tithe, to be computed from the time they were let dry until they were sold or die.

Beasts bought in and sold again, by an agistment tithe, to be computed from the day bought in, until sold, except when kept in the straw yard, and fed with straw; but no exception if fed with hay, though the hay had before paid tithe.

Milk; by the whole of the milk milked on each natural day, as well in the morning as in the evening, to be computed from the time the first cow, after calving, is brought to the pail and milked; and so of every cow after calving, and no regard is paid to what they eat.

The cow-keeper is to give notice to the tithe-owner when and where he goes to milk his cows, and the tithe is to be fetched by him from the place where the cows are milked, unless there be a custom in the parish for the cow-keeper to deliver it to the tithe-owner elsewhere, or at the church porch; and unless he milk his cows in another parish than that in which they are fed; for the tithe of milk is payable to the tithe-owner of the parish in which the cows are fed, and not in that in which they are milked; in which case he is not obliged to fetch it, but the cow-keeper must bring it to the tithe-owner.

9. Of horses. The tithes are taken in the following manner:

Foals; by the tenth, if ten, to be taken at the time of weaning; and by the tenth of the value of all above or under ten, if sold, before used for the plough, by an agistment tithe, to be computed from the time they become yearlings, until sold or removed.

Horses kept for working the farm yield no tithe while working; but if used for hire or profit, or employed in another parish than that in which the owner lives, then by an agistment tithe.

Saddle and pleasure horses. Saddle horses, and horses used for pleasure only, yield no tithe; but if used for hire or profit, by an agistment tithe.

Horses turned up or bought to feed for sale; by an agistment tithe, to be computed from the time turned up or bought in until sold or removed.

Brood mares and horses taken in to feed or agist at so much per week, by an agistment tithe for the tithe kept.

It is to be observed, that the true object of agistment is not the improvement of the animal, but the tenth of what the land is worth to let, for taking in the cattle of another person to agist; and land on which cattle are fed for slaughter should be rated at double the value of the land on which store cattle are fed.

10. Of Pigs, the tithes are to be taken by the tenth pig, if ten, to be taken at the time of weaning, and for all above or under ten, the tenth of the value thereof at weaning.

Bought in and sold again, by the tenth of the clear profit thereof.

11. Of Rabbits and deer. Rabbits, if sold, by the tenth of both skin and carcase at every killing; and in like manner deer also will yield a tithe, if sold for profit, although *feræ naturæ*.

12. Of Fish, no tithe is payable, except in certain places by immemorial usage.

13. Of Pigeons, the tithe is taken by the tenth of the value of all pigeons, when sold.

Pigeon manure, if not used on the farm, but sold, is also titheable by the tenth of the value sold for.

14. Of Wild Fowl taken in decoys, and sold for profit, the tithe is taken by the tenth of the value when sold.

15. Of Honey and Wax the tithe is taken by the tenth measure of honey, and the tenth weight of wax.

16. Of Eggs, the tithe is taken by the tenth egg of all turkeys, hens, geese, ducks, or any other domesticated fowl, and by the tenth weight of the feathers of geese.

17. Of Mills, the tithe of corn-mills shall be paid of the clear yearly gains and profits, after deducting rent, servants wages, repairs, and other real expences, except of ancient mills erected before the 9th year of Edward II.

18. Other parish dues, payable to the minister of the parish, consist of Easter-offerings, mortuaries, and surplice fees.

Easter-offerings are payable for every person in the parish of sixteen years of age and upwards, by the master or mistress of a family, after the rate of two-pence per head.

Mortuaries are for every person dying in the parish, possessed of moveable goods to the value of forty pounds and upwards, his debts first paid—10*s*.

If to the value of thirty pounds, and under forty pounds—6*s*. 8*d*.

If to the value of six pounds thirteen and fourpence, and under thirty pounds—3*s*. 4*d*.

Except for beneficed clergymen, for whom a mortuary is only due to the bishop of the diocese wherein he held his benefice and resided.

Surplice fees are payable for every marriage, whether by licence or by banns, for every funeral, and for every churching, according to the custom of the parish.

By 7 & 8 *W*. 3. *cap*. 6, *s*. 1. it is, for the more easy recovery of small tithes, where the same do not amount to above the yearly value of forty shillings, from any one person, enacted, "that if any person shall fail in payment for twenty days after demand, the parson may make complaint in writing to two justices of the peace, neither being patrons, nor interested, who, after summoning the party, are to hear and determine the complaint, give a reasonable allowance for the tithes and costs not exceeding ten shillings.

If the person complained against insists on any prescription, composition, *modus decimandi*, or other title, delivers the same in writing to the justices, and gives to the party complaining sufficient security to pay costs at law, if the title is not allowed, the justices are not to give judgment. The justices have power to give costs, not exceeding ten shillings, to the party prosecuted, if they find the complaint false and vexatious. The act not to extend to tithes within the city of London, or in any other place, where the same are settled by any act of parliament. An appeal is given to the sessions, and no proceedings or judgment had by virtue of this act, to be removed, or superseded, by any writ of certiorari, or other writ whatsoever, unless the title of such tithes shall be in question.

By 7 & 8 *W*. 3. c. 34. *par*. 4. where any quaker shall refuse to pay, or compound for his great or small tithes, it shall be lawful for the two next justices of the peace of the same county, other than such justice of the peace as is patron of the church, or chapel, to which the tithes belong, or any ways interested, upon the complaint to convene before them such quaker, and to examine upon oath the truth of the complaint, and to ascertain what is due from such quaker, and by order under their hands and seals to direct the payment thereof, so as the sum ordered do not exceed ten pounds; and upon refusal of the quaker to pay, to levy the money. Any person aggrieved, may appeal to the next general quarter-sessions.

No proceedings or judgment had by virtue of this act, shall be removed or superseded by any writ of certiorari, or other writ out of his majesty's courts at Westminster, or any other court whatsoever, unless the title to such tithes shall be in question.

By 1 *Geo*. 1. *st*. 2. *cap*. 6. *par*. 2. the like remedy is given for the recovery of all tithes and all other ecclesiastical dues from quakers, as by the 7 & 8 *W*. 3. *cap*. 34. is given for tithes to the value of ten pounds.

And such justices of the peace, upon complaint of any parson, vicar, curate, farmer, or proprietor of such tithes, or other person who ought to have, receive, or collect any such tithes or dues, may proceed in a similar manner as directed by the former act touching quakers.

TITHING, (*Tithinga*, from the Sax. *Teothunge*, i. e. *Decuriam*.) Was in its first appointment the number or company of ten men with their families, held together in a society, all being bound for the peaceable behaviour of each other. And of these companies there was one chief person who was called teothing-man, at this day tithing-man, but the old discipline of tithings is long since left off. 1 *Black*. 113. 4. 404.

TITHING-MEN. Petty constables, elected by parishes, and sworn into their offices in the court-leet, and sometimes by justices of peace. And there is frequently a tithing-man in the same town with a constable, who is, as it were, a deputy to execute the office in the constable's absence. *Dalt*. 3. When there is no constable of a parish, the office and authority of a tithing-man seems to be the same. See *Constable*.

TITLE, (*Titulus*.) The word title includeth a right, and is thus defined, *titulus est justa causa possidendi quod nostrum est*, and is the means whereby the owner of lands hath that just possession of his property. *Co. Lit*. 345. 2 *Black*. 195.

1. The lowest and most imperfect degree of title consists in the mere naked possession, or actual occupation of the estate; without any apparent right, or any shadow or pretence of right, to hold and continue such possession. This may happen, when one man invades the possession of another, and by force or surprise turns him out of the occupation of his lands; which is termed a disseisin, being a deprivation of that actual seisin, or corporal freehold of the lands, which the tenant before enjoyed. Or it may happen, that after the death of the ancestor and before the entry of the heir, or after the death of a particular tenant and before the entry of him in remainder or reversion, a stranger may contrive to get possession of the vacant land, and hold out him that had a right to enter. In all which cases, and many others that might be here suggested, the wrong doer has only a mere naked possesssion, which the rightful owner may put an end to by a variety of legal remedies. But in the mean time, till some act be done, by the rightful owner to divest this possession and assert his title, such actual possession is, *prima facie*, evidence of a legal title in the possessor; and it may, by length of time, and negligence of him who hath the right, by degrees ripen into a perfect and indefeasible title. And, at all events, without such actual possession, no title can be completely good. 2 *Black*. 196.

2. The next step to a good and perfect title is the right of possession, which may reside in one man, while the actual possession is not in himself but in another. For if a man be disseised, or otherwise kept out of possession, by any of the means before-mentioned, though the actual possession be lost, yet he has still remaining in him the right of possession, and may exert it whenever he thinks proper, by entering, upon the disseisor, and turning him out of that occupancy which he has so illegally gained. See *Limitations*.

And by stat. 32 *H*. 8. *c*. 9. it is provided, that no one shall sell or purchase any pretended right or title to land, unless the vendor hath received the profits thereof for one whole year before such grant, or hath been in actual possession of the land, or of the reversion or remainder; on pain that both purchaser and vendor shall each forfeit the value of such land to the king and the prosecutor.

TITLE OF ACTS OF PARLIAMENT. After the house of commons hath finally agreed (on a third reading) that a bill pass, the title to it is then settled; which used to be a general one, for all the acts passed in the session, till in the fifth year of *Hen*. 8. distinct titles were introduced for each chapter 1 *Black*. 182, 3.

TITLE TO THINGS PERSONAL. As to the title to things personal, or the various means of acquiring, and of losing such property as may be had therein. The methods of acquisition or loss are principally twelve: 1. By occupancy; 2. By prerogative; 3. By forfeiture; 4. By custom; 5. By succession; 6. By marriage; 7. By judgment; 8. By gift; 9. By contract; 10. By bankruptcy; 11. By testament; 12. By administration, which titles see.

TITLES OF CLERGY. A title, is an assurance that the party about to be ordained is to be appointed curate, or otherwise preferred to some ecclesiastical benefice, by certificate from the incumbent, or where the bishop, who ordains him, intends shortly afterwards to admit him to a benefice or curacy then void. *Count. Pars. Comp*. 2. 3.

And no person shall be ordained without a title; and this is required, to keep out those from the ministry who might otherwise for want of maintenance bring disgrace upon the church. And if a bishop shall admit any person into the ministry without any title, he shall maintain him till he prefers him to some ecclesiastical living; or if he refuses so to do, he shall be suspended from giving orders for one year. *Can.* 31.

TITLE TO THE CROWN. The crown is, by common law and constitutional custom, hereditary; and this in a manner peculiar to itself, inasmuch as that right of inheritance may, from time to time, be changed or limited by act of parliament; under which limitations the crown still continues hereditary. 1 *Black.* 191.

TITINYLKS. An old word for talebearers. *Cowell.*

TOALIA. A towel; and there is a tenure of lands by the service of waiting with a towel at the king's coronation. *Ibid.*

TOBACCO. By 12 *Car.* 2. *c.* 34. tobacco shall not be set in seed or plant, in England, Ireland (repealed as to Ireland, 19 *Geo.* 3. *c.* 35. and as to Guernsey, Jersey, or Scotland, by 22 *Geo.* 3. *c.* 73.), on forfeiture of all such tobacco, or of 40*s.* for every pole so planted.

Not to hinder planting tobacco in any physic garden, so as the quantity exceed not one-half of one pole, in any one such place or garden. *Ibid.*

By 15 *Car.* 2. *c.* 7. the penalty is increased to 10*l.* a pole, besides the former penalty.

By 22 & 23 *Car.* 2. *c.* 26. justices of peace shall issue warrants to constables, to search for tobacco sown, planted, or made, and destroy the same. Not destroying it, to forfeit 5*s.* for every rod of ground; and persons resisting the constable, shall forfeit 5*l.*

By 6 *Anne*, *c.* 22. no tobacco of the growth of Europe, or mixed therewith, shall be sold in any ships of war. But the same shall be the produce of the British plantations, whereon the duty has been paid, on pain of the purser's losing his place, and forfeiting 3*s.* for every pound sold.

By 1 *Geo.* 1. *c.* 46. tobacco shall not be adulterated, or mixed with leaves, herbs, or other materials; offering the same to sale, or to obtain drawback on exportation, shall forfeit 5*s.* for every pound weight, together with the leaves, and all utensils.

Houses may be searched at seasonable times, by warrant from two justices, and after seizure and condemnation, the leaves shall be burnt. *Ibid.*

Servants employed in adulterating tobacco, or vending the same, may be imprisoned six months. *Ibid.*

Persons mixing any snuff with oker, umber, or other colouring, or mixing any wood or dirt with snuff, or selling the same, shall forfeit the snuff, with 3*s.* per pound. *Ibid.* Also 5 *Geo.* 1. *c.* 11.

And by 29 *Geo.* 3. *c.* 68. no person shall cut walnut-tree, hop, sycamore, or other leaves, in imitation of *tobacco*, on penalty of forfeiture thereof and 200*l.*

TOBACCO-PIPE CLAY. Is prohibited to be exported, except to the British plantations. 13 & 14 *Car.* 2. *c.* 18. *s.* 8. 6 *Geo.* 1. *c.* 21. *s.* 32.

TOD OF WOOL. Twenty-eight pounds or two stone. 12 *Car.* 2. *cap.* 32.

TOFT, (*Toftum.*) A messuage, or rather a place or piece of ground where an house formerly stood. *West's Symb. par.* 2. Hence

TOFTMAN, (*Toftmanus.*) The owner or possessor of a toft. *Cowell.*

TOILE, (Fr. i. e. *Tela.*) A net to encompass or take deer, which is forbid to be used. See *Deer.*

TOKENS. See *False Tokens* and *Swindlers.*

TOLERATION. See *Dissenters* and *Roman Catholics.*

TOLL. To bar, defeat, or take away; as to toll the entry, i. e. to deny or take away the right of entry. 8 *Hen.* 6. *c.* 9. *Cowell.*

TOLL, (*Tolnetum vel Theolonium.*) Is a Saxon word, and properly a payment in towns, markets, and fairs, for goods and cattle bought and sold. It is a reasonable sum of money due to the owner of the fair or market, upon sale of things tollable within the same. 2 *Inst.* 220. 2 *Jones* 207.

But if the king grants to a man a fair or market, and grants no toll, the patentee shall have no toll; for toll being a matter of private right for the benefit of the lord, is not incident to a fair or market, as a court of piepowder is, which is for the benefit of the public and the advancement of justice, &c. And therefore such a fair or market is free from toll; and, after the grant made, the king cannot grant a toll to such free fair or market, without some proportionable benefit to the subject. And if the toll granted with the fair or market be outrageous, the grant of the toll is void, and the same is counted a free fair and market. 2 *Lutw.* 1336.

Toll is payable only on actual sale, unless by special custom. *Moor* 474. 1 *Wils.* 115. 2 *Str.* 1238. 2 *Inst.* 220. And when by custom a toll is due upon the sale of any goods in a fair or market, and he who ought to pay it refuses, an action on the case lies against him, and this is the proper remedy where goods are fraudulently sold out of the market to avoid the tolls. *Rol. Abr.* 103, 104, 106. *Cowp.* 661. If the king, or any of his progenitors, have granted to any one to be discharged of toll, either generally or specially, this grant is good to discharge him of all tolls at any of the king's *own* fairs or markets; and of the tolls that have been granted for any new fair or market created subsequent to such discharge. 2 *Inst.* 221. Also the king himself is exempt from toll. 2 *Inst.* 221. Likewise tenants in ancient demesne, whether they hold in fee for life, year, or at will. *Ibid.* 4 *Inst.* 269. *Roll. Abr.* 321. But this privilege does not extend to one who gets his living by buying and selling, but is annexed to the person in respect of the land, and to those things which grow and are the produce of the land. *Fitz. N. B.* 228. 2 *Leon.* 191. *Cro. Eliz.* 227.

If excessive toll be taken in a market-town, by the lord's consent, the franchise shall be seized; and if by other officers, they shall pay double damages, and suffer forty day's imprisonment, &c. *Stat. Westm.* 1. 3 *Edw.* I. c. 31.

And what shall be deemed reasonable is to be determined by the judges of the law, when it comes judicially before them.

There is also a prescription to have port oll for all goods coming into a man's port, and this without any consideration, but not to have toll of goods brought into a river, &c. 2 *Lev.* 96. 2 *Lut.* 1519. And the liberty of bringing goods into a port for safety, implies a consideration in itself. 3 *Lev.* 37. Prescription of toll for goods landed in a manor, or to have port-toll for all goods coming into port, is a good prescription. 2 *Mod.* 144.

—— *Toll Traverse,* is where one claimeth to have toll for every beast driven over his ground; for which a man may prescribe and distrain for it *in via Regia.* *Cro. Eliz.* 710. But a man cannot prescribe to have toll-traverse or thorough toll of men passing through a vill in the high street, because it is against the common law and common right; for the high street is common to all. 2 *Rol. Abr.* 522. 25 *Ass.* 58. And toll-traverse being to pass a nearer way, he that has it is to repair the way, because he receives money for it. 2 *Lil. Abr.* 585.

—— *Thorough-Toll,* is where a town prescribes to have toll for such a number of beasts, or for every beast that goeth through their town; or over a bridge or ferry, maintained at their cost, which is reasonable, though it be for passing through the king's highway, where every man may lawfully go, as it is for the ease of travellers that go that way. *Terms de Ley,* 561, 562. Persons may have this toll by prescription or grant; but it must be for a reasonable cause, which must be shewn, viz. that they are to repair and maintain a causeway, or a bridge, or such like. *Cro. Eliz.* 711.

—— *Turn-Toll.* A toll paid for beasts that are driven to market to be sold, and do return unsold. 6 *Rep.* 46.

TOLLAGE, is the same with tallage; signifying generally any manner of custom or imposition. 17 *Car.* I. *cap.* 17. *Cowell.*

TOLL-BOOTH. The place where goods are weighed. *Ibid.*

TOLL-CORN. Corn taken for toll ground at a mill. *Ibid.*

TOLL-HOP. A small dish or measure by which toll is taken in a market. *Ibid.*

TOLSESTER, (*Tolcestrum.*) An old excise, or duty paid by the tenants of some manors to the lord, for liberty to brew and sell ale. *Cowell.*

TOLSEY, (from the Sax. *tol,* i. e. *tributum,* and *see Sedes.*) Is the place where merchants meet, in a city or town of trade. *Ibid.*

TOLT. A writ whereby a cause depending in a court baron is removed into the country court. *Old Nat. Br.* 5.

TOLTA. Wrong, rapine, extortion, any thing exacted or imposed contrary to right and justice. *Cowell.*

TOMBS. See *Monument.*

TOMIN. A weight of twelve grains used by goldsmiths and jewellers. *Cowel..*

TONGUE. See *Felony,* article *Maiming.*

TONNAGE, (*Tonnagium.*) A custom or impost paid to the king for merchandiz carried out, or brought in ships, or suc like vessels, according to a certain rate upon every ton. *Cowell.*

TORCARE, is to comb and cleanse oxen. *Ibid.*

TORRA, (Sax. *Tor.*) A mount or hill. *Ibid.*

TORT, (from the Lat. *Tortus.*) Is a French word for injury or wrong; as, *de son tort de mesne,* in his own wrong. And wrong or injury is properly called tort, because it is wrested or crooked, and contrary to that which is right and straight. *Co. Lit.* 158.

TORTFEASOR, (Fr. *Tortfaiseur.*) A wrong-doer, a trespasser. *Ibid.*

TORTITIUM, signifies a torch. *Cowell.*

TORTURE. See *Paine forte & dure.*

TOTIES QUOTIES. As often as a thing shall happen. *Cowell.*

TOTTED. A good debt to the king, is by the foreign apposer or other officer in the exchequer noted for such by writing the word *tot* to it: and that which is paid shall be totted. Tot *pecuniæ regi debetur.* 42 *Ed.* 3. *c.* 9. 1 *Ed.* 6. *cap.* 15. *Cowell.*

TOURN. The sheriff's court so called. See *Turn.*

TOURNAMENTS. Martial exercises frequent in former ages, wherein the combatants fought with blunt weapons and in great companies; the intent of them was to inure men to the wars. *Cowell.* See *Justs.*

TOUT *tempus prist & encore est,* i. e. always was, and is at present ready; and is a kind of plea by way of excuse for him that is sued for any debt or duty. *Broke* 258.

TOWAGE, (*towagium,* Fr. *tavage.*) Is the drawing a ship or barge along the water by another ship or boat fastened to her, or by men or horses, &c. on land; it is also money which is given by bargemen to the owner of ground next a river where they tow a barg or other vessel. *Cowell.*

TOWN, (*Oppidum, Villa.*) Tithings, towns, and vills, are of the same signification in law. 1 *Black.* 114.

TRABARIÆ. Little boats, so called from their being made out of single beams, or pieces of timber cut hollow. *Cowell.*

TRABES in churches, what we now call branches, made usually with brass, but formerly with iron. *Ibid.*

TRACTUS. A trace by which horses in their gears draw a cart, plough, or waggon. *Ibid.*

TRADE. There is a difference between commerce and trade. The first relates to our dealings with foreign nations or our colonies abroad, the latter to our mutual traffick and dealings amongst ourselves at home together.

Persons serving seven years as apprentices to any trade, have an exclusive right to exercise that trade in any part of England. 5 *Eliz. c.* 4. *s.* 31.

This law, with respect to the exclusive part of it, has by turns been looked upon as a hard law, or as a beneficial one, according to the prevailing manner of the times, which has occasioned a great variety of resolutions in the courts of law concerning it; and attempts have been frequently made for its repeal, though hitherto without success. For at common law every man might use what trade he pleased. But this statute restrains that liberty to such as have served as apprentices: the adversaries to which provision say, that all restrictions (which tend to introduce monopolies) are pernicious to trade; the advocates for it alledge, that unskilfulness in trades is equally detrimental to the public as monopolies. This reason indeed only extends to such trades, in the exercise whereof skill is required: but another of their arguments goes much farther, viz. that "apprenticeships are useful to the common wealth, by employing of youth, and learning them to be early industrious; but that no one would be induced to undergo a seven years servitude, if others, though equally skilful, were allowed the same advantages without having undergone the same discipline. And Lord Coke says, this statute was not enacted only that workmen should be skilful, but also that youth should not be nourished in idleness, but brought up and educated in lawful sciences and trades. 11 *Co.* 54.

However, the resolutions of the courts, upon information for the penalty, which is 40*s.* a month, one half to the king, the other half to the prosecutor, have in general rather confined than extended the restriction; for no trades are held to be within the statute, but such as were in being at the making of it. *Lord Raym.* 514. for trading in a country village, apprenticeships are not requisite. 1 *Ventr.* 51. 2 *Keb.* 583.; and following the trade seven years, without any effectual prosecution, (either as a master or a servant,) is sufficient without an actual apprenticeship. *Lord Ray.* 1179. *Wallen* qui tam *v. Holton. Tr.* 33 *Geo.* 2.

If a bond or covenant restrains the exercise of a trade to a particular place only, if there was no consideration for it, it is void; but if there be a consideration, in that case it will be good. But if the restraint be general throughout England, although there be a consideration, it will be void, 2 *Lill. Abr.* 179. *Lord Raym.* 1436. 2 *Strange* 739.

TRADESMEN must be styled of their proper craft. 1 *Black.* 407. And there is in law, always, an implied contract with a workman, that he perform his business in a workmanlike manner; in which, if he fail, an action on the case lies to recover damages for such breach of his general undertaking. 11 *Rep.* 54. 1 *Saund.* 324. But if I employ a person to transact any of these concerns, whose common profession and business it is not, the law implies no such general undertaking; but, in order to charge him with damages, it must be on a special agreement. 3 *Black.* 160. 5.

TRAGA, A waggon without wheels. *Cowell.*

TRAIT. Bread of trait was formerly what we now call white-bread. *Ibid.*

TRAITORS. Persons guilty of high treason. See *Treason.*

TRANSCRIPT, is the copy of any original writing or deed, where it is written over again, or exemplified. *Cowell.*

TRANSCRIPTO *pedes finis levati mittendo in Cancellariam.* A writ for certifying the foot of a fine levied before justices in eyre, in the chancery. *Reg. Orig.* 669.

TRANSCRIPTO *Recognitionis factæ coram Justiciariis itinerantibus, &c.* is an old writ to certify a recognizance taken by justices in eyre. *Reg. Orig.* 152.

TRANSGRESSIONE. A writ or action of trespass. *Cowell.*

TRANSIRE, (from *transeo.*) Is used for a warrant from the custom-house, to let pass. 14 *Car.* 2. *cap.* 11.

TRANSITORY. Transitory actions are those that may be laid in any county or place; such as any personal action of debt, assumpsit, assault, or the like. See *Local*, and 3 *Black.* 294.

TRANSLATION, (*translatio.*) Is the removal of a bishop to another diocese, which is called translating. A bishop writes not *annus* consecrationis, but *anno* translationis *nostræ*, &c. And a bishop translated is not consecrated *de novo:* for a consecration is like an ordination, it is an indelible character, and holds good for ever. 3 *Salk.* 72. 1 *Salk.* 137.

TRANSPORTATION, is the banishing or sending away a criminal into another country. And by 24 *Geo.* 3. *c.* 56. if any offender shall be ordered by the court to be transported, or shall agree to transport himself, either for life or any number of years, and shall be afterwards at large before the expiration of the term, without lawful excuse, in any part of Great Britain or Ireland, he shall, being lawfully convicted thereof, suffer death without benefit of clergy.

TRANSUBSTANTIATION, (*transubstantiatio.*) Is a converting into another substance. To transubstantiate, i. e. *quid piam in aliam substantiam converto. Lit. Dict.* A declaration against the doctrine of transubstantiation used in the church of Rome is required by the stat. 30 *Car.* 2. *cap.* 1. See *Papists* and *Roman Catholics.*

TRAVELLERS. Innkeepers are by law obliged to receive travellers; and find them lodgings and necessary victuals. And on refusal, (a reasonable price being tendered,) they may be indicted and fined, or an action on the case lies against them. 2 *Hawk.* 225.

TRAVERSE, (from the Fr. *traverser.*) Is the denying of some matter of fact, alledged to be done in a declaration or pleadings; upon which the other side comes and affirms that it was done; and this makes a single and good issue for the cause to proceed to trial. And the formal words of a traverse are in our French *Sans ceo*, in Latin *absque hoc*, and in English without that, that such a thing was done or not, &c. *Kitch.* 217. *West. Symb. par.* 2. *Cowell.*

TRAVERSE OF AN INDICTMENT OR PRESENTMENT, is to take issue upon, and contradict or deny some chief point of it. As in a presentment against a person for a highway overflowed with water, for default of scouring a ditch, &c. he may traverse the matter, that there is no highway, or that the ditch is sufficiently scoured; or otherwise traverse the cause, viz. That he hath not the land, or he and they whose estate, &c. have not used to scour the ditch. *Lamb. Eiren*, 521. *Book Entr.* 4 *Black.* 345.

TRAVERSE OF AN OFFICE, is to prove that an inquisition made of lands or goods by the escheator, is defective and untruly made. *Vaugh* 64. 2 *Lil. Abr.* 590, 591. See *Inquisition of Office.*

TRAVERSUM, signifies a ferry. *Cowell.*

TRAWLERMEN, a kind of fishermen on the river Thames, who used unlawful arts and engines to destroy fish, of which some were termed tinckermen, or others hebbermen, and trawlermen, &c. Hence to trowl or trawl for pikes. *Cowell.*

TRAYLBASTON. Edward the First, in his 32d year sent out a new writ of inquisition, called Trailbaston, against intruders on other men's lands, who, to oppress the right owner, would make over their lands to great men; against batterers hired to beat men, breakers of the peace, ravishers, incendiaries, murderers, fighters, false assisors, and other such malefactors: which inquisition was so strictly executed, and such fines taken, that it brought in great treasure to the king. 4 *Inst.* 186. Afterwards in a parliament 1 *Ric.* 2. the commons petitioned the king, that no commission of Eyre or Traylbaston might be issued during the wars, or for twenty years to come. *Cowell.*

TRAYTOR. See *Treason.*

T. R. E. *Tempore Regis Edwardi.* These initial letters have this continual note of time in the domesday register, where the valuation of manors is recounted, what it was in the time of Edward the Confessor: and what since the conquest. *Cowell.*

TREASON, (from the French *trahir*, to betray, and *trahison*, betraying, contracted into treason. Latin *proditio*,) is a crime of the highest nature, and imports a betraying, treachery, or breach of faith.

It therefore only happens between allies, saith the *Mirror*, c. 1. § 7. for treason is indeed a general appellation made use of by the law, to denote not only offences against the king and government, but also that accumulation of guilt that arises whenever a superior reposes a confidence in a subject or inferior, between whom and himself there subsists a natural, a civil, or even a spiritual relation: and the inferior so abuses that confidence, so forgets the obligations of duty, subjection, and allegiance, as to destroy the life of any such superior or lord. This is looked upon as proceeding from the same principle of treachery in private life, as would have urged him who harbours it to have conspired in public against his liege lord and sovereign, and therefore for a wife to kill her lord or husband, a servant his lord or master, and an ecclesiastic his lord or ordinary; these being breaches of the lower allegiance of private and domestic faith, are denominated petit treasons.

But when disloyalty so rears its crest as to attack even majesty itself, it is called by way of distinction high treason, *alta proditio;* being equivalent to the *crimen laesae majestatis* of the Romans, as Glanvil denominates it also in our English law.

As this is the highest civil crime, which (considered as a member of the community) any man can possibly commit, it ought therefore to be the most precisely ascertained. And yet, by the ancient common law, there was a great latitude left in the breast of the judges, to determine what was treason, or not so: whereby the creatures of tyrannical princes had opportunity to create abundance of constructive treasons; that is, to raise, by forced and arbitrary constructions, offences into the crime and punishment of treason, which were never suspected to be such. Thus the accroaching, or attempting to exercise, royal power (a very uncertain charge) was in the 21 *Edw.* 3. held to be treason in a knight of Hertfordshire, who forcibly assaulted and detained one of the king's subjects till he paid him 90*l.* a crime well deserving of punishment: but which seems to be of a complexion very different from that of treason. Killing the king's father, or brother, or even his messenger, has also fallen under the same denomination. But however, to prevent the inconveniences which began to arise in England from this multitude of constructive treasons, the stat. 25 *Edw.* 3. *c.* 2. was made; which defines what offences only for the future should be held to be treason. This statute comprehends all sorts of high treason under seven distinct branches.

1. "When a man doth compass or imagine the death of our lord the king, or of our lady his queen, or of their eldest son and heir." Under this description it is held that a queen regnant (such as queen Elizabeth and queen Anne) is within the words of the act, being invested with royal power and entitled to the allegiance of her subjects: but the husband of such a queen is not comprised within these words, and therefore no treason can be committed against him, 3 *Inst.* 7. 1. *Hal. P. C.* 106. The king here intended is the king in possession, without any respect to his title: for it is held, that a king *de facto* and not *de jure*, or in other words an usurper that hath got possession of the throne, is a king within the meaning of the statute; as there is a temporary allegiance due to him, for his administration of the government, and temporary protection of the public: and therefore treasons committed against Henry VI. were punished under Edward IV. though all the line of Lancaster had been previously declared usurpers by act of parliament. But the most rightful heir of the crown, or king *de jure* and not *de facto*, who hath never had plenary possession of the throne, as was the case of the house of York during the three reigns of the line of Lancaster, is not a king within this statute against whom treasons may be committed. And by stat. 11 *Hen.* 7. *c.* 1. which is declaratory of the common law, all subjects are excused from any penalty or forfeiture "which do assist and obey a king *de facto*." It is, however, to be observed, that the statute of Henry VII. does by no means command any opposition to the king *de jure*; but only excuses the obedience paid to a king *de facto*. When therefore a usurper is in possession, the subject is excused and justified in obeying and giving him assistance: otherwise, under a usurpation, no man could be safe; if the lawful prince had a right to hang him for obedience to the powers in being, as the usurper would certainly do for disobedience, 4 *Black.* 76. Also a king who has resigned his crown, such resignation being admitted and ratified in parliament, is according to sir Matthew Hale no longer the object of treason. And the same reason holds, in case a king abdicates the government; or by actions subversive of the constitution, virtually renounces the authority which he claims by that very constitution: since, when the fact of abdication is once established, and determined by the proper judges, the consequence necessarily follows, that the throne is thereby vacant, and he is no longer king. 1 *Black.* 212.

As to what is a compassing or imagining the death of the king, these are synonymous terms; the word compass signifying the purpose or design of the mind or will, and not, as in common speech, the carrying such a design to effect. And therefore an accidental stroke, which may mortally wound the sovereign, *per infortunium*, without any traiterous intent, is no treason: as was the case of sir Walter Tyrrel, who, by the command of king William Rufus, shooting at a hart, the arrow glanced against a tree, and killed the king on the spot. But as this compassing or imagining is an act of the mind, it cannot possibly fall under any judicial cognizance, unless it be demonstrated by some open or overt act of a full and explicit nature, to convict the traitor upon. The statute expressly requires, that the accused "be thereof upon sufficient proof attainted of some open act by men of his own condition." Thus, to provide weapons or ammunition for the purpose of killing the king, is held to be a palpable overt act of treason in imagining his death. To conspire to imprison the king by force, and move towards it by assembling company, is an overt act of compassing the king's death; for all force used to the person of the king, in its consequence may tend to his death, and is a strong presumption of something worse intended than the present force, by such as have so far thrown off their bounden duty to their sovereign; it being an old observation, that there is generally but a short interval between the prisons and the graves of princes. There is no question also, but that taking any measures to render such treasonable purposes effectual, as assembling and consulting on the means to kill the king, is a sufficient overt act of high-treason. 1 *Hawk. P. C.* 38. 1 *Hal. P.C.* 119.

And in every indictment for this species of treason, and indeed for levying war, or adhering to the king's enemies, an overt act must be alledged and proved. For the overt act is the charge, to which the prisoner must apply his defence. But it is not necessary, that the whole of the evidence intended to be given, should be set forth; the common law never required this exactness, nor doth the statute of king William require it. It is sufficient, that the charge be reduced to a reasonable certainty, so that the defendant may be apprized of the nature of it, and prepared to give an answer to it. *Fost.* 194.

On this subject Mr. Justice Foster observes that, in the case of the king the statute of treasons hath, with great propriety, retained the rule *voluntas pro facto.* The principle upon which this is founded, is too obvious to need much enlargement. The king is considered as the head of the body-politic, and the members of that body are considered as united and kept together by a political union with him and with each other. His life cannot, in the ordinary course of things be taken away by treasonable practices, without involving a whole nation in blood and confusion; consequently every stroke levelled at his person is, in the ordinary course of things, levelled at the public tranquillity. The law, therefore, tendereth the safety of the king with an anxious concern; and with a concern bordering upon jealousy. It considereth the wicked imaginations of the heart in the same degree of guilty as if carried into actual execution from the moment measures appear to have been taken to render them effectual. And therefore, if conspirators meet and consult how to kill the king, though they do not then fall upon any scheme for that purpose, this is an overt-act of compassing his death; and so are all means made use of, be it advice, persuasion, or command, to incite or encourage others to commit the fact, or join in the attempt; and every person who but assenteth to any overtures for that purpose will be involved in the same guilt. *Fost.* 194.

The care the law hath taken for the personal safety of the king is not confined to actions or attempts of the more flagitious kind, to assassination or poison, or other attempts directly and immediately aiming at his life. It is extended to every thing wilfully and deliberately done or attempted, whereby his life may be endangered. And, therefore, the entering into measures for deposing or imprisoning him, or to get his person into the power of the conspirators, these offences are overt acts of treason within this breach of the statute. For experience has shewn, that between the prisons and the graves of princes the distance is very small. *Fost.* 194.

And this was the species of treason with which the state prisoners were charged, who were tried in 1794. And the question, as stated by the court for the jury to try was, Whether their measures had been entered into with an intent to subvert the monarchy and to depose the king. *Hardy's trial.*

How far mere words, spoken by an individual, and not relative to any treasonable act or design then in agitation, shall amount to treason, has been formerly matter of doubt. We have two instances in the reign of Edward the Fourth, of persons executed for treasonable words: the one a citizen of London, who said he would make his son heir of the crown, being the sign of the house in which he lived; the other a gentleman, whose favourite buck the king killed in hunting, whereupon he wished it, horns and all, in the king's belly.* These were esteemed hard cases, and the chief justice Markham rather chose to leave his place than assent to the latter judgment. But now it seems clearly to be agreed, that by the common law and the statute of Edward III. words spoken amount only to a high misdemeanor, and no treason. For they may be spoken in heat, without any intention, or be mistaken, perverted, or mis-remembered by the hearers; their meaning depends always on their connexion with other words and things; they may signify differently even according to the tone of voice with which they are delivered; and sometimes silence itself is more expressive than any discourse. As, therefore, there can be nothing more equivocal and ambiguous than words, it would indeed be unreasonable to make them amount to high treason. And accordingly in 4 *Car.* 1. on a reference to all the judges, concerning some very atrocious words spoken by one Pyne, they certified to the king, " that though the words were as wicked as might be, yet they were no treason; for, unless it be by some particular statute, no words will be treason. But if words are attended or followed by a consultation, meeting, or any act, then they will be evidence, or a confession, of

* There was even a refinement and degree of subtlety in the cruelty of that case, for he wished it, horns and all, in the belly of him who counselled the king to kill it; and as the king killed it of his own accord, or was his own counsellor, it was held to be a treasonable wish against the king himself. 1 *Hal. P. C.* 115.

the intent of such consultation, meeting, or act; yet loose words not relative to facts, are at the worst no more than bare indications of the malignity of the heart. *Fost.* 202.

If the words be set down in writing, it argues more deliberate intention: and it has been held that writing is an overt act of treason; for *scribere est agere.* But even in this case the bare words are not the treason, but the deliberate act of writing them. And such writing, though unpublished, has in some arbitrary reigns convicted its author of treason: particularly in the cases of one Peachum, a clergyman, for treasonable passages in a sermon never preached; and of Algernon Sydney, for some papers found in his closet; which, had they been plainly relative to any previous formed design of dethroning or murdering the king, might doubtless have been properly read in evidence as overt acts of that treason, which was specially laid in the indictment. But being merely speculative, without any intention (so far as appeared) of making any public use of them, the convicting the authors of treason upon such an insufficient foundation has been universally disapproved. Peachum was therefore pardoned; and though Sydney indeed was executed, yet it was to the general discontent of the nation; and his attainder was afterwards reversed by parliament. There was then no manner of doubt but that the publication of such a treasonable writing was a sufficient overt act of treason at the common law, though of late even that has been questioned. 4 *Black.* 81.

2. The second species of treason is, "if a man do violate the king's companion, or the king's eldest daughter unmarried, or the wife of the king's eldest son and heir." By the king's companion is meant his wife; and by violation is understood carnal knowledge, as well without force as with it: and this is high treason in both parties, if both be consenting; as some of the wives of Henry the Eighth by fatal experience evinced. The plain intention of this law is to guard the blood royal from any suspicion of bastardy, whereby the succession to the crown might be rendered dubious; and therefore, when this reason ceases, the law ceases with it; for to violate a queen or princess dowager is held to be no treason: in like manner as, by the feodal law, it was a felony, and attended with a forfeiture of the fief, if the vassal vitiated the wife or daughter of his lord; but not so, if he only vitiated his widow.

3. The third species of treason is, "if a man do levy war against our lord the king in his realm." And this may be done by taking arms, not only to dethrone the king, but under pretence to reform religion, or the laws, or to remove evil counsellers, or other grievances whether real or pretended.* For the law does not, neither can it, permit any private man, or set of men, to interfere forcibly in matters of such high importance; especially as it has established a sufficient power, for these purposes, in the high court of parliament: neither does the constitution justify any private or particular resistance for private or particular grievances. 4 *Black.* 81, 2.

To resist the king's forces, by defending a castle against them, is a levying of war; and so is an insurrection with an avowed design to pull down all inclosures, all brothels, and the like; the universality of the design making it a rebellion against the state, an usurpation of the powers of government, and an insolent invasion of the king's authority. But a tumult with a view to pull down a particular house, or lay open a particular inclosure, amount at most to a riot; this being no general defiance of public government. So, if two subjects quarrel and levy war against each other, (in that spirit of private war which prevailed all over Europe in the early feodal times,) it is only a great riot and contempt, and no treason. Thus it happened between the earls of Hereford and Gloucester in 20 Edward I. who raised each a little army, and committed outrages upon each other's lands, burning houses, attended with the loss of many lives: yet this was held to be no high treason, but only a great misdemeanor. 1 *Hal. P. C.* 136.

A bare conspiracy to levy war does not amount to this species of treason; but if particularly pointed at the person of the king or his government, it falls within the first, of compassing or imagining the king's death.

4. "If a man be adherent to the king's enemies in his realm, giving to them aid and comfort in the realm, or elsewhere," he is also declared guilty of high treason. This must likewise be proved by some overt act, as by giving them intelligence, by sending them provisions, by selling them arms, by treacherously surrendering a fortress, or the like. By enemies are here understood the subjects of foreign powers with whom we are at open war. As to foreign pirates or robbers, who may

---

* Lord Mansfield declared, upon the trial of Lord George Gordon, that it was the unanimous opinion of the court, that an attempt, by intimidation and violence, to force the repeal of a law, was levying war against the king, and high treason. *Doug.* 570.

happen to invade our coasts, without any open hostilities between their nation and our own, and without any commission from any prince or state at enmity with the crown of Great Britain, the giving them any assistance is also clearly treason; either in the light of adhering to the public enemies of the king and kingdom, or else in that of levying war against his majesty. And, most indisputably, the same acts of adherence or aid, which (when applied to foreign enemies) will constitute treason under this branch of the statute, will (when afforded to our own fellow-subjects in actual rebellion at home) amount to high treason under the description of levying war against the king. But to relieve a rebel, fled out of the kingdom, is no treason: for the statute is taken strictly, and a rebel is not an enemy; an enemy being always the subject of some foreign prince, and one who owes no allegiance to the crown of England. And if a person be under circumstances of actual force and constraint, through a well-grounded apprehension of injury to his life or person, this fear or compulsion will excuse his even joining with either rebels or enemies in the kingdom, provided he leaves them whenever he hath a safe opportunity.

5. "If a man counterfeit the king's great or privy seal," this is also high treason. But if a man takes wax bearing the impression of the great seal off from one patent, and fixes it to another, this is held to be only an abuse of the seal, and not a counterfeiting of it; as was the case of a certain chaplain, who in such manner framed a dispensation for nonresidence. But the knavish artifice of a lawyer much exceeded this of the divine. One of the clerks in chancery glewed together two pieces of parchment; on the uppermost of which he wrote a patent, to which he regularly obtained the great seal, the label going through both the skins. He then dissolved the cement; and taking off the written patent, on the blank skin wrote a fresh patent, of a different import from the former, and published it as true. This was held no counterfeiting of the great seal, but only a great misprision; and Sir Edward Coke mentions it with some indignation, that the party was living at that day. 3 *Inst.* 16.

6. The sixth species of treason under this statute, is, "if a man counterfeit the king's money; and if a man bring false money into the realm counterfeit to the money of England, knowing the money to be false, to merchandise and make payment withal." As to the first branch, counterfeiting the king's money; this is treason, whether the false money be uttered in payment or not. Also, if the king's own minters alter the standard or alloy established by law, it is treason. But gold and silver money only are held to be within the statute. With regard likewise to the second branch, importing foreign counterfeit money, in order to utter it here, it is held that uttering it, without importing it, is not within the statute.

7. The last species of treason ascertained by this statute, is, "if a man slay the chancellor, treasurer, or the king's justices of the one bench or the other, justices in eyre, or justices of assise, and all other justices assigned to hear and determine, being in their places doing their offices." These high magistrates, as they represent the king's majesty during the execution of their offices, are therefore for the time equally regarded by the law. But this statute extends only to the actual killing of them, and not wounding, or a bare attempt to kill them. It extends also only to the officers therein specified, and therefore the barons of the exchequer, as such, are not within the protection of this act.

By the statute 7 *Anne*, c. 21. it is made high treason to slay any lords of session, or lords of justiciary, sitting in judgment; or to counterfeit the king's seals appointed by the act of union. This statute 7 *Anne*, c. 21. has also enacted that the crimes of high treason and misprision of treason shall be exactly the same in England and Scotland; and that no acts in Scotland, except those above specified, shall be construed high treason in Scotland, which are not high treason in England.

And all persons prosecuted in Scotland for high treason, or misprision of treason, shall be tried by a jury, and in the same manner as if they had been prosecuted for the same crime in England.

And by 1 *Mar.* s. 1. c. 1. no act or offence shall be treason, petit treason, or misprision, but such as by 25 *Ed.* 3. s. 5. c. 2. are so declared.

The new treasons, created since the stat. 1 *Mar.* c. 1. and not comprehended under the description of statute of Edw. 3. fall under three heads: 1. Such as relate to papists; 2. Such as relate to falsifying the coin or other royal signatures; 3. Such as are created for the security of the protestant succession in the house of Hanover. 4 *Black.* 87.

1. The first species relates to Papists.

By stat. 5 *Eliz.* c. 1. to defend the Pope's jurisdiction in this realm is, for the first time, a heavy misdemeanor; and, if the offence be repeated, it is high treason. Also by stataute 27 *Eliz.* c. 2. if any popish priest, born in the dominions of the crown of England, shall come over hither from beyond the seas, unless driven by stress of weather, and departing in a reasonable time, or shall tarry here three days without conforming to the church, and taking the oaths, he is guilty of high treason. And by statute 3 *Jac.* 1. *c.* 4. if any natural-born subject be withdrawn from his allegiance, and reconciled to the Pope or see of Rome, or any other prince or state, both he and all such as procure such reconciliation, shall incur the guilt of high treason.

The reason of distinguishing these overt-acts of popery from all others, by setting the mark of high treason upon them, is on a civil, and not on a religious account. For every popish priest of course renounces his allegiance to his temporal sovereign upon taking orders; that being inconsistent with his new engagements of canonical obedience to the pope: and the same may be said of an obstinate defence of his authority here, or a formal reconciliation to the see of Rome, which the statute construes to be a withdrawing from one's natural allegiance; and therefore, besides being reconciled "to the pope," it also adds, "or any other prince or state. 4 *Black.* 87, 8.

2. In consequence of glaring outrages, publicly offered to the person of the king, innumerable seditious publications, tending to the total subversion of the government, and frequent seditious meetings, an act was passed in the 36th year of his present majesty's reign, intitled, "An act for the safety and preservation of his majesty's person and government against treasonable and seditious practices and attempts." By which it was enacted, that if any person shall compass, imagine, or intend death, destruction, or any bodily harm to the person of the king, or to depose him, or to levy war in order by force to compel him to change his measures or councils, or to overawe either house of parliament, or to excite an invasion of any of his majesty's dominions, and shall express and declare such intentions by printing, writing, or any overt-act, he shall suffer death as a traitor. *s.* 1.

And if any one by writing, printing, preaching, or other speaking, shall use any words or sentences to incite the people to hatred and contempt of the king, or of the government and constitution of this realm, he shall incur the punishment of a high misdemeanor; that is, fine, imprisonment, and pillory: and for a second offence he is subject to a similar punishment, or transportation for seven years, at the discretion of the court. *s.* 2. 3.

But a prosecution for a misdemeanor under this act must be brought within six months. And this statute shall not affect any prosecution for the same crimes by the common law, unless a prosecution be previously commenced under the statute. This statute is to continue in force until the end of the next session of parliament after the demise of the crown. 36 *Geo.* 3. *c.* 7.

3. The only two offences made treasons relative to the coin or other royal signatures, by the statute 25 *Edw.* 3. are the "actual counterfeiting the gold and silver coin of this kingdom; or the importing such counterfeit money with intent to utter it, knowing it to be false." But these not being found sufficient to restrain the evil practices of coiners and false moneyers, other statutes have been since made for that purpose. The crime itself is made a species of high treason; as being a breach of allegiance, by infringing the king's prerogative, and assuming one of the attributes of the sovereign, to whom alone it belongs to set the value and denomination of coin made at home, or to fix the currency of foreign money: and besides, as all money which bears the stamp of the kingdom is sent into the world upon the public faith, as containing metal of a particular weight, and standard, whoever falsifies this is an offender against the state, by contributing to render that public faith suspected. 4 *Black.* 88.

And by statute 1 *Mar. st.* 2. *c.* 6. 1. That "if any person falsely forge or counterfeit any such kind of coin of gold or silver, as is not the proper coin of this realm, but shall be current within this realm by consent of the crown; or, 2. shall falsely forge or counterfeit the sign manual, privy signet, or privy seal; such offences shall be deemed high treason.

And by stat. 1 & 2 *P.* & *M. c.* 11. if any persons do bring into this realm such false or counterfeit foreign money, being current here, knowing the same to be false, with intent to utter the same in payment, they shall be deemed offenders in high treason. The money referred to in these statutes must be such as is absolutely current here, in all payments, by the king's proclamation; of which there is none at present, therefore to counterfeit it is not high treason, but another inferior offence.*

---

* That is to say, by 37 *Geo.* 3. *c.* 126. if any person shall coin or counterfeit any kind of foreign gold or silver coin, though not current within this realm, he shall be guilty of felony, and may be transported for seven years; and if any person knowingly and fraudulently shall bring any counterfeit coin into the kingdom, he shall be subject to the same punishment.

And if any person knowingly utter, or tender in payment, or pay any such counterfeit foreign coin, for the first offence he shall be imprisoned six months, and find sureties for his good behaviour for six

Clipping or defacing the genuine coin was not hitherto included in these statutes; though an offence equally pernicious to trade, and an equal insult upon the prerogative, as well as personal affront to the sovereign, whose very image ought to be had in reverence by all loyal subjects. And now, by statute 5 *Eliz. c.* 11. clipping, washing, rounding, or filing, for wicked gain's sake, any of the money of this realm, or other money suffered to be current here, shall be adjudged high treason; and by statute 18 *Eliz. c.* 1. ("because the same law, being penal, ought to be taken and expounded strictly according to the words thereof, and the like offences, not by any equity to receive the like punishment or pains") the same species of offence is therefore described in other more general words, viz. impairing, diminishing, falsifying, scaling, and lightening; and made liable to the same penalties. By statute 8 & 9 *W.* 3. *c.* 26. made perpetual by 7 *Anne*, c. 25. whoever, without proper authority, shall knowingly make or mend, or assist in so doing, or shall buy, sell, conceal, hide, or knowingly have in his possession, any implements of coinage specified in the act, or other tools or instruments proper only for the coinage of money; or shall convey the same out of the king's mint; he, together with his counsellors, procurers, aiders, and abettors, shall be guilty of *high treason*; which is by much the severest branch of the coinage law. The statute goes on farther, and enacts, that to mark any coin on the edges with letters, or otherwise, in imitation of those used in the mint; or to colour, gild, or case over any coin resembling the current coin, or even round blanks of base metal, shall be construed high treason. But all prosecutions on this act are to be commenced within three months after the commission of the offence: except those for making or amending any coining tool or instrument, or for marking money round the edges; which are directed to be commenced within six months after the offence committed.* And lastly, by statute 15 & 16 *Geo.* 2. c. 28. if any person colours or alters any shilling or sixpence, either lawful or counterfeit, to make them respectively resemble a guinea or half-guinea; or any halfpenny or farthing to make them respectively resemble a shilling or sixpence; this is also high treason: but the offender shall be pardoned, in case (being out of prison) he discovers and convicts two other offenders of the same kind.

4. The other new species of high treason is such as is created for the security of the protestant succession over and above such treasons against the king and government as were comprized under the statute 25 Edw. 3. For this purpose, by the stat. 1 *Anne, st.* 2. *c.* 17. if any person shall endeavour to deprive or hinder any person, being the next in succession to the crown according to the limitations of the act of settlement, from succeeding to the crown, and shall maliciously and directly attempt the same by any overt act, such offence shall be high treason. And by stat. 6 *Anne*, c. 7. if any person shall maliciously, advisedly, and directly, by writing or printing, maintain and affirm, that any other person hath any right or title to the crown of this realm, otherwise than according to the act of settlement: or that the kings of this realm, with the authority of parliament, are not able to make laws and statutes, to bind the crown and the descent thereof; such person shall be guilty of high treason.

In cases of high treason, whereby corruption of blood may ensue, (except treason in counterfeiting the king's coin or seals,) or misprision of such treason, it is enacted by statute 7 *W.* 3. c. 3. first, that no person shall be tried for any such treason, except an attempt to assassinate the king, unless the indictment be found within three years after the offence committed: next, that the prisoner shall have a copy of the indictment, (which includes the caption,) but not the names of the witnesses, five days at least before the trial; that is, upon the true construction of the act, before his arraignment; for then is his time to take any exceptions thereto, by way of plea or demurrer: thirdly, that he shall also have a copy of the pannel or jurors two days before his trial: and, lastly, that he shall have the same compulsive process to bring in his witnesses *for* him, as was usual to compel their appearance *against* him. And,

---

more; for the second offence he shall be imprisoned two years; and for the third he shall be guilty of a capital felony.

And if any person, without lawful excuse, shall have more than five such counterfeit pieces in his custody, he may be convicted before a justice, and forfeit from 40s. to 5*l.* for each piece, and for failure of payment may be imprisoned three months.

* If a person is apprehended in the act of coining, or is proved to have made a considerable progress in making counterfeit pieces resembling the gold or silver coin of this realm, yet if they are so imperfect as that no one would take them, he cannot be convicted upon the charge of coining under this statute. *Leach*, 71. 126. But he may be convicted, if he has made blank pieces without any impression to the similitude of silver coin worn smooth by time. *Welch's Case, Ibid.* 293.

by statute 7 *Ann.* c. 21. (which did not take place till after the decease of the late pretender), all persons indicted for high treason or misprision thereof, shall have not only a copy of the indictment, but a list of all the witnesses to be produced, and of the jurors impannelled, with their professions and places of abode, delivered to him ten days before the trial, and in the presence of two witnesses; the better to prepare him to make his challenges and defence. But this last act, so far as it affected indictments for the inferior species of high treason, respecting the coin and the royal seals, is repealed by the stat. 6 *Geo.* 3. *c.* 53. else it had been impossible to have tried those offences in the same circuit in which they are indicted; for ten clear days, between the finding and the trial of the indictment, will exceed the time usually allotted for any session of oyer and terminer. And no person indicted for felony is, or (as the law stands) ever can be, entitled to such copies, before the time of his trial. *Fost.* 250.

It is the practice to deliver the copy of the indictment, and the lists of witnesses and jurors, ten clear days, exclusive of the day of delivery and the day of trial, and of intervening Sundays previous to the trial. *Fost.* 2. 250.

And by the 39 & 40 *Geo.* 3. *c.* 93. it is enacted, that in all cases of high treason, in compassing or imagining the death of the king, or in misprision of such treason, where the overt act of such treason shall be alleged in the indictment to be the assassination of the king, or a direct attempt against his life or person, the person accused shall be indicted and tried in the same manner in every respect and upon the like evidence, as if he was charged with murder. But the judgment and execution shall remain the same as in other cases of high treason.

The punishment of high treason in general, is very solemn and terrible. 1. That the offender be drawn to the gallows, and not be carried or walk; though usually (by connivance, at length ripened by humanity into law) a sledge or hurdle is allowed, to preserve the offender from the extreme torment of being dragged on the ground or pavement. 2. That he be hanged by the neck, and then cut down alive. 3. That his entrails be taken out, and burned, while he is yet alive. 4. That his head be cut off. 5. That his body be divided into four parts. 6. That his head and quarters be at the king's disposal. 1 *Hal. P. C.* 382. 3 *Inst.* 211.

The king may, and often doth, discharge all the punishment, except beheading, especially, where any of noble blood are attainted. For, beheading, being part of the judgment that may be executed, though all the rest be omitted by the king's command. 1 *Hal. P. C.* 351. But where beheading is no part of the judgment, as in murder or other felonies, it hath been said that the king cannot change the judgment, though at the request of the party, from one species of death to another.

In the case of coining, which is a treason of a different complexion from the rest, the punishment is milder for male offenders; being only to be drawn, and hanged by the neck till dead. And in treasons of every kind, the punishment of women, from the decency due to the sex, which forbids the exposing and publicly mangling their bodies, the sentence is now, by the statute 30 *Geo.* 3. *c.* 48. that women convicted in all cases of treason, shall receive judgment to be drawn to the place of execution, and there be hanged by the neck till dead.

For the consequences of this judgment, see *Titles*, *Attainder*, *Forfeiture*, and *Corruption of Blood*.

PETIT-TREASON. See *Homicide*.

TREASURE, (*thesaurus*,) signifies riches and wealth; and as the king's treasure is the honour and safety of the king, for this reason mines of gold and silver belong to the king. *Cowell.*

TREASURER, (*thesaurarius.*) Is an officer to whom the treasure of another is committed to be kept, and truly disposed of. Thus we have the lord treasurer of England, who is a lord by his office, and one of the greatest men of the kingdom. He holds his place *durante bene-placito*, by the delivery of a white staff. He is also treasurer of the exchequer, by letters patent. Under the charge and government of the lord treasurer, is all the king's wealth contained in the exchequer; he has the check of all the officers employed in collecting the customs and royal revenues; all the offices of the customs in all ports of England are in his gift and disposition; escheators in every county are nominated by him; and he makes leases of all the lands belonging to the crown, &c. *Cowell.*

But the high and important post of lord treasurer has of late years, like some other great offices, such as the lord high admiral, been esteemed too great a task for one person, and been generally committed by the crown to the commissioners of the exchequer. *Ibid.*

Besides the lord treasurer, there is a treasurer of the king's household, who is of the privy council, a treasurer of the navy, treasurer of the ordnance, and other treasurers of corporations, &c. *Ibid.*

TREASURER, *in Cathedral Churches.* An officer whose charge was to take care of the vestments, plate, jewels, relics, and other treasure belonging to the churches. *Ibid.*

TREASURER *of the County.* Is he that keeps the county stock. See *County Rates.*

TREASURE-TROVE, (*thesaurus inventus.*) Is where any money is found hid in the earth, but not lying upon the ground, and no man knows to whom it belongs; then the property thereof belongs to the king, or the lord of the manor by special grant or prescription. But if the owner may any ways be known, it doth not belong to the king or lord of the liberty, but such owner. *Bract. lib.* 3. 3 *Inst.* 132. *Kitch.* 80. But nothing is said to be treasure-trove but gold and sliver, and concealing treasure found, and not making it known to the coroner, is punished by fine and imprisonment. *Britton. cap.* 17. *S. P. C.* 25.

TREASURY. The place where the king's treasure is deposited. *Cowell.*

TREATIES. It is the king's prerogative to make treaties, leagues, and alliances with foreign states and princes. 1 *Bl.* 257.

TREBUCHET, *Trebucket, Tribush,* (*terbichetum.*) A tumbrel or cucking-stool. Also a great engine to cast stones, to batter walls. 3 *Inst.* 219. See *Castigatory.*

TREES. See *Trespass* and *Waste.*

TREET, (*triticum.*) Fine wheat. Stat. 51 *Hen.* 3. *Cowell.*

TREMAGIUM, *Tremesium, Termisium.* The season or time of sowing summer corn, being about March, the third month. *Cowell.*

TREMELLOM. A granary. *Ibid.*

TRENCHEATOR, (from the Fr. *trancher,* to cut.) A carver of meat at a table. *Ibid.*

TRENCHIA. A trench, or dyke newly cut. *Ibid.*

TRENTAL, (Fr. *Trentale.*) An office for the dead, that continued thirty days, consisting of thirty masses. *Ibid.*

TREPGET. A great engine to throw stones against a wall in storming a town. *Ibid.*

TRESAYLE. A writ sued on ouster by abatement, on the death of the grandfather's grandfather—now obsolete. 4 *Black.* 186.

TRESPASS, (*Transgressio.*) Is any transgression of the law under treason, felony, or misprision of either. But it is most constantly used for that wrong or damage which is done by one private man to another: and it is of two sorts; 1. Trespass general, otherwise called trespass *vi & armis*: and 2. Trespass special, or upon the case. *Bro. Trespass. Bract. lib.* 4.

Trespass, in its largest and most extensive sense, signifies any transgression or offence against the law of nature, of society, or of the country in which we live, whether it relates to a man's person or his property. Therefore, beating another is a trespass, for which an action of trespass *vi et armis* in assault and battery will lie: taking or detaining a man's goods are respectively trespasses, for which an action of trespass *vi et armis,* or on the case in trover and conversion, is given by the law; so also non-performance of promises or undertakings is a trespass, upon which an action of trespass on the case in assumpsit is grounded; and, in general, any misfeasance, or act of one man, whereby another is injuriously treated or damnified, is a transgression, or trespass in its largest sense; for which, whenever the act itself is directly and immediately injurious to the person or property of another, and therefore necessarily accompanied with some force, an action of trespass *vi et armis* will lie; but if the injury is only consequential, a special action of trespass on the case may be brought. 3 *Black.* 208. 9.

In a limited and confined sense, it signifies no more than an entry on another man's ground without a lawful authority, and doing some damage, however inconsiderable, to his real property. And every entry upon another's lands, (unless by the owner's leave, or in some very particular cases), is an injury or wrong, for satisfaction of which an action of trespass will lie, subject as to the quantum of satisfaction, by considering how far the offence was wilful or inadvertent, and by estimating the value of the actual damage sustained.

Every unwarrantable entry on another's soil the law therefore entitles a trespass by breaking his close; and the words of the writ of trespass command the defendant to shew cause, *quare clausum querentis fregit.* For every man's land is in the eye of the law inclosed and set apart from his neighbour's: and that either by a visible and material fence, as one field is divided from another by a hedge; or, by an ideal invisible boundary, existing only in the contemplation of law, as when one man's land adjoins to another's in the same field. And every such entry or breach of a man's close, carries necessarily along with it some damage or other; for, if no other special loss can be assigned, yet still the words of the writ itself specify one general damage, viz. the treading down and bruising his herbage.

A man must have a property (either absolute or temporary) in the soil, and actual possession by entry, to be able to maintain an action of trespass: or, at least, it is requisite that the party have a lease and possession of the vesture and herbage of the land. Thus, if a meadow be divided annually among the parishioners by lot, then, after each person's several portion is allotted, they may be respectively capable of maintaining an action for the breach of their several closes, for they have an exclusive interest and freehold therein for the time. But before entry and actual possession, one cannot maintain an action of trespass, though he hath the freehold in law. And therefore an heir before entry cannot have this action against an abator; though a disseisee might have it against a disseisor, for the injury done by the disseisin itself, at which time the plaintiff was seised of the land: but he cannot have it for any act done after the disseisin, until he hath gained possession by re-entry, and then he may well maintain it for the intermediate damage done; for after his re-entry, the law, by a kind of *jus postliminii*, supposes the freehold to have all along continued in him. Neither, by the common law, in case of an intrusion or deforcement, could the party kept out of possession sue the wrongdoer by a mode of redress, which was calculated merely for injuries committed against the land while in the possession of the owner. But by the statute 6 *Ann.* c. 18. if a guardian or trustee for any infant, a husband seised *jure uxoris*, or a person having any estate or interest determinable upon a life or lives, shall, after the determination of their respective interests, hold over and continue in possession of the lands or tenements, they are now adjudged to be trespassers; and the reversioner or remainder-man may once in every year, by motion to the court of chancery, procure the *cestuy que vie*, to be produced by the tenant of the land, or may enter thereon in case of his refusal or wilful neglect. And, by the statutes of 4 *Geo.* 2. c. 28. and 11 *Geo.* 2. c. 19. in case after the determination of any term of life, lives, or years, any person shall wilfully hold over the same, the lessor is entitled to recover by action of debt, either a rent of double the annual value of the premises, in case he himself hath demanded and given notice in writing to deliver the possession; or else double the usual rent, in case the notice of quitting proceeds from any tenant having power to determine his lease, and he afterwards neglects to carry it into due execution.

A man is also answerable for not only his own trespass, but that of his cattle also: for if by his negligent keeping they stray upon the land of another (and much more if he permits, or drives them on) and they there tread down his neighbour's herbage, and spoil his corn or his trees, this is a trespass for which the owner must answer in damages. And the law gives the party injured a double remedy in this case, by permitting him to distrain the cattle thus damage feasant, or doing damage, till the owner shall make him satisfaction, or else by leaving him to the common remedy *in foro consentioso*, by action. And the action that lies in either of these cases, of trespass committed upon another's land, either by a man himself, or his cattle, is the action of trespass *vi et armis*, whereby a man is called upon to answer, *quare vi et armis clausum ipsius A. apud B. fregit, et blada ipsius A. ad valentiam centum solidorum ibidem nuper crescentia cum quibusdam averiis depastus fuit, conculcavit, et consumpsit, &c.*: for the law always couples the idea of force with that of intrusion upon the property of another. And herein, if any unwarrantable act of the defendant or his beasts in coming upon the land be proved, it is an act of trespass for which the plaintiff must recover some damages; such however as the jury shall think proper to assess.

In trespasses of a permanent nature, where the injury is continually renewed, (as by spoiling or consuming the herbage with the defendant's cattle) the declaration may alledge the injury to have been committed by continuation from one given day to another, (which is called laying the action with a continuando) and the plaintiff shall not be compelled to bring separate actions for every day's separate offence. But where the trespass is by one or several acts, each of which terminates in itself, and being once done cannot be done again, it cannot be laid with a continuando; yet, if there be repeated acts of trespass committed, (as cutting down a certain number of trees) they may be laid to be done, not continually, but at divers days and times within a given period.

In some cases trespass is justifiable; or, rather, entry on another's land or house shall not in those cases be accounted trespass: as if a man comes there to demand or pay money, there payable; or to execute, in a legal manner, the process of the law. Also a man may justify entering into an inn or public-house, without the leave of the owner first specially asked; because, when a man professes the keeping of such inn or public-house, he thereby gives a general licence to any person to enter his doors. So a landlord may justify entering to distrein for rent; a commoner to attend his cattle, commoning on another's land; and a reversioner, to see if any waste be committed on the estate; for the apparent necessity of the thing. Also it hath been said, that by the common law and custom of England, the poor are allowed to enter and glean upon another's ground after the harvest, without being guilty of trespass: which humane provision seems borrowed from the mosaical law. In like manner the common law warrants the hunting of ravenous beasts of prey, as badgers and foxes, in another man's land; because the destroying such creatures is profitable to the public. But in cases where a man misdemeans himself, or make an ill use of the authority with which the law entrusts him, he shall be accounted a trespasser *ab initio*; as if one comes into a tavern, and will not go out in a reasonable time, but tarries there all night contrary to the inclination of the owner; this wrongful act shall affect and have relation back even to his first entry, and make the whole a trespass. But a bare non-feasance, as not paying for the wine he calls for, will not make him a trespasser; for this is only a breach of contract, for which the taverner shall have an action of debt or assumpsit against him. So if a landlord distreined for rent, and wilfully killed the distress, this by the common law made him a trespasser *ab initio*: and so indeed would any other irregularity have done, till the stat. 11 *Geo.* 2. *c.* 19. which enacts, that no subsequent irregularity of the landlord shall make his first entry a trespass; but the party injured shall have a special action on the case for the real specific injury sustained, unless tender of amends hath been made. But still, if a reversioner, who enters on pretence of seeing waste, breaks the house, or stays there all night: or if the commoner, who comes to tend his cattle, cuts down a tree; in these and similar cases the law judges that he entered for this unlawful purpose, and therefore, as the act which demonstrates such his purpose is a trespass, he shall be deemed a trespasser *ab initio*. So also in the case of hunting the fox or the badger, a man cannot justify breaking the soil, and digging him out of the earth: for though the law warrants the hunting of such noxious animals for the public good, yet it is held that such things must be done in an ordinary and usual manner; therefore, as there is an ordinary course to kill them, viz. by hunting, the court held that the digging for them was unlawful.

A man may also justify in an action of trespass, on account of the freehold and right of entry being in himself; and this defence brings the title of the estate in question. This is therefore one of the ways devised, since the disuse of real actions, to try the property of estates; though it is not so usual as that by ejectment, because that, being now a mixed action, not only gives damages for the ejection, but also possession of the land: whereas, in trespass, which is merely a personal suit, the right can be only ascertained, but no possession delivered; nothing being recovered but damages for the wrong committed.

But in order to prevent trifling and vexatious actions of trespass, as well as other personal actions, it is (*inter alia*) enacted by statutes 43 *Eliz.* *c.* 6 and 22 & 23 *Car.* 2. *c.* 9. *s.* 136. that where the jury, who try an action of trespass, give less damages than forty shillings, the plaintiff shall be allowed no more costs than damages; unless the judge shall certify under his hand that the freehold or title of the land came chiefly in question. But this rule now admits of two exceptions more, which have been made by subsequent statutes. One is by statute 8 & 9 *W.* 3. c. 11. hereafter more fully noticed, which enacts, that in all actions of trespass, wherein it shall appear that the trespass was wilful and malicious, and it be so certified by the judge, the plaintiff shall recover full costs. And every trespass is wilful, where the defendant has notice, and is especially forewarned not to come on the land: as every trespass is malicious, though the damage may not amount to forty shillings, where the intent of the defendant plainly appears to be to harrass and distress the plaintiff. The other exception is by stat. 4 & 5 *W.* & *M.* c. 28. which gives full costs against any inferior tradesman, apprentice, or other dissolute person, who is convicted of a trespass in hawking, hunting, fishing, or fowling upon another's land: and upon this statute it has been adjudged, that if a person be an inferior tradesman, as a clothier for instance, it matters not what qualification he may have in point of estate; but that if he be guilty of such trespass, he shall be liable to pay full costs. *Ld. Raym.* 149.

—— *Trespass, to things personal.* As to damage that may be offered to things personal, while in the possession of the owner, as hunting a man's deer, shooting his dogs, poisoning or otherwise destroying his cattle or living animals, or making them in a worse condition than before, these are injuries, for which the law allows redress in two shapes: 1. by action of trespass *vi et armis*, when the act is in itself immediately injurious to another's property, and therefore necessarily accompanied with some degree of force; 2. and by special action on the case, where the act is in itself indifferent, and the injury only consequential, and therefore arising without any breach of the peace. In both of which suits the plaintiff shall recover damages, in proportion to the injury which he proves that his property has sustained. And it is not material whether the damage be done by the defendant himself, or his servants by his direction, for the action will lie aginst the master as well as the servant. And, if a man keeps a dog or other brute animal used to do mischief, as by worrying sheep, or the like, the owner must answer for the consequences, if he knows of such evil habit.

TRESPASSES RESTRAINED BY STATUTE. There are divers trespasses against which parliament have found it expedient to make special provision, as appears from the following statutes:

I. Pulling down Inclosures. By 13

Ed. 1. *s.* 1. *c.* 46. where sometimes it chanceth that one having a right to improve, doth then levy a dyke or an hedge, and some by night or at another season, when they suppose not to be espied, do overthrow the hedge or dyke, and it cannot be known by verdict of the assise or jury, who did overthrow the hedge or dyke, and men of the towns near, will not indict such as be guilty of the fact; the towns near adjoining shall be distrained to levy the hedge or dyke at their own cost, and to yield damages,

And by 3 & 4 *Edw.* 6. *c.* 3. such person as shall bring an assise hereupon, and have judgment to recover, shall have his damages trebled by the judgment of the court.

2. Cutting growing corn, robbing of orchards or gardens, breaking hedges, pulling up fruit-trees, or spoiling wood growing. By 43 *Eliz.* c. 7. if any person shall cut, or unlawfully take away any corn growing, or rob any orchards or gardens, or break or cut any hedge, pales, rails, or fence, or dig, pull up, or take up, any fruit-trees, to the intent to take the same away, or shall cut or spoil any woods or underwoods, poles or trees standing (the same not being felony by the laws of this realm), every such person, his procurers and receivers knowing the same, being convicted by confession, or one witness, before one justice of peace, mayor, or other head officer, where the offence shall be committed, or the party apprehended, shall give such recompence for the damages as by such justice shall be appointed for the first fault; and if such offenders shall be thought, in the discretion of the justice, not able, or do not make satisfaction for the damages, the justice shall commit the offenders to some constable or other inferior officer, where the offence shall be committed, or the party apprehended, to be whipped: and for every such offence for which the offenders shall be eftsoons committed, to receive the said punishment of whipping, *s.* 1.

And if any constable, or inferior officer, do not, at the command of any such justice, execute by himself, or some other, the punishment limited by this statute, it shall be lawful for the justice to commit him to the common gaol, until the offenders be by him, or by his procurement, whipped. *s.* 2.

But no such justice shall execute this statute for any offences done unto himself, unless he be assisted by one or more other justices, whom the offence doth not concern. *s.* 3.

3. Hedge-breakers and stealers of wood, gates, pales, &c. By 15 *Car.* 2. c. 2. the constable may apprehend, or cause to be apprehended, every person he shall suspect, having or carrying any kind of burden of any kind of wood, underwood, poles, or young trees, or bark, or bast of any trees; or any gates, stiles, posts, and pales, rails or hedgewood, broom or furze. And by warrant of one justice, directed to any officer, such officer shall have power to enter into and search the houses, outhouses, yards, gardens, or other places, belonging to the houses of every person they shall suspect to have any wood, underwood, poles, or young trees, or bark, or bast of any trees; or any gates, stiles, posts, pales, rails, or hedgewood, broom or furze; and where they shall find any such, to apprehend the persons suspected, for cutting and taking the same. And as well those apprehended carrying, as those in whose houses and places the same shall be found, to carry before one justice. And if such person do not then and there give a good account how he came by the same, such as shall satisfy the said justice, or else shall not in some convenient time, to be set by the said justice, produce the party of whom he bought the same: or some credible witness, to depose upon oath such sale thereof, he shall be convicted of cutting and spoiling the same, and punished according to the above statute of 43 *Eliz.* and further by this act. *s.* 2.

That is to say, he shall for the first offence give the owner such recompence or satisfaction for damages, and within such time, as the justice shall appoint; and over and above pay down presently to the overseers, for the use of the poor, such sum, not exceeding 10*s.* as the justice shall think meet; and if he do not make such recompence, and also pay the said sum to the poor, the said justice shall commit him to the house of correction for not exceeding one month, or to be whipped by the constable; and if he shall again commit the said offence, and be thereof convicted as before, he shall be sent to the house of correction for one month, to be there kept to hard labour; and if he shall again commit the said offence, and be thereof convicted as before, he shall be deemed an incorrigible rogue. *s.* 2, 3.

And whosoever shall buy any burdens of wood, or any poles or sticks of wood, or any other the things aforesaid, which may be justly suspected to have been stolen, or unlawfully come by, it shall be lawful for one justice, upon complaint, to examine the matter upon oath: and if he shall find that the same was bought of a person who might justly be suspected to have stolen, or unlawfully come by the same, and that the same was stolen, or unlawfully come by, he may award the party who bought the same, to pay treble value to him from whom it was unlawfully taken;

and in default of present payment, may issue his warrant to levy the same by distress, and in default of distress to commit the party to gaol, at his own charge, there to remain one month without bail. *s.* 4.

But no person shall be punished for any offence upon this law that hath been punished for the same by any former law; nor unless he be questioned within six weeks after the offence. *s.* v.

4. Destroying timber-trees, fruit-trees, or other trees or plantations. By 37 *Hen.* 8. *c.* 6, if any person shall maliciously, willingly, and unlawfully bark any apple-trees, pear-trees, or other fruit-trees, he shall forfeit to the party grieved double damages, by action of trespass, at the common law, and also 10*l.* to the king.

But it is enacted by 1 *Geo.* 1. stat. 2. *c.* 48, to encourage the planting of timber-trees, fruit-trees, and other trees in fields, hedge-rows, gardens, walks, and elsewhere, either for ornament, shelter, or profit, and to prevent the malicious destroying or spoiling thereof; that, if any person shall maliciously break down, cut up, pluck up, throw down, bark, or otherwise destroy, deface, or spoil any timber-tree or trees, fruit-tree or trees, or any other tree or trees, the person damaged shall receive such satisfaction and recompence from the inhabitants of the parish, town, hamlet, villa, or place; to be viewed, and damages and costs to be recovered in the same manner as hedges and ditches overthrown in the night may by the stat. 13 *Ed.* 1. c. 46, unless the party offending shall by such parish or place be convicted of such offence within six months. *s.* 1.

And as doubts had arisen on this last act, whether such offences were punishable if committed in the day-time, the stat. 6 *Geo.* 1, c. 16. was passed, to explain and amend the same, and also to extend the provisions thereof to the destroyers of hedges and other fences: by which said act is enacted as follows: that is to say,

If any person whatsoever shall either by day or by night, cut, take, destroy, break, throw down, bark, pluck up, burn, deface, spoil, or carry away any wood springs, or springs of wood trees, poles, wood, tops of trees, under woods or coppice woods, thorns, or quicksets, without the consent of the owner of such woods, wood-grounds, parks, chases, or coppices, plantations, timber-trees, fruit-trees, or other trees, thorns, or quicksets, or of the person chiefly entrusted with the care and custody thereof; or shall break open, thrown down, level, or destroy any hedges, gates, posts, stiles, railing, walls, fences, dykes, ditches, banks, or other inclosures thereof, the owner may have such satisfaction and recompence from the inhabitants of the parishes, towns, hamlets, villages, or places joining on such grounds, and recover such damages against such place or places, and in the same manner and form, as by the above statute of the 13 *Ed.* 1. c. 46., unless the offender, by such parishes or places, be convicted within six months, 6 *Geo.* 1. *c.* 16. *s.* 1.

But if the offender is known, then the following proceedings shall take place:

That is to say, if any offender shall, in a riotous, open, tumultuous, or in a secret or clandestine manner, forcibly, or wrongfully, or maliciously, and without the consent of the owner, or person chiefly entrusted with the care of the above-mentioned premises, commit any of the offences restrained by the said acts of 1 *Geo.* 1. stat. 2. c. 48. or 6 *Geo.* 1. c. 16, two justices, or the justices in sessions, on complaint made by the inhabitants of such parish or place, or by the owner of the wood or trees, or any other, may cause the offender to be apprehended, and hear and determine the offence, and on conviction shall commit the offender to the house of correction to hard labour for three months; and where there is no house of correction, then to the prison for four months; and shall also order the offender to be publicly whipped by the master of such house of correction once a month during such three months, in the borough or corporation, if the offence be committed therein; or in the market-town where the house of correction stands, or in the next market-town next adjacent to such house of correction, on the market-day: and in the county where such offence shall be committed, on the market-day between the hours of eleven and two; and where there is no house of correction, the said justices shall order him to be whipped by the common hangman, once a month during such four months, on the market day of any borough or corporation where such offender shall be committed; or, on the market-day of some town between the hours of eleven and two o'clock, 1 *Geo.* 1. stat. 2. c. 48. *s.* 2. 6 *Geo.* 1. *c.* 16. *s.* 2.

And before such offender shall be discharged, he shall find sufficient sureties for his good behaviour for two years, 1 *Geo.* 1. stat. 2. *c.* 48. *s.* 3. 6 *Geo.* 1. *c.* 16. *s.* 2.

5. Destroying trees growing on wastes. Also by 29 *Geo.* 2. *c.* 36. if any person shall unlawfully cut, take, destroy, break, throw down, bark, pluck up, burn, deface, spoil, or carry away, any tree growing in any waste, wood, or pasture, in which any person or body politic hath right of common, every such offender shall be in like manner convicted of such offence, and incur the like penalty, as is directed by 6 *Geo.* 1. c. 16. *s.* 8.

And the parties may take their remedy for damages, either against the parish or place where the offence shall be committed, according to the above acts, 1 *Geo.* 1 *c.* 8, and 6 *Geo.* 1. *c.* 16, or on the hundred, according to the stat. 9 *Geo.* 1. *c.* 22. *s.* 7, as to them shall seem most meet. *s.* 9.

6. Destroying timber-trees in forests or chases. By 6 *Geo.* 3. *c.* 48. every person who shall wilfully cut or break down, bark, burn, pluck up, lop, top, crop, or otherwise deface, damage, spoil, or destroy, or carry away, any timber-tree, or any tree likely to become timber, or any part thereof, or the lops or tops thereof, without the consent of the owner thereof first had; or in any of his majesty's forests or chases, without the consent of the surveyor, or his deputy, or person entrusted with the care of the same, and shall be thereof convicted upon the oath of one witness, before one justice, shall, for the first offence, forfeit not exceeding 20*l.* together with the charges previous to and attending such conviction, to be ascertained by such justice; and upon non-payment thereof, such justice shall commit the offender to the common goal, for not exceeding twelve nor less than six months, or until the penalty and charges be paid; and if any person so convicted shall be guilty of the like offence a second time, and shall be thereof convicted in like manner, such person shall forfeit not exceeding 30*l.* together with the charges attending such conviction; and upon non-payment thereof, such justice shall commit the offender to the common goal for not exceeding eighteen nor less than twelve months, or until the penalty and charges be paid. And if any person so convicted shall be guilty of the like offence a third time, and shall be thereof convicted, such person shall be guilty of felony, and the court before whom he shall be tried, shall transport such person for seven years. *s.* 1.

And all oak, beech, chesnut, walnut, asp, elm, cedar, fir, ash, lime, scyamore, birch, (poplar, alder, larch, maple, and hornbeam trees, 13 *Geo.* 3. *c.* 3.) shall be deemed timber-trees within the meaning of this act. *s.* 2.

7. Destroying underwoods, hollies, or the like. Also every person who shall go into the woods, underwoods, or wood-grounds, of any of his majesty's subjects, not being the owner thereof, (or into any of his majesty's forests or chases, 9 *Geo.* 3. *c.* 41. *s.* 8,) or any of the woods or wood-grounds belonging to his majesty in Great Britain, as well in right of his duchy of Lancaster, as otherwise, and whether such woods or wood-grounds shall be within any of his majesty's forests or chases or not, 45 *Geo.* 3. *c.* 6. and shall there cut, lop, top, or spoil, split-down, or damage, or otherwise destroy, any kind of wood, or underwood, poles, sticks of wood, green stubs, or young trees, or carry or convey the same away (or shall by night or day, cut down, destroy, take, carry, or convey away, any hollies, thorns, or quicksets, there growing or being, 9 *Geo.* 3. *c.* 41. *s.* 8.) or shall have in his custody any kind of wood, underwood, poles, sticks of wood, green stubs, or young trees, (or any such hollies, thorns, or quicksets, 9 *Geo.* 3. *c.* 41. *s.* 8.) and shall not give a satisfactory account how he came by the same, and shall be thereof convicted before one justice, on the oath of one witness, shall for the first offence forfeit not exceeding 40*s.* together with the charges attending such conviction; and if the same be not forthwith paid on conviction, the justice shall by warrant commit him to the house of correction for one month, to hard labour, and to be once whipped there:—and if any person shall commit any of the offences aforesaid a second time, he shall forfeit not exceeding 5*l.* together with the charges attending such conviction; and if the same be not forthwith paid on conviction, the justice shall by warrant commit him to the house of correction for three months, and to be whipped there, once in every one of the said three months; and if a third time, such person convicted thereof shall be deemed an incorrigible rogue, and punished as such, *s.* 4. 6.

And the justices for the counties, cities, ridings, divisions, or places wherein any offences against this act shall be done, are to put this act in execution. *s.* 5.

And one moiety of all forfeitures, not otherwise directed, shall go to the informer, and the other to the person aggrieved. *s.* 8.

And if any person shall hinder, or attempt to prevent, the seizing or securing any person employed in carrying away any such timber or other trees, such person shall forfeit 10*l.* to the person who shall convict such offender; and if not paid on conviction, the person convicted shall be committed to the house of correction to hard labour, for not exceeding six calendar months. *s.* 7.

And for the better preventing the destruction of timber-trees, and other trees, underwood and covert in forests and chases, it is enacted by 4 *Geo.* 3. *c.* 31. that it shall be lawful for every surveyor of his majesty's woods, and his lawful deputy, and for the officers and keepers of any forest or chase (besides the penalties for destroying the trees or underwood,) to seize and take away for his own use, any saw, axe, hatchet, bill-hook or other instrument used by any person whom they shall find unlawfully plucking up, sawing, cutting down, topping, lopping, or destroying any timber-tree, or other tree, underwood, or covert, within such forest or chase.

8. Destroying plantations, nurseries, or gardens. Also by the said stat. 6 *Geo.* 3, c. 48, every person who shall pluck up, or cut, spoil, or destroy, or take away, any root, shrub, or plant, out of the fields, nurseries, gardens, or garden-grounds, or other cultivated lands, of any person whomsoever, without the consent of the owner first had, and shall be thereof convicted upon the oath of one witness, before one justice, shall for the first offence forfeit not exceeding 40*s.* together with the charges previous to and attending such conviction, to be ascertained by such justice; and if the same are not paid down upon conviction, forthwith, the said justice shall by warrant commit him to the house of correction for one month to hard labour, and to be once whipped there;—and if any person so convicted shall again commit the like offence, and be convicted in manner aforesaid, such person shall for such second offence forfeit not exceeding 5*l.* together with the charges attending the conviction; which if not paid down upon conviction, forthwith the said justice shall by warrant commit him to the house of correction for three months, and to be whipped there once in every of the said three months. And if any person so before convicted, shall a third time commit the like offence, and shall be thereof convicted, such person shall for such third offence be deemed guilty of felony, and the court before whom he shall be tried, shall transport such person for seven years. *s.* 3. 6.

9. Stealing turnips, potatoes, cabbages, parsnips, pease, or carrots, growing. Also by 13 *Geo.* 3. *c.* 32. and 42. *Geo.* 3. *c.* 67, if any person shall steal and take away, or maliciously pull up, injure, or destroy any turnips, potatoes, cabbages, parsnips, beans, pease, or carrots, growing or being in any garden, lands, or grounds, open or inclosed, and shall be thereof convicted, on a prosecution begun within thirty days after the offence, before any justice, either by the confession of the party offending, or by the oath of one witness, every person so offending, and being convicted, shall forfeit not exceeding 20*s.* over the value of the goods stolen, as to such justice shall seem meet; which shall be distributed between the owner of the goods and overseers, for the use of the poor, in such proportion as such justice shall think fit; or the whole shall be given to the owner or to the overseers, according to the discretion of such justice; and in default of payment, such justice shall commit such offender to the house of correction, to be kept to hard labour for not exceeding two months, unless such penalty be sooner paid. *s.* 1.

And in all informations, and other proceedings, the evidence of the owner and of the inhabitants of the parish shall be taken. 13 *Geo.* 3. *c.* 32. *s.* 2.

But where the conviction shall be upon the oath of the owner, the whole of the penalty shall be paid to the overseer for the use of the poor. *s.* 3.

10. Destroying timber or other trees, or any roots, plants, or shrubs in the night. By 22 and 23 *Car.* 2. c. 7. if any person shall, in the night-time, maliciously, unlawfully, and wittingly destroy any plantations of trees, or throw down any inclosures, he shall forfeit to the party injured treble damages, to be recovered by action of trespass, or upon the case; but upon request of the party injured, three justices of the peace may within six months inquire thereof, as well by a jury as by examination of witnesses upon oath, or by any lawful ways which to them shall seem meet. *s.* 5, 6, 7.

And it is enacted by 6 *Geo*, 3. *c.* 36, that every person who shall in the night-time lop, top, cut down, break, throw down, bark, burn, or otherwise spoil or destroy, or carry away any oak, beech, ash, elm, fir, chesnut, or asp, timber-tree, or other tree standing for timber, or likely to become timber, without the consent of the owner thereof; or shall in the night-time pluck up, dig up, break, spoil, or destroy, or carry away any root, shrub, or plant, roots, shrubs, or plants, of the value of 5*s.* and which shall be growing and being in the garden-ground, nursery-ground, or other inclosed ground of any person; or shall be aiding or assisting therein, or shall buy or receive such root, shrub, or plant, roots, shrubs, or plants, of the value aforesaid, knowing the same to be stolen, shall be guilty of felony and transported for seven years.

11. Damage feasant. Where an injury has been done by the cattle or goods of any one to the lands of another, he who receives the injury, may either distrain them while doing the damage, or bring his action of trespass, and recover for the damage sustained; but he should make his election of his remedy: for if he distrains, and the distress escapes, the action of trespass is gone, unless the escape was not through his fault or neglect; and it is to be observed that this action may be brought against him who has only the care, custody, or possession of the cattle which do the damage.

If the tenant's goods are distrained for tolls or customs pretended to be due, he may bring his action for the taking, in which the right to the tolls will be tried.

12. Hunting. In respect to injuries from hunting, or the pursuit of game, the following points are necessary to be noticed in this place:

Any person may justify going upon the lands of another in pursuit of ravenous beasts, as foxes, badgers, and the like: for the taking of them is of public benefit; but he cannot justify to break the ground or dig for them.

So it will not justify any excessive or unreasonable damage to the land; for the justification is only as to the following, and shall be done with as little damage as possible; and therefore if to trespass for such cause, the defendant justifies for following a fox or such beast, and in fact has committed unnecessary mischief, the plaintiff must, in his pleading, newly alledge and prove excessive and unnecessary injury.

But in general it is trespass at common law for any man to hunt on another's ground; and the owner or tenant of the soil may maintain his action of trespass for the same.

Yet if the party is qualified according to the statutes to kill game, and the damage found be under 40*s.* unless the title to the land was chiefly in question, the defendant shall, in such case, pay no more costs than damages.

But for preventing wilful and malicious trespasses, the stat. 8 & 9 *Will.* 3. *c.* 11. *s.* 4, enacts, that in all actions of trespass wherein, at the trial of the cause, it shall appear and be certified by the judge, under his hand, on the back of the record, that the trespass upon which any defendant shall be found guilty was wilfully and malicious, the plantiff shall recover not only his damages, but his full costs of suit.

Under this statute, therefore, if the owner or tenant of the land expressly forwarns another not to come thereon, he will in an action of trespass, subsequent thereto, be entitled to full costs, notwithstanding the damages recovered be under 40*s.*; for every trespass is wilful where the defendant has notice, and is especially forewarned not to come on the land.

And if a general notice be given, not to trespass on certain lands, and another hunts over a close belonging to the party giving such notice, the judge on the trial of an action for such trespass is bound under the above stat. 8 & 9 *Will.* 3. *c.* 11. *s.* 4, to certify that it was wilful and malicious, in order to entitle the plaintiff to his full costs; notwithstanding it appear upon the trial that the defendant was anxious to avoid trespassing on the ground, and that he made frequent enquiries respecting the plaintiff's boundaries.

TRESPASSANTS, (Fr.) according to *Britton*, c. 29. passengers.

TRESPASSER, is one who commits a trespass; and though the law allows a man to enter a place peaceably, yet if he doth abuse the licence of the law by committing a trespass, the law will adjudge hm a *trespasser ab initio.* 8 *Rep.* 146.

TRESTORNARE, to turn or divert another way. *Cowell.*

TREYTS, (Fr.) Signifies taken out or withdrawn, and was applied to a juror removed or discharged. *F. N. B.* 159.

TRIAL, (*Triatio.*) Is the examination of a cause, civil or criminal, before a judge who has jurisdiction of it, according to the laws of the land; it is the trial and examination of the point in issue, and of the question between the parties, whereupon the judgment may be given. 1 *Inst.* 124. *Finch.* 36.

TRIBUCH and TREBUCHET, (*Terbichetum.*) A tumbrel, or cucking stool, *Cowell.*

TRICENNALE. See *Trental.*

TRICESIMA, an ancient custom in a borough in the county of Hereford, so called, because thirty burgesses paid 1*d.* rent for their houses to the bishop, who is lord of the manor. *Lib. Nigr. Heref. Cowell.*

TRIDINGMOTE, the court held for a triding or trithing. *Cowell.*

TRIENNIAL ELECTIONS. The utmost extent of time that the same parliament was allowed to sit, by the stat. 6 *W.* & *M.* c. 2. was three years; after the expiration of which, reckoning from the return of the first summons, the parliament was to have no longer continuance. But, by the stat. 1. *Geo.* 1. stat. 2, *c.* 38. to prevent heats, animosities, and expence, this term was prolonged to seven years.

TRIGINTALE. See *Trental.*

TRILION, used in accounts, to signify three millions. *Cowell.*

TRIMILCHI. The Anglo Saxons denominated the month of May, *Trimilchi*; because they milked their cattle three times every day in that month. *Beda.*

TRINITY, (*Trinitas*). The number of three persons in the godhead or deity; and denying any one of the persons in the trinity to be God, is subject to divers penalties and incapacities. See *Blasphemy.*

TRINITY-HOUSE. Is a kind of college at Deptford, belonging to a company or corporation of seamen, who have authority by the king's charter to take knowledge of those that destroy sea-marks; also to redress the faults of sailors, licensing pilots, and divers other things belonging to navigation. 8 *Eliz. c.* 13. See *Pilots.*

TRINK. A fishing-net, or engine to catch fish. 2 *Hen.* 6. *c.* 15.

TRINOBANTES. The inhabitants of Middlesex, Essex, and Hertfordshire. *Cowell.*

TRINODA NECESSITAS, signified a threefold necessary tax, to which all lands were liable in the Saxon times, i. e. for repairing of bridges, the maintaining of castles and garrisons, and for expeditions to repel invasions. *Ibid.*

TRIORS, *Triours*, or *Triers*, are such as are chosen by the court to examine whether a challenge made to the panel of jurors, or any of them, be just or not. *Broke* 122.

TRIORS OF JURORS on challenges to the favour; that is, where the party hath no principal challenge, but objects only some probable circumstances of suspicion, as acquaintance, and the like; the validity thereof must be left to the determination of triors, whose office it is to decide whether the juror be favourable or unfavourable. These triors, in case the first man called be challenged, are two indifferent persons named by the court; and if they try one man, and find him indifferent, he shall be sworn; and then he and the two triors shall try the next; and when another is found indifferent and sworn, the two triors shall be superseded, and the two first sworn on the jury shall try the next. *Co. Lit.* 158.

TRIORS OF PEERS. Formerly, on the trial of a peer in parliament, a precept was issued to summon only eighteen or twenty, selected from the body of the peers. But now, by stat. 7 *W.* 3. *c.* 3. upon all trials of peers for treason or misprision, all the peers who have a right to sit and vote in parliament shall be summoned at least twenty days before such trial, to appear and vote therein; and every lord appearing shall vote in the trial of such peer, first taking the oaths of allegiance and supremacy, and subscribing the declaration against popery.

TRIPODIUM. According to *Leg. H.* 1. *cap.* 64. for a small offence, the composition was twenty shillings; and for a great offence, three times twenty shillings, viz. *tripodium. Cowell.*

TRIRODA TERRÆ. Three rods or perches. *Ibid.*

TRISTEGA. The uppermost room in the house, or garret. *Ibid.*

TRISTIS, (from the Fr. *traist*, i. e. trust.) Was an immunity, whereby a man was freed from attendance on the lord of a forest when he was disposed to chase within the forest. *Manwood. Cowell.*

TRISTRA. A post or station, in hunting. *Cowell.*

TRITHING or TRIHING, (Sax. *Trithinga.*) Contains the third part of a county, or three or four hundreds. Also it was a court held within that circuit, of the nature of the court-leet, but inferior to the county-court. *Cambd.* 102. *Magn. Chart.* c. 36. The ridings in Yorkshire are corruptly called by that name, from tridings or trithings. And those who anciently governed those trithings, were termed trithing-reves, before whom were brought all causes which could not be decided in the hundreds; for from the hundred-court suits might be removed to the tithing, and thence to the county-court. *Spelm. Cowell.*

TRIUMVIR. A trithing-man, or constable of three hundreds. *Cowell.*

TRONAGE (*tronagium.*) Is a customary duty or toll for weighing of wool. *Ibid.*

TRONATOR, (from *trona*, i. e. *statera.*) An officer in the city of London, who weighed the wool brought thither. *Ibid.*

TROPE, (*tropus*, of τρόπος, from τρέπω, Gr. to turn.) An elegant turning or application of a word, from its strictly proper signification to another.

TROPER, (*troperium.*) Was a book of alternate turns or responses in singing mass. *Cowell.*

TROPHY-MONEY. Money formerly raised towards providing for the militia. See *Militia.*

TROVER, (from the Fr. *trouver*, i. e. *invenire.*) Is an action which a man hath against one, that, having found any of his goods, refuseth to deliver them up on demand: or if another hath in his possession my goods, by delivery to him, or otherwise, and he sells or makes use of them without my consent, this is a conversion for which trover lies; so if he doth not actually convert them, but doth not deliver them to me on demand. 2 *Lill. Abr.* 618.

This action of trover and conversion was in its original, an action of trespass upon the case, for recovery of damages against such person as had found another's goods, and refused to deliver them on demand, but converted them to his own use; from which finding and converting, it is called an action of trover and conversion. The freedom of this action from wager of law, and the less degree of certainty requisite in describing the goods, gave it so considerable an advantage over the action of detinue, that by a fiction of law actions of trover were at length permitted to be brought against any man, who had in his possession, by any means whatsoever, the personal goods of another, and sold them, or used them without the consent of the owner, or refused to deliver them when demanded. The injury lies in the conversion: for any man may take the goods of another into possession, if he finds them; but no finder is allowed to acquire a property therein, unless the owner be for ever unknown: and therefore he must not convert them to his own use, which the law presumes him to do, if he refuses to restore them to the owner; for which reason, such refusal alone is, *prima facie*, sufficient evidence of a conversion. The fact of the finding, or trover, is therefore now totally immaterial: for the plaintiff needs only to suggest (as words of form) that he lost such goods, and that the defendant found them; and, if he proves that the goods are his property, and that the defendant had them in his possession, it is sufficient. But a conversion must be fully proved: and then in this action the plaintiff shall recover damages, equal to the value of the thing converted; but not the thing itself, which nothing will recover but an action of detinue or replevin. 3 *Black.* 152.

TROY-WEIGHT, *(pondus trojæ.)* A weight of twelve ounces to the pound. *Cowell.*

TRUCE, (*treuga.*) A league or cessation of arms. And by stat. 2 *Hen.* 5. *st.* 1. *c.* 6. conservators of truce and safe-conducts were appointed in every port. See *Safe-Conduct.*

TRUG-CORN, *(truga frumenti.)* A measure of corn; and at Leominster the vicar hath trug-corn allowed for officiating at some chapels of ease. *Cowell.*

TRUNCUS. A trunk set in churches, to receive the oblations of pious people. *Ibid.*

TRUSSA. A truss or bundle of corn. *Ibid.*

TRUST, *(fiducia, confidentia.)* Is a confidence which one man reposes in another, and nothing more than a new name given to an use; but, as generally used in law, it is a right to receive the profits of land, and to dispose of the land itself (in many cases) for particular purposes, as directed by the lawful owner, or pointed out by the deed of settlement, or other conveyance which created the trust: and if a person in whom a trust is reposed, breaks or doth not perform the same, the remedy is by bill in chancery, the common law generally taking no notice of trusts. 2 *Lill. Abr.* 624. See *Resulting Trust* and *Uses and Trusts.*

TUB-MAN, *in the Exchequer.* In the court of exchequer, two of the most experienced barristers, called the Postman and the Tub-man, (from the places in which they sit) have a precedence in motions. 3 *Black.* 28 *n.*

TUMBRELL, (*tumbrellum, turbichetum.*) Is an engine of punishment, which ought to be in every liberty that hath view of frank-pledge, for the correction of scolds and unquiet women. *Kitchen, fol.* 13. See *Castigatory, Cucking-stool.*

TUN, (Sax.) In the end of words signifying a town, or dwelling-place. *Cowell.*

TUN, (Lat. *tunellum.*) A vessel of wine and oil, being four hogsheads. 1 *R.* 3. *c.* 12. A tun of timber is a measure of forty solid feet, cut to a square. 12 *Car.* 2. *c.* 14. And a tun is twenty hundred weight of coals. *Stat.* 9 & 10 *W.* 3. *c.* 13.

TUNNAGE, (*tunnagium.*) A custom or impost granted to the crown for merchandize imported or exported. See *Customs.*

TUN-GREVE, (Sax. *tungerœva,* i.e. *villæ præpositus.*) The town-reeve or bailiff. *Spelm. Cowell.*

TURBAGIUM. The liberty of digging turfs. *Cowell.*

TURBARY, (*turbaria,* from *turba,* an obsolete Latin word for turf.) Is a right to dig turfs on a common or in another man's ground. *Kitch.* 94.

TURKINS. A kind of sky-coloured cloth, mentioned in 1 *R.* 2. *c.* 8.

TURN, or TOURN. Is the king's leet through all the county; of which the sheriff is judge, and this court is incident to his office; wherefore it is called the sheriff's tourn. And it had its name originally from the sheriff's taking a turn or circuit about his shire, and holding this court in several places. *Crompt. Jurisd.* 230. 4 *Inst.* 260. 2 *Hawk. P. C.* 55. It is a court of record. But great part of the business of the turn and leet hath, for several years past, through the negligence of sheriffs and stewards, devolved on the quarter-sessions. 4 *Black.* 274.

TURNIPS. See *Trespass.*

TURNO VICECOMITUM. Is a writ that lieth for those that are called to the sheriff's turn out of their own hundred. *Reg. Orig.* 173.

TURNPIKES. The turnpike roads are placed under the management and direction of certain bodies of trustees, who are usually named and appointed by the respective acts of parliament, which are occasionally passed for the purpose of making, repairing, and sustaining the particular roads therein specified: but the power of these statutes being confined to separate and distinct objects, it was thought expedient to pass some general laws, which should apply in common to all trustees and turnpike roads in general throughout the kingdom. 1 *Hawk. P. C. Leach's Edit.* 423. These provisions are contained in the stat. 13 *Geo.* 3. *c.* 84. the most popular of which are as follows:

By this act it is enacted, that if the driver of any cart, car, dray or waggon, shall ride upon such carriage, in any street or highway, not having some other person on foot or on horseback, to guide the same (such carriages as are conducted by some person holding the reigns of the horses excepted):

Or if the driver of any carriage whatsoever shall, by negligence or misbehaviour, cause any hurt to any person or carriage passing;

Or shall quit the highway, and go on the other side the hedge or fence inclosing the same; or wilfully be at such distace from such carriage, or in such a situation, while it shall be passing on such highway, that he cannot have the direction of such cattle drawing the same:

Or shall, by negligence or misbehaviour, prevent or interrupt the free passage of any other carriage on the said highways:

Or if the driver of any empty waggon, cart, or other carriage, shall neglect or refuse to turn aside for any coach, chariot, chaise, loaded waggon, cart, or other loaded carriage:

Or if any person shall drive any such coach, post-chaise, or other carriage let for hire, or waggon, wain, or cart, not having the owner's name as hereby required, painted thereon, or shall refuse to discover the true christian and sirname of the owner:

Such driver, being convicted of any such offence, either by his own confession, the view of a justice, or by the oath of one witness before any justice, shall for every offence forfeit not exceeding 10*s*.

In case such driver shall not be the owner, and in case the offender be the owner of such carriage, then not exceeding 20*s*.; and in either of the said cases shall, in default of payment, be committed to the house of correction for not exceeding one month.

And such driver offending in either of the said cases, shall, by authority of this act, with or without any warrant, be apprehended by any person who shall see such offence committed, and shall be immediately conveyed to a constable or peace-officer, to be conveyed before some justice; and if such driver shall refuse to discover his name, it shall be lawful for the justice before whom he shall be taken, or to whom such complaint shall be made, to commit him to the house of correction, for not exceeding three months, or to proceed against him for the penalty, by a description of his person and offence, and expressing in his proceedings that he refused to discover his name. 13 *Geo.* 3. *c.* 84. *s.* 40.

And for the better discovering of offenders, the owner of any waggon, wain, or cart, and also of every coach, post-chaise, or other carriage let to hire, shall paint upon some conspicuous part of his waggon, wain, or cart, and upon the pannels of the doors of all such coaches, post-chaises, or other carriages, before the same shall be used upon any turnpike-roads, his christian and sirname, and the place of his abode in large letters, and continue the same thereupon so long as such waggon or carriage shall be used upon such turnpike-road, and the owner of every common stage waggon or cart employed in travelling stages from town to town, shall, above his christian and sirname, paint on the part and in the manner aforesaid the following words: "Common Stage Waggon" (or Cart, as the case may be,) and every person using such carriage without the names and descriptions painted thereon as aforesaid, or who shall paint any false name or abode on such waggon or other carriage, shall forfeit not exceeding 5*l.* nor less than 1*l.* *s.* 68.

If any person shall by day or night pull down, pluck up, throw down, level, or destroy any turnpike-gate, post, rail, wall, chain, bar, or other fence set up to prevent passengers from passing without paying toll, or any house erected for the use of such turnpike-gate, or any crane, machine, or engine for weighing carriages; or shall forcibly rescue any person lawfully in custody of any officer for any of the said offences, every person so offending shall be guilty of felony, and transported for seven years, or committed to prison for not exceeding three years, at the discretion of the court before whom he shall be tried; and any indictment for such offences shall be determined in any adjacent county within England, as if the facts had been therein committed. 13 *Geo.* 3. *c.* 84. *s.* 42.

TURNY, (Fr. *tourney.*) See *Tournament.*

TUTORS. See *Schoolmaster.*

TWAITE, signifies a wood grubbed up, and converted to arable land. *Co. Lit.* 4.

TWANIGHT GESTE, (*hospes duaram noctium.*) Was a guest at an inn a second night. *Cowell.* See *Awnhinde.*

TWELTHIMDI, (Sax.) The highest rank of men in the Saxon government, who were valued at one thousand two hundred shillings; and if any injury were done to such persons, satisfaction were to be made, according to their worth. *Leg. Alf. cap.* 12, 13. *and of H.* 1. *c.* 76. *Cowell.*

TWELVE MEN, (*duodecimo homines legales.*) A number of twelve persons or upwards, by whom and whose oath as to matter of fact all trials pass, both in civil and criminal causes, through all courts of the common law in this realm. They are otherwise called the jury or inquest. See *Jury.*

TWO WITNESSES, when necessary. See *Evidence* and *Treason.*

TWYHINDI, (Sax.) Were the lower order of Saxons, valued at 200*s.* as to pecuniary mulcts inflicted for crimes, &c. *Leg. Alf. c.* 12. *Cowell.*

TYHTLAN. An accusation, impeachment, or charge, of any trespass or offence. *Leg. Ethel. c.* 2. *Cowell.*

TYLWITH, (Brit. derived from *Tyle*, i. e. *locus ubi stetit domus, vel locus ædificandæ domui aptus*, or from *tylath, trabs, tignus.*) Signifies a place whereon to build a house, or a beam in the building. *Cowell.*

TYNMOUTH. There is a customary

descent of lands in the honour of Tynmouth, that if any tenant hath issue two or more daughters, and he die seised in fee, the land shall go to the eldest daughter for life only, and after to the cousins of the male line; and for default thereof to escheat. 2 *Keb.* 111. 114.

TYPE, (*typus.*) A figure, example, or likeness of a thing. *Lit. Dict.* See *Printers.*

TYPOGRAPHIA. The art of printing. *Ibid.*

TYTHES, (*decimæ.*) See *Tithes.*

V

VACANS. Vacant, free, at leisure; void. *Lit. Dict. Cowell.*

VACARIA. A void place or waste ground. *Ibid.*

VACATING RECORDS. Embezzling or vacating records, is felony. 8 *H.* 6. c. 12.

VACATION, (*vacatio.*) The time between the end of one term and the beginning of another; which begins the last day of every term as soon as the court rises. There is also a vacation in the spiritualities, from the death of the bishop or other spiritual person until the appointment of another.

VACATURA. An avoidance of an ecclesiastical benefice. *Cowell.*

VACCARY, (*vaccaria.*) A house or place to keep cows in; a dairy-house, or cow-pasture. *Fleta, lib,* 2. *Cowell.*

VACCARIUS. The cow-herd, who looks after the common herd of cows. *Ibid.*

VADIARE DUELLUM. To wage a combat See *Trial by Wager of Battle.*

VADIUM PONERE. Is to take security, bail, or pledges for the appearance of a defendant in a court of justice. *Cowell.*

VADIUM MORTUUM. A mortgage or pawn of lands for securing to the creditor the repayment of his debt. *Glanv. lib.* 10 *cap.* 8. See 2 *Black. Com.* 157.

VAGABOND, (*vagabundus.*) A wandering beggar or idle person who wanders about, and has no certain place of abode. See *Vagrants.*

VAGRANTS, (*vagrantes.*) The stat. 17 *Geo.* 2. c. 5. called the Vagrant Act, divides these offenders against good order into three classes: 1. Idle and disorderly persons; 2. Rogues and vagabonds; and 3. Incorrigible rogues.

I. Idle and disorderly persons are by 17 *Geo.* 2. c. 5.; 1. Those who threaten to run away, and to leave their families upon the parish. 2. Who return from the parish to which they are removed as paupers, without a certificate. 3. Who refuse to work for the usual wages. 4. Who beg within their own parishes: and 5. by 32 *Geo.* 3 c. 45. who neglect to work, or who spend their money idly, without making a sufficient allowance for the subsistance of their families.

II. Rogues and vagabonds are thus described by 17 *Geo.* 2. c. 5. 1. Gatherers of alms, under pretence of loses, or for prisons or hospitals; 2. Fencers; 3. Bearwards; 4. Players of interludes, tragedies, comedies, operas, plays, farces, or other entertainments of the stage, not being authorized by law; 5. Minstrels; 6. Juglers; 7. Gypsies; 8. Fortune-tellers; 9. Deceivers by subtle craft: 10. Players and betters at unlawful games; 11. Persons who run away and leave their families chargeable to the parish; 12. Unlicensed pedlars; 13, Persons who wander abroad, and lodge in alehouses, outhouses, or in the open air, without giving a good account of themselves, pretending to be soldiers, mariners, or sea-faring men; 14. Persons wandering from home, under pretence of seeking harvest-work, without a certificate from the minister and one churchwarden of their parish; 15. All wandering beggars; 16. Beggars in their own parishes, who being apprehended, shall escape or resist; 17. By 32 *Geo.* 3. *c.* 45 soldiers and mariners begging; 18. By 28 *Geo.* 3. *c.* 88. all persons who are apprehended with any picklock or implement, with intent to feloniously break and enter any dwelling-house, or with any offensive weapon, with intent to feloniously assault any person; or who shall be found in or upon any dwelling-house, outhouse, yard, area, or garden, with intent to steal, shall be deemed rogues and vagabonds; 19. suspected persons and reputed thieves frequenting the Thâmes, and the quays and warehouses adjoining, with a felonious intent, 39 & 40 *Geo.* 3. *c.* 87. *s.* 11. 20. Persons to the number of two or more, who shall assemble together to destroy the game in the night-time, or persons aiding or assisting therein. 39 & 40 *Geo.* 3. *c.* 87. *s.* 1. 21. Every person who shall be found making any light, fire, or blaze, or signal to certain vessels hovering within eight leagues of the coasts. 42 *Geo.* 3. *c.* 82. 22. Persons setting up or playing at any Little Go or other unlawful lottery. 42 *Geo.* 3. *c.* 119.

III. Incorrigible rogues and vagabonds, 1. Who escape when they are apprehended, or refuse to go before a justice, or to be examined: 2. or who give a false account of themselves, after warning of the consequences, or who refuse to be conveyed by a pass; 3. or who escape from the house of correction; or, 4. who commit, after punishment, a second offence: 5. Offenders found with any child after it has been placed out as a servant or apprentice by the sessions; 6. Vagrants passed to Scotland, afterwards found begging: 7. Persons convicted of a third offence, against the acts 6 *Geo.* 3. *c.* 48. 9 *Geo.* 3. *c.* 41. and 45 *Geo.* 3. *c.* 16.—See *Trespass.*

The punishment of idle and disorderly persons is commitment to the house of correction, there to be kept to hard labour, not exceeding a month. Rogues and vagabonds are to be publicly whipped, or sent to the house of correction until the next sessions, or any less time, and after such whipping or commitment may be passed to their last legal settlement or place of birth, or if under fourteen, and have a father or mother living, to the place of abode of such father and mother. And if committed until the next sessions and adjudged a rogue or vagabond, the justices may order him to be kept in the house of correction to hard labour not exceeding six months. 17 *Geo.* 2. *c.* 5. *Ibid.*

A person adjudged at the sessions an incorrigible rogue, may be kept in the house of correction to hard labour, not exceeding two years, nor less than six months, and during the confinement be corrected by whipping, at such times and places as the justices shall think fit, and may then be passed as aforesaid: and if a male, and above the age of twelve years, the justices before his discharge may send him to be employed in the king's service, either by sea or land. If before the expiration of his confinement he shall escape from the house of correction, or offend again in the like manner, he shall be deemed to be guilty of felony, and transported for any time not exceeding seven years. *Ibid.*

Any person may apprehend and carry before a justice any persons going about from door to door, or placing themselves in streets, highways, or passages, to beg alms in the parishes where they dwell, and the justices may order the overseers of the poor to pay such person 5*s.* for every offender, which, on refusal of payment, may be levied on the overseer's goods. Any person may apprehend an offender against this act, and carry him before a justice. *Ibid.*

And the justice, or the court of quarter-sessions, may, if they think proper, order a vagabond, after punishment, to be conveyed to his place of settlement by a pass, but no justice of peace shall order any vagrant to be conveyed by a pass, who has not been actually whipped, or imprisoned for at least seven days, which shall be certified by the pass. 32 *Geo.* 3. *c.* 45. The object of this was to correct an abuse, which much prevailed, of removing paupers by a pass, who had committed no act of vagrancy, and who ought to have been removed by an order of removal. For the effects of an order of removal and a vagrant pass are very different; in the first case, the parish removing bears all the travelling expences of the paupers; but the expence of conveying vagrants by a pass, is borne by each county through which they are carried. And no appeal lies against a vagrant pass, so that the parish to which the vagrant is conveyed, must be at the expence of sending, by an order of removal, the vagrant back again, or to such place as, upon enquiry, may be thought his legal settlement.

VALET, (*valettus vel valecta.*) Was anciently a name denoting young gentlemen, though of great descent or quality; but afterwards attributed to those of lower rank, and now a servitor, or gentleman of the chamber. *Cam. Selden's Tit. Hon. Bract. lib.* 3. *Cowell.*

VALENTIA. The value or price of any thing. *Ibid.*

VALESHERIA. The kindred of the slain, one on the father's side, and another on the side of the mother, to prove that a man was a Welshman. Mentioned in *Stat. Walliæ,* 12 *Ed.* 1. *c.* 4. *Cowell.*

VALOR MARITAGII. Under the ancient tenures, while an infant was in ward, the guardian had the power of tendering him or her a suitable match without disparagement or inequality; which, if the infants refused, they forfeited the value of the marriage, *valorem maritagii,* to their guardian; that is, so much as a jury would assess, or any one would *bona fide* give to the guardian for such an alliance: and if the infants married themselves without the guardian's consent, they forfeited double the value, *duplicem valorem maritagii.* This was one of the greatest hardships of our ancient tenures—but the tenures being taken away, the law is abolished. 2 *Bl.* 70.

VALUABLE CONSIDERATION. See *Consideration.*

VALVASORS. The first name of dignity, next beneath a peer, was anciently that of *vidames, vice domini,* or *valvasors,* who are mentioned by our ancient lawyers as *viri magnæ dignitatis.* Yet they are now quite out of use, and our legal antiquarians are not agreed upon even their original or ancient office. 1 *Black.* 403.

VALUE, (*valentia, valor.*) The value of things is usually set forth in indictments, to distinguish between grand and petit larceny, and in trespass, to aggravate the fault, &c.

VALUE OF LAND. There is a distinction herein, namely, ancient and improved value. 2 *Leon.* 117. *Lutw.* 1304.

VALUE OF MARRIAGE, (*valore maritagii.*) A writ lay for the lord, having offered marriage to an infant without disparagement, if the man refused to take the lord's offer, and married another woman, to recover the value of the marriage. *Reg. Orig.* 164. See *Valor Maritagii.*

VANG, (Sax.) He vanged for me at the vant, *i. e.* stood for me at the font. *Blount.*

VANNUS. A Vane, *Venti Index*; and *vannus,* a fan to winnow corn with. *Lit. Dict. Cowell.*

VANTARIUS, (*præcursor,*) as *vantarius regis,* the king's running footman. *Cowell.*

VARIANCE, (*variantia,* from the Fr. *varier,* i. e. *alterare.*) Signified any alteration of a thing formerly set forth in pleading, or where the declaration in a cause differs from the writ or from the deed upon which it is founded.

But when the pleading is good in substance, a small variance shall not hurt. 2 *Lil. Abr.* 629. 3 *Mod.* 227. 2 *Str.* 1131. Where the original writ varies from the declaration, it is not remedied. See *Amendment.*

VASSAL, (*vassalus.*) Is said to be *quasi inferior socius,* as the vassal is inferior to his master, and must serve him; and yet he is in a manner his companion, because each of them is obliged to the other. 2 *Black.* 53.

VASSALAGE. The state of a vassal, or servitude and dependency on a superior lord. *Cowell.*

VASSELERIA. The tenure of holding of vassals. *Ibid.*

VASTO. A writ that lies against tenants for terms of life or years, committing waste. *F. N. B.* 55. *Reg. Orig.* 72. See *Waste.*

VASTUM. A waste or common lying open to the cattle of all tenants who have a right of commoning. *Cowell.*

VASTUM *Forestæ vel Bosci.* That part of a forest or wood, wherein the trees and underwood were so destroyed, that it lay in a manner waste and barren. *Ibid.*

VAVASOR. Is one who was in dignity next to a baron. *Brit.* 109. *Bract. lib.* 1. *cap.* 8. *Spelm. Gloss. Cowell.*

VAVASORY, (*vavasoria.*) The lands that a vavasor held. *Bract. lib.* 2. *Cowell.*

VEAL MONEY. The tenants within the manor of Bradford, in the county of Wilts, pay a yearly rent by this name to their lord, in lieu of veal paid formerly in kind. *Blount's Ten.*

VECTIGAL JUDICIARIUM. Money or fines paid to the king, to defray the charge of maintaining the courts of justice, and protection of the people. 3 *Salk.* 33.

VEJOURS, (*visores,* from the Fr. *veior,* i. e. *cernere*) Viewers sent by the court, to take a view of any place in question, for the better decision of the right thereto. *Old Nat. Br.* 112, *Bract. lib.* 5. *Cowell.*

VELTRAIA, (*Ministerium de Veltraia.*) The office of dog leader or courser. *Cowell.*

VELTRAIAS. One who leads greyhounds. And lands are held *per servitium inveniend. unum* veltrarium *Canes ducere,* &c. *Blount's Ten.* 9.

VELUM QUADRAGESIMALE. A veil or piece of hanging anciently drawn before the altar in Lent, as a token of mourning and sorrow. *Cowell.*

VENARIA. Beasts caught in the woods by hunting. *Ibid.*

VENATIO. Venison, in Fr. *venaison*: called so from the means whereby the beasts are taken, *quoniam ex* venatione *capiuntur,* and being hunted are most wholesome: and they are termed beasts of venary (not venery) because they are gotten in hunting. 4 *Inst.* 316.

VENDITIONI EXPONAS. A judicial writ, directed to the sheriff, commanding him to sell goods which he hath formerly taken into his hands, for the satisfying a judgment given in the king's court, upon a return made that they remain in his hands for want of buyers. *Reg. Jud.* 33. *Stat.* 14 *Car.* 2 *cap.* 21. 13 *H.* 7. 1. *Dyer* 363. 1 *Roll. Abr.* 894.

VENDITOR REGIS. The king's salesman; being the person who exposed to sale goods and chattels seized or distrained to answer any debt due to the king. *Cowell.*

VENDOR AND VENDEE. Vendor is a person who sells any thing, and vendee the person to whom it is sold. 2 *Chan. Cases* 5. 21 *Vin. Abr.* tit. *Vendor* and *Vendee.*

VENELLA, a narrow or strait way. *Cowell.*

VENIA, a kneeling or low prostration on the ground, by penitents. *Cowell.*

VENIRE FACIAS, a judicial writ awarded to the sheriff to cause a jury of the neighbourhood to appear, when a cause is brought to issue, to try the same: and if the jury come not at the day of this writ, then there shall go a *habeas corpora*, and after a distress until they appear. *Old Nat. Br.* 157.

VENIRE FACIAS *tot Matronas.* See *Ventre inspiciendo.*

VENTER, used for the children by a woman of one marriage; as the issue of first and second venter, &c. as proceeding from the abdomen or belly of the wife.

VENTRE INSPICIENDO, is a writ to search a woman that saith she is with child, and thereby withholdeth lands from the next heir. The trial whereof is by a jury of women. *Reg. Orig.* 227.

VENUE, *(Vicinetum* or *Visnetum)* is taken for a neighbouring place, *locus quem vicini habitant*; it is the county or place from whence a jury are to come for trial of causes. *F. N. B.* 115. In actions of trespass and ejectment, the *venue* is to be from the vill or hamlet where the lands in question do lie. And in all real actions, the *venue* must be laid in that county where the thing is for which the action is brought. 2 *Lill. Abr.* 634, 635. Although the jury now come from the body of the county, in all cases, by virtue of the stat. 4 & 5 *Ann.* c. 16.

In all transitory actions, as debt, assumpsit, trover, and the like, which may be laid in any county, the judges may alter the *venue* from the place where by the law it otherwise may be, if they believe, through any just cause, there cannot be an indifferent trial in the county where the *venue* is laid; and if a defendant will move to change the *venue*, he must make affidavit, that the cause of action (if any be) did arise in the county where he would have the *venue* to be, and not in the county where the plaintiff hath laid his action or elsewhere. And this motion to change it must be made before the rules for pleading are out; and it is a rule not to change a *venue* where necessary evidence arises in two counties to support the action, if the plaintiff will be bound to give some material evidence in the county where he has laid his action. 2. *Salk.* 698, 669. And some persons, such as barristers or attornies, are privileged to lay and keep the *venue* in Middlesex, or move the same into that county. 2 *Strange* 1049. Unless there is another defendant joined with them. 1 *Strange* 610.

With respect to criminal cases it is ordained by the statute 21 *Jac.* 1. c. 4. that all informations on penal statutes shall be laid in the counties where the offences were committed.

VERDEROR, (*Viridarius*, from the Fr. *Verdeur*, i. e. *Custos Nemoris)* is an officer in the king's forest, whose office is properly to look to the vert, and see it well maintained; and he is sworn to keep the assises of the forest, and view, receive, and inroll the attachments, and presentments of trespasses of vert and venison, &c. *Manwood, par.* 1. 332.

VERDICT, *(Veridictum, quasi dictum Veritatis)* is the answer of a jury given to the court, concerning the matter of fact in any cause committed to their trial; wherein every one of the twelve jurors must agree, or it cannot be a verdict. And the jurors are to try the fact, and the judges to adjudge according to the law that ariseth upon it. 1 *Inst.* 226.

In all cases, and all actions, the jury may give a general or special verdict; and the court is bound to receive it, if pertinent to the point in issue; and if the jury doubt, they may refer themselves to the court, but are not bound so to do. 3 *Salk.* 373. And if the jury will take upon them to find against the directions of the court, any thing in matter of law, the court will receive the verdict; but it may afterwards be set aside on a motion for a new trial. And the stat 32 *Geo.* 3. c. 60, in respect to a verdict upon an indictment or information for a libel, (see *Libel*,) seems to be merely declaratory of the law on this subject.

In case a jury acquit a man upon trial against full evidence, and being sent back to consider better of it, are peremptory in and stand to their verdict, the court must take it. And if the jury will by verdict convict a person against or without evidence, and against the opinion of the court, the court may reprieve him before judgment, and certify for his pardon. 2 *Hale's Hist. P. C.* 310.

VERECUNDIUM, is specially used for injury done to any one. *Cowell.*

VERGE, *(Virgata,)* the compass of the king's court, which bounds the jurisdiction of the lord steward of the househould; and that seems to have been twelve miles about. *Stat.* 13 *R.* 2. c. 3. *Britton* 68. *F. N. B.* 24. A verge of land; is an uncertain quantity directed by the custom of the country, from 15 to 30 acres. Also verge has another signification, of a stick or rod, whereby one is admitted tenant to a copyhold estate. *Old Nat. Br.* 17. As to verge of the court, see *Marshalsea.*

VERGERS, (*Virgatores*,) are such as carry white wands before the justices of either bench. Also in cathedrals. *Cowell. Fleta, lib.* 2. c. 38.

VERONICA. It is said that amongst other pretended miracles, there is preserved in St. Peter's church at Rome, an handkerchief called *veronica*, which bears the likeness of our Saviour, which was miraculously impressed thereon while he was led to the cross. *Cowell.*

VERT, (Fr. *Verd.* i. e. *Viridis*, otherwise called *Greenhue.*) in the forest laws signifies every thing that beareth a green leaf within a forest, that may cover a deer; but especially great and thick coverts. 4 *Inst.* 327. And vert is sometimes taken for that power which a man hath by the king's grant to cut green wood in the forest. 3 *Black.* 71.

VERVISE, a kind of cloth, stat. 1. *R.* 3. c. 8.

VERY LORD AND VERY TENANT, (*Verus Dominus & Verus Tenens*) are they that are immediate lord and tenant one to another. *Broke.*

VESSELS. See *Coopers.*

VEST, (*Vestire,*) to invest with, to make possessor of, to place in possession. *Cowell.*

VESTA, the vest, vesture, or crop on the ground. *Ibid.*

VESTED. See *Remainder* and *Legacy.*

VESTRY, a place adjoining to a church, where the vestments of the minister are kept; also a meeting at such place, to consult on the affairs of the church or parish. By custom there may be select vestries, or a certain number of persons chosen to have the government of the parish, make rates, and take the accounts of the churchwardens. 2 *Strange* 728. But in general, if a parishioner be shut out of the vestry room by the clerk of the vestry, and he makes it appear that he hath a right to come into the room, and to be present and vote in the vestry, &c. action of the case lies, as a remedy. *Mod. Ca. in L. & E.* 52. 354.

VESTURA, a crop of grass or corn. *Cowell. Paroch. Antiq. p.* 620.

VESTURE, (*Vestura,*) a garment, but in the law it is metaphorically applied to a possession or seisin. *Stat. West.* 2. c. 5.

VETITUM NAMIUM, is where the bailiff of a lord distrains beasts or goods of another, and the lord forbids his bailiff to deliver them when the sheriff comes to make replevin. The word *namium* signifying a taking or distress, and *vetitum* forbidden; and the owner of the cattle may demand satisfaction for the injury, which is called *Placitum de vetito namio.* 2 *Inst.* 140. *Black.* 148.

VEXATIOUS ARRESTS. By 51 *Geo.* 3. c. 124. after the 1st of November, 1811, no person shall be held to special bail upon any process issuing out of any court where the cause of action shall not have originally amounted to fifteen pounds over and above and exclusive of any costs, charges, and expences that may have been incurred, recovered, or become chargeable, in or about the suing for or recovering the same, (except where the cause of such action shall arise or be maintainable upon any bill of exchange, or promissory note, in which cases the parties liable thereupon may be held to special bail as formerly,) and where the cause of action shall not amount to fifteen pounds exclusive of costs, (except as before excepted) no special writ, nor any process specially therein expressing the cause of action, shall, after the 1st of November, be sued forth in order to compel any person to appear thereon.

VIA MILITARIS, a highway. *Cowell.*

UFFINGI. The kings of the East Angles were so termed from king Uffa, who lived in the year 578. *Ibid.*

VIA REGIA is the highway or common road, called the king's way, because authorised by him, and under his protection. *Cowell.*

VICAR, (*Vicarius, quasi vice fungens rectoris,*) the parson of every parish is called rector, unless the predial tithes are appropriated, and then he is stiled vicar; and when rectories are appropriated, vicars are to supply the rectors' places. *Cowell.* See *Appropriation.*

VICARAGE, (*Vicaria,*) Places which originally belonged to the parsonage or rectory, being derived out of it. 2 *Roll. Abr.* 59. And vicarage or not, is to be tried in the Spiritual Court, because it could not begin to be created but by the ordinary. 3. *Salk.* 378.

VICARIAL TITHES, small tithes. See *Tithes.*

VICARIO DELIBERANDO OCCASIONE CUJUSDAM RECOGNITIONIS, &c. An ancient writ that lay for a spiritual person imprisoned, upon forfeiture of a recognizance, &c. *Reg. Orig.* 147.

VICE-ADMIRALTY COURTS. There are vice-admiralty courts in America, and our other plantations. From those courts appeals may be brought before the courts of admiralty in England, as being a branch of the admiral's jurisdiction, though they may also be brought before the king in council. 3. *Black.* 69.

VICE-CHAMBERLAIN, a great officer next under the lord chamberlain: and in his absence hath the rule and controul of all officers appertaining to that part of his majesty's household, which is called the chamber above stairs. 13 *R.* 2. c. 1.

VICE-COMES, the sheriff.

VICE-CONSTABLE OF ENGLAND. See *Constable.*

VICE-CONSUL. The same as *Vicecomes* or sheriff.

VICE-DOMINUS. The same with *vicecomes.*

VICE-DOMINUS EPISCOPI, the vicar-general, or commissary of a bishop. *Cowell.*

VICE-GERENT, a deputy or lieutenant. *Ibid.*

VICE-MARSHAL is mentioned with vice-constable. 4 *Inst.* 71.

VICE-ROY, (*Pro. Rex.*) the king's lord-lieutenant over a kingdom. *Litt.*

VICE-TREASURER, an officer under the lord-treasurer. See *Under Treasurer of England.*

VICINAGE, (Fr. *Voisinage, Vicinetum,*) the neighbourhood. And there is common because of vicinage, or neighbourhood, where the inhabitants of two townships which lie contiguous, have usually intercommoned with one another; the beasts of the one straying mutually into the other's fields, without any molestation from either. 2 *Black.* 33. See *Jury* and *Venue.*

VICIS ET VENELLIS MUNDANDIS, a writ which lay against a mayor or bailiff of a town, for the clean keeping of their streets. *Reg. Orig.* 267.

VICOUNT, or VISCOUNT, (*Vicecomes*) signifies as much as sheriff. See *Sheriff.* Viscount also signifies a degree of nobility next to an earl; first created in this country by Henry VI. who, in his eighteenth year in parliament, created John lord Beaumont, viscount Beaumont. *Selden* 761.

VICOUNTIEL, or VICONTIEL, is an adjective from viscount, and signifieth any thing that belongeth to the sheriff; as writs vicontiel are such writs as are triable in the county or sheriff's court. *O. N. B.* 109. *F. N. B.* 184. *Cowell.*

VICOUNTIEL JURISDICTION, that jurisdiction which belongs to the officer of a county; as to sheriffs, coroners, escheators, and

VICOUNTIEL, or VISCONTIEL RENTS are mentioned, 22 *Car.* 2. *cap.* 6. *Hale's Sheriff's Accounts*, 40.

VICTUALS, (*Victus*), sustenance, and things necessary to live by, as meat and provisions: victuallers are those that sell victuals; and we call now all common alehouse keepers by the name of victuallers. Selling of corrupt victuals, or exposing them to sale, is punishable by stat. 1. *R.* 3. c. 1. And in some manors they chuse yearly two surveyors of victuals, to see that no unwholesome victuals be sold, and destroy such as are corrupt. 1 *Mod.* 202. See *Forestallers.*

VIDAME was the same as *vice-dominus*, the bishop's deputy in temporal matters. 1 *Black.* 403.

VIDELICET, (viz.) a *videlicet* in a deed may make a separation, as it says *habendum* 100*l.* to them to be equally divided, viz. 20*l.* to one, and so to the rest, &c. 5 *Mod. Rep.* 29.

VIDUITATIS PROFESSIO, the making a solemn profession to live a sole and chaste widow. *Cowell.*

VIDIMUS. See *Innotescimus.*

VI ET ARMIS are words used in indictments, to express the charge of a forcible and violent committing any crime or trespass. 2 *Hawk. P. C.* 179. 1 *Hawk.* 150, 220.

VIEW, (Fr. *Veue*, i. e. *Visus*,) is generally where a real action is brought, and the tenant doth not know certainly what is in demand; in such case he may pray that the jury may view it. *Briton*, c. 45. *F. N. B.* 178. This view is for a jury to see the land or thing claimed, and in controversy; and lies in ejectment, waste, assises of *novel disseisin*, where at least six of the recognitors or jurors must have the view before the assizes. 2 *Lil. Abr.* 655. Stat. 13 *Ed.* 1. c. 48. 12 *Ed.* 2. 4 & 5 *Anne.* c. 16. And upon a view, the thing in question is only to be shewn to the jury; and no evidence can be given on either side. 2 *Lil.* 656.

VIEW OF FRANK-PLEDGE, (*Visus Franci plegii,*) signifies the office which the sheriff in his county court performs in looking to the king's peace, and seeing that every man be in some pledge, &c. Or it is a power of holding a court-leet, in which court formerly all persons at the age of fourteen were bound with their sureties or pledges for their truth to the king, and the steward was to certify on view. *Bract. lib.* 2.

VIGIL, (*Vigilia*) is the eve, or next day before any solemn feast; because then christians were wont to watch, fast, and pray in their churches. 2 & 3 *Ed.* 6. c. 19. *Cowell.*

VI LAICA REMOVENDA, a writ that lay where two parsons contended for a church, and one of them entered into it with a great number of laymen, and held out the other *vi et armis*; then he that was holden out had this writ directed to the sheriff, that he remove the force. But the sheriff ought not to remove the incumbent out of the church, whether he is there by right or wrong, but only the force. *F. N. B.* 54. 3 *Inst.* 161. And the writ was not to be granted until the bishop had certified into the chancery such resisting and force, &c. *New Nat. Br.* 121.

VILL, or VILLAGE, (*Villa*) is sometimes taken for a manor, and sometimes for a parish or part of it. But a vill is most commonly the out-part of a parish, consisting of a few houses, as it were separate from it. 1 *Inst.* 115. And a manor may consist of several villages, or one alone. *Fleta, lib.* 6. c. 51. See *Parish. Down.*

VILLA REGIA, a title given to those country villages where the kings of England had a royal seat, and held the manor in their own demesne, having there commonly a free chapel, not subject to ecclesiastical jurisdiction. *Paroch. Antiq.* 53.

VILLAIN, VILLEIN, (*Vilanus*, Fr. *Vilain*, i. e. *Vilis*,) signified a man of base or servile condition, a bondman, or servant. Of these bondmen or villains there were two sorts in England; one termed a villain in gross, who was immediately bound to the person of the lord, and his heirs. The other, a villain regardant to a manor, being bound to his lord as a member belonging and annexed to a manor, whereof the lord was owner. *Cowell.*

VILLAIN ESTATE or CONDITION, contra-distinguished to free estate. *Stat.* 8 *H.* 6. 11. *Cowell.*

VILLANIS *regis subtractis reducendis*, a writ that lay for the bringing back of the king's bondmen that had been carried away by others out of his manors whereto they belonged. *Reg. Orig. fol.* 87.

VILLANOUS JUDGMENT, (*Villanum Judicium*,) is that which casts the reproach of villany and shame upon him against whom it is given, as a conspirator, &c. And the judgment in such a case shall be like the ancient judgment in attaint, viz. That the offender shall not be of any credit afterwards; nor shall it be lawful for him to approach the king's court; and his lands and goods shall be seized into the king's hands, his trees rooted up, and body imprisoned, &c. *Staundf. P. C.* 157. *Lamb. Eiren.* 63. Stat. 4 *H.* 5.

VILLEIN FLEECES, bad fleeces of wool, shorn from scabbed sheep. 31 *Ed.* 3. *c.* 8.

VILLENAGE, (*Villenagium*,) from villain, a servile kind of tenure belonging to land or tenements, whereby the tenant was bound to do all such services as the lord commanded, or were fit for a villain to do, which tenure was wholly abolished by 12 *Car.* 2. *c.* 24. See *Socage Tenure.*

VINAGIUM, (*Tributum a vino*,) a payment of a certain quantity of wine, instead of rent, to the chief lord, for a vineyard. *Cowell.*

VINCULO MATRIMONII, Divorce, *a.* If a marriage is improper through some cause which existed previous to the marriage, and was such a one as rendered the marriage unlawful *ab initio*, as consanguinity, corporal imbecility, or the like; in this case the law looks upon the marriage to have been always null and void, because contracted *in fraudem legis*, and decrees not only a separation from bed and board, but *a vinculo matrimonii* itself. 3 *Black.* 94. See *Divorce.*

VINNET, (from the Fr. *Vignet*,) a flower or border which printers use to ornament printed leaves of books; mentioned in *Stat.* 14 *Car.* 2. *c.* 33.

VINTNERS. See *Alehouses.*

VIOLATING THE QUEEN. See *Treason.*

VIOLENCE, (*Violentia*.) All violence is unlawful; and if a man assault another with an intention of beating him only, and he dieth, it is felony. And where a person knocks another on the head who is breaking his hedges, or the like, this will be murder, because it is a violent act beyond the provocation. *Kel. Rep.* 64, 131.

VIOLENT PRESUMPTION is many times equal to full proof, from the strong circumstances which appear to have attended the fact. 3 *Black.* 371. See *Circumstancial Evidence.*

VIRGA, a rod or white staff, such as sheriffs, bailiffs, and others, carry as a badge or ensign of their office. *Cowell.*

VIRGATA TERRÆ, a yard land. *Ibid.*

VIRGE, *Tenant by.* A species of copyholders, viz. such as are said to hold by the virge, or rod. *Calthorpe*, 51, 54. 2 *Black.* 147, 148.

VIRIDARIO ELIGENDO, a writ that lies for the choice of a verderor in the forest. *Reg. Orig.* 177.

VIRIDIS ROBA, a coat of many colours; *viridis* being used for *varius. Bract. lib.* 3.

VIRILIA, the privy members of a man; to cut off which was felony by the common law, though the party consented to it. *Bract. lib.* 3. *pag.* 144.

VIS, (Lat.) is any kind of force, violence, or disturbance relating to a man's person, his goods, or right in lands. *Cowell.*

VISCOUNT, (*Vicecomes*) a degree of nobility next to an earl. See *Vicount.* They are now made by patent, as an earl; but their number is small in this kingdom, in comparison with the other degrees of peerage. 1 *Black.* 399.

VISITATION, (*Visitatio*) is that office which is performed by the bishop of every diocese once every three years, or by the archdeacon once a year, by visiting the churches and their rectors throughout the whole diocese. *Noy.* 123. 3 *Salk.* 370.

VISITATION BOOKS OF HERALDS. The original visitation books of heralds, compiled when progresses were solemnly and regularly made into every part of the kingdom, to enquire into the state of families, and to register such marriages and descents as were verified to them upon oath, are allowed to be good evidence of pedigrees. *Comb.* 63.

VISITOR, is an inspector of the government of a corporation. Thus the ordinary is visitor of spiritual corporations; but corporations instituted for private charity, if they are lay, are visitable by the founder, or whom he shall appoint, and from the sentence of such visitor there lies no appeal. 3 *Salk.* 381.

VISITOR OF MANNERS, in ancient time was wont to be the name of the regarder's office in the forest. *Manwood*, 1. *p.* 195.

VISNE, (*Visnetum*,) signifies a neighbouring place, or place near at hand. *Cowell.* See *Venue.*

VISUS, view, or things to be taken by inspection. *Cowell.*

VITA *Justitiæ et Legis*, a sheriff of the county is said to be the life of justice, as no suit begins and no process is served but by him; and after suits are ended, he hath the making execution, which is the life of the law. *Cowell.*

VIVARY, (*Vivarium*) a place by land or water, where living creatures are kept. And in law it is most commonly used for a park, warren, piscary, and the like. 2 *Inst.* 100.

VIVA VOCE, is where a witness is examined personally in open court. *Cowell.* See *Deposition.*

VIVO VADIO, estate in. When a man borrows a sum of another, and grants him an estate until the rents and profits shall repay the sum borrowed, he is then said to have an estate *in vivo vadio*, or a self-dissolving pledge.

ULCUS, a hulk of a ship of burden. *Cowell.*

ULLAGE is when there is want of measure in a cask. *Ibid.*

ULNAGE. See *Alnage.*

ULNA FERREA is the standard ell of iron, kept in the Exchequer for the rule of measure. *Cowell.*

UMPIRAGE is where there is but one arbitrator of matters submitted to award; and is usually when the parties submit themselves to the arbitrament of certain persons; and if they cannot agree, or are not ready to deliver their award in writing before such a time, then to the judgment of another as umpire. 1 *Roll. Abr.* 261, 262. See *Arbitration.*

UMPIRE, (*Arbiter*) one chosen to compromise and deal indifferently between both parties. *Litt.* See *Arbitrament. Award.*

UNA CUM OMNIBUS ALIIS, in the grant of a deed, is a new addition of other things than were granted before; and hath its own conclusion attending it. *Hob.* 175.

UNANIMITY OF JURIES. The necessity of a total unanimity of the jurors, on every trial, seems to be peculiar to our own constitution. 3 *Black.* 376. See *Verdict.*

UNCEASSATH. This is an obsolete word, mentioned in *Leg. Inæ. c.* 37. viz. He who kills a thief, may make oath that he killed him in flying for the fact, *et parentibus ipsius occisi juret* unceassath, that is, that his kindred will not revenge his death. From the Saxon *ceas*, *litis*, and *un*, which is a negative particle, and signifies without, and *ath*, which is oath; that is, to swear that there shall be no contention about it. *Cowell.*

UNCERTAINTY OF THE LAW. It has sometimes been said, that the uncertainty of the law, as it is improperly called, owes its origin to the number of our municipal constitutions, and the multitude of our judicial decisions; which occasion, it is alledged, abundance of rules, that militate and thwart with each other, as the sentiments or caprice of successive legislatures and judges have happened to vary. But although the fact of multiplicity is allowed, yet the people mistake variety for confusion, and complicated cases for contradictory; and the causes of the multiplicity of the English laws are the extent of the country which they govern; the commerce and refinement of its inhabitants; but above all, the liberty and property of the subject. These will naturally produce an infinite fund of disputes; which must be terminated in a judicial way. And it is essential to a free people, that these determinations be published and adhered to, that their property may be as certain and fixed as the very constitution of their state. For though in many other countries every thing is left in the breast of the judge to determine, yet with us he is only to declare and pronounce, not to make or new model the law. Hence a multitude of decisions, or cases adjudged, will arise; for seldom will it happen that any one rule will exactly suit with many cases. And in proportion as the decisions of the courts of judicature are multiplied, the law will be loaded with decrees, that may sometimes (though rarely,) interfere with each other. Either because succeeding judges may not be apprized of the prior abjudication; or because they may think differently from their predecessors; or because the same arguments did not occur formerly as at present; or, in fine, because of the natural imbecility and imperfection that attends all human proceedings. But, wherever this happens to be the case in any material point, the legislature is ready, and, from time to time, both may, and frequently does, intervene to remove the doubt; and, upon due deliberation had, determines by a declaratory statute how the law shall be held for the future. 3 *Black.* 325.

UNCIA TERRÆ, UNCIA AGRI. These phrases often occur in the charters of the British kings, and signify some measure or quantity of land. It was the quantity of 12 *modii*, and each *modius* possibly 100 feet square. *Cowell.*

UNCORE PRIST, is a plea of a defendant in nature of a plea in bar, where being sued for a debt due on bond at a day past, to save the forfeiture of the bond, he says that he tendered the money at the day and place, and that there was none there to receive it; and that he is also still ready to pay the same. 7 *Ed.* 6. 6. 9 *Rep.* 70. 3 *Black.* 303.

UNCUTH, a Saxon word, signifying *incognitus*, unknown. *Bract. lib.* 3. *Cowell.*

UNDE NIHIL HABEAT. See *Dote unde nihil habet.*

UNDER-CHAMBERLAIN OF THE EXCHEQUER, is an officer there that cleaves the tallies, written by the clerk of the tallies, and reads the same, that the clerk of the pell, and comptrollers thereof, may see their entries be true. He also makes searches for all records in the treasury, and hath the custody of domesday book. *Cowell.* See *Exchequer.*

UNDER ESCHEATOR, (*Sub-Escheator.*) See *Escheator.*

UNDER-SHERIFF, (*Sub-Vicecomes.*) See *Sheriff.*

UNDERTAKERS, &c. Persons that undertake funerals. See *Burial.*

UNDER TREASURER OF ENGLAND, (*Vice Thesaurarius Angliæ,*) an officer first created in the time of Hen. VII. His business was to chest up the king's treasure at the end of every term, to note the content of money in each chest, and see it carried into the king's treasury for the ease of the lord treasurer, as being a thing beneath him, but fit to be performed by a man of great trust and secrecy. And, in the vacancy of the lord treasurer's office, he did all things in the receipt, &c. This officer is mentioned in several statutes, and named treasurer of the exchequer till the reign of queen Elizabeth, when he was termed under treasurer of England. 39 *Eliz.* c. 7.

UNDERWOOD. See *Trespass.*

UN DIEU, ET UN ROY, was Littleton's motto. *Cowell.*

UNDRES, a word used for minors, or persons under age; not capable to bear arms, &c. *Fleta, lib.* 1. c. 9. *Cowell.*

UNFRID, one that hath no quiet or peace. *Cowell.*

UNGELD, a person out of the protection of the law, so that, if he were murdered, no geld or fine should be paid, or composition made by him that killed him. *Leg. Ethelred. Cowell.*

UNGILDA AKER. (From the Sax. *un*, without, *gilda*, *solutio*, and *acera*, *ager.* It signifies almost the same as ungeld, viz. were a man was killed attempting any felony, he was to lie in the field unburied, and no pecuniary compensation was to be paid for his death. *Cowell.*

UNIFORMITY, (*Uniformitas,*) one form of public prayers and administration of sacraments, and other rites and ceremonies of the church of England, prescribed by statutes, to which all must submit. 1 *Eliz.* c. 2. 14 *Car.* 2. c. 4. But see *Dissenters.*

UNION, (*Unio,*) is a combining and consolidating of two churches into one. And by assent of the ordinary, patron, and incumbent, two churches lying not above a mile distant one from the other, and whereof the value of the one is not above six pounds a year in the king's books of the first fruits, may be united into one. *Stat.* 37. *H.* 8. c. 21. Also by 17 *Car.* 2. c. 3. in cities and corporation towns, it shall be lawful for the bishops, patrons, and mayors, or chief magistrates of the place, &c. to unite churches therein; but where the income of the churches united exceeds 100*l.* a year, the major part of the parishioners are to consent to the same; and, after the union made, the patrons of the churches united shall present, by turns, to that church only which shall be presentative, in such order as agreed; and notwithstanding the union, each of the parishes united shall continue distinct as to rates, charges, &c. though the tithes are to be paid to the incumbent of the united church. And by 4 & 5 *W.* & *M.* c. 12. it is ordained, that where any churches have been united, by virtue of the 17 *Car.* 2. c. 3. and one of them is demolished; when the other church shall be out of repair, the parishioners of the parish whose church is down, shall pay in proportion towards the charge of such repairs, &c.

UNION WITH IRELAND. See *Ireland.*

UNION WITH SCOTLAND. See *Scotland.*

UNITY OF POSSESSION, (*Unitas Possessionis,*) is where a man hath a right to two estates, and holds them together jointly in his own hands; as if a man take a lease of lands from another at a certain rent, and after he buys the fee-simple, this is an unity of possession, by which the lease is extinguished, because that he who had before the occupation only for his rent, is now become lord and owner of the land. *Terms de Ley.* See *Year's Tenant.*

UNIVERSITY, (*Universitas.*) The universities with us are taken for those two bodies which are the nurseries of learning and liberal science in this kingdom, viz. Oxford and Cambridge; endowed with great privileges. And although each university was a civil corporation before, it is, by 13 *Eliz.* c. 27. enacted, that each of the universities shall be incorporated by a certain name; and that all letters patent, and charters granted to the universities, shall be good and effectual in law. That the chancellor, masters, and scholars, of either of the said universities shall enjoy all manors, lands, liberties, franchises, and privileges, and all other things which the said corporated bodies have enjoyed, or of right ought to enjoy, according to the intent of the said letters patent; and all letters patent, and liberties, franchises, &c. shall be established and confirmed, any law, usage, &c. to the contrary notwithstanding.

Their courts are called the chancellor's courts, and these courts of the two universities of England enjoy the sole jurisdiction, in exclusion of the king's courts, over all civil actions and suits whatsoever, where a scholar or privileged person is one of the parties; excepting in such cases where the right of freehold is concerned. And these, by the university-charter, they are at liberty to try and determine, either according to the common law of the land, or according to their own local customs, at their discretion; which has generally led them to carry on their process in a course much conformed to the civil law. 3 *Black*. 83.

These privileges were granted, that the students might not be distracted from their studies by legal process from distant courts, and other forensic avocations. But these particular jurisdictions, derogating from the general jurisdiction of the courts of common law, are ever taken strictly, and cannot be extended farther than the express letter of their privileges will most explicitly warrant. 3 *Black*. 83.

This privilege, so far as it relates to civil causes, is exercised in the chancellor's court: the judge of which is the vice-chancellor, his deputy, or assessor. From his sentence an appeal lies to delegates appointed by the congregation; from thence to other delegates of the house of convocation; and if they all three concur in the same sentence, it is final, at least by the statutes of the university, *Tit*. 21. *sec*. 19. according to the rule of the civil law. *Cod*. 7, 70. I. But, if there be any discordance or variation in any of the three sentences, an appeal lies in the last resort to judges delegates, appointed by the crown under the great seal in chancery. 3 *Black*. 83.

By the charter of 7 *Jun*. 2 *Hen*. 4. (confirmed among the rest, by the statute 13 *Eliz. c*. 29.) cognizance is also granted to the universities of all indictments of treasons, insurrections, felony, and mayhem, which shall be found in any of the king's courts against a scholar or privileged person; and they are to be tried before the high steward of the university, or his deputy, who is to be nominated by the chancellor of the university for the time being. But, when his office is called forth into action, such high steward must be approved by the lord high chancellor of England; and a special commission under the great seal is given to him, and others, to try the indictment then depending, according to the law of the land and the privileges of the said university. When therefore an indictment is found at the assises, or elsewhere, against any scholar of the university, or other privileged person, the vice-chancellor may claim the cognizance of it; and (when claimed in due time and manner) it ought to be allowed him by the judges of assize: and then it comes to be tried in the high steward's court. But the indictment must first be found by a grand jury, and then the cognizance claimed: for the high steward cannot proceed originally *ad inquirendum*; but only, after inquest in the common law courts, *ad audiendum et determinandum*. 4 *Black*. 277.

When the cognizance is so allowed, if the offence be *inter minora crimina*, or a misdemesnor only, it is tried in the chancellor's court by the ordinary judge. But if it be for treason, felony, or mayhem, it is then, and then only, to be determined before the high steward, under the king's special commission to try the same. The process of the trial is this. The high steward issues one precept to the sheriff of the county, who thereupon returns a pannel of eighteen freeholders; and another precept to the bedels of the university, who thereupon return a pannel of eighteen matriculated laymen, "*laicos privilegio universitatis gaudentes*:" and by a jury formed *de medietate*, half of freeholders and half of matriculated persons, is the indictment to be tried. And if execution be necessary to be awarded, in consequence of finding the party guilty, the sheriff of the county must execute the university process; to which he is annually bound by an oath. 4 *Black*. 278.

There has happily been no occasion for more than a century past, nor will it perhaps ever be thought adviseable to revive them, though it is not a right that merely rests *in scriptis* or theory, but has formerly often been carried into execution. *Ibid*.

UNKNOWN PERSONS. An indictment will lie, for stealing the goods of a person unknown. *Hal. P. C*. 512. See *Larceny*.

UNLAGE, a Saxon word, denoting an unjust law. *Cowell*.

UNLAWFUL ASSEMBLY, (*Illicita Congregatio*.) See *Riots*.

UNNATURAL, (*Præturnaturalis*.) That which is not of or by nature. And what is unnatural to man generally, must be the same to all men, and at all times; but what is unnatural to this or that person, is to him only, and but for the time it is so. *Vaugh*. 224.

UNQUES PRIST, always ready to perform a thing. Used in pleading. *Kitch*. 243. *Cowell*.

VOCIFERATIO, an out-cry, or hue and cry. *Cowell.*

VOIDANCE, (*Vacatio,*) the want of an incumbent upon an ecclesiastical benefice. See *Avoidance.*

VOID AND VOIDABLE. In the law some things are absolutely void and some are voidable. A thing is void which is done against law at the very time of the doing of it, and it shall bind no person. But a thing which is only voidable and not void, will remain good until it is avoided. 2 *Lil. Abr.* 653.

But it hath been adjudged, that a bond of an infant, or of one *non compos*, is void, because the law hath not appointed any thing to be done to avoid such bonds; for the party cannot plead *non est factum*, as the cause of nullity doth not appear upon the face of the deed. 2 *Salk.* 675. 3 *Nels. Abr.* 486.

But a deed of exchange, entered into by an infant, or one *non sanæ memoriæ*, is not void; but may be avoided by the infant, when arrived at age, or by the heir of him who is *non sanæ memoriæ. Perk.* 281.

VOIRE, a French word signifying truly. *Law Fr. Dict.*

VOIRE DIRE, (Fr. *Veritatem dicere,*) is when it is prayed upon a trial at law, that a witness may be sworn upon a *voire dire* before he is examined in chief, which is, that he shall on his oath speak the truth, whether he shall get or lose by the matter in controversy. *Blount.* And this is often done, where a busy evidence, not otherwise to be excepted against, is suspected of partiality. *Terms de Ley.* 581.

VOLUMUS, is the first word of a clause in the king's writs of protection and letters patent. *Co. Litt.* 199.

VOLUNTARY, where any conveyance is made without any consideration, either of money, marriage, or the like, &c. it is found voluntary. And remainders limited in settlements, to a man's right heirs, &c. are deemed voluntary in equity, and the persons claiming under them called volunteers. *Abr. Cas. Eq.* 385. 3 *Salk.* 174. See also *Escape Oaths* and *Waste.*

VOLUNTAS, is when a tenant by lease holds lands at the will of the lessor; or a copyholder holdeth his lands at the will of the lord, by a copy of court-roll, according to the custom of the manor, &c. *Cowell.*

VOTUM, a vow or promise used by *Fleta* for *nuptiæ*; so *dies votorum*, is the wedding day. *Fleta, lib.* 4.

VOUCHE, (Fr. in Latin *Voco,*) Signifies to call one to warrant lands. *Cowell.*

VOUCHEE. The person who is vouched, in a writ of right. *Ibid.*

VOUCHER is a word of art, when the tenant in a writ of right calls another into the court, who is bound to him to warranty; that is, either to defend the right against the demandant, or yield him other lands to the value, &c. He that voucheth is called the voucher, (*vocans,*) and he that is vouched, is called the vouchee, (*warrantatus,*) &c. *Co. Litt.* 101.

A foreign voucher is when the tenant being impleaded within a particular jurisdiction, as in London, voucheth one to warranty in some other county out of the jurisdiction of that court, and prays that he may be summoned, &c. 2 *Rep.* 50. See *Recovery* and *Warranty.*

VOUCHER, is also used for a leger-book, or book of accounts, wherein are entered the acquittances or warrants for the accountant's discharge. *Stat.* 19 *Car.* 2. *c.* 1. Voucher signifies also, any acquittance or receipt, discharging a person, or being evidence of a payment. *Cowell.*

VOX, *Vocem non habere.* One who is not to be admitted to be a witness. *Bract. lib.* 3.

UPHOLSTERS. None shall put to sale any beds, bolsters, &c. except such as are stuffed with one sort of dry pulled feathers, or clean down; and not mixed with scalded feathers, fen-down, thistle-down, sand, &c. on pain to forfeit the same, or the value. And they are to stuff quilts, mattrasses, and cushions, with clean wool, and flocks; without using horse-hair, &c. therein, under the like forfeiture. *Stat.* 11. *H.* 7. c. 19. and 5 & 6. *Ed.* 6. *c.* 23.

UPLAND, high ground, or *terra firma*, contrary to marshy and low ground. *Cow.*

USA is the river Isis. *Blount.*

USAGE differs from custom and prescription. No man may claim a rent, common, or other inheritance by usage, though he may by prescription. 6 *Rep.* 65. See *Prescription.*

USANCE. The limitation for the payment of foreign bills drawn or payable at Amsterdam, Rotterdam, Hamburgh, Altona, Paris, or any place in France, Cadiz, Madrid, Bilboa, Leghorn, Genoa, or Venice; and this usance (instead of the limitation of payments by years, months, or days,) signifying the usage between those places and this country is as follows: An usance between this kingdom and Amsterdam, Rotterdam, Hamburgh, Altona, Paris, or any place in France, is one calendar month from the date of the bill; an usance between us and Cadiz, Madrid, or Bilboa two; an usance between us and Leghorn, Genoa, or Venice, three; A double usance is double the accustomed time, an half usance half, and where it is necessary to divide a month upon an half usance, which is the law where the usance is either one month or three, the divisions, notwithstanding the difference in the length of months, contains fifteen days. *Marius* 23.

USE, (*Usus*), is, in application of law,

the profit or benefit of lands and tenements; or a trust and confidence reposed in a man for the holding of lands. That he to whose use the trust is made shall take the profits thereof. *West. Symb. par.* 1. 1 *Inst.* 272.

USES AND TRUSTS are in their original of a nature very similar, or rather exactly the same; a use being a confidence reposed in another who was tenant of the land, or terre-tenant, that he should dispose of the land according to the intentions of *cestuy que use*, or him to whose use it was granted, and suffer him to take the profits. As, if a feoffment was made to A and his heirs, to the use of (or in trust for) B and his heirs; here at the common law A the *terre-tenant* had the legal property and possession of the land, but B the *cestuy que use* was in conscience and equity to have the profits and disposal of it. *Bacon on Uses*, 306.

And the stat. 27 *Hen.* 8. c. 10. enacts, that, "when any person shall be seised of lands, &c. to the use, confidence, or trust of any other person or body politic, the person or corporation entitled to the use in fee-simple, fee-tail, for life, or years, or otherwise, shall from thenceforth stand and be seised or possessed of the land, &c. of and in the like estates as they have in the use, trust, or confidence; and that the estate of the person so seised to uses shall be deemed to be in him or them that have the use, in such quality, form, manner and condition as they had before in the use." The statute thus executes the use, as our lawyers term it; that is, it conveys the possession to the use, and transfers the use into possession; thereby making *cestuy que use* complete owner of the lands and tenements, as well at law as in equity. 2 *Black.* 332.

USES AND TRUSTS, *covenant, to stand, seized to.* This is a species of conveyance, by which a man, seised of lands, covenants, in consideration of blood or marriage, that he will stand seised of the same to the use of his child, wife, or kinsman; for life, in tail, or in fee. Here the statute executes at once the estate; for the party intended to be benefited, having thus acquired the use, is thereby put at once into corporal possession of the land, without ever seeing it. But this conveyance can only operate, when made upon such weighty aod interesting considerations as those of blood or marriage. *Bacon. Use of the Law.* 151.

DEEDS OF REVOCATION OF USES, are founded in a previous power, reserved at the raising of the uses, to revoke such as were then declared; and to appoint others in their stead, which is incident to the power of revocation.

DEEDS TO LEAD THE USES OF FINES AND RECOVERIES, are necessary deeds to lead, or to declare the uses of fines, and of recoveries. For if they be levied or suffered without any good consideration, and without any uses declared, they, like other conveyances, enure only to the use of him who levies or suffers them. And if a consideration appears, yet as the most usual fine "*sur cognizance de droit come ceo, &c.*" conveys an absolute estate, without any limitations, to the cognizee; and as common recoveries do the same to the recoverer, these assurances could not be made to answer the purpose of family settlements, (wherein a variety of uses and designations is very often expedient,) unless their force and effect were subjected to the direction of other more complicated deeds, wherein particular uses can be more particularly expressed. The fine or recovery itself, like a power once gained in mechanics, may be applied and directed to give efficacy to an infinite variety of movements in the vast and intricate machine of a voluminous family settlement. And if these deeds are made previous to the fine or recovery, they are called deeds to lead the uses; if subsequent, deeds to declare them. As if A, tenant in tail, with reversion to himself in fee, would settle his estate on B for life, remainder to C in tail, remainder to D in fee; this is what by law he has no power of doing effectually, while his own estate-tail is in being. He therefore usually, after making the settlement proposed, covenants to levy a fine (or if there be any intermediate remainders, to suffer a recovery) to E, and directs that the same shall enure to the uses in such settlement mentioned. This is now a deed to lead the uses of the fine or recovery; and the fine when levied, or recovery when suffered, shall enure to the uses so specified and no other. For though E, the cognizee or recoverer, hath a fee-simple vested in himself by the fine or recovery; yet, by the operation of this deed, he becomes a mere instrument or conduit-pipe, seised only to the use of B, C, and D, in succescive order, which use is executed immediately by force of the statute of uses. Or, if a fine or recovery be had without any previous settlement, and a deed be afterwards made between the parties, declaring the uses to which the same shall be applied, this will be equally good as if it had been expressly levied or suffered in consequence of a deed directing its operation to those particular uses. For by stat. 4 & 5 *Anne*, c. 16. indentures to declare the uses of fines and recoveries, made after the fines and recoveries had and suffered, shall be good and effectual in law, and the fine and recovery shall enure to such uses, and esteemed to be only in trust, notwithstanding any doubts that had arisen on the statute of frauds, 29 *Car.* 2. *c.* 3. to the contrary.

And by 39 & 40 *Geo.* 3. *c.* 56. after reciting "that it was the practice of courts of equity, in cases in which money, under the control of such courts, was subject to be laid out in the purchase of lands to be limited to uses capable of being barred by a fine, to direct the money to be paid to the person who could bar the uses by levying a fine, without requiring the actual investment of the money in the purchase of lands; but in cases where a fine would not bar the uses, and it was necessary to suffer a recovery to bar the interests in remainder, it was the practice to require an actual investment of the money in lands, which practice was attended with great expence and inconvenience, and did not materially promote the interests of the parties in remainder:" it is enacted, that upon the petition of such persons who could, by a recovery, or any other mode, bar the estates-tail, and all the interests in remainder, if the money were invested in freehold or copyhold hereditaments, the petitioners being adult, and if *femes covert* being duly examined and consenting, a court of equity may order the money to be paid, and applied in such manner as the petitioners shall appoint, and the court approve.

For the purpose of carrying this into execution, lord chancellor Loughborough consulted the chief justices and the master of the rolls, how this act ought to be executed; and they agreed that it would be proper not to order the money to be paid out of the court, until such time as the tenant in tail might actually have suffered a common recovery of the land: and in consequence a direction is added to the order in such cases, that it shall have no effect unless the tenant in tail shall be living on the second day of the next term. 5 *Ves.* jun. 12. 6 *Ibid.* 116.

But the court will make no order, unless the right of the petitioners is clear and indisputable. 6 *Ves.* jun. 156.

USES, SUPERSTITIOUS. By statute, a devise of lands or goods to superstitious uses, is where it is to find or maintain a chaplain or priest to pray for the souls of the dead, or lamp in a chapel, a stipendary priest, &c. These, and such like, are declared to be superstitious uses; and the lands and goods so devised are forfeited to the king. 1 *Ed.* 6. *c.* 14.

USER DE ACTION, is the pursuing or bringing an action in the proper county, &c. *Broke* 64.

USHER, (Fr. *huissier*, a door-keeper,) is an officer in the king's house, as of the privy chamber, and the like. And there are ushers of the courts of chancery and exchequer.

USUCAPTION, (*usucaptio.*) Signifies the enjoying by continuance of time; a long possession, or prescription. *Terms de Ley.*

USUFRUCTUARY, (*usufructuarius.*) One that hath the use and reaps the profit of a thing. *Cowell.*

USURIOUS CONTRACT. A corrupt bargain or contract, to receive or allow more interest for money than the law allows. See *Usury.*

USURPATION, (*usurpatio.*) The usurpation of a church benefice is, when one that hath no right presenteth to the church, and his clerk is admitted and instituted into it, and hath quiet possession six months after institution before a *quare impedit* brought. It must commence upon a presentation, not a collation; because by a collation the church is not full, but the right patron may bring his writ at any time to remove the usurper. 1 *Inst.* 227. 6 *Rep.* 30. And by usurpation, the fee of an advowson may be gained, as well as the avoidance upon which the usurpation is made. And the true patron cannot remove the incumbent to regain the possession, without a writ of right advowson, which he is driven to for recovery of the inheritance. 6 *Rep.* 49.

USURPATION OF FRANCHISES AND LIBERTIES, is when a subject unjustly uses any royal franchises, &c. And it is said to be an usurpation upon the king, who shall have the writ of *quo warranto* against the usurpers. See *Quo Warranto.*

USURA MARITIMA. See *Bottomree.*

USURY, (*usura.*) Is the interest or profit exacted for a loan beyond what is allowed by statute.

And by the stat. 12 *Anne*, *c.* 16. "no person shall take, directly or indirectly, for loan of any money, or any thing, above the value of 5*l.* for the forbearance of 100*l.* for a year, and so proportionably for a greater or less sum; and all bonds, contracts, and assurances made for payment of any principal sum to be lent on usury, above the rate of 5*l. per cent.* shall be void. And whoever shall take, accept, or receive by way of corrupt bargain, loan, &c. a greater interest, shall forfeit treble the value of the money lent; and scriveners, solicitors, and drivers of bargains, are not to take above 5*s.* for procuring the loan of 100*l.* for a year, on pain of forfeiting 20*l.* &c.

Although, by this statute, if a man give a bond or other assurance for payment of an interest beyond that which is allowed by the statute, yet the receipt of higher interest by virtue of an agreement subsequent to the first contract, doth not avoid an assurance fairly made; and the receipt thereof will subject the party to the forfeiture of treble value only. 1 *Hawk.* 246. 1 *Mod.* 69. For no contract legal at the time it was entered into can by any subsequent event be awarded as usurious. 3 *Tr. Rep.* 539.

And a bill of exchange given on an usurious consideration is void even in the hands of an innocent indorsee for a valuable consideration, without notice of the usury. *Doug.* 736.

And the usury is the same whether the loan be of goods or any other thing, and not money. *Mo.* 398.—Also if the allowance be by a mean, and indirectly, as if a country banker, discounting a bill, takes interest for the whole time it has to run, and instead of paying money for the bill, gives notes payable in London three days after sight, such country banker is guilty of usury. *Peake's N. P.*—So it is usury if there be an agreement for payment of 100*l.* for wares within a month, or otherwise 120*l.* at the end of a year. *Mo.* 397. 5 *Co.* 70 *a.* 2 *Cro.* 508.

But where it is in the power of the borrower of money to pay the principal within a limited time, without interest; on non-payment of the reservation of a larger sum than the statute allows, it is no usury. *Cowp.* 115.; therefore, if a tradesman sell goods at three months credit, and stipulate, in case the money be unpaid, that the vendee shall allow him so much per month till he discharge the debt: this allowance, though above the legal rate of interest, yet being the usage of that particular trade, and the contract being a *bona fide* sale, is not usurious. *Ibid.* 112.

And the loan of money produced by the sale of stock, on an agreement that the borrower shall replace his stock on a certain day, or repay the money on a subsequent day, with such interest in the mean time as the stock itself would have produced, is not usurious, though the interest exceed 5*l.* per cent. unless the transaction be colourable, and a mere device to obtain more than legal interest. As if a wager be to give 40*l.* for 20*l.* paid, if A. should be alive at a certain day, as at the year's end, or the like. *Cro. Eliz.* 643.

Also interest exchange and other incidental expences on a protested bill of exchange beyond 5*l.* interest, if the charges are reasonable and warranted by usage, are not unlawful, provided they are not made a colour for usury. 2 *Ter. Rep.* 52.

So, if there be a hazard of the principal, it will not be usury, 3 *Ter. Rep.* 581, though the interest may, upon a contingency, exceed that allowed.

So when words are colourably added to avoid the statute which may be averted; as if the agreement be to pay for 100*l.* 20*l.* *per ann.* from Michaelmas next, if it be not repaid before Michaelmas, where it was agreed that it should not be repaid before. 5 *Co.* 69.

For if the substance of the contract be a borrowing and lending, a slight colourable contingency only will not take it out of the statute. *Cowp.* 770. And there is no contrivance whatever by which a man may cover usury. *Cowp.* 796.

Thus if the borrower of money give a bond for the principal and interest at 5*l.* *per cent.* and covenant at the same time also to pay to the lender a certain portion of the profits of a trade carried on by him in partnership with another person, it is an usurious contract, and the obligee cannot recover on the bond. 4 *Ter. Rep.* 353.

So, if on a negociation for a loan of money, the lender says he cannot advance the money, but will furnish goods, which the other takes and sells, if the security given be for a sum of money made payable at a future day, greatly exceeding the value of the goods and 5*l.* per cent., this is an usurious loan, and the security and contract are both void. *Doug.* 736.

If there be an agreement to pay legal interest, and a premium be paid down over and above the interest, the agreement is usurious and void. *Doug.* 235.

But the penalty under the statute is not immediately incurred if the premium itself do not exceed legal interest, nor until more than legal interest be actually received. *Ibid.*

And therefore an action may be brought for the penalty, though more than a year has elapsed since the payment of the premium, if it be not a year since what has been paid exceeded legal interest. *Ibid.*

The offence of usury is not complete until the lender has actually received the excess of interest in money or money's worth, therefore if a promissory note be given for repayment of a sum lent, with usurious interest, and the note when due not paid, but another note substituted for it, the offence of usury is not thereby committed, nor is the penalty incurred till the latter note be paid. 7 *Ter. Rep.* 184.

For when the usurious contract, the lending, the forbearance, or interest, concur, then the offence is committed, and the action must be brought on the statute within a year from that day, nor does part of the penalty being to the king avail. 3 *Wils.* 250. 2 *Black. Rep.* 792.

And before a party can entitle himself to relief by a civil action from an usurious contract, he must tender all the money really advanced; therefore when goods are pawned to a broker for a certain sum, and usurious interest agreed to be paid thereon, the pawner of the goods cannot maintain an action of trover for them, in order to get rid of the usurious contract, without first tendering the money which had been first actually advanced, with legal interest. 1 *Ter. Rep.* 153.

And an antecedent *bona fide* debt is not destroyed by being mingled with an usurious contract relating to it. 1 *Hen. Black.* 462.

UTAS, *Octava.* Is, in the return of writs, the eighth day following any term or feast, as the utas of St. Michael, &c.

UTENSIL. Any thing necessary for use and occupation, as household stuff; also things of necessary use in manufactories. See *Excise.*

UTERINUS FRATER. A brother by the mother's side. *Fortes.* 5.

UTFANGTHEF, (*Fur extra captus, scilicet, extra dominium, vel jurisdictionem.*) An ancient privilege or royalty granted to a lord of a manor, by the king, which gives him power to punish a thief dwelling out of his liberty, and committing theft without the same, if he be taken within his fee. *Bract, lib.* 2. *tract.* 2. *cap.* 35.

UTLAGATO CAPIENDO *quando utlagatur in uno comitatu et postea fugit in alium.* A writ noticed in *Reg. Orig. fol.* 133.

UTLEGH, (*uthlagus.*) An outlaw. See *Outlaw.*

UTLAWRY, (*utlagaria, vel utlagatio.*) See *Outlawry.*

UTLEPE, (Sax.) An escape of a felon out of prison. *Fleta, l.* 1. *c.* 47. *Cowell.*

UTRUM. A writ now out of use. *Ter. de Ley.* See *Assise de Utrum.*

UTTER BARRISTERS, (*juris consulti.*) Barristers allowed only to plead without the bar. See *Treason, Barrister.*

UTTERING FALSE MONEY. See *Felony.*

VULGARIS PURGATIO. That by ordeal, distinguished by the appellation of *Judicium Dei;* in contra distinguishment from canonical purgation, by the oath of the party.

ULTIVA. A wound in the face. *Cowell.* See *Mayhem.*

VULTUS DE LUCA. The image of the Saviour kept at Lucca in the church of the Holy Cross. And William I. the Conqueror, often swore *per sanctum vultum de Luca. Cowell.*

UXORIUM. A mulct or fine paid for not marrying. *Lit. Dict. Cowell.*

W

WAFTORS, (*waftores,*) Ancient conductors of vessels at sea. *Cowell.* See *Pilots.*

WAGE, (*vadiare,* from Fr. *Gage,*) To give security, or pledge security for performance of any thing; as to wage or gage deliverance, to wage law, or the like. *Co. Lit.* 294. See *Wager of Law.*

WAGER OF BATTLE. Trial by wager of battle is a species of trial of great antiquity, but now disused; though still in force if the parties chuse to abide by it. See *Battle.*

WAGER OF LAW, (*vadiare legem.*) Is where an action of debt is brought against a man upon a simple contract between the parties, without deed or record; and the defendant swears in court, in the presence of his purgators, that he oweth the plaintiff nothing in manner and form as he hath declared. 2 *Inst.* 45.

And in the trial by wager of law, the defendant gives a pledge, gage, or *vadium,* that is, puts in vadios or sureties, that at such a day he will make his law, that is, take the benefit which the law has allowed him. *Co. Lit.* 295. For our ancestors considered, that there were many cases where an innocent man, of good credit, might be overborne by a multitude of false witnesses; and therefore established this species of trial, by the oath of the defendant himself; who if he will absolutely swear himself not chargeable, and appears to be a person of reputation, he shall go free and for ever acquitted of the debt, or other cause of action. 3 *Black,* 341.

The manner of waging and making law is this: He that has waged, or given security, to make his law, brings with him into court eleven of his neighbours. The defendant then, standing at the end of the bar, is admonished by the judges of the nature and danger of a false oath. And if he still persists, he is to repeat this or the like oath: "Hear this, ye justices, that I do not owe unto Richard Jones the sum of ten pounds, nor any penny thereof, in manner and form as the said Richard hath declared against me. So help me God." And thereupon his eleven neighbours or compurgators shall avow upon their oaths, that they believe in their consciences that he saith the truth; so that himself must be sworn *de fidelitate*, and the eleven *de credulitate*. And by such wager of law (when admitted) the plaintiff is perpetually barred.

It is only in actions of debt upon simple contract, or for an amercement, in actions of detinue, and of account, where the debt may have been paid, the goods restored, or the account balanced, without any evidence of either, that the defendant is admitted to wage his law. *Finch. L.* 423. So that wager of law lieth not, when there is any specialty, as a bond or deed, to charge the defendant; for that would be cancelled if satisfied; but when the debt groweth by word only. Nor doth it lie in an action of debt, for arrears of an account, settled by auditors in a former action. Wager of law lieth however in a real action, where the tenant alledges he was not legally summoned to appear, as well as in mere personal contracts.

A man outlawed, attainted for false verdict, or for conspiracy or perjury, or otherwise become infamous, as by pronouncing the horrible word in a trial by battle, shall not be permitted to wage his law. Neither shall an infant under the age of twenty-one, and the defendant, where an infant is plaintiff, shall not wage his law. But a feme-covert, when joined with her husband, may be admitted to wage her law: and an alien shall do it in his own language. *Co. Litt.* 295.

It is also a rule, that where a man is compellable by law to do any thing, as a goaler for victuals, or debt brought by an attorney for his fees, the defendant cannot wage his law, because the plaintiff as goaler cannot refuse the prisoner sustenance, or as attorney is compellable to be his attorney.

In no case where a contempt, trespass, deceit, or any injury with force, is alledged against the defendant, is he permitted to wage his law. *Raym.* 286.

Executors and administrators, when charged for the debt of the deceased, shall not be admitted to wage their law. The king also has his prerogative; and there shall be no such wager on actions brought by him. And this extends to his debtor and accomptant; for, on a writ of *quo minus* in the exchequer for a debt on simple contract, the defendant is not allowed to wage his law. *Finch, L.* 424.

WAGERING POLICIES. By *Stat.* 19 *Geo.* 2. *c.* 37. All insurances interest or no interest, or without further proof of interest than the policy itself, or by way of gaming or wagering, or without benefit of salvage to the insurer, shall be totally null and void, except upon privateers, or ships in the Spanish and Portugueze trade. See *Insurance.*

WAGERS in general, by the common law, were lawful contracts, and all wagers may still be recovered in an action upon a *mutuaitus assumpsit*, in the courts of justice, which are not made upon games, or which are not such as are likely to obstruct the public peace, or to encourage immorality, or such as will probably affect the interests, characters, and feelings, of persons not parties to the wager, or such as are contrary to sound policy or the general interest of the nation. 3 *Ter. Rep.* 53.

WAGES *of members of parliament.* The rate of these wages established in the reign of Edward III. was four shillings a day for a knight of the shire, and two shillings for a citizen or burgess. See *Parliament.*

WAGGONS and WAGGONERS. See *Carts*, *Highways*, and *Turnpikes.*

WAIFS, (from the Sax. *Wafian*, Fr. *Chose guaive*, Lat. *Bona Waviata*,) are goods which are stolen and waved, or left by the felon on his being pursued, for fear of being apprehended; which are forfeited to the king or lord of the manor, who has the grant thereof from the crown. *Kitch.* 81.

WAIN, (*Plaustrum*) a cart, waggon, or plough to till land. *Cowell.*

WAINABLE, i. e. That may be ploughed or manured; land tillable. *Ibid.*

WAINAGE, (*Wainagium*,) the contenement of a villain: or the furniture of his cart or wain. 2 *Inst.* 28. And the villain of any other, if he fell into mercy, was to be amerced saving his wainage. *Magn. Chart. c.* 14. It has been also used for tillage.

WAIVE, (*Waivare.*) In a legal sense as applied to a woman, is the same as what is termed when applied to a man, to be outlawed. *Reg. Orig.* 132.

WAIVER, signifies the passing by of a thing, or a refusal to accept it. *Lit. Sect.* 710. And an infant, or if he die, his heirs, may by waiver avoid an estate made to him during his minority. 1 *Inst.* 23, 348. But where a particular estate is given with a remainder over, there regularly he that hath it may not waive it, to the damage of him in remainder. Though it is otherwise where one hath a reversion; for that cannot be hurt by such waiver. 4 *Shep. Abr.* 192.

WAKE, the eve feast of the dedication of churches; in many places observed with feasting and rural diversion. *Paroch. Antiq.* 609. *Cowell.*

WAKEMAN, (*Quasi*, watchman,) the chief magistrate of the town of Rippon in Yorkshire, is so called. *Cowell.*

WALES. By the common law, Wales is not considered as a part of England. 1 *Black.* 93.

Wales had continued independent of England, unconquered and uncultivated, in the primitive pastoral state which Cæsar and Tacitus ascribe to Britain in general, for many centuries; even from the time of the hostile invasions of the Saxons, when the ancient and christian inhabitants of the island retired to those natural intrenchments, for protection from their pagan visitants. But when these invaders themselves were converted to christianity, and settled into regular and potent governments, this retreat of the ancient Britons grew every day narrower; they were over-run by little and little, gradually driven from one fastness to another, and by repeated losses abridged of their wild independence. Very early in our history we find their princes doing homage to the crown of England; till at length in the reign of Edward I. who may justly be stiled the conqueror of Wales, the line of their ancient princes was abolished, and the king of England's eldest son became, as a matter of course, their titular prince; the territory of Wales being then entirely re-annexed (by a kind of feodal resumption) to the dominion of the crown of England; or, as the statute of Rhudhlan expresses it. 10 *Edw.* 1. "*Terra Walliæ cum incolis suis, prius regi jure feodali subjecta*, (of which homage was the sign,) *jam in proprietatis dominium totaliter et cum integritate conversa est, et coronæ regni Angliæ tanquam pars corporis ejusdem annexa et unita.*"* By statute also of Wales, very material alterations were made in divers parts of their laws, so as to reduce them nearer to the English standard, especially in the forms of their judicial proceedings: but they still retain very much of their original polity; particularly their rule of inheritance, viz. that their lands were divided equally among all the issue male, and did not descend to the eldest son alone. By other subsequent statutes their provincial immunities were still further abridged: but the finishing stroke to their independency was given by the statute 27 *Hen.* 8. c. 26. which at the same time gave the utmost advancement to their civil prosperity, by admitting them to a thorough communication of laws with the subjects of England. Thus were this brave people gradually conquered into the enjoyment of true liberty; being insensibly put upon the same footing, and made fellow-citizens with their conquerors. A generous method of triumph, which the repnblic of Rome practised with great success, till she reduced all Italy to her obedience, by admitting the vanquished states to partake of the Roman privileges. 1 *Black.* 94.

It is enacted by the stat. 27 *Hen.* 8. 1. That the dominion of Wales shall be for ever united to the kingdom of England. 2. That all Welchmen born shall have the same liberties as other the king's subjects. 3. That lands in Wales shall be inheritable according to the English tenures and rules of descent. 4. That the laws of England, and no other, shall be used in Wales: besides many other regulations of the police of this principality. And the statute 34 & 35 *Hen.* 8. *c.* 26. confirms the same, adds farther regulations, divides it into twelve shires,* and, in short, reduces it into the same order in which it stands at this day: differing from the kingdom of England in only a few particulars, and those too of the nature of privileges, (such as having courts within itself, independent of the process of Westminster-hall,) and some other immaterial peculiarities, hardly more than are to be found in many counties of England itself.

WALESHERIA signifies *Walliæ pars. Cowell.*

WALISCUS, (i. e. *Servus*) a servant, or any ministerial officer. *Ibid.*

WALKERS are foresters with a certain space of ground assigned to their care in forests, &c. *Cromp. Jurisd.* 145. *Cowell.*

---

* Barrington, in his Observations on the Ancient Statutes, p. 74, states, that the *Statutum Walliæ* bears date *apud Rothelanum*, what is now called Rhuydland, in Flintshire. And though Edward says, that *terra Walliæ prius regi jure feodali subjecta*, yet Barrington assures us, that the feudal law was then unknown in Wales, and that there are at present in North Wales, and it is believed in South Wales, no copyhold tenures, and scarcely an instance of what we call manerial rights; but the property is entirely free and allodial. Edward, however, was a conqueror, and he had a right to make use of his own words in the preamble to his law." *Ibid.* 75.

* By this union of Wales with England, twenty-seven members were added to the English house of commons. By the 27 *Hen.* 8. *c.* 26. the county of Monmouth (which till that time had been part of Wales) was enabled to send two members to parliament; but the other counties and the towns in Wales represented in parliment had the privilege granted of returning one only.

WALL, *Sea-Wall*, a bank of earth. *Cowell.* See *Watergage.*

WALSINGHAM. The demesne lands in Walsingham may be let by copy, and shall be copyholds. 35 *Hen.* 8. *c.* 13.

WALTHAM BLACKS. In the reign of *Geo.* 1. there sprung up a set of desperate villains called Waltham Blacks, headed by one whom they stiled king John: who blacking their faces, and using other disguises, robbed forests, parks, and warrens, destroyed cattle, levied money on their neighbours, by threats and menaces to fire their houses, and committing divers other violences and outrages, to the great terror of the people; but they were suppressed and declared felons, by stat. 9 *Geo.* 1. c. 22. See *Felony, Black Act.*

WANDERING *soldiers and mariners.* See *Vagrants.*

WANG, (Sax.) the cheek, or jaw wherein the teeth are set. *Cowell.*

WANGA, an iron instrument with teeth. *Ibid.*

WANLASS, or driving the wanlass, is to drive deer to a stand, that the lord may have a shoot; an ancient customary tenure. *Blount's Ten.* 140.

WANT. A man in extreme want of food or clothing, cannot justify stealing either, the law admitting no such excuse at present. 1 *Hal. P. C.* 54. 4. *Black.* 31.

WAPENTAKE, (from the Sax. *Weapen*, i. e. *Armatura, et Tac, tactus*). The same as what we call a hundred; specially used in the north countries beyond the river Trent. *Bract. lib.* 3.

WAR, (*Bellum*) a contest between nations, in vindication of their just rights; also the state of war, or all the time it lasts. See *Laws of Arms and Soldiers.*

WARA, a certain quantity or measure of ground. *Cowell.*

WARD, (*Custodia*,) is variously used. A ward in London is a district or division of the city, committed to the special charge of one of the aldermen. *Stow's Surv.* A forest is divided into wards. *Manwood. par.* 1. *p.* 97. And a prison is called a ward. Lastly, the heir of the king's tenant, that held *in capite*, was termed a ward during his nonage. But this wardship is taken away by the stat. 12. *Car.* 2. c. 24.

WARDA, the custody of a town or castle, which the inhabitants were bound to keep at their own charge. *Cowell.*

WARDAGE, (*Wardagium*,) the same with *Wardpeny.*

WARDEN, (*Guardianus*, Fr. *Gardin*) is he that hath the keeping or charge of any persons or things by office; as the wardens of the companies in London.

WARDMOTE, (*Wardmotus*,) is a court kept in every ward in London, called the wardmote court. *Cowell.*

WARDPENY, money paid and contributed to watch and ward. *Domesday. Cowell.*

WARDWIT, is to be quit of giving money for keeping of wards. *Terms de Ley. Cowell.*

WARDS was a court first erected in the reign of king Henry VIII. and afterwards augmented by him with the office of liveries; wherefore it was stiled the Court of Wardens and Liveries, now abolished by the 12 *Car.* 2. *c.* 24.

WARD STAFF, the constable or watchman's staff. *Cowell.*

WARECTARE, to plough up land designed for wheat in the spring, in order to let it lie fallow for better improvement; which in Kent is called summer-land. Hence *warectabilis campus*, a fallow field; *campus ad warectum, terra war actata, &c. Cowell.*

WARGUS, a banished rogue. *Ibid.*

WARNISTURA, garniture, furniture, provision. *Ibid.*

WARNOTH, an ancient custom, that if any tenant holding of the castle of Dover failed in paying his rent at the day, he should forfeit double, and for the second failure treble. *Ibid.*

WARRANT, a precept under hand and seal to some officer to bring any offender before the person granting it, or to commit him to safe custody.

WARRANT OF ATTORNEY, is an authority and power given by a client to his attorney, to appear and plead for him; or to suffer judgment to pass against him by confessing the action, by *Nil dicit, non sum informatus, &c. Strange* 526. 2 *Strange* 807. Vide *Stat.* 4. & 5 *Anne*, c. 16.

And it is now very usual, in order to strengthen a bond-creditor's security, for the debtor to execute a warrant of attorney to any one, empowering him to confess a judgment by either of the ways just now mentioned (by *nihil dicit, cognovit actionem*, or *non sum informatus*) in an action of debt to be brought by the creditor for the specific sum due: which judgment, when confessed, is absolutely complete and binding. But if the party is in custody, it will be void unless an attorney on his behalf is present.

WARRANTIA CHARTÆ, a writ that lieth where a man is feoffed of lands with warranty, and then he is sued or impleaded. And if the feoffee be impleaded in assise, or other action, in which he cannot vouch or call to warranty, he shall have this writ against the feoffor, or his heirs, to compel them to warrant the land unto him; and if the land be recovered from him, he shall recover as much lands in value against the warrantor, &c. But the *warrantia chartæ* ought to be brought by the feoffee depending the first writ against him, or he hath lost his advantage. *F. N. B.* 134. *Terms de Ley*, 372, 588.

WARRANTIA DIEI, is an ancient writ, lying where one having a day assigned personally to appear in court to any action, is in the mean time employed in the king's service, so that he cannot come at the day appointed. And it is directed to the justices to this end, that they neither take nor record him in default for that time. *Reg. Orig.* 18. *F. N. B.* 17. See *Essoin.*

WARRANTY, (*Warrantia,*) is a promise or covenant by deed made by the bargainor, for himself and his heirs, to warrant or secure the bargainee and his heirs, against all men for the enjoying of the thing granted. *Bract. lib.* 2 & 5. *West. Symb. par.* 1.

A warranty is real or personal. A real warranty is a covenant real annexed to lands, whereby a man and his heirs are bound to warrant the same to some other and his heirs; and that they shall quietly hold and enjoy the lands, and upon voucher, or by writ of *warrantia chartæ*, to yield other lands and tenements to the value of those that shall be evicted by elder title. And warranty being a covenant real, bindeth to yield lands in recompence. 1 *Inst.* 365, 384.

Personal warranty is when it concerns goods and chattels; and it is created by implication; for the purchaser of goods may have a satisfaction from the seller, if he sells them as his own, and the title proves deficient although there be no express warranty to that purpose.

WARREN, (*Warrenha*, from Germ. *Wahren*, i. e. *Custodire*, or the Fr. *Garinne.*) is a franchise or place privileged, by prescription or grant from the king, for the keeping of beasts and fowls of the warren, which are hares and conies, partridges, pheasants, and some add quails, woodcocks, and water-fowl, &c. *Terms de Ley*, 589. 1 *Inst.* 233.

WARSCOT, a contribution usually made towards armour, in the time of the Saxons. *Cowell.*

WARTH, a customary payment for castle-guard. *Blount's Ten.* 60.

WASH, a shallow part of a river, or arm of the sea; as the washes in Lincolnshire, &c. *Knight.* 1346.

WASSAILE, (Sax.) a festival song, heretofore sung from door to door about the time of the Epiphany. *Cowell.*

WASTE. Whatever does a lasting damage to the freehold or inheritance is waste; and, in treating thereof, it is to be shown that it may be committed; first, in respect of houses; secondly, in respect of gardens, orchards, and the like; thirdly, in respect of land; fourthly, in respect of timber and other trees.

First, as to houses; it is clear from the stat. *Marlb.* 23, and stat. *Glo.* 5, that waste may be done in houses: thus if the tenant pull down the houses demised, it will be waste; so if he suffers a house to be uncovered, whereby the timber decays, though the timber be not thereby thrown down; so if the house was uncovered at the commencement of the lease, yet it will be waste if he pulls it down without the consent of the landlord; or if it was ruinous at the commencement, and he suffers it to be more ruinous; so if the tenant suffers glass windows to be broke or carried away, or the wainscot, benches, doors, furnaces, or the like, which are fixed to the house, to be removed, although they were originally fixed, by the tenant, by nails, screws, or otherwise. It is also waste if he permits the walls of a house to be decayed for want of plastering, whereby the timber is rotted—or the chambers of a house, though the timber be not thereby rotted; so if he does not scour a drain, whereby the ground timber is decayed—so it will be waste if the walls are suffered to go to decay, though the timber was in decay at the commencement of the lease; and it will be waste though there be no timber upon the land demised for repairs; or though the house was uncovered by or damaged by tempest, if it be suffered afterwards to remain in decay; so it will be waste if the tenant pulls down the house and rebuilds it less than before, or if he rebuilds it larger to the prejudice of the landlord; for it is more charge to repair. So if the tenant alters the house to the landlord's prejudice: as, if he converts a parlour into a a stable, or changes a corn-mill to a cotton or fulling-mill, or the like. So it may be waste to turn two rooms into one: for if it would be for the lessor's advantage it may be shown on the other side. So it will be waste if the tenant builds a new house, and afterwards suffers that to be decayed.

However, in all questions respecting waste, it is to be observed that, in regard to the repairs of the houses the tenant is not liable thereto, unless he holds the premises under a lease for a term of years, but the burthen thereof lies on the landlord. Thus, in the case of a tenancy at will, or from year to year, the landlord is under an obligation to keep the premises in tenantable repair; but where there is an actual lease, the charge of repairing, without any express covenant for that purpose, is upon the tenant, reasonable or ordinary wear and use being allowed.

But, if the house was uncovered at the

commencement of the lease, it is no waste if the tenant suffers it to fall into further decay, without pulling it down; or if the walls were uncovered, or insufficiently supported; or if the house was ruinous and the tenant suffers it to be as it was, without permitting it to become more ruinous. So also it is no waste if the tenant removes furnaces, coppers, or other utensils of trade, though fixed to the freehold, if he removes them before the expiration of his term; but if he permits them to remain after the expiration of the term, he cannot remove them, for they are then vested in the reversioner or landlord.

In like manner green and hot-houses are removeable; so a barn erected on the premises upon blocks of timber; and this notwithstanding there be a covenant to leave all buildings which then were or should be erected on the premises in repair; for such covenant means that the tenant shall leave all buildings annexed to and become part of the reversionary estate; but if the tenant will actually build, he must leave the buildings for the benefit of the landlord,—thus if the tenant erect a beast-house, a carpenter's shop, cart-house, pump-house, or fold-yard wall, letting such buildings into the ground, he cannot remove the same; for there is a distinction between erections necessary to the purposes of trade or manufactures, such as hot-houses or the like, and those that are requisite in order to the enjoyment of the land demised, such as beast-houses and the like; and therefore those of the latter description are not removeable by the outgoing tenant, but must remain for the benefit of the inheritance.

Secondly; as to gardens, orchards, and the like: waste may be committed therein, if the tenant cuts down pear-trees, apple-trees, or other fruit-trees: or if they are thrown down by tempest, and the tenant afterward roots them up, or cuts down the germens growing without planting new.

So if the tenant destroys or suffers the stock of a dovecote, warren, park, fish-pond, pool, or the like, to be diminished, or throws down the pales of a park or warren, or stops up the holes of a dovecote, or throws down the banks of a fish-pond. But if the tenant kills or destroys, yet it is no waste if he leaves a sufficient stock.

Thirdly; as to land: it will be waste if the tenant suffers the sea to surround arable land, meadow, or pasture; or if he suffers a wall or bank against the sea, a river, or the like, to be ruinous; by which the water surrounds or overflows the land, and renders it useless; so if he digs up the surface of the land, and carries it away; or if the tenant converts arable land to wood, or wood-land to arable, it will be waste, or meadow to arable or pasture; or meadow to orchard or hop-ground—though it be done for the amelioration of the soil—or a hop-ground to tillage.

So if a tenant for life or years opens new mines in land, demised without mention of mines, it will be waste; so if he digs for gravel, lime, clay, brick-earth, stone, or the like, in pits not open.

But it is not waste if land is surrounded or overflowed by the violence of a tempest, or if pasture be converted to tillage for the improvement of the soil, where it has been sometimes pasture and sometimes arable; or if it was stocked with rabbits, it not being a warren by charter or prescription; so if it was a warren. So it is not waste if the land lies fallow, though it is bad husbandry; or if trenches are dug in a meadow to draw off the water; or if woad or the like be sown against the end of the term, though it is not ripe for several years.

So it is not waste to dig for ore, coal, or the like, in mines open at the time of the lease; or if mines were not demised, if the land was demised with all mines; neither will it be waste for the rector or vicar to dig for or open mines in his glebe.

Fourthly; as to timber and other trees: it is waste if a tenant cuts down timber: and oak, ash, and elm, are timber after the age of twenty years, throughout the realm; and in some counties, where such timber is scarce, beech, willow, hornbeam, and other trees, may be accounted timber, if they have been so deemed by custom and immemorial usage. And therefore if a tenant cuts down trees, which by law, or the immemorial usage and custom of the country, are esteemed timber, it will be waste; so it will be waste if the tenant does an act by which the timber decays, as if he lops and tops them: so if he cuts down birch, willow, maple, or other trees, which are not timber if they are growing in defence of the house; or if he roots up or destroys quicksets of white-thorn and the like; so if he extirpates or destroys the germens of underwood, which may be cut. It will also be waste if the tenant cuts down trees for fuel, when there is dead and decayed wood sufficient; or if he cuts down, for new pales, fences, a house, or the like, where none were before; so it is waste if the tenant sells the trees, and with the money repairs, or afterwards repurchases and uses for repairs; so if he cuts down for repairs which are not necessary, or for repairs when there shall be no occasion, or for repairs which happened by his own default.

But cutting down trees which are not timber, nor stand for the defence of the house, is not waste, nor trees that were timber, when they are dead. So cutting down of trees is justifiable for house-boot, hay-boot, plow-boot, and fire-boot. For by the common law lessee shall have them, though the deed does not express it; but if he takes more than is necessary he shall be punished in waste. So the tenant may take sufficient wood to repair the walls, pales, fences, hedges and ditches, as he found them, but he cannot make new.

So also cutting of timber-trees, by a lessee for necessary repairs, and using the same therein, is not waste, and there is no difference whether the lessor or lessee covenants to repair the houses; for in either case it is not waste, if lessee cuts them.

WASTEL-BOWL, (From the Sax. Was-heal, *i. e.* Health be to you) A large silver cup or bowl, wherein the Saxons, at their entertainments, drank a health to one another, in the phrase of wass-heal: and this wastel or wass-heal bowl, was set at the upper end of the table in religious houses for the use of the Abbot, who began the health or *poculum charitatis* to strangers, or to his fraternity. Hence cakes and fine white bread, which were usually sopped in the wastel bowl were called wastel bread. *Matt. Paris.* 141. *Cowell. Blount.*

WASTERS, were a kind of thieves so called; mentioned among robbers, draw-latches, &c. *Stat.* 4 *Hen.* 4. *c.* 27.

WATCH AND WARD, is to stand sentry or attend as a guard, &c. And watching is properly for the apprehending of rogues in the night, as warding is for like purposes in the day; and for default of watch and ward the township may be punished. In all towns, &c. between the day of Ascension and Michaelmas-day, night-watches are to be kept, in every city with six men at every gate; and six or four in towns; and every borough shall have twelve men to watch, or according to the number of the inhabitants of the place, from sun-setting to sun-rising; who are to arrest strangers suspected, and may make hue and cry after them, and justify the detaining them until the morning: And watches shall be kept on the sea coasts, as they have been wont to be. *Stat.* 13 *Ed.* 1. *c.* 4. 5 *Hen.* 4. *c.* 3. Every justice of peace may cause these night-watches to be duly kept; which is to be composed of men of able bodies, and sufficiently weaponed: And none but inhabitants in the same town are compellable to watch, who are bound to keep it in turn; or to find other sufficient persons for them, or on refusal, are indictable, &c. *Co. Litt.* 70. *Cro. Eliz.* 204. And by a late statute, viz. 52 *Geo.* 3. *c.* 17. (passed in consequence of the riotous behaviour of divers persons in several manufacturing towns) IT IS ENACTED, that in case of disturbance in any county, the *custos rotulorum*, or sheriff, or *five* justices of the peace may by warrant convene a special general sessions of the peace to appoint a special watch and ward for all places disturbed in such county, in the manner prescribed by the act.

WATCHES, made by artificers, are to have the makers names, &c. under the penalty of 20*l.* *Stat.* 9 *and* 10 *W.* 3. *c.* 28.

WATER-BAILIFF, an officer in port towns, for the searching of ships. Also in the city of London, there is a water-bailiff who hath the supervising and search of fish brought thither; and the gathering of the toll arising from the Thames: And he attends on the Lord Mayor, having the principal care of marshalling the guests at his table; and arrests men for debt, or other personal or criminal matters upon the river Thames. 28 *H.* 6. *c.* 5.

WATER-COURSE. A water-course does not begin by prescription, nor yet by assent, but begins *ex jure naturæ*, having taken this course naturally, and it cannot be diverted. *Per Whitlock* J. 3 *Bulst.* 340. in case of *Surrey* v. *Piggot.*

Action on the case lies for diverting a water-course to my prejudice. See *Action on the Case*, and *Het.* 32. *Skin.* 316, 389. 5 *Mod.* 206. and 22 *Vin. Abr.* 525, 528.

WATER-GAGE, a sea wall or bank, to restrain the current and overflowing of the water: and it signifies an instrument to guage or measure the quantity or deepness of any waters. *Cowell. Blount.*

WATER-GANG. *(watergangium)* Is a Saxon word for a trench or course to carry a stream of water; such as are commonly made to drain water out of marshes. *Ordin. Narisc. de Romn. Chart. H.* 3. *Cowell. Blount.*

WATER-GAVEL, was a rent paid for fishing in, or other benefit received from some river. *Chart.* 15 *Hen.* 3. *Cowell. Blount.*

WATER-MEASURE, is greater than Winchester measure, and used for selling of coals in the pool, &c. mentioned in the *Stat.* 22 *Car.* 2. *c.* 11.

WATERMEN. The Lord Mayor and court of aldermen in London, have a great power in the government of the Company of Watermen, and appointing the fares for plying on the Thames; and the justices of peace for Middlesex, and other adjoining counties, have likewise authority to hear and determine offences, &c.

WATER-ORDEAL, a way of purgation used by the Saxons. See *Ordeal*, and 4 *Black. Com.* 336.

WATERSCAPE, (From the Sax. Waeter, *Aqua*, and Schap, *ductus*) An aqueduct, or passage for water. *Cowell. Blount.*

WATLING-STREET, is one of those four ways which the Romans are said to have made here, and called them *Consulares, Prætorios, Militares et Publicas.* This street is otherwise called Werlam Street. *Et strata quam filii Wethe regis ab orientali mari usque ad occidentale per Angliam straverunt.* R. Hov. f. 248. a. n. 10. This street leads from Dover to London, St. Albans, Dunstable, Towecester, Atherston, and the Severn, near the Wrekin in Shropshire, extending itself to Anglesey in Wales. Anno 39 *El. c.* 2. The second is called Ikenild street, so called *ab Icenis*, stretching from Southampton over the river Isis, at Newbridge; thence by Cambden and Litchfield; then it passeth the river Derwent by Derby, so to Bolsover castle, and ends at Tynmouth. The third was called the Fosse, because in some places it was never perfected, but lies as a large ditch, leading from Cornwall through Devonshire, by Tethbury, near Stow in the Wolds, and beside Coventry to Leicester, Newark, and so to Lincoln. The fourth was called Ermine or Erminage-street, beginning at St. David's in West Wales, and going to Southampton. See the laws of Edward the Confessor, whereby these four public ways had the privilege of *Pax Regis.* See *Hollingshed's Chron. vol.* 1. *cap.* 19. And *Henry* of *Huntingdon, lib.* 1. *in principio.* And in *Leg. Will.* 1. *c.* 30. there are three ways mentioned; but Ikenild-street is omitted, which was called Iknild from the Iceni, and streat, which signifies a way. See an old description of these ways, made by Robert of Gloucester, *Dug. Antiq. of Warw. p.* 6. *Cowell.*

WAVESON, is used for such goods as after shipwreck, do appear swimming upon the waves. *Chart.* 18 *Hen.* 8. *Cowell. Blount.* See *Jetson.*

WAX-CHANDLERS. Justices of peace shall examine the goodness of wax candles; and chandlers are to take but 3d. a pound for the candle, &c. more than the common price of the wax, on pain of forfeiture and to be fined by the justices, &c. *Stat.* 11 *H.* 6. *c.* 12. Wax-chandlers mixing with their wax, tallow or other deceitful stuff, shall forfeit the candles; and they are to have stamps or marks, which shall not be counterfeited, under penalties, &c. 23 *Eliz. c.* 8.

WAXSCOT, *(Ceragium)* A duty anciently paid twice a year towards the charge of wax-candles in churches. *Spelm. Cowell. Blount.*

WAY, *(Via)* A passage, street, or road. *Litt.* And where a man has a way to his close, he cannot go further without a prescription; but it is held if he go to a mill or bridge, it may be otherwise. 1 *Lord Raym.* 75. 2 *Black. Com.* 55. 3 *Black.* 241.

WAYS AND MEANS, Committee of. When the commons of Great Britain in parliament assembled, have voted a supply to his Majesty, and settled the *quantum* of that supply, they usually resolve themselves into what is called a committee of ways and means, to consider of ways and means to raise that supply so voted. *Black. Com.* 307, 308.

WEALD, or WALD. In the beginning of names of places, signifies a situation near wood, from the Sax. Weald, *i. e.* a wood: and the woody parts of the counties of Kent and Sussex, are called the Wealds; though misprinted wildes in the statute 14 *Car.* 2. *c.* 6.

WEALREAF, (From the Sax. Weal, *i. e. Strages*, and Reaf *Spoliatio)* Is the robbing of a dead man in his grave. *Leg. Etheldred. cap.* 21. *Cowell. Blount.*

WEAR, a great dam made across a river, accommodated for the taking of fish, or to convey a stream to a mill. And all wears for the taking of fish, are to be put down, except on the sea-coasts, by the statutes 9 *H.* 3. *c.* 23. and 25 *Ed.* 3. *c.* 4. Also commissions shall be granted to justices, to keep the waters, survey wears and mills, and to inquire of and correct abuses; and where it is found by them that any new wears are made, or others altered to the nuisance of the public, the sheriff by *scire facias* is to give the person making them notice of it; and if he do not amend the same in three months, he shall forfeit 100 marks, &c. *Stat.* 1 *and* 4 *Hen.* 4. 12 *Ed.* 4.

WEAVERS. Persons using the trade of a weaver, shall not keep a tucking or fulling-mill, or use dying, &c. Or have above two looms in a house, in any corporation or market-town, on pain of forfeiting 20s. a week: and shall serve an apprenticeship of seven years to a weaver or clothier, or shall forfeit 20l. &c. *Stat.* 2 *and* 3 *P. and M. c.* 11.

WED, (Sax.) A covenant or agreement; whence to wedd, a wedded husband, wedded bond-slave. *Cowell. Blount.*

WEDBEDRIP, the customary service which inferior tenants paid to their lord in cutting down their corn, or doing other harvest duties. From the Sax. Wed, a covenant or agreement (whence to wedd, wedding, a wedded husband, a wedded bondslave, &c.) and biddan to pray or desire, and rippan to reap or mow. As a covenant of the tenant to reap for the lord at the time of his bidding or commanding. *Paroch. Antiq.* 401. *Cowell. Blount.*

WEEK, *(Septimana)* Seven days of

time; four of which weeks make a month, &c. And the week was originally divided into seven days, according to the number of the seven planets. *Skene. Cowell. Blount.*

WEIGH, *(waga)* Is a weigh of cheese or wool, containing two hundred and fifty-six pounds; and in Essex the weigh of cheese is three hundred pounds. A weigh of barley or malt is six quarters, or forty-eight bushels: and we read of a weigh of salt, &c. 9 *H.* 6. *c.* 8.

WEIGHTS, *(Pondera)* and Measures, are used between buyers and sellers of goods and merchandize, for reducing the quantity and price to a certainty, that there may be the less room for deceit and imposition. There are two sorts of weights in use with us, *viz.* troy-weight and avoirdupois: troy-weight contains twelve ounces to the pound, and no more; by which are weighed gold, silver, pearl, jewels, medicines, silk, &c. and avoirdupois contains sixteen ounces in the pound, by which wheaten bread, grocery wares, copper, iron, lead, flesh, cheese, butter, tallow, hemp, wool, &c. are weighed: and here twelve pounds over are allowed to every hundred, so as one hundred and twelve pounds make the hundred weight. *Dalt.* 248. In the composition of troy-weight, twenty pennyweights make an ounce, twenty-four grains a pennyweight, twenty mites a grain, twenty-four droits a mite, twenty perits a droit, and twenty-four blanks a perit: and the troy-weight is said to be 20s. sterling in the pound; and the avoirdupois weight 25s. sterling. 4 *Shep. Abr.* 194. Fleta mentions a weight, called a trone-weight, being the same with what we now call troy-weight; and according to the same author, all our weights have their composition from the penny sterling, which ought to weigh thirty-two wheat-corns of the middle sort; twenty of which pence make an ounce, and twelve such ounces a pound; but fifteen ounces make the merchants pound. *Fleta, lib.* 2. *c.* 12. By *Magna Charta,* 9 *H.* 3. *c.* 25. 14 *Ed.* 3. *c.* 12. 25 *Ed.* 3. *c.* 10. 27 *Ed.* 3. *&c.* There is to be but one weight, &c. throughout the kingdom; but this is to be understood of the same species of goods, otherwise the troy and avoirdupois weights would not be permitted. Every city, borough, and town, shall have a common balance, with common weights sealed; on pain of 10l. in the city, 5l. the borough, and 40s. the town. 8 *H.* 6. *c.* 5. But only cities and market-towns are enjoined to have common balances, weights, and measures, by 11 *H.* 7. *c.* 4. And by this statute, weights are to be marked by the chief officers of places and sealed, &c. Refusing or delaying to do it, is liable to a penalty of 40s. And allowing weights not agreeable to the standard, incurs a forfeiture of 5l. &c. And the mayors and such officers are once a year to view all weights and measures, and burn and destroy those which are defective; also fine the offenders, &c. And two justices of peace have power to hear and determine the defaults of mayors. See the statutes 17 *Car.* 1. *c.* 19. 22 *Car.* 2. *c.* 8. *&c.* and vide *Measures.*

And by a late statute 35 *Geo.* 3. *c.* 102. The justices [at their petty sessions, 37 *Geo.* 3. *c.* 143.] are to appoint persons to examine weights and balances; and the persons so appointed are to visit shops and places, and seize those which are false; and the penalty for having the same is not exceeding 20s. nor less than 10s. *s.* 1, 2.

Penalty for obstructing inspectors, or refusing to produce weights, is not exceeding 40s. nor less than 5s. *s.* 3.

Quarter Sessions to allow a recompence to inspectors out of the county rate, *s.* 4. Persons punished under this act not to suffer by any other, *s.* 5. but not to lessen the authority of persons appointed at the court leet. *s.* 6.

Justices to cause standard weights to be purchased out of the county rate, which shall be produced to persons paying the costs of production. *s.* 7.

No person to be prosecuted unless information be given within one month.

By 37 *Geo.* 3. *c.* 143. the examiners when directed by the justices, may visit shops and other places, and seize false weights and balances; and persons having the same on conviction at such petty sessions, are to forfeit not exceeding 20s. nor less than 5s. to be levied by distress. *s.* 2.

Justices are to cause false weights and balances to be broken, and the produce of the materials, and forfeitures to be paid to the county treasurer. *s.* 3.

If the majority of the inhabitants of the parish wish that any persons should be specially appointed examiners, they may in vestry nominate them for the approbation of the justices. *s.* 4. But no such appointment shall be made till the inhabitants shall have procured standard weights, the costs of which, and the recompence to the examiners shall be paid out of the poor rates. *s.* 8.

WEIGHTS OF AUNCEL, mentioned in statute 14 *Ed.* 3. *st.* 1. *c.* 12. See *Auncel-weight.*

WEND, (Wendus, *i. e.* Perambulatio, from the Sax. Wendam) Signifies a certain quantity or circuit of ground. *Rental. Regal. Maner. de Wye, pag.* 31. *Cowell. Blount.*

WERE, (Sax. *Wera*) is the sum paid

in ancient time for killing a man, when such crimes were punished with pecuniary mulcts, not death: or it is *pretium redemptionis* of the offender. *Leg. Ed. Conf. cap.* 11. *Cowell. Blount.*

WERELADA, (From the Sax. *Were, i. e. Pretium Capitis Hominis Occisi,* and Ladian *purgare)* Was where a man was slain, and the price at which he was valued not paid to his relations; but the party denied the fact; when he was to purge himself by the oaths of several persons, according to his degree and quality, which was called *werelada. Leg. H.* 1. *c.* 12. *Cowell. Blount.*

WERGILD, WEREGILD, *(Wergildus)* The price of homicide; paid partly to the king for the loss of a subject, partly to the lord whose vassal he was, and partly to the next of kin of the person slain. *LL. H.* 1. 4 *Black. Com.* 4. 188, 308, 406.

WEST-SAXONLAGE, was the law of the West-Saxons. See *Merchenlage,* and 1 *Black. Com.* 65. 4, 405.

WESTMINSTER, *(Westmonasterium,* Sax. *West-mynster,* i. e. *Occidentale Monasterium)* The ancient seat of our kings; and is now the well known place where the high court of parliament, and courts of judicature sit: it had great privileges granted by Pope Nicholas; among others, *Ut amplius in perpetuum Regiæ constitutionis locus sit atque repositorium regalium insignium.* 4 *Inst.* 255.

WESTMONY AND ISELAND, fishing vessels not to proceed thither till the 10th of March, 15 *Car.* 2. *c.* 15.

WHARF, *(Wharfa)* a broad plain place, near some creek or haven, to lay goods and wares on that are brought to or from the water. 12 *Car.* 2. *c.* 4.

WHARFAGE, *(Wharfagium)* is money paid for landing of goods at a wharf, or for shipping and taking goods into a boat or barge from thence: it is mentioned in the statutes 17 *H.* 8. *c.* 26. and 22 *Car.* 2. *c.* 11.

WHARFS. By statutes 1 *Eliz. c.* 11. and 13 and 14 *Car.* 2. *c.* 11. *sect.* 14. the crown is enabled by commission to ascertain the limits of all ports, and to assign proper wharfs and quays in each port, for the exclusive landing and loading of merchandize.

WHARFINGER, is he that owns or keeps a wharf. 12 *Car.* 2. and 22 *Car.* 2. And wharfingers commonly keep boats or lighters of their own, for the carrying out and bringing in of goods, in which if a loss or damage happens, they as common carriers are made answerable. *Lex Mercat.* 133.

WHEELAGE, *(Rotagium) Tributum est quod rotarum nomine penditur; hoc est, pro plaustris et carris transeuntibus. Spelm. Cowell. Blount.*

WHERLICOTES, the ancient British chariots, that were used by persons of quality before the invention of coaches. *Stow's Survey Lond. pag.* 70.

WHINIARD, a sword, from the Sax. *Winn, i. e.* to get, and *Are* honour; because honour is gained by the sword. *Cowell. Blount.*

WHIPPING, a punishment inflicted for many of the smaller offences, by divers statutes, and in particular under the vagrant act.

WHITE-ASHES. None shall ship, lade, or convey away any white-ashes, to parts beyond sea, under the penalty of 6s. 8d. a bushel. *Stat.* 2 and 3 *Ed.* 6. *cap.* 6.

WHITEHART SILVER, is a mulct on certain lands in or near the forest of Whitehart, paid yearly into the Exchequer, imposed by King *Hen.* 3. upon Thomas de la Linde, for killing a beautiful white hart which that king before had spared in hunting. *Camb. Brit.* 150. *Cowell. Blount.*

WHITE-MEATS, are milk, butter, cheese, eggs, and any composition of them, which before the reformation were forbid in *Lent* as well as flesh, till *Hen.* 8. published a proclamation allowing the eating of white-meats in *Lent. Anno* 1543. *Cowell. Blount.*

WHITE-RENTS. Payments or chief rents reserved in silver or white money, called white-rents or blanch-farms, *reditus albi;* in contradistinction to rents reserved in work, grain, &c. Also white-rent in *Cowel, Blount,* is a duty or rent payable by the tinners in Devonshire to the Duke of Cornwall. 2 *Black. Com.* 42.

WHITE-SPURS, a kind of esquires called by this name.

WHITSONTIDE, the feast of Pentecost, being the fiftieth day after Easter: and is so called, saith *Blount,* because those who were newly baptized came to the church between Easter and Pentecost in white garments. *Blount's Dict.*

WHITSON-FARTHINGS, mentioned in letters patent of King *Hen.* 8. to the Dean of Worcester. See *Pentecostals.*

WHITE-STRAITS, a kind of coarse cloth in Devonshire, about a yard and half a quarter broad, raw, mentioned in *Stat.* 5 *Hen.* 8. *c.* 2.

WHOLE-BLOOD. A kinsman of the whole blood is he that is derived, not only from the same ancestor, but from the same couple of ancestors. 2 *Black. Com,* 227.

WIC, a place on the sea-shore, on the bank of a river. 1 *Inst.* 4. But it more properly signifies a town, village, or dwelling-place; and it is often in the Saxon language made a termination to the name of the town, which had a com plete name without it, as Lunden-wic, *i. e.* London-town; so Ipswich is written in some old charters Villo de Gippo Wico, which is the same thing, for Gipps is the name, and Gipps Wic. is Gipps Town. *Cowell. Blount.*

WICA, a country house or farm, and there are many such houses now called the *Wick* and the *Wike. Cartular. Abbat. Glaston. pag.* 29. *Cowell. Blount.*

WICHENERIF, a Saxon word for witchcraft, which occurs in the laws of K. *Canut, cap.* 27. *Cowell. Blount.*

WIDOW, *(Vidua Relicta)* a married woman bereft of her husband, left all alone. *Litt.* The widow of a freeman of London, may use her husband's trade, so long as she continues a widow. *Chart. K. Cha.* 1. *Cowell. Blount.*

WIDOWS-CHAMBER. In London the widow of a freeman, is, by the custom of the city, entitled to her apparel, and the furniture of her bed-chamber, called the Widow's Chamber. *Cowell. Blount.*

WIDOW OF THE KING, *(Vidua Regis)* was she that after her husband's death, being the king's tenant *in capite*, could not marry again without the king's consent. *Staundf. Prærog. cap.* 4. *Stat.* 17 *Edw.* 2. and 32 *H. cap.* 46.

WIDOWHOOD, *(Viduitas)* the state and condition of a widow.

WIFE, *(Uxor)* is a woman married; and after marriage the will of the wife, in judgment of law, is subject to the will of the husband; and it is said a wife hath no will, *sed fulget radiis mariti. Plowd.* 344. 4 *Rep.* A wife cannot contract for any thing, or bring actions, &c. without her husband; she is also entitled for life to one third part of the rents and profits of all lands whereof the husband was seized during marriage for her dower, unless there has been a settlement or will making a provision in lieu of dower; and she is entitled likewise to one third of the personal estate of her husband if he dies intestate; also if separated or divorced on account of cruelty, she is entitled to alimony from her husband: and the course of the Ecclesiastical Courts in such cases is usually to decree an allowance of one fifth part of the clear income of the husband's estates. But if the wife commits adultery, even though it be through the cruelty of the husband, she loses her right to dower and her thirds.

WIGREVE (From the Sax. *Wig*, i. e. *Sylva*, and *Greve, Præpositus)* The overseer of a wood. *Spelm. Cowell. Blount.*

WIGHT ISLAND, was anciently called *Guith* by the Britons; whence it had many other names, as *Icta, Wotha,* &c. *Law Lat. Dict.* See *Stat.* 4 *Hen.* 7. *c.* 16.

WILD-FOWL, are not to be destroyed by nets or otherwise, nor their eggs taken, under divers penalties by *Stat.* 25 *Hen.* 8. *c.* 11. 1 *Jac.* 1. *c.* 17. 9 *Ann. c.* 25.

WILL, *Defect of.* An involuntary act, as it hath no claim to merit, so neither can it induce any guilt: the concurrence of the will, when it hath its choice either to do, or to avoid the fact in question, being the only thing that renders human actions either praise-worthy or culpable. 4 *Black. Com.* 20, 21. But note, trespass will lie for an accidental hurt.

WILL, *Estates at.* An estate at will is where lands or tenements are let by one man to another, to have and to hold at the will of the lessor; and the tenant by virtue of this lease obtains possession. Every estate at will is at the will of both parties, landlord and tenant, so that either of them may determine his will, and quit his connections with the other at his own pleasure, giving previous notice according to the contract between them; but if there is no particular agreement on the subject, then there must be six months previous notice, ending on the day when the party first entered. Note, if tenant at will sows his lands, and the landlord before the corn is reaped, puts him out, yet the tenant shall have the emblements and free ingress, egress, and regress, to cut and carry away the profits. 2 *Black. Com.* 145, 146.

WILL OF THE LORD. Though in general copyholders are still said to hold their estates at the will of the lord, yet it is such a will as is agreeable to the custom of the manor; which customs are preserved and evidenced by the rolls of the several courts baron in which they are entered or kept on foot by the constant immemorial usage of the several manors in which the lands lie. 2 *Black. Com.* 95, 147.

WILL, *vicious.* In all temporal jurisdictions an *overt* act, or some open evidence of an intended crime, is necessary, in order to demonstrate the depravity of the will, before the man is liable to punishment. And, as a vicious will without a vicious act is no civil crime, so, on the other hand, an unwarrantable act, without a vicious will, is no crime at all. So that to constitute a crime against human laws, there must be first, a vicious will; and, secondly, an unlawful act consequent upon such vicious will. See 4 *Black. Com.* 20, 21.

WILL, OR LAST WILL AND TESTAMENT, *(Testamentum, ultima voluntas)* is a solemn act or instrument, whereby a person declares his mind and intention, as to the disposal of his lands, goods or effects, and what he would have done after his death. *Co. Litt.* 111.

And the common law calls that a will, when lands or tenements are given; and where it concerns goods and chattels alone, it is termed a testament: in a will of goods there must be an executor appointed, but not of lands only, without goods; an executor having nothing to do with the freehold. 1 *Inst*. 111. If lands are given by will, it is called a devise; and goods and chattels a legacy or bequest: And there is this diversity between lands and goods given by a will, that when lands are devised in fee, or for life, the devisee shall enter without the appointment of others. In case of goods and chattels there must be the assent of the executor, &c. *Swinb*. 24. If lands are given and devised by will, the will ought to be proved in the Chancery; and of goods it must be in the spiritual court: but a will both of lands and goods, may be proved in the spiritual court. *Ibid.*

He who makes the testament, is called the testator; and when a man dies without a will, he is said to die intestate. *Shep. Abr. part* 4, *voc. Testament.*

An infant, until he be of the age of 21 years, can make no will of his lands by statute 32 *H*. 8. *c*. 1. But by special custom in some places, where land is deviseable by custom, he may devise it sooner; and of his goods and chattels, if he be a boy, he may make a will at fourteen years of age, and not before; and if a maid, at twelve years of age, and not before: and then they may do it without and against the consent of their tutor, father, or guardian. 32 *H*. 8, *c*. 1. 34 *H*. 8, *c*. 5. *Swinb. part* 11. *sect*. 2.

A feme covert cannot make a will of her lands and goods, with or without her husband's consent, stat. 32 and 33 *H*. 8. 4 *Rep*. 51. *Bro. Testament*, 13. But of the goods and chattels she has, as executrix to any other, she may make an executor without her husband's consent; 12 *H*. 7. c. 24. *Perk. sect*. 502. *Fitz. Exec*. 40.

A mad or lunatic person, during the time of his insanity of mind, cannot make a will; but such a one as hath his *lucida intervalla*, clear or calm intermissions, may, during the time of such quietness and freedom of mind, make his will, and it will be good; *Swinb*. 11. *s*. 3. So an ideot, or one who cannot number twenty, or tell what age he is, or the like, cannot make a will or dispose of his lands or goods; an old man likewise, who, by reason of his great age, is childish again, or so forgetful that he forgets his own name, cannot make a will. *Id. ibid. par*. 11. *s*. 1. 6 *Rep*. 23. *Marquis of Winchester's case*. So also it seems a drunken man, who is so excessively drunk that he is deprived of the use of his reason and understanding, during that time may not make a will. *Swinb. part* 11. *s*. 1. and *sect*. 6.

A man who is both deaf and dumb, and is so by nature, cannot make a will; but a man who is so by accident, may by writing or signs make a will. *Id. part* 11. *s*. 1. and 10. And so also may a man that is blind. *Id. part* 1. *s*. 1. and 11. But an alien enemy, persons convicted and attainted, and recusants convict, cannot make a testament of lands or goods. *Wood's Inst*. 335.

A traitor attainted of treason or felony, can make no will. *Swinb. part* 11. *s*. 12. 135. and 6 *Edw*. 6. *c*. 11. *s*. 9. And if a man kill himself, his will as to his goods and chattels is void, although as to his lands it is good. *Plowd*. 261. *Hales* v. *Pettit*.

A man likewise, who is outlawed in a personal action, cannot make a will of his goods and chattels, so long as the outlawry continues in force, but of lands he may make a will. *Swinb. part* 11. *s*. 21.

The *Stat*. 32 *H*. 8. *cap*. 1. usually called the statute of wills, enacts, " That every person having manors, lands, &c. shall have power to give, dispose, will, and devise by will, in writing or otherwise, by act executed in his life-time, all his said manors, &c. any law, statute, &c. to the contrary notwithstanding."

And by the statute of frauds and perjuries, 29 *Car*. 2. *c*. 3. *s*. 5. All devises and bequests of any lands or tenements deviseable by the statute of wills, or by any particular custom, shall be *in writing, and signed by the party devising the same, or some other person in his presence, and by his express directions, and shall be attested and subscribed in the presence of the said devisor by three or four credible witnesses*, or else they shall be utterly void and of none effect.

And by *sect*. 6. " No devise in writing of lands, tenements or hereditaments, or any clause thereof, shall be revocable other than by some other will or codicil in writing, or other writing declaring the same, or by burning, cancelling, tearing or obliterating the same by the testator himself, or in his presence, and by his directions and consent: but all such devises and bequests shall remain in force until the same be burnt, &c. in manner aforesaid, or unless the same be altered by some other will or codicil in writing, or other writing of the devisor, signed in presence of three witnesses, declaring the same."

Therefore if a will be of lands or tenements, it must be in writing, and it must be committed to writing at the time of the making thereof; and it is not sufficient that it be put in writing after the death of the testator, being first made by word of mouth only, for then it is but a nuncupative will. See *Wood, part* 1. 798. *Dyer* 72. *Plowd*. 345.

And by 39 & 40 *Geo*. 3. *c*. 98. No person by deed or will shall settle, or dispose of any real or personal property in such manner that the rents or produce shall be accumulated for a longer time than the life of the settler or divisor, or 21 years after his decease, or during the minority of any party living at his decease, or the minorities of persons beneficially entitled: any other division shall be void, and the rents go to such persons as would be entitled thereto, if such accumulation had not been directed, *s.* 1. But nothing herein is to extend to any provision for payment of debts, or for raising portions for children, or touching the produce of timber, *s.* 2, 3. These provisions take effect on all wills made before 28th July 1800.

And by 38 *Geo.* 3. *c.* 87. If at the expiration of twelvemonths after the testator's decease, the executor *shall not be within the jurisdiction* of the King's courts, a creditor may obtain a special administration, *s.* 1. A court of equity also, pending a suit, may appoint a person to collect debts, *s.* 4. and executors returning are to be made parties to the suit, *s.* 5. Also when an infant is sole executor, administration with will annexed shall be granted to the guardian till the infant is 21, *s.* 6.

Devisees, legatees, and creditors, are now made competent witnesses to wills, for by the act of the 25 *Geo.* 2. *c.* 6. for avoiding and putting an end to certain doubts and questions, relating to the attestation of wills and codicils, it is enacted, That if any person shall attest the execution of any will or codicil, to whom any beneficial devise, legacy, estate, interest, gift or appointment of, or affecting any real or personal estate, except charges on lands, for payment of any debt which shall be thereby made, such devise, &c. or appointment, shall, so far only as concerns such persons attesting the execution of such will or codicil, be utterly null and void; and such person shall be admitted as a witness to the execution of such will or codicil; and in case by any will or codicil, any lands shall be charged with debts, and any creditor whose debt is so charged, hath attested the execution, such creditor shall be admitted as a witness to the execution of the said will or codicil.

CODICILS.] The form of a codicil is not material, so that it be expressed to be, or be clearly intended as an addition to the testator's will; and may be used for the purpose of *revoking*, *republishing*, *adding to*, or otherwise varying the dispositions made by such will, or by substituting new executors in the room of any who may have died, &c. since the publication of the will. It is not, however, correct to appoint them originally by this instrument when none have been named in the will.

Of nuncupative Wills.—By the stat. 29 *Car.* 2. *c.* 3. *s.* 19. For the preventing fraudulent practices, it is enacted, "That no nuncupative will shall be good where the estate thereby bequeathed shall exceed the value of 30 pounds, that is not proved by the oaths of three witnesses, at the least, that were present at the making thereof, and bid by the testator to bear witness that such was his will, or to that effect." (And by stat. 4 *Ann.* *c.* 16. *s.* 14. it is declared, "That all such witnesses as are and ought to be allowed to be good witnesses upon trial at law by the laws and customs of this realm, shall be deemed good witnesses to prove any nuncupative will, or any thing relating thereto.) Nor unless such nuncupative will were made in the time of the last sickness of the deceased, and in the habitation where he or she has been resident for ten days next before making of such will, except where such person was surprised or taken sick, being from his own home, and died before he returned. That after six months passed after the speaking of the testamentary words, no testimony shall be received to prove any will nuncupative, except the said testimony, or the substance thereof, were committed to writing within six days after the making of the said will. That no letters testamentary, or probate of any nuncupative will, shall pass the seal of any court, till fourteen days, at the least, after the decease of the testator be fully expired, nor shall any nuncupative will be at any time received to be proved, unless process have first issued to call in the widow, or the next of kindred to the deceased, to the end they may contest the same, if they please. That no will in writing concerning any goods or chattels, or personal estate, shall be repealed; nor shall any clause, devise, or bequest therein, be altered or changed by any words, or will by word of mouth only, except the same be in the life of the testator committed to writing, and after the writing thereof read to the testator, and allowed by him, and proved to be so done by three witnesses at the least."

"Provided that any soldier in actual military service, or any mariner or seaman being at sea, may dispose of his moveables, wages, and personal estate, as before the making of this act."

(Revocation.)—As to what acts of a testator, after the publication of his will, will operate as a revocation of it, it is to be observed:

1. Any material alteration in the devised estate subsequent to the devise, will operate as a revocation of such devise; therefore a recovery suffered of the devised estate by a tenant in tail, or a feoffment by a tenant in fee, will be a revocation of a previous devise of them, although they be by the same instrument limited to the use of the devisor in fee; and the assurance be made for a particular purpose not inconsistent with the devise, as if it be done for the express

purpose of confirming a previous will: for the devisor being divested of the estate by the conveyance, the will has lost the subject of its operation; and the estate although immediately taken back by the same conveyance, is a new estate acquired subsequently to the will.

2. The partition of an estate holden in joint tenantry, coparcenary, or in common, is holden not to be a revocation, unless upon such partition the testator take his part for a different estate from that which he held before: but a very small difference in the two estates will cause a revocation, as if it were before holden in fee simple, and it be taken in the partition to such uses as the owner shall appoint, or the like.

3. The surrender of an old lease for the purpose of a renewal, will be a revocation of a previous will, whether the lease be a freehold or chattel interest, unless in the case of chattel interest, and then the words in the will referring to such interest as the testator may have at the time of his decease must take effect.

4. The alteration of a will, will also be a revocation of a will *pro tanto*, that is, to the extent of the alteration: and will, in some cases, vary the interests of the other devisees.

5. Although the estate still remains in the devisor, yet if he have bound himself by contract for a valuable consideration to convey it, such contract will operate as a revocation of a previous devise, and that although the contract should not be carried into effect for want of title.

6. If the conveyance be by way of mortgage only, for securing the payment of a debt, it will in law be considered as a revecation; but in equity where a mortgage is reckoned merely as a pledge or deposit of the estate, it will be a revocation *pro tanto* only, that is, to the extent of the charge.

7. A commission of bankrupt operates as such revocation, and so will the assignment made of his effects by the commissioners.

8. Any material alteration in the family situation of the testator, subsequent to his will, as the *marriage and birth* of a child, will also operate as a revocation: but both these circumstances must actually occur in order to render a previous will void; as *marriage alone*, without having a child either in the life-time of the testator, or posthumously, will not effect a revocation; unless in the case of a woman, whose marriage alone will be a suspension and revocation of her will during the life-time of her husband; but in case of her surviving him it has been holden *(Plow, Com.* 343,*)* that it will revive: but this does not seem to be clearly settled.

9. The making an advancement for a child by the parent subsequent to his will, will also be considered *prima facie* as an ademption, that is, a revocation of his legacy.

WIN, (Sax.) In the beginning or ending of the names of places, signifies that some battle was fought, and victory gained there. *Cowell. Blount.*

WINCHES. Engines to draw barges against the stream of a river. 21 *Jac.* 1. *cap.* 32.

WINCHESTER MEASURE. A standard originally kept at Winchester: and we find in the laws of King Edgar, near a century before the conquest, an injunction that one measure, which was kept at Winchester, should be observed throughout the realm. 1 *Black. Com.* 274, 275.

WINDAS, or WINDLASS, Corruptly wanlass, is a term for hunting of deer in forests to a stand, &c. See *Wanlass.*

WIND-MILL. A man may not erect a wind-mill within any forest, because it frights deer, and draws company to the disquiet of the game. *W. Jones Rep.* 293.

WINTER-HEYNING, Is a season between the eleventh day of November and the three and twentieth day of April; which is excepted from the liberty of commoning in the Forest of Dean, &c. *Stat.* 20 *Car.* 2. *cap.* 3.

WIRE-DRAWERS. The silver wire to be drawn for silver thread, is to hold eleven ounces and fifteen penny weights, and all silver to be gilt and used in the wire-drawers trade, shall hold eleven ounces and eight penny weights of fine silver on the pound weight troy; and four penny weights and four grains of gold, to be laid upon each pound of silver, on forfeiture of 5s. for every ounce made otherwise. 15 *Geo.* 2. *cap.* 20.

WISTA, A measure of land among the Saxons; being the quantity of half a hide, and the hide 120 acres.—*Octo virgatæ unum hidam faciunt;* wista *vero quatuor virgatis constat. Mon. Ang. Tom.* 1. p. 133. *Cowell.*

WITAM, *Secundum* witam *jurare*, Was for a person to purge himself by the oaths of so many witnesses, as the offence required. *Leg. Inæ, cap.* 63. *Cowell.*

WITCHCRAFT, Using of, was felony by *Stat.* 1 *Jac.* 1. *cap.* 12. repealed by 9 *Geo.* 2. *c.* 5. See *Fortune-tellers* and *Vagrants.*

WITE, A Saxon word, used for punishment; a pain, penalty, mulct, &c. And *witefree* is a term of privilege or immunity from fines and amercements. *Sax. Dict.* From hence come the words *Bloodwite, Lecherwite*, &c. *Cowell. Blount.*

WITENA-GEMOT, or WITTENA-GEMOT, (Sax. *Conventus sapientum*) Was a convention or assembly of great men to advise and assist the king, answerable to our parliament, in the time of the Saxons; or, rather an assembly of the whole nation. See *Diets*, and *Squire's Anglo-Saxon-Government* 165, &c, *Cowell. Blount.*

WITENS, Were the chief of the Saxon Lords or *Thanes*, their nobles and wise men. *Sax. Dict.*

WITERDEN. A taxation of the West Saxons, imposed by the public council of the kingdom. *Chart. Ethelwolf. Reg. Anno* 855.

WITHDRAWING FROM ALLEGIANCE. By 3 *Jac.* 1. *c.* 4. if any natural born subject be withdrawn from his allegiance, and reconciled to the Pope or See of Rome, or any other prince or state, both he and all such as procure such reconciliation shall incur the guilt of high treason.

WITHERNAM, (From the Sax. *Wither*, i. e. *altera*, or, as some say, *contra*, and *Nam*, *captio*) Is where a distress is driven out of the county, and the sheriff upon a replevin cannot make deliverance to the party distrained: in this case the writ of withernam is directed to the sheriff, for the taking as many of his beasts or goods, who did thus unlawfully distrain, into his keeping, till the party make deliverance of the first distress, &c. It is a taking or reprisal of other cattle or goods, in lieu of those that were formerly unjustly taken and eloined, or otherwise withholden. *F. N. B.* 68, 69. 2 *Inst.* 140. *Stat. West.* 2. 13 *Ed.* 1. *c.* 2.

WITHERSAKE, An apostate, or perfidious renegado. *Leg. Canut. cap.* 27. *Cowell. Blount.*

WITNESS, (*Testis*) Is one that gives evidence in a cause; an indifferent person to each party, sworn to speak the truth, the whole truth, and nothing but the truth: and if he will be a gainer or loser by the suit, he shall not be sworn as a witness. 2 *Lill. Abr.* 700. But it is now declared by *Stat.* 46 *Geo.* 3. *c.* 37. that a witness cannot by law refuse to answer on the ground of subjecting himself to a suit for debt.

WITTENA-GEMOTE. See *Witena-gemot*, and *Black. Com.* 1 *V.* 148. 4 *V.* 405.

WOAD, A profitable herb much used for the dying of blue colours, mentioned in the *Stat.* 27 *H.* 8. *cap.* 2.

WOLD, (Sax.) Signifies a down, or open champaign ground, void of wood; as Stow in the Wolds, Cotswold in Gloucestershire, &c. *Cowell. Blount.*

WOLFESHEAD, or WOLFERHEFOD, (Sax.) *Caput Lupinum*, Was the condition of such as were outlawed in the time of the Saxons; who if they could not be taken alive to be brought to justice, might be slain, and their heads brought to the king; for they were no more accounted of than a wolf's head, a beast so hurtful to man. *Leg. Edw. Conf. Bract. lib.* 3. *Cowell. Blount.*

WOMEN. A woman is capable of being a sexton, and of voting at an election for one. 2 *Strange* 1114. She is also liable to serve the offices of church-warden, overseer, or constable in her turn, for she may appoint a deputy. A bastard is within the statute of *P. & M.* against taking away young women. 2 *Strange* 1161. And by 30 *Geo.* 3. *c.* 47. Women convicted of high or petit treason are to be hanged; and women convicted of petit treason are liable to the same punishment as persons convicted of wilful murder under 25 *Geo.* 2.

WONG, A Saxon word for field.——*Tres acras terræ jacentes in le* wongs, i. e. *in Campis opinor seminalibus. Spelm. Cowell. Blount.*

WOOD. If any person purposely burn any pile of wood, or bark any trees, &c. the owner may recover treble damages for it in trespass. *Stat.* 37 *Hen.* 6. *c.* 6. None may destroy any woods, by turning them into tillage or pasture, &c. if two acres or more in quantity, on pain of 40s. an acre: and no person shall suffer his swine to go in a wood unringed, under penalties. Where there is wood or coppice in common, the lord may inclose a fourth part, &c. 35 *H.* 8. *c.* 17. 13 *Eliz. c.* 25. If coppice wood is felled at or under twenty-four years growth, there must be left twelve standils of oaks in every acre, or the like number of ash, elm, &c. on pain of forfeiting 3s. 3d. for every standil wanting; and they are not to be cut down till ten inches square within three foot of the ground, or until so many years after left, under the penalty of 6s. 8d. &c. *Stat.* 35 *H.* 8. *cap.* 17. All woods or coppices felled at fourteen years growth, shall be preserved from destruction for eight years; and no cattle be put into the ground from the time of felling, till five years afterwards, by 13 *Eliz. cap.* 25. The statutes 43 *Eliz. cap.* 7. and 15 *Car.* 2. *cap.* 2. provide against woodstealing, ordaining recompence to be made, and inflicting a forfeiture of 10s. &c. Burning woods, or underwood, is made felony: and persons maliciously cutting or spoiling timber-trees, fruit-trees, &c. are to be sent to the house of correction for three months, and whipt once a month, by 1 *Geo.* 1. *c.* 48. Also where persons destroy trees, woods, or break open hedges, the owners shall have satisfaction from the inhabitants of the place, as for dikes overthrown in the night, provided by 13 *Ed.* 1. under approvement: if the offenders be not convicted in six months, &c. 6 *Geo.* 1. *cap.* 16. It has been adjudged, that if *A.* plants a tree upon his own ground, and in growing its roots extend into the land of *B.* adjoining, they are tenants in common of this tree: but if all the root grows in the ground of *A.* though the boughs overshadow *B.*'s land, yet the branches follow the root, and the property of the whole is in *A.* 1 *Ld. Raym.* 737.

WOOD-CORN, A certain quantity of grain paid by the tenant of some manors to the lord, for the liberty to pick up dead or broken wood. *Cartular. Burgi S. Petri MS.* 142. *Cowell. Blount.*

WOOD-GELD, Is taken to be the cutting of wood within the forest, or rather money paid for the same to the foresters; or it signifies to be free from payment of money, for taking wood in any forest. *Cromp. Juris.* 157. *Co. Litt.* 233.

WOODMEN, Seem to be those in forests, that have their charge particularly to look to the king's woods there. *Cromp. Juris.* 146. *Cowell. Blount.*

WOODMOTE, Is the old name of that court of the forest which is now called the Court of Attachments; and was wont to be held at the will of the chief officers of the forest, without any certain time, till since the statute of *Charta de Foresta. Manwood, cap.* 22. *pag.* 207. 3 *Black. Com.* 71.

WOOD-PLEA-COURT, A court held twice in the year in the forest of Clun in Shropshire, for determining all matters of wood and agistments there. *Cowell. Blount.*

WOODWARD, Is an officer of the forest, whose office consists in looking after the woods, and vert and venison, and presenting offences relating to the same, &c. And woodwards may not walk with bow and shafts, but with forest bills. *Cromp. Juris.* 201. *Manwood, par.* 1. 189.

WOOL, Being a staple commodity of the greatest value in this kingdom, there have been divers statutes made from time to time, to preserve the same entirely to ourselves, and to prevent its being transported to other nations; a matter of sound policy, as the process through which it passes in various ways, in the manufacturing of the different commodities of which wool is the chief substance, gives employment not only to the poor, but to a very numerous and meritorious class of artizans, namely, those who have been wholly brought up in the manufacturing of woollen goods.

By the stat. 9 & 10 *W.* 3. *cap.* 40. entries are to be made of wool shorn, and wool is not to be carried near the sea-coasts, but between sun-rising and sun-setting, &c. Also by 28 *Geo.* 3. *c.* 28. other provisions are made in respect of this article.

WOOL-DRIVERS, Are such as buy wool in the country of the sheep owners, and carry it on horseback to the clothiers, or to market-towns, to sell again. 2 & 3 *P.* & *M. c.* 13.

WOOLFERHEFOD. See *Woolfeshead.*

WOOL-KEY, Its ground, wharf and key, in the parish of All-saints, Barking, in London, vested in trustees for his majesty, his heirs and successors, &c. 8 *G.* 1. *c.* 31.

WOOLLEN, BURIAL IN. By 54 *Geo.* 3. *c.* 108. the acts 30 *Car.* 2. *c.* 3. and 32 *Car.* 2. *c.* 1. for burying in woollen are repealed. See *Burials.*

WOOLLEN-MANUFACTURES. For the protection of this branch of trade, there are numerous statutes, the provisions of which are to be found under the title *Manufactures,* section *Woollen.*

WOOL-STAPLE, Mentioned in *stat.* 51 *H.* 3. *stat.* 5. is, That city or town where wool was sold. See *Staple.*

WOOLWINDERS, Those that wind up every fleece of wool, intended to be packed and sold by weight, into a kind of bundle.

WORCESTERS, and worsted cloths, are mentioned in many of our old statutes, as 17 *R.* 2. 7 *E.* 4. 14 *&* 15 *Hen.* 8. *c.* 3. *&c.* See *Abr. Stat.*

WORDS, Which may be taken or interpreted by law in a general or common sense, ought not to receive a strained or unusual construction: and ambiguous words are to be construed so as to make them stand with law and equity; and not to be wrested to do wrong. And words which are in themselves uncertain, may be made certain by subsequent or following words. A word which is written short or abbreviated, is not good without a dash to distinguish it: and senseless words are void and idle; though they shall not hurt where it is good without them. Nor shall words in deeds that are needless, impeach a clause certain and perfect without such words. 2 *Lill. Abr.* 711, 712, 713, 714. *Hob.* 313. Vide *Scilicet.*

WORDS; TREASONABLE. It seems clearly to be agreed, that by the common law, and the statute of *Edward* 3, words spoken amount only to a high misdemeanor, and no treason. 1 *Black. Com.* 80.

WORK-HOUSES, Are places erected in most parishes for the reception and employment of the poor, and the most considerable work-house in the city of London, is that in Bishopsgate-street; wherein some hundreds of idle persons are constantly employed in beating hemp, &c. and a great many poor children maintained and educated. *Stat.* 13 & 14 *Car.* 2.

WORMTAK. *Item est ibidem, apud, &c. de* Wormtak, *vi sol viii den. solvend annuatim ad Festum* S. Martini. *Inquisic. Heref.* 22 *Rich.* 2.

WORT, or WORTH, (From the Sax. *Weorth*) A curtilage or country farm. *Matt. Westm.* 870. *Cowell. Blount.*

WORTHIEST OF BLOOD. An expression of the lawyers, signifying the preference given in descents, to sons before daughters. *Ibid.*

WORTHINE OF LAND, Is a certain quantity of ground, so called in the manor of Kingsland in the county of Hereford: and in some places the tenants are called worthies. *Consuetud. Maner. de Hedenham in Com. Bucks.* 18 *Edw.* 3. *Cowell. Blount.*

WRECK, (Lat. *Wreccum Maris*, Fr. *Wreck de Mer*, sometimes writ *Wreche*, *Werec*, and *Seup-werpe*, *quasi Sea-up-werp*, i. e. *Ejectus Maris*) signifies in our law such goods as, after a ship-wreck, are cast upon the land by the sea, and left there within some county; for they are not wrecks so long as they remain at sea, in the jurisdiction of the Admiralty. 2 *Inst.* 167. Where a ship perisheth on the sea, and no man escapes alive out of it, this is called wreck: and the goods in the ship being brought to land by the waves, belong to the king by his prerogative, or to the lord of the manor. 5 *Rep.* 106. And by the *Stat.* of *Westm.* 1. 3 *Ed.* 1. *cap.* 4. it is enacted, that when a man or any living creature, escapes alive out of a ship cast away, whereby the owner of the goods may be known, the ship or goods shall not be wreck; but the same shall be kept a year and a day by the sheriff, to be restored to any person that can prove a property in the goods within that time; and if no body comes, then the same shall be forfeited as wreck. The year and day shall be accounted from the seizure; and if the owner of the goods dies within the year, his executors or administrators may make proof: and when the goods are *bona peritura*, the sheriff may sell them within the year; so as he disposes of them to the best advantage, and accounts for them, &c. 2 *Inst.* 167. 5 *Rep.* 106. *Wood's Inst.* 214.

And by 48 *Geo.* 3. *c.* 75. when dead bodies shall be cast on shore from wrecks, the churchwardens and overseers of the poor shall cause the same to be removed and interred in a decent manner, in the churchyard of the parish, by the minister, who is to perform the funeral service at the same fees as paupers. There are also other provisions contained in the act for the preservation of wrecked goods, which are too long to be minutely detailed in this work.

WRECKFREE, Is to be exempt from the forfeiture of ship-wrecked goods and vessels; which K. *Edw.* 1. by charter granted to the Barons of the Cinque Ports. *Placit. temp. Ed.* 1.

WRIT, (*Breve* in Sax. *Writan*, i. e. *Scribere*) In general is the King's precept, in writing under seal, issuing out of some court to the sheriff, or other person, and commanding something to be done touching a suit or action, or giving commission to have it done. *Terms de Ley.* 1 *Inst.* 73.

WRIT OF ASSISTANCE, Is a writ issuing out of the Exchequer, to authorise any person to take a constable, or other public officer, to seize goods or merchandize prohibited and uncustomed, &c. And there is a writ of this name issued out of the Chancery, to give possession of land. *Stat.* 14 *Car.* 2. *cap.* 1.

WRIT OF INQUIRY OF DAMAGES, Is a judicial writ, that issues out to the sheriff upon a judgment by default, in action of the case, covenant, trespass, trover, &c. commanding him to summon a jury to enquire what damages the plaintiff hath sustained *occasione præmissorum*; and when this is returned with the inquisition, the rule for judgment is given upon it; and if nothing be said to the contrary, judgment is thereupon entered. 2 *Lill. Abr.* 721.

WRIT OF REBELLION, A writ out of the Chancery, or Exchequer, against a person in contempt, for not appearing in those courts, &c. See *Commission of Rebellion.*

WRITER OF TALLIES (*Scriptor talliarum*) Is an officer in the Exchequer, being clerk to the auditor of the receipt, who writes upon the tallies, the whole letters of the tellers bills. *Cowell.*

WRITING, (*Scriptum*) A simple writing or declaration, not in the manner of a deed, made to a certain person, &c. shall be good in law. *Hob.* 312.

WRONG, (*Injuria*) Signifies any damage or injury, being in law construction that which is contrary to right. *Co. Litt.* Vide *Tort.*

WRONGLANDS, Seem to be ill grown trees that will never prove timber; such as wrong the ground they grow in. *Kitch.* 169. *Cowell. Blount.*

WUDEHETH, (From the Sax *Wude*, i. e. *Sylva*) a felling of wood. *Leg. Hen.* 1. *c.* 37. *Cowell. Blount.*

WYDRAUGHT, A water-passage, gutter, or watering-place; often mentioned in old leases of houses, in the covenants for repairs, &c. *Cowell.*

WYKE, WYKA,——*Et totam* Wykam *cum hominibus*, &c. *Mon. Ang. tom.* 2. p. 154. See *Wic* and *Wicâ*.

WYTE, *Pœna*, *Mulcta*——*Saxones duo mulctarum genera statuere*, i. e. Weram & Wytam. Vide *Wite.*

X

XANTUS, Is used for Sanctus; Xanta *Dei lex est quæ mortuos vivere doret.*

XENIA, *Dicuntur munuscula, quæ a provincialibus rectoribus, provinciarum efferebantur: vox est in privilegiorum chartis non insueta; ubi quietus esse a Xeniis immunes notat ab hujusmodi muneribus aliisque donis regi vel reginæ præstandis, quando ipsi per prædia privilegiatorum transierint. Chart. Dom. Semplingham. Mem. Scacc. Anno* 20 *Edw.* 3. *Spelm. Gloss. Cowell. Blount.*

XENODOCHIUM, Is interpreted an inn, allowed by public licence for the entertainment of strangers, and other guests: also an hospital, *In qua valetudinarii & senes,* i. e. *Infirmi, recipiuntur et aluntur. Vocab. utriusque Juris. Cowell. Blount.*

XEROPHAGIA, A kind of christian fast; the eating of dry meat. *Litt. Dict.*

XYLOPOLA, A woodmonger, or dealer in wood. *Litt.*

XYSTICUS, Is a wrestler, or champion: and xystus was a covered place or theatre, where men used wrestling and other exercises in the winter. *Ibid.*

Y

YA AND NAY,—*Quod homines de Rippon sint credendi per suum* ya, *et per suum* nay *in omnibus querelis, &c. Charta Athelstan. Reg. Mon. Angl. tom.* 1. *p.* 173. *Cowell.*

YARD, Is a well known measure, three feet in length; by which cloth, linen, &c. are measured: It was ordained by King *Hen.* 1. from the length of his own arm. *Baker's Chron.*

YARDLAND, (*Virgata Terræ*) Is a quantity of land, different according to the place or country; as at Wimbledon in Surrey, it is but fifteen acres, in other counties it is twenty, in some twenty-four, and in others thirty, and forty acres. *Bract. lib.* 2. *c.* 10.

YAUGH, A yacht, or little bark; also a fly-boat, pinnace, &c. In Lat. called *Celox, à celeritudine,* from its swiftness. *Litt. Dict. Cowell. Blount.*

YEONOMUS, *Oeconomus;* an advocate, patron, or defender. *Vit. Abbat. S. Albani. Cowell. Blount.*

YEAR, *(Annus)* In the full extent of the word, contains a system or cycle of several months, usually twelve; and is the time wherein the sun goes round his compass through the twelve signs, viz. three hundred and sixty-five days, and about six hours. A year is twelve months, as divided by Julius Cæsar: and the church begins the year on the first day of January, called New-year's day; but the civil account formerly, not till March the 25th. It appears by ancient grants and charters, that our ancestors began the year at Christmas, which was observed here till the time of William I. commonly called the Conqueror; but afterwards, for some time the year of our Lord was seldom mentioned in grants, only the year of the reign of the King. *Mon. Ang. tom.* 1. *p.* 62.

There is a year of the world, and a year of Christ: and besides the solar year, the lunar year, being the time in which any of the celestial bodies finish their course; and thirty days, by which the Egyptians reckoned. Year is also taken for time in general; and the age of man. *Litt.*

YEAR AND DAY, *(Annus & Dies)* Is a time that determines a right, or works a prescription in many cases by law; as in case of an estray, if the owner challenge it not within that time, it belongs to the lord; so of a wreck, &c. A year and a day is given to prosecute appeals; and for actions in a writ of right, &c. after entry or claim, to avoid a fine: and if a person wounded die in a year and day, it makes the offender guilty of murder, &c. 3 *Inst.* 53. 6 *Rep.* 107.

YEAR, DAY AND WASTE, (*Annus, Dies et Vastum*) Is a part of the King's prerogative, whereby he hath the profits of lands and tenements for a year and a day of those that are attained of petit treason or felony, whosoever is lord of the manor whereto the lands or tenements do belong; and the King may cause waste to be made on the tenements, by destroying the houses, ploughing up the meadows and pastures, rooting up the woods, &c. except the lord of the fee agree with him for the redemption of such waste; afterwards restoring it to the lord of the fee. *Staundf. Prærog.* 44.

YEAR-BOOKS. Reports in a regular series from the reign of King *Ed.* 2. inclusive, to the time of *Hen.* 8. which were taken by the prothonotaries, or chief scribes of the court, at the expence of the crown, and published annually, whence they are known under the denomination of the year-books. 1 *Black. Com.* 71, 72.

YEARS, Estates for. An estate for years is a contract, for the possession of lands or tenements, for some determinate period: and it happens where a man letteth them to another, for the term of a certain number of years, agreed between the lessor and lessee, and the lessee enters thereon. If the lease be but for half a year, or a quarter, or any less time, this lessee is respected as a tenant for years, and is styled so in some legal proceedings. 2 *Black. Com.* 140.

YEMAN, or YEOMAN, or YOMAN, A derivative of the Saxon, *geman*, i. e. *communis.* These *Camd.* in his *Brit. pag.* 105. placeth next in order to gentlemen, calling them *ingenuos*, whose opinion the statute affirms, *Anno* 6 *Rich.* 2. *cap.* 4. and 20 *Rich.* 2. *cap.* 2. Sir *Thomas Smith* in his *Republ. Anglorum, lib.* 1. *c.* 23. calls him a yeoman, whom our law calls *legalem hominem*, which (says he) is in the English a free-born man, that may dispend of his own free-land in yearly revenues to the sum of forty shillings sterling. *Verstegan* in his *Restitution of Decayed Intelligence, cap.* 10. writes, that *gemen* among the ancient *Teutonicks*, and *gemein* among the modern, signifies as much as common, and the letter *g* being turned into *y*, is written yemen, which therefore signifies a commoner. Yeoman also signifies an officer in the king's house, in the middle place between the sergeant and the groom, as yeoman of the chandry, yeoman of the scullery, 33 *H.* 8. *cap.* 12. yeoman of the crown, 3 *E.* 4. 5. The word youngmen is used for yeomen, in the statute 33 *H.* 8. *cap.* 10. *Cowell.* 1 *Black. Com.* 406.

YEME, Is an ancient corruption of *hieme*, winter. *Cowell. Blount.*

YEVEN, or YEOVEN, (as we use at the end of indentures and other instruments, yeoven, the day and year first above written) Is derived from the Saxon, *ceorian*, i. e. dare, and is the same with given. So *Dictum de Kenelworth* concludes with—Yeoven, and proclaimed in the castle of Kenelworth the day before the calends of Nov. *anno* 1256. *Cowell.*

YEW, Is derived from the Greek Ἰίπτω, to hurt, and probably because before the invention of guns our ancestors made bows with this wood, with which they annoyed their enemies, and therefore they took care to plant the trees in the church-yards, where they might be often seen and preserved by the people. *Minshew. Cowell. Blount.*

YIELDING AND PAYING, (*Reddendo et Solvendo*) Comes from the Sax. *Geldan et Gildan;* and in *Domesday*, *Gildare* is frequently used for *Solvere, Reddere*, the Sax. G. being often turned into Y. and the words yielding and paying in leases for years, are words of covenant.

YINGMAN, Mentioned in the laws of King *Hen.* 1. *c.* 15. Spelman thinks may be a mistake for Inglishman, or as we now say Englishman: but perhaps the yingmen were rather youngmen, printed for yeomen and yemen, in *Stat.* 33 *H.* 8. *cap.* 10. *Cowell.*

YOKELET, (Sax. *Jocelet*) Is a little farm, &c. in some parts of Kent, so called from its requiring but a yoke of oxen to till it. *Sax. Dict. Cowell.*

YORK AND YORKSHIRE. Persons inhabiting, or those who have any goods within the province of York, may by will dispose of all their personal estate, &c. 4 & 5 *W. & M. cap.* 2. And a registry of deeds, conveyances, and wills, &c. of lands, is ordained in the West-Riding of Yorkshire, by 2 *Ann. c.* 4. And so in the East and North-Ridings, by subsequent acts.

YORK, Custom of. In the city of London, and province of York, the effects of an intestate after payment of his debts, are in general divided, according to the ancient universal doctrine of the *pars rationabilis.* If the deceased leaves a widow and children, his substance, deducting the widow's apparel and furniture of her bed-chamber, which in London is called the widow's chamber, is divided into three parts; one of which belongs to the widow, another to the children, and the third to the administrator: if only a widow, or only children, they shall respectively, in either case, take one moiety, and the administrator the other; if neither widow nor child, the administrator shall have the whole. And this portion or dead-man's part the administrator was wont to apply to his own use, until the Stat. 1 *Jac.* 2. *c.* 17. declared that the same should be subject to the statutes of distribution. So that if a man dies worth 1800*l.* leaving a widow and two children, the estate shall be divided into eighteen parts; whereof the widow shall have eight, six by the custom, and two by the statute; and each of the children five, three by the custom, and two by the statute: if he leaves a widow and one child, they shall each have a moiety of the whole, or nine such eighteen parts, six by the custom, and three by the statute: if he leaves a widow and no child, the widow shall have three-fourths of the whole, two by the custom, and one by the statute; and the remaining fourth shall go by the statute to the next of kin. If the wife be provided for by a jointure before marriage, in bar of her customary part, it puts her in a state of non-entity, with regard to the custom only; but she shall be entitled to her share of the dead-man's part, under the statute of distributions, unless barred by special agreement. And if any of the children are advanced by the father in his life-time, with any sum of money, (not amounting to their full proportionable part) they shall bring that portion into hotchpot with the rest of the brothers and sisters, (but not with the widow,) before they are entitled to any benefit under the custom; but if they are fully advanced, the custom entitles them to no farther dividend. In the province of York, the heir at common law, who inherits any lands in fee or in tail, is excluded from any filial portion, or reasonable part. 2 *Black. Com.* 518, 519.

YPSIVREMETA, In Latin *Altitonans*, signifies God; the thunderer. *Cowell. Blount.*

YVERNAGIUM, (From the French *Hyvernee*, that is, the winter season) was anciently used for the winter seedness, or season for sowing of corn. *Cowell.* See *Hybernagium*.

YULE. In the North of England, the country people call the feast of the nativity of our Lord by the name of Yule, which is the proper Scotch word for Christmas; and the sports used at Christmas here, called Christmas Gambols, in Scotland they term Yule Games. *Cowell. Blount.*

Z

ZABOLUS, i. e. *Diabolus*, as used in many old writers, *viz. Edgar. in Leg. Monach. Hydens. c.* 4. *Orderic. Vitalis* 460, &c. *Cowell.*

ZABULUM, (Latin, *Sabulum*) Gross sand or gravel *Quinque plaustratas zabuli*, for five wain-loads of land. *Computus temp. H.* 6. *Cowell.*

ZACHINE, A foreign coin of gold. *Merch. Dict.*

ZALA, i. e. *Incendium;* from whence we derive the English word zeal.

ZANCHA, A kind of vesture or garment. *Litt.*

ZANT-KILLOW, A measure containing six English bushels. *Cowell.*

ZATOBIN, Sattin, or fine silk; mentioned in *Mon. Ang. Tom.* 3. *p.* 177. *Cowell.*

ZEALOT, *(Zelotes)* Is for the most part taken in *pejorum sensum*, so that we term one that is a separatist or schismatic from the church of England, a Zealot or Fanatic. *Cowell. Blount.*

ZERETH, An Hebrew measure of nine inches. *Litt. Dict.*

ZETA, A room kept warm like a stove; a withdrawing chamber with pipes conveyed along in the walls, to receive from below either the cool air in the summer, or the heat of fire, &c. in winter: it is called by our English historians a dining-room, or parlour. *Osborn vita S. Elphegi apud* Wharton, *Angl. par.* 2. *p.* 127. *Cowell.*

ZIGARUS, A strolling thief, or gipsey. *Litt.*

ZODIACK, *(Zodiacus)* A circle in the heavens containing the twelve signs through which the sun passes every year. *Litt.*

ZUCHE, *(Zucheus, Stips siccus et aridus)* A withered or dry stock of a tree. *Cowell. Blount.*

ZYGOSTATA, Is a clerk of the market, to see to weights, &c. *Litt. Dict.*

ZYTHUM, A drink mode of corn, used by the old *Gauls;* so called from the seething or boiling it, whence cyder had its name. *Cowell. Blount.*

FINIS.

W. Flint, Printer, St. Sepulchre's, London.